The Dictionary of Art · volume ten

The Dictionary of Art

10

Egypt, ancient,
§XI: Writing
and books
TO
Ferrant

GROVE

The Dictionary of Art

edited by JANE TURNER, in thirty-four volumes, 1996

Reprinted with minor corrections, 1998

This edition is distributed within the United Kingdom and Europe
by Macmillan Publishers Limited, London, and within the United States and Canada by
Grove's Dictionaries Inc., New York.

Text keyboarded by Wearset Limited, Sunderland, England
Database management by Pindar plc, York, England
Imagesetting by William Clowes Limited, Suffolk, England
Printed and bound by China Translation and Printing Services Ltd, Hong Kong

British Library Cataloguing in Publication Data

The dictionary of art
  1. Art - Dictionaries 2. Art - History -
  Dictionaries
I. Turner, Jane
703

ISBN 1-884446-00-0

Library of Congress Cataloging in Publication Data

The dictionary of art / editor, Jane Turner.
  p. cm.
Includes bibliographical references and index.
Contents: 1. A to Anckerman
ISBN 1-884446-00-0 (alk. paper)
  1. Art—Encyclopedias.
  I. Turner, Jane, 1956–
N31.D5 1996   96–13628
703—dc20   CIP

Contents

List of Colour Illustrations

General Abbreviations

The abbreviations employed throughout this dictionary, most of which are listed below, do not vary, except for capitalization, regardless of the context in which they are used, including bibliographical citations and for locations of works of art. The principle used to arrive at these abbreviations is that their full form should be easily deducible, and for this reason acronyms have generally been avoided (e.g. Los Angeles Co. Mus. A. instead of LACMA). The same abbreviation is adopted for cognate forms in foreign languages and in most cases for plural and adjectival forms (e.g. A.= Art, Arts, Arte, Arti etc). Not all related forms are listed below. Occasionally, if a name, for instance of an artists' group or exhibiting society, is repeated within the text of one article, it is cited in an abbreviated form after its first mention in full (e.g. The Pre-Raphaelite Brotherhood (PRB) was founded...); the same is true of archaeological periods and eras, which are abbreviated to initial letters in small capitals (e.g. In the Early Minoan (EM) period...). Such abbreviations do not appear in this list. For the reader's convenience, separate full lists of abbreviations for locations, periodical titles and standard reference books and series are included as Appendices A–C in vol. 33.

A.	Art, Arts	Anthropol.	Anthropology	Azerbaij.	Azerbaijani
A.C.	Arts Council	Antiqua.	Antiquarian, Antiquaries	B.	Bartsch [catalogue of Old Master prints]
Acad.	Academy	app.	appendix		
AD	Anno Domini	approx.	approximately	*b*	born
Add.	Additional, Addendum	AR	Arkansas (USA)	BA	Bachelor of Arts
addn	addition	ARA	Associate of the Royal Academy	Balt.	Baltic
Admin.	Administration			*bapt*	baptized
Adv.	Advances, Advanced	Arab.	Arabic	BArch	Bachelor of Architecture
Aesth.	Aesthetic(s)	Archaeol.	Archaeology	Bart	Baronet
Afr.	African	Archit.	Architecture, Architectural	Bask.	Basketry
Afrik.	Afrikaans, Afrikaner	Archv, Archvs	Archive(s)	BBC	British Broadcasting Corporation
A.G.	Art Gallery				
Agrar.	Agrarian	Arg.	Argentine	BC	Before Christ
Agric.	Agriculture	ARHA	Associate of the Royal Hibernian Academy	BC	British Columbia (Canada)
Agron.	Agronomy			BE	Buddhist era
Agy	Agency	ARIBA	Associate of the Royal Institute of British Architects	Beds	Bedfordshire (GB)
AH	Anno Hegirae			Behav.	Behavioural
A. Inst.	Art Institute	Armen.	Armenian	Belarus.	Belarusian
AK	Alaska (USA)	ARSA	Associate of the Royal Scottish Academy	Belg.	Belgian
AL	Alabama (USA)			Berks	Berkshire (GB)
Alb.	Albanian	Asiat.	Asiatic	Berwicks	Berwickshire (GB; old)
Alg.	Algerian	Assist.	Assistance	BFA	Bachelor of Fine Arts
Alta	Alberta (Canada)	Assoc.	Association	Bibl.	Bible, Biblical
Altern.	Alternative	Astron.	Astronomy	Bibliog.	Bibliography, Bibliographical
a.m.	ante meridiem [before noon]	AT&T	American Telephone & Telegraph Company	Biblioph.	Bibliophile
Amat.	Amateur	attrib.	attribution, attributed to	Biog.	Biography, Biographical
Amer.	American	Aug	August	Biol.	Biology, Biological
An.	Annals	Aust.	Austrian	bk, bks	book(s)
Anatol.	Anatolian	Austral.	Australian	Bkbinder	Bookbinder
Anc.	Ancient	Auth.	Author(s)	Bklore	Booklore
Annu.	Annual	Auton.	Autonomous	Bkshop	Bookshop
Anon.	Anonymous(ly)	Aux.	Auxiliary	BL	British Library
Ant.	Antique	Ave.	Avenue	Bld	Build
Anthol.	Anthology	AZ	Arizona (USA)	Bldg	Building

Bldr	Builder	Chin.	Chinese	Cur.	Curator, Curatorial, Curatorship
BLitt	Bachelor of Letters/Literature	Christ.	Christian, Christianity	Curr.	Current(s)
BM	British Museum	Chron.	Chronicle	CVO	Commander of the [Royal] Victorian Order
Boh.	Bohemian	Cie	Compagnie [French]		
Boliv.	Bolivian	Cinema.	Cinematography	Cyclad.	Cycladic
Botan.	Botany, Botanical	Circ.	Circle	Cyp.	Cypriot
BP	Before present (1950)	Civ.	Civil, Civic	Czech.	Czechoslovak
Braz.	Brazilian	Civiliz.	Civilization(s)	$	dollars
BRD	Bundesrepublik Deutschland [Federal Republic of Germany (West Germany)]	Class.	Classic, Classical	*d*	died
		Clin.	Clinical	d.	denarius, denarii [penny, pence]
		CO	Colorado (USA)		
Brecons	Breconshire (GB; old)	Co.	Company; County	Dalmat.	Dalmatian
Brez.	Brezonek [lang. of Brittany]	Cod.	Codex, Codices	Dan.	Danish
Brit.	British	Col., Cols	Collection(s); Column(s)	DBE	Dame Commander of the Order of the British Empire
Bros	Brothers	Coll.	College		
BSc	Bachelor of Science	collab.	in collaboration with, collaborated, collaborative	DC	District of Columbia (USA)
Bucks	Buckinghamshire (GB)			DDR	Deutsche Demokratische Republik [German Democratic Republic (East Germany)]
Bulg.	Bulgarian	Collct.	Collecting		
Bull.	Bulletin	Colloq.	Colloquies		
bur	*buried*	Colomb.	Colombian	DE	Delaware (USA)
Burm.	Burmese	Colon.	Colonies, Colonial	Dec	December
Byz.	Byzantine	Colr	Collector	Dec.	Decorative
C	Celsius	Comm.	Commission; Community	ded.	dedication, dedicated to
C.	Century	Commerc.	Commercial	Democ.	Democracy, Democratic
c.	*circa* [about]	Communic.	Communications	Demog.	Demography, Demographic
CA	California	Comp.	Comparative; compiled by, compiler	Denbs	Denbighshire (GB; old)
Cab.	Cabinet			dep.	deposited at
Caerns	Caernarvonshire (GB; old)	Concent.	Concentration	Dept	Department
C.A.G.	City Art Gallery	Concr.	Concrete	Dept.	Departmental, Departments
Cal.	Calendar	Confed.	Confederation	Derbys	Derbyshire (GB)
Callig.	Calligraphy	Confer.	Conference	Des.	Design
Cam.	Camera	Congol.	Congolese	destr.	destroyed
Cambs	Cambridgeshire (GB)	Congr.	Congress	Dev.	Development
can	*canonized*	Conserv.	Conservation; Conservatory	Devon	Devonshire (GB)
Can.	Canadian	Constr.	Construction(al)	Dial.	Dialogue
Cant.	Canton(s), Cantonal	cont.	continued	diam.	diameter
Capt.	Captain	Contemp.	Contemporary	Diff.	Diffusion
Cards	Cardiganshire (GB; old)	Contrib.	Contributions, Contributor(s)	Dig.	Digest
Carib.	Caribbean	Convalesc.	Convalescence	Dip. Eng.	Diploma in Engineering
Carms	Carmarthenshire (GB; old)	Convent.	Convention	Dir.	Direction, Directed
Cartog.	Cartography	Coop.	Cooperation	Directrt	Directorate
Cat.	Catalan	Coord.	Coordination	Disc.	Discussion
cat.	catalogue	Copt.	Coptic	diss.	dissertation
Cath.	Catholic	Corp.	Corporation, Corpus	Distr.	District
CBE	Commander of the Order of the British Empire	Corr.	Correspondence	Div.	Division
		Cors.	Corsican	DLitt	Doctor of Letters/Literature
Celeb.	Celebration	Cost.	Costume	DM	Deutsche Mark
Celt.	Celtic	Cret.	Cretan	Doc.	Document(s)
Cent.	Centre, Central	Crim.	Criminal	Doss.	Dossier
Centen.	Centennial	Crit.	Critical, Criticism	DPhil	Doctor of Philosophy
Cer.	Ceramic	Croat.	Croatian	Dr	Doctor
cf.	confer [compare]	CT	Connecticut (USA)	Drg, Drgs	Drawing(s)
Chap., Chaps	Chapter(s)	Cttee	Committee	DSc	Doctor of Science/Historical Sciences
Chem.	Chemistry	Cub.	Cuban		
Ches	Cheshire (GB)	Cult.	Cultural, Culture	Dut.	Dutch
Chil.	Chilean	Cumb.	Cumberland (GB; old)	Dwell.	Dwelling
				E.	East(ern)

EC	European (Economic) Community	figs	figures	Heb.	Hebrew
Eccles.	Ecclesiastical	Filip.	Filipina(s), Filipino(s)	Hell.	Hellenic
Econ.	Economic, Economies	Fin.	Finnish	Her.	Heritage
Ecuad.	Ecuadorean	FL	Florida (USA)	Herald.	Heraldry, Heraldic
ed.	editor, edited (by)	*fl*	*floruit* [he/she flourished]	Hereford & Worcs	Hereford & Worcester (GB)
edn	edition	Flem.	Flemish	Herts	Hertfordshire (GB)
eds	editors	Flints	Flintshire (GB; old)	HI	Hawaii (USA)
Educ.	Education	Flk	Folk	Hib.	Hibernia
e.g.	*exempli gratia* [for example]	Flklore	Folklore	Hisp.	Hispanic
Egyp.	Egyptian	fol., fols	folio(s)	Hist.	History, Historical
Elem.	Element(s), Elementary	Found.	Foundation	HMS	His/Her Majesty's Ship
Emp.	Empirical	Fr.	French	Hon.	Honorary, Honourable
Emul.	Emulation	frag.	fragment	Horiz.	Horizon
Enc.	Encyclopedia	Fri.	Friday	Hort.	Horticulture
Encour.	Encouragement	FRIBA	Fellow of the Royal Institute of British Architects	Hosp.	Hospital(s)
Eng.	English	FRS	Fellow of the Royal Society, London	HRH	His/Her Royal Highness
Engin.	Engineer, Engineering			Human.	Humanities, Humanism
Engr., Engrs	Engraving(s)	ft	foot, feet	Hung.	Hungarian
Envmt	Environment	Furn.	Furniture	Hunts	Huntingdonshire (GB; old)
Epig.	Epigraphy	Futur.	Futurist, Futurism	IA	Iowa
Episc.	Episcopal	g	gram(s)	ibid.	*ibidem* [in the same place]
Esp.	Especially	GA	Georgia (USA)	ICA	Institute of Contemporary Arts
Ess.	Essays	Gael.	Gaelic		
est.	established	Gal., Gals	Gallery, Galleries	Ice.	Icelandic
etc	*etcetera* [and so on]	Gaz.	Gazette	Iconog.	Iconography
Ethnog.	Ethnography	GB	Great Britain	Iconol.	Iconology
Ethnol.	Ethnology	Gdn, Gdns	Garden(s)	ID	Idaho (USA)
Etrus.	Etruscan	Gdnr(s)	Gardener(s)	i.e.	*id est* [that is]
Eur.	European	Gen.	General	IL	Illinois (USA)
Evangel.	Evangelical	Geneal.	Genealogy, Genealogist	Illum.	Illumination
Exam.	Examination	Gent.	Gentleman, Gentlemen	illus.	illustrated, illustration
Excav.	Excavation, Excavated	Geog.	Geography	Imp.	Imperial
Exch.	Exchange	Geol.	Geology	IN	Indiana (USA)
Excurs.	Excursion	Geom.	Geometry	in., ins	inch(es)
exh.	exhibition	Georg.	Georgian	Inc.	Incorporated
Exp.	Exposition	Geosci.	Geoscience	inc.	incomplete
Expermntl	Experimental	Ger.	German, Germanic	incl.	includes, including, inclusive
Explor.	Exploration	G.I.	Government/General Issue (USA)	Incorp.	Incorporation
Expn	Expansion			Ind.	Indian
Ext.	External	Glams	Glamorganshire (GB; old)	Indep.	Independent
Extn	Extension	Glos	Gloucestershire (GB)	Indig.	Indigenous
f, ff	following page, following pages	Govt	Government	Indol.	Indology
		Gr.	Greek	Indon.	Indonesian
F.A.	Fine Art(s)	Grad.	Graduate	Indust.	Industrial
Fac.	Faculty	Graph.	Graphic	Inf.	Information
facs.	facsimile	Green.	Greenlandic	Inq.	Inquiry
Fam.	Family	Gr.-Roman	Greco-Roman	Inscr.	Inscribed, Inscription
fasc.	fascicle	Gt	Great	Inst.	Institute(s)
fd	feastday (of a saint)	Gtr	Greater	Inst. A.	Institute of Art
Feb	February	Guat.	Guatemalan	Instr.	Instrument, Instrumental
Fed.	Federation, Federal	Gym.	Gymnasium	Int.	International
Fem.	Feminist	h.	height	Intell.	Intelligence
Fest.	Festival	ha	hectare	Inter.	Interior(s), Internal
fig.	figure (illustration)	Hait.	Haitian	Interdiscip.	Interdisciplinary
Fig.	Figurative	Hants	Hampshire (GB)	intro.	introduced by, introduction
		Hb.	Handbook	inv.	inventory

Inven.	Invention	m	metre(s)	Moldov.	Moldovan
Invest.	Investigation(s)	m.	married	MOMA	Museum of Modern Art
Iran.	Iranian	M.	Monsieur	Mon.	Monday
irreg.	irregular(ly)	MA	Master of Arts; Massachusetts (USA)	Mongol.	Mongolian
Islam.	Islamic			Mons	Monmouthshire (GB; old)
Isr.	Israeli	Mag.	Magazine	Montgoms	Montgomeryshire (GB; old)
It.	Italian	Maint.	Maintenance	Mor.	Moral
J.	Journal	Malay.	Malaysian	Morav.	Moravian
Jam.	Jamaican	Man.	Manitoba (Canada); Manual	Moroc.	Moroccan
Jan	January	Manuf.	Manufactures	Movt	Movement
Jap.	Japanese	Mar.	Marine, Maritime	MP	Member of Parliament
Jav.	Javanese	Mason.	Masonic	MPhil	Master of Philosophy
Jew.	Jewish	Mat.	Material(s)	MS	Mississippi (USA)
Jewel.	Jewellery	Math.	Mathematic	MS., MSS	manuscript(s)
Jord.	Jordanian	MBE	Member of the Order of the British Empire	MSc	Master of Science
jr	junior			MT	Montana (USA)
Juris.	Jurisdiction	MD	Doctor of Medicine; Maryland (USA)	Mt	Mount
KBE	Knight Commander of the Order of the British Empire			Mthly	Monthly
		ME	Maine (USA)	Mun.	Municipal
KCVO	Knight Commander of the Royal Victorian Order	Mech.	Mechanical	Mus.	Museum(s)
		Med.	Medieval; Medium, Media	Mus. A.	Museum of Art
kg	kilogram(s)	Medic.	Medical, Medicine	Mus. F.A.	Museum of Fine Art(s)
kHz	kilohertz	Medit.	Mediterranean	Music.	Musicology
km	kilometre(s)	Mem.	Memorial(s); Memoir(s)	N.	North(ern); National
Knowl.	Knowledge	Merions	Merionethshire (GB; old)	n	refractive index of a medium
Kor.	Korean	Meso-Amer.	Meso-American	n.	note
KS	Kansas (USA)			N.A.G.	National Art Gallery
KY	Kentucky (USA)	Mesop.	Mesopotamian	Nat.	Natural, Nature
Kyrgyz.	Kyrgyzstani	Met.	Metropolitan	Naut.	Nautical
£	libra, librae [pound, pounds sterling]	Metal.	Metallurgy	NB	New Brunswick (Canada)
		Mex.	Mexican	NC	North Carolina (USA)
l.	length	MFA	Master of Fine Arts	ND	North Dakota (USA)
LA	Louisiana (USA)	mg	milligram(s)	n.d.	no date
Lab.	Laboratory	Mgmt	Management	NE	Nebraska; Northeast(ern)
Lancs	Lancashire (GB)	Mgr	Monsignor	Neth.	Netherlandish
Lang.	Language(s)	MI	Michigan	Newslett.	Newsletter
Lat.	Latin	Micrones.	Micronesian	Nfld	Newfoundland (Canada)
Latv.	Latvian	Mid. Amer.	Middle American	N.G.	National Gallery
lb, lbs	pound(s) weight	Middx	Middlesex (GB; old)	N.G.A.	National Gallery of Art
Leb.	Lebanese	Mid. E.	Middle Eastern	NH	New Hampshire (USA)
Lect.	Lecture	Mid. Eng.	Middle English	Niger.	Nigerian
Legis.	Legislative	Mid Glam.	Mid Glamorgan (GB)	NJ	New Jersey (USA)
Leics	Leicestershire (GB)	Mil.	Military	NM	New Mexico (USA)
Lex.	Lexicon	Mill.	Millennium	nm	nanometre (10^{-9} metre)
Lg.	Large	Min.	Ministry; Minutes	nn.	notes
Lib., Libs	Library, Libraries	Misc.	Miscellaneous	no., nos	number(s)
Liber.	Liberian	Miss.	Mission(s)	Nord.	Nordic
Libsp	Librarianship	Mlle	Mademoiselle	Norm.	Normal
Lincs	Lincolnshire (GB)	mm	millimetre(s)	Northants	Northamptonshire (GB)
Lit.	Literature	Mme	Madame	Northumb.	Northumberland (GB)
Lith.	Lithuanian	MN	Minnesota	Norw.	Norwegian
Liturg.	Liturgical	Mnmt, Mnmts	Monument(s)	Notts	Nottinghamshire (GB)
LLB	Bachelor of Laws			Nov	November
LLD	Doctor of Laws	Mnmtl	Monumental	n.p.	no place (of publication)
Lt	Lieutenant	MO	Missouri (USA)	N.P.G.	National Portrait Gallery
Lt-Col.	Lieutenant-Colonel	Mod.	Modern, Modernist	nr	near
Ltd	Limited	Moldav.	Moldavian		

Nr E. Near Eastern

NS New Style; Nova Scotia (Canada)

n. s. new series

NSW New South Wales (Australia)

NT National Trust

Ntbk Notebook

Numi. Numismatic(s)

NV Nevada (USA)

NW Northwest(ern)

NWT Northwest Territories (Canada)

NY New York (USA)

NZ New Zealand

OBE Officer of the Order of the British Empire

Obj. Object(s), Objective

Occas. Occasional

Occident. Occidental

Ocean. Oceania

Oct October

8vo octavo

OFM Order of Friars Minor

OH Ohio (USA)

OK Oklahoma (USA)

Olymp. Olympic

OM Order of Merit

Ont. Ontario (Canada)

op. opus

opp. opposite; opera [pl. of opus]

OR Oregon (USA)

Org. Organization

Orient. Oriental

Orthdx Orthodox

OSB Order of St Benedict

Ott. Ottoman

Oxon Oxfordshire (GB)

oz. ounce(s)

p pence

p., pp. page(s)

PA Pennsylvania (USA)

p.a. per annum

Pak. Pakistani

Palaeontol. Palaeontology, Palaeontological

Palest. Palestinian

Pap. Paper(s)

para. paragraph

Parag. Paraguayan

Parl. Parliament

Paroch. Parochial

Patriarch. Patriarchate

Patriot. Patriotic

Patrm. Patrimony

Pav. Pavilion

PEI Prince Edward Island (Canada)

Pembs Pembrokeshire (GB; old)

Per. Period

Percep. Perceptions

Perf. Performance, Performing, Performed

Period. Periodical(s)

Pers. Persian

Persp. Perspectives

Peru. Peruvian

PhD Doctor of Philosophy

Philol. Philology

Philos. Philosophy

Phoen. Phoenician

Phot. Photograph, Photography, Photographic

Phys. Physician(s), Physics, Physique, Physical

Physiog. Physiognomy

Physiol. Physiology

Pict. Picture(s), Pictorial

pl. plate; plural

Plan. Planning

Planet. Planetarium

Plast. Plastic

pls plates

p.m. post meridiem [after noon]

Polit. Political

Poly. Polytechnic

Polynes. Polynesian

Pop. Popular

Port. Portuguese

Port. Portfolio

Posth. Posthumous(ly)

Pott. Pottery

POW prisoner of war

PRA President of the Royal Academy

Pract. Practical

Prefect. Prefecture, Prefectural

Preserv. Preservation

prev. previous(ly)

priv. private

PRO Public Record Office

Prob. Problem(s)

Proc. Proceedings

Prod. Production

Prog. Progress

Proj. Project(s)

Promot. Promotion

Prop. Property, Properties

Prov. Province(s), Provincial

Proven. Provenance

Prt, Prts Print(s)

Prtg Printing

pseud. pseudonym

Psych. Psychiatry, Psychiatric

Psychol. Psychology, Psychological

pt part

Ptg(s) Painting(s)

Pub. Public

pubd published

Publ. Publicity

pubn(s) publication(s)

PVA polyvinyl acetate

PVC polyvinyl chloride

Q. quarterly

4to quarto

Qué. Québec (Canada)

R reprint

r *recto*

RA Royal Academician

Radnors Radnorshire (GB; old)

RAF Royal Air Force

Rec. Record(s)

red. reduction, reduced for

Ref. Reference

Refurb. Refurbishment

reg *regit* [ruled]

Reg. Regional

Relig. Religion, Religious

remod. remodelled

Ren. Renaissance

Rep. Report(s)

repr. reprint(ed); reproduced, reproduction

Represent. Representation, Representative

Res. Research

rest. restored, restoration

Retro. Retrospective

rev. revision, revised (by/for)

Rev. Reverend; Review

RHA Royal Hibernian Academician

RI Rhode Island (USA)

RIBA Royal Institute of British Architects

RJ Rio de Janeiro State

Rlwy Railway

RSA Royal Scottish Academy

RSFSR Russian Soviet Federated Socialist Republic

Rt Hon. Right Honourable

Rur. Rural

Rus. Russian

S San, Santa, Santo, Sant', São [Saint]

S. South(ern)

s. solidus, solidi [shilling(s)]

Sask. Saskatchewan (Canada)

Sat. Saturday

SC South Carolina (USA)

Scand. Scandinavian

Sch. School

Sci. Science(s), Scientific

Scot. Scottish

Sculp. Sculpture

SD	South Dakota (USA)	suppl., suppls	supplement(s), supplementary	Urb.	Urban
SE	Southeast(ern)			Urug.	Uruguayan
Sect.	Section	Surv.	Survey	US	United States
Sel.	Selected	SW	Southwest(ern)	USA	United States of America
Semin.	Seminar(s), Seminary	Swed.	Swedish	USSR	Union of Soviet Socialist Republics
Semiot.	Semiotic	Swi.	Swiss		
Semit.	Semitic	Symp.	Symposium	UT	Utah
Sept	September	Syr.	Syrian	v	verso
Ser.	Series	Tap.	Tapestry	VA	Virginia (USA)
Serb.	Serbian	Tas.	Tasmanian	V&A	Victoria and Albert Museum
Serv.	Service(s)	Tech.	Technical, Technique	Var.	Various
Sess.	Session, Sessional	Technol.	Technology	Venez.	Venezuelan
Settmt(s)	Settlement(s)	Territ.	Territory	Vern.	Vernacular
S. Glam.	South Glamorgan (GB)	Theat.	Theatre	Vict.	Victorian
Siber.	Siberian	Theol.	Theology, Theological	Vid.	Video
Sig.	Signature	Theor.	Theory, Theoretical	Viet.	Vietnamese
Sil.	Silesian	Thurs.	Thursday	viz.	videlicet [namely]
Sin.	Singhala	Tib.	Tibetan	vol., vols	volume(s)
sing.	singular	TN	Tennessee (USA)		
SJ	Societas Jesu [Society of Jesus]	Top.	Topography	vs.	versus
Skt	Sanskrit	Trad.	Tradition(s), Traditional	VT	Vermont (USA)
Slav.	Slavic, Slavonic	trans.	translation, translated by; transactions	Vulg.	Vulgarisation
Slov.	Slovene, Slovenian			W.	West(ern)
Soc.	Society	Transafr.	Transafrican	w.	width
Social.	Socialism, Socialist	Transatlant.	Transatlantic	WA	Washington (USA)
Sociol.	Sociology	Transcarpath.	Transcarpathian	Warwicks	Warwickshire (GB)
Sov.	Soviet	transcr.	transcribed by/for	Wed.	Wednesday
SP	São Paulo State	Triq.	Triquarterly	W. Glam.	West Glamorgan (GB)
Sp.	Spanish	Tropic.	Tropical	WI	Wisconsin (USA)
sq.	square	Tues.	Tuesday	Wilts	Wiltshire (GB)
sr	senior	Turk.	Turkish	Wkly	Weekly
Sri L.	Sri Lankan	Turkmen.	Turkmenistani	W. Midlands	West Midlands (GB)
SS	Saints, Santi, Santissima, Santissimo, Santissimi; Steam ship	TV	Television		
		TX	Texas (USA)	Worcs	Worcestershire (GB; old)
		U.	University	Wtrcol.	Watercolour
SSR	Soviet Socialist Republic	UK	United Kingdom of Great Britain and Northern Ireland	WV	West Virginia (USA)
St	Saint, Sankt, Sint, Szent			WY	Wyoming (USA)
Staffs	Staffordshire (GB)	Ukrain.	Ukrainian	Yb., Y.-b.	Yearbook, Year-book
Ste	Sainte	Un.	Union	Yem.	Yemeni
Stud.	Study, Studies	Underwtr	Underwater	Yorks	Yorkshire (GB; old)
Subalp.	Subalpine	UNESCO	United Nations Educational, Scientific and Cultural Organization	Yug.	Yugoslavian
Sum.	Sumerian			Zamb.	Zambian
Sun.	Sunday	Univl	Universal	Zimb.	Zimbabwean
Sup.	Superior	unpubd	unpublished		

A Note on the Use of the Dictionary

This note is intended as a short guide to the basic editorial conventions adopted in this dictionary. For a fuller explanation, please refer to the Introduction, vol. 1, pp. xiii–xx.

Abbreviations in general use in the dictionary are listed on pp. vii–xii; those used in bibliographies and for locations of works of art or exhibition venues are listed in the Appendices in vol. 33.

Alphabetization of headings, which are distinguished in bold typeface, is letter by letter up to the first comma (ignoring spaces, hyphens, accents and any parenthesized or bracketed matter); the same principle applies thereafter. Abbreviations of 'Saint' and its foreign equivalents are alphabetized as if spelt out, and headings with the prefix 'Mc' appear under 'Mac'.

Authors' signatures appear at the end of the article or sequence of articles that the authors have contributed; in multipartite articles, any section that is unsigned is by the author of the next signed section. Where the article was compiled by the editors or in the few cases where an author has wished to remain anonymous, this is indicated by a square box (□) instead of a signature.

Bibliographies are arranged chronologically (within section, where divided) by order of year of first publication and, within years, alphabetically by authors' names. Abbreviations have been used for some standard reference books; these are cited in full in Appendix C in vol. 33, as are abbreviations of periodical titles (Appendix B). Abbreviated references to alphabetically arranged dictionaries and encyclopedias appear at the beginning of the bibliography (or section).

Biographical dates when cited in parentheses in running text at the first mention of a personal name indicate that the individual does not have an entry in the dictionary. The presence of parenthesized regnal dates for rulers and popes, however, does not necessarily indicate the lack of a biography of that person. Where no dates are provided for an artist or patron, the reader may assume that there is a biography of that individual in the dictionary (or, more rarely, that the person is so obscure that dates are not readily available).

Cross-references are distinguished by the use of small capital letters, with a large capital to indicate the initial letter of the entry to which the reader is directed; for example, 'He commissioned LEONARDO DA VINCI . . .' means that the entry is alphabetized under 'L'.

E

[continued]

Egypt, ancient. [continued]

XI. Writing and books.

The hieroglyphic script, a form of picture writing, was in use in ancient Egypt for some 3000 years. All subsequent developments in Egyptian writing were based on it, including the hieratic and demotic scripts, until experiments with the use of the Greek alphabet to write the Egyptian language in the first two centuries AD led to the emergence of Coptic as the native language and script of Christian Egypt.

1. Hieroglyphs. 2. Hieratic and demotic scripts. 3. Scribes, books and literacy.

1. HIEROGLYPHS. The emergence of hieroglyphic writing seems to have taken place not long before the beginning of the Dynastic period (*c.* 2925 BC). It is generally thought that writing had been invented somewhat earlier in Mesopotamia. Egypt may have borrowed the idea of writing from there, but the hieroglyphic system was not, even in its initial rudimentary stages, a simple borrowing.

(i) Historical development and principal features. The first evidence for the writing of connected text, as opposed to mere names and short phrases, is from the 3rd–4th dynasties. Significant developments in orthographic practice can be seen between the Old Kingdom (*c.* 2575–*c.* 2150 BC) and the Middle Kingdom (*c.* 2008–*c.* 1630 BC). Thereafter the system underwent no basic or lasting change until its final extinction in the 4th century AD. The use of cryptography (the writing of such things as kings' and gods' names in a deliberately puzzling way) and the highly contrived orthography of Greco-Roman temple inscriptions (partly derived from cryptography) merely stretched the principles of hieroglyphic writing, rather than introducing new procedures.

The hieroglyphs themselves are pictures of gods, human beings, animals, aspects of the natural world, everyday objects and artefacts associated with religious cults or with kingship. Some depict only part of a being or object, such as a human arm. All obey the general principles of Egyptian art for the representation of objects in two dimensions (*see* §IV, 2 above), although they vary greatly between themselves as to how stylized a form they attain. Some are almost abstract symbols, occasionally because they represent forms of objects no longer seen in daily life; but such an explanation cannot apply, for example, to a quite unrecognizable depiction of three human toes forming one common sign. In a number of cases, it is clear that the Egyptians themselves had lost the knowledge of the origin of a sign, or had reinterpreted it. At the other extreme, the various hieroglyphs representing birds, a very conspicuous feature of the script, normally retained realistic forms, which had to be maintained in order to allow them to be distinguished one from another.

Hieroglyphic texts differ widely in the amount of detail they incorporate into the signs, and this partly depended on the writing surface and method of execution. For example, hieroglyphs on a stone stele might be incised as rough shapes filled with one or more pigments, or carved with more or less interior detailing. Texts on temple or tomb walls might be executed in the same manner as all the various styles of Egyptian relief carving and painting, such as sunk and raised relief. Jewellery and royal gold coffins of the New Kingdom (*c.* 1540–*c.* 1075 BC) often incorporated hieroglyphs formed of inlays of hardstones and glass. Some consistency has been noted in the use of colours, and, in the case of elaborately painted hieroglyphs, many signs were coloured according to the normal principles of Egyptian painting.

(ii) Functions. Various modifications have been suggested to the generally accepted view of the functions of hieroglyphs: even the most consulted account in English, that of Gardiner's *Egyptian Grammar*, was not entirely traditional. The following account is simplified and does not try to do justice to the issues of theory and of terminology. Gardiner's 'Sign list', incorporating brief discussions of the origins and uses of signs, has not been superseded in any language, and its convenient numbering system has become standard.

In general, the use of hieroglyphs may be divided into three types, traditionally referred to as ideograms, phonograms and determinatives. (Some hieroglyphs are employed in only one of these ways, but this is not true of others.) As an ideogram, a hieroglyph may be used to write a whole word, with or without the aid of other accompanying signs belonging to the two following types. The sign may straightforwardly depict the object or action signified by the word, or some looser association may have given rise to its use. Always, however, it 'writes' words, not ideas. As a phonogram, the hieroglyphic may be used to represent sounds, having a fixed value of one, two or three consonants assigned to them. In many cases, it can be seen that the phonetic value of a sign derives from the consonantal skeleton of a word for the object depicted; other cases may be more problematic. This is often described as the 'rebus' principle in the script; but writers were not normally engaged in inventing new phonetic values. The phonetic signs standing for a single consonant may be used to spell out the consonants of a word one by one, or may accompany a multiconsonantal sign, reinforcing one of its constituent consonants. These uniconsonantal signs are frequently called the hieroglyphic 'alphabet', although this term may give a false impression of their role. As determinatives, signs may be used singly or in combinations at the end of a word that is written with signs of the preceding two types, to indicate what kind of word is in question (e.g. a verb of motion or a word for a tree). Many have treated determinatives as a subclass of ideograms. The extent to which the hieroglyphic script may have been intended on occasion to provide clues as to the vowels of a word is still debated. Basically, however, the script does not directly represent vowels, but only consonants.

From the account just given, it may be realized that in theory a word might be written in a large number of ways. Generally, however, at any one period, a given word will have a limited number of correct or acceptable writings. For example, a particular multiconsonantal sign may be expected to occur in a particular word, or it may normally be written without any determinative. This and other features meant that the hieroglyphic script went some way towards permitting whole words to be recognized at one glance, although it was left to hieratic and to a greater extent demotic to develop this tendency further. The order and layout of the signs within a hieroglyphic text followed fairly strict rules, and modifications of these for the sake of appearance were made only in accordance with limited set practices. In hieroglyphic texts, however (unlike those in the derived scripts such as hieratic), there was always sufficient flexibility (including variation in the size of signs) to allow the elegant grouping of the hieroglyphs. They were wherever possible arranged in imaginary square 'blocks', each generally containing from one to four signs, and unsightly gaps (e.g. a long, low sign with an empty space left above it) were avoided.

The corpus of hieroglyphic signs underwent some changes, although in principle the script relied at any one time upon a traditional repertory of signs with an accepted range of uses. A considerable number of Old Kingdom hieroglyphs had fallen out of use by the Middle Kingdom, when only a few hundred signs were in frequent use. New signs were not created in any great numbers until the Late Period (c. 750–332 BC), although the shape of some was modified, and some signs derived from cursive hieratic forms were introduced. There was a general tendency for a common sign to take over the function of similar less common signs, and this tendency perhaps derived from hieratic practice. The many hundreds of new signs created in the Greco-Roman period (332 BC–AD 395) for temple inscriptions were mostly modifications, combinations and elaborations of traditional signs, rather than marking a significant change in the nature of the hieroglyphs.

(iii) Orientation and placement. The hieroglyphic script may be written from right to left or from left to right; a piece of text running from left to right is a precise mirror-image of the same text written from right to left. Hieratic was always written from right to left, and, perhaps for that reason, this seems to have been the norm for hieroglyphic texts when no outside factor influenced their orientation. Signs which have a natural front and back, for example human beings or animals, normally 'face' towards the beginning of the text, and so against the direction of writing. A hieroglyphic text may be arranged either in horizontal bands, or in vertical columns, which always read from top to bottom. Writing within vertical columns has just as much the possibility of 'facing' either to the left or to the right as that in horizontal bands. Except in special kinds of text, a succession of columns of writing that 'face' to the right was written in sequence from right to left, and vice versa for columns 'facing' to the left. Hieroglyphic writing in all contexts paid no attention to the separation of individual words. Punctuation was entirely unknown in inscriptions, and inscribed passages of continuous text very rarely marked even major divisions in the subject-matter. In the interests both of legibility and of appearance, straight lines drawn to separate the bands or columns of text were overwhelmingly common in hieroglyphic texts of all kinds at all periods. Hieroglyphs look so well when framed in this way that single bands or columns of text were frequently provided with a pair of framing-lines, even when there was no need to divide them from other matter.

Sections of text that are arranged in more than one of the four possible formats just described not uncommonly occur together in contexts where they are clearly intended to be seen as related to one another, or where they obviously cannot be supposed to stand in isolation. For example, they may be inscribed upon the same artefact, or together on a statue or stele. A piece of furniture may bear inscriptions, symmetrically arranged, including both horizontal bands running in each direction, and vertical columns facing each way. Symmetry, however, was only one factor governing the orientation of hieroglyphic texts. Texts that accompanied representations of human beings or of gods were arranged to 'face' the same way as the figures to which they belonged. This frequently arose in the case of texts in or alongside scenes on temple or tomb walls. In temple reliefs, the god would usually be shown to 'face' out from the innermost part of the temple, while the worshipper would be shown facing inwards, towards the god's shrine. Such considerations might influence the arrangement of inscriptions even when they were not directly accompanying any representation. The various factors governing the orientation of inscriptions have been particularly investigated in several of Fischer's publications.

(iv) Hieroglyphs and art. Although the Egyptians plainly appreciated and exploited the decorative qualities of the hieroglyphic script, this consideration goes only a short way towards explaining the almost ubiquitous presence of writing, for example in Egyptian relief, on or in association with Egyptian sculpture. Two other factors were more potent, and they are interconnected. First, it has often been pointed out that, from the earliest periods, inscription and representation were more organically linked in Egyptian art than merely as picture and 'caption', and indeed that there was no rigid demarcation between script and art. Fischer (1986) takes as his most basic illustration of this a typical Old Kingdom tomb relief in which the scene depicted may be dissected and the elements 'read' as the determinatives of the words of the hieroglyphic phrase that stands above it. Second, hieroglyphs had magical power in their own right. A standard Egyptian phrase for hieroglyphic writing (as opposed to hieratic) was 'words of god'. At some periods, hieroglyphs in inscriptions within tombs, especially those representing men or animals, were drawn or painted in an altered or incomplete form, or 'mutilated', so that they should not be able to harm the tomb owner. For example, the hieroglyph representing the horned viper might be drawn so as to show the snake neatly cut into two halves. Amulets representing hieroglyphs were extremely common, either as two-dimensional shapes, or extrapolated into three-dimensional forms; they were chiefly made of faience or hardstones. A statue of a tomb owner not only represented him, but also allowed him to come to life, to become immanent in it. The owner's name was essential to give the statue identity and to allow it to serve its purpose in the tomb. It is also clear that a magical papyrus was thought to have power in itself, and not merely when its spells were read aloud. In the later Dynastic period, miniature papyrus rolls, bearing protective magical texts (at this date written in hieratic), might be enclosed in small cylindrical cases and worn strung from the neck as amulets.

2. HIERATIC AND DEMOTIC SCRIPTS. For most of pharaonic history, until the emergence of demotic as a documentary script in the Late Period, hieratic (see fig. 77)

was the script of daily life. Scribes began by learning hieratic rather than hieroglyphs. Although it is difficult to believe that a trained scribe would have been quite unable to read hieroglyphs, he might have had little concern with writing them, unless he was, for example, involved in copying religious books written in hieroglyphs for temple use, engaged in the manufacture of copies of the Book of the Dead (a collection of funerary spells) for wealthy individuals or employed in drafting hieroglyphic texts on temple or tomb walls for subsequent carving or painting. In general it is assumed that many kinds of inscription were composed, or their texts handed down, in hieratic on papyrus, and transcribed into hieroglyphs *in situ*. This can sometimes be demonstrated by the nature of mistakes made. As already mentioned, however, certain kinds of text—by the New Kingdom, virtually only religious texts—were written on papyrus in hieroglyphs. These might be drawn in great detail or very summarily. There was also a distinctive pen-drawn style of simplified and schematized hieroglyphic writing known as 'cursive hieroglyphs'. The form of these hieroglyphs owed little to hieratic, and the orthography—the choice of signs to write a word—was not that of the hieratic script, but that proper to hieroglyphic texts.

(i) Historical development and principal features. The hieratic script was a natural development from the hieroglyphic, each hieratic sign deriving from and having the same value as a particular hieroglyph. It appears to have come into being quickly and the stages of its early development cannot be traced. The earliest evidence for hieratic from the Old Kingdom already shows a fully developed writing system. Some hieratic signs are readily recognizable as rapid versions of their hieroglyphic originals. Others were heavily simplified, or had taken on distinctive abstract shapes, which could hardly have been predicted from the form of the hieroglyphs. Although a hieratic text can be

77. Papyrus fragment, with hieratic script documenting the robbery of a royal tomb, h. 410 mm, late 20th Dynasty, *c.* 1080 BC (London, British Museum, Abbott papyrus, No. 1022. 1)

transcribed sign by sign into hieroglyphs (and this is the normal fashion in which modern scholars publish hieratic texts), separate orthographic habits were developed for hieratic, and words might be written with a different choice of signs in the two scripts. The arrangement of signs might also be different. The divergence between the two scripts increased in several stages from the Old Kingdom to the late New Kingdom. In hieratic, signs might be linked together in writing, and the resulting combined shapes or 'ligatures' could have distinctive shapes. The total repertory of signs became reduced and there grew a risk that simplified forms of signs might be confused one with another. To compensate for this, the writings of many words became 'fuller', that is, they tended to contain a greater number of signs in hieratic than in the hieroglyphic script. A word might include more phonetic signs, and might end with several determinatives rather than just one. By the late New Kingdom, hieratic had progressed far beyond the hieroglyphic script in the extent to which the eye of the reader could take in whole words as recognizable groupings.

(ii) Orientation. The earliest hieratic writing seems to have begun by being written in vertical columns, starting from the right. This may have been a natural consequence of the way in which the Egyptians chose to handle papyrus. Granted that scribes always preferred to write upon the inside surface of the roll (as writing on the outside was easily smudged in handling the roll), it may be suggested that it was simply most convenient to hold the roll in the left hand and unroll it little by little as each vertical column was written. This may be the original reason why hieratic in any format (horizontal or vertical) was always written from right to left, never from left to right. Inevitably, as soon as hieratic could be written with speed and fluency, it will have been perceived to be impracticable or a waste of time to try to acquire the skill of writing in both directions, especially as the shapes of signs came to be strongly influenced by such considerations as which hand- and finger-movements came most naturally, and how the pen most easily moved over the writing surface. Writing in horizontal lines running from right to left, and organized into separate rectangular 'pages', also proceeding from right to left along the roll, soon became the norm for literary and documentary texts, and hieratic was not usually written in vertical columns after the Middle Kingdom.

(iii) Abnormal hieratic and demotic. At the end of the New Kingdom, scribes began to develop the hieratic script into new and rapid styles. There was an exaggeration of the natural tendency of hieratic to modify the form of signs or of linked groups of signs into simpler but still distinctive shapes. The writing of whole words often had to be taken in as one recognizable group, while, in an opposite tendency, some words were spelt out by means of a revised set of uniconsonantal ('alphabetic') signs and a restricted set of determinatives. At Thebes, the relatively short-lived documentary script known as 'abnormal hieratic' was the result. A similar development is assumed to have taken place in the north of Egypt, leading under the 26th Dynasty (664–525 BC) to the emergence of demotic as the documentary script of the whole country. Demotic at most periods was capable of considerable elegance. Some early contracts were extremely handsome, being lavishly set out on large rolls, presumably reflecting the status of those who had them drawn up. At least by the 4th century BC, demotic was employed for secular literary texts. In the Roman period (30 BC–AD 395), the use of demotic for documents had become severely curtailed, both government requirements and social pressure dictating the use of Greek for most purposes. The office of professional demotic scribe had suffered a rapid decline and most writers of demotic were priests. At this period, particularly in the first two and a half centuries AD, the copying of old literary texts in demotic and the production of new ones flourished, as did the preparation of modernized demotic versions of traditional religious texts, alongside the continued use of hieratic, which was now virtually confined to religious texts. A notable exception was provided by the Late Period versions of hieratic word lists, which were not directly derived from the texts current in the New Kingdom. One of the purposes of these new texts was undoubtedly to keep alive a proper knowledge of the hieratic script.

3. SCRIBES, BOOKS AND LITERACY. There is no reason to suppose that literacy in pharaonic Egypt extended beyond a very small élite of about 1% at the most of the total population. Literacy was acquired by learning to write: there is no evidence that any Egyptians were able to read but not to write. It is clear that the highest officials received a scribal training; and there was no social class, even at court, that felt itself to be above the need to learn to write, although there are indications that successful officials would naturally have delegated writing chores to their subordinates. There is adequate evidence that kings were literate, and, as princes, attended school at court with others outside the royal family. Indeed there are references in more than one kind of text to kings writing with their own hands.

78. Scribal palette with a slot containing rush pens and two depressions for cakes of black and red pigment, wood, l. 290 mm, 18th Dynasty, *c.* 1540 BC (London, British Museum)

(i) Scribal equipment. (ii) Scribal education. (iii) Calligraphy. (iv) Libraries. (v) Books.

(i) Scribal equipment. Throughout the pharaonic period, a scribe's equipment remained simple and, above all, portable. The hieroglyph representing a scribe's kit shows the essentials: a cylindrical case to hold a few pens, a small palette (see fig. 78) bearing two cakes of pigment (one black and one red) and, in the commonest form of the sign, a pot to hold water. Already in the Old Kingdom, a longer rectangular palette was becoming standard; it was normally made of wood and had a slot to hold the pens. Artists' palettes, bearing several cakes of different pigments, were basically similar. Scribes presumably needed a sharp knife or razor to cut the papyrus and to shape the points of their pens, but no special form of scribe's knife has been identified. Evidence for pointed pieces of sandstone used as erasers and for any device for polishing the surface of papyrus is problematic.

For Egyptian scribes of all periods, the ideal writing material was the papyrus roll. The typical scribe's posture, sitting cross-legged, with the roll supported on the lap, is well known (*see* §IX, 2(i)(d) above). When making brief notes, scribes were also able to work standing. If only a very short length of papyrus was unrolled, the exposed surface had sufficient stiffness to be written on. There is no evidence for the use of any kind of writing table in pharaonic Egypt. Thus the way in which scribes worked, together with the fact that their pens had necessarily to be of a kind that would not puncture the papyrus (which normally had little firm support beneath it), must have ensured that a certain freehand fluency, rather than precise regularity or painstaking ornamentation, was the aim in hieratic writing. This remained the case as long as hieratic continued to be the script of everyday life: despite the development of various styles in many different periods, hieratic remained essentially one script until extreme cursive forms diverged from it in the Late Period.

Although the use of papyrus was in some ways basic to Egyptian writing, other writing materials were regularly employed. Leather rolls seem to have been confined to limited applications, perhaps for especially luxurious books (*see* §(v) below), and possibly for those that received very regular handling, such as the ritual books used in the temples. The evidence is slight, but does not suggest that leather was in common use, nor that it might have been regarded as a cheaper substitute for papyrus. Rectangular writing boards, made of wood and coated with a thin layer of plaster, were common (e.g. London, BM, 5601; see fig. 79). They seem often to have been used in school, perhaps because the writing could easily be expunged and the board reused an indefinite number of times. They would appear to modern eyes to have the great advantage of rigidity. They were certainly carried around to be used for lists and accounts, but tomb scenes of several periods seem to suggest that scribes recording, for example, the harvest in the fields were just as likely to do so on a papyrus roll. Conveniently sized potsherds or flakes of limestone (both now termed 'ostraca') were commonly used for a wide range of purposes, above all in schools and for brief memoranda and accounts. They would have cost nothing; several large and impressive examples are also known, for example one from Deir el-Medina, which

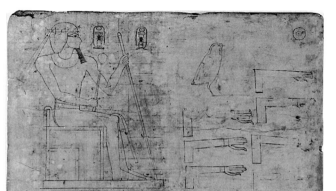

79. Writing board, bearing a representation of King Tuthmosis III (*reg c.* 1479–*c.* 1426 BC) and trial hieroglyphs of an arm and a chick, wood and gesso, h. 354 mm, 18th Dynasty (London, British Museum)

contains most of *Sinuhe*, an adventure story written in the Middle Kingdom, which later attained the status of a classic (*see* §(ii) below).

Hieratic was written with a rush pen consisting of a convenient length (*c.* 200–300 mm) of the stem of the rush *juncus acutus* (frequently referred to as *juncus maritimus*), which is commonly found growing wild in Egypt. The writing end was cut obliquely with a knife, and the fibres that form the sheath of the plant's stem were often lightly chewed to achieve a stiff but almost brush-like point. The rush normally tended to produce thick and thin strokes automatically, according to the direction of movement of the pen, but this effect could be overridden in various ways, both by twisting the pen in the fingers and by changing the angle of the hand, so that Egyptian writing rarely shows an entirely mechanical alternation of thick and thin strokes. To judge from representations of scribes at work, the Egyptian writer seems to have held his pen some 30–60 mm from its writing end, and not to have rested the heel of his hand on the writing surface. He would also use the rush pen for painting illustrations on papyrus; thus, in some respects, the use of the rush pen resembled that of the brush in Chinese calligraphy, although the rush pen was clearly not held vertically, but at an angle, normally with the thumb, first and second fingers, in a grip not unlike that most commonly adopted by modern western writers. Considerable practice must have been required before uniformly attractive results could be achieved. Although plenty of rapidly or carelessly written hieratic survives, there is no evidence to suggest that many Egyptians acquired and were satisfied with a merely rudimentary skill in writing; both the nature of the script and the character of Egyptian education must have discouraged this.

(ii) Scribal education. Many aspects of Egyptian education are poorly documented, but from the large number of surviving texts written in schools, especially texts of New Kingdom date, considerable light has been thrown on how pupils learnt to write. Students acquired writing skills by mechanically copying hieratic texts. Particular attention

seems to have been given to shaping the signs correctly and elegantly, and to setting out the work in a neat and regular fashion. There is no hint that the principles of the writing system were taught. The very nature of the script demanded that scribes had virtually to learn how each individual word ought to be written, both common words and rare or exotic words. There is some indication that both visual copying and dictation were practised.

The texts copied included traditional literary texts, chiefly wisdom texts and narratives. Numerous copies of portions of the Middle Kingdom story of *Sinuhe* survive from the New Kingdom, attesting the story's lasting role as a schoolroom classic. Traditional and systematic word lists (termed 'onomastica' in the modern literature), purporting to list the name of everything that exists, taught in the most direct fashion how words should be written. From the later New Kingdom there survive collections or 'miscellanies' of short texts suitable for school use. Some of the material included may have provided examples of types of letter or report that scribes might actually have had to write in the course of their careers. Other items may have been supposed to have an educational value, for example the texts pointing out the advantages of becoming a scribe and criticizing those who were not diligent in learning to write. Many passages, however, seem to have been included because of the rare and foreign words they contained. It would be wrong to imply that texts were chosen for copying regardless of their subject-matter, but, on the whole, New Kingdom school material suggests that usually little attention was paid to the contents. Many examples combine considerable skill in handling the pen and in forming the signs with great confusion of words and sense. It is debatable whether this would cast doubt upon or lend support to the view that learning passages by heart was an essential element of Egyptian education. Texts copied in school were by no means always written on ostraca or writing boards and discarded. Whole papyrus rolls survive, notably later New Kingdom miscellanies. If it is doubted whether these were retained out of an interest in their contents, they may perhaps have been kept to be produced as proof of scribal skill; but, in any case, some of these rolls included other material. Certainly there is little direct evidence, until perhaps the Late Period, that schoolmasters explained even the meaning of the texts they taught.

New Kingdom school copies are remarkable for the inclusion of various marks of punctuation, which had not previously been a feature of Egyptian writing. Their use does not seem to have spread to scribal practice in general, and it has been suggested that they were intended specifically to assist reciting texts in class. Some word lists of the Late Period show a different system of punctuation, which is clearly designed to bring out the structure of the lists; but this again does not appear to have found any wider employment.

(iii) Calligraphy. It is natural to ask if fine writing—calligraphy—was admired in ancient Egypt, and also whether books of any kind were prized and collected. Well-formed writing was aimed at by all, and an elegant hand was not something to which only a proportion of writers aspired. Although different styles of hieratic hand

for any one period are recognized, and such terms as 'an 18th Dynasty literary hand' or 'a late New Kingdom report hand' are used, there were not separate styles of hand intended to have greater aesthetic appeal than others. The cultivation of personal or idiosyncratic styles of writing would have been foreign to Egyptian attitudes; and scribal 'signatures' at the ends of texts or documents show no distinctive individuality. This does not imply that all the writing at any one time was mechanical or indistinguishable: modern scholars confidently identify and distinguish the hands of individual scribes among large archives of material.

Some official reports and letters of the late New Kingdom begin with a line or more of large and imposing writing, containing in the former case the date and royal titles, and in the latter the name and titles of the addressee. Presumably there was an element of status and prestige in these headings. By the end of some texts the writing often becomes considerably more rapid and careless, but such degeneration occurred gradually and cannot be taken as representing different styles of hand within one document. It is perhaps significant that nothing resembling the contrasting use of larger or more formal writing was common in earlier periods, and that literary texts do not display similar degenerative tendencies. Thus, what we now describe as calligraphy seems to have been taken for granted in ancient Egypt. The items in the school miscellanies that touch on scribal education contain little more than bald references to the need to apply oneself to writing (and also reading), preferring to expatiate on the advantages of a scribal, that is, administrative, career and the disadvantages of other callings, or on the dissipations and obstinacy of the pupil. Even the lengthy *Satirical Letter of the Scribe Hori*, which finds numerous faults with a letter received from a fellow scribe, concentrates its criticisms on the writer's powers of expression, administrative competence, experience of foreign travel and erudition.

(iv) Libraries. There are ample indications of the existence in ancient Egypt of libraries, chiefly temple libraries (Burkard). Greco-Roman period temple inscriptions even specify where within the temple the library was supposed to be located and the titles of the numerous books it was supposed to contain. Other evidence for the contents of libraries, however, is limited and questionable. Two massive finds of papyri from the Faiyum, one from Tebtunis and the other chiefly from Soknopaion Nesos, have often been supposed to represent the remains of temple libraries of the Roman period. In the case of the Tebtunis material the nature of the contents, together with the scant information about the circumstances of its discovery—which took place over a number of years—suggest that it may have chiefly constituted the property of the priests of the Tebtunis temple as individuals—or possibly in some cases of their guilds—rather than a temple library in the strict sense. From earlier periods, there are slight indications that the king himself might have had a collection of books; and several groups of papyri, known or presumed to have been found together, may have been the possessions of private individuals, although the possibility that they might have belonged to institutions cannot be ruled out entirely. Whether or not any kind of book trade existed in pharaonic

Egypt is uncertain. Some scribes appear to have copied books for their own use, and this was perhaps the commonest practice. Scribes who produced copies of books occasionally 'signed' their work, but indications of ownership as such are almost unknown. Two small faience plaques bearing a book title and, in the better preserved instance, the name of Amenophis III (*reg c.* 1390–*c.* 1353 BC) of the 18th Dynasty, are generally interpreted as royal *ex libris* book labels; but, as we have no further evidence of any kind of separate book label until the Greco-Roman period, there must remain some doubt about their purpose.

(v) Books. Books of various types—religious, magical and literary—were valued in a number of different ways for their contents. Respect was also shown for old books, and this must be seen as related to respect for the antiquity of the contents of books. Frequently the authorship or committing to writing of works was ascribed—usually, no doubt, with no justification—to famous figures of the past, or even to the god Thoth himself. A significant development was the reproduction on the walls of the burial chambers of early 18th Dynasty royal tombs (for example, that of Amenophis II (*reg c.* 1426–*c.* 1400 BC)) of funerary texts as though written upon an immense papyrus roll. The papyrus was depicted as old, being discoloured to a shade of yellow. Copies of books often included (or implied) a claim that they were totally accurate copies, although their contents frequently do not appear to substantiate this. Nevertheless, accuracy was evidently recognized as an ideal for some types of material. Examples of faithful transcription—even to the extent of noting lacunae in the exemplar—can be cited, but other instances of a cavalier approach to copying are common.

Except in the case of funerary books, it is difficult to comment on the nature, or indeed on the existence, of *éditions de luxe*. We do not know what a book owned by, for example, the king might have looked like, although we may guess that it would have been no different from the best-written and most spaciously laid-out books that have survived. That leather may have been a prestigious writing material is only a hypothesis, although its use for a copy of the Book of the Dead implies that it had a certain status. With the exception of the two possible royal book labels mentioned above, there is no evidence for any elaborate or costly accessories: no rods around which books might be rolled; no wrappers or special containers. Papyri were probably stored together in baskets or in bags with a string closure. What arrangements were made in large libraries or archives is not known. Rolls were kept closed in the same way as letters were sealed: a few papyrus fibres were freed and tied around the roll, and a small lump of mud could hold the arrangement firm and act as a sealing; it might receive a seal impression, if desired.

The most sumptuous Egyptian books known are copies of 'Books of the Dead'. In the New Kingdom, these might contain a series of elaborate painted illustrations (see figs 75 and 76 above). The quality of the best of these must surely have been admired, quite apart from their ability to emphasize the owner's status, even though their true purpose was to be shut away in the tomb to assist the deceased magically. The richness of the illustrations in this kind of material and in some magical papyri contrasts strongly with the almost total lack of painting in other kinds of books. This suggests that their magical power was a prime motive for their inclusion, even though unillustrated copies of the Book of the Dead were perfectly acceptable at some periods. It is often assumed that the elements of tomb and temple scenes were stored on papyrus in 'pattern books', but no such material has survived. Illustrated narratives seem to have been quite unknown at any period in Egypt, until they appeared in Greek papyri. Even texts of a scientific kind do not normally seem to have been illustrated. However, the Rhind Mathematical Papyrus (London, BM) contains simple and schematic drawings to accompany its geometrical problems. The text also displays considerable sophistication in the use of layout and red ink to make the contents easier to follow. One 26th Dynasty papyrus records a favourable response given to an official's request addressed to the image of the god Amun carried in procession. In addition to the textual matter, the consultation of the 'oracle' is depicted in an elaborate coloured drawing. The nature of the illustration is not surprising—at first glance it might be taken for a copy or draft of a temple-relief scene—but its appearance in a document and its depiction of the affairs of a private individual are extraordinary.

BIBLIOGRAPHY

LÄ: 'Schreiben'
H. Sottas and E. Drioton: *Introduction à l'étude des hiéroglyphes* (Paris, 1922)
A. H. Gardiner: *Egyptian Grammar* (Oxford, 1927, rev. 3/1957)
H. Brunner: *Altägyptische Erziehung* (Wiesbaden, 1957)
N. M. Davies: *Picture Writing in Ancient Egypt* (Oxford, 1958)
W. Schenkel: 'The Structure of the Hieroglyphic Script', *Royal Anthropol. Inst. News*, xv (1976), pp. 4–7
H. G. Fischer: *Egyptian Studies: The Orientation of Hieroglyphs*, i (New York, 1977)
H. Brunner, R. Kannicht and K. Schwager, eds: *Wort und Bild* (Munich, 1979)
G. Burkard: 'Bibliotheken im alten Ägypten', *Bibliothek: Forschung & Praxis*, iv (1980), pp. 79–115
M. J. Raven: *Papyrus van bies tot boekrol* (Zutphen, 1982)
J. Baines: 'Literacy and Ancient Egyptian Society', *Man*, n. s., xviii (1983), pp. 572–99
J. Baines and C. J. Eyre: 'Four Notes on Literacy', *Götting. Misz.*, lxi (1983), pp. 65–96
T. G. H. James: *Pharaoh's People: Scenes from Life in Imperial Egypt* (London, 1984)
M. L. Bierbrier, ed.: *Papyrus: Structure and Usage* (London, 1986)
H. G. Fischer: *L'Ecriture et l'art de l'Egypte ancienne* (Paris, 1986)
H. te Velde: 'Scribes and Literacy in Ancient Egypt', *Scripta Signa Vocis: Studies about Scripts, Scriptures, Scribes and Languages in the Near East, Presented to J. H. Hospers . . .*, ed. H. L. J. Vanstiphout (Groningen, 1986), pp. 253–64
W. V. Davies: *Egyptian Hieroglyphs* (London, 1987)
C. J. Eyre and J. Baines: 'Interactions between Orality and Literacy in Ancient Egypt', *Literacy and Society*, ed. K. Schousboe and M. T. Larsen (Copenhagen, 1989), pp. 91–119

W. J. TAIT

XII. Funerary equipment.

The ancient Egyptians' desire for an afterlife of pleasure, free from physical toil and danger, led them to place in their tombs objects designed to ensure the owner's resurrection and welfare in the afterlife. These included essentially functional items, such as coffins, sarcophagi and a variety of statuettes, amulets and models intended to provide assistance and protection by magical means. A considerable proportion of the funerary equipment also consisted of everyday objects, such as furniture, clothing and tools, not designed specifically for use in a funerary context (*see* §XVI below).

1. Purpose and provision. 2. Containers for the corpse and internal organs. 3. Items for sustenance and protection in the afterlife.

1. PURPOSE AND PROVISION. The funerary practices of the ancient Egyptians were motivated by their belief in man's resurrection after death. Natural phenomena, such as the daily solar cycle and the annual cycle of vegetation, were believed to symbolize rebirth after apparent death. The latter phenomenon was closely linked with the myth of the god Osiris, said to have been restored to life after being murdered by his brother Seth. At first, only kings equated themselves with Osiris, but from the Middle Kingdom (*c.* 2008–*c.* 1630 BC) onwards every Egyptian hoped for a similar rebirth by becoming identified with Osiris after death. The afterlife was envisaged either in the sky, the realm of the sun-god Re, or beneath the earth, in the kingdom of Osiris. These beliefs profoundly influenced the form and decoration of funerary equipment.

The deceased required a constant supply of sustenance and the means to avoid potential hazards in the afterlife. Food and drink were often deposited in the grave, and it was hoped that the deceased's relatives would make regular food offerings in the tomb chapel. However, since these expedients would not guarantee sustenance in perpetuity, various items were devised to satisfy this requirement by magical means; the dangers that the deceased might encounter on the passage to the next life were offset by the provision of amulets and divine figures, and by magical texts inscribed on papyri, coffins and sarcophagi.

Most of the surviving funerary equipment was made for royal personages, important state officials and members of the priesthood, and their families. Poor people normally had to be content with the simplest grave goods or none at all. Throughout the pharaonic period, particularly in the Old Kingdom, highly favoured courtiers sometimes received their tombs and funerary furniture from the king, as a reward for good service. Usually, however, the responsibility for providing the necessary equipment fell to the deceased's relatives. The larger items may sometimes have been manufactured during the owner's lifetime, but most pieces were probably made or bought during the 70-day interval between death and burial, while the corpse was being embalmed.

The design of the objects was usually dictated by current trends. The purchaser probably selected the kind of decoration he desired from a limited number of patterns before the craftsmen began work. At all periods some items, particularly coffins and *shabti*s (funerary statuettes; *see* §3(ii) below), were prefabricated in workshops and completed except for the owner's name. They were relatively cheap, and blank spaces were left in the inscriptions into which the name of the eventual owner was inserted. The finest funerary furniture was made by royal craftsmen, but most was produced locally in workshops attached to the main temples. Substantial items such as coffins were produced by teams of craftsmen; probably only the simplest pieces were made by individuals.

2. CONTAINERS FOR THE CORPSE AND INTERNAL ORGANS. One of the main prerequisites for the attainment of eternal life was the preservation of the body as an abode for the spirit. Thus the process of mummification arose. The most important items of funerary equipment, such as coffins and canopic jars, were primarily intended to protect the embalmed body and viscera from destruction. (*See also* MUMMY, EGYPTIAN.)

(i) Coffins. (ii) Sarcophagi. (iii) Mummy masks. (iv) Cartonnage mummy cases. (v) Ornamentation of the mummy wrappings. (vi) Canopic jars. (vii) Canopic chests.

(i) Coffins. The earliest wooden coffin designs were based on the forms of primitive domestic architecture and emphasized the symbolic function of the coffin as a 'house' for the spirit. Over the course of the Dynastic period there were many different coffin shapes and styles, reflecting the gradual evolution of Egyptian funerary beliefs.

(a) Predynastic period–Old Kingdom (*c.* 6000–*c.* 2150 BC). (b) First Intermediate Period–Middle Kingdom (*c.* 2150–*c.* 1630 BC). (c) Second Intermediate Period–New Kingdom (*c.* 1630–*c.* 1075 BC). (d) Third Intermediate Period (*c.* 1075–*c.* 750 BC). (e) Late Period–Roman period (*c.* 750 BC–AD 395).

(a) Predynastic period–Old Kingdom (c. 6000–c. 2150 BC). The Egyptians of the Predynastic and Early Dynastic periods (*c.* 6000–*c.* 2575 BC) buried their dead in a contracted posture (see fig. 80a), so the first wooden coffins (in the 1st and 2nd dynasties) were relatively short rectangular chests. However, with advances in mummification techniques during the 3rd and 4th dynasties (*c.* 2650–*c.* 2465 BC), it became increasingly common for the body to be laid out with extended limbs. This became the standard pattern and led to the appearance of longer coffins, designed to contain bodies buried in the full-length position.

Rectangular wooden coffins were commonly used during the Old Kingdom. They were usually made of irregularly shaped pieces of wood, dowelled together, and the simplest examples were perfectly plain. Two important decorated types were also in use. The first (2nd–6th dynasties), derived from architectural forms, is distinguished by a vaulted lid with rectangular end boards and by a form of recessed panelling on all four sides (see fig. 80b), known as 'palace façade'. The other major Old Kingdom type of coffin was smooth-sided with a flat lid. A vertical inscription ran down the centre of the lid, while around the upper inside and outside edge of the case was a horizontal band containing the 'offering formula' (a spell intended to provide the deceased with basic necessities). The coffin was traditionally positioned in the tomb with its left side towards the east, so the deceased could face the rising sun (symbolizing rebirth) and look towards the place in the tomb where funerary offerings were made to his spirit. Hence the eastern, left-hand, wall of the coffin became, symbolically, the most important part, and a pair of eyes was regularly painted on its exterior. It was believed that the deceased could look through this eye-panel into the tomb. The interior of the eastern side was also decorated: at its head was a depiction of a 'false door', intended to let the occupant's spirit pass freely in and out to receive his funerary offerings (*see* STELE, §2). A list of

80. Stylistic evolution of ancient Egyptian coffins: (a) 'house' coffin for contracted burial, Early Dynastic period, *c.* 2925–*c.* 2575 BC; (b) smooth-sided, flat-lidded coffin with eye-panel, Old Kingdom, *c.* 2575–*c.* 2150 BC; (c) rectangular coffin, Middle Kingdom, 12th Dynasty, *c.* 1938–*c.* 1756 BC; (d) anthropoid coffin, late Middle Kingdom, *c.* 1800 BC; (e) *Rishi*-coffin, Second Intermediate Period, *c.* 1630–*c.* 1540 BC; (f) anthropoid coffin with decoration on a black background, New Kingdom, 18th–19th dynasties; (g) everyday dress type, New Kingdom, 19th Dynasty, *c.* 1292–*c.* 1190 BC; (h) anthropoid coffin, Third Intermediate Period, 21st Dynasty, *c.* 1075–*c.* 950 BC; (i) cartonnage mummy-case, Third Intermediate Period, 22nd Dynasty, *c.* 950–*c.* 730 BC; (j) anthropoid inner coffin with pedestal, Late Period, 25th–26th dynasties, *c.* 750–525 BC; (k) rectangular outer coffin with vaulted lid and corner posts, Late Period–Roman period, *c.* 750 BC–AD 395; (l) anthropoid coffin, Ptolemaic period, 304–30 BC

these was also painted on the coffin interior. This type of coffin, which first appeared in the 6th Dynasty (*c.* 2325–*c.* 2150 BC), was extremely popular during later periods.

(b) First Intermediate Period–Middle Kingdom (c. 2150–c. 1630 BC). The coffins of the First Intermediate Period and the Middle Kingdom evolved from the painted and inscribed Old Kingdom type, but they display greater stylistic variation. Vertical bands of inscription referring to different deities began to appear on the exterior, together with a painted representation of a false door, at first only below the eye panel but later repeated between the vertical texts. The eye-panel remained the most important feature of the external decoration, constituting a focal point for the orientation of the inscriptions. The internal decoration also became more elaborate, and its function was closely related to that of the decoration of tomb chambers in the Old Kingdom. An offering table laden with food was usually shown, together with a standardized list of offerings and the 'object frieze', a series of painted representations of funerary gifts, often labelled with their names. Additionally, the inner walls of many coffins were inscribed in cursive hieroglyphs with religious texts designed to guarantee the deceased's well-being. This extensive body of religious literature, now known as the Coffin Texts, derives in part from the Pyramid Texts (a series of religious inscriptions inside pyramids) of the Old Kingdom, with a variety of additional spells apparently of provincial origin. Under the general heading of Coffin Texts come a number of self-contained compositions, including the *Book of Two Ways*, found only on coffins from Deir el-Bersha, which includes a map to assist the deceased in finding his way in the Underworld.

These changes in the decoration of coffins were related to developments in their religious significance. The exteriors of the earlier coffins were decorated mainly with images and inscriptions aimed at providing the deceased with material benefits such as 'a good burial' and funerary offerings; in this way the coffin fulfilled much the same role as the tomb. On later examples the vertical inscriptions on the outside and the more complex internal decoration were closely related to the rituals carried out at the funeral, which sought to bring about the rebirth of the dead person through his association with creator gods, notably Orisis and Re.

The poorer quality Middle Kingdom coffins were made of irregular pieces of native wood, their rough construction masked by a plaster coating, but those of high-ranking officials were carefully assembled from large, straight planks of imported timber, secured by mitre joints and wooden dowels. The coffins rested on four battens, to which the sides and floors were attached. The decoration was painted directly on to the finely smoothed wooden surface. Wealthy owners were buried in two rectangular wooden coffins (*see* fig. 80c), while members of the royal family usually had a sarcophagus (*see* §(ii) below) instead of an outer coffin.

The first anthropoid coffins appeared in the early Middle Kingdom. They are believed to have evolved from mummy masks made from cartonnage (layer of linen stiffened with plaster) during the First Intermediate Period. Some of the early examples were made entirely of cartonnage, while others were of wood. Both the lid and the case reproduced the appearance of the wrapped mummy in its linen bandages, wearing a mask and a bead-collar, and a single barrel-shaped bead (Egyp. *seweret*) often decorated the throat (see fig. 80d). The background could be either black or white, as on the coffin of Userhet (Cambridge, Fitzwilliam), or consisted of an elaborate reticulated pattern in several colours, as on the coffins of the brothers Khnumnakht and Nakhtankh (Manchester Mus.). Inscriptions were confined to a single column in the centre of the lid, and plain transverse bands imitating mummy bandages were also sometimes depicted. The religious function of the anthropoid coffin at this date was evidently to act as a substitute body for the spirit to inhabit in case the mummy perished and to emphasize the divine status of the deceased and his identification with Osiris.

(c) Second Intermediate Period–New Kingdom (c. 1630–c. 1075 BC). In the early Second Intermediate Period the stylistic traditions of the late 12th Dynasty were followed with little change, but perhaps from *c.* 1650 BC, a new type of rectangular coffin evolved: long and narrow with a heavily vaulted lid and polychrome external decoration on a black ground. Instead of the traditional four text columns on the long sides, there were as many as ten. The eye-panel was enclosed in a frame shaped like a pectoral, above an elaborate false door. The inscriptions and decoration were clumsily executed.

The most characteristic coffin type of the late Second Intermediate Period was a mummiform case, often carved from a single tree trunk and rather ungainly in shape. The painted decoration of the lid, representing the deceased enfolded in the protective wings of a goddess, has given rise to the term *rishi* (Arab.: 'feathered') for this type of coffin (see fig. 80e). The 'offering formula' was usually inscribed between the wings, and the deceased was adorned with the *nemes* headcloth (a royal headdress with two side lappets) and a large collar. *Rishi*-coffins were apparently developed at Thebes during the 17th Dynasty (*c.* 1630–1540 BC). Besides those made for private persons, several royal examples are known, enhanced with gold leaf and inlaid eyes, such as those of two 17th Dynasty kings, Nubkheperre Inyotef (London, BM, 6652) and Sekhemre-Upmaat Inyotef (Paris, Louvre, E.3019).

During the New Kingdom the use of precious metal for making royal funerary equipment increased. The solid gold inner coffin of Tutankhamun (Cairo, Egyp. Mus., JE 60671) exemplifies the type of equipment produced for kings during this period. The feathered motif was retained for royal coffins at least as late as Tutankhamun's reign, but for private individuals anthropoid mummy cases of a new type became popular in the early 18th Dynasty. These were constructed from planks of wood, with shallower, less rounded lids than those of earlier mummiform coffins, and deeper, flat-based cases. Only the exterior was decorated. The wig was usually of the private tripartite type and a collar was painted on the breast. The crossed hands began to be represented from about the reign of Hatshepsut (*reg c.* 1479–*c.* 1458 BC), as in Hatnefert's coffin (Cairo, Egyp. Mus., JE 66197), although on royal coffins, such as those of Ahmose-Nefertari, Ahhotpe and Queen Merytamun (Cairo, Egyp. Mus., CG 61003,

CG 61006, JE 53140), this feature appeared somewhat earlier. A prayer to the sky-goddess Nut ran down the centre of the lid and a protective deity was frequently shown above it: at first a vulture, and later Nut herself. By this time (*c.* 1500 BC) the transverse bands contained religious formulae and continued from the lid on to the case, dividing the sides into compartments (as on Middle Kingdom rectangular coffins). Indeed, when rectangular coffins declined in popularity, some of their principal decorative features, such as the eye-panel, were transferred to anthropoid coffins. Depictions of the funeral ceremonies were sometimes painted on the case, but from the middle of the 18th Dynasty the compartments were usually occupied by figures of Anubis, Thoth, the Sons of Horus and, frequently, large *wedjat*-eyes (representing the eye of the god Horus). Isis and Nephthys were represented beneath the feet and on top of the head.

These basic elements of coffin decoration remained popular throughout the New Kingdom. The external surfaces were usually more elaborately decorated as time passed and the anthropoid cases conformed more closely to the mummy's shape. The colouring of the coffins is an important dating criterion. Those of the early 18th Dynasty, down to the reign of Tuthmosis III (*reg c.* 1479–*c.* 1426 BC), were characterized by a white ground with polychrome decoration. This type was succeeded by coffins with designs primarily in yellow paint or gold leaf on a black ground (see fig. 80f).

At the end of the 18th Dynasty or the beginning of the 19th, a distinctive new colour scheme was introduced, with polychrome decoration on a yellow ground. This coincided with an increase in the richness of the decoration: the wigs became more elaborate, differing in style according to the owner's sex. Further new distinctions included the modelling of the female breasts and a difference in the representation of the hands: open for women, clenched (often grasping amulets) for men. The spaces between the inscriptions on the lid were filled with figures of deities and offering scenes. This type of coffin was the most frequent during the Ramesside period (*c.* 1292–*c.* 1075 BC).

Wealthier individuals of the 18th and 19th dynasties possessed two or three coffins. The outer cases were sometimes rectangular, either copying the Middle Kingdom type with a vaulted lid, or resembling a shrine, with a sloping roof and sledge-runners. Ostensibly, these were designed for transporting the mummy to the tomb, but examination of the specimen belonging to Yuya, father of Queen Tiye, suggests that the ensemble was actually assembled in the burial chamber.

The frequent use of mummy masks (see §(iii) below) led to the creation at about the end of the 18th Dynasty (*c.* 1300 BC) of a full-length rigid covering placed directly over the mummy. Early examples consisted of two pieces: an upper portion comprising the face mask and crossed arms, and a lower part imitating the decoration of the coffin lids, with a depiction of the sky-goddess Nut and figurative scenes in openwork, bounded by bands of inscription. During the Ramesside period these mummy-boards were also made in one piece from painted wood, sometimes representing the owner as a living individual, wearing everyday costume (see fig. 80g). A few coffin lids

were similarly decorated, and an analogous type occurs in the development of *shabti* figures (see §3(ii) below).

(d) Third Intermediate Period (c. 1075–c. 750 BC). The Third Intermediate Period was characterized by an increase in the richness of coffin decoration, with more protective emblems and symbolic allusions to beliefs about the afterlife (see fig. 80h). Nevertheless, 21st Dynasty coffins followed the basic design patterns of the Ramesside period. The external surfaces were painted primarily in red and in light and dark green on a yellow ground, and covered with an orange-yellow varnish. All the coffins were mummiform. The type wearing daily dress was abandoned and the mummy-boards began to copy the design of coffin lids closely. One or two wooden coffins and a mummy-board were provided for each individual.

The decoration of the lid, below the arms, usually comprised a horizontal zone containing a winged deity, accompanied by many figures or emblems, and an area divided vertically into rectangular compartments adorned with figures. In the early 21st Dynasty the exterior of the case often carried such traditional designs as the Sons of Horus and the figures of Thoth and Anubis, but a much wider repertory of scenes rapidly appeared. Particularly common were depictions of important mythological scenes such as the god Shu raising Nut above the earth-god Geb, episodes in the sun-god's nocturnal journey, the judgement of the dead, the cow-goddess Hathor guarding the necropolis and a tree goddess giving food to the dead. Representations of Osiris were also frequent. Texts played a relatively minor role in the decorative layouts, but the interior of the case was regularly adorned, usually with polychrome designs on a yellow or dark red ground. A large goddess or a *djed*-pillar (hieroglyphic symbol of stability) usually dominated the floor, while around this and on the internal walls were many smaller figures.

Stylistic development during the 21st Dynasty is reflected in details such as the increase in the collar's size and complexity and the multiplication of figures with outspread wings on the lid. From *c.* 1000 BC the crossed arms were normally covered by the collar so that only the hands were visible. In the late 21st Dynasty and the early 22nd there was a tendency for the floor decoration to be divided into registers, while a full-face *ba*-bird (the spirit in the form of a human-headed bird) was often shown in the area above the mummy's head. The decoration of the better quality coffins was influenced by the tomb paintings of the Ramesside period; the poorer specimens generally carried monotonous repetitions of offering scenes and deity figures.

The kings of the 21st and 22nd dynasties, together with some of their courtiers, were buried in inner coffins of solid silver. The coffin of King Psusennes I (*reg c.* 1040–*c.* 997 BC), found at Tanis, resembles the gold coffin of Tutankhamun. King Heqakheperre Shoshenq II of the 22nd Dynasty possessed a silver coffin of a new type, with a falcon's head in place of the face of the King (both Cairo, Egyp. Mus.). At the beginning of the 22nd Dynasty a range of new coffin styles for non-royal persons superseded the yellow type. Wooden coffins of simpler forms were introduced, the crossed hands and the contour of the elbows usually being omitted from the lid; the mummy-board was discontinued and the body was normally enclosed in a one-piece cartonnage mummy case (see fig. 80i).

The new decorative designs were relatively uncomplicated, with large, uncrowded vignettes and boldly drawn figures. Among the more popular of the many layouts was the horizontal and vertical division of the lid into compartments containing gods and offering scenes; solar discs, hawks (often ram-headed) and other winged deities were also common. The painting of a scarab beetle on the top of the head also typified the prominence of solar symbolism. Emblems of the god Osiris, such as the *djed*-pillar and Abydos fetish (a symbol consisting of a pole topped with a beehive-shaped object), appeared in dominant central positions, and allusions to the gods of Memphis were included, with the bark of the god Sokar and the painting of an Apis bull beneath the mummy's feet. Some coffins were very sparsely decorated, with only a single line of inscription on the lid and another around the case. The interior, sometimes completely plain, usually bore a large figure of Nut, drawn full-face with her arms outspread so that the mummy rested in the goddess' protective embrace. Several colour schemes were used, ranging from polychrome decoration on a white ground to more austere types where the decoration was painted directly on to the smoothed wooden surface.

*(e) Late Period–Roman period (*c. *750* BC–AD *395).* The typical coffins of the 25th and 26th dynasties developed gradually from those of the preceding period. A transitional phase, c. 750–680 BC, led to a new range of styles, with relatively uniform decoration. Conscious archaizing was a feature, with a revival of designs popular in the 21st Dynasty, and even much earlier motifs, such as the two eyes on the side. The coffins were usually provided in sets of two or three. The inner and intermediary coffins were anthropoid (see fig. 80j); this shape was sometimes used for the outermost case, but for high-ranking owners a rectangular outer coffin with a vaulted lid and four corner posts was used (see fig. 80k). Intermediary coffins resembled the sparsely decorated examples of the preceding period. By the early 7th century BC cartonnage cases had been superseded by wooden inner coffins, both halves of which were modelled to the mummy's shape, with a dorsal pillar and a pedestal beneath the feet.

Outer and inner mummiform coffins were covered with linen, plastered and painted in bright colours on a white or yellow ground. The decoration of the outer coffin lids consisted mainly of scenes such as the judgement of the soul and the mummy lying on a bier, alternating with columns of text in horizontal bands. A large inscription was usual on the case, while the interior was frequently decorated with the figure of the god Ptah–Sokar–Osiris. The rectangular type of outer coffin was often rich in scenes of solar mythology, as well as the usual figures of protective deities. The inner coffins received the most symbolic decoration, with a figure of Nut below the collar and, beneath this, either a series of registers dominated by scenes of the judgement, the solar bark and the mummy on a bier, or a broad central panel of inscription flanked by divinities with their recitations. A *djed*-pillar or columns

of text normally appeared on the rear, and the interior was often covered with extracts from the Book of the Dead (a collection of spells) or figures of goddesses. Many examples of this type of coffin have been found at Deir el-Bahri (e.g. Cairo, Egyp. Mus., CG 41001–72).

This style continued at Thebes into the late 26th Dynasty. After this date evidence for coffin development is poor and the material has been little studied. The fundamental characteristics of the 26th Dynasty Theban coffins occurred in other parts of Egypt, including the Memphite area and the necropolis of Akhmim. Specimens from Akhmim are distinguished by their voluminous wigs, large collars and decoration dominated by the winged Nut, the mummy on a lion-bier (a bed in the form of two elongated lions), large serpents and rows of knife-bearing divinities. The inscriptions frequently included extracts from the Pyramid Texts, as well as portions of the Book of the Dead.

Wooden coffins from the last centuries of pharaonic civilization were often crudely made. Some specimens copied the shape of anthropoid sarcophagi (see fig. 80l), but many were badly proportioned and decorated with corruptions of the traditional funerary iconography and unintelligible inscriptions. The revival of cartonnage as an inner covering for the mummy at about the end of the 26th Dynasty (525 BC) probably contributed to the decline of the wooden anthropoid coffin. Rectangular coffins, however, adorned with pseudo-Egyptian designs were used well into the Roman period.

(ii) Sarcophagi. In the Old and Middle kingdoms stone sarcophagi were mainly the prerogative of royal personages and high-ranking dignitaries. The principal stones used were limestone, alabaster and black and red granite. In their form the sarcophagi imitated contemporary wooden coffins, a custom also observed in later periods. The simplest form in the Old Kingdom was a plain rectangular chest with a flat lid, but more elaborate specimens had 'palace façade' panelling and vaulted lids. Decoration was otherwise limited to brief inscriptions and occasionally a pair of eyes on the eastern side. In the Middle Kingdom both plain and panelled sarcophagi were used, while figured decoration was sometimes carved in relief. The sarcophagi of Ashayt and Kauit, two of the wives of Nebhepetre Mentuhotpe II (*reg c.* 2008–*c.* 1957 BC), from Deir el-Bahri, which bear scenes of daily life, are excellent examples and are also unusual in being composed of limestone or alabaster blocks instead of being hewn in one piece.

During the 18th Dynasty the sarcophagi of the pharaohs developed from a flat-lidded, strictly rectangular type to a version with a vaulted lid and a chest rounded at one end like a cartouche. The sculpted decoration, at first deliberately copied from that of Middle Kingdom coffins, was developed by the addition of figures of gods and the introduction of texts from the Book of the Dead. A change in style occurred in the reign of Akhenaten (*reg c.* 1353–*c.* 1336 BC), and the sarcophagi of the later kings of the 18th Dynasty (*c.* 1332–*c.* 1292 BC) were purely rectangular, with a cavetto-cornice and figures of the four protective goddesses carved in relief at the corners.

Before the reign of Amenophis III (*reg c.* 1390–*c.* 1353 BC) all 18th Dynasty royal sarcophagi were of quartzite, but in the 19th and 20th dynasties red granite became the standard material. It also became customary for kings to have more than one sarcophagus. The fine alabaster specimen of Sethos I (*c.* 1279 BC; London, Soane Mus.; see ALABASTER, fig. 1) closely resembles a mummiform coffin, but later examples were more massive and carried an effigy of the king, carved in high relief on the lid.

Rectangular sarcophagi were also made for private individuals in the New Kingdom, but from the mid-18th Dynasty (*c.* 1450 BC) mummiform examples began to appear. The earliest, which belonged to Merymose, the viceroy of Kush (London, BM, 1001), were modelled on contemporary wooden coffins. This tendency continued in the 19th Dynasty, although mummiform sarcophagi were often roughly executed. A further innovation of the Ramessid period was the shaping of the lid into an effigy of the deceased, wearing everyday costume.

During the Third Intermediate Period the kings were buried in sarcophagi usurped from earlier owners or hewn from older monuments, while sarcophagi for private individuals were extremely rare. Between the 26th Dynasty and the Ptolemaic period, however, the production of rectangular or cartouche-shaped sarcophagi was revived. These were often massive, with vaulted or bevelled lids. The external surfaces were usually covered with vignettes and inscriptions derived from major funerary compositions. Sarcophagi belonging to the 26th Dynasty divine adoratrices (chief priestesses of Amun) had figures of the deceased carved on the lids, such as those of Nitocris (Cairo, Egyp. Mus.) and Ankhnesneferibre (London, BM).

From the 26th Dynasty a new type of anthropoid sarcophagus became fashionable, particularly in the north of Egypt. Surviving examples are made of basalt, granite, limestone and greywacke. They depict the deceased in mummy form, wearing a tripartite wig. Some specimens (mainly from Lower Egypt) were characterized by sparse decoration and broad, grotesque faces. Others display closer affinity to wooden coffins and bore representations of collars, pectorals and deities, with inscriptions in vertical columns. The chests were often undecorated, although a brief text was sometimes inscribed on the exterior.

(iii) Mummy masks. As embalming techniques developed, attempts were made to render the corpse as lifelike as possible. Particular attention was devoted to the head and, from the 6th Dynasty, the deceased's features were sometimes modelled in plaster directly over the wrappings of the face. Mummy masks subsequently became a standard part of burial equipment. The mask fulfilled the magical function of acting as a substitute for the deceased's head, in case this should be lost. It also identified him with Osiris and Re, besides endowing him with the attributes of various other deities connected with the concept of rebirth.

Masks made from cartonnage, which covered the head and shoulders and often extended as far as the waist, were introduced in the First Intermediate Period. They represent the deceased wearing a wig and collar, and they frequently include the depiction of a beard and moustache.

Such masks, often made in a crude provincial style, are particularly associated with Middle Egyptian cemeteries. They continued to be made in the 12th Dynasty, although often without facial hair. The flesh was often painted yellow and the finest specimens were gilded. Elaborate winged headdresses were represented and collars consisting of plain rows of beads were common. Examples from the Second Intermediate Period include some highly unconventional types with small faces and prominent winged decoration, possibly the precursors of the *rishi*-coffins of the 17th Dynasty.

During the 18th and 19th dynasties cartonnage masks covering the head and shoulders remained standard. Those of private persons represented the deceased wearing a divine or secular type of wig and a falcon-collar. Tutankhamun's solid gold mask (Cairo, Egyp. Mus.), inlaid with lapis lazuli, quartz, cornelian and coloured glass, illustrates the extremely high quality of royal workshop products.

In the Ramesside period masks were superseded by mummy-boards and, apart from the fine metalwork examples made for the 21st and 22nd Dynasty kings buried at Tanis (all Cairo, Egyp. Mus.), they do not appear to have been widely used again until the Late Period, when they occur with the cartonnage plaques frequently placed over the outer mummy wrappings. Cartonnage masks of the Ptolemaic period (304–30 BC) usually had gilded, idealized faces and wigs painted with religious scenes and motifs. In the Roman period Hellenistic influences led to the introduction of painted plaster masks made in moulds, with realistic features and a contemporary hairstyle. Whereas earlier masks of this type fitted over the mummy's skull, later masks showed the head in a raised position, as if resting on a pillow. During the same period gilded plaster busts of the deceased in Greco-Roman costume were also used. The finest masks, however, were the encaustic portraits on wooden panels inserted into the mummy wrappings over the face. These panels, dating from the 1st century AD to the early 4th, carry full-face or three-quarter-view portraits of the deceased in everyday dress. They are surprisingly realistic and display unusual artistic freedom, particularly in the treatment of light and shade. They are painted in coloured wax and some of them were probably executed during the owner's lifetime, displayed in the house for several decades and ultimately trimmed to a size suitable for insertion in the mummy wrappings. Most examples were found in the FAIYUM area (notably at Hawara) and although precise dates are elusive, the changing hairstyles and jewellery shown on the portraits provide useful indications. A fine example, still attached to a cartonnage mummy case, is that of Artemidorus from Hawara (early 2nd century AD; London, BM, 21810).

(iv) Cartonnage mummy cases. The use of cartonnage was at its height during the 9th and 8th centuries BC, when it was employed to make complete mummy cases. These were moulded in one piece over a disposable core and laced together with cord at the rear after the body had been inserted. The smooth plastered exterior was covered with polychrome decoration and often embellished with gold leaf. These one-piece cases may have been invented in the north of Egypt, as they are known to have been

made for kings of the early 22nd Dynasty, buried at Tanis, and are not attested at Thebes until the reign of Shoshenq I (*reg c.* 950–*c.* 929 BC). The finest examples come from Thebes and are decorated in a style similar to that of contemporary wooden coffins. Besides protective divinities and religious symbols, divine figures with outspread wings were a popular decorative motif.

The one-piece cases were superseded by wooden inner coffins in the early 7th century BC, but from about the end of the 26th Dynasty to the Ptolemaic period the outer wrappings of mummies were often adorned with a mask and several decorated plaques, all of cartonnage. These separate pieces usually included a falcon-collar (which had falcon-headed terminals), a breast cover with a Nut figure or funerary scenes, a leg covering and a foot-case. This practice apparently led to the development of a single covering with openwork decoration, which extended over the mummy's front and sides. Such covers were often gilded and are associated with separate masks, while the feet were encased in a rectangular covering, decorated on the base with figures of bound captives. Finally, complete enveloping cartonnage cases were reintroduced during the Greco-Roman period. Some of these bore crude imitations of traditional Egyptian funerary scenes and either an idealized mask or a portrait panel over the head. Others, notably from Akhmim, represented the deceased in everyday dress, with the hands stretched at the sides. These cases possess an additional interest: they were made from discarded papyrus documents.

(v) Ornamentation of the mummy wrappings. From the New Kingdom to the Ptolemaic period the mummy wrappings themselves were sometimes adorned. Sheets decorated with extracts from the Book of the Dead or painted scenes are attested in the New Kingdom, and in the 21st Dynasty a large figure of Osiris was often drawn in ink on one of the outer shrouds. From the 25th Dynasty the mummies of high-ranking officials were frequently adorned with nets of blue faience beadwork. These gradually became larger and more elaborate, and collars, pectorals and figures of deities were applied to or worked into the net. Ultimately, the net extended over the entire body and incorporated a beadwork face. In the Roman period particular care was devoted to the mummy's wrapping; the bandages were arranged in a rhomboidal pattern of many layers, with gilded studs in the intervening spaces. A gilded mask or portrait panel was usually fixed over the face. Also during this period, painted shrouds were used, decorated with Egyptian deities and a portrait of the deceased.

(vi) Canopic jars. In the 3rd Dynasty a major breakthrough in the development of mummification procedures was the introduction of the practice of eviscerating the corpse. Those organs regarded as essential for survival in the afterlife (liver, lungs, stomach and intestines) were removed from the body and separately embalmed. During most of the pharaonic period they were deposited in sets of four vases, known as canopic jars. The name derives from an erroneous association with the Greek legend of Kanopos, the pilot of Menelaos, who was supposed to have been worshipped in Egypt in the form of a human-headed jar.

The earliest jars (5th Dynasty) were limestone, often roughly modelled, with shallow convex lids. They were usually uninscribed. In the First Intermediate Period and early Middle Kingdom the visceral packages were sometimes placed directly in chests, without canopic jars. Occasionally the packages were provided with miniature cartonnage mummy masks. Probably at a slightly later date, canopic jars made entirely of cartonnage appeared, with small masks as lids. These usages reflect the prevailing custom of providing a mask or anthropoid coffin for the mummy and indicate that the canopic containers were regarded as coffins for the viscera.

By the early 12th Dynasty the typical Middle Kingdom canopic jar was firmly established. The most popular material was stone, but wood and pottery were also used. The jars, usually 350–400 mm high, were squat, with a pronounced shoulder and walls tapering sharply to the foot. All four lids were made in the shape of human heads, representing the deceased wearing a wig; the men were often bearded.

From at least the Middle Kingdom the viscera were regarded as being under the protection of four minor deities, the Sons of Horus. Each of these gods ultimately came to be identified with one of the four principal organs. Imsety protected the liver, Hapy the lungs, Duamutef the stomach and Qebehsenuf the intestines. Additional protection was provided by the goddesses Isis, Nephthys, Neith and Selkis, who in turn guarded the Sons of Horus. From about the 12th Dynasty short inscriptions relating to the function of these deities began to appear on canopic jars; occasionally their protective embrace was more graphically illustrated by the carving or painting of human arms on the sides of the jar.

Canopic jars seem to have been more rarely used between the 13th Dynasty and the beginning of the New Kingdom. Those of the 18th Dynasty were mainly limestone and alabaster, but pottery specimens (sometimes painted in imitation of stone) became more common. The jars were similar in form to those of the Middle Kingdom, with human-headed lids and the standard formulae usually inscribed in three or four vertical columns.

Important stylistic changes occurred in the 19th Dynasty. The jars, often of stone and also of faience, became taller and slimmer, lacking the pronounced shoulder of earlier examples. The lids often represented the heads of the Sons of Horus. Imsety's was human in form, while the others depicted a baboon (Hapy), a jackal (Duamutef) and a falcon (Qebehsenuf). Besides the traditional protective formulae, Ramessid jars were sometimes decorated with deities or adoration scenes.

The production of canopic jars declined during the Third Intermediate Period, since the viscera were at this time replaced in the body before burial. The packages were often accompanied by wax figures of the Sons of Horus. Either empty jars or solid, imitation jars of stone, pottery or wood were sometimes still provided, probably out of respect for tradition. From about the reign of Taharqa (*reg c.* 690–664 BC) true canopic jars with cavities were used once more, although not universally, as the viscera were often merely placed between the mummy's thighs. Jars continued to be provided in the 26th Dynasty and are attested as late as the Ptolemaic period, although

81. Canopic jars, with lids depicting the gods Hapy, Imsety, Qebehsenuf and Duamutef, limestone, h. *c.* 510 mm, from the tomb of Djedbastetefankh at Hawara, 30th Dynasty, 380–343 BC (Oxford, Ashmolean Museum)

they were used less frequently. They were often of alabaster and were relatively tall (*c.* 280–470 mm), tapering only slightly. The lids, often rather summarily carved, represented the Sons of Horus, and the jars bore texts in one to seven columns but no figured scenes (see fig. 81).

(vii) Canopic chests. In the Old Kingdom the embalmed entrails were sometimes put into rectangular chests, divided internally into four compartments. The use of chests alone recurred sporadically, but during most of the pharaonic period they served as containers for sets of canopic jars. Until the New Kingdom the canopic chests, like the jars, were regarded as the 'coffins' of the internal organs, and in their form and decoration they imitated the appearance of contemporary rectangular coffins.

The earliest chests were stone. Until the New Kingdom these were mainly the prerogative of members of the royal family, since private individuals were normally provided with wooden chests. Middle Kingdom examples were usually square, the lids flat or (in the 12th–13th dynasties) slightly vaulted with rectangular end-boards. The floor was often supported by two battens. In the 11th Dynasty canopic chests were simply decorated with borders around the edges, a single line of inscription on the lid and a broad band of text running around the sides. In the 12th Dynasty the decoration was often more elaborate, with one to three lines of inscription on the lid, and vertical texts at the corners of the chests (formulae of the Sons of Horus or protective goddesses), in addition to the horizontal bands. Other motifs included false doors, eye-panels and pictures of offerings.

In the late Second Intermediate Period a new type of canopic chest appeared, oblong rather than cubic, and relatively deep, while the sides bore representations of the

Anubis jackal as well as the usual inscriptions. These chests were subdivided internally but did not contain canopic jars. From the New Kingdom the chests no longer directly imitated coffins but were made in the shape of a square shrine with a sloping lid and cavetto-cornice. They were mounted on sledge-runners and in depictions of the funeral procession they are shown being dragged to the tomb by this means. The development of the decoration, however, paralleled that of New Kingdom coffins. Predominantly white chests were succeeded by a black type with decoration in yellow paint or gold leaf. These were followed in the 19th Dynasty by chests with polychrome paintings on a yellow ground. The decoration, which increased in complexity, consisted principally of figures of the Sons of Horus and the tutelary goddesses grouped in pairs on the sides and accompanied by their recitations.

The stone chests made for the pharaohs were more richly decorated, with goddesses sculpted in relief at the corners, their arms outspread across the sides in a protective embrace. These chests contained four cylindrical cavities covered by stoppers carved to represent the king's head. In Tutankhamun's chest (Cairo, Egyp. Mus.) the viscera were further enclosed in miniature gold coffins, inlaid with cornelian and coloured glass. The use of small coffins as canopic containers is also occasionally encountered in Middle and New Kingdom private burials.

The shrine-shaped chest survived until the early 21st Dynasty, after which none is attested until the end of the 8th century BC. Rare examples from the 25th Dynasty and the early 26th are again of the cubic shrine type, although without the cavetto-cornice and sledge-runners. The polychrome decoration included two Anubis jackals flanking a central inscription on the lid and, at the sides, the Sons of Horus receiving libations from their guardian goddesses, with appropriate texts.

The latest type of canopic chest seems to have been in use between the late 26th Dynasty and the early Ptolemaic period. It was of painted wood, again in the form of a shrine but taller than the previous types, with sloping sides and a cavetto-cornice. The lid often bore a wooden model of a falcon. Such boxes were commonly decorated with winged solar discs, friezes of symbols and various figured scenes, often including the Sons of Horus and the *djed*-pillar (symbol of stability). Two closed shrine doors, sometimes flanked by gods, frequently appeared on the front. These chests, which are sometimes (probably erroneously) described as *shabti* boxes, contained four compartments for the visceral packages, which at this period were often buried without canopic jars.

3. ITEMS FOR SUSTENANCE AND PROTECTION IN THE AFTERLIFE. As well as preserving the body by means of mummification, it was also considered essential to supply various items of equipment that would enable the deceased to play a full part in the afterlife.

(i) Servant statues, models and 'soul houses'. (ii) Funerary statuettes (*shabti*s). (iii) *Shabti* containers. (iv) Figures of deities. (v) 'Osiris-beds' and 'corn-mummies'. (vi) Funerary amulets and jewellery.

(i) Servant statues, models and 'soul houses'. To satisfy the tomb owner's need for food, drink, clothing and other comforts in the afterlife, the walls of tomb chapels of the Old and Middle kingdoms were decorated with scenes of servants producing all the essential commodities. These figures, it was believed, could be magically brought to life at the master's command and would then carry out their individual tasks. From the 4th to the 12th Dynasty, the painted and carved scenes were supplemented with, and sometimes replaced by, statuettes or models that fulfilled the same function and were iconographically related.

The statuettes of the 4th Dynasty to the early 6th represent servants performing ordinary tasks such as grinding corn or brewing beer. They are 200–450 mm in height, made of limestone and were found mainly in tombs at Giza and Saqqara. Among Egyptian stone sculptures they are unusual in representing an individual engaged in vigorous activity, often with considerable vitality.

From the end of the 6th Dynasty to the 12th, the stone statuettes were replaced by small wooden figures, plastered and painted, often crudely made and naive in appearance. The activities most frequently shown were making bread, brewing beer and butchering cattle, but ploughing and hoeing also appeared, together with spinning, weaving, carpentry and brickmaking. The figures were usually mounted in groups on a single wooden base, and different stages in the production of a commodity were often depicted simultaneously. Different activities were often represented within a single group. Model granaries were also common; here the complete building was reproduced, with walls and door, but no roof, so that the figures inside could be seen at work.

During the 9th–11th dynasties groups of soldiers were sometimes included, the finest being those from the 11th-Dynasty tomb of Mesehti at Asyut (Cairo, Egyp. Mus.; see fig. 98 below). Offering bearers, bringing food, drink and other necessities, are more common. These are

82. Female servant statue bringing offerings, wood covered with painted plaster, h. 1.23 m, from the tomb of Meketre at Thebes, 11th Dynasty, *c.* 2000 BC (Cairo, Egyptian Museum)

sometimes arranged in groups but the most frequent type represents a single female servant carrying a basket on her head and a bird in her right hand. Several examples of this type are large and excellently made (see fig. 82). These models were mainly found in tombs in Middle and Upper Egypt. The finest collection belonged to the 11th Dynasty Theban noble Meketre (now divided between Cairo, Egyp. Mus., and New York, Met.). They ceased to be produced during the 12th Dynasty, when their role was taken over by the *shabti* (*see* §(ii) below).

Painted wooden boats formed another important category of models found in Middle Kingdom tombs; these continued to be provided in the New Kingdom. Some are propelled solely by oarsmen; on others the mast is erected and the sail set. Two main types of boat model may be distinguished: the first represents the vessels used in daily life for transport and fishing (often including the figure of the owner sitting under a canopy, sometimes with attendants and soldiers), and the second consists of the funerary boats (mainly 12th Dynasty), on which the deceased's coffin or mummy may be represented, accompanied by mourners and attendants. These funerary models symbolized the ritual voyage that the deceased hoped to make to Abydos, the cult centre of Osiris.

In the Middle Kingdom the graves of the less affluent often contained a pottery model of a house, known as a 'soul house', which served as an eternal home for the owner's spirit. Food and drink were usually depicted in the forecourt to provide sustenance for the afterlife—a simpler and cheaper means of ensuring perpetual nourishment than the provision of servant statues.

*(ii) Funerary statuettes (*shabti*s).* Small human figures, generally mummiform, were an important part of the burial equipment from the Middle Kingdom to the Ptolemaic period (see fig. 83). The Egyptian name for this type of statuette varied between *shabti*, *shawabti* and *ushabti*. Although the precise interpretation of the two earlier words remains uncertain, it is clear that the figure was essentially a substitute for the deceased owner. Originally *shabti*s seem to have acted as substitutes for the mummy, but more importantly the figure was intended to take the place of the owner in performing any manual labour in the afterlife (particularly the more unpleasant tasks involved in food production). *Shabti*s thus superseded the servant statues of the Middle Kingdom by assuming their duties.

From the New Kingdom onwards the idea of the *shabti* as a mere slave became predominant (reflected in the term *ushabti*: 'answerer'). Their role is expressed in chapter 6 of the Book of the Dead, known as the '*shabti* formula': 'Oh *shabti*, if the Osiris X is called upon to do any of the work required there [in the necropolis] . . . you shall say: Here I am, I will do it.' The majority of *shabti*s were placed in tombs, but in the New Kingdom it was also customary

83. *Shabti* figures (from left to right): (a) Rensenb, painted limestone, h. 230 mm, 13th Dynasty, *c.* 1700 BC; (b) Heteti, painted limestone, h. 215 mm, New Kingdom, *c.* 1540–*c.* 1075 BC; (c) Nesitanebtasheru, faience, h. 150 mm, Third Intermediate Period, *c.* 1075–*c.* 750 BC; (d) Tjanehebu, faience, h. 195 mm, 26th Dynasty, 664–525 BC (London, British Museum)

for kings and officials to dedicate *shabti*s as votive offerings at the holy site of Abydos and in the Memphite necropolis.

The precursors of *shabti*s, in the 9th–11th dynasties, were small figures of wax or mud, crudely fashioned to represent the naked body, unmummified, with the arms stretched at the sides. Figures in the typical mummiform shape first appeared in the 12th Dynasty. This form was probably intended to express the divine qualities of the deceased, and its adoption for the *shabti* coincided with the introduction of other mummiform representations in the funerary context, such as coffins and statues. The owners were high officials, and usually only one or two figures were provided for each individual. They were made of stone, although examples in wood and faience are known. They vary in height from *c.* 100 mm to *c.* 400 mm and were generally of fine workmanship. The head was adorned with a wig. The hands, although often omitted, were sometimes crossed on the breast, and in 13th Dynasty examples they hold attributes such as vases, *ankh* symbols and sceptres or pieces of cloth. Many Middle Kingdom *shabti*s were uninscribed, but others bore the 'offering formula' or the owner's name and titles, written vertically on the front. At the end of the 12th Dynasty the '*shabti* formula' began to be inscribed on the bodies and legs of the figures.

After an hiatus, the production of *shabti*s was revived in the Theban area in the late 17th Dynasty–early 18th. Some of these were crude imitations of Middle Kingdom examples, but most characteristic of this phase were roughly carved figurines of sycamore wood, *c.* 100–200 mm high, often roughly inscribed in ink with the owner's name or the '*shabti* formula'.

In the New Kingdom *shabti*s increased in popularity. They were provided for kings as well as for private individuals, and there were significant developments in their function and iconography. Early 18th Dynasty *shabti*s resembled those of the Middle Kingdom, but a greater variety of forms soon appeared. Stone and painted wood were the usual materials, but faience and pottery became more popular; bronze figures were occasionally made for persons of very high rank.

From the mid-18th Dynasty the crossed hands were usually represented and the '*shabti* formula' was inscribed horizontally around the legs. But the most important innovation was the representation of agricultural tools with which the *shabti* was supposed to perform its tasks in the afterlife. At first, model implements were buried with the figures, but at least from the reign of Tuthmosis IV (*reg c.* 1400–*c.* 1390 BC) two hoes were represented, held in the hands, while one or two grain baskets were often depicted on the back, suspended on cords over the shoulders.

*Shabti*s continued to be produced during the Amarna period (*c.* 1353–*c.* 1332 BC), despite the absence of a clearly defined role for them in the new solar religion promoted by Akhenaten. Many *shabti*s made for Akhenaten survive, together with a few that belonged to his contemporaries. They are conventional in form, but their inscriptions are purged of references to the orthodox religion. One legacy of this phase was the appearance, in the late 18th Dynasty, of more richly detailed *shabti*s, often with large, elaborate wigs of the kind worn in daily life. Collars were usually

depicted and some *shabti*s had imitations of mummy bandages and even a pectoral ornament, figure of the goddess Nut, or other symbolic device on the breast. At the height of the New Kingdom some unusual forms were created, such as the double *shabti* (often consisting of figures of a husband and wife), the corn-grinding *shabti* and the *shabti* lying on a lion-bier, of which the wooden specimen from Tutankhamun's tomb is the finest (Cairo, Egyp. Mus.).

In the Ramesside period (*c.* 1292–*c.* 1075 BC) there was a marked increase in the number of *shabti* figures owned by one person. The better quality *shabti*s, of stone and painted wood, were usually large, with polychrome decoration on a yellow or white ground. The iconography was basically the same as that of the 18th Dynasty *shabti*s, with crossed arms, hoes, grain baskets and the '*shabti* formula'. However, at the end of the 18th Dynasty or the beginning of the 19th, a new type appeared, showing the deceased in everyday dress, with a fashionable wig and a pleated kilt with a large apron. The crossed hands of these figures sometimes grasp amulets instead of hoes, or they may embrace a *ba*-bird, sculpted in relief on the breast. Some were of high quality. Much smaller *shabti*s were produced in large quantities for persons of moderate means. These were mainly of painted pottery or faience, often crudely modelled. The faience examples often have a white ground, with details in red and a short inscription (usually the owner's name and titles preceded by an introductory formula) in black or blue.

The increase in the number of *shabti*s at this time led to an artificial organization of the figures into gangs of ten, each controlled by an overseer. The *shabti* overseers wore everyday dress, like some 'worker' *shabti*s of the late 18th Dynasty–early 19th, but they are distinguishable by the position of their arms (one at the side, the other flexed across the breast) and by the whips they carry. The number of figures for each burial seems to have varied in the Ramessid period, but by the 21st Dynasty (*c.* 1075–*c.* 950 BC) the ideal requirement was 365 'worker' *shabti*s (one for each day of the year), with 36 overseers to control them.

Blue-glazed faience and pottery *shabti*s became the standard type throughout Egypt in the 21st Dynasty. Hundreds of examples belonging to the priests of Amun have been discovered at Deir el-Bahri; the 21st Dynasty kings buried at Tanis also possessed figures of this type. These *shabti*s (*c.* 80–170 mm high) were mostly of mediocre workmanship, roughly modelled, with large heads, squat bodies, prominent feet and often flat backs. The figures wore tripartite wigs, which, from the mid-21st Dynasty, were encircled by a fillet and tied at the back. The face was usually beardless. The crossed hands grasped hoes and a grain basket was often carried on the back. These statuettes were sometimes inscribed with the '*shabti* formula' but usually carried only the owner's name and titles written vertically below the hands. Overseer figures were still recognizable by their dress, posture and whips.

Similar forms were current in the 22nd Dynasty (*c.* 950–*c.* 730 BC), although the glazed faience was often green. During this period *shabti*s were usually small and of poor quality. Those of the 25th Dynasty royal family show signs of the revival of older traditions, most notably under Taharqa (*reg* 690–664 BC), whose tomb at Nuri yielded large *shabti*s in hard stones (granite, serpentine and alabaster). These display stylistic affinities with examples of the Middle and New Kingdoms. The most influential Theban officials of the late 25th Dynasty–early 26th also possessed *shabti*s of this kind. However, the development was short-lived and these were the last *shabti*s to be made of stone.

From the beginning of the 26th Dynasty (664–525 BC) to the late Ptolemaic period (*c.* 1st century BC) *shabti*s were characterized by an unprecedented stylistic uniformity. There was only one basic design, with no differentiation between overseer and worker (although the distinction was perhaps not forgotten). The figures were of green or blue faience; other colours are probably the result of decay or patination. The body was slender and rested against a dorsal pillar, while a rectangular base supported the feet. The tripartite wig had no fillet and the face, usually bearded, was smiling. The hands grasped a hoe and mattock and a basket was carried over the shoulder. In the 26th Dynasty the inscription consisted either of the '*shabti* formula' in horizontal lines on the legs or the owner's name and title incised in a vertical column.

This latest type was provided both for kings and private individuals. The majority of known specimens were made for men and derive from cemeteries in northern Egypt. The finest examples date to the reigns of Psammetichus II, Apries and Amasis (595–526 BC). After the 26th Dynasty, *shabti*s declined in quality. Among the few stylistic innovations of the subsequent period were the disposition of the text in two framed lines arranged in a T-shape (from the mid-5th century BC) and the incrustation of the inscription in deep blue on a light blue or green ground. Otherwise, the *shabti*s of the 29th–30th dynasties and the Ptolemaic period were inferior imitations of those of the 26th Dynasty, with crudely fashioned faces and inscriptions filled with errors.

(iii) Shabti *containers.* The *shabti*s of the Middle Kingdom and the wax and mud figures that preceded them were placed in small wooden replicas of the contemporary rectangular coffins, complete with eye-panels and inscriptions. This custom continued into the 13th Dynasty. The crude wooden *shabti*s of the 17th Dynasty and the early 18th were provided with miniature wooden or mud coffins, mostly rectangular, but sometimes anthropoid. During the first half of the 18th Dynasty, models of mummiform coffins were often used. The finest examples faithfully reproduce the decoration, colouring and inscriptions of full-size coffins.

From the mid-18th Dynasty special *shabti* boxes were introduced, usually of painted wood, which gradually superseded the miniature coffins. The first major type was the tall, shrine-shaped box (*c.* 300–430 mm high), with upstanding ends and, normally, a vaulted lid. This type evolved during the 19th and 20th dynasties to a box in the form of two, three or four such shrines joined side by side, with multiple cavities. These boxes were mounted on flat or sledge-shaped bases and were variously decorated. The earlier specimens (of the 18th Dynasty–early 19th) had simple 'palace façade' designs, lines of inscription and sometimes mummiform figures, while the boxes of the Ramessid period display an increase in figural scenes (usually polychrome, sometimes yellow on black ground)

84. *Shabti* box of Khabekhnet and Ese, painted wood, h. 300 mm, 19th Dynasty, *c.* 1250 BC (Paris, Musée du Louvre)

showing the deceased seated with his wife (see fig. 84) or in the presence of various deities. These boxes increased in size as the number of *shabti*s gradually rose. The double and triple shrine types continued in use into the 21st Dynasty, although the internal division into compartments was by then abandoned. Contemporaneous with these, in the 21st Dynasty, were simpler rectangular boxes, their ends slightly rounded at the top. They had two or three flat lids and were painted white, with a panel of inscription and, occasionally, figural scenes. The same form, sometimes painted black, was used in the early 22nd Dynasty.

Two other types of *shabti* box can be assigned to the Third Intermediate Period. The first was rectangular, with a single lid and square or rounded end boards; the latter variety usually had one or two boats painted on the lid, and on the box vertical or horizontal texts, sometimes with a figural scene. These boxes were particularly characteristic of the 25th Dynasty. Those of the second type, of approximately the same date, resembled the sarcophagus-shaped coffins used at the time, with a vaulted top and four corner posts.

After the early 26th Dynasty, *shabti* boxes were used less frequently, the figures heaped up or arranged in rows in the tomb. The tall, shrine-shaped chests of the post-Saite and Ptolemaic periods, sometimes described as *shabti* boxes, appear in fact to have been canopic chests. No other type of container designed specifically for *shabti*s can be attributed to this period.

A third category of *shabti* receptacle, the *shabti* jar, dates to the 19th and 20th dynasties. These pottery vessels with lids in the form of the heads of the Sons of Horus bore some resemblance to canopic jars. They normally contained between six and twelve figures and seem to have been most common in the cemeteries of Abydos.

(iv) Figures of deities. Wooden statuettes of divinities frequently formed part of royal and private burial equipment from the New Kingdom onwards. Most were protective in function, such as the figures of genii from New Kingdom royal tombs, and those of the Sons of Horus and Isis and Nephthys, found in some private burials of the 22nd Dynasty and the Late Period respectively. Others were probably designed to contain rolled funerary papyri (*see* §X, 4 above), concealed in a cavity within the figure's body. This function was perhaps fulfilled by the life-size 'guardian' statues of kings, found in several New Kingdom royal tombs, including that of Tutankhamun.

The most important type of divine funerary figure was the wooden mummiform statuette of a god with the attributes of Osiris, common in private burials from the New Kingdom to the Ptolemaic period. These figures fall into two groups: statuettes of Osiris and figures of the syncretistic deity Ptah–Sokar–Osiris.

The earliest examples of statuettes of Osiris, designed to hold a funerary papyrus, were squat figures, holding sceptres in their crossed hands. The god wears the *atef*-crown, with his face coloured green and the rest of the decoration polychrome. These figures were hollow; they were usually made in two halves, although in some cases a separate container for the papyrus was attached to the back. They appeared about the beginning of the 19th Dynasty and were succeeded by a similar black-varnished type, dating to the late 21st Dynasty and the early 22nd. Probably partly contemporary with these were solid black-varnished figures, of slimmer proportions, with a tripartite wig and ostrich feather crown. These statuettes, usually without hands, are attested in burials of the early 22nd Dynasty, but *c.* 900–*c.* 750 BC the figures apparently ceased to be made, a circumstance probably connected with the disappearance of large funerary papyri.

The second group of statues, representing Ptah–Sokar–Osiris, symbolized the deceased's hopes of resurrection. Most contained a miniature 'corn-mummy' (*see* §(v) below), rather than a papyrus. There was usually, therefore, a cavity either in the figure itself or in the base. The figures, generally without hands, represented the god wearing a blue wig, surmounted by an ostrich feather crown with sun-disc and ram's horns. The body was supported by an inscribed back-pillar and the cavity in the rectangular base was covered by a model falcon (probably representing the god Sokar) or, in the Ptolemaic period, a miniature sarcophagus (representing the tomb of Osiris).

These statues were perhaps introduced in the early 7th century BC. The first examples (in the 25th and 26th dynasties) were tall and slender, with green faces and red bodies, often decorated with blue cross-hatching imitating a bead net. Inscriptions appeared on the front and on the dorsal pillar. Later examples were generally larger, with clumsily proportioned bodies and large collars. The faces, although usually gilded, were sometimes painted white or yellow and most specimens were inscribed with a hymn to Ptah–Sokar–Osiris on the front.

(v) 'Osiris-beds' and 'corn-mummies'. Like the Ptah–Sokar–Osiris figures, these objects were symbolic of resurrection. The 'Osiris-bed', found in several tombs in the Valley of the Kings, consisted of a two-dimensional image of the god, either drawn in ink on linen stretched over a wooden frame or hollowed out of a piece of wood, the cavity filled with earth. Shortly before the burial, barley was sown on the cloth or in the wooden silhouette. This seed, sprouting from the god of the dead, was a potent symbol of the rebirth for which the deceased hoped.

The same basic concept led to the creation, during the Ptolemaic period, of small images of Osiris (*c.* 350–500 mm long) made of earth mixed with grains of corn and wrapped to resemble a miniature mummy. The image itself, often ithyphallic, was provided with a wax mask, representing Osiris's face and headdress. It was placed in a small wooden coffin with the head of a falcon. This probably represented Sokar but has often given rise to the erroneous belief that the objects in question are 'falcon-mummies'. The cases were sometimes painted with motifs derived from the decoration of full-size coffins. Such 'corn-mummies' were probably associated with the Osirian mysteries and buried together in pits, rather than in tombs.

(vi) Funerary amulets and jewellery. The placing of amulets on the mummy was a popular method of providing magical protection for the deceased (*see* §XVI, 1 below). The amulets were mainly stone or faience, and whereas some (such as the hieroglyphic symbols of life, protection and stability) fulfilled a general protective function, others played a more specific role and were inscribed with an appropriate magical text. The most important of these was the 'heart scarab', a large representation of a SCARAB beetle carved from dark stone and placed on the mummy's breast. This amulet, common from the Second Intermediate Period, was inscribed with chapter 30b of the Book of the Dead, intended to prevent the heart from disclosing any of the deceased's earthly misdemeanours during the final judgement. Among the most popular amulets of the Late Period and Ptolemaic period were small protective images of deities and the hypocephalus—a disc, usually of cartonnage, which was placed under the mummy's head. Its purpose was to keep the mummy warm, and it bore figures of deities drawn in ink, together with the relevant text from the Book of the Dead.

The numerous items of jewellery that adorned the mummies of wealthy individuals often had amuletic significance. Among the metalwork accoutrements of the mummy were gold sandals and protective casings for fingers and toes. But the most important classes of funerary jewellery were collars of various forms (notably the falcon-collar with hawk-headed terminals) and the pectorals, the design of which often incorporated a scarab beetle. For further detail *see* §XIV below.

BIBLIOGRAPHY

GENERAL

E. A. W. Budge: *The Mummy* (Cambridge, 1894, rev. 2/1925)

J. Garstang: *The Burial Customs of Ancient Egypt* (London, 1907)

H. Carter and G. Herbert, 5th Earl of Carnarvon: *Five Years of Explorations at Thebes: A Record of Work Done, 1907–1911* (London, 1912)

A. C. Mace and H. E. Winlock: *The Tomb of Senebtisi at Lisht* (New York, 1916)

H. Carter and A. C. Mace: *The Tomb of Tut.ankh.Amen*, 3 vols (London, 1923–33)

H. E. Winlock: *Excavations at Deir el-Bahri, 1911–31* (New York, 1942)

P. Montet: *La Nécropole royale de Tanis*, 3 vols (Paris, 1947–60)

H. Bonnet: *Reallexikon der ägyptischen Religionsgeschichte* (Berlin, 1952)

W. C. Hayes: *The Scepter of Egypt*, 2 vols (New York, 1953–9)

E. Bresciani, S. Pernigotti and M. P. Giangeri Silvis: *La tomba di Ciennehebu, capo della flotta del ré* (Pisa, 1977)

A. J. Spencer: *Death in Ancient Egypt* (Harmondsworth, 1982)

D. A. Aston: *Tomb Groups from the End of the New Kingdom to the Beginning of the Saite Period* (diss., U. Birmingham, 1987)

A. M. Donadoni Roveri, ed.: *Egyptian Civilization, Religious Beliefs* (Milan and Turin, 1988)

Mummies and Magic: The Funerary Arts of Ancient Egypt (exh. cat., Boston, MA, Mus. F.A., 1988)

COFFINS AND MUMMY MASKS

LÄ: 'Särge'

P. Lacau: *Sarcophages antérieurs au nouvel Empire*, 2 vols (Cairo, 1904–6)

E. Chassinat: *La Seconde Trouvaille de Deir el-Bahari (sarcophages)*, i (Cairo, 1909)

G. Daressy: *Cercueils des cachettes royales* (Cairo, 1909)

H. Gauthier: *Cercueils anthropoïdes des prêtres de Montou* (Cairo, 1913)

A. Moret: *Sarcophages de l'époque bubastite à l'époque saïte* (Cairo, 1913)

V. Schmidt: *Sarkofager, mumiekister, og mumiehylstre i det gamle Aegypten: Typologisk atlas* [Sarcophagi, mummy-cases and mummy-trappings in ancient Egypt: typological atlas] (Copenhagen, 1919)

A. F. Shore: *Portrait Painting from Roman Egypt* (London, 1962, rev. 2/1972)

G. Grimm: *Die römischen Mumienmasken aus Ägypten* (Wiesbaden, 1974)

J. H. Taylor: *The Development of Theban Coffins during the Third Intermediate Period: A Typological Study* (diss., U. Birmingham, 1985)

A. Niwinski: *21st Dynasty Coffins from Thebes: Chronological and Typological Studies* (Mainz, 1988)

H. Willems: *Chests of Life* (Leiden, 1988)

J. H. Taylor: *Egyptian Coffins* (Aylesbury, 1989)

SARCOPHAGI

LÄ: 'Sarkophag'

G. Maspero: *Sarcophages des époques persane et ptolemaïque*, 2 vols (Cairo, 1914–39)

W. C. Hayes: *Royal Sarcophagi of the XVIII Dynasty* (Princeton, 1935)

M.-L. Buhl: *The Late Egyptian Anthropoid Stone Sarcophagi* (Copenhagen, 1959)

B. Lüscher: *Untersuchungen zu ägyptischen Kanopenkästen, vom alten Reich bis zum Ende der zweiten Zwischenzeit*, (Hildesheim, 1990)

CANOPIC EQUIPMENT

LÄ: 'Kanopen'

G. A. Reisner: *Canopics* (Cairo, 1967)

E. Brovarski: *Canopic Jars*, Boston, MA, Mus. F.A. cat. (Mainz, 1978)

C. Dolzani: *Vasi canopi, N. 19001–19153*, Turin, Mus. Egizio (Milan, 1982)

FUNERARY STATUETTES

LÄ: 'Uschebti'

B. Turaeff: *The Boxes for Egyptian Funerary Figurines: The So-called 'Ushabti'* (Moscow, 1914)

P. E. Newberry: *Funerary Statuettes and Model Sarcophagi*, 2 fasc. (Cairo, 1930–37)

W. M. F. Petrie: *Shabtis* (London, 1935)

J.-F. Aubert and L. Aubert: *Statuettes égyptiennes: Chaouabtis, ouchebtis* (Paris, 1974)

H. D. Schneider: *Shabtis*, 3 vols (Leiden, 1977)

B. Peeters: *De Oesjebtikist in het Nieuwe Rijk* [The *shabti* box in the New Kingdom] (Leuven, 1983)

DIVINE FIGURES

M. J. Raven: 'Papyrus-sheaths and Ptah–Sokar–Osiris Statues', *Oudhdknd. Meded. Rijksmus. Ouden Leiden*, lix–lx (1978–9), pp. 251–96

C. N. Reeves: 'Tutankhamun and his Papyri', *Götting. Misz.*, lxxxviii (1985), pp. 39–45

J. H. TAYLOR

XIII. Ceramics.

All Egyptian pottery vessels share one characteristic: in shape and surface appearance they clearly show the properties of the clay from which they are made. As in other cultures, Egyptian pots may occasionally imitate other materials, such as stone, metal or organic matter, but this imitation was never carried so far that the ceramic nature of the vessels was obscured. Above all, the pottery of ancient Egypt was true to its material.

1. Clay types. 2. Technical processes. 3. Shapes. 4. Decoration.

1. CLAY TYPES. The two basic types of fabric used in Egyptian pottery are Nile clay, from the alluvial sediments of the River Nile, and marl clay, from various beds of calciferous shales and mudstones in the mountains and high desert terraces bordering the Nile Valley. Almost all Egyptian pottery is of the type called 'coarse earthenware'. Only a few of the marl clay wares approach 'stoneware'. Egyptian pottery therefore has a decidedly rustic quality. This rusticity is not accompanied by any of the tendencies to playful embellishment commonly found in the ceramics of agricultural societies.

(i) Nile clay. Egyptian ceramics made with Nile clay fabrics are particularly porous and soft; they constitute roughly two thirds of all pottery used in ancient Egypt. When used for short-term storage (e.g. beer jars) or tableware, such pots have a welcome cooling effect due to their permeability to liquids. The fact that Nile clay pots also broke rather easily did not deter the users, since very low prices were paid for these objects.

The surface colour of Egyptian pots of Nile clay ranges from warm reddish-brown to light brown. It is often intensified by a wash of red ochre as in the case of the Maidum bowl (see fig. 87 below). The red or brown of the clay is due firstly to the presence of finely disseminated iron hydroxides and secondly to the firing of the pots in an oxidizing atmosphere at temperatures between 700° and 800° C. Control of the firing atmosphere was not sufficiently precise to ensure an even colour throughout the thickness of the walls: black, grey, red and variously coloured core zones are common. Non-plastic inclusions consist of sand, mica, rock particles (mainly of Upper Nilotic origin) and organic matter in a wide range of sizes. In the fine Nile fabrics the remains of organic particles are so thin that scholars have argued for a temper of dung. In the coarse variants, the organic temper consists mainly of chaff, while in the medium fine fabrics a large variety of organic tempering materials has been identified.

(ii) Marl clay. For long-term storage and long-distance transportation, the Egyptians used pots made from marl clays. It was only in the 1st millennium BC that potters in Egypt discovered the existence of other alternative clays. Some of these other clay materials, used in the Late Period (*c.* 750–332 BC) and afterwards, seem to have belonged to the kaolin group. The material (calciferous shales and mudstones) from which marl clay was derived was deposited in the desert terraces by pre-Nile rivers or washed

down by Pleistocene wadi torrents from the limestone formations. Consequently, many marl clays are naturally mixed with sand and even alluvial clay from the late Pleistocene Nile. Observations in modern Egyptian workshops also show that potters sometimes mix marl with Nile clay. In fired pottery, therefore, many of the fabrics called 'marl clay' are actually mixtures of marl and Nile clay. But, since the presence of the marly substances gives the fabrics here called 'marl clay' their characteristic properties, the term can be accepted. The subdivisions of the marl clay group, however, to some degree may be caused by an addition—naturally or by human hand—of Nile clay.

All fabrics of marl clay character show a higher percentage of calcium carbonate than Nile clay fabrics. Silica content is somewhat lower in the marl fabrics. Iron oxides are present, so is mica, but again in lesser quantities. All marl clay pots are harder than those of Nile clay, and their fabrics are considerably denser. Their permeability for liquid is lower, and marl clay vessels do not break as easily as those of Nile clay. Sherds of marl clay pots make up only about a tenth of all pottery found in excavations, although the percentage of marl clay pots that were actually in use at a given time can be estimated at roughly a third.

The surface appearance of marl clay pots is significantly different from that of Nile clay vessels. Marl clay pots show a pale yellow or pinkish-white surface colour occasionally with a reddish or greenish tint. This surface zone is not the result of a slip, but forms naturally on the outside of marl clay pots during the firing process. Ceramological studies have shown that salt particles migrating to the surface seem to contribute to this phenomenon.

The wall fractures beneath the surface zone of marl clay pots are either pink, light red or pale brown, but they can also be of the same greenish-yellow colour as the surface. The colour range of the wall thickness is to some degree dependent on the firing temperature: reddish colours result at c. 850° C, pale yellow to greenish-white colours are found in wares fired up to 1100° C. In overview, however, while colour variations within a certain range may be more or less accidental, each locally identifiable Egyptian marl fabric exhibits a specific wall fracture colour. It is uncertain whether this occurs because a local pottery workshop consistently used the same range of firing temperatures (i.e. the same kiln constructions) or because potters knew and exploited the fact that certain clays taken from local beds reached their peak quality at certain temperatures.

Archaeologists have distinguished five groups of marl clay fabrics. One group was certainly of Upper Egyptian origin. All its fabrics are characterized by homogeneity of both the groundmass and the density, and the presence of elongated pores usually arranged parallel to the vessel surface. Some, but not all, fabrics of this group have been fired at temperatures of around 1100° C; fracture colour therefore varies. One distinctive fabric is always greenish-yellow throughout the vessel wall, another shows a pink to pale brown fracture. Sand and limestone admixtures also vary. In one variant the limestone particles are angular: this is certainly an instance of crushed limestone used as temper. This particular fabric was used for prehistoric 'Decorated ware'.

A second group of marl clay fabrics was used in pottery workshops of the region between Memphis and the Faiyum. In this group fractures always show a reddish colour beneath the grey or yellow surface zone. Inclusions of partly decomposed limestone and semi-vitrified ochre are diagnostic of these fabrics. The geographical origins of the remaining three groups of marl clay fabrics, including a group of very gritty fabrics especially common in the Second Intermediate Period and early New Kingdom, and a large group of sand and limestone tempered marl used for New Kingdom storage vessels, have not yet been determined.

2. TECHNICAL PROCESSES. The methods of manufacture of Egyptian pottery span the whole range of technological possibilities from the simplest hand modelling through many varieties of turning devices and simple wheel techniques to the composite wheel (kick wheel) of the 1st millennium BC. This large range of technological methods did not constitute a progressive development in which each new invention was adopted to the exclusion of existing methods. On the contrary, the ceramic history of Egypt presents a picture of gradual enrichment in the technologies available (see fig. 85 below). At the end, in the Roman period, almost all the methods invented were simultaneously in use.

Pottery workshops have only recently begun to be recognized in excavations and have not yet been thoroughly studied. Such workshops seem to have been simple, ephemeral structures. More elaborate installations had a series of rooms or enclosed spaces for preparing the clay, shaping the pots, drying and decorating them. For the shaping and drying process the rooms must have had roofs of reed matting or wood to provide shadow. Tools were usually very simple: there was a heap of round pebbles for burnishing; discs on which pots could be moved while still wet; pieces of string or wire for the removal of pots from the wheel or 'hump'; vessels containing water or lubricant; and a flat instrument (possibly of wood) used to fashion the outside bottoms of pots.

Kilns were all built of mud-brick that, through use, became baked brick. They can be divided into three main types: simple chimney kilns, two-storey kilns and the characteristic Egyptian kilns with flaring walls. The chimney kilns were probably mainly used in the local manufacture of Nile clay pottery. They had a fire hole at the bottom which was closed by a door. It is not known whether this type of kiln had a separate loading chamber. Chimney kilns were always loaded from the top, which was then covered by potsherds or pieces of wood or bark during firing. Two-storey kilns were round and considerably larger than chimney kilns. The lower chamber was for the fire, the upper chamber for loading. The loading again took place from the top, which was then covered. The lower chamber was broader in circumference than the upper. The typically Egyptian kiln with flaring walls had a round, oval or horse-shoe shaped ground-plan. A representation of this kiln (the earliest of which dates to the 5th Dynasty) was used in the hieroglyphic script to designate the words 'to be hot' and 'kiln'. These kilns may have been the ones that produced the temperatures above 1000° C used to fire some marl clay wares. All kilns of this category had two chambers, and many had a firing channel in front of the firing hole. Some may have had separate loading windows. Late Period kilns were roofed by a brick dome. They were loaded from a window and were in other respects similar to two-storey kilns.

The typical kilns, as well as some chimney and two-storey types, were erected in a depression in the ground with the walls supported against the sides of the depression. In front of the firing hole was an area, also on low ground, where the potter sat to control the fire and add more firing material when necessary. The face of the kiln, around and above the firing hole, could be reinforced by brick walls or a row of horizontally arranged sticks. New pots removed from the kiln were placed in general storehouses from which they were distributed to the users. In prehistoric times, and locally in primitive household pottery workshops, pit-firing was surely also used. Evidence for such firing can be seen in the black stains of 5th-millennium BC and very simple later pottery.

Potters were considered among the lowest of Egyptian craftsmen. In texts the potters' work is repeatedly described as dirty and disagreeable. In Deir el-Medina, the New Kingdom Theban village of artisans who prepared the royal tombs, potters were far below painters and builders, at the same level as gardeners, woodcutters and fishermen. Nevertheless, one Middle Kingdom source uses a word for a potter that approaches 'artist' in meaning ('the one who creates life', or 'makes alive'), and the creator-gods Khnum and Ptah are depicted as potters shaping human beings on the wheel. The names of some master potters, such as Amak, Ahawte and Menna, have been preserved.

The custom of shifting workshop personnel from place to place, as work demanded, played an important role in the history of ceramics. While the master–apprentice relationship (surely often a father and son) guaranteed a continuity of tradition in technology and style, the movement of personnel ensured the dissemination of newly found methods and ideas. The widespread distribution of actual pots throughout the country, which resulted from the distribution economy of the centralized Egyptian state, had a comparable effect. All these factors created a uniformity of style during those phases of Egyptian history in which the centralized economy was firmly established. At times of lesser economic cohesion, this exchange of goods and personnel functioned only in circumscribed regions, so that technological and stylistic unity broke down and each region started to develop its own style. The resulting diversity of ceramic styles usually lasted considerably longer than the period of economic and political disunity; this phenomenon can be seen in crafts directly serving simple utilitarian purposes.

3. SHAPES. The simplicity of Egyptian pottery and the customary concentration of ceramologists on vessel typology sometimes obscure the fact that Egyptian potters were masters of the art of conceiving shape. Nine different phases can be distinguished (see fig. 85).

(i) Phases 1 and 2 (c. 4500–c. 2600 BC). During the first phase, from the 5th millennium BC to Naqada I, potters

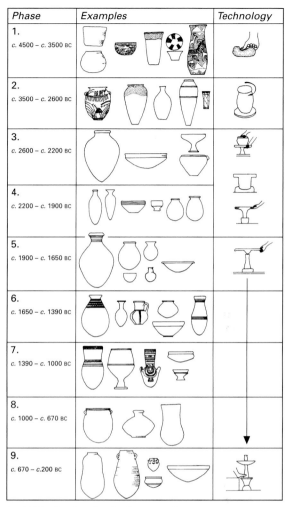

Phase	Examples	Technology
1. c. 4500 – c. 3500 BC		
2. c. 3500 – c. 2600 BC		
3. c. 2600 – c. 2200 BC		
4. c. 2200 – c. 1900 BC		
5. c. 1900 – c. 1650 BC		
6. c. 1650 – c. 1390 BC		
7. c. 1390 – c. 1000 BC		
8. c. 1000 – c. 670 BC		
9. c. 670 – c. 200 BC		

85. Table showing the development of ancient Egyptian pottery shapes in nine phases

imitated the containers made of organic materials which had been used since the beginning of human existence. Only in the second phase (Naqada II to Early Dynastic times) did potters show they understood the vessel of fired clay as a solid object in its own right, a body in the round with a base and an aperture. In many pots of phase 2 the front and back were clearly marked by the presence of small handles. The contour of the vessels then became a precisely controlled line between base and rim. The rims of phase 2 vessels are firmly accentuated. This is due partly to the method of shaping pots on turning devices which reached high speed and allowed firm motion in the round only during the final stages of the shaping process, but it is also a stylistic feature that expressed the new discovery of the pottery vessel's structural framework.

With the end of phase 2, pottery-making in Egypt entered the historic age. Typical vessels at the end of phase 2 had a simplified, almost abstract, contour. The loss in volume was, however, not a degeneration but a reduction to the indispensable in each shape. A similar process can be seen in the formation of the hieroglyphic script, another achievement of the period.

(ii) Phase 3 (c. 2600–c. 2200 BC). The pots of phase 3 are contemporary with the great pyramids of the Old Kingdom. Egyptian potters created ceramic products of the highest artistic and technological quality while still using rather primitive manufacturing methods. All vessel shapes are characterized by a powerful dynamic tension, which results from the subordination of all details under the main accents at the rim and maximum diameter. Old Kingdom pots are characterized by rustic broadness, austerity and refinement, which anticipated the forms of phase 4.

(iii) Phase 4 (c. 2200–c. 1900 BC). After the high quality of phase 3 pottery, phase 4 was a period of degeneration and decline of craftsmanship. There was, however, progress in the technology of wheel construction, and a new diversity in regional pottery styles following the break-up of the centralized Old Kingdom economy.

In the Memphis region, a manneristic degeneration of form was noticeable and shapes became extremely elongated. At the same time, in Upper Egypt, shapes were of a rustic, almost clumsy character. In this pottery, a fresh, hitherto unexpressed artistic potential surfaced. At the end of phase 4, during the last generation of the 11th Dynasty and the first two of the 12th, a new pottery style evolved from a combination of northern and southern elements.

(iv) Phase 5 (c. 1900–c. 1650 BC). The shapes of phase 5 (Middle Kingdom) pots are dominated by aspects of contour rather than volume; the phase 5 contour is, above all, an even one. Any corners, ledges or abrupt changes of the contour line are avoided. Body shapes approximate geometric solids, such as spheres or cones, as much as possible. If dynamic tension characterized Old Kingdom pottery, it is the closed form that typifies Middle Kingdom ceramics. The regional diversity of phase 4 persisted well into phase 5. It was only at the end of the latter phase (during the later 12th Dynasty) that pottery was again of the same style throughout Egypt. This uniform style, however, was broken up during the 13th Dynasty, when the regions of Upper Egypt and the various parts of the Delta again developed their own ceramic styles. The transition from phase 5 to phase 6 was gradual and indistinct. Many phase 5 types continued to be produced in phase 6 with minor alterations, but certain new accentuations were already entering the formal repertory of phase 5 during the 13th Dynasty.

(v) Phase 6 (c. 1650–c. 1390 BC). In phase 6 Egyptian potters finally discovered that vessels are composed of parts and that each part has its own function within the whole. Necks, bodies, bases, upper bodies, lower bodies and shoulders were for the first time firmly distinguished, the structure of the whole vessel being the relation of these parts to each other and the whole. Handles played a more important role, ring bases became more frequent and the decoration served to accentuate the vessel's structure. This was the phase in which the 'Brown and red painted' decorative style was invented and delicate figure vases created *(see §4(ii)(d) and (iv) below).*

86. Phase 7 broad-formed beaker jar, Nile clay painted with cobalt blue, red and dark brown, h. 500 mm, from el-Amarna, 18th Dynasty, *c.* 1400–*c.* 1300 BC (Berlin, Ägyptisches Museum)

(vi) Phase 7 (c. 1390–c. 1000 BC). The change from phase 6 to phase 7 occurred at the beginning of the reign of Amenophis III *(reg c.* 1390–*c.* 1353 BC), that is, definitely before the beginning of the Amarna period (*c.* 1353–*c.* 1332 BC). The emergence of a new ceramic style at this juncture is not easy to explain because there is no apparent economic or political break. The nature of the style suggests that a shift in the preponderance of workshops may have taken place. If the phase 6 style was largely an achievement of the Upper Egyptian potters, phase 7 could again be an expression of Memphite ceramic traditions, which might also explain the remarkable similarity of phase 7 to phase 3. Broad shapes once more dominated the repertory, and the elegance of phase 6 pots was again superseded by large, voluminous vessels (see fig. 86). Bases, handles and rims were thick and heavy in phase 7, transitions often marked by broad ledges; and previously straight contours tended to bulge. The 'Blue painted' style of decoration and applied elements with large faces of the goddess Hathor or the god Bes are diagnostic of the style *(see §4(ii)(d) and (iv) below).*

(vii) Phases 8 and 9 (c. 1000–c. 200 BC). There is insufficient evidence, at present, as to how phase 7 merged into phase 8, the style of which is poorly known. A distinct style certainly existed between phases 7 and 9, which had traits in common with phase 7 but also introduced its own

forms. Egyptian potters received important influences from western Asia during this phase.

All the shapes of phase 9 pottery demonstrate that a new invention had brought further mechanization into pottery manufacture. The kick wheel, for instance, enabled phase 9 potters to produce shapes of a hitherto unknown precision, but the same device led to the loss of much of the previous liveliness of Egyptian ceramics. Phase 9 shapes tend to be stiff and angular. Many details imitate those of metal shapes and even in some genuinely ceramic forms the sharp edges of metal tools are noticeable. Phase 9 ceramic types were among the most long-lived in Egyptian ceramic history—a fact that speaks of Egyptian potters' ability to satisfy their customers, even at the end of their history. It is, however, also a sign of an increase of industrialization and a decrease in creativity.

Phase 9 is the last genuinely Egyptian ceramic style. At its conclusion, pottery production in Egypt merged with that produced in the great centres of the eastern Mediterranean. Pots continued to be made in Egypt and are still made, but their stylistic features cannot be understood separately from Greek and Roman influences.

4. DECORATION. Flinders Petrie called the Egyptian 'the father of the world's ornament', but it has always seemed that Egyptian potters were curiously reluctant to decorate their products. However, the often repeated statement that pottery was decorated only during the Naqada II period (*c.* 3500–*c.* 2925 BC) and New Kingdom (*c.* 1540–*c.* 1075 BC) is incorrect. It can be demonstrated from close observation that in every period Egyptian potters painted or decorated pots when the vessels served certain specific purposes. Decoration was required for funerary, ritual, cosmetic or medicinal functions, as well as for eating and drinking at religious feasts. Otherwise, pots received no decoration beyond the surface finish, and occasionally simple stripes to accentuate the vessel's shape. The reason for the reluctance of the Egyptians to decorate pots for simple embellishment must be sought in their general attitude towards decoration. Egyptian decoration, whether in a temple or on a vessel, is never ornamentation *per se*, but always a means of interpreting the object by evoking its wider context. Earthenware pots used for everyday purposes did not require such interpretation.

(i) Surface finish. (ii) Painted decoration. (iii) Incised decoration. (iv) Applied decoration and figure vases.

(i) Surface finish. A review of Egyptian decorative techniques must begin with the various forms of surface finish: this was the means used most frequently to enhance the appearance of pots, and the techniques used were also often the first steps to more elaborate decoration. The simplest method of surface finish was to smooth the pot with a flat tool and/or to coat it with a thin layer of fine clay diluted in water, a method known as 'self slip'. This method seldom touched the bottom of the pots. Up to the Second Intermediate Period the zone at the bottom of the pot was invariably finished by cutting and scraping on the outside. Thereafter some vessels still received this hand treatment, while others were put back on the wheel for finishing the bottom exterior. Whether finished on the wheel or by hand, the bottom third of Egyptian pots is

87. Maidum bowl, Nile clay coated with ochre and burnished, diam. 277 mm, late 5th Dynasty/6th, *c.* 2350–*c.* 2180 BC (London, University of London, University College, Petrie Museum of Egyptian Archaeology)

usually less smooth than the rest, and if decoration is applied, it is seldom incorporated into the ornamented area.

A red ochre wash provided a more reliable method for concealing unevenness or blemishes in the surface. If this coating was thick, all pores and scraping or cutting marks disappeared. However, large Nile clay vessels seldom show a thick ochre coating because this surface layer would have reduced the desirable evaporation effect of the Nile clay. Tableware and vessels for cosmetic ointments, as well as medium-sized jars for washing water, often have a thick, even coating of ochre which has been burnished to a high lustre (see fig. 87) or rubbed to create a matt sheen. This was an especially appropriate surface finish for the dynamic shapes of phase 3. The ochre coating was also used for simple decorative purposes: broad red stripes appear around the circumference of plates, the upper part of a closed vessel may be coloured red, and red dots or splashes also occur. While the latter serve in most cases to imitate stone, the former could also be influenced by the custom of closing a vessel by covering its mouth and neck with a cloth.

Pharaonic-period vessels with red-washed upper parts are stylistic successors of the 'Black-topped' ware of prehistoric times (dated to both Naqada I and II periods, with precursors at EL-BADARI). Vessels of this ware were coated with red ochre wash, burnished and then (during firing) treated in such a way that the entire inside and the upper part of the outside were finally black. There has been some debate about the method of achieving this effect. The most convincing reconstructions envisage a two-stage process: first red-coloured pots would have been produced and then, directly after firing and while still hot, they would have been placed in a position so that the partly exposed parts were carbonized by smoke (either upside down in smouldering sawdust or buried upright in sand with only the uppermost part of the outside and the inside uncovered).

Both decorative schemes, the reddened upper part and the black top, presuppose an understanding of the pottery vessel as one uniform body. Another decorative scheme, still essentially a variation of surface treatment, suggests a more structural understanding of vessel shape. This decoration consists of brown or black stripes on the rim or at transitional points from one part of the vessel to another, such as the base of the neck, the maximum diameter or the transition from shoulder to body. This type of ochre treatment first appears in the later Middle Kingdom (*c.* 1700 BC) and frequently occurs in the 18th Dynasty (*c.* 1540–*c.* 1292 BC).

(ii) Painted decoration. Red ochre, so often used in surface finish, also played a vital role in painted decoration. Besides red and yellow ochre, other pigments used were gypsum white, a specially developed synthetic cobalt spinel for blue and a manganese oxide for dark red, brown and black. Carbon black appears less often, and green (using the mineral atacamite) least frequently of all. Yellow was most often yellow ochre, but orpiment (18th Dynasty) and jarosite (11th Dynasty) have also been determined in analyses. Whether particular wares were painted before or after firing is still open to debate. As a rule, it seems that funerary vessels were painted after firing; for these gypsum white, carbon black and other more transient pigments were used. Pots for cosmetics and festive eating and drinking were probably painted before firing; manganese black, red ochre and cobalt blue are the most frequently used pigments. There were seven main styles of painted decoration.

(a) 'White crosslined' (Naqada I). In this style (*c.* 4000–*c.* 3500 BC), first identified by Petrie, white gypsum pigment was applied to Nile clay pots that had been coated with ochre and then burnished. The decorative elements are either geometric, in clear imitation of basketwork or woven fabrics, or abstracted figures of animals (see fig. 88), human beings and plants. The geometric designs placed in juxtaposition with such figures seem to represent landscape, fences or animal traps.

(b) 'Decorated' (Naqada II and III). This style occurred on the pink or whitish-yellow surfaces of marl clay pots, dating to the Naqada II and III periods (*c.* 3500–*c.* 2925 BC). The decoration was painted, before firing, in manganese red, dark brown or black. The decorative elements include splashes, dots and spirals imitating stone. There are also undulating lines, rows of Z-signs, crisscrossed rectangles (reminiscent of the 'White crosslined' imitation basketwork) and figures and pictorial scenes. The figurative decoration is dominated by large ships with many oars and usually two cabins. Tree branches, on the prows or bows, and emblems set on poles attached to the cabins show that these ships were meant to carry gods or to symbolize religious voyages. Male and female figures with raised arms may be interpreted as dancers. Rows of animals, plants (especially frequent is an aloe bush) and what appear to be animal traps accompanied by figures of armed men, seem to be magical evocations of man's claim to be the master of the universe rather than actual hunting scenes. The pictorial repertory of the 'Decorated' style was certainly not invented by potters. Scant remains of wall paintings found in tombs of the same period suggest that the elements were originally evolved in large wall paintings. The religious content explains only partly the rather stereotyped character of the paintings on the pots: this ceramic ware was evidently mass-produced in centralized workshops and traded—at least in the later part of its period—all over Egypt.

88. 'White crosslined' decoration on a beaker jar, Nile clay coated with ochre and burnished, painted with white pigment, h. 255 mm, from Naqada, Predynastic period, *c.* 4000–*c.* 3500 BC (Oxford, Ashmolean Museum)

(c) 'White background' and 'Scenic' (First Intermediate Period–Late Period). 'White background' ware (which flourished in the First Intermediate Period, New Kingdom and Late Period) was decorated after firing with paint of various colours on a white background. The elements were again either geometric, emblematic or pictorial. Pictures were often elaborate offering scenes, either carried by male and female bearers or piled up on tables and plates. On some vessels, hunting scenes appear (in one picture the hunter is a Nubian), or desert animals are depicted. There are early instances of animals depicted in

a 'flying gallop', c. 2000 BC. There is also one example of a papyrus thicket with birds and butterflies. All these scenes are derived from wall paintings. The painters of these pots could have been those who usually decorated the walls of tombs or painted coffins and other funeral equipment. This would explain why the ware appears only sporadically and has no continuous history.

The 'Scenic' style of pot painting is closely related to the 'White background' style in its sporadic appearance and predominantly funerary function. In this ware, scenes of mainly religious content (such as offering scenes) are painted directly on to the plain or ochre-coated surfaces of vessels.

(d) 'Brown-and-red painted' and 'Blue painted' (New Kingdom). The 'Brown-and-red painted' style developed at the beginning of the New Kingdom out of the simple striped ware of the late Middle Kingdom to the Second Intermediate Period. Certain foreign influences (including, perhaps, Syro-Palestinian Bichrome ware) may have played an initiatory role in its further development. Although the 'Brown-and-red painted' style seems to have originated earlier than the 'Blue painted', it cannot be described as its predecessor, since 'Brown-and-red painted' vessels continued to be made almost as long as the 'Blue painted' style lasted. The two wares are also functionally very similar: pots of both styles served as festive tableware. The 'Brown-and-red painted' pots were also frequently used as cosmetic containers. When deposited in burials, the same pots were filled with dried fruit or even grain. The main difference between the two wares is their material; while 'Blue painted' pots are predominantly Nile clay, the 'Brown-and-red painted' decoration is found mainly on marl clay vessels. It is therefore probable that different workshop centres produced the two wares.

The 'Brown-and-red painted' style comes nearest of all Egyptian pottery painting to using a distinctive set of patterns. These consist essentially of groups of two, three or four lines. The colours were chosen so that either brown lines frame red ones, or vice versa. The line groups may be supplemented by various other elements, which then occupy the centre, with either two or four lines ranged on each side. Zigzags, wavy lines, a series of dots, triangles and more elaborate patterns serve as central elements. Both simple line groups and compound groups can be horizontally or vertically arranged.

The horizontal arrangement often emphasizes the shape of the vessel and is applied at either the rim, the transition from neck to body, the shoulder or the maximum diameter. When vertically disposed, elements are connected at one end with one of the horizontal elements so that they seem to hang from the horizontal design. In most cases the lower end of such 'hanging' elements remains loose, without a horizontal counterpart, thus further emphasizing the free-hanging effect. Floral elements (lotus buds and flowers) may be similarly 'hung' from horizontal parts of the design. Other pictorial, sometimes rather elaborate, elements include leaping calves or horses and religious emblems, with such meanings as life, prosperity and eternity, common symbols connected with the goddess Hathor. The style is a good indication of the way in which Egyptian decoration grew out of an interpretation of the decorated object enriched by associative elements.

The 'Blue painted' style of pottery decoration predominantly employs cobalt blue pigment. Black, red and, more rarely, yellow are also found. The elements of the decoration are mainly derived from floral garlands (see fig. 86 above). Lotus flowers and buds, as well as petals of various flowers, are arranged as if strung on threads and draped around the necks and shoulders of the pots. Such draping of actual floral garlands was an old custom in Egypt known from many representations of festive scenes. In a sense the decoration perpetuated the ephemeral ornament which thus became a lasting part of the vessel. 'Blue painted' pots also bear pictures of young animals in lively postures, the emblems of the goddess Hathor and the auspicious hieroglyphs found on 'Brown-and-red painted' pots.

In spite of the association with free-hanging elements, the distribution of the 'Blue painted' decoration on the vessel surface basically followed a system whereby horizontal bands vary (in width and elaboration of design) in relation to the pot's contours. Thus the exuberance of the blue and the floral and animal elements are firmly contained within a structural pattern. During the earlier phase of the style (the late 18th Dynasty), the painter's inventiveness and spontaneity prevented the decoration from becoming rigid, but in the later phase (19th and 20th dynasties) the pictures grew more and more stereotyped. Paradoxically, the rigidity of the design became more pronounced as the richness of the single elements increased. The ubiquitous medium-sized amphorae with heavy, oval-shaped garlands painted on their shoulders are an example.

(e) 'Lotus flower and crosslined' (Late Period–Ptolemaic). Pots of this ware—either large bottles, or shouldered two-handled jars—are often covered with decoration from rim to foot. This feature may show some degree of foreign (perhaps Greek) influence because it is contrary to previous Egyptian customs, but single decorated shoulder zones also occur. The decoration consisted mainly of bands of varied width, certainly applied before firing, with dark red or brown pigment on the orange surface of the pots which are probably made of kaolin clay. Two bands are usually filled with a crosslined grid. On the shoulder, one broad zone shows bushes or trees bordered by lotus flowers and grass-like plants. Further down on the vessel, a narrower second pictorial zone shows lotus flowers in horizontal position with the stems rolled into loose spirals. The rest of the pot is covered with dark horizontal stripes. The 'Lotus flower and crosslined' ware represents the last example of a painted decoration using solely Egyptian motifs. Examples so far have been found only in the Theban area.

(iii) Incised decoration. Incising techniques ranged from simple cuts to crescent-shaped marks made with the end of a reed, and elaborate combing. Gouging was also used, often producing a relief effect when the removed piece of clay was left to hang beside the gouged-out cavity. In some cases, incised lines were filled with gypsum white. The best known among the latter was named after the place where it was first found, Tell el-Yahudiya. In this ware,

carbonized vessels with dark brown or black surfaces bear elaborate, incised white-filled decoration, which consists predominantly of geometric elements but also includes fishes, birds and plants. Some vessels actually have the shape of fruit and birds. The ware was manufactured at various centres inside Egypt, as well as others outside (e.g. Palestine and Cyprus); trade was extensive and even reached Nubia. The Upper Egyptian marl clay incised ware of the early Middle Kingdom is an example of a genuine Egyptian ware with a rich variety of incised decoration.

(iv) Applied decoration and figure vases. Applied decoration was sometimes used to transform a vessel into a partial human figure by adding arms, breasts or a head. Other examples of applied decoration show figures of animals attached to the rims of vessels, or in relief on the body of the pot. The application of miniature vessels on to the rim, neck or shoulder of a normal-sized pot was typical for ritual vessels. Such applied miniature pots were sometimes pierced so that they could serve as multiple spouts or hold flower stems. A special decorative feature often found in connection with 'Blue painted' style pots is the addition of a moulded face, usually that of the god Bes or the goddess Hathor. The faces were either modelled free-hand on to the vessel wall (sometimes with additional applied parts) or a mould was pressed against the vessel's wall.

Figure vases (see fig. 89) were first shaped free-hand, then details were added by sculpturing with a flat tool. The elements of the vessel, such as necks and handles,

were produced separately either on the wheel or free-hand, then added to the figure parts. For high quality figure vases and the production of face moulds the potters may well have called on the help of professional sculptors. The same would be true for the fine human-headed lids of canopic jars (see §XII, 2(vi) above), which are closely related to contemporary portrait sculpture.

BIBLIOGRAPHY
LÄ: 'Gefässe', 'Keramik', 'Ton', 'Töpferei'
W. M. F. Petrie: *Corpus of Prehistoric Pottery and Palettes* (London, 1921)
P. J. Ucko: *Anthropomorphic Figures of Predynastic Egypt and Neolithic Crete with Comparative Material from the Prehistoric Near East and Mainland Greece* (London, 1968)
H.-Å. Nordström: *Neolithic and A-group Sites*, 2 vols (Lund, 1972)
R. Holthoer: *New Kingdom Pharaonic Sites: The Pottery* (Lund, 1977)
B. J. Kemp and R. Merillees: *Minoan Pottery in Second Millennium Egypt* (Mainz, 1980)
D. Arnold, ed.: *Studien zur altägyptischen Keramik* (Mainz, 1981)
Umm el-Ga'ab: Pottery from the Nile Valley before the Arab Conquest (exh. cat. by J. Bourriau, Cambridge, Fitzwilliam, 1981)
C. A. Hope: 'Blue Painted Pottery', *Egypt's Golden Age: The Art of Living in the New Kingdom* (exh. cat., Boston, MA, Mus. F.A., 1982), pp. 88–100
B. A. Adams: *Sculptured Pottery from Koptos* (London, 1987)
J. Bourriau: 'Pottery Figure Vases of the New Kingdom', *Cah. Cér. Égyp.*, i (1987), pp. 81–96
C. A. Hope: *Egyptian Pottery* (Aylesbury, 1987)
DOROTHEA ARNOLD

XIV. Jewellery.

In Egypt jewellery was worn from the earliest times. Much of it is characterized by the polychrome splendour of its inlays. A variety of inlay materials was used, ranging from stones, such as lapis lazuli and turquoise, to faience and glass. The Egyptians loved colour in their jewellery, and the various coloured stones that they used provide the best indications for the ancient trade in precious materials. Lapis lazuli was brought from Afghanistan, while turquoise came from the Sinai desert (for further discussion *see* §§I, 3 and VII, 1 above), although, strangely, neither pearls nor diamonds were known in Egyptian jewellery until the Ptolemaic period (304–30 BC). The Egyptians used a variety of manufactured materials (including coloured glazes and glass that would be scorned by modern jewellers), as well as wood, bone, ivory and other organic materials. Many ancient Egyptians would have had little or no access to jewellery of gold, silver or hardstones, and they would have made do with ornaments of base metals and various organic materials.

The setting of stones in most Egyptian polychrome jewellery was never a celebration of the stones themselves but simply a means to an end: the application of pigment to an icon. The stones are meticulously cut and polished to fit their settings, whereas settings are never made specially for a particular stone. The goldwork, and thus the stones or glass, were made according to a strict canon of form and proportion: like other Egyptian art forms, jewellery was not usually a medium for experiment or free expression.

1. Predynastic (*c.* 6000–*c.* 2925 BC). 2. Early Dynastic–Old Kingdom (*c.* 2925–*c.* 2150 BC). 3. Middle Kingdom (*c.* 2008–*c.* 1630 BC). 4. New Kingdom (*c.* 1540–*c.* 1075 BC). 5. Third Intermediate Period (*c.* 1075–*c.* 750 BC). 6. Late Period (*c.* 750–332 BC). 7. Macedonian and Ptolemaic periods (332–30 BC). 8. Roman period (30 BC–AD 395).

1. PREDYNASTIC (*c.* 6000–*c.* 2925 BC). The earliest known Egyptian ornaments were mainly beads but there

89. Figure vase in the shape of a nurse with baby, marl clay coated with ochre, burnished and painted, h. 140 mm, 18th Dynasty, *c.* 1540–*c.* 1400 BC (Berlin, Ägyptisches Museum)

were also bracelets, bangles and various small pendants used as protective amulets. Harder stones, such as cornelian, were often simply drilled with minimal external shaping. Softer stones, such as serpentine, steatite and even malachite, could easily be worked with flint implements. Organic materials, including wood, tortoiseshell, horn and shells, were popular ornaments. Shells were often strung together as necklets and bracelets and this fashion lasted throughout Egyptian history. By the Middle Kingdom (*c.* 2008–*c.* 1630 BC), if not long before, cowries and perhaps other shells had become fertility symbols. Beautiful garlands of flowers and buds were also worn, but few of these survive.

Gold and copper ornaments were being produced in the early 4th millennium BC (the Naqada I period). Faience first appeared at about the same time—perhaps in connection with the development of copper smelting technology. Silver was in use by the second half of the 4th millennium (the Naqada II period) and by then harder stones were more often used.

2. EARLY DYNASTIC–OLD KINGDOM (*c.* 2925–*c.* 2150 BC). By the 1st Dynasty (*c.* 2925–*c.* 2775 BC), the use of coloured inlay became more formalized, particularly with regard to cornelian, faience and turquoise. The representations, either geometric or naturalistic, became more precise, with an increasing use of supplementary engraved or incised decoration.

Garnet (mainly simple beads) and amethyst had been known from earlier times, but by the 1st Dynasty, Egyptian craftsmen were involved in more elaborate stoneworking, such as the production of the toggle-shaped amethyst elements of one of three bracelets found on the arm of an Early Dynastic princess in the tomb of King Djer at Abydos (Cairo, Egyp. Mus., CG 52010). Lapis lazuli was used for the first time (together with turquoise and gold) in two of the three bracelets (Cairo, Egyp. Mus., CG 52009, CG 52011). These can be compared in technique and design with early Sumerian jewellery (*see* ANCIENT NEAR EAST, §II, 4). For example the corrugated form of the lapis beads and the beads of coiled gold wire match jewellery from Ur, although the presence of turquoise is very non-Sumerian and rules out the possibility that the whole item was imported from Sumeria.

The goldsmith of the early Old Kingdom was experienced in working sheet-gold, producing hollow, spherical beads in sheet-gold and soldering the gold components of his work together, sometimes with surprising precision. Sheet-gold could be hammered out and cut into wires or precise forms. These parts could be assembled to imitate natural forms, such as flowers or animals. During the Old Kingdom there was some refinement in skills, including a growing precision in surface embossing and chasing.

Enough jewellery has survived to demonstrate the repertory of the goldsmith's materials and techniques, but a fuller picture of jewellery types is provided by representations in wall painting and sculpture. Both men and women in the Old Kingdom apparently favoured a 'broad collar' (Egyp. *wesekh*) and a pair of wide bracelets, all usually made of beads. Some form of pectoral was probably worn occasionally from an early period, but

90. Reproduction of an Old Kingdom bracelet, silver with stone inlay, from the tomb of Queen Hetepheres I, Giza, 4th Dynasty, *c.* 2540 BC (Boston, MA, Museum of Fine Arts)

representations are rare before the Old Kingdom. (Earrings and finger-rings were not worn.) Other decorations included head ornaments such as diadems and belts.

One very rare, and lucky, survival is a belt belonging to Prince Ptahshepses (*fl c.* 2400 BC; Cairo, Egyp. Mus.), found during excavation of the valley temple of Wenis's pyramid at Saqqara. The main part of the belt is composed of a gold band, the outside of which is covered by a repeating chevron design in attached gold, faience and cornelian beads. The fastener at the front is a near-rectangular gold plate (*c.* 100 mm long) inlaid with cornelian and faience, much like the cloisonné technique that became so characteristic of later Egyptian goldwork. In fact, the inlay is more like champlevé work: the receptacles for the stones are depressions on the surface of the sheet rather than separately made cells with gold-strip walls. The design is in the form of symmetrical mirror images of the seated prince with falcons and his name in hieroglyphs. Some minor details of the design are chased into the gold but other details, such as the faces of the prince, are left as undecorated cornelian surfaces. The silver bracelets of Queen Hetepheres (*fl c.* 2540 BC; Boston, MA, Mus. F.A.; see fig. 90) from Giza have similar champlevé work. This technique of stone inlay, although never forgotten, was later largely superseded by cloisonné work. At least some jewellery, such as the ubiquitous 'broad collar' and bracelets, doubtless continued to be made and worn during the unsettled First Intermediate Period (*c.* 2150–*c.* 2008 BC), but there are no gold ornaments that can be unequivocally dated to this period.

3. MIDDLE KINGDOM (*c.* 2008–*c.* 1630 BC). As peace began to be established under the rulers of the 11th Dynasty (*c.* 2081–*c.* 1938 BC), jewellery production increased, but there is still little extant jewellery from this period apart from beads. Although a wider range of coloured stones was used for beads and pendants, there was little sign of the polychrome splendour of 12th Dynasty inlaid jewellery. Surviving gold and silver items show little technical sophistication. One exception is a silver scarab, beautifully and precisely inlaid with pale gold. Since this scarab, together with other gold, silver and stone jewellery (New York, Met.), was found at Deir el-Bahri in

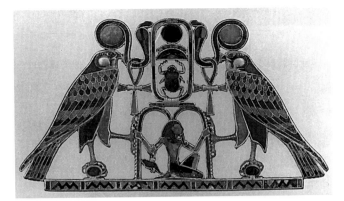

91. Middle Kingdom gold pectoral, from the tomb of Princess Sithathoriunet, el-Lahun, *c.* 1818–*c.* 1770 BC (New York, Metropolitan Museum of Art)

the tomb of Wah, who was only a minor royal official, the original ornaments of the ruling families towards the end of the 11th Dynasty must have been spectacular. Wah's jewellery includes a characteristic 11th Dynasty bead form consisting of a hollow sphere with tube-like projections extending from the threading holes.

During the Middle Kingdom the goldsmiths produced some of the most spectacular work known not only from Egypt but from the entire Ancient Near Eastern world. The most characteristic production of the Middle Kingdom jewellers was cloisonné inlay work. Faience and coloured stones (typically cornelian, lapis lazuli and turquoise) were precisely shaped and set into sheet-gold cells outlining designs. Symmetry plays a large part in the overall effect, although the precision and minuteness of many of the inlays produces a sense of tightness and vitality.

Enough jewellery has survived from this period to allow a wider understanding of motifs and design. There is a fixed repertory of iconographic motifs and a canon of proportions that provide an overall unity. For example, the overall symbolism and coherence of a pectoral from the tomb of Princess Sithathoriunet at el-Lahun (New York, Met.; see fig. 91) is self-evident: it takes the form of confronted falcons, and on each of the falcons' heads is a sun-disc with a royal uraeus. Each falcon grips a symbol of power in one claw, and in the other he supports the hieroglyphic symbol for millions of years. Hanging from the uraei are *ankh*-symbols (signifying life), and between the uraei and *ankh*s, supported by the symbol for millions of years, is the name of Sesostris II (*reg c.* 1844–*c.* 1837 BC). The whole design rests on a base with a zigzag design representing the primeval water from which creation began. Princess Sithathoriunet also owned an almost identical pectoral among a wealth of other jewellery. This second pectoral (Cairo, Egyp. Mus.) is of poorer quality and bears the name of Ammenemes III (*reg c.* 1818–*c.* 1770 BC). Both pectorals are decorated on their backs with chased designs detailing the design as seen from the front, a common feature in Egyptian jewellery.

Not all Middle Kingdom jewellery is so easy to interpret. One charming circle for the hair (Cairo, Egyp. Mus.) was found in the tomb of the princess Khnemt, daughter of Ammenemes II (*reg c.* 1876–*c.* 1842 BC), at Dahshur. It is in the form of interwoven flowers, like a multi-strand daisy

chain. The stalks are of thin gold wire and the flower heads are gold with inlaid petals of turquoise and centres of cornelian. This same princess possibly also possessed a parure of strangely Asiatic appearance including granulated stars (Cairo, Egyp. Mus.). This group of items from Dahshur stands out from other Middle Kingdom jewellery and can best be compared to jewellery from western Asia. The re-examination of the Dahshur excavation records of Jacques De Morgan suggests, however, that this parure might not have been part of the original burial of Princess Khnemt and that it should be re-dated to the years immediately after the Middle Kingdom.

Granulation first appeared in Egypt during the Middle Kingdom. This technique involves soldering a series of minute gold spheres to a sheet-gold background. The more complicated granulated and applied filigree work that began to appear in western Asia by about 2000 BC does not seem to have appealed as much to the Egyptians, although it was not lack of skill that prevented their adoption of it. Middle Kingdom Egyptian granulation work (typically amuletic pendants in the form of vertically hanging cylinders) is just as technically precise as contemporary western Asian work. The Egyptians never combined the typical polychrome inlay (with its representational designs) with granulation or applied filigree. The same applies to most of the pectorals and other polychrome ornaments of the New Kingdom (*c.* 1540–*c.* 1075 BC) and even Tanite period (*c.* 1075–*c.* 960 BC). The recently introduced use of granulation was probably not considered suitable for a whole class of traditional inlaid, 'icon-like' jewellery.

Simple bands of gold and other materials had long been worn on the fingers but during the Middle Kingdom more elaborate rings appeared for the first time. Granulation was used to produce decorative finger-rings from the burial of Queen Mereret (*fl c.* 1840 BC) at Dahshur. Among her jewellery (Cairo, Egyp. Mus.) there is one ring with a repetitive design of chevrons of granules; another has single grains and applied filigree spirals. Both the technique and the non-representative nature of the designs point to inspiration (if not manufacture) outside Egypt. The characteristic form of the Middle Kingdom ring is a scarab beetle mounted on a wire hoop which, in the simplest examples on mummies, was a cord tying a scarab to the finger. Some beautiful inlaid scarab rings of this type have survived, such as those from Queen Mereret's tomb, but many may have been produced only as funerary ornaments.

The technical perfection of the Middle Kingdom jewellers is to be seen in the sliding fasteners, where a T-section bar on one half of the clasp slides into a slot in its companion piece. These clasps usually take the form of cowries and reef-knots, like the gold beads they fasten. One fine cowrie shell is among Queen Mereret's jewellery and others can be seen in various collections, including the British Museum, London, and the Metropolitan Museum of Art, New York. The cowrie shell, whether natural or replicated in gold, was a fertility symbol and the same is probably true of the knot.

The contrast between the intricate, even garish, inlaid jewellery with its strict representational canon, and the smooth rounded contours of the gold shells and other forms, shows the versatility of the Middle Kingdom jeweller. It also reveals a conservatism and adherence to the symmetry and established canons that characterized Egyptian jewellery for the next 1500 years. The occasional granulated gold jewel stands out strongly and reflects—indeed derives from—increasing foreign outlooks and contacts. Little jewellery has survived from the Second Intermediate Period (*c.* 1630–*c.* 1540 BC), even though the dire desolation once attributed to the period has probably been overstated.

4. NEW KINGDOM (*c.* 1540–*c.* 1075 BC). Jewellery design at the very beginning of the 17th Dynasty is strongly reminiscent of Middle Kingdom work, although such items as the inlaid jewellery from the tomb of Queen Ahhotpe (*fl c.* 1540 BC) at Thebes (Cairo, Egyp. Mus.) are not finely executed. The pectoral, for example, in its chunky layout and rather garish use of strong, red-coloured cornelian, has a somewhat barbaric look which is absent from either the Middle Kingdom or mid-New Kingdom examples. Other items from this tomb show distinct Asiatic influence.

Various heroes of the war over the Hyksos rulers in Lower Egypt received gold rewards. One particular military award was the gold fly, three fine and heavy examples of which were found in Queen Ahhotpe's tomb strung on a gold loop-in-loop chain with a hook and eye fastener (Cairo, Egyp. Mus.; see fig. 92). This latter feature is unusual in Dynastic Egyptian jewellery. The presenting of gold to those favoured by the pharaoh continued until the Ptolemaic period. At the beginning of the 18th Dynasty, Ahmose Pennekhbet received gold jewellery from three successive rulers: Amenophis I, Tuthmosis I and Tuthmosis II. According to his inscriptions, the items he was given included rings, necklets and bracelets as well as 'flies of valour'. Surviving jewellery from this period is mostly limited to stray finds from minor burials.

Tangible evidence for the renewed output of a royal atelier is provided by the jewellery from the Theban tombs of three girls (usually given the unsubstantiated title 'princesses'), who belonged to the harem of Tuthmosis III (*reg c.* 1479–*c.* 1426 BC). Unfortunately, since the find was made by thieves (rather than archaeologists) and disseminated on to the market over a long period, the original find (now mainly in New York, Met.) was supplemented by a large number of gold forgeries and a variety of other items which, though ancient, belong to other periods. Some of the pieces have more of a Middle Kingdom appearance, while one so-called tubular pendant with outer spiral decoration looks very like an early Byzantine screw-threaded fastener.

If the contentious items among this jewellery of the 'three princesses' are ignored, the rest comprise a selection of ornaments including rings, headdresses and necklets. The rings are of the scarab type that originated in the Middle Kingdom. The headdresses include elaborate wig-covers that are essentially chain-mail-like sections of inlaid gold rosettes (rosettes of this type, including forgeries of the same form, are spread among various collections, but the reconstruction in the Metropolitan Museum of Art, New York, is probably close enough to the original arrangement of the headdresses). One necklet has a series of drop-shaped pendants with the same type of coloured

92. New Kingdom military decoration gold necklace with three fly pendants, l. 590 mm, from the tomb of Queen Ahhotpe, Thebes, 17th Dynasty, *c.* 1540 BC (Cairo, Egyptian Museum)

inlays as the headdresses and was probably from the same workshop. Markings on the back of some of the headdress sections (presumably giving references for assembly positions) provide an indication of the goldsmiths' working methods. The quality of work and the precision of the fitted inlays attest to their high skill.

Earrings in the form of corrugated hoops are included in the treasure of the 'three princesses' and this type is well known in the mid-18th Dynasty. It occurs at the same time as a chunky penannular hoop earring which, when made of precious metal, is hollow and often of electrum sheet, plated with gold. Many of the well-known penannular hoops of stone, usually red jasper, were probably also worn in the ears and attest to the growing fashion for earrings so noticeable during the 18th Dynasty.

Despite the major impact of the Amarna period on the art styles of the later 18th Dynasty and subsequent period, little gold jewellery has survived from the time of Akhenaten (*reg c.* 1353–*c.* 1336 BC). Akhenaten himself is seldom depicted wearing much jewellery, although he is shown distributing gold rings, necklaces and vessels to his subjects. Gold jewellery dateable to his reign includes a number of gold signets with cartouche-shaped bezels (*see also* §XVII, 15(ii) below), usually engraved with Akhenaten's name or titles. Almost as many of these signet rings seem to have been found in Cyprus as in Egypt. Some of the rings are made from a gold alloy with much added copper, producing a marked red colour.

Evidence of jewellers' workshops has been excavated in Akhenaten's capital at el-Amarna, including moulds, some jewellery and even gold ingots (subsequently melted down by the Egypt Exploration Society). Some gold jewellery was supposedly found in a câche near, if not in, the royal tomb at el-Amarna. Some of this is of the period but other items, such as a gold ear-stud and bracelets

(Edinburgh, Royal Mus. Scotland), are as late as the Ptolemaic and Roman periods.

The wealth and diversity of the large and well-known assemblage of jewellery of TUTANKHAMUN (*reg c.* 1332–*c.* 1323 BC) compensate for the lack of material from his predecessors. The large items such as the pectorals and collars (*see* JEWELLERY, colour pl. IV, fig. 2) may seem much the same as those from the Middle Kingdom, but there are important differences. Tutankhamun's jewellery is less cluttered and busy: design and harmony in layout have become as important as strict iconographic depiction. Symmetry is still important, but sometimes this is abandoned when the central motif or figure is markedly asymmetric. The quality of most of the goldworking is superb, and the quantity makes it possible to identify the characteristics of some of the individual designers and craftsmen. As with the Middle Kingdom jewels, the official repertory of techniques tended to exclude granulation and beaded wire on the more formal items, but granulation was used frequently by the inventive designers or craftsmen on less formal jewels, particularly bracelets, and on items such as small gold beads on a necklet from which a *wedjat*-eye (an amulet representing the eye of the god Horus) hangs. Some of Tutankhamun's magnificent pairs of earrings appear to have some applied decoration in beaded wire—almost its earliest occurrence in ancient jewellery. Another form of decorative wire—a notched strip of gold—is also found on a variety of the jewellery, but, again, mainly on the items that were not so strictly 'icons'. The small counterweight to one necklet (that with a winged scarab pendant) has the cloisonné walls holding the inlay made from either lines of granules or a notched strip.

In many cases coloured glass replaced coloured stones, reflecting the fine quality of glasswork, but the colours were still the same traditional ones, imitating lapis lazuli, cornelian and turquoise. Contrasting with this lack of adventure in glass colours, the goldsmith varied his gold surface by using a reddish coloration in chosen places, such as on alternate pendants hanging from a pectoral. This reddish colour was not produced by alloying gold with copper, as with Akhenaten's rings, but was a surface effect caused by the addition of iron in one form or another to the gold. In other cases the craftsman deliberately used a greyish coloured silver–gold alloy to depict the moon.

The few items of jewellery that survive from the time of Ramesses II include a fine pair of bracelets of gold and lapis lazuli, depicting double-headed geese (Cairo, Egyp. Mus.), which were part of the câches of treasure recovered from Bubastis in 1906. Both bracelets are decorated with granulation and either beaded wires or ribbed gold tubes. A pendant in the form of a seated figure of a king (Boston, MA, Mus. F.A.) is probably of this same period and may represent Ramesses II himself.

A set of gold jewellery found in the Theban tomb of a young princess must date to about the time of Sethos II (*reg c.* 1204–*c.* 1198 BC) since some of the items bear the name of his queen, Tausert. These items are not particularly grand, but one unusual feature is the openwork filigree technique of a series of beads and seed-shaped pendants making up a necklace (Cairo, Egyp. Mus.). Of the later Ramesside rulers little jewellery has remained although there is a pair of earrings (Cairo, Egyp. Mus.) from the mummy of an unnamed woman from the household of Ramesses XI (*reg c.* 1104–*c.* 1075 BC), found by Mariette at Abydos. The goldwork is not as precise as earlier in the New Kingdom, but the earrings include quite accurate granulation work and are also striking examples of the red-coloured gold surface seen in Tutankhamun's jewellery.

5. THIRD INTERMEDIATE PERIOD (*c.* 1075–*c.* 750 BC). The magnificent gold and coloured stone jewellery from the burials of the 21st Dynasty (*c.* 1075–950 BC) pharaohs (now mainly in Cairo, Egyp. Mus.) demonstrates that the Third Intermediate Period did not suffer anything of the artistic poverty of the First and Second Intermediate periods. In both overall splendour and actual technical quality, the pectorals, bracelets and other goldwork from the tombs at Tanis of Psusennes I (*reg c.* 1040–*c.* 997 BC), Shoshenq II and their relatives compare favourably with the finest jewels of the Middle and New kingdoms.

In some ways the tight, sometimes crowded and often very symmetrical designs are more reminiscent of the Middle Kingdom than the New. This is also seen in the return to real stones, particularly lapis lazuli, green feldspar and cornelian, which must indicate continuing trade with western Asia, although there is also clear evidence for the reuse of earlier materials: one necklace of Psusennes (Cairo, Egyp. Mus.) includes an almost spherical bead of lapis lazuli with a cuneiform inscription. In another example a bracelet of Shoshenq II (Cairo, Egyp. Mus.) is actually set with a lapis lazuli cylinder seal of Akkadian date (*c.* 2300 BC). Many of the inlays of lapis lazuli in a cloisonné depiction of a large *wedjat*-eye on a bracelet (Cairo, Egyp. Mus.) found on the mummy of Shoshenq II show, in their colour bandings and qualities, that they were probably slices cut from a single block of lapis. Faience and coloured glass are also used in some of the jewellery, and true enamel makes what is probably its first appearance in Egyptian goldwork.

While the standard, rather two-dimensional jewellery, such as the pectorals, was often of high quality at this time, it is in the three-dimensional items that the most charming work is found. There were, for instance, superb solid gold pendant amulets in the form of deities such as Bastet and Hathor. These were mainly very precise lost-wax castings with some final details chased in place. In some cases, pieces in the round were built up by combining castings with sheet-gold components. The finest example is a triad ornament (Paris, Louvre) from the time of Osorkon II (*reg c.* 929–*c.* 914 BC), showing Isis and a hawk-headed Horus flanking a figure of Osorkon in the form of Osiris squatting on a lapis-encrusted column. The combination of goldwork with carved amulets (usually of lapis lazuli) seems to have been a fashion of the period. The craftsmen's skills can also be seen in the curving inlaid jewels. Stone inlays were precisely cut and set around the periphery of bracelets and rings. Particularly fine examples include a pair of bracelets of Psusennes (Cairo, Egyp. Mus.), each of which takes the form of an annular torus and thus both lapis lazuli inlays and cloisonné cells curve gently in all three dimensions. In concept the torus-like form harks back to the silver bracelets of Hetepheres of the Old Kingdom with their champlevé inlay work, also of lapis.

The finger-rings from the royal tombs at Tanis (Cairo, Egyp. Mus.) are mainly of the swivel type set with scarabs or *wedjat*-eyes. There are also inlaid flat hoops, like miniature bracelets. The technical expertise of the jewellers of the Third Intermediate Period is shown in much of the goldwork, in the fine loop-in-loop chains and exquisite chasing and embossing. Necklets of chains often have no fastener but were long enough to pass over the head. The traditional repertory of techniques allowable on the iconographic jewels still seems to have excluded the use of granulation and beaded wires; even applied filigree decoration of twisted wires is rare.

The gold or other jewellery worn by private individuals is less easy to ascertain, as little has been preserved. Beads in faience and other materials would have been popular as necklaces and bracelets. On 21st Dynasty painted coffins, women are typically depicted wearing large rosette earrings. One woman of the period, Tiye, is shown wearing these rosettes in representations on her coffins and even in her Book of the Dead papyrus: it is interesting to compare the large size of the rosettes depicted with the huge holes distending the ear lobes on the head of her surviving mummy (head, coffins and Book of the Dead all in New York, Met.). In the 22nd Dynasty (*c*. 950–*c*. 730 BC) men were still sometimes shown with pierced ears but later this became less common, except on representations of Asiatics. Earrings are markedly absent in the royal jewellery of the period, but a 22nd Dynasty relief from Memphis (Paris, Louvre) depicts a priest of Ptah wearing hoop earrings with three hanging drops.

6. LATE PERIOD (*c*. 750–332 BC). The huge wealth of bronzework dating from the Late Period is ample evidence of the continuing expertise of the metalworker, but unfortunately surviving goldwork is extremely rare. The only major exceptions are the typical gold and silver signet rings of the period. These differ from the stirrup shapes of the New Kingdom in having a large oval bezel with a separately applied circular section gold hoop. The form may derive from the Phoenician signet types (which in turn were based on the New Kingdom type; *see* PHOENICIAN, §5); these were then adapted for manufacture from sheet-metal. These large gold signets are among the most massive and solidly spectacular of all private Egyptian goldwork and hardly suggest any lack of gold in Egypt at that time. Their survival might well be due to the fact that most of such rings were probably used by priests rather than being accoutrements from royal or noble burials.

Earrings seldom seem to have survived from the period between the 25th Dynasty and the Ptolemaic period (i.e. *c*. 750–304 BC). Exceptions in gold are a few tapered hoops found at various Delta sites. From both provenance and style these relate best to eastern Greek forms. Pierced ears are often shown on 25th and 26th Dynasty women's coffins but the earrings all seem to be rather stylized rosettes like those of the Third Intermediate Period, so this was possibly more of a funerary convention than a representation of a common, everyday type of jewellery.

Statues and wall decorations show types of pectorals, collars and headdresses that might well have been worn by the nobility and priesthood, but no examples have been found. Two dark stone statues of men wearing distinctive Achaemenid Persian-style animal-head jewellery (Rome, Vatican, Mus. Gregoriano Egizio, 196, and New York, Brooklyn Mus., 37.353) date to the Saite period; their provenance is uncertain, but the Brooklyn statue is probably from Memphis.

7. MACEDONIAN AND PTOLEMAIC PERIODS (332–30 BC). In the Macedonian and Ptolemaic dynasties, which followed Alexander the Great's invasion of Egypt, Egyptian and Greek traditions in jewellery existed side by side. In the official representations of pharaohs or deities the traditional forms of Egyptian jewellery were carefully copied, but surviving examples of goldwork are almost entirely in the cosmopolitan Hellenistic forms found throughout the eastern Mediterranean.

Most of the surviving jewellery was probably owned by the middle classes—perhaps mainly the Greeks then living in Egypt—and grander royal items are all but unknown. Typical forms include hoop earrings consisting of a tapering, twisted gold hoop terminating in the embossed, sheet-gold head of an animal (examples in most museum collections). Bulls and gazelles are common, as is the horned lion–griffin. The various types of Hellenistic necklets, usually consisting of stone beads supported in various ways on gold links, and elaborate earrings are less common in Egypt than, for instance, in Asia Minor or southern Italy, but examples are known. Typically Greek gold and silver signet rings are found in Egypt, as are engraved gemstones. In the Ptolemaic period, textual evidence suggests that Alexandria was a thriving centre for jewellery, gem-engraving and fine metalwork, but surviving examples are scarce.

The wealth of simple Hellenistic-style gold jewellery might well reflect the increased amount of gold available to the general populace through the circulation of gold coinage. The forms and techniques used in Egypt during the Ptolemaic period mirror the general chronological development of Hellenistic jewellery elsewhere in the eastern Mediterranean world. There was a gradual increase in the popularity of coloured stones, particularly garnets, emeralds and pearls: the two latter stones occur for the first time in Egyptian jewellery. Gold jewellery seems to have been relatively abundant among the well-to-do Greek inhabitants of Egypt in the first century or so of Ptolemaic rule, but afterwards it became far less common, doubtlessly reflecting the economic problems of the period and the related fact that gold coins ceased to be minted in Egypt.

Of the more traditional Egyptian jewel types, the only item that occurs with some frequency is the amulet of the *ba*-bird (a spirit in the form of a human-headed bird) with outstretched wings. The wings are usually inlaid with stones or sometimes enamelled in a typical Hellenistic filigree enamel technique. These pendants (examples in many collections) were almost certainly for funerary use only, and again they suggest the continuing use of traditional forms for religious depictions or functions. The incorporation of filigree enamelwork in a traditional Egyptian style of jewel shows a newly flexible approach to traditional jewellery. Another interesting hybrid type is the gold *wedjat*-eye amulet, frequently depicted on mummy cases as worn on the brows of women. Surviving examples of gold *wedjat*-eyes retain the traditional shape but some have applied filigree decoration that is purely Hellenistic in concept. From the Ptolemaic period there are also more literary references to jewellery in everyday use, including allusions to signet rings being used to seal documents or goods. There are also many more representations of jewellery actually being worn than in earlier periods.

8. ROMAN PERIOD (30 BC–AD 395). The numerous depictions of jewellery, such as those on funerary masks and portraits, are sufficient indication of its importance to the Romano-Egyptians. All the forms shown can be matched with surviving Roman jewellery types, suggesting a high degree of accuracy among the painters and draughtsmen. Some Roman-period jewellery was probably for funerary use only; this is true of most of the serpentine snake bracelets shown on women's wrists in the 1st century AD. Some examples, normally of flimsy gold sheet, survive (including a pair in Cairo, Egyp. Mus.), but in many cases the depiction on the sarcophagus or mask was probably enough. Little gold jewellery has been found in burials dating to the early Roman period (30 BC–AD 275). Gold coinage was not being minted in Egypt at this time and the burial of gold with the dead would not have suited the Roman officials' ideas of how best to serve the treasuries of Rome.

Typical examples of jewellery from the first half of the Roman period are snake armlets worn on the upper arms, usually in pairs. Normally they have only one or two coils, sometimes with wavy tails and sometimes with a strange smaller head at the tail end. Other popular forms are earrings consisting of wires bent to an S-shape and threaded with emerald, onyx, pearls or glass beads. Animal-head earrings also remained in vogue: they have a series of stone beads threaded behind the head, often that of a dolphin—sometimes diminutive—or a goat. Both the S-hook and animal-head earrings are characteristic of Egypt.

Several non-Egyptian examples of Roman jewellery are known from Egypt. One type of earring consists of hollow gold 'balls'; another consists of a stone setting above two or three free-hanging wire pendants threaded with pearls or emeralds. These have closer stylistic and technical links with Roman jewellery from the Pompeii region and Asia Minor than with the continuing Hellenistic styles of goldwork from Syria and the Levant.

After the Edict of Diocletian (AD 300) and the reorganization of the coinage, gold coins began to be circulated again in Egypt. There was a simultaneous—and presumably not unrelated—increase in surviving jewellery. One typical form is a necklet consisting of an open, loop-in-loop chain with a circular clasp bearing a raised representation of a Medusa-head. Many necklets of this type survive and they are clearly depicted in the numerous funerary paintings in Egypt during the 4th century AD. Another common Egyptian form is a bracelet of twisted tubes terminating in a hinged bezel in the form of a vessel-like container holding a stone. The stone is usually conical and invariably of orangeish-brown onyx or brown or green jasper.

Some of the most magnificent 6th-century AD jewellery from the entire ancient Mediterranean region has been found in Egypt, although the frequently expressed assumption that most was produced in Constantinople rather than Egypt needs more critical assessment. Egypt had been the home of skilled goldsmiths since the 3rd millennium BC and an almost continuous tradition of such skills can be traced from the Predynastic period to Fatimid times.

BIBLIOGRAPHY

E. Vernier: *La Bijouterie et la joaillerie égyptiennes* (Cairo, 1907)
H. Schäfer: *Ägyptische Goldschmiedarbeiten* (Berlin, 1910)
W. Dennison: *A Gold Treasure of the Late Roman Period*, ii of *Studies in East Christian and Roman Art* (New York, 1918)
C. Williams: *Catalogue of Egyptian Antiquities, Numbers 1–60: Gold and Silver Jewellery and Related Objects* (New York, 1924)
A. Lucas: *Ancient Egyptian Materials and Industries* (London, 1926, rev. 4/1962/R 1989)
W. M. F. Petrie: *Objects of Daily Use* (London, 1927)
E. Vernier: *Bijoux et orfèvreries*, 2 vols, Cairo, Egyp. Mus. cat. (Cairo, 1927)
H. E. Winlock: *The Treasure of El Lahun* (New York, 1934)
A. Lansing: *Egyptian Jewellery* (New York, 1940)
W. B. Emery: *Nubian Treasure: An Account of the Discoveries at Ballana and Qustul* (London, 1948)
H. E. Winlock: *The Treasure of Three Egyptian Princesses* (New York, 1948)
P. Montet: *Les Constructions et le tombeau de Psousennes à Tanis* (Paris, 1951)
W. C. Hayes: *The Scepter of Egypt*, 2 vols (New York, 1953–9)
J. R. Harris: *Lexicographical Studies in Ancient Egyptian Minerals* (Berlin, 1961)
C. Desroches-Noblecourt: *Vie et mort d'un pharaon: Toutankhamon* (Paris, 1963; Eng. trans., London, 1963)
A. M. El-Khachab: 'Gems from Egypt in Private Collections', *J. Egyp. Archaeol.*, xlix (1963), pp. 147–56
M. Vilimova: *Egyptian Jewellery* (Prague, 1969)
C. Aldred: *Jewels of the Pharaohs* (London, 1971)
A. Wilkinson: *Ancient Egyptian Jewellery* (London, 1971)
Africa in Antiquity: The Arts of Ancient Nubia and the Sudan, 2 vols (exh. cat., ed. S. Wenig; New York, Brooklyn Mus., 1978)
A Private Collection of Egyptian Gold Jewellery (sale cat., London, Christie's, 1 June 1979)
Jewellery: Ancient to Modern, Baltimore, MD, Walters A.G. cat. (New York, 1980)
C. A. R. Andrews: *Jewellery from the Earliest Times to the Seventeenth Dynasty*, London, BM cat., vi (London, 1981)
J. Ogden: *Jewellery of the Ancient World* (London, 1982)
P. Davidson and A. Oliver: *Ancient Greek and Roman Gold Jewellery in the Brooklyn Museum* (New York, 1984)
Tesori dei faraoni (exh. cat. by S. Curto and A. Roccati, Venice, Doge's Pal., 1984), pp. 84–95
Tanis: L'Or des pharaons (exh. cat., Paris, Grand Pal., 1987); rev. as *Gold of the Pharaohs* (Edinburgh, City A. Cent., 1987–8)
C. A. R. Andrews: *Ancient Egyptian Jewellery* (London, 1990)

JACK OGDEN

XV. Metalwork.

Only a small percentage of Egyptian metalwork has survived, since the constant difficulty in obtaining and working metal (*see* §VII, 2 above), precious or otherwise, has meant that many items over the centuries have been stolen and melted down. Metal funerary equipment (*see* §XIII above) was particularly vulnerable; it might be taken soon after the burial by contemporaries of the deceased, but it might also be stolen from tombs several centuries later, judging from the textual evidence of legal proceedings against bands of pillagers in the 20th Dynasty (*c.* 1190–*c.* 1075 BC). The papyrus recording this trial (London, BM, 10068) notes 'vessels of offerings, which the thieves of the necropolis said they brought away from the tomb that they had violated and which they said they divided among themselves. . .four bronze *keb*-vessels for the toilet, two bronze *nesh*-vessels, two bronze spittoons'. These eight vases were immediately melted down to ensure an equal share of metal for each member of the band, which always included one or more coppersmiths.

Egyptian metalworkers produced numerous types of objects: utilitarian, ritual and magical objects, and items of personal adornment. Apart from statuary, which forms the largest category of metalwork (*see* §1 below), metal was used for countless other objects essential to the celebration of religious cults, including bronze libation situlae decorated with engraving or relief; censers in the form of arms decorated with falcons; heads or statuettes; and musical instruments such as sistra, cymbals and trumpets (*see* §XVII, 12 below), of which Tutankhamun's tomb provided many examples in gold, silver and bronze (Cairo, Egyp. Mus.). The ritual objects and luxury items housed in temples were also particularly susceptible to pillaging. In the treasure chamber of the Temple of Amun at Karnak there are reliefs depicting the many metal objects (including caskets, altars, vases, fans and statuettes) kept in the sanctuary during the reign of Tuthmosis III (*reg c.* 1479–*c.* 1426 BC), none of which survives.

Besides these and the uses discussed in detail below, Egyptians also employed metal for jewellery (*see* §XIV above), arms and armour (*see* §XVII, 2 below) and furniture and fittings (*see* §XVII, 6 below). Metalworkers also often collaborated with sculptors, carpenters, cabinetmakers and even architects. In the Temple of Amun at Karnak, for instance, the walls of certain rooms were lined with gold: the sheets had been applied to screens and then hammered so that the decoration showed through in bas-relief, but only the holes of the tenons have survived. The points of obelisks were also covered with a layer of gold or copper, and many statues of kings, queens and sphinxes originally bore metal crowns (surviving only in the form of a deep groove).

1. Statuary. 2. Vessels. 3. Cosmetic items.

1. STATUARY. Since the Egyptians considered that statues of gods or people were complete substitutes for reality, they appear to have treated metal as a living substance. The earliest religious texts assert that the bones of the gods are silver and their flesh is gold, and the king is often compared to a wall of copper or bronze.

(i) Royal and private. Metal statuary was evidently already being produced in the early 3rd millennium BC, judging from the text of a set of royal annals preserved on a basalt slab known as the Palermo Stone (Palermo, Mus. Reg.), which refers to a great copper statue (untraced) made in the image of the last pharaoh of the 2nd Dynasty, Khasekhemwy (*reg c.* 2600 BC). The earliest surviving copper royal statues date to the reign of Pepy I (*reg c.* 2289–*c.* 2256 BC): two works (Cairo, Egyp. Mus., JE 33034–5), excavated at Hierakonpolis, show that the metalworkers' skill was equal to that of sculptors in basalt and diorite. The larger of the two statues (h. 1.77 m) is inscribed with the name of Pepy I, while the smaller, uninscribed figure (h. 0.7 m) may represent either the same king as a child or possibly his son, Merenre (*reg c.* 2256–*c.* 2246 BC). Both

statues originally consisted of a wooden core (long since destr. by termites) over which copper sheets were hammered and nailed into place. Only the head, hands and feet may perhaps have been moulded. The two figures represent the pharaoh in an upright, walking posture, with the left leg forward. The larger statue has the left arm forward, holding a cane, while the right arm hangs by the side of the body with clenched fist (probably originally gripping a sceptre). A section of the torso above the hips is missing, perhaps because the sculptor had attached a loincloth of a different material, which—judging from the surviving traces of plaster at the edge of the metal—may have been lined with gold leaf. The smaller statue is intact, depicting the King as a naked figure with both arms at his sides. His face is delicate and his inlaid eyes give him a lively expression (see fig. 93). The pupils are of obsidian, the corneas of white calcite and each eye is ringed with metal circles using a different type of copper alloy from the rest of the statue.

The Egyptians continued to make large metal statues after the reign of Pepy I. Unfortunately, however, only a few fragments have survived, such as the bronze figure of a pharaoh excavated in the Faiyum and probably representing Ammenemes III (*reg c.* 1818–*c.* 1770 BC; New

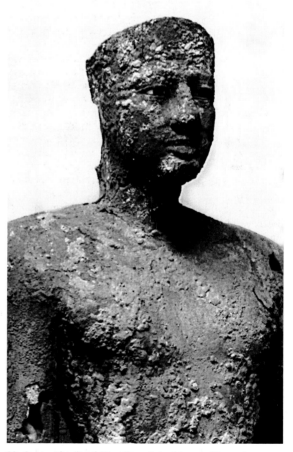

93. Statue (detail) of King Pepy I (or his son Merenre), copper, h. 700 mm, from Hierakonpolis, 6th Dynasty, *c.* 2300 BC (Cairo, Egyptian Museum)

94. Statuette of kneeling Libyan prisoner, bronze and silver, h. 90 mm, 18th Dynasty, *c.* 1500 BC (Paris, Musée du Louvre)

with embroidery imitating feathers, was represented by damascening in threads of gold, silver and electrum. The wig, face, arms and legs were covered with a thin film of gold, of which only a few traces remain.

A century later the same technical dexterity can be seen in a 25th Dynasty gold and copper alloy female statuette, identified as the lady Takushit (Athens, N. Archaeol. Mus.). She is dressed in a long clinging robe decorated with religious scenes embroidered in silver filigree. Although smaller and not damascened, the bronze kneeling statuette of the 25th Dynasty King Shabaka (*reg c.* 719–

York, priv. col., see Wildung, pp. 208–9). This figure, 300 mm high without the headdress, must have belonged to a statue similar in size to Pepy I's smaller statue, although the production technique was very different: it involved pouring metal into a mould rather than hammering sheet-metal over a core. The facial expression, with inlaid eyes, is remarkable. A head has also survived from a statue of somewhat later date (Hildesheim, Pelizaeus-Mus.).

A number of smaller items of statuary have also been preserved, with particularly large numbers of bronze statuettes of kings and private individuals from the Middle Kingdom (*c.* 2008–*c.* 1630 BC) onwards. Metalworkers mastered the lost-wax process, which allowed them greater flexibility in the modelling of the face and body, as in the case of the bronze statuette of a walking man with a shaven head, leaning on a cane (*c.* 1600 BC; New York, Brooklyn Mus.). Another outstanding example is a kneeling bronze statuette of Tuthmosis IV (*reg c.* 1400–*c.* 1390 BC) offering a libation vessel in each hand (London, BM); his eyes and eyebrows are underlined by a rib of silver. Probably contemporary with this is a kneeling bronze figure of a Nubian prisoner (New York, Brooklyn Mus.), his head slightly bent and his arms tied behind his back. The masterpiece of the genre of statuary representing prisoners, however, is the bronze and silver 18th Dynasty statuette of a captured Libyan with his right knee on the ground and his left leg raised (Paris, Louvre; see fig. 94).

The maintenance of quality in metalwork until the end of the Dynastic period is demonstrated by such Late Period examples as the small standing figure of Karomama, divine adoratrice and wife of Takelot II (Paris, Louvre; see fig. 95), in bronze, gold, electrum and silver. The statuette is wearing a heavy round wig, originally surmounted by a crown, and her arms are bent and held forward, in the gesture of the goddess Isis shaking a pair of sistra (now lost). Her long, clinging tunic, decorated

95. Statuette of the divine adoratrice Queen Karomama, bronze, gold, silver and electrum, h. 600 mm, 22nd Dynasty, *c.* 860 BC (Paris, Musée du Louvre)

96. Head of falcon, gold and obsidian, h. 375 mm, from Hierakonpolis, 6th Dynasty, *c.* 2200 BC (Cairo, Egyptian Museum)

c. 703 BC; Paris, Louvre) also shows the virtuosity of Late Period artists, notably in the delicate treatment of the face.

(ii) Deities. A discussion of all the bronze figurines representing animal gods such as falcons, cats, rams and bulls (either in animal form or as humans with animal heads) would involve the enumeration of the entire Egyptian pantheon. Some, however, rank among the masterpieces of Egyptian metalwork, as in the case of the 26th Dynasty bronze statuette damascened with gold, representing the falcon of Horus (Cairo, Egyp. Mus.). A fine bronze falcon-headed figure of Horus (Paris, Louvre)—probably dating to a later phase of the Late Period than the statuettes of Shabaka and Takushit mentioned above—is unusual in having jointed limbs. The standing figure, almost 1 m high, has arms raised and hands clasped together as if holding an object; the gesture is reminiscent of the act of libation performed by Horus and Seth during a ceremony known as the 'Baptism of the pharaoh'. This statue would have been used by a priest to pour purifying water on the head of the king or his representative during important ceremonies.

(iii) Composite. Besides statues and statuettes of individual kings, deities or private individuals, there are also composite metalwork statues portraying several figures or objects, such as the golden head of the Horus falcon (Cairo, Egyp. Mus.; see fig. 96), under whose beak stood a royal bronze statuette. Discovered at Hierakonpolis at the same time as the statues of Pepy I (but in a different location), the falcon is thought to have been used in worship and is generally dated to the 6th Dynasty. However, a later date (probably Middle Kingdom) has also been suggested. When excavated, it was in one piece, but its body, made of fine copper sheets nailed to a wooden core, disintegrated almost immediately and has not been restored. Both the falcon and royal statuette were placed on a rectangular plinth resting on a pottery support. The head of the falcon—a masterpiece of Egyptian metalwork—was created by hammering gold leaf (*c.* 1–2 mm thick) around the core and engraving the details. The eyes are made from a single cylinder of obsidian that passes through the head. Two tall perforated feathers behind a standing uraeus decorate the crown.

2. VESSELS. The Protodynastic Narmer Palette (*c.* 3000 BC; Cairo, Egyp. Mus., JE 32169; for illustration *see* NARMER) bears a relief depiction of a royal sandal-bearer holding a metal vessel—this shows that Egyptian craftsmen of the 4th millennium BC were already making vases with inset handles and copper-leaf spouts. Metal vases with curved inset spouts, used to pour water before and after meals, as well as the bowls that caught the water, demonstrate not only the artist's technical skill (such as his ability to attach the long pouring spout to the vase with rivets) but also the characteristic Egyptian taste for simplicity, expressed in the elegant curve of the spout and the bell-shaped vessel itself, resembling the calyx of a flower. The shapes of metal vases developed substantially over the centuries; some are known only through depictions in reliefs and wall paintings (particularly in 18th Dynasty Theban tombs), which often show production and decorative techniques.

Apart from copper vessels for everyday use, some precious metal vases have been recovered from incompletely plundered tombs. They are all of excellent workmanship and delicate taste, particularly the silver pomegranate-shaped vase from the tomb of Tutankhamun. Most of the vases, and those of the finest quality, come from the royal necropolis at Tanis and the royal burial places of the 21st–22nd dynasties (*c.* 1075–*c.* 730 BC). Among these (all Cairo, Egyp. Mus.) are a cup decorated with underwater scenes of female swimmers among lotus flowers; gold and silver gadrooned paterae; a cup with a stand; a long-necked vase in the shape of a half-opened lotus flower; a spouted ewer; a cup with a handle in the form of a papyrus flower; and plates and bowls often enhanced by an engraved legend in hieroglyphs.

The decoration of metal vases was usually engraved, but occasionally it incorporated sculpture in the round. Heads of birds and animals, such as ducks and gazelles, were sometimes added to handles. In some examples even statuettes were employed, as in a bronze cup (New York, Met.), in the bottom of which stands a small bronze figure of Hathor, or a silver wine jug with a gold handle sculpted to represent a wild goat (Cairo, Egyp. Mus.).

3. COSMETIC ITEMS. Egyptian cosmetic items also provide good examples of metalworking, especially the numerous surviving mirrors. At the beginning of the 20th century the collection in the Egyptian Museum, Cairo, included over 100 mirrors, and others have been acquired since. Together with *shabti*s (funerary statuettes), mirrors are the most widespread type of pharaonic object.

Copper, bronze and silver (as well as bronze and silver alloys) were commonly used for mirrors. Gold and electrum were undoubtedly also employed—judging from models in gilded bronze and Middle Kingdom lists of votive objects—but no such examples have survived. The handles of mirrors were sometimes made from different varieties of wood, bone, ivory and even stone, but usually they were made from the same metal as the reflective disc. From the Old Kingdom onwards many mirrors were decorated with a female head bearing cows' ears, representing the goddess Hathor, or, more rarely, the image of the dwarf-god Bes. From the beginning of the New Kingdom (*c.* 1540–*c.* 1075 BC) the handle often took the form of a bronze female statuette, again probably Hathor (*see* MIRROR, fig. 2). In a more austere style, the handle sometimes represented a papyrus stalk, with the disc of the mirror appearing to emerge from the open flower, like the sun or moon appearing over the horizon. The Upper Nubian tombs of 25th Dynasty pharaohs contained a great deal of high quality Egyptian metalwork, including mirrors made entirely of silver, their handles in the form of figurines representing various deities.

Another cosmetic item, used by both men and women, was the bronze razor. The decoration of the slender handle, often cut out or in delicate relief, usually consisted of depictions of animals, such as a gazelle or ibex rearing up on its hind legs, or very occasionally a human figure, such as a Nubian lute-player (New York, Met.). Finally, the cases that held the fine kohl-stick of wood or haematite used to spread make-up on the eyelids were usually made of highly embellished wood, but some were bronze decorated with statuettes of small naked girls.

BIBLIOGRAPHY
G. Daressy: *Statues de divinités*, 2 vols (Cairo, 1906)
G. Benedite: *Miroirs* (Cairo, 1907)
G. Daressy: 'La Barque d'or du roi Kamès', *An. Service Ant. Egypte*, xxi (1921), pp. 129–37
E. Vernier: *Bijoux et orfèvreries* (Cairo, 1927)
Ch. Boreux: *Guide-catalogue sommaire*, Paris, Louvre, 3 vols (Paris, 1932)
G. Roeder: *Ägyptische Bronzewerke* (Hildesheim, 1937)
P. Montet: *Les Constructions et le tombeau de Psousennès*, i of *La Nécropole royale de Tanis* (Paris, 1951)
D. Dunham: *Nuri*, ii of *Royal Cemeteries of Kush* (Boston, 1955)
G. Roeder: *Ägyptische Bronzefiguren* (Berlin, 1956)
E. Young: 'Note on a Hitherto Unknown Technique in Egyptian Bronze-working', *J. Egyp. Archaeol.*, xlv (1959), pp. 104–5
Ch. Desroches-Noblecourt: *Vie et mort d'un pharaon: Toutankhamon* (Paris, 1963; Eng. trans., New York, 1963)
H. Kayser: *Ägyptisches Kunsthandwerk* (Braunschweig, 1969)
J. Vandier d'Abbadie: *Les Objets de toilette égyptiens au Musée du Louvre* (Paris, 1972)
A. Radwan: *Die Kupfer und Bronzegefässe Ägyptens* (Munich, 1983)

JEAN VERCOUTTER

XVI. Other arts.

1. Amulets. 2. Arms and armour. 3. Basketwork. 4. Dress. 5. Faience and glaze. 6. Furniture. 7. Gardens. 8. Glass. 9. Ivory and bone. 10. Leatherwork. 11. Maps and plans. 12. Musical instruments. 13. Personal art. 14. Plaster and stucco. 15. Seals. 16. Stone vessels. 17. Textiles.

1. AMULETS. Amulets and amuletic jewellery were an essential adornment for the ancient Egyptians both as part of the costume of the living and as funerary equipment set on the mummy for use in the afterlife (*see* §XIII, 3(vi) above). Many amulets were worn in life for their magical properties and then taken to the tomb; others were provided exclusively for the afterlife. They were made from precious metals, hardstones, coloured glass or faience and, less commonly, ivory, wood, bone or shell.

The colour of the material often had particular significance: lapis lazuli was the colour of the all-embracing, protective night sky; red jasper or cornelian resembled life-blood; the green of new vegetation was suggested by feldspar or green jasper; turquoise was the colour of the life-bringing waters of the Nile; gold represented the sun with all its inherent generative powers. Indeed, the material for specific amulets was prescribed in funerary texts. The 'heart scarab' was set in a mummy's wrappings to prevent adverse witness against its owner when his heart was weighed to ascertain his worthiness to enter heaven. It was ideally made of a green stone, tentatively identified as nephrite, but most existing stone 'heart scarabs' are of basalt or serpentine. The 'girdle of Isis', representing the knot and ties of the goddess's belt, had to be of a red material in order to reinforce the amulet's purpose of enriching the blood of the deceased. A hardstone was required for the 'two fingers amulet' which perhaps represented the fingers of the embalmer; most extant examples are of obsidian. For an unknown reason nearly all amulets in the shape of the headrest, by which the head of the deceased would be raised in resurrection, are of haematite.

The first recognizable amulets pre-date by centuries the beginning of the 1st Dynasty. Although their forms are simple—typically, a crouched hawk, animal claws, a tethered hippopotamus, a 'green' beetle—in some instances they mark the first appearance of types that were to continue in use throughout Dynastic history. However, the few pieces from the Early Dynastic period show a great improvement in workmanship; this is exemplified by a royal bracelet from Abydos (Cairo, Egyp. Mus., CG 52008) formed from alternating gold and turquoise hawks, each crouched on a *serekh* palace façade, and by a collection of gold shell shapes and a gold bull and oryx from a contemporary burial at Nag el-Deir. During the Old Kingdom a few new types were added to the repertory, notably the fish (which gave protection against drowning) and the *wedjat*-eye of the hawk-headed god Horus which was considered one of the most powerful sources of protection. But it was essentially at the end of the Old Kingdom and during the First Intermediate Period that amulets buried with the dead increased greatly in range of form and in numbers. Especially common were those in the shape of parts of the body. Amuletic legs, hands, faces and hearts not only endowed their owners with their particular bodily functions, namely the capability of movement and activity and the use of the senses and the intelligence, but could also act as physical replacements should those parts be lost.

During the Middle Kingdom there was a further increase in the repertory of forms. Some were exclusive to the period, such as the oystershell conferring health, the cowrie warding off the evil eye from pregnant women, the knot clasp conferring restraint and control (all of precious metal) and the hardstone crouched *ba*-bird, probably a protective spirit. Amulets of this date are made from either the hardest stones, superbly carved, or precious metal manufactured by every known metalworking technique. Conspicuously few, before the New Kingdom, are amulets of deities (see fig. 97), whether as humans with animal heads or in the form of a sacred animal, but from *c*. 1300 BC until the end of Dynastic history such figures are probably the most numerous. Their material is most often precious metal exquisitely moulded and engraved or a rock-hard faience with superb sharpness of detail for objects so small in scale. Some amuletic deities are characteristic of a period. Groups of the Four Sons of Horus, protectors of the mummified internal organs, do not appear before *c*. 1050 BC, when a change in embalming practices led to the return of the treated viscera to the body cavity, each package with its own appropriate amuletic deity attached. Most popular after *c*. 600 BC are amulets of Isis suckling Horus, Thoth returning the *wedjat*-eye (see fig. 97b) and Isis and Nephthys mourning or with Horus the child, all protagonists in the Osiris legend. Almost as numerous are figures of Bastet (cat-goddess of festivity and fertility), Ptah (craftsman–god of Memphis; see fig. 97d), Sakhmet (Ptah's wife, the lioness), Nefertum (Ptah's son) and Pataikos, the dwarf-form protector.

Attempts have been made to categorize the functions of amulets. Although the distinctions between categories occasionally blur, there are only three basic types: amulets of substitution, of transference of properties (assimilation) and of protection. Amulets shaped like possessions or funerary goods could be a substitute for the actual objects: an amuletic trussed ox or goose, a loaf or a jug would magically provide food and drink in the afterlife; an amuletic broad collar or fringed apron would furnish the dead with adornment and clothing. Amulets in the form of royal regalia, such as crowns, sceptres and the uraeus, endowed their non-royal owners with a pharaoh's capability of dominion and supremacy. By a similar transference of properties from inanimate objects, a plummet granted eternal equilibrium and a set-square everlasting rectitude. Hieroglyphs in amuletic form brought their meaning into being: thus an *ankh* guaranteed life, the papyrus vigour and the *djed*-pillar stability. By assimilation with living creatures, a figure of the lioness Sakhmet, who embodied the burning heat of the sun, would ward off harmful influences; a figure of Min, representing the archetypal procreative urge, would ensure virility; and one of a frog or cat, both noted for their reproductive qualities, would ensure fecundity. Amulets of powerful deities, such as Amun-Re, king of the gods (see fig. 97c), or the sun-god,

97. Egyptian amulets of deities (from left to right): (a) pendant figure of the goddess Mut, gold, h. 29 mm, *c*. 1200–*c*. 1100 BC; (b) pendant figure of ibis-headed Thoth, gold, h. 24 mm, *c*. 1000–*c*. 900 BC; (c) pendant figure of Amun-Re, gold, h. 25 mm, *c*. 600–*c*. 300 BC; (d) figure of Ptah, gold foil, h. 31 mm, *c*. 300–*c*. 100 BC (all London, British Museum)

offered protection through their very supremacy. The more homely Thoeris, hippopotamus-goddess of childbirth, and her dwarfish helper Bes were also able to avert evil. It was thought that amulets of harmful or malevolent forces such as the turtle, creature of darkness, could ward off the very evil represented.

See also §15(ii) below for discussion of 'seal amulets' (or 'design amulets').

BIBLIOGRAPHY

LÄ: 'Amulett' [incl. an extensive bibliog.]
W. M. F. Petrie: *Amulets* (London, 1914)
C. Brunton: 'Amulets', *Introduction to Egyptian Archaeology*, ed. R. Engelbach (Cairo, 1946/*R* 1961), pp. 249–59
C. Andrews: *Amulets of Ancient Egypt* (London, 1994)

CAROL ANDREWS

2. ARMS AND ARMOUR. Most of the Egyptian army consisted of light infantry. Their major weapons were bow and arrow, spear, dagger, sword, axe, sling, throwstick and boomerang. Shields were sometimes carried (see fig. 98) but scale armour was rare and was not used before the New Kingdom (*c*. 1540–*c*. 1075 BC).

(i) Projectiles and missiles. The principal military (and hunting) weapon at all times was the bow. Before the New Kingdom only self bows (or simple bows) were used. They were normally 1–2 m long and made from a single piece of wood of circular section tapering towards the ends. Shorter examples (e.g. New York, Met., 14.1.406) tended to have a single continuous curve, while longer ones were straight with turned-in tips or of the more efficient double convex recurved form (e.g. New York, Met., 36.3.212), already known in Egypt in the Predynastic period. Bows were often wrapped around at intervals with cord and had decorative ferrules on their tips. The strings were made from twisted gut simply lashed to the ends of the bow by wrapping them around several times. The composite bow, made from strips of wood, animal horn and sinew glued together, had better range and power. It was not introduced in Egypt until the early New Kingdom, probably from western Asia. The most common type of composite bow in Egypt was recurved (e.g. Cairo, Egyp. Mus., JE 615). The monuments, however, also illustrate examples in the shape of a very shallow isosceles triangle. Composite bows were prized possessions kept in special

98. Arms and armour carried by Egyptian spearmen, painted wooden model, h. 590 mm, w. 620 mm, from the tomb of Mesehti at Asyut, 11th Dynasty, *c.* 2000 BC (Cairo, Egyptian Museum)

richly decorated bow cases or in bow pockets in chariots. Simple bows remained in use especially for hunting.

Arrows were made from reed, fletched with three feathers and fitted with tapering hardwood points, often of ebony. Chisel-edged flint flakes were sometimes attached to the points or set in the shaft to form barbs. Bronze arrowheads (e.g. Cairo, Egyp. Mus., JE 6155) were used in later periods. Stun arrows with blunt wooden tips covered with cord (e.g. Cairo, Egyp. Mus., JE 61548/24) were used for hunting small game and birds. Quivers (e.g. New York, Met., 21.2.5) were made from leather, coiled basketwork or cartonnage covered in leather. They were usually cylindrical, tapering slightly into a rounded base and decorated. They were fitted with shoulder straps or could be attached to chariots. Leather wrist-guards were made from thick pads of leather and had narrow straps.

Although examples of woven slings with plaited cords have been found, they were probably mainly used in the New Kingdom during sieges of Syro-Palestinian cities. They were certainly less popular than hardwood clubs which had straight handles and were bent over at the end. The boomerang was an ancient weapon especially favoured for hunting birds. The wooden blade was curved at an angle of approximately 140° and was flat on one side but slightly convex on the other. Throwsticks were similar in shape and function.

(ii) Hand-to-hand weapons. One of the earliest weapons in Egypt was the stone mace head (Oxford, Ashmolean; see fig. 51 above). The earliest Predynastic examples were flat disc mace heads but these were replaced by pear-shaped ones. The wooden haft often tapered at the hand end and was bound with fibre to assist grip. The handles were

occasionally covered in thick gold leaf with repoussé depictions of animals. In later periods the mace head became a purely ceremonial weapon.

The spear was used as a short-range weapon thrown from fairly close quarters like a short javelin. The earliest forms were made of copper and had tangs inserted into the wooden shafts (e.g. Berlin, Bodemus., 23277). Early New Kingdom examples were made from bronze and had a central strengthening midrib. Under the Ramesside kings (*c.* 1292–*c.* 1075 BC) socketed spear heads were introduced.

The axe was a common infantry weapon at all periods. It was used for hand-to-hand fighting and for dispatching an enemy already wounded by missiles. It was sometimes used as a two-handed weapon. Although several tanged types evolved, the Egyptians never developed a socketed axe. The earliest axes had blades of copper with a semicircular head (e.g. London, BM, 32580). They were attached to handles by cords or hide lashings passed through perforations along the top edge and wrapped over lugs which projected from either side. From the 1st Dynasty some of the blades were embellished with line engravings. The semicircular form was improved in the Middle Kingdom (*c.* 2008–*c.* 1630 BC): it became taller and had tapering concave sides to a rounded cutting edge. It persisted into the New Kingdom (e.g. London, BM, 36772); gradually the sides became straighter and the cutting edge narrower, giving a taller, thinner axe. The Egyptians also used a 'scalloped' axe which had a rounded cutting edge and was attached to the shaft by three tangs either lashed through perforations in each tang or secured by tubular metal ferrules (e.g. London, BM, 32203). In the New Kingdom ceremonial axes were made. One battle-axe, made of copper set with gold, cornelian, lapis lazuli and turquoise (Cairo, Egyp. Mus., JE 4673), was found in the tomb of Queen Ahhotpe (*fl c.* 1540 BC). They were of archaic form and had openwork designs cut from the blades and would not have been strong enough for use in battle. Such axes were possibly given as rewards for valour or long service.

Daggers were common from the 12th Dynasty (*c.* 1938–*c.* 1756 BC), though knives were used much earlier (e.g. Predynastic example with gold handle, *c.* 3200 BC; Cairo, Egyp. Mus.). Daggers had tapering copper blades riveted to elaborate handles with short, wide grips and broad crescent-shaped pommels (e.g. London, BM, 5426). The bronze daggers of the New Kingdom had a long thin tang cast in one with the blade, and they eventually evolved into a form of short sword (e.g. Oxford, Ashmolean, 1927.4622), possibly under influence from the Sea Peoples. A peculiar scimitar-like sword (Egyp. *khepesh*) with its curved blade cast in one with the hilt (e.g. London, BM, 27490) was introduced in the Second Intermediate Period (*c.* 1630–*c.* 1540 BC). The sword, however, was an uncommon weapon in Egypt.

(iii) Shields and armour. Egyptian shields were basically rectangular although the sides tapered gently outwards to a straight bottom edge; the top was rounded or, more rarely, pointed (e.g. New York, Met., 17.9.3). They were made of stiffened bull's hide stretched over horizontal wooden braces. A grip was carved out of the centre brace. There were two sizes of shield—full-length ones, up to 1.5 m high, which could protect the entire body, and a smaller type, *c.* 1 m high, which was obviously lighter. Shields could be fitted with straps and slung over the shoulder when scaling ladders. A smaller shield, introduced in the New Kingdom, had a rounded top and sides tapering inwards to the straight bottom edge. It was obviously intended to maintain adequate protection for the head while minimizing the overall size and weight. Sherden (i.e. north Syrian) mercenaries attached to the New Kingdom Egyptian armies carried circular shields.

Armour was not introduced until the New Kingdom. Old Kingdom (*c.* 2575–*c.* 2150 BC) soldiers wore a very brief garment consisting of little more than a belt with a triangular flap down the front. Middle Kingdom troops wore simple everyday dress such as the short kilt. Metal scale armour was probably introduced in the Second Intermediate Period but did not become common until the mid-18th Dynasty (*c.* 1400 BC). It was manufactured by sewing small metal plates on to a linen or leather tunic. Both full-length coats of armour and shorter shirts, which protected only the upper body, are depicted. The upper arms were protected but the lower arms were not. The neck was protected by a leather collar. Helmets when worn were probably made of leather rather than metal, but bronze helmets are among lists of booty which the Egyptians took from Syro-Palestinian battlefields.

BIBLIOGRAPHY
W. M. F. Petrie: *Tools and Weapons* (London, 1917)
H. Bonnet: *Die Waffen der Völker des alten Orients* (Leipzig, 1926/*R* 1977)
W. Wolf: *Die Bewaffnung des altägyptischen Heeres* (Leipzig, 1926/*R* 1977)
Y. Yadin: *The Art of Warfare in Biblical Lands* (London, 1963)
E. Kuhnert-Eggebrecht: *Die Axt als Waffe und Werkzeug im alten Ägypten* (Berlin, 1969)
W. E. Mcleod: *Composite Bows from the Tomb of Tutankhamun* (Oxford, 1970)

W. V. Davies: *Tools and Weapons: Axes*, London, BM cat., vii (London, 1988)

PHILIP J. WATSON

3. BASKETWORK. The excellent climatic conditions in Egypt have allowed examples of ancient basketry to be preserved from as early as the Neolithic period (*c.* 6000–*c.* 2925 BC) and many specimens from the Dynastic period (*c.* 2925–30 BC) can be found in museums throughout the world. As versatile containers for storage and transport, the functions of baskets varied from the storing of quantities of grain to the housing of personal clothing, equipment and even corpses (for a representation of a 'basket coffin' see fig. 80a above).

On the basis of form and method of construction, Egyptian baskets can be categorized into three types: coiled, twined and plaited. A coiled basket (see fig. 99) is formed by spirally coiling a continuous foundation of tightly wrapped bundles of fibres to create a circular or oval base and walls. The coiled foundation is then consolidated by stitching, which intersects and binds successive coils to one another. Twined basketry is constructed by weaving horizontal fibres (wefts) around a stationary vertical framework (warps). A wide variety of knots and stitches can be used for securing these elements. In plaited baskets both warp and weft are active: strips of material are woven into baskets by passing under and over each other, usually at regular intervals. The continuous intersection of the plaited constructional elements provides a cohesive unit, and no additional stitching is usually required except, in some examples, to secure the edges. Of these three basketry categories, the coiled variety was by far the most common in ancient Egypt.

Different kinds of plant fibres were exploited by the Egyptians for use in the construction of baskets. The leaves of the date-palm (*Phoenix dactylifera*) and the dom-palm (*Hyphaene thebaica*) were commonly used, especially in plaited baskets and for wrapping and stitching the foundation elements in coiled basketry. Leaf-base fibres

99. Coiled basket with vertical reinforcement ribs, halfa grass and palm-leaves, diam. 205 mm, from Deir el-Medina, New Kingdom (Paris, Musée du Louvre)

from the palms were also used as a basic material in forming the foundation bundles of coiled baskets. Halfa grasses (*Demostachya bipinnata* and *Imperata cylindrica*), however, were a more common bundle material. Such grasses could also be twisted into cordage, which would then serve as one or both sets of elements in a kind of twined basketry. Sedges (*Cyperus papyrus, Cyperus schimperianus*), rushes (*Juncus acutus, Juncus arabicus*), flax (*Linum usitatissimum*) and a woody shrub (*Ceruana pratensis*) were also variously employed.

Ancient Egyptian baskets were produced in a wide variety of shapes and sizes, with oval and circular forms being particularly common. Lids were often made to match, and carrying loops were occasionally attached for ease in handling. The art of basketwork also allowed a degree of artistic expression in terms of construction and decoration. The patterning of the various constructional elements could be manipulated in order to produce not only a useful container but also an aesthetically pleasing object. Smooth, rounded lines and graceful reinforcement ribs can be appreciated in many surviving examples of coiled basketry. Egyptian baskets were often decorated with ornamental or coloured stitching or plaiting incorporated into the design. Chequered, vandyked and other geometric patterns were common, and animal designs were occasionally employed. Black, red and white pigments were frequently used to colour these designs through painted or dyed stitching, plaits or threads. The numerous artistic depictions found in tombs and on other monuments demonstrate their vast range of uses. Baskets also figured prominently in several hieroglyphs.

BIBLIOGRAPHY

A. Lucas: *Ancient Egyptian Materials and Industries* (London, 1926, rev. 4/1962), pp. 128–34
G. M. Crowfoot: 'Textiles, Basketry and Mats', *A History of Technology*, ed. C. Singer, E. J. Holmyard and A. R. Hall (Oxford, 1954), pp. 413–47
J. M. Adovasio: *Basketry Technology* (Chicago, 1977)
Y. Gourlay: *Les Sparteries de Deir el-Médineh*, 2 vols (Cairo, 1981)

DONALD P. RYAN

4. DRESS. Egyptian sculptures, reliefs and paintings feature well-to-do citizens dressed as they wished to be remembered for eternity. Fashion, as represented in these sources, displays a remarkable degree of conservatism over 3000 years, particularly for women. Actual surviving remains of garments are scarce, and those that are preserved often bear little resemblance to the depictions. Evidence of some common types of garment, such as the *shendyt*, is surprisingly lacking. Conversely, there are some surviving examples for which contemporary representations are extremely rare or totally absent. Moreover, when both an actual garment and its representation exist, they often resemble one another only superficially. One striking disparity is that, despite representations of tight garments, surviving clothing is rarely close-fitting. Draping rather than fine tailoring characterized Egyptian fashions throughout the dynasties. Yet these two main sources of evidence provide a picture of a highly developed textile industry, the beginnings of which may be traced back to the Predynastic period (*see* §VII, 4 above for cloth production and §17 below for the decorative techniques used on Egyptian textiles).

Ancient Egyptian dress seems, above all, to have reflected the wearer's status and occupation. Generally the greater amount of the body covered, the higher the wearer's social standing: overseers often wore garments extending from chest to ankle, while workers were naked or clad only in loincloths (see fig. 55 above). Servant women were sometimes shown with exposed breasts (see fig. 72 above) while their mistresses were only occasionally depicted in this way. Young children generally went naked (see fig. 73 above). Priests and viziers were distinguishable by their special garments, such as leopard skins (see fig. 75 above). Other garments, such as the royal *shendyt*, were initially the exclusive clothing of kings but were later 'democratized' and widely adopted. Accessories worn or carried in conjunction with clothing, such as wands or walking sticks, also reflected position or status. Others, such as the bull's tail, sceptres and uraei worn by kings, may have had a symbolic or apotropaic function (for further discussion of the symbolism and iconography of Egyptian dress *see* §V, 2 and 3 above).

(i) Royal and divine. (ii) Private.

(i) Royal and divine.

(a) Representational evidence. Narmer (*reg c.* 3000 BC), the last king of the Predynastic period, is depicted on the ceremonial Narmer Palette (Cairo, Egyp. Mus., JE 32169; for illustration *see* NARMER) wearing an above-the-knee kilt, decorated with a beaded apron and bull's tail, and a corselet held in place by a single shoulder strap. Although the kilt varied in accoutrement and detail, it remained the most popular garment worn by kings in Egypt, from the beginning of Dynastic times to the Roman period.

The royal kilt most frequently depicted was the *shendyt* (see fig. 100a), a rectangle of cloth, usually pleated, gilded or painted gold and rounded at the lower corners. It was wrapped around the king's waist, over a narrow, trapezoidal middle strip, and belted. Most often it reached only just above the knee, thereby permitting free movement. The trapezoidal middle piece was often replaced by an apron, either unadorned or elaborately decorated, often with beadwork (and possibly embroidery), especially during the Middle Kingdom (*c.* 2008–*c.* 1630 BC).

During the New Kingdom (*c.* 1540–*c.* 1075 BC) the royal kilt was frequently longer and fuller, or sometimes a second longer and fuller skirt was worn over the short *shendyt*. This second skirt sometimes also formed part of a tunic which enveloped the king's body from neck to ankle. The king was also shown wearing the tunic alone, especially from the middle of the 18th Dynasty (*c.* 1400 BC).

The beginning of the Late Period (*c.* 750 BC) was characterized by a general trend towards archaism in art, which also extended to royal clothes. After the end of the New Kingdom the long loose garment was abandoned in favour of the traditional kilt (see fig. 65 above). Covering for the royal chest could also take the form of a separate garment, as on the Narmer Palette. The corselet was probably simply a rectangle of cloth or leather, encircling the chest below the armpit and held in place by one or two braces. Another upper body covering worn by the king (in representations from the Old Kingdom onwards)

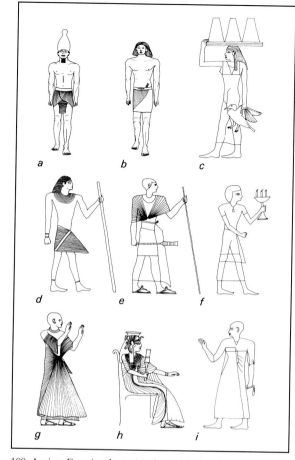

100. Ancient Egyptian dress: (a) *shendyt* kilt, false beard and crown of Upper Egypt, worn by King Mycerinus, 4th Dynasty, *c.* 2480 BC; (b) short wrapped kilt with pleated overlap, worn by Raneferef, 5th Dynasty, *c.* 2419 BC; (c) tight-fitting sheath dress, worn by a female offering-bearer, 5th Dynasty, *c.* 2350 BC; (d) pleated, wrapped kilt with triangular projection, worn by Teti, 6th Dynasty, *c.* 2300 BC; (e) pleated shawl over double skirt, worn by Djehutihotpe, 12th Dynasty, *c.* 1850 BC; (f) 'bag-tunic' with pleated overlap, worn by an unidentified man, mid-18th Dynasty, *c.* 1375 BC; (g) long, loose-fitting, sleeved tunic with overskirt and sandals, worn by Ptahmes, late 18th Dynasty, *c.* 1330 BC; (h) long, flowing cloak over a tight-fitting sheath dress, worn by Queen Nefertari, 19th Dynasty, *c.* 1250 BC; (i) sleeved tunic and wrapped skirt with horizontal roll, worn by Thaasetimu, 30th Dynasty, *c.* 360 BC

decoration. Other parts of the king's costume included one of a variety of crowns and headcloths; a straight, narrow, artificial beard strapped on to the middle of the chin (see fig. 61 above); and sandals and sceptres.

Many gods, such as Amun or Montu, were represented in the same clothing as royalty, thereby strengthening the association between divinity and the office of kingship. They were sometimes differentiated from kings by their accoutrements, including different headgear, staffs or a beard with an upturned tip. Occasionally they are distinguishable from the king only by their relative position in a temple or by an accompanying inscription. In contrast, other gods, including Ptah and Osiris, wore their own very specific garments.

Until the middle of the 18th Dynasty, queens were traditionally represented in sculpture, relief and painting wearing a tight-fitting sheath dress extending from breast to ankle and secured with two shoulder straps (for illustration *see* MYCERINUS). Occasionally, the shoulder straps and upper border of the bodice were decorated in a manner suggesting beadwork. The queens' shoulders were only rarely covered before the New Kingdom. For example, on a 4th Dynasty relief in the rock-cut tomb of Queen Meresankh III (*fl c.* 2530 BC) at Giza, she is shown wearing a garment with pointed shoulders and long, tight-fitting sleeves. Ashayt, one of the minor queens of the 11th Dynasty king Nebhepetre Mentuhotpe II (*reg c.* 2008–*c.* 1957 BC), is depicted in an elbow-length shawl on her painted limestone sarcophagus (Cairo, Egyp. Mus.). In a statue of Queen Sobekneferu (*reg c.* 1760–1756 BC; New York, Met.), the last ruler of the 12th Dynasty, she is shown enveloped in a long cloak.

In the mid-18th Dynasty, when kings began to be represented wearing longer and fuller garments, queens adopted a similar mode of dress. Queen Nefertiti (*fl c.* 1350 BC), for instance, often wore a floor-length, billowy, pleated cloak made from a rectangle of material wrapped around her torso, draped over her shoulders and then tied beneath her breasts or secured with a separate sash. In many representations this garment was worn over the sheath dress. It remained in vogue with other queens until the end of the New Kingdom (see fig. 100h), when, in keeping with the archaizing tendencies at the beginning of the Late Period, it was superseded by the earlier plain sheath.

An all-over, feather-patterned sheath (first associated with a number of deities, including Nekhbet, the vulture-goddess) was occasionally worn by queens and divine adoratrices at least from the 11th Dynasty (*c.* 2000 BC) onwards (see fig. 70 above), and it may symbolize Nekhbet's protective wings. From the 18th Dynasty, the feather motif also decorated the corselet and kilt of kings. It occurred particularly in the contexts of battle, coronation and agricultural festivals, suggesting an association with Horus, the falcon-god, in his role as protector of kings.

(b) Surviving garments. The earliest examples of surviving royal garments are from the tomb of Tuthmosis IV (*reg c.* 1400–*c.* 1390 BC) of the 18th Dynasty (Cairo, Egyp. Mus.), although some of these were heirlooms bearing the name of his father and grandfather. Three fragments

was the 'king's jacket'. This appears to have consisted of bands of material joined to form sleeves, then crossed over the front of the torso, then the back, and finally knotted just above the navel. Sometimes the plain, crossed bands were replaced by falcon wings, symbolic of the king's divine protector, Horus.

On certain occasions, such as the *sed*-festival (royal jubilee), the king was shown in a special garment consisting of a cloak draped around his shoulders and extending to the knee or below (see fig. 109 below). On a statuette of an Early Dynastic king (*c.* 2925–*c.* 2575 BC; London, BM, 37996) the garment bears a lozenge pattern, perhaps representing an embroidered, appliqué or tapestry-woven

(perhaps robes) from this tomb are executed with consummate skill and represent the earliest examples of tapestry-weaving from ancient Egypt. Weft (rather than warp) threads produced a decorative pattern on both front and back consisting of royal names woven in contrasting colours accompanied by floral motifs (see fig. 118 below). A row of embroidered rosettes decorates a fourth fragment.

The richest hoard of royal garments comes from the tomb of Tutankhamun (*reg c.* 1332–*c.* 1323 BC). The garments (Cairo, Egyp. Mus.) are varied in type and manufacturing technique. There are over 100 triangular loincloths, almost 30 gloves (for archery), tunics, shawls, kerchiefs, belts, corselets and countless bundles of cloth, the fragility of which prevents further analysis. Among the small fraction that has been thoroughly studied, three of the King's bag-tunics have embroidered, tapestry-woven bands at the neck, sides and hem. Some motifs, including flowers, flying ducks, geometric designs and hieroglyphs, are purely Egyptian in origin, while others, such as griffins, palmettes, biting animals and winged female sphinxes, suggest Near Eastern influence. The bodies of all the tunics are of fine plain linen, hemmed up the sides to the armhole with openings cut for the head, and, in a few cases, sewn-in sleeves. Some extend just below the knee, while others are ankle-length. One tunic is decorated with over 3000 gold rosettes. Multicoloured stripes made of faience beads adorn a kilt, and two corselets glitter with gold inlay interspersed with cornelian and faience. Tutankhamun took his childhood garments with him into the afterworld, as well as a shirt bearing a date of 'year seven' beside the cartouche of Akhenaten (*reg c.* 1353–*c.* 1336 BC). An imitation leopard skin, made of linen with a gold head and claws, reflects the King's role as high priest.

A long band of tapestry-woven linen (Liverpool Mus., M11156) purchased in Luxor in the 19th century bears the cartouche of Ramesses III (*reg c.* 1187–*c.* 1156 BC) and probably came from his tomb. It is over 5 m long and its width tapers from 130 mm to just under 50 mm, a shape that suggests it was wound around the chest to form the 'king's jacket'. This colourful cloth consists of two tapestry bands separated from each other by a strip of plain linen. Each is decorated with a combination of dots, stripes, zigzags and *ankh*-signs.

(ii) Private. In fashion, as in art, architecture, religion and funerary customs, private people usurped royal styles whenever they could. Noblemen were therefore often represented in royal modes of dress, as well as a great variety of other styles. Their fashions, like those of the kings, gradually became more elaborate. Even the *shendyt*, the quintessential royal garment, was worn by private individuals in Old Kingdom scenes of hunting and trapping, by soldiers in the First Intermediate Period and in a wide variety of contexts from the Middle Kingdom onwards.

(a) Representational evidence.

Old Kingdom–Middle Kingdom (c. 2575–c. 1630 BC). The most commonly depicted private male garment from the Old Kingdom onwards is a simple, short, wrapped kilt made from a wide strip of linen displaying either sharp or rounded bottom corners (see fig. 100b). Both noblemen and workmen wore it in a great variety of contexts, and occasionally female servants and dancing girls are also depicted in it (see fig. 9 above). The kilt varied in length, shape and decoration, especially in the Old Kingdom. The more ornate versions were made for the wealthy, while labourers might wear only a long scarf, wrapped around their waists and legs—if anything at all.

Egyptian inventiveness and artistry is nowhere better exemplified than in the variations on the simple kilt. Parallel, radiating or V-shaped lines indicate plain or herringbone pleats, which may cover all or some of the kilt. One frequently decorated part is the overlap, which could project downward or outward, giving the kilt a triangular shape (see fig. 100d). In the Old Kingdom, both short (knee-length) and longer (mid-calf) kilts were adorned in this way. Horizontal lines, suggesting plaid, beaded aprons and belts, added further variety. On a single monument, the owner was sometimes shown wearing a number of different garments. To complete his costume, the well-dressed man throughout Egyptian history often wore such accessories as an elaborately curled wig, a broad collar, bracelets and sandals and carried a walking stick, sceptre or handkerchief.

For private women of the Old Kingdom, the traditional garment was the same tight-fitting sheath dress (see fig. 100c) worn by queens and goddesses. Occasional traces of paint indicate that these dresses were sometimes coloured. The greatest variation occurred in the shape and decoration of the shoulder straps, and in at least one example in a 5th Dynasty (*c.* 2400 BC) tomb relief at Dishasha, the sheath has long narrow sleeves. In the Early Dynastic period, some women covered one or both of their shoulders with long enveloping mantles. This practice was infrequent, however, before the middle of the 18th Dynasty (*c.* 1400 BC). Like men, they too might wear elegant, curled wigs and abundant jewellery, including broad collars, bracelets, necklaces and anklets.

In the early Middle Kingdom (*c.* 2000 BC), both kings and commoners usually copied Old Kingdom fashions, but by the mid-12th Dynasty (*c.* 1900 BC) new styles also appeared. There was a preference, especially among male officials, for covering more of the body, most often with undecorated garments. The hemlines of skirts sometimes reached ankle length, and the waist, occasionally highlighted by a looped fringe, became higher. The vizier's garment, for example, which first appeared at the end of the 12th Dynasty, was a skirt, extending from upper chest to ankle, held in place by a band around the neck. Short shawls might also be worn (see fig. 100e).

Double kilts worn by kings in relief representations as early as the 5th Dynasty were adopted by the nobility by the mid-12th Dynasty. Usually a longer, transparent, sometimes open skirt covered an opaque knee-length kilt (for illustration *see* THEBES (i), fig. 7). More must have been regarded as better, since in a few delightfully provincial representations on 13th Dynasty stelae, the owner wears three skirts, each longer and higher than the one beneath. The frequent appearance of a long cloak draped over one or both shoulders is another example of the Middle Kingdom trend to cover more of the body. The owner sometimes clutched a corner of the garment to hold it closed.

Women in both Old and Middle Kingdoms (*c.* 2575–*c.* 1630 BC) dressed in an ankle-length white sheath. During the Old Kingdom, however, their shoulder straps tended to meet in the centre of the bodice, forming a V-neck. In the Middle Kingdom the straps were more likely to be separate, and the neckline was trapezoidal. In one instance, in a tomb at Meir, the sheath has a single short sleeve. As in the Old Kingdom, women occasionally wore shawls.

New Kingdom–Roman period (c. 1540 BC–AD 395). Earlier private garment styles remained in vogue in Egypt's New Kingdom, but from the early 18th Dynasty new ones also gained acceptance. A New Kingdom man of high social standing would be represented with his upper torso and shoulders covered. Although known since the Middle Kingdom, it was only in the New Kingdom that the 'bag-tunic' garment slipped over the head and arms (see fig. 100f) gained popularity. It covered at least the chest but could extend to the ankles. A second piece of material was wrapped around the hips like a sporran or wide sash. The tunic was plain and close-fitting at first, but by the reign of Amenophis III (*reg c.* 1390–*c.* 1353 BC) it had acquired greater volume and multiple pleats, the latter indicated by vertical lines or ridges. It was usually long, from this time onwards, often with long, loose sleeves (see fig. 100g). The apron was also sometimes more voluminous: its hem might be tucked under the hem of the tunic to create a puffed effect. This trend toward greater elegance mirrors the opulence of Egypt's empire during the New Kingdom.

For high-ranking officials in the army or security forces, the apron was wrapped around the waist and tied so that the front section assumed a triangular shape. Soldiers and labourers might wear this garment alone, while officers and other dignitaries represented in tomb paintings up to the mid-18th Dynasty sometimes wore shawls, occasionally rippled and fringed at the edge. From the middle of the 18th Dynasty the well-dressed noblewoman wore the billowy frock of contemporary queens. Although superficially it resembled the voluminous pleated tunic worn by men, it was wrapped around the torso rather than slipped over it.

Private fashions at the beginning of the Late Period (*c.* 750 BC) paralleled royal styles by harking back to the garments of the Old and Middle kingdoms. Simple, short, wrapped kilts and *shendyt*s were common for men, while women often wore the plain, tight-fitting sheath with shoulder straps. From the reign of Amasis (*reg* 570–526 BC) officials wore a high-waisted skirt wrapped left over right and secured by looping the initial corner of the material over the upper edge, thereby forming a horizontal roll (see fig. 100i). This garment probably derived from the high skirt of the Middle Kingdom, although it wrapped in the opposite direction.

In Ptolemaic and Roman times (304 BC–AD 395), three traditional Egyptian garments were combined in the costume of the well-dressed male. The first was an unpleated bag-tunic, which usually extended to the knees. A high-waisted skirt over the tunic wrapped generally from right to left in keeping with the most common Dynastic manner.

However, rather than featuring a fringed upper border, the fringed edge fell vertically. The final garment was a fringed shawl, usually draped loosely over one shoulder and beneath the opposite arm. It was held in place with the hand of the covered arm. Since it fell in natural pleats, thereby creating an overall effect reminiscent of garments of the Greek and Roman world, scholars until recently erroneously regarded it as a product of Hellenistic influence.

The characteristic female garment of Ptolemaic and Roman times, like the male costume, also consisted of three Egyptian components worn in an innovative manner. A close-fitting ankle-length tunic came first. On top of it, a long rectangle of cloth was draped around the body like a robe. To hold it in place, it was tied to a fringed shawl which draped down the back. The knot fell either between the breasts or at the right shoulder, adding a decorative touch. In its graceful, flowing effect, this garment resembled the standard female garment of the later New Kingdom.

(b) Surviving garments. Although the earliest surviving fragment of cloth in Egypt dates to the 5th millennium BC (London, U. Coll., Petrie Mus., 2942), the oldest garment is a long-sleeved pleated tunic (London, U. Coll., Petrie Mus., 28614) discovered by Flinders Petrie in a mastaba tomb of the time of Den (*reg c.* 2850 BC) at Tarkhan. This tunic, consisting of a skirt with an attached combination of bodice and sleeves, displays a remarkable degree of sophistication and attention to detail. The skirt was made from a rectangle of linen sewn up the left side in a manner that leaves a decorative edge exposed. Two separate, narrower rectangles of linen folded in half and tightly pleated horizontally were sewn to the upper edge of the skirt so that each formed the bodice and a sleeve. The edges of the sleeves and the V-neck were rolled and finished with tight, neat whip-stitches. Unfortunately the bottom edge is missing, so its original length is unknown. Traces of creases underneath the arm and at the elbows demonstrate that it was worn and not simply made for burial.

This type of tunic is mentioned in lists of linen from the 2nd Dynasty (*c.* 2700 BC) until the First Intermediate Period (*c.* 2100 BC). The only known representation of a figure wearing such a sleeved garment is found in a 5th Dynasty tomb at Dishasha, the same site at which nine dresses were discovered in a woman's tomb. The dresses from Dishasha, only two of which (London, U. Coll., Petrie Mus.) have been closely examined and conserved, display the same basic pattern as the tunic from Tarkhan, but they show coarser workmanship, especially in the finishing details. The Dishasha garments differ in being extremely narrow. This implies that they were specifically made to be placed in the tomb, an implication borne out by the absence of indications of wear.

Similar dresses have been found in private tombs (usually of women) at a number of other sites, including Asyut, Meir, Nag el-Deir and Gebelein (examples in Cairo, Egyp. Mus.; Boston, MA, Mus. F.A.; and Paris, Louvre). Most of these dresses are significantly wider than the Dishasha garments, suggesting that they were intended for use. They also differ from the Dishasha examples by being covered with regular, narrow horizontal pleats held in place at the side by a vertical row of running stitches.

A fine but rare example of a surviving kilt is from the tomb of Wah (TT 1102), estate manager for Meketre in the 11th Dynasty (*c.* 2000 BC). It was dyed red and fringed at the edge. The earliest bag-tunic to be preserved was found in the 11th Dynasty tomb of Meketre. Others date from the 18th Dynasty until Roman times, and their contexts indicate that they were worn by men, women and children. Like Tutankhamun's bag-tunic, they were made from a rectangle of linen folded in half and sewn up the sides to the armhole. A keyhole-shaped opening for the head, cut in the centre, was tied with cords. Some had detachable sleeves for extra warmth. Although early representations of this garment suggest it was form-fitting, the shape of the surviving examples indicates that it was at best loose and bulky.

The richest hoard of non-royal garments (Turin, Mus. Egizio), from the Theban tomb (TT 8) of the 18th Dynasty architect Kha (*fl c.* 1380 BC) at Deir el-Medina, includes knee-length tunics, seven of which were paired with seven triangular loincloths. There were 17 longer tunics, including one of a heavy, warm linen decorated with tapestry-woven bands at the neck, sides and hem. The tapestry bands give it a decorative touch reminiscent of 18th Dynasty royal tunics. Forty-three additional loincloths, four shawls and two large rectangles of fringed linen, possibly cloaks, complete the picture of what a wealthy and prosperous New Kingdom man selected as his ideal wardrobe for eternity. Perhaps Kha's unexpected demise forced his household to prepare his affairs with some haste. Although most of his clothing was freshly washed and folded, a small number of loincloths never reached the 'laundry'. They were packed separately.

As early as the Old Kingdom, professional launderers served on large estates. Clothes to be washed were hauled to the riverbank, moistened and then soaped with natron, a naturally occurring salt used as a bleaching agent until modern times. Tomb scenes (e.g. the wall painting in the tomb of Ipy, at Deir el-Medina, Thebes; TT 217) show workmen beating laundry on stones, rinsing it, wringing it and then laying it out in the sun to dry. The useful life of an ancient Egyptian garment was sometimes extended by patching and mending. Egyptian women also suffered from other apparently 'modern' frustrations: one woman wrote to another seeking a tailor, for, as she complained, she had nothing to wear.

LÄ: 'Tracht'

BIBLIOGRAPHY

B. Cartland: 'The Dress of the Ancient Egyptians (i): In the Old and Middle Kingdoms', *Bull. Met.*, xi (1916), pp. 166–71
——: 'The Dress of the Ancient Egyptians (ii): In the Empire', *Bull. Met.*, xi (1916), pp. 211–14
H. Bonnet: *Die ägyptische Tracht bis zum Ende des neuen Reiches* (Leipzig, 1917)
E. Staehlin: *Untersuchungen zur ägyptischen Tracht im alten Reich* (Berlin, 1966)
R. S. Bianchi: 'Not the Isis Knot', *Bull. Egyp. Semin.*, ii (1980), pp. 9–31
R. Hall: *Egyptian Textiles* (Aylesbury, 1986)
P. J. Watson: *Costume of Ancient Egypt* (London, 1987)
E. Zoffili: *Kleidung und Schmuck in alten Ägypten* (Berlin, 1992)
G. Vogelsang-Eastwood: *Pharaonic Egyptian Clothing* (Leiden, New York and Cologne, 1993)

RITA E. FREED

5. FAIENCE AND GLAZE. Of the wide range of vitreous products prized by the Egyptians for their decorative and symbolic properties, the most characteristically Egyptian was faience. The exact distinctions between faience, FRIT, glass paste and glazed composition, however, have been confused by Egyptologists, and the terms are often used interchangeably in the literature.

(i) Introduction. (ii) Predynastic and Early Dynastic (*c.* 6000–*c.* 2575 BC). (iii) Old Kingdom–Middle Kingdom (*c.* 2575–*c.* 1630 BC). (iv) New Kingdom–Third Intermediate period (*c.* 1540–*c.* 750 BC). (v) Late Period–Roman period (*c.* 750 BC–AD 395).

(i) Introduction. Egyptian faience is a manmade compound with a powdered quartz sintered body and alkaline glaze. It is chemically unconnected with the tin-glazed earthenware produced at Faenza in the early 16th century AD, although the range and brightness of the colours employed by Egyptian craftsmen made the Europeans of the day draw comparisons between the two. The alkaline glazes found on Egyptian faience objects are most frequently blue, green or greenish-blue, though sometimes other colours are found. They are essentially sodium–calcium–silicate compounds, consisting of an alkali, such as natron or plant ash, a small amount of copper or other metallic compound for colouring, some calcium carbonate and a large proportion of silica. Such glazes are chemically close to glass and have no lead content. Lead glazes, which will adhere to ordinary burnt-clay ware, are not found in Egypt until the Late Period (*c.* 750–332 BC); alkaline glazes cannot be used on fired pottery unless the clay is exceptionally high in silica, and hence there is no glazed Egyptian pottery from the Dynastic periods. The Egyptians themselves seem to have regarded glazes (*ṯḥnt š'd*) as by-products of faience (*ṯḥnt*), though in fact the reverse was true; steatite alkaline-glazed objects occurred in Egypt long before faience. The circumstances that led to the discovery of faience in Egypt during the course of the 4th millennium BC are subject to speculation. It is possible, for example, that this new technology was imported into the Nile Valley from the Fertile Crescent. Technological advances, undoubtedly related to the ability to smelt copper, enhanced the potential to manufacture faience.

The production of faience took place from the Predynastic period (*c.* 4th millennium BC) until after the Arab conquest of Egypt in the mid-7th century AD, when the artistic legacy of ancient Egyptian faience was incorporated into the emerging Islamic ceramic industry (*see* ISLAMIC ART, §V, 2(iv)). Faience was worked by hand, cast in moulds but not thrown on the potter's wheel. Once it had been formed into the desired shape, it was fired for several hours at temperatures of *c.* 800° C. The firing caused the porous body to be held together by a glassy 'connective tissue' while the colorants percolated to the surface and fused, producing a vitreously glazed surface. Several faience workshops have been excavated, ranging in date from the 18th Dynasty (*c.* 1540–*c.* 1292 BC) to the Greco-Roman period (332 BC–AD 395). These sites have yielded raw materials, tools, moulds and wasters among other items.

The relationship between faience and glass (probably introduced from the Near East during the 18th Dynasty) is as complex as the distinctions between faience, glaze, frit and 'Egyptian blue', the last now classified as a type of glass rather than faience. Frit (Egyp. *ḫsbd n sš, šsit, w3d* or *ḥmt*) appears more porous than faience, from which it differs in its greater silicate content and lower firing temperature. The technology of frit production, known from early times, was used mainly for smaller objects, such as beads, amulets and inlays, and the only known larger objects of frit are vases (e.g. New York, Brooklyn Mus., 44.175). Frit was also sometimes pulverized to produce colorants for paints and ceramic glazes in ranges from blue to green and from white to grey.

(ii) Predynastic and Early Dynastic (c. 6000–c. 2575 BC). The most common faience objects from the Badarian phase (*c.* 6000–*c.* 4000 BC) are beads. These were manufactured using a body paste coated over a string and rolled into a long cylinder, which was then cut into the desired shapes and sizes. After one firing, the string in each bead was burnt out; the bead was then dipped in glaze and refired. It was perhaps also during the Badarian period that the Egyptians first began to glaze and fire individual beads carved from steatite. The intention of glazed steatite and faience beads, usually blue-green, may have been to imitate green feldspar or turquoise, but it is not known whether the colour was sought for its aesthetic appeal or magical properties (*see* §1 above for a discussion of colour symbolism in amulets). These early beads were intended for personal adornment, perhaps with funerary overtones: excavated examples are strung with other ornaments and served as necklaces adorning the bodies recovered from Predynastic graves. By the end of the Predynastic period, faience had become an integral part of Egypt's material culture.

In the Early Dynastic period Egyptian craftsmen began to manufacture faience statuettes of humans (e.g. the figure seated on a chair, New York, Brooklyn Mus., 57.165.6), as well as animals and birds such as baboons and falcons and perhaps even a pig (New York, Brooklyn Mus., 57.165.2). The archaeological contexts of the faience figurines at Abydos and Elephantine indicate that their purpose was votive and that they may represent deities in the emerging Egyptian pantheon. Faience soon became the chosen medium for amulets of all kinds.

(iii) Old Kingdom–Middle Kingdom (c. 2575–c. 1630 BC). It was at one time assumed that the faience industry was eclipsed during the Old Kingdom, the only extensive work in this material being the tiles used to decorate some of the subterranean chambers of the Step Pyramid complex built by Djoser (*reg c.* 2630–*c.* 2611 BC) at SAQQARA (*in situ* and Cairo, Egyp. Mus., JE 68921; see fig. 101). The excavations of the Czechoslovak Institute of Archaeology, however, have uncovered a vast quantity of faience material in the mortuary complex of Raneferef (*reg c.* 2419–*c.* 2416 BC) at ABUSIR. Some finds (e.g. Cairo, Egyp. Mus., JE 97329) are blue tablets bearing figures and accompanying hieroglyphs, with gilding adhering to the plaster; others are figural inlays, inscribed and predominantly green. Although this material has not been properly assessed, it is possible that it evolved out of the earlier use of 'paste' inlays on the walls of the tomb of Nefermaʿat at MAIDUM (begun *c.* 2600 BC; Cairo, Egyp. Mus., JE 43809, and Munich, Glyp., 103). Paste inlays were also used on the base of the seated statue of Princess Redydjet (*fl*

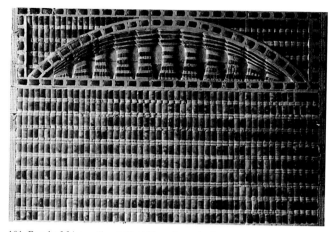

101. Panel of faience tiles, 1.81×2.03 m, from the funerary complex of Djoser at Saqqara, 3rd Dynasty, *c.* 2630–*c.* 2611 BC (Cairo, Egyptian Museum)

102. Faience statuette of a hippopotamus, h. 155 mm, Middle Kingdom, *c.* 2008–*c.* 1630 BC (London, British Museum)

c. 2630 BC; Turin, Mus. Egizio, 3065). Although the paste was not fired, its use in an architectural setting might have led eventually to the architectural use of figural faience plaques.

The production of faience accelerated dramatically during the 11th Dynasty. There are many blue-green faience figurines of hippopotamuses from the Middle Kingdom, often bearing black-painted depictions of riverine plants and occasionally also insects (see fig. 102). The craftsmen of this period also produced female faience figurines known as 'brides of the dead', which were evidently intended to ensure the resurrection of the deceased in the hereafter, an analogy with the posthumous procreative powers of the god Osiris. Among the human faience figurines, the most enigmatic is a figure originally catalogued as 'bedizened catamite' but more probably representing a lyre-player (New York, Brooklyn Mus., 61.164).

At the same time as the resurgence of faience production in Egypt, there appears to have been a similar flowering of the industry in the Nubian KERMA culture, although some of the sherds from faience vessels discovered at Kerma were imported from Egypt. Locally manufactured beads (e.g. Leipzig, Ägyp. Mus., 3845) and plaques, some depicting a scorpion in raised relief (e.g. Khartoum, N. Mus., 1036), attest to the mastery of the Kerma workshops. The Kerma craftsmen also seem to have developed the technology necessary to glaze quartz, assuming that the ram's head from Kerma (Boston, MA, Mus. F.A.) was not an import from Egypt.

(iv) New Kingdom–Third Intermediate Period (c. 1540–c. 750 BC). Faience was put to its most spectacular uses in the New Kingdom. New colours, such as lemon yellow, were introduced, and several colours were often combined in the design of a single object to produce a vivid polychromatic effect (e.g. New York, Brooklyn Mus., 37.123E–124E). Faience was used for many elements of jewellery, particularly beads, pendants, amulets and scarabs (see fig. 97 above). Animal figurines, particularly frogs (e.g. New York, Brooklyn Mus., 58.8.8), continued to be popular. Faience also began to be used for stelae (e.g. Philadelphia, U. PA, Mus., E.13578). At least one stele, perhaps from the New Kingdom, is made of glazed terracotta (Stockholm, Medelhavsmus., 10080). Faience vessels were also common, ranging from different types of chalice to the so-called *Nunschalen* ('vessels of Nun'), which were associated with a particular cult of the goddess Hathor in western Thebes. There were even faience imitations of Aegean vessel forms (e.g. Boston, MA, Mus. F.A., 00.702).

Two other applications of faience became widespread during the New Kingdom: inlay and tiles. Faience inlays were used on *senet* gaming-boards (e.g. Boston, MA, Mus. F.A., 11.3095–7) and, although rare, on stone stelae (e.g. Tübingen, Ebernard-Karls-U., Ägyp. Inst., 1716). The increasing architectural use of faience tiles was particularly dramatic. Although this application had distant antecedents in the Old Kingdom tiles from Abusir and Maidum, it began in earnest only during the reign of Amenophis I (*reg c.* 1514–c. 1493 BC), who used faience tiles to decorate one of his buildings at Karnak. The use of faience tiles—often multicoloured with floral motifs—was widespread during the Amarna period (c. 1353–c. 1332 BC). Such tiles are also common in Ramesside buildings at sites in the Delta region, such as Qantir (*see* PIRAMESSE). A number of large faience tiles with an extraordinary spectrum of colour (e.g. Cairo, Egyp. Mus., and New York, Met.) were introduced on to the art market in the 1920s; the excavations of the Pelizaeus-Museum, Hildesheim, have shown Qantir to have been the source.

Technological advances in the faience industry continued unabated into the Third Intermediate Period, when faience rivalled bronze as the most popular medium for votive offerings. It has been argued that the brownish spots that characterized faience objects in the 22nd Dynasty (c. 950–c. 730 BC) were deliberately introduced during the manufacturing process to create a decorative effect. Glassy faience, a composition with less silica and more alkali than other faience, also first appeared at this time (e.g. New York, Brooklyn Mus., 37.344E). It is identifiable by the gem-like quality of the mass of blue and white crystals visible in a fresh break, and it continued to be used for statuettes until the Roman period, as in the case of a figurine from the reign of Tiberius (*reg* AD 14–37; Paris, Bib. N., Cab. Médailles, 3488). Glassy faience vessels, however, were produced only during the Macedonian and Ptolemaic dynasties (304–30 BC).

The most characteristic faience objects of the Third Intermediate Period were vessels, many in the shape of chalices decorated with registers of relief (e.g. Berlin, Ägyp. Mus., 4563), and numerous *shabti*s (mummiform funerary figurines) in turquoise blue with black inscriptions. There were also faience plaques, pierced as if for suspension (e.g. New York, Brooklyn Mus., 59.17). During this period the technology of faience spread throughout the eastern Mediterranean, and it is often difficult to distinguish between imported Egyptian faience objects, such as scarabs and amulets, and those made locally (*see* ANCIENT NEAR EAST, §II, 5).

(v) Late Period–Roman period (c. 750 BC–AD 395). At the beginning of the Late Period an apple-green faience began to be used for *shabti*s, so-called pilgrims' flasks (e.g. New York, Brooklyn Mus., 37.337EO) and a number of votive offerings, of which the most popular were faience model sistra, the handles of which have survived in large numbers. Faience vessels, particularly alabastra (ointment vessels), came into vogue slightly later. Large figures, such as the upper torso and head of a faience statue identified as the goddess Isis (London, BM, 20449), attest to the craftsmen's technical skill. The primacy of faience as a medium may be gauged by the high quality of a figure of Bes, complete with silver earrings and a gold nose-ring (London, BM, 37401; see fig. 103). During the 30th Dynasty (380–343 BC) blue and green faience began to be used as complementary colours within the same object.

The Egyptian faience industry during the Ptolemaic period is not fully known. There were faience foundation deposits (e.g. New York, Met., 66.99.134), which continue a much older tradition and must be the products of native Egyptian ateliers. Faience figurines continued to be made in small numbers; the statuette of an actor (Alexandria, Gr.-Roman Mus., 28851) is one of the largest and best preserved. Two types of faience vessels became extremely popular during the Ptolemaic period. The first, mainly consisting of hemispherical bowls, was decorated with registers of relief that derived almost exclusively from Classical, non-Egyptian sources. The vessel's function and the significance of its decoration are not known. Although Memphis is thought to have been the primary centre of production, the vessels were probably also produced in Alexandria, judging from the quantity of sherds found in the north-western Delta (Alexandria, Gr.-Roman Mus.). Vessels of the second type—the 'queens' vases'—were probably also produced by Alexandrian Greek ateliers (e.g. London, BM, 73.8–20.389). There was also at least

103. Faience figurine of the dwarf-god Bes, with silver earrings and a gold nose-ring, 33×20 mm, Late Period, c. 750–332 BC (London, British Museum)

one instance of a Hellenistic Alexandrian imitation in faience of a 4th-century BC Attic vessel shape. At about the turn of the 1st millennium BC, plastic black-glazed vessels (e.g. Munich, Staatl. Samml. Ägyp. Kst, 3991) bear glazed depictions of Isis and Serapis, coalescing with the ceramic vessel bodies.

In the Roman period there was continued production of faience vessels (e.g. New York, Brooklyn Mus., 49.31) and figurines. Surviving figurines of the 2nd century AD include representations of Venus (New York, Brooklyn Mus., 44.7) and Nemesis (New York, Brooklyn Mus., 53.173).

BIBLIOGRAPHY
GENERAL
LÄ: 'Fayence', 'Fritte', 'Glasur'
W. Wallis: *Egyptian Ceramic Art* (London, 1900)
W. von Bissing: *Fayencegefässe* (Vienna, 1902)
A. Lucas: *Ancient Egyptian Materials and Industries* (London, 1926, rev. 4/1962), pp. 155–78
J. D. Cooney: 'Glass Sculpture in Ancient Egypt', *J. Glass Stud.*, ii (1960), pp. 10–43
E. Riefstahl: *Ancient Egyptian Glass and Glazes* (Brooklyn, 1968)
P. Derchain: 'La Perruque et le cristal', *Stud. Altägyp. Kult.*, vii (1979), pp. 55–74
A. Kaczmarczyk and others: *Ancient Egyptian Faience: An Analytical Survey of Egyptian Faience from Predynastic to Roman Times* (Warminster, 1983)
C. Herrmann: *Formen für ägyptischen Fayencen* (Göttingen, 1985)

EXHIBITION AND MUSEUM CATALOGUES
J. D. Cooney: *Glass* (1976), iv of *Catalogue of the Egyptian Antiquities in the British Museum* (London, 1976)
Africa in Antiquity: The Arts of Ancient Nubia and the Sudan (exh. cat., New York, Brooklyn Mus., 1978), pp. 145, 153
Meisterwerke altägyptisches Keramik: 5000 Jahre Kunst und Kunsthandwerk aus Ton und Fayence (exh. cat., Horn-Grenzhausen, Rastel-Haus, 1978)
E. Brunner-Traut and E. Brunner: *Die ägyptische Sammlung der Universität Tübingen*, 2 vols (Mainz, 1981)
Egypt's Golden Age: The Art of Living in the New Kingdom (exh. cat., Boston, MA, Mus. F.A., 1982), pp. 140–59
W. Needler: *Predynastic and Archaic Egypt in the Brooklyn Museum*, New York, Brooklyn Mus. cat. (New York, 1984)
25 Years: The Czechoslovak Institute of Egyptology (exh. cat., Cairo, Egyp. Mus., 1985)
Ägyptens Aufstieg zur Weltmacht (exh. cat., ed. A. Eggebrecht; Hildesheim, Pelizaeus-Mus., 1987), pp. 127–8, 136–7
Cleopatra's Egypt: Age of the Ptolemies (exh. cat., ed. R. S. Bianchi; New York, Brooklyn Mus., 1988), pp. 75–80, 174–5

SPECIALIST STUDIES AND EXCAVATION REPORTS
J. Cledat: 'Le Sceptre en verre de Sesostris', *Chron. Egypte*, xi (1936), pp. 484–7
W. C. Hayes: *Glazed Tiles from a Palace of Ramesses II at Kantir* (New York, 1937)
A. Lucas: 'Early Red Faience', *J. Egyp. Archaeol.*, xxiv (1938), p. 245
J. D. Cooney: 'Egyptian Glassy Faience of the 26th Dynasty', *J. Glass Stud.*, ii (1960), pp. 32–9
G. A. Tait: 'The Egyptian Relief Chalice', *J. Egyp. Archaeol.*, xlix (1963), pp. 93–139
B. J. Peterson: 'Ägyptische Stelen und Stelenfragmente aus Stockholmer Sammlungen', *Opuscula Athen.*, ix (1969), pp. 95–123
G. Grimm: 'Two Early Imperial Faience Vases from Egypt', *Misc. Wilbouriana*, i (New York, 1972), pp. 71–100
E. Riefstahl: 'An Enigmatic Faience Figure', *Misc. Wilbouriana*, i (New York, 1972), pp. 137–44
D. B. Thompson: *Ptolemaic Oinochoai and Portraits in Faience* (Oxford, 1973)
J. E. Dayton: 'Appendix D: Faience', *The Sacred Animal Necropolis at North Saqqara: The Southern Dependencies of the Main Temple Complex*, ed. G. T. Martin (London, 1975), pp. 135–7
G. Clerc and others: *Fouilles de Kition* (Nicosia, 1976)
R. S. Bianchi: 'Faience at Kerma', *J. Soc. Stud. Egyp. Ant.*, x (1980), pp. 155–60
H. W. Müller: 'Bemerkungen zu den Kacheln mit Inschriften aus Qantir und zu den Rekonstruktionen gekachelter Palasttore', *Mitt. Dt. Archäol. Inst.: Abt. Kairo*, xxxvii (1981), pp. 339–57
J. Osing: 'Zu einer Fremdvölker Kachel aus Medinet Habu', *Mitt. Dt. Archäol. Inst.: Abt. Kairo*, xxxvii (1981), pp. 389–91
M. A. Hoffmann: *The Predynastic Economy of Hierakonpolis: An Interim Report* (Oxford, 1982)
A. Le Brun: 'Colloque: "Jemdet Nasr, Period or Regional Style?", Tübingen, 26–29 novembre 1983', *Paléorient*, ix (1983), pp. 102–3
C. Castel and G. Soukiassian: 'Dépôt de stèles dans le sanctuaire du Nouvel Empire au Gebel Zeit', *Bull. Inst. Fr. Archéol. Orient.*, lxxxv (1985), pp. 285–93
J. Leclant and G. Clerc: 'Fouilles et travaux en Egypte et au Soudan, 1985–1986', *Orientalia* [Rome], lvi (1987), pp. 292–389

ROBERT S. BIANCHI

6. FURNITURE. Ancient Egyptian houses were simply and sparsely furnished with wooden beds, chairs, low tables and stools and a variety of chests and boxes for storage. Many pieces were flexible in use: beds doubled as couches for daytime use, and multipurpose stands of pottery or latticework supported vessels or trays to create individual dining tables. In keeping with the conservative attitudes of the ancient Egyptians, furniture design changed very little over time. However, surface decoration did vary: in the Old and Middle kingdoms decorative elements were restrained and generally reiterated the bold designs of the furniture, but by the New Kingdom, when elaborately decorated furniture was a mark of social standing, forms were obscured by ornamental detail.

Because of its perishable nature, very little furniture has survived from habitation sites and virtually all the evidence therefore comes from tombs, either in the form of actual pieces interred as grave goods or as representations in reliefs and wall paintings. However, as these practices began only in the Early Dynastic period and died out following the end of the New Kingdom, little is known of furniture outside this period. This has also meant that most pieces are atypical in that they come from royal or noble burials, although vernacular furniture is sometimes depicted in tomb paintings. Additionally, the tomb context can make it difficult to distinguish between objects of everyday use and specifically funerary pieces. What little evidence there is for furniture in the period after the New Kingdom suggests that traditional forms continued in use, only gradually being replaced by foreign types; however, by the Greco-Roman period, wealthy householders had gone over to furnishing their homes in the Hellenistic and Roman styles.

(i) Early Dynastic (*c.* 2925–*c.* 2575 BC). (ii) Old Kingdom and First Intermediate Period (*c.* 2575–*c.* 2008 BC). (iii) Middle Kingdom and Second Intermediate Period (*c.* 2008–*c.* 1540 BC). (iv) New Kingdom (*c.* 1540–*c.* 1075 BC).

(i) Early Dynastic (c. 2925–c. 2575 BC). From the little evidence that survives, it seems that the basic repertory of Egyptian furniture—stools, chairs and boxes—was already in existence at this date. Among the earliest known pieces are fragments of furniture from royal mastaba tombs of the 1st Dynasty (*c.* 2925–*c.* 2775 BC) at Abydos and Saqqara; these include some finely carved ivory chair legs in the form of massive bulls' legs with prominent veins (New York, Met.) and some fragments of an ebony chair that had clearly been carved in imitation of a woven rush prototype (Cairo, Egyp. Mus.). The tomb of King Djer also yielded a finely made compartmented wooden box (Cairo, Egyp. Mus.). A less sophisticated piece from the same period is a rudimentary stool from Grave 415 at Tarkhan that was made from a roughly cut tree trunk with three branches trained to form legs; this form later evolved into the elegant three-legged stool with slender splayed legs popular in the New Kingdom.

Much of the evidence for 3rd Dynasty (*c.* 2650–*c.* 2575 BC) furniture comes from relief carvings in the TOMB OF HESYRE, chief of scribes to King Djoser (*reg c.* 2630–*c.* 2611 BC). Among the items represented is a canopied bed; fragments of a similar canopy were found in a storage chamber at Djoser's funerary complex at Saqqara.

(ii) Old Kingdom and First Intermediate Period (c. 2575–c. 2008 BC). The funerary furniture of Hetepheres I (Cairo, Egyp. Mus.; *see* HETEPHERES I, TOMB OF) included two graceful wooden armchairs richly embellished with gilding and coloured faience (see fig. 104). The first of these is low and broad, to accommodate the customary seated posture in which the legs were drawn up and usually crossed. Its design is a simple rectangle with a supporting strut in the centre of the frame at the back and high arms decorated with delicate palace-façade designs in thin gold. The wooden supports of the armrests are carved in the form of bound papyrus flowers and again sheathed in gold. The lion's legs, all facing forward, have only cursorily sketched musculature; the paws are elevated on conical rilled platforms which were themselves protected by copper shields beneath. The seat and armrests are tilted slightly backwards. The form of the second chair is less

certain; it must have been basically the same in design but was narrower and more elaborately decorated. The lion's legs are bold and sturdy, and attention was given to the modelling of the ankles. The arms were decorated with gold and inlays of faience representing Horus, the god of kingship, standing on a palm column, while the armrests were inlaid with a design of feathers and rosettes, a motif found also on the footboard of the bed and the lid of a box. Across the back of the chair, standards representing the crossed arrows of the goddess Neith were executed in coloured inlays set into a background of blue-green faience (*see* §5 above). Stylized locks of hair outlined the design across the upper frame of the back. The traditional association of these symbols with the north of Egypt suggests that the chairs were made in Memphis, the Old Kingdom capital, although their basic designs were to persist over time in the capitals of Thebes and Akhetaten.

Hetepheres' palanquin seems very small and delicate when compared to the breadth of the armchairs. In design, it is an armchair with solid arms and a high back set on a shallow box. The frame was covered in gold and the carrying poles, probably of ebony, ended in massive gold papyrus flowers. Across the back of the chair, at the height of the arms, is a strip of ebony with the names and titles of the queen inlaid in gold. The design is forthright and pure; as in much Egyptian furniture, neither the clarity of the line nor the functional nature of the piece is obscured. Both the palanquin and the armchairs must have had counterparts that were used during the Queen's lifetime; indeed, they themselves might have been so employed. The construction of a similar palanquin is portrayed in the tomb of Hetepheres' granddaughter Meresankh III (*see* GIZA, §1) along with an armchair in which the arms are supported by the bodies of lions; the famous diorite statue of her grandson Chephren (*reg c.* 2520–*c.* 2494 BC; *see* fig. 52 above) shows him seated on a throne supported by figures of lions.

Further interpretations of royal furniture were carved on the walls of the tomb of the 5th Dynasty (*c.* 2465–*c.* 2323 BC) courtiers Niankhkhnum and Khnumhotpe at Saqqara. In a long limestone chamber, Niankhkhnum was illustrated seated in a palanquin with high arms supported by vertical slats so that his body may be seen through the openings. Old Kingdom furniture frequently recalls architectural forms; this feature is reminiscent of the colonnaded entrance to Djoser's nearby funerary complex. In the same tomb, Khnumhotpe is shown sitting in an armchair with solid arms which, like the seat, were outlined in paint to convey the supporting framework of the chair. Bull's legs replaced those of lions, but the ribbed bases were retained and set on additional triangular bases. An armchair illustrated in a relief carving in the tomb of Iason at Giza was apparently built for a person sitting upright with both feet on the floor. Although of the same general design as Khnumhotpe's chair, the back is high enough to extend above Iason's head, and the bull's legs are unusually long. This variation continued into the Middle Kingdom. Other types shown in 6th Dynasty (*c.* 2325–*c.* 2150 BC) relief decorations include high-backed chairs in the tomb of Sekhemka (Giza, west field, G1029) and palanquins in the tomb of Qar at Giza.

A form of chair or stool found in reliefs in all Old Kingdom private tombs was used specifically for placement in front of an offering table. These chairs were customarily designed with the frame of the seat ending in a large papyrus flower finial, and a modicum of comfort was accorded the seated person by a pillow or cloth at his or her back. In Nefer and Kahay's tomb (late 5th Dynasty) at Saqqara, the stools before the offering table of Werbauw and Khentkawes had bull's legs, a reversion to 1st-Dynasty tradition. The lion's leg reappeared on a stool represented in the tomb of Qar in a very imaginative form: the legs are curved at the top to indicate the lion's shoulders, necessitating a corresponding curve in the seat, with the effect that the stool is rendered as a single animal.

The two main types of stool used in the Old Kingdom were the three-legged stool, known since the Late Predynastic period (c. 3000 BC), and the folding-stool, which must have derived from the kind of furniture easily transported on military expeditions or hunting excursions. The three-legged stool may be the only example of a plebeian object that evolved into an article used by the nobility: other types of furniture, so far as can be ascertained, seem to have originated in furnishings made for the aristocracy and subsequently adapted for citizens of lesser rank.

No evidence of the sleeping arrangements of the common people has survived, but a famous royal canopied bed was found in the tomb of Hetepheres I. The bed is of an early type, a wide, cross-boarded structure which sloped downwards slightly from head to foot. The four corners of the frame were ornamented with boldly protruding papyrus flowers. Virtually the entire structure, including the legs, was cased in gold of considerable thickness. The inner surface of the footboard was sheathed in gold decorated with the feather-and-rosette motif, while its outer surface was left unsheathed. Lion's legs of particularly sturdy appearance served as supports. Presumably some sort of mattress was provided, and a headrest covered in gold was found in a gold box with an inlaid lid. The headrest reflects earlier designs, except that the column has wide, shallow flutes rising to a single abacus which in turn supported the curved head support. The height of the headrest at least theoretically equalled the width of the owner's shoulders; since the design was retained for millennia, it must be assumed that the objects were more comfortable than they appear. While the influence of architecture is clear in this case, the form of headrests in general may have had amuletic significance, as it resembles the hieroglyph for 'horizon'. Some 5th-Dynasty headrests were carved from a single block of wood. The canopy of Hetepheres' bed, which carried the royal curtains, appears to have been a fragile structure. Its design clearly demonstrates the purity of line typical of Old Kingdom furnishings, while the restrained decoration attests to the luxury the Queen expected. The wood was first inscribed with the name of Sneferu and with matt patterns, over which gold was fitted. Each of the poles was covered with a single sheet of gold, even on those parts that abut each other and thus could not have been seen. The upper parts of the support poles were made of separate pieces of wood joined by gold tacks, and the poles were fitted into copper sockets soldered with silver. Similar bed canopies reappeared in the 4th Dynasty, in

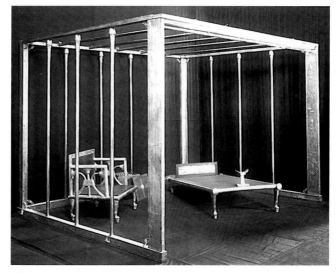

104. Chair, bed and bed-canopy of Queen Hetepheres I, gilded and inlaid wood, chair 795×720 mm, bed 1.78×0.97 m, 4th Dynasty, c. 2551–2528 BC (Cairo, Egyptian Museum)

relief decorations in the tomb of Meresankh and in that of her son, Nebemakhet, at Giza. The powerful 6th-Dynasty courtier Mereruka also possessed a canopy of the same design. While these objects may have had a specific purpose in funerary practice, they must have been in ordinary domestic use as well.

Many examples of boxes, chests and caskets of all kinds have survived, some of which are simple in design, others elaborately ornamented. Hetepheres' curtain box was covered in gold which had been pressed into carved inscriptions and decorative motifs, then inlaid with faience. This use of coloured pastes may have been the inspiration for the inlay work on the curtain box and other pieces in the tomb. A long, narrow inlaid box, encased in gold, offers another example of the familiar feather-and-rosette decoration, while another box, which held the Queen's silver bracelets, was covered inside and out with ribbed sheets of gold and had an ivory button for lifting the lid; the latter was a common feature of the smaller boxes and chests.

Old Kingdom tables are little attested. Those known from wall decorations in tombs are of straightforward rectilinear design with four unembellished legs and sometimes a horizontal strut bracing the legs. They were sometimes embellished with cavetto cornices, a feature that first appeared in a 5th Dynasty tomb at Saqqara. The development of the cavetto cornice for false doors and for other articles of furniture may have occurred at the same time.

(iii) Middle Kingdom and Second Intermediate Period (c. 2008–c. 1540 BC). Few examples of furnishings have been preserved from this period; the main sources are scenes on coffins and sarcophagi. The carved limestone sarcophagus of Kawit from Deir el-Bahri (Cairo, Egyp. Mus., JE 47397) illustrates furniture that had clearly developed from 6th-Dynasty types, and includes an armchair with extremely long legs and a high back which would

have required the user to sit upright with both feet on the floor. A lion-footed chair of the same type is represented on the sarcophagus of Ashait, also from Deir el-Bahri (Cairo, Egyp. Mus., JE 47267), but in this case a platform is provided as a footrest. Fully-modelled lion heads appear to be attached to the seat rather than to the legs, but this may be artistic shorthand. A jewellery casket illustrated on the sarcophagus of Kawit has a cavetto cornice and a gabled lid, a type that was to become common in the New Kingdom. With the treasure of el-Lahun, the funerary equipment of Sithathoriunet, a daughter of Sesostris II (*reg c.* 1844–*c.* 1837 BC), a new attitude towards furniture emerged. The Princess's ebony jewellery casket (New York, Met.) introduced an unparalleled emphasis on surface ornamentation which was to influence the workmanship of the New Kingdom. Gold *djed* columns were set into ivory panels on all four sides of the box to form decorative false doors which were inlaid with blue faience and cornelian; each side was surmounted by an ivory cavetto cornice set off by gold mouldings and Hathor heads. In this way the structure of the casket was obscured; and in general, the pure lines and sturdy animal legs of Old Kingdom furniture increasingly gave way to complicated surface decoration which deliberately detracted from the form.

(iv) New Kingdom (c. 1540–c. 1075 BC). Imported woods, including ash, beech, cedar, cypress, yew and the highly prized ebony, predominated in royal furniture of the New Kingdom. Royal furniture was often covered in gold, and in a new feature figural scenes depicting the owners appeared on the backs of chairs. Sitamun, a daughter of Amenophis III (*reg c.* 1390–*c.* 1353 BC), gave her maternal grandparents Yuya and Tuya (*see* YUYA AND TUYA, TOMB OF) a lion-legged chair with a broad rush seat. On its back are gilded scenes of the Princess receiving a *menat* collar, while the high solid arms have scenes of the domestic deities Bes and Beset; at the top of the legs, where lions' heads might normally appear, are human heads, presumably of Sitamun herself. The subject-matter is both magical and funerary because the object was presented in a funerary context.

The most spectacular examples of gilded chairs come from the tomb of TUTANKHAMUN. The throne (Cairo, Egyp. Mus., JE 62028) is a standard lion-footed chair with lions' heads at the height of the cane seat and solid arms in the form of winged serpents. This type of upright, long-legged chair had been used since the late Old Kingdom in domestic contexts, but here it is adapted for royal use. The entire piece is covered in gold leaf, and a scene of the young King and his wife on the back is ornamented with glass paste and hardstones. However, the architectural quality of Old Kingdom furniture has been sacrificed to the magnificent decoration. A tiny ebony chair made for the King when a child (Cairo, Egyp. Mus.) has lion's feet, between which are latticed supports for the slatted seat. The solid gold arms represent relaxing ibexes, an appropriate theme for the royal nursery. A more formal aspect of design is seen in a full-sized chair in which the figure of the god Heh kneeling on the sign for gold forms the back. The inlaid ebony ceremonial chair (see fig. 105) represents a more complex form as well as a dazzling

105. Ceremonial chair of Tutankhamun, gilded and inlaid wood, 1.02×0.70 m, New Kingdom, *c.* 1325 BC (Cairo, Egyptian Museum)

display of decorative techniques. It basically comprises a folding-stool to which a high back has been added. The seat, curved to accommodate a cushion, has ivory inlays in imitation of a leopard skin. The upper part of the back represents the Aten sun disc above a vulture with outstretched wings flanked by the titles of the King. Entirely covered in gold leaf, it is enhanced with inlays of ivory, ebony, hardstones and faience. Ebony heads of ducks, inlaid with long triangular insets of ivory, form the splayed legs and grasp the floor runners in their bills. In front of the chair was placed a footstool, on which bound captives are depicted in order that the King might symbolically crush them beneath his feet. As the floor runners offered insufficient stability for such an elaborate object, additional broad struts were set vertically at the back, unpleasing to the eye but again masked in gold..

The folding-stool with ducks' heads holding floor runners in their bills was a common article of furniture in wealthy households. The heads were often given graceful, slender inlays of ivory, while carved eyes heightened the sense of a living animal. The seat was made of two broad strips of wood, originally covered with leather, though this has often disappeared (e.g. Berlin, Ägyp. Mus., 12552). In one scene on his golden throne, Tutankhamun is shown seated on a folding-stool with large cushions of punched leather; the same type of leather seat is illustrated in a painted scene in the Theban tomb of Nebamun and Ipuky. In humbler homes the traditional three- and four-legged stools remained in use; elegant variants with splayed legs were produced for the nobility. One type, an example of which was found in Tutankhamun's tomb, had slender latticework supports between the legs. These lattices, formed by vertical and diagonal struts, are familiar from the many painted representations of pot stands in Theban tombs: one actual example comes from Thebes (London, BM, 2476). The lattice design continued into the 19th Dynasty and features on a chair illustrated on the funeral sledge of Khonsu (Cairo, Egyp. Mus., JE 27302) from Deir el-Medina.

Ordinary chairs were commonly made of hardwood and had slatted backs, woven seats and lions' legs. Sturdily built, they recall the boldness of Old Kingdom design combined with the more graceful and presumably more comfortable slanting New Kingdom back. A more utilitarian type was a simple, armless chair with a broad supporting strut at the back and a rush seat woven in a chevron pattern; a rare example is from Deir el-Medina (Paris, Louvre, E 14437). Finally, no discussion of New Kingdom chairs would be complete without mention of the 'easing-chairs' known from el-Amarna (e.g. room 29, House of Nakht). Made of wood or clay, these chairs were either portable or bricked into place. They share the basic form of the classic 18th Dynasty chair but have a keyhole-shaped opening in the contoured seat that enabled the user to urinate or defecate into a sand-filled receptacle below.

Headrests in the form of folding-stools include a fine ivory example from the tomb of Tutankhamun (Cairo, Egyp. Mus., JE 62023). A clumsier version from Akhmim, also in ivory, is decorated with carved heads of Bes as a protection against snakes, scorpions and evil spirits of the night. A more common form, executed in wood, had a broad base supporting a broadly fluted column and was commonly incised with figures of Bes and Thueris.

In humble homes such as the dwellings of the necropolis workers at Deir el-Medina, low mud-brick benches served as seating during the day and sleeping platforms at night. Wealthy residences were equipped with beds; these took various forms, but all basically comprised a wooden frame, with lion's legs, over which matting was stretched. Mattresses and cushions were placed on top. High beds, such as those depicted in the tomb of Ramesses III (*reg c.* 1187–*c.* 1156 BC), were supplied with small steps to enable the user to climb up. There were also various kinds of low beds, including a folding camp-bed from the tomb of Tutankhamun. The animal-headed couches from the same tomb were strictly funerary; similar types are shown on the funeral sledge of Khonsu and in the tomb of Sennedjem where it was found (*see* THEBES (i), fig. 10).

Elegant tables with cavetto cornices, torus mouldings and splayed legs are reminiscent of the entrance pylons of temples; these designs derived in part from furniture of the Old Kingdom. The unembellished straight-legged table also continued in use, but few examples have survived. Chests and boxes of all kinds abounded. Lids may be sloping or vaulted, and cavetto cornices are common; simple flat lids, double lids and gable lids are also attested. Boxes were secured by lashing a cord around one knob on the lid and another on the side; the lashings could be sealed with clay. Boxes in the form of shrines were equipped with knobs on the elevated part of the lid, as in the case of Panhesy's box from Tell el-Amarna. Gabled lids and sliding lids had been used in the Old Kingdom; the latter may have had Predynastic origins. The best examples, however, come from the New Kingdom and include a double compartmented trinket box with a sliding lid (Toronto, Royal Ont. Mus., 931.55) and a multi-compartmented box from Sedment with two sliding lids and a gable lid (see fig. 106). An elegant jewellery casket from the Theban tomb of Yuya and Tuyu is made of gilded wood inlaid with ebony, ivory and blue faience, with a vaulted lid set on a cavetto cornice and bearing the titles of Amenophis III in gold (Cairo, Egyp. Mus.).

106. Multi-compartmented box, wood, 58×94 mm, from Tomb 254, Sedment, New Kingdom, *c.* 1540–*c.* 1075 BC (Philadelphia, PA, University of Pennsylvania, University Museum)

Boxes, chests and caskets, however ornamented, remained utilitarian. Those belonging to the funerary assemblage of Tutankhamun were crammed with objects of all kinds. The King's headgear box was a deep chest set on legs with a hinged lid secured by lashings around two knobs, containing a support for the King's cap (Cairo, Egyp. Mus.; *see* WOOD, colour pl. III, fig. 1). Two cabinets set on long legs so that they resemble tables are relatively plain objects of cedar relieved by openwork friezes of amuletic symbols (Cairo, Egyp. Mus); they were basically objects of daily use, not objects made specifically as funerary furniture. Several little chests were apparently made for the King as a child and were used as toyboxes. Other examples of functional pieces include a chest of ebony and cedar set on retractable carrying poles which slide through bronze rings (Cairo, Egyp. Mus.). Conversely, the design and rich ornamentation of the more famous chests and boxes in Tutankhamun's tomb attest to a symbolic function. The chest in the form of a cartouche, with the King's title boldly stated in ebony and ivory against a gold background (Cairo, Egyp. Mus.), represents a superbly crafted three-dimensional statement of the immortality of the King's name. An alabaster chest covered in hieroglyphs has a jewel-like quality. The small, dark hieroglyphs against the translucent surface tend to deny the solidity of form and emphasize the precious nature of the object. Similarly, in a magnificent wooden chest (Cairo, Egyp. Mus., JE 61467), stuccoed and painted with a series of hunting scenes, emphasis is on the pictorial and thus the two-dimensional aspect; the viewer sees the profusion of colour and movement rather than the form of the object.

BIBLIOGRAPHY
H. Carter and A. Mace: *The Tomb of Tut.Ankh.Amen*, i (London, 1923)
H. Carter: *The Tomb of Tutankamen*, ii–iii (London, 1927–33)
G. A. Reisner: 'The Household Furniture of Queen Hetep-heres I', *Bull. Mus. F. A. Boston*, xxvii (1929), pp. 83–90
: 'The Bed Canopy of the Mother of Cheops, Queen Hetepheres I', *Bull. Mus. F. A. Boston*, xxx (1932), pp. 56–60
——: *A History of the Giza Necropolis*, ii (Cambridge, MA, 1955)
C. Desroches-Noblecourt: *Tutankhamen: Life and Death of a Pharaoh* (New York, 1965)
D. Dunham and W. K. Simpson: *The Mastaba of Queen Mersyankh III, G 7530–7540* (Boston, MA, 1974)
A. Moussa and F. Junge: *Two Tombs of Craftsmen* (Mainz, 1975)
I. E. S. Edwards: *Treasures of Tutankhamun* (New York, 1976)
Egypt's Gold Age: The Art of Living in the New Kingdom, 1558–1085 BC (exh. cat., ed. E. Brovarski; Boston, MA, Mus. F.A., 1982)
E. FINKENSTAEDT

7. GARDENS. Although to an Egyptian the ideal setting for an eternal existence was a field of corn of supernatural growth, a garden was his paradise on earth. Flowers and herbs as well as trees were grown not only for enjoyment but also for the use of cooks, herbalists and scent manufacturers. The ideal garden was walled and laid out around a square pond with fishes and lotus flowers (see fig. 7 above). Trees and plants were arranged symmetrically in relation to the pond, the beds being intersected by paths. Borders of shrubs featured blue cornflowers, red poppies and yellow mandrake fruits. Architectural elements included massive, inscribed stone gates, double rows of columns (supporting climbing vines) and sometimes a 'pleasure house'. There were gardens at most temples (e.g. the Temple of Amun at Karnak and the temple of Hatshepsut at Deir el-Bahri in western Thebes). The tomb of Ineni the architect (TT 81; *c.* 1500 BC), also at Thebes, contained wall paintings showing a garden that included 90 sycamore figs, 31 persea trees, hundreds of date- and dom-palms and many other identifiable plants such as willows and vines. The 'Botanical Room' of Tuthmosis III (*reg c.* 1479–*c.* 1426 BC), to the east of the 'Festival Hall' in the Temple of Amun at Karnak, includes reliefs depicting plants imported by the King from abroad.

For further discussion *see* GARDEN, §II, 2.

BIBLIOGRAPHY
LÄ: 'Garten'
D. Hennebo: 'Betrachtungen zur altägyptischen Gartenkunst', *Archv Gtnbau*, iii (1955), pp. 173–218
M.-F. Moens: 'The Ancient Egyptian Garden in the New Kingdom: A Study of Representations', *Orient. Lovan. Period.*, xv (1984), pp. 11–53
J.-C. Hugonot: *Le jardin dans L'Egypte ancienne* (Frankfurt am Main, 1989)
L. Manniche: *An Ancient Egyptian Herbal* (London, 1989)
LISE MANNICHE

8. GLASS. Despite the early use of glazes and faience (*see* §5 above) in ancient Egypt the use of glass as a medium in its own right came relatively late in Egyptian history; having enjoyed a short flowering during the New Kingdom (*c.* 1540–*c.* 1075 BC) it virtually died out until its revival as part of a new artistic and technological tradition in the later 1st millennium BC.

(i) Introduction. (ii) Techniques. (iii) Stylistic development.

(i) Introduction. One of the earliest uses of glass was probably as a substitute for semi-precious stones in jewellery (*see* §XV above); other products included such small items as beads and amulets, and gradually cosmetic jars and kohl bottles, small figurines and coloured pastes for inlays in wood, stone or metal were introduced. Glazed windows were introduced in the Greco-Roman period (332 BC–AD 395).

Apart from a few pieces believed to be earlier (*see* §(iii)(a) below) it seems that glass appeared in Egypt as a fully developed industry *c.* 1500 BC. Since there are no apparent trial stages, it has been suggested that the introduction of glassworking was the result of the Near Eastern campaigns that marked the beginning of the New Kingdom (*see* §I, 2(v) above). During the campaigns of Tuthmosis III (*reg c.* 1479–*c.* 1426 BC), for example, notably his conquests in Mitanni, glassworkers may have been brought into Egypt as captives. It is possible that these workers depended on their native lands for their basic raw materials, and that in Egypt they served as glassworkers rather than as true glassmakers. Diplomatic correspondence from the site (*see* AMARNA, EL-) mentions the import of raw glass, confirming it as a commodity of sufficient value to be mentioned at the highest levels, and glass ingots, probably bound for Egypt, were discovered in an ancient shipwreck off Ulu Burun on the Turkish coast. That glass was both highly prized and rare is further indicated by the presence of wooden imitations of glass vessels in the tomb of Yuya and Tuyu (Cairo, Egyp. Mus., JE 3686–9). It has also been claimed that glass manufacture was confined to royal workshops as a state-controlled monopoly, although evidence for this is not conclusive. By the middle of the 18th Dynasty (*c.* 1400 BC) some true glassmaking was probably taking place in Egypt; glass workshops of the period are known from Malqata and Tell el-Amarna. Workshops of the 20th Dynasty (*c.* 1190–*c.* 1075 BC) are known from el-Lisht and the vicinity of Manshiya near Dahshur.

Although glassmaking declined from the late 20th Dynasty, it continued on a much reduced scale into the early 21st Dynasty. Apart from a few isolated pieces, the craft then became almost extinct, and was not reintroduced until the revival of Egyptian cultural tradition that took place from the 25th (*c.* 750–*c.* 656 BC) and 26th dynasties onward. By the 30th Dynasty (380–343 BC) the glass industry seems to have been concentrated in Lower Egypt, broadly in the area between the Faiyum and the Delta. Mosaic glass (*see* §(ii) below) was also introduced at this time. In addition, large quantities of eastern Mediterranean glass vessels were imported into Egypt, including rare examples of vessels in classical shapes from Phoenicia. In the Greco-Roman period a greater range of glass forms became known as a result of the incorporation of Egypt into first the Ptolemaic and then the Roman empires. The newly founded capital of Alexandria soon became a thriving centre of glass production with its own specialized repertory, and there was a guild of glassworkers in the city of Oxyrhynchus. Late in the 1st century BC glass-blowing was discovered, probably somewhere on the Syrian coast, and it gradually spread to Egypt. By the early 1st century AD Egyptian and Syrian glassmakers were setting up workshops in Rome itself, and the technique of glassmaking spread rapidly throughout the Roman Empire.

(ii) Techniques. The silica, alkali and lime necessary for glass production were all available in Egypt. Silica was obtained as sand, although crushed flint or quartz could also be used if the sand proved unsatisfactory. To allow the silica to melt at a sufficiently low temperature ancient workers found it necessary to add an alkali to serve as a flux. These alkalis were added in the form of plant ashes, particularly from saltmarsh plants, or as natron. Ancient texts do not mention the addition of lime, and it is to be supposed that this was present as an impurity in sand, making certain deposits more valuable for glassworking than others.

Ancient Egyptian glass furnaces could achieve temperatures of only *c.* 1000°C. Although this heat was adequate to melt the raw ingredients it would not sufficiently reduce their viscosity to allow gas bubbles to be liberated and unmelted raw material to settle out. Glassmaking was therefore a two-stage process. The first stage, 'fritting', involved the heating together of the raw materials at a temperature between 700° and 850°C until they formed a mass. This reaction allowed gases to escape from the mixture; on cooling, it left a solidified mass with a lower sediment fraction, a middle portion of crystallized glass material and a vesicular upper surface. Once the impurities had been chipped away from the upper and lower surfaces, the remaining material was crushed into a fine glass powder. This was melted at a higher temperature, up to *c.* 1000°C, to produce a molten glass ('metal') that could then be formed.

Colours were achieved by adding minerals to the mixture. Copper was used for blue-green and cobalt for blue or violet; mixtures of copper, cobalt and manganese were also common. With lead oxide, copper could be used to produce shades of green, and with sodium or potassium, a turquoise blue. Under reducing (low-oxygen) conditions copper oxide could be used to produce a dull red. Antimony was used for producing yellow and opaque white glass. Although forming processes varied over time and with the type of artefact, all glass had to be annealed after working. This process involved the slow cooling of the vessel, probably in an oven located next to the main melting furnace the residual heat of which it could share, which allowed the gradual release of stresses created in the glass during forming. The New Kingdom glass workshops at Malqata and el-Amarna have yielded evidence of pans that were apparently used in the production of frit, as well as other vessels that served as stands. Numerous glass rods of varying thicknesses, which had been poured or perhaps pulled from the batch of molten glass, were also recovered. Some of these rods (e.g. London, U. Coll., Petrie Mus., 22889A) had been rolled, perhaps to alter their thickness for shaping into vessel parts. Test samplings showing the impressions of pincers were also found (e.g. London, U. Coll., Petrie Mus., 22923).

Vessels of the New Kingdom were generally core-formed, a process that involved the shaping of the vessel's body around a core composed of a mixture of dung or vegetable material with clay and sand, sometimes coated with ground limestone mixed with ferruginous clay. This core, formed around a wooden rod that could be used for handling, was either dipped into molten glass or had glass trailed over it. The viscous material might then be rolled on a flat surface ('marvered') to even the wall thickness. Trails of coloured glass could then be added and marvered into the parent material to give the banded effect of agate or some other hardstone (*see* GLASS, colour pl. IV, fig. 2). Rims, handles and bases could be worked separately and added to the main body once shaped; rims and bases might also be drawn from the body material. After annealing, the cooled piece would have the core removed by chipping it away, although the frequently opaque appearance of ancient Egyptian glass is due to the remains of this core on the inside surface of what is otherwise translucent glass. The vessel was then smoothed and polished to the desired finish. Although workers produced shapes to suit Egyptian tastes they did not develop forms unique to glass.

Pieces combining several techniques are also known, such as a small early New Kingdom kohl vessel (London, BM, 24391) with gold rim and foot bands. Its lid was moulded, whereas the body could be either moulded or cold-worked, and its centre was drilled but was then smoothed with pumice. The shape is directly derived from stone vessels and it may be that some of this technology was also transferred. Cold-working of glass, then, was practised during the New Kingdom, and although this technique is commonly thought to have reached a peak in later times, some fine examples belong to this period. Techniques already well established by gem-cutters were employed; pieces were solid cast and then abraded using quartz or flint. A limited amount of sculpture in the round was produced by these methods, but such small pieces were rare because of the difficulty of working fine detail, and they must always have been highly prized luxury items. No moulds survive; a certain amount of detail would have been included, but how much is uncertain, and most pieces show substantial traces of reworking. Inscriptions were added separately.

More complex pieces were almost certainly cast by the lost-wax technique in which a wax image of the finished form has clay pressed around it. An opening is left at the top or bottom of the clay mould and when this is fired the wax evaporates, leaving a void in the shape of the original image. Molten (or powdered) glass is poured into this void and after cooling and annealing, the clay mould is broken away. A great deal of retouching is necessary on removing the piece from the mould, but the overall effect can be very fine.

A less conventional technique is 'conglomerate glass', in which fragments of coloured glass are melted together in a one- or two-piece mould until they fuse, giving an effect resembling ornamental stone. Again, the interior surface of pieces made in one-piece moulds would have needed extensive finishing after removal. The *millefiori* technique strictly refers to floral patterns but is generally used to refer to simple patterns such as the yellow 'eyes' set against a green background found on some bowls of the Late Period. Mosaic glass is similar but is generally reserved for more complicated patterns. It involves the production of glass rods, sometimes in multiple colours, which are then fused together and pulled into canes. This drawing-out retains the pattern while reducing it in scale, so that delicate yet intricate designs can be produced. The canes are then cut into slices that can be fused together in a mould or used for decoration. These techniques were probably an Egyptian development, and in any case attained their greatest development there.

The manufacture of blown glass, increasingly common in Egypt from the 1st century BC, involves the collecting of molten glass on the end of a hollow pipe; the glassmaker then blows air into this 'gather' of molten glass and shapes it into a vessel by rolling it on a flat surface or blowing it into a mould. The advantage of the technique is that it allows quite elaborate vessels to be produced more quickly and cheaply than with other techniques. Glass-blowing was sometimes combined with cutting techniques to produce cameo glass. In this technique a darkly coloured glass vessel was dipped into glass of a lighter colour, which after cooling and annealing was then delicately carved away to create subtleties of shade and colour.

(iii) Stylistic development.

(a) Old Kingdom–Second Intermediate Period (*c.* 2575–*c.* 1540 BC). (b) New Kingdom–Third Intermediate Period (*c.* 1540–*c.* 750 BC). (c) Late Period and Greco-Roman period (*c.* 750 BC–AD 395).

(a) Old Kingdom–Second Intermediate Period (c. 2575–c. 1540 BC). The manufacture of glass in Egypt before *c.* 1500 BC is not well attested; however there are a few pieces that apparently pre-date the New Kingdom. Many of these pieces are still contentious, and those given here are only the most secure or well known. Some may have been imported, while some of the beads may have resulted from accidents in faience- or glaze-making. A number of beads and amulets ranging between the 5th and 11th dynasties are known, though most of these have not been subject to examination in recent times and so should be treated with extreme caution. There are two scarabs, both inscribed for officials, one in opaque blue glass, the other in turquoise blue, which seem to be securely dated to the 12th Dynasty. There are also numbers of so-called 'crumb-beads' of the same date. Particularly controversial is the so-called 'Bull Mosaic' from the treasure of Princess Khnumet found at Dahshur (Cairo, Egyp. Mus., CG 52975, register 31126) and dated to the 12th Dynasty. It has been suggested that the mosaic is merely paint, covered by a clear layer of quartz. Also of this date, from Abydos, is a glass frog set in a silver ring, as well as several glass eyes from funerary masks. A glass rod with the cartouche of the 12th Dynasty king Amenemhet III (Berlin, Ägyp. Mus.) should be similarly early, though it may be a Roman piece, since this King was commonly regarded as a deity in later times. If the 'Bull Mosaic' is discounted, then true mosaic glass technique is not encountered again until the 1st century BC to the 1st century AD.

A glass inlay in a lotus flower pendant (London, BM, EA 3077) has been confirmed by analysis and may be of Middle Kingdom date, but since the pendant has been re-strung using other pieces of Middle Kingdom jewellery and has no provenance, the date must be regarded as uncertain. The famous blue lion's head amulet inscribed for Nubkheperre and thought to refer to King Nubkheperre Inyotef of the 17th Dynasty (London, BM, 59619) has long been regarded as an early piece of sculpted glass. Scientific examination suggests that the piece is actually of high quality Egyptian Blue, while the date could be as late as the Third Intermediate Period (*c.* 1075–*c.* 750 BC). A blue glass vessel from Qaw el-Kebir dated to the Second Intermediate Period (*c.* 1630–*c.* 1540 BC) comes from a disturbed context and must therefore be treated with caution.

*(b) New Kingdom–Third Intermediate Period (*c. 1540–c. 750 BC*).* A square bead in light blue glass (Boston, MA, Mus. F.A., 1978, 691) bears the names of Ahmose and Amenophis I, the first rulers of the New Kingdom, and, if contemporary with them, predates the established rise of glass by 50 or 60 years. The earliest firmly dated glass vessels from Egypt are fragments (Cairo, Egyp. Mus., 24981) from the tomb of Tuthmosis I (*reg c.* 1493–*c.* 1482 BC), but it was not until the time of Tuthmosis III (*reg c.* 1479–*c.* 1426 BC) that production was greatly expanded. Among the earliest dated pieces of core-formed glass is a jug of Tuthmosis III (see fig. 107), one of a set of seven vessels used to hold the sacred oils used in funerary ritual. The piece, of turquoise-blue glass, has a yellow rim band, below which are two registers of yellow festoons and, at the junction of the neck with the shoulder, a row of white dots between two yellow lines. An inscription on the shoulder giving the King's coronation name was executed in yellow powdered glass, giving an enamelled effect; this is the earliest known example of this technique. Below the inscription is a further yellow band, beneath which are three tamarisk trees, and a foot band, also in yellow. A chalice of turquoise blue glass with dark blue and yellow thread decoration (Munich, Staatl. Samml. Ägyp. Kst., ÄS 630) and gold-mounted lotiform cup, also in turquoise glass (New York, Met., 23.9), are inscribed

107. Core-formed glass jug bearing the coronation name of Tuthmosis III in powdered-glass lettering, h. 87 mm, 18th Dynasty, *c.* 1479–*c.* 1426 BC (London, British Museum)

with the name of the same King. There are a number of similar vessels bearing royal names, notably those of Amenophis II (*reg c.* 1426–*c.* 1400 BC; e.g. Cairo, Egyp. Mus., JE 24753, 24794, 24804).

Three types of core-formed vessel were of particular importance during the New Kingdom: the two-handled jar with a wide neck, the lentoid flask and the kohl tube. They were mainly small and used for storing and applying cosmetics; the wide-necked form was ideally suited to this purpose. The cores of such pieces were easily removed, adding to the overall impression of quality, and some (e.g. London, BM, 4741) are beautifully finished to a high gloss. The decoration is generally in the form of swags or festoons of coloured glass, commonly yellow, white and/ or turquoise against a dark blue background (New York, Met., 91.1.1365; Toledo, OH, Mus. A.; *see* GLASS, colour pl. IV, fig. 2). The lentoid flasks, which copy a form common in pottery and alabaster, often have rims decorated with a rope-like pattern made from prefabricated canes of glass twisted together (e.g. London, BM, 64338). Kohl tubes frequently featured elaborate rims made in the form of palm leaves, so that the whole body of the vessel formed a palm column (e.g. London, BM, 2589, 2590). Their glass applicator rods, some of which survive, are typically in the form of a teardrop. When found, most of the small core-formed vessels showed no trace of having had lids; others were covered by linen or had wax stoppers.

However, it is clear that some originally had glass lids; a particularly fine example of this type was found in the tomb of Kha at Deir el-Medina (Turin, Mus. Egizio, Suppl. 8480). Dating to the early part of the reign of Amenophis III (*reg c.* 1390–*c.* 1353 BC), this piece is uniquely decorated with duck heads, although plain examples are the rule. The ornamental vessels in the form of the *bulti* fish (*Tilapia nilotica*), a popular amulet, were also core-formed. A particularly fine example from the reign of Akhenaten (*reg c.* 1353–*c.* 1336 BC) discovered at el-Amarna (London, BM, 55193) is of matt blue glass decorated in festoons of white and yellow. The dorsal fin is of the same blue as the body with threads of yellow, white and turquoise, while the front fins are made of light and dark blue threads; the mouth is outlined in yellow and the eyes are opaque white glass with black pupils. Less elaborate fish vessels, some with monochrome decoration (e.g. London, BM, 63786) were also made. Like more conventional forms, they probably served as cosmetic containers, although they would have required stands.

Open-form glass vessels were not common during the New Kingdom, but where they occur they are sometimes moulded. One fine moulded example (London, BM, 65774) is of turquoise-blue glass in the form of a clam shell, a shape more common in faience. Of the core-formed bowls a particularly significant example (London, BM, 36342) is believed to have come from the tomb of Amenophis II. Made of dark blue glass, it has a foot that is solid save for a small hole left by a rod: if the dating is correct, it is the earliest known glass footed bowl. More elaborate pieces were moulded and then cold-worked: noteworthy examples include a blue glass stand inscribed for Amenophis III and a turquoise-blue glass headrest of Tutankhamun (*reg c.* 1332–*c.* 1323 BC; Cairo, Egyp. Mus., Tut. 531), one of two glass headrests from his tomb, which was carved in two separate pieces and then joined at the stem, using an inscribed gold band to disguise the join.

Glass sculptures were generally cast and cold-worked; inscriptions were added separately. Only three glass *shabti*s (see §XII, 3(ii) above) are known (all Cairo, Egyp. Mus.). The first and most securely dated, is in turquoise-blue glass; it was made for Qenamun, an official at the court of Amenophis II, and probably came from his tomb at Thebes. It has an inscription running down the centre and five additional inscribed bands across the body. The second dates from the reign of Tuthmosis IV (*reg c.* 1400–*c.* 1390 BC) and was made for the priest Hekareshu. The piece is in light blue opaque glass and, although small, is of exceptionally fine workmanship, having gold leaf on parts of the head and body. Such pieces were almost certainly produced in the royal workshops and presented as gifts of the highest value by the king to his most favoured officials. The third *shabti*, that of Men, dates from the 19th or 20th Dynasty. Made of violet-blue glass, it is of small size and inferior quality with a flat back, indicating that it must have been made in a one-piece mould. Royal pieces include a small head of a king, probably Amenophis II, wearing a *nemes* headcloth in discoloured blue glass (see fig. 108). Another example from the tomb of Tutankhamun is a small figurine of the King in a squatting position in purple-blue glass in a matt finish (Cairo, Egyp. Mus., JE 60719); it is the most

108. Blue glass head, possibly of Amenophis II, h. 40 mm, 18th Dynasty, *c.* 1426–*c.* 1400 BC (Corning, NY, Museum of Glass)

complicated piece of glass sculpture attempted by the ancient Egyptians. Tutankhamun has his right hand raised to his mouth, while the left rests on his knee, and there is a suspension loop on the back of his crown. A similar piece, perhaps also representing Tutankhamun, is less well cast (London, BM, 15767).

Conglomerate glass also became popular during this period. A bowl, one of two complete examples known (London, BM, 27727) contains fragments of opaque white, brick red, purple-blue and black glass, all moulded together; it has a matt finish and a yellow rim. The second example (New York, Brooklyn Mus., 48.162) lacks the yellow rim band. Both were probably made at Malqata, where fragments of such pieces are common. The technique was also used to produce drinking vessels: a particularly fine example in red, green, white and yellow glass with a gold rim and foot band comes from the tableware of the harem of Tuthmosis III (New York, Met., 26.7.1175).

Throughout the New Kingdom glass continued to be used to manufacture amulets and inlays for jewellery (*see* §1 and §§XIII, 3(vi) and XV, 4 above). Notable pieces using glass inlay include several of the most spectacular objects from the tomb of Tutankhamun (*see* JEWELLERY, colour pl. IV, fig. 2), among them the famous gold coffin and funerary mask (Cairo, Egyp. Mus.).

(c) Late Period–Greco-Roman period (c. 750 BC–AD 395). Core-formed glass vessels were made throughout the eastern Mediterranean at this time (*see* ANCIENT NEAR EAST, §II, 2), and many were imported into Egypt, making

recognition of indigenous pieces difficult. Superficially, these late core-formed vessels resemble the earlier pieces: they commonly use a dark blue glass as a background and preserve the use of coloured festoon decoration. However, whereas the earlier vessels have generally suffered little from burial, these later pieces are often patchy or discoloured. Similarly, the festoons are not so carefully applied, the trailed threads of which they are composed often being irregularly spaced and of differing breadth. In the earlier vessels, each band of colour was a separate ring of glass thread, but in later pieces the threads were applied spiral-fashion; sometimes a second colour was applied on top of the first. Similarly, the colours used for the festoons were rather different; orange often replaced the earlier yellow, while turquoise became more common than previously. Such late core-formed vessels mainly comprise tall, slender shapes heavily influenced by the Mediterranean ceramic tradition such as alabastra, amphoriskoi with button feet, oinochoai and aryballoi (*see* GREECE, ANCIENT, §X, 5). Even core-formed vessels made within Egypt conform to this general Classical/Hellenistic tradition.

The *millefiori* and mosaic glass techniques developed during the Late Period. Common patterns included yellow circles or 'eyes' set against a green background for the former technique and sometimes a simple chequer-board pattern of black and white squares for the latter. The cut sections of rod were often backed on to monochrome glass or fitted into a mould to produce larger objects but were mostly used for the production of inlays for jewellery and furniture. Plain glass paste inlays also continued in use; both types were employed in the inlaid inscriptions on the pine coffin of Petosiris from Tuna el-Gebel (Cairo, Egyp. Mus., JE 46592).

Glass-blowing was only slowly adopted in Egypt, and during the Greco-Roman period the majority of the finest Alexandrian work continued to be produced using the sand core technique or by cutting or mosaic work. However, Roman core-formed vessels produced in crude imitation of the work of the New Kingdom and Late Period are often clumsily executed, particularly in the rather haphazard trailed thread decoration. In contrast, the sophisticated cameo glass technique made possible unprecedented subtleties of shade and colour, most outstandingly seen in the Portland Vase (London, BM) which may have been made at Alexandria. The technique of mosaic glass reached a peak in the 1st century BC–1st century AD. Very intricate and complicated patterns were produced involving many different colours of glass and irregular shapes. One of the most intricate is a cane which preserves, throughout its thickness, half of the head of a satyr from which slices would have been cut and mounted side by side to make a full face. The end section of the piece, as preserved, measures only 30×21 mm (Washington, DC, Freer). The themes treated in mosaic are both Classical and Egyptian, and wall plaques made by this technique were common. Workshops for the production of this glass are as yet unknown, although evidence from a studio found at Gumaiyima, near Tanis, suggests that the craft may have been carried out on an itinerant basis. The production of *millefiori* glass also flourished in the

Greco-Roman period, with bowls and dishes being produced in Hellenistic styles.

Some experimentation with glass colouring also took place at this time, and a number of vessels that showed different colours according to lighting conditions were produced. Two fragments of such vessels, one from Tanis (London, BM, 29095) the other from Gebel Kibli, near Memphis (London, BM, 14321), appear to be opaque black until held to the light, whereupon they show a rich ruby red. Cold painting on glass also became quite common.

Gold glass was probably an Alexandrian speciality, although only five certain Egyptian pieces are known (all London, BM). To produce it, gold sheet was usually sandwiched between two pieces of glass which were then melted together at the edges; alternatively, the gold could be stuck to the surface of the vessel while it was slightly viscous, and then covered. A particularly complicated, though badly damaged, piece is the gold glass zodiac from Tanis (London, BM, 29137).

For further discussion of materials and techniques *see* GLASS, §§I–III.

BIBLIOGRAPHY

W. E. S. Turner: 'Studies of Ancient Glass and Glass-making Processes, Part I: Crucibles and Melting Temperatures Employed in Ancient Egypt at about 1370 B.C.', *J. Soc. Glass Tech.*, xxxviii (1954), pp. 436–44

A. Lucas and J. R. Harris: *Ancient Egyptian Materials and Industries* (London, 1962)

B. Nolte: *Die Glasgefässe im alten Ägypten* (Berlin, 1968)

E. Riefstahl: *Ancient Egyptian Glass and Glazes in the Brooklyn Museum* (New York, 1968)

J. D. Cooney: *Glass* (1976), iv of *Catalogue of Egyptian Antiquities in the British Museum* (London, 1968–)

S. M. Goldstein: *Pre-Roman and Early Roman Glass in the Corning Museum of Glass* (New York, 1979)

PAUL T. NICHOLSON

9. IVORY AND BONE. From Neolithic times until the end of the Dynastic period (*c.* 6000–30 BC), ivory and bone—durable and easy to carve—were used for numerous types of object in ancient Egypt, particularly cosmetic items, jewellery and game-pieces. Some uses of ivory and bone were more prevalent during certain phases of Egyptian history. Magic ivory knives, for instance, were produced only in the Middle Kingdom and for a short time afterwards (*c.* 2000–*c.* 1600 BC), while ivory furniture inlay was common until the late Dynastic period.

Hippopotamus ivory was available locally because the hippopotamus was native to ancient Egypt. Elephant ivory, on the other hand, had to be imported from Punt, Nubia, Crete and Syria–Palestine (*see* §I, 3(iv) above). The domain of the African elephant was always far to the south of Aswan and had receded even further by the Dynastic period. Animal bone, always easily available as a waste product, was used to a limited extent during the Predynastic period for awls, punches, needles, beads and finger-rings, but it was rarely exploited later.

(i) Predynastic and Early Dynastic (c. 6000–c. 2575 BC). The huge cemeteries of the Predynastic and Early Dynastic periods (such as Tarkhan, el-Gerzeh, Deir Tasa, el-Badari, Hammamiya, el-Mahasna, Qaw el-Kebir, el-Amra, Abadiya, Naqada and Abydos) were rich in ivory and bone funerary equipment. There were also important sets of ritual and ceremonial ivories excavated from the temple enclosures at Abydos (Oxford, Ashmolean, and Cairo, Egyp. Mus.) and Hierakonpolis (London, U. Coll., Petrie Mus.; Philadelphia, U. PA, Mus.; Cairo, Egyp. Mus.). Throughout the Predynastic period bone and ivory were used primarily for cosmetic items. Long-toothed combs and hairpins (both of which were sometimes found in the hair of the deceased) were often carved with figurative depictions, including gazelles, hippopotamuses and birds engraved on combs (e.g. London, U. Coll., Petrie Mus., 9581, 16108 and 5367) and predominantly birds represented on hairpins (e.g. London, U. Coll., Petrie Mus.,

109. Ivory figure of a king, h. 88 mm, from Abydos, 1st Dynasty, *c.* 2900 BC (London, British Museum)

10156). The cosmetic spoons of the Badarian and Naqada periods had thin handles and small bowls. Small, cylindrical and oval vessels containing cosmetics and oils were placed in Predynastic graves at sites such as el-Badari.

Bone and ivory amulets (in the form of bull's heads and flies) and jewellery (including arm-rings, earrings, earplugs, finger-rings, beads and necklaces) have survived from the earliest times. In Predynastic hunting and warfare, bone and ivory were used for arrow-heads and harpoons with barbed hooks. There are also a number of surviving Predynastic ivory knife-handles, including examples from GEBEL EL-ARAK (Paris, Louvre) and Abu Zaidan (New York, Brooklyn Mus.; see fig. 49 above), bearing engraved depictions of wild animals and battle scenes.

The earliest ivory statues are naked female figurines from the Badarian and Naqada periods (London, BM; London, U. Coll., Petrie Mus.; Baltimore, MD, Walters A.G.). The first surviving statuette of a king is a finely carved 1st Dynasty ivory figure from Abydos, wearing the white crown of Upper Egypt and wrapped in a cloak with a diamond pattern (London, BM, 37996; see fig. 109). Several early ivory animal figurines (Cairo, Egyp. Mus., and London, U. Coll., Petrie Mus.) were found at Hierakonpolis.

From the 1st Dynasty, ivory was used for small tablets or labels bearing engraved representations and hieroglyphs, usually recording inventories, quantities, delivery dates, festivals or momentous events. Each tablet had a hole in the upper edge by which it could be secured to a container with a piece of string. Some of these ivory tablets are important sources for the early historical period, as in the case of the plaque of King Aha (reg c. 2925 BC; Cairo, Egyp. Mus.; for illustration see NAQADA).

Ivory was also used for game-pieces, frequently from the 1st Dynasty, in the form of small rods, flat hemispheres and prostrate lions. The gaming-boards themselves often incorporated ivory, and frequently only the durable ivory components (such as ivory feet in the form of bulls' hooves, e.g. London, U. Coll., Petrie Mus., 15129) survive.

Two Early Dynastic tombs at Qaw el-Kebir were reused until the 19th Dynasty (c. 1292–c. 1190 BC) for specialized ivory and bone refuse deposits, including animal bones (particularly hippopotamus) as well as various artefacts of hippopotamus ivory. The weight of one deposit alone was estimated at two to three tonnes.

See also §IX, 3(i) above for further discussion of Predynastic carving.

(ii) Dynastic (c. 2575–c. 30 BC). Ivory and bone continued to be used for cosmetic items in the Dynastic period. Spoons were often more carefully formed (particularly in the New Kingdom); in some examples the handle was in the form of a naked swimming girl and the bowl in the form of a duck. The ivory cosmetic bowls of the Predynastic phase gradually developed into the richly decorated vessels of the Dynastic period, often in the shape of a human figure (e.g. London, U. Coll., Petrie Mus., 26199–200 and 7906).

Magic knives, always of hippopotamus ivory and used primarily during the Middle Kingdom, were thought to protect mothers and children from illnesses, demons, snakes and other dangers. The corner tusk of the hippopotamus was carved lengthways and its natural curve produced the knife's characteristic sickle shape. The pointed end of the tusk was often carved as a jackal head (e.g. London, U. Coll., Petrie Mus., 16382) and the wide end as a leopard head. The surface of the knife was decorated with engraved figures, usually of the deities Bes and Thoeris, as well as imaginary peoples and animals. There seems to have been a strong connection between the worship of the pregnant hippopotamus–goddess, Thoeris, and the use of the hippopotamus tusk as a raw material. The patches used to repair many magic knives point to the intensity of their use.

Many clappers of hippopotamus and elephant ivory (e.g. Cairo, Egyp. Mus., JE 39765) have survived from the Middle and New kingdoms. These musical instruments, usually in the shape of a forearm with outstretched hand, were produced in pairs, to be struck together rhythmically like castanets (see §12 below).

Ivory continued to be used occasionally in statuary of the Dynastic period, either for statuettes or inlay. A rare ivory enthroned figurine, the only surviving image of King Cheops (reg c. 2251–c. 2528 BC; Cairo, Egyp. Mus., JE 36143), was found at Abydos.

Throughout the Dynastic period, many objects incorporated elements of bone or ivory. The handles of knives, daggers, fans, whips and mirrors were often made of ivory carved with reliefs. Ivory was also used extensively as veneer, fittings and inlay for furniture and cosmetic containers. This use flourished with the craftsmanship of the New Kingdom, as the finds from the tomb of Tutankhamun (reg c. 1332–c. 1323 BC) impressively demonstrate. Ivory, sometimes coloured red, green or brown, was especially used in conjunction with woods such as ebony for the decoration of stools, chests, cabinets and gaming-boards.

BIBLIOGRAPHY

W. M. F. Petrie and J. E. Quibell: *Naqada and Ballas* (London, 1896), pp. 46–8
J. E. Quibell and F. W. Green: *Hierakonpolis*, i (London, 1900), pls v–xvi
W. M. F. Petrie: *Diospolis Parva: The Cemeteries of Abadiyeh and Hu* (London, 1901), pp. 21–2
D. Randall-MacIver, A. C. Mace and F. Ll. Griffith: *El Amrah and Abydos* (London, 1902)
W. M. F. Petrie: *Abydos*, 2 vols (London, 1902–3)
——: *Prehistoric Egypt* (London, 1920), pp. 6–7, 30–33
A. Lucas: *Ancient Egyptian Materials and Industries* (London, 1926, rev. 4/1962), pp. 28, 32–3
W. M. F. Petrie: *Objects of Daily Use* (London, 1927)
G. Brunton, A. H. Gardiner and W. M. F. Petrie: *Qau and Badari*, 3 vols (London, 1927–30)
N. de G. Davies: *The Tomb of Rekh-mi-Re at Thebes* (New York, 1943/R 1973), pls 17–20, 22
E. Massoulard: *Préhistoire et protohistoire d'Egypte* (Paris, 1949), pp. 304–6
B. Adams: *Ancient Hierakonpolis*, 2 vols (Warminster, 1974), pp. 59–75
A. J. Spencer: *Early Dynastic Objects*, London, BM cat., v (London, 1980), nos 447–55, 458, 460–87, 494–6
R. Drenkhahn: *Elfenbein im alten Ägypten: Leihgaben aus dem Petrie-Museum, London* (Hannover, 1986)

ROSEMARIE DRENKHAHN

10. LEATHERWORK. The great diversity of leather artefacts recovered from archaeological contexts as well as their representations in tomb paintings and texts offer much evidence of the importance of leather at every level of Egyptian life. The Egyptians used the hides and skins from a variety of domestic or wild animals, including cattle, gazelles, hippopotamuses, calves, goats, sheep,

leopards and cheetahs. These pelts were then prepared (by 'sweating' or 'scudding') and treated (by chamoising, tawing or tanning). (For a detailed explanation of these technical processes, *see* LEATHER, §3.) The favourable climate in Egypt made the extensive use of dried rawhide possible, but most of the leather artefacts in Egypt were made of the stiff, white leather that resulted from tawing the pelt with a mineral substance containing alum and salt.

The leather produced by the Egyptians was often painted before being processed into objects. The types of paint included red (kermes and madder), yellow (pomegranate rind), blue (indigo), green (pigment or dye unknown), black (iron sulphate) and even gilt. The painting process was often combined with the tanning or tawing of the pelts: alum, for instance, was often used as a mordant as well as a tanning agent. The yellow colouring was probably also thought to have a preservative value, judging from the ancient Egyptian name given to the pomegranate ('leather apple').

(*i*) *Uses.* Although the best-preserved and most beautiful Egyptian leather objects come from funerary contexts, the practical applications of the material in Egyptian society were far more widespread. In addition to the uses outlined below, leather is known to have been employed for waterskins, all kinds of bags, children's playing balls, drumheads, cushions and rolls of writing material.

(*a*) *Binding.* Rawhide, simply cut into strips (with or without the hair still attached) was often applied wet to make joints in woodwork. The shrinkage that occurred as the rawhide dried resulted in a tightly fitting binding. The same principle was widely applied for joining adzes and other tools to their wooden handles. There are several early examples of this application, as well as later developments in which the simple lashings were replaced by elaborate leather plaiting (e.g. Cairo, Egyp. Mus., A6736 and 7+6/324–5). The 18th Dynasty ceremonial axe of Ahmose (*reg c.* 1540–*c.* 1514 BC) has an imitation of plaited leather joints in gold (Cairo, Egyp. Mus., JE 4673).

Leather was also used for making rope, either in the same way as the plying of cordage from vegetable fibres or in more decorative ways, as in the case of one leather cord (Cairo, Egyp. Mus., 56484B), in which tiny thongs were circularly woven into a spiral weft. Leather cordage was especially useful in shipping, since leather does not absorb water.

(*b*) *Footwear and dress.* Tomb paintings suggest that the Egyptian leatherworker's most important product was the sandal. This is confirmed by excavations, which have yielded many examples of leather footwear. Sandals made of rush and papyrus were more common than those made of leather. Beautiful leather sandals were part of Tutankhamun's burial equipment (Cairo, Egyp. Mus., 565); these are decorated with drawings in gold of Egypt's enemies, so that whenever the King wore the sandals he would be crushing his enemies. From the New Kingdom onwards, shoes were worn. In contrast to sandals, the upper material of shoes does not consist of thongs but of leather, cut and sewn into shape.

Leather was also important for items of clothing. Although the only surviving prehistoric finds are leather funerary shrouds, leather was probably also used at that time to clothe the living. By Dynastic times, however, linen had supplanted leather as material for clothing. Nevertheless, certain special items, such as belts (e.g. one made of finely plaited thongs, Cairo, Egyp. Mus., JE 42843) and loincloths for sailors, soldiers, masons and labourers (Hall, p. 34), continued to be made from leather in all periods. Leather gloves are depicted twice at el-Amarna in the 18th Dynasty tomb of King Ay (*reg c.* 1323–*c.* 1319 BC), but no actual examples are known to have survived.

No royal crowns have survived either, but it has been suggested that royal headgear was usually made of leather: the headcloth (*nemes*) was made of pleated and painted fine leather, and the blue, white and red crowns consisted of painted leather and metal studs.

(*c*) *Furniture and household items.* In addition to rawhide's use as leather joints, it could be shaped into hard, more or less watertight, vessels by pulling it around a mould and letting it dry. One such container was found in a Predynastic grave in Nubia.

In domestic furniture, leather had a dual role: it was used to lash pieces together and to provide chair seats, especially for wooden stools. A good example—though the leather itself is decayed—is the folding stool from the tomb of Kha (Turin, Mus. Egizio, 8509). An ebony and ivory imitation of a similar stool, with the 'leopard fur' represented in negative, was among Tutankhamun's funerary equipment (Cairo, Egyp. Mus.).

Some tents in Egypt (*see* TENT, §III, 1) were also made of leather. The earliest reference to a leather tent is in a 19th Dynasty (*c.* 1292–*c.* 1190 BC) inscription, although no examples have survived from that period. One extant example from a later period is the funeral tent of Queen Isiskhemheb (Cairo, Egyp. Mus.), made in the 21st Dynasty (*c.* 1075–*c.* 950 BC) from a patchwork of brightly coloured leather.

(*d*) *Military.* Leather was also widely applied to the production of war gear and horse harnesses (*see* HARNESS AND TRAPPINGS, §1(i)). There are two beautiful examples of finely decorated quivers (Cairo, Egyp. Mus., 4308 and 4305), one decorated with painting in black, blue and red, the other with delicately incised and punched figures. Shields, made out of a wicker frame or wood, were covered with leather or fur. Sheaths for daggers and bracers to protect the archer's wrists were all made of leather (e.g. Cairo, Egyp. Mus., 872). The material was also important for Egyptian chariots: the wheels were lashed with rawhide; the floor consisted of interlaced leather thongs; and the 'tyres' were made of either rawhide or leather (e.g. Cairo, Egyp. Mus.).

(*ii*) *Workshop production.* Information about the production of leather in ancient Egypt is derived from both textual and visual sources. From the following passage from the *Satire of the Trades* (a Middle Kingdom educational text which compares the hardships of several trades to the bliss of that of the scribe; for trans. see Lichtheim), it is apparent that the ancient Egyptian leatherworker was responsible for the initial stages of preparing the hides as well as producing the many types of leather objects:

The cobbler suffers much
Among his vats of oil;
He is well if one's well with corpses.
What he bites is leather.

The major tasks of the leatherworker are splendidly illustrated in a wall painting from the tomb of Rekhmire at Thebes (TT 100). At the left of the painting a man is producing long thongs by cutting a hide spirally; the two men next to him are making leather cordage using weights to swing the thongs into a plied cord. In the scene below, two kinds of leather products are depicted in use: adzes, joined to their handles by plaited leather thongs, are being used by carpenters, and leather bellows are being used by metalworkers.

The next process shown is sandal-making (see fig. 110): at the left a man pierces the straps of a sandal with an awl; to the right a sandal-maker is shown pulling a leather thong through the hole in the middle of the sandal by using his teeth, a scene illustrating the last sentence in the *Satire of the Trades*; the man at the top is pulling and stretching leather in order to make it supple, while the man to his right is cutting out sandals with a half-moon knife. Further scenes show the 'staking' of leather (pulling and stretching it over a beam or stake to make it supple); piercing the sole of a sandal; two men working with 'vats of oil' (probably tawing fur); the rubbing of fat into a pelt; and more cutting and 'staking'. The sequence of scenes ends with the presentation of the finished products, including numerous sandals and some fur-covered shields, at the far right of the painting. In other tomb paintings, just one action, for instance 'staking', is used to represent the entire process of leatherworking.

BIBLIOGRAPHY
LÄ: 'Leopard'
L. Klebs: *Die Reliefs und Malereien des Alten Reiches* (Heidelberg, 1915), pp. 95–6
——: *Die Reliefs und Malereien des Mittleren Reiches* (Heidelberg, 1922), pp. 121–2
A. Lucas: *Ancient Egyptian Materials and Industries* (London, 1926, rev. 4/1962), pp. 28–40
L. Klebs: *Die Reliefs und Malereien des Neuen Reiches*, i (Heidelberg, 1934), pp. 165–71
N. de G. Davies: *The Tomb of Rekh-mi-Re at Thebes* (New York, 1943/*R* 1973), pp. 49–50, pls lii–liv

J. W. Waterer: 'Leather', *A History of Technology*, i, ed. C. Singer, E. J. Holmyard and A. R. Hall (Oxford, 1956), pp. 147–87
H. Junker: *Weta und das Lederkunsthandwerk im Alten Reich* (Vienna, 1957)
R. J. Forbes: 'Leather in Antiquity', *Studies in Ancient Technology*, v, ed. R. J. Forbes (Leiden, 1966), pp. 1–79
M. Lichtheim: *Ancient Egyptian Literature*, i (Los Angeles, 1973), pp. 88–9
R. Drenkhahn: 'Lederhandwerk', *Die Handwerker und ihre Tätigkeiten im alten Ägypten*, Ägyptologische Abhandlungen, xxxi (Wiesbaden, 1976), pp. 1–17
Tutanchamun in Köln (exh. cat., ed. J. Settgast; Cologne, Stadtmus., 1980), p. 98
M. A. Littouwer and J. H. Crouwel: *Chariots and Related Equipment from the Tomb of Tut'ankhamun*, Tut'ankhamun's Tomb Series, viii (Oxford, 1985), pp. 70–74, 93–4, pls lxviii–lxix
R. Hall: *Egyptian Textiles* (Aylesbury, 1986), pp. 34–5 [leather loincloths]
M. Saleh and H. Sourouzian: *The Egyptian Museum, Cairo*, Cairo, Egyp. Mus. cat. (Mainz, 1987), no. 121

WILLEMINA Z. WENDRICH

11. MAPS AND PLANS. It is clear that the Egyptians of the Dynastic period (*c.* 2925–332 BC) were acquainted with the concept of creating a two-dimensional representation of the relative location of topographical features or the ground-plan of a structure. The evidence for Egyptian maps and plans is sparse and unbalanced, deriving mostly from the Theban necropolis, and they occur most often on limestone ostraca (inscribed sherds or limestone flakes, *see* §XI, 3 above), but this may be solely a result of the vagaries of survival rather than evidence of the contexts within which maps and plans were most used.

At the simplest level, some common Egyptian hieroglyphs, attested from the earliest stages of Egyptian writing, show buildings in crude ground-plan (although others show elevations), and the hieroglyph for a village takes the form of a simplified ground-plan. Egyptian art in general contains much that is akin to maps and plans. Tomb paintings, for example, show houses, palaces and gardens, while the walls of temples of the Ramesside period (*c.* 1292–*c.* 1075 BC) bear scenes of warfare being waged in specific places. Various funerary texts contain representations of portions of the topography of the underworld, as well as plans of buildings there. Temple 'building inscriptions' of the Greco-Roman period (332 BC–AD 395), such as those in the Temple of Horus at Edfu, may include the dimensions of rooms. The Egyptians' use of working drawings can be deduced from the elaborate designs of surviving monuments.

(i) *Maps.* Egyptian religious thought involved concrete ideas about the structure of the cosmos, which could be represented by various two-dimensional forms in religious art. There is, however, no indication that this led to any notion of representing the land of Egypt with a map, although it is clear from secular texts that the Egyptians were nevertheless able to form a mental picture of the Nile Valley as a whole. An illustrated hieroglyphic text (e.g. Cairo, Egyp. Mus., P. Boulaq 1) evidently popular in the Faiyum region in the Ptolemaic (332–30 BC) and early Roman (30 BC–AD 395) periods provides a schematic geographical description of the Faiyum and its cult centres, combined with cosmographical elements, but the correspondence with topographical reality is generally obscure. The existence of unillustrated hieratic versions (e.g. Florence, U. Studi, Ist. Papirol. Girolamo Vitelli, P. ierat. Tebt.

110. Leatherworkers making sandals, line drawing after wall painting in the Theban tomb of Rekhmire, 18th Dynasty, *c.* 1450 BC (from left to right): piercing the straps; threading the thongs; pulling and stretching the leather; and cutting out the sandals

A) of the text suggests that the Egyptians may have thought of this description of the Faiyum chiefly in terms of cosmography and as an illustrated list, rather than as a map.

How much use literate Egyptians made of maps is impossible to say. The Turin Mine Plan (Turin, Mus. Egizio, 1879, 1899 and 1969) is the only surviving Egyptian map worthy of the name. Presumably drawn up for a specific mining expedition, the map consists of a number of fragments from a papyrus roll with various topographical features, including roads, quarries and mining areas, along the Wadi Hammamat (a dry valley linking the Nile Valley and the Red Sea). The map is annotated in hieratic script, and the use of various conventions—such as colour coding and indication of features such as a rock-strewn road—hints at an established map-drawing technique.

There are no references in Egyptian texts to maps, nor is their use implied by Egyptian ways of describing topography or giving directions. This is true even in those areas where their value ought to be most apparent: military affairs and land measurement for taxation and crop assessment (for which there is considerable indirect evidence). The surviving copies of the 'onomastica' (elaborate word lists; see §XII, 3(ii) above) are unillustrated and include listings of the towns of Egypt in a more or less set order. The narrowness of the Nile Valley makes a mere list appropriate for Upper Egypt. However in the 'onomastica' and elsewhere the Egyptians also seem to have preferred to think in terms of lists rather than of geographical relationships in the case of the Delta and even of foreign towns, such as those of Syria–Palestine, in which the ordering now seems problematic.

(ii) Plans. The purpose of the surviving architectural plans is generally plain. Some might have been drawn to record structures, as with the plan of the tomb of Ramesses IV (KV 2; Turin, Mus. Egizio, 1885; see fig. 111) and the ink study of a shrine on a fragment of limestone, dating to the 13th or 12th century BC (Cambridge, Fitzwilliam). Others might have been executed as part of the training of apprentices. Most, however, seem to be working sketches designed for a particular task. These plans usually took the

form of ostraca, which were used because they were practical, robust and available at no cost. The inclusion of precise measurements in some plans may indicate that they were records of existing structures, but this is inconclusive. Some plans of New Kingdom (c. 1540–c. 1075 BC) rock-cut royal tombs do not correspond exactly to the final known state of the tomb and thus must represent plans made in the course of the work: the design of a royal tomb could be changed many times during construction.

In method, architectural plans resemble modern ideas of a ground-plan, with the addition of individual features, such as doorways, shown in front elevation. This technique is consistent with general Egyptian methods of two-dimensional representation (see §IV, 2 above). The only fundamental difference between plans and, for example, the depiction of a royal palace in a New Kingdom tomb is that the latter aims to show the contents of the rooms in elevation, the overall effect being similar to the horizontal registers of tomb scenes. This can make the actual plan of the building difficult to decipher. In Egyptian architectural drawings, however, the plan is all-important and never obscured by other detail.

In general, the surviving architectural plans are schematic in intention: they roughly represent the shape and (with varying success) the structural proportions. They are usually not scale drawings from which dimensions can be deduced visually; instead they function essentially as a peg on which to hang hieratic annotations stating the principal dimensions. There are, however, exceptions such as the Gurob Shrine Plan (London, U. Coll., Petrie Mus., 27934.i–ii), which consists of a pair of elevations (front and side) of a portable shrine, drawn in detail on a papyrus roll of unusual breadth. The elevations are placed on a square grid, ruled in advance. Despite the problems posed by the system of measurement adopted in these plans, they are evidently scale drawings, and any dimension needed could be found with the aid of the grid (in this case there are no accompanying annotations). These drawings belong to the New Kingdom or Late Period (c. 750–332 BC). A second exception may be implied by an ostracon (Cairo, Egyp.

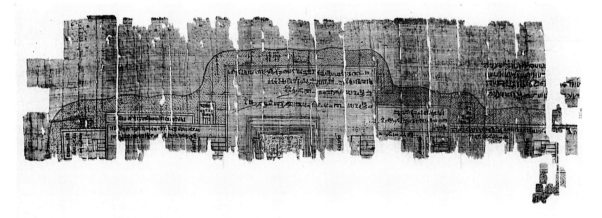

111. Plan of the tomb of Ramesses IV (*reg c.* 1156–*c.* 1150 BC), black, red, brown and yellow inks on papyrus, 0.31×1.05 m, 20th Dynasty (Turin, Museo Egizio di Torino)

Mus., JE 50036) showing a rough sketch of a curved structure, with notes of precise measurements of a kind that were presumably originally derived from an accurate master drawing.

BIBLIOGRAPHY
LÄ: 'Architekturdarstellung', 'Bauinschriften', 'Baupläne', 'Landkarte'
H. Carter and A. H. Gardiner: 'The Tomb of Ramesses IV and the Turin Plan of a Royal Tomb', *J. Egyp. Archaeol.*, iv (1917), pp. 130–58
S. Clarke and R. Engelbach: *Ancient Egyptian Masonry: The Building Craft* (Oxford, 1930), pp. 46–68
A. Badawy: *Le Dessin architectural chez les anciens égyptiens: Etude comparative des représentations égyptiennes de constructions* (Cairo, 1948)
G. Goyon: 'Le Papyrus de Turin dit "des mines d'or" et le Wadi Hammamat', *An. Service Ant. Egypte*, xlix (1949), pp. 337–92
E. Brunner-Traut: *Die altägyptischen Scherbenbilder (Bildostraka) der deutschen Museen und Sammlungen* (Wiesbaden, 1956), pp. 120–23
E. Scamuzzi: *Museo Egizio di Torino*, Turin, Mus. Egizio cat. (Turin, 1963; Eng. trans., New York, 1965), pls 87–8
E. Thomas: *The Royal Necropoleis of Thebes* (Princeton, 1966), pp. 277–85
J. Černý: *The Valley of the Kings* (Cairo, 1973), pp. 23–34
W. H. Peck: *Drawings from Ancient Egypt* (London, 1978), pp. 192–9
H. S. Smith and H. M. Stewart: 'The Gurob Shrine Papyrus', *J. Egyp. Archaeol.*, lxx (1984), pp. 54–64
A. F. Shore: 'Egyptian Cartography', *The History of Cartography*, i, ed. J. B. Harley and D. Woodward (Chicago, 1987), pp. 117–29

W. J. TAIT

12. MUSICAL INSTRUMENTS. The importance of music in ancient Egypt is attested by the large number both of representations of musical scenes (*see* §VI, 18 above) and surviving instruments in museum collections. The latter can be classified into four groups: idiophones, membranophones, aerophones and chordophones. The idiophones, which include clappers, sistra, cymbals and bells, were particularly associated with religious worship. The membranophones included the tambourine, usually played by girls at banquets or in outdoor ceremonies, and also the drum, a military instrument that sometimes appeared in religious processions. The earliest Egyptian aerophone was the flute, but there were also double 'clarinets', double 'oboes' and trumpets or bugles (mostly connected with the army). There were three types of chordophone: the harp (an indigenous Egyptian instrument), the lute and the lyre (both Asiatic imports).

(i) Idiophones. This is the best represented group, with the sistrum predominating, either arched or with its upper part in the shape of a naos or shrine. In the earlier periods both types of sistrum were sacred to the goddess Hathor, whose son Ihy is regarded as an Egyptian god of music. Later, the goddess Isis became associated with the instrument, and its use spread throughout the Roman world, although the naos-sistrum, usually of faience, was confined to Egypt. Plutarch (*On Isis and Osiris*, ccclxxvi.63) maintained that the jangling of the sistrum's metal plates symbolized the perpetual motion of all things.

Many surviving examples are models, designed as votive offerings to a god and often inscribed with a pharaoh's name. A fine alabaster model of a naos-sistrum (New York, Met.) is inscribed with the name of the 6th Dynasty king Teti (*reg c.* 2325–*c.* 2291 BC). A wooden sistrum (Edinburgh, Royal Mus. Scotland) of the New Kingdom (*c.* 1540–*c.* 1075 BC) is an unusually slender sounding instrument and remarkable for the intricacy of its inlay. The arched sistrum was mostly of bronze, but a model might have a flimsy arch of palm fibre (e.g. London, BM). In the

Late Period (*c.* 750–332 BC) large arched sistra were lavishly engraved with representations of Hathor, plant motifs and figures of other goddesses (impressive examples in London, BM; Paris, Louvre; Boston, MA, Mus. F.A.). Music in temple scenes is often concerned with the presentation of sistra to a deity by a pharaoh, as in scenes of the Roman emperors Augustus and Nero in front of Hathor at Dendara.

Among other idiophones, the earliest clappers (many examples in Cairo, Egyp. Mus.) had their ends fashioned in the form of animal or human heads. Later clappers of wood, ivory or bone were elegantly carved in the shape of a human hand, often with a profusion of roundel ornaments or a hieroglyphic inscription. They were used in religious festivals, as shown by the Opet celebrations depicted in the Temple of Amun at Luxor or by the rumbustious procession portrayed on a steatite bowl (London, BM) of the first Persian period (525–404 BC).

Bells, which were usually bronze, appeared late in Egyptian history, often bearing the features of the dwarf-god Bes, bringer of good cheer to the home. Roman examples approximated to the types still used in the Coptic Church. Bronze cymbals (e.g. London, BM; Paris, Louvre; New York, Met.), whether held separately or mounted on a handle similar to a pair of tongs, came equally late to Egyptian music.

(ii) Membranophones. The earliest known drum is from Beni Hasan and dates to the 12th Dynasty (*c.* 1900 BC; Cairo, Egyp. Mus.). Although this example is cylindrical, most elongated drums from Egypt were barrel-shaped and hung from the player's neck; they were used by soldiers or by priests in procession. Round tambourines appeared in the New Kingdom and were often associated with Bes, as in the case of a New Kingdom statuette (London, BM). They were also played by girls in scenes of jubilation, such as that depicted on a 13th-century BC relief block from Saqqara (Cairo, Egyp. Mus.). The skin coverings of tambourines were often richly decorated. One splendid example bears a depiction of a female player in front of Isis (Cairo, Egyp. Mus.); another is decorated with brilliantly painted scenes arranged into four registers (Oxford, Ashmolean). A rectangular tambourine with concave sides (Cairo, Egyp. Mus.) is of the type played by women at banquets, introduced during the reign of Tuthmosis III (*reg c.* 1479–*c.* 1426 BC).

(iii) Aerophones. The end-blown flute dates from at least Protodynastic times (*c.* 2950 BC), judging from the depiction on a slate palette from Hierakonpolis (Oxford, Ashmolean) showing a fox (or possibly a hunter dressed as a fox) playing a flute to a dancing giraffe and ibex. It was common in Old Kingdom (*c.* 2575–*c.* 2150 BC) chamber groups, where the player was always male; but the earliest surviving example of an end-blown flute dates to the Middle Kingdom (*c.* 1900 BC; Cairo, Egyp. Mus.). These flutes varied considerably in size and had three to eight playing holes. The double 'clarinet' with parallel pipes, to which single reeds were attached, is also characteristic of the Old Kingdom; by the Middle Kingdom it had become a rarity. Such instruments, with four to six holes in each pipe, are now in the Egyptian Museum, Cairo and the Bodemuseum, Berlin. They were played in

scenes of male chamber groups or sometimes in rural scenes. By contrast, the double 'oboe' is primarily a New Kingdom instrument, played with a double reed; it featured widely in ensembles of girl musicians at banquets, who often played with crossed hands. A fragment of wall painting from an unnumbered 18th Dynasty Theban tomb (*c.* 1400 BC; London, BM, 37984) clearly shows the double reeds picked out in white, but 'Satirical Papyrus' (London, BM, 10016), dating to the late Ramesside period (*c.* 1100 BC), displays a pair of similar pipes in the paws of a fox herding goats. The finest instruments so far discovered are the two trumpets from Tutankhamun's tomb (Cairo, Egyp. Mus.), decorated with incised reliefs featuring the main gods of the Egyptian army. Similar but less splendid instruments are shown in the hands of soldiers in temple scenes at Deir el-Bahri, Abydos and Abu Simbel.

(iv) Chordophones. The arched harp was the most popular of Egyptian stringed instruments. Representations show it in a remarkable range of shapes and sizes, with soundboxes of varied design. The earliest harps had a soundbox resembling a spade. In the 6th Dynasty (*c.* 2310 BC) tomb of Mereruka at Saqqara, the reliefs depict Princess Seshseshet playing this type of harp while singing to her husband. Later soundboxes were often in the shape of a ladle or narrow boat. Sometimes a harp is as large as the standing player, or might be small enough to be played easily on the shoulder. A falcon or royal head often adorned the upper end of the neck. Of the many surviving Egyptian harps, none is more exquisite than the richly painted and cunningly inlaid models now in the British Museum (see fig. 112) and the Oriental Institute Museum, University of Chicago. Angular harps were brought to Egypt from Asia in the New Kingdom and are superbly represented by a Late Period (*c.* 750–332 BC) example (Paris, Louvre), which has a vertical soundbox covered with green leather and a horizontal neck that can accommodate some 20 strings.

The two types of lute, one with a long wooden soundbox and the other with a round soundbox of tortoiseshell, are finely illustrated on another fragment of 18th Dynasty wall painting from Thebes (London, BM, 37981); it depicts the fingerboard frets and the plectra for striking the strings. The popularity of the delicate lute is shown by toilet spoons carved to the shape of a female lute-player and ornamental faience bowls painted with similar motifs. A lute belonging to the singer Harmose, excavated near Deir el-Bahri, illustrates the shorter type (Cairo, Egyp. Mus.).

The lyre makes its first Egyptian appearance in the 12th Dynasty tomb (*c.* 1900 BC; Tomb 3) of Khnumhotpe II at Beni Hasan, where it is held by an Asiatic bedouin. A lyre with trapezoidal soundbox (New York, Met.) has a hook to fasten the lower end of the six strings. There was a rich variety of lyres during the reign of Akhenaten (*reg c.* 1353–*c.* 1336 BC), none more imposing than the giant lyres played by a pair of men with Asiatic headgear, depicted on a relief block from the Karnak temple (Luxor, Mus.).

Wall paintings in the New Kingdom Theban tombs of Djeserkaresonb (TT 38) and Paser (TT 106) include a rich display of such Egyptian instruments as the harp, lute, lyre and double 'oboe'; to these might be added a rectangular tambourine to accompany a song or the supple dance

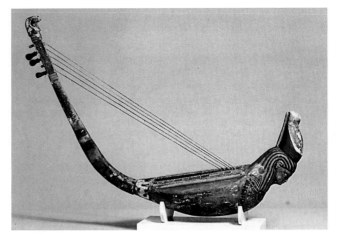

112. Model arched harp, wood, bone and faience, l. 972 mm, from Thebes, New Kingdom, *c.* 1540–*c.* 1075 BC (London, British Museum)

movements of a female slave. There is no more striking tribute to the ubiquity of such music in ancient Egypt than another satirical papyrus (*c.* 1250 BC; Turin, Mus. Egizio, 55001) depicting an ass with a large arched harp, a lion with a lyre, a crocodile with a lute and a monkey with a double 'oboe'.

BIBLIOGRAPHY

Grove 6: 'Egypt' [incl. extensive bibliog.]
H. Hickmann: *Catalogue général des antiquités égyptiennes du Musée du Caire: Instruments de musique, nos 69201–69852*, Cairo, Egyp. Mus. cat. (Cairo, 1949)
——: *45 siècles de musique dans l'Egypte ancienne* (Paris, 1956)
J. Vandier: 'La Musique, la danse et les jeux', *Manuel d'archéologie égyptienne*, iv (Paris, 1964), pp. 364–533
L. Manniche: *Ancient Egyptian Musical Instruments* (Munich, 1975)
R. D. Anderson: *Musical Instruments*, London, BM cat., iii (London, 1976)
L. Manniche: *Musical Instruments from the Tomb of Tutankhamun* (Oxford, 1976)
C. Ziegler: *Catalogue des instruments de musique égyptiens au musée du Louvre*, Paris, Louvre cat. (Paris, 1979)
——: *La Musique égyptienne* (Paris, 1979)

ROBERT ANDERSON

13. PERSONAL ART. The range of Egyptian personal art discussed here encompasses not only body decoration but cosmetics, tattoos and wigs, but also the associated items, particularly toiletry objects, and their iconography.

Most of the evidence for Egyptian personal art comes from funerary contexts, and there is a strong correlation between funerary imagery and the decoration of toiletry items. For example, a naked female lute-player in a marsh setting carved on the handle of an ointment spoon may be regarded as an erotic symbol, reinforcing a link between cosmetics and daily life, but the same motifs may occur in a strictly funerary context, perhaps as an allusion to the desired rebirth and resurrection. Given the close association between particular ancient Egyptian religious tenets and the parts of the human body (especially the eye, which was regarded as the principal port of entry through which both life and death could alternately pass), it would be rash to interpret all ancient Egyptian cosmetics as exclusive manifestations of contemporary fashion.

(i) Predynastic and Early Dynastic (c. 6000–c. 2575 BC). The use of cosmetics by the ancient Egyptians began in

the Predynastic period and is attested by numerous schist palettes, either geometric (New York, Brooklyn Mus., 07.447.601), zoomorphic (New York, Brooklyn Mus., 76.7) or with animal-headed terminals (London, BM, 35501), on which eye paint, usually green derived from malachite (New York, Brooklyn Mus., 09.889.190) but also black from galena, was ground before its application. Later these slate palettes were embellished with relief decoration and the receptacle for the paint took the form of a shallow, bowl-like reservoir (London, BM, 20790, and Cairo, Egyp. Mus., CG 14716).

More problematic is the Predynastic evidence for body decoration, either in the form of body paint or tattoos. The painted decoration on clay figurines of full-figured women, all unprovenanced (e.g. New York, Met., 07.228.71), has been speculatively adduced as proof for both practices.

(ii) Old Kingdom–Middle Kingdom (c. 2575–c. 1630 BC). The evidence for cosmetics from the Old Kingdom is sparse. Grave goods often include elegant stone vessels (e.g. Cairo, Egyp. Mus., JE 34941, 34942, 64886, 65416, 65422) which may have been containers for unguents and ointments (*see also* §16 below). A gold shell found in the pyramid of Neuserre at Giza (Cairo, Egyp. Mus., JE 92656) may have had a cosmetic purpose and demonstrates the copying of a natural prototype in metal. Alabaster vessels, often in the form of an ape and inscribed with the names of the 6th Dynasty kings (e.g. New York, Met., 30.8.134), provide the models on which all subsequent zoomorphic stone examples were based.

The material culture of the 11th to 13th dynasties provides far richer evidence for personal art. There are several engaging scenes of women at their toilette, such as those on the sarcophagus of Queen Kawit in Cairo (Egyp. Mus., JE 47397) and the reliefs of Neferu (New York, Brooklyn Mus., 54.49). Contemporary with these scenes are the tattoos found on the bodies of a group of women associated with the cult of Hathor at Thebes, which provide the first incontrovertible evidence for tattoos in pharaonic Egypt. Rather than representing a secular desire for adornment, these tattoos had religious or cultic connotations. Throughout the pharaonic period they were confined to decorating the bodies of women only. An approximation of their actual appearance can be gained by examining the series of dots and dashes on the thighs and pubic regions of the 'faience' female figurines from the period known as 'brides of the dead' (Cambridge, Fitzwilliam, E.191.2939; *see also* §5 above).

Complete cosmetic kits are now attested, such as the sumptuously appointed examples that belonged to Princess Sithathoryunet (New York, Met., 16.1.1ff) and the Butler Menuny (New York, Met., 26.7.135). That of Senebtisi at el-Lisht included an elaborate ring box. While both sexes owned cosmetic kits, those of men often contained a pair of razors. Contemporary with such kits are zoomorphic vessels, at least one in the shape of an ape (New York, Met., 10.176.54), vividly recalling the Old Kingdom royal prototype. Luxury vessels of similar form, mostly in anhydrite, a pale blue stone employed only at this period, exhibit a consummate skill on the part of the

craftsmen (e.g. Bristol, Mus. & A.G., H.4201). The so-called 'registers of objects', characteristic of painted wooden sarcophagi of the period (e.g. Boston, MA, Mus. F.A., 20.1822), show a rich array of such items, each often accompanied by its hieroglyphic designation.

(iii) New Kingdom–Third Intermediate Period (c. 1540– c. 750 BC). The greatest amount of attention to Egyptian

113. Wooden 'ointment spoon', 635×210 mm, New Kingdom, 18th Dynasty, *c.* 1540–*c.* 1292 BC (London, University of London, University College, Petrie Museum of Egyptian Archaeology)

cosmetics has been focused on the New Kingdom, particularly on the material culture of the 18th Dynasty. At this period the archaeological record complements the visual to provide the most complete documentation of cosmetics from any period of Egyptian history. Crafted from a variety of materials—metals and woods of all sorts as well as faience—the finest of these objects exhibit a harmonic sense of design in which all of the disparate elements are integrated into pleasing compositions. Mirrors, with bronze or silver discs (*see also* §XVI, 3 above), are often equipped with handles in the form of graceful, nude female figures (e.g. New York, Brooklyn Mus., 60.27.1) or heads of the goddess Hathor (*see* MIRROR, fig. 2). Metal razors generally have quinquelateral blades to which handles of like material are attached (e.g. Toronto, Royal Ont. Mus., 929.52.13). Also often called razors, although their actual use has not yet been determined, is a series of small, metal scissor-like objects, one arm of which is often decorated with a rampant beast (London, U. Coll., Petrie Mus., UC 30134), while the other arm fits into a channel forming a cutting edge. Metal tweezers, most used as depilatories, are also known (e.g. Boston, MA, Mus. F.A., 01.7317). Wooden boxes, generally less opulent than their Middle Kingdom antecedents, may have been used to house either cosmetics or jewellery (e.g. Toronto, Royal Ont. Mus., 931.55). Wooden zoomorphic boxes, generally representing gazelles (e.g. Cairo, Egyp. Mus., JE 44744) but sometimes grasshoppers (e.g. priv. col., on loan to New York, Brooklyn Mus., L48.7.1), with slotted backs or movable wings respectively, are suggested to have been deluxe containers for costly balms, as are the numerous figures, mostly in ebony, representing servant girls (e.g. London, U. Coll., Petrie Mus., UC 14210) or dwarfs (e.g. Boston, MA, Mus. F.A., 48.296) carrying a variety of vessel shapes. Among such figures, the most valued are those (in wood, ivory or a combination of materials) depicting a young woman floating on her stomach as she is pulled along the water by aquatic fauna or fowl, the bodies of which are the containers for ointments (e.g. New York, Met., 26.2.47). Of more varied forms are the so-called 'ointment spoons' or dishes (again in either wood or ivory), which are generally ornamented with two-dimensional, openwork scenes forming the handles for the spoon-shaped receptacles. The scenes often depict individuals engaged in activities in the swamp (e.g. London, U. Coll., Petrie Mus., UC 14365; see fig. 113), figures as bearers (e.g. Paris, Louvre, N.1738) or deities (e.g. London, U. Coll., Petrie Mus., UC 14366), but may also consist exclusively of floral arrangements (e.g. London, BM, 5966), or simply a human hand on a shell (e.g. Boston, MA, Mus. F.A., 1974.2).

Containers for kohl, a black eye paint derived from antimony, often take the shape of small pots, usually with bases and flaring lips that support thin disc covers. Although all examples generally conform to one standard shape, the materials range from undecorated polished stone (e.g. Manchester Mus., 11172), rarely embellished with gold (e.g. London, BM, 24391), to examples in faience, usually decorated with relief (e.g. Cambridge, Fitzwilliam, E.72.1932). The shapes of the applicators with which the kohl was applied vary from those resembling drum sticks (e.g. Toronto, Royal Ont. Mus., 910.165.773) to spatula forms (e.g. Boston, MA, Mus.

114. Faience bowl decorated with a woman with a leg tattoo and a monkey, h. 45 mm, diam. 140 mm, New Kingdom, late 18th Dynasty, *c.* 1400–*c.* 1300 BC (Leiden, Rijksmuseum van Oudheden)

F.A., 72.4330). Kohl was also placed in tubes resembling sections of papyrus stalk, which were crafted from bone, wood, ivory or faience. Whereas single tubes for kohl appear to be more common (e.g. Berkeley, U. CA, A. Mus., 5-2100), kohl containers consisting in one unit of from two tubes (e.g. Boston, MA, Mus. F.A., 01.7318) to four (e.g. U. Liverpool, M 11187) are also known. These often have incised decoration combining floral and/or figural motifs (e.g. New York, Brooklyn Mus., 49.52). Somewhat rarer are kohl containers in the form of female or divine images (e.g. Boston, MA, Mus. F.A., 72.4308 and 72.4158).

Many of the motifs used in the design and decoration of these cosmetic implements, such as fish and waterfowl, apes and Nilotic floral elements, belong to a common repertory of forms that also appear in the scenes of fishing and fowling in the marshes in the tombs of nobles (see fig. 8 above) and recur in contemporary literary compositions. Whatever may have been the function, or functions, of these elaborately crafted New Kingdom cosmetic spoons or dishes, not one has ever been found to contain even the slightest trace of unguent, or any other cosmetic substance, perhaps reinforcing the association of cosmetics with the other world. Similarly, razors may not have been used exclusively as a routine depilatory but had some ritual significance. This implement had its own tutelary deity, Duawer, and these elaborate razors may be associated with the obligatory shaving of certain classes of Egyptian priests or transitional rituals involving shaving, such as at adolescence.

Although not attested on New Kingdom mummies, tattoos continued to appear in the cultural record and remained, as earlier, restricted to women. The dots and dashes of the earlier periods were replaced by figural designs, the most common being the so-called Bes-image (see fig. 103 above), which may have been an amulet for warding off evil. Images of women decorated in this way appear on a faience bowl in Leiden (Rijksmus. Oudhd., AD 14/H118/E.xlii.38; see fig. 114) where the theme of a female in a marsh setting appears to have more in common with the amphibolic imagery of contemporary tomb paintings than with secular eroticism.

(iv) Late Period–Roman period (c. 750 BC–AD 395). The evidence from the Late Period for the funerary and cultic functions of cosmetics in ancient Egypt is equally compelling. The tomb of Padyenaset at Saqqara contains inscriptions in which funerary amuletic jewellery is juxtaposed with funerary ointments. The cosmetic implements from the period, mostly bronze, also have non-domestic contexts that reinforce the association of unguent and tomb (see §XVI, 3(ii) above). These bronze implements include toilet spoons (e.g. London, BM, 67218) and spatulas (e.g. Cairo, Egyp. Mus., JE 91498), as well as razors (e.g. London, BM, 68924–5) and mirrors (e.g. Oxford, Ashmolean, 1971.103). Scenes depicting the manufacturing of perfume appear in some of the so-called Neo-Memphite tomb reliefs (e.g. Paris, Louvre, E.11162), the earliest of which date to the 26th Dynasty. The most complete documentation for the uses of unguents and perfumes in ancient Egypt is found in inscriptions from the 'laboratoriam' in the Temple of Horus at Edfu, and Temple of Hathor at Dendara, and in the fragmentary parallels from the Temple at Tod.

During the Roman period, tattooing became more widespread in Egypt and appeared for the first time on males, perhaps influenced by the customs of North European legionaries in Egypt or by African practices. Coptic tattoo designs, which had an exclusively religious significance, preserved a considerable repertory of debased pharaonic and late Roman decorative motifs, such as Isis suckling Horus and equestrian saints derived from figures of emperors. Some of them are still tattooed on Coptic pilgrims.

BIBLIOGRAPHY

LÄ: 'Tätowierung'
I. E. S. Edwards: *A General Introductory Guide to the Egyptian Collection in the British Museum* (London, 1964)
W. C. Hayes: *The Sceptre of Egypt*, 2 vols (New York, 1968)
N. Scott: *The Daily Life of the Ancient Egyptians* (New York, 1973)
J. L. Foster: *Love Songs of the New Kingdom* (New York, 1974)
W. M. F. Petrie: *Prehistoric Egypt: Corpus of Prehistoric Pottery and Palettes Illustrated by the Egyptian Collection in University College, London* (Warminster, 1974)
Egypt's Golden Age: The Art of Living in the New Kingdom, 1558–1085 BC (exh. cat., Boston, MA, Mus. F.A., 1982)
W. Needler: *Predynastic and Archaic Egypt in the Brooklyn Museum* (New York, 1984)
M. Saleh and H. Sourouzian: *Official Catalogue*, Cairo, Egyp. Mus. cat. (Mainz, 1987)
R. S. Bianchi: 'Tattoo in Ancient Egypt', *Marks of Civilization: Artistic Transformations of the Human Body*, ed. A. Rubin (Los Angeles, 1988)
Pharaohs and Mortals: Egyptian Art in the Middle Kingdom (exh. cat. by J. Bourriau, Cambridge, Fitzwilliam, 1988)
R. A. Fazzini and others: *Ancient Egyptian Art in the Brooklyn Museum* (New York, 1989)

14. PLASTER AND STUCCO. Plaster was employed throughout Egyptian history for a wide variety of purposes, including masks, sculptures and casts. Its primary use,

however, was as a simple wall covering and an adhesive for pigments in wall paintings (see §X, 2 above). During the New Kingdom (c. 1540–c. 1075 BC) the interior walls of royal tombs at Thebes and Saqqara were routinely covered with plaster, which was then sculpted and painted. In later periods even architectural detailing was made of plaster.

Since wood, linen, wicker, leather, sandstone and limestone all have porous or irregular surfaces, they were often coated with plaster which served as a foundation for applied decoration. The plaster funerary masks (see §XIII, 2(iii) above) of the Old and Middle kingdoms (c. 2575–c. 1630 BC) were revived in the Late Period (c. 750–332 BC) in the form of cartonnage funerary ensembles in which linen and papyrus provided the support for decorated, moulded plaster.

Because of the paucity of marble in Egypt, many Greco-Roman (332 BC–AD 395) marble sculptures from Egypt were completed in plaster, especially in the area of the hair and the back of the head. Several types of sculpture were made entirely of plaster, including both moulded and handmade statuary and relief. Images of the god Serapis, including an example from the Roman period (Amsterdam, Allard Pierson Mus., 17932), form by far the largest published group of such plaster sculptures. There are numerous plaster busts of kings and heads of lions, which are traditionally—perhaps incorrectly—called sculptors' studies. There are also individual plaster heads representing identifiable pharaohs, such as Apries (reg 589–570 BC), Nectanebo I (reg 380–362 BC) and Ptolemy II Philadelphos (reg 285–246 BC; Budapest, Mus. F.A., 51.2256) in the traditional bland, idealizing style of the Late Period. These heads must derive from complete royal statues made entirely of plaster, similar to certain surviving representations of seated female figures. Independent works in plaster also include animal sculpture and images of deities, many excavated in Middle Egypt and dating to the Dynastic, Greco-Roman and Coptic periods.

There are also a number of small stucco reliefs, which have never been studied as a unit. The earliest among them seem to share stylistic affinities with Neo-Memphite limestone reliefs. They continued to be produced into the Roman period, as the superb example in the Pelizaeus-Museum, Hildesheim (see fig. 115), demonstrates.

The most problematic works in plaster are the masks (Berlin, Bodemus.) excavated in the workshop of the sculptor THUTMOSE at el-Amarna, the realistic features of which have been regarded as evidence for their having been death-masks. It is uncertain whether the Egyptians ever cast from living models, but they certainly made plaster casts from statues, as shown by a cast of a wig from an 18th Dynasty colossal statue (London, BM, 68047) and by the plaster head (Cairo, Egyp. Mus.) of a hippopotamus excavated by Petrie.

The taking of plaster casts from silver or gold vessels was a vigorous industry in Egypt during the Roman period, and possibly earlier. The Classical motifs on the plaster casts found at Memphis (Cairo, Egyp. Mus.; Hildesheim, Pelizaeus-Mus.) are comparable with those on casts found at Baia (anc. Baiae) in Italy, which were evidently intended to copy well-known Classical statues. However, some of the casts from Memphis, ostensibly from metal originals, were evidently considered to be works of art in their own right and were collected as such—a few even apparently bear artists' signatures in ink.

A final category of plaster sculptures—'anatomical donaria'—are separately made parts of the human body, the most common of which is like a half-mask, representing the brow, the eyes and the top of the bridge of the nose. These were probably used as offerings for the cure of ailments contracted in the particular part of the body represented.

BIBLIOGRAPHY

LÄ: 'Gips', 'Stuck'

C. C. Edgar: *Sculptors' Studies and Unfinished Works* (Cairo, 1906), pp. i–xii

W. M. F. Petrie and others: *Meydum and Memphis*, iii (London, 1910), p. 40

D. B. Thompson: 'Pannuchis', *J. Egyp. Archaeol.*, l (1964), pp. 161–2

W. B. Emery: 'Preliminary Report on the Excavations at North Saqqara', *J. Egyp. Archaeol.*, lvi (1970), pp. 8–9

R. S. Bianchi: [review of C. Reinsberg: *Studien zur hellenistischen Tereutik* (Hildesheim, 1980)], *J. Egyp. Archaeol.*, lxxi (1985), pp. 59–61 [review suppl.]

ROBERT S. BIANCHI

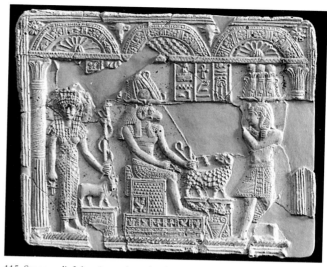

115. Stucco relief showing a pharaoh of the early Roman period (the Emperor Trajan) making offerings to Amun and Hathor, 193×234 mm, from Memphis, *c.* 1st century AD (Hildesheim, Pelizaeus-Museum)

15. SEALS. In ancient Egypt a great many objects with at least one inscribed surface may have been used as seals, even though they might ordinarily be classified as amulets, charms or otherwise. Nevertheless, in the course of the long pharaonic period certain kinds of object were developed specifically for sealing, although even these might sometimes be employed for other purposes, particularly as amulets and ornaments. The main categories are cylinders and stamp seals, the latter including that huge body of small objects known as scarabs.

(i) Cylinder seals. (ii) Stamp seals. (iii) Scarabs and scaraboids.

(i) Cylinder seals. These were possibly already in use before the beginning of the 1st Dynasty (*c.* 2925 BC). Predynastic cylinder seals, few in number but found in reliable archaeological contexts, bear motifs of fishes, eye-ovals and ladders, which are characteristic of cylinders from Babylonia of the Protohistoric period. They were probably imports into Egypt from western Asia and may be considered to be the precursors of, or inspiration for, native Egyptian cylinders.

After the start of the Dynastic period, there is ample evidence, in the form either of actual cylinders or of impressions made by cylinders, to show that the idea of sealing certain kinds of receptacle, and possibly also documents, had taken root in Egypt. Most of the surviving seals are made of steatite or serpentine, but some of wood and ivory have also been found. Royal names dominate the legends inscribed on early cylinders, repeated continuously around the engraved surface. The royal names are often combined with those of high-ranking officials; the names of vineyards are often included, especially for wine-jar sealings.

Other sealings, mostly known only from impressions, contain small ritual scenes of episodes from the *sed*-festival (royal jubilee), showing the king hunting the evil hippopotamus of the god Seth. Files of animals and boats are found on some, less common, impressions. One large category of cylinders from the 1st and 2nd dynasties, all small and made of steatite, was apparently never used for

sealing purposes. They carry private names and signs showing either a man or woman seated at an offering table or a bird, possibly representing the soul. The purpose of both was undoubtedly funerary.

Cylinders continued to be used for sealing to the 6th Dynasty (*c.* 2150 BC), although perhaps only for royal purposes. Strangely few cylinder-seal impressions of the 6th dynasty have been discovered, but on surviving examples of the seals themselves royal names and titles predominate. Official titles are also frequently included, but not the names of officials. During the Middle Kingdom (*c.* 2008–*c.* 1630 BC), occasionally during the New Kingdom (*c.* 1540–*c.* 1075 BC) and briefly during the 25th Dynasty (*c.* 750–*c.* 656 BC), cylinders engraved with royal names and epithets were produced as charms. They were mostly made of steatite and glazed; their legends were cut so lightly, and the cut lines were so filled with glaze, that they could have served no practical function as seals.

(ii) Stamp seals. During the period between the late 5th Dynasty (*c.* 2350 BC) and the late 11th Dynasty (*c.* 1950 BC) the change was made from cylinder seals to stamp seals, that is from seals that were rolled to produce an impression to those that were impressed by stamping. It is possible that the change arose from the usage of certain kinds of inscribed object by ordinary people, while more important people continued to use cylinders. Eventually the practical advantages of stamps led to the abandonment of cylinders. During this time of transition the scarab evolved as seal and amulet (*see* §(iii) below).

The 'seal amulet' (also known as the 'design amulet') was almost certainly the precursor of the stamp seal of the Middle Kingdom. This type of amulet—capable of being used as a sealing instrument—first appeared in burials of people, often women, from modest levels of society, in 4th Dynasty (*c.* 2500 BC) provincial cemeteries of Middle Egypt. It was subsequently found in similar archaeological contexts throughout the Old Kingdom and First Inter-mediate Period. Early examples are pyramidal in form or take the shape of half-cylinders. Later developments show the backs modelled as animal or human heads, with whole animals or other creatures, including the scarab beetle, forming yet later categories. The square, rectangular, oval or circular base carries a design that is usually abstract and linear, consisting of meanders and maze patterns. Such objects were usually made of steatite and glazed, but there are examples in other materials, including bone, ivory, copper and gold. Claims have been made that both the type of object and quite specifically the linear designs should be traced back to Cretan or western Asiatic prototypes, but scholarly opinion now generally accepts their native Egyptian character.

A particular subcategory of these 'seal amulets' takes the more precise shape of flat- or slightly dome-backed 'buttons'. On these the legends are more elaborate and figurative. Humans are shown as stick-figures performing simple actions such as wielding staves, raising arms and running. There are also depictions of various creatures, particularly lions, jackals, lizards and bees. Figures are often arranged *tête-bêche* (head-to-tail); sometimes the field is quartered with parts of creatures arranged in a cruciform pattern. Occasionally common and easily distinguished hieroglyphs are included. Generally, however, the designs, of which no two are precisely alike, are illiterate; if they were used as seals, the likelihood is that their owners were equally illiterate.

Formal and readily identifiable stamp seals emerged during the 12th Dynasty (*c.* 1938–*c.* 1756 BC). Few actual examples have been found (apart from scarabs), but large numbers of mud sealings bearing the impressions of stamps have been excavated. Important official seals produce impressions that are mostly rectangular with one rounded side. A typical legend contains the name of an office or department of state, and possibly the name of the place from which the sealed document originated, the whole almost invariably enclosed within a border of running scrolls. Some impressions of the 13th Dynasty (*c.* 1700 BC) were clearly made by rectangular seals of considerable length, containing royal names. The common material seems still to have been glazed steatite, but there is some evidence to suggest that wood was considered the proper material for official seals.

Stamp seals during the New Kingdom fall into two main types. The most important was the signet, a solid ring of metal on the bezel of which was engraved (or cast) the significant device, usually included within a simple oval surround. The ring of the 18th Dynasty is similar to the modern signet ring. It had developed from the simple scarab fastened by thread or metal wire to the finger, through various stages of elaboration including the setting of the scarab or other carved stone 'bezel' in a metal oval or *funda* which could swivel. Judging from surviving examples New Kingdom metal rings (mostly of bronze, but some of gold or silver) and mud sealings from documents, the devices, although finely engraved, are usually simple, containing royal names. They are certainly seals of authority. Some surviving examples, however, have elaborate scenes showing royal personages engaged in ritual and other acts. Metal rings continued in use as

official stamps for the rest of the Dynastic period and later. As time passed, greater emphasis was placed on the inscribed bezel. In many cases it became almost a separate plate, standing away from the ring; frequently the inside of the bezel was pinched, providing depressions for the thumb and forefinger, making it easier to hold and to apply pressure when in use as a signet. Some late signets are so heavy and awkward in shape that it is most unlikely they were ever worn as rings. (For further discussion of signet rings and their precursors *see* §XIV above.)

Much larger stamp seals were used to seal wine and other jars during the New Kingdom and later. Their legends, including such details as the contents of the jar, its source, the name of the reigning king and sometimes the name of a god associated with the product, were often picked out in colour. Those seals that have been discovered are usually made of limestone and are not particularly handsome, but many of the impressions are striking when the individual hieroglyphic signs are finely shaped and painted.

In the Late Period (*c.* 750–332 BC) a type of metal seal was developed, of which the surviving examples mostly relate to the great Theban Temple of Amun at Karnak. They regularly take the form of a base containing the legend made in openwork, attached to a long handle by metal struts arranged like a pyramid. Some are embellished with little figures of rams, an animal sacred to Amun. The text of the legend reads simply 'House of Amun'. Such implements were probably used by the agents acting on behalf of the Karnak temple on the god's many estates throughout Egypt.

At all times, from the early 18th Dynasty to the end of the pharaonic period, large wooden seals were used to stamp bricks with royal names—the application of a magical imprimatur—and to seal large plastered surfaces, such as the walled-up entrances to royal tombs in the Valley of the Kings. The interest of such seals, like that of so many smaller Egyptian seals, lies not in the instruments themselves, which were usually functional, but in the meaning of the legends.

(iii) Scarabs and scaraboids. Throughout the Dynastic period the scarab beetle occupied a significant place in Egyptian religious symbolism. From the late Old King-dom, small scarab amulets were made for magical and other purposes (*see* §I above). From the late 11th Dynasty, at least, scarabs were used as sealing instruments, and in the two succeeding dynasties became common for this purpose. Scarabs were also often beautiful small objects, finely carved and decorated with small-scale texts and intricate designs (for illustration *see* SCARAB). Some scarabs can be classified as jewels, others as instruments of propaganda. The sacred character of the scarab, which led to its initial importance in Egyptian religious estimation, derived from its association with the sun-god, and in particular the sun-god in the early morning. The theological basis for this lay in the link between the sun's reappearance every morning and the apparent ability of the scarab beetle to regenerate itself. The popularity of the scarab, however, must have been based as much on its neatness of form and its versatility as a vehicle for inscriptions and decorative motifs, as on its divine association.

Scarabs became significant sealing instruments during the 12th and 13th dynasties. One special group were the 'private-name scarabs', on the bases of which were carved inscriptions including the titles and names of important officials of state. These were personal sealing instruments used when their owners were engaged on official business. Many hundreds of examples survive, and many thousands of mud sealings bearing impressions of such scarabs have been excavated. The scarabs themselves, mostly made of glazed steatite, are often finely carved with special attention devoted to the delineation of natural detail. In some cases they are still mounted in gold settings as parts of finger-rings (see fig. 116).

During the Second Intermediate Period (c. 1630–c. 1540 BC) large numbers of private-name scarabs continued to be produced, often duplicated many times. It seems unlikely that these later examples were used as seals; confirmatory evidence from contemporary mud sealings is lacking. They are also less well designed than the fine Middle Kingdom products. The few scarabs with names from later periods were also probably never used as seals, although from their nature and design they could have been so used.

Of the tens of thousands of scarabs that survive from antiquity, large numbers with royal names were made for propaganda purposes. Some exceptionally large scarabs were used to commemorate important royal events and activities, especially in the reign of Amenophis III (reg c. 1390–c. 1353 BC). But most were used for simple amuletic purposes, made chiefly of glazed steatite, although faience was much employed in the later New Kingdom

and for scarabs manufactured outside Egypt. The form was universal in its appeal, often beautifully carved and provided with a well-designed legend. When hardstones were used, the craftsman's skill was specially tested, and remarkable carvings were produced on a small scale. For such, the term 'gem' is an apt description.

BIBLIOGRAPHY
J. de Morgan: *Fouilles à Dahchour*, i (Vienna, 1895)
P. E. Newberry: *Scarabs: An Introduction to the Study of Egyptian Seals and Signet Rings* (London, 1906)
H. R. Hall: *Royal Scarabs* (London, 1913), i of *Catalogue of Scarabs etc in the British Museum*
W. M. F. Petrie: *Scarabs and Cylinders with Names* (London, 1917)
——: *Buttons and Design Scarabs* (London, 1925)
G. Brunton: *Mostagedda and the Tasian Culture* (London, 1937)
——: *Matmar* (London, 1948)
G. A. Reisner: 'Clay Sealings of Dynasty XIII from Uronarti Fort', *Kush*, iii (1955), pp. 26–69
G. T. Martin: *Egyptian Administrative and Private-name Seals* (Oxford, 1971)
P. Kaplony: *Die Rollsiegel des Alten Reichs*, 2 vols (Brussels, 1977–81)
W. A. Ward and O. Tufnell: *Studies on Scarab Seals*, 2 vols (Warminster, 1978–84)
                                                    T. G. H. JAMES

16. STONE VESSELS. From the beginning of Egyptian civilization stone vessels were fashioned with consummate skill and artistry; a combination of fine material, design and workmanship has produced objects of lasting artistic merit. Indeed, the Egyptologist Walter Emery has suggested that 'no country then or since has achieved such perfection . . . in its effort to produce an object of utility which was also a thing of beauty'. Because of their durability and attractiveness, stone vessels can be seen in virtually all major collections of Egyptian art, although many of the finest examples are in the Egyptian Museum, Cairo. The Petrie Museum, in the University of London, includes vessels from Flinders Petrie's private collection, many of which are unprovenanced, while the Ashmolean Museum, Oxford, has a large variety of provenanced vessels, many in storage. There is an excellent display of stone vessels at the British Museum, London. The Museum of Fine Arts, Boston, includes many Predynastic and Old Kingdom vessels from George Reisner's excavations.

(i) Introduction. (ii) Predynastic and Early Dynastic (c. 6000–c. 2575 BC). (iii) Old Kingdom–New Kingdom (c. 2575–c. 1075 BC). (iv) Third Intermediate Period–Roman period (c. 1075 BC–AD 395).

(i) Introduction. In the Predynastic (c. 6000–c. 2925 BC) and the Early Dynastic periods (c. 2925–c. 2575 BC) stone vessels were primarily made for funerary purposes, as more durable substitutes for pottery containers of food and ointments. Gradually, beginning in the Old Kingdom, actual food offerings in the tomb were partly replaced by models, magic formulae and depictions of food preparation in reliefs and paintings. In the late Old Kingdom (c. 2575–c. 2150 BC), stone models of food storage vessels and tableware were made in miniature. By the Middle Kingdom (c. 2008–c. 1630 BC) most stone vessels were containers for cosmetics or scented oils, to which were added in the New Kingdom (c. 1540–c. 1075 BC) drinking vessels, all of which were used in life before accompanying their owner into the tomb.

The method of manufacturing stone vessels (for which *see also* §VII, 1(ii)(b) above) is depicted on tomb walls throughout the Dynastic period in scenes of craftsmen at

116. Scarab seal inscribed for the official 'senior commander Senwosre', unglazed steatite set in a gold *funda* from a signet ring, h. 215 mm, from Egypt, c. 1700 BC (London, British Museum)

work (see fig. 10 above). From the late Predynastic period, the drill employed for hollowing out the vessels (a depiction of which was used as the hieroglyphic symbol for craftsman) was made of a bent stick, weighted at the top, with a notch at the bottom to hold the bit. It was operated with a push–pull motion that caused the weights to swing off balance and rotate the drill. A number of surviving unfinished vessels provide evidence for the various stages of manufacture. The outside of a vessel was first roughed out, then the interior was hollowed using a tubular copper bit fed with an abrasive, or a crescent-shaped flint bit for softer stones. The exterior (and interior in the case of open forms) was then polished by hand. A few labour-saving tricks were employed: rims, for instance, were sometimes made separately, and vessels with a narrow mouth were occasionally made of two or more separate pieces cemented together. In some cases contrasting stone colours were deliberately selected for decorative effect.

(ii) Predynastic and Early Dynastic (c. 6000–c. 2575 BC). The earliest stone vessels from the Predynastic period were of hard, black basalt, a stone prized for durability but correspondingly difficult to work. They were shaped and hollowed by pounding and rubbing by hand, thus producing irregularities in the curved surface. By the Naqada II period (*c. 3500–c. 2925 BC*) stone vessels were more numerous and better made, reflecting the appearance of copper tools and the invention of the drill. A variety of hardstones were popular, including andesite porphyry, diorite, tuff and siltstone or greywacke (Egyp. *bekhen*), as well as softer stones composed of calcium carbonate such as travertine, limestone and red limestone breccia. Characteristic shapes are the tall, cylindrical jars and beakers (often footed; see fig. 117(i)a–d) and the tall and squat ovoid jars that typically have tubular handles and sharp-edged rims (117(i)f–g). A few zoomorphic forms (e.g. Cairo, Egyp. Mus., JE 66628) have also survived, including some shaped like frogs (see fig. 117(i)e) and birds.

In the Early Dynastic period, the old cylindrical jars developed into more open forms that flared slightly at the base (see fig. 117(ii)a). Bowls with an incurved rim, a sharp inner lip and a round, drilled depression in the base of the interior, were characteristic of this period (see fig. 117(ii)b–c). Shouldered jars became more common and their rims more rounded (see fig. 117(ii)d). Among the exceptional pieces were a series of squat, shouldered jars (see fig. 117(ii)e), such as those from the tomb of King Khasekhemwy (*reg c. 2700 BC*) at Abydos, which had covers of gold foil fastened around the mouth of the vessel by gold wire, in imitation of a cloth cover tied with string (Cairo, Egyp. Mus., JE 34941).

The greatest diversity of ornamental stones occurred in Early Dynastic vessels. In particular, the royal tombs of Abydos contained vessel fragments of an astonishing array of colours and compositions, including clear rock crystal, amethyst, obsidian, lapis lazuli, dolomite, diorite, granite, serpentine, pink limestone, black limestone and andesite tuff with purple stripes. Vessels of green ash tuff and green siltstone from the great mud-brick mastaba tombs at Saqqara are among the finest products of the Early Dynastic period. The craftsmen fashioned the hardstone as if it were clay, making thin-walled, delicate vessels with

the forms of leaves, flowers and baskets (e.g. Cairo, Egyp. Mus., JE 71298). Other forms imitate metalwork, complete with imitation rivets.

One of the largest collections of Early Dynastic stone vessels was found in the subterranean chambers of the Step Pyramid of Djoser (*reg c. 2630–c. 2611 BC*) at Saqqara. Two long galleries were packed from floor to ceiling with an estimated 40,000 stone vessels (many in Cairo, Egyp. Mus.). Since these vessels were inscribed only with the names of 1st and 2nd Dynasty kings, it has been suggested that Djoser might have ordered them to be gathered up from the plundered tombs of the preceding dynasties and reburied in greater security beneath his pyramid, thus in a sense returning them to the use of their rightful owners in the afterlife. There were many unusual forms in the Step Pyramid cache, including jars with an imitation netting of knotted ropes carved on the exterior, bowls divided into compartments by wafer-thin vertical partitions fashioned as an integral part of the vessel, and double and even quadruple bowls carved in one piece to represent a stack of shallow bowls nesting one within the other. Some of the forms were unique, such as a stone jar in the likeness of a granary; a tall, fluted, cylindrical jar imitating a column; and a jar decorated with a relief-carving representing the hieroglyphs for 'a million jubilee festivals' (thus wishing the king to reign eternally).

Most of the vessels from the Step Pyramid were of travertine, which was cleverly exploited by craftsmen to enhance the appearance of each vessel. For bowls and jars the preference was for the alternating layers of colour in the travertine to be aligned horizontally, while for shallow dishes and flat-topped tables the layers were aligned vertically to produce stripes across the vessel's broadest surface. Although the percentage of hardstones in the Step Pyramid cache was small, the remarkable variety was a hallmark of the Early Dynastic period.

(iii) Old Kingdom–New Kingdom (c. 2575–c. 1075 BC). The proportion of travertine to hardstones was higher in the private tombs of the first two dynasties than in the royal tombs, and by the Old Kingdom travertine far outnumbered all other stones in both royal and private tombs. Translucent, banded diorite gneiss from a quarry in Nubia was introduced in the Early Dynastic period but it reached its height of popularity in the Old Kingdom. The use of hardstones generally diminished throughout the Old Kingdom as the frequency of travertine increased, although certain stones were retained in use longer for particular types of vessels: for example most of the squat ovoid jars (see fig. 117(iii)e) found in great quantities in the magazines of the Valley temple of Mycerinus at Giza were of mottled black-and-white diorite (Boston, MA, Mus. F.A.). Many of these were only roughly finished and partly hollowed, having been provided as a traditional part of the funerary equipment although no longer functional as containers.

After the Old Kingdom, stone vessels were more frequently objects of daily (rather than funerary) use and were largely restricted to softer stones. A common form in the Middle Kingdom was the concave-sided beaker with flat lid (see fig. 117(iv)a), which held scented oils. These vessels were often made in sets of eight, each for a

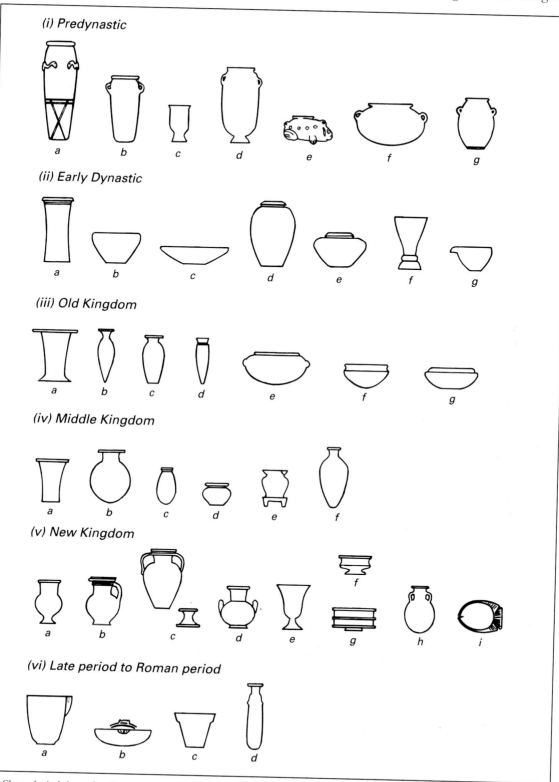

(i) Predynastic

a   b   c   d   e   f   g

(ii) Early Dynastic

a   b   c   d   e   f   g

(iii) Old Kingdom

a   b   c   d   e   f   g

(iv) Middle Kingdom

a   b   c   d   e   f

(v) New Kingdom

a   b   c   d   e   f   g   h   i

(vi) Late period to Roman period

a   b   c   d

117. Chronological chart of ancient Egyptian stone vessel shapes

different oil, neatly fitted into a wooden chest which contained other cosmetic items such as a kohl pot, a mirror and a razor. Small kohl jars (see fig. 117(iv)d) were commonly made from pale blue anhydrite, the characteristic softer stone of the Middle Kingdom which rarely appeared outside this time. Kohl pots were sometimes attached to a four-legged stand, or the stand was carved in one piece with the base (see fig. 117(iv)e). Anhydrite was also used for small ointment jars fancifully carved in the shape of animals such as fish, ducks with curved necks forming handles, and monkeys clasping jars in their paws, all forms that retained their popularity into the New Kingdom (see fig. 117(v)i). Larger Middle Kingdom ointment jars usually had a round base.

In the New Kingdom, stone vessels commonly had a pedestal or ring base and many had loop handles, perhaps a foreign influence. The characteristic forms, with globular body and long neck (see fig. 117(v)a–d), contained ointments and oils. Stone goblets were popular as drinking cups in the New Kingdom (see fig. 117(v)e), and the evidence of tomb paintings suggests that ribbed dishes were probably used to dispense scented ointment at banquets; dishes with one rib (117(v)f) are the earliest, while those with three or four appeared later (117(v)g). Pilgrim flasks (see fig. 117(v)h) first appeared in the 18th Dynasty (c. 1540–c. 1292 BC). Two special types of kohl pot, one of blackened limestone with yellow incised decoration imitating ebony and gold, the other of green-glazed steatite with openwork or incised decoration, date to the early 18th Dynasty. Shortly afterwards, in the reign of Tuthmosis III (reg c. 1479–c. 1426 BC), kohl pots were superseded by kohl tubes. Travertine remained the most common stone for New Kingdom vessels, with another soft stone, a finely mottled green and black serpentine, a popular alternative.

(iv) Third Intermediate Period–Roman period (c. 1075 BC–AD 395). The kings of the Third Intermediate Period (c. 1075–c. 750 BC) were notorious for reusing their predecessors' monuments. King Amenemope (reg c. 998–c. 989 BC) included in his tomb a stone vessel of Sethos I (reg c. 1290–c. 1279 BC) from which he had erased the name of the earlier king. Nevertheless, stone vessels continued to be produced in the Third Intermediate Period, and small cosmetic containers such as beakers with swivel lids (see fig. 117(vi)a) and shallow, round dishes (117(vi)b) were among the possessions of the wealthy. Royal workshops produced large, two-handled storage jars, which were found among the grave goods of the kings' tombs at Tanis and were exported to Phoenicia and Palestine. These Egyptian stone vessels were considered such a valuable commodity that the Assyrians carried them off from Phoenicia as booty over a century after their manufacture, while Phoenician colonists as far away as Spain reused Egyptian Third Intermediate Period vessels as cinerary urns. In the 25th Dynasty (c. 750–c. 656 BC) a reverence for the past and a deliberate copying of earlier artistic styles found their expression in stone vessels that imitated the forms of Early Dynastic vessels.

After the Third Intermediate Period, stone vessels were relatively rare and restricted to only a few forms. The mortar with square lugs (see fig. 117(vi)c), which first appeared in the New Kingdom, became more common from the 26th Dynasty onwards and continued in use throughout the Roman period. The alabastron, in its classic form (see fig. 117(vi)d), was characteristic from the Late Period to Roman times, although it had its precursors in the Third Intermediate Period. By the Late Period the few stone vessels still manufactured as actual containers were all of the softest stones: travertine, steatite and serpentine. However, mortars, designed for grinding, were often made of harder stones such as diorite. In the Roman period they were made from the purple imperial porphyry, much prized by Romans but rarely used earlier.

BIBLIOGRAPHY
W. M. F. Petrie: *Prehistoric Egypt* (London, 1920), pp. 34–6
A. Lucas: *Ancient Egyptian Materials and Industries* (London, 1926, rev. 4/1962), pp. 406–28
G. Reisner: *Mycerinus* (Cambridge, 1931), pp. 130–201
W. M. F. Petrie: *Stone and Metal Vases* (London, 1937)
J.-P. Lauer: *La Pyramide à degrés*, iii (Cairo, 1939)
W. B. Emery: *Archaic Egypt* (Baltimore, 1961), pp. 214–18
R. Hartenberg and J. Schmidt jr: 'The Egyptian Drill and the Origin of the Crank', *Technol. & Cult.*, x (1969), pp. 155–65
A. El-Khouli: *Egyptian Stone Vessels: Predynastic Period to Dynasty III*, 3 vols (Mainz, 1978)
A. J. Spencer: *Early Dynastic Objects*, London, BM cat., v (London, 1980), pp. 17–42
Egypt's Golden Age: The Art of Living in the New Kingdom (exh. cat., Boston, MA, Mus. F.A., 1982), pp. 126–33

BARBARA G. ASTON

17. TEXTILES. Large quantities of textiles have been excavated from Egyptian settlements, such as Kahun (c. 1850 BC) and el-Amarna (c. 1350 BC), and from many private and royal tombs. The two most famous caches of cloth, both from the mid-14th century BC, come from the Theban tombs of the architect Kha (c. 1400 BC; Turin, Mus. Egizio) and King Tutankhamun (reg c. 1332–c. 1323 BC; Cairo, Egyp. Mus.).

The most important use of textiles in pharaonic Egypt was for clothing (for discussion of Egyptian dress see §4 above), but texts and representations indicate a wide range of other uses. Household items made from textiles included towels, curtains, cushions, sheets, bed covers, awnings and dividers. Outside the house, textiles were used for flags, banners, awnings, covers for objects being transported, sails, saddle cloths and other trappings. In warfare, textiles were used for finger stalls, archery ties, quivers, archers' pads and slings. Textiles also formed an important element in the gifts sent by the pharaohs to other kings, and in temples throughout Egypt there was a long tradition of offering textiles to the gods. There were also secondary uses of textiles, such as mummy bandages, wrappings for statues and figurines, bags, sacks, amulet holders, lamp-wicks, hobbles for animals, rags for cleaning or stuffing in wall cracks, as well as constituent parts of door seals.

Although most Egyptian textiles were simply bleached white, the more elaborate examples were decorated using the techniques discussed below. (For the manufacture and production of cloth see §VII, 4 above.)

(i) Dyed. Occasionally some or all of the cloth was coloured using a mineral or plant dye; reds, for example, were produced from ochre, madder or henna; blues from indigotin (probably derived from a type of woad) or sunt; and yellows from saffron, safflower or pomegranate.

Purples, browns and greens were usually produced by double-dyeing the yarn or cloth, as in the case of a purple yarn dating to the mid-18th Dynasty (*c.* 1350 BC) from el-Amarna, which was dyed with madder and indigotin. This method of producing an optical purple was continued in Egypt well into the early Islamic period. These colours had various symbolic meanings, and certain restrictions were placed on their use. Priests, for example, were expected to wear white, the purest of all colours, while certain blues were regarded as the colours of mourning.

There are two types of organic dyes: the substantive or direct types (such as indigo and woad), which can be applied to fibres or cloth with no intermediary, and the adjective types (including madder, sunt, saffron and saf-flower), which can only be successfully applied to fibres treated with a mordant. A wide range of mordants, such as salt, natron and alum, were available in the Dynastic period, but it is virtually impossible to detect any of these substances on a piece of dyed cloth, since they tend to be masked either by natron used for burial purposes or by the naturally occurring salt and alum in sand.

(ii) Fringed. The use of warp fringes (produced by twisting or plaiting together groups of warp threads) and the more complex weft fringes (woven with extra threads that extend beyond the selvedge) as textile decoration can be seen in Middle and New Kingdom tomb reliefs, such as the scenes in the 12th Dynasty tomb of Khnumhotpe III (Tomb 3), at Beni Hasan (Tomb 4; *c.* 1900 BC), and in an early 18th Dynasty depiction in the tomb of User at Thebes (TT 260; *c.* 1450 BC). Weft fringes do not seem to have been used in later periods, although it is not clear when the practice died out. Some examples of weft fringe survive (Oxford, Ashmolean, 1917.52, and U. Chicago, IL, Orient. Inst. Mus., 18284). It seems that weft fringes are found only on cloth woven on the horizontal loom, and it is possible that they ceased to be made when this type of loom fell out of use.

(iii) Looped. Many of the textiles found in the tomb of Kha at Thebes (TT 8; *c.* 1360 BC) were woven with soft loops of flax. These loops were created by adding an extra weft thread to the cloth during weaving. The thread was pulled up (sometimes wrapped around a stick) until the desired length of loop was achieved. Some of the textiles from Kha's tomb have the loop arranged in simple geometric patterns. A more complex design is represented by a rectangular piece of cloth (Cairo, Egyp. Mus., 56279) with an all-over design of loops worked in dots, simple lines, vertical and horizontal chevrons and diamonds. Some textiles have loops made of a hard, palmlike fibre, while others have soft loops (e.g. Cairo, Egyp. Mus., 57174). Such variations in loop texture appear to be due to differences in the intended function of the cloth.

(iv) Woven. One of the simpler forms of woven decoration is illustrated by one of Tutankhamun's shawl (Cairo, Egyp. Mus., 1668), which has rows of alternating light blue and brown ducks. A more complex form of woven decoration is tapestry-weaving, a technique in which the coloured wefts do not pass from selvage to selvage but are changed according to the demands of the design (*see* TAPESTRY, §I, 2). There are a number of tapestry-woven textiles

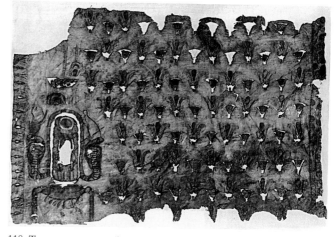

118. Tapestry-woven textile with cartouche of Amenophis II surrounded by lotus flowers and buds, w. 420 mm, from the tomb of Tuthmosis IV, *c.* 1390 BC (Cairo, Egyptian Museum)

associated with two royal tombs, both dating to the mid-14th century BC. A piece from the tomb of Tuthmosis IV at Thebes (KV 43) bears a cartouche of Amenophis II surrounded by lotus flowers and buds (Cairo, Egyp. Mus., JE 46526; see fig. 118). The finds from the tomb of Tutankhamun included several tapestry-woven objects, such as a quiver decorated with red, brown, dark and light blue lotus blooms and buds (Cairo, Egyp. Mus., JE 335) and a large cloth with a warp fringe, a design of quatrefoils, *wedjat*-eye motifs alternating with lotus buds and a border of blocks and circles (Cairo, Egyp. Mus., JE 1666). All the motifs on the cloth have been worked in brown and blue. Both the 'girdle' of Ramesses III (Liverpool Mus., M 111356) and Tutankhamun's collar (Cairo, Egyp. Mus., JE 931) were woven in a tight plain weave, using both coloured and undyed flax yarns to produce simple geometric patterns. The Ramesses III girdle has a design of *ankh*-signs (the hieroglyph for life) and chevrons worked in blue, red, yellow, green and undyed flax. Despite suggestions that it was woven using cards or tablets, it seems to have been produced by a different technique; there is no evidence to suggest that card-weaving was practised in Dynastic Egypt.

The design of the Tutankhamun collar consists of a repeating pattern of crosses, squared triangles and coloured squares in red, brown, yellow and light blue. There is no evidence to suggest that large-scale tapestries (of the type that have survived from the Roman and Coptic periods in Egypt) were ever produced during the Dynastic period. Nor were the vertical looms depicted in Theban tombs used to produce large tapestries, although they are sometimes described as tapestry looms. Since the cloth depicted in the tombs is shown as completely white, large sheets of white (rather than coloured) cloth were probably being produced.

(v) Embroidered and pleated. Although a number of Dynastic textiles were embroidered, it was apparently not a common Egyptian decorative technique. One of the most elaborate surviving examples is a rectangular cloth, from

Tutankhamun's mummy, which has appliqué motifs of lotus flowers and hieroglyphs surrounding a bird (possibly a falcon) with outstretched wings (Cairo, Egyp. Mus., JE 1647). Unfortunately this piece is in such poor condition that it is impossible to identify the original colours.

Some textiles have simple vertical or horizontal pleats, while in more elaborate examples the pleats run in both directions (e.g. Cairo, Egyp. Mus., JE 51513, which has vertical pleats alternating with bands of chevron pleats). Male and female garments with decorative pleats are frequently depicted in tomb paintings. In addition to these depictions, a number of pleated women's dresses have survived (see §4(iv)(b) above). It is clear from these garments that the use of pleats was common on items of daily wear, such as the 1st Dynasty (c. 2850 BC) tunic from Tarkhan (London, U. Coll., Petrie Mus., 28614 Bi) and on dresses that were specially produced for burial in a tomb, such as a 5th Dynasty (c. 2400 BC) garment from Dishasha (London, U. Coll., Petrie Mus., 31183).

It has been suggested that some of the pleats were introduced using changes of tension in the cloth weave, but there is no satisfactory evidence for this theory. The presence of horizontal, vertical and chevron pleats in some textiles indicates that various methods of pleating were employed. It is possible that the pleating took place by wetting the cloth, then hand-folding it or pressing it into shape using 'pleating boards' (e.g. London, BM, 35908).

One form of decoration associated with Egyptian textiles of the Ptolemaic and Roman periods (304 BC–AD 395) is sprang—a process involving the manipulation of a set of stretched threads. Although it does not seem to have been used during the Dynastic period in Egypt, it was a popular form of textile production in ancient Greece and it may have been introduced into Egypt by Greek settlers during the Ptolemaic period.

BIBLIOGRAPHY

E. Schiaparelli: *La tomba intatta dell'architetto Cha* (Turin, 1927)
R. Pfister: 'Les Textiles du tombeau de Toutankhamen', *Rev. A. Asiat.*, x (1937), pp. 207–18
E. C. Riefstahl: *Patterned Textiles in Pharaonic Egypt* (Brooklyn, 1944)
J. Allgrove MacDowell: 'Kahun: The Textile Evidence', *The Pyramid Builders of Ancient Egypt*, ed. R. David (London, 1985)
R. Hall: *Egyptian Textiles* (Aylesbury, 1986)

GILLIAN VOGELSANG-EASTWOOD

XVII. Regional art.

Regionalism was a limited phenomenon in ancient Egypt, since the ethos underlying art was that of a state, the focus and raison d'être of which was the king's rule over the ordered world. Both state and artistic production were in principle centralized. Whereas regional variations existed in prehistoric Egyptian styles—preserved chiefly in ceramics, in small-scale works in other media and in rock drawings—these lessened after the end of the Naqada II period (c. 2925 BC), when Egypt became culturally homogeneous and politically centralized. Characteristically Egyptian art thus originated, together with writing, in the context of a large state. In later times, even when the state was not centralized, conventions of iconography and representation remained essentially uniform (see §§IV–V above). Regional styles nonetheless developed to some extent, but they arose from incompletely assimilated central norms more than from local initiative. Art remained geographically centripetal until the late New Kingdom, when the integrated state gradually declined, opening the way to a more plural regional culture. Artistic individualism was seldom at a premium, and artists usually worked in groups (see §II, 2 above); deliberate regionalism would have gone against norms and practice. Far more significant for variety and innovation than regionalism was the exploitation of the past, with its range of well-known periods and associations, while the different media of relief and statuary, hard and soft stones and wood developed distinctive styles.

Attempts to classify Egyptian art regionally have applied attributional procedures of Western art history to a more fundamentally anonymous tradition. Since few individuals could be identified, hypothetical, often regional 'schools' provided the model. Although artists, groups of artists and local styles can be identified, such constructs are inappropriate and extraneous for most periods. Work of this type will ultimately be essential for detailed study, especially of techniques, but it will not greatly deepen the understanding of Egyptian art's cultural meaning.

Regional art is significant in the First Intermediate Period, the early Middle Kingdom and the Second and Third Intermediate periods, as well as in the Late Period and Greco-Roman period, with their more complex traditions. Among the earlier periods, only the Middle Kingdom was a time of general cultural growth.

1. LATE OLD KINGDOM–EARLY MIDDLE KINGDOM (c. 2350–c. 1950 BC). From the later part of the 5th Dynasty (c. 2465–c. 2325 BC) some high-ranking officials built their tombs in the provinces, both in the Nile Valley and the Delta. This trend increased in the 6th Dynasty (c. 2325–c. 2150 BC), but provincial tombs never achieved the size or artistic quality of those at the capital, from which their scenic repertory was derived. The First Intermediate Period continued these tendencies, but lacked central organization and produced a wide variety of styles, especially in southern Upper Egypt. Reunification in the 11th Dynasty (c. 2081–c. 1938 BC) gradually led to the readoption of the central tradition throughout the country, but in the Theban area, from which the new rulers came, there was an uneasy mixture of the traditions of Memphis (the old capital) and local traditions of the First Intermediate Period. The Memphite forms were probably valued more for historical than for geographical associations, while the more innovative Theban forms displayed the regional basis of the dynasty's power. This brief period was almost the only time when the most creative art was distinctively regional. The kings of the 12th Dynasty (c. 1938–c. 1756 BC) moved the capital back to the Memphite area and abandoned their local origins. The first funerary monuments of the 12th Dynasty rulers were based on the latest major Old Kingdom monument, the pyramid complex of Pepy II (reg c. 2246–c. 2150 BC) at Saqqara. For the next century there were important tombs of local potentates in Upper Egyptian nomes. These too displayed local power, while acknowledging central authority, and are more diverse in style than major Old Kingdom tombs. However, the finest of them, such as

some of those at MEIR and, especially, Qaw el-Kebir, are centripetal in design and aspiration.

The most important single regional sculpture find is a large group of Middle Kingdom statues from the shrine complex of Heqaib on Elephantine Island (Elephantine Island, Aswan, some still *in situ*; see fig. 119). The statues of the local élite, carved in hard stone and of a generally high quality, follow national fashions but reinterpret them in details of iconography and style; the iconography displays considerable pretension. The find included some royal statues (the heads are lost) that may have been produced in royal workshops, unlike the non-royal pieces. It is impossible to assess how widespread similar art with a distinct regional identity may have been. In about 1700 BC, during the weak later 13th Dynasty, an official

119. Statue of Heqaib, son of Sattjenj, grey granite, h. 700 mm, from the shrine complex of Heqaib at Elephantine, late 12th Dynasty, *c.* 1800 BC (Aswan, Elephantine Island)

from Hierakonpolis in the far south went to the capital to fetch a new cult statue for the local temple. This suggests that the capital's artistic pre-eminence, at least for religious works, had outlived its political position.

2. NEW KINGDOM–THIRD INTERMEDIATE PERIOD (*c.* 1540–*c.* 750 BC). The Second Intermediate Period had produced no distinctive regional styles, but, like the First Intermediate Period, had dissolved into technically inferior local workshop styles. Major New Kingdom (*c.* 1540–*c.* 1075 BC) building and artistic projects continued to be centrally funded and directed, but the temples, which were scattered throughout Egypt, acquired great wealth of their own. The two principal centres of power and prestige, Thebes and Memphis, had distinct styles of tomb decoration, conditioned in part by the different normal media, painting and painted relief respectively. Among the provincial monuments, a late 18th Dynasty tomb from Asyut shows a local manner, but, as elsewhere, this may use central models imperfectly rather than provincialize. Other monuments of similar date have been discovered to the south, in the region of Akhmim, and to the north in Middle Egypt. In the aftermath of the Amarna period (*c.* 1353–*c.* 1332 BC; *see* AMARNA STYLE) Memphite tomb art flourished in a diverse, often mannered style that owed much to Amarna. Thebes, where Akhenaten's principal early buildings were constructed, resisted the new style more strongly.

Despite the continued centripetal organization and character of art, the gradual breakdown of central authority led to some regionalization, building on differences between Thebes and Memphis. In the later New Kingdom, much artistic production was in the Delta, but hardly any of this is preserved, and what is known is not regionally distinct from Memphite work. Earlier ascriptions of a style to Tanis in particular have proved erroneous: Tanis was the capital of the succeeding Third Intermediate Period (*c.* 1075–*c.* 750 BC), to which many earlier monuments were transported from elsewhere.

3. LATE PERIOD–ROMAN PERIOD (*c.* 750 BC–AD 395). The chief art form of the Late Period (*c.* 750–332 BC), hardstone sculpture, continued and renewed traditions of the New Kingdom and Third Intermediate Period, while also looking eclectically to other earlier periods. Most statuary was almost certainly produced in temple workshops, but sound criteria for regional attribution have been found in inscriptions on statues rather than in style. Because stone came from a limited number of quarries, statues could have been made, if not completely finished, near the quarries and not near where they were set up in temples. Other contemporaneous art forms are insufficiently studied, and some attempts to discern regional patterns, such as Günther Roeder's regional classification of bronze statuettes of Osiris according to their arm poses, have not met with general acceptance. Stone statuary has been found throughout Egypt, but it is often impossible to tell where pieces were made, as against deposited, and no satisfactory regional classification has been achieved. There is a marked contrast in tomb reliefs between the massive private tombs of Thebes, which look

back principally to New Kingdom models, and the smaller-scale but innovative and eclectic works of northern Egypt (*see* §IX, 3(xi)(b) for discussion of Late Period reliefs). Some of the latter from the Delta are distinctive but not of high quality and may be products of regional workshops. Most were made in the Memphite area, although they may have been distributed elsewhere.

In the Greco–Roman period official Egyptian art prospered greatly in the temples. There may have been regional variation in these, but this is largely invisible because most known temples of the period are in southern Upper Egypt. During the Ptolemaic period there was a great flowering of native Egyptian statuary, which has been found throughout the country. Here again, however, no important regional patterns can be seen.

BIBLIOGRAPHY
J. Capart: *Les Monuments dits Hycsos* (Brussels, 1914)
H. Kees: *Studien zur ägyptischen Provinzialkunst* (Leipzig, 1922)
H. Steckeweh: *Die Fürstengraber von Qaw* (Leipzig, 1936)
W. C. Hayes: 'Horemkhauef of Nekhen and his Trip to It-towe', *J. Egyp. Archaeol.*, xxxiii (1947), pp. 3–11
A. M. Blackman: *The Rock Tombs of Meir*, vi (London, 1953)
G. Roeder: *Ägyptische Bronzefiguren* (Berlin, 1956), pp. 180–92
H. G. Fischer: 'An Example of Memphite Influence in a Theban Stela of the Late Eleventh Dynasty', *Artibus Asiae*, xxii (1959), pp. 240–52
——: *Inscriptions from the Coptite Nome, Dynasties VI–XI* (Rome, 1964)
——: *Dendera in the Third Millennium BC and its Aftermath, down to the Theban Domination of Upper Egypt* (Locust Valley, NY, 1968)
E. Winter: *Untersuchungen zu den ägyptischen Tempelreliefs der griechisch-römischen Zeit* (Vienna, 1968)
J. S. Karig: 'Die Kultkapelle des Amenhotep aus Der Durunka', *Z. Ägyp. Sprache & Altertknd.*, xcv (1969), pp. 27–34
N. Kanawati: *The Egyptian Administration in the Old Kingdom: Evidence on its Economic Decline* (Warminster, 1977)
D. Kurth: *Die Dekoration der Säulen im Pronaos des Tempels von Edfu* (Wiesbaden, 1983)
L. Habachi: *The Sanctuary of Heqaib*, 2 vols (Mainz, 1985)
L. M. Leahy: *Private Tomb Reliefs of the Late Period from Lower Egypt* (diss., U. Oxford, 1988)
B. G. Ockinga and Y. al-Masri: *Two Ramesside Tombs at el Mashayikh*, 2 vols (Sydney, 1988–90)
J. Baines: 'Ancient Egyptian Concepts and Uses of the Past: 3rd to 2nd Millennium BC Evidence', *Who Needs the Past? Indigenous Values and Archaeology*, ed. R. Layton (London, 1989), pp. 131–49
JOHN BAINES

XVIII. Rediscovery.

In the first few centuries AD the civilization of ancient Egypt was already being described and analysed by Roman authors, in works such as Horapollo's *Hieroglyphica*. European interest in Egypt was kindled in the 15th and 16th centuries with the rediscovery of these late Classical texts and the growth of antiquarians' interest in ancient Egyptian monuments. From the 16th to the 18th century early European travellers visited numerous sites throughout the Nile Valley and brought back antiquities, which stimulated further interest in ancient Egypt. The first genuinely art-historical studies of ancient Egypt were compiled by two 18th-century collectors, BERNARD DE MONTFAUCON and A.-C.-P. de Tubières, Comte de CAYLUS.

Napoleon's military campaign in Egypt was accompanied by the first attempt at a comprehensive survey of the surviving ancient Egyptian remains (1798–1801). In the early 19th century, various copies of Egyptian monuments were made by individuals, such as John Gardner Wilkinson (1797–1875) and Robert Hay (1799–1863), but the first true epigraphic survey of Egypt was undertaken by Jean-François Champollion (1790–1832) and Ippolito Rosellini (1800–43) in 1828–9.

The excavation of Egyptian remains was at first primarily in the hands of dealers and collectors, and it was not until the mid-19th century that the transition from pillaging to scientific excavation began to take place. Such excavators as FLINDERS PETRIE, Ludwig Borchardt (1863–1938) and George Reisner laid the foundations of modern excavation in Egypt. The archaeology, epigraphy and art history of ancient Egypt continued to evolve during the 20th century, with periods of more intense activity during the international campaigns of rescue archaeology occasioned by the building and expansion of the Aswan dams, in 1902, 1929 and 1962.

1. Early travellers. 2. Archaeologists. 3. Epigraphers. 4. Art historians.

1. EARLY TRAVELLERS.

(i) 16th–17th centuries. After the Arab conquest of Egypt (AD 641), only a few hardy merchants and pilgrims ventured from Europe to the Mediterranean ports of Egypt and occasionally to Cairo. However, after the Turkish occupation (1517) there was a gradual increase in trade and travellers. Generally 16th- and 17th-century travellers' accounts of Egypt are less scientific and systematic than later investigations. Pierre Belon (1517–65), a French apothecary who visited Egypt in 1547 in the suite of the French ambassador, observed the pyramids at Cairo and his account of this event was published in 1553. In 1551–2, André Thevet (1504–92), a French geographer, visited the same area and on his return published his *Cosmographie de Levant*, with numerous illustrations. Prospero Alpini (1553–1616), an Italian physician and botanist on the staff of the Venetian embassy, lived in Egypt from 1580 to 1584, later publishing several works on the country and its flora. An English traveller, Laurence Aldersey (*fl* 1581–6), left an account of his visit to Alexandria and Cairo. Jacques, Seigneur de Villamont (1558–1628), in Egypt in 1589–90, was the first European to identify the site of ancient Memphis (*see* MEMPHIS (i)). The Italian Pietro della Valle passed through Egypt in 1615–16 on his way east. Apart from his published account, he brought back a number of artefacts and manuscripts. Another notable traveller was George Sandys (1578–1644), who visited Egypt in 1610 and published his account in 1615.

The English astronomer and mathematician John Greaves (1602–52) went to study the pyramids at GIZA in 1638. When published, his *Pyramidographia* of 1646 was the most comprehensive survey of the history and measurements of these monuments yet carried out and can be considered the first scientific investigation of the area. Jean de Thévenot (1633–67), a French traveller, visited Egypt in 1657–9, exploring the area of Saqqara (*see* SAQQARA) where he opened up a tomb. His *Voyage au Levant* appeared in 1664. In 1668 two Capuchin fathers managed to reach as far as Luxor (*see* THEBES (i), §III) although they failed to identify the ancient site. In 1664 Johann Michael Wansleben (1635–79) was in Egypt on an abortive mission to Ethiopia, but he returned in 1672–3 as an agent of the French government to collect manuscripts and antiquities. He explored the Faiyum region and

Middle Egypt as far south as Girga, publishing his account in 1677. Robert Huntington (1637–1702), English chaplain to the Levant Company at Aleppo, visited Egypt twice (1678–9, 1681) and formed a large collection of manuscripts and antiquities, giving the latter to the Ashmolean Museum, Oxford, in 1683.

(ii) 18th century. The French consul general Benoît de Maillet (1656–1738) undertook several journeys during his term of office and sent back to France a large number of Egyptian objects for private collections. In his retirement he wrote the important *Description de l'Egypte* (1735). Paul Lucas (1664–1737), a French adventurer, made several journeys to Egypt, notably in 1716. He travelled to Upper Egypt passing through Luxor, where he was unable to stop, but he was the first European to see the temples of DENDARA and ARMANT. He published entertaining accounts of his various travels and can be considered the first popularizer of Egyptian travel. In 1719 Bernard de Montfaucon published a number of engravings of Egyptian antiquities in France in his *Antiquité expliqué.*

The era of scientific exploration was inaugurated by the Jesuit Claude Sicard (1677–1726), who headed a mission in Cairo. During his 14 years in Egypt he undertook almost yearly voyages throughout the country, notably to Luxor and Esna in 1718 and the cataracts in 1720–21. He was the first person correctly to identify Luxor as ancient Thebes and located other ancient sites. Some accounts of his travels were published by the Jesuits, but his projected volume on the geography of Egypt has been largely lost. His original map of Egypt, now also lost, was forwarded to France and copied by later cartographers and so was more widely circulated. In the course of the 18th century Egypt became part of the Grand Tour for more intrepid travellers, although they rarely strayed much beyond Cairo. William Lethieullier (1701–56), a British collector, was in Cairo in 1721, and John Montagu, 4th Earl of Sandwich (1718–92), toured Giza and Saqqara in 1738–9. A French physician, Dr N. Granger (*d* 1733), ventured into Upper Egypt as far as Edfu, and in 1730 he discovered the temple of Sethos I at Abydos.

RICHARD POCOCKE, an English clergyman, twice visited Egypt in 1737–9 as part of a tour of the Levant. He did not restrict himself to the environs of Cairo but journeyed as far south as Aswan. His detailed maps and plans published in 1743–5 are extremely valuable as many of the monuments are now lost. At the same time Frederik Ludwig Norden (1708–42) was exploring Egypt on behalf of King Christian VI of Denmark. He penetrated into Nubia as far as el-Derr, but his valuable account was not published until 1751–5, when it was the most comprehensive description of Egypt to date. In 1737 Alexander Gordon (1692–1754), a Scottish antiquarian, produced a series of engravings of Egyptian antiquities in Great Britain. In 1741–3 an Egyptian Society was briefly formed in London numbering among its members such travellers as Pocoke, Norden, Lethieullier and the 4th Earl of Sandwich.

In 1763–4 the English traveller and eccentric Edward Wortley Montagu (1713–76) visited Egypt with his secretary Nathaniel Davison (*d* 1809), who supervised his master's excavations at Alexandria and Saqqara. Most of the objects discovered were soon deposited in the British Museum, London. On Montagu's departure in 1764, Davison fell in with the eccentric French nobleman Joseph d'Albert d'Ailly, Duc de Chaulnes (1741–92), whom he later accused of stealing his papers. Two objects from the Chaulnes collection were later illustrated by the Society of Dilettanti and entered the collections of CHARLES TOWNLEY and RICHARD PAYNE KNIGHT. In 1768 James Bruce (1730–94) visited Luxor and the Valley of the Kings on his way to Ethiopia, but his detailed account did not appear until 1790. The French traveller Charles Sonnini de Manoncour (1751–1812) visited Egypt in 1777–8, ascending as far as Aswan, although he did not publish his memoir until 1799. Constantin Comte de Volney (1757–1820) toured the Levant in 1783–5 and published an influential account in 1787. Unsettled conditions in Egypt at the end of the 18th century deterred foreign travellers, but this was soon to change as a result of the French invasion.

MORRIS BIERBRIER

2. ARCHAEOLOGISTS.

(i) 18th–19th centuries. (ii) 20th century. (iii) The Nubian campaigns.

(i) 18th–19th centuries. Napoleon's Egyptian campaign, in 1798–9, was a military failure but a scientific triumph. He took with him a group of 175 savants who, from 1798 to 1801, studied, excavated, copied and explored the monuments of the Nile Valley from the Delta to the Sudan. Their numerous discoveries included the Rosetta Stone (London, BM, 24), which eventually provided the key to the decipherment of the hieroglyphic and demotic scripts. Inspired by the publications of members of the Napoleonic expedition (*Voyage dans la basse et la haute Egypte*, written by VIVANT DENON in 1802, and the monumental *Description de l'Egypte*, edited mainly by Edmé François Jomard in 1809–22), the earliest phase of archaeological work in the Nile Valley was principally concerned with recording the visible monuments (*see* §3 below) rather than excavation.

The first extensively recorded archaeological investigation in Egypt was that conducted by Richard Vyse (1784–1853) and John Shae Perring (1813–69) at Giza, where they measured and surveyed the pyramids. They entered the pyramid of Mycerinus, discovering a panelled stone sarcophagus, which was lost off the coast of Spain while being transported to England. The most successful of the early surveys of Egypt was conducted by the expedition of the King of Prussia, Frederick William IV (*reg* 1840–61), under the direction of Karl Richard Lepsius (1810–84) in 1842. Lepsius's work, however, was primarily epigraphic, and the general pillaging of archaeological sites by antiquities dealers and collectors was the only form of excavation being conducted (*see* §XX, 1 and 2 below).

After the end of the 18th century, there was a move towards controlled excavation as the main focus of archaeological research. Auguste Mariette had been sent to Egypt by the Louvre to obtain Coptic manuscripts, but he was appalled at the widespread plundering of Egyptian sites and became interested in excavation. In 1858 he was appointed as first Director of the Egyptian Antiquities Service and subsequently conducted excavations at 35 different sites. Among his many discoveries was the

Serapeum, the burial place of the sacred Apis bulls at Saqqara. His greatest achievement was the founding of the first Egyptian museum at Bulaq, to house the finds from his excavations.

Mariette was succeeded by Gaston Maspero (1846–1916) in 1881. Under Maspero the Antiquities Service was expanded and became an official part of the Egyptian government. In addition, the excavations of foreign scholars were brought under the control of the Antiquities Service, which rewarded them with exclusive concessions to dig at a site and the gift of a portion of the antiquities found. One of the most important discoveries of the Antiquities Service under Maspero's direction was a cache of royal mummies at Deir el-Bahri (see THEBES (i), §IV) in 1881. A second cache containing the coffins and mummies of the priests of Amun and their families of the 21st and 22nd dynasties (c. 1075–c. 730 BC) was discovered at Deir el-Bahri by Eugène Grébaut (1846–1915) in 1891. During this same period, at Saqqara, the pyramids of Wenis, Pepy I, Teti and Pepy II were opened, and the famous Pyramid Texts were found inscribed on the walls of their burial chambers.

The organization of excavations under the Antiquities Service led to the creation of a number of important foreign institutes; these began annual campaigns of excavation, many of which still continue. In 1880 Flinders Petrie travelled to Egypt to measure the 'Great Pyramid' at Giza, spurred on by his interests in metrology and archaeology. Often described as the father of scientific archaeology, Petrie was certainly the most prolific excavator ever to work in Egypt. In 1883 he joined the Egypt Exploration Fund, an organization founded by the English novelist Amelia B. Edwards to excavate Egyptian sites of importance to biblical and Classical history. The Fund commenced excavating sites in the Delta in 1882, beginning with TELL EL-MASKHUTA, and went on to work at such sites as TANIS (1883), NAUKRATIS (1884–6), Tell Nabesha (1886), TELL EL-YAHUDIYA (1887), BUBASTIS (1887–9), MAIDUM (1890–91), EL-AMARNA (1891–2) and KOPTOS (1893–4). Working for the Egypt Exploration Fund in 1893, Edouard Naville (1844–1926), a Swiss Egyptologist, began the exploration, restoration and publication of the temple of Hatshepsut at Deir el-Bahri. This work was extended in 1903 to the adjoining temple of Nebhepetre Mentuhotpe II of the 11th Dynasty (reg c. 2008–c. 1957 BC; see THEBES (i), §IV).

At the end of the 19th century there was a burgeoning of archaeological work throughout Egypt. In 1894–5, in the area of NAQADA, Petrie discovered a large cemetery of a type not then known to Egyptologists. He recognized that the graves and their contents were radically different from material he knew and he called this culture the 'New Race', suggesting that it had migrated into Egypt during the First Intermediate Period. In March 1897 Jacques de Morgan, then Director of the Egyptian Antiquities Service, discovered a 1st-Dynasty royal tomb at Naqada. He published his findings in Origines de l'Egypte, identifying Petrie's 'New Race' as the Egyptians of the prehistoric period. Convinced by de Morgan's finds, Petrie was able to reconstruct the chronology of the Predynastic period by developing a method called 'sequence dating' or seriation, which he recorded in Diospolis Parva (1901).

In 1895–8 Emile Amélineau (1850–1915) began excavations at ABYDOS and discovered the tombs of the kings of the 1st and 2nd dynasties. Amélineau was slow to publish and his methods were substandard. From 1899 to 1903 Petrie re-excavated this area and was able to salvage a great deal of important information, enabling him to reconstruct the chronology of the first two dynasties. In 1897–9 James Quibell (1887–1935) and Frederick W. Green (1864–1949), working for the Egypt Exploration Fund, excavated another important Early Dynastic site, the ancient town of HIERAKONPOLIS. There they discovered the 'Decorated Tomb', the great slate palette of King Narmer (Cairo, Egyp. Mus., JE 32169; for illustration see NARMER) and other important monuments of the early historic period.

In 1893–5 de Morgan excavated for the Egyptian Antiquities Service around the pyramids of Ammenemes II, Ammenemes III and Sesostris III at DAHSHUR, discovering a large number of smaller tombs containing a wealth of gold and jewellery (New York, Met. and Cairo, Egyp. Mus.) from the burials of royal princesses of the late Middle Kingdom (see §XV above) as well as the tomb of King Awibre Hor of the 13th Dynasty.

In 1898 the German Archaeological Institute began excavation of the 5th Dynasty pyramids at Abusir and their associated sun temples at Abu Ghurab, under the direction of Ludwig Borchardt and Friedrich W. von Bissing (1873–1956). In the same year Victor Loret (1859–1946) became Director of the Egyptian Antiquities Service and began work in the Valley of the Kings (see THEBES (i), §IX). He discovered and cleared the royal tombs of Tuthmosis I, TUTHMOSIS III, Amenophis II and the private TOMB OF MAIHERPRI. In the tomb of Amenophis II, Loret found a cache of mummies that included the remains of Tuthmosis I, Amenophis III, Merneptah, Sethos II, Siptah, Sethnakht and Ramesses IV, V and VI (Cairo, Egyp. Mus.).

(ii) 20th century. By the end of the 19th century archaeologists from many different countries were excavating in Egypt, and several newly established Egyptological periodicals began to publish regular preliminary reports. From the first decade of the 20th century many American archaeologists, notably George Reisner, Theodore Davis (1837–1915) and Herbert Winlock (1884–1950), worked in Egypt. In 1899–1901 George Reisner, sponsored by Phoebe Apperson Hearst and the University of California, began excavations at Quft, Deir el-Ballas and el-Ahaiwah. From 1901 to 1905 he worked with Arthur Mace (1874–1928) at the cemeteries of NAG EL-DEIR and Giza. At about the same time, Maspero granted Davis a special permit to undertake excavations in the Valley of the Kings. Along with Percy Newberry (1869–1949), Howard Carter, Edward Ayrton (1882–1914), Harold Jones (d 1911) and others, he discovered and cleared the intact TOMB OF YUYA AND TUYA (the parents of Queen Tiye) and the tombs of HATSHEPSUT, Tuthmosis IV, HOREMHEB and Siptah. He also excavated a puzzling burial of a late Amarna-period royal personage in tomb KV 55, which has been variously interpreted as the tomb of Queen Tiye, Akhenaten, Smenkhkare or Queen Nefertiti.

In 1903 the French archaeologist Georges Legrain (1865–1917), working at Karnak for the Department of Antiquities, found a great cache of over 17,000 statues, which had been cleaned out of the temple and buried in antiquity (*see* THEBES (i), §II, 2). His work was described as 'fishing for statues' and some of the greatest masterpieces of Egyptian sculpture, ranging in date from the Old Kingdom to the Late Period (*c.* 750–332 BC) came out of this deposit. He also undertook a major campaign of restoration work on the temple complex at Karnak.

The German Archaeological Institute worked at el-Amarna from 1910 until the beginning of World War I, providing a great deal of fresh architectural and art-historical information. In 1920–21 the Egypt Exploration Fund returned to el-Amarna and continued excavating the ruins of the city under the direction of T. Eric Peet (1882–1934), Sir LEONARD WOOLLEY, Francis Newton (1878–1924), F. L. Griffith (1862–1934), HENRI FRANKFORT and John Pendlebury (1904–41). The expedition cleared the palaces, temples and houses in the main city and the north suburb as well as a workmen's village and its associated chapels.

The French Archaeological Institute, under Georges Foucart (1865–1946), worked both at the Temple of Horus at Edfu and at Deir el-Medina in the village of the artisans who built the royal tombs in the Valley of the Kings. Howard Carter continued working in the Valley of the Kings for Theodore Davis and later for George Herbert, 5th Earl of Carnarvon (1866–1923). In 1922 Carter discovered the tomb of TUTANKHAMUN and cleared and recorded it over the next ten years, assisted mainly by Arthur Mace, Harry Burton (1879–1940), Walter Hauser (1893–1960) and Linsey Hall.

In the first half of the 20th century, a number of European and American archaeologists directed excavations on behalf of the Egyptian and Sudanese Antiquities Services. Cecil Firth (1878–1931), for example, continued Quibell's excavations at Saqqara. In 1925–6 Gustave Jéquier (1868–1946) cleared the funerary monuments of Pepy I, the Mastabat Faraun and a number of small pyramids of the late Old Kingdom and Middle Kingdom at South Saqqara. Under Emile Baraize (1874–1952), the Antiquities Service also carried out a systematic plan of conserving and protecting the monuments. From 1940 to 1950 some of the earliest settlement sites in the Nile Valley were discovered by William J. Arkell working for the Sudanese Antiquities Service at Shaheinab and in Khartoum itself.

At Thebes, Herbert Winlock, working on behalf of the Metropolitan Museum of New York, undertook the excavation of the area around the temples at Deir el-Bahri, discovering the broken sphinxes of Hatshepsut and the wooden models in the tomb of Meketre (TT 280; Cairo, Egyp. Mus. and New York, Met.). In 1924 the French Archaeological Institute, under Fernand Bisson de la Roque (1885–1958), began the excavation of the temple of Madamud.

In 1954 there was an incredible number of discoveries in Egypt, including the great wooden boat of Cheops (found by Kamal al-Mallakh and Zaki Nour), the stele of Kamose at Karnak and the pyramid of Sekhemkhet (found by Zakaria Goneim). Work on the Early Dynastic tombs at North Saqqara continued under the British archaeologist W. B. Emery (1903–71) and at the Step Pyramid under Lauer. Ahmed Fakhry cleared the temples and causeway of the Bent Pyramid of Sneferu at Dahshur in 1951. The German and Swiss Institutes, under the direction of Herbert Ricke (1901–76) and Hans Stock (1908–66), continued the excavation of the sun temples at Abu Ghurab.

(iii) The Nubian campaigns. In 1906 the Egyptian government began a project to raise the old dam at Aswan (built between 1898 and 1902) and increase the size of the reservoir. A campaign was therefore launched to record and consolidate the monuments in the area to be flooded. The survey was conducted by George Reisner, Cecil Firth and Aylward Blackman (1883–1956). Also working in Nubia, James Henry Breasted, founder of the Oriental Institute of the University of Chicago, made two epigraphic surveys through Nubia from the 1st Nile cataract to Khartoum in 1905–7.

In 1929, after a proposal to raise the Aswan Dam a second time, plans were made for the continuation of the first Nubian survey southwards to cover the area to be inundated by the enlarged reservoir. This survey was conducted by W. B. Emery and Laurence Kirwan. Excavations were also carried out by Georg Steindorff (1861–1951) at the site of Aniba. The Egyptian frontier fortresses at the Second Nile cataract, including Semna, Kumma, Mirgissa and Uronarti (*see* NUBIA, §II), were excavated by the Harvard-Boston Expedition in 1924–9, under the direction of Alan Rowe.

After a great flurry of excavation in the mid-1950s there was a lull in Egyptian archaeology until the early 1960s, when Lower Nubia was faced with total destruction through a project to expand the Dam further. A great international campaign to record and salvage the monuments of Upper Egypt was launched under the auspices of UNESCO and the Egyptian and Sudanese Antiquities Services. This third campaign was the most intensive archaeological exploration of an area to date and involved an international team of Egyptologists, anthropologists, archaeologists, geologists and engineers. Among the campaign's most illustrious achievements was the salvage of several temples, including those of PHILAE and ABU SIMBEL. The American archaeologist William Y. Adams undertook an exhaustive survey of Lower Nubia, while the Middle Kingdom forts at Buhen and Mirgissa were re-excavated by W. B. Emery and Jean Vercoutter respectively. At the same time the Egypt Exploration Society began a long-term excavation at QASR IBRIM.

The work of the third Nubian campaign has inspired the present generation of archaeologists, who, thanks partly to the interdisciplinary contact brought about by the campaign, are producing a more comprehensive and scientific picture of the archaeology of the Nile Valley.

PETER LACOVARA

3. EPIGRAPHERS. In a narrow sense, Egyptian epigraphy is a method of obtaining exact copies of inscribed or decorated, mainly architectural monuments. Recording techniques have constantly developed in order to satisfy the growing demands of Egyptology and to take advantage

of scientific progress, and they vary according to the character of work and the resources available. The preparation of line drawings is partly subjective, but cannot be satisfactorily replaced by any other recording method known at present.

Epigraphy may be more broadly defined as a complete study of monuments; however the distinction is somewhat theoretical since a good recording inevitably involves preliminary interpretation, and its aim is almost always publication. Modern publications usually consist of reduced facsimile drawings, photographs and a text with additional information and commentary.

(i) 18th–19th centuries. Travel books of the 18th century occasionally included drawings of reliefs *in situ*, such as those in Paul Lucas's *Voyage dans la Turquie, l'Asie, Sourie, Haute et Basse-Egypte* (1724), Richard Pococke's *A Description of the East and Some Other Countries* (1743–5) and Frederick Ludwig Norden's *Voyage de l'Egypte et de Nubie* (1755). These drawings, however, bore only a superficial resemblance to the monuments. The recordings made by Napoleon's scientific survey of Egypt in 1798–1801 represented an enormous leap forward, although the artists found it difficult to adopt unfamiliar representational conventions. A massive corpus of material was published in the volumes of *Description de l'Egypte* (1809–28).

Several copyists perfected the accuracy of recordings through prolonged work in Egypt in the first half of the 19th century. Prominent among them was Henry Salt (1780–1827), the British Consul-General in Egypt, whose training as a portrait painter enabled him to produce the first almost completely faithful handmade copies. Others were William Bankes (?1787–1855), John Gardner Wilkinson, James Burton (1788–1862), Robert Hay and Linant de Bellefonds (1799–1883). In 1828–9 Jean-François Champollion and Ippolito Rosellini led the first epigraphic expedition to record monuments. Among those taking part was the French draughtsman and archaeologist Nestor l'Hôte (1804–42). The results were published by Champollion in both *Monuments de l'Égypte et de la Nubie d'après les dessins exécutés sur les lieux, sous la direction de Champollion le jeune* (1835–45) and *Notices descriptives conformes aux notices autographes rédigées sur les lieux par Champollion le jeune* (1844–89), and by Rosellini in *I monumenti dell'Egitto e della Nubia . . .* (1832–44).

These efforts were crowned in the 1840s by the work of Karl Richard Lepsius and his team: the first real epigraphers. The Lepsius expedition worked in Egypt and Nubia between 1842 and 1845, and the artists Joseph Bonomi (1796–1878), Ernst Weidenbach (1818–82) and Max Weidenbach (*d c.* 1893) were among its draughtsmen. Hand-drawn copies were accompanied by paper squeezes (impressions). Most of the material appeared as the 12-volume *Denkmäler aus Ägypten und Äthiopien . . .* (1849–59). The accuracy, presentation and understanding of the Egyptian representational conventions were such that the publication remains indispensable even now. A significant contribution to the recording of monuments was at this time made by Emile Prisse d'Avennes (1807–79) in *Les Monuments égyptiens* (1847).

In comparison with the achievements of Lepsius's team, the epigraphic work of Auguste Mariette (1821–81) at

such sites as Dendara, Abydos and Karnak is inevitably found wanting. His less satisfactory method of recording reflected the shift of emphasis towards excavation rather than epigraphy. Mariette's handmade copies, probably supplemented by squeezes, were later completed in Europe by Ernst Weidenbach, who was forced to standardize the details since he had few means of verifying them. The accomplished copies of an Italian Egyptologist Luigi Vassalli (1812–87) have never been published.

The prevailing 19th-century attitude to monumental inscriptions was epitomized in the work of Heinrich Brugsch (1827–94) and Gaston Maspero. Both recorded extensively, but almost their only concern was the contents of the texts. These were usually reversed to read horizontally from left to right and the signs were standardized. Later, the greatest exponent of this approach was Kurt Sethe (1869–1934), particularly in his *Die altägyptischen Pyramidentexte* (1908–22). Other great copyists were Emmanuel de Rougé (1811–72), Jacques de Rougé (1842–1923), Johannes Duemichen (1833–94), Karl Fredrik Piehl (1853–1904) and Jacques De Morgan.

A refined but nevertheless similar method of publishing texts (using a hieroglyphic fount) was adopted in the massive volumes on the Greco-Roman temples at Esna, Edfu and Dendara. From 1892 onwards, these have been issued by the Institut Français d'Archéologie Orientale (IFAO) in Cairo and edited by Maxence de Chalvet, Marquis de Rochemonteix (1849–91), Emile Chassinat (1868–1948), F. Daumas, S. Sauneron and others.

(ii) 20th century. A new era was heralded by the much-underestimated copies of the Luxor Temple published by Albert Gayet (1856–1916). Modern epigraphic practices and publications were introduced at the end of the 19th century, and the Egypt Exploration Fund (later the Egypt Exploration Society) played a distinguished part in this process. Edouard Naville, the Fund's first excavator, published *The Temple of Deir el-Bahari* (1894–1908); the copying and the preparation of the plates for these volumes were carried out by Howard Carter and assistants and collated by Naville. This publication faithfully reflects the original texts and representations, as well as their state of preservation, and the appearance of the monument itself. At about the same time, the Fund's Archaeological Survey of Egypt worked in exemplary fashion in Middle Egypt. The driving force behind the project was F. L. Griffith, and the Egyptologists working on the survey were, in turn, Percy Newberry, Norman de Garis Davies (1865–1941) and Aylward Blackman.

An expedition of the Deutsche Orient-Gesellschaft and another sponsored by Friedrich W. von Bissing worked at Abusir and Abu Ghurab between 1898 and 1908. Their epigraphic recordings, and those by Davies at Saqqara (1898–9), set the standard for Old Kingdom reliefs. The same high standards were sought when monuments of the same date were subsequently explored on a large scale at Giza by Hermann Junker (1877–1962) and Selim Hassan, and at Saqqara by Gustave Jéquier. Some of the best copies of wall decoration in Theban tombs of the 18th Dynasty (*c.* 1540–*c.* 1292 BC), many in colour, were made by Norman de Garis Davies, his wife Anna (Nina) de Garis Davies (1881–1965) and their collaborators from the Metropolitan Museum of Art, New York (1907–37). Most of the results were published by the Egypt Exploration Society, the Metropolitan Museum, New York and the Griffith Institute, Oxford (as well as examples on display at Oxford, Ashmolean). An important contribution to the epigraphy of Theban tombs was also made by the copyists of the IFAO, in particular Marcelle Baud and J. Vandier d'Abbadie.

In 1924 the Epigraphic Survey of the Oriental Institute of the University of Chicago was created by Breasted for epigraphic work in the Theban area; subsequent publications have included *Medinet Habu* (1930–70), *Reliefs and Inscriptions at Karnak* (1936–86), *The Temple of Khonsu* (1979–81) and *The Tomb of Kheruef* (1980). Harold H. Nelson (1878–1954) was its first Field Director, and G. R. Hughes and C. F. Nims were among his successors. Another expedition, at Saqqara, was published as *The Mastaba of Mereruka* (1938). As a specialized institution, the Epigraphic Survey remains unique; meticulous recording and impeccable presentation ensure its leading position in Egyptian epigraphy. For temples of the Greco-Roman period, *Das Geburtshaus des Tempels der Isis in Philä*, by Hermann Junker and E. Winter (1965), with drawings by O. Daum, is similarly outstanding.

The use of photography as a means of recording hieroglyphs was mentioned when the invention of Louis Daguerre was presented to the Académie in January 1839. Félix Guilmant's *Le Tombeau de Ramsès IX* (1907) was based on drawings made over photographs. A similar approach was used by A. M. Calverley and Myrtle Broome in *The Temple of King Sethos I at Abydos* (1933–58); this was a joint project of the Egypt Exploration Society and the Oriental Institute of the University of Chicago. Epigraphic methods employed by the Chicago Epigraphic Survey and the Centre d'Etudes et de Documentation sur l'Ancienne Egypte (CEDAE) rely on photographs in their early stages. Purely photographic recording has also been attempted, as in *The Pyramid of Unas* (1968) by Alexandre Piankoff. Colour photography has been used by G. Thausing and H. Goedicke in *Nofretari: Eine Dokumentation der Wandgemälde ihres Grabes* (1971).

The CEDAE was created by agreement between the Egyptian government and UNESCO in 1956. The epigraphic activities of the CEDAE at first concentrated on Nubia, producing such publications as *Le Petit Temple d'Abou Simbel* (1968) by C. Desroches-Noblecourt and C. Kuentz. The results are mainly published in the *Collection scientifique* series. The CEDAE afterwards turned its attention to monuments in the Theban area, such as the Ramesseum, several private tombs and various graffiti.

A great deal of epigraphic work was undertaken in the early 1960s during the campaigns to save the monuments of Nubia threatened by the building of the High Dam at Aswan. Temple reliefs, graffiti and rock drawings were recorded by expeditions from various countries. After the conclusion of the Nubian campaigns, the attention of epigraphers has focused on Egypt proper. Changes in agricultural practices, industrialization, the rapid expansion of towns and villages and the growth of tourism have again made epigraphy a great priority in Egyptology.

JAROMIR MALEK

4. ART HISTORIANS. Egyptian works of art were rediscovered and identified during the Renaissance, chiefly in Rome, and Egyptian subjects featured in the major iconographic handbooks; the earliest collection of hieroglyphic inscriptions dates to *c.* 1620 (Herwart von Hohenburg). Until the 18th century, however, interest in Egyptian objects was more iconographic and archaeological than artistic, and there was hardly any perception that Egyptian art formed a tradition of its own, alien to Western art. This began to change with the publication of the collections of Bernard de Montfaucon and the Comte de Caylus, and of new visual material from Egypt by such authors as Richard Pococke and Frederik Ludwig Norden, as well as illustrations by Piranesi of Egyptian objects in Rome (*see* PIRANESI, GIOVANNI BATTISTA, §1(iv)). The Comte de Caylus's collection was the first pubished work with an art-historical evaluation of Egyptian art, praising architecture more than sculpture. It was followed by the rather more negative, Classically orientated judgement of JOHANN JOACHIM WINCKELMANN, applied chiefly to sculpture—which did, however, discuss Egyptian art as a tradition of its own. His attitude, which probably influenced generalizing views such as those of JOHANN GOTTFRIED HERDER, was countered by Piranesi, who was also the architect of the first EGYPTIAN REVIVAL building, the Caffè degli Inglese in Rome (*c.* 1760). His *Diverse maniere d'adornare i cammini* ... (1769), with a trilingual essay in defence of Egyptian and Tuscan architecture, turned Winckelmann's arguments around, proposing that Greek standards of naturalism were not relevant to Egyptian art; Egyptian architecture should likewise be appreciated on its own terms. This active acceptance of Egyptian style, however fantastic the results, influenced serious as well as less serious examples of Egyptian Revival architecture throughout Europe and North America. This revival was widely paralleled in other art forms, which were also influenced by the ideas of Freemasonry. Egyptian architectural forms contributed much to the grand projects of late 18th-century French architects and writers, such as CLAUDE-NICOLAS LEDOUX and ETIENNE-LOUIS BOULLÉE; everywhere the Egyptian Revival was focused on the idea of Egyptian art as being grandiose and sublime, rather than harmonious or adapted to the human scale. This Revival continues, testifying to an enduring Western cultural concern with Egyptian art. While it has used Egyptological publications for visual stimulus, its evolution has been largely independent from Egyptology, the concern of the rest of this article, but it constitutes a more active and immediate response to Egyptian art.

The integration of Egyptian art into a Western tradition was far ahead of Egyptology. Scholarly analysis could not be attempted until the publication of reliable copies by Napoleon's expedition in the *Description de l'Egypte* (1809–28) and the Franco-Tuscan expedition of Jean-François Champollion and Ippolito Rosellini. The most enduring of these publications was that of the Prussian expedition of 1842–5 led by Karl Richard Lepsius, while such writers as John Gardner Wilkinson and Emile Prisse d'Avennes, who spent many years studying the monuments in Egypt, were also influential. Prisse d'Avennes published the first separate history of Egyptian art (1878–9). These works were roughly contemporary with early photography, which improved knowledge of the appearance of Egyptian art.

The first volume of *Histoire de l'art dans l'antiquité* (1882), by Georges Perrot and Charles-Jérôme Chipiez, is the most important late 19th-century treatment (by non-Egyptologists); it views Egypt as a glorious and pristine introduction to the achievements of later civilizations and particularly praises Egyptian architecture. Knowledge of the primary material was slowly transformed by the publication of museum collections and copies of the monuments. This material needed to be integrated, and Adolf Erman (1854–1937) commented that his *Ägypten und ägyptisches Leben im Altertum* (1885–6), which included a significant treatment of art, involved ordering the representational and textual material into periods before a synthesis could begin. Among museum publications, the most important were the photographic volumes *Le Musée égyptien* for the Cairo Museum, with a principal text by Gaston Maspero, and the Cairo *Catalogue général* (not organized in art-historical terms) initiated by Ludwig Borchardt.

In the 20th century Egyptological approaches to Egyptian art have diverged according to art form—architecture, sculpture, painting—and nationality of author. Several Francophone authors can be grouped around Jean Capart (1877–1947), who published numerous general studies and collections of monuments and transmitted a basically intuitive approach. The first important study of a particular form, *Denkmäler ägyptischer Skulptur* by Friedrich W. von Bissing, used the techniques of connoisseurship and Classical archaeology to interpret Egyptian works but, despite his sympathetic approach to the material, did not progress far in evaluating the works in indigenous terms. Concern with close dating has been essential to subsequent studies of sculpture, partly in default of any consensus on attributing works to schools or individual sculptors. Attribution was a preoccupation of Gaston Maspero, who believed he could identify regional styles. The issue is visible again in *Les Grandes Époques: La Statuaire* (1958) by Jacques Vandier (1804–73), the only systematic repertory of Egyptian statuary. The most precise attributional work was that of George A. Reisner concerning the different sculptors of the 4th Dynasty king MYCERINUS. A great deal of work on sculpture has been published by museum curators.

After World War II, several scholars with close mutual links became prominent, all of them applying methods of connoisseurship and attribution principally to statuary. The group looked to an older scholar, Hans Gerhard Evers (1900–93), who published a single, highly influential work on Middle Kingdom royal sculpture, *Staat aus dem Stein* (1929). Bernard V. Bothmer (1912–93), who moved from Berlin to the United States in 1941, began a corpus of Late Period sculpture with Hans Wolfgang Müller (1907–91) and Herman de Meulenaere, creating a highly influential exhibition of the work in progress in 1960 at the Brooklyn Museum; he later sponsored a major exhibition there of Nubian art (see 1978 exh. cat.). Cyril Aldred (1914–91) published many works principally on statuary and jewellery and was especially influential in his treatment of the Amarna period (see 1973 exh. cat.).

Museum-based art historians have been prominent in the USA, the leading figures being William Stevenson Smith (1907–69), the author of three major works (1946, 1958 and 1965), and John D. Cooney (1905–82), whose achievement is visible in the extraordinary collections of the Brooklyn Museum, New York, and the Cleveland Museum of Art, Ohio, more than in publications. Many Egyptologists have been wrongly sceptical of the interpretive eye of such specialists as Cooney, preferring more limited but 'objective' approaches to dating and analysis.

The leading scholar of Egyptian art, HEINRICH SCHÄFER, focused his work not on dating and attribution but on the interpretation of representation in relief and painting. Among later German authors, the chief figure was Walther Wolf (1900–73), whose monumental but flawed *Die Kunst Ägyptens* (1957) is the most explicitly theoretical major work on Egyptian art. Wolf was heavily influenced by the early theoretical writings of ERWIN PANOFSKY, EDGAR WIND and the historian of Greek art Bernhard Schweitzer (1892–1966). His formalistic sympathies, in which he was opposed to Schäfer, have some parallel in H. A. Groenewegen-Frankfort's *Arrest and Movement* (1951), a prominent work on Near Eastern art in general, which ultimately founders on a negative and extraneous evaluative attitude to its material.

Egyptian architecture has been interpreted in more archaeological terms than other art forms. Ludwig Borchardt was the most prominent earlier excavator and analyst of architecture and was succeeded as Director of the Swiss Institute (until 1933 the German Institute) in Cairo by Herbert Ricke (1901–76), whose studies of primitive architectural forms and their relationships with hypothetical population groups, and of ritual in relation to architecture (especially the 'Step Pyramid' complex of Djoser), were for many years very influential. The most valuable visual presentation of architecture was *L'Architecture et la décoration dans l'ancienne Égypte* (1920–24) by Gustave Jéquier, which was confined to temples. This implies much in its choice of material, but has almost no text. Architecture has continued to be presented with excavations of major monuments, but the general study of Egyptian architecture, its articulation of space, formal vocabulary and symbolism has not advanced very far. Another vital field in Egyptian art that has not been adequately covered is iconography (*see* §V above).

This article excludes living art historians.

JOHN BAINES

BIBLIOGRAPHY

GENERAL

D. Dunham: *The Egyptian Department and its Excavations* (Boston, 1958)
L. Greener: *The Discovery of Egypt* (London, 1966)
Collections de voyageurs occidentaux en Égypte, Institut Français d'Archéologie Orientale, Cairo, 24 vols (Cairo, 1970–84)
W. R. Dawson and E. P. Uphill: *Who Was Who in Egyptology* (London, 1972)
P. Clayton: *The Rediscovery of Egypt* (London, 1982)
T. G. H. James, ed.: *Excavating in Egypt* (London, 1982)

17TH AND 18TH CENTURIES

J. G. Herwart von Hohenberg: *Thesaurus hieroglyphicorum* (n.d. [c. 1620])
B. de Montfaucon: *L'Antiquité expliquée et représentée en figures*, ii (Paris, 1719); *Supplément*, ii (Paris, 1724)
R. Pococke: *A Description of the East and Some Other Countries* (London, 1743–5)

A.-C.-P. de Tubières, Comte de Caylus: *Recueil d'antiquités, égyptiennes, étrusques, grecques, romaines et gauloises*, i (Paris, 1752)

F. L. Norden: *Voyage de l'Egypte et de Nubie*, 2 vols (Copenhagen, 1755; Eng. trans. 1757)

J. J. Winckelmann: *Geschichte der Kunst des Alterthums*, 2 vols (Dresden, 1764/R Baden-Baden, 1966)

G. B. Piranesi: *Diverse maniere d'adornare i cammini. . .con un ragionamento apologetico in difesa dell'architecttura egizia, e toscana* (Rome, 1769); also in *The Polemical Works*, ed. J. Wilton-Ely (Farnborough, 1972)

C. Sicard: *Oeuvres I–II*, 3 vols (Cairo, 1982)

19TH CENTURY

E. Jomard and others, eds: *Description de l'Egypte*, 12 vols (Paris, 1809–22, 2/1820–30)

I. Rosellini: *I monumenti dell'Egitto e della Nubia*, 3 vols (Pisa, 1832–44)

J.-F. Champollion-le-Jeune: *Les Monuments de l'Egypte et de la Nubie*, 4 vols (Paris, 1835–45)

J. G. Wilkinson: *The Manners and Customs of the Ancient Egyptians*, 3 vols (London, 1837, rev. 4/1878)

C. R. Lepsius: *Denkmäler aus Aegypten und Aethiopien*, 12 vols (Berlin, 1849–59)

E. Prisse d'Avennes: *Histoire de l'art égyptien*, 3 vols (Paris, 1878–9) [illus. by Prisse d'Avennes, text by P. Marchandon de la Faye]

G. Perrot and C. Chipiez: *Histoire de l'art dans l'antiquité*, i (Paris, 1882)

A. Erman: *Aegypten und aegyptisches Leben im Altertum* (Tübingen, 1885–7, rev. by H. Ranke, 2/1922)

E. Grébaut and others: *Le Musée égyptien: Recueil des monuments et notices sur les fouilles d'Egypte*, i–iii (Cairo, 1890–1915)

20TH CENTURY

L. Borchardt: *Statuen und Statuetten von Königen und Privatleuten*, 5 vols, Cairo, Egyp. Mus. cat. (Berlin, 1911–36)

F. W. von Bissing: *Denkmäler ägyptischer Skulptur*, 3 vols (Munich, 1914)

G. Jéquier: *L'Architecture et la décoration dans l'ancienne Egypte*, 3 vols (Paris, 1920–24)

J. Capart: *Documents pour servir à l'étude de l'art égyptien*, 2 vols (Paris, 1927–31)

H. G. Evers: *Staat aus dem Stein*, 2 vols (Munich, 1929)

G. A. Reisner: *Mycerinus: The Temples of the Third Pyramid at Giza* (Cambridge, MA, 1931), pp. 127–9

J.-M. Carré: *Voyageurs et écrivains français en Egypte*, 2 vols (Cairo, 1932)

H. Ricke: *Bemerkungen zur ägyptischen Baukunst des alten Reichs*, 2 vols (Zurich, 1944; Cairo, 1950)

W. S. Smith: *A History of Egyptian Sculpture and Painting in the Old Kingdom* (London and Boston, 1946, 2/1949)

H. A. Groenewegen-Frankfort: *Arrest and Movement: An Essay on the Representation of Space and Time in the Art of the Ancient Near East* (London, 1951/R New York, 1972); review by J. Baines in *J. Egyp. Archaeol.*, lx (1974), pp. 272–6

W. Wolf: *Die Kunst Ägyptens: Gestalt und Geschichte* (Stuttgart, 1957)

W. S. Smith and W. K. Simpson: *The Art and Architecture of Ancient Egypt*, Pelican Hist. A. (Harmondsworth, 1958, rev. 2/1981)

J. Vandier: *Les Grandes Epoques: La Statuaire* (1958), iii of *Manuel d'archéologie égyptienne* (Paris, 1952–78)

Egyptian Sculpture of the Late Period (exh. cat. by B. V. Bothmer, M. W. Müller and H. de Meulenaere, New York, Brooklyn Mus., 1960)

W. S. Smith: *Interconnections in the Ancient Near East* (New Haven, CT, 1965)

F. G. Bratton: *A History of Egyptian Archaeology* (New York, 1968)

N. Pevsner and S. Lang: 'The Egyptian Revival', *Studies in Art, Architecture and Design*, ed. N. Pevsner, i (London, 1968), pp. 212–35, 245–8

G. Mokhtar: 'Registration of the Hieroglyphic Texts: The Technique Adopted by Cairo Centre of Documentation', *Textes et langages de l'Egypte pharaonique: Hommages. . .Champollion*, iii (Cairo, 1972), pp. 279–83

C. F. Nims: 'The Publication of Ramesside Temples in Thebes by the Oriental Institute', *Textes et langages de l'Egypte pharaonique: Hommages. . .Champollion*, ii (Cairo, 1972), pp. 89–94

A. Roullet: *The Egyptian and Egyptianizing Monuments of Imperial Rome* (Leiden, 1972)

Akhenaten and Nefertiti (exh. cat. by C. Aldred, New York, Brooklyn Mus., 1973)

R. Caminos: 'The Recording of Inscriptions and Scenes in Tombs and Temples', *Ancient Egyptian Epigraphy and Palaeography*, ed. R. Caminos and H. G. Fischer (New York, 1976), pp. 1–25

R. G. Carrott: *The Egyptian Revival: Its Sources, Monuments and Meaning, 1808–1858* (Berkeley, 1978)

Africa in Antiquity: The Arts of Ancient Nubia and the Sudan, 2 vols (exh. cat., ed. S. Wenig; New York, Brooklyn Mus., 1978)

M. Podro: *The Critical Historians of Art* (New Haven, CT, 1982), pp. 20–26

C. K. Wilkinson and M. Hill: *Egyptian Wall Paintings: The Metropolitan Museum of Art's Collection of Facsimiles* (New York, 1983)

L. Bell: 'The Epigraphic Survey: The Philosophy of Egyptian Epigraphy after Sixty Years' Practical Experience', *Problems and Priorities in Egyptian Archaeology*, ed. J. Assmann, G. Burkard and W. V. Davies (London, 1987), pp. 43–55

JOHN BAINES, MORRIS BIERBRIER, PETER LACOVARA, JAROMIR MALEK

XIX. Forgeries.

1. History. 2. Partial forgeries. 3. Complete forgeries.

1. HISTORY. According to Prisse d'Avennes (1846), the native population of Egypt turned to the manufacture of forgeries after 1836, when Muhammad 'Ali Pasha (*reg* 1805–48) set up the first pharaonic museum in Cairo. The museum filled only a single room, but it entailed restrictions on the excavation and sale of antiquities. Within a few years tourists were being offered surprisingly good imitations of small objects such as *shabtis* (funerary statuettes) in a variety of types of stone. A second French source, A. Clerc, reported in 1847 that this production reached considerable proportions by about 1843 and was supplemented by the more careful workmanship of two or three Levantines as well as by the import of scarabs, jewellery and bronzes from Greece and Italy. This inform- ant found the native forgeries defective in style and material; they were frequently made of plaster.

As early as 1821, however, the Kunsthistorisches Mu- seum, Vienna, acquired a limestone copy (161; Lilyquist, 1988, fig. 68) of a Third Intermediate Period (*c.* 1075– *c.* 750 BC) stele, clumsy in style, but scarcely less so than many later forgeries. The same museum possesses two other limestone copies of similar style but better work- manship (5075–6), both imitating stelae now in the Egyp- tian Museum, Cairo, and both originally from a private collection at Miramar; they were bought after *c.* 1850 and before 1866, along with other forgeries including a lime- stone king, standing 500 mm high described by Reinisch (1865) and Komorzynski (1954). Other early forgeries include the gold bowl of Djehuty, acquired by the Louvre in 1827 (Lilyquist, 1988), two small limestone obelisks of Old Kingdom (*c.* 2575–*c.* 2150 BC) style, which were brought from Egypt in 1839 (Fischer, 1978), and a limestone statuette of the god Amun, itself probably genuine, but bearing a spurious inscription on the back; the last was acquired by Robert Hay between 1828 and 1833 (Dunham, 1933). Considerably earlier imitations of Egyptian art are also known (Lilyquist, 1988). It seems doubtful that many of these were intended to deceive, even though (according to Foissy-Aufrère, 1985) some were duplicated from genuine objects by collectors, and (according to Dewachter, 1986) quite a few came to be regarded as genuine antiquities, subsequently exposed by Champollion and others.

By the last decade of the 19th century, larger statues were being made, such as a limestone statue of Old Kingdom style in the Ägyptisches Museum, Berlin, ac- quired in 1895 (Fischer, 1978; 1987), and probably also the statuette of Queen Tetisheri (*fl c.* 1560 BC), which was acquired by the British Museum in 1890 (Davies, 1984). These examples are much more impressive than those described by Budge in 1894 or the bulk of those illustrated by Wakeling in 1912, but Budge wrote only about scarabs and both were concerned only with native Egyptian production.

Modest as they are, the forgeries produced by native Egyptians at the turn of the century sowed a certain amount of confusion in later years, when they turned up in other corners of the world, mislaid by the travellers who had collected them. The most famous case, exposed by Schäfer in 1906, was a clay statuette discovered in Rhodesia and taken as evidence of ancient Egyptian penetration into Africa. Similar examples are said to have come from a Roman tomb in Morocco and from ruins in Mexico (Fischer, 1963). The same forgers' workshop produced scarabs, cast from a genuine specimen, that have turned up in Beirut, in Jerusalem, in a Roman site at Mandeure (on the eastern border of France) and in Tanis (Yoyotte, 1988). Other likely forgeries of this period include a limestone frog found by a farmer in Lower Austria (Komorzynski, 1963) and a scarab found at Ossimo Superiore in Italy (Schulman, 1975). Both bear the cartouche of Ramesses II (*reg c.* 1279–*c.* 1213 BC), as does a fake scarab discovered in the Austrian Alps (Flucher, 1967).

By World War I the presumed activity of Levantine forgers is attested by some particularly imposing pieces such as a wooden horse and rider purchased by the Metropolitan Museum of Art, New York, in 1915 (Fischer, 1987) and the bust of a woman (New York, Met., 26.7.1391) in the style of the Old Kingdom, bought by Lord Carnarvon a year later (Fischer, 1978). The latter may be the work of Oxan Aslanian, an Armenian who began his activity in Egypt, then continued in Berlin and Hamburg; for some time he was only known as the Berliner Meister (Herzer, 1971; Schoske and Wildung, 1983; Krauss, 1986).

From the series of forgeries published by Borchardt in 1930, it is apparent that they were most frequently influenced by two periods: the classical Old Kingdom (the sculpture of which became well known in 1867, when Mariette exhibited his finds from Saqqara) and the Amarna period (*c.* 1350 BC; *see* AMARNA STYLE), popularized by the discoveries of German archaeologists in 1911–14. Both sources would have been familiar to Aslanian from the museums of Cairo and Berlin. Apart from Aslanian, the only prominent forger who has been identified with certainty is Pierre Bouriant, the son of an eminent Egyptologist and himself an advanced student, who inscribed two large scarabs with a hieroglyphic version of the circumnavigation of Africa by Necho II (*reg* 610–595 BC), based on Herodotus. They were sold to the Musées Royaux d'Art et d'Histoire, Brussels, in 1908, and were exposed the same year by Erman and Schäfer (van de Walle, 1980).

There are also several first-hand accounts of Egyptian forgers at work, mostly in the vicinity of Luxor: Wiedemann on scarabs made in 1880–82; Schäfer (1908) on clay figurines produced during the following decade; Quibell (1932) and Ehlebracht (1931) on sculpture; and Francis (1980) on scarabs and beads.

2. PARTIAL FORGERIES. Antiquities that come on the market are frequently restored in various ways prior to sale so that their authenticity is compromised to a greater or lesser extent. An early example is provided by a painted sarcophagus (London, BM) 'restored' by Giovanni Battista Belzoni (Sharpe, 1862). Reliefs may be enhanced by the addition of paint, as in the case of a number of Amarna reliefs from Hermopolis Magna (New York, Brooklyn Mus.; ex-Schimmel priv. col., now New York, Met.). If they have been broken, the mended cracks may be excessively filled with plaster and the increased lacunae filled with newly incised detail that affects the surrounding surface. When the stone is soaked to remove salt, the plaster restoration comes away, leaving traces that are difficult to distinguish from the original carving (Fischer, 1960a).

A much more serious problem is the restoration of a damaged face by recarving. Some examples are described by Clère (1952), Bothmer (1972), Schoske and Wildung (1983 exh. cat., referring to Munich, Staatl. Samml. Ägyp. Kst, ÄS 4871). An unpublished example is a New Kingdom (*c.* 1540–*c.* 1075 BC) statuette of the god Amun (Chicago, IL, Field Mus. Nat. Hist., 31714). In the case of another statue (ex-MacGregor priv. col.; New York, Met.), this sort of restoration has involved the addition of a royal uraeus-cobra to the brow as well as extensive inscriptions fraudulently identifying it as King Piye (*reg c.* 750–*c.* 719 BC). In another instance the original inscription was removed from an excavated statuette and replaced by one in a style contemporaneous with the original but naming a daughter of Kamose, one of the founders of the New Kingdom (Fischer, 1974). Both of these revisions called for a certain amount of research on the part of the forger, as did the addition of a Greek dedication to an Old Kingdom mirror: the objective was to increase local interest, for the mirror (Bird) is in the Karellopoulos Museum, Athens. On the other hand, a Middle Kingdom (*c.* 2008–*c.* 1630 BC) inscription that was added to a statue of the 27th Dynasty (*c.* 500 BC) or later in the British Museum (Hall, 1930) was carelessly copied from the nearest source at hand. The detection of such problems is complicated by the fact that monuments were often reused, reinscribed or otherwise altered, in antiquity. This explanation has been unconvincingly applied to a relief from Deir el-Bahri (Gilbert, 1965) that formerly displayed the first name (i.e. the 'Horus-name') of Queen Hatshepsut (*reg c.* 1479–*c.* 1458 BC); the name has been removed, isolating the falcon (representing the god Horus) that surmounted it, and the fragment trimmed so as to resemble a complete round-topped stele. A second example of the same kind has been cited by van Siclen (1988). Other reliefs, including those discussed by Borchardt (1930) and Cooney (1963), sometimes show vestiges of ancient figures or inscriptions that have been enhanced by a much more substantial amount of detail.

The most extraordinary composite forgery is a Middle Kingdom statuette of a husband and wife, the top and bottom of which are in the Museum of Fine Arts, Boston, while the centre, in the Petrie Museum of Egyptian Archaeology (London, U. Coll.), has been recarved in the form of a man and woman, crudely imitating the style of the New Kingdom. The recarved portion retains the original inscription on the outer edge at each side, making it possible to join the three pieces (Fischer, 1974). Scarcely less curious, however, is the bust of Queen Ahmose-Nefertari (U. of Chicago, IL, Orient. Inst. Mus.), which is in two pieces, the upper part including a well-preserved head and shoulders, the more damaged lower part identifying the Queen. One of the two parts is certainly added to the other, for the stone does not match and the join is unconvincing, but it seems likely that neither part is ancient and that one forgery has been augmented by another (Fischer, 1987).

Wooden forgeries generally come into the category of partial ones, even if the carving is completely modern, since those of good workmanship are usually of ancient wood. But since wooden statuary is assembled from several parts, the arms and base being made separately, any one of these components may be restored, and sometimes only the base is original, validating the forgery mounted on it. In the case of stone sculpture, it is generally the head or upper part of a statue that is supplemented (Cooney, 1950; Wenig, 1977), sometimes using the surviving head of another ancient statue (Fischer, 1960b). Genuine Predynastic (c. 6000–c. 2925 BC) pots often bear modern decoration (Brunton, 1934; Payne, Kaczmarczyk and Fleming, 1977) and stone objects of this period are occasionally recarved (Arkell, 1955; Fischer, 1974).

3. COMPLETE FORGERIES. While they may be completely of modern workmanship, forgeries of the 20th century have often been conceived as a fragment, in which case they usually show a head or bust, if in the round, or a face, if in relief; but spurious fragments of relief may include one or more entire figures. As a rule, there is enough peripheral damage to make the fragmentary nature of such pieces look convincing, but the more important features are left intact (Schoske, 1984). The advantage of this technique is that it not only reduces the forger's work but spares him the complexities of a hieroglyphic inscription. Many a forgery has initially been suspected because of palaeographic defects. In at least two such cases—a statue identifying a well-known Old Kingdom scribe Rehotpe (fl c. 2575 BC) and another bearing the name of the Middle Kingdom ruler Sesostris III (reg c. 1837–c. 1818 BC)—such suspicion led the dealer to destroy the incriminating evidence, leaving the figure completely uninscribed (Schoske and Wildung, 1983; Fischer, 1987).

The earliest forgeries exemplify the most common and prudent procedure: to copy an ancient model as closely as possible. The duplication of metal objects, which can be cast in a mould, may be extremely difficult to detect. For example, it is uncertain which of two small silver sphinxes of the 17th Dynasty ruler Seqenenre (Morlanwelz-Mariemont, Mus. Royal Mariemont) is original, or whether both were cast from an unknown original (Fischer, 1974, n. 55); additional copies are to be found in the British Museum and the Louvre. The original has yet to be found for five brass casts of an ornamental 18th Dynasty axe head, manufactured before 1891 (Davies, 1987). Scarabs and other small objects have also been cast in clay or faience, using ancient originals or ancient moulds. But copies carved in stone or wood are generally more recognizable, especially if one can identify the model on which they are

based (Riefstahl, 1951; Botti, 1954; Fischer, 1974; Kueny and Yoyotte, 1979; Clère, 1981; Krauss, 1986; Haslauer, 1987). One such forgery is in a private collection in Brussels (Frankfort, 1930). Even though Henri Frankfort recognized the subject as a detail in the tomb of Sethos I (KV 17; reg c. 1290–c. 1279 BC), he assumed that the tomb had been despoiled of this fragment. If it is compared with the same detail in the tomb itself (see fig. 120, right), the stylistic deficiency of the copy (fig. 120, left) becomes apparent, to say nothing of the fact that one of the hieroglyphs is badly distorted. Unfortunately such copies are often made from objects in the forger's possession, which may never come to public attention (e.g. Wiedemann, 1911; Spiegelberg, 1923; Fischer, 1988). In other cases dealers have had single copies made of an antiquity with the more modest goal of doubling their profits (Quibell). Occasionally archaeologists such as Mariette and Garstang have had copies made as souvenirs (Cooney, 1963; Kueny and Yoyotte, 1979), and it is apparent that many equally innocent objects, originally sold as such (Wiedemann, 1916), may ultimately be offered as genuine antiquities.

In the past, copies in stone or wood have rarely, if ever, been exact facsimiles; they usually reflect something of the modern craftsman's style or the taste of his period. This may render the product even more appealing to the prospective buyer but tends to make it more recognizable with the passage of time. In many cases the stylistic difference is so slight, and the model so conventional, that the forgery does not seriously distort our appreciation of Egyptian art. There are, however, a number of pieces that present a more serious problem. An attractive bust that is supposed to be the wife of Menna (fl c. 1380 BC), with its coiffure of unusual zigzag pattern (Cairo, Egyp. Mus., JE 36550), has come under increasing suspicion, to the point that its label has carried a warning in recent years, and the sculpture itself has been intermittently retired from exhibition—this despite the statement of Sir Robert Mond that he excavated it in a shaft near the tomb of Menna, at Thebes, in 1903. Ever since its discovery, there have been persistent but contradictory rumours about how it came to be there. A relief showing the face of Amenophis I (reg c. 1514–c. 1493 BC) has also been withdrawn from exhibition at the Metropolitan Museum of Art, New York, although Myśliwiec (1976) is inclined to think it is genuine. It was acquired at the end of World War II, and its modelling is so admirably executed that, if it is indeed spurious, it signals a distinct and alarming advance in the level of Egyptian forgeries. Thus the authenticity of some works continues to be debated. There is little debate, however, about objects in the Mansoor private collection of Amarna sculpture (see XX, 2 below); these objects have been shunned by nearly every curator of Egyptian antiquities in the latter half of the 20th century (Hochfield, 1978; Schoske and Wildung, 1983; Nolli and Becker-Colonna, 1986).

The steady accumulation of publications reflects the increasing amount of attention that the subject of Egyptian forgeries has received. This situation is also reflected in the Munich exhibition of 1983 (Falsche Faraonen), which was subsequently shown in Hamburg and Brussels.

120. Forgery (left) of a limestone relief (right, detail) in the tomb of Sethos I, Valley of the Kings, Luxor, *c.* 1280 BC; limestone, h. 570 mm, ?*c.* 1930 (Brussels, private collection); published in *Maandblad voor Beeldende Kunsten*, vii (1930), p. 87

BIBLIOGRAPHY

GENERAL

G. Steindorff: 'Fakes and Fates of Egyptian Antiquities', *J. Walters A. G.*, x (1947), pp. 52–9 (52–7)
K. Lange: *Pyramiden, Sphinxe, Pharaonen* (Munich, 1952), pp. 150–54
J. D. Cooney: 'Assorted Errors in Art Collecting', *Expedition*, vi/1 (1963), pp. 20–27 (22, 24–7)
Falsche Faraonen (exh. cat., ed. S. Schoske and D. Wildung; Munich, Staatl. Samml. Ägyp. Kst; Hamburg, Mus. Kst & Gew.; Brussels, Mus. Royaux A. & Hist., 1983)
H. G. Fischer: 'Notes on the Macclesfield Collection', *Götting. Misz.*, xcv (1987), pp. 35–44 [a]
H. Whitehouse: 'A Forgery Exposed', *Disc. Egyp.*, ix (1987), pp. 63–7

HISTORY

A. C. T. E. Prisse d'Avennes: 'Collections d'antiquités égyptiennes au Kaire', *Rev. Archéol.*, ii/2 (1846), pp. 729–52 (729–30)
A. Clerc: 'Lettre à M. de Saulcy', *Rev. Archéol.*, iii/2 (1847), pp. 649–67
S. Reinisch: *Die ägyptischen Denkmäler in Miramar* (Vienna, 1865) [pl. 29 (3) is an extremely inaccurate drawing of Vienna, Ksthist. Mus., 5804]
E. A. W. Budge: *The Mummy* (Cambridge, 1894), pp. 253–5
H. Schäfer: 'Die angebliche Figur aus Rhodesia', *Z. Ethnol.*, xxxviii (1906), pp. 896–904
T. G. Wakeling: *Forged Egyptian Antiquities* (London, 1912)

A. Wiedemann: [review of H. R. Hall: *Catalogue of Scarabs etc in the British Museum* (London, 1913)], *Orient. Litztg*, xxi (1918), cols 91–7
J. E. Quibell: 'Loose Ends', *Studies Presented to F. Ll. Griffith* (London, 1932), pp. 480–81
D. Dunham: 'An Ancient Egyptian Forgery?', *Bull. Mus. F.A., Boston*, xxxi (1933), pp. 79–81
E. Komorzynski: 'Über Fälschungen auf dem Gebiet der ägyptischen Altertumskunde', *Mittbl.: Ver. Bndkrimbeamt. Österreichs*, nos 52–8 (1954) [the last lists 12 forgeries in Vienna; nos 3, 4, 6–11 from the Miramar priv. col.]
H. G. Fischer: 'A Frequently Copied Scarab', *J. Amer. Res. Cent. Egypt*, ii (1963), pp. 39–41
E. Komorzynski: 'Eine altägyptische Frosch- oder Krötenfigur', *Archiv Orientforsch.*, xx (1963), pp. 141–6 [considered genuine]
H. Flucher: 'Skarabäusfund am Hohen Sonnblick', *Jb. Dt. Alpenver.* (1967), pp. 128–32
H. Herzer: 'Ein Relief des "Berliner Meisters"', *Obj. & Mondes*, iv–v (1971), pp. 39–46
A. R. Schulman: 'The Ossimo Scarab Reconsidered', *J. Amer. Res. Cent. Egypt*, xii (1975), pp. 15–17 [thought to be genuine]
H. G. Fischer: 'Quelques prétendues antiquités de l'ancien empire', *Rev. Egyptol.*, xxx (1978), pp. 78–95
P. Francis jr: 'Bead Report III: Beads in Egypt', *Ornament*, iv/4 (1980), pp. 15–17, 49–50

B. van de Walle and others: *La Collection égyptienne* (Brussels, 1980), pp. 35–6, 81–92

P. Ehlebracht: 'Die Meisterfälscher von Ägypten', *Art* [Hamburg], ii (1981), pp. 52–64

W. V. Davies: *The Statuette of Queen Tetisheri: A Reconsideration*, BM Occasional Pap., 36 (London, 1984)

M.-P. Foissy-Aufrère: *Égypte en Provence* (Avignon, 1985), pp. 203–4, 250 [canopic jar and copy, A115a, A115c]

M. Dewachter: 'L'Académie et l'Egypte ancienne', *L'Institut de France dans le monde actuel* (Paris, 1986), pp. 310, 314–15

R. Krauss: 'Zwei Beispiele für Echtheitsuntersuchungen an Aegyptiaca', *Jb. Preuss. Kultbes.*, xxiii (1986), pp. 155–75

H. G. Fischer: 'Encore des faux', *Chron. Egypte*, lxii (1987), pp. 90–107 [b]

C. Lilyquist: 'A Gold Bowl of Djehuty: A Study of Objects and Early Egyptology', *Met. Mus. J.*, xxiii (1988), pp. 5–68 [Paris, Louvre, N713]

J. Yoyotte: 'Une Tentative de "truffage"?', *Bull. Soc. Fr. Fouilles Tanis*, i (1988), pp. 55–9 [example added to Fischer, 1963]

PARTIAL FORGERIES

S. Sharpe: *Egyptian Antiquities in the British Museum* (London, 1862), p. 100

A. Wiedemann: 'Notes on Some Egyptian Monuments', *Proc. Soc. Bibl. Archaeol.*, xxxiii (1911), pp. 167–8

H. R. Hall: 'Two Middle-Kingdom Statues in the British Museum', *J. Egyp. Archaeol.*, xvi (1930), pp. 167–8 [inscr. on second example now acknowledged to be a forgery]

G. Brunton: 'Modern Painting on Predynastic Pots', *An. Service Ant. Egypte*, xxxiv (1934), pp. 149–56

J. D. Cooney: 'A Re-examination of Some Egyptian Antiquities', *Bull. Brooklyn Mus.*, xi/3 (1950), pp. 11–26

J. J. Clère: 'The Statue of an Egyptian Priest', *Mus. Notes: Mus. A., RI*, ix/4 (1952), pp. 1–3

A. J. Arkell: 'Modern Designs on Predynastic Slate Palettes', *J. Egyp. Archaeol.*, xli (1955), p. 126

H. G. Fischer: 'The Inscription of *In-it.f*, Born of *Tfi*', *J. Nr. E. Stud.*, 19 (1960), pp. 258–60[a]

——: 'The Inspector of Youths *Nfr-n-Ḥwfw*', *Oudhdknd. Meded. Rijksmus. Ouden Leiden*, xli (1960), p. 1[b]

P. Gilbert: 'Remploi d'un relief de Deir el-Bahari', *Chron. Egypte*, xl (1965), pp. 17–19

B. V. Bothmer: 'The Head that Grew a Face', *Misc. Wilbouriana*, i (Brooklyn, 1972), pp. 25–31

H. G. Fischer: 'The Mark of a Second Hand on Ancient Egyptian Antiquities', *Met. Mus. J.*, ix (1974), pp. 5–34

J. C. Payne, A. Kaczmarczyk and S. J. Fleming: 'Forged Decoration on Predynastic Pots', *J. Egyp. Archaeol.*, lxiii (1977), pp. 5–12

S. Wenig: *Ägyptische Altertümer aus der Skulpturensammlung Dresden* (Dresden, 1977), p. 34

J. Bird: 'An Inscribed Mirror in Athens', *J. Egyp. Archaeol.*, lxxii (1986), pp. 187–9

C. C. van Siclen: 'IV. Florence 7616: A Re-worked Antiquity?', *Var. Aegyp.*, iv (1988), pp. 249–52; v (1989), p. 23

H. G. Fischer: 'Two Iconographic Questions: Who and When?', *Chief of Seers: Studies in Memory of Cyril Aldred* (London, 1994), pp. 146–53 [a forged Late Period inscription on a Middle Kingdom relief, Brooklyn 37.1355E]

COMPLETE FORGERIES

A. Wiedemann: 'Ein Skarabäus zu Cambridge', *Orient. Litztg*, xix (1916), cols 129–31

W. Spiegelberg: 'Eine merkwürdige Fälschung', *Z. Ägyp. Spr. & Altertknd.*, lviii (1923), pp. 158–60

L. Borchardt: 'Ägyptische "Altertümer", die ich für neuzeitlich halte', *Z. Ägyp. Spr. & Altertknd.*, lxvi (1930) [suppl.]

H. Frankfort: 'Egyptischje Beeldhouwwerken uit de Verzameling A. Stoclet te Brussel' [Egyptian sculptures in the A. Stoclet collection at Brussels], *Mdbl. Beeld. Kst.*, vii (1930), pp. 67–93 [unacknowledged forgeries, ten shown in preceding article]

A. Wiedemann: 'Neuzeitliche Fälscherkünste', *Z. Ägyp. Sprache & Altertknd.*, lxvii (1931), pp. 122–6 [for the Toronto scarab (p. 125) see Yoyotte, 1956]

E. Riefstahl: 'An Egyptian Portrait of an Old Man', *J. Nr E. Stud.*, x (1951), pp. 65–73

G. Botti: 'Raccolto di antichità egizie Wilson-Barker', *Aegyptus*, xxxiv (1954), pp. 63–79

J. Yoyotte: 'Plaidoyer pour l'authenticité du Scarabéc, historique de Shabaka', *Biblica*, xxxvii/4 (1956), pp. 457–76

P. J. Ucko and H. W. M. Hodges: 'Some Pre-Dynastic Egyptian Figurines: Problems of Authenticity', *J. Warb. & Court. Inst.*, xxvi (1963), pp. 205–22

E. J. Baumgartel: 'Some Additional Remarks on the Hierakonpolis Ivories', *J. Amer. Res. Cent. Egypt*, viii (1969–70), p. 10 [Oxford, Ashmolean, 1922.70]

J. F. Aubert and L. Aubert: *Statuettes égyptiennes* (Paris, 1974), pp. 273–5 [*shabtis* in priv. cols and on the market]

H. Goedicke: 'Remarks about a Recent Acquisition', *Götting. Misz.*, xvii (1975), pp. 27–30 [Boston, MA, Mus. F.A., 71.403]

K. Mysliwiec: *Le Portrait royal dans le bas-relief du nouvel Empire* (Warsaw, 1976), pp. 32–4 [New York, Met., 45.2.7]

S. Hochfield: 'The Mansoor Collection: An Insoluble Controversy?', *Art News Annu.*, lxxvii/6 (1978), pp. 50–57

G. Kueny and J. Yoyotte: *Grenoble, Musée des Beaux-Arts collection égyptienne* (Paris, 1979), pp. 178–81

J. J. Clère: 'La Table d'offrandes de l'échanson royale Sa-Rénénoutet surnommé Tchaouy', *Bull. Inst. Fr. Archéol. Orient.*, lxxxi (1981), p. 223 [suppl.]

S. Schoske: 'Fälschungen altägyptischer Kunst-Kriterien ihrer Entdeckung', *Kstjb. Stadt Linz* (1984), pp. 18–22

R. Krauss: 'Besucherberatung: Ein gefälschtes Ushebti', *Ber. Staatl. Mus. Preuss. Kultbes.*, i (1986), n.p.

G. Martin: 'Shabatis of Private Persons in the Amarna Period', *Mitt. Dt. Archäol. Inst.: Abt. Kairo* (1986), pp. 126–9 [vindication of specimens previously doubted]

G. Nolli and A. Becker-Colonna: *In Defense of the Mansoor-Amarna Collection* (Rome, 1986)

W. V. Davies: *Axes*, London, BM cat., vii/1 (London, 1987), pp. 31, 32, 35, 42 [protodynastic relief], 47, 49 [suspect inscrs] and 52 [modern casts]

E. Haslauer: 'Die zweite Stele des Pa-di-asha-ikhet', *Götting. Misz.*, xcviii (1987), pp. 47–8

M. Müller: *Die Kunst Amenophis' III und Echnatons* (Basel, 1988), iv, p. 38 [peculiarities of Brooklyn 59.19, most of them noted by James Romano, who has questioned its authenticity]

B. Williams: 'Narmer and the Coptos Colossi', *J. Amer. Res. Cent. Egypt*, xxv (1988), p. 39 [contra Baumgartel, 1969–70]

D. Franke: 'Anchu, der Gefolgsmann des Prinzen (Grabrelief Boston MFA 1971.403)', *Miszellanea Aegyptologica: Wolfgang Helck zum 75. Geburtstag* (Hamburg, 1989), pp. 67–87 [contra Goedicke, 1975]

B. Lüscher: 'Zwei interessante Fälschungen', *Z. Ägyp. Spr. & Altertknd.*, cxvi (1989), pp. 58–9 ['lion-hunt' scarabs of Amenophis III]

R. M. Boehmer: 'Gebel-el-Arak und Gebel-el-Tarif-Griff: Keine Fälschungen', *Mitt. Dt. Archäol. Inst.: Abt. Kairo*, xlvii (1991), pp. 51-60

HENRY G. FISCHER

XX. Collectors and dealers.

Distinctions between the collector and the dealer are often blurred: a dealer can build a collection and a collector may finance acquisitions by turning to dealing in a limited way. Many dealers in Egyptian art have also tended to be involved in the buying and selling of art from Classical Greece and Rome, Africa and the Pacific Islands. In the 1970s Egyptian antiquities were usually described together with 'Savage art' or African and Oceanic objects, and there was only a small number of dealers (mainly in France and the USA) concentrating solely on Egyptian art. This association with African and Oceanic objects has had some influence on the types of Egyptian antiquities that were sought, with emphasis being placed on the aesthetic value of form and material. This strong sense of aesthetics has permeated the dealing and collecting of ancient Egyptian art to the extent that the collection of objects serially, rather than in terms of artistic merit, is essentially a late 20th-century phenomenon.

1. Collectors. 2. Dealers.

1. COLLECTORS. After the failure of Napoleon's Egyptian campaign, collectors began systematically to

remove Egypt's antiquities. The principal individuals were Bernardino Drovetti (1776–1852), a naturalized French-man, who served as French Consul-General in Egypt from 1814 to 1829; Henry Salt (1780–1827), his British counterpart, appointed in 1816 and succeeded by William Bankes (see BANKES, (3)); and Giovanni Anastasi (1780–1857), the Swedish-Norwegian Consul-General. Salt was urged by JOSEPH BANKS and William Hamilton (ii) to acquire art for the British Museum. Giovanni Battista Belzoni (a former circus strong man; 1778–1823) and his wife Sarah arrived in Egypt in 1815. Their imagination was fired by JEAN LOUIS BURCKHARDT who described the temples of ABU SIMBEL and a colossal head of Ramesses II at Thebes (the 'Young Memnon'; London, BM, 19), which the French had been unable to move. In 1817 Belzoni took the head back to Britain on behalf of Salt, not without opposition by Drovetti. Size was no problem for Belzoni who moved large numbers of heavy works of art including, in 1818, one obelisk from Philae (now Kingston Lacy, Dorset, NT), which he even managed to rescue from the Nile. Salt and Belzoni attempted to sell their finds to the British Museum in 1818; they asked for £8000 and eventually received £2000. However, their prize, the alabaster sarcophagus of Sethos I, went to the collection of JOHN SOANE (London, Soane Mus.). After falling out with Belzoni, Salt collected through the Greek excavator, Giovanni D'Athanasi (1799–?1850). In 1826 he sold his second collection to King Charles X of France for £10,000, through the agency of Jean-François Champollion. In 1835 Salt's final collection, composed of 1083 lots, was sold at Sotheby's, London, for £7000. Three collections were also assembled by Drovetti. These sold to King Charles Felix of Sardinia (1824), King Charles X of France (1827) and Karl Richard Lepsius, acting for the Berlin Museum (1836).

In 1849 an American named George Robins Gliddon (1809–57)—moved by the spoliation of Egypt—wrote *An Appeal to the Antiquaries of Europe on the Destruction of the Monuments of Egypt*. But it was ten years before a concerted effort was made within Egypt to protect the monuments. Auguste Mariette (1821–81), who had been sent to Egypt to acquire early Christian manuscripts but turned his attention to the excavation of the Serapeum (see SAQQARA, §1(iii)–(iv)), established the Egyptian Antiquities Service. Mariette also formed the collection of the Egyptian Musem, Cairo, which was initially housed in an abandoned mosque (see §XXI below). The excavation of the sarcophagus from the tomb of AHHOTPE (1859) in western Thebes and its seizure by a local governor resulted in Mariette's first major test as Director of the Antiquities Service. By means of threat of violence, Mariette finally secured its return, complete with its gold contents (Cairo, Egyp. Mus.). The ruler of Egypt, 'Abbas Pasha (reg 1848–54) was presented with a scarab and necklace for which Mariette was rewarded with a new museum building.

When the Victorian traveller and writer Amelia B. Edwards (1831–92) visited Egypt in 1873, she also sought to rectify the destruction of Egyptian patrimony. In 1882 she founded the Egypt Exploration Fund for the purpose of scientific excavations at a time when new standards were being set by such individuals as the Scottish excavator Alexander Henry Rhind (1833–63). Edouard

Naville and Flinders Petrie excavated on behalf of the Fund (see §XVIII, 2(i) above), but Petrie later excavated independently and funded his work by selling finds. In 1914 he excavated the tomb of Sithathoriunet, a daughter of Sesostris III, at el-Lahun, which contained a royal treasure (New York, Met. and Cairo, Egyp. Mus.). Since the treasure was similar to that found at Dahshur, Petrie was allowed to keep most of the jewellery and this he subsequently sold to the Metropolitan Museum, New York.

Anthony Charles Harris (1790–1869) was both a collector and dealer; after his death, his collection was sold to the British Museum. Some collectors resorted to skulduggery in the interests of their nation, as in the case of the French collector Sébastien Louis Saulnier (1790–1835), who removed the Circular Zodiac (Paris, Louvre) from the ceiling of Dendara and sold it to King Louis XVIII. Emile Prisse d'Avennes (1807–79) removed the Table of Kings (Paris, Louvre) by stealth of night from the Temple of Amun at Karnak and took it to France. Museums have relied to a great extent on acquiring private collections, since the acquisition of scientifically excavated objects, by the 'division' of finds at the end of an excavation, does not ensure a representative collection. It was incumbent even on university museums to acquire objects: James Henry Breasted (1865–1935), for instance, bought much of the collection of the Swiss dealer André Bircher (1838–1926), for the Oriental Institute Museum, University of Chicago.

Apart from the foreign consuls and their agents in Egypt, there were several other noteworthy collectors whose material was either bequeathed or sold to public collections. Among the private collections acquired by the Berlin Musem was that of Jakob Salomon Bartholdi and Giuseppe Passalacqua (1797–1865). The Metropolitan Museum of Art, New York, was given that of Theodore M. Davis (1837–1915) and acquired that of A. E. Gallatin. R. G. Gayer-Anderson (1881–1945) and R. H. Greg (1876–1953) both gave their collections to the Fitzwilliam Museum, Cambridge. Much of the collection of Comte Eustach Tyszkiewicz (1804–73) was given or sold to the Louvre, which also has most of the collection of J. H. Hoffman (1823–97). The Hermitage, St Petersburg, benefited from the bequest of the collection of the Duc de Leuchtenberg (1827–52) as well as part of that of N. K. de Giers (1820–95), while the Pushkin Museum of Fine Arts, Moscow, was given that of V. S. Golenischeff (1856–1947). The collections of Anthony Benaki and Calouste Sarkis Gulbenkian were given to their own museums in Athens and Lisbon respectively, and the Roemer- und Pelizaeus-Museum, Hildesheim, was renamed after its principal donors, Wilhelm Pelizaeus (1850–1930) and Hermann Roemer. Other museums that have benefited from gifts of individual collections include the Boston Museum of Fine Arts (that of John Lowell, 1799–1836) and the Brooklyn Museum, New York (that of Charles Edwin Wilbour, 1833–96). Educational institutions that have received private collections include Eton College (that of W. J. Myers, 1858–99), the Petrie Museum, University College London (that of Henry Wellcome), and the University of Durham, which acquired the collection of Algernon Percy, 4th Duke of Northumberland. Among the collectors whose holdings were bought by museums are Vitaliano Donati (1717–62), whose collection went to the Museo Egizio, Turin; J. B. De Lescluze, whose material was purchased by Leiden in 1826 and is now in the Rijksmuseum van Oudheden; Edward Dodwell (1767–1832), whose collection is now in the Staatliche Sammlung Ägyptischer Kunst, Munich; and R. G. B. Sabatier (1810–79), whose collection was largely sold to the Ny Carlsberg Glyptotek, Copenhagen. Some collections were divided between several institutions: for example that of Giuseppe Di Nizzoli (*fl*1818–28) was distributed between the museums of Vienna, Florence and Bologna, and that of Alessandro Ricci (*d*1832) went to both Dresden (Skulpsamml.) and Florence.

Private collections of note that were sold publicly are those of: Jean François Mimaut (Paris, 1837); Baron James Menascé (Hôtel Drouot, 1891); P. Philip (Hôtel Drouot, 1905); F. G. Hilton Price (London, Sotheby's, 1911); Lady Valerie Meux (dispersed 1911, much to W. R. Hearst); Tigrane Pasha (dispersed 1911); Henry Martin Kennard (London, Sotheby's, 1912); Robert de Rustafjaell (London, Sotheby's, 1906, 1913; New York, 1915); Francis Wallis Grenfell (London, Sotheby's, 1917); Lord William Amherst (London, Sotheby's, 1921); William York MacGregor (London, Sotheby's, 1922); Giovanni Dattari (Paris, 1912); John Evans (London, Sotheby's, 1924); Sir Thomas Carmichael (London, Sotheby's, 1926); Sir John Grenfell Maxwell (1929); Lord Horatio Herbert Kitchener (London, Sotheby's, 1938); William Randolph Hearst (London, Sotheby's, 1939); the Spencer-Churchill family (Christie's, 1965); Lt Gen. Pitt-Rivers (collection dispersed gradually, 1970–80); Comtesse de Béhague (Monaco, Sotheby's, 1987).

2. DEALERS. During the time of Muhammad 'Ali Pasha (*reg* 1805–48), foreigners were allowed to take antiquities out of Egypt. In 1920 the archaeologist Flinders Petrie advised the Egyptian State to consider paying compensation to the finders of antiquities, who might otherwise find it more profitable to melt down precious metal objects. The excavators themselves were not averse to making purchases, and for a time there was a 'salle du vent' at the Egyptian Museum in Cairo, where duplicate material was sold. In 1952, however, President Nasser nationalized all art, prohibiting Egyptians from selling, trading or owning any object made before 1850, although dealers were allowed to sell off their stock until 1979. These restrictive laws, combined with the absence of government compensation for finds of the type requested by Petrie, resulted in a growth in illicit dealing in Egypt.

The UNESCO accords, drafted in 1970 to prevent the illegal import, export and transfer of cultural property, do not designate objects as stolen if they have been taken from as yet unknown sites. Museums that adhere to the UNESCO accords usually insist on a reliable pedigree for any object that they purchase, but documentation of Egyptian antiquities has tended to be poor, ever since they began to be taken out of Egypt in the 19th century. The issue of provenance is complex: it is difficult for a country to establish that an antiquity is legally theirs since the object has to have been documented in the country of origin. Title of ownership is easily challenged and seldom proven.

The three great dealing families in the USA were the Abemayors, the Kelekians and the Brummers. The Abemayor family, which consisted of three generations of dealers, was expelled from Egypt along with other Jews during the 1950s. Michel Abemayor, the last of the family, sold off their antiquities in a piecemeal fashion. The Abemayor collection included two stone statuettes of Pepy I and the alabaster figure of Pepy II on his mother's lap (New York, Brooklyn Mus.).

Khan Dikran Garabed Kelekian (1868–1951), an Armenian American who was at one time a US diplomat to Turkey, opened galleries in Paris and New York during the 1890s and was joined by his son Charles Dikran Kelekian (*d*1981) in 1918. The Kelekians also collected Persian miniatures, Chinese art, carpets and Islamic pottery. It was Khan Kelekian who sold the Assyrian reliefs to the Metropolitan Museum of Art, while his son Dikran sold the famous indurated limestone head of Tutankhamun wearing the blue crown from a coronation group to the same institution. The Kelekians' greatest clients were Everette Macy, the American department store mogul, and Henry Walters (*see* WALTERS, (2)). The Walters Art Gallery, Baltimore, houses Henry Walters's renowned collections of medieval and Egyptian art.

Like the Kelekians, the Brummer family, Joseph (*d*1947) and his younger brothers Imre (*d*1928) and Ernest (*d*1964), also belonged to the tradition of collecting and dealing in many areas, including Egyptian, Classical, Byzantine, medieval and Renaissance. Their collections were sold in three sales, in 1949, 1964 and 1979. The first, in New York, required three sales catalogues.

In France the great connoisseur-dealers from the 1920s were Asher, Altounian, Mallon and Ratton. Asher (*fl*1922/3–78) sold to most major American museums, as did Charles Ratton, who was an expert for the Hôtel Drouot and whose younger brother owned a gallery. Like many successful dealers who sold major works of art, the Mallons and Altounian (in Mâcon) dealt quietly from home. In Britain, Rollin & Feuardent (*fl*1867–83) were among the earliest Egyptian dealers in antiquities, but until the late 20th century the only British dealers in Egyptian material of note were Spinks. Sidney Burney was another St James's dealer (*fl*1928–49) who dealt in Egyptian art as well as early Oceanic art and drawings by Henry Moore.

In Egypt the dealing families were primarily concerned with Egyptian finds rather than material from other cultures. One of the most noteworthy discoveries was the cache of mummies at Deir el-Bahri, which Aḥmad 'Abd al-Rasul and his brother Muhammad located (1881) and sold piecemeal through Mustafa Agha Ayat, a Turkish consular agent for Belgium, Britain and Russia, with diplomatic immunity. Wallis Budge, the Assistant Keeper of Egyptian and Assyrian Antiquities at the British Museum, bought from the al-Rasul family. Despite an Egyptian law, from 1835 onwards, prohibiting the export of antiquities, in 1887 Budge managed to buy 24 large crates of antiquities, which he transported illicitly by means of the military. On a subsequent trip to Egypt, Budge was under suspicion by the Antiquities Service and was kept under police surveillance. His cache of antiquities included the 24 m-long papyrus, the Book of the Dead for Ani (London, BM). Effendi Idris, Muhammad Muhassib and Boulos Todrous were late 19th-century contemporary dealers at Thebes. Todrous, a silversmith by trade, reputedly forged antiquities, as did Constantine Simonides (1824–67), an accomplished forger of papyri and manuscripts. The Khawam family, active as dealers from 1860, supplied the Egyptian royal family with antiquities for official gifts to visiting dignitaries. The Mansoor family based in Shepheard's Hotel, Cairo, also boasted of supplying many gifts to royalty. The family assembled a large Amarna-period art collection (106 stone sculptures and reliefs) the authenticity of which required a vigorous defence (see §XIX above). Nevertheless, Queen Nazli bought an Amarna princess statuette from them, as a birthday gift for King Fārūq I (reg 1936–52). Maurice Nahman (d 1948), a former banker, was a renowned dealer in Cairo. Foreigners dealing within Egypt itself included Edwin Smith (1822–1906), an American; V. Galli Maunier (fl 1840–75), a Frenchman who was even entrusted with the supervision of Mariette's excavations; the Greek-Frenchman Nicolas Tano (d 1924); and an Austrian called Theodor Graf (d c. 1920), who amassed a large FAIYUM portrait collection.

BIBLIOGRAPHY

S. Birch: *Catalogue of the Collection of Egyptian Antiquities at Alnwick Castle* (London, 1880)
E. A. W. Budge: *Some Account of the Collection of Egyptian Antiquities in the Possession of Lady Meux of Theobald's Park, Waltham Cross* (London, 1893, 2/1896)
Art of Ancient Egypt (exh. cat., London, Burlington F.A. Club, 1895)
F. G. Hilton Price: *A Catalogue of the Egyptian Antiquities in the Possession of F. G. Hilton Price Dir. S.A.*, 2 vols (London, 1897–1908)
Antiquités égyptiennes, grecques et romaines appartenant à P. Philip et divers amateurs (sale cat., Paris, Hôtel Drouot, 10–12 April 1905)
Collections de feu M. Jean Lambros d'Athènes et de M. Giovanni Dattari du Caire: Antiquités égyptiennes, grecques et romaines (sale cat., Paris, Hôtel Drouot, 17–19 June 1912)
Catalogue of an Exhibition of Ancient Egyptian Art (exh. cat., London, Burlington F.A. Club, 1922)
W. R. Dawson and E. P. Uphill: *Who was Who in Egyptology* (London, 1951, rev. 2/1972)
J. D. Cooney: 'Egyptian Art in the Collection of Albert Gallatin', *J. Nr E. Stud.*, xii (1953), pp. 1–19
——: *Amarna Reliefs from Hermopolis in American Collections* (Brooklyn, 1965)
B. M. Fagan: *The Rape of the Nile: Tomb Robbers, Tourists and Archaeologists in Egypt* (London, 1975)
Ancient Egypt: An Exhibition of El-Amarna Sculptures and Reliefs of the M. A. Mansoor Collection (exh. cat. by A. Becker-Colonna, San Francisco, U CA, Lib., 1975)

XXI. Museums.

This section discusses museums worldwide with important holdings of ancient Egyptian art. For other collections in Egyptian museums see EGYPT, §VI.

1. Egypt. 2. Europe. 3. USA.

1. EGYPT. The largest collection of ancient Egyptian art is at the Egyptian Museum in Cairo. There were two attempts to create a national museum in Egypt: one in the 1830s and another in 1859. On the first attempt, portable objects were housed in a government building in Cairo, but the viceroy used the collection as a source for gifts to visiting dignitaries. 'Abbas Pasha (reg 1848–54) wiped out the remains of this collection with his gift to the Austrian Archduke Maximilian. In 1859 Auguste Mariette was given a brief from the viceroy of Egypt to create a national museum. His efforts were beset with adversity and the museum changed premises several times, from Bulaq to Giza and Qasr al-Nil, before it was finally installed in 1902 in the present site, a Neo-classical building in central Cairo. The Greco-Roman Museum at Alexandria (essentially a post-pharaonic collection) was inaugurated in 1891, although the building was erected in 1895. The modern Luxor Museum, completed in 1975, displays objects with a Theban provenance.

2. EUROPE. In 1823 the British Museum, London, bought the first of three collections that Henry Salt had amassed with Giovanni Battista Belzoni's help. In the 1830s the museum was enriched from the collections of Anastasi and D'Athanasi and again from the collection of Salt. Numerous benefactions were received in the late 19th century, including a large amount of excavated material from the Egypt Exploration Fund. While E. A. Wallis Budge was Assistant Keeper of Egyptian and Assyrian Antiquities at the British Museum, he aggressively acquired objects personally in Egypt, despite the loud outcry against the undocumented removal of antiquities, the existence of the vociferous Egypt Exploration Fund (1882) and an Egyptian ordinance against the illicit art trade (1835).

The Egyptian collection in what is now known as the Durham University Oriental Museum was acquired in 1950 from that formed by ALGERNON PERCY, 4th Duke of Northumberland, who was keenly interested in the Middle East and collected Egyptian art; he had assembled some 2500 pieces, mostly at auction, including many from the 'third' collection of Salt and that of James Burton. However, the Duke's fine collection of Egyptian gold jewellery and scarabs was sold at auction at Sotheby's, London, in 1875.

The Fitzwilliam Museum in Cambridge has a considerable Egyptian collection, which was amply enlarged by the collection of R. G. Gayer-Anderson (1943), a military major, posted in Egypt, with a keen eye. The Ashmolean Museum, with its interesting collection, together with the Griffith Institute, both in Oxford, form a focal centre for Egyptological studies. Another fine British collection is that created by the archaeologist W. M. Flinders Petrie for University College, London (London, U. Coll., Petrie Mus.). His own collection of bought material (1880–92) packed in 50 tea chests was sold to the museum for £5860 and this collection was augmented annually by division material from his excavations. Other English cities with Egyptian material include Manchester and Liverpool. The Library of Eton College, Berkshire, has a fine collection created from gifts of former students, particularly the collection of W. J. Myers, and Harrow School, London, owes its collection to the generosity of John Gardner Wilkinson. The Royal Museum of Scotland, Edinburgh, has a good collection of Egyptian art, some of which was bequeathed by A. H. Rhind.

The Egyptian collection in Berlin (Berlin, Erdgeschoss, Ägyp. Mus.) was started in earnest in 1828 when Alexander von Humboldt convinced King Frederick William III to buy some 2000 objects from the collection of Giuseppe

Passalacqua, which had already been impressively catalogued by Champollion's brother Jacques Joseph Champollion-Figeac. Passalacqua was hired as Director of the Ägyptisches Museum, Erdgeschloss, Berlin, a position he held until 1865. He was responsible for the acquisition of two other collections, those of Drovetti (1836) and Saulinier (1839). Karl Richard Lepsius, a German Egyptologist, was sent on an expedition to Egypt by King Frederick William IV to survey, excavate and acquire objects for the museum (1842–6). After acquiring 1500 objects, Lepsius returned to prepare his monumental publication: *Denkmäler aus Ägypten und Äthiopien* (1849–59). He had already become *de facto* director of the Egyptian collection at Berlin Museum, but after Passalacqua's death he was appointed Keeper. In 1884 Adolf Erman took over from Lepsius as Keeper, devoting most of his career to the publication of the first lexicon of the hieroglyphic language. Though a philologist, Erman acquired objects of great quality such as a fragment of a Ptolemaic statuette now known as the 'Berlin Green Head' and the 18th Dynasty wooden head of a statuette of Queen Tiye (both Berlin, Ägyp. Mus.). However, it was Ludwig Borchardt, a German architect and architectural historian, who led German excavations in Egypt, installed the Cairo Museum (and conceived its *Catalogue général*) and provided Erman with more excavated objects for the museum. Borchardt also discovered the famous painted limestone bust of Queen Nefertiti (Berlin, Ägyp. Mus.; for illustration *see* NEFERTITI) when excavating el-Amarna with funds from James Simon. Berlin's next director was HEINRICH SCHÄFER (1914), the first art historian of Egyptology (*see* §XVIII, 4 above). Thus, the Berlin Museum produced the first handbooks of Egyptian philology and art history. Schäfer acquired many objects from Friedrich W. von Bissing, who had earlier financed the excavations at the Sun Temple of Neuserre in ABU GHURAB directed by Borchardt and von Bissing himself, in 1898. It remained for Rudolf Anthes to pack the Berlin Museum collections and distribute them to seven underground depots before the city was bombed during World War II. After the war, the objects in three magazines were sent to the USSR and only returned to the Bodemuseum in East Berlin in 1958. The objects in the other depots, except those destroyed in two magazines, were eventually sent to the Ägyptisches Museum in West Berlin, which was housed in an existing late Neo-classical building. Because of the consequent gaps in the range of the collection, the Ägyptisches Museum in Berlin has pursued a relatively aggressive acquisitions policy with great success. Since the unification of East and West Germany the government has decided to reunite the Berlin collections in the former East Berlin.

Several Egyptian collections are scattered throughout Germany. Hildesheim owes its fine collection to Wilhelm Pelizaeus, who lived in Egypt and bought art on behalf of Hermann Roemer for the antique museum. Pelizaeus also supported excavations at Giza under Steindorff (1903–7) and Junker (1912–14), therefore acquiring the superb collection of Old Kingdom material in Hildesheim. In 1911 Pelizaeus bequeathed his collection to Hildesheim, which honoured both museum founders jointly by naming the collection the Roemer- und Pelizaeus-Museum. During

World War II the museum was levelled; a new one was built in 1959 and was entirely restored in 1976, though by the early 1990s the collection had not yet been fully reinstalled. The museum publishes its own series of Egyptological monographs and has hosted numerous major exhibitions.

The superb Egyptian collection in Munich (Staatl. Samml. Ägyp. Kst), started in the 17th century, is one of the oldest in Europe. Ludwig I, King of Bavaria (*reg* 1825–48), was the driving force behind the growth of the Munich collection in the 19th century. Much Egyptian art confiscated by Napoleon from the Roman cardinal Alessandro Albani was sold to Ludwig I in order to finance the cost of transporting the rest back to Rome after the war. Ferdinand Michel, perhaps once part of Napoleon's entourage, sold Munich an important collection of Egyptian monuments (1824), the cost of which impoverished the Bavarian Academy. Ludwig also bought from Drovetti. In 1837 he bought half the royal Meroitic gold treasure from the pyramid of Queen Amanishaketo (*see* NUBIA, §IV, 4). Between 1905 and 1914 Friedrich W. von Bissing expanded Munich's Egyptian collection with material from his excavations. Munich has pursued a vigorous connoisseur's acquisition policy since the 1960s.

The Sammlung Antiker Kleinkunst des Archäologischen Instituts at Ruprecht-Karls-Universität, Heidelberg, was created as a teaching collection under the direction of Hermann Ranke and much of the material is derived from excavations at el-Hiba and from Junker's 1927–8 Delta expedition. The city of Tübingen has another university collection (U. Tübingen, Ägyp. Inst.). The Kestner-Museum in Hannover is an important, largely acquired collection of mainly decorative arts, cult objects and small sculptures.

Vienna's impressive Egyptian collection (Ksthist. Mus.) was derived from benefactions from merchants and diplomats to the imperial collections, as well as the acquisition of the collection of Archduke Maximilian. Junker's excavations at Giza provided the bulk of the Old Kingdom material at Vienna and further material comes from digs in Nubia, the East Delta and Thebes.

Leiden owes its collection to early royal patronage (William I) and to the energies of one of the earliest museologists, C. J. C. Reuvens, who took an interest in lighting and mounting. Through his efforts, Leiden acquired material from J. B. De Lescluze (1826/7); Maria Cimba (325 objects); 5675 objects from Anastasi's collection (1828); and a large part of von Bissing's collection (1939).

The Egyptian collection at the Musée du Louvre, Paris, essentially began with the temporary collection amassed by Napoleon's savants led by VIVANT DENON who subsequently became Directeur-Général of Museums. Jean-François Champollion, best known as the first translator of hieroglyphics, was the original keeper of the Egyptian department of the Louvre. A long tradition of French excavations in Egypt has increased the holdings. Auguste Mariette's excavations at the Serapeum (*see* SAQQARA, §1) yielded 7000 objects for the Louvre. Ironically, it was Mariette who later founded the Egyptian Antiquities Service and the Egyptian Museum, Cairo. The Louvre also acquired several private collections: Salt (1826), Drovetti

(1827), Clot-Bey (1852), Anastasi (1857) and Tyszkiewicz (1862).

Other major Continental Egyptian collections are at Lisbon (Mus. Gulbenkian), Copenhagen (Ny Carlsberg Glyp.), Brussels (Musées Royaux A. & Hist.), St Petersburg (Hermitage), Rome (Vatican, Mus. Gregoriano Egizio) and Florence (Mus. Archeol.). The collection at Florence was mainly created between 1824 and 1838, when Florence was an important centre for the art market.

3. USA. The outstanding American collections are mainly on the eastern seaboard: the Metropolitan Museum and Brooklyn Museum, New York; the Walters Art Gallery, Baltimore, MD; and the Museum of Fine Arts, Boston, MA. There are also good Egyptian collections at Richmond, VA, Cleveland, OH, and Detroit, MI. The relatively comprehensive collections of two excellent university museums (Philadelphia, U. PA, Mus., and U. Chicago, IL, Orient. Inst. Mus.) were mostly created as a result of excavations in Egypt. The universities at Yale, Princeton and Berkeley also have respectable Egyptian collections.

The Egyptian Department of the Metropolitan Museum of Art was founded in 1906 with Albert Lythgoe as its first director. In the same year the Egyptian Expedition was created by the museum to record and excavate Egyptian monuments. The collections were greatly enhanced by the Expedition's excavations at the Middle Kingdom site of el-Lisht (1906–34) and at the mortuary temples of Nebhepetre Mentuhotpe II and Hatshepsut at Deir el-Bahri (1911–31). The museum completed the reinstallation of its entire Egyptian collection in an enhanced wing in 1978, ending the year with the dedication of the Temple of Peteese and Pihor, from Dendur (moved from Nubia to the Metropolitan in return for American aid in the Nubian Salvage Campaign), and the opening of the Tutankhamun exhibition.

At the Brooklyn Museum, it is a policy of the department to have only high-quality objects on view, while the rest is in a study collection. The first acquisitions were made in 1902 from W. M. Flinders Petrie and for the next 36 years the museum supported excavations through the Egypt Exploration Fund, receiving finds in return. The Brooklyn Museum also financed Henri de Morgan's survey and excavations (1906–8) in Upper Egypt which yielded Predynastic material. The museum inherited the collection and library of the amateur Egyptologist Charles Edwin Wilbour, whose family provided an endowment for a separate Egyptian department and library. A subsequent boon was the acquisition in 1948 of over 2000 objects from the collection of Henry Abbott, which had been on loan from the New York Historical Society since 1937. From 1948 the department acquired so many objects of unquestionable aesthetic importance that exceptional pieces on the market may sometimes be described as of 'Brooklyn quality'.

BIBLIOGRAPHY

O. Marucchi: *Il Museo Egizio Vaticano*, Rome, Vatican, Mus. Gregoriano Egizio cat. (Rome, 1899)
A. Ippel and G. Roeder: *Die Denkmäler des Pelizaeus-Museum zu Hildesheim* (Berlin, 1921)
M. Mogensen: *La Glyphothèque Ny Carlsberg: La Collection ègyptienne* (Copenhagen, 1930)
C. Boreux: *Département des antiquités égyptiennes: Guide-catalogue sommaire*, 2 vols, Paris, Louvre cat. (Paris, 1932)
W. C. Hayes: *The Scepter of Egypt*, 2 vols (New York and Cambridge, MA, 1953–9) [Egyp. col. of New York, Met.]
W. Kaiser: *Ägyptisches Museum Berlin* (Berlin, 1967)
Staatliche Sammlung Ägyptischer Kunst (Munich, 1976)
T. G. H. James: *An Introduction to Ancient Egypt* (London, 1979) [intro. to the Egyp. dept of the BM, London]
J. F. Romano and others: *The Luxor Museum of Ancient Egyptian Art: Catalogue* (Cairo, 1981)
S. Hodjash and O. Berlev: *The Egyptian Reliefs and Stelae*, Moscow, Pushkin Mus. F.A. cat. (Leningrad, 1982)
M. Saleh and H. Sourouzian: *Official Catalogue of the Egyptian Museum Cairo* (Mainz, 1987)
P. R. S. Moorey: *Ancient Egypt* (Oxford, 1988) [Egyp. col. at the Ashmolean, Oxford]
R. Fazzini and others: *Ancient Egyptian Art in the Brooklyn Museum* (New York, 1989)

XXII. Exhibitions.

In 1821 Giovanni Belzoni, wishing to gain credence and respectability for his archaeological work in Egypt, exhibited his finds and a complete facsimile of the Theban tomb of Sethos I in the Egyptian Hall, London. This was one of the earliest cases of a public 'vanity' exhibition of a private collection, intended to improve value for the objects at subsequent auction. The Egyptian exhibit at the Exposition Universelle in Paris, in 1867, however, was a different matter. François Auguste Mariette, the Director of the Egyptian Antiquities Service, installed the objects, including gold from the Theban tomb of Queen Ahhotpe. The Egyptian Hall in London was already in decay when Flinders Petrie arranged an exhibition of Faiyum portraits and mummies (*c.* 1887). For several years from 1894, Petrie subsequently hosted annual exhibitions of excavation finds at University College, London. In 1895 and 1922, two major exhibitions of Egyptian objects (mostly privately owned) were exhibited at the Burlington Fine Arts Club, London.

The Brooklyn Museum in New York played a distinguished role in presenting ground-breaking exhibitions of Egyptian art; in 1941 it presented *Pagan and Christian Egypt*, a show of provincial Late Antique material, a relatively neglected area of Egyptian art. *Egyptian Sculpture of the Late Period* (1960) established dating criteria for 800 years of prolific sculpture production, which had previously not been systematically addressed. EL-AMARNA art, especially reliefs, was featured in *Akhenaton and Nefertiti* (1973). The relatively unknown field of Nubian art (*see* NUBIA, §I) was the focus of *Africa in Antiquity*, conceived and executed in collaboration with scholars from East Berlin. Another academic show undertaken at Brooklyn was *Cleopatra's Egypt* (1989), which emphasized portraiture of the Egyptian and Hellenistic Greek idioms during the Ptolemaic period (304–30 BC). Few other exhibitions of the calibre of those at the Brooklyn Museum have been undertaken in the United States. However, *Treasures of Egyptian Art from the Cairo Museum* (1970) presented by the Metropolitan Museum of Art and the Museum of Fine Arts, Boston, produced a superb catalogue with model entries in the field of Egyptian art. In 1982 the Museum of Fine Arts, Boston, also mounted a very large show to illustrate objects of daily life. *Egypt's Golden Age: The Art of Living in the New Kingdom, 1558–1085 BC* (1982) illustrated both utilitarian objects and works of great technical achievement.

The exhibition of objects from the tomb of Tutankhamun began in France and went to several cities, everywhere drawing record crowds. In Britain alone it attracted 1.7 million visitors between March and December 1972. The money raised helped the UNESCO efforts to transfer the monuments from the submerged island of PHILAE to the higher site of Agilqia. Everywhere it went the exhibition had a profound effect on visitors, yet few of the Tutankhamun objects have been properly published.

From the 1960s, in Germany, Egyptian art exhibitions were used as part of a cultural offensive to raise museum profiles. Perhaps because of the large amount of Amarna material in Berlin, *Ägyptische Kunst der Armana-Zeit* was mounted in Hamburg (1965); it included material that had just been exhibited at the Fogg Art Museum, in Cambridge, MA. A similar show originating in Belgium, *Nofretete-Echnaton*, followed in Germany (1975). Rather than initiate instructive exhibitions, the emphasis in Germany in the 1970s and 1980s has been on essentially undigested shows with disparate, though beautiful, material. These exhibitions are nearly always accompanied by glossy catalogues of similar format with brief descriptive entries. *Egyptian Art from the Brooklyn Museum* (1976) was just that—a selection of objects. Similarly, *Von Troja bis Amarna* lured the public to see the disparate material from the private American collection of Norbert Schimmel. Objects from all periods (5000 years), materials and subjects, albeit handsome selections from Cairo and Alexandria, were the focus of *Götter—Pharaonen* (1978). Other broadly conceived exhibitions involving objects closer to home but of three millennia were *Bilder für die Ewigkeit: 3000 Jahre: Ägyptische Kunst* (1983) and *Osiris Kreuz Halbmond* (1984). A gathering of Egyptologists prompted an exhibition of varied material from Bavarian collections: *Entdeckungen* (1985). Images of women formed the basis for *Nofret—Die Schöne* (1985). Egyptian art of Dynasty XVIII was the subject of *Ägyptens Aufstieg zur Weltmacht* (1987), but even this was padded out with material from daily life already catalogued by the Museum of Fine Arts, Boston.

The phenomenon of mounting exhibitions for the sake of drawing crowds is not exclusive to Germany. In the United States, *Ramses II: The Pharaoh and his Time* (1985) was accompanied by a catalogue with colour photographs, printed captions, no interpretative essays and much empty space. Several precious metal objects of Dynasty XXI date from Tanis were included and two of these resurfaced more appropriately in a subsequent show on Tanite objects in Paris, Marseille, Edinburgh and Australia: *Tanis: L'Or des pharaons* (1987). This was an exhibition that explained the history and archaeology of a single site excavated by the French. As an additional lure, it offered a wealth of precious metal objects found at the site. The exhibition was stripped of its character as the history of Tanis when it arrived in Edinburgh without the Louvre material under the new title *Gold of the Pharaohs* (1988).

ELENI VASSILIKA

Egyptian Revival. Neo-classical style of architectural and interior design; as Egyptomania or *Egyptiennerie* it reached

its peak during the late 18th century and early 19th. Napoleon's campaign in Egypt (1798) coincided with emerging tastes both for monumental and for richly ornamental forms, enhanced by the literary and associational concerns of Romanticism. Unlike its Greek and Gothic counterparts, the Egyptian Revival never constituted a coherent movement with ethical or social implications. Indeed, since its earliest manifestations occurred in the later Roman Empire, the Revival itself can be seen as one in a series of sporadic waves of European taste in art and design (often linked to archaeological inquiry), acting as an exotic foil to the Classical tradition with which this taste was and remains closely involved. On a broader plane of inquiry, the study of Egyptian art and architecture has continued to promote a keen awareness of abstraction in design and a decorative vocabulary of great sophistication. These are among the most enduring contributions of ancient Egypt to Western art and design. *See also* EGYPT, ANCIENT, §XVIII, 4.

1. Origins and early developments, to 1760. 2. Interior decoration and furnishings, 1760–1820. 3. Architecture and design since 1810.

1. ORIGINS AND EARLY DEVELOPMENTS, TO 1760. Even before the Roman conquest of Egypt in 30 BC, the forms, rituals and architectural concepts of Egyptian civilization were being gradually absorbed into the Classical world. In time, aspects of the cults of Isis and Osiris were assimilated by early Christianity, while Imperial Rome itself became a major repository for Egyptian monuments and art. This collection of artefacts was to play a considerable role in later phases of the Revival. Hadrian may be considered to have been one of the first Egyptian revivalists through the creation around AD 130 of the Canopus area of his villa at Tivoli. This complex with its Serapeum and its telemon figures—two of which, recovered during the papacy of Pius II (*reg* 1458–64), became major features of the Vatican collections from Raphael's time—commemorated the town on the River Nile where Antinous, Hadrian's favourite, drowned in AD 122.

Although certain motifs, such as obelisks and sphinxes, recur in funerary art during the Middle Ages, the Arab conquest of Egypt in 641 had made access extremely difficult for Europeans in later centuries. This situation encouraged extravagant conceptions to proliferate among scholars and humanists until these were partly dispelled by published accounts of European travellers in Egypt in the 16th century. By this time there was a fresh interest in Egyptian imagery, as can be seen, for example, in Bernardino Pinturicchio's recondite fresco scheme in the Appartimenti Borgia of the Vatican (1492–5), ingeniously tracing Alexander VI's descent from the sacred Apis bull. Apart from scattered motifs in frescoes by Raphael, Giulio Romano and their followers, a major addition to Egyptian Revival iconography was provided by the rediscovery *c.* 1520 of the Mensa Isiaca, also known as the Tabula Bembi after Cardinal Pietro Bembo (Turin, Mus. Civ. A. Ant.). This bronze tablet (itself a revival artefact from the time of Claudius) with its hieroglyphics and decorations contained a wide range of new information, and a description by Enea Vico was first published in 1559 (Lorenzo Pignoria's more sophisticated edition appeared in 1669).

During the 17th century and the early 18th two opposing aspects of Egypt's appeal for Western scholars and artists began to emerge. The imaginative world of fantasy was fuelled by the copious illustrated writings of the German Jesuit Athanasius Kircher, whose tendentious publications, mainly issued between 1643 and 1679, promoted the mystical theories of Rosicrucianism and, much later, those of Freemasonry. Such an approach was to lead to the speculative reconstructions of Egyptian monuments, including the Great Pyramids, in Johann Bernhard Fischer von Erlach's *Entwurff einer historischen Architektur* (1721). This work stimulated architects and landscape designers such as Nicholas Hawksmoor and John Vanbrugh in, for example, their early 18th-century pyramidal structures amplifying the landscape setting of Castle Howard, N. Yorks. On the other hand, far more sober scholarship developed from John Greaves's *Pyramidographia* (1646), which offered the first systematic study of the celebrated tombs at Giza. This academic tradition culminated in a work that greatly deepened the understanding of Egyptian art and architecture for the West—Bernard de Montfaucon's *L'Antiquité expliquée et représentée en figures* (1719–24). In addition to this comprehensive archaeological compendium, various travel accounts were published in the mid-18th century, exemplified by Frederik Norden's *Voyage de l'Egypte et de Nubie* (1755), which, based on his first-hand studies, provided the most accurate images of the monuments hitherto available.

Significantly, a major turning-point in the fortunes of the Revival was reached during the age of Neo-classicism with its concern for the phenomenon of historical styles. By means of his *Recueil d'antiquités égyptiennes, étrusques, grecques, romaines et gauloises* (1752–67), A.-C.-P. de Tubières, Comte de Caylus, not only offered a formidable corpus of detailed illustrations but for the first time analysed the aesthetic properties of Egyptian art. He saw Egypt as representing the cultural roots of European civilization, which subsequently passed through Tuscany to Greece and then to Rome. For him its salient qualities were grandeur, primitiveness, simplicity and massiveness—characteristics that have largely dominated conceptions of the Revival ever since.

2. INTERIOR DECORATION AND FURNISHINGS, 1760–1820. Within this intellectual context occurred the first attempt to create a fully integrated style of interior design, supported by a far more radical theory than that of Caylus. During the early 1760s the Venetian designer Giovanni Battista Piranesi created a highly original painted interior in the Egyptian taste for the Caffè degli Inglesi in the Piazza di Spagna, Rome. He employed a plethora of motifs derived from the Vatican collections and various publications—from those on the Mensa Isiaca to that by Caylus—but Piranesi's novel setting, recorded in two etched plates, excited little enthusiasm at the time. The plates were included, along with 11 bizarre chimney-piece designs in the Egyptian style, among the 67 illustrations of his *Diverse maniere d'adornare i cammini* (1769). This folio treatise, advocating a broadly eclectic style for contemporary designers and their patrons, was preceded by a remarkable essay in which Piranesi not only stressed the decorative range of Egyptian design but also discussed the process whereby their art had been abstracted from nature, keenly observed. While it is often said that Piranesi's compositions have a Rococo levity, this misconception is swiftly corrected once the etched compositions of the *Diverse maniere* are set against earlier work, such as the 'Apis Altar' (1731; Dresden, Grünes Gewölbe), a cabinet made by the goldsmith Johann Melchior Dinglinger for Augustus the Strong, Elector of Dresden. Where Piranesi's designs show a far greater understanding of the potential weight and formal variety of Egyptian decorative forms, Dinglinger's attractively capricious cabinet is embellished with canopic vases, sphinxes, obelisks and hieroglyphics that bear little organic relationship to the supporting structure.

Within the next two decades the tentative signs of a sustained stylistic revival are discernible for the first time, initially in the applied and decorative arts. With the exception of Anton Raphael Mengs's scheme (*c.* 1770) for the Camera dei Papiri in the Vatican, Piranesi's etched compositions were used mainly as a quarry for random ornamental motifs, as seen for example in François-Joseph Bélanger's (unpublished) chimney-piece designs of 1770 or in Pierre Gouthière's furniture of the 1780s. In England, meanwhile, Josiah Wedgwood was also deriving ideas from Bernard de Montfaucon and Caylus, while producing his Egyptian wares from the 1770s onwards.

By the 1790s the taste of Neo-classicists for a more severe and monumental style was growing more sympathetic to the full implications of Piranesi's system of design. The Billiard Room at Cairness House, Grampian—the first Egyptian Revival interior in Britain—which used three-dimensional features such as a stepped chimney-piece and battered doorcases, was devised by James Playfair in 1793, shortly after his return from Rome. In the last three decades of the 18th century, the scope of the architectural imagination to extend these ideas to a sublime scale was realized in the visionary compositions of Revolutionary French designers, notably Louis Jean Desprez, Jean-Jacques Lequeu, Etienne-Louis Boullée and Claude-Nicolas Ledoux. Of all the elemental forms derived from antiquity, the stern geometry of the pyramid was the most favoured (e.g. Boullée's projected design for a Chapelle des Morts (*c.* 1780; Paris, Bib. N.).

After visiting Rome in the mid-1770s and Egypt in 1796, the English designer Thomas Hope produced the most accomplished interior of the Egyptian Revival. Refashioning the main rooms of his house (destr. 1850) in Duchess Street, off Portland Place, London, he created his 'Egyptian' or 'Black Room' (see fig.) between 1779 and 1801:

> happening to possess several Egyptian antiquities, wrought in variously coloured materials, such as granite, serpentine, porphyry, and basalt, of which neither the hue nor the workmanship would have well accorded with those of my Greek statues . . . , I thought it best to segregate the former, and to place them in a separate room, of which the decoration should, in its character, bear some analogy to that of its contents.

A suite of highly imaginative furniture and the decorative setting was set off with 'that pale yellow and that blueish-green which holds so conspicuous a rank among the Egyptian pigments; here and there relieved by masses of black and gold'.

By 1807, when Hope published these comments to accompany illustrations to his *Household Furniture and Interior Decoration Executed from Designs by Thomas Hope*, he was able to pay tribute to a new source—the fruits of Napoleon's campaign in Egypt. In 1798 Napoleon had appointed a commission of scholars, scientists and surveyors to record Egyptian antiquity in all its aspects. The resulting *Description de l'Egypte*, issued in 20 volumes between 1809 and 1828, not only represented a landmark in archaeology but, together with Baron Vivant Denon's equally magnificent *Voyage dans la basse et la haute Egypte pendant les campagnes du Général Bonaparte* (1802), impelled the Revival as far as the third decade of the new century. As had been the case with an earlier phase, new influences were first reflected in the applied arts, ranging from François-Honoré-Georges Jacob-Desmalter's suite of furniture, designed by Charles Percier for Denon himself in 1809, to the highly ambitious 'Service égyptienne' in Sèvres (1810–12), originally made to Napoleon's directions and later given by Louis XVIII to Arthur Wellesley, 1st Duke of Wellington (now London, Apsley House). In both instances, the closeness of the forms concerned to those new published sources is often in marked contrast to the licence taken by Piranesi, and even Hope, in their acts of imaginative transposition. The emerging Egyptian Revival taste proved to be as international a style as the Pompeian and Greek counterparts, as exemplified respectively by the furniture designed by the Sienese Agostino Fantastici and the English Charles Heathcote Tatham.

3. ARCHITECTURE AND DESIGN SINCE 1810. Notwithstanding John Soane's strictures against serving 'that monster, Fashion', by the second decade of the 19th century architects had begun to follow suit. Instances of civic, commercial and engineering structures include William Bullock's Egyptian Hall (1811; destr.), Piccadilly, London, with a façade by Peter Frederick Robinson (1776–1858) that was inspired by the Temple of Hathor, Dendara; the Egyptian Hall by John Foulston (1772–1842) in Devonport Library (1823), Devon; Isambard Kingdom Brunel's Clifton Suspension Bridge (1831), near Bristol; and, perhaps most original of all, the Temple Mill (1842), Leeds, also derived from Dendara by Joseph Bonomi. But it was in funerary architecture that the mature style of the Revival was universally applied in a variety of buildings and tombs at cemeteries from Père Lachaise in Paris and Mount Auburn in Cambridge, MA, to Kensal Green and Highgate, both in London. Predictably, this latter phenomenon incurred A. W. N. Pugin's wrath in *An Apology for the Revival of Christian Architecture in England* (1843) as displaying evidence of pagan utilitarianism.

Parallel with the applied arts and architecture, the romantic imagery of Egypt was also influencing stage design on the one hand and masonic ritual on the other; themes closely allied in Mozart's opera *Die Zauberflöte*, first produced in Vienna in 1791 and given particularly fine panoramic stage sets by Karl Friedrich Schinkel at the Königliches Theater, Berlin, in 1816. Masonic lodges, first associated with Egyptian symbolism and ceremony in the late 18th century, continued to reflect this as late as 1900,

The 'Egyptian Room', 1779–1801, in Thomas Hope's house (destr. 1850), Duchess Street, London; from T. Hope: *Household Furniture and Interior Decoration* (London, 1807), pl. VIII

when P. L. B. Henderson (1848–1912) created the opulent Chapter Room for the Royal Arch Chapter of Scottish Freemasons in Edinburgh.

In contrast, the mystery surrounding the meaning of hieroglyphics had finally been dispelled in the 1820s through Jean-François Champollion's research on the trilingual Rosetta Stone (London, BM). While Egyptology was henceforward to be established on a firm documentary basis, the romantic exploits of Giovanni Belzoni's excavations between 1815 and 1819, under the benevolent rule of Mohammed Ali Pasha, captured the public imagination. The consequent arrival in Britain of the colossal head of Ramesses II (London, BM) and the sarcophagus of Sethos I (London, Soane Mus.), acquired by Soane, helped to inspire the histrionic paintings of John Martin, as exemplified by *Belshazzar's Feast* (1821; version, New Haven, CT, Yale Cent.). Archaeological interest also gave rise to a new generation of illustrated travel books, which reached a high level of accuracy and artistic calibre in the lithographs of David Roberts's *Egypt and Nubia* (1846–9). Salon paintings on evocative themes continued into the later decades of the century: Edward John Poynter's *Israel in Egypt* (London, Guildhall A.G.) was a sensation at the Royal Academy in 1867.

The High Victorian phase of the Revival in England also found a place in the campaign of improved art education promoted by Henry Cole and his circle. Reflecting Gottfried Semper's current design teaching, Owen Jones and Joseph Bonomie provided an Egyptian Court with large-scale exemplars of art and architecture in the Crystal Palace, rebuilt at Sydenham after London's Great Exhibition of 1851 (destr. 1936). Egyptian material also played a major role in Jones's magisterial *The Grammar of Ornament* (1856), in which the author, echoing Piranesi's respect for the Egyptian genius in natural abstraction, wrote that 'we are never shocked by any misapplication or violation of a natural principle'. Jones considered the Egyptian style, although among the oldest, to be the most perfect: 'the language in which it reveals itself to us may seem foreign, peculiar, formal and rigid; but the ideas and the teachings it conveys to us are of the soundest'. Contemporary designers, such as Christopher Dresser, also drew attention to the functional properties he discerned in Egyptian utensils and furniture in his *The Principles of Decorative Design* (1873), and he produced several chairs based on ancient prototypes.

The perennial influence of basic Egyptian forms and patterns continued to recur in the 20th century. Transcending the more ephemeral impact on jewellery and costume, as well as on several Hollywood films, of Howard Carter's discovery of Tutankhamun's tomb at Thebes in 1922, certain formal influences affected design: Art Deco interiors (e.g. the foyer of Oliver P. Bernard's Strand Palace Hotel, London (1930, destr. 1967–8; parts now London, V&A)); Modernist office, cinema and industrial buildings (e.g. J. J. Burnet's Adelaide House, 1924–5; and Collins & Parri's Arcadia Works for Carreras, 1927–8; both in London). The most persistent of all Revival images, the pyramid form, provides the focal point, in glass, of I. M. Pei's controversial extension to the Musée du Louvre, Paris; completed in 1989, it represents a discourse across two centuries with the 'architecture parlante' of Ledoux.

See also PYRAMID, §3.

BIBLIOGRAPHY

J. Greaves: *Pyramidographia* (London, 1646)
B. de Montfaucon: *L'Antiquité expliquée et représentée en figures*, 10 vols (Paris, 1719–24)
J. B. Fischer von Erlach: *Entwurff einer historischen Architektur* (Vienna, 1721)
A.-C.-P. de Tubières, Comte de Caylus: *Recueil d'antiquités égyptiennes, étrusques, grecques, romaines et gauloises*, 7 vols (Paris, 1752–67)
F. Norden: *Voyage de l'Egypte et de Nubie*, 2 vols (Copenhagen, 1755; Eng. trans., 1757)
G. B. Piranesi: *Diverse maniere d'adornare i cammini...* (Rome, 1769); repr. in *The Polemical Works*, ed. J. Wilton-Ely (Farnborough, 1972)
D. V. Denon: *Voyage dans la basse et la haute Egypte pendant les campagnes du Général Bonaparte* (Paris, 1802)
T. Hope: *Household Furniture and Interior Decoration* (London, 1807/R New York, 1971)
E. F. Jomard and others, eds: *Description de l'Egypte*, 20 vols (Paris, 1809–28)
O. Jones: *The Grammar of Ornament* (London, 1856)
C. Dresser: *The Principles of Decorative Design* (London, 1873)
H. Honour: 'The Egyptian Taste', *Connoisseur*, cxxxv (1955), pp. 242–6
J. S. Johnson: 'Egyptian Revival in the Decorative Arts', *Antiques*, xc (1966), pp. 420, 428
N. Pevsner and S. Lang: 'The Egyptian Revival', *Studies in Art, Architecture and Design*, ed. N. Pevsner, i (London, 1968), pp. 212–48
R. Wittkower: 'Piranesi and Eighteenth-century Egyptomania', *Studies in the Italian Baroque* (London, 1975), pp. 259–73
R. G. Carrott: *The Egyptian Revival: Its Sources, Monuments and Meaning, 1808–1858* (London, 1978)
P. Clayton: *The Rediscovery of Egypt* (London, 1982)
J. S. Curl: *The Egyptian Revival: An Introductory Study of a Recurring Theme in the History of Taste* (London, 1982)
The Inspiration of Egypt: Its Influence on British Artists, Travellers and Designers, 1700–1900 (exh. cat., ed. P. Conner; Brighton, A.G. & Mus., 1983)
D. Syndram: *Ägypten-Faszinationen; Untersuchungen zum Ägyptenbild im europäischen Klassizismus bis 1800* (Frankfurt, 1990)
J. Wilton-Ely: *Giovanni Battista Piranesi: The Complete Etchings* (San Francisco, 1984), pp. 886ff
W. L. Macdonald and J. Pinto: *Villa Adriana, Tivoli* (in preparation)
                                                    JOHN WILTON-ELY

Ehn, Karl (*b* Vienna, 1 Jan 1884; *d* Vienna, 26 July 1957). Austrian architect. He trained at the Wagnerschule, Vienna

(1904–7), and emerged as one of its most promising students. After completing military service in 1908, he worked for the city of Vienna as architect to the XXII district until 1914. After World War I he returned to the city architect's office, where, in the aftermath of defeat, social issues and housing problems in particular dominated the city's building programme. He joined the Sozialistische Partei Österreiches (SPOE) and as an architect was drawn into the debate over the rival merits of suburban low-density cottage developments, often self-built, and those of high-density city-centre block housing. He generally identified himself with the policy of the latter although he built some low-density housing. In 1922, when funds for housing first became more readily available, he designed a six-storey block on the Balderichgasse, a restrained interpretation of traditional Viennese urban design. In the next year he planned the Hermeswiese Siedlung, a low-density, predominantly two-storey suburban development in a simplified vernacular manner.

In 1924 Ehn designed the Lindenhof, which was one of the first major projects to establish the form of the tenement *Hof*, so characteristic of Viennese social housing until the mid-1930s. These were generally designed as a series of linked courts of five to six storeys, planned with staircase access to two or three dwellings via a landing; the individual dwellings were arranged with a view into substantial courts, measuring *c.* 80×50 m and sometimes larger. The spartan space standards and equipment of the individual dwellings were offset by the generous provision of communal facilities such as crèches, kindergartens, laundry and drying rooms, and shared services such as direct heating. His subsequent projects included the Bebelhof (1925) and the Svobodahof (1926–7). However, the project that established his reputation was the Karl-Marx-Hof (1928; *see* VIENNA, fig. 6), the most renowned example of high-density municipal housing in Vienna. Over 1 km long, the block is architecturally vigorous, if not distinguished. Ehn abandoned the mannered, angular, almost Gothic detailing that had appeared as a contrast to the large-scale massing of the earlier courts, for a starker and bolder approach exemplified by the towers and the huge semicircular arches of the centre court; yet these towers are essentially formal devices bearing only a tenuous connection to the formal logic of the system of staircase access. Similarly the three great arches directly beneath the towers lead only to a U-Bahn station. The development was widely publicized. It was visited by housing reformers, architects and politicians from across Europe and the USA and provided an influential image of the benefits that enlightened municipal government could achieve for an urban working-class community.

Despite the Depression Ehn continued to build, and even after the Anschluss in 1938 he maintained his position in the city's administration, abandoning his 20-year membership of the SPOE to join the Nazis. Too old for active service during World War II, he remained in Vienna, rising to the Senatsrat but building little before his retirement in 1950.

BIBLIOGRAPHY

K. Mang: *Kommunaler Wohnungsbau in Wien: Aufbruch, 1923–1924, Ausstrahlung* (Vienna, 1977)
H. Hautmann and R. Hautmann: *Die Gemeindebauten des Roten Wien, 1919–1934* (Vienna, 1980)
                                                    NICHOLAS BULLOCK

Ehninger, John W(hetten) (*b* New York, 22 July 1827; *d* Saratoga Springs, NY, 22 Jan 1889). American painter and illustrator. After graduating from Columbia College, New York, in 1847, he immediately departed for Europe to pursue artistic training. He visited Italy and France, but staying in Germany, specifically Düsseldorf, was his main objective. There he studied with Karl Friedrich Lessing, Carl Ferdinand Sohn and Emanuel Leutze, and in Paris Thomas Couture instructed him. During the early 1850s he travelled between America and Europe but finally settled in New York in 1853 until his move to Saratoga Springs after marrying in 1877. Ehninger exhibited regularly at the National Academy of Design, New York, where he was elected a full member in 1860. His work reveals interests shared by the other Americans in Düsseldorf: these were mainly history and genre painting, with occasional forays in European landscape. But he quickly returned to American subject-matter; *Yankee Peddler* (1853; Newark, NJ, Mus.), for example, describes the initiative of an itinerant entrepreneur in the young nation.

Ehninger's work often suffers for being overcrowded with figures, obscuring the effect of the meticulously rendered details. While he was in England Ehninger designed for the *London Illustrated Times*, and in the USA he illustrated works by Washington Irving, Longfellow and Tennyson. He also introduced *cliché-verre*, a new technique for photographic etching, to America in a portfolio published in 1859. Ehninger thrived on diversity; as well as being an artist, he was an accomplished linguist, classical scholar and amateur actor.

BIBLIOGRAPHY
H. W. Williams jr: *Mirror to the American Past* (Greenwich, CT, 1973)
American Artists in Düsseldorf, 1840–1865 (exh. cat., ed. A. Harding and others; Framingham, MA, Danforth Mus. A., 1982)
H. NICHOLS B. CLARK

Ehrenberg, Felipe (*b* Mexico City, 27 June 1943). Mexican painter, performance artist, installation artist, writer, teacher and publisher. He qualified as a printmaker at a very early age, then as a painter and engraver, under the tutelage of several masters among whom the most influential on his life was José Chávez Morado. Although he at first worked with traditional media, he possessed a constantly innovative and critical attitude and experimented with performances, installations, happenings, correspondence and media art, as well as writing, lecturing and publishing on such themes as artistic experimentation, cultural promotion, professional management for artists, collective mural painting and the publishing process. From 1968 to 1972 Ehrenberg lived in England where, with the architect Martha Hellion and the critic and historian David Mayor, he founded the Beau Geste Press/Libro Acción Libre in Devon, to propagate the work of artists involved with the Fluxus movement of the 1970s. He was also instrumental in the rise of many artistic groups, workshops and small publishing houses, such as Grupo H₂O/Talleres de Comunicación, in which tutors gave workshops on editorial work and collective mural painting. He was involved in numerous collective mural projects in Mexico.

BIBLIOGRAPHY
R. Tibol: *Gráfica y neográfica* (Mexico City, 1987)
J. A. Manrique: *Artistas en divergencia* (Mexico City, 1988)
C. Monsiváis: *Entrada libre* (Mexico City, 1988)
N. García Canclini: *Culturas híbridas* (Mexico City, 1990)
JULIETA ORTIZ GAITÁN

Ehrenreich, Adám Sándor [Antal] (*b* Pozsony [now Bratislava, Slovak Republic], 1784; *d* Vienna, 13 July 1852). Hungarian engraver, publisher and dealer. He studied under his father József Ehrenreich (1765–1842), a seal engraver, and in 1800 went to the Akademie der Bildenden Künste in Vienna, where in 1806 he won a prize. In the same year he made a portrait of *Imre Marczibányi*. When he had completed his studies he moved to Buda and worked in the Trattner Press. In 1807 he advertised himself as an engraver, letter engraver and seal engraver, and in 1809 he started dealing. In 1814 he engraved a picture of *King David*, after a drawing by Johann Nepomuk Hoefel (1788–1864). He did portraits of a number of important people in national political and cultural life, including *Johan Spissich, József Ürményi, Miklós Wesselényi, László Kollonits, Archduchess Henrietta, István Ferenczy, Ferdinánd Jakab Miller* and *Benedek Virág*. He also engraved several illustrations for the first Hungarian scientific periodical, the *Tudományos Gyüjtemény* (Scientific Repertory; 1817, 1818, 1830). From 1823 until the early 1840s he undertook the huge task of engraving over 100 portraits of Hungarian historical figures and famous contemporary people; he called the collection *Icones Principum*. Although other engravers also worked on this project, most of the portraits were executed by Ehrenreich. The engravings of historical figures were taken from portraits, while those of contemporary figures were based on drawings and paintings by foreign and Hungarian artists. The majority were made very precisely, and they vary in quality depending on the artistic merit of the original drawing or painting. Although Ehrenreich moved to Vienna in 1825, he continued the series. A bookdealer in Pest republished them in 1904. From 1840 to 1842 he was a dealer and publisher on Szervita Square in Pest, and in 1842–3 he published a series of lithographs about the history of Hungary and Transylvania with the history painter Johann Geiger (1805–70) and the historian Gusztáv Wenzel (1812–91), which ran to three editions.

PRINTS
Icones Principum (Pest, 1904)
BIBLIOGRAPHY
J. Szendrei and G. Szentiványi: *Magyar képzőművészek lexikona* [Hungarian artists' dictionary], i (Budapest, 1915), pp. 421–6
D. Pataky: *A Magyar rézmetszés története* (Budapest, 1951), pp. 106–16
G. Rózsa: 'Ehrenreich Ádám forrásai' [Adám Ehrenreich's sources], *Müveszettörténeti Értesítö*, viii (1959), pp. 61–7
E. Csatkay: *Kazinczy és a képzőművészetek* [Kazinczy and the artists] (Budapest, 1983), pp. 58, 75
JÚLIA PAPP

Ehrenstrahl, David Klöcker (*b* Hamburg, 27 April 1628; *d* Stockholm, 27 Oct 1698). German painter, active in Sweden. 'Ehrenstrahl' was an honorific title received on his ennoblement in Sweden in 1674; his eventual appointment as court steward there in 1690 reflects his status as a founding father of Swedish painting. He initially studied in the Netherlands (1648–50), but his early works, stylistically undecided, reflect contemporary German painting. Such a work is his equestrian portrait of *Field Marshal Carl Gustaf Wrangel* (1652; Stockholm, Skokloster Slott), in whose service he travelled to Sweden in 1652. In 1654 he went to study in Italy. In Rome he learnt from Pietro da Cortona's allegories and his mastery of compositional devices, movement, colour, light and shade; travelling on to Paris, he became acquainted with the work and career of Charles Le Brun. When the artist returned to Sweden in 1661, the influence of Hedvig Eleanora, the Queen Mother, secured him a position as a court painter.

Ehrenstrahl primarily worked as a portrait painter: the penetrating portrait of *Georg Stiernhielm* (1663) and that of *Per Olsson* (1686; both Gripsholm Slott), which combines courtly decorum with lively characterization, are notable examples. But he also engaged in the decoration of royal and aristocratic residences. For Queen Hedvig Eleanora he executed paintings and emblem plates for the royal bed-chamber at Drottningholm Slott (*c.* 1667), works inspired by the contemporary doctrine of humanistic values and conceived in an undramatic style, with subdued colours. In 1669 he presented a sketch for a ceiling painting (1669–74) in the Riddarhus in Stockholm, a patriotic apotheosis illustrating the *Council of the Virtues beneath the Throne of Svecia* in which the composition and handling of figures and light were inspired by Cortona's fresco in the Palazzo Barberini, Rome. His early use of sun symbolism in Swedish royal apotheosis can be seen in his portrait of *Charles XI as Apollo* (1670; Stockholm, Drottningholm Slott).

In the 1670s Ehrenstrahl produced allegories for his royal commissioners, with subjects such as *Truth Revealed by Time* (1675) and *History and Fame* (1677; both Stockholm, Drottningsholm Slott), in which classicizing figures are depicted in diverse attitudes and brilliant colours—a style developed in the group portrait of the *Swedish Royal Family* (1683; Mariefred, Gripsholm Castle, N. Portrait Col.) and allegories commemorating dead princes from the same decade. During the same period he produced one of the earliest genre paintings in Sweden, depicting the *Spa Master of Medevi and his Sons* (1689; Mariefred, Gripsholm Castle, N. Portrait Col.). In the 1690s he painted monumental allegories for Drottningholm Slott, showing the history of the Caroline dynasty (*see* SWEDEN, fig. 9). By this point his work had a fading compositional and coloristic energy also noticeable in his *Last Judgement* and *Crucifixion* (1695), large paintings made for the chapel in the Kungliga Slott, Stockholm. In his large-scale animal and hunting pictures—e.g. *Blackcock Mating* (1675; Stockholm, Nmus.) and *Capercaillie Mating* (1675; Stockholm, Drottningholm Slott)—Ehrenstahl combined a perceptive observation of animals in movement with a remarkable appreciation of the Nordic landscape. In his notes (1694) on his *Self-portrait with Invention and Painting* (1691; Stockholm, Nmus.) he upheld the doctrine of the academies, although he did so more in the spirit of the Rubéniste tradition than by aligning himself with Charles Le Brun and his classicism.

UNPUBLISHED SOURCES
Stockholm, Riksarchv [*Biographica*]

WRITINGS
Certamen equestre caeteraque solemnia Holmiae Suecorum ao: 1672 m. decbr. celebrata . . . Das grosze Carrosel und prächtige Ring-Rännen nebst dem, was sonsten Fürtrefliches zu sehen war, alsz . . . Carl der Eijlffte, die Regierung . . . antratt (Stockholm, n.d.)

Die vornehmste Schildereyen, welche in denen Pallästen des Königreiches Schweden zu sehen sind, inventiret, verfertiget und beschrieben (Stockholm, 1694)

Explication öfwer the twenne stora schilderier, som hoffintendenten David Klöcker Ehrenstrahl hafwer inventerat och förfärdigat uti choret, af Kongl. Slotz Kyrkian i Stockholm [Explanation of the two large paintings that the court steward David Klöcker Ehrenstrahl had invented and completed in the choir of the Royal Castle Church in Stockholm] (Stockholm, 1695)

Disa: Historia von der Königin Disa, kürtzlich beschrieben, und in 8 Kupfer-Bildnussen vorgestellet (n.d.)

BIBLIOGRAPHY
A. Hahr: *David Klöcker Ehrenstrahl* (Uppsala, 1905)
A. Sjöberg: *David Klöcker Ehrenstrahl* (Malmö, 1947)
W. Nisser: *Die italienischen Skizzenbücher von Erik Jönsson Dahlberg och David Klöcker Ehrenstrahl* (Uppsala, 1948)
B. Rapp: *Djur och stilleben i karolinskt måleri* [Animals and still-lifes in Caroline painting] (Stockholm, 1951), pp. 75–145
R. Josephson: '*Ehrenstrahls målarlära*' [Ehrenstrahl's theory of painting], Svenska Humanistiska Förbundet (Stockholm, 1959)
A. Ellenius: *Karolinska bildidéer* [Caroline pictorial ideas] (Uppsala, 1967)

ALLAN ELLENIUS

Ehrensvärd, Carl August (*b* Stockholm, 5 May 1745; *d* Örebrö, 21 May 1800). Swedish naval officer, draughtsman and writer. His father was founder and commanding officer of the Sveaborg Fort in Finland, which belonged at that time to Sweden. There Ehrensvärd grew up and as part of his education was instructed by the most eminent Swedish watercolour painter, Elias Martin (ii). His naval career was broken off by a trip of decisive importance to Italy (1780–82), which resulted in his producing a series of watercolours and writing *Resa til Italien, 1780, 1781, 1782* ('Journey to Italy, 1780, 1781, 1782') and *De fria konsters philosophi* ('Philosophy of the liberal arts'). These were both published in 1786 and are among 18th-century Sweden's most remarkable books on art. They reflected the author's contacts with Neo-classicism throughout Europe, contemporary theories on climate and physiognomy and, not least, ideas that constitute an early manifestation of Functionalism.

Under the influence of a visit to Paestum, Ehrensvärd executed studies of Classical buildings in a Nordic landscape and designs for dockyard buildings at Karlskrona that employ a Greek Doric order of extraordinarily squat proportions. Other works included a series of drawings influenced by English caricature art, parodying the political and moral atrocities of his time, and he frequently collaborated with the draughtsman and sculptor JOHAN TOBIAS SERGEL. He formulated his aesthetic ideas in an extensive series of wash-drawings entitled *Poetens Historia* ('History of the poet'), dedicated to the poet Johan Gabriel Oxenstierna, showing a poet and an artist being trained aesthetically and morally so as to be able to create works to equal those of Classical times. Another, equally personal series was entitled *Snillets lek i svenska historien* ('The genius's game in Swedish history'), comprising watercolour medallions depicting motifs from Sweden's history in a gently ironic and satirical light.

WRITINGS
De fria konsters philosophi (Stockholm, 1786)
Resa til Italien, 1780, 1781, 1782 (Stockholm, 1786/*R* 1948)
Skrifter, 2 vols (Stockholm, 1922–5)

BIBLIOGRAPHY
R. Josephson: *Carl August Ehrensvärd* (Stockholm, 1963)
H. Frykenstedt: *Carl August Ehrensvärd: An Original Swedish Aesthetician and an Early Functionalist* (Uppsala, 1965)
——: *Studier i Carl August Ehrensvärds författarskap* [Studies on Carl August Ehrensvärd's authorship] (Stockholm, 1965)
——: *Carl August Ehrensvärd: Poetens historia* (Stockholm, 1969)
——: *Idé och verklighet i C. A. Ehrensvärds karikatyrer* [Idea and reality in the caricatures of C. A. Ehrensvärd] (Stockholm, 1974)

HOLGER FRYKENSTEDT

Ehrenzweig, Anton (*b* Vienna, 1908; *d* London, 5 Dec 1966). Austrian writer, theorist and teacher. He studied law, psychology and art and was appointed as a magistrate in Vienna in 1936 before leaving for England in 1938. Here he made a substantial reputation for himself as a teacher and lecturer and published a large number of studies, including *The Psycho-analysis of Artistic Vision and Hearing* (1953). At the time of his death he was a Lecturer in Art Education at Goldsmiths' College, University of London, and had just completed his most important work, *The Hidden Order of Art* (pubd 1967).

Ehrenzweig's distinctive contribution to the understanding of the visual arts depended on the fact that he worked at a tangent from traditional art history. He greatly admired the way in which his fellow exile from Austria, E. H. Gombrich, provided a psychological interpretation of stylistic change in *Art and Illusion* (London, 1960). But Ehrenzweig's own engagement as a teacher was with the immediate and practical problems of textile design. It was through pondering the question of what made a particular motif 'fertile'—capable of being repeated without its interest being exhausted—that he came to conclusions that also appeared valid for the advanced art of his own period. An 'over-visualized' motif implied too great a degree of conscious control by the student. It was only by blocking out 'ego rigidity', and involving the lower levels of mental organization, that a dynamic space could be obtained.

In his careful elaboration of this central idea, Ehrenzweig was deeply reliant on the writings of Sigmund Freud, while at the same time he was willing to modify and extend Freud's basic concepts in accordance with his own experience. Similarly he accepted, without repeating, much of the subsequent work on the creative process done by figures such as Melanie Klein (1882–1960), Marion Milner (*b* 1900) and Adrian Stokes. His own specific contribution is summed up in the concept of 'dedifferentiation', which he used to explain the process by which the ego scatters and represses surface imagery, thus achieving a structure that can only be grasped by 'syncretistic vision'. In arguing for the acceptance of this principle, Ehrenzweig was able to point to a range of examples in the art of his time. Although he believed Paul Cézanne might have pioneered the use of the total, undifferentiated field of vision, it was even more evident in the work of a contemporary artist such as Jackson Pollock, or in that of British artists such as Bridget Riley and Eduardo Paolozzi, whom he knew and admired. Ehrenzweig was convinced that the difference between good abstract art and mere decoration hinges upon the possibility of involving the deeper levels of the mind. He therefore offered powerful warnings against the tendency of post-war abstraction to degenerate into an empty mannerism.

WRITINGS
The Psycho-analysis of Artistic Vision and Hearing: An Introduction to a Theory of Unconscious Perception (London, 1953, 3/1975)
The Hidden Order of Art: A Study in the Psychology of Artistic Imagination (London, 1967)

BIBLIOGRAPHY
M. Milner: '1967: The Hidden Order of Art', *The Suppressed Madness of Sane Men* (London, 1988)

STEPHEN BANN

Ehret, Georg Dionysius (*b* Heidelberg, 30 Jan 1708; *d* London, 9 Sept 1770). German draughtsman and painter, active also in England. While working as a gardener, he used his free time to draw plants, persevering until he abandoned gardening altogether. His lifelong patron, Dr Christoph Jacob Trew (1695–1769) of Nuremberg, instructed him in botany and provided him with good-quality paper. Journeying, mainly on foot, through Switzerland and France, he learnt in Paris the technique of painting on vellum. In Holland he met Linnaeus (1707–78), to whose *Hortus Cliffortianus* (Amsterdam, 1737–8) he contributed several botanical illustrations and whose system of plant classification he made known by publishing a '*tabella*' (Leiden, 1736).

In 1736 Ehret settled permanently in England. He first worked with Philip Miller (1691–1771), head of the Chelsea Physic Garden, whose sister-in-law he married, then found patrons among scientists who commissioned him to illustrate their botanical articles and travel books. He published his own engraved and hand-coloured plant-book, *Plantae et papiliones rariores* (London, 1748–62). He was elected an FRS (1757) and a member of the Leopoldina in Germany (1758). The patronage of rich garden-owners, such as the Duchess of Portland, provided him with financial subsistence but never with security. To supplement his income he later 'taught the daughters of the English noblesse flower-painting and botanique', as he writes in his autobiography.

Ehret's unsurpassed plant drawings, painted in gouache on a white background, are on paper, usually 340×210 mm before his settling in England, afterwards on vellum between 450 to 560 mm by 300 to 365 mm, and they are signed G. D. EHRET. The potteries of Chelsea (1754–6) and Tournai (?1775) copied them to decorate their dishes. The largest collection of Ehret's drawings is at Knowsley Hall, Lancs.

BIBLIOGRAPHY
C. J. Trew, ed.: *Plantae selectae* (Nuremberg, 1750–73)
——: *Cedrorum libani historia*, i and ii (Nuremberg, 1757 and 1767)
——: *Hortus nitidissimus* (Nuremberg, 1758–82)
——: 'Herrn Georg Dionysius Ehret bisherige Lebens-Umstände nach seinen eigenem am 22 Oct. 1758 zugeschickten Entwurf mit einigen Anmerkungen ausgefertigt von Dr Christoph Jac. Trew', trans. E. S. Barton, *Linnean. Soc. Proc.* (1894–5), pp. 41ff
A. H. Uggla: 'G. D. Ehret's vaxt planch over sexual systemet', *Svensk. Linné Sällsk. Årsskr.*, xxii (Stockholm, 1939), pp. 108–13
W. Blunt: *G. D. Ehret* (Guildford, 1956)
C. Murdoch: *G. D. Ehret: Botanical Artist* (Inverness, 1970)
W. L. Tjaden 'Georg Dionysius Ehret: Flower Painter Supreme', *J. Royal Hort. Soc.*, xcv (1970), pp. 585ff
G. Calmann: *Ehret: Flower Painter Extraordinary* (Oxford, 1977)

GERTA CALMANN

Ehrlich, Georg (*b* Vienna, 22 Feb 1897; *d* Lucerne, 1 July 1966). British sculptor, printmaker and painter of Austrian birth. He studied at the Kunstgewerbeschule in Vienna between 1912 and 1915. His first mature works date from *c.* 1918. In 1919 he moved to Munich, and then to Berlin in 1921, where, under contract to Paul Cassirer, his work was exhibited alongside that of Ernst Barlach, Oskar Kokoschka and Wilhelm Lehmbruck. He returned to Vienna in 1923, with a considerable reputation as an Expressionist printmaker. Many of his etchings and lithographs are religious in subject-matter, such as the *Crucifixion* (lithograph, 1920; Vienna, Albertina), full of *Angst* born largely of his experiences as a soldier in World War I.

Ehrlich made his first sculpture in 1926, an activity that subsequently took precedence over printmaking, although he was also painting landscapes in oils. In 1928 he executed his first public commission as a sculptor, a monument to the blind organist *Joseph Labor* (Vienna, Cent. Cemetery). He moved to England in 1937 and was joined by his wife, Bettina [née Bauer] (1902–85), also a painter, and he became a British subject in 1947. After 1962, when he was elected an ARA, he lived in Austria, Germany, Italy and Switzerland.

Ehrlich favoured bronze for his sculptures, which comprised mainly portraits—many of them of musical celebrities, such as *Benjamin Britten* (bronze, 1950–52; Peter Pears priv. col., see 1968 exh. cat., no. 28)—quasi-symbolic figure compositions and images of animals. With the exception of the portraits, he never modelled from life. Elegant simplification of form, which in his later works tends towards distortion reminiscent of Wilhelm Lehmbruck or Georg Minne, and a sense of pathos verging on sentimentality are the keynotes of his art.

BIBLIOGRAPHY
E. Tietze-Conrat: *Georg Ehrlich* (London, 1956)
E. Rathenau, ed.: *Georg Ehrlich's Sketchbook* (New York, 1963)
Georg Ehrlich (exh. cat. by Lord Croft and P. Pears, London, O'Hana Gal., 1968)
Georg Ehrlich, Plastiken und Zeichnungen (exh. cat. by R. Mikula, Vienna, Hist. Mus., 1976)
Georg Ehrlich (exh. cat. by A. Haskell, Bruton Gal., 1978)
                    MONICA BOHM-DUCHEN

Ehrlich, Hugo (*b* Zagreb, 31 Jan 1879; *d* Zagreb, 21 Sept 1936). Croatian architect. He studied at the Technische Hochschule, Vienna (1897–1903). He then became an associate of Adolf Loos and also worked until 1909 on the restoration of the Burg Kreuzenstein, near Korneuburg, Austria, under the direction of Friedrich Ohmann. Erlich's most significant undertaking of the period was the completion (1906) of the Villa Karma, Clarens, Switzerland, begun by Loos in 1904 but abandoned after arguments with the client, the psychiatrist Theodor Beer. Ehrlich subtly interpreted Loos's original concept and created a seminal building of modern architecture. He added pergolas to the four corners of the pure cube of the original design, thereby relating the building to the landscape in a way not originally envisaged by Loos. In 1909 Ehrlich returned to Zagreb and until 1918 worked in partnership with VIKTOR KOVAČIĆ. These two architects represented the avant-garde movement in Zagreb at that time, and they achieved important works including the urbanization and layout of Strossmayer Square; the Grand Café Medulić; the Frank House (1913–14); and several villas at Josipovac (all in Zagreb). In 1922, together with Loos, Ehrlich designed an alternative project (unexecuted) for the Hotel Esplanade in Zagreb. On Kovačić's death in 1924, Ehrlich succeeded him as Professor of Architecture at the newly established High Technical School, Zagreb; he also completed the building of the Stock Exchange (1923–4), Zagreb, designed by Kovačić. In the 1920s and 1930s Ehrlich designed a series of prominent buildings in Zagreb, including the Slav Bank (1921–3), Vlaška Street; the Industrial Bank (1924–5), 38 Ilica; the Pension Fund Building (1934), Jelačić Square; and several villas.

BIBLIOGRAPHY
P. Tvrtković: 'Yugoslav Architecture Today', *Archit. Des.*, xxviii (1958), pp. 199–203
——: 'Shades of Zagreb', *Bldg Des.*, 895 (1988), pp. 14–17
                    PAUL TVRTKOVIĆ

Ei, Kyū [Sugita, Hideo] (*b* Miyazaki Prefect., 28 April 1911; *d* Tokyo, 10 March 1960). Japanese photographer, painter, printmaker and critic. In 1925 he entered the department of *yōga* (Western-style painting) at the Japanese School of Art in Tokyo. In 1926 he began writing art criticism and in 1927 he left the School, going on in 1930 to study at the School of Oriental Photography, Tokyo. In 1934 he returned to Miyazaki and studied Esperanto, going back two years later to Tokyo; thereafter he rejected his real name of Hideo Sugita in favour of his pseudonym, which was suggested by Saburō Hasegawa. His first exhibition, a one-man show of photograms (Tokyo, 1936), was based on drawings that used photographic paper. His collection of photograms, *Nemuri no riyū*, was also published in 1936. In 1937 he was a founder-member of the Jiyū Bijutsuka Kyōkai (Independent Art Society) and in Osaka, of the Demokurāto Bijutsuka Kyōkai (Democratic Art Society); from then on he produced etchings, also making lithographs from 1956. In 1957 he exhibited *Travellers* (lithograph; Tokyo, Nat. Mus. Mod. A.) in the first Tokyo International Print Biennale. In 1959 he painted *Pastoral B* (Miyazaki, Prefect. Lib.). An exhibition of his oil paintings was held in 1960 at the Kabutoga Gallery in Tokyo.

PHOTOGRAPHIC PUBLICATIONS
Nemuri no riyū [The reason of sleep] (Tokyo, 1936)
BIBLIOGRAPHY
Gendai bijutsu no chichi Ei Kyū [The father of modern art—Kyū Ei] (exh. cat., essay by T. Kubo; Tokyo, Odakyū Grand Gal., 1979)
Ei Kyū To Sono Shūhen [Kyū Ei and his circle] (exh. cat., essay by S. Segi; Urawa, Saitama, Prefect., Mus. Mod. A., 1986)
                    YASUYOSHI SAITO

Eibisch, Eugeniusz (*b* Lublin, 7 Jan 1896; *d* Warsaw, 7 March 1987). Polish painter. He studied at the Kraków Academy of Fine Arts (1912–20) under Jacek Malczewski and Wojciech Weiss. Formism (*see* FORMISTS) influenced his first works, such as *Swings* (1921; Kraków, Halina Lisowska priv. col.), but soon he moved to Polish Colourism and was faithful to its principles for the rest of his prolific career. His stay in Paris (1923–39) was successful. He had a few exhibitions and dealt with some of the best Paris dealers. He befriended the French novelist Roger Martin du Gard, who used him as a model for one of his characters in *Les Thibault*. He never joined any group, but in 1926 he exhibited in Kraków with the Jednoróg group. On returning to Poland he was appointed a professor at the Academy of Fine Arts in Kraków (1939–50), and then in Warsaw. He painted serene still-lifes, interiors and portraits, such as *Sisters* (1949; Warsaw, N. Mus.). His technique derived from Post-Impressionism; his paintings were carefully composed, based on perspective and the actual relationship between objects, as in *Self-portrait with Wife* (1963; Poznań, N. Mus.). He renounced any interest in abstraction, but some of his works are close to it, with characteristic 'blurred' contours.

BIBLIOGRAPHY
Eugeniusz Eibisch: Obrazy olejne, rysunki [Oil paintings, drawings] (exh. cat., ed. J. Zanoziński; Warsaw, N. Mus., 1967)

ANNA BENTKOWSKA

Eichel, Emanuel, II (*b* Augsburg, 1717; *d* Augsburg, *bur* 12 May 1782). German engraver and draughtsman. He was the son of the ebonist and draughtsman Emanuel Eichel I (1690–1751) and a pupil of the engraver Johann Daniel Herz the elder (1693–1754). He was director and teacher in the drawing department of the Protestant Kollegium of St Anna in Augsburg. Eichel was a versatile, if not particularly original, engraver. His subjects included architecture, landscape, illustrations of historical subjects and saints, portraits, animals and ornament, usually after works by other artists but sometimes, particularly in the case of ornament, after his own designs. The engravings were mainly published by Augsburg firms: deserving of special mention are his engraved view of the organ by Johann Andreas Stein in the Barfüsserkirche, Augsburg (pubd by Johann Esaias Nilson), the print after G. M. Kraus's copy of the Holbein portrait of *Thomas More*, illustrations in Thomas Permont's *Britische Tiergeschichten* (pubd by Johann Elias Haid) and his own ornamental engravings (pubd mostly by Johann Georg Hertel).

BIBLIOGRAPHY
Thieme–Becker
A. Hämmerle: 'Die Familie Eichel', *Schwäb. Mus.*, ii (1926), pp. 57–8

EBBA KRULL

Eichholtz, Jacob (*b* Lancaster, PA, 2 Nov 1776; *d* Lancaster, 11 May 1842). American painter. He trained as a coppersmith and was encouraged to paint by Thomas Sully, who visited Lancaster in 1808 and used his studio. From that point Eichholtz began to paint on canvas instead of panels. Always attempting to improve his work, he visited the portrait painter Gilbert Stuart in Boston about 1811 and soon afterwards turned entirely to painting. He lived in Philadelphia for ten years from 1822, and by the time he moved back to Lancaster he had become one of the leading portrait painters in Philadelphia and Baltimore. His earliest works (*c.* 1808–10) were stiff profile views, but these flat, colourless works gave way to more ornate, even elegant, freshly coloured, three-quarter views. He exhibited almost every year from 1811 to 1833 at the Pennsylvania Academy of the Fine Arts, Philadelphia, which holds the largest group of his paintings.

BIBLIOGRAPHY
R. Beal: *Jacob Eichholtz, 1776–1842: Portrait Painter of Pennsylvania* (Philadelphia, 1969)
Jacob Eichholtz, 1776–1842, Pennsylvania Painter: A Retrospective Exhibition (exh. cat., intro. E. P. Richardson; Philadelphia, PA Acad. F.A., 1969)

DARRYL PATRICK

Eichler, Gottfried, I (*b* Liebstadt bei Pirna, Saxony, 28 March 1677; *d* Augsburg, 8 May 1759). German painter, draughtsman and engraver. The son of the cabinetmaker Heinrich Eichler, he studied with Johann Heiss in Augsburg (1696–1703), then made prolonged study trips to Italy. In Rome he met Benedetto Luti and Carlo Maratti and became friends with Jan Kupecký. In 1705 he painted at Schloss Ludwigsburg for the Württemberg court and in 1707 accompanied Kupecký to Vienna. In 1713 he married and became a master in Augsburg, where from 1742 he was the Protestant director of the academy and also court painter to the Palatinate.

Eichler's oeuvre, which includes many works seemingly produced quickly and consists almost exclusively of painted, drawn and engraved portraits, has yet to be studied as a whole: most of these portraits, notably of high-ranking, usually evangelical personalities from Augsburg, are only known in engraved copies, often by Johann Jakob Haid (1704–67). The majority are rather mediocre, but the *Self-portrait* (Augsburg, Städt. Kstsammlungen) is extremely wittily conceived—the figure examining the onlooker critically through his glasses is close to Kupecký—and there is a series of wonderful early classical portraits (e.g. *Portrait of a Man*, 1744; Prague, N.G.). None of his few religious pictures has survived.

BIBLIOGRAPHY
B. Bushart: 'Augsburg und die Wende der deutschen Kunst um 1750', *Festschrift für Werner Gross* (Munich, 1968), p. 295
Deutsche Barockgalerie: Katalog der Gemälde, Augsburg, Städt. Kstsammlungen cat., ii (1984), pp. 65ff

GODE KRÄMER

Eidlitz. American family of architects of Bohemian origin. (1) Leopold Eidlitz became one of the most influential architects in the USA during the 19th century. Responsible for many New York City churches and for government buildings in the state capital of Albany, he was also a founder of the American Institute of Architects. His son, (2) Cyrus L. W. Eidlitz, is perhaps best known for his New York Times building in Times Square, New York.

(1) Leopold Eidlitz (*b* Prague, 29 March 1823; *d* New York, 22 March 1908). He studied estate management and construction at the polytechnic in Vienna. In 1843 he settled in New York and entered the architectural office of Richard Upjohn. Among the active projects in Upjohn's office during Eidlitz's brief stay were the Gothic Revival style Trinity Church (*c.* 1839–46), New York, and the *Rundbogenstil*-inspired church of the Pilgrims (1844–6), Brooklyn. In 1846 Eidlitz and the German-born architect Otto Blesch received a commission from the evangelical congregation of St George's Episcopal Church, Stuyvesant Square, New York. The use of *Rundbogenstil* motifs on St George's reflects the influence of Upjohn's church of the Pilgrims but, more importantly, indicates both Eidlitz and Blesch's debt to contemporary work in southern Germany, particularly to the *Rundbogenstil* buildings of the Munich architect Friedrich von Gärtner. According to Montgomery Schuyler, Blesch was responsible for the exterior of St George's, while Eidlitz designed the interior. The layout of the interior was unusual for an Episcopal church in that it was an open rectangular space, more akin to a Protestant meeting-house. Eidlitz supervised the construction of the entire building and rebuilt the interior after a fire in 1865.

The success of St George's led to Eidlitz receiving several commissions from Episcopal and Protestant congregations. Each of his churches had exposed timber roofs that clearly expressed the building's structure. Among the finest of Eidlitz's churches are the Congregational Church (1856–9), Greenwich, CT, with its German-inspired openwork stone spire, and St Peter's Episcopal Church (1853–5; chapel, 1867–8; restored by Cyrus L. W. Eidlitz following a fire in 1879), Westchester Avenue, Bronx, New York. Eidlitz was also responsible for one of New York's most important 19th-century synagogues, Temple Emanu-El (1866–8; with Henry Fernbach; destr. 1901), Fifth Avenue, noted for its distinctive combination of Romanesque and Moorish motifs. Eidlitz's most famous church was Holy Trinity Episcopal Church (1870–75; destr. 1901), Madison Avenue and East 42nd Street, New York: its bold polychromatic brick exterior evoked the appellation 'Church of the Homely Oilcloth'. The plan of Holy Trinity was extremely unusual, with an elliptical auditorium set within rectangular walls.

Eidlitz was also active in the design of commercial and civic buildings. His earliest commercial works, such as the Continental Bank (1856–9; destr. 1901), Nassau Street, New York, and the American Exchange Bank (1857; destr. 1899), Broadway, New York, were stone structures with the rusticated bases, arched windows and rusticated voussoirs found on such German buildings as von Gärtner's Staatsbibliothek (1832–43), Munich. The Produce Exchange (1860–61; destr. 1885), Whitehall Street, New York, and the Academy of Music (1860–61; destr. by fire 1903), Montague Street, Brooklyn, were Eidlitz's most successful efforts at manipulating façade elements to reflect interior spaces. Ornament was kept to a minimum on both buildings, but each had a dramatic street presence.

In the mid-1870s Eidlitz received two major civic commissions. In 1875 he joined H. H. Richardson in the completion of the New York State Capitol, Albany. Eidlitz was responsible for the Assembly Chamber, the Golden Corridor and the Senate Staircase. The Assembly Chamber, described by Schuyler as 'perhaps the noblest monument to the Gothic revival in America' (*Archit. Rec.*, xxiv, p. 369), was a medieval-inspired 17-m high room with a stencilled stone-vaulted ceiling supported on granite columns. Ironically, although Eidlitz had a deep concern for structure, both the Assembly Chamber ceiling and the Golden Corridor proved to be structurally unsound and were dismantled in 1888–9. In 1876 Eidlitz was commissioned to complete John Kellum's New York County Courthouse ('Tweed Courthouse'), begun in 1861. Eidlitz added a Romanesque-inspired wing to Kellum's Italianate building. The stylistic contrast between the wings was widely condemned, although Schuyler notes that Eidlitz was 'puzzled by the commotion' (*Archit. Rec.*, xxiv, p. 374). Eidlitz's last major work was undertaken for his first client. In 1886 he designed a Clergy House for St George's. This rough-hewn brownstone structure (now converted into flats), with its clear exterior delineation of interior spaces, is a perfect complement to the church.

Eidlitz's reputation as one of the most influential architects in the USA between the 1840s and 1890s was also due to his role as a founder of the American Institute of Architects and as an active participant in its affairs. He often delivered papers at the Institute's meetings and his comments, printed in *Crayon*, were some of the first architectural criticism and theory published in the USA. Through his talks and papers, the publication of his lengthy theoretical tract *Nature and the Function of Art, More Especially of Architecture* (1881), and his buildings, Eidlitz had a widespread influence on his contemporaries that began to be understood only later. Because so few of Eidlitz's major buildings survive, it is difficult to comprehend fully his career. He was deeply committed to the view, inspired by medieval architecture, that structure should determine form. He believed that a building's mass should grow directly from its plan and that materials should be used in a clear structural manner, with ornament added only to accent structure, material and function. These concerns are evident in his finest work.

WRITINGS

'Christian Architecture', *Crayon*, v (1858), pp. 53–5
Crayon, v (1858), pp. 109–11 [untitled address at the first annual dinner of the American Institute of Architects]
'On Style', *Crayon*, v (1858), pp. 139–442
'Cast Iron Architecture', *Crayon*, vi (1859), pp. 20–24
'The Architect', *Crayon*, vi (1859), pp. 99–100
'On Aesthetics in Architecture', *Crayon*, viii (1861), pp. 111–13
The Nature and Function of Art, More Especially of Architecture (New York, 1881/R 1977)

BIBLIOGRAPHY

M. Schuyler: 'The Evolution of a Skyscraper', *Archit. Rec.*, xiv (1903), no. 5, pp. 329–43
——: 'A Great American Architect: Leopold Eidlitz, I. Ecclesiastical and Domestic Work', *Archit. Rec.*, xxiv (1908), no. 3, pp. 163–79
——: 'The Work of Leopold Eidlitz: II. Commercial and Public', *Archit. Rec.*, xxiv (1908), no. 4, pp. 277–92
——: 'The Work of Leopold Eidlitz: III. The Capitol at Albany', *Archit. Rec.*, xxiv (1908), no. 5, pp. 364–78
W. Weisman: 'Commercial Palaces of New York: 1845–1875', *A. Bull.*, xxxvi (1954), pp. 285–302
H. Brooks: 'Leopold Eidlitz: 1823–1908' (MA diss., New Haven, CT, Yale U., 1955)
W. Jordy and R. Coe, eds: *American Architecture and Other Writings by Montgomery Schuyler* (Cambridge, MA, 1961/R New York, 1964), pp. 3–53
B. Erdmann: *Leopold Eidlitz's Architectural Theories and American Transcendentalism* (diss., Madison, U. WI, 1977; R Ann Arbor, 1978)
A. Bedell and M. Dierickx: *The Tweed Courthouse Historic Structure Report* (New York, 1980)
Master Plan for the New York State Capitol (Albany, 1982)

(2) Cyrus L(azelle) W(arner) Eidlitz (*b* New York, 27 July 1853; *d* Southampton, NY, 5 Oct 1921). Son of (1) Leopold Eidlitz. He was sent to school in Geneva and at the age of 15 enrolled in the department of architecture at the polytechnic in Stuttgart. In 1871 he entered his father's New York office. He continued to share an office with his father even after he established an independent career. Eidlitz's earliest independent works, such as the Buffalo Library (1884–7; destr.), Buffalo, NY, and Dearborn Station (completed 1885; altered after a fire in 1922), South Dearborn Street, Chicago, were monumental Romanesque Revival style works. In the 1880s he became active in the design of skyscrapers. His earliest have Romanesque details, but by the 1890s he was breaking away from his father's medievalism to make use of Renaissance ornament. Eidlitz's most famous works include the New York Times building (1903–5; stripped 1966), Times Square, New York. This trapezoidal tower, with Renaissance- and Gothic-inspired terracotta cladding, had a sophisticated skeletal frame set around a new subway station.

DAB

BIBLIOGRAPHY
M. Schuyler: 'Cyrus L. W. Eidlitz', *Archit. Rec.*, v (1896), no. 4, pp. 411–35

ANDREW SCOTT DOLKART

Eidograph. *See* PANTOGRAPH.

Eidophusokon. 'Moving picture' device invented by PHILIPPE JACQUES DE LOUTHERBOURG and first exhibited in London in 1782. Views of London and scenes such as a storm at sea were shown together with sound effects and various lights and coloured gauzes to imitate the different times of day.

BIBLIOGRAPHY
P. J. de Loutherbourg: *Morning Herald* (25 Dec 1784)
E. Hardcastle: *Wine and Walnuts* (London, 1823) [eyewitness account]

Eiebakke, August (*b* Askim, 25 April 1867; *d* Oslo, 21 July 1938). Norwegian painter. He went to live in Kristiania [now Oslo] when he was 15. He wished to train as a sculptor and enrolled at the Royal School of Drawing in Kristiania in 1883, studying there until 1889 under Julius Middelthun, Mathias Skeibrok (1851–96) and Harald Petersen (1850–1933). At this time Eiebakke grew more interested in painting and from 1886 to 1887 took instruction from the leading Norwegian Naturalist painters Christian Krohg, Hans Heyerdahl and Eilif Peterssen. Eiebakke made his début at the Kristiania Autumn Exhibition in 1887 with a landscape and an interior. He exhibited regularly at this exhibition and won special praise for *Laying the Table* (Oslo, N.G.) in 1891. During this period Eiebakke concentrated on realistic depictions of human subjects and landscape. In 1892 he spent several months at Kristian Zahrtmann's school of painting in Copenhagen and for a time his work showed the influence of his teacher. In 1893 he went to Paris and the following year made the first of many visits to Italy. Here he approached a more stylized, Neo-Romantic form resembling the style that Danish colleagues such as Peter Rostrup Bøiesen (*b* 1882), Karl Schou (1870–1938) and Vilhelm Tetens (1871–1956) were using. For a time he also worked on religious themes, for example *Jesus and Thomas* (Oslo, Frogner Church). Eiebakke won a gold medal at the Exposition Universelle in Paris in 1900.

After the turn of the century Eiebakke's use of colour in landscapes, interiors and portraits became more lively, for example *T. Schjelderup-Ebbe* (1914; Oslo, Bymus.). In 1910 he became a teacher at the Kristiania Royal School of Drawing, where he was director from 1912 to 1937. Although he never had a one-man exhibition, a retrospective was arranged at the Oslo Society of Art in 1939.

BIBLIOGRAPHY
J. Thiis: *Norske malere og billedhuggere* [Norwegian painters and sculptors], ii (Bergen, 1907), pp. 360–63
Catalogue of the Exhibition of Work by Modern Norwegian Artists (exh. cat., Brighton, Pub. A. Gals, 1913), pp. xix, 28, 44, 48
Norges kunsthistorie [History of Norwegian art], v (Oslo, 1981), pp. 243, 246, 453
Norsk Kunstnerleksikon [Encyclopedia of Norwegian artists], i (Oslo, 1982), pp. 547–8 [incl. bibliog.]
Dreams of a Summer Night (exh. cat., ACGB, 1986), pp. 84–6

TONE SKEDSMO

Eiermann, Egon (*b* Neuendorf, nr Berlin, 29 Sept 1904; *d* Baden-Baden, 19 July 1970). German architect and teacher. He studied at the Technische Hochschule, Berlin (1923–7), and was a pupil of Hans Poelzig there (1925–8). In 1931 Eiermann founded his own practice in Berlin with Fritz Jaenecke (1903–78), who moved to Sweden in 1935. They built a number of single-family houses which were aesthetically functional and restrained. Examples include the Haus Hesse (1933), 44 Siemenstrasse, Lankwitz, Berlin, and the Haus Dienstbach (1936), Nikolassee, Berlin, both using painted brickwork with relatively large windows. During the 1930s Eiermann also worked on film and theatre projects and designed a series of strikingly modern shops (1934–7) for the undertakers Grieneisen in Berlin. Despite voicing sharp criticism of the emerging architectural style of the Nazis in 1935, he was able to stay in Berlin during World War II and keep his office going with essential wartime projects. In 1947 he was appointed Professor of the Architectural Faculty at the Technische Hochschule, Karlsruhe. He also established an office there and built up a prolific and influential practice during the period of reconstruction after World War II. He promoted Moderne Sachlichkeit in the public arena and participated in numerous public competitions, also acting as a judge, for example in the competition for the design of buildings for the Olympic Games in Munich in 1972. Although he was artistic by temperament, Eiermann's architectural philosophy was strictly rational, and the conflict between the two occupied him throughout his life. His aim was to avoid using mere intuition to create an effect that he could not justify in the given situation. Instead he investigated various architectural elements which he then perfected in relation to their function and construction, thus achieving architectural order. Eiermann regarded all buildings as functional, and he therefore rejected the language of symbolism by which a building could be specifically defined. His designs and elevations therefore reveal such simple forms as the rectangle or square, similar to those found in the work of Mies van der Rohe.

An early example of Eiermann's additive method of design is the Taschentuchweberei Blumberg (1949–51), where he places the heating plant next to the factory and the chimneys next to the heating plant. Another early example of his additive design is the façade of the headquarters of Vereinigte Seidenwebereien Krefeld (1951–53), which comprises identical elements. The German Pavilion (1958; destr.; reconstructed) at the Exposition Universelle et Internationale, which he designed with Sep Ruf, comprised several individual buildings spread over a large area and linked by open walkways. In this way he was able to leave behind the closed building type. His work was more open and transparent and even the façades developed into spacious open areas carefully formed and technically equipped to cope with the prevailing weather conditions. The most important examples of his personal style in the following period are his own home (1952–62) in Baden-Baden, the lightness and detail of which is reminiscent of Japanese architecture, the Chancellery (1958–64) of the German Embassy in Washington, DC, in which the mass of the structure is broken up by terraces, and the administration and training centre (1968–72) of Deutsche Olivetti in Frankfurt, which reflects his mastery in combining and separating diverse construction elements. The Kaiser-Wilhelm-Gedächtniskirche (1957–63), Berlin, is an exception in its use of non-rectangular forms: having failed to resolve a design based on a series of circles, he grouped around the war-damaged remains of a 19th-century church an arrangement of four starkly Modernist buildings based on geometric forms including the cube and octahedron.

Detailing was important, as it enabled him to express an artistic approach through the use of materials, like a craftsman or engineer. He therefore respected the integrity of such materials as steel, wood and textiles, and he emphasized precision of workmanship and clarity of form. By these means his buildings achieved a distinctive elegance and beauty based on their functionalism. Eiermann's interest in design extended to furniture and even to his own coffin. He received many prestigious national and international awards during his career.

WRITINGS

'Einige Bemerkungen über Technik und Bauform', *Baukst & Werkform*, i (1947), pp. 45–8
'Der arbeitende Mensch und die Technik', *Baukst & Werkform*, x (1951), pp. 13–29
with H. Kuhlmann: *Planungsstudie Verwaltungsgebäude am Beispiel für die IBM-Deutschland* (Stuttgart, 1967)

BIBLIOGRAPHY

'Architekten aus Poelzigs Schule: Häuser und Räume von Egon Eiermann', *Bauwelt*, xxviii (1935), pp. 1–5
A. Leitl: 'Vom Sauerteig des Künstlerischen', *Baukst & Werkform*, iv (1951), pp. 23–44
U. Kultermann: *Architektur der Gegenwart*, Kunst der Welt (Baden-Baden, 1967), pp. 145, 162, 189–90
H. W. Rosenthal: 'Egon Eiermann, 1904–1970', *J. RIBA*, lxxviii (1971), p. 41
'Headquarters of Olivetti Germany', *A & U*, iv/6 (1974), pp. 91–9
E. Lucie-Smith, S. Hunter and A. M. Vost: *Kunst der Gegenwart*, Propyläen-Kstgesch. (Frankfurt am Main, 1978), pp. 133, 308–9
W. Schirmer, ed.: *Egon Eiermann, 1904–1970: Bauten und Projekte* (Stuttgart, 1984)

THOMAS SPERLING

Eiffel, Gustave (*b* Dijon, 15 Dec 1832: *d* Paris, 27 Dec 1923). French engineer and writer. He began his advanced studies at the Ecole Polytechnique in Paris in 1850 but failed examinations during his first year; he subsequently enrolled at the Ecole Centrale des Arts et Manufactures, where he earned a diploma in chemical engineering. In 1856 he received his first major engineering commission, the iron railway bridge (completed 1860) over the River Garonne at Bordeaux. Aged only 26, he was given total control of the project; his use of compressed air to drive the pier foundations was an early application in France of this new technology. His lifelong concern for close site supervision was also already in evidence on this project: when the bridge was finished in 1860, the workers were so grateful for Eiffel's personal involvement that they presented him with a medal.

At the end of 1866 Eiffel established his own company at Levallois-Perret on the outskirts of Paris. Much of the most profitable work produced by the company over the next several decades was in small, demountable bridges that were widely exported, especially to Indo-China and South America. For the Exposition Universelle of 1867 in Paris, Eiffel displayed his talent for more complicated engineering problems by preparing a complete set of calculations for the span of the Galerie des Machines, one of the first such studies on arch behaviour. Between 1867 and 1869 he completed four large-scale viaducts in southern France, one of the most important being the viaduct over the River Sioule, where two iron towers 59 m high support the structure from the valley below. The towers, which are tapered to compensate more efficiently for wind resistance, were early structural precursors of the famous Eiffel Tower completed 20 years later.

In the 1870s Eiffel's firm took on increasingly ambitious and demanding projects, many of them outside France. A rare example of monumental architecture in his career was the central station (1875) in Pest (now Budapest) commissioned by the Austrian State Railways. This station departed significantly from general custom in leaving a considerable portion of the metal structural elements exposed on the façade. For the commission of the Ponte Doña Maria I, a bridge over the River Douro in Oporto, Eiffel's company prevailed over several larger competitors because, with his design making much more efficient use of materials, he could greatly underbid them. Eiffel, who again supervised all work on the site, used five piers of varying length and a central parabolic arch of 160 m span to support a continuous girder 353 m long. Completed in 1877, the Douro bridge was then the largest non-suspension bridge in the world. Its design was repeated in many of Eiffel's later structures, the most significant being the Garabit railway viaduct (completed 1884) over the River Truyère south of Clermont-Ferrand. Here the route was over an unusually deep valley with difficult terrain; the tallest of the supporting piers is 89 m high and the span of the central arch 165 m.

Although still specializing primarily in bridges and viaducts, Eiffel began to work in several other areas of design in the 1870s. In 1875 he built a large church with a cast-iron framework in Tacna, Peru. In 1878 he was a major contributor to the Exposition Universelle in Paris, where he was responsible for the structural design of the pavilion of the city of Paris, and of the iron and glass entrance vestibule on the façade of the main Champ-de-Mars complex. The delicate transparency of its central dome paralleled similar cage constructions executed by Eiffel for the Banque Crédit Lyonnais (1877), Boulevard des Italiens, and the Bon Marché department store (1867–76; *see* BOILEAU, (1); for illustration *see* DEPARTMENT STORE), Rue du Bac, both Paris. He also proposed a covered gallery above the Pont d'Iéna on the Seine to link the two groups of exposition buildings, but this plan was ultimately abandoned as being too expensive. Aware of Eiffel's expertise in the study of wind resistance, the sculptor Frédéric-Auguste Bartholdi asked him to design an armature for his *Statue of Liberty*, New York, in 1881; Eiffel's solution was a variation on the design of the tall iron towers he had employed in his earlier bridges and viaducts. In 1885 Eiffel designed the rotating hemispherical dome for the Nice Observatory (*see* OBSERVATORY, fig. 4), the first major structure in France to employ steel as the primary material.

The 300 m iron tower (see fig.) that became the architectural centrepiece for the Exposition Universelle in Paris of 1889 was probably first conceived by Eiffel's young assistant, the Swiss engineer Maurice Koechlin (1856–1946). Without Eiffel's experience, influence and initiative, however, the tower would certainly never have been built. Although based on Eiffel's earlier viaduct pier designs, this tower required much more complicated calculations and construction methods. The vast number of working drawings, prepared under Koechlin's supervision, were extremely precise, making it possible to assemble the prefabricated components on site with virtually no modification. A group of four pivoting cranes was specially built to hoist the components into position. Eiffel's customary attention to questions of wind resistance was reflected in the complex masonry foundations and the hydraulic presses that compensated for shifting in each leg of the tower. Completed on 31 March 1889, the tower, which now bears Eiffel's name, took 26 months to build but never required more than 250 workmen on the site. During the seven months of the exposition, the tower received nearly two million visitors.

Along with his many engineering triumphs, Eiffel also experienced some major disappointments. The Panama Canal Company, which commissioned Eiffel to construct ten locks, fell into financial ruin in 1889, and although he was ultimately vindicated, Eiffel himself was implicated in the flood of litigation that followed. His practical plans for a low-cost underground railway system for Paris, presented in 1890, were ignored, as was his somewhat more adventurous plan of the same year for an underwater tunnel across the English Channel. In his later years Eiffel increasingly devoted himself to theoretical studies of wind resistance, meteorology and aerodynamics, frequently using the Eiffel Tower as a site for his experiments. In 1912 he established an experimental laboratory at Auteuil, where he continued to work until 1920.

WRITINGS
Exposition universelle de 1878: Notice sur les appareils, modèles et dessins exposés par MM. G. Eiffel et Cie (Paris, 1878)
La Tour de trois cents mètres, 2 vols (Paris, 1900)
Travaux scientifiques exécutés à la tour de 300 mètres, de 1889 à 1900 (Paris, 1900)

BIBLIOGRAPHY
G. Tissandier: *La Tour Eiffel de 300 mètres* (Paris, 1889)
F. Poncetton: *Eiffel: Le Magicien du fer* (Paris, 1939)
R. Barthes and A. Martin: *La Tour Eiffel* (Lausanne, 1964)
D. Billington: *The Tower and the Bridge: The New Art of Structural Engineering* (New York, 1983)
B. Lemoine: *Gustave Eiffel* (Paris, 1984)
B. Marrey: *The Extraordinary Life and Work of Monsieur Gustave Eiffel* (Paris, 1984)
H. Loyrette: *Eiffel: Un Ingénieur et son oeuvre* (Fribourg, 1985); Eng. trans. as *Gustave Eiffel* (New York, 1985)
D. Fremy: *Quide de la Tour Eiffel* (Paris, 1989)

ROBERT JAY

Eiga. *See* TAKUMA, (2).

Eight, the (i) [Cz. Osma]. Group of Bohemian painters established in 1906 with the aim of making colour the dominant element in their art. The members, all graduates of the Academy of Fine Arts in Prague, were Emil Filla, Friedrich Feigl (1884–1965), Antonín Procházka, Willy Nowak (1886–1977), Otokar Kubín, Max Horb (1882–1907), Bohumil Kubišta and Emil Artur Pittermann-Longen (1885–1936). Filla, Feigl and Procházka had undertaken further study journeys in Europe, which had opened up their artistic horizons and convinced them of the need for innovation in Czech art. At their initial meetings, held at a Prague coffee-house, the Union, they planned to publish their own magazine and put on an exhibition in the prestigious Topič salon in Prague. Eventually they succeeded in renting a shop in Králodvorská Street, Prague, where a hastily organized exhibition was opened on 18 April 1907, with a catalogue consisting of a sheet of paper headed *Exhibition 8 Kunstausstellung*. The number 8 in the title of the exhibition was intended to represent the number of members in the group; in fact there were only seven, because Pittermann-Longen was only allowed at his own request to exhibit 'behind the curtain in the cubby-hole', since he was still a student at the Academy. The catalogue was in German as well as Czech, as Nowak, Horb and Feigl were of German birth. The majority of the paintings exhibited showed the artists' tendency towards an expressionism in the manner of Munch (who had an exhibition in Prague in 1905), van Gogh, Honoré Daumier and Max Liebermann. Only Max Brod gave the exhibition a positive review; otherwise the reaction of the public and critics was negative. A second exhibition of the Eight took place in the Topič salon in 1908, though it was without the participation of Horb (who had died) and Kubín (who was in Paris). The new exhibitors were Vincenc Beneš and Linka Scheithauerová

Gustave Eiffel: Eiffel Tower, Champ-de-Mars, Paris, 1887–9

(1884–1960), the future wife of Procházka. The catalogue of exhibitors does not include Pittermann-Longen, and they were therefore once again seven. Among the artists' aims on this occasion was the enhancement of expression (Filla) and the liberation of colour splashes (Procházka). The exhibition produced an even more negative reaction than the first. Although it was never officially disbanded, the members of the group maintained contact until 1911, when some of them were co-founders of the Cubist-orientated Group of Plastic Artists. Kubín and Filla turned to Neo-primitivism, and Nowak to Neo-classicism; Feigl remained in the Expressionist tradition.

BIBLIOGRAPHY
M. Brod: 'Frühling in Prag', *Die Gegenwart* (Berlin, 1907), pp. 316–17
M. Lamač: *Osma a Skupina Výtvarných Umělců* [The Eight and the Group of Artists] (Prague, 1988)

VOJTĚCH LAHODA

Eight, the (ii). Group of eight American painters who joined forces in 1907 to promote stylistic diversity and to liberalize the exclusive exhibition system in the USA. They first exhibited together at Robert Henri's instigation at the Macbeth Galleries, New York, in February 1908, following the rejection of works by George Luks, Everett Shinn, William J. Glackens and others at the National Academy of Design's spring show in 1907, of which Henri was a jury member before resigning in protest. Henri, the driving force behind the group, was joined not only by Luks, Shinn and Glackens but also by John Sloan, Ernest Lawson, Arthur B. Davies and Maurice Prendergast. Henri was a painter of cityscapes and portraits who worked in a dark and painterly, conservative style influenced by Frans Hals and Velázquez; a gifted teacher, he encouraged his students to depict the urban poor with vitality and sensitivity.

Sloan, Luks, Shinn and Glackens had met Henri in Philadelphia in the 1890s while employed as newspaper illustrators. Henri persuaded them to move to New York, where they painted urban realist scenes of prostitutes, street urchins and vaudeville performers, for which they were later called the ASHCAN SCHOOL. Ironically, while these painters were often deemed rebels, all worked in the coarsely brushed academic mode of Henri, and none but Sloan, who espoused Socialism, imposed social criticism. They commonly treated their subjects not as oppressed victims but as colourful and bohemian characters.

Lawson, Davies and Prendergast had little in common with the other members of the Eight; these three were influenced by late 19th-century French painting. Lawson portrayed upper Manhattan and the lower Hudson River with thickly applied impressionist strokes. Davies painted idyllic, symbolist landscapes populated by female nudes. Prendergast used a pointillist technique to depict the middle classes at leisure.

Despite some criticism, the Macbeth exhibition was generally well received and well attended. As a result it travelled to nine major cities, and the National Academy of Design temporarily liberalized its exhibition policies. The historic exhibition of the Eight is considered a milestone in the development of artistic independence, inspiring other independent exhibitions, including the Armory Show (1913; *see* NEW YORK, fig. 7), which radically transformed American art in the early 20th century.

BIBLIOGRAPHY
The Eight (exh. cat. by E. Shinn, New York, Brooklyn Mus., 1944)
B. B. Perlman: *The Immortal Eight: American Painting from Eakins to the Armory Show, 1870–1913* (New York, 1962); rev. as *The Immortal Eight and its Influence* (1983)
A. Goldin: 'The Eight's Laissez-faire Revolution', *A. America*, lxi/4 (1973), pp. 42–9
M. S. Young: *The Eight: The Realist Revolt in American Painting* (New York, 1973)
F. Goodyear: 'The Eight', *In this Academy: The Pennsylvania Academy of Fine Arts, 1805–1976* (exh. cat., Philadelphia, PA Acad. F.A., 1976)
M. Laisson: 'The Eight and 291: Radical Art in the First Two Decades of the Twentieth Century', *Amer. A. Rev.*, ii/4 (1979), pp. 91–106
The American Eight (exh. cat., intro. J. W. Kowelek; Tacoma, A. Mus., 1979)
B. B. Perlman: 'Rebels with a Cause: The Eight', *ARTnews*, lxxxi/18 (1982), pp. 62–7
The Shock of Modernism in America: The Eight and the Artists of the Armory Show (exh. cat. by C. H. Schwartz, Roslyn, Nassau Co. Mus. F.A., 1984)

JANET MARSTINE

Eight, the (iii) [Hung. Nyolcak]. Hungarian avant-garde group founded in early 1909 and consisting of the painters Róbert Berény, Béla Czóbel, Dezső Czigány, Károly Kernstok, Ödön Márffy, Dezső Orbán (1884–1986), Bertalan Pór and Lajos Tihanyi. Later the sculptors Márk Vedres (1870–1961) and Vilmos Fémes Beck and the industrial designer Anna Lesznai (*b* 1885) also became members. The group was originally called the Searchers (Keresők) and had formed the most radical section within MIENK (Hungarian Impressionists and Naturalists), a broad-based group of artists. They left MIENK in order to develop a more modern aesthetic. The name the Eight was adopted on the occasion of the second exhibition in 1911, and its leader and organizer was Kernstok. Unlike the earlier Nagybánya school or other contemporary Western movements, the Eight had no homogeneous style, individual artists being influenced by a variety of sources ranging from Cézanne to Cubism. Though unified by a sense of the social function of art, the details of this belief again varied with each artist.

Essentially, the Eight grew up in opposition to the predominant Impressionist style and aesthetic then current in Hungarian art. In particular they rejected the subjective aspect of Impressionism, which aimed at a depiction of nature as perceived through the mood of the artist. This approach was seen as inappropriate to modern society, and, in the context of the political unrest of the period, this desire for change acquired a strong sense of urgency. In contrast to the subjectivism of Impressionism and its concomitant lack of order and structure, the Eight proposed an art of order and harmony based on permanent values. This aesthetic was furthermore seen as an integral part of a new social order in which the artist would assume a central role. This view was most forcibly expressed in Kernstok's essay 'The Social Role of the Artist' (*Huszadik Század*, 1, 1912, pp. 377–80), in which he claimed that in the future the artist would 'stand on the highest rung of the social ladder where, even if he will not enter into discussion with gods, he will direct the spirit of the masses'.

Though lacking their own periodical, the Eight were supported by such critics as Lajos Fülep (1885–1970) and by the Marxist philosopher György Lukács, both of whom wrote appreciative articles in the radical journal *Nyugat* ('West'). In particular, Lukács's article 'The Ways Have Parted' (*Nyugat*, i, pp. 190–93) was an important exposition of the group's aims. Lukács closed the article with 'a declaration of war on all Impression, all sensation and mood, all disorder and denial of values, every *Weltanschauung* and art that writes "I" as its first and last word'. The group exhibited only three times: first in December 1909 at the publishers Könyves Kálmán Műkiadó, then at the Nemzeti Szalon (National Salon) in Budapest from April to May 1911 and finally at the Nemzeti Szalon again, from November to December 1912.

The social inclination of the Eight was evident through the number of monumental paintings and frescoes executed by the group. Pór, for example, produced a fresco for the People's Opera House in Budapest in 1911, the very nature of such projects revealing a desire to communicate with a wide audience. At the second exhibition, Kernstok's *Horsemen on the River Bank* (1910; Budapest, N.G.) was one of the central attractions, and this work highlights the peculiar mixture of tradition and modernity within the group. Its bright coloration shows the influence of Fauvism, though the brushwork is less expressive, yet the subject-matter is distinctly Neo-classical. The statuesque naked figures and horses gathered by the riverside do indeed form an image of a Golden Age, but it is one rooted in the past not the present.

Other artists reflected the variety of influences that converged within the group. Tihanyi's *Self-Portrait* (1912; Budapest, N.G.) exploits elements of Cubist fragmentation, while Czigány's *Still-life with Apples* (c. 1910; Budapest, N.G.) is reminiscent of Cézanne. Berény, who had earlier also been influenced by Cézanne, later turned to Expressionism, as shown by his *Portrait of Béla Bartók* (1913; New York, Bartók Archvs, see Neméth, pl. 33). By the end of 1912 the Eight had disintegrated through internal pressures and external political events; nevertheless, during its short life it revolutionized aesthetic attitudes in Hungary and paved the way for its successor, the ACTIVISTS.

BIBLIOGRAPHY

K. Passuth: *A Nyolcak Művészete* [The art of the Group of Eight] (Budapest, 1967)
L. Neméth: *Modern Art in Hungary* (Budapest, 1969), pp. 49–62
Z. D. Fehér and G. Ö. Pogány: *Twentieth Century Hungarian Painting* (Budapest, 1975)
The Hungarian Avant Garde: The Eight and the Activists (exh. cat. by J. Szabó and others, London, Hayward Gal., 1980)
S. A. Mansbach: 'Revolutionary Events, Revolutionary Artists: The Hungarian Avant-garde until 1920', *'Event' Arts and Art Events*, ed. S. C. Foster (Ann Arbor, 1988), pp. 31–60
G. Eri and others: *A Golden Age: Art and Society in Hungary 1896–1914* (London, 1990), pp. 41–4

□

Eigil (*d* 15 June 822). Bavarian abbot and patron. He was Abbot of Fulda from 818 to 822. A nobleman related to Sturm (Abbot 744–79), Eigil entered the monastery (*see* FULDA, §1) as a child between 754 and 759. It is thought that he played a leading role in the revolt against RATGAR (Abbot 802–17). After the latter's deposition there was an interregnum until Eigil's election, during which the community was re-established. At his institution Eigil undertook to govern wisely and to restrict the abbey's building programme, which had become over-ambitious under his predecessor. Nevertheless, he not only completed the internal decoration of the 'Ratgar basilica' (his biographer Candidus was responsible for wall paintings in the western apse) but also added a modest crypt at each end of the church before its dedication on 1 November 819. These hall crypts of three by three bays were designed by another monk, Racholf. In 822 two further churches were consecrated, both of them small: an estate church at Grossenlüder and St Michael's in Fulda. The latter, a rotunda with ambulatory and crypt, was the monks' funerary chapel. Eigil's final building project was a new claustral range to the east of the abbey church, sited according to the Roman custom near to the burial place of St Boniface. The foundations had been laid when Eigil died, but it was left to his successor Rabanus Maurus to complete the building. Eigil was buried in St Michael's. His interests had been literary as well as architectural. He wrote a Life of his predecessor, Sturm, encouraged Candidus to write a Life of Baugulf, which has not survived, and appointed Rabanus to run the monastery school.

Thieme-Becker   BIBLIOGRAPHY
Candidus de vita Aegili, ed. E. Dümmler, Mnmt Ger. Hist., Poetae Latini Aevi Carolini, ii (Berlin, 1884), pp. 94–117 [verse Life]
Vita Eigilis abbatis Fuldensis auctore Candido, ed. G. Waitz, Mnmt Ger. Hist., Scriptores, xv/1 (Hannover, 1887), pp. 221–33 [prose Life]
K. Lübeck: *Die Fuldaer Äbte und Fürstäbte des Mittelalters*, Veröffentlichungen des Fuldaer Geschichtsvereins, xxxi (Fulda, 1952), pp. 32–5
                                           DAVID PARSONS

Eigtved [Eigtwedt], **Niels** [Nicolai; Nikolaj] (*b* Haraldsted, nr Ringsted, 4 June 1701; *d* Copenhagen, 7 June 1754). Danish architect. His wide-ranging activities and his personal version of French and German Rococo made him a major figure in European 18th-century architecture.

1. EARLY INFLUENCES, TO 1735. He was trained as a garden designer, working in the gardens of Frederiksberg Palace in the early 1720s. In 1723 he went on a study tour with letters of recommendation from Frederick IV, visiting Berlin, where he found employment in the Royal Parks of Charlottenburg and Oranienburg, and reaching Warsaw in 1725. The following year he became assistant to Karl Friedrich Pöppelmann (c. 1698–1750), the son of Matthäus Daniel Pöppelmann and the personal architectural adviser in Warsaw to Augustus the Strong, Elector of Saxony and King of Poland. Under Augustus's lead, the taste for the opulent, sculptural Baroque typified by the Zwinger in Dresden by Matthäus Daniel Pöppelmann was developing towards the cooler, more disciplined Baroque classicism practised by the French émigré architects such as Zacharias Longuelune and Jean de Bodt. From them Eigtved learnt not only stylistic traits but also a fine draughtsmanship that remained characteristic of his work.

Through the patronage of the Danish ambassador to Berlin, Poul Vendelbo Løvenørn (1686–1740), in 1732 Eigtved received from Christian VI of Denmark a bursary for a journey to Italy to study civil architecture and interior design in preparation for a planned new palace in Copenhagen. After two years in Rome, Eigtved returned by way of Vienna, where, at Christian's request, he studied and measured Schloss Schlosshoff, the country residence of Prince Eugene of Savoy, recently enlarged by Johann

Lukas von Hildebrandt. He also stopped in Munich, where he studied the Residenz, Nymphenburg and Schleissheim palaces. Here the new Rococo suites, particularly the work of François de Cuvilliès the elder, were of great importance to Eigtved's artistic development. His 12-year sojourn abroad made Eigtved, on his return to Denmark in 1735, one of the most knowledgeable architects in the country.

2. COURT ARCHITECT, FROM 1735. Eigtved was immediately appointed court architect, and, although his official areas of responsibility were Funen and Jutland, the King arranged for him also to work in Copenhagen, most importantly, on the erection of Christiansborg Palace, under Elias David Häusser (1687–1745), a solid but old-fashioned architect who was probably responsible for the original designs of 1731–2. Along with his rival Laurids De Thurah, Eigtved was entrusted with the interior decoration of the two main floors. In collaboration with the French sculptor Louis-Auguste Leclerc, Eigtved created many of the main interiors, including the King's suite, gradually gaining ascendancy over Häusser and De Thurah as the King's favourite. His administrative ability, as well as his artistic talent, helped to secure for him the design of several important sections, such as the main staircases, the tower, the chapel and the portals. In 1742 Häusser was ousted, and Eigtved became chief architect. He altered Häusser's U-shaped courtyard and stable wings, and he redesigned the bridge and flanking gate-houses of the main entrance in an elegant, sculptural Rococo. A fire in 1794 destroyed all of Eigtved's interiors, except those in the south wing of the stables, which have marble columns and delicate vaulting. This stable complex around the front court, with its varied skyline and sweeping porticos, is the only part of the early Christiansborg to survive intact. However, the few surviving pictorial sources for the palace interiors show that Eigtved's style, while based in early Bavarian Rococo, had become more subtle and refined under the influence of Leclerc and of the latest pattern books and treatises from Paris.

During the reorganization in 1742 of the administration of the royal buildings, Eigtved was placed in charge of the Copenhagen area and received several important new royal commissions. The Prinsens Palais (now the Nationalmuseet), opposite Christiansborg, was erected in 1743–4 for the newly married crown prince, using parts of an existing building. With a recessed main block and side-wings enclosing a courtyard, and a one-storey entrance wing at the street line, it was the first example in Denmark of the traditional Parisian hôtel. It was aligned on a central axis with an existing formal garden, and the delicate exterior treatment focused on the centre, culminating in the pediment of the main block. The interior plan was somewhat old-fashioned, reminiscent of the German palaces Eigtved had seen on his travels. The high-ceilinged Great Hall is panelled throughout in white and gold but is strangely linear, with rocaille ornaments in the plasterwork of the coved ceiling and the chimney-pieces recalling Longelune's work of the 1720s.

Eigtved also introduced to Denmark the French *maison de plaisance*, only a few years after the publication of Jacques-François Blondel's influential pattern book *De la*

1. Niels Eigtved: Levetzau Palace, Amalienborg Square, Copenhagen, *c.* 1750; on the right is the equestrian statue of *Frederick V* (1753–4) by Jacques-François-Joseph Saly

distribution des maisons de plaisance (Paris, 1737–8). Fred-
eriksdal at Lake Fure was built in 1744 for the Foreign
Minister. Its comparatively modest size and informal
layout are balanced by the elegantly differentiated exteriors: blue-black glazed tiles contrast coolly with the whitewashed low-relief walls and the grey stonework of the
entablature, which is embellished with balustrades and
escutcheons. The white and dainty central salon has rich
rocaille plasterwork on the ceiling and in a slender framework on the walls. The original Sophienberg, built for
Queen Sophie Magdalene on the coast near Rungsted in
1743–4, was similar in style. The plan shows the main
block closed towards the garden, with doors opening on
to the lateral terraces only from the side rooms. A few
years later the palace was extended with an upper *bel-étage*
and a five-part roof with central octagonal dome and
heavy mansard roofs on the pavilions, imparting a richer
Baroque character. The building survives only in truncated
form. The Sophienberg scheme was repeated in the
Chinese Garden Pavilion (1745–6; destr. early 19th century) at Hirschholm. The exterior had Eigtved's characteristic framework of pilaster-strips and roof-balustrades,
while the central pavilion had round-headed door and
window apertures and a tent-like roof with festive finials
recalling the fantastic roof-shapes of Dresden and Warsaw.
The use in the central salon of Eigtved's favourite order,
the Composite, was also reminiscent of the German
Baroque.

Outside Copenhagen, Eigtved remodelled the manor
house (1748–50) of Bregentved for Count Adam Gottlob
Moltke, the Lord Chamberlain, creating a new main wing
with a raised centre and end pavilions to form a grandiose
approach from the east. For the same patron he designed
in 1752–4 a new main building at Turebyholm. This was a
simple, narrow structure with a hipped roof and pediments
and beautifully curved steps up to the central doors. He
was also responsible for important extensions at Fried-
richsruhe (1744) in Schleswig and Fredensborg Palace
(1753–5), Zealand, but a project (1745) for remodelling
Charlottenlund remained unexecuted. All these projects
demonstrate Eigtved's flexibility and ability to subordinate
his ideas to complement existing structures.

The huge East-Asiatic Company warehouse (1748–50;
later restored to house the Foreign Office) on Christianshavn, Copenhagen, has simple but harmoniously arranged
elements enriching and creating rhythmic interest on its
façades and disguising the original utilitarian nature of the
structure. Similarly, Eigtved's Royal Theatre (1748) in
Copenhagen is made to appear from the outside like a
patrician town house. The central projections on both
fronts have pediments, in front of a heavy mansard roof.
Both buildings display Eigtved's characteristic pilaster-
strip framing, which strongly influenced later Danish civil
and military architecture.

Eigtved's major achievement as a town planner, architect and interior designer came in the last five years of his
life, with the development of Frederiksstaden. This was a
former royal park and parade-ground, donated to the city
of Copenhagen in 1749 by the new king, Frederick V.
Eigtved conceived the master-plan of regular cross-axes
of broad streets, meeting in the octagonal Amalienborg
Square. He also laid down unifying rules for the building

2. Niels Eigtved: design for Frederikskirke, Frederiksstaden, Copenhagen,
1752 (Copenhagen, Kunstakademiets Bibliotek)

of the projected town houses and supplied standard
designs and variations for them. More outstanding buildings were planned for the visually important sites. Foremost among these were the four noblemen's residences
flanking Amalienborg Square (see fig. 1), which from 1794
housed the Danish royal family. Eigtved's original plan
with four similar mansions with imposing *corps de logis*,
connecting gate-houses and obliquely set pavilions on the
street corners, created a brilliantly lively and unique skyline,
which was enhanced by the complex recesses of the
classically ordered façades. In a later remodelling in 1794,
the central doors were altered, the gate-houses raised and
a colonnade connecting two of the palaces was added.
Eigtved was responsible for all of the four exteriors, but
undertook the detailed interior decoration only of Moltke
Palace, where he created the richest Rococo interiors that
survive in Denmark. The columned, oval vestibule was
destroyed during the remodelling, but the staircase and
bel-étage have survived. The Great Hall, with its carved gilt
panelling and ceiling, mirrors, royal portraits and decorative paintings by Boucher, is one of the great European
Rococo interiors.

Eigtved made several designs for the commemorative
Frederikskirke (see fig. 2), planned as a focus for the short
axis of Amalienborg Square. All incorporated a rotunda
with a high drum and dome, towers on the transverse axis

and porches on both façades of the main axis, which were strangely domestic in tone, recalling his Royal Theatre designs. The projects for the church show the influence of Eigtved's time in Italy, Dresden and Paris, but they are mainly to be seen as the dramatic focus and culmination of his plans for the area, reflecting the style and proportions of the town houses. The church was not completed to Eigtved's designs, however, being finished by Ferdinand Meldahl only in 1894. The Christianskirke (1755) on Christianshavn was likewise finished posthumously, but here the centralized cruciform plan, focused on the altar, pulpit and organ centrepiece, and the high round-headed windows, perfectly fitted into the wall articulation, are true to Eigtved's design. Eigtved also designed the Frederiks Hospital (1752–7; now the Danish Museum of Decorative Art) with a ward quadrangle and free-standing pavilions on the street fronts, although these were built to De Thurah's design after Eigtved's death. He also played an important role in the early history of the Kongelige Danske Kunstakademi (see DENMARK, §XVI).

BIBLIOGRAPHY

F. Meldahl: *Frederikskirken i København* (Copenhagen, 1896)
C. Elling: *Christiansborg-interiører* (Copenhagen, 1944)
——: *Amalienborg interiører* (Copenhagen, 1945)
H. Lund: 'Frederiks hospital og Frederiks stad', *Kunstindustrimuseet: Virksomhed, 1964–69* [Museum of decorative arts: activities, 1964–69], iv (Copenhagen, 1969), pp. 15–50
K. Voss: *Arkitekten Nicolai Eigtved, 1701–54* (Copenhagen, 1971)
J. Erichsen: *Frederiksstaden* (Copenhagen, 1972)
H. Lund: *Christiansborg Slot* i, (Copenhagen, 1975), pp. 220–97

HANNE RAABYEMAGLE

Eiheiji. Japanese Zen Buddhist monastery of the Sōtō sect, in Fukui Prefecture. Eiheiji's significance derives largely from the place in the history of Japanese Buddhism of its founder, Dōgen (1199–1253), and to his interpretation of Sōtō Zen monastic practice. After 1217 Dōgen joined the dominant Tendai school of Buddhism, but he grew disillusioned with Japanese Buddhism as a feasible human soteriology, although he was much attracted to the practice of Zen meditation. In 1223 he left for China, then under the rule of the Song dynasty (AD 960–1279), to practise Chinese Chan (Jap. Zen) Buddhism under the master Rujing (1163–1228) at Mt Tiantong. After his return in 1227 he advocated Sōtō Zen but was continuously harassed by Tendai-sect monks until he cleared donated land in 1243 in Echizen (western Japan) for the first Sōtō Zen monastery, Eiheiji (Monastery of Eternal Peace). At Eiheiji, Dōgen faithfully reproduced Chinese Chan Buddhism in two important ways: experientially, with daily meditation integrated into such basic activities as eating, walking, working, begging and washing, whereby enlightenment might be attained by the practitioner and by others; and architecturally, the buildings in the temple compound, each unique in structure and function, being tightly integrated into a working site for daily Zen discipline and arranged to fit into the topography of the forested hillside.

Eiheiji is an exact reproduction of a Southern Song-period (1127–1279) Chan Buddhist monastery, specifically that on Mt Tiantong. It is a classic Zen monastic compound, with seven structures aligned along an axis that runs uphill, south–north; it has an area of about 3.31 ha.

At the southern end of the central axis, behind the Bell Tower, is the Mountain Gate (Sanmon), to the east and west of which are the bathhouse and the latrine, respectively. In the centre is the Buddha Hall (Butsuden), with the kitchen (*kuin*) and monks' quarters (*sōdo*) to east and west respectively. The northernmost building is the Dharma Hall. All major structures are connected by extensive roofed but open-sided corridors (*kairō*) to facilitate movement between buildings during daily practice. The third abbot, Gikai (1219–1309), completed the basic layout, although most structures have had to be rebuilt several times because of damage by fires from warfare and natural disasters.

The Imperial Messenger Gate is situated south-west of the Mountain Gate. This was where the emperor's emissary would be received. It was originally in the 'opposed-pillar' format of the Chinese Tang period (AD 618–907) but was rebuilt in 1840 in Tenpō-era (1830–44) style. The Mountain Gate is the main gate to the compound and the oldest extant structure at Eiheiji (rebuilt in 1749). It has two storeys, the ground floor measuring 16.6×9 m, with five bays and three doors. On the ground floor are statues of the *Four Guardian Kings* (Skt Lokapala); on the second floor are groupings of statues of 16 *arhat*s (enlightened beings) and 500 *arhat*s. Between the Mountain Gate and the Buddha Hall on the north–south central axis is the Central Sparrow Gate, the most famous example of a Sōtō Zen monastery structure. Though not distinctive in design, it is the presence and location of the gate within the temple compound that is one of the defining architectural characteristics of Eiheiji. The Buddha Hall is a famed Meiji-period (1868–1912) structure, rebuilt in 1902, with a hip-and-gable pantile roof. It contains statues of the Buddhas *Shaka* (Skt Shakyamuni), *Miroku* (Skt Maitreya) and *Yakushi* (Bhaishajyaguru) on an altar representing Mt Sumeru (*shumidan*; the cosmic mountain and abode of the gods) and a portrait of the emperor (Eiheiji served as an 'imperial prayer temple'). The floor space of the Buddha Hall is 298 sq. m. The Ichimonji (Straight-line Corridor) is open-sided and runs east–west connecting parallel corridors that run north–south between the Buddha Hall and the Dharma Hall. The Dharma Hall (860.6 sq. m) was used for lectures and exchanges between master and disciples. It was rebuilt in 1843 during the Tenpō era in the style of a guest hall.

The kitchen was remodelled in 1837 and more extensively in 1930. It has a floor area of 397.2 sq. m. The monks' quarters constitute the central site for meditation, meals and sleeping. They were rebuilt in 1901 and have a floor area of 602.4 sq. m. To the west is the Reading Hall, a Buddhist scripture study rebuilt in 1951, and the Kounkaku, which was built to honour the second Sōtō-school abbot, Koun Ejō (1198–1280), and rebuilt in 1881. The ground area is 209 sq. m. Directly behind the Kounkaku is the Founder's Hall, built to honour Dōgen and early abbots and patrons. It was destroyed by fire in 1879 and rebuilt in 1881. The abbot's quarters (*hōjō*; to the north of the kitchen), built in 1852, consist of inner quarters for the abbot's personal use and outer quarters for rituals. The Daikōmyōzō (Brilliant Treasury), immediately to the south-west of the abbot's quarters, is a large building (828 sq. m) that was used as the Sōtō school's parishioner interview hall. It was rebuilt in 1930. The Myōkōdai (Platform of Mysterious Light) that lies directly west of the abbot's quarters served as a reception site for special guests. It was rebuilt in 1844.

BIBLIOGRAPHY
H. Yokoyama: *Zen no kenchiku* [Zen architecture] (Tokyo, 1967)
S. Kanaoka: *Kodera meisatsu jiten* [Dictionary of old and famous temples] (Tokyo, 1970)
Zengaku daijiten [Dictionary of Zen studies], Zengaku Daijiten Hensansho, 3 vols (Tokyo, 1978)
M. Collcutt: *Five Mountains: The Rinzai Zen Monastic Institution in Japan* (Cambridge, MA, and London, 1981)
Eiheiji shi [A history of Eiheiji], Daihonzan Eiheiji (Eiheiji-chō, Fukui Prefect., 1982)
H. Sakurai: *Eiheiji* (Tokyo, 1987)

DENNIS LISHKA

Eikoh Hosoe. *See* HOSOE, EIKOH.

Eikonion. *See* KONYA.

Eilbertus of Cologne (*fl* 1129–60). German metalworker and enameller. A monk in the monastery of St Pantaleon, Cologne, he was one of the principal masters of its important workshop and among the most outstanding German metalworkers of the Romanesque period. His name is engraved as part of an inscription on a small portable altar (ex-Welf treasure; Berlin, Tiergarten, Kstgewmus.), produced *c.* 1150–60, which reads: EILBERTUS COLONIENSIS ME FECIT. The form of the altar (see fig.) follows that commonly found in portable altars of the 10th and 11th centuries. Eilbertus's achievement was to replace the silver niello decoration customary on altars up to that date, and perfected by Roger of Helmarshausen, with enamel work; and to do so at about the same time as Mosan masters (*see* ROMANESQUE, §VII). He also prepared the ground for the formal convergence in the 13th century of portable altars with larger shrines. The figures decorating the altar are individually characterized with spare lines, and they show the artist's distinctive use of champlevé enamel with marked ridges separating areas of shaded colour. On the top of the altar the *Twelve Apostles* and scenes from the *Life of the Virgin* and the *Passion* are depicted in reserved gilt copper on blue and green enamel backgrounds. In the centre a rock crystal altar stone covers a *Christ in Majesty* painted on parchment. On the sides this is reversed, showing standing 13 prophets and *Jacob*, *Bileam*, *David*, *Melchizedek* and *Solomon* in coloured enamel against gilt backgrounds. The engraving of the figures on the top, partly enamel-filled, and the ridges around the enamelled backgrounds outlining the figures show Eilbertus's ability to convey emotion and action with sparse, woodcut-like lines, seen especially in the faces. In contrast to Roger of Helmarshausen's tightly packed, dramatic figural friezes on the Abdinghof Altar (after 1115; Paderborn, St Josef; for illustration and further discussion *see* ROGER OF HELMARSHAUSEN), Eilbertus arranged isolated groups and figures within frames or separated those on the sides with architectural pilasters, without losing the overall coherence of the programme. He thus divided up the altar casing while respecting its functional integrity, giving it a character of almost classical tranquillity.

Closely related to the Berlin altar are two others: one (also from the Welf treasure) is decorated with *Cardinal Virtues*; the second, the portable altar of St Maurice (*c.* 1135; Siegburg, St Servatius), has colourfully enamelled figures. A portable altar with *Twelve Apostles* under round-arched arcades (*c.* 1135; Mönchengladbach, St Vitus Münsterkirche) and the damaged shrine of St Victor (1129; Xanten Cathedral) are also attributed to Eilbertus's workshop. The latter is a small-scale copy of a church nave

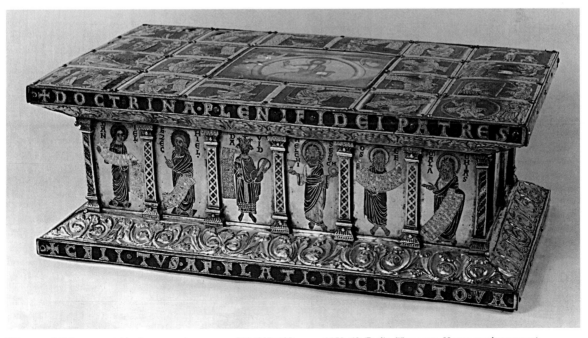

Eilbertus of Cologne: portable altar, enamel on copper, 210×357×130 mm, *c.* 1150–60 (Berlin, Tiergarten, Kunstgewerbemuseum)

with gable roof and repoussé relief ornamentation in silver, a form that would become almost universal in later shrines. Eilbertus's works mediated between Saxon and Rhenish artistic traditions and foreshadowed the masterpieces produced in Cologne by Fridericus and Nicholas of Verdun in the second half of the 12th century.

Thieme–Becker

BIBLIOGRAPHY

M. Rosenberg: *Das Goldschmiede Merkzeichen* (Frankfurt am Main, 1890, rev. 1911), no. 861
O. von Falke and H. Frauberger: *Deutsche Schmelzarbeiten des Mittelalters* (Frankfurt am Main, 1904), pp. 21–6
G. Lehnert, ed.: *Illustrierte Geschichte des Kunstgewerbes*, i (Berlin, [1907])
H. Lüer and M. Creutz: *Geschichte der Metallkunst*, ii, Kunstgeschichte der edlen Metalle (Stuttgart, 1907), pp. 193–7
J. Braun: 'Die Pantaleonswerkstätte zu Köln', *Stimmen der Zeit*, lvi (1925), pp. 21–7
W. Burger: *Abendländische Schmelzarbeiten* (Berlin, 1930), pp. 77–82
Rhein und Maas: Kunst und Kultur, 800–1400 (exh. cat., Cologne, Joseph-Haubrich-Ksthalle, 1972)
G. Schade: *Deutsche Goldschmiedekunst* (Leipzig, 1974), pp. 68–73

G. REINHECKEL

Eileithyiaspolis. *See* KAB, EL-.

Eilshemius, Louis M(ichel) (*b* North Arlington, NJ, 4 Feb 1864; *d* New York, 29 Dec 1941). American painter. After early education in Switzerland and Germany (1873–81), he spent a year at Cornell University, Ithaca, New York (1882–3), before studying painting at the Art Students League in New York. He also studied privately with the painter Robert C. Minor (1840–1904) who influenced his early style derived from the Barbizon school. In 1886 he enrolled in life classes at the Académie Julian in Paris. The death of his father in 1892 left him with the means to travel, notably to Europe and North Africa (1892–3) and to the South Pacific and New Zealand. He also made extensive visits to California (1889, 1893–4) and Rome (1903).

One of the most striking features of Eilshemius's artistic development is the dramatic shift from his charming late-19th-century landscapes in the Barbizon manner, for example *Landscape with Woman and Haystack* (1890; Los Angeles, CA, Co. Mus. A.), to the eccentric, frequently disturbing subjects and idiosyncratic style of the later period, seen in *Jealousy* (*c.* 1915; Philadelphia, PA, Mus. A.). Dominated by female nudes, this work is characterized by a colouristic expressionism in which personal fantasy, growing directly from the experience of his life and travels, is more important than the impact of the Armory Show or modernist theory. Like Albert Pinkham Ryder, the painter with whom he has most in common, his work was stamped by a unique and original poetic vision, seen for example in *Flying Dutchman* (1908; New York, Whitney), derived from Ryder's original. His best work was subjective, literary and metaphorical, and related more to late 19th-century Symbolism than to those aspects of modernism that it might superficially resemble. His work was almost entirely ignored during his productive career, and he stopped painting in 1921. He had been, however, discovered by Marcel Duchamp in 1917, and by the early 1930s Eilshemius's name was established. After being hit by a car in 1932 he was confined to his home where he railed against his misfortunes in an endless flow of letters to the New York press. Despite three simultaneous one-man exhibitions in New York in 1939, the artist was by this time reduced to a state of helpless poverty. He died of pneumonia in 1941.

BIBLIOGRAPHY

D. Phillips: 'The Duality of Eilshemius', *Mag. A.*, xxxii (Dec 1939), pp. 694–7, 724–7
W. Schack: *And he Sat among the Ashes* (New York, 1939)
P. J. Karlstrom: *Louis Michel Eilshemius* (New York, 1978)
——: *Louis M. Eilshemius: Selections from the Hirshhorn Museum and Sculpture Garden* (Washington, DC, 1978)

PAUL J. KARLSTROM

Einbeck, Conrad von. *See* CONRAD VON EINBECK.

Einden, van den. Flemish family of patrons. They belonged to the merchant community who dominated trade and commerce in 17th-century Naples. Jan van den Einden (*d* 1671) traded in Rome and Naples with his brother, Ferdinand (*d* 1630), whose wealth he inherited. He became a business associate of the distinguished collector Gaspar Roomer, and his increasing wealth enabled him to buy the title of Marques of Castelnuovo for his son, Ferdinand van den Einden (*d* 1674), and to collect pictures. His collection was inherited and enriched by Ferdinand, and an inventory of more than 400 pictures was drawn up by Luca Giordano in 1688, when the collection was divided into three parts for Ferdinand's three daughters. It is not possible always to establish which works were commissioned by Jan and which by Ferdinand. The taste of both was formed by Gaspar Roomer, whose will gave to Ferdinand the choice of 90 pictures from his collection. Ferdinand selected Dutch and Flemish pictures, such as those by Pieter van Laer, and the most modern works: Rubens' *Feast of Herod* (Edinburgh, N.G.) passed to his collection. Jan owned works by Rubens and van Dyck (untraced) and also works by classical artists working in Rome, among them Nicolas Poussin's *Holy Family* (New York, Heinemann priv. col.) and paintings by Andrea Sacchi and Simon Vouet (untraced). The van den Einden family were outstanding collectors of Neapolitan painting from 1635 to 1670. The inventory suggests little interest in Caravaggio and his followers, but an ardent admiration for the most recent trends, particularly for the dramatic works of Mattia Preti and Luca Giordano and for the 16th-century Venetian painters who had inspired them. Giordano's *Adoration of the Golden Calf* (Biberach an der Riss, Städt. Samml.) was probably part of their collection. De Dominici recorded that Ferdinand was deeply impressed by a *Marriage at Cana* that Preti painted for Gaspar Roomer and commissioned several works himself. Among paintings by Preti in the van den Einden collection were the *Crucifixion of St Peter* (U. Birmingham, Barber Inst.), the *Beheading of St Paul* (Houston, TX, Mus. F.A.), the *Martyrdom of St Bartholomew* (Manchester, NH, Currier Gal. A.) and the *Feast of Herod* (*c.* 1653–6; Toledo, OH, Mus. A.; for illustration *see* PRETI, MATTIA, fig. 2). Another formative influence on the van den Eindens' taste was their wish to attain prestige through a rich art collection, which resulted in a tendency to be eclectic and also to acquire the work of fashionable painters; hence their large group of works by the highly esteemed but dull classicizing artist Andrea Vaccaro. They were keen collectors of still-life, genre and landscape and owned Flemish and Neapolitan still-lifes, battle paintings by Aniello Falcone, landscapes and marines by Salvator Rosa and Micco Spadaro. The collection included works by Bolognese painters, among them Annibale Carracci and Francesco Albani (untraced).

Such patrons were rare in 17th-century Naples and their collection had a significant influence on Neapolitan artists. The paintings by Rubens and van Dyck introduced such painters as Castiglione, Bernardo Cavallino, Andrea Falcone and Nicolo de Dimone (*fl* 1636–54) to the warm colour, light and brilliant painterly surfaces of Venetian painting; the Flemish still-lifes attracted artists exploring similar themes, while the Bolognese pictures were studied and imitated by the most classicizing of Neapolitan painters.

BIBLIOGRAPHY

F. Haskell: *Patrons and Painters* (London, 1963, rev. London and New Haven, 1980), p. 208

R. Ruotolo: *Mercanti-collezionisti fiamminghi a Napoli: Gaspare Roomer e i Vandeneyden* (Meta di Sorrento, 1982)

Painting in Naples, 1606–1705: From Caravaggio to Giordano (exh. cat., ed. C. Whitfield and J. Martineau; London, R.A., 1982), pp. 211–15

RENATO RUOTOLO

Einhard [Eginhard] (*b c.* AD 770; *d* 837). German patron, writer and possibly metalworker. He received his early education at Fulda Abbey, where he wrote documents between 788 and 791, although he was not ordained or professed as a monk. He then moved to the court at Aachen, which had recently been established, to continue his studies under Alcuin (*c.* 735–804) and others. His most notable product was the *Life* of his patron Charlemagne,

written in the late 820s. Contemporaries recorded his small stature and lively conduct, and his nickname Be(se)leel, after Bezaleel, the worker in precious metals in Exodus 31:2–5.

For a time Einhard oversaw the works at Aachen Palace, and it is possible that he was directly involved in the casting of the bronze doors and gallery grilles that survive in the Palace Chapel (now Cathedral) and are of high aesthetic quality and technical accomplishment. Like other courtiers, he was maintained by grants of churches or monasteries, including St Servatius at Maastricht. There he donated one of the most remarkable works of the so-called Carolingian Renaissance, a reliquary/crossfoot (destr.). This may be reconstructed from 17th- and 18th-century drawings and descriptions (see fig.): a form of triumphal arch with figures of Christ and the Apostles in the upper bands and secular figures in a Late Antique style, perhaps modelled on ivories, below.

Einhard was also given estates at Michelstadt, where he built the monastery of Steinbach (consecrated 827), and Mulinheim, where he established the abbey of Seligenstadt (built 831–40), to which he translated relics from Rome. The church, a basilica with nine bays and a transept, which was modelled on S Stefano degli Abissini in Rome, survives in part. A letter of Einhard's shows his interest in Vitruvius and the possibility of rendering one of his architectural concepts in ivory. Unexpected discoveries of carved ivory fragments at Seligenstadt indicate that this was more than theoretical. Whether Einhard's artistic activities had any impact beyond the immediate court circle is not clear, but the total achievement was remarkable and a distinctive expression of the Carolingian revival.

Embossed silver reliquary, intended as a crossfoot, donated by Einhard to St Servatius, Maastricht, in 815 (destr. after 1794); from a 17th-century drawing (Paris, Bibliothèque Nationale, Cod. fr. 10440)

BIBLIOGRAPHY

R. Krautheimer: 'The Carolingian Revival of Early Christian Architecture', *A. Bull.*, xxiv (1942), pp. 1–38; also in *Studies in Early Christian, Medieval and Renaissance Art* (London and New York, 1971)

R. Büchler and H. Zeilinger: 'Reste einer karolingischen Elfenbeinarbeit in Seligenstadt', *Kst Hessen & Mittelrhein*, xi (1972), pp. 19–31

K. Hauck, ed.: *Das Einhardkreuz: Vorträge und Studien der Münsteraner Diskussion zum arcus Einhardi* (Göttingen, 1974)

D. A. BULLOUGH

Einsiedeln Abbey. Benedictine abbey and Marian pilgrimage site *c.* 35 km south-east of Zurich, in the canton of Schwyz, Switzerland. The original abbey, on the site of the martyrdom of St Meinrad (AD 861), was founded in 934 by Eberhard, provost of Strasbourg Cathedral. The abbey church (consecrated 948) burnt down in 1029 in the first of a series of fires. A new building, erected in 1039, was divided in the middle by twin towers into an upper and lower minster, corresponding to the respective requirements of monks and pilgrims. Baroque rebuilding started in 1674, when Johann Georg Kuen began work on a new monks' choir and a confessional chapel for the upper minster (completed 1684).

Plans for reconstructing the upper minster, then the rest of the church (*see* SWITZERLAND, fig. 2) and finally the whole abbey were commissioned in 1702 from Caspar Moosbrugger, a lay brother of the abbey who had worked as a mason under Kuen. The work was carried out between 1704 and 1735. The medieval abbey was replaced by a symmetrical layout that unified the architecture and gave it a monumental character. The abbey enclosure (156× 136 m) was completed by 1718 with corner pavilions and central projections. The orientated church lies at the centre and is linked to the enclosure by wings forming a cross that extends to the east, north and south (see fig.). The inner courtyards (gardens) thus created contribute to the overall layout, making a grand architectural concept reminiscent of the Escorial, Spain. The refectory and great hall in the south wing and the library in the north wing are imposing public areas.

The church (begun 1719; consecrated 1735) consists of a sequence of three spaces of unequal height and width. The first bay houses the black marble Lady Chapel (rest. 1807), an older *casa santa* on the site of St Meinrad's hut, within which is a late 15th-century image known as the Black Madonna of Einsiedeln. This bay's octagonal form, reflected in the convex west façade, is created by a series of piers from which springs an octagonal vault. The next bay, square in plan, has a sail vault. Originally a drummed dome was intended for the last bay of the lower minster, likewise square, but a drumless dome with a lantern was substituted. Moving east, the height and lightness of the spaces increase, while the width and length decrease. The wall plan follows the normal scheme used in Vorarlberg Baroque, but here it is impressively extended: four free-standing pillars are inserted into the main space, linked to the wall pillars by galleries. This creates the effect of a nave and two double aisles in the relationship 4:2:1. Centrality and a sense of direction are combined, making Einsiedeln one of the most important creations of Baroque spatial design. With its twin towers, convex central portion, frontispiece and restrained articulation, the façade (for illustration *see* MOOSBRUGGER, CASPAR) recalls that of Weingarten Abbey, on which Moosbrugger also worked.

The stuccowork (1724–5), comprising some 100 individual figures, is by Egid Quirin Asam, and the ceiling frescoes of the *Miraculous Consecration*, *Last Supper* (with *quadratura* effects) and *Nativity* are by Cosmas Damian Asam. The stucco figures for the side altars and two

Einsiedeln Abbey by Caspar Moosbrugger, 1704–35; view from the south-west

commemorative plaques at the entrance to the choir (from 1730) are by Diego Carlone, whose brother Carlo Carlone painted the altars of SS Benedict and Meinrad (1739–41). Joseph Anton Feuchtmayer was responsible for the altar of the Holy Cross and the altar of the Mount of Olives. Franz Anton Kraus redesigned the choir in 1746–50 to the plans of Egid Quirin Asam, extending it to the east with a sacristy and upper choir. Kraus also painted the *Assumption* (1749) above the high altar, while Johann Baptist Babel made the over life-size figures of the Apostles, angels and female allegories. The Lady Chapel was given its classical form in 1816–17.

The abbey church was restored between 1975 and 1996. The original Romanesque apse of the choir crypt (1039), which was used as a burial vault from 1674, was excavated in 1980 and incorporated into the modern lower church in 1986.

BIBLIOGRAPHY

L. Birchler: *Kunstdenkmäler des Kantons Schwyz*, i (Basle, 1927), pp. 17–213
A. A. Schmid, ed.: *Corolla Heremitana* (Olten, 1964)
A. von Euw: 'Meisterwerke des 17. bis 19. Jahrhunderts in der Sammlung des Stiftes Einsiedeln', *Aachen. Kstbl.*, xxxix (1969), pp. 1–52
W. Oechslin, ed.: *Die Vorarlberger Barockbaumeister* (Einsiedeln, 1973)
H. J. Lehner: 'Die Ausgrabungen im Chor und in der Sakristei der Stiftskirche Einsiedeln', *Mitt. Hist. Ver. Kant. Schwyz*, lxxiv (1982), pp. 5–67
M. Meyer, B. Davi and S. Polac: 'Die neue Unterkirche im Kloster Einsiedeln', *Meinradsraben*, lxxv (1986), pp. 17–24
J. Salzgeber: *Die schwarze Muttergottes von Einsiedeln* (Einsiedeln, 1986)
G. Holzherr: *Einsiedeln: Kloster und Kirche Unserer Lieben Frau: Von der Karolingerzeit bis zur Gegenwart* (Munich, 1987; Eng. trans., Zurich and Munich, 1988)
R. Paschke: *Cosmas Damian Asam in Einsiedeln: Zur Beurteilung barocker Deckenmalerei* (Berlin, 1987)
H. Böck: *Einsiedeln: Das Kloster und seine Geschichte* (Zurich and Munich, 1989)

P. GABRIEL KLEEB

Einsle, Anton (*b* Vienna, 30 Jan 1801; *d* Vienna, 10 March 1871). Austrian painter of German descent. In 1814 he was admitted to the Vienna Akademie der Bildenden Künste, where in 1817 he was awarded first prize in ornamental design. By 1827 he was already executing commissions for portraits in oils and portrait miniatures, and in 1829 he received the Lampi prize. On the death of his father he moved to Prague, where he quickly established his reputation as a portrait painter. Having exhibited successfully in Prague and Dresden, in 1830 he began to show his work regularly at the Vienna Akademie exhibitions. In 1832 he settled in Budapest, where the patronage of the Archduke Joseph and his consort Maria Dorothea culminated in his appointment as court painter (1838), ensuring his future success and bringing further prestigious commissions from the nobility and the Church.

In 1843, following his departure from Budapest, Einsle was elected a member of the Vienna Akademie. He received commissions from the Austrian imperial family, and on the accession of the Emperor Francis Joseph in 1848 he was appointed official portraitist. He was provided with a studio in the Hofburg, where he painted numerous portraits of the Emperor and the Empress Elisabeth. By this time his elegant work, very much in the English style, was in such demand that he had to decline an invitation

to the court in St Petersburg and found it necessary to employ a team of assistants.

BIBLIOGRAPHY
Thieme–Becker

COLIN J. BAILEY

Eiraku Hozen [Nishimura Zengorō XI; Konan Hozen] (*b* ?Kyoto, *c*. 1795; *d* Ōtso, Tōtōmi Prov. [now Shiga Prefect.], 1854). Japanese ceramicist and member of the Eiraku family. At the age of 13 he was adopted by Nishimura Ryōzen, the tenth-generation head of a family of *doburo* (earthenware braziers) makers for the tea ceremony. In 1827 he was invited to Kii Province (now Wakayama Prefect.) to produce porcelain for the local daimyo, from whom he received the right to use a silver seal bearing the name Eiraku. He obtained national recognition for his *sometsuke* (blue-and-white) and *kinrande* (gold and enamel) wares (*see* JAPAN, §VIII, 3(iii)). Hozen was skilled in the manufacture of many types of ceramic ware, including stonewares and copies of Chinese Ming-period (1368–1644) wares, and his coloured glazes (violet, yellow, red, blue and green) were a major influence on later Kyoto ceramics (*kyōyaki*). He also devoted much effort to mastering the use of underglaze copper red (*shinsha*). After passing the family headship to his son, Wazen, in 1849, Hozen travelled to Edo (now Tokyo), where he planned to open a kiln. The venture failed, but soon after his return to Kyoto he was invited by a patron to build a kiln in Miidera (Ōtsu, Tōtōmi Prov.; now Shiga Prefect.). Hozen spent his last years working there, producing what came to be known as Konan ware, and later, at another kiln, Nagarayama ware. He was succeeded by his son, Wazen (1823–96), and his adopted son, Sosaburō (Dōzen).

BIBLIOGRAPHY
E. S. Morse: *Catalogue of Japanese Pottery*, Boston, MA, Mus. F.A. cat. (Boston, 1900)
H. Gorham: *Japanese and Oriental Ceramics* (Tokyo, 1971)
Y. Tazawa: *Biographical Dictionary of Japanese Art* (Tokyo, 1981)
J. Ayres: *Japanese Ceramics*, Geneva, Col. Bauer cat. (Geneva, 1982)

HIROKO NISHIDA, ANDREW MASKE

Eirene (*b* Athens, *c*. 752; *reg* 797–802; *d* Lesbos, 803). Byzantine empress and patron. On the death of her husband, Emperor Leo IV (*reg* 775–80), she acted as regent for their son Constantine VI (*reg* 780–97). In 796 she had him blinded and took sole power as the first woman in recorded European history to be acknowledged as a sovereign monarch. Her proposed marriage with Charlemagne would have united the two empires. She was responsible for the restoration of images in Orthodox worship after their destruction and removal during the first wave of iconoclasm (726–87; *see* CHRISTIANITY, §III, 2(i)). On her own initiative and against the hostility of the iconoclast church and imperial administration, in 787 she convened the Seventh Ecumenical Council at Nicaea (now Iznik), which suppressed iconoclasm, although it was to break out again in 814.

Despite Eirene's patronage of monasteries and churches, there seems to have been little artistic activity during her reign. She was, however, probably responsible for reinstating the image of Christ above the Chalke Gate of the Great Palace at Constantinople (*see* ISTANBUL, §III, 12). After making an apparently miraculous recovery from illness, she also commissioned portraits of herself and Constantine VI for the church of the Virgin of Pêgê outside Constantinople. Other gifts included vestments, curtains in cloths of gold and liturgical vessels. Her most important work lay in ensuring the survival and continued importance of icons as objects of veneration and worship in the Orthodox church.

BIBLIOGRAPHY

Theophanes: *Chronicle* (early 9th century); Eng. trans. by H. Turtledove (Philadelphia, 1982)
S. Runciman: 'The Empress Eirene the Athenian', *Medieval Women*, ed. D. Baker (Oxford, 1978), pp. 101–18
P. Speck: *Kaiser Konstantin VI* (Munich, 1978)
R. S. Cormack: 'Women and Icons: And Women in Icons', *Gender and Byzantine Studies*, ed. L. James (in preparation)

L. JAMES

Eisen. French family of artists of Flemish origin. (1) François Eisen is chiefly known as a painter of genre scenes. His son (2) Charles Eisen received recognition as a painter and book illustrator. Charles's sons, Christophe-Charles Eisen (*b* 1744) and Jacques-Philippe Eisen (*b* 1747), were also artists.

(1) François Eisen (*b* Brussels, *c.* 1695; *d* Paris, 1778). Painter. He served his apprenticeship (1705–6) with Pierre Roger in Valenciennes and in 1716 was admitted master of the Confrérie de St Luc there. In the same year he married Marguerite Gainse; one of their seven children was (2) Charles Eisen. François Eisen worked for the religious houses of Valenciennes, most notably for the abbey of Vicoigne, making eight paintings (untraced) for the refectory in 1729. He moved to Brussels *c.* 1732 and joined his son Charles in Paris *c.* 1745. In later life he painted numerous genre pictures in a light-hearted Flemish manner (e.g. *The Swing*, 1770; Bourg-en-Bresse, Mus. Ain); these were probably made specifically for dealers.

BIBLIOGRAPHY

Au temps de Watteau, Fragonard et Chardin: Les Pays-Bas et les peintres du XVIIIe siècle (exh. cat., ed. H. Oursel; Lille, Mus. B.-A., 1985), p. 93
F. Machelart: *Peintres et sculpteurs de la confrérie Saint-Luc de Valenciennes aux XVIIe et XVIIIe siècles* (Valenciennes, 1987), p. 67

(2) Charles(-Dominique-Joseph) Eisen (*b* Valenciennes, 17 Aug 1720; *d* Brussels, 4 Jan 1778). Painter, draughtsman and illustrator, son of (1) François Eisen. He went to Paris *c.* 1740 to work in the studio of the engraver Jacques-Philippe Lebas. Eisen himself engraved little, and probably produced the drawings from which Lebas or studio assistants would engrave. In 1745 Eisen was asked to illustrate a volume celebrating the betrothal of the Dauphin Louis to Maria Theresa of Spain. This was his first significant commission and was probably passed to him by Lebas. Two years later he established his reputation and independence by providing 43 drawings for an edition of the works of Nicolas Boileau. In 1748, however, the Académie de St Luc seized Eisen's studio effects because he was refusing to pay the joining fee, arguing that, as an artist of exceptional talent, he should be admitted for a lesser amount. Two years later he sued successfully and was admitted without fee; his *morceau de réception* was a painting of *Daedalus and Icarus* (untraced). Within the Académie de St Luc, Eisen rose from assistant professor (1753) to assistant rector (1774), and

he exhibited paintings and drawings at its exhibitions from 1751 to 1774. His paintings, of which few are known to survive, were of scenes of elegant life and of religious, mythological and historical subjects (e.g. *St Genevieve*, 1764; Paris, St Médard), showing the influence of Carle Vanloo and François Boucher. He also painted two charming rural scenes, a *Shepherd and Shepherdess* and *Villagers Dancing in the Country* (Bordeaux, Mus. B.-A.), and a few portraits (e.g. the allegorical portrait showing the *Apotheosis of Charles of Lorraine*, 1777; Brussels, Mus. A. Anc.). His reputation was, however, based on his talents as a draughtsman, particularly of small scenes for use in book illustrations, in which he combined his light touch with a good grasp of the incident or theme to be illustrated. His drawings were used in nearly 400 books (including multiple editions) during his lifetime and remained in use through to the first decade of the 19th century. The wide range of publications included editions of Lucretius, Ovid, Tacitus, Virgil, Boccaccio, Erasmus and Ariosto. A particularly prestigious commission was one for 80 drawings for the luxurious Fermiers Généraux edition of Jean de La Fontaine's *Contes* (1762). It was a sign of Eisen's importance that his engraved portrait headed the second volume as that of La Fontaine did the first. His drawings were also used to illustrate books by contemporary authors including Charles de Secondat, Baron de Montesquieu, Jean-Jacques Rousseau and Voltaire. In 1767 Voltaire wrote to him that his *Henriade* would reach posterity because of Eisen's prints, while the critic Friedrich Melchoir, Baron von Grimm, said of Claude-Joseph Dorat's *Les Baisers* (1770) that its value lay in the illustrations; other works by Dorat

Charles Eisen: *Cul de lampe*; engraving by Jean Massard from Claude-Joseph Dorat: *Lettres d'une chanoinesse de Lisbonne* (The Hague and Paris, 1771)

illustrated by Eisen include *Lettres d'une chanoinesse de Lisbonne* (see fig.).

Eisen's career was doubtless helped by his finding favour with the d'Argenson family, the protectors of the Académie de St Luc in the 1750s, and it was perhaps this connection that led to his becoming drawing-master to Mme de Pompadour. In 1753 he published a book of ornamental designs for use by artists, with, unusually, most of the engravings done by himself, and in 1757 a book with engravings in the new crayon manner technique. His pre-eminent influence as a book illustrator was implicitly recognized by the publication of the *Recueil de divers petits sujets agréables . . .*, another book aimed at artists. By the mid-1770s, however, book illustration as a genre had ceased to be fashionable, and in 1776 the Académie de St Luc was suppressed. This was presumably the reason why Eisen left Paris for Brussels *c.* 1776–7; he died there insolvent.

PRINTS
Nouveau recueil des troupes qui forment la Garde et Maison du Roy . . . dessiné d'après nature par Eisen (Paris, 1757)
Recueil de divers petits sujets agréables d'après Eisen et autre maîtres (Paris, 1770)

BIBLIOGRAPHY
E. de Goncourt and J. de Goncourt: *Les Vignettistes* (Paris, 1868)
V. Salomons: *Charles Eisen* (London, 1921)
C. Lemoine-Isakan: 'Les Peintures de Charles Eisen', *Gaz. B.-A.*, n. s. 5, lviii (1961–2), pp. 223–36
A. Carlier: *Charles Eisen de Valenciennes* (Valenciennes, 1966)

HUMPHREY WINE

Eisen. *See* OKUDA EISEN.

Eisenburg. *See* HUNEDOARA CASTLE.

Eisenhoit [Eisenhaut; Eisenhut(t); Iserenhod(t)], **Anton** (*b* Warburg, 1553–4; *d* Warburg, 1603). German goldsmith, engraver and draughtsman. Probably from a long-established Warburg family of freemen, he is first fully named in 1578, in an engraving that shows his connections with scholars as an illustrator of academic works. One of these was Michele Mercati, for whom Eisenhoit worked during a stay in Rome *c.* 1580 on the *Metallotheca Vaticana*, a work cataloguing the Vatican's scientific collections. His style draws principally on the Roman Late Renaissance. Back in Germany by *c.* 1582–5, Eisenhoit began to work primarily for patrons residing near Warburg, where he had settled by 1587 at the latest. Commissions of these years show work for the Hessian courts in Kassel and Marburg and the beginning of his cooperation with Jost Bürgi, instrument-maker and mathematician to the Landgrave of Hesse-Kassel. Between *c.* 1582 and 1594 Eisenhoit decorated Bürgi's mechanical celestial globes with engravings and illustrated with etchings a treatise on engineering.

Eisenhoit's first works in gold (1587) were for the Landgrave William IV of Hesse-Kassel (*reg* 1567–92), of whom he cut commemorative medals even after William's death in 1592. From 1588 onwards Eisenhoit supplied work in silver and gold, engraving and even tapestry designs mainly to his sovereign Dietrich von Fürstenberg, Prince-Bishop of Paderborn (*reg* 1585–1618), and his brother Caspar, a leading member of Westphalian aristocracy. Three main pieces of a set made of silver and parcel gilt, created for the Prince-Bishop's divine service, bear

Eisenhoit's full signature: a chalice (1588), an altar cross (1589) and a vessel for holy water (before 1601; all Schloss Herdringen, Westphalia), testifying to Eisenhoit's then unusual artistic self-confidence (he referred to himself as an 'art engraver' in 1588). They also show him as one of the most gifted German Mannerist goldsmiths. His ecclesiastical works in silver sympathetically combined older Gothic formal traditions with the contemporary styles of Roman and Dutch artists such as Cornelis Cort and of Rudolfine artists such as Bartholomäus Spranger, showing a fine sense of line and monumentality in his outstanding embossed reliefs.

BIBLIOGRAPHY
A. M. Kesting: *Anton Eisenhoit: Ein westfälischer Kupferstecher und Goldschmied* (Münster, 1964)
J. H. Leopold and K. Pechstein: *Der kleine Himmelsglobus 1594 von Jost Bürgi* (Lucerne, 1977), pp. 167–93
J. H. Leopold: *Astronomen, Sterne, Geräte: Landgraf Wilhelm IV und seine sich selbst bewegenden Globen* (Lucerne, 1986), pp. 46, 146–7
Prag um 1600: Kunst und Kultur am Hofe Rudolfs II (exh. cat., Essen, Villa Hügel, 1988), pp. 277, 544–5

MARION HAGENMANN-BISCHOFF

Eisen Ikeda. *See* IKEDA EISEN.

Eisenlöffel, Jan [Johannes] (*b* Amsterdam, 10 Jan 1876; *d* Amsterdam, 17 Sept 1957). Dutch decorative artist and draughtsman. After training at the Rijksnormaalschool, Amsterdam, he was appointed head of the metalwork department at the applied-arts studio Amstelhoek in 1896. Here he made a name for himself as one of the most important designers within the Nieuwe Kunst movement. His contribution is characterized in its use of pure, functional forms and by the use of cheap materials such as brass and copper, with which he made, among other things, mass-produced objects such as coffee and tea services and, in particular, lamps. He propagated techniques of machine-production and used constructive elements such as rivets as decorative motifs.

Eisenlöffel also made unique objects in precious materials. He learnt enamel and niello techniques, which he used frequently during a trip to Moscow and St Petersburg. In 1900 he won a distinction at the Exposition Universelle in Paris for his clocks with enamel decoration. After 1902 he also applied the enamel technique to his decorations and in this was inspired by Merovingian and Carolingian examples. Around 1905 he designed silver services and cutlery for the Begeer firm in Utrecht, where a silversmith's studio was built. During this period he also made study trips to Vienna, learning transparent enamel techniques. The later designs of Eisenlöffel are generally more elegant in form, partly because he moved away from rigid functionalism.

BIBLIOGRAPHY
Scheen
Amstelhoek, 1897–1910 (exh. cat., ed. J. D. van Dam and A. Hidding; Leeuwarden, Gemeentelijk Mus. Het Princessehof, 1986)

G. JANSEN

Eisenlohr, (Jakob) Friedrich (*b* Lörrach, 23 Nov 1805; *d* Karlsruhe, 27 Feb 1855). German architect. He studied (1824–6) at the Polytechnische Schule Karlsruhe, under Friedrich Weinbrenner, after whose death he went on a scholarship to Italy (1826–8), where he was in close contact with the Nazarenes. After qualifying in 1830 he was appointed in 1832 as a teacher at the Polytechnische Schule by Weinbrenner's successor, Heinrich Hübsch, becoming a professor there in 1839. One of his first works was the rebuilding in romantic spirit of the castle ruins at Ortenberg (1838–42), but his main works were produced after he joined the building authority in 1839 and took over the planning and execution of all buildings for the Baden railways. The station at Mannheim (1839–40; destr.) was followed by others at Heidelberg (destr.) and Freiburg, as well as that at Karlsruhe (1842–5), which was probably his most important building, in which both the *Rundbogenstil* details and general grouping demonstrate the Italianate influence typical of the period. His love of the traditional timber buildings of the Black Forest led him to construct many of the auxiliary buildings of the Baden railways in timber. In Badenweiler he built the Trinkhalle (1853; enlarged 1932–4). His Protestant ecclesiastical work included not only a thorough redesign of the Early Gothic parish church at Lahr (1848–51) and the church (1855–64) in Augustaplatz, Baden-Baden (the latter a Gothic Revival hall church with a twin-towered façade), but also numerous theoretical designs for centralized churches (1848–54). In 1853 he was appointed director of the Bauschule in Karlsruhe.

UNPUBLISHED SOURCES
U. Karlsruhe, Inst. Baugesch. [MSS and drgs]

BIBLIOGRAPHY
ADB; Thieme–Becker; Wasmuth
J. Clewing: 'Jakob Friedrich Eisenlohr', *Soweit der Turmberg grüsst*, suppl. to *Durlacher Tagbl.*, vi (1954), pp. 5–8

DIETRICH NEUMANN

Eisenman, Peter D. (*b* Newark, NJ, 12 Aug 1932). American architect, theorist, writer and teacher. He graduated from Cornell University, Ithaca, NY (BArch 1955),

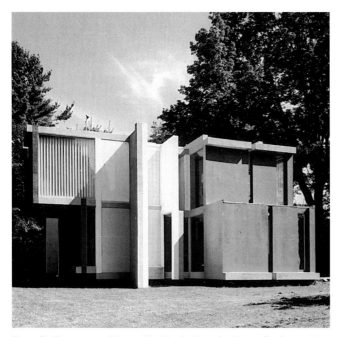

Peter D. Eisenmann: House VI (Frank House), Cornwall, Connecticut, 1972–3

and worked for Percival Goodman in New York (1957–8) and the Architects' Collaborative in Cambridge, MA (1959). He then went to Columbia University, New York (March 1960), and the University of Cambridge, England, where he completed his PhD in the theory of design (1963) and also taught (1960–63). Back in the USA, he was involved in several unexecuted competition entries and projects (1963–5) with Michael Graves and began to teach (1963–7) at Princeton University, NJ, moving to Cooper Union, New York, in 1967. In that year he became the founding director of the Institute for Architecture and Urban Studies, New York, which became a major centre for exhibition and debate in the architectural profession; he also established and edited its influential journal *Oppositions* (1973–82), to which he contributed many writings.

Eisenman's principal role as an architect was mainly that of theorist and *agent provocateur* and his built works total only a fraction of those produced by such contemporaries as Michael Graves. Although a popular lecturer, he did not court popularity with his buildings, which are linked with the modernist but post-Functionalist avant-garde. He was interested in Italian Rationalist architecture of the 1930s and participated in the NEW YORK FIVE exhibition (1969) at MOMA, New York, with some early neo-Rationalist work, the first of a series of numbered houses that began with House I, the Barenholtz House (1967–8), Princeton, House II, the Falk House (1969–70), Hardwick, VT, and House III, the Miller House (1969–70), Lakeville, CT. These were complex, rectilinear geometric compositions; numbered as if they were abstract works of art, they expressed his investigation into the nature and meaning of architectural form. Rejecting functionalism, which he saw as a continuation of the humanist tradition, he increasingly attempted to express a truly 'modernist sensibility' in which buildings were seen and experienced as autonomous and self-referential, independent of human context or function. Thus House VI, the Frank House (1972; see fig.), Cornwall, CT, for example, has a door too narrow to be entered without turning sideways and a staircase that cannot be climbed.

A recurrent feature of Eisenman's work was the archetypal modernist element, the grid, but twisted, rotated and overlaid to create displacements and new possibilities of form. This is evident in the IBA low-cost housing (1981; partly executed), Berlin, whose undeclared grids appear in colour on the surface without explanation of their meaning, and in the Wexner Center for the Visual Arts (1983–9), Ohio State University, Columbus, which may best be described as a non-building. Here Eisenman overlaid the campus grid with the offset grid of the city, locating his scheme where they intersected and creating a new path into the campus on an east–west axis. Forming the north–south axis is a long circulation spine, a diagrammatic, quasi-Miesian galleria, partly glazed and partly enclosed in 'scaffolding' or open, gridded frames whose components do not quite meet; galleries contain the deconstructed elements of the modernist cube projecting from walls, floor and ceiling; stairs lead nowhere and columns are cut off in mid-air. The crossing of the two axes is thus an 'event': a circulation route at a critical junction of the campus that is also a centre for the visual arts, whose 'scaffolding' negates the traditional image of shelter. Built partly below ground level, it also embodies the symbolism of excavation used in other, unexecuted projects, for example housing on the Cannaregio (1978), Venice, and Parc de la Villette (1988; with Jacques Derrida), Paris.

Eisenman's compositional techniques, unlike those of Michael Graves, were not figurative or pictorial, although they may have had a narrative or 'rhetorical' basis. His exploration of formal syntax centred on the development of a modernist 'dialectic' involving fragmentation and the reordering of fragments into a new whole, perhaps revealing suggestions of originals within some new assembly. In this way, for example, the demolished Armory at Ohio State University is recalled in an assembly of fragments of the original tower placed at the entrance to the Wexner Center. Thus Eisenman, within the broad spectrum of POST-MODERNISM, sought to simulate both the known and the unknown. In 1987 he declined the Deanship of the Columbia University Graduate School of Architecture in order to devote himself to the realization of his theoretical ideas, which were expressed in increasingly convoluted and arcane texts. His work was widely exhibited in the USA and Europe.

See also DECONSTRUCTION.

WRITINGS
'White and Gray', *A & U*, 52 (1975), pp. 25–180 [special feature guest-edited by Eisenman with R. A. M. Stern]
Guiseppe Terragni (Cambridge, MA, 1985)
with others: *House of Cards* (New York, 1987)

BIBLIOGRAPHY
M. Gandelsonas: 'On Reading Architecture: Eisenman and Graves: An Analysis', *Prog. Archit.*, liii/3 (1972), pp. 68–87
C. Jencks: 'Peter Eisenman: An Architectural Design Interview', *Archit. Des.*, lviii/3–4 (1988), pp. 49–62
'Peter Eisenman', *A & U*, 8 (1988) [extra edition]
A. Graaflaud, ed.: *Peter Eisenman: Recente Projekten* (Nijmegen, 1989)
Wexner Center for the Visual Arts, The Ohio State University (New York, 1989)
MALCOLM QUANTRILL

Eisenstaedt, Alfred (*b* Dierschau, West Prussia [now Poland], 6 Dec 1898; *d* 23 Aug 1995). American photographer of German birth. He attended Berlin University from 1913 to 1916 and served in the army (1916–18). He survived the world economic crisis after the war as a belt and button salesman for a Berlin firm. He was a self-taught photographer, though a friend taught him enlargement techniques in 1926. In 1927 he began to work for the *Berliner Tageblatt*, which led him to photograph in smaller format; he was soon also acting as a freelance photographer for the *Weltspiegel*, producing work for the Pacific and Atlantic Picture Agency, Associated Press and the *Berliner illustrierte Zeitung* from 1929 until 1935. He photographed Marlene Dietrich in Berlin in 1928, while she was filming *Der blaue Engel* (see Eisenstaedt, 1969, p. 103), and this picture of a woman in a man's black smoking jacket became one of Eisenstaedt's most famous photographs.

In 1935 he emigrated to the USA, where he was naturalized, and worked for *Harper's Bazaar*, *Vogue*, *Town, Country* and others. A year later he travelled to Ethiopia as a photojournalist to record the Ethiopian–Italian war for *Life*. The first issue of this magazine appeared on 21 November 1936, and he supplied the photograph of a young trainee officer from West Point for the cover of the second issue. By 1972, he had taken more than 70 of the magazine's cover photographs.

Eisenstaedt photographed the most important figures of the period—politicians, actors, writers, artists and industrialists—and managed, as in his portrait of *J. Robert Oppenheimer* (1954; see Eisenstaedt, 1966, p. 121), to include signs of the times. As a result his portraits always represent something more than the individuality of the sitters. A work by Eisenstaedt is at once representative of the sitter's class, country, race or profession, whether it is a facial portrait or, for example, a picture of the cracked soles of the feet of an Ethiopian soldier (see Eisenstaedt, 1969, p. 51). His photographs have a power and a symbolic resonance that made him one of the best *Life* photographers.

PHOTOGRAPHIC PUBLICATIONS
Witness of our Time (New York, 1966)
The Eye of Eisenstaedt (New York, 1969)
Martha's Vineyard (New York, 1970)
People (New York, 1973)
Eisenstaedt's Album: 50 Years of Friends and Acquaintances (New York, 1976)

BIBLIOGRAPHY
E. Steichen: *Memorable Life Photographs* (New York, 1951)
S. Rayfield, ed.: *Life Photographers: Their Careers and Favorite Pictures* (New York, 1957)
M. Edey: *Great Photographic Essays from Life* (Boston, 1978), pp. 117–27
REINHOLD MISSELBECK

Eisgrub. *See* LEDNICE.

Eishi. *See* HOSODA EISHI.

Eishin. *See* KANŌ, (13).

Eishōsai Chōki (*fl c.* 1780–early 1800s). Japanese painter and woodblock-print designer. He is thought to have studied under Toriyama Sekien (1712–88), the teacher of KITAGAWA UTAMARO. Chōki specialized in compositions of beautiful women (*bijinga*), sometimes with little or no background but more often with atmospheric backgrounds in which there is a limited sense of depth. He was influenced by Utamaro, Torii Kiyonaga (*see* TORII, (8)) and TŌSHUSAI SHARAKU, but developed his own style of tall, slender figure. He left a number of superbly printed designs. Chōki was particularly skilful at depicting half-length figures; many of his best designs are compositions of two such half-length figures. Examples include the colour woodblock-print *Girl with an Umbrella and a Servant* (*c.* mid-1790s; e.g. Tokyo, N. Mus.), with a background of falling snow and, in the foreground, a girl holding an umbrella and leaning on the back of her manservant as he bends to (presumably) clear the snow from her sandal. In *Hunting Fireflies* (*c.* mid-1790s; Honolulu, HI, Acad. A.) a young woman and a male child engage in the summer pastime of catching fireflies at night. The composition includes irises in bloom, a pond and fireflies lighting up a dark background. Although not all of Chōki's colour woodblock prints reach this quality in design or execution, his best works are well regarded for their composition, colour, atmospheric effects and skilful printing techniques. Some scholars believe that Chōki may have used the art name Shikō, others that this may be the signature of a different print designer.

BIBLIOGRAPHY
M. Ueda and others: *Konsaisu Nihon jinmei jiten* [Concise Japanese bibliographical encyclopedia] (Tokyo, 1976, rev. 1990)
S. Yoshida: *Ukiyoe no mikata jiten* [Encyclopedia of a view of *ukiyoe*] (Tokyo, 1977)
R. Neurer, H. Libertson and S. Yoshida: *Ukiyo-e: 250 Years of Japanese Art* (New York, 1979)

BRENDA G. JORDAN

Eisselburg, Peter. *See* ISSELBURG, PETER.

Eitoku. *See* KANŌ, (5).

Ejagham. Bantu-speaking people, numbering *c.* 100,000, occupying the sparsely populated forest lands of the Nigeria–Cameroon border area to the north-east of Calabar, in the cultural area known as the Cross River region. The Ejagham are often referred to in the literature as 'Ekoi', a derogatory name used by the Efik, that has now largely been abandoned by scholars. The old designation 'Ekoi' is often extended to those of their neighbours—including the Yakö and Mbembe to the west, Bokyi to the north, Widekum to the north-east and BANGWA to the east—who have adopted aspects of Ejagham ritual and material culture. The Ejagham are thus not a single 'tribe' or ethno-linguistic group but, rather, a loose confederation or congeries of peoples sharing major cultural features but with distinct socio-political systems. Many museum collections of African art include examples of Ejagham art (for illustrations see works listed in the bibliography).

1. Mask and masquerade. 2. Stone sculpture. 3. Cement sculpture. 4. Bronzework. 5. Wood-carving. 6. Regalia and personal arts.

1. MASK AND MASQUERADE. The Ejagham are most famous as the makers and users of the unique genre of skin-covered wooden masks, which they are thought to have originated. Animal hide, usually antelope skin, is dehaired and softened with vegetable preparations and then applied to the surface of the wood while still wet and pliant. The skin is secured to the mask with wooden pegs, special care being taken to ensure a close fit between skin and wood, especially around the facial features. Insets of cane, metal or bone, for the teeth, and round-headed wooden pegs, for the coiffure, are often added after the skin-covering process. Vegetable dyes are used as decoration as well as to represent ethnic scarification marks, and, finally, the mask's eyes and teeth are whitened with a suspension of roasted and ground forest snail shells or white clay.

Ejagham skin-covered masks are often highly naturalistic—an effect undoubtedly heightened by the polished appearance of the skin itself. They represent human or animal heads, the latter of antelope or crocodile, for example, or therianthropic forms. The masks are worn on top of the head as caps or headdresses, or, in the case of helmet masks, covering the wearer's head and resting on his shoulders. There are single-, double- and multi-faced forms. In the case of the double-faced mask, a male face almost invariably faces forwards, a female face backwards (see fig. 1). The cap mask is worn with a long cloth gown, formerly of woven string, extending from the top of the head to the ankles and covering the whole of the wearer's face, apart from the eyes. Helmet masks are worn either

1. Ejagham Nsofang age-set masker wearing two-faced, skin-covered helmet mask with feather rods, south Etung people, Ikom, Nigeria; from a photograph by Keith Nicklin

with a woven string costume or a cloth skirt supported by a waist hoop.

Although an individual may gain considerable prestige by introducing a new skin-covered mask into his community, ownership of masks and their associated dance paraphernalia and musical instruments is almost invariably communal. Typical mask-owning institutions include age-sets and associations of hunters or warriors. Dramatic masquerade performances are held on the initiation or death of a member of the group or during routine group meetings. At funerals the masquerades create a continuum between the land of the living and that of the deceased ancestors. By the 1970s only a few artists still made skin-covered masks, the genre having been superseded by cap and helmet masks decorated with brightly coloured, commercially produced paints.

The vestiges of an 'archaic' style of wooden face mask are found throughout Ejagham territory and among some adjacent peoples (Nicklin and Salmons, 1984, pp. 40–42). Although these masks do not resemble the skin-covered masks in any way, they do resemble aspects of the Cross River monoliths (*see* §2 below), especially in the representation of facial scarification. Unlike the skin-covered masks, on which ethnic marks consist of a series of concentric circles on the temple, the face masks often have a vertical row of small keloids in the centre of the forehead, at the temples, and/or on the cheeks. By the

1970s some surviving face masks had passed into secondary use, for example in children's 'plays' at Christmas, while others continued to be used by such surviving traditional regulatory societies as Okua and Etankara. Most such face masks are either imported from the Annang craft centre at Ikot Ekpene, Nigeria (*see* IBIBIO, §1), or copied from them.

Masking is also an important activity of the Ngbe ('Leopard') society. This most prestigious and widely dispersed of Cross River secret societies was once thought to have originated among the Ejagham, but new evidence points to the ancestors of the present-day community of Isangele in the Rio del Rey area of south-west Cameroon (Nicklin, 1991). The association's rituals are concerned with the invocation and propitiation of the spirit of the leopard for the good of the community. Elders control the society's numerous grades and use its authority to enforce their legislative and judicial decisions. Younger members, sometimes masked, administer fines and punishments. Ngbe members meet regularly as a corporate group for eating, drinking, informal discussion and merriment.

For the members of most Ngbe grades the masquerade costume is woven from string, with coloured horizontal stripes, and covers the entire body, with ruffs of dyed raffia around the neck, wrists and ankles. A hat-like structure of cane and cloth is worn over the shoulders, and a feather-rod hangs down over the face from a topknot. A bell is worn around the waist, and the masker may also carry a hippopotamus hide whip with which to chastise non-initiates, or a ceremonial staff used in making customary signs to senior Ngbe members. The movements of the Ngbe masker are intended to simulate the powerful, graceful, cunning and controlled movements of leopards (Leib and Romano, 1984). The masker also tests the esoteric knowledge of those present by employing a sign language. The term for this, *nsibidi*, refers to a complex cultural phenomenon involving not only sign language but also a pictographic script, used in ground drawings and engraved with a hot poker on gourds. *Nsibidi* is also used as a source of decorative motifs for the indigo sew-and-dye cloth used for both dress and banners by Ngbe members. The term *nsibidi* is derived from the Ejagham word for 'to cut' or 'to sever', and nowhere is this given more sinister expression than in the two figures, dressed in black costume, faces obscured by palm fronds, who appear at the installation of the Ntui, the sacred leader of the Ejagham Qua people. Each of these characters strikes a buffalo horn with a machete to emphasize his role as an executioner, should the Ntui exceed the authority afforded him by custom.

Masquerade performances also characterize the Obassi Njom or Basinjom, a complex anti-witchcraft cult with graded membership (1974 exh. cat.; Koloss, 1984, 1985). Obassi Njom appears to have originated among the Ejagham, perhaps in the Oban or Ikom area, and then diffused widely. The Obassi Njom masker wears a carved wooden mask in the form of a stylized crocodile head backed by a fan of blue and yellow feathers, and a loose-fitting dark blue gown with raffia ruffs at the wrists and ankles. Accompanied by drum and rattle music the masker wheels and glides through the settlement searching out witches. He speaks in an esoteric tongue, while bearers follow with guns and a raffia-fringed wooden horn, blown to 'cool' his voice.

2. STONE SCULPTURE. The second best known Ejagham art form is that of the 'Cross River monoliths' (Allison, 1968). Until about 1900 some groups of northern Ejagham, including Akajuk, Nnam, Nselle and Nde, used basalt river boulders to commemorate their deceased 'priest-chiefs' or 'divine kings'. These monoliths were known as *akwanshi* among some groups, *atal* among others. Ranging in height from *c.* 0.3 m to 1.5 m, they are carved with human features: eyes, nose, mouth, beard and ethnic scarification marks—the latter mainly on the cheeks and temples. Most of the stones have a protuberant navel, and the overall configuration is often phallic (see fig. 2). Some have low-relief arms and hands and spiral decoration in the abdominal area, which may represent a no longer extant form of body scarification. Approximately 300 monoliths were recorded in the 1960s (Allison, 1968), since when many have entered the international art market and are no longer *in situ*. The number of known examples has, however, been extended by the work of Ekpo Eyo in the Ikom area. A radiocarbon date of *c.* AD 200 has also been established for some associated sites (Eyo, 1986). Eyo prefers to use the term *atal* rather than *akwanshi* for the carved stones, and, since they are found among sub-clans of the Bakor Clan, now calls this group the 'Bakor monoliths'.

2. Ejagham Cross River monolith, Nnam, near Ikom, Nigeria, *c.* AD 200; from a photograph by Keith Nicklin

3. CEMENT SCULPTURE. This form of commemorative art began to develop in the Ejagham forest lands in the early 20th century. Such monuments commemorated not only 'divine kings' but also those who had sufficient financial or social standing (Rosevear, 1984, p. 44). The most common form of Ejagham cement sculpture has been an abstracted human figure with one hand pointing heavenward, while other forms derived from the Celtic cross and the pointed Gothic window of the Christian missionaries. Many of the first cement sculptors learnt their art while working as migrant labourers in the Gold Coast. During the 1940s and 1950s the standard funerary sculpture for a man became the representation of a sola topi on a rectangular column, while for a woman it became a stylized version of the Celtic cross. In the 1970s the trend was towards realism, with artists working from a photograph of the deceased to produce an accurate rendering of the ancestor as a seated figure.

4. BRONZEWORK. Small, but well-executed, copper alloy castings are found among the Ejagham and other groups of south-east Nigeria and south-west Cameroon. These have been termed the 'Cross River bronzes' (Nicklin, 1982–3). Both anthropomorphic and zoomorphic forms occur, as well as representations of feline, possibly leopard, skulls, skeuomorphs of gourd and horn drinking vessels, and 'waisted' or 'tulip' bells. Bronze figures representing tutelary deities controlling agricultural and human fertility were in the guardianship of the spiritual leaders of the communities in which they were found. The bells were used to form the fringe of hide bags carried in ceremonial procession before village heads, as well as being used in shrines and worn by maskers and members of age-set wrestling groups.

Mid-17th-century and mid-19th-century dates have been established by thermoluminescence dating for a few of these bronzes (Nicklin and Fleming, 1980, 1982). Continuity with the more ancient past is, however, suggested by the decorative motifs, including skeuomorphic string and stitching lines and such geometric motifs as spirals, reversed or figure-of-eight spirals, and concentric circles, that the bronzes share with material from the site of IGBO-UKWU (9th century AD). The hypothesis (Neaher, 1979) that the bronzes of south-east Nigeria were produced in eastern Igboland and distributed by Aro traders would appear to be an oversimplification, in view of the fact that there is increasing evidence of manufacture by indigenous Cross River peoples, who perhaps learnt the skill from itinerant Igbo smiths (Nicklin, 1982–3).

5. WOOD-CARVING. The Ejagham are not renowned for their figure sculpture in wood, except for those carved human and animal forms that constitute parts of mask ensembles. Examples of firmly provenanced Ejagham wooden figure sculpture are rare but include some from the eastern Ejagham, Keaka, area (St Petersburg, Peter the Great Mus. Anthropol. & Ethnog.) described as having a 'sharp nose with flaring nostrils' and 'screw-head eyes' (Olderogge, 1969, p. 35). Others (Los Angeles, priv. col.) are said to have a 'powerful bent knee form' and 'a rudimentary sagittal crest' resembling that found in some mask forms among the Ejagham Keaka and Bokyi (Salmons, 1986). It has been suggested that this type of anthropomorphic carving was used as medicine (enok ateng, 'fighting alone') for protection against witchcraft (Salmons, 1986).

Large-scale sculpture, both house-posts and free-standing pillars, existed in the past (Mansfeld, 1908; Talbot, 1912). Few of these survived into the 1970s, however, by which time mighty monoxylous sculpture was more frequent among such western neighbours of the Ejagham as the Yakö and Mbembe. The same applies to the slit-drums used by Cross River peoples to summon men for war or to announce the death of a chief. In the past the Ejagham pieces were decorated with finials at either end, carved in the round to represent human beings or animals (or their heads), and the sides were carved in low relief with geometric, plant and animal (especially crocodile and snake) motifs. Again, by the 1970s most surviving examples of such drums were to be found among such neighbours of the Ejagham as the eastern Igbo, Widekum and Bangwa.

6. REGALIA AND PERSONAL ARTS. Traditionally, the regalia of an Ejagham chief often included a woven-string cap decorated with elephant-tail bristles, a circlet of leopard claws, a necklace of leopard teeth, a sacred staff and a side-blown horn of elephant ivory, the finial of which might be carved in the round in the form of an animal or human head. The bronze figures representing tutelary deities that the Ejagham chiefs kept (see §4 above) might also be considered part of their regalia.

The Ejagham practise a richly developed form of the so-called 'fatting-house' institution. The pre-nuptial fattening of women is a female rite of passage marking the change in status from girlhood to nubile womanhood. It is characterized by a period of seclusion lasting up to several months, during which the girl is given foods of high calorific value, her body is massaged, and she is instructed in matters of cuisine, deportment, dance and sexual technique. During the rite of incorporation the young woman parades with others of her age-set to display her corpulent body painted with intricate patterns and coloured with earth pigments and red camwood paste. Her hair may be made up into horn- or coronet-like structures, sometimes portrayed in cap masks (see §1 above) worn on such occasions. Waist-beads and brass leg-bangles may also be worn, as well as woollen halters with coloured pom-poms around the breasts, together with ivory or brass bracelets. In contrast to the IBIBIO, among whom the same institution is found, associated figure sculpture is not generally found among the Ejagham.

Members of Ejagham age-sets, comprising coevals of the same sex within a 3–4- year age range, were in the past marked with face or body scarification (see Mansfeld, 1928, for excellent illustrations). The inner portion of the upper and/or lower incisors of both sexes was sometimes removed. Rarely seen in life by the 1970s, such traditional body arts survive in the forms of masks and wooden sculptures.

BIBLIOGRAPHY
A. Mansfeld: Urwald-Dokumente (Berlin, 1908)
J. K. Macgregor: 'Some Notes of Nsibidi', J. Royal Anthropol. Inst. GB & Ireland, xxxix (1909), pp. 209–19

E. Dayrell: 'Further Notes on 'Nsibidi Signs with their Meanings from the Ikom District, Southern Nigeria', *J. Royal Anthropol. Inst. GB & Ireland*, xli (1911), pp. 521–40, pls lxv–lxvii

P. A. Talbot: *In the Shadow of the Bush* (London, 1912)

——: *The Peoples of Southern Nigeria: A Sketch of their History, Ethnology and Languages*, 4 vols (Oxford, 1926)

A. Mansfeld: *Westafrika aus Urwald und Steppe zwischen Crossfluss und Benue* (Munich, 1928)

M. D. W. Jeffreys: 'Some Notes on the Ekoi', *J. Royal Anthropol. Inst. GB & Ireland*, lxix (1939), pp. 95–108, pl. iii

P. Allison: *African Stone Sculpture* (London, 1968), pp. 25–35 and pls 27–49

——: *Cross River Monoliths* (Lagos, 1968)

D. Olderogge: *The Art of Africa: Negro Art from the Institute of Ethnography, Leningrad* (London, 1969)

K. Nicklin: 'Nigerian Skin-covered Masks', *Afr. A.*, vii/3 (1974), pp. 8–15, 67–8, 92

African Art in Motion: Icon and Act (exh. cat. by R. F. Thompson, Washington, DC, N.G.A.; Los Angeles, UCLA, Wight A.G.; 1974), pp. 172–88

K. Nicklin: *Guide to the National Museum, Oron* (Lagos, 1977)

N. C. Neaher: 'Nigerian Bronze Bells', *Afr. A.*, xii/3 (1979), pp. 42–7, 95–6

K. Nicklin: 'Skin-covered Masks of Cameroon', *Afr. A.*, xii/3 (1979), pp. 54–9, 91–2

K. Nicklin and S. J. Fleming: 'A Bronze "Carnivore Skull" from Oron, Nigeria', *MASCA J.*, i/4 (1980), pp. 104–5

K. Nicklin: 'Rape and Restitution: The Cross River Region Considered', *Museum* [Philadelphia], xxxiii/4 (1981), pp. 259–60

J. Salmons: 'Fat Is Beautiful', *A. Links* (Sept 1981), pp. 22–5

K. Nicklin and S. J. Fleming: 'Analysis of Two Bronzes from a Nigerian Asunaja Shrine', *MASCA J.*, ii/2 (1982), pp. 53–7

K. Nicklin: 'The Cross River Bronzes', *The Art of Metal in Africa* (exh. cat., ed. M.-T. Brincard; New York, Afr.–Amer. Inst.; Houston, TX, Sewall A.G.; Santa Ana, CA, Bowers Mus.; 1982–3), pp. 47–51

G. I. Jones: *The Art of Eastern Nigeria* (Cambridge, 1984)

H.-J. Koloss: 'Njom among the Ejagham', *Afr. A.*, xviii/1 (1984), pp. 71–3, 90–93

E. Leib and R. Romano: 'Reign of the Leopard: Ngbe Ritual', *Afr. A.*, xviii/1 (1984), pp. 48–57, 94–6

K. Nicklin: 'Cross River Studies', *Afr. A.*, xviii/1 (1984), pp. 24–7, 96

K. Nicklin and J. Salmons: 'Cross River Art Styles', *Afr. A.*, xviii/1 (1984), pp. 28–43, 93–4

D. R. Rosevear: 'Cross River Tombstones', *Afr. A.*, xviii/1 (1984), pp. 44–7, 94

H.-J. Koloss: 'Obasinjom among the Ejagham', *Afr. A.*, xviii/2 (1985), pp. 63–5, 98–101, 103

E. Eyo: 'Alok and Emangabe Stone Monoliths: Ikom, Cross River State of Nigeria', *Arte in Africa: Realtà e prospettive nello studio della storia delle arti africane*, ed. E. Bassani (Modena, 1986), pp. 101–4

J. Salmons: 'Keaka Figures', *Expressions of Cameroon Art: The Franklin Collection* (exh. cat., ed. T. Northern; Los Angeles, CA, Nat. Hist. Mus.; Baltimore, MD, Mus. A.; Hanover, NH, Dartmouth Coll., Hood Mus. A.; 1986), pp. 74–5

K. Nicklin: 'An Ejagham Emblem of the Ekpe Society', *A. Tribal*, 1 (1991), pp. 3–18

KEITH NICKLIN

Ekaku Hakuin. *See* HAKUIN EKAKU.

Ekeland, Arne (*b* Bøn, Eidsvoll, 14 Aug 1908; *d* 28 Feb 1994). Norwegian painter. He was self-taught, apart from a few months' study at the Kunstakademi in Oslo in 1928, where he was influenced by the artistic concepts of his teacher Axel Revold's decorative compositions, built up of striking colours. He spent his childhood in Bøn's working-class district, and his Communist sympathies were influenced by his father's political convictions. The suffering and struggle of the working-class on the one hand and on the other the Utopia of a free and classless society are constant themes in his work, along with the surroundings of Bøn and references to art history. Ekeland's paintings of the 1930s, for example *We Unemployed* (1934; Oslo, N.G.), were influenced by German Expressionism, Surrealism and Cubism. Their subjects show poor, protesting people, and the dark and brutal colour contrasts correspond to the symbolic undertones of the content; this artistic vocabulary was already setting Ekeland apart from other politically conscious Norwegian painters.

Ekeland was attracted by the Cubism in the works of Pablo Picasso and Georges Braque after a long stay in Paris in 1931. Three years later, a trip to Italy inspired him to become more concerned with aesthetic and decorative values in his work. These he found in the ornamental, decorative narratives of Byzantine ecclesiastical art and the cool formality of Florentine painting. Such impulses indicated the way to his distinctive symbolic form of expression through monumental, imaginative paintings in which great, bleached figures offer easily interpreted messages about oppression and repression, as in *The Drawings* (1937; Oslo, Komm. Kstsaml.), and feelings of joy, freedom and comradeship. *Sisters of Freedom* (1957–8; Oslo, Storting), of which there is a later version (1964; Gjøvik, Rådhus), a competition project for the decoration of the Oslo Town Hall, originally submitted in 1938, shows his concern with aesthetic value and also his wish to depict global, social approaches to problems. The work (a sketch for a later painting) was given a cash prize for its painterly quality but did not win the competition, perhaps because of its social content or its allegorical form. The theme is the brotherhood of the peoples of the world under the shelter of learning and the fruits of the earth. The dry colours, confined to pale pink, blue and grey against a kaleidoscopic background of strong colours, and the constructed landscape combine with the idealized, naked throng of people to form a musical play of lines and colour. Ekeland aroused attention with his very first exhibition, and his exhibition in Kunstnernes Hus, Oslo, in April 1940 established him as one of the most significant painters of the time.

During World War II, Ekeland recreated the despairing mood of the country and manifested its opposition to the occupation of Norway in such works as the expressive *Last Shot* (1940; Oslo, N.G.) and the visionary *Struggle* (1943; Oslo, N.G.). His concern for the depiction of beauty expressed itself in a series of spring scenes with elongated female figures gleaming like mother-of-pearl among children and flowers, for example *Spring Picture* (1941; ex-Hafsten priv. col., see Ekeland and Moe, 1986 exh. cat., p. 15). After his trip to the USSR in 1948 Ekeland experimented with Socialist Realism (e.g. *Dove Flying*, 1953; see Revold, p. 255) in a departure interpreted by the critics as an unfortunate shift towards formalism. Over the years, however, Ekeland's works related more consistently to his perception of space, moving from deep perspective to a more planar representation with horizontal and vertical structures. Thickly and thinly applied brushstrokes came to delineate faceted forms. In the early 1960s Ekeland reduced his colour register and began working Neo-classical buildings and 19th-century factories from Bøn, formerly only background subjects, into a mechanistic pattern (the so-called 'cogwheel style'). In many paintings, in a metal-grey atmosphere, sculptural humans and machines pull and work together in a sort of rhythmic cooperation, as in *Old Dam* (1963; artist's col., see 1986 exh. cat. p. 30).

Shortly after a trip to China in 1966, Ekeland made a general move towards abstraction. Paintings from this period, such as the *White Roof Falls* (1968; artist's col., see Ekeland and Moe, 1986 exh. cat., p. 23), and the use of strengthened colour contrasts and ribbon-like forms, reveal an affinity with Futurism and the clean lines of hard-edge painting compressed into an expressive synthesis. Ekeland participated in two Biennales, in São Paulo (1957) and Venice (1972). In the paintings in his retrospective exhibition (Høvikkoden, Henies–Onstads Kstsent., 1986) the cool power of the pastel colours was stronger, and aesthetic concern was demonstrated through the use of disintegrating, decorative forms. In *The Chain* (1979–85; artist's col., see Ekeland and Moe, 1986 exh. cat., p. 40), the stylized, doll-like figures who, as in his earlier work, symbolized injustice, show the concerns expressed in his subject-matter to have remained unchanged. Later in life Ekeland, who influenced two generations of Norwegian painters, lived at Bøn in self-imposed isolation. He kept in his own possession his large production of drawings, ink washes and watercolours, mostly made in preparation for the paintings. Ekeland did not care for publicity or for exhibiting, and he was never tempted to alter his political convictions in line with the changes in Eastern Europe and the USSR during the 1980s. He also wrote poetry, stories and notes, mostly for private use.

NKL

BIBLIOGRAPHY

A. Revold: *Norges billedkunst i det 19. og 20. århundre* [Norway's pictorial art in the 19th and 20th centuries] (Oslo, 1953), ii, pp. 247–54
K. Berg and others, eds: *Mellomkrigstid* [The inter-war period] (1983), vi of *Norges kunsthistorie* (Oslo, 1981–3), pp. 168, 233–7
——: *Inn i en ny tid* [Into a new era] (1983), vii of *Norges Kunsthistorie* (Oslo, 1981–3), pp. 95, 120–22
Arne Ekeland (exh. cat. by A. Ekeland and O. H. Moe, Høvikkodden, Henies–Onstads Kstsent., 1986)
Arne Ekeland, Paintings: 1937–85 (exh. cat. by K. Frydenlund and O. H. Moe, Edinburgh, City A. Cent.; Jarrow, Bede A.G.; Swansea, Vivian A.G. & Mus.; 1986)
O. Storm Bjerke: *Arne Ekeland* (in preparation)

SUSANNE RAJKA

Ekels, Jan, II (*b* Amsterdam, 28 June 1759; *d* Amsterdam, 4 June 1793). Dutch painter and draughtsman. He was first trained by his father, Jan Ekels I (1724–81), and from 1774 to 1781 attended the Amsterdam Tekenacademie. He won prizes in the annual competition for life drawing in 1779 and 1781. In 1776 he went to Paris for two years to further his studies before returning to Amsterdam. Possibly influenced by the revival of interest in Dutch 17th-century art, he became a painter of portraits, genre pieces and *'moderne gezelschappen'* (modern conversation pieces). In 1783 he travelled along the Rhine in Germany with his friends Daniel Dupré (1752–1817) and Jacques Kuyper (1761–1808), visiting the collections at Düsseldorf and Mannheim. After his return in 1784 he became an active member of the Felix Meritis society.

Ekels left a relatively small oeuvre (some 50 paintings are known), partly because he was financially independent and partly because he died young after a stroke. He enjoyed painting scenes from everyday life; it is not always clear whether his realism contained allegorical meanings.

His most famous pictures of this kind are the *Writer Sharpening his Pen* (1784; Amsterdam, Rijksmus.), the *Draughtsman* and the *Smoker* (both 1787; Frankfurt am Main, Städel. Kstinst.). Their format, composition, colour scheme and lighting are reminiscent of Johannes Vermeer, Pieter de Hooch and Adriaen van Ostade. Apart from these, he painted allegorical themes, such as the Five Senses. He also made many drawings after Old Masters and a few portraits that were engraved by Reinier Vinkeles and Louis E. F. Garreau (*fl* 1782–96). His work, like that of Adriaan de Lelie and Wybrand Hendriks, anticipated the anecdotal paintings of the 19th century. Jacob Smies (1764–1833), the famous cartoonist, was his pupil.

BIBLIOGRAPHY
Scheen; Thieme–Becker
J. Knoef: *Tusschen rococo en romantiek* (The Hague, 1948), pp. 21–36
Dutch Masterpieces from the Eighteenth Century: Paintings and Drawings, 1700–1800 (exh. cat., ed. E. R. Mandle, essay J. W. Niemeijer; Minneapolis, Inst. A.; Toledo, OH, Mus. A.; Philadelphia, Mus. A.; 1971–2), pp. 40–42

P. KNOLLE

Ekelund, (Georg) Hilding (*b* Kangasniemi, 18 Nov 1893; *d* Helsinki, 30 Jan 1984). Finnish architect. He graduated in architecture from the University of Technology in Helsinki in 1916. His earliest works were in the style of Scandinavian Classicism. Following his first journey to Italy (1921–2), he concentrated on the study of *architettura minore*, the anonymous houses of countryside and towns. He became well known for his travel sketches, which he produced throughout his life. After his return to Finland he entered numerous architectural competitions, although few of his entries were executed. After a trip to Italy in 1926 he was commissioned to design the interior of the Capitol cinema in Helsinki, taking his inspiration from the ancient site of Pompeii. In Töölö Church (1927–30) he combined Mediterranean motifs with Functionalist elements and a skilful manipulation of the surrounding space. Ekelund's main work of the 1920s was the Art Exhibition Hall (1927–8) in Helsinki, where one can see the influence of many of the most important exhibition buildings and pavilion projects of Scandinavian Classicism. His airy perspective drawings for the urban planning competition for the Töölö area of Helsinki (1925) also hold an important place in the history of Finnish architecture.

Ekelund contributed to the introduction of Functionalism in Finland, not only through his competition entries but also as editor-in-chief of the journal *Arkkitehti* (1931–4). Executed Functionalist buildings by Ekelund include the Finnish Embassy (1935–8) in Moscow and the cycling and rowing stadiums (1939–40) in Helsinki. From 1941 to 1949 he was city architect in Helsinki. He was deeply influenced by the ideas and works of Heinrich Tessenow. His first opportunity to realize his ideas on housing design came in the Olympic Village (1939–40) in Helsinki. The area became a Nordic variation of the German Siedlung. His later production included schools and housing developments, for example Sahamäki housing (1950–56) in Maunula in Helsinki. From 1950 to 1958 Ekelund was Professor of Housing Design at the University of Technology in Helsinki. Ekelund's wife, Eva Kuhlefelt-Ekelund (1892–1984), was also an architect and produced one of the most successful classicist designs of the 1920s, the Private Swedish Girls' School (1928–9) in Helsinki. Later she concentrated on the building problems of the countryside and worked as architect for Bostadsföreningen för Svenska Finland (Finland's Swedish-speaking Housing Association) between 1936 and 1966.

WRITINGS
'Nykyajan rakennustaide ja traditio' [Modern architecture and tradition], *Abacus*, iii (1983), pp. 167–87 [Fin. and Eng. text of Ekelund's lecture at U. of Technology in 1951]

BIBLIOGRAPHY
Nordisk klassicism/Nordic Classicism, 1910–1930 (exh. cat., ed. S. Paavilainen; Helsinki, Mus. Fin. Archit., 1982)
Arkkitehti/Arkitekten, 8 (1983) [issue ded. Ekelund]
Profiles: Pioneering Women Architects from Finland (exh. cat., Helsinki, Mus. Fin. Archit., 1983)

SIMO PAAVILAINEN

Ekhmim. See AKHMIM.

Ekkei. See TENSHŌ SHŪBUN.

Eklingji and Nagda. Two groups of Hindu temples of the 10th–15th centuries AD on the edge of a small lake near Udaipur in Rajasthan, India. The complex is enclosed by undecorated walls similar to those at Baroli. The main temple at Eklingji is dedicated to Shiva and houses a *linga* regarded as the guardian deity of the Sisodia Maharanas of Mewar. However, the earliest temple in the complex is the Lakulisha Temple (971–2), a simple building consisting of a sanctuary (*vimāna*), a hall (*maṇḍapa*) and a porch. One wall niche contains an image of the goddess Sarasvati (*see* INDIAN SUBCONTINENT, §V, 7(iii)(a)), and inside the sanctum is a seated sculpture of Lakulisha, founder of the Pashupata sect; the doorway has a similar image on the lintel. Although the hall is square, its supporting columns form an octagonal space. Niches on its outer walls contain relief sculptures of a variety of goddesses. The main Eklingji temple dates from the 15th century. The principal sanctuary and the two-storey hall are constructed of marble, and there is a curved tower over the sanctuary. Inside the sanctum is a highly decorated silver doorway and screen preceding the central image, a black marble four-faced Shiva *linga*, faced by a silver figure of the god's vehicle, the bull Nandi. In the corner of the temple is an underground pool from which rises a small *linga*; according to legend, this stone was worshipped by the founder of the Mewar Dynasty, Bappa Rawal.

Some 2 km north of Eklingji are the Vaishnava Sas and Bahu temples of Nagda, the earliest capital of the Mewar rulers. The temples, attributable to the late 10th century, stand on a common platform (*jagatī*). The larger Sas ('mother-in-law') Temple is surrounded by ten secondary shrines, while the smaller Bahu ('daughter-in-law') Temple has four. Each temple consists of a sanctuary with an elaborately carved doorway, a hall and an open porch; the curvilinear brick superstructures have suffered some damage. The sanctuary walls are undecorated but contain images of Brahma, Shiva and Vishnu, above which are representations of Rama, Balarama and Parashvrama. In contrast, the porches and halls have a variety of sculptures and decoration, including relief carvings of auspicious *mithuna* couples, divine nymphs (*apsarasa*s) and episodes from religious narratives. The hall columns are richly decorated, and there are eight brackets in the form of women in the ceiling of the smaller temple.

BIBLIOGRAPHY
J. Tod: *Annals and Antiquities of Rajasthan*, 3 vols (Oxford, 1920)
J. C. Harle: *The Art and Architecture of the Indian Subcontinent* (London, 1986)
G. Michell: *Buddhist, Jain, Hindu*, Penguin Guide Mnmts India, i (London, 1989), pp. 286–7

HEATHER ELGOOD

Ekman, Robert Wilhelm (*b* Uusikaupunki, nr Turku, 13 Aug 1808; *d* Turku, 19 Feb 1873). Finnish painter. Between 1824 and 1837 he studied at the Kungliga Akademi för de Fria Konsterna in Stockholm. From about 1831 he was also a private pupil of Johan Gustav Sandberg (1782–1854), the leading exponent of a type of painting depicting Swedish folk life. Although Ekman succeeded in satisfying the Neo-classical principles taught at the Konstakademi, Sandberg's themes of folk romanticism had a greater impact on his art. In 1837 he received the Konstakademi's substantial travel grant, which enabled him to study in Paris. He travelled to France by way of the Netherlands, where he became familiar with 17th-century Dutch genre painting, which he studied further in Paris. As a student in Paris, he also came into contact with contemporary European art and continued his studies under Paul Delaroche, whose *juste-milieu* style was a decisive influence on him. Ekman's work from this period is not well known, but it seems that both his technical skills and his artistic vision matured significantly. In 1840 he went to Italy, where he remained for three years. He abandoned his formal education and concentrated on visiting the museums and studying the landscape and peoples of the south. The portrayal of colourful folk life (e.g. *Italian Servant*, c. 1841–2; Turku, A. Mus.; see fig.) remained his greatest interest.

Ekman returned to Sweden in 1844 and was elected a member of the Konstakademi. In 1845 he received an important commission to provide frescoes with religious and historical themes for the chancel of Turku Cathedral (*in situ*) and so moved back to Finland, finally completing the project in 1854. His extensive experience and education abroad afforded him a central place in Finland's art world during the 1840s and 1850s. The idealistic form of nationalism dominating Finnish intellectual life from the 1840s to the 1860s provided a favourable atmosphere for his type of artistic expression. In 1845 he settled in Turku, the old cultural capital of Finland, where he taught and had many pupils who became leading painters in the following generation, such as Karl Emanuel Jansson (1846–74) and Alexandra Frosterus-Såltin (1837–1916). He continued to paint Italian themes, but Finnish folk life soon became a more dominant interest. His idealizing style reflected the prevailing intellectual atmosphere, leading to such works as *Theme from 'The Elk-hunters'* (1845; see Reitala and Lauréus, p. 104, fig. 3), *Sunday Morning in a Savo Farmhouse* (1847) and *Pentti Lyytinen Reading his Poems in a Peasant Cottage* (1848; all priv. cols, see Wennervirta, pl. 14). He was much acclaimed for these predominantly genre works and remained financially successful well into the 1860s, although he worked in almost total isolation from other artists.

Robert Wilhelm Ekman: *Italian Servant*, oil on canvas, 720×260 mm, 1846 (Turku, Art Museum)

Ekman first became interested in the Finnish national epic, the *Kalevala*, at the end of the 1850s. He became completely immersed in the idea of creating an extensive series of paintings based on themes from it at a time when national idealism was becoming increasingly unfashionable in Finland. He was thus driven into a spiritual as well as economic impasse that embittered the last years of his life. His incomplete collection of works illustrating the *Kalevala* is nonetheless very interesting, especially from an iconographic point of view. The major painting in the series is the large *Väinämöinen's Music* (*c.* 3.90×2.85 m, 1858–66; Helsinki, Old Student House). In the more liberal and politicized intellectual climate of the 1860s, his idealism came to seem old-fashioned to his students, many of whom left to study in Düsseldorf. In later years he resignedly returned to familiar folk themes. For example, between 1867 and 1869 he produced several versions (Helsinki, Athenaeum A. Mus.; Turku, A. Mus.) of his earlier *Kreeta Haapsalo* painting (1857), which again drew on the *Kalevala*. He retained his eclectic style, a mixture of 17th-century Dutch art, Swedish folk romanticism, Italian influences and the Neo-classicism learnt at the Konstakademi in Stockholm. Towards the end of his life, however, Realist features begin to appear in such works as *Catechism*

Morning (1868; Helsinki, Athenaeum A. Mus.). He also painted a large number of altarpieces, such as the *Deposition* (1855) for the Grenadjärskapskytte-Bataljonenskyrka in Turku. Ekman's nephew Carl Anders Ekman (1833–55) was also a painter.

BIBLIOGRAPHY

B. Hintze: *Robert Wilhelm Ekman, 1808–1873: En konsthistorisk studie* [Robert Wilhelm Ekman: a study in art history] (Helsinki, 1926)
L. Wennervirta: *Suomen taidetta, 1800–luvulla* (Porvoo and Helsinki, 1934, 3/1964), pl. 14
J. Ervamaa: 'R. W. Ekmanin Kreeta Haapsalo-aiheiset maalaukset' [R. W. Ekman's paintings of Kreeta Haapsalo], *Ateneumin Taidemuseo Museojulkaisu*, i–ii (1971), pp. 7–18 [Swed. pp. 36–43]
A. Reitala and A. Lauréus: *Taidehistoriallisia tutkimuksia*, Konsthistoriska studier, i (Helsinki, 1974), p. 104, fig. 3
——: *R. W. Ekmanin ja C. E. Sjöstrandin Kalevalaaiheiden taide* [The *Kalevala* in the art work of R. W. Ekman and C. E. Sjöstrand], Fin. Fornminnesfören. Tidskr./Suom. Muinmuist. Aikak., 81 (Helsinki, 1981)

JUKKA ERVAMAA

Ekphrasis [Gr., pl. *ekphraseis*; Lat. *descriptio*]. Technical term of ancient rhetoric: teachers of rhetoric defined it as a vivid description intended to bring the subject before the mind's eye of the listener. The composition of an ekphrasis was one of the most advanced of the graded preparatory exercises (*progymnasmata*) designed to teach basic rhetorical skills to schoolboys. These texts suggest persons, places, events and times of the year as possible themes for ekphrasis. In practice, however, paintings, sculpture and buildings came to be popular subjects for Greek rhetoricians from the 2nd century AD onwards. Ekphraseis of works of art and buildings survived throughout the Byzantine Middle Ages and reached the West during the Renaissance.

An ekphrasis can be characterized as an extended description of a rhetorical nature. The author displayed his skill with words as well as expressing the qualities of the work described. An ekphrasis generally attempted to convey the visual impression and the emotional responses evoked by the painting or building, not to leave a detailed, factual account. In an ekphrasis of a painting the author did not confine himself to the specific moment represented but was free to discuss the general narrative context, referring both forwards and backwards in time. He was also free to imagine what the characters might be feeling or saying and might even be moved to address them. Since ekphraseis in antiquity and the Byzantine period were often composed for special occasions, to honour the patron, architect or, more rarely, the artist, they set out to praise, not to criticize. The value of ekphrasis as a source for archaeological reconstruction is therefore often limited, but it can provide some indication of contemporary responses to art.

1. The literary tradition of describing works of art. 2. Rhetorical ekphrasis in antiquity. 3. Byzantine ekphrasis. 4. Ekphrasis in the Renaissance West.

1. THE LITERARY TRADITION OF DESCRIBING WORKS OF ART. Ancient literature included descriptions of works of art long before rhetoricians took up the genre. Such passages are related to rhetorical ekphrasis and are in many ways precursors of it, but instead of developing these descriptions for their own sake, authors use them as literary devices tailored to the demands of the narrative

context. The earliest are to be found in the *Iliad*, where Hephaistos is described decorating the shield of Achilles with various detailed scenes of human life: cities at peace and at war, men at work in the fields and a scene of celebration (XVIII). The authors of later epics followed the Homeric example. Such descriptions perform various functions. The scenes depicted on shields or other objects may foreshadow future events: for example, Virgil's Shield of Aeneas (*Aeneid* VIII) bears scenes of the future history of Rome. Like the paintings of the Trojan War that Aeneas finds at Carthage (*Aeneid* I), they may, on the other hand, refer to the immediate past. Other poets exploited this opportunity for creating a scene within a scene. For example, in poem 64 Catullus (*c.* 84–*c.* 54 BC) develops an image of Ariadne on Naxos, depicted on a couch, into a full narrative of her love for Theseus and her abandonment, setting up a complex interplay between this digression and the wedding scene in the main body of the poem. Descriptions of paintings were also used to didactic ends. Cebes' *Pinax* (?1st century AD) is a moral interpretation in dialogue form of an allegorical picture. In such Greek 'novels' as *Daphnis and Chloe* by Longus (*fl* 3rd century AD) and *Kleitophon and Leukippe* by Achilles Tatius (*fl c.* late 2nd century AD), descriptions of paintings play a significant role in the plot, functioning as omens or even inspiring the narrator to begin his tale.

2. RHETORICAL EKPHRASIS IN ANTIQUITY. Greek rhetoricians in the Roman Empire adopted and developed the description of works of art for their own sake. These could either be the subject of a whole piece or might be included as graphic illustrations of a point. In *The Hall*, LUCIAN OF SAMOSATA gave a description of a sumptuous hall, decorated with mythological scenes; his *Hippias*, in praise of an architect, gives an account of the baths he had designed. In *Hercules*, Lucian describes and interprets an unusual representation of the god drawing people by chains to symbolize the force of eloquence. He also introduced descriptions of pictures into short essays on various topics, illustrating *On Calumny* with an account of an allegorical depiction by the painter Apelles. For an example of a new and unusual subject he used a painting by Zeuxis of a family of centaurs in his *Zeuxis*. *Herodotus* features a painting of Alexander the Great's marriage to Roxana.

Philostratos Lemnios composed a collection of ekphraseis of paintings, entitled *Eikones*, or *Imagines* (first half of the 3rd century AD), purporting to be descriptions of works in a private collection in Naples, addressed to the owner's son (*see* PHILOSTRATOS, (1)). Philostratus the younger, his grandson, added a third book (*see* PHILOSTRATOS, (2)). The descriptions concentrate on the narrative subject-matter of the paintings and are rich in literary allusions, paradoxes and appeals to the emotions. They contain a few remarks on illusionistic techniques, such as shading and the effects of depth, but composition is largely ignored. It is impossible to tell if the gallery described by Philostratos Lemnios really existed. None of the artists is named, but some of the individual descriptions are similar to surviving Roman paintings (e.g. *Narcissus* and the *Education of Achilles*; both Naples, Mus. Archeol. N.) or to statues (e.g. *Dwarfs*). In the 4th century AD Kallistratos

composed a series of descriptions of statues with the title *Ekphraseis*. They concentrate on the depiction of emotions and frequently praise the effects of realism attained by the sculptors. The artists are often named, and some of the works described may be identifiable with surviving copies of ancient sculptures (e.g. *Narcissus*). Also in the 4th century, the teacher and sophist Libanios of Antioch (314–93) composed a series of model ekphraseis which include some of paintings.

Despite some opposition to images and to Classical culture, the Greek Church Fathers made use of ekphraseis of works of art in their sermons. Asterios of Amasia (*d c.* 410), for example, described a painting of scenes from the martyrdom of St Euphemia: its realism served to heighten its emotional effect for him. Pagan works could also be turned to a Christian use; thus Gregorius Nazianzenus (4th century AD) used a depiction of Maenads to evoke an image of frenzy.

3. BYZANTINE EKPHRASIS. The Byzantines continued to use *progymnasmata* in schools and to read the examples of ekphrasis in the works of Lucian, the Philostrati and the Church Fathers. Byzantine authors composed ekphraseis in verse and prose as independent works or included them in sermons and in secular literature. Ekphraseis were often composed to be recited on special occasions, such as the inauguration of a church, and thus often describe identifiable monuments. The rhetorical school of 6th-century Gaza produced several notable examples. Choricius of Gaza in his *Laudatio Marciani* described two churches with their decorative schemes. John of Gaza described a cosmological painting in the baths of either Gaza or Antioch with a mixture of Christian and pagan elements. Prokopios of Gaza (*d c.* 550) described, in honour of the patron, a complex programme of paintings of the myth of Phaedra and Hippolytus.

Paulos Silentiarios' verse ekphrasis of Hagia Sophia in Constantinople was recited at the beginning of 563, soon after the second consecration of the church; it celebrated the Emperor Justinian's rebuilding of the dome. He emphasized the effect of light and space in the building and the splendour of the multi-coloured marble. His account corresponds well to what is known of the church at that period and gives useful information, telling us, for example, that the original decorative scheme probably included no figural mosaics. The church of the Holy Apostles in Constantinople (destr. 1469; *see* ISTANBUL, §III, 9(i)) is documented in two ekphraseis that provide valuable evidence for the architecture and decoration of the building. The verse ekphrasis by Constantinus Rhodius, addressed to the Emperor Constantine IX between 931 and 944, concentrates on the architecture. Nikolaos Mesarites' prose ekphrasis (between 1198 and 1203) describes the building from the exterior to the interior, using the mosaics as a starting point for theological discourse. The homilies of the 9th-century Patriarch Photios and the Emperor Leo VI (866–912) also include ekphraseis of churches and their decoration.

Descriptions of real and imaginary works were also included in secular literature. The 10th- or 11th-century ballad *Digenes Akrites* describes the hero's marvellous palace (Book VII), and Eustathios Makrembolites' novel

Hysmine and Hysminias (12th century) contains accounts of allegorical picture cycles. One of the last Byzantine emperors, Manuel II Palaeologos, described a tapestry he had seen in Paris during his visit to the West between 1399 and 1402. Like many Byzantine ekphraseis it shows the influence of a literary model, in this case Libanios' ekphrasis of spring.

4. EKPHRASIS IN THE RENAISSANCE WEST. Interest in Greek studies grew in Italy from the end of the 14th century. The scholar Manuel Chrysoloras passed on the Byzantine taste for Lucian to the early humanists. One of his pupils, the humanist and teacher Guarino da Verona, translated Lucian's *On Calumny* into Latin (probably before 1415), and several more translations were made during the 15th century. Leon Battista Alberti included the description of Apelles' painting in his *De pictura* (1435) as an example of invention.

Artists and patrons soon saw the potential of ancient ekphrasis as a source of subject-matter and as a means of recreating ancient graphic art, which was then almost entirely unknown. Botticelli's *Calumny of Apelles* (1490s; Florence, Uffizi) is based on a Latin translation of Lucian's dialogue. The challenge of recreating Apelles' painting was taken up by several other artists, including Mantegna (drawing, *c.* 1504–6; London, BM), Raphael (drawing;

Ekphrasis from *Imagines* by Philostratus the elder: *Les Amours*; anonymous engraving in Blaise de Vigenère's translation entitled *Les Images ou tableaux de platte peinture* (Paris, 1614), p. 31 (London, University of London, Warburg Institute)

Paris, Louvre) and in the north by Dürer (1521–2; ex-Rathaus, Nuremberg, destr.). The *Marriage of Alexander and Roxana* proved a popular subject, appearing, for example, in drawings by Raphael (1515–16; Haarlem, Teylers Mus.; Vienna, Albertina) and Parmigianino (*c.* 1527–30; Hamburg, Ksthalle; Vienna, Edgar Plan priv. col.) as well as in frescoes by Sodoma (1516–17; Rome, Villa Farnesina), Niccolò dell'Abate (1570; Fontainebleau, Château) and Taddeo Zuccaro (1559–60; Rome, Pal. Caetani) and on tapestries and maiolica. Lucian's *Hercules* was illustrated in drawings from the school of Raphael (Oxford, Ashmolean) and by Giulio Romano (London, V&A) and Dürer (Vienna, Ksthist. Mus.); it also appears in various emblematic contexts. Dürer also drew Zeuxis' *Centaur Family* (1505; Coburg, Veste Coburg), and Joannes Stradanus published a print of the same subject based on a drawing by Hans Collaert (*c.* 1570). In 1658 Poussin based his *Orion* (New York, Met.) on one of the paintings in Lucian's *Hall*.

The *Imagines* of the Philostrati and Kallistratos' *Ekphraseis* were known in Italy by the mid-15th century and were first printed (with an edition of the works of Lucian) in Venice in 1503. Isabella d'Este had the *Imagines* translated into Italian (*c.* 1511); the Elder Philostratos was also the source for several paintings commissioned by Isabella and her brother Duke Alfonso of Ferrara. In the programme for Perugino's *Combat of Love and Chastity* (1503; Paris, Louvre), painted for Isabella, the detail of cupids riding swans comes from *Imagines* I.9. Titian recreated *Imagines* I.6 and I.25 in his *Worship of Venus* (1518–19) and *Andrians* (1523–5; both Madrid, Prado) for Alfonso's Camerino d'Alabastro in Ferrara. Rubens later copied both of these paintings. Alfonso's son Ercole commissioned a painting of *Hercules and the Pygmies* (*Imagines* II.22) from Battista Dossi in 1534 (Graz, Steiermark. Landesmus.). Philostratus also supplied the subject-matter for the decoration of the Villa Madama by Giovanni da Udine and Baldassare Peruzzi. A luxury edition of Blaise de Vigenère's French translation of the Philostrati and Kallistratos, with engravings designed by Antoine Caron and others (see fig.), was printed in Paris in 1614. Apart from these specific instances, the mythological scenes from Lucian and Philostratus were absorbed into the iconographic repertory of the Renaissance and influenced many decorative schemes.

It has been suggested that Giorgio Vasari's descriptions of paintings in his *Vite* and those of Pietro Aretino in his letters on art belong to the tradition of ekphrasis. Although these descriptions show the interest in narrative and emotion familiar from the Philostrati, there are vital differences in their aims. The Renaissance critics show a new interest in the formal aspects of particular paintings, which are treated as ends in themselves. In this they differ from the earlier tradition of ekphrasis, which used works of art as starting-points for displays of rhetorical virtuosity. Rhetoric began to give way to criticism, and the significance of the work lay less in what it represented than in its place in the history of art.

BIBLIOGRAPHY
P. Friedländer: *Johannes von Gaza und Paulus Silentiarius. Kunstbeschreibungen justinianischer Zeit* (Leipzig, 1912)

Philostratus the elder and Philostratus Lemnius the younger: *Imagines*; Callistratus: *Descriptions*; with Eng. trans. by A. Fairbanks, Loeb Class. Lib. (Cambridge, MA, 1931)

E. H. Gombrich: 'The Subject of Poussin's *Orion*', *Burl. Mag.*, lxxxvi (1944), pp. 37–41; *R* in *Symbolic Images* (Oxford, 1985), pp. 119–22

G. Downey: 'Ekphrasis', *Reallexikon für Antike und Christentum*, ed. T. Klausner, iv (Stuttgart, 1959)

S. Alpers: 'Ekphrasis and Aesthetic Attitudes in Vasari's *Lives*', *J. Warb. & Court. Inst.*, xxiii (1960), pp. 190–215

E. C. Harlan: *The Description of Paintings as a Literary Device and its Application in Achilles Tatius* (diss., U. Columbia, 1965)

G. Hohlweg: 'Ekphrasis', *Reallexikon zur byzantinischen Kunst*, ed. K. Wessel and M. Restle, ii (Stuttgart, 1971)

M. Baxandall: *Giotto and the Orators* (Oxford, 1972)

C. Mango: *The Art of the Byzantine Empire: Sources and Documents* (Englewood Cliffs, 1972)

H. Maguire: 'Truth and Convention in Byzantine Descriptions of Works of Art', *Dumbarton Oaks Pap.*, xxviii (1974), pp. 111–40

D. Cast: *The Calumny of Apelles* (New Haven, 1981)

M. Marek: *Ekphrasis und Herrscherallegorie* (Worms, 1985)

N. Land: 'Ekphrasis and Imagination: Some Observations on Pietro Aretino's Art Criticism', *A. Bull.*, lxviii (1986), pp. 207–17

Bacchanals by Titian and Rubens. Papers Given at a Symposium in Nationalmuseum: Stockholm, 1987

D. Carrier: 'Ekphrasis and Interpretation: Two Modes of Art History Writing', *Brit. J. Aesth.*, xxvii (1987), pp. 20–31

R. Macrides and P. Magdalino: 'The Architecture of Ekphrasis: Construction and Context of Paul the Silentiary's Poem on Hagia Sophia', *Byz. & Mod. Gr. Stud.*, xii (1988), pp. 47–82

G. Perini: 'L'arte di descrivere: La tecnica dell'ecfrasi in Malvasia e Bellori', *I Tatti Stud.*, iii (1989), pp. 175–206

N. Land: 'Titian's *Martyrdom of St Peter Martyr* and Ekphrastic Art Criticism', *A. Hist.*, xiii (1990), pp. 297–317

J. M. Massing: *Du texte à l'image: La Calomnie d'Apelle et son iconographie* (Strasbourg, 1990)

D. Rosand: '*Ekphrasis* and the Generation of Images', *Arion*, n.s. 3, i (1990), pp. 61–105

L. James and R. Webb: 'To Understand Ultimate Things and Enter Secret Places: Ekphrasis and Art in Byzantium', *A. Hist.*, xiv (1991), pp. 1–17

J. A. W. Heffernan: *Museum of Words: The Poetics of Ekphrasis from Homer to Ashbery* (Chicago and London, 1993)

RUTH WEBB

Eksperimentalni atelje. *See* EXAT-51.

Ekster, Aleksandra. *See* EXTER, ALEXANDRA.

Ekström, Per (*b* Övre Segerstad, Öland, 23 Feb 1844; *d* Mörbylånga, Öland, 21 Jan 1935). Swedish painter. He studied from 1865 to 1872 at the Konstakademi in Stockholm, where he was influenced more by the French tradition than by the German Düsseldorf tradition, as seen in such works as *Autumn Landscape at Dusk* (1872; Stockholm, Nmus.). There he became the leading personality in a Bohemian circle and met August Strindberg, who used Ekström's character as the basis for the artist Sellén in his novel *Röda rummet* [The red room] (Stockholm, 1879). In spring 1876 Ekström went to France, where he lived until 1890, partly in and around Paris (including Barbizon and Saint-Germain), partly in the village of Carolles, Normandy. He made his début at the Paris Salon in 1878 with a *French Landscape* (priv. col.) and was a gold medallist at the Exposition Universelle in 1889 with several works from the late 1880s, including *Sun Rays on the Water* (priv. col.).

Ekström was one of the first Swedish *plein-air* painters to be influenced by the Barbizon school, most of all by Théodore Rousseau and by Jean-Baptiste-Camille Corot. His handling of light and atmosphere, often pale sunshine in misty air or sunshine reflected through foliage above calm pools or flooded fields, is sometimes Impressionist in style. His choice of subjects was conditioned by his childhood experience of the lonely stretches and barren beaches of his native island of Öland in the Baltic; in France, sodden fields, deserted coastal regions or solitary woodlands were his preferred themes. In this respect he differed from Swedish contemporaries of the 1880s who painted the blander cultivated landscape and village life in Grez-sur-Loing on the outskirts of Fontainebleau Forest.

After returning to Sweden in 1891 Ekström settled in Göteborg. In that year he produced what is probably his most successful winter landscape, *Sun and Snow* (1891; 1.72×1.14 m, Göteborg, Kstmus.), showing the ice-covered Nybro Bay in Stockholm. Until *c.* 1900 the soft, grey-toned colour of Ekström's work in France was replaced by greater colour contrasts, with touches of local colour. At the same time Ekström was also influenced by the contemporary Scandinavian preference for twilight tones, for example in *Scene from Öland* (1901; Göteborg, Kstmus.). From 1909 until his death he lived on Öland, painting local landscapes.

BIBLIOGRAPHY

M. Hofrén: *Per Ekström: Människan och målaren* [Per Ekström: the man and the painter] (Stockholm, 1947)

P. G. Ekström: *Om min far, landskapsmålaren Per Ekström* [My father: Per Ekström, landscape painter] (Kalmar, 1982)

HANS-OLOF BOSTRÖM

Ektachrome. *See under* PHOTOGRAPHY, §I.

Ekweme, Alex (Ifeanyi Chukwu) (*b* Oko Aguata, 21 Oct 1932). Nigerian architect. He studied architecture at the University of Washington, Seattle, between 1952 and 1957. After graduating, and before returning to Nigeria in 1958, he served apprenticeships with Leo A. Daily & Associates, Seattle, and Nickson & Borys, London. He served briefly at Esso (West Africa) Inc., Lagos, as Co-ordinator of Construction Maintenance, before opening his own offices, Ekweme Associates, in 1958. From 1960 to 1978 Ekweme was active in architectural practice. A founder-member of the Nigerian Institute of Architects (NIA) and a fellow from 1970, he served as Assistant Secretary (1958–62), Vice-President (1963–4) and President (1965–6). In 1969 he was registered by the Architects' Registration Council of Nigeria (ARCON), a body he also served as president from 1976 to 1979. He enrolled for a postgraduate programme in housing at the University of Strathclyde, Scotland, in 1976 and was awarded a PhD of that university in 1978. In the period 1960–78 he was very active in his architecture offices; from 1979 to 1983 he was the Vice-President of Nigeria and was called to the Nigerian Bar in 1991.

One of his earlier projects was a 100-bed hospital for the Nigerian Railway Corporation at Ebute Metta, Lagos (1962). In a design employing linear elements with repetitive, but paralleled, wings, he was able to achieve scale control and a visual harmony between the complex and the site. In the period 1958–65 the bulk of the government's building programmes concerned facilities for education. Since most buildings had narrow, linear designs, for ease of cross ventilation, the contrast in style from one architect to the next was interesting and subtle. Ekweme's laboratory buildings (1962) for St Gregory's College,

Lagos, cantilevers at the first level to provide protective cover for students as they change classes. In the United Christian Commercial Secondary School (1961) in Apapa, Ekweme used subtle angularity to control and direct pedestrian movement and views, achieving an exciting and interesting interplay of volume and voids. Between 1970 and 1975 Ekweme's practice, now called Integrated Consultants, was responsible for the design of the prototype for some 21 Federal Government Unity Schools distributed throughout Nigeria. His practice was also responsible for the eight-storey apartment buildings for staff housing (1978) that dominate the Queen's College Campus in Onike, Yaba.

For general discussion of modern Nigerian architecture *see* NIGERIA, §IV.

BIBLIOGRAPHY
U. Kultermann: *New Directions in African Architecture* (New York, 1969)

DAVID ARADEON

el [el-]. For proper names with this prefix, with the exception of El Salvador, *see under* the second part of the name.

Elamite. Inhabitant of Elam, an ancient state that flourished intermittently from the 4th millennium BC to the 1st, in the area that is now Fars and Khuzistan in southwest Iran. The Elamites spoke a language that was neither Semitic nor Indo-European, and its linguistic affinities are problematic. At certain periods of their history they produced a lively and distinctive art, which they transmitted eastwards along one of the great trade routes of antiquity as far as Afghanistan and the Indus valley.

The frontiers of the original Elam are uncertain, but its heart was the city of Anshan (or Anzan; now Tall-i Maliyan in Fars), on the plateau north-west of Shiraz. The other great city that was sometimes under Elam's sphere of influence was SUSA, some 400 km to the north-west of Anshan, the capital of Susiana (now Khuzistan), which was a rich agricultural plain with a mixed population of settled Semitic peasants and townspeople, and nomadic Elamites from the surrounding uplands and from the plateau. During the periods when Susa fell under the influence of Mesopotamia (now Iraq, to the west) the state of Elam lost all political importance. Thus the history of Elam alternates between periods of prosperity, when the Elamites of Anshan controlled Susa and the main east–west trade route, and periods of obscurity when Susa came under Mesopotamian rule and the Elamites returned to a nomadic existence. The Elamites were frequently in conflict with Mesopotamia throughout their history.

In the last centuries of the 4th millennium BC Susa was closely linked with Mesopotamia (i.e. in the Uruk or proto-Sumerian period, *see* MESOPOTAMIA, §I, 2(i)(c)) and had colonies far to the north and north-east (GODIN TEPE and TEPE SIALK). Seal impressions dating from this period, especially those from Susa, show people carrying produce to domed granaries or engaged in weaving and other activities. Some impressions depict a fortified temple decorated with horns.

At the end of the 4th millennium BC the Uruk civilization collapsed in Susiana and was replaced by the Proto-Elamite civilization. This was probably as a result of an incursion of Elamites who had settled in the province of Fars and founded the city of Anshan, where excavations have revealed a palace-like structure with polychrome wall paintings consisting of S-shaped and crenellated patterns. In developing what is known as the Proto-Elamite script for writing their language they were probably aided by scribes from the annexed city of Susa. The Proto-Elamite political entity, with its two capitals, was the forerunner of historic Elam. Colonies were established at sites as far afield as Tepe Sialk, TEPE YAHYA and SHAHR-I SOKHTA. On the seals humans are no longer depicted, but bulls, lions and caprids often assume human postures in well-balanced compositions (*see* ANCIENT NEAR EAST, fig. 12). There are many humorous stone animal and bird figurines and vessels, some of them probably survivals from earlier periods. However, a small sculpture of a lioness standing on its hindlegs has a monumental quality (New York, Brooklyn Mus.; *see* IRAN, ANCIENT, fig. 6). The Proto-Elamite civilization collapsed abruptly *c*. 2800 BC and Anshan was deserted. Susa became a minor city of Sumerian type until it came under direct Mesopotamian rule *c*. 2300 BC during the reign of Sargon of Akkad.

Puzur-Inshushinak, the Elamite ruler of a state called Awan, founded a short-lived empire after the fall of Akkad, *c*. 2100 BC. His bilingual Akkadian and Elamite inscriptions, found at Susa, notably on the statue of a goddess seated on a throne supported by lions (Paris, Louvre), are indicative of Elam's dual culture. The Elamites united against the Sumerian kings of the 3rd Dynasty of Ur, who had recaptured Susa, and caused their downfall in 2004 BC. The Elamite kings, each known as '*sukkalmah* (grand vizier) of Anshan and Susa', are shown on seals beneath a trellised vine; gods wear distinctive headdresses with flaring horns, while men are distinguished by the bulging hairstyle typical of the Elamites. Bowls, made of stone or bitumen, are decorated with reliefs of animals or with animal protomes. Susa shared the Mesopotamian vogue for small terracotta figures, often made in moulds; terracottas of naked, bow-legged lute players are a typical local product. Susa declined towards the middle of the 2nd millennium BC as the neighbouring city of Kabnak (HAFT TEPE) rose to power.

In the 14th century BC there was an Elamite renaissance. During this Middle Elamite period King Untash-Napirisha built Dur-Untash (CHOGHA ZANBIL) *c*. 1340–1300 BC as a state capital where the gods of the two parts of Elam were honoured, and the site is dominated by a huge ZIGGURAT (*see* IRAN, ANCIENT, fig. 4). Excavations at Susa have produced a series of monuments that date to this same period, including a faience panel with deities in relief (Paris, Louvre; *see* ANCIENT NEAR EAST, §II, 5) and a huge bronze statue of Queen Napir-Asu (Paris, Louvre; *see* IRAN, ANCIENT, fig. 11). A stele (Paris, Louvre; see fig.) is framed by snakes, and its four registers, divided by guilloches, depict: the king before a god who, according to Elamite custom, was probably seated on a coiled snake (broken); three figures (upper part missing); two fish-tailed water deities who hold streams of water; and two bull-men on either side of a stylized tree. Towards the middle of the 12th century BC the Elamite kings Shutruk-Nahhunte I and Shilhak-Inshushinak twice conquered Babylonia, and its masterpieces were brought to Susa

Elamite stele of Untash-Napirisha, limestone, h. 2.62 m, from Susa, 14th century BC; reconstruction drawing (original in Paris, Musée du Louvre)

(among them the late 3rd- and early 2nd-millennium BC stelae of Sargon, Naram-Sin and Hammurabi, which were excavated in the 19th century AD and are now in the Louvre in Paris). At the end of the 12th century BC the Babylonians destroyed Elamite power and only Susa remained prosperous.

In the 8th century BC the kingdom of Anshan (Anzan) and Susa emerged from obscurity under Shutruk-Nahhunte II (*reg* 717–699 BC); this period is known as Neo-Elamite. Many faience artefacts and rock reliefs date to this time (*see* ANCIENT NEAR EAST, §II, 5; IRAN, ANCIENT, §IV). By then the population of Susa was mainly Elamite, whereas the nomads of the Anshan region were gradually merging with the Persians who were moving into Fars. The coherence of the Neo-Elamite state was thus undermined from within and was further threatened in the west by an alliance with Babylon that led to conflict with

Assyria. In the middle of the 7th century BC the armies of Ashurbanipal of Assyria destroyed it during a series of campaigns that are depicted on reliefs from Ashurbanipal's palaces at Nineveh (London, BM; *see* MESOPOTAMIA, §III, 6(i)) and that culminated in the sack of Susa in 646 BC. This date effectively marks the end of Elamite history, although Susa was quickly rebuilt and Elamite principalities survived, as attested by the seal of a prince, depicting two dragons (Jerusalem, Israel Mus.).

In the 6th century BC the Persian Cyrus the Great took the title King of Anshan, and traces of Elamite style can be seen in the art of the ACHAEMENID empire that he founded. There are references to Susa and Elam in the Bible (e.g. Genesis 10:22; Ezra 4:9–10; Daniel 8:2), and the name Elam survived in that of the later province and kingdom of ELYMAIS (last centuries BC and early centuries AD).

BIBLIOGRAPHY
P. Amiet: *Elam* (Auvers-sur-Oise, 1966)
E. Carter and W. Stolper: *Elam: Surveys of Political History and Archaeology* (Los Angeles, 1984)
P. Amiet: *L'Age des échanges inter-iraniens, 3500–1700 avant J.-C.* (Paris, 1986)
——: *Suse: 6000 ans d'histoire* (Paris, 1988)

PIERRE AMIET

Elbfas, Jacob Heinrich (*b* Estonia, *c.* 1600; *d* Stockholm, March 1664). Estonian painter, active in Sweden. In 1622 he was resident in Strassburg (now Strasbourg), but by 1624 he was in Sweden, where he painted the half-length portrait of *Anna Margareta Sture* (Stockholm, Stadshuset). He was recorded as an alderman in the artists' guild in 1628, and from 1634 to 1640 he was court painter to the Swedish dowager queen Maria Eleonora (1599–1655), although only workshop versions of his portraits of members of the court survive from this period. His portraits of the young Queen Christina, painted between 1637 and 1641, include a version with the first Swedish landscape background (workshop copy, *c.* 1634; Mariefred, Gripsholm Slott) and a full-length portrait of her in a paved interior (1641; Stockholm, Stadshuset). Only the portrait of *Admiral Carl Carlsson Gyllenhielm* (1641; Stockholm, Karlberg Slott) survives of the work that the Admiral commissioned from Elbfas. Between 1649 and 1655 Elbfas executed, with substantial workshop assistance, a series of full-length portraits of members of the Vasa dynasty, foreign monarchs, eminent men and members of Magnus Gabriel De la Gardie's family for the latter's castle at Läckö, Östergötland (now Kägleholm). For other members of this family he painted the full-length portraits of *Catharina De la Gardie* (1642; Ornö, Stenbock priv. col.) and *Maria Sophia De la Gardie* (1643; Tyresö Slott).

Although Elbfas received further minor royal commissions during the 1640s and 1650s, his position as the leading royal portrait painter in Sweden was usurped by the influx of foreign artists towards the end of the 1640s. His static and decorative portrait style, which perpetuated a tradition established in Sweden during the 16th century, was derived from German Renaissance court art, with some inspiration also from the work of Frans Pourbus the younger.

BIBLIOGRAPHY
SVKL; Thieme–Becker
K. E. Steneberg: *Kristinatidens måleri* [Painting during the time of Queen Christina] (Malmö, 1955), pp. 42–7
B. von Malmborg: *Svensk porträttskonst genom fem århundraden* [Five hundred years of Swedish portraiture] (Malmö, 1978), p. 102
ANTONIA BOSTRÖM

Elbo, José (*b* Ubeda, Jaén, 26 March 1804; *d* 4 Nov 1844). Spanish painter. He began his apprenticeship in Ubeda and, at an early age, he went to Madrid, where he studied with José Aparicio Inglada. As he had been a national conscript, Elbo's work was not recognized by Fernando VII, but both the Duque de Osuna and the English ambassador became his patrons. Elbo was elected an *Académico de mérito* of the Real Academia de S Fernando, Madrid, to which he bequeathed his finest work, *Madrid Bull-ring on the Day of a Bull-fight (in situ)*. Despite frequent claims, his *costumbrista* paintings of everyday life make no references to Goya's work, and their highly detailed finish makes them appear cold (a quality possibly resulting from Elbo's training under the Neoclassical Aparicio Inglada) and lacking in that warmth that characterizes Spanish Romanticism. Elbo was nevertheless an excellent draughtsman, as is seen in his collaboration with Aparicio Inglada on *Madrid Scenes* and *Panorama*. Two of Elbo's most important late paintings are a *Roadside Inn* and *Bulls in the Field* (both 1843; Madrid, Mus. Romántico).

BIBLIOGRAPHY
M. Ossorio y Bernard: *Galería biográfica de artistas españoles del siglo XIX* (Madrid, 1868, 2/1883–4/*R* Barcelona, 1975)
R. Laínez Alacalá: 'El pintor Elbo en el Museo Romántico', *Archv Esp. A.*, xiv/1 (1940–41), pp. 110–18
JOSÉ MANUEL ARNÁIZ

Elchingen, Jakob von. *See* ZWITZEL, (1).

Eldem, Halil Edhem (*b* Istanbul, ?24 June 1861; *d* Istanbul, 16 Nov 1938). Turkish museum director and historian. He was the youngest son of the grand vizier Ibrahim Edhem Pasha (?1818–93), who was one of the first Ottomans to be educated in Europe. Halil Edhem was schooled in Berlin, Zurich, Vienna and Berne, where he received his doctorate in natural sciences and chemistry. He also studied history and archaeology on his own initiative and spoke French, German, Turkish, Arabic and Persian. On his return to Istanbul in 1885, he became a civil servant and taught natural sciences in several schools as a volunteer. In 1892 he became vice-director of the Archaeological Museum in Istanbul and in 1910 on the death of the former director, his brother OSMAN HAMDI, he was promoted to director. Both the Museum of the Ancient Orient and the Topkapı Palace Museum were opened to the public during his tenure. He organized the *International Ottoman Exposition* (1897) and was awarded honorary degrees by the universities of Istanbul, Basle and Leipzig. A lifetime member of the Turkish Historical Society and a founding member of the Permanent Commission of Antiquities, he initiated a tradition of historical preservation in Turkey. He wrote many guidebooks and catalogues, a geology textbook, and numerous articles and books on numismatics, inscriptions and Turkish painting and illumination.

WRITINGS
with M. van Berchem: *Matériaux pour un Corpus Inscriptionum Arabicarum: Troisième partie: Asie Mineure, 1: Siwas, Diwrigi*, Mém.: Inst. Fr. Archéol. Orient. Caire, xxix (Cairo, 1910–17)
Kayseriye şehri [The city of Kayseri] (Istanbul, 1915)
Düwel-i Islâmiyye [The Islamic dynasties; rev. and enlarged trans. of S. Lane-Poole, *The Mohammedan Dynasties*] (Istanbul, 1927)
with G. Mignon: 'Les Collections du Vieux Serai à Stamboul', *Syria*, xi (1930), pp. 91–102
Topkapı Sarayı [Topkapı Palace] (Istanbul, 1931)
Camilerimiz [Turkish mosques] (Istanbul, 1932)
Yedikule hisarı [The fortress of Yedikule] (Istanbul, 1932)
Nos mosquées de Stamboul (Istanbul, 1934)
Niğde kılavuzu [Guide to Niğde] (Istanbul, 1937)
BIBLIOGRAPHY
Enc. Islam/2
Halil Edhem hatıra kitabı [Halil Edhem memorial volumes], 2 vols (Ankara, 1948)
LALE H. ULUÇ

Eldem, Sedad Hakkı (*b* Istanbul, 18 Aug 1908; *d* Istanbul, 7 Sept 1988). Turkish architect. He was descended from an élite Ottoman family. He trained at the Academy of Fine Arts in Istanbul (1924–8) and in the office of Hans Poelzig in Berlin (1929–30). Inspired by Auguste Perret, Le Corbusier and Frank Lloyd Wright, Eldem was a committed Modernist searching for a culturally relevant Turkish architecture. His early works include the State Monopolies General Directorate (1934–7), Ankara, the Faculty of Arts and Sciences (1942–3), Istanbul, and Faculty of Sciences (1943–5), Ankara, the latter two, in their monumentality and use of stone, reflecting the acknowledged influence of Paul Bonatz with whom Eldem collaborated in this period. His paradigmatic Taşlık Coffee House (1947–8; destr. 1988), Istanbul, was modelled after a 17th-century timber house and reflected Eldem's lasting preoccupation: the reinterpretation of the timber-frame Turkish house in modern terms using reinforced concrete. Wide overhanging eaves, modular window patterns and traditional plan types constitute the leitmotifs of his personal style, elaborated over decades in numerous private houses along the banks of the Bosphorous in Istanbul and employed on larger scales in a number of embassy buildings in Ankara. Eldem also directed the architectural department of the Academy of Fine Arts in Istanbul where, in 1934, he established the National Architecture Seminar for the survey and documentation of traditional residential architecture. He published numerous works including his monumental *Türk Evi* (1984–7). Internationally he won recognition for his Zeyrek Social Security Agency Complex (1962–4), Istanbul, a contextualist scheme sensitive to the scale and character of the surrounding urban fabric, which won him a prestigious Aga Khan Award in 1986.

WRITINGS
Türk Evi [Turkish house], 2 vols (Istanbul, 1984–7)
BIBLIOGRAPHY
G. Gerçek, ed.: *Sedad Hakkı Eldem: Büyük Konutlar* [Sedad Hakkı Eldem: House Projects] (Ankara, 1982)
——: *Sedad Hakkı Eldem: Elli Yıllık Meslek Jubilesi* [Sedad Hakkı Eldem: monograph published on the occasion of his 50th year in the profession] (Istanbul, 1983)
S. Bozdogan, S. Özkan and E. Yenal: *Sedad Eldem* (Singapore, 1987)
SIBEL BOZDOGAN

Eldin, Lord. *See* CLERK, (5).

Eleanora of Toledo. *See* MEDICI, DE, (15).

Eleanor of Castile, Queen of England. *See under* PLAN-TAGENET, (3).

Eleanor of Provence, Queen of England. *See under* PLANTAGENET, (2).

Eleanor of Viseu, Queen of Portugal. *See* AVIZ, (5).

Electrography [electrophotography; xerography]. Term for processes involving the interaction of light and electricity to produce images and for the production of original works of art by these processes. Since these processes are used by nearly all photocopiers, the production of such works has also been referred to as 'copy art', although this is misleading, since it suggests the mere replication of already existing works. Artistic photocopies were made in California in the late 1950s, but electrography proper as an international art form dates from the early 1960s, when electrographers developed its basic techniques. Bruno Munari's pioneering works, workshops and publications, starting in 1963, foreshadowed the preponderant role played by Europe in the history of electrography, to which important exhibitions at the Musée National d'Art Moderne in Paris (1980) and in Valencia (1988) later testified. Electrographs vary widely in size and can be over 1 km in length; materials used include not only paper but also canvas and leather. In the mid-1970s xeroradiography (a xerographic process in which an X-ray gun is used to obtain X-ray pictures) and telecopy respectively gave rise to electroradiographic art and fax art. The advent in the 1980s of the digital copier, with its creative programmes, also created new possibilities, and from 1989 the colour laser copier could be connected to a computer or a video camera, thereby increasing the creative potential of electrography. At the end of the 20th century it was one of the most practised technological art forms, with Pol Bury and David Hockney among its prominent exponents. The Museo Internacional de Electrografía in Cuenca, Spain, is the leading institution devoted to the subject.

BIBLIOGRAPHY
2 Bienal internacional electrografía, 3 vols (exh. cat. by C. Rigal and others, Valencia, Ayuntamiento, 1988–91) [texts in Eng. and Sp.; the third vol. is a video cassette]
C. Rigal and others: *Electrografías: La colección Museo Internacional de Electrografía* (Cuenca, 1991) [texts in Eng. and Sp.]
C. Rigal: *L'Art électrographique* (in preparation)

CHRISTIAN RIGAL

Electroplating. Deposition by electrolysis of a layer of metal, often gold, silver or chromium, on to a metal. Experiments into the electrodeposition of metals were carried out from the 18th century, and very soon the commercial potential of this method of gilding or silvering was recognized. However, the electrolytic solutions then available gave disappointing results, since the plated layers were loose and unsightly. By the end of the 1830s a great deal of research had been carried out, notably in Britain, France, Germany and Russia, but without any commercial success. At this point, George Richards Elkington and his cousin, Henry Elkington (*c.* 1810–52), who ran a large firm making silverwares in Birmingham, decided to advance gold and silver cyanide solutions as electrolytes.

1. Electroplating at the works of Elkington, Mason & Co., Birmingham; from J. Cassel's *Universal Exhibitor* (London, 1852)

This led, in the 1840s, to the successful electroplating of copper and other base metals with continuous, durable and shiny layers of precious metal.

In outline, the processes for both gold and silver plating are broadly similar and have not changed appreciably over the years. The favoured base metal, which acted as a cathode, was copper or nickel-silver (a copper-zinc-nickel alloy), hence the familiar EPNS mark. This was carefully cleaned and polished, then either acid-treated or lightly scratch-brushed to create a suitable surface to which the plating would adhere. Items to be silver-plated were treated with mercury salts to prevent ordinary electrochemical deposition, before being placed in vats filled with the appropriate cyanide-solution electrolyte with anodes of gold or silver to replenish the solution (see fig. 1). After careful washing, the plated items were polished or brushed to produce the required finish.

The conditions could be manipulated to give a variety of colours and textures to the plated layer. Sometimes this was done at the plating stage by, for example, varying the composition of the electrolyte to give red, rose or even greenish tinged gilding. A special effect was produced by plating out lead oxides on to steel plates to give beautiful prismatic colorations. These metallo-chromes, as they were called, were quite widely used in the latter part of the 19th century (before the days of stringent health requirements) for colouring the hands and dials of Swiss clocks, and the small ornamental toys made at Nuremberg.

Within a few years electroplating had largely replaced all other plating methods and formed a very substantial industry. Such firms as Elkington, Mason & Co. in Britain, Christofle in France and the Gorham Manufacturing Co. in the USA produced an enormous range of plated goods, which exceeded both in quantity and elaboration those covered by other, earlier forms of plating. This was largely because the traditional form of silver plate, known as SHEFFIELD PLATE, had a number of commercial as well as practical disadvantages. It was wasteful of materials and required a great deal of highly skilled, and thus expensive, labour. Edges naturally come in for heavy wear, but unfortunately the Sheffield plating process left the edges relatively poorly protected, whereas electroplating automatically deposits more metal at extremities. An even more serious drawback was that Sheffield plating could not be applied to castings. This was partially overcome by die-pressing complex components separately and even making electrotypes, but as prevailing taste favoured ever more ornate designs so casting the whole item and then electroplating it became the only commercially viable method of production. The clean, simple, classical designs of the late 18th century were ideally suited to Sheffield plate, but the increasing complexity of late Regency silverware in the following century may well have encouraged the search for a technique better suited to its production. The advent of electroplating certainly encouraged the development of the ornate Victorian style, not least by bringing down the price and encouraging the dissemination of plated wares to a wider sector of the population.

Electroplating also transformed gilding technology, replacing fire-gilding and to a lesser extent leaf-gilding (*see* GILDING, §I, 1 and 3). One especially interesting application was the electrogilding of such large items as statues or even whole roofs. This was developed to a high degree in 19th-century Russia, especially by the St Petersburg Electroforming, Casting and Mechanical Plant set up by Moritz Hermann von Jacobi (1801–74), which gilded the domes on such buildings as St Isaac's Cathedral, St Petersburg, and the Bol'shoy Theatre, Moscow. The gilded layers were much thinner than could have been achieved by any other method, but even so hundreds of kilograms of gold were used on each roof.

Developments in electroplating continued, especially in new alloys that would be cheaper and more resistant to corrosion. There was considerable research into developing a plate that would protect silver jewellery mounts from tarnish. Platinum and palladium platings were used in the 19th century, but they were expensive and looked different from silver. In the 1930s rhodium plating was introduced for diamond settings. It rapidly spread to a wide range of silver and even silver-plated goods, because although rhodium was very expensive, only an extremely thin layer was needed to give full protection, and the colour and finish were held to be indistinguishable from silver itself.

The search for plating metals that would give a cheap, weather-resistant but attractive finish was pursued with vigour. Thus, at the end of the 19th century such plating alloys as Arcas, three-quarters silver and a quarter cadmium, were developed. These resembled silver but were significantly cheaper and had superior resistance to tarnish—so much so that similar alloys were used to plate cycle handlebars. Nickel plating was also widely used to give protection to exposed copper and brass fittings. However, the major advance was made only in the 20th century with the introduction of chromium plating. This made it possible to give metals, including iron and steel, a durable, silvery finish that was both weather-resistant and attractive.

Chromium had been isolated as a metal in 1795, and by the mid-19th century scientists were performing electroplating experiments with it, but without great success. They realized the potential of a shiny plated layer, which was extremely resistant to weathering, but it proved difficult to make the chromium adhere satisfactorily. The problems were not fully overcome until the 1920s, and chromium plating was then rapidly taken up in Europe and the USA, especially by the motor industry.

The iron or steel is first plated with nickel, then cleaned, polished and electroplated from an electrolyte of chromic acid, catalyzed by sulphate and silico-fluoride ions, in a steel bath lined with lead and with lead or lead-alloy anodes. The plated items emerge from the bath in a bright condition and require little or no further polishing. Plating of plastics began in the 1960s, and many minor items, for example buttons, that were traditionally of metal are very often of chromium-plated plastic.

The advent of chromium plating had a profound effect on the appearance of a wide range of iron and steel consumer goods and even buildings. This was especially true of the motor-car. Prior to this, bright finishes had had little place in automobile design—the few areas that were not painted were of brass, possibly nickel-plated, and would tarnish rapidly unless polished. Shortly after the introduction of chromium plating, considerable areas of bright, shiny plating were being emphasized—Oldsmobile radiator shells, for example, were chromium plated by 1926 (see fig. 2)—and the whole of vehicle design underwent a rapid change in response to the new material. Similarly, the brass handles and fittings of many kitchen and bathroom goods were plated, as was the tubular steel used in Modernist furniture. The same was true of buildings, where previously shiny metal had been strictly limited to brass door furniture, and other exposed structural metalwork had been galvanized and painted. With

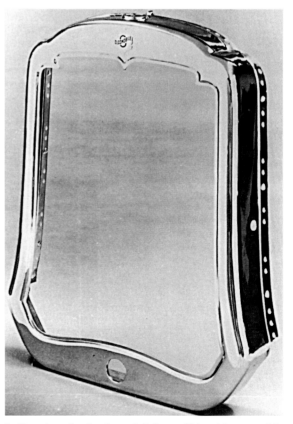

2. Chromium-plated radiator shell for an Oldsmobile automobile, 1926

chromium plating, structural steelwork could be emphasized and purely decorative items added. Indeed, chromium plating became an essential element of modern design.

BIBLIOGRAPHY

G. Langbein and W. T. Brannt: *A Complete Treatise on the Electrodeposition of Metals* (Philadelphia, 1891)

A. Watt and A. Philip: *The Electro-plating and Electro-refining of Metals* (London, 1911)

Handbook on Electroplating, Polishing, Lacquering, Burnishing, Enamelling (Birmingham, 1922)

Electro-plating (Birmingham, [1930s])

E. H. Laister and R. R. Benham: *Rhodium Plating* (London, 1954)

W. G. L. Miller: 'Acceptance Requirements for Nickel–chromium Plating', *Nickel–chromium Plating, London, 1960*, pp. 77–98

O. I. Pavlova: *Electrodeposition of Metals: An Historical Survey* (Moscow, 1963; Eng. trans., Jerusalem, 1968)

S. Bury: *Victorian Electroplate* (London, 1971)

G. Dubpernell: *Electrodeposition of Chromium* (New York, 1977)

J. K. Dennis and T. E. Such: *Nickel and Chromium Plating* (London, 1986)

C. Raub: 'The History of Electroplating', *Metal Plating and Patination*, ed. S. La Niece and P. T. Craddock (Oxford, 1993)

P. T. CRADDOCK

Electrostatic printing. *See under* PHOTOGRAPHY, §I.

Electrotype [galvanoplasty]. Relief printing block in which the plate is made by electrolytically coating a mould with copper. The process (*see* PRINTS, §III, 1(ii)) is the electrical equivalent of casting, and the entire object to be made, known in continental Europe as a galvanoplastic copy, is produced in the plating vat.

Elembrech, Theodoor. *See* HELMBREKER, DIRCK.

Elementarism. Term coined by Theo van Doesburg and applied to painting and architecture to describe the constructive use of line, plane, volume and colour not only as the primary means of art but as an end in itself. In his article, 'L'Elémentarisme et son origine', he stated that the movement had been born in Holland in 1924 via the DE STIJL group. He then listed Elementarist contributors to the arts: 'Georges Antheil in music, César Domela, Vordemberge-Gildewart and the author of this article (the founder of the movement) in painting, Constantin Brancusi in sculpture, Mies van der Rohe, van Eesteren, Rietveld and the author in architecture, I. K. Bonset [one of van Doesburg's pseudonyms] in literature, Friederich Kiesler in the rejuvenation of the theatre'. The term is intimately related to the notion of abstraction and has roots extending back as far as Plato's *Philebus*. In its broader definition it can provide an insight into the development of abstraction. As early as 1915, in his article on the development of modern art, van Doesburg wrote about the 'fundamental elements' of art and analysed how they had been treated during different historical periods.

The publication of Heinrich Wölfflin's *Kunstgeschichtliche Grundbegriffe* (1915) had a profound effect on van Doesburg's ideas, particularly concerning the primary elements of painting and their ability to set the whole canvas in motion. The development of van Doesburg's theory was further supported by the writings of the Dutch Hegelian philosopher Professor G. J. P. J. Bolland, who saw art as elements in relationship. The architect J. J. P. Oud was much impressed by the ideas of van Doesburg and Bolland, and wrote an article 'Over Cubisme, Futurisme, moderne Bouwkunst' (*Bouwkundig Weekblad*, Sept 1916, pp. 156–7) in which he set out to show the ramifications of such an approach for architecture. This second definition of Elementarism gave the initial impetus to the magazine *De Stijl*.

In 1921 Raoul Hausmann, Hans Arp, Jean Pougny and László Moholy-Nagy signed a manifesto which was published as 'Aufruf zur elementaren Kunst' in *De Stijl*. Although these artists had much in common with van Doesburg, they did not constitute a school but had connections with two different movements, Constructivism and Dada. Van Doesburg discussed how the 'profound pioneering work' with the simplest means 'or the elemental means of expression' had been achieved in strict Constructivist terms in his article 'Zur elementaren Gestaltung' published in *G*, the magazine edited by Hans Richter. The point was demonstrated architecturally in the designs and models made by van Doesburg and Cornelis van Eesteren in 1923 for the De Stijl exhibition in Léonce Rosenberg's Galerie de l'Effort Moderne. He later dismissed the identification of the colour plane, architectural plane, visual and literal structure as 'anatomical architecture'.

Van Doesburg described the design for Gerrit Rietveld's Schröder House (1924) in Utrecht as 'the application of our most recent principles' in a letter to César Domela (27 Aug 1925; see Doig, pp. 168–9). He expanded on these principles in 'Tot een beeldende architectur' and 'Vers une construction collective', both published in *De Stijl*. It was in 1924–5 that van Doesburg's experiments in painting produced the transition that was the basis for the narrowest definition of Elementarism, as formulated by the artist himself. In 1924 he painted *Counter-composition V* (Amsterdam, Stedel. Mus.) and *Counter-composition VIII* (Chicago, IL, A. Inst.). Originally these had lozenge formats with horizontal and vertical axes. In June or July 1925 their orientation was changed to a square format, and they became diagonal counter-compositions.

The reintroduction of the diagonal (for illustration *see* DOESBURG, THEO VAN) and implied movement, which occasioned Mondrian's disassociation from De Stijl, to some extent had its roots in El Lissitsky's *Proun* series. Just as Lissitsky had applied the geometrical elements of the series in a *Proun* room for the Berlin Kunstaustellung (1923), van Doesburg's counter-compositions had a corresponding architectural manifestation. Virtually simultaneous with the creation and transformation of *Counter-composition V* and *Counter-composition VIII* was his design of a Flower Room in a villa by Robert Mallet-Stevens for Charles, Vicomte de Noailles, at Hyères, France. There the walls and ceiling were completely covered in diagonal counter-compositions. In his article 'Schilderkunst: Van kompositie tot contra-kompositie', van Doesburg wrote of the need for contrast between the visual structure of painting and the literal horizontal/vertical structure of architecture. From the tension between the two would rise a new 'plastic expression'.

In 1926 van Doesburg was commissioned to rebuild the Aubette, an entertainment complex in Strasbourg, in collaboration with Hans Arp and Sophie Taeuber-Arp. In the complex he again applied the principles of contrast between compositional and counter-compositional methods. The Aubette was the culmination of Elementarism (*see* DOESBURG, THEO VAN). In the issue of *De Stijl* dedicated to the Aubette, van Doesburg published 'L'Elémentarisme et son origine' and the movement was retrospectively invented.

WRITINGS

R. Hausmann, H. Arp, I. Puni and L. Moholy-Nagy: 'Aufruf zur elementaren Kunst', *De Stijl*, iv/10 (1921), p. 156
T. van Doesburg: 'Zur elementaren Gestaltung', *G*, 1 (1923)
H. Richter: 'G', *G*, 3 (1924)
T. van Doesburg: 'Tot een beeldende architectur', *De Stijl*, vi/6–7 (1924), pp. 78–83
——: 'Vers une construction collective', *De Stijl*, vi/6–7 (1924), pp. 89–91
——: 'Schilderkunst: Van kompositie tot contra-kompositie', *De Stijl*, vii/73–4 (1926), pp. 17–28
——: 'Schilderkunst en plastiek: Over contra-compositie en contra-plastiek–Elementarisme (manifest-fragment)' [Painting and plasticism: concerning counter-composition and counter-plasticism-Elementarism (extract from manifesto)], *De Stijl*, vii/75–6 (1926), pp. 35–43; 78 (1926–7), pp. 82–7
——: 'Brancusi', *De Stijl*, vii/79–84 (1927), pp. 85–6
——: 'L'Elémentarisme et son origine', *De Stijl*, viii/87–9 (1928), pp. 20–25
——: 'Elementarisme', *De Stijl*, final issue (1932), pp. 15–16
——: 'Elémentarisme (les éléments de la nouvelle peinture)', *De Stijl*, final issue (1932), pp. 17–19

BIBLIOGRAPHY

J. Baljeu: *Theo van Doesburg* (London, 1974)
S. Bann: *The Tradition of Constructivism*, DMA, ed. R. Motherwell (London, 1974)
A. Doig: *Theo van Doesburg: Painting into Architecture, Theory into Practice* (Cambridge, 1986)
E. van Straaten: *Theo van Doesburg: Painter and Architect* (The Hague, 1988) [good bibliog. and docs]
S. Lemoine, ed.: *Theo van Doesburg: Peinture, architecture, théorie* (Paris, 1990)

ALLAN DOIG

Elephanta [Gharapuri]. Island 10 km from Bombay, India, renowned for its rock-cut temples and sculptures. The name Elephanta is derived from a stone elephant, removed (with other sculptures) to Bombay. The locally popular name Gharapuri is a corruption of *agrahārapurī* (Skt: rent-free village in the possession of brahmins). The names of localities near the present jetty such as Shet Bandar, More Bandar and Raj Bandar indicate the island was used as a port.

The coasts and both of the hills dominating Elephanta were once scattered with antiquities. An image of a horse, reported in the vicinity of the elephant, is no longer extant. Datable finds include large numbers of coins of the 6th-century Kalachuri king Krishnaraja. The style of the characters of an inscription on the base of a Brahma image suggests a date around the 9th century; and an inscribed copper vessel (dated AD 1086) was recovered during the clearance of a cistern. Perhaps the earliest remains (undated) are those of a stupa built of bricks (380× 230×64 mm). Located on the eastern hill of the island, the stupa has cisterns and undecorated caves near by, which may have formed a Buddhist monastery.

The five Brahmanical caves located on the western hill are more impressive in scale and are decorated with sculpture of exceptional beauty. Cave 1, the finest, is unusual in that it is cut into the rock from three different sides. The eastern and western breaches lead to courts that

have entrances to the pillared hall of the main shrine. The central breach enters a portico that leads directly into the hall (approximately 39.6 m across). On either side of the portico are reliefs of Shiva as Lord of the Dance (Nattaraja) and in his form as the supreme teacher (Dakshinamurti). The sanctum within is of the four-door (*sarvatobhadra*) variety and enshrines a *liṅga*.

Large (3.9 m high) door-guardians are carved on the outer walls of the sanctum. Directly across the hall from the central breach and entrance portico is a corresponding blind-portico deep in the rock. This contains a colossal (5.18 m high) triple bust of Shiva in his forms Vamadeva, Tatpurusha and Aghora—one of the most powerful creations of Indian art (*see* INDIAN SUBCONTINENT, fig. 171). On either side are guardian figures and relief panels showing Shiva as the 'lord who is half woman' (Ardhanarishvara) and as the bearer of the River Ganga (Gangadhara). The pillared hall itself has niches in each corner, which contain sculptures of Shiva playing dice with Parvati, the marriage of the divine couple (Kalyanasundara), and Shiva destroying the demon Andhaka and subduing Ravana who shakes Mt Kailasa. These corner niches represent an incorporation of the five-shrined scheme (*pañcāyatana*) within the hall, a configuration seen in later structural temples.

The eastern and western entrances to the cave have additional chapels that also contain reliefs. The eastern shrine, which has a cruciform plan, contains fine images of the Seven Mother Goddesses (*saptamatṛka*s), Bhairava, Ganesha and Kartikeya. A large inscription, apparently from this cave complex, was removed by the Portuguese in an effort to have it deciphered. As the inscription has now disappeared, the patronage and date of the caves are a subject of debate. Iconographic and stylistic considerations suggest the monument was made for the Pashupata sect, probably in the second quarter of the 6th century.

See also INDIAN SUBCONTINENT, §V, 6(iii)(c).

BIBLIOGRAPHY

J. Burgess: *Rock Temples at Elephanta* (Bombay, 1871)
J. Fergusson and J. Burgess: *The Cave Temples of India* (London, 1880), pp. 465–75
Hirananda Shastri: *A Guide to Elephanta* (Delhi, 1934)
S. Kramrisch: 'The Image of Mahadeva in the Cave Temple on Elephanta Island', *Anc. India*, ii (1946), pp. 4–8
M. Neff and R. Von Loyden: 'Homage to Elephanta', *Marg*, xiii (1960), pp. 1–60
P. Chandra: *A Guide to the Elephanta Caves (Gharapuri)* (Bombay, 1962)
K. V. Soundara Rajan: 'Cave Temples of the Deccan', *Architectural Survey of Temples*, iii (New Delhi, 1981), pp. 88–94
C. Berkson, G. Michell and W. O'Flaherty: *Elephanta: The Cave of Shiva* (Princeton, 1983)
W. M. Spink: 'The Great Cave at Elephanta: A Study of Sources', *Essays on Gupta Culture*, ed. B. L. Smith (Delhi, 1983), pp. 235–82
C. D. Collins: *The Iconography and Ritual of Śiva at Elephanta* (New York, 1988)

A. P. JAMKHEDKAR

Elephantine. *See under* ASWAN.

Elers. English family of potters of German birth. David Elers and John Philip Elers were the sons of Martin Elers, a German who had settled in Holland. David is first recorded as a silversmith in London in 1686, and both brothers then made 'Browne muggs and red theapotts' in Staffordshire and Vauxhall, London, from *c*. 1690. In 1693 they were sued by JOHN DWIGHT for infringing his stoneware patent but subsequently made red stoneware under licence from Dwight. In 1698 John Philip gave up the lease of his house at Bradwell Wood, Staffs, where he had been both potter and gentleman farmer, but continued making teapots at Vauxhall with David until they were declared bankrupt in 1700. John Philip became a merchant in Dublin in 1701 and was supplied with Chinese porcelain, imported by the British East India Company, by David during the period 1715 to 1722. The primary importance of the Elers brothers to the history of English ceramics is in their introduction of sprigged, red stoneware to Staffordshire, where it was revived in the 1740s; secondly in their use of slip-casting with plaster of Paris moulds; and thirdly in their use of lathe-turning to achieve lightness and sharp profile. Although David claimed in 1693 that he had learnt the secret of making salt-glazed stoneware at Cologne, excavations on the Bradwell Wood site have proved that the brothers made only redware there and were not responsible for introducing this important process to Staffordshire.

BIBLIOGRAPHY
R. Edwards: 'London Potters circa 1570–1710', *J. Cer. Hist.*, vi (1974) [whole issue]
G. W. Elliott: 'Staffordshire Red and Black Stonewares', *Trans. Eng. Cer. Circ.*, x/2 (1977), pp. 84–94
D. Haselgrove and J. Murray, eds: 'John Dwight's Fulham Pottery, 1672–1978: A Collection of Documentary Sources', *J. Cer. Hist.*, xi (1979) [whole issue]

ROBIN HILDYARD

Eleta, Sandra (*b* Panama City, 4 Sept 1942). Panamanian photographer. She studied art history at Finch College, New York (1961–4), and in the following three years painted in Spain. In 1972–3 she was Instructor of Photography at the Universidad de San José, Costa Rica, and from 1974 worked as a freelance photographer in Panama. Her photographs were not merely reportage, although they provide a documentary record of daily life in Panama. They also give a vivid picture of the character of the Panamanians. This is particularly marked in her photographic study of three peasant women from the Tonosi Valley, and in her series on the village and people of Portobelo.

PHOTOGRAPHIC PUBLICATIONS
Portobelo (Buenos Aires, 1981)

BIBLIOGRAPHY
Contemp. Phots

ERIKA BILLETER

Eleusis. Site on the eastern edge of a row of rocky hills extending along the coast of north-west Attica, to the north of the straits of Salamis and about 20 km from Athens. The town flourished throughout antiquity. Due to its strategic position controlling one of the principal access routes to Attica, it was developed as a stronghold by the Athenians as early as Mycenaean times. However, it was chiefly famous in later eras as the venue for the Eleusinian Mysteries, secret annual rituals held in honour of Demeter and Persephone and open only to initiates of their cult. According to tradition the Mysteries were first celebrated by Eumolpos during the reign of the mythical king Erechtheus. Eleusis was given the status of a panhellenic sanctuary in about 750 BC by a Delphic oracle, and

Solon included the Mysteries in his list of official Athenian rites around 700 BC. The sanctuary reached the height of its religious influence and architectural development in Roman times under Hadrian and the Antonines (2nd century AD). It was sacked in AD 170 by barbarian invaders who burnt the Telesterion (Hall of the Mysteries), but this was repaired in AD 176 by Marcus Aurelius and only ceased to function in AD 392, when the emperor Theodosios I prohibited the continuation of the rites.

The sanctuary was surrounded by strong walls to assure the secrecy of the Mysteries as well as its defence against invaders. In Greek and early Roman times its main entrance was the fortified north gate (5th century BC) where the Sacred Way from Athens ended. Under Hadrian, however, this was replaced by the Greater Propylaia, a marble gateway modelled on the central part of the Mnesiklean Propylaia on the Athenian Acropolis. This ambitious project also included the construction of a large paved court surrounded by arches, stoas and a fountain, with the Temple of Artemis Propylaia and several altars at its centre. To the left of the outer façade of the Greater Propylaia, and at a lower level, are the remains of the Kallichoron well (early 5th century BC), where dances were performed in honour of the goddesses. Immediately inside the sanctuary, next to the Cave of Pluto, was the so-called Lesser Propylaia (*c.* 50 BC; *see* ROME, ANCIENT, fig. 44), a fine building with a unique design that formed

Eleusis, relief depicting *Demeter and Persephone Sending Triptolemos on his Mission to Bring Corn to the World* (the Great Eleusinian relief), marble, h. 2.20 m, *c.* 445 BC (Athens, National Archaeological Museum)

the entrance to the inner precinct. Its unusual architectural features included caryatids on its inner façade, Corinthian columns bearing capitals adorned with animal protomes on its outer façade and a Doric frieze with carvings of bundles of corn and sacred chests (*cistae*) on the triglyphs.

The principal building inside the sanctuary and the focal point for the cult was the Telesterion. The Classical edifice, which replaced several smaller predecessors, was a rectangular hall (inner dimensions: 51.56×51.97 m) with 42 internal columns supporting its roof. In the centre stood the anaktoron or adyton, a chamber housing the sacred objects of the cult, while seating for the initiates was provided by eight steps, partially carved in the rock, lining the inner faces of the walls. A huge Doric porch designed by Philon was added to the front of the building in 345 BC. Finally, along the southern side of the sacred precinct are the remains of a bouleuterion and of the sanctuary's subsidiary entrance, the south gate, providing access from the port.

Few of the numerous works of art that were dedicated to the sanctuary survive. Notable finds, however, include: the Great Eleusinian relief (*c.* 445 BC; see fig.), sometimes attributed to Pheidias, which represents *Demeter and Persephone Sending Triptolemos on his Mission to Bring Corn to the World*; the Niinnion tablet with a ritual scene painted in Red-figure technique (early 4th century BC; Athens, N. Archaeol. Mus.); a splendid statue of *Antinous* (early 2nd century AD; Eleusis Mus.); a series of *kernoi* (unusual ritual vases; Eleusis Mus.); an exquisitely carved ram's head from the gutter of the Peisistratid Telesterion (late 6th century BC, Eleusis Mus.); and the fine capitals and colossal caryatids from the Lesser Propylaia (Eleusis Mus.; one caryatid in Cambridge, Fitzwilliam).

BIBLIOGRAPHY

F. Noack: *Eleusis, die baugeschichtliche Entwicklung des Heiligtumes* (Berlin, 1927)
G. E. Mylonas: *Eleusis and the Eleusinian Mysteries* (Princeton, 1962)
D. G. Giraud: *E kuria eisodos tou ierou tes Eleusinos* [The main entrance to the sanctuary at Eleusis] (Athens, 1986)
J. Travlos: *Bildlexicon zur Topographie des antiken Attika* (Tübingen, 1988)

DEMOSTHENIS G. GIRAUD

Elevation. Diagrammatic line drawing showing the vertical elements of a building, exterior or interior, as a direct projection to a vertical plane. The term is also used for the exterior vertical face of any building.

□

Elgazzar. *See* GAZZAR, ʿABD AL-HADI AL-.

Elgin, 7th Earl of, and 11th Earl of Kincardine. *See* BRUCE, THOMAS.

Elhafen, Ignaz (*bapt* Innsbruck, 1 Aug 1658; *d* Düsseldorf, before 1 June 1715). German sculptor. Having served an apprenticeship in Innsbruck, between 1675 and 1680 he travelled, spending a considerable period in Rome, probably between 1675 and 1678. He moved to Vienna and then, between 1703 and 1704, to Düsseldorf, to the court of John William, the Elector Palatine. Elhafen was an eclectic artist of no outstanding originality, whose talent lay in the field of copying. His importance rests mainly in the wide dissemination of his reliefs on mythological themes, sometimes through mass-production. He was principally a relief sculptor, though he also produced some sculptures in the round. Working in wood and ivory, he concentrated on a few main themes: scenes from the legend of the Sabines, battle scenes from antiquity and the Old Testament, bacchanalia and various mythological episodes.

The style of Elhafen's reliefs is largely based on the graphic material he used, which he took from illustrated Bibles, books of history or the work of Matthäus Merian (i). Until around 1697 each relief was based on a single model. He produced *c.* 1693 a silver gilt and ivory lidded tankard (Baden-Baden, Zähringer Mus.), the ivory part of which, depicting the *Rape of the Sabine Women*, shows clear parallels to the work of Matthias Rauchmiller. One of the earliest works securely attributed to Elhafen is the cedar-wood relief *Samuel Beheading Agag, King of the Amalekites* (*c.* 1685; Kremsmünster, Stiftssamml.); this is an adaptation of an illustration by Matthäus Merian from his *Icones biblicae* (1625). Another relief from the same period, the *Battle of the Israelites against the Amalekites* (ivory, *c.* 1685; Kremsmünster, Stiftssamml.), uses three engravings by Merian on different themes. For the ivory case of the Augsburg Clock (1697; Baden-Baden, Zähringer Mus.) Elhafen used an Italian model: the etching by Pietro Aquila (*fl* 1673–83; *d* 1692) after Pietro da Cortona's *Triumph of Bacchus* (1624; Rome, Mus. Capitolino).

Between 1700 and 1705 Elhafen produced noteworthy composite works made up of groups taken from various engravings. After moving to Düsseldorf he may have found inspiration for his reliefs in the Elector Palatine's collections, which included bronzes by the Florentine court artists Massimiliano Soldani and Giovanni Battista Foggini, small bronzes from the 16th and 17th centuries and plaster casts of famous works of antiquity, as well as engravings and paintings. At the Electoral court he executed some of his best-known works in relief, such as the *Rape of the Sabine Women* (ivory, 1705) and *Bacchanalia* (ivory, 1708; both Munich, Bayer. Nmus.). The reliefs and statuettes of Elhafen's later work are freer in manner: the relief of *Bacchantes* (ivory, signed and dated 1710; Munich, Bayer. Nmus.) shows a certain emancipation from engraved models. In this case he did not copy a complete group but assembled individual figures from a number of original works by Stefano della Bella, François Perrier, Poussin, Raymond La Fage and Pietro da Cortona.

Although Elhafen's reliefs represent his most notable work, his ivory statuettes also deserve attention. These are also rather like reliefs, being designed to be seen from only one point of view. Two of them are the only works on religious themes securely attributed to him: *Mourning Virgin* and *Christ at the Column* (ivory, *c.* 1710–12; Munich, Bayer. Nmus.). In these works Elhafen again used foreign models: the Christ type is taken from the small sculptures of Alessandro Algardi, while the Virgin is based on works by Rubens. Elhafen's statuettes on mythological themes include the only figure marked I.E., *Meleager with the Kalydonian Boar's Head* (ivory, 1708–10; Munich, Bayer. Nmus.), and *Paris with the Apple of Discord* (ivory, 1710–15; London, priv. col., see Theuerkauff, 1968, fig. 125).

BIBLIOGRAPHY
Thieme–Becker
C. Theuerkauff: *Studien für Elfenbeinplastik des Barock: Matthias Rauch-miller und Ignaz Elhafen* (diss., U. Freiburg im Breisgau, 1962)
——: 'Der "Helffenbeinarbeiter" Ignaz Elhafen', *Wien. Jb. Kstgesch.*, xxi (1968), pp. 92–157

THOMAS KLIEMANN

Elharas. Site of a settlement on the left bank of the Amu River 1.5 km east of the Kaparas fortress, Darganata district, Turkmenistan. The site (*c.* 1 ha) is surrounded by a wall of rammed earth. Excavations under L. M. Levina (1973–5) revealed the impressive central building (50× 37 m) of clay and unbaked bricks. The walls and vaulted ceilings survive to a height of 5.5 m. More than 20 rooms were uncovered. A period when the building fell into disuse is marked by a level of sandstone alluvium, when some rooms were carefully filled in with brick rubble. The walls, ceilings and floors of all the rooms and corridors had white plaster covered with red and black paint. Traces of polychrome painting have also been preserved in the wide, arched niches on the northern façade of the building. In the layer of sandstone alluvium, fragments of painted plaster were found, as well as broken pieces of painted clay sculptures and reliefs. The sculpture exhibits no clear signs of Hellenistic influence. One piece bears traces of paint together with small bronze medallions that were used to indicate clothing decoration. The paintings and sculptures may be among the oldest examples of monumental art found in Central Asia, if the suggested date for the building of the last centuries BC is confirmed. This dating by Levina is based on finds of large vessels of the Khwarazm–Kanguy type. Later dates cannot, however, be excluded, since the second earliest stratigraphic level contained a Kushana coin with Khwarazm S-shaped chasing, which can be dated to no earlier than the 3rd century AD. Finds other than sculpture are in the Institute of Ethnology, Moscow.

BIBLIOGRAPHY
L. M. Levina: 'Raskopki na poselenii Elkharas' [Excavations on the Elharas settlement], *Arkheologicheskiye otkrytiya 1973 goda* [Archaeological discoveries for 1973] (Moscow, 1974), pp. 505–6
——: 'Raskopki na poselenii Elkharas' [Excavations on the Elharas settlement], *Arkheologicheskiye otkrytiya 1974 goda* [Archaeological discoveries for 1974] (Moscow, 1975), pp. 525–6

YE. V. ZEYMAL'

Elia de Bissone. *See* GAGINI, (2).

Elias of Dereham (*fl* 1188; *d* 1245). English cleric, sculptor and possibly metalworker. He served in the household of Hubert Walter, Bishop of Salisbury and later Archbishop of Canterbury (1193–1205), and he was employed by other bishops in an executive capacity; he also arranged the distribution of the copies of Magna Carta (1215). With Walter of Colchester (*d* 1248) he organized the translation of the remains of St Thomas Becket to the new shrine at Canterbury Cathedral in 1220, apparently making and setting up the shrine itself. He was 'director of the new fabric' of Salisbury Cathedral (of which he was a canon) from its foundation in 1220 until his death. He built a house for himself in the Close at Salisbury (Leadenhall; destr. 1915). In 1233 and 1236 he was directing the building of Henry III's new hall at Winchester Castle, and in the same decade he supervised construction of the chapel of Clarendon Palace (destr.), Wilts, although, as at Salisbury, his was a purely administrative role.

In 1238 Elias made a marble tomb for Henry III's sister, *Joan, Queen of Scotland* (1211–38; tomb slab possibly in Tarrant Crawford, Dorset, St Mary), and in 1244 Henry defrayed 30 marks towards Elias's costs in making a pyx for Salisbury Cathedral. Elias's skills in marble and metalwork might confirm that he was at least co-author of Becket's great shrine (destr.) at Canterbury Cathedral, which consisted originally of marble steps, an arched marble table-base and an iron coffin enclosed within a gold and silver embossed casket with a hipped roof. The nearby tomb of *Archbishop Walter* resembles the shrine so closely that Elias's hand is again suspected. His interest in cosmography and geometry is witnessed by a *Diagram of the World* in a manuscript from St Albans (London, BL, Cotton MS. Nero D. I, fols 184–5), made 'according to Master Elias of Dereham', and he possibly designed the inflexible geometrical plan of Salisbury Cathedral.

BIBLIOGRAPHY
Harvey: 'Dereham, Elias of '
A. H. Thompson: 'Master Elias of Dereham and the King's Works', *Archaeol. J.*, xcviii (1942), pp. 1–35
H. M. Colvin, ed.: *The Middle Ages* (1963), i of *The History of the King's Works* (London, 1963–82)
N. Stratford, P. Tudor-Craig and A. Muthesius: 'Archbishop Hubert Walter's Tomb and its Furnishings', *British Archaeological Association Conference Transactions: Medieval Art and Architecture at Canterbury before 1220: Canterbury, 1979*, pp. 71–93

FRANCIS WOODMAN

Eliasz., Nicolaes. *See* PICKENOY, NICOLAES ELIASZ.

Eliche, Marqués de. *See* CARPIO, (3).

Eliot, Charles (*b* Cambridge, MA, 1 Nov 1859; *d* Brookline, MA, 25 March 1897). American landscape architect, regional planner and writer. He was the son of Charles W. Eliot, the influential reforming president of Harvard College (1869–1909). He inherited much of his father's broad vision and organizational talent, and he applied these to his interest in landscape preservation.

After completing his basic studies at Harvard in 1882, Eliot decided to attend courses in botany and horticulture at Harvard's Bussey Institute as preparation for a career in landscape architecture. However, in 1883 he was offered an apprenticeship with Frederick Law Olmsted sr, the foremost landscape architect in the USA; he remained with Olmsted until 1885, during which time the office developed plans for several important projects, notably the Boston municipal park system and the Arnold Arboretum, Boston. He then completed his courses at the Bussey Institute, after which he toured abroad for a year, inspecting parks, gardens and natural landscapes from England to Italy and Russia.

In December 1886 Eliot established his practice as a landscape architect in Boston. He became a frequent contributor to popular and professional journals, explaining both the goals and the history of landscape architecture. In his writings and in his early designs he expressed concern for the disappearance of the New England landscape through rapid urbanization. Projects such as White Park (1888) in Concord, NH, were conceived as opportunities to preserve and make accessible the characteristic local landscape.

Eliot soon saw a need to organize more comprehensive conservation efforts. In an article written for *Garden and Forest* (1890) he argued for 'an incorporated association, composed of citizens of all the Boston towns, and empowered by the State to hold small and well-distributed parcels of land free of taxes, just as the Public Library holds books and the Art Museum pictures'. Eliot proceeded to write the legislation and direct the lobbying campaign for a bill enacted in 1891 to establish the Trustees of Public Reservations, a private organization empowered to acquire lands for conservation throughout the state. Using the Trustees as a base, Eliot next conceived of a public metropolitan authority to provide for the recreation and conservation needs of the entire Boston basin. By 1893 he had engineered the creation of the Boston Metropolitan Park Commission and had become the consultant to both the Commission and the Trustees. After an exhaustive survey of the lands within the Commission's jurisdiction, Eliot proposed a landscape preservation philosophy and specific property for acquisition; this report was completed in 1894, and by his death he had overseen the initial development of most of its proposals.

Also in 1893 Eliot accepted an entreaty from Olmsted to establish a new partnership, Olmsted, Olmsted & Eliot; he collaborated on Olmsted projects and accepted major new commissions such as Keney Park in Hartford, CT. *Vegetation and Scenery in the Metropolitan Reservations of Boston*, a statement of his vision for natural area management (1898), was published posthumously.

UNPUBLISHED SOURCES
Cambridge, MA, Harvard U., Frances Loeb Sch. Des. Lib. [pap.]

WRITINGS
'The Waverley Oaks: A Plan for their Preservation for the People', *Gdn & Forest*, iii (1890), pp. 85–6
Vegetation and Scenery in the Metropolitan Reservations of Boston (Boston, 1898)

BIBLIOGRAPHY
[C. W. Eliot]: *Charles Eliot: Landscape Architect* (Cambridge, MA, 1902) [biog. by his father, incl. substantial quotations from Eliot's rep. and corr.]
N. Newton: 'Charles Eliot and his Metropolitan Park System', *Design on the Land* (Cambridge, MA, 1971), pp. 318–36

KEITH N. MORGAN

Elisabeth-Charlotte, Duchesse d'Orléans. *See* ORLÉANS, (2).

Elizabeth, Electress Palatine of the Rhine and Queen of Bohemia. *See* STUART, House of, (5).

Elizabeth, Empress of Russia. *See* ROMANOV, (2).

Elizabeth, Queen of Spain [Farnese, Elizabeth]. *See* BOURBON, §II(2).

Elizabeth I, Queen of England. *See* TUDOR, (3).

Elizabethan Revival. Term used to describe an antiquarian style popular in England from the 1830s to the 1860s, inspired by the ELIZABETHAN STYLE of the 16th century. Designs for Elizabethan-style furniture first appeared in Rudolf Ackermann's *Repository of Arts* in 1817, although the style was not widely popular until the 1830s. The

English architect most closely identified with the style was ANTHONY SALVIN, who designed Harlaxton Manor, Lincs (1831–8). The entire vocabulary of gables, octagonal turrets, tall chimney-stacks, pinnacles, leaded-paned windows and heraldic ornament was used at Harlaxton, which was based on the Elizabethan E-plan. Salvin's other notable works in this style include Mamhead (1828–33), Devon, and Scotney Castle (1835–43), Kent. Mentmore Towers (1851–4), Bucks, was designed by Joseph Paxton and George Henry Stokes for Baron Mayer Amschel de Rothschild (1818–74) and is possibly the most elaborate manifestation of the Elizabethan Revival style.

In interiors the great hall was revived as the most important room in the house. Fireplaces were 16th century in style: the wainscot was oak, and plaster ceilings were of lozenge design with pendant bosses. By the 1850s there was a preference for furniture in darker woods; early oak pieces were collected or new furniture was made that incorporated the Elizabethan and Jacobean styles. Buffets, cupboards and four-poster beds were popular; high-backed chairs had spool- or spiral-turned uprights and carved cresting in the spirit of 17th-century vernacular furniture. A large collection of Elizabethan Revival furniture can be seen at Charlecote Park, Warwicks, NT. Two manufacturers well known for their production of Elizabethan Revival furniture were John Gregory Crace and W. Gibbs Rogers (1792–1872).

In silverware and ceramics there was a revival of Elizabethan-style covered salts, beakers and tankards. Plain surfaces are predominant, the decoration being confined to coats of arms, strapwork, bands of cinquefoils, egg-and-tongue or overlapping laurel leaves. Women's toilet cases from this period have silver or silver-gilt mounts imitating Flemish strapwork, and travelling writing cases were often shaped like caskets. Snuff-boxes in the shape of a boar's head or pointed Elizabethan shoes were also popular. Potteries in Staffordshire reintroduced salt glazes, which gave an authentic mottled appearance to stoneware jugs, mugs and tankards. A few studio potteries made tiles and platters decorated with coloured earthenware slip trailed or combed in the manner of such 17th-century potters as Thomas Toft (*d* 1689). The style persisted in the decorative arts until the 1920s and 1930s.

BIBLIOGRAPHY
C. Hussey: 'Harlaxton Manor, Lincolnshire, 1831–8', *Country Life*, cxxi (April 1957), pp. 704–7, 764–7
H. Bridgeman and E. Drury: *Encyclopedia of Victoriana* (London, 1975)

☐

Elizabethan style. Term used to describe British art and architecture produced during the reign (1558–1603) of Elizabeth I. The dominant characteristics in all media are flatness and linearity; in representational art, surface decoration, high colour and complex silhouettes are preferred over plastic form or naturalistic three-dimensional depiction. There is evidence that Nicholas Hilliard, Elizabeth I's favoured portrait miniaturist, and such other court painters as George Gower, Marcus Gheerhaerts (ii) and Isaac Oliver consciously suppressed their knowledge of contemporary Italian and Flemish naturalism to produce their own distinctive iconic portraits. As for sculpture, the Dutch and Flemish masons who visited or settled in

England, such as Garat Johnson (i) and Richard Stevens, tended to dominate. Their recumbent effigies carved for alabaster funerary monuments (often richly coloured) were conventional in design and modelling, while ornamental motifs owed much to the influence of Mannerist Flemish pattern books, such as those by Hans Vredeman de Vries. Among the decorative arts, embroidery in particular was highly prized and widely practised to an exemplary standard in later 16th-century England: the realistic portrayal of fruits and flowers, boldly coloured and within complex formed designs, epitomizes the Elizabethan style in textiles.

The leading architect of the Elizabethan period was Robert Smythson, who synthesized traditional English planning and Renaissance classicist detailing and external symmetry. At such prodigy country houses as Longleat House (from 1570), Wilts, Wollaton Hall (1580–88), Notts, and Hardwick Hall (1590–97), Derbys, working with masons associated with the Office of Works, he created a style of architecture that is characterized by symmetry and clear, blocky massing as well as extensive fenestration and carved ornamental strapwork.

BIBLIOGRAPHY
J. Summerson: *Architecture in Britain, 1530–1830*, Pelican Hist. A. (Harmondsworth, 1953, rev. 7/1983)
E. K. Waterhouse: *Painting in Britain, 1530–1790*, Pelican Hist. A. (Harmondsworth, 1953, rev. 4/1978)
E. Mercer: *English Art, 1553–1625*, Oxford Hist. Eng. A. (Oxford, 1962)
M. Whinney: *Sculpture in Britain, 1530–1830*, Pelican Hist. A. (Harmondsworth, 1964, rev. 2/1988 by J. Physick)

ALICE T. FRIEDMAN

Elk, Ger(ard Pieter) van (*b* Amsterdam, 9 Mar 1941). Dutch conceptual artist. From 1959 to 1961 he studied in Amsterdam, then at the Immaculate Heart College in Los Angeles (1961–3) and at the University of Groningen in the Netherlands from 1965 to 1966. His work examined the structures that pervade both art and reality through a variety of media: photography, painting, sculpture and installations. In *About the Reality of G. Morandi II* (1971; Rotterdam, Boymans–van Beuningen), for example, he displayed a reproduction of a still-life by Giorgio Morandi, flanked by two photographs of objects such as matches, spectacles and ink bottles that might have been found in his studio. He thus emphasized the process of selection and rejection of everyday objects that was involved in the still-life. The existence of dualities was featured in works such as *The Symmetry of Diplomacy I* (1971; Amsterdam, Stedel. Mus.), which consisted of a pair of photographs, each showing a pair of chairs. In one of the photographs, based on clichéd images of diplomatic meetings, the left-hand chair is occupied by a man talking to the adjacent empty chair, the positions being reversed in the other photograph. Examining the media of art, in *Rolled-up Palm Lane at Middelharnis, California* (1975; Paris, Pompidou) van Elk presented a rolled-up landscape image in front of a curling photograph of a landscape. Made from photographs partly painted over with acrylic he emphasized the two-dimensional nature of images, using two-dimensional images to do so.

In his later work van Elk introduced allusions to 17th-century Dutch painting, making mocking use of past styles, as in *The Western Stylemasters* (1987; Rotterdam, Boymans–van Beuningen). The title is a punning reference to Rembrandt's famous *Syndics of the Amsterdam Drapers' Guild* ('The Staalmeesters', 1662; Amsterdam, Rijksmus.) and also the De Stijl movement, while in style it imitates Frans Hals. After 1972 he taught at Ateliers 63 in Haarlem.

BIBLIOGRAPHY
Ger van Elk (exh. cat. by W. Beeren, Basle, Ksthalle, 1980)
On the Nature of Genre: Ger van Elk (exh. cat. by F. Kaiser and J. Svestka, Düsseldorf, Kstver., 1988)

Elkington, G(eorge) R(ichards) (*b* Birmingham, 17 Oct 1801; *d* Pool Park, Denbs, 22 Sept 1865). English silver manufacturer. In 1815 he was apprenticed to a small, family-owned silver manufacturing business in Birmingham, which he eventually inherited. The firm made spectacle-frames, snuff-boxes and silver-gilt 'toys' and bottle mounts. Between 1829 and 1836 he was in partnership with his cousin Henry Elkington (*c.* 1810–52), during a period of much interest in electrometallurgy. G. R. Elkington hired a metallurgist, Alexander Parkes, and patronized chemists in the attempt to develop the electrogilding and ELECTROPLATING of base metal articles for commercial production. From 1836 to 1838 he registered several patents and in 1840 took out a patent on an improved method of electroplating discovered by John Wright, a Birmingham surgeon. Elkington's electroplate, perfected by Parkes, revolutionized the manufacture of plated silver and by the late 1850s had superseded almost all of the trade in Sheffield plate. Elkington opened a new factory in 1840, and in 1842 a wealthy pen manufacturer, Josiah Mason (*d* 1859), joined the firm, which became Elkington, Mason & Co. until Mason's retirement in 1856 and Elkington & Co. thereafter. Determined to retain exclusive rights, Elkington bought others' patents or hired his competitors and for large fees granted other firms, notably Christofle et Cie in France, licences to manufacture electroplate under his patent.

By 1847 Elkington, Mason & Co. was mass-producing large, electroplated silver wares, for example salvers, trays, dishes and meat covers. The firm also produced a wide range of brassware. The trade catalogues illustrate electroplated silver and brass tableware in revival styles offered by the firm, finished and polished in the factory by hand. Elkington also engaged sculptors and designers, including Léonard Morel-Ladeuil (*c.* 1820–88) and Auguste Willms (*fl* 1848–99), to design electrotype versions of ancient Greek and Roman, Renaissance and 18th-century pieces (e.g. 'Inventions' vase, 1863; London, V&A). The company passed to Elkington's son, Frederick Elkington, upon his death and continued in production into the 20th century. The business changed hands in the 1950s and in 1963 became part of British Silverware.

BIBLIOGRAPHY
P. Wardle: *Victorian Silver and Silver-plate* (London, 1963)
S. Bury: *Victorian Electroplate* (Feltham, 1971)
J. Culme: *Nineteenth-century Silver* (Feltham, 1977)

Elle. French family of painters. Ferdinand Elle (*b* Mechelen, *c.* 1580; *d* Paris, 1649) is documented in 1609 in Paris, where he worked under the name of Ferdinand; in that year he was paid 400 livres for a large group portrait (untraced) of the *Echevins, procureurs et greffiers* of Paris (untraced). In 1612 Nicolas Poussin was his pupil for three months. Elle was principally a portrait painter; most of his portraits are known only from mediocre engravings, which nevertheless indicate that he developed an extensive practice and enjoyed considerable success. Among his sitters were *Henry IV* (*c.* 1600; engraved *c.* 1660 by Jean Morin) and *Marie de' Medici* (untraced). He subsequently became a court painter to Louis XIII, and painted portraits of some notable persons about the court, such as the surgeon *Jacques de Marque* (1616; engraved by Michel Lasne, 1637). One surviving example of his work is the portrait of *Henri de Lorraine, Marquis de Mouy* (1631; Reims, Mus. St-Denis).

Louis [Ferdinand I] Elle (*b* Paris, 1612; *d* Paris, 12 Dec 1689), Ferdinand Elle's elder son and pupil, succeeded him as court painter. In 1648 he was one of the founder-members of the Académie Royale, and in 1659 he was appointed professor. He was obliged to resign his membership in 1681 because he was a Protestant; he resumed it in 1686, having renounced his faith. Although he is recorded as a painter of mythologies and allegories, such as *Portrait of a Lady as Minerva* (1655; Marseille, Mus. Grobet-Labadié), like his father he chiefly painted portraits, most of which are known only from engravings. His earliest work, such as the portrait of *Charles II Gonzaga, Duke of Mantua* (*c.* 1640; engraver unknown, see Wildenstein, fig. 6), was stiff and conventional, but his style developed steadily, and his work of the 1650s is much more individual. In such portraits as *Gaspar de Fay de Saint-Jouin, Maître des Requêtes* (*c.* 1655; engraved in 1659 by Jean Fresne), he shows considerable powers of characterization and perception. He was associated with the Précieux circle, and made portraits (known from engravings) of the *Marquise de Sévigné, Ninon de Lenclos* and *M. de Montausier* among others. Of his later work, *Charles d'Orléans, Comte de Dunois* (engraved by Robert Nanteuil, 1660), is a charming and relaxed portrait of a child; in this and other portraits, Elle was well served by Nanteuil, whose master he may have been. He exhibited three portraits (untraced) at the Salon of 1673.

Pierre Elle (*b* Paris, 20 March 1617; *d* Paris, 4 Sept 1665), Louis Elle's younger brother, began as a painter, but increasingly turned to print-publishing, sharing business interests with such figures as François Langlois, Pierre Mariette (i) and Pierre Mariette (ii); he published the work of Jacques-Samuel Bernard and that of his brother Louis. His son and pupil Louis [Ferdinand II] Elle (*b* Paris, 1648; *d* Paris, 1717) followed him as Peintre du Roi. He was elected to the Académie Royale in 1681 on presentation of three-quarter length portraits of some distinction of *Jacques-Samuel Bernard* and of *Thomas Regnaudin* (both Versailles, Château).

BIBLIOGRAPHY

E. and E. Haag: *La France protestante*, v (Paris, 1855), pp. 90–92
G. Wildenstein: 'Les Ferdinand Elle: A propos de deux inventaires inédits', *Gaz. B.-A.*, n. s. 5, 1 (1957), pp. 225–36
R.-A. Weigert: *Inventaire du fonds français: Graveurs du dix-septième siècle*, Paris, Bib. N., Dept Est. cat., iv (Paris, 1961), pp. 165–74 [as Ferdinand]
S. Hanappier: *Les Elle: Peintres de portraits* (diss., U. Paris IV, 1983)
M. Préaud, P. Casselle, M. Grivel and C. Le Bitouzé: *Dictionnaire des éditeurs d'estampes à Paris sous l'Ancien Régime* (Paris, 1987), p. 122

Ellerker & Kilburn. Australian architectural partnership formed by W(illiam) H(enry) Ellerker (*b* Birmingham, 1837; *d* Melbourne, 30 March 1891) and E(dward) G(eorge) Kilburn (*b* Australia, 1859; *d* 1894), active in Melbourne from 1886 to 1891. Ellerker came to Melbourne with his parents in 1853 and in 1856 was engaged as a draughtsman by Thomas Kemp. From 1858 he worked as a draughtsman in the Railways Department and then the Public Works Department. In 1863 he went to Queensland, where his design for Parliament House was recommended by a royal commission but did not proceed. He returned to Melbourne in 1867 and established a general practice in partnership with his brother John Ellerker, which was productive but designed nothing notable. He was a considerable investor in the Melbourne land boom of the 1880s and seems to have largely withdrawn from practice. The first major city buildings pre-date the partnership and were designed in association with William Pitt: the Federal Coffee Palace (1884–8), a grandiose combination of Baroque and Mannerist elements, and Oxford Chambers (1885), both in Melbourne. These seem unlikely to be attributable to Ellerker, who may have been involved only because of his financial interests.

In 1886 Ellerker entered partnership with E. G. Kilburn, a skilled draughtsman. Kilburn's characteristic work reveals an American influence. The house Coornor (1888) in Kew was described by a contemporary as German Gothic but seems closely related to Richard Morris Hunt's Linden Gate (1873), Newport, RI. In 1890 the firm produced two Romanesque Revival designs in the American manner, for competitions for the Commercial Bank of Australia headquarters in Melbourne and for the Broken Hill municipal buildings, New South Wales, although neither project was built. The more modest Priory school in St Kilda was begun the same year and was the first thoroughgoing example of the American Romanesque Revival in Australia, followed by the house Cestria (1891), similarly in red brick with cement dressings. After the partnership dissolved Kilburn seems to have gained no significant work.

BIBLIOGRAPHY

S. Clements: *W. H. Ellerker* (diss., U. Melbourne, 1973)
H. Fryday: *W. H. Ellerker* (diss., U. Melbourne, 1979)

MILES LEWIS

Ellesmere, 1st Earl of. *See* EGERTON, (2).

Ellice Islands. *See* TUVALU.

Elliger. Family of painters of German origin. Ottmar Elliger (i) (*b* Göteborg, 1633; *d* Berlin, 1679) painted still-lifes of flowers and fruits. He studied with Daniel Seghers in Antwerp, then worked in Amsterdam *c.* 1660 before settling in Hamburg in 1666 and entering the service of the Great Elector Frederick William of Brandenburg in Berlin in 1670. Ottmar Elliger (ii) (*b* Hamburg, 19 Feb 1666; *d* St Petersburg, 19 Feb 1735) was a history painter and engraver. He trained under his father; when his father died he left for Amsterdam to study under Michiel van Musscher until 1686. He then joined the studio of Gérard de Lairesse, whose classicizing tendencies had a profound impact. He became painter to the court of the Prince-Elector of Mainz *c.* 1716. Finally he moved to St Petersburg, where his engravings won him some renown.

Unlike his father, who was essentially a realist painter, Ottmar Elliger (ii) (by far the most talented of the family) devoted himself to painting in the grand decorative and idealist manner. Influenced by Lairesse's theoretical teaching, he created a pleasant, light, harmonious art that did not achieve the monumentality of Lairesse's work but was nonetheless a worthy precursor of 18th-century European developments. His colouring was stronger than that of Lairesse, as can be seen in the *Adoration of the Shepherds* (Münster, Westfäl. Landesmus.). His son Antonie Elliger (*b* Amsterdam, 1701; *d* Ede op de Veluwe, 1781) worked as a historical and portrait painter. His work was derivative of his father's but did not achieve the same quality.

BIBLIOGRAPHY
Thieme–Becker
A. Houbraken: *De groote schouburgh* (1718–21), ii, p. 293

ALAIN ROY

Elliot, Archibald (*b* Ancrum, Roxburghshire [now Borders], Aug 1760; *d* Edinburgh, 16 June 1823). Scottish architect. He was a successful Edinburgh architect with no formal education. He trained as a joiner and may have worked as a contractor for the building of Castle Mona (1801–6), Isle of Man, designed by George Steuart (*c.* 1730–1806) for the 4th Duke of Atholl, who later became Elliot's patron. From 1794 to 1799 he exhibited architectural drawings at the Royal Academy. In 1800 he set up in joint practice with his brother James Elliot (1770–1810), running offices in London and Edinburgh. Elliot cannot be considered an architectural innovator. His usual style for country houses was castellated and derived directly from Roger Morris's conception at Inveraray Castle (from 1745), Argyll, for the 3rd Duke of Argyll and from the Adam castle style. Loudoun Castle (1804–11; gutted 1941), Strathclyde, for the Marquess of Hastings, is an exercise in post-Adam castellated design, while Taymouth Castle (1806–10), Tayside, for the 1st Marquess of Breadalbane, and Stobo Castle (1805), Borders, for Sir James Montgomery, are dramatic examples in the Inveraray tradition, with their large central staircase saloons decorated with elaborate Gothic Revival plasterwork. The Calton Gaol (1815–17; destr. *c.* 1938) and Governor's House (1815–17), Edinburgh, the County Buildings and Gaol (1818–20; destr. 1970), Paisley, Strathclyde, and Jedburgh Gaol (1820–23), Borders, confirm his sense of the picturesque castellated composition. His best town work in Edinburgh, mostly Greek Revival, contributed to Edinburgh's fame as the 'Modern Athens'. It included the Regent Bridge (1815–19) and Waterloo Place (1819), an ensemble in the best Nash manner; twin Ionic porticos flank the end of Waterloo Place and lead the eye past palace fronts, across the triumphal arch, past the Doric arches of the Regent Bridge that lie parallel to the road, to the prospect of the Calton Hill. His ambitious design for a National Monument on the Calton Hill, Edinburgh, was a grand rotunda based on the Pantheon, Rome. It is probable that his design would have been accepted but for his death.

BIBLIOGRAPHY
Colvin; Papworth
J. Macaulay: *The Gothic Revival, 1745–1845* (Glasgow, 1975)

CATHERINE H. CRUFT

Elliott, Charles Loring (*b* Scipio, NY, 12 Oct 1812; *d* Albany, NY, 25 Aug 1868). American painter. Resolved to become an artist, he moved from Syracuse, NY, to New York City around 1830, reportedly bearing a letter of introduction to John Trumbull and receiving some brief instruction from him. Elliott spent six months in the studio of the genre painter John Quidor but returned to upstate New York, where he worked for several years as an itinerant portrait painter. Back in New York City by 1839, his art steadily improved; Henry Inman met him around 1844–5, whereupon he predicted: 'When I am gone that young man will take my place'. Elliott's portrait of *Capt. John Ericsson* (*c.* 1845; untraced) won praise in 1845 as 'the best American portrait since [Gilbert] Stuart', and from that date he was acknowledged as New York's leading portrait painter. His facility for capturing a vivid, characteristic likeness and his genial personality assured a constant stream of private patrons and public commissions. In 1867 it was reported that he had executed nearly 700 portraits.

Elliott painted with a vibrant palette and a somewhat more fluid brush than his contemporaries, creating direct, unsentimentalized likenesses often relentless in their accuracy. The materiality of his approach is most evident in *Mrs Thomas Goulding* (1858; New York, N. Acad. Des.), a portrait in which forceful character shines through a factual rendering of features and costume. He was intrigued by the new science of photography and based some of his later portraits on daguerreotypes. His best works, such as the full-length *Matthew Vassar* (1861; Poughkeepsie, NY, Vassar Coll. A.G.), transcend photographic realism through their robust modelling and grand-manner style.

BIBLIOGRAPHY
H. Tuckerman: *Book of the Artists* (New York, 1867/*R* 1966), pp. 302–5
T. Bolton: 'Charles Loring Elliott, an Account of his Life and Work'; 'A Catalogue of Portraits Painted by Charles Loring Elliott', *A. Q.*, v (1942), pp. 59–96

SALLY MILLS

Elliott, Julian (Arnold) (*b* Cathcart, 27 Aug 1928). South African architect. He studied at the University of Cape Town (1948–53) and spent a year in London working for Frederick Gibberd and Partners (1953–4). He then formed a partnership with Philippe Charbonnier at Elisabethville, Congo (now Lubumbashi, Zaire), which became Charbonnier and Elliott (1955–8). He was responsible, with Charbonnier, for several buildings in Elisabethville, including the Bocskay Flats (1956) and a group of variegated, interconnected one-family houses of concrete and brick (1956–7), which adapted a traditional African vernacular to modern forms. An innovative private house (early 1960s) built at Itawa, near Ndola, Zambia, displayed Elliott's sensitivity to climate and terrain with its curving, independent rain-roof poised like a bird's wing over the structure to provide deep shade. He established a private practice in Ndola (1959–68), where his designs included the Kasama Cathedral. He was best known for his buildings (1964–8) for the University of Zambia, Lusaka, planned as a linear complex of linked buildings allowing for future growth. In 1969 he moved his practice to Newlands, South Africa. As a spokesman for a heterogeneous modern architecture in Africa, he was active as a teacher and became Director of the University of Cape Town Planning Unit in 1969. His design (1984–6) for the new Middle Campus, University of Cape Town, was linked to African *kraals* (huts grouped in a compound), with its low-profile clusters of gable-roofed buildings with deep balconies like horizontal slits, planned with regard to older buildings, walks and trees. It expressed his dislike of megastructures and his philosophy for a humane architecture that responded to the needs of its users.

WRITINGS
'UCT Campus, 1918–81: A Case Study in University Planning', *Archit. SA*, 15 (1981), pp. 56–9 [reprinted extract from lecture]

BIBLIOGRAPHY
U. Kultermann: *New Architecture in Africa* (London, 1963)
——: *New Directions in African Architecture* (London, 1969)

Ellis. English family of patrons and collectors.

(1) Welbore Agar Ellis (*d* 1805). He was one of the leading English collectors of the 18th century and purchased mainly French and Dutch 17th-century works, including Claude Lorrain's *Pastoral Landscape with the Arch of Titus* (1661; Eaton Hall, Ches) and *Landscape with Hagar and the Angel* (Winterthur, Samml. Oskar Reinhart), and Poussin's *Achilles among the Daughters of Lycomedes* (1650s; Boston, MA, Mus. F.A.) and *Moses Striking the Rock* (*c.* 1637; Duke of Westminster, on loan to Edinburgh, N.G.). Much to his subsequent regret, Ellis refused the offer of Maria Laura to sell him Poussin's first series of the *Seven Sacraments* (1638–9; Belvoir Castle, Leics; *Baptism* in Washington, DC, N.G.A.), and it was acquired in 1784 by the Duke of Rutland. Ellis was less resigned about Benjamin West's refusal of his offer for a *Death of Actaeon* (1560s; London, N.G.) attributed to Titian and, according to Paul Sandby, paid a French artist to visit London and pronounce the picture a copy. Ellis welcomed visitors to view his collection, including the young Thomas Lawrence in 1787. His collection, numbering 65 works, was announced for sale at Christie's, London, on 2–3 May 1806 but was bought prior to the sale by Robert, 2nd Earl Grosvenor, for approximately £30,000.

BIBLIOGRAPHY
The Catalogue of Paintings the Property of a Nobleman, Being Part of the Collection of W. E. Agar (London, 1808)
G. Waagen: *Treasures of Art in Great Britain*, i (London, 1854), p. 16
G. Redford: *Art Sales: A History of Sales of Pictures and Other Works of Art*, i (London, 1888), p. 95
A. Maclaren: *The Dutch School* (London, 1960), pp. 452–3
M. Röthlisberger: *Claude Lorrain: The Paintings, I: Critical Catalogue* (New Haven, CT, 1961), pp. 234, 321
A. F. Blunt: *The Paintings of Nicolas Poussin: A Critical Catalogue* (London, 1966), pp. 73, 89, 174, 177

R. WINDSOR LISCOMBE

(2) George James Welbore Agar-Ellis, 1st Baron Dover (*b* London, 14 Jan 1797; *d* London, 10 July 1833). He was obviously a kinsman of (1) Welbore Agar Ellis, but the exact relationship has not been established. Elected to Parliament in 1818, he rose in the ranks of the Whig party until ill health forced his retirement. Guided by Sir George Beaumont, whom he met in 1821, he was instrumental in the establishment of a purpose-built National Gallery in London and subsequently he served as a trustee of the National Gallery and of the British Museum. He was a friend of Thomas Lawrence, whose portrait of him (New Haven, CT, Yale Cent. Brit. A.) was exhibited at the British Gallery in 1833.

Agar-Ellis's own collection was dominated by the works of contemporary British painters and included John Jackson's portrait of *John Flaxman*, but it also featured Francesco Guardi's *Gondola on a Lake near Mestre* and *Caprice* (both London, N.G.), a portrait then supposed to be by Rembrandt but later attributed to Ferdinand Bol, and a drawing by van Dyck after Rubens's sketch for the *Martyrdom of St Ursula and her Companions* (London, BM).

UNPUBLISHED SOURCES
Northampton, Northants Record Office, Annaly of Holdenby Col. [diaries]

WRITINGS
Catalogue of the Principal Pictures in Flanders and Holland (London, 1822)
ed.: *Letters of Horace Walpole, Earl of Orford, to Sir Horace Mann, British Envoy at the Court of Tuscany*, 3 vols (London, 1833)

BIBLIOGRAPHY
DNB
C. Holmes and C. H. Collins Baker: *The Making of the National Gallery* (London, 1924)
F. Owen and D. B. Brown: *Collector of Genius: A Life of Sir George Beaumont* (London, 1988)

DAVID BLAYNEY BROWN, R. WINDSOR LISCOMBE

Ellis, Harvey (*b* ?Rochester, NY, Dec 1852; *d* Syracuse, NY, 2 Jan 1904). American architect, painter and designer. Between 1879 and 1885 he and a brother, Charles Ellis, maintained an architectural partnership in Rochester that produced commercial buildings and fashionable residences. Simultaneously he exhibited traditional representational drawings and watercolours in the Rochester Art Club. In 1885 Harvey Ellis won first prize and considerable fame with a beautiful perspective for a monument to *General Ulysses Grant* (1822–85), sponsored and published by *American Architect and Building News* (xvii (1885), p. 175). Ellis worked as an architectural draughtsman and occasional designer for a succession of Midwestern firms, including LeRoy Sunderland Buffington in Minneapolis, MN (1887–9); Eckel & Mann in St Joseph, MI (1889–91); and, when the latter partnership was dissolved, until 1893 with George R. Mann in St Louis, MO. During this period a number of his perspectives of various projects were published in *American Architect and Building News* and *Inland Architect*, where they had a considerable influence. They were delightfully imaginative, romantic interpretations of current 19th-century styles, picturesquely interpreted by Ellis's pictorial vision. By 1895 Ellis had returned to Rochester. He concentrated on painting, in a moderately avant-garde style that stressed abstract two-dimensional pictorial organization (e.g. *The Hourglass*, 1898; Rochester, NY, Strong Mus.; see 1972–3 exh. cat.) rather than the earlier illusionism, graphic designs for posters (e.g. Third National Cycle Exhibition, 1897; Rochester, NY, Strong Mus.) and magazine covers, and designs for stained glass and furniture (e.g. side chair designed for Gustav Crafts, *c.* 1903–4; Newark, NJ, Mus.; library table, *c.* 1903–4; New

York, Brooklyn Mus.). He helped to organize the Rochester Arts and Crafts Society in 1897 and, at the invitation of GUSTAVE STICKLEY, publisher of the *Craftsman*, he moved to Syracuse to become its editor in 1903, a position he held until his death the following year.

WRITINGS

Regular contributions to *Craftsman* (1903–4) [articles; house and furniture designs]

BIBLIOGRAPHY

Macmillan Enc. Architects

C. Bragdon: 'Harvey Ellis: A Portrait Sketch', *Archit. Rev.* [Boston], xv (1908), pp. 173–86

F. Swales: 'Master Draughtsman III: Harvey Ellis, 1852–1907 [sic]', *Pencil Points*, vii (1912), pp. 49–55, 79

E. Manning: *The Architectural Designs of Harvey Ellis* (diss., Minneapolis, U. MN, 1953)

R. Kennedy: 'The Long Shadow of Harvey Ellis', *MN Hist.*, xl (1966), pp. 97–108

——: 'Long, Dark Corridors: Harvey Ellis', *Prairie Sch. Rev.*, v/1–2 (1968), pp. 5–18

A Rediscovery: Harvey Ellis: Artist, Architect (exh. cat., U. Rochester, NY, Mem. A.G.; Rochester, NY, Strong Mus.; 1972–3)

The Arts & Crafts Movement in New York State, 1890s–1920s (exh. cat. by C. Ludwig, Oswego, SUNY, Tyler A.G., 1983), pp. 75–7

EILEEN MICHELS

Ellora [Elura, Marathi Verul; anc. Elāpura]. Site of outstanding cave temples, datable between *c.* AD 575 and the end of the 9th century, 20 km north of Aurangabad in the Sahyadri Hills, Maharashtra, India. The caves were excavated into volcanic rock along a 2-km stretch of west-facing embankment; there are 34 major caves, numbered consecutively rather than chronologically, starting with the Buddhist group (Caves 1–12) in the south. Other groups are dedicated to the Brahmanical pantheon (Caves 14–29) and to Jainism (Caves 30–34). The most notable monument is Cave 16, the Kailasa Temple.

1. History and development. 2. Kailasa Temple.

1. HISTORY AND DEVELOPMENT. The caves contain some of the best examples of large-scale sculptured reliefs in India. The earliest caves, which are Hindu, were excavated between *c.* 575 and 600, when the KALACHURIS OF MAHARASHTRA and CHALUKYAS OF BADAMI were struggling for supremacy of the Deccan. Cave 29 is largely modelled on Cave 1 at Elephanta but without the three-faced relief of Mahadeva and the central positioning of the four-doored *liṅga* shrine. Both caves have prominent reliefs of Lakulisha, the founder of the Pashupata sect of ascetics, whose influence persisted at Ellora until the 9th century. A local idiom remarkable for its emphasis on goddess iconography is best evidenced in Caves 21 and 14, which combine influences from the Konkan and further north with those from Badami to the south. Cave 21 has an unequalled group of life-size mother goddesses (*saptamātṛkā*s), carved almost in the round, and exquisitely rendered reliefs of the river goddesses Ganga and Yamuna at each end of the façade. The verandah with a carved balustrade and massive piers adorned with large bracket figures is similar to the roughly contemporary caves at Badami. Cave 14 is dedicated to the goddess Shakti; although the image in the shrine is missing, the five massive reliefs on each side of the pillared hall contain various aspects of the goddess in her role as divine consort

(*śakti*), of Shiva on the south wall and Vishnu on the north. Seated mother goddesses, accompanied by Ganesha and Virabhadra, on the south wall of the passage (*pradakṣiṇa*) beside the shrine, hold a child on their lap, emphasizing their benevolent aspect; their power to destroy evil is suggested by their proximity to an over life-size group of skeletons portraying Kala, the God of Death, with his attendants. Caves 14, 20, 21 and 26 bear a close stylistic resemblance to the earliest Buddhist caves at the site, particularly in the decoration of the shrine doorways and the giant guardian flanking figures. These excavations can probably be attributed to the same workmen. Traces of Buddhist decoration on the pilasters and window frames of Cave 27, which was later transformed into a Vaishnava cave, suggest that the Buddhist caves originally extended to the Velganga waterfall but that the Buddhist monks were relocated between *c.* 600 and 730 to the southern end of the escarpment, where they excavated an interrelated, densely packed group of 12 caves.

The Buddhist caves are important landmarks in the development of Mahayana Buddhism. Cave 5, the earliest, has a rare example of a parallel row of raised narrow rectangular platforms extending nearly the length of the cave (*c.* 37 m), a feature seen at Kanheri and which remains unexplained. Iconographically, the image of the Buddha develops from the Vairocana form—with his hands in the teaching position (*dharmacakra mudrā*)—in the earlier caves to the more Tantric Akshobhya—shown with his hand touching the ground (*bhūmisparśa mudrā*) calling the earth as witness when he resisted temptation—in some of the later ones (*see* INDIAN SUBCONTINENT, §II, 2). A new use of space was also developed. The images of Buddhas that were portrayed in two-dimensional reliefs on the walls of Cave 6 were disposed in three-dimensional space along the side galleries of Cave 2, in order that the worshipper could walk through the cave, experiencing and meditating on the sculpture. The latest Buddhist caves (11 and 12) were excavated in three storeys of increasing size and complexity, where each floor is adapted in layout and iconography to a different level of spiritual development. The shrine chambers on the topmost floor contain a unique arrangement of four over life-size *bodhisattva*s on either side of the Buddha image. Female imagery is prominent. A unique panel of Mahamayuri exists in Cave 8, while the images of the ascetic goddess Brikuti are derived from Tapasvini, a form of Parvati. Cave 10, with a unique broken horseshoe-shaped arch above the major entrance (*see* INDIAN SUBCONTINENT, fig. 47), is the last major rock-cut *caityagṛha* (hall for the worship of a stupa) in India.

From *c.* 750 the site became the showpiece of the RASHTRAKUTA dynasty. A copperplate inscription of the first ruler, Dantidurga (*reg c.* 730–54), records his worship of Shiva as Lord of the Cave and describes his military conquests and visit to Ellora with his army. The free-standing hall (*maṇḍapa*) of Cave 15, which bears a further inscription of Dantidurga, is hewn out of the rock in the forecourt and seems to have been a prototype for the Kailasa Temple. Its pierced, rock-cut windows with elaborately carved superstructures are modelled largely on those of the Papanatha Temple at Pattadakal, while the numerous monumental mythological scenes carved in high relief on the top floor of the temple surpass the panels at Pattadakal, on which their style and iconography were based. These Hindu sculptures were incorporated into what was originally a three-storey Buddhist excavation. Only two of the storeys were completed, but small Buddha figures remain on the elaborately carved façade pilasters of the top floor. Cave 16 is the celebrated Kailasa Temple, the main body of which was carved out of the hillside during the reign of Krishna I (*reg c.* 758–73). Major caves (e.g. 22 and 25) were added or modified by the Rashtrakutas until about the early 9th century.

With the accession of Amoghavarsha I (*reg c.* 814–73) Rashtrakuta activity moved about 800 m to the north, to a hill sacred to the Jainas. Five Jaina temples were excavated at that time, including the Chota Kailasa (Cave 30A), a small, unfinished copy of the Kailasa Temple. The Indra Sabha (Cave 32) is a two-storey cave facing a courtyard with a shrine surmounted by a southern-style superstructure. The courtyard contains a pillar, a life-size elephant and a southern-style gateway, or *gopura*, and screen in imitation of the arrangement at the Kailasa Temple. The Jaina sculptures are remarkable for their fine surface detail and heavily decorated style. Iconographically their imagery belongs to the Digambara sect of JAINISM, with exceptional emphasis on asceticism. The image of Bahubali, a warrior saint who attained enlightenment by standing naked in meditation, rooted to the ground, makes its first appearance at the site. Jainism continued at Ellora after the Rashtrakutas, as evidenced by a monumental image of Parshvanatha dated AD 1234 at the top of the hill.

The area above Caves 14–29 contains numerous smaller excavations datable to *c.* 7th–13th century, frequently with an image of Lakulisha above the shrine entrance and a large relief of the three faces of Shiva behind the *linga*. Two noteworthy groups, the Yogeshvari Caves and the Ganesha Lena, lie on the banks of the Velganga River before it enters the plain.

Extensive unexcavated remains and a large stepped tank may prove to be the site of the early capital of the Rashtrakutas, visited by al-Masudi in 915. In the 12th and 13th centuries the area formed part of the religious and cultural milieu of the Yadava dynasty; their capital, Devagiri (mod. Daulatabad), was only 10 km away. Ellora is associated with the rise of mysticism in Maharashtra; Jnanadeva (writing from 1290), the first Maratha mystic, frequented the site, as did Janardana Swami (*b* 1504) and Ekanath (*fl c.* 1590). It became a holy centre for Muslims, whose incursions into the Deccan in the late 13th century were at Devagiri. The continuing importance of Ellora under Muslim rule is indicated by the fact that the Mughal emperor Aurangzeb (*reg* 1658–1707) was buried at Khultabad above the caves in a modest tomb beside that of his Sufi preceptor. Ellora was an important centre of Hindu revival: around 1776 the Ghrishneshvara Temple was built by the Maratha queen of Indore, Ahalyabai Holkar, to house a *jyotirlinga*, one of the 12 'Lingas of Light' that are still worshipped throughout India.

2. KAILASA TEMPLE. The most notable rock-cut temple of India, it is dedicated to Shiva and is datable mainly to the last quarter of the 8th century with some subsidiary shrines added later. A copperplate inscription (812) attributes the temple's establishment to Krishna I (*reg c.* 758–73) as a celebration of the victory of the Rashtrakuta dynasty over the Chalukyas of Badami. The Kailasa is partly modelled on the Virupaksha and Mallikarjuna temples at Pattadakal, buildings that were themselves conceived as rivalling the Kailasanatha Temple in Kanchipuram. Even the architect–builder was struck with astonishment at the temple's perfection, according to the inscription. Local legends of the Skanda Purana of considerable antiquity maintain that the architect came from the south.

The Kailasa Temple represents the culmination of rock-cut architecture, with huge sculptural reliefs heightening the overall symbolism of the temple as cosmic mountain and as the home of Shiva. An entire temple complex in the southern manner, the Kailasa comprises the main building (Skt *vimāna*), the Nandi pavilion and the entrance doorway (*gopura*), sculpted *in situ* from the escarpment (see fig.). Additional temples and shrines were sculpted from the vertical sides of the compound at different periods, and a recessed gallery comprising monumental reliefs is contained on three walls at the back of the compound. Structurally and stylistically the temple is uniquely adapted to its position in a deep, rectangular cut in the hillside (about 30×45×90 m). Entrance is gained only at second-storey level and the temple stands on a solid base (h. 7m) carved with massive elephants in high relief that alternate with lions. The elephants on the north and east sides are frontal, as at Karle, while those on the south side are engaged in lively combat with the lions as in the smaller friezes in the temples at Pattadakal. Two free-standing, over life-size elephants, symmetrically placed in the courtyard, are symbols of military might frequently found in such Rashtrakuta foundations as the caves at Jogai Amba, although the earliest example is found among the rock-cut temples at Mamallapuram belonging to the Pallava king Mahendravarman I (*reg c.* 570–630). Beside each elephant is a carved, square-based pillar (*dhvaja stambha*) about 14 m high, one of which, on the north, retains what is likely to be a depiction of a *trisūla* at the top. At the front ends of the plinth, beside the steps that lead up to the second storey, are important narrative reliefs in eight tiers depicting scenes from the *Mahābhārata* and the *Rāmāyana*, on the north and south side respectively. The lower two rows of the northern side reveal a complex and innovative rendering of the childhood of Krishna.

A rock-cut screen forming an impressive façade almost blocks the view of the temple from outside the compound. The screen consists of a central two-storey gateway with a balcony on the upper level and eight pillared niches below containing life-size figures of the guardians of the directions (*dikpāla*s). The doorway is flanked with purifying water symbols: over life-size sculptures of male and female serpent deities (*nāga*s and *nāginī*s) and of the river goddesses Ganga and Yamuna. To the left of the doorway are six shallow, pilastered niches, each containing a benevolent form of a deity, mostly Shiva, while the corresponding deities to the right represent violent, destructive forms of both Shiva and Vishnu. This disposition of beneficence contrasting with destruction is repeated on the inner side of the screen wall. Facing the left side of the courtyard is

Ellora, Kailasa Temple, last quarter of the 8th century AD to mid-9th

a rare panel of Kama, the god of love, with his wife Rati, contrasting with a rendering of Durga killing the buffalo–demon (*Mahiṣāsuramardinī*), and facing the right side of the courtyard is a monumental relief, sweeping across the inner corner of the gateway, of Shiva destroying the three cities (*tripurāntaka*) contrasting with several damaged portrayals of Shiva as an ascetic.

An extraordinarily powerful relief of Ravana shaking Mt Kailasa, on which Shiva and Parvati are seated (*see* INDIAN SUBCONTINENT, fig. 190), is placed at basement level on the south side of the main temple (*vimāna*), a visual pun on its identification with Mt Kailasa itself. Above it, large flat areas of temple wall are perfectly balanced with recessed niches containing mythological scenes, flying figures in deep relief, and finely carved pilasters. On the south elevation are some combat scenes from the *Rāmāyaṇa*, including one of the bird Jatayu attempting to prevent the abduction of Sita by Ravana. A standing sculpture of Lakulisha indicates the continued influence of the Pashupata sect at Ellora.

The temple interior consists of a hall (*maṇḍapa*) with sixteen pillars arranged in groups of four; cruciform aisles leading to three entrances resemble the arrangement at Elephanta and at Cave 29, Ellora. Three porches with massive overhanging eaves and immense door guardians mark these entrances, which once linked the temple to other shrines at second-storey level. The front entrance opens towards the Nandi pavilion; the southern porch, facing the three-storey Parlanka Cave, which is carved into the southern wall of the pit and was originally used for the

consecration of the image, was connected to it by a stone bridge that has collapsed. On the north side of the cliffs is the Lankeshvara, a later excavation (started *c.* 821) that rivals the interior of the Kailasa in size. It was reached by a wooden bridge, now lost.

The main shrine is surmounted by a pyramidal, southern-style superstructure of four horizontal stages topped by an octagonal cupola (*śikhara*). It is surrounded by an exterior circumambulatory platform with five smaller shrines at its outer edges. The exterior walls of the main shrine chamber are adorned with reliefs of Shiva and the Goddess. At the base of the superstructure, framed in a horseshoe arch, is the image that sets the theme for the entire temple, that of Shiva as Mahayogi, the Great Ascetic. Directly below, inside, on the ceiling of the antechamber to the shrine, is a corresponding relief of the goddess Annapurna, the provider of sustenance on earth. In the antechamber, flanking the shrine, are the two most important iconographic themes of the temple: on the north wall, Shiva and Parvati playing dice, representing the separation of the elements *puruṣa* and *prakṛti* that leads to dissolution of creation and to the reabsorption of the individual soul into the Universal Soul; on the opposite wall, Somaskanda, showing Shiva and Parvati with their son, representing their reunion and the recreation of the worlds. On the north side of the compound, the shrine of the river goddesses, in a sinuous, richly decorated style, may commemorate the victorious incursions *c.* 790 into the Gangetic doab of the Rashtrakuta king Dhruva (*reg c.* 780–93). The 'Hall of Sacrifice' on the south side, containing exquisitely carved but damaged mother goddesses, may have been added by the powerful Rashtrakuta king Govinda III (*reg c.* 794–813). Carved fully in the round, three female figures (who may be queens) seem to preside over a sacrifice represented by altars sculpted out of the floor of the cave. Each is faced by three lifelike seated figures of deities: Kaushiki, the highest form of the Goddess, in the centre flanked by Durga on her lion and the skeletal Kala, god of death, with a corpse and a hyena at his feet. Fragmentary traces of painting dating from the 8th century to the 14th survive on the ceiling of the entrance porch and elsewhere on the building (*see* INDIAN SUBCONTINENT, §VI, 3(i)(a)).

See also INDIAN SUBCONTINENT, §§III, 5(i)(d) and IV, 7(iii)(b).

BIBLIOGRAPHY
J. Burgess and J. Fergusson: *The Cave Temples of India* (London, 1880)
R. G. Bhandarkar: 'The Rāshtrākūṭa King Krishṇarājai and Elāpura', *Ind. Antiqua.*, xii (1883), pp. 228–30
J. Burgess: *Report on the Elura Cave Temples and the Brahmanical and Jain Caves of Western India*, Archaeol. Surv. W. India, Rep., v (London, 1883/R Delhi, 1970)
K. de B. Codrington: 'Ancient Sites near Ellora, Deccan', *Ind. Antiqua.*, lix (1930), pp. 10–13
A. S. Altekar: *The Rashtrakutas and their Times* (Poona, 1934)
S. K. Dikshit: 'Ellora Plates of Dantidurga: Saka 663', *Epig. Ind.*, xxv (1939–40), pp. 25–31
H. Goetz: 'The Kailasa of Ellora and the Chronology of Rashtrakuta Art', *Artibus Asiae*, xv (1952), pp. 84–107
O. C. Gangoli: *The Art of the Rashtrakutas* (Bombay, 1958)
R. Sengupta: 'The Panels of Kalyāṇasundaramūrti at Ellora', *Lalit Kala*, vii (1960), pp. 14–18
——: 'The Yajñaśālā of the Kailāsa at Ellora and Identification of Some of its Sculptures', *Ind. Hist. Q.*, xxxvi (1960), pp. 58–67
R. S. Gupte and R. D. Mahajan: *Ajanta, Ellora and Aurangabad Caves* (Bombay, 1962)
R. S. Gupte: *Iconography of the Buddhist Sculptures (Caves) of Ellora* (Aurangabad, 1964)
W. Spink: *Ajanta to Ellora* (Bombay and Ann Arbor, 1967)
——: 'Ellora's Earliest Phase', *Bull. Amer. Acad. Benares*, i (1967), pp. 11–22
S. J. Czuma: *The Brahmanical Rashtrakuta Monuments of Ellora* (diss., Ann Arbor, U. MI, 1968)
K. Kumar: 'The Buddhist Origin of Some of the Brahmanical Cave-Temples at Ellora', *E. & W.*, n. s. xxvi/3–4 (1976), pp. 359–73
D. C. Chatham: *The Stylistic Sources and Relationships of the Kailasa Temple at Ellora* (diss., Berkeley, U. CA, 1977)
J. Pereira: *Monolithic Jinas* (New Delhi, 1977)
T. V. Pathy: *Elura: Art and Culture* (New Delhi, 1980)
P. V. Ranade: *Ellora Paintings* (Aurangabad, 1980)
D. C. Chatham: 'Pratīhāras from Paṭṭadakal to Ellora: The Early Western Chālukya Basis for the Sculpture Style of the Kailāśa Temple', *Chhavi-2*, ed. A. Krishna (Banaras, 1981), pp. 71–9
J. S. Hawley: 'Scenes from the Childhood of Krṣna on the Kailāsanātha Temple, Ellora', *Archvs Asian A.*, xxxiv (1981), pp. 74–90
M. B. Heston: 'Iconographic Themes of the *Gopura* at the Kailāsanātha Temple at Ellora', *Artibus Asiae*, xliii/3 (1981–2), pp. 219–35
M. K. Dhavalikar: 'Kailasa: The Stylistic Development and Chronology', *Bull. Deccan Coll. Res. Inst.*, xli (1982), pp. 35–45
——: *Masterpieces of Rashtrakuta Art: The Kailas* (Bombay, 1983)
K. V. Soundara Rajan: *Cave Temples of the Deccan* (1983), iii of *Architectural Survey of Temples* (Delhi, 1964–)
S. Huntington: *The Art of Ancient India: Buddhist, Hindu and Jain* (New York and Tokyo, 1985)
R. Parimoo, ed.: *Ellora Caves: Sculpture and Architecture* (Delhi, 1988)
G. H. Malandra: *Unfolding a Mandala: The Buddhist Cave Temples at Ellora* (New York, 1993)
M. Soar: *The Hindu Cave Temples at Ellora and Sanskrit Traditions: With Special Reference to the Śivālaya Māhātmya of the Skanda Purāṇa* (diss., U. London, SOAS [in preparation])

M. SOAR

Ellwood, Craig (*b* Clarendon, TX, 22 April 1922). American architect. Between 1946 and 1948 he studied structural engineering at the UCLA Extension and worked for a construction company, where he was involved with designs by Richard Neutra, Charles Eames and other Los Angeles Modernists. He established his own design office in 1948. Three years later he emerged on the national and international scene through his well-published design of the *Arts and Architecture* Case Study House 16 (1811 Bel Air Road, Los Angeles, CA). This was followed by two additional Case Study Houses: 17 (1954; 9554 Hidden Valley Road) and 18 (1955; 1129 Mirdero Road) both in Los Angeles, CA.

As with other architects who participated in the Case Study House projects, Ellwood was a strong exponent of the rectangular grid steel frame, following the successful practice of Mies van der Rohe and Eames. Ellwood's interpretation of this material tended to be delicate, light and refined, striking a remarkable balance between Mies and Eames. His Smith house, Crestwood Hills, Los Angeles (1957–8), is framed by a rectangular steel grid on thin legs of steel, which hovers over a steep hillside; its plan is in the form of a T. His Rosen house, 910 Oakmount Drive, Los Angeles (1961–3), is in the form of a square, with a central open atrium. Its steel members are heavier than those he had used in earlier houses. In the Art Center School in Pasadena, CA (1977), Ellwood used a truss form of structure, which allowed the building to become a bridge spanning two hills. In the late 1970s he essentially gave up the full-time practice of architecture and turned his attention to painting.

WRITINGS
'Who Really Designs our Buildings?', *Archit. Forum*, cxvi/1 (1962), pp. 96–9

BIBLIOGRAPHY
E. McCoy: *Craig Ellwood: Architecture* (New York, 1962)
——: *Modern California Houses: Case Study Houses, 1945–1962* (New York, 1962), pp. 54–67
H. Weisskamp: *Beautiful Homes and Gardens in California* (New York, 1964), pp. 26–39

DAVID GEBHARD

Elmalı. Town in the district of Antalya, south-west Turkey. Elmalı is set in a fertile plain *c.* 1100 m above sea-level, which is dotted with ancient sites that belonged to Lycia or the Milyad in Classical times. Roads from Lycian coastal sites lead through mountains and river valleys to Elmalı, from where connections upland to Pisidia and Burdur are easy. Excavations of a site of the 3rd millennium BC and of two painted tombs of *c.* 500 BC were carried out by M. Mellink from 1963 onwards on behalf of Bryn Mawr College, PA. Finds are in the Archaeological Museum in Antalya; the wall paintings remain *in situ*. In 1986–7 two tumuli excavated by a team from Antalya Museum produced Phrygian and other grave goods of *c.* 700 to *c.* 600 BC.

At Karataş-Semayük, excavations revealed a fortified mansion of the early 3rd millennium BC and a village of megaron-shaped houses in which the extensive use of timber is noticeable. In the burial grounds individual and family burials were contained in large jars. Early art is evident in metalwork (e.g. a silver pendant in double-axe shape and a silver pin with boar's head finial), in designs on terracotta stamp seals and in incised and applied animal figures on pottery. Red polished pottery is decorated with white painted ornament.

Several tumuli were excavated in a necropolis near Bayındır, north-east of Elmalı. Tumulus D contained a collapsed wooden chamber of Phrygian type. A young woman had been buried there with grave goods including Phrygian equipment: a large bronze cauldron, smaller silver and bronze cauldrons, ladles, omphalos bowls, some with graffiti in Phrygian, and silver belts of the finest Phrygian workmanship. Lydian affinities are evident in several ivory figurines and a silver one, notably a woman in Anatolian costume holding a girl by the hand and carrying a nude boy on her shoulder. There were also iron horsebits, silver horse trappings and many silver appliqués, the last paralleled in bronze in an Ankara tumulus. Other Bayındır tumuli covered cremations and had few Phrygian traits: Tumulus C had fine gold jewellery with granulation and a bronze cauldron with cast griffin protomes.

An archaic tumulus south-east of Elmalı, at Kızılbel, has a small gabled chamber (2.3×2.0×2.4 m) built of trapezoidal and ashlar masonry in limestone. It was plundered in ancient times. The burial had been laid on a stone *kline* against the west wall. Walls, floor and ceiling had been decorated with red (in various shades), blue (some greenish), white and black paint. All designs were painted directly on the stone. The walls have superposed friezes of varying height, with the main frieze over the *kline* showing a warrior's departure by chariot and a banquet scene, in reference to the tomb owner. Mythological scenes on the south wall depict fleeing Gorgons and

Elmalı, head of a banqueter, detail of Greco-Persian wall painting from tomb chamber at Karaburun, *c.* 475 BC

the decapitated Medusa with Pegasus and Chrysaor rising from her neck. A scene of Achilles and Troilos is less well preserved. Other themes are sports and hunting, seafaring, parades of soldiers, horsemen and court life. The style is archaic with strong East Greek affinities, dating the tomb to *c.* 525 BC. Resemblance to archaic Etruscan wall paintings is to be explained by separate dependence on East Greek schools of wall painters, some of which also worked at Gordion.

There is a second tomb chamber at Karaburun, north-east of Elmalı. Here the gabled chamber was built of large rectangular blocks (3.00×2.60×2.66 m), and a *kline* stood against the rear wall. The walls were prepared for painting by the application of a sandy *intonaco* with a coat of fine white plaster. Among the new colours used extensively are green and purple. The main wall, behind the *kline*, has a large banquet scene showing a bearded nobleman (see fig.) reclining on a couch and attended by servants in Persian costume. A woman in Greek dress stands behind him. On the right wall, the nobleman appears on horseback in a battle scene, in which he defeats the chieftain of an army of Greek hoplites. On the left wall the nobleman rides in a throne–chariot on an official journey (not necessarily a funeral voyage), accompanied by servants, horses and a baggage chariot. In style these paintings are Greco-Persian and date to *c.* 475 BC. They must have had counterparts in Persian palaces and mansions, and fragments survive in other tombs in western Anatolia. They are related to Greco-Persian relief sculpture best known from Daskyleion, the site of a Persian satrapal palace near the Hellespont.

BIBLIOGRAPHY

Amer. J. Archaeol., lxviii (1964), pp. 269–78; lxix (1965), pp. 241–51; lxx (1966), pp. 245–57; lxxi (1967), pp. 251–67; lxxii (1968), pp. 243–59; lxxiii (1969), pp. 319–31; lxxiv (1970), pp. 245–53; lxxv (1971), pp. 245–55; lxxvi (1972), pp. 257–69; lxxvii (1973), pp. 293–303; lxxviii (1974), pp. 351–9; lxxix (1975), pp. 349–55; lxxx (1976), pp. 377–84 [excavation reports of Karataş-Semayük and Elmalı by M. J. Mellink]
Antalya Museum (Ankara, 1988), pp. 32–49 and covers

M. J. MELLINK

Elmes, Harvey Lonsdale (*b* Oving, W. Sussex, 1814; *d* Jamaica, 26 Nov 1847). English architect. Elmes was responsible for one of the finest Neo-classical public buildings in Europe, St George's Hall and Assize Courts, Liverpool; a remarkably convincing re-creation of the grandeur of imperial Rome for someone who had never visited Italy or Greece. Elmes was a pupil of his father James Elmes (1782–1862) and of his uncle Henry John Elmes, a London builder. Author of the first documented life of Sir Christopher Wren (1823) and founder of a pioneering art journal, *Annals of the Fine Arts* (1816–20), James Elmes doubtless gave his son a firm grounding in architectural history as well as practice. In 1834 Harvey Elmes passed from the Royal Academy Schools, London, to the Bath office of H. E. Goodridge (1797–1864), with whom he remained for three years. At this time Goodridge was engaged on designs for the Roman Catholic procathedral in Bristol (building of which was never completed). The grandeur of Goodridge's scheme of 1834 seems to have influenced Elmes's designs for St George's Hall and Assize Courts at Liverpool, for this is also on a sloping site and features largely windowless walls and a massive Corinthian portico with sculptured pediment.

The complicated story of Elmes's Liverpool masterpiece began in July 1839, when he won the first premium of 250 guineas in a competition for a concert hall to be known as St George's Hall. This was in direct emulation of Birmingham, which had begun a monumental new town hall in 1832. Liverpool's population had grown from 80,000 inhabitants in 1800 to over 286,000 in 1840, a period during which the city became the country's principal Atlantic port and chief entrepôt for cotton for the Lancashire mills. In 1840 Elmes won the premium of £300 in a second competition, also arranged by the city corporation, for new Assize Courts. Elmes's buildings were grouped round two sides of a piazza approached through a triumphal arch. In 1840 the corporation decided to unite the two functions, somewhat incongruously, in a single building. Elmes now made a new design, approved in October 1840, that consisted of a great barrel-vaulted central hall flanked by the crown court at the south end and the civil court at the north. At the north end of the whole building, and on a higher level than the courts, was an elliptical concert hall, expressed externally by a huge apse with attached columns. The complex external articulation of the long side walls is a brilliant and original system in which pilasters in the upper parts of the building become giant, free-standing square piers. This grid-like treatment and Grecian detail are in the manner of Karl Friedrich Schinkel although Elmes did not visit Germany until 1842, by which time construction of the building had already been in progress for a year.

Elmes's health had by now begun to give way under the strain of preparing detailed drawings for so enormous and complex a building without adequate assistance. He died in 1847, and the structure was completed between 1847 and 1851 by the engineer Sir Robert Rawlinson (1810–98), with C. R. Cockerell completing the interior decoration (1851–4). The colossal barrel vault of the Great Hall, constructed by Rawlinson of hollow wedge-shaped bricks, was inspired by the Baths of Caracalla, Rome, as restored in 1828 by Guillaume-Abel Blouet. Owing to his early death Elmes designed few buildings apart from St George's Hall. The largest of them, the Collegiate Institution (1840–43), Liverpool, in the late Perpendicular Gothic Revival style, was inspired by Charles Barry's King Edward VI Grammar School (completed 1838), Birmingham.

BIBLIOGRAPHY
G. Hemm: St George's Hall, Liverpool (Liverpool, 1949)
Q. Hughes: Seaport: Architecture and Townscape in Liverpool (London, 1964)
——: 'Neo-classical Ideas and Practice: St George's Hall, Liverpool, by Harvey Lonsdale Elmes', Archit. Assoc. Q., v/2 (1973), pp. 36–44
D. Watkin: The Life and Work of C. R. Cockerell, RA (London, 1974)
S. Bayley: 'A British Schinkel', Archit. Assoc. Q., vii/2 (1975), pp. 28–32
J. Olley: 'St George's Hall, Liverpool', Architects' J., clxxxiii (1986), no. 25, pp. 36–57; no. 26, pp. 36–61
DAVID WATKIN

Elmore, Alfred (b Clonakilty, Co. Cork, 1815; d London, 24 Jan 1881). English painter of Irish birth. The son of a doctor, Elmore moved to London and attended the Royal Academy Schools from 1832. He also studied at a French atelier and travelled to Munich and Italy, spending two years in Rome and returning to England in 1844. He began exhibiting at the Royal Academy in 1834 and continued to exhibit there between his travels. His large historical subjects such as *Rienzi in the Forum* (exh. RA 1844; sold London, Sotheby's, 16 March 1988) led to his election as ARA in 1845 and RA in 1857. The historical settings of his paintings ranged from 14th-century Florence to absolutist France, and his subject-matter was often unusual (e.g. *Invention of the Combing Machine*, exh. RA 1862; Nottingham, Castle Mus.). He also painted literary subjects, especially from Shakespeare. Elmore's brief experimentation with modern life subject-matter resulted in *On the Brink* (exh. RA 1865; Cambridge, Fitzwilliam), which depicts a woman in distress outside the notorious gaming salon at Homburg. Although ambiguous in implication, Elmore's painting seems to suggest the potential fall of a woman through seduction, following the tradition of Holman Hunt's *Awakening Conscience* (1853; London, Tate) and Augustus Egg's *Past and Present* (1858; London, Tate).

Elmore's skill appeared more noticeably in his watercolours, which reveal the influence of the Troubadour style, and have often been mistaken for the work of Richard Parkes Bonington. Elmore's *Two Women on a Balcony* (London, V&A) is reminiscent of Bonington's *On the Balcony, Venice* (Port Sunlight, Lady Lever A.G.) in its use of rich colour and vaguely medieval subject-matter.

BIBLIOGRAPHY
Redgrave; Wood
Obituary, A. J. [London] (1881), p. 95
M. Hardie: Water-colour Painting in Britain, ii (London, 1968), pp. 186–7
J. W. Goodison: Fitzwilliam Museum, Cambridge: Catalogue of Paintings, iii (Cambridge, 1977), pp. 70–71
L. Nead: 'Seduction, Prostitution, Suicide: On the Brink by Alfred Elmore', A. Hist., v/3 (1982), pp. 310–22
SHEARER WEST

Elmslie, George Grant. *See under* PURCELL & ELMSLIE.

Eloy, Mário (Jesus de Pereira) (b Lisbon, 16 March 1900; d Telhal, nr Lisbon, 5 Sept 1951). Portuguese painter and actor. Following a family tradition, he began his artistic career in the theatre. In 1922 he was an assistant to a theatre designer, and in 1923 he worked as an actor with a professional company in Lisbon. He lived in Paris in 1926, and from 1927 to 1932 in Berlin. His leaning towards Expressionism, nourished by the sojourn in Germany, was innovative in Portugal where Paris was usually looked to as the cultural point of reference. From 1932 to 1939, when he retired from public view, his output was large; he concentrated on figures and melancholy portraits, often of contemporary artists and intellectuals. His last important works were imaginary group compositions with a disturbed and frenzied atmosphere, for example *The Poet* (1939; Lisbon, Mus. N. A. Contemp.). He had six solo exhibitions and took part in many official and independent salons. In 1945 he was interned at the sanatorium of the Order of St John in Telhal, where, lonely and ill, he eventually took his life.

BIBLIOGRAPHY
D. de Macedo: Mário Eloy (Lisbon, 1958)
J. Segurado: Mário Eloy (Vila da Maia, 1982)
RUTH ROSENGARTEN

El Portón. *See under* SALAMÁ VALLEY.

El Salvador, Republic of [Sp. República de El Salvador]. Central American country bordered to the north and east by Honduras, to the south-east by the Gulf of Fonseca, to the south by the Pacific Ocean and to the west by Guatemala (see fig. 1). It covers an area of 21,200 sq. km and has a population of over five million; c. one million live in the capital, San Salvador, which is located in the central southern region of the country. The territory is subdivided politically into 14 departments. El Salvador gained independence from Spanish colonization in 1821. This article covers the art and architecture produced since colonial times. For a discussion of the arts of pre-colonial times, *see* MAYA, §2.

The Spanish colonial conquest and rule began with the discovery of El Salvador by Andrés Niño in 1522. Within the Viceroyalty of Guatemala, El Salvador was of immense value for its agricultural wealth. In the struggle for independence in Central America, San Salvador was the first city to rebel, and the country played a leading role in Central American integration, with the establishment in 1951 of the Organización de Estados de Centro América (ODECA), the headquarters of which were in San Salvador. The capital was founded in 1525 by Pedro de Alvarado near a volcano. The early adobe and thatch settlement was destroyed by an earthquake in 1575 and reconstructed on its present site in the second half of the 17th century. When Antigua was destroyed in 1773 San Salvador became the largest city in Central America, and in 1786 it became the seat of an Intendancy within the Audiencia of Guatemala. Further earthquakes in 1789, 1854 and 1873 wiped out virtually all of the capital's colonial architecture, including the cathedral and town hall; little remains from the 16th and 17th centuries, although a few buildings survive from the 18th. One of the most significant is the massively constructed church del Pilar (1762–9) at San Vicente, whose nave arcades and barrel-vaulted roof have survived successive tremors. A unique pentagonal arch over its entrance doorway and a single octagonal opening above it enhance the impression of strength, though the highly original façade with its bolster (*almobadillado*) pilasters is reminiscent of architecture in Antigua. The church at Metapán (1743) has nave walls strengthened by pilasters and centrally placed columns, suggesting Mexican influence. Also of interest are the parish churches around San Salvador with roofs framed and decorated in *Mudéjar* style. Santa Cruz in Panchimalco (see fig. 2), 15 km south of the capital, is perhaps the best known. Rebuilt and enlarged in the mid-18th century, it has fine carved and painted column-brackets, cross-ties and rafters and unusual octagonal framing to the roof of the main chapel reminiscent of Los Dolores (1732), Tegucigalpa, Honduras. A low and wide entrance archway is the only opening in a sturdy façade that emphasizes the horizontal and rises to a voluted third storey whose modest termination reflects the suggestion of towers at either end. Other examples are the nunnery churches of S Sebastián (*c.* 1880) and Santiago, now in the San Salvador suburbs of the same name, and at Jocoro in the east, where a scalloped pediment is enlivened with stucco Baroque reliefs.

In a plan of 1788 for the Casa Reales (Seville, Archv Gen. Indias), Pedro Guerrero aimed to bring together in a single block of domestic scale all the administrative sections for the new intendancy, contained within a square of the San Salvador city grid. Uniform, arcaded, single-storey façades to the surrounding streets gave access through decorated portals via common vestibules to the house for the Intendente, the Cajas Reales, Renta de Tabaco and Aduana. 18th-century urban houses survive

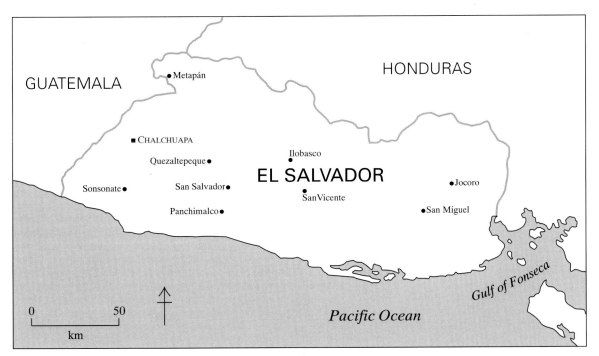

1. Map of El Salvador; the site CHALCHUAPA has a separate entry in this dictionary

2. El Salvador, Panchimalco, Santa Cruz, main façade, mid-18th century

of the highest quality were commissioned from the capital of the Viceroyalty, Guatemala, whose school of painting rivalled those of Mexico and Peru. In both churches and private collections there are paintings from the Spanish period executed by Guatemalans. Outstanding among these are the altarpieces of several colonial churches, such as that of the church of Sonsonate, executed in 1582 by Quirio Cataño (1550–1622) and Antonio Rodas, and that of Panchimalco. Painting was almost entirely anonymous and eclectic, while candid and naive in style. The artists, often monks or people of mixed race, showed the latent influence of native motifs and elements of the natural environment in repeated patterns and elaborate foliage. Much of the decorative work on sculptures was executed by anonymous local craftsmen. The influence of indigenous skills in sculpture also led to the use of such materials as corn and bone, in addition to cedar and mahogany. Imagery was simplistic but vigorous, and the style echoed the elaborate realism of European Baroque sculpture.

Silvestre Antonio García (d 1807) carved the renowned image of Christ, *Salvator mundi* (1777) that is housed in San Salvador's cathedral (begun 1950s; designed by José María Durán). Francisco W. Cisneros (1823–78) reached prominence following independence, but few of his works remain in El Salvador, as he settled abroad. Pascasio González (1848–1917) was a sculptor, architect, painter and quilter; in collaboration with his former pupil Marcelín Carballo (1874–1949) he painted images in the capital's cathedral. The real initiator of a post-Independence artistic style was the painter and sculptor Carlos Alberto Imery (1879–1949), a student of Carballo, who studied in Rome, France and Spain before returning in 1912 to found the Escuela Nacional de Artes Gráficas in San Salvador, which produced many successful artists. In 1936 the Spanish master Valero Lecha (1894–1976) founded another academy of painting from which many successful artists emerged to promote modernism in El Salvador. Other leading painters included Mauricio Aguilar (1919–78), whose *Pear* (1973; see 1985 exh. cat., p. 161) is typical of his expression of the effect of light on natural objects, and Benjamín Cañas (1933–89), whose interest in the absurd is shown in the series *Kafka: Letters to Milena* (1976; see 1985 exh. cat., p. 163).

The most prominent 20th-century sculptor was Valentín Estrada (1902–84). While displaying an academic realism in portraits and idealized monuments (e.g. portrait of the hunting Indian *Atlacatl*, 1924–5; see Mariño Sánchez and others, fig. 78), he also adapted the formal vocabulary of ancient native traditions in such works as the open-air sculpture *Shiutetl, God of Fire* (1955; San Salvador, Planes de Renderos). The Spanish artist Benjamín Saúl (1924–80) settled in El Salvador in 1964. His contorted and playful female nudes (e.g. *Woman Lying Down*, 1968; San Salvador, Edificio de la Centroamericana priv. col.) had a lasting influence on his pupils, who included Dagoberto Reyes, Mauricio Jiménez Larios, Osmín Muñoz, Carlos Velis, Alberto Ríos Blanco, René Ocón and Andrés Castillo, and with whom he formed the short-lived sculpture cooperative Grupo UQUXKAH for the purpose of executing the abstract work *Monument to the Sea* (bronze, 1971; San Salvador, 25 Avenida Norte). The metal sculptures of Rubén Martínez, notably the passion cycle *Via*

in San Miguel and elsewhere. Towards the end of the 19th century the city became dominated by structures of timber and stamped metal sheeting, a fine example of which is the Candelaria church, San Salvador (completed 1891). Neo-classical design continued into the 20th century even after the introduction of reinforced concrete and steel-framed structures in such buildings as the Teatro Nacional (1930).

Increased American influence brought a period of progress and development in the 1950s and the introduction of the International Style. Housing the increasingly numerous landless poor brought the introduction of suburban and rural rehousing under such agencies as the Fundación Salvadoreña de Desarrollo y Vivienda Mínima (FUNDASAL). The earthquake of 1986 destroyed many urban buildings of the 1950s and 1960s, even though they were intended to be earthquake-resistant.

Among the indigenous population various arts and crafts continued to be practised following colonization. Prominent among these was pottery, which had a strong tradition influenced by Mexican ware but with distinctive linear and geometric patterns. Basketry, matmaking and weaving were also practised. Painting and sculpture were practised only by the Spanish colonizers, as were decorative arts such as leatherwork, gold- and silversmithing and cabinetmaking. Traditional items continued to be manufactured in the late 20th century at a number of sites, including Ilobasco, where erotic miniatures of painted clay were made in pottery workshops using modern designs, and Quezaltepeque, which produced crockery.

As in other Latin American countries, colonial painting and sculpture in El Salvador had a strong religious content, through the influence of Spain, and many leading painters were also prominent sculptors. Unfortunately, natural disasters have destroyed much of what existed. The works

Crucis (1980; San Salvador, Iglesia del Rosario) brought him considerable acclaim.

The Museo Nacional David J. Guzmán in San Salvador was founded in 1883 and houses archaeological, ethnological and historic collections. Artistic institutions promoting the plastic arts include the Asociación de Artistas Plásticas de El Salvador, the Asociación Salvadoreña de Trabajadores del Arte y la Cultura and the Unión General de Autores y Artistas Salvadoreños. Non-profit-making private institutions exist to support the arts, such as the Patronato Pro-Patrimonio Cultural y Asociación del Patrimonio Cultural de Santa Ana, which supports government efforts in the preservation of and research into the national heritage. The Patronato Pro-Cultura fosters the plastic arts, music and dance, and the Patrimonio Pro-Arte is dedicated to music and the theatre. The Universidad Dr José Matías Delgado in San Salvador was founded in 1977 and has departments of fine and applied arts. The Consejo Nacional para la Cultura y el Arte (CONCULTURA) was created in 1991 by the Ministry of Education with the aim of contributing to the investigation, preservation, patronage, advancement and dissemination of culture and the arts.

BIBLIOGRAPHY

A. Guerra Triqueiros: 'The Colonial Churches of El Salvador', *Bull. Pan Amer. Un.*, lxxii (1938), pp. 271–9

Ars, 1 (1951) [issue on El Salvador]

D. Angulo Iñíguez: *Historia del arte hispanoamericana*, iii (Barcelona, 1956), pp. 62–74

J. Sanz y Díaz: 'Pintores salvadoreños contemporáneos', *Ars*, 8 (1957), pp. 53–69

O. M. Monedero: *Historia de la arquitectura contemporánea en El Salvador* (San Salvador, 1970)

J. Casin de Montes: 'Arte colonial de El Salvador: Criterios de valorización estética', *Estud. Centamer.*, xxviii (1973), pp. 243–5

C. Mariño Sánchez and others: *Desarrollo de la escultura en El Salvador* (San Salvador, 1974)

Selections from the Permanent Collection (exh. cat. by J. C. Baena Soares, R. Novey and M. Traba, Washington, DC, Mus. Mod. A. Latin America, 1985)

J. R. Cea: *De la pintura en El Salvador* (San Salvador, 1986)

CLAUDIA ALLWOOD DE MATA

Elscheid, Nikolaus (*b* Niederscheidweiler, nr Wittlich, 1835; *d* Cologne, 1874). German sculptor. Early in his career he worked in Cologne with the neo-Gothic sculptor Christoph Stephan (1797–1864). Alexander Schnütgen, the Domkapitular of Cologne Cathedral, recommended him to August Ottmar von Essenwein, who from 1868 had been restoring St Maria im Kapitol in Cologne. For this church Elscheid sculpted the life-size *Pietà* (*c.* 1870) for the south transept (now in the crypt) and the over-life-size wooden *Triumphant Crucifixion* group (*c.* 1870; Bonn-Poppelsdorf, St Sebastian), the latter inspired by the late Romanesque group depicting the same subject in the chapel of Schloss Wechselburg. A *Vesperbild* in the Katholische Pfarrkirche Mariae Himmelfahrt in Mönchengladbach and one in Kempen (Städt. Kramer-Mus.) are so similar stylistically that they can be attributed to Elscheid. A *Heart of Jesus* (*c.* 1870) in the narthex of St Maria im Kapitol may also be by Elscheid. In addition to these commissions, he carved small hard-wood statues in the High Gothic style that was prevalent in Cologne. They were rendered with such skill that in later years they were assumed to be either authentic Gothic works or fakes. It

is uncertain, however, whether he intentionally intended these sculptures to deceive the viewer. The controversy over their origins has resulted in a renewed interest in them and has led to the rediscovery of several that were previously little-known. Such works (all 1860–70) as the box-wood *Virgin* (examples Frankfurt am Main, Mus. Ksthandwk; Antwerp, Mus. Mayer van den Bergh; Florence, Mus. N. Bargello), the *Virgin Enthroned* (Cologne, Schnütgen-Mus.) and the *Magdalene* (ex-priv. col., Basle) have as their prototype the 14th-century *Virgin of Milan* (*c.* 1290) in Cologne Cathedral. In these small sculptures he was able to represent a stylistic position between the neo-Gothic aspects of the earlier 19th-century art of the Nazarenes and the more flamboyant characteristics of the later Rhenish Gothic Revival, which shows the influence of the neo-Baroque. In the last year of his life, through the efforts of Christian Mohr, he received the commission for the portrait bust of *Alexander Schnütgen* (1874; untraced) for Cologne Cathedral.

BIBLIOGRAPHY

P. Bloch: *Skulpturen des 19. Jahrhunderts im Rheinland* (Düsseldorf, 1975)

——: 'Neugotische Statuetten des Nikolaus Elscheid', *Festschrift für Otto von Simson zum 65. Geburtstag* (Berlin, 1977), pp. 504–15

PETER BLOCH

Elsden, William [Guilherme] (*fl* 1760–78). English architect, active in Portugal. It is probable that he was invited to Portugal by Wilhelm, Graf von Schaumburg-Lippe (*b* London, 1724), Commander-in-Chief in 1762–3 of the Portuguese army, in which Elsden served as a military engineer. It is certain that in 1763 Elsden was promoted from Captain to Major, that he taught mathematics at the Real Academia Militar, Lisbon, and that in 1771 he was appointed Quartermaster General with the rank of Lieutenant-Colonel.

Elsden's work as a cartographer included plans for the defence of the region of Rio Frio (1767–8). He was also responsible for making the designs for the pantheon (1770) in the Benedictine monastery of Alcobaça, an early example of the Gothic Revival movement in Portugal. In 1773 the Marquês de Pombal sent Elsden to supervise the large-scale remodelling of the university buildings at Coimbra, necessitated by Pombal's programme of educational reforms that were first conceived in 1772. In his capacity as chief architect and director of building works Elsden produced numerous drawings and plans, including those for restructuring the schools and opening up the Via Latina (a covered gallery containing the rector's residence and the principal lecture rooms). He made changes to the Gerais (the cloister adjoining the university classrooms) and to the gallery at the north that surrounds this building. He made plans (all 1773) for the Jesuit College, the Public Hospital, the Anatomy Theatre, the Pharmaceutical Dispensary, the Laboratory of Experimental Physics, the Natural History Museum (*in situ*, façades remain as built), the Chemistry Laboratory (*in situ*), and for the adaptation of the Arts College, which became a hospital in 1853. Assisted by Teodoro Marques Pereira da Silva, he made the designs for the Observatório Astronómico (1773; not completed), and he adapted the cloister and annexes of the old cathedral, Coimbra, for use as the university press (defunct by 1934, destr. shortly after) as well as laying the foundation for the Jardim Botânico (1773; *in situ*). All these plans and buildings show the innovative mark of Neo-classicism along Palladian lines.

After February 1777 the death of King Joseph led to the fall of his Minister Pombal and of the Rector (Reformador Reitor) of Coimbra University, D. Francisco de Lemos (1735–1822); the continuation and completion of this major project was disrupted. Elsden's activities after 1777 are unknown.

BIBLIOGRAPHY

S. Viterbo: *Diccionario historico e documental dos architectos, engenheiros e constructores portugueses ou a serviço de Portugal*, i (Lisbon, 1899), pp. 10–12, 297–99; ii (Lisbon, 1922), pp. 255–6, 351

M. Lopes de Almeida: *Documentos da reforma pombalina*, i (Coimbra, 1937), pp. 52, 69, 70–71, 80–82, 90–91, 104–5, 115, 133, 139, 164, 208, 214

M. Pessoa de Figueiredo Sousa Franco: *Riscos das obras da Universidade de Coimbra: O valioso álbum da reforma pombalina*, Coimbra, 1983 [reproduces Elsden's accounts, ground-plans and elevations for the U. of Coimbra]

L. Craveiro: 'Guilherme Elsden e a introdução do Neo-classicismo em Portugal', *Actas do Simpósio: Portugal e Espanha entre a Europa e além-mar: Coimbra, 1987*

LURDES CRAVEIRO

Elsheimer, Adam (*b* Frankfurt am Main, *bapt* 18 March 1578; *bur* Rome, 11 Dec 1610). German painter, printmaker and draughtsman, active in Italy. His small paintings on copper established him after his brief life as the most singular and influential German artist to follow Dürer. Their grand conception in terms of monumental figures and poetic landscape and their meticulous, miniature-like execution were admired by Rubens and came to influence many 17th-century artists, including Rembrandt. Most were produced in Rome after 1600: the limits of this oeuvre and its chronology are extremely hard to establish.

1. Life and work. 2. Working methods and technique. 3. Posthumous reputation.

1. LIFE AND WORK.

(i) Before 1600: Frankfurt, Bavaria and Venice. (ii) 1600 and after: Rome.

(i) Before 1600: Frankfurt, Bavaria and Venice. The eldest son of a Frankfurt tailor, Elsheimer may first have trained as an artist with Johann Vetter I (*fl* 1575; *d* 1620), the head of the city's stained-glass-painting guild. He probably visited Strasbourg in 1596 in the company of Vetter's son Johann Vetter II (*fl* 1596–1619) to meet Friedrich Brentel I, a local artist, and the glass-painting workshop of the Lingg family. This would explain the obvious dependence on South German and Swiss prototypes seen in his earliest surviving drawing, *Fama* (Karlsruhe, Staatl. Ksthalle), and the design for an armorial window (1596; Düsseldorf, Kstmus.), both made in collaboration with the younger Vetter. Frankfurt was not an artistic centre at this time, apart from the flourishing publishing trade for which another teacher of Elsheimer's, Philipp Uffenbach, supplied prints. Through Uffenbach he obtained a commission to provide etched illustrations (Hollstein, no. 21) for an account of Cornelis Houtman's expedition (1595–7) to the East Indies, which were published in the *Messrelationen* (1598), a news-sheet issued twice a year for the Frankfurt trade fairs. They are somewhat clumsy works, based on recently published Dutch prototypes, and yet there are signs of an individual style, notably in the only surviving

preliminary drawing (Copenhagen, Stat. Mus. Kst). No doubt prints by Dürer and Albrecht Altdorfer were freely available in Uffenbach's studio, for their influence is very clear; a painted copy (London, Hampton Court, Royal Col.) of Dürer's engraving *The Witch* (1507; Hollstein, no. 68) is possibly Elsheimer's earliest surviving painting. Other early works are the recently recovered *St Elizabeth Visiting the Sick* (?*c*. 1598; London, Wellcome Inst. Hist. Med., Lib.) and a domestic altar with scenes from the *Life of the Virgin* (Berlin, Gemäldegal.). The former shows an individuality and sensitivity astonishing for a youth of about 18, though there are passages of pentiment, and the perspective (some of it carefully incised into the wet paint) is often misconceived. He used two of its figures again in the Berlin altar, which is modelled on Dürer's *Heller Altar* (1507–9; destr.), then still in the Dominican Church in Frankfurt.

Elsheimer probably left Frankfurt soon after completing the *Messrelationen* etchings to travel through Bavaria, for he made an allegorical drawing, *Genius of Painting* (1598; Brunswick, Herzog Anton Ulrich-Mus.), in a Munich album. There he would have seen the great altarpieces by Altdorfer, whose impact remains visible in his work thereafter. The dramatic compositions *Jacob's Dream* and the *Conversion of Saul* (both Frankfurt am Main, Städel. Kstinst. & Städt. Gal.) date from this 'apprentice' journey; both still depend on earlier German models. It is thought that he arrived in Venice in 1598, where he is said to have associated himself with the Munich painter Hans Rottenhammer I. The influence of the great Venetian painters Palma Giovane, Veronese and Jacopo Bassano, always filtered, so to speak, through Rottenhammer's eyes, is discernible in works that very likely date from this Venetian interlude: the *Flood* (Frankfurt am Main, Städel. Kstinst. & Städt. Gal.)—particularly in its repoussoir figures—the *Baptism* (London, N.G.; see fig. 1) and the *Holy Family with St John* (1599; Berlin, Gemäldegal.). What is notable in these, and to some extent in some of the panels of the earlier Berlin altar, is the role and treatment of landscape: a mixture of northern (Flemish) and newly observed Italian influences. Landscape was to remain more than mere background decoration: it enveloped the figures within it and brought out the painting's distinctive atmosphere.

Such a conception of landscape was transmitted in paintings which shared with Elsheimer's few prints (e.g. the *Mocking of Ceres*, Hamburg, Ksthalle) the use of copper as a support. This practice was common in such print-making centres as Flanders or Venice: to Elsheimer it offered a smooth surface which allowed for miniature-like delicacy of the brush. Only the unusually large *Self-portrait* (Florence, Uffizi) adopts canvas instead. Some of Elsheimer's smaller paintings were very likely intended to be let into furniture. Whereas their size is small, the monumentality of the figures vies with the most elaborate and ambitious of the great Venetian masters. Such a tiny panel is the *St Christopher* (probable original, St Petersburg, Hermitage), perhaps a transitional work, as it shows the influences of both Dürer and Tintoretto. The composition was known in Rome (and hence may have been taken there by Elsheimer himself), for Orazio Borgianni's *St Christopher* (*c*. 1609; Edinburgh, N.G.) is obviously based

1. Adam Elsheimer: *Baptism*, oil on copper, 281×210 mm, *c.* 1598–1600 (London, National Gallery)

on it, and Rubens made a drawing of the heads of the *Christ Child and St Christopher* (*c.* 1611–14; London, BM).

(ii) 1600 and after: Rome.

(a) Early development. (b) Middle period. (c) Ovidian and other late works.

(a) Early development. Elsheimer arrived in Rome in April 1600 and remained there till his death. He joined the circle of humanists around Johannes Faber (*fl* 1600–1628), an erudite doctor from Bamberg who had become herbalist to Pope Paul V and had treated Rubens during a severe illness; besides Rubens, the circle included the philosopher Justus Lipsius (1547–1606) and Kaspar Schoppe (Scoppius; 1576–1649), who was probably responsible for Elsheimer's conversion to Catholicism in 1606. In the same year Elsheimer joined the Accademia di S Luca and married the widow of the Lorraine painter Nicolas de Breul (*d* 1606), a woman probably of Scottish origin referred to as Carola Antonia Stuarda. His working life in the city was bound up with that of HENDRICK GOUDT, a problematic and somewhat mysterious figure who seems to have been both his patron and his pupil. Goudt lived in the Elsheimer household for several years, supporting the family and engraving several of Elsheimer's pictures, but then appears to have quarrelled and moved away. Some sources hint that he finally put the artist into the debtors' prison for not delivering enough work in recompense.

Elsheimer himself was seemingly of a nervous, melancholic and neurotic disposition, working slowly and meticulously at his little copper plates, often putting them aside to complete them later and sometimes even leaving them unfinished (to be worked over, in some cases, by other hands). There is no record of his patrons or commissions in Rome, apart from Goudt, though collectors such as the cardinals Barberini and del Monte appreciated his type of small cabinet picture. He was evidently appreciated within his small humanist circle but when he exhibited with other artists, according to Baglione (1642), his little paintings were overshadowed by their more flamboyant works. None of his paintings are signed, and of his Roman works only the *Flight into Egypt* is inscribed with a date (1609). From the inventory of his possessions drawn up for his widow a few days after his death, it is clear that he lived in abject poverty; she was subsequently beset by creditors and had to pawn some of his paintings. Needing to sell them, she may have got other painters to overpaint incomplete works. The small *Pietà* (priv. col.) seems to have undergone such a process.

These circumstances make it hard to define what constitutes Elsheimer's Roman oeuvre and to establish its chronology. But *St Paul on Malta* (London, N.G.) and the *Burning of Troy* (Munich, Alte Pin.) seem to show a technical progress from the Venetian work, suggesting they were produced in Rome. However, the first definitely Roman work is the *Preparation for the Martyrdom of St Lawrence* (London, N.G.), which incorporates, very freely, the Temple of Vespasian. The group of attendant figures in the middle distance, a feature of the earlier *Baptism of Christ*, became a hallmark of Elsheimer's subsequent compositions. The turbans they wear are Elsheimer's characteristic way of giving an oriental setting to biblical subjects. Crowd scenes, hitherto managed with varied skill, become an integral part in the *Stoning of St Stephen* (Edinburgh, N.G.; *see* PERSPECTIVE, colour pl. VII, fig. 1), probably the next picture chronologically. Elsheimer's obvious delight in narrating a dramatic scene transmutes the gruesome incident into a colourful spectacle. The central group is isolated by a theatrical spotlight of heavenly rays, which also catches some of the riders in the middle distance. Rubens copied figures from the painting and regrouped them in the drawing *Turkish Prince Looking on, with Attendants* (*c.* 1600–1608; London, BM), which became famous through being engraved in two editions, with the caption 'Elsheimer inv.'. A document of 1659 (Bodart) suggests that the Flemish artist Paul Bril supplied the painting's landscape background; although this is unlikely, it suggests that Elsheimer was impressed by the older painter's treatment of landscape. The influence was later reciprocated.

Among other influences, much has been made of Caravaggio's strong contrasts of light and dark, but those characteristics were already apparent in the works Elsheimer produced before arriving in Rome and having an opportunity to see Caravaggio's paintings. His 'night pieces' and his dramatic exploitation of light (or its absence) derive from Altdorfer and Bassano. Caravaggio's source of light is always invisible, mysterious and theatrical, whereas Elsheimer's, whether earthly or celestial, is always discernible. As to the so-called 'poetic landscapes' alleged to derive from Annibale Carracci, these too were already present in his Venetian paintings and indeed prefigured in some panels of the Berlin altar.

The *St Lawrence* and *St Stephen* compositions led towards the seven sections of the tabernacle with the story of the *Finding and Exaltation of the True Cross* (Frankfurt am Main, Städel. Kstinst. & Städt. Gal.), probably the most ambitious work Elsheimer ever attempted. The original appearance of this ensemble, including the framing and positioning, is known from a sketch among letters (Florence, Archv Stato) sent by the agent of Grand Duke Cosimo II de' Medici, when the latter acquired it in 1619. It is probably of the same period as Rubens's treatment of the same theme (1602; Grasse Cathedral) for the Roman church of Santa Croce in Gerusalemme. In his version, Elsheimer grouped six small panels depicting the search for and discovery of the cross around the largest, central section depicting its glorification by figures of the Old and New Testament (see fig. 2). Compared with his other Roman works, there are fewer attendant figures in each scene, the action being concentrated on the essentials and the landscapes more elaborately worked out. Yet the narrative is vivid, and so are some of the details, some of which almost border on genre. The central panel obviously contains reminiscences from his stay in Venice: Dürer's *Virgin of the Rose Garlands* (1506; Prague, N.G.), Titian's *Gloria* (c. 1554; Madrid, Prado, engraved by Cornelis Cort, 1566), Tintoretto's *Paradise* (1588–92; Paris, Louvre) and

Rottenhammer's *All Saints* (London, N.G.). Yet from all this material Elsheimer conceived a totally original composition, with such attention to detail that the eye is constantly arrested as it scans the multitude of figures without ever losing a sense of cohesion. The coronation of the Virgin, usually the central incident of such a composition, is hardly visible in the extreme upper-left corner of the main panel, and although the *Elevation of the True Cross* is the titular subject here, it is towards the great event up above that all the panel's figures directly, or by implication, direct their glance. As in his previous religious pictures, Elsheimer enhanced the importance of his theme by colourful draperies and by the hieratic appearance of the participants, who are nevertheless shown in an intimate, even tender, relationship with one another. None of the figures is idealized, and yet they are quite different from the somewhat theatrical earthiness of Caravaggio: it was exactly this almost anecdotal realism that so much appealed to Elsheimer's northern followers, who were to transmit it to Rembrandt.

(b) Middle period. A similar impact on the younger generation of northern artists who knew Elsheimer and probably worked with him in Rome was generated by the *Three Marys at the Tomb* (Bonn, Rhein. Landesmus.), a work datable to the middle period of Elsheimer's life in Rome but formerly ascribed to Jan Pynas and Pieter Lastman. Its gestures of lamentation stem from High Renaissance sources and were also used by Caravaggio in his *Entombment* (Rome, Pin. Vaticana). Also datable to this 'middle period' is *Il Contento* (Edinburgh, N.G.), a work claimed by Joachim von Sandrart, Elsheimer's chief biographer, to have been his masterpiece. It was left unfinished, with some of the foreground figures overpainted by another hand. Its curious title derives from an interpolated story in the Spanish picaresque novel *Guzman de Alfarache* (Madrid, 1599; Italian trans., Venice, 1606) by Mateo Alemán (1547–?1609), relating the abduction of the goddess 'Content' (self-satisfaction) by Mercury at the behest of Jupiter who finds that the people, indulging in pleasurable activities, pay him insufficient homage. The zigzag of the crowd's movement being halted by Jupiter's wrathful gesture is separated from the background by a kind of window-opening which frames the pleasure-seeking people, seen moving in the opposite direction. Pieter Lastman in his *Paul and Barnabas at Lystra* (1614; ex-N. Mus., Warsaw) transmitted this strikingly novel compositional device to his pupil Rembrandt, who copied it in a drawing, and the contemporary Dutch poet Joost van den Vondel (1587–1679) celebrated it in a poem. (For further discussion of *Il Contento*, see §2 below.)

The drama and rhetorical gestures contained in *Il Contento* can also be seen, not only in the *Three Marys*, but in another work probably of the same period, the gruesome *Judith and Holofernes* (London, Apsley House)—though its violence is contained within an almost comfortable domestic setting. This picture once belonged to Rubens. This is of more than academic interest, for Rubens himself based his rendering of this scene (1609–10), now known only through an engraving (c. 1621; B. 31) by Cornelis Galle (i), on Elsheimer's copper. Rembrandt too may have had knowledge of this work, for the agonies of the

2. Adam Elsheimer: *Exaltation of the True Cross*, oil on silver-coated copper, 485×350 mm, c. 1603–5 (Frankfurt am Main, Städelsches Kunstinstitut und Städtische Galerie)

3. Adam Elsheimer: *Tobias and the Angel* (the *Small Tobias*), oil on copper, 116×184 mm, *c.* 1607–8 (Frankfurt am Main, Historisches Museum)

tormented hero in his *Blinding of Samson* (1636; Frankfurt am Main, Städel. Kstint. & Städt. Gal.) imitate the pose of the butchered commander in Elsheimer's picture.

From now on, the drama and rhetoric are contained in single figures or smaller groups. It is likely that this was the period of the tiny panels with *Biblical Figures and Saints* (eight, Petworth House, W. Sussex, NT; one, Montpellier, Mus. Fabre). Cornelis van Poelenburch made copies of these (Florence, Pitti), and it is even possible that there were originally others in the series, for copies of three more, very much in van Poelenburch's style, are let into an early 17th-century Dutch cabinet (Penshurst Place, Kent). These little panels of one or two figures ultimately derive from similar sets of saints in engravings by Dürer and Martin Schongauer. Here an artist by now steeped in Italian art is recalling his earlier upbringing in the old German tradition, in fact a rethinking of some of the figures which had been included in the very early Berlin altar. Yet a comparison between the two works shows how greatly Elsheimer had matured during the intervening years. The landscape backgrounds, with their high and dual viewpoints, are a synthesis of Flemish and Venetian traditions. It was these backgrounds, pastoral and un-tamed, often with wide vistas, that made such an impres-sion on the next generation, in particular David Teniers I: the jungle-like vegetation and broken tree-trunks in the background of Teniers's painting *Tobias and the Angel* (1604–5; Paris, Fond. Custodia, Inst. Néer.) were taken, with few variations, from Elsheimer's panel (Petworth House, W. Sussex, NT) of the same subject. These

backgrounds, so often imitated, have led to innumerable misattributions to him.

The story of Tobias was the subject of two composi-tions, known as the *Small Tobias* (probable original, Frankfurt am Main, Hist. Mus.; see fig. 3) and the *Large Tobias* (original destr.; close copy, Copenhagen, Stat. Mus. Kst), that seem to have established Elsheimer's fame in Rome. Not only were many copies and adaptations made but Goudt made the first (1608) of his famous and influential seven engravings after Elsheimer from the *Small Tobias*. Here a delightful subject, Tobias with his fish, led by the Archangel Raphael, set in a poetic and atmospheric landscape, became almost a hallmark by which he was judged through generations. The *Large Tobias* is set on higher ground, with the middle distance consisting of a densely wooded slope. The charming, genre-like details of the smaller version—the little dog and the frogs at the water's edge—have now gone and the focus is on Tobias, trailing the enormous fish, and the accompanying angel. Although, as always in his works, the figures are at the centre, the landscape assumes a more dominant role, enveloping the figures and setting them off.

(c) Ovidian and other late works. This development is even more striking in Elsheimer's most Virgilian (or Horatian) landscape, *Aurora* (Brunswick, Herzog Anton Ulrich-Mus.), in which for once nature appears as the chief protagonist. The left side of this panel, which contains the two figures, is much damaged and overpainted, so as

to obscure the true theme of the work: scientific examination has revealed that underneath this puzzling passage loom other, larger figures and that the crown of one of the trees, silhouetted against the morning sky, originally contained the head of what looks like a giant, so that what Elsheimer intended to depict may have been the story of Acis and Galatea with the Cyclops. Goudt's engraving of the painting (1613; Hollstein, no. 7) omitted this whole left section (the right in the print), obviously because already he could not comprehend it. Perhaps it was already damaged, or perhaps Elsheimer once again left the work partly unfinished.

Aurora may thus refer to a story by the Latin poet Ovid. Elsheimer's widow's inventory shows that he owned a copy of Ovid's *Metamorphoses*, and no fewer than four of his works deal with Ovidian subjects. *Apollo and Coronis* (Liverpool, Walker A.G.) was so often copied that it has been hard to conclude which version is the original. Here he fused figures and landscape as hardly ever before. There is also the recently recovered, much damaged *Latona* (London, David Barclay Ltd), a composition etched by Wenceslaus Hollar in 1649. The *Mocking of Ceres*, made famous through Goudt's engraving (1610; Hollstein, no. 5), was a subject that occupied Elsheimer greatly, for he also made an etching and gouache (both Hamburg, Ksthalle) of the story of Proserpina's mother who roamed the world in search of her. The best available painting

(Madrid, Prado), though once in Rubens' collection, cannot be Elsheimer's original as it has all the hallmarks of a contemporary copy, but even from this one can gauge the grandiose, almost antique statuesqueness of the chief figure. It is a 'night piece' in the most magical and majestic vein. In contrast, the indoor subject of *Jupiter and Mercury in the House of Philemon and Baucis* (1608–9; Dresden, Gemäldegal. Alte Meister) is a mysterious and claustrophobic composition, in which the clutter of a humble hut and its two old inhabitants are illuminated and hallowed by the light that falls on them not merely from two oil-lamps but from the presence of the two gods that will transform their lives. Rembrandt, who knew the composition (in reverse) from Goudt's engraving (1612; Hollstein, no. 6), was so impressed with the regal pose of Jupiter that he transformed it into the figure of Christ in his *Supper at Emmaus* (1628–30; Paris, Mus. Jacquemart-André). Even more claustrophobic is *Minerva*, one of three panels depicting the goddesses Paris judged (she and *Venus*, Cambridge, Fitzwilliam; *Juno*, untraced, but etched by Hollar, 1646), symbolizing the *vita triplex* or contemplative, sensual and active modes of life. Possibly the suggestion of this theme arose out of the circle of learned men with whom Elsheimer associated, as it is largely based on the works of Fulgentius (AD 468–533) and Vincenzo Cartari.

Elsheimer's last work was the spellbinding *Flight into Egypt* (1609; Munich, Alte Pin.; see fig. 4). Although, as

4. Adam Elsheimer: *Flight into Egypt*, oil on copper, 310×410 mm, 1609 (Munich, Alte Pinakothek)

always, the central core of the composition is the group of the fleeing Holy Family, the vastness and complexity of nature nearly dominate the whole. The most magical touch is the starry sky, with the first-ever representation in landscape painting of the Milky Way, depicted a year before Galileo published his observations. This painting was in Elsheimer's studio at the time of his death, and Rubens, in a memorable letter to Johannes Faber on hearing of his friend's death (see Andrews, 1977, p. 51), mentioned it specifically.

2. WORKING METHODS AND TECHNIQUE. The only painting by Elsheimer for which preparatory drawings survive is *Il Contento* (two, Paris, Louvre; one, Edinburgh, N.G.). They give valuable indications of how he developed his compositions. An item in the inventory drawn up by his widow shows that, like Tintoretto and Poussin, he experimented with little wax figures, which he moved about like puppets on a miniature stage. For *Il Contento* he seems to have concentrated on the arrangement of the foreground, and he is seen in his drawings experimenting with grouping, positioning and the impact of light. Two of the drawings show the outlines incised for transfer. This usually indicates that the composition, or single figure, was to be used for a cartoon or a print, but in this case he probably moved his wax figures and retraced the relevant changes of position on to a new sheet. The Paris drawing that comes nearest to the final design is drawn almost wholly with the stylus.

The fact that the painting itself was left unfinished (one of several abandoned works) affords an opportunity to examine Elsheimer's painting methods. The uncompleted figures in the middle distance were broadly sketched in, whereas the fully completed background and some of the foreground reveal how carefully he painted within strictly confined areas, never 'laying in' broad sequences of forms. To achieve such fine details on such a minute scale, he must have worked, like a miniaturist, with the thinnest of brushes and probably with a magnifying glass. Yet none of the tiniest detail is ever sacrificed to a strong overall impression. As Edward Norgate reported in 1650, the Italians called him 'il diavolo per gli cose piccole'.

3. POSTHUMOUS REPUTATION. Elsheimer's fame really only began after his death. Goudt's seven prints after his pictures were partly responsible for establishing it, but also the younger generation of Netherlandish artists in Rome, such as Pieter Lastman, Jan and Jacob Pynas, Adriaen van Stalbemt and David Teniers I carried his style into Holland and Flanders, thus making an impact on such artists as Rembrandt and Claes Moeyaert. Cornelis van Poelenburch and Bartholomeus Breenbergh, who also went to Italy, copied his works and transmitted his novel feeling for nature to such painters as Agostino Tassi, Carlo Saraceni and Claude Lorrain. As so often with artists who died young, his name has been attached to a host of works that were vaguely conceived in his style.

BIBLIOGRAPHY

Hollstein: *Ger.*

G. Baglione: *Vite* (1642); ed. V. Mariani (1935)

E. Norgate: *Miniatura, or the Art of Limning* (1650); ed. M. Hardie (Oxford, 1919), p. 43

J. von Sandrart: *Teutsche Academie* (1675–9); ed. A. R. Peltzer (1925)

A. von Bartsch: *Le Peintre-graveur* (1803–21) [B.]

H. Weizsäcker: *Adam Elsheimer, der Maler von Frankfurt*, i (Berlin, 1936), ii, ed. H. Möhle (Berlin, 1952)

D. Bodart: 'Les Tableaux de la succession de Paul Bril', *Mélanges d'archéologie et d'histoire de l'art offerts au professeur Jacques Lavalleye* (Leuven, 1970), pp. 11–14

K. Andrews: *Adam Elsheimer* (Oxford, 1977; enlarged German trans., Munich, 1985)

KEITH ANDREWS

Elsinore. *See* HELSINGØR.

Elsken, Ed(ward) van der (*b* Amsterdam, 10 March 1925; *d* Amsterdam, 20 Dec 1990). Dutch photographer and film maker. He was mainly self-taught in photography, but he took a correspondence course from the Nederlandse Fotovakschool, The Hague. From 1947 to 1950 he worked as a freelance photographer in Amsterdam before moving to Paris. In the 1950s he produced highly subjective images of the district of Saint-Germain. This series, which was shown at various international exhibitions, was published in book form as *Love on the Left Bank* (Amsterdam, 1954). The subject is the 'Lost Generation' of the 1950s, depicted in the form of a love story with images and short texts. Thereafter he photographed people all over the world. These travels often resulted in books such as *Bagara, Central Africa* (Amsterdam, 1959), a report about the people and their way of life; *Sweet Life* (Amsterdam, 1963), images produced during a 14-month world tour; and *The Discovery of Japan* (Amsterdam, 1988), which contains photographs from his many visits to that country.

Van der Elsken was successful in conveying not only the fun and excitement of city life but also the boredom and depression. His direct approach to human life, captured in informal compositions printed in dark tones, influenced a generation of Dutch and Japanese photographers. In addition, he held a place as an unconventional but talented photographer, noted for his cinéma-vérité-like approach. His last film, *Bye*, is an impressive account of the progress of his terminal illness from cancer.

BIBLIOGRAPHY

Ed van der Elsken (exh. cat., Amsterdam, Stedel. Mus., 1966)

Fotografie in Nederland, 1940–1975 (exh. cat., ed. E. Barents; Amsterdam, Stedel. Mus., 1978)

Once upon a Time [monograph on the occasion of a retro. in the Stedel. Mus., 1991] (Amsterdam, 1991)

HRIPSIMÉ VISSER

Elsner, Jakob (*fl* ?Konstanz, *c.* 1486; *d* Nuremberg, 1517). German painter and illuminator. Although there is no documentary reference to him in Nuremberg, he may have been the son of the wealthy Sebald Elsner, who became a citizen there in 1456. Elsner had apparently established his reputation as a portrait painter by *c.* 1490, but there is no evidence of his activity as a miniaturist before 1500. His skill as a lutenist led to friendship with Sebastian Imhof, Wilhelm Haller and Lorenz Staiber, whose patronage probably promoted his work. The earliest portraits attributed to him, of long-since-dead participants in the Council of Konstanz (1414–18), suggest that he began his journeyman years in the Upper Rhine area, in Konstanz. In the portrait of the councillor *Heinrich Schilther* (*c.* 1486; Vienna, Akad. Bild. Kst.) the head fills out the picture, with highly lifelike features; *Thomas Reuss* (*c.* 1486; Austrian priv. col.) presents the first front-view portrait in German painting, pre-dating Dürer's *Self-portrait* (1500; Munich, Alte Pin.); and *Bertruid Reuss* (Austrian priv. col.) has a delicate smile on her full mouth. Although these portraits are archaic in effect, they are less so than the portrait triptych of *Conrad Imhof* (*c.* 1486; Munich, Alte Pin.) and the splendid ornamental portrait of *Jörg Ketzler* (*c.* 1499; Nuremberg, Ger. Nmus.), in which the drawing of the eyes, nose and mouth is fairly crude.

In the latter portrait Elsner added hands for the first time, here touching and forming a barrier between the figure and the balustrade. The inscription on the reverse gives Ketzler's exact age (to the day) when painted, as well as the price paid for the portrait.

In the *Portrait of a Man* (*c.* 1490; ex-Louis Jay Col., Frankfurt am Main) the space around the gaunt half-figure of the subject is widened for the first time. A portrait of a *Young Man* (Nuremberg, Ger. Nmus.) who holds a forget-me-not in his right hand surpasses all other demonstrations of Elsner's capabilities, presumably as the result of his examination of Dürer's early *Self-portrait* (1493; Paris, Louvre): the young man's vivacity can be seen in his dark, bright eyes, and his face is framed by a splendid mass of wavy hair. By contrast, in the portrait of *A Woman* (Berlin, Gemäldegal.) the face is almost drowned in her enormous headdress. Among his later work, a second portrait of *Jörg Ketzler* (1507; Hannover, Niedersächs. Landesmus.; see fig.) bravely tries to keep up with Dürer, at least in

Jakob Elsner: *Jörg Ketzler*, oil on panel, 393×280 mm, 1507 (Hannover, Niedersächsisches Landesmuseum)

technique: the shapes of the subject are softer than in the earlier portrait, and more three-dimensional in effect; this can be seen even in the letters and the figures of the date, with their strong shadows.

While Elsner was one of the most successful predecessors of Albrecht Dürer in portrait painting, by *c.* 1500 he had also so distinguished himself in miniature painting that Frederick III, Duke of Saxony, awarded him commissions comparable with those given to Nikolaus Glockendon. In 1504 in Nuremberg Elsner began work on a two-volume gradual, the *Gänsebuch* (New York, Pierpont Morgan Lib.), commissioned by the provost of St Lorenz, Dr Anton Kress. He completed the first volume (Winter) in 1507, the second (Summer) in 1510. Both contain border decorations and initial scenes in light colours, and pictures of animals on the lower edge which reveal a comic quality that progresses beyond Late Gothic naturalism. Meanwhile Elsner had also worked on several illuminated books for the Duke, including two volumes of pericopes (1507; Jena, Ubib.) which contain full pages with a large central picture and a rich ornamental border incorporating angels, cherubs and flowers; the pervasive Late Gothic prick-work distinguishes these from their Netherlandish models. Elsner is also attributed with a large portrait miniature, with rich landscape which shows Netherlandish influences, produced to commemorate Duke Frederick's pilgrimage to the Holy Land in 1493. A missal (1513; Nuremberg, Ger. Nmus.) which represents the final high point of his activity as an illuminator was another commission from Dr Anton Kress. Its full-page pictures of the Trinity and of Kress also incorporate animal grotesques, and Netherlandish influence is again apparent in the borders of the initial pages with their floral decoration.

BIBLIOGRAPHY

R. Bruck: *Friedrich der Weise als Förderer der Kunst* (Strasbourg, 1903), pp. 184–203

E. Buchner: *Das deutsche Bildnis der Spätgotik und der frühen Dürerzeit* (W. Berlin, 1953), nos 153–60

HANS GEORG GMELIN

Elstrack [Elstracke], **Renold** [Renier] (*b* London, before 5 Nov 1570; *d* ?London, after 1630). English engraver. The son of a glazier, his earliest signed works are three maps for Jan Huygen van Linschoten's *Discourse of Voyages into ye Easte and West Indies* (1598), made in collaboration with William Rogers (i), with whom Elstrack may have trained. By 1604 such line engravings as *James I in Parliament* show his work had lost its early awkwardness and that he was under the growing influence of the de Passe family of engravers. A full-length of *Henry, Prince of Wales*, probably engraved soon after Henry's death in 1612, a double portrait of *James I and Anne of Denmark* (*c.* 1604) and equestrian portraits of the *Infanta Maria of Spain* (*c.* 1618–20) and *Charles I* (*c.* 1614–15, 1620 and 1625) are among his best works.

One of Elstrack's most important commissions was a collaborative work for Henry Holland's *Baziliologia* (1618), a series of portraits of English monarchs, each of which is set in a decorated oval within a rectangular frame. His title-pages, for which he often made elaborate designs, and which include that for the *Baziliologia*, are to be found in Sir Walter Ralegh's *History of the World* (1614), James

I's *Works* (1616) and elsewhere, and there are examples of his work in the British Museum, London.

BIBLIOGRAPHY

DNB

A. F. Johnson: *A Catalogue of Engraved and Etched English Title-pages down to the Death of William Faithorne, 1691*, Bibliog. Soc. (Oxford, 1934)

H. M. Hind: *The Reign of James I*, 2 vols (1955), ii of *Engraving in England in the Sixteenth and Seventeenth Centuries* (Cambridge, 1953–64)

R. T. Godfrey: *Printmaking in Britain: A General History from its Beginnings to the Present Day* (Oxford, 1979), p. 16

SUSAN JENKINS

Elte, Harry (*b* Amsterdam, 3 Sept 1880; *d* Theresiënstadt, 1 April 1944). Dutch architect. He trained at the Ambachtsschool (Technical School) and at the Avondtekenschool voor Gezellen (Evening School of Drawing for Craftsmen) in Amsterdam. Between 1896 and 1899 he worked for various offices including that of Gerrit van Arkel. From 1899 to 1909 he worked for H. P. Berlage, after which he established himself as an independent architect. Most of his work is in Amsterdam, for example the house at Stadionweg 44 (1928–9), which is characteristic of his architecture. His style was influenced by that of Frank Lloyd Wright, which can be seen in the synagogue on the Jacob Obrechtplein (1928). Elte composed the component volumes of his buildings in an emphatically plastic manner and made use of strongly horizontal overhanging roofs and canopies. This phase of his work corresponds with other orthogonal styles then current in the Netherlands, particularly in The Hague, which form a bridge between the Amsterdam school and the Rationalist architecture of the 1930s. Elte joined Groep 32 in 1932 and then Architectengroep de 8. In 1941 he worked with other members of the latter, including Ben Merkelbach and Mart Stam, on reconstruction plans for the Hofplein and Blaak areas of Rotterdam. Elte died in a concentration camp.

BIBLIOGRAPHY

G. Fanelli: *Architettura moderna* (1968)

H. F. de Roy van Zuidewijn: *Amsterdamse bouwkunst, 1815–1940* [Amsterdam architecture, 1815–1940] (Amsterdam, 1970), p. 187

B. Rebel: *Het nieuwe bouwen* [The new architecture] (Utrecht, 1980)

FRANK VAN DEN HOEK, DIANNE TIMMERMAN

Eltham Palace. Former royal palace in south-east England. Eltham, once rural, is now surrounded by the south-east London suburbs. The old de Vesci manor was rebuilt between 1295 and 1311 by Bishop Bek of Durham, who bequeathed it to Prince Edward, later Edward II (*reg* 1307–27), from whom it passed to Queen Isabella. She made additions to it under the supervision of Michael of Canterbury. Before 1360 Edward III spent over £2500 on new buildings; by this time Eltham had a great hall, chambers and chapels for the king and queen, a court and a 'long chamber', all moated and walled. Eltham remained popular with Richard II, who added a 'dancing chamber', an outer court and further accommodation. Henry IV added new royal chambers fitted with stained glass and elaborate wooden ceilings, stretched over a cloister leading to his chapel, and in 1445 Henry VI built an additional great hall and chambers for Queen Margaret. Edward IV, however, demolished and rebuilt much of the palace, and the principal remnant of royal building at Eltham is the

Eltham Palace, Great Hall, *c.* 1475–83

Great Hall (see fig.) erected by him between *c.* 1475 and his death in 1483. No evidence survives concerning its designers, although Thomas Jordan and Edmund Graveley were respectively the King's chief mason and carpenter at the time. Henry VIII rebuilt the main chapel, added a 'clerestoryed' and embattled gallery and an embattled timber cloister.

Two 16th-century plans of the Tudor palace survive, which compensate somewhat for the ruinous and fragmentary state of the remains and enable the Tudor layout to be established. One plan (London, PRO) is signed by John Thorpe and dated 1590, the other (Hatfield House, Herts) is to the same scale but unsigned. There were two irregular courts on different axes, *c.* 300×140 m, with an inner moated enclosure of *c.* 110×95 m, making Tudor Eltham about the same size as Hampton Court. The probably 15th-century stone bridge to the inner Great Court survives, with three angular, four-centred arches. The walled court was aligned north–south and had brick angle towers. A large six-bay chapel measuring 36×13 m with flanking western stair-turrets projected into the court. A pentise and cloister connected the west end of the chapel to the royal apartments. On the south side of the court stood the Great Hall of Edward IV and other chambers. South of this range were five irregular courts, the Great Kitchen and many other chambers. The outer Green Court skewed east of the main axis and contained numerous apartments, including the Lord Chancellor's, which may survive in part within an existing structure. A Parliamentary Survey of 1649 lists a 'fair chapel', hall and nearly 100 chambers in the inner court alone. Eltham was allowed to decay from this time.

The restored Great Hall measures 31×11 m, with a screens passage to the east and flanking square oriels to the west. The structure is brick with stone facing. Stepped buttresses divide the side walls into five bays, each with twin four-centred clerestory windows with Y tracery. The oriel windows are similar but full height with embattled transoms; internally, they have blind panelling and stone vaults. The magnificent timber roof stands on embattled stone corbels. It follows the hammerbeam form, though unconventionally. Moulded principals with hammer-beams, hammerposts, double butt-purlins and upward and downward wind braces create a rich effect with a minimum of applied decoration. The hammerposts have simple, embattled pendants. The hall is a perfect example of late medieval English domestic architecture and has parallels in many Oxford and Cambridge colleges and in contemporary structures such as Crosby Hall, London.

BIBLIOGRAPHY

Harvey
A. W. Clapham and W. H. Godfrey: *Some Famous Buildings and their Story* (London, 1913)
H. M. Colvin, ed.: *The History of the King's Works*, i, ii (London, 1963)
J. H. Harvey: *The Perpendicular Style* (London, 1978) [pls]

FRANCIS WOODMAN

Eluard, Paul [Grindel, Eugène(-Emile-Paul)] (*b* Saint-Denis, 14 Dec 1895; *d* Charenton-le-Pont, Seine, 18 Nov 1952). French writer and collector. He was an innovative poet and was intimately involved with the Surrealist movement from its inception. He maintained a lasting friendship with Max Ernst, and his first wife Gala later married Salvador Dalí. He counted Pablo Picasso as one of his closest friends and dedicated more poems to him than to any other artist. Surrealist painters constantly stressed the importance of the inspiration they derived from the poets in their circle, in which Eluard was a central figure, largely because of his great sensitivity to the ways in which art and language could enhance each other. Not only did he publish numerous works dedicated to contemporary artists—notably *Capitale de la douleur* (Paris, 1926), *La Vie immédiate* (Paris, 1932) and *Donner à voir* (Paris, 1939)—but on many occasions he commissioned them to illustrate his poems: his collaborations with Max Ernst (*Les Malheurs des immortels*, Paris, 1922), Pablo Picasso (*Les Yeux fertiles*, Paris, 1936) and Man Ray (*Facile*, Paris, 1935; *Les Mains libres*, Paris, 1937) were particularly successful.

Eluard's views on art were most clearly expressed in his writings on Picasso (e.g. *A Pablo Picasso*, 1944; Eng. trans., London, 1947; 'Picasso, bon maître de la liberté', 1948; 'Picasso, dessins', 1952; see *Oeuvres complètes*, ii, pp. 161–70, 447–54), in *Donner à voir* and in his selection of articles for the posthumously published three-volume *Anthologie des écrits sur l'art* (Paris, 1952–4). Picasso exemplified Eluard's artistic credo in that he refused to be constrained by external reality but accepted the autonomy of the imagination and in his creative activity mirrored the dynamic of nature: it was this life-giving quality that gave art its ethical dimension. Eluard saw both poet and painter as enabling others to see afresh, and the theme of seeing was a leitmotif in his oeuvre. This ability to liberate the vision of others, thereby enabling them to integrate a world of the imagination with external reality, was the quality he most admired in the work of Picasso and sought to achieve in his own writing. Eluard believed that creation was far from being art for art's sake: instead, he equated

the passion for painting with a love of life. Eluard's sympathy for the visual arts enabled him to transpose successfully the visual into the verbal, and his writing demonstrated a keen awareness of such pictorial qualities as space, light and colour. It was largely due to Eluard that the vision and beliefs of the Surrealists found verbal expression, in prose and in poetry. He was a key figure at all points where literature and art met during the 1920s, 1930s and 1940s, and was one of the main figures responsible for allowing this cross-fertilization to take place.

Eluard was a bibliophile and collector, notably of African and other non-Western art, and of works by De Chirico, MAX ERNST, Picasso and other contemporaries. He collected numerous Surrealist works, but his collection was constantly changing. As an entrepreneur, too, he played a significant role, for example in his editorial work for the periodical *Minotaure*, and in helping to organize such events as the International Surrealist Exhibition at the New Burlington Galleries in London in 1936.

See also SURREALISM.

WRITINGS
M. Dumas and L. Scheler, eds: *Oeuvres complètes*, 2 vols (Paris, 1968)

BIBLIOGRAPHY
R. D. Valette: *Eluard, livre d'identité* (Paris, 1967)
A. Mingelgrün: *Essai sur l'évolution esthétique de Paul Eluard* (Lausanne, 1977)
J.-C. Gateau: *Paul Eluard et la peinture surréaliste (1910–1939)* (Geneva, 1982)
Eluard et ses amis peintres (exh. cat., Paris, Pompidou, 1982)
J.-C. Gateau: *Eluard, Picasso et la peinture (1936–1952)* (Geneva, 1983)

VALERIE HOLMAN

Elura. *See* ELLORA.

Elvas. Portuguese city in the province of Alto Alentejo, located on the frontier with Spain in eastern Portugal, and with a population of *c.* 12,500. Situated in an area rich in evidence of prehistoric occupation, its first defences were built by the Romans. Traces also remain of the adobe walls erected during its domination by the Moors (from AD 711), but Elvas did not achieve importance until the Middle Ages. It was captured from the Moors by Afonso Henriques I in 1166, in the course of the Christian reconquest of the whole Iberian peninsula, but did not become a Portuguese possession until 1230, under Sancho II (*reg* 1223–48). The town's strategic position, on the summit of a small hill controlling one of the natural entrances to Portugal on the Castilian frontier, resulted in its becoming the strongest fortress in the Alentejo. The nucleus of the medieval fortification, although much altered, dates from the first half of the 13th century. Almost contemporary with it is the convent of S Domingos (begun 1267), one of the most expressive Gothic buildings in Portugal, with a nave and two aisles, a wooden ceiling, a chevet with five side chapels, and many windows (*see* PORTUGAL, fig. 2).

In 1513 Elvas was raised to the status of a city, and in 1570 it became the seat of a bishopric (which was suppressed in 1881). The ensuing period of expansion was marked by a number of buildings, of which the former cathedral (now the parish church) is the most important. Designed by Francisco de Arruda (*see* ARRUDA, (2)), it

Elvas, Aqueduto das Amoreiras, attributed to Francisco de Arruda, 1543–1622

was begun in 1517 on the site of an earlier Gothic church. The façade, quite original in Portuguese architecture, is designed to resemble a tower, and inside, the ogival vaulting, decorated with symbols of royal power, exemplifies the characteristic use of Late Gothic structures in MANUELINE architecture. Another important construction dating from the same period is the Aqueduto das Amoreiras (1543–1622). Its design is also attributed to Arruda, and it is notable for its exuberant engineering and elegance, with several rows of arches supported by semi-cylindrical buttresses (see fig.). The octagonal Dominican convent was begun the same year as the Aqueduto and completed in 1547. It has a segmented cupola, which was decorated with *azulejos* (glazed tiles) during the 17th century.

During the long War of Restoration against Spain (1640–68), when Elvas was at the centre of military operations, the defensive walls around the city were designed by the Dutch engineer Cosmander, a pupil of Descartes. They form an irregular perimeter of 11 bastions with a proliferation of outworks including the fort of Santa Luzia, which was built on an adjoining hill between 1641 and 1687. Graf Wilhelm von Schaumburg Lippe-Bückeburg, who was responsible for reorganizing the Portuguese army in the 1760s, built another important bastion to the north, the fort of Nossa Senhora da Graça (1763). The nucleus of the town remains largely unaltered since the late 18th century.

BIBLIOGRAPHY

G. Pereira: 'Elvas', *A arte e a natureza em Portugal*, viii (Lisbon, 1908)
Teatro das antiguidades de Elvas, com a história da mesma cidade e descrição das terras da sua comarca (Elvas, 1915)
M. Pinheiro Chagas: *Elvas* (Elvas, 1930)
L. Keil: *Inventário artístico de Portugal: Distrito de Portalegre* (Lisbon, 1943)

MIGUEL SOROMENHO

Ely, Reginald of. *See* REGINALD OF ELY.

Ely Cathedral. Cathedral in Cambridgeshire, England. It began as the minster church for the city of Ely, having been founded in AD 673 on an island in the Fens by Queen Etheldreda (*reg* 630–79). After being sacked by the Danes in 870, the minster was reconsecrated and re-endowed by Bishop Aethelwold and King Edgar (*reg* 959–75) in 970 as the church of a Benedictine monastery. Before the Norman Conquest of 1066 Ely was one of the richest English monasteries. Little is known of the undoubtedly sizeable Anglo-Saxon church, which possibly lay on the north side of the present nave, because the first Norman abbot, Simeon (*reg* 1081–93), founded a new church in 1082. In 1109 Ely was made an episcopal see, and the endowments were divided between the bishop and the monastery. The monastery was dissolved in 1539, and the cathedral church refounded in 1541, when the dedication to SS Etheldreda and Peter was changed to the Holy and Undivided Trinity.

Ely Cathedral has important Romanesque, High Gothic and Decorated architecture, while the later medieval period is represented principally by chantry chapels. Major restorations took place in the mid-18th century under James Essex and in the mid-19th century under Sir George Gilbert Scott.

1. Architecture. 2. Sculpture.

1. ARCHITECTURE. The west front of the cathedral is dominated by the tall, Late Romanesque axial tower and the south arm of a western transept with apsidal chapel; little but the foundations remain of the northern arm of this transept, which probably collapsed in the late 14th century. A 12-bay Romanesque nave leads to the 14th-century octagonal crossing tower, from which extends the Romanesque transept, three bays to each arm. To the east is a 14th-century choir, adjoining a mid-13th-century presbytery. To the north of the choir is a large, rectangular,

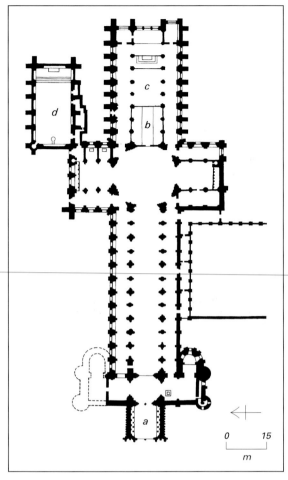

1. Ely Cathedral, begun 1082, ground-plan: (a) galilee porch; (b) choir; (c) presbytery; (d) Lady Chapel

14th-century Lady Chapel (see fig. 1). The cathedral, which has an overall length of 157.6 m, was built of clunch, Purbeck and limestone, the last largely from quarries at Barnack, Cambs.

(i) Romanesque church. Begun in 1082 by Abbot Simeon, formerly Prior of Winchester, work had progressed sufficiently by 1106 for the dedication and translation of relics from the Anglo-Saxon church. Simeon's ambitious plans placed Ely among the largest of early Romanesque buildings. Ferguson's analysis of the building postulated six design phases in a more or less continuous campaign between 1082 and 1140.

In the first phase of work, lasting into the early 1090s, the essential elements of the plan of the whole east end were established. It comprised the ground-storey levels of the south transept, the eastern elevation of the north transept and the choir. Stylistically, this work is characterized by arches without mouldings, attic bases and volute capitals in the interior and by details such as the torus mouldings of the window arches to the exterior. The plan of the church closely resembled that of Winchester Cathedral, begun in 1079 by Simeon's brother, Bishop Walkelin

(reg 1070–98). Winchester may also have provided the model for the three-storey elevation, but it was not the source of the system of alternating compound and columnar piers nor of the clerestory passage with tripartite groups of stepped arches on the inner plane. Many features of the first phase, notably the absence of vertical articulation, as well as some of the decorative details and the poor quality of the masonry, indicate that a local workforce was employed.

The second phase, extending from the 1090s to *c.* 1103, included the upper two storeys of the south transept, the remainder of the choir and the continuation of work on the north transept, with its western arcade. A new decorative vocabulary was introduced: the abaci and base shapes, cushion and scalloped capitals, arched corbel tables and the appearance of arch mouldings. Subsequent phases involved the completion of the north transept, the beginning of work on the nave and the construction of the gallery bridges of the transept terminal walls. Much of the south side of the nave was completed by 1109.

The fifth phase is datable to 1109–1118/25 by stylistic comparison with the choir of Peterborough Cathedral. There was an increasing standardization of forms and simplification of construction techniques. The alternation of compound and cylindrical piers, the use of cushion capitals, the vertical articulation by means of half-shafts, the triforium design of twin openings under an enclosing arch and the tripartite openings of the clerestory passage continue through the nave (see fig. 2). The massively thick lower stages of the western transepts have an exuberant decorative treatment, with tiers of ornamental arcading and rows of superposed passages. Building on the western

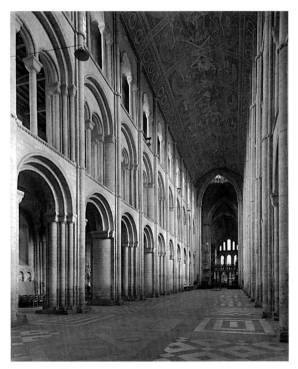

2. Ely Cathedral, begun 1082, nave looking east

transepts continued into the 1130s, but it probably stopped in 1140 with the outbreak of civil war, which badly affected Ely. The later portions of the western transepts should be dated after 1154, when the see and monastery of Ely began to recover their lost possessions, rights and lands. The change to pointed arches, keeled mouldings and new capital shapes is clearly visible at the higher levels of interior and exterior, and Bishop Ridel (*reg* 1174–89) is recorded as having completed the west end. Bishop Northwold (*reg* 1229–54) added a spire to the west tower, which was replaced in the late 14th century by the present octagon, probably causing the collapse of the north-west transept.

(ii) Galilee porch. The Ely chronicler attributed the construction of the new galilee porch to Bishop Eustace (*reg* 1198–1215). It must have replaced an earlier building (of which Essex claimed to have found traces), since this would be structurally necessary to abut the west tower. Although Stewart and Pevsner postulated a later dating, the chronicler's account places the galilee in the context of St Hugh's choir at Lincoln Cathedral, the probable source of the double tier of syncopated arcading inside the porch.

The two-storey galilee was extensively restored by Scott, Essex having earlier removed the room above the vaulting and lowered and rebuilt the roof. Many features, including the employment of Purbeck marble shafts, the sunk foils, tall lancet windows and the lavish mouldings with dogtooth and stiff-leaf capitals, are important as models for the presbytery. The rib vault of the porch is also the first in the cathedral.

(iii) Presbytery. Following the example of Canterbury Cathedral and other great churches in extending the east end to give more space and emphasis to shrines, a presbytery was added to the four-bay Norman chancel between 1234 and 1252 (see fig. 3). It was funded by Bishop Northwold, whose accounts survive (London, BL, MS. Cotton Tiberius B.ii). The flat east front of the three-storey, six-bay, rectangular extension has inserted Perpendicular windows in the aisles but is otherwise little altered. The central vessel and aisles were decorated with corner turrets and lit by groups of lancets, decorated with shafts and dogtooth. The interior elevation has an arcade, tribune gallery and clerestory, the proportions dictated by those of the Romanesque bays to the west. Most of the north and south aisle windows have been altered, and only two tribune windows survive, on the west end of the north side. They now appear as an exterior screen, because Bishop Barnet (*reg* 1366–73) removed the gallery roof and rebuilt and glazed the interior tracery to give more light to the shrines. The 13th-century clerestory survives intact, with its trios of stepped lancets grouped under an enclosing arch on the exterior. All but three of the flying buttresses were rebuilt when the tribune was refenestrated.

Details suggest that construction of the presbytery proceeded from east to west, with the north side slightly in advance of the south. Both the interior elevation and the vault design have been connected with Lincoln Cathedral nave, but Timms suggested that certain elements (e.g. the Purbeck marble piers with a circular core and eight detached shafts linked by shaft rings, the main arcade

3. Ely Cathedral, the choir, begun *c.* 1323, and presbytery, begun 1234, looking east

mouldings studded with dogtooth and the foliate corbels with grotesque heads) may be related to the cathedrals of Salisbury and Worcester. The Ely presbytery differs from its sources in the astonishing richness of the architectural and decorative treatment. The tribune gallery is subdivided, as was that of the Romanesque chancel, but the dividing shafts are Purbeck, and the enclosing arch is heavily moulded and crocketed. Sunk foiled shapes decorate the tympanum and the spandrels of both tribune and arcade. The capitals have distinctive embossed stiff-leaf foliage, and the foliate brackets to the vaulting shafts are increasingly elaborate around the main shrine area at the west end. In front of the clerestory wall passage are trios of stepped lancets, while Purbeck shafts and dogtooth enrich the lancets of the east wall. Many of the details of Ely Presbytery reappear in modernized form in the Angel choir of Lincoln Cathedral, started shortly after Ely was finished, and it was also an important model for the choir of Old St Paul's Cathedral, London.

(iv) Octagon, choir and Lady Chapel. The last major phase of building activity at Ely comprised the three Decorated style structures, the Octagon, choir and Lady Chapel (*see* GOTHIC, fig. 14), all of which were essentially complete by 1349 when the Black Death devastated the monastic community. Work started with the Lady Chapel in 1321, but construction was severely affected by the collapse in

February 1322 of the Anglo-Norman crossing tower and its subsequent replacement. As the choir-stalls were housed under the crossing tower, work on the new octagon, funded by the sacrist, started immediately: the masonry base was complete by 1328. By 1339–40 the timber lantern was nearly complete; bells were hung in the bell chamber in the 1340s and the exterior covered with lead in 1352–3.

The octagon absorbed a bay of each arm of the cathedral. There are tall arches to the main vessels and a three-tier arrangement on the diagonal sides with a 'blind triforium' of image niches above the arcade arches and a tall clerestory with Flowing tracery windows. At the angles are image niches above reliefs of the *Legend of St Etheldreda*. A wooden tierceron vault rises from the capitals of the vault shafts to the lantern, designed by WILLIAM HURLEY. The outer sides of the lantern face the inner angles of the masonry octagon base. The lantern itself has blind tracery below large windows restored by Scott and a tierceron vault, above which is the bell chamber. The structure is supported by a framework of timbers concealed above the lower vault. The technical sources for the octagon's design are still unclear.

The three-bay choir adjoining the octagon replaced the remaining Anglo-Norman bays, and many of its features were intended to harmonize with Bishop Northwold's presbytery to the east. This is clearest in the internal elevation: the piers are of Purbeck marble with arches of complex moulding; the subdivision of the gallery, foliate corbels and the sunk foiled shapes in the spandrels all point to a sensitive attempt to integrate the new work with the old. The main differences are the clerestory (now lit by large windows with Flowing tracery, the forward trio of lancets echoed only in the residual cusping of the rere arch) and the exterior, where to conform to the 13th-century elevation would have produced a gallery of unacceptably squat proportions.

Work progressed from west to east, with the south side earlier than the north, as can be seen by such changes as the move from a tierceron vault in the south aisle to the liernes of the north aisle and high vault, the alteration in the form of the spandrels at arcade and gallery level, the variations in tracery design and the rationalization of complex mouldings visible in the earlier work. Since the building was separately funded by Bishop Hotham, its construction probably went on simultaneously with the octagon; it was complete by 1337 when the Bishop was buried in the building.

The rectangular Lady Chapel to the north of the presbytery has an interior of extraordinary richness. Every surface, from the sedilia running round three sides of the building, with relief sculptures in the spandrels, to the walls encrusted with image niches, shows the dominance of the sculptural conception. Although image niches had been placed between windows in such buildings as St Etheldreda's, London, and the Lady Chapel of St Alban's Abbey, they had not been permitted to cover the whole wall surface. The large-scale sculpture was smashed by iconoclasts and the relief cycle of the *Life of the Virgin* severely mutilated. The building is illuminated by four-light traceried windows on the north and south walls and by huge seven- and eight-light windows to the east and west respectively, sometimes wrongly thought to be later additions. Although the wide lierne vault sits unhappily on the walls, it almost certainly dates from the 14th century. The dominance of curving line and sculptural plasticity separate the chapel from the first buildings in the Perpendicular style; it may already have seemed old-fashioned by the time it was finished in 1349.

(v) Chantry chapels and other late medieval work. Bishop Alcock's chapel, at the east end of the north aisle of the presbytery, was started in 1488 and completed by 1500, when the Bishop was buried in it. Its distinguishing features are the tiers of image niches and the fan vault with its openwork pendant. Only a single figure, repainted in the 19th century, survives from the great sculptural programme. Bishop West's chapel, at the east end of the south aisle, finished in 1534, was possibly designed by JOHN LEE. The screen walls have two tiers of niches with reliefs above. All but a few fragments of the sculpture, some of which was certainly carved by an English sculptor, have been removed. As with the related work at Hengrave Hall, Suffolk, the decorative vocabulary of the minor sculpture combines Gothic with Renaissance details, the latter particularly prominent on the lierne vault and its pendant bosses. The only other late medieval work of any importance at Ely comprised the addition of the octagon to the western tower and the subsequent strengthening of the tower arch (late 14th century), a 15th-century refenestration campaign and the rebuilding of parts of the cloister.

BIBLIOGRAPHY

J. Bentham: *The History and Antiquities of the Conventual and Cathedral Church of Ely* (Cambridge, 1771)
W. Stevenson: *A Supplement to the First Edition of Mr Bentham's History and Antiquities of the Cathedral and Conventual Church of Ely* (Norwich, 1817)
D. J. Stewart: *On the Architectural History of Ely Cathedral* (London, 1868)
T. D. Atkinson: *Cambridge and the Isle of Ely*, Victoria Hist. Co. England, iv (1953/*R* London, 1967), pp. 50–77
N. Pevsner: *Cambridgeshire*, Bldgs England (Harmondsworth, 1954, rev. 2/1977)
D. Purcell: *The Building of Ely Cathedral* (Ely, 1973)
British Archaeological Association Conference Transactions: Medieval Art and Architecture at Ely Cathedral: Ely, 1976 [contains pap. by T. Cocke, N. Coldstream, P. Draper, E. Fernie, J. Fletcher]
J. A. F. Timms: *The Architectural Sources of the Presbytery at Ely* (MA thesis, U. London, Courtauld Inst., 1981)
F. Woodman: 'The Vault of the Ely Lady Chapel: Fourteenth or Fifteenth Century?', *Gesta*, xxiii/2 (1984), pp. 137–44
E. C. Wade and J. Heyman: 'The Timber Octagon of Ely Cathedral', *Proc. Inst. Civ. Engin.*, lxxviii (1985), pp. 1421–36
S. Ferguson: *The Romanesque Cathedral of Ely: An Archaeological Evaluation of its Construction* (diss., New York, Columbia U., 1986)
P. G. Lindley: 'The 14th-century Architectural Programme at Ely Cathedral', *England in the 14th Century*, ed. W. M. Ormrod (Woodbridge, 1986), pp. 119–29

PHILLIP LINDLEY

2. SCULPTURE. The best-preserved sculpture at Ely Cathedral is the Romanesque work, dated *c.* 1090–1170, and divisible into three groups. The enriched volute capitals (*c.* 1090) in the south-east transept are the earliest: their low-relief carvings are among the first of this type to be produced in Britain after the Conquest. Three kinds of ornament are used: simple geometric designs; elaborate foliate motifs, some symmetrical, others asymmetrical, rich in lanky tendrils and fleur-de-lis endings; and stylized creatures shown in profile, alone or in pairs. Each type of

4. Ely Cathedral, nave, south aisle, dragon capital, *c.* 1090

motif derives from a different stylistic source. The geometric designs are, like the volute capital itself, purely Norman in origin, while the foliage recalls a still vigorous Anglo-Saxon style. The animals resemble those found in the borders of the Bayeux Tapestry (*c.* 1080) and represent an emerging Anglo-Norman style. An additional capital of this group in the first bay of the nave's south aisle (isolated when the octagon was built) is carved with an attenuated dragon with clawed feet and a trifid tongue (see fig. 4). This dragon also closely resembles those in the Bayeux Tapestry, particularly the one below Aelgyva and the cleric, where the resemblance between the embroidery and the carving is close enough to suggest a common stylistic source.

The three cloister doorways, known by their 19th-century names, are the next group. They can all be attributed to a single distinguished master sculptor active at Ely in the 1130s, who was also responsible for most of the cathedral's corbel-table heads, five capitals in the east transept galleries and at least one fragment now loose in the south gallery of the nave. He was English and may have worked briefly in Norwich. The Vestry doorway, of which only half survives, is the simplest of the three, a single arch and jamb shaft, both richly carved with alternating spirals of beaded bands and luxuriant leaves and blossoms. At the apex is an elegant human head rising from a sea of gracefully unfurled leaves. Near by, the distinctive trefoil arch of the Monks' doorway provides still further opportunities for elaborate carving. There the fantastic and the commonplace are juxtaposed. A pair of dragons crouch over the central opening locked in playful combat, while in each of the two spandrels below is a kneeling monk with crook and tonsure.

The Prior's doorway, used not by the prior but by his distinguished lay guests, is dominated by its carved lintel and tympanum (see fig. 5), which contain the doorway's theological significance. An unusually youthful, unbearded

Christ in Majesty sits within a mandorla supported by two angels. The great dignity and grace of the seated figure as well as the careful treatment of small details such as hands, feet, wing feathers and drapery all demonstrate the sculptor's skill. On the jambs below is a marvellous iconographical hotchpotch characteristic of the period. Two slightly startled male heads jut from the upper inside corner of each inner jamb. The adjacent shafts are thick with spirals of foliage alternating with paired birds. On the outer jambs are roundels containing carvings. The subjects of these are enormously varied. Many are drawn from zodiacs and bestiaries, while others are genre figures relating to feasting, entertainment and popular pastimes. On the right side are four musicians, a juggler and an acrobat who, as a group, probably represent a troupe of *jongleurs*. All these subjects are very well observed: the musicians hold their instruments in a convincing way, and the non-mythical animals are easily recognizable. This immediacy gives the small roundel figures a timeless poignancy that counter-balances the more remote elegance of the tympanum.

The third and last group of Romanesque sculpture is in the ruins of the monastic infirmary, now flanking a lane south-east of the cathedral. The remains consist of a simple aisled hall, nine bays long, with an adjoining chapel entered through a low ornamental doorway. Part of the chapel's chancel arch is embedded in the far wall beyond. The arcade of both hall and chapel are richly carved with complicated sequences of mouldings, and the ornamental motifs found on the pier capitals are no longer figurative.

5. Ely Cathedral, Prior's doorway, *c.* 1135

The use of geometric forms, whether concave or convex, has become a major preoccupation. The technical skills displayed are very great. Angles and curves are crisp and precise. The capitals of the chancel arch and unusual north doorway, with joggle-jointed lintel and reticulated tympanum, are particularly fine. This work cannot be ascribed to a single sculptor, but it is attributable to a workshop also active at nearby Denny Abbey, a priory belonging to the monks at Ely, which can be reliably dated (1160–70).

The handsome Tournai tombslab in the north aisle of the cathedral choir also belongs to this period. Carved with *St Michael* holding the naked soul of a bishop, it was probably ordered by Bishop Nigel before his death in 1169 (*see* TOMB, fig. 9). There are good Purbeck effigies of *Bishop Northwold* and *Bishop Kilkenny* (*d* 1257), and the tomb of *Bishop de Luda* (*d* 1298) is by the same designer as the tomb of *Edmund Crouchback, Earl of Lancaster* (*d* 1296) at Westminster Abbey, London. Besides the chapels of bishop Alcock and West, the finest late medieval monuments are those of *John Tiptoft* (*d* 1470) and his two wives, and *Bishop Redman* (*d* 1505). Later monuments include brasses to *Bishop Goodrich* (*d* 1554) and *Dean Tyndall* (*d* 1614), and the tombs of *Sir Robert Steward* (*d* 1570) and *Sir Mark Steward* (*d* 1603).

The 14th-century choir-stalls, probably designed by William Hurley, were removed from their original position under the octagon to the east end of the nave by James Essex during the 18th century, entailing the destruction of the Romanesque pulpitum. They were transferred to their present position by Sir George Gilbert Scott in the 19th century.

BIBLIOGRAPHY

G. Zarnecki: *The Early Sculpture of Ely Cathedral* (London, 1958)

J. Coad: *Denny Abbey* (London, 1984)

P. Lindley: 'The Tomb of Bishop William de Luda: An Architectural Model at Ely Cathedral', *Cambridge Antiqua. Soc. Proc.*, lxxiii (1984), pp. 75–87

D. Wilson: *The Bayeux Tapestry* (London, 1985)

F. Johnson: 'A Romanesque Capital at Ely Cathedral', *Antiqua. J.*, lxvi/1 (1986), pp. 130–31

P. Lindley: 'The Imagery of the Octagon at Ely', *J. Brit. Archaeol. Assoc.*, cxxxix (1986), pp. 75–99

K. Powell: 'Ely Cathedral Close, Cambs.', *Country Life* (3 March 1994), pp. 48–51

FAITH JOHNSON, with PHILLIP LINDLEY

Elymais. Name given in later antiquity (2nd century BC onwards) to an area in south-western Iran that originally probably covered the geographical region of the Bakhtiari Mountains, linking lowland and highland Iran. One route, coming from Susiana, led over the Bakhtiari Mountains through Izeh (Malamir) towards central Iran; another route, passing further south through Behbehan, led to the province of Fars.

Classical authors, rock inscriptions and the coins of Elymaian kings (*see* ANCIENT NEAR EAST, §II, 8) provide information on the history of this area. Although some Elymaian kings from the 2nd century BC to the 2nd century AD are known, the exact sequence of their rule is uncertain. The Elymaians were regarded by Strabo as different from the people of Susiana. They successfully withstood attacks by the Seleucids in the first half of the 2nd century BC, briefly conquered the Greek city of Susa under the Elymaian king Kamnaskires I in 147 BC, but were soon defeated by the army of the Parthian king Mithradates I in 139–138 BC. Elymaian temples, such as those of Athena and Artemis, were reported to be extremely wealthy and were looted by the Parthians. Nevertheless, the Elymaian kingdom continued to exist, as evidenced by coins struck by their local kings, though remaining part of the Parthian empire. From the mid- to late 1st century AD the kingdom of Elymais seems to have regained some of its previous importance, and it is assumed that the Elymaians even recaptured Susa from the Parthians.

Three major sites and a number of rock-reliefs are located in Elymais. They show that the art of this region was strongly influenced by PARTHIAN art (240 BC– c. AD 224).

See also IRAN, ANCIENT, §IV.

1. Shami. 2. Masjid-i Solaiman and Bard-i Nishandeh. 3. Hung-i Nauruzi. 4 Bid Zard. 5. Hung-i Kamalvand Aždar. 6. Hung-i Yar Alivand. 7. Shimbar. 8. Kuh-i Tina. 9. Tang-i Sarvak. 10. Mehrenan.

1. SHAMI. Sir Aurel Stein visited the site of Shami near Izeh (Malamir) in the remote Bakhtiari Mountains in the late 1930s and found stone foundations of walls belonging to a rectangular building that had been burnt down and plundered in antiquity. Within the enclosure a small platform built of bricks probably served as an altar, and square stones with holes were probably statue bases. The sanctuary, the cella and the temple do not seem to have been roofed. Poor preservation makes dating difficult, although fragments of sculpture found outside the enclosure suggest that the sanctuary may already have been in use in the 2nd and 1st centuries BC. Its final destruction probably took place in the late Parthian period. Dug into the hillside below the shrine a stone grave was also found.

Many fragments of sculpture, some made of marble but mostly in bronze, were uncovered. These include a small marble male head with a diadem tied around it, the bronze 'Mask of Antiochus' and a small bronze statue (Tehran, Archaeol. Mus.). The outstanding piece among the finds from Shami, however, is the large bronze male statue, usually described as a Parthian prince (Tehran, Archaeol. Mus.). Measuring 1.92 m high, it was found by local workmen who claimed to have discovered it inside the rectangular enclosure. The bearded and moustached male statue was made in two parts with the small head manufactured separately but closely fitting on to the body. The figure has a headband tied across the forehead and stands upright in frontal position. The left arm is bent with the left hand broken, and the right arm is missing. The figure wears the Parthian costume: a short belted and crossed-over jacket, short trousers and tube-shaped leggings. The leggings were probably attached to a hidden suspender-belt underneath the back part of the jacket. A cushion-type support appears at the back. A dagger is worn on the rear right side with the hilt sticking out of the legging. The iconography of the statue compared with Parthian works indicates that it was probably made in the late 1st century BC or the beginning of the 1st century AD (*see also* IRAN, ANCIENT, §III, 3, and PARTHIAN, fig. 2).

2. MASJID-I SOLAIMAN AND BARD-I NISHANDEH. Some 90 km west of Shami are the two large Elymaian sites of Masjid-i Solaiman and Bard-i Nishandeh. The

ruins of Masjid-i Solaiman consist of a large terrace built on top of a natural mound. Four large stairways gave access to the buildings on the terrace: the podium, the Great Temple and the Herakles Temple. The Great Temple consisted of a central square hall leading to the antecella and cella. Corridors surrounded the central complex with the main entrance being on the east side, which at one point was refurbished with a portico of 21 columns. The Herakles Temple, named after a relief of *Herakles* found inside the temple (see fig.), was smaller. It consisted of a broad-type cella and antecella. The outer façade of the antecella had three stairs on either side of the main entrance. A fragmentary dedicatory inscription, engraved on a stone bench in front of the façade, dates the temple to the late 2nd century AD or early 3rd. Numismatic evidence suggests that the destruction of the site took place during the reign of Shapur II in the early 4th century AD. The many fragments of statues and reliefs (Tehran, Archaeol. Mus.; Paris, Louvre) found on the terrace mostly represent worshippers who are shown in the familiar Parthian pose of adoration, with raised right hand and open palm.

Elymais, stone slab with a representation of *Herakles*, h. 304 mm, Parthian period, late 2nd–early 3rd century AD (London, British Museum)

Similar worshipping figures, usually wearing the Parthian tunic and trousers, were also found at neighbouring Bard-i Nishandeh. The site covered an area of 250×700 m and included a palace, a fort, a terrace and a temple built on a lower terrace. This temple consisted of a square cella with its roof supported by four columns. It was surrounded by rectangular rooms on three sides and a double portico with eight columns on the fourth side. A large hoard of coins, found in one of the rectangular rooms adjoining the cella, dates the last building phase of the temple to the 1st and 2nd centuries AD.

3. HUNG-I NAURUZI. The large rock carving at Hung-i Nauruzi is one of the best-preserved. The scene is set within a rectangular panel and shows a mounted male figure in profile facing a row of four frontally standing male figures. The bearded rider has a large head and relatively small body, a short hairstyle and a diadem with long floating ties. The horse, with its left foreleg lifted, faces a large figure who occupies the maximum height of the relief panel. This princely figure with tripartite hairstyle and diadem wears the Parthian costume of tunic and trousers. Those standing behind him are dressed in a similar fashion but do not wear a diadem. In addition to the figures, there are two birds between the rider and the large standing figures. One of these clutches a small ring in its claws; the other carries a ring in its beak with which it touches a bunch of the large figure's hair, its outstretched claws and the open wings probably indicating flight.

The presence of a figure in profile on the relief of the Hung-i Nauruzi and the similarity of the head of the rider figure and busts of Mithradates I on his coins have led some scholars to date the relief to the early Parthian period and to see it as a commemorative monument set up by Mithradates I after his victory over Elymais in 139–138 BC. But coins of Elymaian rulers with busts similar to that of the rider figure were struck between 82–81 BC and AD 75. In addition, stylistic and iconographic features suggest a 1st-century AD date. It is thus likely that the scene of the large relief at Hung-i Nauruzi shows a local Elymaian ruler, who was either worshipping the central divine figure or handing the ring of power to a petty prince. It is also possible that a local king, the central figure, received the ring from a divine ancestor on horseback.

A second incomplete relief from Hung-i Nauruzi shows a standing figure with halo-shaped hairstyle, a belted tunic and trousers; the head is damaged and the arms are missing.

4. BID ZARD. At Bid Zard, near Hung-i Nauruzi, there is a relief showing a seated royal figure with a diadem tied around his head and two figures standing on either side. The central figure seems to hold an object resembling a cup, and his right hand is raised. The relief may depict a sacrificial scene and probably dates to the 2nd century AD.

5. HUNG-I KAMALVAND AŽDAR. Situated close to Hung-i Nauruzi, this badly eroded relief shows two figures, one on horseback and the other standing. The latter has his right arm stretched towards the horse and holds a jug in his hand. The Aramaic inscription carved above the heads of the two figures has been translated 'Phraates, the

priest, son of Kamnaskires'. The rider figure could perhaps have been the Elymaian king Phraates (*reg ?c.* AD 100), son of Orodes I.

6. HUNG-I YAR ALIVAND. Situated less than 2 km west of Hung-i Nauruzi and carved some 2 m above the ground, this badly eroded relief shows two standing figures in frontal position, each holding a ring. Although no details are visible, a 2nd-century AD date is possible because of its geographical proximity to the relief of Hung-i Kamalvand Aždar.

7. SHIMBAR [Tang-i Botan]. Shimbar is an enclosed valley some 60 km north-east of Masjid-i Solaiman. A large panelled rock-relief was cut into the mountains at Tang-i Botan, and traces of a stone building, known as Qaleh Dokhtar, were found near by; extensive terracing and two water tunnels used for irrigation were also noted. The 2 m-high panel shows a row of standing male figures in four separate groups; a separate smaller panel appears on the far right side. The nude figure has been identified as the god Herakles, who appears with figures dressed in the Parthian tunic and trousers. All figures have a halo-shaped hairstyle and are shown frontally. The smaller panel on the far right consists of three half-size standing figures with their right hands lifted, perhaps in sign of adoration. They are dressed in the same manner as the others. Although inscriptions were carved on to the rock, they cannot be read; the style of the Elymaian script, however, suggests a 2nd-century AD date. The five groups are thought to have been carved successively between AD 100 and 200, the one on the far left perhaps being the earliest.

8. KUH-I TINA. This badly eroded rock-relief north-west of Shimbar shows two male figures. One is reclining and holds an object, perhaps a bowl, in his left hand, while the other, who is probably seated, seems to carry a cornucopia in his right hand. The relief probably dates to the 2nd or 3rd century AD.

9. TANG-I SARVAK. At Tang-i Sarvak, 54 km north-west of Behbehan, reliefs were carved on four blocks of rock. Some architectural remains near the rocks, and ancient walled terraces probably used for cultivation, may have been connected with the various rock-reliefs.

The first rock, Tang-i Sarvak I, has reliefs carved on all three sides. These show a nude figure with halo-shaped hairstyle and stylized lion skin wrapped around the left arm, identified as Herakles (north side); two frontally standing figures on different levels with an altar placed in front of the one on the higher level (north-west side); and two badly eroded figures standing side by side, with perhaps an altar separating them (east side).

The second and main rock, Tang-i Sarvak II, is *c.* 2 km from the first rock and has sculptures on three sides. The upper panel of the north-east side shows a reclining banquet scene. The royal figure who holds a ring in his raised right hand is resting on a *kline* (bed) with eagle's feet. He is flanked by deities carrying their various attributes. The scene probably depicts the investiture of the reclining king, Vorod, named in the inscription above, who receives the ring of power in the presence of various

deities. He has been identified as the Elymaian king Orodes III or IV of the 2nd century AD.

On the north-east side of the same rock, three men stand side by side. The north side shows a bearded and moustached figure standing frontally with one arm raised next to an altar, which is set on a triple base. He has two full bunches of hair and a pointed hat, and he wears a tunic, cloak and trousers. A diadem with long floating ties is fastened around the top part of a conical sacred stone. The top register of the north-west panel shows the 'court assembly', with nine figures, two seated and seven standing (two deities, or an enthroned king and attendants). The middle register of the north-west panel consists of four large and two small standing figures, with the larger figures raising their right hands. Hardly any details are visible. To the right, in a separate scene, a mounted hunter with a lance slays an animal, perhaps a lion, a boar or a bear. On the lower register of this panel a standing male figure is slaying a roaring lion.

The third rock, Tang-i Sarvak III, has figures carved on its south-western side only. Here the scene is dominated by a large rider holding a lance and his smaller horse; both wear chain mail. To the left are some smaller figures. Traces of a figure shooting an arrow and possibly also on horseback have been discovered at the far right. On Tang-i Sarvak IV two standing figures in frontal position are shown on the north side. The east side consists of a badly eroded relief of a reclining figure.

The reliefs at Tang-i Sarvak were probably not all carved at the same time, and the scenes on the first rock were probably earlier than the others. Although inscriptions in Elymaian script do appear, they are mostly badly eroded and hardly legible. The inscription naming Vorod and a comparison of the Tang-i Sarvak sculptures with those from other Elymaian sites suggest a late 2nd- or early 3rd-century AD date.

10. MEHRENAN. The village of Mehrenan near the River Karun lies some 23 km north of Izeh, and here three hills with traces of walls were discovered. The finding of rectangular stone slabs perhaps indicates the presence of a necropolis. A badly eroded, oval-shaped stele shows a frontally standing male figure with thick bunches of halo-shaped hair, wearing tunic and trousers, with a dagger on his right side; in his right hand he is grasping what might be a sword-hilt, and in his other hand he holds a cone or a palm. The stele probably dates to the 2nd century AD.

BIBLIOGRAPHY

A. M. Stein: *Old Routes in Western Iran* (London, 1940)
W. B. Henning: 'The Monuments and Inscriptions of Tang-i Sarvak', *Asia Major*, ii (1952), pp. 151–78
R. Ghirshman: *Iran: Parthians and Sasanians* (New York, 1962)
W. Hinz: 'Zwei neuentdeckte parthische Felsreliefs', *Iran. Antiq.*, iii (1963), pp. 169–73
A. D. H. Bivar and S. Shaked: 'The Inscriptions at Shimbar', *Bull. SOAS*, xxvii (1964), pp. 265–90
R. Ghirshman: *Terrasses sacrées de Bard-e Nechandeh et de Masjid-i Solaiman* (Leiden, 1976)
M. A. R. Colledge: *Parthian Art* (London, 1977)
G. Herrmann: *The Iranian Revival* (Oxford, 1977)
L. Vanden Berghe: *Reliefs rupestres de l'Iran ancien* (Brussels, 1984)
L. Vanden Berghe and K. Schippmann: *Les Reliefs rupestres d'Elymaïde (Iran) de l'époque parthe* (Ghent, 1985)

T. S. Kawami: *The Monumental Art of the Parthian Period in Iran* (Leiden, 1987)

H. E. Mathieson: *Sculpture in the Parthian Period*, 2 vols (Aarhus, 1992)

VESTA SARKHOSH CURTIS

Emanuel-Philibert, Prince of Carignan. *See* SAVOY, §II(5).

Emanuel-Philibert, 10th Duke of Savoy. *See* SAVOY, §II(2).

Emar. *See* MASKANA, §1.

Emberton, Joseph (*b* Audley, Staffs, 23 Dec 1889; *d* London, 20 Nov 1956). English architect. He was articled to Chapman and Snape and studied at evening classes at Burslem Art School near Stoke-on-Trent, before winning a scholarship to the Royal College of Art, London, in 1911. While working as an assistant to Trehearne and Norman, he met Thomas Tait, whose partnership with J. J. Burnet Emberton he joined after service in World War I. Tait's style influenced his early work (in partnership with P. J. Westwood (1878–1958), 1922–6). They designed kiosks for the British Empire exhibition at Wembley, London (1924), and Summit House (1925), Red Lion Square, London. Emberton visited the Exposition Internationale des Arts Décoratifs et Industriels Modernes in Paris in 1925 and was one of the earliest English architects to work in the Art Deco style (e.g. shopfronts for Lotus and Delta shoes, *c.* 1927; see Ind, pl. 38). His unified scheme for the Advertising Exhibition (1927), Olympia, London, was a notable step towards high-quality exhibition design, and he added a streamlined façade to the Olympia Exhibition Hall in 1930.

Emberton's breakthrough to the Modern Movement was signalled by the Royal Corinthian Yacht Club (1931; with George Fairweather (1906–86)), Burnham-on-Crouch, Essex, a functionalist building in reinforced concrete. His interest was in structural efficiency rather than aesthetics, and he developed early British glass curtain walls at Universal House (1933; destr.; see Ind, pls 57–8), London, and Timothy Whites Chemists shop (1934; destr.; see Ind, pl. 81), Southsea, Hants. In rebuilding the shop for Simpson's (1956), Piccadilly, London, Emberton employed a novel steel-frame system devised by the engineer F. J. Samuely (1902–59), and designed elegant shopfittings and a neon-lit façade. He designed the temporary Soleil Pavilion at the Exposition Internationale des Arts et Techniques dans la Vie Moderne in Paris in 1937, and the black granite-faced HMV shop (1939), Oxford Street, London. At Blackpool Pleasure Beach, Lancs, Emberton rebuilt rides and attractions including the Fun House and Grand National (1935), showing how modern architecture could also promote pleasure. The Casino at the Pleasure Beach, a circular concrete building, was a major work of pre-war modernism, with a near-Constructivist spiral stair and viewing platform on the exterior. Emberton spent World War II as Housing Officer to the Ministry of Aircraft Production and a consultant to the Ministry of Supply on the design of steel houses. After 1945 he designed the flats of Stuart Mill House in Killick Street and the Stafford Cripps Estate, Old Street (1954),

London. He was interested in Le Corbusier's ideas on urban planning and developed them as visionary schemes.

BIBLIOGRAPHY

R. Ind: *Joseph Emberton* (London, 1983)

ALAN POWERS

Emblem book. Artistic genre that flourished in Europe particularly in the 16th and 17th centuries, though it continued beyond this. An emblem (Gr. *emblema*, originally meaning 'inlaid work', 'mosaic') combines both words and images, the interpretation of which requires intellectual effort and results in the communication of a moral lesson. Emblems generally consist of three parts: a short, often Classical, motto (*lemma, inscriptio*), a pictorial representation or icon (*pictura*) and the explanation of the link between them in an epigram (*subscriptio*). The earliest and most important emblem book is the *Emblematum liber* (Augsburg, 1531) by ANDREA ALCIATI. Though its meaning derives largely from the work of Alciati, the emblem was from the beginning an ambiguous concept, covering a variety of connections between word and image. These interrelations arose from the fashionable idea of UT PICTURA POESIS and were propagated by the techniques of printing. The term continues to be applied and defined in different ways and is in some cases used in tandem with that of the SYMBOL. Like the latter, emblems constitute an important area of study in ICONOGRAPHY AND ICONOLOGY.

1. Sources and distinctions. 2. History. 3. Fields of application. 4. Problems of definition.

1. SOURCES AND DISTINCTIONS. The term used for the explanatory text reveals its origin in Classical epigram, the form and content of which exercised a strong influence after the publication of the *Anthologia Graeca* (Florence, 1494), based on the 13th-century collection made by Maximus Planudes (40 of Alciati's original epigrams are based on texts from the *Anthologia Graeca*). Here the moral intention is absent, as it is in the related form of the illustrated poem (*Bilddichtung*) and that of the literary description of a picture (ekphrasis).

The motto often consists of a proverb, slogan or the like, such as those collected in Erasmus' *Adagia* (Paris, 1500). Devices and imprese (symbolic pictures with a personal motto, such as were popular in France and at the Burgundian court; *see* IMPRESA) became fashionable in Italy after the French invasion of 1499. They provided many models for mottoes and icons but were distinguished from emblems by their personal character and the absence of an explanatory inscription. In particular Paolo Giovio's *Dialogo dell'imprese* (Rome, 1555) contains numerous rules that were applied also to the theory of emblems: for instance the comparison of picture and text with body and soul, the requirement of a motto in a foreign language and a formulation that should be enigmatic but not too obscure. Sources for icons are also found in the numerous symbolic representations on the reverse side of Renaissance medals, which were often based on ancient hieroglyphs. The rediscovered *Hieroglyphica* (1419; printed Venice, 1505) by the Late Classical Horapollo (*fl* early 5th century BC) was believed to provide a key to Egyptian picture-writing and the ancient hermeneutic tradition, understood as a kind of rebus or script based on phonetic similarities.

Connected with rebus and epigram is the riddle, the solution of which may involve icons from emblems. However, it lacks the moralizing element and reverses the sequence of depiction and explanation. Alciati used many fable motifs in his emblems. These, like exempla, often use the threefold division of emblems, but both have a dynamic character, whereas emblems are generally static. The 'pre-scientific' natural history of the Middle Ages (lapidaries, bestiaries etc), with its interpretation of the natural world, was by no means dead in Renaissance times and provided many models for emblems, though not couched in the same form. The writings of Ulisse Aldrovandi on biology contain extensive emblematic interpretations. Allegories (*see* ALLEGORY) and iconographic handbooks, such as the *Iconologia* (Rome, 1593; first illustrated edn, Rome, 1603; *see* ICONOGRAPHIC HANDBOOK) by Cesare Ripa, often include emblems. However, allegory is not restricted to moral messages, and many emblematists (as in the theory of personal devices) rule out the representation of the human figure.

2. HISTORY. Andrea Alciati is considered the founder and chief exponent of the emblematic art. A lawyer with a humanistic background, from *c.* 1518 he translated Greek epigrams that, from the 1520s, he designated as emblems, meaning a text describing a thing or event (*res vel historia*). The threefold pattern is first found in his *Emblematum liber* (Augsburg, 1531), containing woodcuts after Jörg Breu (ii), though the genesis of this work is not wholly clear. Other illustrated editions were published (see fig. 1), but in later years, perhaps for financial reasons, unillustrated editions (*emblemata nuda*) also appeared. Alciati's book comprises a multiplicity of forms and types of emblems (mythological, exemplary, hieroglyphic etc), which were much varied and added to in the course of nearly 200 editions. That of 1548 is arranged in sections corresponding to moral ideas and also includes a separate group of 11 tree emblems. The definitive number of 211 emblems was reached in 1550. Later revisions comprised refinements of technique and terminology, which were often projected back to the early history of the genre. Humanistic learning is displayed in the commentaries by Sebastian Stockhamer (from 1565), Claude Mignault (from 1571) and others, leading to the *editio optima* (Padua, 1621) edited by Johannes Thuilius (*fl* 1617–29). The types and possibilities of Alciati's emblem book were to some extent systematized by his many successors, with varying aims in view.

The tradition of the humanistic-encyclopedic emblem book in Alciati's style was followed in the first French emblem book, *Le Théâtre des bons engins* (Paris, 1539) by Guillaume de la Perrière (*c.* 1490–1553), as well as in, among others, the *Emblemata* (Antwerp, 1564) by Johannes Sambucus (1531–84), *Sinnepoppen* (Amsterdam, 1614) by Roemer Visscher (*c.* 1547–1620), *Speculum imaginum veritatis* (Cologne, 1650) by Jacob Masen (1606–81) and the great encyclopedia *Mundo symbolico* (Milan, 1653–4; Lat. edn 1681) by Filippo Picinelli (1604–*c.* 1667). (To this group also belong several 'realistic' emblem books, i.e. those that convey their messages more through the use

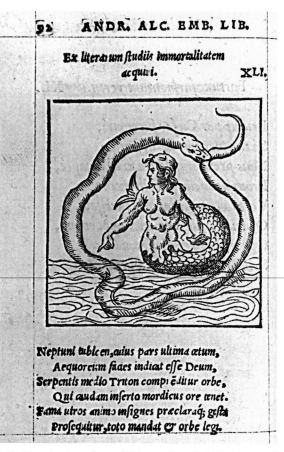

1. Emblem showing a figure of Triton and a snake biting its own tail (illustrating the eternal fame that can be attained through art); woodcut from Andrea Alciati: *Emblematum libellus* (Paris, 1542), p. 92 (London, British Library)

of 'realistic' pictorial means than through a complex process of encoding.) Such encyclopedic collections, as Alciati's tree emblems show, may also be arranged in terms of natural history, as in *Symbolorum et emblematum I [–IV] centuria* (Nuremberg, 1590–1604) by Joachim Camerarius (1500–1574), or they may illustrate occult sciences such as alchemy or Rosicrucianism, as does the *Atalanta fugiens* (Oppenheim, 1617) by Michael Maier (1568–1622).

From the realm of history and mythology come materials akin to exempla, such as the *Mikrokosmos sive parvus mundus* (Antwerp, 1579) by Gerard de Jode (i) with texts by Willem van Haecht II, Joost van den Vondel (1587–1679) and others; or *Picta poesis ovidiana* (Frankfurt am Main, 1580) by Nicolas Reusner (1545–1602). Reusner followed Classical literature in his use of the material, as did Otto van Veen in *Q. Horatii Flacci emblemata* (Antwerp, 1607). Proverbs etc are treated emblematically in the *Hecatomgraphie* (Paris, 1540) by Gilles Corrozet (1510–62) and in *Spiegel van den ouden en nieuwen tijdt, bestaende uyt spreekwoorden ende sinspreuken* (The Hague, 1632; see fig. 2) from Jacob Cats.

Ethical emblem books present difficulties in that many of them must be assigned to neighbouring genres such as imprese or celebratory volumes (*Festbücher*). Just as personal mottoes could easily be broadened into emblems of general validity, so general emblematic truths were often applied to a specific person, for example in the *alba amicorum* (friends' commonplace-books): many emblem books contained blank spaces for this purpose, or blank sheets were inserted at the binding stage. The connection with family albums is evident in Theodor de Bry's *Emblemata nobilitati* (Frankfurt am Main, 1593) and the *Emblemata physico-ethica* (Nuremberg, 1595) by Nicolaus Taurellus (1547–1606). Taurellus was a doctor of medicine in the Altdorf Academy, one of the bodies that published corporate emblem books, as did the Italian linguistic societies and German poets' associations (often in connection with the striking of medals). Ethical teaching aimed at a particular social class is found in books related to the 'mirror for princes' type of treatise, such as the *Emblemata politica* (Strasbourg, 1618) by Johannes à Bruck and *Idea de un príncipe cristiano* (Munich, 1640) by Diego de Saavedra Fajardo (1584–1648).

Typical of bourgeois emblematology in 17th-century Holland is the half-moralizing, half-playful type of amatory emblem, often making use of motifs from Petrarch, the origin of which can be traced back to *Délie* (Lyon, 1544) by Maurice Scève (?1505–64). The genre began on an academic and mythological note in *Queris quid sit amor* (Amsterdam, 1601) by Daniel Heinsius (1580–1655). *Emblemata amatoria* (Amsterdam, 1611) by Pieter Cornelisz. Hooft (1581–1647), with its systematic linking of everyday *exempla* and symbolic scenes depicting Cupid, was aimed at an upper middle-class public. *Maechden-plicht* (Middelburg, 1618) by Jacob Cats was much in vogue as a handbook of female education at the popular level.

Compared to other types, the religious emblem book has not as yet been much explored. The first Protestant emblem book was *Emblemes, ou devises chrestiennes* (Lyon, 1571) by Georgette de Montenay (1540–*c*. 1581); high-points of the genre are *Jesus en de ziel* (Amsterdam, 1678) by Jan Luyken (1649–1712), *Levendige herts-theologie* (Amsterdam, 1686; from a German original) by Christian Hoburgh (*d* 1700) and Jan Luyken's *Vonken der liefde Jesu* (Amsterdam, 1687), which, like his previous book, was influenced by the mysticism of Jakob Böhme (1575–1624). Catholic emblem books were more widespread than Protestant ones and took many specific forms. Their importance was enhanced by the role assigned to pictures in the Counter-Reformation, as exemplified by the illustrations, for purposes of meditation, in the *Exercitia spiritualia* of St Ignatius Loyola, and was reflected in many ways in the educational system, through *dissertationes emblematicae* and festive occasions. A counterpart to the emblematology of worldly love is found in Otto van Veen's *Amoris divini emblemata* (Antwerp, 1615), the enormously popular Jesuit editions of *Pia desideria* (Antwerp, 1624) by Herman Hugo (1588–1629) and *Emblemes* (London, 1635) by Francis Quarles (1592–1644). Comparable works are the 'course' of spirituality in the *Schola cordis* (Antwerp, 1628) and *Regia via crucis* (Antwerp, 1635), both by Benedictus van Haeften (1588–1648).

All parts of the Bible found their way into emblematic literature, either in historical sequence or according to subject, such as the life of Christ and the mysteries of the

2. Emblem from Jacob Cats: *Schoon voor-doen is half verkocht* ('A good display is half sold'), engraving after Adriaen van de Venne, from *Spiegel van den ouden en nieuwen tijdt* ('A mirror of the old and new time') (The Hague, 1632), p. 29 (London, British Library)

Virgin; the same is true of saints' lives and the histories of religious orders. Examples include *Vita beatae Mariae virginis* (Paris, 1646) by Jacques Callot and *Emblemata sacra S. Stephani* (Rome, 1589) by Julius Roscius Hortinus.

The emblematic art enjoyed a second blossoming, chiefly of a religious character, in Victorian Britain, having been poorly represented in the 17th century, except by the work of Quarles. This fashion derived its strength from various elements: theology (the Oxford Movement); the practical needs of Christian art, with the Gothic Revival in search of a vocabulary of symbols; and the needs of artists (e.g. the Pre-Raphaelites), bibliophiles (e.g. the Holbein Society and its president, the collector William Stirling-Maxwell), and such scientific writers as Henry Green (1801–73).

3. FIELDS OF APPLICATION. The applications of emblematology are extremely wide and various. It was used in literature, as a form of illustration or a structural principle in many genres, from preaching to drama, and maintained continued vitality in the form of children's books. Pedagogical elements were already present in the original and revised versions of Alciati's work and were made explicit by Jan Amos Comenius (1592–1670); thanks to them, later 'realistic' emblem books were especially well

suited to didactic purposes. Late 18th-century editions of 'children's games' by Jacob Cats and Jan Luyken were absorbed, almost without change, into early children's books. *Delight for the Ingenious* (London, 1684) by Nathaniel Crouch (*c.* 1632–*c.* 1725) appeared as late as the 19th century as a children's book entitled *Choice Emblems* (London, 1832). Christian Friedrich Weise (1642–1700), in his *Kleine Gedichte für Kinder* (Leipzig, 1765), used many older *emblemata* that decisively influenced a whole category of children's books.

The emblematic art also constituted a 'pattern book' with a broad influence on all the arts; this 'extra-literary' or 'practical' use of emblems took the most varied of forms. In close connection with literature it was used in various ceremonial forms of the Renaissance and Baroque periods, such as processions and festivities (*see* PAGEANT AND FESTIVAL ARTS). Such *Festbücher* as Rubens's *Pompa introitus Ferdinandi* (Antwerp, 1635) and Claude François Menestrier's homage to Louis XIV, King of France, had an immediate reciprocal effect on the production of emblems; the same was true of such decorative programmes as the pictures for the principal chamber of the Nuremberg town hall, published as *Emblemata politica* (Nuremberg, 1617). The rich decorative programmes of churches and monasteries have been a major field for the application of religious emblems. Emblematic forms are found in modern advertising serving a function similar to their use in political or religious propaganda. In applied art, inscriptions and icons on articles of daily use give them a didactic and moral function.

Besides this use of emblems in accordance with a more or less codified iconography, which also includes emblematic quotations in historical pictures and portraits, the deciphering of emblems in 'realistic' still-lifes and genre pictures has come to occupy a central place in recent research. In line with the 'disguised symbolism' (Erwin Panofsky) perceived in the work of the Flemish primitives, the Dutch art historians Jan Ameling Emmens (1924–72) and Eddy de Jongh (*b* 1931) have proposed ingenious readings of 'realistic' paintings in which emblems are the principal key to a (moralistic) interpretation. The popularization of these scholars' cautious methods, *inter alia* with the help of modern indexes, has led to uncritical and arbitrary translations of supposed emblematic motifs. In these cases the same problems arise as those encountered in attempts to define emblems more closely.

4. PROBLEMS OF DEFINITION. The Victorian use of emblems constitutes a link in the transition to modern research in this field, which may be said to begin with Henry Green and Anne Gerard Christiaan de Vries. It is distinguished by a general interest in the Renaissance and the approach, in that period, to hieroglyphs as riddles. After work by Walter Benjamin and Bertolt Brecht (1898–1956) in the 1920s, the problem of defining the emblem was once again raised in Mario Praz's *Studi sul concettismo* (1934–9). Starting from literary forms of concettism, Praz defined the emblem as a concettist pictorial form, the combining of unconnected elements in such a way as to excite surprise and wonder. This definition derives additional justification from the *ars memoria* and philosophical depth from *Il Cannocchiale Aristotelico* (Turin, 1670) by Emanuele Tesauro (1572–1675).

The definition by William S. Heckscher (*b* 1904) and Karl-August Wirth (see *RDK*) derives the riddle character of the emblem from its structure in three parts: the motto and the icon stand to each other in a relationship that is not clear until explained by the epigram. This definition is often serviceable in practice, but, like that of Praz, its scope is limited to typically humanistic emblems. On the other hand, the ontological definition of the emblem as formulated by Albrecht Schöne (*b* 1925), going far beyond the sphere of the plastic arts, relates to the medieval concept of the significance of the thing portrayed, based on research by Friedrich Ohly (*b* 1914) into medieval semantics. Such a concept of meaning results in ideal definitions instead of descriptive ones, which excludes a large part of the historical use of emblems. New definitions on the basis of semantics, as formulated for example by Bernard Scholz (*d* 1943), operate with a limited number of models. The comprehensive attempts of D. Sulzer to define the nature of the emblem from the context of word–picture art forms have remained incomplete.

Such attempts to define the emblem seem no less presumptuous than necessary, and the results inevitably vague. Looking at the typical form the genre took between 1530 and the end of the 18th century, while adhering to the above-mentioned 'practical' definition, a shift of emphasis is evident. The humanistic emblem seeks, by means of verbal and pictorial paraphrase, to represent a coded message with a moral content. Subsequently the emblem developed in two directions. In one, the process of encoding became more of an object in itself (with esoteric or purely amusement value), while in the other, in the later emblems, in the interests of greater clarity this process became subordinated to didactic objectives.

The problem of interpretation posed by the 'realistic' emblem can be resolved by suggesting that the subject-matter (with its constituent objects etc) bears its intended meaning before the occurrence of any artistic manipulation. The humanistic emblem uses, in addition to pictorial language, a language of signs, the 'hieroglyphs', which makes the emblem highly concise and gives it its enigmatic character. When, under the influence of new rules of art and thought, the representation becomes largely pictorial ('realistic'), it may comprise more redundant and misleading elements, which derive from the requirements of representation rather than those of signification. Such a definition, while highly provisional, also makes it easier to understand the value of emblems in the interpretation of genre and still-life painting. On the one hand it is assumed that the process of representation is always effective; on the other that the work must, as a rule, have a meaning over and above the representation. Both of these initial hypotheses are probably too extreme. Only the study of particular examples, the conditions of their production and reception, can clarify the position, and in each case the multiform concept of an 'emblem' must be defined in precise and concrete terms.

RDK

BIBLIOGRAPHY

H. Green: *A. Alciati and his Books of Emblems* (London and Manchester, 1872)

A. G. C. De Vries: *De Nederlandsche emblemata* (Amsterdam, 1899)

M. Praz: *Studi sul concettismo* (Milan, 1934, rev. Rome, 1964)

——: *Studies in Seventeenth-century Imagery* (London, 1939, rev. Rome, 1974) [vol. 2 of *Studi sul concettismo*]

K. L. Selig: 'La teoria dell'emblema in Ispagna', *Convivium*, n.s. 3 (1955), pp. 409–21

E. F. von Monroy: *Embleme und Emblembücher in den Niederlanden, 1530–1630: Eine Geschichte der Wandlungen ihres Illustrationstils*, Biblioteca emblematica, ii (Utrecht, 1964)

A. Schöne: *Emblematik und Drama im Zeitalter des Barock* (Munich, 1964, rev. 1968)

A. Henkel and A. Schöne: *Emblemata: Handbuch zur Sinnbildkunst des 16. und 17. Jahrhunderts* (Stuttgart, 1967, rev. 1976)

J. Landwehr: *German Emblem Books, 1531–1888*, Biblioteca emblematica, v (Utrecht and Leiden, 1972)

J. E. Shell: *The Role of the Emblem and the Fable in the Didactic Literature of the Sixteenth Century* (diss., Rice U., Houston, TX, 1972; microfilm, Ann Arbor, 1988)

F. J. Stopp: *The Emblems of the Altdorf Academy: Medals and Medal Orations, 1577–1626*, Publications of the Modern Humanistic Research Association, vi (London, 1974)

J. Landwehr: *French, Italian, Spanish and Portuguese Books of Devices and Emblems, 1534–1827: A Bibliography*, Biblioteca emblematica, vi (Utrecht, 1976)

Tot lering en vermaak: Betekenissen van Hollandse genrevoorstellingen uit de seventiende eeuw [For instruction and pleasure: the interpretation of 17th-century Dutch genre scenes] (exh. cat. by E. de Jongh and others, Amsterdam, Rijksmus., 1976)

K. Porteman: *Inleiding tot de Nederlandse embleemliteratuur* [Introduction to Dutch emblematic literature] (Groningen, 1977)

P. M. Daly: *Emblem Theory: Recent German Contributions to the Characterization of the Emblem Genre*, Wolfenbütteler Forschungen, ix (Nendeln, 1979)

P. Buchwald-Pelcowa: *Emblematy w drukach polskich i polski dotyczących XVI–XVIII wieku: Bibliografia* [Emblems in Polish and in Poland's prints concerning the 16th–18th centuries: a bibliography] (Wrocław, Warsaw, Kraków, Gdańsk and Łódź, 1981)

C. Kemp: *Angewandte Emblematik in süddeutschen Barockkirchen*, Kunstwissenschaftliche Studien, liii (Munich, 1981)

D. Sulzer: 'Bemerkungen zu einer Soziologie des Emblems', *De poeticis medii aevi quaestiones: Käthe Hamburger zum 85. Geburtstag*, ed. J. Kühnel and others, Göttinger Arbeiten zur Germanistik, cccxxxv (Göttingen, 1981), pp. 209–40

——: 'Emblem', *Enzyklopädie des Märchens*, iii (Berlin, 1981), cols 1379–91

Y. Giraud and others: *L'Emblème à la Renaissance* (Paris, 1982)

B. F. Scholz: 'Emblematisches Abbilden als Notation: Überlegungen zur Hermeneutik und Semiotik des emblematischen Bildes', *Poetica*, xvi (1984), pp. 61–90

D. S. Russell: *The Emblem and Device in France*, French Forum Monographs, lix (Lexington, 1985)

Goya, clxxxvii–clxxxviii (1985) [contributions on emblems and their use in Spain]

K. J. Höltgen: *Aspects of the Emblem: Studies in the English Emblem Tradition and the European Context*, Problema semiotica, ii (Kassel, 1986)

Emblemata: An Interdisciplinary Journal for Emblem Studies (1986–)

I. Höpel: *Emblem und Sinnbild: Vom Kunstbuch zum Erbauungsbuch* (Frankfurt am Main, 1987)

A. Saunders: *The Sixteenth-century French Emblem Book: A Decorative and Useful Genre* (Geneva, 1987)

J. Landwehr: *Emblem and Fable Books Printed in the Low Countries, 1524–1813: A Bibliography* (Utrecht, 1988)

P. M. Daly, ed.: *The English Emblem and the Continental Tradition* (New York, 1989)

P. M. Daly, L. T. Duer and A. Raspa, eds: *The English Emblem Tradition* (Toronto, 1989)

A. Saunders: *The Sixteenth-century French Emblem Book* (Geneva, 1989)

B. F. Scholz: 'Emblematik: Entsehung und Erscheinungsweisen', *Literatur und bildende Kunst: Ein Handbuch zur Theorie und Praxis eines komparatistischen Grenzgebiets*, ed. K. Weisstein (Berlin, 1992), pp. 113–37

D. Sulzer: *Poetik synthetisierender Künste und Interpretation der Emblematik: Studien zu einer Geschichte der Emblemtheorie*, ed. G. Sandner (St Ingbert, 1992)

JOCHEN BECKER

Emborio [Emporio]. Modern and perhaps ancient name of a site on the south coast of Chios. It was excavated by the British School at Athens in 1952–5. The first settlement, at the foot of a rocky hill by the harbour, revealed an occupation sequence with ten periods (X–I) from Neolithic (before *c.* 4000 BC) to Early Bronze Age (Troy I–II; *c.* 3000–*c.* 2000 BC); traces of Middle and Late Bronze Age habitation (*c.* 2000–*c.* 1050 BC) were noted on the hill above. Settlers using Late Helladic IIIC (*c.* 1180–*c.* 1050 BC) pottery occupied the site at the end of the Bronze Age (*c.* 1200 BC): they may have been Abantes from Euboia. In the 8th century BC, Ionian Greeks founded a Sanctuary of Apollo on the edge of the former Mycenaean settlement but built their town on the slopes of Prophitis Elias Hill north of the harbour, below a walled acropolis with a ruler's house and Sanctuary of Athena. The town was abandoned by the end of the 7th century BC in favour of settlement in the plain below. Cult in the Athena sanctuary continued, however, into the 4th century BC. The Apollo sanctuary by the harbour flourished throughout the Greek period and into Roman times, providing the material for a basilica church built there in the 6th century AD. A small fortress was erected on the rocky hill above as a defence against the Arabs, who destroyed it shortly before their attack on Constantinople (now Istanbul) in AD 674. It was reoccupied but was finally abandoned in the 11th or 12th century.

BIBLIOGRAPHY

J. Boardman: *Excavations in Chios, 1952–1955: Greek Emporio* (London, 1967)

S. Hood: *Excavations in Chios, 1938–1955: Prehistoric Emporio and Ayio Gala*, 2 vols (London, 1981–2)

M. S. F. Hood: 'Mycenaeans in Chios', *Chios: A Conference at the Homereion: Chios, 1984* (Oxford, 1986), pp. 169–80

M. Ballance and others: *Byzantine Emporio* (London, 1989)

SINCLAIR HOOD

Embossing [Fr. *papier gaufré*; Ger. *Blinddruck, Blindpressung*]. Term used in printmaking and the decorative arts to describe an intentional relief produced by stamping or moulding. It is derived from 'boss' (Mid. Eng. boce, bose), meaning a convex protuberance. The following article discusses the process in the context of printmaking; for embossing in metalwork *see* METAL, §IV; GOLD, §2; and SILVER, §2.

1. METHODS AND TECHNIQUES. The process is usually carried out on dampened paper, but materials such as lead or leather can also be embossed (*see* LEATHER, §2(ii)), and the vacuum-forming of sheet plastic gives comparable effects. Although colour can be used, embossed prints are often made without ink, a method known as blind embossing, which has affinities with Braille. Paper can be embossed by causing it, when damp and under pressure, to expand into incisions or broader areas cut out of plates of metal or blocks of wood, or it can be debossed by pressing it from above with a stamping device. The technique is still popular for wallpaper, and during the 19th century it was used in 'oleographs' (reproductions of paintings stamped with a texture to imitate canvas). Die stamping, used for high-quality visiting cards or letterheads, involves compression between 'male' and 'female' plates, one plate being incised with the image in intaglio,

the other bearing its counterpart in relief. Lever-operated, desktop machines that blind stamp notepaper with an address are based on this principle. Similar devices, known as chops, are used to emboss symbols indicating artists, printers or publishers on 20th-century prints.

2. HISTORY. The earliest inkless prints to survive in the West are the rare 15th-century 'seal prints', imitating bone or ivory reliefs. Embossing was first systematically used in the mid-18th century by Arthur Pond and Elisha Kirkhall (*c*. 1682–1742). Working in Venice in the 1740s, the English artist John Baptist Jackson made several unusual reproductive mural prints combining colour woodcut with passages of uninked embossing. These prints preceded by almost 20 years the full-colour Japanese *ukiyoe* woodcuts, often refined by blind embossing called 'gaufrage' (Fr. *gaufrer*: 'to goffer or emboss'), a technique that had been used on monochrome Japanese prints from *c*. 1730. Examples of these Japanese prints, imported into Europe from the mid-19th century, inspired French Art Nouveau artists, among them Alexandre Charpentier, Maurice Dumont (1870–1899) and Pierre Roche. To illustrate *La Loïe Fuller* (Evreux, 1904), Roche employed gypsography, a Victorian technique of 1837 based on the use of incised plaster as a mould for stereotyping.

Intaglio experimentation between World War I and World War II resulted in greater awareness of paper's sculptural potential. In 1925 Rolf Nesch accidentally bit a hole in an etching plate and exploited it pictorially after realizing it would create a bubble in the paper. S. W. Hayter, at his Parisian workshop, Atelier 17, also capitalized on the ability to model paper three-dimensionally by the use of deep-etched plates. Etienne Hajdu, who worked with Hayter in the late 1950s, found a graphic equivalent for his polished marble sculptures by smoothing the rugosity of a heavy paper with loose zinc shapes placed on the bed of the press (see fig.). Hajdu's 'estampilles' marked a revival of white-on-white and were used, for example, to adorn a book of Pierre Lecuire's poetry, *Règnes* (Paris, 1961). The Colombian Omar Rayo (*b* 1928), the Yugoslav Marjan Pogačnik (*b* 1920), the German Günther Uecker, the Japanese Kazumasa Nagai (*b* 1929) and the Americans Boris Margo (*b* 1902) and Romas Viesulas (1918–86) are among innumerable artists who exploited inkless embossing around the same time. The Swedish artist Birgit Skiöld (1923–82) won the *Aigle d'or* at the 1970 Festival Internationale du Livre in Nice with an interpretation of Dante Gabriel Rossetti's *Chimes* (Guildford, 1969). Both *Chimes* and her *Zen Gardens* (Guildford, 1973) utilized blind printing from cut lino, the latter framing photo-etchings within wide embossed borders suggesting raked Japanese gardens. In 1969, Josef Albers and Jasper Johns exploited embossing at Gemini GEL Workshop in Los Angeles; Johns tried it on paper and lead, while Albers, the former Bauhaus master, had precision drawings for his *Embossed Linear Constructions* translated into digital tape to direct an automatic engraving mill to cut the plates, making images not imposed on the surface of the sheet, but 'drawn out of its very substance'.

BIBLIOGRAPHY

T. P. Herrick, ed.: *Embossing, Blocking and Die Stamping: A Practical Guide to these Processes* (London, n.d., rev. 2/*c*. 1908)
A Practical Guide to Embossing and Die Stamping, Maclean-Hunter Publishing Corp. (Chicago, 1908)
S. W. Hayter: *About Prints* (London, 1962)
T. R. Newman: *Innovative Printmaking: The Making of Two and Three-dimensional Prints and Multiples* (New York, 1977)
Paperwork (exh. cat. by P. Gilmour and A. Willsford, Canberra, N.G., 1982)
A. Stohlman: *The Art of Embossing Leather* (Fort Worth, n.d. [*c*. 1986])

PAT GILMOUR

Inkless embossed print by Etienne Hajdu: *Bird*, paper size: 520×430 mm, 1973 (courtesy Pat Gilmour); printed by the artist

Embriachi [Ubriachi]. Italian family of entrepreneurs and carvers. The precise location and the organization of the workshop is unknown, although *c*. 1431 there was evidently a workshop in Venice, in the area of S Luca, where various members of the family are recorded. The family had links with Florence until the end of the 15th century, particularly with the church of S Maria Novella, where Baldassare Embriachi was recorded as a benefactor, and where his descendant Lorenzo d'Antonio di Messer Manfredi degli Embriachi was buried in 1483.

The workshop completed a number of prestigious commissions for patrons in north Italy and Burgundy and is known also for its production of domestic objects, which were mass-produced in numbers comparable with 14th-century Nottingham alabasters. In choosing Venice as a centre for production, the workshop profited from the existing casket and altarpiece industries and employed the skills of local workers specializing in *certosina* (inlay of stained woods, bone and horn). Articles were sold as stock items, carved in the readily available material, bone (usually horse or ox), and embellished with inlaid woods.

The earliest documented member of the family workshop was Baldassare di Simone d'Aliotto degli Embriachi (*fl c*. 1390–1409), a Florentine of Genoese extraction. He was an entrepreneur and manager of a large workshop of bone-carvers but is unlikely to have been a practising craftsman. He is recorded as a dealer in jewels trading in Spain, France and England, and he also served as the political and banking agent (*cambiatore*) for Gian Galeazzo Visconti, Duke of Milan, in Venice. Between 1400 and 1409 the Prior of the Certosa di Pavia made final payments to Baldassare for a large carved bone triptych with scenes from the *Life of the Virgin*, the *Legend of the Three Magi* and the *Life of Christ* (Pavia, Certosa, Sacrestia Vecchia; see fig.) and two coffers (now dismantled; New York,

Met.); the latter are decorated with carved bone plaques depicting the seated *Virtues* and scenes from *Pyramus and Thisbe*, the *Story of Mattabruna* and other mythological subjects. Other large triptychs can be attributed to this workshop by stylistic comparison with the Pavia altarpiece. They are two altarpieces (the so-called *Oratoires des Duchesses de Bourgogne*; now much restored, Paris, Mus. Cluny) depicting scenes from the *Life of Christ* and the *Life of St John the Baptist*, which were donated in 1393 by Philip the Bold, Duke of Burgundy, to the Charterhouse of Champmol. A triptych (Paris, Louvre) with similar

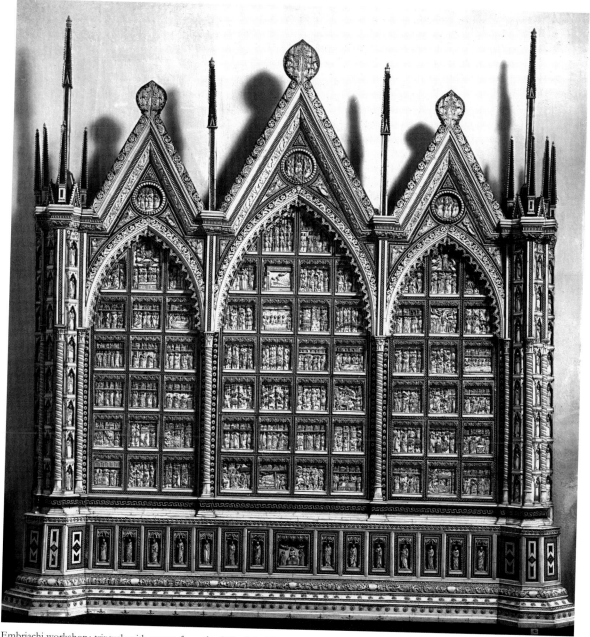

Embriachi workshop: triptych with scenes from the *Life of the Virgin*, the *Legend of the Three Magi* and the *Life of Christ*, bone and inlaid wood, h. 2.60 m, *c.* 1400–09 (Pavia, Certosa, Sacrestia Vecchia)

subjects and donor portraits of *Jean, Duc de Berry*, and his wife, *Jeanne de Boulogne*, was donated to the abbey of Poissy in 1408 or 1409, and a triptych with scenes of the *Lives of Christ and SS John the Baptist and John the Evangelist* (*c.* 1400–10; New York, Met.), formerly in the abbey of Cluny, can also be attributed on stylistic grounds. All are examples of the most elaborate works produced by the workshop and were intended for public display in the institutions with which the patrons had close associations. The compositions are carved in small convex panels of bone (h. *c.* 50–100 mm) and are framed by rich *certosina* work. The multiple panels are arranged within the three arched divisions of each triptych. The carving is uniformly low relief, partly dictated by the convex profile of the material itself, with little attempt to illustrate form or depth, and architectural settings are arranged with buildings and figures piled up in friezelike compositions. Intricately carved pinnacles and crockets on the frames, borders of angels, and the figures of saints and prophets in niches recall the ornate frames of 14th-century Venetian polyptychs.

The workshop also made caskets, which were produced as bridal gifts to hold jewels or documents. Scenes from mythology (such as the legends of Jason and Paris) and chivalric romances (such as Lancelot du Lac) decorate the sides and are drawn from north Italian and French illuminated manuscripts. The caskets were produced in rectangular, octagonal and hexagonal formats, with domed lids often decorated with panels depicting the Virtues. The earliest documented piece from the workshop is a small casket (*c.* 1375–80) in the chapel of St Sigmund in Prague Cathedral. The best examples retain traces of gilding and polychromy, such as the casket with scenes from the *Legend of Paris* (*c.* 1400–25; ex-Ste-Chapelle, Paris; London, V&A). Mirrors, game-boards and other domestic objects produced by the workshop are all decorated in the typical combination of carved bone and inlay. The workshop also produced portable house-altars for domestic use, and these diptychs and triptychs vary considerably in size and quality. They were made to the requirements of the prospective purchaser, who would select the saints and religious scenes for inclusion on the wings and central panels, as for example an altarpiece with scenes from the *Life of Christ* (*c.* 1400–25; Turin, Mus. Civ. A. Ant.).

Though never rivalling the elegance of 14th-century French ivory carvings, the finest works of the Embriachi workshop depend on French models and iconography, although the more crudely carved and naive depiction of figures and architecture retains a wholly Italian charm.

Under Baldassare's son Benedetto (legitimized in 1389), who was an authority on glass mosaic and maiolica glazing, the workshop continued to operate in Venice until *c.* 1420. Another branch of the family (all described as ivoryworkers) is recorded in Venice in 1431, when the three sons of an Antonio Ubriachi (*d c.* 1431), Geronimo (*fl* 1431), Domenico (*fl* 1431) and Lorenzo (*c.* 1400–83), with the help of the Florentine ambassador Giuliano Davanzati, liquidated the contents of the workshop of their father and his brother Giovanni (*fl* 1400–33). It is also probable that other north Italian workshops were producing articles based on their models for a considerable period after 1430. A sufficient number of forgeries exist in public and private collections and on the art market to suggest that Italian and Tyrolese workshops continued to produce altarpieces, caskets and other domestic items in the Embriachi style well into the 19th century.

BIBLIOGRAPHY

D. Sant'Ambrogio: 'Il trittico in dente d'ippopotamo e le due arche o cofani d'avorio della Certosa di Pavia', *Archv Stor. Lombardo*, xxii (1895), pp. 417–68
——: 'Il grande trittico d'osso scolpito dell'abbazia di Poissy', *Archv Stor. A.*, ix (1896), pp. 288–305
L. Beltrami: *Storia documentata della Certosa di Pavia* (Milan, 1896)
H. Semper: 'Über ein italienisches Beintriptychon des XIV. Jahrhunderts im Ferdinandeum und diesem verwandte Kunstwerke', *Z. Ferdinandeums, Tirol & Vorarlberg*, iii, 40 (1896), pp. 145–78, figs vi–viii
J. von Schlosser: 'Die Werkstatt der Embriachi in Venedig', *Jb. Allhöch. Kr.*, xx (1899), pp. 220–82
Medioevo e produzione artistica di serie: Smalti di Limoges e avori gotici in Campania (exh. cat., ed. P. Giusti and P. Leone de Castris; Naples, Mus. N. Cer., 1981–2), pp. 49–54, 118–43
G. A. Dell'Acqua: *Embriachi: Il trittico di Pavia* (Milan, 1982) [excellent pls]
K. Benda: 'Časná Embriachiovská truhlička 2. Kaple Sr. Zikmunda ve Svatovítském Chrámv' [An early Embriachi chest from the second chapel of St Sigmund in St Vitus Cathedral], *Umění*, xxxv (1987), pp. 483–9
A. Boström: *Catalogue of the Embriachi and Other Northern Italian Workshops in the Victoria and Albert Museum* (in preparation)

ANTONIA BOSTRÖM

Embroidery. Method of decorating a ground material by stitching, cutting or withdrawing threads or by applying beads, pieces of fabric etc. Embroidery has been used throughout the world from the earliest times. From the beginning its form varied according to climatic and social conditions and the local availability of materials. These long-established differences persisted, though archaeological evidence shows that embroidered goods and materials were widely traded as early as the 5th century BC. Techniques and styles were also spread by migration and conquest, though they were often modified by local practice, as in the two-way exchange between England and India in the late 17th century and early 18th.

The importance of embroidery has fluctuated with the availability of other decorated textiles, such as patterned silks, and with changing fashions in dress and furnishings. Embroidery has been used to decorate churches, temples, palaces and the robes of princes of church and state (see colour pl. I, fig. 1), yet it has also existed within poor and isolated communities. It has been made by both skilled professionals and amateurs and has always been done by men as well as women. When worked for the leaders of society and the international market, embroidery has reflected stylistic developments as accurately as other luxury goods. It has been a major means of expression for styles as varied as those of the Early Horizon in the Central Andes (*c.* 900 BC–*c.* 200 BC), Gothic Europe (*c.* 1000–1450) and the Mughal empire (*c.* 1550–1700; see colour pl. I, fig. 2). It is also a medium in which styles and techniques have been preserved over long periods, as on the dress and household furnishings that distinguish peasant communities, tribal groups and minority populations in many parts of the world. The following Western historical survey concentrates on the tradition. For embroidery of other cultures and geographical areas see under the relevant headings elsewhere in this dictionary.

1. BEFORE 1850. The earliest surviving embroideries show an outstanding mastery of technique; the saddle-cloth and hanging discovered at Pazyryk (4th century BC; St Petersburg, Hermitage), for example, are decorated in brightly coloured felt appliqué with kings, horsemen, fighting animals and mythical beasts. A Chinese silk cloth embroidered with birds and foliage in chain stitch was found with them, and the existence of an established trade in embroidery is confirmed by a similar find of woollen embroidery decorated in couched work with a cavalcade of horsemen between borders of fighting griffins and dragons, probably from Bactria or southern Russia, to-gether with Chinese chain stitch embroideries, in the tombs of Noin Ula in northern Mongolia, which date from the 1st century BC to the 1st century AD.

The oldest European embroideries include two from France: a gold-embroidered border of *c.* AD 590–600 from a tomb formerly believed to be that of Queen Arnegunde at Saint-Denis and a silk robe of *c.* 660–64, associated with Queen Bathilde, embroidered with motifs imitating jewellery, from the treasury at Chelles (Chelles, Mus. Mun. Alfred-Bonno). From England there survive the chasuble of SS Harlindis and Relindis (*c.* 800; Maaseik, St Katharina-kerk), worked with silk and gold and silver thread, and the stole and maniple of St Cuthbert (909–16; Durham Cathedral; *see* ANGLO-SAXON ART, fig. 15), which are densely embroidered with couched gold thread and coloured silks. Three mantles associated with the Holy Roman Emperor Henry II and his wife Kunigunde (Bamberg, Domschatzkam.), of silk embroidered with gold thread and coloured silks, were worked in southern Germany, perhaps in Regensburg, as was possibly the chasuble that was later converted into the coronation mantle of the Hungarian kings (1031; Budapest, N. Mus.). The 12th-century coronation mantle of the Holy Roman emperors (Vienna, Schatzkam.) is spectacularly decorated with two enormous lions attacking camels, worked in couched gold, enamels, beads and jewels on a red silk ground. The kufic inscription embroidered on it states that it was made in the royal workshops in Sicily in 1133–4. The chasuble formerly associated with Thomas Becket (Fermo Cathedral), which was embroidered in Almería in Islamic Spain in 1116, is also dated by its kufic inscription. In contrast to these rich embroideries are those made of wool and linen, notably the BAYEUX TAPESTRY (Bayeux, Mus. Tap.), which was worked in England, possibly at Canterbury *c.* 1080, with brightly coloured wools on linen. The large hanging in Girona Cathedral, which shows *Christ* surrounded by scenes of the *Creation*, was produced at about the same time but in a very different style; the whole surface is covered with laid and couched coloured wools.

Fine linen entirely covered with underside-couched gold thread and silk embroidery in split stitch is a feature of Italian, French and English ecclesiastical embroidery from the late 12th century to the 14th. OPUS ANGLICANUM was greatly prized for the quality of its work and the delicacy of its coloured figurative subjects set against gold-embroidered silk or velvet grounds. Metal thread embroidery in a different style was made in Germany, for example the antependium of *c.* 1230 from Rupertsberg (see fig. 1), which is decorated with majestic figures in silver and gold on a ruby-red silk ground. *Opus teutonicum* was made in

1. Embroidered antependium from Rupertsberg, detail depicting *Christ in Glory* with the symbols of the Four Evangelists, red silk ground with gold threads and silk: satin, stem and gobelin stitches, *c.* 1230 (Brussels, Musées Royaux d'Art et d'Histoire)

German-speaking areas, notably Switzerland, Hessen, Lower Saxony and Lübeck: this was white linen embroidered with white linen thread and sometimes a little coloured silk or wool in a variety of stitches, including drawn-thread work. Early examples of whitework survive in many European countries.

During the 14th century plain velvet began to be used as a ground. At first the embroidery was worked through fine silk or linen laid on the surface of the velvet, but later, in a quicker but coarser technique, it was worked separately and applied. At the same time fine silk embroideries, skilfully shaded in the needle-painting technique, were made in the Italian city states, notably Florence and Venice, and also in central Europe. Produced initially in Bohemia but influencing a wide surrounding area, this embroidery had a distinctive style marked by the emotional power of its figurative subjects.

In the south Netherlands the needle-painting technique was combined, in the early 15th century, with a new way of shading laid gold threads with coloured silks to achieve a metallic, shot-silk effect known as *or nué*. The most famous example is probably the large mass set (*c.* 1425–75; Vienna, Schatzkam.; see colour pl. II, fig. 2; *see also* BELGIUM, fig. 49), almost certainly worked in Brussels, which was commissioned by Philip the Good of Burgundy and given by him to the Order of the Golden Fleece. The designs were based on the work of contemporary artists, as was also the practice in Italy, where the *or nué* technique was employed to work pictorial pieces in sharp perspective, as for example the scenes from the *Life of St John the Baptist* designed by Antonio del Pollaiuolo for a set of vestments (1466–79) for Florence Cathedral (Florence, Mus. Opera Duomo). The use of raised or padded embroidery also developed at this date. It was sometimes confined to the moulded borders of pictorial pieces, as in many Spanish embroideries, but it was also used in three-dimensional figurative work, particularly in Bohemia and Austria.

The number of surviving secular embroideries increases from the mid-16th century. Many were made domestically or within insular communities, where they later formed the basis of peasant traditions, but the majority come from professional workshops established in the major centres to serve a discerning clientele. During the 16th, 17th and 18th centuries embroiderers provided vestments and items of secular dress (see colour pl. II, fig. 1), wall coverings for whole rooms, pictorial hangings, canopies, valances and bed curtains, a variety of covers, cushions, carpets and, by the late 17th century, upholstery, as well as a host of smaller items, in a wide variety of techniques. Thus, during the 16th century and early 17th, Renaissance ornament designs were embroidered in outline stitches on linen covers and items of dress; furnishings of silk and velvet were decorated in appliqué with Renaissance strapwork or swirling Baroque foliage; needle-painting techniques were used on large woollen hangings and on more delicate silk pieces (*see* NETHERLANDS, THE, fig. 63); and canvas-based seat furniture and wall and screen panels were worked in cross and tent stitches (*see* FRANCE, fig. 97). By the mid-18th century the old technique of inlaid appliqué had begun to change its form, and by the end of the century European printed cottons were widely used in a combination of appliqué and patchwork techniques.

Despite time-lags and regional variations, professional workshops followed the general stylistic progression from Renaissance to Baroque, from Rococo to Neo-classicism, and embroidery shared common design sources with woven silks, printed cottons, ceramics and other decorative arts. The controlled use of decoration in the Neo-classical period sharply reduced the amount of embroidery applied to furnishings and dress and also led to a simplification of techniques and patterns. Some elaborate room settings in the Etruscan and Egyptian styles (e.g. Lyon, Mus. Hist. Tissus and Paris, Mobilier N.) were produced in France in the early 19th century, worked largely in appliqué and chain stitch, but they were not typical of embroidery as a whole.

Professional workshops were mainly engaged in working vestments for the Catholic Church, ceremonial and military furnishings and dress (often almost entirely in metal threads) and, in contrast, exceptionally fine whitework. In the first half of the 19th century there was a steady decline in standards of design in a coarsening of techniques. Thus delicate whitework gave way to broderie anglaise, and needle-painting with silk threads gave way to canvas work.

2. 1850 AND AFTER. In the mid-19th century avant-garde church architects in England, notably A. W. N. Pugin and G. E. Street, strove to improve standards of embroidery. Many later architects were to follow their lead in seeing textile furnishings as an essential feature of secular and ecclesiastic interiors. Embroidery was the first textile craft with which William Morris became involved: during the late 1850s and the 1860s he experimented with woollen threads on wool and linen grounds to make hangings decorated with floral and pictorial subjects. Morris drew his inspiration from historical embroideries, but his designs were never simply derivative. This is also true of the followers of the Arts and Crafts Movement throughout Europe and the USA in the latter part of the century. Most were influenced by the simpler embroideries of the past; linen and wool were favoured over silk, though plain silk was used to considerable effect in some of the bold appliqué pieces by such designers as M. H. Baillie Scott (see fig. 2). At the end of the century embroidery was used by several designers working in the Art Nouveau style, for which the fluidity of the technique was particularly suited. Progressive colleges of art and design throughout Europe emphasized the importance of design, while techniques, though worked to a high standard, were usually relatively simple. By contrast, the professional workshops were again using a full range of rich materials and techniques for both secular and ecclesiastical furnishings and dress. Elaborate effects were also created by embroidery machines, which had been used for the commercial production of white cotton and coloured silk embroidery from the mid-19th century.

2. Embroidered screen panel, silk appliqué on a cotton and hemp ground, designed by M. H. Baillie Scott and worked by Mrs Scott, 1896 (London, Victoria and Albert Museum)

The developments of the late 19th century continued into the 20th with an increasingly marked separation, in design and technique, between commercial work (both hand and machine) and that of artist-craftsmen and amateurs. Although within the schools, colleges and artistic communities there was an emphasis on the craft aspect of the technique, there was also an increasing tendency to follow the stylistic developments in fine and graphic art. From the late 1950s there was a resurgence of interest in embroidery, and although initially based on ecclesiastical work this spread to all branches of the craft. In the late 20th century methods have become increasingly experimental: hand- and machine-embroidery are frequently combined; photographic, paint and dye techniques are incorporated; and a variety of materials is used, from traditional textiles to wood and plastic. Embroidery has become a recognized form of gallery art.

See also ANGLO-SAXON, §VIII; ARRAIOLOS; BEADWORK; GOTHIC, §IX; PATCHWORK; QUILTING; ROMANESQUE, §X; SAMPLER; VESTMENTS; and under articles on textiles or embroidery in country surveys.

BIBLIOGRAPHY

L. de Farcy: *La Broderie du XIe siècle jusqu'à nos jours*, 4 vols (Paris, 1890–1919)

E. Chartraire: *Inventaire du trésor de l'église principale métropolitaine de Sens* (Paris, 1897)

H. B. Southwell: *A Descriptive Account of Some Fragments of Medieval Embroidery Found in Worcester Cathedral* (n.p., 1914)

M. Symonds and L. Preece: *Needlework through the Ages* (London, 1928)

A. Branting and A. Lindblom: *Medeltida vävnade oche broderier i Sverige*, 2 vols (Uppsala, 1928–9); Eng. trans. as *Medieval Textiles in Sweden* (Uppsala, 1932)

E. Iklé: *La Broderie mécanique, 1828–1930* (Paris, 1931)

Mrs A. H. Christie: *English Medieval Embroidery* (Oxford, 1938)

G. M. Crowfoot: 'The Tablet-woven Braids from the Vestments of St Cuthbert at Durham Cathedral', *Antiqua. J.*, xix (1939), pp. 57–122

V. Trudel: *Schweizerische Leinenstickereien des Mittelalters und der Renaissance* (Berne, 1954)

A. Geijer: 'Engelske broderier av romansk typ', *Nordenfield. Kstindustmus. Åb.* (1956), pp. 43–69

Y. Hackenbrock: *English and Other Needlework, Tapestries and Textiles in the Irwin Untermeyer Collection* (New York and London, 1960)

A. Nahlik: *Tkaniny welniane importowane i meijscowe Nowogrodu Wielkiego X–XV wieku* [Woollen fabrics, 10th–15th centuries: imported and local products found in Old Novgorod] (Warsaw, 1964)

M. Schuette and S. Müller-Christensen: *The Art of Embroidery* (London, 1964)

A. Nahlik: *Tkaniny wsi wschodnioeuropejskiej, X–XIII w* [Eastern European textiles, 10th–13th centuries] (Łódź, 1965)

R. Kroos: *Niedersächsische Bildstickereien des Mittelalters* (Berlin, 1970)

H. Bridgeman and E. Drury, eds: *Needlework: An Illustrated History* (New York and London, 1978)

J.-P. Laporte: *Le Trésor des saints de Chelles* (Chelles, 1988)

K. S. Robinson: 'The Textiles from Pazyryk: A Study in the Transfer and Transformation of Artistic Motifs', *Expedition*, xxxii (1990), pp. 49–61

P. Périn: 'Pour une révision de la datation de la tombe d'Arégonde, épouse de Clotaire Ier, découverte en 1959 dans la basilique de St-Denis', *Archéol. Méd.*, xxi (1991), pp. 21–50

K. Staniland: *Embroiderers*, Medieval Craftsmen (London, 1991)

LEONIE VON WILCKENS

Embu. Effect of paint colours sinking into the canvas, which results in the image appearing dull.

□

Embury, Aymar, II (*b* New York, 15 June 1880; *d* Long Island, NY, 14 Nov 1966). American engineer, architect and writer. He trained as an engineer at Princeton University, NJ (MS 1901), and during his career built more than 70 bridges including the Triborough Bridge (1937), New York. In the 1920s and 1930s he became a principal designer for Robert Moses (1888–1981) who, as Chairman of the State Council of Parks (1924–63), instigated a large number of public works projects whose 'Moses aesthetic' defined much of the architectural style of the public realm in the New York City area. Designs included buildings in Central Park Zoo, Brooklyn Zoo (1935), the New York City building at the New York World's Fair (1939), the redesign of Herald Square (1940) and many private houses. He was one of the foremost architects of the Beaux-Arts renaissance in the USA at this time. He was also a prolific writer: works included a book on Dutch colonial houses (1913) that popularized this style among American house builders. He was an authority on the aesthetic expression of concrete and steel, about which he wrote a series of articles in *Pencil Points* (1938). Perhaps his crowning achievement was the campus of Hofstra University in Hempstead, Long Island, where he was campus architect for 30 years.

WRITINGS

One Hundred Country Houses: Modern American Examples (New York, 1909)

The Dutch Colonial House (New York, 1913)

Early American Churches (Garden City, NY, 1914)

'Engineering and Architecture', *J. Amer. Inst. Architects*, i/5 (1944), pp. 223–33

BIBLIOGRAPHY

R. A. M. Stern, G. Gilmartin and T. Mellins: *New York, 1930: Architecture and Urbanism between the two World Wars* (New York, 1987)

PETER S. KAUFMAN

Emden, Hans von. *See* STEENWINCKEL, (1).

Emeric-David, Toussaint-Bernard (*b* Aix-en-Provence, 20 Aug 1755; *d* Paris, 2 April 1839). French writer. He gained a law degree at Aix-en-Provence in 1775 and intended to enter the legal profession. However, several years' residence in Florence and Rome awakened his interest in the visual arts. He returned to Aix in 1787 and inherited the family printing business. During the French Revolution he was elected mayor of Aix (1791) but left for Paris when the political situation deteriorated and went into hiding during the Terror. He settled in Paris permanently and embarked on a second career as an art historian. In 1816 he was elected to the Académie des Inscriptions et Belles-Lettres. His first work, *Musée olympique de l'école vivante des beaux-arts* (1796), caused a considerable stir. He believed existing art institutions—the Salon, the Institut de France and the Louvre—gave inadequate encouragement to contemporary artists and argued that the creation of a special museum to house works by living painters and sculptors would remedy this; with artists competing to have their work accepted, he assumed progress would be inevitable. The idea impressed the authorities and was a factor in the establishment of the Musée du Luxembourg in the early 19th century.

Emeric-David is best known for his *Recherches sur l'art statuaire* (1805). Written as an entry for the Institut's 1799 competition essay 'What were the reasons behind the perfection of antique sculpture, and how might it be achieved?', the article appealed to the contemporary desire to emulate the Ancients through a theory that harmonized with the confident optimism of the era. He rejected 18th-century cultural and climatic explanations, which emphasized conditions the modern world could not hope to reproduce. He saw the progress of Greek art as the result of a vigorous tradition that transmitted correct artistic principles and rules of excellence down the centuries through the important master–pupil relationship. Improvements thus lay in the hands of the artist, for whom Emeric-David provided the 'correct' aesthetic. He attacked Johann Joachim Winckelmann's interpretation of ideal beauty as an imaginative quality existing beyond nature, declaring that the fundamental principle of Greek art was, on the contrary, truth to nature. Ideal beauty was the product of visible reality refined through careful selection, a theory that was bitterly opposed by the antiquarian and theorist Antoine-Chrysostome Quatremère de Quincy. With detailed instructions on how to achieve perfection, *Recherches* became a popular manual with art students, contributing to the revival of realism during the First Empire.

Emeric-David subsequently worked with the antiquarian Ennio Quirino Visconti to challenge Winckelmann's assumption of a decline in Greek art after the 5th and 4th centuries BC. Following Napoleon's victorious Italian campaigns, the finest examples of later Classical antiquities entered the Louvre collection. The French disliked the theory that these statues were inferior, and Emeric-David's interpretation of Greek art helped bolster their status. He attributed new refinements and perfections to Greek art of the 3rd century BC and later, and, with his definition of ideal beauty based on observation of nature, postponed the beginning of artistic decline until after the Antonines in the 1st century AD.

Emeric-David's pioneering work on the neglected medieval period, though marred by a complete failure to understand its art, placed France at the centre of the European tradition. This, together with his belief in the pre-eminence of modern French art, injected nationalism into art history. He collaborated with Visconti on the catalogue of the Louvre collection (1803–9) and contributed many articles to contemporary journals. He also helped to prepare for publication the *Histoire de l'art par les monuments* of Jean-Baptiste Séroux de l'Agincourt and provided information on artists for the *Biographie universelle*.

WRITINGS

Musée olympique de l'école vivante des beaux-arts (Paris, 1796)
with E. Q. Visconti and S.-C. Croze-Magnan: *Le Musée français: Recueil complet des tableaux, statues et bas-reliefs qui composent la collection nationale* (Paris, 1803–9), 4 vols
Recherches sur l'art statuaire, considéré chez les anciens et chez les modernes (Paris, 1805)
Discours historique sur la peinture moderne (Paris, 1807, rev. 1812)
Essai sur le classement chronologique des sculpteurs grecs les plus célèbres (Paris, 1807)
Contributions to *Biographie universelle, ancienne et moderne* (Paris, 1811–53), 83 vols, *Moniteur Univl* (all articles on the history of art, 1817–21), *Rev. Eur.*
Recherches sur les sculpteurs en France jusqu'en 1632 (Paris, 1826)

DBF

BIBLIOGRAPHY

M. A. Shedd: *T.-B. Emeric David and the Criticism of Ancient Sculpture in France: 1790–1839* (diss., Berkeley, U. CA., 1980)

YVONNE LUKE

Emerson, P(eter) H(enry) (*b* Cuba, 13 May 1856; *d* Falmouth, Cornwall, 12 May 1936). English photographer. He lived in Cuba and the United States until his widowed English mother took her two sons to England in 1869. He studied medicine at King's College Hospital, London (1879), and later received a BA (1883) and a Bachelor of Medicine degree (1885) from Cambridge University. While at Cambridge he studied photography, and after a brief medical practice he left the profession in 1886 for photography and writing. After becoming a member of the Photographic Society of Great Britain in 1883, he achieved recognition writing for such journals as *Amateur Photographer*.

In East Anglia Emerson used his nautical skills and knowledge of natural history while photographing the fen country and its people. The results were albums such as *Life and Landscape on the Norfolk Broads* (London, 1886), which he co-authored with the English painter Thomas F. Goodall (1856–1944), *Pictures of East Anglian Life* (London, 1888), *Wild Life on a Tidal Water* (London, 1890), *On English Lagoons* (London, 1893) and *Marsh Leaves* (London, 1895). These limited edition albums, which contained either platinotype (platinum) prints or photogravures, reveal Emerson's sensitivity to pictorial values and his knowledge of country people and fishermen. The picturesque photographs, such as *Gathering Water Lilies* (1886; New York, MOMA), are balanced by careful descriptions, including some accounts of mistreatment of women and problems created by absent landlords and encroaching tourists. Photographs, such as the platinotype *Towing the Reed* (1885; Rochester, NY, Int. Mus. Phot.), suggest Emerson's interest in French realist artists, particularly Jean-François Millet.

Emerson's claim that photography was a pictorial art, 'superior to etching, woodcutting [and] charcoal drawing' (Emerson, 1886, p. 139), rested on his idea of Naturalism. He considered his theory scientific and called for 'differential focusing', which, supposedly, would give effects similar to human vision. Through use of a long focus lens, diaphragm and camera-back swings, the main subject could be made relatively sharp while other areas were rendered softer. Achieving a faithful impression satisfied his belief that nature was the scientific first principle of art. He advanced this theory, along with diatribes on other photographic approaches, in articles and in lectures before the Royal Photographic Society and the Camera Club (London), which he helped to found in 1885, as well as in his book *Naturalistic Photography for Students of the Art* (1889). He scorned the art-like combination print and took issue with its chief proponent Henry Peach Robinson in the photographic press. He also opposed retouching, 'dodging' and gum bichromate printing. He advocated platinum printing or photogravure and suggested new exhibition techniques. In 1890 the chemists Ferdinand Hurter and Vero Charles Driffield published experiments on the relationship of exposure and development that Emerson mistakenly interpreted as proving the mechanical limitations of photography in controlling tones. A conversation with a noted artist, possibly Whistler, led him to renounce photography as art, in a black-bordered pamphlet entitled *The Death of Naturalistic Photography* (1890), which he had printed privately. With the third edition of

Naturalistic Photography (1899) he reiterated that photography was mechanical and not art.

As the photographic contest judge for the *Amateur Photographer* in 1887, Emerson discovered Alfred Stieglitz and awarded him first prize for *A Good Joke* (1887). In later years Emerson published lists of medallists, designating silver or bronze medals to photographers whom he admired, among them Julia Margaret Cameron and Nadar. The Royal Photographic Society awarded him its prestigious Progress Medal in 1895. He remained bound to his purist aesthetic, and, although he continued to photograph in the early 20th century, he was no longer a leading force. The straight photography aesthetic, however, has prevailed in much 20th-century photographic art.

WRITINGS
'Photography: a Pictorial Art', *The Amateur Photographer*, iii/74 (1886), pp. 138–9
Naturalistic Photography for Students of the Art (London, 1889/*R* New York, 1975)

BIBLIOGRAPHY
N. Newhall: 'P. H. Emerson: Artist; photographer; writer', *The Complete Photographer*, iv/23 (1942), pp. 1484–8; *Encyclopedia of Photography*, vii (1963), pp. 1254–7
R. S. Kahan and J. B. Colson: 'Peter Henry Emerson', *Lib. Chron.*, n. s., v (1972), pp. 69–75
P. Turner and R. Wood: *P. H. Emerson: Photographer of Norfolk* (Boston, 1974)
N. Newhall: *P. H. Emerson: The Fight for Photography as a Fine Art* (Millerton, 1975)
B. Newhall: *The History of Photography* (New York, 1982, rev. London, 1982/*R* London, 1986), pp. 141–5, 152–3
N. McWilliams and V. Sekules, eds: *Life and Landscape: P. H. Emerson Art and Photography in East Anglia, 1885–1900* (Norwich, 1986)
J. Taylor: 'Aristocrats of Anthropology: A Study of P. H. Emerson and Other Tourists on the Norfolk Broads', *Image*, xxxv/1–2 (1992), pp. 2–23

JOHN FULLER

Emerson, Sir William (*b* Whetstone, London, 3 Dec 1843; *d* Shanklin, Isle of Wight, 26 Dec 1924). English architect. He trained first under William Habershon (1818–92) and Alfred Pite (1832–1911) and then under William Burges. He went to India in 1864 with Burges's drawings for a new building for the School of Art in Bombay, but in the event they were too expensive to use. His own family connections secured him work in India, where he designed the Crawford Markets (1865–71), Bombay. His church (1870–73) at Girgaum, near Bombay, is in a French Gothic style. His other work in India in this period includes Allahabad Cathedral (1871–1929), in a Gothic Revival style, and Muir College (1872–8), also in Allahabad, combining Gothic and Saracenic elements. On his return to England he won the first competition (later abandoned) for Liverpool Cathedral in 1886 and designed the church of SS Mary and James (1887), Brighton, the Clarence Wing (1892) of St Mary's Hospital, Praed Street, London, and Hamilton House (1898–1901), Victoria Embankment, London, an imposing office in Portland stone for an insurance company. He was President of the Royal Institute of British Architects from 1899 to 1902 and was knighted in 1902. On Queen Victoria's death (1901), Lord Curzon, Viceroy of India, commissioned him to design the Victoria Memorial (1903–21) in Calcutta. Built to celebrate the British Raj, the Memorial is a large building containing a museum and galleries (*see* CALCUTTA, fig. 2). It has four corner towers with domes, and a large central dome crowned with a revolving bronze statue of *Victory*. The building, clad in marble, is an impressive symbol of authority in the contemporary British Baroque Revival style, especially striking seen across the ornamental lake, and was intended, in part, to emulate the Taj Mahal.

For an example of his work *see* CALCUTTA, fig. 2.

BIBLIOGRAPHY
A. B. Pite: Obituary, *Builder* (2 Jan 1925), p. 5
J. Morris: *Stones of Empire: The Buildings of the Raj* (Oxford, 1983)
P. Davies: *Splendours of the Raj: British Architecture of the Raj, 1660 to 1947* (London, 1985)
J. Morris and others: *Architecture of the British Empire* (London, 1986)
P. Davies: *The Penguin Guide to the Monuments of India*, ii (London, 1989)
T. R. Metcalf: *An Imperial Vision: Indian Architecture and Britain's Raj* (Berkeley, 1989)

BETZY DINESEN

Emerson, William Ralph (*b* Alton, IL, 11 March 1833; *d* Milton, MA, 23 Nov 1917). American architect. He trained in the office of Jonathan Preston (1801–88), a little-known architect–builder in Boston. In 1857–61 he was in partnership with Preston then practised on his own for two years. There followed an association with the Boston architect Carl Fehmer (*b* 1838), which lasted until 1873. A few projects from this early period have been identified, mostly in partnership with Fehmer, which are in the popular historical styles of the period and exhibit little that became characteristic of Emerson's later work.

From 1874 until his retirement in 1909 Emerson practised alone. During this period he became well known with the public and respected among his fellow architects for his suburban and summer residences, mostly in New England. He departed from traditional, symmetrical floor-plans and avoided elaborate exterior ornamentation, which was then popular, by exploiting the potential of the building materials. His most important projects were built on generous plots that allowed picturesque siting of the house. He made frequent use of wood shingles for roofs and walls, often in conjunction with a first storey of rubble, to make his houses harmonious with their suburban or country sites.

Emerson was one of the chief practitioners in the SHINGLE STYLE, and his Redwood, the Charles J. Morrill cottage at Bar Harbor, ME (1879), is considered the first fully developed example of the style; it also displays features of Queen Anne Revival, such as stylized half-timbered gables.

In Bar Harbor, Redwood was quickly followed by several outstanding examples of Emerson's work, all of which have been destroyed: Edgemere (1881), Thirlstane (1881–2), Beau Desert (1881–2) and Mossley Hall (1882–3). Each of these large cottages had an open plan organized around a large entry hall with windows framing magnificent scenic views. The use of a spacious entry hall or 'living hall' as a focal-point was characteristic of the period and made innovative floor-plans in domestic design possible. In his work at Bar Harbor, Emerson used shingles cut in a variety of patterns and complex roofing plans to achieve striking picturesque effects.

One of Emerson's most important early projects was the Charles G. Loring house at Pride's Crossing, MA (1881), typical of his best work in its masterful use of a rocky coastal site, in which the house's picturesque asymmetrical exterior responds to the location. Its exterior ornamentation is based on American Colonial architecture, providing an early example of Emerson's interest in the style and an indication of his later development. The gambrel roof derives from Early American architecture and enabled Emerson to treat a large portion of the sweeping roof like a wall, shingling both portions and thereby disguising the transition between two normally sharply delineated sections of a building. His own house in Milton, MA (1886), is a notable example of this technique.

The last phase of Emerson's career began when his vernacular-inspired designs lost favour among wealthy clients, who came to prefer more palatial country homes based on elaborate historical styles and formal plans. From the 1890s Emerson obtained fewer large-scale commissions offering scope for innovative treatment. With a number of small projects, however, he continued his evolution towards sparsely ornamented shingled buildings. One of his last important projects was Felsted, Deer Isle, ME (1896), a summer cottage for Frederick Law Olmsted. Located at an isolated site on a rocky promontory, it was formed somewhat like the stern of a ship resting on massive granite blocks. Designed in perfect harmony with its site, Felsted is a masterpiece of the Shingle style.

BIBLIOGRAPHY

V. J. Scully jr: *The Shingle Style and the Stick Style: Architectural Theory and Design from Downing to the Origins of Wright* (New Haven, 1955, rev. 1971)
C. Zaitzevsky: *The Architecture of William Ralph Emerson, 1833–1917* (Cambridge, MA, 1969)
R. G. Reed: *A Delight to All who Know it: The Maine Summer Architecture of William R. Emerson* (Augusta, ME, 1990)

ROGER G. REED

Emona. *See* LJUBLJANA.

Empire style. Term used to describe a French style of artistic production that lasted from the mid-18th century until *c.* 1840. The name derives from the first French Empire under Napoleon I (*see* BONAPARTE, (1)). The dates defining the period of the Empire historically (1804–14) and the duration of the style itself are at variance: the early phase, referred to by contemporaries as 'le goût antique', was a late form of Neo-classicism and became more developed as the chaos resulting from the French Revolution subsided *c.* 1796. The DIRECTOIRE STYLE and the CONSULATE STYLE—terms similarly derived from political periods in France—were both part of the development of the Empire style.

The term was originally applied to architecture, but because Napoleon rejected the building of new castles and palaces as wasteful, the style was especially used in interior design and decoration, later being extended to other decorative arts and fashion. There was strong conscious allusion to the civilization of ancient Rome through the building forms and motifs used by the first Roman emperors, who pursued goals of internal peace and a new order together with an expansionist military policy, as did Napoleon. Personal taste and comfort became of secondary importance to the demonstration of wealth and power. The Empire style spread throughout Europe and acquired fresh impetus with the Napoleonic conquests.

1. FORMULATION AND EARLY PHASE. The formulation of the style was the work of two architects, CHARLES PERCIER and PIERRE-FRANÇOIS-LÉONARD FONTAINE, and the first use of the term was linked directly with them (Delacluze, p. 400). Their refurbishment of the Hôtel de la Victoire, Paris (1797), Percier's designs for the redecoration of the house (1798) of the banker Récamier (see fig.) and their collaboration at the Château de Malmaison, the country residence of Napoleon and Josephine Bonaparte (1800–02; for illustration *see* FONTAINE, PIERRE-FRANÇOIS-LÉONARD) represented the decisive beginning of the Empire style. At Malmaison (*see* BONAPARTE, (3)) they had under their direction a team of craftsmen that included François-Honoré-Georges Jacob-Desmalter, Bernard Molitor, Pierre-Philippe Thomire, Jean Baptiste Claude Odiot and Martin-Guillaume Biennais, who subsequently adhered to the style (for illustration *see* PERCIER, CHARLES).

Architectonic structure and ornament were subordinate to a strict axial symmetry that united the ensemble and defined the hierarchy of its component parts. Conspicuously expensive and elaborately worked materials were combined with a massiveness of scale and a 'truth to materials' aesthetic. There was a clear distinction between the flat surfaces of the walls and furniture cases and the ornament applied to them, in terms of materials, colour and texture. Percier and Fontaine's album of designs, the 'bible of the Empire style', *Recueil de décorations intérieures comprenant tout ce qui a rapport à l'ameublement* (Paris, 1801), played a vital part in establishing the new decorative

Empire style bedchamber of Madame Récamier, as depicted in a watercolour sketch by Robert Smirke (ii), 1802 (London, Royal Institute of British Architects)

language, based on a repertory of antique forms (*see* FRANCE, fig. 59). They introduced the vogue for chaises longues with scrolled ends, X-framed stools, klismos chairs and the Egyptian throne-chair with lion monopode legs, as well as circular tripod stands and sarcophagus-shaped cabinets and wine coolers. They also set the fashion for walls, windows and beds draped or hung with plain or patterned silks or damasks, with seat furniture upholstered *en suite* to match (*see* FRANCE, §V, 4 and 5). Patterned wallpapers by such companies as Zuber & Cie became increasingly fashionable and often imitated the effect of draped fabrics (*see* WALLPAPER, fig. 3). Symbols of majesty and abundance were fully exploited in furniture, ceramics (*see* SÈVRES PORCELAIN FACTORY), metalwork (*see* FRANCE, §IX, 1(iv)), textiles and wallpaper; motifs included eagles, swans, cornucopias, fasces of arms, winged torches and such Napoleonic motifs as bees and large Ns within laurel wreaths. The arms and front legs of chairs were often decorated with carved and gilded wood or cast-bronze figures of caryatids or terms, winged griffins or sphinxes. Sofas of huge proportions were placed against walls; important suites of sofas and chairs were upholstered in satin-silk woven in Lyon or in tapestry (e.g. side chair upholstered in Beauvais tapestry, 1804; Malmaison, Château N.). The *méridienne*, a sparsely upholstered day bed with curled, upturned ends, became fashionable for ladies' boudoirs and was popularized by David's portrait of *Madame Récamier* (1800; Paris, Louvre). Other popular furniture types were the *athénienne*, a tripod-based stand for holding wash-basins or jardinières (e.g. *c.* 1804–10; New York, Met.), and the *psyché*, a free-standing mirror in an ornate frame, probably introduced by Percier. *Lits bateaux* were moved from their traditional position at right angles to walls or in alcoves and positioned with their long sides against the wall, surmounted with tentlike draperies of silk and muslin. The commode was increasingly used as bedroom furniture, while circular pedestal tables, console tables and secrétaires graced drawing-rooms.

2. SUBSEQUENT DEVELOPMENT. As the Empire style developed it moved away from the lively, linear use of grotesque ornament that typified the period around 1800. From 1804–5 the overall architectonic forms became heavier, and ornament became increasingly simple and subordinated to the display of luxurious materials: 'she [Josephine] no longer wants chimaera, lions' heads and gilded arabesques . . . she wants a new, completely smooth mahogany dressing-table, . . . a piece of furniture in solid gold would cost no less' (St Hilaire, 1831).

The style was disseminated throughout Europe in the imperial palaces, for example the salons of the Casa del Labrador at the Aranjuez Palace, Spain (1805; *in situ*), the Royal Palace, Amsterdam (1808; *in situ*), and the restoration of the palace at Laeken, near Brussels (*in situ*). Such students of Percier and Fontaine as Louis Joseph Adrien Roelandt adhered to the strict Empire style in their own projects (e.g. auditorium for Ghent University, 1826). Important decorative schemes in France included the Caryatid Rooms at the Tuileries (destr. 1870) and those at the châteaux of Fontainebleau and Compiègne (1806), the Grand Trianon and the Hôtel de Rambouillet. It was popularized by such journals as *Meubles et objets de goût*

(Paris, 1802–35), *Journal des Luxus und Moden* (Weimar, 1793–1810) and *Konst och Nyhetmagazin* (Stockholm, 1818–). In America, the cabinetmaker DUNCAN PHYFE was producing furniture with Empire details in 1808 and subsequently produced suites of furniture in the Empire style that *c.* 1815 followed the American Federal style.

However, the dominance of the established, academically based repertory of forms propagated by Percier and Fontaine meant that there was little evolution in the Empire style, and it is often impossible to use formal stylistic criteria as a basis for deciding the date of a work of art from the first decades of the 19th century. Even from the beginning, this canon of official good taste resulted in the creation of subsidiary styles such as the Troubadour style, the 'goût turc' and, most important of all, the Egyptian style (*see* EGYPTIAN REVIVAL). As the industrial revolution got under way, craftsmen trained over a long period were drawn into the growing number of factories, where they continued to work to the high standards obtaining for luxury goods under the *ancien régime*. Only as the craft-trained older generation gradually left the factories was there a clear and noticeable decline in quality.

BIBLIOGRAPHY

M. de St Hilaire: *Les Petits Appartements des Tuileries, de Saint-Cloud et de la Malmaison*, vol 2 (Paris, 1831), p. 35
E. Delacluze: *Louis David: Son école et son temps* (Paris, 1855)
F. Benoit: *L'Art français sous la Révolution et l'Empire* (1897)
P. Lafond: *L'Art décoratif et le mobilier sous la République et l'Empire* (Paris, 1900)
J. Vacquier: *Le Style Empire*, 2 vols (Paris, 1912)
W. Hessling: *Style Empire: Meubles et intérieurs* (Paris, 1913)
M. von Boehn: *Das Empire: Die Zeit, das Leben, der Stil* (Berlin, 1925)
P. Marmottan: *Le Style Empire*, 3 vols (Paris, 1925–30)
E. Bourgeois: *Le Style Empire: Son origine, ses caractères* (Paris, 1930)
P. Lavedan: 'Napoléon I, urbaniste', *Histoire de l'urbanisme*, iii (Paris, 1952)
L. Hautecoeur: *Histoire de l'architecture classique en France*, v of *Révolution et Empire, 1793–1815* (Paris, 1953)
G. Hubert: *La Sculpture dans l'Italie napoléonienne* (Paris, 1964)
S. Grandjean: *Empire Furniture, 1800–1825* (London, 1965)
G. Jannear: *L'Empire* (Paris, 1965)
H. Honour: *Neo-classicism* (Harmondsworth, 1968, rev. 1977)
W. Becker: *Paris und die deutsche Malerei, 1750–1840* (Munich, 1971)
C. Isermayer: *Empire* (Munich, 1977)

HANS OTTOMEYER

Empoli, Jacopo da [Chimenti, Jacopo] (*b* Florence, 30 April 1551; *d* Florence, 30 Sept 1640). Italian painter and draughtsman. He lived and worked in Florence all his life, and he followed Santi di Tito in the return to the clarity of the Florentine High Renaissance. He absorbed the ideas of his more innovative contemporaries and became one of the most popular painters of altarpieces for churches in Florence and Tuscany. He was also a distinguished still-life painter and received many commissions from private patrons, among them the Medici. Empoli's painting is distinguished by simple, lucid forms, strong colour and direct and clear interpretation of the subject.

1. Life and work. 2. Working methods and technique. 3. Critical reception.

1. LIFE AND WORK.

(i) Training and early works, to 1600. He was the son of Chimenti di Girolamo, a cloth merchant, and of Alessandra Tatti, the daughter of the sculptor Jacopo Sansovino. He

trained under the Mannerist painter Maso da San Friano. The *Adoration of the Shepherds* (Plymouth, City Mus. & A.G.) is one of a small number of paintings attributed to his earliest years (Bianchini, 1980). The two framing figures and the hooded shepherd on the left echo Maso's style, while the full, sharply modelled forms suggest that Empoli had studied the art of Giorgio Vasari. However, these sources are modified by Empoli's greater naturalism, and the ruined hut, the simple, devout shepherds and demure little angels recall the accessible and direct religious paintings of Santi di Tito. In the *Virgin in Glory between SS Ivo and Luke* (1579; Paris, Louvre), the first work securely attributed to Empoli, the softer yet more monumental forms show the artist moving away from his teacher's influence, though the lively little angels and some of the faces, such as the woman's profile on the right, still recall Maso da San Friano. Like Santi di Tito, he was both returning to the naturalism of late 15th-century Florentine art, with its emphasis on drawing from life, and inspired by the classicism of the early 16th-century Florentine tradition. He studied ceaselessly from the art of Fra Bartolommeo, Andrea del Sarto and Jacopo Pontormo. Cardinal Carlo de' Medici commissioned him to make a copy (untraced) of Fra Bartolommeo's *Resurrection of Christ* (Florence, Pitti). Empoli paid particular attention to the work of Andrea del Sarto and made copies (untraced) of his famous frescoes in the atrium of SS Annunziata. But he felt the closest affinity with Pontormo and copied many of his works, of which the only ones remaining (Florence, Certosa del Galluzzo, Pin.) are of Pontormo's five frescoes of scenes from the *Passion* (1523–4) in the Certosa del Galluzzo. Through such studies Empoli formed his own 'firm style, with fine drawing, without errors, with excellent drapery, good facial expression, and sometimes also very good use of colour' (Baldinucci, p. 12).

In the last quarter of the 16th century the influence of Venetian art spread to Florence, mainly through the Veronese artist Jacopo Ligozzi and through Domenico Passignano. From the beginning of the 1590s these trends were encouraged by the art of Lodovico Cigoli and of Gregorio Pagani. Florentine painters developed a freer, more painterly technique and a more sensitive treatment of light and shade. The *Immaculate Conception* (1591; Florence, S Remigio), with its dramatically foreshortened figures, enveloped in radiant light, reveals Empoli's response to this new influence. Yet, although the effects of light are Venetian, in other respects the painting remains within a Florentine tradition. The arrangement of the figures around the Virgin recalls Vasari and Federico Zuccaro, while the startling three-dimensionality of the figures against the light is reminiscent of Agnolo Bronzino's frescoes in the chapel of Eleonora di Toledo in the Palazzo Vecchio. Empoli's study of Bronzino, though undocumented, was undoubtedly intensive, for his drawing, his analysis of form and his approach to his subject-matter became increasingly lucid. This aspect of his art, which nonetheless remained indebted to his earlier sources, found its fullest expression in *Our Lady of Help* (1593; Florence, Pitti), which reveals an interest in Raphael, and in the works painted towards the end of the 16th century, such as the *Assumption of the Virgin* (Florence,

1. Jacopo da Empoli: *Susanna Bathing*, oil on canvas, 2.29×1.72 m, 1600 (Vienna, Kunsthistorisches Museum)

SS Annunziata), the *Annunciation* (1599; Pontedera Cathedral), the *Stigmatization of St Francis* (Florence, Convento dei Cappuccini di Montughi) and *Susanna Bathing* (1600; Vienna, Ksthist. Mus.; see fig. 1). The *Susanna*, one of Empoli's most beautiful and famous paintings, still evokes the art of the early 16th century, yet the emphasis on objects carefully selected and lucidly described looks forward to the art of Orazio Gentileschi.

(ii) Mature and late works, 1600–40. Between 1600 and 1610 Empoli painted a series of large canvases for churches in Florence and elsewhere in Tuscany. These are noble works, executed in confident style in which it is no longer possible to identify the stylistic sources. The series includes the *Annunciation* (1603; Florence, Santa Trìnita, Strozzi Chapel), where the patch of sky surrounding the angel and breaking through the walls of the cell looks forward to the Baroque; the *Presentation in the Temple* (1604; ex-Empoli, Collegiata; destr. World War II); the *Healing of the Cripple* (1605; Florence, SS Annunziata, Brunaccini Chapel); the *Delivery of the Keys to St Peter* (1607; Florence, Santa Trinita, Usimbardi Chapel); and *St John the Baptist Preaching* (1608; Florence, S Niccolo sopr'Arno, Gianni Chapel). These imposing works are distinguished not only by the dignity and nobility of the figures but also by the spatial clarity, the new emphasis on landscape and the lively realism of expression and costume. The colours are bright and strong, and the forms modelled by a clear light.

After 1610 Empoli's work shows signs of contact with the rich, florid painting introduced into Florentine circles by the pupils of Cigoli and Pagani, among them Cristofano Allori, Giovanni Biliverti and Matteo Rosselli. This new influence appears in *St Carlo and the Rospigliosi Family* (1613; Pistoia, S Domenico) and *St Eligius the Goldsmith* (1614; Florence, Uffizi) painted for the goldsmiths' and silversmiths' guild. In these canvases there are more ample forms, a richer brushwork, more spacious settings and compositions, and more sumptuous costumes and accoutrements, derived from Matteo Rosselli. Empoli's most important works date from 1610–20. They include the *Calling of St Peter* (Impruneta, S Maria dell'Impruneta), which retains the classic clarity and balance of his early works, *St Ivo, Protector of Orphans* (1616; Florence, Pitti; see fig. 2), which has always been considered Empoli's masterpiece, and the *Baptism* (1620; Pisa, S Francesco). In the same period Empoli also painted secular works, including *Michelangelo Presenting the Plans for S Lorenzo to Pope Leo X* (1617–19) for the Casa Buonarroti, Florence (*in situ*), which is close to works by Tuscan Caravaggisti.

Few works can be dated to Empoli's final years, in which his pace of work seems to have slowed. Between 1621 and 1625 he painted still-lifes, of which about ten are known. These include two *Kitchen Scenes* (both Florence, Pitti), one dated 1621, the other 1624; a *Larder with Hare, Game and Pig's Head* (Bergamo, priv. col.; see 1986–7 exh. cat., i, p. 133) and a pair of still-lifes in the Molinari–Pradelli collection in Bologna; *Larder with Fruit, Vegetables and Ham* (1625; see 1986–7 exh. cat., i, p. 135) and its pendant, *Larder with Vegetables, Eggs and Fish* (see

1986–7 exh. cat., i, p. 136). In all of these works the abundant still-life objects are arranged parallel to the picture plane in clear and lucid compositions, whose severity recalls contemporary still-lifes by Alejandro de Loarte. These paintings have always surprised critics because of their divergence from the dominant trends of contemporary Florentine painting. They may have been painted purely for Empoli's own amusement, yet they were widely influential.

In 1628 Empoli painted the *Virgin in Glory with Saints* (Florence, SS Annunziata, del Palagio Chapel) and the *Nativity* (Florence, S Michele Visdomini). The latter work seems to be a résumé of all Empoli's art: the figure of the Virgin recalls his early contacts with Santi di Tito, the shepherds derive from Cigoli, while the ample forms and richly textured fabrics are indebted to more recent influences. In his last decade Empoli painted two versions of the *Creation of Adam* (1632; Florence, Depositi Gal., 1633; priv. col.). The *Virgin Presenting the Child to St Francis* (after 1633; Florence, S Gaetano, Franceschi Chapel) may be considered his last work. By then he was almost completely inactive and was forced to sell his numerous drawings in order to live.

2. WORKING METHODS AND TECHNIQUE. Empoli found in drawing a congenial form of expression and drew constantly from life. A justly famous group of drawings in pen and black chalk, among them the *Young Man Viewed from Behind* (Florence, Uffizi) and the *Lute Player* (Amsterdam, Rijksmus.), show young men in contemporary costumes drawing, writing and making music. They recall a 15th-century tradition of drawing from nature and may have been stimulated by Maso Finiguerra's drawings.

Sketches recording Empoli's first conception of a composition are rare, for he translated his ideas into images only after fully elaborating them in his mind and after a repeated study of every figure and detail. Most of his drawings are related to paintings and consist of studies of the human figure, nude, clothed or draped, each with its pose and gestures on a separate sheet. A good example is the *Study for the Figure of Isaac* (Rome, Gab. N. Stampe), a careful drawing from the live model, with details of drapery, feet and hands on the same sheet. It was for this type of drawing that he used the tinted papers for which he has become well known, thus emphasizing the significance he attached to them. He learnt the use of tinted papers from 15th-century artists, and from Maso da San Friano and Alessandro Allori, but transformed the practice into a highly individual and personal technique. He preferred rather dark colours, such as an almost ultramarine blue, golden-yellow, dark red, brown, dark grey and green, and laid these colours on white paper with great care, using long vertical brushstrokes that let the light background show through here and there. On these prepared papers he generally drew with a very soft black pencil, almost charcoal, adding highlights with white chalk to obtain a suggestive effect of tone on tone. The *Handmaiden Kneeling* (Florence, Bib. Marucelliana), a preparatory study for *Susanna Bathing*, is a celebrated example.

After carefully studying the single details, Empoli made a series of compositional studies, continuing to make these even after he had established the final form. These

2. Jacopo da Empoli: *St Ivo, Protector of Orphans*, oil on panel, 2.91×2.15 m, 1616 (Florence, Palazzo Pitti, Galleria Palatina)

drawings are distinguished by a confidence and felicity that have few rivals even in the rich field of Florentine drawing. For his sketches of the entire composition, such as the *Annunciation* (Florence, Uffizi), he normally used pen and watercolour. In most cases these were modelli intended to be shown to the client. The precise definition of the details and the frequent squaring of the paper suggests that Empoli proceeded directly to the full-scale cartoon and the painting. Most of Empoli's voluminous legacy of drawings (*c.* 400 sheets) is in the Gabinetto dei Disegni, Uffizi, Florence. This collection probably comes in part from that of Leopoldo de' Medici, who assisted the painter when he was old and poor by purchasing many of his drawings.

3. CRITICAL RECEPTION. The oldest and most authoritative source of information on Empoli's work is the ample and vivid life of the painter included by Filippo Baldinucci in his *Notizie de' professori del disegno* (1681–1728). All later criticism has been heavily influenced by this source. Throughout the 18th and 19th centuries Baldinucci's biography was repeated fragmentarily and slavishly, with its anecdotes, its precise list of works and even its critical evaluation of the artist. Only in the 20th century has there been a renewal of interest in the Florentine painting of the late 16th century and early 17th. As a result Empoli's work has been studied afresh. The first complete 20th-century study of Empoli was the well-informed essay (1933) by Simonetta De Vries. No less important were the various articles that appeared in dictionaries and periodicals, especially in relation to exhibitions. Bianchini's unpublished thesis (1962) on Empoli has been summarized by the author in an article (1980), and this is the fullest and most up-to-date study of the artist.

BIBLIOGRAPHY

Thieme–Becker

F. Baldinucci: *Notizie* (1681–1728); ed. F. Ranalli (1845–7), iii, pp. 5–18
O. H. Giglioli: 'Un quadro dell'Empoli per la chiesa di San Felice e la sua storia', *Riv. A.*, x (1917–18), pp. 107–17
S. De Vries: 'Jacopo Chimenti da Empoli', *Riv. A.*, xv (1933), pp. 329–98
P. Bacci: '*L'Annunciazione* e *L'Eterno Padre* dipinti dall'Empoli nel 1614 per Sant'Agostino di Massa Marittima', *Riv. A.*, xxii (1940), pp. 108–18
S. Bottari: 'Due nature morte dell'Empoli', *A. Ant. & Mod.*, 3 (1960), pp. 75–6
G. Delogu: 'Nature morte dell'Empoli', *Emporium*, cxxxi (1960), pp. 195–8
M. A. Bianchini: *Jacopo da Empoli* (diss., Florence, U. Studi, 1962)
Disegni di Jacopo da Empoli (exh. cat. by A. Forlani, Florence, Uffizi, 1962)
U. Procacci: *La Casa Buonarroti a Firenze* (Milan, 1965)
A. W. Vliegenthart: *De Galleria Buonarroti: Michelangelo en Michelangelo il Giovane* (Rotterdam, 1969)
Feste e apparati medicei da Cosimo I a Cosimo II (exh. cat. by G. Gaeta Bertelà and A. M. Petrioli Tofani, Florence, Uffizi, 1969)
Disegni fiorentini (1560–1640) dalle collezioni del Gabinetto Nazionale delle Stampe (exh. cat. by S. Prosperi Valenti Rodinò, Rome, Villa Farnesina, 1977)
Painting in Florence, 1600–1700 (exh. cat. by C. McCorquodale, London, R.A., 1979), pp. 26–30
M. A. Bianchini: 'Jacopo da Empoli', *Paradigma*, iii (1980), pp. 91–146 [fullest study]
Firenze e la Toscana dei Medici nell'Europa del cinquecento: Il primato del disegno (exh. cat., ed. A. Forlani Tempesti; Florence, Pal. Strozzi, 1980), pp. 112–16
S. Neuburger: 'Paggi, Passignano oder Empoli: Ein Konkurrenzentwurf zum *Paradies* in San Remigio in Florenz', *Mitt. Ksthist. Inst. Florenz*, xxv/3 (1981), pp. 383–90
Dessins baroques florentins du Musée du Louvre (exh. cat. by C. Monbeig Goguel and F. Viatte, Paris, Louvre, 1981–2)
G. Cantelli: *Repertorio della pittura fiorentina del seicento* (Florence, 1983)
M. Chiarini: 'Jacopo da Empoli: Un soggetto mitologico', *Ant. Viva*, xxiv (1985), pp. 67–9
Il seicento fiorentino, 3 vols (exh. cat., Florence, Pal. Strozzi, 1986–7), i, pp. 21–5

ELENA TESTAFERRATA

Emporiae [Gr. Emporion; now Ampurias]. City on the Gulf of Rosas on the Catalan coast of Spain, founded in the 6th century BC by Greek settlers from the Phokaian colony of Massalia (Marseille). The site may have been occupied earlier by the native Indiketes, but the only evidence is furnished by graves at Parralli and Muralli. The first Greek settlement was on a small island off the coast now covered by the village of San Martín. Early excavators claimed to have found architectural remains on its beach, but these have vanished. The 4th-century AD antiquary Avienus, however, mentioned that there was both a city and a temple on the island, and a section of an Archaic frieze showing two opposed sphinxes (Ampurias, Mus. Monográf. Excav.) may come from the temple. By the time the Romans occupied the region in 218 BC, a new city, Neapolis, had been established on the mainland. This may have been the *dipolis* ('double city') referred to by ancient authors, indicating a native quarter. The small city was surrounded on its inland side by a cyclopean wall. The numerous finds of Greek pottery at the nearby native town of Ullastret clearly indicate an association between native and colonial settlements. Buildings at Emporiae included a sacred precinct (mid-1st century BC) with temples to Serapis and Asklepios, the latter containing a fine cult statue (3rd century BC; Barcelona, Mus. Arqueol.). There was probably also a temple to Artemis of Ephesos, whose cult the Phokaians had brought with them from Asia Minor. Remains of an agora, a stoa and several houses have also been found.

The arrival of the Romans did not end Greek influence in the region. The development of Neapolis shows the influences of Hellenistic urban design, while emblemata-type mosaics in *opus vermiculatum* (in which the tesserae follow the flowing lines of the shapes) depicting such subjects as the *Sacrifice of Iphigenia* were imported, perhaps from south Italy, as late as the 1st century BC. Under Roman rule the settlement expanded, and an upper city was developed during the 1st century BC. This area had its own walls, outside which stood the amphitheatre. The upper city was laid out on a grid plan dominated by a forum–temple complex with a basilica and tabernae. During the 1st century AD large houses were constructed in blocks around the forum. They included one with Third Style wall paintings (*c.* 15 BC–AD 62) and another containing marble portraits (Ampurias, Mus. Monográf. Excav.) of the 1st century AD. Other important finds from the city are a bronze portrait head of a woman (*c.* AD 69–*c.* 96) and a small marble torso of a nude *Aphrodite* (Hellenistic; both Barcelona, Mus. Arqueol.). Never important during the Roman period, Emporiae began to decline after the Germanic invasions of the 3rd century AD, although a basilica was built in the lower city in Early Christian times.

BIBLIOGRAPHY

J. Puig i Cadafalch: 'Les excavacions d'Empuries', *Anu. Inst. Estud. Catalans* (1908), pp. 150–94

——: 'Els temples d'Empuries', *Anu. Inst. Estud. Catalans* (1911–12), pp. 3–22

E. Ripoll i Perelló: *Ampurias: Guía itineraria*, 7th edn (Barcelona, 1982)

J. Aquilué Abadias and others: *El fórum romà d'Empuries: Excavacions de l'any 1982* (Barcelona, 1984)

R. J. Harrison: *Spain at the Dawn of History: Iberians, Phoenicians and Greeks* (London, 1988)

S. J. Keay: *Roman Spain* (London and Berkeley, 1988)

WILLIAM E. MIERSE

Emporio. *See* EMBORIO.

Emulsion. Apparently homogeneous mixture made up of two distinct liquid substances that would not normally mix, one existing in the form of finely divided particles, suspended in and surrounded by a continuous phase of the other. Naturally occurring emulsions include egg and milk, both of which are composed of fats and water. Invariably, an emulsifying agent is also present, either occurring naturally or specifically introduced. This acts on the interface between the two substances, allowing them to co-exist without repelling each other. The small size of the dispersed particles and the characteristics of the film formed around their surfaces prevent their coming together when a stable emulsion is formed. In egg, for example, lecithin, present mostly in the yolk, acts as an emulsifying agent for the oils, fats and water that the yolk contains. The gelatinous colloids present in solutions of various natural gums and glues with water are also effective emulsifying agents, and any of these substances will emulsify drying oils into mixtures that can be thinned with water. Alkalis and compounds derived from them also act as emulsifying agents, soap being a simple example.

Emulsions do not form spontaneously: the ingredients must be stirred or shaken vigorously to break down the particle size and achieve an even distribution of one liquid throughout the other. The surrounding liquid (the external phase) will determine how the emulsion behaves. The practical value of an emulsion usually lies in its combination of the properties of each parent liquid in a single medium. In an emulsion of glue size and oil, for example, the size contributes fast drying and ease of use, with water used as thinner, while the oil imparts a degree of water-resistance and flexibility to the film formed as the emulsion dries out. The term 'emulsion' may also be used to describe the dried film, and the term 'emulsifying agent' is sometimes loosely applied to any substance performing a stabilizing function.

Egg tempera painting employs a natural emulsion (*see* TEMPERA) and may be distinguished from other emulsions manufactured specifically for painting. Evidence of the use of these before the 19th century is scarce. Modern scientific analysis of paint media, however, has supported the traditionally held view that tempera and oil paint were sometimes used together in the same work, particularly during a transitional period in the 15th century but quite possibly extending from before that date until perhaps as late as the mid-17th century. Egg and oil are occasionally detected in the same sample dating from this time, but more often they are found separately, and at best it can be tentatively supposed that slight modifications of egg tempera with oil were not unusual. Whether this was an established practice or merely an experimental response to the increasing dominance of oil painting is difficult to determine. In the 19th century Charles Lock Eastlake also quoted two recipes for the preparation of wax and size emulsions involving the use of alkali; he suggested that these recipes were invented in the Middle Ages, though the documents in which they originally appear are not that old. In any event, they illustrate the use of relatively sophisticated emulsions at an early date, and it seems almost inconceivable that the painters of the time should not also have been acquainted with the possibilities of other, more easily formed emulsions involving drying oil and the tempera media of egg, glue and gum.

Despite evidence of their use in the late medieval period, subsequent records of emulsions in painting did not occur until the mid-16th century, when Vasari referred to a canvas priming made of flour paste, oil and white lead. Similar recipes were given in the 17th century by Francisco Pacheco and at the beginning of the 18th century by Antonio Palomino. A starch paste is convenient for filling the pores of a loosely woven canvas, but it is evident from Vasari's descriptions that the flexibility introduced by the addition of oil was also important. The use of emulsion grounds (*see* GROUND) was not confined to Italy and Spain: they occur also beneath paintings by Rembrandt and Vermeer, though the composition varies. An animal glue and resin binder was used in the ground of Rembrandt's *Feast of Belshazzar* (*c.* 1635; London, N.G.); that of Vermeer's *Guitar Player* (*c.* 1672; London, Kenwood House) is bound with a glue size and oil emulsion.

In the 19th century the rediscovery of tempera painting led to many fanciful experiments with emulsion paints (*see* PAINT, §I) by such artists as Arnold Böcklin; this trend, also promoted through the technical writings of Max Doerner (1870–1939), influenced artists well into the 20th century. Emulsion paints were also employed as household and industrial paints, and the technology of their commercial manufacture may well have influenced the artists' colour trade of the time. Egg and oil emulsion tempera paints were probably available in tubes from the late 19th century.

In the late 20th century emulsions were represented by acrylic paints (*see* ACRYLIC PAINTING, §1) and the acrylic and PVA media that are used as glues in various arts and crafts. Aqueous emulsion acrylics were first introduced in the 1950s and became available as artists' materials soon afterwards. The Pop artists of the early 1960s, including David Hockney and Andy Warhol, were among the first to adopt them. Although technically emulsions, acrylic paints are unrelated to the other types of emulsions discussed and represent more advanced technology. The light-sensitive coatings used in photography are also known as emulsions and are based on particles of silver bromide or other photosensitive chemicals dispersed within a matrix of pure gelatine. The 'compo' used in decorative arts from the 18th century can also be identified as an emulsion. The usual formula combined animal glue, boiled oil and resin, which was then packed with powdered chalk to make a dough-like substance that could be pressed into moulds.

BIBLIOGRAPHY

G. Vasari: *Vite* (1550, rev. 2/1568); ed. G. Milanesi (1878–85), intro. trans. by L. S. Maclehose as *Vasari on Technique* (London, 1907, rev. New York, 1960)

C. L. Eastlake: *Methods and Materials of the Great Schools and Masters*, 2 vols (London, 1847/R New York, 1960)

M. Doerner: *Malmaterial und seine Verwendung im Bilde* (Stuttgart, 1933); Eng. trans. by E. Neuhaus as *The Materials of the Artist* (London, 1934/R 1979)

R. J. Gettens and G. L. Stout: *Painting Materials: A Short Encyclopaedia* (New York, 1965)

N.G. Tech. Bull. (1977–)

Z. Veliz, ed. and trans.: *Artists' Techniques in Golden Age Spain* (Cambridge, 1986)

J. Stephenson: *The Materials and Techniques of Painting* (London, 1989)

JONATHAN STEPHENSON

En. School of Japanese sculpture that flourished during the 12th century. It was founded by and named after Ensei (*d* 1134) and was one of the two major schools of Japanese Buddhist sculpture of the later Heian period (794–1185), the other being the IN school (*see also* JAPAN, §V, 3(iii)(c)). Ensei was a pupil of Chōsei (*d* 1091), the chief disciple of JŌCHŌ, who had developed a refined, elegant style that satisfied both the secular and spiritual pretensions of the 11th-century aristocracy. Sculptors of both the En and In schools were patronized by the most influential figures of the capital of Heian (now Kyoto), at whose behest they rejected innovation in favour of close replication of the formal qualities of Jōchō's imagery. They worked mainly in wood. Ensei's only surviving work is a seated *Healing Buddha* (Jap. Yakushi, Skt Bhaishjyaguru; 1103, Kyoto, Ninnaji). The details of his numerous commissions, however, are known from records. Ensei seems to have favoured a highly detailed style. He was succeeded by his sons Chōen (*d* 1150) and Ken'en (*fl* 1114–50), who received many commissions from the retired emperors GoShirakawa (*reg* 1072–86) and GoToba (*reg* 1107–23). Ken'en's most famous commission, a *Seated Amida* (Skt Amitābha; Buddha of the Western Paradise) (destr.) was executed for GoToba in 1136 and was reputed to be an exact copy of Jōchō's *Amida* in the Hōōdō (Phoenix Hall) of the Byōdōin (*see* JAPAN, fig. 61). Other sculptors of the En school include Myōen (*d* 1200), who participated in the restoration of the temples of Tōdaiji and Kōfukuji in Nara (*see* NARA, §III, 4 and 7), after they were burnt during the Taira–Minamoto War.

BIBLIOGRAPHY

Kodansha Enc. Japan

SAMUEL C. MORSE

Enamel. Vitreous or glass paste used in a variety of ways to decorate a metal or, more rarely, ceramic surface. The word 'enamel' is of obscure origin. It probably derives from *smelzan* (Old High Ger.: 'to smelt') and *esmail* (Old Fr.). The Greek philosopher Philostratos Lemnios wrote that 'barbarians. . .pour these colours into bronze moulds, so that the colours become hard as stone' (*Imagines* I. xxviii); the 'colour' probably refers to molten glass. This may have been a description of a process which was not enamelling but its precursor. The art of enamelling was a logical progression in the artistic alliance between the goldsmith and the glassworker. During the 15th century BC in Egypt coloured, cut-glass pieces were decoratively embedded into gold *cloisons* (cells); the inclusion of molten glass may have been a later refinement of the Greeks and the Celts.

1. Materials. 2. Techniques. 3. Conservation.

1. MATERIALS. The enamelling process is the fusing of a vitreous substance on to a prepared metal surface, either in a kiln (furnace) or with the application of intense local heat (e.g. with a blowtorch), at temperatures ranging from 300°C for the softest (opaque) enamels to 850°C for the hardest (transparent) enamels. The vitreous compound is itself called enamel, but it is the bipartite, heat-bonded combination of often noble metal with it that is referred to as enamel.

The vitreous substance is composed of sand or flint, soda or potash and sometimes red lead. These ingredients are heated together (fritted) for 15 hours to form an almost colourless transparent flux. Metallic oxides are added to the mixture to produce the colours. The first known true enamel, found in small quantities on Greek gold jewellery (4th century BC), was blue, made by the addition of cobalt oxide. Copper oxide gives turquoise and some greens; gold oxide gives red and oxides of antimony or uranium give yellow. Different quantities of ingredients produce enamels that are 'soft' or 'hard': soft enamel, containing a higher proportion of red lead, fuses at a lower temperature but can be scratched easily. Transparent and translucent enamels fuse at the highest temperature and are the most durable; all enamels, however, are damaged by shock, scratching and flexing. Variations in the combination of ingredients or of additives result in the four accepted categories of enamel: opaque, opalescent, translucent and painted transparent, terms that indicate their fired visual and physical state.

The metal base to which enamel is fused was historically noble (i.e. gold or silver). Platinum is rarely used, except in a 5% alloy in platinum-silver. In its pure state, even keyed, platinum shows poor adherence to enamel. This is due to its extremely high melting point (1630°C) and rapid rates of expansion and contraction. Copper was increasingly used as a base from the 1740s. It became particularly fashionable in England at the Battersea Enamel Factory, London (est. 1753), which produced wares including enamelled snuffboxes and wine-labels. Such alloys as bronze have also been extensively used.

Before the addition of enamel, the metal surface is prepared to remove oxides or grease: it is annealed (heated to red hot) and then immersed in an acid bath (pickled). The acid, which is usually diluted, may be nitric (undiluted), for copper, or sulphuric, for gold or silver. The metal is then alkalized and the powdered enamel applied as soon as possible to arrest renewed oxidation. Pure gold does not oxidize, hence its popularity as a metal base. As some colours react chemically with certain metals during firing, the metal is often first coated with a flux.

The enamel is ground to a fine powder from the frit by pulverization, washed under water and then dried. It is then mixed to a paste with water or, for painted enamel, a volatile oil such as spike (lavender oil) and applied to the prepared metal surface, which may also have been worked (etched, engraved, modelled, formed and soldered) and finally fired. Enamel fuses at a lower temperature than the metals to which it is applied, although *grand feu* colours (those that have a melting point of *c.* 850°C) approach the melting point of silver. Due to the different expansion co-efficients of glass and metal (metal contracts at a faster rate than the enamel), fired objects are subject to enormous stresses on cooling. To counteract the buckling and cracking, the metal 'back' is counter-enamelled with a layer of flux of equal thickness to the surface enamel, which minimizes the problem.

2. TECHNIQUES.

(i) Cloisonné [Fr.: 'cell-work']. A metal surface, usually of finely beaten gold, is decorated by soldering, edge-on, metal fillets of flattened wire. These delicate cells (*cloisons*) are filled with coloured and powdered enamel, fired and then ground flat with carborundum, exposing the gold pattern beneath. *Cloisons* mimic jewels, create rigidity and also break the surface of the item; it is very difficult to enamel a large surface (*en plein*) evenly. Byzantine enamels, developed from Greek antecedents, were generally cloisonné (*see* EARLY CHRISTIAN AND BYZANTINE ART, §VII, 7(ii)). From the 9th to the 12th century AD precious cloisonné enamelling, as seen in the Pala d'Oro altarpiece (AD 976; present setting 1342–5; Venice, S Marco; *see* VENICE, fig. 20), was extensively used. In the later Middle Ages, the technique was also referred to as *email de plique.* Historically, both opaque and translucent enamels have

been used for cloisonné. In China the technique was introduced during the Yuan period (1279–1368) by Islamic artisans (*see* CHINA, §XIII, 6; *see also* colour pl. III, fig. 2); in India the technique was well established by the 16th century, although no extant objects predate *c.* 1600 (*see* INDIAN SUBCONTINENT, §VIII, 15(iv)); early Islamic cloisonné enamelling was possibly inspired by Byzantine enamelling and was used from the 10th to the 15th century and again in the 18th and 19th centuries (*see* ISLAMIC ART, §VIII, 3). In Russia the earliest enamels date from the 11th to the 12th century and were influenced by Byzantine enamels. From the 16th century fine, twisted gold or silver wire filigree *cloisons* were used to produce an effect resembling complex indigenous embroidery (*see* RUSSIA, §X, 1).

(ii) Champlevé [Fr.: 'raised field']. This is a potentially economical alternative to cloisonné enamelling and is therefore often used on larger objects. Into a thicker metal base—which can be gold but is more often bronze—troughs are gouged, or in modern champlevé, of which Surrey enamel (*see* §(viii) below) is a precursor, cast. The depressions are then filled with powdered enamel, which is fired, and the surface ground flat. In champlevé the metal areas are left plain, engraved, gilded or decorated in other ways, including cloisonné enamel. In Gothic and Chinese champlevé enamelling, the surface metal is generally mercury or fire gilded. Romano-Celtic artists also

1. Dunstable Swan Jewel, opaque white enamel used *en ronde bosse* over gold, h. 32 mm, English or French, *c.* 1400 (London, British Museum)

2. Goblet with *plique à jour* enamelling, designed by Torolf Prytz and made by Emil Saether, h. 325 mm, Norwegian, 1900 (Oslo, Kunstindustrimuseum)

Royal Gold Cup of the Kings of France and England (*c.* 1380–90; London, BM; see colour pl. III, fig. 1). The Russian goldsmith CARL FABERGÉ developed a method of 'water-marking' precious metals by engraving them with repetitive wavelike patterns, known as *guilloché*, on a rose-engine lathe. Translucent enamels were then applied over the decorated surface (see colour pl. IV, fig. 3).

(iv) En ronde bosse [Fr.: 'in rounded relief'; encrusted enamel]. In France at the end of the 14th century it became possible to decorate three-dimensional objects or very high-relief surfaces with an enamel covering. The objects were often small but precious, as in such Gothic emblems as the Dunstable Swan Jewel (*c.* 1400; London, BM; see fig. 1 and ENGLAND, §I, 9(i)(a)), or the exquisite Goldenes Rössel (1403–4; Altötting, SS Philipp und Jacob, Schatzkam.; *see* GOTHIC, fig. 95), the most lavish of all *en ronde bosse* enamels. Technical difficulties necessitated keying (roughing) the metal in order to support the enamel covering. There were also problems achieving naturalistic flesh tones, as seen in the figure of the *Virgin* in the house-altar of Albert V, Duke of Bavaria (1573–4; Munich, Residenz), in which the gold and polychrome work contrasts with the glaring, milky-pink skin tones.

(v) Plique à jour [Fr.: 'against the light']. In the late 14th century, under the patronage of the courts of France and

3. Pendant with *en résille sur verre* enamelling, *Adoring Shepherds*, attributed to Valentin Sezenius, 68×42 mm, Paris or Prague, *c.* 1620 (London, Wallace Collection)

filled some cells with designs of tiny patterns known as *millefiori* (It.: 'thousand flowers'). The Alfred Jewel (9th century; Oxford, Ashmolean, *see* JEWELLERY, colour pl. IV, fig. 1), aesthetically in the 'Celtic' style associated with champlevé, is actually cloisonné. Spectacular Romanesque champlevé, enamelling from Limoges (*see* LIMOGES, §1), southern France, Christian Spain and the Meuse and Rhine valleys (*see* ROMANESQUE, §VII; *see also* colour pl. IV, fig. 2), often using gilded copper or bronze, survives from the 12th and 13th centuries. During the Middle Ages large chasses (chests) and reliquaries made in the Limousin were in demand throughout Europe (*see also* GOTHIC, §VI).

(iii) Basse taille [Fr.: 'shallow cut'; It. *lavoro di basso rilievo*]. Chased or engraved metal (often silver or silver gilt) with bas-relief compositions or patterns is entirely covered with translucent enamel. A rich tonal quality is created by the varying degrees of engraving and depth of enamel. Chasing the object also provides key (grip) for the enamel and facilitates application to larger areas. The earliest surviving example of *basse taille* is the chalice of Pope Nicholas IV (1288–92; Assisi, Tesoro Mus. Basilica S Francesco; *see* GOTHIC, fig. 94) made by the Italian goldsmith GUCCIO DI MANNAIA. One of the most spectacular examples is the

1. Embroidered dress, coral, silver and silver gilt on velvet, from Hungary, mid-17th century (Budapest, Museum of Applied Arts)

2. Embroidered cope of the Order of the Golden Fleece (detail), gold and silver thread, silk, velvet, pearls on linen, 3.3×1.64 m (whole cope), ?from Brussels, c. 1425–75 (Vienna, Kunsthistorisches Museum)

PLATE I

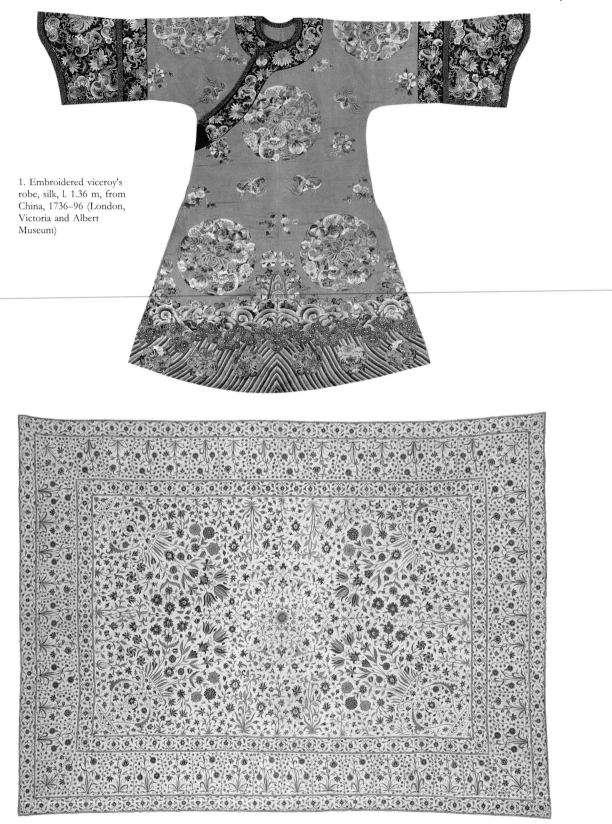

1. Embroidered viceroy's robe, silk, l. 1.36 m, from China, 1736–96 (London, Victoria and Albert Museum)

2. Embroidered hanging, silk thread on cotton, 2.03×2.69 m, from India, Mughal, *c.* 1700 (London, Victoria and Albert Museum)

PLATE III   Enamel

1. *Basse taille* enamelled cup and cover, known as the Royal Gold Cup, gold, h. 236 mm, from Paris, *c.* 1380–90 (London, British Museum)

2. Cloisonné enamelled lobed basin, diam. 500 mm, from China, mark and reign period of Wanli, 1573–1620 (London, British Museum)

1. Painted enamel portrait of *Anne, Duc de Montmorency* by Léonard Limosin, copper and gilt-wood setting, 720×560 mm, from Limoges, 1556 (Paris, Musée du Louvre)

2. Champlevé enamelled reliquary cross with five scenes from the Old Testament, from Mosan region, h. 372 mm, *c.* 1160–70 (London, British Museum)

3. *Guilloché* enamelled cigarette case by Fabergé, red gold and rose diamonds, l. 93 mm, from Moscow, 1899–1908 (British Royal Collection)

Burgundy, this technique developed to fully display the 'stained glass' potential of translucent enamel. In a technique related to cloisonné, a network of metal wires or strips is created and set against a metal backing. These cloisons are then filled with translucent enamel and fired; when the backing melts, the enamel is left suspended in the *cloisons*. The Mérode Cup (*c.* 1430; London, V&A), made in Burgundy or France, incorporates a band imitating stained-glass windows and is the only extant medieval example of this technique. The Chinese made exceptional *plique à jour* vases. René Lalique incorporated the technique in his jewellery, and at the end of the 19th century the firm of J. Tostrup in Oslo also created magnificent *plique à jour* tableware (see fig. 2). In the case of small *cloisons*, surface tension holds the enamel in place as it is fired, so backing is not required.

(vi) En résille sur verre [Fr.: 'in grooves on glass']. This is a rare form of enamelling that is closely related to the cloisonné technique. A design is cut into a glass ground which is coloured blue or green; the grooves are then lined with gold foil and filled with powdered enamel of extremely low fusibility. The process was introduced by French goldsmiths in the late 16th century and early 17th, on such highly ornamental, valuable objects as pendants and mirror backs. The German engraver Valentin Sezenius is also attributed with works in this technique dating from 1619 to 1625 (see fig. 3). Roman glassworkers of the 1st century AD may have attempted a similar technique, possibly by pressing molten glass into the *cloisons*.

(vii) Painted. The object, usually made of copper, is covered in a layer of white, opaque enamel and then fired; it is then gradually decorated with coloured enamels, which require different firings. The earliest surviving examples are Netherlandish (*c.* 1425; *see* SILVER, fig. 3). By the early 16th century Limoges had become the centre for painted enamels on copper (*see* LIMOGES, §1), and the PÉNICAUD family from this town are particularly associated with its development. Nardon (Léonard) Pénicaud used polychrome enamels on a clear, fluxed ground, outlined with dark enamels. The wet enamel is also often scratched with a needle to create delineation or uses *paillons* (small pieces of gold foil) for details. Limoges enamels from *c.* 1535 to *c.* 1575 were principally decorated with grisaille (grey-toned) enamels, which gave a relief effect created by repeated firings of white, translucent enamels over a dark ground. Coloured enamels were found to be suitable for painting small portraits (see colour pl. IV, fig. 1), jewelled boxes and plaques, and their popularity spread throughout Europe; the Swiss miniature painter JEAN PETITOT, for example, introduced the technique into England (*see* ENGLAND, §X, 2). Painted enamels were introduced into China at the court of the Kangxi emperor (*reg* 1662–1722) by Jesuits (*see* CHINA, §XIII, 9). Enamel painting eventually led to transfer-printed enamelling in England, first at the York House in Battersea (1753–6) and then at Bilston, in Wednesbury and in Birmingham in the late 18th century.

(viii) Surrey [Stuart]. A short lived, rarely described class of enamelling using cast-brass objects of sometimes substantial size as ground for the enamel. The surfaces of the objects were cast in low-relief and generally filled with a bichrome palette of enamel, especially black-and-white or blue-and-white (e.g. Warwick Candle, 1650–60; London, BM). Surrey enamels were made in England in the second half of the 17th century, probably near the brass mill (est. 1649) at Esher, Surrey. Two Germans, Daniel Diametrius and his partner Joseph Momma, may have influenced the production of such items as fire-dogs and candlesticks.

BIBLIOGRAPHY
L. F. Day: *Enamelling* (London, 1907)
L. E. Millenet: *Enamelling on Metal* (Kingston Hill, 1927/*R* 1951)
K. F. Bates: *Enameling: Principles and Practice* (New York, 1951)
P. Michaels: 'Technical Observations on Early Painted Enamels of Limoges: Their Materials, Structure, Technique and Deterioration', *J. Walters A.G.*, xxvii–xxviii (1964–5), pp. 21–43
B. Newble: *Practical Enameling and Jewelry Work* (London, 1967)
J. Cherry: 'The Dunstable Swan Jewel', *J. Brit. Archaeol. Assoc.*, xxxii (1969), pp. 38–53
A Thousand Years of Enamel (exh. cat. by K. Snowman, London, Wartski, 1971)
S. Benjamin: *Enamels* (New York, 1983)
M. Campbell: *An Introduction to Medieval Enamels* (London, 1983)
H. Tait, ed.: *The Art of the Jeweller* (London, 1984)
Contemporary British Enamels (exh. cat., Gateshead, Shipley, A.G., 1985)

MARIT GUINNESS ASCHAN

3. CONSERVATION. The conservation of enamel requires caution, as both the vitreous material and the metal support must be taken into account when carrying out a treatment. In some cases, the object can be cleaned simply by dusting with a soft brush. If this is not adequate, and the enamel is in very good condition, it can be cleaned with a mild, aqueous detergent in de-ionized water, but metal areas should be avoided, and the object should be allowed to air dry immediately after cleaning to avoid corrosion to the underlying metal. Enamels may also be cleaned with a 50:50 mixture of ethanol and acetone, applied with a swab or soft brush. Dirt and grime in cloisonné enamel can be mechanically removed using a soft, pointed wooden stick, followed by the ethanol and acetone mixture, which will also serve to degrease the metal.

If the enamel has deteriorated, due to burial conditions or inherent chemical instability, it can be consolidated with synthetic resins, for example the acrylic resin Paraloid or Acryloid B-72 (manufactured by Rohm and Haas). However, when the deterioration is due to chemical instability, consolidation may provide initial visual improvement, but the deterioration will probably continue. If possible, the cause of the deterioration should be determined, and the object stored in a stable environment.

In contrast to the repair of glass, the adhesives used for enamels do not usually require great structural strength, nor is the refractive index of as much importance. As the repair usually includes returning the enamel to place on a metal substrate, acrylic resin adhesive is used in preference to epoxies, which are corrosive to metal and should be avoided unless structural strength is required. If epoxies are used, an isolating layer of an acrylic resin over the metal will prevent corrosion. The repair of metal parts may consist of straightening cloisonné bands or adhering metal pieces, again using an acrylic resin adhesive. Heat or soldering is not used, as the application of heat can cause further damage to the enamel.

For opaque enamels, restoration of missing parts may be carried out using one of the commercially available vinyl-based fill materials, after first applying an isolating layer of acrylic resin over the metal substrate. The fill can then be inpainted with acrylic or natural resin colours. For translucent enamels, acrylic resins toned with dry pigment may be used, but if the missing area has greater depth, a toned epoxy or polyester is more suitable, once the metal has been isolated with an acrylic resin. Epoxies and polyester resins can be toned with dyes, but these tend to alter in colour over time. Hard waxes have also been used for enamel fills: a hard synthetic wax should be used instead of a natural wax, which may have organic acids that cause corrosion to metal.

BIBLIOGRAPHY

L. Bacon and B. Knight, eds: *From Pinheads to Hanging Bowls: The Identification, Deterioration and Conservation of Applied Enamel and Glass Decoration on Archaeological Artifacts* (London, 1987)
R. Newton and S. Davison: *Conservation of Glass* (London, 1989)

RIKA SMITH McNALLY

En camaieu. *See* CAMAIEU.

Encaustic painting. Method of painting with molten wax first used by ancient Greek and Roman artists. The word derives from the Greek *enkaustikos*, 'to burn in'. The term encaustic is also used occasionally to designate certain types of ceramics, but these are unrelated to encaustic painting.

1. Materials and techniques. 2. History. 3. Conservation.

1. MATERIALS AND TECHNIQUES. The basic method calls for dry pigments to be mixed with molten wax on a warm palette and then applied to any ground or surface, including wood, plaster or canvas. It is traditional to pass a heat source close to the surface of a finished painting to 'burn in' the colours (see fig. 1) by fusing and bonding them to the support. Once hardened, encaustic paint is as durable as any other paint surface. No additional varnish is necessary, but the surface can be polished to a dull sheen with a soft cloth.

Wax is resistant to moisture and does not yellow, properties that make it an ideal medium for painting. It has a pleasing translucency and a matt finish favoured by some artists, and it is both economical and clean. White, refined beeswax is the type most commonly employed in encaustic painting, and this can be supplemented with small portions of carnauba wax, which acts as a hardener, or microcrystalline wax, a plasticiser. A small amount of damar resin may also be added to the beeswax to improve its consistency and hardness. All pigments suitable for oil painting can be used successfully with wax. The proportion of pigment to wax varies, but in general less is needed to colour a wax than an oil medium. Batches of coloured wax may be mixed in advance and kept in small containers, which can easily be reheated on the warm palette. Molten colours are applied either with brushes or with palette knives.

Modern encaustic painting has been greatly facilitated by electrically heated equipment. Although wax has a fairly low melting-point (beeswax melts at approximately 60–65°C while carnauba wax requires a higher temperature of 83–86°C), the ideal temperature for keeping wax colours fluid is around 200°C. For this purpose electrically heated

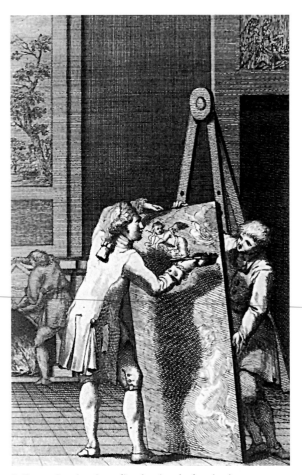

1. Encaustic painter's studio, showing the burning-in process; engraving from Vincenzo Requeno: *Saggi sul ristabilimento dell'antica arte de' greci e romani pittori* (Parma, 1787)

aluminium palettes are available commercially. These are generally quite small and ill-suited to making large batches of colour for sizeable paintings. Larger palettes can be improvised by placing sheets of iron or stainless steel over an electric stove or hot plate. The final burning-in is the most challenging part of the encaustic painting process. It can be accomplished by laying the painting flat on a table and passing a reflector light bulb or an infra-red heat bulb above it slowly and evenly, which is very time-consuming, by using an ordinary clothes iron or by adapting a hot plate or other heating element. Most artists use an electrically powered heat gun. Whatever is chosen, it is important to guard against bringing the heating element too close to the finished surface.

This is the classic method of encaustic painting as it uses melted wax colours and heat in the final burning-in process, but the wax can also be dissolved, saponified or emulsified and then used in combination with oil, casein or tempera paints. It is soluble in turpentine, mineral spirits or carbon tetrachloride and can be saponified and made water-soluble through the addition of alkali. One recipe for a wax-oil emulsion recommends melting equal parts of white beeswax in castor oil and thinning the resulting mixture with five parts of turpentine. A cold wax medium (Dorland's Wax Medium) made of waxes, resins and oils, which has the consistency of lard, is available commercially in the USA. This may be mixed directly with tube oil paints or with dry pigments, then fused with a final application of heat in imitation of classic encaustic, though heat is not essential. There is much disagreement as to whether other painting methods involving wax can properly be classified as encaustic (*see* WAX, §II, 2).

2. HISTORY.

(i) Pre-Renaisssance. The earliest references to encaustic painting are found in the works of a number of Roman authors of the 1st century AD, including Pliny the elder, Vitruvius and Plutarch. The most extensive references are in book XXV of Pliny's *Natural History*. Pliny states that 'We do not know who first invented the art of painting with wax colours and burning in the painting'. He mentions several Greek artists—including Aristeides, Praxiteles and Polygnotos—who can be credited with the earliest use of the medium and says that Pausias was the first well-known master in this style, having learnt the process from Pamphilos, the master of Apelles. Pausias painted small pictures on wood, which he was able to execute very rapidly, probably owing to the speed with which the wax hardened as it cooled. In another section of book XXV, Pliny indicated that there were three different methods of encaustic painting: 'one with wax, the other further on ivory—by means of a *cestrum* or a sharp point', and the third, introduced when it became fashionable to paint ships of war, 'of melting the wax by fire and using a brush'. This third method attests to the medium's impermeability and permanence.

Vitruvius offered another variation on the encaustic methods described by Pliny, in his description of a process for protecting paintings on plaster with a coat of wax varnish. He recommended the application with a strong brush of 'Punic wax melted in the fire and mixed with a little oil. Then putting charcoal in an iron vessel, and heating the wall with it, let the wax first be brought to melt, and let it be smoothed over with waxed cord and clean linen cloths, the same way as naked marble statues.' The actual composition of Punic wax has given scholars much cause for debate. Pliny described its preparation as follows: yellow beeswax was exposed to the air for some time, then cooked with repeated boilings and additions of sea water and potassium carbonate. The foamy mass was then poured into cold water and afterwards exposed in a basket to the bleaching action of sunlight. However, the actual proportions are not indicated, and it is unclear from this reference whether Punic wax was merely a form of purified beeswax or whether the addition of potassium carbonate actually caused it to become saponified.

The tools of the encaustic painter included the stylus or *cestrum* (a long-handled instrument with a spoon-like end), the *cauterium* (a pan of coals used for the final burning-in process), a spatula and cakes or tablets of coloured waxes. The tomb of a 3rd-century AD woman painter excavated at Saint-Médard-des-Prés, France, in the mid-19th century contained a number of materials for encaustic painting, of which two bronze *cestri* were of special interest. Another,

slightly later, tomb, excavated at Herne-Saint-Hubert, Belgium, contained a number of coloured waxes in which oil had also been used as a binder.

The earliest surviving examples of encaustic painting are portraits from the 2nd century AD on small wooden panels that were attached to mummy cases or the wrappings of the deceased (see fig. 2). They are believed to have been executed by Greek artists residing in Egypt. From the beginning of the 19th century over 600 have been excavated in the Faiyum district (*see* FAIYUM, §1). Most are painted directly on ungessoed wooden panels, and the well-preserved paint surfaces exhibit a remarkable degree of naturalistic observation and detail. Greek artists in North Africa continued to practise encaustic painting during Late Antiquity, receiving patronage from the Christian court at Constantinople in particular. In the Byzantine Empire encaustic was used for icons in the 6th and 7th centuries, after which it was largely replaced by egg tempera (*see* EARLY CHRISTIAN AND BYZANTINE ART, §III, 1). Wax was also used throughout the early Middle Ages as a wall varnish in fresco painting and to treat marble sculpture. For example, the records of Orvieto Cathedral contain a reference to a wax vehicle or varnish used by Andrea Pisano in 1345 and to the varnishing of a marble statue of the *Virgin* in 1351.

For the most part, however, the practice of encaustic painting was superseded in the West by the use of tempera, fresco and ultimately oil painting. There is some evidence that encaustic may have enjoyed a minor revival during

2. Encaustic paint on the wooden mummy case of Artemidorus (detail), h. 1.67 m, from Faiyum, Egypt, early 2nd century AD (London, British Museum)

the Renaissance period, when Lucas Cranach (i) and Andrea Mantegna reputedly experimented with the medium. Scholars have speculated that Leonardo da Vinci's *Battle of Anghiari* may also have been a failed experiment with encaustic, ruined in the final burning-in process. The texts by Pliny and Vitruvius were certainly available for consultation, though the early translators of Pliny's *Natural History* were largely content to translate without interpreting. Some implied that encaustic was a form of enamel since it involved the use of fire, while others suggested that it was a way of moulding coloured wax reliefs. Louis de Montjosieu, writing in 1585, called for a practical demonstration to settle the question but never attempted one himself.

(ii) Post-Renaissance revival. Encaustic painting did not enjoy its first full-scale revival until the mid-18th century, when the French antiquarian the COMTE DE CAYLUS took issue with earlier translators of Pliny and set out to demonstrate the art of encaustic painting. Encouraged by the discoveries made at Herculaneum in 1738 and Pompeii in 1748 of beautifully preserved fragments of wall paintings, Caylus hired a chemist named Majault and engaged the artist Joseph-Marie Vien to experiment with the wax medium. Vien successfully painted a small *Head of Minerva*

(St Petersburg, Hermitage) on panel in the encaustic medium, which Caylus proudly exhibited at the Académie Royale des Inscriptions in 1754. However, since he did not immediately reveal the details of his encaustic process, a number of experiments were made by other enthusiasts. One of these, in an anonymous treatise entitled *L'Histoire et le secret de la peinture en cire*, challenged Caylus's claim to have rediscovered the encaustic process. The author of this treatise (recognized by his contemporaries as none other than the philosopher Denis Diderot) condemned Caylus for his secrecy and championed instead the experiments of the artist Jean-Jacques Bachelier. The ensuing controversy between supporters of Caylus and of Diderot is demonstrated by the large number of articles, letters and pamphlets published on this matter between 1755 and 1757.

Vien exhibited six paintings in encaustic at the Salon of 1755. Several other artists also showed wax paintings, including Alexandre Roslin, who exhibited a self-portrait in Caylus's process, and another of Caylus's protégés, Louis-Joseph Le Lorrain, who exhibited two encaustics. Jean-Jacques Bachelier exhibited four paintings using his own, rival method of painting with wax. The revival of encaustic painting in France was connected with the new

3. George Stubbs: *Lady and Gentleman in a Carriage*, encaustic paint on panel, 825×1016 mm, 1787 (London, National Gallery)

interest throughout Europe in the art of antiquity. In Sweden Carl Gustaf Pilo tried Bachelier's technique, and in England the process was communicated to the Royal Society and employed by the illustrator and naturalist George Edwards (1694–1773), and by Johann Heinrich Müntz, who conducted his experiments with wax under the supervision of Horace Walpole at Strawberry Hill. Müntz later published an English translation and interpretation of Caylus's treatise. Inspired by the general interest in encaustic painting, George Stubbs (see fig. 3) and Joshua Reynolds both experimented with wax media; and Stubbs also worked with Josiah Wedgwood to develop a technique for painting with matt enamel on flat ceramic plaques. Wedgwood, who took out a patent in 1769 for 'encaustic' vase painting (a process used to imitate Greek red-figure vases), was well aware of the French experiments and eager to rival them (see WEDGWOOD, §1). Vincenzo Valdré (1742–1814) and John Francis Rigaud used encaustic for large, classicizing mural decorations at Stowe, Bucks, and Packington Hall, Warwicks, respectively.

In Germany, Benjamin Calau (1724–85) and Joseph Fratrel (1730–83) introduced wax painting to a number of other German artists, including Christian Bernhard Rode and Johann Christoph Frisch. Their technique called for a pre-emulsified liquid wax substance and did not require a final burning-in. Jacob Wilhelm Christian Roux (1775–1831) and Franz Xavier Fernbach (1793–1851) also experimented with encaustic painting. In Munich, it attracted the attention of Ludwig I, who commissioned JULIUS SCHNORR VON CAROLSFELD to paint several scenes in encaustic in the Residenz in 1831. Other Munich artists also employed the encaustic media described by Fernbach in his manual *Die enkaustische Malerei* of 1845.

In Italy, in 1784, Vincenzo Requeno (1743–1811) published a treatise on encaustic painting that attracted a flurry of criticism and controversy not unlike that which had greeted Caylus's work in France three decades earlier. Requeno later revised and expanded his work into two volumes, published in 1787. A number of Italian artists experimented with wax media, including Vincenzo Martinelli, Giovanni David and Andrea Appiani. In Rome, Christoph Unterberger supervised the production of a small cabinet painted in encaustic with designs borrowed from Raphael and supplemented with antique motifs, for Catherine the Great. The Italian artists Giuseppe Cades, Felice Giani, Luigi Campovecchio and Giovanni Battista dell'Era (1765–98) assisted him. Destined for Catherine's summer palace Tsarskoe Selo in St Petersburg, the cabinet was destroyed, along with much of the palace, during World War II.

With so much attention focused on Italy during this period of classical revival, the Italian experiments with encaustic attracted considerable notice. Jacques Nicolas Paillot de Montabert travelled to Italy, met Campovecchio and dell'Era and compiled a monumental, eight-volume treatise on painting techniques published in 1829, one volume of which was dedicated to encaustic. Paillot de Montabert was closely affiliated with a group of Jacques-Louis David's students known as Les Primitifs for their radical interest in primitive painting styles, to which the encaustic medium was particularly well suited.

By the mid-19th century encaustic techniques derived from Paillot de Montabert's formulae were in common use, especially for mural decorations. In France, such artists as Pierre Puvis de Chavannes, Eugène Delacroix and Hippolyte Flandrin experimented with wax medium techniques. The Swiss artist Arnold Böcklin also worked with wax. The inclusion of a chapter on encaustic in Charles Blanc's popular *Grammaire des arts du dessin* and the publication in 1884 of César-Isidore-Henri Cros and Charles Henry's *L'Encaustique et les autres procédés de peinture chez les Anciens* demonstrate the wide acceptance that the medium enjoyed. In England, W. B. Sarsfield Taylor documented the process in *A Manual of Fresco and Encaustic Painting*, and Charles Eastlake included a chapter on encaustic and fresco in his influential history of oil painting.

Several 20th-century painters have used encaustic painting, including Georges Rouault and Diego Rivera. It enjoyed a modest popularity in the 1940s in the USA, largely due to the efforts of Karl Zerbe, the head of the Painting Department at the Boston Museum School, but this cannot compare with the prominence encaustic received through the work of Jasper Johns. Johns is one of the most devoted practitioners in this medium, and his bold use of the technique, recorded in the film *Painters Painting* (1972), has been a source of inspiration to many younger artists. Wax and encaustic media are found in the work of contemporary artists as diverse as Julian Schnabel and Mimmo Paladino, but a comprehensive account of the use of encaustic in 19th- and 20th-century art has yet to be written.

3. CONSERVATION. Judging by the state of preservation of many of the Faiyum mummy portraits, classic encaustic paintings are extremely durable. Surface cleaning with swabs moistened in distilled water is generally sufficient, but for more tenacious dirt, a solution of beeswax and carbon tetrachloride is recommended. One of the challenges in the proper identification and treatment of wax or encaustic paintings is the large number of different waxes used and the many materials they can be mixed with, such as resins and oils. Wax may be identified by its physical properties (i.e. its melting point, specific gravity and refractive index), but there is often not enough wax in the medium to allow for ready identification through physical examination alone. Infra-red photography and gas chromatography have been used successfully to identify wax media. A knowledge of the history of the medium and of the variety of different recipes for encaustic painting is also of assistance in proper identification.

BIBLIOGRAPHY
A.-C.-P., Comte de Caylus: *Mémoire sur la peinture à l'encaustique et sur la peinture à la cire* (Geneva, 1755)
[D. Diderot]: *L'Histoire et le secret de la peinture en cire contre le sentiment du Comte de Caylus* (n.p., [1755])
J. Müntz: *Encaustic or Count Caylus's Method of Painting in the Manner of the Ancients* (London, 1760)
V. Requeno: *Saggi sul ristabilimento dell'antica arte de' greci e romani pittori*, 2 vols (Parma, 1784; rev. 1787)
J.-N. Paillot de Montabert: *Encaustique* (Paris, 1829), viii of *Traité complet de la peinture*
W. B. Sarsfield Taylor: *A Manual of Fresco and Encaustic Painting* (London, 1843)
C. L. Eastlake: *Materials for a History of Oil Painting*, 2 vols (London, 1847–69); rev. as *Methods and Materials of Painting of the Great Schools and Masters*, 2 vols (New York, 1960)

C. Blanc: *Grammaire des arts du dessin* (Paris, 1870)

H. Cros and C. Henry: *L'Encaustique et les autres procédés chez les anciens, histoire et technique* (Paris, 1884)

A. P. Laurie: *Greek and Roman Methods of Painting* (Cambridge, 1910)

H. Schmid: *Encaustik und Fresko auf antiker Grundlage* (Munich, 1917)

——: *Neuzeitliche Enkaustik* (Munich, 1932)

R. Mayer: *The Artist's Handbook of Materials and Techniques* (New York, 1940, rev. London, 4/1987)

F. Pratt and B. Fizec: *Encaustic Materials and Methods* (New York, 1949)

M. Borda: *La pittura romana* (Milan, 1958)

P. R. Büll: *Wachsmalerei: Enkaustik und Temperatechnik unter besonderer Berücksichtigung antiker Wachsmalverfahren* (Frankfurt, 1963), i of *Vom Wachs*

R. Beyer: *Enkaustik* (Stuttgart, 1967), v of *Reallexikon des deutsches Kunstgeschichte*

D. Rice: *The Fire of the Ancients: the Encaustic Painting Revival, 1755 to 1812* (diss., New Haven, CT, Yale U., 1979)

DANIELLE RICE

Encaustic tile. *See under* BRICK, §I, 1(iii).

Encke, Erdmann (*b* Berlin, 26 Jan 1843; *d* Neubabelsberg, 7 July 1896). German sculptor. He studied (1860–65) at the Akademie in Berlin under Albert Wolff, and he first exhibited in 1864 at the Akademie exhibition. In 1866 he won the competition for a design for a monument to *Jahn, the Father of Gymnastics* for the Volkspark Hasenheide in Berlin, the first open space for gymnastics established by Jahn in 1811; Encke's sculpture was unveiled in 1872. After establishing his own studio in Berlin, Encke travelled to Italy. From 1882 he taught at the Akademie in Berlin, and he regularly showed at the Akademie exhibitions until 1890. Among Berlin sculptors he remained one of the most faithful to the earlier 19th-century tradition established by Christian Daniel Rauch.

Among the many important official commissions Encke received were those for a marble monument to *Queen Louise* for the Tiergarten (1876–80; now Berlin, Lapidarium; copy in original location), for the large-scale statues of *Elector Frederick William* (1883) and *Frederick II* (1886) for the Berlin Zeughaus (now in Burg Hohenzollern bei Hechingen), for the bronze statue of the *Elector Joachim II* (1889; Berlin-Spandau, Reformationsplatz), and for the bronze group *Electoral Princess Elisabeth Teaching the Christian Scriptures to her Son Joachim* (1890; Berlin, Neue N.G.). In 1894 statues of the Hohenzollern dynasty for the Kaiser-Wilhelm-Gedächtniskirche were commissioned but not executed; but in the same year Encke had the honour of providing the sarcophagus figures of *Emperor William I* and *Empress Augusta* for the Charlottenburg Mausoleum in Berlin. One of Encke's last works is among his freer and more charming compositions: the bronze *Page with a Pony* of 1896 (Berlin, Neue N.G.).

UNPUBLISHED SOURCES

Berlin, Akad. Kst., Archv [personal papers]

BIBLIOGRAPHY

Bénézit; Thieme–Becker

P. Bloch and W. Grzimek: *Das klassische Berlin: Die Berliner Bildhauerschule im 19. Jahrhundert* (Berlin, 1978)

Berliner Kunst von 1770 bis 1930 (exh. cat., W. Berlin, Berlin Mus., 1982)

M. Arndt: *Die Ruhmeshalle* (Berlin, 1985)

BRIGITTE HÜFLER

Enckell, (Knut) Magnus (*b* Hamina, 9 Nov 1870; *d* Stockholm, 26 Nov 1925). Finnish painter and designer. He was the leading figure in the generation of Finnish Symbolist artists that included Ellen Thesleff. After studying in Finland he travelled to Paris in 1891 and enrolled at the Académie Julian. He remained in Paris almost uninterruptedly until the spring of 1894. He was immediately attracted by the current in contemporary French painting that modelled itself on primitive art, the work of Pierre Puvis de Chavannes and the work of Manet at the time of his *Olympia* (1865; Paris, Mus. d'Orsay). Enckell was also strongly influenced by the literary mysticism of the Soleil d'Or groups and of Joséphin Péladan. He firmly rejected Realism and developed a sculptural and synthetist style, adopting extreme asceticism in his treatment of colour, which was limited almost entirely to various shades of grey, black and ochre.

In the early 1890s Enckell's preferred subjects were solitary figures, usually nude, androgynous boys (e.g. *Reclining Boy*, 1892; Helsinki, Athenaeum A. Mus.), as well as psychologically expressive portraits. In 1894 Enckell travelled to Italy, where his work took on a deeply mystical dimension. He was especially interested in Renaissance art, in particular the work of Masaccio and Leonardo, and he was also impressed by Arnold Böcklin's mystical interpretation of Classical mythology.

Towards the end of the 1890s Enckell returned to Italy to prepare himself for a monumental cycle. The Symbolist elements in his work began to disappear and his colour spectrum softened. This is evident in his large-scale compositions from this period, such as his mural for Helsinki University library in 1904, on the theme of the *Golden Age*. In 1906–7 Enckell produced the *Resurrection* altarpiece for the recently completed Jugendstil St John's church, Tampere (now Tampere Cathedral), to complement the mural decorations by Hugo Simberg. In 1909 Enckell adopted a markedly different style, which brought him closer to the Post-Impressionist treatment of colour. With other proponents of heightened Post-Impressionist colour he founded a short-lived exhibition group, Septem. This approach characterized all his later work, for example a *Music Hall in Paris* (1912; Helsinki, Athenaeum A. Mus.). In addition to painting landscapes and portraits Enckell continued to explore themes of religious mysticism of a deeply personal nature: Pori church contains his last great work, a sequence of stained glass depicting the story of the *Passion* and the *Redemption*.

BIBLIOGRAPHY

N. G. Hahl: *Om konst och konstindustri* [On art and the arts industry] (Helsinki, 1924)

J. Puokka: *Magnus Enckell, ihminen ja taiteilija* [Magnus Enckell, the man and the artist] (Helsinki, 1949)

S. Sarajas-Korte: *Suomen varhaissymbolismi ja sen lähteet 1890–1895* [Early Finnish Symbolism and its origins 1890–1895] (Helsinki, 1966)

——: 'Magnus Enckell ja kahlittu Prometheus' [Magnus Enckell and Prometheus bound], *Ateneumin Taidemuseo Museojulkaisu*, 21 (1979)

——: *Vid symbolismens källor. Den tidiga symbolismen i Finland 1890–1895* [At the source of Symbolism: early Symbolism in Finland, 1890–1895] (Pietarsaari, 1981)

——: 'Magnus Enckellin Melankolia' [Magnus Enckell's melancholy], *Ateneumin Taidemuseo Museojulkaisu*, 27 (1985)

Dreams of a Summer Night (exh. cat., London, ACGB, 1986)

SALME SARAJAS-KORTE

Encolpion. *See under* CROSS, §III, 2(i).

Encyclopedia, manuscript. Term anachronistically applied to a wide range of antique and medieval works of a compendious character, which were often provided with extensive cycles of didactic illustration. The boundaries of the genre are difficult to set, for the content, scale, structure, stated aims and intended audiences of the works vary considerably. All contain comprehensive descriptions of the natural world—celestial and terrestrial—often in conjunction with information from other fields, for example history or ethics. The material, drawn from sources approved by tradition, is normally presented not alphabetically but according to systems of the author's devising. The compilations are often simply called 'On the nature of things', but sometimes more evocative metaphoric titles are employed: 'image' or 'mirror' of the world, 'garden of delights', 'treasure'. The works, each containing a library of information in small compass, were intended to be of practical use, especially to commentators on the Bible. They served an edifying function by bringing the reader to the knowledge and love of the Creator.

Images in these books were used to reinforce or summarize the content of given texts or as substitutes for verbal explanation. Diagrams appear early on in medieval copies of Late Antique encyclopedic works. The descriptions of the heavens and the earth included in Macrobius' commentary (4th–5th century AD) on Cicero's *Dream of Scipio* were regularly accompanied by five line drawings referred to in the text, namely diagrams of the zodiac, falling rain, the five zones of earth and the five zones of heaven with the ecliptic, and a world map. Cassiodorus' handbook of Christian education, the *Institutiones* (mid-6th century AD), was also provided with visual aids: in five manuscripts of the late 8th century and the 9th, which are likely to reflect Cassiodorus' original, no fewer than 32 ornamented schemata were used to set out the divisions and subdivisions of each of the seven liberal arts. Copies of Isidore of Seville's brief cosmological tract, *De natura rerum*, probably completed by 613, regularly contain seven diagrams, six of which are mentioned in the text; all but one of these are circular, giving the work its popular title, the 'Book of wheels' (*Liber rotarum*).

Another of Isidore's works, the *Etymologiae*, was far more ambitious in scale; it became a source upon which most later encyclopedists would draw, directly or indirectly. Divided into 20 books after the author's death in 636, the compendium contains etymological definitions of a multitude of concepts: it begins with the liberal arts and continues with treatment of terms associated with medicine and law, time and the ages of world history, scripture and ecclesiastical offices, God, the angels and the faithful, the church and sects, pagan philosophers, poets, magicians and gods, peoples and social structures, man and monsters, animals, the heavens and the earth, buildings and fields, stones and metals, agriculture, warfare and games, ships, food, tools and furnishings. Many hundreds of manuscripts are preserved, normally containing no more than a scattering of schemata (e.g. geometrical figures, drawings of the phases of the moon, consanguinity tables, a world map). A manuscript produced in Zwiefalten (*c.* 1130–40; Stuttgart, Württemberg. Landesbib., MS. poet. et phil. 2° 33), in which 17 of 43 initials contain small scenes related to the content of the text, is exceptional.

By the 11th century, however, an encyclopedia based on Isidore's *Etymologiae*, compiled in the 840s by Rabanus Maurus, Abbot of Fulda, was fully illustrated. The work,

Encyclopedia illustration: *Lily among Thorns*; from Lambert of Saint-Omer: *Liber floridus*, *c.* 1120 (Ghent, Bibliotheek van de Rijksuniversiteit, MS. 92, fol. 230*v*)

in 22 books, called *De rerum naturis*, deals chiefly with the mystical significance of things; Rabanus gives spiritual interpretations of concepts Isidore defined. Six fully or partially illustrated manuscripts (11th–15th centuries) survive, some fragmentary, all believed to descend from a common archetype. The earliest, a codex produced *c.* 1023 in the South Italian monastery of Montecassino (Montecassino Abbey Lib., MS. Cas. 132), contains 360 images at the chapter headings that illustrate Isidorian subjects. Since the images are found only in manuscripts containing an interpolated version of Rabanus's text, it is unlikely that they date from the author's time.

Between *c.* 1112 and 1121 Lambert, a canon at the collegiate church in Saint-Omer, compiled a copiously illustrated compendium, the *Liber floridus*. The autograph manuscript (Ghent, Bib. Rijksuniv., MS. 92; see fig.) and nine creative copies (12th–16th centuries) survive. Lambert, writing shortly after the successful completion of the

First Crusade, was concerned with the meaning of history—traced from its beginning to its approaching end—and he included in his 190 chapters not only historical chronicles but also discussions of celestial and terrestrial phenomena, marvellous creatures, signs and wonders and much else. He himself seems to have been responsible for the brilliantly coloured images and text-bearing diagrams that adorn the work, many of them forming the sole content of chapters.

In the last quarter of the 12th century the Abbess Herrad von Landsberg in Alsace completed her HORTUS DELICIARUM (MS. destr. 1870, reconstructed from 19th-century notes and copies). Into a chronological framework, beginning with Old Testament history and ending with a treatment of last things, Herrad inserted information on such subjects as cosmology, the muses, the liberal arts and the virtues and vices. Imposing narrative and diagrammatic images worked in conjunction with the texts.

Smaller, more practical and more widely distributed compendia were also produced in the 12th century. Honorius Augustodunensis's *Imago mundi*, divided into three books devoted respectively to the earth and heavenly bodies, the divisions of time, and world history, survives in several recensions, the first completed *c.* 1110, the last in 1139. Like William of Conches's cosmological handbook, the *Philosophia mundi* (1120s), with which it was often bound, this text was occasionally provided with schemata.

In the 13th century large numbers of encyclopedias were produced both in Latin and in the vernacular. Authors began to incorporate newly available Greek and Arabic learning into their works: Alexander Nequam cited and praised Aristotle in his *De naturis rerum* (*c.* 1200), a description of the natural world, man and society rich in anecdotes and moralizations. In this period compilers were often members of the preaching orders: Bartholomeus Anglicus, a Franciscan, prepared his very popular encyclopedia in 19 books, *De proprietatibus rerum* (*c.* 1230), as an aid to Bible study; the Dominican Thomas of Cantimpré, author of the *Liber de natura rerum* (before 1244), intended the information that he had assembled about the properties of created things to be used by preachers 'for the confirmation of faith and the improvement of morals'. The grandest of the 13th-century encyclopedias was compiled from many hundreds of sources by the Dominican Vincent of Beauvais in the middle of the century: his vast *Speculum maius* consisted of three parts—the 'Speculum naturale', the 'Speculum doctrinale' and the 'Speculum historiale'—to which a fourth, the 'Speculum morale', was added by a later writer. Illustration in all these Latin encyclopedias, when it existed, was generally confined to historiated initials at the main text divisions. The earliest surviving luxury copy of Vincent's work (Brussels, Bib. Royale Albert 1er, MS. II 1396), produced in Tournai *c.* 1260, contains only an author portrait; certain later copies, especially of the 'Speculum historiale', have fairly extensive series of initials.

Contemporary writers in the vernacular adapted Latin encyclopedic learning for lay audiences. The cleric Gossuin of Metz, for example, produced the first redaction of his popular *Image du monde*, a poem in 6600 verses, in 1245; among his sources were Honorius's *Imago mundi* and Alexander Nequam's *De naturis rerum*. Manuscripts of the verse and prose redactions regularly contain a series of artful cosmological diagrams, referred to in the text and deemed essential ('without which the book cannot be easily understood'). Gossuin's work was a source for later encyclopedias, including two widely circulated works that contain extensive cycles of illumination: Bruno Latini's *Li Livres dou tresor* and Matfre Ermengau's *Breviari d'amors*. The *Tresor*, written in French before 1267 and translated into Italian soon after, contains a chronicle of world history, a description of the physical world, a translation of part of Aristotle's *Ethics* within a treatment of the virtues and vices and discussions of rhetoric and politics. Many illustrated copies exist (13th–16th centuries) that contain small images, framed or enclosed in initials, identifying the matter discussed in the chapters they precede. The *Breviari d'amors* (1288–92), an encyclopedic work of 34,597 verses in Provençal concerning the nature of love, relies on images—narrative and diagrammatic—to communicate ideas: the plan of the entire work is set out at the beginning in a 'Tree of Love'.

Latin encyclopedias were themselves translated into vernacular languages. Copies of the translations, made for secular patrons, normally received more lavish illustration than the originals. Seven of the surviving eleven copies of Jacob van Maerlant's *Der naturen bloeme* (*c.* 1270), a Flemish translation of Thomas of Cantimpré's compendium, contain illustrations. Luxury copies of Jean de Vignay's French version of Vincent of Beauvais's 'Speculum historiale' (*c.* 1332) contain hundreds of framed miniatures. Manuscripts of the French translation of Bartholomaeus Anglicus's work made by Jean Corbechon for King Charles V in 1372 are adorned with large miniatures before each of the compendium's 20 books.

Encyclopedias continued to be written in Latin in the 14th century. The learned Petrus Berchorius (Pierre Bersuire) completed his massive *Reductorium morale* in the 1340s while resident in Avignon; this book of moralizations for the use of preachers, based in part on Bartholomaeus Anglicus, remained unillustrated. The *Omne bonum*, however, an alphabetically ordered encyclopedia produced in London before 1375 by one James le Palmer, a clerk of the exchequer, was provided with large miniatures and hundreds of historiated initials representing unusual subjects; the manuscript survives as a unicum (London, BL, Royal MSS 6. E.VI–VII). Older encyclopedias—medieval and antique—continued to be copied and illustrated in the late Middle Ages. Pliny's *Natural History* (1st century AD), a vast compendium of observations about the natural world in 37 books that was an important source for medieval encyclopedists, was provided with historiated initials in Bologna *c.* 1300. A full cycle of 37 initials executed in Venice by 1425 would be copied in Renaissance manuscripts and early printed books.

BIBLIOGRAPHY

F. Saxl: 'Illustrated Mediaeval Encyclopaedias', *Lectures*, 2 vols, ed. G. Bing (London, 1957), pp. 228–54

J. Fontaine: *Isidore de Séville: Traité de la nature* (Bordeaux, 1960)

M. de Gandillac and others: *La Pensée encyclopédique au moyen âge* (Neuchâtel, 1966)

A. Derolez, ed.: *Lamberti S. Audomari canonici Liber Floridus: Codex autographus bibliothecae universitatis Gandavensis* (Ghent, 1968) [facs.]

C. Segre: 'Didattica scientifica—Enciclopedie', *La Littérature, didactique, allégorique et satirique*, ed. H. R. Jauss, 2 vols, Grundriss der romanischen Literaturen des Mittelalters, 6 (Heidelberg, 1968–70), pp. 134–41, 190–95

K. Laske-Fix: *Der Bildzyklus des Breviari d'amors* (Munich, 1973)

P. C. Mayo: 'The Crusaders under the Palm: Allegorical Plants and Cosmic Kingship in the *Liber Floridus*', *Dumbarton Oaks Pap.*, xxvii (1973), pp. 29–67

A. Derolez: *Lambertus qui librum fecit: Een codicologische studie van de Liber Floridus-Autograaf* (Brussels, 1978) [Eng. summary]

R. Green and others, eds.: *Hortus deliciarum*, 2 vols, Stud. Warb. Inst., xxxvi (London, 1979)

D. Byrne: 'Rex imago Dei: Charles V of France and the *Livre des propriétés des choses*', *J. Med. Hist.*, vii (1981), pp. 97–113 [bibliog.]

V. I. J. Flint: 'Honorius Augustodunensis: Imago mundi', *Archvs Hist. Doctr. & Litt. Moyen Age*, xlix (1982), pp. 7–153

I. Kratzsch and J. Flemming: *Über die Eigenschaften der Dinge: Die Enzyklopädie des Bartholomaeus Anglicus in einer illuminierten französischen Handschrift der Universitätsbibliothek der Friedrich-Schiller-Universität Jena* (Jena, 1982)

L. Armstrong: 'The Illustration of Pliny's *Historia naturalis*: Manuscripts before 1430', *J. Warb. & Court. Inst.*, xlvi (1983), pp. 19–39

B. C. Barker-Benfield: 'Macrobius', *Texts and Transmission*, ed. L. D. Reynolds (Oxford, 1983), pp. 222–32

C. Meier: 'Grundzüge der mittelalterlichen Enzyklopädik: Zu Inhalten, Formen und Funktionen einer problematischen Gattung', *Literatur und Laienbildung im Spätmittelalter und in der Reformationszeit. Symposion: Wolfenbüttel, 1981* (Stuttgart, 1984), pp. 467–500 [bibliog.]

M. Reuter: *Text und Bild im Codex 132 der Bibliothek von Montecassino 'Liber Rabani de originibus rerum'* (Munich, 1984)

J. B. Holloway: *Brunetto Latini: An Analytic Bibliography* (London, 1986)

Actes du XIVe colloque de l'Institut d'études médiévales: Vincent de Beauvais: Intentions et réceptions d'une oeuvre encyclopédique au moyen âge: Montréal, 1988 [esp. articles by A. Stones and C. A. Chavannes-Mazel]

M. Evans: 'The *Ysagoge in theologiam* and the Commentaries Attributed to Bernard Silvestris', *J. Warb. & Court. Inst.*, lv (1991), pp. 1–42

L. F. Sandler: *'Omne bonum': A Fourteenth-century Encyclopedia of Universal Knowledge* (in preparation)

ELIZABETH SEARS

Encyclopedias and dictionaries of art. Alphabetically arranged art reference works of varying size and scope. They may treat the entire history of art and architecture, including its chief figures, monuments, movements and national manifestations, or focus on some specific aspect, such as biography, terminology or iconography, usually with further chronological or geographical limits. Strictly speaking, a dictionary is a reference book about words whereas an encyclopedia explains things and concepts. The term 'dictionary', however, which has been in usage since the 17th century, has been applied to many types of alphabetically arranged reference works, including encyclopedias and compendia of biographical information.

BIBLIOGRAPHY

J. Schlosser: *Die Kunstliteratur* (Vienna, 1924/*R* 1985)

L. Fowler and E. Baer, eds: *The Fowler Architectural Collection of the Johns Hopkins University* (Baltimore, 1961)

R. Collison: *Encyclopaedias: Their History throughout the Ages: A Bibliographical Guide* (New York, 1966)

J. M. Crook: 'John Britton and the Genesis of the Gothic Revival', *Concerning Architecture: Essays on Architectural Writers and Writing Presented to Nikolaus Pevsner*, ed. J. Summerson (London, 1968)

J. M. Pérouse de Montclos: *Architecture: Méthode et vocabulaire*, Principes d'analyse scientifique, 2 vols (Paris, 1972)

J. Dobai: *Die Kunstliteratur des Klassizismus und der Romantik in England*, 4 vols (Berne, 1974–84)

K. Hardesty: *The Supplément to the Encyclopédie* (The Hague, 1977)

M. Baudry: *La Sculpture: Méthode et vocabulaire*, Principes d'analyse scientifique (Paris, 1978, 2/1984)

R. Darnton: *The Business of Enlightenment: A Publishing History of the Encyclopédie, 1775–1800* (Cambridge, MA, 1979)

E. Arntzen and R. Rainwater: *Guide to the Literature of Art History* (Chicago, 1980)

J. Coover: 'Dictionaries and Encyclopedias of Music', *The New Grove Dictionary of Music and Musicians*, ed. S. Sadie, v (London, 1980), pp. 430–59

A. K. Placzek, ed.: *Macmillan Encyclopedia of Architects*, 4 vols (New York and London, 1982)

A. Ross: 'State of the Art Sources: Visual Arts Encyclopedias', *Ref. Serv. Rev.*, xi/4 (1983), pp. 55–8

A. Simowitz: *Theory of Art in the Encyclopédie* (Ann Arbor, 1983)

K. Harrington: *Changing Ideas on Architecture in the Encyclopédie, 1750–1776* (Ann Arbor, 1985)

E. Goldberg: *After Vasari: History, Art, and Patronage in Late Medici Florence* (Princeton, 1988)

The Foundations of Architecture: Four Essays from the Dictionnaire raisonné of Viollet-le-Duc, intro. by B. Bergdoll (New York, 1990)

E. Byrne and S. Klos: '[Review of] Encyclopedia of Architecture: Design, Engineering and Construction [1988–89]', *A. Libs J.*, xv/4 (1990), pp. 32–7

E. Harris: *British Architectural Books and Writers, 1556–1785* (Cambridge, 1990)

I. Before 1700. II. 1700–50. III. 1751–1800. IV. 1801–50. V. 1851–1900. VI. After 1900.

I. *Before 1700.*

Some of the proto-encyclopedic compendia of the ancient and medieval periods contain information about the visual arts. In *Natural History* (*c.* AD 77) PLINY THE ELDER provides an extensive survey of the development of various art forms in Greece and Rome from the 7th century BC, naming notable artists and relating anecdotes about them and their work. The 7th-century *Etymologiae*, a compendium by Isidore of Seville (*d* 636), includes extensive coverage of architecture, with chapters on houses, public buildings, sacred buildings, factories and workshops, furnishings and tombs (*see* ENCYCLOPEDIA, MANUSCRIPT). Entries for many early artists, craftsmen and inventors are contained in the *Suidae lexicon*, a widely used encyclopedic dictionary compiled in the 10th or 11th century. It was one of the first reference sources to have an alphabetical arrangement rather than one based on a sequence of subjects organized according to a judgement of their affinities and relative importance.

The most authoritative source of practical art information from the medieval period is the 12th-century treatise *De diversis artibus* (?1110–40) by THEOPHILUS. His highly technical descriptions of painting, glassmaking and metalworking techniques seem so immediate and authentic that some art historians have been convinced that he was a practising artist, not merely a compiler of information based on the experience of others, and have attempted to identify him with Roger of Helmarshausen, an early 12th-century metalworker.

Much information on colour theory and on the manufacture and mixing of colours and inks was included in *De proprietatibus rerum* (1220–40) by the English Franciscan scholar Bartholomeus Anglicus (*fl* early 13th century). According to Collison it was the most popular encyclopedia in Europe for three centuries and was widely translated, although it was the Latin text that first appeared in printed form, published by Koelhoff in Cologne *c.* 1470.

The gradual increase in the number of alphabetically arranged encyclopedias was apparently due—after the invention of printing—to the influence of certain dictionaries in Latin, the definitions of which had become detailed enough to qualify them as encyclopedias. Notable among these publications were the encyclopedic dictionaries produced in Paris by Charles Estienne (1504–64). Concurrently there was also a trend towards publication of encyclopedias and dictionaries in the vernacular languages of the burgeoning, literate middle class, rather than the Latin of scholars or the clergy. In his English translation (1664) of *Parallèle de l'architecture antique et de la moderne* (1650) by Roland Fréart (*see* FRÉART, (1)), the diarist John Evelyn included a glossary of architectural terms to assist his readers. In the preface to the glossary, Evelyn explained that although *De verborum Vitruvianorum significatione* (1612), an excellent dictionary of architectural terms by BERNARDINO BALDI, already existed, it was in Latin and he was therefore afraid that his readers would be unable to use it. Evelyn's glossary of architectural terms was organized not alphabetically but in the form of an essay, with the explained terms printed in italics. Harris suggests that Evelyn's purpose in doing this was didactic: his readers would be obliged to peruse large sections of his essay in order to find specific terms. This was, however, an exception to usual practice; normally, the glossaries of architectural terms that accompanied translations of important late 17th-century architectural treatises were arranged in alphabetical order. For example, the English translation (1692) of Claude Perrault's abridged version of *On Architecture* by Vitruvius contained an alphabetically arranged glossary, 'explication of the hardest terms in architecture', with brief definitions of terms representing architectural features.

In continental Europe the development of dictionaries of art and architectural terminology seems to have been fairly advanced by the late 17th century. *Principes de l'architecture, de la sculpture, de la peinture* (1676), by ANDRÉ FÉLIBIEN, presented brief definitions of terms used in architecture, sculpture and painting. The dictionary section of Félibien's work was preceded by three, heavily illustrated essays, one on each of the art forms, which provided usage in context and an illustration for many of the terms in the dictionary. As an architect, Félibien appears to have been more confident with architectural terms than with those from other media, and he was clearly more comfortable defining words for objects rather than concepts; he was particularly good on artists' and architects' implements and tools. Félibien stated in his preface that one of his motives for compiling the dictionary was to help provide an understanding of contemporary art for future researchers. This concern for posterity can also be seen in the *Vocabolario toscano dell'arte del disegno* (1681) by FILIPPO BALDINUCCI. It was sponsored by the Accademia della Crusca, an organization founded in 1582 to promote the purity of Tuscan Italian. It accomplished this in part by supporting such projects as Baldinucci's specialized lexicon and by publishing (from 1612) its own official dictionary of the language.

Baldinucci concentrated in the *Vocabolario* on terms for artists' and architects' materials and techniques. He provided antecedent Latin words, sometimes showed variant terms and supplied many cross-references. In his youth he had been an art student conversant with the terminology in use in studios and workshops in Florence; and consequently his dictionary conveys a feeling of authenticity.

The tradition of producing collections of brief biographies of notable artists and architects, arranged chronologically, was quite strong in the second half of the 17th century. Successors of Vasari produced some of their most important work during this period: *Le vite de' pittori, scultori ed architetti ed intagliatori* by GIOVANNI BAGLIONE was first published in 1642 and appeared in later editions in 1649 and 1733; *Le vite de' pittori, scultori ed architetti moderni* by GIOVANNI PIETRO BELLORI was published in 1672, with a second edition in 1728; and *L'Academia todesca della architectura, scultura et pittura* by JOACHIM VON SANDRART was published in two volumes between 1675 and 1679. These works provided a precedent and a source of data for the production of biographical dictionaries of artists and architects, conveniently arranged in alphabetical order, that began in the early 18th century.

There were some late 17th-century transitional works between these biographical collections and biographical dictionaries: *Noms des peintres* (1679), compiled by Félibien, presents a very brief paragraph about each artist but is arranged in the traditional chronological form. At the end, however, an alphabetical index by forename of all the artists is included. In 1694 Sebastiano Resta's brief biographies of painters with descriptions of some of their works were translated into English and published as *The True Effigies of the Most Eminent Painters*; engraved, full-page portraits of 120 of the painters were included. The biographies are arranged first by nationality and then chronologically; no index is provided.

The manuscript of the *Catalogus architectorum* by the Dutch philologist Franciscus Junius was also first published in 1694. It was the long-awaited companion volume to Junius's treatise on art *De pictura veterum* (Amsterdam, 1637). Junius, who for many years was librarian to Thomas Howard, 2nd Earl of Arundel, presents in the *Catalogus* alphabetically arranged entries for Classical and biblical figures credited with broadly interpreted artistic or architectural activity. The entries are a compendium of quotes from Classical, Byzantine and early medieval writers about each artist or architect.

BIBLIOGRAPHY

Pliny: *Natural History*
Isidorus Hispalensis [Isidore of Seville]: *Etymologiae* (c. 600; Augsburg, 1472); ed. in *PL*, lxxxi–lxxxiv; ed. W. Lindsay (Oxford, 1911/*R* 1962)
Suidae lexicon (c. 1050; Milan, 1499); ed. I. Bekker (Berlin, 1854)
Theophilus: *De diversis artibus* (?1110–40); Eng. trans. by C. Dodwell (London, 1961)
Bartholomeus Anglicus: *De proprietatibus rerum* (1220–40; Cologne, 1470; Eng. trans. 1398/*R* 1975)
B. Baldi: *De verborum Vitruvianorum significatione* (Augsburg, 1612)
G. Baglione: *Le vite de' pittori, scultori ed architetti ed intagliatori, dal pontificato di Gregorio XIII del 1572, fino a' tempi di Papa Urbano VIII nel 1642* (Rome, 1642, rev. 3/1733); facs. ed. with marginal notes by Bellori, ed. V. Mariani (Rome, 1935)
R. Fréart: *Parallèle de l'architecture antique et de la moderne* (Paris, 1650; Eng. trans., 1664/*R* 1970)
G. P. Bellori: *Le vite de' pittori, scultori ed architetti moderni* (Rome, 1672); ed. E. Borea, intro. G. Previtali (Turin, 1976)
C. Perrault: *Abrégé des dix livres d'architecture de Vitruve* (Paris, 1674; Eng. trans., London, 1692)
J. von Sandrart: *L'Academia todesca della architectura, scultura et pittura; oder, Teutsche Academie der edlen Bau-, Bild- und mahlerey-künste von 1675: Leben und berühmten Maler, Bildhauer und Baumeister*, 2 vols (Nuremberg, 1675–9/*R* 1971)
A. Félibien: *Principes de l'architecture, de la sculpture, de la peinture et des autres arts qui en dépendent avec un dictionnaire des termes propres à chacun de ces arts* (Paris, 1676, 3/1699/*R* 1966)

——: *Noms des peintres* (Paris, 1679/*R* 1972)
F. Baldinucci: *Vocabolario toscano dell'arte del disegno* (Florence, 1681/*R* ?1976)
F. Junius: *Catalogus architectorum* (Rotterdam, 1694; Eng. trans., 1991)
S. Resta: *The True Effigies of the Most Eminent Painters* (London, 1694, 2/1739)

II. 1700–50.

During this period a market for reference books was created by the increasing number of literate people who felt the need for conveniently accessible sources of information. Several notable general encyclopedias had been published in the last decade of the 17th century: the *Dictionnaire universel* (1690) by Antoine Furetière (1619–88); the *Dictionnaire des arts et des sciences* (1694) by Thomas Corneille (1625–1709) and the *Dictionnaire historique et critique* (1697) by Pierre Bayle (1647–1706). In 1703 *The City and Country Purchaser's and Builder's Dictionary*, compiled by Richard Neve (*d* 1764), was published. A 300-page volume with detailed entries containing many technical definitions, formulae for estimating costs and specific instructions to builders, its intended audience was obviously workmen, not antiquarians. Harris describes it as 'the first proper dictionary of builders' terms in English' and believes that Neve's work may have been stimulated by the detailed announcement in 1702 of another general encyclopedia, the *Lexicon technicum* (1704) by John Harris (?1667–1719). Two other notable general encyclopedias soon followed: the *Curieuses Natur- Kunst- Gewerck- und Handlungs-Lexicon* (1712) by Paul Jacob Marperger (1656–1730); and the *Cyclopedia* (1728) by Ephraim Chambers (*c.* 1680–1740). Although each of these general encyclopedias had only minimal art and architectural coverage, it is certainly possible that this international publication of general encyclopedias provided stimulus to the production of encyclopedic works in such specialist areas as art and architecture.

Architectural glossaries continued to be published in the early 18th century as parts of larger works, but rather than elucidating classic treatises they were now used to supplement manuals or contemporary theoretical works. *Palladio Londinensis* (1734), by William Salmon (*c.* 1703–79), was a popular manual for artisans who aspired to be builders. It includes an alphabetically arranged glossary that supplies brief definitions of architectural procedures and features. A glossary of contemporary architectural features and construction terminology is included in *Les Loix des bâtimens suivant la coûtume de Paris* (1748), a manual of property law by Antoine Desgodetz. The second edition (1714) of the *Nouveau Traité de toute l'architecture* (1706) by JEAN-LOUIS DE CORDEMOY, an architectural theorist who argued for the integration of aspects of Gothic and Greek architectural styles in church construction, contains a 67-page 'dictionary of all the terms used in this treatise' as a sort of appendix.

During the first half of the 18th century, compilers of biographical reference works on artists seemed ambivalent about the organizational concept of arranging entries alphabetically by surnames. Throughout the century there was much agonizing over this issue by writers who, while conceding that alphabetical order was more convenient for readers, argued that it obscured an overall view of

artistic development provided by a chronological arrangement. The *Abecedario pittorico* (1704) by the historian PELLEGRINO ANTONIO ORLANDI arranged artists alphabetically by forename but also provided an end index that listed them alphabetically by surname. Orlandi's coverage was international, but since he relied heavily on 16th- and 17th-century Italian biographers (e.g. Vasari, Bellori and Baglione) for his information, most of the painters, sculptors and architects he includes are Italian. He generally only supplies a few lines on each artist, saying little about specific works. The book was one of the first biographical reference works to include several engraved plates illustrating facsimiles of artists' monograms. The art-loving public must have been ready for a convenient source of biographical information about artists: the *Abecedario pittorico* was often republished in Italy throughout the 18th century and was also issued in an English translation in 1730.

The other important biographical reference work on artists produced in the first half of the 18th century was the *Abrégé de la vie des plus fameux peintres* (1745–52), by the apparently well-travelled Antoine-Joseph Dezallier d'Argenville (*see* DEZALLIER D'ARGENVILLE, (1)). He lists paintings by major artists in collections he had visited, without, however, providing very precise identification of individual works; he also lists the names of prominent engravers of well-known artists' works. Italian, Netherlandish/German and French painters are covered in separate volumes, arranged according to their date of birth, but detailed indexes arranged alphabetically by surname are also supplied so that entries for specific painters can be found more easily. Dezallier's biographies are far more detailed than those of Orlandi, and he claimed in his preface to the first volume to have coverage of 'nearly a hundred' artists whose biographies appeared in no other reference book. While Orlandi's *Abecedario* is badly designed and difficult to use, Dezallier's biographies must have been relatively accessible because of the detailed index and intelligent use of different typefaces.

Around the mid-18th century some highly interesting books were published that represented new types of art reference works and new solutions to art information problems. *Tables historiques et chronologiques des plus fameux peintres anciens et modernes* (1742), by Antoine Frédéric Harms (*fl* early 18th century), appears to have been the first biographical index of painters; it indicates which of several potentially appropriate sources of biographical information contained data on a particular artist. Harms indexed the biographical data contained in the works of Vasari, Félibien, Orlandi and several other writers. The *Dictionnaire des monogrammes* (1750) was one of the first dictionaries of artists' monograms published as a separate book. Its longest section is the collection of monograms from a slightly earlier German compendium written by Johann Friedrich Christ (1700–56). It also contains entries on artists and accompanying monograms from several other sources, including Orlandi's *Abecedario*; the editor who compiled this material was, however, anonymous.

The idea of presenting several different categories of art information in the same alphabetical sequence also began to develop during this period. The impetus was evidently to provide travellers interested in art and architecture with a versatile, portable source of information. The *Dictionnaire abrégé de peinture et d'architecture* (1746), by François Marie de Marsy (1714–63), presented in two slim, unillustrated volumes, contains entries that survey the architectural attractions of large cities, brief biographies of deceased artists and architects and art/architectural terminology.

It was also during the early 18th century that the first dictionary-style reference works devoted to Classical mythology and iconography were published. Among them was the *Grundliches Lexicon mythologicum* (1724), by Benjamin Hederich (1675–1748), the entries of which explain how particular mythological beings were portrayed in art works, without, however, listing specific works.

BIBLIOGRAPHY

A. Furetière: *Dictionnaire universel*, 3 vols (The Hague, 1690/*R* 1970, rev. 4/1727/*R* 1972)

T. Corneille: *Dictionnaire des arts et des sciences*, 2 vols (Paris, 1694/*R* 1968, rev. 2/1731)

P. Bayle: *Dictionnaire historique et critique*, 2 vols (Rotterdam, 1697; Eng. trans., 1734–41; rev. 11/1820–24)

R. Neve: *The City and Country Purchaser's and Builder's Dictionary; Or the Complete Builder's Guide* (London, 1703, rev. 2/1726/*R* 1969, rev. 3/1736)

J. Harris: *Lexicon technicum* (London, 1704/*R* 1966, rev. 5/1736), suppl. (1744)

P. A. Orlandi: *Abecedario pittorico* (Bologna, 1704/*R* 1980; Eng. trans., 1730)

J.-L. de Cordemoy: *Nouveau Traité de toute l'architecture ou l'art de bastir utile aux entrepreneurs et aux ouvriers* (Paris, 1706, 2/1714/*R* 1966)

P. J. Marperger: *Curieuses Natur- Kunst- Gewerck- und Handlungs-Lexicon* (Leipzig, 1712, rev. 3/1755)

B. Hederich: *Grundliches Lexicon mythologicum* (Leipzig, 1724, rev. 2/1741)

E. Chambers: *Cyclopedia*, 2 vols (London, 1728, rev. 7/1751–2)

W. Salmon: *Palladio Londinensis: Or, the London Art of Building* (London, 1734/*R* 1969, rev. 8/1773)

A. F. Harms: *Tables historiques et chronologiques des plus fameux peintres anciens et modernes* (Bronsvic, 1742)

A.-J. Dezallier d'Argenville: *Abrégé de la vie des plus fameux peintres*, 3 vols (Paris, 1745–52, rev. 2/1762/*R* 1972)

F. M. de Marsy: *Dictionnaire abrégé de peinture et d'architecture*, 2 vols (Paris, 1746/*R* 1972)

A. Desgodetz: *Les Loix des bâtimens suivant la coûtume de Paris* (Paris, 1748, rev. 3/1777)

J. F. Christ: *Dictionnaire des monogrammes, chiffres, lettres initiales, logogryphes, rébus etc*; trans. from the German by M. de l'Acad (Paris, 1750/*R* 1972, 3/1762)

III. 1751–1800.

During this period, the majority of significant art and architectural dictionaries and encyclopedias were produced in France. The first editions of the *Encyclopédie* (1751–72) by Diderot and Jean Le Rond d'Alembert (1717–83) had a general clarity of exposition and combination of text and plates (*see* PARIS, fig. 28) to convey information that set a new standard in the production of encyclopedias. Although the *Encyclopédie* is a general work, its coverage of the visual arts (including architecture) is more extensive than any previous general encyclopedia. For the first time, as Simowitz explains, it gave the visual arts a prominent location in an encyclopedia's classification of knowledge, which was then carried through by providing hundreds of articles on art and architectural subjects by such authorities as the architect Jacques-François Blondel and the connoisseurs Paul Landois (*fl* late 18th century) and Claude-Henri Watelet.

During the same period some dictionaries of architectural terms began to include terminology from related disciplines, thus becoming technical dictionaries rather than purely architectural ones. In addition to architectural terms the *Dictionnaire portatif de l'ingénieur et de l'artilleur* (1755) by Bernard Forest de Bélidor (?1697–1761), especially in its second edition (1768), revised and enlarged by Charles-Antoine Jombert (1712–84), includes definitions of military and marine architectural terms and mathematical terms. The three-volume *Dictionnaire d'architecture* (1770) by Charles François Roland Le Virloys (1716–72) includes terms from civil, military and naval architecture. Although it was not particularly portable, its improvements on the Bélidor–Jombert dictionary include polyglot entries with Latin, Italian, Spanish, English and German translations of the terms, 99 engraved plates and splendid illustrations (to which the text is keyed) elucidating many of the terms, and brief biographies of deceased architects from all countries and periods. The *Diccionario de las nobles artes para instrucción de los aficionados, y uso de los profesores* (1788), which contains mostly architectural terminology, with some painting, sculpture and engraving terms, was compiled by Diego Antonio Rejon de Silva (1740–96). Rejon was scrupulous in citing his sources for the terms; most of the architectural ones were culled from the late 17th-century writings of the Spanish Augustinian architect Lorenzo de San Nicolás.

The foundation of a new, higher standard of thoroughness in biographical dictionaries of artists and architects was established with the publication of the *Allgemeines Künstlerlexicon* (1763), the first in a long series of works by the Füssli family of Zurich. Johann Rudolf Füssli (1709–93) was responsible for the first and second editions, and his son Johann Heinrich Füssli (1745–1832) produced a much-expanded third iteration (1806–24). The first and second editions contain largely rehashed data from old sources, but in the third (although designated 'zweyter Theil' on its title page) Johann Heinrich introduced entries on living artists and rewrote and enlarged existing articles, discussing more individual works of art and expanding bibliographical sources to include many recent publications.

According to Dobai, *The Gentleman's and Connoisseur's Dictionary of Painters* (1770) by Matthew Pilkington (?1700–84) was the first British art dictionary. Although its entries are rather brief and uninformative, it became a staple source of biographical information on artists for readers of English and was reissued in many further editions through the 1850s. In 1777 the *Dictionnaire des artistes* by FONTENAI was published in Paris. As well as containing biographical entries (some fairly extensive) for architects, painters, sculptors, printmakers and decorative artists, this dictionary includes coverage of musicians, actors, dancers, printers, clockmakers, scientists and engineers and also has a few entries on art subjects.

Between 1767 and 1785 several significant, biographical reference works on printmakers were published: the *Dictionnaire des graveurs anciens et modernes* (1767) by Pierre-François Basan; the *Dictionnaire des artistes dont nous avons des estampes* (1778–90) by KARL HEINRICH VON HEINECKEN; and *A Biographical Dictionary Containing an Historical Account of All the Engravers* (1785–6) by Joseph

Strutt (1749–1802). These all present the printmakers alphabetically by surname and supply brief biographical information on each artist and a list of their prints. Part of the stimulus for Strutt's work, according to his preface, was to correct such deficiencies in Basan's volumes as the failure to illustrate artists' monograms or comment on their styles of printmaking. Heinecken's dictionary was the most detailed and accurate of the three, but it also took the longest to complete, and only four volumes, covering artists whose surnames began with 'A' to 'Diz', were produced by the time of his death.

In the format of Marsy's *Dictionnaire abrégé* (1746), which presented art and architectural information in several different categories—terminology, biographical data and longer articles on a variety of topics—were several works of the 1750s and 1760s. The *Dictionnaire portatif des beaux-arts* (1752) by Jacques Lacombe (1716–1801) presents architectural, literary and a few secular iconographical terms in addition to brief biographies of poets, composers and visual artists. A reference work that provided many more entries than Lacombe's for broader art subjects was the *Dictionnaire portatif de peinture, sculpture et gravure* (1757) by Antoine Joseph Pernéty (1716–1801). In addition to covering art forms, techniques, materials and artists' biographies, Pernéty includes substantial articles on such subjects as 'Perspective', 'Original', 'Connoissance', 'Inventeur', and 'Clair-Obscur'. His *Dictionnaire*, which did not cover architecture, is equipped with over sixty illustrations of artists' implements on eight engraved plates, with references from the entries to the appropriate illustrations.

An attempt at a complete one-volume dictionary of the arts was the *Handlexicon, oder, kurzgefasstes Wörterbuch der schönen Wissenschaften und freyen Künste* (1760) by Joachim Christoph Gottsched. It contains biographical entries for artists and writers, composers and figures from Classical antiquity and brief articles for terms and important works from literature, music and the visual arts.

A similar broad spectrum of art subjects was covered by J. G. SULZER in *Allgemeine Theorie der schönen Künste* (1771–4), an arts dictionary with a heavy emphasis on aesthetic theory. About 60 of Sulzer's articles (e.g. 'Architekt', 'Expression', 'Clair-Obscur' and 'Aesthetik') were translated into French and published in the *Supplément à l'Encyclopédie* (1776–7), a collection of amplifications and corrections to Diderot's *Encyclopédie*. A revised and enlarged edition (1792–9) of Sulzer's original work contained the most extensive scholarly apparatus that had so far appeared in an art dictionary or encyclopedia, including long, apparently exhaustive bibliographies appended to major articles; for example that for 'Portrait' appears to have been an attempt to list every published collection of engraved portraits to date.

One of the criticisms of Diderot's *Encyclopédie* was that its arrangement in one long alphabetical sequence scattered information on related topics. In 1782 the editor and publisher Charles Joseph Panckoucke (1736–98) brought out the first volume of his *Encyclopédie méthodique, ou par ordre de matières* (1782–1832), a project to revise the articles in the original *Encyclopédie* and rearrange them by subject. Watelet, who had written many of the articles on painting and drawing in the *Encyclopédie*, collaborated with Pierre

Charles Lévesque (1736–1812) to write the two-volume *Beaux-arts* section (1788–91) for the Panckoucke project. *Architecture* (1788–1825) was written by ANTOINE QUATREMÈRE DE QUINCY, a prominent theoretician at the Académie des Beaux-Arts. Companion collections of plates were planned for both sets. Those for *Beaux-arts* were finally published in 1805, but the ones for *Architecture* were never made. The *Encyclopédie méthodique* progressed slowly because of the disruption caused by the French Revolution and the chronic lack of capital of Panckoucke's firm.

In addition to the usual biographical entries and definitions of terms, the Quatremère de Quincy volumes contain articles on cities of architectural interest, periods in western European architectural history and some coverage of the history of architecture in various non-European countries. In the *Beaux-arts* set, Watelet and Lévesque appear to have been preoccupied with providing long discussions of aesthetic concepts (e.g. 'Agréable', 'Beau', Variété), although there is also selective coverage of artists' materials and implements, and many brief biographical entries for painters, printmakers and sculptors collected under the headings *Peintres*, *Graveurs* and *Sculpteurs*.

In the *Dictionnaire iconologique* (1756), which may have been the first reference source to present Classical, Christian and secular iconographical information in a dictionary format, Honoré Lacombe de Prezel (*b* 1725) provides brief entries for gods and other mythological beings, allegorical figures, liturgical objects, animals and other entities with representational significance in the visual arts. Lacombe's focus was primarily on Classical antiquity, and his examples of specific art works in which the themes he covered appeared were usually ancient or Renaissance medals.

BIBLIOGRAPHY

D. Diderot and J. d'Alembert, eds: *Encyclopédie, ou dictionnaire raisonné des sciences, des arts et des métiers, par une société de gens de lettres: Mis en ordre et publié par M. Diderot . . . et quant à la partie mathématique, par M. d'Alembert*, 17 vols and suppls (Paris, 1751–72/R 3/1986–9)

J. Lacombe: *Dictionnaire portatif des beaux-arts* (Paris, 1752, rev. 4/1759)

B. Forest de Bélidor: *Dictionnaire portatif de l'ingénieur et de l'artilleur* (Paris, 1755, rev. 2/1768/rev. 3/1775)

H. Lacombe de Prezel: *Dictionnaire iconologique* (Paris, 1756, rev. 3/1779/R 1972)

A. J. Pernéty: *Dictionnaire portatif de peinture, sculpture et gravure* (Paris, 1757/R 1972, 2/1767)

J. C. Gottsched: *Handlexicon, oder, kurzgefasstes Wörterbuch der schönen Wissenschaften und freyen Künste* (Leipzig, 1760/R 1970)

J. R. Füssli: *Allgemeines Künstlerlexicon*, 3 vols (Zurich, 1763, rev. 2/1779–1824)

P. F. Basan: *Dictionnaire des graveurs anciens et modernes, depuis l'origine de la gravure*, 3 vols (Paris, 1767, 3/1791)

M. Pilkington: *The Gentleman's and Connoisseur's Dictionary of Painters* (London, 1770, rev. ?10/1857)

C. F. Roland Le Virloys: *Dictionnaire d'architecture, civile, militaire et navale, antique, ancienne et moderne*, 3 vols (Paris, 1770)

J. G. Sulzer: *Allgemeine Theorie der schönen Künste*, 2 vols (Leipzig, 1771–4, rev. 2/1792–9/R 1967), suppl. (1792–1808)

J. Robinet, ed.: *Supplément à l'Encyclopédie*, 4 vols (Amsterdam, 1776–7)

L. A. de Bonafons [Fontenai]: *Dictionnaire des artistes ou notice historique et raisonnée des architectes, peintres, graveurs, sculpteurs, musiciens, acteurs et danseurs, imprimeurs, horlogers et mécaniciens*, 2 vols (Paris, 1777/R 1972)

K. H. von Heinecken: *Dictionnaire des artistes dont nous avons des estampes*, 4 vols (Leipzig, 1778–90/R 1970)

C. J. Panckoucke, ed.: *Encyclopédie méthodique, ou par ordre de matières*, ?199 vols (Paris, 1782–1832)

J. Strutt: *A Biographical Dictionary Containing an Historical Account of All the Engravers*, 2 vols (London, 1785–6/R 1972)

D. A. Rejon de Silva: *Diccionario de las nobles artes para instrucción de los aficionados, y uso de las profesores* (Segovia, 1788/R 1985)

C. H. Watelet and P. C. Lévesque: *Beaux-arts*, 2 vols (1788–91, 2/1792/R 1972), *Encyclopédie méthodique ou par ordre de matières*, ed. C. J. Panckoucke (Paris, 1782–1832)

A. Quatremère de Quincy: *Architecture*, 3 vols (1788–1825), *Encyclopédie méthodique ou par ordre de matières*, ed. C. J. Panckoucke (Paris, 1782–1825)

IV. 1801–50.

The dominance in France of art and architectural dictionary and encyclopedia production declined as disruptions caused by the French Revolution and Napoleonic Wars affected the art infrastructure and publishing industry. An exception to this was the publication in 1806 of one of the most interesting art reference works published during this period: the *Dictionnaire des beaux-arts* (1806) by AUBIN-LOUIS MILLIN DE GRANDMAISON. This was another attempt (like that of Pernéty half a century before) to compile something approaching a complete encyclopedia of the arts by providing a number of different categories of art and architectural information in the same book. Millin explained in his preface that his aim was to combine information on the history of the arts (he included music as well as the visual arts and architecture) with Sulzer's excellent coverage of aesthetic theory in his work of 1771. Many of Millin's articles are quite substantial and are provided with the most thorough bibliographies to have appeared so far in an art reference source; a large number of citations were, however, undoubtedly culled from Sulzer. Millin does not include biographical entries but provides extensive coverage of secular, iconographical themes.

A new trend in biographical dictionaries of artists and architects was represented by the publication of such works devoted to figures from a single country as the *Diccionario histórico de los más ilustres profesores de las bellas artes in España* (1800), by Juan Augustín Ceán Bermúdez; the *Dictionnaire des artistes de l'école française au XIXe siècle* (1831), by Charles Henri Joseph Gabet (1793–1860); and *De levens en werken der Hollandsche en Vlaamsche kunstschilders* (1842–3), by Johannes Immerzeel (1776–1841). One advantage of focusing biographical research on a single country was that compilers could provide better information about locations of artists' individual works. The lists of works and locations supplied by Ceán Bermúdez, for example, were the most extensive ever to have been published in a biographical dictionary of artists and architects. Gabet's *Dictionnaire* was a new kind of biographical reference work. Instead of attempting to document only long-dead artists, its purpose was to supply information about artists, architects and composers in France between 1800 and 1830. As most were still active in 1831, when the *Dictionnaire* was published, it functioned as a handbook of recent artistic activity.

Comprehensive, biographical dictionaries of artists and architects were also produced during this period, although it was the last time that this monumental task was attempted by lone compilers. The successors of these works did not appear until the early 20th century and were the result of large teams of scholars and researchers. The

Dizionario degli architetti, scultori, pittori (1830–33) by STEFANO TICOZZI attempted to cover artists and architects of all western countries and from all periods. The *Neues allgemeines Künstler-Lexikon* (1835–52) by G. K. NAGLER did the same, but in much greater detail. Nagler was a book- and print-dealer who worked on the *Lexikon* in his shop between serving customers. His professional experience with prints is reflected in the fairly lengthy entries for printmakers and extensive lists of their work. The works of neither Ticozzi nor Nagler, however, contain many bibliographical references, in contrast to the scrupulous documentation of such compilers as Johann Heinrich Füssli and Millin de Grandmaison.

An extremely popular reference work at this time was *A Biographical and Critical Dictionary of Painters and Engravers* (1816), by Michael Bryan, which was republished in revised and enlarged forms several times during the next 90 years. Bryan and his revisers supply at least rudimentary lists of works (sometimes with locations) for major painters and printmakers. *The Picture Collector's Manual* (1849) by James R. Hobbes has brief, uninformative biographical entries but includes a section classified by broad subject ('River Views', 'Battle Pieces'), in which painters are arranged according to their specialities.

International biographical coverage of printmakers, including some then still living, was provided in *Le classiche stampe* (1836) by Giulio Ferrario (1767–1847), which lists a few of each artist's prints with varying levels of information, usually including dimensions and sometimes the condition of the works and recent prices. The real progress in cataloguing prints in the 19th century was made not by compilers of biographical dictionaries but by such connoisseurs as Adam von Bartsch and his successors, whose massive catalogues concentrated more on the prints than their makers, the latter being arranged chronologically.

The *Dictionnaire de monogrammes* (1817) of Franz Brulliot (1780–1836), especially in its enlarged, three-volume edition (1832–4) with over 7000 entries, was the first significant attempt since that of J. F. Christ in 1750 to present a comprehensive collection of artists' marks and adumbrated the even longer anthologies of Nagler and Oscar Edmond Ris-Paquot (*b* 1835) that appeared later.

The *Architectural Dictionary* (1811–19), issued in parts by Peter Nicholson, contains long, well-written articles that cover aspects of architectural history and include a very detailed and technical presentation of construction practice; the entries on carpentry and bricklaying amount to concise manuals. It was, however, in the quality and imaginative use of illustrations that Nicholson's dictionary was so progressive: in no previous art or architectural reference work did the plates so effectively supplement and explicate the text.

Other architectural reference works of this period range from such unadorned dictionaries of terms as the *Rudimentary Dictionary* (1850) by John Weale (1791–1862), to such works as *A Dictionary of the Architecture and Archaeology of the Middle Ages* (1838) by John Britton, which catered for, and helped promote interest in, the Gothic Revival. Britton, a publisher and self-taught antiquarian, includes entries for medieval architectural features, early construction methods, liturgical objects and practices and biographical articles on medieval architects and ecclesiastics. He often supplies succinct, etymological histories of terms and gives their counterparts in other European languages. According to John Mordaunt Crook, however, Britton's dictionary was criticized by contemporary reviewers for 'a number of errors and omissions, particularly with regard to foreign terms'. Another, more popular, dictionary of historical architectural terminology was *A Glossary of Terms Used in Grecian, Roman, Italian and Gothic Architecture* (1836), compiled by John Henry Parker (1806–84). It went through many subsequent, enlarged editions and included so many illustrations that publication of a concise version began in 1846.

In the category of Christian iconography, two of the most significant dictionary-style reference works published in this period were compiled by Louis Jean Guénebault (1789–1878). His *Dictionnaire iconographique des monuments de l'antiquité chrétienne et du Moyen Age* (1843–5), which covers Byzantine as well as western ecclesiastical art and architecture, includes entries for biblical figures, saints and other historical individuals from the early Christian and medieval periods, liturgical objects and specific churches and other religious buildings. Guénebault discusses particular art works and supplies much bibliographical documentation and references to published illustrations. His *Dictionnaire iconographique des figures, légendes et actes des saints* (1850) was brought out as part of the series of reference works called the *Encyclopédie théologique* (1845–73) issued by Jacques Paul Migne (1800–75), the enormously productive publisher of religious materials. It was a prototype of a kind of art reference work that became very familiar in the late 20th century. In addition to the usual index of saints' attributes, Guénebault includes such useful features as an index of artists, listing their specific works in which saints are portrayed. Both Guénebault's works are unillustrated.

BIBLIOGRAPHY

J. A. Ceán Bermúdez: *Diccionario histórico de los más ilustres profesores de las bellas artes in España*, 6 vols (Madrid, 1800/*R* 1965)

J. H. Füssli: *Allgemeines Künstlerlexicon*, 4 vols (Zurich, 1806–21), suppl. (1824)

A. L. Millin de Grandmaison: *Dictionnaire des beaux-arts*, 3 vols (Paris, 1806, 2/1838)

P. Nicholson: *Architectural Dictionary*, 2 vols (London, 1811–19, rev. ?3/1854)

M. Bryan: *A Biographical and Critical Dictionary of Painters and Engravers*, 2 vols (London, 1816); rev. ed. G. C. Williamson: *Bryan's Dictionary of Painters and Engravers*, 5 vols (4/1903/*R* 1920)

F. Brulliot: *Dictionnaire de monogrammes* (Munich, 1817, rev. 2/1832–4/*R* 1969)

S. Ticozzi: *Dizionario degli architetti, scultori, pittori, intagliatori in rame ed in pietra, coniatori di medaglie, mosaicisti, niellatori, intarsiatori d'ogni età e d'ogni nazione*, 4 vols (Milan, 1830–33)

C. H. J. Gabet: *Dictionnaire des artistes de l'école française au XIXe siècle* (Paris, 1831)

G. K. Nagler: *Neues allgemeines Künstler-Lexikon oder Nachrichten von dem Leben und den Werken der Maler, Bildhauer, Baumeister, Kupferstecher, Formschneider, Lithographen, Zeichner, Medailleure, Elfenbeinarbeiter, etc.*, 22 vols (Munich, 1835–52/*R* Leipzig and Vienna, 1924)

G. Ferrario: *Le classiche stampe* (Milan, 1836/*R* 1978)

J. H. Parker: *A Glossary of Terms Used in Grecian, Roman, Italian and Gothic Architecture* (London, 1836, rev. 5/1850)

J. Britton: *A Dictionary of the Architecture and Archaeology of the Middle Ages* (London, 1838)

J. Immerzeel: *De levens en werken der Hollandsche en Vlaamsche kunstschilders, beeldhouwers, graveurs en bouwmeesters*, 3 vols (Amsterdam, 1842–3, rev. 2/1855/*R* 1974)

L. J. Guénebault: *Dictionnaire iconographique des monuments de l'antiquité chrétienne et du Moyen Age*, 2 vols (Paris, 1843–5)

J. R. Hobbes: *The Picture Collector's Manual*, 2 vols (London, 1849)

L. J. Guénebault: *Dictionnaire iconographique des figures, légendes et actes des saints*, Encyclopédie théologique (Paris, 1850)

J. Weale: *Rudimentary Dictionary of Terms Used in Architecture* (London, 1850, rev. 2/1860)

V. 1851–1900.

In the second half of the 19th century two groups of dictionaries of art and architectural terminology were developed that were aimed at very different audiences. This was the period of comprehensive, but rather superficial, dictionaries of terms intended for a large, general readership. Such works as *A Dictionary of Terms in Art* (1854) by Frederick William Fairholt (1814–66), *An Illustrated Dictionary of Words Used in Art and Archaeology* (1883) by John William Mollett (*fl* late 19th century) and *Lexique des termes d'art* (?1881) by Jules Adeline (1845–1909) cover, although very sketchily, almost every area in the visual arts and architecture. The other group of dictionaries was intended for an audience of scholars and antiquarians. They define terms, mostly associated with the decorative arts and domestic furnishings of the nobility, from the late Middle Ages and Renaissance. The publications *Glossaire français du Moyen Age* (1872) by Léon de Laborde (1807–69), the *Glossaire archéologique du Moyen-Age et de la Renaissance* (1887–1928) by Victor Gay (*d* 1887) and Henri Stein (*b* 1862) and other such publications supply precise, detailed definitions in addition to examples of the terms' uses in context in early documents.

Architectural dictionaries ranged from such simple, unillustrated compendia of undocumented definitions of polyglot terms as the *Dictionnaire général des termes d'architecture* (1868) by Daniel Ramée (1806–87) to heavily illustrated, multi-volume works with longer articles equipped with bibliographies such as the *Dictionnaire raisonné d'architecture* (1877–80) by Ernest Bosc (*b* 1837). Dictionaries of contemporary art or architectural terminology that focused on a single art form or a smaller geographical entity than a country began to appear during this period. For example the *Real-Lexikon der Kunstgewerbe* (1884) by Bruno Bucher (1826–99) provided definitions for terminology in the decorative arts and crafts, including printing and bookbinding. Architectural terminology in use in Naples during the late 19th century is covered in *Vocabolario di architettura* (1874) by Francesco Jaoul.

In a different league in terms of length, detail and wealth of illustration were the architectural encyclopedias by EUGÈNE-EMMANUEL VIOLLET-LE-DUC and Paul Amédée Planat (1839–1911). The two encyclopedias also differed from each other in purpose, coverage and presentation of information. Viollet-le-Duc's *Dictionnaire raisonné de l'architecture française du XIe au XVIe siècle* (1854–68), far from representing an attempt to compile an objective reference work, is essentially a vehicle for promoting his convictions about the superiority of the structural principles of Gothic architecture and their suitability as a modern system of design and construction. His entries in the *Dictionnaire*, mainly for building types, major architectural features, construction procedures and aspects of medieval decorative art, are generally quite long, so that there is sufficient space to develop his argument. The system of illustration in the *Dictionnaire*, as Bergdoll points out, was remarkably innovative, breaking with academic conventions for drawing buildings just as sharply as Viollet-le-Duc's ideas on the relative merits of Gothic and Classical architecture countered the conventions of the Establishment.

The Académie des Beaux-Arts began publication of its own well-illustrated *Dictionnaire* in 1858. It contained long, scholarly entries for a wide variety of art, architectural and musical terms, including decorative arts forms and motifs, artists' implements, building types and construction techniques. Pérouse de Montclos points out that many of the architectural entries were taken directly from the earlier dictionary written by Quatremère de Quincy. According to Bergdoll, the progress of the Académie's *Dictionnaire* was plagued by in-fighting and disputes over format; by the time it was discontinued in 1896, only six volumes (reaching the letter 'G') had been published.

The *Encyclopédie de l'architecture et de la construction* (1888–92), edited by P. A. Planat, was one of the first major art or architectural encyclopedias to be written by a large team of contributors. It contained signed articles on periods in architectural history, architecture in foreign countries, building types, biographical entries for architects and theorists and entries for notable buildings. Illustrations, although more conventional than Viollet-le-Duc's bird's-eye views and cutaways, were plentiful and included many plates and gatefolds. Some reversal of fortune must have forced Planat to finish the *Encyclopédie* in haste as articles representing the second half of the alphabet (N–Z) are crammed into the final volume in abbreviated form.

The most imposing architectural encyclopedia published in the 19th century, the *Dictionary of Architecture* (1852–92; 8 vols, plus plates), was British and mainly the work of one man, the versatile Wyatt Papworth. Papworth's interest in the recording of architectural information led him to found the Architectural Publication Society in 1848. From the beginning, the main purpose of the Society appears to have been the planning and production of the *Dictionary*, with Papworth as editor and principal contributor. This work is by far the most comprehensive and authoritative architectural enyclopedia to have been produced up to that time, with more than 18,000 articles on the architecture of all periods and places, and hundreds of full-page lithograph illustrations.

Biographical dictionaries of artists and architects continued the trend, begun early in the century, towards concentration on more circumscribed groups of subjects: for example *A Dictionary of Artists of the English School* (1874) by Samuel Redgrave and the *Dictionnaire général des artistes de l'école française* (1882–5) by Emile Bellier de La Chavignerie and LOUIS AUVRAY provide biographical coverage of artists and architects from all periods. Bellier–Auvray, as it is known, contains more information about individual art works than any previous biographical dictionary. The entries have minimal biographical data and concentrate instead on lists of artists' works, particularly paintings that had appeared in the Salons, the official exhibitions held in Paris since 1667 by the Académie des Beaux-Arts. Incidental, but important, information about many works, including their locations and provenance, is

also supplied. The same kind of data was supplied for sculptures by artists included in the *Dictionnaire des sculpteurs de l'école française* (1898–1921), by Stanislas Lami (*b* 1858).

Another notable biographical dictionary of this period was the *Malerwerke des neunzehnten Jahrhunderts* (1891–1901) by Friedrich von Boetticher, which covers 19th-century European painters, most of them German. As the title of the work suggests it resembles Bellier–Auvray in its emphasis on lists of works. Information on individual paintings and drawings sometimes includes date of execution, dimensions, exhibition, collection and auction history and even occasional references to illustrations in periodicals.

Towards the end of the 19th century art history had existed as a discipline long enough for a significant body of information on individual art works to have accumulated in catalogues and journals, which became available to the compilers of biographical dictionaries of artists and other art reference works. Consequently there was a new preoccupation with the documentation of individual works. The first dictionary-style, art reference work to include illustrated entries for specific works of art in addition to biographical articles was the *Cyclopedia of Painters and Paintings* (1885–7), by the Americans John Denison Champlin (1834–1915) and Charles C. Perkins. The illustrations were only small line blocks but were sufficient to convey some idea of a painting's composition and portrayal of subject-matter. The accompanying entry provided a verbal description and a bibliography. Champlin and Perkins cited over 900 items in their main bibliography, and their preface made it obvious that they regarded current printed information on individual works of art as extremely important. In addition to the most recent monographs and issues of art journals they claimed that 'the latest catalogues of all the great art museums of the world, and of many private collections, have . . . been carefully collated, so that the information given is the best and fullest accessible up to the date of publication'.

The writer HENRI BERALDI compiled, or co-compiled, two excellent biographical dictionaries of printmakers: *Les Graveurs du XVIIIe siècle* (1880–82) with Roger Portalis (1841–1912) and *Les Graveurs du XIXe siècle* (1884–92). In addition to biographical information these works supplied catalogues, or at least a list, of printmakers' works. Since they include many more artists (most of them French) than the leading catalogues that covered the work of French 18th- and 19th-century printmakers (by Prosper de Baudicour and Loys-Henri Delteil respectively), or the incomplete series *Inventaire du fonds français* by the Bibliothèque Nationale, they are extremely useful. The two most comprehensive dictionaries of artists' marks were produced during this period: *Die Monogrammisten* (1857–78) by G. K. Nagler, which contains *c.* 15,000 monograms in addition to significant, biographical information on the artists to whom they belonged, and the *Dictionnaire encyclopédique des marques et monogrammes* (1893), by Oscar Edmond Ris-Paquot, with over 12,000 entries. The Nagler work was eventually supplemented by the *Monogramm Lexikon* (1964) by Franz Goldstein, which began its coverage at 1850.

Guénebault's iconographical reference works (1843–5; 1850) were intended for a scholarly audience. Later in the 19th century some dictionaries of Christian iconography for the educated, general reader began to be published. *Christliche Symbolik* (1854) by Wolfgang Menzel contains brief but substantive entries for events, things, animals, saints and biblical figures, including references to specific art works in which they appear and citations to illustrations of those art works. In the 1870s and 1880s Clara Erskine Clement Waters (1834–1916) produced several iconographical dictionaries that dealt principally with saints and their representation in the visual arts; her entries describe how saints were portrayed but usually stop short of naming specific works. The iconography of Classical art was given detailed, scholarly coverage in such late 19th-century Classical dictionaries as the *Ausführliches Lexikon der griechischen und römischen Mythologie* (1884–1937), edited by Wilhelm Heinrich Roscher (1845–1923); *Denkmäler des klassischen Altertums* (1885–9), edited by August Baumeister (1830–1922); *Dictionnaire des antiquités grecques et romaines* (1877–1919), edited by Daremberg and Saglio; and *Paulys Realencyclopädie der classischen Altertumswissenschaft* (1894–1978), edited by Wissowa, Kroll and Mittelhaus. Each of these dictionaries cites specific art works in which Classical figures or themes are represented and also supply bibliographical references to illustrations of the art works in books and journals. Roscher and Pauly–Wissowa provide the fullest information on the iconography of mythological figures, while the works of Baumeister, Daremberg and Saglio contain the fullest articles on other aspects of ancient art and architecture. Baumeister contains the best entries on archaeological sites; Daremberg and Saglio provide the fullest coverage of the history of ancient art forms, such as sculpture and vase painting.

In *Allgemeiner Portrait-Katalog* (1860), Wilhelm Eduard Drugulin (1822–79) provides a listing, alphabetical by sitter, of almost 24,000 printed portraits. In most cases he supplies the name of the original artist who painted or drew the portrait as well as the printmaker.

BIBLIOGRAPHY

W. Papworth, ed.: *Dictionary of Architecture*, 8 vols (London, 1852–92)

F. W. Fairholt: *A Dictionary of Terms in Art* (London, 1854/*R* 1969, 3/1903)

W. Menzel: *Christliche Symbolik*, 2 vols (Regensburg, 1854)

E. Viollet-le-Duc: *Dictionnaire raisonné de l'architecture française du XIe au XVIe siècle*, 10 vols (Paris, 1854–68/*R* 1967)

G. K. Nagler: *Die Monogrammisten und diejenigen bekannten und unbekannten Künstler aller Schulen, welchen sich zur Bezeichnung ihrer Werke eines figürlichen Zeichens, der Initiale des Namens, der Abbreviatur desselben, etc.*, 5 vols (vols 1–4, Munich, 1857–76, vol 5, Leipzig, 1878; rev. Munich, 2/1860–79/*R* 1966)

Dictionnaire de l'Académie des Beaux-Arts, 6 vols (Paris, 1858–96)

W. E. Drugulin: *Allgemeiner Portrait-Katalog*, 2 vols (Leipzig, 1860/*R* 1961)

D. Ramée: *Dictionnaire général des termes d'architecture* (Paris, 1868)

L. de Laborde: *Glossaire français du Moyen Age* (Paris, 1872/*R* 1975)

F. Jaoul: *Vocabulario di architettura* (Naples, 1874)

S. Redgrave: *Dictionary of Artists of the English School* (London, 1874, rev. 2/1878/*R* 1970)

E. Bosc: *Dictionnaire raisonné d'architecture*, 4 vols (Paris, 1877–80, 2/1883)

C. Daremberg and E. Saglio, eds: *Dictionnaire des antiquités grecques et romaines*, 5 vols (Paris, 1877–1919/*R* 1962–3)

R. Portalis and H. Beraldi: *Les Graveurs du XVIIIe siècle*, 3 vols (Paris, 1880–82/*R* 1970)

J. Adeline: *Lexique des termes d'art* (Paris, ?1881, 2/1884; Eng. trans., 1891)

E. Bellier de La Chavignerie and L. Auvray: *Dictionnaire général des artistes de l'école française depuis l'origine des arts du dessin jusqu'à nos jours*, 2 vols (Paris, 1882–5/*R* 1979), suppl. (Paris, 1887)

J. W. Mollett: *An Illustrated Dictionary of Words Used in Art and Archaeology* (London, 1883/*R* 1987)

H. Beraldi: *Les Graveurs du XIXe siècle*, 12 vols (Paris, 1884–92/*R* 1981)

B. Bucher: *Real-Lexikon der Kunstgewerbe* (Vienna, 1884)

W. H. Roscher, ed.: *Ausführliches Lexikon der griechischen und römischen Mythologie*, 6 vols (Leipzig, 1884–1937/*R* 1965), suppls (1904–21/*R* 1965)

J. D. Champlin and C. C. Perkins: *Cyclopedia of Painters and Paintings*, 4 vols (New York, 1885–7/*R* 1969, 7/1927)

A. Baumeister, ed.: *Denkmäler des klassischen Altertums*, 3 vols (Munich, 1885–9)

V. Gay and H. Stein: *Glossaire archéologique du Moyen-Age et de la Renaissance*, 2 vols (Paris, 1887–1928/*R* 1967)

P. A. Planat, ed.: *Encyclopédie de l'architecture et de la construction*, 6 vols (Paris, 1888–92)

F. von Boetticher: *Malerwerke des neunzehnten Jahrhunderts*, 2 vols (Dresden, 1891–1901/*R* 1969, ?3/1944–8)

O. E. Ris-Paquot: *Dictionnaire encyclopédique des marques et monogrammes*, 2 vols (Paris, 1893/*R* 1964)

G. Wissowa, W. Kroll and K. Mittelhaus, eds: *Paulys Realencyclopädie der classischen Altertumswissenschaft*, 34 vols in 68 (Stuttgart, 1894–1978/*R* 1981)

S. Lami: *Dictionnaire des sculpteurs de l'école française*, 8 vols (Paris, 1898–1921/*R* Nendeln, 1970)

F. Goldstein: *Monogramm Lexikon: Internationales Verzeichnis der Monogramme bildender Künstler seit 1850* (Berlin, 1964)

VI. After 1900.

Numerous art dictionaries and encyclopedias were published after 1900, and detailed information on most of them is available in such excellent art bibliographies as *Guide to the Literature of Art History* (1980) by E. Arntzen and R. Rainwater. One of the most widely used general dictionaries of art terms in the 20th century was the *Dictionnaire polyglotte des termes d'art et d'archéologie* by Louis Réau, which was first published in 1928. Its 1977 edition includes alphabetical lists of German, English and Italian art terms with their French equivalents. A similar polyglot work, but with a main lexicon in Italian, was the *Dizionario di termini artistici* (1967) by Michelangelo Masciotta. Dictionaries of German art and architectural terminology include the *Bildwörterbuch der Kunst* (1950) by Heinrich Lützeler (*b* 1902), which has been republished in several subsequent editions. Some projects attempted to establish the correct definitions for art and architectural terms on a large scale. The *Glossarium artis* series of dictionaries sponsored by the Comité International d'Histoire de l'Art began publication in 1972. Each of the dictionaries published covers the terminology of a relatively circumscribed branch of art or architectural history, such as military architecture, Christian liturgical objects or urban design. Early volumes in the series give terms in both German and French, with the definitions in German, while the later ones also include corresponding English terms. In 1971 the Inventaire Général des Monuments et des Richesses Artistiques de la France published *Tapisserie: Méthode et vocabulaire*, the first of a series of heavily illustrated, classified dictionaries of terminology related to various art forms.

One of the most popular English-language dictionaries of architectural terminology was the *Illustrated Glossary of Architecture, 850–1830* (1966), by John Harris (*b* 1931) and Jill Lever; it includes excellent photographic illustrations on which architectural features have been clearly designated; a second edition called *The Illustrated Dictionary of Architecture, 850–1914* was published in 1989. *English Architecture: An Illustrated Glossary* (1977) by James Stevens Curl (*b* 1937) presents well-illustrated definitions of terms, many of them specific to British architectural history. The *Wörterbuch der altchristlichen Kunst* (1959) by Heinrich Laag (*b* 1892) is a small dictionary of German and Latin words that one might encounter in the study of early Christian art. *Glossaire des termes techniques* (1965) by Melchior de Vogüé provides definitions and equivalents from other European languages for terms associated with Romanesque art and architecture; it is illustrated with well-keyed photographs. Definitions of contemporary art terminology are supplied in the *Glossary of Art, Architecture and Design since 1945* (1973) by John Albert Walker (*b* 1938). Terms for painters' materials and implements and other technical terms are defined in *Materia Pictoria: An Encyclopedia of Methods and Materials in Painting and the Graphic Arts* (1939) by Eric Hesketh Hubbard (*b* 1892), but in the late 20th century the standard dictionary of the technology of art was *A Dictionary of Art Terms and Techniques* (1969) by Ralph Mayer (*b* 1895).

The major 20th-century biographical dictionary of artists and architects was the *Allgemeines Lexikon der bildenden Künstler* (1907–50), edited by Ulrich Thieme and Felix Becker (*see* THIEME-BECKER), and the supplement for artists and architects born after 1870, *Allgemeines Lexikon der bildenden Künstler des XX. Jahrhunderts* (1953–62), edited by Hans Vollmer (*b* 1878). Thieme–Becker includes artists and architects from all periods and countries. No other biographical dictionary comes close to its comprehensive coverage and the detail of its major articles and their bibliographies. A distant second place belongs to the *Dictionnaire critique et documentaire des peintres, sculpteurs, dessinateurs et graveurs* (1913–22), edited by Emmanuel Bénézit, which was republished in several, successively larger editions. A new edition of Thieme–Becker, begun by the Leipzig publisher E. A. Seemann and edited by G. Meissner in 1983, faltered after the publication of three volumes, but the project was taken over in 1992 by the firm of K. G. Saur, which issued reset versions of the Seemann volumes and added some of its own as it continued the series.

One of the best visual arts biographical dictionaries published in the late 20th century was the *Macmillan Encyclopedia of Architects* (1982), edited by Adolf K. Placzek, which contains substantive articles by specialist scholars on the major figures. Among the outstanding 20th-century biographical dictionaries devoted to the artists and architects of a single country were the *Dictionary of British Sculptors, 1660–1851* (1953) by Rupert Gunnis and *A Biographical Dictionary of English Architects, 1660–1840* (1954) by Howard Montagu Colvin, both of which have excellent topographical indexes. The *Dictionnaire biographique des artistes contemporains, 1910–1930* (1930–34) by René Edouard-Joseph covers a brief but important chronological period and includes not only French artists but also foreign artists working in France during those years. *French Sculptors of the 17th and 18th Centuries: The Reign of Louis XIV* (1977–), edited by François Souchal, contains useful biographical entries for the sculptors included, but its primary purpose is to provide illustrated catalogues of their work. In its later editions *I pittori italiani dell'ottocento: Dizionario critico e documentario* (1934) by Agostino Mario Comanducci (1891–1940) was expanded to include 20th-century figures and became the most comprehensive national biographical dictionary of modern painters. The *Niederländisches Künstler-Lexikon auf Grund archivalische Forschungen bearbeitet* (1906–11) by ALFRED VON WURZBACH is an important, scholarly work that covers painters, printmakers and some sculptors from the 15th century to the 19th. Entries for major figures conclude with useful, widely cited lists of their works; titles of works are given, as well as such information as whether they were dated or signed and the birth and death dates and occupations of the subjects of portraits. Separate lists of prints by an artist or after an artist's work (in the latter case supplying information about who made the engraving and who invented the original image) are also included.

Additions to the significant dictionaries of monograms and other marks in the 20th century were *Les Marques de collections de dessins et d'estampes* (1921–56), a compendium of collectors' marks by Frits Lugt, and *The Classified Directory of Artists' Signatures* (1976) by H. H. Caplan.

The potential hinted at in the mid-18th century works by Lacombe, Pernéty and others, who appeared to be attempting to compile comprehensive encyclopedias of art, was for the first time realized in the 20th century. Comprehensive surveys of art and architectural history were presented in encyclopedias of varying size, from the huge *Encyclopedia of World Art* (1959–68) to the one-volume *Oxford Companion to Art* (1970), edited by Harold Osborne (*b* 1905). The *Encyclopedia of World Art* and the *Reallexikon zur deutschen Kunstgeschichte* (1937–) are very different kinds of encyclopedia. The *Encyclopedia of World Art*, a translation of the Italian *Enciclopedia universale dell'arte* (1958–67), is an alphabetically arranged sequence of long survey articles on major subjects, such as art-historical periods, the history of art in large countries and such monographic topics as 'Historiography', 'Museums and Collections' and 'Perspective'. Bibliographies at the end of articles are usually very full. The last volume contains a very detailed, 650-page analytical index to information in all the articles, which somewhat mitigates the monolithic effect of the longer entries. Half of each volume, except the index, comprises a section of large black-and-white and colour illustrations, which are keyed to the articles.

Articles in the *Reallexikon zur deutschen Kunstgeschichte* are shorter and more discrete than those in the *Encyclopedia of World Art*. It is particularly strong in its coverage of Christian and Jewish liturgical objects and paraphernalia; the iconographical entries are also excellent. The bibliographies are exhaustive, and the text is heavily studded with parenthetical references to supporting textual and illustrative material. Although it is nominally an encyclopedia of Germanic art, its entries (especially those written since 1945) cover art-historical developments in non-Germanic areas; unfortunately the publication progressed very slowly. Smaller, general art and architectural encyclopedias of the 20th century include the *Lexikon der Kunst* (1968–78), a then East German publication of generally high quality with particular strength in the art and architecture of Central and Eastern Europe, and the *McGraw-Hill Dictionary of Art* (1969), edited by Bernard Samuel Myers (*b* 1908), which has broad biographical coverage as well as excellent coverage of cities of architectural importance and their monuments.

Four large architectural encyclopedias were published in the 20th century: the *Dictionary of Architecture and Building* (1901–2), edited by Russell Sturgis, which is still occasionally helpful for illustrated explanations of 19th-century construction technology; *Wasmuths Lexikon der Baukunst* (1929–37), which is especially strong in its illustrated historical entries and articles on building types, major European cities and early 20th-century building design and technology; the *Dizionario enciclopedico di architettura e urbanistica* (1968–9), edited by Paolo Portoghesi and known for its strong conceptual articles (e.g. 'Eclettismo', 'Moderno', 'Proporzioni'), biographical entries for architectural historians and theorists and excellent lists of works in its entries on architects; and, most recently, the *Encyclopedia of Architecture: Design, Engineering and Construction* (1988–9), edited by Joseph A. Wilkes, which has strong technical articles on materials and procedures but a rather erratic coverage of architectural history.

Notable encyclopedias devoted to a particular period in art and architectural history have also been compiled in the 20th century. For example the *Enciclopedia dell'arte antica, classica e orientale* (1958–66) provides scholarly coverage of a huge portion, both topographical and chronological, of the ancient world, including articles on archaeological sites, iconographical themes and individual artists. The *Dictionnaire d'archéologie chrétienne et de liturgie* (1907–53), edited by Fernand Cabrol (1855–1937), is an enormous work covering the history and development of early Christianity and includes a great deal of material on art, architecture and iconography. The *Reallexikon zur byzantinischen Kunst* (1966–), edited by Klaus Wessel (*b* 1916) and Marcell Restle (*b* 1932), is a carefully produced encyclopedia that covers all aspects of Byzantine art and architecture, including significant sites, iconographical themes, art forms and notable figures.

The elevation of iconography to a major tool of art-historical research in the 1930s and 1940s helped stimulate the production of many excellent reference works, not all of them alphabetically arranged; for example, Réau's survey of the Old and New Testaments in *Iconographie de l'art chrétien* (1955–9) follows the episodic order of the Bible. The identification of iconographical themes, however, with human or divine beings, animals, well-known legends, historical events or common objects, lends itself most readily to an alphabetical presentation of information. The most authoritative dictionary of Christian iconography is the *Lexikon der christlichen Ikonographie* (1968–76), edited by Engelbert Kirschbaum (*b* 1902), which, in its first four volumes, has lengthy entries that give motifs' sources in scriptural or other early writings, detail their appearances in specific works of art (with citations to illustrations of the works in other publications) and provide exhaustive bibliographies of books and articles about them. The same high scholarly standard is maintained in the dictionary of saints in volumes five to eight. The series *Saints in Italian Art* by George Kaftal, which was begun in 1952 with the publication of *Iconography of the Saints in Tuscan Painting*, eventually covered all of Italy in four volumes and is the most richly illustrated treatment of saints' iconography. Each of the Kaftal volumes is equipped with an 'Index of attributes, distinctive signs and scenes', which, with such generic entries as 'Departure, Departing, Leaving' or 'Prostrate Figure', can lead a puzzled researcher from the image of an anonymous figure to the correct identification of a saint. *Attributs et symboles dans l'art profane, 1450–1600* (1958–64) by Guy de Tervarent supplies entries for Renaissance secular themes, giving examples of art works in which they appear. The *Lexicon iconographicum mythologiae classicae* (1981–) provides a heavily illustrated source of information about the iconography of figures from Classical mythology for scholars who, previously, were forced to resort to such antiquated reference works as Roscher's *Ausführliches Lexikon*.

Major dictionary-style sources of information about portraits include the *A. L. A. Portrait Index* (1906), which indexes the portraits in books and journals of the late 19th century; the *Allgemeiner Bildniskatalog* (1930–36) and *Neuer Bildniskatalog* (1937–8) by Hans Wolfgang Singer (*b* 1867), which record portraits in German public art collections; and the *Dictionary of British Portraiture* (1979–81), edited by Richard Ormond and Malcolm Rogers, which indexes portraits in British public collections. None of these works is illustrated.

BIBLIOGRAPHY

R. Sturgis, ed.: *Dictionary of Architecture and Building*, 3 vols (New York, 1901–2/*R* 1966)

A. L. A. Portrait Index (Washington, DC, 1906/*R* 1967)

A. von Wurzbach: *Niederländisches Künstler-Lexikon auf Grund archivalische Forschungen bearbeitet*, 3 vols (Vienna and Leipzig, 1906–11/*R* Amsterdam, 1974)

U. Thieme and F. Becker, eds: *Allgemeines Lexikon der bildenden Künstler von der Antike bis zur Gegenwart*, 37 vols (Leipzig, 1907–50); 2/1983–90, ed G. Meissner, 3 vols; rev. Munich, 3/1992–) [only 3 vols of 2nd edn pubd]

F. Cabrol, ed.: *Dictionnaire d'archéologie chrétienne et de liturgie*, 15 vols (Paris, 1907–53)

E. Bénézit, ed.: *Dictionnaire critique et documentaire des peintres, sculpteurs, dessinateurs et graveurs*, 3 vols (Paris, 1911–24, rev. 1913–22 in 10 vols, rev. 3/1976)

F. Lugt: *Les Marques de collections de dessins et d'estampes* (Amsterdam, 1921), suppl. (The Hague, 1956)

L. Réau: *Dictionnaire polyglotte des termes d'art et d'archéologie* (Paris, 1928, rev. Osnabrück, ?3/1977)

Wasmuths Lexikon der Baukunst, 5 vols (Berlin, 1929–37)

R. Edouard-Joseph: *Dictionnaire biographique des artistes contemporains, 1910–1930*, 3 vols (Paris, 1930–34), suppl. (Paris, 1936)

H. W. Singer: *Allgemeiner Bildniskatalog*, 14 vols (Leipzig, 1930–36/*R* 1967)

A. M. Comanducci: *I pittori italiani dell'ottocento: Dizionario critico e documentario*, 2 vols (Milan, 1934/*R* 1991, rev. 4/1970–74)

O. Schmitt, ed.: *Reallexikon zur deutschen Kunstgeschichte* (Stuttgart, 1937–)

H. W. Singer: *Neuer Bildniskatalog*, 5 vols (Leipzig, 1937–8/*R* 1967)

E. H. Hubbard: *Materia Pictoria: An Encyclopedia of Methods and Materials in Painting and the Graphic Arts* (London, 1939)

H. Lützeler: *Bildwörterbuch der Kunst* (Bonn, 1950, rev. 4/1989)

G. Kaftal: *Saints in Italian Art*, 4 vols (Florence, 1952–85)

R. Gunnis: *Dictionary of British Sculptors, 1660–1851* (London, 1953, rev. 2/1968)

H. Vollmer, ed.: *Allgemeines Lexikon der bildenden Künstler des XX. Jahrhunderts*, 6 vols (Leipzig, 1953–62)

H. M. Colvin: *A Biographical Dictionary of English Architects, 1660–1840* (London, 1954, rev. 2/1978)

L. Réau: *Iconographie de l'art chrétien*, 3 vols (Paris, 1955–9/*R* 1974–7)

G. de Tervarent: *Attributs et symboles dans l'art profane, 1450–1600*, 3 vols (Geneva, 1958–64)

Enciclopedia dell'arte antica, classica e orientale, 7 vols (Rome, 1958–66), suppls (1973, 1981–5)

Enciclopedia universale dell'arte, 15 vols (Rome, 1958–67); Eng. trans. as *Encyclopedia of World Art* (New York, 1959–68), suppls (1983, 1987)

H. Laag: *Wörterbuch der altchristlichen Kunst* (Kassel, 1959)

M. de Vogüé: *Glossaire des termes techniques* (Paris, 1965, rev. 4/1989)

J. Harris and J. Lever: *Illustrated Glossary of Architecture, 850–1830* (London, 1966); rev. as *The Illustrated Dictionary of Architecture, 850–1914* (London, 1989)

M. Restle and K. Wessel, eds: *Reallexikon zur byzantinischen Kunst* (Stuttgart, 1966–)

M. Masciotta: *Dizionario di termini artistici* (Florence, 1967)

P. Portoghesi: *Dizionario enciclopedico di architettura e urbanistica*, 6 vols (Rome, 1968–9)

E. Kirschbaum, ed.: *Lexikon der christlichen Ikonographie*, 8 vols (Rome, 1968–76)

Lexikon der Kunst: Architektur, bildende Kunst, angewandte Kunst, Industrieformgestaltung Kunsttheorie, 5 vols (Leipzig, 1968–78/R 1983)

R. Mayer: *A Dictionary of Art Terms and Techniques* (New York, 1969, rev. 2/1991)

B. S. Myers, ed.: *McGraw-Hill Dictionary of Art*, 5 vols (New York, 1969)

H. Osborne, ed.: *Oxford Companion to Art* (Oxford, 1970)

N. Viallet: *Tapisserie: Méthode et vocabulaire*, Principes d'analyse scientifique (Paris, 1971)

Glossarium artis (Tübingen, 1972–)

J. A. Walker: *Glossary of Art, Architecture and Design since 1945* (London, 1973, rev. 3/1992)

H. H. Caplan: *The Classified Directory of Artists' Signatures* (Detroit, 1976, rev. 2/1982)

J. S. Curl: *English Architecture: An Illustrated Glossary* (Newton Abbot, 1977, rev. 2/1986)

F. Souchal, ed.: *French Sculptors of the 17th and 18th Centuries: The Reign of Louis XIV* (Oxford, 1977–)

R. Ormond and M. Rogers, eds: *Dictionary of British Portraiture*, 4 vols (London, 1979–81)

Lexicon iconographicum mythologiae classicae (Zurich, 1981–)

A. K. Placzek, ed.: *Macmillan Encyclopedia of Architects*, 4 vols (New York and London, 1982)

J. A. Wilkes, ed.: *Encyclopedia of Architecture: Design, Engineering and Construction*, 5 vols (New York, 1988–9)

ALEX ROSS

Endara Crow, Gonzalo (*b* Quito, 1936). Ecuadorean painter and sculptor. He studied at the Faculty of Arts of the Universidad Central in Quito (1971) and then taught at the Escuela de Bellas Artes de Loja. From 1977 he gave up teaching to concentrate on his career as an artist. He was a proponent of the naive style of fantastic realism, which corresponded in Latin American visual art to magic realism in literature and constituted a typically Latin American expression of the paradoxes of everyday reality. In his studies of the life of the mestizo population of the Andean world, Endara Crow chose themes based on people's daily lives, depicting, for example, horses pulling bells up the sides of mountains and animals and birds peering out from the upper floors of picturesque provincial houses, in images bordering on magic and the bizarre. In his painting Endara Crow worked mostly in acrylic. He also created colourful sculptural monuments and murals. His work was exhibited internationally to great critical acclaim, and he was awarded many prizes, including the Swiss International Naive Painting prize in 1982 and an award at the 1st Bienal de La Habana, Cuba, in 1984. He was a member of the Henri Rousseau group.

BIBLIOGRAPHY

H. Rodríguez Castelo: 'Gonzalo Endara Crow', *Rev. Diners*, 15 (1983), pp. 44–8

Gonzalo Endara Crow (exh. cat., Quito, La Manzana Verde, 1984)

C. Suárez: *Endara Crow* (Quito, 1986)

CECILIA SUÁREZ

Ende & Böckmann. German architectural partnership formed in 1859 by Hermann Ende (*b* Landsberg am Warthe, 4 March 1829; *d* Wannsee, Berlin, 10 Aug 1907) and Wilhelm Böckmann (*b* Eberfeld, 29 Jan 1832; *d* Berlin, 22 Oct 1902). The practice was one of the most successful commercial firms of architects in Berlin during the latter half of the 19th century. From 1859 until their dissolution in 1895, Ende & Böckmann were instrumental in the architectural development of the city. They participated in the development of such new and elegant residential areas as Wilmersdorf and Neubabelsberg with their palatial villas. Active in the design of commercial buildings, banks and offices for the booming capital, one of their first commercial projects, the so-called Rotes Schloss (1864), was an exemplary office building. Other commercial buildings included the Preussische Bodenkreditbank (1871–4) and the Deutsche Unionbank (1872–5). The firm had a large output, designing buildings as varied as the Museum für Völkerkunde (1880–86; destr.), the Lessing-theater (1887–8; destr.) and the ministry and palace of justice (1886–91; destr.), all in Berlin. The practice provided a stepping stone for such young architects as Hermann Muthesius, who designed the Gothic Revival German church (1887–91) in Tokyo during his period with the firm. In the 1870s the controversy over appropriate architectural styles became more and more acute. Ende & Böckmann took the lead in the propagation of the German Renaissance Revival, a style they used sensitively, acknowledging its local as well as national overtones. This was illustrated in their design for the synagogue (1885–7) in Danzig (now Gdańsk, Poland), which used motifs of the local Renaissance style, asserting individuality in a national context. Their reputation reached as far as Japan: Ende & Böckmann were invited to design for Tokyo the monumental public complex comprising buildings for the Diet (parliament) and the ministry and palace of justice (1886–95; Diet building unexecuted). In Japan, however, their Western-orientated eclectic approach failed: early designs showed superficial attempts to integrate Japanese motifs, mainly through pagoda towers, but the final Renaissance and Baroque Revival mixture was completely alien to the surrounding townscape.

For illustration of work *see* ZOO.

BIBLIOGRAPHY

Thieme–Becker: Wasmuth

V. Hammerschmidt: *Anspruch und Ausdruck in der Architektur des späten Historismus in Deutschland, 1860–1914* (Frankfurt am Main, 1985)

☐

Endell, August (*b* Berlin, 12 April 1871; *d* Berlin, 13 April 1925). German architect, designer, writer and teacher. After moving to Munich in 1892, he abandoned his plan to become a teacher, deciding on a career as a freelance scholar. He then studied aesthetics, psychology and philosophy, being particularly influenced by the lectures of the psychologist Theodor Lipps. He also studied German literature, art and music. In 1895 he intended to write a doctorate on the theme of 'The Construction of Feeling'. In spring 1896 he met Hermann Obrist, who persuaded him to abandon his proposed academic career and become a self-taught artist. As well as book illustrations and decorative pieces for the art magazines *Pan* and

Dekorative Kunst, he produced decorative designs for wall reliefs, carpets, textiles, coverings, window glass and lamps. In 1897 he designed his first furniture for his cousin, the historian Kurt Breysig. His first architectural work, the Elvira photographic studio in Munich (1896–7; destr. 1944; *see* ART NOUVEAU, fig. 4), decorated on its street façade by a gigantic, writhing dragon, was a quintessential work of Jugendstil architecture. It was followed by a contract for a sanatorium in Wyk auf Föhr (1898).

At first Endell was heavily influenced by Obrist, his work characterized by an expressive ornamentation, the bizarre idiom of which seems to be derived from a microscopically observed world of submarine flora and fauna. In Munich, with Otto Eckmann, Obrist, Richard Riemerschmid, Otto Pankok, Bruno Paul and Peter Behrens, Endell was one of the founders of Jugendstil (*see* ART NOUVEAU). In 1897 he collaborated on two small rooms at the art exhibition in the Glaspalast. With Obrist he acted as spokesperson for the new Arts and Crafts movement. At the same time, with texts such as 'Um die Schönheit' (1896), he paved the way for abstract art. In his new art theory based on a psychological aesthetic of perception, he proclaimed a purely formal art divorced from the imitation of nature, an art that evoked strong feelings through freely invented forms, as music does through sounds.

Endell's move to Berlin in 1901 introduced a new phase to his creative work. The Buntes Theater (1901) built for the dramatist Ernst von Wolzogen in the Köpenicker-strasse was, however, still tied stylistically to the work of his Munich period. From then on he gradually evolved from the revolutionary ornamentist to the shaper of architectural space. In the Neumannsche Festsäle at 40 Rosenthalerstrasse (1905–6) a calming of forms is discernible with the emergence of geometrical elements in the interior decoration. In the Haus am Steinplatz (1906–7), an important work in the history of the Berlin apartment building, ornamentation was confined to the entrance, while the whole façade formed a cohesive unity. The villas in Westend, Berlin (e.g. the Pension Müller, Kastanienallee 32, 1908; Haus Nelson, 15 Eichenallee, 1910 and Haus Kühl, 14 Akazienallee, 1910), no longer achieved their overall effect through details, but through masses, a clear articulation of the whole structure. Simplicity, objectivity and utility are the dominant concerns in their design. This was still more true of the engineering structures of the trotting racecourse in Mariendorf, Berlin (1911–13), at which Endell created the first artistic racecourse architecture. In 1916 he took part in a competition for a German House of Friendship in Constantinople (now Istanbul), and in 1917 he produced plans for an imperial war museum in Berlin. He also taught at the Schule für Formkunst, Berlin, which he founded in 1904 and which survived until 1914. He achieved late recognition in 1918, when he was appointed Director of the Akademie für Kunst und Kunstgewerbe in Breslau (now Wrocław, Poland).

WRITINGS
Um die Schönheit (Munich, 1896)
Die Schönheit der grossen Stadt (Stuttgart, 1908)

BIBLIOGRAPHY
K. Scheffler: *Die Architektur der Grossstadt* (Berlin, 1913)
R. G. Köhler: 'Programmatische Künstlerschriften', *Jugendstil: Der Weg ins 20. Jahrhundert*, ed. H. Seling (Munich, 1959), pp. 420–24
K. Reichel: *Vom Jugendstil zur Sachlichkeit: August Endell (1871–1925)* (diss., U. Bochum, 1974)
August Endell: Der Architekt des Photoateliers Elvira, 1871–1925 (exh. cat., Munich, Villa Stuck, 1977)
T. Buddensieg: 'Zur Frühzeit von August Endell: Seine Münchener Briefe an Kurt Breysig', *Festschrift für Eduard Trier zum 60. Geburtstag* (Berlin, 1981), pp. 223–50

GISELA MOELLER

Ender, Thomas (*b* Vienna, 3 Nov 1793; *d* Vienna, 28 Sept 1875). Austrian painter active in Brazil. He studied at the Akademie der Bildenden Künste in Vienna, where from the start he was interested in recording landscape, especially in watercolour. As a protégé of Chancellor Metternich he was appointed artist to the Austrian scientific mission that left for Brazil in 1817 accompanying Dona Leopoldine, the Archduchess of Austria and the Imperial Brazilian princess. During his ten-month stay in Brazil, spent mainly in Rio de Janeiro, São Paulo and in trips between the two cities, he depicted landscapes, people, architecture, everyday implements and the flora and fauna of the region in nearly 800 watercolours and drawings (Vienna, Bib. Akad. Bild. Kst.). Careful detail outweighs the intrusion of a certain exoticism in these works, as can be seen, for example, in *Guanabara Bay* (1817; São Paulo, Mus. A.). On his return to Austria, and after a sightseeing and study trip through Italy, he became professor of landscape painting in the Akademie der Bildenden Künste in Vienna between 1836 and 1851.

BIBLIOGRAPHY
J. F. de Almeida Prado: *Thomas Ender: Pintor austriaco na corte de D. João VI* (São Paulo, 1955)
G. Ferrez: *O velho Rio de Janeiro através das gravuras de Thomas Ender* (São Paulo, 1957)
——: *O Brasil de Thomas Ender* (Rio de Janeiro, 1976)

ROBERTO PONTUAL

Enderle, Johann Baptist (*b* Ulm-Söflingen, 15 June 1725; *d* Donauwörth, 15 Feb 1798). German painter. He was presumably trained by his uncle, Anton Enderle (1700–61), whose works include the ceiling frescoes in the Pfarrkirche built by Dominikus Zimmermann at Günzburg. Johann Baptist arranged to work under Franz Martin Kuen *c*. 1750, and it may be assumed that he visited the Augsburg academy under Johann Georg Bergmüller. In 1755 he married Theresia, widow of the painter Johann Benedikt Reismiller (*d* 1753/4) in Donauwörth and took over his predecessor's workshop and clientele. The frescoes in St Stephan, Kirchdorf (1753), St Clemens, Herbertshofen (1754) and St Martin, Schwabmühlhausen (1759) show Enderle developing his own unmistakable style, with a pale, light palette and fine detailed line. His chief works are at Unterrammingen (Pfarrkirche St Magnus, 1769), Zaisertshofen (Pfarrhaus, 1770), Scheppach (Wallfahrtskirche Allerheiligen, 1770–71), Mainz (Augustinerkirche, 1771/2), Mainz (St Ignaz, 1773/4; substantially overpainted 1902) and Oberndorf am Neckar (former Augustinerklosterkirche, 1776/8). Although Enderle was slightly influenced by Neo-classicism, he was not able to adapt to the new style: his later work shows rather the influence of Matthäus Günther and Gottfried Bernhard Göz. This retardative quality can be seen in the former Deutschordenshaus in Donauwörth (1780) and the Augustinerkirche in Lauingen (1791).

BIBLIOGRAPHY

R. Weser: 'Die Freskomaler Anton und Johann Baptist Enderle von Söflingen' *Archv Christ. Kst*, xxxv (1917), pp. 12–22, 29–51; *Ulm, Oberschwaben*, xxi (1918), pp. 1–87

K. L. Dasser: *Johann Baptist Enderle (1725–1798): Ein schwäbischer Maler des Rokoko* (Weissenhorn, 1970)

KARL LUDWIG DASSER

Enderlein, Caspar (*b* Basle, *bapt* 24 June 1560; *d* Nuremberg, 19 April 1633). Swiss pewterer, *Formschneider* and painter, active in Germany. He was probably apprenticed to the pewterer Hans Friderich in Basle in 1574. By 1583 Enderlein was registered as a journeyman in Nuremberg, which was an important centre for the production of pewter in the 16th century (*see* NUREMBERG, §III, 2). In 1585 he executed his masterpiece, and a year later he was listed as a master and a citizen of the imperial city of Nuremberg. He created models of pewter pots, candlesticks and sconces and may also have produced *Amtsformen* (official patterns or moulds) that masters could lend to each other; according to his own account he was a *Formschneider* (maker of patterns or moulds) and a painter. Enderlein enriched the repertory of form in pewterware by using elements from French Renaissance ornament. He introduced many technical innovations into his craft, and he is credited with producing the first pewter chandelier (untraced) in the Nuremberg area, although no pewter pieces bearing his stamp have been discovered, and thus it is mainly in the field of pattern-cutting that his abilities can be judged. He probably did not employ many journeymen in his workshop, but his idiosyncratic style of ornament appears on pewter tankards, bowls and plates made from the early 17th century until the late Baroque period. Enderlein was more concerned with producing *Edelzinn* (show pewter) pieces than with domestic pewter items. He was twice elected for a three-year period (1603–6, 1613–16) as one of the three jurors or senior masters of his guild.

BIBLIOGRAPHY

H. Demiani: *François Briot, Caspar Enderlein und das Edelzinn* (Leipzig, 1897)

H. Häussler: 'Caspar Enderlein: Zinngiesser, 1560–1633', *Berühmte Nürnberger aus neun Jahrhunderten*, ed. C. von Imhoff (Nuremberg, 1984), p. 157

O. LOHR

Enfilade. Alignment of internal doors in a suite of rooms so that a long, continuous vista is obtained when the doors are all left open.

Engebrechtsz., Cornelis (*b* 1460–65; *d* between 11 Feb and 26 Aug 1527). North Netherlandish painter. Archival research by Bangs has established that he probably was born earlier than 1468, the birthdate given by van Mander; the earlier date would allow Cornelis to have reached majority (25 years) when he married, *c.* 1484. His wife was Elysabeth Pietersdr., who bore him three daughters and three sons, the latter of whom all became painters: PIETER CORNELISZ. KUNST, Cornelis Cornelisz. Kunst (1493–1544) and Lucas Cornelisz. de Cock (1495–1552). Cornelis Engebrechtsz. may have travelled between 1482 and 1487, but after 1487 his name appears regularly in Leiden tax and militia company records, making it unlikely that he spent long sojourns in Antwerp or Brussels, as proposed by various scholars. At his death he had amassed a considerable estate, to judge by the inheritance quarrels that broke out. His wife was described as a widow on 26 August 1527.

Cornelis Engebrechtsz. was probably apprenticed in Leiden, where several as yet unidentified masters were active. Claims that he studied with Colijn de Coter in Brussels are based on questionable stylistic evidence. The first record of him as a master dates from 1482, when he received payment from the monastery of Hieronymusdal, near Leiden. Few works remain from this early period, during which he trained his eldest son, Pieter, and the young Lucas van Leyden. Cornelis taught many of the next generation's artists, including Aertgen Claesz. His acclaim may have attracted students from outside Leiden. Gibson, among others, has suggested that an unidentified apprentice from Antwerp joined Cornelis's studio *c.* 1512, bringing with him the more mannered tendencies that are apparent in Cornelis's art after this date. These elements of ANTWERP MANNERISM may have liberated the painter from North Netherlandish traditions and stiffness.

Cornelis Engebrechtsz.'s pre-eminent position in Leiden brought him commissions from the town council: one in 1522, executed with his son Pieter, for an accurate map of the city, another in 1525 to design banners for the city's trumpeters. Of the four works mentioned by van Mander, two are untraced—what was described as a badly damaged *Adoration* on canvas and an altarpiece that was then owned by the van Lochorst family of Utrecht, of which only the wings survive (Leiden, Stedel. Mus. Lakenhal). The other two works (both Leiden, Stedel. Mus. Lakenhal)—a triptych with the *Lamentation* (also called the *Seven Sorrows of the Virgin*; *c.* 1508) and another with the *Crucifixion* (*c.* 1517–22; see fig.)—form the basis, with the van Lochorst shutters, for the attribution of other works to Cornelis. The painter executed both these altarpieces for Jacob Maertensz. Schout (*d* 1526), the regent of the Augustinian convent of Marienpoel, near Leiden. The large-scale *Crucifixion* was probably intended for the high altar; the *Lamentation* may have been commissioned for the St Barbara Chapel (Bangs), a space traditionally dedicated to all virgins. Cornelis's style, as revealed in these pieces, is characterized by languid line and exaggerated emotionalism. His compositions, while playful, lack the nervous energy associated with Antwerp Mannerism. The slender, charming figures, with their small, expressive hands, strike gracefully curved poses, yet the bodies remain bulky, and delicate features are set between wide brows and knobbly chins. The women often gaze wistfully; costumes are fanciful, and draperies fly about in arbitrary swirls. His technique was refined and controlled, and he favoured an enamelled glaze, which he applied in several layers to create glistening surfaces. He used warm colours, often interspersing a distinctive deep green among the reds and blues. Although his conception and composition are often monumental, his figures remain small in proportion to their space. Cornelis's later works display such diverse influences that it is difficult to isolate workshop participation on the large commissions and to decide whether paintings traditionally attributed to the master should in fact be assigned to pupils. In a work such

Cornelis Engebrechtsz.: triptych with the *Crucifixion*, oil on panel, 2.13×2.78 m (closed), *c.* 1517–22 (Leiden, Stedelijk Museum De Lakenhal)

as *Christ Summoning St Matthew* (1520–25; Berlin, Gemäldegal.), the forms' bulk, the simplification of the details and the naturalistic interior space seem to reflect the work of his former pupil Lucas van Leyden, but the figures remain mannered. The piece was thus executed either by the old established master who continued to experiment with recent developments or by a young pupil whose figures are somewhat retardataire.

Cornelis created few independent portraits, yet the pendants of a husband and wife from the van Zyl family of Leiden (1518; Brussels, Mus. A. Anc.) summarize his contribution to North Netherlandish art. They are rooted in close observation of both the sitters' individual features and their setting. The pair are portrayed as pious, pensive people, who exhibit a restraint appropriate to their inscribed ages of 42 and 40. Their solid bulk fills the foreground, and each is framed by a Renaissance niche, the stately grandeur of which is modified by the fanciful monkeys perched atop the Corinthian columns. In the background is painted the view from the couple's house in Leiden: the convergence of the Nieuwe Rijn and the Gangetje rivers. Cornelis Engebrechtsz. combined old mannerisms with new motifs—and close observation with a greater sense of simplification; his art straddles two styles simultaneously and embodies the transformation of North Netherlandish art during the first quarter of the 16th century.

BIBLIOGRAPHY
K. van Mander: *Schilder-boeck* ([1603]–1604), fol. 210*r–v*
M. J. Friedländer: *Die altniederländische Malerei* (Berlin, 1924–37), x (1932); Eng. trans. as *Early Netherlandish Painting* (Leiden, 1967–76), x (1973), pp. 34–46
Middeleeuwse kunst der noordelijke Nederlanden (exh. cat., Amsterdam, Rijksmus., 1958)
J. R. J. van Asperen de Boer and A. K. Wheelock jr: 'Underdrawings in Some Paintings by Cornelis Engebrechtsz.', *Oud-Holland*, lxxxvii (1973), pp. 61–94
W. S. Gibson: *The Paintings of Cornelis Engebrechtsz.* (New York, 1977)
J. D. Bangs: *Cornelis Engebrechtsz.'s Leiden: Studies in Cultural History* (Assen, 1979)
The Age of Bruegel: Netherlandish Drawings in the Sixteenth Century (exh. cat. by J. O. Hand and others, Washington, DC, N.G.A.; New York, Pierpont Morgan Lib.; 1986), pp. 134–5

JANE L. CARROLL

Engel, (Johann) Carl Ludwig (*b* Berlin, 3 July 1778; *d* Helsinki, 14 May 1840). German architect, active in Finland. He was one of the most important Nordic representatives of early 19th-century Neo-classicism. He carried out his life's work in Finland, and in Helsinki he built the city's homogeneous monumental centre in the Empire style of St Petersburg. He graduated as an architect from the Bauakademie in Berlin in 1804 where Friedrich Gilly had been a teacher and his contemporaries had included Karl Friedrich Schinkel. During the Napoleonic Wars (1803–15) commissions were difficult to find and Engel, like many other young architects and artists, went abroad to seek his fortune. In 1808 he became city architect

1. Carl Ludwig Engel: Senate House, Helsinki, 1818–22; from a photograph of the 1890s

in Reval (now Tallinn, Estonia). From there he made his first visit to St Petersburg and thence his first journey to Finland, in 1814, to Turku, where the university commissioned him to design an observatory, still extant (drawings completed 1817–19; see Pöykkö, 1972, pp. 101, 138). This commission signalled an incipient change of taste in Finland: drawings for the observatory had already been commissioned from Carlo Bassi (1772–1840), an Italian architect who had moved to Finland from Sweden. The Swedish-influenced style that he represented, however, had begun to seem old-fashioned in comparison with that of St Petersburg, capital of the new mother country.

In 1814–15 Engel revisited St Petersburg, thoroughly familiarizing himself with its architecture and learning the latest building techniques. The great era of Empire-style architecture there was already over by this date, although among the important architects still active were Carlo Rossi (1775–1849) and Auguste Ricard de Montferrand (1786–1858). St Petersburg nevertheless made a great impression on Engel. In 1816 he moved to Helsinki, which had become the capital of the autonomous Grand Duchy of Finland in 1812. An ambitious street plan to correspond with the town's new status had been laid out by Johan Albrecht Ehrenström (1762–1847), who had assigned sites for a number of the more important public buildings. Because it was believed that there were no competent architects in Helsinki, Giacomo Quarenghi was asked to

approve the designs of the proposed buildings. His age and poor health, however, meant that he did not carry out the task. Engel was then asked to join the rebuilding committee as its architect with the responsibility of designing an entire city. By 1824, when he was appointed director of the Board of Public Works and Building, the Empire-style architecture that he had introduced from St Petersburg had become a national style.

Senate Square had already received its closed, symmetrical Baroque-classical form in Ehrenström's plan. The buildings that Engel designed to surround it—St Nicholas (1830–40; now the cathedral), the Senate House (1818–22; see fig. 1), the main university building (1828–32) and library (c. 1836–40)—constitute the city's monumental centre. Engel made his central buildings strictly symmetrical: the Senate House and the university opposite are identical in their volume and general articulation. They represent very clearly a type familiar from St Petersburg, a three-storey Palladian palace-type with central and side spaces, the central space with pillars and pediment; the Senate House also had a cupola.

The overall plan included a number of smaller buildings, such as the stone guard-house (1818) which originally stood in front of the cathedral, the former Governor General's house or Bock house (1816–18) and some 18th-century stone houses on the south side of the square that were modernized in the Neo-classical style under Engel's influence. At the same time as the design for the guard-house, Engel's design for the extension of the Bock house into a residence for the Governor General was completed. A narrow façade was decorated with Ionic columns reaching to the second and third storeys with entablatures and pediments. The ballroom in the courtyard wing was barrel-vaulted. In a letter about the building Engel expressed one of his central architectural concepts, which he had consistently attempted to put into practice: 'Here, just as in great music, there has to be a theme with which everything is in harmony' (repr. in Wickberg, 1981, p. 34).

The central building of Senate Square is the Lutheran cathedral, formerly St Nicholas (*see* HELSINKI, fig. 1). Engel designed it over a period of years; the first plans date from the guard-house design of 1818. The church was almost completed during his lifetime but was consecrated only in 1852. Its site and its Greek cross plan were defined in Ehrenström's plan. The architectural concept, a church on a high terrace fronted by a colonnade, appears to have been inspired by Friedrich Gilly's design for a monument to *Frederick the Great*. The church itself is a distant interpretation of the central cupola design, born during the Renaissance, seen in the Empire style of St Petersburg. In some of the letters that Engel wrote about church architecture he stressed the superiority of Neo-classical over Gothic designs which, in his view, aroused a feeling of oppression; he believed the neo-Gothic designs of Schinkel and of students from the Bauakademie in Berlin to be passing phenomena caused by the then ascendancy of France. Nevertheless Engel too experimented a little with the Gothic style, for example in the restoration of Turku Cathedral after the fire of 1827, and in the parish church of Laukaa.

Engel designed the University Library (*c.* 1836–40) to face the main entrance of the cathedral. The building is outwardly harmonious, if heavy, with its strong half columns, pilasters, entablatures and Attic elements (see fig. 2). Its Corinthian style is linked to the church and to the generally Roman structure of the building: its interior was covered by barrel vaults and cupolas. The university library and main buildings were not the only designs by Engel that echoed their harmonious and impressive exterior designs internally; in the Senate House the stair room and throne room are particularly striking. In the former, handsome Doric pillars carry cross-vaulting that Engel claimed to have constructed without iron reinforcement. The staircase is covered by a shallow cupola placed under the one visible from outside. The long throne room behind the central space on the second floor is furnished with Corinthian pillars set in a semi-circle. Rooms of this form were as familiar to Engel from Berlin as from St Petersburg. The most impressive of his interior spaces, however, is the vestibule of the main university building, in which he sought the effect of a central courtyard open from top to bottom with a central stone parterre lower than the rest of the floor.

Despite the closed Baroque-classical design of the square by Ehrenström, Engel sought to treat the eastern and northern sides of the space in the new Romantic spirit of the era, following Schinkel's architectural fantasies of perceiving buildings partly through trees. He thus placed trees in the courtyard of the university and around its

2. Carl Ludwig Engel: University Library, Helsinki, *c.* 1836–40

library; for the church terraces he envisaged decorative shrubs. Behind these monumental buildings there was evidently the intention to let loose a freer, Romantic spirit in contrast to the strict stone architecture of the square. In designing Senate Square he also had the opportunity to put into practice an iconographic programme: the Senate House, as representative of the Tsar's power, is of the Roman-Corinthian order, whereas the university main building is Greek-Ionic, with details referring to the statue of Apollo that was intended as its emblem. To reflect the statue of *Tsar Alexander I* as a Roman emperor, which embellished the great hall of the university, this semi-circular space is Roman in tone, with Roman-Corinthian columns. The guard-house that stood on the site of the monumental steps in front of the cathedral (also designed by Engel) was Doric. At the request of Alexander I (1801–25) he altered the columns making up the colonnade to resemble those at the ancient site of Paestum, Italy.

Engel designed many other buildings for Helsinki: next to the library is the former Cantonists school (1826; now a hospital) with its deliberately heavy and peaceful proportions; opposite stands the small Orthodox Church of the Holy Trinity (1826), whose form brings to mind Russian garrison churches; the Old Clinic (1832) is also in this street. In Market Square he designed the Town Hall (1827–33; formerly a casino) and the nearby Cabinet Banqueting Rooms (1824), a smallish two-storey palace once the Division Commander's and subsequently the Governor General's. Its top storey carries a deeply incised, rhythmical Ionic colonnade. In addition he designed numerous barracks, hospitals and other buildings. The resemblance of Helsinki to St Petersburg led to it sometimes being referred to as an 'Alexandria of the North'. When St Petersburg neared completion Tsars Alexander I and then Nicholas I (*reg* 1825–55) both showed interest in Helsinki. Both appreciated the propaganda value of architecture: another of Engel's designs was for a magnificent customs- and post-house for Eckerö (built 1826), in the humble surroundings of Åland, the archipelago between

Finland and Sweden, as the first sign of the Russian empire for travellers coming from the West.

On appointment as director of the Public Works office in 1824 Engel took it upon himself to improve building techniques and to spread good, that is, Neo-classical taste throughout Finland. He succeeded excellently in his endeavours. As director of the office he was responsible for the design and supervision of designs for public buildings and for a large number of churches. As a result, under his direction the cross-plan churches developed by vernacular builders from models in Stockholm generally continued on the same plan but with the addition of a cupola and Neo-classical detailing.

See also HELSINKI, §1.

UNPUBLISHED SOURCES

Helsinki, City Archv [letters]
Helsinki, N. Board Ant. [various documents]
Helsinki, N. Archv [various documents]
Helsinki, U. Lib. [various documents]

BIBLIOGRAPHY

C. Meisner: *Carl Ludwig Engel: Deutscher Baumeister in Finnland* (Berlin, 1937)
N. E. Wickberg: *Empirestudier: Uppsatser om arkitekturen i Finland och Baltikum under förra hälften av 1800-talet och om bevarandet av empiretidens byggnads minnen i Helsingfors* [Empire studies: essays on Finnish and Baltic architecture of the first half of the 1800s and on the preservation of recollections of Empire-period buildings in Helsinki] (Helsinki, 1945)
C. Lindberg and G. Rein: *Asemakaavoittelu ja rakennustoiminta* [Town planning and building], III/i of *Helsingin kaupungin historia* [The history of the city of Helsinki] (Helsinki, 1950), pp. 9–155
L. Pettersson: *Engelin kirjastorakennus: Bibliotheca Renovata, Helsingin yliopiston kirjasto* [Engel's library building: Bibliotheca Renovata, Helsinki University Library] (Helsinki, 1957), pp. 27–48
Y. Blomstedt: *Giacomo Quarenghi ja empiren Helsinki* [Giacomo Quarenghi and the empire of Helsinki] (Helsinki, 1962), pp. 13–20
——: *Johan Albrecht Ehrenström, kustavilainen ja kaupunginrakentaja* [Johan Albrecht Ehrenström, Gustavian and city-builder] (Helsinki, 1963)
K. Pöykkö: *Helsingin tuomiokirkko* [Helsinki Cathedral] (Vammala, 1971)
——: 'Das Hauptgebäude der Kaiserlichen Alexander-Universität von Finnland', *Fin. Fornminnesfören. Tidskr./Suom. Muinmuist. Aikak.*, 74 (1972) [whole issue]
——: *Valtioneuvoston juhlahuoneisto* [The Cabinet Banqueting Rooms] (Helsinki, 1980)
N. E. Wickberg: *Senaatintori—Senatstorget—The Senate Square—Der Senatsplats* (Rungsted, 1981)

KALEVI PÖYKKÖ

Engelberg, Burkhard (*b* ?Hornberg, Germany, *c.* 1450; *d* Augsburg, 11 Feb 1512). German architect. He was one of the most important masons in south Germany around 1500. Apart from his extensive work at Augsburg he was also in general demand as a specialist in the construction of vaults and towers, providing designs and assessments for alterations and new buildings. His well-organized building practice produced high-quality ashlar parts and architectural decoration for many public and private patrons. An unusual epitaph in the Benedictine abbey church of SS Ulrich und Afra, Augsburg, praises him as a *vilkunstreichen Architectoren* ('most ingenious architect').

Engelberg is first mentioned in 1477 as *parlier* (warden) at SS Ulrich und Afra, which had been destroyed in a storm in 1475. Shortly afterwards he took over control of the building work and from 1509 his lucrative contract was extended to life tenure. A woodcut of 1516 shows that Engelberg's new plan for the church envisaged a pair of lavish towers beside the massive basilican nave at the beginning of the chancel, but only the nave was completed at his death. From 1478 Engelberg paid taxes in Augsburg; he married well, acquired a house and enjoyed a high social standing. In the first decade of the 16th century he was by far the wealthiest mason in the city. He became senior master of works at Augsburg probably in 1494, and in 1506 his contract was confirmed for life on very favourable terms which allowed him to accept commissions outside his official work.

In 1488 the Augsburg Cathedral chapter commissioned him to heighten the south tower of the Cathedral. With the chapter's master of works Hans Kramer (*fl* 1488–1514), Engelberg provided high-quality stonework (branch-work corbels, window jambs, tracery) for the cloister (built from 1470 onwards) and the west choir screen (1501). In 1511 he was commissioned to advise on the proposed erection of a funerary chapel by the Cathedral provost Matthäus Lang. Other ecclesiastical patrons used his designs: those of the new cloister for the Dominican nuns of St Katharina date from 1496; between 1502 and 1508 Engelberg built the hall church of Holy Cross. The basilican church of St Georg (1494–1505/6), a small-scale version of SS Ulrich und Afra, is probably based on his designs.

The sources for the tabernacle for St Moritz, Augsburg (1503–8; destr. by 1542), document the division of labour between mason, sculptor, painter and goldsmith in the Late Gothic period: the elevation was prepared by the goldsmith Jörg Seld, while the architectural parts were the work of Engelberg's lodge. The tabernacle can be compared with the one in the parish church of Our Lady, Donauwörth (Swabia), completed *c.* 1503, which is attributed to Engelberg: its elaborate stone casing is an important example of south German miniature architecture. Masons from his workshop evidently also worked on the early Renaissance Fugger chapel, founded in 1506 at St Anna, Augsburg, but Engelberg's personal contribution to it is uncertain. From 1490 he executed a prestigious new office and residence in the centre of Augsburg for the brothers Ulrich, Georg and Jakob Fugger, the remains of which were built into the Fuggerei after its destruction in World War II. The splendid oriel on the residence of the merchant Ambrosius Höchstetter (now also in the Fuggerei) dates from *c.* 1504.

Engelberg was most famous for his work outside Augsburg. As master of works at Ulm Minster from 1493 he renovated the enormous west tower, which was in danger of collapse. Between 1498 and 1508 he transformed the side aisles into two-aisled halls with elegant columnar piers and net vaults (*see* ULM, fig. 1). He provided designs for the openwork spire of the parish church at Bolzano (Ger. Bozen; now Bolzano Cathedral), Italy (1500); for the openwork of the parish church at Schwaz, Austria (1508); the minsters of Konstanz (1502) and Berne (1507) in Switzerland, and the parish church of Heilbronn (1508). His foreman Stephan Weyrer (*d* 1528) executed his designs (1495) for the vaults of St Georg, Nördlingen. The attribution of other works, in Freising, Upper Swabia, and perhaps in the service of Graf Eberhard von Württemberg is doubtful, owing to the absence of documentary evidence. The direct influence of the Augsburg lodge is

Burkhard Engelberg: Simpertus arch in the south aisle of SS Ulrich und Afra, Augsburg, c. 1493–6

apparent in the nave vaulting of Holy Cross church, Schwäbisch Gmünd, at the beginning of the 16th century.

The Augsburg lodge had considerable influence, Engelberg's assistants disseminating his style in Swabia, the Tyrol and the Upper Rhine. The well-organized workshop enabled Engelberg to cope with his many commissions, his official duties as the city master of works at Augsburg, and his posts at SS Ulrich und Afra and Ulm Minster, as well as numerous consultations (e.g. his expert advice on the Salzbrunnen at Reichenhall, from 1498). The designs drawn in Augsburg were executed on the site by qualified foremen. Small-scale architectural works, such as the pulpit at Ulm (1498–9), were sent from Augsburg in the form of individually carved pieces ready for assembly. As had long been the practice of architects south of the Alps, Engelberg probably used three-dimensional models for design and demonstration, a method that was practised particularly by goldsmiths.

When Engelberg was not constrained by pre-existing buildings and structural difficulties and could design freely, he was original and inventive. Typical are the Augsburg decorative forms, which are clearly distinguished from previous Late Gothic decoration. He characteristically used the *Bogenstückwerk*, abstract ornament composed of cut-off, intersecting fragments of arches. This appears particularly in tracery (e.g. windows at SS Ulrich und Afra) and decorative elements (e.g. the Donauwörth tabernacle; the top of the spire at Bolzano). The principle of fragmentation is also a feature of the net vaults where the ends of the ribs are pierced and truncated. The Simpertus arch in SS Ulrich und Afra, completed in 1496, is a showpiece that demonstrates the full range of Engelberg's abilities (see fig.). It sweeps freely forwards into space in the south aisle and the treatment of its vertical wall elements and mouldings has the delicacy of goldsmith's work and very refined craftsmanship; but the rich decoration of the lateral buttresses was later destroyed and can be inferred only from fragments.

Two silverpoint portrait drawings by Hans Holbein the elder show Burkhard Engelberg in profile (Berlin, Kupferstichkab.; Copenhagen, Stat. Mus. Kst).

See also JAKOB ZWITZEL, HANS LUTZ and HANS HIEBER.

BIBLIOGRAPHY
N. Lieb: 'Burkhard Engelberg', *Lebensbilder Bayer. Schwaben*, iii (1954), pp. 117–52
J. Julier: *Studien zur spätgotischen Baukunst am Oberrhein*, Heidelberger Kunstgeschichtliche Abhandlungen, n. s., xiii (Heidelberg, 1978)
W. Baer, ed.: *Augsburger Stadtlexikon* (Augsburg, 1985), p. 97
F. Bischoff: *Burkhard Engelberg und die süddeutsche Architektur um 1500: Anmerkungen zur sozialen Stellung und Arbeitsweise spätgotischer Steinmetzen und Werkmeister* (diss., U. Bamberg, 1987)
——: 'Burkhard Engelberg und Tirol', *Schwaben und Tirol von der Römerzeit bis zur Gegenwart* (Rosenheim, 1989), pp. 378–84
——: 'Anmerkungen zum Umbau der Seitenschiffe des Ulmer Münsters unter Burkhard Engelberg', *Geschichte des Konstmierens IV. Wölbkonstruktionen der Gotik 1*, xxviii (Stuttgart, 1990), pp. 155–99
FRANZ BISCHOFF

Engelbrecht II, Count of Nassau. *See under* NASSAU.

Engelmann, Godefroy (*b* Mulhouse, 17 Aug 1788; *d* Mulhouse, 25 April 1839). French lithographer and publisher of German birth. After commercial training in Switzerland and in France at La Rochelle and Bordeaux, he studied painting and drawing in Jean-Baptiste Regnault's atelier in Paris. In July and August 1814 he visited Munich to study the new art of lithography. In March 1815 he founded La Société Lithotypique de Mulhouse, and in June 1816 he opened a workshop in Paris. Engelmann was instrumental in introducing lithography to France. He developed numerous improvements (*see* LITHOGRAPHY, §§I and II), including lithographic wash in 1819 and a frame for registration (patented in 1837), which gave chromolithography the technical means needed for its commercial and artistic development. His presses produced large numbers of prints; particularly noteworthy are numerous plates for Baron Taylor's monumental work *Voyages pittoresques et romantiques dans l'ancienne France* (1820–63).

WRITINGS
Manuel du dessinateur lithographe (Paris, 1823)
Traité théorique et pratique de la lithographie (Paris, 1839)

BIBLIOGRAPHY
M. Twyman: *Lithography, 1800–1850* (London, 1970)
L. Lang: *Godefroy Engelmann, imprimeur-lithographe: Les Incunables, 1814–1817* (Colmar, 1977)
ARSÈNE BONAFOUS-MURAT

Enghien [Flem. Edingen]. Belgian town in Hainault, approximately halfway between Brussels and Tournai. Tapestry production in Enghien probably began in the late 14th century or early 15th. Michiel Betten is mentioned as early as 1410 as a tapestryworker, and Herman Betten in 1445, although it is not clear whether or not the industry was well established at this time. The weavers of Enghien had, however, already gained a certain reputation: during the first half of the 15th century two tapestryworkers were resident in Brussels who may have originally come from Enghien.

In 1457 Jan de Doeve and Bartholomeus vander Hage were contracted by Jacques de Riva Mertijn, a Spanish merchant in Antwerp, to deliver 160 ells of *verdures* for which he provided the cartoons. In 1469 Louis de Luxembourg, Count of Saint-Pol and Lord of Enghien, increased the privileges of the tapestry-weavers by setting up an annual fair. The Count was beheaded on the orders of Louis XI in 1475, and his goods, including more than 20 tapestries, were confiscated. It can be assumed that several of them came from Enghien.

Enghien was virtually destroyed by a fire in 1497, and as a result many of the inhabitants emigrated, probably including many weavers. Gradually, however, work was resumed and the weavers returned. In 1503 the government gave a series of locally woven wall hangings to Philip of Cleves, Lord of Enghien, in whose castle hung the famous tapestry depicting the *Story of King Modus and Queen Ratio* (ex-Arenberg col.), a moralistic story of the eternal struggle between hunters and falconers; it is uncertain whether or not this was made in Enghien.

On 18 October 1513 Philip gave the weavers a statute, which was further amplified in 1520 and again in 1527: the weavers were forbidden to use bad or black-dyed wool and silk thread, and every finished piece had to be shown to the dean and chapter of the guild to have it marked with a lead token. One side of the token showed the arms of the city, the other the letter E. In this way it was intended to keep lower-quality work from the towns of Lessen, Viane, Grammont and Galmaarden from being passed as work from Enghien. It can also be deduced from this action that Enghien quickly followed the example of Brussels, probably no later than 1535, by adding the city and weaver's marks to the borders of tapestries. The city monogram was now flanked by the initials E and N.

In the second decade of the 16th century there was a vigorous expansion of the tapestry industry, which lasted until *c.* 1560. Due to good relations with the Antwerp merchants, the tapestries were easily marketed. The two regents of the Netherlands, Margaret of Austria, Duchess of Savoy, and Mary, Queen of Hungary, and many other prominent figures ordered one or more series. In 1559 Nicolaas Hellinck recorded (Brussels, Rijksarchf, no. 90) that the workers of Enghien produced work of a quality equal to that of Brussels, and that it could easily be mistaken for such work. Other important tapestryworkers and merchants included Philips van der Cammen (1576–*c.* 1607) and Jan van der Cammen (*fl* 1567–1618), Laurent Flascoen (*fl* 1525–77) and Quentin Flascoen (*fl* 1577) and Claas de Dobbeleer (*fl* 1566–77).

The religious conflict of 1566 and the looting of Antwerp in 1576 severely affected the tapestry industry in Enghien, and many weavers left the city. In 1604 Hans van der Biest went to Munich to work for Maximilian I, Duke of Bavaria. On 8 August 1685 Nicolaas van der Leen, the last tapestryworker in the town, gave all of the guild's income to the Brotherhood of Our Lady and the poor of Enghien.

It is unlikely that tapestry cartoons were ever produced in Enghien as the industry was not big enough, and workshops used cartoons from other cities or borrowed them from the client who commissioned the work. Producers therefore found it more economical to make large-leaved *verdures* (e.g. *c.* 1550; Vienna, Ksthist. Mus.). The designs for these were cheaper, and their execution far less time-consuming. Pictorial tapestries were also produced at Enghien; a particular characteristic of these tapestries was the flesh tints, which the weavers in Oudenaarde tried to emulate in the 16th century. Although the work from Enghien was often mediocre, several handsome pieces have been preserved that are comparable with Brussels tapestries. These include the *Armorial Tapestries of Margaret of Austria* (1528; Budapest, Mus. Applied A.), the *Fall of Phaeton* (*c.* 1560; Landshut, Burg Trausnitz) and the colourful tapestries made by Claas de Dobbeleer, with large leaves, flowers and birds (examples in Vienna, Ksthist. Mus.).

BIBLIOGRAPHY

H. Göbel: *Wandteppiche I: Die Niederlande*, 2 vols (Leipzig, 1923–34; Eng. trans. of vol i, New York, 1924)

E. Duverger: 'Een bestelling van groenwerk te Edingen in 1457', *A. Textiles*, vii (1971), pp. 206–10

J. Duverger: 'Tapijten van Claes de Dobbelaer van Edingen', *A. Textiles*, viii (1974), pp. 189–94

G. Delmarcel: *Tapisseries anciennes d'Enghien* (Mons, 1980)

ERIK DUVERGER

Engilberts, Jón (*b* Reykjavík, 23 May 1908; *d* Reykjavík, 12 Feb 1972). Icelandic painter, printmaker and illustrator. He studied art privately in Iceland (1921–2) and then at the Kunstakademi, Copenhagen (1927–30), under Axel Jörgensen (*b* 1883) and the Kunstakademi, Oslo (1931–3), under Axel Revold. He lived in Copenhagen from 1933 to 1940.

Engilberts was one of the second generation of modern Icelandic artists who turned their attention from landscape to the new realist subject of the fishing villages and their people. His early paintings and prints are much influenced by German Expressionism and bear the mark of his involvement in left-wing politics. During the 1930s he began to employ a strong streak of sensuous Romanticism, producing paintings that display a mixture of Munch's introspection and some of his compositional techniques, and Revold's colouristic flair; e.g. *Evening in a Seaside Village* (1935–7; Reykjavík, N.G.).

After his return to Iceland in 1940, Engilberts became an important figure on the Icelandic art scene, as a teacher, printmaker, campaigner for artists' rights and an illustrator. He was a particularly effective interpreter of Romantic literature, and his illustrations to poems by Jónas Hallgrímsson, a leading figure in 19th-century Icelandic literature, are among his most popular works. Engilberts was one of the founders of the Society of Icelandic Printmakers (Íslensk grafík) in 1954 and produced a number of important woodcuts and linocuts. In 1965 he began to paint large-scale, thickly impastoed Abstract Expressionist works, combining private fantasies with references to Icelandic nature and mythology.

BIBLIOGRAPHY

Ó. Kvaran and B. Óskarsson: *Jón Engilberts* (Reykjavík, 1988)

AÐALSTEINN INGÓLFSSON

England. Largest of the constituent parts of the United Kingdom. Located on the island of Great Britain, England (see fig. 1) has a population of *c.* 49 million; LONDON is the capital of both England and the UK.

DETAILED TABLE OF CONTENTS

I. Introduction. II. Architecture. III. Painting and graphic arts. IV. Sculpture. V. Interior decoration. VI. Furniture. VII. Ceramics. VIII. Glass. IX. Metalwork. X. Objects of vertu. XI. Textiles. XII. Patronage. XIII. Collecting and dealing. XIV. Museums. XV. Art education. XVI. Art libraries and photographic collections. XVII. Historiography.

I. Introduction.

The highest area in England lies in the north-west where such peaks as Scafell and Skiddaw rise over 900 m above the lake-filled valleys (the Lake District). Further south is the excellent farming land of the Midland plain; here, the splendid cathedrals of Chester, Worcester, Hereford and Lincoln provide evidence of the region's prosperity in medieval times, and, to the east, some small towns have extraordinarily grand 15th-century churches, built when there was a flourishing wool trade. Many Dutch and Flemish weavers arrived at this time to teach the English their craft. In the south-east lies the London basin of the River Thames; to the south-west lie Salisbury Plain and the fertile Hampshire basin wherein some of the oldest British settlements such as Stonehenge and Avebury are found. Beyond lies the peninsula of Devon and Cornwall; here there are many good fishing havens, and the harbour at Plymouth has been one of the most important naval bases since the reign of Elizabeth I. No part of England is more than 100 miles from the sea, which has prevented attack from foreigners and has a considerable effect on England's climate. The winds frequently bring rain, resulting in a more temperate climate than in much of central Europe.

The geology of England also explains the great variety in the type and quality of building stone available. The changes in the character of the rock are far greater than in other European countries of a comparable size, and consequently the landscape, although less spectacular than other parts of mainland Europe, offers a remarkable variety within a small area. The geological pattern of England runs predominantly from the south-west to the north-east and, generally speaking, the younger rocks lie to the east and south-east, the older to the west and north-west. The outstanding feature is the limestone belt, the long and relatively narrow band of rock that runs from Portland Bill in Dorset to the Humber, terminating in the Cleveland Hills of Yorkshire. It is from this belt that the majority of the most famous English stone is quarried. The limestone makes excellent building material, especially in the Cotswolds, where there are beautiful villages and small towns with fine stone churches, such as Broadway and Chipping Campden.

Most of the stone used for English buildings is limestone and sandstone, but granite and marble, which can both be polished, are also used. Marble is rarely found in Britain, although Purbeck marble was very popular with the cathedral builders and sculptors of the Middle Ages. Regional building styles are inevitably based on the materials available locally. The limestone belt produces only one group of vernacular building materials, and the older geological formations to the north and west provide a variety of stone from the red, grey, brown and yellow sandstones of the West Midlands to the tough carboniferous limestones of the north and the hard granites of Devon and Cornwall.

The invasion of the Romans, who incorporated Britain into the Roman Empire after AD 43, led to the establishment of numerous large towns connected by an elaborate network of roads. Indigenous tribes that resisted the Romans' presence were pushed back to the frontiers of Wales and Scotland, Hadrian's Wall (constructed c. AD 121) providing a great defensive barrier across Britain between the Tyne and Solway. Luxury goods were introduced, and for over three centuries Britain remained a relatively peaceful outpost of the Roman Empire. By the late 4th century AD the Empire had begun its decline, and gradually the Roman legions were recalled. After the departure of the Romans there were numerous invasions by Nordic peoples such as the Angles, Saxons and Jutes, but an event of more enduring significance for the arts was the arrival of Christianity with St Augustine in AD 597. The new religion stimulated painting, sculpture and architecture and gave a huge impetus to the decorative arts (see ANGLO-SAXON ART). The rituals of the church required the production of an extraordinary array of garments, vessels and other precious objects, and this in turn helped establish a concern for the preservation and display of works of art. Indeed the clergy (and especially the monastic orders) played the leading role in the promotion of the arts, from the extraordinary calligraphic achievements of the Lindisfarne Gospels to the splendours of ecclesiastical architecture (see also INSULAR ART).

In the Middle Ages the State, or more properly the king, acquired greater powers, and royal influence on the arts significantly increased. This was especially the case under Henry III (reg 1216–72), who lavished money on religious foundations, particularly Westminster Abbey in London. Indeed, the 13th century was a golden age for building as the Romanesque style was replaced by the Gothic not only in ecclesiastical architecture but also at the universities of Oxford and Cambridge and, as the legal profession began to flourish, at the Inns of Court in London. The large fortunes made by sheep farmers in East Anglia and merchants in Kent during the late 13th century are reflected in the exceptional Perpendicular style churches

1. Map of England; all the sites named have separate entries in this dictionary

built by the former and the castles and brick manor houses erected by the latter.

After the Wars of the Roses (1455–85), in which the succession to the throne was contested, the influence of the Italian Renaissance became evident in the early 16th century: Henry VIII employed large numbers of foreign craftsmen to decorate such royal residences as Hampton Court and Nonsuch Palace, and Holbein, one of the most distinguished portrait painters of the century, worked at Henry's court. On the other hand, the Reformation and the dissolution of the monasteries in the late 1530s, and the transfer of their lands to the Crown, caused many distinguished buildings to fall into disrepair and ruin; some of the money from their sale, however, was used to endow such charitable and educational establishments as Trinity College, Cambridge, and Christ Church, Oxford. The reign of Elizabeth I was characterized by a wide range of cultural activity, with dramatists, musicians and artists from Shakespeare to Nicholas Hilliard establishing reputations alongside such adventurers as Sir Francis Drake and Sir Martin Frobisher, who returned with riches from their voyages to the New Lands, while such courtiers as William Cecil, 1st Baron Burghley, at Burghley House near Stamford, Lincs, and Theobalds, Herts, spent huge sums on new houses in which to entertain the Queen and her enormous entourage.

The early part of the reign of Charles I (1625–49) was characterized by a great cosmopolitanism in the arts, with the first great collections of European art formed during these years as well as the emergence (first under Inigo Jones) of Palladianism in architecture. However, during the Civil War (1642–9) and the Commonwealth period (1649–60) that followed, building and the production of both fine and decorative arts virtually ceased. In 1660 the Stuart monarchy, despite its Roman Catholic sympathies, was restored, but after the 'Glorious Revolution' of 1688 the Protestant ascendancy was secured under King William III and Queen Mary II. During their reign many Huguenots sought refuge in England.

After the Act of Union with Scotland (1707), Great Britain emerged as a world power and as a trading nation of great economic significance. The ascendancy brought about by the victories of the Seven Years War (1756–63) in Canada and India was offset by the loss of the American colonies in the early 1780s, but the wealth of empire expanded the home market for luxury goods as such artists and craftsmen as Gainsborough, Reynolds and Thomas Chippendale the elder flourished. The Industrial Revolution of the late 18th century and the early 19th and the great growth in England's population had profound consequences for the arts. The increased sense of nationalism fuelled the Gothic Revival in architecture, and the rise of a more anecdotal type of painting, for example, reflected the tastes of the bourgeois industrialists. The arts suffered during the economic decline of the first half of the 20th century, and after World War II artists fared notably less well than in previous generations. State support for the arts, under the aegis of the Arts Council of Great Britain (est. 1946), began to redress the imbalance, and the 1960s was a decade of enthusiasm and experimentation in the arts. Towards the end of the 20th century, however,

economic depression returned, leading to a mood of austerity.

BIBLIOGRAPHY

T. Boase, ed.: *The Oxford History of English Art*, 9 vols (Oxford, 1952–78)
A. Clifton-Taylor: *The Pattern of English Building* (London, 1962)
N. Pevsner: *The Englishness of English Art* (Harmondsworth, 1964)
K. Morgan, ed.: *The Oxford Illustrated History of Britain* (Oxford, 1984)
B. Ford, ed.: *The Cambridge Guide to the Arts in Britain*, 9 vols (Cambridge, 1988–91)
C. Hibbert: *The Story of England* (London, 1992)

BRIAN ALLEN

II. Architecture.

1. Before 1066. 2. 1066–c. 1530. 3. c. 1530–c. 1660. 4. c. 1660–c. 1830. 5. c. 1830–c. 1914. 6. After c. 1914.

1. BEFORE 1066. Before the Roman period there was little in England that could be described as architecture, although the stone circle of Stonehenge (c. 3200–1600 BC; for illustration see STONEHENGE), Wilts, was a monumental achievement. Prehistoric England was otherwise characterized by the thatched round hut, built of timber or stone, while masonry was also used to reinforce the banks and ditches of hill-forts (see PREHISTORIC EUROPE, §VI, 2(i)).

Monumental civic architecture was introduced into England by the Romans. Towns developed from the mid-1st century AD, with military buildings in stone by the 80s. The careful planning of the forts associated with Hadrian's Wall (after 122; for illustration see HADRIAN'S WALL), with their barracks and bath buildings, was matched in towns, some of which, for example CHESTER, were very military in aspect. By the late 3rd century the big towns featured a central administration building and a rectangular grid of streets, with a forum block, insulae of houses, baths, theatres, aqueducts and sometimes walls and gates, as at Lincoln (see LINCOLN, §1). The houses were either long or with courtyards and were built of timber or wattle-and-daub on stone foundations. Small country houses and huts continued to be circular and thatched, but the villas (farms) could be partly two-storey, with several rooms, mosaic floors and hypocausts, the most elaborate example being the palace of Fishbourne, W. Sussex, rebuilt after 73. Temples were of masonry, and the Romano-Celtic examples combine Roman building techniques with Celtic plans. Although there is written evidence of urban churches, none certainly survives; parts of a house could be converted to Christian use, as at the villa at Lullingstone, Kent.

With the collapse of the Roman Empire between the early 4th century and the late 6th, towns went out of use, not reviving until the 9th century, with particularly strong development from the 10th, when *burhs*, defended against Viking incursions, were planned with street grids. The large, rectangular, timber-framed halls of the Anglo-Saxons can be dated back to the 6th century. A stone hall was built, perhaps under Carolingian influence, at Northampton in the 9th century, and stone was used at such 11th-century sites as Sulgrave, Northants (see ANGLO-SAXON ART, §II), but timber remained the favoured building material. The main hall was grouped with other buildings, sometimes within a defended enclosure, as at Goltho (c. 900), Lincs.

Stone churches began to be built by Christian missionaries immediately after their arrival in the late 6th century, and the type then established (e.g. St Martin's Chapel (now part of St Martin's Church), Canterbury), with aisleless nave, apsidal chancel and flanking chambers (*porticus*), continued throughout the Anglo-Saxon period, later buildings having towers (e.g. Sherborne Abbey, Dorset; destr.) and decoration (e.g. St Lawrence, Bradford-on-Avon, Wilts). Anglo-Saxon architecture remained largely detached from developments in mainland Europe, although there is evidence of Carolingian influence and that of the 10th-century reform movements. Building was mostly in rubble, with small windows, but there are notable 9th-century crypts (e.g. Cirencester Abbey, Glos; St Wystan, Repton, Derbys), and aisled plans were introduced in the 9th century. Towers and sculptured decoration became quite common in the 10th century, and the Old Minster at Winchester was rebuilt with apses, transepts and a westwork (*see* WINCHESTER, §III, 1(i)). The abbeys at Glastonbury and Canterbury show the Anglo-Saxon tendency to build several small churches on a site rather than one large one.

2. 1066–*c*. 1530. Although the Romanesque style of Normandy had appeared before the Norman Conquest (1066) at Westminster Abbey (rebuilt from 1394; *see* LONDON, §V, 2(i)), the effects of the Conquest on architecture were highly visible and long-lasting (*see* RO-MANESQUE, §II, 6(i)). The Normans inaugurated a huge programme of castle-building and rebuilt cathedrals and abbey churches on a larger and more rational scale, with carefully massed volumes and ashlar masonry. The rapid growth of the Cistercian Order in the 12th century also led to the building of many new monasteries (*see* CISTER-CIAN ORDER, §III, 1). Within a century of the Conquest, imposing stone buildings were visible throughout England. Building stone was imported from French quarries: that from Caen in Normandy is the most readily identifiable (e.g. at Canterbury Cathedral) and was used throughout the period. The Normans had conquered a land rich in good stone, however, and local quarries were increasingly used, many being associated with particular buildings, such as Doulting (Somerset) for Wells Cathedral and Tadcaster (N. Yorks) for York Minster. In the south-west, granite was the most readily available material, while limestone was predominant in a line running north-east through the Cotswold Hills, Lincolnshire and Yorkshire, and some of the famous medieval quarries lie on this curve: Chilmark (Wilts), Ketton (Leics), Barnack (Cambs) and Ancaster (Lincs). Sandstone was ubiquitous; it was quarried especially in the south-east (at Reigate, Surrey), the west Midlands, where Old Red sandstone was used for Hereford Cathedral, and Yorkshire, where the abbeys of Rievaulx and Whitby were built with Jurassic sandstone. Owing to the scarcity of stone in East Anglia, brick became popular from the late 12th century, and flint was used in England, particularly in the south-east, more than in any other country. The quarries of Purbeck (Dorset), Bethersden (Kent) and Frosterley (Tyne and Wear) yielded coloured limestones, known as marble, that took a high polish and were used for decorative work, as were the alabasters of Nottinghamshire, which were suitable only for interiors.

The Conquest did not, however, destroy the Anglo-Saxon past, nor did it link Britain exclusively to Normandy. The traditional European areas of influence, the Rhine and Meuse regions, continued to be strong sources of inspiration to church architects, and after about one generation a certain illogicality crept into Anglo-Norman architectural decoration, which has been ascribed to the re-emergence of Anglo-Saxon decorative tastes. Anglo-Norman architecture was, however, so forceful in character that in many ways it left its mark until the late Middle Ages, even though styles had completely changed.

In domestic architecture the hall remained the essential element of the house, whether rural or urban, of stone or timber. Houses acquired more rooms and floors, and town houses were long and deep, often with oversailing upper floors, as in the 15th-century houses of Exeter. Later halls, such as Penshurst (1340s), Kent, and Westminster Hall (rebuilt 1390s; *see* LONDON, §V, 3(i)(a)), London, were roofed with spectacular carpentry. In castles, the hall, at first a separate building in the bailey (defended courtyard), was incorporated into the main building, until by the late 14th century at Kenilworth, Warwicks, the domestic function of the castle was beginning to overshadow the military. The castles, the sign of conquest, had always been fortified residences, and the towers that stood on the artificial mounds (mottes) were extremely sophisticated from an early date (*see* CASTLE, §I). The square donjon (begun 1127) of the bishops of Rochester, Kent, had five storeys, with two sets of living-quarters and with stairways, passages and fireplaces in the thickness of the outer walls. It was articulated with four corner turrets and a central pilaster on each wall. Set on the edge of or within the bailey, the donjon, later combined with the gate-house, remained the essential element in castle design, and it adopted many different plans: square (Newcastle upon Tyne; 1170s; for illustration *see* NEWCASTLE UPON TYNE), cylindrical (Conisbrough, S. Yorks; 1180–1200) or polygonal (Orford, Suffolk; 1165–73). The late 11th-century donjons at Colchester (Essex) and the Tower of London (the White Tower; *see* LONDON, §V, 4 and fig. 40) were of palatial standard. Under Edward I (*reg* 1277–1307) the castle achieved its greatest development as a fortified residence (*see* MILITARY ARCHITECTURE AND FORTIFICA-TION, fig. 10). Edward's castles in north Wales (*see* JAMES OF ST GEORGE) and the Clare family castle at Caerfili, Mid Glam., based their strength on a combination of mural towers and a twin-towered gatehouse. The Anglo-French donjon, however, persisted until the 15th century, as can be seen in the great brick tower at Tattershall (Lincs; for illustration *see* TATTERSHALL), while the gate-house, the common feature of castles and less fortified dwellings (*see* GATE-HOUSE), was developed into a grand entrance, as at Thornton Abbey (1382), Lincs.

In church architecture, the Anglo-Norman legacy, apart from the emphasis on fine ashlar masonry, is visible in persistent forms of both elevation and structure. Despite strong regional variations, Anglo-Norman great churches are generally identifiable by their three arcaded storeys with a deep, high gallery and a clerestory with a passage in the thickness of the wall (e.g. Winchester Cathedral, begun

1079; see fig. 2). The Norman THICK-WALL STRUCTURE, which occasioned the passage, consisted of two skins of ashlar enclosing a rubble core. It could be more than 3 m thick and was very stable but too inflexible to respond to the skeletal engineering of 13th-century French Gothic. The retention of both the thick wall and the high gallery must have been a matter of taste: although proportions were often matched when buildings were extended, as at Ely Cathedral from 1234 (see ELY, fig. 2), new 13th-century buildings such as Salisbury Cathedral (1220s), Wilts, or Westminster Abbey (from 1246), London, were deliberately designed with high galleries and (at Salisbury) a clerestory passage (see SALISBURY, fig. 4).

From the late 12th century the strongest single influence on English Gothic was France, and on its first appearance at the cathedrals of Canterbury and Wells from the 1170s the style did not diverge greatly from the source. Anglo-Norman arches and ribbed vaults had contributed to the formation of French Gothic, and the high, skeletal structures of 13th-century France were yet to come. From the 1190s, however, it was clear that English architects would pursue their own preoccupations, adopting the appearance of French Gothic but not its substance (see also GOTHIC, §II, 1). English buildings remained squat, thick and copiously decorated with rich, delicate foliage, contrasting marbles and crocketing (see EARLY ENGLISH). The effects were less stern and decisive: on exteriors especially, in contrast to the strong, assertive towers and carved doorways of their French mentors, the wide façades, small doors and busy sculptural decoration of the cathedrals of Wells and Salisbury had less precision and visual clarity (see WELLS, fig. 4).

Surface pattern was a preoccupation throughout the period, from the blind arcading and chevron ornament at Durham Cathedral (c. 1100; see DURHAM, fig. 2); but where early Anglo-Norman ornament had more or less adhered to architectural logic, by the mid-12th century the distinction between architecture and ornament was becoming less clear. In the so-called West Country group of buildings, extending from Malmesbury Abbey, Wilts, to Llanthony Abbey, Gwent, and St David's Cathedral, Dyfed, applied decoration and decorative mouldings invaded the structural members in a manner that anticipated the developments from the 1190s, when in St Hugh's choir at Lincoln Cathedral the vault ribs were split to make a pattern on the ceiling.

The introduction of window tracery from France in the 1240s caused significant change. English masons soon outstripped their French counterparts in ingenuity of design; but owing to the short clerestories, the only large expanses of window were the flat east walls of the newly fashionable rectangular choirs that had replaced their apsed Anglo-Norman predecessors. Tracery dominated the east façades of the Angel choir at Lincoln Cathedral (begun 1256; see LINCOLN, §2(i)(c)) and Old St Paul's (begun c. 1258; destr.), London. The need for larger, more visible windows caused the demise of the high gallery: at Exeter Cathedral (begun c. 1279), where window tracery and patterned vaulting reached new excesses, the gallery was reduced to a narrow arcaded band, and in many 14th-century churches, such as Selby Abbey (1330s), N. Yorks, it was suppressed altogether. These buildings still had thick walls and deep window embrasures, and they responded well to the encrustation of undulating foliage, niches and tracery that enveloped such buildings as the Lady Chapel (begun 1320s; see DECORATED STYLE) of Ely Cathedral.

Finally, however, the logic of the thin, skeletal walling of French Rayonnant made itself felt in the PERPENDICULAR STYLE, which developed from the early 14th century. Composed of various French elements, Perpendicular was unique to Britain, and because many parish churches were rebuilt or extended in the 15th century, the wide, panelled windows, crenellated flat roofs and tall square towers that characterize the style are still prevalent. The rectilinearity extended from wall and window-panelling to the flattened, four-centred arches and the vaulting: it is seen in the rectilinear nets in the nave of Winchester Cathedral (c. 1390) and St George's Chapel (begun 1474; see fig. 3), Windsor, and in the great fans at Peterborough Cathedral (completed c. 1518). The idea of surface decoration and the fusion of architectural and sculptural motifs were not lost: the early Tudor buildings manage to look both back to past tradition and forward to the following generations. The crinkled window angles of the south front of Thornbury Castle (c. 1511–21), Avon, and Henry VII's Chapel (1502–9), Westminster Abbey, show the old desire to manipulate the wall surface; but the succession of rectilinear forms that characterizes late Perpendicular buildings

2. Winchester Cathedral, begun 1079, interior of the north transept, west side

3. Windsor Castle, St George's Chapel, begun 1474, interior of the nave looking east

anticipates at least one strand of development of the later 16th century.

BIBLIOGRAPHY
J. Evans: *English Art, 1307–1461*, Oxford Hist. Eng. A. (Oxford, 1949)
T. S. R. Boase: *English Art, 1100–1216*, Oxford Hist. Eng. A. (Oxford, 1953)
G. Webb: *Architecture in Britain: The Middle Ages*, Pelican Hist. A. (Harmondsworth, 1956, rev. 1965)
P. Brieger: *English Art, 1216–1307*, Oxford Hist. Eng. A. (Oxford, 1957/R 1968)
P. Kidson, P. Murray and P. Thompson: *A History of English Architecture* (London, 1962, rev. Harmondsworth, 1979)
H. M. Taylor and J. Taylor: *Anglo-Saxon Architecture*, 3 vols (Cambridge, 1965–78)
S. S. Frere: *Britannia* (London, 1967)
R. Willis: *The Architectural History of Some English Cathedrals*, 2 vols (Chicheley, 1972–3) [contains reprints of Willis's writings pubd between 1841 and 1863]
J. Harvey: *The Perpendicular Style, 1330–1485* (London, 1978)
J. Bony: *The English Decorated Style* (Oxford, 1979)
J. Ward-Perkins: *Roman Imperial Architecture*, Pelican Hist. A. (Harmondsworth, 1981)
E. Fernie: *The Architecture of the Anglo-Saxons* (London, 1983)
English Romanesque Art, 1066–1200 (exh. cat., ed. G. Zarnecki and others; London, Hayward Gal., 1984)
The Age of Chivalry (exh. cat., ed. J. J. G. Alexander and P. Binski; London, RA, 1987–8)
C. Platt: *The Architecture of Medieval Britain* (London, 1990)

NICOLA COLDSTREAM

3. *c.* 1530–*c.* 1660. During the 16th century and the early 17th, two fundamental and interrelated developments in English architecture occurred. First, following the Reformation, there was a shift away from ecclesiastical towards secular forms of building, at a time when advances were being made in construction technology. Second, by 1660 the foundations had been laid, largely in London, for a style of building and for preferred materials that suggested a form of 'polite' architecture, especially for grand and public buildings, that was to challenge and supplant many vernacular traditions over the next two centuries (*see* VERNACULAR ARCHITECTURE, §II, 1(i)). The Reformation brought an end to the complex interaction of ritual, fabric and decoration of the medieval parish church after a century during which many churches had been renewed and extended. The building of churches did not entirely cease after the 1530s, however: a significant number of new churches were constructed, for example St Nicholas (1590), Holcot, Beds, and many west towers of older churches were completed during the later 16th century (*see* GOTHIC SURVIVAL). Most churches, however, were kept merely in minimal good order and decorated, by statute, with the royal arms, as well as with the heraldry of local gentry and aristocracy, particularly on their tombs.

Royal building activity was more intensive during the 1530s and 1540s than at any other time in English history. The palaces of Henry VIII (*reg* 1509–47), mainly concentrated in the south-east, signalled, through their huge spreading courtyards and increasingly complex sets of royal apartments, the new importance of the court as the centre of the nation's political life. Whitehall Palace (destr. 1698; *see* LONDON, §V, 5) and HAMPTON COURT PALACE, both seized from Cardinal Thomas Wolsey by 1529, NONSUCH PALACE, Surrey, begun by the King in 1538 (destr. after 1687) and Oatlands (destr.), Surrey, were the palaces where work was most extensive; at some of these their ranges of buildings constantly changed according to royal needs. Brick was used at these palaces and led the fashion for large domestic buildings in this material (*see* BRICK, §II, 3(i)(d)). In other ways, too, these palaces set the tone for large-scale domestic architecture until after 1600: selfconscious references to the medieval past were made through the construction of lofty gatehouses and complex roof-lines; deference to the symbols of dynastic power was achieved through external heraldry; and the impression of wealth was conveyed by large windows. The Office of Works during these years retained the basic organization of medieval times (*see* CLERK OF WORKS), although the chief administrative posts were now granted to leading, working craftsmen: James Nedeham, the master carpenter who designed the hammer-beam roof for the Great Hall (1532–4; *see* HAMPTON COURT PALACE, fig. 1) at Hampton Court, became Clerk and Surveyor of the Works in 1532.

Former monasteries had an important history. Some, by their dismemberment, provided stone for new structures, both urban and rural, which was especially significant in those parts of the country where building stone was not locally abundant; others were recast into new houses. Some significant courtier houses, which grew from former monastic sites around the mid-16th century, turned cloisters into courtyards, the latter being highly fashionable for the plan of the great house. Grand courtyards remained the dominant feature of many large courtier houses even beyond 1600, as at Audley End, Essex, which was transformed from an earlier house *c.* 1603–16 for Thomas Howard, 1st Earl of Suffolk (outer court and gate-house destr. 1721; see fig. 4). Some great houses adopted a compact plan, however, with service, state and private rooms arranged into distinctively stacked storeys, notably in the series of houses built by Robert Smythson in the east Midlands: Worksop Manor (completed 1585) and Wollaton Hall (1580–88; *see* SMYTHSON, (1), fig. 1), both Notts, and Hardwick Hall (1590–97; *see* COUNTRY HOUSE, fig. 2), Derbys. The gentry, who needed less space since they no longer entertained on a large scale, led the way in establishing smaller and ultimately more practical types of country-house plan, including the familiar E-shape of the ELIZABETHAN STYLE and the JACOBEAN STYLE (e.g. Stibbington Hall (1625), Cambs), and others square in plan, a form that was also adopted occasionally by the aristocracy for hunting-lodges.

Although debated by historians, surviving structures and written evidence together suggest that there was a raising of standards in the provision of domestic housing and an expansion and structural renewal of public buildings in the late 16th century and during the first half of the 17th. Such buildings, which sometimes were radical transformations of pre-existing structures, are the oldest surviving domestic buildings in most of the English towns that enjoyed a period of prosperity before the Industrial Revolution. Shrewsbury, for example, retains important (restored) examples of the half-timbered and gabled town mansions of leading Shropshire merchants of the later 16th century. The addition of private rooms on upper floors, the glazing of window-openings, formerly only shuttered, and the abandonment of central hearths for fireplaces, all mark the improvement of houses at this time, as William Harrison observed in his *Description of England* (1577). In rural areas, the addition of wings to medieval hall-houses marked the decisive break between

a housing stock principally made up of single-space dwellings to one of multi-unit houses. The emergence at this time of the lobby-entry house, with its characteristic feature of a centrally arranged back-to-back fireplace serving a room on either side is found in many parts of the country. The foundation of new colleges at the universities of OXFORD and CAMBRIDGE, numerous grammar schools and the many surviving rows of modest almshouses bear witness to a renewed concern for buildings of public utility, with municipal authorities and private individuals playing a greater role than previously alongside the established role of the church. At Guildford, Surrey, are two impressive examples of larger foundations: the Grammar School (1557–86) and the brick almshouses known as Abbot's Hospital (1619–22).

While the ground-plans of many examples of buildings of the same type can be usefully compared across the country at this time, their elevations bear witness not only to the survival but also to the consolidation of local building styles and materials. The accident of survival can be deceptive, but the evidence suggests a more aggressive assertion of the potential of local materials than ever before, from the advanced technology of brick in East Anglia (e.g. Roos Hall (1593) at Beccles, Suffolk) to the black-and-white half-timbered houses of north-west England and along the Welsh border (e.g. the additions of 1559 to Little Moreton Hall, Ches, or those made to Pitchford Hall; see fig. 5).

The history of the assimilation in England of the pervasive style of continental architecture, Renaissance classicism, into local traditions is a complex one. The chief interest of Henry VIII and his courtiers with Italian and French ideas lay in the decorative splendour of surface ornament; this is even true of the programmatic scheme

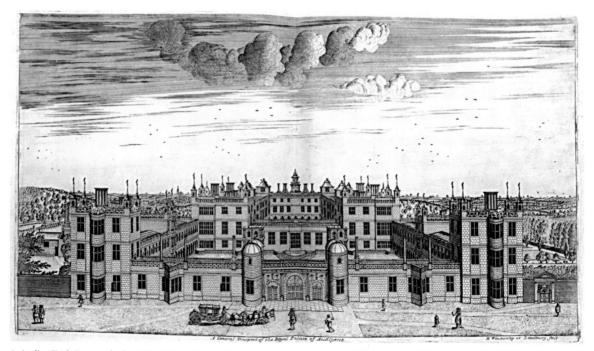

4. Audley End, Essex, rebuilt *c*. 1603–16 (partly destr.); from an engraving by Henry Winstanley, *c*. 1678 (London, British Library)

5. Pitchford Hall, Shropshire, entrance façade (added 1560s)

in stucco, edged with slate borders, on the exterior walls of Nonsuch Palace. Around 1550 courtiers began to reach a more fundamental understanding of classical architecture as a system of rule, proportion and decorum. The chief monument to this phase was (Old) Somerset House (destr.) in the Strand, London, the symmetrical street façade of which was built in 1547–51 for Edward Seymour, 1st Duke of Somerset. The Reformation did not completely sever England's cultural links with Italy, but the stronger trading links with the Protestant Low Countries as well as the immigration of refugee HUGUENOTS meant that the dominant source of foreign influence in the late 16th century was Flemish. This influence continued into the 17th century, particularly in the domestic architecture of the wealthy urban, merchant classes, as in the shaped gables of the brick Dutch House, also known as Kew Palace (1631), just west of central London.

Through his European travels and collection of foreign architectural treatises, Inigo Jones came to understand more profoundly than anyone before him in Britain the principles on which contemporary Italian architecture was based. He was to be influential later, not only through the classical language of the façades of his London buildings (e.g. the Banqueting House, 1619–22, Whitehall; *see* JONES, INIGO, fig. 1), but also in terms of his innovative building types and choice of facing materials. Jones and his close associates, including Isaac de Caus and John Webb (i), worked for the courts of James I and Charles I and their immediate circle, for example for the Herbert family at Wilton House, Wilts (*see* WILTON, §1). Other architects, however, looked at the possibility of applying elements of classicism to native styles and forms of architecture. In such buildings as the Leathersellers' Hall (1620s; destr.), London, designed by the guild's own carpenter, the use of

classical detail was subject at each stage to English tradition. The rule of proportion was here not permitted to override the need for marking out the traditional raised and well-lit hall, with its large and close-set windows; the porch, too, was a prominent feature, suggesting a form of architecture that still allowed significant points of access to dominate the whole. This quite widespread inventiveness of leading craftsmen, masons and carpenters (*see* ARTISAN MANNERISM) stands alongside the legacy of Jones in the formation of the deepening preference for classicism that was to become more prominent in the late 17th century.

BIBLIOGRAPHY
J. Summerson: *Architecture in Britain, 1530–1830*, Pelican Hist. A. (Harmondsworth, 1953, rev. 7/1983)
F. Jenkins: *Architect and Patron* (Durham, 1961)
M. Girouard: *Robert Smythson and the Architecture of the Elizabethan Era* (London, 1962), rev. as *Robert Smythson and the Elizabethan Country House* (London, 1983)
E. Mercer: *English Art, 1553–1625*, Oxford Hist. Eng. A. (Oxford, 1962)
H. M. Colvin, D. R. Ransome and J. Summerson: *1485–1660* (1975), iii of *The History of the King's Works*, ed. H. M. Colvin (London, 1963–82)
E. Mercer: *English Vernacular Houses* (London, 1975)
M. Airs: *The Making of the English Country House, 1500–1640* (London, 1978)
——: *The Buildings of Britain: Tudor and Jacobean* (London, 1982)
M. Howard: *The Early Tudor Country House: Architecture and Politics, 1490–1550* (London, 1987)
J. Schofield, ed.: *The London Surveys of Ralph Treswell* (London, 1987)
S. Thurley: *The Royal Palaces of Tudor England* (New Haven and London, 1993)
MAURICE HOWARD

4. *c.* 1660–*c.* 1830.

(i) English Baroque. (ii) Palladianism and the classical revival. (iii) The Picturesque and later revival styles.

(i) English Baroque. During the later 17th century such amateur architects as Roger Pratt, who designed Coleshill

(c. 1658–62; destr. 1952), Berks, for his cousin Sir George Pratt, began the practice of designing country houses for family and friends, thereby enhancing the position of the architect relative to those working in the other building trades. The most famous 17th-century amateur architect was CHRISTOPHER WREN, a mathematician and astronomer. In 1663–9 he built the Sheldonian Theatre, Oxford, and in 1665 he made a prolonged visit to France, where he studied the architecture in and around Paris, including the royal palaces of the Louvre and Versailles. His opportunity to concentrate exclusively on architecture came after the Great Fire (1666), which destroyed a large area of the City of London, including such public buildings as Old St Paul's Cathedral and the parish churches.

An increase in the London Coal Tax provided the funds for rebuilding St Paul's and for 51 other City churches. Wren's early designs for a domed, centralized cathedral were rejected, but in 1675 his third plan, known as the Warrant Design, won royal approval, and from this the final form developed until the completion of the building in 1711 (see LONDON, §V, 1(ii)(a) and fig. 25). At St Paul's, Wren produced a classical building that incorporated a dome, never seen before in what had hitherto been a medieval city of spires. Like St Paul's, Wren's City churches, including St Bride's, Fleet Street (1671–8), St Stephen Walbrook (1672–9) and St Clement Danes (1680–82), display a classical decorative system, although the churches themselves often follow the ground-plan of the earlier Gothic structures.

Wren gathered around him a group of architects and craftsmen to form the reconstituted Office of Works, which carried out building programmes for successive monarchs. For Charles II, Wren built Chelsea Hospital (1682–92), London, and Winchester Palace (1683–5; destr.); for William and Mary, he designed extensions to HAMPTON COURT PALACE (begun 1689; see WREN, CHRISTOPHER, fig. 3), and during their reign he also designed the Royal Naval Hospital (1696–1716; for illustration see GREENWICH), Greenwich, which incorporated classical colonnades and Baroque domes into the earlier scheme for the palace begun by John Webb (see WEBB, JOHN (i)).

Two architects strongly influenced by Wren at the Office of Works were John Vanbrugh and NICHOLAS HAWKSMOOR. Vanbrugh's early major works, Castle Howard (1701–24; for illustration see CASTLE HOWARD), N. Yorks, and BLENHEIM PALACE (1705–16; see VANBRUGH, JOHN, fig. 2), Oxon, show him in command of a well-developed French Baroque style. He continued to design dramatically composed country houses, including Kings Weston (1710–11), Avon, Eastbury Park (1716; largely destr. 1755), Dorset, and Seaton Delaval (1720–29; destr. 1822; see VANBRUGH, JOHN, fig. 4), Northumb. His own house at Greenwich, Vanbrugh Castle (1718–25; see VANBRUGH, JOHN, fig. 3), is distinguished by its proto-Romantic, castellated roof-line; his imaginative style was possibly informed by his second occupation as a playwright. Hawksmoor also developed a distinctive style, while retaining the classical form. Easton Neston (begun 1680s; façades remodelled c. 1700–02; see HAWKSMOOR, NICHOLAS, fig. 1), Northants, with its long dramatic staircase, was his first independent work. Hawksmoor became involved in the project to build new parish churches under the Act for Building Fifty New Churches (1711), and was responsible for such original buildings as Christ Church, Spitalfields (begun 1714), and St George's, Bloomsbury (begun 1716), both in London. Although Hawksmoor took a keen interest in the archaeology of antique architecture, his own work displays a fascination with oversized details of striking geometric form, such as those he employed at the Clarendon Buildings (1711–13), Oxford (see OXFORD, fig. 4). In the north quadrangle of All Souls College (1714), however, he demonstrated that he could also adapt the Gothic style to suit the prevailing rational taste.

Another architect to work in the English Baroque style was THOMAS ARCHER, who, in addition to several country houses, is remembered for his churches, including St Philip's (1710–25), Birmingham, and St Paul's, Deptford (see fig. 6), and St John's, Smith Square (1714–28), both in London, in which he demonstrated his first-hand knowledge of the Roman Baroque. James Gibbs also visited Rome, where he worked with Carlo Fontana (iv) and acquired an eclectic style incorporating 16th-century Mannerism and the Baroque. Gibbs was a Scot and a Tory Catholic who did not always find it easy to gain commissions, but he managed to steer his own course in such buildings as St Mary-le-Strand (1714) and St Martin-in-the-Fields (1720–26; see GIBBS, JAMES, fig. 1), both in London. The latter established the accepted form of the 18th-century church, with a portico and pediment surmounted by a spire. Gibbs was also responsible for Senate

6. Thomas Archer: St Paul, Deptford, London, 1713–30

House (1722–30) and the Fellows Building (1724–30), King's College, both in Cambridge, and the circular, domed Radcliffe Camera (1739–49; *see* GIBBS, JAMES, fig. 2) in Oxford.

(ii) Palladianism and the classical revival. In the early 18th century, the Whig ascendancy encouraged the development of a new style based loosely on the work of Inigo Jones and his interpretation of the work of Palladio (*see* PALLADIANISM). The Whig appreciation of Jones as an English architect free from the influence of the French Baroque led to a revival of interest in his work, and the English Palladian style was encouraged by the publication of the first volume of Colen Campbell's *Vitruvius Britannicus* (London, 1715), in which the author compared recent buildings with the work of Jones and with his own Palladian villa, Wanstead House, Essex (*c.* 1715–20; destr. 1824; *see* CAMPBELL, COLEN, fig. 1). The Palladian villa dominated the design of the country house in England for most of the 18th century. The houses consisted of a rusticated ground floor housing the kitchens, storerooms and servants' quarters; a *piano nobile* housing the hall and public rooms; and one or two upper floors housing the more private rooms of the family, including the bedrooms. The *piano nobile* was usually approached directly by external stairs leading to a portico surmounted by a pediment; the hall was often formal in its proportions and severe in its decoration. The houses were intended to enhance the status of their owners and were placed to advantage within the landscape of their estates. The style could be adapted for houses large or small; in addition to Wanstead, Campbell designed STOURHEAD (1721–4; *see* CAMPBELL, COLEN, fig. 2), Wilts, Houghton Hall (1722), Norfolk, and a version of Palladio's Villa Rotonda, near Vicenza, at Mereworth (1723), Kent. Another influential supporter of Palladianism was Richard Boyle (ii), 3rd Earl of Burlington, who designed Chiswick House (1725–9); for illustration *see* CHISWICK HOUSE, London, inspired partly by Palladio's Villa Rotonda, and the Assembly Rooms (1731–2; *see* BOYLE, (2), fig. 4), York, derived from the so-called Egyptian Hall of Vitruvius as interpreted by Palladio. He was assisted by William Kent, a talented interior designer whom Burlington had met in Italy. Kent was responsible for Holkham Hall (*c.* 1731–5; *see* PALLADIANISM, figs 1 and 3), Norfolk, which, although restrained externally, has an apsidal entrance hall with a dramatic staircase up to the first floor that reveals his scenographic talents. Kent also demonstrated his originality in landscape design at STOWE (*c.* 1730–36), Bucks, and Rousham (1738–41; for illustration *see* ROUSHAM), Oxon, where he evoked the antique ruins of Italy.

The development of Palladianism followed the agricultural reforms of the 18th century as landowners enclosed land and built new houses on their expanded estates. Architects were engaged throughout the country; for example, JAMES PAINE designed Kedleston Hall (1757), Derbys, and Wardour Castle (1770–76), Wilts, and John Carr designed Harewood House (1758), W. Yorks. While architectural developments were most noticeable in their impact on the appearance of the country house, they also affected the appearance of the town. The city of Bath flourished from 1725 under the joint efforts of the architects John Wood I and his son John Wood II (*see* WOOD (ii)), with the quarry owner Ralph Allen. Bath provided England with its own Roman archaeological remains, and the Woods laid out the town with formal squares, crescents and a circus (*see* BATH (i), fig. 3) in recognition of its Roman origins. Their houses were built in the Palladian style, with a ground floor, *piano nobile* and proportioned façades, some with Classical orders, while Grosvenor Square (1727; *see* LONDON, fig. 5), London, by Edward Shepherd (*d* 1747), set the standard for elegant residential districts in the later expansion of provincial towns.

Although the Palladian style endured, the taste for something less severe began to emerge during the second half of the 18th century. Discoveries of antique remains in Italy suggested to architects ways in which they could decorate the interiors of their houses with motifs derived from domestic Roman ruins discovered at Pompeii and Herculaneum. The Scottish architect Robert Adam (*see* ADAM (i), (3)) followed his other countrymen by building in England after a visit to Italy had brought him into contact with the exciting finds that were being made at the archaeological sites there. He designed such houses as Syon House (1760–69; *see* ADAM, fig. 2) and Kenwood (1767–9), both in London, with interiors that depend on delicate, flat plasterwork inspired by the so-called ETRUSCAN STYLE, which was better suited to intimate domestic spaces than the work of the Italian stuccoists active in England earlier in the century. By introducing moulds and instructions through detailed drawings, Adam was able to produce intricate interior designs for such houses as Harewood House (1759–71), W. Yorks, and Kedleston Hall (1760–71), Derbys, both well beyond the confines of fashionable London, where he had also designed fine interiors, for example at Home House (1773–7), 20 Portman Square.

The towns provided an opportunity for architects to design other building types. George Dance (i) (*see* DANCE, (1)) built the Mansion House (1739–53) in the City of London as the official residence of the Lord Mayor, while his son George Dance (ii) designed Newgate Prison (1768–75; destr. 1902; for illustration *see* DANCE, (3)), London, in a style that graphically expressed the building's purpose, with blind rusticated walls and festoons of chains. William Chambers designed the first purpose-built offices at Somerset House (begun 1776), London, for a variety of government departments and as a permanent location for the Royal Academy of Arts (*see* CHAMBERS, WILLIAM). Chambers was also significant because he brought back from France the sort of professionalism exemplified by the Académie d'Architecture, thereby providing an example for a generation of younger architects.

(iii) The Picturesque and later revival styles. The dominance of the classical style in architecture, while never completely abating, began to lift during the second half of the 18th century. Influence from abroad inspired such buildings as the Chinese Pagoda (1761–2) at Kew Gardens, London, by William Chambers. More significantly, the Gothic began to be appreciated once more, albeit as a curiosity, as at Lacock Abbey (see fig. 7), Wilts, by SANDERSON

7. Sanderson Miller: Great Hall, Lacock Abbey, Wiltshire, 1753–6

MILLER, and at Strawberry Hill (begun 1753), Twickenham, built for Horace Walpole, 4th Earl of Orford (*see* WALPOLE, (2)). There was no attempt at this time to reproduce authentic Gothic structures, but rather to produce examples of the PICTURESQUE.

The two most prominent exponents of the Picturesque were JOHN SOANE and JOHN NASH. Soane, while remaining true to the classical style, became the master of the dramatically lit interior, whether in the public banking halls of the Bank of England (1792–1827; interiors destr. 1930s), London, or in the intimate spaces of his houses, including his own (begun 1792; now Sir John Soane's Museum) in Lincoln's Inn Fields and Pitshanger Manor (1801–3), both in London. He reduced the classical detail almost to a point of abstraction and increased the sense of attenuation by introducing suspended ceilings.

Another major example of his public buildings is Dulwich Picture Gallery (1811–14), the first purpose-built art gallery in Britain (*see* MAUSOLEUM, fig. 4), which incorporates a mausoleum to its benefactor, Sir Peter Francis Bourgeois. Nash was another scenographic architect who sought to produce theatrical effects through his dramatic exteriors. From 1795 he worked with HUMPHRY REPTON in producing Picturesque designs for rural estates, such as the castellated Luscombe (1800–04), Devon, and the Italianate villa of Cronkhill (*c.* 1802), Salop. Nash later entered the circle of the Prince Regent (later George IV), and he took the opportunity to develop the Picturesque to a high degree with such works as the Royal Pavilion (1815–22), Brighton, in an Indian style (for illustration *see* BRIGHTON), and the Regent's Park terraces (1812–27), London, derived from Roman palaces. The latter scheme, which included

8. Robert Smirke (ii): British Museum, London, south façade, 1823–48

not just the park and terraces but also Regent's Street and Carlton House Terrace, was greater than any of the urban projects undertaken by his contemporaries.

A tendency towards eclecticism arose at the end of the 18th century, the chief exponent of which was probably James Wyatt. His early work included Heaton Hall (1772), Manchester, built in a style reminiscent of Adam, but at Dodington (1798–1813), Glos, he also mastered the increasingly fashionable Neo-classical style, which reduced decoration to a minimum and emphasized the giant order. Wyatt also worked in the Gothic style, for example at Fonthill Abbey (1795–1807; destr.; *see* WYATT, (2), fig. 2), Wilts, a folly built for William Beckford.

During the first three decades of the 19th century there was a spate of public building, much of it in the GREEK REVIVAL style, characterized by a preference for a horizontal composition with heavy porticos using the Doric or Ionic orders. One of the early exponents of the style was THOMAS HARRISON at Chester Castle (1788–1822), built to accommodate county courts, a prison and barracks, the forecourt of which is guarded by a version of the Propylaea on the Acropolis, Athens. The Greek Revival style was also used by William Wilkins for Downing College (1806), Cambridge, and by Robert Smirke (ii) (*see* SMIRKE, (2)) for the British Museum (see fig. 8), London. St Pancras New Church (1819–22), London, by William Inwood and his son Henry William Inwood, is a major example of the Greek Revival style, with its direct quotations from the Erechtheum and the Tower of the Winds in Athens.

Even while Greek classicism continued to dominate public building, the Gothic, an interest in which began as an academic study, soon came to be considered an appropriate style for certain building types (*see* GOTHIC REVIVAL). Some of the 174 churches erected under the Church Building Act of 1818 (*see* RICKMAN, THOMAS) displayed a transitional style, such as St Luke's (1820–24) in Chelsea, London, by James Savage (1779–1852), which retained the galleries of the classical church while introducing Gothic elements, including stone vaulting. At the time of the competition for the new Houses of Parliament after the fire of 1834, a Gothic or Tudor style was stipulated (*see* LONDON, §V, 3(iii)), marking the beginning of the Gothic Revival, which developed throughout the rest of the 19th century.

BIBLIOGRAPHY

Colvin
J. Summerson: *Architecture in Britain, 1530–1830*, Pelican Hist. A. (Harmondsworth, 1953, rev. 8/1991)
J. Lees-Milne: *Earls of Creation* (London, 1962)
K. Downes: *English Baroque Architecture* (London, 1966)
J. M. Crook: *The Greek Revival: Neo-classical Attitudes in British Architecture, 1760–1870* (London, 1972)
R. Wittkower: *Palladio and Palladianism* (New York, 1974)
B. Little: *Sir Christopher Wren: A Historical Biography* (London, 1975)
K. Downes: *Hawksmoor* (London, 1979)
J. Summerson: *The Life and Work of John Nash, Architect* (London, 1980)
T. Friedman: *James Gibbs* (New Haven, 1984)
D. Stroud: *Sir John Soane, Architect* (London, 1984)
K. Downes: *Sir John Vanbrugh* (London, 1987)
M. McCarthy: *The Origins of the Gothic Revival* (New Haven, 1987)
E. Harris: *British Architectural Books and Writers, 1556–1785* (Cambridge, 1990)
D. King: *The Complete Works of Robert and James Adam* (Oxford, 1991)

TANIS HINCHCLIFFE

5. *c*. 1830–*c*. 1914. By the early Victorian period architecture had emerged as a recognizable profession, regulated and supported by such bodies as the Institute of British Architects, founded in 1834 (from 1837 the Royal Institute of British Architects), and the Architectural Association, founded in 1847. From 1843 architects also had their own weekly magazine, *The Builder*. The concept of the architect as an independent professional was consolidated in the course of the 19th century as the industrial wealth, political power and social and artistic developments that resulted from the Industrial Revolution led to the creation of the modern building industry, to the emergence of new types of building and to more complex methods of planning (*see* URBAN PLANNING, §IV), servicing and construction (*see* CONSTRUCTION MACHINERY, §2). This period was also notable, however, for the stylistic variety of its architecture. Indeed, in terms of buildings, ideas and trends, the contribution to the construction industry of the English architecture of this period is surpassed only by that of the 18th century, and such buildings as the Crystal Palace (1851; destr. 1936), London, by Joseph Paxton (for further discussion and illustration *see* PAXTON, JOSEPH, §2), and the Red House (1859), Bexleyheath, Kent, built for William Morris by Philip Webb, have frequently been singled out for their pioneering role, in terms of their use of materials or from a stylistic viewpoint. Towards the end of the 19th century, however, a number of late Victorian architects, including Richard Norman Shaw, attempted to emancipate themselves from the more commercial concerns of their profession and of the building industry, and to insist on the recognition of the architect as an artist.

(i) Building types. Building in the 18th century was still largely a localized activity, but by the early 19th century, accompanying the developments of the Industrial Revolution, a vast expansion of building activity occurred together with a diversification in the types of buildings required. Previously, for an office and for most manufacturing activities an adapted dwelling house had been sufficient, but already by the later 18th century separate FACTORY buildings were developed, and after *c*. 1830 an increasing number of separate purpose-built urban offices were constructed (*see* OFFICE BUILDING), for example London and Westminster Bank (1837; destr.), Lothbury, London, by C. R. Cockerell. Similarly, before the 19th century there was only a small number of buildings in England devoted to the tasks of central or regional administration, but with the Municipal Corporations Act of 1835, which provided for a more democratic, efficient and uniform method of government for 178 boroughs and cities in Britain, the construction of municipal buildings was undertaken on an unprecedented scale. The town hall became the focal building of every major English town, especially in those that had risen to prominence through industrialization, where their civic buildings were signs of their newly acquired social, economic and political respectability (*see* TOWN HALL, §3(i)). Many such buildings combined administration with law courts and halls for cultural events, for example Birmingham Town Hall (1832–60s; *see* BIRMINGHAM, fig. 1) by Joseph Aloysius

Hansom, St George's Hall (1841–56), Liverpool, by HARVEY LONSDALE ELMES and C. R. Cockerell (*see* COCKERELL, (2)), and Leeds Town Hall (1853–8) by Cuthbert Brodrick (1822–1905).

During the early Victorian period a succession of legislative measures helped to improve the social condition of the population; this led to the requirement for new or improved buildings for public welfare and health, which, in turn, excelled in the new ingenuity of their planning. The Poor Law Amendment Act (1834) created the system of workhouses, while, in turn, attempts were also made to humanize lunatic asylums and prisons. At the Pentonville Model Prison (1840–42; *see* PRISON), London, by Sir Joshua Jebb (1793–1863) and Charles Barry, new types of warm-air heating and ventilation were introduced, and each cell contained its own wash-basin with running water and its own toilet. The Health of Towns Act (1848) and its subsequent amendments led to improvements to and the further provision of hospitals, public baths and wash-houses, cemeteries and housing. The hospitals built after *c.* 1860 according to the theories of Florence Nightingale adopted the pavilion plan (e.g. St Thomas's Hospital (1868–71; partly destr.), London, by Henry Currey (1820–1900)), which ensured maximum levels of light and natural ventilation (*see* HOSPITAL, §1 (iii)). Among the largest constructions of the later 19th century were the drainage systems: together with the fresh water supply, they gave rise to some of the most spectacular technical as well as ornamental buildings, such as the Crossness Sewage Works (1865), London, by JOSEPH BAZALGETTE. The railways were the chief signposts of 19th-century architecture: their stations constituted completely new types of buildings, exemplified by the great variety of combinations of sheds and reception buildings, as at Paddington Station (1850–54; *see* RAILWAY STATION, fig. 2), London, by ISAMBARD KINGDOM BRUNEL, assisted by the architect Matthew Digby Wyatt.

Traditionally, only small quantities of building materials had been transported over long distances, with the exception of timber, but the development of extensive transportation networks, particularly the railways, led to the increasing movement of building materials around the country during the 19th century. Slates from North Wales replaced the use of local tiles in most regions in England; stone from Bath, often machine-cut at the quarry, could be cheaply transported to all parts of the country; Peterborough (Fletton) and Bedfordshire bricks began to replace locally made bricks throughout England in the late 19th century. In addition, the greater availability and cheapness of cast iron and wrought iron due to new industrial manufacturing processes (*see* IRON AND STEEL, §II, 1) led to the widespread use of such metals instead of timber in the construction of roofs, greenhouses and railway stations, and very occasionally for whole buildings, of which the best known was the Crystal Palace, London, built for the Great Exhibition of 1851 and relocated to a permanent site in Sydenham, Kent, in 1852–4. At the same time, the quality and reliability of buildings began to be subjected to stricter controls, by the demands of clients, by the building industry itself through more stringent contractual and competitive procedures, and through government legislation, particularly the Public Health Acts of 1848 and 1875, which ensured that even the smallest new house was subject to detailed planning and building regulations.

(ii) Architectural styles. The architecture of the 19th century and the early 20th in England was characterized by the unparalleled variety of styles that appeared. Different forms of plan and elevation as well as different forms of external decoration were even proposed for the same project, for example in the 218 submitted competition designs (1857) for the Foreign Office, London. The reason for such variety lay ultimately in the continuation of the 18th-century British aesthetic of the Picturesque, the Beautiful and the Sublime, and the new relativism it brought regarding the laws of beauty. By 1850 English architecture was characterized by its stylistic eclecticism. Designers strove to demonstrate their competence in all styles: for example Charles Barry (*see* BARRY, (1)) used a whole range of styles for various types of buildings, such as the Renaissance Revival (*see* RENAISSANCE REVIVAL, §1) style for the Reform Club (1837–41), Pall Mall, London, and the GOTHIC REVIVAL style for the Houses of Parliament (see fig. 9; *see also* PUGIN, (2); and LONDON, figs 37 and 38), London. Even such relatively minor architects as John Brown (1805–76), surveyor of the county of Norfolk, followed suit. The knowledge of the history of architecture was expanding rapidly. Spectacular architectural drawings by such artists as David Roberts and Samuel Prout, and attractive reproductions in books about old buildings, for example by John Britton, abounded (*see also* §XVII below). However arbitrary the choice of style might seem at first, there were attempts to relate the decoration of a building to its material and symbolic functions. Stylistic eclecticism in the late 18th century had been used in ephemeral buildings in parks and had later been applied most notably to country houses and villas. In 1864 the critic and architect Robert Kerr published *The Gentleman's House; or How to Plan English Residences, from the Parsonage to the Palace*; based on such books by John Claudius Loudon as his *Encyclopedia of Cottage, Farm and Villa Architecture and Furniture* (London, 1833), Kerr's work lists 10 styles from which the patron and designer of any domestic project 'had' to choose. For other types of buildings there was a seemingly more plausible set of alternatives: administration buildings erected by municipal authorities and central government continued to demand the classical style into the 1860s (with the important early exception of the Gothic Houses of Parliament), as did urban commercial structures such as banks (*see* BANK, §2). Churches, however, and a few related building types, including church-run primary schools, parsonages and cemetery buildings, were deemed to be most appropriately designed in the medieval Gothic style.

The choice between the Gothic and classical styles dominated architectural thought in England in the 19th century. Of the two, Gothic was the more 'recent' style, and many writers on architecture concerned themselves principally with preaching the 'progress' of the GOTHIC REVIVAL, which played a greater role in England than in any other country; eminent defenders of the classical style, such as C. R. Cockerell (*see* COCKERELL, (2)), were rare.

9. Charles Barry and A. W. N. Pugin: Houses of Parliament, London, 1837–67

The success of Gothic was largely due to A. W. N. Pugin (*see* PUGIN, (2)), who around 1840, in several incisive books, made out what seemed an overwhelming case for the style: Gothic, to Pugin, represented the pre-Reformation Church and 'true' faith, with its emotional appeal and liturgical, artistic and architectural splendour, but it was also associated with Englishness; classical forms appeared 'foreign'. Moreover, Gothic architecture provided the most rational, practical and 'truthful' solution; the inherent irregularity of a building programme dictated by its various functions could not be forced to adhere to a symmetrical, classical layout.

Although Pugin was a convert to Roman Catholicism, his work and influence found an immediate application in the enormous amount of church building that began in the 1840s, in particular for the Church of England; the Nonconformists, in their even larger output of buildings, were less orthodox in their choice of style. The new Gothic church, frequently accompanied by a vicarage and a church school, is as characteristic an expression of Victorian England as the new factories and banks. A devoted party of young Gothic Revival practitioners, including G. E. STREET, WILLIAM BUTTERFIELD and WILLIAM WHITE, together with Oxford- and Cambridge-educated clergy and patrons, congregated in the Cambridge Camden (from 1845 the Ecclesiological) Society, founded c. 1836; in the widely read and influential publications of the society, including pamphlets and the periodical *The Ecclesiologist* (1841–68), church architecture was debated, and detailed prescriptions were published for the building

of churches that were very much in accordance with the ideas of Pugin. Designers were also meticulous in the details of church interiors, as at All Saints' (1849–59), Margaret Street, London, by William Butterfield, the model church of the Ecclesiological Society, built of red brick with Bath stone detailing, and with a richly decorated interior that uses a wide variety of materials, including polished granite, glazed tiles and terracotta (*see* BUTTERFIELD, WILLIAM, fig. 1). The Gothic Revival reached a peak in the 1860s and 1870s with such buildings as St Pancras Hotel (1866–76), London, by George Gilbert Scott I (*see* SCOTT (ii), (1), §3), the Bradford Wool Exchange (1871–3) by the partnership of Lockwood & Mawson, and the Royal Courts of Justice (1874–82), London, by G. E. Street (*see* STREET, G. E., §4). The most widely respected of all the Gothic Revival practitioners was probably ALFRED WATERHOUSE, for the way in which he combined lavish decoration and picturesqueness of outline with sound planning, for example at Manchester Town Hall (1868–77).

From *c*. 1850 it was felt that the polarization of the Gothic and the classical could be avoided by selecting the best elements from all periods of the past and combining them in a way that suited the present, a concept known as eclecticism. This also provided, at least temporarily, an answer to the question of why Victorian England lacked its own style. Favourite compromise styles were Elizabethan and Jacobean, which had already begun to play an important role in the 1820s and 1830s: the ELIZABETHAN REVIVAL style was chosen by Henry Herbert, 3rd Earl of

10. Richard Norman Shaw: Cragside, Northumberland, 1870–*c*. 1885

Carnarvon, when he decided to remodel (1839–42, by Charles Barry) his Georgian country house, Highclere, Hants. Architects of the Gothic Revival branched out from the narrow fields of English Gothic, as prescribed by Pugin, into a variety of foreign medieval styles, including the Romanesque of France, Germany, Spain and especially Italy. Two notable ROMANESQUE REVIVAL churches are SS Mary and Nicholas (1840–45), Wilton, Wilts, by Thomas Henry Wyatt and David Brandon (1813–97), which incorporates a free-standing Italianate campanile, and Christ Church (1840–42), Streatham, London, by James William Wild (1814–92), an externally bare building of yellow brick. Pugin's successor as a powerful architectural critic was JOHN RUSKIN, who, in his writings of the 1850s and 1860s, developed Pugin's demand that building materials not be concealed and advocated the use of different textural materials of different colours. This device, known as constructional polychromy (*see* BRICK, §V, 3(ii)(c) and POLYCHROMY, §1(ii), and colour pl. I, fig. 2), was applied particularly in church architecture, for example at Keble College Chapel (1867–83), Oxford, by William Butterfield (*see* BUTTERFIELD, WILLIAM, §4, and fig. 2). Also in the 1850s and 1860s the SECOND EMPIRE STYLE, promoted in France by Napoleon III, was adopted in England, combining French late medieval and Renaissance high roofs, in the manner of the French château, with classical Mannerist decoration, for example at the Grosvenor Hotel (1860–62), London, by James Thomas Knowles (*see* KNOWLES, (1)). In the mid-19th century a large number of architects began to explore alternatives to the mainstream styles at the centre of the architectural

debate. In particular, by the 1860s they began to emancipate themselves from the religious–moralistic attitudes of Pugin and the early Ruskin, adopting more hedonistic attitudes that culminated in the AESTHETIC MOVEMENT and the idea of 'Art for Art's Sake'. Pugin had already pronounced his hatred of commercialized building and design, and of the mass production of decoration. WILLIAM BURGES, an ardent Gothicist, although chiefly interested in the application of the Gothic to secular buildings, went further, however, and termed himself an 'art architect'. Increasingly, individual styles among architects, especially among those associated with the Gothic Revival, were adopted, for example by William Butterfield, William White, EDWARD BUCKTON LAMB, J. L. PEARSON and JAMES BROOKS (i). The most notable representative of the Aesthetic Movement, however, was E. W. GODWIN, who designed the White House (1877–9; destr.), Tite Street, Chelsea, London, for another of the movement's protagonists, the painter James McNeill Whistler. The house was built of whitewashed brick, unusual in an urban setting.

Also by the 1860s another new mode of thinking had entered avant-garde architecture: the revival of the vernacular. Attention turned away from the 'High Styles' to the levels of the local builder and of the 'English tradition'. The love of the simple rural cottage or OLD ENGLISH STYLE, chiefly manifested in half-timbering, had already begun by *c*. 1820, but from the 1860s the style was used much more comprehensively in the large villas and country houses designed by a group of architects in London centred around RICHARD NORMAN SHAW and W. E. NESFIELD. Notable examples include Cragside (see fig. 10), Northumb., by Shaw, a large, isolated, asymmetrical stone house that rises through a range of timber-framed gables to a crenellated tower, itself topped by a half-timbered gabled roof. Many of the architects associated with the revival of the vernacular, including W. R. LETHABY, E. S. PRIOR and Philip Webb, were closely associated with the ARTS AND CRAFTS MOVEMENT, most notably in their common concern with the building crafts. For example, at Standen (1892–4), W. Sussex, by Philip Webb (for illustration *see* WEBB, PHILIP), the variety of materials and techniques used, including brick, stone, tilehanging and weatherboarding, is a reflection of local buildings. What was entirely new in the 1870s was the combination of the vernacular with the style of urban brick structures of the 17th and 18th centuries, known as the Queen Anne Revival. The term originally applied to the work of Shaw and Webb, to their specific use of red-brick façades with white timber detail, for example at Bedford Park (begun 1878; *see* QUEEN ANNE REVIVAL, fig. 1), Turnham Green, London, a planned Victorian suburb of modest red-brick houses designed by Shaw with Edward John May (1853–1941) and MAURICE B. ADAMS. Various regional vernacular revivals subsequently dominated suburban and even urban domestic architecture, with a number of architects, including M. H. BAILLIE SCOTT, C. F. A. VOYSEY, PARKER & UNWIN and ERNEST NEWTON, devoting themselves to one or another version of the style in the 1890s. Some of them also allied themselves with the new GARDEN CITY movement, which was influential throughout western Europe and the USA.

At the end of the century there was also, in the area of public buildings, the last important revival of a major textbook style of the past. Some architects considered it necessary to return to the values of classicism, and this led to a revival of the Baroque style. One of the most successful examples of the Late Victorian Baroque Revival is Colchester Town Hall (see fig. 11) by John Belcher: above a rusticated ground floor the façade is articulated by giant columns supporting a central triangular and two flanking segmental pediments, the whole decorated with classical architectural elements and allegorical sculpture and surmounted by a tall, slender tower. The style was also widely used in London, as a result of a widespread conviction that the capital failed to match the planned splendours of Paris or Rome and needed aggrandizement in order to reflect the prosperity, extensive empire and national pride of the period. Notable examples from the Edwardian period include the Old Bailey (1900–06; *see* BAROQUE REVIVAL), London, by E. W. Mountford, the central dome of which is derived from Christopher Wren's Royal Hospital at Greenwich, London, and the Piccadilly Hotel façades (1905–8) on Piccadilly and Regent Street, London, by Richard Norman Shaw. The Edwardian Grand Manner thus firmly established itself as the predominant style for English building, although from *c.* 1910–20 it was usually tempered with a NEO-GEORGIAN sobriety, evident, for example, in the offices for the Bennett Steamship Co. (1908), Southwark, London, by S. D. ADSHEAD.

The two major styles, the informal vernacular and the grand classical, dominated English architecture in the later 19th century and the early 20th; in addition, Gothic remained valid for churches, although English Gothic

11. John Belcher: Colchester Town Hall, Essex, 1897–1902

models were preferred. The stylistic dilemmas of the 19th century seemed finally to be solved. Traditionalism, with which both classicism and the vernacular were associated, was approved, while Victorian revival styles were condemned by early 20th-century English designers and critics and their Modernist contemporaries on the Continent, although there was little demand to break away completely from historical styles. In a more general sense, however, English architecture between 1830 and 1914 contributed to the MODERN MOVEMENT, through the commercialization and industrialization of the building process and in the creation of a new kind of designer, who combined conviction of truth and even social reform with an insistence on artistic independence.

BIBLIOGRAPHY

The Builder; *Bldg News*; *The Architect* ; *Archit. Rev.* [London]; *Civ. Engin. & Architect's J.*; *The Ecclesiologist*, *J. RIBA*; *RIBA J.*; *Trans. RIBA*
H. Muthesius: *Das englische Haus* (Berlin, 1904; Eng. trans., London, 1987)
H. R. Hitchcock: *Early Victorian Architecture in Britain* (New Haven and London, 1954)
P. Ferriday, ed.: *Victorian Architecture* (London, 1963)
J. Summerson: *Victorian Architecture: Four Studies in Evaluation* (New York and London, 1970)
M. Girouard: *The Victorian Country House* (Oxford, 1971)
R. Macleod: *Style and Society: Architectural Ideology in Britain, 1835–1914* (London, 1971)
G. L. Hersey: *High Victorian Gothic: A Study in Associationism* (Baltimore, 1972)
S. Muthesius: *The High Victorian Movement in Architecture, 1850–1870* (London, 1972)
Marble Halls: Drawings and Models of Victorian Secular Buildings (exh. cat. by J. Physick and M. Darby, London, V&A, 1973)

V. Glasstone: *Victorian and Edwardian Theatres* (London, 1975)
A. Service: *Edwardian Architecture and its Origins* (London, 1975)
J. Fawcett, ed.: *Seven Victorian Architects* (London, 1976)
M. Girouard: *Sweetness and Light: The Queen Anne Movement* (Oxford, 1977)
A. Service: *Edwardian Architecture* (London, 1977)
R. Dixon and S. Muthesius: *Victorian Architecture* (London, 1978)
P. Davey: *Arts & Crafts Architecture* (London, 1980)
R. Gradidge: *Dream Houses: The Edwardian Ideal* (London, 1980)
A. D. King, ed.: *Buildings and Society* (London, 1980)
D. Pearce and M. Binney: *Railway Architecture* (New York, 1980)
C. Cunningham: *Victorian and Edwardian Town Halls* (London, 1981)
J. Franklin: *The Gentleman's Country House and its Plan, 1835–1914* (London, 1981)
S. Muthesius: *The English Terraced House* (New Haven and London, 1982)
J. F. White: *The Cambridge Movement, the Ecclesiologists and the Gothic Revival* (Cambridge, 1982)
R. H. Harper: *Victorian Architectural Competitions: An Index to British and Irish Architectural Competitions in 'The Builder', 1843–1900* (London, 1983)
J. Bassin: *Architectural Competitions in 19th-century England* (London, 1984)
E. Jones: *Industrial Architecture in Britain, 1750–1939* (London, 1985)
I. Toplis: *The Foreign Office: An Architectural History* (London, 1987)
M. W. Brooks: *John Ruskin and Victorian Architecture* (London, 1989)
P. Howell and I. Sutton: *Faber Guide to Victorian Churches* (London, 1989)
C. M. Smart jr: *Muscular Churches: Ecclesiastical Architecture of the High Victorian Period* (Fayetteville, AR, 1989)
J. Stevens Curl: *Victorian Architecture* (Newton Abbot, 1990)

STEFAN MUTHESIUS

6. AFTER *c.* 1914. Architecture in England after World War I showed tendencies towards both traditional conservativism and the avant-garde. Immediately after the war, the trend in architecture, as in other aspects of English cultural life, was to recapture what was perceived as pre-war 'normality', and architects who had been influential before 1914 continued to work during the 1920s and 1930s. By unspoken consent, architectural style was divided between Arts and Crafts for country building and classical for the town. EDWIN LUTYENS was able to work successfully in both styles, and in the 1920s he reached

12. C. H. James and S. Rowland Pierce: Norwich City Hall, 1932–8

the peak of his career, completing the Viceroy's House (1912–31; now the Rashtrapati Bhavan; *see* LUTYENS, EDWIN, fig. 3), New Delhi, and the unexecuted design (1929) for the Roman Catholic Cathedral, Liverpool. Among the other architects who continued to be influential after World War I were William Curtis Green, whose Wolseley showroom (1921; now Barclays Bank) in Piccadilly, London, carried on the opulent Edwardian classical style, and J. J. BURNET, whose firm, Sir John Burnet, Tait & Lorne, was responsible for many distinguished commercial buildings, including Adelaide House (1924–5), London Bridge Approach, London.

During the same period the architectural schools, such as that at Liverpool University under Charles H. Reilly and the one at the Architectural Association under Howard Robertson, assumed a greater influence in the education of a new generation of architects. Through Robertson and F. R. Yerbury (1885–1970), during the 1920s English architects learnt of the architectural experiments in form and structure in both continental Europe and North America. Of particular interest was the Swedish example, the influence of which can be seen in the work of CHARLES HOLDEN, one of the new generation of architects, who, in his stations for the Northern and Piccadilly underground railway lines in London, broke free from the constraints of historical styles to provide a functional but nonetheless monumental form for contemporary building types. The use of traditional brick by the Swedes, and also by such Dutch architects as W. M. Dudok, suggested a way in which modern buildings could satisfy contemporary requirements without the need for fundamental changes in the building industry, and this influenced such buildings as Norwich City Hall (1932–8) by C. H. James and S. Rowland Pierce (1896–1966) (see fig. 12). With the publication of books by Le Corbusier, notably *Towards a New Architecture* (translated into English by Frederick Etchells in 1927), a new influence emerged, intimating that unfamiliar materials such as reinforced concrete and glass need not be used only to reproduce earlier forms.

Despite the prevalence of the NEO-GEORGIAN style after 1918, the architecture of the 1930s showed a marked tendency towards eclecticism. Grey Wornum's headquarters (1931–4) for the Royal Institute of British Architects at 66 Portland Place, London, is in a stripped-down classical style, while Hays Wharf (1929–31; largely destr.), London, by H. S. GOODHART-RENDEL was influenced by Art Deco, made popular by the Exposition Internationale des Arts Décoratifs et Industriels Modernes held in Paris in 1925. The influence of German Expressionism is evident in the distinctive churches designed by Welch & Lander, and N. F. Cachmaille-Day, such as St Saviour's (1932–3), Eltham, London, as well as in the Shakespeare Memorial Theatre (1928–32), Stratford-upon-Avon, by Elizabeth Scott (ii) (*see* SCOTT (ii), (6)). At the same time, the *Daily Express* Building (1931) in Fleet Street, London, by Ellis & Clarke with Owen Williams as engineer, was a startling demonstration of the use of curtain-walling in a London setting. Giles Gilbert Scott (ii) (*see* SCOTT (ii), (4)) perhaps epitomized the architect of the 1930s, seeking a monumental style that would be contemporary without being historicist, as can be seen in structures as diverse as

Cambridge University Library (1930–34) and Battersea Power Station (1930–34; altered), London.

Eclecticism was evident, too, in private houses built during the 1930s by such architects as OLIVER HILL, but it was also through houses for private clients that the Modern Movement first made an impression in England. A series of houses designed with the characteristic flat roof, white walls and horizontal windows began with New Ways (1923–5), Northampton, by Peter Behrens. The greatest impetus to the adoption of the ethos of the Modern Movement came from young architects recently arrived from the former British Colonies and the Continent. Amyas Douglas Connell, who helped to initiate the movement in England with his house High and Over (1928–9) in Amersham, Bucks, was from New Zealand, as were Basil Robert Ward (*see* CONNELL, WARD & LUCAS) and George Checkley; Raymond McGrath was from Australia, while Wells Coates was Canadian. During the mid-1930s refugees from the Continent introduced into England a mature form of modern design, and while Walter Gropius and Marcel Breuer stayed in England only briefly before travelling to the USA, Erich Mendelsohn spent seven years there, and such émigrés as Berthold Lubetkin and Ernö Goldfinger remained.

In 1933 the MARS (Modern Architectural Research) Group was formed to advance the ethos of the new modern design (*see* MARS GROUP). Lubetkin, a leading member of MARS, had joined with six other young architects in 1932 to form TECTON, a practice that was responsible for such pioneering works as the Penguin Pool (1934; for illustration *see* ARUP, OVE) at London Zoo, Highpoint I (1933–6) at Highgate and the Finsbury Health Centre (1935–8), all in London. Tecton was aided in its innovative work in concrete by the engineer Ove Arup. Another engineer significant in the development of concrete structures was Owen Williams, who was responsible for the Boots Wets Factory (1930–32), Beeston, Nottingham (for illustration *see* WILLIAMS, OWEN), the Empire Pool (1934), Wembley, London, and the Pioneer Health Centre (1935), Peckham, London.

After World War II the young architects who had been enthusiastic champions of the Modern Movement in the 1930s assumed responsibility for many of the public construction projects undertaken by local authorities in the fields of housing and schools. The Architects' Department of the London County Council was particularly important in providing an opportunity for innovative projects, first under Robert Matthew and then under Leslie Martin (*see also* LONDON, §II, 6). The Roehampton Housing Estate (1952–9) in west London was probably the most successful implementation of Le Corbusier's concept of towers in the park. Another important development was the employment by Hertfordshire County Council of a young team of architects under Stirrat Johnson-Marshall (*see* ROBERT MATTHEW, JOHNSON-MARSHALL & PARTNERS) to design a series of new schools of light construction. This led to the development for Nottingham County Council of the CLASP (Consortium of Local Authorities Special Programme) system of building, subsequently used extensively in schools and in the construction of the University of York (1962–70) by Robert Matthew, Johnson-Marshall & Partners.

In 1954 Alison and Peter Smithson (*see* SMITHSON) challenged the functional ethos of the emerging Modern

13. Foster Associates: Stansted Airport, Essex, 1991

Movement in England with the formal arrangement and industrial finish of their steel-frame Secondary Modern School (1950–54) at Hunstanton, Norfolk. In reaction to the MARS Group and to the international group CIAM (Congrès Internationaux d'Architecture Moderne), to which the MARS group was affiliated, the Smithsons helped to set up in 1956 a group called TEAM TEN, which was intended to undertake research into the architectural needs of modern life. The influence of the Smithsons was greatest through their unbuilt projects, such as their competition scheme (1952) for 'streets in the air' at Golden Lane, London, and their publications, including *Team Ten Primer* (1962).

The expansion in education during the 1960s gave architects the opportunity to design new schools and universities; the character of the latter led them to adopt the Modernist style, nowhere more aggressively than at the University of Essex (1963–8), Wivenhoe, near Colchester, Essex, designed by Kenneth Capon of Architects' Co-Partnership. New building work was also undertaken at Oxford and Cambridge to provide additional residences for the colleges and new faculty buildings, such as the Law Library (1959–64) at Oxford by LESLIE MARTIN and COLIN ST JOHN WILSON and New Hall (1962–5) at Cambridge by CHAMBERLIN, POWELL & BON.

There were further opportunities for large-scale building as other institutions were rebuilt. DENYS LASDUN added the National Theatre (1967–76; now the Royal National Theatre; for illustration *see* LASDUN, DENYS) to London's South Bank arts complex, which already comprised two concert halls, the Royal Festival Hall (1950–51) and the Queen Elizabeth Hall (1961–8), both designed by the London County Council Architects' Department. Two new cathedrals, Coventry Cathedral (consecrated 1962) by BASIL SPENCE and the Metropolitan Roman Catholic Cathedral (consecrated 1967; for illustration *see* GIBBERD, FREDERICK), Liverpool, by Frederick Gibberd, each in its own way introduced modern ideas into a traditional building type. Much of the new commercial building during the 1960s was strongly influenced by contemporary American architecture; for example, the podium and glass curtain-walling of Castrol House (1960), Marylebone Road, London, by Gollins, Melvin, Ward, referred to Skidmore, Owings & Merrill's Lever Building (1952) in New York.

As the glass curtain-walling typical of the International Style and the exposed concrete characteristic of BRUTALISM were becoming established as the accepted method of building in the mid-20th century, the desire for a more referential architecture, manifest in Robert Venturi's influential *Complexity and Contradiction in Architecture* (1966), eventually destroyed its hegemony and led to a return to eclecticism. From the late 1970s architecture split into various styles, including High Tech, exemplified by the Lloyd's Building (1979–86), London, by Richard Rogers (for illustration *see* ROGERS, RICHARD), the *Financial Times* Printing Works (1987–8), London, by Nicholas Grimshaw, and Stansted Airport (see fig. 13) by Foster Associates. JAMES STIRLING, who, with James Gowan, employed a constructivist style in the Engineering Building (1959–63) at the University of Leicester, continued to develop more historical references in his architecture, for example at the

Clore Gallery (1980), an extension to the Tate Gallery, London. The decorative Post-Modern style was adopted for some developments by TERRY FARRELL, and even the classical style saw a revival, for example in the Howard Building (1988) at Downing College, Cambridge, by QUINLAN TERRY. Perhaps one of the most significant developments during the 1980s, however, was the internationalization of architecture. Some of the most important works by English architects were built abroad, for example the headquarters of the Hong Kong and Shanghai Bank (1981–6; for illustration *see* FOSTER, NORMAN), Hong Kong, by Foster Associates, and the gallery and theatre (1977–84) for the Staatsgalerie, Stuttgart, by James Stirling (*see* CLASSICISM, fig. 3). Conversely, the prestigious commission to design the Sainsbury Wing (1987–91) of the National Gallery, London, went to the American architects Venturi, Rauch & Scott Brown (*see also* §XIV below).

BIBLIOGRAPHY

Architects' J.; *Archit. Rev.* [London]
T. Dannatt: ~~*Modern Architecture in Britain* (London, 1959)~~
A. Jackson: *The Politics of Architecture: A History of Modern Architecture in Britain* (London, 1970)
J. Gould: *Modern Houses in Britain, 1919–1939* (London, 1977)
G. Stamp, ed.: 'Britain in the Thirties', *Archit. Des.*, xxiv (1979) [whole issue]
The Thirties: British Art and Design before the War (exh. cat., ed. J. Hawkins and M. Hollis; London, Hayward Gal., 1979)
L. Esher: *A Broken Wave: The Rebuilding of England, 1940–1980* (London, 1981)
A. Saint: *Towards a Social Architecture: The Role of School-building in Postwar England* (London, 1987)
J. Glancey: *New British Architecture* (London, 1989)

TANIS HINCHCLIFFE

III. Painting and graphic arts.

1. Before *c.* 1450. 2. *c.* 1450–*c.* 1620. 3. *c.* 1620–*c.* 1830. 4. *c.* 1830–*c.* 1855. 5. *c.* 1855–*c.* 1914. 6. After *c.* 1914.

1. BEFORE *c.* 1450. No prehistoric painting in England has been discovered, and the earliest known works are Roman, for instance the 1st-century AD black-and-white geometric mosaic floors and Pompeian-style paintings at FISHBOURNE (W. Sussex). Throughout the medieval period manuscripts provide the primary evidence for painting, although examples of wall and panel paintings as well as stained glass survive in progressively increasing numbers in the later period.

(i) Before *c.* 1066. (ii) *c.* 1066–*c.* 1450.

(i) Before c. *1066.* The early missionaries to England, led by St Augustine in 596–7, brought with them illustrated manuscripts to help convey the Christian message. The success of their missionary activity ensured a continuing need for new manuscripts, the decoration of which produced some of the finest painting of the medieval period. The difficulty in establishing the precise origins within Great Britain and Ireland of these Insular manuscripts (e.g. the BOOK OF KELLS) has led to much controversy (*see* INSULAR ART, §§1 and 3). The importance of the Gospel book in this period is reflected in its sumptuous ornamentation. Its decorative programme typically includes a pair of elaborately patterned 'carpet' and *incipit* pages introducing each Gospel and consisting of interlace, strapwork, biting animals and swirling motifs,

adapted from native pre-Christian traditions and closely related to contemporary metalwork (*see* §IX, 1(i) below); these are preceded by stylized, linear Evangelist portraits (e.g. *see* BOOK, fig. 3), derived in their iconography ultimately from Mediterranean models. An outstanding example from Northumbria, one of the principal centres of manuscript production, is the LINDISFARNE GOSPELS (*c.* 698; London, BL, Cotton MS. Nero D. IV). Mediterranean influence possibly reached Lindisfarne through the neighbouring communities of Monkwearmouth and Jarrow, which had strong connections with Italy. Their abbots Benedict Biscop and Coelfrith bought back manuscripts and panel paintings after visiting Rome (*c.* 678 and 684–6). The Codex Amiatinus (before 716; Florence, Bib. Medicea-Laurenziana, MS. Amiatinus 1), one of three Bibles commissioned by Coelfrith, has miniatures in a painterly, illusionistic style reminiscent of Early Christian wall painting in Rome.

Another important centre of English manuscript production was at Canterbury. The 6th-century Italian ST AUGUSTINE GOSPELS (Cambridge, Corpus Christi Coll., MS. 286; *see* EARLY CHRISTIAN AND BYZANTINE ART, fig. 57), traditionally thought to have been brought to England by St Augustine, was influential on manuscripts produced in Kent. This is evident, for example, in the naturalistic and modelled figures in the VESPASIAN PSALTER (*c.* 730; London, BL, Cotton MS. Vesp. A. I), which are combined with Northumbro-Irish decorative motifs. The Psalter is an early example of the so-called Tiberius group of manuscripts, which were produced in Kent and Mercia during the 8th and 9th centuries. Missions to northern Europe throughout this period, for example St Willibrord's foundation (697–8) of a monastery at ECHTERNACH, ensured that Insular painting styles were carried to the Continent. As a result such motifs as interlace were absorbed in a 'Franco-Saxon' style (*see* CAROLINGIAN ART, §IV, 3) and eventually reimported to Britain during the 10th century.

During the Anglo-Saxon period monasteries continued to be the primary centres of artistic production (*see* WINCHESTER, §II; CANTERBURY, §II). Examples of early work at Winchester are the wall-painting fragments discovered reused in the foundations of the New Minster; the figures (before 901–3; Winchester, City Mus.; *see* ANGLO-SAXON ART, fig. 7) are in a bold, linear style, close to the paintings in some slightly later manuscripts, for example Bede's *Lives of St Cuthbert* (after 934; Cambridge, Corpus Christi Coll., MS. 183), and dependent on Carolingian figure types. Painting particularly flourished in association with the 10th-century monastic reformers. Under Bishop Aethelwold, the so-called Winchester school style of painting evolved: the dedicatory miniature in the New Minster Charter (966; London, BL, Cotton MS. Vesp. A. VIII), commemorating his new regime there, is the earliest expression of this style in its fully developed form. The characteristic solid, three-dimensional figures, enlivened by fluttering, agitated drapery folds and set within heavy, fleshy acanthus-leaf frames (for illustration *see* ACANTHUS (i)), receive their most accomplished treatment in the lavish Benedictional of St Aethelwold (*c.* 980; London, BL, Add. MS. 49598) but are also found in wall paintings, for instance those *in situ* (*c.* 1000) at the parish church in nearby Nether Wallop (*see* ANGLO-SAXON ART, figs 8 and 9 respectively).

In sharp contrast to the fully painted, heavily modelled miniatures of this style are the various drawing techniques employed in other Anglo-Saxon manuscripts. An outline drawing (mid-10th century) associated with another reformer, St Dunstan, and added to a composite text known as Dunstan's Classbook (Oxford, Bodleian Lib., MS. Auct. F.4.32, fol. 1*r*), is in a monumental style, the figures with round faces and bulbous, staring eyes reminiscent of Carolingian figure types found in manuscripts of the Court school (*see* CAROLINGIAN ART, §IV, 3). The evolution of drawing techniques, which became such a feature of English manuscripts, was significantly affected by the arrival in Canterbury *c.* 1000 of the Carolingian UTRECHT PSALTER (816–34; Utrecht, Bib. Rijksmus., MS. 32). Quite different from the monumental style, the Psalter's small, spirited and calligraphic figures exerted a continuing influence on Canterbury manuscripts, beginning with the first copy of the Psalter (London, BL, Harley MS. 603; *see* ANGLO-SAXON ART, fig. 10), in which the monochrome drawn narratives of the original were transformed by the Anglo-Saxon artists into coloured outline versions (*see* MANUSCRIPT, colour pl. II). Drawing techniques were not limited to Canterbury manuscripts: an ambitiously decorated Psalter associated with Winchester (mid-11th century; London, BL, Cotton MS. Tib. C. VI) and containing the earliest narrative cycle to preface a Psalter, is executed in shadowed outline drawing (*see* WINCHESTER, fig. 2).

Evidence that some Anglo-Saxon artists were itinerant is provided by similarities between the illustration of the Ramsey Psalter (London, BL, Harley MS. 2904), possibly made at Winchester for use at Ramsey Abbey, and several manuscripts from Fleury in northern France, for example a copy of Cicero's *Aratea* (late 10th century; London, BL, Harley MS. 2506). Such Classical texts, transmitted through Carolingian copies, formed part of a vigorous tradition of secular illustration in England, which also included scientific works (e.g. medical compendium, London, BL, Cotton MS. Vitel. C. III).

(ii) c. 1066–c. 1450. By the mid-11th century Anglo-Saxon painting had begun to show a hardening of line and solidity of form (e.g. Troper, *c.* 1050–75; London, BL, Cotton MS. Calig. A. XIV) that foreshadowed stylistic developments in the Romanesque period. With the importation of Norman monasticism after the Conquest, a yet drier version of this style was introduced into England along with an emphasis on the use of decorated and historiated initials. Norman illumination was also influential on wall painting in southern England, where gesticulating figures with parallel drapery folds are typical of the 'Lewes group' paintings (*c.* 1100) in Sussex. Indigenous and Norman styles were fused in the manuscripts produced at Christ Church, Canterbury; this Anglo-Norman tradition reached its peak in the second quarter of the 12th century, when impressive series of decorated initials such as those in a copy of Flavius Josephus' *Jewish Antiquities* (*c.* 1130; Cambridge, U. Lib., MS. Dd. 1. 4; Cambridge, St Johns Coll., MS. A. 8; *see* ROMANESQUE, fig. 61) reveal Canterbury artists at their most inventive. Related in style to such manuscripts are the apsidal paintings (*c.* 1125–30)

in St Gabriel's Chapel, Canterbury Cathedral. In both manuscripts and wall paintings the nested V-fold draperies echo the style of the German metalworker Roger of Helmarshausen.

St Albans Abbey became a focus of manuscript painting from the 1120s (*see* ST ALBANS, §2). The first English manuscript with an extensive cycle of miniatures in a fully developed Romanesque style is the St Albans Psalter (*c.* 1120–30; Hildesheim, St Godehardikirche; *see* ROMANESQUE, fig. 63), which was painted by the Alexis Master, probably an itinerant layman. It is the first of a series of Psalters illustrated with narrative cycles, which became something of an English speciality: for example the second version of the Utrecht Psalter, the Eadwine Psalter (Cambridge, Trinity Coll., MS. R. 17. 1; *see* CANTERBURY, fig. 6), and the Winchester Psalter (London, BL, Cotton MS. Nero C. IV), both dated to the mid-12th century.

The principal patron of manuscripts during the 12th century, however, was the abbey at Bury St Edmunds, which attracted several leading artists. The Alexis Master, for example, contributed to the *Life and Miracles of St Edmund* (*c.* 1130; New York, Pierpont Morgan Lib., MS. M. 736; *see* BURY ST EDMUNDS, fig. 2). His characteristic elongated, hieratic figures with prominent profiles are rendered more naturalistically by another artist present at Bury, MASTER HUGO, whose work on the BURY ST EDMUNDS BIBLE is one of the masterpieces of English Romanesque (see fig. 14; *see also* ROMANESQUE, fig. 64). His figures are articulated by draperies with sinuous double lines, the 'clinging curvilinear style', a version of Byzantine dampfold, which became standard in English art in the period *c.* 1140–70. The LAMBETH BIBLE (*c.* 1150; London, Lambeth Pal. Lib., MS. 3; Maidstone, Mus. & A.G.), produced at either St Albans or Canterbury, is in a similar but more mannered version of this style; in the tradition of such English 'Giant' Bibles it is illustrated with initials and miniatures before each book (*see* BIBLE, fig. 4). A wall painting in Canterbury Cathedral of *St Paul and the Viper* displays the same drapery style as the Bury Bible combined with expressive facial modelling.

During the last quarter of the 12th century the artistic links between England and France became stronger, and the influence of Byzantine art was renewed, introducing a more naturalistic figure style. Byzantine influence, perhaps deriving from the mosaics (1140s) of the Cappella Palatina at Palermo, is clear in the calm, modelled figures painted by the Master of the Morgan Leaf, one of the later artists working *c.* 1170–80 on the Winchester Bible (Winchester, Cathedral Lib.; for illustration *see* WINCHESTER BIBLE), and in the last Canterbury version (*c.* 1180–90; Paris, Bib. N., MS. lat. 8846) of the Utrecht Psalter. This classicizing 'TRANSITIONAL STYLE', in which monumental figures with heavily modelled faces are clothed in bulky drapery with looped folds (*muldenfalten*), is also characteristic of the Master of the Gothic Majesty (another artist of the Winchester Bible), the Westminster Psalter (*c.* 1200; London, BL, Royal MS. 2 A. XXII), the wall paintings (*c.* 1170–80) of the Holy Sepulchre Chapel at Winchester Cathedral and the closely related paintings (*c.* 1180–1200) in the chapter house at SIGENA MONASTERY in Aragon, thought to be the work of English artists, perhaps from Winchester (*see* ROMANESQUE, figs 54 and 55).

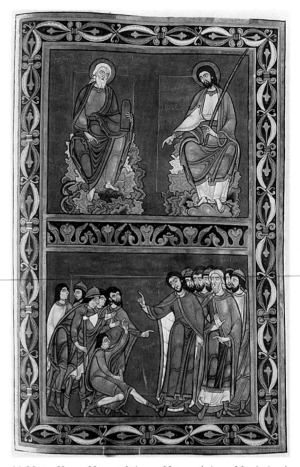

14. Master Hugo: *Moses and Aaron*; *Moses and Aaron Numbering the People*, miniature from the Bury St Edmunds Bible, 514×353 mm, *c.* 1135 (Cambridge, Corpus Christi College, MS. 2, fol. 70*r*)

A contemporary yet contrasting style, characterized by slender, dramatically posed figures, is evident in some manuscripts (e.g. Bestiary, *c.* 1200; Cambridge, U. Lib., MS. li. 4. 26) and in stained glass (e.g. *Miracles of St Thomas Becket*, *c.* 1200–20; *see* CANTERBURY, §III, 3 and GOTHIC, fig. 68). It prevailed in mid-13th-century works, for instance the tinted drawings of the St Albans monk MATTHEW PARIS (e.g. *Life of St Alban*, Dublin, Trinity Coll. Lib., MS. 177; *see also* GOTHIC, fig. 65) and the refectory paintings at Horsham St Faith. The decorative elements associated with this style are delicate, elastic foliage forms and the use of framing medallions. In manuscripts of this period greater emphasis was placed on borders, which in England were typically combined with marginalia and grotesques (*see* BORDER, MANUSCRIPT). Early examples are seen in the work of WILLIAM DE BRAILES (e.g. *c.* 1250; Oxford, New Coll., MS. 322; *see also* GOTHIC, fig. 64). As a professional artist working in Oxford, where the university promoted a flourishing book trade (*see* OXFORD, §2), William de Brailes exemplifies the shift away in this period from monastic scriptoria towards urban lay workshops for the production of manuscripts.

Medieval painting in England in the following centuries was shaped by successive waves of continental influence that were assimilated into regional traditions. The most important source of influence in the 13th century was Paris. From here a drapery style with crisp, broad folds was introduced into such English works as the Bible of William of Devon (*c.* 1266–70; London, BL, Royal MS. 1. D. I), which was probably illustrated by French artists working in Oxford, and, in a more exaggerated form, the Lambeth Apocalypse (London, Lambeth Pal. Lib., MS. 209). As the location of government became more fixed, metropolitan royal patronage flourished. Works emanating from the court are characterized by a heavily mannered version of the broad-fold style. The Douce Apocalypse (*c.* 1270–75; Oxford, Bodleian Lib., MS. Douce 180; *see* GOTHIC, fig. 73), for instance, was made for Edward I and Eleanor of Castile and is another example of the lavishly illustrated APOCALYPSE manuscripts that were particularly popular in England. The Westminster Retable (Westminster Abbey; *see* GOTHIC, fig. 71), perhaps the most outstanding court monument of the period, has elegant, attenuated figures standing in sinuous curves beneath elaborate gables. Fictive painted enamel and decorative glass around the retable frame contribute to the sumptuous effect; such a combination of different media became a feature of Gothic painting, anticipating Italian developments. The decoration of the Painted Chamber (destr. 1834; two surviving panels, London, BM) at the palace of Westminster is another example of this French-inspired court style (*see* LONDON, §V, 2(iii) and 3(i)). Towards the end of the century a new Parisian style, associated with the circle of the illuminator Master Honoré, began to influence English painting. Squatter figures and softer, more rounded drapery folds are seen in the stained glass at Merton College, Oxford, and at York Minster (*see* YORK, §III, 1(iii)). The slightly later wall paintings of *St Faith*, *St Thomas* and *St Christopher* (*c.* 1300–1310) in Westminster Abbey are in a similar style.

During the 14th century painters drew on an increasingly eclectic range of sources, while certain regional traditions were strengthened. The growing concentration of wealth in eastern England, for instance, fostered the patronage of ostentatious manuscripts in East Anglia (e.g. the Peterborough Psalter, *c.* 1310–20, Brussels, Bib. Royale Albert 1er, MSS 9961–2). Northern French styles permeated East Anglian manuscripts through the influence of the possibly peripatetic workshop of the QUEEN MARY PSALTER (*c.* 1310–20; London, BL, Royal MS. 2 B. VII); its delicate and refined figures are close to the work of the French illuminator Jean Pucelle. The Gorleston Psalter (London, BL, Add. MS. 49622), a manuscript from Norwich begun in an indigenous style, shows a rare instance of Italian influence in the added miniature of the *Crucifixion* (*c.* 1325, fol. 7*r*; *see* GOTHIC, fig. 79), possibly a reflection of documented imported Tuscan panels. English painting in this period often displays closer links to south Netherlandish work, for example in the figure style of the LUTTRELL PSALTER (*c.* 1330–40; London, BL, Add. MS. 42130), although here the profusion of marginal decoration is typically English.

One of the most ambitious late medieval decorative programmes was that instigated by Edward III for St Stephen's Chapel (destr. 1834) in the palace of Westminster. The glazing and painting (fragments, London, BM) were carried out *c.* 1350–63 by artists from a wide area, including the Netherlands, and the resulting works show a variety of sources ranging from Avignonese to Bohemian and, especially, Italian. Italian influence is also reflected in the *Last Judgement* paintings (1372–1404) in the chapter house of Westminster Abbey. In the same building the *Apocalypse* paintings are strongly German in character, close to the style of Master Bertram, as are the paintings (*c.* 1390–1400) in the Byward Tower of the Tower of London. The transmission of Bohemian styles, the result of Richard II's marriage to Anne of Bohemia, is seen *c.* 1390–1400 in the *Liber regalis* (London, Westminster Abbey, Muniment Room & Lib., MS. 38) and more controversially in the portrait of *Richard II* (London, Westminster Abbey; *see* LONDON, fig. 33). The hybrid nature of court works at the end of the 14th century is one reason why the Wilton Diptych (1390–1410; London, N.G.), with stylistic similarities to French, Italian and Netherlandish painting, has proved so difficult to place.

BIBLIOGRAPHY

F. Wormald: *English Drawings of the Tenth and Eleventh Centuries* (London, 1952)
M. Rickert: *Painting in Britain: The Middle Ages*, Pelican Hist. A. (Harmondsworth, 1954, 2/1965)
O. Demus: *Romanische Wandmalerei* (Munich, 1968; Eng. trans. London, 1970)
J. J. G. Alexander, ed.: *A Survey of Manuscripts Illuminated in the British Isles* (London, 1975–)
C. Nordenfalk: *Celtic and Anglo-Saxon Painting: Book Illumination of the British Isles, 600–800* (London, 1977)
R. Marks and N. Morgan: *The Golden Age of English Manuscript Painting, 1200–1500* (London, 1981)
C. R. Dodwell: *Anglo-Saxon Art: A New Perspective* (Manchester, 1982)
English Romanesque Art, 1066–1200 (exh. cat., ed. G. Zarnecki, J. Holt and T. Holland; London, Hayward Gal., 1984)
The Golden Age of Anglo-Saxon Art, 966–1066 (exh. cat., ed. J. Backhouse, D. H. Turner and L. Webster; London, BM, 1984)
The Age of Chivalry: Art in Plantagenet England, 1200–1400 (exh. cat., ed. J. Alexander and P. Binski; London, RA, 1987–8)
S. Carthar, D. Park and P. Williamson, eds: *Early Medieval Wall Painting and Painted Sculpture in England*, BAR British Series, 216 (Oxford, 1990)
M. P. Brown: *Anglo-Saxon Manuscripts* (London, 1991)
The Making of England: Anglo-Saxon Art and Culture, AD 600–900 (exh. cat., ed. L. Webster and J. Backhouse; London, BM, 1991)

TANYA ALFILLÉ

2. *c.* 1450–*c.* 1620.

(i) Painting. Despite the periodic immigration of artists from the Low Countries during this period, English artists continued to reinvent the native medieval tradition of line and clear colour. The rejection of naturalistic illusion was a persistent aspect of English artistic practice. The religious scenes portrayed (*c.* 1490) on the walls of Eton College Chapel have close affinities with the courtly Late Gothic style, which was characterized by elegant figures depicted with graceful, flowing lines. However, those images also reveal an English resistance to the more painterly approach and use of naturalistic space that appeared on the Continent in the second half of the 15th century. Henry VII (*reg* 1485–1509) appropriated the magnificent ceremonies of the Burgundian court with its emphasis on medieval chivalry. On his accession he brought with him a large group of Flemish artists who formed a permanent and

15. Hans Holbein the younger: *Henry VIII*, black ink and watercolour on paper mounted on canvas, 2.58×1.37 m, 1537 (London, National Portrait Gallery)

influential community in England. Henry VIII (*reg* 1509–47) spent more lavishly than his father on courtly ceremonies (*see* TUDOR, (1) and (2)). Native and Flemish artists were engaged in the painting of temporary structures for revels, tilts and triumphal processions, with easel painting initially playing only a secondary part. The *Field of the Cloth of Gold* (*c*. 1545; London, Hampton Court, Royal Col.), by an unknown artist, presents a panoramic view of such chivalric ceremonies.

The painting of portrait miniatures, developed from the techniques of manuscript illumination, was brought to England from Bruges by Lucas Horenbout. Hans Holbein the younger (*see* HOLBEIN, (3)) learnt the miniature technique from Horenbout and introduced a practice that flourished well into the 17th century in the work of such artists as Nicholas Hilliard (*see* HILLIARD, (1)) and Isaac Oliver (*see* OLIVER, (1)). The miniature, encased in expensive and elaborate covers, was a precious object and

required close-up viewing, eventually influencing the way large-scale paintings were viewed. Holbein, employed by Henry VIII, painted many of the important figures of the court (e.g. *Sir Thomas More*, 1527; New York, Frick), and many of his portrait drawings survive (Windsor Castle, Berks, Royal Col.). Following the break with the Church in Rome in the 1530s, imagery was used to affirm royal authority. In his portrait of *Henry VIII* (see fig. 15) Holbein created a portrait of dynastic power, the supreme head of both church and state: the life-size and massive body of the King, legs astride, confronts the spectator with a figure of absolute power. After Holbein's death in 1543, Guillim Scrots portrayed the young *Edward VI* (*c*. 1546–7; Windsor Castle, Berks, Royal Col.) in Henry's image, full-length with legs planted firmly apart, his hand grasping his dagger. Holbein had only one close follower, John Bettes (i) (*see* BETTES, (1)), but his continuing influence on English portraiture throughout this period can be observed in the strong linear projection of the figure against the background, which can be seen in the work of such painters as HANS EWORTH.

While Protestant distrust of idolatry led to the prohibition of religious imagery, portraits were spared destruction because of their perceived association with a commemorative function. However, images of royalty frequently assimilated and transformed a familiar religious iconography. In the book *Acts and Monuments* (1563) by John Foxe (1516–87), Queen Elizabeth I (*see* TUDOR, (3)) is given the attributes of the Roman Emperor Constantine: she is seated on her throne, carrying the sword of justice, the Pope entwined with serpents beneath her feet. Unlike her father, Elizabeth I, conscious of shrinking crown revenues, was not a patron of the arts. Nevertheless, she carefully controlled the content of her portraits. Images of Elizabeth incorporated various symbols that referred to her problematic role as an unmarried queen: the pelican, which tears its own breast to feed its young, appears on a jewel worn by Elizabeth in a large-scale painting attributed to Hilliard (*c*. 1585; Liverpool, Walker A.G.). In William Segar's portrait (*c*. 1597; Hatfield House, Herts), she appears with an ermine, a symbol of chastity. Many paintings allegorize the virtues of her reign: in the *Family of Henry VIII* (*c*. 1570; Sudeley Castle, Glos), now attributed to Hans Eworth, Elizabeth is accompanied by the figures of Peace and Plenty, in contrast to Mary I (*reg* 1553–8) and the Spanish king Philip II, who appear with Mars. The chivalric code also determined the iconography of the paintings of her courtiers, whose portraits display symbols and devices associated with the Queen. In the portrait of *Sir Walter Raleigh* (*c*. 1588; London, N.P.G.) by the Monogrammist H, a crescent moon refers to Elizabeth as Diana, the virgin goddess. The 'Armada Portrait' of *Elizabeth I* (see fig. 16) by GEORGE GOWER illustrates important aspects of Elizabethan and Jacobean portraiture. Each element is minutely defined and structured as if on a heraldic shield. The figure of Elizabeth is almost life-size but, with no illusion of distance between viewer and object, the painting could be 'a miniature blown up under glass' (Piper, 1975, p. 102). On either side of Elizabeth are emblematic references to the defeat in 1588 of the invading Spanish Armada. Emblems (images with accompanying

16. George Gower: *Elizabeth I* (the 'Armada Portrait'), oil on panel, 1.05×1.32 m, *c.* 1588 (Woburn Abbey, Beds)

mottoes), popular in England, accustomed viewers to seeing a picture as depicting something to be read.

There were no master texts in England that prescribed an aesthetic canon; rather, painting absorbed aspects of tapestry design, goldsmiths' patterns, heraldry, emblems and continental prints and miniatures, without making distinctions between high and low, decorative and figurative art. Indeed, both emblems and heraldry were included in contemporary definitions of painting. Heraldry, with its emphasis on line and bright, symbolic colour, was especially important, its pervasive use in portraits reflecting a mobile society in which displays of rank played a critical role. English sumptuary laws defined rank through dress, and in Elizabethan and Jacobean portraits the precise description of fabric and jewels reveals the wealth and status of the subject, as in the portrait of *Richard Sackville, 3rd Earl of Dorset* (1613; London, Ranger's House) by WILLIAM LARKIN.

With the accession of James I in 1603, the court again became the centre of artistic patronage. In 1605 Inigo Jones introduced Italianate elements and perspective scenes in his designs for the masques at court, and this seems to have influenced some portraits by ROBERT PEAKE: in *Henry Frederick, Prince of Wales, and Robert Devereux, 3rd Earl of Essex* (*c.* 1605; New York, Met.), spatial themes and classical elements are incorporated into the linear figures and bright unshadowed colours of the Elizabethan style. An interest in naturalistic illusion and classical models led Queen Anne of Denmark and Henry, Prince of Wales, to recruit artists from abroad. The Dutch artist Paul van Somer portrayed *Queen Anne in Hunting Attire outside Oatlands House* (1617; Windsor Castle, Berks, Royal Col.) in a setting of continuous space and also showed James I standing in front of the classical façade of Jones's Banqueting House (1620; British Royal Col.).

(ii) Graphic art. In the late 15th century WILLIAM CAXTON published 19 books with woodcut illustrations. Prints and book publishing were closely connected throughout this period. While some continental prints seem to have been available in England, English engraving did not appear until the mid-16th century and was associated with the large print workshops in the Low Countries. Foreign and native artists in England produced title-pages, maps and prints of notable and contemporary events. Marcus Gheerhaerts (i), for example, executed a series of nine etchings of the *Procession of the Knights of the Garter* (1576; London, BL). In 1589 WILLIAM ROGERS (i) executed the first

portrait engraving by an Englishman. His image of *Queen Elizabeth as 'Eliza Triumphans'* (1589; e.g. Exeter, Devon Rec. Office, City Archv) celebrates the defeat of the Spanish Armada with elaborate detailing of the Queen's costume and the display of emblematic figures of Victory and Plenty on either side. A series of portraits of English monarchs, the *Baziliologia* (London, BM), appeared in 1618, engraved by RENOLD ELSTRACK, and a companion set of British worthies, the *Heroologia* (London, BL), was published in 1620, engraved by Willem van de Passe. The work of the English engraver WILLIAM HOLE is of interest because of the subjects of his portraits and title-plates, including the title-page for Ben Jonson's *Workes* and the portrait frontispiece to George Chapman's translation of *The Whole Works of Homer* (both 1616).

BIBLIOGRAPHY

A. Hind: *Engraving in England*, i (Cambridge, 1952)
O. Millar: *Tudor, Stuart and Early Georgian Pictures in the Collection of Her Majesty the Queen*, 2 vols (London, 1963)
R. Strong: *The English Icon: Elizabethan and Jacobean Portraiture* (London, 1969)
D. Piper: 'Tudor and Early Stuart Painting', *The Genius of British Painting*, ed. D. Piper (New York, 1975), pp. 62–110
G. Kipling: *Triumphs of Honour: Burgundian Origins of the Elizabethan Renaissance* (The Hague, 1977)
Holbein and the Court of Henry VIII (exh. cat. by J. Roberts, London, Queen's Gal., 1978–9)
L. Gent: *Picture and Poetry, 1560–1620: Relations between Literature and the Visual Arts in the English Renaissance* (Leamington Spa, 1981)
The English Miniature (exh. cat. by J. Murdoch, J. Murrell, P. J. Noon and R. Strong, New Haven, CT, Yale Cent. Brit. A.; Toronto, A.G. Ont.; Fort Worth, TX, Kimbell A. Mus.; 1981–2)
E. Honig: 'Lady Dacre and Pairing by Hans Eworth', *Renaissance Bodies*, ed. L. Gent and N. Llewellyn (London, 1990), pp. 60–110
Henry VIII: A European Court in England (exh. cat., ed. D. Starkey; London, N. Mar. Mus., 1991)

ELLEN K. CHIRELSTEIN

3. *c.* 1620–*c.* 1830.

(i) Portraiture and subject painting. (ii) Landscape painting and graphic art.

(i) Portraiture and subject painting. The arrival of ANTHONY VAN DYCK in England in 1632 (after a previous brief visit in the winter of 1620–21) heralded a more sophisticated and cosmopolitan phase in the development of British painting, which lasted until his death in 1641. Van Dyck rapidly established himself as the leading portrait painter to the court of Charles I (*see* STUART, House of, (6)). He was heavily influenced by Titian and his own master, Rubens, who himself came to England, painting the influential *Apotheosis of James I, with Justice, Zeal, Religion, Honour and Victory* (1630–34) in the ceiling compartments of the Whitehall Banqueting House. Van Dyck's style was in sharp contrast to the comparatively rigid and archaic mannerisms of the previous generation of native-born portrait painters. Such other notable émigré painters as Paul van Somer had either recently died or, like the accomplished Dutchman Daniel Mijtens I, were quickly eclipsed. Van Dyck's greater naturalism, elegance and delicacy of touch brought about the most dramatic change in British portrait painting and had a profound effect on subsequent generations of artists. The enormous advantage of his training in the studio of Rubens gave van Dyck the confidence to work on a large scale in both portraiture and subject painting, and those works executed for Charles I and such other prominent patrons as the Pembroke

family are magnificent statements in a theatrical manner previously unwitnessed in England. No other painter was so adept in understanding and projecting the image that the society desired of itself for posterity: the atmosphere of glamour, and, in the case of depictions of the King, romantic melancholy that pervades these images is synonymous with the age.

Van Dyck's influence was astonishingly pervasive, although such native-born painters as Gilbert Jackson (e.g. *John Belasyse*, later 1st Baron Belasyse; see fig. 17), Edward Bower and, in the provinces, John Souch appear to have remained immune to it. The work of WILLIAM DOBSON, despite a certain coarseness, provides a convincing testament to van Dyck's legacy, but the only other painter of real quality among van Dyck's contemporaries was the miniaturist Samuel Cooper (*see* COOPER, (1)), whose technique had more in common with the oil painter's method than the traditional stippling technique of the limner. Because he always painted from life, Cooper produced miniatures of great character and vivacity. The emergence of the role of the studio in portrait production, which developed under van Dyck, was encouraged by PETER LELY, who arrived in England probably in 1641 or 1643. After abandoning the small historical and mythological pictures so redolent of his Dutch background, Lely pursued a lucrative career as a portrait painter: his work of the 1640s demonstrates his debt to van Dyck, but he

17. Gilbert Jackson: *Lord Belasyse*, oil on canvas, 1892×1295 mm, 1636 (London, National Portrait Gallery)

later established a more distinctive, languorous style best represented by the portraits executed for the Duke of York in the 1660s, collectively known as the *Beauties* (London, Hampton Court, Royal Col.). The reign of Charles II (1660–85) is characterized by the presence of a succession of relatively undistinguished foreign painters, from Lely's pupil Willem Wissing to such artists as Gerard Soest, Jacob Huysmans, Henri Gascar and the Verelst family. With the German-born GODFREY KNELLER and the Swede Michael Dahl, portrait painting became largely standardized in its denial of individual character or likeness, with the sitters concealed by the polite 'masks' that idealize their features.

In 1685 William Aglionby, in his *Painting Illustrated*, lamented England's failure to produce 'an Historical Painter, Native of our own Soyl'. In fact, only a couple of decades earlier ROBERT STREETER had painted the elaborate ceiling of the Sheldonian Theatre in Oxford with *Truth Inspiring the Arts and Sciences* (1669), but it is nevertheless true that history painting did not flourish in England during the 17th century, despite the impetus provided by Rubens's work at the Banqueting House. However, after the Restoration, late Baroque elements from France and Italy emerged in the hands of minor talents such as Antonio Verrio and Louis Laguerre, whose highly illusionistic and pompous allegorical and mythological subjects decorate the walls and staircases of the many great houses built or remodelled in the aftermath of the Glorious Revolution of 1688. In the early 18th century, a wave of Venetian painters led by Giovanni Antonio Pellegrini and the Ricci family quickly and deservedly gained ascendency, but for nationalistic reasons James Thornhill was awarded the most prestigious commissions of the day at the Royal Naval Hospital (now College), Greenwich (for illustration *see* THORNHILL, JAMES), and St Paul's Cathedral (*see* ILLUSIONISM, colour pl. V). History painting, which was considered intellectually superior to other categories of painting, continued to occupy the thoughts of more serious artists and such theorists as Jonathan Richardson in the first half of the 18th century. Paradoxically, WILLIAM HOGARTH fought vigorously to support the genre throughout his career, although he is more commonly associated with the invention of a new type, the 'modern moral subject', in which an episode from contemporary life is related in a series of paintings designed to be engraved. Hogarth also did much to popularize the conversation piece or small-scale informal group portrait, which had been introduced into England by the German-born but French-trained Philippe Mercier. This essentially private art form remained popular throughout the 18th century, undergoing something of a revival in the years after 1760 in the hands of JOHAN ZOFFANY, FRANCIS WHEATLEY and JOHN HAMILTON MORTIMER.

In the second quarter of the 18th century, visits by such French artists as Gravelot and an awareness of engravings after French paintings influenced many English painters, particularly those under the guidance of FRANCIS HAYMAN, who were associated with the St Martin's Lane circle. This group produced the most exuberant expression of the Rococo in England with the decoration of Vauxhall Gardens in the 1740s. English Rococo painting can be characterized by an emphasis on frivolity of subject-matter combined with the brightness of palette found in contemporary French painting. Portrait painting remained the dominant genre: by the 1740s it showed a positive response to developments on the Continent, especially in the work of such artists as ALLAN RAMSAY, whose stylish adaptation of European Rococo ensured his success. Ramsay and his less distinguished rival THOMAS HUDSON dominated portraiture in the mid-century, but Hogarth's own considerable achievement as a portrait painter, which lay in his fresh, direct and solid appreciation of the sociability of his sitters, should not be underestimated.

Hogarth and his contemporaries also did much to promote the status of the artist from the rank of craftsman to that of professional gentleman. Although a few artists (van Dyck, Lely, Kneller and Thornhill) had been knighted by successive monarchs for their services, it was the establishment of academies of art in London, beginning in 1711 with Kneller's Academy in Great Queen Street, that liberated the artist from an antiquated and almost feudal system of patronage. This process culminated with the establishment in 1768 of the Royal Academy, with its important annual public exhibitions (*see* LONDON, §VI, and EXHIBITION, fig. 3). By the mid-century new types of patron were emerging in significant numbers, most notably among the professional classes, whose occupations had flourished since the late 17th century, and the Grand Tourists, who filled their houses with booty from Italy but also wanted the native product (*see* §XII, 4 below). Artists had to be increasingly aware of the forces of supply and demand as patrons discovered a wide variety of sources of art overseas, provided by the dealers and their agents. With several years of study in Italy behind him, JOSHUA REYNOLDS was ideally placed to exploit this changing market. Reynolds was the most original and creative portrait painter of the century in England, despite his technical shortcomings. In attempting to elevate portraiture from the mundane level of 'face painting' to the more highly esteemed genre of history painting, Reynolds used his breadth of learning and knowledge of the Old Masters to achieve an almost inexhaustible variety of pose in the Grand style, provoking Thomas Gainsborough to exclaim 'Damn him, how various he is!' Gainsborough himself, whose mature style (to some extent based on van Dyck) was formed in Bath in the 1760s, worked in a very different manner. Whereas Reynolds employed studio assistants for the 'mechanical' part of painting, such as draperies, Gainsborough revelled in painting sumptuous surface textures and shimmering reflections on silks and satins, with a delicacy and natural ease of handling rarely found in the work of his compatriots (*see* GAINSBOROUGH, THOMAS). GEORGE ROMNEY, who, despite never exhibiting at the Royal Academy, seriously challenged his older rivals during the late 1770s, seems to have modelled his style on the nonchalance of Pompeo Batoni, whose works he saw in Rome in 1773–5. However, after the death of Reynolds and Gainsborough, WILLIAM BEECHEY and JOHN HOPPNER were the most notable portrait painters until the rise of Thomas Lawrence at the end of the century. Lawrence was the most gifted and successful portrait painter of the late 18th century and the early 19th. He first displayed his natural gift for representing dazzling silks and satins at the Royal Academy in 1790, with his ravishing portrait of *Queen Charlotte* (*see* LAWRENCE, THOMAS, fig. 1).

The most important painter to pursue a career primarily outside London in the 18th century was JOSEPH WRIGHT OF DERBY. Wright's highly individual candlelit and industrial pictures, influenced indirectly by the Utrecht Caravaggisti and the mezzotints of THOMAS FRYE, are a fascinating attempt to promote a kind of epic subject painting in contrast to the more academically acceptable stoic history paintings practised by those artists, such as the American-born Benjamin West, who had benefited from a Roman training. In truth West, a notable exponent of Neo-classicism, was one of the few artists, thanks largely to royal patronage, who managed to make a successful living from history painting, while many, such as JAMES BARRY and BENJAMIN ROBERT HAYDON, died in despair at the lack of patronage for this most elevated of art forms. Even the few commercial ventures that attempted to redress this imbalance, such as John Boydell's Shakespeare Gallery, which opened in London in 1789, ultimately failed.

One genre that did flourish in the second half of the 18th century was sporting art, which was patronized by the nobility. This had emerged as a distinct genre in England after the Restoration, reflecting the growth in popularity of sport among the landowning classes. In the early 18th century, in the work of such artists as JOHN WOOTTON and Peter Tillemans, the emphasis was decidedly on depicting the landscape with sport as a heroic activity. However, from the 1760s the genre reached new heights in the work of GEORGE STUBBS, not only because of Stubbs's profound understanding of the anatomy of animals (especially thoroughbred racehorses) but also through his ability to strike a poetic and occasionally sublime note in his grander compositions. In the early 19th century sporting art became increasingly marginal in the hands of such artists as Ben Marshall, J. F. Herring and J. N. Sartorius, primarily because the intricacies and accoutrements of horse-racing became more important to them than any attempt to engage, as Stubbs had done, with prevailing artistic theory (*see also* SPORTING SCENES).

Literary subject-matter also had an enduring role in English painting, and from the 1760s and 1770s British artists began to explore with remorseless zeal a huge repertory of literary sources in search of dramatic themes with which to involve their audience. In a more anecdotal vein, the young Scot DAVID WILKIE, active in England, became the most important British genre painter in the early 19th century. Wilkie's humorous style, based on the peasant scenes of David Teniers (ii) and other 17th-century Netherlandish painters, was immensely successful, attracting such patrons as the Prince Regent (the future George IV). Later in his career Wilkie turned to a more conventional type of history painting and, to a lesser extent, to portraiture, occasionally with memorable results.

(ii) Landscape painting and graphic art. Landscape painting began to emerge in the 17th century as a lesser genre, dominated by Flemish and Dutch artists. Among the earliest landscapes are topographical works by Claude de Jongh and Adriaen van Stalbemt, executed in London in the 1620s and 1630s. Although van Dyck's few landscape watercolours exhibit a highly personal and emotive response to their subject (*see* WATERCOLOUR, colour pl. VII, fig. 1), more characteristic of the age are the drawings and etchings of the Bohemian Wenzel Hollar, whose work is the main source for views of London before the Great Fire. Hollar and most of the landscape painters before *c.* 1725 were essentially concerned with the imparting of information about the scene portrayed. In this context the vogue for bird's-eye topographical views of country estates and their great houses, many of them executed by the Dutchman Leonard Knyff and engraved by his compatriot Johannes Kip, is important. Landscape painting was also commonly used in a decorative context in overdoors and overmantels, and it is in this form that the fashion for

18. George Lambert (i): *Box Hill*, oil on canvas, 908×1084 mm, 1733 (London, Tate Gallery)

19. George Cruikshank: *Little Boney Gone to Pot*, 1814 (London, British Museum)

'ideal' landscape (usually referring to classical landscape and literature) first took root.

In the second quarter of the 18th century the two notable landscape painters JOHN WOOTTON and George Lambert (i) managed to earn their living as specialists in both ideal and topographical landscape (e.g. Lambert's *Box Hill*; see fig. 18), often blending elements from both in their pictures. Topographical painting was given a considerable boost by the arrival of Canaletto from Venice in 1746; however, although he remained in England, with a brief interruption, until 1755, his impact was not great, despite the enduring images of the Thames painted mainly for his noble clients. In the work of Richard Wilson (*see* WILSON, RICHARD (i)) there is a more profound understanding of Claude, Poussin and Dughet than is to be found in Wootton or Lambert, and this led to a more dramatic conception of classical landscape in harmony with Reynolds's Grand style portraiture. Gainsborough's considerable achievements as a landscape painter, on the other hand, range from early, carefully wrought, Dutch-inspired interpretations of his native Suffolk to the Arcadian pastorals of his middle period, inspired by his awareness of Rubens, and finally to intensely poetic and freely brushed paintings and drawings, in which his own nostalgic feelings towards nature and the delights of rustic life emerge. Gainsborough was unusually prolific as a draughtsman: he considered drawing as a medium in its own right, entirely independent of painting, whereas for

most of his compatriots, drawing had hitherto been perceived merely as a genteel activity for men of taste. By Gainsborough's day watercolour painting had begun to emerge not only as a means of enhancing line but as a technique with its own special skills and effects (*see* WATERCOLOUR, §2). With Paul Sandby, who also used gouache to match the effects of oil, the medium began to reach maturity, and John Robert Cozens (*see* COZENS, (2)) was among the first to use watercolour to achieve the kind of emotional appeal that the next generation, led by J. M. W. TURNER and Thomas Girtin, were to exploit.

By the early 19th century landscape painting was established as a serious genre, and artists increasingly looked to nature itself, as open-air sketching in oils became a common practice among such artists as William Henry Hunt, William Delamotte and John Linnell (ii) as well as its most notable exponents, Turner and JOHN CONSTABLE. Constable immortalized his native Stour Valley in Suffolk with an obsessive emotional involvement with the scenery. In the series of large canal scenes (exhibited at the Royal Academy in the 1820s) on which his reputation was based after his death, Constable synthesized his years of studying nature at first hand. His later works, however, with their heavily overworked and agitated surfaces, are more deeply introspective. By contrast, the precocious Turner established himself at a very early age and developed a range of subject-matter unmatched by any of his contemporaries, from classical history to sublime landscape (*see* WATER-COLOUR, colour pl. VIII, fig. 1). His reputation, however, is based mainly on his ability to evoke the subtlety and intensity of natural light in a style that had no following in England but that influenced French art at the end of the 19th century.

Printmaking also played an important role in popularizing landscape painting and drawing, and indeed other forms of art. Hollar, for instance, established the practice of etching in 1636, and mezzotint, which became something of a national speciality after it was introduced by Prince Rupert of the Rhine (1619–82) in 1662, was particularly suited to the reproduction of portraits in the 18th century. Hogarth achieved enormous success with his series of satirical engravings (e.g. *A Harlot's Progress* (1732), based on his paintings on the same subject). Especially original contributions to graphic art in the 18th and 19th centuries were made by caricaturists, with JAMES GILLRAY, THOMAS ROWLANDSON and George Cruikshank (*see* CRUIKSHANK, (3)) the most tireless exponents of this savagely satirical genre (e.g. Cruikshank's *Little Boney Gone to Pot*; see fig. 19). Many other technical processes, such as stipple engraving and aquatint, were introduced in the late 18th century and the early 19th, but the introduction of the durable steel plate in the 1820s was of great significance in widening the market for engravings. Perhaps the most original printmaker of this period was WILLIAM BLAKE, whose work included hand-printed books combining prophetic poetry and visual imagery. His influence was felt in particular by the group of painters and engravers known as the ANCIENTS, led by SAMUEL PALMER.

BIBLIOGRAPHY

L. Binyon: *Drawings of British Artists in the British Museum*, 4 vols (London, 1898–1907)
C. H. Collins Baker: *Lely and the Stuart Portrait Painters*, 2 vols (London, 1912)
W. T. Whitley: *Artists and their Friends in England, 1700–1799*, 2 vols (London, 1928)
F. D. Klingender: *Art and the Industrial Revolution* (London, 1947)
E. Waterhouse: *Painting in Britain, 1530–1790*, Pelican Hist. A. (Harmondsworth, 1953, rev. 1978)
M. Whinney and O. Millar: *English Art, 1625–1714*, Oxford Hist. Eng. A. (Oxford, 1957)
T. S. R. Boase: *English Art, 1800–1870*, Oxford Hist. Eng. A. (Oxford, 1959)
E. Croft-Murray: *Decorative Painting in England, 1537–1837*, i (London, 1962)
W. Gaunt: *A Concise History of English Painting* (London, 1964)
D. Piper, ed.: *The Genius of British Painting* (London, 1975)
J. Burke: *English Art, 1714–1800*, Oxford Hist. Eng. A. (Oxford, 1976)
J. Sunderland: *Painting in Britain, 1525–1975* (London, 1976)
R. Godfrey: *Printmaking in Britain: A General History from its Beginnings to the Present Day* (London, 1978)
S. Deuchar: *Sporting Art in Eighteenth-century England: A Social and Political History* (New Haven and London, 1988)
The Great Age of British Watercolours, 1750–1880 (exh. cat. by A. Wilton and A. Lyles, London, RA, 1993)

BRIAN ALLEN

4. *c.* 1830–*c.* 1855. At the beginning of the 1830s the noteworthy painters were mature Academicians born in the preceding century. With the death of the President of the Royal Academy, Sir Thomas Lawrence, portraiture declined as the principal genre. Chief among the masters were the landscape painters JOHN CONSTABLE and J. M. W. TURNER; the genre painters DAVID WILKIE, William Mulready (*see* MULREADY, (1)) and C. R. LESLIE; the animal painter Edwin Landseer (*see* LANDSEER, (4)); and the watercolourists PETER DE WINT, DAVID COX and JOHN SELL COTMAN. With the exception of BENJAMIN ROBERT HAYDON and WILLIAM ETTY, history painting in the 1830s and 1840s was nearly moribund. Instead, artists and the public preferred literary subjects from the works of Cervantes, Molière, Goldsmith and Shakespeare, with sentiment being considered at least as important as technique. Meanwhile, in his experiments with the calotype, an important contribution was being made by WILLIAM HENRY FOX TALBOT to the development of photography.

The most significant event concerning the fine arts in the 1830s was a disaster: the burning of the Houses of Parliament on 16 October 1834. By September 1841, a parliamentary Select Committee recommended the establishment of a Royal Commission to develop a plan for the interior decoration of the new Palace of Westminster (*see* LONDON, §V, 3(iii)). With Albert, the Prince Consort, as chairman, the Royal Commission—comprising members of Parliament, men of letters and Charles Lock Eastlake—determined that murals should be used and that the participating artists would be selected through a series of competitions. So great was the anticipation surrounding the plan that 500,000 people visited Westminster Hall during an eight-week period in the summer of 1843 to view the cartoons submitted in the first competition. A second contest, of frescoes, was staged in 1844, followed by a third, of oils, in 1845. Allegorical themes and subjects from John Milton, Edmund Spenser, Shakespeare and British history were designated for the decorations, which were completed without fanfare, mostly by the 1860s.

As plans progressed for the new Palace of Westminster in the 1840s, Prince Albert and Queen Victoria selected WILLIAM DYCE to execute decorations (1844; destr.) for a garden pavilion in Buckingham Palace. Dyce, who also painted subjects from Arthurian legend (1848–63) in the Queen's Robing Room in the new Parliament, was a key figure in promoting early or 'primitive' Italian and Netherlandish art, an interest he shared with Prince Albert. In his position as arts educator (he served as Superintendent of the Government Schools of Design from 1838 to 1843), Dyce had travelled throughout Europe, meeting the German Nazarenes and studying early Italian painting, and his biblical subjects, crisp draughtsmanship and clear colour were informed by these sources.

Around this time the interest in 15th-century Italian and Netherlandish art was also stimulated by such publications as Alexander Lindsay's *Sketches of the History of Christian Art* (London, 1847), while at the same time the Arundel Society promoted the study of early painting in order to improve public taste. Indeed, throughout the Victorian period great value was attached to education in art, since art itself was seen as having an important role in the moral education of society. The view that the improvement of society was dependent on the understanding and application of beauty in art was most forcefully expressed by JOHN RUSKIN, and it influenced a whole generation of artists in the mid-19th century. In 1848 a group of young Londoners joined together to form the Pre-Raphaelite Brotherhood (PRB), a name reflecting their admiration for the early Italian 'primitives' (*see* PRE-RAPHAELITISM).

20. Richard Redgrave: *The Governess*, oil on canvas, 700×900 mm, 1844 (London, Victoria and Albert Museum)

Of the seven original members, the three most significant painters were WILLIAM HOLMAN HUNT, JOHN EVERETT MILLAIS and Dante Gabriel Rossetti (*see* ROSSETTI, (1)). Painting on a wet white ground in strong local colours, the PRB eschewed conventional composition and chiaroscuro and were disdainful of the conventions of the art establishment. Instead, inspired and supported by the writings of John Ruskin, they postulated sincerity in art, achieved by an exacting study of nature, the pursuit of genuine ideas and a refusal to avoid the ungainly in order to present dramatic truth. Allegations of blasphemy in such religious works as Millais's *Christ in the Carpenter's Shop* (1844–50; *see* MILLAIS, JOHN EVERETT, fig. .1) plagued the group at first, but they gained wider acceptance after 1851, when they began to concentrate on subjects from English literature, particularly the works of Keats, Tennyson and Shakespeare (e.g. Millais's *Ophelia*, 1851–2; London, Tate). The group also produced a short-lived journal, *The Germ*, but by the mid-1850s the Brotherhood had virtually disbanded.

The Pre-Raphaelite circle included Rossetti's teacher FORD MADOX BROWN. Trained on the Continent, Brown had successfully participated in the cartoon competition for the new Palace of Westminster and painted such historical subjects as *Chaucer at the Court of Edward III* (1846–51, Sydney, A.G. NSW; smaller version, 1867–8,

London, Tate). His landscapes, including *The Pretty Baa-lambs* (exh. RA 1852; Birmingham, Mus. & A.G.), promoted the development of *plein-air* painting in England, and his allegorical *Work* (1852, 1856–63; Manchester, C.A.G.; *see* BROWN, FORD MADOX, fig. 1), showing the stratification of labour in mid-Victorian society, was perhaps the most important moralizing picture of the period. Among the significant followers of the Pre-Raphaelites were Elizabeth Siddal, ARTHUR HUGHES, HENRY WALLIS, FREDERICK SANDYS, and the landscape painters JOHN BRETT, J. W. Inchbold and Thomas Seddon. Although independent of the group, the watercolour paintings of John Frederick Lewis (i) and William Henry Hunt further promoted the Pre-Raphaelite cause through their meticulous technique. In the 1840s and 1850s there was a proliferation of modern narrative subjects. These were intended to convey moral messages, whether dealing with the plight of the working woman, as in Richard Redgrave's *The Governess* (see fig. 20), the theme of the fallen woman, as in Rossetti's *Found* (begun 1854; unfinished; Wilmington, DE, A. Mus.), or the emigration problem, as in Brown's *The Last of England* (1855; Birmingham, Mus. & A.G.; *see* BROWN, FORD MADOX, fig. 2). William Powell Frith's anecdotal works, including *Life at the Seaside* or *Ramsgate Sands* (exh. RA 1854; London, Buckingham Pal., Royal Col.; for illustration *see* FRITH, WILLIAM POWELL), were also enormously popular, earning him large sums in selling the rights to the engravings after the designs. Other painters who became well known in mid-century for their narrative pictures included RICHARD DADD, AUGUSTUS EGG, Henry Nelson O'Neil and JOHN PHILLIP, who with Frith were members of THE CLIQUE, founded in the late 1830s.

5. *c*. 1855–*c*. 1914. A second wave of Pre-Raphaelitism was born in 1857–8, when EDWARD BURNE-JONES and WILLIAM MORRIS met as undergraduates and worked with Rossetti on the decoration of the debating chamber of the Oxford Union, depicting Arthurian themes (now faded). Although the project failed, the Pre-Raphaelites continued to exert an important indirect influence in the second half of the 19th century. The PRB's *The Germ* together with Edward Moxon's edition of Tennyson's poems in 1857, to which nine artists including the leading Pre-Raphaelites contributed illustrations, helped rejuvenate the art of book illustration and led to a proliferation of magazines and books in the 1860s. During this period a generation of talented illustrators appeared, including GEORGE DU MAURIER and ARTHUR BOYD HOUGHTON, while the watercolourists FRED WALKER, MYLES BIRKET FOSTER and Helen Allingham depicted the life of the British countryside in their minutely painted works. The developing art of photography also began to attract such exponents as JULIA MARGARET CAMERON.

The 1860s also marked the beginning of a classical revival that flourished throughout the rest of the 19th century. FREDERIC LEIGHTON, EDWARD JOHN POYNTER and G. F. Watts idealized form, painting classical myths and subjects removed from contemporary life. From the time of his success at the Royal Academy in 1855 with *Cimabue's Celebrated Madonna Carried through the Streets of Florence* (Brit. Royal Col., on loan to London, N.G.) up to his later single-figure compositions, such as *Flaming June* (*c*. 1895; Ponce, Mus. A.), Leighton was a pillar of the art establishment. Both he and Poynter served as Royal Academy presidents, yet both were schooled on the Continent, thereby promoting academic, but not necessarily British, training. Watts, who had been a prize-winner in the Houses of Parliament competition of 1843 and painted social realist subjects during the 1840s and 1850s (e.g. *The Irish Famine*, *c*. 1849–50; Compton, Watts Gal.) began painting portraits and classical and allegorical subjects, for which he later became internationally renowned (e.g. *Hope*, 1886; version London, Tate; for illustration *see* WATTS, G. F.). Another classicizing artist, Lawrence Alma-Tadema (*see* ALMA-TADEMA, (1)), combined the Victorian love of detail with the taste for the ancient world in his works, which were popularized through engravings.

Another artist involved in the classical revival was Albert Joseph Moore (*see* MOORE, (1)), who depicted languid figures in classicizing costume, engaged in repose and music-making (e.g. *A Musician*, *c*. 1867; New Haven, CT, Yale Cent. Brit. A.). Among Moore's closest associates was the American expatriate painter JAMES MCNEILL WHISTLER, and together these two artists were leading figures in the AESTHETIC MOVEMENT, which was also fuelled by such paintings as Rossetti's *Bower Meadow* (1871; Manchester, C.A.G.) and Burne-Jones's *Laus Veneris* (1873–

8; Newcastle upon Tyne, Laing A.G.). These depictions of ethereal and allegorical women, based loosely on ideal female types originated by Titian and Botticelli, indicated the enduring influence of Pre-Raphaelitism. Whistler's work did not meet with the immediate approval of the art establishment, but such paintings as *Nocturne in Black and Gold: The Falling Rocket* (*c*. 1875; Detroit, MI, Inst. A.) radically altered the course of English art, supplanting the preference for anecdote and detail with more evocative, tonal and non-narrative treatments. With his friendships on both sides of the Channel, Whistler was also crucial in promoting the taste for French art that dominated later 19th-century English painting. His work, and that of other members of the Aesthetic Movement, was promoted by Sir Coutts Lindsay and Lady Blanche Lindsay (1844–1912), who from 1877 organized exhibitions at their Grosvenor Gallery, London, as an alternative to those at the Royal Academy. One of Whistler's paintings exhibited that year provoked Ruskin to accuse the painter of duping the public, leading to a notorious libel suit in which Whistler was awarded damages of one farthing, or a quarter of a penny.

The late 19th century was a period of great diversity, both in style and subject-matter. Social realist painting depicting the plight of the poor became popular in the 1870s and 1880s in works by Luke Fildes, Frank Holl (ii) and Hubert von Herkomer. Large paintings such as Fildes's *Applicants for Admission to a Casual Ward* (1874; Egham, U. London, Royal Holloway & Bedford New Coll.; for illustration *see* FILDES, LUKE) and Herkomer's *Eventide: A Scene in the Westminster Union* (exh. RA 1878; Liverpool, Walker A.G.) first appeared as designs in the magazine *The Graphic* and later influenced such artists as van Gogh. Genre painting became more specialized, with such artists as William Quiller Orchardson and JAMES TISSOT concentrating on high society, and LADY BUTLER focusing on military scenes. Various artists' colonies developed. The CRANBROOK COLONY (*c*. 1855–1900), whose senior member was THOMAS WEBSTER, settled in Kent and painted light-hearted scenes of village life in the manner of David Wilkie and William Mulready. The members of the urbane ST JOHN'S WOOD CLIQUE, formed in the 1860s by Royal Academy members, including Henry Stacy Marks, shared a common humorous approach to art. The NEWLYN SCHOOL, perhaps the most serious of these groups, was founded in the early 1880s in a remote fishing village in Cornwall. Inspired by the *plein-air* painters of the Barbizon school, members of the Newlyn School, including STANHOPE FORBES and FRANK BRAMLEY, represented scenes of the hardship of fishing life (see fig. 21).

A break with the past came with the founding in 1886 of the NEW ENGLISH ART CLUB (NEAC), a group whose focus was anti-academic and anti-narrative, and whose members admired Whistler, French Impressionism and the French painter Jules Bastien-Lepage. Chief among the NEAC were PHILIP WILSON STEER, JOHN LAVERY, HENRY HERBERT LA THANGUE and GEORGE CLAUSEN. While some members also showed at the Royal Academy and at other galleries, they were united in their admiration for working *en plein-air*, looser handling of paint and the atmospheric effects of contemporary French painting. Whistler's growing reputation was consolidated in 1886,

21. Frank Bramley: *A Hopeless Dawn*, oil on canvas, 1.23×1.68 m, 1888 (London, Tate Gallery)

when he was elected President of the Society of British Artists. Six years earlier, his estranged brother-in-law, the physician Francis Seymour Haden, had been elected the first president of the Royal Society of Painter–Etchers and Engravers, formed to promote etching as a fine art.

The 'Gilded Age' of the 1890s was the high point of book and magazine illustration. Especially noteworthy is *The Works of Geoffrey Chaucer* (1892–6), illustrated by Burne-Jones and produced by Morris at his Kelmscott Press. The illustrations by AUBREY BEARDSLEY for Oscar Wilde's *Salomé* (1894) and Beardsley's other designs for the magazine the *Yellow Book* became synonymous with *fin-de-siècle* decadence and the Art Nouveau style (*see also* BOOK ILLUSTRATION, fig. 7). A new generation of promising artists at the turn of the century were trained at the Slade School by professors FREDERICK BROWN and HENRY TONKS. These young artists included Augustus John, Gwen John (*see* JOHN, (1)), WILLIAM ROTHENSTEIN and William Orpen, all of whom were brilliant draughtsmen and portrait painters. Augustus John, the most radical and talented of the group, epitomized anti-academicism and bohemianism with his long hair and beard, unconventional lifestyle, and gypsy subjects.

In 1905 Sickert returned to London after seven years in Dieppe and Venice. He settled in Fitzroy Square, where he attracted a circle of realist painters that included SPENCER GORE and HAROLD GILMAN. With the addition of CHARLES GINNER, ROBERT BEVAN, Lucien Pissarro (*see* PISSARRO, (2)) and others, these artists, known as the CAMDEN TOWN GROUP, staged three exhibitions at the Carfax Gallery in London in 1911 and 1912. Their work had in common a bright palette inspired by the Post-Impressionists and subject-matter drawn from the urban landscape and working-class life in Camden and other parts of London (see fig. 22). Around the same time, two ground-breaking shows, both organized by the critic ROGER FRY and both held at the Grafton Galleries in London, were introducing the English public to French modernism. Impressionist, Post-Impressionist, Fauvist and Cubist art were all included in *Manet and the Post-Impressionists* and *The Second Post-Impressionist Exhibition*, and the latter also contained works by several members of the future Bloomsbury Group and Omega Workshops, including Duncan Grant and Vanessa Bell (*see* §5 below). Furthermore, a rearrangement of the second exhibition in 1913 also included the future Vorticist Wyndham Lewis, indicating the co-existence of a variety of styles and groups in London at this time. A final aspect of the period involved those British artists who were attracted to the dynamism of Futurism. While Fry had not included the Italian Futurists in his important exhibitions, works by Marinetti and Severini had been exhibited in London at that time. Futurism was particularly influential on the work of Christopher Nevinson, and on the artists who adhered to VORTICISM during World War I.

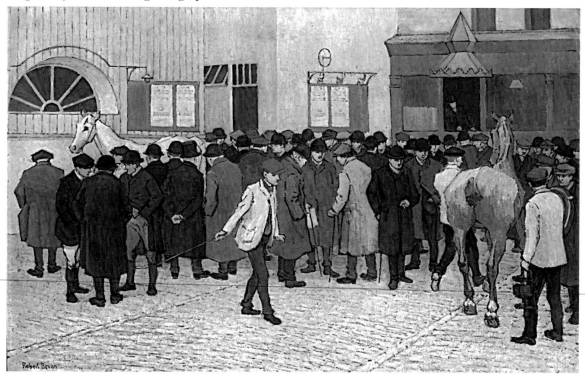

22. Robert Bevan: *Horse Sale at the Barbican*, oil on canvas, 0.79×1.22 m, 1913 (London, Tate Gallery)

BIBLIOGRAPHY
Engen; Wood
J. Ruskin: *Modern Painters*, 5 vols (London, 1843–60)
A. P. Oppé: 'Art', *Early Victorian England*, ii, ed. G. M. Young (London, 1934), pp. 101–77
T. S. R. Boase: *English Art, 1800–1870*, Oxford Hist. Eng. A. (Oxford, 1959)
G. Reynolds: *Victorian Painting* (London, 1966, rev. New York, 1987)
M. Hardie: *Water-colour Painting in Britain*, iii (London, 1968)
J. Maas: *Victorian Painters* (London, 1969)
J. Steegman: *Victorian Taste: A Study of the Arts and Architecture from 1830 to 1870* (Cambridge, MA, 1971)
H. Beck: *Victorian Engravings* (London, 1973)
C. Wood: *Victorian Panorama: Paintings of Victorian Life* (London, 1976)
D. Farr: *English Art, 1870–1940*, Oxford Hist. Eng. A. (Oxford, 1978)
D. Robertson: *Sir Charles Eastlake and the Victorian Art World* (Princeton, 1978)
Great Victorian Pictures: Their Paths to Fame (exh. cat. by R. Treble, Leeds, C.A.G.; Leicester, Mus. & A.G.; Bristol, Mus. & A.G.; London, RA; 1978)
C. Wood: *Olympian Dreamers: Victorian Classical Painters, 1860–1914* (London, 1983)
The Pre-Raphaelites (exh. cat., ed. L. Parris; London, Tate, 1984)
J. Treuherz, ed.: *Hard Times: Social Realism in Victorian Art* (London and Mount Kisco, NY, 1987)
Victorian Landscape Watercolors (exh. cat. by S. Wilcox, New Haven, CT, Yale Cent. Brit. A., 1992)

HILARIE FABERMAN

6. AFTER *c.* 1914. From 1914 English art was dominated by members of the BLOOMSBURY GROUP and the former CAMDEN TOWN GROUP, the two groups most closely associated with the establishment of modernism in England. Both set the tone for particular strains of art that continued to hold sway in their country during the 20th century. Bloomsbury artists such as VANESSA BELL and DUNCAN GRANT accentuated the literary bias of much of the art that followed and also, through the OMEGA WORKSHOPS, suggested the application to the decorative arts of design principles that originated in painting. Sickert (in both his paintings and prints) and his colleagues from the Camden Town Group, such as HAROLD GILMAN and CHARLES GINNER, were instrumental in developing an unsentimental urban realism with a radical formal approach that combined a flattening of space with sombre but anti-naturalistic colour schemes. Shortly before World War I, Gilman was one of the moving forces behind the formation of the LONDON GROUP, which began championing an anti-academic, anti-naturalistic stance but eventually, like the New English Art Club, became little more than an exhibiting society.

The REBEL ART CENTRE, founded in London in 1914, became the focus of activity of the most self-consciously avant-garde English movement of the period, VORTICISM. This was led by WYNDHAM LEWIS, who published his *Vorticist Manifesto* in the short-lived journal *Blast* in 1914. While heavily influenced by foreign art, in this case Cubism and especially Futurism, such Vorticist painters as Lewis, DAVID BOMBERG, EDWARD WADSWORTH and CHRISTOPHER NEVINSON (*see* SPORTING SCENES, fig. 3) proposed a strident and dynamic art, linear and geometric in effect, with its own distinct character. The movement's name derived from the frequent arrangement of the compositional elements around a central point or vortex. Although stopping short of full abstraction, through the extreme stylization of their representational art and ready embrace of the Machine Aesthetic, the Vorticists anticipated qualities of the most advanced forms of European art. Their militarist ideology determined the subject-matter and form of much of their work: for example Wadsworth's use of camouflage motifs in such woodcuts as *S.S. Jerseymoor* (1918; Liverpool, Walker A.G.). The movement lost its impetus after World War I, but it remained a striking example of the possibility of an uncompromising modern art in a country that during most of the 20th century remained noted for its upholding of solid figurative traditions.

Unlike their counterparts on the Continent, English artists tended to shy away both from official groupings and from manifestos. On the whole, they also proved slow to respond to the challenge posed by European movements, although artists operating on their own sometimes proved exceptions: MATTHEW SMITH, for instance, was virtually alone in taking up the high-keyed colour of Matisse and the Fauves. Instead, native traditions of landscape and figure painting continued to exert a strong influence on English artists in the period between the World Wars. After painting desolate landscapes symbolizing the destruction of World War I, Paul Nash (*see* NASH, (1)) developed a stylized form of landscape that carried forward the English notion of a sense of place, by the 1930s exaggerating the enigmatic atmosphere of his pictures as a personal response to Surrealism. Bomberg, having abandoned his Vorticist style, returned during the 1920s to direct observation and in so doing developed a materialist approach to nature that proposed an equation between the chosen subject and its reformulation in paint; although neglected during much of his life, after World War II he proved highly influential as a teacher of such painters as FRANK AUERBACH and LEON KOSSOFF. Yet another approach to landscape was exemplified by IVON HITCHENS, one of the exhibitors with the 7 & 5 Society,

founded in 1919 (*see* SEVEN AND FIVE SOCIETY). Hitchens's luscious abstractions from nature in panoramic formats helped prepare the way for more fully abstract work after World War II by such painters as Patrick Heron.

The 7 & 5 Society also included in its membership Ben Nicholson (*see* NICHOLSON, (3)) and CHRISTOPHER WOOD, both of whom in the 1920s were among those who developed a fresh and spontaneous form of representational painting, in their case inspired largely by the naive art of ALFRED WALLIS. Much of the most memorable figurative art produced by English painters during the 1920s and 1930s was created by artists who remained stubbornly eccentric or impervious to outside influences, for example STANLEY SPENCER, with his unlikely marriages of the spiritual and the sexually profane, and EDWARD BURRA, whose large-scale watercolours were full of quirky observations of human behaviour. This recalcitrance supplied such art with much of its emotional charge and also won it consistent local support, but at the same time it gave it a provincial character that limited its appeal abroad. Even the early contribution to Surrealism by such English artists as EILEEN AGAR and ROLAND PENROSE remained essentially peripheral. The conscious attempt in the 1930s by WILLIAM COLDSTREAM and his colleagues in the EUSTON ROAD SCHOOL to evolve an objective and measured form of realism from the example of Cézanne and French Post-Impressionism was also conditioned by its 'Englishness', and in particular by its extreme reserve. Their photographer colleagues in MASS OBSERVATION, while explicitly limiting themselves to the study of their local situation, perhaps proved more influential in their

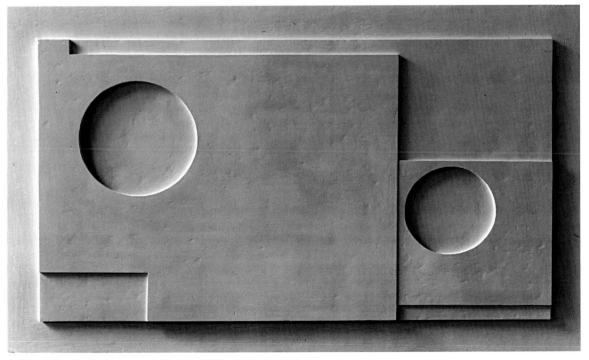

23. Ben Nicholson: *White Relief,* oil on panel, 1.02×1.67 m, 1935 (London, Tate Gallery)

reconsideration of the social and political possibilities of documentary photography. The ARTISTS INTERNATIONAL ASSOCIATION, established in 1933, favoured an aesthetically conservative approach to realism but proved politically active for 20 years, until a change in its constitution left it with little purpose other than as an exhibiting society.

During the 1930s and 1940s the greatest inroads into modernist internationalism were made by English painters and sculptors associated with abstract art and especially Constructivism, notably members of UNIT ONE (such as Ben Nicholson and Barbara Hepworth) and JOHN PIPER. Nicholson's most extreme geometrical abstractions of the mid-1930s, such as *White Relief* (see fig. 23), were as rigorous in form as the work of Piet Mondrian, by whom he was in part inspired. By contrast with the practitioners of OBJECTIVE ABSTRACTION, who provided an interesting episode in the mid-1930s, these artists and those who followed in their tradition in the 1950s, such as VICTOR PASMORE, demonstrated the possibility of an elegant art of radical simplicity that acknowledged its debts to European art while maintaining its separate identity (*see* CONSTRUCTIVISM, §2). No single approach, however, was ever dominant, with the result that highly divergent attitudes often took hold simultaneously. During the 1940s, for instance, much attention was given to NEO-ROMANTICISM, perhaps the most studiedly English of 20th-century movements, with its concentration on the spirituality of the pastoral landscape. During the 1950s the stranglehold of London was briefly broken by the painters based at the artists' colony of ST IVES, such as PATRICK HERON, ROGER HILTON and PETER LANYON, who took the landscape as a starting-point for a sensuous form of abstraction that provided the closest equivalent in England to Abstract Expressionism or *Art informel*.

Other artists working in the 1950s reacted against these various approaches, which they saw as a form of escapism. The painters of the short-lived KITCHEN SINK SCHOOL, such as JOHN BRATBY and JACK SMITH, created a gritty if rather dreary realism from the circumstances of impoverished domestic existence, while such members of the INDEPENDENT GROUP as RICHARD HAMILTON and EDUARDO PAOLOZZI proposed new areas of inspiration in their examination of subject-matter from the mass media and popular culture, paving the way in the late 1950s for POP ART, an international movement to which English artists made a vital early contribution. It was Pop artists, too, who were especially active and innovative as printmakers, particularly in their adoption of silkscreen printing, a medium previously considered suitable purely for commercial purposes but not for fine art; the master printer Christopher Prater at the Kelpra Studio in London played a highly influential role in this respect, effectively collaborating with such artists as PATRICK CAULFIELD, R. B. KITAJ, Hamilton and Paolozzi, among many others, on a steady production of silkscreen prints during the 1960s and 1970s. Another painter initially associated with Pop art, DAVID HOCKNEY, produced a highly significant body of graphic work, using the more traditional processes of etching and lithography.

During the 1960s the provincialism of English art finally began to be swept away. American abstract painting, particularly Abstract Expressionism, which was shown at the Tate Gallery in London in 1956 and 1959, replaced the work of the artists of the Ecole de Paris as the example against which English artists tended to measure their own achievement. Hard-edge painting, colour field painting and Post-painterly Abstraction all had equivalents in England, notably in the work of the painters of the SITUATION group. English artists also made important contributions to other international currents of the 1960s, including Op art (one of whose major figures was the English painter BRIDGET RILEY), Minimalism (e.g. PETER JOSEPH), process art, performance art (e.g. STUART BRISLEY and BRUCE MCLEAN), conceptual art (e.g. ART & LANGUAGE), feminist art and video art. English artists, notably RICHARD LONG and HAMISH FULTON, were also prominent among those who found non-sculptural applications for LAND ART in their use of photographs and texts as equivalents to their experience of nature. It was perhaps in the realm of figurative painting, however, that artists working in England after World War II, notably FRANCIS BACON, made the greatest impression, revitalizing traditions that were often played down elsewhere and confirming the sense in which contrariness and even a form of provincialism served them proudly as strengths. Bomberg's former students Auerbach and Kossoff, along with LUCIAN FREUD (see fig. 24), Hockney and Kitaj, were among the major figures within a loosely knit group for which Kitaj coined the term 'School of London'. Many of these painters were of foreign birth, confirming another constant in 20th-century English art, the vitality with which its traditions respond to a wide range of influences.

24. Lucian Freud: *Naked Girl with Eggs*, oil on canvas, 750×605 mm, 1980–81 (London, British Council)

BIBLIOGRAPHY

J. Rothenstein: *Modern English Painters*, 3 vols (London, 1952–74, rev. 1984)

R. Alley: *British Painting since 1945* (London, 1966)

Arte inglese oggi, 2 vols (exh. cat., essays by N. Lynton and others; Milan, Pal. Reale, 1976)

R. Shone: *A Century of Change: British Painting since 1900* (Oxford, 1977)

D. Farr: *English Art, 1870–1940*, Oxford Hist. Eng. A. (Oxford, 1978)

C. Parry-Crooke, ed.: *Contemporary British Artists, with Photographs by Walia*, intro. N. Lynton (London, 1979) [dictionary with entries on 201 artists]

Kelpra Studio: The Rose and Chris Prater Gift: Artists' Prints, 1961–1980 (exh. cat., intro. P. Gilmour; London, Tate, 1980)

C. Harrison: *English Art and Modernism, 1900–1939* (Bloomington and London, 1981)

F. Spalding: *British Art since 1900* (London, 1986) [with annotated bibliog.]

British Art in the 20th Century (exh. cat., ed. S. Compton; London, RA, 1987) [incl. select bibliog.]

A. Hicks: *The School of London: The Resurgence of Contemporary Painting* (Oxford, 1989)

F. Spalding: *20th Century Painters and Sculptors* (Woodbridge, 1991), vi of *Dictionary of British Art*

MARCO LIVINGSTONE

IV. Sculpture.

1. Before *c*. 1530. 2. *c*. 1530–*c*. 1660. 3. *c*. 1660–*c*. 1830. 4. *c*. 1830–*c*. 1914. 5. After *c*. 1914.

1. BEFORE *c*. 1530. Following the departure of the Romans in the 5th century AD, stone sculpture was not practised by the Anglo-Saxons until the introduction of Christianity in the 7th century. The principal patrons were the monasteries, with the façades, columns and friezes of the new buildings providing the main opportunities for carved ornamental decoration, although the High Cross later became the most characteristic Anglo-Saxon sculptural monument (*see* CROSS, §II, 1(i)). Stylistic influences were absorbed from numerous contemporary continental sources as well as, in some cases, from remaining Roman models (*see* ANGLO-SAXON ART, §III). Initially, the most important centres were in Northumbria, for example at MONKWEARMOUTH ABBEY, but later the most notable developments of the form were in the midland region of Mercia and (after the Viking invasions of the 10th century) the southern region of Wessex. Romanesque influence is visible in English sculpture from the 11th century, with Norman canons of taste affecting the architectural placing, functions and handling of sculpture (*see* ROMANESQUE, §III, 1(v)), although elements of the Anglo-Saxon tradition remained in evidence until the early 12th century. The decoration of not only religious but also secular buildings continued to provide the focus for sculptural work in the 12th and 13th centuries, with new elements such as the CHEVRON pattern and the BEAKHEAD being introduced.

Throughout the Middle Ages, English sculpture continued to be profoundly affected by influences from the Continent. However, while the remarkable figure sculpture of St Mary's Abbey, York (*see* YORK, §III, 2), from the second half of the 12th century may have belonged to the first full-scale portal programme in England, stylistic influences from France were not generally accompanied by an acceptance of the portal as the dominant area for complex iconographic schemes. Instead there was a recurring tendency in English Gothic to arrange sculpture in tiers of niches; this contrast is illustrated by a comparison

of the west fronts of the cathedral of Notre-Dame in Amiens and Wells Cathedral. Even the closest English follower of Amiens, the north transept façade of Westminster Abbey (remodelled 1879–90 by J. L. Pearson), departed in many important ways from its model and, like the architecture of the Abbey, is a hybrid of indigenous and French models. This is further seen in the pair of statues representing the *Annunciation* (see fig. 25), probably by William Yxeworth. French sources are indicated by such details as the rose decoration, recalling examples at the cathedrals of Amiens and Rheims, but the posture of the Westminster angels, among other aspects, is a direct development of sculptural styles seen at Wells.

English effigial sculpture testifies to an originality and experimentation in both style and materials that are hard to parallel elsewhere in western Europe. The importation of Tournai 'marble', probably pioneered by Bishop Henry of Blois, produced a taste for grave-slabs made from such

25. William Yxeworth (attrib.): *Gabriel*, from the *Annunciation*, stone, *c*. 1253 (London, Westminster Abbey, Chapter House)

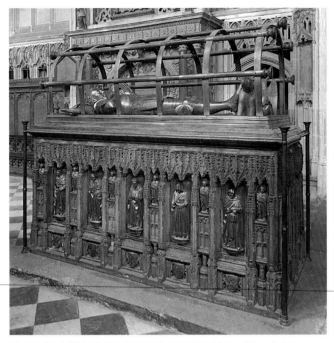

26. Tomb of *Richard Beauchamp, Earl of Warwick*, marble and gilt-copper, *c.* 1447 (Warwick, St Mary)

dark stones as Purbeck marble, mined near Corfe in Dorset, which would take a high polish. The development of the effigy from low-relief slabs reached a high level of technical accomplishment in the mid-13th century Purbeck marble effigies of ecclesiastical figures (e.g. *Hugh of Northwold, d* 1254; Ely Cathedral). Equal virtuosity is evident in the effigies of lay men and women appearing from the early 13th century, and in particular in the cross-legged knights, whose pose gradually became more agitated and mannered. The demand for complex detailing, however, and an increasing taste for polychromy ultimately ended the trade in Purbeck effigies, and some of the most remarkably articulated knightly effigies from the late 13th century, such as those at Dorchester Abbey (Oxon) and Gloucester Cathedral, were carved from freestone or wood. The naturalism often attributed to these effigies is unequivocally evident in the foliage sculpture of the late 13th century. The early 14th-century effigies of ladies at Much Marcle and Ledbury (both Hereford & Worcs) reveal an interest in the depiction of the recumbent figure and in the realistic disposition of drapery that is unsurpassed until the 16th century. By the 1330s, alabaster, which was to enjoy great popularity as a material for relief panels, was increasingly in demand for high-status effigies, and it continued in vogue until the end of the period. Alabaster figures of both *Edward II* and *Henry IV* were produced, but following the casting of effigies of *Henry III* and *Eleanor of Castille* (both London, Westminster Abbey) by WILLIAM TOREL in the 1290s the principal material for royal effigies was gilt-bronze. Brasses (actually made of latten) set into marble slabs provided a cheaper but splendid commemoration for lesser laity and ecclesiastics, and relief effigies also enjoyed a short vogue in the

13th century; brasses could be set flat into the floor surface and therefore did not restrict the circulation within a building in the same way as a free-standing effigy on a tomb-chest. More obstructive still were the free-standing chantry chapels that first appeared in the 14th century and which in their most spectacular manifestations (e.g. in the series at Winchester Cathedral; *see* WINCHESTER, §III, 3) provided ample opportunity for the figure sculptor.

In the 14th century a distinctively English deployment of figure sculpture was illustrated by the interior of the Lady Chapel of Ely Cathedral, where a huge programme (destr.) of figure sculpture in tiers of niches covered the walls above an extensive Marian relief cycle. The inventiveness of English designers in the first half of the 14th century and their taste for schemes orchestrated in different media, as in the east end of Dorchester Abbey or the octagon at Ely (where the master carpenter, probably from 1322, was WILLIAM HURLEY), were replaced with the dominance of the Perpendicular style and a stricter subordination of sculpture to its architectural context. One new area for the display of major programmes of sculpture in the later Middle Ages, however, was the great reredos, which remained popular until the end of the period. The last was possibly that of Southwark Cathedral, London, erected *c.* 1520 by Bishop Fox, where Renaissance stylistic influences are evident. Italian influences were also evident in the 14th century (e.g. Exeter Cathedral façade), but France was the dominant continental source until the 15th century, when Burgundo-Netherlandish norms became more important. This influence is seen in the drapery and tragic facial expressions of the figures set in niches along the tomb of *Richard Beauchamp, Earl of Warwick* (see fig. 26). The figures were cast in copper by William Austen and gilded by Bartholomew Lambespringe, although the designer remains anonymous.

The death of Henry VII in 1509 led to the arrival of Renaissance influences in English sculpture. The commission for the tomb of the King and his queen, Elizabeth of York, was eventually given to the Italian sculptor Pietro Torrigiani (*see* TORRIGIANI, PIETRO, fig. 1), who also received the order for the monument to the King's mother, *Lady Margaret Beaufort*, the Countess of Richmond, who died in the same year as her son. Both monuments, resting on black-and-white tomb-chests, are in Westminster Abbey. There are Renaissance details in the decoration of the Countess's tomb-chest, but her partly gilded bronze effigy and the niche's architectural repertory are partly compromised by dependence on a two-dimensional model supplied by a Netherlandish painter. The gilded effigies of the King and his consort are not compromised in this way, and the monument features boy angels perched on the corners of the tomb-chest, naked putti supporting the coats of arms and circular wreaths carved with bay leaves, flowers, fruit and ribands, each enclosing gilt-bronze plaques of two saints in high relief. Other Florentine sculptors active in England in the 16th century included Giovanni da Maiano II (*see* MAIANO, DA, (3)) and BENEDETTO DA ROVEZZANO. The alabaster tomb-makers of the Midlands sometimes introduced ill-understood Renaissance motifs and ill-formed putti into their works, but these still remained Gothic in concept until well into the 16th century.

It was the Reformation and the changed attitudes that came with it, rather than the coming of the Renaissance, that caused the demise of medieval sculpture in England. Indeed, it has been argued (Stone) that less than 10% of medieval sculpture remains, as a result of two main periods of image destruction, during the Reformation in the 16th century and during the Commonwealth (1649–60). Some types, including the formerly ubiquitous rood images and sculpture in precious materials, effectively disappeared altogether, although effigies, which received considerable state protection during periods of religious upheaval, survive in large numbers. Iconoclasm also had other distorting effects: vaulting bosses remain abundant, but some of the largest programmes of full-scale imagery, as in the 14th-century Lady Chapel (destr.) of Ely Cathedral (*see* ELY, §1(ii)), have disappeared; wood sculpture was largely burnt, apart from misericords and such fragmentary pieces as the 12th-century head of *Christ* from South Cerney (Glos). Neglect in the post-medieval period affected external sculpture in particular, while important metropolitan programmes such as that from the early 16th century on the exterior of Henry VII's Chapel at Westminster Abbey disappeared in the early 18th century. Later restorations also resulted in the loss of damaged medieval sculpture or in stylistic incongruity (e.g. the 19th-century figure of the *Virgin* in the Judgement Portal of Lincoln Cathedral). Furthermore, while from the mid-13th century lay specialists had emerged as major suppliers of tomb sculptures and religious imagery, their status had apparently always remained much lower than that of the master masons; the change in perception heralded by the arrival of the Italians in the early 16th century was never effected because of the iconophobic attitudes of so many English Reformation thinkers.

BIBLIOGRAPHY

E. S. Prior and A. Gardner: *An Account of Medieval Figure Sculpture in England* (Cambridge, 1912)
A. Gardner: *Alabaster Tombs of the Pre-Reformation Period in England* (Cambridge, 1940)
L. Stone: *Sculpture in Britain: The Middle Ages*, Pelican Hist. A. (Harmondsworth, 1955, rev.2/1972)
G. Zarnecki: *Studies in Romanesque Sculpture* (London, 1979)
H. A. Tummers: *Early Secular Effigies in England: The Thirteenth Century* (Leiden, 1980)
F. H. Thompson, ed.: *Studies in Medieval Sculpture* (London, 1983)
P. Williamson: 'Sculpture', *The Age of Chivalry* (exh. cat., ed. J. J. G. Alexander and P. Binski; London, RA, 1987–8), pp. 98–106

PHILLIP LINDLEY

2. *c.* 1530–*c.* 1660. The staple trade of providing religious imagery came to an abrupt end in the 1530s, with the Reformation, the dissolution of the monasteries and the first wave of iconoclasm. The main preoccupation of sculptors therefore became the provision of sepulchral monuments, although there was a small market for secular architectural decoration, as at Cardinal Thomas Wolsey's palace at Hampton Court, where there remain terracotta busts of Roman emperors within roundels by Giovanni II da Maiano (*see* MAIANO, DA, (3)). French influence is probably visible in East Anglia during the first half of the 16th century, where terracotta was used for a small group of tombs by unknown artists. In the church of St Mary the Virgin, Layer Marney, Essex, the tomb of *Henry, 1st Lord Marney* (*d* 1523), while conventionally 15th-century

in appearance, has early Renaissance rather than Gothic detailing. The church of St Michael, Framlingham, Suffolk, houses the best group of early Renaissance tombs in the country, notably that of *Thomas Howard, 3rd Duke of Norfolk* (*d* 1554; see fig. 27), with finely carved clunch statues on the limestone tomb-chest depicting the Apostles standing in shell-headed niches separated by balusters. Almost contemporary and also with shell-headed niches—but between Ionic columns—and with kneeling children in contemporary dress, is the much restored alabaster tomb of *George Brook, 9th Lord Cobham* (1561; Cobham, Kent, St Mary Madgalene). Such fine work was, however, exceptional at this time.

In the mid-16th century the rise of the new aristocracy of the Tudors, replacing that of the Plantagenets, gave a fresh impetus to tomb-making. This coincided not only with the influx of sculptor refugees from the Netherlands but also with a proclamation by Elizabeth I in 1560 ordering the protection of monuments from destruction or damage, although the Queen was not inspired by any artistic motive. The new landowners, many living in former monastic buildings, needed to establish their lineage, and the commemorative monuments inspired by Elizabeth's proclamation were therefore flamboyant in their heraldry, with effigies not only of husband and wife but also of all their children, whether living or dead. The refugee sculptors, many of whom settled on the fringe of the City of London and became known as the Southwark school, brought new ideas from the Continent, their pattern-books and other designs being handed on to their sons. So similar was their work that it is impossible to distinguish between the families concerned; those with the anglicized names of Cure, Johnson and Colt were, however, the most important. The degeneration meanwhile of the work of the native alabaster tomb-makers was marked. Their carving became inept, and their use of Renaissance detail demonstrated a lack of understanding; this is particularly evident in the work of Richard Royley (*d* 1589), of Burton-on-Trent, Staffs, and his son Gabriel Royley. Monuments by them are in St James's, Somerton, Oxon (*Thomas Fermor, d* 1580), and St Mary's, Breedon-on-the-Hill, Leics (*John Shirley, d* 1585).

The Southwark school and its followers, whose work is found throughout the country, made great display of alabaster, lavishly painted, with Corinthian columns and strapwork. There was no overt religious imagery but much symbolism of death, such as hour-glasses, skulls and scythes. Their effigies, in contemporary dress (often attempts at portraits), were initially recumbent with hands at prayer but gradually became reclining, with head on hand, or kneeling, and very occasionally seated. Narrative was rarely introduced, but one example, in Canterbury Cathedral, of the *Hales Family* (*c.* 1596), not only shows a committal of a body to sea but also has a painting of a suicide (by drowning in a river). Much of the school's work comprised relatively small-scale mural memorials, but the grandest and most expensive were enormous, extending from floor to roof (e.g. *George Talbot, 6th Earl of Shrewsbury, d* 1590; alabaster; Sheffield Cathedral) or else free-standing, beneath large decorated canopies. Probably their finest and most sophisticated monuments are those to *Elizabeth I* (1605–7) by MAXIMILIAN COLT and

27. Tomb of *Thomas Howard, 3rd Duke of Norfolk*, limestone and marble, *c.* 1554 (Framlingham, Suffolk, St Michael)

to *Mary, Queen of Scots* (1605–*c.* 1613) by Cornelius Cure and William Cure (ii) (*see* CURE, (2) and (3)), both commissioned by James I (*reg* 1603–25) for Westminster Abbey. In these alabaster is abandoned in favour of black and white marble. (Colt, who came from Arras in the 1590s, was undoubtedly familiar with the use of marble in contemporary French and Netherlandish sculpture, and he probably influenced the Cures.)

The work of the first native Renaissance sculptor of note, EPIPHANIUS EVESHAM, while still in the Southwark tradition, was much more individual in manner (e.g. memorial to *Christopher Roper, 2nd Lord Teynham, d* 1622; alabaster with plaster; Lynsted, Kent, SS Peter and Paul). This individualism, together with the use of marble, heralded the great change brought about by Nicholas Stone (*see* STONE (ii), (1)), who studied under Hendrik de Keyser, in the Netherlands, and who was the first major English sculptor and the first whose work is known in quantity. With his skilled portraiture and ability to suggest new and, for the period, surprising poses, Stone set the fashion during the reigns of James I and Charles I (*reg* 1625–49) for greater sophistication, restraint and exceptional refinement of Renaissance detail; he also worked from the designs of the architect Inigo Jones. His monument to *Lady Carey* (*c.* 1620, marble; Stowe-Nine-Churches, Northants, St Michael) is a very sensitive work and a fine portrait, while the effigy on the marble monument to *John Donne* (*d* 1631; London, St Paul's Cathedral)

stands upright in a shroud. Working at the same time as Stone the CHRISTMAS family, while producing decorations for the Lord Mayor of the City of London or carving ornament on ships, also created a fashion for monuments decorated with bones or with bases revealing charnel-houses. Edward Marshall (*see* MARSHALL, (1)) worked in Stone's tradition in the mid-17th century and popularized the shrouded figure, of which the most poignant example, possibly by Marshall, was on the marble monument to *Lady Kinlosse* (*d* 1627; Exton, Leics, SS Peter and Paul).

The main centre for sculptors was London, and works were transported on the Thames and by sea to other rivers, from where they could be delivered to the nearest convenient location and then conveyed by horse and cart. The workmen who accompanied the crates added their costs to the bill, and if the sculpture was a monument it was often left to them to decide where it was to be set up in the church. Although the most accomplished work generally came out of London, there is a distinguished group of monuments from the 1620s and 1640s, within a radius of *c.* 40 miles of Gloucester, by or ascribed to SAMUEL BALDWIN of Stroud. Some are in Gloucester Cathedral, others in St Andrew's, Miserden; St Mary's, Berkeley; St John the Baptist's, Cirencester; St Bartholomew's, Much Marcle; St Mary's, Elmley Castle; and All Saints', Wroxton.

There was little court patronage before the reign of Charles I. He introduced foreign artists, among them

FRANCESCO FANELLI from Florence, FRANÇOIS DIEUS-SART from Flanders and HUBERT LE SUEUR from Paris. Surviving examples of Le Sueur's work include the bronze equestrian statue of *Charles I* (1633; London, Trafalgar Square), a bronze bust, also of *Charles I* (see fig. 28), and his two vast memorials of marble and bronze to *George Villiers, 1st Duke of Buckingham* (*d* 1628) and *Ludovick Stuart, 2nd Duke of Lennox and 1st Duke of Richmond* (*d* 1624; both h. *c.* 7 m), both in Westminster Abbey. In architectural sculpture the period's main innovation was the standing figure in a niche, among the earliest and most important of which were the statues of sovereigns for the Royal Exchange, London, commissioned *c.* 1622 from Nicholas Stone. The outbreak of the Civil War in 1642 interrupted court patronage, and the subsequent Commonwealth (1649–60) under Oliver Cromwell was too unsettled for the production of innovative sculpture. Only one Commonwealth sculptor, WILLIAM WRIGHT, was of note: his recorded work is slight, and his monument to Cromwell's son-in-law *Henry Ireton* in Westminster Abbey was destroyed by order of Charles II in 1660. It was not until the Restoration that year that sculpture again received encouragement, impetus and opportunity.

BIBLIOGRAPHY
K. A. Esdaile: *English Monumental Sculpture since the Renaissance* (London, 1927)
J. G. Mann: 'English Church Monuments, 1536–1625', *Walpole Soc.*, xxi (1933), pp. 1–22, pls i–xxvi
E. Mercer: *English Art, 1553–1625*, Oxford Hist. Eng. A. (Oxford, 1962)
M. D. Whinney: *Sculpture in Britain, 1530–1830*, Pelican Hist. A. (London, 1964, rev. 1988)
B. Kemp: *English Church Monuments* (London, 1980)
A. White: 'Classical Learning and the Early Stuart Renaissance', *Ch. Mnmts*, i (1985), pp. 20–33
B. Kemp: 'England c. 1560–c. 1660: A Hundred Years of Continental Influence', *Ch. Mnmts*, vii (1992), pp. 24–74

3. *c.* 1660–*c.* 1830. The Restoration of the monarchy in 1660, after the dour period of the Commonwealth, provided a new impetus for sculpture, although there was some continuity from the previous reign. Joshua Marshall (*see* MARSHALL, (2)), for example, carried on the practice established by his father, Edward Marshall, and PETER BESNIER successfully applied for reinstatement as Sculptor in Ordinary to the Crown. Court patronage was, however, less significant than under Charles I. Many people had, through exile or travel, become much more aware of trends in sculpture in such countries as France, Italy and the Netherlands, and more of the sculptors active in England after the Restoration had either been born in Europe or had visited or worked there. JOHN BUSHNELL, during his 10 years of enforced exile, had certainly been employed in Venice and probably elsewhere in Italy. He was the first English sculptor to demonstrate an awareness of the Baroque, as in his monument to *John, Viscount Mordaunt* (*d* 1675; see fig. 29), but increasing mental deterioration affected his output. Other artists equally aware of the Baroque dominated until the early 18th century, including GRINLING GIBBONS from Rotterdam; his partner Artus Quellinus from Antwerp (*see* QUELLINUS, (6)); CAIUS GABRIEL CIBBER from Denmark; John Nost the elder (*see* NOST, VAN, (1)) from Mechelen; and two Englishmen, Edward Pierce (*see* PIERCE, (2)) and FRANCIS BIRD. Of the last two only Bird had been to the

28. Hubert Le Sueur: *Charles I*, bronze, h. 868 mm, 1636 (Oxford, Bodleian Library)

Continent, working in both Italy and the Netherlands. All these sculptors seem to have designed their own works, although they were as happy taking designs from others, as is demonstrated by the greater survival of drawings for sculpture from this period onwards. There is also evidence to suggest that Bird made use of engravings; the mural monument in marble to *Christopher Hewer* (*d* 1715) in St Paul's, Clapham, London, which is a direct if slightly modified copy of Bernini's monument to *Maria Raggi* (1643; Rome, S Maria sopra Minerva) although unsigned, could well be by him.

Throughout the latter part of the 17th century, and especially for the many requirements of Christopher Wren in rebuilding London after the Great Fire of 1666 (*see* LONDON, §II, 3), there also developed a group of mason–sculptors that included Thomas Cartwright (*c.* 1617–1702), Christopher Cass (1678–1734), Thomas Dunn (*c.* 1676–1746), Christopher Horsnaile and THOMAS STAYNER. The three members of the STANTON family, who besides providing architectural sculpture were equally capable of producing original sculpture of quite high quality and originality, were particularly significant. In 1694 William Stanton employed eight men, most of whom were probably labourers rather than sculptor-assistants. The first

29. John Bushnell: monument to *John, Viscount Mordaunt*, marble, *c*. 1675 (Fulham, London, All Saints)

architect regularly to design for sculpture was JAMES GIBBS. He provided the Roman Giovanni Battista Guelfi, protégé of Richard Boyle, 3rd Earl of Burlington, with the design for the standing figure in indeterminate classical drapery on the marble monument to the Secretary of State *James Craggs* (*d* 1721) in Westminster Abbey. Also in Westminster Abbey and from Gibbs' designs are marble memorials to *John Dryden*, *Alexander Pope* and *Ben Jonson*, as well as the towering marble construction (1723) by Francis Bird dedicated to *John Holles, 1st Duke of Newcastle*; John Nost the elder had also produced a design (London, BM) shortly after the Duke's death in 1711. Michael Rysbrack (*see* RYSBRACK, (2)) from Antwerp was also used by Gibbs as well as by WILLIAM KENT. Another sculptor to produce monuments from Kent's designs was Peter Scheemakers (*see* SCHEEMAKERS, (2)), also from Antwerp, whose early career was spent in partnership with LAURENT DELVAUX, another immigrant from the Low Countries. Together they brought the narrative sculptural monument in marble to Westminster Abbey, with that to *John Sheffield, 1st Duke of Buckingham and Normanby* (*d* 1721), where the Duke in Roman armour reclines on a sarcophagus, his mourning wife at his feet, while above, the figure of Time bears away portrait medallions of their children. Working later independently Scheemakers was overshadowed by Rysbrack until 1740, when from Kent's design he carved the greatly acclaimed marble memorial in Westminster

Abbey to *William Shakespeare*. Both artists executed small mural monuments, usually with a bust, as well as vast ones, sometimes with many statues, of the dead persons, their family and (usually female) allegorical figures. Like most 18th-century sculptors they also produced numerous busts—some portraits, others of sets of Worthies and so on—as well as chimney-pieces for the Palladian houses of the aristocracy.

By the mid-18th century, both Rysbrack and Scheemakers had been eclipsed by the Frenchman LOUIS-FRANÇOIS ROUBILIAC from Lyon. Probably a pupil of Balthasar Permoser in Dresden and then of Nicolas Coustou in Paris, Roubiliac soon became associated with the circle of artists that included William Hogarth. He developed dramatic Rococo monuments of his own and seems never to have worked from anyone else's designs; his busts were more Rococo than those produced by his two main rivals. Several of his memorials are in Westminster Abbey, that to *Joseph and Lady Elizabeth Nightingale* (1758–61) justly being the most famous. There is evidence to suggest that Roubiliac was not afraid to tone his marbles in order to produce effects of perspective. After arriving in England Roubiliac had worked for Henry Cheere (*see* CHEERE, (1)), a sculptor who created his own style of Rococo monument, making much greater use of coloured marbles than had previously been the fashion. Like Rysbrack and Scheemakers, Cheere had a profitable business providing chimney-pieces, on which he used delicately carved panels of pastoral subjects. His brother John Cheere produced lead garden-figures, continuing a fashion begun by Cibber and Nost at Hampton Court for William III; these had initially been of stone or marble, but Nost switched to lead, which was more suited to resist the English weather.

When the Royal Academy was founded by George III in 1768, only three sculptors were among the first members: Agostino Carlini, William Tyler and JOSEPH WILTON. Only the last of these is noteworthy, but even though he was capable of producing large works such as the memorial to *General James Wolfe* (1772; for illustration *see* WILTON, JAMES) for Westminster Abbey, he was inconsistent and cannot be compared with his immediate predecessors. Of the following generation of Royal Academician sculptors, the most important were Joseph Nollekens (*see* NOLLEKENS, (2)), John Bacon (*see* BACON, (1)) and THOMAS BANKS. Nollekens became the leading portrait sculptor, with a vast practice that lasted until the 1810s. But Bacon, who specialized in depicting lightly clad women weeping beside urns and coffins beneath willow trees or beside broken columns, was widely copied, with growing sentimentality, until the mid-19th century. His influence extended to the baleful memorials in newly founded cemeteries and remained painfully apparent in the late 20th century. The only sculptor with an international reputation was the coldly classical JOHN FLAXMAN, who had been a student at the new Royal Academy Schools. Like Bacon, he modelled work for ceramics (Wedgwood) and for silver and gold (Rundell, Bridge & Rundell). Although his grandiose sculpture is very obvious in St Paul's Cathedral or Westminster Abbey—for example, on the monument to *William Murray, 1st Earl of Mansfield* (*d* 1793; see fig. 30)—his great strength was in producing relatively low-relief sculpture.

During the 1760s a manufactory of very durable artificial stone had been founded in London by ELEANOR COADE, who provided sculptured architectural decoration, statues and monuments. Not only did she wisely select architects as designers, but she was also careful to select well-known and successful sculptors as modellers, among them Bacon and Flaxman. Among those architects of the late 18th century who provided designs for sculpture were William Chambers (Westminster Abbey; St Michael's, Chenies, Bucks); Robert Adam (i) (Westminster Abbey; St Edmund's, Warkton, Northants; All Saints, Kedleston, Derbys); James Stuart (Westminster Abbey; St Andrew's, Wimpole, Cambs); and James Leoni (*d* 1746; Westminster Abbey; St Mary and Holy Cross, Quainton, Bucks). Towards the end of the century it became quite common for much routine work to be carried out by sculptors' assistants, aided by such instruments as the pointing machine, invented by Bacon and improved by Francis Chantrey. Without such mechanical and personal help Nollekens would not have been able to produce large numbers of replicas of sought-after busts of such figures as William Pitt or Charles James Fox, and other sculptors whose work was exported to the colonies would not have been able to undertake their great number of commissions. Inevitably, London remained the centre of focus for sculptors, but many relatively minor artists were established in the regions; none achieved great significance as their work was usually inspired by the major artists, but their businesses might extend for several generations. Among towns that had local sculptors were Bath (the King family, established by Thomas King, 1741–1804), Bristol (the Paty family, led by Thomas Paty, 1718–89, and his son William Paty, 1758–1800), Birmingham (*see* HOLLINS, PETER), York (*see* FISHER), as well as Northampton, Gloucester and Liverpool. In Norwich there were two sculptors, Thomas Rawlins and Robert Page (1707–78), and in Shrewsbury, Thomas Farnolds Pritchard (1723–77), whose Rococo works can easily be mistaken for those of Henry Cheere.

Around the time of the arrival in London in 1816 of the Elgin Marbles (the 5th-century BC frieze and pedimental sculpture from the Parthenon, Athens), there came a decline in private but an increase in public patronage, not only for monuments but increasingly for statues, at first of the sovereign and then of parliamentarians, national heroes and civic leaders. The principal sculptors of this period were FRANCIS CHANTREY and Richard Westmacott (*see* WESTMACOTT, (2)). Chantrey was the more successful, and his many commissions for statues, portrait busts and monuments allowed him to amass a considerable fortune. The Chantrey bequest is still used for the purchase of works of art executed within the shores of Great Britain. Westmacott's output included the first public male nude statue in London, the bronze *Achilles* (1822; Hyde Park), paid for by English ladies who subscribed in honour of the 1st Duke of Wellington; the figure was based on one of the Dioscuri on Monte Cavallo in Rome. The rise of the monumental mason to cope with the public demands for cemeteries led to the decline of monuments in churches, and during the 19th century most sculptors had to turn elsewhere for business.

30. John Flaxman: figure of *Death*, detail from the monument to *William Murray, 1st Earl of Mansfield*, marble, erected 1801 (London, Westminster Abbey)

BIBLIOGRAPHY

Gunnis

K. A. Esdaile: *English Monumental Sculpture since the Renaissance* (London, 1927)

M. D. Whinney: *Sculpture in Britain, 1530–1830*, Pelican Hist. A. (London, 1964, rev. 1988)

J. Physick: *Designs for English Sculpture, 1680–1860* (London, 1969)

N. Penny: *Church Monuments in Romantic England* (London, 1977)

B. Kemp: *English Church Monuments* (London, 1980)

J. Bryant: 'The Church Memorials of Thomas Banks', *Ch. Mnmts*, i (1985), pp. 49–64

I. Roscoe: 'Flemish Sculptors and Adjustments for the English Market: The Case of Peter Scheemakers', *Ch. Mnmts*, vii (1992), pp. 75–84

4. *c.* 1830–*c.* 1914. A gradual change occurred in British sculpture in the 19th century, in the training of sculptors and in a greater experimentation in the use and mixture of different materials. Public patronage, both national and local, became more predominant, with statues of statesmen, national heroes such as Horatio, Lord Nelson, and Arthur Wellesley, 1st Duke of Wellington, and local worthies appearing in city and town squares and parks in quite large numbers. Interest in sculpture generally was enhanced by competitions, the most important being those set up for the sculptural decoration of the new Palace of Westminster (1844; *see* LONDON, §V, 3(iii)), the monument to Lord Nelson in Trafalgar Square, London (1838; set aside and held again in 1839), and for the national memorial to the Duke of Wellington in St Paul's Cathedral, London (*see* LONDON, §V, 1(ii)(b)). The deaths of Sir Robert Peel in 1850 and Wellington in 1852, and most importantly that of Albert, the Prince Consort, in 1861 resulted in a large number of statues throughout the country. Figures could be equestrian or standing, and either dressed in uniform or in the robes of an order of chivalry. These accoutrements were usually not available, however, for a mayor, a member of parliament or a local benefactor, who had to be content with a frock-coat and shapeless, wrinkled trousers, sometimes mercifully disguised beneath civic or academic gowns. To overcome

this difficulty sculptors often used classicizing drapery. The more important works were accompanied by groups, as in Edward Hodges Baily's memorial to *Sir Robert Peel* (see fig. 31), or by reliefs on the pedestals representing activities connected with the person commemorated. The epitome of commemorative sculpture was the memorial to *Prince Albert* (completed 1876) in Kensington Gardens, London, which brought together all these features beneath an immense Gothic ciborium lavishly decorated with mosaic, and standing on a frieze composed of representations in high relief of 169 musicians, painters, architects, poets and sculptors through the ages. The general form was designed by the architect George Gilbert Scott (*see* SCOTT (ii), (1)); 11 sculptors were involved in the figure-work, including John Henry Foley (for illustration *see* FOLEY, JOHN HENRY) and Henry Hugh Armstead.

Sculptural decoration for buildings provided much opportunity as the century progressed. In addition to the Palace of Westminster there were new town halls and other civic buildings, as well as many churches. In the latter Gothic reigned supreme, but public buildings could be in either classical or Gothic style. The main decorative feature of a classical town hall was the allegorical group in the pediment (for example that of *c.* 1870 by William Calder Marshall at Bolton Town Hall, Lancs). Gothic

buildings were often influenced by John Ruskin's books *The Seven Lamps of Architecture* (1849) and *The Stones of Venice* (3 vols; 1851–3) and by his dictum that architectural ornament should derive from natural form (e.g. the work of the O'SHEA family at the University Museum, Oxford, in the late 1850s). Buildings in a Gothic idiom provided ample opportunity for figures of kings and queens and heroes of local history to decorate both the exterior and the interior. Sculptors who worked on a classical building had no qualms about providing Gothic work when asked, especially for the numerous new churches and restorations (e.g. John Birnie Philip: Lichfield Cathedral reredos, after 1857). In order to cope with the demand for this ecclesiastical work—which controversially included saints (for example Bristol Cathedral, in G. E. Street's north porch)—firms such as Farmer & Brindley (Worcester Cathedral reredos, 1860s), Thomas Earp (1828–93; Oxford, Magdalen College reredos, *c.* 1865; London, the Charing Cross, 1863) and Harry Hems (1842–1916; St Albans Abbey reredos, 1884–90) were established; examples of their work exist throughout England. A revival in the use of terracotta for architectural decoration at South Kensington (the Victoria and Albert Museum, the Royal Albert Hall and the Natural History Museum) illustrated its usefulness for easily reproduced ornament.

After the founding in 1837 of the School of Design, Somerset House, London, further schools were set up throughout England (*see also* §XV below), and in the second half of the century numerous French sculptors were appointed to important teaching posts. Alphonse Legros, for example, was appointed professor at the Slade School of Fine Art in London, and Aimée Jules Dalou taught at the National Art Training School (now the Royal College of Art) before moving to Lambeth School of Art and the South London Technical Art School. Most of the foremost English sculptors of the Victorian period trained either at one of these schools or at the Royal Academy, but two artists who trained outside the conventional academic system were the Italian CARLO MAROCHETTI, who fled from France after the Revolution of 1848, and Matthew Cotes Wyatt (*see* WYATT, (5)). Marochetti, favoured by the English court, aroused the antagonism of native artists, but he nevertheless executed the monument to *Queen Victoria and Prince Albert* (1864–8) at Frogmore, Windsor. Wyatt, the son of the architect James Wyatt, had no formal sculptural training. In 1846 he produced a statue of *Wellington* that became the most reviled and lampooned statue of the period; it was soon banished to Caesar's Camp, near Aldershot.

Probably the most controversial English sculptor of the 19th century was ALFRED GILBERT. His figure of *Eros* (London, Piccadilly Circus) is of aluminium, and Gilbert did not hesitate elsewhere to mix such materials as marble, bronze, ivory, polychromy (*see* POLYCHROMY, colour pl. IV) and semi-precious stones. Other sculptors, such as HARRY BATES (see fig. 32), did the same and also designed for jewellery and manufacture. A notable manifestation of this fashion for sculptural innovation, which came to be known as NEW SCULPTURE, was in the architectural decoration (often with the swirling lines of Art Nouveau) of Baroque Revival buildings in the early 20th century.

31. Edward Hodges Baily: *Sir Robert Peel*, bronze, 1852, Market Place, Bury, Lancashire

sculptor, a criticism that could be levelled at much of the sentimental and banal output of the 19th century. Although several sculptors were knighted the only one to be given an hereditary award (a baronetcy) was the Viennese JOSEPH EDGAR BOEHM, who in 1880 was appointed Sculptor-in-Ordinary to Queen Victoria.

BIBLIOGRAPHY

Gunnis
British Sculpture, 1850–1914 (exh. cat., London, F.A. Soc., 1968)
E. Manning: *Marble & Bronze: The Work and Life of Hamo Thornycroft* (London, 1982)
B. Read: *Victorian Sculpture* (New Haven and London, 1982)
S. Beattie: *The New Sculpture* (New Haven and London, 1983)
R. Dorment: *Alfred Gilbert* (London, 1985)
M. Stocker: 'The Church Monuments of Joseph Edgar Boehm', *Ch. Mnmts*, iii (1988), pp. 61–75

JOHN PHYSICK

5. AFTER *c.* 1914. Although traditions of Victorian sculpture continued well into the 20th century, most conspicuously in the memorial sculptures by Sargeant Jagger, Eric Kennington and others that proliferated after World War I, the influence of Cubism and the modernist dynamism of Vorticism paved the way for more avant-garde approaches. The most important figures in this respect were both of foreign origin: HENRI GAUDIER-BRZESKA, who died in action in 1915, and JACOB EPSTEIN, whose *Rock Drill* (1913–14; London, Tate; for illustration *see* EPSTEIN, JACOB), exhibited in that year with the London Group, provided a radical departure both through the mechanistic style of the figure and in its use of a real mining drill as its base. In general, however, the stylized naturalism of such sculptors as ERIC GILL and FRANK DOBSON (see fig. 33) dominated the 1910s and 1920s. The primitivist tendencies in such work were much more openly pursued in the early 1930s by both Epstein (e.g. in his earth-mother figure of *Genesis*, 1931; Granada Television Ltd, see 1987 exh. cat., pl. 99) and HENRY MOORE, whose sources included ancient Egyptian, Archaic Greek and Mayan art.

Moore was the towering example for English sculptors as late as the 1950s, when the controversy of his modernist stance finally began to fade and he became an establishment figure considered worthy of comparison with Michelangelo. By the time he helped found UNIT ONE in 1933 he had, under the influence of Picasso and Surrealism, moved towards an abstract biomorphism of form. Like the other great English sculptor of the period, his friend BARBARA HEPWORTH, he came close at that time to international currents in abstract art while remaining faithful to a peculiarly English involvement with nature and the landscape. Both were among the sculptors featured in *Circle*, a survey of Constructivism published in 1937, in which the Russian Naum Gabo and his brother Antoine Pevsner were also represented. Gabo, who moved to London from Paris in 1936 and followed Hepworth and Ben Nicholson to the artists' colony of ST IVES in 1939, remained in England until 1947 and was one of the first to use synthetic modern materials such as perspex in his work. The full repercussions of these explorations of abstract and geometric sculpture were, however, felt only in the 1960s.

32. Harry Bates: *Mors Janua Vitae*, bronze, ivory and mother-of-pearl, h. 940 mm, 1899 (Liverpool, Walker Art Gallery)

Some sculptors specialized in this genre, among them Henry Fehr (1867–1940), William Silver Frith (1850–1924), Frank Lynn Jenkins (1870–1927) and Frederick Schenck (*fl* 1896–1918). The death of Queen Victoria in 1901 provoked a spate of memorials, the largest of which (h. *c.* 25 m), outside Buckingham Palace, London, was a collaboration (1901–24) between the architect Aston Webb and the sculptor THOMAS BROCK, an overwhelming and eclectic work that earned Brock a knighthood. The *Architectural Review* (xxviii, 1910) thought that this might be regarded as a mausoleum for the reputation of the

both in the spiky figurative works, sometimes referred to as the 'geometry of fear', produced after World War II by such sculptors as KENNETH ARMITAGE, REG BUTLER and LYNN CHADWICK, and in the totemic figures produced during the 1950s by WILLIAM TURNBULL, EDUARDO PAOLOZZI and others. Paolozzi's incorporation of *objets trouvés* into his maquettes before casting them in bronze, as in *The Philosopher* (1957; London, Brit. Council Col.), brought him to international prominence as a practitioner of junk art, but the references in such works to science-fiction monsters and other popular sources also made them important forerunners of Pop art in the early 1960s. His robotic and much more machine-made sculptures initiated in 1962, together with sculptures produced then by other English artists, notably the chromed objects of Clive Barker (*b* 1940) and Colin Self (*b* 1941) and the humorous fibreglass figures of Nicholas Monro (*b* 1936), were highly individual contributions to the movement.

During the 1960s and 1970s only a few sculptors working in England, such as Turnbull, his Singaporean wife, Kim Lim (*b* 1936), and Garth Evans (*b* 1934) worked within the terms of Minimalism, which remained essentially an American movement. The dominant tendency in English sculpture in the 1960s was, instead, the abstract constructed work pioneered at the beginning of the decade by ANTHONY CARO under the influence of American art, notably of David Smith's sculptures, Kenneth Noland's paintings and Clement Greenberg's formalist criticism. By eliminating the conventional pedestal and using such things as steel girders as undisguised elements of his sculpture, Caro made a strong case for a more democratic relationship between the sculptural object and its environment. Through his teaching at St Martin's School of Art in London he also exerted an enormous influence on such younger sculptors as PHILLIP KING, TIM SCOTT and WILLIAM TUCKER, who were among a group that came to prominence in the exhibition *The New Generation: 1965*

33. Frank Dobson: *Two Heads*, 1921 (London, University of London, Courtauld Institute Galleries)

The impact of Surrealism on the work of English sculptors in the 1930s was varied but short-lived, encompassing the assemblages of Roland Penrose and Eileen Agar. The influence survived in modified form, however,

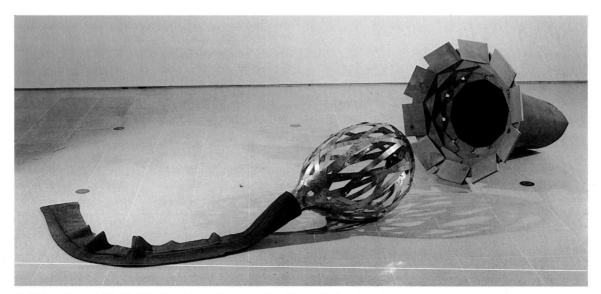

34. Richard Deacon: *The Eye Has It*, stainless and galvanized steel, brass, cloth and wood, 0.80×3.44×1.70 m, 1984 (London, Arts Council of Great Britain)

(London, Whitechapel A.G.). It was in reaction against their example, however, that subsequent sculpture students at St Martin's and their peers in the late 1960s and 1970s created alternative forms closely related to Conceptual art, all of which they presented as sculpture: the team of GILBERT AND GEORGE (the 'living sculptures') and BRUCE MCLEAN within the terms of Performance art; the land art of HAMISH FULTON and RICHARD LONG (*see* LAND ART); the soft art forms of BARRY FLANAGAN, an important contribution to process art similar in spirit to Arte Povera; and the environmental art installations of TIM HEAD, which combined real objects with projected images.

By the early 1980s a greater pluralism of approach was visible, and artists were again prepared to work in more traditional ways; even Flanagan, while retaining his mischievous sense of humour, began to produce cast bronzes representing hares and other animals. The concept of the avant-garde, although often declared dead, continued to find adherents, but openly historicist styles were also brought into play, as in the work of MICHAEL SANDLE, who made provocative reference to pre-modernist war memorials in exquisitely crafted bronzes as a means of countering formalism with a psychological and sometimes erotic exploration of modern institutionalized violence. The most visible presence internationally, however, was that of the sculptors associated with the Lisson Gallery, London, who did much to recharge earlier approaches with a new sense of purpose: TONY CRAGG and BILL WOODROW, for example, inventively returned to some of the strategies of junk art in an urban reworking of Long's land art, while RICHARD DEACON, assembling a variety of materials in a depersonalized and workman-like manner (e.g. *The Eye Has It*; see fig. 34), demonstrated the continuing possibility of an art rich in metaphor.

BIBLIOGRAPHY
J. L. Martin, B. Nicholson and N. Gabo: *Circle: International Survey of Constructive Art* (London, 1937/*R* 1971)
D. Farr: *British Sculpture since 1945* (London, 1965)
The New Generation: 1965 (exh. cat., preface B. Robertson, intro. I. Dunlop; London, Whitechapel A.G., 1965)
A. M. Hammacher: *Modern English Sculpture* (London, 1967)
British Sculpture in the Twentieth Century (exh. cat., ed. S. Nairne and N. Serota; London, Whitechapel A.G., 1981)
F. Spalding: *British Art since 1900* (London, 1986)
Entre el objeto y la imagen (exh. cat., Madrid, Pal. Velázquez, 1986)
Sculpture in Britain between the Wars (exh. cat., intro. B. Read; London, F.A. Soc., 1986)
T. Neff, ed.: *A Quiet Revolution: British Sculpture since 1965* (London, 1987)
British Art in the 20th Century (exh. cat., ed. S. Compton; London, RA, 1987)
MARCO LIVINGSTONE

V. Interior decoration.

1. Before 1485. 2. 1485–*c.* 1660. 3. *c.* 1660–1720. 4. 1721–90. 5. 1791–1830. 6. 1831–1900. 7. After 1900.

1. BEFORE 1485. Although the general perception of domestic interiors in England during the Middle Ages is one of profound discomfort, only slightly tempered for those in the upper levels of society, there is much evidence that for all but the lowest classes a considerable degree of comfort could in fact be enjoyed. The means by which this was achieved were usually easily portable, so that

when the king, great ecclesiastic or lord travelled around the country, as then frequently happened, he was accompanied by a train of waggons carrying hangings, furniture, plate and even kitchenware. When the lord was away, however, his home was bare. English interior decoration from the 11th century to the 14th was chiefly influenced by France, succeeded in the mid-14th and 15th centuries, during the Hundred Years War (1337–1453), by Burgundy, with its brilliant ducal court and its possessions in the Low Countries. Contemporary illuminated manuscripts are a fruitful source of information about the decoration and furnishings of the medieval house. Throughout the period furniture was simple and largely comprised trestle tables, stools and chests. Only the master of the house would have a chair, and bedsteads were owned by the upper classes.

Although medieval households were largely communal organizations centred on the great hall, the search for privacy is evident from the 12th century. Broughton Castle (*c.* 1300), Oxon, is an early surviving example of a house where private rooms were built behind the dais in the hall, with fireplaces and comparatively small windows, which may have been glazed from the beginning, but otherwise were certainly shuttered. Glass was expensive throughout the Middle Ages and was certainly a new luxury in the 13th century, judging by the frequency with which King Henry III ordered that it be installed in royal buildings.

Henry III's Close Rolls, which list alterations and improvements to the royal properties, also describe painted wall decorations, and it is likely that the upper classes probably followed his example. Walls were covered with plain boards (there is no suggestion of framing or panelling) and then painted, the Queen's Chamber (1240) in the Tower of London being decorated with roses on a white ground. About the same time, the king's lower chamber at Clarendon, Oxon, had a green wainscot with borders painted with the heads of kings and queens; the upper chamber contained on the upper walls the story of St Margaret and the four Evangelists, while the green wainscot below was spotted with gold and painted with the heads of men and women. Archaeological investigations have revealed that the gold spots were small, gilded lead stars and crescents with hooks to attach them to the woodwork. Secular subjects were more popular in a domestic setting than religious ones. The chimney-breast of the Queen's Chamber (1237–8) at the Palace of Westminster, London, for example, was adorned with a figure of Winter 'which as well by its sad countenance as by miserable distortions of the body may be deservedly likened to Winter itself'. The programme of subjects was carefully worked out; Henry II ordered that a room in Winchester Castle (1222–35) should be decorated with an eagle attacked by its four young to symbolize the rebellions of his four sons. Lesser houses were decorated with geometrical painting, one extant example being that in the former buttery of Stokesay Castle, Salop, which has a red scroll pattern on a white ground dating from the late 13th century or the early 14th.

Despite the increasing use and number of private rooms, the hall remained the spiritual as well as the physical heart of the medieval household. At meal-times, the master of the house sat on a dais at one end, while entry was through a door at the other. A surviving example of this layout is at Haddon Hall, Derbys, where the 15th-century screen stands in a 14th-century hall (see fig. 35). On occasion, the screen could be moveable, a unique extant example being the one at Rufford Old Hall, Lancs, which dates from the late 15th century. Over the master's seat would hang a canopy, usually in fabric, but Rufford Old Hall is one of several houses where a solid, wooden-coved canopy was attached to the wall. The fabric could be either painted or woven with a pattern, the actual material depending on the status and wealth of the master, certainly imported silks for the king and perhaps only linen for a knight. A variety of fabrics was available for furnishings, ranging from cotton, imported from the Mediterranean, linen, mostly home produced, silks and velvets, mostly from Italy, and of course wool—England's staple export in the 14th and 15th centuries.

Other textiles used in the house included tapestries. At first hung behind the dais to emphasize its importance, they were soon hung in the private rooms. The fashion for life-sized, figurative tapestries began in France and Burgundy and soon spread to England. Often they were given as diplomatic gifts. In 1393 Philip the Bold, Duke of Burgundy, gave Henry of Lancaster (later Henry IV; *reg* 1399–1413) a set showing *Clovis, Pharaoh and Moses* (untraced), which was woven in the Low Countries of English wool. Sometimes specific subjects were commissioned. One of the many tapestries owned by Sir John Fastolf at Caister Castle, Norfolk, depicted the *Siege of Falaise* (untraced), in which he had participated. For those who could not afford tapestries, painted hangings were available.

Ornate floors composed of glazed, encaustic or *sgraffito* tiles were at first a luxury, but by the 14th century they were commonly available (*see* TILE, §II, 1). Plain glazed tiles could be arranged in a chequerboard pattern or they could be decorated with animals or heraldic devices. The lower classes made do with beaten earth. Carpets were not completely unknown; when Eleanor of Castile came to the Palace of Westminster in 1255, her rooms were carpeted. The most likely covering for floors were loose rushes and sweet herbs for most levels of society. Woven rush matting, plaited and then stitched to the appropriate size, was not uncommon in great households. Carpets very occasionally appear in illuminated manuscripts, and it is known that Henry VI had a leather carpet. As John II of France had a bedside rug of green sendal, which matched the hangings in his chamber, such matched items were also probably used in England.

BIBLIOGRAPHY

N. Lloyd: *History of the English House* (London, 1931, 2/1975)
C. McCorqudale: *The History of Interior Decoration* (London, 1983), pp. 35–46

2. 1485–*c*. 1660. During the period between the accession to the throne of Henry VII and the Restoration of Charles II there were tremendous advances in the levels of sophistication of interior decoration in England, largely in response to developments in Europe. In the late 15th century foreign influences were chiefly Burgundian, but the employment by Henry VIII of the Italian sculptor Pietro Torrigiani in 1512 to design his father's tomb in Westminster Abbey, London, clearly indicates the source of future influences on English culture, even if, for much of the period, it was reflected through a Netherlandish prism. The break with Rome in 1536 tended to discourage direct contact with Italy, and developments in what became the Protestant United Provinces were more relevant to the English, united as the two countries were by trade and political interest. Consequently, the Renaissance reached England through Holland, Flanders and Germany rather than Italy, and most commonly through published treatises or pattern books by, among others, Sebastiano Serlio, Hans Vredeman de Vries, Wendel Dietterlin and Jacques Androuet Du Cerceau (i) (*see* PATTERN BOOK, §I). The nature of these sources meant inevitably that much Tudor and Jacobean decoration was an accumulation of decorative fragments rather than the new unity of conception developed from the late 15th century by Italian and later even some French architects. Although the occasional Italian or Frenchman was recorded working in England, the vast majority of foreign craftsmen were Flemish, such as Giles de Witt at Cobham Hall (1590s), Kent, Gerard Holleman at Kyre Park (1592), Worcs, and Maximilian Colt at Hatfield House (1607–12), Herts, who all supplied chimney-pieces. In court circles from the 1620s until the opening skirmishes of the Civil War in 1642, the revolution in architecture and interior design based on Italian models and introduced by Inigo Jones (e.g. the Queen's House, Greenwich, begun 1615, fitted up by 1638) was limited in

35. Banqueting Hall of Haddon Hall, Derbyshire, *c*. 1370; screen, *c*. 1450

36. Dining-room at Haddon Hall, Derbyshire, c. 1500

its effect on the national taste, and it was the Low Countries that continued to exert the strongest influence on interior decoration.

Rooms were not generously furnished by modern standards. Inventories reveal that most houses contained tables, benches, stools and coffers for storage. From the late 16th century, cupboards became increasingly common. The higher a household stood in the social scale, the more likely it was to have a chair or chairs, used by the master of the house and honoured guests. As time went on, these were more usually upholstered, rather than made of solid wood and softened by cushions.

Throughout this period, most of the colour given to interiors came from fabrics, either figurative tapestries of which Henry VIII, for example, owned over 2000 pieces, or embroidered hangings (e.g. a set of early 17th-century Florentine stitch hangings at Chastleton House, Oxon). For those who could not afford tapestries, canvas was often painted to resemble them; an extremely rare survival of this type of hanging depicting the *Acts of the Apostles* (late 16th century), probably painted by John Ballechouse, who was paid for such work in 1599, is a set hanging in the Chapel of Hardwick Hall (1590–97), Derbys. Even in their present faded state, the interiors of Hardwick and of Knole, Kent, give a good idea of the vital contribution of fabrics to late 16th- and early 17th-century interiors. They are virtually unique survivals from this period. The reconstructed interiors and contents of a prosperous Kentish yeoman's house, Bayleaf Farm (c. 1540; Singleton, Weald & Downland Open Air Mus.), which was recreated from documentary evidence, demonstrates how fabrics brightened lesser houses.

Plasterwork, particularly on ceilings, assumed a growing importance in English interior decoration until the end of the 16th century (see STUCCO AND PLASTERWORK, §III, 10(i)(c)). Thereafter it tended to become simpler; in court

circles the barbaric splendours of a generation earlier were tamed to the cool, Palladio-derived order of the new style propagated by Jones. At the beginning of the period, ceilings were of a simple type, often with applied carved wooden decoration (e.g. the late 15th-century hall ceiling at the Bede House, Lyddington, Leics). The room popularly known as Wolsey's Closet (c. 1525, although now largely a recreation of the 1880s) at Hampton Court Palace demonstrates a later development, having shallow ornament of papier mâché and lead. Ceilings were often divided up by mouldings into panels, occasionally converging as pendants. They became increasingly elaborate and heavy, some of the most lush examples surviving at Langleys (c. 1620), Essex, and the Long Gallery (c. 1640), Lanhydrock House, Cornwall. Their late date demonstrates how little court taste filtered outside court circles. Plaster friezes were also common throughout the period, from the rather simple but lively example (c. 1565) in the dining-room at Grove Place, Nursling, Hants, to the extraordinary frieze (c. 1592) with life-size figures, probably by Abraham Smith, around the High Great Chamber, Hardwick Hall.

These elaborate ceilings appear to have been painted white, but earlier ceilings were often painted in colours. Probably the best surviving example is the dining-room ceiling (c. 1500) at Haddon Hall, Derbys, which has a red-and-white chequer-board pattern with panels containing heraldic emblems (see fig. 36). This is one of the latest examples of the medieval tradition of painted ceilings. Walls, however, continued to be painted in colours. The great frieze at Hardwick, for example, was painted naturalistically. At 3 Cornmarket, Oxford, two walls survive painted c. 1570 in reticulated panels containing flowers or grapes, surmounted by pious inscriptions. An interior (mid- to late 16th-century) at Barhams Manor House, Higham, Suffolk, is painted with interlaced octagons in black on a white ground, with fruit and foliage in red and green.

The early 16th-century wainscot or panelling in the Council Chamber, Compton Wynyates, Warwicks, is still of the flush boarded (i.e. unframed) type popular since the Middle Ages. Wainscot, usually of oak, consisting of a framework enclosing small panels, soon achieved an almost universal popularity. These panels were frequently carved and, from the resemblance of one common type to folded fabric, it acquired the name 'linenfold' panelling in the 19th century. An early example of this type is in the Abbot's Lodgings (c. 1530), Thame Park, Oxon. Sometimes the resemblance to fabric was enhanced by the incised and punched representation of a stitched border (e.g. early 16th-century farmhouse, Kingstone, Somerset). During the second half of the 16th century, all sorts of elaborations were developed based on foreign pattern books, including elaborate carved work (the Long Gallery, c. 1580, Haddon Hall, Derbys), inlay (a room from Sizergh Castle, c. 1575, Cumbria; now London, V&A) and such eccentric techniques as columns of translucent size containing spirals of wood shavings (e.g. a room in the Old House, c. 1580, Sandwich, Kent). Wainscoting could be left bare or painted. The Little Castle (1608–17) at Bolsover Castle, Derbys, retains original, rich painted decoration in several rooms. A room in Sutton House, Hackney, London, contains late 16th-century linenfold panels painted c. 1630 in corn yellow against a field of emerald green. About the same time, the staircase at Sutton House was painted with strapwork decoration (*in situ*). An alternative type of decoration can be seen in the High Great Chamber, Hardwick, where the wainscot (1590s) has contemporary Flemish and German engravings, coloured, pasted on and varnished over as part of the decorative scheme.

The earliest example of European printed wallpaper was discovered on the beams in the Master's Lodgings, Christ's College, Cambridge. Printed in black on white on the back of paper containing textual matter of 1509, it has a design of highly conventionalized pomegranates and was apparently meant to be seen as a frieze above wainscoting. The printer was Hugo Goes (his rebus flanks the pomegranate), who worked in Beverley and York. Like other early wallpapers, it was intended to imitate, however crudely, the designs of brocades or velvets. An elaborate heraldic wallpaper (c. 1550–75; *see* WALLPAPER, fig. 3) survives from Besford Court, Hereford & Worcs, and fragments of surviving papers demonstrate that wallpapers of increasing sophistication were becoming available. By 1600 coloured wallpapers were being produced, and a paper of about that date (destr.) from Borden Hall, Sittingbourne, Kent, was printed in black on a red ground, with jade green and turquoise foliage and flowers. Although papers were usually pasted to walls, this example had been nailed to the plaster with large flat-headed nails.

37. Lady's bedchamber, c. 1640; engraving by Edmond Marmion, 125×172 mm, c. 1640 (Cambridge, Magdalene College)

Documentary evidence from the late Middle Ages indicates that painted wallpapers were known, but none earlier than the late 17th century appears to survive.

In lesser houses floors continued to be of beaten earth, as they were occasionally even in greater houses. Erasmus, in a letter written before 1530, commented that English floors were commonly of clay strewn with rushes, and in a contract of 1595 for building new offices at Woolavington, Sussex, the kitchen was to be floored with Purbeck stone, the larders with tiles and the rest were beaten earth. A popular and more solid alternative was a hard plaster, of which surviving examples include floors at Burghley House (1570s) and Hardwick (early 1590s). Otherwise wooden floors became common for the first time, particularly of oak, which was valued for its hardness. They were not polished but kept dry scrubbed, a process which was either done with damp sand or with such herbs as mint, tansy or balm. The use of bricks for flooring was rare, but tiles, which had become popular in grander houses during the Middle Ages, continued in use. For the chapel in The Vyne, Sherborne St John, Hants, tin-glazed blue, yellow, orange and green tiles (c. 1525; in situ) were ordered from the workshop of GUIDO ANDRIES in Antwerp. In 1535 Flemish paving-tiles in green and yellow were ordered for Hampton Court Palace, at a cost of 5d. per 100. Increasingly common by the early 17th century was the use of marble, either English or imported, such as the black-and-white floor (c. 1610) of the Marble Closet at Bolsover Castle.

Carpets were still uncommon, but documentary evidence suggests that they were no longer acquired exclusively by rich or aristocratic households (e.g. they were recorded in 1603 in the Great Chamber of Hengrave Hall, Suffolk), as an inventory of the goods of a prosperous farmer, John Andrews of Bepton, Sussex, taken in 1577, records that he had a carpet in his parlour. Carpets were usually used to cover seats, chests and tables, as seen in The Ambassadors (1533; London, N.G.; see HOLBEIN, (3), fig. 2), a use suggested by the listing of Andrews's carpet between a table and a coffer. Carpets intended for use on the floor were often called 'fote' cloths. One owned in 1541 by Sir Richard Weston of Sutton Place, Surrey, was described as 'a grete carpet to lay under the Kyngs fete'. Many must have been imported from the Middle East, for they were known as Damascene, Venetian (i.e. Anatolian imported through Venice) or Turkey carpets, but they were also made in England and known as 'turkey-work' (see §XI, 6 below). In an inventory of Cardinal Thomas Wolsey's goods made after his downfall in 1529, 11 were described as of English manufacture, and from their descriptions they were evidently virtual copies of Eastern patterns. Many carpets were embroidered, and a fine mid-16th century English carpet in petit-point survives (London, V&A).

Illustrations of English interiors of this period are virtually non-existent, unlike Dutch interiors, which were frequently depicted in oils. What may be the earliest surviving representation of an English interior (see fig. 37), depicts a fashionable bedchamber (c. 1640), closely modelled on the latest Paris styles. It therefore probably represents the type of furnishings to be found in buildings designed by Jones and his circle. Characteristically, the walls are hung with tapestry, and, as was now the fashion,

also hung with paintings. The back stools stand against the wall, as moveable furniture always stood from the Middle Ages to the late 18th century.

BIBLIOGRAPHY
L. Turner: *Decorative Plasterwork in Great Britain* (London, 1927)
M. St Clare Byrne: *The Elizabethan Home* (London, 1949)
B. Greysmith: *Wallpaper* (London, 1976)
M. Girouard: *Life in the English Country House* (New Haven and London, 1978)
P. Thornton: *Seventeenth-century Interior Decoration in England, France and Holland* (New Haven and London, 1978)
——: *Authentic Decor: The Domestic Interior, 1620–1920* (London, 1984)
M. Girouard: *Hardwick Hall* (London, 1989)
G. Beard: *The English House Interior* (London, 1990)
T. Mowl: *Elizabethan and Jacobean Style* (London, 1993)
S. Thurley: *The Royal Palaces of Tudor England: Architecture and Court Life, 1460–1547* (New Haven and London, 1993)

CHARLES WHEELTON HIND

3. *c.* 1660–1720. The return of Charles II from exile on the Continent revived court life in England and stimulated interest in the arts and architecture. Dutch influence was dominant, as many aristocrats had found refuge in the Netherlands during the Commonwealth; the 'double pile' houses of the architects Hugh May and William Winde, for example, were indebted to Dutch architecture. Other supporters of Charles II, as well as the King himself, had spent time in France and were open to French ideas. Robert Hooke, for instance, designed a house (1674–9; destr.) in Bloomsbury, London, in the French style with corner pavilions for Ralph Montagu, later 1st Duke of Montagu, ambassador to the court of Louis XIV. The remodelling (1675–85) of the interiors and the design of new state rooms (now largely destr.) at Windsor Castle by May showed the influence of the French Baroque style (see WINDSOR CASTLE, §3), which became predominant during the reigns of William III and Anne. The fashions, etiquette and magnificence of Versailles, symbolizing the glory of Louis XIV, became the model for an international court style that affected planning and decoration of English interiors until the beginning of the 18th century. It was only after the Hanoverian succession, when the Whig politicians rejected the Baroque style as a symbol of absolute monarchy, that a renewed interest in the works and publications of the Italian Renaissance architect Andrea Palladio took place. After 1660 continental engravings and pattern books became more readily available and contributed greatly to the improvement of the standard of English craftsmanship. The large-scale rebuilding of London after the Great Fire of 1666 not only required the training of native craftsmen but also provided the opportunity for the adoption of the latest continental fashions. Many foreign artists were also working in England. During the Restoration they were mostly Dutch, including such craftsmen as the carver Grinling Gibbons and the cabinetmaker Gerrit Jensen, as well as the portrait painters Peter Lely and Gerard Soest. After the revocation of the Edict of Nantes in 1685, many French Huguenot craftsmen also arrived in England. One of these exiles, who played an important role in the dissemination of the Louis XIV style, was the architect and designer Daniel Marot I (see MAROT, (2)). He came to England via the Netherlands, where he had designed

the interiors of the palace Het Loo for William and Mary, and was employed at Hampton Court Palace, London. Marot's engraved work, illustrating such architectural elements as wall elevations, ceilings and chimney-pieces as well as designs for furniture and upholstery, contributed greatly to the decorative unity of the English interior.

As in France, the grand English houses were designed to contain several *appartements*, consisting of a bedchamber, preceded by one or more antechambers and followed by several small rooms or closets. The state apartments at such large Baroque houses as Chatsworth, Derbys, and Castle Howard, N. Yorks, were each laid out in a single, long *enfilade* with their doors aligned to provide magnificent vistas. The *enfilade* also created an impressive approach to the main room of the apartment, the richly decorated bedchamber with its state bed.

From the reign of Charles II until the end of the 17th century magnificent plasterwork was used for the decoration of ceilings. Divided into compartments, most ceilings of the period display scrolls, foliage, festoons and other ornament framed by moulded ribs. Especially impressive is the drawing-room ceiling at Astley Hall, Lancs, with its large shells, palm branches and festoons in high relief executed by an unknown master *c.* 1666. Among well-known plasterers were Robert Bradbury (*fl* 1675–6) and James Pettifer (*fl* 1675–1702), who were responsible for the elaborately decorated ceilings (1675–6) at Sudbury Hall, Derbys. Outstanding plasterwork was also executed by Edward Goudge at Belton House, Lincs, in the 1680s. Plastered decoration declined in use towards the end of the century because of the increasing popularity of allegorical painting. The interior decoration of Windsor Castle, with the illusionistic paintings by the Italian artist Antonio Verrio and his assistants, set a pattern that was followed by wealthy aristocrats. Verrio, who had come to England from France in 1672, was also employed at Burghley House, Cambs, where he painted the so-called Heaven Room (1687–98; for illustration *see* VERRIO, ANTONIO), and later at Hampton Court (1700–04). Verrio's successors, among them the Frenchmen Louis Laguerre and Louis Chéron, worked in the style of Charles Le Brun, covering the ceilings and walls of halls and staircases with complex mythological and allegorical scenes in deep, rich colours set against illusionistic architectural backgrounds. The painted hall (1692–4) at Chatsworth with scenes from the life of Julius Caesar by Laguerre is typical. The most talented English-born painter was James Thornhill, whose decoration of the hall at Blenheim Palace, Oxon, in 1716 glorified John Churchill, 1st Duke of Marlborough.

Walls were generally lined with oak panels framed by bolection mouldings and crowned by a carved cornice. Panelled doors were surrounded with similar mouldings

38. Blue Drawing-room, Ham House, Surrey, *c.* 1670s, with grained panelling and damask wall hangings bordered with velvet

and surmounted by an architrave decorated to match the woodwork of the walls. Most of the panelling was left unpainted to display the natural grain of the wood, and, as a result, rooms tended to be dark. The carved decoration of the woodwork sometimes had gilt details, and such less expensive woods as fir were often grained (e.g. the King's Dining-room, Drayton House, Northants) or marbleized, as at Ham House, Surrey, or the Balcony Room at Dyrham Park, Avon.

Walls were sometimes covered above the dado with textile hangings, and some rooms were supplied with different sets for summer and winter. Designs by Marot illustrated hangings embellished with elaborate gathered valances and tassels. It was fashionable to use two different kinds of fabric or to alternate panels of the same fabric in contrasting colours. Colourful effects were also created by bordering a panel of one type of material with a differently patterned fabric (see fig. 38). Especially magnificent are the red and yellow wall hangings of silk damask and velvet at Penshurst Place, Kent, dating from c. 1695 and executed in appliqué technique. Tapestries, the most expensive of all wall hangings, were made in England at the Mortlake Factory (1619–1703) and, after its closing, in the Soho district of London (see §XI, 1 below). Such Mortlake tapestry sets as the *Acts of the Apostles*, after cartoons by Raphael, and the *Playing Children* are at the family seat of Ralph Montagu, who acquired these works in 1674 (Duke of Buccleuch priv. col.). Fine tapestries were also woven by John Van-derbank the elder, who headed the Great Wardrobe tapestry workshop in Great Queen Street, London, from 1689. He was responsible for wall hangings with chinoiserie designs (examples in New York, Met. and London, V&A) and for the series of *The Four Elements* at Burghley House, which were adapted from designs by Le Brun for tapestries executed at the Gobelins in Paris. Imported mostly from Holland and Spain, panels of decorated gilt leather were popular as wall decoration until the beginning of the 18th century (e.g. at Dyrham Park and Dunster Castle, Somerset). Although wallpaper was not common during this period, flock paper, patterned with powdered wool in imitation of cut velvet, was regularly used.

An important role in the creation of a unified décor was played by upholsterers. Many of the upholsterers who worked in England at this time were French, such as Francis Lapierre (1653–1714). Upholsterers were not only responsible for the wall hangings and bed and window curtains in a particular room but also for the matching upholstery of the seat furniture, which was usually arranged along the walls. Initially found only in the most important rooms, single or symmetrically divided draw curtains became widely used towards the end of the century. A new type of pull-up or festoon curtain, supplied with a richly decorated pelmet, was introduced around 1700. The sliding sash window with wooden glazing bars, common at the turn of the century, was set flush with the outside wall to allow space for folding interior shutters and a window seat.

English interiors of the late 17th century were renowned for their decorative carvings, and some of the most exquisite examples were executed by Grinling Gibbons. Mostly surrounding picture frames or embellishing overdoors and overmantels, his work displays swirling scrolls, flowers,

39. Great staircase, Sudbury Hall, Derbyshire, 1675–6, with balustrade by Edward Pierce, plasterwork by Robert Bradbury and James Pettifer, and paintings by Louis Laguerre, c. 1691

fruits, birds and other deeply undercut ornament in unpainted lime-wood; examples can be found at Windsor Castle, Chatsworth, Kensington Palace, London, and Petworth House, W. Sussex. Other distinguished carvers were Jonathan Maine (fl c. 1680–1709) and Edward Pierce. Pierce was responsible for the balustrade panels carved with foliated scrolls that were set between newels of the staircase at Sudbury Hall (see fig. 39). Wood staircases with similar balustrades are at Eltham Lodge, Kent, and formerly at Cassiobury Park, Herts (now New York, Met.). Other balustrades consisted of turned balusters (e.g. at Coleshill, Berks, and Ashburnham House, Westminster, London). After the publication of Jean Tijou's designs for ironwork in *A New Book of Drawings* (1693), wrought-iron balus-trades, combined with stone stairs, became fashionable in grand houses. Some balustrades, as at Easton Neston, Northants, imitated the florid style of Tijou, while others (Hampton Court Palace, Chatsworth and Drayton) were executed by the master ironworker himself.

Floors were generally made of unpolished oak or of deal boards in various widths. Parquet floors were intro-duced from France; among the first English examples were those laid in 1661 at Somerset House, London, for Queen Henrietta Maria. Floors with both geometrical patterns (parquetry) and naturalistic patterns (marquetry) were executed at Ham House in the 1670s. The landings and treads of some staircases were also inlaid. Stone and marble were reserved for the floors in halls or for passages and chapels. Although Turkish and Persian carpets were available for both floors and tables, they were not common. Imitations of these Oriental pile carpets, called Turkey work, were made in England; a good example is the Molyneux Carpet of 1672 (London, V&A). Thin mats with brightly coloured patterns, imported from Africa but frequently called Portugal, Tangiers or Barbary mats, were often found in bedchambers.

As one of the most important elements in the room, the chimney-piece was generally designed by the architect and was usually made of wood or coloured marble and decorated with simple mouldings (see fig. 38). The fireplace was fitted with a cast-iron fireback, a metal fender, a pair of andirons, fire-irons or a coal grate. The overmantel was often panelled to match the woodwork of the walls and usually incorporated a painting, which in some houses was surrounded by decorative carving, as at Petworth and Chatsworth. At the end of the 17th century, when larger plates of mirror glass were not only imported but also produced at the Vauxhall and other London glass manufactories, a mirror was frequently inserted directly above the mantel. The early 18th-century gilt frames of overmantel mirrors frequently matched those of the pier-glasses placed between the windows in the same room. Corner chimney-pieces, based on designs by Marot and often found in small rooms such as those at Hampton Court and Beningborough Hall, N. Yorks, probably originated in England. Expressing contemporary enthusiasm for East Asian porcelain, several of Marot's designs show a tiered arrangement of vases, cups and saucers on the overmantel (see DISPLAY OF ART, fig. 10). Porcelain or Delftware was also displayed on brackets along the walls and on the cornice, above the doors, on the mantel shelf and, during the summer, in the fireplace. The taste for the exotic was sometimes shown by lining the walls of a cabinet or closet with panels of East Asian or imitation lacquer, of which some examples still exist at Drayton House and at Honington, Warwicks. Another expression of this vogue was the use of chintz, printed or painted cotton imported from India, as bed and wall hangings and curtains, mostly in small rooms.

BIBLIOGRAPHY

J. Harris: *English Decorative Ironwork* (London, 1960)
E. Croft-Murray: *Early Tudor to Sir James Thornhill*, i of *Decorative Painting in England, 1537–1837* (London, 1962/*R* 1970)
O. Hill and J. Cornforth: *English Country Houses: Caroline, 1625–1685* (London, 1966)
J. Lees-Milne: *English Country Houses: Baroque, 1685–1715* (London, 1970)
P. Thornton: *Seventeenth-century Interior Decoration in England, France and Holland* (New Haven and London, 1978)
C. Gilbert and A. Wells-Cole: *The Fashionable Fire Place, 1660–1840*, Temple Newsam Country House Studies, ii (Leeds, 1985)
C. Gilbert, J. Lomax and A. Wells-Cole: *Country House Floors, 1660–1850*, Temple Newsam Country House Studies, iii (Leeds, 1987)
P. Clabburn: *The National Trust Book of Furnishing Textiles* (London, 1988)
G. Beard: *The Work of Grinling Gibbons* (London, 1989)

For further bibliography *see* §§4–6 below.

DANIËLLE GROSHEIDE

4. 1721–90. Interior decoration during the 18th century closely paralleled the continuing evolution in architectural taste of the middle and upper classes. The Court or Baroque taste of Christopher Wren and his younger associates John Vanbrugh and Nicholas Hawksmoor began to disintegrate with the revival of the work of Andrea Palladio, as interpreted by the 17th-century English architect Inigo Jones, and by Colen Campbell under the patronage of such Whig peers as Richard Boyle, 3rd Earl of Burlington and 4th Earl of Cork. Although the detail of interiors was designed by architects or builders, the actual furnishing of them was generally left to an upholsterer, who usually worked directly for the client and sometimes in opposition to the architect. At Blenheim Palace, Oxon, Vanbrugh was superseded by a cabinetmaker, James Moore sr (1670–1726), after the architect fell out with his client, the Duchess of Marlborough. The most famous of the upholsterers was Thomas Chippendale (*see* CHIPPENDALE, (1)), who could supply a complete decorating service from painting and paper-hanging to the supply of fabrics and furniture. By the mid-18th century architects were increasingly aware of the possibilities of decoration and the contribution it could make to the success or otherwise of their designs. William Kent, a protégé of Lord Burlington, established a precedent for architects also designing the contents of a room (Houghton Hall, Norfolk, is a particularly complete survival of his work), a process taken to its ultimate length by the Adam brothers, who could supply designs for anything from a complete house to a picture frame or lock-plate. As architecture was a polite accomplishment of many gentlemen, so clients of both sexes took a close interest in the decorating of their houses, as shown by Lord Chesterfield's letter of 1743 to Solomon Dayrolles: 'The rest of the day is employed in riding, and fitting up my house [Chesterfield House in Mayfair, London; destr.]; which I assure you, takes a great deal of time, now that we are come to the minute parts of finishing and furnishing.' The client's intervention in matters of taste as well as expense was often a significant influence.

By the 1740s the strict orthodoxy of the first generation Palladians was beginning to relax as the Rococo style was introduced from France, and the formal symmetrical plan of detached houses was giving way to ingeniously varied layouts, often organized around a top-lit staircase. Under the umbrella term 'Rococo', such exotic styles as Gothic, Chinese or Moorish became fashionable, even more so in furniture, fabrics and accessories than in architecture. The most famous Gothick interiors were at Strawberry Hill, Twickenham, created by Horace William Walpole, 4th Earl of Orford, between 1749 and 1776, and notable interiors in the Chinese style survive at Claydon, Bucks. Designs for furniture in all these Rococo styles were published by Chippendale in his book *The Gentleman and Cabinet-maker's Director* (1754) and were widely imitated and adapted. The publication by James Stuart and Nicholas Revett of their *Antiquities of Athens* in 1762 and Robert Adam's *Ruins of Emperor Diocletian's Palace at Spalato* two years later popularized the Neo-classical style that had already begun to emerge in the 1750s. Neo-classicism spawned such offshoots as the Etruscan and Pompeian styles, of which notable examples are at Osterley Park

40. Arthur Devis: *John Bacon and his Family in a London Drawing-room*, oil on canvas, 766×1311 mm, *c.* 1742 (New Haven, CT, Yale Center for British Art)

House, Middx (1775, Robert Adam), and Packington Hall, Warwicks (1786, Joseph Bonomi), where even the furniture was derived from the decoration of ancient Greek vases. In the second half of the 18th century the pace of change in all fields of decoration began to speed up, and the rapidly increasing wealth of the country provided the means for such extravagancies as Adam's Glass Drawing-room at Northumberland House (1773–5; London, V&A), London. In the 1780s French taste was once again a significant influence under the patronage of the Prince of Wales (later George IV), with the introduction by Henry Holland of the Louis XVI style into Carlton House (destr.), the Prince's residence in London.

At the beginning of the 18th century walls were usually covered in wainscoting or panelling, and more luxurious rooms with tapestry. Wainscoting was generally of oak or cedar in the principal interiors and in pine or deal in less important rooms, often painted to imitate the more expensive woods. Two houses in Shropshire, Mawley Hall and Davenport House, contain panelling elaborately inlaid and veneered with exotic woods with parquetry floors to match. There were variants on simple graining to provide a more luxurious finish. At Canons Ashby, Northants, the Painted Parlour preserves a rare marbled decoration with *trompe l'oeil* details, while the upper room at Swangrove, a park pavilion at Badminton, Glos, has simple, early 18th-century panelling painted with chinoiserie scenes in imitation of oriental lacquer. Tapestries, particularly those depicting heroic figures, were declining in popularity by the 1720s, although Francis Dashwood, 15th Baron Le Despenser, hung an early set of Brussels tapestries at West Wycombe Park, Bucks, as late as 1765. The Soho Tapestry Works produced lighter designs: an arabesque set was hung at Squerryes Court, Kent, in 1720. By the late 1740s the Soho works were producing fashionable Rococo-style hangings (e.g. set at Hagley Hall, Worcs). There was a brief revival in the 1760s, when a number of rooms designed by Robert Adam were hung with Gobelins tapestries woven to order, one of the finest of which was made for Croome Court, Worcs (now New York, Met.).

Wall and ceiling paintings, popular during the Baroque period (*see* §3 above), survived at least into the 1730s. In the 1720s and 1730s the art was dominated by Gaetano Brunetti (active in England in the 1730s) and the Venetians Jacopo Amigoni, Giovanni Antonio Pellegrini and Sebastiano Ricci and his nephew Marco Ricci, many from Venice, were greatly influenced by Giambattista Tiepolo and introduced a lightness of touch unknown to the earlier Baroque painters. Their only serious English rival was James Thornhill, much of whose work dates from before 1720 (a later example is the Chapel at Wimpole Hall, Cambs, *c.* 1724), but whose greatest work was the Painted Hall at Greenwich Hospital (1708–27; for illustrations *see* THORNHILL, JAMES, and ILLUSIONISM, colour pl. V). His style became increasingly unfashionable during the 1720s, to the extent that, despite his position as Sergeant Painter to George I, the commission to paint the interiors at Kensington Palace (executed 1722–8), London, was given to William Kent. Kent's work shows a move away from the sprawling gods and goddesses of Baroque illusion towards the confinement of decorative paintings within a strongly architectural framework, often with grotesque decoration inspired by Raphael's loggias in the Vatican, Rome, which reflected the rising ascendancy of Palladianism under the auspices of his patron, Lord Burlington. Francis Dashwood continued to commission grand frescoed decoration by the Piedmontese artist Giuseppe Borgnis until the late 1750s (West Wycombe Park), by which time most other clients either favoured the Rococo singeries of Andien de Clermont (*fl*?1717–83), as at Kirtlington Park, Oxon, or had abandoned frescoes altogether. In the late 18th century there was a brief fashion for 'landscape' rooms, intended to give the impression that the viewer was in a forest glade, of which the earliest complete surviving example (Norbury Park, Surrey) was painted by George Barret and others in 1783. Wall paintings could either be executed in oils on plaster or on huge canvases nailed to battens and attached to the wall. The staircase at Moor Park, Herts, contains decorations on canvas (*c.* 1732) by Francesco Sleter (1685–1775), while his splendid painted ceiling (*c.* 1739–40) at Mereworth Castle, Kent, was applied directly on to the plaster.

Stuccowork was a fashionable form of decoration during the first half of the 18th century. Stucco required the use of marble dust and supporting armatures, while the more traditional British method of plastering called for animal hair mixed with the plaster to give strength. Again, the most brilliant stuccoists were Italian, almost exclusively from the Ticino area of northern Italy. The two best known were Giovanni Bagutti (1681–after 1730) and Giuseppe Artari (*d* 1769), who worked principally for Vanbrugh, James Gibbs and Colen Campbell. There is some evidence from Ditchley Park, Oxon, by Gibbs that they actually supplied designs for plasterwork and did not simply execute the designs of others. Some stuccoists established a local practice, such as Giuseppe Cortese (*fl* 1725–78) and Francesco Vassalli (*fl* 1724–63) in Yorkshire, again often working to their own designs. English

plasterers were perhaps less successful in adopting the Baroque manner of the Italians, but with the rise of Palladianism and the consequent relative restraint in decoration they came into their own. By the middle of the century Thomas Roberts of Oxford and Thomas Stocking (1722–1808) of Bristol were the equal of any plasterer in the country, and by the 1770s almost no foreign plasterers were working in England.

In the 18th century there was a steady move away from a stiff and formal public way of life for the upper classes towards an intimacy and informality that was reflected in interior decoration. The thick damasks and cut velvets of the first three decades of the century were gradually replaced by lighter cottons and silks, in clothing as well as for interiors. Furniture also became lighter and less architectural, although throughout the period its arrangement continued to be formal, with chairs and tables stood against the wall, leaving the floor clear. Dining-tables were generally stored in passages or folded down until needed, and the 'cosy' arrangements around fireplaces seen in conversation pieces were strictly temporary (see fig. 40). Wallpaper became a fashionable and cheaper alternative to heavy hangings. Painted Chinese wallpaper, known as 'India' paper from its importers, the East India Company, was used in England from the late 17th century, the earliest surviving example probably being at Saltram House, Devon, which was hanging by 1720 (see fig. 41). The most common type showed exotic birds flitting through vegetation (*see* WALLPAPER, colour pl. VI; extra birds could be cut out and pasted on), but depictions of figures or activities are known also. One of the Saltram rooms shows the growing, curing and packing of tea for export. Chinese wallpaper continued to be fashionable into the early 19th century. Printed wallpapers are known from the 16th century but became common only during the 18th century (*see* WALLPAPER, colour pl. IV, fig. 1). Early in the century flock papers were fashionable, imitating the much more expensive damasks. In the 1740s John Baptist Jackson introduced oil-based colours in the place of distempers, which enabled him to achieve more intense colours, and by 1750 his factory in Battersea, London, was producing a wide range of patterns. Thirty years later the Eckhardt brothers of Chelsea—Francis, Frederick and George—were printing their patterns on to silk and linen as well as paper, allowing the integration of wall coverings and fabrics within a single room. Specialists in retailing and hanging wallpapers had emerged in the middle of the century; Thomas K. Bromwich of Ludgate Hill, London, who worked with Chippendale, was one of the best known. On walls, papers and fabric were usually applied to linen or scrim, rather than directly on to the walls. The nailheads on the battens to which the backing was attached needed to be covered, and from the 1730s braid or fillets were used. Fillets were often gilded or painted to match the predominant colours of the paper and were made of cast lead, papier mâché, composition or, most expensively, carved wood (*see* DRESS, fig. 44). With wallpapers, printed borders were used to give the same effect.

The most expensive upholstery fabrics were silk velvets and damasks. Other silk fabrics were brocade, satin, taffetas, lutestring, tabby and sarsnet, producing a wide variety of price and finish. Woollen fabrics were generally moreen, camlet, harateen, tammy and caffoy. Fabric was

41. Dressing-room with Chinese wallpaper, Saltram House, Devon, *c.* 1720

often used on walls as well as for seat furniture and curtains. As the century progressed printed cottons became increasingly popular because they were light, easily cleaned and inexpensive. Furniture upholstery was usually protected by case covers in a cheaper fabric, which were only removed on the grandest occasions. Curtains throughout the period were generally reefed or festoon, although draw curtains, first used in France in the mid-17th century, remained in use. During the 1780s festoon curtains dropped out of fashion, and by the end of the century draw curtains were almost universal. As festoon curtains blocked the light to some extent, reefed curtains were more common in rooms with lower ceilings where there was little room for the festoons to be pulled up to the 'dead light' above the window. Reefed curtains were also often used on beds, and Chippendale illustrated a number in his *Director*. Venetian or slatted blinds were not uncommon, nor were roller blinds, which were often painted with landscapes or decorative *trompe l'oeil* designs.

Bare marble floors and timber floors with small rugs were superseded in living-rooms by fitted carpets produced at Axminster, Exeter and Wilton (see §XI, 6 below). Popular alternatives were painted floors (a rare survival of *c.* 1760 is at Crowcombe Court, Somerset) or floor cloths, where designs imitating stone or inlay were painted on to canvas and sealed; this type of floor covering was in use until late in the 18th century. Inlaid floors declined in popularity as carpets became more common, although they were sometimes used on staircases. The finest staircase, dating from the 1760s, is at Claydon, inlaid with ebony, holly and ivory. Carpets were sometimes designed by architects to harmonize with specific rooms: Robert Adam had several made for his clients by the carpet factory in Moorfields, London, established by Thomas Moore (*c.* 1700–88). Syon House and Osterley Park House, both in Middlesex, and Sir Watkin Williams-Wynn's town house at 20 St James's Square in London all contained 'Persia carpets' to match the ceilings, and Raby Castle in Durham retains part of a rare 'Gothick'-style carpet of *c.* 1785, ordered to harmonize with John Carr's remodelling of the drawing-room for the 2nd Earl of Darlington.

BIBLIOGRAPHY

A. V. Sugden and J. L. Edmondson: *A History of English Wallpaper, 1509–1914* (London, 1926)

M. Jourdain: *English Interior Decoration* (London, 1950)

E. Croft-Murray: *Decorative Painting in England, 1537–1837* (London, 1962/R 1970)

J. Fowler and J. Cornforth: *English Decoration in the 18th Century* (London, 1974)

G. Beard: *Decorative Plasterwork in Great Britain* (London, 1975)

For further bibliography see §§5 and 6 below.

5. 1791–1830. This period of English design was dominated by the corpulent figure of the Prince Regent, George, Prince of Wales, later George IV. With his palace in London, Carlton House (destr.), his country retreat, the Royal Pavilion, Brighton, and the rebuilding of Buckingham Palace, London, and Windsor Castle, Berks, he led fashion as few of his predecessors had done. The period was one of transition between the formality of aristocratic 18th-century life and the increasingly bourgeois nature of the 19th-century world, as the collapse of the *ancien régime* in France and the Napoleonic Wars combined with the

Industrial Revolution to undermine the old certainties of the Age of Reason. There was a more eclectic approach to design and a greater willingness to accept the conveniences brought by improving domestic technology, including central heating, efficient water supplies, cast-iron conservatories attached to houses and even gas lighting. The domestic emphasis was increasingly on comfort. New houses were less likely to contain under-used rooms of parade, and the term 'living-room' appeared for the first time in 1812. In many smaller houses the library ceased to be the reserve of the gentlemen and was commonly used as a family room (see fig. 42). Furniture began to be moved away from the walls, and pieces were grouped together to provide different areas within a room, allowing a number of separate activities—music, talking, reading and sewing—to go on simultaneously.

Fashions in the 1790s were particularly influenced by the French Directoire style, a form of simplified Louis XVI, of which the finest surviving example (Southill, Beds, 1796–1800) was designed by Henry Holland, who also created new interiors in the same style at Carlton House (*c.* 1783–96, destr. 1827; *see* UPHOLSTERY, colour pl. XIV, fig. 2). An increasingly archaeological approach to interior decoration was encouraged by the publication of Charles Heathcote Tatham's *Etchings of Ancient Ornamental Architecture* (1799–1800), a major sourcebook based on discoveries in Pompeii, Herculaneum, Tivoli and Rome in the previous decade. Through his brother Thomas and a relation, John Linnell (i), both leading cabinetmakers, he had an important influence on furniture design; this was reinforced after 1807 following the appearance of Thomas Hope's *Household Furniture and Interior Decoration*. Hope, a wealthy connoisseur, drew extensively on Tatham's work, and his book depicts the interiors of his town house in Duchess Street, London (for illustration *see* EGYPTIAN REVIVAL), and his country seat, the Deepdene, Surrey. By allowing winged griffins to end sofas or Egyptian figures of Isis to bear clocks, he showed how the objects of ancient civilization could be copied and adapted. These two books were an influence on Napoleon's favourite architects, Charles Percier and Pierre-François-Léonard Fontaine, who were prominent in establishing the Empire style, the French equivalent of the English Regency style. This archaeological approach encouraged increasingly rich and dark effects. In paintwork, strong reds, greens and yellows were used; these are seen with particular effect in the domestically scaled interiors of John Soane's house (now Sir John Soane's Museum, London). Black was often used to imitate antique decorative patterns, and by the 1820s elaborate treatments using graining, marbling and bronzing were at the height of their popularity on furniture as well as in architectural details. Furniture also became richer and more elaborate with cabinetmakers reviving boullework and other complex surface treatments (*see* MARQUETRY, colour pl. VIII, fig. 1). Woods with rich grains such as rose-wood, amboina and calamander became popular, often with gilt mounts or carved or inlaid ornament derived from the fashionable classical vocabulary. The use of textiles also became more extravagant as the popularity of full-length and bow windows finally caused draw curtains to triumph over festoon curtains and to acquire swagged and draped pelmets (*see* UPHOLSTERY,

42. John Buckler: *Library–Drawing-room at Bromley Hill, Kent*, watercolour, 267×368 mm, 1816 (London, Guildhall Library, Print Room)

colour pl. XII), which degenerated by the 1820s into wastefulness and vulgarity. This tendency was encouraged by the publication of a number of pattern books, of which the best known were George Smith's *A Collection of Designs for Household Furniture and Decoration* (1808) and his *Cabinet-maker's and Upholsterer's Guide* (1826), which provide an interesting chart of the decline in standards. Tented rooms, possibly deriving from the fashion for matters military brought on by the Napoleonic Wars, appeared about 1800 and were much used for bedrooms and boudoirs into the 1830s.

By the 1820s there were signs of a Rococo Revival based on the Louis XV style rather than on the English version of the mid-18th century. Such rooms as the Elizabeth Saloon (*c.* 1825) at Belvoir Castle could be created using authentic French *boiseries* reset or in a straightforward revival style, as in the Waterloo Gallery (*c.* 1828) at Apsley House, London. Taste in interior decoration was increasingly eclectic from the turn of the century. An important thread running through this period was the interest in the Middle Ages and the ensuing Gothic Revival. Horace Walpole's brand of Rococo Gothic was abandoned in favour of a more archaeological, though still frequently pasteboard, approach that could sometimes be taken to extremes. The trend towards antiquarianism is shown particularly in the interiors of Fonthill Abbey (1796–1813; destr. 1825), Wilts, built to house a great collection of medieval and later furniture and *objets d'art*

acquired by William Beckford, and of Sir Samuel Rush Meyrick's Goodrich Court (1828–31; destr. 1950), Herts, which, with its collections of medieval armour and furniture, was part house and part museum.

BIBLIOGRAPHY
T. Hope: *Household Furniture and Interior Decoration* (London, 1807/*R* 1971)
Ackermann's Regency Furniture and Interiors (London, 1809–28/*R* 1984)
G. Beard: *Craftsmen and Interior Decoration in England, 1660–1820* (Edinburgh, 1981)
C. Wainwright: *The Romantic Interior: The British Collector at Home, 1750–1850* (New Haven and London, 1989)

For further bibliography *see* §6 below.

6. 1831–1900. Throughout the 19th century the trend in interior design and furnishing was towards greater privacy and comfort, with rooms decorated in a variety of styles that grew increasingly eclectic as the century wore on. At the beginning of the period the impact of the Industrial Revolution was apparent in the progressive debasement of workmanship and design as a greater range of mechanical processes were employed in the mass production of furniture and textiles. In reaction, a Gothic Revival based on archaeological research developed, with an emphasis on hand craftsmanship that in various forms, including the ARTS AND CRAFTS MOVEMENT, survived into the 20th century. In interior decoration, as in architecture, the rules of classical order established in the previous century rapidly broke down, as can be seen in the rising popularity of the Elizabethan Revival style with its combination of classical and Gothic motifs in the 1830s and 1840s, moving towards a mixed Renaissance Revival from the 1850s. The 1840s and 1850s were the years of the 'battle of styles', with the Gothic Revival architects pitted against the classicists. The Goths on the whole won the battle if not the war, and classicism, or at least a freely interpreted Italianate style, survived primarily because it was seen as more acceptable in urban contexts, where it suited the long rows of terraced houses that surrounded the rapidly expanding industrial centres. The evenhanded approach of some clients was typified by the millionaire Robert Stayner Holford, who commissioned the architect Lewis Vulliamy (1791–1871) to build both the palatially Italianate Dorchester House (1851–7; destr. 1929) in Park Lane, London, and the equally palatial neo-Elizabethan Westonbirt (1863–7) in Gloucestershire.

Developments in interior decoration were driven by the enormous social and economic changes of the 19th century. The growth of a larger and more moneyed middle class, allied to the rapid expansion of the industrial cities, generated a huge demand for furniture and decorating materials. Nine out of ten houses in England were privately rented, and rents were not particularly high. Decorating was regarded as a way of personalizing a landlord's property. In an increasingly status-conscious society, decoration was a means of indicating social position or aspirations, and the restless search for novelty also helped stimulate demand. Paralleling this change in the demands of the decorating classes was a revolution in the technology for supplying them. Methods were devised for producing more luxurious and expensive-looking goods more cheaply. In furniture, the introduction from the 1830s of machines that could cut veneers meant that valuable timbers could be sliced more thinly and therefore go further in covering cheap pine or deal carcases. Papier mâché, in use since the mid-18th century as a substitute for plaster ornaments on ceilings, was used from the 1830s as a cheap and easily moulded material for making furniture, often on an iron frame. The invention of springing in the 1820s resulted in a softer and deeper upholstery that undercut the costs of traditional stuffing. Press-moulding, introduced into the glass industry in the 1830s, allowed the mass production of glass with a handmade effect. On ceramics, the use of polychrome transfer printing (instead of the former single colours, usually blue) increased opportunities for decorative effects on cheaper tableware. Improved printing techniques meant that wallpapers, which were expensively hand-blocked until the 1830s and subject to various taxes until their repeal in 1836, dropped in price within 20 years from $1\frac{3}{4}$d. per yard to only $\frac{1}{4}$d. per yard (see WALLPAPER, colour pl. IV, fig. 2).

At the beginning of the 1830s the two most popular styles of decoration were the Elizabethan and Louis Revivals. The Elizabethan Revival was characterized by strapwork decoration (in the form of carving, inlay or crestings on panelling and furniture), barleysugar twists, bulbous legs and general references to historic sources that could date from any time between about 1580 and 1690. The Louis Revival, also known as 'tous-les-Louis', was an amalgamation of the French styles of the Louis XIV to Louis XVI periods, frequently decorated in white and gold with weighty and elaborate details (see fig. 43). It was this style in particular that such polemicists as A. W. N. Pugin condemned while advocating the 'honesty' of Gothic Revival furniture, built of solid wood with the jointed and pegged construction clearly visible. Desire for reform in design and attempts to raise standards first became apparent in the 1830s, and, as a result of a government Select Committee report in 1836, government-sponsored schools of design were established in London, Manchester, Birmingham and other industrial centres, and taxes on glass and wallpaper were repealed. The effect of the Great Exhibition of 1851 in London was to reinforce the impression that British technical achievements were as high as anywhere in Europe, but that British design was lagging far behind. Under the influence of reformers, design for the first time became a political issue with moral overtones: classicism was reviled as foreign, debased, unchristian and immoral, while the Gothic style was lauded as English, Christian and morally sound. Pugin's work at the New Palace of Westminster, together with the publication of his principles in *Contrasts: Or a Parallel between the Architecture of the 15th and 19th Centuries* (1836), was enormously influential in propagating the belief that, in line with Gothic practice, ornament should be simple, flat, geometric and, where applied to fabrics and wallpapers, two-dimensional. Ornament should also be appropriate, significant and purposeful, and where possible hand-crafted, not machine-made. In practice, this approach was only possible in the few houses built and furnished from new. The interiors of the New Palace of Westminster survive largely intact or have been restored to their original state, but no domestic interiors by Pugin remain complete with contents. Only Victorian photographs of such houses as Abney Hall (1852–7), Ches, decorated by Pugin's friend J. G. Crace, indicate how they looked. The Great Exhibition, promoted by such reformers as Henry Cole, helped stimulate interest in design still further and led to the foundation of the South Kensington Museum, later the Victoria and Albert Museum, London. Initially the museum contained a number of exhibits from the Crystal Palace (site of the exhibition), chosen as examples of good and bad design; its mission was to collect objects of the highest quality from around the world with the purpose of raising the standard of contemporary British design.

The post-Pugin Goths were less interested in the revival of the 15th-century Perpendicular Gothic used at Westminster and they turned instead to the earlier, more vigorous Gothic of the 13th century and the early 14th. A number of architects, including William Burges, William Butterfield and J. P. Seddon, were also designers for a wider market, although their more extravagant creations were for wealthy private clients. The Gothic Revival entered the mass market through the work of two architects, Charles Locke Eastlake, the author of *Hints on Household Taste* (1868), and Bruce J. Talbert, whose designs were published in *Examples of Ancient and Modern Furniture, Metalwork, Tapestry, Decoration, etc.* of 1876. As their publications reached a wider audience, the ideals of 'truthful' construction and handcraft production were compromised, and veneers, plated metalwork and machine-made tiles appeared on their furniture. Talbert was employed as a designer by the two London furniture-making firms of Holland & Sons and Gillow's, and by the late 1860s mass-produced Gothic designs had achieved considerable popularity. The foundation in 1861 of the firm that became known as Morris & Co. provided an alternative to the mainstream styles in British interior design. Dissatisfied with what was available commercially when seeking to decorate his own house in 1860, WILLIAM MORRIS sought to make artistic furnishings available to all classes of society. Although he employed such artists as Edward Burne-Jones and Philip Webb to design products for the firm, Morris himself was responsible for a vast range of stained glass, furniture, embroideries and fabrics, tiles and ceramics produced by Morris & Co (see DYE, colour pl. IV, fig. 2 and TAPESTRY, colour pl. III, fig. 2). The keynote was simplicity of form combined with rich colours and patterns.

From the 1850s onwards design elements from other cultures became increasingly important, and the publication in 1856 of *The Grammar of Ornament* by Owen Jones provided a rich sourcebook for polychromatic decoration drawn from ancient Egypt, Greece and Rome, Islam, the Orient and elsewhere. One of the more extravagant interiors is the Arab Hall (1877–9) added by the architect George Aitchison to the house in Holland Park, London, of Frederic Leighton, President of the Royal Academy. It was, however, the influence of the Far East and particularly Japan that had a profound effect on British interiors over the next two decades, the period of the AESTHETIC MOVEMENT. Japanese textiles, ceramics and prints began to arrive in Europe after the signing of the Treaty of Edo in 1858, which ended two centuries of Japanese isolation from social and commercial contact with the West. The International Exhibition of 1862 in London was a landmark in the widespread dissemination of Japanese influence, and soon oriental fans, birds, bamboo and other exotic motifs were added to the Gothic and Renaissance design vocabulary. When handled sensitively, Aesthetic interiors could be very revolutionary (see fig. 44). E. W. Godwin and W. E. Nesfield were both Gothic Revival architects whose work after the 1860s was significantly influenced by Japan. The catalogue of the Art Furniture Warehouse, founded by Godwin in 1867, was a manifesto for the new style as well as a useful source for other manufacturers to copy. Furniture, often stained black or green, tended to be spindly, with incised gilt decoration and turned elements that were inexpensive to produce. Oriental motifs were freely applied, and interiors often displayed Japanese vases (or copies of them), peacock feathers and muted colours. The harsh colours produced by the aniline dyes of the 1850s and 1860s gave way to softer, more natural greys and greens in paintwork

43. Library at Wrest Park, Bedfordshire, from a watercolour by Thomas Scandrett, *c.* 1835 (Collection of Lady Lucas)

44. Dining-room of the artist Linley Sambourne, 18 Stafford Terrace, London, c. 1875

and textiles. Aesthetic interiors, which were closely associated with the Queen Anne Revival in architecture, were
popular in many middle- and upper-class homes as a
reaction against the gloomy solidity of the previous
generation. One of the most notable expressions of the
new style was *Harmony in Blue and Gold: The Peacock
Room*, created for the London house of F. R. Leyland.
Originally commissioned from Thomas Jeckyll, the room
was sumptuously painted with blue and gold peacocks by
James McNeill Whistler in 1876 (partially re-installed;
Washington, DC, Freer). Founded by ARTHUR LASENBY
LIBERTY in 1875, Liberty's initially specialized in the
import of Oriental goods, expanding after 1883 to sell a
wider range of Aesthetic furnishings. The art fabrics
commissioned by Liberty's from such designers as Walter
Crane and Arthur Silver achieved a lasting popularity.
Another prominent designer and a product of one of the
government schools of design was Christopher Dresser,
who established himself in 1862 with his book *The Art of
Decorative Design* and later worked for a number of firms
with products ranging from silverware to wallpaper and
ceramics. Although the Aesthetic Movement lasted only
for 20 years or so, it raised the standard of public taste
and established the idea that the domestic interior could
be a work of art.

By the 1880s a revival of 18th-century fashions was
becoming apparent, and versions of the 'Adam' style were
introduced, based loosely on Neo-classical designs made
popular by Robert Adam and James Adam 100 years
earlier. At the same time the Arts and Crafts Movement
drew again on Gothic forms, much modified by the taste
of the decades intervening since Pugin's death. As a result
of the Aesthetic aversion to commercial novelties, it
became more common to furnish houses with antiques.
The introduction of electric light into domestic interiors
accelerated a trend towards lighter and simpler interiors,
as the increased light levels did not suit rich, and dust-
catching, decorations. The Arts and Crafts Movement
evolved a 'cottage style' as practised by M. H. Baillie Scott,
C. F. A. Voysey and W. R. Lethaby, among others. This
formed part of the English domestic revival lauded by
such foreigners as Hermann Muthesius and subsequently
described in his *Das englische Haus* (Berlin, 1904–6). At
the end of the century, continental experiments with the
vegetative forms of Art Nouveau attracted a small following, although British designers were never as enthusiastic
as their European contemporaries.

BIBLIOGRAPHY
C. L. Eastlake: *Hints on Household Taste* (London, 1868)
B. J. Talbert: *Examples of Ancient and Modern Furniture, Metalwork,
    Tapestry, Decoration, etc.* (London, 1876)
R. W. Edis: *Decoration and Furniture of the Town House* (London, 1881)
E. A. Entwisle: *The Book of Wallpaper* (Bath, 1970)
N. Cooper: *The Opulent Eye: Late Victorian and Edwardian Taste in
    Interior Design* (London, 1976)

M. Girouard: *Sweetness and Light: The 'Queen Anne' Movement, 1860–1900* (New Haven and London, 1977)

J. Cornforth: *English Interiors, 1790–1848: The Quest for Comfort* (London, 1978)

M. Girouard: *The Victorian Country House* (London, 1979)

P. Thornton: *Authentic Decor: The Domestic Interior, 1620–1920* (London, 1985)

C. Gere: *Nineteenth Century Decoration: The Art of the Interior* (London, 1989)

J. Banham and others: *Victorian Interior Design* (London, 1991)

CHARLES WHEELTON HIND

7. AFTER 1900. The Arts and Crafts aesthetic continued to exert a predominant influence in England until well after World War I. As at the Orchard, Chorleywood, Herts, completed in 1900 by C. F. A. Voysey, whitewashed walls, low-beamed ceilings, seating fitted into window bays and inglenooks around fireplaces and wooden doors and window-frames enhanced by decorative metalwork all continued to evoke the traditional English cottage. Heal & Son manufactured furniture in the vernacular style to furnish such interiors, in which electricity and other modern services were discreetly incorporated. The Omega Workshops, a collaboration between artists Roger Fry, Duncan Grant and Vanessa Bell that lasted from 1913 until 1921, attempted to reconcile the handcraft ideal with commercial reality. In 1925 the fashionable decorator Basil Ionides (1884–1950) chose to treat his weekend retreat at White Hall, Howbridge, near Witham in Essex, in the Arts and Crafts manner. Many of the mid-century designers, such as Gordon Russell and Oliver Hill, were also schooled in this tradition. This 'Old English' rural style reached a wider audience in the housing developments built to provide functional and healthy dwellings for the working and suburban classes. The designs of M. H. Baillie Scott won the Letchworth Garden City Cheap Cottages competition in 1905, and the style continued to be used in Garden City schemes after World War I. Associated with the extension of railway and underground networks, these 'Metroland' ribbon developments were characterized by asymmetrical mock Tudor elevations with projecting gables and diamond-paned windows that often contained stained glass. Interiors boasted natural materials and featured brick or glazed-tiled fireplaces. Woodwork, however, was painted glossy chocolate brown, and linoleum in imitation of marble, tiles or parquet covered the floor. Patterns of both jazzy geometric shapes and naturalistic floral motifs in primary colours appeared on carpet squares, frilled curtains and on the upholstery of deeply sprung furniture. The living-room might also have had a walnut-veneered gramophone or a wireless in a bakelite case with a sunburst motif over the sound box. Consumers obtained decorating advice from a variety of sources. Sponsored by the national newspaper *The Daily Mail*, the first Ideal Home exhibition was held at Olympia in London in 1908, and the magazine of the same name was launched in 1920.

German Modernism and French Art Deco of the inter-war years were not immediately popular in England. It was largely due to manufacturers and retailers in collaboration with progressive designers, many of whom came to England during the early 1930s to escape persecution in Europe, that stylistic innovation reached mainstream taste. In 1928 Waring & Gillow appointed Serge Chermayeff

Director of Design in their Modern Art department, assisted by Paul Follot. The first English steel-framed furniture was marketed in the 1930s: items shown by the Birmingham-based company Practical Equipment Ltd (PEL) at the 1931 Ideal Home exhibition were well-received. During the early 1930s, annual exhibitions of applied arts at Dorland Hall, Bayswater, prompted the work of progressive designers such as Oliver Hill, Serge Chermayeff, Wells Coates and Raymond McGrath, featuring chrome, glass and mirror, as well as schemes for interiors by such painters as Rex Whistler. English taste, however, was more receptive to modern forms in traditional materials as exemplified by contemporary Scandinavian design. Pieces in plywood manufactured by The Makers of Simple Furniture to designs by Gerald Summers (1899–1967), during the early 1930s, reflected the influence of Alvar Aalto.

During the inter-war years interior decoration became a profession for society figures. Syrie Maugham (1879–1955) was noted for her all-white interiors that featured rectilinear forms and reflective surfaces combined with sculptured-pile carpets and deeply upholstered sofas with numerous cushions. Betty Joel (1896–1985) was another decorator who had business premises in Knightsbridge, London. The photographer Cecil Beaton invented settings of extravagant theatricality, while the painter Paul Nash created Surrealist schemes through the incongruous juxtaposition of disparate elements. Sibyl, Lady Colefax (1874–1950), who opened a business in 1933, advised the owners of stately homes on creating environments in which period antiques could be integrated sympathetically with the requirements of modern life. Decorative paint effects simulating marble or fabric were in vogue, as were murals by contemporary artists.

After World War II the country-house look was applied in both rural and urban contexts. Interiors created by Lady Colefax with the assistance of the decorative painter John Fowler (1906–77; incorporated as Colefax & Fowler in 1945) epitomized a style in which colour, texture and ornament were carefully combined to create an impression of natural and ageless comfort. Characteristic features included glazed chintzes with floral patterns contrasting with checked fabrics, in combination with 18th-century 'Gothick' or chinoiserie elements (see fig. 45). Typical colour schemes consisted of clear yellows, blues, pinks and apricots with natural greens. Antique furniture was often the key feature, and increasing importance was attached to period authenticity. From 1956 Fowler was consulted on the treatment of historic interiors by the National Trust. The close association between the professions of interior decorator and antique dealer dates from this period, as London assumed a leading position in the auction-house world. Beautifully photographed country-house interiors appeared regularly in such magazines as *Country Life* (founded 1897), *House and Garden* (1947–) and *World of Interiors* (1981–), reflecting the continuing popularity of this traditional style.

The only new furnishings available during and immediately after World War II were those produced under the strictly controlled Utility Scheme under the authority of the Board of Trade. Although Utility furniture appeared drab to some, the principles of sound construction and

45. Interior of the Hunting Lodge, Odiham, Hampshire, by John Fowler; from a watercolour by Alexander Serebriakoff, c. 1948 (London, private collection)

simplified form determined by the design consultant Gordon Russell ensured a basic standard of quality. With the Festival of Britain in 1951 marking the end of wartime austerity, the development of an innovative contemporary style was strongly influenced by Scandinavian and American modern design. The open-plan living area was widely adopted in England, often with the television set replacing the traditional hearth as a focal point. Wallpapers, frequently with patterns derived from such self-consciously modern sources as chemical diagrams, were a distinctive feature. Furniture of such modern materials as chromed tubular steel, plywood, plastic and glass was arranged informally, and 'found' objects in seemingly random 'tablescape' arrangements served as ornaments. Furniture design was characterized by thin structural elements complemented by 'free form' shapes, as seen in the steel legs and moulded plywood seat of the 'Antelope' chair by Ernest Race. The streamlined look suggested a concern for efficiency in the design of domestic household objects and interiors, particularly with regard to bathrooms and fitted kitchens. Other designers were inspired by the classic forms and bold colours of the Regency period. The interiors of David Hicks combined areas of bold, unbroken colour with patterns of geometric motifs; his style was quickly imitated in commercial design in the 1950s and 1960s.

During the 1950s manufacturers and retailers attempted to address the needs of an expanding consumer market by developing the Do-It-Yourself (D.I.Y.) concept initiated in the USA. The direct marketing of coordinated furnishings was epitomized by Arthur Sanderson & Sons Ltd, whose ranges of wallpapers and fabrics were displayed from 1960 in purpose-built showrooms and who became retailers in 1975. Home decoration was also catered for by D.I.Y. Homebase centres opened by major retailers after 1972, following the lead of the Texas chain.

Interiors of the last 40 years of the 20th century reflected increasingly varied lifestyles and greater freedom of individual expression. During the 'Swinging Sixties' English Pop culture centred on London and achieved the status of an international phenomenon. 'Throw away' paper furniture and inflatable or water-filled plastic furniture in amorphous shapes and psychedelic colours expressed an attitude of rebellion towards traditional styles and values. Alternatively, the fashion for sprigged floral prints, pastel colours and stripped pine, popularized from the mid-1950s by Laura Ashley (1925–85), is an up-to-date version of the country cottage look with overtones of ecological concern. Terence Conran's Habitat shops and mail-order service, inaugurated in 1964, offered a choice of coordinated solutions for interiors, from re-issued 1930s and contemporary Italian designs to ethnic imports from non-European cultures. Progressive interiors of the 1970s made use of the industrial materials, functional mass-produced items and the palette of tertiary tones or strong primary colours found in the High-Tech architecture of Norman Foster, James Stirling and Richard Rogers. This minimalist style was countered by a craft revival and an increasing importance given to historic preservation. Historicist conceits in interiors by Charles Jenks (b 1939), for example in his own Holland Park house, exemplify the Post-modernist trend of the 1980s in interiors in England.

BIBLIOGRAPHY
P. Garner: *Twentieth Century Furniture* (Oxford, 1980)
S. Calloway: *Twentieth Century Decoration* (London, 1988)
A. Massey: *Interior Design of the 20th Century* (London, 1990)

CLAIRE BRISBY

VI. Furniture.

1. Before 1450. 2. 1450–*c.* 1660. 3. *c.* 1660–1720. 4. 1721–80. 5. 1781–1830. 6. 1831–1900. 7. After 1900.

1. BEFORE 1450. The quantity of medieval English furniture that survives is small and unrepresentative. The only item available in sufficient quantity to be able to judge its development and variety is the chest. No medieval beds exist at all. Most extant furniture of the period is found as the furnishings of cathedrals and churches, but there is no evidence to suggest that furniture made for ecclesiastical patrons differed markedly from that made for secular settings. Almost all surviving furniture is constructed in oak, evidence of the popularity and endurance of this timber, though other woods of a less durable nature must have been used extensively. Because of the paucity of examples, the historian of medieval furniture must rely on illustrative and documentary sources. Most of the illustrations of interiors and furniture that survive are of French or Netherlandish origin. This does not invalidate such sources as there were close contacts between England and both of these regions. Such documentary evidence as inventories, though of immense value, can mislead as they can omit significant items of medieval furnishings and can give the impression of cold, bare and sparsely furnished interiors, which may not have been the case (*see* §V, 1 above). Surviving furniture, illustrations and documents are likely to be of late medieval date, and for earlier periods much uncertainty exists.

The main influence on English furniture design and decoration before *c.* 1200 was from Romanesque architecture and art. An armchair of turned construction (*c.* 1200) in Hereford Cathedral incorporates Romanesque arcading below the seat at the front and was intended as a seat for a person of authority. Gothic influence followed and is evident in all but the very simplest of surviving furniture. The contacts between England and the Continent in the Middle Ages were close; the long period of warfare with France in the 14th and 15th centuries cemented an alliance with the Dukedom of Burgundy, which included much of the Low Countries, and the brilliance of its Valois court and its patronage of the arts would have fundamentally affected the taste of the English court and richer citizens at large. The cloth trade would have reinforced this cultural interchange.

The survival of the chest in sufficient quantity to enable a study of the progression in craft skills both in construction and decoration is a testimony to the usefulness and sturdiness of this item of furniture. The crudest form of chest that exists is merely a log, roughly squared, hollowed out and provided with a lid. Examples exist in a number of English churches, including Wimborne Minster, Dorset, Milton Bryan, Beds, Somersham and Wistow, Cambs, and Orton, Cumbria. Their general ruggedness provides little guide to age. Another early development was the chest of boarded construction using broad, oak planks, the large flat surfaces providing space for decoration in the form of carving or for the application of decorative ironwork. Both plain and carved chests might be painted. Such chests often have vertical stiles at the corners: these extend down below the base to provide legs, keeping the bottom of the chest off the ground. Typical of such chests are an example decorated with Gothic arcading (see fig. 46) at St Mary's

46. Oak chest with Gothic arcading, 0.64×2.00 m, from St Mary's, Climping, West Sussex, *c.* 1280–1300; engraving by Henry Shaw from his *Specimens of Ancient Furniture* (London, 1836), pl. xxix

Climping, W. Sussex, and one decorated with iron straps at Merton College, Oxford, both dating from c. 1280–1300. Chests of simple construction were liable to damage because of timber warpage or splitting, and by the beginning of the 15th century the more sophisticated frame and panel construction was in evidence in chests and other items of furniture.

For larger-scale storage, armoires were made, either free-standing or built-in, such as the four incorporated below the Watching Loft at St Alban's Abbey (1413–29) and a splendid series in the Zouche Chapel at York Minster of c. 1400. Tables of various sizes and for different functions existed, some with fixed tops and others consisting of boarded tops supported on trestles, such as those in the Hall of Penshurst Place, Kent, with elm board tops, 8.1 m long, supported on cruciform pillar supports and thought to be late 15th century in date. Examples of seating furniture are few, but evidence suggests that they range from impressive seats of authority, such as the Coronation Chair (1299–1301) of Edward I in Westminster Abbey (see THRONE, fig. 4), to simple turned stools or boarded chairs, such as that at St James, Stanford Bishop, Hereford & Worcs, which is believed to be 12th century or earlier. Although the most important patrons of furniture-makers were the court, the feudal nobility and the Church, the growing middle class commissioned furniture, and it was not entirely missing from the homes of the peasantry (although no examples survive). Worcestershire court rolls dated between 1346 and 1434 contain inventories of house contents made on the change of agricultural tenancies: these mention tables, chests, stools and 'standes' among other house furnishings.

In the households of the wealthy, wooden furniture was of low value compared with such items as fabrics and plate, which were much more prestigious. In the Middle Ages families of importance often moved from estate to estate, leaving manor houses largely unoccupied for long periods. Also, certain parts of houses, such as the hall, were open to public access. For these reasons furniture and furnishings had to be of one of two types—either light and portable, if valuable, so that security could be provided, or built-in or heavy in order to frustrate theft. Heavy furniture of simple form could be transformed by being covered with rich fabrics, often imported, which could at other times be kept locked in the wardrobe. Plate could be displayed on tables and cupboards (buffets), the wood similarly covered with fabrics. There is evidence that bedclothes and hangings were not placed on beds until immediately before use. Rich furnishing materials, tapestries and plate were the means by which status or estate was indicated; no man was judged by the quality of his timber furniture. On formal occasions the estate of an important person could be indicated by the provision of a canopy above his seat with a cloth of estate behind. At a feast he would be seated centrally behind the table on a raised dais at the end of the hall. Beds also denoted status, through the richness of the fabrics used and the form of the bed itself. A bed for a person of importance would have a canopy above, curtains and a coverlet. For persons of lesser importance beds with half canopies might be provided. In the household of Sir John Fastolf at Caister Castle, Norfolk, in the mid-15th century, beds with testers and hangings were confined to the owner and family and senior officers of the household. Those of yeoman status and servants had beds without hangings. Carpets beside a bed were another indication of status. On formal occasions chairs, especially those of X-frame design, implied status, and people of lesser social distinction sat on benches or stools. Outside this formal context, chairs were not uncommon, and simpler examples might be found in the houses of the middle classes or even artisans and peasants.

A number of craft guilds were involved in the manufacture of furniture. The earliest craft involved in furniture-making was carpentry; the guild of carpenters in London can be traced back to 1333. Although the members of this guild were mainly involved in the structural woodwork of buildings, they manufactured furniture of boarded construction, including the built-in furniture that would be needed in new structures. They were to a degree eclipsed when late in the 14th century the new and more sophisticated techniques associated with frame and panel construction were introduced from the Continent. A joiners' guild existed in London in 1373 and was given the right to elect wardens and granted powers of search in 1400. In York a guild of joiners existed in 1413. Turning as a craft was practised at an early date and was certainly being employed in London by the beginning of the 14th century. Chair production, as well as the manufacture of a wide range of such household equipment as buckets and bowls, was closely associated with the guild of turners. Coffer-makers producing chests, especially those used for travelling and covered in leather (trussing coffers and standards), are first mentioned in London in 1328. Although London upholders (upholsterers) had obtained an ordinance as early as 1360 recognizing their independence as a separate trade, they did not at this early date have much association with furniture manufacture. Their main role in the Middle Ages appears to have been the sale by auction or retail of second-hand goods.

For bibliography see §2 below.

BRIAN AUSTEN

2. 1450–c. 1660. As in the years before 1450, wooden furniture remained less highly prized than such portable items as plate or textiles. Contemporary wills and inventories describe in detail the silver that was displayed on a buffet and the textile hangings of a bed, and give their worth, while scant reference is made to the wooden structures supporting them. By the 16th century the peripatetic nature of medieval society meant those wealthy enough to own properties and have interests in several places were likely to move entire households around with them. Huge quantities of luggage were taken on these progresses, not only personal belongings but textile hangings, plate and valued household furnishings, which were displayed to indicate their owners' estate in each new setting. Only a bare minimum of immovable furniture was left behind. By the 16th century a more settled way of life was emerging; nonetheless, Elizabeth I set forth on a progress through her realm each summer. She was received by William Cecil, 1st Baron Burghley, at Theobalds Place, Herts, and Sir Christopher Hatton at Holdenby House, Northants, great houses built during her reign in expectation of a royal visit. Despite the preparations that had

47. Sea-dog or Chimera table, walnut, with supports based on a design by Jacques Androuet Du Cerceau (i), 0.85×1.47×0.85 mm, late 16th century (Hardwick Hall, Derbys, NT)

been made, she took with her a quantity of belongings, including household furnishings.

Occasional items of display furniture, comparable to plate and textiles, are referred to from an early date. The X-frame chair was a symbol of estate throughout the Middle Ages, a tradition dating back to the *sella curulis* of the Roman magistrate (*see* CHAIR, §1). Medieval examples were often made from or ornamented with precious materials: reference is made in an inventory of the Duchess of Suffolk's possessions taken in 1466 to 'a chaire of tymbre of astate covered wt blue cloth of gold and panells of copper' and 'a case of lether thereto'. Examples dating from the 1550s survive at York Minster and Winchester Cathedral. Such display furniture gradually became more common, especially at the highest level of society. In 1598 the traveller Paul Hentzner was impressed by the royal beds, silver cabinets and jewel chests he saw at the Palace of Whitehall, London. At Hardwick Hall, Derbys, built for Elizabeth Talbot, Countess of Shrewsbury (*see* TALBOT, (1)), between 1590 and 1597, a few elaborate items of furniture can still be identified from an inventory taken in 1601. Among these is the Sea-dog or Chimera table (see fig. 47), the supports of which were based on a design by Jacques Androuet Du Cerceau (i). The inventory makes clear that even at this date textiles in the form of cushions, table-covers and wall hangings remained the most highly prized elements in fashionable interiors.

In the Elizabethan period there was a great increase in the wealth of the country, which was reflected in a boost in building. This in turn led to a new demand for furniture, even at a comparatively humble level. The best-known piece of furniture to survive from this time, the Great Bed of Ware (see fig. 48), was apparently made about 1590, its enormous size intended to draw custom to a posting inn. The fine carving and inlaid decoration would originally have been almost hidden beneath hangings.

The craft of the joiner, as distinct from that of the carpenter, was by the late 15th century well established in England. Instead of constructing furniture from riven planks held together by wooden pegs or wrought-iron nails, thinner panels of sawn wood were dropped into frames united by mortice and tenon joints. Furniture of frame and panel construction was lighter and less likely to warp; it was suitable for chests, settles, cupboards and some kinds of chair.

The wood most frequently used for furniture-making during this period was oak, due to its strength and ready availability, followed by elm, ash and walnut. However, exotic woods were being imported in increasing quantities: cypress and cedar, for instance, were favoured for chests that were to be used for storing textiles, since these woods were believed to have moth-repellant qualities. Carving was a popular form of decoration, as were scrolling wrought-ironwork and painting. The latter two forms of ornament seem to have fallen from favour in the 16th century, when the technique of inlaying was adopted, as found on the Great Bed of Ware. Ash, holly, sycamore, ebony, bog oak and fruit-wood were among the woods that were set into a carcase of oak or walnut, and ivory, mother-of-pearl and marble were also used. Examples of intarsia work, in which the materials are built up into a mosaic, are to be found in a group of chests inlaid with architectural designs that in the 19th century became known as 'Nonsuch' chests because of a supposed resemblance to Henry VIII's palace (destr.) of that name. An outstanding example of this type of chest, probably made for the merchant Hugh Offley in 1588, may be seen in Southwark Cathedral, London. They are closely related to chests made in south Germany, and many of them may have been directly imported from there or made by immigrant craftsmen working in Southwark, where they were outside the jurisdiction of the City of London guilds.

Chests and coffers were still the principal items of furniture used for storage. (The modern distinction between the two is that a chest has a flat lid, while a coffer, usually covered in leather, has a domed lid to throw off rain when travelling.) Chests often owe their survival to the fact that they remained in the same place, frequently being used to store records and other valuables, for long periods. Chests with drawers are mentioned in inventories of the late 16th century; at first the drawers were of simple nailed construction, but it was not long before crude dovetails were being used. By about 1650 chests-of-drawers had appeared, usually with doors enclosing the drawers and a box compartment at the top. The original 'cupboard', or buffet, has a shelved structure used for the display of plate and the ceremonial service of food and drink. It was draped with textiles when in use, and precious objects were displayed on it, their number and the number of tiers suggesting the rank of the owner. The court cupboard developed from the buffet and sometimes had a lower portion enclosed by doors. The armoire, a simple shelved or unshelved storage space enclosed by doors, became the modern cupboard.

Trestle tables, which could be stored away when not in use, were gradually replaced with tables on fixed frames, which were left in their permanent position. These were supplemented by tables with folding tops (which had

48. The Great Bed of Ware, oak with carved and inlaid decoration and traces of pigment, 2.67×3.35×3.35 m, c. 1590 (London, Victoria and Albert Museum)

appeared by the beginning of the 16th century), draw-tables with extending leaves (by the middle of the century) and the gate-leg type with two hinged flaps (by about 1600). Table-legs, bedposts, 'thrown' chairs (some of extremely intricate design), small vessels and some types of ornament were produced by turners on a lathe. Lathes continued to be used throughout the medieval period, but the Turners' Company was not incorporated in the City of London until after 1604. Guild regulations in some towns let a craftsman work as turner and joiner as well as carpenter (in York, for instance, the Joiners' and Turners' Companies were amalgamated in 1530, and in 1563 they were joined by carvers, sawyers and workers in various other trades). In London, however, attempts were made to keep the trades separate, the Court of Aldermen seeking to assign specific categories of furniture to specific trades as late as the 1630s as a result of disputes between joiners, turners and carpenters.

The Upholders' Company is mentioned in the records of the Carpenters' Company in London in 1549. Upholders, or upholsterers, were involved in the manufacture of bedding, particularly mattresses and bolsters, and increasingly with the production of furniture. Sir John Fastolf's inventory of about 1460 lists 'Pillowes of Grene silk' and 'A cover of Grene silke to a bedde lined with blue silk', while Henry VIII's inventory of 1547 mentions various velvet-embroidered beds. The development of upholstered seating was a new feature, and lavishly upholstered X-frame chairs were made throughout the period. In the royal inventory reference is also made to upholstered chairs and stools covered in rich materials with fringes of silk and gold thread. Around 1596 Sir John Harrington wrote of 'easy quilted and lyned formes and stools', commenting that plain wainscot stools were 'so hard that since great breeches were layd aside, men can skant endewr to sit upon them'. A simple form of upholstered furniture was covered in Turkey work, an English imitation of the knotted-pile carpets being imported from Turkey.

On the whole, in furniture as in architecture, the English were slow to assimilate Renaissance ideas, and Late Gothic carved details remained popular until the mid-16th century. Continental influence was for the most part confined to decorative motifs, such as romayne work (loosely based on Classical medallions), acanthus foliage and strapwork, and the bulbous cup-and-cover uprights used for table-legs and bed-posts. Geographical proximity, the ties of Protestantism and the trade in wool between the two countries meant that Flemish influences were strong, as is

49. X-frame chair of state and stool, beech, upholstered in purple velvet with silk fringes, 1270×889×686 mm (chair), 368×551×501 mm (stool), mid-17th century (London, Victoria and Albert Museum)

evident from the comparison of surviving pieces of furniture with the engravings of Cornelis Floris, Hans Vredeman de Vries and Cornelis Bos among others. In the early 17th century there was an influx of more sophisticated ideas from France and Italy, centring round the court, where artists of the stature of Inigo Jones, Peter Paul Rubens, Francesco Fanelli, Francis Cleyn and Isaac de Caus were employed under James I and Charles I. Some idea of the splendid and sophisticated furnishings of this era can still be glimpsed at such houses as Knole, Kent, Ham House, Surrey, Wilton House, Wilts, and the Queen's House at Greenwich, London. An X-frame chair of state and a stool (see fig. 49) that belonged to Archbishop William Juxon (1582–1663) exemplify the luxurious upholstered furniture produced for court circles. A painted and gilded set of chairs (London, V&A; Birmingham, Mus. & A.G.) from Holland House, London, where Cleyn worked, clearly derives from the Italian *sgabello*, indicating a knowledge of Renaissance design. The Civil War (1642–51) and the Commonwealth (1649–60) were times of austerity traditionally exemplified by a very plain type of leather-upholstered 'Cromwellian' chair. It seems likely, however, that more highly decorated pieces of furniture also continued to be made, although documentary evidence is lacking.

BIBLIOGRAPHY
E. Mercer: *Furniture, 700–1700* (London, 1969)
L. Boynton: 'The Hardwick Hall Inventory of 1601', *Furn. Hist.*, vii (1971), pp. 1–40
B. M. Forman: 'Continental Furniture Craftsmen in London, 1511–1625', *Furn. Hist.*, vii (1971), pp. 94–120
S. Jervis: *Printed Furniture Designs before 1650* (London, 1974)
P. Eames: 'Furniture in England, France and the Netherlands from the Twelfth to the Fifteenth Century', *Furn. Hist.*, xiii (1977) [whole issue]
V. Chinnery: *Oak Furniture: The British Tradition* (Woodbridge, 1979)
G. Beard: *The National Trust Book of English Furniture* (London, 1985)
C. Graham: *Ceremonial and Commemorative Chairs in Great Britain* (London, 1994)

CLARE GRAHAM

3. *c*. 1660–1720. In this period English furniture developed to a state where it could compare favourably with what was being produced in the Netherlands and France; by 1715 Elizabeth Charlotte of Orléans, a niece of Louis XIV, was forced to concede, 'One can no longer send such fashions because the English have their own, which are followed here now.' The cabinetmaker's skill came to the fore, and it was increasingly to such a tradesman, particularly if he was London-based, that the property-owner turned when he wished to refurbish his house, rather than to the craftsman in his locality. Previously the craftsman had provided everything from joint-stools to farm woodwork, with little opportunity for specialization, but gradually he was supplanted by the London cabinetmaker, who could provide the latest fashions for those who could afford it. In the provinces, meanwhile, sturdy oak pieces reflecting regional styles continued to be made for farmhouses and cottages. A number of factors helped English furniture to flourish; expanding trade, particularly in East Asia, and rising prosperity certainly played their part. Two events can be singled out as contributory factors: the Restoration of the English monarchy in 1660 and the Revocation of the Edict of Nantes in 1685, which resulted in an influx of Huguenot craftsmen, particularly after the 'Glorious Revolution' of 1688. Charles II endured an exile of ten years in France and the Netherlands, and both he and his followers acquired a taste for the fashions of these countries. His return brought about what John Evelyn called 'a politer way of living', even if it gave way to 'intolerable expense', doubtless aided by the vulgar tastes of his courtiers and mistresses.

Certain characteristics associated with the early part of this period in fact preceded the Restoration. Walnut now became the most popular wood for veneer or joinery (although furniture made in this timber is to be found in the inventories of Henry VIII). Lacquered and japanned cabinets became very fashionable in Charles II's reign, furnishing the apartments of courtiers and houses of merchants, judging from entries in Evelyn's diaries, and in 1688 John Stalker and George Parker published *A Treatise of Japanning and Varnishing* for those trying to produce imitations of the costly Eastern originals; these cabinets had, however, appeared in England as early as 1614, being listed in the inventory of the 1st Earl of Northampton's London house. The gateleg-table had appeared at the beginning of the 17th century, as a convenient object that could be used for dining in any room and then be folded up when not wanted, but by Charles II's reign it prevailed over the more bulky draw-table. Inlay, brought to high levels in marquetry cabinets and tables by such craftsmen as Gerrit Jensen (see below) and Cornelius Gole (*fl c*. 1689–91), had been used in the 16th century for the architectural views on 'Nonsuch' chests (*see also* MARQUETRY, fig. 2). There is evidence that the Commonwealth was not as philistine and barren a period as has sometimes been assumed. There can be no doubt, however, that the Restoration added a great impetus to developments already under way and helped bring about as great a change in the decorative arts as in architecture.

Houses became more richly furnished, comfort was more sought after and pieces of furniture took on more specialist functions. There developed tall-front scriptors, at which one could write at greater ease and in which one could conceal documents, and cabinets in which collections of curiosities could be stored. The elaborate decoration, often in marquetry or inlay of king-wood and amboina with silver mounts, indicates the great value of these pieces. Not only did gateleg-tables become popular but also tea-tables, mostly imported from East Asia until the beginning of the next century, and toilet-tables. Chairs became more generously upholstered, even if the techniques were somewhat primitive compared with those that developed later, and in the late 17th century much attention was paid to fringes. Sleeping-chairs, with adjustable backs and closed in at the sides to exclude draughts, became fashionable. John Paudevin (*fl* 1677–88) supplied a number for the queen, Catherine of Braganza, and it has been suggested that he also made the surviving examples at Ham House, Surrey (see fig. 50). Cane, a simple innovation introduced in England in 1664, proved to be more comfortable than wooden seats and backs, and seat furniture of this type remained popular well into the 18th

50. Sleeping-chair with original upholstery, h. 1.4 m, attributed to John Paudevin, made for Ham House, Surrey, mid-1670s (London, Victoria and Albert Museum)

century. Innovations in horology resulted in the popularity of the bracket and longcase clock—a fashionable device whose precision exercised endless fascination in owners, mathematicians and, not least, Charles II himself (*see* CLOCKS AND WATCHES, fig. 5).

There survive invoices for upholstery for Charles II from his restoration onwards, but no pieces can be identified with certainty. John Casbert (*fl* 1660–76) provided seating and canopies of state for Whitehall Palace, London, Windsor Castle, Berks, and Somerset House, London, between 1660 and 1676, and John Whitby (*fl* 1660–67) supplied '18 French Chair frames' and a large bedstead in 1661. There survives an animated petition from Robert Morris (*fl* 1660–70) of that year for his account to be settled following the supply of extensive furnishing for the King and his mother, Queen Henrietta Maria, and 75 chairs of Turkey work for the House of Commons, London. Perhaps the leading cabinetmaker of this period was GERRIT JENSEN, a man of obscure but probably Flemish or Dutch origin, greatly influenced by Pierre Gole. His activity spanned from 1680, when he is recorded as making a set of furniture for the Emperor of Morocco, until his death in 1715. Not only was he patronized by royalty but also by the aristocracy. There are records of his working as far afield as Hamilton Palace, Lanarks, Boughton House, Northants, Petworth House, W. Sussex, and Knole, Kent, where his famous suite of silver furniture remains *in situ*. Fortunately, a few documented pieces have survived: a glass-fronted cabinet and marquetry table at Kensington Palace, London, a pier-glass with a royal cypher and crown in blue glass at Hampton Court Palace, London, a pair of *verre églomisé* glasses for the 6th Duke of Somerset at Petworth and a fine pair of metal inlaid cabinets at Boughton. His great contemporary was Thomas Roberts (*fl* 1685; *d* 1714), who was perhaps the leading joiner, providing seating, screens and state beds for royalty and the aristocracy. Roberts's work shows an abundance of putti and flowers, carved in fine detail, and in the Venetian Ambassador's Room at Knole there survives the famous suite of matching chairs and stools made for James II shortly before he fled to France in 1688. Roberts also made Queen Anne's coronation throne, acquired as a perquisite by the 5th Earl of Salisbury and now at Hatfield House, Herts. Contemporary descriptions of the highly ornate bed that he made for the Great Bed Chamber at Windsor Castle strongly suggest the influence of Daniel Marot I (*see* MAROT, (2)), who worked sporadically in England after he was exiled from France by the Revocation of the Edict of Nantes. Marot's designs for elaborate half-tester beds within an architecturally unified interior were highly influential, not just on Roberts but among such upholsterers as Francis Lapierre, even though they were not published until the 1700s, and then only in the Netherlands. His style reflects the grandeur and architectural unity of French court decoration, but it developed, particularly with regard to state beds, into something far more elaborate, with the simple, rectilinear bed preferred by the French court acquiring a lofty, flamboyant, flared tester (e.g. the bed designed for the 1st Earl of Melville, 1690; London, V&A).

51. Gilt-gesso table, 788×865 mm, attributed to James Moore sr, *c.* 1714 (London, Victoria and Albert Museum)

In France architects aimed at external and internal unity, with furniture playing an important part in decorative schemes, but in England there is less evidence of this being the case. Perhaps it is an accident of survival, but few designs for interiors are known prior to the arrival of Marot. Of these, the design of 1666 by John Webb (i) for a bedchamber at the Queen's House, Greenwich (London, RIBA), is the only one to include a piece of furniture, a French-style state bed. Another, albeit isolated, example is John Talman's drawing for a cabinet of curiosities (*c.* ?1702; London V&A) for Ranworth, the family seat in Norfolk, to house the vast collections of William, his father, an architect in the circle of William III. The pieces consist of a chest-on-chest with a drop front, a cabinet with two inlaid doors set on a flamboyant Baroque stand, similar to Venetian examples, and stools of similar design.

In the reign of Queen Anne (*reg* 1702–14) there emerged outstanding craftsmen such as John Gumley (*fl* 1691–1727) and James Moore sr (1670–1726). Gumley specialized in the manufacture of plate-glass, but his firm provided furniture of all kinds for Hampton Court Palace, for the 1st Duke of Montrose's lodgings in the Drygate, Glasgow, and for a Mr Paul Foley, from whom an extensive bill exists. The furnishings are predominantly mirrors, but desks and bureaux survive (London, Hampton Court, Royal Col.). James Moore sr, who formed a partnership with Gumley, is known for his gilt-gesso furniture (see fig. 51), mostly in the form of side-tables and stands, such as have survived at Kensington Palace, and a chest with a design loosely based on an Italian cassone, at Blenheim Palace, Oxon. He is recorded as having provided furniture for the 2nd Duke of Buccleuch at Dalkeith Palace, Edinburgh, for the 1st Duchess of Marlborough at Marlborough House, London, and for North Cray, Lincs. His good working relationship with the Duchess of Marlborough, who referred to him as her oracle, gave him control over the building of Blenheim Palace following the dismissal of John Vanburgh in 1716. Other important cabinetmakers included John Belchier (*fl* 1717; *d* 1753), who supplied furniture for Erddig, Clwyd, and the prolific firm of John and G. Coxed and T. Woster, whose activities date from 1700 to 1736. At Erddig there still exist Belchier's state bed, a pair of gilt girandoles and a glass-topped table with the Meller coat of arms. A large number of desks, bureaux, secretaires and chests-of-drawers from the period also survive, bearing the trade labels of Coxed & Woster. The bureaux, which frequently incorporate mirrors, are embellished with king-wood, crossbanding and pewter. Pieces such as these made their way as far afield as Williamsburg, VA.

Mention should be made of stylistic developments during this period. As has been said above, precious few designs survive, let alone published ones, in England before Marot's arrival. However, a development in style can be traced in extant work, with radical changes appearing at the beginning of the 18th century. Furniture of what roughly comprises the first 40 years of this period was essentially rectilinear with an abundance of surface decoration. Cabinets were set on stands with columns, usually Doric, solomonic or in the form of a term, joined by stretchers above ball feet. The same is the case with tables. The stands that supported lacquer cabinets were usually gilt and often curvaceous, frequently in the form of Auricular or foliate scrolls. The legs of such stands were sometimes joined by floral swags with putti at the top, as well as by curved stretchers at the bottom. Chairs were normally raised on turned legs joined by stretchers, the front stretcher often echoing the crest of the back, particularly in the high cane chair backs with 'boys and crowns' characteristic of William III's reign. The back increased in height as the century progressed, and by the early 18th century the gap between the seat and back had disappeared. The great innovation in design was brought about by the elegantly curved cabriole leg, with its origins in East Asia. This serpentine member, strengthened at the top by a 'knee', was strong enough to support the seat, so stretchers became obsolete. To harmonize with the cabriole leg, the seat frame and back broadened and became more curvilinear until the feet took on a greater variety of form, with the claw-and-ball and the lion's-paw making their appearance. The harsh winter of 1709 resulted in a shortage of French walnut, so sought after by cabinetmakers, and although the shortfall was compensated for by Virginia walnut, mahogany, first recorded in the Customs House ledgers of 1699, became popular; it was to come to the fore in the 18th century.

BIBLIOGRAPHY

J. Moxon: *Mechanick Exercises* (London, 1703/*R* New York, 1970)
R. Edwards and P. MacQuoid: *The Dictionary of English Furniture from the Late Middle Ages to the Late Georgian Period*, 3 vols (London, 1924–7, rev. 1954)
R. W. Symonds: *English Furniture from Charles II to George II* (London, 1929)
——: *Veneered Walnut Furniture, 1660–1760* (London, 1946)
——: *Furniture-making in Seventeenth and Eighteenth Century England* (London, 1955)
R. Edwards and L. G. C. Ramsey, eds: *The Stuarts*, Connoiseur Period Guide (London, 1957)
Oak Furniture from Yorkshire Churches (exh. cat. by A. Wells-Cole, Leeds, Temple Newsam House, 1971)

Oak Furniture from Lancashire and the Lake District (exh. cat. by A. Wells-Cole, Leeds, Temple Newsam House, 1973)

C. Gilbert: 'Regional Traditions in English Vernacular Furniture', *Arts of the Anglo-American Community in the Seventeenth Century*, ed. I. Quimby (Winterthur, DE, 1974), pp. 43–77

Oak Furniture from Gloucestershire and Somerset (exh. cat. by A. Wells-Cole, Leeds, Temple Newsam House, 1976)

P. Thornton: *Seventeenth-century Interior Decoration in England, France and Holland* (New Haven and London, 1978)

P. Thornton and M. Tomlin: 'The Furnishing and Decoration of Ham House', *Furn. Hist.*, xvi (1980) [whole issue]

4. 1721–80. Within this period the dominant architectural trends were Palladian, Rococo, Neo-classical and to a lesser extent the Gothic Revival, a movement that was to gain momentum in the latter half of the 18th century and become the main force of the 19th century. Architecture influenced furniture styles, with WILLIAM KENT, James Wyatt, Robert Adam (*see* ADAM (i), (3)) and WILLIAM CHAMBERS regarding furniture as an integral part of their interiors. At the same time, upholsterers, cabinet-makers and carvers began to compete for control over schemes, and several published large collections of furniture designs. Even if Palladian architecture (*see* PALLADIANISM) prevailed during the reigns of George I (*reg* 1714–27) and George II (*reg* 1727–60), the architect had to accept the fact that his patrons would often want the latest fashion in furniture and upholstery, and from *c.* 1740 until 1765 this was Rococo. While the Palladian architect might have felt that his interiors would have been better complemented by large marble-topped tables with woodwork of a massive sculptural quality, he would have to include furniture with an abundance of S scrolls and rocaille motifs in his publications if he was to attract wealthy patrons. Hence, designers and furniture-makers became remarkably eclectic in their styles, making use of Palladian, Rococo, Gothic and chinoiserie elements.

Mahogany became the most widely used wood. Robert Walpole not only exempted Jamaican mahogany from import duty, making it cheaper than the more sought after Cuban or 'Spanish' mahogany, but he also had the staircase and panelling at Houghton Hall, Norfolk, made in this material. Mahogany was popular with cabinetmakers as it enabled crisp, high-quality carving, it was stable and resistant to warping and woodworm and it came in large planks, making it suitable for all kinds of furniture. Walnut still had its devotees in the earlier decades of the century, but by 1776 William Hunter wrote in his edition of John Evelyn's *Silva*, 'Formerly the walnut tree was much propagated for its wood, but since the importation of mahogany and the Virginia walnut it has considerably decreased in reputation.' Native woods such as oak, ash, elm and beech were often used, as is evidenced in the large numbers of Windsor chairs, many of which were made at High Wycombe, Bucks, owing to the abundance of beech in the neighbourhood. In the 1720s marble-topped tables became prized status symbols, although they had occasionally appeared in the 16th century (as in the Leicester House and Lumley inventories). Under Italian influence, encouraged by the Grand Tour, this material became highly fashionable. Matthew Brettingham (ii) despatched from Italy seven cases containing marble slabs in 1764. At Badminton House, Glos, in 1754, Dr Richard Pocoke noticed several tables, 'some of alabastro fioret, one or

two of porphyry'. An important table (see fig. 52), an early essay in the Neo-classical style designed by Chambers and executed by GEORG HAUPT, has a top inlaid with specimens of antique marble; it is also one of the first examples of the use of satin-wood. This timber, from the West Indies, became highly fashionable towards the end of the century, with Thomas Sheraton commending it for its 'cool, light and pleasing effect on furniture'.

As travel became more popular, the Grand Tour, culminating in a sojourn in Rome, became *de rigeur* for the patron. This resulted in a growing awareness of and appreciation for all things Italian. Architects and draughtsmen made thorough studies and went further afield to study the ancient Classical remains at Palmyra, in the case of Robert Wood, Greece, in the case of James Stuart and Nicholas Revett, and Split in Dalmatia, in the case of Adam. Chambers, in his capacity as a merchant, went as far as China and promoted himself to no small degree through bringing back drawings of Chinese furniture and architecture, which differed greatly from the fancies of chinoiserie. James 'Athenian' Stuart's designs initiated a taste for all things Greek: but for his life-style and indolence, which often exasperated his patrons and dissipated his talents, his ideas could have had wide-reaching results. Adam, on the other hand, concentrated on the

52. Table, marble and satin-wood, h. 852 mm, made by Georg Haupt to a design by William Chambers, 1769 (London, Victoria and Albert Museum)

ornamental detail of Classical architecture and on surviving examples of Roman interior decoration, particularly the grotesque element. This provided a novelty that was to be much in demand, and his use of talented craftsmen for every element of a scheme, his attention to detail and his organizational abilities established him as the leading architect and decorator of the day. His ideas were highly influential on cabinetmakers and were responsible for some of the finest pieces created in this period (see fig. 92 below).

William Kent spent some ten years both studying and painting in Italy, where his talents came to the notice of the rich, powerful and energetic Richard Boyle, 3rd Earl of Burlington. In 1719 he returned to England, and under Lord Burlington's influence he became an architect. With Burlington he was responsible for the building and decoration of Chiswick House, London. Through his patron's political connections as much as through his abilities as a designer, he won scores of prestigious commissions. His furniture for Houghton (c. 1730), in the form of gilt chairs with Genoese silk upholstery, a fine state bed with a shell headboard, side-tables and other pieces, survives in situ. His furnishings for Chiswick House (also c. 1730), including a fine library table adorned with gilt owls, are now at Chatsworth, Derbys. The term 'Kentian' is used to describe a type of heavy, sculptural furniture incorporating pediments, masks and architectural features. Tables are often set on massive scrolled consoles (see fig. 53) and the chairs enriched with fishscale ornament. Kentian furniture was by no means invariably massive, gilt and marble-topped: the architect was well aware of the possibilities offered by

mahogany, using it extensively at Houghton and Chiswick, for example. Kent's designs are known mainly through John Vardy's *Some Designs of Mr Inigo Jones and Mr William Kent* (London, 1744), but his legacy of architectural drawings include some for furniture. Although he died in 1748, his influence on the design of furniture persisted, a good example being a series of massive tables from Wimpole Hall, Cambs, featuring the mask of Hercules draped with the skin of the Nemean lion, with others at Wentworth Woodhouse, S. Yorks, and Ditchley Park, Oxon, after a design by MATTHIAS LOCK.

The most fashionable cabinetmakers of this period were GILES GRENDEY, Benjamin Goodison (c. 1700–67), James Moore jr (b c. 1690; d before 1734), Lock, William Hallet sr (c. 1707–81) and JOHN CHANNON. These men were for the most part active well after the death of Kent and were patronized by wealthy connoisseurs, even if they were not necessarily working in conjunction with the architects best known to posterity. James Moore benefited from the reputation of his father, James Moore sr, providing furniture for Kensington Palace, London, to Kent's designs and enjoying the patronage of Frederick, Prince of Wales. Giles Grendey, as well as securing commissions for Stourhead, Wilts, and Kedleston Hall, Derbys, exported furniture to Spain. Benjamin Goodison and John Boson (fl 1720–43) were particularly connected with Kent, and the output of William Hallett ranged from Kentian work at Badminton House, Rousham, Oxon, and Holkham Hall, Norfolk, to Gothic furnishings for Horace Walpole at Strawberry Hill, London, in 1755.

Running concurrently with the Palladian vogue from the 1740s was the Rococo, with its Chinese and Gothic tributaries. It was better suited to interior decoration and the applied arts than to external architecture. Lock not only executed fine gilt furniture but also published in London such suites of Rococo designs as *Six Sconces* (1744), *Six Tables* (1746) and *New Book of Ornaments* (1752). Lock studied the work of such French designers as François de Cuvilliés I and Nicolas Pineau, and drawings by Thomas Chippendale the elder (*see* CHIPPENDALE, (1)) in his collection suggest that the two men may have worked together. James Pascall (fl 1733–54), another carver, produced work in the Rococo style in the form of console tables, candlestands and seating for the 7th Viscount Irwin at Temple Newsam House, W. Yorks, and unspecified work at Stourhead, Wilts. John Channon, of Exeter and London, provided furniture for Powderham Castle, Devon, and Hornby Hall, Lancs. A pair of monumental bookcases at Powderham Castle bears his signature, and such pieces as the library desk (London, V&A) and the Murray Writing-cabinet (Leeds, Temple Newsam House) show that mahogany with gilt mounts was well suited to the curvaceous quality of Rococo. The fashion for all things Rococo went hand in hand with strong anti-French feelings, partly propagated by the Antigallican Association, and an urge among craftsmen to outdo the French in this style.

The middle decades of the 18th century were marked by the publication in London of Thomas Chippendale's *Gentleman and Cabinet-maker's Director* of 1754, with a second edition the following year and a response from INCE & MAYHEW in the form of their *Universal System of*

53. Pedestal table, h. 890 mm, designed by William Kent, c. 1728 (London, Victoria and Albert Museum)

54. Chair, h. 1.07 m, made by Thomas Chippendale to a design by Robert Adam, *c.* 1765 (London, Victoria and Albert Museum)

Household Furniture (1759). Chippendale swiftly produced a third edition in 1762, with a co-edition in French and a somewhat defensive preface. The early editions refer on the title page to 'furniture in the Gothic, Chinese and Modern taste', but the third edition reflects the progressive Neo-classical ideas of Stuart, Chambers and Adam, introducing such motifs as rams' heads and caryatids. Chippendale supplied furniture for an enormous number of houses throughout England, and the French edition gave him an international reputation. So influential were his designs that the term 'Chippendale' is used to describe work often only remotely inspired by the *Director*, rather than produced in his workshop. Although he provided furniture to houses decorated by Adam, the only time he worked to Adam's designs was at the London residence of Sir Lawrence Dundas in 1765 (see fig. 54).

Although Ince & Mayhew were rivals of Chippendale, their designs are very close to his. Sheraton judged their work as 'much inferior to Chippendale's'. Despite this, the firm prospered in the 1760s and 1770s and enjoyed fruitful relationships with fashionable clients and architects of the day. With the 4th and 5th Dukes of Bedford they worked on an exclusive basis, and in the case of the 4th Earl of Coventry at Croome Court, Worcs, they worked alongside Vile & Cobb (see below) and other firms. They showed a less independent spirit towards architects than Chippendale, often following to the letter the designs of Chambers, Adam and later 'Capability' Brown and Henry Holland. For other commissions, for example the chairs in the Tapestry Room at Croome Court, they were given a free hand. As Rococo waned, Ince & Mayhew were well able to provide work of a more severe style and to reach high levels of skill in marquetry. Theirs is an example of a fruitful relationship between cabinetmakers and architects, as they were able to profit from the designs of others, while their own, as published in the *Universal System*, had enjoyed only a modest success.

William Vile, who initially worked under William Hallett, formed a partnership with John Cobb from *c.* 1750 until *c.* 1767. The firm's most prestigious work was at the royal palaces and Croome Court. Their pieces are marked by exuberant foliate decoration, oval wreaths on flat surfaces and fine architectural detailing, particularly on bookcases.

William Linnell (1703–63) and JOHN LINNELL (i), father and son, worked together from 1749 until William's death. The father's early work was mainly as a carver, and his name appears on documents relating to the Radcliffe Camera, Oxford, and Woburn Abbey, Beds. John was a talented draughtsman, educated at the St Martin's Lane Academy, London. He designed the chairs and probably the other pieces of chinoiserie furniture for the Chinese Bedroom at Badminton House, and he published a *New Book of Ornaments Useful for Silversmiths* (London, 1760). With his uncle, Samuel Butler, he designed a new state coach for George III, and even though it was not executed, the fact that it was dedicated to Nathaniel Curzon, the 1st Baron Scarsdale, resulted in his producing two pairs of spectacular gilt sofas for the State Drawing-room at Kedleston Hall. Linnell made the sideboard and urns designed by Adam for the Eating-room at Osterley Park House, London, and it has been suggested that Haupt and Christopher Fuhrlohg (*b c.* 1740; *d* after 1787), two important cabinetmakers who had worked in France, produced the library furniture for Osterley that reflected the *goût grec*, which had become fashionable in France during the 1750s. Linnell supplied furniture to houses where Adam worked, either executing his own designs, such as the triton sofas at Kedleston, or those of Adam. His style, recorded in a large number of drawings at the Victoria and Albert Museum, London, reflects a development from chinoiserie and Rococo to mature Neo-classical.

Kent pioneered the use of Gothic Revival at Rousham Park, Oxon, between 1738 and 1740, and yet his style follows strict classical symmetry. It was Horace Walpole who consciously developed it in the building of Strawberry Hill, stating that he was 'almost as fond of the Sharawaqqi or Chinese want of Symmetry'. Batty Langley published designs for Gothic chimney-pieces, which met with Walpole's disapproval. Gothic furniture appears in Matthias Darly's *New-book of Chinese, Gothic & Modern Chairs* (London, 1751), Chippendale's *Director* (1754) and Robert Manwaring's *Cabinet and Chair-maker's Real Friend and Companion* (London, 1765). In all these cases the designs are essentially classical and symmetrical, with Gothic elements added on. Frequently Gothic and Rococo blend, as is the case with Ince's 'Sofa in an Alcove' (*c.* 1760) or Chippendale's Gothic library bookcases. One suspects that A. W. N Pugin's later designs would have been looked upon with some sympathy by Walpole but regarded as barbarous by any other connoisseur of this period.

There are various other strands of taste running through these years. Along with massive architectural furniture, which was far more consistent with the architectural drawings of Andrea Palladio than with anything produced in Italy at the time, went curvaceous furniture with cabriole legs and bureaux with japanned decoration. A restrained version of continental Rococo was successfully adapted to English interiors and furniture (particularly to the carved work) in a rather whimsical manner. The Neo-classical ideal, first evident in Chambers's presidential chair of 1759 for the Royal Society of Arts, London (*in situ*), sometimes resulted in stark, austere furniture and sometimes in highly elaborate surface decoration, almost as if the full repertory of classical motifs had to be used. Alongside this enthusiasm for all things classical, there developed an increasing awareness of Gothic art and architecture. It is ironic that Adam, subject to frequent censure from Walpole, should have been involved in the design of Strawberry Hill and have been willing to provide Gothic chairs for Syon House, London. This period was perhaps the golden age of English furniture, when tastes were remarkably eclectic and each style was handled with elegance and fluency.

BIBLIOGRAPHY

R. Edwards and M. Jourdain: *Georgian Cabinet Makers* (London, 1944, rev. 3/1955)

A. Heal: *London Furniture Makers from the Restoration to the Victorian Era, 1660–1840* (London, 1953)

C. Musgrave: *Adam, Hepplewhite and Other Neo-classical Furniture* (London, 1958)

E. Harris: *The Furniture of Robert Adam* (London, 1963)

H. Hayward: *Thomas Johnson and the English Rococo* (London, 1964)

A. Coleridge: *Chippendale Furniture: The Work of Thomas Chippendale and his Contemporaries in the Rococo Taste, circa 1745–1765* (London, 1968)

M. Tomlin: *Catalogue of Adam Period Furniture* (London, 1972)

J. Fowler and J. Cornforth: *English Decoration in the Eighteenth Century* (London, 1974)

G. Beard: *The Work of Robert Adam* (London, 1978)

C. Gilbert: *The Life and Work of Thomas Chippendale*, 2 vols (London, 1978)

H. Hayward and P. Kirkham: *William and J. Linnell, Eighteenth-century London Furniture Makers* (London, 1980)

Rococo: Art and Design in Hogarth's England (exh. cat., ed. M. Snodin; London, V&A, 1984)

M. Wilson: *William Kent: Architect, Designer, Painter, Gardener, 1685–1748* (London, 1984)

JAMES YORKE

5. 1781–1830. During the late Neo-classical period there was a greater emphasis on designs derived from antique Greek and Roman prototypes as well as fundamental advances in techniques of production. The era was dominated by the 'Francophile' tastes of George, Prince of Wales, who became Prince Regent in 1811 and succeeded to the English throne as George IV (*see* HANOVER, (4)) in 1820. His passionate interest in the decorative arts, his own collections of French furniture and the Parisian craftsmen that he patronized all influenced the spread of French ideas in fashionable circles. Among the French craftsmen engaged by the Prince at Carlton House (destr. 1827–8), London, was François Hervé (*fl* 1780–90), who designed various pieces of seat furniture (examples dated 1782–3; Chatsworth House, Derbys). HENRY HOLLAND, in his remodelling and refurbishment of Carlton House between *c.* 1783 and *c.* 1796 (*see* UPHOLSTERY, colour pl. XIV, fig. 2), confirmed his admiration for chaste French Neo-classicism. Holland, with the designer C. H. TATHAM, was most influential during the early phase of the Regency period. His interiors and furniture designs were executed in an understated Anglo-French style that was evolved in part from Tatham's studies of architectural fragments seen at ancient sites in Italy (e.g. side-chair with carved Roman motifs, attrib. to Holland, *c.* 1800; British Royal Col.). The animal monopodia, lion's-paw feet and other motifs much employed in Regency furniture were partly based on Tatham's *Etchings of Ancient Ornamental Architecture*, published in 1799 and 1800 (e.g. chair by GEORGE SMITH (ii), *c.* 1805; London, V&A). The Gothic, Egyptian, 'Hindoo' and chinoiserie styles, however, were all characteristic of the Regency period, together with the Rococo Revival in the 1820s. Besides animal forms, typical Regency features were reeded and fluted supports, carved acanthus-leaf scrolls, paterae, stars and a central fan motif of inlaid woods. Imitation bamboo turning was used in chinoiserie pieces.

Pattern books were important in the dissemination of fashionable styles, and they found eager subscribers among members of the furniture trade. The several books of designs published by THOMAS SHERATON, in particular his four-part *The Cabinet-Maker and Upholsterer's Drawing Book* (1791–3; 1794; 1802), spread his style beyond the British Isles to America, Germany, Russia, Scandinavia, Spain and Italy. *The Repository of Arts* (1809–28), published by RUDOLPH ACKERMANN, *Household Furniture and Interior Decoration* (1807), published by Thomas Hope (*see* HOPE, (1)), and *A Collection of Designs for Household*

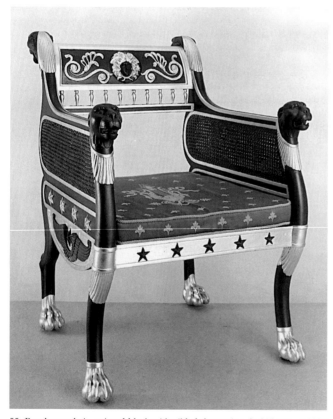

55. Beech armchair, painted black with gilded decoration, h. 915 mm, *c.* 1805 (London, Victoria and Albert Museum); from a design dated 1804 in George Smith: *A Collection of Designs for Household Furniture and Interior Decoration* (1808), pl. 56

Furniture and Interior Decoration (see fig. 55), published by Smith, also had a great impact and popularized such pieces characteristic of the Regency period as long, Grecian couches, X-frame stools, sabre-leg Klismos and scroll-back chairs, tripod pedestal tables and boat-shaped beds.

Two important manufacturers catering for the demands of the middle classes for modish, high-quality furniture were GILLOW of Lancaster, established *c.* 1730, and George Seddon & Co. in London, founded *c.* 1750 (*see* SEDDON, (1)). Gillow, which opened a branch in London in 1769, was credited with originating the whatnot (*c.* 1790) and the Davenport (*c.* 1816), as well as pieces adapted from designs by Sheraton and those of GEORGE HEPPLE-WHITE published in the *Cabinet-maker and Upholsterer's Guide* (1788; 1789; 1794). From *c.* 1796 the firm produced Hepplewhite's Carlton House table (*c.* 1793), with a superstructure of tiered drawers and a writing-slope, which is probably the best-known piece of Regency furniture (e.g. Uppark, W. Sussex, NT). Seddon's had extensive premises in London and survived through several generations of the family until 1868. Between 1827 and 1832 the cabinetmaker Nicholas Morel (*fl* 1790–1832) was commissioned in partnership with Seddon's to remodel the interiors at Windsor Castle, Berks, and provide furnishings.

By the early 19th century, English cabinetmakers had brought a full-bodied refinement to Classical forms and design. Furniture was more solid, with elegant, functional shapes. The preference in England for mahogany continued, but rose-wood, amboina, maple and zebra-wood were favoured for their colour and figured grains. Floral marquetry was replaced by panelled veneers, decorative stringing and crossbanding, and ormolu was generally used with restraint. Grilles, mounts and inlays of brass were popular, frequently in combination with rose-wood, and painted effects and japanning were revived. New forms were developed incorporating greater flexibility to meet particular domestic needs. Tables were supplied with extra leaves so that they could be extended for dining; dressing-tables were fitted with fold-down mirrors, pull-out trays and drawers to conceal bidets and chamberpots. Among the innovations were the tiered revolving bookcase on casters, the nest of four small tables known as the 'quartetto', the convex mirror, the ottoman, and the chiffonier. Patent mechanical furniture, often combining two functions, appeared in many forms, including the 'gouty' mahogany armchair with a carpeted footrest that could be raised.

After 1815, when the British were once again able to travel to France, there was a renewed interest in 18th-century French styles, particularly Louis XIV and Louis XV. GEORGE BULLOCK and the Frenchman Louis Constantin Le Gaigneur, who was recorded in London between *c.* 1814/15 and 1820/21, were both associated with the revival in England of boullework furniture, and Le Gaigneur supplied pieces to the Prince Regent (e.g. writing-table, *c.* 1815; British Royal Col.). The Royal Pavilion, Brighton, rebuilt for the Prince by JOHN NASH between 1815 and 1822, exemplifies the late Georgian taste for chinoiserie. The Regency was a richly inventive yet scholarly style, and the essential elegance of the furniture has ensured its continued popularity.

BIBLIOGRAPHY
I. Hall: 'A Neoclassical Episode at Chatsworth', *Burl. Mag.*, cxxii (1980), pp. 400–14
F. Collard: *Regency Furniture* (Woodbridge, 1985)
P. Kirkham: *The London Furniture Trade, 1700–1870* (London, 1988)
George Bullock: Cabinet Maker (exh. cat., London, Blairman & Sons; Liverpool, Sudley A.G.; 1988)
M. Levy: 'Sincerest Form of Flattery', *Country Life*, clxxxiii (15 June 1989), pp. 178–81
C. Wainwright: *The Romantic Interior: The British Collector at Home, 1750–1850* (New Haven and London, 1989)
Carlton House: The Past Glories of George IV's Palace (exh. cat. by G. De Bellaigne, London, Queen's Gal., 1991)

FRANCES COLLARD

6. 1831–1900. In this period there was a greater demand for domestic furniture, in a wider range of styles, than previously. Historicism—the revival of period styles—and ornament are key features of Victorian furniture design, giving a richness and variety in contrast to the perceived severity of much Regency furniture. Such new or unexpected materials as papier-mâché, cast-iron, horn, slate and coal were used, as well as the more familiar mahogany, walnut, rose-wood and oak. London was the major centre of production, employing about two-fifths of all furniture-makers in England and Wales in the 1850s and two-thirds by 1881. Furniture was, however, made in most other cities, especially ports. The towns of Barnstaple, Bath, Bristol, Lancaster, Leeds, Manchester, Newcastle upon Tyne and Warwick all produced high-quality furniture. Chair-making was concentrated in High Wycombe and Birmingham, and the West Midlands specialized in metal bedsteads, furniture hardware and papier-mâché furniture.

From the 1840s the London furniture-makers split into two geographically distinct groups, known as the 'honourable' and 'dishonourable' (or 'slop') trade. The former comprised such West End makers as Holland & Sons and Gillow & Morant, whose staff were apprenticed in large manufactories to learn all aspects of their craft. In contrast, most furniture-making in the East End was 'sweated' labour in small workshops, without benefit of apprenticeships or trade societies; labour was subdivided so that cabinetmakers made only particular items or parts of furniture, for example boxes, wardrobes or table legs. The growing demand by department stores and such retail shops as Maples for ever-cheaper furniture encouraged the East End trade, which by the 1870s had outstripped the West End in quantity produced. In the last quarter of the century many established West End firms went out of business, refusing to compromise on quality and thus unable to compete on price.

Numerous wood-working machines were patented from the 1840s, but much cabinetmaking was done by hand until the end of the century, particularly in the East End. From the 1850s machinery was regularly used to saw logs into planks and cut veneers. It was the large, high-quality firms, such as Holland & Sons and Jackson & Graham, that used steam-powered machines the earliest, in the 1850s and 1860s, at the same time as conserving the more specialized hand skills that were gradually lost in the East End. Much carving was done by patent machinery from the 1840s, including work at the New Palace of

Westminster, London, although it still had to be finished by hand.

The four major early Victorian furniture styles were listed by John Claudius Loudon in his *Encyclopedia of Cottage, Farm and Villa Architecture and Furniture* of 1833. These are the 'Grecian or modern style, which is by far the most prevalent', the 'Gothic or perpendicular style', the 'Elizabethan' and the 'Louis XIV'. Furniture in the Classical Grecian style, which displayed a continuation of Regency forms, was popular for many years, gradually losing elegance while gaining bulk. Two of the main advocates of Gothic were A. W. N. Pugin and John Ruskin. Gothic was chosen in 1835 for the New Palace of Westminster and was the most progressive design style until the 1870s. Pugin's designs show a development from Regency Gothick to an increasing concern with the structural honesty of furniture, where construction is clearly revealed. Influenced by Pugin, Charles Bevan, William Burges, R. Norman Shaw and J. P. Seddon worked in this Reformed Gothic manner in the 1860s, often in oak with geometrical painted or inlaid decoration. Sir Walter Scott's historical novels and the decoration of his house, Abbotsford (nr Melrose, Borders), by George Bullock helped to popularize furniture in an Elizabethan or Tudor style, with carved strapwork and spiral turning. Richard Bridgens's *Furniture with Candelabra and Interior Decoration* (1838) was an important source of Elizabethan designs. Curvaceous Rococo Revival furniture, inconsistently called Louis XIV, Louis XV or Old French, became increasingly popular among decorators and commercial manufacturers, and by the time of the Great Exhibition of 1851 in London it was the dominant style. Much classic mid-Victorian drawing- and dining-room furniture, for example the mahogany balloon-back chair or the over-stuffed curved sofa, was inspired by Rococo forms (*see* MARQUETRY, colour pl. VIII, fig. 1).

Naturalistic decoration, based on plant or animal forms, is a major feature of much mid-19th-century furniture. A prerequisite for such ornament was that it should be 'appropriate'; for example, dining-room sideboards were carved with fish and game. The *trompe l'oeil* naturalistic style appealed most to an unsophisticated domestic market and was condemned by such design reformers as Henry Cole. In the 1850s there was also a revival of interest in Renaissance decoration, promoted by Alfred Stevens (i) and by such foreign designers as Gottfried Semper. By 1862, when the International Exhibition took place in London, both naturalistic and Rococo Revival designs had begun to give way to a new Neo-classicism, confirmed at the Paris Exposition Universelle of 1867 when Wright & Mansfield's satin-wood 'Adam' cabinet won the only gold medal for English furniture. The Medieval Court at the International Exhibition included painted furniture by Burges, Shaw and William Morris's recently formed firm, Morris, Marshall, Faulkner & Co. Philip Webb designed much early furniture, both plain and painted sturdy oak pieces, for Morris. Cheaper, rush-seated chairs based on traditional Sussex types were sold by the firm from the mid-1860s into the 20th century and were copied by a number of other companies (*see* MORRIS, WILLIAM, fig. 1).

Two influential publications of the late 1860s, Bruce J. Talbert's *Gothic Forms Applied to Furniture* (1867) and

Charles Locke Eastlake's *Hints on Household Taste* (1868), inspired some commercial manufacturers to produce simple oak furniture in a modern Gothic style, with chamfered edges and chip-carved decoration. Eastlake's book was particularly influential in the USA. Japanese arts and crafts also interested AESTHETIC MOVEMENT designers at this time, particularly E. W. Godwin, whose *Art Furniture* (1877) includes sophisticated, rectilinear, Anglo-Japanese designs. T. E. Collcutt's cabinet (see fig. 56) was the model for much ebonized 'art furniture' for the next 20 years. Mass-produced sideboards and overmantels in this style incorporated painted panels, tiles, rows of spindles, brackets, turned supports and bevelled mirror-glass.

The rise of the craft guild in the 1880s was influenced by the writings of Morris and Ruskin; A. H. Mackmurdo's Century Guild of 1882 was followed by the Art Worker's Guild (1884) and the Guild of Handicraft (1888). Many of the best-known furniture designers of the ARTS AND CRAFTS MOVEMENT showed work at the Arts and Crafts Exhibition Society from 1888. These artists included C. F. A. Voysey, who made oak dressers with capped uprights and high-backed chairs with pierced heart motifs, and Ernest Gimson, co-founder of Kenton & Co. in 1890.

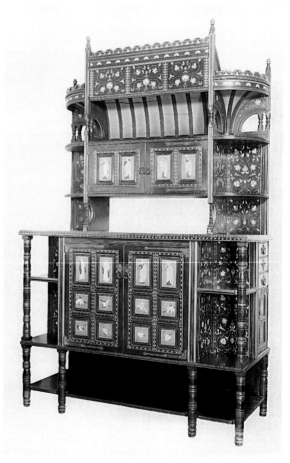

56. Ebonized cabinet with painted decoration, designed by T. E. Collcutt and made by Collinson and Lock, 1871 (London, Victoria and Albert Museum)

In 1892 Gimson, Ernest Barnsley and Sidney Barnsley (1865–1926) moved from London to the Cotswolds, where they made such Arts and Crafts furniture as rush-seated, ladder-backed chairs, plain oak pieces and more elaborate inlaid cabinets. In London Heal & Son produced similar furniture on a commercial scale.

Numerous pattern books and trade and exhibition catalogues were produced in the 19th century, particularly in the second half, illustrating the immense range of furniture types and styles concurrently available. Such works as Blackie's *Cabinet-Maker's Assistant* (1853) and C. & R. Light's *Cabinet Furniture* catalogue (1880) are more typical of general household furniture than the *Illustrated Exhibition Catalogues* (1851, 1862) published by the *Art Journal*, but all display the richly eclectic mix of design popular throughout the Victorian period.

BIBLIOGRAPHY

E. Aslin: *Nineteenth Century English Furniture* (London, 1962)
R. Symonds and B. Whineray: *Victorian Furniture* (London, 1962/R 1987)
C. Handley-Read: 'England, 1830–1901', *World Furniture*, ed. H. Hayward (London, 1965, rev. 7/1975), pp. 207–29
S. Jervis: *Victorian Furniture* (London, 1968)
Victorian and Edwardian Decorative Art: The Handley-Read Collection (exh. cat. by S. Jervis, London, RA, 1972)
E. Joy: *English Furniture, 1800–1851* (London, 1977)
Pictorial Dictionary of British Nineteenth Century Furniture Design, intro. E. Joy (Woodbridge, 1977)
P. Agius: *British Furniture, 1880–1915* (Woodbridge, 1978)
Architect-Designers: Pugin to Mackintosh (exh. cat., London, F.A. Soc., 1981)
S. Jervis: *High Victorian Design* (London, 1983)
Truth, Beauty and Design: Victorian, Edwardian and Later Decorative Art (exh. cat. by A. J. Tilbrook, London, Fischer F.A., 1986)
J. Cooper: *Victorian and Edwardian Furniture and Interiors* (London, 1987)
P. Kirkham, R. Mace and J. Porter: *Furnishing the World: The East London Furniture Trade, 1830–1980* (London, 1987)

ROSAMOND ALLWOOD

7. AFTER 1900. Because of the difficult economic conditions in the years leading up to World War I, the mechanization of the furniture industry was limited. An aversion to mechanization was shared by furniture designers allied with the Arts and Crafts Movement, who sought to promote soundly crafted (and thus expensive) furniture in vernacular styles. The outlook of such designers as Sidney Barnsley (1865–1926), ERNEST GIMSON and AMBROSE HEAL was opposed to that of larger-scale producers who catered for mass taste at competitive prices and sold their goods through a variety of retail outlets, particularly the new furniture stores that became increasingly widespread. From 1918 the furniture industry expanded considerably, aided by two significant developments: the increasing proportion of furniture bought through Hire Purchase schemes and the considerable improvement in plywood fabrication, which lowered production costs. Expansion was also marked by a trend towards larger, more mechanized factories whose output was clothed in a multiplicity of styles, traditional and novel. Mainstream commercial furniture was treated with disdain by those who sought to improve standards of design, including such retailers as Dunn's of Bromley, Crofton Gane of Bristol and Peter Jones and Bowman's in London. By the late 1920s there was a greater awareness of progressive design on the Continent. Such exhibitions as the *Exhibition of Modern Art in Decoration and Furnishing* (1928) held at Waring & Gillow's in Oxford Street, London, introduced the public to fashionable, decorative and exotic French furniture that was imitated at the lower end of the market by cheap, superficial derivatives. This had considerably more public appeal than the stark, modern, tubular-steel furniture seen in Germany in the 1920s, but the impetus for such furniture in Britain was provided by the Austrian Thonet Co. (est. 1819), which opened its London showrooms in 1929. Two English firms also led the way: Cox & Co. (est. 1927) and Practical Equipment Ltd (PEL, est. 1931; e.g. tubular-steel-frame dining furniture made for Prudential Assurance, mid-1930s; London, V&A). A third, Steelchrome (1932–64), specialized in furniture for the beauty and hairdressing industries and hospital equipment. Many such modern designs of the 1930s found outlets in contract furnishing. In 1938 Geoffrey Dunn (*b* 1909), Crofton Gane and GORDON RUSSELL formed the Good Furniture Group, which sought to commission, produce and sell modern furniture. Before 1939 other progressive influences from the Continent made themselves felt. Scandinavian design received increasing attention during the 1920s and 1930s; the sculptural plywood designs of Alvar Aalto were undoubtedly an influence on furniture designed for the Isokon Furniture Co. (est. 1931).

World War II marked a hiatus in furniture design and manufacture because of government restrictions on the use of timber. The state-imposed Utility Scheme (1943–52) legislated precise methods of construction and amounts of timber to be used in furniture production (e.g. utility tallboy chest in light oak; London, Geffrye Mus.). Its austere aesthetic was unpopular with the public, which, when restrictions were eased in the later 1940s, favoured the more familiar styles available a decade earlier. After 1945 the Council of Industrial Design (COID, est. 1944) did much to promote modern furniture. The *Britain Can Make It* exhibition of 1946 and, more particularly, the Festival of Britain of 1951, helped to introduce the public to what was termed 'Contemporary style' furniture. A new group of forward-looking designers began to attract international attention, including ROBIN DAY and Clive Latimer (*b* ?1916), who won a prize in 1949 in an international competition held at MOMA, New York. The Milan Triennali also provided opportunities for international recognition: in 1951 Day won a gold medal and in 1954 a silver medal; in the same year ERNEST RACE was awarded a gold medal. Furniture designers soon began to explore the possibilities of new materials, including steel rods, plastics, laminated paperboard and fibreboard. From the late 1950s there were more opportunities for design consultants in the furniture industry; these included Robert Heritage (*b* 1927), who worked for Archie Shine Ltd, Robin Day for Hille (see fig. 57), and John Reid (*b* 1925) and Sylvia Reid for the Stag Cabinet Co. By the early 1960s the principal English manufacturers involved in furniture production were located in the London and High Wycombe areas. In London these included Harris Lebus Ltd of Tottenham, Beautility Furniture Ltd of Edmonton and Cabinet Industries of Chingford; in High Wycombe

57. 'Hillestak' chair by Robin Day, moulded plywood seat and back, 1950 (Brighton, Art Gallery and Museum)

there was a recession in furniture manufacture and retailing, but also the emergence of furniture warehouses located on out-of-town sites with easy access by road and good parking. Among the earliest of these companies were Harris Queensway and MFI, whose superstores provided furniture ensembles in a wide variety of styles, from historicizing to modern. Such outlets acknowledged the concept of 'lifestyle' as an aspect of conspicuous consumption, a phenomenon that became increasingly dominant during the 1980s. Other companies diversified their product ranges to include furniture as an aspect of 'lifestyle' marketing, ranging from such firms as Laura Ashley to Marks & Spencer.

BIBLIOGRAPHY
J. C. Rogers: *Modern English Furniture* (London, 1930)
The Working Class Home: Its Furnishing and Equipment, Council for Art and Industry (London, 1937)
Working Party Report on Furniture, Board of Trade (London, 1946)
E. Goldfinger: *British Furniture Today* (London, 1951)
D. Joel: *The Adventure of British Furniture* (London, 1953)
M. Farr: *Design in British Industry: A Mid-century Survey* (Cambridge, 1955)
D. Young and B. Young: *Furniture in Britain Today* (London, 1964)
J. L. Oliver: *The Development and Structure of the Furniture Industry* (Oxford, 1966)
Utility Furniture and Fashion, 1941–51 (exh. cat., London, Geffrye Mus., 1974)
PEL and Tubular Steel Furniture of the Thirties (exh. cat., ed. D. Sharp and others; London, Archit. Assoc., 1977)
P. Agius: *British Furniture, 1880–1915* (Woodbridge, 1978)
A. J. Coulson: *A Bibliography of British Design, 1851–1970* (London, 1979)
S. Worden: *Furniture for the Living Room: An Investigation of the Interaction between Society, Industry and Design in Britain from 1919–1939* (diss., U. Brighton, 1980)
F. MacCarthy: *British Design since 1880* (London, 1982)
P. Sparke: 'The Furniture Retailer as Taste-maker', *Did Britain Make It?*, ed. P. Sparke (London, 1986), pp. 128–42
P. Dormer: *The New Furniture: Trends and Traditions* (London, 1987)

JONATHAN M. WOODHAM

VII. Ceramics.

1. Before 1600. 2. 1600–1700. 3. 1701–1830. 4. 1831–1900. 5. After 1900.

1. BEFORE 1600.

(i) Saxo-Norman. In the late 9th century and the 10th several factors stimulated both the establishment of new potteries and generally increased production. Foremost among these was the demand created by growing urban communities, combined with an increasingly sophisticated commerce in which goods were traded through market networks. Many of the production centres were located in towns, and the evidence from such places as Norwich and Thetford, both in Norfolk, suggests that there were concentrations of potters in certain areas. However, the evidence for production sites is very sparse, and documentary sources are non-existent before the *Domesday Book* (1086), in which there are three references to potters.

It seems likely that only local clays and tempering materials were used, but the evidence is so far very limited. In the Danelaw of eastern England the potters mostly aimed at producing fully reduced grey wares (wares that reduced to a grey colour in the kiln), but at Stamford, Lincs, a finer, off-white body was produced (*see* STAMFORD, §2). Both wheel-throwing and hand-building (using

E. Gomme Ltd and Parker-Knoll were the most significant. In the 1960s there were considerable changes in the way in which furniture was marketed, with the emergence of design-conscious boutiques that catered for a growing youth market for whom durability and practicality were of less concern. In 1964 Terence Conran's first Habitat store opened in the Fulham Road, London, growing rapidly to a network of more than 30 British outlets by 1980. The company also developed expertise in the growth areas of mail order and the drive-away market from where furniture could be transported in flat-packs for subsequent home assembly. Specialist furniture retailers became interested in Italian and Scandinavian design, putting further pressure on an industry that moved increasingly towards large-scale manufacturing units at the expense of smaller, often more innovative companies.

Although few British firms employed furniture designers, a number of designers maintained close personal links with furniture-making as an expression of creative autonomy. The crafts provided an opportunity for continuity as well as experimentation in furniture design through such makers as John Makepeace (*b* 1939) and the more flamboyant Fred Baier (*b* 1941), who experimented with bright, stained colours and veneers and drew on a wide range of cultural sources, including Pop and science fiction, to provide a Post-modern alternative to mainstream styles. Ron Arad (*b* 1951), founder of the One-Off design company in 1981, is another maker who is opposed to the conformity of mass-production and seeks to blur the barriers between art and furniture design. In the 1970s

slab or coil construction) techniques were used. The kick-wheel has been associated with production in towns both in and on the borders of the Danelaw, such as Stamford and Norwich. Its adoption, along with glazes and red-painted decoration, was an innovation that probably originated with foreign craftsmen settling in eastern England, with clear continental influences from the Rhineland and northern France. Kick-wheels were also used in such places outside the Danelaw as Exeter, Devon and Gloucester, but the use of turntables and simpler coiling techniques characterize ceramics in much of England beyond the Danelaw. The vessels were fired in either a single-flued, up-draught kiln or in clamp or bonfire kilns. The latter have been identified in Chichester, W. Sussex, and strongly suspected elsewhere, but the former were more distinctive and widely distributed from Exeter to Torksey, Lincs.

The main forms were small jars, known as cooking pots from their assumed function, and bowls; the latter were occasionally provided with spouts, perhaps for separating cream. Other forms included cresset lamps, crucibles, ring-vases, costrels, storage jars and spouted pitchers with handles. The largest and most elaborate vessels were Thetford ware storage jars, criss-crossed with applied strips, which were sometimes impressed with stamps. Winchester wares were among the most ornate vessels and included such wheel-thrown forms as cups, strainers, tripod pitchers, bottles and costrels with yellow, orange and pale green lead glazes (see fig. 58). Additional decoration included rouletting, applied strips, incised lines and stamps. Although the production site has not been located, it seems certain that this high-quality fabric owes much to the important royal associations with the town of Winchester. With the exception of Stamford and Winchester wares, plain, unglazed pottery was produced at other sites. At production centres where kick-wheels were in use, rouletted decoration occurs on the shoulders of cooking pots, but where pots were handmade, stamps and applied strips were occasionally used.

(ii) The Middle Ages. The combined evidence from historical and archaeological sources suggests that many craftsmen were operating all over the country, in both towns and rural areas. A number of potters are known by name from documentary sources, but little else was recorded before the 16th century apart from the sparse details of rents, fines or disputes. There was certainly a lack of patronage and investment in the industry, which conspired to inhibit experimentation and innovation. Advances in ceramic production in other European countries, such as the use of high-firing temperatures, tin glazes and lustres, were not adopted by potters in England before the post-medieval period.

Generally, local clays and fuels were used, and the tempering material tended to be of local origin. The trend for potters to become more selective in their choice of clays and therefore less dependent on tempers became more pronounced in the 15th and 16th centuries, when such ceramic types as the reduced green wares of northern England or glazed red earthenwares contain nothing that can be claimed as a deliberate temper. There is considerable variation in the colours of medieval pots, even though many vessels were neither fully oxidized nor fully reduced. At the kilns at Mill Green, Essex, and Nash Hill, Wilts, attempts were made to conceal the colour of the body with a white slip, in imitation of contemporary French wares. Vessels were fired in kilns with multiple flues normally fuelled with wood, though coal and peat were also used. In the 12th and 13th centuries kilns with two opposed flues were commonly used, but from the late 13th century kilns with between three and five flues, foreshadowing post-medieval bottle kilns, were widely adopted in the Midlands and Yorkshire.

The most commonly made forms were cooking pots and jugs, followed by bowls and dishes. In the 12th and 13th centuries cooking pots were frequently large with a sagging base, which contrast with the smaller, Late Saxon cooking pots. In the later Middle Ages there was a growing preference for smaller footed and handled cooking pots known as pipkins, in shapes that reflect the growing popularity of Dutch redwares and metal cauldrons. In the 12th and 13th centuries many jugs and pitchers were large, and one of the more distinctive regional types was the tubular-spouted tripod pitcher produced in Oxfordshire and the west Midlands (e.g. 12th century; Gloucester, City Mus. & A.G.). By the 14th century most jugs had assumed more elegant shapes, including the baluster form. Bowls and dishes were less common, and in such areas as Devon they were not made in earthenware before the 16th century. Over 60 other forms were made including lamps, costrels, money boxes, chafing dishes, aquamaniles, condiment

58. Winchester ware costrel, punched and incised, h. 265 mm, 10th century (Winchester, City Museum)

dishes, salts, lobed cups, urinals, horns, plant pots and watering pots, as well as industrial wares, such as those used for distilling, and roof furniture, notably finials, louvres and chimney pots as well as plain tiles (see TILE, §II, 1).

One of the most important forms from the 14th century was the cistern used for brewing and storing beer. Previously drink had been consumed from small bowls or metalwares, but from the 14th century small jugs, including many Rhenish stonewares, were used for drinking. Cups became increasingly important after the late 15th century. Potters on the Surrey–Hampshire border produced whitewares, including jugs and cups, with a rich green glaze known as Tudor green wares. Among the other common regional types of the 16th century was the distinctive brown-glazed Cistercian ware, which was produced in many areas, especially Yorkshire (see WRENTHORPE). Cups were the speciality of the Cistercian ware potters, but they also made jugs, costrels, candlesticks, chafing dishes, salts and bowls.

Medieval potters sometimes decorated their wares, especially during the 13th and 14th centuries. While such domestic wares as cooking pots and bowls were occasionally provided with an internal glaze, applied strips or incised lines, these features were probably functional rather than purely decorative. As a means of enhancing the appearance of the pot, glaze was widely used on the external surface of jugs and other tablewares throughout the Middle Ages. Apart from on Stamford wares, glaze was used very sparingly, at first applied as a powder to create a splashed appearance. The range of coloured glazes included olive green, yellow, brown and red. Some glazes had copper filings added to produce emerald greens, the earliest of which is found on the fine 13th-century 'developed' Stamford ware jugs (see fig. 59). Other forms of decoration were normally confined to jugs, pitchers and such roof furniture as face finials, although the majority were plain. Little is known about the ways in which the decoration was applied or the schemes laid out. Occasionally, as on LYVEDEN ware, design lines can be seen beneath the glaze and decoration. At the kilns at Rye, E. Sussex, earthenware jugs were decorated with a wide variety of incised figures, which were randomly applied.

Many of the most elaborately decorated vessels may have been one-offs. Outstanding examples are the 'Knight' jugs made in such centres as Scarborough, N. Yorks, in the 13th and 14th centuries. Mounted knights wearing helmets and shields were modelled in the round and appear above a frieze of animals (e.g. 14th century; Winchester, City Mus.). Another common motif, usually attached to the rim, is the bearded face-mask, which takes various forms: at Carlisle, Cumbria, the mask and long beard were modelled in the round and attached to the jug at the rim and shoulder like a handle. At Doncaster, S. Yorks, and Grimston, N. Yorks, the masks have short beards on the side of the jug rim; at LAVERSTOCK, Wilts, the masks have short beards that form a very prominent part of the spout. Less common instances of anthropomorphic decoration include male figures such as those on wares from Nottingham with erect phalluses. Animal, fish and bird motifs rarely appear on medieval English wares. Aquamaniles imitated the shapes of metal ewers and were

59. 'Developed' Stamford ware jug, speckled green glaze, h. 315 mm, late 12th century or early 13th (London, British Museum)

modelled in the form of rams (e.g. late 13th century; Scarborough, Rotunda Mus. Archaeol. & Local Hist.) or horses and riders. Jugs from the Rye kilns have incised fish. Other elaborate vessels are the London ware polychrome jugs produced in the late 12th century and the 13th, and the 13th-century Mill Green ware. These were decorated with stripes in white, green and red slip on glazed jugs, combined with a number of other abstract motifs. The inspiration for this type of decoration was derived from Rouen ware. Design also included heraldic motifs with letters, in imitation of metal personal seals. Other heraldic devices can be identified on jugs from the Burley Hill kilns, Derbys, emblazoned with the arms of the de Ferrers family. The wares of the Toynton All Saints kilns in Lincolnshire have applied designs including fleur-de-lis and horseshoes thought to be heraldic in origin, but they also bear a wide range of other motifs including ladder-like devices. Other decorative techniques included roletting, which was more complex than that used on Saxo-Norman wares and which originated in the Low Countries. In addition, other devices include scales, stamps, bosses, iron-coloured strips, incising, sgraffito, applied strips, pads and thumbing, combined in an endless variety of ways in abstract designs.

The production of highly decorated pottery in England faded out in many areas from the mid-14th century. However, sgraffito motifs on wares from Essex and Cambridgeshire, brown and black painting on Sussex wares and the use of white slips at St Germans, Cornwall, continued to be used. Cistercian wares were often decorated with white slip, floral designs, pads and incised faces that appear yellow beneath the clear glaze. In general, however, decoration after the mid-14th century is less exuberant or absent: the reasons for this are complex and probably relate to the impact of the plagues and their consequences for society, as well as the increasing availability of metalwares.

The late 15th century and the 16th were transitional periods in which the range of forms differed from earlier wares. Tablewares included cups, mugs, drinking jugs, sweetmeat dishes, porringers, posset pots, chafing dishes and candlesticks. Other domestic wares included an increasing variety of such forms as colanders, watering pots, storage jars, chamber pots and pancheons. German stonewares were imported from the 15th century, but the manufacturing techniques were not adopted until the 17th century. Imported maiolicas were also well known in wealthy homes during the Tudor period, but the technique of tin-glazing, which was not introduced until the end of the 16th century, had no impact on production until the 17th century.

BIBLIOGRAPHY

J. W. G. Musty: 'Medieval Pottery Kilns', *Medieval Pottery from Excavations: Studies Presented to Gerald Clough Dunning*, ed. V. Evison, H. Hodges and J. G. Hurst (London, 1974), pp. 41–65

J. G. Hurst: 'The Pottery', *The Archaeology of Anglo-Saxon England*, ed. D. M. Wilson (London, 1976), pp. 283–348

S. A. Moorhouse: 'The Medieval Pottery Industry and its Markets', *Medieval Industry*, ed. D. W. Crossley (London, 1981), pp. 95–125

M. R. McCarthy and C. M. Brooks: *Medieval Pottery in Britain, AD 900–1600* (Leicester, 1988)

MICHAEL R. MCCARTHY

2. 1600–1700. At the beginning of the 17th century, despite the prosperity and stability of the Elizabethan period, England was still largely dependent on the Continent for all but the most functional pottery. Tudor green mugs, copied from the ubiquitous 16th-century stonewares imported from Raeren and Cologne/Frechen, were the first English ceramic mugs. Continental eating habits and their specialized pots—for example handled bowls, braziers and pipkins—were gradually introduced through trade and by Netherlandish refugees escaping from religious persecution. The impact of Chinese porcelain, which reached Europe in quantity only through cargoes captured by the Dutch in 1602 and 1604, had not yet taken effect, nor was the civilizing habit of tea- and coffee-drinking established in England before the mid-17th century.

Utilitarian earthenware pots continued to be made throughout the 17th century in rural areas where fuel and suitable clay could be found, and while more refined continental pottery was imported into London for redistribution, coarse pottery from the west of England was largely exported to captive markets in Ireland and the American colonies. Apart from the Tudor green wares of the Surrey kilns, tall, conical, multi-handled cups of lustrous black Cistercian ware were made in the Midlands and the north, while copies of Netherlandish forms were also made in Midlands yellow ware and Midlands black ware. Decorated pottery was made in several places: Metropolitan trailed slipware was made in the Harlow area of Essex; commemorative tygs with applied decoration were made in Wrotham, Kent, throughout the century (see fig. 60a); at Donyatt in Somerset and Barnstaple and Bideford in North Devon elaborate sgraffito decoration was practised until the end of the 19th century; and in North Staffordshire slipware was more highly developed. The inspiration for all these wares came from imported slipwares from North Holland, Beauvais in France and Weser in Germany, from the fine sgraffito dishes of Werra in Germany and even, at Wrotham, from the stamped and applied decoration of Rhineland stonewares.

In the second half of the century the natural and cultivated advantages of the STAFFORDSHIRE area became apparent: abundant coal, red and white clays, access by river to the sea, an established system of 'cratemen' for pottery distribution, highly developed skills, the first use of press-moulded designs for slipwares, and enough commercial drive to extinguish the existing Midlands potting centres. The last three decades of the century produced the magnificent trailed slipware chargers of such potters as Thomas Toft (d 1689), William Talor (b c. 1630), Ralph Simpson (1651–1724) and Samuel Malkin (1668–1741), who used contrasting clay lines with 'jewelled' or 'stitched' edges reminiscent of embroidery. Of more lasting significance were the thinly potted dipped slipware tygs and cups, and especially the treacle-coloured wares with lead-manganese-iron glaze that were the precursors, in form and colour, of the brown salt-glazed stonewares made from c. 1700.

Tin-glazed earthenware or delftware—known until the 18th century as 'galleyware'—was not yet affected by developments in Staffordshire. Introduced first as a popular import from Antwerp, and later, in the late 16th century, as a native manufacture at Norwich and Aldgate, London, by such Netherlandish potters as Jaspar Andries, who was of recent Italian descent, this material was light, with a white ground suitable for a large variety of painted decoration, was fired with wood and could be made with clays from Norfolk and tin from Cornwall. The range of high-temperature 'in-glaze' colours consisted of cobalt-blue, manganese-purple, iron-red, copper-green and antimony-yellow.

Apart from the Aldgate Pottery, which closed c. 1615, two other important factories were established: the first by Edmund Bradshawe (fl 1611–17) and Hugh Cressey (fl 1595/6–1626) at Montague Close, Southwark, London, and the other by Christian Wilhelm (fl 1604; d 1630) at Pickleherring Quay, also in Southwark, c. 1618, both presumably making the 'bottel(es) basons & ewers salt(es) dishes drinkinge pott(es) pavinge tyles Apothecaries & Comfittmakers pott(es)' mentioned in Wilhelm's patent of 1628. In addition to these either plain white wares or

60. 17th-century English ceramics, from left to right: (a) red earthenware candlestick decorated with white slip (slipware), h. 184 mm, made at Wrotham, Kent, 1649; (b) tin-glazed earthenware dish or charger, painted with a figure of *William III*, diam. 340 mm, probably made in London, *c.* 1690–1700; (c) salt-glazed stoneware bottle with inlaid marbling and white sprigs, h. 172 mm, made by John Dwight at the Fulham Pottery, London, *c.* 1685; (d) red stoneware mug, unglazed, slip-cast and lathe turned, with applied sprigs, h. 95 mm, made by the Elers brothers at Bradwell Wood, Staffordshire, *c.* 1690–98 (London, Victoria and Albert Museum)

wares with rudimentary blue and purple decoration, a series of inscribed pots with blue bird-on-rock decoration in the style of blue-and-white porcelain made in China during the Wanli period (1573–1620) was made at Pickle-herring in the 1620s. Besides a wide range of white or blue-and-white pottery, from *c.* 1630 large dishes for display ('blue-dash chargers') with bold polychrome painting were made by the London potteries, which were inspired by Italian maiolica, Chinese porcelain patterns and Netherlandish engravings.

If the Thirty Years War in the Low Countries and the consequent depression of the Dutch and German pottery industries during the 1620s and 1630s were crucial in establishing the production of English delftware, the Civil War (1642–9) must have brought a period of austerity to the pottery trade, expressed in the notably sparse decoration of the mid-17th century; documented orders for replacing melted-down silver would have been small compensation. Possibly because of the conditions in London *c.* 1650, potters migrated from Southwark to found a delftware pottery at Brislington, moving in the early 1680s to Bristol itself, where the business flourished.

The Restoration (1660) brought a demand for colourful commemorative pots, chargers with royal portraits (see fig. 60b) or tulips, such luxury articles as 'sack' bottles (given as New Year presents), flower vases, posset pots, handwarmers and wall tiles, for which a patent was granted to the potter Jan Ariens van Hamme (*fl* 1676; *d* 1679/80), who had emigrated from Delft, in 1676. A period of prosperity is certainly indicated by the successful prohibition by the potters of 'painted earthenwares' from abroad

in 1672 and 1676 and by the establishment of six more pothouses, mainly in Southwark and Lambeth, London, during the period 1663–83. The Dutch influence was still strong and was then combined with that of France, which inspired the white painting on a dark-blue ground, imitating the *bleu persan* style of decoration of wares from Nevers. By 1698 the London potters were strong enough to remove successfully the excessive duty of earthenware and stoneware that had depressed the trade; and it must have been clear that the cultivated English taste for blue-and-white Chinese patterns would guarantee the future expansion of the industry in the 18th century.

Attempts in the 17th century to make brown, salt-glazed Rhineland stoneware, which was in constant demand due to its durability, were closely connected to conditions in the Frechen potteries; these were dependent on the English trade and on the difficulties of the Dutch and German shippers, who retained control despite the monopoly granted to Henry Noell (*d* 1597) in 1593. The difficulties of unravelling the technical process, of obtaining suitable clay and of building high-temperature kilns were indeed great: neither the patent obtained by Thomas Browne (*fl* 1614; *d* 1636) and Toby Steward (*fl* 1614; *d* before 1633) in 1614 to make 'stone pott(es) stone jugg(es) and stone bottles', nor that of the immigrants Thomas Rous (*fl* 1617; *d* 1640) and Abraham Cullen (*fl* 1618; *d* 1658), who in 1626–7 attempted to import German expertise, seem to have produced any stoneware. The excavated but undocumented mid-17th century stoneware pottery at Woolwich, London, was short-lived, and by the 1660s, after both the imposition of heavy taxation and disruption to the stoneware bottle trade caused by the Dutch Wars, the new practice of storing wine in glass bottles rapidly gained favour, a fact that caused at least one main Dutch importer to cease operations.

The spirit of enquiry during this period produced not only George Ravenscroft's lead glass but also the first successful stoneware pottery. In 1672 JOHN DWIGHT obtained, entirely through his own experiments, his first patent for 'transparent Earthen Ware' and 'Stone ware vulgarly called Cologne ware', just before a rival application by William Killigrew, who had already made stoneware with assistance from German potters. Dwight's main objective was, however, the making of luxury wares and especially porcelain, and it was only in 1674 that he resigned himself to making salt-glazed stoneware (see fig. 60c) as a staple product at the Fulham Pottery, London, contracting with the Worshipful Company of Glass Sellers to supply them with his bottles of traditional Rhineland type in 1676. His continuing experiments soon led him to produce a red stoneware of the Yixing type, which he patented in 1684 among his other claims and actual achievements: 'White gorges Marbled Porcellane Vessels Statues and Figures . . . transparent Porcellane and opacous redd and darke coloured Porcellane or China and Persian Wares'. Although Dwight narrowly failed (from lack of china stone) to make porcelain, his surviving stonewares display technical mastery combined with crisp potting, lathe turning, fine brown, near-white or marbled clay bodies and sharp sprig decoration made with brass moulds.

Once the secret of salt-glazing was known, potters with access to stoneware clays quickly began to exploit it, and through Dwight's litigation of the 1690s much is known about these infringements of his patents. In Staffordshire the ELERS brothers made slip-cast red stoneware in the 1690s at Bradwell Wood under licence from Dwight (see fig. 60d), while James Morley (fl 1682–95) at Nottingham openly continued making fine, lustrous mugs, and the Wedgwood brothers at Burslem claimed that they made only lead-glazed copies. In London, the Southwark potters Matthew Garner (fl 1680–1718) and Luke Talbot (fl 1683/4–1726/7) at Gravel Lane and Moses Johnson (fl 1675–1715) at the Bear Garden undoubtedly produced bottles and tavern mugs. By about 1700 the technique had finally taken root in Staffordshire, where it was developed and refined into the tablewares that fuelled the massive expansion of the Potteries in the 18th century.

BIBLIOGRAPHY

A. J. B. Kiddell: 'Wrotham Slipware and the Wrotham Brickyard', Trans. Eng. Cer. Circ., iii/2 (1954), pp. 105–18
R. G. Cooper: English Slipware Dishes, 1650–1850 (London, 1968)
S. Moorhouse: 'Finds from Basing House (c. 1540–1645)', Post-med. Archaeol., i/4 (1970), pp. 31–90
P. C. Brears: The English Country Pottery (Newton Abbot, 1971)
L. Weatherill: The Pottery Trade and North Staffordshire, 1660–1760 (Manchester, 1971)
R. Edwards: 'London Potters Circa 1570–1710', J. Cer. Hist., 6 (1974) [whole issue]
I. N. Hume: Early English Delftware from London and Virginia (Williamsburg, 1977)
D. Haselgrove and J. Murray, eds: 'John Dwight's Fulham Pottery, 1672–1978: A Collection of Documentary Sources', J. Cer. Hist., 11 (1979) [whole issue]
F. Britton: English Delftware in the Bristol Collection (London, 1982)
R. Jackson, P. Jackson and R. Price: 'Bristol Potters and Potteries, 1600–1800', J. Cer. Hist., 12 (1982) [whole issue]
A. Grant: North Devon Pottery: The Seventeenth Century (Exeter, 1983)
L. L. Lipski and D. M. Archer: Dated English Delftware (London, 1984)
J. G. Hurst, D. S. Neal and H. J. E. van Beuningen: Pottery Produced and Traded in North-West Europe, 1350–1650, Rotterdam Papers, vi (Rotterdam, 1986)
R. Coleman-Smith and T. Pearson: Excavations in the Donyatt Potteries (Oxford, 1988)
D. Haselgrove: 'Steps towards English Stoneware Manufacture in the 17th Century', London Archaeologist, vi/5 (1989), pp. 132–8; vi/6 (1990), pp. 152–9
J. Pearce: Border Wares, Post-Medieval Pottery in London, 1500–1700, i (London, 1992)
M. Biddle, ed.: The Palace of Nonsuch (in preparation)
C. Green: Excavations at John Dwight's Fulham Pottery, 1971–79 (in preparation)

For further bibliography see §§3 and 4 below.

3. 1701–1830.

(i) Earthenware and stoneware. (ii) Porcelain.

(i) Earthenware and stoneware. At the beginning of the 18th century various branches of the ceramic industry were already well established in England, and the technical discoveries of John Dwight together with the slip-casting technique developed by the Elers brothers (see §2 above) showed further avenues of possible development. Most tableware and household goods were provided by the delftware potteries, supplemented by imported Chinese porcelain; tavern, kitchen and cottage utensils were either German or English brown salt-glazed stoneware or some type of coarse lead-glazed earthenware. The main types of pottery were continuously refined and adapted during the 18th century until the introduction of porcelain in the 1740s provided the spur for Staffordshire potters to develop the durable, light, smooth earthenware that culminated in the production of Josiah Wedgwood's 'Queen's Ware' in 1765.

Traditional slipware tygs continued to be made in the early 18th century at Wrotham, Kent, while their Staffordshire counterparts displayed masterly potting and simple but assured decoration in black slip: dishes with press-moulded outline patterns were early attempts to save labour. At Barnstaple, Devon, 'Harvest' jugs of local red clay, used for bringing beer or cider to the harvesters, were covered in white slip and decorated with lively sgraffito designs. From the late 18th century several potteries in Sussex made inlaid slipware, and in many country potteries combed or slip-trailed dishes, money-boxes and puzzle jugs were made well into the 19th century, when competition from industrialized Staffordshire reduced them to the level of novelties.

By 1700 delftware potteries at Southwark and Lambeth in London and at Bristol and nearby Brislington were making large quantities of plates, bowls, mugs and drug jars, mostly with cobalt-blue or manganese-purple decoration, generally inspired by Dutch and Chinese motifs. Towards the mid-18th century a delftware pottery was started at Wincanton, Somerset, while earlier in the 18th century an important industry had been founded at Liverpool (see LIVERPOOL, §3). However, London was perhaps the biggest centre of production and made vast numbers of plates with lively painting and bold patterns until the early 19th century. The Bristol potteries (see BRISTOL, §3(i)) suffered an early decline in the 1780s but are noted for their use of chinoiserie and bianco-sopra-bianco decoration. At Liverpool, where the painted patterns were comparatively dull but meticulous, production ceased at approximately the same time except for tiles—often printed by the firm of Sadler & Green (*see* TILE, fig. 1)—which remained an area immune from Staffordshire competition. Although many attempts had been made to improve the appearance of delftware—powdered blue and manganese ground colours, polychrome patterns and even, at Liverpool, the rare use of *petit feu* enamels and transfer-printing—by the mid-18th century the material was clearly unsuitable for further development. The advent of creamware, the waning popularity of blue-and-white chinoiserie patterns in the 1780s and the labour-intensive manufacturing process, as well as the tendency of the glaze and body to chip and crack, all combined to cause the demise of a type of ware that, at its best, was highly decorative, cheap and popular both in England and as an export to North America. In terms of social status it ranked, beside pewter, below Staffordshire earthenware and the plainest Chinese porcelain.

Before his death Dwight's patented salt-glaze process for 'Fulham Ware' was being exploited by potteries in Southwark, Staffordshire, Nottingham, Crich (Derbys) and then in Bristol and Liverpool. In London, riverside potteries made a complementary range of delftwares and heavy-duty stoneware mugs and bottles, which supplanted the traditional stonewares imported from Frechen and the Westerwald. The few decorated wares included commemorative sprigged hunting mugs made at the Vauxhall Pottery and later versions at Mortlake. Bristol stonewares consisted of sprigged mugs and refined cider or beer jugs in addition to the mass-produced bottles of the 19th century. At Nottingham light, lathe-turned pots ('Nottingham Ware') with a brown lustrous glaze were made throughout the 18th century, sometimes with pierced, incised or sprigged decoration, while the associated contemporary potteries in Derbyshire—centred on Denby and Brampton—used local clay and coal to expand hugely after 1800.

By 1700 in STAFFORDSHIRE the skilled potters of Burslem, using their abundant local clay and coal to make brown salt-glazed stonewares and lead-glazed earthenwares streaked with iron and manganese, were laying the foundations for a great industry. Brown stoneware was abandoned as soon as a white-clay body was developed, either whitened with slip or further improved after *c.* 1720 by the addition of calcined flint and clays from Dorset and Devon (an invention attributed to either JOHN ASTBURY or Thomas Heath). Cheaper, lighter and stronger than any other type of British ceramics, the material was soon used to provide tewares, mugs, small dishes and, later, dinner-services for the mass market. During the second quarter of the 18th century much use was made of the contrast between a drab-coloured body and applied white or blue details or white oil-gilded sprigs. During the early 1740s Staffordshire potters, no doubt stimulated by the establishment of the London porcelain factories at Chelsea, Bow and Limehouse (*see* §(ii) below), but lacking their entrepreneurial and artistic capabilities, began a period of major innovation: press-moulding, slip-casting from plaster of Paris moulds (first practised in England by the Elers brothers), enamelling in colours supposedly introduced by

Dutch immigrants working at Cobridge, scratch-blue decoration, early attempts to make figures and a range of new, clay bodies were all introduced. Other potting centres were quick to follow, so that until the 1780s huge quantities of cheap, moulded or thrown stoneware were made and largely exported to the Continent and the Americas. Press-moulded designs tended to be sharp but linear, often based on shell- and basketwork, while slip-casting encouraged the production of three-dimensional forms in the Rococo spirit. Of the many Staffordshire salt-glaze stoneware makers, Thomas Wedgwood (1703–76) and John Wedgwood (1705–80) were perhaps the most productive, while Aaron Wedgwood (1717–63) in partnership with William Littler (1724–84) developed a translucent blue dip ('Littler's Blue') during the late 1740s. During the 1750s and 1760s, before the perfection of plain creamware, the colourful and inventive enamelling of stoneware by independent decorators in, for example, Cobridge, Leeds and London could equal that of Bow porcelain, but thereafter stoneware seems to have become increasingly utilitarian.

Of the new ceramic bodies, red stoneware was re-introduced almost 50 years after the Elers' experiments, perhaps as a development of the red earthenware with white sprigs ('Astbury Ware') made in the 1730s and of the marbled red earthenware patented by Samuel Bell (1684–1744) in 1729. Unglazed red stoneware imitating Chinese teapots from Yixing, engine-turned or sprigged, carried on through the century, until it was revived by Josiah Wedgwood as 'Rosso Antico' in 1776. The red-clay body could also be stained black with a lustrous glaze ('Jackfield Ware'), either painted or oil-gilded to resemble lacquer or decorated with white-sprigged trailing vines. However, the most important development of the 1740s was the refinement of the white stoneware body into a type of cream-coloured earthenware by such pioneers as Enoch Booth (*fl* 1740–54) of Tunstall, who attempted underglaze blue painting and who in 1750 invented an improved liquid lead-glaze and introduced to creamware the biscuit-firing process. THOMAS WHIELDON of Fenton Vivian gave his name to a sponged oxide colour decoration, although, like many other potters during this period, he made a wide range of solid agate, red and black wares; he is also noteworthy for his partnership (1754–9) with Josiah Wedgwood (*see* WEDGWOOD, §1), which allowed Wedgwood to perfect the green and yellow glazes that complemented the improved cream body and the elaborate vegetable forms produced by the influential blockcutter, decorator and potter William Greatbatch (1735–1813).

Wedgwood's experiments at his own pottery in Burslem resulted in 'Queen's Ware', the creamware that earned him the patronage of Queen Charlotte in 1765 and which, with its pale body and perfectly matched glaze, was ideal for reproducing the elegant Neo-classical boat and vase shapes of silver and Sheffield plate. Although his 'Black Basalt' (1768) and 'Jasper' (1775) were materials capable of imitating gems, medallions, coloured marble and Greek vases, it was the more humble creamware that was to transform the English pottery industry and extinguish the production of tin-glazed earthenware in many parts of Europe. The new material was light and resistant to cracking and provided a perfect ground for decoration, which Wedgwood fully exploited by securing in the 1760s the exclusive services of the Leeds enameller David Rhodes (*d* 1777) and the Liverpool printers Sadler & Green, rather in the same way as he engaged John Flaxman as modeller for some of the ornamental wares, including the 'Frog' service made for Catherine II of Russia in 1773–4 (see fig. 61). As the leading and best-documented potter of his period, Wedgwood has overshadowed such contemporaries as John Turner (*d* 1787) of Lane End, William Adams (*d* 1805) of Tunstall and James Neale (*b* 1739–40), all of whom were happy to purchase each others' products to fill urgent orders. Other creamware centres were soon established in Yorkshire at Leeds, Castleford, Rotherham, Swinton, Rothwell and Ferrybridge, as well as at Liverpool, Derby and Bristol and in the north-east. The Yorkshire potteries excelled in pierced creamwares ('Leeds Ware'), which were sometimes enamelled in a limited palette of strong colours by Robinson & Rhodes at Leeds or printed in black. At Sunderland and Newcastle upon Tyne decoration was restricted to simple border patterns and bold printing. During the 1770s, in response to changing public taste, Staffordshire potters introduced a whiter body with a bluish glaze called 'Pearlware', which was intended to imitate the greyness of Chinese porcelain and which was either painted or later printed in underglaze blue. From this development, which effectively replaced delftware,

stemmed the massive output of blue-and-white printed wares of the 19th century, the best of which were made by such firms as the SPODE CERAMIC WORKS in the early years of the century. Copper plates for these transfers were engraved by specialists and widely distributed: to the range of patterns in the Chinese taste was added the ever-popular 'Willow' pattern and a variety of overall prints of Indian and Classical views copied from book illustrations. Meanwhile, pale, almost white creamware with enamelled borders continued to be made in the early 19th century by such factories as the Spode, Davenport, Minton and Wedgwood. A parallel development was that of 'Ironstone China', patented by the potter Charles James Mason (1791–1856) of Lane Delph in 1813 and consisting of a heavy, tough body ideal for dinner services, decorated with Imari patterns copied from Arita porcelain.

During the late 18th century and the early 19th the pottery trade expanded greatly, primarily to cope with the export trade, which in 1785 was estimated at five-sixths of the total Staffordshire production. New types of white earthenware with banded decoration were followed by 'Mocha' ware (decorated with moss-like traceries) in the 1790s, and from this period lustre was made in many areas, either with an overall silver coating (platinum) copying metalwork forms, or painted with pink (gold),

61. Creamware plate (a 'second') from the 'Frog' service, h. 298 mm, made by Wedgwood and painted at his Chelsea decoration workshop, 1773–4 (London, Victoria and Albert Museum)

which was used at Sunderland until well into the 19th century. 'Prattware', a type of inexpensive pearlware decorated with high-temperature colours, notably green and orange, was similarly made throughout England from the late 18th century until the 1830s. The coloured stonewares pioneered by Wedgwood were gradually adapted and popularized at the end of the 18th century. His 'Caneware' of the 1770s was matched by John Turner's invention in 1780 of a refined, unglazed, buff stoneware that was ideal for sharp modelling in low relief and was soon copied by William Adams and others. Coloured dry-bodied or smear-glazed (with salt) stoneware tea and ornamental wares were made in quantity until the early 19th century, carrying on the stoneware tradition until it was used for the Staffordshire and Shropshire floor-tile industry and for the moulded jugs made from the 1840s. By about 1820 glazed blackware had replaced black basalt and the moulded 'Castleford' ware teapots of white felspathic stoneware with blue enamel borders.

The great tradition of Staffordshire earthenware figures began in the 1740s with the hand-built, salt-glazed stoneware 'Pew Groups' and earthenware musicians, once attributed to Astbury. The new moulding techniques soon enabled such potters as Thomas Whieldon and, later, members of the Wood family of Burslem (see WOOD (iii)) to reproduce lead-glazed figures streaked with coloured oxides cheaply. A great variety of animals, 'Toby' jugs, busts and classical figures were made by many potteries, notably John Walton (*fl* 1810–35), who later made naive earthenware copies of 18th-century porcelain bocage groups. Elaborate groups of animals on table bases were

62. Porcelain group of Chinese musicians, h. 354 mm, made by Chelsea, probably modelled by Joseph Willems, *c.* 1755 (London, Victoria and Albert Museum)

also made, but from the 1830s Staffordshire figures degenerated into flat-backs (figures made in moulds with flat backs), which, together with model cottages, have continued to be made ever since.

(ii) Porcelain. After the failure of John Dwight's experiments to produce porcelain at Fulham, no serious attempt seems to have been made until, in 1743–4, separate patents were registered by William Steers and Thomas Briand (*d* 1747), and three unconnected factories were established in London. That they chose this moment to launch their new soft-paste formulae was perhaps partly due to such recent technological advances in Staffordshire as slip casting and enamel painting and partly to the availability of venture capital and artistic expertise, fuelled by the demand for imported East Asian and German porcelain. Around 1744 NICHOLAS SPRIMONT began making a frit porcelain at the CHELSEA PORCELAIN FACTORY, using his considerable talents as a silversmith to supply expensive luxury porcelains to a discerning, wealthy London clientele. At the BOW PORCELAIN FACTORY a partnership of merchants including Thomas Frye, who in 1749 obtained a bone-ash porcelain patent, set out to capture the market in enamelled East Asian porcelain, also producing, like Chelsea, white wares influenced by the *blanc-de-Chine* wares from Dehua, Fujian Province, to show off the new material to the best advantage. A less ambitious factory at Limehouse, under Joseph Wilson, made mainly blue-and-white wares (*c.* 1744–8). The success of Chelsea was aided by a Flemish sculptor, Joseph Willems (*c.* 1715–66), and the availability in London of the best porcelain painters in England. Tablewares, and figures (see fig. 62) that were used as table adornment in the German fashion, imitated wares from the Meissen porcelain factory (*see* MEISSEN, §3), but from the 1750s the rich ground colours of Vincennes and Sèvres were reproduced. The production, which represented the English Rococo in both form and decoration, was stock-piled and sold for extravagant prices at annual auctions. Bow, styled 'New Canton', achieved commercial success with tablewares, vases and figures aimed at a middle-class market, using enamelled 'Kakiemon style' patterns in addition to underglaze blue and 'powder-blue' grounds. Despite a flourishing export trade, Bow did not long outlast Chelsea, which was taken over by WILLIAM DUESBURY in 1770 and finally moved to Derby in 1784.

The second wave of porcelain ventures occurred *c.* 1750: the London 'Girl-in-a-swing' factory managed by Charles Gouyn, formerly associated with the Chelsea factory, made mostly 'toys' (trifles) and figures. Vauxhall made mostly blue-and-white tablewares; Lund & Miller produced porcelain briefly at Bristol; the Worcester Porcelain Co. (*see* WORCESTER) concentrated on tablewares; the DERBY factory made notable figures under André Planché (1727/8–1805) and tablewares under Duesbury; the LOWESTOFT PORCELAIN FACTORY made tablewares in imitation of Chinese export wares; at Liverpool several factories made large quantities of tablewares; and at Longton Hall, Staffs, figures and ambitious moulded tablewares were attempted. Some of these provincial factories, benefiting from lessons learnt by the pioneers in London, aimed their products at an undemanding public

63. Two porcelain garniture vases, h. 150 mm, made by Chamberlain of Worcester, possibly painted by Thomas Baxter, *c*. 1810 (London, Victoria and Albert Museum)

who might otherwise have bought Chinese export porcelain. In the 1750s and 1760s the Vauxhall and Liverpool factories made similar wares, with some technical difficulties, while Lowestoft survived until the 1790s by concentrating on a limited range of blue-and-white and polychrome patterns. Worcester flourished under Dr John Wall (1708–76) after adopting the Lund & Miller soapstone (steatite) formula, which made the porcelain impervious to hot liquids, and mass-produced fine painted tablewares and pioneered the use of printing under Robert Hancock; blanks or partly decorated wares were also supplied to the noted London decorator James Giles (1718–80). Imitations of Worcester blue-and-white were successfully made at the CAUGHLEY PORCELAIN FACTORY in Shropshire, which was later absorbed by the COALPORT PORCELAIN FACTORY. Derby continued to make its popular figures (except for the more sophisticated biscuit models) well into the 19th century and, like Worcester, adopted Neoclassical ornamental forms. In Staffordshire, William Littler gave up his pottery in 1751 to manage the Longton Hall Factory, which, after the patents of Briand and Steers and the experiments at the Pomona factory (*c*. 1746–54) in Newcastle-under-Lyme, was the first serious porcelain venture in the Potteries. Prolific but lacking a reliable porcelain formula, it survived only until 1760.

In addition to the Bow bone-ash and the Worcester soapstone porcelain formulae, hard-paste porcelain was made by WILLIAM COOKWORTHY at Plymouth in 1768, moving in 1770 to Bristol, where tablewares and figures were made until 1781. Richard Champion (1743–91), who had acquired this important patent in 1774, at first tried to interest Wedgwood and then managed to sell it to the consortium of Staffordshire potters that set up the New Hall factory in 1782, at a time when the north Staffordshire

potteries were benefiting from the opening of the Trent and Mersey Canal and the installation of steam-power and were able to draw from a pool of experienced porcelain painters. The combination of a hard-paste porcelain, fine Staffordshire potting and restrained, elegant patterns proved so successful that others imitated the formula, notably the Turners of Lane End, John Davenport at Longport and Miles Mason (*d* 1822) at the beginning of the 19th century. After the successful use of bone-ash at Lowestoft, Chelsea, Derby and Liverpool, and after Champion's extended hard-paste formula patent had expired in 1796, potters were able to combine the ingredients and the virtues of both types of porcelain to produce the new bone china, which was developed by James Neale and perfected by Josiah Spode (i) *c*. 1800. Further boosts were given to the English porcelain makers, now increasingly centred on the Potteries, when the East India Company ceased importing Chinese porcelain in 1791 and by the restricted import on porcelain from France during the Revolution.

From this period the manufacture of blue-and-white was taken over by the earthenware potters, while the established porcelain makers embraced the rich effects that comprised the Regency style, combining shapes copied from metalwork or from Paris porcelain with peculiarly English 'watercolour' painting, which was well-suited to the hard, greyish hybrid paste favoured by the Worcester factories of Robert Chamberlain (*b* 1735), Grainger & Co., the soapstone of the Flight & Barr factory and the soft-paste of Derby. Historical scenes, topographical views, botanical specimens and flowers were painted, often in reserve on a coloured or gilt ground (see fig. 63), by such highly competent artists as Thomas Baxter (1782–1821), who, as independent decorators or artists employed by several factories, raised to a peak the general standard of porcelain painting.

The new factories of Minton, Coalport and Spode soon established themselves by using a huge variety of simple, bold patterns including 'Japan' patterns, painted vignettes or grey stippled bat-prints for their smooth, white, metal-work-shaped, bone-china teawares. After these successes New Hall, Miles Mason, Davenport and even, for a brief period, the Wedgwood factory changed over to bone china, and from about 1810 yet more factories were started, notably Hilditch, Bourne & Co., Riley, Daniel, RIDGWAY and Machin. In addition many minor factories now made cheap, functional bone china for a popular market, decorated with plain or hand-coloured prints, lilac sprigging and even pink lustre. The English taste for Sèvres soft-paste porcelain, which had made bone china popular, also encouraged serious attempts to imitate both the style and material. To satisfy demand, Coalport, Spode and Minton improved their bone chinas in the 1820s by adding feldspar, so that as the Rococo Revival took hold of English porcelain manufacturers, it was also possible to make spirited imitations of mid-18th-century Meissen porcelain styles, in particular assymetrical forms and clustered, applied flowers. This style, perfected at such factories as the Coalport porcelain factory and the ROCK-INGHAM CERAMIC FACTORY, which made china from 1825, long remained popular and mingled in the 1830s with chinoiserie, Gothic and the remnants of Neo-classical taste in a way that heralded the eclecticism of the mid-19th century.

BIBLIOGRAPHY

GENERAL

L. Jewitt: *The Ceramic Art of Great Britain* (London, 1878, rev. 1972)
B. Rackham: *Catalogue of the Glaisher Collection of Pottery and Porcelain in the Fitzwilliam Museum, Cambridge* (Cambridge, 1934, rev. Woodbridge, 1987)
G. Godden: *An Illustrated Encyclopedia of British Pottery and Porcelain* (London, 1966)
B. Hillier: *Pottery and Porcelain, 1700–1914* (London, 1968)
J. Thomas: *The Rise of the Staffordshire Potteries* (New York, 1971)
D. Edwards: *Neale Pottery and Porcelain: Its Predecessors and Successors, 1763–1820* (London, 1987)
P. Atterbury and M. Batkin: *The Dictionary of Minton* (Woodbridge, 1990)
R. Reilly: *Wedgwood*, 2 vols (London, 1990)

EARTHENWARE AND STONEWARE

D. Towner: *The Leeds Pottery* (London, 1963)
A. Mountford: *Staffordshire Salt-glazed Stoneware* (London, 1971)
F. H. Garner and M. Archer: *English Delftware* (London, 1972)
D. Towner: *Creamware* (London, 1978)
A. Oswald, R. J. C. Hildyard and R. G. Hughes: *English Brown Stoneware* (London, 1982)
Stonewares & Stone Chinas of Northern England (Stoke, 1982)
J. Lewis and G. Lewis: *Pratt Ware* (Woodbridge, 1984)
F. Britton: *London Delftware* (London, 1986)
J. Horne: *English Tin-glazed Tiles* (London, 1989)
D. Barker: *William Greatbatch: A Staffordshire Potter* (London, 1990)

PORCELAIN

B. Watney: *Longton Hall Porcelain* (London, 1957)
H. Sandon: *Illustrated Guide to Worcester Porcelain* (London, 1969, rev. 1980)
A. L. Thorpe and F. Barrett: *Derby Porcelain* (London, 1971)
G. Godden: *British Porcelain* (London, 1974, rev. 1990)
H. Sandon: *Flight and Barr Worcester Porcelain, 1783–1840* (Woodbridge, 1978)
P. Bradshaw: *18th Century English Porcelain Figures* (Woodbridge, 1981)
G. Godden: *Eighteenth-Century English Porcelain* (London, 1985)
E. Adams and D. Redstone: *Bow Porcelain* (London, 1987)
P. Bradshaw: *Derby Porcelain Figures* (London, 1990)
For further bibliography *see* §4 below.

ROBIN HILDYARD

4. 1831–1900. By 1831 the Industrial Revolution was entering its final phase, and porcelain and earthenware factories were becoming larger and increasingly specialized. The industry had become firmly wedded to the Rococo Revival style, which, with its loosely defined rules and the improved technology available, provided ample scope for designers to produce larger, more flamboyant shapes demanded by a growing and increasingly affluent middle class. With the end of the East India Company's monopoly of the tea trade in 1830, the price of tea fell, giving an impetus to the demand for teawares.

From the early years of the 19th century pure white, highly translucent bone china had become the standard body used by English porcelain manufacturers, and extravagances of size and design were no longer limited by the plasticity of the body or its stability in the kiln. This freedom was fully exploited by the major factories, including the Staffordshire potteries of Minton, Copelands, Davenport & Co., Samuel Alcock & Co. and H. & R. Daniel; Rockingham, in Yorkshire; Coalport, in Shropshire; and Grainger & Co. and Chamberlain's, both in Worcester. In the 1830s the chiefly ornamental, fussy, flower-encrusted 'Coalbrookdale' wares, made in imitation of Chelsea figures and vases of the 1760s, were introduced (e.g. Coalport porcelain vase, *c.* 1830; London, V&A). These were by no means confined to Coalport as their generic name might imply, and the massive 'Rhinoceros' vases of the Rockingham ceramic factory offer an impressive example of the genre (e.g. of *c.* 1830; London, V&A).

While the later established factories enjoyed sustained growth, the few 18th-century porcelain manufacturers who had survived into the 19th century found the competition increasingly difficult: C. J. Mason & Co., in Fenton, Staffs, had ceased manufacturing porcelain by 1830; New Hall, in Shelton, Staffs, by 1835; and production ceased in Derby by 1848. The Rockingham and Daniel factories also failed in the 1840s, and the factory of Flight, Barr & Barr in Worcester was taken over by William Chamberlain in 1840 to become Chamberlain & Co. During the 1830s there was a reaction against the strong ground colours of the Regency period of the 1820s, and a range of new underglaze or high-temperature ground colours (formerly confined to cobalt blue) was introduced, which reduced decorating costs. These new colours included a subdued range of greys, drabs (stone colours), fawns and buffs, often dignified with the name of 'Adelaide' in honour of the new queen.

The dichotomy of earthenware and porcelain became irrevocable during this period. The rich, cream-coloured ware, introduced by Wedgwood in the 18th century, was first replaced by the whiter pearlware (a type of earthenware with additions of white clay and flint, and cobalt oxide in the glaze, which gave it a bluish tinge), and then by a cheap white earthenware, the quality of which could be enhanced by covering the entire surface with an underglaze-blue, transfer-printed pattern. As good-quality bone china became more widely available, cheaper earthenwares were relegated to the kitchen and sent to the colonies. Earthenwares for the table never again reached the position of eminence, relative to porcelain, that they had enjoyed throughout most of the 18th century.

The introduction of a range of high-temperature colours for porcelain was matched by a range of coloured printing inks. By 1840 it was possible to print a large range of engraved patterns not only in cobalt blue but also in brown, green, pink or purple. This soon led to experiments, probably initiated at Davenport & Co., for use on both earthenware and bone-china bodies, of multi-colour printing. Originally this was achieved by applying different coloured inks to the same copper plate but later led to a full, four-colour separation, building up the print by applying each colour from a separately engraved plate. The technique was perfected in time for examples to be entered for the Great Exhibition of 1851 in London by F. & R. Pratt of Fenton, Staffs.

The fashion for drab colours established at the beginning of the decade was not to continue after the accession of Queen Victoria (1837). The freedom of the Rococo Revival style permitted, and indeed encouraged, eclecticism. The search for inspiration in the porcelain of 18th-century Sèvres led to much deliberate copying, and a full range of ground colours was reintroduced, including a rich turquoise copying *bleu céleste* and a deep rose colour called 'rose du Barry', which imitated *rose Pompadour*. The factory marks of both Sèvres and Meissen were also freely copied. Coalport teawares came very close to the French originals in both shape and colouring. Herbert Minton (1793–1858) went a stage further, creating superb copies of Sèvres *vases à elephants* and *vaisseaux à mat* (a type of pot pourri vase in the shape of a ship), which are visually barely distinguishable from the originals.

A new porcelain body, 'Parian' or 'statuary' porcelain, was developed by Copeland's in 1842. A dense body with a silky, marble sheen, it was the ideal medium for reproducing antique marble figures. As it needed no glaze, the sharpness of detail in the modelling could be retained. In 1843 Benjamin Cheverton (1794–1883) invented a reducing pantograph, which opened up the possibility of reproducing Classical sculptures for a mass market, a project encouraged by Henry Cole and his Felix Summerly's Art-Manufactures. The educational potential of Parian figures was diluted by the preferences of manufacturers for commissioning new models from such fashionable sculptors as John Bell, John Gibson (i), Albert-Ernest Carrier-Belleuse and Raffaelle Monti. Their designs frequently took the form of partially clad females in submissive poses, which appealed to the Victorian market and were sold in great numbers. Notable public figures were also commemorated (see fig. 64).

The Manchester Exhibition of Industrial Art of 1846, the Birmingham Exhibition of 1849 and the Great Exhibition of 1851 all served to introduce English ceramics to a wider public. Competition for medals led manufacturers to create increasingly imaginative and dynamic designs, which, by their sheer size and technical virtuosity, were aimed at blinding the critics to their often brash vulgarity. For the next 20 years self-confidence was to remain the hallmark of Victorian style. The gold medals won by the firms of Coalport and Minton in 1851 and at the Exposition Universelle in Paris in 1855 may have owed more to

64. Parian porcelain 'Nelson' vase, made by S. Alcock & Co., 1851 (London, Victoria and Albert Museum)

plagiarism than to innovation. New technical advances in the industry were not always matched by fresh aesthetic inspiration. A new earthenware body called 'majolica', decorated with brilliantly coloured glazes, was introduced at that time as a recreation of the 16th-century glazed wares of Bernard Palissy. It proved immensely popular, and a wide variety of objects, from whimsical teapots to garden ornaments and colossal fountains, ensured its popularity until the end of the century (e.g. majolica ewer and plateau by Minton & Co., *c.* 1862; London, V&A).

The development of tile manufacture owed much to majolica glazes. The factory of William Chamberlain, then in decline, was making tiles in Worcester in the 1840s. In 1850 John Hornby Maw (1800–85) purchased these tile works and a few years later moved the concern to Broseley, Salop, a town long associated with the clay industries. There he experimented with encaustic and glazed tiles and in 1883 moved to nearby Jackfield, where Craven Dunnill had already established a large tile works. In 1855 Herbert Minton had patented a method of making encaustic tiles. After his death in 1858 the firm of Minton & Hollins

65. Salt-glazed stoneware vase, h. 216 mm, made by the Martin brothers, London, *c.* 1886 (London, Victoria and Albert Museum)

porcelain created a new demand for simplicity, exemplified in the hand-thrown stoneware decorated with traditional glazes of the Arts and Crafts Movement.

This new movement was fuelled by several unrelated factors. There was an influx of French designers and decorators into the Staffordshire Potteries following the outbreak of the Franco-Prussian War (1870–71). This immigration was partially due to the influence of Léon Arnoux (1816–1902), who had been Minton's art director since 1849. Antoine Boullemier (1840–1900), Paul Comolera (1818–97) and William Mussill (*d* 1906) were recruited to the Potteries at this time, joining Emile Lessore (1805–76) and Charles Hurten (1818–97). In 1870 MARC-LOUIS-EMANUEL SOLON introduced the *pâte-sur-pâte* technique at Minton: a series of applications of white slip were applied to a coloured Parian body until the design was raised in slight relief; the design was then carved back before firing. His compositions, executed with an almost frivolously light touch, blended Classical and amorous themes and were immensely popular (e.g. Minton vase of Sèvres form decorated with *pâte-sur-pâte* panels, 1898; London, V&A).

Also during the 1870s there was a revived interest in Japanese culture, diversely reflected in contemporary majolica, in the blue-and-white wares collected by such artists as Whistler and Dante Gabriel Rossetti associated with the Aesthetic Movement, in Royal Worcester porcelain, in the designs of Christopher Dresser for the Linthorpe Art Pottery, near Middlesborough, Cleveland, and in the products of Minton's short-lived South Kensington Art Pottery Studio, which opened in Kensington Gore, London, in 1871. Henry Doulton (1820–97) was largely responsible for the revived interest in salt-glazed stonewares for ornamental use and began employing at his factory in Lambeth students from the Lambeth School of Art, including George Tinworth (1843–1913), Hannah Barlow (1859–1913), Arthur Barlow (*d* 1878) and Florence Barlow (*d* 1909). The four Martin brothers (*see* MARTIN (iii)) began potting at Fulham, London, in 1873, moving to Southall, also in London, in 1877. They specialized in bizarre and grotesque animal forms as well as more conventional vases (see fig. 65).

The art pottery produced by the DOULTON CERAMIC FACTORY, the Martin brothers, Sir Edmund Elton (*d* 1920), William De Morgan (*see* DE MORGAN, (1)), Maw & Co., Burmantofts Faience, Leeds, and Edward Bingham (1829–*c.* 1900) at CASTLE HEDINGHAM had little in common and followed no readily definable style. As the Pre-Raphaelite Brotherhood looked back to the 14th century, the art potters looked back to the days before Josiah Wedgwood. They rejected precise potting, moulding and lathe-turning and all the refinements and mechanical techniques that had successfully established Wedgwood. Only Christopher Dresser seemed to look forward to the new century with Japanese-inspired designs that were unashamedly modern. At the same time the international exhibitions, which proliferated during the second half of the century, had induced manufacturers to concentrate, in their efforts to win medals, on virtuoso performances, *tours de force*, which had little relevance to utilitarian wares made for the popular market. This was no doubt a factor in divorcing, in the public mind, the concept of art pottery

broke away from the parent company and became a major producer of tiles in competition with the two Jackfield concerns. Between them they supplied tiles to a growing market throughout the world, tiling almost every major public building in the British Empire, including the New Palace of Westminster (*in situ*). The tile industry was given a fresh impetus by the fashion for extensive restoration of medieval churches and by the victory of the Gothic style for ecclesiastical and public buildings; this movement was passionately advocated by the architect A. W. N. Pugin, who also designed tiles for Minton in the late 1840s (*see* TILE, fig. 5).

In reaction to the earlier encrusted and elaborately decorated Victorian ceramics, at the International Exhibition of 1862 in London the exhibits were less flamboyant, characterized for the most part by a technical perfection, a meretricious slickness that lacked vigour and could stylistically lead nowhere. Copelands, Minton & Co. and Coalport continued to manufacture enormous quantities of tableware for the world market, but they had become the followers of fashion rather than the arbiters of public taste. New aesthetic principles were being propounded by John Ruskin and William Morris, who saw mass production and the specialization of labour as the ultimate social and artistic evil. The ideal of the individual craftsman, the potter who throws, fires and decorates his own pots, proved an impossible dream in an expanding market. Nonetheless, the reaction against slick, mass-produced

from objects made purely for domestic use. Paradoxically the Art Nouveau movement, which so infused the designs commissioned by Arthur Lasenby Liberty for Liberty's at this time, made little impact either on art pottery or on ceramics made for domestic use. During the last decades of the century designs for tablewares largely followed established traditions in manufacturing methods, design and decoration and continued to become increasingly derivative and debased.

BIBLIOGRAPHY

R. G. Haggar and W. Mankowitz: *The Concise Encyclopedia of English Pottery and Porcelain* (London, 1957)

G. A. Godden: *Minton Pottery and Porcelain of the First Period, 1793–1850* (London, 1968)

——: *Coalport and Coalbrookdale Porcelain* (London, 1970)

L. Whiter: *Spode* (London, 1970, rev. 1990)

D. Holgate: *New Hall and its Imitators* (London, 1971)

D. G. Rice: *An Illustrated Guide to Rockingham Pottery and Porcelain* (London, 1971)

J. Barnard: *Victorian Ceramic Tiles* (London, 1972)

G. A. Godden: *An Illustrated Guide to Ridgway Porcelains* (London, 1972, rev. 1990)

——: *British Pottery: An Illustrated Guide* (London, 1974)

E. Lloyd Thomas: *Victorian Art Pottery* (London, 1974)

D. Eyles: *The Doulton Lambeth Wares* (London, 1975)

R. Haggar and E. Adams: *Mason Porcelain and Ironstone, 1796–1853* (London, 1977)

M. Messenger: *Pottery and Tiles of the Severn Valley* (London, 1979)

M. Berthoud: *H. & R. Daniel, 1822–1846* (Bridgnorth, 1980)

G. A. Godden: *Godden's Guide to Mason's China and Ironstone Wares* (Woodbridge, 1980)

J. Twitchett: *Derby Porcelain* (London, 1980)

G. A. Godden: *Chamberlain-Worcester Porcelain, 1788–1852* (London, 1981)

M. Batkin: *Wedgwood Ceramics, 1846–1959* (London, 1982)

A. W. Coysh and R. K. Henrywood: *The Dictionary of Blue and White Printed Pottery, 1780–1880*, 2 vols (Woodbridge, 1982–9)

Alwyn Cox and Angela Cox: *Rockingham Pottery and Porcelain, 1745–1842* (London, 1983)

D. Drakard and P. Holdway: *Spode Printed Ware* (Harlow, 1983)

G. A. Godden, ed.: *Staffordshire Porcelain* (St Albans, 1983)

P. Miller and M. Berthoud: *An Anthology of British Teapots* (Bridgnorth, 1985)

G. A. Godden: *Encyclopaedia of British Porcelain Manufacturers* (London, 1988)

T. A. Lockett and G. A. Godden: *Davenport: China, Earthenware, Glass, 1794–1887* (London, 1989)

H. Sandon and J. Sandon: *Grainger Worcester Porcelain* (London, 1989)

MICHAEL BERTHOUD

5. AFTER 1900. Pottery production in the 20th century can be divided into two groups: commercial wares produced by the pottery industry, based mainly in the Potteries around Stoke-on-Trent, Staffs; and the work of individual studio potters or clayworkers.

(i) Commercial pottery. The majority of factories were in Stoke-on-Trent, with other manufacturers including the Denby Pottery, Denby, Derbys; the Royal Crown Derby Porcelain Co., Derby; the Poole Pottery, Poole, Dorset; and Royal Worcester, Worcester. The industry maintained two strands in its production: traditional and modern. Traditional shapes and the decorative patterns continued to be made, and various designs reworked and reissued. Popular patterns included such underglaze, transfer-printed designs that originated in the early 19th century as landscapes and the 'Willow' pattern. Border patterns of various widths and colours often echoed 18th-century

designs and proved to be enduringly popular. Classic 18th- and 19th-century shapes for table and ornamental ware also remained in use.

At the beginning of the century the sinuous Art Nouveau style was dominant in Europe. Such English potters as WILLIAM MOORCROFT used the style predominantly for surface decoration as seen in his range of raised-slip decorated 'Florian' wares, while the firms of Doulton and Minton produced ranges specifically designed for this style. At Minton, under the art director John William Wadsworth (1879–1955), Art Nouveau toiletwares and tablewares were produced and often decorated with raised-slip designs with coloured glazes in the reserves. The Art Deco style became popular after the 1925 Exposition Internationale des Arts Décoratifs et Industriels Modernes in Paris and was employed by many factories and potters. Most firms merely added bold, bright, hand-painted slabs of colour in geometric or abstract designs to existing shapes, but some created new ones. CLARICE CLIFF, who ran the Newport Pottery, adjacent to the firm of A. J. Wilkinson Ltd, Burslem, Staffs, produced a highly popular range of such geometric and angular forms as 'Bizarre' and 'Fantasque' decorated with brightly coloured designs including 'Crocus'. Teawares, vases and bowls were conical, while handles were triangular, either solid or with an awkward, small hole. During the 1930s factories were influenced by the International Modern Movement in architecture. Vases, bowls, mugs and jugs became increasingly functional and rational in shape with minimal decoration and neutral matt glazes. This trend is evident in the work of the architect Keith Murray (1892–1981), who worked for Josiah Wedgwood and Sons Ltd from 1933, producing simply shaped wares that were decorated with lathe-turned bands (e.g. coffee service, c. 1935; Barlaston, Wedgwood Mus.). A particularly successful mass-produced range by Murray was the cane-coloured 'Bournvita' drinking set produced for Cadbury by Wedgwood in 1933; more than a million beakers were sold in 14 months.

During World War II regulations introduced by the government Utility Scheme prevented the creation of new designs; production for the home market was limited to plain white or ivory wares until August 1952 when the restrictions were lifted. During the 1950s the freedom to use colour and shape led to a huge range of new designs. The greatest innovation of this period was the coupe-shaped plate, which had no rim for salt and mustard. Decorative patterns included such motifs as exotic holiday locations, furniture, cutlery, stars, spots and gingham plaids. The primary colours or maroons and greys were dominant. Shapes became softer, and vases and bowls featured undulating edges. From about 1957, however, wares with crisp, geometric outlines were introduced, for example in the work of SUSIE COOPER, and dominated design during the 1960s and early 1970s. Shapes became more streamlined and were often decorated with transfer-printed, silk-screened or inlaid designs, many of which were regular to emphasize the shape (e.g. Wedgwood bone-china plate decorated with 'Variations on a Geometric Theme', designed by Eduardo Paolozzi, 1971; Barlaston, Wedgwood Mus.). Stylized floral designs also became popular, for example the 'Nevada' range of tablewares

66. Earthenware sugar bowl (h. 95 mm), teapot (h. 130 mm) and 'Boo Boo' cream-jug (h. 155 mm), designed by Mabel Lucie Attwell, made at the Shelley Pottery, Longton, Staffordshire, 1926 (London, Victoria and Albert Museum)

introduced by Hostess Tableware Ltd in Longton, Staffs, in 1972.

A new ceramic ware, known as oven-to-table ware, was introduced in many factories in the mid-1960s to compete with the heat-resistant glassware 'Pyrex'. This hard-wearing ovenware was made in a variety of functional, solid shapes and wares, including casserole, soufflé and pizza dishes. Decoration was often limited to brown or speckled glazes and reflected the influence of studio potters on the industry (e.g. 'Romany' oven-to-table wares, Denby Pottery, 1972). By the end of the 1970s further technical advances enabled factories to produce wares that could be used in the microwave oven, freezer and dishwasher. Colours were lightened, and shapes were softened.

Wares specifically designed for children also flourished in the 20th century and included not only dishes, bowls, plates and cups but also figures, mobiles, money-boxes, Christmas-tree ornaments and teasets. Decoration included designs by such artists as Mabel Lucie Attwell, who designed a range of nursery wares including a toadstool sugar bowl and teapot and 'Boo Boo' character cream-jug for the Shelley Pottery in Longton, Staffs (see fig. 66). Since 1949 Wedgwood has owned exclusive rights to the manufacture of wares decorated with reproductions of Beatrix Potter's watercolour drawings of Peter Rabbit, which were lithographed in colour.

(ii) Studio pottery. Handmade pottery by individuals working away from the main factories is a 20th-century phenomenon. In the first half of the century studio pottery was influenced by East Asian wares and medieval and 17th-century English slipwares. The movement began in London with such potters as George Cox and WILLIAM STAITE MURRAY, but spread throughout the country under the influence of BERNARD LEACH and MICHAEL CARDEW. Potters interested in East Asian wares strove to produce the temmoku, celadon and *jun* glaze effects of Korean, Chinese and Japanese potters (e.g. stoneware vase with temmoku glaze by Leach, 1959; London, V&A). Stoneware clays were dominant and often fired in East Asian style kilns. Potters producing slipwares, including Cardew,

intended to revive the traditional style of English earthenwares. These wares were made in red clay and decorated with brown and cream slips (e.g. slipware jug by Cardew, 1938; London, V&A).

During the late 1940s and early 1950s studio potters were influenced by such potters from continental Europe as LUCIE RIE, HANS COPER and Ruth Duckworth (*b* 1919), who had settled in Britain in the late 1930s. They produced elegant, vigorous wares in muted colours with minimal decoration. ALAN CAIGER-SMITH revived the techniques

67. Stoneware 'Optical' pot, h. 313 mm, made by Elizabeth Fritsch, 1980 (London, Victoria and Albert Museum)

of tin-glaze and lustre decoration, using silver and copper to produce stunning effects.

The desire to create new surface textures and glazes encouraged such potters as KATHERINE PLEYDELL-BOU-VERIE, who was a pupil of Leach, and Norah Braden to experiment with a variety of glazes produced by wood and plant ashes (e.g. stoneware bowl with box-ash glaze by Pleydell-Bouverie, 1937; Bath, Holburne of Menstrie Mus.). The use of saltglaze, produced in Britain during the 18th century, had lapsed until the 1960s when Denise Wren (1891–1979) reintroduced it. Many potters used this revived technique and combined it with coloured washes.

Potters working with such hand-building techniques as slab-building and coil-building include ELIZABETH FRITSCH, ALISON BRITTON and Martin Smith (b 1950); Fritsch concentrated on flattened forms, which combined balance with geometric decoration (see fig. 67); Britton's assembled sheets of clay are asymmetrical and decorated with bold, abstract designs. In the late 20th century domestic wares continued to be made by such potters as David Leach (b 1911) and Sophie McCarthy, who attempted to reinterpret and re-design traditional shapes, surface textures and decoration. Some studio potters produced standard wares, as well as their studio wares, for mass production by small industrial units: Janice Tchalenko worked for Dart Pottery in Dartington, Devon, producing designs in a range of shapes, and Carol McNicoll (b 1943) designed slip-cast forms for Next Interiors.

BIBLIOGRAPHY
G. Forsyth: *20th Century Ceramics* (London, 1934–5)
M. Casson: *Pottery in Britain Today* (London, 1967)
N. French: *Industrial Ceramics: Tableware* (Oxford, 1972)
E. Cooper and E. Lewenstein: *New Ceramics* (London, 1974)
J. Spours: *Art Deco Tableware* (London, 1988)
P. Rice and C. Gowing: *British Studio Ceramics in the 20th Century* (London, 1989)
K. Niblett: *Dynamic Design: The British Pottery Industry, 1940–1990* (Stoke-on-Trent, 1990)

KATHY NIBLETT

VIII. Glass.

1. Before 1592. 2. 1592–*c*. 1725. 3. *c*. 1725–1830. 4. 1831–1900. 5. After 1900.

1. BEFORE 1592. The earliest glassmaking in England was after the Roman invasion in the 1st century AD. The glass made was a soda-lime glass, the alkali obtained from marine plant ash imported from the Mediterranean, a formula that continued to be used for the next 1000 years. There were several glassmaking sites during this early period in Essex, Norfolk and Cheshire. Some glass made from the 5th century to the 7th has survived due to the custom of burying goods with the dead. Forms include cone-shaped beakers with finely trailed decoration called claw-beakers; jars, bottles and palm-cups were made during the 7th century. In 675 Benedict Biscop, Abbot of Monkwearmouth Abbey, Tyne & Wear, sent a request for Gaulish glassworkers to come to England to make window glass for the new monastery; the abbot of the nearby Jarrow Monastery sent a similar request to the Archbishop Lullus of Mainz in the Rhineland in 758. About 1000 the composition of glass changed due to increasing problems in communication with the Mediterranean, and glassmakers changed the fluxing agent to potash obtained from

beech or bracken ash. The new more durable formula known as *Waldglas* was used to make vessels, apothecary flasks and beakers with applied or moulded decoration.

During the 13th century French glassmakers came to the Weald area of Surrey, Sussex and Kent, which remained the most important centre of glassmaking production in England until the end of the 16th century. In 1226 Laurence Vitraerius (*fl* 1220–40) from Normandy set up a glasshouse at Dyers Cross, near Chiddingfold, Surrey, where he made vessel glass. About 1350 John Alemayne (*fl* 1350–55) arrived in the Weald area and, although not

68. Soda-glass goblet by Jacopo Verzelini, h. 215 mm, from the Crutched Friars glasshouse, London, diamond-point engraved, possibly by Anthony de Lysle, 1581 (London, Victoria and Albert Museum)

a glassmaker, he leased his property near Chiddingfold to John Schurterre, whose glassmaking family came from Normandy *c.* 1343. The industry was dominated by the production of window glass and simple, utilitarian vessels. Other glasshouses in Shropshire, Staffordshire and Cheshire were also in production during the 14th century. From the 11th century to the 16th various vessel types were made, including ampullae, funnel-shaped lamps and goblets. Beakers became popular during the 15th century. Urinals were produced as chamber pots and for uroscopy. These items were made in *Waldglas* and may have been influenced by Venetian glass, which was imported from *c.* 1399.

The influence from Venice continued when a number of Huguenot craftsmen who could produce Venetian-type glass came to England from the Continent after 1550. In 1567 Jean Carré (*d* 1572) arrived from Arras via Antwerp. He built two furnaces in Alford, Sussex, for the production of window and vessel glass and he employed the de Hennezell family from Lorraine and Peter Bungay and John Bungay from Normandy. In 1570, with his partner Peter Briet, he established the Crutched Friars glasshouse in London for the production of glass *à la façon de Venise*. The types of vessels produced were tapering conical or cylindrical medicine-bottles, stemmed goblets and ribbed beakers. At first predominantly Flemish workers were employed at Crutched Friars, but Italians from Antwerp were increasingly hired, including Jacopo Verzelini (1522–1616). He managed Crutched Friars until Carré's death and then took over the factory. In 1574 he obtained a licence granted by Elizabeth I for the production of Venetian-style glass for 21 years, which also prohibited the import of Venetian glass and the production of glass *à la façon de Venise* by other glasshouses. The only surviving items made by Verzelini are a number of thinly blown soda-glass goblets. Some have funnel-shaped bowls, and some have hollow, moulded, knop stems and a folded foot. Although one is gilded, the remainder are decorated with diamond-point engraving bearing a name, date or inscription, as in the goblet made for Jon and Jone Dier (see fig. 68). Anthony de Lysle (*fl* 1577–90) is thought to have done some diamond-point engraving for Verzelini's factory.

For bibliography *see* §4 below.

2. 1592–*c.* 1725. Following the retirement of Jacopo Verzelini (*see* §1 above) in 1592, his licence was taken over by Sir Jerome Bowes (*d* 1616). This was the start of the era of the Monopolists, a group that controlled the industry through obtaining licences and patents that restricted glass production. In 1595 Bowes was granted a 12-year monopoly for importing Venetian glass and for manufacturing glass *à la façon de Venise*. About 1600 he built a new furnace on the site of Blackfriars Monastery in London and leased it to William Robson and William Turner. In 1605 he was granted a new patent, and in 1607 a reversion of his monopoly was agreed to be transferred on his death to Percival Hart and Edward Forcett. After 1605 Robson took sole charge of the Blackfriars Glasshouse; he also acquired Winchester House glasshouse in Southwark, London, which had been established *c.* 1608 by Edward Salters. Robson was a dominant producer of *cristallo* from

1610 until 1612, when a patent was issued to Sir Edward Zouch to make all types of glass; this did not infringe on previous licences, because Zouch used a coal furnace rather than a wood one. In 1615 a royal proclamation prohibited the use of wood furnaces, and coal was used as the permanent replacement.

Sir Robert Mansell (1573–1656) was the next Monopolist. About 1617 he built the Broad Street Glasshouse in the City of London, which was managed by Robson. By 1618 Mansell was the sole proprietor and in 1623 obtained a patent for various sorts of glassware made in coal furnaces, which he maintained until 1642. The production was dominated by flat glass for mirrors, spectacles and bottles. Mansell employed predominantly Italian craftsmen, such as Antonio Miotti (*fl* 1616–23), and eventually he owned glasshouses in England, Wales and Scotland.

The Civil War had a devastating effect on the glass industry, and it was not until the Restoration in 1660 that George Villiers, 2nd Duke of Buckingham (1628–87), emerged as the next Monopolist. He dominated the industry for 14 years due to his wealth and his influence at the court of Charles II. In 1660 he acquired a glasshouse at Greenwich and employed Venetians and the Frenchman John de la Cam (*fl* 1660–68) to make glass *à la façon de Venise*. About 1663 he acquired the Vauxhall Glasshouse, London, where sheet glass and mirrors were made. His establishments were eventually taken over by the Worshipful Company of Glass Sellers of London. In 1662 Christopher Merrett translated *L'Arte vetraria* (Florence, 1612) by Abbot Antonio Neri (1576–1614), which discusses the principles of Italian glassmaking. From 1667 to 1673 the Company imported glass from the works of Alessio Morelli (*fl* 1667–72) in Murano, made to designs by John Greene (*d* 1703). From 1670 the Company promoted research, and its fundamental aim was to develop a native glass.

In 1674 the Company authorized GEORGE RAVENSCROFT to set up a glasshouse and research establishment at Henley-on-Thames, Oxon. By 1676 Ravenscroft had developed a new metal called lead glass, which was made by the addition of lead-oxide as a flux. The new metal was thick, oily, brilliant and light-refractive. The creation and development of lead glass enabled England to become the dominant glass-producing country in the 18th century. Items made included jugs, bowls and goblets with hollow stems, decorated with raspberry prunts (blobs of glass that have the appearance of a raspberry). Roemers for the consumption of hock (see fig. 69) and flutes were also introduced; these showed stylistic influences from Germany and the Netherlands. The influence from the Continent continued until 1685 with the use of such decoration as gadrooning, ball knops, raspberry prunts and tear knops. The number of glasshouses in operation by the late 17th century increased due to the success of lead glass. Although production was centred in London, many provincial glasshouses were established, including those at King's Lynn, Norfolk; Bristol, Avon; Stourbridge, W. Midlands; and Newcastle upon Tyne, Tyne & Wear.

The first completely original English design was the baluster glass. The baluster period started in 1690 and

18th century and used on candlesticks, tapersticks and sweetmeat dishes.

For bibliography *see* §4 below.

3. *c.* 1725–1830. The introduction of wheel engraving was a new way of decorating glass in England in the 1720s and showed the continuing influence from Germany. This development became significant from 1725 and lasted into the 19th century. During the early part of the 18th century engraving was applied only to the thickest parts of glasses, such as the stems and rims of sweetmeat dishes, which were scalloped. The real significance of wheel engraving, however, is evident in wares from later in the century.

The Baroque-style curved stems used for baluster glasses became increasingly angular. Influence from the late 17th century (the Anglo-Venetian period) lingered on in the gadrooned bowls, but English styles developed in the extended solid-bowl with a tear-drop in the stem. The feet changed from the folded to the domed and folded. The bowl forms varied from a round funnel, bucket or a Rococo-style double ogee, which was a particularly dominant feature of sweetmeat glasses.

The success of English lead glass led to an expansion in the variety of items available. The most extensive range of glassware was made for drinking; there were different types of glasses for wine, cordials, ale and champagne. Toastmasters' glasses were trumpet shaped with thin stems. Firing glasses had a trumpet-shaped bowl and a very thick foot for thumping on the table after a toast. Mirrors, wine and beer bottles, decanters, cruet bottles, dishes, plates, sugar casters, tea caddies, teapots, cups and saucers were all being produced in glasshouses throughout the country.

From 1725 the distinctive 'Newcastle' style appeared. The glasshouse established by the Dagnia family in Newcastle upon Tyne made balustroids, which were more complex and lighter in form than the baluster glass. The metal was of a very high quality, thinly blown, and the stems were decorated with air-beaded knops. From 1730 the style began to spread, and balustroids were made in most glasshouses until 1760. From 1725 to 1749 large quantities of English glass (the majority of which came from Newcastle upon Tyne) were exported to the Netherlands for engraving. Dutch engravers used the diamond-point to decorate glass with stippling; one of the most prominent engravers was Frans Greenwood (1680–1761), who used this method of decoration from *c.* 1722. In 1745 the Glass Excise Act was enforced. The tax was levied on the weight of dry materials and resulted in the production of lighter forms and styles. In an attempt to reduce the weight, some glasshouses reduced the lead content in the glass and replaced it with soda as the fluxing agent. Alternative methods of decoration resulted in the popularity of hollow stems, air-twists and cotton twists and the growing fashion for coloured glass in the second half of the 18th century.

Stem decoration was very popular during the 18th century. From *c.* 1730 to *c.* 1770 the air-twist stem was used in a variety of forms. Single, double and multiple series air twists were inserted into the stem and were often used in conjunction with engraved bowls. From 1760 to 1790 cotton-twist stems were made using canes of opaque

69. Lead-glass roemer with raspberry prunts by George Ravenscroft, h. 165 mm, made at the Savoy Glasshouse, London, *c.* 1676 (London, Victoria and Albert Museum)

continued until *c.* 1725. Initially the stem was inverted and later (*c.* 1715–25) it was decorated with a single or multiple tear drop. The number of knops also varied. The early bowl forms were a round funnel, which was followed by a drawn trumpet and finally a bell shape. During the early 18th century various types of drinking glasses appeared for different drinks; gin became available during the reign of William and Mary, and in 1703 a treaty was signed with Portugal allowing the import of port at a reduced duty. This resulted in smaller glasses being used for stronger drinks, in addition to ale flutes and beaker glasses for beer. Stem cutting and the introduction of the moulded, shouldered stem, called the 'Silesian' stem, replaced the baluster stem. The Silesian stem was at first four-sided. It was made to celebrate the coronation of George I in 1714 and was decorated with a crown and his cypher. The six-sided stem was popular from 1718 to 1725, and the poorer-quality, eight-sided stems were produced until the late

white glass. (Opaque white glass and cullet had been excluded in the tax of 1745.) There were many variations in form, including cables, corkscrews, gauze, lace and multiple spiral twists. The cotton twists were a continuation of techniques developed in Venice in the 16th century. The coloured twist became popular from 1770. In 1777 the tax on glass was doubled and included enamel, which brought about the demise of the cotton-twist stem.

Many glasshouses, particularly those in the provinces, did not adopt the moulded pedestal glasses. Jacobite glasses, for drinking toasts, were wheel-engraved with decoration that displayed sympathy and loyalty to the exiled James II and later to James Edward Stuart (the Old Pretender) and Charles Edward Stuart (the Young Pretender). Until 1745 bowls were engraved with the English rose with between six and eight petals, buds and such mottoes as *Fiat* and *Redeat*. From *c.* 1746 to 1760 decoration consisted of disguised Jacobite symbols. It was probably during this period that 'Amen' glasses were made. These were wine glasses with a drawn stem. The bowl was diamond-point engraved with a crown and reversed cypher, verses of the Jacobite hymn and the word 'Amen'. After 1770 secrecy was abandoned, and the glasses were decorated with portraits and overt Jacobite symbols.

In the 1760s enamelled decoration was carried out almost exclusively in Newcastle upon Tyne. The Dagnia Williams glassworks supplied glass for decoration to the Beilby family. William Beilby and his sister Mary Beilby enamelled glassware from *c.* 1762 to 1774. They decorated decanters, wine glasses and goblets with armorial devices (see fig. 70) and, later, Rococo motifs with floral subjects, naturalistic birds, classical ruins and rustic scenes.

Coloured glass was made at many glasshouses during the 18th century. Glasshouses in Bristol (*see* Bristol, §3(ii)) made blue and amethyst-coloured glass, and items produced included scent bottles, finger bowls and decanters. Green and opaque white glass was also produced. The glass was decorated by cutting, engraving, gilding and enamelling. Michael Edkins (1734–1811), a freelance glass painter, was based in the Bristol area from *c.* 1762. He worked for various glasshouses in Bristol and painted opaque white glass and gilded blue glass with chinoiseries and other Rococo motifs.

The influence of the Neo-classical style as interpreted by the architects Robert Adam and James Adam is seen in the work of James Giles (1718–80), who was a freelance porcelain painter in London. He decorated coloured glass decanters, scent bottles and vases with gilding and enamelling using exotic birds, Rococo motifs and then Neo-classical motifs. The items were made by the Falcon glassworks in Southwark and the Parker Cut Glass factory in Fleet Street, London.

Decanter bottles had been made in green and brown glass from the mid-17th century. However, the form developed further during the 18th century and was manufactured for serving not only wine but also sherry, port and later cordials and spirits. From 1725 to 1750 shapes were similar to the short-necked and broad-bodied decanter bottles. From 1730 the glass stopper came into use in various forms. From *c.* 1775 decanters became more slender with disc stoppers, and by the end of the 18th century they had broad, bulbous bodies with mushroom

70. Enamelled glass goblet with cotton-twist stem by William Beilby, h. 210 mm, *c.* 1762 (Cambridge, Fitzwilliam Museum)

stoppers. They were usually made of clear glass, which was sometimes faceted or engraved with vines and a label. Coloured glass decanters, especially blue glass with a gilded bottle label, were also made.

During the late 18th century the manufacture of glass was dominated by high-quality cut glass. From the mid-18th century cut glass had become more elaborate, and wares were faceted with diamonds and triangles. From 1760 to 1770 cutting became very rich and then more sober with the influence of the Neo-classical style, when the vertical flute and low-relief diamond cutting were popular. In 1777 the tax on basic materials was increased, and in 1780 the right of free trade was granted to Ireland (*see* Ireland, §VIII), which led to many glasshouses being set up there and employing English and European workers.

In the 18th century and the early 19th one of the largest ranges of glassware was made for lighting. Candlesticks and candelabra were produced, but the quality and brilliance of cut glass was best demonstrated in the CHANDELIER. During the first half of the 18th century chandeliers were made of a shaft consisting of globe-shaped members and a bowl to which S-shaped arms were attached, terminating in a pear-shaped pendant. During the second half of the century the chandelier became two-tiered with more elaborate faceting on all the members and drops. The Neo-classical style gave rise to urn-shaped members, swags of pear-shaped drops and plain-cut arms. By 1810 the chandelier had developed into an extravagance of tiered curtains of vertical strings of drops, ormolu fittings and fixed S-shaped arms. During the early years of the 19th century there was an increase in the variety of glass objects, in particular the jug, which became an item for everyday use.

For bibliography *see* §4 below.

4. 1831–1900. This period of glass production is marked by a variety of individual achievements, designers, companies and new technology, which resulted in the most eclectic age of English glass. The increased use of steam-power enabled cutters to produce an enormous variety of richly cut glass by an efficient mechanical means. Relief-diamond cutting gave way to more intricate and deeper cutting, and vertical motifs gained popularity with the revived interest in the Gothic style. However, this phase was ephemeral, and relief-diamond cutting was revived during the 1840s. English cut glass was very popular and enormously influential across Europe.

During the 1830s Bohemian coloured glass began to be copied by English glass factories in a wide variety of styles and colours. After the repeal in 1845 of the Glass Excise Act (1745), which had inhibited research, experiment and innovation, there was an increased use of cased glass, in which two or more layers of different coloured glass were used together for a purely decorative effect. By 1849 good-quality coloured glass was being produced by such firms as W. H., B. & J. Richardson in Stourbridge, but most output concentrated on white or coloured opaline glass, which was inspired by the French and decorated with transfer-printing, enamelling and gilding.

The influence of France is also seen in the work of Apsley Pellatt (1791–1863), who owned the Falcon glassworks in Southwark, London. In 1819 he had obtained a patent for producing sulphides (encrusted cameos). The process had been introduced at the end of the 18th century by the Frenchman Barthélemy Desprez (*fl* 1773–1819), and Pellatt called the technique 'crystallo-ceramie'. Production included goblets, paperweights and scent-flasks, which incorporated an embedded medallion made of a porcellanous material decorated with profile portraits, busts, coats of arms and landscapes. In 1831 he developed a similar technique called 'Crystallo Engraving', which was imitative of wheel engraving, in which a mould-blown object was decorated with an intaglio impression achieved by the inclusion of a plaster motif in the mould (see fig. 71). During the 1850s Pellatt revived ice-glass.

In 1851 window tax was abolished, and in the same year Joseph Paxton designed the Crystal Palace (destr.) in

71. Cut-glass scent-bottle with a 'Crystallo Engraving' portrait of *William IV* by Apsley Pellatt, h. 110 mm, made at the Falcon glassworks, London, 1834 (London, Victoria and Albert Museum)

Hyde Park, London, to house the Great Exhibition. It was an iron-framed construction incorporating *c.* 300,000 panes of glass and demonstrated the possibilities of glass in an architectural context. The glass for the building was made by the Spon Lane glassworks at Smethwick, Birmingham. The focal point of the exhibition was a 6 m high glass fountain (destr.) made by the F. & C. Osler Glasshouse in Birmingham.

During the 19th century several publications were influential in glass production: in 1849 Pellatt published his *Curiosities of Glass Making*, and in 1856 Owen Jones produced his *Grammar of Ornament*, which depicts various historical styles but with most emphasis on the Classical. The latter was used by students who attended the government-sponsored design schools founded during the 1840s. At the Great Exhibition the preference was for extravagantly coloured and cut glass. However, the London company of J. G. Green had exhibited classically inspired wares. Engraving became increasingly popular, and by the International Exhibition of 1862 in London this style of decoration prevailed. Classical engraving was most popular during the 1860s and 1870s. Blanks were made by such firms as THOMAS WEBB of Stourbridge and sold to retailers who employed highly skilled Bohemian engravers. Etching, using hydrofluoric acid, was a technique that was intended as a cheap alternative to copper-wheel engraving and became very significant during the 19th century. In 1857 Benjamin Richardson of Stourbridge, who had been experimenting with acid-etching, was granted a patent for the production of acid-etched glass using sulphuric and hydrofluoric acids and an Indian-rubber resist. In 1859 John Northwood (1836–1902), who had been working with Richardson, set up a workshop at Wordsley, near Stourbridge, where he decorated blanks, concentrating on naturalistic and Classical styles (e.g. vase, 1878; Kingswinford, Broadfield House Glass Mus.). Northwood was also responsible for such technical innovations as the template etching machine (1861) and the geometrical etching machine (1865).

In Stourbridge another development that took place was the revival of the Roman art of cameo glass. In 1783 the Portland Vase (early 1st century AD; London, BM; see GLASS, fig. 5) had been brought to England by Sir William Hamilton (i). Early attempts to reproduce it in glass were unsuccessful. In 1873 the Red House glassworks in Stourbridge made the blank, and Northwood executed the carving, completing it in 1876. Northwood employed George Woodall (1850–1902), who proved to be a most proficient cameo sculptor. From 1874 Woodall was employed by Thomas Webb & Sons as a glass engraver. The Classical elements in his work were inspired by Antonio Canova and John Flaxman. However, he also used Chinese, Greek and Roman ornament for inspiration. The demand for cameo glass was greatly increased, and in 1880 the Stourbridge firms developed more cost-effective methods of production: these included the increased use of wheel-engraving and the production of smaller pieces on which the white casing was applied more thinly to aid acid removal.

The most important technological development to affect the glass industry was the introduction of press-moulding. It was first used in the USA during the 1820s and spread to Europe during the 1830s. The Birmingham-based firm of George Bacchus & Sons made pressed glass during the 1830s, when production was centred in Birmingham and Stourbridge. The main centres in the 1850s were Manchester and the north-east. The most original designs were produced between 1880 and 1900. The pressed glass produced by the Sowerby Ellison Glassworks in Gateshead, Tyne & Wear, in the 1870s was clearly influenced by the display of Japanese art at the International Exhibition. In 1879 it introduced an opaque white pressed glass known as 'Patent Queen's Ivory' ware. Other technological developments included the introduction of the threading machine, which was patented in 1876 by Hodgetts, Richardson & Son of Stourbridge, and in the 1880s the development of a semi-automatic bottle machine. In the 1890s the traditional method of polishing glass with wheels was superseded by acid polishing, where a combination of hydrofluoric and sulphuric acids was used to give cut glass a glossy finish.

At the end of the 19th century fundamental changes in the principles of design were influenced by the Arts and Crafts Movement, led by William Morris. The movement encouraged a shift away from excessive ornament to a simpler, more functional style, opposed industrial mass production and promoted craftsmanship. During the 1870s the Venetian Revival encouraged such glass factories as the Whitefriars Glass Works of JAMES POWELL & Sons in London to produce glass à la façon de Venise. Powell made the glass for Morris's house, the Red House in Bexleyheath, Kent. In the 1880s and 1890s the Art Nouveau style became popular. CHRISTOPHER DRESSER designed elegant goblets and vases, often in 'Clutha' glass, which were made by James Couper & Sons of Glasgow (see also fig. 81 below). Dresser's linear approach was inspired by the geometry of plants, but he also produced copies of Pre-Columbian and Roman shapes and original designs.

BIBLIOGRAPHY
English Glass (exh. cat. by R. J. Charleston, London, V&A, 1968)
H. Newman: *An Illustrated Dictionary of Glass* (London, 1977)
R. J. Charleston: *English Glass and the Glass Used in England, c. 400–1940* (London, 1984)
C. Truman: *An Introduction to English Glassware to 1900* (1984)

K. SOMERVELL

5. AFTER 1900. At the beginning of the 20th century Stourbridge and Birmingham were the main centres for the production of handmade table and ornamental glass, while the pressed-glass industry was based in Manchester and the north-east. The styles of the late Victorian period remained popular until the beginning of World War I, modified to a certain extent by the influence of Art Nouveau. The one important firm outside these areas was the Whitefriars Glass Works of JAMES POWELL & Sons in London. Their fragile, thinly blown vessels emphasized the ductile nature of molten glass and successfully combined the sinuous curves and elongated forms of Art Nouveau with a historicist tendency.

During World War I factories were forced to make scientific, industrial and medical glass. After the war the industry was flooded with cheap imports from such countries as Belgium, Germany, Czechoslovakia and the USA. The pressed-glass industry was particularly badly affected, while the handmade sector chose to abandon many of its cheaper lines, particularly its coloured glass, and concentrate on good-quality cut and engraved glass, where the foreign competition was not quite so strong. Survival was therefore the main concern rather than experiment and innovation. In 1926, however, Mrs Graydon-Stannus (1873–1961) set up a small glass works in Battersea, London, making brightly coloured vases and bowls not dissimilar to the 'Monart' glass made by the Moncrieff Glassworks in Perth.

The introduction of tariffs (1931) on imported domestic goods, coupled with falling unemployment, brought about a gradual recovery, and factories began to look at ways of expanding their product range. These were looking increasingly old-fashioned compared to the exciting new designs being introduced by such artists and companies as René Lalique in France and the Orrefors Glasbruk in Orrefors, Sweden; during the early 1930s there was much discussion among design pundits as to how the standard of design could be improved. The time-honoured solution was to encourage artists to work within the industry, and this was the approach adopted by the Stourbridge firm of Stevens & Williams, which in 1932 employed the New Zealand-born architect Keith Murray (1892–1981) as a designer. The collaboration lasted for seven years and resulted in some highly distinctive decorative vases, many of which betray the architect's admiration for contemporary Swedish glass (e.g. wheel-engraved vase, c. 1935–40;

London, V&A). Stuart & Sons, another Stourbridge firm, tried a slightly different approach, employing a whole team of artists including Paul Nash and Laura Knight to design table glass for an exhibition at Harrods Ltd, London, in 1934. This, however, seems to have been more a publicity stunt than a serious attempt to introduce more modern design, and none of the artists were retained on a permanent basis. The bulk of Stuart's glass therefore remained in the traditional style. The Whitefriars Glass Works had no need to resort to outside designers, having an established 'in-house' team of James Hogan (1883–1948), Barnaby Powell (1891–1939) and W. J. Wilson; the design of their glass was consistently better than any other English firm during the inter-war period.

The pressed-glass industry also underwent a revival during the 1930s. From utilitarian products in patterns imitating cut glass, such factories as Jobling of Sunderland, Sowerby of Gateshead and Bagley in South Yorkshire branched out into colourful Art Deco vases, figures and trinket sets in a characteristic palette of pink, amber, pale blue and green, which had been influenced by Lalique and contemporary French and Czechoslovakian production. Jobling even produced a successful imitation of Lalique's opalescent glass, which was called 'opalique'. The only area, however, in which outside designers were used to any extent was in the production of heat-resistant 'Pyrex' glass, introduced by Jobling in 1921 under licence from the USA. This careful design element, coupled with the fact that the glass was machine produced and therefore cheap, led to the unlikely situation of heat-resistant glass being championed by such leaders of the Modern Movement as Herbert Read and E. Maxwell Fry as an outstanding example of contemporary British industrial design.

The trend towards cut glass, at the expense of coloured, gathered pace after World War II, and by 1960 the use of colour was virtually non-existent in the Stourbridge industry. Cut patterns became increasingly traditional in design, although there were isolated attempts to introduce a more contemporary note, as with some ranges designed by David Douglas, 12th Marquess of Queensberry (b 1929), for Webb Corbett Ltd in Amblecote near Stourbridge, during the early 1960s. The Whitefriars Glass Works made more effort to change with the times, launching for example in the 1960s a range of brightly coloured vases, with a surface texture imitating wood bark, by the designer Geoffrey Baxter (b 1922). This firm closed in 1980, and ten years later Thomas Webb & Sons of Stourbridge also closed due to the collapse of the owners, Coloroll. New firms appeared, notably Dartington Glass in Dartington, Devon, which was founded in 1967 with a Swedish managing director and workforce and which concentrates on plain, well-designed glass in the Scandinavian style.

The general lack of imagination shown by the industry after World War II was compensated for by progress in other areas. From the 1940s there was a revived interest in glass engraving inspired by such artists as David Peace (b 1915) and Laurence Whistler (b 1921; see fig. 72); this eventually led to the founding of the Guild of Glass Engravers (1975), with Whistler as its first president. While engraving gradually died out as a decorating technique in the factories, the number of independent engravers continued to increase, and the work of the Guild's

72. Engraved glass bowl by Laurence Whistler, h. 223 mm, 1973 (Kingswinford, Broadfield House Glass Museum)

leading members has been highly acclaimed both at home and abroad. The most significant post-war development, however, was the emergence of the studio-glass artist. Since the Industrial Revolution, glass had been produced in the factory; experiments in the USA in the 1960s proved that it was possible to devise glass mixtures with comparatively low melting-points using small furnaces, which could be operated by one person. Glass thus became a material with which individual artists could work, free from the constraints of the factory system. The first studio established in England was the Glasshouse in Covent Garden, London, in 1969. Glass courses were set up in colleges such as Leicester Polytechnic under John Cook to cater for the growing interest in studio glass as an artistic medium. The range of glass made varied from studio to studio. Such firms as Okra Glass at Stourbridge concentrated on small-scale production of coloured vases, paperweights and scent-bottles, while such artists as David Reekie (b 1947) and Colin Reed (b 1953) explored the sculptural possibilities of the material.

BIBLIOGRAPHY

G. Janneau: *Modern Glass* (London and New York, 1931)
L. M. Angus-Butterworth: *British Table and Ornamental Glass* (London, 1956)
A. Polak: *Modern Glass* (London, 1962)
R. Stennett-Wilson: *Modern Glass* (London, 1975)
G. Beard: *International Modern Glass* (London, 1976)
Thirties: British Art and Design before the War (exh. cat., London, Hayward Gal., 1979–80)
Pyrex: 60 Years of Design (exh. cat., Newcastle upon Tyne, Tyne & Wear Joint Museums Cttee, 1983)
J. Baker and K. Crowe: *Jobling 1930s Decorative Glass* (Tyne and Wear, 1985)

R. Dodsworth, ed.: *British Glass between the Wars* (Dudley, 1987)
D. Klein: *Glass: A Contemporary Art* (London, 1989)

ROGER DODSWORTH

IX. Metalwork.

1. Gold and silver. 2. Base metals.

1. GOLD AND SILVER.

(i) Before 1450. (ii) 1450–1660. (iii) 1661–1729. (iv) 1730–80. (v) 1781–1895. (vi) After 1895.

(i) Before 1450. In the 5th and 6th centuries AD Anglo-Saxon peoples introduced a highly developed art of ornamental work in precious metals (*see* ANGLO-SAXON ART, §V), as illustrated by many extant brooches, clasps, pendants and crosses, dating from *c.* 600, from burial sites. These objects are of gold with inlaid garnets, coloured glass and filigree decoration or of cast gold with niello decoration. The garnets are set in geometric patterns formed of gold *cloisons*, occasionally with interlace patterns and animal and bird motifs. The best examples of this type of object from the first half of the 7th century are the clasp and belt buckle (London, BM; *see* SUTTON HOO, fig. 1) from the burial site at Sutton Hoo, Suffolk, the Kingston Brooch (Liverpool Mus.) and the Ixworth and Wilton Crosses (Oxford, Ashmolean; London, BM).

From late 7th- and early 8th-century Northumbria there are fragments of silverwork, sometimes gilded, with figures and ornament in low relief, for example a portable altar (Durham, Cathedral Treasury) and a plaque from Hexham with a profile of a saint (London, BM). Other fine examples of such work dating from the second half of the 8th century are the large St Rupert Cross (1580×940 mm; Salzburg, Dommus.), decorated with both vine scroll and interlace relief ornament and with polychrome glass roundels, and the Ormside Bowl (York, Yorks Mus.). Reliquaries from the 9th century with ornamental and figural decoration include a purse-shaped reliquary (Winchester, City Mus.) and the Mortain Reliquary (Mortain, St Evroult).

In the 9th century a type of silver brooch, partly gilded and decorated with niello, evolved, with deeply engraved or openwork patterns of animal and interlace ornament. Examples of this type include the brooches from the Pentney Hoard, Norfolk, and the Strickland Brooch (all London, BM). The Fuller Brooch (late 9th century; London, BM; *see* ANGLO-SAXON ART, fig. 12) is also of silver with niello decoration but is less deeply engraved and has little openwork; it is decorated with personifications of the *Five Senses*. The design of the gold Alfred and Minster Lovell Jewels (late 9th century; Oxford, Ashmolean; *see* JEWELLERY, colour pl. IV, fig. 1), decorated with cloisonné enamel and filigree, suggests influence from contemporary Carolingian goldsmiths' work (*see* CAROLINGIAN ART, §V).

Relatively few pieces of goldsmiths' work that date from the early 10th century to the Norman Conquest in 1066 have survived, as almost all English medieval ecclesiastical goldsmiths' work was destroyed at the Reformation and during the Civil War. The majority of objects produced were probably liturgical vessels and Gospel-book covers. Surviving examples in continental collections include a silver portable altar (*c.* 1025–50; Paris, Mus.

Cluny) engraved with the Evangelists' symbols and depictions of angels, and a cross (*c.* 1000–25), also engraved with the Evangelists' symbols, in the treasury of Brussels Cathedral. The use of engraved figural ornament continued after the Conquest, for example in the gilt-copper Lundø Crucifix (*c.* 1050–75; Copenhagen, Nmus.).

The majority of surviving metalwork of the period from the Conquest to 1200 is of copper and bronze, sometimes gilded (*see* ROMANESQUE, §VI, 6, and §2(i) below). The Gloucester Candlestick (*c.* 1107–13; London, V&A), made for the Benedictine abbey of Gloucester, is of a gilt-copper alloy incorporating much silver and has niello decoration and coloured glass insets. The base and stem are of cast openwork foliage, animals and human figures, imitating the decoration of contemporary illuminated manuscripts.

In the second half of the 12th century champlevé enamelling, influenced by Mosan work, was practised on goldsmiths' work in England. Examples include the Morgan, Warwick and Balfour Ciboria (*c.* 1160–80; New York, Pierpont Morgan Lib.; London, V&A), decorated with Old and New Testament scenes in medallions separated by foliate scrolls. In a related style and of the same period are a series of rectangular enamelled plaques (one London, V&A) depicting the *Lives of SS Peter and Paul*. A number of silver-gilt bowls and cups with niello decoration, for example the cups from the Dune Treasure (Stockholm, Stat. Hist. Mus.), also date from the second half of the 12th century. A silver-gilt ciborium with low-relief figural work in roundels in the treasury of the abbey of St Maurice d'Agaune, Switzerland, was produced *c.* 1200.

The amount of surviving English goldsmiths' work from the 13th century is small (*see* GOTHIC, §V, 7). A few silver-gilt chalices and patens have engraved foliage and figures, and the finest of these is the Dolgelley Chalice and Paten (*c.* 1230–50; British Royal Col., on loan to Cardiff, N. Mus.). The silver-gilt sceptre of Richard, Earl of Cornwall (*c.* 1260; Aachen, Domschatzkam.), and the girdle of Ferdinando de la Cerda (*c.* 1270; Burgos, Monastery of Las Huelgas), decorated with sapphires, pearls and champlevé enamels, are the only two surviving pieces connected with the patronage of the English court.

In contrast, a number of important works have survived from the 14th century. As elsewhere in Europe, the technique of *basse taille* enamel for goldsmiths' work was revived in England from the early 14th century. Examples include the Swinburne Pyx (*c.* 1310–25; London, V&A), now mostly lacking its enamel and decorated with depictions of the *Lamb of God*, the head of *Christ*, the standing figure of the *Virgin and Child* and the *Nativity*, and the Savernake Horn (*c.* 1325–50; London, BM). The finest piece is undoubtedly the silver-gilt secular King's Lynn Cup (see fig. 73), decorated with standing figures of men and women, some engaged in hawking and hunting, in blue, green and purple *basse taille* enamel framed with foliate ribs. The crosier (*c.* 1367; Oxford, New Coll.) of William of Wykeham, Bishop of Winchester, which is one of the few English croziers in precious metals to have survived from the medieval period, also has *basse taille* enamel decoration. Several relatively plain silver pieces, including several chalices and patens, sometimes with relief or engraved decoration, also date from the 14th

73. King's Lynn Cup, silver gilt and *basse taille* enamel, h. 380 mm, *c.* 1340 (King's Lynn, Guildhall of the Holy Trinity)

century. Of greater importance is a silver-gilt censer (*see* GOTHIC, fig. 91) and incense boat (*c.* 1325–50; London, V&A) with ram's head decorations, indicating that it was probably from Ramsey Abbey. Secular cups, mazers, horns and dishes have survived in greater numbers than liturgical vessels: the 'Guy of Warwick' Mazer (*c.* 1300–50; Harbledown, St Nicholas), the Bermondsey Dish (*c.* 1335–45; Bermondsey, St Mary Magdalen), the Corpus Christi Swan Mazer (*c.* 1350–75; Cambridge, Corpus Christi Coll.), the Queen's College Wassail Horn (*c.* 1341–9; Oxford, Queen's Coll.) and the Studley Bowl (*c.* 1400; London, V&A) are the finest examples.

The newly invented Parisian technique of enamel *en ronde bosse* was adopted in England for goldsmiths' work in the early 15th century. The earliest English example of this technique is the small Dunstable Swan Jewel (*c.* 1400; London, BM; *see* ENAMEL, fig. 1), the form of which, a small strutting swan, was possibly the livery badge of Henry of Lancaster, later Henry IV (*reg* 1399–1413). The

most important work in this technique, controversially attributed to English craftsmen, is the elaborate Reliquary of the Order of the Holy Spirit (Paris, Louvre), a gift from Joanna of Navarre, Queen of Henry IV, to her son John V, Duke of Brittany (*reg* 1399–1442), in 1412. It has seated and standing figures in *en ronde bosse* enamel of the *Trinity* and the *Virgin and Saints* set in a jewelled structure of tabernacles and pinnacles. Several chalices, patens, mazers, cups, salts, brooches and pendants from the first half of the 15th century survive, but they are not exceptional and give little impression of the rich treasure of gold, silver and enamel objects described in numerous 15th-century inventories. Two outstanding objects, however, are a silver SS Lancastrian livery collar (*c.* 1422–61; London, Mus. London) and the bridal crown of Margaret of York (Aachen, Domschatzkam.), made before her marriage to Charles the Bold, 4th Duke of Burgundy, in 1468. It is decorated with the white roses of the House of York in *en ronde bosse* enamel.

BIBLIOGRAPHY

C. Oman: 'The Goldsmiths of St. Albans Abbey during the 12th and 13th Centuries', *Trans. St Albans & Herts Archaeol. Soc.* (1932), pp. 215–36
N. M. Penzer: 'The King's Lynn Cup', *Connoisseur*, cxviii (1946), pp. 12–16, 64, 79–84, 120
C. Oman: 'The Swinburne Pyx', *Burl. Mag.*, xcii (1950), pp. 337–41
——: *English Church Plate, 597–1830* (London, 1957)
D. M. Wilson: *Anglo-Saxon Ornamental Metalwork, 700–1100, in the British Museum* (London, 1964)
J. Cherry: 'The Dunstable Swan Jewel', *J. Brit. Archaeol. Assoc.*, xxxii (1969), pp. 38–53
C. Oman: *British Rings, 800–1914* (London, 1974)
D. M. Wilson: 'Tenth Century Metalwork', *Tenth Century Studies*, ed. D. Parsons (Chichester, 1975), pp. 200–07, 247–8
M. Campbell: 'The Campion Hall Triptych and its Workshop', *Apollo*, cxi (1980), pp. 418–23
N. Stratford: 'The Henry of Blois Plaques in the British Museum', *Medieval Art and Architecture at Winchester Cathedral*, British Archaeological Association Conference Transactions, vi (1983), pp. 28–37
——: 'Metalwork', *English Romanesque Art, 1066–1200* (exh. cat., London, Hayward Gal., 1984), pp. 232–95
——: 'Three English Romanesque Enamelled Ciboria', *Burl. Mag.*, cxxvi (1984), pp. 202–16
A. Borg: 'The Gloucester Candlestick', *Medieval Art and Architecture at Gloucester and Tewkesbury*, British Archaeological Association Conference Transactions, vii (1985), pp. 84–92
N. Stratford: 'Niello in England in the Twelfth Century', *Art and Patronage in the English Romanesque*, ed. S. Macready and F. H. Thompson (London, 1986), pp. 28–49
M. Campbell: 'English Goldsmiths in the Fifteenth Century', *England in the Fifteenth Century: Proceedings of the 1986 Harlaxton Symposium* (Woodbridge, 1987), pp. 43–52
——: 'Metalwork in England, *c.* 1200–1400', *Age of Chivalry* (exh. cat., ed. J. Alexander and P. Binski; London, RA, 1987), pp. 162–8
——: 'Gold, Silver and Precious Stones', *English Medieval Industries*, ed. J. Blair and N. Ramsay (London, 1991), pp. 107–66
R. W. Lightbown: *Mediaeval European Jewellery* (London, 1992)

For general bibliography see §(vi) below.

NIGEL J. MORGAN

(ii) 1450–1660.

(a) History and uses. (b) Form and decoration.

(a) History and uses. During this period London was the centre of a goldsmiths' craft that was burgeoning nationally; such towns as Exeter recorded over 100 goldsmiths between 1550 and 1650. Sixteenth-century master goldsmiths were often wealthy men; Robert Amadas (*d* 1532), Henry VIII's Royal Goldsmith and Master of the Jewel House (a rare distinction for a goldsmith),

had a large household and estates in Essex. Foreign craftsmen, particularly from Germany, Italy and the Netherlands, arrived in London, bringing new styles, forms and techniques from the Continent. The manufacture of secular plate grew more important than that of religious plate after the Reformation, and the range of domestic vessels steadily increased.

The fashionable aesthetic criterion was workmanship rather than design (the term 'curiously wrought' being the highest praise), although few English pieces matched the finish and technical command of plate from Antwerp and Nuremberg. Conspicuous consumption and display remained the signs of power and status: Henry VIII spent £24,943 on goldsmiths' work between 1509 and 1518. Church lands were transferred to secular owners after the Reformation, and the new gentry demanded silver as befitting their status.

A well-furnished cupboard of plate was evidence of solvency as well as status; plate could be melted into coin or pledged for cash at the goldsmith's. The gradual growth in the possession of material goods, particularly plate and textiles, in many social groups was largely due to the decline in the price of precious metals. Gold objects dressed the monarch's table, buffet and private apartments (i.e. casting bottles, toilet implements and comfit-boxes) but were infrequently found outside court circles, and few survive. For others wealth and status could be expressed by means of small gold accessories and jewellery and the use of double and treble gilding on silver objects to simulate gold. Owners of silver, however, remained a tiny minority; in most homes pewter, latten (brass), ceramics or wooden vessels were used. Goldsmiths' booths at regional fairs in the late 16th century offered a range of simple, lightweight articles: small salts, boxes, low-grade spoons and thimbles. Travelling 'chapmen' or hawkers bought wholesale in London and passed off substandard silver at such fairs.

The provision of precious metals increased in the late 15th century and the 16th, supplied by mines in central Europe and the New World, payments in bullion for cloth exports to the Netherlands and quantities of Spanish silver entering the Mint. In the late 1540s and 1550s, after the Dissolution of the Monasteries, imported silver and gold, particularly from Flanders, augmented the national supply. There was no legitimate export trade in wrought silver, though the relative purity of English gold and silver coinage made both desirable on the Continent. Much elaborate English silver was sent abroad as ambassadorial plate or regal exchanges of gifts. The large collection of late 16th- and early 17th-century English silver in the Kremlin Museum, Moscow, mostly results from gifts (reciprocated in furs) from English ambassadors to the Tsars of Russia. Foreign gifts to the monarch were held by the Jewel House, London, which was responsible for maintaining the royal plate and supplying the monarch's gifts, including the annual stock for the New Year exchange of gifts between monarch and courtiers. The latter often purchased their gifts at goldsmiths' shops in Cheapside, London. The monarch also received gold and silver objects on his official 'progress' around the realm (a medieval tradition), which could then be given to foreign magnates; a cup (Moscow, Kremlin) given to James I at

Warwick on his progress in 1617 was presented to Tsar Mikhail Romanov in 1620.

Lacking objects from which to make stylistic judgements—due to the melting down of plate in the mid-16th century and the 17th—scholars are dependent on inventories to reconstruct both secular and religious holdings of plate. Royal collections are particularly well recorded from 1521 to c. 1649, though not as much is known about the holdings of the lesser nobility and gentry. Objects surviving in any quantity do so by default; mazers, drinking horns, coconut cups and Rhenish stoneware jugs with silver mounts bear a negligible amount of precious metal. The largest category of extant silver objects is spoons.

Ewers and basins, flagons and steeple-cups enhanced buffet displays, and rules of rank based on those of the 15th-century Burgundian court dictated the number of its stages. It was usual for colleges, livery companies and even the monarch to borrow or hire plate to achieve the required effect. A large number of late 16th- and early 17th-century display and presentation pieces, many with armorials, are preserved by livery companies and colleges in Oxford and Cambridge, to which they were given on admission to the freedom of the city or on graduation (e.g. tankard, c. 1596; Cambridge, Christ's Coll.).

Monarchs established strict eating rituals, and distinctions of rank governed both secular and religious dining habits. The magnificent standing salt dominated the table, marking the place of the host. Sixteenth-century royal tables would be dressed with silver trenchers and serving dishes (uncommon outside court circles), the sovereign's trencher-of-state, drinking vessels, voiding knives and baskets—for cleaning the tablecloth between courses (e.g. silver and crystal voiding knife; King's Lynn, Town Hall)—knives, spoons with fig-shaped bowls, cream bowls and wine-fountains, for example the one (untraced) given as a New Year's gift by Henry VIII to Anne Boleyn (1501–36) in 1534, for which drawings survive (Basle, Kstmus.); the air in the dining chamber would be sweetened by silver cassolettes. The use of fingers as well as spoons and knives necessitated handwashing before and during meals, and ewers and basins were used for this purpose; forks were scarcely used in the Middle Ages and later only for the dessert course. The earliest surviving table fork (London, V&A) is dated c. 1640. Dessert plate—spice-plates and boxes, sugar boxes (for sweetening wine, an English custom) and dessert cutlery—were elaborately decorated and gilded; some incorporated verre eglomisé. They were used after the voidée and at the meals of spiced bread, wine and candied fruit taken in special rooms, for example the banqueting houses on the roof of Longleat House, Wilts, at rites of passage and the election of masters of livery companies. In the 17th century more complex menus and the influx of such exotic fruit and vegetables as artichokes, cucumbers and squashes stimulated the production of specialized plate, for example artichoke dishes and sets of 'sallat' plates.

It has been estimated that bullion, plate and other treasures worth over £1 million, including spoils from the shrine of St Thomas Becket at Canterbury, were sent to the Mint between 1536 and 1540 during the Dissolution of the Monasteries. Men were employed at the Tower of London to coin money from ecclesiastical silver. The process continued under Edward VI (*reg* 1547–53), and on her accession Mary I (*reg* 1553–8) attempted, but failed, to reverse it. In 1548 the first pieces of Protestant plate were made, for example a communion-cup from St James's Garlickhythe (*c.* 1549; London, St Paul's Cathedral).

In the 1560s and 1570s Elizabeth I and her bishops mounted a systematic campaign of reform throughout the dioceses, commanding that all existing chalices be converted into communion-cups. The design was imposed from London by Matthew Parker, Archbishop of Canterbury, and the Goldsmiths' Company coordinated the programme. Some remote parishes managed to retain pre-Reformation chalices; the Nettlecombe Chalice and Paten (1479; Nettlecombe, St Mary, on loan to London, V&A) is the earliest set of church plate with a date letter. Other pre-Reformation chalices survived by concealment; Corpus Christi College, Oxford, retains the gold chalice given by Bishop Richard Fox in 1507. Elizabethan communion plate represents the only substantial documented body of provincial silver before 1700 and has formed the basis for attributions of marks to provincial goldsmiths of that period, for example William Mutton (*fl c.* 1555–70/80) of Chester and Nicholas Goston (Gorston; *fl c.* 1546–70/75) of Nottingham. Recusant plate, made for Roman Catholics celebrating mass in secret, is rare. Usually unmarked and without inscriptions, it is comparable in form to Late Gothic types (examples in London: V&A; St Etheldreda, Ely Place; Westminster Cathedral).

Charles I's record of extracting revenue and converting royal plate into coin has been linked with Oliver Cromwell's melting of plate to finance the parliamentarian army as an explanation for the relative paucity of early 17th-century plate. In the 1620s large quantities of royal plate, for example a pair of ewers (*c.* 1604; Moscow, Kremlin), were sold to the Tsars of Russia. Both sides in the Civil War were obliged to ask supporters for plate and cash, and sequestrations in the late 1640s and 1650s made a concerted attack on the goods and landed property of noblemen and others who were perceived as royalists. Not all of the treasures were lost; some colleges and livery companies concealed plate, some of the wealthy nobility had large reserves, and the growing cult of antiquarianism encouraged the preservation of medieval plate.

See also LONDON, §IV, 2.

(b) Form and decoration. The group of medieval gold and silver that survives is so small and random that the evolution of style and ornament is difficult to assess. The majority of extant objects are mounted drinking vessels, for example a coconut cup (1490; Oxford, New Coll.), with silver-gilt mounts forming a naturalistic oak tree with branches enclosing the nut, and the Three Kings Mazer (*c.* 1490; Cambridge, Corpus Christi Coll.), with 'writhen' work (i.e. spiralling lobes) forming the silver stem. One of the finest examples of an hour-glass salt is Bishop Fox's Salt (1494–1501; Oxford, Corpus Christi Coll.), with lush foliage decoration, animals and pelicans in openwork tracery (originally laid over enamel), pearls and scenes of the *Coronation of the Virgin*.

Marks are rare on late 15th- and early 16th-century pieces, and attributions are, therefore, tentative. Such objects as medieval spice-plates, powder-boxes, candlesticks and chargers are known only through records. Drinking vessels are described in inventories as 'bells', 'bolepeces' (chalice-shaped cups) and 'flatpeces' (font-shaped cups), perhaps like the Campion Cup (1500; London, V&A). Cups and salts in the shape of fruit, vegetables, animals and men illustrate the Gothic taste for fantasy and naturalism. A salt in the shape of a tower decorated with roses is listed in Sir John Fastolf's comprehensive inventory of 1459, and Edward IV's gold and gem-set elephant- and castle-shaped salt was recorded in 1468. Most medieval plate bears the armorials, often enamelled, of the donor, his ancestors, his livery company and the king. Lady Margaret Beaufort's Cup (*c.* 1500; Cambridge, Christ's Coll.) is engraved with the Beaufort and Tudor badges, and its foot is in the shape of a Tudor rose.

In the late Middle Ages the style of designs and motifs that were applied to English goldsmiths' work was derived from Flemish Gothic architecture. Castings of miniature tracery, buttresses and other architectural elements appear on such objects as a pastoral staff (*c.* 1487–1501; Oxford, Corpus Christi Coll.). Manuscripts were another source for decoration; the border decoration on a silver pax (*c.* 1510; Oxford, New Coll.) relates closely to an engraving in a Parisian Book of Hours of *c.* 1500 (repr. in Harthan, pp. 170–71). Surfaces could be embossed with fruit and foliage (e.g. Warden's Grace Cup, *c.* 1480; Oxford, New Coll.), lobate forms (e.g. font-cup, 1515; Oxford, Corpus Christi Coll.) or were left plain and burnished, contrasting with gilt crestings (e.g. Lacock Cup, mid-15th century; Lacock Abbey, Wilts, on loan to London, BM). Ropework, bands of pierced trefoils or quatrefoils, engraved lettering (e.g. Campion Cup, 1500; London, V&A) or narrow strips of punched ornament, for example on the rims of Bishop Fox's ablution basins (1493 and 1514; Oxford, Corpus Christi Coll.), were also used. It was customary to name distinctive and outstanding pieces of plate; one type of cup called the 'Shepherd', made of gold and crystal and decorated with stones, was presumably a figural piece. Another type, the 'Swan', possibly incorporated heraldic devices. Rich texturing of surfaces, with overlapping scales, pine-cones and honeycomb patterns, appeared on standing-cups (e.g. of *c.* 1520; Cambridge, Christs' Coll.).

In the 1520s ornament emanating from Italy via Flanders and France gained popularity in England, resulting in a sharp change from the Gothic to the Renaissance style in both form and decoration. The Italian artists and craftsmen employed by Henry VIII aided this process. Virtually no Italian silver appears to have reached England at this time, the transmission of styles coming through the designs of Hans Burgkmair I and Nicoletto da Modena (*fl* 1500–12) that were circulating in England. With little extant plate dating from 1515 to 1525 it is impossible to date precisely the introduction of the new 'antique work' into the goldsmiths' workshops. The earliest surviving example, the Howard Grace Cup (see fig. 74), traditionally a relic of St Thomas Becket, bears cast Renaissance motifs derived from a design by Burgkmair. The application of such designs, for example the plaquettes after Peter Flötner on a salt (*c.* 1569; London, Vintners' Co.), is rare on plate of this period.

74. Howard Grace Cup, silver gilt and ivory, h. 320 mm, 1525–6 (London, Victoria and Albert Museum)

All-over surface decoration with moresques, foliage masks, urns, relief busts in roundels, acanthus, fleshy foliage and putti characterizes English Renaissance silver. Hans Holbein the younger's English sketchbook (*c*. 1532–5; Basle, Kstmus.) shows salts with stems of putti and grotesques in the 'antique' manner. Holbein's designs for the English court (1532–43) influenced the adaptation of Renaissance ornament to established English forms, but his work had no lasting influence on English goldsmithing. His carefully finished design (first sketch, London, BM; final version, Oxford, Ashmolean) for the gold and jewelled cup (untraced) presented by Henry VIII to Jane Seymour (1509–37), probably in 1536, incorporates many

elements of fashionable Renaissance ornament. Holbein's name also appears, with that of Hans van Antwerpen (*fl c*. 1515–50), on a commission for a silver cradle for Princess Elizabeth (later Elizabeth I). Innovations in form and ornament seen on plate from 1520 to 1560 were largely due to such foreign craftsmen. Designs from Vitruvius published *c*. 1543 by Sebald Beham, with borders of guilloche, laurel leaves, ovolo and scalework, were adopted by goldsmiths in England as standard motifs for the edges of feet and covers and as banded ornament, and their use continued into the 17th century.

In the late 1540s the Renaissance style was superseded by Antwerp Mannerism, which dominated the ornament of court plate until the turn of the 17th century, largely fuelled in the 1550s and 1560s by the influx of engraved designs by Erasmus Hornick, Adriaen Collaert and Cornelis Floris from Antwerp. An early example of the Mannerist style (*c*. 1525) is the Barber Surgeons' instrument box (London, Barbers' Co.), engraved with mermen and dolphins. Mannerist decoration on English plate is characterized by intermingled, disparate themes: religious, marine, grotesques and fruits and foliage. This eclecticism is demonstrated by a set of six spice-bowls (1573; London, V&A), each engraved in three zones: scenes from the life of Abraham in the centre, marine creatures and monsters, ships, shells and grotesques around the bowl, and animals and birds enclosed in floral scrolls on the rim. Strapwork and cartouches were combined with embossed fruit, squashes, gourds and masks, for example on the Mostyn Salt (*c*. 1566; London, V&A) and the Vyvyan Salt (*c*. 1592; London, V&A; for illustration *see* SALT). Marine subjects were associated with salts and vessels for liquids; the Simon Gibbon Salt (*c*. 1576; London, Goldsmiths' Co.) incorporates a figure of Neptune enclosed in a crystal cylinder. The Game-cock Salt (*c*. 1560–70; London, V&A)—a nautilus shell mounted in silver gilt—continues, like the Glynne Cup (1579; priv. col., on loan to London, V&A), the Gothic conceit of cups and salts formed as birds. Chased and embossed sea creatures continually featured on ewers and basins, for example mermaid ewers paired with shell basins (*c*. 1610; Toledo, OH, Mus. A.).

Moresque and arabesque ornament, popular in the late 16th century and the early 17th, was derived from late 15th-century Veneto-Saracenic metalwork; a compilation of such designs, *Morysse and Damashin Renewed and Encreased Very Profitable for Goldsmiths and Embroderars*, was published by Thomas Geminus (*fl* 1540–70) in London in 1548. Continuous bands of engraved scrolling foliage terminating in cross-hatched leaves were used on rims, borders and bands, for example on a silver-gilt, font-shaped standing-cup (*c*. 1557; Moscow, Kremlin) and on mounts on a stoneware pot (*c*. 1566; Oxford, Ashmolean). Floral designs enclosed in strapwork, for example on the Stoke Prior Double Salt (*c*. 1594; London, V&A), were an English invention, as was the flowing floral design covering a silver-gilt livery pot (*c*. 1606; Moscow, Kremlin). A high proportion of late 16th- and early 17th-century plate is chased and engraved. The more adroit and ambitious engraved schemes are often attributed to such foreign craftsmen as Theodor de Bry from Liège and Nicasius Roussel (*fl c*. 1567–1640) from Bruges. Roussel, who supplied James I and Anne of Denmark with silver and published a book of ornament, *De Grotesco* (London, 1623), has been attributed with the engraving of grotesques on a flagon of *c.* 1587 (London, St Mary Woolnoth, on loan to London, St Paul's Cathedral).

In the early 17th century traditional forms, for example cups and salts, remained popular, there were no radical innovations in ornament, and foreign influences declined until the accession of Charles I in 1625, when French and Dutch trends flowered briefly under his patronage. Christiaen van Vianen (*see* VIANEN, VAN, (3)) from Utrecht (largely credited with the importation of the Dutch and German Auricular style) was the only goldsmith of international repute working for the English court in the early 17th century. Van Vianen's audience was confined to a small court circle, for whom he produced sophisticated embossed work, for example the Dolphin Basin (1635; London, V&A).

At the same time plainer plate—drinking vessels, scroll salts and candlesticks (e.g. set of *c.* 1637; London, Sotheby's, see Glanville, 1990, fig. 207)—was produced. There was a considerable market for cheap and thinly embossed porringers, sweetmeat dishes (e.g. of *c.* 1633; London, Goldsmiths' Co.) and wine tasters. Ornament generally consisted of matted or 'pounced' patterning, sometimes used as all-over decoration or alternating with plain panels, for example on a standing-cup of 1635 (Goldsborough, St Mary), or flat-chasing to outline simple conventional

patterns, for example on a child's drinking pot (*c.* 1646; Los Angeles, CA, Co. Mus. A.). The new technique of cut-card work appeared during the reign of Charles I, sometimes masking the joint between bowl and stem on chalices.

The plainness of plate, the decline in the use of engraving and gilding, and the reduced amount of provincial work is usually ascribed to the economic depression of the 1640s and the impact of Puritanism. Assay office figures, however, indicate that trade continued to flourish. Foreign craftsmen continued to work in England, and engraved ornament from the Continent was utilized, as can be seen on an Auricular covered cup and salver (1658; Richmond, VA, Agecroft Hall) and the French designs on the Thirkleby Flagon (see fig. 75). In the more stable religious climate, church plate resumed its traditional role as a staple product for goldsmiths until the Civil War (1642–9), and there was a flood of gifts of secular plate into the churches. A 'Gothic' revival under the influence of the High Church royalists adopted late medieval forms, for example on an altar set of 1653 (Staunton Harold priv. col., on loan to London, V&A). From the 1650s the Baroque influence from France and the Netherlands began to appear, with engraved and embossed botanical ornament used as decoration on cups, porringers and similar objects (e.g. two-handled cup and cover, *c.* 1658; London, V&A).

BIBLIOGRAPHY

C. Oman: *The English Silver in the Kremlin, 1557–1663* (London, 1961)
P. Glanville: 'The Parr Pot', *Archaeol. J.*, cxxvii (1971), pp. 147–55
J. Hayward: 'The Restoration of the Tudor Clock-Salt', *Goldsmiths' Rev.* (1972–3), pp. 27–31
T. F. Reddaway and L. E. M. Walker: *The Early History of the Goldsmiths' Company, 1327–1509* (London, 1975)
J. F. Hayward: *Virtuoso Goldsmiths and the Triumph of Mannerism, 1540–1620* (London and New York, 1976)
J. Harthan: *Books of Hours and their Owners* (London, 1977)
M. L. Campbell: 'Bishop Fox's Salt', *The Pelican* (1983–4), pp. 39–72
P. Glanville: 'Bishop Fox's Ablution Basins', *The Pelican* (1983–4), pp. 73–86
J. R. ter Molen: 'The Van Vianen Family: Utrecht Silversmiths of International Renown', *Catalogue of the International Silver and Jewellery Fair and Seminar: London, 1986*, pp. 22–31
M. L. Campbell: 'English Goldsmiths in the 15th Century', *England in the Fifteenth Century: Proceedings of the 1986 Harlaxton Symposium* (Woodbridge, 1987), pp. 43–52
P. Glanville: *Silver in Tudor and Early Stuart England* (London, 1990)
M. L. Campbell: 'Gold, Silver and Precious Stones', *English Medieval Industries*, ed. J. Blair and N. Ramsay (London, 1991), pp. 107–67

For general bibliography *see* §(vi) below.

(iii) 1661–1729.

(a) History and uses. (b) Form and decoration.

(a) *History and uses.* During the late 17th century the dramatic drop in silver production of 1642–3 caused by the Civil War was reversed, as expenditure on plate continued to rise. Plate that had been converted into coin in the 1640s was replaced, and silver was eagerly acquired for status and investment. The fashion for plate spread, as wealthy landowners, corporations and colleges had money to spare. Livery companies acquired more plate as gifts or fines, and churches, cathedrals and private chapels were replenished with pieces of plainer design. The urban middle class and yeomen began to purchase more silver. Demand was so great that the practice of clipping and

75. The Thirkleby Flagon, silver, h. 260 mm, *c.* 1646 (London, Victoria and Albert Museum)

melting coinage became widespread and threatened to undermine the economy. In 1697 a higher silver content for wrought plate was introduced to protect the coinage, and new marks denoting the Britannia standard replaced the sterling mark (see MARKS, §4(i)). The late Stuart monarchs and aristocracy set a luxurious standard of living, imitating the splendour of Louis XIV's court at Versailles. Continental influence on the design of plate gained impetus as new ideas and fashions from the Netherlands and France were introduced with the return of Charles II's court from exile, and designs became more sophisticated in the late 17th century and the early 18th with the influx of Huguenot craftsmen fleeing religious persecution in France. Mercantile companies, for example the East India Company, imported new commodities, including tea, coffee and chocolate, that revolutionized social drinking habits and challenged goldsmiths to create new forms. The importance of the morning *levée* during this period introduced another new form of silverware: the *en suite* toilet service, a matrimonial gift usually from husband to wife, consisting of 30 items or more and sometimes incorporating a tea, coffee or chocolate service. The toilet service evolved in the mid-17th century and was popular among the nobility and wealthy gentry until *c.* 1730. Charles II gave Catherine of Braganza (1638–1705) a toilet service (untraced) valued at £4000.

Table silver was desirable for display, and the use of armorials on tableware became fashionable; those without a coat of arms devised a rebus or cipher. Feet, handles and finials cast as crests provided three-dimensional armorials, for example the peacocks supporting the handles of a cistern (1682; Belvoir Castle, Leics) for John Manners, 1st Duke of Rutland (*d* 1711). Dining became more refined, and a gradual change in the structure of dinner began, from a number of dishes served at once to the modern system of courses served sequentially. By 1700 refinements in tableware included sets of casters and cruets, sauceboats, dish rings, cutlery, tiered centrepieces and the caddinet—used only by royalty—all imitating French practice. The great standing salts of the 16th century and the early 17th were replaced by sets of smaller, plainer receptacles.

Wine was distributed from side-tables, and lead glasses began to replace silver for wine-drinking. Salvers were used for presenting food and drink. Some also had a ceremonial function, recording the honour of high-ranking office by the use of engraved, obsolete seal matrices, for example one of *c.* 1695 engraved with mantling by Simon Gribelin II (Glasgow, Burrell Col.). Other vessels—monteiths, punch-bowls, wine-funnels and orange-juice strainers—were created for preparing and serving punch. One of the earliest surviving punch-bowls, probably by Philip Rollos (1685; Stamford, Lincs, Town Hall), is decorated with gadrooning and stands on four dolphin feet.

The demand for silver extended, for those who could afford it, to such utilitarian household articles as chamber pots, warming-pans and cooking utensils. A fashion for cooking at the table led to the introduction of silver saucepans, skillets and chafing dishes. The aristocracy indulged in silver andirons with embossed decoration and surmounted by a figure or a vase (examples at Knole, Kent, NT; Ham House, Surrey, NT) and spectacular silver furniture. Charles II provided Louise de Kérouaille, Duchess of Portsmouth (1649–1734), with a large suite of silver furniture and Nell Gwynn (1650–87) with a bed made in 1674, probably by Jean Gérard Cooqus (Cockus, Cooques; *d* 1697). These do not survive, but they would have been made of thin sheets of embossed silver applied to wooden cores. The solid silver mirror and table by Andrew Moore (*fl* 1690–1700), presented by the Corporation of London to William III (*c.* 1695; British Royal Col.), is decorated with the royal arms and bands of flowers and fruit; caryatids form the legs of the table.

State reception rooms with large silver garnitures on chimney-pieces and side-tables were lit by columnar candlesticks, (e.g. by JACOB BODENDICK, *c.* 1665; London, V&A), sets of sconces, chandeliers and tall candlestands. A set of 12 cartouche-shaped sconces made for Charles II (*c.* 1670; four in British Royal Col.; Colonial Williamsburg, VA; priv. cols) is richly embossed with floral sprays and putti. Massive wine-cisterns and fountains, for example a cistern of 1699 by Philip Rollos for Evelyn Pierrepont, 1st Duke of Kingston (1699; St Petersburg, Hermitage)—for cooling wine and washing glasses and cutlery between courses—stood on the crowded buffet or the floor. Mounted pieces of porcelain were also fashionable for interior decoration, for example a blue-and-white jar (*c.* 1665; London, V&A) with silver-gilt mounts by WOLFGANG HOWZER, with a chased cover imitating motifs painted on the jar.

A fire at the Goldsmiths' Hall in London in 1681 destroyed records of goldsmiths' marks; the only official record is marks struck on a copper plate (London, Goldsmiths' Co.) between 1675 and 1697, although no names accompany the marks. It is, therefore, difficult to identify goldsmiths in this period. The term goldsmith designated membership of the Goldsmiths' Company, though craftsmen worked mainly in silver, and the term covered a range of activities related to the precious metals. Among the diverse activities engaged in by goldsmiths, banking was the most profitable. Alderman Edward Backwell (*fl* 1654–83; *d* 1683) and Sir Robert Vyner (1631–88) were high-ranking financiers who supplied plate and jewels and were able to make recommendations to patrons and to solicit orders. Vyner was appointed Royal Goldsmith in 1660 and also held the offices of Sheriff and Lord Mayor of London. It seems likely that Thomas Jenkins (*fl* 1688–1705/6) also included banking as a profitable sideline, as did the Huguenot DAVID WILLAUME at his premises in St James's Street, London.

After the Restoration several foreign craftsmen skilled in the techniques of cagework, chasing and embossing, including Jacob Bodendick of Limburg and Wolfgang Howzer of Zurich, came into prominence. The 'Engraver Extraordinary' to the crown was a Frenchman, John Destach, and Christiaen van Vianen returned to England from Utrecht. In 1663 he was appointed 'Silversmith in Ordinary' to Charles II for chased work. Though his work was greatly admired, his influence on English silver was confined to the occasional use of Auricular ornament (e.g. perfume burner, 1663; Moscow, Kremlin). He was succeeded in his royal post by his son-in-law, Jean Gérard Cooqus from Liège. Royal support enabled foreigners to work in London despite petitions from the Goldsmiths'

Company and native craftsmen. In 1664 a letter from Charles II ensured that Bodendick and Howzer had their wares assayed. In 1678 an Act of Parliament enabled foreign Protestants to trade and to enter apprenticeships, and Charles II intervened personally in 1681, issuing 'Letters of Denization' and permitting them to travel to England. Another petition in 1682, against foreign goldsmiths obtaining the freedom of the Goldsmiths' Company, included among its signatories such prominent English goldsmiths as George Garthorne (*d* 1730).

The harassment of Protestants in France leading up to and following the Revocation of the Edict of Nantes in 1685 brought numerous Huguenot craftsmen to England in the late 1670s and 1680s, one of the first and most prominent being PIERRE HARACHE, who arrived in 1682. In 1687 James II (*reg* 1685–9) proclaimed his 'Declaration of Indulgence', promising his subjects free exercise of religion, and more emigrés arrived. Some Huguenot goldsmiths found work as journeymen to their English counterparts, and others submitted their work for assay through them, possibly paying for this favour. Several Huguenots succeeded in becoming freemen of the Goldsmiths' Company, including Harache, Willaume, Pierre Platel, PHILIP ROLLOS and Daniel Garnier (*fl* 1696–1710). There were many complaints of undercutting, as the Huguenots proved more skilful, particularly in the technique of castwork, and quickly attracted aristocratic patronage. During the early 18th century a number of women goldsmiths were active in London, including Alice Sheene (*fl* 1700–*c*. 1715), Sarah Holaday (*fl* 1719–*c*. 1740) and Mary Rood (*fl* 1721). Many were of Huguenot origin, for example Anne Tanqueray (1691–1733), wife of DAVID TANQUERAY and daughter of David Willaume.

After 1720 there was considerable duty-dodging after the introduction of a 6d. per ounce duty on wrought silver. The simplest method was to avoid taking the wares for assay, but the most prevalent was to cut the hallmarks from a small object and transpose them into the base of a larger, heavier piece, of which the cost in duty would be considerable; George Wickes (1698–1761), PAUL DE LAMERIE and Peter Archambo (*fl* 1721–50) were all guilty of this malpractice. Robert Dingley (*d* 1747), a goldsmith and jeweller, regularly sold unmarked plate and managed to export 18,600 ounces of silver, mainly wrought by Huguenot goldsmiths, to Russia in 1726.

(b) Form and decoration. The floral Baroque style dominated English silver from the 1650s to the 1690s, reinforced by the presence of foreign craftsmen and the availability of German and Dutch plate. The most popular form of decoration was elaborately embossed ornament on thin, finely finished silver, combining flowers and foliage with putti, birds, beasts and monsters (e.g. pilgrim bottle by Robert Smythier (*c*. 1638–84/9), 1663; Moscow, Kremlin). The floral Baroque style also appeared in cagework, for example on the standing cup that Samuel Pepys presented to the Clothworkers' Company (*c*. 1677; London, Clothworkers' Co.), and on engraved pieces (e.g. peg tankard by John Plummer (*fl* 1648–72) of York, 1663; London, V&A). Acanthus leaf ornament appeared constantly on silverware throughout this period in many forms—embossed in bands and running scrolls, chased

and engraved, applied to handles and candlesticks and on church plate (e.g. silver-gilt ewer and communion-cup, 1683; London, St James's Piccadilly, on loan to London, V&A).

Topical narratives were often engraved on plate, for example scenes of the Great Plague of 1665 and the Fire of London (1666) engraved on a tankard (1675; London, Mus. London), as were such topographical subjects as the view of Ripon Cathedral on a covered paten (Ripon Cathedral). Engravers, like chasers, were specialist craftsmen, and their skills were in demand as the engraving of armorials on presentation pieces became fashionable. Pouncing, an easier and cheaper form of surface decoration, can be seen on a nest of travelling tumblers (*c*. 1670; Colonial Williamsburg, VA) and continued to be used in the 1680s.

Chinoiserie ornament was popularized in England from *c*. 1675 to 1720 by the imports of East Asian decorative art. Chinoiserie decoration was frequently flat-chased (e.g. Gubbay Toilet Service, *c*. 1680; London, V&A), engraved (e.g. covered cup, 1671; Boston, MA, Mus. F.A.; salver by Ralph Leake (*fl* 1679–1714), 1691; Boston, MA, Mus. F.A.) or chased into high-relief panels giving an encrusted effect, for example on a chafing dish (1698; Toronto, Royal Ont. Mus.) by Anthony Nelme (*fl* 1681–1722). Fanciful scenes incorporated Chinese and Indian figures, exotic birds, architectural elements, plants and foliage (e.g. inkstand by Anthony Nelme, 1685; London, V&A). This fashion affected form as well as decoration: silver garnitures were inspired by Oriental vases (e.g. of *c*. 1675; London, V&A). Charles de Moelder (*fl* 1694), probably a plate engraver, published chinoiserie ornament in *Proper Ornaments to be Engraved on Plate* (London, 1694), which includes designs for components of toilet services derived from French plate of the 1670s.

The presence of the Huguenots effected a marked change to the character of silver produced in London and encouraged the spread of the French court style, though most of the goldsmiths came not from Paris but from the French provinces. They maintained links with France, and the origins of their style can be found in published designs of ornament by French engravers who contributed to the creation of the Louis XIV style—Jean Le Pautre (*see* LE PAUTRE, (1)), JEAN BERAIN I, Daniel Marot I (*see* MAROT, (2)) and Paul Androuet Du Cerceau—and specialist designs for metalwork published by Michel Mouton (*fl* 1670) and 'le Sieur' Masson. Le Pautre's and Berain's Baroque designs for figure candlesticks, helmet-shaped ewers and harp handles were widely imitated in England by both French and English goldsmiths. Examples include female figure candlesticks (e.g. by Anthony Nelme, *c*. 1680; Oxford, Ashmolean), a magnificent ewer and basin by Pierre Harache (1697; Chatsworth, Derbys) and a harp-handled cup and cover by Pierre Platel (1705; Oxford, Ashmolean). Le Pautre had published elaborate teapot designs in Paris in the 1660s, although the earliest English teapots date from the 1680s and 1690s (London, V&A; Burghley House, Cambs; Boston, MA, Mus. F.A.).

Marot's published designs for silver were adapted rather than copied by goldsmiths. The sculptural upper rim, scrolled handles with lion masks, armorial cartouches and gadrooning and fluting on a monteith (1703; Philadelphia,

76. Silver gilt waiter by Benjamin Pyne, diam. 124 mm, 1698 (London, Victoria and Albert Museum)

ornament and technique that are completely in the Huguenot manner. Whether such pieces were in fact the work of Huguenot journeymen in English employ or immigrant goldsmiths submitting their work for assay under English goldsmiths' marks remains unclear.

Plate characterized by sparse decoration and simplicity of form was also produced during the late 17th century, for example an inkstand by Robert Smythier (1685; untraced). Around 1700 the simple, elegant Queen Anne style became predominant in silverware. Many objects were based on geometrical forms—rectangles, hexagons and octagons—and their outstanding features are the lack of applied ornament, harmonious proportions and faceted surfaces. Teapots and tea kettles became more common, and from c. 1700 the faceted, pear-shaped teapot with carved wooden handle emerged, often supplied with a lamp and stand. An outstanding example is SIMON PAN-TIN's hexagonal silver tea kettle and lamp stand on a silver tripod (1724; New York, Met.). Bullet-shaped teapots (e.g. by James Smith, 1719; London, V&A) were introduced c. 1710. Cylindrical tapering chocolate-pots with domed lids differ from coffeepots only by the addition of a small aperture in the lid for the insertion of a swizzle-stick. Plain surfaces relieved by mouldings distinguished salvers (e.g. by Pierre Platel, 1710; see Hayward, 1959, fig. 59a), bowls (e.g. sugar bowl by William Fleming (fl 1697–1727), 1718; Manchester, Assheton Bennett priv. col.), salts (e.g. by Paul de Lamerie, 1712; Oxford, Ashmolean) and casters (e.g. set by Simon Pantin, c. 1716; London, V&A).

From 1715 these plain pieces were accompanied by more expensive examples in the Régence style. Huguenot goldsmiths were responsible for most of this highly finished ornamental plate, decorated with intricate chasing or engraving. The Walpole Salver by de Lamerie (1727; London, V&A) has oblong trellised border panels, separated by shell and husk medallions containing busts and ciphers, and the surfaces of a cruet stand by Paul Crespin (1721; Colonial Williamsburg, VA) are richly chased with subjects from *Aesop's Fables* and hunting scenes. Bands and panels of diaper and classical patterns were sometimes combined with armorials, for example on an octagonal wine bucket (1716; New York, Met.) by William Lukin (fl 1699–1751). On more ostentatious pieces these designs provide the background to late Baroque cast ornament and relate closely to earlier designs by Marot, for example a wine-cooler by de Lamerie overstruck with the mark of Paul Crespin (see fig. 77) and a wine-fountain (1728; London, Goldsmiths' Co.) by Peter Archambo. In some of this plate from the 1720s the earliest hints of the Rococo style can be detected.

PA, Mus. A.) by Samuel Lee (fl 1701–23) are typical of Marot's style. Stefano della Bella's earlier etchings of ornament, for example *Ornamenti di fregi e fogliami*, influenced the decoration of silver made in the 1690s. His delicate friezes of dogs and putti evolving into foliage appear on the borders of a set of hexagonal waiters by BENJAMIN PYNE (see fig. 76). These were possibly engraved by SIMON GRIBELIN II, one of the few identified Huguenot engravers, who specialized in heraldic ornament and the decoration of salvers. A comfit-box (c. 1690; London, V&A) is probably the earliest surviving piece decorated by him.

From the 1680s designs for silver tea equipages, mustard pots and cruets were all copied from objects made in Paris. New types of ware, for example the écuelle (e.g. by Pierre Platel, 1704; priv. col., see Hayward, 1959, fig. 69a) and the double-lipped sauceboat (e.g. by Samuel Margas, 1726; priv. col., see 1985 exh. cat., no. 337), were introduced by the Huguenots, as were large-scale architectural pieces for buffet displays, sculptural decoration and layered cut-card work, for example on a gold ewer and basin by Pierre Platel (1701; Chatsworth, Derbys). Many Huguenot goldsmiths' marks were of the French type with a crown over the initials, for example those of Harache and Platel, and, in some cases, a fleur-de-lis (e.g. that of Willaume).

English goldsmiths were compelled to imitate the French forms and to learn the techniques of casting and applying ornament to heavy-gauge wrought silver. The new style did not generally penetrate to the provinces, where there were fewer emigré craftsmen. The English and the French styles gradually merged, though French features predominated. From the 1690s the work of leading English goldsmiths, for example George Garthorne (e.g. chandelier, 1690; London, Hampton Court, Royal Col.) and Benjamin Pyne (e.g. standing-cup, c. 1705; London, Pewterers' Co.), exhibits characteristics of form,

BIBLIOGRAPHY

J. Evans: 'Huguenot Goldsmiths in England and Ireland', *Proc. Huguenot Soc. London*, xiv/4 (1933), pp. 496–654

J. Hayward: *Huguenot Silver in England, 1688–1727* (London, 1959)

J. Bannister: 'Pepys and the Goldsmiths', *Proc. Soc. Silver Colrs*, i/10 (1968), pp. 9–16

J. Hayward: 'A William and Mary Pattern-book for Silversmiths', *Proc. Soc. Silver Colrs*, ii/1 (1970), pp. 18–21

H. Tait: 'Huguenot Silver Made in London (c. 1690–1723): The Peter Wilding Bequest to the British Museum', *Connoisseur*, clxxx (Aug 1972), pp. 267–77; clxxxi (Sept 1972), pp. 25–36

A. Grimwade and J. Bannister: 'Thomas Jenkins Unveiled', *Connoisseur*, cxcv (July 1977), pp. 172–81

The Quiet Conquest: The Huguenots, 1685–1985 (exh. cat., ed. T. Murdoch; London, Mus. London, 1985)
Courts and Colonies: The William and Mary Style in Holland, England and America (exh. cat. by D. Revere McFadden, New York, Cooper-Hewitt Mus., 1988)
P. Earle: *The Making of the English Middle Class, 1660–1730* (London, 1989)

For general bibliography *see* §(vi) below.

(iv) 1730–80.

(a) History and uses. (b) Form and decoration.

(a) History and uses. In this period there was a substantial increase in middle-class consumption of luxury goods. Greater importance was attached to dining, for which a separate room was allocated, along with more utensils. Knives and forks and, under French influence, tureens and sauceboats with ladles and the surtout or épergne were generally in use. Silverware gradually replaced pewter in middle-class homes and was equalled in popularity by porcelain and creamware. The English tendency to display all of the plate at mealtimes was deplored by the French. From the 1720s complete matching dinner services came into fashion, although their expense precluded their acquisition by any but the very rich.

Through surviving court, fire insurance and business records and correspondence, more detail is available about the operation of the goldsmiths' trade at this time. By the mid-18th century retailers were known as goldsmiths and the working craftsmen as silversmiths. In 1773 the gold- and silversmiths operating in London alone numbered 688. Some goldsmiths ran large retail businesses, and success meant balancing costs of labour and materials against the credit required by clients and the large amounts of bullion invested in wrought objects. The production of Rococo silver in particular was labour-intensive, 'fashioning' charges were high, and aristocratic clients often kept retailers waiting two or three years for payment.

It is evident that objects previously accredited to the craftsmanship of one individual—as thought to be evidenced by the presence of the maker's mark—were actually the result of subcontracting work to specialist craftsmen, and that the identifying mark was that of the retailer rather than the maker or makers. The existence of a tripartite system—an interaction of artist-designer, plateworker and retailer—was acknowledged in both contemporary and 19th-century writings. This makes it easier to explain, for example, the large body of work attributed to Paul de Lamerie on the basis of his mark. It also accounts for the repetition of designs and cast ornament bearing a variety of maker's marks. Casting moulds were probably shared, and modellers worked for several goldsmiths. It is likely that the closely-knit Huguenot community supplied each other with unmarked wrought plate to be stamped or overstamped with the retailer's mark (*see* LONDON, §IV, 2).

In 1743 a new means of producing cheaper wares that resembled silver appeared with the invention of Sheffield plate by the cutler Thomas Boulsover (1704–88). This was successfully applied by Joseph Hancock (*c.* 1711–91) to the manufacture of candlesticks and hollowware in Sheffield, and by 1765 MATTHEW BOULTON was producing high-quality Sheffield plate and silver at his new factory in

77. Silver wine-cooler by Paul de Lamerie, h. 265 mm, 1727 (London, Victoria and Albert Museum)

Soho, Birmingham, becoming its largest single manufacturer. London's position as the leading centre of plate production was thus challenged by Birmingham (*see* BIRMINGHAM, §3) and SHEFFIELD. Machinery was introduced in the 1760s that could repeat stamping, embossing or piercing operations with great precision. With the introduction of steam-powered machines, parts could be mass-produced quickly and cheaply from thinner-gauge sheets of 'flatted' or rolled silver (a silver flatting mill had been invented in the 1720s).

By the 1770s plated wares had become fashionable in London and the provinces. They were often of identical design to silver wares, as the same steel dies were used for the manufacture of both. The makers of Sheffield plate identified their goods so closely with traditional silver that they adopted marks in imitation of those for goldsmiths. Provincial workshops adhering to traditional methods were unable to compete. Candlesticks in Sheffield plate became so popular that some retailers in London bought them in large quantities and overstamped the Sheffield mark with their own. As so many shops in London were obtaining their stock from commercial businesses, it was expedient for makers of wrought plate to announce that they also offered silver that was made on the premises. In addition, they proposed, without success, that there should be a duty of 6d. per ounce payable on all plated goods that had silver strips, edges and ornaments added to prevent the copper showing through.

The improvements in the availability and quantity of cheaper domestic plate meant that it was now affordable by the less wealthy. In 1777 there were 63 new categories of silverware and 79 types of small silver items recorded. Catalogues published by firms manufacturing Sheffield plate illustrate the wide range of objects that were available in popular designs. There was, nevertheless, a limit to the types of ware that could be made commercially, and the goldsmith was still required to produce commissioned objects using traditional methods.

(b) Form and decoration. Silver played an important and pioneering role in the promotion of the Rococo style in England, which was introduced via the imported continental pattern books that were circulated in the trade by itinerant craftsmen and by aristocrats on the Grand Tour who brought back French silver and designs. The production of Rococo silver was largely dominated by the second-generation Huguenot goldsmiths, principally PAUL DE LAMERIE and PAUL CRESPIN, who were influenced by their French contemporaries and who were, together with the Englishman George Wickes, the leading goldsmiths working in the style by the 1730s. A candelabrum and a kettle stand by de Lamerie (1731; Los Angeles, CA, Gilbert Col.) are set with small cast elements, including asymmetrical cartouches, characteristic of French silver, and swirling 'raffle' leaves. A pair of ice buckets by Crespin (1733; Blenheim Palace, Oxon) for Charles Spencer, 3rd Duke of Marlborough (*d* 1758), are indicative of Crespin's close interpretation of French sources: the design is inspired by the work of JUSTE-AURÈLE MEISSONNIER and incorporates wave ornament used by Thomas Germain (*see* GERMAIN, (1); e.g. tureen and plateau; priv. col.) in the same year.

By the mid-1730s English silversmiths were adopting ornamental motifs drawn from French engravings and pattern books. Some copied directly from French pieces that were circulating on the London market. Meissonier's *Livre de légumes* (1734) provided models for the naturalistic

78. Silver candlesticks (two of a set of four) after a design by George Michael Moser, h. 370 mm, *c.* 1740 (London, Victoria and Albert Museum)

cast vegetables and crustacea used as decoration on tureens, for example one by de Lamerie (*c.* 1736; priv. col., see 1990 exh. cat., p. 127). The influence of Jacques de Lajoue's *Recueil de différents cartouches* can be seen in the asymmetrical cartouches on a ewer and basin by George Wickes (1735; priv. col., see Barr, fig. 4). An inkstand by de Lamerie of 1738 (Blenheim Palace, Oxon) has a base modelled as an irregular cartouche.

Works of art from the 16th and 17th centuries also influenced the design of Rococo silverware: Jean Le Pautre's etchings of caryatid candlestick forms and Bernini's marble group of *Apollo and Daphne* (1625; Rome, Gal. Borghese) together inspired figure candlesticks (see fig. 78) after a design (London, V&A) by George Michael Moser (1704–88), where they are combined with rocaille ornament. The work of de Lamerie also incorporated Auricular motifs of the 17th-century Dutch silver made by the van Vianen family, for example on a serpent-handled cup and cover (*c.* 1737; London, Fishmongers' Co.) chased and embossed with Auricular masks on the foot and cover.

The essentially sculptural character of the Rococo style is exemplified by the work of NICHOLAS SPRIMONT. His reputation as one of the most celebrated 18th-century English goldsmiths is based on relatively few pieces of the 1740s, before he relinquished the manufacture of silver in favour of that of porcelain (*see* §VII, 3(ii) above). His crayfish salts (*c.* 1742; British Royal Col.) and figured sauceboats (*c.* 1743; British Royal Col.), from the dinner service for Frederick, Prince of Wales, were reworked in porcelain when he was director of the Chelsea porcelain factory. Another group of innovative goldsmiths who contributed to the development of the Rococo style *c.* 1740 were John Edwards (*fl* 1723–53), Aymé Videau (*fl* 1733–73), CHARLES KANDLER, Pézé Pilleau (1696–1776) and Christian Hillan (*fl* 1736). A creamboat by Hillan (*c.* 1740; priv. col., see 1984 exh. cat., p. 110), depicting the legend of Zeus and Io, is characteristic of the use of Greek mythological figures in Rococo silverware.

The predominant marine theme encompassed rocaille ornament, representations of flowing water and foam, marine creatures and vegetation, tritons, nereids, reptiles and grotesques, juxtaposed with scrolls, cartouches, putti, masks, naturalistic flowers, leaves and insects. The ubiquitous shell performed a structural as well as a decorative role. It was used particularly for salts and baskets. A basket by de Lamerie (1747; Oxford, Ashmolean) consists of a pierced scallop shell resting on dolphin feet.

William Kent's designs for silver in *Some Designs of Mr Inigo Jones and Mr William Kent* (1744), though incorporating classical elements, were used by such goldsmiths as Wickes—on a Rococo épergne (1745; Brit. Royal Col.) for Frederick, Prince of Wales—Crespin and Edward Wakelin (*fl* 1748–84). By the 1750s a renewed fashion for chinoiserie was combined with the Rococo, notably in épergnes and in William Chambers's designs for teaware. An épergne (*c.* 1762; Colonial Williamsburg, VA) by Thomas Pitts, on an openwork floral frame with scroll feet, has two bell-hung pagoda canopies surmounted by a pineapple. By the 1760s heavy, curvaceous but restrained forms, for example a tureen by Thomas Heming (*c.* 1762; Camden, NJ, Campbell Mus.), which were similar to those of French silver of the 1730s, became popular.

By 1770 the Rococo style had been replaced by Neoclassicism, although vestigial traces of the former remained, for example on the handles cast as plant stalks on a tureen (*c.* 1771; priv. col., see Young, 1986, p. 31) by Sebastian Crespel (*fl* 1762–1806) and James Crespel (*fl* 1762–1806) derived from designs in Meissonier's *Livre de légumes* and a coffeepot (1776; London, V&A) by Charles Wright (*fl* 1757–90; *d* 1815), which incorporates Rococo and Neo-classical motifs. Chambers's designs of the 1770s combine Neo-classical forms with organic naturalism. He also provided designs for Thomas Heming, when the latter was goldsmith to the royal household, that anticipate the Regency style in the combination of naturalism with bold classical ornament.

The architects Robert Adam, James Wyatt and James Stuart, as well as Chambers, designed Neo-classical silver and subscribed to the concept that plate, like furniture, should be designed to complement the interior in which it was placed. Adam owned a scrapbook containing 180 prints by Stefano della Bella, whose *Raccolta di vasi diversi* (Paris, *c.* 1646), based on the work of the Florentine Mannerists, was an important source for Neo-classical form and ornament in silver. A vase and cover by Parker & Wakelin (1770–71; London, V&A) is derived from an etching in the *Raccolta* of a vase with rising hooked handles. Adam's design (1773) for a two-branched tripod candelabrum was closely interpreted by John Carter (*fl* 1769–77) in a candelabrum with a pine-cone finial, ram's heads, scrolling foliage, palmettes and guilloche borders (London, Lloyds'). This design is preserved in Sir John Soane's Museum, London, along with others, including two for urn-shaped tureens designed for Hugh Smithson Percy, 1st Duke of Northumberland, in 1779.

Matthew Boulton adopted the Neo-classical style for both wrought and plated silver. Adam, Wyatt and Stuart all designed wares for him (see fig. 79). The urn and the vase were the principal forms chosen for silverware; the urn shape was particularly appropriate for tureens, which were made by Boulton and John Fothergill (*d* 1782), Parker & Wakelin, Thomas Heming and others, as well as sauceboats, wine-coolers (e.g. by Charles Kandler, 1775; London, V&A) with ram's heads, Vitruvian scrolls and bound reeding, and small tea caddies and sugar and condiment containers. The vase shape was suitable for ewers, flagons, jugs, coffee- and chocolate-pots (e.g. of 1777 by Henry Greenaway (*fl* 1775–90; *d* 1818/22); London, V&A; based on a Greek amphora with tripod support). The classical column was an apposite form for the candlestick, as was the tripod for candelabra and cassolettes. Objects unsuited to these shapes, for example salvers and bread baskets, incorporated decorative Neo-classical motifs. The border of a salver by Charles Kandler (1775; Birmingham, Mus. & A.G.) is decorated with husk festoons, ram's heads and paterae.

Forms were regular and symmetrical with graduated curves, delicate shallow fluting and relief ornament derived from archaeological publications. Such elements were economically reproduced by casting, and engraving was mainly restricted to armorials. As certain motifs became

79. Silver sauceboat (one of a set of eight) designed by Robert Adam (i) and made by Matthew Boulton and John Fothergill, 130×250×118 mm, 1776–7 (London, Victoria and Albert Museum)

popular, for example guilloches, egg-and-dart mouldings, palmettes and acanthus leaves, steel-die makers supplied variants that could be assembled at minimum cost in diverse combinations. A characteristic treatment of plain surfaces was a pattern of regular, alternate vertical panels of burnished and matt metal in imitation of ancient Greek ceramics, for example on a tea service for the actor David Garrick (1774; London, V&A) by James Young (*fl* 1760–93) and Orlando Jackson (*fl* 1759/60–74). The applied medallions employed by Andrew Fogelberg (*c.* 1732–1815), for example on a cauldron-shaped sugar basin with hoofed feet (1777; London, V&A), were based directly on James Tassie's reproductions of Renaissance gems and cameos (Tassie and Fogelberg were neighbours in Soho).

BIBLIOGRAPHY
R. Rowe: *Adam Silver* (London, 1965)
E. Barr: *George Wickes: Royal Goldsmith, 1698–1761* (London, 1980)
K. Quickenden: 'Boulton & Fothergill Silver: Business Plans and Miscalculations', *A. Hist.*, iii (1980), pp. 274–94
Rococo Art and Design in Hogarth's England (exh. cat., ed. M. Snodin; London, V&A, 1984)
K. Quickenden: 'Boulton & Fothergill Silver: An Epergne Designed by James Wyatt', *Burl. Mag.*, cxxxviii (1986), pp. 417–21
H. Young: 'Sir William Chambers and John Yenn: Designs for Silver', *Burl. Mag.*, cxxxviii (1986), pp. 31–5
——: 'Sir William Chambers and the Duke of Marlborough's Silver', *Apollo*, cxxv (1987), pp. 396–400
Paul de Lamerie: The Work of England's Master Goldsmith (exh. cat. by S. Hare, London, Goldsmiths' Co., 1990)

For general bibliography *see* §(vi) below.

PHILIPPA GLANVILLE

(v) 1781–1895. At the end of the 18th century the design of English silver was affected by two principal factors. The first was the increasing use of machine-produced parts, often made from rolled plate of thin gauge. By these means of production greater quantities of primarily domestic wares—cruets, candlesticks, cutlery and teapots—characterized by simple shapes and decorated with precise piercing, embossing and engraving, became more widely available at a considerably lower cost. The establishment in 1773 of assay offices in Birmingham, where MATTHEW BOULTON was one of the most important silversmiths, and in SHEFFIELD facilitated the development of these cities as important centres for the mass production of

80. Goodwood Cup by Paul Storr, silver gilt, h. 445 mm, 1829 (British Royal Collection)

silverware. The monopoly on silver manufacture enjoyed by goldsmiths in London was threatened by such cheaper wares, but larger pieces or services in heavier gauge metal, with complex casting and chasing or in inventive designs, continued to be hand made at greater cost.

The second, stylistic, factor affecting silver design resulted from the decline of the so-called 'Adam' style, characterized by the use of boat-shaped or urn-derived forms, tripods, low-relief decoration, bright-cutting, cut-card work, gadrooning, fluting and reeded edges, which had been fashionable from about 1770, and the consequent introduction of forms that closely reflected the growing interest in the development of a type of Neo-classicism based more accurately on the designs and forms of such archaeological finds as the Warwick, Buckingham and Lanti Vases, many of which were acquired by English aristocrats on the Grand Tour. These, together with published engravings of antiquities, notably those by Piranesi, inspired the work of the leading goldsmiths of the first quarter of the 19th century. The architect Charles Heathcote Tatham, in his *Etchings of Ancient Ornamental Architecture* (1799) and in his highly influential *Designs for Ornamental Plate* (1806), advocated 'massiveness' as the principal characteristic of 'good plate'. Pieces made after Tatham's designs exemplifying this quality and exhibiting high standards of chasing include a candelabrum (Althorp House, Northants) made by William Pitts II (1790–1840) for George Spencer, 2nd Earl Spencer, the candelabra (before 1810) for the gallery at Castle Howard, N. Yorks, and another magnificent candelabrum (before 1810; Castle Howard, N. Yorks) for Frederick Howard, 5th Earl of

Carlisle. New designs were further stimulated by the acquisition in 1802 by the British Museum, London, of Egyptian antiquities collected by Napoleon and captured by the British in Cairo.

Silver of the Regency period is characterized by the continued use of elegant classical models combined, however, with extravagant decoration. The Prince Regent (later George IV) continued the patronage begun by his father, George III, of the firm of RUNDELL, BRIDGE & RUNDELL, which pursued policies similar to those later adopted by Liberty & Co., whereby many of the leading silversmiths of the day were subcontracted to produce pieces that were sold under the firm's name. Such work includes the set of eight silver-gilt wine-coolers (1808; British Royal Col.) made for the Prince Regent by PAUL STORR, Benjamin Smith (1764–1823) and James Smith, the design of which, although with modified frieze and base, is clearly based on Piranesi's etching of the Medici Krater. In a similar manner, the set of eight silver-gilt ice-pails (1812; British Royal Col.), also by Storr for the Prince, are based on the Warwick Vase.

The naval and military victories of Nelson and the Duke of Wellington resulted in the production of large-scale, commemorative services and centrepieces. The Trafalgar Vases (1805–6; London, V&A), for example, presented to admirals and captains present at the Battle of Trafalgar, were designed by the sculptor John Flaxman and executed by Benjamin Smith and Digby Scott (*fl* 1802–7). Flaxman's extensive designs for Regency silver also included two silver-gilt candelabra (1809; British Royal Col.), representing the *Three Graces*, made by Storr for the Prince Regent's Grand Service, the Theocritus Cup (1812; London, V&A), also by Storr, and the Shield of Achilles (1821–2; Windsor Castle, Berks, Royal Col.), executed by Rundell, Bridge & Rundell. Flaxman also produced designs in the Gothic Revival style, for example the National Cup (1824; British Royal Col.). A sideboard dish (1814), representing the *Triumph of Bacchus and Ariadne*, and a shield (London, V&A) for the Duke of Wellington, presented in 1822, both designed by Thomas Stothard, include strong sculptural elements that combine architectural and figurative forms with naturalistic detail, which are also characteristic features of Flaxman's influential classical designs. The architect Charles Robert Cockerell also produced designs (1821) for plate, including a vase presented by the Duke of Wellington's staff to General Alava, that were executed by Rundell, Bridge & Rundell. Sporting achievements were celebrated in the ornate Weymouth Regatta Cup (1827–8; London, V&A), the Doncaster Gold Cup (1828; Leeds, Temple Newsam House), both by Rebecca Emes (*fl* 1808–29) and Edward Barnard (1781–1846), and the Goodwood Cup (see fig. 80) by Paul Storr, the last two also derived from Piranesian models. Other types of presentation piece include the massive rectangular tray (Woburn Abbey, Beds), designed by the painter Edwin Henry Landseer and embossed with agricultural scenes, for John Russell, 6th Duke of Bedford.

Throughout the Regency period many leading craftsmen, including Storr, the two Smiths, Joseph Preedy, John Edward and William Edwards, continued to produce utilitarian pieces, for example teapots, salt-cellars, sugar bowls, coasters, salvers, tea-caddies, candlesticks and sauce-tureens. An impressive example of the last type (1819; London, V&A) in the Rococo Revival style was made by Storr to a design almost certainly by Edward Hodges Baily. Other utilitarian pieces of this period often combine classical, Egyptian and chinoiserie, as well as Rococo, elements, for example a silver-gilt tankard and cover (1817; priv. col.) by Edward Farrell (1779–1850). The manufacture of 'toys'—small decorative artefacts in gold, silver and steel, for example snuff-boxes, *étuis*, toilet articles, inkstands, snuffers, buckles and watch-chains—was centred on Birmingham, where the most prominent firms were those of Boulton, Edward Thomason (1769–1849) and Samuel Pemberton. Production of these small, utilitarian items increased enormously after the economic depression of the 1780s and 1790s, reaching a peak by about 1840.

From the 1830s there were attempts to improve the standards of design and manufacture of plate, although eclectic styles continued to be popular. The foundation *c.* 1836 of the Cambridge Camden Society resulted in the stricter control of the manufacture of ecclesiastical plate, under the supervision of William Butterfield. From the late 1830s chalices, patens, censers, ciboria, monstrances and reliquaries were made to the designs of A. W. N. Pugin, many by the firm of John Hardman & Co. of Birmingham. In 1841 Pugin published the *True Principles of Pointed or Christian Architecture*, in which he deplored the uniformity of machine-made artefacts and the vulgar styles of much contemporary silverwork. He advocated a revival of medieval methods of manufacture that emphasized the metallic nature of the material and that involved the processes of hammering, soldering, piercing, chasing, engraving and, where appropriate, enamelling. As with classical models of the early 19th century, however, many practitioners of the Gothic Revival style did not produce slavish imitations of medieval pieces. Work by Francis Skidmore the elder and younger of Coventry, some in the 'Geometric' Gothic Revival style and designed by Sir Giles Gilbert Scott (ii), is different from that of Pugin, as are pieces designed in the 1860s by the architects William Burges, who favoured the use of parcel gilding and gemstones with contrasting plain and engraved surfaces, and G. E. Street, who frequently incorporated niello in otherwise plain bodies with restrained mouldings. The Gothic Revival style was used for domestic wares at this time: tea and coffee services designed and made by John Hardman Powell in the 1860s, for example, clearly show the influence of ecclesiastical work in the same style, as do jugs and flagons, some of glass mounted with silver feet, collars, handles and knops.

Despite Pugin's attempts to revive craft production of silver, industrially produced wares in a wide variety of styles were manufactured in the mid-19th century. Prince Albert, who designed a silver-gilt centrepiece (1842; London, V&A) made by the leading firm of GARRARD, was one of the prime instigators, together with HENRY COLE, of the Great Exhibition of 1851 in London, at which it was evident that improved industrial methods had made possible the manufacture of virtually any form in silver, particularly elaborate, naturalistic pieces. Developments in electroplating techniques, of which the successful firm of G. R. ELKINGTON was the leading exponent, enabled the

production of items that were even cheaper than those in Sheffield plate. The growing interest in antiquarianism among designers and silversmiths was also reflected in the revival in the mid-19th century of Italian Renaissance and 16th-century German forms and ornament. Pieces by Benvenuto Cellini and Nicholas Schmidt, designs by Rosso Fiorentino incorporating nautilus shells or strapwork, and 16th-century English steeple-cups and repoussé work inspired many High Victorian pieces in the Renaissance Revival style by such designers as Walter Langley. The eclectic nature of these historicist styles, the use of such continental techniques as oxidization and enamelling and the employment by leading manufacturers of such French designers and craftsmen as Antoine Vechte (1799–1868) almost certainly militated against the development of a national style from the 1850s to the 1870s.

With the emergence of the Arts and Crafts Movement in the 1870s, CHRISTOPHER DRESSER, in his *Principles of Decorative Design* (1873), emphasized utility and economy of construction and ornament in silverware, resulting, in his own work—jugs (see fig. 81), tea services, bowls and other utilitarian pieces—in functionalist forms of often astonishing severity and abstraction that were probably inspired by the simplicity of Japanese design. In the 1880s W. A. S. BENSON produced silver items characterized by

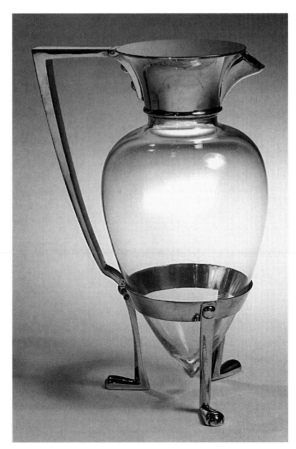

81. Claret jug designed by Christopher Dresser, glass with silver mounts, 1879 (London, Victoria and Albert Museum)

simplicity of design and hammered surfaces, as opposed to the mechanically produced finish by which all tool marks were removed by an abrasive process. C. R. ASHBEE, the founder in 1888 of the Guild and School of Handicraft, London, the first late 19th-century guild devoted to the production of silver and metalwork, also left hammer-marks visible and favoured polishing to a tactile and soft, rather than a glittering, sheen. Many of his pieces, both domestic and ecclesiastical, are simple in form, but others are elaborately decorated with embossing, chasing, casting, enamelling and wirework (*see also* §(vi) below). Despite Ashbee's aim of making such pieces widely available, the handmade silver produced by his Guild was often so costly as to be considered only as luxury items, although the forms and techniques were often imitated by amateur silversmiths. Although more overtly commercially orientated than Ashbee's Guild, the Birmingham Guild of Handicraft, founded in 1895 by Arthur Dixon (1856–1929), a silversmith trained as an architect, produced work that is equally simple in form and finish.

BIBLIOGRAPHY

C. Oman: *English Domestic Silver* (London, 1934, 7/1968)
S. W. Turner: 'The Establishment and Development of the Silver Plate Industry in Sheffield', *Apollo*, xlvi (1947), pp. 143–5, 149
C. Oman: *Regency Domestic Silver* (London, 1952)
——: *Royal Plate* (London, 1954)
——: *The Wellington Plate* (London, 1954)
N. M. Penzer: *Paul Storr* (London, 1954)
G. Taylor: *Silver* (Harmondsworth, 1956, London, 3/1964)
C. Oman: *English Silversmiths' Work* (London, 1965)
——: 'A Problem of Artistic Responsibility: The Firm of Rundell, Bridge & Rundell', *Apollo*, lxxxiii (1966), pp. 174–83
H. Honour: *Goldsmiths & Silversmiths* (London, 1971)
Birmingham Gold and Silver, 1773–1973 (exh. cat., Birmingham, Mus. & A.G., 1973)
D. Udy: 'Piranesi's "Vasi": The English Silversmith and his Patrons', *Burl. Mag.*, cxx (1978), pp. 820–37
Sporting Glory: The Courage Exhibition of National Trophies (exh. cat., London, V&A, 1992)

RICHARD RIDDELL

(vi) After 1895. At the turn of the 19th century the Guild of Handicraft, which epitomized the values of the Arts and Crafts Movement under the leadership of its founder, C. R. Ashbee, continued to produce an innovative range of silverware. Ashbee's elegant use of twisted wirework, for example the loop handles attached to plain silver dishes and the silver collars and slim cordon of wires encasing green glass decanters (*see* ARTS AND CRAFTS MOVEMENT, fig. 1), is one of the most original features of his silverware of this period. Other distinguishing characteristics of silver made by the Guild are plain, unpolished surfaces, with visible planishing marks, occasionally decorated with areas of rich, monochrome enamel. Ashbee's designs occasionally incorporate traditional elements, for example the Painter-Stainer's Cup (1900; London, V&A), which is in the form of a 17th-century English steeple-cup, but his interpretation of historical forms was always in a characteristically modern and idiomatic style.

Ashbee's ideas, much to his discontent, were successfully exploited by large commercial manufacturers and retailers. In 1899 William Hutton & Sons of Sheffield and then, more spectacularly, Liberty & Co. of London, in conjunction with the firm of W. H. Haseler of Birmingham, began to produce a range of silver hollowware and jewellery under the 'Cymric' label, which was considerably

influenced by, but not directly imitative of, Ashbee's pioneering work. There are certain characteristics in common between silver made by Liberty's and that by Ashbee, for example large areas of plain silver with concentrated ornament, including clusters of coloured hardstones and enamelled work, and the use of planished surfaces, which in the case of Liberty's were achieved by machine stamping. The 'Cymric' style is a rich blend of the English Arts and Crafts and continental Art Nouveau styles. While it was Liberty's policy for its designers to remain anonymous, subsequent research has revealed that ARCHIBALD KNOX was responsible for the most distinguished designs in the 'Cymric' range, probably from 1899 to 1912. His work displays a fluent mastery of interlaced ornament that is both strikingly modern and yet inspired by Celtic scroll-work (e.g. biscuit-box, 1901–2; London, V&A). Other designers associated with Liberty's at this time included Olive Baker, Bernard Cuzner (1877–1956) and Jessie M. King.

At the beginning of the 20th century the Guild of Handicraft enjoyed a modest prosperity, but Ashbee was forced to declare bankruptcy in 1908. From 1900 to 1910 others adopted and extended his ideas, for example HENRY WILSON (1864–1934), Nelson Dawson (1859–1942), John Paul Cooper (1869–1933), Alexander Fisher (1864–1936) and Arthur Gaskin (1862–1928), who were beginning to produce work that was richer than the austere simplicity of that made by the Guild of Handicraft. OMAR RAMSDEN was another silversmith who successfully exploited Ashbee's stylistic mannerisms. Ramsden went into partnership with his fellow student Alwyn Carr (1872–1940) on the completion of his training in 1899, when they moved from Sheffield to London. Like Liberty's, the predominant characteristics of their early work can best be described as a combination of Arts and Crafts (e.g. silver dish with red enamel boss, 1911–12; Leeds, Temple Newsam House) and Art Nouveau. After Carr departed from the partnership in 1918 Ramsden's style was moderated into a pleasing, if unchallenging, Arts and Crafts style. In the 1920s, however, Ramsden's work enjoyed a considerable reputation for consistent high quality.

In the 1920s and 1930s the popularity of Arts and Crafts metalwork gradually declined. Liberty's continued with their 'Cymric' range until 1927, although their association with Haseler's continued until just after World War II. Although the Arts and Crafts Movement was no longer fashionable, its influence on the silversmithing trade continued to be powerful. Some of the most original and innovative silver of this period was produced in small workshops, run by such artist-craftsmen as Ramsden, almost all of whom had been trained by leading figures in the Arts and Crafts Movement. Other silversmiths in the generation that succeeded Ashbee and his contemporaries, however, had an altogether more prosaic outlook and attempted to address the problems of British manufacturing design. The impetus for this had come from abroad, when several members of the British Arts and Crafts Society had visited the Deutscher Werkbund exhibition of 1914 in Cologne. The immediate result was the foundation in 1915 of the Design and Industries Association, which was intended to promote a new, progressive spirit in British industrial design. One of its founder-members was the silversmith HAROLD STABLER, who had started his career producing silver that is entirely in the Arts and Crafts style. A loving-cup (c. 1908; London, V&A) by Stabler, for example, decorated with painted enamel and mythological scenes, is comparable to the work of Henry Wilson. Stabler's mature work of the 1920s and 1930s, however, shows the formal properties that were closely related to the Modernist preoccupations of contemporary avant-garde architects in Britain and Europe. Other silversmiths who promoted the Modern Movement in silver included Henry George Murphy (1884–1939), who had a profound influence as a teacher at the Central School of Arts and Crafts, London, and who worked closely with the designer R. M. Y. Gleadowe (1888–1944). The latter was responsible for extremely refined designs, often incorporating engraving, a technique that enjoyed a revival in the 1930s. The designs were executed principally by Murphy (see fig. 82) or the workshop of Wakeley & Wheeler in London.

English silversmithing after World War II continued to show the same harmonious equilibrium between ornament and form and material and technique that had been established in Arts and Crafts silver by Ashbee and that is also evident in Modernist silver of the 1930s. Stylistically, the immediate post-war generation of silversmiths adopted the latter style, although the characteristic use by Gerald Benney (b 1930) of textured surfaces resulted in a richly

decorative quality in some of his pieces. Silversmiths also benefited considerably from institutional support provided principally by two sources. The Goldsmiths' Company of London was active in support of the craft through sponsorship of exhibitions, scholarships and its collecting policies. Secondly, the renaissance of the Royal College of Art in London in the 1950s contributed enormously to the success of British silversmithing and such related disciplines as industrial design. Such distinguished silversmiths as Benney and ROBERT WELCH enjoyed international reputations. DAVID MELLOR also began a successful career as a silversmith in the 1950s and later established himself as one of the foremost industrial designers in England. In the late 20th century silversmiths incorporated a richer vocabulary of ornament in their work. These craftsmen included Rod Kelly (b 1952), an exceptionally gifted chaser (e.g. silver bowl, 1984; London, V&A), Howard Fenn (b 1953), who used abstract elements, and Lexi Dick, who incorporated anthropomorphic details into her work.

BIBLIOGRAPHY

GENERAL

A. Heal: *The London Goldsmiths, 1200–1800* (Cambridge, 1935)
G. Taylor: *Silver* (London, 1956, rev. 3/1968)
C. Oman: *English Church Plate, 1597–1830* (London, 1957)
Y. Hackenbroch: *English and Other Silver in the Irwin Untermeyer Collection* (London, 1963)
C. Oman: *Caroline Silver* (London, 1970)
A. Grimwade: *London Goldsmiths, 1607–1837: Their Marks and Lives* (London, 1976, rev. 1990)
C. Hernmarck: *The Art of the European Silversmith, 1430–1830*, 2 vols (London and New York, 1977)
C. Oman: *English Engraved Silver, 1150–1900* (London and Boston, 1978)
Touching Gold and Silver: 500 Years of Hallmarks (exh. cat., London, Goldsmiths' Co., 1978)
C. Oman: 'College Plate', *New College, Oxford, 1379–1979*, ed. J. Buxton and P. Williams (Oxford, 1979), pp. 293–305
A. Gruber: *L'Argenterie de maison: Du XVI au XIX siècle* (Fribourg, 1982); Eng. trans. as *Silverware* (New York, 1982)
Pattern and Design: Designs for the Decorative Arts, 1480–1980 (exh. cat. by S. Lambert, London, V&A, 1983)
H. Tait: 'Huguenots in Britain and their French Background, 1550–1800', *Contributions to the Historical Conference of the Huguenot Society of London, 1985*, ed. I. Scouladi, pp. 89–113
The Quiet Conquest: The Huguenots, 1685–1985 (exh. cat., ed. T. Murdoch; London, Mus. London, 1985)
C. Blair, ed.: *The History of Silver* (London, 1987)
P. Glanville: *Silver in England* (London and New York, 1987)
L. Weatherill: *Consumer Behaviour and Material Culture in Britain, 1660–1760* (London, 1988)
P. Glanville and J. Faulds Goldsborough: *Women Silversmiths, 1685–1845* (London, 1990)
E. J. L. Packer: *Silver Toilet Services, circa 1660–1780* (diss., U. Leeds, 1990)
Fake?: The Art of Deception (exh. cat., ed. M. Jones; London, BM, 1990)
English Silver Treasures from the Kremlin (exh. cat., ed. I. Rodimtseva; London, Sotheby's, 1991)

AFTER 1895

S. Bury: 'The Liberty Metalwork Venture', *Archit. Rev.*, cxxxiii (1963), pp. 108–11
——: 'A Craftsman who Used the Machine', *Country Life*, cxxxvii (18 March 1965), pp. 624–7
The Worshipful Company of Goldsmiths as Patrons of their Craft, 1919–1953 (exh. cat., ed. G. Hughes; London, Goldsmiths' Co., 1965)
G. Hughes: *Modern Silver* (London, 1967)
'An Arts and Crafts Experiment: The Silverwork of C. R. Ashbee', *V&A Mus. Bull.*, iii (Jan 1967)
Liberty's, 1875–1975: An Exhibition to Mark the Firm's Centenary (exh. cat., ed. S. Bury; London, V&A, 1975)
A. Crawford: *C. R. Ashbee* (New Haven, 1985)

82. Silver beaker designed by R. M. Y. Gleadowe and made by Henry George Murphy, h. 110 mm, 1933–4 (London, Victoria and Albert Museum)

E. Turner: 'Modernism and English Silver', *V&A Mus. Album*, 5 (1986), pp. 240–48
S. Calloway, ed.: *The House of Liberty* (London, 1992)
Silver of a New Era: International Highlights of Precious Metalware from 1880 to 1940 (exh. cat., ed. J. Willink; Rotterdam, Boymans–van Beuningen, 1992), pp. 9–43
20th Century Silver (exh. cat. by H. Clifford and others, London, Crafts Council Gal., 1993)

ERIC TURNER

2. BASE METALS.

(i) Before 1450. (ii) 1450–1600. (iii) 1601–1800. (iv) After 1800.

(i) Before 1450.

(a) Copper alloys. From early Anglo-Saxon times in the 7th century AD copper alloys were used for buckles and helmet decorations that were often gilded (e.g. the Benty Grange Helmet; Sheffield, City Mus.). Decorative gilt copper alloy bands with interlace ornament appear on the York Helmet (see fig. 83) of the second half of the 8th century. Gilt copper alloys were also used for Anglo-Saxon reliquaries and shrines; two of the few surviving examples are a male head from an 8th-century shrine (London, BM) and a late 9th-century burse reliquary (Winchester, City Mus.). Bronze was used for censers, and three survive in part from the Anglo-Saxon period: the 9th-century North Elmham Censer and the 10th-century Canterbury and Pershore Censer Covers (all London, BM).

In the Romanesque period images of Christ, the Virgin and saints in gilt copper alloys were probably common; the few surviving examples include the standing figures of

a *Saint* and the *Virgin* (*c*. 1050; York, Yorks Mus.) and a figure of *Christ* in high relief on the cover of the Sandford Reliquary (*c*. 1100; Oxford, Ashmolean). Figures of three soldiers guarding the Tomb of Christ (*c*. 1140–50; Glasgow, Burrell Col.) were also probably part of a reliquary. The most common form of figure was that of the *Crucifixion*, of which there are several extant examples dating from the late 11th century and the 12th: the Lundø Crucifix (*c*. 1050–75; Copenhagen, Nmus.) and the Monmouth Crucifix (*c*. 1170–80; Monmouth, St Mary) are the only ones with the original cross. The Gloucester Candlestick (1107–13; London, V&A; *see* ROMANESQUE, fig. 76) is one of the finest pieces of Romanesque gilt metalwork and is formed of cast, entwined beasts, human figures and foliage. Church door-knockers, usually formed of a lion's head, as elsewhere in Europe, were made of bronze, and examples survive at Durham Cathedral (*c*. 1133) and St Peter, Dormington, Hereford & Worcs (*c*. 1150); an early 13th-century example from St Mary, Lindsell, Essex, is in the British Museum, London. In later centuries door-knockers seem mainly to have been imported from north Germany, and an example of *c*. 1300 in Gloucester (City Mus. & A.G.) is one of the few produced in England.

Copper alloys were used extensively for crosiers and liturgical vessels in the 13th, 14th and 15th centuries. Chalices were usually in silver for the practical reason that the Eucharistic wine would soon cause the poisonous substance, verdigris, to form on a chalice made of copper alloys. Gilt copper was used for holy water stoups, pyxides and chrismatories, which sometimes have simple, engraved foliage decoration, and for the tablets for the pax, which are engraved or have a scene of the *Crucifixion* in relief (e.g. of *c*. 1400; Bury St Edmunds, St Edmundsbury Museums). Altar and processional crosses survive mainly from the 15th century, but there is a fine extant example of *c*. 1220–50 (London, V&A). Book covers were often of gilt bronze, for example the remnants of the cover of the Book of Llandaff (*c*. 1250–65; Aberystwyth, N. Lib. Wales). Aquamanilia, usually in the form of lions, seem in the main to have been imported from Flanders or Germany, but a late 13th-century English example (London, BM) survives. Numerous 14th-century MONUMENTAL BRASSES are also extant (*see* LONDON, fig. 14). Bronze was also used for large-scale tomb effigies, but very few remain. In Westminster Abbey, London, are the bronze effigies (*c*. 1292–4) of *Henry III* and *Eleanor of Castile* (*c*. 1222–91), at Canterbury Cathedral that (*c*. 1376) of *Edward, Prince of Wales* (1330–76), and at St Mary, Warwick, that (*c*. 1447; see fig. 26 above) of *Richard Beauchamp, Earl of Warwick* (1382–1439).

(b) Tin, lead, pewter and iron. From the 12th to the 15th centuries tin was occasionally used for statuettes of Christ, the Virgin and the saints. Lead was most commonly used as the material for pilgrim badges (*see* PILGRIM BADGE) but also for fonts, of which many survive from the 12th century and the early 13th. These are decorated with high-relief foliage patterns and figural work and are important examples of English Romanesque sculpture. The finest examples are at St Peter, Walton-on-the-Hill, Surrey (*c*. 1150–60), St Mary, Wareham, Dorset (*c*. 1150), St Mary, Frampton-on-Severn, Glos (*c*. 1150–75), the Abbey of SS

83. The York Helmet, iron and copper alloy, h. 246 mm, second half of the 8th century (York, Castle Museum)

Peter and Paul, Dorchester, Oxon (c. 1170–80), and St Augustine, Brookland, Kent (c. 1200). In the 13th and 14th centuries pewter was occasionally employed for candlesticks and liturgical vessels, particularly for chalices and patens used in the burial of priests, but its main use seems to have been for simple, undecorated domestic tableware and drinking vessels.

It is questionable whether, before the 12th century, anything other than such functional items as shield bosses, helmets and other military equipment was made of iron. From the 12th to the 15th centuries, however, it was widely used as decoration for chests, wooden doors, locks, grilles and railings. Hinges are the main part of medieval ironwork decoration of doors, although patterns often extend from the hinge straps to cover part or even the whole of the door. In 12th-century examples at St Mary, Little Hormead, Herts; All Saints, Staplehurst, Kent; St Helen, Stillingfleet, N. Yorks; and St Andrew, Willingale Spain, Essex, there is much variety of ornamentation, incorporating dragons, geometric patterns, foliage and other motifs. From the second half of the 12th century foliage patterns were used almost exclusively, for example on a door at St Albans Cathedral and on the Slype Door, St Andrew, Sempringham, Lincs.

In the early 13th century certain innovations, involving the use of moulded dies and punches for stamping and the introduction of deeply grooved stems of foliage, occurred in French ironwork (e.g. west doors of Notre Dame, Paris); the earliest English example of these techniques is the entrance door to St George's Chapel, Windsor Castle, Berks (1240–49). The new forms were used by the blacksmith Thomas de Leghtone, who made the grille (1292–3) for the tomb of *Eleanor of Castile* in Westminster Abbey. A simple grille from Chichester Cathedral (c. 1250–75; London, V&A) also survives.

In the late 13th century and the early 14th blacksmiths tended to employ cutting and filing methods to work cold iron rather than use a hammer and anvil to shape hot iron. Sheet iron for grilles and other items was pierced to create patterns resembling the tracery fashionable in Gothic architecture. Pierced and stamped ironwork ornaments a chest (c. 1300) at All Saints, Icklingham, Suffolk, and the entrance gate (1304–9) of the choir of Canterbury Cathedral.

In the 14th and 15th centuries carved woodwork on doors supplanted the ironwork decoration, which was reduced to simple hinges, although occasionally quite elaborate patterns were used around the locks. The main forms of decorative ironwork in this period were rails and grilles around tombs; these incorporate such architectural motifs as turrets and castellation in the design, for example those on the tombs of *Bishop Beckington* (d 1465) at Wells Cathedral and *Edward IV* (d 1483) at St George's Chapel, Windsor Castle. The latter, by John Tresilian, is extremely elaborate, incorporating delicate tracery, buttresses and pinnacles, similar to contemporary wood-carving in choir-stalls. With this important work the tradition of English medieval ironworking came to an end.

See also ROMANESQUE, §VI, 6 and GOTHIC, §V, 7.

BIBLIOGRAPHY

J. Tavenor-Perry: *Dinanderie: A History and Description of Mediaeval Art Work in Copper, Brass and Bronze* (London, 1910)

O. Hoever: *An Encyclopaedia of Ironwork* (London, 1927); repr. as *A Handbook of Wrought Iron* (London, 1962)

J. Starkie Gardner: *Ironwork: From the Earliest Times to the End of the Mediaeval Period* (London, 1927/R London, 1978)

G. C. Druce: 'Lead Fonts in England with Some Reference to French Examples', *J. Brit. Archaeol. Assoc.*, xxxix (1934), pp. 289–329

R. Lister: *Decorative Wrought Ironwork in Great Britain* (London, 1957/R Newton Abbot, 1970)

G. Zarnecki: *English Romanesque Lead Sculpture* (London, 1957)

C. C. Oman: 'English Medieval Base-metal Church Plate', *Archaeol. J.*, cxix (1962), pp. 195–207

J. Hatcher and T. C. Barker: *A History of British Pewter* (London, 1974)

U. Mende: *Die Türzieher des Mittelalters* (Berlin, 1981)

English Romanesque Art, 1066–1200 (exh. cat., ed. G. Zarnecki; London, Hayward Gal., 1984), pp. 232–97

The Golden Age of Anglo-Saxon Art, 966–1066 (exh. cat., ed. J. Backhouse, D. H. Turner and L. Webster; London, BM, 1984), pp. 30–37, 88–112, 203–7

J. Geddes and D. Sherlock: 'The Church Chests of Icklingham, Suffolk and Church Brampton, Northamptonshire', *Proc. Suffolk Inst. Archaeol. & Hist.*, xxxvi (1987), pp. 202–6

The Age of Chivalry (exh. cat., ed. J. Alexander and P. Binski; London, RA, 1987–8), pp. 162–7, 174–5

W. J. Blair and N. L. Ramsay, eds: *English Medieval Industries: Craftsmen, Techniques, Products* (London, 1991), pp. 57–106, 167–87

The Making of England: Anglo-Saxon Art and Culture, A.D. 600–900 (exh. cat., ed. L. Webster and J. Backhouse; London, BM, 1991), pp. 21–34, 47–62, 79–100, 132–43, 167–76, 220–39, 268–83

NIGEL J. MORGAN

(ii) 1450–1600. During the 15th century calamine (zinc ore), raw brass and finished copper and brass goods, known as 'battery', were imported via Antwerp and Amsterdam from mining towns and centres of brass production on the banks of the River Meuse (*see* BELGIUM, §IX, 2), and copper ore came from Germany. Domestic brass objects were then made in York, London and other towns using tin and lead mined in Cornwall. In the mid-16th century Elizabeth I encouraged both the immigration of foreign brassworkers and attempts to discover native deposits of copper and zinc ore in order to establish a self-sufficient brass industry, mainly for the production of cannon. In 1565 Elizabeth I granted the right to mine calamine, found principally in the Mendip Hills, Somerset, to the assay-master William Humphrey and Christoph Schulz from Saxony. At the same time they secured a monopoly on the manufacture of brasswork in England and in 1568 formed the 'Society for the Mineral and Battery Works'. The earliest brassworks were established at Isleworth and Rotherhithe in London, although the brass produced was of a low quality. In the same year another German, Daniel Hochstetter, founded the 'Mines Royal Societie', which built copper mines at Keswick, Cumbria, and employed German miners. This venture also was not entirely successful, as merchants continued to buy copper ore imported from the Continent.

The production of bronze began in England in the late Middle Ages and was controlled by the Founders' Company; in the 15th century the membership of this guild varied between 85 and 100. John Stow (1525–1605), in his *Survey of London* (1598), recorded that the founders were centred at Lothberry and that their products included candlesticks, chafing dishes and spice mortars, which were also probably manufactured outside London. No makers' marks have been identified, although a number of extant

84. Cast-iron 'Armada' fire-back, h. 870 mm, 1588 (London, Victoria and Albert Museum)

although most extant cast-iron English fire-backs date from the 16th century. These were produced on the Kent and Sussex Wealds and in the Forest of Dean, Glos. One of the most notable examples is the so-called 'Armada' fire-back (see fig. 84), dated 1588 and decorated with nautical motifs and foliage.

BIBLIOGRAPHY
J. Mainwaring-Baines: *Wealden Firebacks* (Hastings, 1958)
H.-U. Haedeke: *Metalwork* (London, 1970)
A. C. Jones and C. T. Harrison: 'Cannock Chase Ironworks, 1590', *Eng. Hist. Rev.*, 93 (1978), pp. 795–810
P. Hornsby: *Collecting Antique Copper and Brass* (Ashbourne, 1989)
Pewter: A Celebration of the Craft, 1200–1700 (exh. cat. by P. R. G. Hornsby, R. Weinstein and R. Homer, London, Mus. London, 1990)

PETER HORNSBY

(iii) 1601–1800.

(a) Brass. The discovery of raw materials used in the manufacture of brass in south-west England, Wales and the Lake District at the end of the 16th century led to the development of the brass industry in England. The principal use for brass was initially for wire, pins and such small wares as thimbles and buckles. The development of successful casting techniques in the 1630s led to the extensive use of brass for sword-hilts, mounts for fire-arms and small vessels. A number of early 17th-century English warming pans with lids made from thin sheet brass are preserved (e.g. of *c.* 1600; London, V&A). Brass from this period was rarely marked or stamped, although some small brass sealing-wax cases dating from the 1650s (e.g. of *c.* 1650; London, V&A) were signed by a maker named Maden of Sheffield (*fl* 1650–55). By the second half of the 17th century there was a substantial brass trade in England, based mainly in London (*see* LONDON, §IV, 2), Bristol (*see* BRISTOL, §3(iii)) and Birmingham (*see* BIRMINGHAM, §3). The wares produced included sconces, candlesticks, chandeliers, boxes, clocks and door furnishings. There was a vogue for lantern clocks, the cases of which were made from sheet brass, usually finely engraved (e.g. of *c.* 1650; London, V&A), as well as scientific instruments, for example rulers, nocturnals and sun-dials.

In the 18th century domestic wares were often made in brass. These include various forms of skimmer, sugar casters (examples in London, V&A), cream jugs, trivets, dishes, graters and occasionally large tankards. The forms of many of these vessels are often similar to that of contemporary silverware. Many brass objects were silvered (e.g. salver; London, V&A) and were direct copies of silver wares. Candlesticks formed an important part of the production of brass-founders in Birmingham throughout the 18th century. Luxury items made in brass, for example watchcases, étuis, nutcrackers and snuff-boxes, often finely engraved or embossed, are also common.

Engraved brass tobacco-boxes were made throughout the 17th and 18th centuries (see fig. 85). Some late 18th-century English boxes, probably made in Lancashire (e.g. of *c.* 1790; A. North priv. col.), have a series of combination dials that have to be correctly set to open them. Brass boxes are often engraved with patriotic verses or carry portraits of contemporary figures, for example Nelson and the Duke of Wellington.

items have cast makers' symbols, more easily recognizable by illiterate workmen and buyers than a signature or name. One fine example is the Mortar (1308; York, Yorks Mus.) made by William of Towthorpe, but such cast inscriptions and signatures are rare. The most frequently recorded bronze objects in 16th-century domestic inventories are pots, pans, cooking-pots (e.g. at Hampton Court) and skillets (83% of named items), although candlesticks were also found in significant numbers.

By 1450 pewter was manufactured in London and most large provincial towns in substantial quantities. The Pewterers' Company had formal control over the operations of all English pewterers, but in practice it was difficult to supervise provincial makers. There was an average of 54 master pewterers at work in London in the mid-15th century, and by the 1550s this number had risen to about 128. In addition there were several hundred pewterers in Bristol, York, Coventry and Norwich during this period. In the 15th century pewter was mostly owned by ecclesiastical institutions and the aristocracy, but gradually it became available to gentlemen, yeoman farmers and merchants. Although a variety of objects was made, plates, dishes, chargers and saucers (e.g. of *c.* 1500; London, Mus. London), known as flat- or sadware, and such other eating utensils as porringers with trefoil or fleur-de-lis shaped 'ears' (handles), spoons and salts were the most common. A study of 528 household inventories dating from 1575 to 1625 shows that 82% of recorded items were of these forms. Other pewter objects that were introduced during this period included candlesticks, ewers and basins, flagons and baluster measures for selling ale, which were of a bellied shape and were stamped with a mark indicating the capacity. A bulbous type of flagon with a knopped lid (e.g. of *c.* 1590–1610; London, Pewterers' Co.) was popular in the late 16th century.

Unlike the manufacture of pewter, that of cast iron was relatively limited. Iron pots, mortars, fire-backs, stove-plates and fire-dogs were produced from the 15th century,

,

(b) Pewter. Although a vast amount of English pewter has been lost or melted down, enough survives from the early 17th century to indicate the types of vessels produced. Beakers, porringers, chargers, plates and dishes seem to have been common, and there are also a number of lidded baluster measures. Although most pewter from this period is plain, one form of decoration fashionable in the second half of the 17th century consists of cast relief ornament incorporating strapwork and heraldic badges. The Grainger Candlestick (1616; London, V&A), made for a member of the Pewterers' Company of London, is decorated in this manner. By the mid-17th century broad-rimmed dishes and large, lidded, tapering flagons (e.g. London, Pewterers' Co.) had become popular. Porringers were also produced throughout the 17th century. Many examples have handles or 'ears' cast in elaborate designs (e.g. with 'dolphin' ears, *c.* 1650–80; London, Pewterers' Co.). Pewter vessels tended to follow the design of silver, particularly the fine lidded tankards produced from the 1670s, although wrigglework decoration usually was used only on pewter (*see* PEWTER, fig. 1; *see also* METAL, colour pl. II, fig. 2). More is known about pewterers after the 1660s, and such Huguenot makers as the Taudin family introduced new alloys, incorporating antimony, to the London trade.

In the 18th century there was increasing competition from earthenware manufacturers, but English pewterers continued to produce such wares as tavern mugs, plates, dishes, spoons and salts, which remained popular because they were relatively inexpensive. Such larger items as candlesticks, although popular in the 17th century, were replaced by brass in the 18th, and later pewter examples are comparatively rare. The English pewter trade was extensive, and large amounts of pewter were made outside London in such centres as Wigan, York, Bristol and Bewdley. In the 18th century pewterers attempted to follow contemporary trends by producing plates and dishes in the Rococo style (e.g. of *c.* 1750; London, V&A). Pewter was usually manufactured by casting in a mould, which led to the persistence of styles over long periods; the design of plates, for example, changed little from 1730 to 1800.

(c) Copper and copper alloys. In the 17th century copper was used for such larger domestic wares as buckets and kettles. Some of these have been found in shipwrecks and indicate that items were built up from large sheets rivetted together. Smaller copper articles from the second half of the 17th century, for example watchcases and boxes, are extant. Copper was regularly used for weathervanes, because of its weather-resistant qualities (e.g. London, V&A). In the 18th century many domestic wares were made from copper, often tinned on the inside. These include kettles, coffeepots, preserving pans and water containers. In the last quarter of the 18th century copper tea-urns became fashionable (e.g. of *c.* 1800; London, V&A). Two designs are most commonly found: a large globe supported on four feet and a Neo-classical urn shape. A tap was fitted to the front from which water or tea, which was kept hot by means of a piece of red-hot iron inserted in a sleeve at the top, could be drawn off.

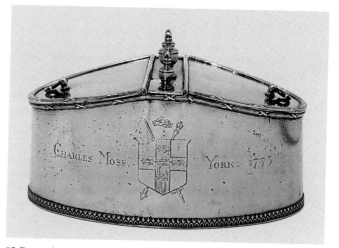

85. Brass tobacco-box, from York, 1775 (London, Victoria and Albert Museum)

Copper was also used at the end of the 18th century for tobacco-boxes engraved with patriotic mottoes.

During the 18th century alloys that were used for the manufacture of small luxury items, for example jewellery, boxes and watchcases, were introduced. One of the best known is 'pinchbeck', an alloy of about five parts of copper to one of zinc. It was named after Christopher Pinchbeck, a watchmaker working in London in the 1740s. In appearance this alloy resembles gold and was widely used, especially by craftsmen in London, for cheaper items of jewellery. Another alloy used in the jewellery and watch trade during the 18th century was 'Prince's metal'. This seems to have been an alloy of copper and zinc that resembled brass. It is said to have been invented by Prince Rupert of the Rhine and is also referred to, in contemporary sources, as 'Rupert's metal'.

Paktong, consisting of copper, zinc and nickel, was imported from China (*see* CHINA, §X, 1), probably as early as 1730. Paktong varies considerably in colour depending on the amounts of nickel and copper incorporated in the alloy. It is light, hard and ideal for casting and is also known as 'tutenag'. The most commonly found objects made from paktong are candlesticks. The forms vary from the familiar 'petal-base' shape fashionable in the 1730s and 1740s, which is more commonly found in brass and silver, to the square-based Neo-classical shapes of the late 18th century (e.g. of 1770; London, V&A). Fire-grates, fenders and fire-irons made from paktong and cast iron were designed by Robert Adam (for illustration *see* FIREPLACE FURNISHINGS). Kettles, tea-urns and mounts for fire-arms were also produced.

(d) Iron and steel. The use of Gothic motifs characterizes much English wrought ironwork in the first half of the 17th century. The majority was intended for architectural use: gates, window-grilles, screens and door furnishings. Many examples from the late 17th century and the early 18th are documented, so it is possible to attribute these to individual craftsmen. Nicholas Paris (*d* 1716), a gunsmith and inventor as well as a blacksmith, supplied the choir-gates and other wrought ironwork (*in situ*) for the church of St Mary in Warwick. The gates, balustrades and window-grilles (1676; *in situ*) of the Wren Library in Trinity

86. Jewel casket of Queen Mary II by Robert Bickford, blued steel and gilt brass, 1688–94 (London, Victoria and Albert Museum)

College, Cambridge, incorporating scrollwork and floral motifs, were made by Partridge, a blacksmith in London, at the end of the 17th century.

One of the best-known blacksmiths to have worked in England at the end of the 17th century was the Huguenot JEAN TIJOU. His work includes screens and gates (1689–96; *in situ*) made for the Fountain Garden at Hampton Court, London, screens for St Paul's Cathedral, London, and examples at Burghley House, Cambs. Unlike his contemporaries, Tijou used repoussé work, usually in the form of skilfully wrought masks of sheet iron set at intervals within the design.

In the reign of William III and Mary II (1689–1702) the art of the locksmith reached high standards with the work of such craftsmen as Robert Bickford of London (*fl* 1680–1700). He supplied some fine locks and keys for the royal household in the 1690s, and his masterpiece is a jewel casket made for Queen Mary between 1688 and 1694 (see fig. 86). The surface is covered with pierced quatrefoils of blued steel, mounted on gilt brass. This type of decoration is one of the characteristic features of Bickford's work.

In the 18th century the blacksmith's art flourished with the work of ROBERT BAKEWELL of Derby, who produced some fine, large-scale wrought-iron arbours (1706–11; *in situ*) for Melbourne Hall, Derbys, and ironwork for the Radcliffe Camera, Oxford. Cast-iron architectural features were introduced, for example the railings (*c.* 1710) around St Paul's Cathedral, London, and those around the Senate

House, Cambridge (1730). In the late 18th century Neo-classical motifs, for example urns, garlands and columns, appeared in wrought and cast ironwork. Stoves, fire-grates and balconies were designed by James Adam (i) and Robert Adam (i) (examples in London, V&A). The factory established by MATTHEW BOULTON and John Fothergill (*d* 1782) at Soho, Birmingham, in the 1770s manufactured a variety of steel wares, including buckles and sword-hilts. Workshops in Woodstock, Oxon, specialized in watch-chains, chatelaines and sword-hilts (e.g. steel buckle, *c.* 1790; London, V&A). All these products were made in highly polished steel, the surface being set with a series of faceted studs.

BIBLIOGRAPHY

J. Harris: *English Decorative Ironwork from Contemporary Source Books, 1610–1836* (London, 1960)
H. Hamilton: *The English Brass and Copper Industries to 1800* (London, 1967)
R. Gentle: *English Domestic Brass, 1680–1810, and the Story of its Origins* (London, 1975)
P. Hornsby: *Pewter of the Western World, 1600–1850* (Exton, 1983)
C. A. Peal: *Pewter of Great Britain* (London, 1983)
S. Dunkerley: *Robert Bakewell: Artist, Blacksmith* (Cromford, 1988)

(iv) After 1800. In the early 19th century there was a great demand for trinkets and souvenirs made from copper and brass. Tobacco- and snuff-boxes embossed with figures and engraved with patriotic mottoes were popular during the Napoleonic Wars. In the 1820s base-metal ornaments were produced in the Gothic Revival style. These included

small containers for spills and elegant chimney ornaments that could be converted into fire-screens. These were produced by B. Day & Co., a manufacturer in Birmingham, and were in the form of tall Gothic pinnacles of cast brass with black lacquered stems (e.g. pair of 1820; London, V&A). Brass candlesticks continued to be produced in the early 19th century; Neo-classical designs were gradually replaced by squat, baluster stems with exaggerated mouldings. Chamber candlesticks with broad trays of sheet brass were also made in large quantities in the first quarter of the 19th century. Many of these were fitted with patented ejectors for removing the stubs of candles. Special holders for wax-covered tapers were also popular.

Tavern mugs and medical equipment continued to be made in pewter by traditional methods, but the introduction of mass-produced Britannia metal articles (*see* PEWTER, §1) in the 19th century, as well as an influx of cheap porcelain and earthenware after the 1830s, led to a rapid decline in the industry. Britannia metal was produced by manufacturers in Birmingham and Sheffield, for example G. R. Elkington & Co. and James Dixon & Sons.

In the 1840s the Gothic Revival in base metalwork was promoted by such designers as A. W. N. Pugin, who worked in collaboration with John Powell Hardman of Birmingham. Pugin's designs include brass candelabra (1846) with 'wrythen' stems and 'bough' Gothic arms made for the House of Lords, Palace of Westminster,

London (*see* LONDON, fig. 38). Pugin also designed relatively simple forms, for example a pair of gilt-brass candlesticks (1844–5; London, V&A) made by Hardman for his own house at Ramsgate, Kent. The central support consists of a pierced oval plate engraved with his coat of arms.

During the 19th century cast iron was used extensively for architectural and decorative purposes. Alfred Stevens (ii) produced a number of designs for fire-grates and stoves in the 1850s. Some of his work, made by Henry Hoole & Co. of Sheffield, was shown at the Great Exhibition of 1851 in London (e.g. cast-iron fire-grate with cast bronze firedogs, *c.* 1850; London, V&A). In the mid-19th century there were a number of commissions for altar plate in base metalwork. Candlesticks and altar crosses in the Gothic style were made by such firms as Hardman's, gilt copper and brass being the favoured materials.

The use of cast brass for a huge variety of ornamental objects had become widespread. Much was sold by means of trade catalogues. Those produced by such firms as G. R. Elkington & Co. (e.g. London, V&A) show that, apart from the large number of brass candlesticks available, desk furniture, including pentrays, inkstands and letter racks, was also popular. Most of these were mass-produced in the Renaissance Revival style.

William Morris and other members of the Arts and Crafts Movement rejected these types of ware and revived

87. Copper chafing dish and stand by W. A. S. Benson, *c.* 1895 (London, Victoria and Albert Museum)

the production of hand-made brass and copper objects. Designs were plain and functional. Candlesticks and dishes based on plain medieval forms were especially popular, the decoration limited to simple piercing, casting and engraving. Philip Webb designed copper candlesticks (c. 1861; London, V&A) in the style of the 16th century, with wide bases and drip pans. A number of English designers and craftsmen, however, accepted the inevitability of mass production in an industrialized society; many of Christopher Dresser's wares, for example, were designed to be manufactured in brass or electroplate. One of his better-known designs is for a simple stand for fireplace furnishings designed to be made in cast brass.

In the last quarter of the 19th century a number of influential workshops were established by artists and designers to produce domestic base-metal wares. These workshops included the Guild of Handicraft, set up by C. R. Ashbee in London in 1888, and the Keswick School of Industrial Art. W. A. S. BENSON, who worked in Hammersmith, London, in the 1890s, produced some fine copper trays, kettles and dishes (see fig. 87) of plain but striking design. Brass objects were produced by Arthur Dixon (1856–1929), who made plain teapots and jugs. C. F. A. Voysey specialized in wares with plain surfaces (e.g. teapot, c. 1896; London, V&A) and used rivets as decorative features. Traditional methods of production are evident on the wares: surfaces are covered with a series of hammer marks, and the use of abrasives produced a dull satin finish. Highly polished surfaces were commonly used on copper wares, and both copper and brass were treated with transparent lacquers to preserve the desired finish.

The Art Nouveau style did not often appear in copper and brass, although letter racks, mirror-frames and decorative vases in these materials were produced. In the 1890s Liberty & Co. began to sell pewterware under the trade name of 'Tudric', which was made by the firm of W. H. Haseler in Birmingham. Many pieces were designed by Archibald Knox (e.g. hot water jug, 1904; London, V&A). There was a great demand in the early 20th century for Jacobean Revival objects in copper and brass. The catalogues of firms in Birmingham, for example Pearson Page, illustrate candlesticks, lamps, dishes and warming-pans in the style of the 17th century. This mass-produced ware has tended to obscure the work of such innovative designers as Gertrude Hermes (1904–83).

Plastics have tended to replace copper and brass for domestic use in the late 20th century. A revival in blacksmiths' work, however, occurred in the 1970s and 1980s with the work of such artists as Antony Robinson and Stuart Hill, who rejected revival styles to produce ironwork with sculptural qualities (e.g. fire-grate by Robinson, 1979; London, V&A). Firms in London specializing in pewterware, for example Englefields, also maintained high standards of design and manufacture with commissions for ceremonial pieces, as well as a vigorous export trade.

BIBLIOGRAPHY

J. S. Lindsay: *Iron and Brass Implements of the English House* (London, 1964)
Art Nouveau Pewter (exh. cat., London, V&A, 1969)
H.-U. Haedeke: *Metalwork* (London and New York, 1970)
Towards a New Iron Age: The Art of the Blacksmith Today (exh. cat., London, V&A, 1982)
I. Anscombe and C. Gere: *Arts & Crafts in Britain and America* (New York, 1983)
J. M. Burks: *Birmingham Brass Candlesticks* (Charlottesville, 1986)

A. R. E. NORTH

X. Objects of vertu.

1. Jewellery. 2. Enamels. 3. Gold boxes.

1. JEWELLERY. From the 6th century AD colourful and striking rings, brooches, belt-buckles, hairpins and necklaces of gold, silver or bronze were made in a wide range of techniques. An example of fine craftsmanship is the jewellery found at the SUTTON HOO ship-burial (7th century; London, BM). Brooches, rings and pendants made after the Norman Conquest of 1066 are of severe design with settings shaped to fit the irregular contours of cabochons. Matthew Paris illustrated rings of this period in his marginal drawings in the *Liber Additamentorium*, a list of gifts compiled for St Albans Abbey (1251–9; London, BL, Cotton MS. Nero D.I, fols 146v–147r). Such jewels are often inscribed with French or Latin invocations to the Virgin, magical charms or love mottoes in Lombardic characters. The love motif with two clasped hands first appears on the bezel of a silver ring (London, BM) dating from the reign of Henry II (1154–89), found near Lark Hill, Worcester. (*See also* ROMANESQUE, §VI, 6.)

By the mid-14th century the wearing of jewels became so widespread that sumptuary laws were enacted to restrict it to specific ranks. In 1363, for example, it was decreed that knights were not to wear rings or brooches made of gold or set with gemstones. During this period such techniques as enamelling—champlevé, *basse taille, en ronde bosse*—and faceting were refined, and gems were set in more regular, neat collets. Throughout the medieval period cameos and gemstones were popular (e.g. Oxwich Brooch, c. 1320–40, Cardiff, N. Mus.; M Jewel, late 14th century, Oxford, New Coll.). The designs of coronets, cauls, hat-badges, girdles, chains, collars and pendants were influenced by Gothic architecture and express themes derived from magic, religion, romance and heraldry (e.g. the Dunstable Swan Jewel, badge of the Bohun family, enamelled white *en ronde bosse*, c. 1400; London, BM; *see* ENAMEL, fig. 1). A type of devotional jewellery found only in England and Scotland was named by Victorian collectors as 'iconographic'. Each piece is engraved with one or more images of the Virgin, Holy Trinity and the saints, the lines often being filled with niello. The most common pieces, however, are rings made from the mid-14th century to the 16th (examples in London, V&A). A gold rosary of c. 1490 belonging to the Catholic Langdale family of Yorkshire is engraved with 110 figures depicting saints, each identified in Gothic characters (London, V&A).

Portraits and inventories from the 16th century (e.g. Hieronimos Custodis's portrait of *Elizabeth Brydges*, 1589; Woburn Abbey, Beds) reveal the popularity of elaborate jewellery among the wealthy. The influence of the Italian Renaissance was absorbed through the activities of foreign merchants and craftsmen, particularly from Hans Holbein the younger, who worked at the court of Henry VIII from

1532 to 1543. Holbein's designs (c. 1540; London, BM) for jewellery incorporate such classical motifs as acanthus, putti, caryatids and grotesques, although no jewellery known to have been designed by him has survived. Most Tudor jewellery follows the styles of European court jewellery, although some groups are of particularly English design, for example a series of historiated hat-badges with figures enamelled *en ronde bosse* (e.g. a roundel depicting Christ with the Woman of Samaria, c. 1540; London, BM). After the foundation of the Anglican Church in 1533 reliquaries and rosaries were forbidden, although crosses and jewels of the sacred monogram, IHS, continued to be worn. *Memento mori* symbols are found on rings and pendants, of which the most interesting is the Tor Abbey Jewel: a black enamelled coffin enclosing an articulated white enamelled skeleton; the sides of the coffin are inscribed THROUGH THE RESURRTION OF CHRISTE WE ALL BE SANCTIFIED (c. 1550; London, V&A). Carved gemstone and cameo portraits of Elizabeth I were made from c. 1575 and were set in rings, pendants and brooches (see fig. 88).

From the beginning of the 17th century the design emphasis shifted from settings to stones; the Cheapside Hoard (c. 1640–50; London, Mus. London and BM), containing a jeweller's stock hidden at the time (c. 1650) of the Civil War, provides a conspectus of the variety of gems available and the principal types of ornaments—bodkins, earrings, chains, rings—stocked during this period. Portraits by Peter Lely and Godfrey Kneller show the popularity of pearls and gem-encrusted jewellery during the second half of the 17th century, although few examples of this jewellery survive. Many sentimental jewels, however, are extant. These are commonly heart-shaped or oval gold lockets incorporating locks of hair and gold wire monograms with *memento mori* or amorous symbols (*see* JEWELLERY, fig. 3). Some are set beneath a crystal face and are framed by pearls or rose-cut diamonds. Others commemorate such events as the execution of Charles I (examples of c. 1650; London, BM), or the refusal of the Bishops of Chichester and Peterborough to sign the oath of allegiance to William III and Mary II in 1688. After the Revocation of the Edict of Nantes in 1685 many Huguenot jewellers, such as Elias Russell and Peter Duval, emigrated to London; their skilful craftsmanship transformed the quality of English jewellery, although they had to adapt both to the conservative taste of their clients and to the latter's preference for diamonds rather than coloured gemstones. The Swiss gold chaser and enameller George Michael Moser, who emigrated to England in 1726, excelled at the chatelaines, watchcases and étuis worn with less formal clothes (e.g. watch; Grimsthorpe Castle, Lincs).

In the 1770s sentimental and memorial jewellery was produced in the Neo-classical style. Locks of hair, miniatures and monograms, sometimes combined with images of weeping-willows, urns, obelisks and allegorical female figures in flowing drapery, were set in lockets and rings. Cut-steel jewellery was a speciality of workshops in Woodstock, Oxon, and Wolverhampton, W. Midlands, and of Mathew Boulton's factory in Soho, Birmingham. Wedgwood's jasper-ware plaques decorated with white Neo-classical figures and mounted in frames of cut steel (e.g. clasp, c. 1780; London, V&A; *see also* METAL, colour pl. II, fig. 3) were popular in Britain, and much was exported.

The victory of Waterloo in 1815 was celebrated in jewellery designs with such patriotic symbols as sprays of laurel and oak leaves, the Prince of Wales's feathers, Maltese crosses and portraits of Admiral Nelson and the Duke of Wellington. Designs inspired by the Garter insignia with the emblems of the rose, thistle and shamrock express similar nationalistic sentiments; many were made to commemorate the coronation of George IV in 1821 (e.g. jewelled gold Garter collar; see Scarisbrick, 1989, pl. 101). During the early 19th century the firm of Rundell, Bridge & Rundell manufactured jewellery in a wide range of styles; its jewellery was influential on the Continent, and the firm maintained a flourishing export trade to Russia, Turkey and Haiti. From the 1820s quality declined as production became more mechanized and the industry expanded, especially in Birmingham. From the 1840s a number of craftsmen designed pieces that revived past styles (e.g. Gothic Revival parure designed by A. W. N. Pugin, 1848; 3 pieces in London, V&A). The

88. Barbor Jewel, enamelled gold pendant, with rubies, diamonds and pearls, set with an onyx cameo of *Elizabeth I*, c. 1600 (London, Victoria and Albert Museum)

increasing rigidity of mourning conventions led to a greater demand for black jewellery, especially from 1850 to 1875. It was most commonly of jet (*see* JET, §2) or such imitations as vulcanite and black glass (examples in London, V&A). Most jet jewellery was produced at workshops in Whitby, N. Yorks, near the main source of the material. Regional specialities of jewels in such materials as Irish bog oak and Derbyshire hardstones were made in both traditional and contemporary designs; examples were displayed at international exhibitions, including the Great Exhibition of 1851 in London. The parures of diamonds, pearls and coloured gemstones that were shown by such leading London jewellers as Garrard & Co. Ltd and Asprey & Co. were also popular, more on account of their cost than their aesthetic qualities. Designs were mainly based on such naturalistic motifs as butterflies, stars, crescents, lizards and horseshoes, although jewellery sometimes consisted of simple rows of gemstones. The Arts and Crafts Movement reacted to this trend by using cheaper materials to produce jewellery that emphasized design and craftsmanship rather than the expense and brilliance of the gemstones. The leading exponents of this movement in Britain were Henry Wilson and C. R. Ashbee of the Guild of Handicrafts (for illustration *see* ASHBEE, C. R.). This movement was influential on the Continent through the work of René Lalique, who was in England from 1878 to 1880, and Josef Hoffmann. In the late 19th century the firm of Liberty & Co. sold 'Cymric' designs (e.g. necklace, 1902; see Bury, ii, pl. 769) that were mass-produced, although with a hand-finished appearance, in Birmingham.

Throughout the 20th century English jewellery designs followed those of such large French firms as Cartier & Co. who established branches in London. The outstanding jeweller of the 1920s and 1930s was Charles Bruno (*d* 1955), who was appointed the chief designer for R. G. Hennell & Sons in 1928. He specialized in a distinctively architectural version of Art Deco (see Scarisbrick, 1993, pp. 202, 221). The most interesting developments in the second half of the century were from the studio craftsmen of the 1960s, notably John Donald (*b* 1928), Gerda Flockinger (*b* 1927) and Wendy Ramshaw (*b* 1939). In the final decades of the 20th century the emergence of Laurence Graff as the world's leading dealer in precious stones, which he incorporates in his own designs, has attracted an international clientele comparable with that of Rundell, Bridge & Rundell in the period after Waterloo.

BIBLIOGRAPHY
J. Evans: *A History of Jewellery, 1100–1870* (London, 1953)
H. Newman: *An Illustrated Dictionary of Jewellery* (London, 1981)
P. Hinks: *Twentieth Century British Jewellery, 1900–1980* (London, 1983)
Y. Hackenbroch: *Renaissance Jewellery* (London, 1984)
D. Scarisbrick: *Jewellery* (London, 1984)
——: *Ancestral Jewels* (London, 1989)
S. Bury: *Jewellery, 1789–1910*, 2 vols (Woodbridge, 1991)
R. Lightbown: *Mediaeval European Jewellery* (London, 1992)
D. Scarisbrick: *Rings* (London, 1993)
——: *Jewels in Britain, 1066–1837* (Norwich, 1994)

DIANA SCARISBRICK

2. ENAMELS. Early examples of enamelling dating back at least to the 1st century AD have been excavated in England, but their origins are obscure. Outstanding among them are the 7th-century Celtic champlevé treasures from the SUTTON HOO ship-burial (London, BM) and the late 9th-century cloisonné Alfred Jewel (Oxford, Ashmolean; *see* JEWELLERY, colour pl. IV, fig. 1). Champlevé liturgical objects from the 12th century (e.g. Balfour Ciborium, *c*. 1160–80; London, V&A) have been ascribed to English makers, however, as have a group of small 14th-century *basse taille* diptychs and triptychs (London, V&A).

Enamelling flourished during the late 15th century and the 16th, by which time the *en ronde bosse* method was practised (e.g. Phoenix Jewel, *c*. 1570–80; London, BM). Later 'Surrey' or 'Stuart' enamels were made at the brass mills founded in 1649 at Esher, Surrey (e.g. Warwick Candle, *c*. 1650–60; London, BM). In all of the preceding examples the treatment of the metal was essential to the design, but *c*. 1637 a technique was brought to England from France by JEAN PETITOT, whereby the metal was entirely covered in white enamel and overpainted with polychromed enamels. This technique was used for portraiture and for the decoration of gold watchcases and other small, precious objects. Production of gold boxes and small objects decorated with painted enamel greatly increased in the mid-18th century (see fig. 89 below). Designs were often inspired by the work of such painters as Watteau and Boucher (e.g. gilt-bronze jewelled cabinet with painted panels, *c*. 1775; New York, Met.).

From *c*. 1747 enamel-on-copper, hand-painted snuffboxes were made, but their manufacture was soon transformed by the invention of transfer-printing, allowing the works of accomplished artists to be reproduced on enamelled surfaces. A Dublin engraver, John Brooks (*c*. 1710–60), who claimed to have invented the transfer-printing process, became a partner of the enamelling factory at York House, Battersea, founded in 1753 by Stephen Theodore Janssen (*c*. 1705–77). Among the renowned engravers who worked for Janssen were Simon François Ravenet (i) (*see* RAVENET) and ROBERT HANCOCK. Enamel snuff-boxes, framed plaques and wine labels (examples by Ravenet, *c*. 1754; London, V&A) produced at Battersea were transfer-printed in soft monochrome shades or gold, and some were over-painted in delicate translucent colours. The enterprise, however, was short-lived. By 1756 Janssen was declared bankrupt and the factory had closed, its equipment and stock being sold at auction.

This dispersal undoubtedly contributed to the spread of the enamelling industry, which developed rapidly, especially in Birmingham and in Bilston and Wednesbury, Staffs. In these areas enamelled domestic and personal items were produced in diverse styles, culminating in the 1770s with vivid colours and gold-encrusted Rococo cartouches framing transfer-printed and richly overpainted genre scenes and landscapes. Nécessaires, étuis and bonbonnières were a speciality (examples in Wolverhampton, Bantock House Mus.), while small snuff- and patch-boxes were made in large numbers. Enamel-on-copper objects of vertu were produced in London workshops and were also made—or at least decorated—in Liverpool by Sadler & Green, a firm specializing in transfer-printed ceramics for many companies. Production declined in all areas towards the end of the 18th century and by 1840 had entirely ceased due partly to the economic effects of the Napoleonic Wars and a change in fashion.

In the mid-19th century the Birmingham firm G. R. Elkington & Co. produced gilded and electro-plated metal ornaments decorated with champlevé and cloisonné enamel influenced by medieval, Renaissance and Moorish models. The Arts and Crafts Movement fostered enamelling skills, and much Art Nouveau design featured softly coloured enamels, many of them made by the London firm of Liberty & Co. At the turn of the century Alexander Fisher (1864–1936) became England's premier enameller and inspired other artists to adopt the medium; among his works is an enamelled sconce (c. 1896; London, V&A). Mass-produced enamelled dressing-table sets, cigarette cases and powder compacts were popular in the 1920s and 1930s, the more vibrant enamel colours being admirably suited to the hard-edged Art Deco style.

In 1956 Stefan Knapp (b 1921) revolutionized enamelling by inventing massive enamel-on-steel panels to cover the exteriors of public buildings (e.g. Reading, Rowney Office Building, 1973). In 1969 Marit Guinness Aschan (b 1919), who developed the plique-à-jour technique to form abstract, sculptural works of art (e.g. Méditerranée, 1973; Raleigh, NC, Mus. A.), became a founder-member and president of the Society of Artist-Enamellers, and in 1970 Halcyon Days Ltd, a London antique shop, in collaboration with Bilston and Battersea Enamels PLC in Bilston, revived enamelling-on-copper in the 18th-century manner. In the 1990s most enamelling techniques continued to be employed to embellish jewellery and objects of vertu (e.g. 18ct gold egg containing clock, 1993; Asprey PLC, London).

BIBLIOGRAPHY

R. J. Charleston: 'Battersea, Bilston or Birmingham', V&A Mus. Bull., 3 (1967), pp. 1–12

E. Benton: 'John Brooks in Birmingham: The Bilston Enamellers', Trans. Eng. Cer. Circ., vii/3 (1970), pp. 162–6

——: 'The London Enamellers', Trans. Eng. Cer. Circ., viii/2 (1972), pp. 137–63

B. Watney: 'English Enamels in the 18th Century', Antiques International, ed. P. Wilson (Feltham, 1973), pp. 287–96

S. Benjamin: English Enamel Boxes (London, 1978)

——: Enamels (Washington, DC, 1983)

SUSAN BENJAMIN

3. GOLD BOXES. Gold snuff-boxes have been made in England from the late 17th century, particularly by Huguenot craftsmen, such as the Harrache family and Michael Cabaret Lagarene (d 1725), who came to England after the Revocation of the Edict of Nantes in 1685 (see Snowman, 1990, pl. 564). A number of boxes with repoussé work in high relief made c. 1700, for example the gold box-lid in the Franks Collection (London, BM), have similar decoration to that employed on many Italian and German gold-enamelled Renaissance hat-badges.

During the first quarter of the 18th century silver and gold boxes were usually rectangular, oval or bow-fronted, and the decoration, if any, was generally confined to an engraved coat of arms (e.g. by Philippe-Antoine Magimel, 1745; Lugano, Col. Thyssen-Bornemisza) or a monogram. From c. 1700 to c. 1715 it became fashionable to set carved pieces of agate of attractive striation into the lids of boxes (see fig. 89), and often also the body of the box would consist of cornelian, jasper or chalcedony. The gold work provided a mount, often reeded, that secured the hardstones. Shells or mother-of-pearl were also used as decoration.

Boxes with cagework mounts set with tortoiseshell, decorated en piqué in the French and Italian manner, but modified to English taste with a rather more controlled decorative discipline, became popular (e.g. of c. 1760; Leeds, Temple Newham House). During the 1750s rectangular, oval or shaped gold snuff-boxes were elaborately embossed with classical or mythological scenes in relief. This type of box was also popular in the Netherlands, as well as in England, and it is difficult to determine the precise origin of some examples owing to their striking similarity of design. English examples, however, tend to be irregular in shape (e.g. of c. 1750; Boston, MA, Mus.

89. Gold boxes: (left) snuff-box by Michael Cabaret Lagarene, yellow gold, set top and bottom with striated agate panels, 14×71×67 mm, London, c. 1710 (London, private collection); (right) rectangular box, burnished and dull gold, set with an enamelled grisaille plaque depicting the Muse Clio after Boucher, 32×74×51 mm, London, c. 1755 (private collection)

F.A.), with scrollwork and shell motifs on all surfaces. Dutch examples have chasing on the lids. The subject-matter on many English boxes, especially those with figures forming part of the composition, derives from designs by Gravelot, who worked in England from 1733 to 1744. The work of Juste-Aurèle Meissonnier also influenced English goldsmiths. Rustic or mythological scenes in the style of Watteau and Boucher were framed in graceful Rococo scrollwork (see fig. 89).

The most distinguished gold chaser working in London during the second half of the 18th century was George Michael Moser, who was born in Schaffhausen. He was also a skilful enameller and specialized in the elaborate decoration of freedom-boxes (e.g. Copenhagen, Rosenborg Slot). Gold boxes from the 1760s to the 1790s are usually oval, with the decoration composed of gold panels with engine-turned patterns (e.g. by Melchior-René Barre, 1780/81; see Snowman, 1990, pl. 464): barley, fox head, honeycomb, waves, lines or basketwork, bounded by raised and boldly chased foliate or floral borders. Some gold boxes of this period were decorated with enamels by Peter Wirgman (*fl* 1784–96) and Thomas Pepper (*fl* 1790–96), who both trained in Geneva. James Morisset (*d* 1815), a Huguenot working in London, produced some elaborate enamelled and chased boxes (e.g. of 1798; London, N. Mar. Mus.), as well as sword-handles, towards the end of the 18th century.

In the early 19th century the increased use of the engine-turned lathe enabled the cheaper production of gold boxes. Birmingham became an important centre of production in the 19th century. Boxes manufactured there are characterized by floral borders and pattern on all surfaces. Chased oakleaf and acorn borders are found on many boxes produced *c.* 1815. This type of decoration is a feature of the work of Alexander James Strachan (*fl* 1799; *d* 1842–50).

BIBLIOGRAPHY

P. A. S. Phillips: *John Obrisset and his Works in Horn and Tortoiseshell, 1705–1728* (London, 1931)
A. Heal: *The London Goldsmiths, 1200–1800* (Cambridge, 1935)
C. Le Corbeiller: *European and American Snuff Boxes, 1730–1830* (London, 1966)
A. K. Snowman: *Eighteenth Century Gold Boxes of Paris: A Catalogue of the J. Ortiz-Patiño Collection* (London, 1974), pls 532, 533, 564
——: *18th Century Gold Boxes of Europe* (London, 1990), pls 464, 532–3, 539, 540, 567
C. Truman: *The Gilbert Collection of Gold Boxes* (Los Angeles, 1991)

A. KENNETH SNOWMAN

XI. Textiles.

1. Tapestry. 2. Embroidery. 3. Lace. 4. Printed cotton. 5. Silk. 6. Carpets.

1. TAPESTRY.

(i) Before 1590. (ii) 1590–1720. (iii) After 1720.

(i) Before 1590. 'Tapitors' and 'tapicers' are mentioned in English records from the early 14th century, and in 1331 a guild of tapisiers received its statutes in London. The regulations of the guild, however, imply that it was for cloth-, not tapestry-weavers, and the lack of inventory references to tapestries of English origin during the 14th century suggests that there was little native industry in this period. The first indisputable references to tapestries in England occur in inventories of the second half of the 14th century and indicate that they were imported, such as the set of 'tapestries of arras work' recorded in 1369, which was among the possessions of Queen Isabella, wife of Edward II (*reg* 1307–27). This was a period of rapid expansion for the Flemish industry, and from this point English inventories record increasing numbers of its products. In addition to purchases made directly from tapestry merchants or fairs in the Low Countries, the collections of the crown and leading nobility were enlarged with gifts from the Burgundian dukes and with booty from the Hundred Years War (1337–1453). On his death in 1399 Richard II possessed *c.* 50 tapestries, while the inventory taken on the death of Henry V (1422) lists more than 100. Many included gold thread, and they varied in size from small, decorative furniture covers to panels more than 30 yards in length, with a wide variety of religious, classical, romance and genre subject-matter. The majority of these hangings were described as 'arras'. The exact role of this Flemish centre of tapestry production (*see* ARRAS, §2) is still a matter of debate, and, while many of these importations may well have been produced or traded through the town, the word seems to have become a synonym for high-quality tapestry in England, irrespective of its origin, fairly early in the 15th century.

With the exception of some hunting tapestries (*c.* 1430; formerly Hardwick Hall, Derbys, NT, now London, V&A), almost nothing of these early collections survives, and knowledge of them is largely dependent on documentary evidence. The royal collection was inevitably the richest of the day, and Henry VI, Edward IV and Henry VII all made significant tapestry acquisitions. While there is some evidence of designs being sent from London to be made in the Low Countries (e.g. armorial fragments in Winchester Cathedral and Haddon Hall, Derbys, and inventory references to tapestries depicting English kings and Henry VII's accession to the throne), the majority of these purchases appear to have been woven from existing cartoons. A well-documented example is Henry VII's set of the *History of Troy*, purchased from Jean Grenier (*d* 1519) in 1488. Duplicate sets are recorded in the collections of, among others, Charles the Bold, 4th Duke of Burgundy, and Federigo II, Duke of Urbino (fragments of this design in New York, Met.; Glasgow, Burrell Col.).

Via the annual fairs in the Low Countries, the Flemish industry continued to find a ready market for its products in England in the 16th century. Tapestry was one of the principal forms of decoration for the rich, with medium-quality genre and *millefleurs* hangings being used daily and finer hangings being used for important rooms and on special occasions. Those cathedrals and churches that possessed tapestries would display them on feast days (e.g. *Life of Christ* series for Canterbury Cathedral, woven 1511; now Aix-en-Provence, St Sauveur Cathedral). Tapestry also played a central role in the display and propaganda associated with the court and its rival factions. The use of tapestry by Cardinal Thomas Wolsey was particularly extravagant, and in the course of his life he accumulated a collection of *c.* 600 pieces (examples at London, Hampton Court, Royal Col.). The Venetian ambassador to England reported the frequency with which tapestries were changed in his palace as one of the most visible expressions of his wealth and power.

The greatest collection at this time, however, belonged to Henry VIII, who increased his inheritance by numerous purchases, as well as by appropriating tapestries from the dissolved monasteries and attainted courtiers. Descriptions of such contemporary events as the meeting of Henry and Francis I in July 1520 at the Field of the Cloth of Gold, near Calais, reflect the contribution that tapestry made to the magnificence of the Tudor court, and the inventory taken after Henry's death (1547) lists over 2000 tapestries. These included examples of many of the most up-to-date Italianate and Flemish designs available, including a set of the *Acts of the Apostles* (formerly Berlin, Kaiser-Friedrich Mus., destr. 1945) based on Raphael's cartoons (London, V&A), another of the *Triumphs of the Gods*, woven from designs that Vasari attributed to Giovanni da Udine (two London, Hampton Court, Royal Col.), and an extremely lavish weaving of the *History of Abraham* (London, Hampton Court, Royal Col.), the design of which is attributed to Bernard van Orley or one of his pupils.

Henry's children did not make significant additions to the collection, but contemporary records reveal the care and respect with which it continued to be used, and this practice exerted a strong influence on the decoration of the Elizabethan 'prodigy' houses. The quality and nature of contemporary patronage is indicated by tapestries purchased by Sir John Thynne for Longleat, Wilts; by Sir Christopher Hatton (1540–91) for Holdenby House, Northants (now at Hardwick Hall, Derbys, NT), and by Robert Dudley, 1st Earl of Leicester, for Kenilworth, Warwicks (armorials at London, V&A; Glasgow, Burrell Col.).

Throughout the first two-thirds of the 16th century the majority of tapestries in England continued to be imported from centres in the Low Countries. The first documented factory in England was that established by William Sheldon (*d* 1570) in Barcheston, Warwicks, and Bordesley, Worcs, shortly after 1560. The director Richard Hyckes (*c.* 1524–1621) had served an apprenticeship in Holland and, according to Sheldon's will, he was the 'only author and beginner of this art [tapestry] within this realm'. After Sheldon's death the works were continued by his descendants well into the 17th century. The majority of Sheldon products were small tapestries for cushions or seat covers, with biblical and allegorical subjects (examples London, V&A; Glasgow, Burrell Col.). Only a few larger pieces were woven, and these appear to have been commissioned either for the Sheldon family or for other local landowners. The most accomplished of these are a series of tapestry maps (e.g. map of *Worcestershire*, 1570–99; London, V&A; *see* TAPESTRY, fig. 7).

(ii) 1590–1720. For high-quality tapestries the English nobility continued to turn to continental centres, especially those set up in Holland by weavers who had left the Southern Netherlands as a result of the religious troubles of the last third of the century. The most important of these was the workshop established in Delft by Frans Spiering (*c.* 1550–1630) in the early 1590s, which received numerous commissions from English patrons in the course of the next 30 years. The most notable was that from Charles Howard, 2nd Baron of Effingham, the Lord

High Admiral (1534–1624), for a set depicting the *Armada* (woven 1591–5; destr. 1834), which from 1650 was hung in the House of Lords in the Palace of Westminster, London. Other Spiering tapestries woven for English patrons are at Knole in Kent, Warwick Castle and the Rijksmuseum, Amsterdam. During the same period other commissions were directed to workshops in Antwerp and Brussels by English agents in these towns.

The virtual monopoly that the Low Countries enjoyed over English patronage came to an end in 1619. In the early 17th century Henry IV of France had established a factory in Paris, and the success of this provided James I and his son Charles, Prince of Wales (later Charles I), with the stimulus to establish a similar venture in England. An abstract of the founding contract of the Paris works was obtained as a guide, and in 1619 Charles's secretary, Sir Francis Crane (*c.* 1579–1636), agreed to establish a workshop. In return he received financial grants and a 21-year monopoly over tapestry manufacture (exclusive of existing British workshops). Crane purchased a site at Mortlake (nr London) on the Thames, and by 1620 the premises were ready for production, staffed with at least 50 Flemish weavers who had been brought to England with great secrecy and placed under the direction of the master weaver Philippe de Maecht (*d* 1655).

The first tapestries woven at Mortlake were copies of an antique series originally purchased by Henry VIII. Between 1620 and 1623 sets of *Vulcan and Venus* (London, St James's Pal., Royal Col.) and the *Twelve Months* (London, V&A) were woven for the Prince of Wales and George Villiers, Marquis of Buckingham (later 1st Duke of Buckingham). This repertory was expanded in 1623 when Charles managed to purchase from Genoa the original *Acts of the Apostles* cartoons by Raphael (London, V&A). The task of executing new working cartoons and designing new borders was entrusted to the chief designer, FRANCIS CLEYN. At first he was engaged on a variety of tasks, but his aptitude for tapestry design led to his appointment as chief designer to the Mortlake factory in 1626. The first set of *Acts* was woven for Charles between 1625 and 1630 (Paris, Mobilier N.; *see* fig. 90), and in this period Cleyn supplied original cartoons for several new sets, including those of *Hero and Leander* (*c.* 1625–30; fine early weavings in Stockholm, Kun. Husgerådskam. and Lyme Park, Ches.), the so-called *Horses* (*c.* 1630; extant example London, V&A) and the *Five Senses* (*c.* 1630; fine early set Haddon Hall, Derbys).

At first the financing of the industry appears to have been uneven, but after the accession of Charles I (1625) Crane was granted an annual subsidy of £2000, exclusive of purchase costs, and in the subsequent 12 years the industry flourished. The high cost of the tapestries purchased by the Crown in these years led to considerable grants of land and property to Crane, and in 1628 he was made Chancellor of the Order of the Garter. This success bred resentment, which resulted in accusations of fraud, but these appear to have been unfounded. After Crane's death the works were briefly administered by his brother, Captain Richard Crane (*d* 1645), before being purchased by the King in 1638, to be known thenceforth as the King's Works under the direction of Sir James Palmer.

90. Tapestry of the 'Miraculous Draught of Fishes' from the series *Acts of the Apostles* (after Raphael), wool, silk and gold and silver thread, 5.3×5.8 m, woven at the Mortlake Tapestry Factory, London, 1625–30 (Paris, Mobilier National)

During the 1630s a number of commissions were undertaken for such leading courtiers as Philip Herbert, 4th Earl of Pembroke and 1st Earl of Montgomery (e.g. a series of *Acts*; Duke of Buccleuch priv. col.; Urbino, Pal. Ducale), and Henry Howard, Earl of Holland (*Vulcan and Venus*; Paris, Mob. N.).

The Civil War (1642–9) precipitated the decline of the factory. By 1643 the King owed it considerable sums of money, and the subsequent defeat of the royalist forces resulted in the death or exile of almost all of its previous patrons. During the Commonwealth (1649–60), the Council of State made belated attempts to maintain production, but weaving activity during these years was limited and many weavers left to seek work elsewhere.

Following the execution of Charles I (1649) many of his possessions were sold, and the tapestry collection that Charles II inherited at the Restoration (1660) was about half the size (*c.* 800 tapestries) of that of his father. The highlights of the collection remained in constant use, and the example being set by Louis XIV's patronage of the Gobelins in Paris ensured that tapestry remained a fashionable feature in British court decoration. While Charles II continued to purchase new tapestries he appears, however, to have been unwilling or unable to subsidize the Mortlake works as his father had done, and during the 1660s control of the factory passed through various hands. The financial problems it faced were compounded by its dependence on old cartoons and the competition of tapestries from Brussels and Antwerp.

In 1674 Mortlake was acquired by Ralph Montagu (later 1st Duke of Montagu), who had also purchased the Mastership of the Royal Wardrobe in 1671. Montagu had served as ambassador in Paris and he may have hoped to persuade the King to patronize Mortlake as Louis XIV had done at the Gobelins. His period of office, however, led to the consolidation of new workshops in London at the expense of Mortlake. Many weavers had already left before the Restoration, and by 1670 at least one ex-Mortlake weaver, William Benood (*fl* 1645–75), had established himself at new premises in Lambeth, where he continued to weave from old Mortlake cartoons (examples London, V&A; New York, Met.). Other ex-Mortlake workers went to work for the Great Wardrobe under the direction of the royal 'yeoman arras maker'. From the 1660s this position was held by Francis Poyntz (*d* 1685), who drew a daily wage for executing repairs to the royal tapestry collection but whose workshop also wove new tapestries. In the 1670s he was entrusted with several royal commissions, including a royal portrait series (1672–5; Houghton Hall, Norfolk) and a historical series of the *Battle of Solebay* (*c*. 1673–8; London, Hampton Court, Royal Col.). During these years a limited production was maintained at Mortlake, but without royal patronage it lacked the edge to compete with the London workshops. Montagu resigned his interest in the factory in 1691 to a corporation with the hopeful title of the 'Tapestry Makers of England', but their plans to revive the works came to nothing and a licence to use the premises for other purposes was granted in 1703.

Well before the closure of the Mortlake works English patrons had reverted to the old practice of ordering high-quality tapestries from other European workshops, and during the reigns of William III and Mary II and of Queen Anne (*reg* 1702–14) numerous series were imported from Brussels and other Flemish centres. Military scenes by Lambert de Hondt and mythologies by Jean van Orley were well suited to the contemporary taste for large-figure tapestries in formal rooms (examples at Blenheim Pal., Oxon; London, V&A). For more informal settings genre scenes derived from paintings by David Teniers (ii) were extremely popular (many extant examples, e.g. at London, Marlborough House; Uppark, W. Sussex, NT).

A native industry continued to co-exist with this import trade, producing medium-quality and cheaper tapestries for the domestic market. After the closure of Mortlake all native production was based in London, and because of the location of several of the workshops English tapestries of this period are generally, and sometimes misleadingly, referred to as 'Soho' tapestries. The most important workshop was that of John Vanderbank the elder (*d* 1717), who had obtained the office of Royal Arras Maker in 1689 and who, like Poyntz, combined his official duties with the administration of a commercial enterprise. Many of Vanderbank's early tapestries were copied from Gobelins and Brussels designs, such as the *Elements* series (Duke of Buccleuch priv. col. and Burghley House, Cambs), after cartoons by Charles Le Brun. The weaving of these is coarse in comparison with their continental models, but Vanderbank's factory was to enjoy great success producing cheaper decorative tapestries, such as the chinoiserie designs first produced for Kensington Palace, London, in the early 1690s, of which numerous examples survive (London, V&A; New York, Met.; The Vyne, Hants).

(iii) After 1720. Vanderbank's successors in the office of yeoman arras weaver did not continue commercial production on the same scale, but several new independent workshops developed in London during the 1720s and 1730s. These were run by upholsterers who combined their other business activities with tapestry production. The most significant were those of Joshua Morris (*fl c*. 1720–28), best known for decorative floral panels (examples at Grimsthorpe Castle, Lincs; Hagley Hall, Hereford & Worcs; and Squerryes Court, Kent); William Bradshaw (*fl* 1728–*d* 1775), whose most distinguished tapestries were derived from pastoral scenes by Antoine Watteau and Jean-Baptiste Pater (examples in Holkham Hall, Norfolk, and Ham House, Surrey, NT; see fig. 91); and Paul Saunders (1722–71), one of the leading London upholsterers of the mid-18th century, who held the position of Tapestry Maker to George III and is best known for East Asian style landscapes woven in the 1750s and 1760s after designs by Francesco Zuccarelli (examples in Holkham Hall; Petworth House, W. Sussex, NT).

In the second third of the 18th century the market for tapestry began to decline as a result of the increasing interest in collections of paintings and the taste for wallpapers and lighter styles of decoration. Saunders was the last important native tapestry producer of the period, although decorative chambers of Gobelins tapestry, after designs by François Boucher, enjoyed a considerable vogue in the 1760s and 1770s, especially among patrons of Robert Adam (examples at Newby Hall, N. Yorks, woven 1766–71; and Osterley Park House, London, woven 1775–6; *see* TAPESTRY, fig. 10).

While there is evidence of the use of antique tapestry to create a romantic medieval atmosphere in some country houses in the late 18th century and the early 19th (e.g. at Cotehele, Cornwall, NT) and while a tapestry room remained a standard feature of many houses throughout this period, there was little demand for new tapestry. Interest in the medium revived only in the second half of the 19th century and resulted in various attempts to re-establish the craft. In 1876 a workshop was set up under royal patronage at Windsor, Berks, largely staffed by French weavers, with Michel Brignolas (*fl c*. 1870–96) as the head weaver. In 1882 the factory became known as the Royal Windsor Tapestry Factory and at its peak it employed *c*. 100 workers producing historical and land-scape tapestries (examples at Windsor Castle, Berks, Royal Col.; London, Mansion House and V&A) from cartoons by such artists as E. M. Ward and H. A. Bone (1854–1932). Despite the worthy intentions of its founders the factory was not a commercial success and it closed in 1890. Brignolas subsequently established a workshop in Poland Street, London, where the *History of the Clan MacIntosh* (*c*. 1896; now dispersed) was woven for the 28th Chief of that name. Other weavers went to work at the factory of William Baumgarten (1845–1906) in New York; his studio (est. 1893) had been partially inspired by the Windsor tapestries shown in such exhibitions as the World's Columbian Exposition of 1893 in Chicago.

The Windsor factory also provided an example and object of derision for WILLIAM MORRIS, whose interest in tapestry had been awakened during journeys on the Continent in his university days. Morris taught himself to weave in 1879 and founded the Merton Abbey Tapestry Works in Merton, Surrey, in 1881. Rejecting the weaving technique of the Gobelins and Windsor factories, which

91. Tapestry of *The Swing* (after Antoine Watteau), wool and silk, 2.6×4.9 m, from a set of four tapestries woven at the Bradshaw factory, London, *c.* 1774 (Ham House, Surrey, NT)

took pains to reproduce a painterly cartoon with a large range of silks and wools, Morris sought to return to the simplicity of palette and design of the medieval age. These ideals were embodied in cartoons designed by Edward Burne-Jones (*see* TAPESTRY, fig. 13) and woven under the direction of John Henry Dearle (1860–1932). The most ambitious of these works was the *Holy Grail* series commissioned by the industrialist William Knox D'Arcy (1849–97) for Stanmore Hall, Stanmore, Middx (woven 1890–94; the original set now dispersed in priv. cols; a later weaving now Birmingham, Mus. & A.G.; *see* TAPESTRY, colour pl. III, fig. 2). In 1976 a tapestry workshop was established by Edward James at West Dean, near Chichester, W. Sussex, where designs by John Piper (e.g. *Tapestry of the Trinity*; Chichester Cathedral, W. Sussex) and Henry Moore (examples at Much Hadam, Henry

Moore Found.) were woven. The workshop continued production in the late 20th century.

BIBLIOGRAPHY

W. G. Thomson: *A History of Tapestry from the Earliest Times until the Present Day* (London, 1906, rev. East Ardsley, 3/1973)
——: *Tapestry Weaving in England from the Earliest Times to the End of the XVIIIth Century* (London, 1914)
H. C. Marillier: *History of the Merton Abbey Tapestry Works Founded by William Morris* (London, 1927)
——: *English Tapestries of the Eighteenth Century: A Handbook to the Post-Mortlake Productions of English Weavers* (London, 1930)
——: *Handbook to the Teniers Tapestries* (London, 1932)
H. Göbel: *Die germanischen und slavischen Länder* (Leipzig, 1934), ii of *Wandteppiche* (Leipzig, 1923–34)
G. W. Digby: 'Tapestries by the Wautters Family of Antwerp for the English Market', *Het herfsttijd von de Vlaams tapijtkunst* (Brussels, 1959)
E. A. Standen: 'The Croome Court Tapestries', *Decorative Art from the Samuel H. Kress Collection at the Metropolitan Museum* (Aylesbury, 1964)

M. P. Havinden: 'The Soho Tapestry Makers', *Greater London Council Survey of London*, xxxiv: *The Parish of St Anne, Soho* (London, 1966), app. 1, pp. 515–20

A. Wace: *The Marlborough Tapestries at Blenheim Palace and their Relation to other Military Tapestries of the War of the Spanish Succession* (London, 1968)

A. Haynes: 'The Mortlake Tapestry Factory', *Hist. Today*, xxiv (1974), pp. 32–40

Les Tapisseries de la Vie du Christ et de la Vierge d'Aix-en-Provence (exh. cat., Aix-en-Provence, Mus. Tap., 1977)

G. C. Cullingham: *The Royal Windsor Tapestry Manufactory, 1876–90: An Illustrated Handlist of Tapestries Woven at the Old Windsor Works* (Windsor and Maidenhead, 1979)

W. G. Digby: *Victoria and Albert Museum: The Tapestry Collection: Medieval and Renaissance* (London, 1980), pp. 71–83

E. A. Standen: 'English Tapestries after the Indian Manner', *Met. Mus. J.*, xv (1980), pp. 119–42

E. P. Thompson: *Tapestry: Mirror of History* (London, 1980)

L. Martin: 'Sir Francis Crane: Director of the Mortlake Tapestry Factory and Chancellor of the Order of the Garter', *Apollo*, cxiii (1981), pp. 90–96

W. Hefford: 'The Chicago Pygmalion and the English Metamorphoses', *Mus. Stud.*, x (1983), pp. 93–117

——: 'Soho and Spitalfields: Little Known Huguenot Tapestry Weavers in and around London', *Proc. Huguenot Soc. London*, xxiv (1984), pp. 103–12

T. Campbell: *A Consideration of the Career and Work of Francis Clein: Including a Survey of Tapestry Designs Used at Mortlake whilst Clein was Artistic Director* (MA thesis, U. London, 1987)

S. McKendrick: 'Edward IV: An English Royal Collection of Netherlandish Tapestry', *Burl. Mag.*, cxxix (1987), pp. 521–4

A. Garrould and V. Power: *Henry Moore Tapestries* (London, 1988)

W. Hefford: 'Introducing James Bridges: New Light on an English Series of Eucharist Tapestries', *A. VA*, xxviii (1988), pp. 34–47

J. Cornforth: 'Surprises of the Silver Age', *Country Life* (9 March 1989)

D. King: 'Tapestries and Other Hangings', *The Late King's Goods: Collections, Possessions and Patronage of Charles I in the Light of the Commonwealth Sale Inventories* (London and Oxford, 1989), pp. 308–14

W. Hefford: 'Cleyn's Noble Horses', *NACF Rev.* (1990), pp. 97–102

S. McKendrick: 'Tapestries from the Low Countries in England during the Fifteenth Century', *Merchants and Artists: England and Europe in the Fifteenth Century: Proceedings of the Royal Holloway and Bedford New College Conference: London, 1991*

W. Hefford: 'Ralph Montagu's Tapestries', *Boughton House: The English Versailles*, ed. T. Murdoch (London, 1992), pp. 96–107 [good bibliog.]

T. Campbell: 'Cardinal Wolsey's Tapestry Collection', *Antiqua. J.* [in preparation]

T. CAMPBELL

2. EMBROIDERY. References to high-quality English embroidery pre-date the Norman Conquest (1066), and surviving examples include the Maaseik embroideries, panels associated with SS Harlinde and Relinde (*c.* AD 800; Maaseik, St Katharinakerk), and the Durham embroideries, the stole and maniple of St Cuthbert (909–16; Durham, Cathedral Treasury; *see* ANGLO-SAXON ART, fig. 15). By the 13th century gold embroideries on grounds of twill-woven silk (*see* OPUS ANGLICANUM) were appearing in inventories throughout Europe, and the silk grounds were beginning to be replaced with linen, which was entirely covered with delicate, figurative embroidery worked with coloured silks in split stitch and with gold thread in underside couching (e.g. Syon cope, *see* TEXTILE, fig. 2). Quite unlike the ecclesiastical vestments, by which *opus anglicanum* is almost entirely represented, is the BAYEUX TAPESTRY (1066–97; Bayeux, Mus. Tap.), which was embroidered in England. Made of linen and wool, it is a unique example of the less luxurious but lively embroideries made for secular and religious use throughout the medieval period.

From the mid-14th century English embroidery declined in quality; if no longer superlative, however, good work was still produced both professionally and within large households, for embroidery was an expected accomplishment even for women of privileged backgrounds. More embroideries survive from the 16th century, when larger disposable wealth was reflected in personal possessions including wall- and bed-hangings, table-covers and cushions decorated with embroidery. Most heavy furnishings were worked with coloured wool or silk on canvas; sometimes individual cut-out motifs were applied to grounds of wool or velvet. Linen was used for a variety of covers and for such items of dress as coifs, shifts and shirts (examples in Hardwick Hall, Derbys, NT; London, V&A).

From the mid-16th century the influence of the Renaissance is evident in many designs. Flowers, arranged within coiling stems or standing as single sprigs, continued to dominate English embroidery in the 17th century, although the velvet and fine linen grounds were replaced by satin and fustian (a linen and cotton mix), which was worked with crewel wools rather than silk. Late 16th- and early 17th-century table-carpets, valances and cushions often incorporated pictorial scenes taken from a variety of printed sources and illustrating biblical, classical and mythological stories. By the 1630s such scenes were embroidered to hang on the wall; at first they were worked on a fine canvas, but by the 1650s satin was also used, and a wide variety of techniques including raised work was employed. These recurring scenes and motifs were supplied by London print-sellers.

From the 1650s the style of the floral motifs became increasingly Baroque, and fustian curtains were decorated with huge, exotic leaves, usually in monochrome. In the 1690s, however, as the Indian Tree of Life became the dominant motif, polychrome wools took over. Flowers remained a preoccupation of English embroiderers, and during the early 18th century furnishings were decorated with delicate floral trails or isolated sprigs. Some were worked in chain stitch and in shades of red and green in imitation of imported Indian work. During the 1720s and 1730s flowers increased in size and were featured on many objects, including superb bed-sets worked with metal threads and skilfully shaded silks. By the 1740s the finest dresses worn at court were entirely covered in polychrome floral embroidery.

Canvaswork was used for carpets, panels and seat furniture, at first decorated with pictorial scenes set within floral surrounds, but later entirely floral. During the 1750s embroidery was largely replaced by patterned silks, and its use declined further as the Rococo style gave way to the Neo-classical. Embroidery was, however, an effective means of producing restrained ornament, as on the State Bed (see fig. 92) at Osterley Park House, near London, designed by Robert Adam (i) in 1776. Only court dress, including men's suits, provided an outlet for elaborate effects, although the simple muslin dresses worn from the end of the 18th century were embroidered or tamboured with sprig motifs and floral trails, usually in white but also in coloured silk.

Two important techniques in the 18th century were patchwork and quilting. Quilting was used from the late 17th century for such linen accessories as stomachers and nightcaps; later it was applied to larger garments, including

92. Embroidered State Bed, designed by Robert Adam, 1776 (London, Osterley Park House, NT)

men's waistcoats, which were popular from the 1730s to 1750s. Quilted petticoats were worn throughout the century, and those of silk were fashionable from the 1730s to 1780s. Furnishings were also quilted, and flat-quilted grounds feature on many elaborate silk embroideries. The shell pattern popular in quilting forms the basis of a set of hangings of 1750 to 1775 (London, V&A), which is one of the earliest-known examples of patchwork made with printed cottons. Silk pieces had been used earlier, but it was the availability of brightly printed cottons that led to the patchwork craze, which in the early 19th century encouraged manufacturers to print centrepieces and borders especially for the covers. Throughout the 19th century patchwork was made mainly by amateurs; the use of hundreds of tiny hexagons was a typically English style of design.

Until the 1840s the most flourishing form of embroidery was whitework, which was used to decorate large collars, handkerchiefs and other accessories. Coloured silkwork was used to decorate court dress and some small items. Some carpets and cushions were worked on canvas, but this was not employed for upholstery until the mid-19th century, by which time it was dominated by Berlin woolwork. This ever-coarsening technique had a deadening effect on embroidery. By the 1850s whitework had also coarsened, and coloured silk embroidery began to be mixed with beads and other materials to create very elaborate effects.

It was against such work that reformers, including A. W. N. Pugin and William Morris, campaigned. Pugin turned to military embroiderers to work his vestments, and later ecclesiastical architects were largely responsible for the revival of technical skills. Also influential was the School of Art Needlework (est. 1872; now known as the Royal School of Needlework), for which Morris, Selwyn Image and others designed. Embroidery was the first textile technique with which Morris experimented, and, under the care of his daughter May Morris (1862–1938) and John Henry Dearle (1860–1932), it remained an important part of Morris & Co.'s output into the 20th century. Many of the Arts and Crafts designers of the late 19th century and the early 20th appreciated embroidery as an expressive medium. Styles and techniques varied widely from the bold linen appliqués of Godfrey Blount (1859–1910) to the panels of dense swirling foliage designed by LEWIS FOREMAN DAY and embroidered by his wife in floss silks (examples in London, V&A).

By 1900 embroidery teaching was established in many schools and art colleges, and the importance of design continued to be emphasized by such organizations as the Needlework Development Scheme (est. 1934). One of its first advisers, Rebecca Crompton (1895–1947), showed how imaginative embroideries could be created using only simple materials and techniques. She was also one of the first to promote the use of the domestic sewing machine for embroidery. Another important teacher was Constance Howard (b 1910), who established the influential embroidery course at Goldsmith's College, University of London, which she ran between 1947 and 1975. An innovative approach continues to distinguish the work of many of the embroidery departments.

As in the 19th century, the church provided important commissions for embroiderers, especially after World War II. Some pieces were made to designs by such artists as John Piper (examples in London, V&A), but increasingly they were the work of such creative embroiderers as Beryl Dean (b 1911). Traditional skills have not been neglected, and, since the 1970s, quilting and patchwork have enjoyed a revival that has passed from the amateurs to the professionals. In the hands of such artists as Pauline Burbidge (b 1950), they have been used to create gallery works of great strength and beauty.

BIBLIOGRAPHY

R. Crompton: *Modern Design in Embroidery* (London, 1936)
A. G. I. Christie: *English Medieval Embroidery* (Oxford, 1938)
B. Dean: *Ecclesiastical Embroidery* (London, 1958)
C. Risley: *Machine Embroidery* (London, 1961)
B. Morris: *Victorian Embroidery* (London, 1962)
G. W. Digby: *Elizabethan Embroidery* (London, 1963)
D. King: *Opus Anglicanum* (London, 1963)
A. F. Kendrick: *English Needlework* (London, 1967)
P. Wardle: *Guide to English Embroidery* (London, 1970)
S. M. Levey: *Discovering Embroidery of the 19th Century* (Princes Risborough, 1971, 3/1983)
K. Brett: *English Embroidery in the Royal Ontario Museum, 16th–18th Centuries* (Toronto, 1972)
H. Bridgeman and E. Drury, eds: *Needlework: An Illustrated History* (London, 1978), pp. 31–82
M. Swain: *Figures on Fabric* (London, 1980)
C. Howard: *Twentieth-century Embroidery in Great Britain*, 4 vols (London, 1982–6)
D. Wilson: *The Bayeux Tapestry* (London, 1985)
L. Parry: *Textiles of the Arts and Crafts Movement* (London, 1988)
M. Swain: *Embroidered Stuart Pictures* (Princes Risborough, 1990)
K. Staniland: *Embroiderers*, Medieval Craftsmen series (London, 1991)
X. Brooke: *Catalogue of Embroideries* (Stroud, 1992)

SANTINA M. LEVEY

3. LACE. The making of both bobbin (bone) lace and needlepoint lace was established in England by 1600. Flemish immigrants may have contributed to its introduction. In the 17th century the main centres of commercial bobbin lacemaking were already the East Midlands, around Bedfordshire and Buckinghamshire, and Devonshire. Documentary evidence indicates that English lace followed Flemish modes, but it is difficult to identify. Lace in clumsy versions of Flemish designs and a coarser thread on collars and cuffs of the 1630s is thought to be English. Bobbin lace was also made domestically, and girls were taught to make both bobbin and needlepoint lace, of which the latter figured in samplers until the early 18th century. Needlepoint lace with floral designs or coiling stems has been identified as English. By the end of the 17th century lacemaking in England had been sufficiently expanded to give the English lace manufacturers enough weight to press the government for protectionist measures. Although an act was passed in 1697, it failed to stem the flood of imports. The English industry was incapable of competing with the industries in France and Flanders, either then or later, and in general it concentrated on the cheaper end of the market. A completely different branch was the gold and silver lace industry that developed in London, particularly around the parish of St Giles in Cripplegate, during the second half of the 17th century and that continued into the 18th. Needlepoint lacemaking died out commercially in the 18th century, but it continued to be made domestically in the form of hollie point—lines of knotted, buttonhole stitches worked over straight threads with gaps at intervals to form a pattern; it was used to decorate baby clothes.

The two centres of bobbin lace production acquired clearer definition in the 18th century. Lace of the Mechelen type made in Flanders (now Belgium) became the chief product of the East Midlands, while producers in Devonshire concentrated on part lace based on the Brussels model. Both industries fluctuated in size according to demand and were encouraged by protectionist measures, royal patronage and a ready-made export market in the American colonies. The mid-18th-century fashion for a coarse lace called 'trolly' also favoured the East Midlands industry, and Mechelen eventually also spread to Devonshire.

England pioneered the development of machine lace. The first Nottingham manufacturer to produce plain and patterned net by machinery was probably Robert Frost (*fl c.* 1765–1810) *c.* 1770, and silk machine net was being made in quantity by the 1780s, giving rise to a large embroidered net industry in Nottingham. John Heathcoat (1793–1861) invented the bobbin-net machine (1808), which eventually made it possible to produce cotton net and opened the way for the development of patterned machine lace.

The handmade lace industry prospered throughout the blockade during the Napoleonic Wars (1803–14), but it declined thereafter and began to revive only *c.* 1830. The East Midlands industry benefited from a number of good designers and enterprising manufacturers around the middle of the century. In addition to the standard, narrow laces of Mechelen and Lille types, innovations were adopted: large pieces were produced by joining narrow

93. Bobbin-lace handkerchief, cotton, designed by Lady Trevelyan and made by Miss S. Sanson, Honiton, *c.* 1860 (London, Victoria and Albert Museum)

strips together, black silk lace was introduced, and, after 1850, such coarser laces as Bedfordshire Maltese, Cluny and Yak were made. The Devonshire industry was less well-organized, but its products took on a distinctive character; Honiton motifs applied to machine net were made in addition to bobbin-made Honiton guipure (see fig. 93). Despite strenuous efforts to raise the standard of design, it was never able to compete successfully with Brussels lace or the growing threat from machine lace.

The machine lace industry, however, was not spared booms and slumps: the disastrous slump in embroidered net in the 1830s led to the development of various types of patterned machine lace. These began to appear in the 1840s, and in the following decades imitations of most types of bobbin lace were perfected, while the lace-curtain industry burgeoned as a special branch on its own. The main competition to the Nottingham industry came from France, although the Swiss and German imitations of needle lace caused a minor slump in the 1890s. The industry weathered all these vicissitudes, however, and continued as a leading force in the late 20th century. Handmade lace, however, could not withstand the competition from machine-made items, despite a brief resurgence at the end of the 19th century. There was a revival of Honiton, Buckinghamshire and Bedfordshire lace in the late 20th century, as an amateur pursuit on a traditional basis.

BIBLIOGRAPHY

W. Felkin: *A History of the Machine-wrought Hosiery and Lace Manufactures* (Cambridge, 1867/*R* Newton Abbot, 1967)

T. Wright: *The Romance of the Lace Pillow* (Olney, 1919)

C. Freeman: *Pillow Lace in the East Midlands* (Luton, 1958)

Z. Halls: *Machine-made Lace in Nottingham in the 18th and 19th Centuries* (Nottingham, 1964)

P. M. Inder: *Honiton Lace* (Exeter, 1971)

A. Buck: *Thomas Lester, his Lace and the East Midlands Industry* (Carlton, 1981)

K. Staniland and S. M. Levey: 'Queen Victoria's Wedding Dress and Lace', *Costume*, xvii (1983), pp. 1–32

H. J. Yallop: *The History of the Honiton Lace Industry* (Exeter, 1992)

PATRICIA WARDLE

4. PRINTED COTTON. Textiles were first block-printed in England in factories established on the rivers around London in the late 17th century. Although both cottons and linens have survived from this period, none has a certain London provenance. The two printed banyans or nightgowns (St Petersburg, Hermitage) printed in madder colours, the first with patterns reminiscent of imported Indian cottons and the second much closer to the designs of contemporary woven silks, which belonged to Peter the Great, may be English or Dutch. There are some tiny samples in the Alexander Papers (New York, Hist. Soc.) of madder-printed cottons and fustians, which are almost certainly English, dating from the 1720s. From 1721 all-cotton cloth was forbidden, and printed fustian in the papers of John Holker (*c.* 1750; Paris, Mus. A. Déc.) proves that English block-printing had developed to the point where naturalistic Rococo designs in imitation of woven patterns could be produced in lively colours on fustian. Indigo blue had to be 'pencilled' on the fabric until English printers pioneered the use of the 'China blue' technique, by which indigo could be printed when made into a paste with iron sulphate and a thickener, usually gum arabic. The cloth was then dipped alternately in baths of lime and iron sulphate until the desired depth of colour was reached.

About 1752 Francis Nixon (*d* 1765), an Irish printer, first used copperplate printing at the Drumcondra print-works, outside Dublin, Ireland, and he introduced it in England at Merton, Surrey, soon after. Large-scale mon-ochrome designs were produced, sometimes with additional colours added by pencilling. At the factory of Robert Jones at Old Ford, Poplar, some of the most graceful Neo-classical designs were printed, two of the most famous of which are signed and dated 1761 and 1769 respectively (London, V&A). Birds, flowers, chinoiseries and pastoral scenes were typical, often based on well-known published engravings. Surviving plate-impressions permit the identification of many cottons printed at Bromley Hall on the River Lea, Middx, by the firm of Talwin & Foster. Many of these have survived as cotton furnishings in the USA, whence they had been exported in the 18th century—together with a group of blue resist textiles long mistakenly thought to be French. In the resist technique, the white ground was reserved by a coating of wax prior to dipping, and the mention of 'wax-houses' in the insurance policies of English calico printers indicates that they were using this method.

The Manchester Act of 1736, which legalized the printing of linen and cotton mixtures, was followed in 1774 by an act that permitted the production and printing of all-cotton cloth, provided it had three blue threads woven into the selvages to indicate that it was English cotton. Thus English cottons can be distinguished from French imitations, although the English in turn borrowed French designs. Among those who campaigned for copy-right on designs was William Kilburn (1745–1818), a calico printer from Wallington, Surrey, who had illustrated the *Flora Londiniensis* (1777–98) by William Curtis. Kilburn made exquisite block-printed designs, drawing on his botanical knowledge (*see* COTTON, fig. 3). Such printers as the Ware family of Crayford, Kent, produced both dress and furnishing cottons (*see* COTTON, fig. 2). During the last quarter of the 18th century printed patterns led fashion in textiles, copying and improving on woven design.

The ends of printed cotton pieces were stamped to prove the payment of duty, and thus many can be assigned to particular printers. Some printers, however, such as Richard Ovey (*fl c.* 1790–1831), the leading London linen draper, were wholesalers who had work printed for them by sub-contractors. Once the technique of roller-printing had been mastered, much cheaper but still very beautiful cottons were printed, such as the set based on the book *The Birds of America* (1826–39). Equally, some of the most garish cottons ever printed were the work of English calico printers, especially after the discovery by Perkin of the coal-tar dyes. One cotton decorated with life-sized sprays of lilac and rose in mauve, blue, green, red, pink and cream on a brown ground, which was condemned as a 'direct imitation of nature' in the exhibition *False Principles in Design* (1852), organized by the Department of Practical Art in London, has, however, been in production virtually ever since. It was against such commercial design that William Morris and the later members of the Arts and Crafts Movement reacted so strongly. Morris restricted his palette to a limited and harmonious range of colours, which he based as far as he could on natural dyestuffs, especially indigo. An acute observer of natural form, he nevertheless subordinated this to the structure of the design as a whole, as in the 'Tulip' design (*see* MORRIS, WILLIAM, fig. 3). Others followed his example, notably C. F. A. Voysey, Lindsay Butterfield and LEWIS FOREMAN DAY. Their designs were in the forefront of the Art Nouveau style; many were sold at Liberty's, London, and were very influential. While there have been important English designers of printed textiles in the 20th century, their work has formed part of a European context, while the best have used modern dyestuffs in a controlled manner.

See also COTTON.

BIBLIOGRAPHY

D. King: 'Textiles and the Origins of Printing in Europe', *Pantheon*, xx (1962), pp. 23–30

F. Montgomery: *Printed Textiles: English and American Cottons and Linens, 1700–1850* (London, 1970)

W. Hefford: *The Victoria and Albert Museum's Textile Collection: Design for Printed Textiles in England, 1750–1850* (London, 1992)

NATALIE ROTHSTEIN

5. SILK. Broad-silk weaving in England developed from the silk ribbon industry and the production of mixed fabrics. The enormous growth in the production of pure silk in the mid-17th century made it a sizeable industry in such centres as London and Canterbury, with immigrant Huguenots contributing to its development. By 1700 the London silk industry had spread out from the City to Spitalfields to the east.

In the first half of the 18th century production was mainly of dress silks, stimulated by continuous innovation in fashion design and a considerable export market. The designs and silks by James Leman (1688–1745) and Anna Maria Garthwaite (1690–1763; see fig. 94; *see also* TEXTILES, colour pl. X, fig. 3) testify to the technical proficiency and artistry achieved in the English silk industry at this time. Between the 1680s and 1770s there was almost continuous progress, aided by legislation, including the prohibition of printed calicoes in 1721, the prohibition of imported French silks in 1766 and, in 1773, the first of a series of Spitalfields Acts agreeing rates of pay, so securing several decades of industrial peace. In the later 18th century weaving developed in the Midlands in such towns as Macclesfield and Leek, which were established as silk-throwing centres. The industry adapted to the fashion for smaller patterns, although this reduced wages, and was reasonably stable until 1824, when under Free Trade reform the Act of 1766 and the Spitalfields Acts were repealed. Effective from 1826, the legislation brought immediate and crippling results: French silks flooded the market, and Spitalfields and other communities faced bankruptcies and starvation. Those to survive were largely the producers of cheaper, lightweight or low-quality silks (in which the industry in Manchester specialized) or such

accessories as shawls and handkerchiefs produced in Norwich and Macclesfield and ribbons in Coventry.

In the 1830s tariffs were introduced to protect the textile trades, and for a few years such British firms as Daniel Walters & Sons in Braintree, Essex, made significant advances in furnishings. Use of the Jacquard loom had first been investigated in England between 1816 and 1820; it was gradually introduced in the 1830s and was established for silk weaving by 1840.

In 1860 the abolition of duty on foreign silks led to the immediate doubling of imports, and the industry once more suffered with many firms going out of business. Nevertheless, a small group of silk-weavers continued to weave for the growing interior-design market; in 1870 Benjamin Warner (1828–1908) started production in Spitalfields, and his firm became a leading silk manufacturer. In 1887 the Silk Association of Great Britain was founded, and in the 1890s and early 1900s a number of exhibitions of English silk were held to promote the industry. Such firms as Warner & Sons maintained high technical standards, and a new generation of designer-weavers, such as Edmund Hunter (1866–1937), produced high-quality, hand-woven silks. Artificial silk was also patented and developed, initially by Samuel Courtauld & Company in London, and by the 1920s it was established as a successful competitor to natural silk, the production of which continued but did not regain its former place in the industry.

BIBLIOGRAPHY

N. Rothstein: 'The Introduction of the Jacquard Loom to Great Britain', *Studies in Textile History in Memory of Harold B. Burnham*, ed. V. Gervers (Toronto, 1977), pp. 281–304
——: *Silk Designs of the Eighteenth Century in the Collection of the Victoria and Albert Museum* (London, 1990)
V. Mendes: *British Textiles from 1900 to 1937* (London, 1992)
L. Parry: *British Textiles from 1850 to 1900* (London, 1993)
N. Rothstein: *Woven Textile Design in Britain to 1750* (London, 1994)
——: *Woven Textile Design in Britain from 1750 to 1850* (London, 1994)

CLARE WOODTHORPE BROWNE

6. CARPETS. Pile carpets were imported into England from the Near East and Spain from at least as early as the mid-15th century, and by 1546 Henry VIII had a collection of 800 pieces. It is possible that by this time knotted carpets (Turkey work) were being made in England using a hemp ground and a woollen pile, which were imitative of carpets from the Middle East ('turkie carpetts') (*see* CARPET, §I, 1). At first the patterns were also based on Eastern models, as seen on the earliest dated European carpets, a group of four at Boughton House, Northants. Three are Star Ushak carpets and one an arabesque or 'Lotto' design; the two that retain their flat-woven ends are dated 1584 and 1585. The Boughton carpets are decorated with the Montague and Harrington coats of arms, and heraldry is a feature of many other Turkey work pieces, from large carpets to small upholstery panels. From the early 17th century the Middle Eastern patterns were largely replaced by floral designs related to those of contemporary English embroideries. Turkey work (*see* CARPET, fig. 8) was made by both amateurs and professionals, with Norwich being cited as a place of manufacture in a number of inventories. Although it continued to be made into the early 18th century, there was no direct link between Turkey work and the later production of hand-knotted pile carpets (see fig. 95), first at Fulham and then

94. Silk dress (remade 1770s), from silk designed by Anna Maria Garthwaite, 1744 (London, Victoria and Albert Museum)

95. Knotted pile carpet, 3.75×4.98 m, made in Exeter, 1757 (London, Victoria and Albert Museum)

Wilton or Brussels (*see* CARPET, fig. 4); both types were also made in such other centres as KIDDERMINSTER. The Jacquard attachment was applied to the looms in 1825. Another form of patterned pile carpeting, made without the help of the Jacquard, was 'Venetian' or 'Tapestry' carpeting, in which the pattern was pre-printed on to the pile warp. It was developed in the 18th century but was most successfully promoted by the firm of Crossley's of HALIFAX in the 19th century. During the later 19th century new and cheaper methods of weaving imitation pile carpets were introduced; these included chenille carpets (Patent Axminsters; *see* CARPET, §I, 5) and machine-tufted carpets (Royal Axminsters; *see* CARPET, §I, 8), which soon came to dominate the market.

Another branch of the carpet industry was based on the production of relatively cheap, flat-woven woollen carpeting, which was made by joining together strips of reversible double or triple cloth. Ultimately made in several centres including Kendal and Barnard Castle, it was known, after the main production areas, as Scotch or Kidderminster carpet and also, because of its use of pre-dyed yarns, as 'Ingrain' carpet (*see* CARPET, §I, 3). It was woven from as early as the late 16th century and grew in importance during the 18th and 19th centuries; by the 1840s it was being made on power looms with Jacquard attachments, but other forms of carpeting had largely replaced it by the early 20th century.

Quite distinct from the hand-knotted and woven carpets were those embroidered by hand on canvas. Those of the 16th century and the early 17th were made mostly as table-carpets, but, by the early 18th century, embroidered floor carpets became increasingly common. Worked by both professionals and dedicated amateurs, they were decorated with floral motifs increasingly arranged symmetrically within the central and border areas. By the late 18th century plain or diaper-patterned grounds were more common, with the flowers confined to central medallions and corner segments.

After a period of decline, there was a marked revival from the 1830s to the 1860s, spurred partly by the return of large-patterned fabrics and partly by the growing popularity of Berlin woolwork. Amateur enthusiasm for working carpets declined in the later 19th century, but the commercial industry was successfully revived by J. M. Pontremoli (1888–1952) of London, whose workshops produced a range of carpets in historical styles from the 1920s to World War II.

at Moorfields in London, and at Exeter (*see* EXETER, §2) and AXMINSTER.

From the mid-1750s the production of hand-knotted carpets was dominated by Thomas Moore (*c.* 1700–88) of Chiswell Street, Moorfields, and Thomas Whitty (*d* 1792) of Axminster. Both worked for the leading upholsterers and designers of the day, including Robert Adam (i); among the carpets woven to his designs were those for Syon House, London, and Saltram House, Plymouth, produced respectively by Moore and Whitty in 1769. Moore's business survived only until 1793, but that of Whitty was continued by his descendants until it went bankrupt in 1835. The production of hand-knotted carpets was then transferred to Wilton, where it continued until the 1950s.

The technique of producing pile strip carpets on the loom ('Brussels' carpet), by a method akin to that of velvet weaving, was introduced in Britain *c.* 1740 and quickly became established. The first looms were set up at Wilton (*see* WILTON, §2), and, depending on whether the pile loops were cut or uncut, the carpeting was known as

BIBLIOGRAPHY

C. E. C. Tattersall: *A History of British Carpets* (London, 1934)
M. J. Mayorcas: *English Needlework Carpets, 16th to 19th Centuries* (London, 1963)
C. E. C. Tattersall and S. Reed: *A History of British Carpets from the Introduction of the Craft until the Present Day* (Leigh-on-Sea, 1966)
B. Jacobs: *Axminster Carpets (Hand-made), 1755–1957* (Leigh-on-Sea, 1970)
W. Hefford: 'Thomas Moore of Moorfields', *Burl. Mag.*, cxix (1977), pp. 840–48
Country House Floors, 1660–1850 (exh. cat., Leeds, Temple Newsam, 1987)
I. Bennett and M. Franses: 'The Early European and Oriental Carpets at Boughton', *Boughton House*, ed. T. Murdoch (London, 1992), pp. 108–117

SANTINA M. LEVEY

XII. Patronage.

1. Before c. 1000. 2. c. 1000–c. 1500. 3. c. 1500–c. 1700. 4. c. 1700–c. 1800. 5. After c. 1800.

1. BEFORE c. 1000. The Roman invasion of AD 43 introduced into England the extraordinary variety of the culture of the Classical world, including such new art forms as sculpture in stone and bronze, mosaic work, fresco painting and plasterwork. It also changed the context in which art was produced. While art in Iron Age Britain (see PREHISTORIC EUROPE, §VI, 1) had largely been for an élite, there was a wider range of patrons in provincial Roman society (see also ROME, ANCIENT, §I, 3). In the cities, and especially in London, the erection of such large public buildings as basilicas with forums, the first example of which was built in the late 1st century, was not matched until the great increase in public building in the 19th century. Perhaps the most significant patron of architecture during the Roman occupation was the army, which commissioned not only substantial barracks but also such exceptional pieces of military architecture as Hadrian's Wall (AD 122–8). By the early 4th century, however, the enhancement of the private residence, particularly the villas built by native Britons, as well as Romans, gradually began to replace public munificence as a means of stimulating the production of arts and crafts, particularly that of mosaic work, gold and silver and other precious objects.

With the departure of the Romans in the 5th century AD, the important patronage by the central authorities disappeared, and in the 5th and 6th centuries only such small-scale works as jewellery and other objects in precious metals were commissioned, due to the uncertain economic conditions. The conversion of Britain to Christianity affected every area of Anglo-Saxon life, and within a century the construction of many new churches, initially of timber but later of stone, completely changed the form of English architecture; such buildings as Jarrow Abbey were embellished by foreign craftsmen. Apart from the new forms of art, the introduction of Christianity resulted in a new type of patronage: metalworkers, carpenters, painters and embroiderers were commissioned to furnish churches with liturgical items and reliquaries. Although illuminated Gospel books were initially imported from Italy, native production soon flourished. Monasticism was the main conduit for artistic, as well as religious, ideas but by the 9th century was in decline.

A few Anglo-Saxon rulers, for example Athelstan, King of Wessex (reg 924–39; see WESSEX, (2)), were notable patrons. His court had a distinctly international atmosphere, and the revival of monasticism in his reign was largely due to his numerous foundations and the influx of foreign scholars. The Benedictine reform movement in the reign of Edgar (reg 959–75), with its emphasis on elaborate liturgy and ceremony, resulted in new features in ecclesiastical architecture, for example complex west ends and transept galleries, and in the continued production of illuminated manuscripts, liturgical vessels and reliquaries (see BENEDICTINE ORDER, §II).

2. c. 1000–c. 1500. After the Norman invasion of 1066, a new generation of patrons embarked on a dramatic programme of castle and church building, and French rather than Scandinavian influences were dominant. The largest stone keeps constructed in England, at London (begun c. 1080), Colchester (c. 1085) and Canterbury (c. 1086), date from the reign of WILLIAM I. The growth in the number of monasteries and their endowments in the 11th and 12th centuries, as well as gifts by secular chapters, made possible the erection of many of the great English cathedrals of the Middle Ages, for example those at Canterbury (begun c. 1070), Lincoln (1073–92) and York (begun c. 1080). During the 12th century artistic production became increasingly secular, although monasteries continued to play a role. The monarchy, meanwhile, became increasingly powerful, and royal influence on the arts was particularly pronounced in the 13th century in the extensive activities of such monarchs as Henry III (see PLANTAGENET, (2)): his building of some 13 royal palaces was emulated by the nobility, and the construction of castles to contain the Welsh and Scots stimulated technical progress in military architecture. Henry III's most important project, however, was the rebuilding (from 1246) of Westminster Abbey, London, which absorbed a sizeable part of the national revenue (see LONDON, §V, 2(i)).

The growth of royal power also produced a new type of patron: the powerful bureaucrat, often recruited from an ecclesiastical background. A typical example was WILLIAM OF WYKEHAM, Bishop of Winchester, Keeper of the Privy Seal and Lord Chancellor. In the 1350s he entered the service of Edward III, and his main task was to transform Windsor Castle, Berks, into a sumptuous royal palace. His subsequent clerical appointments made him a wealthy man, and he epitomized the new type of patron, funding the arts by establishing educational foundations, for example New College (begun 1379), Oxford. The presence of shrines in cathedrals also encouraged the wealthy to commission elaborate tombs. These were no longer the prerogative of royalty but were also ordered by knights and gentry and were the type of personal investment (along with memorial brasses and chantry chapels) in which non-aristocratic patronage began to emerge from about the 1350s. Alabaster figures also began to be produced for a wide range of patrons.

Later medieval English kings, for example Richard II (reg 1377–99; see PLANTAGENET, (6)), were often notable patrons, although Richard aimed primarily to enhance his personal status by such ostentatious commissions as the Wilton Diptych (London, N.G.; see DIPTYCH, fig. 2) and the immensely expensive gilt-bronze effigies in Westminster Abbey of himself and Queen Anne of Bohemia. By the mid-15th century, however, the most important influences on artistic production were being exerted by an increasingly affluent merchant class, who commissioned large houses in such cities as London, Bristol and Norwich. Some parish churches, for example those at Lavenham and Long Melford, Suffolk, were also paid for by merchants, and the guilds that commissioned splendid meeting halls comparable to the great town houses of the aristocracy also emerged as patrons of significance. In domestic architecture, the construction of such mansions as Oxburgh Hall (begun c. 1481), Norfolk, illustrates the increased patronage by the gentry.

3. *c.* 1500–*c.* 1700. The patterns of patronage in the 16th century were firmly established by Henry VII (*reg* 1485–1509; *see* TUDOR, (1)). The most novel feature was the King's patronage of Burgundian artists, whom he employed primarily to promote pageantry, thereby enhancing the status of the Tudor monarchy. His son Henry VIII (*reg* 1509–47; *see* TUDOR, (2)) brought Pietro Torrigiani from Florence to create a tomb (1512–18) in Westminster Abbey for his parents, resulting in the introduction of the Italian Renaissance style in England (*see* TORRIGIANI, PIETRO, fig. 1; *see also* §IV, 1 above). Teams of foreign craftsmen, mostly French and Italian, were also employed by Henry VIII on his royal palaces, particularly Nonsuch Palace (destr. 1682; *see* NONSUCH PALACE, §1), which offered the most radical architectural innovations in competition with the palaces of his rival, Francis I, King of France. In Hans Holbein the younger (*see* HOLBEIN, (3)), whom he employed from 1536, Henry had at his court one of the most distinguished artists in northern Europe, although Holbein's influence was short-lived.

The dissolution of the monasteries in the late 1530s and the accumulation of wealth by those associates of the King who benefited from the redistribution of lands fuelled a building boom and, with it, more luxurious ways of living. In the reign of Elizabeth I (*reg* 1558–1603) magnificent houses, known as 'prodigy' houses, were built throughout England, which were intended to express the increased wealth and status of their owners (*see also* ELIZABETHAN STYLE). The Queen had no new palaces to compare with those of Elizabeth Talbot, Countess of Shrewsbury (*see* TALBOT, (1)), at Hardwick Hall, Derbys (1590–97), William Cecil, 1st Baron Burghley (*see* CECIL, (1)), at Burghley House, Cambs, or Sir Francis Willoughby at Wollaton Hall, Notts (begun 1580; *see* SMYTHSON, (1), fig. 2). The most important factor concerning the construction of these houses was the working partnership between patrons and such craftsmen and architects as Robert Smythson. Church building, on the other hand, all but ceased between the 1530s and Christopher Wren's rebuilding of the City churches in London after the Great Fire of 1666.

As the use of religious imagery in painting was also restricted (unless it was blatantly anti-papal), the demand for portraits, particularly miniatures, which included the sort of emblematic devices previously reserved for religious subject pictures, increased. The full-length portrait, which could be displayed in the great long galleries of the 'prodigy' houses, gained in popularity from the mid-16th century. Although during the reign of Elizabeth spending on the arts was considerably reduced, by comparison with that of her father's court, the Queen commissioned numerous portraits of herself (see fig. 16 above), the production of which was strictly controlled and which helped promote the cult that grew up around her (*see* TUDOR, (3)). The patronage of her favourites, Robert Dudley, 1st Earl of Leicester (*see* DUDLEY, (2)), and ROBERT DEVEREUX, 2nd Earl of Essex, however, was also central to the development of the arts and to the introduction of continental models in this period.

The first half of the 17th century was one of the most important periods in the history of patronage in England. James I (*see* STUART, House of, (2)) attempted to promote London as a centre of Renaissance culture. To this end he commissioned Inigo Jones to build the new Banqueting House (1619–22; *see* JONES, INIGO, fig. 1) at Whitehall, London. This and the Queen's House at Greenwich (begun 1616), for Anne of Denmark (*see* STUART, House of, (3)), were the first buildings in England to show the influence of Palladio. The elegance of the Stuart court under James's successor, Charles I (*see* STUART, House of, (6)), is best represented in the work of the northern artists that he employed, notably PETER PAUL RUBENS and ANTHONY VAN DYCK. Charles's attempts to glorify the monarchy are also evident in such works as van Dyck's *Charles I on Horseback with M. de St Antoine* (1633; British Royal Col.). In addition, Charles commissioned a number of bronze portrait busts of himself from such foreign sculptors as Hubert Le Sueur (see fig. 28 above) and Francesco Fanelli.

The Civil War (1642–9) and its aftermath resulted in little significant artistic and architectural patronage in the mid-17th century—Roger Pratt's Coleshill (destr.), Berks, was one of the few buildings of distinction commissioned in the late 1650s—but the Restoration of 1660 was followed by a burst of enthusiastic patronage in the upper ranks of society. Hugh May's elaborate remodelling for Charles II (*see* STUART, House of, (8)) of the north range (1675–88) of Windsor Castle, Berks, was the most conspicuous act of royal patronage during this period. The King never managed to emulate the building activities of Louis XIV, King of France, at the château of Versailles, as the vast palace at Winchester (begun 1683), designed by CHRISTOPHER WREN, remained unfinished at his death. The Office of Works, under Wren's Surveyorship for almost half a century from 1669, became an influential institution of architectural patronage. Only the reluctance of property owners, determined to maintain their previous holdings after the Great Fire of 1666, prevented the implementation of Wren's grand urban plan for London in the late 17th century. The increased wealth and status of the aristocracy in the Restoration period were also manifested in the new mansions of Piccadilly, London, for example that built (1664–7) for EDWARD HYDE, 1st Earl of Clarendon. The erection of town houses in St James's Square by Henry Jermyn, 1st Earl of St Albans (*d* 1684), heralded the early stages of a boom in speculative house building by the landed gentry who owned considerable areas of London. This was to continue throughout the 18th century. Meanwhile William and Mary (*see* ORANGE NASSAU, (5) and (6)) had Wren rebuild part of the old Tudor palace at Hampton Court, London (*see* HAMPTON COURT PALACE), and remodel Nottingham House, renamed Kensington Palace, from 1689. William, however, failed to implement the ostentatious plans for the new Whitehall Palace in London that Wren drew up after the fire of 1698 destroyed the old palace. The King and Queen also shared a passion for gardening and decorating their various residences, resulting in the development of what is known as the WILLIAM AND MARY STYLE. In the sphere of public building they commissioned Wren to rebuild the Royal Hospital at Greenwich (founded 1694; *see* GREENWICH, §2), a maritime counterpart to the Royal Hospital (1682–92) at Chelsea, begun by Charles II.

Although Hampton Court was not complete at the end of the 17th century, the decoration of the state apartments and those of many of the grandest late 17th-century houses, including CHATSWORTH HOUSE, Derbys, for William Cavendish, 4th Earl and 1st Duke of Devonshire (*see* CAVENDISH, (1)), was enhanced by the taste for Baroque decorative painting executed mainly by such émigré French and Italian painters as Antonio Verrio and Louis Laguerre (see fig. 40 above). The most prominent painters employed at the Stuart courts of the late 17th century, for example Peter Lely, Willem Wissing and Godfrey Kneller, also introduced European artistic influences, and the influx of many talented Huguenot craftsmen after the Revocation of the Edict of Nantes in 1685 stimulated the production of decorative arts, especially metalwork. This resulted in numerous commissions for silver tableware from the aristocracy (*see* §IX, 1(iii) above).

4. *c.* 1700–*c.* 1800. At the accession of Queen Anne in 1702, artists were still restricted by an inadequate system of patronage that left them dependent on the support of an individual or a small group that employed the artist as a member of the household. Aristocratic patronage provided, for example, by JAMES BRYDGES, 1st Duke of Chandos, remained important, but a new type of patron emerged in significant numbers in the second quarter of the 18th century: the professional banker, lawyer, physician or clergyman, whose occupations had become more prominent from the late 17th century. The organization of a more formal banking system during the reign of William and Mary was particularly important in the creation of some of the great private fortunes, such as that of the Hoare family (*see* HOARE (i)), that benefited the arts in the 18th century (*see also* BANK, §1). By the mid-18th century the distinction between the aristocratic and middle classes had greatly lessened both socially and culturally, with those patrons that Daniel Defoe dubbed 'the middle sort, who live well' deriving much of their cultural information from the expanding book and periodical trade, which helped to create work for illustrators and engravers.

Although many painters were forced to diversify their output and derived much of their income from prints, some English artists attempted to respond to the changing conditions of patronage by developing better methods of training for their profession. The St Martin's Lane Academy, revived by William Hogarth in 1735 (*see* §XV below), was the forerunner of the Royal Academy of Arts (est. 1768), which did so much to enhance the status of the artist and increase direct patronage through its annual exhibitions (*see* LONDON, §VI). Demand for portraits by such prominent artists as Joshua Reynolds and Thomas Gainsborough, however, continued unabated throughout the 18th century, both from traditional aristocratic sources and from the rising professional classes. Many of the Grand Tourists also gave commissions to foreign artists through the network of English dealers and agents in Italy. In the mid- and late 18th century intense competition was supplied by such sculptors as Joseph Nollekens, whose portrait busts were inspired by antique sculpture, fashionable among collectors. Demand for history painting from English artists remained negligible until such artists as Benjamin West and John Singleton Copley began to capture the public imagination with episodes from contemporary history that could be engraved for a wider audience. Meanwhile, the Grand Tour and the rise of tourism within the British Isles encouraged the popularity of landscape painting and gardening. The gardens at STOWE, Bucks, for RICHARD TEMPLE, 1st Viscount Cobham, and STOURHEAD, Wilts, for the Hoare family, reflected the taste for paintings by Claude Lorrain, although relatively few patrons could either find or afford genuine paintings by that artist.

In architecture, the rise of the Palladian style in the first half of the 18th century, fostered by Richard Boyle, 3rd Earl of Burlington and 4th Earl of Cork (*see* BOYLE, (2)), and his circle, including William Kent, was a vehicle for the expression of the wealth, derived from colonies and trading, acquired by the English aristocracy and gentry. The great country houses dating from the first half of the 18th century, for example Houghton Hall (1722–35), Norfolk, for Robert Walpole, 1st Earl of Orford (*see* WALPOLE, (1)), and Holkham Hall (begun 1734), Norfolk, for Thomas Coke, 1st Earl of Leicester (*see* COKE, (1)), include opulent interiors and furnishings. This tendency towards lavish display remained evident in the architectural patronage of the mid- and late 18th century: in 1762 Hugh Smithson, later 1st Duke of Northumberland (*see* PERCY, (3)), commissioned Robert Adam to rebuild Syon House, Middx, with rich Neo-classical interiors. WILLIAM BECKFORD employed James Wyatt to construct the magnificent Fonthill Abbey (1796–1813; destr.), Wilts, in the Gothic Revival style.

There was a dearth of commissions for secular public building in the early 18th century, both in London and in the provinces, although in ecclesiastical commissions the Act of Parliament of 1711 for the building of 50 new churches in London was notable. By the mid-18th century, however, a tide of philanthropy had led to the establishment of several new hospitals that had connections with the arts, such as the Foundling Hospital, London, founded in 1739 (*see also* §XIV below). The most important public building constructed in London in the 18th century was William Chambers's Somerset House (begun 1776), built as government offices on the site of the old Tudor palace, but many provincial civic authorities, for example that of Doncaster, W. Yorks, built elaborate mansion houses or town halls around this time.

5. AFTER *c.* 1800. A significant change in patronage took place in the early 19th century, when a new breed of patron–collector, whose wealth was often derived from the expansion of industry at this time, specialized in patronizing British artists. Such patrons included ROBERT VERNON, an army contractor, and JOHN SHEEPSHANKS, a cloth manufacturer from Leeds. George O'Brien Wyndham, 3rd Earl of Egremont (*see* WYNDHAM, (2)), however, was also a notable patron of J. M. W. Turner. These three were among the first of many northern industrialists whose philanthropy resulted in bequests to the nation or to the many provincial museums that sprang up in the second half of the 19th century. One of the last significant royal patrons was the Prince Regent (later George IV; *see* HANOVER, (4)). He employed JOHN NASH to extend Carlton House (1814; destr.), London, and the Royal

Pavilion at Brighton (1815–22; for illustration *see* BRIGH-TON); the latter has elaborate and bizarre Indian-style and chinoiserie decoration, the exuberance of which reflected the Prince's temperament. During the 1820s Nash was also employed to carry out a series of metropolitan improvements in London that transformed the architecture of the city. Both Queen Victoria and her husband, Prince Albert (*see* HANOVER, (6) and (7)), however, also showed a deep concern for the arts, with the Prince playing a vital role in the organization of the Great Exhibition of 1851 in London. They also employed such well known artists as Edwin Landseer and Franz Xaver Winterhalter.

A number of artistic institutions established in the 19th century also provided direct and indirect patronage for British artists. The British Institution was founded in London in 1805 as an exhibiting body for living artists and helped to promote their work. Following the recommendation of a Parliamentary Select Committee in 1836, the Art Union of London (which later had equivalents in the provinces) was founded in 1837. Primarily concerned with the improvement of public taste, it held lotteries with paintings and prints, usually bought direct from the artist, as the prizes.

The state and civic authorities also began to play an increasingly prominent role in the promotion of the arts and art education in the 19th century. The National Gallery, London, was established in 1824, and the new British Museum, London, was constructed (1823–48). Parliamentary Select Committees were established in 1835, leading to the foundation of the Government School of Design two years later, and in 1841 to the '[consideration of] the promotion of the fine arts ... in connexion with the building of the Houses of Parliament', which resulted in one of the few opportunities since the early 18th century for history painters to decorate a public building (*see* LONDON, §V, 3(iii)). This commission was emulated by the civic authorities at Manchester: in the late 1870s Ford Madox Brown was employed to decorate the newly completed town hall (1867–77) with murals depicting the history of Manchester. Many other civic authorities erected such public buildings as libraries, museums, town halls, offices and new churches in a variety of styles from Gothic to classical. Such figures as Charles Lock Eastlake (*see* EASTLAKE, (1)), who occupied the posts of Director of the National Gallery (from 1843), President of the Royal Academy (from 1850) and Secretary of the new Royal Fine Arts Commission (1841–8), provided important patronage for English artists through these powerful institutions. By the late 19th century interest in art had become so widespread that huge incomes could be earned by the most popular artists. John Everett Millais, for example, is said to have made between £25,000 and £40,000 a year in the 1870s and 1880s, and street and trade directories from around the end of the century reveal the names of hundreds of artists in London alone.

At the beginning of the 20th century it was clear that aristocratic patronage on a grand scale had largely been superseded by that exercised by merchants, manufacturers and such art dealers as JOSEPH DUVEEN, 1st Baron Duveen of Millbank, who paid for the addition of new rooms at the Tate Gallery, initiated and named after Sir HENRY TATE, on Millbank in London. Artists, meanwhile, fared rather less well than their 19th-century counterparts, although exhibitions held at the Leicester Galleries and Arthur Tooth & Sons in London gave many their first 'one-man' shows, and the Contemporary Art Society was founded in 1910 to promote the development of contemporary art. Such patrons as the art historian KENNETH CLARK, later Lord Clark of Saltwood, supported young artists, including Henry Moore and Graham Sutherland, at his own expense in the 1930s, and as Chairman of the War Artists' Advisory Committee in 1939 he was able indirectly to exert considerable patronage.

Other acts of government patronage in the 20th century included the establishment in 1940 of the Committee for the Encouragement of Music and Arts (CEMA) and in 1946 of the Arts Council of Great Britain. The foundation of the latter enabled the arts to receive and distribute government finance without the intervention of the State, and it sponsored exhibitions of both contemporary and historic art after World War II. Not until 1965, however, did a British government set out a policy for public funding of the arts, which attempted to counteract the negative attitudes of the interwar years. From 1979 the government encouraged significant changes in arts funding, shifting importance from public funding to business sponsorship.

BIBLIOGRAPHY
W. T. Whitley: *Artists and their Friends in England, 1700–1799*, 2 vols (London, 1928/*R* 1968)
——: *Art in England, 1800–1837*, 2 vols (Cambridge, 1928–30)
T. Boase, ed.: *The Oxford History of English Art*, 9 vols (Oxford, 1952–78)
Support for the Arts in England and Wales: A Report to the Calouste Gulbenkian Foundation by Lord Redcliffe-Maud (London, 1976)
H. Baldry: *The Case for the Arts* (London, 1981)
B. Denvir: *A Documentary History of Taste in Britain*, 4 vols (London, 1983–8)
B. Ford, ed.: *The Cambridge Guide to the Arts in Britain*, 9 vols (Cambridge, 1988–91)

XIII. Collecting and dealing.

1. Before 1700. 2. 1700–1840. 3. After 1840.

1. BEFORE 1700. In 16th-century England there were few collections remotely comparable in quality to those formed by such continental rulers as Cosimo I, Grand Duke of Tuscany, Ferdinand, Archduke of Austria, or Augustus, Elector of Saxony. By the time English collectors began to respond to European developments, the more enlightened continental nobility (especially the Italians) had already begun to concentrate on forming picture galleries, rather than cabinets of curiosities. In the early 16th century Cardinal THOMAS WOLSEY was the only collector in England whose acquisitions, which included Netherlandish paintings and tapestries, were comparable to those of continental collectors; his visits to Rome no doubt gave him delusions of grandeur that were ultimately to lead to his fall from power, and the dispersal of his collection benefited such institutions as Christ Church, Oxford. The desanctification of relics and other ecclesiastical objects that followed Wolsey's demise and the break with the Roman Catholic Church did not diminish the demand for these works: many passed into secular collections.

There was no real lead from the English Crown in collecting in the 16th century. The collections of Henry VIII (*see* TUDOR, (2)) were more in keeping with the medieval concept of the *Schatzkammer*—a treasure store of jewels, plate and curiosities—rather than an art collection in the modern sense, although inventories taken in 1542 and 1547 list a considerable number of paintings, including both secular and religious works by Netherlandish artists, at the palaces of Greenwich, Hampton Court and Westminster in London and at Oatlands, Surrey. Few names, however, are mentioned, making identification difficult. Apart from assembling a gallery of portraits of her royal forebears, Elizabeth I (*see* TUDOR, (3)) seems to have added relatively little to the royal collection, although she must have had an interest in pictures other than portraits, since the Calvinist rebels in Ghent intended to offer her the Ghent Altarpiece (*c.* 1423–32; Ghent, St Bavo; for illustration *see* EYCK, VAN, (1)) by Hubert and Jan van Eyck in 1579. She also apparently attempted to purchase the great *St John* altarpiece (1508–11; Antwerp, Kon. Mus. S. Kst; *see* METSYS, (1), fig. 1) by Quinten Metsys. The royal collection at the end of Elizabeth's reign was probably not superior to those assembled by her illustrious subjects JOHN, 1st Baron LUMLEY, and Robert Dudley, 1st Earl of Leicester (*see* DUDLEY, (2)).

One of the most important periods in English collecting was that from the reign of James I to the outbreak of the Civil War in 1642, when a number of patrons in court circles, as well as the royal family, formed magnificent collections of Classical, Renaissance and contemporary art. Henry, Prince of Wales (*see* STUART, House of, (4)), the heir to James I, seems to have had a particular passion for pictures. In January 1611, on seeing the gallery or 'Cabinet Room' at St James's Palace newly fitted out by Inigo Jones for the Prince, the Venetian Ambassador remarked that the paintings were for 'the large part brought out of Venice'. After Prince Henry's death in 1612, the entire collection, which also included Flemish and Dutch paintings and Italian bronze statuettes, was housed at Whitehall Palace, London, for some years, until it passed to the Prince's younger brother Prince Charles, later Charles I (*see* STUART, House of, (6)), who became the most outstanding of English royal collectors.

Charles's taste for pictures must have been influenced by those of his father's favourites, ROBERT CARR, 1st Earl of Somerset, and GEORGE VILLIERS, later 1st Duke of Buckingham, and by Thomas Howard, 2nd Earl of Arundel (*see* HOWARD (i), (1)), who were known as the 'Whitehall Cognoscenti'. Arundel owned one of the finest English art collections, which he kept at Arundel House (destr.) near the Strand, London, in the early 17th century. The German artist and writer Joachim von Sandrart, who saw the Arundel collection on a visit to England in 1627, described it as being 'resplendent with the finest ancient statues of marble, of Greek and Roman workmanship'. The sculpture gallery is depicted in the background of the portrait of *Thomas Howard, 2nd Earl of Arundel* (*c.* 1618; Arundel Castle, W. Sussex; *see* LONDON, fig. 16) by Daniel Mijtens I. Arundel's knowledge of art, his connoisseurship and the size and range of his collections, which, apart from ancient marbles, included paintings by Hans Holbein the

younger and high-quality Venetian pictures, were exceptional in England at this time. One of the most important Venetian pictures acquired by an English collector during this period was Titian's *Vendramin Family* (mid-1540s; London, N.G.), purchased by Algernon Percy, 10th Earl of Northumberland (*see* PERCY, (2)), from the collection of Anthony van Dyck.

The Duke of Buckingham was an even more enthusiastic collector of Venetian pictures, and among the 19 Titians that he is said to have owned was a version of the *Ecce homo* (Vienna, Ksthist. Mus.) that BALTHAZAR GERBIER secured for him in Venice in 1621. Buckingham's holdings, mostly housed at York House (destr.) in London, were considerably enriched by collections of Roman antiquities purchased from Peter Paul Rubens when Buckingham visited Antwerp in 1625. The Duke and Prince Charles vied with one another in their connoisseurship and his enlargement of their collections; Buckingham accompanied the Prince on his visit to Spain in 1623, in an attempt to win the hand of the Spanish Infanta, when many works of art were acquired, some of them through the offices of ENDYMION PORTER. The Prince made one great purchase in the early 1620s, paying £700 for the celebrated eight cartoons of the *Acts of the Apostles* by Raphael, known as the Raphael Cartoons (London, V&A; *see* RAPHAEL, fig. 5), which were used as designs for tapestries woven at the Mortlake factory (*see* §XI, 1(ii) and fig. 90 above).

Even before Charles's accession in 1625, his collection was impressive, and Rubens referred to him as the 'greatest amateur of paintings among the princes of the world'. Until 1642 Charles continued to spend vast sums enriching his collections. Some works were acquired through exchanges with courtiers, others were gifts. Ambassadors, special envoys and diplomatic agents, for example HENRY WOTTON, Sir DUDLEY CARLETON, Sir Henry Vane the elder (1589–1655) and Francis, Baron Cottington (?1578–1652), as well as Endymion Porter, scoured the Continent for works of art and gave commissions to foreign artists on behalf of the King and his courtiers. The agents NICHOLAS LANIER and DANIEL NYS achieved perhaps the greatest coup in the history of art collecting: the acquisition for Charles of a large part of the collections owned by Vincenzo Gonzaga II, 7th Duke of Mantua, including Mantegna's *Triumphs of Caesar* (London, Hampton Court, Royal Col.) and works by Leonardo, Raphael, Titian, Correggio and Caravaggio, which were sold by the Duke in two instalments in 1627 and 1628 for £25,500.

After Charles's execution in January 1649, the House of Commons resolved to sell the late King's possessions in what came to be known as the 'Commonwealth Sale'. Some pictures were bought by the late King's friends, and a few were returned to the royal collection at the Restoration in 1660. Many, however, were given in lieu of cash to the King's creditors and were later sold on to dealers with continental clients, including royalty. Other works, including the Raphael Cartoons and Mantegna's *Triumphs*, remained in the royal collection. The 'Dutch Gift' of important paintings from the collection of the Reynst family to Charles II at the Restoration in 1660 was one of the few additions of Italian pictures to any English collection in the mid-17th century, although in the late

17th century important Italian pictures were acquired by Robert Spencer, 2nd Earl of Sunderland (*see* SPENCER, (1)), some of which are still at Althorp House, Northants, by Sir THOMAS ISHAM, whose collection (except two untraced works) remains at Lamport Hall, Northants, and by John Cecil, 5th Earl of Exeter (*see* CECIL, (3)), for Burghley House, Cambs.

Lord Exeter's political affiliations led him to break with the court and London society; his collection is particularly interesting because the pictures were specifically intended to be housed at Burghley at a time when it was the usual practice among aristocratic collectors to hang pictures in their London house. His acquisition of works by Carlo Maratti, Giuseppe Bartolomeo Chiari, Carlo Dolci, Luca Giordano and other outstanding contemporary Italian artists in the 1680s (all Burghley House, Cambs) suggests a remarkably advanced taste for an English collector. Other important private collections created in the late 17th century include that of the Dukes of Devonshire (*see* CAVENDISH), which was later housed at Chatsworth (*see* CHATSWORTH HOUSE), Derbys, that of the MONTAGU family at Boughton House, Northants, and Montagu House, London, and that of Charles Seymour, 6th Duke of Somerset (1662–1748), at Petworth House, W. Sussex. These eventually rivalled the few collections that had survived the Civil War, such as that of the Earls of Pembroke (*see* HERBERT), which includes Dutch, Flemish and 16th-century Venetian works, at Wilton House, Wilts. Even at the end of the 17th century, however, most collections in England consisted of cabinets of curiosities of the kind formed by John Tradescant the elder (*see* TRADESCANT) and presented by ELIAS ASHMOLE to Oxford University in 1679 or collections of natural objects such as that built up over 25 years of continental travel by Sir William Charleton (1642–1703) and shown in his rooms at the Temple in London.

2. 1700–1840.

(i) Trends in collecting. (ii) Growth of the art trade.

(i) *Trends in collecting.* The greatest stimulant to collecting in 18th-century England was undoubtedly the almost obligatory GRAND TOUR, a lengthy journey around Europe with Italy as the ultimate goal. Although guidebooks to Italy had appeared from 1670, Jonathan Richardson's *An Account of Some of the Statues, Bas-reliefs, Drawings and Pictures in Italy &tc. with Remarks* (London, 1722) was the work most widely used for reference by Grand Tourists. This book and others by Richardson, for example his *Essay on the Theory of Painting* (1715), also did much to improve the education of the English aristocracy and gentry, laying the foundations for a more scholarly connoisseurship based on recent developments in French art theory, expressed particularly in the writings of Roger de Piles. The SOCIETY OF DILETTANTI, established in 1732 by a group of young men who had visited Italy on the Grand Tour, eventually played an important role in furthering scholarship of Classical art.

Another important factor in the development of collections was the increased dispersal of works of art from London to country houses. In the early 18th century some country houses were designed to incorporate and display art collections. Even the initial designs of Blenheim Palace, Oxon, for example, included a grand picture gallery to house the magnificent works by Rubens and van Dyck owned by JOHN CHURCHILL, 1st Duke of Marlborough. From the 1730s such collectors as Sir ANDREW FOUNTAINE gave up their London house altogether and moved to the country, and this tendency was probably given further impetus as the fashion for Palladian country houses with purpose-built galleries took hold in the second quarter of the 18th century. The London house of Thomas Coke, 1st Earl of Leicester (*see* COKE, (1)), in Thanet Street, for example, could not match the splendour of the interiors at Holkham Hall, Norfolk, as a setting for the display of his collection of paintings and sculpture, even if fewer visitors could see the important works of art shown there. Although many of the great houses were open to visitors, this lack of easy public access caused some concern among artists and scholars, including Joshua Reynolds and Johann Joachim Winckelmann; the latter, after visiting England in 1760, noted that 'those barbarians, the English, buy up everything and in their own country nobody sees it but themselves'. A number of important collections, however, remained in London. Only when he resigned from political office in 1742 did Sir Robert Walpole, 1st Earl of Orford (*see* WALPOLE, (1)), remove part of his collection from his house in Arlington Street to Houghton Hall, Norfolk, and as late as 1766 Devonshire House in Piccadilly, and not Chatsworth, Derbys, contained the finest of the paintings owned by the Cavendish family.

By the mid-18th century a remarkable number of collections containing works of high quality had been formed or were being assembled, not all of them aristocratic. The most important were listed in Thomas Martyn's two small volumes entitled *The English Connoisseur* (London, 1766), which were based on earlier inventories, principally the researches by Robert Dodsley (1703–64) in the late 1750s, published in his *London and its Environs* (1761). The extensive collections of the celebrated physician Dr RICHARD MEAD were all located in his town house in Great Ormond Street in London. Mead spent much of his sizeable income buying paintings, bronzes, coins and medals, as well as forming a magnificent library, and his collections were a testament to the growing prestige of his profession. From the early 18th century there had been a steadily growing taste for Dutch paintings, not least because they were available in enormous quantities and at reasonable prices, and in the 1740s Mead's gallery contained paintings by van Dyck, Rembrandt and Frans Hals, as well as works by Holbein and Rubens and such contemporary continental painters as the fashionable Canaletto and Watteau; the latter had come to London in 1719–20 to seek a cure from Mead for his tuberculosis. Mead's collection was dispersed in a series of auction sales held at Langford's (see §(ii) below) after his death in 1754.

By the mid-18th century high-quality Dutch pictures, including landscapes, had also been acquired by such collectors as the immensely wealthy CHARLES JENNENS, Dr Mead's neighbour in Great Ormond Street and better known as Handel's librettist. By the early 1760s Jennens owned more than 100 Dutch pictures, including 17 van de Veldes and 11 Ruisdaels, as well as works then attributed to Rembrandt. The nobility, for example Richard Boyle,

3rd Earl of Burlington, and William Cavendish, 2nd Duke of Devonshire, had also acquired works by Rembrandt, Nicolaes Berchem, Hals, Ruisdael and other celebrated artists. Rembrandt was particularly admired by British collectors, a taste promoted by Joshua Reynolds.

Works by such Italian artists as Leonardo, Raphael, Correggio, Annibale Carracci, Domenichino and Guido Reni were the most prized by English collectors *c.* 1760, but few authentic examples appear to have been in English collections. The only significant work by Raphael in England was the early *Ansidei Madonna* (London, N.G.), which was bought in Italy in 1764 for Lord Robert Spencer and given to his brother George Spencer, 4th Duke of Marlborough (1739–1817), for the collection at Blenheim Palace, Oxon. JOHN GUISE had several pictures by Annibale Carracci, which after his death were given to Christ Church, Oxford, and Sir Robert Walpole owned a particularly celebrated work by Guido Reni, the *Virgin and the Doctors of the Church* (St Petersburg, Hermitage), which was displayed at Houghton.

In the 18th century works by Claude Lorrain made a significant impact on many areas of British taste, especially landscape painting and gardening. The exemplary English collection of his work was that of the Earl of Leicester at Holkham Hall, where in the 'Landscape Room' seven paintings by Claude were displayed. Claude's works were rapidly promoted to the highest-priced on the market: in 1786 JOHN JULIUS ANGERSTEIN, whose collection later formed the nucleus of the National Gallery in London, paid the dealer NOEL JOSEPH DESENFANS £2500 for the *Seaport with the Embarkation of St Ursula* (1641; London, N.G.; *see* CLAUDE LORRAIN, fig. 3), but this purchase was soon eclipsed by that of the pair of paintings depicting a *Landscape with the Father of Psyche Sacrificing at the Milesian Temple of Apollo* (1663) and a *Landscape with the Arrival of Aeneas at Pallanteum* (1675; both Anglesey Abbey, Cambs, NT; for the latter *see* CLAUDE LORRAIN, fig. 6), known as the Altieri Claudes, for which William Beckford paid £6825 in 1799. Nine years later Hart Davis paid £12,600 for them, but it is an interesting reflection on the fluctuations of taste that they fetched only £2625 at auction in 1940.

In addition to paintings, English collectors spent enormous sums on sculpture. By the mid-18th century sculpture galleries had been incorporated into a number of country houses: that at Newby Hall, N. Yorks, was designed by Robert Adam in 1767 to house William Weddell's collection of sculpture (*see* WEDDELL, WILLIAM), including the Barberini *Venus*, purchased from the dealer Thomas Jenkins. Other notable sculpture collections included that of Sir RICHARD WORSLEY, a diplomat and amateur archaeologist who published his collection in two important volumes known as the *Museum Worsleyanum*, and that of CHARLES TOWNLEY, depicted by Johan Zoffany in *Charles Townley's Library in Park Street* (*see* ZOFFANY, JOHAN, fig. 2). Townley's collection of sculpture was purchased in 1805 by the British Museum, London, which had also acquired the outstanding collection of Greek vases (then believed to be Etruscan) belonging to Sir WILLIAM HAMILTON (i). The Museum's later purchases of Classical art included the Parthenon Marbles (*see* BRUCE, THOMAS, 7th Earl of Elgin; ATHENS,

fig. 14; and GREECE, ANCIENT, fig. 43) between 1814 and 1816.

The heyday of English collecting from *c.* 1770 to *c.* 1830 resulted mainly from the increased affluence of the English gentry and aristocracy, coinciding with the decline of many of the aristocratic and royal families of Europe. The French Revolution and numerous European wars at the end of the 18th century led to a huge influx of works of art of the highest quality for sale in England. The immensely complicated and protracted sale in London between 1792 and 1800 of the Orléans collection, consisting of hundreds of paintings mostly acquired between 1715 and 1723 by Philippe II, Duc d'Orléans, when Regent of France, resulted in a consortium, led by the enormously wealthy Francis Egerton, Duke of Bridgewater (*see* EGERTON, (1)), his nephew George Granville Leveson-Gower, 2nd Marquess of Stafford (1758–1833), and Frederick Howard, 5th Earl of Carlisle (*see* HOWARD (ii), (3)), purchasing the outstanding Italian pictures from the collection for £43,000 in 1798. The works included Titian's *Rape of Europa* (Boston, MA, Isabella Stewart Gardner Mus.; *see* TITIAN, fig. 8). High-quality pictures continued to be imported long after peace was restored in 1815.

The passion for collecting also found expression in the early 19th century with the establishment in 1805 of the British Institution in London. Although initially founded to exhibit contemporary art, from 1813 it began an important series of exhibitions of Old Master paintings, with most of the works lent by the members, for example Charles Long, 1st Baron Farnborough (*see* LONG, (1)). These were the forerunners of the exhibitions begun at Burlington House, London, at the end of the 19th century. Despite hostility from the Royal Academy, dominated by artists, the Institution, with George III as its Patron, the Prince Regent (later George IV) as Vice-patron and John Young, the author of illustrated catalogues of several leading collections of the time, as Keeper, did much to promote the interests of English collectors.

In the early 19th century Dutch paintings continued to be popular among collectors; one of the most important purchases was that of Rembrandt's portrait of the *Shipbuilder and his Wife* (Brit. Royal Col.) for the enormous sum of £5250 by the Prince Regent in 1811 (*see* HANOVER, (4)). Sir ROBERT PEEL also specialized in collecting 17th-century Dutch pictures, for example Meindert Hobbema's *Avenue at Middelharnis* (1689; London, N.G.; *see* HOBBEMA, MEINDERT, fig. 2), but his contemporaries, especially those newly enriched by the Industrial Revolution, were increasingly inclined to reject traditional tastes in collecting in favour of contemporary British art. Surprisingly, the precedents for this trend were found among the nobility and gentry. Sir JOHN FLEMING LEICESTER, who divided his holdings between his London house and Tabley Hall, Ches, and George O'Brien Wyndham, 3rd Earl of Egremont (*see* WYNDHAM, (2)), at Petworth House, W. Sussex, both bought English paintings, particularly works by J. M. W. Turner, and sculpture. Galleries of contemporary sculpture were also created by John Russell, 6th Duke of Bedford (*see* RUSSELL, (4)), at Woburn Abbey, Beds, in 1815 and by William Spencer Cavendish, 6th Duke of Devonshire (*see* CAVENDISH, (5)), at Chatsworth in 1818. In both galleries works by Antonio Canova (e.g.

the *Three Graces* for Woburn Abbey, 1815–17; Edinburgh, N.G. and London, V&A; *see* CANOVA, ANTONIO, fig. 4) were included along with those of contemporary English and German sculptors who had visited Rome.

By 1840 the rise of the middle-class patron–collector had become a notable phenomenon. Perhaps the most typical collectors of those who became rich as a result of the most intensive phase of industrialization or through the Napoleonic wars were JOHN SHEEPSHANKS, a Yorkshire cloth manufacturer, and ROBERT VERNON, who, from humble origins, made a fortune as a horse dealer and supplier to the army. Both bought almost exclusively contemporary art, usually direct from the artist.

(ii) Growth of the art trade. In the 18th century English dealers, for example ANDREW HAY, were often rather enigmatic figures who assembled a collection on the Continent and brought it back to London for sale by private treaty or through the auction rooms. By the mid-18th century, however, a considerable number of British painters and antiquarians had settled in Italy, especially in Rome, and had become prominent figures there. Many artists had gone abroad to study the arts but found it easier to make their living acting as guides and mentors for young Grand Tourists or as agents or dealers in art and antiquities. The most celebrated of the artist-dealers was GAVIN HAMILTON, who was also a distinguished archaeologist; his patrons included Charles Wyndham, 2nd Earl of Egremont, Henry Temple, 2nd Viscount Palmerston, William Petty, Marquess of Lansdowne and 2nd Earl of Shelburne, and John Spencer, 1st Earl Spencer. Other antiquarians and artists who turned to dealing included JAMES BYRES, THOMAS JENKINS and George Augustus Wallis.

English dealers in Italy included diplomats, bankers and political exiles (usually Jacobites). Of the first group JOSEPH SMITH is the best known. He became British Consul to Venice in 1744 and is best remembered for the sale in 1762 to the young George III of his own collection of pictures formed in Venice, including over 40 works by Canaletto (e.g. *see* VEDUTA, fig. 1). Among other diplomat-collectors and dealers were Horace Walpole's friend and correspondent Sir HORACE MANN, active in Florence from 1738 and appointed Envoy and Plenipotentiary in 1782; Sir William Hamilton (i), Plenipotentiary to Naples from 1764; Robert Udney (*see* UDNEY, (1)), the Consul at Livorno from 1754 to 1766; and, somewhat later, ROBERT FAGAN, especially active as a dealer while British Consul-General in Sicily from 1809.

From the 1730s, however, the auction houses handled the largest share of the art market in England. EDWARD MILLINGTON had held sales at premises in Covent Garden, London, from 1689; the auction room of CHRISTOPHER COCK, also in Covent Garden, was flourishing by 1726, and Abraham Langford (1711–74) held regular picture sales by the mid-18th century. James Christie (1730–1803), founder of the firm that eventually dominated the market for paintings (*see* CHRISTIE'S), was in business in Pall Mall, London, by 1766; the firm of SOTHEBY'S was established earlier (1744), but it initially specialized in selling literary property. Other notable auction houses in business by the end of the 18th century were those of Skinner & Dyke,

JOHN GREENWOOD, H. Phillips of Bond Street, London, PETER COXE (from 1794), George Robins (1778–1847), who had rooms in Covent Garden, Thomas Winstanley and George Stanley. The last two were both art dealers as well as auctioneers.

By the early 19th century the extremely lucrative art trade had become much more organized, and a number of professional picture dealers were operating alongside the auction houses. One of the most important was WILLIAM BUCHANAN, the author of *Memoirs of Painting* (1824), which contains important information concerning the import of works of art into England at this time. Buchanan, who campaigned tirelessly for the foundation of the National Gallery, London, had agents in Italy, Spain and the Netherlands and kept a relatively small stock of high-quality, expensive pictures. In 1896 it was noted that one-third of the paintings in the National Gallery had passed through his hands. JOHN SMITH (ii), another dealer interested in Dutch and Flemish painting, was responsible for the publication between 1829 and 1842 of a remarkable nine-volume *Catalogue Raisonné of the Works of . . . Dutch, Flemish and French Painters.* The principal dealer in drawings was SAMUEL WOODBURN, who helped to form the spectacular collection of Italian Renaissance drawings and prints assembled by the painter THOMAS LAWRENCE. Several of the best-known firms of picture dealers in the 20th century began operating in the more humble but lucrative market of print dealing: COLNAGHI'S was founded in London in 1760 and THOS AGNEW & SONS in Manchester in 1817, moving to London in 1860.

In addition to the professional dealers and auction houses, there was a large contingent of gentlemen collector-dealers active in the late 18th century and the early 19th, for example MICHAEL BRYAN, who imported the Orléans collection, and NOEL JOSEPH DESENFANS, who left the collection he formed for Stanislav II Poniatowski, King of Poland, to his friend the amateur artist Sir PETER FRANCIS BOURGEOIS, who in turn bequeathed it to Dulwich College in 1811 (resulting in the establishment of the Dulwich Picture Gallery, London, in 1814). Alexis Delahante, an émigré from France, also became a successful dealer in London. WILLIAM YOUNG OTTLEY was a well-known connoisseur and writer who in his last years became Keeper of Prints and Drawings at the British Museum. During his visit to Italy from 1791 to 1798, Ottley built up an important collection of early Italian paintings, including Botticelli's *Mystic Nativity* (see BOTTICELLI, SANDRO, fig. 5). This previously neglected but increasingly fashionable area of collecting was also promoted by the activities of EDWARD SOLLY, a Baltic timber merchant and one of the most important *marchands-amateurs*, who owned one of the largest collections of early Italian pictures. By 1819 he had acquired 3000 paintings, which were stored at his house in Berlin. In 1821, when he moved back to England, he sold most of them to the Prussian state, and they formed the basis of the collections in the royal gallery in Berlin (most works now in Berlin, Gemäldegal.). The collection of early Italian paintings formed by the banker and lawyer WILLIAM ROSCOE, with the assistance of the dealer and auctioneer Thomas Winstanley, was also notable; much of it survives in the Walker Art Gallery, Liverpool.

3. AFTER 1840.

(i) Trends in collecting. By the time of the death of Sir Robert Peel in 1850, the number of English collectors of Old Master paintings had diminished. One of the last large-scale purchases of such paintings was that of the collection of the artist and dealer Vincenzo Camuccini by Algernon Percy, 4th Duke of Northumberland (*see* PERCY, (4)), in 1856 for Alnwick Castle, Northumb. Among the Venetian pictures in this collection was the *Feast of the Gods* by Giovanni Bellini and Titian (Washington, DC, N.G.A.). Existing collections were, however, astonishingly rich in Old Master paintings. When the huge exhibition of the *Art Treasures of the United Kingdom* opened in Manchester in 1857, the French critic Théophile Thoré remarked that the 'collection of pictures . . . is about on a level with the Louvre'.

The art critic F. G. Stephens drew attention to the large number of mid-19th-century middle-class collectors of British art in an important series of articles on 'The Private Collections of England', published in *The Athenaeum* between 1873 and 1884. These mention F. R. LEYLAND, JAMES LEATHART, George Rae and many other self-made magnates from such industrial northern cities as Liverpool and Newcastle upon Tyne, who favoured the work of the Pre-Raphaelites and their followers rather than Old Masters. Even Queen Victoria (*see* HANOVER, (6)) was a fervent admirer of contemporary British painting and occasionally bought pictures, usually with a strong narrative content, at the annual exhibition at the Royal Academy, London.

The most notable trend in collecting in the late 19th century and the early 20th was the growth of interest in the decorative arts. The vast collection of medieval and Renaissance glass, maiolica and gems assembled by RALPH BERNAL and sold at auction in 1855 possibly indicates the beginning of the trend, along with the loan of the collection of GEORGE SALTING to the Victoria and Albert Museum, London. The great houses of the ROTHSCHILD family, for example Waddesdon Manor, Bucks, with fine 18th-century furniture and objects of vertu, are a testament to the revival of interest in 18th-century decorative arts in the 1870s. Although a few collections of Old Master paintings, for example those of EDWARD CECIL GUINNESS, 1st Earl of Iveagh (London, Kenwood House), and the Cook family, were still being formed in the late 19th century with the help of such dealers as Agnew's, such works were not generally popular among collectors in the 20th century. Nevertheless, the collection formed by Sir John and Lady Heathcote Amory with the help of Sir Geoffrey Agnew was notable. Relatively few English collectors bought works by the French Impressionists: one notable exception was Samuel Courtauld (*see* COURTAULD, (1)), whose collection, possibly influenced by that of the Irishman Sir Hugh Lane, was donated to the University of London and housed in the Courtauld Institute Galleries from 1931. The collection includes such well-known works as Manet's *A Bar at the Folies-Bergères* (*see* MANET, EDOUARD, fig. 3). Roger Fry, Sir Michael Ernest Sadler (1861–1943) and Clive Bell all purchased works by French Post-Impressionist painters in the first decade of the 20th century.

A notable development in the 20th century was the formation of collections of Chinese ceramics by such Englishmen as Sir PERCIVAL DAVID, who spent much of his business career in East Asia and who presented his holdings to the University of London. The International Exhibition of Chinese Art held at the Royal Academy, London, in the winter of 1935–6 undoubtedly encouraged this trend. Numerous collections of East Asian ceramics were bequeathed to English museums in the mid-20th century, and the collecting of English ceramics and glassware also became fashionable. In the fine arts, the Leicester Galleries in London helped to promote the works of modernist English artists of the inter-war years. Around this time there were two prominent collectors of Surrealist art: ROLAND PENROSE and EDWARD JAMES. With Old Master paintings being sold for enormous sums, many English collectors in the mid-20th century concentrated on acquiring drawings and watercolours, particularly by British artists. Among these scholar-collectors were Sir Robert Witt (1872–1952), Sir Bruce Ingram (1877–1963), who donated 700 drawings by Dutch marine artists to the National Maritime Museum, London, in 1957, A. PAUL OPPÉ, Iolo Williams and Martin Hardie, some of whom indulged their passion for collecting with the organizing of exhibitions for the Arts Council of Great Britain after World War II. During the mid- and late 20th century a number of corporate art collections were formed, many of which include works by 20th-century British artists. Such businessmen as ROBERT SAINSBURY and CHARLES SAATCHI also formed important private art collections.

(ii) Dispersal of collections and art legislation. By the time of Queen Victoria's Golden Jubilee in 1887, a number of large collections were being dispersed. The sale of the collection of Richard Plantagenet Temple Nugent Brydges Chandos Grenville, 2nd Duke of Buckingham and Chandos (1797–1861), at Stowe, Bucks, in 1848, although large, was less important than the earlier sale of 174 paintings from Sir Robert Walpole's collection to Empress Catherine II of Russia in 1779, and it was relatively unusual for a nobleman to part with art treasures in the mid-19th century. The decline of English agriculture and the subsequent drop in land values and rents, however, meant that many families, unable to sell off settled land or heirlooms, found it impossible to maintain their homes. To counteract this emergency, the Settled Lands Act was passed in 1882, making it possible for the trustees of settlements, on application to the Chancery, to sell land and chattels, providing the proceeds remained in trusteeship. As a result of this legislation, a large number of country-house collections were sold, notably most of that at Blenheim Palace in 1884. Numerous other collections were sold to foreign dealers during the late 19th century, and many works were acquired by immensely wealthy American collectors, including Henry Clay Frick, Daniel Huntington, J. Pierpont Morgan and Andrew W. Mellon, who were supplied by the dealer JOSEPH DUVEEN, later 1st Baron Duveen of Millbank, and ROBERT LANGTON DOUGLAS. Although concern about the export of important works of art led to the foundation of the National Art-Collections Fund in 1903, it was not until the Waverley criteria were drawn up in 1952 that any serious effort was

made by a British government to stem the flood of exports. The Waverley criteria empowered a committee appointed by the government temporarily to stop the export of works of art that were first 'so closely associated with our national life that departure would be a misfortune', second 'of outstanding aesthetic importance' and third 'of outstanding significance for the study of some particular branch of art, learning or history'. The issue of an export licence could be delayed for a few months in order to give British public (or private) collections the opportunity to match the purchase price. This legislation continues to operate throughout the United Kingdom.

BIBLIOGRAPHY
F. H. Taylor: *The Taste of Angels: A History of Art Collecting from Rameses to Napoleon* (London, 1948)
F. Simpson: 'Dutch Paintings in England before 1760', *Burl. Mag.*, xcv (1953), pp. 39–42
G. Reitlinger: *The Economics of Taste: The Rise and Fall of the Picture Market, 1760–1960* (London, 1961)
F. Herrmann: *The English as Collectors: A Documentary Chrestomathy* (London, 1972)
O. Millar: *The Queen's Pictures* (London, 1977)
F. Haskell: 'The British as Collectors', *The Treasure Houses of Britain: Five Hundred Years of Private Patronage and Art Collecting* (exh. cat., Washington, DC, N.G.A., 1985), pp. 50–59
I. Pears: *The Discovery of Painting: The Growth of Interest in the Arts in England, 1680–1768* (New Haven and London, 1988)
A. Braham: 'Towards a National Gallery', *National Art-Collections Fund Annual Report: Eighty-sixth Year* (London, 1989), pp. 78–92
For further bibliography *see under* the entries for those individuals indicated by cross-references.

XIV. Museums.

1. Before 1820. 2. 1820–*c.* 1845. 3. *c.* 1845–90. 4. After 1890.

1. BEFORE 1820. The origins of the numerous public museums now found throughout England can be traced back to the great private collections of the 16th, 17th and 18th centuries. The earliest rooms designed specifically for the display of collections of curiosities were the cabinets (*see* CABINET (i)) of the aristocracy in the 16th and 17th centuries. In 1611 Inigo Jones built a 'Cabinet Room' at St James's Palace, London, for the collection of paintings of Henry, Prince of Wales. With a few exceptions, for example Thomas Howard, 2nd Earl of Arundel (*see* HOWARD (i), (1)), there were no English collectors with private 'museums' as renowned as those of contemporary French and Italian cardinals and German princes in the early 17th century. Gradually, however, a new type of collection emerged, the gentleman scholar dedicated to the pursuit of learning. By 1660 there was widespread interest in collecting and systematically classifying specimens and rarities of nature. It was within this tradition that the Ashmolean Museum at Oxford University—possibly the first museum, in the modern sense, in England—was established. It was housed in a repository, built between 1679 and 1683 and designed specifically for the preservation and display of antiquities and curiosities collected by John Tradescant the elder (*see* TRADESCANT) and presented to the University by ELIAS ASHMOLE.

From the beginning of the 18th century connoisseurs of painting and sculpture came to dominate the field of collecting, and matters of taste and aesthetics displaced a fascination for the bizarre and curious. The gradual transition from private to public collections, however, which began in the mid-18th century, was far from straightforward, as illustrated by the history of the establishment of the British Museum, London. The collections of the British Museum originated in the multifarious private collections of HANS SLOANE, which were housed first in Great Russell Street and later in Cheyne Walk, London. In 1749 Sloane made his will, bequeathing his collections, including manuscripts, coins and medals, to the nation, in exchange for payment of £20,000 to his family, and in 1753 an Act of Parliament permitted the use of a lottery to finance the deal. In addition, the manuscripts collection of Sir ROBERT BRUCE COTTON and the outstanding collection of books and manuscripts of Edward Harley, 2nd Earl of Oxford (*see* HARLEY, (2)), were acquired. The elegant but otherwise unsuitable Montagu House in Bloomsbury was then purchased from George Montagu-Dunk, 2nd Earl of Halifax (1716–91), and refurbished; the Museum opened in January 1759. Although this was the first museum in Europe specifically intended to be open to the public, in practice entry was severely restricted. For years after its foundation there was a limit of 60 visitors per day, and only in the early 19th century were several of the other restrictions concerning public access lifted. Although Parliament provided a meagre annual grant, money was made available (albeit under pressure) for especially important purchases, the most significant of these being the acquisition of the collection of Greek vases belonging to Sir WILLIAM HAMILTON (i) in 1772, the collection of sculpture, bronzes and gems owned by CHARLES TOWNLEY in 1805 and 1814, and the Parthenon Marbles (collected by THOMAS BRUCE, 7th Earl of Elgin) in 1814–15. The purchase of the last in particular enhanced the Museum's international reputation in the field of Classical antiquities, which had been established by the creation of a Department of Antiquities in 1807.

There were no public picture galleries in England in the mid-18th century. The privileged could gain access to private collections both in London and in country houses, but for the artist and those lower down the social order the main opportunity to see Old Master paintings was provided by the auction houses or the collections (containing relatively few paintings) of churches and cathedrals. From the mid-1740s the Foundling Hospital in Bloomsbury, London, displayed contemporary art presented by the leading artists associated with William Hogarth's St Martin's Lane Academy, but public access was again limited.

In 1777 the controversial John Wilkes (1727–97) suggested the foundation of a national gallery at the British Museum, in an unsuccessful attempt to prevent the sale of most of the collection of Robert Walpole, 1st Earl of Orford, from Houghton Hall, Norfolk, to Empress Catherine II of Russia. Wilkes was also concerned at that date about George III's removal of the celebrated Raphael Cartoons (London, V&A) from Hampton Court Palace to Buckingham House in London. The Cartoons had gradually been made available for public inspection in Christopher Wren's purpose-built gallery at Hampton Court, where they had been installed since 1699. Another failed scheme for a national gallery that would have comprised works by members of the Royal Academy is described in Joseph Farington's *Diaries* in 1799, and a year later the painter John Opie also conceived a plan for a 'National Gallery of Art' that was not executed. The display of such important collections as the Orléans Collection before sale in London in the 1790s and the installation of part of the French royal collection in the Palais du Luxembourg, Paris, as early as 1750 also increased interest in the creation of a permanent collection of Old Master paintings accessible to the British public.

One of the earliest purpose-built galleries, however, was that designed in 1788 by George Dance the younger on the north side of Pall Mall, London, for JOHN BOYDELL's short-lived Shakespeare Gallery, where works by Joshua Reynolds, Benjamin West and Joseph Wright of Derby were displayed, and which was later used as the premises of the British Institution, founded in 1805. The interior consisted of three amply proportioned interconnecting rooms lit from the top. This suite of rooms provided the inspiration for Sir JOHN SOANE's design for Dulwich Picture Gallery, London, one of the first galleries open to the public, built in 1811 to house the collection of Sir PETER FRANCIS BOURGEOIS, bequeathed to Dulwich College, and opened in 1814. Three years earlier Soane had built, albeit on a smaller scale, a similar arrangement of rooms at the back of No. 13 Lincoln's Inn Fields, London, to form the rear gallery of what is now Sir John Soane's Museum (*see* §2 below). The gallery contained a library, a 'plaister room' and a 'catacomb' in the basement, but Soane collectively called it a museum in order to distinguish it from the house that he built in front of it, facing Lincoln's Inn Fields, in 1812.

2. 1820–*c*. 1845. From the 1820s increased interest in the visual arts and the development of middle-class provincial culture, exemplified by the profusion of literary and philosophical societies, gave impetus to the establishment of a number of public and university museums and galleries in London and the provinces. One of the earliest and most imposing of these was the Royal Institution of Fine Arts at Manchester (now the Manchester City Art Gallery). In 1823 it was suggested that an institute based on both the British Institution and the Royal Academy in London should be created to organize exhibitions of works by contemporary British artists and to establish a school of art. Although the response from northern nobility was cool, the businessmen of Manchester, persuaded by the potential economic benefits to the city, were immensely enthusiastic. In 1824 a museum was established in the same building as the gallery designed by the young Charles Barry, who had won the architectural competition for the new building. The classical style of this building (completed 1835) is less indebted to English versions of the Greek Revival than to French styles, resulting in one of the best examples of medium-sized Neo-classical museums in England. Although most of its interiors have been remodelled, the entrance hall, with its conspicuous attic storey, is similar to the dramatic proportions of Schinkel's Museum (1823–30; now the Altes Museum) in Berlin.

In 1823 the Trustees of the British Museum also approved a design for a complete rebuilding of Montagu House in Bloomsbury. The original holdings of the Museum had grown considerably, and the prestige of the institution was such that the government was persuaded that a building commensurate with the quality of the holdings was appropriate. The design was entrusted to Robert Smirke (ii), rather than his older colleagues at the Board of Works, Soane and John Nash (i). By the time of its completion in 1848, Smirke's Greek Revival building was decidedly old-fashioned in style, but the galleries and especially the entrance hall and staircase possess a strength and unity for which the architect has infrequently been credited. In the early 19th century the idea of establishing a national gallery was of increasing popular interest and was realized in 1824, when Parliament purchased for the nation 38 paintings from the collection of the banker JOHN JULIUS ANGERSTEIN, together with the lease of his house at 100 Pall Mall, for £57,000. The National Gallery was, however, one of the last of the great European galleries to be established, following the Louvre, Paris (1793), the Royal Museum, Stockholm (1794), and the Rijksmuseum, Amsterdam (1808). In 1832 WILLIAM WIL-KINS won the architectural competition for the design of a building to house the National Gallery (shared with the Royal Academy until 1869), which was erected, in contrast to the slow construction of the new British Museum, between 1834 and 1837 on the north side of what subsequently became Trafalgar Square in London. In 1838 the collections of the Gallery, with additional bequests from Sir GEORGE BEAUMONT, who had encouraged the purchase of the works from Angerstein's collection, and the Rev. WILLIAM HOLWELL CARR, were moved to the new building. Wilkins's building was one of the last English museum buildings to be designed in the Greek Revival style.

Sir John Soane's Museum (*see* SOANE, JOHN) in his London house was opened to the public after his death in 1837, but for some years he had been considering its purpose as an educational institution promoting the study of painting, sculpture and architecture. His private Act of Parliament, passed in 1833, by which the collection was given to the nation, required that free admission be given to the house 'at least two days in every week throughout the months of April, May and June . . . to Amateurs and Students in Painting, Sculpture and Architecture, and to such other persons as shall apply for and obtain admission thereto'. In the first brief guidebook to the collection, Soane explained that he was hoping to illustrate the close connections between painting, sculpture, architecture, music and poetry by arranging his collection in a certain way; he stipulated that the objects should not be moved 'from the positions relatively assigned to them; they having been arranged as studies for my own mind, and being intended similarly to benefit the Artists of future generations'. Soane also hoped that his collection would help visitors to educate themselves.

In the years following the establishment of the National Gallery and other public galleries and museums, significant progress was also made in the development of museums at the universities of Oxford and Cambridge. On his death in 1816, RICHARD FITZWILLIAM, 7th Viscount Fitzwilliam of Merrion, had bequeathed to Cambridge University, his *alma mater*, his collection of Old Master paintings, prints and his library, as well as considerable funds for a 'substantial and convenient Museum'. The winner of the competition to design the new building was Soane's former pupil George Basevi. Work began on the building of the Fitzwilliam Museum in 1837: the exterior, with its continuous colonnade breaking forward to form an eight-column portico, was inspired by Smirke's design of the new British Museum. The portico, hall and staircase formed almost half the total area of the original building, the remaining space being occupied by the top-lit galleries or 'picture rooms', which are among the finest in Britain; the design of these may have been derived from that of the principal gallery at the Alte Pinakothek (1825–36) in Munich by Leo von Klenze.

After Basevi's death in 1845, work on the Fitzwilliam, which was almost completed by this date, was continued by C. R. Cockerell, who was already at work on the new Ashmolean Museum and Taylorian Institution (1839–45; see COCKERELL, fig. 2) in Oxford, replacing the 17th-century building on Broad Street with one in a curious hybrid style, combining elements of Greek Revival with Italian Mannerism. The new Ashmolean and Fitzwilliam Museum buildings have much in common: construction was begun in the same decade by the same builders, and the same ornamental sculptors were employed to execute the decoration. Unlike the Fitzwilliam, however, which consists almost entirely of galleries, the Ashmolean was primarily designed to contain lecture rooms and a library, and the most urgent requirement was a purpose-built space for the Arundel Marbles, which had not been properly housed since they were presented to the University in the 18th century. By comparison with the collections of the Fitzwilliam, the holdings of paintings at the Ashmolean were negligible in the mid-19th century.

3. *c*. 1845–90. In 1845 the Museums Act was passed, empowering local boroughs to use a proportion of the rates to establish 'Public Museums of Art and Science'. The bill was introduced by William Ewart (1798–1869), who had been associated with the Parliamentary Select Committee of 1835–6 that had recommended that 'the opening of public galleries for the people should, as much as possible, be encouraged'. The Act stipulated that entry to museums should not exceed one penny; this stricture was superseded by the Museums and Libraries Act of 1850, which insisted on free entry. As a result a considerable number of municipal museums were created in the 1850s and 1860s. The building of a museum was often due to the presentation of an important collection; if this was not offered, local councillors generally preferred to construct a library or another civic building of more practical purpose. The great trade exhibitions of the mid-19th century also affected the development of museums. In 1852 a museum that included works purchased from the Great Exhibition of 1851 in London was established by HENRY COLE at Marlborough House, London, with the aim of improving public taste. This became the basis of the South Kensington Museum (later the Victoria and Albert Museum), which became one of the most influential museums in the 19th century. Prince Albert was the moving force behind the creation of the South Kensington Museum, and his original idea was to create a cultural centre in South Kensington that embraced all the arts and sciences. Although a group of autonomous institutions was eventually established, the increased awareness of the value of culture and the necessity of the arts in mid-19th-century Britain must be partly credited to him. The National Portrait Gallery, the creation of which may have been inspired by the two exhibitions of portraits at South Kensington, was also established in 1856.

From about 1860 the most progressive museum design was evident in the South Kensington Museum building. The supremacy of the classical style as the most suitable for museum buildings had, however, already been challenged by Deane & Woodward's Oxford Museum (1855–61; now the University Museum, Oxford), executed in Ruskinian Gothic. The innovations at South Kensington included the use of iron construction and the application of high-quality sculptural ornament, often in terracotta and ceramics, for both interior and exterior features. A good example is the South Court and the Quadrangle, where both Gothic and classical styles are employed.

Many of the provincial galleries and museums established in the late 19th century were inspired by Henry Cole's ideas concerning the educational purpose of museums, put into practice at Marlborough House and South Kensington. Another influence was John Ruskin's writings, which promoted the idea of providing, by means of drawings, prints, photographs and casts, images of a more beautiful and civilized world for those living in particularly deprived areas. These philanthropic concepts contrasted sharply with the élitist ideas prevalent at the beginning of the 19th century. Among the museums created at this time were the Royal Albert Memorial Museum in Exeter (1865), another example of High Gothic, Brighton Art Gallery and Museum (1873), the Walker Art Gallery, Liverpool (1877), York City Art Gallery (1879), Wolverhampton Art Gallery (1884) and the City of Birmingham Museum and Art Gallery (1885). The establishment of the Museums Association in 1889 was a further indication of the growing professionalism and changing attitudes in the museum world.

4. AFTER 1890. By the end of the 1890s the number of new provincial museums being built had begun to decline, although the elaborate Bury Art Gallery and Museum (founded 1897) and Cartwright Hall in Bradford are indicative of the confidence of the civic authorities of major northern cities at the end of the 19th century. In London, meanwhile, the idea of a national gallery of British art finally reached fruition with the establishment of the Tate Gallery. Although the idea had been current for many years, successive governments had failed to provide funds for a building to house the collections of ROBERT VERNON and JOHN SHEEPSHANKS (that of the latter now forms part of the collection of the Victoria and Albert Museum), as well as the few British paintings in the National Gallery. In 1889 the sugar magnate Sir HENRY TATE offered to the National Gallery his collection of modern British art, which was refused due to lack of space. Tate then offered to provide funds for a building to house the collection, provided the government allocated the land; the site of the former Millbank Penitentiary was eventually chosen. Tate chose the architect, the obscure Sidney R. J. Smith

(1858–1913), who, after numerous modifications, designed a building with Beaux-Arts classical features. The Gallery was opened in 1897. The national art collections were also enhanced at the turn of the 19th century by the government's acceptance of the Wallace Collection, bequeathed by Lady Wallace, widow of Sir Richard Wallace (see SEYMOUR-CONWAY, (3)), in 1897. This includes many high-quality 18th-century French paintings (of which there were few in the National Gallery) and decorative arts, notably Sèvres porcelain.

In 1901 the additions to the South Kensington Museum were begun, using Aston Webb's winning entry in the design competition, and the Museum was finally re-opened in 1909 by Edward VII as the Victoria and Albert Museum. The design echoes that of Alfred Waterhouse's neighbouring Natural History Museum (1872; opened 1881; for illustration see WATERHOUSE, ALFRED) without imitating it, resulting in a Renaissance-style building without columns and pilasters. A similar design, on a much smaller scale, had been conceived by Ewan Christian for the St Martin's Lane façade of the new building for the National Portrait Gallery (opened 1895), London, which resulted in an elevation similar to that of a Florentine Renaissance palazzo, together with a dash of Romanesque.

The few museums built between the two World Wars were frequently the result of private munificence. The Lady Lever Art Gallery (opened in 1922) at Port Sunlight, near Liverpool, was part of the model village built by WILLIAM HESKETH LEVER, 1st Viscount Leverhulme, to house workers at his soap factory. Lord Leverhulme believed passionately in the importance of a visually stimulating environment, and his gallery is one of the last products of late 19th-century philanthropic attitudes. Other museums and galleries founded by individual benefactors include the Usher Art Gallery, Lincoln (1927); the Williamson Art Gallery and Museum, Birkenhead (1928); the Graves Art Gallery, Sheffield (1934); and the Barber Institute of Fine Arts at the University of Birmingham (1939). The building housing the Barber Institute in particular shows a pronounced shift away from classicism: Robert Atkinson was appointed to provide a building, financed by Lady Barber's bequest, for 'the study and encouragement of art and music', and he produced a striking Modernist design using high-quality materials. A flexible approach to the design of galleries is evident, with a conscious rejection of the notion of the temple, palace or great private house, which had been popular in museum design in the 18th and 19th centuries. The galleries, arranged in rows around a central core, are divided into bays separated by V-shape partitions, avoiding the potentially wearying effect of a continuous wall of paintings.

Styles of picture-hanging had also changed radically by the inter-war years. The decorative and cluttered arrangements that British collectors had adopted from the great continental collections of the 17th and 18th centuries were common in the early public galleries, including the National Gallery when it was located in Angerstein's house in Pall Mall. By the 1840s this had been superseded by arrangement with national schools. Less crowded arrangements gradually became fashionable, and by the 1880s the single-row hang was generally accepted. The tendency from the 1930s and 1940s was towards obliterating the character of older galleries in favour of false ceilings, neutral colours and artificial lighting, but from the late 1970s the works in the Wallace Collection and National Gallery were displayed using traditional arrangements.

With a few exceptions, for example the Sainsbury Centre for the Visual Arts at the University of East Anglia in Norwich, the development of English museums and galleries after World War II largely involved additions to older galleries. The Sainsbury Centre, opened in 1978, is an enormous hanger-like High Tech structure designed by NORMAN FOSTER. It has the dual purpose of displaying a wide variety of art objects from the collection of Sir ROBERT SAINSBURY as well as housing the art history department of the University. James Stirling's Clore Gallery for the Turner Collection at the Tate Gallery, opened in 1985, and the Sainsbury Wing at the National Gallery by Venturi, Rauch & Scott Brown, opened in 1991, both use traditional materials, although in quite different ways: the Post-modernist elements of the former contrast with the cool serenity of the latter, the design of which, redolent of a Florentine church, is appropriate for the early Renaissance paintings that it houses. In the late 20th century there was also a trend towards decentralizing national museums, and branches of the Tate Gallery were established in Liverpool (1988) and St Ives (1993).

BIBLIOGRAPHY

J. Jones: 'Museum and Art Gallery Buildings in England, 1845–1914', *Mus. J.*, lxv (1965), pp. 230–38; (1966), pp. 271–80
K. Hudson: *A Social History of Museums: What the Visitors Thought* (London, 1975)
——: *Museums of Influence* (Cambridge, 1985)
J. Summerson: 'The Architecture of British Museums and Galleries', *The Fine and Decorative Art Collections of Great Britain and Ireland*, ed. J. Chapel and C. Gere (London, 1985), pp. 9–19
Palaces of Art: Art Galleries in Britain, 1790–1990 (exh. cat., ed. G. Waterfield; London, Dulwich Pict. Gal.; Edinburgh, N.G.; 1991–2)

BRIAN ALLEN

XV. Art education.

1. Before 1768. 2. 1768–1920. 3. After 1920.

1. BEFORE 1768. From the Middle Ages until the 18th century the principal artistic organization in England was the Painter-Stainers Company, which oversaw apprenticeships and laid down rules for professional painters; other guilds included the masons, carpenters, goldsmiths and tilers. Before 1711 many fine artists were trained abroad or were apprenticed to court painters, while cathedral workshops and those of individual artists and craftsmen also provided tuition. Attempts to form art schools in the 17th century, such as the Museum Minervae (1635) in Covent Garden, London, were intended for the gentleman or connoisseur and included draughtsmanship among other 'manly arts' such as fencing and riding. From the 17th century, the Society of Virtuosi of St Luke and later the Rose and Crown Club had professional artists among their members, but their aims were to encourage convivial exchange of artistic ideas, with no formal instruction given. The very existence of such clubs implied, however, that artists were starting to feel the need to band together.

The first organized institution for professional artistic training in Britain was Godfrey Kneller's Academy in Great Queen Street, London, formed in 1711 to promote drawing and painting from life, and attendance at which cost a small fee. Other founder-members included Giovanni Antonio Pellegrini, JAMES THORNHILL and George Vertue. Thornhill succeeded Kneller as Governor in 1716 but was deposed by Louis Chéron and John Vanderbank, who re-established the Academy in St Martin's Lane in 1720. The new Academy instituted the use of the female model, purportedly to attract business. Hogarth, Kent and Joseph Highmore, among others, attended classes there, and the Academy existed until embezzlement led to its closure.

In competition, Thornhill opened a new academy in Covent Garden in October 1722, and Hogarth later opened a second St Martin's Lane Academy in 1735. Although this institution likewise stressed draughtsmanship and study from life, its egalitarian structure gave all subscribers an equal vote, and a sub-committee selected potential students. The St Martin's Lane Academy was taken over by the Incorporated Society later in the century. In addition to these institutions George Michael Moser (i) opened a school for painting and drawing from life c. 1735, and WILLIAM SHIPLEY ran an art school in the Strand, London, in the 1750s and 1760s. Artists also continued at this time to begin their training through contractual apprenticeships, and in addition they were sometimes able to study works in private collections. Dr Richard Mead opened his house in Great Ormond Street to students, giving them access to master works until his death in 1754, when his collection (see §XIII, 2(i)) was dispersed. At the Duke of Richmond's Gallery in Whitehall, opened to students in 1758, teaching was more structured. Giovanni Battista Cipriani and Joseph Wilton instructed, and private drawing schools sent students. The Incorporated Society later took control of the gallery in 1770, but poor student conduct, including mutilation of casts, led to its closure in the 1780s. In the 17th century and the early 18th sculptors usually trained in the studios or yards of other sculptors, sometimes family businesses such as that of the Stantons (see STANTON). Michael Rysbrack worked for Michiel van der Voort, and Peter Scheemakers worked for his father Peter Scheemakers (i) and then for Francis Bird and Denis Plumier (1688–1721). Joseph Nollekens was in turn apprenticed to Scheemakers, whom the young Thomas Banks also visited each evening. Architectural training remained largely a matter of a craft apprenticeship, although in the 16th and 17th centuries some craftsmen who had served apprenticeships began to establish themselves as craftsmen–architects. Indeed, the medieval system of building, whereby a group of skilled craftsmen collaborated on both design and construction, continued until well into the 18th century, although by this time the roles of designer and builder were starting to diverge.

2. 1768–1920.

(i) The Royal Academy Schools. (ii) The growth of new schools. (iii). Architectural education. (iv) Outside the institutions: amateur art training and the education of women.

(i) The Royal Academy Schools. The Royal Academy Schools were established in Pall Mall in 1768, moving to Old Somerset House in 1771; they charged no tuition fee and were funded by profits from annual exhibitions. The training programme was laborious and rigid, reflecting both the hieratic nature of the Academy and its devotion to an encouragement of history painting, which was considered intellectually superior to other genres. Initially students drew from plaster casts in the 'antique school' before passing on to life classes, which were restricted to married men aged over 20. Public lectures were also delivered by professors of anatomy, architecture, painting, perspective and geometry, and, after 1810, sculpture; a painting school was created in 1815 for the copying of Old Masters. The first professorships were held by William Hunter for anatomy, Edward Penny for painting, Samuel Wale for perspective and geometry, and Thomas Sandby for architecture. John Flaxman became the first professor of sculpture in 1810. The first students of the Royal Academy Schools, who included William Hamilton (ii), Joseph Farington, Francis Wheatley and Flaxman, were primarily men who had previously been apprenticed to manufacturers, scene painters and other artisans. Only a few exceptional students achieved membership of the Royal Academy. From 77 students at the end of the first year, the number of students enrolled had increased to 814 by 1800. Incentives for students included free admission to Royal Academy exhibitions, medals and travel scholarships. The annual summer exhibitions also provided the opportunity for sculptors, in particular, to show portrait busts and even designs for monuments, in the hope of receiving new commissions.

From the beginning, however, the Royal Academy Schools attracted much criticism. In 1799 Academicians complained about indiscriminate acceptance of students, although stricter entrance and examination requirements did not come into force for many years. Direct criticism came from reports made to the Royal Commissions of 1836 and 1863. The Academy Schools were first censured for their obsession with life classes to the detriment of architectural studies and industrial application of art. Laxity of professors was also criticized, and Turner, among others, was admonished for neglecting his lectures. In the wake of Liberal reforms the second Commission was more thorough in its consideration of structure, and Edward Armitage submitted a revised organization of the Schools based on the French *atelier* model. However, only minor changes were adopted, arousing much indignation and paving the way for the opening of competitive fine art training institutions. The Schools moved to Burlington House in 1869, and in 1887 an internal committee was appointed to suggest reforms.

See also LONDON, §VI.

(ii) The growth of new schools. As part of his campaign to encourage state support of the visual arts and to break the virtual monopoly of art education exercised by the Royal Academy, Benjamin Robert Haydon was from the 1820s one of the most vigorous supporters of a national art school, prompting the establishment in 1836 of the Select Committee on Arts and their Connections with Manufacture. The Committee recommended setting up a new Government School of Design under the Board of Trade, and this opened in Somerset House in 1837 under the architect J. B. Papworth. The students, however, were more interested in becoming fine artists than designers, although the Royal Academicians among the school's

governors ensured that there would be no life-drawing classes that might rival their schools, and industrialists were unwilling to send their apprentices. In these dispiriting circumstances the proposals for reform made by WILLIAM DYCE were greeted with approval. In 1838 Dyce was appointed Superintendent, and, having studied art education in France and Germany, he introduced a course based on scientific principles of design and their direct application to industry. Even at the final stage of the course, however, students were obliged to copy engraved examples from Dyce's *Drawing Book* (1843) rather than actual flowers or fruit. Those who expressed ambitions to become fine artists were frowned upon.

In his *Journal of Design and Manufactures* (1849–52) HENRY COLE attacked the failures of the School of Design, which was widely blamed for the poor standard of British products at the Great Exhibition in London in 1851. The School closed in 1852, to be replaced by the Department of Practical Art (from 1853 the Department of Art and Science), with Cole as its head, and this moved to South Kensington in 1857. Cole and his art superintendent, Richard Redgrave (*see* REDGRAVE, (2)), dominated art education for the next two decades. Although Cole's avowed aims were utilitarian his regime increasingly emphasized mastery of a narrow range of drawing techniques rather than broader or more practical design skills. His principal instrument was the National Course of Instruction devised by Redgrave for all the state schools of art. The course prepared students for the National Competition, held annually between 1852 and 1915; its methodical nature was reflected in the drawings submitted for competition medals, which often took over a year to produce and were generally lifeless or unoriginal, although a few medal-winning National Scholars became leading artists (e.g. Luke Fildes and Hubert von Herkomer). Those seeking practical training in industrial design, for whom the Schools had originally been set up, were gradually forced out by the fees, and few professional designers were produced by the system (Christopher Dresser being a notable exception). The central National Art Training School (as it became in 1863) concentrated increasingly on training art teachers, particularly those destined for regional art schools. In addition, women were permitted to study sculpture theory; early students included Ruby Levick (*fl* 1894–1921), Esther Mary Moore (*fl* 1890–1911) and Florence Steele (*fl* 1896–1918).

One of the earliest and most important regional art schools was established in Manchester in 1838. Under John Bell (until 1843) it provided lectures, a museum of approved examples and a course of instruction. Despite Dyce's protests, life drawing was included, as local industrialists, on whom the school depended heavily for support, considered a broad artistic training would be more useful for their designers. Schools were subsequently set up in York (1842), Birmingham (1843), Norwich (1845) and elsewhere. From the 1850s Cole attempted to bring the regional schools under more central control and impose a standardized curriculum, but local government and private sponsors retained considerable freedom to develop their schools as they wished. In 1838 Haydon set up a rival School for Promoting Practical Design, in which life drawing was central to the curriculum. Many other, mostly minor, artists also set up private art schools in the 19th century, and while these provided an alternative to a Royal Academy or state education, they also bolstered the status quo. The first was Henry Sass (1788–1844), whose drawing school in London principally prepared young artists for the Royal Academy Schools in a traditional manner; it continued from 1842 under F. S. Carey, whose rival James Mathews Leigh (1808–60) opened his own school in 1845 with a group of dissatisfied ex-students of the Schools of Design. Leigh was succeeded in 1860 by T. J. Heatherley, one of the most successful art teachers of the late 19th century. Their students, who included Edward Burne-Jones, Albert Joseph Moore, Edward John Poynter and Alfred Gilbert, copied antique casts but were also allowed to draw from the nude model without restriction. The St John's Wood School of Art and the school opened by Byam Shaw and Rex Vicat Cole (1870–1940) in 1910 (*see* SHAW, BYAM, (1)) continued to direct their pupils towards the Royal Academy. Hubert von Herkomer, however, sought a more independent stance for his school (opened in 1883) in Bushey, Herts, in which no particular style was advocated and greater emphasis was placed on oil sketching.

In the late 19th century, new developments in art education reflected new influences at work in English art theory and practice. Although the chief inspiration of the Arts and Crafts Movement, William Morris, had only a limited interest in art education, he had considerable influence on such organizations as the ART WORKERS' GUILD (founded 1884), many of whose members (notably WALTER CRANE and W. R. LETHABY) became influential teachers. In such books as *The Claims of Decorative Art* (1892) Crane attacked Richard Redgrave's rigid and, as he thought, spuriously scientific system of instruction at South Kensington, believing instead that artistic creativity and originality could be found only through direct practical experience of handicrafts. In 1893 he became part-time Director of Design at the Manchester School of Art, and in 1898 he was appointed principal of the Royal College of Art (formerly the National Art Training School), where he introduced practical classes in enamelling, bookbinding, handicrafts, pottery and stained glass.

The Technical Instruction Act (1899) gave power to local councils to levy a rate for technical instruction, and, as a result, in the following years many municipal authorities took over their local schools of design, introducing more vocational training and responding more readily to local industrial needs. In London W. R. LETHABY became Principal of the Council's newly established Central School of Arts and Crafts in 1896. He set up well-equipped workshops to teach principally those crafts that had been revived by the Arts and Crafts Movement—bookbinding, book production and illustration, metalwork, jewellery, cabinet-making and stained glass—and he drew on the Arts and Crafts Movement for his teachers. Lethaby and his staff brought a new professionalism to the teaching of practical design skills, but they were deeply equivocal in their attitude towards the place of the machine (and particularly mass production) in the design process. Nevertheless, the Central School rapidly established an international reputation for the quality of its workshop training.

Lethaby remained in charge until 1901, when he moved to the Royal College of Art to introduce similar ideas.

Another important institution founded in the late 19th century was the Slade School of Fine Art, which opened in 1871 as part of University College, London. Its character was first established by the French Realist artist Alphonse Legros, who succeeded Edward John Poynter as professor in 1876. Legros introduced French academic ideas, most notably the mastery of rapid oil sketching, memory training and figure draughtsmanship, in which contour rather than outline and hatching expressed three-dimensional form; the latter became a hallmark of the Slade's training. Legros also introduced competitions, prizes and travel scholarships, as well as an etching class. FREDERICK BROWN, a critical but open-minded teacher at the Westminster School of Art from 1877 to 1892, introduced to the Slade an appreciation of developments at the New English Art Club by his appointments of HENRY TONKS and Philip Wilson Steer, who taught such artists as Ambrose McEvoy, Augustus John and William Orpen; the Camden Town Group painters Harold Gilman, James Dickson Innes and Spencer Gore; the Bloomsbury Group artists Duncan Grant and Mark Gertler; and the Vorticists Wyndham Lewis, Christopher Nevinson, Edward Wadsworth, William Roberts and David Bomberg.

(iii) Architectural education. In the late 18th century many aspiring architects began to be trained through the emerging practice of pupilage. ROBERT TAYLOR is believed to have first established this system, and pupils in his London office in the 1770s included Samuel Pepys Cockerell and John Nash (i). Additional guidance in drawing was often undertaken at an art school, and regular attendance of classes and lectures at the Royal Academy Schools remained a significant part of architectural education until the mid-19th century; both the Royal Academy and the Society of Arts included architectural drawings in the annual exhibitions.

Architectural students at the Royal Academy were, however, given less opportunity than their peers in the fine arts, and in 1810 one former pupil, James Elmes (1782–1862), attempted unsuccessfully to initiate a royal academy of architecture that would, among other things, grant students levels of facilities equal to those of the fine arts counterparts. In 1831 the Architectural Society was founded with the long-term aim of setting up a library and a museum of drawings, architectural models and other aids, as well as holding exhibitions and establishing professorships. Three years later the Institute of British Architects (IBA) was formed, with J. B. Papworth as a founder-member. This was to develop into the more powerful organization, later absorbing the Architectural Society. The IBA (from 1866 the Royal Institute of British Architects, or RIBA) increasingly became the profession's regulatory body, defining the architect's responsibilities.

In the 19th century, as new building types and materials were developed and as architecture became increasingly competitive, efficient office practice became fundamental. Working drawings became increasingly detailed, and contracts became more specific with regard to materials and workmanship. In the 1840s London colleges began to increase the amount of training that articled pupils received in offices, and in 1842 the Association of Architectural Draughtsmen—formed by junior architects who had insufficient experience to join the IBA—was set up in London, in part to meet the new educational requirements; this developed in 1847 into the Architectural Association. In 1887 the RIBA instituted exams for those wishing to become associate members. The RIBA's influence was enormous; nevertheless, only *c.* 10% of architects were RIBA members at the end of the 19th century, and the Institution had a number of enemies, including R. Norman Shaw and Thomas Graham Jackson, joint editors of *Architecture: A Profession or an Art?* (1892), who opposed the RIBA's attempts through state legislation to force stricter professional exams on all practising architects.

(iv) Outside the institutions: amateur art training and the education of women. The appointment of drawing masters in schools was widespread by the end of the 18th century and had long been customary among the wealthy and the nobility. The development of watercolour painting from the second half of the 18th century provided the amateur with a simpler medium in which to work, and many drawing masters began as watercolour painters, including J. B. Malchair, who took groups of students on sketching tours around Oxford. Increased amateur art production in the provinces was evidenced by the number of members of the Norwich Society, including John Sell Cotman and John Crome, who were able to earn a living by teaching. Students generally learnt by imitating the style of the master. This method stimulated the publication of drawing manuals, which flourished from the early 19th century. Typical was *Aqua Pictura* (1813) by John Hassell (1767–1825), which used watercolours by John Varley, Thomas Girtin and others to exhibit progressive stages in the development of a landscape view. While most drawing books were concerned with landscape, still-life painting was also popular.

Although women had been active as drawing teachers from the 18th century, artistic training was generally considered to be merely a vehicle for them to foster a genteel 'accomplishment'. Women were further excluded from training by a popular conception of genius, which saw them as capable only of technical ability. Women were thus admitted into regional schools of design rather than of fine art, and in 1842–3 the Government School of Art for Females was opened in Gower Street, London. The high enrolment in this school reflected the fact that it was the only place where middle-class women could gain training. The majority of women artists, however, learnt through their families. They were excluded from studying at the Royal Academy Schools until 1860, when Laura Herford (*fl* 1860–70) gained admittance by submitting drawings anonymously. Although the Schools were again closed to women students in 1863, they were soon forced to accept women once more, but men and women were placed in different painting schools. From 1893 women were allowed to make life drawings, albeit from a male model draped with a voluminous loincloth, but it was not until 1903 that life-drawing classes were totally permitted to them. The growing realization of women's potential led to their admittance to the Slade School of Fine Art, where they could pursue fine art without apology, and their former association exclusively with applied art was broken down.

3. AFTER 1920. From 1920 to 1935 the principal of the Royal College of Art was the painter William Rothenstein, who emphasized painting, sculpture and graphic arts and sought, in competition with the Slade, to provide a full training for the intending professional artist. This more liberal and non-doctrinaire regime helped foster such outstanding sculptors as Henry Moore and Barbara Hepworth. It also subconsciously relegated design training (especially that relevant to industry) to a subordinate place as essentially less creative; there was little investment in machinery, and the design subjects taught were primarily pottery (by William Staite Murray), textiles (by Reco Capey) and illustration (by Eric Ravilious, John Nash and Paul Nash). A number of universities, meanwhile, such as Liverpool, London, Sheffield, Durham and Manchester, created architecture courses of several years' duration, earning exemption from the RIBA's own examinations.

Walter Gropius, who was in Britain from 1934 to 1937 as a refugee from Nazi Germany, was unsuccessful in bringing the revolutionary Bauhaus experiment to British art education, failing to find work at the Royal College of Art and elsewhere. Only after World War II were the lessons of the rigorous and all-embracing Bauhaus training applied in Britain. The foundation in 1937 of what became known as the EUSTON ROAD SCHOOL represented a more positive, if short-lived, response to European modernism. Its principal teachers, Victor Pasmore, Claude Rogers (1907–79), WILLIAM COLDSTREAM and Graham Bell, claimed not to impose a style, but they encouraged students to observe and record contemporary urban life in an undemonstrative and sombre-toned realism.

Having spent the inter-war years largely in the doldrums, the Slade was dominated in the post-war period by Coldstream (Slade professor, 1949–75), who fostered the school's tradition of sober draughtsmanship by the example of his own work. He also brought with him from the Camberwell School of Art (where he had taught from 1945 to 1949) such like-minded colleagues as Rogers and Keith Vaughan. The most invigorating force in British art education in the immediate post-war period, however, was Robin Darwin (*b* 1910), who was Principal of the Royal College of Art from 1948 to 1971 and brought a new enthusiasm to the practical problems of training the industrial designer while retaining fine arts as the core of the curriculum. He encouraged teachers and students to specialize but allowed them considerable freedom within their chosen field. By judicious use of publicity-generating public commissions, such as the *Lion and Unicorn* mural for the 1951 Festival of Britain, Darwin raised the status of the Royal College of Art and gave to the life of the art student and teacher a glamour they had never previously enjoyed. This era culminated in the Pop art generation trained at the Royal College of Art in the late 1950s and early 1960s. David Hockney and R. B. Kitaj were among those who responded to the freedom that the College offered while rejecting much of the formal curriculum. Richard Hamilton, another pioneer of Pop art in England, taught design at King's College, University of Durham, from 1956 to 1958, and together with Victor Pasmore, Ian

Stephenson (*b* 1934) and Harry Thubron (*b* 1915) he created a basic course called 'The Developing Process'. A 'New Generation' of British sculptors was also fostered in the welding studio that Anthony Caro introduced to St Martin's School of Art in 1959, with one of its members, Phillip King, later teaching at the same institution.

The first Coldstream Report (1960) of the National Advisory Council on Art Education proposed a new Diploma in Art and Design to replace the National Diploma in Design set up in 1946. This would consist of a one-year pre-Diploma general course followed by a three-year specialized diploma. These recommendations were the most thorough attempt since the time of Henry Cole to impose centralized state control on British art schools. In attempting to set predetermined and uniform standards, which many colleges failed to meet, the Report provoked widespread unrest and uncertainty about the status of art education within education as a whole. The growth of Higher and Further Education following the Robbins Report (1963) and the relative economic prosperity of the 1960s partially masked these difficulties, as demand remained strong for art graduates not only as teachers but also in advertising, publishing and the fashion, film and music industries, for which the art schools began to cater.

Student unrest in English art schools during the late 1960s reflected widespread youth protest and mirrored profound conflict at the Ecole des Beaux-Arts in Paris in 1968. As many artists advocated the primacy of unfettered self-expression, students questioned the relevance of an academic tradition to their training and the extent to which creativity could be taught. From the late 1970s these protests were muted by the combined effect of economic recession and political demands for greater vocational relevance from the art school system. The victors in the so-called 'palace revolution' at the Royal College of Art in the mid-1980s advocated a return to William Dyce's principle of art education as the servant of industry and Henry Cole's value-for-money utilitarianism; a re-evaluation of traditional academic figure drawing also began to emerge at the same time. Changes to the Royal Academy Schools in the 20th century, meanwhile, were often in response to war or financial problems rather than to reconsideration of the curriculum; even after the introduction of fees in 1977, six free places were still retained. Education cutbacks, however, closed or threatened with closure many of the smaller art schools.

BIBLIOGRAPHY

A. Pasquin [J. Williams]: *An Authentic History of the Professors of Painting, Sculpture and Architecture . . .* (London, 1796)
E. Edwards: *Anecdotes of Painters* (London, 1808/*R* 1970)
R. Wornum, ed.: *Lectures on Painting by Royal Academicians* (London, 1847)
A. Beaver: 'The Progress of Academies of Art in Great Britain', *Mag. A.*, iv (1881), pp. 517–19
F. Brown: *South Kensington and its Art Training* (London, 1912)
W. T. Whitley: 'The Central School of Arts and Crafts', *The Studio*, lxxx/330 (1920), pp. 51–8
——: *Artists and their Friends in England, 1700–1799*, 2 vols (London, 1928/*R* 1968)
J. A. Gotch, ed.: *The Growth and Work of the RIBA, 1834–1934* (London, 1934)
N. Pevsner: *Academies of Art Past and Present* (Cambridge, 1940, rev. New York, 1973)

First Report of the National Advisory Committee on Art Education (London, 1960)

H. C. Morgan: *A History of the Organization and Growth of the Royal Academy Schools from the Beginning of the Academy to 1836* (diss., U. Leeds, 1964) [copy in RA Lib., London, which also contains an unpublished reference work by Morgan on the Royal Academy Schools, 1837–78]

S. MacDonald: *The History and Philosophy of Art Education* (London, 1970)

The Slade, 1871–1971 (exh. cat. by B. Laughton, London, RA, 1971)

H. C. Morgan: 'The Schools of the Royal Academy', *Brit. J. Educ. Stud.*, xxi/1 (1973), pp. 88–103

J. Wilton-Ely: 'The Rise of the Professional Architect in England', *The Architect: Chapters in the History of the Profession*, ed. S. Kostof (Oxford, 1977), pp. 180–208

T. P. Cowdell: *The Role of the Royal Academy in English Art, 1918–30* (diss., U. Leeds, 1980), pp. 38–84

A. Powers: 'Edwardian Architectural Education: A Study of Three Schools of Architecture', *AA Files*, v (1984), pp. 49–59

C. Frayling: *The Royal College of Art: One Hundred and Fifty Years of Art and Design* (London, 1987)

P. Gerrish Nunn: *Victorian Women Artists* (London, 1987)

Gilpin to Ruskin: Drawing Masters and their Manuals, 1800–60 (exh. cat. by P. Bicknell, Cambridge, Fitzwilliam, 1987)

OLIVER GARNETT, SHEARER WEST

XVI. Art libraries and photographic collections.

The first collections in England of books on art and architecture were in libraries belonging to royalty or to wealthy individuals. Many of these collections still exist, for example at Windsor Castle and Chatsworth House, although they are not always readily accessible to the public. It was not until the second half of the 18th century that libraries began to be established at such institutions in London as the Royal Academy and the British Museum. These were followed in the 19th century by an increase in libraries related to art education, among other places at the South Kensington (now the Victoria and Albert) Museum in London and in schools of design, later schools of art. Public and university libraries then developed in the major cities, often with substantial donations from industrialists and landowners. In the 20th century the provision of art libraries was consolidated through a more widespread public library service and the establishment of a large number of educational institutions.

Collections of national importance exist in the British Library in London and in other copyright deposit libraries at the universities of Oxford and Cambridge. The two major specialist national libraries, the National Art Library in the Victoria and Albert Museum and the British Architectural Library in the Royal Institute of British Architects, London, provide the most comprehensive research libraries on these subjects in Britain. Aside from its extensive collection relating to fine art, the National Art Library has an increasing holding of books and periodicals relating to design. Important collections covering particular subjects also exist in the libraries of some larger galleries and museums, with the emphasis often on the collection of art held by the institution, as is the case with the National Gallery Library in London. Of exceptional quality is the library of the Tate Gallery in London, whose collection of material on modern art is of international standing and includes comprehensive holdings of periodicals and exhibition catalogues.

Academic libraries provide the bulk of art and architecture resources in England. While architecture is taught only in a small number of institutions of higher education, which form the main centres for architectural information, architectural history is also included with art and design in a much wider spectrum of universities, polytechnics and colleges. With some notable exceptions, such as the Courtauld Institute in London, the major collections relating to the arts are in institutions that originated in the schools of art established in the 19th century. All of these libraries are open to the public, at least on a reference basis, and tend to act as focal points for arts information in their regions. While many art libraries contain collections of photographs or slides, major libraries specifically of visual material include the National Art Slide Library, which in 1992 moved from the Victoria and Albert Museum to De Montfort University in Leicester, and the Witt Library at the Courtauld Institute in London. Central to the collection of the latter are *c.* 150,000 photographs of works of art amassed in the 1890s by Sir Robert Witt and his wife and bequeathed in 1944 to the University of London.

Public libraries, and particularly those in large cities, almost invariably include collections relating to the arts, but with changes in funding to local authorities the role of these may alter as some fail to keep pace with purchasing or redefine their status as major resources for research. The range of interest in the arts and their diversity mean that no one sector of libraries can be self-sufficient, and there has therefore been a tendency towards cooperation with some attempts at coordination, leading to a (largely informal) network of information provision through specialist institutions. The development of this network has taken place partly under the auspices of the British Library, as well as through the activities of the Art Libraries Society of the United Kingdom & Eire, established in 1969. There still remains scope, however, for further coordination in arts information, particularly at a local and regional level.

BIBLIOGRAPHY
J. Honer: *The Art Directory* (London, 1993), pp. 469–511

JOHN KIRBY

XVII. Historiography.

The lack of native artists and art patronage discouraged historical awareness of English art until the 17th century, when halting attempts were made to provide biographical information about artists working in England. The *Lives of the English Painters* by BAINBRIGG BUCKRIDGE appeared in 1706 as an English version of Roger de Piles's *Abrégé de la vie des peintres* (1699), but it includes mostly foreign painters living in England; John Evelyn's translation (1664) of Roland Fréart's *Parallèle de l'architecture antique et de la moderne* (1650) contains a general historical account of architects and architecture; and in the more ponderous *Chronologia architectonia* (*c.* 1670) John Aubrey attempted a history of British medieval architecture. These tentative beginnings were reinforced in the 18th century, when a more lively artistic environment promoted greater interest in the nation's art and its history. The opening (1711) of Godfrey Kneller's academy in London and its successors, as well as the establishment of the Society of Antiquaries (1717) and the Society of Dilettanti (1732), led to a more precise documentary approach in such works as *The Antiquities of England and Wales* (4 vols, 1773–87) by FRANCIS GROSE. The most important study of English art in the early 18th century was initiated by GEORGE VERTUE, an engraver and member of the Society of Antiquaries, whose *Notebooks* (from 1713) contain invaluable jottings about contemporary and past art. In 1757 Vertue's manuscripts were acquired by Horace Walpole (*see* WALPOLE, (2)), who used them to compile his *Anecdotes of Painting in England* (4 vols, 1762–71), a more discursive history. In the tradition of Vasari's *Vite*, Walpole interpreted the history of English art as a progression towards perfection, creating the first coherent 'story' of it; he also included architecture and landscape gardening. The rapid changes in English art, however, with the founding of the Royal Academy (1768), left Walpole's scrupulous research behind.

The strength of the Royal Academy and the expansion of patronage in the 19th century coincided with increasing literacy and a proliferation of illustrated books. Art historiography diversified: works such as Allan Cunningham's *Lives of the Most Eminent British Painters, Sculptors and Architects* (6 vols, 1829–33) adopted a sweeping biographical approach, and Cunningham's inclusion of sculptors was a significant addition to the literature. E. Hamilton's *The English School* (4 vols, 1831) represented an early attempt to establish a native 'school' of art parallel to those of France and Italy. General histories of architecture were dominated by a renewed interest in medieval buildings and debates on the classification of architectural styles. John Britton, in his massive *Architectural Antiquities of Great Britain* (5 vols, 1807–26), catalogued architecture by means of plans, elevations and cross-sections, contrasting with THOMAS RICKMAN who, in *Attempt to Discriminate the Styles of English Architecture from the Conquest to the Reformation* (1817), assumed a more argumentative stance. General histories of the decorative arts began appearing in the late 19th century, after William Morris and the Arts and Crafts Movement helped make them respectable and popular subjects for consideration. Such works as Llewellyn Jewitt's *The Ceramic Art of Great Britain* (1878) exemplify this new concern with what had formerly been seen as 'minor' arts. A new interest in prints was also manifested in such works as J. Smith's *British Mezzotinto Portraits* (1878–83).

Biographies also acquired more importance in the 19th century, and such early attempts as S. Gwynn's *Memorials of an Eighteenth-century Painter* (1898), a study of James Northcote, adopted a chatty informal approach, while more serious chronological accounts were provided by the genre painter C. R. Leslie in, for example, his *Memoirs of the Life of John Constable* (1843). Biographies often allowed writers to re-evaluate the work of recent artists and to compare it with contemporary fashions; for example, in his *Life and Writings of Henry Fuseli* (3 vols, 1831), J. Knowles attempted to re-evaluate the work of a much misunderstood painter. The increasing willingness to be critical or evaluative was also demonstrated by A. W. N. Pugin's comparisons of modern with medieval architecture (*see* PUGIN, (2)) and by such books as John Pye's *Patronage of British Art* (1845), a dry account of

English art exhibitions and societies unexpectedly enlivened by his outrage at the exclusion of engravers from membership of the Royal Academy.

Art historiography at the turn of the century was dominated by amateurs, who took advantage of a flourishing interest in particular artists within the art market. The general interest in English art, however, was stimulated by a nationalist feeling that intensified during World Wars I and II. The founding of *Country Life* magazine in 1897 inspired a new concern with preservation, which eventually led to such works as the Shell Guides, a series of county histories edited from 1933 by John Betjeman. This attention to Englishness instigated rediscoveries of such artists as Samuel Palmer. An emphasis on the stylistic analysis of art and architecture arose with the new aesthetics of Modernism. The *Architectural Review* (from 1896) promoted a stylistic rather than documentary analysis of architecture, while the *Burlington Magazine* was founded in 1903 by ROGER FRY to further the aesthetic appreciation of art. A more rigorous and academic approach followed in the 1930s, when German refugee art historians founded the Courtauld Institute (1932) and the Warburg Library was brought to London (1933). Although Fritz Saxl, Rudolf Wittkower and Ernst Gombrich devoted little attention to British art, NIKOLAUS PEVSNER, in his *Pioneers of the Modern Movement* (1936), traced Modernism back to William Morris, while his mammoth Buildings of England series (46 vols, 1951–74) offered, county by county, an exhaustive and idiosyncratic account of extant buildings and monuments. The *Walpole Society* journal, begun in 1930 to publish Vertue's manuscript notebooks, became an invaluable source for other primary documentation. The new academic approach was characteristic of the work of such art historians as ELLIS WATERHOUSE, whose quirky but insightful *Painting in Britain, 1530–1790* (1953) formed part of the Pelican History of Art series, edited by Pevsner. Other publishing ventures encouraged a monographic approach to British artists and a scholarly survey of its history, while new dictionaries and general histories of sculpture, architecture and the decorative arts, including Rupert Gunnis's *Dictionary of British Sculptors, 1660–1851* (1953), Howard Colvin's *Biographical Dictionary of English Architects* (1954), Martin Hardie's *Water-colour Painting in Britain* (3 vols, 1966–8) and E. Croft-Murray's *Decorative Painting in England* (2 vols, 1970), compiled previously unpublished information in sound and useful formats. This documentary approach resulted in new scholarship in such diverse areas as textiles, furniture, book illustration, miniature painting and gardening.

In the 1970s and 1980s increasingly thorough catalogues accompanying art exhibitions contributed to the growth of art-historical scholarship. These placed English art in an international context by exploring such stylistic categories as Neo-classicism (London, RA, 1972) and the Rococo (London, V&A, 1984); catalogues such as those on *Reynolds* (London, RA, 1986), *Francis Hayman* (London, Kenwood House, 1987) and *Francis Danby* (London, Tate, 1989) also began replacing standard monographs on individual artists, and from the 1970s new methodologies, often based on literary criticism, emerged. Early efforts were made by Ronald Paulson, whose *Emblem and Expression* (1975) angered conventional art historians by its strained literary interpretations of 18th-century English painting. More successful were books that attempted to see art history in its social and commercial context: Judith Hook's *The Baroque Age in England* (1976), among others, considers aspects of patronage, art institutions and the impact of economic forces. Marxist methodology is to be found in such works as John Barrell's *Dark Side of the Landscape* (1980), while feminist art history dominates the re-evaluation of Victorian painting in such works as Pamela Gerrish Nunn's *Victorian Women Artists* (1987) and Lynda Nead's *Myths of Sexuality* (1989). The monographic and documentary approach has been augmented, rather than superseded, by these new methods, resulting in an enrichment of academic scholarship about British art.

BIBLIOGRAPHY

J. Dobai: *Die Kunstliteratur des Klassizismus und der Romantik in England, 1700–1840*, 4 vols (Berne, 1974–84)
D. Watkin: *The Rise of Architectural History* (London, 1980)

SHEARER WEST

Engleheart [Engelheart]. English family of artists, of German origin. Francis Engelheart (*b* Silesia, 1713; *d* Kew, 1773) was a plaster modeller. He came to England *c.* 1721 and later worked as a decorative plasterer at Kew Palace for Frederick, Prince of Wales (1707–51), and his widow Augusta, the Princess Dowager (1719–72). He seems also to have produced decorative ceilings for Hampton Court Palace. After his death, his family changed the spelling of their name to Engleheart.

Two of Francis's sons, John Dillman Engleheart (1735–1810) and Paul Engleheart (*d* 1774), carried on the business, while two others found success in other fields. Thomas Engleheart (*b* ?London, 1745; *d* ?London, 1786) was a sculptor and wax modeller, and George Engleheart (*b* Kew, ?Nov 1753; *d* Blackheath [now in London], 21 March 1829) was a painter. Thomas studied from 1769 at the Royal Academy schools, London, where he won a gold medal in 1772 for a relief of *Ulysses and Nausicaa* (untraced). From 1773 he exhibited busts, portraits in wax (e.g. *Edward, Duke of Kent*, 1786; London, N.P.G.) and medallions at the Royal Academy. Early in his career George was influenced by the miniaturist Jeremiah Meyer, who introduced him to George Romney. He entered the Royal Academy schools, London, in 1769, and was a pupil of George Barret sr and Joshua Reynolds, whose work he copied. As his fee books for 1775 to 1813 (see Williamson) attest, he was a prolific miniaturist, exhibiting regularly at the Royal Academy between 1773 and 1822. His early work, which was almost exclusively on ivory, was small and cool in hue with finely shaded plain backgrounds. From the 1780s (during which decade he produced *c.* 2000 miniatures), his brushstrokes became more evident and his colours richer. Large eyes with prominent pupils and lids are characteristic of his faces, for example in *A Woman, Said to be Mrs Dicksee* (*c.* 1780; London, V&A). He also produced single eye miniatures (e.g. priv. col., see Foskett, pl. 102). From the mid-1790s he increasingly used larger (*c.* 76 mm h.) and rectangular ivories in place of the more traditional oval format of his earlier work. His nephew, John Cox Dillman Engleheart (1782/4–1862), was an equally successful portrait miniaturist in the same style, serving as his pupil and assistant.

Thomas Engleheart's son Francis Engleheart (*b* ?Egham, Surrey, 1775; *d* London, 15 Feb 1849) was primarily a book illustrator who learnt his craft of line engraving under Joseph Collyer (1748–1827), to whom he was apprenticed in 1790, and James Heath (1757–1834). He engraved designs after Thomas Stothard, Richard Cook (1784–1857), Robert Smirke (i), William Mulready and Francis Philip Stephanoff, many of which were published in annuals, such as *Amulet* (London, 1826–36), *Keepsake* (London, 1828–56) and *Literary Souvenir* (London, 1825–37). Sir David Wilkie employed him to engrave *Duncan Gray* (1828) and *The Only Daughter* (1838), both published by Francis G. Moon. His last and most important work was *Serena Rescued by the Red Cross Knight* (1846; London, N.G.) after William Hilton.

BIBLIOGRAPHY

DNB [Francis Engleheart]; Gunnis [Thomas Engleheart]
A. J. [London] (1849), p. 206 [Francis Engleheart]
G. C. Williamson: *George Engleheart* (London, 1902)
M. Bryan: *Bryan's Dictionary of Painters and Engravers* (London, 1926–34), ii [Francis Engleheart]
J. H. Slater: *Engravings and Their Value* (London, 1929), p. 304 [Francis Engleheart]
G. Reynolds: *English Portrait Miniatures* (London, 1952), pp. 162–5 [George Engleheart]
D. Foskett: *A Dictionary of British Miniature Painters* (London, 1972) [George Engleheart]
G. Beard: *Decorative Plasterwork in Great Britain* (London, 1975), p. 218 [Francis Engleheart]

BASIL HUNNISETT

English Renaissance. *See* BAROQUE REVIVAL.

Englund, Lars (*b* Stockholm, 1933). Swedish sculptor and painter. He studied under Vilhelm Bjerke-Petersen in Stockholm (1950–51) and under Léger in Paris (1952). In the late 1950s he produced abstract paintings in white and in the early 1960s paintings in lacquered oil on film. These had gentle gradations of sombre colours in a rigidly rectilinear abstract design, which was vertically divided in half by a line formed by tonal contrasts, as in *Communication* (1963; Stockholm, Mod. Mus.). At the same time he produced relief works using cardboard or plastic, as in *Tool* (plastic, 1964; Stockholm, Mod. Mus.), a minimal curved form that emerges from the mounting surface. He then began working with rubber, which he fixed into various forms and inflated, so distorting the rectilinear structure, as in the relief *Rubber Object* (1967; Stockholm, Mod. Mus.). Other rubber sculptures were free-standing and could dominate a gallery space. In the early 1970s he experimented with large structures constructed from identical sections, often curved polycarbonate elements, as in *Fragment, Berry Work* (1973; Stockholm, Mod. Mus.), inspired by Baroque architecture, which he saw as a means of organizing large, complex structures according to simple mathematical laws. The same spirit pervaded his later work, which consisted of repeated painted metal structures similar to molecular models, as in *Part of the Whole* (1979; see Granath, 1982, p. 33).

BIBLIOGRAPHY

Lars Englund (exh. cat. by H. Eklund, Stockholm, Gal. Burén, 1965)
Englund (exh. cat. by O. Granath, Paris, Gal. Ileana Sonnabend, 1968)
O. Granath: *Another Light: Swedish Art since 1945* (Stockholm, 1974, 2/1982), pp. 30–35

Engonopoulos, Nikos (*b* Athens, 21 Oct 1910; *d* Athens, 31 Oct 1985). Greek painter, stage designer and poet. He spent his school years in Constantinople (now Istanbul) and Paris. Between 1932 and 1938 he studied at the Higher School of Fine Arts in Athens under Konstantinos Parthenis and Yannis Kefallinos (1893–1957). At the same time he worked with Fotis Kontoglou. The publication in 1938 of his first collection of surrealistic poems, and the first exhibition of his paintings the following year, were enthusiastically received by the most authoritative members of the Greek literary and artistic avant-garde, such as Andreas Embirikos (1901–75) and Odysseas Elytis (*b* 1911). From 1941 to 1972 he held the post of professor of painting at the School of Architecture of the National Technical University of Athens. He was one of the first exponents of Surrealism in Greece, combining the universal principles of the movement with the Greek artistic and cultural tradition. Deeply influenced by de Chirico's metaphysical painting, he attempted to create an imagery of unexpected combinations, based upon poetic imagination and colour. His paintings are characterized by the presence of mannequins placed in Neo-classical houses overlooking the Parthenon or within strange Greek interiors. The female figure is almost always present in his works, as in *The Poet and his Muse* (1938; see Papastamos, p. 221). He published nine collections of poems between 1938 and 1984. He lectured on architecture, illustrated books and designed sets and costumes for the Greek National Theatre, for example for Sophocles' *Electra* in 1939. He also worked as a painter of icons and executed frescoes for the church of St Spyridion, New York.

BIBLIOGRAPHY

D. Papastamos: *Painting, 1930–40: The Artistic and Aesthetic Vision of the Decade* (Athens, 1986), pp. 220–23

FANI-MARIA TSIGAKOU

Engraving. Technique of intaglio printmaking in which an image is cut with tools into a plate from which multiple impressions may be made; the term is also applied to the resulting print, which has characteristic lines created by the tools and techniques of cutting. The incised image, which lies below the plate's surface, is filled with ink, and then pressure is used to force the paper into the inked lines, creating a slightly raised three-dimensional line and an embossed platemark.

The printing of images from engraved metal plates began in the 15th century and spread to Asia from the 16th. Woodblock engraving had been used in Japan from the 8th century to make prints of religious texts under the auspices of Buddhist temples and the aristocracy, but the earliest copperplate engravings in Japan date to the 16th century. In China the influence of European graphic art spread as early as the Ming period (1368–1644), continuing in the Qing (1644–1911). Western engravings were the model for the *Chengshi moyuan* given to Cheng Dayue by Matteo Ricci (1552–1610), and the Jesuits were involved in printmaking activities in China in the 17th and 18th centuries (*see* CHINA, §XIII, 19(ii)). The technique of copperplate-engraving was introduced into South-east Asia in the 16th century by Portuguese, Spanish and Dutch colonizers. The history of engraving is based predominantly in the West, however, and it is on this that this article concentrates.

I. Materials and techniques. II. History.

I. Materials and techniques.

The preferred metal for engraving plates is copper, which is easily incised, yet strong enough to withstand repeated passes through a press under pressure. Silver, zinc, steel and plastic plates are also used. Metal plates can also be steel- or chrome-faced by electrolysis. This protective layer, consisting of a microscopically thin coating of a stronger metal, is useful in large editions, in which the line quality gradually deteriorates. Since the 1950s some artists have engraved on transparent plastics, with the advantage that a drawing placed underneath can be seen.

Specialized engraving tools are used, and each has a characteristic cut that produces a distinctive printed line (see fig. 1). The graver or burin (1a–d) is a steel shaft, square or lozenge in section, mounted in a rounded wooden handle. Burins come in a variety of sizes. The end of the shaft, which can be straight or bent, is sliced off at a 35–45° angle. The resultant line has an innate formality resulting from the method of cutting. The engraver holds the tool with the palm of the hand, low to the plate, and cuts straight ahead, turning the plate against the tool as the line curves. The burin is capable of a range of strokes, from the most delicate to rather wide, depending on the pressure exerted. As the tool moves in a V-shaped cut, it produces a curl of metal ahead of the engraver; the line swells and tapers according to the depth of the cut and

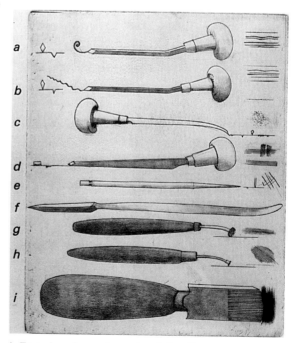

1. Engraving of engraving tools and the effects they produce: (a) square burin or graver; (b) lozenge burin or graver; (c) stipple graver; (d) multiple line graver; (e) drypoint needle; (f) scraper and burnisher; (g) roulette; (h) roulette; (i) mezzotint rocker

whether the graver is held straight or is rotated to the side. The end of a line appears to come to a point. If the cut is not absolutely clean, a sharp burr remains, which is generally scraped away. Burr left along the line will hold ink and adds richness to the print. This richness is characteristic of the earliest impressions from a plate, for burr will soon be flattened by repeated printings.

Other tools used for engraving include drypoint needles or scribers (1e) for lightly scratching the design on the plate; and compasses and dividers for measuring and scribing. Tools for producing tones and textures include stipple gravers (1c); multiple lining tools (1d); roulettes (1g-h), tools with small wheels that perforate; mattoirs (or mace heads), whose end has irregular points, and mezzotint rockers (1i), which have curved blades with serrated edges. Machine oil and good whetstones are necessary to maintain the sharpness of engraving tools. The engraver also uses files for bevelling the edges of the plate, scrapers and burnishers, callipers, hammers and pumices and fine grits for correcting errors. Many engravers rest their plates on a leather cushion or ball to assist in turning the plate. Some engravers use magnifying lenses or eyepieces, worn on a headband or supported by a stand.

The design for an engraving can be transferred from paper to a plate in a variety of ways. One method is to rub the verso of a drawing on paper with chalk. The plate is then coated with wax or asphaltum, or carbon paper can be placed between a drawing and the coated plate. A scriber is used to retrace the outlines of the drawing, imprinting a transferred line on to the plate in the same direction as the original drawing. The resulting print will be a mirror image of the original drawing. A second method enables the engraver to produce a print in the same direction as the original drawing. The plate is coated with wax or asphaltum, and a soft graphite drawing or ungummed ink on a smooth surface such as tracing paper is placed face down on the plate. The drawing is either rubbed or run through the press, and the transferred drawing prints in reverse on to the plate. After engraving, when the plate is printed, the impression is in the same direction as the original drawing. Ungummed-ink transfers to engraving plates were used as early as 1605.

During the course of the engraving process, engravers often print trial prints or 'proofs' to show the progress of the work, and these can be drawn on to explore alternatives for further engraving. A counterproof (a print made from a freshly printed proof) is sometimes made to reverse the reversal of the original design.

Papers for printing engravings must be able to be soaked or dampened to remove the sizing and relax the fibres, and be strong enough to withstand the reshaping of the sheet under pressure without tearing. Lightweight, translucent, laid and heavier opaque mould-made papers are suitable. Evenness of pulp is desirable, and coloured papers have often been used. Paper is an important factor in the appearance of an impression. Alternatives to paper, used especially in the 19th century, include satin, which is extremely receptive to the printed image, and silk. Decals printed with ceramic inks from engraved plates have been transferred to porcelain and fired, fusing the ink into the glaze. In the 20th century S. W. Hayter introduced the process of printing engraved plates by casting them in plaster.

Printing inks are prepared from well-ground pigments that are worked into reduced linseed oil (burnt-plate oil) until the mixture is very stiff and well saturated with pigment. Both black and coloured inks are used. It can take a week or more for oil-based inks to dry. Additives used in modern commercial inks include driers, varnishes and fillers. Solvents for cleaning include paint-thinner and turpentine; some formerly used, such as benzine, are now banned as health hazards.

The plate is inked with one of a number of devices for spreading it across the surface and forcing it down into the lines. An inking ball of leather or a *poupée* (a cylinder of tightly wound felt) are traditional, and brayers and squeegees are often used today. Fabrics, such as stiffly starched mesh, called 'tarlatan' cloth, and newspaper are used to wipe the surface. The printer can wipe the plate's surface perfectly clean or leave a film of plate tone either all over or in selected areas. Wiping is finished using the heel of the hand with whiting (calcium carbonate). Multiple colour prints are made using separate plates for each colour and printed wet on wet (to avoid registration problems arising from paper shrinkage) or *à la poupée*, that is all the colours carefully applied and blended on a single plate.

The press used for printing engravings consists of a structure that supports two heavy cylinders arranged horizontally, one above the other, separated by a flat pressbed that moves horizontally between them. In modern presses the cylinders are attached to powerful springs that are tightened by pressure screws. A flywheel drives the cylinders either directly or by means of gears. Formerly presses were built of wood, but since the 19th century they are of cast-iron or steel; since the late 20th century plastic laminates have also been used.

The wiped plate is placed face up on the press bed, and dampened, blotted paper laid on top of the plate. Felts (blankets) are placed on top of the paper, and then the bed passes between the rollers, forcing the paper into the inked lines. For each impression made, the plate must be re-inked and wiped.

Engraving can combine in the same plate with any other of the intaglio methods such as drypoint, etching, mezzotint and aquatint. Since engraved plates are printed by intaglio, they cannot be printed simultaneously with cast type in the same printing run. Early illustrated books were illustrated by relief-printed blocks and metal plates, but in the 16th century engraved metal plates were recognized as having greater endurance, finer detail and greater ability to show certain pictorial effects of atmosphere. By the second quarter of the century engraving and typography were routinely combined in books and single sheets printed by means of two different presses. In the 20th century experimental printmakers began combining engraving with woodcut, lithography, serigraphy and monotype printed on the same sheet.

A tradition of signing and inscribing titles and publishing information has grown up with engraving. Early engravers used a hallmark or monogram and later personal names, sometimes inscribed in a plaque or tablet within the image. The work of producing an engraving was divided among specialists, and the artist, engraver, printer and publisher were frequently different individuals. By the 16th century an inscriptional space was frequently left on the lower edge of a plate, where a variety of customary Latin words and phrases were used to identify the work and claim rights of publication: the artist *invenit* (invented), *delineavit* (drew) or *pinxit* (painted) the image; the engraver *sculpsit* (engraved) or *fecit* (made) the plate; the publisher *excudit* or *divulgavit* (published) the print, often *cum privilegio* (with the permission and copyright protection) of a governmental authority for a certain period of time. Works were also frequently *D.D.* (dedicated) to some valued patron. The engraving of lettering was a speciality and was often done by someone other than the pictorial engraver. The idea of limiting the size of editions arose in the 18th century, and the custom of autographing original prints in the lower margin outside the platemark began in the 19th century, as did the concept of artist's proofs. The practice of fractional numbering of the impressions in an edition (for example, '3/50', i.e. third impression of an edition of 50) began *c.* 1900.

BIBLIOGRAPHY

A. Bosse: *Traicté des manières de graver en taille douce sur l'airin par le moyen des eaux fortes* (Paris, 1645/*R* Bologna, 1937)
J. Evelyn: *Sculptura* (1662); ed. C. F. Bell (Oxford, 1906) [with previously unpubd second part]
W. Faithorne: *The Art of Graveing and Etching* (London, 1662 and 1702/both *R* New York, 1970; ed. J. Kainen)
S. W. Hayter: *New Ways of Gravure* (New York, 1949, rev. 1966)
A. Floçon: *Traité du burin* (Paris, 1952, rev.1981)
A. Brittain and P. Morton: *Engraving on Precious Metals* (London, 1958/*R* 1980) [traditional craft techniques for goldsmiths)
G. Peterdi: *Printmaking: Methods Old and New* (New York, 1959)
J. Ross and C. Romano: *The Complete Printmaker* (New York, 1972, rev. 2/1990)
J. B. Meek: *The Art of Engraving: A Book of Instruction* (Montezuma, IA, 1973)
F. Eichenberg: *The Art of the Print: Masterpieces, History, Techniques* (New York, 1976)
R. Leaf: *Etching, Engraving and other Intaglio Printmaking Techniques* (New York, 1984)

II. History.

The incising of images into metal and other hard materials was practised long before engraved surfaces were used as printing matrices (*see* METAL, §V; *see also* GOLD, §2, and SILVER, §3). Engraved stone, bone, ivory and shell objects from Palaeolithic sites are evidence that incising an image is old and widespread. Mesopotamian engraving, for example, was highly developed in technique, style and subject-matter, and cylinder seals impressed into clay of *c.* 3300 BC are perhaps the earliest examples of printed, engraved images. The art of niello, in which a powder of sulphur, mineral oxides and borax was rubbed into the lines of an engraved design and then heated to form a shiny black deposit, was a precursor of printed engravings. It was practised by the ancient Egyptians and was popular among the Greeks, Romans, Byzantines and Anglo-Saxons and throughout the Renaissance. The Florentine niellist and draughtsman Maso Finiguerra is credited by Giorgio Vasari with inventing the idea of printing engravings on paper from niello plates, but scholars question whether he was actually printing on paper from the casts (*see* NIELLO PRINT, §2).

BIBLIOGRAPHY

Hollstein: *Dut. & Flem.*; Hollstein: *Ger.*
A. P. F. Robert-Dumesnil: *Le Peintre-graveur français* (1835–71)
A. von Bartsch: *Le Peintre-graveur* (1803–21) [B.]
A. M. Hind: *A History of Engraving and Etching from the 15th Century to the Year 1914* (London, 1923, rev. New York, 3/1963)
A. H. Mayor: *Prints and People: A Social History of Printed Pictures* (New York, 1971)
L. Mason and J. Ludman: *Print Reference Sources* (New York, 1975, rev. 2/1979)
R. Godfrey: *Printmaking in Britain: A General History from its Beginnings to the Present Day* (New York, 1978)
M. Melot and others: *Prints: History of an Art* (Geneva, 1981)
T. Riggs: *The Print Council Index to Oeuvre-catalogues of Prints by European and American Artists* (New York, 1983)
A. Griffiths and R. Williams: *The Department of Prints and Drawings in the British Museum: User's Guide* (London, 1987)

1. Before *c.* 1430. 2. *c.* 1430–*c.* 1500. 3. *c.* 1500–*c.* 1600. 4. *c.* 1600–*c.* 1750. 5. *c.* 1750–*c.* 1900. 6. *c.* 1900 and after.

1. BEFORE *c.* 1430. The invention of printing engravings on paper was connected to three factors: the idea of using an engraved plate as a means of reproducing an image, the availability of paper and the means of applying pressure. The precise location at which these came together has been the subject of debate, with both Germany and Italy having its proponents. Most scholars believe that the practice of impressing paper on engraved plates originated in the workshops of south German goldsmiths in the Rhine Valley in the second quarter of the 15th century. Goldsmiths would make a record of designs incised in metal by filling the lines with ink and impressing paper against it. These printed designs could be used to help in the transfer of symmetrical and repeated elements and for training and record-keeping.

The first important centre of paper manufacture in Italy was set up at Fabriano *c.* 1276. Other mills were established in northern Italy during the 14th century, supplying not only Italian but also south German demand. Paper mills were first established in Germany *c.* 1320 near Cologne and Mainz, and in the Netherlands by the beginning of the 15th century. The use of paper for writing became common throughout Europe by the second half of the 14th century, essentially replacing vellum in the 15th. This new availability of paper was the key to the 'invention' of printing in Europe and first appeared in connection with relief printed blocks. Vertical pressure presses (wine presses) existed in the Rhineland and had already been adapted for printing woodcuts *c.* 1400. The dual cylinder or 'etching' press seems to have come into use by 1500. Oil-extended solid inks were also a German invention.

BIBLIOGRAPHY
Rhein und Maas: Kunst und Kultur, 800–1400 (exh. cat., Cologne, Josef-Haubrich-Ksthalle, 1972)

2. *c.* 1430–*c.* 1500.

(i) Northern Europe. (ii) Italy.

(i) Northern Europe. Important engraving centres developed along the Upper Rhine from Konstanz and Basle to Colmar and Strasbourg. The earliest engravers did not generally sign and date their prints, and their works have been attributed to various hands on stylistic grounds. Scholars have 'named' hundreds of these anonymous engravers after characteristic elements or subjects in their prints, such as the Master of 1446, after the earliest date

on an engraving, and the Master of the Playing Cards. Although their real names remain unknown, individual styles and hands are distinguishable, and many of them were highly accomplished artists. Later engravers began signing works with monograms, hallmarks and symbols, and eventually their names. The increasing importance of the engraving and the individual who designed it is reflected in the fact that by *c.* 1460 Master E.S. was the first printmaker to sign some of his prints with his monogram, and from *c.* 1470 Martin Schongauer monogrammed almost all his prints.

Because engraving was not so much invented as joined to the new technology of printing, one cannot speak of a 'primitive' phase; goldsmith-engravers continued to use techniques developed previously. Fifteenth-century northern European engraving is firmly rooted in the Gothic style. The earliest engravings are not purely linear but incorporate texture, shadow, modelling and pattern, which is unsurprising, since goldsmiths had been dealing with such pictorial problems for centuries. While many early engravers were trained as goldsmiths, others, however, seem to have been trained as painters, judging from their broader handling of form and detail. In the work of such an engraver-painter as the Master of the Playing Cards, contours were firmly engraved with a descriptive and restless line, and internal forms, such as facial features, were cut with delicacy. Certain mannerisms taken from drawing and also seen in early woodcuts, such as the 'fish-hook' end to a line in drapery, were used by this master and his contemporaries. Early engravers used a variety of cuts to create tonality and modelling. These include laying down hundreds of tiny straight strokes, with no particular reference to the direction of a plane, long hatchmarks and random crosshatching, with or without stippling.

The Master E.S., believed to have been a goldsmith, was active near Lake Constance and produced over 200 prints. He seems to have been the first to turn his plate against the burin as he cut modelling lines, resulting in a more logical system that followed and expressed form sculpturally. He also developed a systematic method of crosshatching that responds to form and produces a greatly enriched range of darks. Developments in northern European engraving after 1450 included increased interest in light, shade and environment, construction of pictorial space and use of the expanded narrative series as a focus for human drama.

Many early engravings were scenes from the Life of Christ, the Passion and images of the saints. These were sold as souvenirs at pilgrimage sites and were often used for personal devotion. Other prints had secular functions, such as New Year's greetings, playing cards and amorous and chivalric images. Although most engravers would have been well trained in drawing, the engraver did not necessarily design the image. Some engravings clearly reproduce paintings and have strong stylistic connections with known painters active in a given locale. Goldsmith designs were handed down through copying, so the reproduction of an image was intrinsic to the goldsmith-engraver's craft. Engravings were frequently copied by other engravers and so exist in more than one version. Engraving became a medium of stylistic diffusion, as these portable objects were used as reference material in artists' workshops. Early

engravings have been identified as the sources of images produced by 15th-century artists working in other media, such as book illumination and sculpture. In comparison with early woodcuts, engravings were a luxury item, more expensive to produce and made by more highly trained artist-engravers. Perhaps because of their relative value, more engravings were preserved at the time, pasted into books or boxes. Early engravings have survived, often in more than one impression. The cheaper, ephemeral, early single-sheet woodcuts were less likely to have been saved by their original users and consequently are rarer today, with many known only in unique impressions.

The most important northern European engraver in the last quarter of the century was Martin Schongauer (*see* Schongauer, (1)). The son of a goldsmith, he worked primarily as a painter but also produced about 100 engravings. His early graphic technique stressed black line against the white ground of the paper, with form articulated by hundreds of tiny strokes and dots. He gradually incorporated some of the Master E.S.'s innovations, eventually surpassing him and developing an immaculately crafted, masterful graphic language capable of expressing form, tone, space and surface. As his art developed, he moved from complexity to clarity and monumentality, exploring both Flemish gravity and Germanic expression, for example in his mature engraving, the two-part *Annunciation* (*c.* 1490; see fig. 2). His engravings are characterized

2. Engraving by Martin Schongauer: *Archangel Gabriel*, from the two-part *Annunciation*, 167×116 mm, *c.* 1490 (Paris, Bibliothèque Nationale)

by a feeling of constant movement as the eye is led by the gesturing figures and the ceaselessly exploring contour line. Schongauer extended engraving's range of tonalities, creating visually rich images, which were often copied and much imitated. Artists strongly influenced by Schongauer include the south German Master L.Cz., whose energetic and spontaneous burin work created colouristic surfaces that sparkle with contrasts and whose style combines the delicate solemnity of Schongauer's figure types with a greater sense of landscape space and delight in the luxuriance of the natural world. The prolific Israhel van Meckenem (ii) was the son of the engraver Israhel van Meckenem (i), known as the Master of the Berlin Passion (an identification that is now in question). Van Meckenem (ii)'s works comprise mainly copies after such engravers as the Master E.S., but he also engraved c. 150 images after his own designs. Many of these show a great interest in secular subjects and contemporary life and style, drawn in a lively manner. After c. 1480 he used a very dense crosshatching system, introducing new levels of rich blackness. Many of his later works have a breadth of conception comparable to panel painting but exploit engraving's ability to show the tiniest details. His enormous output shows that engraving was well established commercially by the late 15th century. It has been plausibly suggested that another engraver in this workshop was his wife, Ida van Meckenem, known from his engraved self-portrait with her, making her the earliest-known woman engraver.

In the Lower Rhine Valley and the Netherlands engraving developed in a manner similar to the Upper Rhine, with its major artists appearing slightly later. The Dutch Master IAM of Zwolle engraved animated, startlingly expressive compositions containing angular, rigid and flattened figures. Master FVB produced important works in which the figures were strongly influenced by Schongauer but with less interest in psychological interaction and more in incidental decorative detail. He excelled in contrasting intricate, highlighted forms against dark cross-hatched backgrounds.

By the last quarter of the 15th century northern European engraving was capable of a greatly expanded range of pictorial effects. It evolved from a predominantly linear mode, which described static form in an uncolouristic way, to the expression of a rich range of contrasts, as well as textures, by means of linear systems, of which contour was only one element.

(ii) Italy. Italian engraving was also rooted in and influenced stylistically by goldsmithing and niello. Florence was the first major centre, with Ferrara, Bologna, Mantua, Milan and Venice having significant activity later in the 15th century. All the major early Florentine engravers had a background in goldsmithing and were in contact with the niellist Finiguerra. Most, however, did not merely reproduce the niello manner of engraving light against dark but worked in a more open style, emphasizing outline and form against a light ground. Many 15th-century engravings are printed in a pale grey ink, in contrast to the more densely pigmented German inks, so the overall print has less contrast between the line and the paper.

From the outset, Italian engraving was closely connected with drawing in pen and wash. Early Italian engraving shares with contemporary drawing clarity of design, monumentality of form, firmness of outline and rational space. Early Italian engraving prints are traditionally grouped in two categories: 'fine manner' and 'broad manner'. In fine-manner prints contour lines define forms, and fine, delicate hatching and crosshatching strokes express modelling, imitating the effect of pen and wash, as in the work of Baccio Baldini. Broad-manner engraving reflects vigorous pen drawing, with the back-and-forth hatching reproduced by the burin; Francesco Rosselli was one of the most important practitioners of this style. Some engravers worked in both manners, making attributions problematic. The style of well-known artists is often reflected in early Italian engraving, and such artists as Botticelli designed specifically for engraving, including his series illustrating Dante's *Inferno*, engraved by Baldini. In addition to imitating drawing, engravers copied other engravings, including northern European prints. The subject-matter of Italian prints is highly varied, including religious, secular, amorous and erotic subjects. Series, such as the planets, the *Trionfi* of Francesco Petrarch and 'Tarocchi' cards, were popular.

Antonio del Pollaiuolo, painter, sculptor and goldsmith, designed and engraved only one surviving print, the *Battle of the Ten Nudes* (c. 1470–75; *see* POLLAIUOLO, (1), fig. 3). It is one of the most important 15th-century engravings and was the largest, most complex plate and also the earliest to be fully signed. Much speculation has taken place on its meaning. The image reveals Pollaiuolo's ability to render the nude in a variety of positions and views. Although the shallow space and friezelike design owe

3. Engraving by Antonio del Pollaiuolo: *Battle of the Ten Nudes* (detail), 383×595 mm, c. 1470–75 (London, British Museum)

much to antique relief and to niello, the engraving technique is in the looser 'broad manner' (see fig. 3). This rain of fine parallel hatching defining the musculature, systematically laid down from left to right with little reference to the direction of the form, imitates the pen work of the original drawing.

The Florentine engraver Robetta is associated with *c.* 40 engravings. The figures in these show the influence of Filippino Lippi and other Italian sources. Robetta often combined these with landscapes derived from prints by Schongauer and Dürer. His original and vigorous engraving style is related to drawing rather than painting. His cutting technique was less systematic than that of many of his contemporaries, and he employed short bursts of fine, curving, parallel lines and flecks to model form. Outlines were built up with multiple cuts, describing outer contours without dominating the tonal areas.

An important group of prints is associated with ANDREA MANTEGNA and the Mantegna school engravers Zoan Andrea and Giovanni Antonio da Brescia, among others. Mantegna has traditionally been thought to have engraved only seven prints himself, but his drawings were the basis for many others. In the late 20th century the question of attribution was under re-examination (Boorsch, Landau). Stylistically, many of the Mantegna prints are 'broadmanner' engravings and show much influence of Pollaiuolo, but many of the later prints are in a 'fine' style. Whether this is a question of evolution or reflects the different backgrounds of the engravers, it is clear that these engravings were meant to imitate Mantegna's pen drawings. In contrast to those of Pollaiuolo, in such prints as the *Risen Christ* (early 1470s; Hind, no. 7) and the *Battle of the Sea Gods* (1470s; Hind, nos 5, 6) the outlines are less fluid, more angular, more varied in width of line and have more interior drawing. The device of leaving white space between hatching and a contour to help round a form is frequently employed, and some of Mantegna's engravers used it with less understanding than others. Mantegna's *Virgin and Child* (*c.* 1480–85; Hind, no. 1), in which the image appears to have been developed as it was engraved, is convincing as an autograph work. Mantegna and Mantegna school prints include innovative narrative scenes from the Passion, and classicism permeates his vision of both Christian and ancient mythology and history. Mantegna prints were widely influential in Italy, Germany and the Netherlands.

BIBLIOGRAPHY

M. Lehrs: *Geschichte und kritischer Katalog des deutschen, niederländischen und französischen Kupferstichs im 15. Jahrhundert*, 9 vols (Vienna, 1908–34; New York, 1970)
A. M. Hind: *Andrea Mantegna and the Italian Pre-Raphaelite Engravers* (London, 1911)
——: *Nielli, Chiefly Italian of the XV Century, Plates, Sulphur Casts and Prints, Preserved in the British Museum* (London, 1936)
——: *Early Italian Engraving: A Critical Catalogue with Complete Reproduction of All the Prints Described*, 7 vols (London, 1938–48)
Fifteenth-century Engravings of Northern Europe (exh. cat. by A. Shestack, Washington, DC, N.G.A., 1967)
A. Shestack: *The Complete Engravings of Martin Schongauer* (New York, 1969)
A. Hyatt Mayor: *Prints and People* (New York, 1971), pp. 138–140
Early Italian Engravings from the National Gallery of Art (exh. cat. by J. Levenson, K. Oberhuber and J. Sheehan, Washington, DC, N.G.A., 1973)
R. Field, L. Richards and A. Shestack: *A Census of Fifteenth-century Prints in Public Collections of the United States and Canada* (New Haven, 1985)
S. Boorsch: 'Mantegna and his Printmakers', *Andrea Mantegna* (exh. cat., ed. J. Martineau; New York, Met.; London, RA; 1992), pp. 56–66
D. Landau: 'Mantegna as Printmaker', *Andrea Mantegna* (exh. cat., ed. J. Martineau; New York, Met.; London, RA; 1992), pp. 44–54
D. Landau and P. Parshall: *The Renaissance Print, 1470–1550* (New Haven and London, 1994)

3. *c.* 1500–*c.* 1600. The 16th century was dominated by Albrecht Dürer, Marcantonio Raimondi, Lucas van Leyden and Hendrick Goltzius and their differing conceptions of engraving. The print's function as an original work of art was firmly established, notably by Dürer. Two major approaches to engraving technique evolved: one stressed contour, texture and light by a complex but often unsystematized linear vocabulary; the other stressed the rendering of solid form rather than surface and light, depending on geometric, abstract line systems. This second approach dominated 16th-century reproductive engraving, and its graphic language of evenly spaced, unmodulated lines and dots influenced the way in which styles, paintings and sculptures were known and understood. The beginnings of etching *c.* 1510 were also crucial for important interrelationships; printmakers often worked in both media, even in the same plate. At first most artists saw etching primarily as a fast way to make engravings and drew on plates in ways that imitate engraving. Etching gradually achieved independence and developed its own language (*see* ETCHING, §II).

(i) Major exponents and their influences. (ii) Commercial growth.

(i) Major exponents and their influences.

(a) Dürer. (b) Raimondi. (c) Lucas van Leyden. (d) Goltzius. (e) Duvet and other French engravers.

(a) Dürer. In the evolution from line to tone, the work of Albrecht Dürer far exceeded what had been achieved by his predecessors (*see* DÜRER, (1)). He not only perfected engraving technique and expanded its subject-matter but also made it a fully independent art form. Dürer's earliest engravings, such as the *Oriental Family* (*c.* 1496; B. 85), are firmly in the 15th-century northern European tradition and show the influence of Schongauer in their use of line and of the Housebook Master in the intimate informality of their subjects. The burin work of the technically innovative *Prodigal Son amid the Swine* (*c.* 1496; B. 28) imitates the specific textures of the barnyard, and Dürer exploited the burr's ability to catch ink. In this early work his understanding of musculature is evident, and the representation of landscape and pictorial space is ambitious. Classical and mythological subject-matter and a continuing study of the nude began appearing in such prints as *Nemesis* (1501–3; B. 77).

By 1500 Dürer was engraving grey tones composed of tiny lines and flecks that smooth transitions into an ever deeper pictorial space. Landscape and naturalistic details, such as the animals in *St Eustache* (*c.* 1501; B. 57), became more important, and first-hand observation of towns, castles and ruins gave a new realism to his images. The *Fall of Man* (1504; B. 1), the only print that he fully signed and dated, demonstrates his skill as an engraver and his mastery of the nude, and it achieved a synthesis between sculptural Italian classicism and northern realism with its emphasis on description, texture and light. In a trilogy of images exploring human temperament he created his masterworks: *Knight, Death and the Devil* (1513; B. 98), *St Jerome in his Study* (1514; B. 60; see fig. 4) and *Melencolia I* (1514; B. 74; *see* DÜRER, (1), fig. 9). In his engravings after 1515, including the new subject of portraiture, Dürer simplified and monumentalized his compositions, which he achieved with subtle tonal range and deliberate use of the paper as light; he used parallel lines that filter the white of the paper, and intermingled delicate hatching and dotting to create greys.

Dürer's realism and his technique influenced the works of his contemporary Albrecht Altdorfer and the next generation of Nuremberg artists, George Pencz, Sebald Beham, Barthel Beham and Heinrich Aldegrever, known collectively as the LITTLE MASTERS, after the size of their prints. Their works also show knowledge of Marcantonio Raimondi's line system and understanding of Classical form. Among this group, Aldegrever remained closest to a purely northern tradition.

(b) Raimondi. One of the most influential engravers of the 16th century, MARCANTONIO RAIMONDI, was a student of Francesco Francia, a painter. Raimondi was a product of Bolognese humanism and antiquarianism, and his interest in antique sculpture is evident in his mastery of plasticity. By *c.* 1506 Raimondi was working in Venice, which was emerging as an important centre for engraving, influenced by the colourism and atmospheric effects of Venetian painting, and for such engravers as Jacopo de' Barbari, Girolamo Mocetto, Giulio Campagnola and his son Domenico Campagnola. Jacopo de' Barbari, the first important Italian engraver to travel and work in Germany and the Netherlands, influenced Dürer; their relationship has been carefully studied. His work is characterized by figures with elongated insubstantial bodies engraved with long, elegant, massed parallel strokes that give his prints a silvery, atmospheric quality. In Venice, Raimondi engraved copies of Dürer's engravings and woodcuts; in 1506 Dürer brought a legal complaint against him. Raimondi was, in a sense, Dürer's greatest student, learning from his prints a more refined and orderly technique, and incorporating a greater range, delicacy and expressiveness of cuts. Raimondi seems to have learnt something of the use of stipple from Giulio Campagnola, a highly original artist, who made prints after his own designs and borrowed from such sources as Dürer's prints. Campagnola developed a method of engraving that was flexible enough to imitate and interpret painterly tone and atmosphere through the predominant use of stipple. His design after Mantegna's *St John the Baptist* (Hind, no. 5) sets a tightly outlined figure, modelled entirely with dots, into a stippled Giorgionesque *sfumato* landscape.

Raimondi left Venice *c.* 1508, and it is assumed that he travelled via Florence, where he recorded Michelangelo's *Battle of Cascina* (1504–5; destr. *c.* 1515). In his engraving depicting *The Climbers* (1510; B. 487), he combined figures from Michelangelo's large cartoon with a landscape from the engraving *Muhammad and the Monk* (1508; B. 126) by Lucas van Leyden. Settling in Rome, he engraved after drawings by artists there. His most important working relationship was with Raphael. Although their specific

4. Engraving by Albrecht Dürer: *St Jerome in his Study* (detail), 248×191 mm, 1514 (London, British Museum)

arrangement remains unclear, Raimondi frequently used working drawings of projects in progress in Raphael's shop, which often reflect a conception that differs in certain respects from the finished painting. The engravers did not go to the site of an installed canvas or fresco to copy the model. Some images, such as the *Judgement of Paris* (*c.* 1517–20; B. 245; see fig. 5), seem to have been made specifically to be engraved. This print is a highpoint of Raimondi's mature style. He used a highly disciplined engraving technique to clarify three-dimensional form: masses of evenly spaced, curving parallels and dots create forms and shapes that abut each other, eliminating the need for contour line; paper also shows through, playing the role of light. After Raphael's death (1520), Raimondi made engravings after Giulio Romano and Baccio Bandinelli. Gaoled in 1524 for engraving Giulio Romano's erotic series *I modi*, he was released the next year but lost all his possessions during the Sack of Rome (1527). He is thought to have returned to Bologna.

Raimondi's engraving style was adaptable and easy to learn. His workshop included a number of engravers who closely followed his style and copied his prints, including Marco Dente, Agostino dei Musi and the Master of the Die. Raimondi's prints diffused the authoritative version of High Renaissance style throughout Europe. Through them not only Raphael's but also his own manner became widely imitated. His great contribution was to make engraving the pre-eminent means of pictorial transmission.

5. Engraving by Marcantonio Raimondi: *Judgement of Paris* (detail), 292×433 mm, *c.* 1517–20 (Paris, Musée du Louvre)

important work, the *Marriage of Cupid and Psyche* (1575; B. 40), after Giulio Romano, is a long three-plate engraving representing sections of the Palazzo del Te fresco, engraved with perfect understanding of Raimondi's technique half a century after its formulation.

Giorgio Ghisi refined Raimondi's manner, adding more variety and delicacy, making it more tonal. His prints often have a granular, tactile, though never sensuous quality, the result of the extensive use of dots intermixed with hatching and diagonal lines that create lozenge crosshatching and concentric and curving parallels. His minutely spaced cuts function optically, filtering the light of the paper overlaid with plate tone, producing the perception of different tones of black. Primarily a reproductive engraver, he worked after designs by many artists, including Raphael, Giulio Romano, Luca Penni, Bronzino, Francesco Primaticcio and Michelangelo. His most important and complex image, executed with an engraving technique of ultimate richness, was the enigmatic *Allegory of Life* (1561; B. 67). He is significant as the personal conveyor of Raimondi's reproductive engraving style to the most important publishing centres in the north.

(c) Lucas van Leyden. The most important body of work in the Netherlands was produced by LUCAS VAN LEYDEN, whose career overlapped Dürer's and Raimondi's; it included *c.* 180 engravings that reflect major technical and stylistic transformations throughout his career. His early engraving technique involved the use of minute strokes, producing an all-over lightness and delicacy that were quickly noted by Raimondi in Italy. Later van Leyden began to incorporate delicate crosshatching into his linear vocabulary. He was strongly influenced by prints of such northern engravers as Schongauer, and later by Dürer, whom he met. Van Leyden's interest in the natural world is striking, and he was a gifted observer of figures and landscape. His portrait of *Holy Roman Emperor Maximilian I* (*c.* 1520; B. 172) was one of the first prints to combine preparatory line work in etching with engraving. By the 1530s his awareness of Raimondi was reflected in his shift to a more abstract linear system that stresses form rather than the nature of material and to Classical subject-matter and a thorough understanding of the nude. His late style is almost Mannerist in its conception of the figure.

Van Leyden's engraving style formed the basis for Dirk Vellert's work. A glass painter and dean of the painters' guild of Antwerp, he made *c.* 21 fascinating prints, including mixed etchings and engravings, and woodcuts. These combine a late northern Gothic sense of line, light and penchant for detail with Italian Renaissance classical motifs, as in his *St Luke Painting the Virgin* (1526; B. 9). Vellert is unusual in that he often signed and dated his prints with the day, month and year.

(d) Goltzius. By the end of the 16th century Haarlem and Amsterdam had become important centres for print publishing; many artists and intellectuals fled the southern Netherlands. The best-known Haarlem printmaker was HENDRICK GOLTZIUS. He was trained in Xanten by the engraver, writer, political agitator, statesman and humanist Dirck Coornhert, who had worked for Hieronymous Cock. Goltzius followed his teacher to Haarlem and settled

Among the engravers under Raimondi's influence who worked in Rome after the Sack was Giovanni Jacopo Caraglio, who made prints after designs of Raphael, Parmigianino and Rosso Fiorentino, producing vigorously engraved models of Mannerist style. Enea Vico produced over 500 engravings, applying Raimondi school techniques to Mannerist images, costume studies, portraits and title-pages. Giulio di Antonio Bonasone made hundreds of engravings after Raphael, Michelangelo and Parmigianino as well as after his own compositions. Martino Rota was active in Rome, Florence and Venice, and brought Raimondi's technique north to Vienna, where he worked for the Imperial court. His very fine and orderly technique combined etching with engraving, as in his portrait of the Holy Roman Emperor *Rudolf II* (1570s; B. 96). Raimondi's controlled and delicate manner was continued by a group of Mantuans and north Italians in the circle of Giulio Romano. These were Giovanni Battista Scultori, his children Adamo Scultori and Diana Scultori, and Giorgio Ghisi. Diana Scultori worked in Mantua and Rome, where she engraved after her own designs and after paintings and stuccos by Giulio Romano and others. Her most

there in 1577. Many of his earliest engravings were religious and allegorical subjects after Coornhert, Joannes Stradanus and Maarten van Heemskerck, and they were published by Cock's widow and by Philip Galle. While some of Goltzius's early prints are delicate and descriptive, others are engraved in a bolder linear system in the style of Cornelis Cort. Goltzius mastered many engraving styles, employing linear languages appropriate to the images engraved.

Goltzius began publishing independently in Haarlem c. 1578, producing both original works and reproductions. He delicately engraved portraits that capture personality as well as the sheen of satin and intricacies of decoration. He also began to incorporate elegantly flourished, italic engraved calligraphy in his inscriptional spaces. Towards 1580 swelling, curving and serpentine line and lozenge crosshatching became more important in his work. He tempered Cort's and Agostino Carracci's abstract reproductive manner with extraordinary delicacy and a greater sense of light. His reproductive technique found its perfect vehicle in the late Mannerist style of Bartholomäus Spranger, whose anti-naturalistic, elongated figures, postures and gestures and implied eroticism became the basis for his mid-career engraving and drawing styles from c. 1585 to 1593. The *Wedding of Cupid and Psyche* (1587; B. 277; see fig. 6; after a wash drawing by Spranger), a remarkable *tour de force*, is Goltzius's most important reproductive work in this style. The virtuosity of Spranger's draughtsmanship in the musculature and billowing clouds is complemented by the curving, swelling lines of Goltzius's engraving technique. Goltzius's bravura series of Sprangeresque *Roman Heroes* (1586; B. 94–103) and his prints of contemporary military leaders and standard-bearers (mid-1580s) can be connected with the disintegrating political situation in the Netherlands. The monumental figure standing in close foreground against a deep landscape space filled with tiny figures in combat was to become a standard compositional formula for single-figure prints.

Goltzius achieved wide fame throughout Europe, and in 1590 he travelled incognito to Italy, where he studied and drew for about a year. His Italian experience is evident from new subject-matter in such prints as the numerous engravings by him and his students after Polidoro da Caravaggio's frescoes. The inherent three-dimensionality of his engraving style gave a new impetus to the use of engraving to depict actual works of sculpture, for example his *Farnese Hercules* (c. 1592; B. 143) and *Apollo Belvedere* (c. 1592, dated 1617; B. 145). His experience in Italy is also apparent in the relaxing of his Sprangeresque style in favour of a greater naturalism.

In 1593–4 Goltzius engraved a series of six scenes from the *Life of the Virgin* (B. 15–20), known as the 'Master Prints', which he designed in the manner of various painters: Federico Barocci, Parmigianino, Jacopo Bassano, Raphael, Lucas van Leyden and Dürer. He used not only the imagery and style associated with each of these artists but also the appropriate manners of engraving, so effectively that his *Circumcision* (1594; B 18) in the manner of Dürer fooled his contemporaries into thinking it was an authentic, previously unknown work. Throughout the 1590s Goltzius worked in a variety of contemporary and historic styles of engraving. In his *Passion* (1596–8; B. 27–38) he drew on Lucas van Leyden's Dürer-influenced style of the 1520s. Goltzius also engraved a number of magnificent portraits from life, such as *Frederick de Vries* (1597; B. 190), in which he combined different engraving techniques in a single plate. He had ceased engraving by 1600, probably because his eyesight had deteriorated, and turned to painting. His dazzling mastery of the various burin techniques set the direction and standards of excellence for the next generation.

Goltzius's students and other engravers under his influence worked well into the next century. Jacob Matham, Jacques de Gheyn II, Jan Saenredam and Willem Swanenburgh produced important reproductive and original prints. The prints by Matham, Goltzius's stepson, are characterized by a dryness and sculptural quality, with much use of crosshatching. Jacques de Gheyn II stressed colouristic effects and produced many works after Goltzius and Karel van Mander I. He also designed extraordinary original images that were engraved by himself and by Zacharias Dolendo and Andries Jacobsz Stock (*b c.* 1580; *d* after 1648).

Saenredam made engravings after Goltzius's designs and also became a gifted interpreter of the drawings of the young Abraham Bloemaert. Saenredam's original engravings include the *Beached Whale at Beverwijck* (1602; B 11) and the beautiful, nocturnal series the *Wise and Foolish Virgins* (1605; B. 2–6). Late Dutch Mannerist delight in artifice and virtuosity reached a highpoint in the works of the virtuoso engraver Jan Muller, a master of the swelling, serpentine line. He had an extraordinary ability to define three-dimensional form and was admired for his ability to engrave using no more than two intersecting lines in crosshatching. He engraved swelling, tapering, curving lines that intersect at angles and dot the lozenge interstices. His line system sometimes produced moiré patterns and optical vibrations; this system of engraving persisted in portrait and banknote engraving into the 20th century. In some of Muller's works, however, such as the *Adoration of the Magi* (1598; B. 2), he suppressed optical effects in favour of a more delicate and descriptive technique, with long parallels, converging lines and dense, rich crosshatching, which create a dark nocturnal scene with dramatic lighting.

(e) Duvet and other French engravers. In France the goldsmith and engraver JEAN DUVET knew the work of Mantegna, Raimondi's prints after Raphael, and Michelangelo. Dürer's woodcut series *Apocalypse* (1496–8) inspired Duvet's own visionary series (completed 1555). These dark images reflect his goldsmith's delight in textures and details and are richly expressionistic and personal. Such compositions as *St Michael and the Dragon* (1546–55; B. 25) are completely packed in a wonderful, driving, hallucinatory chaos. From c. 1557 Etienne Delaune engraved delicate ornament prints and illustrations. His inventive designs contain slender, elongated figures. He is notable for using stipple to show dematerialized figures and landscapes. In Lyon, Jean Gourmont (i) engraved images of small figures in monumental, dark, arched interiors, using a technique that showed considerable knowledge of Marcantonio Raimondi. Georges Reverdy

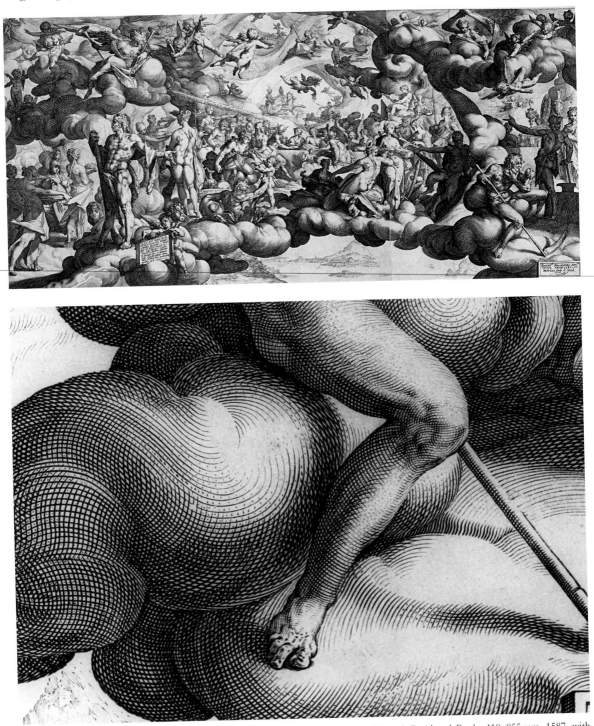

6. Engraving by Hendrick Goltzius after a drawing by Bartholomäus Spranger: *Wedding of Cupid and Psyche*, 410×855 mm, 1587, with (below) a detail of the right foreground figure (Amsterdam, Rijksmuseum)

made prints influenced by both Gourmont and Duvet, with a similar compression of space and sense of anxiety. Most of the printmakers associated with the Fontainebleau school were primarily etchers, but Domenico del Barbiere's engravings include striking original and reproductive images that are close to Raimondi's school technique. Pierre Milan made reproductive engravings of Rosso Fiorentino's images (*see* FONTAINEBLEAU SCHOOL, fig. 1) in a detached, mechanical, unsensuous style that shows considerable disparity between image and technique.

(ii) Commercial growth. During the 16th century engraving became an important international cultural and commercial activity (*see* PRINTS, §IV, 2). As engravings and engravers began to circulate, prints became the primary agent of the transmission and interchange of image, style and graphic technique. In Italy by the middle of the century print publishing was well established in Rome with the publishers Antoine Lafréry, Tommaso Barlacchi (*fl* 1540–50), Antonio Salamanca, Nicholas van Aelst (*b* 1526; *d* after 1612) and Philippe Thomassin. In addition to reproductive prints, they produced views of Classical ruins and Roman churches, maps and illustrated guidebooks. Engravings began to be used for book illustrations, with the engraved title-pages first appearing in Venice *c.* 1518 and every year from 1548 (*see* BOOK ILLUSTRATION, §I, 2). Despite the need for passing a sheet through two different presses, one for the text in relief and the other for the intaglio image, engraving gradually replaced the woodcut for book illustration. Engraving was capable of producing more impressions and was favoured for its greater ability to represent three-dimensional form, details and tone. The development of engraving technique was greatly affected by the expansion of the commerce in prints. Publishers needed plates that could withstand large print runs or could be easily reworked. This favoured the use of Raimondi's regularly spaced line systems and impersonal styles.

The engraver and etcher Hieronymus Cock of Antwerp went to Italy in the 1540s. In Rome he made drawings of Classical ruins and probably met Giorgio Ghisi whom he invited to work for him. He began his publishing business Aux Quatre Vents *c.* 1548 in Antwerp and gradually turned from engraving to running it, with the height of its activity between 1555 and 1565. It was a melting-pot in which his international staff of engravers and etchers made prints in different styles for a varied and far-flung market. Northern European engravers by mid-century were trained in the artist-engraver tradition of Dürer and Lucas van Leyden with its original images and personal repertories of strokes, rich texture and tone and an emphasis on description; they were, however, also exposed to a more abstract linear system that emphasized form, through the primarily reproductive prints coming from Italy and through Ghisi. The result was a cross-fertilization, with the Italian system becoming more delicate and varied, the northern more regularized.

Unlike publications from many engraving shops, those of Hieronymus Cock (*see* COCK, (3)) were characterized by variety rather than uniformity of style. Cock's chief engravers included Cornelis Bos, the brothers Jan and Lucas van Doetechum, Pieter van der Heyden, Dirck Volkertsz. Coornhert, Cornelis Cort and Philip Galle, each working in an individual manner. Contemporary Dutch and Flemish artists provided designs, and Joannes Stradanus sent drawings from Florence. His prints after Frans Floris and Maarten van Heemskerck document the changes taking place in Netherlandish art as it was totally transformed by Italian Renaissance and Mannerist influences. Cock's publications after Hieronymus Bosch and Pieter Bruegel I were important for the future development of Dutch art. Landscape was an important element in

prints from his circle, and the rise of independent landscape painting in Dutch and Flemish art owed much to these works. The works that his engravers produced included single images and cycles from the Bible and Lives of the Saints, allegories, Classical and mythological subjects, portraits, architectural views, maps, ornament and reproductions of Italian paintings. These prints were often issued with inscriptions in two or more languages. Prints from Aux Quatre Vents were sent as far as South America and were found in the *Nova Zemblaya* shipwreck off the northern coast of Russia, bound for Japan.

Antwerp became the most important centre for map and topographical engraving, in association with the work of Gerard Mercator (1512–94) and Abraham Ortelius. Christoph Plantin's publishing house, the Golden Compasses, printed engraved maps, title-pages and book illustrations. Map engraving's allied speciality of lettering engraving enabled the first engraved calligraphy manual, *Esercitatio alphabetica*, after the work of the scriptor Clement Perret and engraved by Cornelis de Hooghe, to be issued by Plantin in 1569. Antwerp was also the home of Jan Wierix, Jerome Wierix and Anton Wierix II. These engravers massed tiny, delicate strokes so that the eye perceives silvery tones capable of infinite nuances of light, colour and texture. Their workshop production of over 2000 engravings included portraits, reproductions of paintings, copies of older prints and many small devotional images of their own design that found their way around the world under the auspices of the Jesuit Order. One of these was the model for one of the earliest copperplate engravings made in Japan in 1597 by a Jesuit near Nagasaki.

Throughout Europe family workshops produced thousands of engravings for local and international trade. Crispijn van de Passe (i) founded a dynasty that was active well into the next century in Utrecht, Cologne, London and Paris. Flemish engravers travelled and worked throughout Europe, spreading various Antwerp engraving styles to England, France and Germany. Members of the engraving dynasty including Raphael Sadeler I worked in Munich, and his nephew Aegidius Sadeler II was active in Prague and engraved after Spranger.

Dutch and Flemish engravers were the first to be active in England, where the earliest engravings were published in the 1540s. Early engraving commerce centred on the production of maps, topographic illustration and portraits of Elizabeth I and the nobility. Theodore de Bry engraved John White's drawings of the expedition of Sir Walter Raleigh to Virginia, 1585–6. William Rodgers (i) was the first important native English engraver. His images of Elizabeth I combine a goldsmith's love of ornament with Christian iconic conventions, realistic portraiture, Flemish landscape, classical victory iconography and Mannerist strapwork. His engraving technique recalls Cock's atonal linear work of a generation earlier, and his prints do not reflect any of the major changes that had taken place in engraving style by his time.

Many of the engravers who passed through Cock's shop went on to have independent careers. Cornelis Cort left *c.* 1560 for Italy, where he worked for Titian for several years. Titian favoured his colouristic northern burin style, which more closely approximated to the qualities of Venetian painting, over the flatter Roman engraving.

Under Titian, Cort developed a new manner of using the burin, cutting lines that swell and taper: intersecting groups of swelling, curving parallels meet to form lozenge cross-hatching, setting up moiré patterns that catch light and also produce optical vibrations that stimulate a near-perception of colour. Outline became redundant, since form and light created contour. Cort's new technique was the result of blending Italian systematization with a northern sensibility, capturing the black-and-white equivalent of colour and light in an abstract, all-purpose system. It opened new possibilities for reproduction of paintings but required a higher level of skill on the part of the engraver in calibrating the spacing, and controlling the curvature and swell of the line. The virtuosity of an engraver therefore became a crucial factor, and the linear language of the medium headed in a new direction.

In Rome Cort's style influenced Francesco Villamena. Villamena learnt to engrave parallel lines that flow over a form like a contour map, for this new swelling line gave engravers the ability to model form, imply contour and modulate tone without resorting to outline and crosshatching. Villamena engraved many images of beggars, introducing to printmaking a new subject, which was taken up in the 17th century by many etchers. Agostino Carracci, the foremost follower of Cort in Italy, adopted Cort's swelling, curving burin technique in Bologna *c.* 1578. He purged it of its northern and Venetian colourism, contrast and texture by opening up the spacing between lines and intersections, letting more paper show. Carracci is credited with over 200 engravings, including reproductive prints, portraits, coats of arms and ornament. Annibale Carracci began to etch *c.* 1590. Etching offered a greater freedom in drawing and softer atmospheric effects than engraving, but he successfully combined both techniques to achieve a looser, more painterly engraving style. Agostino Carracci followed his lead, and his later engravings also combine etching.

BIBLIOGRAPHY

Hollstein: *Dut. & Flem.*; Hollstein: *Ger.*
A. von Bartsch: *Le Peintre-graveur* (1803–21) [B.]
C. Dodgson: *Albrecht Dürer: Engravings and Etchings* (London, 1926/R New York, 1967)
A. F. Johnson: *A Catalogue of Italian Engraved Title-pages in the Sixteenth Century* (Oxford, 1936)
A. M. Hind, M. Corbett and M. Norton: *Engraving in England in the Sixteenth and Seventeenth Centuries: A Descriptive Catalogue with Introductions*, 3 vols (Cambridge, 1952–64)
Die Kunst der Graphik: Das Zeitalter Albrecht Dürers (exh. cat. by A. Strobl, Vienna, Albertina, 1964)
Die Kunst der Graphik IV: Zwischen Renaissance und Barock, das Zeitalter von Bruegel und Bellange (exh. cat. by K. Oberhuber, Vienna, Albertina, 1967)
H. Zerner: *The School of Fontainebleau* (New York, 1969)
Albrecht Dürer: Master Printmaker (exh. cat., Boston, MA, Mus. F.A., 1971)
T. Riggs: *Hieronymous Cock: Printmaker and Publisher in Antwerp at the Sign of the Four Winds* (New York, 1977) [with earlier bibliog.; cat. rai. of prts & drgs, checklist of prt pubns] [R]
W. Strauss: *Hendrik Goltzius: The Complete Engravings and Woodcuts*, 2 vols (New York, 1977)
I. M. Veldman: *Maarten van Heemskerck and Dutch Humanism in the Sixteenth Century* (Maarssen, 1977)
H. Mielke: *Manierismus in Holland um 1600: Kupferstiche, Holzschnitte und Zeichnungen aus dem Berliner Kupferstichkabinett* (exh. cat., W. Berlin, Kupferstichkab., 1979)
Prints and Related Drawings by the Carracci Family (exh. cat. by D. G. Bohlin, Washington, DC, N.G.A., 1979)
Incisori mantovani del '500; Giovan Battista, Adamo, Diana Scultori e Giorgio Ghisi dalle collezioni del Gabinetto Nazionale delle Stampe e della Calcografia Nazionale (exh. cat. by S. Massari, Rome, Calcografia N., 1980)
The Engravings of Marcantonio Raimondi (exh. cat. by I. Shoemaker and E. Broun, Lawrence, U. KS, Spencer Mus. A., 1981)
The Prints of Lucas van Leyden and his Contemporaries (exh. cat. by E. Jacobowitz and S. Stepanek, Washington, DC, N.G.A.; Boston, MA, Mus. F.A.; 1983)
The Engravings of Giorgio Ghisi (exh. cat. by S. Boorsch, M. Lewis and R. E. Lewis, New York, Met., 1985)
Mannerist Prints: International Style in the Sixteenth Century (exh. cat. by B. Davis, Los Angeles, CA, Co. Mus. A., 1988)
The World in Miniature: Engravings by the German Little Masters, 1500–1550 (exh. cat. by S. Goddard, Lawrence, U. KS, Spencer Mus. A., 1988)
Una dinastia di incisori: I Saedeler (exh. cat. by C. L. Virdis, F. Pellegrini and G. Piccin, Padua, Mus. Civ., 1992)
N. Orenstein and others: 'Print Publishers in the Netherlands, 1580–1620', *Dawn of the Golden Age* (exh. cat., Amsterdam, Rijksmus., 1993)
R. Ralkenburg, J. P. Filedt Kok and H. Leeflang: *Nederlands kunsthistorisch jaarboek, 1991–1992*, xlii and xliii of *Goltzius Studies: Hendrick Goltzius (1558–1617)* (Zwolle, 1993)
Giulo Romano pinxit et delineavit: Opere grafiche autografe di collaborazione e bottega (exh. cat. by S. Massari, Rome, Ist. N. Graf., 1993)
Graven Images: The Rise of Professional Printmakers in Antwerp and Haarlem, 1540–1640 (exh. cat. by T. Riggs and L. Silver, Evanston, IL, Northwestern U., 1993)

4. *c.* 1600–*c.* 1750. Although a small group of engravers worked in a richly tonal and descriptive style, engravers throughout Europe favoured parallel-line or lozenge-hatched line systems. Fewer artists executed original engravings, preferring the freedom of etching for their printmaking. Engraving became largely concerned with reproduction, portraiture, book illustration, maps and music. After *c.* 1620 printmakers trying to create a graphic equivalent for dark tone turned to mixed techniques such as etching in combination with drypoint and engraving, monotype and tonal wiping and finally to mezzotint.

(i) Callot, Bosse and the status of engraving. (ii) Engraved lettering and cartography. (iii) Reproductive engraving. (iv) Portrait engraving.

(i) Callot, Bosse and the status of engraving. Although JACQUES CALLOT of Nancy is best known as an etcher, he was first trained as an engraver. Callot's understanding of engraving greatly affected his practice of etching. Even after he took up etching, he continued to work with the linear systems of Mannerist engraving, rather than in the freer drawing style possible in etching. The two major technical contributions to etching with which Callot is traditionally credited, the *échoppe* and reliable hard ground, were the result of his attempts to make etching more like engraving. Callot's most important follower, Abraham Bosse, the author of the *Traicte des manieres de graver en taille douce* (Paris, 1645), the first truly useful printmaking shop manual, stated that 'The etcher's chief aim is to counterfeit engraving'.

Encouragement of the arts in general by Louis XIV, King of France, stimulated the demand for more engravings. The commerce of prints, by then centred in Paris, led to the amassing of the first great collections, such as that of Michel de Marolles with over 123,400 prints. The King's purchase in 1660 of Marolles's collection became the nucleus of the Calcographie du Louvre. Important print dealers and publishers such as the Mariette family began the documentation of prints, which laid the foundations for the first catalogues and print histories of the

18th century. Engravers were admitted to the Académie in 1655.

(ii) Engraved lettering and cartography. During the early 17th century a remarkable flourishing of calligraphy existed in the Netherlands, and Amsterdam and Haarlem continued to be important centres for the specialized skill of engraved lettering. Jodocus Hondius I, Cornelis Boissens (1567–1635), Gerard Gauw (*c.* 1580–1638) and Simon Frisius engraved writing-books after their own and other scriptors' exemplars, including those of the great calligrapher Jan van den Velde II. Cartography was another Dutch speciality, with vast wall maps, globes and celestial spheres, bound maps and navigational charts by engravers and publishers such as Jodocus Hondius and Hendrik Hondius 'II', Pieter van den Keere (*b* 1570/71; *d* after 1645) and Willem Jansz. Blaeu (*fl* 1571; *d* 1638).

(iii) Reproductive engraving. Pictorial developments in early Baroque painting began to have an impact on Mannerist engraving from *c.* 1600. Renewed naturalism in art produced interest in the problem of the representation of specific time and light conditions, such as the nocturnal and candle-lit scenes of Caravaggio in Italy and his northern European followers. Engravers attempted to translate such effects into graphic terms, but the glittering Mannerist linear systems were not adequate for the expression of the darkest tonalities. The nocturnal paintings of Adam Elsheimer, active in Rome, were transmitted to the north through the influential reproductive engravings of Hendrik Goudt, a Dutch engraver working in Rome and Utrecht. He developed an engraving style that involved the building-up of deep blacks through countless minutely crosshatched and parallel lines. In his nocturnal *Flight into Egypt* (1613; Hollstein, no. 3) after Elsheimer, he achieved the effects of fire, starlight and moonlight reflected in water. He also incorporated beautiful engraved calligraphic inscriptions in the lower margins of his prints. In the 1620s Jan van de Velde II began to engrave in Goudt's manner, increasing the contrast between dramatic lighting and velvety blackness. Also in the 1620s Magdalena van de Passe in Utrecht engraved in a very dark manner after Jan Pynas under the influence of Elsheimer.

In Antwerp the brothers Boetius Bolswert and Schelte Bolswert engraved in a style that blended a traditional northern delicacy and emphasis on drawing, details and light with current reproductive technique. Schelte produced many engravings after Rubens as well as after such 16th-century artists as David Vinckboons. Rubens designed hundreds of images to be engraved, including title-pages for books published by Christoph Plantin's press. Rubens employed and closely trained or retrained engravers to reproduce his designs, including Pieter Soutman, Cornelis Galle (i), Willem (Isaacsz.) van Swanenburgh (*d* 1612) and Lucas Vorsterman (i). The difference between the Dutch engravers who continued to follow Goltzius and the engravers of the Rubens school is that, although both groups used linear systems, the Antwerp engravers had less interest in engraving that primarily displayed the engraver's virtuosity. The painting or drawing to be reproduced was the paramount reason for the engraving, and Rubens's close involvement is evident in these prints. Rubens's engravers concentrated on translating the effects of light and colour into the black-and-white graphic language of line. Lucas Vorsterman, who was originally trained by Goltzius, used delicate strokes organized in groups of curving and concentric parallels and short dotted lines that disintegrate into areas of white highlights. He laid straight lines over curved ones to create crosshatched reticulations. Vorsterman eventually left Rubens's studio and went to England, where from 1624 to 1630 he engraved after van Dyck. Vorsterman's student Paulus Pontius continued to work for Rubens. Both Vorsterman and Pontius collaborated with van Dyck on his *Iconography* (*c.* 1632–44), a series of portraits of his contemporaries etched in a free drawing style in the preliminary states and then formally finished in engraving by Vorsterman, Pontius, the Bolswerts and Pieter de Jode (ii), among others.

Compositions by Raphael and the Bolognese Baroque painters Annibale Carracci, Domenichino and Guido Reni were important subjects for reproductive engraving. French reproductive engravers became more experimental in their use of mixed techniques and sought alternatives to the standard formulas of line-engraving. Underdrawing in etching prior to engraving allowed engravers to move away from rigid geometric linear reticulations towards a more fluid and intuitive drawing style. The burin added a crisp black in contrast to the corroded etched line. Girard Audran prepared his plates by underdrawing in etching and did not hide the etched line but exploited its variety in combination with the crisp engraved line. Much of his work was after paintings by Simon Vouet and Charles Lebrun. Towards 1700 mixed engraving and etching was used by Audran's descendants and other engravers for the reproduction of Watteau's paintings and drawings. Nicolas-Henry Tardieu and Charles-Nicolas Cochin I dominated engraving in Paris in the 1720s and 1730s. They perfected the combination of etching and engraving, using the *échoppe* to simulate engraving in the underdrawing but engraving with the openness and freedom possible in etching. Cochin's *Village Bride* (1729; see 1984 exh. cat., no. 14) and Tardieu's *Embarkation for Cythera* (1733; see 1984 exh. cat., nos 15a and 15b), both after Watteau, represent a new, more spontaneous and less mechanical approach to reproductive engraving.

Great experimentation took place in France in the 18th century. New tools and techniques for reproductive printmaking were developed. The collecting of drawings and watercolours stimulated a market for new types of prints. The old line systems that had served to translate painting were inadequate to replicate chalk, pastel and wash. Stipple tools, roulettes and mattoirs were used in combination with engraved line and etching in a new direct technique known as CRAYON MANNER. Gilles Demarteau excelled in imitating the chalk drawings of François Boucher and printed his plates in red and brown inks. Multiple-plate colour printing simulating pastel was perfected by Louis-Marin Bonnet, working after Boucher and other contemporary painters. The *Encyclopédie, ou dictionnaire raisonné des sciences, des arts et des métiers*, edited by Denis Diderot and Jean d'Alembert (Paris, 1751–72), contained detailed articles written by engravers on both the history and techniques of engraving. The illustrations included the latest tools and methods and are important documents of 18th-century printmaking (see fig. 7).

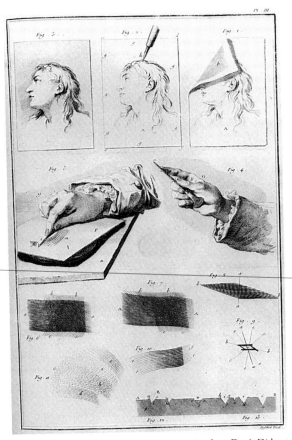

7. Copperplate-engraving techniques; illustration from Denis Diderot and Jean d'Alembert, eds: *Encyclopédie* (Paris, 1751–72), pl. iii (London, British Library)

copper plates using a stipple technique of dots and flecks along with longer lines, maintaining the quality of chalk on rough paper. His engravings have a naturalness, immediacy and freedom that set them apart from those by his contemporaries, and the subjects look out of oval and octagonal frames. In France during the late 16th century and early 17th century portrait engravers worked in the very delicate manner of the Wierixes. The Flemish engraver Thomas de Leu produced hundreds of small portraits, as did the very prolific Léonard Gaultier. In Paris, Claude Mellan combined the portrait form with a personal style, which brought the systematization of engraved line to its ultimate development. He had worked in Rome from *c.* 1624 to 1636, where he mastered Francesco Villamena's manner of defining form with swelling parallels and concentric lines, completely eliminating crosshatching. He opened up Villamena's spacing, letting more white paper show through. In Mellan's work the calibration of thickness of line and spacing determines the illusion of form. His incredible virtuosity is demonstrated in the face of Christ in the *Sudarium* (1649), which is engraved with one spiralling, varying line that begins at the tip of the nose. His unique engraving style was taken up by Johann Jakob Thourneysser I (1636–1718) in Basle. Mellan was responsible for bringing Leoni's manner of portrait engraving to France, where it was developed in a more naturalistic manner by Jean Morin; his prints show the influence of van Dyck's method of beginning a plate with a freely sketched, etched underdrawing before engraving.

Robert Nanteuil, one of the greatest French portrait engravers, was not only a superb engraver but also had the artistry to penetrate the character of his subjects, depicted as if in a framed 'living' painting. In his prints the space between the oval frame of the portrait and the print's outer edge was characteristically filled in with evenly ruled horizontal light lines that read as a middle grey, representing a wall on which the frame casts a shadow. This device creates the transition from the two-dimensional space of the paper to the three-dimensional illusion of the portrait itself. Lettering appears in an inscriptional space either on the frame or in the traditional space below, which is sometimes drawn to simulate a plinth. Nanteuil used different types of line work to distinguish between the border areas and the portrait space. The portrait is engraved with delicate parallel, flowing, swelling lines and crosshatching, which produce rich tonal areas from dark blacks to pure white. Contour is suppressed, and the image is defined through light and texture. In 1658 he was appointed Dessinateur et Graveur Ordinaire du Roi to Louis XIV, who in 1660 passed an edict raising engraving from an 'industrial art' to a 'liberal art'. Nanteuil produced over 200 engravings of members of the court, including 11 of the King. The engraved portrait became a status symbol in mid-17th century France, as the aristocracy, clergy and other public figures had themselves depicted, but only towards the end of the century did the middle class appear in copperplate portraits.

Portrait engraving was also important in the Netherlands. Goltzius's followers, such as Jan Muller, had engraved important portraits of royalty. As portrait painting became popular in the 17th-century Netherlands, luminaries of the Dutch Republic were recorded by painters such

In England the prolific and innovative engraver WILLIAM HOGARTH conceived of prints as having a didactic and moral function. Due to the success of his images, his work was pirated, and one of his major contributions to engraving was his soliciting Parliament to pass an Act in 1735 protecting artists' publication rights for 14 years. In original narrative dramatic series such as *A Harlot's Progress* (pubd 1732) and *A Rake's Progress* (1735), Hogarth combined underdrawing in etching with engraving. His prints were the means to disseminate morally improving subject-matter to the public, and his engraving style did not call attention to technique, although he incorporated many types of cuts, including swelling parallels, delicate stipple and gridlike crosshatching. As his success grew, he employed others to engrave after his designs. The French engravers Gérard Scotin II, Simon François Ravenet I (1706–74) and Bernard Baron executed the plates for his *Marriage à la mode* (1745), which are among the most delicate in technique and brilliant in tonal contrasts of Hogarth's prints.

(iv) Portrait engraving. Throughout Europe portrait engraving became a characteristic speciality of 17th-century engraving. Ottavio Leoni, active in Rome, was the first engraver to specialize in portrait engraving. He drew his sitters in chalk and engraved these designs on to tiny

as Michiel van Mierevelt and engraved by Willem Delff. Cornelis van Dalem I and Abraham Blooteling were active in the middle of the century. Blooteling became involved in the search for new ways to engrave dark tone and was one of the first engravers to use a mezzotint rocker and scraper.

Many of the Flemish engravers who were established in Paris in the late 17th century show the influence of the Rubens school, and their engraving was dedicated to capturing effects of light, atmosphere, texture, wide tonal range and colour. For them, the highest achievement of the engraver lay in the total dedication of means to the painterly image reproduced. Such displays of engraving ability as Mellan's, whose line functions on two levels, are antithetical to this style. The Flemish portrait engraver Gérard Edelinck expanded portraiture's standard compositional formulae to include standing and seated figures in Baroque settings. He massed lines together densely to create deep shadows, enlivened by brilliant highlights. Many of his portraits are after paintings by Hyacinthe Rigaud. Pierre Drevet (1663–1738) also worked after Rigaud and excelled in capturing movement and the effect of flickering light on such textures as velvet, silk and fur. His son Pierre-Imbert Drevet (1697–1739) surpassed him in the rendering of textures and light effects on luxurious materials, as in his masterpiece, the portrait of *Jacques-Bénigne Bossuet* (1773; see 1984 exh. cat., no. 8).

In England, William Faithorne engraved portraits in Mellan's style of parallel, uncrossed lines. In Paris *c.* 1649 he came under the influence of Nanteuil, in whose complex manner he later engraved. Faithorne's work spans the period from Charles I to the Restoration (1625–60). In 1662 he published *The Art of Graveing and Etching* (London), based on Bosse's *Traité*.

Copperplate-engraving was introduced in the Americas by the Spanish, and one of the earliest American prints known, the *Catafalque of Philip IV in the Cathedral*, was published in Mexico in the *Llanto del occidente* (Mexico City, 1666) by Isidro Sariñana (1630–96). In the late 17th century a flourishing publishing industry was turning out hundreds of books illustrated with copperplate-engravings. In the New England colonies the first known engraving, a portrait of *Increase Mather* (1701; Stauffer, no. 982) was made by Thomas Emmes and was copied from an earlier English engraving.

BIBLIOGRAPHY
D. Stauffer: *American Engravers upon Copper and Steel*, 2 vols (New York, 1907/*R* 1974)
J. Adhémar: *Graphic Art of the Eighteenth Century* (New York, 1964)
E. Rouir: *La Gravure originale au XVIIe siècle* (Paris, 1974)
Rubens and his Engravers (exh. cat., London, Colnaghi's, 1977)
Printmaking in the Age of Rembrandt (exh. cat. by C. Ackley, Boston, MA, Mus. F.A., 1980)
Regency to Empire: French Printmaking, 1715–1814 (exh. cat. by V. Carlson and J. Ittman, Baltimore, U. MD, Mus. A.; Minneapolis, MN, Inst. A.; 1984)
Mirror of Empire: Dutch Marine Art of the Seventeenth Century (exh. cat. by G. Keyes, Minneapolis, MN, Inst. A., 1990)

5. *c.* 1750–*c.* 1900. By the mid-18th century pure engraving had largely been replaced by mixed etching-engraving techniques, the tonal engraving processes of mezzotint, roulette and stipple and the tonal etching processes of soft ground and aquatint. The word 'engraving' had come to mean any intaglio process, as opposed to 'line-engraving', which referred to burin-engraving. Paris remained the most important centre for line engraving, while London became important for mezzotint, stipple engraving and mixed intaglio prints.

(i) Pure and mixed reproductive engraving. (ii) Historical revival and William Blake. (iii) Steel engraving. (iv) Engraving and the Etching Revival. (v) Decline of reproductive engraving.

(i) Pure and mixed reproductive engraving. Mixed techniques became popular in Paris and London, but pure line engraving continued to be practised by Charles Dupuis (1685–1742) and Nicholas-Gabriel Dupuis. In France engraving enjoyed official patronage, and many foreign engravers were attracted there. Georg Friedrich Schmidt (1712–75), who later worked in Berlin, and Jean-Georges Wille were among the most masterful burin-engravers of the 18th century. Wille's disciplined technique involved the use of regularly spaced crosshatching filled with dots and flecks, and alternating dark and light lines.

In Britain printmaking was held in lower esteem than in France. British engravers were excluded from full membership in the Royal Academy on the grounds that engraving was completely devoid of the 'intellectual qualities of invention and composition'. Engraving gained prominence, however, through the important genre of landscape. The leading landscape engravers were Francis Vivares and William Woollett, both of whom worked in mixed etching and engraving. Woollett's distinctive method consisted of several etched bitings of preliminary wormlike lines, after which lines were cut with the burin. His dramatic landscape print *Destruction of the Children of Niobe* (1761; see 1980 exh. cat., no. 36) after Richard Wilson was commissioned by the publisher John Boydell, for whom it achieved great success as an export item to France. Woollett later turned to engraving history paintings. He was sought after by painters who wanted him to help make their reputations through his reproductions, for example his engraving after Benjamin West's *Death of Wolfe* (1776; see 1983 exh. cat., no. 10). John Boydell was the most important English publisher at that time, and his many projects included the famous Shakespeare Gallery, a group of paintings of Shakespearean subjects. His intention was to make a profit from the sale of portfolios of engravings after these paintings, but they were not commercially successful.

Robert Strange, one of Britain's greatest reproductive engravers after the Old Masters, had an international career in Edinburgh, Paris, London and Italy, where his technique was particularly influential. His method involved etching and then re-engraving the lines with a burin, achieving a controlled softness and light. Although most of his works were engraved after masterpieces of the Renaissance and Baroque, such as works by Raphael, Guercino and Guido Reni, his *Apotheosis of the Princes Octavius and Alfred* (1786; see 1980 exh. cat., no. 62), after Benjamin West, was an important engraving in the new Neo-classical style. His rigorous and delicate, silvery engraving style, capable of expressing nuances of light, was to prove well suited to the formal concerns of Neo-classical style. William Sharp also worked after Benjamin

West, as well as van Dyck, Joshua Reynolds, Thomas Lawrence and John Singleton Copley.

These new and large history prints, with their intricate networks of under-etching, engraved lines, dots and lozenge crosshatching, took many years to complete; for example, James Heath took over 11 years to engrave Copley's *Death of Major Peirson* (1796). In North America engraving was still at an unsophisticated level, but engraved prints helped propagate revolutionary consciousness and popularized the iconography of federalism. Copley's contemporary, the silversmith and patriot Paul Revere, engraved a print of the *Boston Massacre* (1770; Stauffer, no. 2675), which sought to spread outrage. After the Revolution (1775–83), engravers helped promote the ideals of the young republic through Neo-classical images and iconic portraits of George Washington (1732–99).

In Italy leading mid-18th-century reproductive engravers were Andrea Zucchi (?1675–1740), Anton Maria Zanetti (i) and Joseph Wagner (1706–80) in Venice, Giovanni Volpato in Rome and the Remondini workshop in Bassano. Joseph Wagner's student Francesco Bartolozzi settled in Britain in 1764, where he specialized in stipple engraving and engraved after decorative Rococo and Neo-classical themes by Giovanni Battista Cipriani (for illustration *see* BARTOLOZZI, FRANCESCO) and Angelica Kauffman. He also worked in pure line, as in his *Holy Family among the Ruins* (1789), after Nicolas Poussin. Volpato's student and son-in-law Raphael Morghen was perhaps Italy's greatest reproductive engraver. His engravings after Old Masters, such as Leonardo da Vinci and Nicolas Poussin, have an extraordinary control and delicacy of technique, with an even texture and silvery grey tonality. Morghen taught at the Accademia di Belle Arti in Florence, and his prints came to the attention of Napoleon, who attempted to lure him to France to establish an academy of engraving.

(ii) Historical revival and William Blake. A historical print revival parallel to the Gothic Revival took place from *c.* 1800 in Britain, Germany and Italy, centred in Venice and Rome. A renewed interest in 15th- and early 16th-century prints resulted in the stylistic influence of artists from Dürer to Michelangelo affecting Romantic and Neo-classical art. At the same time many imitations and forgeries of 15th-century prints and niellos were made. Engraving enjoyed a brief association with Romanticism and original printmaking through the works of two visionary artists, James Barry and William Blake. James Barry is a unique figure in British printmaking for the scale, conception and execution of his original prints. His etchings of the 1770s and 1790s are deeply bitten and reinforced with burin work, and they evoke the sublime through a mystical romantic and heroic classical vision. WILLIAM BLAKE, probably the most important engraver of the 19th century, transformed engraving into an original medium once again. He brought back pure line's function as drawing, re-orientating engraving with a direction that had been abandoned since the 16th century. He was apprenticed (1771–8) as a reproductive engraver with James Basire I (1730–1802), for whom he drew and engraved Gothic monuments for *Sepulchral Monuments in Great Britain* (London, 1786) by Richard Gough. Blake's

experience with antiquarianism was formative, and the 16th-century prints he collected helped shape his vision and technique. The young Blake knew early 16th-century engravings and was much influenced by Michelangelo. He mastered conventional reproductive technique, including the use of etched worm-line backgrounds combined with burin work. Although he made his living etching and engraving after the designs of others, he also made prints after his own visionary and mystical designs. His personal engraving style is characterized by a rich tonal range built up of long strokes of varying weights that emphasize flowing form and contour, with the occasional use of minute lozenge crosshatching. *Glad Day* (1780; Binyon, no. 9) was the first of his prints to incorporate pure line drawing as independent contour against blank paper, creating a radiant and joyous figure. In 1810 he asserted that 'Engraving is drawing on Copper and Nothing Else.'

After spending many years experimenting with relief and colour printing, the ageing William Blake took up engraving again in 1818, inspired, he said, by 'Albrecht Dürer and the old Engravers'. John Linnell (ii) commissioned his major work in engraving, the 21 illustrations to the *Book of Job* (1825; Binyon, nos 105–26), including *When the Morning Stars Sang Together* (see fig. 8). These illustrations are richly worked images set in sketchy drypoint linear borders, and their unorthodox, 'unfinished' format departs radically from contemporary practice. Blake went further with his use of the burin in seven unfinished engravings after his designs for Dante's *Inferno* (1826; Binyon, nos 127–33). His work failed to have wide influence, but he was followed by a small group of younger artists who worked in a variety of print techniques. Two engravers were Edward Calvert, who made dark images inspired by Blake's wood-engravings for *The Pastorals of Virgil* (London, 1821) of the physician Robert John Thornton (1768–1837) and by early Italian prints; and George Richmond, who made a few silvery engravings in which figure types and long burin cuts are reminiscent of the 16th-century Venetian Jacopo de' Barbari.

(iii) Steel engraving. In the 1820s and 1830s the growing market for reproductive prints demanded increased speed and cheapness of production and promoted the invention of hundreds of new printing processes. Engraving and etching were challenged by the new, wide acceptance of LITHOGRAPHY, which could be autographic or reproductive and which could resemble pen, wash or crayon drawings or imitate engravings. Traditional engravers justified their laborious production on grounds of the sheer beauty of the engraved line, but they also began to use such time-saving devices as mechanical ruling combs. Around 1822 Thomas Goff Lupton introduced the steel plate, which was capable of printing an effectively unlimited edition of 20,000–30,000 impressions. The use of steel plates also affected engraving style and size of the image. The hardness permitted the cutting of thousands of tiny, closely laid lines that read as pale greys, their delicacy most effective in small prints. Hundreds of British steel engravers produced reproductions for fashionable annual albums of paintings. The steel printing plate also enabled the more rapid and tonally rich mezzotint to yield huge editions of large-scale works. By 1830 the painterly MEZZOTINT

Canst thou bind the sweet influences of Pleiades or loose the bands of Orion

14

Let there Be

Light

Let there be A

Firmament

Let the Waters be gathered together into one place

& let the Dry Land appear

And God made Two Great Lights

Sun

Moon

Let the Waters bring forth abundantly

Let the Earth bring forth

Cattle & Creeping thing & Beast

When the morning Stars sang together, & all the
Sons of God shouted for joy

W. Blake Inventt & Sc

London, Published as the Act directs March 8: 1825 by Will: Blake N 3 Fountain Court Strand

Proof

8. Engraving and drypoint by William Blake: *When the Morning Stars Sang Together*, 460×347 mm, from his illustrations to the *Book of Job*, 1825 (London, British Museum)

became a commercially viable and fashionable competitor of line-engraving.

Small-scale steel engraving was particularly suited to the reproduction of watercolour. J. M. W. Turner, who also etched preliminary original designs to be finished in mezzotint, closely directed an entire industry of reproductive engraving after his watercolours and paintings. 'Turner engravings' were actually etched landscapes with mechanically ruled engraved skies, which captured the most subtle tones and washes with a glossy sameness of finish. Many of these were printed on *chiné collé*, a receptive and luminous delicate tissue backed with a stronger sheet of paper. The large number of Turner's engravers included James Basire II (1769–1822), Robert Brandard (1805–62), William Bernard Cooke (1778–1855), John Cousen, William Miller (1796–1882), John Pye, Charles Turner (1774–1857) and James Tibbetts Willmore (1800–1863).

Victorian engraving was the ultimate development of printmaking technique, in which both the painter's and engraver's personalities were subsumed by the technique. Pure engravers considered the rigorousness of their medium particularly suited to elevated subjects and heroic themes. Pure line-engravers such as James Henry Watt (1799–1867) continued to work for up to eight years on a single copper plate, such as his *Christ Blessing the Little Children* (1855; see 1973 exh. cat., no. 1) after Charles Lock Eastlake. Such 'noble' subjects as the classical nude became a speciality of line-engraving, such as George Thomas Doo's engraving after William Etty's *Combat—Woman Pleading for the Vanquished: An Ideal Group* (1848; see 1973 exh. cat., no. 11).

(iv) Engraving and the Etching Revival. In addition to the growth of lithography during the first half of the 19th century, etching was revived in the mid-19th century. These new printmakers made original works, not surrogates for paintings, and their use of the various media was often highly experimental in contrast to the traditional craftsmanship of professional engravers. French printers working with artists of the Etching Revival developed the process of steel-facing copperplates, which enabled fragile drypoints, as well as etchings and aquatints, to be printed in large editions, making possible the publication of original prints on a large commercial scale. The attitude of the artists of the Etching Revival towards burin-engraving was wittily expressed by the French artist Félix Buhot, who occasionally combined burin work with his etching, drypoint, roulette and aquatint. His etched frontispiece for *L'Illustration nouvelle* (Paris, 1877), the *Burial of the Burin* (Lavan and Adhémar, no. 88), depicted the demise of engraving as a burin being carried up to heaven by putti. Wiliam Strang, a Scottish printmaker of the Etching Revival, worked with mixed intaglio techniques. He invented a new type of burin that was turned back at the end, allowing the engraver to pull the tool with almost the freedom of the etching needle, yet maintain the line quality possible in engraving.

(v) Decline of reproductive engraving. Pure engraving was gradually replaced by mixed techniques, mezzotint and ultimately photogravure, which permitted rapid and accurate reproduction of art works even though it lacked beauty of surface. At the end of the 19th century British engravers were reduced to ruling engraved skies on etched plates, due to lack of other work. One branch of burin-engraving that remained viable was the BOOKPLATE, associated with silversmithing and heraldic tradition, of which Charles William Sherborn (1831–1912) was one of the leading practitioners. Line-engravers also found employment for their swelling line and dot techniques in the new field of banknote, certificate and postage-stamp engraving, in which reproductive line-engraving style remains fossilized in the late 20th century. Security watermarks and engraving machines that generated geometric swirls were invented to discourage counterfeiting, leaving only the portraits, scenes and lettering for the banknote engraver to execute by hand. A method was devised for multiplying the original copper plates, which wore down quickly, by taking an impression on soft steel that in turn was impressed into other plates and hardened.

In France burin-engraving remained significant into the 20th century, due to official support by the Ecole des Beaux-Arts and the Chalcographie du Louvre. Claude Ferdinand Galliard (1834–87), Alphonse François (1811–88) and Jules Jacquet (1841–1913) were among the leading reproductive engravers of the late 19th century. Also in France steel-engraving had prompted a change in taste away from the rich and colouristic engraving style produced by deep and broad cutting to one that was simpler and more highly finished in its range of greys. In Berlin an engraver associated with the Nazarenes was Friedrich-Edward Eichens (1804–77). Also in Berlin, Karl Stauffer-Bern engraved so delicately that his lines appear to dissolve into tone. Others, such as Friedrich Zimmermann (1826–87) of Dresden and Joseph Kohlschein (1841–1915) of Düsseldorf, continued to use a broader style for their reproductive works. A number of artists combined burin work with etching in original prints, such as Max Klinger in his series *Brahms Fantasy* (1894; Varnedoe and Streicher, nos 66–70). In Italy a few line-engravers continued to work, but there, as everywhere but France, by the first decade of the 20th century reproductive line-engraving had virtually disappeared.

BIBLIOGRAPHY

D. Stauffer: *American Engravers upon Copper and Steel*, 2 vols (New York, 1907/R 1974)

A. M. Hind: *Bartolozzi and Other Stipple Engravers Working in England at the End of the Eighteenth Century* (New York, 1912)

M. Fielding: *American Engravers upon Copper and Steel: Biographical Sketches and Checklists of Engravings: A Supplement to. . .Stauffer's American Engravers* (Philadelphia, 1917/R New York, 1971)

L. Binyon: *The Engraved Designs of William Blake* (London, 1926/R New York, 1967)

J. Lavan and J. Adhémar: *Inventaire du fonds français après 1800*, iii, Paris, Bib. N., Cab. Est. cat. (Paris, 1942)

Victorian Engraving (exh. cat. by H. Beck, London, V&A, 1973)

J. K. T. Varnedoe and E. Streicher: *Graphic Works of Max Klinger* (New York, 1977)

B. Hunnisett: *A Dictionary of British Steel Engravers* (Leigh-on-Sea, 1980)

——: *Steel-engraved Book Illustration in England* (Boston, 1980)

Painters and Engraving: The Reproductive Print from Hogarth to Wilke (exh. cat. by D. Alexander and R. Godfrey, New Haven, CT, Yale Cent. Brit. A., 1980)

Pictures for the Parlour: The English Reproductive Print from 1775 to 1900 (exh. cat. by B. D. Rix, Toronto, A.G. Ont., 1983)

Colour into Line: Turner and the Art of Engraving (exh. cat. by A. Lyles and D. Perkins, London, Tate, 1989)

6. *c.* 1900 AND AFTER. Freed from its reproductive role, burin-engraving regained vitality in the early 20th century and developed in two radically different ways. One direction was associated with the avant-garde and formalism, which emphasized pure line as an element of interest in itself. Such printmakers were involved with abstraction, technical experimentation and colour printing and often used engraving in combination with other techniques. The second direction, centred in Britain and figurative in content, looked back to engraving's early history for inspiration. The artists of such prints often specialized in engraving and did not mix techniques. Less formalist in their approach, they tried to recapture the line quality of 15th-century engraving, and for these engravers line did not exist independent of image.

(i) Modernism and Cubism. Despite the burin's capacity to incise the most elegant and flowing of lines, its association with the mechanical drudgery of engraving tonal equivalents meant that artists did not consider it a tool for creative use. Artists favoured other techniques for reflecting the flowing linearity characteristic of European art *c.* 1900. The idea that an engraving could be an original print returned under the auspices of Cubism, with its geometric rather than organic line quality. Picasso's early prints were etchings and drypoints, but in such later Cubist prints as *Man with Guitar* (1915; see 1981 exh. cat., no. 28) he used the burin to rework an etched image in a completely novel way; he exploited the rich blackness of the engraved line, showing its crisp directionality, graceful arcs, sharpness and burr. To this he added heavy plate-tone and spot wiping to achieve a new context for the engraved line. Throughout his career Picasso enjoyed and used aspects of engraving that had never been admitted before, such as the resistance of the metal. He often worked with an unsharpened tool, which stuttered its way through the copper, kicking up sharp burr. He also deliberately signed and dated his plates, so that his script prints in reverse.

The Cubist Emile Laboureur (1877–1943) experimented with a variety of etching techniques before taking up the portable technique of engraving during his war service (1914–16). He engraved his distinctive stylized images using crisp lines and arcs against white paper, which were interspersed with hatching that flattens and patterns rather than modelling form. Paul Dubreuil also worked in a manner reminiscent of Laboureur's style. John Marin, one of the few American artists influenced by Cubism who engraved, made six prints using the burin in the 1920s. The Polish artist Joseph Hecht (1891–1952) studied in Kraków and in Norway before moving to Paris in 1921. Along with other Polish engravers, he incorporated elements of folk art and decorative patterning in his manner of drawing animals and landscapes with the burin. Despite his traditional craft training as a professional engraver, he came to see the engraved line as interesting in itself apart from what it described and was interested in how it functioned with white paper. His approach to engraving was profoundly to influence printmaking.

(ii) Historical revival. In Britain engravers approached engraving in a very different manner from the modernists, sustaining a connection with the past through a high level of craftsmanship, a sense of historicism and preservation of the print's intimate scale. Robert Sargent Austin (1895–1973), the leading British engraver in the 1920s, emulated Dürer's early style with great delicacy and rigorous drawing. Many of the British engravers active in the 1920s and 1930s were associated with the Royal Society of Painter-Etchers and Engravers (which admitted engravers only in 1926) and with the Bank of England. They included Stanley Anderson (1881–1966), Henry John Fanshawe Badeley (*b* 1874), Enid Butcher (*fl c.* 1930), Stephen Gooden (1892–1955), William Morgan (*b* 1903) and Harry Morley (1881–1945). David Jones engraved copperplate illustrations for private press books using a very open, elegant, wiry line.

During the 1930s, while many American artists were making lithographs, the American scene-painter and etcher Reginald Marsh learnt to engrave in a formal style by taking private lessons from a retired banknote engraver. By 1939 he was making pure engravings that startlingly combined his Realist drawing style with the lozenge crosshatching of banknote engraving. Armin Landeck (1905–84) was another printmaker who found engraving well suited to his expressive architectural imagery, drawn with closely massed parallels and spider-web line networks.

(iii) S. W. Hayter, abstraction and experimentation. Under the influence of Surrealism and Automatism, S. W. HAYTER, who had studied engraving with Joseph Hecht in Paris (1926), liberated line from literal pictorial description. He created abstract, non-objective images through the constant turning of the plate as the burin passed through the copper. He engraved over passages of textured soft ground (see fig. 9), combined engraving with lift-ground etching and gouged out areas (*gauffrage*) that print as uninked three-dimensional relief. He introduced the idea of surface and intaglio printing from the same plate, perfected colour viscosity printing and took casts of engravings in plaster.

In 1927 Hayter founded Atelier 17 (Paris, 1927–40; New York, 1945–50; Paris, 1950–) as a workshop for experimental intaglio printmaking. Hundreds of artists who worked at Atelier 17 tried engraving but most found the medium too disciplined and indirect. Engravers there included John Buckland-Wright (1897–1954), Dorothy Dehner (*b* 1901), Gabor Peterdi (*b* 1915), Sue Fuller (*b* 1914), André Racz (*b* 1916), Ian Hugo (1900–1984) and Mauricio Lasansky. Hayter's personal engraving style, based on improvisation and chance, influenced Jackson Pollock, who made seven engravings with Hayter in 1944–5. Hayter's experimental approach and his bringing together intaglio printmaking and abstraction were major influences on European and American printmaking in the 1940s and 1950s.

Affected by the large scale of Abstract Expressionist paintings, printmakers expanded the scale of their works. This encouraged changes in burin technique, such as the use of powerful, deeply cut, expressive, long, sweeping strokes and violent jabs. The virtuosity, control and strength required to cut such lines is, in some ways, reminiscent of Mannerist engraving.

The practice of engraving in the USA after World War II was due largely to Hayter. Many of the artists who

9. Engraving and soft-ground etching by S. W. Hayter: *Combat*, 490×399 mm, 1936 (New York, The Brooklyn Museum)

worked with him set up their own printmaking workshops in art schools and universities, such as Gabor Peterdi at Yale University, New Haven, CT. Mauricio Lasansky made large, mixed intaglio colour prints containing powerful passages of engraving, and his grotesque, mythic, apocalyptic and political images were drawn with impassioned intensity. He established an important centre of experimental intaglio printmaking at the University of Iowa, Iowa City. He saw engraving as a central skill and insisted that his students master it. Although most of Lasansky's students did not continue to use engraving, by the late 20th century the majority of American artists working with the burin were Iowa-trained. Some printmakers combined electric engraving tools, dental tools and multiple-line gravers with the traditional burin, for example Virginia Myers (*b* 1927), who also used engraving with a metallic-foil stamping process in her gesturally drawn figure and landscape prints.

(iv) Late 20th-century engraving. Intaglio printmaking branched in two distinct directions *c.* 1970: artists who made their own prints, and those who worked collaboratively. Printmakers who made their own prints became associated with 'academic' printmaking. Most contemporary engraving falls in this category. Publisher-financed collaborative printmaking, involving well-known painters working with master printers, favoured complicated, innovative and expensive processes but produced little in the way of engraving. Since engraving is image-oriented

rather than process-oriented, solitary, technically demanding and time-consuming it has no need of a collaborative situation. One artist who worked collaboratively, Frank Stella, updated Hayter's approach by combining engraving with computer-generated imagery, relief, aquatint and etching in enormous, multiplate prints produced at Tyler Graphics in the 1980s.

In the late 20th century many American printmakers were using engraving in combination with other intaglio techniques, including Peter Milton (*b* 1930), who combined elegant burin work with photosensitive ground, aquatint and lift-ground etching in his black-and-white prints. Pure engraving at the end of the 20th century had moved beyond the earlier formalist focus on line *per se* to focus on figurative imagery with a renewed interest in rich tone. The few artists working as engravers selected the burin for its unique ability to produce its characteristic lines and tones and for its simplicity of means. In the USA they included Beth van Hoesen (*b* 1926), Evan Lindquist (*b* 1936), Brian Paulsen and Amy Worthen (*b* 1946). The situation in Britain was more diverse. Such Hayter-trained engravers as Jean Lodge (born in the USA) flourished, while traditional engravers in the Royal Society of Painter-Etchers and Engravers continued to dominate the British conception of the medium. Henry Wilkinson, David Wickes, Ann Le Bas (*b* 1930) and Lawrence Jossett (*b* 1910) made delicate engravings executed with the highest craftsmanship. Britain remained the one place where traditional engraving techniques for silversmiths, gunmakers and banknote engravers as well as artists continued to be taught. Students from Britain and other countries came to study engraving in the three-year silversmiths' course at the City of London Polytechnic (now London Guildhall University), Sir John Cass College of Art, intended primarily for students planning to qualify by examination for the guilds.

Burin-engraving flourished perhaps most conspicuously in France, where the country's rich and varied tradition of engraving was reflected in the strength and variety of its engravers, including Albert Flocon (*fl* mid-century–1980s), a major practitioner and theorist of modernist burin engraving and its relationship to geometry and curvilinear perspective. Both experimental and traditional engraving techniques were taught to printmakers trained in the fine arts academy system. At the Ecole Nationale des Beaux-Arts burin engraving became a required part of the training of printmakers. To qualify for the Prix de Rome, students were required to execute a plate engraved with a burin. In central France, at the Ecole Régionale des Beaux-Arts in Saint-Etienne, the traditional craft of gun engraving, long associated with that city, continued to be taught side by side with engraving for printmakers.

Surrealism continued to inspire some of the most interesting European engraving, including the work of a number of French artists outside the Hayter circle. Marc d'Autry engraved grotesque and mythological creatures with a technique inspired by Dürer. Philippe Mohlitz (*b* 1941) of Bordeaux, a spiritual successor to Jean Duvet and Rodolphe Bresdin, made obsessive Surrealist fantasies designed with grim humour. His lines are delicately engraved but densely packed, creating rich, velvet blacks. Surrealism also influenced the Italian engraver Carla Horat (*b* 1938). The Italian artist Luce Delhore (*b* 1952), born in Belgium, is an exception to the generally figurative style of contemporary engraving: he combined burin, drypoint and roulette in rich, luminous abstractions. Engraving and mezzotint became popular in Japan, with an emphasis on contemporary design and craftsmanship. Mitsuru Ishibashi (*b* 1951) engraved mechanical and graphlike abstractions, using straight, rich burin lines with impressive effect.

BIBLIOGRAPHY
Engravings-USA (exh. cat., St Joseph, MO, Albrecht A. Mus., 1974)
S. W. Hayter and Atelier 17 (exh. cat. by J. Moser, Madison, U. WI, Elvehjem A. Cent., 1977)
The Cubist Print (exh. cat. by B. Wallen and D. Stein, Santa Barbara, U. CA, A. Mus., 1981)
J. Watrous: *A Century of American Printmaking, 1880–1980* (Madison, WI, 1984)

AMY NAMOWITZ WORTHEN

Engström, Leander (*b* Ytterhogdal, Hälsingland, 1886; *d* Stockholm, 6 Feb 1927). Swedish painter and sculptor. He studied under Richard Bergh, Nils Kreuger and Karl Nordström and also spent a year studying under Matisse in Paris. In 1905 he made a trip to Lapland, where the landscape deeply impressed him. Later he also made trips to Denmark, Italy and France, and he was influenced by Cézanne and the Italian Primitives. He painted mainly landscapes and townscapes, executed with a firm structure and strong modelling, as in *The Mill* (1913; Stockholm, Mod. Mus.). Many of his works were inspired by his travels, including *Scene from Lapland* (1916; Stockholm, Mod. Mus.). In his later work he simplified forms and strengthened compositional structures, as in such stylized works as *Golden Evening in Assisi* (1920; Stockholm, Mod. Mus.). Sculptures, such as the powerful *Wolf Killer* (1915; Stockholm, Mod. Mus.) show the same simplification of form. Engström's two sons, the identical twins (*b* 1914) Leander Engström and Tord Engström, were both painters.

Vollmer
BIBLIOGRAPHY
Katalogen: Över Moderna Museets Samlingar av Svensk och internationell 1900-talskonst [Catalogue of the Modern Museum's collection of Swedish and international 20th-century art], Stockholm, Mod. Mus. cat. (Stockholm, 1976), pp. 41–2

□

Enguidanos, Tomás López. See LÓPEZ ENGUIDANOS, TOMÁS.

Enkomi. Bronze Age site at the mouth of the River Pedieos in eastern Cyprus, *c.* 8 km north-west of Famagusta. The settlement, the ancient name of which is uncertain, was founded towards the end of the Middle Cypriot period (*c.* 1700 BC) and subsequently became one of the principal Late Cypriot (LCYP) cities in the island. It was destroyed by fire and earthquake *c.* 1050 BC, when its surviving inhabitants moved to nearby Salamis. The site was first explored in 1896 by scholars from the British Museum; later Swedish, French and Cypriot expeditions (1930–70) unearthed an extensive area of the ancient city.

The prosperous unwalled city of the mid-14th century BC was fortified a century later, when it was surrounded by a Cyclopean wall made of two parallel rows of large unhewn blocks with a superstructure of mud-brick; several towers were built at regular intervals against the south

wall. At the same time the area within the walls was laid out on a regular grid plan that foreshadowed Hellenistic cities: 11 straight streets crossed the single north–south main street at right angles and served 24 residential blocks, while at the centre of the town there was a rectangular paved open space or public square (*see also* CYPRUS, §II, 2(ii)). Enkomi's domestic and sacred architecture of *c.* 1250–*c.* 1150 BC is best illustrated by the outstanding buildings constructed of ashlar blocks. Building 18, probably an official residence, fills an entire plot; its façade on the south is more than 40 m long and has large ashlar blocks (3.0×0.7 m) topped by smaller blocks set parallel to one another like orthostates and covered by horizontal slabs. The House of the Pillar and Sanctuary of the Great Horned God have rectangular pillars and capitals with a stepped profile. These two shrines, with a gateway or main porch and a cella, may be compared with the contemporary Temple 1 at KITION and the Sanctuary of Aphrodite at Old Paphos (*see* PAPHOS, OLD). The later Sanctuary of the Ingot God (*c.* 1150–*c.* 1050 BC) had rubble walls with benches set against them for the deposit of offerings; two double-headed terracotta figurines of centaurs or sphinxes were found there, as well as a hearth altar and two free-standing stone-block altars. The bronze 'Ingot God' statuette (see below) was found in a small room at the north-east corner.

Most of the tombs at Enkomi are rock-cut chamber tombs, although a few tholos tombs have also been found. The ground-plan of the main one (15th century BC) is oval, the lower two courses made of stone blocks on which rest nine other courses of baked bricks. Several rectangular chamber tombs were constructed of fine ashlar limestone blocks covered with large slabs and provided with stepped entrance passages; they are contemporaneous with the Syrian-built tombs of Ugarit (14th–13th century BC).

Enkomi has yielded numerous works of art in bronze, gold, silver, ivory, faience and terracotta, all in typically Cypriot styles that successfully combine Oriental, Egyptian and Aegean elements. Outstanding items include a bronze four-sided stand (12th century BC; London, BM) decorated on each side with two female heads looking out of a window surrounded by rows of spirals; it may be a symbolic representation of a shrine. The two standing male gods from the sanctuaries described above are masterpieces of the Enkomi bronzesmiths. The youthful, muscular 'Horned God' (h. 540 mm; *c.* 1200 BC; Nicosia, Cyprus Mus.) has been identified as Apollo Kereatas, or as the Reshef of Alasia; it is the tallest LCYP bronze statuette so far discovered. The slender 'Ingot God' (*c.* 1150–*c.* 1050 BC; Nicosia, Cyprus Mus.; see fig.), whose helmet has smaller horns, is fully armed with spear and shield; he has been identified as the god who protected the island's mines and copper production. Among the jewellery from the site are gold finger-rings with a bull or lion engraved on an oval bezel, many gold diadems and mouthpieces with stamped decoration, gold pins, and earrings with pendants in the shape of bulls' heads. A hemispherical silver cup (*c.* 1400 BC; Nicosia, Cyprus Mus.; *see* METAL, fig. 14) is decorated in gold and niello with six bulls' heads alternating with lotus flowers, and a frieze of arcaded rosettes below; a similar

BIBLIOGRAPHY

A. S. Murray, A. H. Smith and H. B. Walters: *Excavations in Cyprus* (London, 1900)
E. Gjerstad and others: *The Swedish Cyprus Expedition*, i (Stockholm, 1934)
E. Sjöqvist: *Reports on Excavations in Cyprus* (Stockholm, 1940)
J.-C. Courtois: *Les Tombes d'Enkomi: Le Mobilier funéraire*, ii of *Alasia* (Paris, 1952, 2/1986)
——: *Les Objets des niveaux stratifiés d'Enkomi: Fouilles C. F. A. Schaeffer, 1947–1970*, iii of *Alasia* (Paris, 1952, 2/1986)
J. Lagarce and E. Lagarce: *Deux tombes du Chypriote récent d'Enkomi (Chypre): Tombes 1851 et 1907*, iv of *Alasia* (Paris, 1952, 2/1986)
C. F. A. Schaeffer: *Enkomi-Alasia*, i (Paris, 1952)
P. Dikaios: *Enkomi: Excavations, 1948–1958*, 3 vols (Mainz, 1969–71)
C. F. A. Schaeffer and others: *Alasia [fouilles]: Mission archéologique d'Alasia*, i (Paris, 1971)
J.-C. Courtois, J. Lagarce and E. Lagarce: *Enkomi et le bronze récent à Chypre* (Nicosia, 1986)

JACQUES-CLAUDE COURTOIS

Enkū (*b* Mino Province [now Gifu Prefecture], 1632; *d* 1695). Japanese sculptor and Buddhist itinerant monk (*hijiri*). He was active during the early Edo period (1600–1868). He entered the priesthood of the Tendai sect (*see* BUDDHISM, §III, 10) at an early age, this being one of the few means of advancement within feudal society for individuals of the lower classes. Enkū began sculpting images in the early 1660s for both Buddhist temples and Shinto shrines in his home province. In the later 1660s he made an important missionary expedition to the Tōhoku region of Honshu and to the northern island of Hokkaido, which had only recently come under the control of the Tokugawa shogunate, introducing Buddhism and Buddhist imagery to that still remote island. Thereafter he travelled extensively, carving icons for rural temples and wayside shrines in Honshu, especially in the Kantō and Chūbu regions. He also carved images on living trees on mountain-tops. For more than 300 years his works were little known outside their localities; to local people they were objects of worship, imbued with magical powers to heal and protect.

Legend has it that Enkū vowed to carve 120,000 icons. Some 7000 of his works are extant, depicting a vast range of Buddhist, Shinto and folk deities. In contrast with the rather uninteresting orthodox sculpture produced by his immediate predecessors and contemporaries, they are fresh and dynamic in style, showing constant variation and experimentation. While his images were made as devotional objects for local people, Enkū clearly approached his carving with the imagination and visual sensitivity of an artist. He worked in a pure wood technique, exploiting the qualities of the block. He employed the *nata* (a kind of hatchet) with virtuoso skill, excising an image with the utmost economy of strokes and often leaving the split planes untouched except for some light etching to suggest facial features. For a softer effect, he also carved with flat, V-point and round chisels. In a single day he could complete one image larger than life-size or hundreds of *koppa-butsu* ('chip Buddhas'). Acclaimed as masterpieces are the *Ryōmen Sukuna* (legendary two-headed mountain demon of legend) at Senkōji, Gifu Prefecture; the *Shōtoku Taishi* at Naka Kannondō in Hashima, Gifu Prefecture, near Enkū's birthplace; the three *Kannon* (Skt Avalokiteshvara) figures at Seihōji in Kokubu, Gifu Prefecture; the great congregation of figures at Arako Kannonji and

Enkomi, bronze statuette of the 'Ingot God', h. 350 mm, *c.* 1150–*c.* 1050 BC (Nicosia, Cyprus Museum)

contemporary bowl is known from Dendra in mainland Greece, and the Enkomi example may be an import. Ivory-carving includes a fine ivory games box carved with royal hunting scenes (*c.* 1200 BC; London, BM) and an ivory mirror handle decorated in high relief on both sides, one showing a warrior slaying a griffin and the other a lion attacking a bull (*c.* 1200 BC; London, BM; *see* CYPRUS, fig. 19). Other finds include faience vases (*see* CYPRUS, §II, 5(ii)), fine Pictorial-style Mycenaean bell kraters and their local Pastoral- (or Rude-) style imitations (*see* CYPRUS, §II, 4(iii)), terracotta figurines, and cylinder seals that show Egyptian and Minoan influences.

the distinctive *Nata Yakushi* group, both in Nagoya. Many fine carvings remain jealously guarded in rural temples and shrines.

See also JAPAN, §V, 3(v).

BIBLIOGRAPHY
Kodansha Enc. Japan
T. Tsuchiya: *Enkū no chōkoku* [The sculpture of Enkū] (Tokyo, 1962)
Enkū kenkyū [The study of Enkū], Enkū Gakkai [Enkū study association] (Tokyo, 1973)
M. Honma: *Enkū to Mokujiki* [Enkū and Mokujiki], Butsukusu obu butsukusu [Book of books], xxxv (Tokyo, 1974)
N. Maruyama: *Enkū fudoki* [Enkū and his environment] (Tokyo, 1974)
G. F. Dotzenko: *Enkū: Master Carver* (Tokyo, 1976)
K. Tanahashi: *Enkū: Sculptor of a Thousand Buddhas* (Boulder, 1982)
DONALD F. McCALLUM

Enlarging. *See under* PHOTOGRAPHY, §I.

Enlart, Camille (*b* Boulogne-sur-Mer, 22 Nov 1862; *d* Paris, 14 Feb 1927). French art historian. He studied at the Ecole des Beaux-Arts and the Ecole des Chartes in Paris and was a member of the Ecole Française in Rome. He was director of the Trocadéro museum of comparative sculpture in Paris from 1903 and was elected a member of the Académie des Inscriptions et Belles-Lettres in 1926. He was primarily a specialist in the medieval architecture of Italy and the eastern Mediterranean and in the Flamboyant style. His writings aimed to demonstrate the diffusion of French styles of architecture throughout Europe, carried particularly by the Cistercian order, although he was also the first to recognize the English origins of the Flamboyant style. His greatest celebration of French medieval culture is his *Manuel d'archéologie française* on religious, civil and military architecture. The volume on furniture was completed after Enlart's death by Jean Verrier.

WRITINGS
Les Origines françaises de l'art gothique en Italie (Rome, 1894)
Monuments de l'architecture romane et de transition dans la région picarde: Anciens diocèses d'Amiens et de Boulogne (Amiens, 1895)
L'Architecture gothique et de la Renaissance en Chypre, 2 vols (Paris, 1899); Eng. trans., ed. D. Hunt, 1 vol. (London, 1987)
Manuel d'archéologie française depuis les temps mérovingiens jusqu'à la Renaissance, 4 vols (Paris, 1902–27)
'Origine anglaise du style gothique flamboyant', *Bull. Mnmtl*, lxx (1906), pp. 38–81; lxxiv (1910), pp. 125–67
L'Art roman en Italie: L'Architecture et la décoration (Paris, 1924)
Regular contributions to *Bull. Mnmtl*, *Rev. A. Chrét.* and *Mnmts Piot*
BIBLIOGRAPHY
Camille Enlart, 1862–1927 (Paris, 1929)
ANNE PRACHE

Enlightenment, the [Age of Reason; Fr. Siècle des lumières, Ger. Aufklärung]. Term characterizing the cultural prevalence in western Europe and North America of certain shared ideas during the 18th century. Though not a single unified movement, the Enlightenment was founded on a belief in progress and in the power of reason. Recent achievements in science encouraged the belief that, through the acquisition of knowledge and the application of reason, social, intellectual and moral reforms could be effected. The Enlightenment's intellectual leaders included Voltaire (1694–1778), Denis Diderot and Jean-Jacques Rousseau in France, David Hume in Britain, Immanuel Kant and Gotthold Ephraim Lessing in Germany, and Thomas Jefferson and Benjamin Franklin (1706–90) in America. Their differing temperaments and the varied contexts in which they lived led to varying results from the same basic premise.

Some of the foundations of the Enlightenment developed in 17th-century England. In the *Essay Concerning Human Understanding* (1690) the philosopher John Locke (1632–1704) asserted that there were no innate ideas (in opposition to the theory of René Descartes). This formed the basis of empiricism and led to the conclusion that humans were the product of their environment. The workings of that environment itself were thought to have been uncovered in the universal, mechanistic theories (*Philosophiae naturalis principia mathematica*, 1687) of Sir Isaac Newton (1643–1727). These two developments prompted the notion that laws could be found that governed not only nature, but man and society also. Further, the continued success of science in this period led to a widespread belief that, through a reliance on reason, progress in general was possible. Enlightenment theorists thus vigorously attacked whatever seemed to them to be outmoded, irrational or empirically unjustified, as shown by Voltaire's polemics against prejudice, superstition and the apparent excesses of the Roman Catholic Church. The methodology of reason was employed in the accumulation and codification of knowledge, leading, most impressively, to the monumental *Encyclopédie* (1751–65), edited by Diderot and Jean Le Rond d'Alembert (1717–83).

The impact of the Enlightenment on the arts took various forms. One of the clearest was the homage paid by some artists to science, as in Joseph Wright of Derby's *Experiment on a Bird in the Air Pump* (1768; London, Tate; see fig.). Together with the effect of the light emerging from the apparatus (which serves both dramatic and symbolic ends), this depiction of communal engagement in science forcefully reflects Enlightenment ideals. Etienne-Louis Boullée's *Design for a Cenotaph to Newton* (1784; Paris, Bib. N.; for illustration *see* BOULLÉE, ETIENNE-LOUIS) represents a more personal glorification of science, while also attempting to embody its order and grandeur. The more characteristic Enlightenment images are, however, those of Classical antiquity, which relate the movement to NEO-CLASSICISM. The renewed study of the Classical past, particularly that of Greece and Republican Rome, is evident in the writings of such figures as Johann Joachim Winckelmann and Lessing and was also stimulated by the discoveries of Herculaneum (1738) and Pompeii (1748). The perceived nature of Classical art—its realism, restraint, harmony and order—was in tune with Enlightenment ideology. The culture of that earlier age was seen to embody an ideal to which the progress of man could be directed and also provided historical proof of its achievability. Furthermore, the fact that it was pagan appealed to the anti-religious tendencies of some Enlightenment theorists. Using both its style and subject-matter, contemporary depictions of Classical scenes were seen as a means of morally improving the viewer, so giving art a socially beneficial role.

The Enlightenment desire to foster progress fitted well with the contemporary understanding of Classical art. Its apparently fixed aesthetic norms and grounding in nature allowed the possibility of training artists to imitate it. The

Joseph Wright of Derby: *Experiment on a Bird in the Air Pump*, oil on canvas, 1.83×2.44 m, 1768 (London, Tate Gallery)

belief in the malleability of the individual further encouraged this. Thus in the later 18th century numerous academies were founded, in which Classical art was the sole inspiration and model. The desire to codify art into sets of rules motivated, among others, Joshua Reynolds's *Discourses* (1769–90). One corollary of the notion of objective distinctions between good and bad art was that educated laymen, rather than just artists, philosophers and historians, were attracted into art criticism. Like the artist, the critic could also learn and apply the rules: there was no ineffable secret or rare intuitive sense that required the specialist.

The range of ideas covered by the Enlightenment is well illustrated by the writings of Rousseau (e.g. *Discours sur les sciences et les arts*, 1750). Though in agreement on many issues with such contemporaries as Voltaire and Diderot, there is a strong anti-rational and subjective strain in Rousseau's thinking that sets him apart from the mainstream. In many respects, his influential ideas look forward to ROMANTICISM, a movement whose very different outlook is especially apparent against the backdrop of the Enlightenment. Political events, such as the French Revolution (seen by some as the logical conclusion of Enlightenment theory), further helped to undermine the governing belief in progress through reason.

BIBLIOGRAPHY

E. Cassirer: *Die Philosophie der Aufklärung* (Tübingen, 1932; Eng. trans., 1951)

P. Gay: *The Enlightenment: An Interpretation,* 2 vols (London, 1967–70)

N. Hampson: *The Enlightenment* (Harmondsworth, 1968/R 1986)

H. Honour: *Neo-Classicism* (Harmondsworth, 1968)

L. Eitner: *Neoclassicism and Romanticism, 1750–1850,* i (Englewood Cliffs, NJ, 1970)

The Age of Neo-Classicism (exh. cat., London, RA and V&A, 1972)

R. Porter and M. Teich, eds: *The Enlightenment in National Context* (Cambridge, 1981)

La Révolution française et l'Europe, 1789–99 (exh. cat., Paris, Grand Pal., 1989), pp. 338–45

VALERIE MAINZ

Enneking, John Joseph (*b* Minster, OH, 4 Oct 1841; *d* Hyde Park, nr Boston, MA, 17 Nov 1916). American painter. He received his first art instruction in Cincinnati, OH. He moved to Boston, MA, in 1865, where he received further instruction while earning his livelihood in business. In 1873 he determined to make art his full-time profession and spent the following three years in Europe, studying for nine months in Munich and for two years in Paris with Charles-François Daubigny and Léon Bonnat. Settling in Hyde Park, MA, in 1876, he established himself as a landscape painter of picturesque New England scenery and of hazy winter twilight scenes. He occasionally painted genre subjects and was especially noted for his large-scale and sympathetic portrayals of children and the elderly, as can be seen, for example, in *Removing a Splinter* (1894; New York, Arden priv. col.).

Enneking had his first major success when a large exhibition of his pictures was held in Boston in 1878. The sale of these paintings launched him as one of the most popular landscape painters in New England. While his early landscapes reflect the influence of his Barbizon training, his later images of brightly coloured, sunlit scenes reveal the influence of American Impressionist artists such as Theodore Robinson and John Twachtman.

BIBLIOGRAPHY

J. Davol: 'The Work of John J. Enneking', *Amer. Mag. A.*, viii (1917), pp. 320–23

John Joseph Enneking: American Impressionist Painter (exh. cat. by P. J. Pierce and R. H. Kristiansen, North Abington, MA, Pierce Gal., 1972)

John J. Enneking: American Impressionist (exh. cat., Brockton, MA, A. Cent., 1974)

LEE M. EDWARDS

Eno, Brian (*b* Woodbridge, Suffolk, 15 May 1948). English musician and video artist. He studied fine art at Ipswich and Winchester art schools from 1964 to 1969 before becoming a rock musician with Roxy Music in 1971; from 1973 he recorded on his own and with other musicians. In 1979, he turned to video, producing such contemplative non-narrative works as *Mistaken Memories of Mediaeval Manhattan* (1980–81) and *Thursday Afternoon* (1984) with his own 'ambient' music as soundtrack. Other pieces for gallery installation employed concealed video monitors as internal light sources. He collaborated with the artist Peter Schmidt (1931–80) in 1975 on *Oblique Strategies: Over One Hundred Worthwhile Dilemmas*, a set of oracle cards, and with Russell Mills (*b* 1952) on *More Dark than Shark* (London, 1986), a book of illustrations to his songs.

BIBLIOGRAPHY

Place 13 (exh. cat., ed. J. Hutchinson; Dublin, Trinity Coll., Hyde Gal., 1986)

A. Korner: 'Aurora musicalis', *Artforum*, xxiv/10 (1986), pp. 76–9

RICK POYNOR

Enrico di Tedice (*fl* 1254). Italian painter. A painted *Crucifix* in S Martino, Pisa, once bore his signature, and he was a witness in Pisa on 12 October 1254. He was the brother of Ugolino di Tedice, the painter of a signed *Crucifix* (St Petersburg, Hermitage). The Passion scenes at the sides of the S Martino *Crucifix* illustrate Enrico's expressive style, which is distinguished by the dramatic and emotional quality of the narration, very different from Giunta Pisano's style, and by a very free pictorial technique, using short brushstrokes and strong contrasts of light and colour. Other works attributed to him include a *Crucifix* from the oratory, Castellare (now in S Giovanni alla Vena, Vicopisano, Pisa), and the *Virgin and Child Enthroned with Four Passion Scenes* (Florence, Bargello); the latter had been tentatively attributed by Garrison to the 'Castellare Crucifix Master'. These works show that although Enrico adopted certain characteristics from Berlinghiero and Bonaventura Berlinghieri and even from Giunta Pisano, the origins of his style lie not in the Byzantine courtly tradition but rather in other cultural sources, usually identified as those of the Byzantine provinces of Cappadocia and the Balkan Peninsula. Enrico's expressive style and varied use of colour seem to have influenced the S Martino Master of the following generation in Pisa.

BIBLIOGRAPHY

G. Sinibaldi and G. Brunetti: *Pittura italiana del duecento e trecento: Catalogo della mostra giottesca di Firenze del 1937* (Florence, 1943), pp. 65–7

E. B. Garrison: *Italian Romanesque Panel Painting: An Illustrated Index* (Florence, 1949), pp. 14, 17

C. L. Ragghianti: *Pittura del dugento a Firenze* (Florence, 1955), pp. 8–10

E. Carli: *Pittura medievale pisana* (Milan, 1958), pp. 48–52

A. Caleca: 'Pittura del duecento e del trecento a Pisa e a Lucca', *La pittura in Italia: Le origini*, ed. E. Castelnuovo (Milan, 1985), p. 197

ANGELO TARTUFERI

Enrigus. *See under* GRUAMONTE.

Enrique, Master (*fl c.* 1240–77). French architect, active in Spain. The death of 'Master Enricus of the works of the church of Burgos' is recorded in a calendar of Burgos Cathedral on 6 July 1277. The 'Enricus master of the works' whose death is noted in an obituary of León Cathedral on 7 July 1277 is probably the same man. He may have lived in Burgos, as the death of his wife Mathia is recorded in the calendar of Burgos Cathedral on 18 June 1308.

Master Enrique is unlikely to have been the original architect of Burgos Cathedral, because the foundation stone was laid 56 years before his death; but he could have been responsible for beginning work on the second campaign there in the 1240s and for starting León Cathedral in 1255. As Lambert has pointed out, the fact that features characteristic of Reims Cathedral are present both in the second campaign at Burgos and at León supports this contention: the tracery of the south transept rose at Burgos is derived from that of the north transept of Reims Cathedral, and the plan of León is a reduced version of that of Reims. It also indicates where Master Enrique was trained and reveals that he was responsible for introducing the style of a leading French Gothic cathedral into Castile. The presence at León of such Parisian Rayonnant features as the interior wall passage prompted Branner to suggest that Master Enrique was sent to Paris in 1253 or 1254 to study the most recent achievements there. Not surprisingly, Parisian Rayonnant designs also occur in the contemporary work at Burgos (west towers, cloister).
See also BURGOS, §2(i)(a) and LEÓN, §II, 1(i).

BIBLIOGRAPHY

E. Lambert: *L'Art gothique en Espagne aux XIIe et XIIIe siècles* (Paris, 1931)

R. Branner: *St Louis and the Court Style in Gothic Architecture* (London, 1965)

H. Karge: 'La Cathédrale de Burgos. Organisation et technique de la construction', *Les Bâtisseurs des cathédrales gothiques* (exh. cat., ed. R. Recht; Strasbourg, Musées Ville, 1989), pp. 139–63

C. P. G. Welander: 'The Architecture of the Cloister of Burgos Cathedral', *Medieval Architecture and its Intellectual Context: Studies in Honour of Peter Kidson*, ed. E. Fernie and P. Crossley (Hambledon, 1990), pp. 159–68

CHRISTOPHER WELANDER

Enríquez, Carlos (*b* Zulueta, nr Remedios, 3 Aug 1900; *d* Havana, 2 May 1957). Cuban painter. He studied painting in secondary school in Cuba and then for a short time in 1924 at the Pennsylvania Academy of Fine Arts in Philadelphia. In the USA he met and married the American painter ALICE NEEL; they were divorced some years later. Upon his return to Cuba in 1925 he continued painting on his own and became involved with the group of avant-garde painters and writers seeking to break with the

Academy. Enríquez's unconventional, erotic drawings and paintings focused on subjects such as a nude woman on a horse (pen and ink drawing, 1930; Miami, FL, Cub. Mus. A. & Cult.). They shocked even the most open-minded and were withdrawn from various exhibitions in the late 1920s. From 1930 to 1933 Enríquez lived in Spain and France, where he became interested in Surrealism. His first individual exhibition took place at the Lyceum in Havana in 1934, soon after his return to Cuba, but it was closed almost immediately because of its scandalous content.

In paintings such as *Horsewoman* (1932; Havana, Mus. N. B.A.), contact with Surrealism led Enríquez to depict disembodied forms, X-ray images of body parts and scenes of violence and sexuality in veil-like areas of tan, white and green. After 1934 he dealt increasingly with Cuban rural folklore and myths in such paintings as the *Abduction of the Mulattas* (1938) and the *King of the Cuban Fields* (1934; both Havana, Mus. N. B.A.). Enríquez used the term 'romancero guajiro', which can be translated as 'the romantic spirit of the Cuban peasant', to describe his interest in folklore. This preoccupation with Cuban themes can also be found in Enríquez's novel *Tilín García* (Havana, 1939) and other writings by him. The 1940s and 1950s were a period of great productivity, characterized by female nudes in which tones of green predominate.

BIBLIOGRAPHY

A. de Juan: 'Carlos Enríquez en Cuba', *Pintura cubana: Temas y variaciones* (Havana, 1978, 2/Mexico City, 1980), pp. 71–4

Carlos Enríquez (exh. cat., Havana, Mus. N. B.A., 1979)

Carlos Enríquez (exh. cat., ed. C. Luis; Miami, FL, Cub. Mus. A. & Cult., 1986)

J. Martínez: *Cuban Art and National Identity: The Vanguardian Painters, 1925–50* (Gainesville, 1994)

GIULIO V. BLANC

Enríquez de Cabrera. *See under* CASTILLA (ii).

En ronde bosse. Figure or decorative device modelled in the round and covered with opaque enamel (*see* ENAMEL, §2(iv) and fig. 1). ☐

Enryakuji [Hieizanji; Hieizan Enryakuji; Sanmon]. Japanese Buddhist temple on Mt Hiei (Hieizan), north-east of Kyoto, in the city of Ōtsu, Shiga Prefecture.

1. HISTORY. Enryakuji was founded in AD 785 by the Tendai-sect patriarch Saichō [Dengyō Daishi] (767–822). Enryakuji is the head temple of the Sanmon branch of the Tendai sect, and, together with the Shingon-sect temple KONGŌBUJI in Wakayama Prefecture, it is one of the two principal seats of Japanese Esoteric Buddhism (*mikkyō*). Hie Shrine is its major tutelary Shinto shrine. Enryakuji occupies *c.* 4 sq. km on the slopes of Mt Hiei, a sacred mountain long worshipped as the abode of some of the main guardian deities of Kyoto. In the Heian period (AD 794–1185) it comprised 3000 buildings, and although these now number only about 70 it remains an imposing temple–shrine complex. It is divided into three compounds, called 'pagodas' (*tō*)—the Tōtō (East Pagoda), Saitō (West Pagoda) and Yokawa—which are themselves divided into sections called 'ravines' (*tani*). Another section, Sakamoto, at the eastern foot of Mt Hiei, near the

western shore of Lake Biwa, is Enryakuji's administrative centre and also the site of its museums, which contain a number of national treasures and important cultural properties, such as calligraphy by Saichō. Many of Enryakuji's icons were, however, lost owing to fire or destruction at the hands of Oda Nobunaga.

Throughout its long and venerable history Enryakuji has been home to a strong community of activist monks, whose ideologies and politics affected, sometimes even defined, larger trends in mainstream culture. Most of the founding figures of Kamakura-period (1185–1333) Buddhist sects—from the temple's founder Saichō to Kūya (903–72), Ryōnin (1072–1132), Hōnen (1133–1212), Eisai (1141–1215), Dōgen (1200–53), Shinran (1173–1262), Nichiren (1222–82) and Ippen (1239–89)—lived and studied at Enryakuji. For several centuries Enryakuji hosted lively ideological and philosophical discourse—on Tendai-type worship of the Lotus Sutra (Jap. *Hokkekyō* or *Myōhō renge kyō*; Skt *Saddharmapuṇḍarīkasūtra*), on meditative practices such as *nenbutsu* (Buddha ideation), on Jōdo (Pure Land) teachings and the role of personal faith as a path to salvation. In time these discussions worked a profound influence on Heian- and Kamakura-period Buddhist culture in general and on the production, aesthetics and religious import of Buddhist art in particular.

The temple has its origins in a small chapel built by Saichō on Mt Hiei for the practice of meditation and religious austerities. It was not until 788, however, that this chapel, a *Yakushidō* (Yakushi hall; hall for the worship of Yakushi (Skt *Bhaishajyaguru*)) called Ichijō Shikan'in (chapel of One-vehicle Meditations), was formally consecrated as Hieisanji. Its *honzon* (principal object of worship) was an icon of Yakushi (the Buddha of healing) carved by Saichō himself. On his return from China in 805 Saichō introduced a system of belief and practice that he called *Tendai hokke* ('Tendai teachings'). Saichō requested permission from Emperor Kanmu (*reg* 781–806) to establish on Mt Hiei an autonomous Tendai-sect ordination dais, independent of the Nara 'national' dais at Tōdaiji (*see* NARA, §III, 4). Permission was granted after Saichō's death in 822, and in 823, by imperial decree, his temple was renamed Enryakuji (Enryaku Temple), apparently in reference to the Enryaku era (782–806) and thus to Kanmu's reign.

By the late 10th century, when the abbot Ryōgen (912–85) held tenure, the temple had emerged as a rich, powerful and increasingly bellicose monastic enclave. It had strong ties with the royal house and the civilian aristocracy in Kyoto, whose members numbered among its priestly leaders. Like its similarly powerful contemporaries (and enemies) ONJŌJI, Tōdaiji and Kōfukuji (*see* NARA, §III, 7), Enryakuji at this time developed its own standing army of soldier–monks (*sōhei*) to protect its immense portfolio of tax-immune landholdings (*shōen*), to intimidate the civilian government and especially to wage war on its primary rival, Onjōji, head temple of the Jimon branch of the Tendai sect. That little remains of the original Enryakuji complex seems largely due to the existence of this army and to the temple's willingness to deploy it. In 1571, in a ruthless bid to destroy its power, the warlord ODA NOBUNAGA set fire to Enryakuji, utterly destroying it, and slaughtered thousands of its monks. Enryakuji was reconstructed, first under TOYOTOMI HIDEYOSHI, one of the unifiers of the nation, and later under the Tokugawa shoguns Ieyasu (1543–1616) and Iemitsu (1604–51). Modern Enryakuji dates from 1600.

2. ARCHITECTURE AND LAYOUT. Most scholars agree that the Tokugawa builders sought to preserve the original appearance of Enryakuji. Unlike the ordered temples constructed on flat ground for the great Nara sects, Enryakuji consists of groups of relatively small buildings, most with cypress-bark roofing (*hiwadabuki*), placed randomly in the mountainous, wooded landscape. For many this represents an articulation of the mystical aspects of Tendai-type Esoterism, with its emphasis on reflection and retreat.

The three compounds at Enryakuji evolved chronologically and in tandem with the activities of prominent abbots. The Tōtō emerged first, from Saichō's tenure until 824. On one side of the Ichijō Shikan'in was a *kyōzō* (*sūtra* repository), on the other a *Monjudō* (hall for the worship of Monju (Skt *Manjushri*)). The compound also included a *Hokkedō* (*Hokkezanmaidō*; hall for meditations on the *Hokkekyō*) and the Daikōdō (Great Lecture Hall; see fig.).

In 827 the precinct's *kaidan'in* (ordination hall) was completed. During the tenure of Enchin [Chishō Daishi] (814–98; *see also* ONJŌJI), the Ichijō Shikan'in, then called the Chūdō (Middle Hall), the *kyōzō* and the *Monjudō* were merged into one building, the Konpon Chūdō (Root Hall), as the main hall of Enryakuji. A one-bay extended aisle (*magobisashi*) was attached to the old façade of the Chūdō to form an additional worship area. In 978 the Chūdō was renovated, and another one-bay extended aisle was added to the earlier aisle, again to supply extra worship space. Although the present Konpon Chūdō dates from the Kan'ei era (1624–44) and has since been renovated every 40 years, it is regarded as a faithful reconstruction of the Konpon Chūdō as it existed in 978.

The Konpon Chūdō is regarded as the principal architectural monument at Enryakuji. Built in the *irimoya zukuri* ('hip-and-gable roof construction') format, the 11×6-bay building is one of the largest traditional wooden structures in Japan. It is a typical 10th-century main-hall construction, for example in the contrasting use of planked wood flooring in the outer sanctuary (*gejin*) and hard-packed earthen floors in the inner sanctuary (*naijin*). The hall with its worship areas afforded by the extended aisles is a notable example of the type of building that in the 11th century, as a free-standing construction, came to be known as the *raidō* ('worship hall').

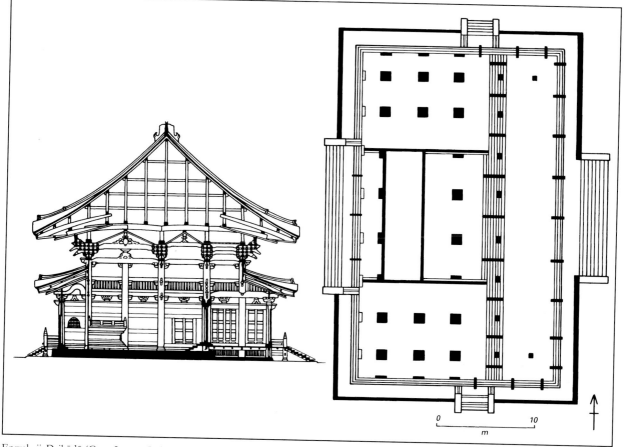

Enryakuji, Daikōdō (Great Lecture Hall), cross-section and plan (roof construction hypothetical), *c.* AD 824

The Saitō was developed during the tenure of Enchō (771–836) and included a *Hokkedō*, *jōgyōdō* (*jōgyō zanmaidō*; hall for the practice of ambulatory meditation on Amida (Skt Amitabha)) and *Shakadō* (hall for the worship of Shaka (Skt Shakyamuni)). Although the *Hokkedō* and the *jōgyōdō* were reconstructed in 1595, they preserve the late Heian-period format known as *hōgyō zukuri* ('pyramidal roof construction'), which was typical of the small, square buildings used for the worship of the Lotus Sutra or Amida, and occasionally as mausolea. The oldest structure at Enryakuji is the Shakadō, also called Denpō-rindō, originally built (completed 1347) as the *kondō* ('golden hall'; image hall) of Onjōji but moved to Enryakuji by Hideyoshi in 1595 as part of his reconstruction project.

The Yokawa was erected during the tenure of Ennin (Jikaku Daishi; 794–864) and inaugurated on his return from China in 848. It included its own main hall, called the Shuryōgon'in (or the Yokawa Chūdō), a *kōdō* (lecture hall) and a pagoda called the Konpon Myohōtō (Root Pagoda of the Marvellous Law), where Ennin is said to have practised the four varieties of Tendai meditation (*shishū zanmai*).

BIBLIOGRAPHY

Eizan daishi den [The life of Hieizan patriarch Saichō] (824)
Tendai zasu ki [The record of the Tendai abbots] (9th–19th centuries)
Sanmon dōsha ki [History of the buildings of Enryakuji] (1417)
T. Fukuyama: *Tendai Shingon shū no kenchiku* [Architecture of the Tendai and Shingon sects] (Tokyo, 1936)
T. Sawa: 'Mikkyō no bijutsu' [The arts of Esoteric Buddhism], *Nihon no bijutsu*, viii (Tokyo, 1964); Eng. trans. by R. L. Gage as *Art in Japanese Esoteric Buddhism*, Heibonsha Surv. Jap. A., viii (New York and Tokyo, 1972)
K. Suzuki: 'Jōdai no jiin kenchiku' [Early Buddhist architecture], *Nihon no bijutsu*, lxvi (Tokyo, 1971); Eng. trans. by M. N. Parent and N. S. Steinhardt as *Early Buddhist Architecture in Japan*, Japanese Arts Library, ix (Tokyo, New York and San Francisco, 1980)
Z. Tsukamoto and others, eds: *Tendai no hihō: Hieizan* [Tendai secret treasures: Mt Hiei] (Tokyo, 1971)
H. Kageyama: *Hieizan to Kōyasan* [Mts Hiei and Kōya], Kyoiku rekishi shinsho: Nihonshi [Educational Publishers new history series: Japanese history], xxix (Tokyo, 1980)
J. Hiroaka: *Nihon jiin shi no kenkyū* [Research in the history of Japanese Buddhist temples] (Tokyo, 1981)
                                                    MIMI HALL YIENGPRUKSAWAN

Ens, Joseph. *See* HEINTZ, (4).

Ensei. *See under* EN.

Ensenada, Marqués de la [Somodevilla y Bengoechea, Zenón] (*b* Hervías, 25 April 1702; *d* Medina del Campo, nr Valladolid, 2 Dec 1781). Spanish politician and collector. Of humble origins, he served in the navy, taking part in the conquest of Oran in 1732 and in 1733 in the expedition to Naples. From 1741 he was Secretary of State and War to the Infante Philip in Parma and in 1743 became Spain's Minister of Finance, the Indies, the Navy and War. In 1754 he was removed from office, exiled, and his goods were confiscated. He never held another post of importance. Ensenada was an important legislator, promoter of science and, with his love of music, was a friend of the castrato Carlo Broschi Farinelli.

In his private life Ensenada surrounded himself with an atmosphere of refinement, with rare objects and with a collection of 238 paintings that he began in Italy. It contained works by Italian, Netherlandish and Spanish masters. When his possessions were returned to him in 1760, he was old and without direct heirs, and he began to sell the paintings to private collectors, among whom were the Bourbon Charles III and the Prince of the Asturias, Don Carlos (later Charles IV). The first inventory of his collection (1754), drawn up by the painter Andrés de la Calleja, valued it at 100,000 pesos; it comprised religious and mythological works, still-lifes, landscapes and portraits.

In 1768 Anton Raphael Mengs chose 30 paintings for the King, costing 147,200 reales de vellón, among which were: *Artemisa* by Rembrandt, the *Conde Duque de Olivares* by Diego Velázquez, *Homage to Rubens* by Luca Giordano and *Judith and Holofernes* by Tintoretto (all Madrid, Prado); and *Innocent X*, bust length, by Velázquez (London, Apsley House, Wellington Mus.) as well as works by Bartolomé Esteban Murillo, Andrea Sacchi, Carlo Maratti and Claudio Coello. The collection shows Ensenada's admiration for 17th-century painting, especially by Spanish artists, by whom he owned a surprising number of mythological paintings. The almost complete absence of works by contemporary artists is also interesting.

UNPUBLISHED SOURCES

Alcalá de Henares, Archv Gen. Cent. [*Inventario de los bienes del Marqués de la Ensenada*, comp. A. de la Calleja, 1754]
Madrid, Archv Escorial [*Inventario de las pinturas del Marqués de la Ensenada compradas por el Rey*, comp. A. R. Mengs, 1768]

BIBLIOGRAPHY

M. Fernández de Navarrete: *Noticia biográfica del Marqués de la Ensenada* (Madrid, 1842)
A. Rodríguez Villa: *Don Zenón de Somodevilla, Marqués de la Ensenada* (Madrid, 1878) [cites inventory by Calleja]
A. G. de Amezúa y Mayo: *Un modelo de estadistas: El Marqués de la Ensenada* (Madrid, 1917)
C. E. Ruiz: *El Marqués de la Ensenada según un confidente* (Madrid, 1922)
C. R. Bouvier y Soldevilla: *Ensenada et son temps: Le Redressement de l'Espagne au XVIIIe siècle* (Paris, 1941)
F. Abad León: *El Marqués de la Ensenada, su vida y su obra*, 2 vols (Madrid, 1985)
M. Agueda: 'Una colección de pinturas en el Madrid del siglo XVIII: El Marqués de la Ensenada', *Actas de las III jornadas de arte: Centro de Estudios Históricos, Madrid, 1990*, pp. 168–98
                                                    MERCEDES AGUEDA

Enshū. *See* KOBORI ENSHŪ.

Ensinger. German family of artists. They worked in the late 14th century and the 15th as master masons mainly at buildings in Germany and Switzerland. (1) Ulrich von Ensingen was Master of the Works at Ulm Minster and Strasbourg Cathedral. He had three sons, Kaspar (*fl* 1427-30), (2) Matthäus Ensinger and Matthias (*d* 1438), all of whom became masons. One of his two daughters married Hans Kun, who succeeded his father-in-law as master at Ulm in 1417. (2) Matthäus Ensinger was married twice, and of his four sons, (3) Vincenz Ensinger and (4) Moritz Ensinger became architects. They were born in Berne and were trained by their father. Matthäus and Moritz were masters of the works at Ulm Minster, and Vincenz became master at Konstanz Minster. Ulrich von Ensingen's mason's mark resembles a small 'h', tilted; Moritz added two x's to the lower end of the vertical stroke, and Vincenz added a cross stroke to it.

(1) Ulrich von Ensingen (*b* Swabia, 1360s; *d* Strasbourg, 1419). Architect and sculptor. The influence of the Parler family on Ulrich's early work suggests that he completed his training in Swabia, but he must also have been at the cathedrals of Prague and Strasbourg, for his work shows significant knowledge of both buildings. In 1392 he became Master of the Works at Ulm Minster, before which he had been involved with the cathedral works in Milan. In 1397, the five-year contract usual at Ulm was changed to life tenure. In 1399 he was also Master of the Works at Strasbourg, where he went to live, and at about this time he became Master of the Works at the Frauenkirche in Esslingen. In 1414 he produced a design for the north tower of Basle Minster.

When Ulrich von Ensingen began work in Ulm, the eight eastern bays of the nave were already standing. He was chiefly responsible for finishing the nave and for the west tower, although he left the nave unvaulted. One version of his plans, in the lower part of the St Martin window (in the west tower), shows that he adopted the lower height of the nave, probably established by Michael Parler von Ulm, but in the actual construction he raised it by *c.* 4 m. A drawing of the tower, probably autograph (Drawing A), is preserved (Ulm, Ulm. Mus.) though this does not show the lower levels. Ulrich completed the tower to the beginning of the first upper level. He bound the lower portions of the massive tower closely into the nave, but the eastern side was supported only by free-standing piers, perhaps on insufficient foundations, so that by the end of the 15th century the lower levels had to be almost completely walled up, separating the tower from the nave. At Esslingen, Ulrich completed the nave and added a western tower, the lower portion of which with its western portal was built under his direction. The south-west portal is also his work.

At Strasbourg, Ulrich planned the north tower, building the octagon up to the beginning of the tracery. Its four stairtowers were planned and built by him only up to first storey level. Two studies for the octagon survive (Strasbourg, Mus. Oeuvre Notre-Dame). The four small and badly preserved figures on the parapet are the only sculptures that can be ascribed to Ulrich von Ensingen. As one of these figures bears a shield with Ulrich's mason's mark it has been identified as a self-portrait.

In his early work Ulrich manipulated and transformed ideas from the Parlers, but later he developed High Gothic forms, articulating his designs with geometric motifs and strongly emphasized verticals. He began to divide the tracery into ever more layers, often independent of each other. By this he achieved greater plasticity, but at the same time individual forms were richer and more refined. This enrichment of the tracery initiated developments that remained influential to the end of the 15th century.

BIBLIOGRAPHY
A. W. F. Carstanjen: *Ulrich von Ensingen* (Munich, 1893)
A. Conradt: *Ulrich von Ensingen als Ulmer Münsterbaumeister und seine Voraussetzungen* (diss., U. Freiburg im Breisgau, 1959)
B. Schock-Werner: *Das Strassburger Münster im 15. Jahrhundert* (Cologne, 1983)
Les Bâtisseurs des cathédrales gothiques (exh. cat., ed. R. Recht; Strasbourg, Mus. A. Mod., 1989)

(2) Matthäus Ensinger (*b c.* 1390–1400; *d* Ulm, 1463). Architect and sculptor, son of (1) Ulrich von Ensingen. He was Master of the Works in Berne, Esslingen and Ulm. He was apprenticed to his father in Strasbourg and returned there not long before his father's death in 1419. He worked, perhaps as a foreman, under the new Master of the Works, Johannes Hültz, until in 1420 he was called to Berne to plan the new Minster, the foundation stone of which was laid in 1421. He directed the works until 1453.

His design for Berne was a basilical nave, leading to a single-cell choir, flanked by side chapels. The west tower was to be integrated into the nave, as at Ulm. Matthäus built the choir and chapels and began the nave arcades.

In 1424 he made for Johann von Freiburg a standing figure of his father, Konrad, for the tomb of the *Counts of Neuenburg* in the collegiate church in Neuenburg. Several years later he also produced a statue of *Johann von Freiburg*. The statues, in the round, realistic and full of life, represent the Counts with folded hands and upward gazes. The arguments surrounding the production of the Heilsspiegel Altar (1433/4) in Basle suggest that Matthäus must also have worked in wood; he probably carved the figures for the shrine.

In 1435 he was called to Ripaille to build a church for a chivalric order next to the castle of Duke Amadeus VII of Savoy. A wooden model was made from his plans and building began but ceased at the death of the patron. The building collapsed in the 15th century.

Matthäus Ensinger was also Master of the Works at the Frauenkirche, Esslingen, in succession to his father. The complete change in the masons' marks and the enlistment of a foreman only after 1424 suggest there was a break in the works. Matthäus directed work on the tower from the second storey (see fig.). Officially he remained Master of the Works until his death, but it is likely that Hans von Böblingen I, who became foreman in 1440, took over most of the work.

In 1446 Matthäus became Master of the Works at Ulm Minster and moved to Ulm, returning to Berne only occasionally. Although between 1449 and 1451 he also tried to become Master of the Works at Strasbourg, the people of Strasbourg would not allow him to hold his position at Ulm simultaneously; so he remained in Ulm, directing the works there until his death.

Matthäus vaulted the choir and the aisles at Ulm (the latter replaced by Burkhard Engelberg). He was also responsible for several chapels: the Neithard Chapel on the north, and the brick Rembold Chapel (1448) to the south-east. The Rothsche Chapel, built in 1447 under his direction, was pulled down in 1817.

Matthäus built the west tower from the upper level of the St Martin window to the beginning of the window of the storey above. The three great traceried ogee arches in front of the St Martin window are attributable to him, as are the blind ogee arches on the buttresses at about the same level. Matthäus worked in his father's building tradition, which was characterized by the sculptural articulation of the whole structure, with fantastic tracery forms. At first he was strongly tied to this tradition and used some identical details; but from *c.* 1440 his forms became harder and were characterized by numerous angular profiles and sharp bends. His sculpture is characterized by a

Matthäus Ensinger: Frauenkirche, Esslingen tower, ?1420s and later

realistic and strongly modelled style, which is at its best in the figures in Neuenburg. His stone monument in Ulm Minster, dated 1463, bears a shield with three superimposed compasses.

(3) Vincenz Ensinger (*b* Berne, after 1420; *d* Konstanz, after 1493). Architect, son of (2) Matthäus Ensinger. His mother was from Berne. He worked with his father until Matthäus went to Ulm in 1446. In 1448 Matthäus was able to appoint Vincenz as his representative in Berne. Vincenz directed the works until 1453, from 1449 with relative independence, as his father did not visit Berne again. Vincenz, however, visited Ulm twice during this period to seek his father's advice. He even worked with his father in Ulm for very short periods. In 1450 he accompanied Matthäus to Strasbourg, where the latter hoped to obtain the position of Master of the Works.

In the spring of 1453 Vincenz became Master of the Works at Konstanz, but he was documented in this position only in 1459, when he took part in the meeting of masons in Regensburg (*see* MARKS, §1).

At Konstanz he first vaulted the eastern range of the cloister and adjacent buildings: the wine cellar, and the school and library that lay over it. The southern chapels of the minster, those of SS Christopher and Mary Magdalen, were built alongside this in 1483. The vaults of the St Maurice rotunda and the antechapel of the Konradi Chapel were also built under Vincenz's direction. His masterpiece is surely the columned chapter house in Konstanz, formerly the library.

In 1487 the foreman was commissioned to make the west portal of the minster, though Vincenz was to act as adviser. Differences arose over this commission, but it is uncertain whether his dismissal on 22 October 1489 was the result of these differences or simply of his age. The patrons retained the right to seek his advice, guaranteeing payment for each occasion. The documents mention Vincenz as a citizen of Konstanz up to 1493.

Vincenz Ensinger was called repeatedly to other places to give advice: in 1469/70 he went to Basle to prepare for the completion of the Martin tower, and in 1477 he advised the Master of the Works at Weingarten. He was a competent and technically perfect architect, but his work shows little individuality.

(4) Moritz Ensinger (*b* Berne, *c.* 1430; *d* Lenzburg, Switzerland, 1493). Architect, son of (2) Matthäus Ensinger. He is first mentioned in 1449 as a journeyman at Ulm Minster, and he was for many years an assistant to his father there. In 1465, two years after his father's death, he was made Master of the Works at Ulm Minster for five years, an appointment then converted to life tenure; he left Ulm in 1477.

At Ulm, Moritz built the upper storey and windows, the nave vaults and the eastern end of the nave. His mason's mark and the date 1471 can be seen on the east wall of the nave below the crown of the vault. The nave vaults are very simply formed, divided by transverse ribs; the diagonals meet a little below the crown of the vault and are connected by a short rib.

Moritz frequently acted as adviser to other cities: in 1472 he went to Nördlingen and Geislingen, in 1474 to Munich and in 1478 to Weingarten. In Munich he advised on the vaulting of the Frauenkirche, while in Nördlingen he was consulted about the tower and the nave vaulting of St George's. He recommended that the square storey of the tower be completed with blind tracery and a decorated string course; that above this should be built, slightly set back, an octagonal belfry decorated with eight rich windows; and finally that the tower be topped by a pierced wooden lantern. He sent a plan (now lost) to Nördlingen, with a plan for the construction of a horse-driven lifting device, recommended as a cost-cutting measure. It is uncertain whether the tower was built according to his plans: in comparison with the tower project at Ulm it is very plain, and the octagon windows could certainly not be described as rich. Yet even the nave vaults at Ulm are very little decorated for the period.

In 1478 Moritz is mentioned as a house owner and citizen of Konstanz, where he joined his brother Vincenz. In that year, however, he went to Berne, where he was Master of the Works again for a short time. A portrait of Moritz originally from Ulm Minster is preserved in Mainz; dated 1483 it shows him with compass in hand. The coat of arms also represented shows two compasses on the shield.

BIBLIOGRAPHY

A. Klemm: *Württembergische Baumeister und Bildhauer bis ums Jahr 1750* (Stuttgart, 1882)

B. Pfeiffer: 'Zur Baugeschichte von Weingarten im 15. Jahrhundert', *Württemberg. Vjhft. Landesgesch.*, n. s. 5 (1896), pp. 422–8

E. Buchner: *Das deutsche Bildnis der Spätgotik und der frühen Dürerzeit* (Berlin, 1953)

L. Mojon: *Der Münsterbaumeister Matthäus Ensinger*, Berner Schriften zur Kunst, i (Berne, 1967)

R. Wortman: *Das Ulmer Münster*, Grosse Bauten Europas, iv (Stuttgart, 1972)

E. D. Schmidt: *Nördlingen: Die Georgskirche* (Stuttgart, 1977)

B. Schock-Werner: *Das Strassburger Münster im 15. Jahrhundert* (Cologne, 1983)

BARBARA SCHOCK-WERNER

Ensor, James (Sidney Edouard), Baron (*b* Ostend, 13 April 1860; *d* Ostend, 19 Nov 1949). Belgian painter, printmaker and draughtsman. No single label adequately describes the visionary work produced by Ensor between 1880 and 1900, his most productive period. His pictures from that time have both Symbolist and Realist aspects, and in spite of his dismissal of the Impressionists as 'superficial daubers' he was profoundly concerned with the effects of light. His imagery and technical procedures anticipated the colouristic brilliance and violent impact of Fauvism and German Expressionism and the psychological fantasies of Surrealism. Ensor's most memorable and influential work was almost exclusively produced before 1900, but he was largely unrecognized before the 1920s in his own country. His work was highly influential in Germany, however: Emil Nolde visited him in 1911, and was influenced by his use of masks; Paul Klee mentions him admiringly in his diaries; Erich Heckel came to see him in the middle of the war and painted his portrait (1930; Cologne, Wallraf-Richartz-Mus.); Alfred Kubin owned several of his prints, while Marc Chagall and George Grosz also adapted certain elements from Ensor. All the artists of the Cobra group saw him as a master. He influenced many Belgian artists including Léon Spilliaert, Rik Wouters, Constant Permeke, Frits van den Berghe, Paul Delvaux and Pierre Alechinsky.

1. Life and work. 2. Working methods and technique.

1. LIFE AND WORK.

(i) Training and early work, before 1881. (ii) 1881–1900. (iii) After 1900.

(i) Training and early work, before 1881. Ensor's family circumstances may help to account for the atmosphere of anxiety which pervades his work. His English father was a social failure and alcoholic, but was idolized by Ensor. His mother was a materialistic middle-class Fleming, and his younger sister Mariette ('Mitche'), to whom he was very close, was a constant source of concern; eventually, in 1892, she impetuously married a Chinese who abandoned her before the birth of their daughter. Ensor later recalled in a letter to André de Ridder of 1928 that at the age of three he had a nightmare of a big black bird sweeping down on his cot, a dream that has been interpreted as a symbol of the fear of castration.

Ensor enrolled at the Academy in Brussels in the autumn of 1877. Among his fellow students were Fernand Khnopff, Darío de Regoyos, Guillaume Vogels, Guillaume van Strijdonck (1861–1937) and Alfred William Finch, who was influenced by Ensor and also had his portrait painted by him (*c.* 1882; Antwerp, K. Mus. S. Kst.). Ensor became a friend of Théo Hannon (1851–1917), a painter and later a poet and art critic, who introduced him to the circle of anarchist intellectuals around Ernest Rousseau, rector of Brussels University. Ensor's early work shows him as the extremely gifted heir of Louis Dubois and the other artists of the Société Libre des Beaux-Arts, although even as early as *Beach Hut* (1877; Antwerp, K. Mus. S. Kst.) he was interested in light effects. He painted life-size portraits of ordinary people such as *Woman with Turned-up Nose* (1879; Antwerp, K. Mus. S. Kst.) and the *Lamp Boy* (1880; Brussels, Mus. A. Mod.). Such paintings as *The Colourist* (1880; Brussels, Mus. A. Mod.) and *Lady with Fan* (1880; Antwerp, K. Mus. S. Kst.) anticipate the Intimist work of Edouard Vuillard. In 1880 Ensor returned to Ostend, where he remained for most of his life.

(ii) 1881–1900. In the early 1880s Ensor showed his work for the first time at two exhibitions in Brussels at the Chrysalide gallery and with Vogels at the Cercle Artistique, where *The Cabbage* (1880; Brussels, Mus. A. Mod.) was criticized for its 'turpitude'. He also exhibited at L'Essor and at the Paris Salon. Between 1881 and 1882 Ensor produced the great works of his so-called 'bourgeois' period, including *Afternoon in Ostend* (1881; Antwerp, K. Mus. S. Kst.), *Middle-class Drawing-room* (1881; Antwerp, K. Mus. S. Kst.), *Russian Music* (1881; Brussels, Mus. A. Mod.) and *Woman Eating Oysters* (1881; Antwerp, K. Mus. S. Kst.), which was rejected by the Salons of both Antwerp and Paris. In *Sombre Lady* (1881; Brussels, Mus. A. Mod.) and *Lady in Distress* (1882; Paris, Mus. Orsay) Ensor approached Symbolism in the oppressive atmosphere created by the suggestion of a disturbing situation not represented directly in the picture itself. Concurrently he produced quasi-Impressionist paintings of Ostend such as the *Roofs of Ostend in Mist* (1885; priv. col., see 1983 exh. cat., p. 121).

In 1883 Ensor was one of the founder-members of the avant-garde group Les XX (*see* VINGT, LES), whose goal was to promote new artistic developments throughout Europe. He had acute differences of opinion with Octave Maus, the secretary of Les XX, although some members of the group considered him to be a leader. Ensor's concern with identity and the role of the artist led him to paint self-portraits throughout his career. In *Ensor in a Flowered Hat* (1883; Ostend, Mus. S. Kst.) he modelled himself after a famous self-portrait by Rubens. This canvas was among those that he later reworked. At this time he also introduced grotesque and exaggerated masks directly inspired by the Ostend carnival and Chinese theatre masks sold in his family's souvenir shop in paintings such as *Scandalized Masks* (1883; Brussels, Mus. A. Mod.).

Ensor suffered from an ulcer in the mid-1880s and consequently his productivity decreased for a time. In

1. James Ensor: *Old Woman with Masks*, oil on canvas, 540×475 mm, 1889 (Ghent, Museum voor Schone Kunsten)

1887 he is thought to have made his first visit to England and to have studied Turner's paintings, some of which he had already sketched from reproductions (sketchbooks in Antwerp, K. Mus. S. Kst.). On the death of his father in 1887, he assumed responsibility for the family, thereby aggravating his financial worries. His battles with Les XX continued in bitter letters to Maus about Khnopff, a fellow member, and Whistler, who had been proposed as a member. Ensor was also treated harshly by the critics, the Belgian Symbolist poet Fernand Séverin remarking that 'the visions of the illiterate Ensor are more ridiculous than terrifying'.

To express his anxiety and at the same time to escape from mundane reality, Ensor began to treat religious subjects in a highly subjective way. The *Tribulations of St Anthony* (1887; New York, MOMA; *see* BELGIUM, fig. 19) for instance, in which the figure is assailed by devils, can be interpreted as a metaphor of Ensor's own sense of persecution. Alfred H. Barr jr was later to say with reference to this work: 'Indeed, at this moment of his career, Ensor was possibly the boldest living painter.' In many of these religious paintings, including *Adam and Eve's Expulsion from Paradise* (1887; Antwerp, K. Mus. S. Kst.), light dissolves form into calligraphic marks and signs. Ensor's flight into a private world became acute in his identification with Christ. Each drawing in the series *Christ's Haloes* or the *Sensitivities of Light* has a subtitle describing the particular light effect in the drawing, for example *Lively and Radiant, Christ's Entry into Jerusalem*

(1885; Ghent, Mus. S. Kst.) and *Sad and Broken, Satan and the Legions of Hell Tormenting Christ on the Cross* (1886; Brussels, Mus. A. Mod.). In the latter, Christ has Ensor's facial features, and Ensor's name is written across an open tomb prophesying the Resurrection. Skeletons are part of the drama, and became a perennial motif in Ensor's work. In the *Dead Christ Watched over by Angels* (pencil on wood with white ground, 1886; Knokke-Het Zoute, priv. col., see 1983 exh. cat., p. 147) and many of the drawings and small paintings that followed, Ensor's use of sinuous line prefigured the arabesques of Belgian Art Nouveau. His oriental sources included Chinese bric-à-brac from the family shop and Japanese prints, and such motifs can also be found in his sketchbooks of *c.* 1881 (Antwerp, K. Mus. S. Kst.).

Ensor had been prevented by illness from sending new paintings to the Les XX exhibition of 1888 and was represented only by drawings and prints. His unhappiness extended also to his personal life, when his family forbade him to marry Augusta Boogaerts, whom he had nicknamed 'La Sirène'. He again alluded to his situation by identifying with Christ, this time in a major canvas, the *Entry of Christ into Brussels in 1889* (2.53×4.31 m, 1888; Malibu, CA, Getty Mus.). In spite of his halo, Christ is ignored by the thronging crowd, many of whom wear threatening masks. Above the crowd is a political banner bearing the legend *Vive la sociale* ('Long live the Welfare State'); the implication is that Christ's message, like Ensor's, is not being heeded. Parody becomes nightmare when one notices, lurking among the masks on the left foreground, the figure of Death in a top hat.

In Ensor's work masks are often used to disclose hidden motives and characteristics, to reveal rather than to conceal identity. Regarding masks as symbols of alienation and the evasion of reality, Ensor seems to have been drawn to such images partly for autobiographical reasons. In *Strange Masks* (1892; Brussels, Mus. A. Mod.), for instance, it is tempting to identify the masked violinist lying prone on the ground as a metaphorical portrait of the artist himself, taunted by grotesque figures representing colleagues from his artistic circle. *Old Woman with Masks* (1889; Ghent, Mus. S. Kst.; see fig. 1), on the other hand, was originally conceived as a straightforward portrait of the mother of Ensor's hairdresser in Ostend. Her refusal to accept or pay for the completed work led Ensor to wreak revenge by surrounding her image with threatening masked heads that emphasize the ugliness of her features.

Skeletons frequently act as personifications of death in Ensor's pictures, acting on human emotions and suffering as if alive, even feeling the cold, as in *Skeletons Trying to Warm themselves* (1889; Fort Worth, TX, Kimbell A. Mus.). They fight over new recruits to the world of the dead, as in *Skeletons Fighting over a Hanged Man* (1891; Antwerp, K. Mus. S. Kst.). Another image of determined aggression, *Skeletons Fighting over a Red Herring* (1891; Brussels, B. Goldschmidt, priv. col.; see Legrand, 1971, p. 74), is also a satire, and an instance of a frequently repeated pun on Ensor's name ('hareng saur' is pronounced the same as 'art Ensor' in French). *Skeleton Looking at Chinoiseries* (1885; New York, J. J. Aberbach priv. col., see 1983 exh. cat., p. 129) was originally a portrait of Ensor's father but was reworked after his death between 1889 and 1891. Ensor bore a marked physical resemblance to his father and identified with his social failure and mental collapse.

In 1890 further difficulties developed with Les XX. A letter from Ensor to Maus reveals how close his torments had brought him to becoming unbalanced. The *Man of Sorrows* (1891; Ghent, Mus. S. Kst.), the most extreme case of his identification with Christ, was painted at the time of this crisis. This exaggerated image of pain, in which mask and flesh are merged in a blood-soaked grimace, is a highly personal reworking of a devotional image familiar in early Netherlandish painting. As Ensor wrote in an unpublished letter to Jules Dujardin of 1897 (Brussels, Archvs A. Belge, no. 981): 'For me, art is the daughter of pain and except for rare moments I have been in league with bitterness and disillusion.'

A journey to the Netherlands with Eugène Demolder, the author of the first monograph on Ensor (Brussels, 1892), seems to have brought him some relief. In 1892 he is thought to have spent four days in London, which may account for the late Pre-Raphaelite aspect of the *Consoling Virgin* (1892; Belgium, priv. col., see 1983 exh. cat., p. 271), in which he portrayed himself, palette in hand, dead fish next to him on the ground, in supplication before the Virgin Mary. Les XX disbanded in 1893, to be succeeded in 1894 by La Libre Esthétique, with Octave Maus as its director, but with Ensor excluded from full membership. In despair Ensor put the contents of his studio up for sale for 8500 francs but was unable to find a buyer. It was nevertheless during this period that he began to secure his reputation. He was invited to take part in several Libre Esthétique exhibitions between 1894 and 1914. The Belgian State purchased one of his major paintings, the *Lamp Boy*, in 1896, and he had his first one-man show in Brussels in the same year. In 1898 an exhibition of his work was organized in Paris by the magazine *Plume*, which also published a special issue that brought together a number of exceptional testimonials, not only by Hannon and Maus but also by the internationally respected Belgian writers Maurice Maeterlinck (1862–1949) and Emile Verhaeren. The Paris exhibition was a fiasco, however; the mixture of tragedy and comedy in his art was met with incomprehension.

(iii) After 1900. It is generally agreed that Ensor's creativity waned after 1900. For the rest of his life the artist repeated himself with slight variations, predating his work, exhibiting old canvases as new ones and even tracing old drawings. His *Self-portrait Surrounded by Masks* (1899; Japan, priv. col., see Legrand, p. 27) suggests that he was aware of his growing inability to communicate. He portrayed himself isolated, surrounded by masks and the advancing figure of death.

Nevertheless, some of his later works are strikingly successful. The *Double Portrait* of Ensor and Augusta Boogaerts (1904; Brussels, M. Mabille priv. col., see Janssens, p. 88), known as the '*Ensor de glace*' (Ensor in the mirror/Ensor made of ice), a pun playing on the presence of the mirror, reflects Ensor's apparent indifference to sex. He continued to paint religious subjects, albeit in a more decorative, less intense manner: *Moses and the Birds* (*Pharaoh's Daughter Discovering Moses*) (1924;

2. James Ensor: *My Mother Dead*, oil on canvas, 750×600 mm, 1915 (Ostend, Museum voor Schone Kunsten)

Berkeley, U. CA, A. Mus.), still-lifes (e.g. *Flowers*, 1909; Otterlo, Kröller-Müller Sticht.) and straightforward landscapes and town views, notably a version of *Afternoon in Ostend* (*c.* 1910; ex-Brussels, Daelemans priv. col., see Haesaerts, p. 156). Ensor did not, however, abandon his more macabre themes, as seen in *Hop Frog's Revenge* (dated 1896, probably 1910; Otterlo, Kröller-Müller Sticht.), a subject taken from a story by his favourite author, Edgar Allan Poe, and the extremely personal *My Mother Dead* (1915; Ostend, Mus. S. Kst.; see fig. 2), a painting of his recently deceased mother in which the dispassionately observed body forms a mere backdrop for the meticulously executed still-life in the foreground. As he grew older he increasingly painted intimate and often humorous portraits of those close to him: *Comical Smokers* (1920; Kortrijk, priv. col., see 1983 exh. cat., p. 317), a portrait of La Sirène, and *Alex in Chinese Costume* (1899; Chicago, IL, A. Inst.), a portrait of Mitche's daughter, are the most outstanding.

Ensor finally won acclaim and respectability at the start of the 20th century. In 1903 he was made a Knight of the Order of Leopold, and in 1908 Verhaeren published a monograph on him. After receiving a harmonium in 1906 as a gift from Emma Lambotte, who collected his paintings, Ensor became increasingly preoccupied with music. In 1911 he produced both the music and designs for a one-act ballet-pantomime, *The Scale of Love*, first performed in 1920. Between 1910 and 1914 he was occupied with music and projects for theatre productions and costumes. World War I did little to affect Ensor, although in 1915 he was arrested and briefly jailed for portraying the Kaiser as a vulture.

Several theories have been put forward to explain Ensor's decline. In Haesaerts's opinion the collapse was psychological: Ensor's self-doubts were heightened by a family atmosphere adverse to creativity and by his inability to earn a living from his art. It is also possible, according to Haesaerts, that Ensor had nothing new to contribute after 1900. Piron believes, however, that Ensor's tendency to masochism and self-disgust found expression in sexual repression, which is particularly apparent in his submission to his family's objections to his proposed marriage with La Sirène. Even when Ensor became financially independent, however, he did not marry, thus placing his virility in question. Various pictures suggest allusions to a sexual impotence that must have been a source of anguish and self-doubt, the physiological equivalent to the artistic impotence that he experienced in later life.

Haesaerts wonders whether Ensor would have continued to paint if he had not been encouraged to do so, by both the public and those close to him. La Sirène, with whom he maintained a lifelong relationship, prepared his canvases and brushes, arranged objects for his still-lifes and looked through old drawings in search of models. Ensor continued to paint, despite the mediocrity of much of his production. Laden with honours, including a baronetcy in 1929, he played at being a famous painter. In fact he had become a stranger to himself. His cynicism was more apparent than ever, despite the slackness of his brush. Ensor declined, and debased himself artistically at the very time that he began to receive widespread acclaim. He acted out to the fullest the artistic self-importance that he mockingly referred to as 'la finale crevaison grenouillère' (*Mes écrits*, pp. 19, 82).

2. WORKING METHODS AND TECHNIQUE.

(i) Paintings and drawings. It has been said that Ensor had 'a hundred and one manners' and that 'he wanted to take up all styles, all subjects, all feelings, all techniques' (Haesaerts). Delevoy speaks of his 'multiplicity of styles', of chance linked with improvisation and of a 'casual acceptance of chance'. Like many artists, he learnt by copying others, notably Callot, Delacroix, Doré and Turner (sketchbooks, Antwerp, K. Mus. S. Kst.); it was perhaps Turner's example that directed him towards light as a means of expression. During his 'bourgeois' or 'dark' period he relied heavily on palette knife techniques, for example in *Still-life* (c. 1880; Brussels, Mus. A. Mod.), which is composed of thick paint with prominent ridges. However, he also painted in an Impressionistic manner during this period, as in *Vlaanderenstraat in Sunlight* (1881; Antwerp, priv. col., see Legrand, p. 20). In the *Roofs of Ostend in Mist* forms begin to dissolve. The *Entry of Christ into Brussels in 1889* contains passages of thick paint that look almost trowelled on, possibly with an admixture of sand. Photographic enlargement reveals a layering of rectangular marks as well as scrawls in all directions.

The *Astonishment of the Mask Wouse* and the *Destruction of the Rebel Angel* (both 1889; Antwerp, K. Mus. S. Kst.),

although contemporaneous, are totally different in technique. The former is painted in a straightforward, relatively smooth manner, while the latter prefigured techniques of Action painting, using rubbing, squirting and crushing. In drawings such as the *Dead Christ Watched over by Angels* the serpentine line anticipates Art Nouveau. Ensor not only reworked his own paintings but also painted over canvases bought in flea markets, as in the *Adoration of the Shepherds* (c. 1887; Brussels, Mus. A. Mod.).

After 1900 Ensor continued to use his previous range of techniques, with the exception of the impasto of the dark period. However, there can often be seen a search for bright, transparent colours, while the hand often seems slack and hesitant, the line confused and the composition chaotic.

(ii) Prints. Even if he had not been a great painter Ensor would have gained a substantial reputation as a printmaker. Most of his 133 prints were produced between 1886 and 1889 and between 1895 and 1899, including 117 etchings, 14 drypoints, one soft-ground etching and one lithograph. After this his activity declined; he produced two or three plates a year. After 1933 he became more productive again but the work was weak in every respect. The series the *Seven Deadly Sins* (1902; Gstaad, L. Franck priv. col., see Janssens, pp. 82–3) are the most inventive and original of his late prints.

Ensor was as influential technically in his prints as in his paintings, as is evident from his first dazzling etching, *Christ Presented to the People* (1886; see Taevernier, p. 24) in which he captured the animation of a surging crowd in a richly detailed surface. He usually worked in a pure linear technique, creating vibrant, radiant or supernatural effects of light: the *Dock, Ostend* (1888; see Taevernier, p. 116); *Boats Aground* (1888; see Taevernier, p. 126); *My Portrait Skeletonized* (1889; see Taevernier, p. 174) and *Ensor Teased by Demons* (1895; see Taevernier, p. 230). Later in life, when he was short of subjects, he produced paintings based on these prints.

WRITINGS

Lettres à André de Ridder, ed. A. de Ridder (Antwerp, 1960)
Mes écrits, ed. F. Hellens (Liège, 1974)

BIBLIOGRAPHY

MONOGRAPHS AND EXHIBITION CATALOGUES

E. Verhaeren: *James Ensor* (Brussels, 1908/*R* 1974)
L. Delteil: *Leys, De Braekeleer, Ensor: Le Peintre graveur illustré*, xix (Paris, 1925)
P. Fierens: *James Ensor* (Paris, 1943)
James Ensor (exh. cat. by L. Tannenbaum, New York, MOMA, 1951/*R* 1966)
P. Haesaerts: *James Ensor* (Brussels, 1953; Eng. trans., New York, 1959)
M. de Maeyer: *Ensor, Maestri Colore* (Milan, 1963)
F.-C. Legrand: *Ensor cet inconnu* (Brussels, 1971)
J. D. Farmer: *Ensor* (New York, 1976)
G. Ollinger-Zinque: *Ensor par lui-même* (Brussels, 1976)
J. Janssens: *James Ensor* (Paris, 1978; Eng. trans., New York, n.d.)
R. L. Delevoy: *James Ensor* (Antwerp, 1981; Ger. trans., 1981)
James Ensor (exh. cat. by H. Szeemann and others, Zurich, Ksthaus; Antwerp, K. Mus. S. Kst.; 1983)
D. Lesko: *Ensor: The Creative Years* (Princeton, 1985)
X. Tricot: *Catalogue raisonné des peintures d'Ensor* (Antwerp, 1992)

DRAWINGS AND PRINTS

P. Fierens: *Les Dessins d'Ensor* (Brussels, 1944)
A. Croquez: *L'Oeuvre gravé de James Ensor* (Geneva, 1947)
L. Lebeer: *James Ensor aquafortiste* (Antwerp, 1952)
—— (pref.): *The Prints of James Ensor* (New York, 1971)

A. Taevernier: *James Ensor: Catalogue illustré de ses gravures, leur description critique et l'inventaire des plaques* (Ghent, 1973) [Fr., Dut. and Eng. text]
James Ensor: Etchings (exh. cat., intro. L. Cooke; London, Fr. Inst., 1979)
Ik James Ensor: Tekeningen en prenten [I, James Ensor: drawings and prints] (exh. cat., Ghent, Mus. S. Kst.; Amsterdam, Rijksmus.; 1987)

SPECIALIST STUDIES

W. Vanbeselaere: *James Ensor: 'L'Entrée du Christ à Bruxelles'* (Brussels, 1957)
H. Defrance: 'James Ensor: Essai de bibliographie commentée', *Bib. Belg.*, 53 (1960)
F.-C. Legrand: 'Les Lettres de James Ensor à Octave Maus', *Mus. Royaux B.-A. Belgique: Bull.*, n.s. xv (1966), pp. 69–88
H. T. Piron: *Ensor: Een psychoanalytische studie* (Antwerp, 1968)
S. C. McGough: *James Ensor: The 'Entry of Christ'* (New York, 1985)

FRANCINE-CLAIRE LEGRAND

Entablature. Term used in Classical architecture for the superstructure carried by columns and divided horizontally, top to bottom, into cornice, frieze and architrave. The proportions and details of the entablature, which are strictly prescribed, differ for each order (*see* ORDERS, ARCHITECTURAL, §I, 1(ii), and fig. 1ii; GREECE, ANCIENT, fig. 9k). By extension, the term is applied to any feature similar to a Classical entablature, used as the crown of a wall.

□

Entartete Kunst [Ger.: 'degenerate art']. Term used by the Nazis in Germany from the 1920s to refer to art that did not fall into line with the arts policies of National Socialism, chiefly avant-garde work. The term 'degenerate art' has been used generally to describe art perceived as signifying decay, and usually forms of art production in chronological proximity (*see also* DECADENCE AND DECLINE). It has been used in a polemical context to enhance the value of a specific aesthetic viewpoint. The first known example is the assessment made by the Italian bourgeoisie of the 14th century of medieval art as a barbaric relapse when compared with antiquity. The Italian writer and statesman Niccolò Machiavelli employed the term 'degeneration' (*corruzione*) in his *Discorso* of 1581. It was used by Giovanni Pietro Bellori in his polemic against Giorgio Vasari and Michelangelo. It is also used generally to mean irregular or against the rules, in contrast with the dominant aesthetic trend, which is set up as the rule. In this sense the term 'Baroque' was also initially intended to be disparaging. At the end of the 19th century the term was used in association with Nietzsche's concept of decadence. It was later used in this sense by Thomas Mann, who regarded the artist as 'a social outsider prone to be tired of life' (1987–8 exh. cat.) and considered this predisposition to be the basis of the need for artistic creativity. Familiarity with crises and melancholy was viewed as the cause and driving force of artistic genius, which found its expression in a new artistic subjectivity. In contrast, in his book *Entartung* (1892–3), Max Nordau viewed Naturalism, Symbolism and Realism as decadent art movements that had originated in the 'degeneracy' of their founders, and he proposed that they be combated in the interest of health. This perception was essentially in line with Emperor William II's ideas on art and with the imperial criticism of art, which, on occasion, even stigmatized Impressionism as 'gutter painting' (*Gossenmalerei*). William II had attempted to regulate art, claiming, in his speech at the inauguration of Siegesallee in Berlin in 1901: 'Art that goes beyond the laws and limits imposed on it by me ceases to be art.' In 1913 a resolution 'Against degeneracy in art' was passed in the Prussian house of representatives. In Germany these defamations were always closely linked to nationalistic tendencies.

With the growth of German nationalism from the end of the 1920s, the term was increasingly present in the art propaganda of the National Socialist Party and applied to everything that did not conform to Nazi goals. It became the central concept of their art policy, being used in the battle against 'foreign infiltration' (*Überfremdung*) of art. Citing petit-bourgeois artistic taste as 'popular sentiment' (*gesundes Volksempfinden*), the Nazis had instigated a wide campaign of defamation within all the arts. It was directed against avant-garde tendencies, both national and international, which had developed from the late 19th century. By 1930 the Minister for Culture and Education, von Thüringen Frick, had already proclaimed his programme 'Against Negro culture—for German national traditions', aimed particularly at the Expressionists, and he ordered the removal of 70 paintings from the permanent exhibition of the Schlossmuseum at Weimar. Also in 1930 Hildebrand Gurlitt, the museum director in Zwickau, was dismissed for promoting such artists as Emil Nolde, Heinrich Zille, Ernst Barlach, Otto Dix and others. In March 1933 Bettina Feistel-Rohmeder, the director of the Deutsche Kunstkorrespondenz, called for the removal from the museums of all works revealing 'cosmopolitan and Bolshevik aspects'. The purpose of this propaganda was the bringing-in-to-line (*Gleichschaltung*) of the arts within a Nazi state. Art's only task was to illustrate the ideas of National Socialism and the glorification of the State. Feistel-Rohmeder demanded the seizure of 'degenerate works of art'. Museum directors were either forced out of office or relieved of their duties following the first defamatory exhibitions of 1933: *Regierungskunst von 1918 bis 1933* in the Staatliche Kunsthalle, Karlsruhe; *Novembergeist im Dienste der Zersetzung* in Stuttgart; *Kulturbolschewismus* in Mannheim; *Schreckenskammer der Kunst* in Nuremberg; *Kunst, die nicht aus unserer Seele kam* in Chemnitz; and *Spiegelbilder des Verfalls in der Kunst* in Dresden. The latter was sent by the Mayor of Dresden, Zörner, as a touring exhibition in Germany. The Law for the Restoration of Civil Service with Tenure, passed on 7 April 1933, facilitated the dismissal of directors for 'the promotion of degenerate art'. In October 1936 the 'temporary' closure of the modern wing in the Kronprinzenpalais in Berlin was ordered, though intended to be final. All these actions were arranged and coordinated by the Reich Ministry of the Interior for Information and Propaganda under Goebbels, in conjunction with the Gestapo. In 1937, under the newly elected President of the Reichskammer für Bildende Künste, Professor Adolf Ziegler, a commission was set up to select works for a planned exhibition of *Entartete Kunst* upon orders from Goebbels. One day after Hitler opened the first Grosse Deutsche Kunstausstellung in the Haus der Deutschen Kunst (now the Haus der Kunst), in Munich, the *Entartete Kunst* exhibition in the Archeologisches Institut in Munich began (19 July 1937). The skilfully anti-aesthetic hanging and the defamatory commentary on the works did not fail to achieve propagandistic success. In a reduced form, this exhibition toured to Leipzig, Berlin and Düsseldorf (1938), and to Chemnitz, Frankfurt am Main and Vienna (1939).

By August 1937 the wide-scale confiscation of all works of art in museums designated 'degenerate' had already begun. According to records, a total of 15,997 works of fine art were confiscated from 101 German museums. This action was justified by the Law on the Confiscation of Products of Degenerate Art, passed belatedly on 31 May 1938. Works affected were those of classical modernity, works by artists of Jewish descent and works of social criticism. Only a few were retained and hidden through the brave manoeuvring of individual members of museum staff. The artists themselves, assuming they had not already left Germany, were forbidden to paint or exhibit. In addition to confiscation, destruction took place of murals and architectural monuments, among others. In May 1938 Goebbels instigated the establishment of the Kommission zur Verwertung der Beschlagnahmten Werke Entarteter Kunst. Confiscated works were stored in depots and from there sold to interested parties abroad (the Nazis hoped for a source of revenue for foreign currency, which was needed for the rearmament programme), and sometimes exchanged (Hermann Goering made exchanges with older works of art for his private collection). In 1939, 125 works were put up for auction in Lucerne, including works by van Gogh, Gauguin, Franz Marc, Macke, Klee, Kokoschka and Lehmbruck. The end of the *Aktion entartete Kunst* was signalled by the burning of 4829 art works in the courtyard of the Berlin Fire Brigade.

BIBLIOGRAPHY

M. Nordau: *Entartung*, 2 vols (1892–3/*R* Berlin, 1992–3)
P. Renner: *Kulturbolschewismus* (Zurich, 1932)
Entartete Kunst: Führer durch die Ausstellung (Munich, 1937)
W. Willich: *Säuberung des Kunsttempels: Eine kunstpolitische Kampfschrift zur Gesundung deutscher Kunst im Geiste nordischer Art* (rev. Munich, 1938)
A. Behne: *Entartete Kunst* (Berlin, 1947)
P. O. Rave: *Kunstdiktatur im 3. Reich* (Hamburg, 1949, rev. Berlin, 1992)
F. Roh: *Entartete Kunst: Kunstbarbarei im 3. Reich* (Hannover, 1962)
H. Brenner: *Die Kunstpolitik des Nationalsozialismus* (Reinbeck bei Hamburg, 1963)
J. Wulf: *Die bildenden Künste im Dritten Reich: Eine Dokumentation* (Gütersloh, 1963)
G. Busch: *Entartete Kunst: Geschichte und Moral* (Frankfurt am Main, 1969)
A. Hentzen: *Die Berliner Nationalgalerie im Bildersturm* (Cologne, 1971)
Die Beschlagnahme-Aktion im Landesmuseum Hannover, 1937 (exh. cat., intro. K. Sello; Hannover, Kstver., 1983)
Verboten-Verfolgt: Kunstdiktatur im 3. Reich (exh. cat., intro. S. Salzmann; Duisburg, Lehmbruck-Mus.; Hannover, Kstver.; Wilhelmshaven, Ksthalle; 1983)
Das Schicksal einer Sammlung: Die neue Abteilung der Nationalgalerie im ehemaligen Kronprinzenpalais (exh. cat., W. Berlin, Staatl. Museen Preuss. Kultbes., 1986)
Künstlerschicksale im Dritten Reich in Württemberg und Baden (exh. cat., Stuttgart, 1987)
Nationalsozialismus und entartete Kunst, 2 vols (exh. cat., ed. P. K. Schuster; Munich, Haus Kst, 1987–8)
Angriff auf die Kunst: Faschistische Bildersturm von 50 Jahren (exh. cat., Weimar, Ksthalle, 1988)
Stationen der Moderne (exh. cat., foreword J. Merkert; W. Berlin, Berlin. Gal., 1988)
Degenerate Art: The Fate of the Avant-garde in Nazi Germany (exh. cat. by Stephanie Barron, Los Angeles, CA, Co. Mus. A., 1991)

ANITA KÜHNEL

Entasis. Architectural term used to describe the almost imperceptible convex curve of the taper between the top and bottom of a column shaft. Entasis is derived from the Greek verb *enteinein*, which contains the idea of tension, but its first recorded use in this specialized sense was by the Roman writer Vitruvius (*On Architecture* III.iii.13). In a column with entasis the distance between the curve of the convex taper and the chord (the imaginary straight line joining points on the circumference of the shaft at its top and bottom) is greatest about halfway up the column.

Together with the practice of making the corner columns of peripteral buildings thicker than flank columns, which Vitruvius discussed in the same section of his treatise, entasis forms an integral part of those Greco-Roman architectural features that have, since the beginning of the 20th century, been classified as 'refinements' and that imply a deviation from formal regularity and rationality (*see* GREECE, ANCIENT, §II, 3(vi)). Entasis is almost certainly the most complex of these. However, unlike the curvature of horizontal lines (e.g. of a temple platform) or the inwards inclination of peristyle columns, which are part of this same group of deviations, neither its existence nor its intentionality have ever been questioned or attributed to later displacements of a building. Indeed, the pronounced entasis of the 'Basilica' (Temple of Hera) columns at Paestum (for illustration of Sanctuary of Hera *see* PAESTUM) was calculated and drawn at the end of the 18th century by P. A. Paoli. Since the beginning of the 19th century successive measurements by both architects and archaeologists have confirmed the presence of entasis in many ancient buildings, dating from the 6th century BC to Imperial Roman times. It occurs in Doric, Ionic and Corinthian columns, usually in temples but also in other great monuments. Nevertheless, entasis was not a regular or even usual feature, as both Vitruvius and various modern writers on Greek architecture have suggested. There was frequently no trace of it at all, and a temple that might include a curvature of the horizontal lines or some deviation of the columns from the vertical might well not incorporate entasis, for the several types of refinement did not form a single, indissoluble set of features.

Since a form of entasis occurs on Egyptian obelisks, it has been thought that it was derived by the Greeks from the Egyptians and, indeed, that the architectural refinements in general originated in Egypt, where curvature of horizontal planes is well attested in temples. The connection, however, is far from certain. In fact, Egyptian columns appear not to have had entasis in the true sense, and its earliest occurrence in the Greek world is in the 'Basilica' at Paestum, in South Italy; it is therefore possible that entasis was invented there in the mid-6th century BC. In the 'Basilica' the maximum offset between the curving taper and the chord reaches 31–72 mm, and the curve never forms the arc of a circle (it flattens out at both the base and the top). This point of maximum offset is slightly higher than the middle of the shaft, while in Hellenistic and Roman examples it is either in the middle or, more usually, below it, at about $\frac{1}{3}$ or $\frac{2}{3}$ of its height. Also in the Greek colonies in South Italy, further examples of entasis occur in two temples at Metapontion, of Apollo and of Hera (the 'Tavole Palatine'), and in the Temple of Athena at Paestum. However, except for the Temple of Hera at

Akragas and the Temple of Hera at Selinus, it was unknown in Sicily. (The fact that the temple at Segesta was never completed poses a problem, since entasis was not determined until the final carving of the columns in the last stages of construction.) It was in the 5th century BC that the use of entasis reached mainland Greece, in particular Attica, though still as a feature only of Doric buildings. It occurs first in the Temple of Aphaia on Aigina, then at Athens in the Parthenon, the Propylaia of the Acropolis and the Temple of Hephaistos. Later examples of entasis are found in the Temple of Zeus at Nemea (4th century BC) and in Asia Minor in the Temple of Athena at Priene (the earliest Ionic building to show entasis) and in the Temple of Apollo at Didyma (3rd century BC). Finally, it occurs on the Corinthian columns of the Temple of Olympian Zeus (Olympieion) at Athens (2nd century BC).

In Greek architecture at least, the maximum diameter of the shaft was always at its base. Although it was accentuated in the 6th century BC, as at Paestum, entasis subsequently became less marked, to the point of being difficult to discern and plot. In columns of the Classical or Hellenistic periods the maximum offset of the curve was generally 0.9–2.4 thousandths of the height of the shaft (1.6 thousandths in the case of the Parthenon). In Roman columns the entasis once again became more marked, the maximum offset ranging from 2 to 4.3 thousandths of the height. This degree of variation suggests that entasis was calculated in each case with extreme care.

Vitruvius's sketches showing his method of outlining entasis no longer survive; thus numerous different methods have been suggested. An empirical method proposed by D. Mertens (based on the method he deduced for the horizontal curvature of the temple at Segesta) involved drawing the axis of the column as a horizontal line on one wall of the cella; a line representing the upper radius of the shaft would be dropped from one end of this, and a line representing the lower radius from the other. A string stretched between the free ends of the two radii would represent the slightly curving taper of the shaft, and the radius of the column at any height would correspond to the vertical distance between the string and the appropriate point on the axis line. A more complex method, discovered by L. Haselberger at Didyma, involved drawing the column axis vertically to $\frac{1}{16}$th scale, with its radii at top and bottom drawn horizontally to full scale; the arc of a circle was drawn between the free ends of the radii so as to give the maximum offset desired. In actual construction the horizontal measurements would be taken unchanged from the diagram, but the vertical measurements would be multiplied 16 times, which would convert the arc of a circle on the drawing to an actual entasis equivalent to the arc of an ellipse. Other suggested methods of outlining entasis employ the conchoid, discovered by Nicodemes (for the Roman forum at Dougga), or the use of a large wooden template.

The original reasons for the use of entasis have been much discussed. Since Vitruvius ranked it among various 'additions' necessitated by optical distortions in the view of a building and intended to restore overall symmetry and harmony, the explanation that prevailed for a long time was that entasis was needed to correct the illusion that an isolated straight-sided column seems to curve inwards slightly at its centre and thus appears weak. This impression is relative, however, and does not apply in the case of engaged columns or cylindrical piers with parallel sides. The use of entasis, clearly derived from Roman models, continued in these types of support into the Middle Ages, in Romanesque though not in Gothic churches, and carried through into the Renaissance. Marked entasis can also be seen in Baroque buildings. It might, therefore, be more accurate to regard it as an aesthetic taste or stylistic effect, since entasis gives columns an attractive appearance of vitality, imparting to them a vigorous 'muscular' tension under the weight of their burden. This is notably true of the 'Basilica' in Paestum, exemplifying the way in which the achievements of this small Achaian colony show, in architecture as in sculpture, both a striving for a high degree of plasticity and a decorative awareness that reveals Ionian influence.

BIBLIOGRAPHY

W. H. Goodyear: *Greek Refinements: Studies in Temperamental Architecture* (London, 1912)
D. Mertens: 'Zur Entstehung der Entasis griechischer Säulen', *Bathron: Festschrift H. Drerup* (Saarbrücken, 1988), pp. 307–18 [with detailed bibliography]
L. Haselberger: 'Aspekte der Bauzeichnungen von Didyma', *Rev. Archéol.*, n.s., i (1991), pp. 99–113
H. Haselberger and H. Seybold: 'Seilkurve oder Ellipse? Zur Herstellung antiker Kurvaturen nach dem Zeugris der didymeischen Kurvenkonstruktion', *Archäol. Anz.* (1991), pp. 165–88
MARIE-CHRISTINE HELLMANN

Environment. *See* INSTALLATION.

Environmental art. Art form based on the premise that a work of art should invade the totality of the architecture around it and be conceived as a complete space rather than being reducible to a mere object hanging on a wall or placed within a space. This idea, which became widespread during the 1960s and 1970s in a number of different aesthetic formulations, can be traced back to earlier types of art not usually referred to as environments: the wall paintings of ancient tombs, the frescoes of Roman or of Renaissance art and the paintings of Baroque chapels, which surround the spectator and entirely cover the architectural structure that shelters them. Indeed, the whole of art history prior to the transportable easel picture is linked to architecture and hence to the environment. A number of artists in the 1960s conceived environmental art precisely in order to question the easel painting.

In the first half of the 20th century, numerous antecedents of modern environments were created. The Futurists, notably Giacomo Balla, studied spatial ambience. In 1917 in Moscow, Aleksandr Rodchenko, Vladimir Tatlin and Georgy Yakulov designed the Café Pittoresque where the constructions seemed to be projected into space. Another collaboration between several artists in a public place, the Aubette entertainment complex in Strasbourg (1926; destr.) designed by Hans Arp, Sophie Taeuber-Arp and THEO VAN DOESBURG, showed a kind of explosion of geometric forms in space. Closer still to the idea of an environment was El Lissitzky's use of the exhibition space at the van Diemen Gallery in Berlin in 1922 at the Erste Russische Kunstausstellung, which resulted in his *Proun*

Space (1923; reconstruction Eindhoven, Stedel. Van Abbemus.); reliefs in painted wood were scattered over the walls and in the corners of a room the dimensions of which were very precisely calculated. Painting had emerged from the frame of the picture to fill the entire space. Piet Mondrian similarly transformed his studio in Paris into a virtual environment in accordance with his theories of Neo-plasticism. From 1923 to 1937 Kurt Schwitters constructed his *Merzbau*, a type of three-dimensional collage that gradually filled his living area in Hannover (destr. 1943; *see* SCHWITTERS, KURT, fig. 2). In this way, the idea of the environment began with the application in space of theories expressed in painting but which could no longer be contained within a two-dimensional surface. This was still true of the participation by LUCIO FONTANA in the exhibition *Spatial Ambience* (Milan, Gal. Naviglio, 1949), in which he created luminous spaces with fluorescent or neon light.

When the concept of the environment proper appeared in the 1960s, it was generally in the context of live PERFORMANCE ART and Happenings, and in this respect it had its roots also in the international Surrealist exhibitions held during the 1930s and 1940s. These had been conceived as theatrical events, which made use of new materials or unlikely objects, such as the kilometres of string strung about the *First Papers of Surrealism* exhibition at the Reid Mansion, New York, by Marcel Duchamp in 1942. When Yves Klein exhibited *The Void* at the Galerie Iris Clert in Paris (1958), and when Arman responded by designing *Fullness* (1960) in the same place, transforming the gallery into an enormous dustbin, they were inaugurating a kind of environmental work that could be neither transported nor transposed. These were ephemeral, provocative creations, non-commercial by definition although exhibited in a gallery. They are manifestos forming a basis for all the artists' other work. At the same time in New York, Allan Kaprow was creating environments: *Yard* (1961) filled the Martha Jackson Gallery with car tyres. Together with other artists such as Jim Dine, Robert Whitman (*b* 1935) and Claes Oldenburg, he transformed and adorned premises, creating spaces for Happenings. In 1961 Oldenburg exhibited *The Store*, an exhibition and sale of painted sculptural replicas of food and other consumer items. Pop artists, Nouveaux Réalistes and other sculptors of the period were thus major exponents of environmental art in the early 1960s: examples include Christo's *Windows*, Edward Kienholz's *Tableaux* and George Segal's life-size figures in architectural settings. An entire exhibition, *Dylaby* (Amsterdam, Stedel. Mus., 1962), was presented as a succession of ludic environments designed by Robert Rauschenberg, Martial Raysse, Jean Tinguely and others. With Niki de Saint Phalle and Per Olof Ultvedt, Tinguely also made *She* (1966; Stockholm, Mod. Mus.), a giant sculpture of a woman into which the visitor entered.

At almost the same time, another category of environmental art emphasized the optical or sonorous nature of the space created. Kinetic artists willingly abandoned the easel painting for the complete space: Jesús-Rafael Soto created *Penetrables*, cubes of plastic shafts among which

observers could lose themselves. The Groupe de Recherche d'Art Visuel invented uncertain pathways, implying an invitation for spectator participation. Several Italian artists (Getulio Alviani, Gianni Colombo and Enrico Castellani) perfected pared-down spatial environments, while others, such as Takis, linked sculpture and sound (*see* SOUND AND ART).

During the 1970s environmental art developed further still. Joseph Beuys and such Arte Povera artists as Jannis Kounellis and Mario Merz filled their spaces with humble materials not normally associated with sculpture. Dan Flavin and Californian artists such as Robert Irwin, James Archie Turrell (*b* 1943) and Doug Wheeler (*b* 1939) created spaces of light where volume is barely perceptible. Others created large-scale paintings directly on walls (e.g. Sol LeWitt's *Wall Drawings*) or linked to the space around them. Daniel Buren developed the idea of the *in situ* work of art, conceived specifically in relation to the architecture around it (see fig.). American artists of the same generation explored the concept of site-specificity, for example Richard Serra's large-scale sculptures, Walter De Maria's *New York Earth-room* (1977; New York, Dia A. Found.) and Bruce Nauman's corridors: narrow spaces through which spectators were led in order to find, for example, their own image reflected in a television set.

Environmental art thus covers a number of extremely diverse visual tendencies culminating in an extension of the object to incorporate the surrounding space. The idea that spectators could enter the painting or sculpture, and that in being surrounded by it they are in some way part of it, has emerged as a more significant and unifying factor

Environmental art: Daniel Buren, French Pavilion, Venice Biennale, 1986

in the art of the second half of the 20th century than any single aesthetic formula.

BIBLIOGRAPHY

12 Environments (exh. cat., Berne, Ksthalle, 1968)

Räume und Environments (exh. cat., Cologne; Opladen; 1969)

G. Kepes: *Arts of the Environment* (New York, 1972)

G. Celant: 'Artspaces', *Studio Int.*, cxc/977 (1975), pp. 114–23

F. Popper: *Art: Action and Participation* (New York, 1975)

G. Celant: *Ambiente/Arte: Dal futurismo alla Body art* (Venice, 1977)

Le stanze (exh. cat., ed. A. Bonito Oliva; Genazzano, Castello Colonna, 1979) [It./Eng. text]

Pittura-Ambiente (exh. cat. by R. Barilli and F. Alinova, Milan, Pal. Reale, 1979)

Für Augen und Ohren (exh. cat., E. Berlin, Akad. Kst. DDR, 1980)

ALFRED PACQUEMENT

Environmental design [Building technology]. Term used to characterize those aspects of architectural design that contribute to the control of the artificial environment in buildings and thus determine the comfort and efficiency of their occupants. The term came into common use in the 1950s, and it relates to one of the primary functions of a building: to act as a modifier of the natural environment. The building fabric operates as a filter to reduce the ingress of the inimical and to admit the desirable elements of climate (passive control); any predicted shortfall in the resulting internal conditions, taking into account the environmental variables associated with human occupation itself, is then corrected by technological means (active control).

Traditional methods of environmental control have a direct effect on the appearance of buildings. Examples of the architectural result of passive techniques include the thick-walled courtyard houses of arid climates, capable of diurnal heat storage and re-radiation at night, with small, deep openings controlling solar radiation and glare, and often with carefully orientated wind-catchers for local ventilation; the lightweight, open-sided buildings of hot, humid zones, sited to capture every breeze for evaporative cooling; and the use of the VERANDAH as an element to control heat gain and glare. It is often important to reconcile environmental factors that may conflict: the larger windows needed to enhance the daytime environment in darker and colder regions, for example, may result in unacceptable levels of additional heat loss in winter (and heat gain in summer), requiring a greater input of active methods of thermal control, traditionally expressed in a proliferation of chimneys.

As the technology of heating and ventilation advanced in the late 19th century and early 20th, greater reliance was placed on active environmental design techniques, particularly in the USA, where the extremes of a continental climate were more demanding. While energy to drive the equipment remained cheap and apparently plentiful, the appearance of buildings was increasingly affected by the desire for good natural lighting. In Britain, for example, lighting levels in schools were fixed by statute in 1907 and were the governing factor in the environmental design of classrooms. This approach was facilitated by the development of new building materials and techniques, but the worldwide spread after World War II of the steel-and-glass architecture of the International Style, regardless of climate, was responsible for many environmentally untenable buildings.

The development of larger buildings and increasingly deep rooms, in schools as in office buildings, led to the concept of Integrated Environmental Design (IED), which allowed smaller windows and the use of sophisticated permanent supplementary artificial lighting systems for use in daylight as well as in darkness. In some regions, such as Brazil, Mexico and Australia, the effects of excessive solar radiation were controlled by the use of increasingly sophisticated *brises-soleil* as a fundamental element of design, whether as lightweight, movable attachments to the façade, as permanent fixed screens or as a function of the structural frame itself (*see* AUSTRALIA, §II, 2). In late Modern architecture louvres gave way to the use of tinted and reflective glass to minimize solar heat gain and thus the loads on air-conditioning systems. This produced a new range of crystalline forms expressive of passive environmental control, seen particularly in the work of I. M. PEI, CESAR PELLI and Helmut Jahn, and in the skyscrapers of such cities as Dallas and Houston—for example, the faceted mirror-glass of the Allied Bank Plaza (now First Interstate Tower; 1986; by I. M. Pei & Partners) in Dallas.

There have also been memorable architectural expressions of active environmental control systems, from the corner-tower ventilation ducts of Frank Lloyd Wright's Larkin Building in Buffalo (1903–6; destr.) to the service towers of the Richards Medical Research Laboratories (1957–61; by Louis I. Kahn) in Philadelphia, and the exposed service ducting of the Centre Georges Pompidou (1971–7), Paris by RENZO PIANO and RICHARD ROGERS. Other buildings incorporate interiors that derive directly from the requirements of acoustic design (*see* ACOUSTICS): notable examples include the auditorium of the Grosses Schauspielhaus (1918–19; by Hans Poelzig) in Berlin, featuring fantastic stalactite forms (*see* EXPRESSIONISM, fig. 3), and the Aula Magna (1952) at the Ciudad Universitaria, Caracas, Venezuela, by Carlos Raúl Villanueva, which features floating acoustic reflectors designed by Alexander Calder (with Robert B. Newman).

After the international energy crisis of 1973–4, sophisticated IED systems were invented to reduce energy use in buildings, and by the end of the 20th century highly engineered environments, sometimes wholly sealed from polluted urban atmospheres, were controlled by computers in so-called 'intelligent' buildings. Many urban buildings of the second half of the century nevertheless developed unacceptable environmental characteristics that became known as 'sick building syndrome', and radical redesign or systems demanding excessive energy consumption were needed to maintain them in use. Meanwhile, a renewed interest in passive control and in the development of more cost- and energy-efficient active techniques using renewable resources, including direct and indirect solar-powered systems, began to change the appearance of many small and medium-sized buildings, and the autonomous house became theoretically possible.

See also GLASS, §IV, 2; LIGHTING; and VERNACULAR ARCHITECTURE, §I.

BIBLIOGRAPHY

S. Giedion: *Mechanisation Takes Command* (London and Cambridge, MA, 1950)

M. Ingels: *Willis Carrier: Father of Air Conditioning* (Garden City, 1952)

R. G. Hopkinson: *Architectural Physics: Lighting* (London, 1963)
R. Breugmann: 'Heating and Ventilation in the 19th Century', *J. Soc. Archit. Historians*, xxxvii/3 (1968), pp. 143–66
P. R. Banham: *The Architecture of the Well-tempered Environment* (London and Chicago, 1969)
R. Knowles: *Energy and Form* (Cambridge, MA, 1975)
H. J. Cowan: *The Masterbuilders: A History of Structural and Environmental Design from Ancient Egypt to the Nineteenth Century* (New York, 1977)

Enzo, Joseph. *See* HEINTZ, (4).

Enzola, Gianfrancesco (di Luca) (*b* Parma, *fl* 1455–78). Italian goldsmith and medallist. He is recorded in Parma between 1467 and 1471 and was master of the mint in Ferrara in 1472–3 under Ercole d'Este, Duke of Ferrara. Although no coins with his signature have been identified, it is quite likely that he engraved dies for some of the Duke's coins of Ferrara and Reggio, in particular a number of fine portrait pieces, including those of his principal patrons, *Francesco Sforza, Duke of Milan, Cecco Ordelaffi of Forlì, Taddeo Menfredi of Faenza* and *Pier Maria Rossi of Berceto*. Many of his early medals (1455–71) are struck from engraved dies and are small, but only a few struck examples survive; most known specimens are cast from struck originals. In later years he changed his method and in 1474–5 produced a splendid series of large cast medals of *Costanzo Sforza, Lord of Pesaro*. One of these is dedicated to the memory of Costanzo's father, Alessandro Sforza, who is portrayed on the reverse. The other reverse types eulogize Costanzo's military prowess but suffer from over-elaboration of detail. Characteristic is the representation of the castle of Pesaro with its pinnacled towers fully manned, many windows, drawbridge and gateway surmounted by a coat of arms. Of his largest medal (92 mm), of *Federigo da Montefeltro*, only an impression in leather is extant (Rome, Vatican, Bib. Apostolica).

Most of Enzola's medals are dated (1455–78) and signed (IOHANNIS FRANCISCI (ENZOLAE) PARMENSIS OPVS, with various abbreviations). His cast medals carry the legend on a raised band, possibly produced by impressing a lettered metal ring into the mould. Other works by Enzola include several signed and unsigned plaquettes, the *Virgin Enthroned*, the *Martyrdom of St Sebastian, St Jerome, St George, Child on a Lion*, and a *Horseman Attacked by Three Lions*, as well as a signed seal of Parma. Other unsigned but stylistically similar seals (e.g. of *Lorenzo Rovorella* and *Niccolò Perotto*) have also been attributed to him.

BIBLIOGRAPHY
Forrer; Thieme–Becker
A. Armand: *Les Médailleurs italiens* (Paris, 1879, rev. 2/1883–7), i, pp. 43–6; iii, p. 7
J. Friedländer: *Die italienischen Schaumünzen des 15. Jahrhunderts, 1430–1530* (Berlin, 1882), pp. 115–20
E. Molinier: *Les Bronzes de la Renaissance: Les Plaquettes, catalogue raisonné* (Paris, 1886), i, p. 60; ii, p. 199
G. F. Hill: *Medals of the Renaissance* (London, 1920; rev. and enlarged by G. Pollard, 1978), pp. 29, 54
G. Habich: *Die Medaillen der italienischen Renaissance* (Stuttgart, 1922), pp. 78–9
H. Nussbaum: 'Fürstenporträts auf italienischen Münzen des Quattrocento', *Z. Numi.*, xxxv (1925), pp. 145–92
G. F. Hill: *Corpus* (1930), i, pp. 70–74
J. Pope-Hennessy: *Renaissance Bronzes from the Samuel H. Kress Collection in the National Gallery of Art* (London, 1965), nos 62–8
G. F. Hill and G. Pollard: *Renaissance Medals from the Samuel H. Kress Collection in the National Gallery of Art* (London, 1967), pp. 22–3
G. Pollard: *Medaglie italiane del rinascimento*, Florence, Bargello cat., i (Florence, 1985), pp. 159–67

MARK M. SALTON

Eosander [Göthe], **Johann Friedrich** (*b* Stralsund, W. Pomerania [now in Rostock], 1669; *d* Dresden, 1729). Swedish–German architect. He first trained with his father, Nils Eosander, a military engineer, and served on Swedish fortification until 1697, when he left for similar work in Brandenburg. After a study tour in France and Italy (1698–9), he was appointed Court Architect to Frederick I of Brandenburg (later King of Prussia) in 1699, First Building Director in 1702 and Quartermaster-General in 1705. Under Frederick, Eosander succeeded Andreas Schlüter on the building of the Berlin Königliches Schloss, the latter having been forced to resign in 1708 because of engineering failures.

Eosander's most prominent extant work is the Charlottenburg Palace in Berlin (*see* DISPLAY OF ART, §VI), which he extended in 1704–12 with wings, an orangery and a central salon under the cupola. His most important commission in Berlin, however, was the completion of the Königliches Schloss, to which he added the western wings round a grand courtyard and a monumental entrance archway known as the Eosanderbau (1707–13, destr. 1951). These works, and his commissions for town and country houses (e.g. Oranienburg and Monbijou, Berlin), employed the vocabulary of the French Baroque combined with the more austere Roman style of Nicodemus Tessin (ii), whose projects for the Royal Palace in Stockholm Eosander had studied while in Sweden.

Eosander was used for secret diplomatic missions as well as for military engineering during the Great Northern Wars (1700–21), returning to Swedish service in 1713. He was granted a family patent of nobility in 1712, with the name Göthe (not von Göthe), and he became a baron in 1713. He was in exile from 1715 in Frankfurt, where he was in charge of the Marian Theatrum Europaeum publishing works (which belonged to his wife's family), and he ended his architectural career in the service of Augustus II of Saxony from 1722.

BIBLIOGRAPHY
C. Gurlitt: *Geschichte des Barockstiles und des Rokokos in Deutschland* (Stuttgart, 1889)
R. Biederrstedt: 'Johann Friedrich Eosander: Grundzüge einer Biographie', *Antikva. Arkv*, 17 (Stockholm, 1961)
R. Josephson: *Barocken* (Lund, 2/1967)

Epano Englianos. *See* PYLOS.

Epen, J(ohannes) C(hristiaan) van (*b* Amsterdam, 14 March 1880; *d* Hilversum, 28 Dec 1960). Dutch architect. After work experience in the offices of Adolf Leonard van Gendt in Amsterdam and J. W. Hanrath (1867–1932) in Hilversum, he worked in Paris (1902–4). On his return to the Netherlands (1905) he began building individual country houses; from the outset his work was influenced by the sober designs of H. P. Berlage, with whom he worked on a low-rise workers' housing complex at Nachtegaalstraat in Amsterdam for the Algemene Woningbouwvereeniging (AWV) in 1914. This led to a series of commissions for housing complexes in Berlage's Amsterdam South Plan, executed during the 1920s for social-democratic housing societies, such as Rochdale, the AWV and De Samenwerking. His work was exemplary for its good construction and adherence to rational plans that provide a maximum of daylight and fresh air, but he also devised a variety of elegant details to enliven the rows and prevent visual monotony and worked out especially well-formed versions of the common features of city houses in the Netherlands, such as entry stairs and hoisting beams. A particularly effective motif that he originated was a brick buttress with a diagonal edge, which was placed at a 45° angle (in plan) at building corners to forestall any tendency towards a box-like appearance. While a series of skyscraper fantasies (see Nooteboom, pp. 38–9), drawn c. 1920, show the influence of German Expressionism, van Epen's executed work continued to strike a balance between dramatic architectural imagery and rational organization of space, between the luxuriousness of the Amsterdam school and the sobriety of Berlage. He maintained a modest practice in Hilversum until the late 1940s; his last executed work was a housing complex for Rochdale (1947).

BIBLIOGRAPHY

H. J. F. de Roy van Zuydewijn: *Amsterdamse bouwkunst, 1815–1940* (Amsterdam, [1969]), pp. 138–9
D. Grinberg: *Housing in the Netherlands, 1900–1940* (Rotterdam, 1982)
W. de Wit, ed.: *The Amsterdam School: Dutch Expressionist Architecture, 1915–1930* (Cambridge, MA, and London, 1983), p. 165
C. Nooteboom: *Unbuilt Netherlands* (New York, 1985)

HELEN SEARING

Epergne [Fr. *épargne*: 'saving']. Type of dining-table centrepiece. Usually made in silver, it has a large central basin or basket with branches supporting candle holders and small baskets or dishes for fruit, sweetmeats and pickles. Epergnes appeared in France and England after 1700, when the most elaborate versions included a tureen, casters, salts, cruets and spice-boxes. From the 1760s cheaper versions with cut-glass bowls were also available. The epergne continued in popularity in the 19th century and was possibly the forerunner of the dessert stand. □

Ephemera, printed. Term used to describe heterogeneous, insubstantial, printed (and less commonly manuscript) matter that was produced for short-term use and then disposal. It may embrace such disparate material as valentines; bill-headings; posters; trade cards; advertisements; temperance and electioneering literature; street ballads; book prospectuses; bookmarks; noteheadings; concert and theatre bills; tickets; seedsmen's lists; religious broadsheets; labels; and packaging. The precise parameters of the term have occasioned much discussion, but the distinguishing feature of ephemera is that it was not intended to survive. (Souvenirs and cigarette cards, produced for collectors, should properly be excluded, although in practice they seldom are and thus are included in this discussion.) Interest in ephemera is predominantly British and North American, though in Australia in the late 20th century enthusiasm was growing significantly. This article therefore draws mainly on British examples in its discussion of interest in printed ephemera.

1. Social and historical value. 2. Collections and institutions.

1. SOCIAL AND HISTORICAL VALUE. The appeal of ephemera is in the glimpse that it affords of the past, devoid of any interpretation. Historians increasingly value these rescued evidential data, through which human nature is seen in all its various aspects: from the cruelty of exhibitions of 'freaks' to the benevolence of charity; from the mundane label for chutney, for instance, to the entrance ticket to a coronation. To take one isolated example, a Covent Garden playbill of 1814 (Oxford, Bodleian Lib., Douce. S. 848; see fig. 1) provides a wealth of information about contemporary theatrical practices and performances, as well as actors and musicians in London. It is also representative of the variety of typography of the period and of the work of E. MacLeish (printer) of 2 Bow Street, London. In some cases the record offered by a surviving piece of printed ephemera may be unique, revealing the existence of a business through its trade card; the price of venison through a butcher's bill; or the occurrence of a lecture at an obscure society through a handbill.

1. Printed ephemera: playbill for the Theatre Royal, Covent Garden, London, 1814 (Oxford, Bodleian Library, Douce. S. 848)

The art of ephemera is inevitably tied to the development of display typefaces and illustrative printing techniques, although much ephemera is entirely unadorned. The techniques of woodcut, wood- and copper-engraving, lithography and chromolithography were all lavishly employed in ephemera, which, being transitory and generally insubstantial, had little time or space to convey its message. There are points in the history of ephemera where fine art stoops to ephemera and ephemera is elevated to fine art. These include William Hogarth's early work as an engraver of trade cards, although many are now ascribed to W. H. Ireland (1777–1835). Hogarth's own trade card of April 1720 (London, BM; see fig. 2) is said to be his earliest work.

Eminent illustrators, such as Walter Crane, Kate Greenaway and Aubrey Beardsley, frequently turned their attentions to 'jobbing art', such as bookplates, bookmarks, book prospectuses and greeting cards. In the 1890s such artists as Henri de Toulouse-Lautrec were employed to create designs for the art form of the poster, and the hoardings were hailed as the poor man's art gallery (*see* POSTER, §II). One of the most celebrated cases of the use (or abuse) of a work of fine art in advertising is that by A. & F. Pears, British soap manufacturers. They acquired John Everett Millais's painting of his grandson, *A Child's World* (1886; A. & F. Pears Ltd, on loan to RA, London), and obtained the artist's permission to add a bar of soap, creating the advertisement now known as *Bubbles* (see fig. 3); despite huge commercial success, it caused a furore in the contemporary art world.

While ephemera is undoubtedly of art historical interest, the fascination for the ephemerist lies in the imperfections as much as in the perfections of the material: printing errors and poor colour registration, for example. Jobbing printers and commercial artists, who proliferated before the ascendancy of photographic reproduction, intimately encapsulated their era through their output.

There is scarcely a subject that has not generated its own ephemera. The ephemera of art, for example, is represented in collections, most often in departments of

3. Printed ephemera: *Bubbles*, 1887; soap advertisement, adapted from the painting *A Child's World*, by John Everett Millais, 1886 (London, A. & F. Pears Ltd)

prints and drawings, whose holdings of ephemera (if any) are likely to have been selected and indexed for their relevance to the field of art. It may include such material as artists' and engravers' trade and calling cards; advertisements for artists' colours and materials; invitations to private views; notices of exhibitions; announcements of print subscriptions; tickets for lectures and *conversazioni*; and prospectuses for art schools and journals. The most intimate connection with art and design lies in ephemera's emphasis on the importance of presentation, as well as the mere recording of facts.

2. COLLECTIONS AND INSTITUTIONS. The very preservation of ephemera, particularly of contemporary examples that survive by design rather than by chance, poses an inherent philosophical problem. Few, however, would now question the validity of collecting what has provided primary information for social historians, illustrations for history books and, latterly, sources for nostalgic reproductions of Victoriana and Edwardiana, for example.

(i) Pioneering collectors. Although the term 'printed ephemera' was not commonly employed until after the publication in 1962 of John Lewis's book on the subject, interest in ephemeral material was not new. Early pioneering collectors in the UK include John Selden (1584–1654), whose collection of ballads was acquired and continued by the diarist Samuel Pepys (1633–1703) and preserved,

2. Printed ephemera: engraved trade card by William Hogarth, 1720 (London, British Museum)

together with Pepys's 'vulgaria' and trade cards, in the Pepys Library at Magdalene College, Cambridge; John Bagford (1650–1716), whose collections of ballads and title-pages are preserved in the British Library, London; and Thomas Percy, Bishop of Dromore (1729–1811), whose great-granddaughter Constance Meade gave some of his papers to John Johnson (see below); in the USA Isaiah Thomas (1749–1831) was one of the earliest collectors.

The first to conceive of comprehensive collections of printed ephemera were John Johnson (1882–1956) in Oxford, England, and, contemporaneously, Bella C. Landauer (1875–1960) in New York. Johnson's aim, stated repeatedly in his correspondence, was to create a 'little museum of common printed things to illustrate at one and the same time the historical development of our social life and the development of printing'. From 1925 to 1946 Johnson was Printer to the University of Oxford, and the Constance Meade Memorial Collection of Ephemeral Printing (named after his benefactress) was housed at Oxford University Press; in 1968 the collection was transferred to the Bodleian Library and renamed the John Johnson Collection of Printed Ephemera.

JULIE ANNE LAMBERT

(ii) European areas of interest. In Europe the concentration of interest in ephemera is far less coherent, and holdings are widely scattered. There are, however, some well-established concepts. One of the earliest is the bill of lading, a mainspring of early international trade that appears in half a dozen languages with the same basic wording ('. . . *the good ship [. . .] now riding at anchor in this port and bound for . . .*') with virtually identical layout. Among the earliest known commercial documents, manuscript papyri are recorded from the 5th and 6th centuries BC; in its printed form it spans the last few centuries, including the 20th.

The trade card appeared in sets of *c.* 50, which were calculated to encourage consumers' product loyalty; the Paris house of Bon Marché is notable for its extensive trade card series. The 'series card', the collectible product insert, most notably created by Suchard, Lefèvre-Utile, Menier and Van Houten, is by far the biggest portion of ephemera collecting. It was pioneered in Central Europe. Those put out by the Liebig Meat Company are internationally famous. From 1872 to 1975 the company produced more than 1871 sets, ranging in subject from poultry to Zeppelins. They appeared in 10 languages for distribution to *c.* 24 countries. With the growth of chromolithographic printing in the second half of the 19th century, the convention was exported to the USA by Louis Prang, whose printing enterprise flooded the country with the process, together with the concept of the collectible card. (It is from these origins that the American 'trade card' and the baseball card spring.)

European ephemera reflects the continent's industrial context; European collections make a feature of such items as wine labels, fruit wrappers and violin labels. They are often highly decorative, and they are valued as much abroad as at their point of source. Many have established design idioms of their own, extending their recognizability all over the world and providing a basic grammar for

imitators. Embossed chromolithographic cigar labels proliferate. The cigar label was also exported from Central Europe. Its design and production techniques have an obviously common source. The convention of cigar box presentation, with its classic trimmings in the forms of labels, bands and box flaps, for example, left no doubt as to the nature of the product, regardless of its actual origin.

A similarly international idiom, though in a radically different vein, has pervaded the engraved tax stamp. This has also applied to the BANKNOTE, involving the security printing aspect familiar to the public in paper currency, and has extended to subjects as disparate as medicine taxes and electricity receipts. Further examples of internationally accepted conventions include chromolithographic matchbox labels, widely produced in France, Belgium, Spain and Italy. Letterpress examples are widespread in the same countries, as well as in Sweden, India, China and Japan; production was in many millions. Labels form another genre. Those for baggage, produced by hotels, shipping companies, airlines and resorts, have acquired international recognition on the world travel scene. Perfume labels are also firmly established worldwide. Rarer, though no less picturesque in their design treatment, are chromolithographic fez labels. These were produced in Central Europe for the international Muslim trade. The abolition of the fez in the 1920s resulted in an accumulation of carton labels, thousands of which survive. Airmail stickers, devoid of decoration, have similarly received world acceptance, emerging by force of administrative circumstance rather than by way of promotional collectibility. Popular European series ephemera also include, especially in Switzerland and Austria in the 1930s, weighing machine tickets, confectionery wrappers and, latterly, miniature cream carton tops.

MAURICE RICKARDS

(iii) Official collections and institutions. The often haphazard collecting of ephemera by institutions can be understood in terms of the difficulties that it presents in acquisition and storage. Ephemera falls on the fringes of the activities of libraries, museums, archives and local history collections. In general it is deficient in bibliographical data, and, indeed, traditional methods of cataloguing are often inappropriate. It suggests varying kinds of access by subject, form (e.g. greeting card, bookmarks), topography, typography, artist, author or publisher, and it defies standardization. Usually flimsy, ephemera is best mounted, either singly or in guard books, ideally with similar materials. Perhaps the most fruitful sources of ephemera are in the named 'special collections' that proliferate in major institutions, but access to ephemera is also afforded by classification systems devised for books. Much discussion has been devoted to the peculiar problems of ephemera, resulting in investigations and reports in the UK by John E. Pemberton, the Advisory Committee on Ephemera and Minor Publications, Alan Clinton, and Kenneth Gibson and John Goldfinch (*see* bibliography). In the late 20th century significant developments included the formation in the UK of the Ephemera Society (1975) by Maurice Rickards (*b* 1919); he was also instrumental in establishing the Foundation for Ephemera Studies in London (1984), to which he donated his collection of ephemera. He was

closely associated with Professor Michael Twyman in the setting up of the Centre for Ephemera Studies (1993) at the University of Reading. His own collection forms a major part of the Centre's holdings. Rickards was also influential in the founding of ephemera societies in the USA (1980), Australia (1987) and Canada (1987); societies have since been formed in Austria and Norway. In 1984 in Gloucester, England, Robert Opie (*b* 1947) established a public collection of packaging called The PackAge Revisited.

In the UK there are a number of major collections of printed ephemera: in London the British Library; the British Museum's Department of Prints and Drawings; the Guildhall Library's Department of Prints and Maps; the Museum of London; the Victoria and Albert Museum's Department of Prints and Drawings; and the National Art Library. Additionally, such specialist museums and libraries as the Theatre Museum, the London Transport Museum, the Wellcome Institute and St Bride's Printing Library have important holdings of ephemera. Other major national collections are held at the Bodleian Library, Oxford, and the University of Reading. The PackAge Revisited in Gloucester displays a permanent exhibition of a collection of packaging. In the USA notable collections include those at the New York Historical Society, the New York Public Library, Lincoln Center, and the Metropolitan Museum of Art in New York, and the American Antiquarian Society in Worcester, MA. European holdings are widely scattered. They include collections held by Helsinki University Library, the University Library in Amsterdam, the Bibliothèque Nationale in Paris, and extensive collections in major museums in Berlin, Rome, Madrid and St Petersburg.

Useful sources for locating ephemera collections in the UK include the *Directory of Rare Book and Special Collections* and *The Picture Researchers' Handbook*, and in Australia the *Directory of Australian Ephemera Collections*. In the 1990s the Centre for Ephemera Studies at the University of Reading was also planning a directory.

BIBLIOGRAPHY

A. Heal: *London Tradesmen's Cards of the XVIII Century* (London, 1925/*R* New York, 1972)
——: 'The Trade Cards of Engravers', *Prt Colr Q.*, xiv (July 1927), pp. 219–50
J. N. C. Lewis: *Printed Ephemera* (Ipswich, 1962/*R* Woodbridge, 1988)
M. Twyman: *Printing, 1770–1970: An Illustrated History of its Development and Uses in England* (London, 1970)
J. E. Pemberton: *The National Provision of Printed Ephemera in the Social Sciences*, University of Warwick Library, Occasional Publication 1 (Coventry, 1971)
The John Johnson Collection (exh. cat. by M. L. Turner, Oxford, Bodleian Lib., 1971)
D. Hindley and G. Hindley: *Advertising in Victorian England, 1837–1901* (London, 1972)
H. Evans, M. Evans and A. Nelki: *The Picture Researchers' Handbook* (Newton Abbot, 1975, rev. 1986)
The Ephemerist, 1– (1975–)
J. N. C. Lewis: *Collecting Printed Ephemera* (London, 1976)
M. Rickards: *This Is Ephemera: Collecting Printed Throwaways* (London, 1977)
M. Dempsey, ed.: *'Bubbles': Early Advertising Art from A. and F. Pears Ltd* (Glasgow, 1978)
G. Herscher: *L'Art et les biscuits: Lefèvre-Utile advertisements, 1897–1914* (Paris, 1978)
A. Clinton: *Printed Ephemera: Collection, Organisation and Access* (London, 1981)
A. Gould: *Named Special Collections in the Department of Printed Books*, British Library Reference Division, Reader Guide No. 9 (London, 1981)
G. Renoy: *Les Etiquettes du vin: Un Monde merveilleux* (St Sulpice, 1981)
O. Sanguinetti and O. Sanguinetti: *Figurine Liebig* (Milan, 1981)
T. R. Nevett: *Advertising in Britain: A History* (London, 1982)
C. Pieske: *Das ABC des Luxuspapiers* (Berlin, 1983)
L. S. Marcus: *An Epinal Album: Popular Prints from Nineteenth-century France* (Boston, 1984)
P. J. Philips: *Kill or Cure: Lotions, Potions, Characters and Quacks of Early Australia* (Richmond, 1984)
M. I. Williams, ed.: *A Directory of Rare Book and Special Collections in the United Kingdom and the Republic of Ireland* (London, 1985)
K. Gibson and J. Goldfinch: 'A National Register of Ephemera Collections?', *The Ephemerist*, 53 (June 1986), pp. 150–51
R. Opie: *The Art of the Label* (London, 1987)
J. G. Johnsen: *Iddisar* [Sardine-tin labels] (Oslo, 1988)
M. Rickards: *Collecting Printed Ephemera* (Oxford, 1988)
H. M. Bien and U. Giersch: *Reisen in die grosse weite Welt* (Harenberg, *c.* 1989) [luggage labels, 1900–60]
M. Anikst and E. Chernevich: *Russian Graphic Design, 1880–1917* (London, 1990)
D. Richlieu: *Papier de collection* (Paris, 1990)
F. Wolaskowitz: *Deckelikatalog* [Catalogue of cream-tub lids] (Langnau, 1990)
H. Notaker: *Den Norske menyen* [Norwegian menus] (Oslo, 1991)
A. Robertson: *Directory of Australian Ephemera Collections* (Sydney, 1992)

JULIE ANNE LAMBERT, MAURICE RICKARDS

Ephesos [Ephesus]. Site of an important Classical city on the west coast of Turkey, *c.* 2 km south-west of modern Selçuk. It has been occupied since perhaps as early as the 10th century BC, and its Late Classical Temple of Artemis (Artemision), built on the site of an earlier temple from the Archaic period, was regarded as one of the Seven Wonders of the World.

I. History and urban development. II. Temple of Artemis.

I. History and urban development.

According to Greek tradition, Ephesos was founded in the 10th century BC by Ionian settlers near the mouth of the River Cayster. From the mid-6th century BC it was ruled successively by the Lydians, Croesus of Lydia extending the unfortified city inland, and the Persians. It was conquered by Alexander the Great in 334 BC, and throughout antiquity Ephesos was an important trading centre, its prestige enhanced by the construction of the colossal Temple of Artemis (6th century BC, rebuilt 4th century BC) on the plain to the north-east of the city. In the early 3rd century BC Ephesos was re-established and fortified by Lysimachos on the nearby slopes of Mts Koressos (Bülbüldağ) and Pion (Panayırdağ), with a new urban plan around an oval harbour (*see* §1(i) below), and thereafter it became the primary port and commercial centre of western Asia Minor. Ephesos came under Roman rule *c.* 133 BC, and in 29 BC it attained the rank of provincial capital of Asia; the population in early Imperial times has been estimated at *c.* 250,000. The apostles Paul and John resided briefly in the city, the latter allegedly accompanied by the Virgin Mary, while emperors from Augustus to Justinian financed the construction of numerous public buildings (*see* §2(i) below). The decline of Ephesos began with the gradual silting of the harbour allied to the economic decline of the Roman Empire; it was exacerbated by invasions by the Goths in the mid-3rd century AD. It nevertheless remained one of the most important cities of the Byzantine empire in the 4th and 5th centuries;

two important church councils were held there (AD 431 and 449), and large churches were built, including that of St John on Ayasuluk Hill above the ancient Temple of Artemis (see §3 below). Ephesos was apparently devastated by an earthquake c. AD 614 and was rebuilt on a much smaller scale within a new fortification wall. It continued to serve as an administrative centre, but increasing attacks by Arabs in the 7th and 8th centuries led the centre of population to shift north-east to the more easily defensible Ayasuluk Hill, which was fortified with walls and a fortress; by the 12th century the ancient city had been largely abandoned. The settlement that grew up around Ayasuluk Hill, which was finally captured by the Turks in 1304, experienced a brief revival under the principality of Aydın, when the mosque of Isa Bey (1374) was built just below the church of St John (see §4 below); the modern town, known as Selçuk after 1914, marks the continued occupation of this area. Excavations were first undertaken by J. T. Wood in 1869 and later by D. G. Hogarth at the Temple of Artemis (see §II below). Since 1895 members of the Austrian Archaeological Institute have been systematically exploring both the temple area and the ancient city, where they have reconstructed several buildings. Finds from the early excavations are in the British Museum, London, and the Kunsthistorisches Museum, Vienna, while those from later excavations are in the Archaeological Museum, Izmir, and the Ephesos Archaeological Museum, Selçuk. Unless otherwise stated, all examples given below are in the latter.

BIBLIOGRAPHY

J. T. Wood: *Discoveries at Ephesus* (London, 1877)
Forschungen in Ephesos: Veröffentlicht vom Österreichischen Archäologischen Institut in Wien (Vienna, 1906)
D. C. Hogarth, ed.: *Excavations at Ephesus* (London, 1908)
J. Keil: *Ephesos: Ein Führer durch die Ruinenstätte und ihre Geschichte* (Vienna, 1915, rev. 5/1964)
F. Miltner: *Ephesos: Stadt der Artemis und des Johannes* (Vienna, 1958)
W. Alzinger: *Die Ruinen von Ephesos* (Berlin, 1972)
C. Foss: *Ephesus after Antiquity: A Late Antique, Byzantine and Turkish City* (Cambridge, 1979)

M. RAUTMANN

1. Greek. 2. Roman. 3. Christian. 4. Islamic.

1. GREEK.

(i) Architecture. Mycenaean walls have survived at two places near Ephesos: on the Ilıcatepe Hills south of Kuşadası and on the Büyükkale Hills in the direction of Tire. The Mycenaean fortress on the Ilıcatepe can presumably be identified as the town of Apasa in Arzawa mentioned in Hittite texts. The earliest remains of Greek Iron Age architecture are in the vicinity of the Temple of Artemis (see fig. 1i; see also GREECE, ANCIENT, fig. 8f). Here a peripteral building of the 8th century BC, which may be the oldest and best-preserved structure of its type yet known in the Greek world, has been uncovered beneath the central base excavated by Hogarth. It had four columns on its front and eight on each flank, as well as a wide door in the west side of its cella. The cella may have been an open court containing a structure similar to a baldacchino, comprising a rectangular base flanked by six columns. This may have contained the oldest cult statue of Artemis, a wooden *xoanon*, since a pectoral made largely of amber has been discovered. Soundings beneath the peripteral

building uncovered Mycenaean and sub-Mycenaean remains, and although these provide no proof of continuity of worship, they do raise the possibility. There are more architectural remains from the 7th century BC, though again only in the Temple of Artemis (see §II below): a cult base from the northern area, a temple (so-called Temple C) from the centre and the 'Hekatompedos' ('hundred-footer') to the west. The construction of the first two buildings is characteristic of the 7th century BC, with beautifully jointed, long split slabs of yellow marble. The 'Hekatompedos' is the earliest Ephesian building with a marble superstructure. Round and rectangular houses of the 7th century BC, perhaps from a village called Smyna, have been excavated below the lower Roman agora.

Among the scant architectural finds is an Ionic corner capital with rosettes in the spandrels discovered near the church of St John, which supports the old reconstruction of capitals from the Archaic Temple of Artemis (London, BM). The characteristics of 6th-century BC Ephesian architecture are again mainly illustrated by buildings in the Artemision. These show the frequent use of spolia in foundations, such as the marble spolia in the south area of the Archaic temple and reused green slate blocks in a later reconstruction of the peripteros. The marble masonry of this period is characterized by blocks with bevelled outer edges and smooth drafted margins.

The only structures in the area to survive from the 5th century BC are two tumuli with the remains of lantern roofs: one above the Mausoleum of Belevi; the other on a hill that was once the island of Syrie. Late Classical architecture other than that of the Artemision includes some notable archaizing Ionic capitals of the 4th century BC, presumably from a peripteral temple. Further 4th-century BC material has been found, reused in a Byzantine villa by the sea near Pamucak; a tumulus with rusticated walls near Kuşdur must also belong to the 3rd or 4th century BC. In general, Late Classical Ephesian architecture is characterized by an archaizing tendency: its technical and stylistic details also occur in the Sanctuary of Artemis at Sardis (3rd century BC) and on the Great Altar at Pergamon.

The first evidence of a planned city at Ephesos dates from the Hellenistic period, when the site was moved. Its new layout was based on a Hippodamic grid, in which some older street courses such as 'Kouretes Street' (Embolos; see fig. 1ii), were preserved. The Embolos was part of a procession road around the Panayirdag Hills to the Artemision. A great city wall was also built, and parts are still well preserved on the surrounding hills. The few other architectural remains include the stage building of the theatre (1iii) with its small fountain house, a round building next to the auditorium and some retaining walls. The most important Hellenistic monument in the vicinity of Ephesos is the Mausoleum at BELEVI (see GREECE, ANCIENT, fig. 30).

BIBLIOGRAPHY

A. Bammer: 'Zur Topographie und städtebaulichen Entwicklung von Ephesos', *Jhft. Österreich. Archäol. Inst. Wien*, xlvi (1961–3), pp. 136–57
——: 'Beiträge zur ephesischen Architektur', *Jhft. Österreich. Archäol. Inst. Wien*, xlix (1968–71), pp. 1–40
——: 'Beobachtungen zur ephesischen Architektur', *Archäol. Anz.*, (1972), pp. 440–57

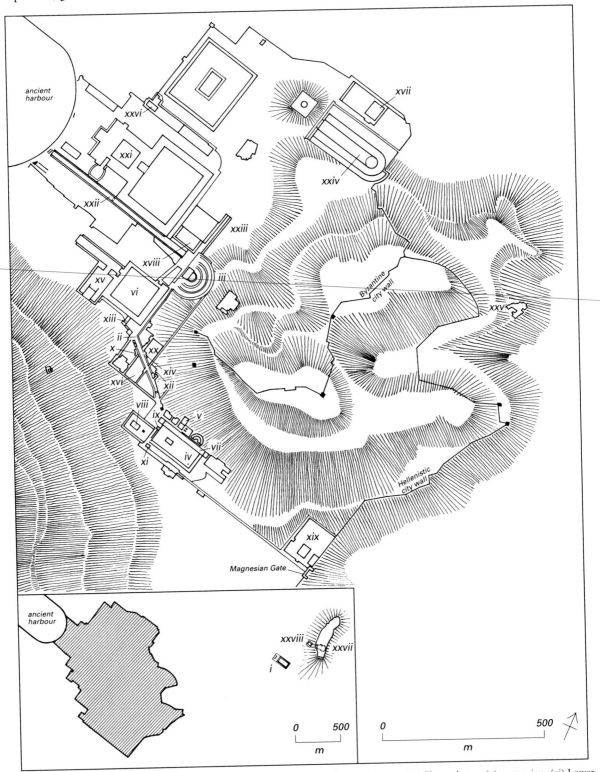

1. Ephesos, plan of site: (i) Temple of Artemis; (ii) 'Kouretes Street' (Embolos); (iii) theatre; (iv) Upper Agora; (v) prytaneion; (vi) Lower Agora; (vii) basilica; (viii) Flavian temple; (ix) Fountain of Domitian; (x) octagonal funerary building; (xi) Fountain of Laecanius Bassus; (xii) Nymphaeum of Trajan; (xiii) Library of Celsus; (xiv) Temple of Hadrian; (xv) Serapeion; (xvi) Slope Houses 1 and 2; (xvii) Vedius Gymnasium; (xviii) Theatre Gymnasium; (xix) 'East Gymnasium'; (xx) Baths of Varius; (xxi) Harbour Gymnasium; (xxii) Arkadiane; (xxiii) Stoa of Servilius; (xxiv) stadium; (xxv) cemetery of the Seven Sleepers; (xxvi) St Mary; (xxvii) St John; (xxviii) Mosque of Isa Bey

——: 'Architecture et société en Asie Mineure au IVe siècle av. J.C.', Architecture et société de l'archaïsme grec à la fin de la république romaine: Collection de l'École française de Rome (1983), pp. 271–300

——: Architektur und Gesellschaft in der Antike (Vienna, 1985)

——: 'Ephesos in der Bronzezeit', Jhft. Österreich. Archäol. Inst. Wien, lvii (1986/87), pp. 1–38

Ö. Özyigit: 'Spätarchaische Funde im Museum von Ephesos und die Lage von Alt-Ephesos', Istanbul. Mitt., xxxviii (1988), pp. 83–96

A. Bammer: 'A Peripteros of the Geometric Period in the Artemision of Ephesus', Anatol. Stud., xl (1990), pp. 137–60

——: 'Die Geschichte des Sekos im Artemision von Ephesos', Jhft. Österreich. Archäol. Inst. Wien, lxii (1993), pp. 137–68

——: 'Fouilles à l'Artémision d'Éphèse', Rév. Archéol. (1993), no. 1, pp. 187–99

D. Knibbe and G. Langmann: 'Via Sacra Ephesiaca I', Berichte und Material, 3 (1993)

(ii) Sculpture. The oldest Greek sculpture found in Ephesos is a bronze group (13th century BC) related to Hittite work and representing a man placing a pot on a tripod (USA, priv. col.). The most important Archaic sculptures are those from the Temple of Artemis (*see* §II below). These include reliefs of ritual processions on the sculpted columns (*c.* 560–520 BC; London, BM; Selçuk, Ephesos Archaeol. Mus.) and friezes (*c.* 530–480 BC; London, BM; Selçuk, Ephesos Archaeol. Mus.) comprising individual scenes of carts and sieges and more extensive depictions of mythological subjects such as centauromachies and gigantomachies. Examples of free-standing Archaic sculpture include fragments of kouroi, cloaked figures and korai from the excavations by Wood and Hogarth (London, BM), as well as from later, unpublished finds. Particularly numerous are the ivory figurines (late 7th century–6th BC; London, BM; Istanbul, Archaeol. Mus.; Selçuk, Ephesos Archaeol. Mus.) found at the Temple of Artemis. Its cult statue by Endoios (Pliny: *Natural History*, XVI.lxxix.213–14) was probably the model for two Roman figures of the Artemis Ephesia (2nd century AD). A colossal lion (late 6th century BC) may have served as a grave marker, while two small heads (late 6th century BC; Selçuk, Ephesos Archaeol. Mus.; London, BM) resemble Cypriot works.

A notable example of Early Classical sculpture is a relief with the seated figure of a cybele (*c.* 460–450 BC), while important Roman copies of works of the period in the Severe style found at Ephesos include a head of 'Aspasia' type (Izmir, Archaeol. Mus.), a headless statue of the Hestia Giustiniani type (Rome, Villa Albani), both dating to the late 2nd century AD, and a head of the Candia type (Rome, Mus. N. Romano). Roman copies of works from the period 450–400 BC include part of a general's head, a head of the Athena Medici type, based on an original sometimes attributed to Pheidias and a sphinx group (Vienna, Ksthist. Mus.; London, BM), made of pebbly conglomerate and based on the armrests of the throne of Zeus at Olympia. Pliny (XXXIV.xix.53) records that Polykleitos, Pheidias, Kresilas, Phradmon and perhaps a fifth sculptor named Kydon competed to produce statues of Amazons for the Temple of Artemis, and these may have been copied in various Roman sculptures. Their attributions and dates are disputed, but a Late Classical architectural relief, apparently from the altar of the Temple of Artemis, depicts an Amazon of the Sciarra type (Vienna, Ksthist. Mus.).

The most significant sculpture of the 4th century BC again comes from the Temple of Artemis. The sculpted columns (London, BM; see fig. 6 below) of the Late Classical temple are decorated with cult scenes as well as representations of *Herakles*, *Theseus* and female deities, while several further sculptures have been ascribed to its altar, including a relief of horses and fragments of free-standing chariot groups. There is also a torso of a female dancer and fragments of over life-size statues. Several other works may belong to this period, although the dates of some are disputed. The bronze statue of a man scraping himself (Vienna, Ksthist. Mus.) may be an original of *c.* 350 BC or an early Imperial copy, while a boy with a goose from the same building is a Roman copy. Other copies that are definitely Roman include the so-called *Hera of Ephesos*, the head, arms and hands of a version of the *Eros of Lysippos* and a head of the Artemis Colonna type.

Hellenistic portraits include a head (*c.* 300 BC) probably representing *Lysimachos*, and a herm bust; the group the *Blinding of Polyphemos* (1st century BC), reused in the Fountain of Domitian (*see* §2(i) below), may originally have come from the pediment of a temple in the Upper Agora. A frieze showing a battle against the Gauls may have been cut to celebrate the Pergamene victory of 166 BC. Sacred sculpture includes a statuette of Cybele and two reliefs (late Hellenistic); grave reliefs also survive, including some depicting funerary feasts.

BIBLIOGRAPHY

F. Eichler: 'Nochmals die Sphinxgruppe aus Ephesos', Jhft. Österreich. Archäol. Inst. Wien, xlv (1960), pp. 5–22

——: 'Die österreichischen Ausgrabungen in Ephesos im Jahre 1962', Österreich. Akad. Wiss.: Anz. Philos.-Hist. Kl., c–ci (1963–4), pp. 45ff

V. M. Strocka: 'Ein ephesisches Urkundenrelief', Jhft. Österreich. Archäol. Inst. Wien, xlix (1968–71), pp. 41–9

S. Lattimore: 'The Bronze Apoxyomenos from Ephesos', Amer. J. Archaeol., lxxvi (1972), pp. 13–16

A. Bammer, R. Fleischer and D. Knibbe: Führer durch das archäologische Museum in Selçuk-Ephesos (Vienna, 1974)

W. Oberleitner: 'Ein hellenistischer Galterschlachtfries aus Ephesos', Jb. Ksthist. Samml. Wien, lxxvii (1981), pp. 57–104

U. Muss: 'Das Wiener Amazonrelief', Jb. Ksthist. Samml. Wien, lxxx (1984), pp. 7–34

E. Atalay: 'Un Nouveau Monument votif hellénistique à Éphèse', Rev. Archéol., ii (1985), pp. 195–204

U. Muss: 'Silen und Gigant auf dem ephesischen Simenfries', Jhft. Österreich. Archäol. Inst. Wien, lvii (1986–7), pp. 29–38

A. Rügler: Die columnae caelatae des jüngeren Artemisions von Ephesos (Tübingen, 1988)

2. ROMAN.

(i) Architecture. (ii) Sculpture.

(i) Architecture. Several monuments date from the Republican period: these include the Monument of C. Memmius (1st century BC), an architectural frieze depicting a *Cavalry Battle* belonging to the heroon close to the octagon at the Embolos and the foundations of a temple in the Upper Agora (see fig. 1iv above). Remains of the Augustan period are more numerous: they include the aqueduct for the Marnas water supply; the Doric vestibule of the prytaneion (1v) with the Hestia hall; the double temple next to the prytaneion; the west and south gates of the Lower Agora (1vi); the monument of Augustus and his grandsons; and the basilica (1vii) in the Upper Agora, which has columns alternately in the Corinthian and Ionic orders, the latter with bull protomes.

In the 1st century AD the intense building activity continued. Under Nero were built the east stoa of the Lower Agora, in the Doric order, and, in the Ionic order, the west end of the basilica, which projects into the Square of Domitian. In the Flavian period a great Corinthian pseudo-dipteral temple (1viii) was built on the south side of the Square of Domitian. It stands on a large terrace with a two-storey façade on the north side; the lower storey is Doric, and the upper storey has supports in the form of atlantids (see fig. 2). At the east end of the temple stood an altar decorated with a weapon frieze (see below). The organization and dating of this complex are disputed. The north terrace may be Antonine rather than Domitianic, and the atlantids have been interpreted as representing barbarians. The Fountain of Domitian (or Fountain of Pollio; 1ix), built in AD 92–3 on the east side of the Square of Domitian, consists of two parts: a baldachin-like structure facing the Upper Agora, and a large apse facing the square, to which group the sculptural *Blinding of Polyphemos (see* §1(ii) *above)* was moved.

The function of the remarkable vine-leaf columns from 'Kouretes Street' is uncertain, and the dating of both an octagonal funerary building (1x) in 'Kouretes Street' and a circular building on Panayirdağ is disputed, with suggestions ranging from Late Hellenistic to Flavian. The octagon consists of a square socle supporting an octagonal Corinthian peripteral structure with a pyramidal roof, possibly the tomb for Arsinoe IV, killed by her sister Cleopatra VII. The circular building has a round lower storey with engaged Doric half-columns, above which is an Ionic colonnade with the volutes of the capitals covered with plant decoration.

2. Ephesos, terrace of the Flavian temple, showing atlantids, ?late 1st century AD

The Doric order is rare at Ephesos. In addition to the Hellenistic fountain house at the theatre, the east stoa of the Lower Agora, the lower storey of the Domitian terrace and the lower part of the circular building, it is found on the vestibule of the prytaneion. In contrast, by the end of the 1st century AD the Corinthian order was already being employed for great showpiece façades at the theatre, the east stoa of the Fountain of Laecanius Bassus (1xi) and the Fountain of Domitian. The full development of façades, however, comes in the 2nd century AD, with the Nymphaeum of Trajan (1xii), the fountain on the Magnesian road and the Library of Celsus (1xiii), which was also a funerary monument. Most of these façades consisted of tiers of aedicules formed by columns supporting projecting sections of the entablature (for illustration of the restored Library of Celsus *see* ROME, ANCIENT, fig. 46). The aedicules often contained statues, and those of the upper storeys were surmounted by small pediments of various forms. In addition, three Corinthian temples date from the 2nd century AD: that of Hadrian (xiv), originally built for Trajan, with a Syrian arch and a figural frieze partly added in Late Antiquity; the Serapeion (xv), and a large peripteral structure on the harbour plain.

Besides the buildings incorporating arches, such as the Monument of C. Memmius, the south gate of the Lower Agora, the Fountain of Domitian, the Gate of Hadrian and the Temple of Hadrian, the centrally planned buildings with square, polygonal or round ground-plans are also noteworthy. Among these are the circular building next to the auditorium; the octagon; the circular building on Panayirdağ; a circular tomb on Bülbüldağ; and a 2nd-century AD funerary building on the road to Aydin.

The Romans also adopted Greek-style altars, decorated with figural friezes, colonnades and courtyards, particularly for the imperial cult. Examples include the altar of the Flavian temple, with its weapon frieze, and the Altar of Lucius Verus or 'Parthian monument'. The lower part of this U-shaped structure, perhaps erected in honour of a victory over the Parthians, has a long figural frieze (Vienna, Ksthist. Mus.), above which there must have been a colonnaded superstructure; it may have been situated south-east of the Library of Celsus (*see* §(ii) *below*). Architectural ornament of the simpler early Roman kind, based mainly on Classical precedents, continues to occur, as on the Monument of C. Memmius and the south gate of the Agora. It did not become richer until the Flavian period, when it was based rather on examples in Rome itself, as in the case of the Fountain of Domitian. A high point in Roman architectural ornament was reached in the Hadrianic period in the Temple of Hadrian and the Library of Celsus. Here the whole repertory of contemporary ornament appears: strigilation, fish-scale pattern, vegetal and animal motifs. Column capitals also demonstrate a development from the pure Corinthian form to the more elaborate Composite order found in the Trajanic period at the Nymphaeum of Trajan.

The most striking feature of Ephesian domestic architecture is the frequent use of peristyle courts, which have been discovered at various places in the city, although only those south of 'Kouretes Street' on the slope of the Bülbüldağ have been systematically excavated. These peristyle courts with their surrounding rooms were situated in two contiguous apartment buildings (Slope House 1 and Slope House 2; 1xvi), which formed a block covering several terraces. Slope House 2 comprised seven dwellings: two on an upper terrace, three on the middle and two on a lower one. The access to the apartments was usually from steep alleys at the side of the block. As can be seen from the surviving internal stairs, they had several storeys, and, since the upper storeys must have belonged to apartments at ground-level, the floor area of individual dwellings must have varied from a few hundred to one thousand sq. m. Some rooms had floor heating, and there were also baths and toilets. Walls were painted and floors laid with mosaics; surviving fittings include bronze and marble furniture, statues and decorative objects. All rooms opened on to the colonnades of the peristyle courts. The inner walls range in date from the 1st to the 3rd century AD; wall paintings occur from the 1st century AD, though most date from the 2nd and 3rd centuries AD, as do the mosaics. In the 4th century AD many dwellings were demolished and later built over with workshops. Each of the two apartment buildings incorporates a large private basilica extending through two storeys, and the name of one of the owners is known: C. Flavius Furius Aptus. The basilicas exemplify the tendency in Roman architecture to develop what had originally been public areas into enclosed elements in private dwellings. Luxurious decoration, with wall paintings clearly intended for an educated public, mosaics depicting scenes from nature and exotic animals, and vaults with plaster reliefs, shows that the apartments belonged to members of the Ephesian upper classes.

From the 2nd century AD onwards, gymnasia combining palaestras and baths occupied a large area of the city of Ephesos. Their strong walls and vaults made them expensive to build, and the large quantities of water needed to operate them had to be supplied through reinforced pipes. Surviving buildings include the Vedius Gymnasium (1xvii), the Theatre Gymnasium (1xviii), the 'East Gymnasium' (1xix), the Baths of Varius (1xx; renovated in Late Antiquity by a certain Scholastikia) and the Harbour Gymnasium (1xxi) (all mainly 2nd to 3rd century AD). The most usual masonry for walls and vaults in the 1st century AD was rough stonework bonded with lime mortar. In the early 2nd century AD construction in brick began, using square bricks the size of a Roman foot. At the end of the 2nd century AD the bricks became larger, and broken bricks are also found in the *opus caementum* filling of the great walls of bath buildings. Stone masonry in conjunction with brickwork first occurs in Late Antiquity.

There are fewer building inscriptions in the 3rd century AD than in the 2nd, but many large buildings, such as gymnasia, may not have been completed until the 3rd century. Changes in the nature of artistic activity can also be seen in portraiture. From the 1st and 2nd centuries AD there are 18 surviving portraits of emperors and 32 of private citizens; from the 3rd century AD one Imperial portrait but 61 private ones survive. This indicates that in the 3rd century AD there was a decrease in public commissions but a sharp increase in private ones. Thus the economic changes at the beginning of the 3rd century AD did not reduce artistic and architectural activity but brought about a reorientation of social and economic interests. In the Slope Houses too there was much building and artistic work in the 3rd century AD.

In Late Antiquity the large public squares were reduced in size and built over with dwellings, and their function was taken over by streets lined with arcades, such as 'Kouretes Street', the Arkadiane (1xxii and §3 below) and the Stoa of Servilius (1xxiii). New areas were selected for major buildings, for example the district between the harbour and the stadium (1xxiv), where palaces, baths, churches and fountains were constructed. However, the basic feature of Late Antique Ephesos was not the expansion of the city but its renovation, in particular following the 3rd-century invasion by the Goths. Every district was revitalized, and older buildings were restored. Reuse of building materials was practised for the first time on a grand scale: some buildings were constructed entirely of spolia, and holes were bored in walls to search for metal clamps. Even so, the total built-up area of the city was reduced.

BIBLIOGRAPHY

W. Wilberg: *Die Bibliothek* (1953), V/i of *Forschungen in Ephesos* (Vienna, 1906–)

A. Bammer: 'Die gebrannten Mauerziegel von Ephesos und ihre Datierung', *Jhft. Österreich. Archäol. Inst. Wien*, xlvii (1964/5), Beiblatt, pp. 289–300

W. Alzinger and A. Bammer: *Das Monument des C. Memmius in Ephesos* (1971), VII of *Forschungen in Ephesos* (Wien, 1906)

M. Wörrle: 'Zur Datierung des Hadrianstempels an der "Kuretenstrasse" in Ephesos', *Archäol. Anz.* (1973), pp. 470–77

W. Alzinger: *Augustische Architektur in Ephesos* (Vienna, 1974)

M. Wegner: 'Gewundene Säulen von Ephesos', *Jhft. Österreich. Archäol. Inst. Wien*, li (1976–7), suppl. pp. 49–64

A. Bammer: 'Elemente flavisch-trajanischer Architekturfassenden aus Ephesos', *Jhft. Österreich. Archäol. Inst. Wien*, lii (1978–80), pp. 67–90

W. Koenigs and W. Radt: 'Ein kaiserzeitlicher Rundbau (Monopteros) in Pergamon', *Istanbul. Mitt.*, xxix (1979), pp. 317–54

D. Knibbe: 'Der Asiarch M. Fulvius Publicianus Nikephoros, die ephesischen Handwerkszünfte und die Stoa des Servilius', *Jhft. Österreich. Archäol. Inst. Wien*, lvi (1985), pp. 71–7

G. J. Lang: 'Zur oberen Osthalle der Agora, der "neronischen Halle" in Ephesos', *Lebendige Altertumswissenschaft: Festgabe H. Vetters* (Vienna, 1985), pp. 176–80

H. Vetters: 'Ephesos: Vorläufiger Grabungsbericht für die Jahre 1984 und 1985', *Österreich. Akad. Wiss. Anz. Philos.-Hist. Kl.*, cxxiii (1986), pp. 75–110

A. Bammer: *Ephesos, Stadt an Fluss und Meer* (Graz, 1988)

M. Torelli: 'Il monumento efesino di Memmius ad Efeo', *Sci. Ant.*, ii (1988), pp. 403–26

V. M. Strocka: 'Zeus, Marnas und Klaseas: Ephesische Brunnenfiguren von 93 n.Chr.', *Festschrift für Jale Inan* (Istanbul, 1989), pp. 79–92

H. Thür: *Das Hadrianstur in Ephesos* (1989), XI/i of *Forschungen in Ephesos* (Vienna, 1906–)

'Ephèse, la cité d' Artémis', *Le Monde de la Bible*, lxiv (1990)

H. Thür: 'Arsinoe IV, eine Schwester Kleopatras VII: Grabinhaberin des Oktogons von Ephesos?', *Jhft. Österreich. Archäol. Inst. Wien*, lx (1990), pp. 43–56

G. M. Rogers: *The Sacred Identity of Ephesus* (London and New York, 1991)

H. Engelmann: 'Zum Kaiserkult in Ephesos', *Z. Papyrologie & Epig.*, xcvii (1993), pp. 279–89

C. P. Jones: 'The Olympieion and the Hadrianeion at Ephesus', *J. Hell. Stud.*, cxiii (1993), pp. 149–52

St. J Friesen: 'Twice Neokoros: Ephesus, Asia and the Cult of the Flavian Imperial Family', *Etud. Préliminaires Relig. Orient. Empire Romain*, cxvi (1993)

ANTON BAMMER

(ii) *Sculpture.* Two portrait heads (2nd quarter of the 1st century BC and mid-1st century BC) were apparently produced in the Republican period, while a relief on the attic storey of the Monument of C. Memmius may also be of this period and not Augustan, as originally thought.

From the Fountain of Laecanius Bassus come fragments of three figures of *Triton* of early Imperial date; its other statues included three of *Aphrodite*, two of the Venus Genetrix type, perhaps ultimately based on a work by Kallimachos and one (1st century AD) based on a Hellenistic development of a late 4th-century BC original.

In addition to the Hellenistic *Blinding of Polyphemos* group (*see* §1(ii) above), figures found at the Fountain of Domitian include a torso of *Aphrodite* and an over life-size reclining nude warrior (late 1st century or early 2nd AD) with an added skull-cap and headband. The warrior's pose is based on Pergamene models, while its scale and headband suggest that the figure represents a hero. A head of Zeus, about twice life-size, also with skull-cap added, resembles Greek High Classical works but was probably produced in the late 1st century AD. The sculptural decoration of the 2nd-century AD Nymphaeum of Trajan also varied in date. It included a statue of *Androklos* (2nd century AD), the mythical founder of Ephesos, based on

a *Meleager* by Skopas of *c.* 340–330 BC; an eclectic *Dionysos* (1st century AD) with a pose based on the '*Tiber Apollo*' (Rome, Mus. N. Romano); and the statue of a woman that was probably part of the original decoration of the Nymphaeum and may represent Julia Lydia Laterane, who is mentioned in the dedicatory inscription.

The altar of the Flavian temple was decorated with a frieze of weapons, while the long relief panels (Vienna, Ksthist. Mus.) from the Altar of Lucius Verus or 'Parthian monument', most of which were found in the Library of Celsus, combine battle scenes with groups of the imperial family. The panels commemorate the Parthian campaign of Lucius Verus (AD 163–6). In contrast, the frieze blocks from the Temple of Hadrian depicting *Androklos Hunting the Wild Boar* and the settlement of Ephesos by the Greeks were later additions to the building, perhaps of Tetrarchic or even Theodosian date (for illustration of the *Androklos* sculpture *see* IONIA).

A sculpted head and forearm from the Flavian temple may have belonged to a colossal statue of the Emperor Domitian, and other material from Ephesos attests to the existence of an important local workshop producing portrait sculpture. Such sculptures include two life-size portraits of *Tiberius* and *Livia*, an over life-size bust of *Marcus Aurelius* and a life-size Late Antique replacement head (see fig. 3) that strongly resembles the head of *Eutropius* (second half of 5th century AD; Vienna, Ksthist. Mus.).

For further illustration *see* ROME, ANCIENT, fig. 118.

BIBLIOGRAPHY

B. Brenk: 'Die Datierung des Reliefs am Hadrianstempel in Ephesos und das Problem der tetrarchischen Skulptur des Ostens', *Istanbul. Mitt.*, xviii (1968), pp. 238–58
R. Fleischer: 'Zwei eklektische Statuen aus Ephesos', *Pro Arte Antiqua: Festschrift für H. Kenner* (Vienna, 1982), pp. 123–9
M. Aurenhammer: 'Römische Portraits aus Ephesos: Neue Funde aus dem Hanghaus 2', *Jhft. Österreich. Archäol. Inst. Wien*, liv (1983), pp. 105–46
B. Andreae: 'Die Polyphem-gruppe von Ephesos', *Lebendige Altertums-wissenschaften: Festgabe H. Vetters* (Vienna, 1985), pp. 209–15
T. Ganschow: 'Überlegungen zum Partherdenkmal von Ephesos', *Archäol. Anz.* (1986), pp. 209–21
M. Aurenhammer: *Die Skulpturen von Ephesos, Bildwerke aus Stein, Idealplastik*, Forschungen in Ephesos, x/1 (Vienna, 1990)

ULRIKE MUSS

3. CHRISTIAN. Between the 4th and the 6th centuries AD Ephesos was the capital of the province of Asia, a major port serving the wealthy agricultural plains of western Asia Minor and a leading religious and pilgrimage centre. St Paul had preached in the city, and St Timothy, St John, the martyr Hermione (daughter of the Apostle Philip), St Mary Magdalen and the Virgin were all associated with Ephesos. Of these the most important cults were those of the Virgin and St John, especially the latter, who was thought to have lived on the hill above the Temple of Artemis, to have written the fourth gospel there and been buried in the same place. Also important were the 'Seven Sleepers of Ephesos', a group of young men who took refuge in a cave just outside the city walls during the anti-Christian persecutions of Emperor Decius (*reg* 249–51) and allegedly awoke during the reign of Emperor Theodosios II (*reg* 408–50). The cave is identified with one to the east of the city (see 1xxv above) that was a favoured burial site in the 5th and 6th centuries and a

3. Ephesos, marble replacement head, h. 380 mm, 5th century AD (Selçuk, Ephesos Archaeological Museum)

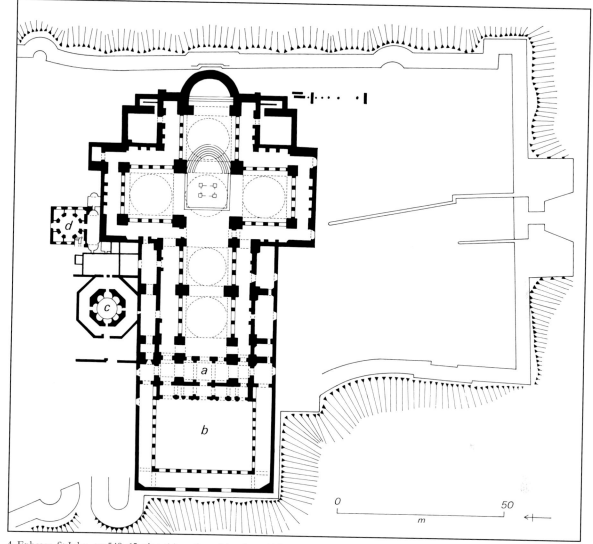

4. Ephesos, St John, AD 548–65, plan: (a) narthex; (b) atrium; (c) baptistery; (d) *skeuophylakeion* (sacristy)

centre of pilgrimage thereafter, with a crypt, church and mausolea built at several levels in the natural ravine. The Metropolitan of Ephesos ranked second in the patriarchate of Constantinople after the See of Caesarea in Cappadocia. The city's ecclesiastical status was enhanced by the holding there of the Church Councils of 431 and 449.

From the 4th century until the early 7th the city continued to occupy its Hellenistic walls, and its core remained the main street known as the Embolos ('Kouretes Street') linking the Upper Agora to the Lower, still lined as in the Roman period with statues and public buildings (*see* §2(i) above). The other principal artery, the Arkadiane—named in honour of Emperor Arkadios (*reg* 395–408)—was about 500 m long, marble-paved and flanked by covered colonnades decorated by geometric floor mosaics and terminated by a monumental gateway at the harbour (1xxii). About halfway along the street stood four massive columns upon which stood statues of

the four evangelists. The street is a typical if grandiose example of late Roman city planning. Major churches of the 4th century to the 6th include the cathedral church of St Mary inside the city near the harbour (xxvi), and the church of St John, lying on the hill associated with the saint *c.* 2 km to the north-east (see figs 1xxvii and 4). The church of St Mary was converted in the 4th century from a huge Roman market (early 2nd century AD) into a three-aisled, apsed basilica with a narthex and large atrium and a baptistery on its north side. The church of St John was founded by Justinian I and replaced two earlier churches on the same site. Work was begun before 548 and completed by 565. An enormous vaulted structure, it was built to a cruciform plan close to that of the Holy Apostles in Constantinople (*see* ISTANBUL, §III, 9(i)), with six domes, a narthex and an atrium. It is flanked on the north side by an octagonal baptistery (?5th century) and a domed octagonal *skeuophylakeion* (sacristy; late 6th century or early 7th). Internal decoration included mosaics, marble revetments and *opus sectile* floors. The church is closely related in style to Justinian's other foundations of Hagia Sophia and Hagia Eirene in Constantinople (*see* ISTANBUL, §III, 1(ii)(a) and 5). Secular monuments of the 4th to 6th centuries include several baths—the largest being the Harbour Gymnasium, restored on imperial orders in the mid-4th century; other work included the Library of Celsus, which, after standing a ruin for over a century, was converted in the late 4th century into a monumental fountain.

Although in the 7th century Ephesos, in common with other Byzantine cities, suffered the effects of the empire's economic collapse as well as an apparent earthquake, it survived as a continuously occupied site. Strong new walls, probably built in the second half of the 7th century, enclosed only a small part of the Early Christian city; they excluded such formerly important areas as the Embolos and the Upper and Lower Agorai but included the church of St Mary, where a much smaller cross-domed basilica was built, probably in the 8th century, inside the ruins of the older church. The church of St John also survived as an important pilgrimage centre and at some date after the 6th century became the city's cathedral. Possibly in the 8th century the hill on which the church stands was given defensive walls, and gradually the centre of Ephesos moved there, so that by the 12th century it had effectively become a fortified settlement around the church of St John and the old city site was largely abandoned. From the 10th century onwards Ephesos benefited from the general revival of the Byzantine economy. In 1090 the city was occupied by the Turks, but it was retaken in 1096 and remained in Byzantine hands until 1304. Monuments from the 10th century onwards include a third and even smaller church on the site of St Mary, and a small chapel decorated with wall paintings on the north side of the church of St John. Neither of these buildings has been closely dated.

BIBLIOGRAPHY

J. Keil and H. Hörmann: *Die Johanneskirche* (1951), IV/iii of *Forschungen in Ephesos* (Vienna, 1906–)
P. Verzone: 'Le fasi costruttive della basilica di S Giovanni di Efeso', *Atti Pont. Accad. Romana Archeol.*, li-lii (1978–9), pp. 213–35
C. Foss: *Ephesus after Antiquity: A Late Antique, Byzantine and Turkish City* (Cambridge, 1979)
M. Büyükkolancı: 'Zwei neugefundene Bauten der Johannes-Kirche von Ephesos: Baptisterium und Skeuophylakion', *Istanbul. Mitt.*, xxxii (1982), pp. 236–57
U. Peschlow: 'Konstantinopel und Kleinasien', *Actes du XIe congrès international d'archéologie chrétienne: Lyon, Vienne, Grenoble, Genève, Aoste, 1986*, ii, pp. 1584–8

MARK WHITTOW

4. ISLAMIC. In 1304 the town that had grown up around the church of St John on Ayasuluk Hill was taken by the Turks. It became known as Ayasuluk, and it reached the height of its prosperity in the 14th century under the principality of Aydın. The Moroccan traveller Ibn Battuta, who visited the town in 1333, noted that it had 15 gates. The church of St John was used as a mosque until the mid-14th century, after which it fell into ruin. The most important monument of the Islamic period is the mosque of Isa Bey (1374; see fig. 1xxviii above and ISLAMIC ART, fig. 53), built just below St John for 'Isa ibn Muhammad ibn Aydın (*reg* 1360–90), the amir of Aydın, by 'Ali ibn al-Dimishqi ('Ali the son of the Damascene). A rectangular stone building (53×57 m), it has a central court bordered on three sides by two-storey arcades. The prayer-hall on the fourth (south) side has two aisles parallel to the qibla wall, which are intersected by a transept of two domed bays leading to the mihrab. The walls are constructed of ashlar; the minarets are of brick, and the magnificent western façade is faced with marble. Much of the material was taken from the ruins of ancient Ephesos, although such elements as the *muqarnas* and joggled voussoirs were obviously made specifically for the mosque. Many of its features, including its spacious plan, elevation and decoration with marble inlay, are foreign to Anatolian architecture and derive from earlier buildings in Syria, notably the Umayyad mosque of Damascus. The integral court of the mosque is a feature adopted by Ottoman architects for imperial mosques. In the 15th century the Aydinid amirate was annexed by the Ottomans (*reg* 1281–1924), and the town gradually fell into decline.

BIBLIOGRAPHY

Enc. Islam/2: 'Aya Soluk'
K. Otto-Dorn: 'Die Isa Bey Moschee in Ephesus', *Istanbul. Mitt.*, xvii (1950), pp. 115–31
A. Ogan: 'Aydın ogullarından Isa Bey camii' [The Aydinid mosque of 'Isa Bey], *Vakıflar Derg.*, iii (1956), pp. 73–81

☐

II. Temple of Artemis.

The remains of two major temples, of the Archaic and Late Classical periods, were discovered by Wood between 1869 and 1874. Earlier structures, excavated by Hogarth, also survive. These include the small Temples A, B and C within the Archaic temple, in an area that has produced coins and ivory figurines. In 1987, however, Temple A was shown to be the latest structure, while B enclosed an earlier (8th century BC) *peripteros*. A 7th-century BC small square base under the north of the Archaic temple platform served a ritual purpose, while a marble building 100 Ionian feet long to the west of the temple is the 'Hekatompedos' ('hundred-footer').

The Archaic temple (*c.* 560–460 BC), also known as the Croesus Temple because King Croesus of Lydia (*reg c.* 560–547 BC) apparently paid for most of its columns, is one of the largest Greek temples ever built, although its length is still unclear (width 59.93 m). It was in the Ionic order with a total of 106 columns and, like the Heraion on Samos (*see* SAMOS, §1), was a dipteral structure. It had an adyton behind the cella, which was apparently unroofed and had a small marble shrine at its centre housing the cult statue of the goddess. The front intercolumniations were graduated, as in Egyptian temples, to make the central opening the widest. This was spanned by a 24-ton block belonging to one of the earliest known marble architraves. Pliny (*Natural History* XXXVI.xxi.96) described how the latter was raised on a ramp of sandbags and gently lowered into position by letting out the sand. The building faced west, in the Asiatic tradition. The architects were said to be the Cretan Chersiphron and his son, Metagenes, and the Samian Theodoros whose name is linked with the Heraion on Samos.

The flutes on the column shafts of the Archaic temple are separated by Doric-style arrises, rather than conventional Ionic fillets. The bases varied in form but provide early examples of the Asiatic spira (moulding), while the capitals had elongated profiles, some bearing rosettes on their volutes. The columns also incorporated sculpted blocks and drums ranging in date from *c.* 560 to 525 BC, but since they are very fragmentary and the column diameters varied considerably, it is difficult to demonstrate exactly where the latter were placed. The temple apparently established the pattern of use of Ionic mouldings, notably the cyma reversa, but also had unusually high marble simas (gutters) decorated with figural friezes. These were inspired by Asiatic terracotta simas and were begun in 530–525 BC columns. The figures themselves varied in height, indicating that there were two friezes. The larger presumably ran around the exterior of the building, while the smaller one probably faced inwards and surrounded the cella alone. This temple was burnt down by Herostratos in 356 BC.

The Late Classical temple (*c.* 350–300 BC; see fig. 5) was built with its columns placed directly above their Archaic predecessors, so that reconstructions of its plan are based largely on that of the Archaic building; again, its exact length is unclear, although it was substantially wider than its predecessor (71.74 m). It stood on a stepped base, which raised it 2.76 m above the earlier level, although the cella was sunk to its original level. The substructure itself was formed by masonry 'ribs', often incorporating Archaic material, aligned on the axes of the columns. The temple was again essentially dipteral, but a third row of columns was added to the west front. Meanwhile, the eight pronaos columns were supplemented by six in the opisthodomos that replaced the earlier adyton, giving a probable total for the building of 120 columns. The façade again had widened central intercolumniations, and ancient coins show a doorway flanked by two windows in the tympanum of the pediment to relieve the architrave over the giant spans. The columns were essentially of canonical Ionic type, but also incorporated sculpted blocks and drums that are better preserved than their Archaic counterparts (see fig. 6). The blocks clearly served as pedestals, but how the drums were used is uncertain. They may also have been pedestals or may have stood directly on top of the blocks; but they probably formed decorative tops to the column shafts, immediately below the capitals, since this scheme is attested at the Hellenistic Temple of Apollo Smintheus at Chryse in the Troas. The temple's architects were Paionios and Demetrios, the 'slave of Artemis'.

The fullest account of the Artemision was provided by Pliny (*Natural History* XXXVI.xxi.95–7 and lvi.179), but it raises numerous problems. The fact that he referred to Chersiphron (*fl* 6th century BC) as the temple's architect and to Skopas (*fl* 4th century BC) as the carver of one of the sculpted column drums without alluding to their different dates makes it unclear which elements of his account apply to which buildings. The figure of 36 sculpted columns that he cited presumably applied to the Late Classical temple but might also apply to the Archaic one; while his assertion that the temple took 120 years to complete also probably applied to the later structure but could apply to the earlier. His statement that the columns' heights were equivalent to eight lower diameters also presents problems: again it is not clear whether he is referring to the Archaic or the Late Classical temple, but

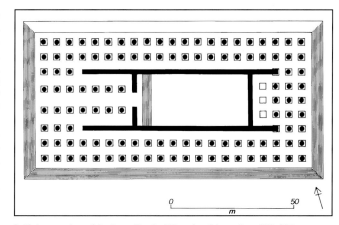

5. Ephesos, plan of the Late Classical Temple of Artemis, *c.* 350–300 BC

even for Archaic columns these proportions would be unusually squat. Finally, his figures for the temple's length and width (425×220 ft) and the columns' absolute height (60 ft) are hard to reconcile with either the Archaic or Late Classical remains.

The altar (*c.* 39.75 m×20.70 m) was of courtyard type, with a rectangular space enclosed on three sides by a podium and containing earlier foundations, probably belonging to a statue base and sacrificial hearth. Although it lay along the front of the temple and was aligned on its axis, it opened away from it, towards the west. The podium itself apparently consisted of a stone socle carved to resemble a fence, surmounted by a figural frieze and a

6. Ephesos, section of sculpted marble column from the Late Classical Temple of Artemis, h. 1.8 m, *c.* 350–300 BC (London, British Museum)

columnar structure. The temple was sacked by the Goths in the mid-3rd century AD and was abandoned after the official adoption of Christianity, subsequently becoming a source of building material for later Byzantine and Islamic structures.

BIBLIOGRAPHY

A. Bammer: *Die Architektur des jüngeren Artemision von Ephesos* (Wiesbaden, 1972)
W. Schaber: *Die archaischen Tempel der Artemis von Ephesos* (Waldsassen, 1982)
A. Bammer: *Das Heiligtum der Artemis von Ephesos* (Graz, 1984)
G. Kuhn: 'Der Altar der Artemis in Ephesos', *Mitt. Dt. Archäol. Inst.: Athen. Abt.*, xcix (1984), pp. 199–216
A. Bammer: 'Plinius und der Kroisostempel', *Jhft. Österreich. Archäol. Inst. Wien*, lvii (1986–7), pp. 13–28

ULRIKE MUSS

Ephrussi, Charles (*b* Odessa, 24 Dec 1849; *d* Paris, 30 Sept 1905). Russian collector and writer. He studied in Odessa and Vienna before settling in Paris in 1871. The following year he visited Italy and started collecting Italian Renaissance work. His interest in drawings and engravings and his desire to provide information for an enthusiastic public led to his collaboration on a catalogue of a collection of drawings bequeathed to the Louvre by Horace His de La Salle in 1878. Between 1879 and 1881 he bought about 20 contemporary paintings, including Monet's *Bathers at La Grenouillère* (1869; London, N.G.), and he was represented in Renoir's *Luncheon of the Boating Party* (1881; Washington, DC, Phillips Col.). In 1881 he stopped buying and writing about contemporary work and returned to his Renaissance studies, helping the Louvre to acquire two frescoes by Botticelli from the Villa Lemmi, Florence, in 1882 (*Lorenzo Tornabuoni Presented by Grammar to Prudentia and the Liberal Arts* and *Giovanna degli Albizzi Receiving Flowers from Venus*; both *c.* 1486). He was an early admirer of Japanese art and in 1892 organized an exhibition of early 19th-century work before it became fashionable in France. He had been writing for the *Gazette des Beaux-Arts* since 1875 and was its effective director from October 1894, at a time when it became a focus for art scholarship in Paris.

BIBLIOGRAPHY

'Bibliographie des ouvrages de Charles Ephrussi', *Chron. A. & Curiosité*, xxxiii (1905), pp. 275–7
A. Marguillier: 'Charles Ephrussi', *Gaz. B.-A.*, 3rd ser., xxxiv (1905), pp. 353–60
P. Kolb and J. Adhemar: 'Charles Ephrussi (1849–1905); ses secrétaires: Laforgue, A. Renan, Proust: "Sa" Gazette des Beaux-Arts', *Gaz. B.-A.*, 6th ser., ciii (1984), pp. 29–41

☐

Ephyra. Sanctuary in Thesprotia, north-western Greece, near the mouth of the River Acheron. It includes an acropolis with the remains of a Late Bronze Age settlement and cemetery, but it was chiefly important in Classical and Hellenistic times for its Nekyomanteion ('oracle of the dead') dedicated to Persephone and Hades. This was situated at the confluence of the Acheron and Kokytos, where Odysseus was supposed to have entered the underworld to meet the shade of Teiresias (*Odyssey* X.513–15), and though the sanctuary's remains date to the 3rd century BC they provide evidence for a ritual strikingly similar to that followed by Odysseus himself. They comprise a large irregular enclosure containing a series of rooms round a courtyard on the west side of the hill, and the main sanctuary building to the east, on the very top of the hill. The shrine building, with massive side walls, was approached by a corridor running along its north and east sides before turning along the south side through a maze-like sequence of arched doorways. Consultation of the oracle was preceded by ritual incubation and bathing in rooms off the north corridor, burnt sacrifices in the east corridor and offerings of white barley in the maze. From here the suppliant entered the central hall, which is flanked by three rooms on each side containing storage jars, wheat, barley and other foodstuffs. Under the central hall was a vaulted crypt representing the underworld. The sanctuary was destroyed in 168 BC during the Roman sack of Epiros.

BIBLIOGRAPHY

S. I. Dakaris: 'The Dark Palace of Hades', *Archaeology*, xv (1962), pp. 85–93
——: 'Das Taubenorakel von Dodona und das Totenorakel bei Ephyra', *Neue Ausgrabungen in Griechenland*, ed. H. A. Cahn and others (Basle, 1963), pp. 35–54
——: 'Anaskaphe sto Nekyomanteio tou Acherontos' [Excavation of the oracle of the dead on the Acheron], *Praktika Athen. Archaiol. Etaireias* (1976), pp. 146–9

Epidamnos. *See* DYRRHACHION.

Epidauros. Site on the south side of the Saronic Gulf in Greece that flourished especially in the 4th and 3rd centuries BC. Though traces of the ancient city exist, its fame derives from the Sanctuary of Asklepios *c.* 10 km inland from Epidauros town, which was the principal cult-centre of the healing god in mainland Greece (see fig. 1). Here there are remains of a Bronze Age settlement, later abandoned, and an early sanctuary of Apollo. Until the end of the 5th century BC the place was of little importance and architecturally undistinguished. The cult of Asklepios began to develop significantly only at this time, perhaps because of the plague that devastated Athens and adjacent regions in the early 420s BC and the general malaise that resulted from the Peloponnesian War between Athens and Sparta (431–404 BC). With the exception of the theatre, the sanctuary buildings are badly ruined. The site was excavated principally by the Greek archaeologist P. Kavvadias.

1. ARCHITECTURE. The architectural development of the sanctuary at Epidauros belongs to the 4th and 3rd centuries BC, when the efficacy of the healing ritual attracted funds from a wide area (Epidauros, an unimportant city, could not have afforded to develop the sanctuary from its own resources). The level of support never equalled that enjoyed by the major established sanctuaries such as Delphi, and many of the buildings were constructed from comparatively cheap material; marble, which had to be imported from Athens, was used sparingly.

The Temple of Asklepios (1a; *see also* GREECE, ANCIENT, fig. 10) was built largely of Corinthian limestone in the space of four years, as the building accounts attest. Its exact date is uncertain, but it was probably built between 387 and 371 BC. It is in the Doric order (6 by 11 columns), the width being approximately half the length; these proportions are found in earlier temples in this part of Greece, though here there is no opisthodomos (rear false porch) to the cella. Its internal columns were probably

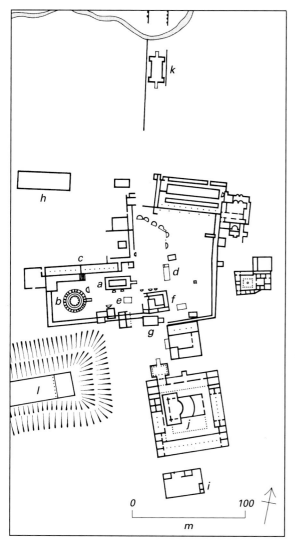

1. Epidauros, plan of the Sanctuary of Asklepios, 4th–3rd centuries BC: (a) Temple of Asklepios; (b) thymele; (c) abaton; (d) Altar of Asklepios; (e) Altar of Apollo; (f) early precinct of Asklepios; (g) Temple of Artemis; (h) cistern; (i) bath building; (j) banqueting hall and Roman odeion; (k) propylon; (l) stadium

Corinthian, and it was approached at the east end by a ramp. (For its sculptural decoration *see* §2 below.)

Close to the west end of the temple was an elaborately decorated circular Doric building, the thymele (or tholos; 1b), again with a ramped approach. Its peristyle and interior had ornamental ceilings with carved flowers inside stone coffers (for illustration *see* COFFERING), and the metopes outside were carved with rosettes. The cella had a compass-patterned floor of black limestone and white marble with an internal Corinthian colonnade; an opening in the centre of the floor gives access to a circular pit, from which it was possible to enter the concentric rings of the foundations. The size and splendour of this building emphasise its importance in the cult. Its exact function is disputed, but it was probably a cenotaph for the mortal

Asklepios, while the temple belonged to Asklepios the god. Its construction (between *c.* 360 and *c.* 320 BC) was protracted because of a shortage of funds.

On the north side of the temple is the abaton (1c), a 4th-century BC stoa extended in Roman times, in which the sick who had come to Epidauros to be healed passed the night, during which they hoped to receive a curative visitation from the god. There are two altars in this part of the sanctuary. One, in front of the temple, was that of Asklepios himself (1d), the other, by the south side, is significantly earlier and belonged to Apollo (1e). East of this is an earlier building (later 5th century BC; 1f), square in plan, with porticos on the north and east side of an inner courtyard. Its function is uncertain, but it may have been the precinct for the cult of Asklepios before the 4th-century BC embellishment of the sanctuary. By its south side is a small late 4th-century BC Temple of Artemis (1g) with six prostyle Doric columns.

These buildings form the nucleus of the sanctuary and are surrounded by other structures. Some of these were utilitarian, providing the abundant water supply apparently essential to the cult. They include a large cistern (1h), its roof supported by transverse arches; deep wells, possibly provided with lifting machinery to raise the water; and fountain houses fed from natural springs. The special water supply arrangements near the abaton were presumably for ritual cleansing, and a pressurized fountain in the form of a statue stood in front of the temple. A building at the southern extremity of the sanctuary appears to have housed baths (1i). These facilities existed in the earliest days of the sanctuary, though they were enlarged and improved in the 4th or 3rd century BC; most of them received later reconstruction.

Between the bath building and the centre of the sanctuary is a large courtyard structure (1j), probably dating from *c.* 300 BC, with an interior peristyle of 16 by 16 Doric columns fronting rooms on all four sides. A splendid entrance porch faced the temple, with a ramped approach and Doric façade. Kavvadias interpreted this building as a gymnasium. The ramped approach, however, found also at the temple and thymele, suggests a sacred function involving processions. The dimensions of several rooms, the position of their doors, and supports for plank couches show that the building was used for the ritual feasting so important in Greek religion. In the 2nd century AD a small odeion was constructed in the courtyard, incorporating some of the colonnade. The main entrance was then converted into a temple, and a new entrance constructed through one of the dining-rooms on the east side. Also from the early 3rd century BC is the propylon on the north side of the sanctuary (1k), marking the end of the processional road from Epidauros. This was a formal architectural flourish, with inner and outer hexastyle Ionic façades; but there is no separating crosswall and no actual doors, and the whole building could be passed on either side.

Athletic and artistic contests were an important part of the festival in this sanctuary. The running track was developed as a formal stadium (1l), with stone seating, probably in the 3rd century BC. On its north side it was linked to the heart of the sanctuary by a vaulted tunnel. The most important surviving structure at Epidauros is without doubt the great theatre (*see* GREECE, ANCIENT, fig. 26). Its auditorium, still virtually intact, was built in the second half of the 4th century BC. The seating, of local limestone, is divided into lower and upper sections, the lower extending beyond the upper, perhaps as a result of later work. The stage building is ruined, though its essential arrangement, with side ramps leading to the stage, is clear enough. Pausanias (*Guide to Greece* II.xxvii.5) attributed the theatre (and the thymele) to Polykleitos. This cannot be the 5th-century BC Argive sculptor but may be his grandson.

The sanctuary flourished throughout the Hellenistic period but was plundered in the 1st century BC. By the 2nd century AD many of the buildings were ruined, particularly those with mud-brick walls. Thoroughgoing reconstruction, much of it in baked brick and mortar, was financed by wealthy Roman devotees. The small theatre in the large courtyard of the banqueting building was part of this and may reflect the earlier use of the courtyard for musical or dramatic performances. Two substantial bath buildings were constructed by the abaton and on the east side of the sanctuary, and the sanctuary was well provided with rectangular and semicircular stone seats. After the 2nd-century AD renewal the sanctuary continued to flourish, even surviving the Roman acceptance of Christianity (4th century AD). The cult, however, associated with resurrection and with a god who was also once a man, came to be seen as a blasphemous parody of Christianity, which probably caused the thorough destruction of the sanctuary. Only the theatre remained well preserved, perhaps because it was buried by landslips.

BIBLIOGRAPHY

A. Defrasse and H. Lechat: *Epidaure: Restauration et description des principaux monuments du sanctuaire d'Asclépios* (Paris, 1895)
P. Kavvadias: *To ieron tou Asklepiou en Epidauro* [The Sanctuary of Asklepios at Epidauros] (Athens, 1900)
F. Robert: *Thymele* (Paris, 1939)
E. J. Edelstein and L. Edelstein: *Asclepius: A Collection and Interpretation of the Testimonies* (Baltimore, 1945)
A. von Gerkan and W. Müller-Wiener: *Das Theater von Epidauros* (Stuttgart, 1961)
G. Roux: *L'Architecture de l'Argolide aux IVe et IIIe siècles avant JC* (Paris, 1961)
A. Burford: *The Greek Temple Builders at Epidauros* (Liverpool, 1969)
R. A. Tomlinson: 'Two Buildings in Sanctuaries of Asklepios', *J. Hell. Stud.*, lxxxix (1969), pp. 106–17
——: *Epidauros* (London, 1983)

R. A. TOMLINSON

2. SCULPTURE. The fragmentary sculptural remains from the Temple of Asklepios at Epidauros are of special interest because of an incomplete inscription pertaining to specific expenditures made during its construction. This inscription, from the first quarter of the 4th century BC, suggests that Hektoridas and another artist whose name is lost carved the two pediments, that TIMOTHEOS (who later collaborated with other sculptors on the Mausoleum of Halikarnassos) and a second artist, Theo- (incomplete), sculpted the two sets of acroteria, and that Timotheos executed other reliefs, the purpose of which is unknown. Payments made for *typoi* (?models) in the inscription have led to suggestions that Timotheos supplied the models for the pedimental sculptures.

Battle scenes decorated the pediments: an *Amazonomachy* on the western pediment (*see* GREECE, ANCIENT, fig. 63) and either the *Fall of Troy* or a *Centauromachy* on the east. Fragments suggest that the figures were slightly over life-size; those of the western pediment were smaller than those of the east. It is probable that the metopes were painted rather than sculpted. Two of the three best preserved acroteria (of six) represent *Nereids* or *Aurai* (breezes) (see fig. 2); the delicacy of their drapery has been compared with that of the figures of the Athena Nike balustrade in Athens (*c.* 415 BC), although its density in some areas anticipates the fully developed Late Classical style. These equestrian figures, each mounted sideways with an arm around her horse's neck, were most likely the corner acroteria from the western side and are generally attributed to Timotheos. A figure of *Nike* holding a bird was probably the central acroterion from the same side.

Thrasymedes of Paros is believed to have executed the lost chryselephantine cult statue of Asklepios (Pausanias: *Guide to Greece* II.xxvii.2). Not mentioned in the building inscription, it was most likely produced after the completion of the temple; stylistic considerations both from Pausanias' description and from representations on coinage suggest that it was executed *c.* 375 BC. Asklepios, his dog by his side, sat on a throne holding a staff in one hand and held his other hand above a serpent. The throne reliefs depicted *Bellerophon and the Chimera* as well as *Perseus*

2. Epidauros, marble acroterion of an *Aurai* or a *Nereid* on horseback, probably by Timotheos, h. 781 mm, from the west façade of the Temple of Asklepios, *c.* 380 BC (Athens, National Archaeological Museum)

Decapitating Medusa. According to Pausanias, Thrasymedes' figure was half the size of the 'Olympian Zeus at Athens', perhaps the Athenian copy of Pheidias' cult statue in the Temple of Zeus at Olympia.

Some of the sculptures from the Temple of Asklepios remain in the local museum, but most have been moved to the National Archaeological Museum in Athens. Other sculptures from Epidauros (all 4th century BC; Athens, N. Archaeol. Mus.) include figures (mostly statues of Nike) from the Temple of Artemis, lion-headed spouts from the thymele, a statue of *Hygieia* and a small statue of *Asklepios*.

BIBLIOGRAPHY

G. M. A. Richter: *The Sculpture and Sculptors of the Greeks* (New Haven, 1929, 4/1970)

J. F. Crome: *Die Skulpturen des Asklepiostempels von Epidauros* (Berlin, 1951)

ANN THOMAS WILKINS

Epigonos. *See under* ISIGONOS, EPIGONOS, STRATONIKOS AND ANTIGONOS.

Epikman, Refik (Fazıl) (*b* Istanbul, 1902; *d* ?Ankara, 1974). Turkish painter. He studied at the Fine Arts Academy in Istanbul, graduating in 1924 and then went to Paris where he worked under the painter Paul-Albert Laurens (1870–1934) at the Académie Julien until 1928. On returning to Istanbul he was a founder-member of the Association of Independent Painters and Sculptors (Müstakil ressamlar ve heykeltraşlar birliği) in 1928 and became assistant teacher at the Fine Arts Academy. His paintings of this period, for example *The Bar* (c. 1930; Istanbul, Mimar Sinan U., Mus. Ptg & Sculp.), were notable for introducing new European ideas, and Epikman was acknowledged as at the forefront of modernism in Turkey. He settled in Ankara in 1932 to teach in the new art department at the Gazi Teachers' College, where he was influential on a younger generation of Turkish painters. His works included a number of large-scale paintings dealing with the Turkish War of Independence and Atatürk. After World War II he participated with several other Turkish artists at the Exposition Internationale d'Art Moderne, organized by UNESCO at the Musée d'Art Moderne in Paris in 1946. He continued to keep abreast of modern developments in painting and from *c.* 1962 began to work in a geometric abstract style. His later work included *Antique Abstraction* (c. 1958; Istanbul, Mimar Sinan U., Mus. Ptg & Sculp.).

BIBLIOGRAPHY

S. Tansuğ: *Çağdaş Türk sanatı* [Contemporary Turkish art] (Istanbul, 1986)

G. Renda and others: *A History of Turkish Painting* (Geneva, Seattle and London, 1988), pp. 183–4, 288

Epiktetos. *See* VASE PAINTERS, §II.

Epinay, Prosper, Comte d' (*b* Port Louis, Mauritius, 13 July 1836; *d* Paris, 23 Sept 1914). French sculptor. He was born a British subject and was the son of a prominent advocate in Mauritius. From 1857 to 1860 he studied caricature with the sculptor Jean-Pierre Dantan in Paris, and in 1861 he worked in the Rome studio of Luigi Amici (1813–97). He was active in Rome and London between 1864 and 1874 but from the mid-1870s increasingly turned his attention from London to Paris. He maintained a studio in Mauritius, producing statues of his father and of the late governor, *Sir William Stevenson* (bronze, 1865; Port Louis, Jardins de la Compagnie). In England his bust of *Edward, Prince of Wales* (bronze, 1912; Port Louis, Champ de Mars), executed from memory, was purchased by Queen Victoria, and from then until 1881 he exhibited at the Royal Academy, London. With the exhibition of the coquettish nude the *Golden Girdle* (exh. Salon 1874; marble version, St Petersburg, Hermitage), reminiscent of the 18th century and the FONTAINEBLEAU SCHOOL, Epinay won the attention of the Paris public. He shared with his equally well-connected contemporary, the sculptress Marcello, a tendency to period pastiche, especially in his female portrait busts, which imitate the emphatic verticality and elaborate coiffures of Jean-Antoine Houdon and Augustin Pajou. A concession to Realism is found in the stress on ethnicity in some of his biblical and literary subjects, such as the *Young Hannibal Strangling the Eagle* (exh. RA 1869; bronze version, Duke of Westminster priv. col.).

BIBLIOGRAPHY

P. Roux: *Prosper d'Epinay: Sa vie, son oeuvre* (MA thesis, U. Paris IV, 1981)

PHILIP WARD-JACKSON

Epiphania. *See* HAMA.

Episcopius, Joannes. *See* BISSCHOP, JAN DE.

Episkopi. *See under* KOURION.

Epistolary. *See under* SERVICE BOOK.

Epistyle [epistylium]. Structural beam or architrave, sometimes wood, laid horizontally over the capitals of a column to form a central interior support.

□

Epitaph [Gr.: 'on a tomb']. Term commonly applied in France, Germany, the Low Countries and Central Europe to a church funerary monument of modest dimensions bearing a memorial inscription. (In English usage, 'epitaph' signifies the inscription alone.) From the mid-16th century increasing numbers of clerics, scholars and members of the middle classes came to be commemorated by monuments in churches; accordingly, a variety of forms of memorial arose. The rise of the epitaph was largely owing to the demand for cheaper monuments that reflected the social hierarchy of burial and remembrance: small tablets took up less space than the effigial tombs of the gentry and nobility, and their modesty reflected an attitude of social deference. Continental epitaphs tended to portray the commemorated persons, sometimes with their family, generally kneeling in supplication before representations of sacred themes; they thus continued the medieval tradition of sepulchral portraiture and thereby provided an important place for religious iconography in Protestant—above all Lutheran—churches. Like Catholic ex-votos, epitaphs combined secular portraiture with sacred representations. They succeeded in surviving the iconoclasm of the Reformation by emphasizing the piety of the

1. Epitaph to *Sigismund Pucher* by an anonymous artist, stone relief, *c.* 1580 (Moosburg, St Castulus)

Sigismund Pucher (*c.* 1580; Moosburg, St Castulus, see fig. 1). In depicting his subject at prayer at the foot of the cross the anonymous sculptor followed a very common pattern, which remained popular well into the next century. The baptism of Christ was yet another popular subject, owing to the Lutheran emphasis on baptism as a token of salvation: Spranger's painted *Hannewaldt* epitaph (*c.* 1600; Wrocław, N. Mus.) is a particularly distinguished example. Other subjects included the coronation of the Virgin, a sculpted relief of which occurs on the epitaph (Passau, Cathedral) by Christoph Murmann (1564/5–1630) to *Canon Johann Gienger von Wolfsegg* (*d* 1612), and the prophet Ezekiel's vision of the valley of dry bones (Ezekiel 37). This subject was well suited to a memorial, since the resurrection of the bones was taken to prefigure the rising of the dead at Doomsday; it is depicted, flanked by kneeling figures, on the painted *Schadius* epitaph of 1588 in St Mary, Gdańsk. Such representations tended to be formulaic, with local workshops producing numerous repetitions of established patterns.

Epitaphs of this kind were most commonly carried out in stone. Cast reliefs in metal were very rare, while epitaphs painted on board were comparatively infrequent and prone to later destruction. A very rare English example of this essentially continental type of monument is the epitaph to deceased rather than the worship of holy images. Protestant epitaphs fostered remembrance rather than veneration; with the abolition of the concept of purgatory they, as well as other types of monument, ceased to request prayers of intercession.

The most common religious subjects represented on epitaphs were those that alluded to man's salvation through Christ and the resurrection on the Day of Judgement. Christ's resurrection was perhaps the most popular subject: an example is Pieter Pourbus's painted epitaph of *Soyer van Marle* (*d* 1578; Bruges, St Jacobskerk). Bartholomäus Spranger's epitaph of *Nikolaus Müller* (*d* 1588; Prague, N.G., convent of St George) depicted the risen Christ triumphing over sin and death, with the deceased and his family portrayed beneath. This painting on canvas was originally set within a sculpted framework by Adriaen de Vries, a notable instance of the combination of painted and sculpted components by celebrated artists that was most frequently encountered in the late 16th century. Another very popular image for epitaphs was the crucifixion, a good instance of which is the relief epitaph to

2. Design for an epitaph by Nicolas Blasset, engraved by Jean Lenfant, from *Les Epitaphes inventés par N. Blasset d'Amiens* (Paris, 1640s) (London, Victoria and Albert Museum)

Edmund Bunny (*d* 1618) in York Minster, depicting this cleric at prayer beside an open grave, a reference to his professed contempt for the fear of death. This stoical sentiment is frequently found on epitaphs, serving to deflect the criticism that memorials celebrated worldly achievement rather than hope of heaven. In the 17th century painted epitaphs became less common throughout Europe, because of the reaction against bright colouring in church monuments and the desire to commemorate individuals in a more sober, classicizing way. Parallel to this was the general tendency of church monuments to expand their variety of format and their range of sepulchral imagery. This became less specifically Christian and was concerned as much with a retrospective celebration of the virtues and accomplishments of the deceased as with the prospect of the life to come. The relatively humble nature of epitaphs made for an innate conservatism in appearance and content; in both aspects they lagged behind tendencies in the monumental style of the 17th century.

Stylistically, epitaphs reflected prevalent architectural tastes and invited comparisons with contemporary architectural designs. In the 16th century they tended to consist of predominant visual elements and an inscription, set within a modest frame or cartouche. In the 17th century this setting tended to become more elaborate, at the expense of pictorial imagery. This development is reflected in a number of 17th-century books of designs for epitaphs, such as Nicolas Blasset's *Les Epitaphes inventés par N. Blasset d'Amiens* (1640s; see fig. 2).

BIBLIOGRAPHY
A. Weckwerth: 'Der Ursprung des Bildepitaphs', *Z. Kstgesch.*, xx (1957), pp. 147–85

ROGER BOWDLER

Epitaphios [*epitaphion*; Gr.: 'on the tomb']. Term used to indicate a number of related items, first among them the iconographical theme of the Lamentation (Gr. *epitaphios threnos*), the earliest example of which is on an 11th-century Byzantine ivory panel (Konstanz, Rosgtnmus.). In Lamentation scenes Christ is usually depicted lying flat on a stone, clothed only in a loincloth, surrounded by the mourning figures of Joseph of Arimathaea, Nicodemus, the Virgin and St Mary Magdalene. This iconography gradually developed out of depictions of the Entombment, but whereas in the latter scene Joseph is shown holding Christ, in the Lamentation it is the Virgin who embraces him.

The epitaphios (Rus. *plashchanitsa*) is also the cloth used during the liturgy on Good Friday in Orthodox churches. It is first recorded in the 14th century, when it served the same function as an *aër*: a cloth with a representation of the dead Christ that was used during the liturgy to cover the Eucharist. The ceremony of bringing the bread and wine to the altar symbolizes the entombment of Christ and is illustrated by representations of the Divine Liturgy in domes of Byzantine churches from the 14th century. In these representations Christ is shown acting as a bishop receiving the holy gifts from a procession of angels, some of whom are carrying the *aër* or epitaphios on their heads, as in the 16th-century painting of the *Divine Liturgy* by Theophanes the Cretan in the dome of the Katholikon in Stavronikita Monastery, Mt Athos. The function of the *aër* has since changed, and it has become a much smaller, more simply decorated cloth, worn on the shoulders of the priest carrying the eucharist, while the epitaphios has kept its original shape and is only used on Good Friday. It can vary in size from *c.* 600×500 mm to 1.50×1.20 m, and is embroidered, often in silver and gold thread, with the *epitaphios threnos*. Lamentation scenes have been divided into historical and liturgical types. In the historical epitaphios the Lamentation is depicted as described above, whereas in the liturgical epitaphios the dead Christ is surrounded by cherubim, serafim and angels holding rhipidia with the symbols of the Evangelists in the corners (e.g. 14th century; Kynii, Euboia, St Athanasios; Athens, Byz. Mus.). Numerous embroidered epitaphioi combine elements from both types (*see* EARLY CHRISTIAN AND BYZANTINE ART, fig. 95).

During the evening service on Good Friday in the Orthodox Church the epitaphios is carried through the northern door of the iconostasis and put on a flower-covered shrine in the middle of the church symbolizing the burial of Christ. This ritual is also called epitaphios.

BIBLIOGRAPHY
K. Weitzmann: 'The Origin of the Threnos', *De Artibus Opuscula XL: Essays in Honour of Erwin Panofsky*, ed. M. Meiss (New York, 1961), pp. 476–90
J. Myslivec: 'Epitaphios', *Lexikon der christlichen Ikonographie*, ed. E. Kirschbaum, i (Freiburg im Breisgau, 1968), cols 654–5
M. Theochari: 'Ta chrysokentita amphia tis I. Monis Stavronikita' [The gold embroidered vestments of the Holy Stavronikita Monastery], *Moni Stavronikita*, ed. Ch. Patrineli (Athens, 1974), pp. 143–6
H. J. Schulz: *Die byzantinische Liturgie* (Trier, 1980), pp. 181–2
K. Onasch: *Kunst und Liturgie der Ostkirche in Stichworten* (Vienna, 1981), p. 107
Byzantine and Post-Byzantine Art (exh. cat. by M. Acheimastou-Potamianou and others, Athens, Mus. U., 1985–6)
M. Chatzidakis: *The Cretan Painter Theophanes* (Mt Athos, 1986)

KAREL C. INNEMÉE

Epstein, Sir Jacob (*b* New York, 10 Nov 1880; *d* London, 19 Aug 1959). British sculptor of American birth. Although he spent his childhood in New York, Epstein defined his identity as an artist only after moving to London in 1905. He had studied at the Arts Students League in New York before moving to the Académie Julien in Paris. His first two years in London remain relatively obscure, but in 1907 the architect Charles Holden invited him to execute a major commission for the new headquarters of the British Medical Association in The Strand (now Zimbabwe House). Holden and Epstein were united by their enthusiasm for Walt Whitman's poetry, and they agreed that 18 large figures should be carved for the building's façade, celebrating nakedness in the spirit of Whitman's poems. Epstein himself announced that the scheme would celebrate 'the great primal facts of man and woman', and he managed to fuse the 'medical' side of the commission with his own most personal preoccupations: erotic delight, mortality, motherhood, virility and above all an uninhibited celebration of humanity in dignified nakedness. The National Vigilance Society, affronted by his figure of *Maternity*, started a vituperative press campaign to have the carvings removed. The assault nearly succeeded, and Epstein became notorious. However, the combined support of eminent artists, critics and museum directors saved

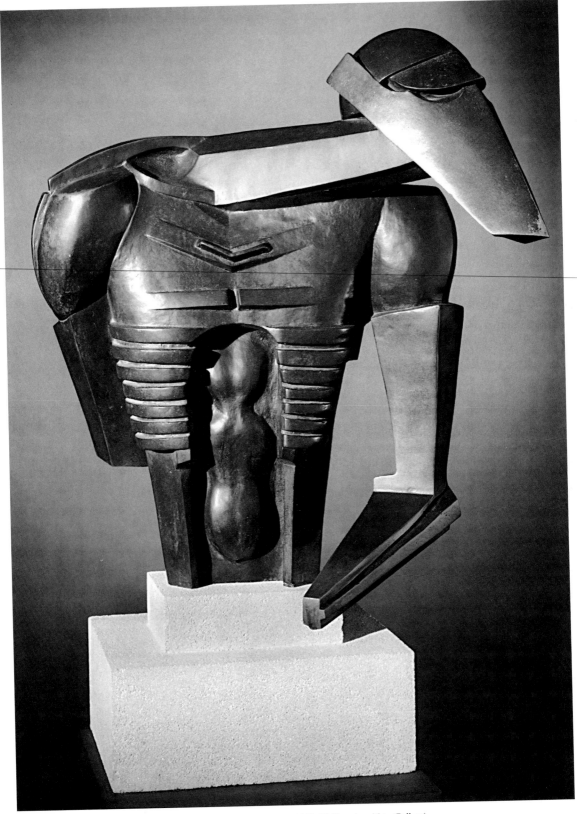

Jacob Epstein: torso in metal from *Rock Drill*, bronze, h. 940 mm, 1913–16 (London, Tate Gallery)

the statues for the time being, although they were severely mutilated 20 years later, when the building's disapproving new owners declared that their condition was unsafe.

At this early stage in his career Epstein's prime loyalties lay with an awkward blend of Classical, Renaissance and Rodinesque sources. His monumental tomb of *Oscar Wilde*, installed in Père-Lachaise Cemetery in Paris in 1912, relied on an overt quotation from the British Museum's Assyrian half-human winged sculptures, which served as guardian-figures at gates. The contrast between the ornate cluster of images on the flying figure's bizarre headdress and the austere cubic simplicity of the tomb's overall masses is symptomatic of a conflict in Epstein's own imagination. Attracted by severe restraint and outspoken symbolism alike, he was determined to incorporate both in the tomb. Having viewed the work at Epstein's Cheyne Walk studio in London before it was transported to Paris, one critic in the *Evening Standard* (3 June 1912) decided that 'There is nothing to destroy the effect of a rectangular block of stone that has felt itself into expression.'

Epstein's desire to honour the existing identity of the stone, and to cultivate a close relationship with his materials through direct carving, was shared by his friend Eric Gill. While Gill was attracted by Indian sculpture, Epstein's trip to Paris for the installation of the Wilde tomb brought him into contact with Modigliani, Picasso, Brancusi and other radical artists. They confirmed his interest in the non-Western carvings that he had already admired in the British Museum. In 1913 his flenite figures of pregnant women took on an openly 'barbaric' identity. His sequence of copulating doves in marble proved no less controversial, but Ezra Pound was quick to defend them when Epstein found himself under attack during his first one-man show at the Twenty-One Gallery, London (Dec 1913–Jan 1914). He also befriended T. E. Hulme and many of the Vorticists, contributing two illustrations to the first issue of *Blast* in 1914.

Epstein never became a member of the Vorticist movement, preferring like David Bomberg to remain independent of Wyndham Lewis's leadership. However, in the successive stages of his most ambitious pre-war sculpture, *Rock Drill*, he explored concerns that brought him very close to the Vorticists' involvement with the machine age. The first stage of the sculpture, developed in a series of powerful drawings, presents the driller as a heroic figure straddling the drill in gaunt yet epic surroundings. The forcefulness was retained when Epstein, with great audacity, purchased a second-hand drill on a tripod and mounted his own plaster figure of a driller on the ready-made base. This version of the sculpture, which was exhibited in all its unsettling starkness at the London Group in March 1915, already contained the figure of an embryo inside the driller's mechanistic rib-cage. Epstein was anxious to explore, in symbolic terms, his fears about the future of the human race in the machine age, and his alarm was confirmed by the devastation of World War I. By the time he displayed the final version of *Rock Drill* (1913–16; London, Tate; see fig.) in June 1916 at the London Group show, the drill had been discarded and the driller himself reduced to a maimed, pitiful victim, hunched and deprived of his legs and hands.

Epstein's shifting attitude towards the machine age is summarized in the various stages of *Rock Drill*, and after the war he moved away from angular semi-abstraction to develop a more figurative and warmly humanist vision. He began modelling portrait busts, establishing so great a reputation that a long succession of distinguished sitters commissioned him to depict them in vigorously characterized bronzes. In 1954 he was knighted. Alongside his portraiture, embracing notable figures from Joseph Conrad to Winston Churchill, Epstein continued to carve on a monumental scale with much of his earlier interest in brusque distortion and brazen sexuality. Some of his finest later carvings were executed for public locations, such as the *Rima* memorial in Hyde Park, London, and the colossal figures of *Night* and *Day* commissioned by Charles Holden for the headquarters of the Underground Railway Company at St James's Park Station, London, in 1928. Both these ventures proved so controversial that Epstein received few public commissions in succeeding years, however. Great carvings such as *Elemental* (1932; priv. col., see 1987 exh. cat., p. 67) or *Jacob and the Angel* (1939–40; Granada Television Ltd, on loan to London, Tate) were essentially private works, mocked by many and only now admired as intense expressions of his sensual yet profoundly religious vision. After World War II he enjoyed a greater degree of acclaim, and among his many commissions perhaps the most outstanding are a *Madonna and Child* (1950–52) in Cavendish Square, London, and the *TUC War Memorial* (1959) in Great Russell Street, London.

WRITINGS

with A. L. Haskell: *The Sculptor Speaks: Jacob Epstein to Arnold L. Haskell: A Series of Conversations on Art* (London, 1931)
Let There Be Sculpture: An Autobiography (London, 1940)

BIBLIOGRAPHY

L. B. Powell: *Jacob Epstein* (London, 1932)
Jacob Epstein: Memorial Exhibition (exh. cat., ed. J. Rothenstein; ACGB, 1961)
Lady Kathleen Epstein and R. Buckle: *Epstein Drawings* (London, 1962)
R. Buckle: *Jacob Epstein: Sculptor* (London, 1963)
Jacob Epstein: The Rock Drill Period (exh. cat. by R. Cork, London, Anthony d'Offay Gal., 1973)
R. Cork: *Vorticism and Abstract Art in the First Machine Age*, 2 vols (London, 1975–6)
Epstein Centenary, 1980 (exh. cat. by A. Haskell, London, Ben Uri A.G., 1980)
E. Silber: *The Sculpture of Jacob Epstein* (Oxford, 1986)
E. Bassani and M. D. Mcleod: *Jacob Epstein, Collector* (London, 1987)
Jacob Epstein: Sculpture and Drawings (exh. cat., ed. T. Friedman and E. Silber; Leeds, C.A.G.; London, Whitechapel A.G., 1987)
S. Gardiner: *Epstein: Artist Against the Establishment* (London, 1992)

RICHARD CORK

Equatorial Guinea, Republic of [República de Guinea Ecuatorial; formerly Spanish Guinea]. Country in West Africa consisting of the island of Biogo (formerly Macias Nguema Biyoga; Fernando Po(o)) in the Bight of Biafra, Pagalu Island (formerly Annobon) in the Gulf of Guinea, the Corisco Islands (Corisco, Elobey Grande and Elobey Chico) and Rio Muni, a square area on the mainland between Cameroon and Gabon. The total area of the country is 26,051 sq. km and the total population 341,000 (UN estimate, 1989). The capital is Malabo (formerly Santa Isabel) on the island of Biogo; it is an attractive port city, with Spanish-style plazas with churches, situated on the slanting base of a huge volcano, Mt Malabo. The territories of modern Equatorial Guinea were formerly Spanish colonies. They were constituted as two provinces of Metropolitan Spain in 1960 and became independent in 1968. The anglicized creole population compete with the local Bubi people for the coffee wealth of Biogo, while the Fang dominate Rio Muni and the surrounding areas of Gabon and Cameroon.

Equatorial Guinea's best-known artist is the sculptor Leandro Mbomio Nsue (b 1938). Both his father and his grandfather were sculptors in the FANG tradition, but he himself received his formal art training in Spain, where he was an exile for many years. He later returned to Equatorial Guinea to become his country's Minister of Culture. Unusually for a modern African sculptor, Mbomio Nsue works in wood, and his works may be placed within the European modernist tradition. Information on other practising artists and the art scene in general is very limited (for a list of practising artists and art institutions see Guez, pp. 78–9).

For discussion of the art of the region see AFRICA, §VII, 5.

BIBLIOGRAPHY

C. Arean: *Leandro Mbomio en la integración de la negritud* (Madrid, 1975)
Africa Explores: 20th Century African Art (exh. cat. by S. Vogel, New York, Cent. Afr. A., 1991), pp. 179, 195
N. Guez: *L'Art africain contemporain/Contemporary African Art: Guide Edition, 92–94* (Paris, 1992)

DANIEL J. CROWLEY

Equestrian monument. Form of sculpture featuring a horse and rider. The problem with any statue of a quadruped is the lack of support in the legs for the weight of the body, and this is exacerbated if the animal has a rider. Such an image, if genuinely free-standing, is all but impossible to carve in stone or marble. In Verona the sculptors of the stone tombs of the della Scala family (c. 1277–1387; front of S Maria Antica; see VERONA, fig. 5) dealt with the need for extra physical support in two ways: in the statue of *Cangrande I della Scala* (d 1329) the caparison of the horse is draped over all four legs and serves to stabilize them, while in the monument to *Cansignorio della Scala* (d 1277) the horse's legs are free, but a small column unashamedly supports its chest. Most other equestrian figures of the early Renaissance period were erected over wall-tombs, so that they could be keyed back into the rear wall and supported by hidden struts; moreover, they were often fashioned in wood, which is lighter and more resilient than stone (e.g. monument to *Paolo Savelli*, c. 1406; Venice, S Maria Gloriosa dei Frari). By contrast, for a true free-standing equestrian monument out of doors, with no artificial support for its legs, neither wood nor stone is suitable, owing to rotting or weathering; since ancient times sculptors have had to resort to bronze, the material hallowed by antiquity and recommended by its evident capacity for survival. This alloy has great tensile strength, enabling the horse's legs to withstand the strains imposed by the weight of horse and rider, especially when buffeted by the wind. Furthermore, it is possible—indeed, it is a fundamental part of the process of modelling and casting—to have a stout iron armature running up inside the bronze; its extremities, projecting downwards from the legs, can be firmly cemented into the pedestal. The same technique can be applied to a rearing horse: there the tail is usually contrived to touch the ground behind the rear legs, thus permitting a third, concealed prop.

1. Classical. 2. Early Renaissance. 3. High Renaissance and Baroque. 4. 18th century and after.

1. CLASSICAL. From a technical point of view, the equestrian monument is the most challenging form of sculpture to have survived from antiquity. Of the two known Classical examples, the monument to the Roman emperor *Marcus Aurelius* (AD 166–80; Rome, Mus. Conserv.; see ROME, ANCIENT, fig. 61) seems to have survived the iconoclasm of pagan monuments in the early Middle Ages because it was traditionally believed to represent Constantine the Great, the first Christian emperor. For centuries it enjoyed great international authority as one of the wonders of the Eternal City, owing to its former prominent location in the Piazza del Campidoglio, Rome. The other example, the *Regisole* ('Sun King'), formerly in Pavia (destr. 1796), is known only from a woodcut of 1505 and from descriptions. The other important examples of Classical horses—but without riders—are the *Horses* of S Marco, Venice, a group of four horses originally yoked to a *quadriga* (four-horse chariot), which the Venetians looted in 1204 from the Hippodrome in Constantinople and erected c. 1265 on the façade of the basilica. These horses, made some time between 300 BC and AD 400 (the date is debated), became widely known through the dissemination of small-scale bronze copies made during the early Renaissance; the influence they exerted in Venice and Padua, as significant as that of the *Marcus Aurelius* in Rome, is to be seen in the earliest surviving equestrian monuments in these cities, the work of the early Renaissance masters Donatello and Verrocchio.

2. EARLY RENAISSANCE. For best effect, one of the horse's forehooves in an equestrian monument should be suspended in mid-air, as was done in most of the Classical prototypes mentioned in §1 above. This has the drawback, however, of reducing the sculpture's supports to only three, rather irregularly disposed. In the earliest surviving Renaissance bronze monument, fashioned in Padua by Donatello to commemorate the condottiere Erasmo da Narni, known as *Gattamelata* (c. 1447–53; Padua, Piazza del Santo; see DONATELLO, fig. 4), the sculptor introduced a cannon-ball to prop up the tip of the horseshoe on the left forehoof; this was also a reference to artillery, the new, revolutionary means of warfare. In Donatello's image, a pioneering and virtuoso feat of bronze-casting, the horse seems to plod forward rather than to spring, and the rider sits squarely back in his saddle.

A generation later the Venetian republic erected a huge equestrian statue of another condottiere, *Bartolomeo Colleoni* (1495; Venice, Campo SS Giovanni e Paolo). It was modelled in clay by Verrocchio, Donatello's Florentine successor (see VERROCCHIO, ANDREA DEL, fig. 4), but was cast after his death by Alessandro Leopardi. Responding to the implicit challenge to outdo Donatello, Verrocchio produced a model with the horse's forehoof in mid-air, and a rider in a much more animated pose (contrapposto): they look as though they are actually advancing, conveying a more dramatic effect. At much the same period, Ludovico Sforza, Duke of Milan, was planning to commission a statue of himself on a rearing horse, presumably to surpass the monuments to the other two condottieri. Another Florentine bronze specialist, Antonio Pollaiuolo, produced two drawings but had to resort to the artificial support lent by a fallen and gesticulating foe. Owing to Pollaiuolo's death, this design was never executed, but it was a vital stimulant to Leonardo da Vinci, whose equestrian monuments would have been a wonder of the world, had they not been destroyed midway or interrupted by hostilities. Leonardo had been in Verrocchio's Florentine workshop when the initial wooden model for the statue of *Colleoni* was being prepared for despatch to Venice as an entry in the competition for the commission (1479–81). In 1482 he wrote a bold letter of self-recommendation to Sforza, advertising his own abilities in bronze-casting and offering to undertake an equestrian monument. Leonardo was employed by the Duke, but not until 1489 did he begin modelling the horse in clay (destr. 1494); the monument was never cast. Leonardo's drawings in the second Madrid Codex (Madrid, Bib. N. MS. 8936) show that while he was fascinated by the drama of a horse and rider rearing over vanquished foes (to provide support), he eventually confined himself to designing a normal, walking horse. His subsequent project (*c.* 1508–11) for an equestrian monument to *Gian Giacomo Trivulzio* had also to be abandoned; thus there exists no three-dimensional remains of Leonardo's ideas, unless some are embodied in a series of dynamic terracotta models (Florence, Bargello, and Paris, Louvre), perhaps by Giovanni Francesco Rustici, Leonardo's associate. Later, in France, Rustici projected an equestrian monument to *Francis I* but cast only the horse (1529–31).

3. HIGH RENAISSANCE AND BAROQUE. In the High Renaissance many other sculptors toyed with the alluring idea of equestrian figures and were able to create them for ephemeral festive decorations, but not in permanent form. Two planned equestrian monuments for the emperor Charles V, by Leone Leoni (1546) and Guglielmo della Porta, came to nothing. The most influential such project of the period, which was partly completed, was for a memorial to *Henry II* of France, commissioned by his widow, Catherine de' Medici, in 1560 from Michelangelo. The elderly sculptor made a few drawings but delegated the modelling to an associate, Daniele da Volterra. The great horse, a spirited, rotund steed stepping bravely forward, was cast, but not its rider; it remained in Rome until 1622, when it was finally removed to Paris, to be given a new rider. It was destroyed in the French Revolution but is known from a sketch by Michelangelo and a contemporary engraving.

In Florence in the early 1560s GIAMBOLOGNA began to solicit his patron Francesco de' Medici, later Grand Duke of Tuscany, to commission a monumental horse, presumably intended to carry a rider; he produced some wax models and anatomical studies, including an *écorché* horse in bronze (Florence, Pal. Vecchio), but it was not until much later that he had the chance to execute it. He finally received the long-awaited commission in 1587 on the accession of Ferdinand I de' Medici; he cast the horse

in 1592 and its rider, *Cosimo I de' Medici*, in 1593, while the whole monument was unveiled in June 1594 in the Piazza della Signoria, Florence (*in situ*). Meanwhile, in 1567 Catherine de' Medici had tried, in vain, to get her brother Francesco to release Giambologna to make the statue of Henry II for the Michelangelesque horse. Giambologna inherited from Michelangelo the bold concept of having a hindhoof as well as a forehoof raised off the ground, as was done in his statuettes (*c.* 1575). In his equestrian monument to *Cosimo I* the tip of the rear horseshoe had in fact to be steadied by contact with a hump of ground conveniently rising below, added after World War II.

The monument to *Cosimo I* was an immediate success, and the Holy Roman Emperor Rudolf II requested a similar statue of himself, to be cast from the same moulds. However, all Giambologna produced was a splendid large statuette (*c.* 610 mm; Stockholm, Nmus.). A similar, signed statuette of *Ferdinand I* himself was cast in 1600 (Vaduz, Samml. Liechtenstein), and a full-scale monument to him on a variant, mirror-image horse (Florence, Piazza SS Annunziata) was commissioned and carried out between 1601 and 1608. In 1604 Marie de' Medici, Queen of France, commissioned an equestrian monument to her husband, *Henry IV*. The monument (destr. 1796) was cast by Pietro Tacca, who had succeeded to Giambologna's studio, and was subsequently erected on the Pont Neuf in Paris by Pietro Francavilla, another of Giambologna's associates. King Philip III of Spain was the next European ruler to request from Tacca a similar statue (1610–16; Madrid, Plaza Mayor). Another such monument was commissioned in 1630 by the Lord Treasurer of England, showing *Charles I* (London, Trafalgar Square): he employed the French court sculptor recently arrived in London, Hubert Le Sueur.

Meanwhile, in Florence the fascination with rearing equestrian figures once more took hold, and Tacca produced large, handsome bronze statuettes of this sort of *Louis XIII* (*c.* 1615; Florence, Bargello) and of *Charles Emanuel I, Duke of Savoy* (1619–21; Kassel, Löwenburg). These culminated in Tacca's rearing monument to *Philip IV*, King of Spain (1634–40; Madrid, Plaza de Oriente; for illustration *see* TACCA, (1)). This statue is a classic example of a flowing tail being used to disguise the third iron armature that was technically necessary to reinforce the two armatures inside the hind legs in supporting the huge weight of horse and rider. The rearing pose was allegorically interpreted (by analogy with the art of equitation) as a prince properly governing his people. The first Baroque equestrian monument in Austria, *Archduke Leopold V*, surmounting the Leopold Fountain (1623–30; Innsbruck, Rennweg) by Caspar Gras, also had a rearing horse, anticipating Tacca's in Madrid by a decade. In Piacenza at the same period Francesco Mochi produced a pair of truly Baroque walking equestrian monuments (1612–29; both Piacenza, Piazza dei Cavalli; for illustration *see* PIACENZA) to two of the Farnese dukes: *Ranuccio Farnese I* and his father, *Alessandro Farnese*. Here the horses' sinuously curling manes and the deliberate stylistic contrast between the two, with the boldly windswept cloak of the later monument, *Alessandro Farnese*, added vivacity and drama to Giambologna's earlier, more classicizing conception.

The master of the Baroque, Gianlorenzo Bernini, addressed the subject twice, preferring to follow Tacca in having his riders on rearing horses (*see* BERNINI, (2), §I, 1(v) and 3(iv)). His statue of *Constantine the Great* (1654–70) dramatically invigorates the arch at the end of the portico of St Peter's, Rome; it is strongly illuminated by concealed but natural light, its white marble contrasting with a background of a billowing curtain sculpted from coloured stone. Here the use of marble presented less of a technical problem, as the statue could be supported from behind. However, when Bernini wished to portray *Louis XIV*, King of France, on a rearing steed, he had to resort to supporting the horse's belly with an outcrop of rocks. This did not turn out happily, and the King rejected the final statue; in 1687 François Girardon altered the subject to *Marcus Curtius Throwing himself into the Flames*, and it was then banished to the bottom of the gardens at Versailles (*in situ*). Louis XIV preferred the more pacific, walking horse for the series of bronze monuments with which he began from 1685 to promote his image throughout the great cities of France. Each of his principal court sculptors produced such a monument: Girardon (1685–92; Paris, Place Louis-le-Grand [now Place Vendôme]); Etienne Le Hongre (1686–91; Dijon, Place d'Armes); Antoine Coyzevox (1686–93; Rennes, Place Royale); and Martin Desjardins (1688–91; Lyon, Place Bellecour). All were destroyed *c*. 1792, during the French Revolution, but their appearances are variously recorded in the artists' preliminary sketches or by engravings, statuettes or small images on the reverses of medals struck to commemorate the unveilings. The King was usually portrayed in Roman armour, which contrasted strangely with his fashionable full-bottomed wig. The sculptors expended much effort on the scientific study of the anatomy and mechanics of movement of real horses, observing them at exercise, as well as on the dissection table.

4. 18TH CENTURY AND AFTER. Evidently marble was not the right material for a rearing statue, and so Etienne-Maurice Falconet reverted to bronze when he was commissioned by Catherine the Great, Empress of Russia to commemorate Emperor Peter the Great in St Petersburg, the city he had founded. The French Rococo sculptor must have been familiar with Bernini's original drawings for the *Louis XIV* statue, which show the monarch dramatically reining in his horse at the summit of an upward-sloping rocky crag. For his *Peter the Great* (the 'Bronze Horseman', 1766–82; see fig.), Falconet used a 1600-tonne block of local granite, its contour echoing the forward thrust of a rearing horse, as a base from which to launch his twice-life-size horse and rider heavenwards. A writhing serpent, trodden under the rear hooves, provides the third point of contact with the base. This was the apogee of the rearing type of equestrian monument.

Thereafter equestrian monuments became a normal appurtenance of city squares, with many variations on the theme, particularly for modern equivalents of conquering Roman generals, such as the Duke of Wellington or Giuseppe Garibaldi. In the 19th century, under the influence of the Romantic movement, more emphasis was

Equestrian monument to *Peter the Great* by Etienne-Maurice Falconet, bronze, twice life-size, 1766–82 (St Petersburg, Decembrists' [Dekabristov] Square)

given to the implicit conflict of wills between the fiery steed and its heroic rider, the subject often being chosen from mediaeval history. Examples are to be found in the works of Carlo Marochetti, such as *Emanuel-Philibert of Savoy* (bronze, 1833–7; Turin, Piazza Carlo) and *Richard Coeur de Lion* (bronze, 1851; London, Pal. Westminster).

BIBLIOGRAPHY

H. Friis: *Rytterstatuens historie i Europa* (Copenhagen, 1933)
J. Pope-Hennessy: *Italian Renaissance Sculpture* (London, 1958, rev. Oxford, 3/1986), pp. 52–60
——: *Italian High Renaissance and Baroque Sculpture* (London, 1963, rev. Oxford, 3/1986), pp. 103–6
F. Souchal: *French Sculptors of the 17th and 18th Centuries: The Reign of Louis XIV*, 3 vols (Oxford, 1977–87)
I cavalli di S Marco (exh. cat. by M. Pallottino, A. Scattolin, G. Perocco and others, Venice, S Apollonia, 1977; Turin, Pal. Madama, 1977–8); Eng. edn as *The Horses of San Marco, Venice* (London, RA, 1979; New York, Met., 1980)
Glorious Horsemen: Equestrian Art in Europe, 1500–1800 (exh. cat., Springfield, MA, Mus. F.A.; Louisville, KY, Speed A. Mus., 1982)
C. Avery: *Giambologna: The Complete Sculpture* (Oxford, 1987), pp. 157–65

CHARLES AVERY

Equicola, Mario (*b* Alvito, nr Frosinone, *c*. 1470; *d* Mantua, 1525). Italian writer. He was a courtier and man of letters, first in the service of the Cantelmo family of Sora, then at the Este court in Ferrara, and finally, for many years, at that of the Gonzaga in Mantua. His writings, not numerous but varied in subject, reflect the interests and manners prevailing in the Italian courts during the 15th and 16th centuries. He occasionally served the Gonzaga as an iconographic consultant, and in the *Chronica di Mantua* (1521) he wrote with admiration of Lorenzo

Costa and enthusiastically cited the masterpieces of Mantegna and Alberti. It has been demonstrated (Shearman) that he conceived the subject-matter of the bacchanalian pictures by Giovanni Bellini, Titian and Dosso Dossi, intended for the *camerino d'alabastro* of Alfonso I d'Este, Duke of Ferrara. In the *Libro di natura d'amore* (1525) he considered themes dear to Renaissance artists, such as the theory of colour and the theory of proportion. However, he did not grant figurative art a more illustrious place than that usually assigned to it by contemporary men of letters—a place well below that of literature. The *Istitutioni di Mario Equicola al comporre in ogni sorte di rima della lingua volgare*, published posthumously in 1541, makes this clear. But the fact that the work is presented as 'an erudite discourse on painting' at the frontispiece suggests the increasing status of that art among educated readers. Equicola's interest in emblems, coats of arms and devices, already evident in the *De opportunitate* (1507), returns in almost all his later works, providing original contributions regarding the theory of symbols and useful material for precise historical documentation.

WRITINGS

De opportunitate (Naples, 1507)
Chronica di Mantua (Mantua, 1521)
Libro di natura d'amore (Venice, 1525)
Istitutioni di Mario Equicola al comporre in ogni sorte di rima della lingua volgare, con un eruditissimo discorso della pittura (Milan, 1541)

BIBLIOGRAPHY

D. Santoro: *Della vita e delle opere di Mario Equicola* (Chieti, 1906)
J. von Schlosser: *Die Kunstliteratur* (Vienna, 1924); 3rd Ital. ed. (Florence, 1964), p. 233
A. Blunt: *Artistic Theory in Italy, 1450–1600* (Oxford, 1940, rev. 1959), pp. 50, 52, 82
P. Barocchi: *Scritti d'arte del cinquecento*, 3 vols (Milan and Naples, 1971–7), i, pp. 259–60, 1088; ii, pp. 1613–27, 2153–8
G. Romano: 'Verso la maniera moderna: Da Mantegna a Raffaello', *Storia dell' arte italiana*, ed. P. Fossati, 12 vols (Turin, 1979–83), VI/i, pp. 5–85
J. Shearman: 'Alfonso d'Este's *camerino*', *'Il se rendit en Italie': Etudes offerts à André Chastel* (Rome and Paris, 1987), pp. 209–30
A. Colantuono: '*Dies Alcyoniae*: The Invention of Bellini's *Feast of the Gods*', *A. Bull.*, lxxiii/2 (1991), pp. 237–56

MARCO COLLARETA

Equipo Crónica [Sp.: 'the chronicle team']. Spanish group of painters formed in 1964 and disbanded in 1981. Its original members were Rafael Solbes (1940–81), Manuel Valdés (*b* 1942) and Juan Antonio Toledo (*b* 1940), but Toledo left the group in 1965. They worked collaboratively and formed part of a larger movement known as Crónica de la Realidad, using strongly narrative figurative images that were formally indebted to Pop art and that had a pronounced social and political content directed primarily against Franco's regime.

Both Solbes and Valdés studied at the Escuela de Bellas Artes de San Carlos in Valencia, but they came into close contact only in summer 1964 when they were included by the Valencian critic Vicente Aguilera Cerni in an exhibition, *España libre*, staged in Italy. This and another exhibition at the Ateneo Mercantil in Valencia, in which they participated with other young Valencian artists, led them to formulate a new concept of painting, Valdés having previously practised a kind of *Art informel* and Solbes an expressionism with subject-matter related to socially-committed literature.

From 1964 to 1966 the Equipo Crónica was heavily influenced by the theorist Tomás Llorens and closely involved with another group, Estampa Popular, with whom they participated in several demonstrations and anti-Franco activities. They remained in Valencia and from 1967 until the dissolution of the group on the death of Solbes in 1981 explored the narrative implications of their earlier pictures by working in series. The generic titles and subject-matter of these groups of works, such as *Recovery* (1967–9; see 1974 exh. cat., pp. 12–22), *Guernica 69* (1969; see 1974 exh. cat., pp. 23–7), *Police and Culture* (1971; see 1974 exh. cat., pp. 33–42) and *The Poster* (1973; see 1974 exh. cat., pp. 57–62), consciously reflected the political climate of the period and the evolution of Spanish society. Characteristically they recycled images that were already familiar from the history of European painting, freely and ironically making reference to styles as diverse as Impressionism, Expressionism and Cubism and to particular works by modern masters such as Paul Cézanne and Pablo Picasso, and appropriating from the mass media a formal language of flat colours, unusual perspectives and techniques derived from photographs. Their use of confrontational methods such as deconstruction, deliberate anachronisms and irrational collage, especially in their later pictures, owed much to the experimental work of Gilles Aillaud (*b* 1928), Antonio Racalcati and Eduardo Arroyo, not only in stylistic terms but in their political stance and questioning of the concept of the avant-garde.

BIBLIOGRAPHY

T. Llorens: *Equipo Crónica* (Barcelona, 1972)
Equipo Crónica (exh. cat. by T. Llorens, Saint-Etienne, Maison Cult.; Rennes, Maison Cult.; Pau, Mus. B.-A.; 1974)
Equipo Crónica (exh. cat., Seville, Cent. A. M-11, 1975) [with text by the group]
Equipo Crónica (exh. cat., intro. G. Busmann; Frankfurt am Main, Kstver.; Karlsruhe, Bad. Kstver.; 1977)
Equipo Crónica (exh. cat. by V. Bozal, T. Llorens and J. F. Yvars, Madrid, Bib. N., 1981)
Equipo Crónica: Sèries 1979/81: Paisatge urbà; Els viatges; Crónica de transició (exh. cat. by V. Bozal, T. Llorens and J. F. Yvars, Barcelona, Gal. Maeght, 1981)

M. DOLORES JIMÉNEZ-BLANCO

Eran [anc. Airikina]. Site of a ruined city and temple complex in Sagar District, Madhya Pradesh, India, 80 km north-west of Vidisha. The site first drew the attention of archaeologists in the mid-19th century but was excavated only in the 1960s, by a team from the University of Sagar that set the origin of the settlement to *c.* 1750 BC. Eran was an important religious centre in the eastern Malwa region in the 4th and 5th centuries AD; as with many ancient cities, the sacred complex was set apart from the town proper. By the 8th century Eran had been largely superseded by BADOH.

The monumental remains at Eran, clustered together on a gentle curve of the Bina River, consist of a row of four ruined shrines, two standing pillars and numerous sculptural and architectural fragments. The oldest stone sculpture at the site is a broken image of a *yakṣī* (female nature spirit) that dates to the second half of the 4th century AD. It appears to have served as a bracket for a gateway (*toraṇa*), similar to older examples preserved *in situ* at Sanchi. The *yakṣī* may be part of an edifice that, according to an inscription, was built at Eran by Samudra-gupta (*reg c.* 335–76).

Remains from the 5th century include a small ruined temple (*c.* 435) dedicated to Narasimha (Vishnu's incarnation as lion-man). Only doorjambs and other fragments survive. Richly carved pillars and abaci suggest the temple had a porch (*prāggrīva*). The main Narasimha image, much worn and broken off below the waist, is set up a few metres from the ruins. A massive (3.4×4.2 m) figure of Vishnu as the Cosmic Boar (Varaha) is all that survives from a second Vishnu temple. It shows the earth goddess clinging to the boar's tusk, while all the sages and gods take refuge in the boar's body. An inscription on the image records that it was set up by one Dhanyavishnu in the first regnal year of the Huna king Toramana (*c.* 500). Also from the 5th century is an impressive monolithic column (13.11 m high) bearing an inscription that describes it as a *dhvaja stambha* of Janardana (flagstaff of an aspect of Vishnu) and states that Maharaja Matrvishnu erected it in 485. The pillar carries a bell capital and cubical abacus carved with lions. On top are two addorsed figures of Garuda with a nimbus-like discus (*cakra*).

A third shrine dedicated to Vishnu is badly ruined, though the porch (*c.* 9th century) is reasonably well preserved. Parts of the porch's doorframe are perhaps original, but a medley of other fragments were added in the 19th century as a conservation measure. Within the ruined sanctum is a four-armed image of Vishnu (h. 4.11 m). This sculpture is probably not a product of the Gupta period, as generally believed, but a rare example of a revival style or copy dating to around the 10th century. Little remains of the fourth shrine at the site.

An 11th-century column east of the large Varaha image may have been part of a monumental gateway. Evidence for other temples is provided by numerous architectural fragments and sculptures ranging in date from the 8th to 11th centuries (not yet systematically studied). An impressive sculpture of Varaha (U. Sagar, Archaeol. Mus.), variously dated, was probably produced in the first half of the 6th century. On the north side of the ruins is a low platform built in the 20th century for the performance of a large ritual.

See also INDIAN SUBCONTINENT, §§III, 4(i) and IV, 6(iv)(b).

BIBLIOGRAPHY
A. Cunningham: 'Eran', *Archaeol. Surv. India Rep.*, vii (1871–4), pp. 88–90
——: 'Eran, or Erakaina', *Archaeol. Surv. India Rep.*, x (1874–7), pp. 76–90
K. Bajpai: *Sagar through the Ages* (Sagar, 1964)
U. V. Singh: 'Eran—A Chalcolithic Settlement', *Bull. Anc. Ind. Hist. & Archaeol.*, i (1967), pp. 29–38
J. Harle: *Gupta Sculpture* (Oxford, 1974)
J. Williams: *The Art of Gupta India: Empire and Province* (Princeton, 1982)
R. Salomon: 'New Inscriptional Evidence for the History of the Aulikaras of Mandasor', *Indo-Iran. J.*, xxxii (1989), pp. 1–36
MICHAEL D. WILLIS

Erard, Charles. *See* ERRARD, CHARLES.

Erardi. Maltese family of painters. Stefano Erardi (*b* 1630; *d* 1716) was of French extraction and would seem to have been trained in the workshop of a Mannerist artist, though much of his apprenticeship probably consisted of copying paintings in Maltese collections and studying prints after works by famous artists. This may account for his eclecticism, but it would be wrong to dismiss him as a plagiarist. His best works reveal him to have been an excellent draughtsman with a good sense of colour, who never completely renounced his Mannerist formation. His contacts with Mattia Preti broadened his artistic horizons and introduced him to Neapolitan Baroque art. His work had great popular appeal and helped to stimulate the emergence of a Maltese school of Baroque painting in the 18th century. His most prestigious commission, and one of his best works, is the *Adoration of the Magi* (Valletta, St John). Equally remarkable are the huge altarpiece of the *Shipwreck of St Paul* (Rabat, Parish Church) and that of the *Martyrs of Nagasaki* (Valletta, Jesuit Church). There are paintings by him in most Maltese churches and in public and private collections.

Stefano's son Alessio Erardi (*b c.* 1671; *d* 1727) was less gifted than his father, and his works are often marred by an unpleasant dryness and rigidity. He seems, nonetheless, to have understood Mattia Preti much better, and Maltese painting of the 18th century is heavily indebted to his example. His most significant achievement, the ceiling decoration of the Victory Church in Valletta, is now a sad ruin. Among his known altarpieces the most notable is the *Virgin of the Rosary* (1702; Lija, Parish Church), which shows him drifting away from the anachronistic idiom of Stefano towards a theatrical and exuberant style. Alessio had business as well as artistic interests and married a rich woman of a higher social class than his own. His lifestyle may have helped improve the status of painters in Malta.

MARIO BUHAGIAR

Erasmus. German family of cabinetmakers, designers and architectural theorists. Georg Caspar Erasmus (*b* Bopfingen; *fl* Nuremberg, 1663–95) was the municipal cabinetmaker in Nuremberg. The main part of the altar of St Stephen in the church of St Sebald, Nuremberg, donated by the Muffel family in 1663, is traditionally attributed to him, although it has also been described as being in the manner of George Schweigger. In 1666 Erasmus produced an architectural treatise, published in Nuremberg, entitled *Seülen-Buch, oder gründlicher Bericht von den fünff Seülen, denen beygefügt fünff Termes*; the 53 plates were engraved by Wilhelm Pfann (*fl c.* 1665–90). New editions that appeared in 1667, 1672 and 1688, and an undated enlarged edition, published in Nuremberg, indicate that the work attracted widespread interest. Erasmus produced a second volume containing 16 engravings in 1695, also published in Nuremberg, entitled *Neues Zierathen Büchlein von allerhand Schreinwerk*. His work was influenced by that of Rütger Kassmann, and the essentially symmetrical Baroque designs with Auricular shapes also relate to those published by the cabinetmaker Donath Horn (*fl c.* 1640–70) of Frankfurt in his *Zierathen-Buch*, which appeared between 1650 and 1670. Erasmus also drew on the works of the publisher Gottfried Müller, for example the *Neuws Compertament Buchlein* (Brunswick, 1621), and Friedrich Unteutsch's furniture designs (*c.* 1640–45). Erasmus was one of the important designers of architectural ornament, intended for cabinetmakers as well as masons, who established an independent northern European decorative style, characterized by Auricular forms, within the framework of the early Baroque. Johann Georg Erasmus (*b* Nuremberg, 19 Sept 1659; *d* Nuremberg, 24 March 1710), son of Georg Caspar Erasmus, left Nuremberg in 1678 but returned in 1684. His surviving works include sketches of Nuremberg Castle (1677) and an etching (1689; Nuremberg, Stadtbib.) of the Triton Fountain (1687) by Hans Leonhard Bromig (*fl c.* 1680–1725) in the Maximiliansplatz, Nuremberg. He also produced a *Seullen-Buch* (*c.* 1690), containing 12 pages of text and 12 plates engraved by Wilhelm Pfann. The work displays the stylistic influence of Hans Blum but also adopts elements from the work of the Imperial Cabinetmaker Johann Indau, who had published his *Wiennerisches Architectur- Kunst- und Säulenbuch* in 1686. The seven plates of the appendix to the *Seullen-Buch* were designed by Georg Caspar Erasmus. Ludwig Christoph Glotsch (*d* 1719) produced engravings of a Temple of Honour for Emperor Leopold I and a triumphal arch for Emperor Joseph I (*reg* 1705–11) to designs by Johann Georg Erasmus.

BIBLIOGRAPHY

Thieme–Becker
W. K. Zülch: *Entstehung des Ohrmuschelstiles* (Heidelberg, 1932), p. 120
E. Forssman: 'Säule und Ornament: Studien zum Problem des Manierismus in den nordischen Säulenbüchern und Vorlageblättern des 16. und 17. Jahrhunderts', *Acta U. Stockhom*, i (1956), pp. 5, 151, 222–6, pl. 61
R. Zöllner: *Deutsche Säulen-, Zieraten- und Schild-Bücher, 1610–1680: Ein Beitrag zur Entwicklungsgeschichte des Knorpelwerkstils* (diss., U. Kiel, 1959), pp. 119–32
E. Forssman: 'Dorisch, ionisch, korinthisch: Studien über den Gebrauch der Säulenordnungen in der Architektur des 16.–18. Jahrhunderts', *Acta U. Stockhom*, v (1961), pp. 55, 101
H.-W. Kruft: *Geschichte der Architekturtheorie: Von der Antike bis zur Gegenwart* (Munich, 1985), pp. 192, 596
H. Günther, ed.: *Deutsche Architekturtheorie zwischen Gotik und Renaissance* (Darmstadt, 1988), pp. 96, 146, 148–9

JÜRGEN ZIMMER

Erasmus (of Rotterdam), Desiderius (*b* Rotterdam, 28 Oct ?1466; *d* Basle, 12 July 1536). Dutch Classical and patristic scholar. He was educated by the Brethren of the Common Life at Deventer (1475–83) and 's Hertogenbosch. In 1487 he entered the Augustinian monastery at Steyn, near Gouda. Ordained in 1492, he became secretary to the Bishop of Cambrai in 1494 and studied in Paris from 1495. He was in England from 1499 to 1500 and from 1505 to 1506, where he befriended Thomas More, William Warham and John Colet, who led him towards biblical and patristic studies. This is reflected in the *Handbook of a Christian Soldier* (1503). He visited Italy from 1506 to 1509, obtained a theological doctorate, re-edited the *Adagia* with Aldo Manuzio in Venice and perfected his Greek, the basis for his magisterial *New Testament* edition of 1516 and those of the Church Fathers. In England again, as the house guest of More, he wrote his most popular work, the *Praise of Folly* (1511). He also lectured at Cambridge. In 1514 Erasmus moved to Basle, where Johann Froben became his principal publisher. Appointed counsellor to Charles V in 1516, he wrote for him the *Instruction for a Christian Prince*, followed by the *Complaint of Peace* (1517). Both works capture the pacifist views that eventually led to his break with Luther. After publishing the *Colloquia* (1518) and teaching at Leuven he returned to Basle in 1521, where he lived until his death, excepting a stay at Fribourg from 1529 to 1535 to avoid the Reformation unrests. His enormous scholarly productivity and ubiquitous correspondence make him the central figure of northern humanism.

Erasmus' interest in the visual arts was limited and centred around portraits of himself. The first is part of a diptych with his humanist friend Petrus Aegidius [Pieter Gillis] (1486–1533), painted in Antwerp in 1517 by Quinten Metsys and presented by both sitters to More (London, Hampton Court, Royal Col.; *see* METSYS, (1), fig. 3) Erasmus is shown writing the initial phrases of his then current project, the *Paraphrase on St Paul's Epistle to the Romans*. The titles on the page-ends of the books behind him document his recent scholarship and his friendship with More. Two years later Metsys designed a bronze medal of Erasmus in profile, the reverse of which depicts the god Terminus with the motto *Concedo nulli*. This controversial device was also painted and drawn by Hans Holbein the younger (Cleveland, OH, Mus. A.; Basle, Kstmus.). Albrecht Dürer used the medal and its Greek inscription for his 1526 engraved portrait (B. 107), which disappointed Erasmus. While visiting the Netherlands, Dürer met Erasmus repeatedly and drew him twice, but only one unfinished charcoal drawing survives (1520; Paris, Louvre). Although the scholar praised the artist in a eulogy for his excellent draughtsmanship (*De recta Latini Graecique sermonis pronuntiatione*, Basle, 1528, pp. 68–9), he preferred Holbein. As an apprentice in Basle, Holbein illustrated a copy of the *Praise of Folly* with witty, marginal pen drawings (1515; Basle, Kstmus.) including two portraits of Erasmus, which amused him. Eight years later Holbein painted the knee-length panel (Longford Castle, Wilts) showing him behind a parapet, holding the *Labours of Hercules*, which was a gift to Archbishop Warham, and the bust-length portrait (Paris, Louvre), which depicts him writing the *Adagia*. Other portraits by Holbein are the small tondo portrait (Basle, Kstmus.), a profile medallion in woodcut as title-page for the 1533 edition of *Adagia* and a print of Erasmus standing behind the Terminus emblem in an archway. Persuasive connections have been made between the text of the *Enchiridion* and Dürer's engraving *Knight, Death and the Devil* (1513; B. 98) and between the *Praise of Folly* and some secular images by Metsys, such as the *Grotesque Old Woman* (*c.* 1513; London, N.G.; *see* METSYS, (1), fig. 4).

WRITINGS
Opus epistolarum Des. Erasmi Roterodami, eds P. S. Allen, H. P. Allen and H. W. Garrod, 12 vols (Oxford, 1906–58)

BIBLIOGRAPHY
G. Marlier: *Erasme et la peinture flamande de son temps* (Damme, 1954)
R. H. Bainton: *Erasmus of Christendom* (New York, 1969)
Erasmus en zijn tijd (exh. cat., intro. by J. C. Ebbinge-Hubben, Rotterdam, Boymans–van Beuningen, 1969)
A. Gerlo: *Erasme et ses portraitistes* (Nieuwkoop, 1969)
E. Panofsky: 'Erasmus and the Visual Arts', *J. Warb. & Court. Inst.*, xxxii (1969), pp. 200–27
J. McConica: 'The Riddle of Terminus', *Erasmus Eng.*, ii (1971), pp. 2–7
B. Radice: 'Holbein's Marginal Illustrations to the Praise of Folly', *Erasmus Eng.*, vii (1975), pp. 8–17
J. Rowlands: 'Terminus, the Device of Erasmus of Rotterdam: A Painting by Holbein', *Bull. Cleveland Mus. A.*, lxvii (1980), pp. 50–54
H. Reinhardt: 'Erasmus und Holbein', *Basl. Z. Gesch. & Altertknd.*, lxxxi (1981), pp. 41–70
L. Silver: *The Paintings of Quinten Massys* (Montclair, 1984), pp. 105–33
L. Jardine: *Erasmus: Man of Letters* (Princeton, 1993)

ROSEMARIE BERGMANN

Erberg [Syunnerberg], **Konstantin (Aleksandrovich)** (*b* Orel, 20 Sept 1871; *d* Leningrad [now St Petersburg], 24 May 1942). Russian theorist, critic and poet. He graduated from the St Petersburg Institute of Jurisprudence (1895), travelled in western Europe (1895–8), then worked in the Russian Ministry of Communications (1899–1917). There his friendship with his colleague the artist Mstislav Dobuzhinsky prompted him to turn to art criticism and theory. He first worked for the modernist periodical *Iskusstvo* (1904–5), but it was in the pages of the Symbolist *Zolotoye runo* ('Golden fleece') that he began from early 1906 to elucidate his rejection of the 'formula' art of the realists and his conception of the creative process as a free, intuitive and pure expression of the artist's consciousness. This aesthetic, with its call for an art freed from preconceptions, external conditioning and utilitarian demands, was echoed in the ideas of Nikolay Kul'bin, Vladimir Markov and the Union of Youth artists, and it was most fully expressed as 'exnormism' (Rus. *innormizm*) in Erberg's book on the aim of creative work (1913). Here, the emphasis on the creative process rather than the end product, and with it the promotion of the 'alogical' and intuitive, led Erberg to the conclusion that the art of improvisation was the most effective means of self-realization. This, combined with his vehement theomachism, allied him with the approach of the Cubo-Futurists. After the 1917 Revolution Erberg was appointed co-chairman of the pedagogical section of the theatrical department of Narkompros; he joined the new Petrograd Institute of the Living Word, of which he was later head until it closed in 1924; he became a member of the philosophical association 'Vol'fil', where he headed the philosophy of art section, giving lectures on such themes as 'Art Is Revolt' and 'Dogmas and Heresies in Art'; and he edited two anthologies on aesthetics (1921 and 1922) in which he continued to proclaim the ideas already pronounced in his earlier work.

WRITINGS

Tsel' tvorchestva: Opyty po teorii tvorchestva i estetiki [The aim of creative work: attempts at a theory of creative work and aesthetics] (Moscow, 1913)

ed.: *Iskusstvo staroye i novoye* [Art old and new] (Petrograd, 1921)

ed.: *Iskusstvo i narod* [Art and the people] (Petrograd, 1922)

Krasota i svoboda [Beauty and freedom] (Berlin, 1923)

JEREMY HOWARD, SERGEY KUZNETSOV

Ercolani [Hercolani]. Italian family of patrons. The Bolognese branch of the family was descended from Andrea Ercolani, who settled in Bologna early in the 15th century. In the second quarter of the 16th century Conte Vincenzo Ercolani became a senator in Bologna and was ennobled by Pope Clement VII. For the family chapel in S Maria del Baraccano he commissioned a *Disputation of St Catherine* (*c.* 1551–60; *in situ*) from Prospero Fontana (i), and according to Vasari he was the owner (perhaps the first) of Raphael's *Vision of Ezekiel* (Florence, Pitti) and the *Noli me tangere* by Correggio (*c.* 1520–28; Madrid, Prado). In 1560 the writer Pietro Lamo noted these paintings in the collection of Conte Agostino Ercolani. In the 17th century the family continued its patronage of painters, including Guercino. In 1699 Filippo Ercolani was made a prince of the Holy Roman Empire by the Emperor Leopold I. In Bologna Filippo was a patron of the painters

Domenico Maria Viani, Angelo Michele Monticelli (1678–1749) and Cesare Giuseppe Mazzoni (1678–1763); the latter painted three pictures of him as Imperial Ambassador to Venice.

In the later 18th century the Marchese Filippo Ercolani, imperial chamberlain and son of Marc'Antonio Ercolani, was a notable patron who was also a collector of art and of art books. He owned several editions of Vasari's *Vite* and an autograph manuscript of notes by Conte Carlo Malvasia on his *Felsina pittrice*. He was closely acquainted with art critics and biographers and under the pseudonym of Doriclo Dioneo composed a sonnet to Luigi Crespi (ii); on the death of Giovan Pietro Zanotti he published a collection of poems, the *Rime in morte di Giampietro Zannotti fra gli Arcadi Trisalgo Larisseate* (Bologna, 1766). In 1792 he commissioned Angelo Venturoli to rebuild the family palazzo (now 45, Via Mazzini), which became a focus of architectural design in Bologna. Jacopo Alessandro Calvi assisted the Ercolani in acquiring the 16th-century altarpiece by Innocenzo da Imola of the *Virgin and Child in Glory with SS Petronio, Francesco, Clara, Caterina de' Vigri and a Donor* (Munich, Alte Pin.), which the family presented to King Ludwig I of Bavaria (*reg* 1825–48) in 1829. Several of the cadet branches of the Bolognese Ercolani died out, and following the marriage of Antonio Ercolani to Mariana Fava-Ghislieri-Simonetti, the family name was changed in 1913 to the Ercolani-Fava-Simonetti.

UNPUBLISHED SOURCE

Bologna, Bib. Com. Archiginnasio, MS. B. 16–17 [notes for Malvasia: *Felsina pittrice*]

BIBLIOGRAPHY

G. Vasari: *Vite* (1550, rev. 2/1568); ed. G. Milanesi (1878–85), iv, p. 116, n. 2 [Correggio]; p. 350, n. 2 [Raphael]

——: *Felsina pittrice* (1678); ed. G. Zanotti (1841), ii, p. 320

G. P. Zanotti: *Storia dell'Accademia Clementina di Bologna* (Bologna, 1739), i, pp. 360, 367; ii, pp. 172, 181

L. Crespi: *Felsina pittrice: Vite de' pittori bolognesi*, iii (Rome, 1769, rev. Bologna, 1970), pp. xviii–xix

G. Giordani: *Sei lettere pittoriche. . .Nozze Hercolani-Angelelli* (Bologna, 1836)

P. Lamo: *Graticola di Bologna ossia descrizione delle pitture, sculture e architetture di detta città fatta l'anno 1560* (Bologna, 1841); ed. G. Roversi, intro. F. Rodriguez (Bologna, 1977), pp. 12–13, 20, n.

V. Spreti: *Enciclopedia storico-nobiliare italiana*, iii (Milan, 1930), pp. 30–31; pp. 663–4 [Hercolani]

L. Marzocchi, ed.: *Scritti originali del Conte Carlo Cesare Malvasia spettani alla sua 'Felsina pittrice'* (Bologna, [1983])

JANET SOUTHORN

Ercolano. *See* HERCULANEUM.

Ercolano, Pietro di Galeotto di. *See* PIETRO DI GALEOTTO.

Ercole de' Roberti [Ercole de' Grandi]. *See* ROBERTI, ERCOLE DE'.

Erdély, Miklós (*b* Budapest, 4 July 1928; *d* Budapest, 22 May 1986). Hungarian architect, sculptor, conceptual and performance artist, teacher, theorist and film maker. He came from a Jewish–Christian family, many of whom were killed during World War II. In 1947 he began training as a sculptor at the College of Fine Arts in Budapest, but he left and continued his studies in the studio of Dezső Birman Bokros (1889–1965), before training as an architect from 1947 to 1951 at the Technical University in Budapest.

During the 1950s and early 1960s he worked as an architect and began experimenting with painting and graphic art, as well as writing poems and short stories. During this period he became acquainted with such artists as Dezső Korniss, László Latner and, most importantly, Béla Kondor and Sándor Altorjai (1933–79), with whom he began a lifelong friendship. In 1959 and 1963 he also enrolled at the Budapest College of Theatre and Film Arts but was advised to leave both times.

From 1962 Erdély lived with his family at Buda in a house that he later rebuilt and that was a venue for artistic events and a meeting-place for artists in the 1960s and later. These included such figures as Tamás Szentjóby (b 1944) and Gábor Atorjay (b 1944). Erdély became interested in many of the artistic developments of the time, such as 'happenings' and the work of the Fluxus group. He himself, however, felt a greater affinity with conceptual art and took part in the late 1960s and early 1970s in a number of avant-garde exhibitions with his conceptual 'textual actions' and series of photographs accompanied by texts. He also began to make films, although none of his films was shown officially in Hungary until the 1980s. The theoretical background to his films was his theory of montage, published in 1966, with its emphasis on repetition and change, its principle of 'meaning negation' and its admission of the role played by intuition and inspiration.

In 1975–6 he ran a series of 'creative exercises', which in 1978 led to the formation of the group known as Indigo (Interdiszciplináris Gondolkodás; Hung.: 'interdisciplinary thought'). This was conceived as an experimental teaching studio, drawing on modern artistic processes, educational methods influenced by Eastern philosophical traditions and many other sources, and it provided an important forum for a new generation of Hungarian artists, such as Ildikó Enyedi (b 1955), András Böröcz (b 1956) and László Révész (b 1957). It was only in the 1980s, however, that Erdély achieved public recognition for his work, which encompassed both social and spiritual concerns and emphasized the underlying affinities between art and science. These thoughts were represented in his huge installation 'Hadititok' ('Military Secret'), in the 1984 exhibition entitled 1984: Orwell und die Gegenwart in Vienna. 'Hadititok' was built from different symbolically interpreted materials (glass, tarpaulin, bitumen), on the surfaces of which the Müllet-Lyer diagram referred to the limited character of the human perception; a built-in digital unit displayed sentences referring to biblical secretiveness and prohibition as reinterpreted by Erdély for modern society.

WRITINGS
'Superstition as Folk Art', New Hung. Q. (1976), no. 64, pp. 219–21

BIBLIOGRAPHY
Erdély Miklós (exh. cat., Budapest, Óbuda Gal., 1986)
L. Beke: 'Die Alternative in der ost- und mitteleuropäischen Kunst der sechziger und siebziger Jahre. Ungarische Beispiele: Miklós Erdély und Tibor Hajas', Dagegen: Verbotene Ostkunst, 1948–1989 (exh. cat., Vienna, Bundesmin. Unterricht & Kst, 1991), pp. 97–102, 154
Miklós Erdély: Opere dagli anni '50 al 1986 (exh. cat., Rome, Spicchi E., 1992)

ANNAMARIA SZŐKE

Erdmann, Kurt (b Hamburg, 9 Sept 1901; d Berlin, 30 Sept 1964). German historian of Islamic art. After taking his doctorate under Erwin Panofsky, he entered the Islamic department of the Staatliche Museum, Berlin. From 1930 he dedicated himself entirely to Islamic art, although he returned occasionally to the theme of its reception in Europe. In 1938 he became guest professor at Fu'ad I University, Cairo; after World War II he lectured at Hamburg, and in 1949 he was guest professor at Bonn. In the tradition of Julius von Lessing, WILHELM BODE and FRIEDRICH SARRE, Erdmann was a dominant figure in Islamic carpet scholarship. He occupied the chair of Islamic art at Istanbul University from 1951 to 1958, although his inability to gain access to the carpet stores in the Museum of Turkish and Islamic Art inclined his attention to other aspects of Turkish art, especially Anatolian architecture. In 1958 he returned to Berlin to become director of the Islamic department of the Staatliche Museum. His writings, which total over 400 books and articles, include Der orientalische Knüpfteppich, a concise history of the carpet, and Der türkische Teppich des 15. Jahrhunderts, in which he challenged the prevailing taste for Safavid carpets by emphasizing the importance of the Turkish tradition of design. He also wrote on Islamic architecture, ceramics, metalwork, rock crystal and glass as well as Sasanian art.

WRITINGS
Der orientalische Knüpfteppich (Tübingen, 1955/R 1975); Eng. trans. by C. G. Ellis as Oriental Carpets: An Account of their History (London, 1962/R Fishguard, 1976)
Der türkische Teppich des 15. Jahrhunderts (Istanbul, 1957); Eng. trans. by R. Pinner as The History of the Early Turkish Carpet (London, 1977)
Das anatolische Karavansaray des 13. Jahrhunderts, 3 vols (Berlin, 1961–76)
Siebenhundert Jahre Orientteppich (Herford, 1966); Eng. trans. by M. H. Beattie and H. Herzog as Seven Hundred Years of Oriental Carpets, ed. H. Erdmann (Berkeley and Los Angeles, 1970)

BIBLIOGRAPHY
R. Ettinghausen: 'Kurt Erdmann', Der Islam, xli (1965), pp. 253–60
Forschungen zur Kunst Asiens in Memoriam Kurt Erdmann (Istanbul, 1969) [contains bibliog. of Erdmann's writings]

S. J. VERNOIT

Erdmannsdorff, Friedrich Wilhelm (von) (b Dresden, 18 May 1736; d Dessau, 9 March 1800). German architect, designer and writer. He studied ancient and modern languages at Dresden and Leipzig and, from 1754 to 1757, mathematics, physics, chemistry, history and philology at Wittenberg. In 1757 he met the young Prince Francis of Anhalt-Dessau and, after journeys on his own to Italy, he travelled with the Prince to England and Scotland (1763) and to Italy and France (1765–6). In Rome he explored the ancient buildings, made contact with Johann Joachim Winckelmann and studied the fundamentals of architecture with Charles-Louis Clérisseau. After returning via Antibes, Paris, London and Edinburgh, the Prince decided to have a palace and garden built at WÖRLITZ in the style of an English Palladian mansion. Schloss Wörlitz (1769–73) was Erdmannsdorff's first important work and probably his masterpiece. His models were Duddingston House (1763–8), Edinburgh, by William Chambers, and Lancelot ('Capability') Brown's preliminary studies for Claremont House (1772–4) in Surrey. The decoration over the windows and doors was derived from archaeological publications on the ruins at Baalbek and Palmyra. While construction was under way, he made further foreign journeys with the Prince and then carried out several works in Dessau, including Schloss Luisium and its gardens (from 1774) and a small theatre (1777) installed in the palace at Dessau. Schloss Georgium, Dessau, was built in 1780, while from that year he was entrusted with the decoration of seven rooms in the Berlin Schloss, Berlin, and two at Schloss Sanssouci, Potsdam. On 1 December 1786 the Berlin Academy admitted him as an honorary member. On a further journey to Italy, accompanying Frederick William, Prince of Brandenburg (later Frederick William III), he bought a number of ancient objects for Frederick William II, King of Prussia. In Italy he met, among others, Angelica Kauffman, Antonio Canova and Philipp Hackert. After his return he built a new theatre at Magdeburg (since rebuilt) and, in addition to an orangerie (1793–4), another theatre (1795; destr. 1855) at Dessau, the completion of which, like that of his town hall (begun 1795) at Wörlitz, he did not live to see. Erdmannsdorff's house in Dessau frequently served as a sort of academy, one of his pupils being Friedrich Gilly, and on his advice the Chalkographische Gesellschaft was founded in 1795; it was widely held in high esteem. Erdmannsdorff's buildings are now regarded as among the most important works of early German Neo-classicism.

WRITINGS
Architektonische Studien in Rom (Dessau, 1797)
W. Hosäus, ed.: *Gedanken über eine allgemeine vorbereitende Unterrichtsanstalt zu mechanischen Gewerben und zu bildender Kunst für Dessau* (Dessau, 1890)

BIBLIOGRAPHY
A. Rode: *Beschreibung des fürstlichen Anhalt-Dessauischen Landhauses und englischen Gartens zu Wörlitz* (Dessau, 1788)
——: *Leben des Herrn Friedrich Wilhelm von Erdmannsdorff* (Dessau, 1801)
E. P. Riesenfeld: *Erdmannsdorff: Der Baumeister des Herzog Leopold Friedrich Franz von Anhalt-Dessau* (Berlin, 1913)
R. Alex: 'Friedrich Wilhelm Erdmannsdorff: Zum 250. Geburtstag', *Bild. Kst.*, xxxiv (1986), pp. 354–6
R. T. Speler: 'Friedrich Wilhelm von Erdmannsdorff und die Herausbildung des Klassizismus in Deutschland', *Burgen & Schlösser*, xxvii (1986), pp. 8–20, 32
Friedrich Wilhelm von Erdmannsdorff, 1736–1800 (exh. cat. by R. Alex, Wörlitz, Schloss, 1986)
Friedrich Wilhelm von Erdmannsdorff, 1736–1800: Sammlung der Zeichnungen (exh. cat. by H. Heise, Dessau, Staatl. Gal., 1986)
R. Alex: *Schlösser und Gärten von Wörlitz* (Leipzig, 1988)
ANDREAS KREUL

Erech. *See* URUK.

Ererouk [Ereruk, Ereruyk]. *See* YERERUYK'.

Eressos. *See under* LESBOS.

Eretria. Greek city on the south-west coast of Euboia, east of Lefkandi and Chalkis and facing north-eastern Attica. Eretria was important in two periods: the Late Geometric and Archaic (c. 750 BC until its sack by the Persians in 490 BC) and the Late Classical and Hellenistic (from c. 400 BC until the Roman sack in 198 BC). Greek and Swiss excavations have uncovered many finds from these periods.

On a site of Bronze Age settlement, Eretria in the first half of the 8th century BC grew into a leading Greek city with active overseas connections, surpassing most in its architecture, urban development and metalworking. Having inherited certain architectural and artistic traditions and perhaps population from Lefkandi, Eretria and Chalkis traded from Italy to Al-Mina and jointly founded the first Greek overseas colony at Pithekoussai in Italy. They were key intermediaries in the interaction of Greece, Italy and the Near East. Some of the earliest Greek alphabetic inscriptions come from Euboia and its colonies.

Burials, architectural remains and Near Eastern imports testify to Eretria's growth. Eighth-century BC settlement was dense in places, with oval and apsidal houses; rectangular ones began c. 700 BC. Houses were of mud-brick on stone socles; the apsidal 'bay hut' (c. 750 BC) with a porch and wooden posts against the walls is probably one such, rather than a temple. There are traces of a 7th-century BC fortification wall and of extensive water-channelling works. The triangular base of a heroon (c. 680 BC) marked off a wealthy group of graves (c. 720–c. 690 BC), some burials of which were in bronze cauldrons and accompanied by iron weapons. A gold hoard of the early 7th century BC, including small ingots, provides evidence for goldworking and exchange. One house (c. 750 BC) contains evidence of bronzeworking near the Sanctuary of Apollo. Several Late Geometric (c. 750–c. 700 BC) gold diadems, of which the 'Eretrian' type is distinguished by a small central tongue-like projection, contain crowded repoussé scenes of warriors, hunts or animals; a later example (early 7th century BC; Eretria, Archaeol. Mus.) is fully Orientalizing in style.

Eretria was distinguished by its early and successive Archaic temples of Apollo Daphnephoros ('laurel-bearer'). The first hekatompedon ('hundred footer', c. 725–c. 700 BC) rivalled the first Temple of Hera (Heraion) on Samos. Disproportionately long (100 Ionic feet) in the Archaic fashion (34.5–35×7–8 m), it had an internal row of posts along its long axis and an apsidal end. In the first half of the 7th century BC this was replaced by a long rectangular temple of megaron form (34×7 m) with a peristyle (6×19 columns) of wooden posts, on an Ionic plan. A Doric peripteral temple (6×14 columns; stylobate, 46.40×19.15 m) with Ionic elements succeeded it (c. 510–c. 500 BC), only to be destroyed in 490 BC. The masterful sculpture from its western pediment (Chalkis, Archaeol. Mus.) included a group of *Theseus Carrying the Amazon Antiope* (see fig.), no doubt into a chariot; some horse fragments survive. A central *Athena* (Chalkis, Archaeol. Mus.) with archaizing tresses stood aloof from the action. The Theseus group formed part of an *Amazonomachy* to which a kneeling Amazon archer belongs (Rome, Mus. Conserv.). Dated c. 510–c. 500 BC, or arguably later, the figures in Parian marble show Attic influence and can be compared with the work of the Athenian sculptor Antenor. Archaic kouroi (Chalkis, Archaeol. Mus.) and the base of an acroterion of two warriors also come from the sanctuary.

Eretria's growth in the Hellenistic period occurred under Macedonian domination. A number of large houses with peristyle courtyards include the earliest in Greece (4th and 3rd centuries BC). Two are so large that they have been labelled palaces. Many have dining-rooms of similar sizes with pebble-mosaic floors, notably the four polychrome mosaics with mythical scenes in the House of Mosaics (c. 400–c. 363 BC). Eretria's theatre had a vaulted tunnel (c. 300 BC) giving access to the centre of the *orchestra* from the stage-building. A Macedonian vaulted tomb

Eretria, Temple of Apollo Daphnephoros, marble pedimental sculpture of *Theseus Carrying the Amazon Antiope*, h. 1.10 m, *c.* 510–*c.* 500 BC (Chalkis, Archaeological Museum)

(*c.* 200 BC) with marble furnishings is north-west of the city. Other features, of varied dates, include the city's fortifications and impressive west gate, its agora bounded by stoas, a tholos, fountain-house, two gymnasia and sanctuaries of Dionysos, Isis and Demeter. Roman and late Roman finds are few.

BIBLIOGRAPHY

Eretria (Berne, 1968–)

P. Auberson and K. Schefold: *Führer durch Eretria* (Berne, 1972)

P. Ducrey and I. R. Metzger: 'La Maison aux mosaïques à Erétrie', *Ant. Kst*, xxii (1979), pp. 3–21

E. Touloupa: *Ta enaetia glypta tou naou tou Apollonos Daphniphorou stin Eretria* [The pedimental sculptures of the temple of Apollo Daphnephoros at Eretria] (Ioannina, 1983)

A. Mazarakis Ainian: 'Geometric Eretria', *Ant. Kst*, xxx (1987), pp. 3–24

JOHN R. LENZ

Eretria Painter. *See* VASE PAINTERS, §II.

Erevan [Yerevan]. Capital of Armenia in the south-eastern foothills of Mt Ararat in the district of Kotayk. Erevan is first recorded in AD 607, but the name is probably derived from the much earlier Urartian fortress of Erebuni, which was founded in 782 BC by King Argishti I (*reg* 785–760 BC) on Arinberd Hill in the south-eastern part of the city.

Erevan's oldest Christian buildings were a subterranean cross-plan tomb (?4th–5th century AD; destr. 1930s) and the church of SS Peter and Paul (?5th–7th century; rebuilt 17th century; destr. 1930s). Although it remained a relatively small town, by the 13th century it had begun to benefit from its trading connections with Ani. The domed, single-nave chapel of the Holy Mother of God probably dates from the 13th century, as is suggested by an inscription of 1264 and such architectural and decorative features as its elongated proportions (most notably of the drum, which is cylindrical on the inside and dodecagonal on the exterior) and its stalactite, interlace and vegetal carved ornament. In the 15th century Erevan became the capital of Erevan province. The depredations caused by the Turkish and Iranian invasions of 1554 and 1635 were brought to an end when in 1639 Erevan became part of the Iranian empire. The city suffered further damage in the earthquake of 1679. Under Catholicos Nahapet of Urfa (*reg* 1691–1705) a major period of reconstruction was begun, which included that of the churches of St Gethsemani (1690s; destr. 1930s), Kat'oghikē (1693; destr. 1930s) and Zōrawor ('the powerful'; 1693). This last church was founded by a rich merchant near the earlier mausoleum of St Anania. It is a small, three-aisled basilica with four piers. The cruciform carving around the double windows on the east façade and the rectangular porch surmounted by an octostyle rotunda on the west façade are characteristic of 17th-century Armenian architecture. Extant buildings of the 18th century include the church of St John (1710) on Kond Hill and the Blue Mosque with an adjoining madrasa (1768; now Mus. Hist. City).

At the end of the 18th century warfare returned, ending with the destruction of Erevan's Iranian citadel and the city's capture in 1827 by the Russian army. Erevan then began to take on the appearance of a provincial Russian town, with western European-style buildings and a regular street plan. During the Soviet period (1917–90) many changes were made to this layout. In 1924 the first General Plan for the reconstruction of Erevan was drawn up by ALEK'SANDR T'AMANYAN; its subsequent growth from a city with 30,000 inhabitants to its present population of 1,000,000 forced the authorities to reassess the plan in 1939, 1951 and 1971. In the plan of 1924 Erevan was conceived as a garden city with a radial circular communication system springing from a central nucleus and precisely divided into zones that included an administrative centre, a students' quarter, a hospital area, leisure areas, industrial districts and so on. Many ancient buildings were demolished to make way for the new. The favoured building material was the local tufa, but from the end of the 1950s reinforced concrete has also been widely used.

The rebuilt central square of Erevan is surrounded by public buildings that combine classical elements with features from medieval Armenian architecture, as in the

Erevan, A. Spendiarov Theatre of Opera and Ballet, by Alek'sandr T'amanyan, 1926–53

Matenadaran Library of Ancient Manuscripts (1949), the Hotel Armenia (1955), the Ministry of Communication (1956) and the Council of Trade Unions (early 1960s; the last three all built by MARK GRIGORYAN). Among the most prominent buildings of the late 1960s to the 1980s are the Palace of Youth (1966–80s) and the House of Chamber Music (1977–8). Other major buildings are the A. Spendiarov Theatre of Opera and Ballet (1926–39, completed 1953; see fig.) by Alek'sandr T'amanyan and the wine cellars of the Ararat Trust (1936–44) by Gevork' B. Kochar (1901–73) and RAFAYEL ISRAYELYAN.

The city contains several museums; the State Picture Gallery holds a rich collection of Armenian, Russian and West European art dating from medieval to modern times. The Matenadaran Library of Ancient Manuscripts houses a renowned collection of manuscripts that were transferred to Erevan from Êdjmiadzin in 1939. It has over 12,000 items in Armenian, almost a third of which are illustrated (see ARMENIA, §III, 1(ii)). Among these are the ÊDJMIAD-ZIN GOSPELS, the Gospels of 1038 (MS. 6201), the Mughni Gospels (11th century: MS. 7736), the Haghpat Gospels (1211; MS. 6288), the Targmantchats Gospels (1232; MS. 2743) and the Book of Hours of the Cilician king Hetum II (1286; MS. 979).

BIBLIOGRAPHY

K. Ghafadaryan: *Erevan: Midjnadaryan Hushardzanner* [Erevan: medieval monuments] (Erevan, 1975)

S. Khodjash, N. Trukhtanova and K. Oganessian: *Erebuni* (Moscow, 1979)

H. Hovhannessian: *The Museums of Yerevan* (Erevan, 1986)

R. Ananikian: *Erévan: Guide touristique* (Moscow, 1989)

PATRICK DONABÉDIAN

Erfurt. German city and capital of Thüringia on the River Gera, at the southern edge of the Thüringian Basin; population *c.* 212,000 (1986). It possesses some fine examples of late medieval urban architecture.

1. HISTORY AND URBAN DEVELOPMENT. From prehistoric times there was a settlement on the site. After the dissolution of the Thüringian empire (531) the area became a centre of Frankish dominion, gaining importance with the Christianization of Thüringia. In the early 8th century the monastery of St Peter was built on the Petersberg, and on a small adjacent hill (Domberg) the baptismal church of St Mary was founded by St Boniface (*c.* 680–754), later replaced by the cathedral (*see* §2 below). In 742 Boniface asked Pope Zacharias (*reg* 741–52) to confirm 'Erphesfurt' as a bishopric, although it is unclear whether he succeeded; after his death Erfurt was incorporated into the bishopric of Mainz. The nunnery of St Paul was mentioned in 836 and 858, and in 836 the relics of St Severus (Bishop of Ravenna, *c.* 340) were translated to the Benedictine monastery (founded beginning 8th century). Situated on early medieval trade routes, the town acquired importance in the 9th century as the frontier trading post to the Slav areas. Trading settlements grew up near the Domberg, the Anger, the Wenigenmarkt and on the Krämerbrücke, a wooden bridge (first mentioned 1156; replaced in stone 1293). A defensive wall was built between the Domberg and the River Gera in 1066, and in 1167 the city was enclosed by a wall (subsequently extended; destr. 19th century).

The city's several churches were built from the 12th century. The city centre is dominated by the cathedral and St Severus on the Domberg (see fig. 1), each with three conjoined towers crowned with spires, facing the town. They are approached by a fine 14th-century stairway. The collegiate church of St Severus (1278–1330) is a hall church with double side aisles (vaulted 1400), rising above the Benedictine monastery. Both the cathedral and St Severus were the seat of an archdeacon. Together they form one of the most important and most memorable medieval urban ensembles. The Romanesque monastic church of SS Peter and Paul on the Petersberg is an aisled basilica (begun 1103; consecrated 1147), one of the largest buildings of the Hirsau tradition to have survived in Thüringia. The Schottenkirche of the Irish Benedictine monks from Regensburg (monastery est. 1136) is an aisled basilica, built in the second half of the 12th century (choir rebuilt from 1472; Baroque façade 1727). The Dominicans, who arrived in 1229, built another aisled basilica with a $\frac{5}{8}$ choir (second half of 13th century; completed 1370). The Franciscans (resident from 1224) built a brick church (partially destr. 1291; rebuilt late 13th century; choir consecrated 1316; nave destr. 1944; choir rest. after 1950); the Augustinian monastery was built between 1277 and the mid-14th century, and the Reglerkirche of the former Augustinian Canons dates from the end of the 12th century (rest. 14th century).

In 1244 the archbishop of Mainz had to recognize the independence of the city, although it never achieved Imperial Free status. The first town hall was mentioned in 1275. In 1331 Ludwig IV (*reg* 1314–47) granted Erfurt the right to hold a market, and in the 14th and 15th centuries it became one of the richest and most populous cities in the empire. Of its forty churches four were collegiate and eleven monastic. The university was founded in 1392 (dissolved 1816).

At the beginning of the 16th century Erfurt was a centre of humanism in Germany. Martin Luther lived there, first as a student and then as a teacher at the Augustinian monastery, and the Reformation reached the city in 1521. In the second half of the 16th century trade, industry and

1. Erfurt, the Domberg, with the cathedral (mid-12th century to mid-15th) on the left and St Severus (1278–1330) on the right

architecture flourished, although urban development subsequently stagnated. In the 17th century, after a siege, the archbishop's sovereignty was restored (1664), and Johann Philipp von Schönborn (1605–73), Elector–Archbishop of Mainz, started immediately to build a fortification (completed 1702) around the city. Among the surviving Baroque buildings two are outstanding: the palatial Waage (1705–11), erected for trade and commerce, and the Statthalterei (seat of government), rebuilt c. 1711–20 by Maximilian von Welsch. The city had a faience factory between 1712 and 1792.

In 1870–81 a new Gothic Revival Rathaus by Sommer replaced the extended medieval building. At the end of the 19th century industrialization gave rise to magnificent historistic residences and commercial buildings, particularly in the Anger area, and to planned suburbs. Erfurt suffered little damage in World War II, and consequently most of its 18th- and 19th-century buildings survive. The city's art collections (founded 1886 as Angermus. and housed in the Waage) are particularly strong in medieval sculpture and painting, 19th-century painting and local crafts.

BIBLIOGRAPHY
A. Overmann: *Erfurt in 12 Jahrhunderten* (Erfurt, 1929)
Die Kunstdenkmale der Provinz Sachsen, i, ii/1, ii/2 (Burg, 1929–32)
R. Lucke and G. Kaiser: *Erfurter Krämerbrücke* (Leipzig, 1971)
H. Giesecke: *Das alte Erfurt* (Leipzig, 1972)
H. Müller, H. Schoder and R. Ziebler, eds: *Denkmale in Thüringen* (Weimar, 1973)
K. Mertens: *Die St Severikirche zu Erfurt* (Berlin, 1974)
G. Kaiser: *Die Predigerkirche zu Erfurt* (Berlin, 1980)
C. Richter: *Das Augustinerkloster zu Erfurt* (Berlin, 1983)

LUTZ UNBEHAUN

2. CATHEDRAL.

(i) Architecture. The cathedral of St Mary was built in three phases. After the collapse of the earlier church founded by St Boniface (*see* §1 above) in 1153, construction of the basilical church was begun: the lower storeys of the towers flanking the choir and parts of the transept of this church still stand. The Gothic cathedral is first mentioned in an indulgence of 1282, and it was consecrated in 1290; this building was soon enlarged to provide for the rapidly expanding city. A huge substructure (completed after 1320) was extended east into the square, allowing the foundation stone for the new choir to be laid in 1349 (see fig. 1 above). This choir, with rectangular bays and a polygonal east end was completed and dedicated c. 1372. The exquisite execution and decoration of the choir make it one of the most important High Gothic works in Germany. At the same time a new portal (triangular in plan) was added to the north front of the transept at the head of the stairway. Its two entrances have stepped porches with two figure cycles (c. 1330) by an unidentified

2. Erfurt Cathedral, Abraham window, stained glass, detail showing (from left to right) *Lot and his Daughters*, the *Birth of Isaac*, *God Demanding Abraham's Sacrifice* and the *Sacrifice of Isaac*, *c.* 1370

workshop: *Apostles* to the east and the *Wise and Foolish Virgins* to the west. After the collapse of the Romanesque nave in 1452, an aisled hall with star vaulting was built (in use by 1465). Two outstanding sculptures of *c.* 1160 remain from the Romanesque church: the high altar with a seated *Virgin* in stucco, and the bronze candelabrum, known as 'Wolfram', consisting of a free-standing figure (*see* ROMANESQUE, §VI, 4(ii)(e)). From the 14th century are the stained glass (*see* §(ii) below) and the choir-stalls (*c.* 1370).

(ii) Stained glass. Thirteen windows of the 14th-century high choir retain original stained glass, as do three windows of the sacristy and one of the cathedral archive. The nave may once have been completely glazed, and some of the later choir windows may have replaced others belonging to an earlier campaign. Documents, however, indicate that since the 15th century there has been no change in location or replacement of any of the windows. In the thorough restoration of all the glass between 1897 and 1911 most of the windows were carefully cleaned and repaired, but some were treated inappropriately, with colours distorted and the overall appearance disturbed.

Johannes Orthonins, prior of the Augustinian canons regular at Dorla, left money for the glazing of the 14th-century choir in 1375. Based on practical considerations and stylistic comparisons with earlier works, the glazing on the south side of the choir is generally believed to have been largely completed by the time of its consecration in *c.* 1372. The windows were all made within about 50 years; each successive campaign has some stylistic relationship to the earlier windows, but there is nevertheless a marked change from the many narrative scenes with small figures in the earlier windows, to the larger, later compositions, with very large figures. There appears to have been an overall iconographic programme, as the scenes are organized according to the three divisions: *ante legem*, the Old Testament scenes at the beginning of the cycle; *sub lege*, Salvation windows devoted to the Virgin and the Passion of Christ; and *sub gratia*, the period after Christ, with scenes of the Apostles and saints.

Of the 'small figure' group, the Old Testament scenes of the south side are distinguished by the use of detail from everyday life and imaginatively conceived architecture, which fills the entire background of each scene and helps to maintain narrative continuity (see fig. 2). The painted and scratched buildings are relatively flat, functioning as frames for the figures and closely related to those found in some Italian 14th-century painting. A second group of 'small figure' scenes, from the north side of the choir, including Apostles and saints, is characterized by more individualized and livelier figures, with highly articulated and expressive faces, set against architecture that is rendered more vertically.

A document of 1403 mentioning an agreement to allow the depiction of Johannes Tiefengruben with his coat of arms on one of the glass panels provides a *terminus post quem* for the earliest of the 'large figure' windows. The size of these representations, which also appear against architectural backgrounds, allows greater characterization, enriched by the depiction of emotions and moral qualities. The narrative feeling of these scenes is maintained by a clear chronological sense.

Stylistic parallels and perhaps sources for the 'small figure' windows are found in sculpture associated with the Parler workshop (at the Stephansdom, Vienna, and throughout south Germany), in stained glass from Alsace (Strasbourg Cathedral; Colmar Dominican church), and in a group of Bohemian paintings, which may have been related to the lost 14th-century stained glass of Prague Cathedral. Of this group the *Liber Viaticus*, the *Laus Mariae* (Prague, N. Mus. Lib., MSS XIII A 12 and XVI D 13, respectively), the Glatz *Madonna* (Berlin, Akad. Kst.) and the Kosatsky *Death of the Virgin* (Boston, MA, Mus. F.A.) share many features, including the characteristic individualization of figures and fantastic play of architectural motifs. Historical evidence also suggests a close relationship between Erfurt Cathedral and Emperor Charles IV, who built Prague Cathedral. The 'large figure' windows have also been related to Bohemian painting, including works of the Master of Trebon.

See also GOTHIC, §VIII, 4(ii).

BIBLIOGRAPHY
K. Mertens: *Der Dom zu Erfurt* (Berlin, 1979)
E. Drachenberg: *Die mittelalterliche Glasmalerei im Erfurter Dom*, 2 vols, Corp. Vitrearum Med. Aevi: Deutsche Demokratische Republik, i/2 (Berlin, 1980)

VIRGINIA ROEHRIG KAUFMANN

Erfurth, Hugo (*b* Halle, 14 Oct 1874; *d* Gaienhofen, 14 Feb 1948). German photographer. He studied at the Kunstakademie in Dresden from 1892 to 1896 while also completing his photographic training with the court photographer Höffert. During the following ten years he ran the Schröder studio, acquiring the Palais des Grafen Lüttichau in 1906, where he set up his studio and later an art gallery. Dresden, the home of the painters' group Die Brücke and the workshops of Otto Dix and Oskar Kokoschka, attracted many artists and writers, who visited the studio to have their portraits taken. Erfurth was considered their equal and was acquainted with many of them, notably Kokoschka, Erich Heckel, Dix and Klee, whom he photographed in 1920 (see Tausk, 1980, p. 64).

In 1919 Erfurth was one of the founder-members of the Gesellschaft Deutscher Lichtbildner (GDL) and presided over its jury (1924–48). The GDL owed its reputation as an organization of leading German art photographers to his criticism and powers of judgement. In 1934 Erfurth moved to Cologne, where his studio and many of his negatives and pictures were destroyed by bombs in 1943; his portraits, however, were preserved. After this he moved to Gaienhofen on Lake Constance.

For half a century Erfurth shaped German portrait photography, uninfluenced by contemporary tendencies, remaining faithful to oil pigment printing and the use of natural lighting, which enabled him to avoid 'uncomfortable clarity', as he once called it, in his photographs. A collection of his work was published as *Porträts: Hugo Erfurth–Porträtphotograph*.

PHOTOGRAPHIC PUBLICATIONS
Porträts: Hugo Erfurth—Porträtphotograph (Dresden, 1930)

BIBLIOGRAPHY
B. Lohse, ed.: *Hugo Erfurth 1874–1948: Der Fotograf der goldenen zwanziger Jahre* (Seebruck, 1977)
Documenta 6, ii (exh. cat. by K. Honnef and E. Weiss, Kassel, Mus. Fridericianum, 1977), pp. 40–41

P. Tausk: *Photography in the 20th Century* (London, 1980), pp. 63
L. F. Gruber and R. Gruber: *Das imaginäre Photomuseum* (Cologne, 1981), pp. 86, 290, 309

REINHOLD MISSELBECK

Erhard, Johann Christoph (*b* Nuremberg, 21 Feb 1795; *d* Rome, 20 Jan 1822). German painter and printmaker. He studied with the Nuremberg artist Ambrosius Gabler (1762–1834) from 1809. His first etchings (1811–14; e.g. *A Peasant on Horseback*, 1814; Essen, Mus. Flkwang) show the influence of Ferdinand Kobell. His fellow pupil Johann Adam Klein aroused his interest in animal studies and military scenes. In June 1816 the two friends went to Vienna. In the summer of 1817 he went on a walking tour in the Schneeberg region near Vienna with Heinrich Reinhold and Ernst Welker (1788–1857); in the summer of 1818 he walked to Salzburg with Klein, Welker, Reinhold and Reinhold's brother, Friedrich Philipp (1779–1840). The landscape etchings he produced immediately after these trips show his intense feeling for nature.

In the autumn of 1819 he travelled to Rome, where he frequented the circle of landscape painters around Johann Christian Reinhart. A recurrent mental disorder prompted an attempt at suicide in 1820; a stay in Olevano in the summer of 1821 brought relief, but he died soon afterwards in a second attempt.

Erhard's landscapes are realistic in conception but animated by deep feeling. The last works produced in Italy are distinguished by simplicity and delicate light effects, as in the etching *Ponte Salario* (*c.* 1821; Essen, Mus. Flkwang).

BIBLIOGRAPHY
A. Apell: *Das Werk von Johann Christoph Erhard, Maler und Radierer* (Dresden, 1866)
B. Golz: *Johann Christoph Erhard* (Hamburg, 1926)
Johann Christoph Erhard und Johann Adam Klein (exh. cat., ed. H. Froning; Essen, Mus. Flkwang, 1980)

HELLA ROBELS

Erhart. German family of sculptors. (1) Michel Erhart, whose rise to the position of leading sculptor of Ulm was rapid, was married to Margarethe, the daughter of the architect Vincenz Ensinger. Two of their sons, (2) Gregor Erhart and Bernhard Erhart (documented 1515–17), followed Michel's craft. Gregor must have trained in his father's workshop. The extent of collaboration and the division of the two sculptors' work in the years before 1494 are matters of dispute; although clear preferences have been expressed, no generally accepted solution has been found. Gregor soon rose to be the leading sculptor of Augsburg. After his marriage in 1496 to Anna Mair, who was from a rich family of linen-weavers, he was able to establish his workshop, which he led until 1531, when he handed it over to his son, Paulus Mair.

(1) Michel Erhart (*b* ?1440–45; *d* Ulm, after 8 Dec 1522). He is recorded in Ulm from 1469, having probably spent part of his apprenticeship in the Netherlands. By 1474 he was commissioned to carve the greater part of the sculptures for the high altar retable in the Minster, one of the most prestigious contracts in 15th-century Ulm. His reputation also spread beyond the city: he received commissions from such important churches as SS Ulrich and Afra Abbey, Augsburg, and Weingarten Abbey. Towards the end of the century he seems to have been in charge of one of the largest sculpture workshops in southern Germany, and his activities ranged as far as Franconia and Switzerland. When during 1516–17 the Ulm authorities erected a gigantic Mount of Olives (destr. 1807; fragments in Ulm, Ulm. Mus.) with over-life-size figures and a baldacchino more than 6 m high, Michel and Bernhard were commissioned to supply numerous stone sculptures. Most of Erhart's documented works have disappeared.

The scope of his work in both wood and stone is not nearly as clearly defined as that of other Late Gothic sculptors. The starting-point for the stylistic analysis of his work is the sole remaining signed piece: an over-life-size Crucifix at St Michael, Schwäbisch Hall, dated 1494. Although his oeuvre grows steadily, controversy persists over attributions. Erhart's authorship of the Ulm choir-stall busts (*see* ULM, §2(i)(b)) is disputed. The choir-stalls were commissioned from the resident carpenter, Jörg Syrlin (i), in 1469. Otto (1943) and Deutsch (1977) thought that the 18 busts were an early major work by Michel Erhart, which instantly made him one of the leading sculptors north of the Alps. Müller (1966) disagreed with this attribution. Schneckenburger-Broschek (1973, 1986) argued that Erhart made only a secondary contribution to the choir-stalls: the unmistakable facial similarity between Erhart's known figures and several of the busts could be due to the influence of, or a period of apprenticeship with, the sculptor of the choir-stall busts, who latest researches suggest was of Netherlandish origin (Schneckenburger-Broschek, 1986).

The *Virgin of Mercy* (Berlin, Skulpgal.; see fig.) was probably made *c.* 1480. It is one of the finest works of German Late Gothic sculpture: expression and extended flowing lines of a lyric smoothness remain bound in a lucid compositional structure. With this work Michel Erhart achieved a high level of maturity. Compared with later works, with their inclination towards stereotyping, it possesses the freshness and individuality of original invention, despite being influenced by the painting of Rogier van der Weyden.

Three further works, the *Martyrdom of St Catharine* and the *Mass of St Gregory* (h. 740 mm; both Berlin, Skulpgal.) and a *St Onofrio* (h. 675 mm; reworked during the 19th century into one of the Magi; Düsseldorf, Kstmus.), are stylistically close to the *Virgin of Mercy* and must have been made at about the same time, probably all for the same altar shrine. The narrative content of the scenes is portrayed through vertically elongated figures whose strict proportional harmony continues the use of both curvilinear and straight verticals that is so pronounced in the *Virgin of Mercy*. The agitated, spatially dispersed drapery with angular breaks and deep undercutting corresponds to the emotional content of the martyrdom scene and suggests knowledge of the style of Nicolaus Gerhaert.

About 1490 Erhart's style grew harder. This was already manifest in the figures from a dismantled altarpiece with *Christ on the Cross*, the *Virgin and SS Dominic and Peter Martyr* (h. 1.4 m, Wimpfen am Berg, former Dominican friary church), made in the late 1480s. The Dominicans personify the opposing aspects of medieval piety: St Dominic, founder of the Order and fighter of heretics, shows energy and the ardour of faith on his angular face

Michel Erhart: *Virgin of Mercy*, lime-wood with polychromy, h. 1.35 m, *c.* 1480 (Berlin, Skulpturengalerie mit Frühchristlich–Byzantinischer Sammlung)

as well as in the sharp angles and diagonal thrust of the lines of his habit. The mortally wounded St Peter Martyr dwells in contemplation on the Passion of Christ; the loosely falling borders of drapery and crumpled pleats descending in soft undulations characterize the enfeebled martyr.

Erhart's workshop style is ever more clear in the 1490s, a period of heightened productivity: together with the harder, more linear drapery, the presentation was more formally perfect but also accomplished with more flourish. Definite figure types developed, with recurring formulae of folds and drapery schemes, regardless of material (stone or wood) or scale. Workshop production and autograph work seem separated only by a difference of quality. The Schwäbisch Hall Crucifix belongs to this phase, and it demonstrates the finesse of autograph work. Both the intensified expression of suffering and the heavy, deeply

undercut locks of hair that are consonant with the halves of the loin-cloth are characteristic of Erhart himself.

The Schwäbisch Hall Crucifix may be a prototype of a long succession of Erhart crucifixes that continues into the 16th century. They were evidently a speciality of the workshop and much in demand. In 1495 alone three crucifixes left the workshop, two acquired by SS Ulrich and Afra Abbey in Augsburg and a third (three times life-size) commissioned by the Schönbrunn family for St Martin, Landshut. In the Heiligkreuzkapelle in Weil der Stadt a version was discovered that had been specially prepared for passion plays connected to the Good Friday liturgy.

The stylistic demarcation between Michel and his son (2) Gregor becomes problematical precisely during the successful 1490s. The altarpiece (*c.* 1493–4; for illustration *see* SCHNITZALTAR) of Blaubeuren Abbey, the only large Late Gothic Swabian altarpiece that is preserved almost undamaged, is central to the discussion. It has five over-life-size shrine figures, wing reliefs of the *Nativity* and *Adoration of the Magi*, and paintings by Bartholomäus Zeitblom and his workshop. Regarded for a long period as an early work of Gregor Erhart, the altarpiece was first attributed to Michel Erhart by Müller (1956). Other sculptures, attributed to Gregor by Otto (1943), who estimated his birth date too early, may be associated with it, including a *Virgin and Child* (Weissenau Abbey Church) and altarpiece figures in St Maria, Thalkirchen. Schädler attributed the *Virgin and Child* (Munich, Bayer. Nmus., 19/144) to Michel Erhart, dating it to 1475–80 and grouping it with the figures of *SS Cosmas and Damian* in St Martin, Kaufbeuren, together with figures in an altarpiece in the church. The question arises whether this enriched oeuvre can still be seen as stylistically unified and following a process of logical development. It would have to begin with his figures of the 1480s, vertically aligned and formed of small elements, leading to the Blaubeuren altarpiece with its discernibly opulent, space-creating and more expansively arranged figures. These difficult questions can clearly be answered only by a revision in our understanding of both Michel's development and the early work of Gregor.

Michel Erhart's influence on the development of German Late Gothic sculpture cannot be compared with that of Hans Multscher or Veit Stoss. His strength lies in the polished, precise formulation of compositions as well as in the power of his figures and heads, which inspired increasing dissemination and imitation. He influenced the early style of Tilman Riemenschneider. The model of his crucifixes lives on in the work of his grandson, Hans Daucher (*see* DAUCHER, (3)) in Augsburg, and the Kefermarkt Altar (*see* MASTERS, ANONYMOUS, AND MONOGRAMMISTS, §I: MASTER OF KEFERMARKT ALTAR) shows knowledge of the types common in the Erhart workshop.

For further illustration *see* GOTHIC, fig. 56.

BIBLIOGRAPHY

G. Otto: *Die Ulmer Plastik der Spätgotik* (Reutlingen, 1927), pp. 100–11
H. Rott: *Bodenseegebiet* (1933), i of *Quellen und Forschungen zur südwestdeutschen und schweizerischen Kunstgeschichte im XV. und XVI. Jahrhundert* (Stuttgart, 1933–8), pp. 89, 241

——: *Altschwaben und die Reichsstädte* (1934), ii of *Quellen und Forschungen zur südwestdeutschen und schweizerischen Kunstgeschichte im XV. und XVI. Jahrhundert* (Stuttgart, 1933–8), pp. 56–9

G. Otto: 'Der Bildhauer Michel Erhart: Ein Vorbericht', *Jb. Preuss. Kstsamml.*, lxiv (1943), pp. 17–44

——: *Gregor Erhart* (Berlin, 1943), pp. 14–32

H. Müller: 'Michel und Gregor Erhart', *Lebensbilder Bayer. Schwaben*, v (1956), pp. 16–27

W. Paatz: *Süddeutsche Schnitzaltäre der Spätgotik* (Heidelberg, 1963), pp. 32–8

A. Schahl: 'Michel Erhart: Der Meister des Haller Kruzifixus', *Württemburgisch-Franken*, xlvii (1963), pp. 37–58

A. Schädler: 'Oberschwäbische Bildhauerkunst der Zeit Hans Holbeins des Älteren', *Hans Holbein der Ältere und die Kunst der Spätgotik* (exh. cat., Augsburg, Rathaus, 1965), pp. 43–5, 181–5

T. Müller: *Sculpture in the Netherlands, Germany, France and Spain, 1400–1500*, Pelican Hist. A. (Harmondsworth, 1966), pp. 114–16, 172–3

A. Miller: 'Der Kaufbeurer Altar des Michel Erhart', *Münchn. Jb. Bild. Kst*, n. s. 3, xxii (1971), pp. 46–62

A. Broschek: *Michel Erhart: Ein Beitrag zur schwäbischen Plastik der Spätgotik* (Berlin and New York, 1973)

J. Rasmussen: 'Ein wiedergefundenes Bildwerk Michel Erharts', *Pantheon*, xxxii (1974), pp. 351–4

W. Deutsch: 'Der ehemalige Hochaltar und das Chorgestühl, zur Syrlin- und zur Bildhauerfrage', *Festschrift: 600 Jahre Ulmer Münster* (Ulm, 1977), pp. 242–322

M. Baxandall: *The Limewood Sculptors of Renaissance Germany* (New Haven and London, 1980), pp. 104–6, 164–72, 255–8

H. Beck: *Michel Erhart*, Liebighaus Monographie Band 6 (Frankfurt am Main, 1980)

M. J. Liebmann: *Die deutsche Plastik, 1350–1550* (Leipzig, 1982), pp. 179–82

W. Deutsch: 'Ein Kruzifix in Weil der Stadt und andere Werke Michel Erharts', *Heimatver. Weil Stadt, Ber. & Mitt.*, xxxiv (1985), pp. 2–15

A. Schneckenburger-Broschek: 'Ein Niederländer als schwäbisches Genie: Neues zum Ulmer Chorgestühl', *Z. Dt. Ver. Kstwiss.*, xl (1986), pp. 40–68

(2) Gregor Erhart (*b* ?Ulm, ?1470; *d* Augsburg, 1540). Son of (1) Michel Erhart. The first documentary evidence for him is in 1494, when the 'sculptor Gregorius' was granted citizenship of Augsburg. The attributional difficulties surrounding his work arise from the narrow basis for a reconstruction of his oeuvre: the only known authenticated work was the *Virgin of Mercy* (Berlin, destr. 1945), which probably came from the high altar retable (1502) of the Cistercian abbey church at Kaisheim. Otto's attribution (1943) of an impressive group of early works to Gregor was based on an untenable birth date, *c.* mid-1460s, and these works have now been attributed to Michel Erhart. The group includes the Blaubeuren altarpiece (*see* (1) above). The Blaubeuren shrine sculptures are not, however, obviously consistent with Michel Erhart's slim, elaborately formed figure types. Schädler (1965) assigned the altarpiece to the 'group style' of the workshop, and Broschek (1973) argued in favour of a strong contribution by the workshop, including that of Gregor.

The commission of 1509 for a life-size stone equestrian monument to Emperor Maximilian I highlights the regard in which Gregor was held and contributed to his reputation as imperial sculptor, even though the work was not completed. Among the nobility and citizens of Augsburg, Jettingen and Dinkelsbühl he made a name for himself as a sculptor of epitaphs. The Augsburg oeuvre has been reconstructed in outline on stylistic grounds. Opinion on Gregor's activity between 1510 and 1531 is, however, varied. The core of the oeuvre is a series of over-life-size statues of the Virgin, which illustrate his evolution towards

the figure style of the Renaissance. His move to Augsburg at this period was significant in that, while Ulm was beginning to stagnate in the Late Gothic tradition, Augsburg was developing into a leading German town of the Renaissance. A *Virgin* in SS Ulrich and Afra Abbey in Augsburg is regarded as Gregor's earliest Augsburg work; the figure is more than 2 m high and may have come from the shrine of the matutinal altar (1493–9). The pose is still marked by the Gothic curve, but the monumental heaviness and roundness of the figure and the spacious, clear, generous fall of the folds show a new feeling for volume.

A chronicle of the Cistercian monastery at Kaisheim from 1531 records that the 'three best masters in Augsburg' (Adolf Daucher (*see* DAUCHER, (2)), Gregor Erhart and the painter Hans Holbein the elder) collaborated on the high altarpiece of the monastery church in 1502. In Gregor's *Virgin of Mercy* (h. 2.16 m), such traditional features as the old pillar-like figure type are still apparent, yet the body has a more stable, tectonic construction, with strong emphasis on the vertical and the horizontal. The upper forms rest securely on the lower, while a splendid new contrapposto gives movement to the figure of the child. Nonetheless the left knee, which is set too low, indicates that Gregor did not achieve the new monumentality entirely without effort.

The *Virgin of Mercy* (h. 1.85 m) in the Wallfahrtskirche at Frauenstein, Upper Austria, represents the next stage of development. The Virgin is shown enthroned, a monumental Queen of Heaven in a representative frontal pose, slightly raised above six sheltering worshippers arranged in a hierarchical order. The calm and equilibrium of the broad-based triangular composition is given freshness and individuality by the strong, energetic Christ Child and the mild, softly sensuous features of the Virgin. The work is generally considered to be an imperial commission, as Maximilian I kneels, opposite his wife Maria Bianca, in front of the Christ Child. As the Emperor himself put the finances of this church in order in 1514, Otto (1943) dated the figure *c.* 1515, but Schädler (1975) suggested a date soon after 1500.

The *Mary Magdalene* (Paris, Louvre; see fig.) is probably Gregor Erhart's most daring wood-carving. The nude female figure looks as natural as if it had been worked from a live model. Even if the sculptor received inspiration from the woodcut of Albrecht Dürer's *Assumption of the Magdalene* (B. 121), the work remains an astonishing advance towards a new autonomy in the field of sculpture. The subject of the work is the elevation of Mary Magdalene to the seven hours of prayer during her thirty years of penance. Otto dated the piece to *c.* 1525, Schädler (1975) proposed 1510–15, and Baxandall put it as early as 1500–10. This implies a much quicker artistic development for Gregor, which has been reinforced by Schädler's attributions of works made after 1510, some of them dramatic. These include the model for the bronze statue of *Elisabeth von Görz* from the Maximilian monument in the Hofkirche in Innsbruck (1509–11), the monument of St Willibald in Eichstätt Cathedral (limestone, *c.* 1514), and a limestone relief of the Virgin (after 1520; London, V&A, 7957–1862).

Gregor Erhart's work developed directly from the Late Gothic tradition in Ulm. In Augsburg he was one of the

vitality, a feeling for monumental construction and an entirely individual, thoroughly Swabian physiognomy. If Schädler's attributions become accepted, Erhart can also be seen to approach a classical quality in the style of the Italian Renaissance, like Peter Vischer the younger and Gregor's nephew, Hans Daucher. The viability of Schädler's attributions will be determined by the results of investigations into the generation of Augsburg sculptors following Gregor Erhart.

BIBLIOGRAPHY

J. Knebel: *Die Chronik von Kaisheim* (Stuttgart, 1531); ed. F. Hüttner (Tübingen, 1902), p. 354
W. Voge: 'Der Meister des Blaubeurer Hochaltars und seine Madonnen', *Mhft. Kstwiss.*, ii (1909), pp. 11–21
J. Baum: *Die Ulmer Plastik um 1500* (Stuttgart, 1911), pp. 81–95, 160–63
E. Spaeth: 'Quellenkundliche Beiträge zur Augsburger Plastik um 1500', *Mhft. Kstwiss.*, xv (1922), pp. 180–92
F. Winkler: 'Der Meister der Schönen Deutschen im Louvre', *Jb. Preuss. Kstsamml.*, xlv (1924), pp. 62–5
K. Feuchtmayr: 'Über Gregor Erhart', *Z. Bild. Kst*, lx (1926–7), pp. 25–31
G. Otto: *Die Ulmer Plastik der Spätgotik* (Reutlingen, 1927), pp. 67–100
——: *Gregor Erhart* (Berlin, 1943)
W. Boeck: *Der Hochaltar in Blaubeuren* (Munich, 1950)
H. Müller: 'Michel und Gregor Erhart', *Lebensbilder Bayer. Schwaben*, v (1956), pp. 16–44
W. Paatz: *Süddeutsche Schnitzaltäre der Spätgotik* (Heidelberg, 1963), pp. 32–8
A. Schahl: 'Michel Erhart: Der Meister des Haller Kruzifixus', *Württembergisch-Franken*, xlvii (1963), pp. 37–58
W. Deutsch: 'Die Konstanzer Bildschnitzer der Spätgotik und ihr Verhältnis zu Niklaus Gerhaert', *Sonderdruck Schrift. Ver. Gesch. Bodensees & Umgebung*, lxxxii (1964), pp. 106–9
A. Schädler: 'Oberschwäbische Bildhauerkunst der Zeit Hans Holbeins des Älteren', *Hans Holbein der Ältere und die Kunst der Spätgotik* (exh. cat., Augsburg, Rathaus, 1965), pp. 43–5, 183–7
T. Müller: *Sculpture in the Netherlands, Germany, France and Spain, 1400–1500*, Pelican Hist. A. (Harmondsworth, 1966), pp. 172–4
A. Broschek: *Michel Erhart: Ein Beitrag zur schwäbischen Plastik der Spätgotik* (Berlin and New York, 1973), pp. 133–52
A. Schädler: 'Das Eichstätter Willibalddenkmal und Gregor Erhart', *Münchn. Jb. Bild. Kst*, xxvi (1975), pp. 65–88
M. Baxandall: *The Limewood Sculptors of Renaissance Germany* (New Haven and London, 1980), pp. 127–32, 291–5
W. L. Strauss: *Sixteenth-century German Artists*, 10 [VII/i] of *The Illustrated Bartsch*, ed. W. Strauss (New York, 1980)
Sculptures allemandes de la fin du Moyen Age dans les collections publiques françaises 1400–1530 (exh. cat., Paris, Louvre, 1991/92), pp. 43f, 202–8
A. Schädler: 'Gregor Erharts "La Belle Allemande" im Louvre: Festschrift Hermann Fillitz zum 50. Geburtstag', *Aachen. Ksthl.*, 60 (1994)

ANJA SCHNECKENBURGER-BROSCHEK

Erh-li-t'ou. *See* ERLITOU.

Erichsen, Thorvald (*b* Trondheim, 18 July 1868; *d* Oslo, 23 Dec 1939). Norwegian painter. He began his studies in 1888 at the painting school of Knud Bergslien (1827–1908) in Kristiania (now Oslo); at the same time he attended the Royal School of Design there. In 1892 he studied for a few months with Kristian Zahrtmann in Copenhagen and the next year with Fernand Cormon in Paris. His paintings from the 1890s show how his naturalism yielded to more synthetic and symbolic tendencies, in keeping with the general trend. The summer landscape *From Telemark* (1900; Oslo, N.G.) marked a turning-point in his career and introduced a new era in Norwegian art. The subject is a typical Norwegian valley with wooded hillsides and cultivated patches between scattered farm buildings. In the background can be seen bluish mountains

Gregor Erhart: *Mary Magdalene*, lime-wood with polychromy, h. 1.77 m, *c.* 1510 (Paris, Musée du Louvre)

first to change from employing Late Gothic forms to those of the Renaissance, notably in the decoration, the style of the folds and the plasticity of form centred on the human body. His work is characterized by its great plastic

under a lightly clouded sky. With its forms tending towards abstraction, conveyed with paint-laden brushstrokes in a wide range of colours, the landscape shimmers with light and warmth. Here Erichsen's earlier experiences, including that of Impressionism and of Cézanne, are fused into a coherent unity.

Erichsen wished to become a figure painter and worked drawing models with the sculptor Victor Segoffin in Paris in 1902. In the following years he painted some large figure compositions, among them *Naked Man and Two Women* (1903; Oslo, N.G.). It was, however, as a landscape painter that he reached his leading position in Norwegian art. By around 1910, he had attained his characteristic style. With wide and rapid but carefully considered strokes of varying character in a broad colour spectrum, he concentrated on Norway's natural landscape and especially its light, which became increasingly important in his work. He spent several months a year in Lillehammer, where he painted the view from the Breiseth Hotel at least 40 times in different light conditions (e.g. *Winter Sun*, 1909; Oslo, N.G.). *From Holmsbu* (1937–9; Oslo, N.G.), a small place on the Oslo fjord where he spent many summers, is characteristic of his late work. Together with younger artists around Henrik Sørensen he belonged to the 'Lysaker Circle'.

NKL

BIBLIOGRAPHY
J. Thiis: 'Malerkunsten i det 19. og 20. Aarhundrede' [Painting in the 19th and 20th centuries], *Norsk kunsthistorie*, ed. H. Aars, ii (Oslo, 1927), pp. 515–18, 521–2, 546, 553, 557, 571–3, 588, 598
R. Revold: *Norges billedkunst i det 19. og 20. århundre* [Norway's pictorial art in the 19th and 20th centuries], ii (Oslo, 1953), pp. 10–11, 13, 15, 30–46
H. Gran: 'Et hovedverk av Thorvald Erichsen' [A major work by Thorvald Erichsen], *Kst & Kult.* [Oslo], li (1968), pp. 1–16
L. Østby, ed.: *Nasjonalgalleriet: Katalog over norsk malerkunst* (Oslo, 1968)
A. Rolfsen: 'Thorvald Erichsen', *Kst & Kult.* [Oslo], lii (1969), pp. 1–12
M. Lange and N. Messel: *Nasjonal vekst* [National growth] (1981), v of *Norges kunsthistorie*, ed. K. Berg and others (Oslo, 1981–3), pp. 262–9
INGEBORG WIKBORG

Erichsson, Nielss [Eriksson, Nils] (*fl c.* 1660/65–80). Swedish stuccoist. He was apprenticed to the German stuccoist Anthonius Lohr, who was in the service of Sweden's commander-in-chief, Carl Gustav Wrangel (1613–76), for whom Lohr made ceilings (*c.* 1660–65) in Schloss Spieker on the island of Rügen. Erichsson's earliest commission may have been to collaborate with Lohr on these ceilings. Erichsson is best known for his 14 stucco ceilings (1670–77), in Wrangel's castle at Skokloster, the majority of which are in the style of *c.* 1580–1600, resembling stucco ceilings in Schloss Ludwigsburg, Pomerania, and Svaneholm in Skåne. In these ceilings the carrying beams are exposed and, like the intervening spaces, are clad in a stucco layer with stylized flowers and acanthus-leaf ornaments, which are wound round the beams where they are round in section and scattered where they are right-angled. Erichsson's idiosyncratic treatment of the leaves makes them resemble the intertwining paws of animals rather than botanical specimens. Despite their old-fashioned style, the ceilings are striking and give the rooms a real feeling of the previous century. This was apparently Wrangel's intention: in building and decorating Skokloster, he wanted to create the archaic quality of a venerable family seat. However, in the ceiling of the dining-room on the first upper floor Erichsson was allowed to imitate a more modern and fashionable style, copying a plate by Jean Le Pautre but substituting his own 'paws' ornament for the plate's elegant acanthus leaves.

BIBLIOGRAPHY
J. Le Pautre: *Oeuvres d'architecture*, i (Paris, 1751/R), pl. 38:9
E. Andrén: *Skokloster* (Stockholm, 1948)
G. Eimer: *Carl Gustaf Wrangel som byggherre i Pommern och Sverige* [Carl Gustav Wrangel as building master in Pomerania and Sweden] (Stockholm, 1961)
TORBJÖRN FULTON

Erickson, Arthur (Charles) (*b* Vancouver, 16 June 1924). Canadian architect. His early fascination with natural form and his admiration for Frank Lloyd Wright led him to study architecture at McGill University, Montreal (1946–51). Upon graduating he embarked on an extended tour of the Mediterranean basin (1950–53), which aroused his awareness of monumental structure (Greek architecture in particular) and the importance of site, light and material. Returning to Vancouver he worked for several firms including Thompson, Berwick, Pratt and Partners; he also taught at the universities of Oregon and British Columbia (1955–64) and initiated his interpretation of the 'West Coast' style represented by the Filberg House, Comox, British Columbia (1958). Its cross-axial plan was subtly integrated with the landscape, while the structure of concrete pillars and elliptical vaults, counterpointed by local stone, echoed the work of both Paul Rudolph and Wright as well as revealing the picturesque and formal well-springs of his concept of design. Those polarities were further nurtured by a tour of Japan and the Far East (1961), which introduced him to another version of the post-and-beam system that became a fundamental theme.

In 1963 with Geoffrey Massey (*b* 1924) he won the competition for Simon Fraser University, Burnaby, British Columbia. They reconstituted historical and current university layouts by siting the faculty and ancillary accommodation around a processional way following the grade level. The ensemble is dominated by the central covered mall and climaxes in the academic quadrangle, which recalls medieval models but is elevated on Le Corbusian pilotis. His historically conscious Modernism emerged in a series of major commercial and institutional buildings awarded to the partnership of Erickson/Massey, notably the massive diminishing grid of concrete piers and beams of the MacMillan Bloedel headquarters, Vancouver (1967–9), described by Erickson as 'Doric' in its powerful rhythmic form. The contemporary University of Lethbridge, Alberta, concentrates academic facilities alongside a continuous corridor, bridging a shallow prairie valley to evoke permanence and integration as well as providing protection against the extremes of local climate; the elevated ideals of higher learning are celebrated in the angular triumphal openings ascending at the middle through the deep horizontal bands of concrete.

Equally admirably related to its site is the Museum of Anthropology, University of British Columbia, Vancouver (1971–6; see fig.), where the north-west coast post-and-beam structure is adapted into an expanding series of flat arches enclosed by glass walls. Visitors enter through a lower portal and descend, rather than ascend as is customary in museums, past successively larger display bays

Arthur Erickson: Museum of Anthropology, University of British Columbia, Vancouver, rear view, 1971–6

advancing towards the magnificent panorama of the Strait of Georgia, thereby participating in an interaction that is visual and also allegorical in its suggestion of descent through valleys to the sea. By contrast, in the extension of the Bank of Canada, Ottawa (1971–3), Erickson deferentially encased the extant late Beaux-Arts edifice with chamfered reflecting glass blocks, linked across the rear by an updated conservatory to serve as a weather-proof concourse. The solution evolved from his brilliant glass envelope for the Canadian Pavilion at Expo '70, Osaka, Japan, enlivened internally by parasols of revolving coloured discs. These and many other artistic collaborations were created with the painter Gordon Smith (*b* 1919), for whom he designed a house-cum-studio in west Vancouver (1964), among a second spate of sophisticatedly naturalized domestic designs, reaching a zenith in that for Helmut Eppich, West Vancouver (1971–4), which took inspiration from Japanese architecture and Richard Neutra.

In 1972 Erickson went into independent practice as Arthur Erickson Associates. He developed an innovative scheme for the Courthouse and Provincial Office, Vancouver (1973–9), where the offices occupy a low-rise tiered fabric, commanded at one end by a grand sloping glass canopy above the courts and at the other by the old Courthouse (by Francis Mawson Rattenbury), suavely converted into the City Art Gallery (1979–83). Between, the external areas provide a garden oasis, with flowing water and a space for public entertainment. His concern that architecture should enrich the pattern of human life is evident in two commissions in Toronto from that

decade: the sheer-glazed amphitheatral Roy Thomson Hall (1976–82), encircling an auditorium, Modernist in form but Baroque in spirit, and the more Functionalist Yorkdale Subway Station (completed 1977), where a faceted Hi-Tech aluminium and glass building simulates the appearance of a fast train, the sense of movement accentuated by internal polychromatic neon tubes illuminated on the arrival and departure of actual trains.

Such imaginative pragmatism increasingly brought Erickson commissions outside Canada, commencing in the Middle East with a remarkable series of variations upon the Arabic heritage, as in the Fintas town centre, Kuwait (1979), derived from the *souk* or market but transposed into the automobile age by buttressing parking towers. Of those projects, which included a geometrical pavilion plan for the Science Halls, Riyadh (1982–3), only the Etisalat Headquarters, Abu Dhabi (1985–6), a polygonal tower bearing quasi-Arabic ornament topped by a dome containing microwave equipment, has been completed. In Britain the Napp Laboratories at Cambridge (1979–83) house advanced facilities in an elegantly reticent structure of compressed concrete arches sandwiching glass panels. In the USA the huge Bunker Hill/California Plaza development in Los Angeles (from 1980), with its dominant curved glass and granite tower, is in marked contrast to the plastic massing yet distilled classicism of the Canadian Chancery, Washington, DC (1982–7). Besides major commissions such as the San Diego Convention Center (1984–7), CA, he designed houses, fascinating for their welding of overt formalism of plan and motif with the landscape, for example the dynamic cross-axial, post-and-beam Haggen House, Bellingham, WA, and the static, Palladian-like and templar Beare Residence, Bel Air, CA, both begun in 1986. Another phase of Erickson's career began after the closure in 1992 of his firm heralded by a series of significant commissions in his native province, notably for the Koesner Library at the University of British Columbia (scheduled to begin in 1994) representing a further synthesis of Modernist principle with more historical, monumental and symbolic themes.

WRITINGS

'The Weight of Heaven', *Can. Architect*, ix (1964), pp. 48–53

'The Architecture of Japan I: The Roots', *Can. Architect*, xii (1966), pp. 28–36

The Architecture of Arthur Erickson (Montreal, 1975); rev. as 2 vols (Montreal, 1986)

'Architecture, Urban Development, and Industrialization', *Can. Architect*, xx (1975), pp. 35–8

BIBLIOGRAPHY

C. M. Ede: *Canadian Architecture, 1960–1970* (Toronto, 1971), pp. 36–45, 146–57, 228–38

J. M. Vastokas: 'Architecture as Cultural Expression: Arthur Erickson and the New Museum of Anthropology', *A. Canada*, xxxiii (1976), pp. 1–15

L. Wright: 'City Colossus 2: Law Courts and Provincial Government Office, Vancouver', *Archit. Rev.*, clxvii (1980), pp. 346–53

E. Iglauer: *Seven Stones: A Portrait of Arthur Erickson, Architect* (Seattle and Vancouver, 1981)

H. Helfeld: 'Bunker Hill Development Generating Income for L.A.', *Urban Design International*, iv/1 (1982), pp. 14–19

R. W. Liscombe and B. E. Shapiro: *Arthur Erickson: Selected Projects, 1971–1985* (New York, 1985) [Crit. study with comprehensive list of works and bibliog.]

C. Bergeron: *Canadian Architectural Periodicals Index* (Quebec, 1986), p. 303

R. WINDSOR LISCOMBE

Ericson, Sigfrid (*b* Fritsla, 7 Oct 1879; *d* Göteborg, 1958). Swedish architect. He trained at the Chalmers Institute of Technology in Göteborg and the Academy of Arts in Stockholm in 1895–1902, and he worked in Göteborg, from 1913 as the head of the Arts and Crafts College. His most important work was in the field of ecclesiastical architecture. Masthuggskyrka in Göteborg (1910–14) is Ericson's most notable church, an impressive amalgam of Swedish medieval motifs executed in brick and roughly finished stone. The church and parish hall form a group with a walled courtyard, and the centre of the composition is a massive tower with a baroque cupola creating a city landmark. The dominating feature of the interior is the unusual dark timber roof, whose jointing forms part of a decorative scheme with carvings of Old Norse subjects.

Ericson was leader of the team of architects who designed the Göteborg Jubilee Exhibition (1923), a feast of buoyant 20th-century classicism. With Arvid Bjerke (1880–1952) he designed the Göteborg Konstmuseum, and the adjoining art exhibition hall (1917–23) which was opened in connection with the exhibition. The gallery is the centrepiece of Götaplatsen, which was planned with inspiration from the City Beautiful Movement. It is a homogenous volume in yellow brick with seven high arches on to the square, and has an unusually heavy sense of monumentality.

WRITINGS

with A. Bjerke: *Jubileumsutställningen i Göteborg 1923: Utställningens arkitektur* [The Jubilee exhibition in Göteborg 1923: exhibition architecture] (Göteborg, 1930)

BIBLIOGRAPHY

Nordisk Klassicism/Nordic Classicism, 1910–1930 (exh. cat., ed. S. Paavilainen, Helsinki, Mus. Fin. Archit., 1982)

H. O. Andersson and F. Bedoire: *Swedish Architecture* (Stockholm, 1986)

☐

Eridu [now Tell Abu Shahrein]. Ancient Mesopotamian city that flourished between *c.* 5000 and *c.* 2100 BC. Eridu once lay on the shore of a tidal lagoon created by the Euphrates estuary but is now a table-shaped mound remotely situated in the desert in Iraq. It was regarded by the Sumerians as their oldest city, respected as the religious centre of the god Enki (Sum.: 'Lord Earth') rather than as a political power.

In 1855 and 1918–19, the British archaeologists Consul J. G. Taylor and Reginald Campbell-Thompson respectively conducted unproductive excavations at Eridu. The 1946 to 1949 excavations of the Iraq Antiquities Directorate, under Fuad Safar and Seton Lloyd, were more successful, showing that the main mound covered a rectangular precinct (200×150 m) that was raised several metres above ground level and supported by a mud-brick retaining wall. At one end were the ruins of an unfinished ziggurat built by a late king of Ur (*c.* 2100 BC), evidently anxious to revive the cult of Enki. Beneath the foundations of the Ur III ziggurat were remains dating to the Uruk period (late 4th millennium BC) when, for the last time, the whole precinct was occupied by buildings (some still standing approximately 2 m high) surrounding a platform-temple, the surviving foundations and fallen ornament of which suggest remarkable sophistication. This citadel and its dependencies seem to represent the culmination of Eridu's prehistoric development.

Excavations have also revealed pre-Uruk phases of occupation, including (under a corner of the ziggurat) the standing walls of a temple of the Ubaid period (5th millennium BC). The sanctuary of Temple VII (see fig.) yielded large quantities of Ubaid painted pottery as well as

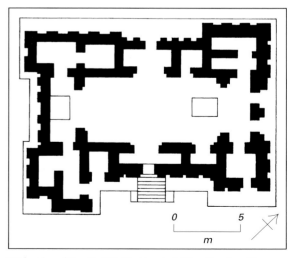

Eridu, plan of Temple VII, Ubaid period, 5th millennium BC

piles of fish-bones, indicating the form of votive offering favoured by marsh-dwelling people. Deeper excavations have produced a sequence of earlier temples stretching back to a primitive chapel, built on virgin sand by the earliest settlers at Eridu *c.* 5000 BC. This evidence of architectural precocity, supplemented by an improved and extended schedule of ceramic typology, has helped to reshape the conception of Mesopotamian prehistory (*see* MESOPOTAMIA, §II, 2).

A cemetery of about 1000 graves, outside the retaining wall of the precinct on the south-west side, also dates to the Ubaid period. These graves are contemporary with the latest building of the Ubaid phase (Temple VI), and their number and uniformity give the impression of a genuine necropolis, such as would be expected in the vicinity of a shrine. Some 200 were excavated, each consisting of a rectangular shaft lined with mud-brick containing a skeleton in an extended position. A second burial was often added to the same grave and, in several cases, the bones of a dog were laid over those of its master.

Among the grave goods was a rare collection of painted pottery vessels, many of them unbroken. All were handmade, the designs freely painted with a soft brush and closely matching those from the type site (*see* UBAID, TELL AL-). Other objects included examples of the painted terracotta figurines that were at first described as 'mother-goddesses' until a male counterpart was found in an Eridu woman's tomb. These objects are now recognized as a common convention in the cult imagery of Near Eastern prehistory, but those from Ubaid and Eridu are of a distinctive type found only at a few sites. One particular find was significant: a model of a sailing-boat (l. 250 mm; Baghdad, Iraq Mus.), with a socketed mast and pierced holes for stays. The boat, like other finds at Eridu, suggests a settled community dependent on fishing and hunting rather than the farming economy of early village life elsewhere.

In a final season Safar uncovered outside the main mound roomy palace buildings, the planning of which was appropriate to the Early Dynastic period, when the main precinct had been largely abandoned. The life-size basalt figure of a lion (Baghdad, Iraq Mus.), found on the surface at Eridu, is less easily datable.

BIBLIOGRAPHY
S. Lloyd and F. Safar: 'Excavations at Eridu', *Sumer*, iii (1947), iv (1948), v (1949), vi (1950)
S. Lloyd: 'Ur, Al 'Ubaid, 'Uqair and Eridu', *Iraq*, xxii (1960), pp. 23–31
J. Oates: 'Ur and Eridu: The Prehistory', *Iraq*, xxii (1960), pp. 32–50
S. Lloyd: 'Abu Shahrein: A Memorandum', *Iraq*, xxxvi (1974), pp. 129–38
F. Safar, M.-A. Mustafa and S. Lloyd: *Eridu* (Baghdad, 1982) [final pub. of the Eridu excav.]

SETON LLOYD

Eriksen, Christian. *See* SKREDSVIG, CHRISTIAN.

Eriksen [Erichsen], Vigilius (*b* Copenhagen, 2 Sept 1722; *d* Copenhagen, 23 or 24 May 1783). Danish painter, active also in Russia. He was apprenticed to the portrait painter Johann Salomon Wahl in Copenhagen. In 1755 he competed unsuccessfully for the gold medal at the Royal Academy of Art in Copenhagen with a historical painting, *Lot and his Wife* (untraced). In a letter he complained that the rules did not allow him to enter a portrait, a genre more suited to his talents. Presumably in 1756 he completed the portraits of the registrar of the royal art collections, *Lorenz Spengler and his Wife* (Copenhagen, Stat. Mus. Kst). These portraits already show the specific features of Eriksen's style, characterized by precise rendering of the sitter, distinct modelling of form and a cool virtuosity in the unemphatic treatment of dresses and accessories.

In 1757 Eriksen went to St Petersburg. During his first difficult years there he managed to obtain commissions for a portrait and several miniatures of the *Empress Elizabeth* (untraced). Shortly after Catherine the Great's *coup d'état* in 1762, Eriksen was asked to execute a large-scale portrait of her. He chose to represent her on the day of mutiny, on horseback, dressed in the uniform of the regiment that had given her support (*Catherine the Great on Brilliante*, 1762; Moscow, Tret'yakov Gal.). The painting was hung in the Winter Palace and secured Eriksen several other commissions from the court. Among the best of his Russian portraits are *Catherine II in Coronation Gown* (1762–3; ex-Academy of Art, St Petersburg; replicas were given to the courts of Prussia, England and Denmark), *Catherine II in Front of a Mirror* (1764; St Petersburg, Hermitage), *Prince Paul* (1764; Copenhagen, Davids Saml.) and *Prince Paul in his Classroom* (1765; St Petersburg, Hermitage). Eriksen's position as the favourite court painter at this time led also to commissions from the leading figures in St Petersburg, for example Aleksandr Golitsyn, Nikita Panin, Grigory Orlov, Aleksey Orlov, Caspar van Saldern and Christopher von Burckhardt, Count Münnich. In 1771 Eriksen sold an unusual painting to Catherine, *A 108-year-old Peasant Woman from Tsarskoye Selo Surrounded by her Family* (St Petersburg, Rus. Mus.). He was paid no less than 12,100 roubles for this and other works in 1771–2.

In 1772 Eriksen returned to Copenhagen, where he became painter to the Danish court. He painted two life-size portraits of *Queen Juliana Maria* (1777; Copenhagen, Stat. Mus. Kst) and *Prince Frederik* (1777; St Petersburg, Hermitage), which were presented to the Russian court. Among his last works is the portrait (1778; Copenhagen, Kon. Kstakad.) of the painter *Peter Cramer* (1726–82), in which the sitter's grey-and-white costume contrasts strikingly with the dark red background. Eriksen was the first Danish portrait painter to achieve an international reputation. In his best works he equals and occasionally surpasses such European rivals as Louis Tocque and Alexandre Roslin.

BIBLIOGRAPHY
A. Pander: 'Vigilius Erichsen, 1722–82: Nogle bidrag til hans virksomhed i Rusland' [Vigilius Eriksen, 1722–82: some contributions to his activity in Russia], *Samleren*, 7 (1930), pp. 97–110
T. Andersen: 'Vigilius Eriksen in Russia', *A.: Period. F. A.*, i (1965), pp. 45–87
——: 'Vigilius Eriksen, List of Paintings, 1757–1772', *A.: Period. F. A.*, iii (1970) [offprint]
T. H. Colding: 'Om Vigilius Eriksen og hans vaerksted i Rusland' [About Vigilius Eriksen and his workshop in Russia], *C. L. Davids Samling*, iv (Copenhagen, 1970), pp. 1–19

TROELS ANDERSEN

Eriksson, Nils Einar (*b* Stockholm, 19 July 1899; *d* Göteborg, 1978). Swedish architect. He trained in Stockholm at the Royal Institute of Technology and at the Royal

College of Arts from 1918 to 1925. He travelled to Greece and Italy to study Classical architecture and while in Europe, designed a winning entry for the Palace of the League of Nations competition in Geneva (1927; unexecuted). On his return to Stockholm he practised for two years under Gunnar Asplund.

Eriksson's early work, such as the Tiden Publishing House, Stockholm (1929), displayed his interest in the radical Functionalism of the time. His mature work, however, represents a restrained modern style that derives its character from elegant proportioning and from attention to detailing both inside and outside. He favoured white Swedish marble and yellow brick façades.

Eriksson's major work is Göteborg Concert Hall (competition 1932; completed 1935). It is situated on Götaplatsen, and the modernist simplicity of the marble-faced, glazed loggia containing the foyer and the surrounding promenade are in keeping with the City Beautiful, 20th-century classicism of the square. The auditorium's acoustics were carefully studied, and the cladding of veneered plywood on walls and ceiling forms a continuous surface free of ornament, giving a sense of dignified calm.

Park Avenue Hotel in Göteborg (1950) and the Folksam Insurance building, Stockholm (1955), are slab blocks with wings of lesser height. The Insurance building has curtain-wall façades of white marble with strictly partitioned windows, some of blue glass; it forms a prominent city landmark. Eriksson also contributed to the development of modern housing c. 1930 in Stockholm and later in Göteborg, where he also designed the People's Hall, containing a theatre, in 1952.

BIBLIOGRAPHY

SVKL

G. E. Kidder Smith: *Sweden Builds* (London, 1950)
H. O. Andersson and F. Bedoire: *Swedish Architecture* (Stockholm, 1986)

☐

Erith, Raymond (Charles) (*b* London, 7 Aug 1904; *d* London, 30 Nov 1973). English architect. The son of a mechanical engineer, his architectural vocation developed during long periods of childhood illness. He entered the Architectural Association School, London, in 1921, then served in the office of Percy Morley Horder (1870–1944), and commenced practice in 1928, in partnership with Bertram Hume (1901–77) until 1939. A curious early work, with Hilda Mason (1880–1955), is the church of St Andrew, Felixstowe (1931), a modernized Perpendicular Gothic design with concrete frame and brick panels. Erith's adherence to classicism was manifested in numerous competition designs, but he had few opportunities to build. In 1936 he rebuilt Great House, Dedham, Essex, for his father-in-law, closely following the original style of *c.* 1825. His lodges and cottages for Windsor Great Park, Berks (1939; see Archer, pl. 69), were destroyed by a bomb soon after completion and were altered in reconstruction.

Erith spent World War II farming in Essex, returning to practice in Ipswich, Suffolk, in 1946, transferring to Dedham in 1958. His career developed slowly in these years; he exhibited imaginative projects at the Royal Academy but built only small, insignificant works. His interest in early 19th-century architecture is shown in

designs such as the unexecuted factory, warehouse and offices in Ipswich (1948; see Archer, pl. 77), and his first substantial post-war work, 15–19 Aubrey Walk, London (1951). After revisiting Italy he became increasingly influenced by Palladio and other Mannerist architects of the 16th century, as can be seen in the remodelling of Morley Hall, Wareside, Herts (1955–7), The Pediment, Aynho, Northants (1956–7), and his severe design for the Provost's Lodgings at The Queen's College, Oxford (1959–60). The Library and Wolfson building, Lady Margaret Hall, Oxford (1959–61, 1963–6), constitute one of Erith's largest groups of buildings, using classicism with originality. The severe entrance façade and the more decorative library interior were particularly successful. His major project during this period was the reconstruction of 10–12 Downing Street, London (1959–63). The rebuilding of Jack Straw's Castle, a public house in Hampstead, London (1963–4), was an ingenious revival of timber structure with vernacular weatherboard cladding and Gothick details.

Erith's main projects of the 1960s were for country houses. Some of them, such as Bentley Farm, Halland, Sussex (1960–71), were remodellings, while others, such as Wivenhoe New Park, Essex (1962–4), were new. Wivenhoe New Park, the re-creation of a Veneto villa, contrasts with the French style of Joscelyns, Little Horkesley, Essex (1969–70), stylistic tendencies which in each case reflected the client's preference. King's Walden Bury House, King's Walden, Herts (1969–71), is an elaborate neo-Georgian mansion with complex historical references, contrasting an ornamental centrepiece with plain wings and revealing Erith's intellectual approach to classicism. His smaller buildings in East Anglia show a sensitive response to vernacular and country Georgian work.

Throughout his career Erith worked against the prevailing tide of Modernism. In 1967 he took into partnership QUINLAN TERRY, who had been his assistant from 1962 and who continued the practice after Erith's death.

BIBLIOGRAPHY

DNB

J. Gowan, ed.: *A Continuing Experiment: Learning and Teaching at the Architectural Association, 8: Raymond Erith Interview—Quinlan Terry and James Gowan* (London, 1975), pp. 71–7
Raymond Erith, RA (1904–1973) (exh. cat. by L. Archer, London, RA, 1976)
W. A. Coles, ed.: 'The Architecture of Raymond Erith, RA', *Classical America IV* (New York, 1977), pp. 125–52
L. Archer: *Raymond Erith, Architect* (Burford, Oxon, 1985)

ALAN POWERS

Erixson, Sven (*b* Tumba, nr Stockholm, 23 Nov 1899; *d* nr Stockholm, 17 May 1970). Swedish painter, draughtsman, tapestry and stage designer. After studying under various artists in Tumba and elsewhere, in 1922–3 he attended the Konsthögskolan in Stockholm and in 1922 visited Berne, Nuremberg and Berlin. His early works, such as *Jeårj* (1923; Stockholm, Mod. Mus.), were loosely painted and naive in appearance and drew on vernacular art. In 1924 he visited Paris and Italy, and in 1924–5 he helped decorate the cinema in Malmö, one of numerous early decorative projects. In 1925 he was a founder-member of the Fri Konst group of artists, which included Carl Alexandersson (1897–1941), Sven Hempel (1896–1944) and others. The following year the membership was expanded to nine by the addition of such artists as Gustav Alexanderson (*b* 1901) to form the Nio Unga (Nine Young Men) group. Erixson travelled extensively around Europe in the late 1920s, and in 1932, after the dissolution of Nio Unga, he was a founder-member of Färg och Form (Colour and Form) with whom he exhibited thereafter. His painting of this period retained the earlier naivety but became more expressive, as in *Dance Hall at Telemarken* (1931; Stockholm, Mod. Mus.). After travels in Spain and Morocco in 1935–6 Erixson designed two large tapestry cartoons for the Konserthus in Göteborg, which were executed by the Gobelins. In 1938–40 he executed two large frescoes for the chapel at Skogskyrkogardens crematorium in Stockholm. From 1942–3 he produced painted glass windows for the St Gertrud chapel at Malmö crematorium, and in 1943 he became a professor at the Konstakademi in Stockholm. Erixson produced numerous theatrical set designs in the 1940s and 1950s, such as those for Federico García Lorca's *Blood Wedding* (1944), and Shakespeare's *Richard III* (1946) and *Romeo and Juliet* (1953), which were performed at the Dramaten theatre in Stockholm. He continued to paint interior scenes, townscapes and landscapes in this period, such as *Autumn in Tattby* (1944; Göteborg, Kstmus.), which still showed the influence of folk art. His later work was of much the same style though the details were pared away as in the powerful *Memory of Nacka Hospital* (1965; see 1969–70 exh. cat.). He was also involved in further decorative projects, producing cartoons, painted windows and theatre designs. Together with Bror Hjorth, Erixson was influential in revitalizing the folk art tradition in Sweden.

BIBLIOGRAPHY

J. P. Hodin: *Sven Erixson* (Stockholm, 1940)

Sven Erixson (exh. cat. by U. Linde, Stockholm, Mod. Mus., 1969–70) [unpaginated]

Sven Erixson, Bror Hjorth (exh. cat. by U. Linde, Oslo, Kstnernes Hus, 1973)

Erlach, Fischer von. *See* FISCHER VON ERLACH.

Erlau. *See* EGER.

Erler, Fritz (*b* Frankenstein, nr Breslau [now Wroclaw], 15 Dec 1868; *d* Munich, 1940). German painter, illustrator and interior designer. He studied at the Kunstschule in Breslau under the German painter Albrecht Bräuer (1830–97), and later at the Pinakothek in Munich, absorbing the work of the Old Masters. He continued his training in Paris at the Académie Julian (1892–4), and established a studio in Munich (1895). With other non-academic painters of the period he rejected the influence of the French Impressionists and allied with the Symbolist painters of the late 19th century. He drew inspiration from wild places and as a young man travelled to the Baltic Sea and to the Riviera and Brittany coasts. He was fascinated by Norse legends, Grimms' fairy tales and Johann Gottfried Herder's *Stimmen der Völker*, all of which had an impact on his subject-matter. His early paintings of bucolic landscapes with figures were executed in flat, calm colours with well-defined outlines, reminiscent of the work of Pierre Puvis de Chavannes. In a long, prolific career he designed costumes and stage sets, stained glass, ceramics and bookbindings.

Erler's particular talent, however, was for interior decoration: he painted walls with huge, ornamented allegorical figures, incorporating motifs from the Rococo and Baroque; from Japanese art, and from contemporary paintings. In 1898–9 he designed the interior of a music room in the Breslau house of Dr Albert Neisser in a strong, Germanic Art Nouveau style. The wood wainscot, beams and furniture were elaborately carved, and painted murals represented musical themes such as 'Dance', 'Adagio', 'Allegro' and 'Scherzo'. The room was noteworthy enough to be discussed in *The Studio* of 1899, with photographs and a detailed analysis. Erler also painted eminent figures of his day, including a portrait of Richard Strauss (1898). In 1900 he produced posters in the manner of Alphonse Mucha; in his later decorative work for restaurants (1900–14), his giant-sized figures became more stylized, anticipating Art Deco. His brother Erich Erler (*b* 1870) was also a painter.

BIBLIOGRAPHY

F. Gos: 'Fritz Erler', *A. & Déc.*, xxviii (July–Dec 1910), pp. 81–96

F. von Ostini: *Fritz Erler* (Leipzig, 1921)

Erlitou [Erh-li-t'ou]. Early Bronze Age Chinese culture (first half of the 2nd millennium BC) distributed throughout Henan Province and surrounding areas, named after the village of Erlitou, situated in Yanshi County, Henan Province, near the modern city of Luoyang, where the largest site pertaining to the culture was found. The distribution and dating of the Erlitou culture largely corresponds to information in historical texts about the XIA DYNASTY, said to be the first dynasty in China, and some scholars identify the Erlitou culture at least partially with the Xia.

Excavation began at Erlitou in the 1960s, revealing a cultural layer 3–4 m thick divided into four chronological periods, each lasting *c.* 100 years, beginning *c.* 1900 BC and terminating *c.* 1500 BC.. The site covers 3 sq. km. In the centre are the remains of two palatial structures (*gongdian*), and in the south a bronze manufacturing area. Specialized workshops for ceramics and bone implements, pottery kilns, small house foundations, storage pits, wells and human burials have also been excavated.

The two palatial complexes are remarkable. Complex 1 consists of a walled enclosure elevated *c.* 1 m above ground-level, measuring *c.* 100 m on a side and orientated nearly north–south. The surrounding wall was once bordered both inside and out by wooden porticos. In the northern part of the complex was an elevated platform (h. 3 m) and on it a hall (30.0×11.5 m) constructed of wood. In the southern part of the complex was a gate some 34 m wide. Complex 2 is almost identical to this, though smaller; both were built in the third period of the Erlitou culture.

The largest grave at Erlitou is situated north of the hall of Complex 2. A rectangular pit grave (5.25×4.25 m at the top, and 6 m deep), it unfortunately has been almost completely plundered. In the upper half of the site a dozen rectangular, vertical pit graves (generally 2×1 m), orientated north–south, have been excavated. The most important grave goods are objects in bronze and jade primarily from the third period of the Erlitou culture. The

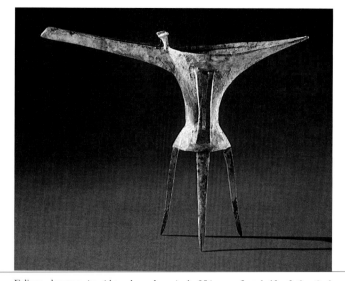

Erlitou, bronze *jue* (three-legged cup), h. 254 mm, first half of the 2nd millennium BC (New York, Metropolitan Museum of Art, on loan from the People's Republic of China)

cast-bronze vessels are the earliest found in China, dating from *c.* 1700 to *c.* 1500 BC. Around 15–20 bronze examples of the ritual *jue* vessel were found, manufactured by a piece-mould casting method that later became standard. The *jue* is a three-legged cup with a handle, a long pouring spout and at this period almost no decoration (see fig.). The tallest found at Erlitou measures 254 mm (*see* CHINA, fig. 146). A few examples of the three-legged *jia* vessel were also found (*see* CHINA, §VI, 3(ii)). Bronze ornaments from Erlitou include small plaques (*c.* 150×70 mm) inlaid with pieces of turquoise, some in an early form of *taotie* animal-mask. A few tools and weapons cast in simple moulds were also found. Ritual jade objects include large ceremonial blades with finely carved decorations, up to 500 mm in length.

BIBLIOGRAPHY
K. C. Chang: *The Archaeology of Ancient China* (New Haven, 1963, rev. New Haven and London, 4/1986), pp. 307–17
The Great Bronze Age of China: An Exhibition from the People's Republic of China (exh. cat., ed. Wen Fong; New York, Met.; Los Angeles, CA, Co. Mus. A.; 1980–81), pp. 69–83
R. L. Thorp: 'Origins of Chinese Architectural Style: The Earliest Plans and Building Types', *Archvs Asian A.*, xxvi (1983), pp. 22–6

SUSANNE JUHL

Ermels, Johann Franz (*b* Reilkirch, ?1621 or 1641; *d* Nuremberg, 7 Dec 1693). German painter and engraver. After training in Cologne under Johann Hulsmann (*fl* 1634–44) he went to Holland, where he devoted himself mainly to landscape painting under the influence of Jan Both and other Dutch Italianates. He lived in Nuremberg from 1660, becoming a master in 1661 and a freeman in 1662. He belonged intermittently to the circle of artists in Joachim von Sandrart I's Künstlerakademie. Ermels's early work includes the masterly *Christ and the Samaritan at the Well* (1661) as well as the *Resurrection* (1663; both Nuremberg, Sebalduskirche). Under the influence of Wilhelm van Bemmel (1630–1708), for whose landscapes he occasionally provided figures, Ermels executed delicate, idealistic landscapes in which powerful light and shade create a rhythmized illusion of space and depth: notably *Landscape with a Thunderstorm* and *Italian Landscape* (both Frankfurt am Main, Städel. Kstinst.) designed as counterparts, and one landscape (Mannheim, Städt. Ksthalle) to which Johann Heinrich Roos added animals. His skies, foliage and staffage of ruins were praised universally. Engravings were still being made from his paintings in the 18th century, by François de Cuvilliés II (1731–77), Johann Christoph Dietzsch (1710–69) and Johann Balthasar Bullinger I, among others. Since then they have been less highly prized, owing to their largely dark colouring.

Ermels also produced etchings, including a series of nine views from the Colosseum in Rome (Andresen, nos 6–14), and drawings (Cologne, Walraff-Richartz Mus.; Nuremberg, Ger. Nmus.).

BIBLIOGRAPHY
Hollstein: *Ger.*; Thieme–Becker
A. Andresen: *Der deutsche Peintre–Graveur* (Leipzig, 1878), pp. 230–41
J. J. Merlos: *Kölnische Künstler in alter und neuer Zeit* (Düsseldorf, 1895), pp. 224–6
G. Adriani: *Deutsche Malerei im 17. Jahrhundert* (Cologne, 1977), pp. 107, 179–80 [with secondary bibliog.]

IRENE HABERLAND

Ermenonville. French landscape garden near Senlis, at the edge of the forest of Chantilly, Oise. Laid out by its owner, LOUIS-RENÉ GIRARDIN, between 1766 and 1776, it became one of the most influential examples of the Picturesque garden in 18th-century France. In contrast to the flat terrain of many French parks, Ermenonville (approx. 850 ha) was varied and had an abundant water supply. Girardin made a large lake to the south of his modernized château; this flowed into two cascades, becoming a meandering stream north of the château. The lake and stream together defined the central north–south axis. The park itself he divided into four areas, in order to maintain the distinctly varied character of Ermenonville's topography: the farm, east of the château, was essentially a *ferme ornée*, whereas the Désert, to the west, was a rocky landscape of sandhills, pine trees and boulders. The fine views to the north and south of the château, improved by the lake and stream, encouraged Girardin to exploit his domain—recomposing the landscape so as to resemble the scenery to be found in the works of celebrated landscape painters. Consequently, southerly views from the château—an area that included an 'Arcadian' field framed by the woods surrounding the lake, cascade and grotto—suggested paintings by Claude Lorrain; those to the north, a flat, marshy area containing a rustic mill, canal and windmill, evoked in the spectator's imagination 'northern, meditative' landscapes. This latter area also included the Tower of Gabrielle (destr.), a Gothick tower dedicated to the mistress of Henry IV. Elsewhere, the views recalled the types of scenery associated with paintings by Hubert Robert, Salvator Rosa and Jacob van Ruisdael.

Among the important features of Ermenonville were the numerous poetic inscriptions taken from Classical and contemporary poetry. These were incised upon altars and other memorials, such as the brick obelisk dedicated to poets of pastoral verse (including William Shenstone),

Marie-Antoinette's bench, funerary monuments and the Altar of Reverie. The Temple of Modern Philosophy, based on the form of the Temple of the Sibyl at Tivoli, was intentionally left ruined. As such it marked the imperfections of human knowledge and, like the Temple of Modern Philosophy at Stowe in England, was dedicated to various humanist and Enlightenment worthies: William Penn, Isaac Newton, René Descartes, Voltaire, Montesquieu, JEAN-JACQUES ROUSSEAU and Montaigne.

In 1778 Girardin invited Rousseau to live at Ermenonville, Rousseau's *Julie, ou la nouvelle Héloïse* (Amsterdam, 1761) having provided Girardin with a model for the development of his estate. Ermenonville's Rustic Temple, the Monument to Old Loves, the Tower of Clarence and the Bocage—a grove by the stream north-west of the château—were all based upon descriptions of Clarence, the fictional estate in Rousseau's novel. Girardin provided Rousseau with a rubble-built thatched cabin that overlooked the lake in the Désert. Following Rousseau's death at Ermenonville in July of the same year, Hubert Robert was commissioned to design a commemorative tomb in the form of a Roman sarcophagus. Constructed on the Isle of Poplars, a small island south of the château, it quickly became something of a pilgrimage site.

From 1874 Ermenonville was gradually broken up and sold off. The woods are now state-owned, the Désert and Rousseau's cabin belong to the Institut de France, and the château is private property. The south lake and surrounding landscape (approx. 60 ha) became the Parc Jean-Jacques Rousseau in 1938 under the ownership of the Touring Club de France; in 1983 it was sold to a group of municipal bodies, one of which is the Commune of Ermenonville.

BIBLIOGRAPHY
L. R. Girardin: *Guide d'Ermenonville* (Paris, 1786)
S. Girardin: *Promenade ou itinéraire des jardins d'Ermenonville* (1788)
A. L. J. de Laborde: *Description des nouveaux jardins de la France et de ses anciens châteaux* (Paris, 1808–10/*R* London, 1971), pp. 83–94
E. de Ganay: *Les Jardins de France* (Paris, 1949), pp. 206–9
D. Lambin: 'Ermenonville et le jardin paysager en France', *Jardins et paysages* (exh. cat., ed. A. Parreaux and M. Plaisant; Lille, 1977), pp. 281–310
D. Wiebenson: *The Picturesque Garden in France* (Princeton, 1978), pp. 81–9
D. Lambin: 'Ermenonville Today', *J. Gdn Hist.*, viii (1988), pp. 42–59
SUSAN B. TAYLOR

Ermont. *See* ARMANT.

Ernst, Archduke of Austria. *See* HABSBURG, §I(11).

Ernest [Ernst], Elector of Saxony. *See* WETTIN, (1).

Ernest [Ernst]-**Ludwig**, Grand Duke of Hesse and the Rhine (*b* Darmstadt, 25 Nov 1868; *reg* 1892–1918; *d* Langen, 9 Oct 1937). German ruler and patron. He was a grandson of Victoria, Queen of Great Britain, who supervised much of his education, and consequently he developed strong anglophile leanings. He was a liberal and politically enlightened ruler, interested in the natural and social sciences but above all in the arts, particularly architecture. He introduced English interior design to Germany by inviting M. H. Baillie Scott and C. R. Ashbee to decorate rooms at the Neue Palais, Darmstadt (1897; destr.). In 1899 he founded an artists' colony on the Mathildenhöhe in Darmstadt (*see* DARMSTADT, §2). Together with the influential publisher Alexander Koch, Ernest-Ludwig envisaged a correlation of the colony and Hessian industry to raise design standards. The seven members of the colony included Peter Behrens and Joseph Maria Olbrich. The exhibitions of the colony made Darmstadt an internationally acclaimed centre for Art Nouveau art and architecture. Ernest-Ludwig also instigated numerous artistic, musical and theatrical organizations, such as a dance school founded by the American dancer Isadora Duncan (1878–1927) on the Marienhöhe in Darmstadt. He himself painted, wrote poetry, composed music and designed many of the ducal gardens.

BIBLIOGRAPHY
Prince Ludwig of Hesse and the Rhine: 'Die Darmstädter Künstlerkolonie und ihr Gründer Grossherzog Ludwig', *Vom Geist einer Stadt: Ein Darmstädter Lesebuch*, ed. H.-W. Sabais (Darmstadt, 1956), p. 309
Ein Dokument deutscher Kunst, 1901–1976, 6 vols (exh. cat., Darmstadt, Hess. Landesmus., 1976)
M. Knoth: *Ernst Ludwig—Grossherzog von Hessen und bei Rhein: Sein Leben und seine Zeit* (Darmstadt, 1978)

Erni, Hans (*b* Lucerne, 21 Feb 1909). Swiss painter, draughtsman, sculptor and stage designer. He took an apprenticeship as a draughtsman-architect (1924–7) and then studied at the Ecole des Arts et Métiers in Lucerne (1927–8). Between 1928 and 1929 he stayed for the first time in Paris, where he attended the Académie Julian. He continued his training at the Vereinigte Staatsschulen für freie und angewandte Kunst, Berlin (1929–30). The works of this period are signed *François Grècque*, a pseudonym that shows his admiration for ancient Greek art, traces of which are found in his works. In the course of many visits to Paris between 1932 and 1934, he had contacts with many artists, including Brancusi, Alexander Calder, Kandinsky, Mondrian and Henry Moore, and he was strongly influenced by the works of Braque and Picasso. In October 1933 he joined the Abstraction–Création group. In 1935 he collaborated in the exhibition *Thèse, antithèse, synthèse* at the Kunstmuseum in Lucerne, and in the same year he won a competition organized by that city, which involved the creation of a fresco, *The Three Graces of Lucerne*, to decorate the railway station. He received a commission for a fresco, *Switzerland: The People's Holiday Country*, for the Landesausstellung in Zurich in 1939, 100 m×5 m in size (Zurich, Schweizer. Landesmus.), and many official commissions for frescoes or mural reliefs followed.

In 1945 Erni designed the costumes and sets for a production of Aeschylus' *Prometheus* in Avenches, following up these incursions into the world of theatre with the sets and costumes for Mozart's *La clemenza di Tito* at the Salzburg Festival in 1949 and for Stravinsky's *Histoire du soldat* at Zurich in 1961. In 1949 he made his first postage stamp designs and in 1950 his first ceramics, the latter winning him the international ceramics prize at Cannes (1955). Between 1950 and 1951 he participated as draughtsman on the research trips made by the ethnologist Jean Gabus in Mauretania and French Guinea. He went on his own account to India (1957 and 1972), to Senegal (1965) and to the Red Sea (1966), from which he brought back many studies and drawings. He worked extensively as a designer and also wrote and lectured on art.

WRITINGS

Considération sur la peinture abstraite (1936)
Wo steht der Maler in der Gegenwart? (Zurich, 1947)
Hans Erni et André Bonnard, Promesse de l'homme (Paris, 1953)

BIBLIOGRAPHY

C. Roy: *Hans Erni* (Geneva, 1955)
J. C. Amman: *Hans Erni: Ein Weg zum Nächsten* (Lucerne, 1975)
J. Matheson: *Hans Erni* (Frauenfeld, 1981)
Hans Erni: Art non-figuratif 1933–1938 abstraction-figuration (exh. cat., Lucerne, Hans-Erni Mus., 1982)

ANNE PASTORI

Ernst, Max(imilian) (*b* Brühl, nr Cologne, 2 April 1891; *d* Paris, 1 April 1976). German painter, printmaker and sculptor, naturalized American in 1948 and French in 1958. He was a major contributor to the theory and practice of SURREALISM. His work challenged and disrupted what he considered to be repressive aspects of European culture, in particular Christian doctrine, conventional morality and the aesthetic codes of Western academic art. Until the mid-1920s he was little known outside a small circle of artists and writers in Cologne and Paris, but he became increasingly successful from *c.* 1928 onwards. After 1945 he was respected and honoured as a surviving representative of a 'heroic' generation of avant-garde artists.

1. Life and work. 2. Working methods and technique. 3. Sources and influences.

1. LIFE AND WORK.

(i) 1891–1914. (ii) 1914–24. (iii) 1924–38. (iv) 1938–43 (v) 1943–76.

(i) 1891–1914. Ernst was the eldest son of Roman Catholic parents. His father was a teacher of the deaf and dumb in the small town of Brühl. According to Ernst's own account (*View*, 1942), his childhood was 'marked by some dramatic incidents but was not particularly unhappy'. Certain of these incidents later formed the basis of a personal mythology, which he incorporated into his work. He became interested in the visual arts as a boy, partly through his father who was a keen amateur painter. He received no formal training in art, however, and at his parents' insistence, after grammar school, he enrolled at the University of Bonn (1909–12). He followed a wide range of courses there, in philosophy, psychiatry and art history, and he was deeply affected by exposure to the ideas of Freud, Nietzsche and the extreme individualist Max Stirner (1806–65). He also came into contact with August Macke and his artistic circle, including Heinrich Campendonck, and developed his own painting sufficiently for the *Crucifixion* (1913; Cologne, Wallraf-Richartz-Mus.) to be included in the Erster Deutscher Herbstsalon in 1913. His painting at this time showed an

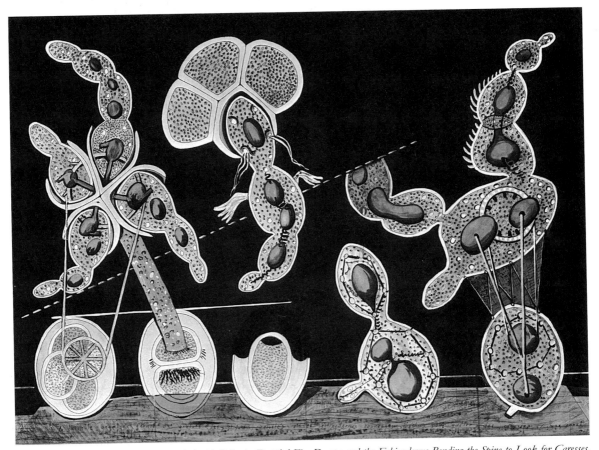

1. Max Ernst: *Gramineous Bicycle Garnished with Bells the Dappled Fire Damps and the Echinoderms Bending the Spine to Look for Caresses*, botanical chart altered with gouache, 743×997 mm, 1920–21 (New York, Museum of Modern Art)

ability to assimilate fashionable practice rapidly and thoroughly: he was influenced by van Gogh, Campendonck, Macke, Robert Delaunay and the Italian Futurists. His later, more personal themes had not yet become evident, although several paintings represent scenes of bourgeois life in a satirical manner, as in *Hat in the Hand, Hat on the Head* (*c.* 1913; London, Penrose priv. col., see Diehl, 1975, p. 10).

(ii) 1914–24. Ernst served in the German Army from 1914 to 1918 but continued to paint meanwhile, temporarily following a semi-Cubist, semi-abstract path under the influence of Delaunay, Arp and Apollinaire (e.g. *Laon*, 1916; Cologne, Wallraf-Richartz-Mus.). In 1916, when on leave, he held a joint exhibition with Georg Muche at the Sturm-Galerie in Berlin, which specialized in international Expressionist art. Like many German writers and artists he was scarred by his experience of the war; it led him to reject the values of his family and class and to join in with the provocative, critical stance of the nascent DADA movement.

Ernst married the art historian Louise Strauss in 1918. In Cologne during 1919 and 1920 he collaborated with Johannes Baargeld on an exhibition and a series of publications similar in style and spirit to the Dada activities in Zurich and Berlin. He was in touch with Arp, whom he had first met in 1914, and through him with Tristan Tzara and, after 1921, the Parisian Dada circle, including André Breton and Paul Eluard. From 1919 to 1921 he worked mostly on collages, initially in reaction to the work of Giorgio de Chirico and Francis Picabia, but he soon attained a level of startling originality, combining images abstracted from magazines with ambiguous visual devices and, in many instances, long, poetic, nonsense titles (e.g. see fig. 1). The Parisian group held an exhibition of his collages in May 1921; Eluard was so impressed (as was Breton) that he and his wife Gala visited Cologne in November specifically to meet Ernst. An exceptional intimacy grew up between the three, and as a result Ernst left his wife and young child and moved illegally to Paris in 1922. Before leaving he provided illustrations for Eluard's collection of poems *Répétitions* (1922) and collaborated with him on *Les Malheurs des immortels* (1922), a combination of jointly written prose poems and collage illustrations drawn from old engravings. In Paris Ernst lived with the Eluards, and in 1923 he decorated their new home at Eaubonne (Val d'Oise) with a number of mural paintings (ex-Gal. André-François Petit, Paris, see Spies, 1974–9, ii, pls 636–52), including *At the First Limpid Word* and *Natural History*. Between 1921 and 1924 he produced a series of paintings evoking the irrational, portentous qualities of dreams, a subject much in vogue at this time in the nascent Surrealist group. This series includes the *Elephant Celebes* (*c.* 1921; London, Tate; see fig. 2), *Oedipus Rex* (1921–2; Paris, priv. col., see Schneede, 1972, pl. 90), *Pietà* or *Revolution by Night* (1923; London, Tate), *Woman, Old Man and Flower* (1923–4; New York, MOMA) and *Two Children Are Threatened by a Nightingale* (1924; New York, MOMA). All of these paintings are related to incidents or images from his childhood.

(iii) 1924–38. In March 1924 Eluard went alone to the Far East. In August Ernst and Gala met him in Saigon

2. Max Ernst: *Elephant Celebes*, oil on canvas, 1.25 × 1.08 m, *c.* 1921 (London, Tate Gallery)

and persuaded him to return to France. The Eluards travelled back together, and Ernst stayed on alone. When he returned to Paris, he moved into a studio in the Rue Tourlaque. During 1925 the Surrealist group, which had been officially launched by André Breton's first *Manifeste du surréalisme—poisson soluble* (1924), was engaged in a debate about the status of painting in the movement and the possibility of applying the practice of automatism to picture-making. Partly in response to this, Ernst developed the technique of *frottage*, which he claimed to be a form of automatism; it first appeared in *Histoire naturelle*, a series of 34 *frottage* drawings that he exhibited and published in 1926 (Eng. edn, London, 1972, 2/1986). For several years he employed variations on the technique in most of his paintings, notably the *Forest* series. These paintings, in which natural forms predominate, revealed his sense of affinity with Romanticism and with certain of his German predecessors, particularly Albrecht Altdorfer and Caspar David Friedrich (e.g. the *Great Forest*, 1927; Basle, Kstmus.).

Ernst was briefly under contract to Jacques Viot in 1925; in 1926 he held a successful exhibition at the Galerie van Leer; this led to a further exhibition at the Galerie Georges Bernheim in 1928, which confirmed his status as a fashionable artist in Paris. In 1926 he had made his first attempt at theatrical design, painting sets for Diaghilev's production of Prokofiev's *Romeo and Juliet* in collaboration with Miró, which made his name in the eyes of the Parisian public. In 1927 he married Marie-Berthe Aurenche and painted *After Us—Motherhood* (1927; Düsseldorf, Kst-samml. Nordrhein-Westfalen), using calm, harmonious forms and warm colours. This painting, along with the three versions of *Monument to the Birds* (1927; version, Paris, Vicomtesse de Noailles priv. col., see Schneede, 1972, pls 156–8), also illustrates Ernst's growing preoccupation with bird imagery during this period.

Ernst returned to collage in 1929, when he composed a 'novel', *La Femme 100 têtes* ('The woman with 100 heads' or, as a pun, 'The woman with no head'), consisting of 124 captioned pictures, all of which had been made by adapting images taken from late 19th-century illustrated magazines, usually adventure or love stories (see fig. 3). The sequence does not follow an evident narrative, although Stokes (1977) suggested that it constitutes a symbolic autobiography. He used the technique again in *Rêve d'une petite fille qui voulut entrer au Carmel* (Paris, 1930; Eng. trans., New York, 1982) and *Une Semaine de bonté* (Paris, 1934; Eng. trans., New York, 1976). Each of these books projects recurrent themes of sexuality, anti-clericalism and violence, by dislocating the visual significance of the source material to suggest what has been repressed.

Between 1929 and 1932 Ernst also produced a series of collages featuring 'Loplop, the Bird-Superior', who had first appeared in *La Femme 100 têtes*. In these and other collages Loplop represents the artist himself and presents a sequence of tableaux illustrating Ernst's technical methods and ideas. Throughout this period Ernst was sensitive to the ideas of the Surrealist group: in 1929–30 Breton's novel *Nadja* (1928) and Dalí's advocacy of the 'paranoiac-critical' method were important background influences on his work. After Breton had 'excommunicated' numerous early Surrealists, Ernst renewed his solidarity with the group in his collage *Loplop Introduces Members of the Surrealist Group* (1931; New York, MOMA); he had already made an act of homage in his painting *At the Rendezvous of Friends* (1922; Cologne, Wallraf-Richartz-Mus.).

Although some of his paintings and collages of 1925–31 had a lyrical and decorative character, the imagery in many of them was violent and menacing. This aspect of his work became more prominent after 1933, partly in reaction to the political and social climate of the time—for example the various versions of the *Angel of Hearth and Home* (1937; see Schneede, 1972, pls 306–8). Like many other German artists and writers Ernst was condemned by the Nazi cultural authorities. He was also influenced at this time by the widespread interest of his circle in non-European art, as reflected in his sculpture of 1934–5, made after his stay at Maloja, near St Moritz in Switzerland, with Alberto Giacometti. In his paintings of this period he explored the theme of metamorphosis and the fascinating cruelty of nature (e.g. *La Joie de vivre*, 1936–7; London, Penrose priv. col., see 1978 ACGB exh. cat., pl. 12.62). Some parallels to this can be found in the contemporary work of André Masson. During the 1930s Ernst became increasingly well known: he exhibited at the Julian Levy

3. Max Ernst: *La Sève Monte*, collage, 107×157 mm, 1929 (London, British Museum); from chapter 3 of *La Femme 100 têtes*

4. Max Ernst: *Europe after the Rain*, oil on canvas, 548 × 1478 mm, *c.* 1940–42 (Hartford, CT, Wadsworth Atheneum)

Gallery in New York and participated in the large international exhibitions of Surrealism held in London, New York and Paris in 1936 and 1938; a special issue of *Cahiers d'Art* was devoted to his work in 1937, the year in which he designed the sets for Sylvain Itkine's production of *Ubu enchaîné* at the Comédie des Champs-Elysées.

(iv) 1938–43. Politics had been a strong motivation of Surrealist activity throughout the 1930s. Ernst had remained sympathetic to the goals and actions of the group without involving himself directly in polemics. In 1938, however, he chose to break with Breton and the remaining group rather than accept the condemnation of Paul Eluard. In the same year he moved to St-Martin d'Ardèche (nr Orange) with the English writer and painter Leonora Carrington, whom he had met in London in 1937. He again experimented with sculpture, decorating the exterior of their house with concrete sculptures and bas-reliefs. At the outbreak of the war he was interned as an enemy alien: after considerable difficulties, and separation from Carrington, who underwent a severe mental illness in 1940–41, he succeeded in fleeing to New York in July 1941. After the USA entered the war, Ernst married Peggy Guggenheim, who had helped him to leave France. He became a leading figure among the émigré art community in New York: Peggy Guggenheim's Art of this Century gallery exhibited his and other European artists' work and also acted as an outlet and source of encouragement to young American artists interested in Surrealist ideas.

In New York, Ernst developed a technique using paint dripped from a suspended, swinging can. It has some similarities to the 'drip' technique used by Jackson Pollock after 1947, although any direct influence remains a matter for conjecture. Ernst reaffirmed his belief in the unconscious sources of his work in *Surrealism and Painting* (1942; priv. col., see Schneede, 1972, pl. 348), in which a hybrid bird creature is represented in the act of making a drip image. Many of his paintings of this period employ the technique of decalcomania, first advocated as a form of automatism by Oscar Domínguez. Ernst used it to represent vegetation, petrified rock formations and organic metamorphosis. A number of pictures, of which the most notable is *Europe after the Rain* (*c.* 1940–42; Hartford, CT,

Wadsworth Atheneum; see fig. 4), use decalcomania to suggest devastated landscapes and a return to a primordial chaos. Reminiscences of the style of Gustave Moreau are probably deliberate: Ernst's practice of quoting previous art was particularly evident in this period. The *Robing of the Bride* (1939–41; Venice, Guggenheim) employs Renaissance perspective devices and Cranach-like figures to represent a pagan marriage; the *Temptation of St Anthony* (1945; Duisburg, Lehmbruck-Mus.) incorporates references to the visionary tradition of Bosch and Grünewald. *Vox angelica* (1943; New Haven, CT, Yale U., A.G.), on the other hand, is an anthology of Ernst's own technical and thematic preoccupations after 1945.

(v) 1943–76. Ernst spent the summer and autumn of 1943 in Arizona with the painter Dorothea Tanning. In 1946 they settled in Sedona (nr Flagstaff, AZ), and two years later he obtained American citizenship. Between 1943 and 1950 he produced a series of paintings in a controlled geometric style. Some of them, such as *Euclid* (1945; Houston, TX, De Menil priv. col., see Schneede, 1972, pl. 360), recall the Mannerist devices of Giuseppe Arcimboldo and Giovanni Battista Bracelli. Ernst also made a number of sculptures for his house in Sedona, the most important of which, *Capricorn* (1948; *in situ*, see Russell, 1967, p. 146), represents a male figure and a female figure surrounded by masks and combines Egyptian, Cycladic and Pre-Columbian influences. *A l'intérieur de la vue: Paramythes* (text by Eluard, Paris, 1947; Eng. trans., Beverly Hills, 1949) and *La Brebis galante* (text by Benjamin Péret, Paris, 1949) use collage images that recall his early collaborations with Eluard. From the 1950s his paintings again made extensive use of automatic techniques, principally drawings over which he laid precisely drawn forms and images to organize and pattern the whole, as in *Father Rhine* (*Old Man River*) (1954; Zurich, priv. col., see Russell, 1967, p. 141).

In 1953 Ernst returned to France with Dorothea Tanning and had his first major post-war retrospective at Knokke-Het Zoute the same year. Between 1955 and 1964 the couple lived near Chinon (Indre-et-Loire); they then moved to Seillans (Var). Ernst became a naturalized French citizen in 1958. His reputation grew steadily after his return to Europe: in 1954 he was awarded a Grand Prix at the Venice Biennale and major exhibitions of his work were held in New York (1961), Cologne (1962) and Stockholm (1969). He generally avoided close involvement in the artistic debates of the period, distancing himself, in Paris, from both the Tachistes and the group of young acolytes who had gathered around Breton. In 1964 Ernst published *Maximiliana ou L'Exercice illégal de l'astronomie* in homage to the astronomer Wilhelm Tempel, which contained his last invention, a secret hieroglyphic script. A major retrospective of his work was held in New York and Paris in 1975.

2. WORKING METHODS AND TECHNIQUE. After 1918 Ernst rarely employed conventional techniques in his paintings. His early work shows that he was a technically skilled painter and draughtsman. Between 1918 and 1924 virtually all his paintings and prints were based on the principle of collage, and this practice remained central to his later work. His use of collage was very different from that of the Cubists and had more in common with the photomontage of John Heartfield, Hannah Höch and Raoul Hausmann. Cubism played with shape, texture and different kinds of mimesis, within a formally and thematically coherent whole. In his collages, however, Ernst abstracted figurative elements from their original context in order to create new forms, in which the familiar became strange and fantastic. This technique did not always involve literally cutting and sticking; some of his earliest collages were made by painting out much of the original—typically a technical illustration—and elaborating on what was left, changing its meaning in the process, as in *Stratified Rock Gift of Nature Composed of Gneiss . . .* (1920; New York, MOMA).

Ernst's major paintings of 1921–4 do not employ collage, but their composition is based on the collage principle. *Oedipus Rex* and *La Belle Jardinière* (1923; ex-Düsseldorf, Kstmus., destr. 1937, see Schneede, 1972, pl. 100), a Surrealist adaptation of Raphael, reworked images originally created in the collages *Parole* (1921) and *Sacra conversazione* (1921); *Pietà* or *Revolution by Night* fuses two figures derived from paintings by de Chirico and Ernst himself, in a pose taken from the iconographic conventions of Christian art. The *Elephant Celebes* (see fig. 2 above) is represented in a landscape setting reminiscent of de Chirico. The main body of the 'elephant' (Ernst entitled the painting 'Célèbes'; 'elephant' is a later nickname) is closely based on a photograph of an African grain store; a hose 'trunk' ending in a bull's head, and a mechanical eye, have been effectively 'stuck on' to this. The phallic tree on the right-hand side of the painting is derived from Ernst's collage the *Hat Makes the Man* (1920; New York, MOMA). The composition as a whole corresponds to Ernst's definition of collage as 'the culture of systematic displacement' and 'the exploitation of the chance meeting of two distant realities on an unfamiliar plane' (*Beyond Painting*, paraphrasing Breton and Lautréamont).

The collages for *Répétitions* and *Les Malheurs des immortels* were based on wood-engravings from 19th-century illustrated magazines. Ernst returned to this technique in the collage novels of 1929–34. These were made by pasting images from different sources on to a single base illustration. In many cases his intervention was minimal; in the *Oedipus* sequence to *Une Semaine de bonté*, for instance, several images have been changed only in the replacement of a human head by that of a bird. The completed collages were sent to the printer to be reproduced by photo-engraving; the actual pasting cannot be discerned in the published plates, and this greatly enhances their impact.

Ernst achieved a comparable level of refinement in the *frottage* technique. The drawings for *Histoire naturelle* were made by placing sheets of paper over different objects such as floorboards and leaves, and rubbing with a stick of graphite. Through precise selection, combination, control of texture and some discreet additions, he was able to build up delicate, surprising images of fantasy landscapes, plants and creatures. He adapted this fundamentally simple technique to painting in the form of *grattage*, by which textures and patterns were made through simultaneously rubbing and scraping off layers of paint. Representational forms were then extracted from the whole by means of overpainting.

Decalcomania was another way of achieving similar results. Rich, unpredictable patterns were obtained by either taking an impression from, or sponging, layers of liquid paint: figurative motifs were then developed by overpainting. In *Europe after the Rain* (see fig. 4 above) the basic division of sky and earth was achieved by painting over the sky area entirely. The exposed sections of decalcomania have been patterned using different materials and worked up by hand to represent vegetation, rock and a number of encrusted, mutilated human forms. The idea behind the technique, using chance textures to suggest forms and images, is similar to that of his early collages. All of Ernst's technical methods had the same goal of evading conventional expression of authorial intention. In his theoretical texts of the 1930s he equated these practices with the concept of 'automatism', which Breton had stated in 1924 to be the touchstone of Surrealism.

3. SOURCES AND INFLUENCES. In the *Dictionnaire abrégé du surréalisme* (1938) Ernst was defined as a 'Surrealist painter, poet and theorist from the origins of the movement to the present day'. Besides his deep affinity with Paul Eluard, he acknowledged the influence of the Symbolist poets Rimbaud and Lautréamont, and much of his work was poetic in the sense that it was verbal as well as visual. His contribution to a theory of Surrealism consisted of a series of texts, written between 1926 and 1936, in which he combined an account of his own development with an exposition of the principles on which it was based. The longest and most important of these was 'Beyond Painting', which appeared in the issue of *Cahiers d'Art* dedicated to Ernst in 1937.

Ernst argued that the task of the artist was to liberate the human imagination. This could be achieved by attacking all constraints on its functioning, notably those imposed by conventional notions of reality, morality and reason, and those embedded in the mind in the form of inhibitions. He justified the techniques of collage and *frottage* as devices for evading these constraints and releasing the creative forces of the unconscious ('He who speaks of collage speaks of the irrational.'). These ideas were developed through contact with the Surrealist circle, but his interest in the relationship between art and the unconscious mind predated his arrival in Paris. He had studied the art of the insane in Bonn before the war, and he acquired a copy of Hans Prinzhorn's pioneering book *Bildnerei der Geisteskranken* (1922) as soon as it appeared. Freud's theory of image formation in the 'dream-work' was a major influence on the development of Ernst's collage. Virtually all the paintings he executed in Paris between 1922 and 1924 have characteristics that parallel those of symbolism, condensation and displacement that Freud identified in dreams. Ernst provided clues to the enigmatic meanings of these and later paintings in his autobiographical fragments. These suggest that he found the basic principles of psychoanalysis useful in understanding his own personality and his motivations as an artist: a 'fever vision' or daydream that he experienced as a child, in which his father appeared as a frightening, lugubrious painter, is central to all these accounts.

In the special Ernst issue of *View* (1942) Ernst listed his favourite poets and painters of the past. The Romantics predominate among the poets, but most of the painters were from the Renaissance period. He apparently felt a particular admiration for Leonardo da Vinci, possibly because Leonardo's obsessive energy and cerebral character were similar to his own. He knew Freud's essay *Eine Kindheitserinnerung des Leonardo da Vinci* (Leipzig, 1910; Eng. trans., New York, 1947) and made an explicit reference to it in *One Night of Love* (1927; Paris, priv. col., see Siegel, 1983), which is based on a reverse image of Leonardo's *Virgin and Child with SS Anne and John the Baptist* (Paris, Louvre). Pfister suggested that this painting contains a hidden image of the 'vulture' that figured in Leonardo's childhood memory. Ernst's own preoccupation with birds dated from his childhood. They are represented throughout his work as victims and as symbols of the instincts and of liberty. In an autobiographical note of 1942 he referred to himself as the child of an eagle: this reflected his interest in shamanism, which exemplified for him and for other Surrealists the superiority of so-called 'primitive' attitudes to the world over modern European ones. He believed that the best European art of the past drew on the resources of the unconscious, even when it conformed to a repressive social code. In 'Beyond Painting' Ernst quoted at length a passage in the *Trattato della pittura*, in which Leonardo suggested that indeterminate visual structures, such as clouds and stains on a wall, could be used as starting-points for artistic invention. This was the essential principle of *frottage*, and confirmed in Ernst's view that the theory on which it was based had permanent validity.

WRITINGS

Cah. A., 6–7 (1937) [issue ded. Ernst, incl. 'Beyond Painting']
R. Motherwell, ed.: *Beyond Painting, and Other Writings by the Artist and his Friends* (New York, 1948)
R. Bertelé, ed.: *Ecritures* (Paris, 1970)

BIBLIOGRAPHY

MONOGRAPHS AND GENERAL EXHIBITION CATALOGUES

View, n. s., i (1942) [issue ded. Ernst]
Max Ernst (exh. cat., Knokke-Het Zoute, Casino Com., 1953)
P. Waldberg: *Max Ernst* (Paris, 1958)
Max Ernst (exh. cat., ed. W. S. Lieberman; New York, MOMA, 1961)

Max Ernst: Oeuvre sculptée, 1913–1961 (exh. cat., Paris, Gal. Point Cardinal, 1961)
Max Ernst (exh. cat., Cologne, Wallraf-Richartz-Mus., 1962)
J. Russell: *Max Ernst: Life and Work* (New York, 1967)
Max Ernst (exh. cat., Stockholm, Mod. Mus., 1969)
C. Sala: *Max Ernst et la démarche onirique* (Paris, 1970)
S. Alexandrian: *Max Ernst* (Paris, 1971; Eng. trans., London, 1972)
U. M. Schneede: *The Essential Max Ernst* (London, 1972)
P. Schamoni: *Maximiliana* (Munich, 1974)
W. Spies and others: *Max Ernst Oeuvre-Katalog*, 4 vols (Cologne, 1974–9)
G. Diehl: *Max Ernst* (Näfels, 1975; Eng. trans., New York, 1975)
Max Ernst (exh. cat. by P. Hulten, W. Spies and G. Viatte, Paris, Grand Pal., 1975)
Max Ernst: A Retrospective (exh. cat. by D. Waldman, New York, Guggenheim, 1975)
E. Quinn, ed.: *Max Ernst* (Boston, 1977)
Max Ernst: Retrospektive, 1979 (exh. cat., ed. W. Spies; Munich, Haus Kst.; W. Berlin, N.G.; 1979)
Max Ernst: A Retrospective (exh. cat., ed. W. Spies; London, Tate; Stuttgart, Staatsgal.; Düsseldorf, Kstsamml. Nordrhein–Westfalen; 1991)

COLLAGES, GRAPHIC WORK AND BOOK ILLUSTRATIONS

W. Spies: *Max Ernst: Frottagen* (Stuttgart, 1968, rev. 2/1986; Eng. trans., London, 1986)
——: *Max Ernst Collagen: Inventar und Widerspruch* (Cologne, 1974)
Max Ernst: Estampes et livres illustrés (exh. cat. by J. Adhémar and M. Frèrebeau, Paris, Bib. N., 1975)
C. V. Stokes: '*La Femme 100 têtes*' by Max Ernst (diss., Charlottesville, U. Virginia, 1977)
Max Ernst: Bücher und Grafiken (exh. cat., ed. W. Spies and W. Konnertz; Stuttgart, Inst. Auslandsbeziehungen, 1977)
Max Ernst: Frottagen, Collagen, Zeichnungen, Graphik, Bücher (exh. cat. by U. Perucchi and W. Spies, Zurich, Ksthaus; Frankfurt am Main, Städel. Kstinst.; Munich, Lenbachhaus; 1978–9)
C. V. Stokes: 'Collage as Jokework', *Leonardo*, xv/3 (1982), pp. 199–204
Max Ernst's 'Histoire naturelle' (exh. cat., intro. R. Penrose; Billingham, A.G., 1982)
Max Ernst: Beyond Surrealism (exh. cat., ed. R. Rainwater; New York, Pub. Lib.; Ann Arbor, U. MI, Mus. A.; 1986–7)

SPECIALIST STUDIES

P. Waldberg: 'La Jeunesse de Max Ernst', *Mercure France*, 1126 (1957), pp. 267–99
——: *Max Ernst: Peintures pour Paul Eluard* (Paris, 1958)
J. Ernst: 'The Artist Speaks: My Father Max Ernst', *A. Amer.*, cvi/6 (1968), pp. 54–61
W. Spies: *Max Ernst, 1950–1970: Die Rückkehr der schönen Gärtnerin* (Cologne, 1971; Eng. trans., New York, 1972)
R. Penrose: *Max Ernst: 'The Elephant Celebes'* (Newcastle upon Tyne, 1972/*R* London, 1987)
G. Hinton: 'Max Ernst: *Les Hommes n'en sauront rien*', *Burl. Mag.*, cxvii (1975), pp. 292–9
Max Ernst in Köln: Die rheinische Kunstszene bis 1922 (exh. cat., ed. W. Herzogenrath; Cologne, Kstver., 1980)
J. Siegel: 'Max Ernst's *One Night of Love*', *A. Mag.*, lvii (Jan 1983), pp. 112–15
W. Spies: *Max Ernst: Loplop* (London, 1983)
E. Legge: *Conscious Sources of the Unconscious: Ernst's Use of Psychoanalytic Themes and Imagery, 1921–1924* (diss., U. London, 1985)
M. Gee: *Ernst: 'Pietà or Revolution by Night'* (London, 1986)
E. Legge: 'Max Ernst's *Oedipus Rex* and the Implicit Sphinx', *A. Mag.*, lxi (Sept 1986), pp. 50–53
D. Hopkins: *The Bride Shared: Structures of Belief and Gender in Duchamp and Ernst* (Oxford, 1966)

GENERAL WORKS

A. Breton: *Le Surréalisme et la peinture* (Paris, 1928, rev. 3/1965; Eng. trans., London and New York, 1972), pp. 23–31, 155–68
Dada and Surrealism Reviewed (exh. cat. by D. Ades, ACGB, 1978)
E. Maurer: 'Dada and Surrealism', *Primitivism in 20th Century Art: Affinity of the Tribal and the Modern*, ii (exh. cat., ed. W. S. Rubin; New York, MOMA, 1984), pp. 535–94

MALCOLM GEE

Erős [Erőss], **Gábor** (*b* Debrecen, 1779; *d* Debrecen, 30 Jan 1815). Hungarian engraver. He studied drawing, engraving and carving under Isaiah Budai (1766–1841) at the Debrecen Reform College. In 1800 he helped to make the first Hungarian language school map, the *Oskolai új átlás* (New school atlas). He and his fellow students Jozsef Pap and István Halász engraved the maps of Europe, Africa, North America, Spain, Italy, Germany, Poland and Hungary. In 1801 a 12-page antiquarian atlas was published for which he, among others, made the 'Orbis terrarum veteribus cogniti Typus' and the maps of Asia Minor. He also made the maps of Great Britain, Norway, Switzerland and Prussia for the 15-page Gatterer map repertory, along with Imré Vajai and Dávid Pethes. After the success of the Debrecen engraving students' maps the 12-page *Oskolai Magyar új átlást* (New school Hungarian atlas) was published in 1804. For this Erős engraved the five continents, Spain, Portugal, Great Britain and Germany. He also made his own original engravings and etchings. In 1800 he engraved an allegory of Mihály Csokonai Vitéz's poem *A szépség ereje a bajnoki szivenn* (The victory of beauty over my valorous heart), and in 1803 he engraved a bust of Anacreon for his collection of verses *Számára Anakreon* (Songs of Anacreon). In the same year he made engravings of the drawings done by his relation János Erős illustrating Jozsef Szentgyörgyi's book *A legnevezetesebb természeti dolgok esméreti* (Important natural history facts), and he engraved an inscription for the silver offertory cup in the Reform Church in Szalacs. When he had completed his studies in Debrecen he went on to study in Pest and Vienna, gaining much practice in letter engraving. His efforts to purchase the Sarospatak and Komárom press were unsuccessful: he had to give up his engraving and typography career because of financial difficulties. Although he still took on etching, printing and stereotypography jobs, he made his meagre living as a clerk.

BIBLIOGRAPHY

L. Naményi: 'Erős Gábor rézmetsző' [Gábor Erős engraver], *Művészet*, iii (1904), p. 204

D. Pataky: *A magyar rézmetszés története* [The history of Hungarian engraving] (Budapest, 1951), pp. 48–9, 117–18

B. Toth: *A debreceni rézmetsző diákok* [The Debrecen engraving students] (Budapest, 1976)

JÚLIA PAPP

Erotic art. Term applied to art with a sexual content, and especially to art that celebrates human sexuality. It is derived from *eros*, the Greek word for human, physical love for another person (as opposed to *agape*, the spiritual, unselfish love for a god). The imagery of erotic art may be either explicitly or implicitly sexual, instances of the latter being more common in many cultures because of such factors as codes of behaviour, prudery and censorship. The majority of sexually explicit works of art in the Western world have been produced as part of an overall desire to express the totality of human experience: very few artists have made eroticism their only motivation. In many other societies and cultures, however, sex has provided a far more evident source of inspiration.

I. Historical survey. II. Historiography and collections.

I. Historical survey.

1. Ancient cultures. 2. Western world. 3. Asia and the Islamic world.

1. ANCIENT CULTURES. All ancient cultures sought to humanize and sexualize their universe by 'projecting' their emotions and activities on to the spiritual powers thought to control nature. A basic concern of many ancient religions was the ritual promotion of fertility in humanity and its food supply. Sexual magic was also widely used as a defence against malignant forces, and sexuality permeated the beliefs and rites marking the human life-cycle. Thus the myths, rituals and arts of ancient cultures, and of many continuing traditions rooted in them, express a wide variety of sexual themes. Erotic images are among the earliest surviving indications of human culture in the Paleolithic period between *c.* 30,000 and 10,000 BC. It is generally assumed that this art reflects beliefs relating to hunting and fertility magic and totemism. Carved reliefs and paintings in caves at such sites as La Ferassie, ANGLES-SUR-L'ANGLIN, La Magdaleine and Le Portel in southern France include figures with pronounced vulvas and phalluses, often juxtaposed with hunting images. Paleolithic 'Venus' statuettes found at LAUSELL, France, and WILLENDORF, Austria, focus attention on enormous breasts, swelling stomach and vulva and are probably emblems of the veneration of female sexuality and childbearing.

Many erotic images and artefacts survive from the Neolithic period between *c.* 9000 and 7000 BC. A carved stone from Ain Sakri in the Judaean Desert (London, BM) represents perhaps the earliest image of human copulation. With the advent of stock-breeding, the male role in procreation must have been well understood and highly valued: many Neolithic figurines of women, usually obese and with vulva emphasized, show associated images of

1. Erotic image of the ithyphallic god Bes (Selçuk, Ephesos Archaeological Museum)

bulls and other horned animals. Some of the most impressive Neolithic images of the fertility cult have been excavated at the sites of Çatal Hüyük and Hacılar on the Anatolian plateau of Turkey. These have been interpreted as representations of the Mother Goddess, the Mother of Beasts and the Sacred Marriage (ritual copulation to promote the fertility of humanity, animals and all nature). Crudely carved figurines and chalk phalluses have been found at various Neolithic sites in England, such as Maumbury Rings, Dorset (examples in Dorchester, Dorset Co. Mus.); at Grimes Graves, Norfolk, a chalk statuette of an obese woman with associated phallus and testicles was found (London, BM) that is thought to be evidence of a fertility ritual.

By 3000 BC the great Bronze Age civilizations of Egypt and Mesopotamia had evolved from Neolithic village cultures. Whereas the interpretations of earlier art can only be a matter of conjecture, the written texts of these ancient civilizations illuminate the religious and sexual symbolism of their art. Egyptian creation myths are represented in many papyri depicting copulating couples with exaggerated sexual organs, such as the Papyrus of Tameniu from the 21st Dynasty (c. 1075–c. 950 BC; London, BM). Large ithyphallic statues of Min of Coptos, god of male creativity and sexual pleasure, have been found at Coptos, and the same figure also appears with the Pharaoh Ramesses III (12th century BC) in the latter's mortuary temple. The cult of Isis and Osiris was celebrated in many erotic images, and the ithyphallic god Bes, patron of prostitutes and initiator of sexual magic, was also frequently depicted (see fig. 1). Mesopotamian art is rich in cylinder seals and moulded terracotta plaques: collections of these objects (e.g. New York, Met.; Paris, Louvre; Oxford, Ashmolean; and London, BM) contain numerous nude images of the goddess Inamia-Ishtar, often in various positions of intercourse, as well as scenes of sexual activity among her priests (see fig. 2).

Bronze Age and Celtic European art is sometimes concerned with the Earth Mother as a sexual fertility symbol, but more frequently found are ithyphallic warriors: many examples are seen in the rock engravings of Sweden and southern Europe. Bronze figurines and jewellery with clear sexual significance have been found throughout Europe. One of the most remarkable erotic images once thought to be of the period is the Cerne Abbas Giant, an ithyphallic hillside figure in Dorset that was thought to represent the Romano-British deity Hercules-Ogmios (see fig. 3). Research in the mid-1990s indicated that it is probably of much later date.

In Africa, initiation ceremonies and fertility rites have provided sexual imagery for many millennia, although it is unclear whether such imagery is intended to be erotic. Rock engravings dating from c. 5000 BC at Ti-n-Lalan in Libyan Fezzan depict a semi-human creature with an enormous penis and canine head and tail, sometimes copulating with a woman. Among the Dogon of western Sudan, the design of masks, clothing and even houses exhibits strong sexual symbolism. In southern Ethiopia there are an estimated 10,000 phallic stone columns, some as tall as 6 m, that are of ancient origin but are still venerated in the 20th century. The phallus has long been seen as a symbol of male power, and images of such deities

2. *Sacred Prostitute and Client*, terracotta plaque, from the Ishtar Temple at Assur, 8th–7th centuries BC (Berlin, Museum für Vor- und Frühgeschichte)

3. Cerne Abbas Giant, chalk hill-figure at Cerne Abbas, Dorset

as Legba and Eshu, with their prominent penises, can still be found throughout West Africa. Similarly the Yoruba of Nigeria have made bronze sculptures of the female deity

Onile displaying her vulva, and such images are also incorporated into ceremonial masks. Much sexually explicit sculpture in Africa, however, is intended to be educational rather than erotic, and in many cultures the most erotically charged art form is scarification.

The legends of the Australian Aborigines continue to be illustrated in rock engravings and bark paintings, often with a strong sexual content. Examples on rock walls at Djilgu in north-western Australia depict phallic lightning spirits and the wild-yam spirit Ungamin, whose ejaculating penis resembles an enormous yam. In other Pacific islands, erotic imagery was found mainly in ceremonial buildings. For example, an elaborately carved wooden pole supporting the gable of the *haus tambaran* in the Sepik River area of New Guinea showed a naked woman displaying her vulva (*see* PACIFIC ISLANDS, §II, 1), and similar images (known as *dilukai*) were the main features of the façades of the sacred clubhouses of unmarried men's fraternities in Palau in Micronesia. The *dilukai* were accompanied by processions of ithyphallic men bearing gifts. In Polynesia, Maori legends were illustrated on carved wooden panels of ceremonial buildings and often included copulating ancestors and women with tattooed vulvas. Such erotic images were also found on other carved objects, including flutes and the handles and lids of sacred wooden boxes.

Sexual divinities were frequently depicted in ancient Mesoamerican art. The Dresden Codex of the Classic Maya period (*c.* AD 250–*c.* 900) shows the elderly god Mam copulating with the youthful goddess of procreation and love Ix Chel, and the same couple often appear embracing on contemporary terracottas. By contrast, grossly ithyphallic ceramic statuettes were produced in the cultures of the modern western states of Colima and Michoacán. A magnificent Aztec figure of a naked crouching woman in childbirth dating from the 15th century (Washington, DC, N.G.A.) is thought to represent Tlazoltéotl, the goddess of fertility and sexuality, giving birth to the maize god Cintéotl.

In Peru, numerous tombs dating from a succession of cultures have been excavated, and most have been found to contain figurative erotic drinking vessels that held alcoholic beverages for the comfort of the dead in their afterlife. The Moche civilization of the 1st to the 8th century AD was the most prolific and varied for such ceramic production, and many of these erotic vessels are now in the Museo de Arte, Lima, and the Institute for Sex Research at Indiana University, Bloomington, IN. Pots with stirrup-shaped spout-handles represent the male and female genitals. A favourite motif is a seated man holding his enormous phallus. The main opening is in the top of his headdress, but liquid would dribble from the perforations below the rim if one tried to drink from there, and instead one would be forced to suck from the small hole in the glans of the phallus-spout. Other pots show copulating couples in various positions, scenes of fellatio and both homosexual and heterosexual intercourse. In Mexico, in a priest's grave at Awatobi, a bowl was found that depicts an ancient Hopi Indian fertility rite (ex-Berlin Mus., Berlin): dancers with enormous erections perform before the Maize Maid.

In the religion and mythology of Classical Greece and Rome, the love stories of the gods were vitally important, both as powerfully erotic inspiration and as the symbolic representation of fertility in nature. Sex, religion, and magic were closely interwoven: art objects, from lamps and vases to paintings and sculptures, show explicit sexual activities in a completely open manner. Zeus or Jupiter, king of Mount Olympus, is the divine hero of many Classical legends, and his amorous conquests are depicted in many Greek vases and Roman lamps and cameos. Especially popular was the story of his love-making in the form of a swan with Leda, wife of King Tyndarus of Sparta. Marble reliefs from the 2nd century AD in the Archaeological Museum in Irakleion, Crete, and the National Archaeological Museum in Athens show the nude figure of Leda helping the swan to penetrate her, encouraged by a naked cupid. Jupiter's affection for the beautiful youth Ganymede was also the subject of many images, for homosexual love was considered not only normal but indeed desirable in certain contexts. Thus the seductive figures of Eros, the god of love, produced by Praxiteles in the 4th century BC were greatly admired, as were the images of Aphrodite, the goddess of beauty (e.g. *Aphrodite of Knidos*, *Aphrodite of Delphi*), which show her with one hand lowered towards her vulva to emphasize her femininity.

Vases, dishes, bowls and cups were the most common gifts in ancient Greece, and since many were directed towards lovers and courtesans, explicit scenes of love-making were common. A cup attributed to Skythes (Paris, Louvre) shows scenes of a wild orgy with various types of intercourse depicted in vivid detail. Religion justified all kinds of sexual love, and erotic excitement was endowed with a sacred character largely because of its association with the cult of Dionysus, god of fertility as well as pleasure. Thus two Attic bowls (London, BM) show Dionysiac rituals, with the god surrounded by sexually excited followers. The worship of Dionysus was characterized by the cult of the phallus, which was probably taken over from the Egyptian deity Min of Coptos. It found expression in the phallic monuments at the Dionysiac temples, such as those erected by Karystios at Delos at the beginning of the Hellenistic era, and also in the crude figures of Hermes with erect phalluses that were popular as fertility symbols in the fields (*see* HERM).

Similar figures depicting the fertility god Priapus were favoured by the intensely superstitious Romans, who considered such phallic images to be powerful talismans. Much evidence of such beliefs was found in the ruins of Pompeii, destroyed by the eruption of Mt Vesuvius in AD 79; examples include amulets and good luck charms in the form of phalluses with wings and hind legs with bells attached to them (London, BM). Domestic lamps had phallus-shaped pendants, and tables were supported by carved ithyphallic figures. Mosaic floors often depicted a phallus, and such images were often incorporated into the walls of buildings, and also into tombstones. The Etruscans had earlier associated death with a renewal of sexual powers, and the Tomb of the Bull at Tarquinia (6th century BC) includes two wall paintings of copulating figures accompanied by animals. Parallels between human and animal sexuality were depicted in bestial scenes on the walls of Roman temples in honour of Priapus, and a famous sculpture found at Pompeii (now in the Museo e Gallerie Nazionali di Capodimonte, Naples) shows Pan having intercourse with a goat. The English sculptor Joseph Nollekens made a terracotta copy (London, BM) while living in Naples in the 1760s.

Wall paintings at Pompeii give valuable insights into Roman erotic art in the mid-1st century BC. In the House of the Vettii is a painting of a deity weighing his enormous phallus with a pair of scales counterbalanced with fruit and crops. No doubt it served a dual purpose as both a talisman against evil and an emblem of fertility. The brothel paintings show intercourse of all possible types and in all positions, representing a philosophy of human love derived from now lost Hellenistic illustrated treatises on modes of copulation. Around the walls of a room in the Villa of Mysteries, 29 life-size figures are depicted on a rich red background, enacting what are believed to be the secret initiation rites of the cult of Dionysus. The god is shown tenderly caressing Ariadne while a woman unveils a basket containing an enormous phallus, and a half-naked female with enormous black wings wields a long thin whip over the arched back of a young girl. The quality of the work is outstanding.

EWA

BIBLIOGRAPHY
J. Marcadé: *Eros Kalos: Essay on Erotic Elements in Greek Art* (New York, Geneva, Paris and Hamburg, 1962)
R. L. Hoyle: *Checan: Essay on Erotic Elements in Peruvian Art* (Geneva, Paris and Munich, 1965)
J. Marcadé: *Roma Amor: Essay on Erotic Elements in Etruscan and Roman Art* (Geneva, Paris and Munich, 1965)
J. Mellaart: *Earliest Civilisations of the Near East* (London, 1965)
P. J. Ucko and A. Rosenfeld: *Paleolithic Cave Art* (London, 1967)
B. Rachewiltz: *Black Eros: The Sexual Customs of Africa from Prehistoric Times to the Present Day* (London, 1968)
G. R. Scott: *Phallic Worship* (London, 1970)
P. Rawson, ed.: *Primitive Erotic Art* (London and New York, 1973)
C. Johns: *Sex or Symbol: Erotic Images of Greece and Rome* (London, 1982)

2. WESTERN WORLD. In Western art the whole concept of eroticism is coloured by a background of taboos. The female nude seems to dominate erotic art in the West since most painting has been executed by men. Rarely is the nude painted dispassionately, for by its very nature it arouses the senses. However, the power of the attraction has led it to be feared in a Judaeo-Christian civilization, and the resulting censorship of explicit sexuality in art has resulted in works whose eroticism is deliberately veiled and whose erotic power is thereby greatly increased. Whereas other world religions have regarded sexual pleasure as an important part of worship and have treated the sexual adventures of gods and goddesses as sacred texts, Christianity is a non-sexual religion. Jesus was sympathetic towards women and the state of matrimony, but St Paul's antipathy to the union of the sexes became the stronger influence. Since the Church was one of the main patrons of the arts in the West until the 18th century, this process had a deep effect on painting and sculpture and led to a distinctive artistic tradition in which the erotic content of many works was presented in an implicit or coded form.

(i) The Middle Ages. (ii) *c.* 1500–*c.* 1700. (iii) *c.* 1700–*c.* 1900. (iv) After *c.* 1900.

(i) The Middle Ages. Eroticism is not common in the art of the Early Christian period and the Middle Ages. Representations of erotic scenes are to be found, however, in both secular and religious contexts. They occur in articles of value owned by the rich such as jewellery,

decorated furniture and manuscripts. Examples include a set of silver plates (St Petersburg, Hermitage), the ivory and bone Veroli casket (late 10th century–early 11th; London, V&A; *see* EARLY CHRISTIAN AND BYZANTINE ART, fig. 9) and a 13th-century gilt mirror (Frankfurt am Main, Städel. Kstinst. & Städt. Gal.), all decorated with scenes of love-making or erotic motifs. Politely erotic miniatures appear in manuscripts relating to Chaucer and Boccaccio or the *Fountain of Life* and the *Garden of Love* (e.g. the *Douce Manuscript*, 15th century; Oxford, Bodleian Lib.; or the Très Riches Heures of the Duc de Berry, *c.* 1411/13–16; Chantilly, Mus. Condé). More robust is the *Roman de la Rose* or a scene in the Bayeux Tapestry (11th century) that shows a nude couple with the man having an erection and stretching his arms out to the woman. Many other medieval manuscripts include marginal scenes that are highly erotic.

Churches throughout Europe were provided with erotic images of various sorts, many of which have since been destroyed. Most obvious are the *Shelah-na-Gig* fertility figures of nude women exposing their vulvas that are

4. Fertility figure, *Shelah-na-Gig*, corbel, from SS Mary and David, Kilpeck, Hereford and Worcestershire, early 12th century

found on some English, and especially Irish, Saxon and Norman churches. These were usually taken from pagan places of worship and incorporated into the fabric of Christian churches. Good English examples are to be found in the 12th-century church of SS Mary and David at Kilpeck, Hereford & Worcs (see fig. 4), and in Oaksey Church, near Leicester. Many Irish examples are now in the Museum of the Royal Society of Antiquaries of Ireland in Dublin. An unusual variant over the window of the church at Whittlesford, Cambs, shows a *Shelah-na-Gig* on one side and an ithyphallic man opposite her. Similar female figures are found elsewhere in Europe (e.g. capitals in the Romanesque cathedral of Piacenza). *Shelah-na-Gig*s have striking resemblances to the heraldic female figures from the Sepik River area of New Guinea and are related in conception to the ithyphallic Cerne Abbas Giant (*see* §1 above).

Erotic imagery can also be found on the capitals, bosses, and misericords of Romanesque and Gothic churches throughout Europe. Examples include a devil with a large erection at Hereford Cathedral; couples in the '69' position in the choir school of the château at Montreuil Bellay (Maine-et-Loire) and in the church of S Gregorio at Valladolid; embracing nude couples at Modena Cathedral and Chichester Cathedral; and copulating couples at Toledo Cathedral and the church of St Martin at L'isle-Adam (Val d'Oise) in France. These scattered erotica are not so much proof of the Church's liberality as of the wily artfulness of the craftsmen it employed.

(ii) c. 1500–c. 1700. The new humanism of the Renaissance in Italy during the 15th century, with its renewal of interest in the world of Classical antiquity, led to dramatic changes in the progress of the arts. The shameful connotations associated with nudity *per se* began to disappear, and with the rise of enlightened secular patronage the hold of the Church over the arts weakened, although it continued to be a major source of patronage in both northern and southern Europe. Religious subject-matter is predominant in the art of the period, but erotic themes or undertones are frequently present. Certain Old Testament stories were ideal for erotic treatment, such as *Susanna at her Bath Spied on by the Elders* (painted by such artists as Tintoretto, Domenichino and Guido Reni), *Joseph Tempted by Potiphar's Wife* (Titian, Guercino, Veronese) and *Lot Committing Incest with his Daughters* (Raphael, Francesco Furini). The most powerfully erotic is the story of Judith, who seduced the enemy commander Holofernes and then cut off his head while he was recovering from the physical exertions of intercourse. This was a favourite subject of such northern artists as Lucas Cranach the elder and Hans Baldung, and in Italy it was painted by Mantegna, Giorgione and Titian, among others. Tintoretto's version (*c.* 1555; Madrid, Prado) conveys the erotic undertones of the violent death, and the painting by Artemesia Gentileschi (*c.* 1613–14; Florence, Uffizi) is especially interesting as one of the earliest erotic paintings by a female artist.

The most obvious figure for erotic portrayal in the New Testament was Mary Magdalene. Francesco Furini portrayed her (Dublin, N.G.) as a full length frontal nude in a state of excitement, clutching a crucifix and stroking a skull. More usually, however, she is shown half-length, with her hands clasped over her naked breasts and a look of ecstasy on her features, as in versions by Tintoretto and Guercino. A painting by Elisabetta Sirani (Besançon, Mus. B.-A. & Archéol.) shows her clutching a whip to her naked breasts, and in Titian's portrayal (1554; Florence, Pitti) she is shown gazing rapturously up to heaven as she clutches her long silky tresses to her body, leaving her full breasts provocatively exposed. Martyrdom scenes also provided erotic subjects. SS Barbara, Christine, Catherine and Margaret were often painted nude being whipped by excited torturers. St Agatha was depicted by Sebastiano del Piombo (1520; Florence, Pitti) with two men attacking her breasts with tongs.

Homosexual patrons often commissioned the *Martyrdom of St Sebastian*. Examples by Sodoma (1525; Florence, Pitti; *see* SODOMA, fig. 1) and Guido Reni (Rome, Mus. Capitolino) show a beautiful idealized male nude transfixed by arrows and struggling to free himself as he gazes upwards with an expression that mingles agony with ecstasy. Homosexuality was condemned by Christian doctrine, but such artists as Perugino and Sodoma were able to cater for such interests. Perhaps the most significant homosexual icon was Michelangelo's *David* (1501–4; Florence, Accad. B.A. & Liceo A.), which in retrospect can be clearly seen as the expression of the artist's own sexual preference. It embodies the epitome of male sexual attraction and excitement, and it is therefore understandable (though no less regrettable) that a fig-leaf was added, to Michelangelo's horror, in order to hide the figure's powerful maleness. The offence was not rectified until the early 20th century. Many of Caravaggio's paintings of young nude male saints and mythological figures show a similar degree of homosexual involvement, the most provocative being *Victorious Cupid* (*c.* 1603; Berlin, Gemäldegal.; for illustration *see* GIUSTINIANI (i)).

Figures from Greek mythology rivalled saints and biblical characters in Renaissance art, providing endless opportunities for erotic portrayals. Of these, Venus was the most popular. Botticelli's *Birth of Venus* (*c.* 1484; Florence, Uffizi), Giorgione's *Sleeping Venus* (1505–10; Dresden, Gemäldegal.) and Titian's *Venus of Urbino* (*c.* 1538; Florence, Uffizi) can all in their different ways be recognized as personifications of sexual beauty. Jupiter's appetite for love was notoriously inexhaustible, and the imagination he put into his courting inspired most painters of the period in northern and southern Europe. Thus *Danaë and the Shower of Gold* was the subject of erotic images by Jan Gossart, Titian, Correggio, Tintoretto and Veronese among others, and *Leda and the Swan* was painted by Titian, Correggio, Bronzino, Lorenzo di Credi and Perino del Vaga. Raphael executed a drawing of *Leda* (Windsor Castle, Royal Lib.) after a famous painting (*c.* 1510; untraced) by Leonardo of the nude princess standing in a flowery meadow embracing the swan. Michelangelo painted the nude *Leda* in 1529 with the swan between her legs after the act of intercourse, its neck between her breasts and its beak touching her lips. One wing fluttered in the air while the princess sank into her pillows in post-coital exhaustion. In the 17th-century the painting was destroyed as obscene and is only known through copies and reproductive prints (see fig. 5).

Formofa hec Leda eft, egmus fit Iuppiter illam
Comprimit, hoc geminum quis credat/parturit ouum,

Ex illo gemini pollux, cum paftore fratres;
Ex ifto trumpeus Helene pulcherrima prodit.

5. *Leda and the Swan*, 16th-century engraving by Cornelis Bos after Michelangelo (London, Royal Academy)

The most notorious of Raphael's erotic works are his frescoes on the theme of the *History of Venus*, executed *c.* 1515 for Cardinal Bibbiena's bathroom in the Vatican. They were whitewashed over in the 19th century and are now in poor condition and out of bounds to visitors. One of the most celebrated of all artistic scandals in 16th-century Italy involved Raphael's pupil Giulio Romano. This was the publication *c.* 1524 of *Aretino's Sonnets* or *Postures*, a book consisting of engravings by Marcantonio Raimondi after lost drawings by Giulio, with accompanying sonnets in bawdy language by Pietro Aretino. Each picture showed a man and a woman in a different position of intercourse. All copies of the original publication seem to have been destroyed, although a single plate is in the Graphische Sammlung Albertina, Vienna, and another single plate survives, with other heavily mutilated plates, in the British Museum, London. Giulio's erotic interests can be seen in his mythological frescoes at the Palazzo del Te in Mantua (*see* GIULIO ROMANO, fig. 3). The missing Aretino drawings were probably a set of *Loves of the Gods*. Such erotic scenes were also produced by Titian, Francesco Primaticcio and Perino del Vaga but are known today only through engravings. The most prolific engraver of erotic subjects at this time was Agostino Carracci (examples in London, BM; Paris, Bib. N.; and Lyon, Mus. B.-A.). The British Museum also has erotic prints by Enea Vico after Parmigianino, by an unknown artist after Jacopo de' Barbari and by Giovanni Battista del Porto.

In France in the 16th century Francis I formed a collection of erotic art at the château of Fontainebleau that included the above-mentioned *Leda and the Swan* by both Michelangelo (destr.) and Leonardo (untraced), as well as Bronzino's *Venus, Cupid, Folly and Time* (*c.* 1544–5; London, N.G.; *see* BRONZINO, AGNOLO, fig. 2), until recently retouched. The King encouraged erotic art, and the Fontainebleau school produced many mythological scenes (e.g. *Venus at the Mirror* and *Mars and Venus*; both Paris, Louvre), as well as nude portraits of the mistresses of Francis and his successor, Henry IV (*Diane de Poitiers as Diana the Huntress* and *Two Court Ladies in the Bath*; both Paris, Louvre). This gallantry in French art continued in the 17th century with Poussin's many erotic drawings and his mythological scenes, such as *Satyr Uncovering the Sleeping Venus* (London, N.G.) and *Leda and the Swan* (Chantilly, Mus. Condé).

In northern Europe during the 17th century there was a trend towards particularized naturalism in erotic art. Rembrandt's *Danaë* (1636; St Petersburg, Hermitage; *see* REMBRANDT VAN RIJN, fig. 3) and *Bathsheba* (1654; Paris, Louvre) suggest intimate glimpses into the artist's private life and were posed for by his wife and mistress respectively. His engraving entitled *'Ledikant'* (*'Le lit à la française'*) (1646; see fig. 6) shows a couple having intercourse and is believed to represent the artist and his mistress Hendrickje Stoffels. Rubens portrayed his wife in many mythological disguises, and in *Hélène Fourment in a*

6. Rembrandt: *'Ledikant'* (*'Le lit à la française'*), etching, engraving and drypoint, 130×230 mm, 1646 (London, British Museum)

Fur Wrap (1630–33; Vienna, Ksthist. Mus.; *see* PORTRAI-TURE, fig. 2) he depicted her almost naked, perhaps having just got out of bed. Thus he was probably the first artist who dared to paint an erotic portrayal of the woman he loved without concealing it behind a biblical or mytholog-ical story. Such freedom was not found elsewhere: Italian art of the Baroque period includes many representations of swooning and ecstatic saints, suggesting repressed sexuality. The most famous example is perhaps Bernini's life-size coloured marble sculpture of the *Ecstasy of St Theresa* (1647–52) in the Cornaro Chapel in the church of S Maria della Vittoria in Rome, in which the Saint appears to be in the throes of orgasm as she reclines beneath the beautiful young angel (*see* BAROQUE, fig. 1). Closer to the northern tendency is the *Rokeby Venus* by Velázquez (*c.* 1650; London, N.G.; *see* VELÁZQUEZ, DIEGO, fig. 8), where the nude goddess seems a very contemporary example of Spanish beauty as she presents her rear view to our gaze and looks at us via a mirror held by a naked cupid.

(iii) c. 1700–c. 1900. The 18th century was not only the Age of Reason but also the Age of Pleasure. French painting of the period reflects the amoral, fun-loving atmosphere of court life; the joys of love-making were celebrated with official approval, and Francis I and Henry IV were succeeded as patrons by the hedonistic Louis XV and his mistresses. Artists who specialized in engravings of erotic subjects included Niclas Lafrensen, Charles Eisen, Louis Binet (1744–*c.* 1800) and Pierre-Antoine Baudouin,

all of whom enjoyed court patronage. The British Museum, London, has an album of 68 watercolours (the *Histoire universelle*) that shows explicitly erotic scenes from biblical history and mythological legend, with the coat of the Orléans family on every page. Philippe II, Duc d'Orléans, was a great admirer of Antoine Watteau, whose *Pilgrimage to the Isle of Cythera* (1717; Paris, Louvre; *see* WATTEAU, (1), fig. 3) is a wistful and poetic allegory of love but whose *Lady at her Toilet* (*c.* 1716–17; London, Wallace) is an intimate glimpse of a voluptuous nude undressing in her bedroom. The archetypal 18th-century French painter was François Boucher, court painter to Louis XV, whose favourite subject was the sexual adventures of Venus. The King's mistress Madame de Pompadour commissioned a set of four *Loves of Venus* in 1754 (London, Wallace) as well as *Venus, Mercury and Cupid* (Berlin, Dahlem Skulp-samml.), in which Mercury is shown with an erection. The King presented his mistress with six explicitly erotic rustic scenes by Boucher, which are believed to have been destroyed in 1871 in the fire at the Tuileries Palace, Paris, and are known only through old photographs. Another of the King's mistresses, Louise O'Murphy, may have been the subject of Boucher's *Reclining Nude* (1752; Munich, Alte Pin.; *see* PORTRAITURE, fig. 4); here the 18-year-old girl lies provocatively nude on her stomach, her enticing buttocks demanding to be fondled, in what has come to be considered one of the most erotic depictions of the female nude in Western art. The King's last mistress, the Comtesse Du Barry, favoured Jean-Honoré Fragonard, who specialized in erotic bedroom frolics with such titles as *Useless Resistance* (*c.* 1770; Stockholm, Nmus.) and *Cupid Stealing a Nightgown* (Paris, Louvre). For Madame Du Barry's château at Louveciennes he painted a scene showing *The Progress of Love* (New York, Frick), but his most famous work is *The Swing* (1767; London, Wallace; *see* FRAGONARD, (1), fig. 2), in which a pretty girl on a swing kicks up her legs and reveals her satin stockings to an excited young man.

Jewellery and small *objets d'art* frequently used sexual themes during this period in France, Germany and England; for example, a small snuff-box from Birmingham (*c.* 1765; Wolverhampton, A.G.) has a false lid showing a soldier copulating with a nun on an altar. However, English art more often treated sex in a moralistic manner, as with William Hogarth's *Harlot's Progress* series of 1732 (paintings destr. 1755). Hogarth's fascination for sexual matters is very clearly reflected in the two series of paintings named *Before* and *After* of 1730–31 (version, Cambridge, Fitzwilliam), which relate to the violation of a young girl. Engravings were the more usual form of erotica: James Gillray's *Fashionable Contrasts, or the Duchess's Little Shoe Yielding to the Magnitude of the Duke's Foot* of 1792 is a satirical view of the Duchess of York, showing a pair of legs with female shoes in a horizontal position with a male pair between them. The erotic prints of Thomas Rowlandson form a small but important part of his total output. Rowlandson was a friend of the fast-living Prince Regent (later George IV), for whom he produced a series of erotic drawings (Windsor Castle, Berks, Royal Col.). His erotica date from his later years and often contain a strong voyeuristic element, with older men observing young girls or copulating couples. He could also work in a comic vein, however: a set of ten prints of love-makers from 1810 entitled *Pretty Little Games for Young Ladies and Gentlemen: With Pictures of Good Old English Sports and Pastimes* (London, BM) includes *The Country Squire New Mounted, Rural Felicity or Love in a Chaise* and *New Feats of Horsemanship*. The Swiss artist Henry Fuseli was also producing erotica in London at this time. His famous paintings entitled *The Nightmare* (1781; Detroit, MI, Inst. A.; and 1782–91; Weimar, Goethe-Nmus. Frauenplan) relate to folk legends and show a woman swooning on her bed with a devil squatting on her body. He also produced hundreds of erotic drawings, many of which were burnt by his widow: those that have survived include an image from the 1820s of three nude girls on a bed servicing a nude man with an erection (London, V&A). The girls have exotic hairstyles that relate to Fuseli's known fetish for women's hair. Another example of *c.* 1815–29 (see fig. 7) shows two elegantly coiffured nude girls in a lesbian activity in front of a mirror.

The open celebration of sexuality in much 18th-century art found little parallel in the 19th century, which paradoxically proved to be a period more obsessed with sex than any that had gone before. In England John Ruskin's intense prudery had a significant influence on the arts. After the death of J. M. W. Turner, Ruskin destroyed certain of the artist's drawings that he considered objectionable, but fortunately some items, including two paintings of nude couples making love (e.g. *Venus and Psyche*; London, Tate), have survived, and the collection of Turner sketchbooks in the British Museum, London, includes at

7. Henry Fuseli: *Lesbian Couple, c.* 1815–29 (London, Maclean-Hobart Fine Art)

least some containing erotic drawings. Outstanding is a separate sheet with on one side a woman performing fellatio on a man and on the other side a pen-and-ink close-up of a man's penis entering the vulva of a woman whose legs are over his shoulders; also on this sheet is a watercolour sketch of a nude Silenus kneeling beside a nude nymph whom he is kissing while manipulating her vulva with his fingers. Elsewhere in Europe, Neo-classical art contained strong erotic undertones. Antonio Canova's *Cupid and Psyche* (1789–93; Paris, Louvre) deeply shocked Wordsworth but sexually excited Flaubert, while Bertel Thorvaldsen's marble reliefs, such as *Cupid Received by Anacreon* (1823–4; Copenhagen, Thorvaldsens Mus.), were highly valued in some quarters for their strong homoerotic implications. The nudes painted by Ingres, such as the Valpinçon *Bather* (1808; Paris, Louvre) and the *Grande Odalisque* (1814; Paris, Louvre), betray an obsession with the sexual attraction of the female body, and the *Turkish Bath* (completed 1863; Paris, Louvre; *see* INGRES, JEAN-AUGUSTE-DOMINIQUE, fig. 4), with its mass of nude and intertwined females, seems to represent a vision of the lustful yearnings of an old man. In the Musée Ingres at Montauban is a collection of the artist's careful copies of erotic 16th-century Italian prints.

For Romantic artists in France violence added an essential ingredient to eroticism, for example in Eugène Delacroix's *Massacres at Chios* (1824; Paris, Louvre). The obvious example is Théodore Gericault, whose bedroom scenes of nude couples, such as *The Lovers* (1815–16;

Paris, Dubaut priv. col.) and *The Kiss* (1822; USA, priv. col.), display a disquieting undercurrent that is still clearer in *Nude Being Tortured* (*c.* 1817; Bayonne, Mus. Bonnat) and his two sculptures of *Nymph Attacked by a Satyr* (*c.* 1818–19; Paris, Rollin priv. col.; and Buffalo, NY, Albright–Knox A.G.). Later in the century, the Realism of Gustave Courbet was a direct reaction against the excesses of Romanticism, and Courbet's erotic nudes, such as *Woman with a Parrot* (1866) and *Nude in the Waves* (1868; both New York, Met.), shocked many people through their alleged 'ugliness' and outspokenness. Khalil Bey, former Turkish ambassador to St Petersburg, commissioned from Courbet two paintings that caused scandals in the 1860s. *The Sleepers* (1866; Paris, Petit Pal.) shows two entwined nude women relaxing on a bed after making love and is one of the few major works of Western art on the theme of lesbianism. *Origin of the World* (*c.* 1867; Japan, priv. col.) depicts the torso of a nude woman with legs apart, concentrating attention on the vulva. This painting, which was eulogized by Edmond de Goncourt in 1889, was untraced until the late 20th century, when it was found to be in the collection of the philosopher Jacques Lacan.

Controversy also bedevilled Edouard Manet. His *Déjeuner sur l'herbe* (1863; Paris, Mus. d'Orsay; see MANET, EDOUARD, fig. 1) provoked a violent outcry because it showed naked women picnicking with clothed men in a contemporary rather than mythological setting. Similarly, his *Olympia* (1863; Paris, Mus. d'Orsay) was attacked at the official Salon of that year on the ground that its mythological title was intended to obscure the painting's subject, a prostitute reclining on her bed. These two paintings were highly significant for the subsequent development of modern art, and yet the most acclaimed work at the 1865 Salon was the *Birth of Venus* (1862; Paris, Mus. d'Orsay) by the highly respected Alexandre Cabanel, a titillating and provocative pin-up pretending to represent a Classical goddess. This was bought by the Emperor Napoleon III, who had publicly condemned both Courbet and Manet as obscene. Such hypocrisy also reigned at this time at the Royal Academy in London, where such paintings as Lawrence Alma-Tadema's *In the Tepidarium* (1881; Port Sunlight, Lady Lever A.G.) were praised as classical and noble in spite of their clear intention to titillate. The prettiness and superficiality of these paintings contrast strongly with efforts of artists who were trying to gain an insight into the nature of sexuality. Edgar Degas, for example, made a series of monotypes depicting life in Paris brothels in the 1880s; these showed real compassion for the inmates and often depicted the lesbian relationships that flourished among them. Henri de Toulouse-Lautrec shared Degas's fascination for the world of the prostitute and painted at least 50 brothel scenes in the 1890s, of which *Au Salon: Rue des Moulins* (1895; Albi, Mus. Toulouse-Lautrec) is outstanding. It depicts some of Lautrec's favourite prostitutes languidly awaiting their clients under the watchful eye of the Madame. *Rue des Moulins: The Inspection* (1894; New York, Chester Dale priv. col.) shows prostitutes parading for a medical inspection, and both *Two Friends* (1894; London, Tate) and *Friends* (1895; Zurich, Schins priv. col.) show the lesbian relationships that had also intrigued Degas. These brothel images exhibit no repugnance or condemnation but also no glorification—merely a sympathetic reportage.

Towards the end of the 19th century the association of sex with death became characteristic of artists associated with DECADENCE AND DECLINE. One of their characteristic themes was that of woman as a mysterious goddess, using her sexuality to dominate men. Early examples include Dante Gabriel Rossetti's *Beata Beatrix* (*c.* 1863) and *Proserpine* (1874; both London, Tate), which seem to exude a brooding eroticism. In France, Gustave Moreau embodied his vision of woman in the historical character Salome, and his paintings of *Salome Dancing* (1876; Los Angeles, CA, Armand Hammer Mus. A.) and *The Apparition* (1876; Paris, Louvre; see MOREAU, GUSTAVE, fig. 2) were made famous by Joris-Karl Huysmans in his novel *A Rebours*. In *The Apparition* an almost naked Salome gesticulates towards the severed head of John the Baptist, which hovers in front of her, dripping blood. In 1894 Oscar Wilde published a play entitled *Salome* that was illustrated with 17 drawings by Aubrey Beardsley. *J'ai baisé ta bouche* (1893; London, V&A) shows the girl fondling the severed head, which she has just kissed, thus triumphing over the saint whose death she has caused. Other drawings in the series were censored because of suggested androgyny and masturbation. Beardsley's illustrations to Aristophanes' *Lysistrata* were issued in a secret limited edition in 1896 and are the most sexually explicit of all his works with their transvestism, masturbating cupids and hugely exaggerated phalluses. The one artist whose work proved more shocking was the Belgian etcher Félicien Rops. In 1884 Rops produced a series of images entitled *The Satanic Ones*, a fantasy involving a naked woman carried off to Hell, where she has intercourse with Satan on an altar. In the final image, the association of eroticism with death reaches its apotheosis as the woman is strangled with her own hair by Satan, imitating Christ on the cross. Gazing upwards, she dies in orgasm.

(iv) After c. 1900. The sexual hypocrisy that required so many artists to disguise or make polite the eroticism in their work during the 19th century waned considerably during the 20th century, when a compulsive degree of self-revelation became characteristic of erotic art. The fervent womanizer Auguste Rodin executed 20 extremely frank lithographs in 1902 for Octave Mirbeau's *Le Jardin des Supplices* and produced many drawings around this time of both heterosexual and lesbian intercourse and women masturbating (e.g. *Reclining Female Nude*, *c.* 1905; U. London, Courtauld Inst. Gals). Similar subjects were drawn by the Austrian artist Gustav Klimt. Klimt's illustrations to *Lucian's Dialogues of Courtesans* (pubd 1907) and his other graphic work of 1910–17 include many lesbian lovers, heterosexual couples in various positions of copulation and women exploring their bodies and masturbating (see fig. 8). Klimt was haunted by the image of the *femme fatale*, which appears in his *Judith I* (1901; Vienna, Mus. 20 Jhts), a depiction of a half-naked woman with open mouth clutching the severed head of Holofernes, and in his *Myth of Danaë* (*c.* 1905; Graz, priv. col.), in which a nude woman is depicted masturbating in the foetal position.

8. Gustav Klimt: *Woman Masturbating*, *c*. 1916 (London, British Museum)

Klimt's contemporary Egon Schiele also lived in Vienna, where the writings of Sigmund Freud and Otto Weininger were newly published. Schiele's erotic work reflects the inner emotional stresses of the period with none of Klimt's sensual excitement. Whether depicting women, men, his own body or young girls (a subject that brought him 24 days imprisonment in 1912), Schiele concentrated on the essential sexuality of the figure, taking great care to show the genitals. His images depict an anguished and lonely eroticism: for example, in *Reclining Girl in a Blue Dress* (1910; New York, Stefan Ellis priv. col.) the vacantly staring girl has pulled her dress up to reveal the vivid red lips of her vulva, and in *Nude Self-portrait* (1911; London, Richard Nagy priv. col.), the culmination of a whole series of such self-examinations, the artist depicted himself grasping his erect penis in a solitary attempt at self-gratification as a temporary relief from unhappiness. Occasionally Schiele's erotic images are more positive. *Observed in a Dream* (1911; New York, Met.) shows a smiling nude woman opening the lips of her vulva, while in *The Red Host* (1911; New York, priv. col.) the artist depicts himself with a large red erection, which is being reverentially caressed by a nude woman. Another artist whose eroticism mirrored the times in which he lived was the German George Grosz. His contempt for mankind in general, but for the Weimar Republic in particular, is revealed in acidly satirical drawings published as *Ecce homo* (1923) and *Der Speisser Spiegel* (1924). Here Grosz unmasked the private life of the ruling classes, reducing them to their common animal nature in visions of jaded sexuality: a sex murderer scrubs his hands after committing a revolting crime, and prostitutes parade their charms in streets and cafés or cater to the perverse tastes of bloated capitalists.

For Pablo Picasso, eroticism was a conscious obsession throughout his long career. His work concentrated on the female form consistently, from his early Barcelona sketches to his last engravings and paintings, and his concern was with the whole range of erotic feelings from love to hate. Sexual subjects appeared intermittently during his Blue Period and especially in the neo-classical works, such as a series of drawings from 1920 of a centaur abducting a woman. By the mid-1920s the multiple aspects of sexual experience had become the main theme of extraordinarily inventive sculptures, drawings and paintings (e.g. *Figures by the Sea*, 1931; Paris, Mus. Picasso; *Two Figures*, 1933; Paris, priv. col.). During the late 1940s Picasso produced a number of paintings and drawings of a copulating couple and a series of the artist painting and making love to his nude model. This subject was continued in engravings of 1963–5 and also in his *Suite 347*, a series of etchings of 1968 on the theme of Ingres's *Raphael and La Fornarina*. Here Picasso appears as an old man watching the young copulating couple with an expression that mixes excitement with wistfulness: the fantasies of an elderly painter looking back to the excitements of his youth.

Picasso's concentration on his erotic feelings was much appreciated by the Surrealists, perhaps the 20th century's most avid explorers of sexuality (*see* SURREALISM). The Surrealists were aware of the revolutionary nature of unfettered erotic expression, and they were inspired by

Freud's argument that sexuality lay at the root of all creativity. Thus Surrealist erotic art has a compulsive intensity that can have a deep effect on the viewer, communicating often on a direct subconscious level. Dreams and nightmares (in the work of Paul Delvaux and Max Ernst), and personal fetishes and sexual games (in the work of Pierre Molinier and Hans Bellmer) all play an important part in Surrealist erotic imagery. Rather than concentrate on genital organs, the Surrealists preferred to transform the whole body into an erotic arena for exciting experiences. For example, the subject of René Magritte's *Rape* (1934; Houston, TX, Menil Col.) is a woman's face where breasts and pubic hair stand in for eyes and mouth, and the neck and face are also a phallus entering the vagina. Salvador Dalí's *Young Virgin Autosodomized by her own Chastity* (1954; New York, Alemany priv. col.) depicts a woman's nude body made up of detachable parts to be passed around and admired. Pierre Molinier used photomontage to create multiple images of fetishized male and female bodies (e.g. *Sur le Pavois*, 1950s). Hans Bellmer, the only member of the group to concentrate his attention entirely on creating erotic imagery, constructed the articulated figure of a young girl whose parts could be assembled in various different ways. *Die Puppe*, a series of photographs he took of this doll in 1934, expressed a powerful and disturbing eroticism that has provoked controversy ever since. Bellmer's later drawings and engravings (e.g. *A Short Treatise on Morals*, 1968) illustrate the sexual dreams of young girls and at the same time explore the sexual fantasies of their author. Fascination with the sexuality of young girls is also characteristic of the work of the French artist Balthus, for example in *Thérèse Dreaming* (1938; California, priv. col.) and *Girl with Cat* (1937; Chicago, IL, priv. col.). In *The Guitar Lesson* (1934; Boston, MA, priv. col.) a seated woman fondles a young girl lying across her lap.

British artists were apparently less concerned with eroticism than their continental counterparts in the 20th century, an exception being D. H. Lawrence, whose paintings were confiscated by the police from his exhibition at the Warren Gallery in London in 1929. However, certain British artists showed a definite interest in erotic imagery in their more private work. The religious artist Eric Gill considered that there should be no conflict between Roman Catholicism and sexual honesty. *Ecstasy*, a stone carving of 1910–11 (London, Tate), shows two lovers, and many of Gill's drawings in the Victoria and Albert Museum and the British Museum, both in London, concentrate on penises (both flaccid and erect), vaginas and copulating couples (sometimes with the Hand of God blessing them). Stanley Spencer saw a definite connection between sex and religion: for him, spiritual and sexual ecstasy were the same, and references to fetishism and masturbation can be found in such religious works as *Love on the Moor* (1949–54) and *Love among the Nations* (1935–6; all Cambridge, Fitzwilliam; see SPENCER, STANLEY, fig. 2). The latter was a series of eight paintings intended for Spencer's never-realized 'Church-house' for which he also painted *Self-portrait with Patricia* (1937; Cambridge, Fitzwilliam) and the *Leg of Mutton Nude* (1937; London, Tate), both of which are nude depictions of the artist with Patricia Preece, who later became his second wife.

David Hockney did not concentrate exclusively on erotic subjects, but his paintings of nude boys by swimming pools, such as *Sunbather* (1966; Cologne, Mus. Ludwig), and related images, such as that of his semi-nude lover Peter on a bed (*The Room, Tarzana*, 1967; USA, priv. col.), express a fascination with homosexual love. This is made more explicit in his *Illustrations for Fourteen Poems from C. P. Cavafy* (for illustration see HOCKNEY, DAVID) and his etching for Peter Webb's book *The Erotic Arts* (1975). Lucian Freud painted *Naked Man and his Friend*, depicting two men asleep on a sofa, in 1979–80 (London, priv. col.), but more often he has depicted nude women, focusing on the genitals, in such works as *Rose* (1978–9; Tokyo, Sukejiro Itani). The works of Allen Jones relate directly to the sexual imagery of popular culture. Jones concentrated on the fascination of the female form in leather or rubber with stockings and high heels in such works as *Desire Me* (1968; London, V&A) and *Table* (1969; London, Tate). The American-born artist R. B. Kitaj, who settled in London, exhibited in 1977 a series of works that attempted to marry the intellect and the senses. These explicitly erotic paintings included *Communist and Socialist*, *This Knot of Life* and *His Hour* (all London, Marlborough F.A.), and featured oral sex, copulation and voyeurism.

In the late 20th century there was a more sustained interest in erotic art in the USA than in Great Britain. The paintings of Richard Lindner are often images of colossal women in tight corsets and high-heeled shoes, full of a menacing sexuality that perhaps relates to the artist's early years as a Jew in Nazi Germany (e.g. *Woman*, 1970; England, priv. col.). Erotic images of women also dominate the work of Tom Wesselmann, whose neatly painted series of *Great American Nudes* unveil their mysteries in matter-of-fact bedroom scenes. Wesselmann's cool detachment is in marked contrast to the involvement of Lindner. The humour of Pop art permeates his work, as in *Bedroom Painting No. 20* (1969; New York, Sidney Janis Gal.), an image of an enormous, brightly coloured penis. Many other American Pop artists have concentrated on the forbidden subject of the penis, including Robert Rauschenberg, Jasper Johns, Brigid Polk and Andy Warhol. Jim Dine exhibited his *London Series* of pretty watercolour penises at the Robert Fraser Gallery in London in 1966, an effort to divorce the subject from its usual pornographic context, but the show was closed by the police. Robert Graham created miniature wax models of copulating couples, and John De Andrea specialized in life-size fibreglass and resin nude girls and copulating couples. In 1975 Claes Oldenburg exhibited drawings of sexual fantasies involving women sucking and caressing giant penises that sprouted from their own and their partners' bodies. One of the most controversial experiments in eroticism was the exhibition of work by Jeff Koons at the Venice Biennale in 1990. Koons's series of life-size sculptures and enormous photo-screen prints were entitled *Made in Heaven* and depicted in explicit detail the artist and his wife, La Cicciolina, the Hungarian-Italian pornography star and Member of Parliament, making love.

Modern erotic art in Denmark includes the obsessive drawings of copulating couples by Ernst Hansen and the

Surrealist collages and paintings of Wilhelm Freddie. Modern works from Sweden include the collages of Max Walter Svanberg and the cartoon drawings of Ulf Rahmberg. In Belgium, Roland Decol painted startlingly photographic nudes in domestic scenes, while in France Mario Tauzin produced explicit etchings of lesbians and copulating couples, and Léonor Fini continued to paint strangely erotic and mysterious images. Many Dutch artists use sexual themes: Karel Appel painted startling scenes of animals copulating with women, Cornelis Doolaard painted a strange fantasy involving himself and various women and animals, and Melle produced meticulously painted stories full of sexual implications. Erotic art in Germany meanwhile tended to accentuate the implicit violence of sex, for example in the graphic works of Horst Janssen and in Paul Wunderlich's images of violation. Wunderlich also produced many works on the theme of lesbian and homosexual love. In Austria Ernst Fuchs etched intricate images that conjure up a rather nightmarish world of demonic sexual energy, and a group of artists practised body art. Günter Brus, Otto Muehl, Hermann Nitsch and Vito Acconci decorated and at times damaged their naked bodies in ritualized and often sensational performances. Such ideas were taken further in various parts of the world by Rudolf Schwarzkogler, Stuart Brisley and Mickey Greenhall.

Another phenomenon characteristic of the late 20th century was a strong concern with gay and lesbian eroticism (*see also* GAY AND LESBIAN ART). With the growing demand for homosexual rights, such painters as David Hockney felt encouraged to create explicitly gay imagery, and other artists concentrated on expressing their preference for men. These included Robert Crowl and Lowell Nesbitt (*b* 1933) in the USA, Phillip Core, Mario Dubsky, Michael Leonard and Jean-Marc Prouveur in England, Francisco Lopez in Spain, Charles Beauchamp in France, Rainer Fetting and Salomé in Germany, and Marcel Joosen and Hans van Manen in the Netherlands. In England, Gilbert and George produced many huge photo-pieces of young men in a grid format and bright colours, recalling ecclesiastical stained glass. The titles explain the subject-matter: *Cock, Arse, Coming, Buggery Faith, Holy Cock.* In *Naked Love* (see fig. 9) the faces of the artists gaze spellbound at two naked boys, while a falling angel fills the centre of the composition. The American photographer Robert Mapplethorpe set out to create images that would be artistically beautiful but also erotically charged. *Man in a Polyester Suit* (1981) shows a black man seen only from chest to knee, with an enormous flaccid penis casually hanging out of the open zip of his suit. *Marty and Hank* (1982) shows two men having oral sex. Much of Mapplethorpe's work explores New York's sado-masochist subculture: in *Self-Portrait* (1978), the photographer wears leather boots and waistcoat and has a bullwhip inserted into his rectum. *Brian Ridley and Lyle Heeter* (1979) are dressed in black leather and heavy chains, while *Elliot and Dominick* (1979) are taking part in a bondage ritual.

Whereas most earlier lesbian imagery had been produced by men, in the late 20th century lesbian women began to create their own erotic images, inspired by the works of Léonor Fini and Tamara de Lempicka. Examples

9. Gilbert and George: *Naked Love*, photographs, 3.02×3.01 m, 1982 (London, Anthony d'Offay Gallery)

include Kate Millet, Nancy Fried, Tee Corinne and Joan Semmel (*b* 1932). The American artist Betty Dodson also produced meticulous drawings of nude women engaged in intercourse or masturbation. In England Christina Berry explored sado-masochistic themes in her soft black leather assemblages, and the Swedish-born artist Monica Sjoo painted nude women in intimate embraces (e.g. *Lovers*, 1975; artist's col.). The Dutch photographers Diana Blok and Marlo Broekmans celebrated their own relationship and those of other lesbian couples in their work: in *Bind me so that I might be Free* (1980) white ribbons form the bond between the nude bodies, and in *The Bite* (1980) the bodies are superimposed on each other as one gently bites the other's ear.

Judy Chicago's *Dinner Party* (1979), a triangular table containing place settings in the form of vaginal icons for 39 famous women, was one of the most influential examples of the feminist critique of patriarchy. Feminist artists often sought to avoid creating imagery that mimicked male sexual fantasies, and some preferred to avoid eroticism altogether, but others chose to concentrate on the image of the male (*see also* FEMINISM AND ART). Nancy Grossman in the USA and Mandy Havers in England produced leather sculptures with elements of sado-masochism that led to accusations that these artists were sensationalist and anti-men, both of which they denied. Other artists preferred the nude male. Sylvia Sleigh painted *Phillip Golub Reclining* (1971; New York, Solo 20 Gal.), in which the model is presented from behind, lying on a sofa and looking into a mirror that reflects not only his face but also the artist painting him. The traditional roles of such works as Velázquez's *Rokeby Venus* are thus reversed. The later *Double Images* shows a young man covered with a generous amount of body hair seen from the front and from behind as he gazes at the view from another mirror. The virility of such male images is far removed from the androgynous beauty of homoerotic nudes in Classical and Renaissance art. Erotically inspired male nudes have also been painted by Martha Edelheit, Connie Greene, Jillian Denby and Alice Neel, while Eunice Golden has concentrated on phallic fantasies involving erect penises and masturbation that express her fascination with the way a man experiences his own sexuality.

EWA

BIBLIOGRAPHY

L. Dunand: 'A propos d'une estampe rare du Musée des Beaux-Arts de Lyon appartenant à la suite du Lascavie d'Augustin Carrache', *Bull. Mus. & Mnmts Lyon.*, ii/1 (1957), pp. 1–20
——: *Les Compositions de Jules Romain 'Les Amours des dieux' gravés par M.-A. Raimondi* (Lyons, 1964)
——L. Dunand: 'Les Estampes dites découvertes et couvertes', *Gaz. B.-A.*, lxix (April 1967), pp. 225–38
F. Haskell: 'Eroticism and the Visual Arts', *Censorship Mag.*, iii/1 (1967)
L. Dunand: 'A propos des dessins dits secrets légués par J.-D. Ingres au Musée de Montauban', *Bull. Mus. Ingres*, 23 (1968), pp. 27–38
Picasso: 347 Gravures (Paris and London, 1968; 2/New York, 1970)
L. Dunand: 'Les Rapports de l'amour et de l'argent dans les estampes des 16. et 17. siècles', *Bull. Mus. & Mnmts Lyon.* (1969)
G. Schiff: *The Amorous Illustrations of Thomas Rowlandson* (New York, 1969)
'L'Image érotique', *Opus Int.*, 13/14 (1969) [special issue]
R. T. Peterson: *The Art of Ecstasy: Teresa, Bernini and Crashaw* (New York, 1970)
X. Gauthier: *Surréalisme et sexualité* (Paris, 1971)
D. Posner: 'Caravaggio's Homo-erotic Early Works', *A. Q.* [Detroit], xxxiv/3 (1971), pp. 301–24
E. Lucie-Smith: *Eroticism in Western Art* (London and New York, 1972)
D. Posner: 'The True Path of Fragonard's *Progress of Love*', *Burl. Mag.*, cxiv/833 (1972), pp. 526–34
N. Powell: *Fuseli's 'The Night-Mare'* (London, 1972)
R. Melville: *Erotic Art of the West* (London and New York, 1973)
F. Nora: 'Degas et les maisons closes', *L'Oeil*, 219 (1973), pp. 26–31
M. Peppiatt: 'Balthus, Klossowski, Bellmer: Three Approaches to the Flesh', *A. Int.*, xvii/8 (1973), pp. 23–8
D. Posner: *Watteau: A Lady at her Toilet* (London, 1973)
L. Nochlin: 'Some Women Realists—Painters of the Figure', *A. Mag.*, xlviii/8 (1974), pp. 29–33
L. Steinberg: 'Eve's Idle Hand', *A.J.* [London], xxxv/2 (1976), pp. 130–35 [on Michelangelo's *Temptation* in the Sistine Chapel]
J. Andersen: *The Witch on the Wall: Medieval Erotic Sculpture in the British Isles* (Copenhagen and London, 1977)
L. Dunand and P. Lemarchand: *Les Amours des dieux: L'Art érotique sous la renaissance* (Lausanne, 1977)
'La Femme surréaliste', *Obliques*, xiv/xv (1977) [whole issue]
M. Walters: *The Nude Male: A New Perspective* (New York and London, 1978)
G. Greer: *The Obstacle Race* (London, 1979)
H. Hofstätter: *Gustav Klimt: Erotische Zeichnungen* (Salzburg, 1979; Eng. trans., London, 1980)
A. Ellenzweig: 'The Homosexual Aesthetic', *Amer. Photographer* (Aug 1980)
Dix-huitième siècle: Soixante-neuf gravures interdites (Paris, 1980)
Kstwk, xxxiv/5 (1981) [issue on erotic art]
L. Steinberg: *The Sexuality of Christ in Renaissance Art and in Modern Oblivion* (London, 1984)
E. Cooper: *The Sexual Perspective: Homosexuality and Art in the Last 100 Years in the West* (London, 1986)
L. Lawner: *'I modi': The 16 Pleasures: An Erotic Album of the Italian Renaissance* (London, 1988)
E. Cooper: *Fully Exposed: The Male Nude in Photography* (London, 1990)

3. ASIA AND THE ISLAMIC WORLD. India, China and Japan have produced a great wealth of erotic art, most of which is little known in the West. The Hindu, Islamic and Daoist philosophies all accept human physical relations as natural, admirable and beautiful. The creation of the world is seen in some philosophies as resulting from a process analogous to human sexual activity, with the deity manifesting a dual sexual role. Thus icons of a male and female nature, representations of phalluses and vulvas, are worshipped as embodiments of aspects of the deity, and sexual activity can be considered as having a religious aspect and as an end in itself rather than the mere means of procreation. Thus in some cultures sex has become a ritual that has to be learnt, as can be seen from the numerous sex manuals and illustrations of sexual positions.

(i) India. From possibly as early as the Indus civilization (*c.* 2550–2000 BC), and certainly from the time the Vedas were codified (*c.* 1500–1200 BC), sexuality was conceived in India as intrinsically divine and the sexual impulse understood as an indication of the presence of divine creativity. Thus sexual pleasure (Skt *kāma*) is one of the prescribed 'aims' of orthodox Hindu life (*see also* INDIAN SUBCONTINENT, §I, 7). Within this context, the sexual impulse took expression in four interrelated ways in the arts. Devotees of the god Shiva worship the sexual and creative impulses in two forms: the *liṅga*, representing the penis, and the *yoni*, representing the vulva. The earliest examples probably date to the 1st or 2nd century AD, and from no later than the 7th century there are examples depicting the two combined in one icon, a round-topped cylinder standing in a shallow basin.

Erotic imagery is also evident in much Indian sculpture. The earliest suggestions of erotic sculpture are the *dampati* scenes, representing a man and woman embracing, seen at Buddhist sites from the 2nd century BC to the 2nd century AD. At Mathura in particular, in the early centuries AD, there are many images of couples and attractive *yakṣis* ('female nature spirits'), forerunners of the celestial nymphs (*apsarasas*) often found in later sculpture. From the Gupta period (4th century AD), a time of great artistic and cultural achievement, representations of the ideal aristocratic lifestyle began to emerge in literature. Incorporating the ancient 'aim' of sensual pleasure (*kāma*), these depictions of courtly life were erotically charged, often being modelled on a noble life in the celestial realms where divine nymphs provide heroes with every form of erotic pleasure. The ambience of this literature is visually captured in the Ajanta paintings (*see* INDIAN SUBCONTINENT, §VI, 3(i)(a)). This period also saw the composition of the earliest extant erotic manual, the *Kāmasūtra* of Vatsyayana. Temples decorated with sculpture depicting erotic scenes appeared in the 5th century and continued as late as the 17th century in south India. Perhaps the most famous erotic sculpture is found at KHAJURAHO and KONARAK. Inscriptions indicate that some temples had prostitutes known as *devadāsī*s ('servants of the god'). The temple reliefs show single nude figures, couples performing a variety of sexual acts, and complex groups, apparently engaged in orgiastic rites. The fantastic sexual feats illustrated in these sculptures can only be understood with reference to the *Kāmasūtra*.

Another important influence on the development of erotic art in India was the appearance in the 6th century AD of the esoteric belief known as Tantrism. Through a highly developed ritual, this formalized the idea of the divine nature of the sexual impulse. The goal was spiritual and the practice fundamentally yogic: adepts were aroused and engaged in ritual copulation, but rather than achieving orgasm they were trained to withdraw their energy back into the self and transmit it up through the central nervous system to the brain, thereby experiencing divine bliss. Tantrism became part of Buddhism and gave rise to the 'Vehicle of the Thunderbolt' (*vajrayāna*), a school that predominated in Tibet from the 8th century, and resulted in brightly coloured carvings and wall paintings of radiant golden couples seated together in sexual union. In the centuries that followed, many erotic album paintings referred to Tantric practices (e.g. *Lovers on a Terrace*, late 18th century; London, V&A). Lastly, the merging of sex and religion found full expresion in the representation of the loves of Krsna and became a common theme in miniature painting in Rajasthan and the Punjab hills. Often imbued with deep erotic feeling, these charming miniatures transform ordinary sexuality into divine love and thus offer instruction to educated devotees.

(ii) China. Eroticism in Chinese art is often religiously inspired, although the imagery is often allusive and philosophical rather than explicit. The main influence behind such art is Daoism as embodied in the *Yijing* of the 12th century BC. The concept of *yin* and *yang*, literally 'shade' and 'light', reflects a belief in the union of opposites as a fundamental component of creation. Female (*yin*) and male (*yang*) are another expression of this essential complementarity. The coming together of the two in sexual intercourse provides contact with the cosmic force of the Dao. Ancient Daoist books on the art of love-making, such as *Chen kao* ('The arts of the bedchamber'), are only known by their texts now, for their explicit illustrations have all been destroyed, but erotic symbolism appears frequently in Chinese imagery. The celestial dragon on the robes of the aristocracy and on imperial porcelain and decorative items represents *yang*, while the female dragon with the *lingzhi* fungus in her mouth is *yin*. They represent Heaven and Earth, and their intercourse is manifested in the rain. Thus clouds and rain (*yunyu*) are an image of sexual intercourse in Chinese literature and painting. In the same way metaphors for the male organ include a stallion and a tree, and for the female organ, a deer, a lotus and a peach. Statues of embracing couples found in temples of the Tibetan Buddhist tradition, such as the 18th-century Lama Temple (Yihegong) in Beijing, use the erotic image of the father-and-mother (*yab-yum*) union to represent the union of compassion and wisdom (*see also* TIBET, fig. 8). Explicit scenes of love-making occur in watercolours of the 16th to 19th centuries, for example *Intimate Scene of Leisurely Love* (*c.* 1550) by the Ming artist Jin Ying, and illustrations to such erotic novels as *Rou putuan* ('The prayer-mat of flesh'). The knowledge of anatomy tends to be perfunctory in comparison with similar imagery from India or Europe.

(iii) Japan. Japanese art and literature have from the earliest times concerned themselves with the act of love. The Shinto religion gives a sexual explanation for the creation of the world, and giant phalluses and representations of a vagina are carried in Shinto processions. Phallic fertility symbols and talismans, Mother Goddess figures and erotic amulets are all still found in Shinto shrines. Japan's outstanding contributions to erotic art are the

shunga, coloured wood-engravings glorifying sexual pleasure. These developed from the pillow-books (scrolls of erotic prints designed as manuals of sexual knowledge to be kept inside the pillow) that were already common in Japan by the 8th century. *Shunga* often depicted courtesans, who provided an essential service in Japanese life and often attained high social rank. They combined the tasks of fashion-plate, publicity for the courtesan and pillow-book. Some of the earliest, such as the *Yoshiwara Pillow Pictures* of 1660 by the Kanbun Master (*fl* 1660–73), which was virtually a guide to the pleasures of sex in 48 positions, were actually commissioned by brothel-keepers. *Shunga* rarely depict nudity, however. The universality of communal bathing in Japan has divested nudity of any erotic implications, and beautiful garments that partly conceal or emphasize sexual organs are considered truly voluptuous. Since exposure of the genitals is thus not uncommon among the Japanese, artists have tended to exaggerate them to obtain a dramatic effect.

The first great master of *shunga* was the late 17th-century artist Hishikawa Moronobu, who pioneered the use of clothing for decorative effect in his *Stylish Yoshiwara Pillow Book* (*c.* 1683). In the 18th century Suzuki Harunobu developed the four-colour block-printing technique, which enabled him to give a poetic atmosphere to his scenes of love-making. Probably the greatest *shunga* artist was KITAGAWA UTAMARO, who produced the finest

10. Katsushika Hokusai: *Dream of the Fisherman's Wife*, colour woodblock print, *c.* 1820 (London, British Museum)

examples of the genre with such albums as *The Song of the Pillow* (1788) and *Twelve Hours of the Green Houses* (*Seirō juniji tsuzuki, c.* 1795). His art is frankly sexual as a result of working from the model, which was not the usual practice in Japan, and it shows a very well-developed sense of design together with striking colour effects. In the 19th century KATSUSHIKA HOKUSAI produced *Models of Loving Couples* (*c.* 1810) and also the most sensational of all Japanese *shunga*, the *Dream of the Fisherman's Wife* (see fig. 10), which shows two octopuses making love to a nude woman.

(iv) Islamic world. Although Islam is associated with strict moral codes of behaviour, the Arab world has produced a great deal of erotic art and poetry. Islamic society accepted sex as a natural and necessary part of human activity, and sex manuals such as *The Perfumed Garden*, by Sheik Nefzawi, were popular because they brought about harmony and satisfaction in marriage. Illustrated manuscripts of love poems and sex manuals are the main source of Islamic erotic art and show the strong influence of Indian miniatures on the same themes. The restraints imposed by Islam discouraged the study of human anatomy, and nudity is very rare, but poets and artists made use of erotic metaphors (such as erect cypress trees, ruby lips and succulent fruit) alongside the depiction of the love-makers. Examples include pages in the style of the Persian master Riza Abbassi (16th–17th centuries; London, V&A) and illuminated volumes of the love poems of the Persian poets Saadi (Edinburgh, U. Lib.) and Nizami (Paris, Bib. N.), both from the 17th century. In a society where the sexes were segregated and adultery was strongly condemned, it was natural for same-sex relationships to flourish, and both lesbian and male homosexual scenes appear in sex manuals and love poems (Turkish examples include the translation of the Indian *Koka Shastra* (11th century) and the poems of Atai (19th century; both Istanbul, Mus. Turk. and Islam. A.)).

BIBLIOGRAPHY
EWA
L. E. Glichner: *Erotic Aspects of Hindu Sculpture* (Washington, DC, 1949)
R. H. van Gulik: *Erotic Colour Prints of the Ming Period* (Tokyo, 1951)
P. Chandra: 'The Kuala-Kāpālika Cults at Khajurāho', *Lalit Kalā*, ii (1955–6), pp. 98–107
M. Fouchet: *The Erotic Sculpture of India* (London, 1959)
P. Thomas: *Kama Kapla* (Bombay, 1959)
R. H. van Gulik: *Sexual Life in Ancient China: A Preliminary Survey of Chinese Sex and Society from circa 1500 B.C. to 1644 A.D.* (Leiden, 1961)
F. Leeson: *Kama Shilpa: A Study of Indian Sculpture Depicting Love in Action* (Bombay, 1962)
M. R. Anand: *Kama Kala: Some Notes on the Philosophical Basis of Hindu Erotic Sculpture* (Hamburg, Geneva and Paris, 1963)
C. Grosbois: *Shunga, Images of Spring: Essay on Erotic Elements in Japanese Art* (Geneva, Paris and Munich, 1966)
R. Surieu: *Sarv e naz: An Essay on Love and the Representation of Erotic Themes in Ancient Iran* (Munich, Geneva and Paris, 1967)
P. Rawson, ed.: *Erotic Art of the East: The Sexual Theme in Oriental Painting and Sculpture* (New York, 1968, 2/London, 1973)
M. Beurdeley: *The Clouds and the Rain: The Art of Love in China* (Fribourg, 1969)
G. Tucci: *Rati-Lila: An Interpretation of the Tantric Imagery of the Temples of Nepal* (Munich, Paris and Geneva, 1969)
R. Etiemble: *Yun Yu: An Essay on Eroticism and Love in Ancient China* (Geneva and Munich, 1970)
P. Rawson: *The Art of Tantra* (London and New York, 1973)
——: *Erotic Art of India* (London and New York, 1977)
T. Evans and M. Evans: *Shunga: The Art of Love in Japan* (New York and London, 1979)

II. *Historiography and collections.*

Sexually explicit works of art have often been termed pornographic, and this has led to attempts by many writers to differentiate between erotic art and pornography. James Joyce, for example, believed that art was an aesthetic experience that precluded the disturbing emotions aroused by pornography; art and pornography for him were therefore at opposite poles. D. H. Lawrence wrote: 'You can recognize [pornography] by the insult it offers, invariably, to sex and to the human spirit.' For him, pornography led to masturbation, which in turn led to 'mob self-consciousness', whereas erotic art redirected the viewer from mob self-consciousness to 'true individuality'. Steven Marcus wrote that art was largely concerned with 'the relations of human beings among themselves', whereas pornography 'is not interested in persons but in organs'. Peter Webb described pornography as 'any material whose sole purpose is to excite sexual appetite with no concern for aesthetic response', and went on: 'to confuse eroticism with pornography vitiates against our ability to appreciate some of art's most rewarding experiences'. Other commentators, however (see Peckham; and Kronhausen and Kronhausen), found it impossible or unnecessary to make any distinction between erotic art and pornography.

The pioneer of studies in erotic art was Eduard Fuchs, who published a series of learned and controversial books in the early 20th century. His liberal ideas were attacked by some critics (see Alexander), but Kenneth Clark defended the artistic potential of erotic subject-matter in *The Nude*: 'All good nude painting and sculpture is sexually stimulating . . . No nude, however abstract, should fail to arouse in the spectator some vestige of erotic feeling, even though it be only the faintest shadow.' Lo Duca analysed erotic art from a psychoanalytic viewpoint as being rooted in the collective unconscious of sexual myths and fantasies. Georges Bataille expressed a philosophy of eroticism as a consciously intellectualized feeling that is possible only in a context where sexuality is repressed: 'Eroticism, unlike simple sexual activity, is a psychological quest independent of the natural goal of reproduction and the desire for children.'

Many contributions to serious research in the area of erotic art were published from the late 1960s onwards. By the 1980s critical views on the subject were being expressed both by some members of the moralistic puritan right and by some on the political left, including numerous feminists, such as Andrea Dworkin. Both groups were united in seeing no reason to distinguish between erotic art and pornography and in supporting CENSORSHIP. Feminist writers concentrated their research on forgotten or undervalued women artists to counterbalance the patriarchy they saw at the root of all histories of art and particularly underpinning the images of women created by men for men (*see also* WOMEN AND ART HISTORY and FEMINISM AND ART). Other late 20th-century writers concerned themselves with discussing gay and lesbian erotic imagery (Feinstein, Cooper) and the role of women artists in creating erotic art for women (Nochlin; Chicago and Hill; Pollock, 1982; Kent and Moreau).

For a long time the collecting of erotic art was the private fascination of the rich and powerful. Famous collectors included the Medici family in Renaissance Florence, the Holy Roman Emperor Rudolf II, Francis I, Henry IV and Louis XV of France, Philippe II, Duc d'Orléans, Lord Houghton, the 27th Earl of Crawford, the 2nd Marquess of Milford Haven, George IV, Edward VII and Edward VIII of England, Richard Payne Knight, Charles Townley, Sir William Hamilton (i) and George Witt. In the late 20th century most collections of erotic art still tended to be private, but museums of erotic art were opened in the 1970s in the USA (San Francisco) and Sweden (Lund), and most of the world's major museums now contain works of an erotic nature. In Paris both the Musée du Louvre and the Bibliothèque Nationale possess items that are not considered suitable for public exhibition, ranging from Greek pottery to European prints and drawings. The Vatican in Rome is said to have a private museum of erotic art, and it is certain that the Vatican Palace contains a bathroom with erotic frescoes by Raphael (*see* §I, 2(ii) above). The Museo e Gallerie Nazionali di Capodimonte, Naples, has a 'secret cabinet' in which sexual objects and paintings found at Pompeii are kept (*see* §I, 1 above). The Museo Nacional de Arte, Mexico City, has a 'salon segreto' that contains sexual images from Pre-Columbian Mexico (*see* §I, 1 above). The Museo de Arte, Lima, has a collection of erotic terracottas from Moche tombs (*see* §I, 1 above). In the USA the Institute for Sex Research at Bloomington, IN, has been gathering art objects of a sexual nature.

London has two interesting public collections of erotic art, but little is on show. The Print Room of the Victoria and Albert Museum houses a fine selection of Japanese *shunga* by such artists as Harunobu and Utamaro (*see* §I, 3(iii) above), all of which are kept in the Restricted Collection. The same museum's Indian Department has a variety of erotic drawings, paintings and sculptures, and all are available on application. The British Museum has one of the finest collections of erotica in the world. The Greek and Roman Department has a Museum Secretum, which contains Greek vases and plates, phallic amulets from Pompeii, ithyphallic figurines of Priapus or Hermes and phalluses removed (as an alternative to fixing a fig-leaf) from Classical statues. The Ethnographical Department has a gilt penis from an Egyptian mummy, erotic drinking vessels from Peru and erotica from Australia, Yucatán, Africa and Easter Island, none of which are on view to the public. Interesting items in the Department of Medieval and Later Antiquities include a stone *Shelah-na-Gig* fertility figure from Ireland, various watches and snuff-boxes with erotic decorations, and a terracotta sculpture of a satyr copulating with a goat made by Joseph Nollekens in the 1760s (*see* §I, 1 above). All are in the Restricted Collection. Chinese and Japanese erotica, including albums by Harunobu, Utamaro (*Poem of the Pillow*), Hiroshige and Hokusai (*Dream of the Fisherman's Wife*), are locked away in the Departments of Oriental Antiquities and Oriental Manuscripts. The Print Room's Restricted Collection includes erotic Italian 16th-century engravings by or after Raphael, Giulio Romano, Agostino Carracci, Jacopo de' Barbari and Enea Vico, and the remains of a set of the famous *Postures* by Marcantonio Raimondi after

Giulio Romano (*see* §I, 2(ii) above). Other rarities include the 18th-century *Histoire universelle*, with its erotic water-colour illustrations (*see* §I, 2(iii) above), and erotica by Félicien Rops, Aubrey Beardsley and Gustav Klimt. Especially interesting are the erotic drawings of J. M. W. Turner, some very explicit drawings by Eric Gill, and the eight etched plates for Thomas Rowlandson's *Pretty Little Games for Ladies and Gentlemen* together with a set of the prints (*see* §I, 2(iii) above).

See also GAY AND LESBIAN ART.

BIBLIOGRAPHY

E. Fuchs: *Die Karikatur der europäischen Völker von 1848 bis zur Gegenwart* (Berlin, 1903)

——: *Das erotische Element in der Karikatur* (Munich, 1904)

C. von Karwarth: *Die Erotik in der Kunst* (Vienna and Leipzig, 1908)

E. Fuchs: *Illustrierte Sittengeschichte vom Mittelalter bis zur Gegenwart*, 3 vols (1909–11)

——: *Geschichte der erotischen Kunst*, 4 vols (1912–26)

——: *Die grossen Meister der Erotik: Ein Beitrag zum Problem des schöpferischen Malerei und Plastik* (Munich, 1928)

Bilder-Lexikon der Erotik, 4 vols (Vienna, 1928–31)

S. Alexander: *Beauty and Other Forms of Value* (London, 1933)

G. Bataille: *L'Erotisme* (Paris, 1957; Eng. trans., London, 1962, 2/New York, 1987)

K. Clark: *The Nude* (Harmondsworth, 1960)

G. Lo Duca: *Histoire de l'érotisme* (Paris, 1960; Eng. trans., London, 1966)

J. Reichardt: 'Censorship, Obscenity and Context', *Studio Int.*, clxxii/883 (1966), pp. 222–3

D. H. Lawrence: *A propos of Lady Chatterley's Lover and Other Essays* (Harmondsworth, 1967)

P. Kronhausen and E. Kronhausen: *Erotic Art: A Survey of Erotic Fact and Fancy in Fine Arts*, 2 vols (New York, 1968–70)

S. Marcus: *The Other Victorians* (London, 1969)

T. Bowie and C. V. Christenson, eds: *Studies in Erotic Art* (New York and London, 1970)

T. B. Hess and E. C. Baker, eds: 'Art and Sexual Politics: Why Have There Been No Great Women Artists?', *ARTnews*, lxix/9 (1971); as booklet (New York and London, 1973)

M. Peckham: *Art and Pornography: An Experiment in Explanation* (New York and London, 1971)

T. B. Hess and L. Nochlin, eds: 'Woman as Sex Object: Studies in Erotic Art, 1730–1970', *ARTnews Annu.*, 38 (1972)

B. Rose: 'Vaginal Iconology', *NY Mag.* (Feb 1974)

D. Seiberling: 'The Female View of Erotica', *NY Mag.* (Feb 1974)

P. Webb: *The Erotic Arts* (London and New York, 1975; rev. 1983)

C. Beurdeley: *L'Amour bleu* (Fribourg, 1978; Eng. trans., New York, 1978) [on homosexuality in art]

J. Chicago and S. Hill: *Embroidering our Heritage: The Dinner Party Needlework* (New York, 1980)

A. Dworkin: *Pornography: Men Possessing Women* (New York, 1981)

R. Parker and G. Pollock: *Old Mistresses: Women, Art and Ideology* (London, 1981)

S. Feinstein: 'Our Bodies, Ourselves', *Gay News*, 245 (1982)

G. Pollock: 'Theory and Pleasure', *Sense and Sensibility in Feminist Art Practice* (exh. cat., Nottingham, Midland Group, 1982)

S. Kent and J. Moreau: *Women's Images of Men* (London, 1985)

E. Cooper: *The Sexual Perspective: Homosexuality and Art in the Last 100 Years in the West* (London, 1986)

PETER WEBB

Erp, Theodoor van (*b* Ambon, Indonesia, 23 June 1874; *d* Laren, Netherlands, 7 May 1958). Dutch archaeologist. Educated in the Netherlands, he trained for the Civil Engineering Corps in Breda (1892–6) and left as an officer for the Dutch East Indies (now Indonesia) to design fortifications. As an accomplished painter he was interested in ancient monuments and became a member of the Borobudur Commission in 1900, completing a survey and technical drawings for a preservation report (1902) on this early 9th-century Central Javanese Buddhist monument. Thereafter van Erp's name remained closely associated with Borobudur, which was restored for the first time between 1907 and 1911. Meanwhile he worked on many other restoration projects and wrote numerous illustrated reports on monuments in Java and Bali for the Archaeological Survey. He returned to the Netherlands in 1912 and continued publishing after his retirement in 1918. His major achievement was the architectural description of Borobudur published in 1931.

WRITINGS

Bouwkundige beschrijving [Architectural description] (1931), ii of N. J. Krom and Th. van Erp: *Beschrijving van Barabudur* (The Hague, 1920–31)

H. I. R. HINZLER

Errante, Giuseppe (*b* Trapani, 19 March 1760; *d* Rome, 16 Feb 1821). Italian painter. His father was a merchant in animal skins, and because of his habit of drawing on the hides Giuseppe was nicknamed 'guastacuoi'. He had a period of apprenticeship with the sculptor Domenico Nolfo in Trapani and continued his studies in Palermo with the painter Padre Fedele da S Biagio (1717–1801) and later with Gioacchino Martorana. On returning to Trapani, he painted the picture the *Virgin of Carmel Liberating the Souls in Purgatory*. After a brief stay in Naples he moved to Rome, where, under the protection of Canova, he studied perspective and architectural drawing with the architect Giuseppe Barberi (1749–1809). Errante became moderately prosperous because he also executed miniatures, as well as making copies of—and restoring—Old Master paintings.

The first painting Errante completed in Rome is dated 1784: *St Vincenzo*, the altarpiece for SS Vincenzo e Anastasio alla Regola, which is characterized by its neat drawing and smooth tonal transitions. In the same period for the Palazzo Altieri he painted a fresco showing *Cupid and Psyche*, in which the Rococo sense of decoration is marked by a fine and soft colouring. In 1786 he began the fresco of the cupola of the Chiesa della Morte at Civitavecchia, completed in 1788, following a period of interruption during which he was married in Trapani. This major work depicting the *Souls in Purgatory* recalls Baroque decoration and is enriched with festive Rococo elements showing garlands of flowers and diminutive angels. Also in the same church are two other works that have been attributed to Errante (see 1972 exh. cat.): a banner with the *Madonna and Child and Souls in Purgatory* on one side and the *Archangel Michael Appearing to SS Gregory the Great and Roch* on the other, as well as a canvas with the *Madonna and Child and St Joseph* (both 1786–8).

Errante returned to Rome for the conclusion of his studies, receiving an annual pension and living at the Palazzo della Farnesina, both privileges from Ferdinand IV, King of Naples. In 1791 he was given the task of painting one of the state rooms in the royal palace of Caserta, but the political turbulence forced him to flee under a false name (Giuseppe Pellegrino). He stayed in Ancona, where for the bishop, Cardinal Vincenzo Ranuzzi, he executed various portraits and the painting of *SS Philip and James* (finally completed in Milan, 1796; Ancona, church of St James). He arrived in Milan at the end of August 1795. There his painting style moved towards Neo-classicism, passing from delicate colours and shading

to work that is smooth and sleek but without chiaroscuro. He painted a large body of pictures on a wide variety of themes, thus achieving considerable popularity. Among his many portraits are those of his patron the *Duca di Monte Leone* and that of *Dr G. A. Borgnes*, in whose collection there were at least 15 pictures by Errante.

In 1804 three of Errante's works were sent to Paris: the *Mourning Artemisia*, *Sleeping Endymion* and *Psyche*. In 1806 he contributed two pictures, the *Death of Count Ugolino* and another *Mourning Artemisia* (both untraced), to the exhibition at the Accademia di Belle Arti, held on the occasion of Napoleon's visit to Milan. His picture depicting the *Death of Antigone* was one of his most celebrated works. The climate of Milan affected his delicate health, and he decided to return to Rome. There he renewed contacts with Ferdinand IV, who proposed to him the opening of an academy and also commissioned a ceiling in one of the rooms in the royal palace at Caserta. Neither of these projects was realized by the artist, who was unwilling to leave Rome. In 1815 he published a letter on colour and in 1817 an essay on the same subject; during the same period he wrote a plan for a new Accademia di Belle Arti.

WRITINGS

Lettera sui colori ['Lettera del signor cavalier Guiseppe Errante al barone D. Alessandro Recupero su' i colori adoperati dai famosi coloristi italiani e fiamminghi ne' bei secoli dell'arte pittorica'] (Rome, 1816)
Saggio sui colori (Rome, 1817)

BIBLIOGRAPHY

Bolaffi; Thieme–Becker
F. Cancellieri: *Memorie raccolte da F.C. intorno alla vita ed alle opere del pittore cavaliere Giuseppe Errante di Trapani* (Rome, 1824)
M. Accascina: *Ottocento siciliano: Pittura* (Rome, 1939/*R* Palermo, 1982), pp. 9, 24–6, 129–31
A. Schiavo: *Palazzo Altieri* (Rome, 1964), pp. 131–3
Soprintendenza alle gallerie e alle opere d'arte per il Lazio: Restauri, 1970–71 (exh. cat., Rome, Pal. Venezia, 1972), pp. 64–6
S. Rudolph: *La pittura del '700 a Roma* (Milan, 1983), p. 764
A. Cera, ed.: *La pittura neoclassica italiana* (Milan, 1987), p. 670, figs 363–5
G. Barbera: 'Giuseppe Errante', *La pittore in Italia: L'ottocento* (1991), pp. 812–13

ANA MARIA RYBKO

Errard [Erard], **Charles**, *le fils* (*b* Nantes, *c.* 1606–9; *d* Rome, 25 May 1689). French painter, draughtsman, architect and writer, active also in Italy. He first studied under Charles Errard *le père* (*c.* 1570–1630), a Mannerist portrait painter and engineer. From 1627 he was in Rome, working under the protection of François de Créqui, French Ambassador to the papal court. There he came into contact with an influential circle of scholars, artists and patrons, including Joachim von Sandrart, Paul Fréart, Sieur de Chantelou, secretary to the French Surintendant des Bâtiments du Roi, François Sublet des Noyers and Giovanni Pietro Bellori. During this period he made copies after paintings by Titian and Annibale Carracci and drawings of Roman antiquities, while learning the idealized, classicizing style that was upheld in academic circles. In 1633 he became a member of the Accademia di S Luca.

In 1643 Errard returned to Paris as a Peintre Ordinaire du Roi and became one of the most fashionable painters in the capital. Over the next two decades he undertook a series of commissions for the crown and for wealthy bourgeois patrons. In February 1648 Errard was among the 12 founder-members of the Académie Royale de Peinture et de Sculpture (*see* PARIS, §VI, 1), established to promote painting and sculpture as intellectually respectable liberal arts. He did much to imbue the Académie with the classical and rationalist conception of painting and sculpture with which it was to become associated in the latter part of the 17th century. In addition, he collaborated with Fréart de Chambray on the architectural treatise *Parallèle de l'architecture antique et de la moderne* (1650) and the translation of Leonardo da Vinci's manuscript *Trattato della pittura*, published as the *Traité de la peinture* in 1651, for both of which Errard provided illustrations that were engraved by others. The latter book was one of the first works of art theory published in French and a seminal academic text throughout the 17th century. A profile portrait in red chalk of Fréart de Chambray by Errard survives (Paris, Louvre).

During the 1640s and 1650s Errard received a series of prestigious commissions. In 1645 he painted the devotional May of Notre-Dame de Paris, the religious painting presented each year to the cathedral of Notre-Dame by the Goldsmiths' Corporation. The following year he made designs for Luigi Rossi's *Orfeo*, one of the first operas to be presented in Paris. Other commissions included decorative schemes for the appartements of Cardinal Jules Mazarin and Louis XIV within the Palais du Louvre, Paris (destr.). Between 1656 and 1665 he and the painter Noël Coypel were in charge of decorating the Grande Chambre of the Palais du Parlement de Bretagne at Rennes (now the Palais de Justice) with arabesques and personified figures, among the few examples of Errard's work to survive. He also contributed to the decoration of the Petit Château at Versailles (destr.) and to the château of Saint-Germain-en-Laye, although the considerable prestige he had enjoyed at court was beginning to wane in favour of Charles Lebrun.

The latter part of Errard's career was spent mostly in Italy, following his appointment in 1666 as the first director of the newly established Académie de France in Rome. Towards the end of the decade he began to work on designs for the church of the Assumption, Rue St Honoré, Paris (1670–76; destr. 1898). For this, his only recorded venture as an architect, Errard depended heavily on antique examples, particularly the Pantheon in Rome; planned on a Greek cross, the church consisted of a drum supporting a dome, the whole fronted by a Corinthian portico. During the 1670s and 1680s he continued to play an important administrative role in the Académie at Rome, and he was responsible for its collaboration with the Accademia di S Luca. He was elected as the Accademia's principal in 1672 and re-elected in 1678, having served as Charles Lebrun's deputy in 1676 and 1677. The death of Jean-Baptiste Colbert, Surintendant des Bâtiments du Roi from 1664 and Errard's protector, prompted his resignation as director of the Académie in Rome in 1683. Errard was buried at Rome in the church of S Luigi dei Francesi.

WRITINGS

with R. Fréart de Chambray: *Parallèle de l'architecture antique et de la moderne* (Paris, 1650)

trans., with R. Fréart de Chambray: Leonardo da Vinci: *Trattato della pittura* [MS. notes] as *Traité de la peinture de Léonard de Vinci* (Paris, 1651)

BIBLIOGRAPHY

A. de Montaiglon: *Correspondance des directeurs de l'Académie de France à Rome* (Paris, 1887)
A. Fontaine: *Les Doctrines d'art en France* (Paris, 1909)
——: *Académiciens d'autrefois* (Paris, 1914)
H. Lapauze: *Histoire de l'Académie de France à Rome* (Paris, 1924)
D. Mahon: *Studies in Seicento Art and Theory* (London, 1947)
J. Thuillier: 'Charles Errard, peintre', *Rev. A.*, xl–xli (1978), pp. 151–72

STEVEN ADAMS

Erri [degli Erri; Herri; de Ler; del R]. Italian family of painters. The family comprised several generations of painters, of whom the most important were the brothers Angelo [Agnolo] Erri (*fl* Modena, 1442–97) and Bartolomeo Erri (*fl* Modena, 1450–79), who worked together. It has proved impossible to distinguish the hand of each in individual works, most of which were commissioned from both of them and probably executed in collaboration.

The Erri brothers' tripartite altarpiece depicting the *Coronation of the Virgin with Saints* and scenes from the *Life of St John the Baptist* (1462–6; Modena, Gal. Estense) contains Late Gothic narrative elements organized according to a rationale that is wholly Renaissance. This can be attributed both to their familiarity with Ferrarese culture and to their free elaboration of Tuscan elements, drawn from the tradition of Domenico Veneziano. Through comparison with that altarpiece, the brothers have been attributed with the altar frontal depicting scenes from the *Life of St Thomas* (after 1466; ex-S Domenico, Modena), of which only eight fragments have survived (Washington, DC, N.G.A.; San Francisco, CA, M. H. de Young Mem. Mus.; New Haven, CT, Yale U. A.G.; New York, Christie's Int.; Brno, Morav. Gal.; several priv. cols). Perhaps another member of the Erri family, if not Angelo and Bartolomeo, worked on the earliest of the three altar frontals for the church of S Domenico, Modena, this one depicting the *Life of St Peter the Martyr* (c. 1450; Parma, G.N.). In 1467 Bartolomeo Erri was commissioned to paint an altarpiece for S Domenico's main altar; in 1480 it was still unfinished, and in 1710 it was removed from the altar and dismantled. All that is known to survive is a fragment depicting the *Virgin Enthroned* and part of the main panel, depicting the *Virgin and Saints* (Strasbourg, Mus. B.-A.), and one of the sections of the predella depicting a *Miracle of St Dominic* (New York, Met.). Compared with the earlier works, the style is more developed and characterized by the geometricizing of the forms and a clearer and stronger illumination of the figures; this indicates a reference to Piero della Francesca.

During the 1480s the Erri brothers worked on the third altar frontal for S Domenico, this one depicting the *Life of St Vincenzo Ferrer* (Modena, Semin. Vesc.; Vienna, Ksthist. Mus.; Oxford, Ashmolean). The whole composition is governed by an absolute obedience to the laws of visual perspective, but the individual elements display an exceptional narrative wealth, with extremely convincing realistic details, particularly in the representation of contemporary Modena.

BIBLIOGRAPHY

A. Venturi: 'L'Oratorio dell'Ospedale della Morte', *Atti & Mem. R. R. Deput. Stor. Patria Prov. Modern. & Parm.*, iii (1885), pp. 245–77
A. M. Chiodi: 'Bartolomeo degli Erri e i polittici domenicani', *Commentari*, ii (1951), pp. 17–25

D. Benati: *La bottega degli Erri e la pittura del rinascimento a Modena* (Modena, 1988)

DANIELE BENATI

Erró [Guðmundsson, Guðmundur] (*b* Ólafsvík, 19 July 1932). Icelandic painter. He studied at the Myndlista-og handíðaskóli Íslands (Icelandic School of Arts and Crafts, Reykjavík, 1949–51) and the Kunstakademi, Oslo (1952–4), where he specialized in fresco painting and printmaking. He undertook further studies in painting and mosaic at the Accademie in Florence and Ravenna (1954–7). He settled in Paris in 1958, later dividing his time between Paris, Bangkok, the Mediterranean island of Formentera and Reykjavík. During his period of study he undertook numerous experiments with style, which coalesced in Italy as a polemic figuration in the *Carcasses* series (e.g. *Black Bull*, 1956; Jerusalem, Israel Mus.).

A cosmopolitan and eclectic artist, Erró developed his work from his study of Old Masters such as Uccello and Bosch, and his close association with the Chilean Surrealist Roberto Matta in 1959. Photomontages and assemblages of found objects underlay his continued interest in Surrealist techniques. In the early 1960s, prompted by repeated visits to the USA, Erró began using popular imagery. In common with other artists associated with Pop art, he began with adaptations of advertising and magazine images, but these were later juxtaposed with quotations from 'high art' sources, from the Old Masters to Picasso. He played a significant part in the development of Happenings in France in 1962–4, and he was also active in the field of experimental filmmaking. Erró used his material non-judgementally, seeking to discover its latent possibilities. Though maintaining a neutral stand vis-à-vis his sources, Erró's accumulations (e.g. *Foodscape*, 1962–3; Stockholm, Mod. Mus.), painted with the highest precision, frequently give expression to a terrifying vision of the modern world, where objects bereft of meaning have crowded out every human emotion. There are murals by Erró in Reykjavík (1957 and 1960), Angoulême (1982) and the Cité des Sciences et de l'Industrie at La Villette, Paris (1990).

BIBLIOGRAPHY

G. Brownstone: *Erró* (Paris, 1972)
Erró: Tableaux chinois (exh. cat., text J.-C. Ammann, Lucerne, Kstmus., 1975)
P. Tilman: *Erró* (Paris, 1976)
Catalogue général 'Erró' (Milan, 1976) [cat. rais., illus.]
M. Johannessen and B. Ásgeirsson: 'Erró: Icelandic Artist', *Iceland Rev.*, iii (1978), pp. 46–53
Catalogue général II 'Erró' 1974–1986 (Paris, 1986) [cat. rais., illus.]
A. Ingólfsson: *Erró: Margfalt Líf* [Erró: Multiple life] (Reykjavík, 1991)

AÐALSTEINN INGÓLFSSON

Erskine, John, 6th and 11th Earl of Mar (*b* Alloa, Central, Feb 1675; *d* Aix-la-Chapelle, May 1732). Scottish patron and amateur architect. He inherited the title of Earl of Mar in 1689, having completed his education and a Grand Tour. Although a Catholic, Mar's political sympathies wavered between loyalty to George I and support for the King's Jacobite enemies. Despite the fact that he inherited immense debts, Mar became the first patron of the architect James Gibbs and commissioned from him Comley Bank Lodge (unexecuted) for his estate at Alloa (*c.* 1710; design in Oxford, Worcester Coll. Lib.), as well as other alterations and improvements. Mar and Hugh Campbell, 3rd Earl of Loudoun (*d* 1731), became Secretaries of State for Scotland, and again Gibbs was employed to divide a house in London at Privy Gardens, Whitehall, to make a home for each of them (1715; destr.). As Gibbs's first British patron, Mar played an important part in his early success and in 1713 helped him gain the post of Surveyor to the Fifty New Churches Commission. With Gibbs's assistance, Mar developed some skill as an amateur architect; he showed imagination, if impracticality, in his prolific, although unexecuted, designs. He worked with Gibbs on alterations to his seat at Alloa and possibly designed houses at Tullibody (destr.) and Tillicoultry (rebuilt 1806), also in Central (formerly Clackmananshire). In 1715 Mar was forced into exile after the defeat of the Jacobite armies at Sherrifmuir. While abroad he corresponded regularly with Gibbs, using this line of communication for sending cryptic political messages as well as for keeping up with architectural developments in Britain. He sent assorted designs to Gibbs, among which were plans for rebuilding at Wilton House and Longleat House (both Wilts), Drumlanrig and his own former estate at Alloa. His letters also included a suggestion for a programme of bridge-building in Edinburgh that was realized after his death. Although he always hoped to return to favour in Britain, he remained in France for the rest of his life. His generous patronage of Gibbs was rewarded when the architect willed Mar's penurious son, Thomas, Lord Erskine, a substantial part of his estate.

BIBLIOGRAPHY

Colvin; *DNB*
C. T. Smout: 'The Erskines of Mar and the Development of Alloa, 1689–1825', *Scot. Stud.*, vi (1963), pp. 57–74 (57–61)
T. Friedman: *James Gibbs* (New Haven, 1984)
M. C. H. Stewart: 'Lord Mar's Gardens at Alloa, *c.* 1700–1732', *Aspects of Scottish Classicism: The House and its Formal Setting, 1690–1750*, ed. J. Frew and D. Jones (St Andrews, 1988)

SHEARER WEST

Erskine, Ralph (*b* London, 24 Feb 1914). English architect, active in Sweden and Britain. He trained at the Regent Street Polytechnic in London (1932–8) and went to Sweden in 1939. After working in Stockholm in the offices of G. Birch-Lindgren and others, he attended the Kungliga Akademien för de fria Konsterna for a year (1945–6) and established his own practice. Early projects for recreational facilities, for example Lida ski-sport centre (1942; with Birch-Lindgren) and Borgafjäll ski-resort hotel (1947–50), showed his interest in adapting architecture to the climate and natural setting as well as a freedom in design and use of simple construction and materials, which became characteristics of his architecture. During the 1940s and 1950s commissions included workers' housing, such as at Gyttorp (1945–55), with protective vaulted roofs and a variegated colour scheme, and the timber workers' village at Jädraås (1951), and industrial buildings such as the Pulp Factory (1950–53) at Fors near Aresta. From 1959 Erskine was a member of Team Ten. His larger housing schemes include Brittgården (1959–61) at Tibro, which combines terrace houses and low-rise blocks of flats with concrete balconies. For Nya Bruket (1973–8) in Sandviken he adapted the redevelopment scheme to the pre-existing grid plan. In housing for the mining community at Svappavaara (1963) Erskine's consideration of harsh climatic conditions as part of his design is illustrated. In Britain a notable work was the Byker redevelopment scheme (1969–80) in Newcastle upon Tyne, where he established a branch office and attempted to involve local people in the planning process. A multistorey, long, meandering wall of flats in variegated brickwork encompassed a low-rise development with gardens. He also planned housing, recreation facilities and city redevelopment projects in Austria, Finland, France and Italy. Versatility, variegated colours, forms and materials, and an architectural eloquence on the verge of loquacity characterize Erskine's always very personal and inventive architectural style. His later projects include the Students' Centre, Auditorium and Library of Stockholm University (1979–82) and the high-rise, red-and-white Skanska office building (1989), Göteborg. He was awarded the Wolf Foundation Prize in 1984 and the RIBA Gold Medal in 1987.

BIBLIOGRAPHY

M. Egelius: 'Ralph Erskine, the Human Architect', *Archit. Des.*, xi–xii (1977)

Arkitektur DK, vii (1981) [issue on Erskine]

P. Collymore: *The Architecture of Ralph Erskine* (London, 1982)

M. Egelius and others: *Recent Developments in Swedish Architecture: A Reappraisal* (Stockholm, 1982)

F. Bedoire and P. Thullberg: *Stockholm University: A History* (Stockholm, 1987)

Ertborn, Florent (Joseph), Ridder **van** (*b* Antwerp, 4 April 1784; *d* The Hague, 28 Aug 1840). Flemish government official, writer, collector and patron. As the Orangist burgomaster of Antwerp (1817–28) in the Unified Greater Netherlands, established after the Congress of Vienna (1815) united the Spanish Netherlands and the Dutch Republic into a single kingdom under William I of Orange Nassau, van Ertborn was instrumental in the economic revival of the city. At the instigation of his friend, the writer, philologist and Flemish activist Jan Frans Willems (1793–1846), Flemish, instead of French, became the official administrative language of Antwerp. The correspondence between van Ertborn and Willems testifies to the ideological affinity between the two men. In 1828 William I appointed van Ertborn Governor of the Province of Utrecht. He was honourably discharged from this position in 1830, when the anti-Dutch Belgian Revolt broke out. After the Kingdom of Belgium was granted independence in 1830, van Ertborn was again elected Burgomaster of Antwerp, but he refused the post out of loyalty to his former king, the House of Orange and the Greater Netherlands. Van Ertborn then lived intermittently in The Hague and Paris, frequently visiting Germany and devoting himself almost exclusively to the study and collection of Old Master paintings, the majority of which were early Netherlandish.

The core of van Ertborn's collection, which was bequeathed to the city of Antwerp, includes such 15th-century masterpieces as Jean Fouquet's *Virgin and Child Surrounded by Angels*, Jan van Eyck's *St Barbara* and the *Virgin at the Fountain*, Rogier van der Weyden's portrait of *Philippe de Croÿ* and the altarpiece of the *Seven Sacraments*, Gerard David's *Quod scripsi, scripsi* panels, Hans Memling's *Portrait of a Man* and many others by anonymous masters, amounting to 115 works in all, now in the

Koninklijk Museum voor Schone Kunsten. This taste as well as the selection was highly unusual for the period. Early Netherlandish painting was unfashionable in the first half of the 19th century and van Ertborn was able to acquire his collection relatively inexpensively. A portrait of *Ridder van Ertborn* (*c.* 1805) by an unknown painter is owned by Graaf J. de Marnix (Kasteel Eyzer, Overijse). Another (untraced) was painted by Jean-Baptiste Greuze *c.* 1810. A portrait bust in marble was carved by Jozef Geefs (1808–85) in 1849 (Antwerp, Kon. Mus. S. Kst.).

UNPUBLISHED SOURCES

Antwerp, Stadsarchf [misc. notes and pap.]

Brussels, Bib. Royale Albert 1er, Handschrkab. II 910 [seven letters from van Ertborn to L. P. Gachard and three replies, dated 1834–7, mentioning a biog. of Jacoba of Bavaria (untraced) that van Ertborn had prepared for pubn]

WRITINGS

Puyn-hoopen rondom Antwerpen [Heaps of ruins around Antwerp] (Antwerp, 1814)

Excursion à l'abbaye d'Altenberg et au château de Nesselrath dans le pays de Berg: Légendes de 13e et 14e siècles (Paris, 1842) [travel diary pubd by van Ertborn's widow]

NBW

BIBLIOGRAPHY

J. Bols: *Brieven aan Jan-Frans Willems* (Ghent, 1909), nos 236, 243, 264, 285, 344, 370

A. H. Cornette: *Een Antwerpsch Maeceen: Ridder Florent van Ertborn* (Antwerp, 1938)

J. De Coo: 'Florent Ridder van Ertborn, gouverneur van Utrecht', *Jb. Kon. Mus. S. Kst.* (1954–60), pp. 35–64

P. Vandenbroeck: *Catalogus schilderijen 14e en 15e eeuw*, Antwerp, Kon. Mus. S. Kst. cat. (Antwerp, 1985), pp. 25–8, 67–71, 134–8, 150–58, 168–78

HANS J. VAN MIEGROET

Ertinger, Franz Ferdinand (*b* Immenstadt, 18 Aug 1669; *fl* 1697). German sculptor and writer. He is known only from his journal *Rais Beschreibung* (Munich, Bayer. Staatsbib; CCM 3212), which begins in 1682 and ends abruptly in 1697. According to the journal Ertinger, after visiting Salzburg, Munich and Augsburg among other places, began an apprenticeship as a sculptor in Kempten in 1683. In 1690 he set off on a walking tour, recording his impressions. During the journey he worked for various masters, probably only as an assistant, as no works of his own are known. The journal is an important source on the cultural history of the late 17th century, including accounts of cities and works of art in southern Germany, Austria, Hungary, Moravia, Silesia and Bohemia, and of such artists as Andreas Faistenberger (1646–1735) and Johann Baptist Fischer (*fl* 1626–76). It throws light not only on workshop practice at the time but also on the oeuvres of particular masters. For example, part of the work of the painters Joachim von Sandrart and Tobias Bock is recorded here, as is the contribution (1685) of Mathias Rauchmiller to the frescoes in Passau Cathedral.

BIBLIOGRAPHY

E. Tietze-Conrad, ed.: *Des Bildhauergesellen Franz Ferdinand Ertinger Reisebeschreibung durch Österreich und Deutschland. Nach der Handschrift CGM 3312 der Kgl. Hof- und Staatsbibliothek München*, n. s. xiv of *Quellenschriften für Kunstgeschichte und Kunsttechnik des Mittelalters und der Neuzeit* (Vienna and Leipzig, 1907)

DORIS KUTSCHBACH

Ertvelt, Andries van. *See* EERTVELT, ANDRIES VAN.

Ervi [Elers], **Aarne (Adrian)** (*b* Forssa, 19 May 1910; *d* Helsinki, 26 Sept 1977). Finnish architect and urban planner. He studied at the Technical University of Helsinki (1930–35). In 1934–5 Ervi worked on the design for the Viipuri Town Library building in the office of Alvar Aalto, and although there was not much visible evidence, Aalto's influence on Ervi's way of thinking and aspirations in architecture can be traced to this period. Even his work as a student shows clear traces of the new tendencies. Before he was 30 Ervi had found his own striking style, and, in competition with J. S. Sirén and Aalto among others, his design for the Helsinki University Library (unexecuted) won first prize in 1937. He was then able to establish his own office in Helsinki in 1938. The functionalist tendencies of the 1930s were evident in Ervi's design for a cap factory (1938) at Kurikka on the west coast of Finland, and the softer forms, characteristic of Ervi's work, were to be seen at this early stage in his design for a block of flats at Lauttasaarentie 9 (1938) in Helsinki and a commercial building in Heinola (destr. 1970s; see Solla, 1970, p. 17).

In the years after World War II, until *c.* 1950 an idealized romanticism found expression in architecture. Ervi's versatility was expressed in various ways during these years. He was one of the founders of the Institute of Building Standards and its first Director. With infallible instinct, Ervi completed the back-stage-like interior of the 'Kestikartano', which, until demolished in 1967, was a popular restaurant with an old Finnish atmosphere. The bar of 'Finland House' in New York, which was renovated in 1947, was also very popular. At the same time Ervi was using industrial manufacture and prefabrication at the Oulujoki power station (1942–6), also designing their housing areas at Pyhäkoski, Jylhämä, Nuojua and Pälli. In urban planning Ervi took an unequivocal stand on the general building plans for Oulu in 1951 in favour of a form of relaxed construction, which implied that humanity was in communion with nature, interpreted by open spaces and well-used forest. Ervi believed that by this approach he could open up to people in their surroundings. Two of Ervi's most beautiful buildings of *c.* 1950 are his own house at Kuusisaari, Helsinki, and the clubhouse of a commercial bank at Otaniemi in Espoo, Helsinki. Both are excellent examples of his desire to express a natural harmony between structural elements and the inhabitants, integrating interior and exterior, incorporating privacy and the wide view and developing different levels in harmony with nature including fences and walls, furniture and plants.

New rational principles, in keeping with the general development in Finland and continuing the functions of the 1930s, guided Ervi in his choice of materials and construction from 1950. In Porthania (1951), the Helsinki University building, a 'total' method of construction was used for the first time in Finland with prefabricated reinforced concrete.

Ervi's constant need to renew and his constant self-criticism were apparent in all his projects. Planning on the University of Turku and the garden city of Tapiola were begun in the early 1950s. As well as the overall plan for Tapiola, he designed buildings there, including the swimming hall (1962), flats, villas and row houses (1952–64) and the department store Heikintori (1965). These projects, as well as the flats at Myllytie 3 in Helsinki and all Ervi's early plans, were clear expressions of his basic principle of relating humanity with nature in all situations. At Tapiola he made full use of the natural features of the site, which was a forest by the sea, punctuated by granite formations and surrounded by low hills. Water is present in most of Ervi's plans, whether from natural sources or artificially created ones.

In 1965 the Association of Finnish Architects asked Ervi to take on the position of leading the newly founded town-planning department of the City of Helsinki. He accepted, despite recognizing that his own architectural office would retreat into the background. In the following years his work on the Töölö Library (1968) in Helsinki was his only work of renown, proving that the decision had been crucial to his career.

BIBLIOGRAPHY

Contemp. Architects
'Habitations en bande continue à Tapiola, Helsinki', *Archit. Aujourd'hui*, 93 (1960–61), pp. 38–41
P. Solla: 'Aarne Ervi: Ein Ritter der alten Schule', *Dt. Bauztg*, ix (1968), pp. 674–86
P. Solla, ed.: *Raportti rakennetusta ympäristöstä, Aarne Ervi arkkitehtuuria* [Report on the built environment, the architecture of Aarne Ervi] (Helsinki, 1970)

PERTTI SOLLA

Erwin [von Steinbach] (*d* Strasbourg, 17 Jan 1318). German architect. The designation 'von Steinbach' is derived from an inscription probably set up at the beginning of the 15th century on the north portal of the façade of Strasbourg Cathedral. Over the centuries Erwin has represented the archetype of the medieval architect; to him has been attributed the whole façade of Strasbourg Cathedral (*see* STRASBOURG, §III, 1), if not the entire fabric, a myth assured wide diffusion by Johann Wolfgang von Goethe's essay *Von deutscher Baukunst* (1772). Erwin's personality and his part in the construction of the cathedral are, however, difficult to determine. Contemporary evidence mentions the name Erwin and his title Master of the Works, while his epitaph (1316–39) adds Administrator of the Fabric (*gubernator fabrice*). His name has been added to a contract of 1284; he is mentioned in a deed of sale of 1293 and in the Book of Donations (Strasbourg, Archvs Mun.), as well as in his epitaph and that of his son Johannes (*d* 1339), and that of another son (*d* 1330) in Niederhaslach. His name also appears on an inscription in the chapel of the Virgin (1316). Few historians still go so far as to attribute to him the design of the whole façade, but it is generally accepted that Erwin headed the façade workshop *c.* 1285, when an attempt was made to hasten the works undertaken until then in conformity with Plan B (Strasbourg, Mus. Oeuvre Notre-Dame). It was in modifying this plan that Erwin finished the portal stage and began the rose. He was very likely responsible for façade Plan C (known through a copy in Nuremberg, Ger. Nmus.) and for Plan D (Strasbourg, Mus. Oeuvre Notre-Dame), which shows the interior elevations of the narthex. In 1316 he was still building the Virgin Chapel (destr. 1682) in the nave, on the north side of the choir screen.

Thieme-Becker

BIBLIOGRAPHY

J. W. von Goethe: *Von deutscher Baukunst: D. M. Erwin a Steinbach* (Frankfurt am Main, 1772)
F. X. Kraus: *Kunst und Alterthum im Unter-Elsass* (Strasbourg, 1876), pp. 365, 375–7, 687–93
P. Wentzcke and H. Kunze: 'Von Meister Erwin in Strassburg, 1284–1318', *Z. Ges. Oberrheins*, n. s., xxviii (1913), pp. 213–38
R. Will: 'Les Inscriptions disparues de la porta sertorum de la cathédrale de Strasbourg et le mythe d'Erwin de Steinbach', *Bull. Cathédrale Strasbourg*, xiv (1980), pp. 13–20
Nouveau dictionnaire de biographie alsacienne, ii (Strasbourg, 1987), pp. 853–4
R. Liess and A. Köpke: 'Zur ehemaligen Erwin-Inschrift von 1277 an der Westfassade des Strassburger Münsters', *Z. Gesch. Oberrheins*, cxxxvii (1989), pp. 105–73 [summary in *Bull. Cathédrale Strasbourg*, xix (1990), pp. 90–92]

ROGER LEHNI

Erwitt, Elliott (*b* Paris, 26 July 1928). American photographer and film maker. He studied film at the New School for Social Research, New York, from 1948 to 1950. From 1951 to 1953 he worked as a photographic assistant for the US Army Signal Corps and under Roy Stryker (1882–1975) at the Standard Oil Company, New Jersey, from 1950 to 1952. From 1953 he was a freelance photographer and film maker and a member of the Magnum photographic agency. Although he was highly successful in the field of advertising, his international reputation was based on his personal work. His street photographs, wry and quirky narratives, concentrated on the vagaries of human existence. They often relied heavily on visual puns. Unrelated and sometimes bizarre events, for example the small dog captured in mid-air in *Ballycotton, Ireland* (1968; see *Photographs and Anti-photographs*, p. 48), are held together within the 35 mm frame by strong graphic and formal compositions. Erwitt's films include *Dustin Hoffman, Arthur Penn: The Director, Beauty Knows No Pain* and *Red, White and Bluegrass*.

PHOTOGRAPHIC PUBLICATIONS

Photographs and Anti-photographs (Connecticut, 1972)
The Private Experience: Elliott Erwitt (Los Angeles, 1974)
Personal Exposures (Ontario, 1988)

BIBLIOGRAPHY

Concerning Photography (exh. cat. by J. Bayer and others, London, Photographers' Gal. Ltd; Newcastle upon Tyne, Spectro A. Workshop; 1977)

ALEXANDRA NOBLE

Erzincan. See ALTINTEPE.

Erzurum. City in eastern Turkey. Located on the main route between Iran and Turkey, it has been an important military and commercial centre since antiquity. Possession of the city passed between the Byzantines, who knew it as Theodosiopolis, and the Arabs, who called it Arz(an) al-rum ('Arz(an) of the Byzantines') after a nearby commercial centre. In 1080 it became the capital of the Saltuqid principality and in 1201 a provincial seat under the Saljuqs of Rum (*reg* 1077–1307). In the mid-13th century it came under the control of the Ilkhanids (*reg* 1256–1353) and subsequently it became part of the principality under Eretna (*see* BEYLIK). The city was captured *c.* 1520 by the Ottomans, for whom it held great commercial and strategic importance. The monuments from these centuries exemplify most of the major types of Anatolian architecture and are remarkable for their construction and decoration in finely cut stone (*see* ISLAMIC ART, §II, 5(iii) and 6(ii)(a)).

The Citadel Mosque (Kale Cami, 12th century) is a small rectangular building with a mihrab fitted into a turret of the citadel walls; the bay in front of the mihrab is surmounted by a hemispherical dome contained within a cylindrical structure with a conical cap. The congregational mosque (Ulu Cami, 1179; rest. 17th–19th centuries) is a large enclosed rectangle (42×55 m) with seven parallel aisles and a domed bay in front of the mihrab. The Çifte Minareli Madrasa (mid-13th century; rest. 1958; *see* ISLAMIC ART, fig. 43), located in the south-east angle of the city wall, is the largest (35×48 m) madrasa in Anatolia. Paired minarets (whence the name of the building) surmount the vaulted portal, which leads to a central court enclosed on three sides by two storeys of rooms and iwans. Opposite the entrance, a large iwan stands before a dodecagonal tomb with a conical cap. The Yakutiye (Yaqutiyya) Madrasa (1310), built by the Ilkhanid governor Khwaja Yaqut, repeats such features as the monumental façade and the polygonal tomb tower, but the open courtyard has been roofed with eight vaults surrounding a *muqarnas* cross-vault with a small lantern.

Several free-standing tomb towers remain in the city, including a group of three south of the Çifte Minareli Madrasa. The tomb of Emir Saltuq (late 12th century) is an octagon surmounted by a high cylindrical drum and a conical cap. Constructed of alternating courses of yellow and brown stone, it is decorated with paired blind windows and a string course. The other two towers are more conventional in shape, material and decoration: they are cylindrical structures with conical caps, built of monochrome masonry with blind arcading. In later centuries the city benefited from the caravan trade between Iran and Bursa, and several notable buildings were constructed under the Ottomans, such as the Rüstem Pasha Caravanserai. The Lala Mustafa Pasha Mosque (1562), designed by Sinan (*see* SINAN (ii)), has a central dome supported on octagonal piers. The Ibrahim Pasha Mosque (1748) is a simple domed square with a triple-vaulted portico.

BIBLIOGRAPHY

J. M. Rogers: 'The Çifte Minare Medrese at Erzurum and the Gök Medrese at Sivas', *Anatol. Stud.*, xv (1965), pp. 63–85
R. H. Unal: *Les Monuments islamiques anciens de la ville d'Erzurum et de sa région* (Paris, 1968)
J. M. Rogers: 'The Date of the Çifte Minare Medrese at Erzurum', *Kst Orients*, viii (1974), pp. 77–119
T. A. Sinclair: *Eastern Turkey: An Architectural and Archaeological Survey*, 3 vols (London, 1987–9), ii, pp. 185–216

LALE BABAOĞLU

Er'zya [Nefyodov], **Stepan (Dmitriyevich)** (*b* Bayevo, Simbirsk province [now Ardatov region], 8 Nov 1876; *d* Moscow, 24 Nov 1959). Russian sculptor. He was by birth a member of the small Mordvinian national group, the Er'zya, and their name became his pseudonym. He studied in Moscow at the Stroganov School (1901–2) and at the School of Painting, Sculpture and Architecture under Sergey Volnukhin (1859–after 1910) from 1902 to 1906. He went to Italy in 1906 and became a member of the Milan group of Futurist artists Nuove Tendenze in 1914, but in his own work he combined characteristics of realism and Art Nouveau. Recollections of the first Russian

Revolution in 1905 formed the basis of a number of his early works, such as *The Prison Priest* (1906; Nice, Mus. B.-A.). Er'zya returned to Russia in 1914 and after the Revolution of 1917 he actively participated in the realization of Lenin's Plan for Monumental Propaganda [1918]. He created a series of poetic portrait sculptures of women and symbolic mythological figures (e.g. *Eve*, marble, 1919; Saransk, Sychkov Mordov. Pict. Gal.).

In 1926 Er'zya went to Paris with an exhibition of his work, then moved to Argentina, where he lived and worked from 1927 to 1950, using the local hardwoods. He achieved decorative effects in the carving and polishing of wood, creating romantic forms displaying a tendency towards Symbolism, for example *Beethoven* (1929; St Petersburg, Rus. Mus.), *Terror* (1933; Saransk, Sychkov Mordov. Pict. Gal.) and *Youth* (1940–43; Moscow, Tret'yakov Gal.). In 1950 he returned to Moscow, where he worked successfully in the same style until the end of his life. Most of his work is in the Sychkov Picture Gallery in Saransk.

BIBLIOGRAPHY
Stepan Er'zya (Leningrad, 1975)
M. N. Baranova: *S. D. Er'zya* (Saransk, 1989) [with English résumé]

SVETLANA M. CHERVONNAYA

Es [Esch; Fobsen; Foppes van Essen; Fossen; Fossens], **Jacob van** (*b* ?Antwerp, *c.* 1596; *d* Antwerp, *bur* 11 March 1666). Flemish painter. Together with Osias Beert and Clara Peeters, he was one of the leading representatives of the archaizing trend in Flemish still-lifes. His birthplace is known from the text on an engraving by Wenceslaus Hollar after a painting by Jan Meyssens (1612–70). Van Es became a master in Antwerp in 1617 but did not join the Guild of St Luke until 1645. Jacob Gillis and Jan van Thiene were his pupils in 1621 and 1623 respectively. He enjoyed a certain esteem among fellow artists, for Jacob Jordaens, Cornelis Schut the elder and Deodaat del Monte were godfathers to his children. Numerous mentions of works by van Es in inventories of 17th-century Antwerp collectors further testify to his success; the inventory of Rubens's collection, for instance, includes two still-lifes by van Es.

Most of van Es's still-lifes contain groupings of food (fruit, fish, lobster, oysters, cheese, ham, bread, olives, lemons and oranges) with other objects, including glass and silver, and occasionally a butterfly or a carnation. The compositions are characterized by a sober arrangement of the objects on a pale, sloping surface. A gentle sense of movement is achieved by contrasting light and shade and differing shapes. Very occasionally there is a tendril of a vine wound round the stem of a glass or the spiral of a lemon or orange peel. The dramatic lighting and generous range of colours saturated with light ochres, creamy whites and red-orange tints increase the sense of three-dimensionality. His signed works include *Oysters, Fish and Rusks with a Glass* (Brussels, Mus. A. Anc.), *Scales with Plums* (Madrid, Mus. Thyssen–Bornemisza) and *Oysters, Crab and a Lemon* (Kortrijk, Stedel. Mus. S. Kst.). He also executed a few flower-pieces, distinguished by their exceptional simplicity, adventurous colours and powerful technique, as in the *Vase with Flowers* (Paris, Fond. Custodia, Inst. Néer.), with three roses and an iris in an earthenware jug on a wooden table.

BIBLIOGRAPHY
C. Sterling: *La Nature morte de l'antiquité à nos jours* (Paris, 1952), p. 51
M. L. Hairs: *Les Peintres flamands de fleurs au XVIIe siècle* (Brussels, 1955; rev., 1985), pp. 353–6
E. Greindl: *Les Peintres flamands de nature morte au XVIIe siècle* (Brussels, 1956; rev. Sterrebeek, 1983), pp. 49–53
J. Adhémar: 'Eléments de repas par Jacob van Es', *Rev. A.*, x (1960), pp. 45–6

CHRISTINE VAN MULDERS

Esad Yesari [Mehmed Esad Yesari; Yesari; As'ad Yasārī] (*d* Istanbul, 1798). Ottoman calligrapher. Born paralysed on the right side of his body and palsied on the left, he was given the nickname 'Yesari' (left-handed). He learnt the art of calligraphy from Mehmed Dedezade, gaining his diploma (Turk. *icazet*) in 1753–4. Appointed calligrapher at the Topkapı Palace in Istanbul by Mustafa III (*reg* 1757–74), Esad Yesari achieved fame for his mastery of *nasta'liq* script (e.g. a calligraphic specimen, Istanbul, Topkapı Pal. Lib., G.Y. 325/4488), and his inscriptions adorn mosques, tombs, fountains and hospices in Istanbul. He was buried in the vicinity of the Fatih Mosque, Istanbul. Among his many pupils was his son Mustafa Izzet Yesarizade (*d* 1849), who received his diploma from his father. Mustafa Izzet wrote a beautiful *nasta'liq* script and his inscriptions also adorn buildings in Istanbul.

BIBLIOGRAPHY
Ş. Rado: *Türk hattatları* [Turkish calligraphers] (Istanbul, n.d.), pp. 182–4, 209
A. S. Ünver: *Mehmed Esad Yesarî: Hayatı ve eserleri* [Mehmed Esad Yesari: his life and works] (Istanbul, 1955)
A. Schimmel: *Calligraphy and Islamic Culture* (New York, 1984), pp. 53, 175

☐

Escalante, Constantino (*b* Mexico City, 1836; *d* Mexico City, 1868). Mexican illustrator and printmaker. Although a portrait by him of his music teacher Pedro Picasso was accepted into the Academy's exhibition of 1855, his work as an illustrator did not take an academic route. He became involved with liberal politics at the close of the Guerra de los Tres Años in 1861 and was the first caricaturist on the bi-weekly review *La Orquesta*, which was founded in that year.

Escalante worked for the magazine until his death in 1868, producing 514 lithographs that provide a detailed vision of Mexico's history through his critical eyes; he dealt most frequently with foreign invasions and the relationship between the Church and State. Working largely for an illiterate public, he used his caricatures to draw attention to some of the problems that oppressed his fellow countrymen. He also produced independent albums of lithographs such as National glories (*Glorias nacionales*), which was sponsored by Vicente Riva Palacio (1832–96), the director of *La Orquesta*. He died in a streetcar accident at an early age.

WRITINGS
Glorias nacionales (Mexico City, 1863, rev. 1867)

BIBLIOGRAPHY
R. Carrasco Puente: *La caricatura en México* (Mexico City, 1953), pp. 37–8, 63–7
E. Acevedo: *Constantino Escalante en el periódico 'La Orquesta'* (diss., Mexico City, U. Iberoamer., 1975)

ESTHER ACEVEDO

Escalante, Juan Antonio de Frías (*b* Córdoba, 16 Nov 1633; *d* Madrid, 1670). Spanish painter. He was an outstanding figure in decorative Baroque art. When quite young he moved from Andalusia to Madrid, where he apparently worked with and was influenced by Francisco Rizi. His artistic development reveals an increasing admiration for Veronese, Tintoretto and Titian, although elements of the style of Alonso Cano persist. Among his first works is *Andromeda and the Dragon* (*c.* 1659; Madrid, Prado), whose mannerist elements derive from an engraving of the subject by Agostino Carracci. The two brilliant works *St Catherine of Alexandria* (Madrid, Las Maravillas) and *Road to Calvary* (Madrid, Real Acad. S Fernando), signed and dated 1660, are executed with an agile and self-assured technique, in colours that stem from Venetian painting. Like other Spanish painters of the period, he painted numerous versions of the *Immaculate Conception* (e.g. 1660, Colegio de Villafranca de los Barros; 1663, Budapest, Mus. F.A.; *c.* 1666, Benedictine monastery of Lumbier, Navarre), which are more Baroque in style and expression than those of José Antolínez and Mateo Cerezo. In these the faces, surrounded by luxuriant hair, is expressed an innocent candour that contrasts with the turbulent appearance of the cherubs. Also characteristic of his style are the versions of the *Annunciation* (1653; New York, Hisp. Soc. America Mus; Béziers, Mus. B.-A.). He treated the theme of St Joseph with great nobility, as in the *Dream of St Joseph* (1666; New York, Chrysler Col.). His deep lyrical feelings pervade the various paintings of the *Infant St John* (Madrid, Prado).

Escalante developed an increasing admiration for the art of Rubens, to the extent of almost copying his works through etchings, which he interpreted in his own brilliant technique, as in the *Conversion of St Paul* (Madrid, Mus. Cerralbo). Under the influence of Flemish art, he began to paint allegories, the most characteristic of which is the Eucharistic series (1667–8) executed for the Order of La Merced Calzada, Madrid, and now distributed among various Spanish museums (e.g. Madrid, Prado; Villanueva y Geltrú, Mus. Balaguer). One of the works from this series, *Elias and the Angel*, exists in another version in the delicate painting in the Museum of Berlin, where until recently it was attributed to Francesco Maffei. Others of his works have been confused with those of Italian painters. The surprising *St Rose of Viterbo* (*c.* 1668; Madrid, Prado), like other works of his final years, heralded a brilliant future cut short by his early death. Escalante's agitated, brightly coloured paintings show a departure from the dourness and severity prevalent in Spanish Baroque painting.

BIBLIOGRAPHY
E. Lafuente Ferrari: 'Escalante en Navarra y otras notas sobre el pintor', *Príncipe de Viana* (1941), pp. 8–23
J. Rogelio Buendía: 'Sobre Escalante', *Archv Esp. A.*, xliii (1970), pp. 33–50
——: 'Recordatorio de Escalante en los trecientos años de su muerte', *Goya*, 99 (1970), pp. 146–53
——: 'Escalantes inéditos en El Escorial', *Real Monasterio de El Escorial: Estudios inéditos en el IV centenario de la terminación de sus obras* (Madrid, 1987), pp. 279–84

J. ROGELIO BUENDÍA MUÑOZ

Escamilla, Luis Tristán de. *See* TRISTÁN DE ESCAMILLA, LUIS.

Esch, Jacob van. *See* ES, JACOB VAN.

Esch, Vincent (Jerome) (*b* London, 20 July 1876; *d* Charlwood, Surrey, 9 Dec 1950). English architect. He qualified under articles before sailing for India in 1898 to take up an appointment (1899–1909) as architect to the Railway Board for work on the Bengal–Nagpur Railway. As well as numerous railway and other buildings Esch designed the race stand, dining hall and clock tower for the Royal Calcutta Turf Club and the simple, neo-classical Allahabad Bank (both 1905–6), Calcutta. He had just completed a new headquarters building for the railway company (1907) at Garden Reach on the Hugli River when he won the competition for the Bengal Club (completed 1908), also in Calcutta. Both of these buildings have Edwardian Baroque façades but are nevertheless very different: the former is faced entirely in common bricks, while the elegant Bengal Club is rendered in the *chunam* (fine, polished stucco) more characteristic of the Neo-classical masterpieces built in Calcutta half a century before, and it boasts a giant Ionic order. In 1910 Esch was appointed consulting architect for the Victoria Memorial (completed 1921) on the Maidan at Calcutta, having earlier been recommended by its architect, Sir William Emerson, to oversee construction. Esch himself designed the garden features and probably the Mughal elements such as the *chhatrī*-like corner domes and filigree marble arch spandrels of this impressive Indian Neo-classical building. In the same decade he produced a spectacular series of works in Hyderabad in the popular Indo-Saracenic style. The Railway Station (1914), the imposing granite High Court (1916) facing the Musi River and the City High School (1918; now part of the university) are all memorable examples of this hybrid style, as is the somewhat later Osmania Hospital (completed 1925). He left India in 1921, leaving behind him a remarkably extensive oeuvre for so short a period, but he designed little after returning to England.

WRITINGS
'Examples of Modern Indian Architecture Mainly in Hyderabad State', *India A. & Lett.*, xvi (1942), pp. 49–59
BIBLIOGRAPHY
'The New Head Office of the Bengal–Nagpur Railway', *The Empress*, xxiii/2 (1909), pp. 1–3
'The All India Victoria Memorial', *The Builder*, cxxi/4113 (1921), pp. 742–8
P. H. Davies: *Splendours of the Raj: British Architecture in India, 1660–1947* (London, 1985), pp. 200–01, 212, 254
The Raj: India and the British, 1600–1947 (exh. cat., London, N.P.G., 1990–91), pp. 330–31   □

Eschauzier, F(rits) A(dolf) (*b* The Hague, 9 June 1889; *d* Bussum, 7 Aug 1957). Dutch architect and teacher. After two years' study at the Technische Hogeschool in Delft, he went to the Architectural Association School in London (1913–15). He also studied for a further year (1927), in Vienna with Professor Oskar Strnad. He gained recognition chiefly through building a large number of country houses. His design method and language were clearly influenced by the work of the English architects Edwin Lutyens and Charles F. A. Voysey. The country houses in Leersum (1933) and 'Noordeinde' (1940) in Vierhouten are characteristic of this: a hierarchical grouping of spaces such that the landscape setting firmly defines the form. Outwardly very closed, the country houses are light and open inside because of their large windows and white plasterwork. Flowing linearity governs the smallest element and is evident in the interconnected spaces. The work is strongly related to that of Gunnar Asplund in its attention to detail and ironic use of historical forms. He managed to develop this elegant style until the end of his career, as in the house (1953) on the Schouwweg in Wassenaar. After the war, Eschauzier's work included extensions to and interior layouts of some important museums, the high point being the Gemeentemuseum (1952) in Arnhem. Here he brought about a synthesis of the design method of his firmly traditional country houses and the white abstract architecture of Nieuwe Bouwen. This approach greatly influenced the younger generation of architects owing to his appointment in 1948 as lecturer in decorative arts at the Technische Hogeschool, Delft.

WRITINGS
Veranderingen in de moderne kunst (Amsterdam, 1937)

BIBLIOGRAPHY
'Professor F. A. Eschauzier', *Forum*, xiii (1958), pp. 216–50
JOUKE VAN DER WERF

Escher, Hans Caspar (*b* Zurich, 9 Aug 1775; *d* Herrliberg, nr Zurich, 29 Aug 1859). Swiss architect and industrialist. He began training in commerce at Livorno, Italy, but broke off to study architecture (1794–7) with Friedrich Weinbrenner in Rome. He went to Germany to supervise the building of Weinbrenner's synagogue (1798) in Karlsruhe, and he later worked in Strasbourg and Stuttgart but did not succeed in establishing himself as an architect. After 1803 he became involved in the textile industry and was co-founder (1805) and director of the Maschinenfabrik Escher, Wyss & Co. in Zurich. His subsequent involvement in architecture was as an amateur but was considerable and included such buildings in Zurich as the Casino (1807), built to heavily modified plans dating from 1796; the Villa Schönenhof (1811; destr.); the asylum for the insane (1813; destr.); the Villa Freudenberg (1822–5; destr.); the police station; and the slaughterhouse (1823–4; partly destr.). He also acted as adviser to Hans Conrad Stadler (1788–1846) in the construction of the post-office building (1832–5), Zurich, and he prepared designs for monuments and bridges. With his training in Rome, he was a central figure in Swiss Neo-classicism, encouraging its emergence in Zurich.

BIBLIOGRAPHY
A. Mousson: 'Lebensbild des Joh. Caspar Escher im Felsenhof', *Neujbl. Waisenhauses*, xxxi (1868), pp. 3–33
H. Hoffmann: 'Die klassizistische Baukunst in Zurich', *Mitt. Antiqua. Ges. Zürich*, xxxi (1930), pp. 18–26
H. von Meyenburg: *Die Schipf in Herrliberg* (Zurich, 1957), pp. 82–103
B. Carl: *Klassizismus* (Zurich, 1963)
H. M. Gubler: 'Architektur ohne Auftraggeber: Zu den frühen Idealprojekten Hans Caspar Eschers', *Neue Zürch. Ztg.*, lx (1988), pp. 69–70
HANS MARTIN GUBLER

Escher, M(aurits) C(ornelis) (*b* Leeuwarden, 17 June 1898; *d* Hilversum, 27 March 1972). Dutch printmaker. After studying at the School voor Kunstnijverheid (School of Applied Arts) in Haarlem (1919–22) he lived in Italy until 1935. There he refined his printmaking skills in woodcuts, wood-engravings and lithographs. His figurative work consisted mainly of representations of nature and had a severe, stylized aloofness, exaggerated by techniques such as the scratch drawings in which he made incisions into an inked surface on parchment-type paper, as in *Self-portrait* (1943; Tokyo, priv. col.). After a visit in May 1936 to the Alhambra, Granada, where he was fascinated by the regular divisions of the plane characteristic of Moorish art, he was prompted to change their abstract patterns into recognizable representation.

From that moment Escher became increasingly involved with invented images, his attention shifting from nature to its underlying mathematical principles. The second half of his life was dedicated to problems such as the structuring of space, in prints dealing with the interpenetration or combination of different worlds; the division of the plane, in prints concerned with metamorphosis and approaches to infinity; and the relationship between illusions of space and the flatness of the picture plane, characterized by perspectival games and prints visualizing impossible worlds or objects. Playful and serious, with imagination and dazzling technical skill, he bridged the gulf between the fine arts and science.

For an illustration of his work *see also* SCIENCE AND ART, fig. 2.

WRITINGS
Regelmatige vlakverdeling [Regular division of the plane] (Utrecht, 1958)
The Graphic Work of M. C. Escher (London, 1961/*R* New York, 1976)

BIBLIOGRAPHY
F. H. Bool, ed.: *M. C. Escher: His Life and Complete Graphic Work* (New York and London, 1982)
D. Schattschneider: *Visions of Symmetry: Notebooks, Periodic Drawings and Related Work of M. C. Escher* (New York, 1990)
J. W. Vermeulen: *Maurits Escher, een eigenzinnig talent* [Maurits Escher, a wayward talent] (Kampen, 1995)
JAN WILLEM VERMEULEN

Eschwege, Wilhelm Ludwig, Baron von (*b* Aue, Near Wanfried, 15 Nov 1777; *d* Wolfsanger, near Kassel, 1 Feb 1855). German engineer, mineralogist and army officer, active in Portugal. A son of a noble family, he attended the University of Göttingen (1796–9). After practical engineering experience, he was appointed director of an iron foundry in Portugal. He then went as a mining engineer to direct various undertakings in Brazil, where he remained from 1807 until the proclamation of independence in 1822. In the meantime he entered the Portuguese army, subsequently attaining the rank of lieutenant-general. He wrote numerous technical and scientific papers on mineralogy, mining and engineering subjects, including the supply of water to Lisbon, but his significance in the history of Portuguese art depends on a single important architectural commission, the Palácio da Pena (1839–49), near Sintra, for Ferdinand II, King of Portugal. This involved the rebuilding and enlargement of the ruined monastery of Nossa Senhora da Pena, which Ferdinand acquired for a summer residence. Situated on a spectacular mountain-top near Sintra, the new royal palace was among the earliest and most important examples of 19th-century Portuguese eclectic architecture. The design was inspired by contemporary English and German Gothic Revival buildings, but at Ferdinand's suggestion this style was combined with Manueline influences, particularly from the Palácio Nacional, Sintra, and the famous window in the Sala do Capítulo, Tomar Abbey. Eschwege's building is a striking symbol of a past age when architecture was required to provide fantastic and magnificent spaces for aristocratic patrons.

BIBLIOGRAPHY

J.-A. França: *A Árte em Portugal no século XIX*, i (Lisbon, 1966), pp. 297–306

J. Teixeira: *Dom Fernando II: Rei-artista, artista-rei* (Lisbon, 1987), pp. 304–8, 317–20

RAQUEL HENRIQUES DA SILVA

Escobar, Luis (*b* Villagordo del Júcar, nr Albacete, 1887; *d* Albacete, 1963). Spanish photographer. He was self-taught as a photographer, and set up his first studio in Albacete in 1910. His principal activity was as a travelling photographer, touring the towns and villages of the region, improvising his studio in the streets, squares and inns. He took pictures of groups, fairs, celebrations and typical rituals of La Mancha, images that are an important source of historical documentation. When the Spanish Civil War began in 1936, he accumulated a large number of pictures of the struggle; these were later seized under the Franco regime.

BIBLIOGRAPHY

P. López Mondéjar: *Retratos de la vida* (Madrid, 1982)

——: *Crónica de la luz: Fotografía en Castilla-La Mancha* (Madrid, 1984)

Idas y caos: Aspectos de las vanguardias fotograficas en España (exh. cat., ed. J. Fontcuberta; Madrid, Salas Picasso; New York, Int. Cent. Phot.; 1984–6)

MARTA GILI

Escobar, Marisol. *See* MARISOL.

Escobedo, Helen (*b* Mexico City, 28 July 1934). Mexican sculptor and museum administrator. She studied in 1950–51 at Mexico City College (now Universidad de las Américas), where she was introduced to sculpture by the renowned abstract artist, Germán Cueto. Awarded a travelling scholarship to the Royal College of Art, London (1951–4), Escobedo met luminaries of European sculpture, including Henry Moore, Jacob Epstein and Ossip Zadkine, who profoundly influenced her sense of organic integrity in form and material. It became clear to her that sculpture as museum piece or domestic ornament did not fulfil her objectives. During the 1960s and early 1970s Escobedo created works on a monumental scale and became well known for such ambitious urban sculptures as *Signals* (painted aluminium, h. 15 m, 1971), sited at Auckland Harbour, New Zealand, and *Doors to the Wind* (painted reinforced concrete, h. 17 m, 1968) at Anillo Periférico and Calzada del Hueso on the Olympic Friendship Route, Mexico. From the 1980s she directed her work towards ecological and humanitarian issues. A number of site-specific installations and performances explored the theme of the densely populated metropolis of Mexico City. While conscious of the social meaning of art, her approach was abstract and conceptual rather than overtly realist. She used natural materials, such as interwoven branches and grass, or the detritus of urban life. As a cultural promoter, she held such positions as director (1958–82) of the museum of the Universidad Nacional Autónoma de México, and director (1983–5) of the Museo de Arte Moderno, Mexico City.

BIBLIOGRAPHY

C. Gorostiza: *Escultura mexicana contemporánea* (Mexico City, 1960)

R. Eder: *Helen Escobedo* (Mexico City, 1982)

Helen Escobedo: Lawn Figures (exh. cat., Oxford, MOMA, 1992)

RITA EDER

Escoffery, Gloria (*b* Gayle, St Mary, Jamaica, 22 Dec 1923). Jamaican painter and writer. She studied at McGill University, Montreal, and the Slade School of Fine Art, London. She began painting in the 1940s and is best known for her depictions of life in rural Jamaica. Other works have surreal imagery and often include art historical and literary references. Typically, even her genre scenes have surreal overtones: slightly distorted figures appear alienated and isolated and are placed in desolate settings. In many works she combined figurative elements with abstract geometrical elements such as patterned borders or geometrically structured backgrounds. A fine colourist, she worked in oil and acrylic as well as watercolour and gouache. One of her masterworks is the five-panel *Mirage* (1987; Kingston, Inst. Jamaica, N.G.). She was perhaps Jamaica's most important art critic and for many years wrote for *Jamaica Journal*.

BIBLIOGRAPHY

Jamaican Art 1922–1982 (exh. cat. by D. Boxer, Washington, DC, Smithsonian Inst.; Kingston, Inst. Jamaica, N.G.; 1983), pp. 18–19, 62

VEERLE POUPEYE

Escomb Church. Anglo-Saxon church dedicated to St John the Evangelist in Co. Durham, northern England. The church today consists of a simple rectangular nave, typically Northumbrian in its tall, narrow proportions (1:1.6), and a chancel that is almost square. But excavation has revealed further complexities. A porticus was added north of the chancel and overlapping the north-east corner of the nave, with access both from the chancel and probably also from outside. A second porticus was butted on to the west wall; there was probably an outside entrance at its north-east corner, and apparently no access from the nave. The height of the roof-line on the west gable suggests that it was two-storey.

The nave itself measures 13.25 × 4.42 m internally. It has a square-headed door in the centre of the north wall; the east jamb of another door (altered later) survives near the west end of the south wall, forming part of the present entrance. The nave was lit by four small windows with monolithic heads and single internal splays, square-headed on the north, round-headed on the south. Between the southern pair externally is a sundial, apparently *in situ*, decorated with a serpent lying over it and an animal's head projecting above. A fifth window is placed high in the west gable, and there may have been a sixth in the chancel east wall, later obliterated by the present one. The elegant arch between nave and chancel has neat radial voussoirs, chamfered imposts, and jambs made from alternately horizontal and vertical stones.

Escomb is built of sandstone, and the technical skill of the masonry is remarkably high. Much of it was probably reused from a nearby Roman fort. (Several stones with Roman broached tooling are visible in the fabric, along with a Roman inscription.) A similar origin has been suggested for the chancel arch. Other features, such as the slight inward slope of the door jambs and window splays and the accurate setting out, must be due to the skill of the Anglo-Saxon masons.

No written evidence dates the fabric, nor is it closely datable stylistically; but its constructional details find their closest analogies in Northumbrian churches that can be dated to between the late 7th century and the late 9th. The plan is comparable to those used in England for secular timber halls from the 6th century to the 9th.

Escomb is generally assumed to have been built by a lord as his private estate church, a view often supported by reference to its modest dimensions. But this is perhaps an anachronistic evaluation: its nave and chancel are two-thirds the length and half the area of the equivalent parts of the principal church at Jarrow, built within the same date range by a monastic community of the first rank. And the fact that Escomb was of masonry at all—let alone ashlar of such high quality—must have distinguished it as a comparatively important building by contemporary standards. More probably it was intended to house a religious community.

BIBLIOGRAPHY

M. Pocock and H. Wheeler: 'Excavations at Escomb Church, County Durham 1968', *J. Brit. Archaeol. Assoc.*, xxxiv (1968), pp. 11–21

E. Fernie: *The Architecture of the Anglo-Saxons* (London, 1983), pp. 54–9

ERIC CAMBRIDGE

Escorial [San Lorenzo el Real de Escorial]. Royal monastery and palace, *c.* 50 km north-west of Madrid, Spain.

1. History. 2. Architecture. 3. Decoration.

1. HISTORY. Emperor Charles V (*reg* 1516–56) left a final codicil in his will for the establishment of a religious foundation in which he was to be buried beside his wife, Isabella of Portugal (1503–39). His son, Philip II (*see* HABSBURG, §II(2)), undertook the task after his return from Flanders in 1559 and appointed JUAN BAUTISTA DE TOLEDO as the royal architect. In 1560 a site was chosen in a farming area at the foot of the Guadarrama Mountains, 2 km from the town of El Escorial, and entrusted to the Hieronymite Order in the following year. The new monastery, which received its foundation charter in 1567, was named S Lorenzo el Real del Escorial, after St Lawrence of Rome, a martyr of supposed Hispanic origin, and was intended to serve as the royal pantheon. Tradition, however, also holds that it was dedicated to S Lorenzo de la Victoria, in fulfilment of a vow made by Philip II to atone for the destruction of a church dedicated to St Lawrence at the Battle of San Quintín (1557).

The first stone was laid on 23 April 1563, and the complex was officially completed on 13 September 1584. The present town of San Lorenzo del Escorial gradually developed around the royal residence. A fire at the monastery in 1671 led to the construction of new roofs, which were built by Gaspar de la Peña and Bartolomé Zumbigo y Salcedo (*d* 1682), and there was further damage from fire in 1731, 1763 and 1825. The Hieronymite Order was expelled three times (1808, 1837 and 1854) and finally replaced in 1885 by the Augustinians, who now occupy the monastery, although the building is under the administration of the Patrimonio Nacional. In 1939 many paintings were transferred to the Museo del Prado in Madrid. Substantial restoration work was carried out from 1953 under the direction of the architect Ramón Andrada (*d* 1992). In 1963 a new gallery (Nuevos Museos) was established in the royal palace for the art collection, together with an architectural museum showing material relating to the construction of the building.

2. ARCHITECTURE.

(i) 16th century. (ii) Later developments. (iii) Sources, symbolism and influence.

(i) 16th century.

(a) Building history. The planning of the monastery of the Escorial was begun in 1561, one year before its final site was marked out. Fray JOSÉ DE SIGÜENZA stated that this was a rectangular area (226×177 m) with a subsidiary area to the east (40×55 m) intended for royal apartments, in accordance with the traditional Spanish custom of joining residences for the monarch to the principal royal monasteries. The ground-plan, the 'universal' design (1561–2) made by Juan Bautista de Toledo, has been regarded as representing the grid on which St Lawrence was martyred. It is surrounded by a portico (*lonja*) at the north-west, by the royal gardens to the east and by the monastery gardens to the south.

This layout was retained throughout the numerous subsequent modifications. The entire western area, planned as the monastery house (*casa conventual*) and college (*Colegio*), was to have been at a lower level than the rest of the building and separated from the eastern area by two towers; the latter were removed from the plan in 1564, leaving only those at the four corners of the complex. Similarly the church, based on Michelangelo's design (1546–64) for St Peter's, Rome, was to have had two eastern towers flanking the sanctuary and over the rooms of the king and queen, and two others on the west façade of the complex. These towers, with cupolas characteristic of formal palace architecture, can be seen in the designs attributed to Juan Bautista (ex-Archv Escorial, Madrid; see Ruiz de Arcaute, 1936, figs 3 and 4), which show alternative designs, one with a double order, the other with a giant order. Other designs (Madrid, Bib. Pal., X-M-242, fasc. 1) show the future Patio de los Reyes (between the main portal and the church) with an open gallery. Juan Bautista's initial design for the church was criticized in 1562 by FRANCESCO PACIOTTO, who deemed its 2:3 proportions to be unsuitable. Paciotto submitted a design for a 'square' church, eliminating the transept apses, introducing pedestals to correct the problems produced by the high level of the presbytery, removing the upper choir above the entrance and raising the overall height of the church to 30 m.

In January 1563, before building began, the members of the advisory Council of Architects, Pedro Fernández de Cabrera y Bobadilla (*d* 1576), 2nd Conde de Chinchón, Martín Cortés, 2nd Marqués del Valle de Oaxaca (1532–89), and Pedro de Hoyo, the Secretary, decided to use the overall design of Juan Bautista with the church design of Paciotto and some details of a design (untraced) by Gaspar de Vega. Further changes were made in 1564, when it was decided to double the number of monks from 50 to 100. Rodrigo Gil de Hontañón and Hernán González de Lara visited the construction and, from the viewpoint of architects trained in Gothic building techniques, criticized details of the overall plan and of the church plan by Juan Bautista. Finally, on the advice of the Obrero Mayor (foreman), Fray Antonio de Villacastín (1512–1607), the whole complex was brought to the same level as the east side. This required changes to several elevations and modifications to the church design, which were incorporated into a section drawing by Juan Bautista known as project 'C' (Madrid, Bib. Pal., X-M-242, fasc. 1; for illustration see TOLEDO, JUAN BAUTISTA DE).

By the death of Juan Bautista in 1567 the foundations of the whole of the south section had been laid, and work had begun on the south and west façades, the Patios Chicos, the Old Church and the pantheon crypt, the Patio de los Evangelistas and the private royal apartments, including the Patio de los Mascarones and perhaps also the Galería de los Convalecientes, which is next to the south-west tower and undoubtedly of Serlian character. All of these reflect the style of Juan Bautista. There was an interval in the planning process until JUAN DE HERRERA took complete charge of the building (c. 1570). Meanwhile, Giovanni Battista Castello (see CASTELLO (i), (1)) had begun work on the main staircase (1568) to his own design, but this was demolished in 1571 to make way for the open-well imperial stairway (1571–4; see fig. 4 below) designed by Herrera. Various plans for the church, including the 'C' design, had been sent to Florence for submission to the Accademia del Disegno in May 1567, and contacts were maintained with Italian architects. In 1571 Pellegrino Tibaldi (see TIBALDI, (1)) sent a design for the church, and Philip II commissioned Barone Gian Tommaso Marturano to collect further plans, including designs (all untraced) by Galeazzo Alessi, Andrea Palladio and an oval design by Vincenzo Danti. These were submitted, probably with others by Spanish architects, for consideration by the Accademia in Florence and were then reworked by Jacopo Vignola in Rome into a new design that was presented to Pope Gregory XIII in 1572 and sent to Spain in 1573.

Work nevertheless continued, and the foundations of the basilica church were laid (1569–74). Two models were constructed in 1570 by Diego de Alcántara (1538–87) and in 1573–4 by Martín de Aciaga. The first stone of the church was laid in 1574; it was completed in 1584 and consecrated on 30 August 1586. From 1571 the conventual buildings were occupied by the Hieronymite Order, and during 1573–4 the mortal remains of several royal persons were temporarily translated to the Old Church. Revised instructions for the organization of the building were issued in 1572, and a new system of construction was introduced in 1575, with the stone being cut at the quarries to allow building work to be carried out more speedily. Work on the north façade began in 1573 and on the courtyards of the Colegio and seminary in 1581, being completed here and at the royal palace to the north-east in 1587. A contract was drawn up for the principal west façade in 1574. The Doric tempietto in the Patio de los Evangelistas was built between 1586 and 1591, also to designs by Herrera.

(b) Plan. From a functional point of view, the monastery can be divided into three main sections from north to south, each with an independent entrance from the west front (see fig. 1). The central section of the western elevation, which is occupied by the library, is higher than the rest of the façade in the manner of Spanish university

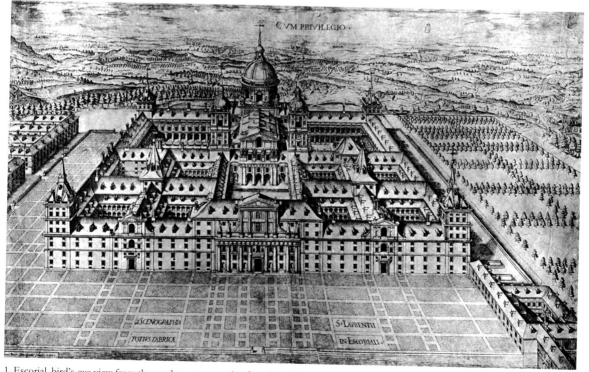

1. Escorial, bird's-eye view from the north-west; engraving from Juan de Herrera: *Sumario y breve declaración* (Madrid, 1589), plan 7

2. Escorial, south façade, completed 1587

libraries. Its façade is of an ecclesiastical type derived from Serlio, with two orders of superimposed columns and a pediment. Beyond the bare, austere, rectangular Patio de los Reyes are the basilica and the private royal apartments built around the Patio de los Mascarones. The church is flanked by two towers, and its façade has two main storeys, a triple arched portico, Doric half columns for the lower level and pilaster-strips supporting a pediment for the upper one. This does not correspond to the elevation of the church interior: the design recalls elements from such Italian prototypes as Alberti's façade at S Sebastiano (begun 1460), Mantua, Bramante's drum (1506–14) for St Peter's, Rome, and Cesare Cesariano's reconstruction of Vitruvius' basilica at Fano. The church, with its centralized planning and Roman character, broke decisively with Spanish traditions of ecclesiastical design. Through the narthex is a public chapel, a centralized area situated beneath the monks' choir and covered by a remarkable flat sail vault, with a floor-plan that repeats the main and private body of the basilica, but on a much smaller scale. The church is organized as a Greek cross within a square, and this main area was inspired, although to a lesser extent than in Juan Bautista's former designs, by Michelangelo's St Peter's, but with the original apses squared in the manner of Alessi's S Maria Assunta in Carignano, Genoa. The cupola of the latter had a direct influence on that of the Escorial, which was the first in Spain to be built with a drum. The main arms of the cross have barrel vaults, the corner areas have sail vaults, and a high gallery runs around the inner perimeter. The interior is articulated with fluted Doric pilasters, without pedestals, and as a result there are inconsistencies at the juncture of the raised presbytery, which is flanked by the imperial and royal sepulchres (see

fig. 3 below). This leads on the east to the oblong Sagrario, open towards the principal retable and giving access to the monstrances. The church is connected to the austerely decorated private royal apartments (the king's chambers) on the south side, and an opening to the presbytery allowed the king to contemplate the high altar from his bedroom. The focal point of the palace is the two-storey Patio de los Mascarones, with arches supported by columns on one level and galleries on three sides. It is reached through a long room on the east side and gives access to the queen's chamber on the north side.

The monastery occupies the south sector (see fig. 2) and has a simple entrance in the western elevation, with a projecting attic crowned by a pediment. The western part of this zone has a cross-shaped layout with four courts (the Patios Chicos) of a simple Tuscan design. The first two belong to the hospice (north) and infirmary (south), while the eastern pair forms part of the monastery itself. At the centre is a tall vestibule, topped by a tower and spire, leading to four rectangular halls housing the kitchens (west) and the refectory (south), with dormitories above. The eastern half of this zone is occupied by the great Patio de los Evangelistas (nearly 50×50 m), enclosed by two storeys of arches upon piers with Doric and Ionic half columns, in a composition derived from the courtyards of the Palazzo Venezia (begun 1455, completed 16th century) and the Palazzo Farnese (1540s), both in Rome. At the centre is the small, octagonal tempietto, with a granite exterior and marble and jasper interior, topped by a cupola and surrounded by four square pools. The north arcade runs alongside the basilica: the others correspond with the locutory, the principal staircase and the provisional chapel (the Old Church) to the west; the chapter houses to the south; and the prior's quarters and the sacristy to the east. Most of the upper storey accommodates dormitories, cells and the scriptorium.

The seminary and Colegio of the northern sector are also entered from the west front and organized in the shape of a cross. The western arm of the cross contains the latrines; the southern arm, with its open gallery, became an ambulatory; the eastern arm housed the refectory and the northern arm the kitchen. Lecture halls were arranged along the west front with lodgings above. The eastern range was set aside for the royal palace. It had two entrances through the north façade and a large central courtyard, similar to that of the Patio de los Evangelistas, although with pilasters rather than half columns. It was divided in its western part into two small courtyards to provide access on both levels to the lodgings of officials, noblemen and royal persons. The north wing included the palace staircase and rooms for ambassadors, while the upper floor of the south wing became a private walk or royal gallery (1.37 m), providing access to the private apartments of the palace and the church.

In the 1580s building work began on various annexes and service areas. Herrera designed the first two Casas de los Oficios (1581–8) to the north-west, bordering the *lonja*, and the Casa de los Doctores (1583–5; destr.) farther to the north. Francisco de Mora (i) designed the Botica (pharmacy) and the stairway and orchard pond (1589) at the south-west corner of the monastery, next to the Galería de los Convalecientes. During the 1590s he also built the Casa de la Compaña to the west and the smaller Cachicanía (gardener's cottage) and Pozo de Nieve (ice-house) to the south. Work was completed in the same decade on the various buildings, both farms and for recreation, in the surrounding areas of El Campillo, La Herrería, El Castañar and Monasterio. This programme had been initiated by Gaspar de Vega with the construction of austere and functional houses for the king and the monks at La Fresneda (1563–9).

(ii) Later developments. The most important addition to the monastery in the 17th century under Philip III (*reg* 1598–1621) was the Panteón de los Reyes, designed by Giovanni Battista Crescenzi in 1617–18. Its construction was supervised by Juan Gómez de Mora (i), Fray Nicolás de Madrid (1600–60) and Alonso de Carbonel, who was responsible for some details. The octagonal, subterranean chamber, decorated with pilasters, inlaid marble and jasper, and bronze-gilt capitals and other ornament, represents the reintroduction of an ornamented style in Spanish architecture and is one of the sources of Spanish Baroque decoration. Gianlorenzo Bernini's *Crucifix* (1654), now in the Colegio chapel, was to have been placed here, but that by Domenico Guidi was substituted in 1659.

The Escorial expanded under Juan de Villanueva (*see* VILLANUEVA, (2)) the Arquitecto Jefe, who built the third service building, the Casa de Oficios, the Casa de Infantes, the Casitas de Arriba y Abajo and the residences of the French consul and the Marqués de Campo Villar during the 1770s and 1780s. Alterations were made to the north front and the interior of the royal palace of the Bourbons, with its new staircase (1793). In the reign of Isabella II

(*reg* 1833–68) work began on the Panteón de Infantes (1862–88), under the architect José Segundo de Lema (*d* 1892), with sculptural decoration and tombs by PONCIANO PONZANO Y GASCON and Giuseppe Galleotti.

(iii) Sources, symbolism and influence. From the 1570s until the mid-17th century, and even beyond, the Escorial exercised an enormous influence on Spanish architecture. It epitomizes the classicism of the age of Philip II and the figurative arts as practised then by both Spanish and foreign artists. It is also a testimony to the continuous evolution of Spanish art up to the 19th century. Its influence on the planning of major architectural projects elsewhere in Europe during the 17th and 18th centuries was widespread.

The Escorial's layout has been linked with various possible precedents, including Diocletian's Palace (AD 295–305) at Split. The cross-shaped hospitals built during the reign of Ferdinand of Aragón and Isabella of Castile and shortly after, such as the Hospital Tavera (1541–99), Toledo, and the Hieronymite monastery at San Miguel de los Reyes (1546), could have inspired Juan Bautista's 'universal' design, which is a logical response, despite its complexity, to the multiple functions and special needs of the monastery.

The Escorial's sober and monumental architectural style, with its treatment of the Classical orders, has been placed within the framework of international Mannerism (Taylor, 1967), in the tradition of the ESTILO DESORNAMENTADO (Kubler, 1982) and in the movement from the Renaissance to the Baroque. It is, however, generally accepted as an example of the classical style advocated by Philip II, who controlled all the planning and construction processes, based on an orthodox handling of the models established in ancient Rome and contemporary Italy, and submitted, principally by Herrera, to a process of geometric abstraction and formal simplification. There has been extensive discussion concerning the ultimate responsibility for the edifice, with critics attributing the onus of the design variously to Juan Bautista de Toledo or to Juan de Herrera. Despite some subtle qualifications, the 16th-century construction is characterized by its coherence and would seem to be the work of one team, led by the King. The building history suggests that Juan Bautista established the outlines of the design and that Herrera, who was trained by Juan Bautista, accepted the legacy and only introduced modifications.

The ideology behind the design has also been the subject of debate. Traditionally it has been considered the embodiment of the most orthodox spirit of the Counter-Reformation and a reflection of the rigid mentality of Philip and Herrera. The possible influence of hermetic thought and the mysticism of the philosopher Ramón Lull (1235–1316) has been suggested (Taylor, 1967), with the Escorial being conceived as a new Temple of Jerusalem, despite Sigüenza's rejection of formal links between the monastery's design and the Temple of Solomon. It has also been seen as relying on Early Christian principles, especially on such early models as the aesthetics of St Augustine (354–430), as embodied in his *City of God* (Kubler, 1982). Another suggestion, drawing on the writings of both Sigüenza and Herrera, is that it revived a

Christian tradition of classical architecture, evident in its use of orders, its system of proportions and its 'cubism' or block-like design. This was believed to emanate from Divine Wisdom and to be present in nature and in various constructions, from Noah's Ark to the Temple of Solomon, that certain circles attributed to God: the Escorial was seen as the last link in this chain (Bustamante and Marías).

3. DECORATION. The monastery was decorated with an enormous number of frescoes, altarpieces, paintings (both commissioned and donated), some 7500 relics in 507 reliquaries, mostly designed by Herrera and the silversmith Juan de Arfe (*see* ARFE, (2)), and collections of books and manuscripts that now number *c.* 45,000 and 5000 respectively. Many of these items have changed location or have been lost. Some of the iconographic schemes for the decorations were conceived by the librarian and humanist BENITO ARIAS MONTANO and were described by Sigüenza and Fray FRANCISCO DE LOS SANTOS.

The fixed and movable decoration of the church at the centre of the monastery, with its celebration and veneration of the saints, martyrs, images, the deceased and the sacraments, and its emphasis on the Virgin as Mother of God, is very much in keeping with the didactic spirit of the Counter-Reformation and its use of images as an exhortation to prayer. Continuing concern over clarity and appropriateness is reflected in contracts and written reports and resulted in successive substitutions of works that had already been executed and continuous corrections of detail, such as that by Juan Gómez Villaseñor (*c.* 1553–1597) in the 1590s.

The first major commission for the church was to JUAN FERNÁNDEZ DE NAVARRETE in 1576 for 32 altarpieces of saints arranged in pairs. He had painted seven by his death in 1579, including that of *SS John the Evangelist and Matthew* (*in situ*). A total of 33 retables, all pairs of saints, were completed *c.* 1584 by ALONSO SÁNCHEZ COELLO, Diego de Urbina (*d* 1594) and LUIS DE CARVAJAL. Five further retables were commissioned: the *Martyrdom of St Maurice* by Romulo Cincinnato, intended to replace El Greco's painting of the same subject (1580–83; now in the Nuevos Museos), the *Sermon of St John the Baptist* and *St Anne* (both 1583–5) by LUCA CAMBIASO, and *St Michael the Archangel* and the *Martyrdom of St Ursula* by Pellegrino Tibaldi, who was in Spain between 1586 and 1596 and painted them to replace pictures of the same subjects by Cambiaso. Federico Zuccaro (in Spain 1585–8) decorated the two large reliquary cupboards (4.9×2.9 m) with two pairs of the *Annunciation* and *St Jerome in Penitence* (exterior and interior panels; both 1586), the latter largely reworked by Juan Gómez Villaseñor

Cambiaso painted frescoes of the *Coronation of the Virgin* on the chancel vaults, a *Gloria* and *Annunciation* on the choir vaults and, with Cincinnato, scenes from the *Lives of SS Lawrence and Jerome* on the walls of the choir. The choir-stalls were designed by Herrera and José Frecha (1540–91). Between 1586 and 1587 Tibaldi decorated the walls of the Sagrario behind the main altar with Old Testament themes referring to the Eucharist: on the walls are the *Gathering of Manna*, the *Meeting of Abraham and*

Melchizedeck, *Elijah Visited by an Angel*, the *Paschal Lamb* and, on the vault, a *Rainbow of the Covenant* supported by cherubim and seraphim, all in a style that imitated manuscript illumination.

In the oratories on either side of the chancel are the funerary monuments of *Charles V*, his wife *Isabella of Portugal*, his daughter the *Empress Mary*, and his sisters *Eleanor* and *Mary* on the Gospels side (1592–7; see fig. 3), and of *Philip II* with his wives, *Maria Manuela of Portugal*, *Elizabeth of Valois* and *Anne of Austria*, and his son *Charles* on the Epistle side (1597–1600). The kneeling figures made by Pompeo Leoni, in gilt-bronze with partial polychrome, are set in marble-vaulted niches that were designed by Herrera after Cardinal Antoine Perrenot de Granvelle unsuccessfully attempted to engage Michelangelo in 1560.

The principal altarpiece (1579–85; 26×14 m), also designed by Herrera and constructed by Leone Leoni, Pompeo Leoni, Jacopo da Trezzo I and Giovanni Battista Comane (*fl* 1579–81), is made of precious marbles and jasper, with gilded bronze pedestals and capitals for its four columniated storeys. The over life-size statues (1579–89), which increase in size the higher they are placed, were mainly executed by Pompeo Leoni and represent the four *Fathers of the Latin Church*, the *Evangelists* (*St John* by Adriaen de Vries), *SS James and Andrew* (both by de Vries), *Peter* and *Paul*, the *Virgin*, *St John the Evangelist* and *Christ on the Cross*. The great tabernacle for the high altar (1579–86), carved by Trezzo from designs by Herrera,

3. Escorial church, chancel and north oratory, with statues of *Charles V* and his family by Pompeo Leoni, gilt-bronze, 1592–7

also employs marble and gilt-bronze (for the small figures of the *Apostles* and the crowning *Salvator mundi*), as did the small tabernacle (destr. 1808). The eight paintings for the high altar, which were originally commissioned from Navarrete in 1579, were entrusted successively to Cambiaso, Zuccaro and Tibaldi. Tibaldi's *Adoration of the Shepherds* and *Adoration of the Magi* occupy the lower section, replacing paintings by Zuccaro—which themselves had replaced an *Annunciation* by Veronese and an *Adoration of the Shepherds* (1575) by Tintoretto (both now in Madrid, Escorial, Nuevos Mus.). The next level has Tibaldi's *Martyrdom of St Lawrence*—replacing the same subject as painted by Titian (1564–7; now in the retable of the Old Church in the Escorial), Cambiaso and Zuccaro (both untraced)—and Zuccaro's *Flagellation* and *Road to Calvary*. The third level has the *Resurrection*, *Assumption* and *Pentecost*, all by Zuccaro.

The monastery's most important decorations are in the Patio de los Evangelistas, which is named after the four marble statues of the *Evangelists*, carved by JUAN BAUTISTA DE MONEGRO, set in the tempietto. The figures represent the propagation of the faith, while the garden and the four pools symbolize Paradise and its rivers. The cloister walls and the staircase are painted with 62 episodes from the lives of the Virgin, Christ and the Apostles: there are 8 on the north wall, from the *Meeting at the Golden Gate* to the *Circumcision*; 16 on the east wall, from the *Baptism* to *Christ and the Woman Taken in Adultery*; 16 on the south wall, from the *Entry into Jerusalem* to the *Deposition*; 15 on the west wall, from the *Entombment* to *Christ Appearing to the Disciples*; and the final 7, completing the circuit on the north wall, from the *Preaching of St Peter* to the *Last Judgement*. Begun by Cambiaso, two of whose paintings remain, most of the work was carried out (1587–93) by Tibaldi, in collaboration with Luis de Carvajal, Miguel Barroso (1538–90) and Cincinnato. These painters were also responsible for the eight altarpieces (*estaciones*) that were placed in pairs at the four corners of the cloister, repeating the iconography of the adjacent frescoes. The frescoes and panels have lost much of their original appearance through repeated restoration, especially the former. The upper level of the cloister is decorated with 11 scenes from the *Life of St Lawrence* (1598) by Bartolomé Carducho.

The sacristy contains Titian's *Christ on the Cross* (*c.* 1555). The vault was painted with grotesques by Nicolás Granello and Fabrizio Castello (i), as were the chapter rooms, where Titian's *Gloria* (1551–4; now Madrid, Prado) was hung in 1574, together with Navarrete's *St Jerome in Penitence* (1569), *Flagellation*, *Martyrdom of St James* (1571), *Adoration of the Shepherds* and *Holy Family* (both 1575; all *in situ*). The vault in the lower level of the prior's cell is decorated with grotesques and a *Judgement of Solomon* (1581) by Francesco da Urbino (*d* 1582), while in the upper level was Navarrete's *Baptism* (1574; now Madrid, Prado). Titian's *Last Supper* (1557–84), now in the Nuevos Museos, was formerly on the main wall of the refectory, while Navarrete's *Abraham and the Three Angels* (1576; Dublin, N.G.; for illustration *see* NAVARRETE, JUAN FERNÁNDEZ DE) was in the locutory.

The only decoration on the main west façade is Monegro's colossal statue of *St Lawrence* (1583). The statues of the *Kings of Judah* (1580–84; *Jehoshaphat, Hezekiah, David, Solomon, Josiah* and *Manasseh*), also by Monegro, are even larger (h. *c.* 5 m) and were placed on the façade of the church at Arias Montano's instigation. The *Crucifix* (1562) of white and black marble by BENVENUTO CELLINI, now in an interior chapel, was originally placed in the central window of the church façade, facing the Patio de los Reyes.

The enormous library behind the west front is decorated with frescoes (1587–92) by Tibaldi depicting allegorical themes to a programme attributed to Arias Montano, Sigüenza and Herrera (*see* SPAIN, fig. 27). The vault is occupied by personifications of the *Liberal Arts and Sciences*, painted *di sotto in sù* and surrounded by giants. In the lunettes are representations of individuals, from antiquity onwards, who had cultivated these disciplines. Scenes on the friezes refer to the trivium and quadrivium. Of the former, Grammar is represented by the *School of Babylon* and the *Tower of Babel*, Rhetoric by *Hercules the Gaul* and *Cicero Defending Gaius Rabirius*, and Dialectics or Logic by *SS Ambrose and Augustine* and *Zeno of Elea Showing the Gates of Truth and Error*. Of the quadrivium, Arithmetic is represented by the *Gymnosophists* and *Solomon and the Queen of Sheba*, Music by *Orpheus Rescuing Eurydice* and *David Playing the Harp before Saul*, Geometry by the *Death of Archimedes* and the *Priests of Egypt Dividing the Lands* and Astronomy by the *Solar Eclipse at Heliopolis after the Death of Christ* and *King Hezekiah Contemplating the Orbit of the Sun*. Philosophy on the north wall (the *School of Athens with Zeno and Socrates*) and Theology on the south (*Constantine the Great at the Council of Nicaea*) complete the programme as the basis and goal of knowledge. The upper library is decorated with a comprehensive series of portraits of saints, pontiffs, sages and artists.

The most impressive of the staterooms in the royal palace is the Galería or Sala de Batallas, with fresco decorations by Granello, Castello, Cambiaso and Lazzaro Tavarone depicting the *Battle of Higueruela*, copied from a 15th-century fabric wall-hanging (destr.), and scenes from the Battle of San Quintín and the conquests of Portugal and the Azores. According to Sigüenza, the Queen's chamber was decorated with drawings of animals and plants of the Indies and engravings by Herrera. These and many other rooms, including the Casa del Rey, had fine German marquetry doors (*see* SPAIN, §V, 2). Throughout the complex were hung devotional paintings from the collection of 1150 works, mainly Flemish and Italian, that the King bequeathed between 1571 and 1598. These included such works as Hieronymus Bosch's triptychs with *The Haywain* and the '*Garden of Earthly Delights*' (both Madrid, Prado; *see* BOSCH, HIERONYMUS, figs 1 and 3), Rogier van der Weyden's *Crucifixion* (after 1454; *in situ*) and *Deposition* (*c.* 1443; Madrid, Prado; *see* WEYDEN, VAN DER, (1), fig. 4) and 14 paintings by Titian, including *St Jerome* (1575) and the *Agony in the Garden* (*c.* 1563; both *in situ*). Many other paintings were added in the 17th century, including works by Velázquez, his Spanish contemporaries and Italian masters.

In the 1650s Velázquez coordinated the decoration and rehanging of paintings in the chapter room, the sacristy and the scriptorium. The sacristy was remodelled in order to house the retable of the *Sagrada Forma*, made to contain

4. Escorial, the imperial stairway by Juan de Herrera, 1571–4, with frescoes by Pellegrino Tibaldi, 1586–8, and by Luca Giordano (vault and frieze), 1692–4; engraving from F. Bambilla: *Colección de las vistas* (Madrid, 1832), p. 7

Claudio Coello's painting of that name (1685–90), and a Crucifix by Pietro Tacca. Between 1692 and 1694 LUCA GIORDANO was working in the monastery, where his frescoes include the *St Lawrence in Glory, Adored by Charles V and Philip II* on the large vault of the great main staircase (see fig. 4) and, below, scenes relating to the Battle of Saint-Quentín and the building of the Escorial. His paintings on the vault of the church include the *Incarnation*, the *Last Judgement*, allegories relating to the *Immaculate Conception* and the *Church Militant*, Old Testament scenes connected with the Eucharist, the victories of God's Chosen People and the four *Fathers of the Latin Church*. These are characteristic of Baroque decoration and detract from the original iconographic conception of the church.

During the reigns of Charles IV and Ferdinand VII, the ceilings in the new rooms of the royal palace were frescoed by Mariano Salvador Maella, Felipe López (1765–1828) and Juan Gálvez (1774–1847), hung with tapestries from Flanders and the Real Fábrica de S Bárbara (made to designs by Goya, Ramón Bayeu or José del Castillo), and decorated with fine intarsia work, for example in the apartments known as the Habitaciones de Maderas Finas.

For further illustrations *see* SPAIN, fig. 26 and TILE, fig. 9.

BIBLIOGRAPHY

EARLY SOURCES AND DESCRIPTIONS
J. de Herrera: *Sumario y breve declaración de los diseños y estampas de la Fábrica de San Lorenço el Real del Escurial* (Madrid, 1589); ed. L. Cervera

Vera in *Las estampas y el sumario de El Escorial por Juan de Herrera* (Madrid, 1954)
J. de Sigüenza: *Historia de la Orden de San Jerónimo*, 2 vols (Madrid, 1600–05/R 1905); ed. as *Fundación del monasterio de El Escorial* (Madrid, 1963/R 1986)
F. de los Santos: *Descripción del Real monasterio de San Lorenzo del Escorial, única maravilla del mundo* (Madrid, 1657/R 1984; Eng. trans., London, 1760)
A. Ximénez: *Descripción del Real monasterio de San Lorenzo del Escorial: Su magnífico templo, panteón y palacio* (Madrid, 1764/R 1985)
D. Bermejo: *Descripción artística del Real monasterio de S Lorenzo del Escorial y sus preciosidades después de la invasión de los franceses* (Madrid, 1820)
E. Llaguno y Amírola: *Noticias* (1829)
V. Poleró y Toledo: *Catálogo de los cuadros del Real Monasterio de San Lorenzo, llamado del Escorial* (Madrid, 1857)
Documentos para la historia del monasterio de S Lorenzo el Real de El Escorial, 9 vols (Madrid and El Escorial, 1916–85)
A. Prieto Cantero: 'Inventario razonado de los documentos referentes al monasterio de El Escorial en la sección de casa y sitios reales del Archivo General de Simancas', *Rev. Archvs, Bib. & Mus.*, cxxi (1963), pp. 7–127
A. Casanovas: 'Catálogo de la colección de grabados de la Biblioteca de El Escorial', *An. & Bol. Mus. A. Barcelona*, xvi–xvii (1963–6) [whole issue, 2 vols]
G. de Andrés: 'Catálogo de las colecciones de dibujos de la Real Biblioteca de El Escorial', *Archv Esp. A.*, xli (Jan 1968), pp. 77–95
——: 'Inventario de documentos sobre la construcción y ornato del monasterio del Escorial', *Archv Esp. A.*, xlv–l (1972–7) [suppl. issues]
——: 'Inventario de documentos sobre El Escorial que se conservan en el Archivo del Instituto "Valencia de Don Juan", Madrid', *Ciudad Dios*, cxciv/2–3 (1981), pp. 511–95

GENERAL
J. de Quevedo: *Historia del Real monasterio de San Lorenzo desde su origen y fundación hasta fin del año 1848* (Madrid, 1849/R 1985)
A. Rotondo: *Descripción de la gran basílica del Escorial* (Madrid, 1861/R 1985)
——: *Historia artística, pintoresca y descriptiva del Real monasterio de San Lorenzo del Escorial* (Madrid, 1862/R 1985)
J. Zarco Cuevas: *El monasterio de San Lorenzo el Real de El Escorial* (El Escorial, 1935)
M. López Serrano: *Trazas de Juan de Herrera y sus seguidores para el monasterio del Escorial* (Madrid, 1944)
A. Portabales Pichel: *Los verdaderos artífices de El Escorial y el estilo indebidamente llamado herreriano* (Madrid, 1945)
——: *Maestros mayores, arquitectos y aparejadores de El Escorial* (Madrid, 1952)
El Escorial, 1563–1963: IV Centenario, 2 vols (Madrid, 1963)
Goya, 56–7 (1963) [whole issue on the Escorial]
Monasterio de San Lorenzo el Real: El Escorial en el cuarto centenario de su fundación, 1563–1963 (San Lorenzo de El Escorial, 1964)
F. Iñiguez Almech: *Las trazas del monasterio de San Lorenzo de El Escorial* (Madrid, 1965)
F. Chueca Goitia: *Casas reales en monasterios y conventos españoles* (Madrid, 1966)
El Escorial: La octava maravilla del mundo (Madrid, 1967)
M. Calì: *Da Michelangelo all'Escorial: Momenti del dibattito religioso nell'arte del cinquecento* (Turin, 1980)
G. Kubler: *Building the Escorial* (Princeton, 1982)
El Escorial en la Biblioteca Nacional (exh. cat., ed. E. Santiago; Madrid, Bib. N., 1985)
Fragmentos, iv–v (1985) [whole issue on the Escorial]
F. Chueca Goitia: *El Escorial: Piedra profética* (Madrid, 1986)
IV Centenario del monasterio de El Escorial, 4 vols (exh. cat., ed. J. Hernández Ferrero; Madrid, Escorial, 1986)
Fábricas y orden constructivo: La construcción (exh. cat., ed. J. M. Hernández de León; Madrid, Real Acad. S Fernando, 1986)
Ideas y diseño: La arquitectura (exh. cat., ed. G. Allende; Madrid, Min. Obras Púb. & Urb., 1986; Spanish ed., Madrid, 1992)
Real monasterio—Palacio de El Escorial: Simposio conmemorativo en el IV centenario de la terminación de las obras: Madrid, 1986
F. Marías: *El largo siglo XVI: Los usos artísticos del renacimiento español* (Madrid, 1989)
——: *El monasterio del Escorial* (Madrid, 1990)
A. Bustamante García: 'El Panteón del Escorial: Papeletas para su historia', *Ann. Dept. Hist. & Teor. A.*, iv (1992), pp. 161–215

SPECIALIST STUDIES

J. Zarco Cuevas: *Pintores españoles en San Lorenzo el Real de El Escorial, 1566–1613* (Madrid, 1931)

——: *Pintores italianos en San Lorenzo el Real de El Escorial, 1575–1613* (Madrid, 1932)

A. Ruiz de Arcaute: *Juan de Herrera, arquitecto de Felipe II* (Madrid, 1936)

L. Cervera Vera: *Las estampas y el sumario de El Escorial por Juan de Herrera* (Madrid, 1954)

R. Taylor: 'Architecture and Magic: Considerations on the Idea of the Escorial', *Essays in the History of Architecture Presented to Rudolf Wittkower* (New York, 1967), pp. 81–109

——: 'Juan Bautista Crescencio y la arquitectura cortesana española', *Academia: Bol. Real Acad. B.A. S Fernando*, xlviii (1979), pp. 63–126

C. von der Osten Sacken: *San Lorenzo el Real de El Escorial: Studien zur Baugeschichte und Ikonologie* (Munich, 1979)

J. J. Martín González: 'El Panteón de El Escorial y la arquitectura barroca', *Bol. Semin. Estud. A. & Arqueol.*, xlvii (1981), pp. 265–84

J. J. Rivera Blanco: *Juan Bautista de Toledo y Felipe II: La implantación del clasicismo en España* (Valladolid, 1984)

A. Bustamante and F. Marías: 'La Révolution classique: De Vitruve à l'Escurial', *Rev. A.* [Paris], lxx (1985), pp. 29–40

C. Wilkinson: 'Proportion in Practice: Juan de Herrera's Design for the Façade of the Basilica of the Escorial', *A. Bull.*, lxvii (1985), pp. 229–42

M. Scholz-Hänsel: *Eine spanische Wissenschaftsutopie am Ende des 16. Jahrhunderts: Die Bibliotheksfresken von Pellegrino Pellegrini im Escorial* (Tübingen, 1987)

C. Wilkinson-Zerner: *Juan de Herrera: Architect for Philip II* (New Haven and London, 1992)

R. Mulcahy: *For the Greater Glory of God: The Decoration of the Basilica of San Lorenzo el Real de El Escorial for Philip II of Spain* (Cambridge, 1993; Spanish ed. Madrid, 1992)

A. Bustamante García: *La octava maravilla del mundo: Estudios sobre el Escorial de Felipe II* (Madrid, 1994)

FERNANDO MARÍAS

Escuelas de Pintura al Aire Libre. Open-air painting schools developed in Mexico as artistic teaching projects for broad sections of the population during the period of the Revolution (1910–17). The first phase of their existence took place under Victoriano Huerta's government (1913–14), and their structure was established under the government of Alvaro Obregón (1920–24). Alfredo Ramos Martínez was the project's main promoter, and he was supported by civil servants, intellectuals and artists. The precepts by which art was to be taught were based on those of John Dewey's Action School in the USA; children and adolescents, farmers and factory workers were to meet and develop their own ideas with sincerity and simplicity, taking as their model the Barbizon school of landscape painting, with its devotion to contact with untamed nature. The first of the *escuelas*, situated at Santa Anita Ixtapalapa on the outskirts of Mexico City, was named Barbizon. Impressionism, a great deal of naive art and a certain involuntary expressionism were all blended together in the works of the students, who needed no formal qualifications to enter the schools. David Alfaro Siqueiros was among them. The project was extended to Chimalistac and moved on in 1921 to Coyoacán, where an attempt was made to involve native Mexicans and mestizos in order to encourage the production of a uniquely Mexican art. Under the government of Plutarco Elías Calles (1924–8), the open-air painting schools system was expanded to include branches in Xochimilco, Tlálpan and Guadalupe Hidalgo. This expansion, which reached the states of Michoacán and Puebla in the 1930s, was due to the enormous need for expression that arises in periods of transition and social upheaval, when a society's cultural traditions are under attack. In 1932 the schools' name was changed to Escuelas Libres de Pintura; entry requirements were also changed. In 1935 government subsidies, already reduced, finally ceased, and the schools went into decline. The Tasco school, under the Japanese director Tamiji Kitagawa (1894–1990), was the last to disappear in 1937, having survived for two years on local resources. Several thousand students attended the open-air painting schools, and their works were exhibited in Berlin, Paris and Madrid in 1926 with great success. During their rise to fame, the schools were enthusiastically supported by Diego Rivera, Alfonso Reyes (1889–1959), Pierre Janet (1859–1947), Eugenio d'Ors and Dewey; during their decline, they were criticized by Siqueiros and Rufino Tamayo.

BIBLIOGRAPHY

R. Martínez and others: *Monografía de las Escuelas de Pintura al Aire Libre* (Mexico City, 1926)

Homenaje al movimiento de Escuelas de Pintura al Aire Libre (exh. cat. by S. Pandolfi and others, Mexico City, Inst. N. B.A., 1981)

Escuelas de Pintura al Aire Libre y Centros Populares de Pintura (exh. cat., Mexico City, Inst. N. B.A., 1987)

RAQUEL TIBOL

Escurialene style. *See* ESTILO DESORNAMENTADO.

Esdaile, William (*b* 6 Feb 1758; *d* Clapham, London, 2 Oct 1837). English collector. He was the fourth son of Sir James Esdaile of Great Gains, Essex, sometime Lord Mayor of London. Commercially trained in the bank of Ladbrooke & Co. in London, he joined the family bank of Esdaile, Hammet & Co. on its foundation (*c.* 1780), at which time he also began tentatively to acquire minor prints. With growing affluence and professional advice he became one of the most ambitious saleroom purchasers and, towards the end of his life, an audacious bidder. He settled at Clapham Common, London, and first visited Italy in 1825 (returning there in 1827 and 1835–6). By 1832, prevented by malaria and weakening health from attending to business, he was occupied chiefly in savouring and ordering what had become one of the supreme collections of his time. Apart from some paintings, ceramics, coins, manuscripts and rare books, this was centred on prints and drawings. The extent of his acquisitions and catholicity of interest became evident in eight posthumous sales in London in 1838 and 1840, although prices made were often far below those originally paid. The series of 100 drawings each by Rembrandt and Claude Lorrain and his imitators (from the collection of Thomas Lawrence) were spectacular, along with a comprehensive group of Rembrandt etchings (some very fine), but the collection contained important and interesting graphic works, both original and reproductive, from all major schools from the 15th century to the collector's own day. The calligraphic pen monogram *WE* (more rarely the full surname) is seen on his prints and master drawings, which became widely scattered throughout the world, often with the previous provenance inscribed *verso*.

DNB
                    BIBLIOGRAPHY
F. Lugt: *Les Marques de collections* (Amsterdam, 1921), pp. 147, 491–3

HARLEY PRESTON

Esdin [**Esdun**]**, Jacquemart de.** *See* JACQUEMART DE HESDIN.

Eseler, Niclas, the elder (*b* Alzey, Rhine Hesse, *c.* 1400–10; *d* Frankfurt am Main, after 24 March 1482). German architect. His style is characterized by clarity of form and a unified effect and by an emphasis on structure, enhanced by an economical use of ornament and a high standard of craftsmanship. It is unlikely, as has been supposed, that he was also a sculptor.

In 1436 and 1448 Eseler worked for the Elector of Mainz in Amorbach, and from 1438 to 1442 he continued the work on the nave of St Michael, Schwäbisch-Hall, begun in 1427 by Konrad von Nürnberg (*fl* 1427–38). His applications for the vacant post of Master of the Works at the Frauenkirche in Esslingen were unsuccessful, but in 1442 he was appointed to a similar post at St Georg, Nördlingen (*see* NÖRDLINGEN, §1). Eseler completed the chancel walls, built the walls and piers of the nave, began the west tower and probably designed the high altar retable. In addition, between 1442 and 1444 he built the dance hall at Nördlingen, and in 1449 he worked on the city fortifications, having already begun, in 1448, his main work, the hall church of St Georg, DINKELSBÜHL. The walls of this building were standing by 1469. In 1453 Eseler was in the service of the city of Mainz and began the west choir of St Jacob, Rothenburg-ob-der-Tauber (finished *c.* 1467; *see* ROTHENBURG-OB-DER-TAUBER). In 1456 he became an adviser for the Johanneskirche in Crailsheim, and from 1456 to 1458 he worked at Schloss Rödelheim in Frankfurt. At the meeting of masons in Regensburg in 1459 Eseler, although Master of the Works at Mainz Cathedral, was refused his master's diploma, and this caused a quarrel. In 1461 there was a further quarrel when he was dismissed from his post at Nördlingen for having absented himself from the city too often since the middle of the century. In that year he worked in Höchst, and two years later he became Master of the Works for life at Mainz Cathedral, as well as architect to the city and diocese of Mainz. He left the city after he was found negligent in installing the bell cage in the east tower of the cathedral. In 1467 he worked in Heidelberg as an adviser. In 1475 he was in Frankfurt am Main, where his son Michael was taken on as a craftsman in 1477, on the condition that Niclas should live in the city. After his son was dismissed in 1481 Eseler had to make an official plea on his behalf. Between 1492 and 1499 his other son, Niclas the younger, produced vaulting for the walls built by his father for St Georg, Dinkelsbühl.

NDB

BIBLIOGRAPHY

W. Lergen: *Die Sippe der Eseler* (Darmstadt, 1940)

H. Koepf: *Die Baukunst der Spätgotik in Schwaben* (Stuttgart, 1958)

E. D. Schmid: *Nördlingen—die Georgskirche und St Salvator* (Stuttgart and Aalen, 1977)

W. Helmberger: *Architektur und Baugeschichte der St Georgskirche zu Dinkelsbühl (1448–1499)* (Bamberg, 1984)

FRIEDRICH KOBLER

Esfahan. *See* ISFAHAN.

Eshnunna. *See under* DIYALA REGION.

Esir. *See* ALI ACEMI.

Eski Krym. *See* STARYY KRYM.

Eskimo peoples. Indigenous inhabitants of the Arctic coasts of Siberia, Alaska, Canada and Greenland. They are biologically classified as Arctic Mongolians and are descended from peoples of a region in north-east Asia, who probably began to migrate *c.* 12,000 BC. Such peoples generally do not use the term 'Eskimo' ('eaters of raw meat') of themselves, which was the Canadian Algonquin name for them adopted by European explorers. There are instead three main groups, the largest of whom are the Inuit of Canada and Greenland.

For main discussion *see under* NATIVE NORTH AMERICAN ART.

Eski Mosul region. Area in north-western Iraq that was the subject of intense archaeological investigation between 1978 and 1987 as a result of the construction of a dam across the River Tigris. In the course of the Eski Mosul (or Saddam) Dam Salvage Project, numerous sites were excavated along both sides of the River Tigris from a few kilometres upstream of the town of Eski Mosul to the Syrian border. Although the area was not agriculturally wealthy and did not contain the remains of important historical cities, much information about the art and archaeology of the region was recovered.

The earliest works of art from the Eski Mosul region come from the pre-pottery Neolithic site of Nemrik, which is dated to the 8th millennium BC. There several schematic stylized animal, bird and human sculptures have been found carved out of stone (Baghdad, Iraq Mus.; see fig.).

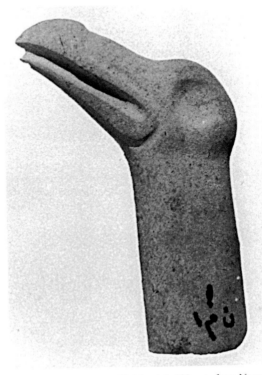

Eski Mosul region, stone bird head, h. 102 mm, from Nemrik, 8th millennium BC (Baghdad, Iraq Museum)

The investigations also cast new light on the attractive painted and incised pottery styles of the first half of the 3rd millennium BC, called Ninevite 5 because they were first found in the fifth period of occupation at the site of NINEVEH, the later Assyrian capital. Many sites belonging to this period were found, and it could be shown that crowded painted designs with naturalistic representations were the earlier style and were replaced by a fine grey ware pottery decorated with incised geometric designs.

From the site of Tell Karana 1 came a cache of votive pottery objects belonging to the second half of the 3rd millennium BC, perhaps contemporary with the Akkadian period in southern Mesopotamia. There were six hollow cylindrical pottery objects, including five phalli; the sixth ended in a gaunt human head very different from the fine naturalism of contemporary royal Akkadian art, as seen for example in the stele of Naram-Sin (Paris, Louvre) or the bronze head from Nineveh (Baghdad, Iraq Mus.; *see* AKKADIAN, figs 1 and 2).

From the later periods, much information was gained about the glyptic art of the region. Sites excavated included a small Late Assyrian provincial palace with outer court-yard and throne-room at Tell Baqaq 2; a 7th-century AD church and monastery built of cut-stone masonry at Museifneh; and an Abbasid caravanserai with carved stucco decoration at Tell Kharabok.

BIBLIOGRAPHY
'Excavations in Iraq, 1979–80', *Iraq*, xliii (1981), pp. 167–198
'Excavations in Iraq, 1981–82', *Iraq*, xlv (1983), pp. 199–224
'Excavations in Iraq, 1983–84', *Iraq*, xlvii (1985), pp. 215–39
M. Roaf and R. Killick: 'A Mysterious Affair of Styles: The Ninevite 5 Pottery of Northern Mesopotamia', *Iraq*, xlix (1987), pp. 199–230
'Excavations in Iraq, 1985–86', *Iraq*, xlix (1987), pp. 231–51
Researches on the Antiquities of Saddam Dam Basin Salvage and Other Researches (Baghdad, 1987)
E. Rova: *Distribution and Chronology of the Nineveh 5 Pottery and of its Culture*, Contributi e materiali di archeologia orientale II (Rome, 1988)
MICHAEL ROAF

Esna [anc. Egyp. Ta-senet, Gr. Latopolis]. Egyptian city *c.* 55 km south of Luxor on the Nile. Inhabited since ancient times, Esna remains important as the terminus of one of the main caravan routes between Egypt and the Sudan, and as a centre of textile production. The only ancient building to survive is part of the Greco-Roman Temple of Khnum, but Deir Manayus wa Shuhada (the 'Monastery of the Martyrs'), a 4th-century AD Coptic foundation, lies 6 km to the south-west, and the Ottoman mosque of el-Amri in the town centre retains a brick-built minaret of the Fatimid period (AD 969–1171).

The Temple of Khnum, now reduced to its hypostyle hall, formed the core of a complex including a quay (*in situ*) and a processional approach (untraced); this was related to four further complexes (almost entirely lost) in the region. The earlier, inner part of the temple is represented by its front wall, which was incorporated into the hall and now forms its rear wall. It has carved relief decoration dating to the reigns of Ptolemy VI Philometor (*reg* 180–164 BC; 163–145 BC) and Ptolemy VIII Euergetes II (*reg* 170–163 BC; 145–116 BC) on its northern face; the southern face was not decorated. The rest of the hall includes some of the latest temple reliefs in Egypt, dating from the reigns of Claudius (*reg* AD 41–54) to Decius

Esna, Temple of Khnum, relief decoration showing a Roman emperor of the 2nd century AD presenting offerings to Shu and Tefenet; detail from Gustave Jequier: *Les Temples ptolémaïques et romains* (Paris, 1924), pl. 78

(*reg* AD 249–51). Since the temple never had an entrance pylon, the motif of the destruction of enemies traditionally placed there to safeguard symbolically the sanctified area was placed instead on the hall's exterior side walls, producing a unique juxtaposition of scene types. Inside, the chief novelty is on the columns, which have extensive texts describing the festivals of the local religious year. They include important liturgical compositions and have a complex spatial organization, probably implying an approach to design similar to that seen in the outer hypostyle hall of the Temple of Horus at Edfu. The wall reliefs include fine scenes, such as one of the king and gods netting birds and fish, and the ceiling is carved with a zodiac, unusually arranged in linear fashion along the architraves. While some of the temple's hieroglyphic texts, which are written in the most elaborate form of the script, show a steep decline in graphic composition and legibility, the reliefs maintain more successfully the standards of other Greco-Roman temples (see fig.).

BIBLIOGRAPHY
S. Sauneron: *Esna*, 6 vols (Cairo, 1959–82)
O. Neugebauer and R. A. Parker: *Egyptian Astronomical Texts*, iii (Providence and London, 1969)
JOHN BAINES

Espagnat, Georges d' (*b* Melun, Seine-et-Marne, 14 Aug 1870; *d* Paris, 17 April 1950). French painter, illustrator and stage designer. Disdaining the traditional art schools, he studied part-time at the Académie Colarossi in Paris under Gustave-Claude-Etienne Courtois (1852–1923) and Jean-André Rixens (1846–1924) but was mostly self-taught. In 1891 he exhibited at the Salon des Refusés and the following year at the Salon des Indépendants. His early works, such as *Suburban Railway* (*c.* 1895; Paris, Mus. d'Orsay), showed a strong debt to Impressionism. He was a friend of Renoir as well as of Paul Signac, Henri Edmond Cross, Louis Valtat and later Maurice Denis, Bonnard and Vuillard. In 1898 he visited Morocco where he painted such works as *Moroccan Horseman* (1898; see Cailler, p. 7). After his return to France, he concentrated on studies from nature, paintings of women, children and flowers and decorative projects for private patrons. In 1904 he exhibited at the Salon d'Automne, becoming its Vice-President in 1935. Between 1905 and 1910 he made several trips with Valtat to visit Renoir on the Côte d'Azur as well as travelling to Spain, Italy, Portugal, Britain, Germany and elsewhere. In 1906 he illustrated Remy de Gourmont's book *Sixtine*, published in Paris. In the early 1910s he painted a number of portraits including several musician friends, including *Albert Roussel* (1912; see Cailler, p. 13), by which time his work was more simplified, fluid and intimate. In 1914 he provided the decor for a production of Alfred de Musset's play *Fantasio* at the Théâtre de Batignolles in Paris. After working in a camouflage unit during World War I, in 1920 d'Espagnat bought a country house in the Quercy region and over the next decade painted numerous landscapes and interiors there (e.g. *Interior*, 1925; Metz, Mus. A. & Hist.). During the 1930s he worked in various media. He illustrated Alphonse Daudet's *L'Immortel* (Paris, 1930) and also produced theatre designs. In 1936 he decorated the Mairie in Vincennes; in 1938 the Palais de Justice in Toulouse and in 1939 the ceiling of the Salle Victor Hugo in the Palais du Luxembourg in Paris. Ironically, considering his earlier attitudes, from 1936 to 1940 he was a professor at the Ecole des Beaux-Arts in Paris. Though disrupted by World War II, he continued to paint until his death and with his pupil Suzanne Humbert, illustrated Francis Jammes's *Clairières dans le ciel, 1902–1906* (Paris, 1948).

BIBLIOGRAPHY
Georges d'Espagnat (exh. cat., London, Wildenstein's, 1934)
P. Cailler: *Georges d'Espagnat* (Geneva, 1959)

ALBERTO CERNUSCHI

Espérandieu, Jacques-Henry [Henri] (*b* Nîmes, 22 Feb 1829; *d* Marseille, 11 Nov 1874). French architect and writer. He showed a notable aptitude for mathematics and line drawing at school and was first employed to copy drawings in the office of Charles-Auguste Questel, who was building the church of St Paul (1838–49) in Nîmes. Between 1846 and 1853 Espérandieu made the drawings for Questel's work on St Paul's, the Romanesque St-Gilles-du-Gard Abbey and the restoration of St Martin d'Ainay in Lyon. Questel's friendship and support was shown by his recommendation of Espérandieu to Léon Vaudoyer, under whom he studied (1846–52) at the Ecole des Beaux-Arts, Paris. Coming from a relatively poor family, Espérandieu had to finance part of his studies by working for both Questel, who opened an office in Versailles in 1851, and Vaudoyer during these years. His time at the Ecole was marked by numerous distinctions and medals, but on completing his studies he first devoted himself to three church projects: the completion of the Capuchin church of Ste Perpétue, Nîmes, designed by Léon Feuchères (1804–57); and in Marseille, where he moved in 1853, his own designs (adopted 1852) for Notre-Dame-de-la-Garde (1853–74) and Vaudoyer's new cathedral (projected 1852; begun 1855; *see* VAUDOYER, (2), fig. 2), for which Espérandieu drew the final plans. In 1854 he was made cathedral inspector and on Vaudoyer's death in 1872 he succeeded him as cathedral architect, completing the dome before his own death two years later.

It was in Marseille that Espérandieu executed his greatest works, which included Notre-Dame-de-la-Garde, the Palais Longchamp (1862–9) and the Ecole des Beaux-Arts et Bibliothèque de la Ville (1864–74). These projects, as well as his unsuccessful entries in national competitions (all 1860) for the church of St Baudille, Nîmes, the Paris Opéra and the stock exchange in Le Havre, testify not only to his talents as a builder, but also to his rational approach to designing and planning in two and three dimensions and to his interest in the history of architecture. His formula of reasoned eclecticism was well suited to his intellectual and artistic outlook, summed up in a number of texts published posthumously by his brother. His buildings are full of personality, combining rationalism, knowledge of cultural history, imagination and subtlety as well as a concern for their setting. Adjoining the church of Notre-Dame-de-la-Garde, who is supposed to protect sailors, he built a watchtower surmounted by a monumental statue of the Virgin in an almost military style, which harmonizes with the remains of a fort that serves it as a base. The crossing of the basilica is crowned by an elegant Romano-Byzantine dome with refined polychrome geometrical decoration outside and mosaics inside completed by Henri-Antoine Révoil (1820–1900), who succeeded Espérandieu as architect to Marseille Cathedral.

Espérandieu's second great project in Marseille, the Palais Longchamp, was one of the most accomplished and theatrical buildings of its period. The perspective along the Boulevard Longchamp emphasizes the central Château d'Eau, the outflow of the Canal de Marseille, which is a domed triumphal arch, from which the water flows, flanked by open quadrant colonnades. Below them the fluid forms of the staircases and fountain basins are flanked by the museums of fine arts and natural history, which enclose a space devoted to the celebration of water. Espérandieu's sculpted and painted decorations are a triumph; the benefits and prosperity brought by the waters of the Canal de Marseille are evoked by images that rejuvenated the iconography of the fountain as a monument. With the Ecole des Beaux-Arts et Bibliothèque de la Ville, Espérandieu played on the different materials used in construction (stone for the façades, brick and stone in the main courtyard) and on the iconography of the buildings, expressing both his dedication to architecture and his tribute to those figures whom he considered had played an essential role in the history of art.

WRITINGS
Chroniques posthumes (Nîmes, 1877)

BIBLIOGRAPHY
E. Parrocel: *L'Art dans le Midi*, iii (Marseille, 1883)
D. Jasmin: 'Le Palais Longchamp et ses images', *Provence Hist.*, xxxiii/125 (1982), pp. 224–34
——: 'Le Palais Longchamp "une des gloires architecturales du Nouveau Marseille"', *Culture et création dans l'architecture provinciale de Louis XIV à Napoléon III* (Aix-en-Provence, 1983)
——: *La Ville, l'administration et l'architecte: Commande publique et architecture à Marseille, 1830–1870* (diss., U. de Provence, 1991)

DENISE JASMIN

Espercieux, Jean-Joseph (*b* Marseille, 22 July 1757; *d* Paris, 6 May 1840). French sculptor. The son of a carpenter, he moved to Paris in 1776 and entered the studio of Charles-Antoine Bridan. He also attended, on an irregular basis, the studios of the sculptors Jean-Joseph Foucou, Pierre Julien and Philippe-Laurent Roland, but he seems to have been chiefly influenced by David. His career is obscure before the French Revolution, in which he played an active role as one of the presidents of the Société Républicaine des Arts, attracting attention through his speeches in favour of patriotic subjects and the use of antique costume. From 1793 he was a regular exhibitor at the Salon, principally showing portrait busts. Although he was a Republican of strong convictions, the climax of his career came during the Consulate (1799–1804) and the Empire (1804–14), when he received a number of state commissions, including a bust of *Cicero* (plaster, 1803; Fontainebleau, Château), a statue of *Mirabeau* (plaster, 1804–5; untraced) for the Palais du Luxembourg, Paris, and a relief of *The Victory of Austerlitz* for the Arc de Triomphe du Carrousel, Paris (marble, 1810; *in situ*). Particularly successful were the allegorical reliefs for the Fontaine de la Paix in the Marché Saint-Germain, Paris (marble, 1810; now Paris, Rue Bonaparte).

Espercieux's popularity gradually diminished after the Restoration in 1815, although his statue of *Philoctetes* (marble, 1814–19; Compiègne, Château) was bought by the State, and he received commissions for a statue of *Sully* for the Pont de la Concorde, Paris (marble, 1816–17; Rosny-sur-Seine) and a decorative relief for the Arc de Triomphe de l'Etoile, Paris (stone, 1830; *in situ*). His last Salon appearance was in 1836 with the marble statue *Young Greek Preparing to Enter the Bath* (Avignon, Mus. Calvet), a work based on a model made in 1806 and a belated proclamation of his unshakable faith in Neo-classicism.

Lami
H. Jouin: *David d'Angers: Sa vie, son oeuvre, ses écrits et ses contemporains*, 2 vols (Paris, 1878), pp. 175–89

PHILIPPE DUREY

Espínola Gómez, Manuel (*b* Solís de Mataojo, Lavalleja, 5 July 1921). Uruguayan painter. Having shown an early talent as a portrait painter, he was encouraged by the Uruguayan composer and violinist Eduardo Fabini, who posed for him several times, to study formally. With Fabini's help he obtained a scholarship to study, briefly, at the Círculo de Bellas Artes of Montevideo under the Uruguayan master Guillermo Laborde (1886–1940) and later under José Cúneo. In 1946 he won second prize at the Salón Nacional de Bellas Artes in Montevideo, and in 1948, together with Washington Barcala, Luis Solari and Juan Ventayol (1911–71), he founded the Grupo Carlos Federico Sáez, which had a dynamic effect on local art circles. Espínola Gómez was much affected by his visit to the São Paulo Biennale in 1954, where he saw Pablo Picasso's *Guernica* (1937) and tapestries by Henri-Georges Adam, and by his first trip to Europe in 1957. The range of his subject-matter, as indicated by major paintings such as *Fat Man* (1960; Montevideo, Mus. N. A. Plást. & Visuales), *Portrait of a Tall Man* (1947; see 1980 exh. cat., pl. 5) and *Most Serene Landscape with Head* (1975; see 1980 exh. cat., pl. 53), indicates a strong attachment to the human figure and landscape. He created unreal landscapes with crystallized figures tempered by real light. He was awarded major prizes at the Salón Nacional de Artes Plásticas in Montevideo in 1961 and 1962.

BIBLIOGRAPHY
Retrospectiva Espínola Gómez 1980 (exh. cat., Montevideo, Gal. Latina, 1980)
Arte contemporáneo en el Uruguay (exh. cat., ed. A. Kalenberg; Montevideo, Mus. N. A. Plást. & Visuales, 1982), pp. 35–6
A. Kalenberg: 'El transrealismo: La paralogía de Espínola Gómez', *A. Colombia*, 30 (1986), pp. 28–31
UABC (exh. cat., ed. W. Beeren; Amsterdam, Stedel. Mus., 1989), pp. 30–31

ANGEL KALENBERG

Espinós, Benito (*b* Valencia, 1748; *d* Valencia, 1818). Spanish painter. He was the son of the painter José Espinós (1721–84), who was his first teacher, and he later went on to study at the Academia de San Carlos, Valencia, where he became an accomplished painter of flowers.

In October 1778, following an order from Charles III, the Academia de San Carlos instituted a flower-painting course with close links to the Valencian silk manufacturing industry, which from 1784 onwards ranked equal with the other classes there. In 1784 Espinós was appointed director of the flower-painting and decorative art course. This appointment occurred a year after he had won first prize in the Academia's competition. These were his most active years, when he was well-known at court and received commissions from Charles III, including, in 1783, the design for a sumptuous wall-hanging intended as a gift for Queen Mary I of Portugal (untraced). Around 1785 he began his collaboration with the Fábrica do los Cinco Cremios de Madrid established in Valencia. For 31 years Espinós was responsible for teaching flower painting as well as heading the course, and for producing drawings for his students to copy. Many of his students, such as José Antonio Zapata (1763–1837) and José Romá (1784–1847), went on to take a significant part in the development of 18th-century Spanish still-life painting that lasted into the next century.

The paintings of Espinós's early period have a chromatic transparency and light backgrounds, and they deploy architectural settings and include sculpture, while those of the second period have darker backgrounds. His flower paintings were much admired and collected at court. Three flower paintings were sent by Espinós as a gift in 1788 to the Prince of the Asturias, the future Charles IV; these included *Vase of Flowers* (Madrid, Prado). Another late work also sent was *Vase of Flowers* (Madrid, Cason Buen Retiro), which shows his study of 17th-century flower painting as well as his light and delicate touch and method of exploiting the effects of light falling on flowers seen against a dark background.

BIBLIOGRAPHY
J. Cavestany: *Floreros y bodegones en la pintura española* (Madrid, 1936–40), pp. 146, 167, 169
S. Aldana Fernández: 'Benito Espinós, pintor académico', *Archv A. Valenc.* (1968), pp. 29–40
——: *Pintores valencianos de flores* (Valencia, 1970), p. 172
Pintura española de bodegones y floreros de 1600 a Goya (exh. cat. by A. E. Pérez Sánchez, Madrid, Prado, 1983), pp. 179–82

ADELA ESPINÓS DíAZ

Espinosa, Jerónimo Jacinto (*b* Cocentaina, Alicante, *bapt* 20 July 1600; *d* Valencia, 1667). Spanish painter. He was the son of Jerónimo Roderiguez de Espinosa (1562–

1638), a modest painter of Valladolid who in 1596 was established in Cocentaina and from 1612 in Valencia. He probably began his training in his father's studio and by 1616 was a member of the Colegio de Pintores of Valencia. His earliest known work is the large *Ransomed Christ* (1623; Valencia, priv. col., see Pérez Sánchez, pl. 5), which depicts the miraculous ransoming of a statue of Christ that had been captured by Algerian pirates; its naturalism and tenebrist lighting are characteristic of his style, as is its sense of composition and colour, which is similar to that of his contemporaries Francisco and Juan Ribalta.

During the 1620s Espinosa worked for several religious houses in Valencia. His depiction of the Dominican *Padre Jerónimo Mos* (Valencia, Mus. B.A.) exemplifies his exceptional skill at portraiture, notably in its intensity of expression, the sober and personal range of colour and the masterly painting of the still-life detail. In the following decade he combined the painting of portraits with that of religious subjects. His *Don Juan Vives de Cañamás* (1634; Madrid, priv. col.) and *Don Francisco Vives de Cañamás, Conde de Fauras* (c. 1635; Kingston Lacy, Dorset, NT) are both fine examples of early 17th-century naturalistic portraiture, similar in character to the portraits painted by Diego Velázquez in Madrid between 1622 and 1630.

Espinosa is documented in Valencia in 1640, as working for the Ayuntamiento, and again in 1646, when he is mentioned in connection with the plague; between those years he may have travelled, particularly to Seville, which would explain the similarity of his later work to that of Francisco de Zurbarán. After 1648 Espinosa remained active for the religious orders, producing the *Death of St Luis Beltrán* (1653; Valencia, Mus. B.A.) and a series of episodes from the life of that saint (1655) for the Dominican convent in S Domingo, Valencia; for the Jesuits he painted the *Apparition of Christ to St Ignatius Loyola* (1658; Valencia, Mus. B.A.).

From 1659 Espinosa worked for the Mercedarians of Nuestra Señora de la Merced, Valencia, as well as at the monastery of El Puig, at the suggestion of José Sánchis, whose portrait he painted (U. Valencia). The canvases painted for the Mercedarian Order are among his best and most mature works, including the *Mass of St Pedro Pascual* (1660), *St Pedro Nolasco and the Sick Monks* (1661), the *Discovery of the Virgin of El Puig* (1661) and the *Virgin of the Mercedarian Order in the Choir* (1661; all Valencia, Mus. B.A.), which show his ability to organize monumental compositions, his mastery in the handling of colour in a restricted palette of white and earthy tones and his capacity to depict devotion in the friars' facial expressions. He also painted isolated figures of saints, including *St John the Baptist* and *St Mary Magdalene* (both c. 1650–60; Madrid, Prado).

Espinosa painted the *Immaculate Conception* several times (e.g. 1660; U. Valencia; and 1661; Valencia, Lonja Seda). The severe frontal presentation of the figures in these works is old-fashioned and very different from the dynamic Baroque interpretations by Bartolomé Murillo in Seville or by painters such as José Antolínez in Madrid. The example at Lonja Seda is a votive painting executed for the Ayuntamiento and is particularly interesting for its portraits of city officials and for the figure of the Virgin,

represented in hieratic form because it is a faithful rendering of a piece of sculpture. In 1659 the cathedral chapter of Valencia commissioned Espinosa to paint the portrait of *Archbishop Pedro de Urbina* and in 1666 that of *Archbishop Martín López de Hontiveros* (both Valencia Cathedral). In the *Virgin of the Rosary* (1663; destr. 1936), painted for the Augustinian nuns of the convent of St Martin, Segorbe, Castellón, he again used a rigidly symmetrical composition, though delicately executed. The *Communion of St Mary Magdalene* (1665; Valencia, Mus. B.A.; see fig.), painted for the Capuchins of Massamagrell, Valencia, is one of his finest works, notable for the solemnity of its composition, the sureness of touch in conveying expression and the masterly handling of detail, despite its old-fashioned traits of naturalism and tenebrist lighting.

From Pedro Orrente and the Ribaltas, Espinosa derived a taste for warm colours reinforced by the red ground he gave his canvases that now shows through in almost all his paintings. He was an excellent draughtsman; all his compositions are carefully composed, each figure expressing its own personality. The arrangement of complex scenes is often rigid and sometimes awkward, as is occasionally the case with Zurbarán, with whom he has much in common, particularly excellent monastic scenes. Espinosa had a strong influence on succeeding Valencian painters, and figure types influenced by his work can be traced well into the 18th century.

Espinosa's son, Jacinto Espinosa de Castro (1631–1707), was his pupil and a modest follower.

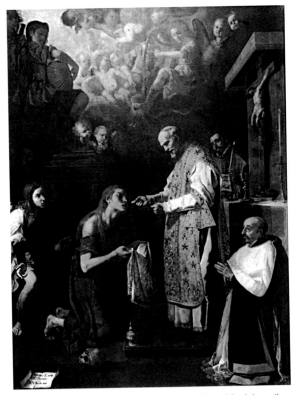

Jerónimo Jacinto Espinosa: *Communion of St Mary Magdalene*, oil on canvas, 3.13×2.26 m, 1665 (Valencia, Museo de Bellas Artes)

BIBLIOGRAPHY
A. E. Pérez Sánchez: *Jerónimo Jacinto de Espinosa* (Madrid, 1972)
Los Ribalta, y la pintura valenciana de su tiempo (exh. cat. by F. B. Domenech, Valencia, Lonja Seda; Madrid, Prado; 1987–8)

ALFONSO E. PÉREZ SÁNCHEZ

Espinosa, Juan Bautista de (*b* ?*c*. 1590; *d* Madrid, before 1641). Spanish painter. Details of his life are scarce. He is documented in Madrid and Toledo between 1612 and 1626, and while he is recorded as having painted religious pictures and portraits (untraced), he is only known today for his still-life paintings. Documents relating to another artist of the same name, known as Juan de Espinosa, dating from 1645 to 1677, concern a different painter.

Juan Bautista de Espinosa seems to have had a traditional training that led to a rigid and rigorously symmetrical arrangement in his still-life compositions; the objects are rendered in minute detail, which aims to bring out their true qualities. Metals and glass are painted with a refined technique that is reminiscent both of Flemish painting and, in Spain, of the technique of van der Hamen y Leon. The directed light and the neutral backgrounds contribute to the almost sculptural roundness of the objects. His subject-matter, like that of van der Hamen y Leon, relates to an affluent and courtly life. These qualities are all seen in the remarkable *Still-life with Silver Gilt Salvers* (signed and dated 1624; ex-Bergen, Reksten Found.), with its severely symmetrical composition and fine evocation of light reflected from the surfaces of the white tablecloth and variously shaped metal objects that are probably of Toledan craftsmanship. He also painted two *bodegones*, which may have been a pair (ex-Duchess of Valencia priv. col., see 1985 exh. cat., figs IV.1 and IV.2), one of which is signed (untraced); the other (Madrid, priv. col., see 1985 exh. cat., figs IV.1 and IV.2) shows the same skilful modelling but has been damaged.

BIBLIOGRAPHY
E. Harris: 'Obras españolas de artistas desconocidos', *Rev. Esp. A.* (1934–5), p. 259
J. Cavestany: *Floreros y bodegones en la pintura española* (Madrid, 1936–40), p. 76
Pintura española de bodegones y floreros, de 1600 a Goya (exh. cat., ed. A. E. Pérez Sánchez; Madrid, Prado, 1983), pp. 45, 58, 206
Spanish Still-life in the Golden Age, 1600–50 (exh. cat., ed. W. B. Jordan; Fort Worth, TX, Kimbell A. Mus., 1985), pp. 90–93
Pintores del reinado de Felipe IV (exh. cat. by D. M. Orihuela, Madrid, Prado, 1994–5), p. 52, no. 10

MERCEDES ORIHUELA

Espinoza, Eugenio (*b* San Juan de los Morros, 29 Nov 1950). Venezuelan sculptor. He studied at the Escuela de Artes Plásticas 'Cristóbal Rojas' and at the Instituto de Diseño Neumann, both in Caracas (1968–71). From 1977 to 1980 he lived in New York, where he studied at the Pratt Institute and at the School of Visual Arts. Espinoza began exhibiting in 1969, participating in the Salón Arturo Michelena de Valencia, Venezuela. From then on he showed his work in one-man and group shows in Venezuela and abroad. The net, represented with canvas stretched to different tensions, was a constant theme of Espinoza's work. In 1985 he represented Venezuela in the São Paulo Biennale in Brazil.

BIBLIOGRAPHY
F. Paz Castillo and P. Rojas Guardia: *Diccionario de las artes plásticas en Venezuela* (Caracas, 1973)

M. Hernandez Serrano, ed.: *Diccionario de las artes visuales en Venezuela*, 2 vols (Caracas, 1982)
CCS-10. Arte venezolano actual (exh. cat., Caracas, Gal. A. N., 1993)

Espinoza, Manuel (*b* San José de Guaribe, nr Zaraza, 1 Jan 1937). Venezuelan painter and engraver. He studied in Venezuela at the Escuela de Artes Plásticas 'Arturo Michelena' in Valencia (1953) and at the Escuela de Artes Plásticas 'Cristóbal Rojas' in Caracas (1955–7). From 1958 to 1966 he participated in national paint salons, exhibiting work that focused on the aesthetic interpretation of indigenous nature. In 1962 Espinoza represented Venezuela at the Venice Biennale. Two years later he was nominated Director of the Círculo del Pez Dorado in Caracas, a competition group that sought to promote art and culture in Venezuela. From 1976 he was involved in creating the Galería de Arte Nacional, also in Caracas, which he directed for eight years. Also in 1976 he helped establish in Caracas the Centro de Enseñanza Gráfica (CEGRA) and the Taller de Artes Gráficas (TAGA). In 1980 he was awarded the Premio Nacional de Artes Plásticas.

BIBLIOGRAPHY
F. Paz Castillo and P. Rojas Guardia: *Diccionario de las artes plásticas en Venezuela* (Caracas, 1973), p. 89

ELIDA SALAZAR

Espinoza Dueñas, Francisco (*b* Lima, 1926). Peruvian painter, printmaker and ceramicist, active in Europe. He studied at the Escuela Nacional de Bellas Artes in Lima until 1953 and then began to exhibit paintings, prints, murals and ceramics on an annual basis in Lima. He continued his studies in Spain in 1956, and from then on remained in Europe, mainly in Paris and Madrid. In Paris he became an assistant at the printmakers' workshop at the Ecole Nationale Supérieure des Beaux-Arts. Following a period in Cuba where he worked at the Taller de Grabado de Cubanacán, Espinoza Dueñas returned to France to study ceramics at Sèvres, executing sculptural, symbolic works reminiscent of Pre-Columbian Peruvian ceramics. His paintings, which are expressionistic in style, are colourful, energetic and full of symbolism (e.g. *Pampa Road*, 1955; Lima, Mus. A.)

BIBLIOGRAPHY
J. A. de Lavalle and W. Lang: *Pintura contemporánea*, Colección arte y tesoros del Perú, ii (Lima, 1976), pp. 158–9

W. IAIN MACKAY

Espirito Santo, Domingos António de. *See* SEQUEIRA, (1).

Esplugas, A. (*fl* 1888). Spanish photographer. He is known mostly from his photographs of the Exposición Internacional in Barcelona (1888). Working in the Plaza del Teatro, in the heart of that city, he captured the hustle and bustle of all stages of the fair, from its construction to its diversions. He had a varied vision of a vast urban scene, so he was concerned with the fair as monument and as humanity, as well as scientifically. In his extensive series on the great feature of the fair, the aerostatic balloon El Cautivo, he focused not only on the balloon as scientific object but also on the fearless public who rode in it. These photographs, including some taken aerially from the balloon, reveal Esplugas's concern to depict the human, scientific and monumental aspects of the fair. He also made studio cartes-de-visite and many views of Barcelona's port.

LEE FONTANELLA

Esposito, Gaetano (*b* Salerno, 17 Nov 1858; *d* Sala Consilina, 8 April 1911). Italian painter. He first studied privately with Gaetano D'Agostino (1837–1914) and later enrolled at the Reale Istituto di Belle Arti in Naples, where he was a pupil of Filippo Palizzi, Domenico Morelli and Stanislao Lista (1824–1908). From 1875 to 1906 he regularly participated in the exhibitions organized by the Naples Società Promotrice di Belle Arti and had his first real success at the Esposizione Nazionale held in Naples in 1877 with three genre paintings, *A Sad Presentiment*, *Daughter of Guilt* and *Kitchen Filled with Smoke* (all untraced). Esposito's genre pictures, particularly those involving children, were clearly influenced by the work of Antonio Mancini, particularly in their sentimental attitude towards squalor or poverty. At the 1880 Esposizione Nazionale in Turin his *Christ among the Children* (Rome, G.N.A. Mod.) was bought by the Ministry of Education, while at exhibitions in Rome (1893), Florence (1896–7), St Petersburg (1902) and the Universal Exhibition in St Louis (1904) he was awarded several prizes.

Esposito's most significant works are portraits and seascapes. Among his portraits are the engraver *Francesco Pisante* (1876; Naples, Accad. B.-A.) and numerous delicately rendered portraits of women, some of which are executed in pastel, a medium that emphasizes his mastery of tonal techniques. His skill in the use of chiaroscuro in all his works was largely a result of years of study of the 17th-century Neapolitan tradition, particularly the work of Jusepe de Ribera and Massimo Stanzione. Esposito's most notable seascape is *From the Rocks of Frisio* (or *Palazzo Donn'Anna*, 1893; Rome, G.N.A. Mod.), showing the unfinished Baroque palace in which he had established his home. This palace became a recurrent theme for him, almost to the point of obsession; various versions of the subject are known, each painted under different light and weather conditions. Such works display Esposito's virtuosity but have little in common with the contemporary experiments of Impressionism and Post-Impressionism; his studies of light had little impact on the plasticity of his forms or their confidently drawn contours. He also painted decorative schemes, for example the large symbolic figure in the central room of the Palazzo della Borsa in Naples (1896; *in situ*).

BIBLIOGRAPHY

E. Giannelli: *Artisti italiani viventi* (Naples, 1916), pp. 232–5
S. Di Giacomo: *Gaetano Esposito* (Naples, 1919)
Il paesaggio nella pittura napoletana dell'ottocento (exh. cat., Naples, 1936), pp. 24–5, 70
O. Casella: 'Gaetano Esposito pittore del mare', *Rass. N.* (Feb 1942), pp. 91–5
C. Siviero: *Questa era Napoli* (Naples, 1950), pp. 177–84, 367–9
P. Ricci: *Arte e artisti a Napoli, 1800–1943* (Naples, 1981)

MARIANTONIETTA PICONE PETRUSA

Esquivel, Antonio María (*b* Seville, 8 March 1806; *d* Madrid, 9 April 1857). Spanish painter. He was trained at the Real Escuela de Tres Nobles Artes in Seville, and he started his artistic career at the age of 21 in an environment of mediocre standards, where he stood out for his great ability in drawing. After working for ten years in Seville, Esquivel went, in 1831, to Madrid, establishing himself rapidly in a privileged position among the painters who worked at the Court. He soon acquired a great reputation as a portrait painter, although he also created lavish religious compositions and colourful scenes of local life. After his triumph in Madrid, Esquivel returned to Seville in 1838 ready to profit from the brilliant reputation he had acquired. In the following year, however, progressive blindness dramatically curtailed his development, and brought him to such despair that he twice tried to commit suicide. These circumstances moved the artistic circles of Madrid and Seville to organize collections of money to provide enough for the artist to live on, and also to cover the cost of treatment, which happily allowed his sight to be restored in June 1840. After this grievous experience Esquivel decided to return to Madrid where he soon recovered his prestige, his career culminating in his being appointed Pintor de Cámara by Isabella II in 1843 and being elected to the Real Academia de San Fernando in 1847. In the following year he published his famous *Tratado de anatomía pictórica*, in which he summarized his teaching on this subject. Esquivel's untiring activity of the last ten years of his life produced both a large number of paintings and many undertakings to promote and defend the fine arts.

Esquivel's principal talent was for drawing the figure from life; but his finished work suffers from a certain coldness in facial expression. His greatest success was in the painting of portraits, although the quality of these is uneven. This imbalance was largely due to the differing levels of interest aroused in the painter by his models, and also to the size of the fee that had been agreed. In his most successful works Esquivel was careful to capture not only physical appearance but also the characteristics of the clothing with all kinds of textures and sheens. Esquivel's self-portraits are of great interest; among these are the *Self-portrait* in the uniform of an Academy Member (1847; Madrid, Mus. Lázaro Galdiano) and a later *Self-portrait* (*c*.1850; Madrid, Casón Buen Retiro), the best that survives. Esquivel also painted a touching *Self-portrait with Wife* (*c*.1827; Seville, Marqués de Aracena priv. col.). In his female portraits Esquivel showed the clear influence of 19th-century English painting, a style imbibed during his period of training in Seville through contact with his English patron, Julian Williams. Such an influence is reflected in the several versions of the *Portrait of the Artist's Wife and Daughter* (e.g. 1830s–40s; see Guerrero Lovillo, pls 20 and 21). Other female portraits of high quality are that of *Doña Concha Argüelles* (Barcelona, Mus. A. Catalunya) and that of the *Señora de Carriquirre* (1845; Seville, Mus. B.A.). Equally attractive are Esquivel's portraits of children, where he catches the innocence of infancy. The early portraits of *Isabella II* and of her sister *Luisa Fernanda* at the ages, respectively, of eight and six years (both 1838; both Sanlucar de Barrameda, Prince Alvaro de Orleans priv. col., see Valdivieso, 1981, figs 30 and 31) show great technical skill. There is also a magnificent portrait of *Isabella II* as Infanta (1838; Madrid, Banco de España). In 1845, Esquivel again painted the two sisters (Seville, Alcázar; see fig.).

Antonio María Esquivel: *Isabella II and her Sister Luisa Fernanda*, oil on canvas, 2.25×1.45 m, 1845 (Seville, Alcázar)

As Esquivel was one of the most important portrait artists of the Madrid Court, he was often called upon to paint the most notable politicians, military men, aristocrats and intellectuals of his time. Among his works of this kind is the equestrian portrait of *General Prim* (Madrid, Mus. Romántico). Among the most important members of the aristocracy painted by Esquivel were the *Conde de Cabarrús* (1842; Jerez de la Frontera, priv. col., see Guerrero Lovillo, pl. 41) and *Don Juan Dómine* (1838–40; Seville, priv. col., see Valdivieso, 1981, pl. 314). This last portrait is a work of particular interest in Esquivel's development, as he started to paint it shortly before going blind and finished it after recovering his sight. Esquivel was also active as a painter of portrait miniatures; and of particular interest as records of Esquivel's cultural setting are the group portraits, *A Reading of Ventura de la Vega on the Stage of the Príncipe Theatre* (1845; Madrid, Casón Buen Retiro) and *A Meeting of Literary Men in the Painter's Studio* (1846; Madrid, Mus. Romántico). Both paintings contain a large number of portraits of the principal actors and literary men of the time.

Esquivel was also deeply committed to religious painting. Although the technical execution of his religious work is always correct, it lacks spiritual feeling. Among the more powerful works are *Transfiguration* (1837; parish church of Santa Cruz de la Palma) and the *Fall of Lucifer* (1841; untraced). Esquivel's skill at drawing from the nude is amply demonstrated in his figures of *Adam and Eve* (1842), *Susanna and the Elders* (2 versions, 1843 and 1854) and *Joseph with Potiphar's Wife* (1854; all Seville, Mus.

B.A.). In all three works, however, the rhetorical, declamatory attitudes of the figures cause them to lose sincerity and verisimilitude. Esquivel's *Mary Magdalene* (1856; Seville, Mus. B.A.) is of high quality, combining accurate drawing with concentrated spiritual feeling. As a typically Romantic artist, Esquivel also painted historical subjects, although this was a minor aspect of his oeuvre (e.g. the *Bell of Huesca*, 1850; Seville, Mus. B.A.). Most of these are colourful, small in scale and successful in terms of composition; but once again overemphatic gesture and expression detracts from their effectiveness as historical scenes. Esquivel painted several works on mythological themes, the most successful being the *Birth of Venus* (1838; Barcelona, priv. col., see Valdivieso, 1981, fig. 33). This is a work of exceptional quality, in which Esquivel established the most admirable type of feminine beauty to be found in all his work.

On occasions Esquivel attempted compositions whose main scenes were subtly erotic, in defiance of the rigid moral principles of the bourgeois society of his time. Only a few of these paintings are known. Among them is the *Young Girl Taking off her Stockings* (1842; Dallas, TX, S. Methodist U., Meadows Mus. & Gal.). Among Esquivel's more successful scenes of local life is his picture of the dancer *Josefa Vargas* (1850; Seville, Col. Alba).

WRITINGS

Tratado de anatomía pictórica (Madrid, 1848)

BIBLIOGRAPHY

J. Guerrero Lovillo: *Antonio María Esquivel* (Madrid, 1957)
J. A. Gaya Nuño: *Arte del siglo XIX*, A. Hisp., xix (Madrid, 1966)
E. Valdivieso: *Pintura sevillana del siglo XIX* (Seville, 1981)
——: *Historia de la pintura sevillana* (Seville, 1986)

Esquivel, Miguel de (*b* Seville, *c.* 1595; *d* Seville, 1621). Spanish painter. He was the son of a painter, Diego Esquivel (*fl* 1593–1618), and probably trained in his father's workshop. He married in Seville in 1616 and died young. Only one signed painting of his has survived, the large *SS Justa and Rufina* in Seville Cathedral (*c.* 1620). It is an example of provincial Baroque naturalism: the two saints are portrayed as solemn, monumental figures with sweet faces; stylistically they are derived from the work of Juan de Roelas. Between the two saints is the Giralda, the tower of Seville, painted in great detail so that the paintings that once adorned its walls (now obliterated) are visible. No other work by Esquivel has survived, although it is recorded that in 1620 he painted an altarpiece for the lower choir of the church of S Pablo (now La Magdalena), Seville, and in the same year he contracted to paint three views of Seville (all untraced).

BIBLIOGRAPHY

E. Valdivieso and J. M. Serrera: *Pintura sevillana del primer tercio del siglo XVII* (Madrid, 1985), pp. 378–83
A. Pérez Sánchez: *Pintura barroca en España, 1600–1750* (Madrid, 1992), p. 160

ENRIQUE VALDIVIESO

Esselens, Jacob (*b* Amsterdam, *c.* 1627; *d* Amsterdam, *bur* 15 Jan 1687). Dutch draughtsman and painter. He was referred to as a 'painter' on the occasion of his (late) marriage on 11 April 1668, but in the will drawn up after the death of his wife in 1677 he is called a 'merchant'. He did indeed trade in silks and velvets. As an artist, he was

Jacob Esselens: *Farmhouse by the Water*, pen and brown ink, with brown and grey wash, 104×185 mm (Amsterdam, Historisch Museum)

self-taught and should probably be considered an amateur. His textile business occasioned visits, among other places, to Italy, France, England and Scotland, where he made accomplished landscape drawings. Panoramic views of English towns (Chatham, Greenwich, London, Rochester and Rye) dating from the 1660s were later included in the Atlas van der Hem (Vienna, Österreich, Nbib.; *see* HEM, LAURENS VAN DER). In 1663 he journeyed along the Rhine with Gerbrand van den Eeckhout and Jan Lievens, as is evident from the many drawings by all three artists of the same locations, including Rhenen, Arnhem and Cleve (e.g. Amsterdam, Rijksmus.; Edinburgh, N.G.; Haarlem, Teylers Mus.; St Petersburg, Hermitage). Besides these topographical views, Esselens also drew imaginary landscapes, for example of riverbanks and coastlines with fishermen or tradesmen in the manner of Simon de Vlieger, woody landscapes suggesting the influence of Anthoni Waterlo and hilly landscapes in the style of his travelling companions van den Eeckhout and Lievens. Some works (see fig.) seem to have been inspired by etchings and drawings of the Dutch countryside made by Rembrandt in the 1640s and 1650s. It would, however, be an exaggeration to consider Esselens a pupil of Rembrandt, as has often been suggested since the 19th century. Despite a clearly recognizable personal style of drawing, Esselens was often inspired by the work of other draughtsmen. This is also true of his paintings, which are somewhat eclectic in nature but sometimes of a surprisingly high artistic standard. His seaside views (e.g. Amsterdam, Rijksmus.; Copenhagen, Stat. Mus. Kst), with their characteristic atmosphere, betray the influence of Adriaen van de Velde, but the use of silver-grey tints also suggests that of Simon de Vlieger. He painted arcadian landscapes, in a rather uninspired style, that are reminiscent of Cornelis van Poelenburgh (e.g. Brunswick, Herzog Anton-Ulrich-Mus.), but he also occasionally produced charming landscapes bathed in southern light, for instance the *Landscape with Hunters* (Amsterdam, Rijksmus.) and the *'Scottish' Landscape* (The Hague, Mus. Bredius). In his non-topographical landscapes, animals and, especially, figures play an important role: fishermen or townspeople are seen buying fish in his beach views, while in other works elegantly dressed ladies and gentlemen are involved in recreational pursuits (e.g. *Elegant Hunting Party on the Bank of a River*; Rotterdam, Mus. Boymans–van Beuningen). He died a wealthy man; his friend and fellow silk merchant Abraham Rutgers (*b* Amsterdam, 1632; *d* Amsterdam, 1699), who was also an avid amateur draughtsman, was appointed guardian of his children. Rutgers was also the administrator of Esselens's estate, which included many of the latter's drawings, which he repeatedly copied.

BIBLIOGRAPHY
P. H. Hulton: 'Drawings of England in the Seventeenth Century by Willem Schellinks, Jacob Esselens and Lambert Doomer', *Walpole Soc.*, xxxv (1954–6), 2 vols
Rembrandt en tekenaars uit zijn omgeving [Rembrandt and draughtsmen of his circle] (exh. cat. by B. P. J. Broos, Amsterdam, Hist. Mus., 1981), pp. 118–26

B. P. J. BROOS

Essen. German city and industrial centre in the Ruhr, North Rhine-Westphalia. It has been a bishopric since 1958 and has a population of 670,000 (1977). Of particular artistic significance is the city's Minster, begun in Carolingian times.

1. MINSTER. About AD 850 Altfried, later Bishop of Hildesheim (851–74), built a convent for noblewomen on his own estate. The first church, dedicated to St Quintin, was a small, rectangular hall with a west gallery and a narrow chancel bay. Between 852 and 870 Altfried built an aisled basilica with a transept, a tripartite chancel with

a central apse and a small west narthex. After a fire in 946 the nave, aisles and chancel were rebuilt on the old plan, preserving the main Carolingian structure. By 965 the west side with an atrium and the baptismal chapel of St John the Baptist was built, and an outer crypt had been added to the chancel. A completely new building was erected under Abbess Theophanu (*reg* 1039–58), granddaughter of Otto II, on the plan of its Carolingian–Ottonian predecessor. Its outstanding feature was the west end, which combined a triple-towered westwork, centralized construction and west chancel with a monumental west entrance and choir galleries to create a unique monument that the patroness must consciously have modelled on Charlemagne's palatine chapel at Aachen (*see* AACHEN, §2(ii)(a) and ROMANESQUE, §II, 2). The crypt was consecrated in 1051, and the atrium was built from 1060 to 1070. The eastern parts were vaulted *c.* 1180. In 1260 the baptismal chapel became a parish church (in 1471 it was replaced by the present building, a Late Gothic, aisled hall church with groin-vaulting).

After a fire in 1275 Theophanu's building was replaced by a Gothic aisled hall church, dedicated to SS Maria, Cosmas and Damian and erected on the same foundations. The walls of the chancel and the south wall of the nave were built by Master Martin by 1304; the north wall was raised and the hall vaulted by a second, unknown architect by *c.* 1327. The nave has four groin-vaulted rectangular bays and simple columns following the type of the Elisabethkirche in Marburg. The aisled fore-chancel is as wide as the transept; the straight-ended hall chancel above the late Ottonian crypt is narrower. The High Gothic gallery below the windows of the side aisles is reminiscent of the cathedrals of Burgundy and the Champagne region. The influence of the Cologne building lodge under Master Martin is seen in the south compound piers and in the ornamentation of the capitals, while the Westphalian influence introduced by the second architect is discernible on the north side. At the western termination of the nave is the elaborate rectangular late Ottonian structure surviving from Theophanu's church, its hexagonal central tower flanked by two octagonal staircase towers. Inside, its groin-vaulted lower storey opens into the nave through three round-headed arches forming three sides of a hexagon, in imitation of the Aachen palatine chapel. Pairs of columns are inserted on two levels into the tall round arches of the gallery above (see fig.). Behind the spandrels, between the piers, are small additional galleries. Adjoining the west end is an atrium, closed in by the parish church of St John the Baptist. The treasury contains outstanding examples of Ottonian goldwork (*see* OTTONIAN ART, §V).

BIBLIOGRAPHY
K. Wilhelm-Kästner: *Das Münster in Essen* (Essen, 1929)
W. Zimmermann: *Das Münster zu Essen* (Essen, 1956)
G. Dehio, H. Thümmler and R. Schmitz-Ehmke, eds: *Rheinland*, Hb. Dt. Kstdkml. (Munich and Berlin, 1967)

BETTINA GEORGI, ERNST ULLMANN

Essen, Jacob van. *See* ES, JACOB VAN.

Essenwein, August Ottmar von (*b* Karlsruhe, 2 Nov 1831; *d* Nuremberg, 13 Oct 1892). German architect and art historian. He was an important exponent of historicism. After studying architecture and art history up to 1851 (graduated 1855) at the Polytechnikum (now Technische Universität), Karlsruhe, he visited Berlin in 1852/3 and travelled in Europe, gaining knowledge that would later be valuable in his work on the conservation of monuments. His first post (1857) was as architect to the Austrian Staatseisenbahn-Gesellschaft. At about that time he designed churches, public buildings and houses, especially in Banat (Hungary; now Romania), and produced plans (1860–61) for the urban development of Franzdorf. In the early 1860s he also produced ornamentation in the Romanesque style for churches, including those at Leiden (Hungary), Berchtoldsdorf, near Vienna, S Antonio, Padua, and Trento Cathedral. In 1864 he became a city architect at Graz and in 1865 Professor of Architecture at the Technische Hochschule, Graz. His publications on architectural history and the conservation of monuments, as well as his practical and theoretical work on problems in the arts and crafts, led to his appointment (1866) as Director of the Germanisches Nationalmuseum, Nuremberg. He extended the collections considerably, laying the foundation of the museum's present importance. The post also gave him wide scope as an architect: he made additions to the building, a medieval Carthusian monastery, in the Romanesque and Gothic Revival styles, and moved parts of the Augustinian monastery in Nuremberg to the museum site. In so doing, he showed complete mastery of the historical material, creating an ensemble with a historical atmosphere well adapted to the character of the city.

Essen Minster, *c.* 850–*c.* 1327, view from the nave towards the polygonal arcade with inset arches that separates it from the western parts of the building

In addition to his museum work, he restored (from 1878) the Frauenkirche in Nuremberg; created new interior furnishings (1879) for Konstanz Cathedral, the Gereonskirche (1883–91) in Cologne and Brunswick Cathedral (1881); designed the mosaic floors (1880–99) at Cologne Cathedral; and extended (1884–9) the Nuremberg Rathaus. All this was undertaken with a wide knowledge of medieval architecture and decoration, applied in a mature historicist manner.

WRITINGS

Norddeutschlands Backsteinbau im Mittelalter (Karlsruhe, 1855)
Die innere Ausschmückung der Kirche Gross-St.-Martin in Köln (Cologne, 1866)
Die mittelalterlichen Kunstdenkmale der Stadt Krakau (Graz, 1866)
Katalog der im Germanischen Museum befindlichen Bautheile und Baumaterialien aus älterer Zeit (Nuremberg, 1868)
Quellen zur Geschichte der Feuerwaffen (Leipzig, 1872–7)
Der Bildschmuck der Liebfrauenkirche zu Nürnberg (Nuremberg, 1881)
Die Sicherstellung der Zukunst des Germanischen Museums (Nuremberg, 1884)
Die romanische und die gotische Baukunst, Handbuch der Architektur, 2 vols (Darmstadt, 1889, 1893)

BIBLIOGRAPHY

ADB; *NDB*; Thieme–Becker
Obituary, *Anz. Ger. Nmus.* (1892), pp. 69–78
G. von Kress: 'Erinnerungen an Geheimrat August von Essenwein', *Mitt. Ver. Gesch. Stadt Nürnberg*, xv (1902), pp. 133–67
J. Bahns: 'Die Museumsbauten von der Übernahme der Kartause im Jahre 1857 bis gegen 1910', *Das Germanische Nationalmuseum Nürnberg, 1852–1977*, ed. B. Deneke and R. Kahsnitz (Berlin, 1978), pp. 357–469
K. Holzamer: *August Essenwein, 1831–1892: Architekt und Museumsmann, seine Zeichnungen und Entwürfe in Nürnberg* (diss., U. Regensburg, 1985)

JÖRN BAHNS

Essex, Earl of. *See* CROMWELL, THOMAS.

Essex, 2nd Earl of. *See* DEVEREUX, ROBERT.

Essex, James (*b* Cambridge, *bapt* 25 Aug 1722; *d* Cambridge, 14 Sept 1784). English architect. He was an enthusiastic antiquary as well as a reliable architect; he built in both the classical style of the mid-18th century and the Gothic. He was educated at the grammar school in the shadow of King's College Chapel; at 18 years old he was already drawing ancient Cambridge buildings, including the castle and Barnwell 'leper chapel'. On leaving school he joined the family business, which undertook general building work and joinery; when his father died in 1749 Essex took sole control. He received a more academic architectural training from James Burrough (1691–1764), the Caius College don and the city's leading amateur architect, and soon he became Burrough's chief assistant and collaborator. In 1753 he married the daughter of a Cambridge bookseller, and in 1756 he was commissioned to build an eleven-bay range along the river front of Queens' College. Only the south-west pavilion (the present Essex building) was constructed, but it established his reputation as a designer of convenient and well-lit college rooms. During the same period Essex reconstructed the decayed Jacobean ranges of Neville's Court in Trinity College. He retained the existing structure but modernized it by making the attic into a proper second floor and removing strapwork ornament. His major classical work (his last in association with Burrough) was the new chapel and domed ante-chapel for Clare College in 1764–9. Although both woodwork and plasterwork are restrained

they are of the highest quality, and he continued to restore or rebuild college buildings in Cambridge in the same manner for the rest of his life.

Essex became the acknowledged authority on architectural matters in and around Cambridge, and acquired a reputation as both a building surveyor and an author and expert on Gothic; this was to bring him commissions from further afield. From 1757 he acted as surveyor for a major restoration of Ely Cathedral in the same county. When the choir was relocated at the extreme east end, Essex designed a new reredos and organ screen. For King's College Chapel, Cambridge, he installed woodwork at the east end in an authentic Gothic style, which had been accepted in preference to schemes by James Adam. From 1762 to 1765 he designed new furnishings for Lincoln Cathedral as well as alterations to the fabric, including the cresting on its central tower and the stone screen across the west end of the nave.

In 1772 Essex became a member of the Society of Antiquaries, and its secretary Richard Gough encouraged his archaeological research on Crowland Abbey (Lincs) and elsewhere. His circle of fellow antiquarians in the Cambridge area included William Cole, who had retired to Milton Lodge (Cambs), altered for him (1768–9) by Essex, the poet Thomas Gray and his friend William Mason, the amateur artist Michael Tyson (1740–80) and James Bentham, minor canon and historian of Ely Cathedral. Through Cole, Essex was introduced to Horace Walpole, and in 1776 he added several of the later and more faithfully medieval embellishments to Walpole's home and garden at Strawberry Hill, Twickenham. Essex's interest in Gothic had led him to take advantage of a restoration of King's College Chapel to make accurate measured drawings of the building, which he planned to have engraved and published. This project, though never abandoned, was never published, and gradually it was overshadowed by his more ambitious plan to write a history of Gothic architecture. At first Essex hoped to find collaborators for this scheme, with Walpole or Cole and Tyson contributing sections on the general history of medieval architecture and society while he dealt with the technical aspects of building, but it never came to fruition. However, Essex continued to assemble materials and to make drafts until the end of his life.

In spite of his professional reputation and financial success (Essex amassed property worth over £15,000), his last years were overshadowed by ill-health and disillusionment. Yet he was active to the last: he promoted a scheme to improve Fenland navigation and in 1782–4 rebuilt the Cambridge Guildhall (destr.).

UNPUBLISHED SOURCES

London, BL, Add. MS. 6771–2 [*History of Gothic Architecture in England*]

WRITINGS

W. M. Fawcett, ed.: *Journal of a Tour through Part of Flanders and France*, (Cambridge, 1888)

BIBLIOGRAPHY

R. Willis and J. W. Clark: *The Architectural History of the University of Cambridge*, 3 vols (Cambridge, 1886)
W. M. Palmer: *William Cole of Milton* (Cambridge, 1935)
D. R. Stewart: 'James Essex', *Archit. Rev.* [London], cviii (1950), pp. 317–21
T. H. Cocke: 'James Essex, Cathedral Restorer', *Archit. Hist.*, xviii (1975), pp. 12–21

Y. Jerrold: *A Study of James Essex of Cambridge, Architect and Antiquarian* (diss., U. Cambridge, 1977)

A. Doig: 'James Adam, James Essex and an Altarpiece for King's College Chapel, Cambridge', *Archit. Hist.*, xxi (1978), pp. 79–82

T. H. Cocke: 'James Essex, 1722–1784', *The Architectural Outsiders*, ed. R. Brown (London, 1985), pp. 98–113

THOMAS COCKE

Essor, L'. Belgian exhibiting society (1876–91), originally founded as the Cercle d'Elèves et anciens Elèves des Académies des Beaux-Arts. A group consisting of Emile Hoeterickx (1858–1923), Julien Dillens, Amédée Ernest Lynen (1852–1938) and 17 other artists adopted the name L'Essor in November 1879 to avoid the academic associations of its previous title. Organized like the official Salon, with numerous rules enforced by a president and a 20-member governing committee, which also acted as a jury, the society sponsored 15 exhibitions between 1876 and 1891, drawing inspiration and members from the previous Société Libre des Beaux-Arts and the coexisting La Chrysalide. Its motto 'Unique art, unique life' stressed originality and the link between art and life; as a society it was anti-academic yet eclectic, admitting conservative artists. It was liberal enough to produce an immediate breakout of conservative members, who formed their own group, Union des Arts, in 1876. Dedicated to selling numerous works of art to large audiences, L'Essor ran a successful lottery and a raffle of art works. This encouraged artists to please the public; L'Essor's receptivity to both conservative and avant-garde artists accounts for its longevity. King Leopold II's purchase of paintings in 1881 and 1882 marked the end of the official ostracism of previous independent exhibition groups and assured public success. Open at first to young artists like James Ensor, its rejection in 1882 of his Impressionist style in favour of Realism led to a division in the group. The inclusion of paintings such as *Psyche* (1882; Tournai, Mus. B.-A.) by Léon Herbo (1850–1907) caused more advanced artists like Frantz Charlet (1862–1928), Théo Van Rysselberghe and Willy Schloboch (1864–1951) to join with 17 other artists including Ensor, Fernand Khnopff, Georges Lemmen and Guillaume Vogels in withdrawing and founding Les XX. Conservative artists like Lynen and Léon Frédéric (1856–1940) remained with L'Essor, which became a foil to the more liberal faction in Les XX. While L'Essor lost many of its most adventurous members to Les XX, it also influenced it, providing a pool of members, including Jan Toorop and Henry De Groux, and a model for the notion of accompanying art exhibitions with musical events and lectures.

BIBLIOGRAPHY

S. M. Canning: *A History and Critical Review of the Salons of 'Les Vingt', 1884–1893* (diss., Philadelphia, U. PA, 1980), pp. 20, 462, 484

J. Block: *Les XX and Belgian Avant-gardism, 1868–1894* (Ann Arbor, 1984), pp. 5–8, 13–15, 18–20, 43, 142–52

JULIUS KAPLAN

Este (i). Italian dynasty of rulers, patrons and collectors (see fig.). Azzo I d'Este was Lord of Ferrara from 1209 to 1212, but the family's power in the city became firmly established only in 1242, when Azzo II d'Este, 2nd Marchese of Ferrara (*reg* 1215–22; 1240–64), defeated the Ghibelline faction with Venetian help. Modena came under Este control in 1288 and (2) Niccolò III d'Este

added Reggio and other cities to the family's territories, (4) Borso d'Este becoming 1st Duke of Ferrara, Modena and Reggio. FERRARA was governed by the Este until 1598, when it was annexed by the papacy, while both MODENA and Reggio remained under Este control until 1796, when the family was deposed by the French. The Este court at Ferrara was one of the most notable in northern Italy, commissioning works from and attracting numerous important artists, musicians and writers. Especially outstanding among the Este as patrons and collectors were (6) Isabella d'Este, (8) Alfonso I d'Este and (16) Francesco I d'Este.

BIBLIOGRAPHY

L. Chiappini: *Gli Estensi* (Milan, 1967)

(1) Niccolò II d'Este, 10th Marchese of Ferrara (*b* Ferrara, 1331; *reg* 1361–88; *d* Ferrara, 1388). He was the son of Marchese Obizzo III d'Este (*d* 1352) and Lippa di Jacopo Ariosti of Bologna. He was known as 'lo Zoppo' (the Lame) because of his infirmity caused by gout. In 1362 he married Verde della Scala, sister of Cangrande II della Scala of Verona. Niccolò's court attracted poets and humanists; Francesco Petrarch was a guest in 1370 and Benvenuto da Imola, a friend of Petrarch and pupil of Boccaccio, dedicated his commentary on Dante's *Divine Comedy* to Niccolò. Niccolò's main undertaking as a patron was to improve Ferrara's civic centre and defences. He employed, in 1385, the military architect BARTOLINO DA NOVARA to construct a fortified castle within the city, borrowing 25,000 ducats from his neighbour and ally Francesco I Gonzaga of Mantua to finance the project. The Castello di S Michele, now known as the Castello Vecchio or Estense (*see* FERRARA, fig. 1), although still ostensibly a medieval fortification, was the first great monument of Renaissance architecture in Ferrara. Niccolò's other projects included paving the main piazza and streets, building a new customs house, erecting a bell tower for the Palazzo della Ragione and fortifying the suburbs, thus transforming Ferrara into an attractive urban centre. The eminent Paduan humanist Giovanni Conversino da Ravenna praised Niccolò's civic improvements in his *Dragmalogia de eligibili vitae genere* (Paris, Bib. N., MS. Lat. 6494; Venice, Fond. Querini–Stampalia, MS. IX, II), which was written in 1405 after Niccolò's death.

BIBLIOGRAPHY

L. Chiappini: *Gli Estensi* (Milan, 1967), pp. 68–73

W. L. Gundersheimer: *Ferrara: The Style of a Renaissance Despotism* (Princeton, 1973)

J. E. Law: 'Popular Unrest in Ferrara in 1385', *Il rinascimento a Ferrara e i suoi orizzonti europei*, ed. J. Salmons and W. Moretti (Cardiff and Ravenna, 1984), pp. 41–60

□

(2) Niccolò III d'Este, 12th Marchese of Ferrara (*b* Ferrara, 1383; *reg* 1393–1441; *d* Milan, 26 Dec 1441). Nephew of (1) Niccolò II d'Este. He became ruler before his tenth birthday, and over the years he added Modena, Rovigo, Reggio and other smaller cities to the Este territorial holdings. Politically astute and praised for his commitment to learning, he could also be cruel and implacable. He made distant pilgrimages to Jerusalem, Vienne (south of Lyon) and Loreto; when at SS Annunziata in Florence, he gave (1435) a large wax relief that represented him on horseback. In 1429 he invited the

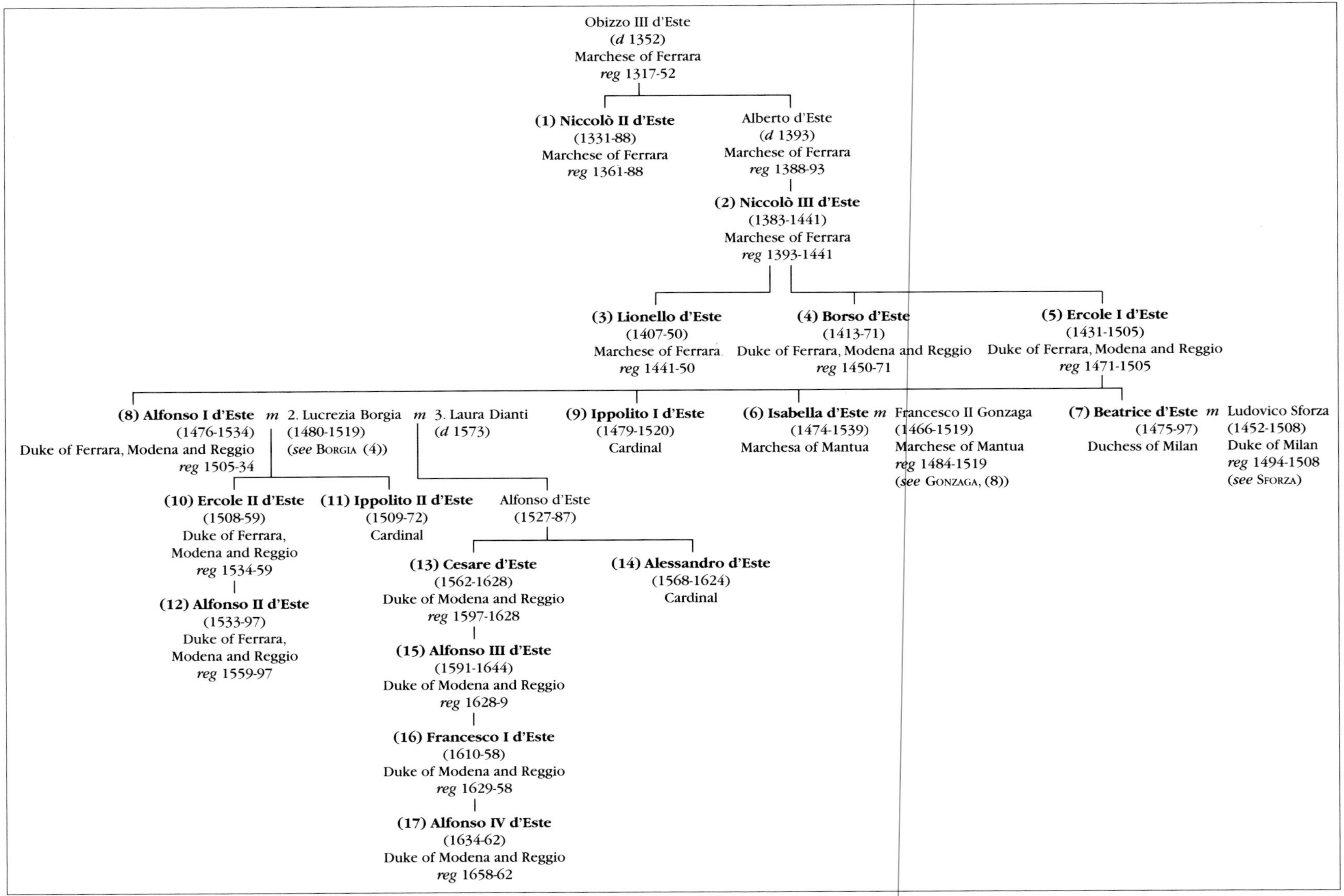

Obizzo III d'Este
(d 1352)
Marchese of Ferrara
reg 1317-52

(1) Niccolò II d'Este
(1331-88)
Marchese of Ferrara
reg 1361-88

Alberto d'Este
(d 1393)
Marchese of Ferrara
reg 1388-93

(2) Niccolò III d'Este
(1383-1441)
Marchese of Ferrara
reg 1393-1441

(3) Lionello d'Este
(1407-50)
Marchese of Ferrara
reg 1441-50

(4) Borso d'Este
(1413-71)
Duke of Ferrara, Modena and Reggio
reg 1450-71

(5) Ercole I d'Este
(1431-1505)
Duke of Ferrara, Modena and Reggio
reg 1471-1505

(6) Isabella d'Este m Francesco II Gonzaga
(1474-1539)   (1466-1519)
Marchesa of Mantua   Marchese of Mantua
reg 1484-1519
(see GONZAGA, (8))

(7) Beatrice d'Este m Ludovico Sforza
(1475-97)   (1452-1508)
Duchess of Milan   Duke of Milan
reg 1494-1508
(see SFORZA)

(8) Alfonso I d'Este m 2. Lucrezia Borgia   m 3. Laura Dianti
(1476-1534)   (1480-1519)   (d 1573)
Duke of Ferrara, Modena and Reggio (see BORGIA, (4))
reg 1505-34

(9) Ippolito I d'Este
(1479-1520)
Cardinal

(10) Ercole II d'Este
(1508-59)
Duke of Ferrara,
Modena and Reggio
reg 1534-59

(11) Ippolito II d'Este
(1509-72)
Cardinal

Alfonso d'Este
(1527-87)

(13) Cesare d'Este
(1562-1628)
Duke of Modena and Reggio
reg 1597-1628

(14) Alessandro d'Este
(1568-1624)
Cardinal

(12) Alfonso II d'Este
(1533-97)
Duke of Ferrara,
Modena and Reggio
reg 1559-97

(15) Alfonso III d'Este
(1591-1644)
Duke of Modena and Reggio
reg 1628-9

(16) Francesco I d'Este
(1610-58)
Duke of Modena and Reggio
reg 1629-58

(17) Alfonso IV d'Este
(1634-62)
Duke of Modena and Reggio
reg 1658-62

Family tree of the Este dynasty of rulers, patrons and collectors

humanist Guarino da Verona to teach at the University of Ferrara, bringing fame to that institution.

Niccolò ordered the completion of the Castello Estense in Ferrara, initiated the first phase (1412) of the cathedral's campanile, commissioned the Este rural retreat of Belriguardo (1435; largely destr.), *c.* 15 km north-east of Ferrara, frescoes and amenities at the Palazzo Schifanoia, Ferrara, and continued construction of the villa of Belfiore (begun by Alberto d'Este; destr.), Ferrara, as well as adding to it the Dominican church of S Maria degli Angeli (destr.). For the latter he ordered a terracotta pala (1440–41) for the main altar from Michele da Firenze, while in the narthex was his equestrian statue made of polychromed cloth and wax (destr. 1484). Niccolò III had a sizeable library, including illuminated manuscripts. In 1400 Jacopo di Cassola (*fl* 1400–30) produced for him a copy of Caesar's *De bello Galico* (Modena, Bib. Estense, MS. Lat. 421) with miniatures by Paduan illuminators. A more important commission was the Bible (1434; Rome, Vatican, Bib. Apostolica, MS. Barb. Lat. 613) with decoration by Belbello da Pavia. Amadio da Milano (*fl* 1437–83) and Sperandio were Niccolò's goldsmiths and medallists, and a medal of Niccolò is attributed to the former (e.g. *c.* 1432; Ferrara, Mus. Civ. A. Ant. Pal. Schifanoia; Modena, Gal. & Mus. Estense). From 1419 Giacomo da Sancino (Sagramoro; *d* 1456/7) was the painter most closely connected to Niccolò's court. When the Marchese hosted the abortive Council of Churches in 1438, Pisanello was on hand executing portraits of his children, but when the artist competed (1441) with Jacopo Bellini to portray his elder son (3) Lionello d'Este, Niccolò III favoured Bellini (*see* (3) below).

Niccolò also sought northern European art; an altarpiece of the *Passion*, made in Nottingham alabaster (Ferrara, Mus. Civ. A. Ant. Pal. Schifanoia) is thought to originate from an Estean oratory of his time. In 1433–41 two Brabantine sculptors, Arrigo [Henri] di Brabante and Guillaume di Brabante (both *fl* 1431–41), were commissioned to carve stone altarpieces in S Francesco, Ferrara, and elaborate ornaments for the cathedral sacristy. An alabaster head of *John the Baptist* (*c.* 1435; Modena, Gal. & Mus. Estense) is by a Brabantine sculptor, the Master of the Rimini Crucifixion (*fl* 1430–42). JEAN FOUQUET executed a portrait of Niccolò's jester, *Gonella* (*c.* 1440; Vienna, Ksthist. Mus.), and from 1436 the Flemish weavers Jacomo de Flandria de Angelo and Pietro di Andrea di Fiandra (both *fl* 1436–41) were employed by Niccolò III.

BIBLIOGRAPHY
A. Venturi: 'I primordi del rinascimento artistico a Ferrara', *Riv. Stor. It.*, i (1884), pp. 591–631
O. Pächt: 'Die Autorschaft des Gonella-Bildnisses', *Jb. Ksthist. Samml. Wien*, lxx (1974), pp. 39–88
N. Gramaccini: 'Wie Jacopo Bellini Pisanello besiegte: Der Ferrareser Wettbewerb von 1441', *Idea: Jb. Hamburg Ksthalle*, i (1982), pp. 27–31
P. de Winter: *Renaissance Sculpture in Ferrara* (Ferrara, 1995)

PATRICK M. DE WINTER

(3) Lionello d'Este, 13th Marchese of Ferrara (*b* Ferrara, 21 Sept 1407; *reg* 1441–50; *d* Ferrara, 1 Oct 1450). Son of (2) Niccolò III d'Este. During his brief rule he used the revenue from family properties and taxes to give lavish support to art and scholarship. His interest, which had developed under the influence of the humanist

Guarino da Verona, who came to Ferrara in 1429, and the condottiere Braccio Fortebraccio (1368–1424), was genuine and discriminating. He established Ferrara as a virtually unrivalled centre for humanism. A reliable guide to cultural life in Ferrara at this time is given in the *De politia litteraria* of ANGELO DECEMBRIO (extant MS. 1462), a dialogue on scholarly, literary and artistic topics, set in Lionello's court. The Marchese appears from this to have favoured poetry and drama above the other arts.

Lionello's portrait was painted in 1441 by Pisanello (Bergamo, Accad. Carrara B.A.) and Jacopo Bellini (possibly the *Virgin and Child with Lionello d'Este*; Paris, Louvre), and in 1449 by Piero della Francesca and Andrea Mantegna (both untraced). Pisanello painted a view of the country villa of Belriguardo (destr.), as well as producing various medals, including five small pieces (?1443) and a superb example to commemorate Lionello's marriage in 1444 (*see* MEDAL, fig. 1). The villa of Belfiore (destr.) was frescoed with a decorative cycle of the *Muses* by Angelo del Macagnino and enriched with intarsie by Cristoforo Canozzi da Lendinara (*fl* 1454–91), Lorenzo Canozzi da Lendinara (*fl* 1434–77) and Arduino da Baisio (*fl* 1406–*c.* 1454). A triptych of the *Lamentation* (untraced) by Rogier van der Weyden (*see* WEYDEN, VAN DER, (1)) is recorded there in 1449. Alberti, held in high esteem by Lionello, was asked to judge the bronze equestrian monument to *Niccolò III d'Este* (1444; destr. 1796) by Antonio di Cristoforo (a pupil of Donatello) and NICCOLÒ BARONCELLI. Alberti also advised on the designs for the pedestal of the Arco del Cavallo and the campanile of Ferrara Cathedral. Lionello continued his father's policy of improving and extending fortifications within the Este territory, and furthered Niccolò's projects for the church and villa at Belfiore and the villas at Cappara, Migliaro and Belriguardo.

BIBLIOGRAPHY
G. Pardi: *Lionello d'Este* (Bologna, 1904)
G. Bertoni: *Guarino da Verona fra letterati e cortigiani a Ferrara, 1429–60* (Geneva, 1921)
M. Baxandall: 'A Dialogue on Art from the Court of Leonello d'Este: Angelo Decembrio's *De politia litteraria* pars LXVIII', *J. Warb. & Court. Inst.*, xxvi (1963), pp. 304–26
W. L. Gundersheimer: *Ferrara: The Style of a Renaissance Despotism* (Princeton, 1973), pp. 92–126, 229–71

(4) Borso d'Este, 1st Duke of Ferrara, Modena and Reggio (*b* Ferrara, 1413; *reg* 1450–71; *d* Ferrara, 20 Aug 1471). Son of (2) Niccolò III d'Este. He held many important mercenary military commands from 1430 to 1450. His art partronage was strategic, pragmatic, centralizing and intimate. Unlike his brother (3) Lionello d'Este, he had only a rudimentary education and little empathy with the thought and literature of the ancient world. His main interest was the development of the Ferrarese state, and his control of the terms in which he wished to be seen by contemporaries and by posterity was absolute. Artists and scholars to him were functionaries, concerned with propaganda and entertainment, undeserving of special consideration, and arts and letters were tools of propaganda, which, shrewdly manipulated, would produce his image as a powerful, just, pious and magnanimous ruler. Borso returned to Ferrara in 1445 to assist Lionello in the administration of the Este territories. In 1452 he was invested as Duke of Modena and Reggio by the Holy

Roman Emperor, Frederick III. The vital difference between Borso and his brother as patrons was revealed at this point. On becoming Marchese, Lionello's first act had been to reform the University of Ferrara; Borso's was to replace the coinage. Thus his presence was seen and felt intimately throughout Ferrarese territory.

The humanists Baptista Guarini (1458–1505), son of Guarino da Verona, and Ludovico Carbone (1435–82) received Borso's support. Their literary style—articulate, eloquent and unoriginal—suited him. Baptista was equally important as a diplomat. Carbone recorded court life in his orations and verse; his translation of Sallust's *Catilinarian* reveals an interest in Republican Roman history and indicates the important role of the vernacular at court. Borso knew no Latin; unlike Lionello, he did not attempt to write sonnets or give orations in Latin. Books were valuable as enhancers of his image. The BIBLE OF BORSO D'ESTE (Modena, Bib. Estense, MS. V.G. 12–13, lat. 422–3) required eight years to complete and ensured work for illuminators and miniaturists. Yet by 1468 the number of books held in Borso's library had declined to 148 compared with the 276 possessed during the reign of Niccolò III.

Borso's desire for flattery gave rise to an intensification of antiquarian researches on Ferrara and the Este territories. Pellegrino Prisciani (1435–1518), humanist, astrologer, antiquarian and historian, was engaged on this and skilfully combined courtly diplomacy with a thorough approach to the subject-matter. It was probably Prisciani who devised the programme for the frescoes of the Palazzo Schifanoia, Ferrara. In this complex work, painted by Cosimo Tura, Francesco del Cossa, Antonio Cicognara and Baldassare d'Este, Borso was portrayed as dispensing sound justice in the presence of the gods and the people. A bronze statue of *Borso d'Este* enthroned (destr. 1796) was completed by Giovanni Baroncelli in 1453–4 and stood outside the Palazzo della Ragione, Ferrara.

In January 1471 Borso attempted to build an artificial mountain at Monte Santo, an unpopular and futile project. On 14 August 1471 he was invested as Duke of Ferrara by Pope Paul II, a mere six days before his death and characteristically magnificent funeral.

BIBLIOGRAPHY
G. Pardi: 'Borso d'Este, Duca di Ferrara', *Stud. Stor.*, xv–xvi (1906–7)
W. L. Gundersheimer: *Ferrara: The Style of a Renaissance Despotism* (Princeton, 1973), pp. 127–72, 229–71

(5) Ercole I d'Este, Marchese of Este, 2nd Duke of Ferrara, Modena and Reggio (*b* Ferrara, 26 Oct 1431; *reg* 1471–1505; *d* Ferrara, 25 Jan 1505). Son of (2) Niccolò III d'Este. From 1445 to 1463 he served as Lieutenant-General under three successive rulers of Naples: Alfonso, Ferdinand and John of Anjou. Borso d'Este recalled him to Ferrara to assist in governing the Este territories and made him ruler of Modena. He was a shrewd and effective statesman, and his experience of the Neapolitan court had influenced his vision of his role and power. He was also compelled by virtue of his position to maintain a grand public image. To this end he held lavish parties and ceremonies and was a generous patron—of the theatre, of literature, music (Josquin Desprez wrote two masses for him), and of the visual arts. His leading court painter from 1486 was ERCOLE DE' ROBERTI, who received a generous salary and considerable encouragement from the Duke,

who may have taken an active part in planning the iconography of the decorations for the Sala di Psyche, Palazzo di Belriguardo (destr.), which Ercole painted in the 1490s (Gundersheimer, 1976).

A pious man, Duke Ercole encouraged the illumination of devotional books and initiated a vast amount of church building and redecoration, most of which has not survived. Of equal importance was the Herculean Addition, the extension of Ferrara (see FERRARA, §1) carried out under his patronage in the 1490s. Biagio Rossetti, who also designed the churches of S Francesco (1494–1515) and S Maria in Vado (1495–6), was the architect. His best-known work is the Palazzo dei Diamanti, Ferrara (begun 1493; remodelled 1565; see ROSSETTI, BIAGIO, fig. 1).

There are portraits of Ercole I d'Este on three medals struck by Baldassare d'Este in 1472 and on medals (1473) by Sperandio, who also made two marble relief portrait busts (c. 1475; one Paris, Louvre). Dosso Dossi's painted portrait (Modena, Gal. & Mus. Estense) conveys the image of majesty that Ercole desired.

BIBLIOGRAPHY
E. G. Gardner: *Dukes and Poets in Ferrara* (London, 1904)
W. L. Gundersheimer, ed.: *Art and Life at the Court of Ercole d'Este* (Geneva, 1972)
W. L. Gundersheimer: *Ferrara: The Style of a Renaissance Despotism* (Princeton, 1973), pp. 173–271
——: 'The Patronage of Ercole I d'Este', *J. Med. & Ren. Stud.*, xi (1976), pp. 1–18

GORDON MARSHALL BEAMISH

(6) Isabella d'Este, Marchesa of Mantua (*b* Ferrara, 18 May 1474; *d* Mantua, 13 Feb 1539). Daughter of (5) Ercole I d'Este. She was brought up in the cultivated atmosphere of her parents' court at Ferrara, where she studied with tutors including the humanist scholars Giovanni Battista Guarino and Mario Equicola. Her intelligence was particularly noted by the envoys sent to assess her by Francesco II Gonzaga, Marchese of Mantua (see GONZAGA, (8)), whom she married in 1490, when she was 16. Her private quarters in Mantua were in the tower of the Castello di S Giorgio, part of the complex of buildings which make up the Ducal Palace. The apartment included her first STUDIOLO and the cave-like *grotta* beneath, which housed her collection of antiquities. Her fame as a patron is due to the decorations she commissioned for her *studiolo*, a set of paintings of classical and allegorical subjects, rather than the religious works associated with other female patrons. She commissioned the first picture from a painter particularly sympathetic to classical subjects, her husband's court artist, Andrea Mantegna, who executed the great *Parnassus* (begun 1495/6, completed 1497; Paris, Louvre) for her. Mantegna's second painting for the *studiolo*, *Pallas Expelling the Vices from the Garden of Virtue* (c. 1499–1502; Paris, Louvre; see ALLEGORY, fig. 4), was only completed several years later (see MANTEGNA, ANDREA, §I, 2(ii)). In the interim, perhaps because of Mantegna's delays, she decided to seek works from the best painters in Italy. Leonardo da Vinci refused, but he did draw her portrait (Paris, Louvre; see fig.) when he visited Mantua in 1499. Giovanni Lorenzo Bellini failed to produce the requested work, objecting to the complex literary programmes she devised with the help of the Mantuan poet Paride Ceresara. Negotiations with Perugino in Florence continued over a period of ten

Isabella d'Este by Leonardo da Vinci, black and red chalk, pastel highlights, 630×460 mm, 1499 (Paris, Musée du Louvre)

years, and more than 70 of the letters survive (Mantua, Archv Stato) as well as a contract for the work (Florence, Archv Stato). Her instructions to him included not only a detailed programme for the picture but also a drawing and an admonition not to add anything of his own invention. The lack of narrative clarity in the painting Perugino finally produced, the *Battle between Love and Chastity* (1503–5; Paris, Louvre; *see* ICONOGRAPHIC PROGRAMMES, fig. 1), may reflect its difficult gestation. By about 1504, Isabella seems to have begun to treat the *studiolo* paintings as a frieze on the theme of virtue and vice, through which her own virtue could be emphasized by association. She turned to a Ferrarese painter, Lorenzo Costa (i), who executed the *Triumph of Poetry* or *Coronation of a Lady* (1505; Paris, Louvre), in which the central figure is probably Isabella. Costa was appointed court painter at Mantua after the death of Mantegna in 1506 and his second work for her, the *Comus* or *Triumph of Music* (Paris, Louvre), was produced only in 1510–11, completing the decoration of the first *studiolo*.

In 1522, a few years after the death of her husband, Isabella moved to the Corte Vecchia of the Palazzo Ducale. Her new quarters included a walled garden and a second *grotta* and *studiolo* with space for an additional two pictures. The new Marchese, her son Federico II Gonzaga (*see* GONZAGA, (9)), preferred works of an overtly erotic character, particularly those of Titian and Correggio, and his taste may have influenced his mother's. Titian painted a flagrantly flattering portrait of Isabella in 1529 (Vienna, Ksthist. Mus.), and about this time she commissioned

Correggio to execute the two additional paintings for the second *studiolo*. The playful sensuality of Correggio's pictures, the *Allegory of Vice* and *Allegory of Virtue* (both *c.* 1531; Paris, Louvre; *see* CORREGGIO, §1(iv)), is a curious contrast to the moralizing tone of the earlier *studiolo* paintings. The decorations of the second *studiolo* included a marble doorway (*c.* 1523) by Tullio Lombardo, marquetry panelling (Mantua, Mus. Pal. Ducale) and cabinets housing her library of over 200 volumes.

Isabella's other abiding passion, her collection of antique and classical art, is virtually without precedent for a woman of her rank. The inventory (Mantua, Archv Stato, Archv Gonzaga, b. 400) of her second *grotta* and other rooms made in 1542, three years after her death, lists 1620 items, mainly coins and medals but also 72 vessels and 46 engraved gems. She built her collection with the help of agents throughout Italy and expert advisers, including Mantegna, Jacopo Sansovino and Gian Cristoforo Romano. Romano, who executed her gold portrait medal (Vienna, Ksthist. Mus.; for illustration *see* GIAN CRISTO-FORO ROMANO), probably designed the elaborate marble doorframe in her second *grotta*. One of her early acquisitions (1501) was a Hellenistic marble relief with two dancing satyrs (Mantua, Mus. Ducale). Her ambitions as a collector were restricted by lack of funds, although in 1506 she paid a significant sum for an onyx vase, traditionally identified with a cameo vase now in Brunswick (Herzog Anton Ulrich-Mus.). Also in 1506 she bargained with the dying Mantegna to obtain his treasured Roman marble bust of the *Empress Faustina*, often identified (probably incorrectly) with the bust in the Palazzo Ducale in Mantua. Other antique busts included one of *Octavian* (untraced), admired in 1572 by Gerolamo Garimberto. Many works were acquired as gifts. Cesare Borgia gave her an antique *Venus* as well as an *all'antica Cupid* by Michelangelo (untraced), which he had appropriated from her Montefeltro relations. She displayed Michelangelo's marble figure with another *Cupid* (untraced) attributed to Praxiteles, acquired through Pope Julius II. In 1515 she acquired part of the collection of antiquities of the recently deceased Galeazzo Sforza of Pesaro (*fl* 1497; *d* 1515). Her son Federico II presented her with a marble Roman relief of *Proserpina in Hades* (Mantua, Pal. Ducale) in 1524, which was given to him by Pope Adrian VI. She owned various antique bronze heads and busts and commissioned contemporary works to complement them: bronze statuettes from Antico, including the *Hercules* and *Antaeus* (Vienna, Ksthist. Mus.). The decoration of the first *grotta* included an elaborate marquetry ceiling (*in situ*) by the Mantuan brothers Antonio and Piero Mola. Isabella's collection and apartments were much visited in her lifetime and were noted in numerous 16th-century guidebooks. Her example inspired the famous *camerino* of her younger brother Alfonso I d'Este, Duke of Ferrara (*see* (8) below) and the Camera del Costo in Federico II's Palazzo di S Sebastiano. Her sons Federico II, Ercole and Ferrante (*see* GONZAGA, (10) and (11)) also became notable patrons.

BIBLIOGRAPHY

J. Cartwright: *Isabella d'Este*, 2 vols (London and New York, 1903)

M. Biachedi, ed.: *La figura e l'opera di Alessandro Luzio* (San Severino, 1957) [includes Luzio's extensive and important publications on Isabella d'Este]

E. Verheyen: *The Paintings in the Studiolo of Isabella d'Este at Mantua* (New York, 1971)

Lo Studiolo d'Isabella d'Este (exh. cat., ed. S. Béguin; Paris, Louvre, 1975)

C. M. Brown and A. Lorenzoni: 'The Grotta of Isabella d'Este', *Gaz. B.-A.*, 6th per., lxxxix (1977), pp. 155–71; xci (1978), pp. 72–82

Splendours of the Gonzaga (exh. cat., ed. D. Chambers and J. Martineau; London, V&A, 1981) [entries by C. Elam and J. Fletcher]

C. M. Brown: *La grotta di Isabella d'Este: Un simbolo di continuità dinastica per i duchi di Mantova* (Mantua, 1985)

Isabella d'Este, Fürstin und Mäzenatin der Renaissance (exh. cat., ed. S. Ferino Pagden; Vienna, Ksthist. Mus., 1994)

——: 'Isabella d'Este's Apartments in the Corte Vecchia at the Palazzo Ducale in Mantua', *The Court of Gonzaga in the Age of Andrea Mantegna, 1450–1550*, ed. R. Oresko and C. Mozzarelli, Biblioteca del cinquecento (in preparation)

CLIFFORD M. BROWN

(7) Beatrice d'Este, Duchess of Milan (*b* Naples, 29 June 1475; *d* Milan, 2 Jan 1497). Daughter of (5) Ercole I d'Este. In 1491 she married Ludovico Sforza ('il Moro'), Duke of Milan. Her forceful and resolute personality was astutely expressed through an affable approach to peers and employees, and was manifest in the splendour of her clothes and jewels and in the numerous poets and musicians of her court. Her support for the applied arts included the commissioning of superb musical instruments from Atalante Migliorotti and Lorenzo Gusnasco di Pavia. Especially noteworthy is the clavichord made by the latter in 1494. This was coveted, and eventually acquired, by (6) Isabella d'Este after Beatrice's death. As far as the fine arts are concerned, GIAN CRISTOFORO ROMANO made a marble bust of her (1490; Paris, Louvre), as strikingly objective as that he created in terracotta of *Francesco II Gonzaga* (*c.* 1498; Mantua, Pal. Ducale). Both Beatrice and Ludovico were enthusiasts for the theatre and had one built in Milan, providing employment for courtiers, writers and scenographers. After Beatrice's death, Ludovico commissioned Christoforo Solari to create a sepulchral monument in her honour. Although the monument was never finished, Solari's marble effigies of Beatrice and Ludovico have survived (for illustration *see* SOLARI (i), (5)).

BIBLIOGRAPHY

J. Cartwright: *Beatrice d'Este, Duchess of Milan, 1475–97: A Study of the Renaissance* (London, 1905/*R* Milan, 1938)

R. de la Sizeranne: *Béatrice d'Este et sa cour* (Paris, 1920; London and New York, 1924)

Le muse e il principe: Arte di corte nel rinascimento padano (exh. cat., Milan, Mus. Poldi Pezzoli, 1991)

GORDON MARSHALL BEAMISH

(8) Alfonso I d'Este, 3rd Duke of Ferrara, Modena and Reggio (*b* Ferrara, 21 July 1476; *reg* 1505–34; *d* Ferrara, 31 Oct 1534). Son of (5) Ercole I d'Este. In 1502 he married Lucrezia Borgia (*see* BORGIA, (4)) and became a ruler of notable military and diplomatic ability. His chief claim to fame as patron was his employment of the poet Lodovico Ariosto, but he also patronized some of the outstanding artists of his day. His most important artistic commissions involved the decoration of his rooms in the so-called Via Coperta, the block linking the Palazzo del Corte (now Palazzo Comunale) with the Castello Estense in Ferrara, which he enlarged. No trace of the original decoration survives *in situ*, and the precise disposition and content of the rooms, which were later known as the Camerini Dorati and the Camerini d'Alabastro, remain matters of controversy. The two Camerini d'Alabastro contained marble reliefs (*c.* 1507–15) by Antonio Lombardo, of which the largest surviving group is in St Petersburg (Hermitage). These reliefs include panels with grotesque decoration as well as large figurative compositions featuring pagan deities.

One of the Camerini d'Alabastro also contained a series of paintings of pagan subjects. The earliest of these was the *Feast of the Gods* (Washington, DC, N.G.A.), completed by Giovanni Bellini in 1514 and subsequently repainted first by Dosso Dossi and again by Titian. Also in 1514 Alfonso seems to have commissioned a *Triumph of Bacchus* from Raphael; this was never completed, nor was a second painting ordered later, a *Hunt of Meleager*. In 1516 Fra Bartolommeo was in Ferrara, and was then apparently given a commission for a *Worship of Venus*, a subject taken from the *Imagines* of Philostratos Lemnios. After his death in 1517 the commission was transferred to Titian, whose picture (Madrid, Prado; *see* TITIAN, fig. 3) was finished in 1519. A second work by Titian, *Bacchus and Ariadne* (London, N.G.; *see* TITIAN, fig. 4), based on a passage of Catullus (84–54 BC), was painted between 1520 and 1523, and a third, *Bacchanal of the Andrians* (Madrid, Prado; *see* TITIAN, fig. 5), again after Philostratos Lemnios, was finished in 1524 or 1525. The same room also contained a frieze of subjects from the *Aeneid* by Dosso Dossi (1518–22; surviving sections, Washington, DC, N.G.A.; U. Birmingham, Barber Inst.; Ottawa, N.G.), and a larger mythological composition that can no longer be identified.

Alfonso's model for this group of paintings seems to have been the ensemble of pictures by Pietro Perugino, Andrea Mantegna and others owned by his sister, (6) Isabella d'Este, in Mantua; but unlike those examples, Alfonso's pictures were without edifying content. His intention was evidently to assemble a group of masterpieces by the foremost Italian painters of the day, emulating the picture galleries of Classical antiquity. The pictures themselves seem not to have been easily accessible in the 16th century, but after their removal to Rome by Cardinal Pietro Aldobrandini in 1598, Titian's bacchanals in particular were immensely influential; there is a copy by Peter Paul Rubens (Stockholm, Nmus.) and one that has been attributed to Nicolas Poussin (Edinburgh, N.G.).

Alfonso also commissioned from Titian the *Tribute Money* (?1516; Dresden, Gemäldegal. Alte Meister), which was almost certainly displayed on the door of a coin cabinet, a portrait of himself (copy in New York, Met.), and one of his mistress *Laura de' Dianti* (*c.* 1527; Kreuzlingen, Heinz Kisters). In addition he is known to have received two other works from Raphael as gifts, the cartoons (untraced) for the *St Michael* and for the portrait of *Joanna of Aragon* (both 1518; Paris, Louvre). Alfonso also commissioned a painting from Michelangelo in 1512, shortly after having inspected the ceiling of the Sistine Chapel from the scaffolding; but this was never delivered. Four years earlier he had acquired the bronze head of *Julius II* (untraced), the only part of Michelangelo's statue of the Pope in Bologna to have been preserved. Alfonso also obtained the bronze used for the rest of the figure, from which he made a large cannon. Besides seeking works by artists living outside Ferrara, Alfonso employed Dosso Dossi and Battista Dossi on a regular basis, though little of their work for him can be identified; the most important examples are some ceiling panels from the Camerini Dorati (Modena, Gal. & Mus. Estense, and elsewhere). Another artist in his service was the decorative painter Tommaso Sellari (1470–1545). A complete account of Alfonso's energetic and informed artistic patronage cannot be provided, because of the dispersal of the d'Este collection and the incomplete preservation of his archive.

BIBLIOGRAPHY

G. Vasari: *Vite* (1550, rev. 2/1568); ed. G. Milanesi (1878–85), vii, pp. 172, 194–5, 199–202
A. Luzio: 'Federico Gonzaga ostaggio di Giulio II', *Archv Soc. Romana Stor. Patria*, ix (1886), pp. 540–41
L. Venturi: 'Saggio sulle opere d'arte italiana a Pietroburgo: II—La scultura', *L'Arte*, xv (1912), pp. 305–13
A. Mezzetti: *Il Dosso e Battista ferraresi* (Milan, 1965), pp. 57–64
C. Hope: 'The "Camerini d'Alabastro" of Alfonso d'Este', *Burl. Mag.*, cxiii (1971), pp. 641–50, 712–21
A. Mezzetti: *Girolamo da Ferrara detto da Carpi* (Milan, 1977), pp. 51–54
G. Cavalli-Björkman, ed.: *Bacchanals by Titian and Rubens*, Nmus. Skrser., 10 (Stockholm, 1987) [articles on the Camerini d'Alabastro, with bibliog.]
J. Shearman: 'Alfonso d'Este's Camerino', *Il se rendit en Italie: Etudes offertes à André Chastel* (Rome, 1987), pp. 209–30
D. Bull and J. Plesters: 'The Feast of the Gods': Conservation, Examination and Interpretation, Stud. Hist. A., 40 (Washington, 1990)
A. Colantuono: 'Dies Alcyoniae': The Invention of Bellini's *Feast of the Gods*, A. Bull., lxxiii (1991), pp. 237–56

CHARLES HOPE

(9) Cardinal Ippolito I d'Este (*b* Ferrara, 20 Nov 1479; *d* Ferrara, 2 Sept 1520). Son of (5) Ercole I d'Este. Destined from birth for an ecclesiastical career, he was named Archbishop of Esztergom at the age of seven through the influence of his aunt, Beatrice of Aragon, wife of King Matthias Corvinus of Hungary. In 1487 Ercole de' Roberti was paid for a painting possibly executed for Ippolito, whom he may have accompanied on a journey to Hungary soon afterwards. Ten years after being appointed archbishop, Ippolito was made apostolic legate and cardinal by Pope Alexander VI. Exchanging Esztergom for the more lucrative seat of Eger, he soon accumulated further benefices: the archbishopric of Milan (which he later renounced), and the bishoprics of Ferrara, Modena, Narbonne and Capua, while also being Abbot of Pomposa, Tellonica and S Faustino. He lived in a princely manner, and, adept in military affairs, sank part of the Venetian fleet in 1509. An epicurean and collector of antique sculpture, he protected Antonio Elia (*fl* 1502–15), a Ferrarese gem-engraver who, while living in his palace in Rome, made copies of antiques, notably the *Laokoon* (Rome, Vatican, Mus. Pio-Clementino). The Cardinal's offices were sought in the expansion of his brother Duke Alfonso I d'Este's collection of antiquities. Tommaso da Carpi (*fl* 1503–23) worked in Ippolito's villas at Ro, Codigoro and Sabioncello, and painted cases for his firearms and musical instruments. Ippolito surrounded himself with men of letters; Ludovico Ariosto wrote *Orlando furioso* while in his service but declined to follow the Cardinal to Hungary in 1517.

BIBLIOGRAPHY

A. Frizzi: *Memorie per la storia di Ferrara*, iv (Ferrara, 1848)
A. Venturi: *La Regia Galleria Estense in Modena* (Modena, 1882)
G. Gruyer: *L'Art ferrarais à l'époque des princes d'Este*, 2 vols (Paris, 1897)

(10) Ercole II d'Este, 4th Duke of Ferrara, Modena and Reggio (*b* Ferrara, 4 April 1508; *reg* 1534–59; *d* Ferrara, 5 Oct 1559). Son of (8) Alfonso I d'Este. He steered a prudent political course, strengthening relations with the papacy that had been strained as a result of the support of Calvinism by his wife Renée, the daughter of King Louis XII of France, whom he married in 1528. He also was an avid collector. Among his acquisitions were ancient reliefs (Bacchic scenes; now Modena, Gal. & Mus. Estense), antique coins and many gems, some carved by Luigi Anichini (?1500–10–after 1559). In 1536 he founded a tapestry workshop in Ferrara, employing weavers from Brussels, including Nicolas Karcher, Giovanni Karcher (*fl* 1517–62) and Jan Rost. Among sets woven (fragments Paris, Louvre) were the *Labours of Hercules* and episodes from Ovid's *Metamorphoses* after cartoons by Battista Dossi, and *White Eagles* after Camillo Filippi. Giulio Romano provided preparatory drawings, while Leonardo da Brescia gave models for panoramas of Este cities and fortresses. Ercole was also an important patron of sculpture; over 40 pieces graced the *studio di marmo* and *adorato* in the Castel Vecchio, Ferrara. In 1536 he commissioned a sculpture (untraced) from Antonio Begarelli, and in 1540 Benvenuto Cellini executed in Ferrara a medal of Ercole, with the personification of Peace on its reverse (untraced). The trenchant personality of Duchess Renée is captured in a medal (Florence, Bargello) by Pastorino Pastorini (1508–92), while Leone Leoni executed a portrait of the ruler in silver (untraced). In 1550, on ducal commission, Jacopo Sansovino began an over life-size statue of Hercules. Originally destined for the Porta Ercolea of Modena's newly built walls, Ercole subsequently had it brought to Brescello, which he intended to transform into a model city and where the statue stands in the main square. In 1552 Alessandro Vittoria sent a sketch (untraced) for a bust of the Duke, while Prospero Spani produced a relief depicting him in profile (Modena, Gal. & Mus. Estense).

Ercole also employed important painters for the decoration of his various residences. Tommaso da Carpi (*fl* 1503–23) and Garofalo executed wall paintings with heraldic subjects and battle scenes for Ercole. Tommaso's son Girolamo da Carpi became principal court painter, producing a full-length portrait of the Duke in armour, a probable portrait of the Duchess (Frankfurt am Main, Städel. Kstinst. & Städt. Gal.), and wall paintings with the 16 Este rulers of Ferrara (1544–7), the *Labours of Hercules* and other themes. He and Battista Dossi also produced canvases, notably those for the Stanze Nuove in the Via Coperta that unite the older and newer parts of the castle. Moreover, Girolamo designed the *giardino pensile* (hanging garden) above the battlements of the Castello Estense. From 1545 Lucas Cornelisz. was landscape painter for the Duke, producing views of the Este *delizie* (pleasure-houses). He was succeeded in 1554 by Guglielmo Boides, and a year later by Leonardo da Brescia (*d* 1598). By 1553 Ercole had taken 'Patience' as his personal emblem. He commissioned a Camera della Pazienza within the Castello Estense in Ferrara, arrayed with large paintings by Girolamo da Carpi and Camillo Filippi (now Dresden and Modena, Gal. & Mus. Estense) and his bust on a socle carved by Spani with an image of Patience (Modena, Gal. & Mus. Estense). Pompeo Leoni's medal of the Duke of

1554 bore the same imagery. Ercole also saw to the expansion of Ferrara's fortifications and to the upkeep of his artillery. He had in his service Annibale Borgognoni (*fl* 1537–68), who in 1556 cast a large double culverin, known as *La regina*, bearing the ducal arms (destr., recorded in line drawings by Sardi). A bronze mortar (Washington, DC, N.G.A.), on which are depicted the four ages of man, bears the Duke's arms within the collar of the French Order of St Michael, which Ercole was granted in 1554. It is probably by Antonio Gentili da Faenza, and was produced in Rome.

BIBLIOGRAPHY

Documenti inediti per servire alla storia dei musei d'Italia, Ministero della Pubblica Istruzione, Direzione generale Antichità e Belle Arti, ii (Florence, 1878)

L. Chiappini: *Gli Estensi* (Varese, 1967)

A. Mezzetti: *Girolamo da Ferrara detto da Carpi* (Ferrara, 1977)

P. de Winter: *Renaissance Sculpture in Ferrara* (Ferrara, 1995)

PATRICK M. DE WINTER

(11) Cardinal **Ippolito II d'Este** (*b* Ferrara, 25 Aug 1509; *d* Tivoli, 2 Dec 1572). Son of (8) Alfonso I d'Este. At the age of ten he was already Archbishop of Milan, his uncle, (9) Cardinal Ippolito I d'Este, having renounced the title. He later held archbishoprics in Lyon, Autun, Auch, Orléans and Morienne and was proclaimed cardinal by Pope Paul III on 5 March 1539, partly through the efforts of the French king Francis I. On several occasions Ippolito was forwarded, unsuccessfully, by the French as papal candidate. Paul IV, however, banished Ippolito from Rome in 1555 on account of his simony, and confiscated the governorship of Tivoli from him. This was restored to him on the accession of Pius IV in 1559. Ippolito's most important mission was as *legato a latere* on behalf of Pius IV in the latter's dealings with Catherine de' Medici from 1561 to 1563, at the time of religious disorders in France. His diplomatic skill and personal contacts ensured some success. In 1566 Ippolito's nephew, (12) Alfonso II d'Este, departed for Hungary to fight the Turks and entrusted the duchy of Ferrara to Ippolito.

Throughout his life, Ippolito shared the Este love of display, which revealed itself in his enthusiastic patronage of the arts, especially music and architecture: for example, he engaged Pirro Ligorio to excavate Hadrian's Villa and to build the sumptuous Villa d'Este at Tivoli (*see* TIVOLI, §§2(iv) and 3). Although Ippolito bought property at Tivoli as early as 1550 for the purpose of laying out the spectacular gardens there, it was not until his return from exile that substantial work was undertaken. Ippolito also enjoyed a fine residence at Monte Cavallo in Rome, where he amassed an almost unrivalled collection of antique sculptures, to be seen by private admirers. This palace also had fine gardens, designed by Girolamo da Carpi, whom Ippolito had summoned to Rome in 1549.

BIBLIOGRAPHY

F. Brioschi: *Villa d'Este* (Rome, 1902)

V. Pacifici: *Ippolito II d'Este*, 2 vols (Tivoli, 1920–23)

C. Marcova: 'Ippolito II, Arcivescovo di Milano', *Mem. Stor. Dioc. Milano*, xi (1959)

GORDON MARSHALL BEAMISH

(12) Alfonso II d'Este, 5th Duke of Ferrara, Modena and Reggio (*b* Ferrara, 28 Nov 1533; *reg* 1559–97; *d* Ferrara, 27 Oct 1597). Son of (10) Ercole II d'Este. Having spent the years from 1552 to 1559 at the French court, once he succeeded to the Este territories his desire to outshine the Medici made him a generous patron of the arts. His court was maintained in great splendour, renowned for virtuosic theatrical productions and for the Duke's patronage of poets (Torquato Tasso and Giovanni Battista Guarini among them), musicians and makers of musical instruments. A richly decorated harp (Modena, Gal. & Mus. Estense) was made for him in Rome in 1581 by Giovan Battista Giacomelli and subsequently inlaid in Ferrara (1587) by the Ferrarese Giulio Marescotti.

As a collector Alfonso II took a particular interest in antiquities, often buying up entire studios formed by earlier collectors in Brescia, Bologna and Parma. In 1563 Enea Vico was appointed curator of these collections, and after his death (1567) PIRRO LIGORIO, who worked in various capacities for the Duke. At the start of Alfonso's reign Leonardo da Brescia (*d* 1598) was commissioned to fresco in grisaille the inner court of the Castello Estense, Ferrara, with images of over 200 Este forebears. The project was short-lived (1559–60) but was resumed in *c.* 1577 by Ludovico Settevechi (*c.* 1520–*c.* 1590) under the direction of Ligorio, who made preparatory drawings. By this time Ferrara had suffered the earthquake of 1570 and much rebuilding, renovating and redecoration was in progress. Settevechi also assisted Sebastiano Filippi II, Alfonso's principal court painter, in decorating the Salone dei Giochi in the Castello Estense with colourful sporting scenes (*c.* 1574; *in situ*). There are various other decorative frescoes in the Castello by Filippi, all done after 1570. Another painter who worked for the court was Giuseppe Mazzuoli (il Bastarolo; *c.* 1536–89), who was commissioned by Alfonso's second wife, Barbara of Austria (*d* 1572), to paint two altarpieces.

As for Alfonso's patronage of sculpture, Prospero Spani was employed by the Duke episodically; he carved a statue of *Alfonso d'Este as Hercules* (Modena, Gal. & Mus. Estense) and also created large figures of *Hercules* and *Marco Emilio Lepito* for the façade of the Palazzo Estense in Modena (both *in situ*). Orazio Grillenzoni (*d* 1592), painter and sculptor, produced a bust for the *gran sala* of the same palazzo. A small bronze bust of *Alfonso II*, known in several casts (e.g. Modena, Gal. & Mus. Estense), portraying him in armour shortly after his accession, was probably made in Milan and not by Hubert Gerhard, to whom it has sometimes been attributed. Francesco Casella (*fl* 1585–1610) was awarded the major sculptural commissions of Alfonso's late years. He was in Ferrara by 1591, working on the ducal chapel and on the long-delayed tomb of *Barbara of Austria* in the Gesù, Ferrara. The tomb was probably designed by GIOVANNI BATTISTA ALEOTTI, who in 1575 became architect to Alfonso II, in succession to Galasso Alghisi, and helped restore the buildings of Ferrara after the earthquake of 1570. The architect ALESSANDRO BALBAS also worked for the Duke from 1574 and was notably responsible for the large tribune (1590–94) in the chapel of the Presiosissimo Sangue in the transept of S Maria in Vado.

BIBLIOGRAPHY

G. Medri: 'La scultura a Ferrara', *Atti & Mem. Deput. Ferrar. Stor. Patria*, xvii (1957) [whole issue]

Bastianino e la pittura a Ferrara nel secondo cinquecento (exh. cat., Ferrara, Pin. N., 1985)

J. Bentini and L. Spezzaferro, eds: *L'impresa di Alfonso II: Saggi e documenti sulla produzione artistica a Ferrara nel secondo cinquecento* (Bologna, 1987)
P. de Winter: *Renaissance Sculpture in Ferrara* (Ferrara, 1995)

PATRICK M. DE WINTER

(13) Cesare d'Este, 6th Duke of Modena and Reggio (*b* Ferrara, 1562; *reg* 1597–1628; *d* Modena, 11 Dec 1628). Grandson of (8) Alfonso I d'Este. In 1597 he inherited the dukedoms of Ferrara and Modena from his cousin, (12) Alfonso II d'Este; but in 1598 the papacy, on the pretext that Cesare was illegitimate, annexed Ferrara. Cesare's surrender of it was attributed by some contemporaries to piety but by most to weakness, a judgement that his apparently careless attitude towards the Este collections seems to confirm. He is chiefly remembered for allowing Cardinal Pietro Aldobrandini in 1598, and Cardinal Scipione Borghese in 1608, to acquire paintings by Titian and Dosso Dossi that had been left behind in Ferrara: Titian's *Bacchanals* paintings (London, N.G.; Washington, DC, N.G.A.; Madrid, Prado) and Dosso's *Aeneas* cycle (Ottawa, N.G.; U. Birmingham, Barber Inst.; Washington, DC, N.G.A.) and five ceiling paintings (Rome, Gal. Borghese). Cesare was not, however, indifferent to art, having in 1592 been the owner of the Palazzo dei Diamanti in Ferrara, for which paintings had been commissioned from artists including Scarsellino and the Carracci family, who painted four panels; Agostino Carracci painted *Pluto*, Annibale Carracci painted *Venus* and *Flora*, and Ludovico Carracci painted *Galatea* (all Modena, Gal. & Mus. Estense). In Modena his patronage was restricted by lack of money; he enlarged but did not rebuild his residence, the Castello di S Pietro (destr. 1634). However, from 1602 to 1606 he was the patron of Bartolomeo Schedoni, from whom he ordered portraits and decorative and devotional paintings. Schedoni's departure for Parma in 1607 left Cesare without a regular artist. From 1609 he frequently borrowed from his son-in-law, Alessandro I Pico della Mirandola, the Venetian artist Sante Peranda (1566–1638), who painted portraits, including one of *Cesare d'Este* (Mantua, Pal. Ducale).

In 1605 Cesare commissioned and eagerly awaited altarpieces by Annibale Carracci and Caravaggio in Rome; had these paintings arrived, his standing as a patron might now be rather higher than it is. Neither artist, however, completed the commission, though it has been suggested that Caravaggio's *Madonna of the Rosary* (Vienna, Ksthist. Mus.) was begun for Cesare and that the Carracci painting is the *Birth of the Virgin* (Paris, Louvre). Consequently, the best example of his taste is the chapel he had built within the Castello and decorated with Titian's *Tribute Money*, salvaged from Ferrara, Schedoni's *Holy Family* and Scarsellino's *Holy Family with SS Barbara and Carlo Borromeo*, ordered by Cesare in 1615 (all Dresden, Gemäldegal. Alte Meister).

BIBLIOGRAPHY
A. Venturi: *La Real Galleria Estense in Modena* (Modena, 1882), pp. 113–78
R. Marchiori Ascione: 'Sante Peranda alla Mirandola e a Modena', *A. Veneta*, xii (1958), p. 126–33
M. A. Novelli: *Lo Scarsellino* (Ferrara, 1964), p. 20
A. Mezzetti: *Dosso e Battista Ferraresi* (Milan, 1965), pp. 74, 99–100, 135
A. G. Lodi: *Bartolomeo Schedoni: Notizie e documenti* (Modena, 1978)
J. Southorn: *Power and Display in the Seventeenth Century: The Arts and their Patrons in Modena and Ferrara* (Cambridge, 1988), pp. 9–18

(14) Cardinal **Alessandro d'Este** (*b* Ferrara, 1568; *d* Rome, 22 May 1624). Half-brother of (13) Cesare d'Este. He was created a cardinal in 1599 and Bishop of Reggio Emilia in 1621. Though no better suited than Cesare to new responsibilities, he adapted more easily to his role, but lack of inclination as much as poverty made him at first an infrequent visitor to Rome. He joined the circle of Cardinal Scipione Borghese, whom he entertained in 1620 at the Villa d'Este at Tivoli, where repairs and alterations to the palace and gardens had been taking place over the previous 15 years; Alessandro's executants included the architect Francesco Peparelli. Alessandro was himself a draughtsman and may have been taught by Bartolomeo Passarotti, whose work he often copied. His art collection was modest by Borghese standards, certainly as regards Old Master paintings, but interesting for the broad taste in contemporary art that it revealed. Artists patronized by Alessandro included the Bolognese Lavinia Fontana (to whom he gave accommodation in Rome), Leonello Spada and Alessandro Tiarini, and in Rome, Bartolomeo Manfredi, whose *Soldier with a Glass* and *Soldier with a Flask* (both Modena, Gal. & Mus. Estense) were in his collection. He was also a patron of Guercino, whose *Four Evangelists* (*c.* 1615; Dresden, Gemäldegal. Alte Meister) he acquired. Alessandro's collection, arranged in 1624 in the rented Palazzo de Cupis in Piazza Navona, Rome, was partly dispersed on his death in that year; the remainder, including the Guercino and Manfredi paintings, was in 1625 sent to the ducal residence in Modena, where it became part of the main Este collection.

BIBLIOGRAPHY
G. Campori: *Raccolta di cataloghi ed inventarii inediti* (Modena, 1870), pp. 57–63
D. Coffin: *The Villa d'Este at Tivoli* (Princeton, 1960)
J. Southorn: *Power and Display in the Seventeenth Century: The Arts and their Patrons in Modena and Ferrara* (Cambridge, 1988), pp. 18–22

(15) Alfonso III d'Este, 7th Duke of Modena and Reggio [Padre Giovanni Battista d'Este] (*b* Ferrara, 22 Oct 1591; *reg* 1628–9; *d* Castelnuovo di Garfagnana, nr Lucca, 24 May 1644). Son of (13) Cesare d'Este. He succeeded to the dukedom in December 1628, but abdicated in July 1629. The abdication, apparently prompted by the death of his wife Isabella of Savoy (1591–1626), whom he had married in 1608, was surprising, given Alfonso's previous determination to be an exemplary ruler. On joining the Capuchin Order in 1629 he renounced his former interests in poetry, jousts, hunting and art (he was himself a draughtsman). Though as a ruler he had intended to rebuild the Castello di S Pietro (destr. 1634) of Modena, he advised his son (16) Francesco I d'Este, who succeeded him, against spending on palaces; and he gave to his second son, Obizzo (1611–44), his collection of drawings that included works by, or attributed to, Raphael, Giulio Romano and Titian. Among those attributed to Titian was a *Vision of St Gregory* (Paris, Louvre), now attributed to Nicolò dell'Abate.

However, art was not entirely dismissed from his new life. Among the devotional paintings commissioned by him for the monastery that he founded at Castelnuovo di Garfagnana was the *Virgin and Child with the Blessed Felice* by Guercino (1641; Modena, Gal. & Mus. Estense). He also commissioned a remarkable series of portraits, painted and engraved, to record the stages of his 'rebirth' and to urge observers to profit by his example: the most notable of these is the portrait of him by Matthew Lowes (*fl* 1615–35), an English pupil of Guercino (1635; Modena, Gal. & Mus. Estense; see also Bravi, pp. 54, 57, 94). Alfonso III's part in the Este patronage in Modena was small, but represents an interesting inversion of the princely patronage of his day.

BIBLIOGRAPHY

G. Campori: *Raccolta di cataloghi ed inventarii inediti* (Modena, 1870), pp. 56–7
F. Bravi: *Il Principe Frate* (Bolzano, 1972)
R. Lecchini: *Alfonso III duca di Modena e di Reggio* (Modena, 1979)
J. Southorn: *Power and Display in the Seventeenth Century: The Arts and their Patrons in Modena and Ferrara* (Cambridge, 1988), pp. 22–7

(16) Francesco I d'Este, 8th Duke of Modena and Reggio (*b* Modena, 5 Sept 1610; *reg* 1629–58; *d* Mortara, Piedmont, 14 Oct 1658). Son of (15) Alfonso III d'Este. Francesco's determination to restore the reputation of the House of Este changed the style of government and patronage in Modena. In 1638 he negotiated an alliance with Spain; in 1643–4 he joined the league of Italian princes and Venice against Pope Urban VIII. Then in 1646 he abandoned Spain in favour of France; acting as a French general in Italy, he fought against Spain until his death on campaign. His marriages to Maria Farnese in 1631, to her sister Vittoria in 1648 and to Lucrezia Barberini in 1654 strengthened his position in Italy. Patronage of art formed part of Francesco's political policy. Since funds were limited (he sometimes borrowed from Genoese bankers), his patronage was characterized by caution, but he was ready to spend lavishly when necessary. He paid the considerable sum of 3000 scudi for the marble portrait bust of himself (Modena, Gal. & Mus. Estense) commissioned in 1650 from Gianlorenzo Bernini and carved from portraits (untraced) by Giusto Suttermans and Jean Boulanger; this bust established both his image as a ruler and his name as a patron (*see* BUST, fig. 4).

Disregarding Modenese artists, Francesco borrowed the services of artists and architects from his peers, or obtained them through his agents abroad. In 1631 he borrowed Girolamo Rainaldi from his brother-in-law Odoardo Farnese, 5th Duke of Parma and Piacenza, to advise on plans for a new palace in Modena, to replace the Castello di S Pietro. In 1635 he borrowed the engineer Carlo di Castellamonte from his uncle Victor Amadeus I, Duke of Savoy, to advise him on the construction of the new fortress of Modena (destr. *c.* 1780). The new Palazzo Ducale was finally begun in 1634 by Francesco's architect, the Roman Bartolomeo Avanzini; further opinions were obtained in 1651 from Bernini, Francesco Borromini and Pietro da Cortona. Despite an often stormy relationship between patron and architect, Avanzini also built Francesco's country palace (begun 1634) at Sassuolo, near Modena. Francesco's Superintendent of Works (from 1635) was Gaspare Vigarani, who also designed the Teatro della Spelta (1654–6; destr. 1780) in Modena and scenery for Francesco's court festivals, of which the most famous was *La gara delle stagioni* of 1652, engraved by Stefano della Bella in 1652–3.

Francesco's taste for the Bolognese style of decorative painting was first shown by his patronage in Modena of Angelo Michele Colonna and Girolamo Curti, who in 1631–2 carried out decorations (destr. 1634) for the old Castello di S Pietro. Then at Sassuolo, from 1645, Francesco employed Colonna and his new partner Agostino Mitelli and their assistants Giovanni Giacomo Monti (1620–92) and Baldassare Bianchi (1614–78) to decorate the principal room, the Salone delle Guardie. Monti and Bianchi remained in his service, to paint for the court festivals and collaborate at Sassuolo (most notably in the Gallery of Bacchus) with Boulanger, since 1638 working as Francesco's reliable but underpaid staff painter.

Francesco's patronage of sculptors was stimulated by contact with Bernini: Francesco never actually met him, but corresponded with him through agents, in particular through his own brother, Cardinal Rinaldo d'Este (1617–72). With Bernini's help, Antonio Raggi was persuaded to visit Modena in 1653; there, using Bernini's sketches, he made terracotta models, which Lattanzio Maschio (*fl* 1650s–1660s) used to carve statues for Sassuolo. In 1654 Francesco ordered designs for ornamental carriage nails (untraced) from Alessandro Algardi.

Francesco's agents and his travels brought him into contact with other artists, including Diego Velázquez, who painted his portrait in 1639 (untraced; oil sketch Modena, Gal. & Mus. Estense). Salvator Rosa contributed three landscape paintings to a group ordered for Sassuolo in 1640 in Rome; they included *Landscape with Erminia* and *Harbour Scene* (both Modena, Gal. & Mus. Estense). Suttermans was frequently borrowed from Ferdinand II de' Medici, Grand Duke of Tuscany, to paint Este portraits, such as that of Alfonso (Modena, Gal. & Mus. Estense), Francesco's son and heir (*see* (17) below). Francesco developed an especially high regard for Guercino, commissioning from him an altarpiece of the *Virgin with SS John the Evangelist and Gregory the Wonderworker* (1629–30; Modena, S Vincenzo), portraits of himself and Maria Farnese (both 1632; untraced) and many subject paintings. When Guercino's brother Paolo Antonio Barbieri died in 1649, Francesco invited the painter to Sassuolo to recover.

By this time Francesco's taste was turning from patronage of painting to collecting. He admired Peter Paul Rubens, whose work he would have seen on his visits to Brussels in 1628 and to Madrid in 1638; and on a visit to Venice in 1650 he bought Rubens's *St Jerome* (Dresden, Gemäldegal. Alte Meister), probably in the shop of the painter–dealer Nicolas Régnier. He was still more interested, however, in 16th-century painting, as was Geminiano Poggi (1600–62), his assistant most concerned with artistic matters. By means of gifts, exchanges, payment by fief and sometimes forced acquisitions from churches, and with the help of agents, including the painter and picture-restorer from Parma Gabriele Balestrieri (*d* 1648), Francesco built up an impressive collection. Among his acquisitions were Albrecht Dürer's *St Jerome* (untraced) and Hans Holbein the younger's portrait of *Charles de Solier* (1534–5) and also works by Italian masters: Andrea del Sarto's *Sacrifice of Isaac* (1529); Giulio Romano's *Madonna of the Ewer* (*c.* 1525); four paintings by Veronese made for the Coccinà family, including the *Adoration of the Magi* (1570s); Parmigianino's *Madonna of Casalmaggiore* (1539–40) and several works by Correggio, including the *Madonna of St Sebastian* (1525–6) and the *Adoration of the Shepherds*

(1529–30). All of these are now in the Gemäldegalerie Alte Meister in Dresden.

In the 1650s, the arrangement of Francesco's gallery in the unfinished Palazzo Ducale in Modena inspired the physician and connoisseur Francesco Scanelli to write *Il microcosmo della pittura*, in praise of the Lombard school, as exemplified by Correggio. The book was dedicated to Francesco as an 'heroic' patron of the arts.

BIBLIOGRAPHY
F. Scanelli: *Il microcosmo della pittura* (Cesena, 1657); ed. G. Giubbini (Milan, 1966)
A. Venturi: *La Real Galleria Estense in Modena* (Modena, 1882)
E. Grandi: *Armi e nozze alla corte di Francesco I d'Este* (Alessandria, 1907)
L. Zanugg: 'Il Palazzo Ducale di Modena: Il problema della sua construzione', *Riv. Ist. Archeol. & Stor. A.*, ix (1942), pp. 212–52
R. Lightbown: 'Princely Pressures: 2. Francesco I d'Este and Correggio', *Apollo* (1963), pp. 193–9
M. Pirondini: *Giovanni Boulanger: Un pittor francese nel ducato di Modena* (Modena, 1969)
C. Gould: *The Paintings of Correggio* (London, 1976), pp. 203–7
J. Southorn: *Power and Display in the Seventeenth Century: The Arts and their Patrons in Modena and Ferrara* (Cambridge, 1988), pp. 28–71

(17) Alfonso IV d'Este, 9th Duke of Modena and Reggio (*b* Modena, Jan 1634; *reg* 1658–62; *d* Modena, 16 July 1662). Son of (16) Francesco I d'Este. Alfonso's reign was overshadowed by that of his father. From the age of 16 he had his own residence, the Casino Pentetorri, near Modena (destr. 1944), designed for him by the ducal Superintendent of Works, Gaspare Vigarani, and decorated by the court painters Jean Boulanger, Giovanni Giacomo Monti and Baldassare Bianchi. As Duke of Modena, Alfonso continued Francesco's policies, as an ally of France (having married in 1656 Laura Martinozzi, a niece of the French statesman Cardinal Jules Mazarin), and as patron and collector. He retained Monti and Bianchi as his court painters, but also employed the Modenese Francesco Stringa. Through the agency of his uncle, Cardinal Rinaldo d'Este (1617–72) in Rome, he was a patron of Gianlorenzo Bernini, who designed the *Bicchierone* fountain (1661) at the Villa d'Este, Tivoli. Alfonso collected altarpieces two of which, the *Assumption of the Virgin* and the *Alms of St Roch* (both Dresden, Gemäldegal. Alte Meister) by Annibale Carracci, he appropriated from S Rocco, Reggio Emilia. He also had a particular admiration for Veronese, no doubt stimulated by his father's acquisition (1644–5) of the four Coccinà paintings by Veronese (Dresden, Gemäldegal. Alte Meister).

BIBLIOGRAPHY
A. Venturi: *La Real Galleria Estense in Modena* (Modena, 1882), pp. 261–314
E. Feinblatt: 'A Note on Bianchi-Monti', *Burl. Mag.*, cxiv (1972), pp. 17–22
M. Canova: 'La villa ducale delle Pentetorri', *Natura e cultura urbana a Modena* (exh. cat., Modena, Musei Civ., 1983), pp. 183–215
J. Southorn: *Power and Display in the Seventeenth Century: The Arts and their Patrons in Modena and Ferrara* (Cambridge, 1988)

JANET SOUTHORN

Este (ii). Italian family of sculptors and museum officials. In 1779 Antonio d'Este (*b* Venice, 1754; *d* Rome, 13 Sept 1837) married Teresa Arrigoni in Rome. They had two sons, Giuseppe d'Este (*b* 1779) and Alessandro d'Este (*b* Rome, 10 Aug 1783; *d* Rome, 8 Dec 1826), both sculptors who also assisted their father in various tasks of museum administration in Rome. A nephew, also called Alessandro d'Este, edited and wrote an introduction to Antonio's *Memorie di Antonio Canova* (Florence, 1864).

In 1769 Antonio d'Este was studying in Venice in Giuseppe Torretti's studio, where he began a friendship with fellow-student Antonio Canova that was to be decisive for his whole career. After 1773 he settled in Rome, working until 1790 in various sculpture studios and as a restorer for the Vatican Museums. From 1787 he also assisted Canova in the management of his studio. D'Este sculpted chiefly portrait busts, including many of Canova, whose image he wanted to disperse throughout Italy (e.g. plaster bust, 1795; Rome, Pal. Cancelleria; *Canova*, 1795; Possagno, Gip. Canoviana). His most noted work is the marble stele of *Leonardo Pesaro* (1797; Rome, S Marco), which follows Canova's style. In 1805 d'Este became Director of the Museo Chiaramonti in Rome. He was made an honorary member of numerous Italian academies, including the Accademia Reale delle Belle Arti, Venice (1808), and the Accademia di S Luca, Rome (1810). In 1815 he was appointed Director of the Vatican Museums, where he had been Custodian since 1807.

Alessandro d'Este studied from an early age in the studio of Canova, who became his most important patron. From 1802 to 1805 Alessandro assisted his father and his brother with the re-ordering of the Museo Chiaramonti, Rome, of which he was appointed Vice-Director in 1805. During the period of French administration from 1809 to 1814 he was Vice-Custodian of the Imperial Museums of the Vatican. In 1813 he sculpted a series of busts of famous Italians (*Dante*, *Tasso* and others) to add to the sculpture collection in the Museo Capitolino. In 1815 he became Vice-Director of the Vatican Museums and also accompanied Canova to Paris to recover works of art that had been confiscated from the Vatican by Napoleon. He was elected to membership in the Accademia di S Luca in 1816. His last work, commissioned in 1822, was a statue of *Canova* (Rome, Gal. Accad. N. S Luca). In 1823 he married Matilde Salviucci.

DBI   BIBLIOGRAPHY
G. Pavanello: 'Antonio d'Este, amico di Canova, scultore', *Antol. B.A.*, xiv/35–8 (1990), pp. 13–22

NINA LÜBBREN

Este, Baldassare d'. *See* BALDASSARE D'ESTE.

Este, Borso d', Bible of. *See* BIBLE OF BORSO D'ESTE.

Este art. Style of prehistoric European art that flourished around Este in the province of Padua, Italy, in the 7th–4th centuries BC. In antiquity this area of the Po Valley was partially swamp and prone to floods, but it was nevertheless well-placed to draw traffic from central Italy up into the foothills of the Alps. This largely accounts for the fact that by the late 7th century BC, ETRUSCAN influences had led to the development of an independent style of figurative art. Este art is typified by bronze vessels, belts and weapons, which were decorated with beaten and engraved figures. Earthenware vessels with similar decoration are found less frequently. Almost all the objects to which the term Este art is usually applied were found in tombs.

To begin with, images of animals with only a few human figures were most common, but from the 4th century BC, in the final phase of this art style, metal votive objects from shrines in the Veneto included representations of the shrines' founders. Gravestones with comparable scenes are also known from this period, mainly from the Padua region. Some fully modelled votive objects from the 6th century BC onwards are also known. The majority of the production centres were probably located in Este, where most of the discoveries were made. The distribution of objects ranges north from the Apennines over the Alps and from the lakes of Lombardy to Slovenia. Other production centres can be discerned from stylistic differences, particularly in the early period; these were probably in the region of Verona or Padua. In more distant areas there were local imitations of Este art.

In the older Este art of the 7th–6th centuries BC there are, in addition to other animals, representations of lions, sometimes winged, and of griffins, sphinxes and centaurs. Their origins in ancient Mediterranean and Near Eastern art is clear, while the motifs of the falcon-headed griffin or lion with a half-devoured animal in its jaws find their best direct parallels in Etruscan art. Occasionally, as on the Benvenuti Situla from Este (Este, Mus. N. Atestino), there are figural scenes: in this case, distinguished revellers seated on Etruscan thrones, a boxing match and soldiers with prisoners. The form of the vessel and the animal images prove that this situla was manufactured in Este; the other scenes show a connection with SITULA ART, which later flourished in the 5th and 4th centuries BC in the south-eastern Alpine region. The Este art of the late 6th century BC to the 4th century BC has occasional examples of figural scenes that reveal Etruscan influence, although most works are decorated only with animal friezes. In contrast to the older Este art, in which the animals appear to move ponderously, they now speed gracefully. Ornamental effects, such as spirals growing between the animals and from their mouths, also occur. From the metal belts decorated with animals that have been incised and otherwise worked, it is clear that the metal votive objects from the shrines belong to the final phase of Este art (all Este, Mus. N. Atestino). However, more detailed stylistic comparisons are made difficult by the wide range of the subject-matter. Individual themes on metal objects from shrines, such as equestrian scenes, can be compared with other animal representations, revealing that the growing votive art tradition continued into later times. The greatest collection of works in this style is held at the National Museum of Este.

BIBLIOGRAPHY
Mostra dell'arte delle situle dal Po al Danubio (VI–IV secolo a.C.) (exh. cat., Padua, 1961)
O.-H. Frey: *Die Entstehung der Situlenkunst: Studien zur figürlich verzierten Toreutik von Este*, Römisch-Germanische Forschungen (Berlin, 1969)
H.-W. Dämmer: *Etrusco-italische Bronzevotive*, Studien zu vor- und frühgeschichtlichen Heiligtümern (Mainz, 1988)
G. Fogolari and A. L. Prosdocimi: *I Veneti antichi: Lingua e cultura* (1988)
O.-H. FREY

Esterházy. Austro-Hungarian family of statesmen, collectors and patrons. The family, whose genealogy can be traced to the 12th century, rose to prominence during the Turkish wars of the 16th and 17th centuries to become one of the leading, most influential and richest families of eastern Europe. Their absolute loyalty to the Habsburgs secured for them great power and wealth. The main family branch was that of Fraknó, from which the princes were descended. There were three cadet branches, those of Csesznek, Zólyom and Fraknó, the last of which was divided in the early 18th century into the two smaller branches of Tata, founded by Count József Esterházy (1682–1748), and Cseklész (now Bernolakovo, Slovakia).

I. Main Fraknó branch. II. Cadet branches.

I. Main Fraknó branch.

(1) Count **Miklós Esterházy I** [the Palatine] (*b* Galánta [now Galanta, Slovakia], 8 April 1582; *d* Nagyhöflány, Grosshöflein, nr Eisenstadt, Austria, 11 Sept 1645). Born into a family of country gentry, he prospered by fighting courageously against the Turks, by astute political instinct, by ardent Catholicism (to which he converted in 1600) and by two marriages of convenience to become a leading member of the aristocracy and the founder of the Esterházy dynasty, as it is best known. He determined the ways and loyalties of the family as supporters of the Habsburgs, of the Counter-Reformation and as propagators of the Baroque style. He became a baron in 1613, palatine of Hungary in 1625, count in 1626 and knight of the Order of the Golden Fleece in 1628. The estate of Kismarton and Fraknó (now Eisenstadt and Forchtenau, nr Vienna, Austria), with its fortified castle, Schloss Forchtenstein, at Forchtenau was granted to him in 1623 and became the family's centre. In the 1630s Miklós rebuilt the castle (subsequently known as Schloss Esterházy) in the early Baroque style.

Miklós was also involved in the building of the influential Baroque Jesuit Church (1629–36) in the archbishopric of Nagyszombat (now Trnava, nr Bratislava, Slovakia), designed by the Italian Giovanni Pietro Spazzo (*fl* 1618–44). Its plan follows those of Il Gesù, Rome, and of the Jesuit church of Vienna, and its wide, twin-towered façade, with restrained decoration, became an important model for ecclesiastical architecture in Hungary until the 19th century. The rich ornamentation in stucco and fresco was carried out in the mid-17th century by the Italians Giovanni Battista Rosso (*fl* 1639–55) and Jacopo Tornini (*fl* 1639–55) and the Austrians Christian Kern and Julius Keller. The nave ceiling is decorated with scenes from the *Life of St John the Baptist*, patron saint of the church, by Pietro Antonio Conti and Johann Erhardt Gruber (both *fl c.* 1700), commissioned by Miklós's son (2) Prince Pál. The inventory (1645) made at the death of Miklós lists 13 chests in the treasury at Fraknó containing numerous precious objects (most in Budapest, Mus. Applied A.). The identifiable objects include a 17th-century *Cupid* pendant, possibly made in Germany; a 15th-century Hungarian silver-mounted clay cup, the Matthias Flask (1470–80); and the Prudentia Cup (1612) by Hans Petzolt of Nuremberg.

(2) Prince **Pál Esterházy** [the Palatine] (*b* Kismarton [now Eisenstadt, Austria], 8 Sept 1635; *d* Kismarton, 26 March 1713). Son of (1) Count Miklós Esterházy I. He followed his father as a soldier and politician. For his part in successfully promoting the Habsburg succession to the

Hungarian throne in 1687, he was created a prince of the Holy Roman Empire in that year. He was an active patron; his commissions emphasize his family's part in helping to deliver Hungary from Turkish rule in 1686, for example the print of the *Triumph of Emperor Joseph I and the Esterházy Family* (1691) by Jonas Drentwett (*c.* 1650–*c.* 1720) and Philipp Kilian. He built the first Hungarian Baroque country house (Schloss Esterházy; 1663–72) at Kismarton, designed by the Imperial Architect of Vienna, Carlo Martino Carlone (1616–67), probably following the plans of Philiberto Luchese. The four protruding corners of the plan show that it was built on the site of a medieval castle, but the open, decorated façade with large windows initiated a new type of country house symbolizing power and wealth. The ceiling frescoes (1665–71) of the ceremonial hall, painted by Carpoforo Tencala, show the story of *Cupid and Psyche* (symbolizing the advantageous marriages of the Esterházys), the *Garden of the Hesperides* and allegorical female figures representing the various provinces of Hungary. The interior was decorated with portraits of the Hungarian nobility and royalty, emphasizing the historical role of the Esterházys. Hans Matthias Mayr carved the busts of Hungarian heroes, including those of Prince Pál and his father, on the main façade in 1667. The other buildings that Prince Pál commissioned in and around Kismarton are the finest examples of early Baroque architecture in Hungary, for example the cathedral, parish and pilgrimage church at Frauenkirchen, begun 1702, by the Italian architect Francesco Martinelli (1651–1708). The equestrian statue of *Prince Pál* (1691) by the Austrian sculptor Martin Filser in the courtyard of Schloss Forchtenstein shows the prince in a regal pose.

The great collection built up by Prince Pál, consisting of some 800 unidentified paintings, was kept at Kismarton, with a *Kunst- und Wunderkammer* at Fraknó, where the arms collection remains. Among the works commissioned were family portraits, as well as seven large canvases depicting the Turkish wars by an unknown Central European painter (early 18th century; Forchtenau, Schloss Forchtenstein). He also made important additions to the treasury, including a huge silver-gilt plate (1654; Budapest, Mus. Applied A.) and a tankard with a large finial in the form of an equestrian statuette (dismantled; part sold Geneva, Christie's, 1989), made by the silversmiths Philipp Jacob Drentwett I and Abraham Drentwett I of Augsburg to commemorate the Battle of Vezekény (1652), in which Prince Pál's elder brother, László Esterházy, and three cousins died. The figure of László is realistically portrayed, and he is associated with the heroic virtues of Hercules. In 1687 Prince Pál commissioned from Bernhard Strauss in Augsburg a miniature triumphal column in ivory (damaged; Budapest, Mus. Applied A.), carved with 33 scenes from Ovid's *Metamorphoses*, which represent the rise to prominence of the Esterházy family; the decorative scheme was probably devised by the Prince. The collection (Budapest, Mus. Applied A.) of gold- and silverware, jewellery, embroidery and needlework includes many objects that were either gifts from the Habsburg emperors or items confiscated from rebellious Hungarian nobles. Prince Pál was also an accomplished composer of music

(e.g. *Harmonia caelestis*, 1711) and author of *Mars Hungaricus* (MS., 1664) and *Tropheum nobilissimae et antiquissimae domus Estorasianae* (Vienna, 1700).

(3) Prince **Miklós (József) Esterházy I** [the Magnificent] (*b* Vienna, 19 Dec 1714; *d* Vienna, 28 Sept 1790). Grandson of (2) Prince Pál Esterházy. He studied in the early 1730s at the University of Leiden with his elder brother before embarking on the Grand Tour. From 1738 to 1758 he lived in Vienna, holding important posts at court. In 1762 he inherited the family fortune from his brother Pál Antal Esterházy, and to sustain his luxurious lifestyle he spent extravagantly.

Prince Miklós commissioned and closely supervised the rebuilding (1764–84) of the country house (first built 1721) that he named Eszterháza (now FERTŐD, Hungary), influenced by the château of Versailles and the palace of Schönbrunn, Vienna. It consisted of a Rococo, U-shaped main building (the only surviving part), two wings for the winter garden and the picture gallery, as well as a puppet theatre, music-house and numerous garden pavilions. The French garden (destr.) and park, together with the neighbouring villages, formed a grand scheme that became the setting for festivities, concerts and opera performances (Joseph Haydn was Kapellmeister from 1761). Few documents concerning the construction of the building survive, and the design cannot be attributed to one architect. Prince Miklós may have incorporated ideas from his Italian stage designer, Girolamo Bon (*fl* 1731–61). Melchior Hefele, a pupil of Balthasar Neumann, also worked at Fertőd; he may have designed the garden façade and the exquisite wrought-iron railings. The façade of the main building (1766) is relatively restrained, despite its Rococo ornament.

The interior has gold and white marble as well as stucco and fresco decoration. Prince Miklós employed several artists from the Akademie der Bildenden Künste, Vienna, including Josef Ignaz Mildorfer, a follower of Paul Troger, who painted the dome of the chapel (1764), with the *Holy Trinity* and *St Stephen of Hungary Offering the Crown of Hungary to the Virgin*; the ceiling of the Banqueting Hall (1766–7), with the *Triumph of Light*, including allegorical figures of *Morning* and *Evening* and *Apollo Driving his Chariot*; and the frescoes of the Sala Terrena (see HUNGARY, fig. 16). The Banqueting Hall contains statues of the *Four Seasons* (*in situ*) by Johann Joseph Rössler and 12 urns, bought by Prince Miklós from the estate of the Marquise de Pompadour. More than 300 paintings decorated the 126 rooms of the house, and 350 paintings were moved from Kismarton to the picture gallery at Eszterháza in 1779. Prince Miklós took up residence in 1768. The garden cascade was completed in 1784, the year a detailed description of the building was made. This emphasizes the quantity of porcelain objects in the Prince's rooms, as well as the size of his clock collection. There were also many 'Chinese' rooms, furnished with oriental objects and chinoiserie panels. The fashion for chinoiserie at Eszterháza culminated in the visit of Maria-Theresa, Queen of Hungary and Bohemia, in 1773, when a masked ball with oriental costumes was held in one of the 'Chinese' rooms.

(4) Prince **Miklós Esterházy II** (*b* Vienna, 12 Dec 1765; *d* Como, Italy, 24 Nov 1833). Grandson of (3)

Bernardo Bellotto: *Kaunitz-Esterházy Palace*, Vienna, oil on canvas, 1.34×2.37 m, *c.* 1760 (Budapest, Museum of Fine Arts)

Prince Miklós Esterházy I. His interest in building was concentrated on the family seat, Schloss Esterházy, at Kismarton, to which his father moved from Eszterháza. Miklós commissioned Karl Moreau to remodel it (1795–1805) in the Neo-classical style and to add wings to accommodate an opera house and gallery. The Napoleonic Wars prevented the completion of this work, and only the garden façade and opera house were built. Miklós's main interest, however, was the formation of his art collection, which became one of the most comprehensive collections of European paintings at this time, and the largest and most impressive in Hungary. He spent several months annually in Italy, and in 1794 he returned with more than 50 paintings, many prints and books, antique vases and alabaster statues. He also acquired coins and shells. He may have bought Correggio's *Madonna del latte* (1523–4; Budapest, Mus. F.A.) at this time, and it is not known whether he or his grandfather acquired Raphael's Esterházy *Madonna* (Budapest, Mus. F.A.).

Prince Miklós also commissioned artists to make portraits of his family, including his wife, *Princess Maria Josefa von Lichtenstein* (1795; Vaduz, Samml. Liechtenstein), by Angelica Kauffman, and his daughter *Leopoldina* (1805–18), by Antonio Canova, which remains in the temple built for it in the park at Kismarton. Through agents in Italy and Vienna, Prince Miklós purchased important paintings and drawings, including Agnolo Bronzino's *Adoration of the Shepherds* (*c.* 1539) from the Borghese collection, the *Portrait of a Youth* (attrib. Raphael; *c.* 1503–4) from the Barberini collection and Claude Lorrain's *Pastoral Landscape* (*c.* 1646) from the Doria-Pamphili collection (all Budapest, Mus. F.A.). In 1802 he employed as curator of his collections József Fischer (1769–1822), an engraver and landscape painter with a knowledge of Dutch and

Flemish painting, which complemented the Prince's interest in Italian works.

By 1806 the collection at Kismarton had become so large that many paintings were removed to the recently acquired palace at Pottendorf, where a picture gallery was opened in 1812. In 1814 the whole collection was taken to the summer palace in Vienna that had recently been purchased from Prince Wenzel Anton Kaunitz-Rietburg (renamed the Kaunitz-Esterházy Palace; destr.; see fig.), where from 27 April 1815 it was opened twice a week to the public. The first catalogue (published 1812) included 528 paintings, although more than 1000 are known to have been in the collection. Of the 348 canvases in the inventory of 1796 made at Kismarton only 23 were displayed in Vienna. The character of the collection was formed by 1812: it excluded Spanish paintings and, because of Prince Miklós's Neo-classical taste, French Rococo paintings. Many Spanish paintings, however, were purchased by his son Pál Esterházy (1786–1866), who in 1819 and 1821 acquired 46 paintings in London and Paris from the collection of Edmund Bourke, the former Danish Ambassador in Naples, Madrid and London. These were mostly Spanish and included works by Bartolomé Esteban Murillo (e.g. *Virgin and Child with Angels Making Music*, *c.* 1660; Saarbrücken, Margot and Albert Ernst priv. col.), Alonso Cano (e.g. *Noli me tangere, c.* 1646–50), Francisco de Zurbarán and Juan Carreño de Miranda (all Budapest, Mus. F.A.). Fischer acquired from the Kaunitz-Rietburg Collection two works by Goya: *The Watercarrier* and *The Knife-grinder* (both *c.* 1808–12) and the *Martyrdom of St Andrew* (1628) by Jusepe de Ribera (all Budapest, Mus. F.A.).

The prints and drawings were mostly acquired through two firms of dealers in Vienna, Artaria and Mollo. In 1803 prints and fine Dutch drawings, including Rembrandt's

Dutch Farmhouse (pen and brown ink, *c.* 1636) and *Woman with Crying Child and Dog* (pen and brown ink, *c.* 1635; both Budapest, Mus. F.A.), were bought from Count Nowohratsky-Kollowrath, Prague, and from 1804 a large part (some 300 sheets) of the collection of Paulus Praun in Nuremberg was acquired, including landscape drawings by the Germans Hanns Lautensack and Augustin Hirschvogel, 17th-century Bolognese drawings, nature studies by Hans Hoffmann, drawings in black and brown pen and wash by Pietro Faccini, and Annibale Carracci's *Study of Two Figures* in red chalk (all Budapest, Mus. F.A.). The collection of Antonio Cesare Poggi, which included three sketches by Leonardo da Vinci (two for the *Battle of Anghiari*, black and red chalk, 1503–5) and drawings by Raphael (e.g. *Study for a Venus*, metalpoint, 1512–13), Nicolas Poussin and Claude Lorrain, was bought in Paris in 1810 (all Budapest, Mus. F.A.).

Due to his heavy expenditure during the Napoleonic Wars, when he raised a regiment, and the spending on his extensive collecting, Prince Miklós suffered financial difficulties, and in 1821 regular purchases of works of art stopped. His grandson Prince Miklós Esterházy III (1817–94), after succeeding to the title in 1866, was forced to sell part of the collections; the sculpture was sold in Vienna, and paintings from the Pottendorf Palace were auctioned in 1867. In the same year jewellery was auctioned in London. From 1865 an assemblage of 636 paintings, about 3500 drawings and about 50,000 prints was on display in Pest (now Budapest) and was purchased by the Hungarian government in 1870 to form the core of the collections of the Szepművészeti Muzeum (Museum of Fine Arts), Budapest.

II. Cadet branches.

(1) Count **Imre Esterházy** (*b* 17 Dec 1663; *d* Pozsony [now Bratislava, Slovakia], 6 Dec 1745). Member of the Csesznek branch. He was Cardinal and Archbishop of Esztergom (1725) and built numerous churches. He commissioned the decoration for many of them, including that for Veszprém Cathedral, in which Antonio Galli-Bibiena painted the illusionistic frescoes of the nave (e.g. the *Assumption of the Virgin*; 1726), which were the first paintings of this type in Hungary. Georg Raphael Donner (*see* DONNER, (1)) worked as Count Imre's Court Sculptor and Superintendent of Works (1728–39). He produced a portrait of his patron in white marble (1732) and the high altar with *St Martin and the Beggar*, both for Bratislava Cathedral (1734–5; both *in situ*). In 1738 Donner and Galli-Bibiena made a triumphal arch for the 50th anniversary of Count Imre's ordination. Franz Anton Palko painted altars in the Trinity Church, Bratislava, in the 1730s and Count Imre's portrait (1743; Bratislava, convent of the Order of St Elizabeth). Galli-Bibiena also painted the illusionistic architectural fresco of the dome of the Trinity Church, Bratislava (1744–5): the coffered dome has at its base the four *Fathers of the Church* and in the top centre the *Eye of God* surrounded by heads of putti.

(2) Count **Miklós Esterházy II** (*b* Tata, 1711; *d* ?Tata, 1764). Member of the Tata branch. During his extensive travels throughout Europe as a diplomat, he commissioned many portraits of himself and his family, including an informal portrait (1758; Budapest, N.G.) by Louis Tocqué. The portrait of his wife, *Maria Ana Lubomirska*, was painted *c.* 1764 by Alexander Roslin, and that of his son, *János Esterházy* (*c.* 1785–90), by Heinrich Friedrich Füger (both Tata, Kuny Mus.).

(3) Count **József Esterházy** (*b* 1714; *d* 1762). Member of the Tata branch, cousin of (2) Count Miklós Esterházy II. He was interested in building and engaged JAKOB FELLNER, Hungary's most talented late Baroque architect. Fellner built the parish church (1751–83), following plans by Franz Anton Pilgram, and the palace (1765–9) at Tata. At Majk, near Tata, a Carmelite church was founded in the first half of the 18th century, and hermits' dwellings were built. Little of this work at Majk survives, but many prominent artists are known to have worked there, including Pilgram and Franz Anton Maulbertsch. József also founded a faience factory (1758–62, 1768–1824) in Tata, mostly with craftsmen from Holić, Slovakia, who developed a distinctive style of decoration incorporating loose bunches of flowers. Figurines designed by the sculptor Antal Schweiger (1728–1802) were also made.

(4) Count **Károly Esterházy** (*b* ?4 May 1725; *d* ?Tata, 14 March 1799). Member of the Tata branch, brother of (2) Count Miklós Esterházy II. He was Bishop of Eger and built about 40 churches in his diocese; the Baroque character of most of the buildings in the city of EGER is mainly due to his patronage. He was an enlightened nobleman, who introduced the teaching of drawing and engraving in Eger. The most important work in Eger that he commissioned is the Lyceum (1765–80), which he intended to be a university on the model of the Sapienza, Rome, but which became a school as a result of the centralizing policies of Emperor Joseph II. Jakob Fellner designed this building after plans by Joseph Gerl, in the Louis XVI style, which is also evident in the decoration of the interior. The Bishop's belief that science flourished under the patronage of the Church is expressed in the ceiling frescoes by leading Austrian artists. The library depicts the *Council of Trent* (1778) by Johann Lukas Kracker, painted in the sober style of the building. The ceremonial hall contains the *Four Faculties* (1781) by Franz Sigrist, one of the finest late Baroque frescoes in Hungary, and the chapel ceiling the *Glorification of All the Saints* (1793–1800), in which Hungarian saints are prominent, designed by Franz Anton Maulbertsch and possibly executed by his assistant, Martin Michl (*fl c.* 1800). At the end of the 18th century the members of the Tata branch of the Esterházy family also created an English-style park, with Roman and medieval ruins from Vértesszentkereszt, on their estate at Tata.

BIBLIOGRAPHY
[?Niemecz Primitivus]: *Beschreybung des hochfürstlichen Schlosses Esterhas in Königreich Ungern* (Pressburg, 1784) [contemp. description of Eszterháza]
J. Fischer: *Catalog der Gemählde-Gallerie des durchlantigen Fürsten Esterházy von Galantha, zu Laxenburg bei Wien* (Vienna, 1812)
Z. de Bulach: *L'Ambassade de Prince Louis de Rohan à la cour de Vienne, 1771–4* (Strasbourg, 1901) [description of life in Eszterháza]
J. Esterházy: *Az Esterházyak története* [History of the Esterházys] (Budapest, 1901)
S. Meller: *Az Esterházy képtár története* [History of the Esterházy gallery] (Budapest, 1915)
M. Horányi: *The Magnificence of Eszterháza* (Budapest, 1962)

A. Pigler: Katalog der Galerie Alter Meister, Budapest, Mus. F.A. cat. (Budapest, 1967) [incl. ptgs from the Esterházy col.]

J. Harich: 'Über das Schloss Esterházy zu Eisenstadt und die Burg Forchtenstein', *Burgenländische Heimatsblätter*, 1, 3, 4 (1972) [incl. an inventory of 1721–5]

A. Héjjné-Détári: 'A fraknói Esterházy kincstár a történet forrásók tükrében' [The Esterházy treasury of Frakno as mirrored in historical sources], *Magyarországi reneszánsz és barokk* [Renaissance and Baroque in Hungary], ed. G. Galavics (Budapest, 1975), pp. 473–551

M. Sallay: *The Esterházy Palace at Fertőd* (Budapest, 1979)

Joseph Haydn in seiner Zeit (exh. cat., ed. G. Mraz and G. Schlag; Eisenstadt, Schloss Esterházy, 1982)

Leonardo to Van Gogh: Master Drawings from Budapest (exh. cat., ed. T. Gerszi; Chicago, IL, A. Inst., 1985) [incl. drgs from Esterházy col.]

G. Galavics: *Kössünk kardot az pogány ellen: Török háborúk és képzőművészet* [Let's get swords against the pagans: Turkish wars and art] (Budapest, 1986) [17th-century Hungarian art and patronage]

ISTVÁN BARKÓCZI

Estes, Richard (*b* Kewanee, IL, 14 May 1932). American painter. He moved with his family to Chicago, where he studied at the Art Institute (1952–6), before going to New York, where most of his paintings are set (although later works were often finished in his house in Maine). His first one-man show was held at the Allan Stone Gallery, New York, in 1968. He sustained a careful commitment to an unvarying subject-matter, usually the built environment of Manhattan, and to PHOTOREALISM. His realism is deceptive in that he rearranges the structure of what he originally sees and records through photographs, which form the basis of the final easel-size paintings, to reconstruct reality. He also expands the viewer's information and sensory field beyond the powers of the naked eye, giving a depth and intensity of vision that only artistic transformation can achieve. Since the paintings are based on more than one photograph, the viewer of an Estes painting perceives, for example, a shop-front window, with a richness that is created by the artist's technical skills. We can see the surface of the window glass, what it is reflecting, and what is behind it. This characteristic effect is wittily achieved in his *Double Self-portrait* (1976; New York, MOMA), which shows the artist, a street with parked cars, building façades across the street and commercial signs, all mirrored in a restaurant window. He tries to avoid using obvious New York landmarks, although many of the distinguishing visual characteristics of his work can be seen in his painting of one of the most celebrated art icons of New York, the *Solomon Guggenheim Museum* (1979; New York, Guggenheim). The scene is devoid of people, giving a Sunday feeling, a clear blue sky and a tonal range of shadow at street level. There is also no litter, which Estes said he found hard to depict. Although he admired the work of Edward Hopper, he was not interested in evoking human moods, and he avoided night scenes. When reconstructing the original scene for the final oil painting in the studio, he used an acrylic ground, which he overpainted in oils.

BIBLIOGRAPHY

Richard Estes: The Urban Landscape (exh. cat. by J. Arthur, Boston, MA, Mus. F.A.; Toledo, OH, Mus. A.; Kansas City, MO, W. Rockhill Nelson Gal.; Washington, DC, Hirshhorn; 1978)

L. Meisel: *Richard Estes: The Complete Paintings, 1966–1985* (New York, 1986)

CHRISTOPHER BROOKEMAN

Estevan [Esteban], **Martín** (*b* late 16th century; *d* 17th century). Spanish sculptor. He was almost certainly Aragonese and was known as Maestro Estevan. His sole documented work is the altarpiece he made in 1607 for the church of the Asunción de Nuestra Señora in the medieval Cistercian monastery in Rueda, near Escatrón. The work was executed in the Plateresque style, which had by then fallen out of use, since artistic taste was turning towards the Baroque, and so it marked out the artist as a traditionalist. In collaboration with Domingo Borunda, who seems to have been a stonemason, Estevan carved it as a magnificent work of white alabaster. Around 1940 the altarpiece was dismantled and transferred to the parish church of Escatrón; it must have been then that the reliefs of the plinth were lost, the ornaments of flowers, fruit and angels alone remaining. In the principal niche Estevan represented the *Immaculate Conception*, and in the pediment was the *Coronation of the Virgin*. The large reliefs on either side represented, on the left, the *Annunciation* and the *Visitation*, and on the right, the *Adoration of the Shepherds* and the *Adoration of the Magi*.

BIBLIOGRAPHY

A. Ponz: *Cartas del viage de España* (Madrid, 1785), xv, letter 5a

Conde de la Viñaza: *Adiciones al diccionario histórico de los más ilustres profesores de bellas artes en España de Céan Bermúdez*, ii (Madrid, 1788, rev. 1890)

G. Weise: *Die Plastik der Renaissance und des Frühbarock im nördlichen Spanien*, ii (Tübingen, 1959), pp. 42–4

CARLOS CID PRIEGO

Esteve. Spanish family of artists.

(1) José Esteve Bonet (*b* Valencia, 22 Feb 1741; *d* Valencia, 17 Aug 1802). Sculptor, stuccoist and administrator. He began to sculpt at an early age, as he belonged to a family connected with the Gremio de Carpinteros of Valencia. He trained in the workshops of the sculptors Ignacio Vergara (1715–76) and Francisco Esteve (1682–1766). From 1762 he began to write *Libro de la verdad*, a detailed record of his works. He was awarded many commissions owing to his good nature, extraordinary capacity for work and relations with influential people in Valencia. He soon received great recognition and was considered the best sculptor working in Valencia. He successively occupied all positions at the Real Academia de Bellas Artes de S Carlos, Valencia, eventually becoming Director-General (1781–4). He sometimes visited the royal court in Madrid and was nominated honorary Escultor de Cámara (1790) for his figures (untraced) for the *Belén del príncipe*, a nativity scene made for King Charles IV when he was Prince of the Asturias. It consisted of about 5950 pieces, of which about 180 were made by Bonet from 1788. He worked in stone and plaster and specialized in religious images done to satisfy the devout tastes of his clients. His delicate Rococo touch, showing the influence of the work of Vergara, is seen in such sculptures as *St Joseph* (1800; Seville Cathedral). On the other hand, Neoclassical elements are present in his 1775–81 stucco reliefs and statues for Valencia Cathedral (e.g. *St Matthew*) and in the marble statues of *St Vincent Ferrer* (1797) and *St Vincent the Martyr* (1798) for the main altar of the basilica of the Nuestra Señora de los Desamparados in Valencia.

BIBLIOGRAPHY

J. V. Martí Mallol: *Biografía de D. José Esteve Bonet* (Castellón, 1867)
M. A. Orellana: *Biografía pictórica valentina* (Valencia, 1967), pp. 394–6, 587–9
A. Igual Ubeda: *José Esteve Bonet: Imaginero valenciano del siglo XVIII* (Valencia, 1971) [includes complete version of *Libro de la verdad*]
A. E. Pérez Sánchez: 'Valencia: Arte', *Tierras de España: Valencia* (Madrid, 1985), pp. 325–6
D. Vilaplana: 'La escultura: El influjo academista y neoclasicista', *Historia del arte valenciano*, ed. V. Aguilera Cerni, iv (Valencia, 1985), pp. 275–8

ANA MARÍA BUCHÓN CUEVAS

(2) Rafael Esteve Vilella (*b* Valencia, 1 July 1772; *d* Madrid, 1847). Engraver, son of (1) José Esteve Bonet. He trained at the Real Academia de Bellas Artes de S Carlos in Valencia and from 1789 studied with a grant at the Real Academia de S Fernando, Madrid. He contributed engravings to Nicolás Barsanti's *Retratos de los Españoles ilustres, con un epítome de sus vidas* (Madrid, 1791), *Real Picadero de Carlos IV* (Madrid, 1799) and *La artillería volante* (Madrid, 1796); and engraved portraits for *Guía de Forasteros* (Madrid, 1800). In 1800 he made portraits of *Charles IV* and *Queen Maria Luisa*, and from 1802 he was Grabador de Cámara. He is known for his engraving of the *Miracle of the Waters*, after the painting by Bartolomé Esteban Murillo (1821; Seville, Hosp. Caridad). He travelled to Italy and in 1834 was in Paris and London. His fine technique was recognized in his appointment in 1839 as *académico de mérito* at the Real Academia de Bellas Artes de S Carlos, where he became Director de Grabado in 1841. He was also made *grabador de honor* at the Academia de S Carlos, Valencia.

BIBLIOGRAPHY

V. Boix: *Memorias para escribir la biografía de don Rafael Esteve, primer grabador de cámara de su Magestad* (Valencia, 1848)
——: 'Un grabador español', *Rev. Ideas Estét.*, xi (1848), pp. 139–61
P. Najera Colino: *Rafael Esteve grabador, 1772–1847* (Valencia, 1986)
J. Carrete, F. Checa and V. Bozal: *El grabado en España, siglos XV al XVIII*, Summa A.: Hist. Gen. A., xxxi (Madrid, 1987)

BLANCA GARCÍA VEGA

Estève, Maurice (*b* Culan, Cher, 2 May 1904). French painter, draughtsman and lithographer. Like Jean Bazaine and Charles Lapicque, Estève belongs to the generation whose early work was influenced by late Cubism. He himself particularly admired Fernand Léger. Estève became aware of his vocation extremely early in life and had already begun to paint when he arrived in Paris at the age of 15. Extreme attention to execution, already evident in early paintings such as *Still-life with Basket of Eggs* (1927; Paris, Conchon priv. col., see Vallier and others, p. 8), was to characterize all his work. Gradually Estève abandoned post-Cubist rigour and the sharp, flat colour that he used until the early 1930s in works such as *First Steps* (1930; Bourges, Mus. Estève); he began to follow Pierre Bonnard's example, working towards softened forms enriched by a profusion of colour, as in *The Meal* (1937; Bourges, Mus. Estève). The problem of subject-matter concerned Estève increasingly as abstraction came to dominate the post-war period. In his paintings the powerful presence of colour invading the entire composition made the subject less and less legible, as in *Sicilian Chair* (1953; Paris, J. Verroust priv. col., see Vallier and others, p. 58). Estève was not, however, convinced of the validity of abstract painting; in his view the external world had to be taken

Maurice Estève: *Combraille*, oil on canvas, 920×730 mm, 1970 (Bourges, Musée Estève)

into account and to be filtered through the artist's sensibility.

Working in this spirit, Estève became the most notable representative of a typically French style of painting that looks abstract but takes figurative subjects as a point of departure. Most of his paintings are landscapes designed as an amalgam of memories, their titles derived from non-existent words or combinations of real place-names, as in *Combraille* (1970; Bourges, Mus. Estève; see fig.). Remaining faithful to his concept of painting, Estève concentrated his efforts on mastering ever more intense colour. Apart from oil paintings, his work includes watercolours, such as *Watercolour, No. 997* (1968; Paris, C. Bernard priv. col., see Vallier and others, p. 84), heightened charcoal drawings, lithographs, tapestries and collages. In each of these media, techniques are subtly combined to enrich the surface and to guard against repetition and routine.

BIBLIOGRAPHY

J. Lescure: *Estève ou les chemins silencieux de la réalité* (Paris, 1945)
P. Francastel: *Estève* (Paris, 1956)
F. Elgar: *Estève: Dessins* (Paris, 1960)
Estève (exh. cat. by J.-L. Ferrier, Düsseldorf, Kstmus., 1961) [retrospective]
Aquarelles d'Estève (exh. cat. by D. Vallier, Zurich, Gal. Nathan, 1973)
J. E. Müller: *Estève* (Paris, 1974)
D. Vallier and others: *Hommage à Maurice Estève* (Paris, 1975)
Estève (exh. cat. by J. Leymarie, Paris, Grand Pal., 1986–7)
M. Prudhomme-Estève: *Catalogue du Musée Estève* (Bourges, 1990)

DORA VALLIER

Esteve y Marques, Agustín (*b* Valencia, 1753; *d* Madrid, *c.* 1820). Spanish painter. He may have been the son of a Valencian sculptor of the same name, Agustín Esteve, documented between 1764 and 1767. He attended the school of the Academia de Bellas Artes de San Carlos, Valencia, and in 1772 went to Madrid to the Real Academia de Bellas Artes de San Fernando, where he won a prize, although he was not to have an important academic career. He established himself in Madrid, where the ducal houses of Osuna and Alba were the first to give him commissions. One of these was for the portrait of *Doña Joaquina Tellez-Girón* (1784; Madrid, Prado), daughter of the 9th Duque de Osuna, painted when she was 13. For more than 25 years Esteve y Marques painted portraits, mainly for aristocratic circles, among whom his simple, flattering and uncritical style was well accepted.

From 1780 Esteve y Marques was an assistant to Francisco de Goya, who influenced his art, as had the work of Antonio Raphael Mengs previously. In Goya's workshop he made replicas of his master's portraits, especially those of *Charles IV* and *Maria Luisa*. He also excelled at painting in miniature, with the technical skill and ability to capture the features of his sitters. In 1800 he was appointed Pintor de Cámara to Charles IV and shortly after became *académico de mérito* at the Academia de San Carlos, Valencia. His fortunes were changed by the political situation in 1808, the year of the King's abdication, by the Napoleonic invasion and the War of Independence (1809). Although after 1814 he continued to paint portraits of Ferdinand VII, his brother Don Carlos and other members of the royal family, the quality of his late work declined, and he lost prestige in society and suffered financially.

BIBLIOGRAPHY

M. S. Soria: 'Agustín Esteve and Goya', *A. Bull.*, xxv, 3 (1943), pp. 239–66
——: 'Agustín Esteve y Goya' (Valencia, 1957)

JUAN J. LUNA

Esthetics. *See* AESTHETICS.

Estienne, Robert (*b* Paris, 1503; *d* Geneva, 7 Sept 1559). French printer and publisher. After training with his father, the printer and publisher Henri Estienne (?1460–1520), and then with his stepfather, Simon de Colines (*fl* 1520–48), he checked and proofread the family editions of the *Epistles*, *Apocalypse*, *Acts* and *Psalms* in 1522–3. Between 1525 and 1530 he produced the Latin Grammar of Philipp Melanchthon (1497–1560). In 1526 he produced the works of Terence, which ran to four editions, the last with notes by Erasmus (other early Classical texts produced subsequently include editions of Plautus in 1529 and Virgil in 1532). His first major work was the 1527 *Bible*, reissued in 1528 and 1532. In 1528 he embarked on a major project: a *Thesaurus linguae latinae*, the definitive edition of which appeared in 1543. Estienne's entire output is estimated to have been between 460 and 470 editions, and he printed books for other publishers as well as his own works. From 1537 he received a royal privilege for every edition. His friendship with Francis I, King of France (*reg* 1515–47), resulted in his nomination in 1539 as 'Printer to the King in Hebrew and Latin' and a similar title in 1544 for works in Greek. His first edition (1544) of the works of Eusebios of Caeserea used the Royal Greek type cut by Claude Garamond (*c.* 1500–1561) based on the handwriting of Angelo Vergerio (*d* 1571). From 1540 Estienne was involved in the acquisition of Greek manuscripts for the royal collection. In 1550 he moved to Geneva, where he produced Protestant texts, including the *Institution de la réligion chrétienne* of Jean Calvin (1509–64), as well as continuing to produce philological works.

BIBLIOGRAPHY

E. Armstrong: *Robert Estienne, Royal Printer: An Historical Study of the Elder Stephanus* (Cambridge, 1954, rev. 1986)
F. Schreiber: *The Estiennes: An Annotated Catalogue of 300 Highlights of their Various Presses* (New York, 1982)

LAURA SUFFIELD

Estienne de Bonneuil. *See* ETIENNE DE BONNEUIL.

Estilo desornamentado [Sp.: 'stripped or unornamented style']. Term used to describe a phase in Spanish architecture in the 16th century and the early 17th, which developed in reaction to the excessive decoration of the PLATERESQUE STYLE. Emphasis was placed on the correct use of Classical orders, the composition of masses, walls and spaces and contemporary Italian practice. *Estilo desornamentado* owed much to the influence of Italian and Portuguese military engineers and to the anti-decorative functionalism of the first Jesuits. Starting in the 1540s, it reached its summit with Juan de Herrera's work (1563–84) at the Escorial (see ESCORIAL, §2), spreading thereafter throughout almost all of Spain (except Andalusia) and differing from the Portuguese *Estilo chão* ('plain style') in that it enjoyed less freedom from academic rules and the styles derived from Italy.

The term was apparently in use in Spain in the later 19th century; it was subsequently applied by C. Justi (1908) to describe the monastery of the Escorial and was taken up by G. Kubler. It was coined to replace the various terms—Herreran, Escurialene, Viñolesco, Tridentine and Mannerism—used by Spanish architectural historians to describe the Escorial and its sequels. Its use has been limited to English and American historians, although J. B. Bury declared himself radically opposed to it (1986). Spanish writers have preferred to use the term 'classicism' to describe this last phase of 16th-century architecture in Spain, keeping the phrase *estilo desornamentado* to designate Renaissance detailing before the construction of the Escorial, where decoration (known as Plateresque) using candelabra and grotesques was abandoned. This detailing is then contrasted with that of the Renaissance buildings that employed such ranges of decoration and were dubbed *ornamentado* ('ornamental').

The tendency to reject the practice of superimposing such decoration on Renaissance structures, leaving the Classical orders as the only decorative element in this type of architecture, seems to have been encouraged by the publication in 1537 and 1540 of books II and IV of Sebastiano Serlio's *Regole generali di architettura sopra le cinque maniere degli edifici* (Venice, 1537–51) and their translation into Spanish by Francisco de Villalpando (1552). Architects from the 1540s, such as Alonso de Covarrubias and Luis de Vega, or Diego de Siloé later on, tried to forgo the use of superficial decoration and limit themselves to employing the orders, together with rustication, as the sole characteristics of a style of architecture that they claimed was 'Roman' or 'ancient'. During the same period, architects such as Rodrigo Gil de Honañón, working in a Gothic Survival tradition, tried to divest their

Gothic structures of any kind of ornament, including the orders, as they considered decoration to be superfluous and prized the structural design ('the plan') above any type of additional element ('art').

Although this state of affairs did not apply uniformly, an important departure in Spanish architecture clearly occurred towards 1560, centred on the court of Philip II. The arrival of Juan Bautista de Toledo from Naples and the brief presence of Francesco Paciotto (1562) signified a renewal of Italian models (the last Spaniards to come from Italy, such as Diego de Siloé or Pedro Machuca, had returned c. 1520). In an attempt to apply the principles of Vitruvius and the 16th-century theory of Classical orders correctly, stress was laid on architecture composed of well-proportioned masses, walls and spaces. There was wide use of Italian forms (not excluding, however, contributions from Flanders), where surfaces were articulated by using Classical orders or linear ensembles of very simple geometric figures, thereby producing a gradual simplification of the orders that reduced them often to a minimum, giving rise to the expression 'reductive classicism'.

The most direct disciples of Herrera's school—Juan de Valencia and Francisco de Mora—continued to work in the style established by Herrera at the monastery of the Escorial. Within court circles in Madrid, the Carmelite Fray Alberto de la Madre de Dios (fl 1610) and Juan Gómez de Mora also continued the style until the mid-17th century. An important centre for the style was also formed in Toledo by other disciples or assistants of Herrera, such as Diego de Alcántara (d 1587), Nicolás Vergara (ii) and Juan Bautista Monegro and their respective followers. Herrera's plans for Valladolid Cathedral (1580) gave rise to another centre in that city, whose chief representatives, Juan de Ribero Rada (d 1600), Juan de Nates (fl 1620) and Diego and Francisco de Praves (1586–?1637), transmitted its characteristics to the architecture of old Castile, León, Asturias, Cantabria, the Basque country and, through Salamanca, to Galicia. Herrera's influence, through both his own designs and those of certain disciples, reached regions such as Valencia and soon touched Andalusia and even Aragon. Here, as in Catalonia, architecture developed characteristics similar to those encouraged by the court, thus promoting exceptional stylistic consistency throughout Spain.

Despite some local opposition and divergences around 1600 and 1620, the style, with its geometrical characteristics and stress on mathematical elements, prevailed throughout the 17th century. From the 1640s, however, the notion of enriching buildings began slowly to be accepted via a new wave of decorative art, which nevertheless respected the composition of the structures and the treatment of the orders.

BIBLIOGRAPHY

J. de Castilho: Lisboa antiga: O bairro alto (Lisbon, 1879, 3/1954–62)
C. Justi: Miscellaneen aus drei Jahrhunderten spanischen Kunstlebens, 2 vols (Berlin, 1908)
G. Kubler and M. Soria: Art and Architecture in Spain, Portugal and their American Dominions, Pelican Hist. A. (Harmondsworth, 1959)
——: Portuguese Plain Architecture, between Spices and Diamonds, 1521–1706 (Middletown, CN, 1972)
C. Wilkinson: 'The Escorial and the Invention of the Imperial Staircase', A. Bull., lvii (1975), pp. 65–90
G. Kubler: Building the Escorial (Princeton, 1982; Sp. edn, Madrid, 1983)
A. Bustamante García: La arquitectura clasicista del foco vallisoletano: 1561–1640 (Valladolid, 1983)
F. Marías: La arquitectura del renacimiento en Toledo: 1541–1631, 4 vols (Toledo and Madrid, 1983–6)
J. Rivera Blanco: Juan Bautista de Toledo y Felipe II: La implantación del clasicismo en España (Valladolid, 1984)
C. Wilkinson: 'Planning a Style for the Escorial: An Architectural Treatise for Philip of Spain', J. Soc. Archit. Hist., xliv (1985), pp. 37–47
El Escorial en la Biblioteca Nacional (exh. cat., Madrid, Bib. N., 1985)
J. B. Bury: 'Juan de Herrera and the Escorial', A. Hist., ix/4 (1986), pp. 428–49
Herrera y el clasicismo (exh. cat., Valladolid, Pal. Santa Cruz, 1986)
F. Marías: El largo siglo XVI: Los usos artísticos del renacimiento español, (Madrid, 1989)

FERNANDO MARÍAS

Estípite. Column or pilaster that tapers towards its base, often overlaid by a sequence of geometric solids that obscure the basic structure; it is characteristic of the CHURRIGUERESQUE style used in 17th- and 18th-century Spanish and Latin American architecture.

☐

Estonia [Est. Eesti; Ger. Estland; Rus. Estonskaya SSR]. Republic in Eastern Europe. It is bounded to the north by the Gulf of Finland, to the east by Russia, to the west by the Baltic Sea and to the south by Latvia (see fig. 1). The country is mainly flat and covers some 45,000 sq. km including numerous offshore islands, the largest of which are Saaremaa and Hiiumaa; it has a population of around 1.5 million. The capital is TALLINN (formerly Reval). Estonians form about 61% of the population, and 30% is Russian-speaking. The Estonian people, who are related to the Finns, have lived in the area for over 5000 years, having migrated there from the east. Their language belongs to the Finno-Ugric group.

Because of its strategic importance, Estonia has been the site of numerous conflicts from the beginning of the 13th century. By 1227 it was divided into small feudal states between Denmark, the bishops of Tartu and Saare Lääne and the Brethren of the Sword (later joining the Teutonic Order and becoming known as the Livonian Knights), who conquered southern Estonia (the historical Livonia) and brought about the conversion of the inhabitants to Christianity in the early 13th century. The Germans and Danes formed the aristocracy and most of the urban population, while the rural population was indigenous. German rule continued under the Teutonic Order, and Lutheranism reached Estonia by 1523. In 1629, after the Livonian and Polish-Swedish wars, Estonia came under Swedish control that lasted until 1710, when the country was conquered by Russia. The Baltic-German aristocracy preserved its privileges. In 1739 the Bible was published in Estonian for the first time, and Estonian schools were established throughout the country. Between 1740 and 1820 serfdom was general.

The era of national awakening began in the 1860s. Numerous peasants bought their own land, periodicals started to appear in Estonian, an interest in folklore developed, and between the mid-1890s and 1917 Estonia became one of the most industrialized parts of the Russian empire. In 1918 Estonia proclaimed its independence, which was recognized by the USSR in 1920. In the 1920s and 1930s Estonian culture was able to develop freely for the first time. In 1939, as a result of the Nazi–Soviet pact,

1. Map of Estonia; those sites with separate entries in this dictionary are distinguished by Cross-reference type

Estonia became part of the USSR's sphere of influence, and in June 1940 the Red Army occupied Estonia. From August 1941 until September 1944 the country was occupied by Nazi Germany. In 1944 the Soviet occupation was restored and lasted until August 1991, when Estonia became independent.

This article covers the art of Estonia from the 13th century AD. For the earlier history of the area *see under* Prehistoric Europe.

I. Architecture. II. Painting, sculpture and graphic art. III. Collecting and art institutions.

I. Architecture.

After conquering Estonia at the beginning of the 13th century the Danish and German invaders began to construct castles, churches and monasteries in styles that varied according to the separate regions. Builders came from Scandinavia and northern Germany as well as other parts of Europe, bringing the influence of their different schools with them. The Romanesque style dominated for a short period at the beginning of the 13th century, but from the 13th century until the 16th the Gothic style prevailed. In northern and central parts of the country local limestone became the primary building material, dictating simple, monumental and rather heavy forms.

The asceticism of the Dominicans and Cistercians also had a strong impact. Examples of Early Gothic buildings in limestone that survive in their original form are small village churches on the island of Saaremaa, such as those at Valjala, Karja and Põide (second half of 13th century–beginning of 14th), each with an aisleless nave, two or three bays and rich sculptural decoration. More typical for mainland, northern and central Estonia is the three-aisled hall church, as at Ambla, Koeru, Järva-Peetri and Suure-Jaani. In southern Estonia, where brick was the main building material, the buildings are lighter and the architectural forms richer, as in the church of St John (14th century) in Tartu, with its terracotta decorations.

By the late Middle Ages there were 50 forts in Estonia, of which the best preserved is the Bishop's Castle (14th century) at Kuressaare on Saaremaa, built according to the construction techniques of the Teutonic order. By the 15th century Tallinn was an important Hanseatic town surrounded by city walls (begun third quarter of 13th century) with numerous strategic towers. The old part of the city is one of the best preserved architectural ensembles of the Middle Ages. Its three large churches, the Toom Kirik (cathedral of St Mary), St Olav Church and St Nicholas Church, were built in the 13th century as hall churches but were rebuilt as basilicas in the 15th century (for illustration *see* TALLINN). The Town Hall (1404), the Main Guildhall (Suurgildi hoone, 1410), St Olav's Guildhall (1422) and numerous merchants' houses are examples of Late Gothic architecture in Tallinn and are characterized by a general simplicity of form, unadorned façades and deep portals.

The influence of the Renaissance reached Estonia between 1510 and 1520 and lasted until the 1630s. Its impact was modest compared to that of the Gothic style, and it was usual to add Renaissance elements to existing buildings. The outstanding architectural monument of the period in Tallinn is the House of the Schwarzhäupter Brotherhood (1597), designed and decorated by Arent Passer (*d* 1637) from Holland. The Baroque style was introduced in the 1630s, and in the 17th century Dutch influences predominated. A fine Baroque ensemble was built in Narva, but apart from the Town Hall (1671; by Georg Teuffel) it was completely destroyed in World War II. Numerous small wooden manor houses were constructed, while the fortifications of Tallinn, Tartu and Narva were rebuilt according to the system devised by SÉBASTIEN LEPRESTRE DE VAUBAN. Baroque chapels were added to several churches, such as the Clodt Chapel (1673) at St Nicholas Church in Tallinn.

In the 18th century, impulses that came from Russia predominated. One of the most remarkable architectural monuments of the period is the Kadriorg Palace (1718–23; now owned by the Art Museum of Estonia), designed by Niccolò Michetti. The elegant stucco decorations of its main hall are characteristic of the architectural forms of the new era. The Rococo style appeared only in interior design, and Neo-classicism dominated Estonian architecture from the 1780s until the mid-19th century. The first example of the style was the interior of the Governor's Palace (1767–73; by Johann Schultz) in Tallinn. Tartu, which had been destroyed by fire in 1775, was rebuilt in Neo-classical style. The Town Hall (1772–89; by Johann Heinrich Bartholomäus Walter) and buildings in the Town Hall Square represent early Neo-classicism. Tartu University (1803–9), by Johann Wilhelm Krause (1757–1828), with its monumental simple forms, is an example of High Classicism. Several large manor houses were built at this time, such as those at Hõreda, Saku and Riisipere.

In the mid-19th century historicism began to inform Estonian architecture: the Gothic Revival style of northern Germany was used in several buildings, including Sangaste Castle (1881) by Otto-Pius Hippius (1826–83). In Tallinn the Gothic Revival style had a Romanesque touch, as in the Charles (Kaarli) Church (1862–70) by Hippius and Rudolf Bernhard (1819–87). Architects of Baltic-German origin who had studied at the Riga Politechnicum were the most active builders. In the early 20th century the work of Finnish architects building in National Romantic style became popular, for example the Vanemuine Theatre (1906; destr. World War II) in Tartu by Armas Lindgren and the Estonia Theatre in Tallinn (1909–13; partly rebuilt after World War II) by Lindgren and Wivi Lönn. In 1913 Eliel Saarinen devised an impressive urban plan for the centre of Tallinn, but it was not realized (*see* SAARINEN, (1)). At the beginning of the century the first Estonian architects educated at Riga Politechnicum became active. Their work, such as the Students' Society building (1902)

in Tartu by Georg Hellat (1870–1943) and the Kalev Society building (1912; destr.) at Pirita by Karl Burman, was influenced by Finnish National Romanticism as well as by Art Nouveau.

The style that prevailed in the architecture of the Estonian Republic of the 1920s has been defined as Traditionalism. Elements of Neo-classicism and Art Nouveau were used with Nordic pragmatism by Estonian as well as Baltic–German architects. The schoolhouse (1923) in Raua Street by Artur Perna (1881–1940) and the Parliament Building in the Upper Town (Toompea) in Tallinn, with its Expressionistic interior (1920–22) by Herbert Johanson (1884–1964) and Eugen Habermann (1884–1944), are characteristic of the era. Functionalist ideals dominated the 1930s. The spirit of Estonian Functionalism is well expressed in the Tallinn Art Hall (1933–4; see fig. 2) by Edgar Johan Kuusik (1888–1974) and Anton Soans (1885–1966), and the Beach Café (1938–9) in Pärnu by Olev Siinmaa (1881–1948), with its elegant mushroom-shaped balcony, as well as in numerous villas in Pärnu and Tallinn. In the 1930s limestone was widely used in buildings with massive, simple forms such as the chapel at Metsakalmistu Cemetery (1935–6) by Herbert Johanson.

During World War II numerous architectural monuments were destroyed, and many architects were killed or escaped from the Communist terror. In 1945–55 Stalinist architectural dictates were followed, although relatively few Stalinist buildings were constructed, while Functionalist ideas were surprisingly often used, as in the Railway Hospital (1945–55), Tallinn, by Nikolai Kusmin (*b* 1906). From the end of the 1950s cheap industrial building methods were introduced in housing. Original projects by talented Estonian architects include the Song Festival

2. Edgar Johan Kuusik and Anton Soans: Tallinn Art Hall, Tallinn, 1933–4

Amphitheatre (1960) by Alar Kotli (1904–63) and Henno Sepmann (1925–85) and the Flower Pavilion (1960) in Tallinn by Valve Pormeister (b 1922), which is influenced by international modernism. In the 1960s and 1970s most of the young architects of note followed neo-Functionalist principles, reminiscent of the period when Estonia was independent. There were more opportunities to realize these ideas in provincial centres than in the capital. The design for the residential area and social centre of Pärnu EKE (Estonian Collective Farm Administrative Building; 1970) by TOOMAS REIN, the administrative building of the Tsooru collective farm (1970–7) by Rein, the new complex of the Tervis sanatorium (1975–7) in Pärnu by Vilen Künnapu (b 1948) and the school (1979–83) in Muraste by Tiit Kaljundi, as well as numerous designs by Leonhard Lapin, Jüri Okas (b 1950) and others, represent the avant-garde spirit of the era. The Sailing Centre (1980) at Pirita near Tallinn by Peep Jänes (b 1936), Ago-Himm Loover (b 1941), Henno Sepmann and Ants Raid is of interest. In the 1980s a Post-modernist approach became evident in the work of Estonian architects.

II. Painting, sculpture and graphic art.

Unusual trapezoid tombstones and memorial stones with pagan symbols date to the periods immediately before and after the Danish-German invasion, but from the 13th century the history of Estonian art is linked with the development of Western European art, particularly its northern regions, until the second half of the 19th century, when the first professional Estonian artists appeared.

Art in Estonia showed the impact of the Romanesque style at the beginning of the 13th century, but the Gothic style began to establish itself from c. 1250. The most remarkable example of the Romanesque style is the ornamental decoration (c. 1260) on the west portal of the Valjala Church on Saaremaa. A particularly fine example of wooden Gothic sculpture is the late 14th-century *Crucifixion* group, originally in Risti Church in Western Estonia, which now belongs to the Art Museum of Estonia and is exhibited at St Nicholas Church Museum, Tallinn.

The sculptures in the church at Karja (14th century; see fig. 3), also on Saaremaa, show similarity with work from Gotland, Sweden. The terracotta sculptures forming an *Apocalypse* cycle (mid- and second half of 14th century) in the church of St John at Tartu initially consisted of over 1000 sculptural heads and decorative forms. Churches were frequently adorned with fine wooden sculptures, while fragments of wall paintings influenced by various German or Scandinavian schools have been found in several Saaremaa churches.

The earliest secular works of art are the carved oak benches (1374 and 1410–30) in Tallinn Town Hall. The liveliest period in the history of Tallinn coincides with the most influential period of the Hanseatic League (1350–1500): numerous stone- and wood-carvers worked in Tallinn, while churches, municipalities and fraternities commissioned several works from well-known painters of the Hansa region. HERMEN RODE of Lübeck created the impressive double-winged altarpiece (1482) for St Nicholas Church, Tallinn. BERNT NOTKE of Lübeck painted the small, double-winged altarpiece (1483) for the church

3. *Crucifixion*, stone relief, Karja Church, Saaremaa, 14th century

of the Holy Spirit (Pühavaimu), and the fragment with 13 figures from the *Dance of Death* (1463 or 1466) in the chapel of St Anthony in St Nicholas Church has been attributed to him. During the Renaissance period (beginning of the 16th century–second quarter of the 17th) secular art became increasingly important. Sculpture flourished, and the popularity of memorial sculpture (epitaphs, coats of arms and tomb monuments) spread. The best-known Renaissance sculptor in Tallinn was Arent Passer (d 1637). His work, which includes the monument to *Pontus de la Gardie* (1589–95) in the Toom Kirik (cathedral of St Mary) and the decorations (1600) for the House of the Schwarzhäupter Brotherhood in Tallinn, was influenced by the Fontainebleau school. Several paintings in Tallinn are attributed to MICHEL SITTOW.

The early Baroque (mid- and second half of the 17th century) was the last productive period of stone sculpture, the tradition dying out in the 18th century. New materials became popular: stucco decorations (1720s) of the Kadriorg Palace are particularly noteworthy. Wood-carving maintained its importance throughout the period. Elert Thiele (d 1674), who carved the frieze of the Tallinn Town Hall in the 1660s–70s, successfully adopted the northern European Auricular style. At the turn of the 17th and 18th centuries acanthus and floral motifs became fashionable. An outstanding and highly productive wood-carver was Christian Ackermann (*d c.* 1710); the pulpit (1686) and altar (1696) of the Toom Kirik and the altar (1700) of the church at Vigala are examples of his most accomplished work. In painting, portraiture prevailed, but religious and allegorical painting was also popular. Ernst Wilhelm Londicer (1655–97), Johann Heinrich Wedekind (1674–1736), Anton Graff and, later, Christian Gottlieb Welté (1748–1823) are the most notable painters of the Baroque period.

The period of Neo-classicism in Estonia (end of the 18th century–mid-19th) coincides with the activation of local Baltic–German culture. A drawing school was founded at Tartu University in 1803. Portrait, landscape and genre painting were favoured by the teachers, including KARL AUGUST SENFF and August Matthias Hagen (1794–1878), as well as by their pupils. An academic approach predominated, but from the 1830s the influence of the Biedermeier style and Romanticism is evident. Georg Friedrich Schlater (1804–70), who specialized in townscapes, founded the first lithography workshop in 1832. The wood-engraving workshop of Friedrich Ludvig von Maydell (1795–1846) followed in 1835. Views of Tallinn, especially panoramas, became popular, and Karl Buddeus (1775–1864) and Johannes Hau (1771–1838) were highly regarded masters of the genre. August Georg Pezold (1795–1859) and Friedrich Siegmund Stern (1812–89) were the first artists who systematically depicted Estonian peasants and their milieu. Several artists born in Estonia became known in Western Europe, including Gustav Adolf Hippius (1792–1856), GERHARD VON KÜGELGEN and Carl Timoleon von Neff (1804–76). The sculpture of the period is less accomplished, and most of the remarkable works are by sculptors from St Petersburg: Giacomo Quarenghi designed the monument to *Admiral S. Greigh* (end of 18th century) in the Toom Kirik, and Vasily Demut-Malinovsky executed the monument to *Barclay de Tolly* in his mausoleum at Jõgeveste as well as his monument in Tartu (1846–9).

In the second half of the 19th century the first indigenous Estonian artists began work, having studied and worked abroad, although Estonian art life was still dominated by Baltic Germans, many of them of international standing, including Eduard von Gebhardt (1838–1925), Rudolf Julius von Zur Mühlen (1845–1913) and EUGEN DÜCKER. JOHANN KÖLER, who had studied and worked in St Petersburg, painted academic portraits (see fig. 4) as well as historical scenes and landscapes, many of which depict Estonian subjects. The sculptor August Weizenberg (1837–1921), who worked for many years in Rome, favoured marble and followed classical ideals. The work of AMANDUS ADAMSON varies in style and material. He sculpted monuments in Estonia, St Petersburg and the Crimea, as well as allegorical figures and portraits. Paul Raud, a student of the Düsseldorf Kunstakademie, was a founder of Estonian *plein-air* painting (see RAUD, (2)).

In the early 20th century modernist ideas began to influence Estonian art. Several artists returned home after studying abroad, and the first general exhibition of Estonian art took place in 1906 (see YOUNG ESTONIA). Ants Laikmaa (1866–1942) and Kristjan Raud were the first to turn their backs on academicism and to open their studios to pupils. Laikmaa's pastel portraits and Estonian landscapes combine Düsseldorf realism with elements of Impressionism. Kristjan Raud developed his own version of National Romanticism in a series of monumental charcoal drawings depicting scenes from the Estonian epic *Kalevipoeg* (see RAUD, (1)). From 1910–20 Estonian artists were orientated towards Paris, Munich and the art of northern Europe. Nikolai Triik (1874–1940) was the most talented portraitist of the time. KONRAD MÄGI was an outstanding colourist, whose treatment of landscape showed increasingly Expressionist qualities. The sculptor JAAN KOORT was strongly influenced by monumental ancient Egyptian sculpture. Ado Vabbe (1892–1961) created several abstract and Futurist works between 1910 and 1920. During World War I contacts with the international avant-garde became closer, and Expressionist and Cubist influences dominated experimental work in the decade before the 1920s. Arnold Akberg (1894–1984), Eduard Ole (*b* 1898) and Märt Laarman (1896–1979) were members of the ESTONIAN ARTISTS' GROUP, founded in 1923. Interest in geometrical abstraction was strong until the end of the decade. Later, Art Deco and *Neue Sachlichkeit* also became important influences. In the art life of the 1920s and 1930s the art school Pallas, founded in Tartu in 1919, played a decisive role. Among its pupils, the printmaker EDUARD VIIRALT had the widest international reputation. From 1925 to 1938 he lived mainly in Paris, where he produced visionary commentaries on contemporary society, such as *Hell* (etching and engraving, 1930–32) and *Cabaret* (etching and engraving, 1931; both Tallinn, A. Mus. Estonia).

In the 1930s late Impressionism dominated Estonian art, which was more conservative than in the 1920s. Ado

4. Johann Köler: *Self-portrait*, oil on canvas, 630×503 mm, 1859 (Tallinn, Art Museum of Estonia)

5. Jüri Arrak: *Town of Towers*, oil on canvas, 0.98×1.70 m, 1979 (Tallinn, Tallinn Art Hall)

Vabbe, Aleksander Vardi (1901–83), Andrus Johani (1906–41) and Kaarel Liimand (1906–41) painted poetical views of scenes from Estonian life. In sculpture the portrait and the female nude were popular. The granite sculptures of ANTON STARKOPF reveal a clear and powerful interpretation of form. In printmaking there were fine examples of woodcuts as well as of intaglio printing. Artistic development was interrupted in 1939 by Soviet intervention and World War II, in the course of which many artists were killed or forced into exile. Realistic war scenes are exceptional in Estonian art. The Expressionist paintings of Johannes Greenberg (1887–1951) represent the depressing atmosphere, while artists connected with the Pallas tradition continued in their earlier manner. After the war the Stalinist concept of art was introduced by artists who had spent the war years in Russia, and from 1949 to 1955 SOCIALIST REALISM was heavily imposed. The more liberal atmosphere of the second half of the 1950s resulted in the revival of the ideals of the 1930s, and there were also some new developments. Elmar Kits (1913–72) created colourist abstractions in the mid-1960s. Leppo Mikko (1911–78) created decorative Constructivist abstractions. Numerous experiments based on modernist experience were carried out in the 1960s, while figurative art with a stress on aestheticism was the official requirement, but this contradiction did not lead to the formation of an artistic underground. The painters Henn Roode (1924–74) and Olav Maran (*b* 1933) and the printmakers Vive Tolli (*b* 1928) and Peeter Ulas (*b* 1934) were among the innovators of the period.

Post-war international developments had an immediate impact on the young artists of the late 1960s and early 1970s, led by TÕNIS VINT. A local version of POP ART developed, and the first Estonian land art projects and happenings took place. By the mid-1970s most artists had turned to more traditional and officially acceptable forms. Symbolist images were used by the painters Peeter Mudist (*b* 1942), Jüri Palm (*b* 1937), Toomas Vint (*b* 1942), Jüri Arrak (*b* 1936; see fig. 5) and Tiit Pääsuke (*b* 1941), the sculptor Jaak Soans (*b* 1943) and the printmakers Marju Mutsu (1941–80) and Silvi Liiva (*b* 1941). The work of LEONHARD LAPIN anticipated the geometric minimalist approach of his contemporaries. Jüri Okas (*b* 1950) showed his adherence to CONCEPTUAL ART in his photo-based intaglio prints; Raul Meel (*b* 1941) was another exponent of Conceptual art. In the 1980s a National Romantic trend, represented by Lembit Sarapuu (*b* 1930), Jaak Arro (*b* 1957) and Epp-Maria Kokamägi (*b* 1959), appeared in response to the impact of Post-modernist ideas as well as the national liberation movement, and from the mid-1980s the liberal atmosphere stimulated an increased range of creative work.

III. Collecting and art institutions.

During the Middle Ages and afterwards the Church and merchants' guilds were the primary patrons of art in Estonia, while in the 18th and 19th centuries there were numerous collectors among the Baltic–German nobility and townspeople. The biggest collection belonged to the von Lipharts family at Raadi manor in Tartu. During World War I numerous works of art were destroyed or disappeared, and few ended up in the collections of Estonian museums. Collectors of German origin who left the country in 1939 took with them numerous works connected with Estonian art history. In the 1920s and 1930s there were few systematic collectors among individual Estonians, and even fewer in the years of Soviet occupation. The two main collectors at that time were the

State (the Ministry of Culture bought works for museums) and the Estonian Art Fund: its collection is now in the Tallinn Art Hall. After independence, rich institutions such as Eke Sadolin and the Saku Beer Factory began to collect art seriously.

The main collector in Estonia is the Art Museum of Estonia in Tallinn. Its forerunner, the Estonian Museum, was founded in 1919; in 1928 it was renamed the Art Museum of Estonia, while during the Soviet occupation it was the State Art Museum of the ESSR. It houses a collection of Estonian, Western European and Russian painting, prints, sculpture and applied art. The main collection is in the old town of Tallinn at Lossi plats 1, where there is a small permanent exhibition of Estonian national art as well as space for temporary exhibitions. The most important examples of medieval art are exhibited in the St Nicholas Church Museum, while items of Estonian applied art are displayed in the Museum of Applied Art in Tallinn. The memorial museums of Kristjan Raud in Nõmme and of Adamson-Eric (1902–68) in Tallinn, as well as an exhibition space at Kohtla-Järve, are run by the Art Museum of Estonia.

The second most important art museum is the Tartu Museum of Art, founded in 1940 as the Tartu State Art Museum. It is housed in two buildings in the centre of the town. The permanent exhibition is dedicated to the work of the most important artists of the Pallas Art School of the 1920s and 1930s, as well as to the contemporary art of Tartu. Both art museums have libraries, photographic collections, documents and slides. The oldest museum in Estonia is the Museum of Classical Archaeology at Tartu University; it was founded in 1803 and opened to the public in 1862. It has an important collection of copies and original works and an art historical library. Several provincial museums house art collections, for example that of Russian art in the Narva Regional Museum.

The most important promoter of contemporary art in Estonia is the Tallinn Art Hall, which puts on about 25 exhibitions a year. Around two-thirds of the shows display the work of contemporary Estonian artists, while a third is of international origin. Built by Estonian artists in 1934, the Art Hall became an independent institution in 1991. It houses a collection of Estonian art from the 1960s onwards; it also organizes exhibitions of Estonian contemporary art abroad. The Tallinn Print Triennales, initiated by Estonian printmakers in 1968, are known throughout the Baltic and Scandinavian areas, as are the Triennales of the applied art of the Baltic countries, held in Tallinn since 1979.

The Estonian Museum of Architecture was founded in 1991 and has organized several remarkable exhibitions in Estonia as well as abroad, even though it does not have an exhibition space of its own. The Estonian Park Museum near Tallinn, which was founded in 1957 and opened in 1964, demonstrates the traditions of Estonian vernacular architecture: farm complexes as well as pubs, mills and so on from different regions of the country have been transferred there. The Estonian National Museum, which houses very valuable ethnographic collections, was founded in Tartu in 1909.

Private galleries began to appear in the 1990s. Among the first was the Vaal Gallery in Tallinn, founded by a group of young graphic designers. Art life in the two main art centres, Tallinn and Tartu, is lively, although an art market has not yet taken shape. There are sections on art history in the three main libraries, the Estonian National Library (Tallinn), the library of Tartu University and the library of the Academy of Sciences in Tallinn. The last contains rare original materials on Baltic history, while the library of Tartu University owns a remarkable collection of Western European prints. To promote the exchange of information on contemporary art, the Estonian Soros Centre for Contemporary Art was established in Tallinn in 1993 along the lines of similar institutions founded by George Soros (b 1930) in the former Socialist countries of Eastern Europe.

BIBLIOGRAPHY

GENERAL

A. Vaga: *Eesti kunsti ajalugu* [A history of Estonian art], i (Tartu, 1932)

V. Vaga: *Eesti kunst* [Estonian art] (Tartu, 1940)

Eesti kunsti ajalugu [A history of Estonian art], 2 vols (Tallinn, 1975–7)

R. Loodus: *Eesti kunstielu kroonia XIX saj. II poolest kuni 1940.a.* [A chronicle of Estonian art life from the second half of the 19th century to 1940] (Tallinn, 1976)

E. Pütsepp: *Kunstielu Eestimaal* [Art life in Estonia], i (Stockholm, 1991)

ARCHITECTURE

Eesti arhitektuuri ajalugu [A history of Estonian architecture] (Tallinn, 1965)

V. Raam: *Arkhitekturnye pamyatniki Estonii* [Architectural monuments of Estonia] (Leningrad, 1974)

T. Habicht: *Rahvapärane arhitektuur* [Folk architecture] (Tallinn, 1977)

L. Künnapuu: *Estonian Architecture: The Building of a Nation* (Helsinki, 1992)

Eesti arhitektuur [Estonian architecture], i (Tallinn, 1993)

Toisin (Otherwise): Functionalism and Neofunctionalism in Estonian Architecture (exh. cat., Tallinn, Estonian Mus. Archit., 1993)

PAINTING, SCULPTURE AND GRAPHIC ART

W. Neumann: *Baltische Maler und Bildhauer des XIX. Jahrhunderts* (Riga, 1902)

——: *Lexikon baltischer Künstler* (Riga, 1908)

S. Karling: *Medeltida träskulptur i Estland* [Medieval wooden sculpture in Estonia] (Göteborg, 1946)

A. Tuulse: *Die spätmittelalterlichen Steinskulpturen in Estland und Lettland* (Helsinki, 1948)

Eesti skulptuur [Estonian sculpture] (Tallinn, 1967)

Estonskaya grafika [Estonian graphic art] (exh. cat. by B. Bernshteyn, Moscow, Cent. House Artists, 1970)

V. Vaga: *Kunst Tartus XIX sajandil* [Art in Tartu in the 19th century] (Tallinn, 1971)

Jaan Vahtra ja kubism eesti kunstis [Jaan Vahtra and Cubism in Estonian art] (exh. cat., Tartu, Mus. A., 1972)

V. Raam: *Gooti puuskulptuur Eestis* [Gothic wooden sculpture in Estonia] (Tallinn, 1976)

V. Vaga: *Kunst Tallinnas XIX sajandil* [Art in Tallinn in the 19th century] (Tallinn, 1976)

T. Nurk: *Korgem Kunstikool 'Pallas', 1919–1940* [The art school 'Pallas', 1919–1940] (Tallinn, 1977)

Düsseldorfi koolkond eesti kunstis [The Düsseldorf school in Estonian art] (exh. cat., Tallinn, A. Mus., 1980)

J. Keevallik: *Märkmeid portreemaalist Eestis 18. sajandil* [Notes on portraiture in Estonia in the 18th century], Töid kunstiteaduse ja kriitika [Works on art history and criticism], iii (Tallinn, 1980)

R. Kangropool and M. Lumiste: *Tallinna maalijad ja puunikerdajad 14. ja 15. sajandil* [Painters and wood-carvers in Tallinn in the 14th and 15th centuries], Kunstiteadus, kunstikriitika [Art history, art criticism], iv (Tallinn, 1981)

Eesti maal [Estonian painting] (Tallinn, 1982)

K. Hagen: *Lexikon deutschbaltischer Künstler: 20. Jahrhundert* (Cologne, 1983)

V. Erm: *Lähtemeistrid* [The founding masters] (Tallinn, 1984)

W. Hütt: *Die Düsseldorfer Malerschule, 1819–1879* (Leipzig, 1984)

R. Loodus: *Tartu kunstielust 19. saj. esimesel poolel* [On art life in Tartu in the first half of the 19th century], Kunstiteadus, kunstikriitika [Art history, art criticism], vi (Tallinn, 1986)

H. Üprus: *Raidkivikunst Eestis XIII–XVII sajandini* [Stone-carving in Estonia in the 13th to 17th centuries] (Tallinn, 1987)

Kunstist ja kunstielust Eestis 19. sajandil [On art and art life in Estonia in the 19th century] (Tallinn, 1988)

M. Levin: *Rahvusromantism Eestis: Kogude teatmik* [National Romanticism in Estonia: collected writings] (Tallinn, 1988)

Struktuur/metafüüsika [Structure/metaphysics] (exh. cat., Pori A. Mus., 1989)

Mythos und Abstraktion: Aktuelle Kunst aus Estland (Karlsruhe, 1992)

Oväntat möte: Estnisk och Lettisk modernism från mellankrigstiden [Unexpected meeting: Estonian and Latvian modernism in the inter-war years] (exh. cat., Stockholm, Liljevalchs Ksthall, 1993)

ANU LIIVAK

Estonian Artists' Group [EKR; Est. Eesti Kunstnikkude Rühm]. Estonian group of painters and sculptors active from 1923 to *c.* 1930. The group continued the progressive internationalist orientation of their predecessors in the YOUNG ESTONIA movement and united a new generation of painters committed to Cubist experimentation. The group was founded in Tartu by Eduard Ole (*b* 1898) and Friedrich Hist (1900–41), joined by Felix Randel (1901–77, named Johansen until 1936). Their work, like that of much of their colleagues, was primarily distinguished by modest geometricized abstraction and decorative colourism suggested by Synthetic Cubism, rather than by explorations of simultaneity, collage etc. It also often displayed strong characteristics of NEUE SACHLICHKEIT and PURISM. The earliest Estonian practitioners of Cubism were among the group's members: Jaan Vahtra (1882–1947) and Hist, who from 1921 studied in Latvia, where he kept company with the modernists of the RIGA ARTISTS' GROUP. In 1924 EKR exhibited in Tartu and Tallinn with the Latvians, by which time membership had grown with the critical additions of Märt Laarmann (1896–1979), Arnold Akberg (1894–1984) and Henrik Olvi (1894–1972). Akberg and Olvi created some of EKR's most radical work, with Akberg investigating non-objectivity in a Cubo-Constructivist manner and Olvi executing rigorous architectonic compositions. Laarmann is credited as the group's ideologue, having written their manifesto, *The New Arts Book*, published in 1928. Other members included the sculptor Juhan Raudsepp (1896–1984) and Edmond-Arnold Blumenfeldt (1903–46). While Blumenfeldt's art was more Expressionistic, Raudsepp worked in the group's distinctive abstract geometric style, which was revived in the 1970s by Estonian nonconformist artists such as TÕNIS VINT and LEONHARD LAPIN.

BIBLIOGRAPHY

Kunst in Tallinn und Estland, vom Mittelalter bis zur Gegenwart (exh. cat., Kiel, Christian-Albrechts U., Ksthalle; Schleswig-Holstein. Kstver.; 1976)

E. Komissarov: 'Estniska konstnärsgruppen' [The Estonian Artists' Group], *Oväntatmöte: Estnisk och lettisk modernism från mellankrigstiden* [Unexpected meeting: Estonian and Latvian modernism from the period between the wars] (exh. cat., Stockholm, Liljevalchs Ksthall, 1993), pp. 27–36

MARK ALLEN SVEDE

Estouteville, Guillaume d' (*b* Normandy, *c.* 1412; *d* Rome, 22 Jan 1483). French cardinal and patron. He became Bishop of Angers and Cardinal Presbyter of S Martino ai Monti (1439–40), Archbishop of Rouen (1453), Cardinal Bishop of Porto (1457) and Cardinal Bishop of Ostia (1461). In 1461 he was also appointed Arch-Presbyter of one of Rome's principal basilicas, S Maria Maggiore (*see* ROME, §V, 20), and in this capacity he embellished the building fabric and installed a sculpted marble ciborium over the high altar. The original appearance of this ciborium, which was dismantled in 1747, is recorded in an engraving in *Basilicae Sanctae Mariae Majoris descriptio ac dilineato* (Rome, 1621) and a detailed written account of it made on the day of its dismantling (MS., Rome, Bib. Vallicelliana). Following a well-established convention for such monuments, it comprised four narrative reliefs of religious subjects of especial relevance to the church's foundation and dedication. In one of them—the *Assumption of the Virgin*—the Cardinal appears on his knees witnessing the scene. Elsewhere, the ciborium was decorated with sculpted figures of saints, symbols of the evangelists and putti supporting the d'Estouteville coat of arms. Remains of the ciborium are now housed in S Maria Maggiore itself and in the USA (*Virgin and Child*; Cleveland, OH, Mus. A.). In a guide to Rome of 1510 the sculptures were attributed to MINO DA FIESOLE—an attribution generally accepted by modern scholars, although some authorities (e.g. Callisen) ascribe the work to Mino del Reame. D'Estouteville was also a patron of architecture, commissioning Jacopo da Pietrasanta to build the Roman church of S Agostino (1479–83). The speed at which the church was constructed and its boldly asserted Renaissance architectural style denote a patron of some determination and vision. The elevation, in two orders, built from Travertine robbed from the Colosseum, is in fact one of the earliest examples of a Renaissance church façade, and the dome was the first to be built in Rome since antiquity. D'Estouteville also commissioned a palace (destr.), adjacent to S Agostino, which was built, according to one contemporary account, in the 'modern manner'. Two portrait medals of the Cardinal survive, one as *Archbishop of Rouen* (London, BM), attributed to Andrea Guazzalotti (1435–?1494/5) and the other as *Cardinal Bishop of Ostia* (London, V&A), attributed to Cristoforo di Geremia. On the basis of these likenesses a 15th-century marble portrait bust (New York, Met.) has been identified as *Cardinal d'Estouteville*; it originated possibly from his funerary monument in S Agostino.

BIBLIOGRAPHY

DBI

S. A. Callisen: 'A Bust of a Prelate in the Metropolitan Museum, New York', *A. Bull.*, xviii (1936), pp. 401–6

C. Seymour jr: *Sculpture in Italy, 1400–1500*, Pelican Hist. A. (Harmondsworth, 1966), pp. 156–8

DIANA NORMAN

Estrada, Jerónimo Hernández. *See* HERNÁNDEZ ESTRADA, JERÓNIMO.

Estrada, José María (*b* Guadalajara, Mexico, *c.* 1800; *d* Guadalajara, *c.* 1860). Mexican painter. He was a pupil of José María Uriarte, the director of the Academia de Guadalajara, but his links with academic painting seem to have been only rudimentary, since his work was in a more popular spirit related to naive art. He was a fine portraitist, generally showing his sitters in three-quarter view, turned towards the left and with their hands usually holding some object. He rendered their expression gracefully and sometimes humorously with a fresh naturalism; he treated the background in a very sober way in marked contrast to his obvious delight in detail in painting the figure. In his portrait of *Matilde Gutiérrez* (1838; Mexico City, Mus. N. A.), for example, greys, blacks and whites are used to underline the warmth of the child's flesh, her small body glimpsed through the delicate fabrics of her clothes; her lips and eyes are shaded in such a way as to contribute to her sweet expression. One of her hands holds a richly dressed doll, while the other seems to be calling a dog towards her. Another notable work is the portrait of *Miguel Arochi y Baeza* (c. 1840; Mexico City, Mus. N. A.), in which the young man's elegance is emphasized by his erect posture and by the tall hat emphasizing his slimness. The buttons, the folds of his cravat, the flowers in his buttonhole and the watch chain hanging from his pocket provide an opportunity for the painter to show his command of detail.

BIBLIOGRAPHY
R. Montenegro: *Pintura mexicana, 1830–1860* (Mexico City, 1933)
J. Fernández: *Arte mexicano de sus orígenes a nuestros días* (Mexico City, 1958)
——: *El arte del siglo XIX en México* (Mexico City, 1983)
MARGARITA GONZÁLEZ ARREDONDO

Estridentismo. Mexican group of writers and artists, active between 1921 and 1927. The group's members included Silvestre Revueltas (1899–1940), Fermín Revueltas, Leopoldo Méndez, Ramón Alva de la Canal and Germán Cueto, and the writers Arqeles Vela and Germán List Arzubide, with Diego Rivera and Jean Charlot as sympathizers. All were keen to stress the importance of cosmopolitanism. They followed Futurism in a complete rejection of academicism and Symbolism in the arts, although no limits were imposed on what should replace these, and their ideal of making art public and accessible corresponded with that of the mural movement in Mexico. This aim at a cultural revival was initially expressed through a manifesto published in the first issue of the periodical *Actual*, written by the poet Manuel Maples Arce. The manifesto included a directory of avant-garde artists and writers of all contemporary styles, probably compiled with the help of Rivera and Charlot, who had recently returned from Paris. It called on Mexican intellectuals to unite and form a society of artists, claiming 'the need to bear witness to the vertiginous transformation of the world'. Maples Arce recommended rapid action and total subversion as an immediate strategy, and looked to the USSR for ideological inspiration. Taking an iconoclastic attitude, he condemned religiosity and patriotism. The generally incoherent and aggressive manifesto borrowed from Marinetti's Futurist manifestos and Spanish Ultraist ideas. The group's ideas were further propagated by the periodicals *Irradiador* (1924) and *Horizonte* (1926–7), the latter being published by their own publishing house, Ediciones Estridentistas. Public meetings and casual exhibitions at the Café de Nadie, Mexico City, were also held.

WRITINGS
M. Maples Arce: 'Hoja de vanguardia comprimido estridentista', *Actual*, 1 (1921)
G. List Arzubide: *El movimiento estridentista* (Mexico City, 1926)

BIBLIOGRAPHY
L. M. Schneider: *El Estridentismo: Una literatura de la estrategia* (Mexico City, 1970)
S. Faucherau: 'The Stridentists', *Artforum*, xxiv (Feb 1986), pp. 84–9

Art in Latin America: The Modern Era, 1820–1980 (exh. cat. by D. Ades and others, London, Hayward Gal., 1989), pp. 131–2, 306–9 [contains reprint of manifesto]
ELISA GARCÍA BARRAGÁN

Estruch. Spanish family of engravers and painters. Domingo Estruch y Jordán (*b* Muro, Alicante, 1796; *d* Madrid, 1851) trained in Valencia with his uncle, Francisco Jordán (*c.* 1778–1832), and after living in Mallorca and in Havana, Cuba, he established himself in Barcelona. He was an *académico de mérito* at the Academia de S Carlos in Valencia and a corresponding member of the Real Sociedad de Fomento in Havana. He engraved many religious prints, the funerary monument of *Mariano Alvarez de Castro* (1816) and illustrations for Alonso de Ercilla's *La Araucana* (Barcelona, 1827) and for José Oriol y Bernadet's *Tratado elemental completo de dibujo lineal* (Barcelona, 2/1850), as well as maps. His son Juan Estruch (*b* Barcelona, 1820; *d* Madrid, 1883) was his father's pupil and between 1836 and 1840 also trained in Italy. Juan became the leading engraver for the Dirección de Hidrografía, Madrid, and engraved many maps and plans. His engraved portraits include those of the artist *Vincente López y Portaña*, of *Manuel Ruiz Zorrilla* and of the *Conde Dunois*.

BIBLIOGRAPHY
M. Ossorio y Bernard: *Galería biográfica de artistas españoles del siglo XIX* (Madrid, 1868, 2/1883–4/R Barcelona, 1975)
I. Albert Berenguer: *Grabadores de Alicante y su provincia* (Alicante, 1958)
A. Gallego: *Historia del grabado en España* (Madrid, 1979)
E. Páez Ríos: *Repertorio* (1981–3), i, pp. 326–7
BLANCA GARCÍA VEGA

Esturmio, Hernando de [Storm; Sturm, Ferdinand] (*b* Zieriksee; *fl* 1537–56; *d* ?Seville). Netherlandish painter, active in Spain. Arriving in Seville in 1537, he became a prolific and successful artist. His work was, however, conservative in nature, and the use of prints (a standard practice among painters in Seville) and the help of workshop assistants reinforced this aspect. His style, formed in his native land in the 1520s, displays the mixture of Netherlandish and Italian elements characteristic of northern Renaissance masters such as Jan van Scorel and Maarten van Heemskerck. Esturmio's earliest dated work is the altarpiece of *St Peter* (1539; Arcos de La Frontera, S Pedro). Other significant paintings include the altarpiece (1548), with the *Annunciation, Nativity, Adoration of the Magi* and images of saints, in the chapel of the university in Osuna and the *Allegory of the Immaculate Conception* (1555; Osuna, Colegiata, chapel of the tombs of the duques de Osuna). His most important work is the altarpiece of the *Evangelists* (1553–5; Seville Cathedral, Capilla de los Evangelistas). Its main panels, the *Mass of St Gregory* (based on the woodcut of 1511 by Albrecht Dürer) and the *Resurrection of Christ*, exemplify Esturmio's dry, nervous and rather mannered style. The predella panels, especially those depicting female saints, are given a softer treatment. The panel depicting *SS Justa and Rufina* contains a view of the old Giralda, the cathedral tower, in the background.

BIBLIOGRAPHY
J. M. Serrera: *Hernando de Esturmio* (Seville, 1983)
N. Dacos: 'Ferdinand Storm, da Ysenbrant a Campaña', *Prospettiva* [Florence], xxxiii–xxxvi (1983–4), pp. 175–80

J. Brown: *The Golden Age of Painting in Spain* (New Haven and London, 1991), p. 48   □

Esztergom [Lat. Solva Mansio, Strigonium; formerly Ger. Gran]. Town in Komárom county in northern Hungary on the right bank of the Danube, where it forms the international boundary with Slovakia. As the seat of the Archbishop of Esztergom, primate of Hungary, the town is the most important ecclesiastical centre in the country.

1. HISTORY AND URBAN DEVELOPMENT. The town was the site of Neolithic and Bronze Age settlements and from the 2nd to the 5th century AD was occupied by a Roman military encampment, Solva Mansio, belonging to the *limes* of Pannonia. Esztergom's history in the early Middle Ages is unclear, but from the 10th century its name appears in city records. After Prince Géza (*reg* 972–97) reached a settlement with the German Empire in 972, he built his capital on the site. In his castle he founded a church dedicated to the protomartyr St Stephen, which from the 14th century became a priory belonging to the chapter of the cathedral. King Stephen I was born in the castle after 975 and was crowned there in 1001. The archbishop's seat was founded at that time, and its cathedral was consecrated to St Adalbert. From the 11th century the castle was the centre of the Royal Mint, and the royal town developed to the south. Because of the presence of the mint, Esztergom developed into an important centre for gold- and silversmithing. From the 12th century the royal town disposed of a staple right, and most of its revenue was gradually expropriated by the chapter of the cathedral. Another settlement, Viziváros ('Watertown'), was founded in 1239 below Castle Hill on the bank of the Danube for the servants of the archbishop. The parish churches of the royal town were consecrated to St Lawrence and St Nicholas, the Franciscan church (before 1233) was dedicated to the Virgin and the Dominican church (before 1228) to St Catherine. On an island in the Danube were a Benedictine nunnery and a convent (completed before 1281) founded by King Géza II (*reg* 1141–62) for the Knights Hospitaller of St John. The priory of St Thomas, dedicated to Thomas Becket, Archbishop of Canterbury, and the Augustinian monastery of St Anne (last third of the 13th century) were both located near the town. In 1242 the Mongols destroyed the entire settlement except the castle, which in 1256 was definitively handed over to the archbishop by the king, and thereafter the city ceased to be the seat of the monarchy.

Esztergom's medieval layout is known from archaeological excavations. The ruins of the royal castle, which have been partially restored, sit on top of significant remains of the 11th and 12th centuries. The second building at the south end of Castle Hill was constructed in the last quarter of the 12th century. In 1198 the castle was recorded as being incomplete. One of its principal rooms was the Early Gothic court chapel (*c.* 1200; see fig. 1) with a ceiling of cross-vaults in the nave and eight ribs resting on each of the slender double columns in the apse. During the political uncertainties of 1300–07 that followed the eclipse of the Arpad Dynasty, both the castle and the cathedral were considerably damaged, and reconstruction may have been completed in the 1330s by

1. Esztergom, Royal Castle, west façade of the chapel, *c.* 1200

Archbishop Csanád Telegdi (*reg* 1330–49). In the second half of the 15th century the castle was rebuilt by archbishops Dénes Szécsi (*reg* 1440–65) and JOHANNES VITÉZ; the latter remodelled the castle in Renaissance style. Archbishops Ippolito I d'Este (i) and Tamás Bakócz (1497–1521) also added Renaissance buildings to the complex.

In 1526 the Turks unsuccessfully besieged Esztergom and its castle, and in 1530 the archbishop fled to Pozsony (now Bratislava). The city was finally captured by Sulayman II the Magnificent (*reg* 1520–66) in 1543. After a damaging siege in 1594–5, Esztergom was in Christian hands until 1600, and when it was recaptured from the Turks in 1683 it was in ruins. The castle was last fortified between 1707 and 1729, and in 1761 Maria-Theresa made Esztergom an archbishop's seat once again. From 1763 a vast levelling of the ground on Castle Hill was begun, and in 1821–2 the entire area of the medieval cathedral was levelled. The excavation and partial restoration of the medieval castle were begun between 1934 and 1938 (under Géza Lux (1910–45)), and remains of a fresco (after *c.* 1450), probably by a Florentine artist, were found in the Hall of Virtues, a room of one of the Renaissance buildings. Female figures representing the Four Cardinal Virtues are depicted standing or sitting in painted niches between columns. The royal town and Viziváros, both of which had fallen into decay, were rebuilt in the first half of the 18th century as a new urban district. Churches, town houses, the County Hall (1747) and City Hall (1778) were built mostly by such late Baroque architects from Pest (now in Budapest) as Andreas Mayerhoffer, Ignać Oracsek and Anton Hartmann. The principal architect of the archiepiscopal cathedral of St Adalbert (1822–69) was JÁNOS PACKH (*see* §2 below), who also designed the church of St Anne (1828–31) on a central plan with a dome.

The treasury and library of the cathedral and the Museum of Christianity contain important collections of art. The Museum of Christianity, founded in 1875 by Archbishop János Simor, is in Vizivaros, below Castle Hill. It has a large collection of paintings from the 14th to the 16th century, including many medieval altarpieces from all regions of Hungary (*see* HUNGARY, §XIII).

BIBLIOGRAPHY

L. Pálinkás: *Esztergom XVIII. századi müvészeti emlékei* [Eighteenth-century monuments of art in Esztergom] (Budapest, 1937)

I. Genthon, ed.: *Esztergom*, i of *Magyarország müemléki topográfiája* [The topography of monuments of Hungary], ed. T. Gerevich (Budapest, 1948)

D. Dercsényi and L. Zolnay: *Esztergom* (Budapest, 1956)

I. Horváth, M. Kelemen and I. Torma: 'Komárom megye régészeti topográfiája: Esztergom és a dorogi járás' [The archaeological topography of Komárom county: Esztergom and the district of Dorog], *Magyarország régészeti topográfiája* [The archaeological topography of Hungary], v (Budapest, 1979)

2. CATHEDRAL. Built on a hill north of the royal castle, the original cathedral of St Adalbert—the first in Hungary—was contemporary with the founding of the archiepiscopate of Esztergom; its construction, therefore, must have begun in 1001. The ruins of the medieval building disappeared when, in the mid-18th century, the ground was levelled for the construction of the new cathedral. The only reliable sources for the original building are drawings made for surveying purposes, in particular a ground-plan by Anton Hartmann published in J. N. Máthes's book *Veteris arcis Strigoniensis* (Esztergom, 1827), and a section (1756; Vienna, Staatsarchv, Kriegsarchv) by Andreas Krey (*d* 1782). Apart from these, only a small number of architectural sculptures have survived (Esztergom, Castle Mus.), mostly 12th-century capitals in a classicizing or figurative style. These were most probably part of the second building (no definite information about the first cathedral and its decoration is available). The altar of the Virgin in front of the *chorus minor* was consecrated before 1156, and the west part of the nave was built after this time. On the west door, the *porta speciosa*, Archbishop Job (*reg* 1185–1203) and King Béla III (*reg* 1172–96) were depicted as donors. Sculpted fragments surviving from the entrance seem to indicate that the sculptor trained around 1180 in the Emilian circle of Benedetto Antelami. Finishing touches in marble incrustation were added by masters from northern France, who also worked on the royal castle in the 1190s, at which time they introduced the Early Gothic style to Esztergom. The rebuilding of the medieval cathedral in Gothic style is mentioned in a written record of 1307; the work must have been completed by the time of Archbishop Csanád Telegdi (*reg* 1330–49). In the course of the remodelling, the main apse was replaced by a Gothic polygonal chancel, and the entire building was vaulted. A Late Gothic reconstruction

2. Esztergom, archiepiscopal cathedral of St Adalbert by Pál Kühnel, János Packh and József Hild, 1822–69; engraving from A. Vambéry: *Hungary in Ancient, Mediaeval and Modern Times* (London, 1890)

took place from 1449 to 1453 on the orders of Archbishop Dénes Szécsi (*reg* 1440–65). In 1543 Pasha Sinan converted the cathedral into a mosque. In the Turkish siege of 1594 it was reduced to ruins, the remains removed in 1763 and finally levelled in 1822–3. The only part that survived was an auxiliary building housing the red marble centrally planned and domed sepulchral chapel (1506–7) of Archbishop Tamás Bakócz (*reg* 1497–1521), built in the style of the Florentine Renaissance and showing a close affinity with the work of Giuliano da Sangallo in particular. The white marble multipartite altar (1519) was sculpted by the Florentine Andrea di Piero Ferrucci (*see* FERRUCCI, (2)); Johannes Fiorentinus (*fl* early 16th century) also worked on the sculptural decoration of the chapel.

Archbishop Ferenc Barkóczy commissioned Isidore Canevale and Franz Anton Hillebrandt to rebuild the cathedral and the Archbishop's residence, but only a small Baroque church dedicated to the protomartyr St Stephen was constructed between 1768 and 1771 on the designs of Hillebrandt and overseen by Anton Hartmann. In 1820 Archbishop Sándor Rudnay (*reg* 1820–31) reinstated the building programme after eliminating all remains except Hillebrandt's Baroque church and the Bakócz Chapel, which was disassembled and rebuilt as a side chapel of the cathedral. In 1820–21 plans for the cathedral and the Archbishop's residence were drawn up by Pál Kühnel (*d* 1824), who oversaw its construction until his death, after which time JÁNOS PACKH became the chief architect of the project. The new church, the largest in Hungary, was built (1822–69) in Neo-classical style on a cross-shaped ground-plan and dominates Castle Hill overlooking the Danube (*see* fig. 2). It has a central dome 72 m high and a porticoed entrance with Corinthian columns facing an elliptical square. The tomb monument for *Prince Primate Ambrus Károly* (1826) by Giuseppe Pisani (1757–1839), the white marble altar of *St Stephen* (1831) by István Ferenczy (1792–1856) and *St Stephen Baptized by St Adalbert* (1824–7; Esztergom, Cathedral Treasury) by János Mihály Hesz (1768–after 1833)—the painting for the main altar—were all completed during Rudnay's archiepiscopate. After the death of Rudnay in 1831 and Packh in 1839, construction of the cathedral proceeded at a slower pace, although Archbishop József Kopácsy (*reg* 1838–47) commissioned JÓZSEF HILD to continue with the work. Hild's most important contributions were the erection of the dome (completed 1845) and the completion of the west front. The cathedral was consecrated on 31 August 1856, but its actual completion and the decoration of its interior in a historicist style continued. The reliefs (1841–5) on the exterior and in the nave were executed by Marco Casagrande (1804–80). The crypt contains tomb monuments (e.g. those of Archbishops *Dénes Szécsi* (*reg* 1440–65) and *Johannes Vitéz*) from the earlier cathedral and the church of St Stephen. The cathedral treasury, open to the public since 1886, has the remains of the medieval treasury, the first inventory of which is known from 1528, and includes such works of art as an early votive cross (*c.* 1250), the cloisonné chalice (*c.* 1450) of Dénes Szécsi and the 'Calvary of Matthias' of Paris (1402) and Italy (1469–90), as well as several gold objects (*see* GOTHIC, fig. 89). The library, housed in a building erected in 1853 in Viziváros, below Castle Hill, contains medieval manuscripts and a

significant collection of early printed works, including 738 incunabula.

BIBLIOGRAPHY

J. N. Mathés: *Veteris arcis Strigoniensis, monumentorum ibidem erutorum, aliarumque antiquitatum lythographicis tabulis ornata descriptio* [Description of the ancient architecture at Esztergom, of excavated monuments there, and of other antiquities, enriched with lithographic tables] (Strigonii [Esztergom], 1827)

G. Edvi-Illés: *Az esztergomi főszékesegyház* [The archiepiscopal cathedral of Esztergom] (Budapest, 1929)

J. Balogh: 'L'Origine du style des sculptures en bois de la Hongrie médiévale', *Acta Hist. A. Acad. Sci. Hung.*, iii (1956), pp. 231–54

A. Zádor: *Az esztergomi főszékesegyház* [The archiepiscopal cathedral of Esztergom] (Budapest, 1970)

E. Marosi: *Die Anfänge der Gotik in Ungarn: Esztergom in der Kunst des 12.–13. Jahrhunderts* (Budapest, 1984)

ERNÖ MAROSI

Eszterháza. *See* FERTŐD.

Etampes, Notre-Dame. Former collegiate church in Seine-et-Oise, France. The church was founded by King Robert II (*reg* 996–1031), but only the crypt of this building survives. Construction of the existing building extended from the second to the third quarter of the 12th century. The importance of Etampes for sculpture lies in its Early Gothic portal, situated in the second bay on the south side of the nave (*see* fig.). It was erected after the nave and aisles were completed but before the construction of the south transept arm, which truncates the portal massif. The south portal combines the newly invented column statue with a strong interest in narrative and a distinctive sculptural style.

The *Ascension* occupies the tympanum of the portal, with the eleven Apostles and the Virgin flanked by two witnesses to the Ascension on the lintel below. The Elders

Etampes, Notre-Dame, south portal, mid-12th century

of the Apocalypse on the inner archivolts introduce a reference to the Second Coming. The outer archivolt bears Old Testament prophets. The angels in the spandrels refer to the Ascension and are reminiscent of the victories of Roman triumphal arches. The column statues, which derive from Saint-Denis, include Old Testament kings, queens and patriarchs.

The capitals of the portal form a frieze, providing a field for narrative. The closest counterpart to this unusual feature appears on the west portal at Chartres Cathedral. The frieze depicts the *Life of Christ*, with *Infancy* scenes on the west and the *Passion* on the east. The capitals of the jambs juxtapose the *Temptation of Christ* with the *Temptation of Adam and Eve*. On the capitals of the east and west embrasures are paired New Testament scenes, so that the frieze reads both narratively and symbolically.

The carving of the portal exhibits a metallic incisiveness, in which projecting, circular drapery folds accentuate the forms beneath. The combination of a strong sense of volume with linear mannerisms is exceptional in the Ile-de-France, and the style has been linked to Burgundy, to Berry and to Palestine. The closest stylistic affinities lie, however, with Romanesque sculptural traditions in north France and Belgium, such as the column statues from the destroyed church of St Géry-au-Mont-des-Boeufs in Cambrai (Cambrai, Mus. Mun). The fine grained limestone employed for the sculpture came from quarries south of Paris. In sheltered areas there are traces of medieval colouring.

The sculptors also contributed to the west façade portal of Chartres, and there is controversy over the question of whether Etampes was the model for the larger Chartrain portal or a reduced copy of it (*see* CHARTRES, §I, 2). No firm evidence resolves the debate, although subtle differences in style, iconography and design suggest that Etampes was earlier. The usual dating of Chartres to 1145–55 supplies the only chronology for Etampes. The destruction of all the heads on the portal is attributed to Huguenot iconoclasm in 1562. Restoration at Notre-Dame has excluded the south portal, apart from repairs to masonry. In the late 1980s the portal sculpture was cleaned and consolidated using a technique employed at Chartres.

BIBLIOGRAPHY
B. Fleureau: *Les Antiquitez de la ville et du duché d'Estampes* (Paris, 1683/*R* Marseille, 1977)
W. Vöge: *Die Anfänge des monumentalen Stiles im Mittelalter* (Strasbourg, 1894)
E. Lefèvre-Pontalis: 'Les Campagnes de construction de Notre-Dame d'Etampes', *Bull. Mnmtl.*, lxxiii (1909), pp. 5–31
L.-E. Lefèvre: *Le Portail royal d'Etampes et la doctrine de Saint-Irénée sur la rédemption* (Paris, 1915)
A. Priest: 'The Masters of the West Façade of Chartres', *A. Stud.*, i (1923), pp. 37–40
W. S. Stoddard: *The West Portals of Saint-Denis and Chartres* (Cambridge, MA, 1952, rev. 1986)
L. Grodecki: 'La "Première Sculpture gothique": Wilhem Vöge et l'état actuel des problèmes', *Bull. Mnmtl*, cxvii (1959), pp. 265–89
A. Lapeyre: *Des façades occidentales de Saint-Denis et de Chartres aux portails de Laon* (Paris, 1960)
C. Grosset: 'Les Sculptures du portail sud de Notre-Dame d'Etampes', *Cah. Civilis. Méd.*, vii (1964), pp. 53–61
B. Kerber: *Burgund und die Entwicklung der französischen Kathedralskulptur im 12. Jahrhundert* (Reckinghausen, 1966)
W. Sauerländer: 'Sculptures on Early Gothic Churches: The State of Research and Open Questions', *Gesta*, ix (1970), pp. 32–48
——: *Gothic Sculpture in France, 1140–1270* (New York, 1972)
K. D. Nolan: *The Early Gothic Portal of Notre-Dame in Etampes* (diss., Columbia U., 1985)
——: 'Narrative in the Capital Frieze of Notre-Dame at Etampes', *A. Bull.*, lxxi (1989), pp. 166–84

KATHLEEN D. NOLAN

Etchells, Frederick (*b* Newcastle upon Tyne, 14 Sept 1886; *d* Folkestone, 16 Aug 1973). English painter and architect. He studied at the Royal College of Art from *c.* 1908 to 1911, before renting a studio in Paris where he met Pablo Picasso, Georges Braque and Amedeo Modigliani. Roger Fry invited him to submit a design for a large-scale mural scheme for the Borough Polytechnic, London, in 1911 and included his work in the *Second Post-Impressionist Exhibition* (London, Grafton Gals, 1912). He had already collaborated with Duncan Grant on a mural for Virginia Woolf's house in Brunswick Square. In the autumn of 1913 Etchells joined the OMEGA WORK-SHOPS; disillusioned with Fry, he joined Wyndham Lewis, whose interest in Cubism and Futurism he shared, in walking out of the Omega. They exhibited with other emergent Vorticists in the 'Cubist Room' section of the *Camden Town Group and Others* exhibition in Brighton (December 1913–January 1914).

Etchells joined Lewis at the REBEL ART CENTRE and contributed illustrations to the first issue of *Blast* magazine (1914). The following year he participated in the Vorticist Exhibition (June 1915) in London. Few of his Vorticist works survive, but a gouache, probably called *Stilts* (Brit. Council Col.), shows the girder-like architectural language of Vorticism in its most urban phase. Medical disability prevented Etchells from fighting in the war, but he painted a large picture called *Armistice Day, Munitions Centre* for the Canadian War Committee (Ottawa, N.G.).

After the war Etchells gave up painting, despite Lewis's encouragement, to pursue his interest in architecture, already apparent in watercolours like *Gunwalloe* (*c.* 1922; priv. col., see Cork, 1975, p. 545). He studied for an ARIBA and achieved success in 1930 with his building for the Crawford Advertising Agency in Holborn, one of the first buildings in London of the Modern Movement. Etchells revealed his interest in Le Corbusier by translating his highly influential work as *Towards a New Architecture* (London, 1927).

WRITINGS
Original Woodcuts and Drawings by Edward Wadsworth (exh. cat., London, Adelphi Gal., 1919)
BIBLIOGRAPHY
Obituary, *The Times* (18 Aug 1973)
J. Betjeman: Obituary, *Archit. Rev.* [London], cliv/920 (1973), pp. 271–2
R. Cork: *Vorticism and Abstract Art in the First Machine Age*, 2 vols (London, 1975–6)
For further bibliography *see* VORTICISM.

RICHARD CORK

Etching [Fr. *eau-forte*; It. *acquaforte*; Ger. *Ätzung*; Sp. *aguafuerte*]. Type of intaglio print, the design of which is printed from grooves corroded into a plate by acid; the term is applied also to the process by which the composition is bitten into the printing plate.

I. Materials and techniques. II. Historical survey.

I. *Materials and techniques.*

The usual material for the etching plate is copper, although the earliest German etchings, at the beginning of the 16th century, were made on iron plates. Since the third quarter of the 19th century zinc has often been used, being cheaper and more sympathetic to coarser effects. Brass, aluminium and even composite metals, such as tinned or chromed steel, have also been employed. To prepare the plate, it is highly polished, then coated with an acid-resistant ground, dry to the touch but soft and flexible enough to be drawn through with a metal point without flaking.

The usual ground is formed from wax, asphalt and a resin such as mastic. A harder ground in which a drying oil is substituted for wax was developed in the second quarter of the 17th century for etchings produced in imitation of engraving. In the 18th century a softer, sticky ground was invented, which included tallow or, more recently, petroleum jelly. This so-called 'soft ground' is used under a membrane such as thin paper on which the drawing is executed with a pencil or stylus (*see* ETCHING, SOFT-GROUND). Thus instead of being scraped from the metal plate by the point itself, the ground is lifted from the plate where the pressure of the point has adhered the ground to the reverse of the paper; the resulting line reproduces the texture of the overlaying paper. In the 20th century other substances, such as fabric, string etc have been used to pick up the ground, imprinting their individual silhouettes and textures.

The conventional wax-based ground is traditionally formed into a small ball wrapped in lint-free silk or other cloth and applied by rubbing the ball over the surface of the metal plate, which has been warmed. The melted ground is smoothed and thinned with a dabber, a pad for dabbing ink on plates or blocks, which is also wrapped in lint-free cloth or leather. Melted etching ground may also be spread with a roller made of hard rubber, linoleum or leather, or dissolved in a rapidly drying solvent and brushed or poured over the tilted plate.

After the ground is laid, it is usually coated with soot from a smoking flame to increase the contrast between the uncoated ground, which is luminous brown, and the metal exposed by drawing. It is thought by some that the smoking action enables the ground to resist the action of acid better. Alternatively, a white pigment may be incorporated into the ground, to simulate on copper the effect of a line drawn in red on white paper.

Preliminary drawings may be transferred to the grounded plate by means of carbon paper (or some comparable intermediary pigment layer), or a drawing in loose pigment (such as graphite or chalk) may be laid face down on the grounded plate and run through the roller press. This latter process obviates the need for the composition to be designed in reverse. The artist draws on the grounded plate with an etching needle or metal point sharp enough to penetrate the ground but polished so that it does not catch on the plate. Points may be of various thickness, but the width of the etched line is usually determined by the process of biting rather than drawing.

Alternatively, in a process possibly invented by the 17th-century Dutch etcher Hercules Segers and greatly developed in the 19th century, the artist may execute his drawing on the ungrounded plate in water-soluble ink, usually containing a high proportion of sugar syrup, then covering it with a water-permeable ground. The plate is then immersed in water so that the areas of ground above the ink lift away as the ink dissolves. If the drawn lines are of substantial width, they may be covered with an AQUATINT ground, which ensures better retention of printing ink. Once the design has been executed on the grounded plate, the plate is exposed to the action of acid, so that all areas of bare metal are corroded. This acid, known as the mordant, may be nitric acid, usually diluted to half strength or less, or a combination of chemicals, such as hydrochloric acid and potassium chlorate (so-called Dutch mordant), ferric chlorate, potassium dichlorate, dilute sulphuric acid, hydrochloric acid (for aluminium) etc. It is the action of the mordant that gives printed etched lines their characteristic coarseness compared to engraved lines of equal strength; bitten grooves always retain a degree of roughness compared to the sharp incisions made by a burin or engraving tool, and this characteristic is transmitted to the ink lines formed in the grooves.

The various mordants each have restrictions as well as advantages; the by-products of such chemicals include the release of gas. Nitric acid, depending on its concentration, can bite very rapidly, forming gas bubbles along the lines. These must be continually brushed away for the bite to continue evenly, although their presence is a useful guide to where and how rapidly biting is progressing, so that foul biting or lack of reaction may be detected early on. In the case of ferric chloride, a gentle and predictable mordant, the action of biting forms sediment in the grooves, impeding its continuation. To forestall this, the plate is usually bitten while suspended upside down in the acid bath, so that the sediment falls away from the grooves. Thus the benefit of a dependable mordant is somewhat offset by the inability to monitor its action. Dutch mordant, another easily controlled agent, tends to bite more directly downward rather than also eating away at the sides (a characteristic of nitric acid). It is therefore preferred especially in areas of close hatching where individual lines are at risk of merging into a broader pit. However, as Dutch mordant does not release gas as it bites, its action cannot so easily be followed except by periodic probing of the lines to determine their depth. In sum, mordants are selected depending upon the type of metal plates, the sequence of intended biting procedures and the ultimate technical and visual effect desired.

Acid may be applied in various ways. Traditionally, a grounded plate was edged with a wax lip forming a shallow pan into which the acid was poured. Another method was to lay the plate, its edges and underside coated with an acid-resistant varnish, into a wooden or earthenware tray set at an angle over a receptacle: acid was repeatedly poured over the plate, which was rotated so that the acid affected all lines equally.

From the 19th century it became more common for the plate, its edges and back protected, to be immersed in an acid bath. Acid may also be applied directly to local areas of the plate with a brush or feather, the plate ungrounded in the *lavis* process (in which the plate is worked to create tonal areas imitative of ink and wash drawing): or it may be mixed into a paste which is spread on to the plate. These techniques permit local areas to be bitten with varying degrees of strength. Using acid in tandem with a viscous liquid (such as saliva), the action of the acid and the area affected may also be modified. After the lines have been bitten to the desired width and depth (determined by probing the grooves with a needle as they form or by timing the bath in a mordant of known strength), the plate is rinsed to halt the action of the acid and the ground removed, traditionally by polishing with charcoal or by the use of a suitable solvent.

Plates are commonly executed in a sequence of bitings in order to obtain tonal gradation through variation of line width. After the first biting, those lines that have been shallowly bitten and that are to remain the lightest in the final composition are covered with an acid-resistant substance, such as grease, fluid ground or varnish, in a procedure called stopping out, so that those lines which are to appear darker are further exposed to acid. Alternatively, additional lines are drawn on the grounded plate, so that lines already bitten will bite more deeply in a second bath compared to the new lines, whose exposure to the mordant action is shorter; or the plate may be re-covered completely with a transparent ground on which new lines are drawn to be bitten in a completely separate operation. A combination of these sequences of biting, stopping-out, redrawing and regrounding may also be undertaken. Each acid bath exposes the plate to additional risk of foul biting, and the more complex the process the greater the chance of technical miscalculation.

Once the plate is bitten and the ground removed, it is printed in the usual manner of all intaglio plates, by wiping ink into the lines, wiping clean the surface of the plate and passing the inked plate together with dampened paper through a roller press under concentrated pressure. Similarly, corrections to the plate are prepared in the same manner as in other intaglio processes: the faulty area is burnished or scraped down, the plate being pounded level from behind if a substantial amount of metal has been removed; its surface is polished before regrounding and re-etching. There is no technical obstacle to combining etching with other intaglio processes on the same plate. The final printed image may therefore contain etching, engraving, drypoint, aquatint and mezzotint in any combination, although different artists and schools of printmaking have held vastly differing ideas about the value of purity of technique.

II. Historical survey.

1. Origins. 2. 17th century. 3. 18th century. 4. The 19th-century Etching Revival. 5. 20th century.

1. ORIGINS. Etching as a printed art form is believed to have been derived from the use of etching to decorate iron (steel) armour in northern Europe in the 15th century, or even earlier. Technical instructions appear in early 15th-century manuscripts (London, BL, MS. Sloane 962; Oxford, Bodleian Lib., MS. Ashmole 1397), and surviving specimens date from the last decades of the century.

(i) Germany and the Netherlands. The earliest printed etchings are believed to have been made by Daniel Hopfer I, Hieronymus Hopfer and Lambert Hopfer of Augsburg at the beginning of the 16th century. The earliest dated etching that survives, a *Girl Washing her Feet* (1513; Hollstein, no. 9), is by the Swiss Urs Graf. Another early, though undated, example, *Venus and Mercury* (Hollstein, no. 834), by Hans Burgkmair I, is of special interest due to its origin in Augsburg, the centre of the German armourers' industry. Contemporary impressions from these plates are extremely rare; the Urs Graf etching survives in only a single example.

The first notable artist to use the process for original compositions, and whose etchings survive in contemporary impressions in significant numbers, was Albrecht Dürer. He executed six etchings; the *Man of Sorrows* (Hollstein, no. 22), which by its technical simplicity is probably the earliest, is dated 1515, and the latest, *The Cannon* (Hollstein, no. 96), is dated 1518. These experiments with a new printmaking technique were virtually simultaneous with Dürer's even fewer ventures into drypoint; they came immediately after his extended concentration on the publication of his four great woodcut series and his production of three iconographically elaborate, technically virtuosic engravings. It may be surmised that he felt the need of a change, but, by the evidence of the very limited numbers of etchings that he produced, the new process did not satisfy him. Like his few predecessors in etching, Dürer used only a single bite.

Most of Dürer's etched plates are notable for an unprecedented vigour of line, which is dramatically more bold in his *Abduction of Proserpine* (Hollstein, no. 67; see figs 1 and 2), for instance, than that of Hieronymus Hopfer in his etched copy, also on iron, of Dürer's plate (Hollstein, no. 47). Thus the effect from a clean-wiped impression of a Dürer etching would be exceptionally stark in the contrasts of line with blank paper. However, many impressions of his etchings (produced by the artist himself) that show no signs of having been printed from a rusted plate and are presumably early were printed with significant amounts of plate tone (that is, with a film of ink left on the surface of the plate to darken areas of the print). Perhaps regretting the absence in these single-bite etchings of the subtle transitions possible in engraving, Dürer exploited the emotive device in the intaglio printer's repertory that would become the hallmark of several master etchers of later centuries.

At virtually the same time as Dürer abandoned etching, other northern European printmakers brought technical innovations to the process and applied it to subjects in ways that likewise would have consequences to this day. Lucas van Leyden and Albrecht Altdorfer were among the first to adopt for etching the copper plates traditional for engraving and to combine the two intaglio techniques: van Leyden's portrait of the *Emperor Maximilian I* (1520; B. 172) is considered the earliest dated example of etching on copper. In this plate the general composition is laid in with etching, with engraving reserved for areas of subtle tonal transitions such as the flesh, establishing a systematic division of the two processes that would be developed and exploited to its ultimate refinement in reproductive

1. Albrecht Dürer: *Abduction of Proserpine*, etching, 310×215 mm, 1516 (London, British Museum)

2. Albrecht Dürer: *Abduction of Proserpine* (detail), etching, 1516 (London, British Museum)

'engravings' in 18th-century Britain, which were in fact based entirely upon etching.

Only a decade later the Italian artist Parmigianino, working in combination with a cutter of chiaroscuro blocks, combined etching for line and woodcut for tone in a reproduction of the tapestry design by Raphael *Peter and John Healing the Lame Man* (*c.* 1523–7; B. 7). This combination of etching with a relief process, more complex in its production requirements, was far more rare over succeeding centuries than the combination of etching and engraving, or other intaglio techniques, in a single plate.

The early application of etching by the Germans Albrecht Altdorfer, Hanns Lautensack and Augustin Hirschvogel to landscape subjects prefigured the development of the technique as a special province of landscape artists. Furthermore, the use of multiple biting was first clearly exploited in landscape etchings by Hirschvogel, in the strengthening of foreground details to enhance the illusion of recession into space. An additional technical advantage of etching, which was realized early by German etchers, was its speed of execution, so that it was employed to record topical events. Thus Nicolas Hogenberg (*fl* 1527; *d* before 23 Sept 1539) represented on 38 plates the entry of the Holy Roman Emperor Charles V into Bologna in 1529. The process was also quickly taken up for pattern and ornament books, manuals, representations of costume etc, in which artistic subtlety counted for less than clarity of detail and economy of production. The first dated book illustrated by etching was Hirschvogel's *Geometria* ([Nuremberg], 1543). The brothers Jan and Lucas van Doetechum invented a mode of etching that closely resembled engraving, foreshadowing the work of Jacques Callot and Abraham Bosse.

(ii) Italy. In Italy, Dürer's role as innovative pioneer was assumed by Parmigianino. Although Marcantonio Raimondi and other far less consequential early 16th-century printmakers were acquainted with etching as a preliminary to engraving, the first independent and significant etched plates were executed by Parmigianino, a pre-eminent painter and not a professional engraver. Some time after 1527, when Parmigianino fled Rome for Bologna, he executed *c.* 16 plates on copper in a single-bite technique, which were often finished by burin touches. They are notable for the openness of their graphic structure, and, far more even than the deftly linear landscapes of Hans Sebald Lautensack, they imitate the rapid line possible in pen sketching. The informality and breadth of handling of Parmigianino's etchings, combined with a compositional exploitation of broad areas of white paper untouched by printed lines, set the style for much of Italian etching for the next 200 years.

A chain of influence from Parmigianino through the Venetian painters Andrea Schiavone, who copied Parmigianino's etchings, and Battista Franco leads to the other great innovator among 16th-century Italian etchers, Federico Barocci of Urbino, a pupil of Franco. He executed only four prints, all in the 1580s, which demonstrate a systematic use of rebiting far more ambitious than anything previously attempted. Even repeated biting did not, however, forestall additional work with the burin to blend the linear networks and enrich the tonal complexity of his plates further, which in a work such as the very large *St Francis in the Chapel* (1581; B. 4) approaches that of painting. As a painter and not a professional engraver, Barocci, like Parmigianino before him and many other etchers to follow, seems to have preferred etching as the fundamental printmaking process because of the direct relation of the use of the needle to that of draughtsman's and painter's tools. Indeed, bundles of close hatching in Barocci's prints approximate brushed passages. His use of the burin remained a subtle adjunct to the basic etched work and was never systematized for specific kinds of depicted surfaces or effects in the manner of professional printmakers.

(iii) France. Etching was probably imported into France by a Bolognese pupil of Parmigianino, Antonio Fantuzzi, who emigrated to Fontainebleau with other Italian and also Flemish painters to join with native artists in establishing a new style in the decoration of the royal country residence. Many of their etchings, all created between 1542 and 1548, reproduce compositions by the Italian painters Rosso Fiorentino, Francesco Primaticcio and Luca Penni for this project. The most important etchers were Fantuzzi, Léon Davent, trained as an engraver, Jean Mignon and Domenico del Barbiere. Their works are characterized by a rough, open, single-bite technique applied on to imperfectly polished plates on which highlight areas are sometimes burnished. In early impressions the result is a tonal effect of coarse black lines on a grey background, accented occasionally with paler modelling. Ornamental effect is emphasized, as in the case of Fantuzzi's landscape views, in which decorative borders dominate naturalistic central motifs. In the case of figural etchings by Justin de Juste (*fl c.* 1537; *d c.* 1559), the antics of acrobats and contortionists are assembled on the printed page as entirely fantastic tableaux coalesced into a single ornament.

2. 17TH CENTURY.

(i) France and Italy. The divergent paths of 17th-century etchers who continued the technical development of the medium are epitomized by the two leading French practitioners: Jacques Callot and Claude Lorrain. Significantly both artists, natives of Lorraine, learnt to etch in Rome, where at the end of the 16th century and beginning of the 17th there was a large and varied international colony of painters, printmakers and publishers. The most prominent among the painters who etched were the Italians Pietro Testa and Giovanni Benedetto Castiglione, the Fleming Paul Bril and the Dutchman Bartholomeus Breenbergh. Callot, in Italy from *c.* 1608 to 1621, was presumably introduced by the Florentine painter and prolific etcher Antonio Tempesta into Medici circles, where he obtained the patronage that set the style for his witty, exact and mannered art. Whether he learnt etching from Tempesta, with whom he collaborated in a set of 29 etchings, the

Funeral Book of the Queen of Spain (Florence, 1612), or from Giulio Parigi (1571–1635), as was asserted by Filippo Baldinucci, he rapidly extended the technique the better to serve his developing manner.

In one procedural development Callot substituted a hard ground made from oil and mastic (lute-maker's varnish) for the by-then traditional, softer, wax ground. In another he bevelled the tip of the etcher's round steel needle to form the oval-faceted *échoppe*, which could be rotated between the fingers to cut a smoothly tapered line in the new hard ground in easy emulation of engraving but which retained the greater flexibility of etching. Yet another potential inherent in etching was perhaps even more important to Callot, a professional, production-orientated print designer whose court and clerical patronage in Florence and, after 1621, in Nancy and Paris demanded the intricate, systematic rendering of elaborate iconographies. He exploited multiple biting to an innovative degree of technical complexity, again to the end of gaining speedily for his plates the rich colouration of traditional, tediously elaborated, prestigious engraving. While his larger compositions, such as the two versions of the *Fair at Impruneta* (1620, *c.* 1622; Lieure, nos 361, 478) and the *Temptation of St Antony* (1611, *c.* 1635; Lieure, nos 188, 1416) and the six-plate *Siege of Breda* (1628; Lieure, no. 593), are more obvious *tours-de-force*, miniature images such as those of the *Balli di Sfessania* (*c.* 1621–2; Lieure, nos 379–402) and the *Large Miseries of War* (1633; Lieure, nos 1339–56) offer equally virtuosic demonstrations of a fully realized etched style dependent upon absolute mastery over its materials.

All these technical developments were widely disseminated by their description by Abraham Bosse in *De la manière de graver à l'eau forte et au burin* (1645), which became the manual for generations of etchers. His book has given Callot a false position as the inventor of tools and techniques that he only standardized and popularized. Even more of a barrier to a correct understanding of technical developments in etching in the 17th century is Bosse's dearth of praise for painterly expedients, which in fact were the primary innovative focus of 17th-century etching. Two painters (and, significantly, not professional printmakers), Claude and Jacques Bellange, another native of Lorraine but of an earlier generation, played important roles in these developments. They followed the lead of Barocci towards greater tonal complexity achieved not through systematic rebitings but through complex interweavings of bitings, burnishing and additions of tone and line by other intaglio means than conventional etching.

Bellange was painter to the court of the duchy of Lorraine at Nancy by 1602; thus his prominence as a leading creative artist antedated by a decade the introduction of intaglio printing to the court in 1610. Before his death, however, he produced at least four dozen plates in less than ten years. His characteristic images are distinguished by extensive reworkings with needle and burin and by burnishing. This burnishing, together with an almost compulsive use of stippling derived from Barocci and the innovative willingness to let the contour of brushstrokes of stop-out varnish stand as positive passages of light, resulted in surfaces of a peculiarly lunar luminosity, especially in early impressions, in which highlights shine

3. Claude Lorrain: *Landscape with Country Dance*, etching, early impression of 1st state, 195×255 mm, 1639 (London, British Museum)

against a grey tone surviving from residual plate-polishing scratches. All these characteristics are seen in *St James* (Robert-Dumesnil, no. 24) and *St John* (Robert-Dumesnil, no. 29). Far more elaborate compositions, such as *Christ Carrying the Cross* (*c.* 1616; Robert-Dumesnil, no. 7) and the *Adoration of the Magi* (*c.* 1610–16; Robert-Dumesnil, no. 2; for illustration *see* BELLANGE, JACQUES), demonstrate Bellange's technical mastery of etching, which hitherto had never been used reliably for such complex conceptions.

Claude, like Barocci before him, seems to have turned to etching early in his artistic career when he was without important commissions. After producing *c.* 40 plates up to *c.* 1640, when demand for his paintings was strong, he abandoned printmaking for at least a decade, resuming with five plates over the next 13 years, which are among the most fully realized compositions of his printed works. His etched output is distinctive for its survival in many states. Although the trivial addition or correction of numbering and the nature of the paper in later states often point to posthumous reworking and reprinting, study of earlier-state sequences makes clear his interest in developing the effect of the plate even after the composition was fully established (usually in the first state) through rebiting, redrawing, burnishing and even, in the case of the *Shepherd with Goats* (*c.* 1634; Robert-Dumesnil,

nos 26–7), cutting a completed image into halves. His etched work, especially his rework, is the antithesis of the clear and concise graphic idiom perfected by Callot. In Claude's work individual lines are suppressed into tone, whether in the mossy shadows of a copse or the sheen of a becalmed harbour. To achieve his rugose woodland textures, he often used a blotched or pitted line; in order to represent sun-struck clouds without lines, he even resorted in the large *Landscape with Country Dance* (1639; Robert-Dumesnil, no. 24; see fig. 3) to brushing acid directly on to the plate. These technical expedients, equivalent to the exquisite adjustment of glazes in his painted landscapes, did not bite deeply into the copper plate, and their intention and effectiveness can be gauged only in early impressions. When he combined his etching methods with individualistic plate wiping, the effect in a few impressions is comparable to his drawings executed in blended brown and black inks and washes and crumbled black chalk. His etchings demonstrate the affinity with drawing that the medium seemed uniquely to hold for painters; that is, the effect of his plates seen in their best impressions is to his chalk and wash drawings as, for example, the open etched style of Parmigianino is to his quill-pen drawings. The two painters' etching techniques, diametrically opposite from each other, are equally distant from the commercially more viable idiom of deeply bitten, clearly structured linear systems of the professional etcher Callot.

The subordination of the etched line into idiosyncratically blended touches, the development of actual etched tones and the exploitation of white line and tone masses, all non-commercial techniques in that they could produce only a few fully realized impressions per plate, were characteristic of many 17th-century artists. The Italians Giovanni Benedetto Castiglione and Stefano della Bella, who worked in Paris, and the Czech Wenceslaus Hollar, who worked in Strasbourg, Cologne, London and Antwerp and travelled elsewhere, are notable for their success in conveying the flickering shadows of wooded glades and torch-lit ruins, and the soft textures of fur, hair and delicate textiles in what a later century can rightfully describe as an impressionistic etched style.

(ii) The Netherlands. In the work of two Dutch etchers of the 17th century, Hercules Segers and Rembrandt, technical expedients adopted and, indeed, invented to enhance the tonal potential of etching brought this intaglio print form into command of its full resources. These two pre-eminent etchers were preceded and joined in the Netherlands by others of great technical capacity, notably Esaias van de Velde, his cousin Jan van der Velde II, Willem Buytewech, Jan Lievens, Jan Both, Jacob van Ruisdael and Simon de Vlieger. All these, and most of the other etchers in the Netherlands, were also painters. Their common preoccupation with tone, often achieved at the expense of orderly linear structure or at least through the means of stippling and other alinear graphic systems, conveys their attentiveness to effects of light, reflection and atmosphere developed by the 17th-century Dutch schools of landscape, interior and still-life painting. In such an etching as *Cottage and Clump of Trees near a Small Stream* (1646; Hollstein, no. 7) by van Ruisdael, line can fairly be said not to exist. This is not, however, to overlook the vigour of Dutch painter-etchers' line, liberated from the conventions of the reproductive printmaker. While *Bathsheba Reading David's Letter* (c. 1615; Hollstein, no. 4) by Buytewech is modulated by stippling, the contour and hatching lines dramatically force the figure to the very edges of the plate. The sketched peasants by Cornelis Bega are so boldly needled into the ground, in their lumpy clothes and hunched forms, that they become granitic.

In the rare works by Hercules Segers etching is brought through several technical innovations into an actual approximation of painting. First he often printed his etchings on cloth, adopting the physical support of painting; and

4. Rembrandt: *Joseph and Potiphar's Wife*, etching, 1st state of two, 1634 (Haarlem, Teylers Museum)

he frequently toned his support, whether cloth or paper, often with several hues, to provide a coloured ground for the printing ink, which frequently in his works is itself not the conventional black but blue, green, burnt orange or even yellowish white. The colouring of his etchings is supported by a tonal complexity generated by his innovative use both of stop-out varnish to provide detailed highlights to entire compositions, as in the *Large Tree* (Haverkamp-Begemann, no. 34), and of LIFT-GROUND ETCHING, apparently his own invention, as seen in the *Large Tree* and a *Road Bordered by Trees* (Haverkamp-Begemann, no. 26), to produce a full range of painterly values. Whether Segers was attempting in his prints to reproduce paintings for commercial ends is doubtful, however, as so few of his prints survive: only 183 impressions are known from 54 plates. There are very few duplicates among the multiple impressions from a given plate: he experimented with colour schemes of ground and ink, often supplementing them with plate tone and added washes, to individualize every example.

This obsessive interest in variation of impression, which ran counter to the contemporary commercial development in Flanders of etching as a formulaic basis for finished engravings after painting, was brought to its highest pitch by Rembrandt. He converted etching from a linear medium to a tonal one, particularly in his experimentation with wiping a film of ink overall or in strategically blended locales to focus on a character or an action or to modulate the mood or atmosphere of a scene. Such effects of wiping are, however, potential in the printing of any intaglio plate; and, indeed, in his later years Rembrandt's 'etchings' were in fact amalgams of engraving and drypoint (usually) superimposed on an etched basis, which might well be almost obliterated in the process. Thus it may fairly be said that the usual estimate of Rembrandt as the consummate creative etcher should be revised to rate him as the consummate creative intaglio printmaker; his accomplishment thus falls outside the scope of this article.

Three aspects of Rembrandt's achievement nevertheless derive purely from the etched process. First, throughout his career, from the tangled netting of such early prints as the *Great Jewish Bride* (1635; B. 340) through the unelaborated scrawl of such sketches as *Six's Bridge* (1645; B. 208) to the hatched screens of such late prints as the transcendant *Christ Appearing to the Apostles* (1656; B. 89), his etched lines exploit as do no other artist's the technique's potential for conveying the idiosyncratic touch of the draughtsman at a particular instant with a specific intention. Secondly, Rembrandt used the process of biting to exquisite variety of effect. From the tender portrait of *Saskia* (1641–2; B. 359), in which his dying wife is portrayed with the delicacy of silverpoint, to the brusque large *Christ at Emmaus* (1654; B. 87), he adjusted the action of his acid as carefully as he did his etching needle, wiping rag, paper and press. Thirdly, the building of black through repeated overlays of cross-hatching (achieved, presumably, through repeated groundings and bitings, although successive states do not usually survive) marks a new extension of the tonal resources of etching. The prints in which he used only etching for this effect, with no added drypoint, such as the *Annunciation to the Shepherds* (1634; B. 44) and *Joseph and Potiphar's Wife* (1634; B. 39; see

fig. 4), date from the earlier years of his career. His willing recourse later to drypoint to establish a full tonal range, rather than for accents or correction, operated in tandem with his ever-deepening commitment to exploration of the potential of the individual impression at the expense of the durability or reproductiveness of the image, which etching would have been more suited to preserve.

Over the next 200 years Rembrandt's demonstration of the aesthetic and spiritual power of black would be appropriated by the masters of other, new intaglio processes, notably the mezzotint artists Valentine Green, Richard Earlom and David Lucas and the aquatint artist Goya. Rembrandt's exploitation of the capacity of the etched line faithfully to mirror the draughtsman's touch, however, an emphasis shared by his painter-etcher contemporaries of every nationality, was maintained by artists through the 18th century.

3. 18TH CENTURY. By this time etching had become the indispensible basis to reproductive engraving. Practically every commercial plate, invariably known as an engraving, a technical term by then synonymous with the concept of the reproduction of a painted composition, was in fact largely an etching. Although the burin was conventionally employed to complete and enrich the preliminary etched design, the visual effects of the etched line (its irregular outline, variously rugged or tremulous, and its potential for opaque and crusty blacks) were exploited in the finished impression as counterpoint to the metallic or velvety sheen of engraved passages.

Should he seek to make an original print, the 18th-century artist who employed pure etching, such as the Italians Giambattista Tiepolo, Giandomenico Tiepolo, Canaletto and Giovanni Battista Piranesi, and the Frenchman Jean-Honoré Fragonard, would rarely fully escape the linear conventions of contemporary reproductive engraving. Only occasionally, as in Fragonard's *Small Park* (1763; Wildenstein, no. 2), was the touch free from formulized stippling and hatching. These artists could and did, however, transform the linear conventions derived from reproductive engraving into idiosyncratic representational schemes for foliage, masonry and cloth and, more distinctively, water, cloud and light. Such etchings as Canaletto's *A la Porte del Dolo* (c. 1735–after 1744; de Vesme, no. 5), Giandomenico Tiepolo's series of the *Flight into Egypt* (1753; de Vesme, nos 1–27) and, in an extreme manifestation of pure graphicness, Piranesi's view of the foundation blocks of the column of Antoninus Pius (Focillon, no. 581; see fig. 5) are dominated by the effects special to etching: the uniform weight of clusters of lines all bitten at a single pass; the easy replication of a cultivated tremor of stroke, the subliminal roughness of both the edge and the surface of the inked line. At its best, 18th-century original etching participates in the contemporary blond, colouristic aesthetic with an added potential for lively surface and sonorous blacks, a combination as unattainable in the mezzotints and engravings as it was unanticipated in the painted confections of the period.

Etching, with its capacity for rapidly executed clear line, its relative ease of technical mastery and its durability compared to mezzotint and engraving, was the medium chosen for the new idiom of the caricature, which developed first in mid-18th-century Britain and then spread

5. Giovanni Battista Piranesi: etching of the foundation blocks of the column of Antoninus Pius, Rome; from *Trofeo o sia magnifica colonna coclide* (Rome, 1775)

rapidly to Europe and even the New World by the end of the century. Social, commercial and political revolutions drove and depended upon this visual arm of the popular press, and William Hogarth, Thomas Rowlandson, James Gillray and countless lesser-known and anonymous followers produced a new style of etching, stripped of ornament and modulation, suited for cheap production and gaudy hand-colouring.

SOFT-GROUND ETCHING, a mid-18th-century technical innovation comparable in its easy replication of the draughtsman's touch to the graphic quality of caricature but thoroughly aesthetic in its application, was also a predominantly British phenomenon. It appealed primarily to draughtsmen, such as Thomas Gainsborough, Thomas Girtin and John Crome, who sought in a reproductive medium the picturesque sensibility of their chalk or graphite landscape renderings. The technique barely became known, however, before it was rapidly displaced by LITHOGRAPHY, which was even more suited to the purposes of the draughtsman who wanted to reproduce his designs without technical re-education and who relished the suggestive tonality of crayon over the strict linearism of pen.

Another English artist, William Blake, nevertheless perfected RELIEF ETCHING at the end of the 18th century, a technical advance tailored to his need as an impoverished poet to publish verse united with illustration and ornamentation. Although his exact materials and method remain unclear (the issue has been argued in the Blake literature since 1920), it is possible that he devised a means to transfer text and decoration applied in an acid-resisting fluid to copper plates; the image being reversed by the transfer process, it would print in the correct orientation. The grounded plates were bitten to reduce the level of areas that were to remain uninked, and to print, the highest surface of the plate (that is, the unetched areas) would be inked, often in Blake's prints with a coloured ink. The resultant monochromatic page would be further enriched with watercolour applied by hand. In his most elaborate productions, such as copies of *The First Book of Urizen* (London, 1794–6), Blake experimented with multicoloured printing, applying inks of varying viscosities to all levels of the plate; the impression was then pulled with sufficient pressure to draw ink from the etched grooves and pits as well as from raised surfaces, creating multicoloured, dappled effects marked by reticulations of pulled points of stiffened pigment.

4. THE 19TH-CENTURY ETCHING REVIVAL. Such idiosyncratic and fragile processes as William Blake's version of relief etching and also the more widely practised soft-ground etching, all tending towards tone and colour and none suited to long press runs and commercialization, anticipated in artistic intention, if not technique and effect, a dramatic revitalization of etching as a popular creative process. After tentative beginnings by Adolph Friedrich Erdmann von Menzel in Germany and Rodolphe Bresdin, Charles Jacque and Charles Meryon in France, an etching revival gathered momentum in the third quarter of the 19th century; pure etching overwhelmed lithography as the print medium favoured by creative artists throughout Europe and North America for original expression. The Etching Revival movement was promoted as much by critics, printers and publishers as by the artists themselves, an alliance that was doubtless modelled on its major commercial competitor, the reproductive print unions (*lotteries*), which were promoted by painters and their critical supporters and publishers. The expressive potential of the pure etched line, in its reflection of the artist's idiosyncratic touch, and also tonal wiping, in its enhancement of each impression as a unique art object, were assets for advocates of the original print in their aesthetic and economic battle against reproductive prints.

The Etching Revival can also be seen as a complement to the renewed favour found by Rembrandt among painters and collectors of the Romantic and Realist generations and as a reaction against both the cold perfection of earlier Neo-classical engraving and the invention of photography. Indeed, in his preface to the first portfolio (1863) of the French Société des Aqua-fortistes, the critic Théophile Gautier raised etching to the status of moral imperative: 'The necessity of reacting against the positivism of the mirror-like apparatus has made many a painter take up the etcher's needle.'

While adherents of the Etching Revival movement were united against the reproductive print industry, they soon fell into dissension among themselves. The pre-eminent artistic talent among them, James McNeill Whistler, practised a style of interpretive printing of the plates of his mature years, such as those of his *Venice* sets (1880, 1883)

6. Seymour Haden: *Dundrum River*, etching, 4th state, 152×140 mm, 1863 (London, British Museum)

and the *Amsterdam* series of the late 1880s, in which the etched lines are often only scantlings for the pictorial structure's cladding of ink tone. This metaphor takes literal form in his *Savoy Scaffolding* (*c.* 1886; Kennedy, no. 267), a bare sketch of builders' staging printed with gradated tone to establish the height and distance of the viewer from the scene and also to enhance the dematerialization of form already implied by the absence of any suggestion of the structure against which the scaffolding rests.

The surgeon Seymour Haden, Whistler's relative by marriage and eventual personal and professional antagonist, took the opposite stance. Like Meryon before him, he came to abjure plate tone and other artefacts of printing. Primarily an etcher of landscape, he developed his representations of scenic detail and atmosphere through expressive line, which in his plates moves quickly from dense hatching to summary sketching after the manner of Rembrandt, his graphic *atavus*.

Both Whistler and Haden, leaders of the British Etching Revival, made innovations in the techniques of biting in order further to refine the capacity of line to respond as sensitively as a pen to the draughtsman's touch. Whistler preferred to bite his plates by dabbing acid on them, so that instead of all his needled lines being exposed to acid for the same duration, each could be individually bitten, the depth varying from line to line and even along the extent of a single line. Haden and Maxime Lalanne, the French author of a highly influential treatise on etching, developed a method of needling the plate while it was immersed in the acid bath, calculating which lines ultimately were to print darkest so drawing them first and which were to print lightest so drawing them last, with a continuous range of intermediate intensity being drawn in

the interval. Such a plate as Haden's *Dundrum River* (1863; Salaman, no. 49; see fig. 6) was simultaneously drawn and bitten before the scene, thus assimilating the gradation of light and shade that the artist observed in the river prospect.

Whistler was a painter and a master etcher; Haden was, however, purely a printmaker. Comparable diversity was found among the French etchers, where '*peintres-graveurs*' (artists who etched their own designs) such as Meryon, Bresdin and (the supreme technician) Félix Bracquemond were printmakers, while Jacque, Jean-Baptiste-Camille Corot, Edgar Degas and Camille Pissarro were primarily painters. Within the work of the last two the most significant technical advances were made, although, as both Degas and Pissarro consistently employed a mixture of intaglio techniques on their plates, they cannot be considered pure etchers. The usage of the period nevertheless stipulated that the more original the print, both in the sense of the design being the etcher's own and in the sense of the impression being individualized through printing technique, the more it merited the designation 'etching'. Degas and Pissarro were therefore among the most important etchers of the period.

Degas was introduced to the monotype by the minor etcher Ludovic Lepic, who, carrying the potential of creative printing to its extreme, used bitten lines simply as suggestive guides for compositional variations executed entirely by plate wiping. The subsequent progress of Degas in monotype (*see* MONOTYPE, fig. 2) is but one aspect of the greater artist's preoccupation with the evolution of his image on the plate, which in his etchings often resulted in multiple states, up to a dozen or more in some cases, of which only one or two impressions might be pulled. In a print such as *Leaving the Bath* (*c.* 1880; Reed and Schapiro, no. 42), for which 22 states have been identified and 33 impressions are known, it seems by the end of the life of the plate that Degas had exhausted rather than realized the potential of his etched expression. Camille Pissarro was equally devoted to developing his images through multiple states and unconventional manipulations of intaglio processes. His most innovative achievement as an etcher was the adaptation of four-colour printing applying the three primary hues and black to the Impressionist aesthetic. The technique had been developed for intaglio prints in 18th-century France, but only with such etchings as Pissarro's *Church and Farm at Eragny* (1890; Delteil, no. 96) did it move from approximations of painted effects to the expression of a creative image and idea.

Almost as quickly as etching asserted the value of printmaking as an original art form, it was displaced by other techniques. The broader effects of colour lithography and woodcut seemed more appropriate in the European responses to Japanese aesthetics and to the sculpture crafts and painted imagery of cultures that had not arisen in urbanized European or Asian contexts and that were newly appreciated by scholars and aesthetes from the colonial powers. Together with drypoint, colour lithography and woodcut seemed to allow even greater scope for individualistic expression. Partly because of its gross overcommercialization, etching, as caricatured by second-generation etching-revival advocates' emphasis on wiping, preciosity of line and paper choice, was viewed as effete and corrupt by most truly creative printmakers at the beginning of the 20th century.

5. 20TH CENTURY. In the 20th century a number of technical advances were made in etching, which derived both from modern materials and from a modern enthusiasm for disrupting conventions of technical usage. From the 1920s, for instance, the German Rolf Nesch capitalized on the accidental overbiting of a plate in which a hole was eaten through the copper; he developed designs that depend upon the contrast of bulging white, uninked positive forms, haloed by ink caught in their corroded edges, with conventional black etched lines (see fig. 7). The idea of voids led Nesch and other etchers logically to the build-up of forms on printing plates, so that ultimately a three-dimensional surface was wiped, with ink held both by lines below the surface and by the contours of super-imposed forms, with the final impression produced as much by the low relief pressed into the paper as by the ink deposited within and across its topography. When complex relief/intaglio plates were inked in several coloured inks of differing viscosity with rollers of varying elasticity, in a systematic development in the 1950s by S. W. Hayter of Blake's innovations, images of tremendous colouristic and textural density could be produced.

A technical enlargement of the potential of soft-ground etching dependent upon modern materials was the idea of automatically establishing registration for colour printing by drawing in successive colours on a sheet of transparent plastic film laid over each of the grounded plates in turn; it was first proposed to Picasso by his printers, the brothers Albert-Jean Crommelynck and Robert-Hubert Crommelynck. The concept was ultimately realized in the 1970s by David Hockney. Softground etching and many other tonal bitten techniques (expanding on traditional and sugarlift aquatint into lavis and spitbite) became an accepted part of the conventional etched repertory. Many artists collaborated with master printers, such as the Crommelyncks in Paris and Kathan Brown in San Francisco, who provided versatile technical resources, not only to printmakers who were familiar with traditional etching practices but also to painters and others who wanted to incorporate into prints effects that initially they could visualize only in terms of work in other media. The most significant and productive advance in modern etching was probably, however, the assimilation into the artist's technical and creative repertory of that process against which 19th-century printmakers had revolted, that (to quote a 19th-century reproductive engraver) 'foe-to-graphic' art, the photograph. Indeed, the first fixed image created by the exposure to light of photosensitive material through an image that was opaque in areas that read as dark and translucent in areas that read as light was for the purpose of producing an etching plate.

7. Rolf Nesch: *Black Chorus Line*, etching with aquatint and monotype colouring, 334×448 mm, 1930 (London, British Museum)

In 1827 the Frenchman Nicéphore Niépce applied bitumen, which hardened when exposed to light, as a ground to a pewter plate and laid over it a 17th-century engraving on paper, which in this application acted as a photographic negative. After light had selectively hardened the 'white' areas of the image transmitted on to the bitumen, the still-soluble 'black' areas were washed away and the plate was bitten in acid to create a functional printing plate, which reproduced the engraving.

The technology of photoreproduction developed rapidly, so that within half a century reproductive engravers on wood and copper were virtually displaced. Photogravure, an etching process, was perfected for luxury productions (see PHOTOGRAPHY, §I, 2; see also PRINTS, §III, 4), and in popular illustration the ubiquitous wood engraving was replaced by 'line-cuts', black-and-white drawings photographically reproduced as relief etchings. In another aspect of the photographic revolution, artists, including etchers, quickly adopted the photographic imagery as models. A 19th-century example that transcends the etching revival's valorization of successive states is a Self-portrait (1889; Delteil, no. 67) by the Belgian James Ensor, closely drawn in its first state after a conventional portrait photograph. In a profound penetration of the appearance of reality provided by the photograph, the print in its third state became My Portrait Skeletonized.

Although photogravure portraits were occasionally surrounded by hand-drawn and etched framing motifs in the 19th century, only in the 20th century did artists fully integrate photographically produced etchings within their plates. In his series Miserere et guerre (1927), Georges Rouault reworked photogravures of his own drawings with etching, roulette and aquatint to produce prints in which the heavy blend of optical and tactile textural effects contribute substantially to the hallucinatory power of his morbid imagery.

The direct transfer of 'real-world' photographic imagery on to an intaglio printing plate as an element in a composition may have begun in 1948 with an isolated example, Attack on Marshall Gilbert, by Kenneth Kilstrom, working in Hayter's New York Atelier 17. Lithography and silkscreen artists of the 1960s incorporated photographic images into their prints far more avidly than those working in etching, and it was not until the 1980s that it became common in the intaglio medium. By this time, however, some artists had forgone hand-drawn revisions of the photographic image. In the Razorback series (1981) by Robert Rauschenberg, each print comprises several photo-etched plates of photographic images, which are printed in different-coloured inks on variously coloured layers of chine appliqué, leaving the white margins of the backing sheet to frame the silhouette of joined oblongs that the combined images present. The artist's creation lies in the choices he has made and in their realization by his printer. In a completely different creative procedure, yet one equally dependent upon photo-etching processes, Peter Milton (b 1930) drew in opaque ink on transparent films and photo-etched his designs, often composites of individual pictorial elements that could also incorporate photographic imagery, on to lift ground. Through reuse of the films, fragments of one print could reappear in another, even in reverse, as in the bust of the

writer Henry James, derived from a photograph, which appears facing right in the Jolly Corner III:3 and left in the Jolly Corner III:5 (1971; McNulty, nos 78, 80).

Thus, while it cannot be said that etching dominates creative printmaking of the late 20th century in the sense that it did the late 19th century, certainly its adaptibility to technical innovation has encouraged its use to express the modernist disruption of traditional forms. Likewise, in such prints as the linear grids of calculated density by Sol LeWitt, etching in its simplest, most conventional conjunction of the artist's touch and the uniform bite continued into the late 20th century to serve as a vehicle for new visual concepts.

BIBLIOGRAPHY

Hollstein: Dut. & Flem.; Hollstein: Ger.; RDK
A. Bosse: Traicté des manières de graver en taille douce sur l'airin, par le moyen des eaux fortes. . . (Paris, 1645)
A. von Bartsch: Le Peintre-graveur (1803–21) [B.]
A. P. F. Robert-Dumesnil: Le Peintre-graveur français (1835–71)
M. Lalanne: Traité de la gravure à l'eau-forte (Paris, 1866, 2/1878; rev. and Eng. trans. as A Treatise on Etching, Boston, 1880)
A. de Vesme: Le Peintre-graveur italien (Milan, 1906/R London, 1979)
L. Delteil: Le Peintre-graveur illustré (Paris, 1906–30)
A. M. Hind: A Short History of Engraving and Etching: From the 15th Century to the Year 1914 (London, 1908, rev. 3/1923)
H. Focillon: Giovanni-Battista Piranesi: Essai de catalogue raisonné de son oeuvre (Paris, 1918)
M. C. Salaman: The Etchings of Sir Francis Seymour Haden PRE (London, 1923)
J. Lieure: Jacques Callot, 6 vols (Paris, 1924–7)
R. S. Lumsden: The Art of Etching (Philadelphia, 1925)
G. Wildenstein: Fragonard aquafortiste (Paris, 1956)
C. White: Rembrandt as an Etcher (London, 1969)
H. Zerner: The School of Fontainebleau: Etchings and Engravings (New York, 1969)
J. Bailly-Herzberg: L'Eau-forte de peintre au dix-neuvième siècle: La Société des Aquafortistes, 1862–1867 (Paris, 1972)
H. D. Russell: Rare Etchings by G. B. and G. D. Tiepolo (Washington, DC, 1972)
E. Haverkamp-Begemann: Hercules Seghers: The Complete Etchings, 2 vols (Amsterdam, 1973)
E. G. Kennedy: The Etched Work of Whistler (New York, 1974)
H. D. Russell, J. Blanchard and J. Krill: Jacques Callot: Prints and Drawings (Washington, DC, 1975)
The Etchings of Jacques Bellange (exh. cat. by W. R. Reed and A. N. Worthen, Des Moines, IA, A. Cent.; Boston, MA, Mus. F. A.; New York, Met.; 1975)
K. M. Guichard: British Etchers, 1850–1940 (London, 1977)
K. McNulty: Peter Milton: Complete Etchings, 1960–1976 (Boston, 1977)
D. Bindman: The Complete Graphic Works of William Blake (New York, 1978)
P. Gilmour: The Mechanised Image: An Historical Perspective on 20th-century Prints (Twickenham, 1978)
I. de Groot: Landscape Etchings by the Dutch Masters of the Seventeenth Century (Amsterdam, 1979)
C. S. Ackley: Printmaking in the Age of Rembrandt (exh. cat., Boston, MA, Mus. F. A., 1981)
H. D. Russell: Claude Lorrain, 1600–1682 (exh. cat., Washington, DC, N. G. A., 1982)
V. Carlson and others: Regency to Empire: French Printmaking, 1715–1814 (Minneapolis, 1984)
K. J. Lochman: The Etchings of James McNeill Whistler (New Haven, 1984)
S. W. Reed and B. S. Shapiro: Edgar Degas: The Painter as Printmaker (Boston, 1984)
R. Hauff and others: Radierungen im 20. Jahrhundert (Stuttgart, 1987)
S. W. Reed and R. Wallace: Italian Etchings of the Renaissance and Baroque (exh. cat., Boston, MA, Mus. F. A., 1989)
D. Landau and P. Parshall: The Renaissance Print (New Haven and London, 1994)

M. B. COHN

Etching, lift-ground [sugarbite or sugar-lift aquatint]. Intaglio printmaking technique and type of print made by such a process. The design is drawn on to an intaglio plate with a pen or brush and water-soluble ink mixture, of which ordinary sugar is usually the main component, although many recipes exist. (Other ingredients can be soap, gum arabic or honey.) The whole plate is then covered with fluid, acid-resistant etching ground. When soaked in water, the special ink mixture dissolves and lifts the ground from the plate, thus exposing the metal of the plate where the image has been drawn. Before or after this step the bare plate may be covered with a substance such as aquatint. As well as the basic technique, a number of variations exist. The whole plate may be covered with the special ink and left to dry. A design is then scraped into this with an etching needle, the plate grounded and then lifted. The ground is left where the design is scraped away. The resulting etching reveals white lines on a dark background. In another method the bare metal is greased, so that when the drawing is made the ink contracts, giving structured lines.

Between 1620 and 1640 the Dutch artist Hercules Segers experimented with processes similar to the 'pen method', first described by Maxime Lalanne in 1866. In this method the design is made with plain India ink and pen and the metal bitten only once. The resulting etching resembles a pen-and-ink drawing. Although the Frenchman Jean-Baptiste Le Prince applied a sugar solution to make powdered resin stick to the plate for his aquatints, this was not a lift ground proper (*see* AQUATINT, §2(ii)). It was the Englishman Paul Sandby who invented the sugar-lift process (see fig.). Having etched the outlines of his drawing in the ordinary way, he then cleaned the plate and applied a liquid aquatint ground. He drew all the shadows with the special sugar solution, grounded, lifted and etched the plate like an aquatint. Thomas Gainsborough learnt the technique from Sandby and went one step further: he first painted all the outlines with special ink, lifted and etched them; he then proceeded as Sandby. Other British artists followed, and Theodore Henry Adolphus Fielding published a description in 1841.

Evidence of the use of lift ground has been found in areas of Europe where aquatint was known. Before 1800 the Flemish artists Louis Bernard Coclers (1741–1817) and his sister Marie Lambertine Coclers (1761–?after 1815) used it, as did the Dutchman Hermanus Fock (1766–1822); in France Claude Aimé Chenavard (1798–1838) applied it in 1832 and Zacheé Prévost (1797–1861) in 1834. Charles Jacque gave a description of it in 1852 and Jean Martin Herman Hammann in 1857. Camille Pissarro used a form of lift ground in 1880, and Arman Séguin applied it in 1894.

Around 1890 the Belgian Armand Rassenfosse developed a refined recipe for a special ink. Around 1923 he also developed a technique whereby the problem of printing a mirror image was avoided, by drawing on smooth paper with the special ink and then immediately laying this on the plate and running it through the press. After offsetting the drawing he powdered the plate with whiting or zinc oxide. The excess powder would then be removed and the plate covered with a very thin layer of

Lift-ground etching by Paul Sandby: *Part of Warwick Castle from the South-east*, 330×487 mm, 1776 (London, British Museum)

varnish. The acid would attack the particles that stuck through the varnish and then the metal underneath each particle. In this way he obtained crayon-like lines.

In Germany, Heinrich Ludwig, Freiherr von Gleichen Russwurm (1836–1901), used lift ground before 1900, and Käthe Kollwitz from 1903. After the French printmaker Roger Lacourière (1892–1966) taught Picasso and S. W. Hayter the process, it became a popular and much-used intaglio technique. Hayter created his own version of the technique at Atelier 17, probably before 1980, in which a paste of whiting and alcohol is used to make the design. Once the alcohol has evaporated the whiting is sprayed with fixative or diluted varnish. When dry the plate is laid in vinegar or acetic acid, which dissolves the whiting to reveal the metal.

Detecting the use of lift ground in reproductive prints is difficult, since it is almost always mixed with other techniques. Furthermore, a skilful printmaker will try not to leave any brushmarks in his reproductions. It is therefore difficult to see what has actually been done in reproductive prints, which formed the bulk of printmaking before 1850.

UNPUBLISHED SOURCE

Amsterdam, Rijksmus. [*Manier om op de Engelsche wijze in het koper te graveeren door hun genoemd Aqua Tinta* (Manner to engrave into the copper in the English way by them called Aqua Tinta), 1810]

BIBLIOGRAPHY

A. M. Perrot: *Manuel du graveur* (Paris, 1830, rev. 3/1865/*R* 1988)
T. H. A. Fielding: *The Art of Engraving, with the Various Modes of Operation* (London, 1841, 2/1844)
C. Jaque: 'Gravure et imprimerie en taille-douce', *Mag. Pittoresque*, xx (1852), p. 333
J. M. H. Hammann: *Des arts graphiques* (Geneva, 1857)
F. A. M. Lalanne: *Traité de la gravure à l'eau forte* (Paris, 1866, 6/1897; Eng. trans. 1880/*R* 1981)
J. Hedon: *Jean Le Prince et son oeuvre* (Paris, 1879)
W. Ziegler: *Die Techniken des Tiefdrucks* (Halle an der Saale, 1901, rev. 4/1923)
E. S. Lumsden: *The Art of Etching* (London, 1925/*R* 1961)
S. W. Hayter: *New Ways of Gravure* (London, 1949, 3/1981)
W. van Leusden: *The Etchings of Hercules Seghers and the Problem of his Graphic Technique* (Utrecht, 1961)
E. Rouir: *Armand Rassenfosse: Catalogue raisonné de l'œuvre gravé* (Brussels, 1984)
A. Griffiths: 'Notes on Early Aquatint in England and France', *Prt. Q.*, iv (1987), p. 269

AD STIJNMAN

Etching, relief. Relief printmaking process in which a metal block is prepared by etching and the design is left in relief. It was first used by Leonardo da Vinci and then most notably by William Blake. Interested in all aspects of printmaking, Leonardo was aware of the lack of a method of making blocks that would give impressions nearer to original drawings than the somewhat crude woodblocks then available. Intaglio engravings could give a close approximation but presented many difficulties, such as the necessity either of putting the leaves through two presses—one for the relief type, another for the intaglios, which required greater pressure—or printing type and illustrations on separate leaves. Relief etching would make it possible to print everything simultaneously and provide lines sufficiently sharp to reproduce a drawing with considerable accuracy.

Leonardo's method involved coating an iron or copper plate with a water-soluble mixture of albumen and white lead. The design was scratched through this in reverse, following which the whole surface was coated with a brittle, acid-resisting varnish containing minium (red lead) or *giallorino*, an opaque lead approximating to Naples yellow (lead antimoniate). Once dry, it was soaked, allowing the varnish to break away from the clear areas. The plate was then bitten with nitric acid, leaving the design in relief. Alternatively, the varnish consisted of minium and hard resin applied warm; being more brittle, this broke away more easily. Although Leonardo's relief etching did not progress beyond experiments, it was shown to be a feasible technique by the Italian artist Attilio Rossi; using Leonardo's receipt, he reproduced a Leonardo drawing of the bones of the human hand and of part of the forearm (Windsor Castle, Berks, Royal Col., 19009*v*).

Little, if any, relief etching was done after Leonardo until it was used by WILLIAM BLAKE, mainly for the production of his illuminated books between 1788 and 1822. Blake's technique has not been finally ascertained, but there are two main hypotheses. In 1947 S. W. Hayter experimented with a technique he considered identical to Blake's. Lettering and design were applied in a solution of asphaltum and resin in benzine on paper coated with a mixture of soap and gum arabic. This was transferred in a press to a heated clean copperplate. The paper was dampened and removed, the lettering and design remaining on the plate, which was then bitten for about nine hours in a mordant of one part nitric acid to two parts water; this left the lettering and design in relief. Alternatively the design (but not the lettering) might be painted directly on to the plate. Hayter concluded that Blake used some such transfer method, since his lettering is not always correctly aligned on the plate. However, the art historian Robert N. Essick asserted that Blake's method was closer to Leonardo's, both design and lettering being painted directly on to the plate in reverse with a fine brush, in a resist of asphaltum and linseed oil, or of olive oil boiled with purified suet. This is now the more generally accepted hypothesis.

The problem of ascertaining Blake's method is exacerbated by the fact that only one remnant of his original plates has survived: a corner of a rejected plate for *America: A Prophecy* (1793). This shows that the biting left an average depth of 0.12 mm on a plate 1.41 mm thick. Blake probably inked his plates with an inking ball, using home-made inks of various colours (their composition is unknown), and probably pulled impressions on dry paper.

According to John Thomas Smith, in *Nollekens and his Times* (London, 1829), Blake characteristically claimed that the process was revealed to him by his dead brother, Robert, in a vision. Blake probably partly derived the idea from experiments by his friend the dilettante George Cumberland, who engraved texts on copperplates and took counterproofs from them. From this to a reversal of the standard etching process was but a step. To Blake, relief etching assumed a spiritual dimension; in his book *The Marriage of Heaven and Hell* (*c.* 1790–93) he said he would print 'in the infernal method, by corrosives, which in Hell are salutary and medicinal, melting apparent surfaces away, and displaying the infinite which was hid'.

Blake made 12 books in relief etching in addition to several single prints. Two other books, *The Book of Ahania* and *The Book of Los* (both 1795), were realized in a combination of relief and intaglio etching. The 12 books vary from small, simple designs, closely resembling early emblem books, such as *All Religions Are One* (*c.* 1788) and *There Is No Natural Religion* (?1784), through such poetic gems as *Songs of Innocence* and *The Book of Thel* (both 1789), to titanic conceptions, such as *America: A Prophecy* (1793; see fig.), *The [First] Book of Urizen* (1794), *Milton: A Poem* (1804) and *Jerusalem* (1804–20). No other artist made such wide, varying and convincing use of the technique.

During the 19th century, many chemical, mechanical and photographic relief techniques were invented and widely used. Typical was the French method, *aciérage* or *en épargne*, in which a master die is engraved in intaglio, from which a mould is made in papier mâché or plaster; in this, relief blocks are made by casting or by electrolytic deposit. *Aciérage* was useful if it was necessary to have a number of identical impressions at one printing, as in postage-stamp production. The highly successful Comte process relied on more traditional methods: a zinc plate was spread with a ground of zinc white and Dutch pink (a yellow lake). The design was scratched through this, the plate coated with acid-resisting ink and placed in water, in which the ground floats off from the clear areas. It could then be bitten. The Comte method was used notably by Karl Bodmer for illustrations in quality magazines, such as the *Monde illustré* and the *Magasin pittoresque*. Among engravers who successfully used photo-mechanically produced etchings were Firmin Gillot of Paris (1820–72), who patented his process, and his son Charles Gillot (1853–1903).

Relief etching has taken its place among modern printmaking techniques and was used with conspicuous success in combination with intaglio by Picasso's master printer, Roger Lacourière (1892–1966), and John Buckland-Wright (1897–1954); S. W. Hayter also used it in conjunction with other techniques achieved by pressing different materials into the ground before etching it. Nylon, cotton, silk, leaves, string, crumpled paper, even wood-shavings have been used thus. J. G. Lubbock (*b* 1915) used relief etching integrated with intaglio etching, engraving, aquatint, grinding and drilling for illustrations to his own books. These include *Aspects of Art and Science* (Leicester, 1969) and *From the Snows to the Seas* (London, 1986).

BIBLIOGRAPHY
S. W. Hayter: *New Ways of Gravure* (London, 1966)
L. Reti: 'Leonardo da Vinci and the Graphic Arts: The Early Invention of Relief-etching', *Burl. Mag.*, cxiii (1971), pp. 188–95
J. Wright: 'Towards Recovering Blake's Relief-etching Process', *Blake Newslett.*, vii (1974), pp. 32–9
R. Lister: *Infernal Methods: A Study of William Blake's Art Techniques* (London, 1975)
R. N. Essick: *William Blake: Printmaker* (Princeton, 1980)
R. Lister: *Prints and Printmaking: A Dictionary and Handbook of the Art in Nineteenth-century Britain* (London, 1984)
J. Viscomi: *Blake and the Idea of the Book* (Princeton, 1993)

RAYMOND LISTER

Etching, soft-ground. Intaglio printmaking technique in which a particularly soft ground is used; the term is also applied to the type of print made by such a process.

1. MATERIALS AND TECHNIQUES. Soft ground is a mixture, usually in equal parts, of ordinary etching ground

Relief etching by William Blake, 240×170 mm, from his *America: A Prophecy* (London, 1793), pl. 5 (England, private collection)

and a greasy substance, such as tallow or petroleum jelly, although many recipes exist. The etching ground is carefully melted and the greasy component stirred in. The mixture may be poured into pots while still warm, or, once cool, may be formed into balls, which are then wrapped in fine cloth. The soft ground is made fluid by dissolving in turpentine or petrol. It is rolled or brushed on to the plate as ordinary etching ground, but no degreasing is necessary, since it is greasy in itself. Nor is smoking of this ground necessary because of the techniques used. Soft ground is also sold ready-made.

There are many techniques that may be used with soft ground. In one the soft ground is covered with paper, on which a drawing is then made or traced. Since the paper adheres to the ground, when removed, it takes the soft ground with it, laying bare the metal and the impression of the drawing. The etching made from this has the appearance of a crayon drawing. In another method the plate is placed on the bed of a roller press and the soft ground covered with some kind of texture. Waxed paper is then laid over it, the pressure reduced and the plate run through the press; the plate is to be etched like an aquatint. Alternatively, the plate is placed on the bed of a roller press and a flat object or material (e.g. leafs, rope or wrinkled paper) laid on the soft ground and waxed paper laid on top. The pressure is reduced and the plate is run through the press; once etched, the image gives the effect of nature printing. Drawing may also be made in the soft ground by such means as match, thumbprint or comb, and soft ground may also be applied to a fabric, which is then laid on a clean plate, or covered with waxed paper and run through the press.

A craquelure effect may be achieved by covering the soft ground with a quick-drying varnish, which, when dry, starts to crack, taking the ground underneath with it. A marbled or 'bubbled' appearance is obtained by covering the soft ground with varnish and heating the plate until ground and varnish begin to move and contract.

Multiple-plate colour prints are produced using two or more plates of equal size. A drawing is made on a piece of paper. After each colour is drawn, the paper is changed to another plate. Drawing with coloured crayon makes the intended result visible. For perfect register, a rectangular or L-shaped frame, with the paper stretched over it, is used. The plates fit within the rectangle or in the corner of the L. Zinc may be etched with a weak nitric acid, copper with 'Dutch mordant' or a ferrochloride solution. Printing is executed like an aquatint.

2. HISTORY. As early as the 16th century line engravings and line etchings were printed in red or brown, possibly to give them the appearance of drawings. This also strengthened their reproductive qualities. From the 16th to the 18th century several attempts were made to imitate a crayon line by means of dotting or scribbling with a burin or etching needle. Arthur Pond even used a roulette. Early successful experiments were executed by Marcello Fagolino (*fl* 1519–48), who used some kind of transfer etching technique. Around 1760 Jean-Etienne Liotard used a technique in which he pressed a fabric into ordinary etching ground while this ground was still warm. He then etched it like an aquatint.

Jean-Charles François invented the crayon manner, using roulettes and other instruments to reproduce high-dotted, crayon-like lines. He published his first print in

this technique in 1757. Besides other inventions he developed a 'secret' etching process in 1757. It was probably similar to that used by Cornelis Ploos van Amstel and others, who tried to reproduce crayon drawings. It has since become known as 'sand-grain'. In 1756 Ploos van Amstel started experimenting successfully with this technique, employing assistants from 1765. For the sand-grain method a normal grounded plate is covered with a piece of paper, to the back of which is glued a hard, powdered material (e.g. sand or copper filings). The drawing is made in the normal way, the hard particles are pressed through the ground, the plate is etched and the print shows finely dotted lines. (In the 20th century ordinary sandpaper is used, giving the same results.) Johann Heinrich Tischbein II (1742–1808) used sand and pulverized tartaric acid, which he melted on top of an ordinary etching ground. Paper was laid on this ground. When drawing, the hard particles were pressed through, the plate was etched and the print showed finely dotted lines. The Dutch chemical engineer Marius Holleman (1878–1926) perfected Tischbein's form of sand-grain technique.

Credit for the invention of soft-ground etching should go to Benjamin Green (*c.* 1736–1800), who showed his first results in 1771. He was followed by Thomas Gainsborough (see fig.) and Paul Sandby *c.* 1775. Paul Sandby gave the first description of this technique. Soft ground became popular in Britain, where it was used mainly for drawing-books, the technique being excellently suited to reproducing drawing techniques. It was applied by such artists as Thomas Rowlandson, Thomas Girtin and Richard Parkes Bonington after 1800. Scottish-born William Charles went from London to Philadelphia, where he made some soft-ground etchings before his death in 1820, the first of this kind on the American continent.

By the end of the 18th century the process became known to non-English artists. In 1792 the Dutch painter Hendrik Meyer (1737–93) had published a set of 12 landscapes in soft ground while working in London. Around 1800, soft ground became known in France when Michel Vauthier (*fl c.* 1800) and Jacques Couché (1750/59–?after 1820) published a *Collection de gravures dans la manière du crayon* in this technique. A second enlarged edition was published in 1802 as *Recueil de paysages enrichis de figures et animaux*.

The use of soft ground as a reproductive medium diminished, however, after 1825 when it was replaced by lithography. In 1817 Ernst Willem Jan Bagelaar (1775–1837) published a small treatise in which he described the soft-ground process, among others. From 1840 the technique is usually mentioned in books and articles about etching and engraving, and from that period French artists used soft ground regularly, first in reproductive prints, often combining it with aquatint, line etching and roulette, and shortly afterwards as a medium for originals. Louis Marvy (1815–50) and Charles Jacque, for example, cooperated in the production of two sets of etchings, partly in soft ground, in 1843. Charles-François Daubigny used the second technique outlined above (*see* §1) in combination with line etching.

In 1862 the Société des Aquafortistes was founded in France. Several of its members applied soft ground in

Soft-ground etching with aquatint by Thomas Gainsborough: *Watering Place*, 279×349 mm, *c.* 1776–7 (London, British Museum)

their etchings, including Maxime Lalanne, whose influential manual on etching contains a paragraph on soft ground. The Impressionists Camille Pissarro and Edgar Degas, guided by Félix Bracquemond, taught themselves etching, and by 1879 they were familiar with soft ground. They were soon followed by other Impressionists. From *c.* 1890 onwards soft ground etching was fairly popular among French printmakers, and some even used it in multiple-plate colour prints. The Belgian Félicien Rops started using soft ground in the 1870s, developing a method in which he used several kinds of paper for one plate. He also had his crayon drawings photomechanically transferred to intaglio plates. The ordinary soft ground mixture did not suit him well for reworking such plates, and so he developed a special soft ground in cooperation with Armand Rassenfosse. By 1892 they worked out the final recipe, which they called 'Ropsenfosse'. Rassenfosse mixed many different soft-ground recipes and was probably the first to make colour prints with soft ground, using two or more plates, from 1900.

In 1885 the Nederlandsche Etsclub was founded. Some of its leading members, including Jan Pieter Veth and Philip Zilcken, taught themselves etching. They certainly used Lalanne's manual, and thus soft ground became known in the Netherlands. In 1890 Veth met Max Liebermann, whom he taught the soft-ground process and who used it in 1890–92. He was followed by several Germans and Austrians, including Otto Gampert (1842–after 1920), Walter Ziegler (1859–1932) and Käthe Kollwitz. The Danish artist Carl Locher (1851–1915), who arrived in Berlin in 1892, made his first print in soft ground in 1897. In 1895 and 1896 the Swedish artist Carl Larsson tried soft ground, stimulated by Axel Tallberg, who had spent several years in London. The Polish artist Wojciech Weiss (1875–1950) learnt soft-ground etching in Paris in 1899–1900, and he later became a teacher and rector at the Kraków Academy of Fine Arts. Yelizaveta Kruglikova came to Paris shortly before 1900 and made her first attempt at soft ground in 1903. She set up her own graphic studio in Paris and trained other Russian artists, who spread the knowledge to Russia.

In the 1920s the use of soft ground spread further, being used by the American Arthur Davies, the Czech František Kobliha (1877–1962) and (probably) the Japanese artist K. Takekoshi. It was S. W. Hayter and his students from Atelier 17 (in Paris from 1927, in New York during World War II) who made the use of this technique truly international. By the late 20th century soft ground was an intaglio technique much in use. Its most prominent exponents included David Hockney, Jasper Johns and Jim Dine.

BIBLIOGRAPHY

J. H. Tischbein II: *Kurzgefaszte Abhandlung über die Aetzkunst* (Kassel, 1790)

A. Fokke Simonsz.: *De graveur* (Dordrecht, 1796)

E. W. J. Bagelaar: *Verhandeling over een nieuwe manier om prenttekeningen te vervaardigen* [Treatise about a new way of making print drawings] (Haarlem, 1817)

F. A. M. Lalanne: *Traité de la gravure à l'eau forte* (Paris, 1866, 6/1897; Eng. trans., 1880/*R* 1981)

A. Delâtre: *Eau forte, pointe sèche et vernis mou* (Paris, 1887)

A. M. Hind: 'Notes on the History of Soft-ground Etching and Aquatint', *Prt Colr Q.*, viii (1921), pp. 377–405

M. Holleman: *Nieuwe etstechnieken* [New etching techniques] (Utrecht, 1927)

M. Hardie: 'Letters from Paul Sandby to John Clerk of Eldin', *Prt Colr Q.*, xx (1933), pp. 362–4

M. Guérin, ed.: *Lettres de Degas* (Paris, 1945), p. 53

A. J. M. van Moorsel: 'Een vergeten Toorop' [A forgotten Toorop], *Oud-Holland*, xc (1976), pp. 275–6

E. Rouir: *Armand Rassenfosse: Catalogue raisonné de l'œuvre gravé* (Brussels, 1984)

S. Lambert: *The Image Multiplied* (London, 1987)

P. D. Cate and M. Grivel: *From Pissarro to Picasso: Color Etching in France* (Paris, 1992)

AD STIJNMAN

Etching on glass. *See* CLICHÉ-VERRE.

Etex, Antoine (*b* Paris, 20 March 1808; *d* Chaville, Seine-et-Oise, 14 July 1888). French sculptor, painter, etcher, architect and writer. The son of a decorative sculptor, he entered the Ecole des Beaux-Arts, Paris, in 1824 as a pupil of Charles Dupaty (1771–1825), moving in 1825 to the studio of James Pradier. Ingres also took an interest in his education, and Etex's gratitude towards him and Pradier was later expressed in projects for monuments to them (that to Pradier not executed, that in bronze to Ingres erected Montauban, Promenade des Carmes, 1868–71).

Etex failed three times to win the Prix de Rome, but in the aftermath of the Revolution of 1830 his Republican sympathies gained him a government scholarship that enabled him to spend two years in Rome. There he sculpted the intensely tragic group *Cain and his Children Cursed by God*, the plaster version of which (Paris, Hôp. Salpêtrière) was one of the great successes of the 1833 Paris Salon. During this period Etex asserted the Republican views that were to earn him the distrust of many of his fellow artists and of the establishment but also gain him the support of the influential critic and politician Adolphe Thiers. He behaved in Romantic fashion as a misunderstood artist, but nevertheless displayed a remarkable tenacity in forwarding his pet projects, including, for instance, schemes for sculptures representing *Napoleon Scaling the World* and the *Genius of the 19th Century* (drawings, Paris, Carnavalet), both intended for the Place de l'Europe, Paris, on which he worked from 1839 until 1878.

On his return to Paris in 1832, Etex received regular state commissions for nearly 30 years beginning with a prestigious contract for two stone high-reliefs for the Arc de Triomphe de l'Etoile: the *Resistance of 1814* and the *Peace of 1815* (1833–6), which although composed in a classical pyramidal shape are full of Romantic expressive force. He subsequently executed monumental marble statues for the Galeries Historiques at the château of Versailles (1837) and in Paris at the church of La Madeleine (1838), the Luxembourg Palace (1847) and the church of the Invalides (1852). Among his other state commissions were the bas-reliefs for the statue of *Henry IV* in the Place Royale, Pau (bronze, 1848), the statue of *General Lecourbe* in the Place de la Liberté, Lons-le-Saunier (Jura) (bronze, 1852–7), and the equestrian monument to *Francis I* in the Place François 1er, Cognac (bronze, 1864).

Etex also produced a number of important allegorical works, including the statue originally called *Poland in Chains* but renamed *Olympia* when it was purchased by Louis-Philippe's government (marble, 1848; Versailles,

Château), the group of the *City of Paris Praying for the Victims of the Cholera Epidemic of 1832* (marble, 1848–52; Paris, Hôp. Salpêtrière) and the group *Maternal Sorrow* (marble, 1859; Poitiers, Parc de Blossac). All these works display Etex's characteristic combination of Neo-classical form, derived from Pradier, with Romantic intensity of emotion, qualities also apparent in the most striking of his tombs, that of the *Raspail Family* (marble, 1854; Paris, Père-Lachaise Cemetery). Tirelessly active, he also produced a large number of portrait busts and medallions of his contemporaries, including, most notably, a colossal bust of *Pius IX* (marble, 1862; Rome, Vatican Pal.), as well as painting such pictures as the *Death of the Proletarian* (1854; Lyon, Mus. B.-A.), etching a suite of 40 plates called *La Grèce tragique* and producing designs for the reconstruction of the Paris Opéra (exh. Salon 1861). He also transposed a number of paintings as bronze reliefs. These included a version (untraced) of his own *The Medici* (1831; Montauban, Mus. Ingres), versions of Géricault's major works for his tomb in Père-Lachaise cemetery, Paris (bronze; *in situ*), and of Ingres's *Apotheosis of Homer* (Paris, Louvre) for his monument in Montauban.

Of his numerous writings on art, which included a review of the Exposition Universelle of 1855 and lives of Paul Delaroche, Pierre-Jean David d'Angers, Pradier, Ary Scheffer and others, his most ambitious work was the *Cours élémentaire de dessin*, in which he stressed the harmony that should exist between painting, sculpture and architecture.

WRITINGS
Revue synthétique de l'Exposition Universelle de 1855 (Paris, n.d.)
Cours élémentaire de dessin, appliqué à l'architecture, à la sculpture, à la peinture, ainsi que tous les arts industriels (Paris, 1859)
Souvenirs d'un artiste (Paris, 1877)

BIBLIOGRAPHY
Lami
P. E. Mangeant: *Antoine Etex* (Paris, 1894)
The Romantics to Rodin: French Nineteenth-century Sculpture from North American Collections (exh. cat., ed. P. Fusco and H. W. Janson; Los Angeles, CA, Co. Mus. A., 1980–81), pp. 250–54
A. Le Normand-Romain: 'Le Séjour d'Etex à Rome en 1821–1832: Un Carnet de dessins inédits', *Bull. Soc. Hist. A. Fr.* (1981, pub. 1983), pp. 175–88
La Sculpture française au XIXème siècle (exh. cat., ed. A. Pingeot; Paris, Grand Pal., 1986)
B. Chenique: 'Une Oeuvre inspirée par André Chénier: Le Damalis d'Etex au Musée de Lille', *Rev. Louvre*, xl/1 (1990), pp. 26–36

ANTOINETTE LE NORMAND-ROMAIN

Ethelwold. *See* AETHELWOLD.

Ethiopia [Amharic Ityopyā; anc. Abyssinia] **and Eritrea.** Countries in north-east Africa, bordered by Sudan to the west, Kenya to the south, Somalia and Djibouti to the east and the Red Sea to the north-east. Ethiopia covers 1,133,882 sq. km and Eritrea (independent from Ethiopia since 24 May 1993) 117,400 sq. km. The population is composed of over 30 ethnic groups. Nearly 70 languages are spoken, falling into the Semitic (e.g. Ge'ez, Tigrinya, Amarinya, Harari), the Cushitic (e.g. Orominya, Somali and Konso), the Nilotic and Omotic language groups. Amarinya is the official language. In the northern and central mountain provinces the Christian Tigray (Tegray) and Amhara practise crop- and cattle-farming. Historically, the Tigray maintained the city state of AKSUM until its decline in the 10th century, while the Amhara supplied the theocratic rulers of Ethiopia from 1270 until the Socialist Revolution in 1974. After the overthrow of the central government in May 1991, a provisional government was formed (July 1991), which remained in 1995. From the 4th century AD until 1974, Monophysite Christianity was the state religion; popular Christianity is influenced by belief in demons and spirits. The southern and eastern provinces are populated mainly by Cushitic-speaking peoples, for example the Oromo. Their traditional religion was overlaid by Christianity in the south and Islam in the east.

For further discussion and illustration of the art of the region *see* AFRICA, §VII, 2.

BIBLIOGRAPHY
G. W. Huntingford: *The Galla of Ethiopia, the Kingdoms of Kafa and Janjero*, Ethnographic Survey of Africa (London, 1955/2nd *R* with suppl. biblio., 1969)
I. M. Lewis: *Peoples of the Horn of Africa: Somali, Afar and Saho*, Ethnographic Survey of Africa (London, 1955/2nd *R* with suppl. biblio., 1969)
E. Ullendorff: *The Ethiopians: An Introduction to Country and People* (London, New York, Toronto, 1960/R 1961, 1962, 2/1965/R 1966, 1967)
W. A. Shack: *The Central Ethiopians: Amhara, Tigriña and related Peoples*, Ethnographic Survey of Africa (London, 1974)

I. Architecture. II. Painting and graphic arts. III. Sculpture. IV. Megalithic art. V. Patronage, museums and collections.

I. Architecture.

1. Before *c.* AD 600. 2. *c.* AD 600–*c.* 1600. 3. After *c.* 1600.

1. BEFORE *c.* AD 600. In the first millennium BC, Semitic Sabean settlers and merchants from South Arabia migrated to northern Ethiopia and influenced considerably the culture (social institutions such as theocratic kingship, astral religion, language, writing, architecture and art) of the indigenous Cushitic Agew-people. The period from around the 5th century BC to the 1st century AD in Ethiopia is termed the Pre-Aksumite period and related to the highlands of Tigray. In the Melazo region (south-east of Aksum), remains of a temple (8.90×6.75 m) with fireplaces, incense altars and an enclosing wall (18.1×12.3 m) have been identified as a shrine dedicated to the Sabaean moon god Almaqah. Dating from about the 5th century BC, it is probably the oldest known temple in Ethiopia. In Yeha (probably an important city in pre-Aksumite times, *c.* 50 km north-east of Aksum) is another temple dedicated to a southern Arabian deity and dating from the 5th or 4th century BC. It is a rectangular (18.6×15.0 m), two-storey building with a stepped podium and walls *c.* 13 m high in smooth-dressed, dry-stone masonry.

The period during which the city of AKSUM attained and maintained dominance as a political centre in the highlands of Tigray and Eritrea is known as the Aksumite period (*c.* 1st–10th centuries AD). Its culture was shaped by southern Arabian elements as well as influences from the Nile valley, the Mediterranean region and the Byzantine Empire, and trade links with India have been demonstrated. The adoption of Christianity in the 4th century marked a cultural turning-point.

Of the élite palaces excavated in Aksum—Ta'aka Maryam, Enda Mika'el, Enda Sem'on—Ta'aka Maryam (120×80 m, central pavilion 24×24 m) was the largest. All these residences were basically, it seems, of one plan: a central lodge or pavilion, raised on a high podium approached by broad staircases, surrounded and enclosed by ranges of buildings on all four sides (for reconstructions see Krencker 1913, pp. 112–21). Except in very rare cases, only the podia have survived and embody the chief distinguishing marks of Aksumite architecture: rebated walls with re-entrants and salients of rubble bound with mud mortar and furnished at the corners with large and carefully cut granite blocks. The necropoleis on the edge of the town, characterized by many monolithic granite stelae, are evidence of a highly developed cult of the dead.

The stelae, which are probably representations of idealized royal residences, imitate in stone a second type of Aksumite construction technique: walls of rubble covered in earth mortar were reinforced at regular intervals by horizontal, square wooden beams, supporting rounded cross-members, the projecting ends of which formed 'monkey heads'. The window and door structures of Aksumite buildings, with openings framed on all four sides and linked by cross-members through the thickness of the walls, are likewise reproduced. The same characteristics are shown by some of the elaborate tombs near the main group of stelae, such as the 'Mausoleum' and the 'Tomb of the False Door' (both late 4th century AD or 5th), probably the burial places of royal personages.

2. *c.* AD 600–*c.* 1600. Remains of Early Christian churches, which were probably built on the stepped podia of temples, have been excavated at various sites, including Aksum, Adulis (Eritrea), the harbour town of the Aksumite empire, in the highlands of Eritrea, and in Takonda' and Kohayto. The wall remains indicate a basilican plan with a semicircular or rectangular apse to the east, often flanked by square side rooms, and at least one narthex to the west.

The earliest surviving free-standing structure is the largest of the two churches of the mountain monastery of Debre Damo (Tigray), between Adwa and Addigrat; both churches are called after the founder of the monastery, Abuna Aragawi (one of the Nine Saints; probably Syrian missionaries who founded monasteries in Ethiopia in the 5th century). The three-aisled basilica (20×9 m) has a square apse, two side rooms and an inner and an outer narthex. It is tentatively dated to the 6th–10th centuries AD. Its construction and style show a synthesis between Aksumite architecture and a Christian, probably mainly Syrian, style (*see* EARLY CHRISTIAN AND BYZANTINE ART, §II, 2(i)(d)). The wall construction, with recesses and salients and internal pillars with cushion-shaped capitals, is of Aksumite origin, as is the decorative wooden frieze resting on the architrave directly below the ceiling, and featuring rows of ornamentally carved blind windows. The wooden doors and windows, the latter with ornamental fillings and openings for light, are also of Aksumite construction. The wooden coffered ceiling (?7th–11th century), decorated with carved animal motifs in the inner narthex, may have come from an Aksumite palace. Christian architectural influence is evident in the basilican plan, the dome above the apse, the carved triumphal arch between nave and apse, and the saddle roof with a flattened ridge. Other churches survived more often when they

were built within the shelter of caves: for example the church of Yemrehenna Krestos (*c.* 12th century), called after a ruler of the Zagwe dynasty (kings from the Lasta region of central Ethiopia; 1170–1270); and the church of Medhane 'Alem (Saviour of the World) (*c.* 13th or 14th century), situated on a slope of the Makina, a part of the massif of Abuna Yosef, both near Lalibela.

From probably the 10th century to the 15th or later, rock-cut churches were constructed in Ethiopia, first in the north and then also in the south; hundreds of examples occur within latitudes 6–16°N and longitudes 37–40°E. Some consist merely of simple rooms cut into the rock, others are partly shaped out of the rock with one or more formed façades. The most sophisticated are free-standing monolithic churches, of which both exterior and interior have been carved from a single block. This architectural style may have evolved from burial chambers or hermits' caves and may also possibly be connected to rock architecture in other parts of the Christian world, for example Cappadocia (*see* CAPPADOCIA, §2(i)(a) and ROCK CHURCH).

The twelve rock-cut churches in Lalibela, four of which are monoliths, date from the 13th century to the early 14th, when rock-cut church art was at its height. Legend ascribes their building to the Zagwe ruler Lalibela (*reg* late 12th century). Erected on stepped podia, the rock-cut churches imitate earlier and contemporary built churches, including the Aksumite wood-and-stone building style (i.e. pillars with cushion-shaped stepped or bracket capitals, carved, coffered ceilings and lantern roofs). However, the roof structure sometimes resembles the barrel vault of Christian churches, and in most churches arches replace the Aksumite architrave. The ornamental wood-carvings on the arches, in the vaulting, in the frieze and on the ceilings of built churches are imitated in rock-cut churches in low relief in stone, or in paint.

The largest monolithic church, Beta Medhane 'Alem (House of the Saviour of the World) (33.7×23.7×11.5 m), is a five-aisled basilica with ambulatory. It is thought to be a copy of the 4th-century cathedral of Maryam Seyon (Māryām Seyon; the Virgin of Zion) in Aksum, which was destroyed in the 16th century, possibly in an attack by the Imam of Harar, Ahmad ibn Ibrahim al-Gazi—called Grāñ (the Left-handed) by the Ethiopians—who destroyed many churches and monasteries in 1527–43. The two monolithic churches of Beta Amanu'el and Beta Maryam are related to Yemrehenna Krestos; the latter has extensive schemes of plaster decoration in geometric and plant patterns. The monolithic church of Beta Giyorgis (see fig. 1), standing by itself in a deep pit, is distinguished by an unusual ground-plan in the form of a Greek cross, and the relief crosses on its roof suggest the form of a wooden portable altar. The second-order ogee-arch windows derive from Islamic architecture. The church of Beta Golgota, with its ornamental façade and Sellasé (Šellāsē; Trinity) Chapel, has the same type of windows. The chapel is significant for its three monolithic stone altars with low-relief carvings. Near Wegro (south-west of Addigrat) are some important, almost monolithic, basilican churches: the church of Abreha Asbeha (possibly 11th century), which bears the names of two mythical Aksumite kings, the Cherqos (Kyrikos) church and the Mika'el Ambo

1. Church of Beta Giyorgis, Lalibela, Ethiopia, 13th century–early 14th

church (both 14th century). All three churches have Aksumite pillars with stepped capitals and architrave. In each basilica the transept is accentuated, creating a cruciform ground-plan.

3. AFTER *c.* 1600. From about the 15th century until the end of the 16th, Ethiopian rulers moved their capitals from place to place and lived in tents. Around the end of the 16th century permanent residences were established on Lake Tana, and the probable beginnings of the 'Gondarene' style are seen in the remains of the palaces and the churches, built by Jesuits in collaboration with Indian master builders for Emperor Susenyos (*reg* 1607–32), in Gorgora (north-western shore of Lake Tana) and to the south of Gondar in Denqez and Azezo, renamed Genneta Iyasus (Gannata Iyasus; Garden of Jesus). This style is considered by most scholars to be a synthesis of Portuguese, Indian and northern Ethiopian elements, and it characterized both secular and religious architecture in and around Gondar, as well as in the region of Lake Tana, until the mid-18th century.

The one- and two-storey palaces have rectangular or square ground-plans; round, domed towers at the wall angles; square observation towers on the roofs; round and square domed towers in compound walls; roof terraces with battlements; and fully arched doors and windows, the arches being decorated with coloured stones; string courses; and wooden balconies. The churches are mostly

round, less often square, often surrounded by arcades and sometimes by a compound wall with towers. All walls are made of stone and, previously unknown, lime mortar.

In the capital Gondar, founded by Emperor Fasiledes (*reg* 1632–67), every ruler had new buildings erected, giving rise to a walled palace district containing secular buildings and churches. The best preserved are the restored palace of Fasiledes and the 'Reception Hall' of Emperor Bakaffa (*reg* 1721–30). Ruins exist of the library of Emperor Yohannes I the Just (*reg* 1667–82), of the 'Saddle Castle' (so called for the shape of the helm of its main tower) of Emperor Iyasu I (*reg* 1682–1706), and of the palace of the Empress Mentewab (*reg* 1730–55), who ruled for her under-age son Iyasu II. Remains also survive of the churches of Gemjabet Maryam (Gemǧābēt Māryām; Treasury of Mary), Elfen Giyorgis (Chapel of George), built by Fasiledes, and Attatami Qeddus Mika'el (Attatami Qeddus Mikā'ēl; St Michael the Beautiful), erected by Dawit III (*reg* 1716–21). Outside the town stands the well-preserved 'Bath of Fasiledes', attributed to Fasiledes, a small palace in the middle of a water reservoir. Also well preserved are churches on the islands of Lake Tana, for example Gabre'el on Kebran (1687), and Sellasé Church on Narga, built by Mentewab in 1747. In Aksum a new basilica, also in the Gondarene style, was built under Fasiledes in 1655, to replace the cathedral of Maryam Seyon.

The most widespread church type in the north after the 16th century, however, was the rectangular church without side aisles, narthex or apse. The function of the apse was taken over by a square sanctuary at the centre of the building, around which priests could walk. In addition, from the early 19th century, churches with a circular floor-plan were built. This type had predominated in central and southern Ethiopia from about the 16th century and probably derived from the Ethiopian round house with conical roof. The walls consist either of stone or wattle and daub, the daub composed of a mud, dung and straw plaster known as *chikka* (čeqa). Older churches were roofed with thatch, while in the 20th century corrugated iron was sometimes used. The interior was divided into three: two ambulatories around the centre; and a quadrangular sanctuary, built of stone or clay, with a tambour supporting the roof.

The traditional house of the peoples of Ethiopia is round, sometimes rectangular, with a brushwork conical thatch roof; there is a growing tendency for rectangular houses with tin roofs. The building material depends on what is available. In the highlands of Tigray and Eritrea, where there is an abundance of stones lying loose on the surface of the land, most of the houses are constructed of stone. They can be rectangular or circular, of one or two storeys, with outside staircases leading to the upper storey. In Lalibela the little drystone houses are circular and two-storey, also with outside staircases. Amhara have square or round houses consisting of stone, particularly in the mountains, or of thin poles stuck in the ground, with cross withies laced to them and then plastered with *chikka* (čeqa). Especially in the southern regions, there are elaborate houses like the bee-hive shaped bamboo houses of the Dorze (in the mountainous areas west of the lakes

Abaya and Chamo) and of the Sidama (between Lake Abaya and Lake Awassa).

Architecturally, Harar presents a special case, having an urban culture shaped by Islamic–Arabic influences. The town wall with five gates dates from the 16th century, and a further gate from the 18th. The mosque known as al-Jami' (al-Ğāmi') was also built in the 16th century; it has two minarets, one of which was replaced in the 18th century. The one- or two-storey houses surrounded by stone walls are traditionally of stone with a flat timber roof. In the 19th century Arab merchants built houses with balconies and gabled roofs in the style prevalent along the Turkish and Egyptian coasts of the Red Sea.

The capital, Addis Ababa, is particularly rich in both traditional and modern forms of architecture. Until about 1910, the architecture of its churches, public buildings, royal residences and homes of the nobility and of foreigners was influenced mainly by Arab and Indian architects, who took account of local stylistic elements. Glazed or open verandahs with supports, arcades and wooden balconies are typical of these rectangular, octagonal or circular buildings, which were made of stone or, from c. 1907, brick. Examples from this period include the churches of Entoto Ragu'el (1885) and Elfen Gabre'el (1897), the banquet hall of Menelik's palace (1897–8) and residences of nobles, for example Ras Biru's house (c. 1900).

From 1910, churches, palaces and public buildings were built by European architects in eclectic, historicist styles. In ecclesiastical architecture, centrally planned buildings with a dome and decorative elements taken from Renaissance and Baroque styles predominated. The octagonal St George (Qeddus Giyorgis) Church (1906) and the rectangular Menelik Mausoleum (Bä'äta Church; 1930) are two examples. The Trinity Church, a Rococo-inspired basilica and the largest church in the city, was completed in 1941. The palace of Haile Selassie (Hāyla Śellasē), Guenet Le'ul (gannata Le'ul), was built in 1935 in a neo-classical style (since 1960 it has been the Institute of Ethiopian Studies, Addis Ababa University). The monumental Jubilee Palace (the imperial residence from 1960–74; now the National Palace) was built in 1955 using an imposing, classicist formal vocabulary. Neo-classicism was also a popular style for such public buildings as banks, post offices, schools and railway stations until c. 1930. It was replaced first by Art Deco, as in the Parliament Building (1934), and after the 1950s by an international, functionalist style. Examples of the latter include the National Bank (1955), Africa Hall (1961) and the Municipality (City Hall; 1961–4). One of only a few practising Ethiopian architects, Michael Tedros (Mikā'ēl Tēwodros) was involved in the building of the Filwoha (Fel Wehā) thermal bath complex (1965). Since 1974, most new buildings have been either dwellings or offices, and their design and supervision have been the responsibility of the Ethiopian Building Construction Authority.

BIBLIOGRAPHY

D. Krencker: Ältere Baudenkmäler Nordabessiniens, ii of Deutsche Aksum-Expedition (Berlin, 1913)
E. Littmann, D. Krencker and T. von Lüpke: Deutsche Aksum-Expedition, 4 vols (Berlin, 1913), pp. 132–67(i); 592–607, 619–42(iv)
O. Jäger and I. Pearce: Antiquities of North Ethiopia (Stuttgart, 1965, rev. 2/1974)
G. Gerster, ed.: Kirchen im Fels (Stuttgart, 1968, rev. Zurich and Freiburg im Breisgau, 2/1972); Eng. trans. as Churches in Rock: Early Christian Art in Ethiopia (London, 1970) [excellent pls]
D. R. Buxton: 'Äthiopische Architektur im Mittelalter', Kirchen im Fels, ed. G. Gerster (Zurich and Freiburg im Breisgau, 2/1972), pp. 51–60
J. Leclant: 'Archäologie der äthiopischen Frühgeschichte', Kirchen im Fels, ed. G. Gerster (Zurich and Freiburg im Breisgau, 1972), pp. 29–35
Ethiopie millénaire (exh. cat., Paris, Petit Pal., 1974)
F. Anfray: 'Les Monuments gondariens des XVIIe et XVIIIe siècles: Une Vue d'ensemble', Proceedings of the Eighth International Conference of Ethiopian Studies: Addis Ababa, 1984, i, pp. 9–45
M. Gervers: 'The Mediterranean Context for the Medieval Rock-cut Churches of Ethiopia', Proceedings of the Eighth International Conference of Ethiopian Studies: Addis Ababa, 1984, i, pp. 171–83
F. Anfray: 'Des Eglises et des grottes rupestres', An. Ethiopie, xiii (1985), pp. 7–34
R. Pankhurst: History of Ethiopian Towns: From the Mid-nineteenth Century to 1935, Äthiop. Forsch., xvii (Stuttgart, 1985)
R. Plant: Architecture of the Tigre, Ethiopia (Worcester, 1985)
L. V. Berry: 'Gondar-style Architecture and its Royal Patrons', Proceedings of the First International Conference on the History of Ethiopian Art: London, 1986, pp. 123–30 [notes pp. 156–7, pls 201–12]
Amare Dawit and Fassil Ghiorgis: 'Early Architectural Development in Addis Ababa', Proceedings of the International Symposium on the Centenary of Addis Ababa: Addis Ababa, 1986, pp. 173–98
Dejene H. Mariam: 'Architecture in Addis Ababa', Proceedings of the International Symposium on the Centenary of Addis Ababa: Addis Ababa, 1986, pp. 199–218
R. Fattowich: 'Some Remarks on the Origins of the Aksumite Stelae', An. Ethiopie, xiv (1987), pp. 43–74
S. Munroe-Hay: Aksum: An African Civilisation of Late Antiquity (Edinburgh, 1991)

II. Painting and graphic arts.

1. Materials and techniques. 2. Historical survey.

1. MATERIALS AND TECHNIQUES. Manuscripts consist of sheets of parchment bound in wooden covers, which are often covered in leather with embossed cross ornament. Most of the text is written in black ink, with the names of certain saints and the punctuation in red ink. Illustrations are either painted on separate folio pages and subsequently bound into the text, or they are scattered within the text. The colophon often gives information on the calligrapher, the patron and the date of production. Painter and calligrapher were usually not the same person. Inks and paints were made from minerals and local plants, apart from indigo, which was imported from India. Egg white, egg yolk, and plant and animal glue were used as a binding medium. Since the second half of the 19th century, imported paints have predominantly been used.

Wall paintings in rock-cut churches were originally applied directly to the rock or to a covering layer of plaster, as in the remains of paintings from the 12th to the 16th centuries on the cupolas, columns and walls of the rock-cut churches of Lalibela (on the south-west flank of Mt Abuna Yosef in Lasta) or in Tigray. Since about the 17th century, the pictures have been painted on canvas and glued on to a smoothed wall surface. This technique is widespread in circular churches, in which pictorial decoration is found mainly on the outer wall of the sanctuary and on the dome drum. Many churches no longer contain their original paintings, and the dating is often uncertain. New rulers often replaced the old paintings; wars, weathering and bird droppings have also destroyed many paintings.

Paintings on wood are found as single panels, diptychs or triptychs. The paintings were either applied directly to a layer of plaster covering the panel, or, from the 17th century onwards, to primed cotton material stretched over the panel. In panels from the 15th and 16th centuries the final varnish is absent. From the 17th century vegetable lacquers (e.g. made from aloe) can be identified.

Among the products of the magico-religious folk art are the magic scrolls made by the *debtera*s (*dabtarā*s), traditional scholars with magical and occult knowledge. These strips of parchment painted with Christian and magic images (e.g. eye motifs, eight-pointed stars, crosses, angels, saints) and prayers are intended for healing and protection against demons. Scrolls are used, above all, by the common people, whereas priests, nobles and *debtera*s use books with similar content. Although magic art goes back to the beginnings of Christianity, most of the scrolls in the collections date from the 19th and 20th centuries.

2. HISTORICAL SURVEY.

(i) Before *c.* 1400. (ii) *c.* 1400–*c.* 1600. (iii) *c.* 1600–*c.* 1900. (iv) After *c.* 1900.

(i) Before c. *1400.* The incised drawings, high reliefs and paintings in caves and under overhanging cliffs in Ethiopia and Eritrea have much in common with rock art throughout Africa (*see* AFRICA, §VI, 15). Examples of such works are the high reliefs and scratched drawings (undated) of cattle in a gorge at Chabe (Çabé), *c.* 10 km west of Dilla in southern Ethiopia, the 4000-year-old paintings of cattle, antelopes, jackals and hyenas near Dire Dawa and Harar and other finds in Tigray and in Eritrea. Stelae from various times, incised with designs, depictions and inscriptions, are also extant (*see* §I above). Most significant is the highly distinctive Christian painting that developed from the 4th century in Ethiopia and is peculiar to that country. The development of Christian painting reflects the various forms of contact—pilgrimages to Jerusalem, missionary work, trade—between Ethiopia and the worlds of Christianity, East and West, of Islam and the Far East. Ethiopian painters copied primarily the iconography of their models, which included illustrations in Greek, Coptic and Arabic manuscripts, icons, pictures by western European painters and prints, but they always reduced the representation to its essence. Sometimes they combined elements of different models in one painting or transformed a scriptural subject in terms of the indigenous oral tradition, and they always translated the models into their own local style. Other features of these works are that all saints are depicted in light colours and that the figures and themes are explained by captions.

No paintings have survived from the Aksumite period (*c.* 1st–10th centuries AD). The painted animals and hybrid creatures decorating the medallions on the ceiling of the church of Yemrehenna Krestos near Lalibela (?12th century) are somewhat similar to the carved motifs on the ceiling of the basilica at Debre Damo (?7th–11th centuries). In these paintings, however, interpretations based on Christian typology seem to be uppermost, in keeping with the *Physiologus* (before mid-2nd century AD; e.g. Berne, Stadt- & Ubib.; Milan, Bib. Ambrosiana), a picture-cycle bestiary that was also translated into Ge'ez (the Ethiopic language, since the 10th century liturgical only). In rock-cut churches of the 11th–16th century (*see* §I above) the ornament may consist of low-relief sculpture,

though more often it is painted. It includes interlace, knots, swastikas, arabesques, rosettes and diversely shaped crosses. Many of the decorative devices derive from ancient Eastern and Mediterranean cultures and came to Ethiopia via Coptic and Nubian models; others, particularly since the 11th century, can be traced to Islamic influences. For example, the painted ornament of both Yemrehenna Krestos and the rock-cut church of the Virgin, also known as Kidana Mehret (Kidāna Meḥrat; Covenant of Mercy) in Debre Seyon, Ger'alta district, Tigray (late 14th century or early 15th), is strongly influenced by Islamic art. In churches, ornament is found mainly on arches, ceilings and vaults and in niches for images of saints.

These niches find their counterpart in the architectural scenery painting that was especially popular in Ethiopian book illustrations of the 14th and 15th centuries, where an arch was usually depicted supported by two columns, often with a richly embellished tympanum. Especially elaborate arabesques form part of the architectural framework into which the canon tables are set (*see* CANON TABLE). The manuscript headpieces are embellished, often on a large scale, with interlace, some with floral and ornithomorphic abstractions at the ends or with arabesques, as is the ornamental frame around the columns of text at the beginning of a chapter (*hāreg*).

Until the end of the 14th century, figure painting was influenced principally by contemporary or earlier Byzantine painting, mediated by the Christian art of Coptic Egypt, Nubia, Syria, Palestine, Mesopotamia and Armenia. The rock-cut churches contain remains of early figural wall paintings, though their dating is often uncertain. The Maryam Church in Lalibela has numerous badly damaged paintings, with remains of figural depictions on the frieze and vault of the nave. These have biblical subjects, such as the *Visitation*, the *Annunciation* and the *Flight into Egypt*, as well as scenes from the Life of Christ, dating from the 12th or 13th century and showing the influence of Coptic painting of the 8th–10th century (e.g. at Bawit and Saqqara; *see* COPTIC ART, §IV, 1). Coptic and Nubian influences can be seen in a *Virgin and Child Enthroned* (13th or 14th century), with the Child in a clipeus (shield-shaped medallion), and other paintings in the Maryam Church on Mount Korkor, Ger'alta district, Tigray. Other churches with preserved figural paintings are: Genneta Maryam (Gannata Māryam; Paradise of the Virgin) (13th century), near Lalibela; Cherqos (Kyrikos) (*c.* 13th century) in Bilbela district, north-west of Lalibela; and Kidana Mehret (late 14th century or early 15th) in Debre Seyon, Tigray.

Among better-preserved examples of early painting are manuscript illustrations, especially Gospel books from the late 13th century and the 14th, influenced by the illustrations in Greek Gospels, which were translated into Ge'ez during the Aksumite period (*see* GOSPEL BOOK). They usually begin with canon tables, which end with the *Fountain of Life*. Each Gospel opens with a portrait of the seated or standing Evangelist, and there are illustrations, varying in number, of scenes from the Life of Christ. One 14th-century Gospel book (Paris, Bib. N., MS. Ethiopia 32) is limited to three illustrations of symbolic character, apart from the canon tables and portraits of Evangelists.

2. *Crucifixion*, miniature from a Gospel book, parchment, 293×184 mm, from Ethiopia, 14th century (Paris, Bibliothèque Nationale, MS. Ethiopia 32, fol. 7*v*)

In the *Crucifixion* (see fig. 2) depicted in an architectural scenery painting, the bare cross ('Golgotha Cross') stands at the centre as a symbol of Christ's victory over death. This depiction is based on Palestinian predecessors, such as are identifiable in the 6th-century souvenir ampullae now in Bobbio and Monza (Italy), but the Ethiopian rendering also diverges from the Palestinian models: the Christ medallion at the point of intersection is replaced by the Sacrificial Lamb (John 1:29) in the tympanum.

The sun and moon as ancient symbols of power, placed above god-like rulers, are a legacy of Early Christian iconography. These astral symbols have survived, if in a more obscure form, in traditional Ethiopian representations of the Crucifixion until the present. Another Gospel book, probably from the late 14th century (Gabre'el Church, Kebran Island, Lake Tana, MS. Lake Tana no. 1), is decorated with 18 illustrations from the Life of Christ.

Typical stylistic features of book and wall painting are: frontal, hieratic representation of figures, which seem flat and without volume and are often reduced to geometrical forms, and a monochrome background. The basic colours red, green, blue and yellow predominate; gold is the exception.

(ii) c. 1400–c. 1600. The 15th century, especially during the rule of Zara Yakob (*reg* 1434–68), and the beginning of the 16th century, under Lebna Dengal (*reg* 1508–40), were periods of strong central power and artistic flowering. Iconography and style in painting were enriched by new influences, which were absorbed and adapted differently by different scriptoria. There is documentary evidence of the work of three European painters: the Venetians Nicolò Brancaleone (Brancaleon; in Ethiopia ?1480–1520) and Gregorio Bicini, neither probably a professional artist, and the Portuguese Lázaro di Andrade (in Ethiopia from 1520), all of whom had arrived with European artisans at the ruler's court. Attributions are not possible to Bicini and di Andrade, who remained anonymous, but some of Brancaleone's works in monasteries and churches in Gojjam have been identified through signatures, for example various paintings on wood, and a book of miniatures with about 50 illustrations (angels, prophets, saints and New Testament scenes) but no text (Wafa Iyesus Church, in the area of Mota, on the edge of the plateau declining to the Blue Nile Gorge). The influence of western European painters is evident in the replacement of frontal by three-quarter views, in a pronounced corporeality in the figures and in attempts to render light and shade and to give more volume to folds in clothing.

More significant, however, are iconographic innovations that can be traced back to European painters and foreign models. The subject of the Trinity, popular in Ethiopia in the form of three identical seated men, was probably first depicted there by European painters at the beginning of the 16th century. A devotional image influenced by Flemish painting of the 16th century, *Ecce homo* (John 19:5), shows the figure of Christ crowned with thorns and giving a blessing; it may have been brought into the country or painted in Ethiopia by a European (?di Andrade). This painting was called *Kwer'ete re'esu* ('The striking of his head'; a paraphrase of Matthew 27:30 and Mark 15:19) and was much venerated; it was taken on military campaigns and adopted by Gondarine kings as their imperial Palladium. Ethiopian artists used it as a model, and replicas were repeatedly copied with variations, especially in the 17th and 18th centuries.

The iconography of the Virgin, much revered as Theotokos ('Mother of God'), was also enriched by new variants in the 15th century. Most representations from the 14th century were based on variants of the principal Virgin type, known as Hodegetria ('She who points the way'), in which the Child may sit on the left or the right arm of the enthroned Virgin. Most examples, of all dates, show two flanking angels, whose presence is intended to accentuate the royal dignity of the Mother of God. By the early 14th century a Greek influence was detectable in allusions to the type of the Virgin known as Eleousa ('merciful'). Cretan or Italo-Cretan icons of the Virgin were held to have been based on a half-length portrait from life of the Virgin on the Mountain of Jerusalem, holding the Child in her arms, traditionally attributed to the Evangelist LUKE; such icons seem to have arrived in Ethiopia at the beginning of the 16th century, and were especially venerated there, exerting a lasting influence. Works based on Italian Renaissance painting include those in which the Virgin is shown crowned or holding a flower in her hand, and the Child naked or playing with a tame bird. The type of the Virgin Suckling the Infant Child seems to have been adopted only in the mid-15th century, as a result of Western influences, although it is documented in Coptic painting of the 9th and 10th centuries.

All these influences are particularly noticeable in panel painting, newly established in Ethiopia in the 15th century and probably received from the West. The Virgin was depicted especially often, on single panels, diptychs and triptychs, after the institutionalizing of the Marian cult by Emperor Zara Yakob. Other important subjects of panel paintings on wood in the 15th century and early 16th were the Crucifixion, the Twelve Apostles and the saints, most notably St George. From the second half of the 16th century onwards, the symbolic representation of the Resurrection also appeared, specifically the Descent into Limbo, widely disseminated in the Eastern Church, where it was known as the Harrowing of Hell, and the Flight into Egypt.

The scriptoria around Lake Tana seem to have assimilated not only Greek and Western but also Armenian and possibly Indian–Islamic and even Japanese influences. The masterpieces of this school include a panel (1.77×1.02 m) from the Estifanos (Estifānos; St Stephen's) Church on the island of Daga, Lake Tana (*c.* 1445–68). Very exceptionally, this work has a signature, which reveals that it was painted by a monk called Fré Seyon, who had worked for Zara Yakob. The upper register contains a depiction of the Virgin, flanked by two angels and suckling the Christ Child, who is playing with a dove, and below are SS Peter, Stephen and Paul; all the figures have slightly Eastern facial features.

Two further stylistic traditions, which can be distinguished in Tigray and Eritrea, were connected with two religious orders active there and developed during the second half of the 15th century. The Gunda Gundé style took its name from the site of the most important find, the monastery of Debre Gerzen in Gunda Gundé (Tigray), a monastery of the Estifanos (Estifānos; Stephanite) community. This rather heterogeneous style, documented primarily in manuscript illustrations, developed before the 15th century and continued until the mid-16th century. Among its characteristics are round faces with high foreheads and elongated eyes, possibly derived from Islamic or Armenian influences, and a wealth of geometric ornament (triangles, zigzags) covering the garments of the saints.

The second style is linked to the Ewostatewos (Ēwostātēwos) Order, of which the most important centre was the monastery of Debre Maryam in Kohayen (Eritrea), where the Psalter made for the local governor Belin Segged was probably produced in 1476–7 (Paris, Bib. N., MS. d'Abbadie 105). The 33 miniatures show mounted saints and the two biblical kings *David and Solomon*, as well as scenes of the *Passion* and depictions of the *Virgin, Apostles* and *Evangelists*. The biblical kings are dressed like the contemporary rulers, and their status symbols (headdress, ear pegs) are shown in elaborate detail. In *David Playing the Harp* (see fig. 3) the harp is in the form of an Ethiopian *begena* (*baganā*). The kings are followed by a court official with the sunshade reserved for kings, and a fly-whisk, also a sign of rank. Many religious paintings reflect the hierarchical social structure in iconography and style, the size of the figures depending on their importance and rank, not

3. *David Playing the Harp*, miniature from the Psalter for Belin Segged, parchment, 300×210 mm, from Ethiopia, 1476–7 (Paris, Bibliothèque Nationale, MS d'Abbadie 105, fol. 13*v*)

on the rules of perspective. Some of the models for this Psalter were probably of Byzantine, possibly Syrio-Palestinian origin; others seem to have been popular western European prints. The three-quarter view and indications of movement are characteristic of this time. However, the figures are two-dimensional, and the drapery folds are decorative rather than naturalistic.

The cultural flowering came to an end in 1527–43, when Christian Ethiopia was devastated by the Muslim Imam of Harar, Ahmad ibn Ibrahim al-Gazi (1506–43), called by the Ethiopians Grāñ (the Left-handed), and many churches, monasteries and manuscripts were destroyed. The art of the period *c.* 1550–1665 has been little researched and is difficult to date. Some paintings reproduce the iconography and style of the 15th century, while others anticipate the stylistic tradition of the 17th. The latter include, for example, portraits of the Twelve Apostles and of the Nine Saints, probably Syrian missionaries, who had founded monasteries in the 5th century. These wall paintings (?16th century) are in the rock-cut church of Abune Yem'ata, named after one of the Nine Saints, on Mt Guh (Ger'alta, Tigray).

(iii) c. *1600–c. 1900.* In the permanent capital, Gondar, a centre of trade, painting and theology was established from the time of Emperor Fasilides (*reg* 1632–67). The town remained a cultural centre until its destruction by

the dervishes from the Sudan (1888–9), although it had forfeited its political position in the mid-18th century. In the early 17th century the First Gondarene style evolved, giving way *c.* 1730 to the Second Gondarene style, which survived until the early 20th century; various foreign influences contributed to the characteristics of both styles.

(a) Growing foreign influences and indigenous developments. The influence of Indian painting, already discernible in the 16th century, grew stronger in the 17th. Details of Eastern buildings, costumes or headdresses were based on Hindu Rajput painting and the Islamic–Hindu Mughal tradition (*see* INDIAN SUBCONTINENT, §V, 4(i)).

Western European models further enriched the iconography, as seen for example in the *Evangelium arabicum*, which is decorated with engravings by Antonio Tempesta (1555–1630), a Renaissance artist influenced by Albrecht Dürer, and which was printed at the end of the 16th century in Rome. Copies were distributed in Ethiopia, and its influence is especially noticeable in various 17th-century illustrated Gospels, such as the *Evangeliar* (1665–70; London, BM, MS. Or. 510), produced in a Gondarene scriptorium, probably for Emperor Yohannes I (*reg* 1667–82).

The painting that most decisively shaped Ethiopian representations of the Virgin from the 17th century onwards is the Byzantine icon *Salus Populi Romani*, of the Hodegetria type, attributed to St Luke (Rome, S Maria Maggiore). Jesuit missionaries disseminated prints of this image throughout the Eastern world, and in Ethiopia this type of the Virgin has been predominant until the present. It was translated by Ethiopian artists into their contemporary local idiom and iconographically transformed until, in the mid-18th century, its adaptation to the Ethiopian context was complete. The inclusion of two archangels, usually Gabriel and Michael, flanking the Virgin was the most important contribution of Ethiopian artists.

The Mother of God remained the most popular subject for Ethiopian painting on walls, panels and manuscripts. In wall paintings she was depicted on the main wall of churches, along with the knight St George, also very popular in Ethiopia; her portrait also appeared in manuscripts, even when unrelated to the text. In triptychs her image occupied the main panel, while other subjects were depicted on the wings. In one such example (17th century; U. Zürich, Vlkerkndmus., Inv. no. 13984; see fig. 4), the right wing shows *St George Slaying the Dragon* at the top and the Ethiopian saint and martyr *Fasilides*, also on horseback, at the bottom. These knight–saints were often depicted with other mounted saints, such as Téwodros (Theodore) and Merkoréwos (Mercury), on the north wall

4. Ethiopian triptych, tempera on gesso-covered canvas glued to wood, 315×415 mm, 17th century (Zurich, Universität Zürich, Völkerkundemuseum)

of churches. The left wing represents in traditional iconography *Tekle Haymanot* (above) and *Ewostatewos* (below), two monastery founders, who were venerated as saints.

Tekle Haymanot in particular, along with the ascetic saint Gebre Menfes Keddus, enjoyed growing popularity from the 17th century onwards, assuming in the 18th century a new iconographic form, which continues to endure. Tekle Haymanot is depicted with three pairs of wings and standing on one leg, the other leg, so legend tells, having withered through his rigid stance at prayer, and Gebre Menfes Keddus appears in the desert, surrounded by lions and leopards.

Among the most important subjects dating from the 17th century onwards are illustrations of the Miracles of Mary (Ta'āmra Māryām), of which the prototypes may go back to Brancaleone. These legends of the Virgin, which originated in France and were taken abroad by the crusaders, were translated into Ge'ez at the beginning of the 15th century, underwent local transformations and in the 15th and 16th centuries were decorated only by a portrait of the Mother of God. An innovation of the 17th century was the insertion into the text of illustrations of the miracles. In Gospel books, too, the images of the life of Christ no longer appeared at the beginning of the book but were spread throughout the Gospel.

In the 17th and 18th centuries in Ethiopia, illustrated 'books' consisting of long parchment strips, folded in pleats, were common; they probably first appeared in the 15th century and were used for devotional purposes. Apart from explanatory inscriptions and short hymns, they consist solely of illustrations. Also in the 17th and 18th centuries, small diptychs painted on both sides, also for devotional purposes, were widespread, probably being worn by monks on a cord round their necks. Favoured illustrations included the Virgin and St George on one side and the Crucifixion and another subject on the other.

(b) First Gondarene style. Apart from numerous panel paintings and manuscripts, the paintings from the church of Abba Antonios (now in Paris, Mus. Homme), dating from the time of Emperor Yohannes I (*reg* 1667–82), are among the most important examples of the First Gondarene style. The partly damaged paintings of the church of Debre Sina in Gorgora on Lake Tana, dating from the reign of Iyasu I (*reg* 1682–1706), are still *in situ*. Characteristic of the First Gondarene style were the elongated faces of the saints, the drapery folds in the form of parallel lines, some with ornaments and imitating Indian or Islamic textiles, and the predominance of the colours yellow, green, red and blue. From the 17th century to the early 20th there was an increasing predilection, perhaps arising from fear of the evil eye, for depicting enemies of Christ in profile.

(c) Second Gondarene style. While the First Gondarene style retained the linearity of earlier stylistic traditions, particularly in Tigray, the Second Gondarene style showed features of an ostentatiously ceremonious court style. Artists attempted to achieve three-dimensionality by light-and-shade effects and by drapery folds, although they stopped short of striving for an illusion of space, and the saints were dressed exactly like the nobility in brocade and velvet garments. The background was no longer monochrome but painted in tones of yellow, red and green. Increasingly, schematically drawn churches and buildings, recalling the castles of Gondar, characterized the locality of an event, and elements of a landscape suggested Lake Tana and its islands. Trees were represented only if they had symbolic meaning or served to articulate space; no true landscape painting emerged.

In the 18th and 19th centuries scenes from the lives of saints were common; new themes included the illustration of the martyrdom of St George. Legends and other themes, such as the Flight into Egypt, had been given actuality by the inclusion of genre elements (domestic objects, weapons, jewellery, church paraphernalia etc) as early as the 17th century; this tendency grew more pronounced from the 18th century, with the result that the paintings acquired a narrative aspect. Donor portraits were executed more frequently in the 17th century and in the 18th century enjoyed growing popularity. The donors usually had themselves shown in prostrate positions, or standing below the figure of a saint with their arms crossed before the breast. These traditional gestures of submission and modesty echoed those performed in front of rulers. Initially, most donors were themselves rulers; later they were also nobles and clerics, as shown, for example, in the lower part of the door to the sanctuary in the church of Kidane Mehret on the Zegé Peninsula, Lake Tana (late 19th century), on which *Gebre Menfes Qeddus Riding on a Cock and Surrounded by Wild Animals* is depicted on the right wing (see fig. 5). The most important motifs on the doors are the armed archangels (Michael and Gabriel, or Raphael and Uriel), the sanctuary guardians. The winged heads of angels, a popular motif of the Second Gondarene style, were inspired by Italian Baroque painting.

From the 18th century, portraits appeared in manuscripts and on church walls, first of earlier rulers who had played an important part in Ethiopian history, then also of more recent rulers. Scenic paintings with non-religious subject-matter first emerged at the beginning of the 19th century, when wall paintings showed episodes from the life of the founder of a particular church. Popular themes were coronation ceremonies, royal processions, burials and, especially, battles, hunts or banquets.

The Second Gondarene style occurs in numerous manuscripts, panel paintings and wall paintings. The latter survive, for example, in the Sellasé (Śellāsē; Trinity) Church, Narga Island, Lake Tana (*c.* 1747); the church of Debre Berhan Sellasé (Dabra Berhān Śellāsē; Light of the Trinity), north-east of Gondar (*c.* 1815–20); the church of Kidane Mehret, Zegé Peninsula, Lake Tana (late 19th century); and the Gebre'el (Gabriel) Church, Kebran Island, Lake Tana (late 19th century).

The First and Second Gondarene styles were also adopted by other scriptoria. The imposing Second Gondarene style, in particular, seems to have been popular at the centres of power, namely at the courts of emperors or local rulers. Examples include hunting scenes (*c.* 1800) in Sellasé Church in Chalaqot (Enderta, Tigray), placed there on the orders of Ras Welde Sellasé, then the ruler of Tigray; paintings in the church of Kidane Mehret in Wayname, near Bichena, Gojjam (*c.* 1800); the royal

5. Painted sanctuary door, probably gesso-covered canvas glued to wood, *c.* 2.7×1.3 m, church of Kidane Mehret, Zegé Peninsula, Ethiopia, late 19th century

procession of Tekle Haymanot, King of Gojjam, in the church of Debre Markos, Gojjam (*c.* 1890); paintings including a battle scene in the rock-cut church of Abreha Asbeha, Tigray, from the time of Yohannes IV (*reg* 1872–89); and manuscripts produced for King Sahle Sellasé of Shewa (*reg* 1813–47).

(d) Other styles. In Shewa, Welo and Tigray, manuscripts and wall paintings were produced in the 18th and 19th centuries that were not influenced by the Second Gondarene style. Many of these recall images on magic scrolls, with such features as outsize eyes and hands, bodies reduced to geometric figures and distortions. Sometimes, too, the ornamental treatment of figures and background suggests the influence of 14th- and 15th-century models. Such images were probably produced in local scriptoria, many of them by *debteras*, for the local clergy or nobility. The Yohannes Church in Me'ekuddi (Ger'alta, Tigray) has examples from the 17th century. From the 19th century onwards, religious themes were supplemented by historical ones, such as portraits of rulers, battle scenes, hunts and banquets.

(iv) After c. 1900. At the beginning of the 20th century church painters, especially from Gondar and Gojjam, were concentrated in Addis Ababa, the capital founded in 1886 by Emperor Menelik II (*reg* 1889–1913). Alongside their paintings for churches, they started to produce large canvases for sale to foreigners. Many features of these popular paintings are derived from traditional scriptoria techniques. For example, pictures are often conceived in a narrative manner with sequences of pictures in a comic-strip format or integral compositions containing a story. Furthermore, rather than using perspective to create an illusion of space, people standing behind one another are shown above one another, and the size of the figures is based not on their position in space but on their social standing, which is emphasized by the use of symbols denoting status. Composition is structured by means of building or plant elements, and traditional subjects (e.g. religious and historical themes and legends) and scenes from everyday life are widely used, one of the most popular being the legend of the Queen of Sheba. From the 1920s, traditional paintings began to be produced in serial runs in commercial studios and also, from 1931, at the newly founded Empress Menen Handicraft School in Addis Ababa. Such traditional handicrafts as basket-weaving, carpet-weaving, embroidery, jewellery and hand and neck crosses are also pursued at the school (which since 1978 has been known as Handicrafts of Ethiopia). Balăččaw Yemar (?1894–1962), his son Salamon Balăččaw (*b* ?1923), Qaññgēta Ğanbarē Ḥāylu (*b* 1913) and Barhānu Yemanu (1908–91) are some of the best-known traditional painters, producing also for the tourist market.

An academic style of painting began to be developed in Ethiopia during the 1930s. This was the result of the fusing of established traditions with Western techniques brought to Ethiopia by artists with Western art training. The development of Ethiopian art was helped by the establishment of the Fine Arts School, Addis Ababa, in 1957. By the end of the 1960s, its own graduates were replacing the foreign teaching staff. Until the 1950s, traditional religious and secular themes, mainly commissioned by the Church or the State, were reproduced in a fairly conventional academic way, by such artists as Agañ-ñahu Engedā (1906–47), who also painted portraits, and Ala Fallaga Salām (*b* 1929). Tendencies towards stylization and abstraction are present in works by Afa Warq Taklē (*b* 1932), although his work was primarily realistic (for illustrations see Pankhurst, 1987). He was the foremost artist of the 1950s and the period of the socialist regime (1974–91) and received government commissions for such projects as the stained-glass windows for Africa Hall (1959–61), which proclaim pan-African ideals. In socialist Ethiopia the government used posters and other visual media to convey political ideas. This enhanced the importance of graphic design in the country.

New forms of expression became established in the 1960s, encouraged by the patronage of an emerging middle class and of foreign residents. The first work in this area came from Gabra Krestos Dastā (1932–81). Influenced by his experience of German Expressionism while in Cologne (1958–61), he adopted abstractionist forms of expression and worked in oil on hardboard and mixed media. Another lasting influence was that of Alexander Boghossian, known as Eskender (*b* 1937), who was exposed to Surrealism and the art and philosophy of Negritude while in Paris (1957–66), before emigrating to the USA in 1969. He took up residence in Washington, DC, in 1974. His partly abstract compositions assimilate inspirations derived from magic scrolls, illuminated manuscripts, representations of legends and black African art, and he used a variety of techniques and media. The Museum of Modern Art, New York, and the Musée d'Art Moderne de la Ville de Paris house works by Eskender. Two of his best-known pupils were Wasanē Kosrof (*b* 1950) and Zarihun Yatemgētā (*b* 1941). Yatemgētā's *Research from the Art of Magic* (see fig. 6) took up the style and motifs of traditional magic scrolls.

Other representatives of 20th-century Ethiopian painting include Dāne'ēl Ṭwāfē (*b* 1935), who was influenced by Salvador Dalí; Abdurāhmān M. Šarif (*b* 1939), who used expressionistic painting and collage techniques; Dastā Ḥagos, among the first women graduating from the Fine Arts School (1969), who specialized in themes showing the hard life of women; Tašoma Baqala (*b* 1950), influenced by Skunder's style; and Ṭebaba Tarffā (*b* 1948), whose work included linear abstractions and expressive paintings especially of life in the city of Harar. Such artists as Warqu Māmmo (*b* 1936), Tāddasa Masfen (*b* 1952) and Ešatē Ṭrunah (*b* 1953) preferred to cultivate a conventional, realistic style, and after 1974 the advent of Socialist Realism gave a boost to works depicting the life of ordinary workers, peasants and soldiers and the struggle against capitalism and imperialism. The woodcut technique was popularized by the German artist Hansen-Bahia (Karl-Heinz Hansen; *b* 1915), who taught at the Fine Arts School from 1963 to 1966. His expressionistic, coloured woodcuts influenced those of Zarihun Yatemgētā and Falaka Armide (*b* 1935). Late 20th-century developments in popular paintings, encouraged by the tourist boom in the 1960s, included the miniaturization of paintings on both canvas and parchment and a standardization of both figures and compositions, although more carefully painted versions were produced by artists who had trained at the Fine Arts School.

BIBLIOGRAPHY

TRADITIONAL RELIGIOUS PAINTING

E. A. W. Budge: *One Hundred and Ten Miracles of our Lady Mary* (London, 1933)
U. Monneret de Villard: 'La Madonna di S Maria Maggiore e l'illustrazione dei miracoli di Maria in Abissinia', *An. Lateranensi*, xi (1947), pp. 9–90
W. Staude: 'Etude sur la décoration picturale des églises Abbā Antonios de Gondar et Dabra Sinā de Gorgorā', *An. Ethiopie*, iii (1959), pp. 185–250
J. Leroy, S. Wright and O. A. Jäger: *Ethiopia: Illuminated Manuscripts* (Paris, 1961)
J. Leroy: *La pittura etiopica durante il medioevo e sotto la dinastia di Gondar* (Milan, 1964; Eng. trans. as *Ethiopian Painting in the Late Middle Ages and under the Gondar Dynasty*, London, 1967)
G. Gerster, ed.: *Kirchen im Fels* (Stuttgart, 1968, rev. Zurich and Freiburg im Breisgau, 2/1972); Eng. trans. as *Churches in Rock: Early Christian Art in Ethiopia* (London, 1970)
E. Hammerschmidt and O. A. Jäger: *Illuminierte äthiopische Handschriften*, Verzeichnis der orientalischen Handschriften in Deutschland, xv (Wiesbaden, 1968)
G. Annequin: 'L'Illustration des ta'amra Maryam de 1630 à 1730: Quelques remarques sur le premier style de Gondar', *An. Ethiopie*, ix (1972), pp. 193–226
E. Hammerschmidt: *Äthiopische Handschriften vom Tānāsee 1: Reisebericht und Beschreibung der Handschriften in dem Kloster des heiligen Gabriel auf der Insel Kebrān*, Verzeichnis der orientalischen Handschriften in Deutschland, xx/1 (Wiesbaden, 1973)
Religiöse Kunst Äthiopiens/Religious Art of Ethiopia (exh. cat., ed. W. Raunig; Stuttgart, Inst. Auslandsbeziehungen, 1973)
Ethiopie millénaire (exh. cat., ed. A. Cacan and J. Leclant; Paris, Petit Pal., 1974)
G. Annequin: 'De quand datent l'église actuelle de Dabra Berhan Sellasé de Gondar et son ensemble de peintures?', *An. Ethiopie*, x (1976), pp. 215–26
E. Hammerschmidt: *Illuminierte Handschriften der Staatsbibliothek Preussischer Kulturbesitz und Handschriften vom Ṭānāsee*, Codices Aethiopici, i (Graz, 1977)
Ethiopia: The Christian Art of an African Nation: The Langmuir Collection, Peabody Museum of Salem (exh. cat., ed. E. Cross Langmuir, S. Chojnacki and P. Fetchko; Salem, MA, Peabody Essex Mus., 1978)
J. Mercier: *Rouleaux magiques éthiopiens* (Paris, 1979; Eng. trans. as *Ethiopian Magic Scrolls*, New York, 1979)
S. Chojnacki: 'Major Themes in Ethiopian Painting: Indigenous Developments, the Influence of Foreign Models and their Adaptation from the 13th to the 19th Century', *Äthiop. Forsch.*, x (Wiesbaden, 1983) [standard work]
——: 'A Note on the Costumes in 15th and Early 16th-century Paintings: Portraits of Nobles and their Relation to the Images of Saints on Horseback', *Ethiopian Studies Dedicated to Wolf Leslau* (Wiesbaden, 1983), pp. 521–53
M. E. Heldman: 'An Ēwosṭāthian Style and the Gundā Gundē Style in Fifteenth-century Ethiopian Manuscript Illumination', *Proceedings of the First International Conference on the History of Ethiopian Art: London, 1986*, pp. 5–14, 135–9, figs 1–29
S. Uhlig: 'Bedeutung und Funktion der Ornamente in äthiopischen Kodizes', *Proceedings of the First International Conference on the History of Ethiopian Art: London, 1986*, pp. 56–8, 153, figs 95–104
C. Lepage: 'Prototypes de deux tétraévangiles du XIVe siècle à cycle court de trois miniatures', *Abbay*, xiii (1986–7), pp. 59–75
R. Pankhurst: 'Secular Themes in Ethiopian Ecclesiastical Manuscripts: A Catalogue of Illustrations of Historical and Ethnographic Interest in the British Library', *J. Ethiop. Stud.*, xxii (1989), pp. 31–64
E. Biasio: 'Art, Culture and Society: Considerations on Ethiopian Church Painting Focusing on the 19th Century', *Proceedings of the Eleventh International Conference of Ethiopian Studies: Addis Ababa, 1991*, pp. 541–62
R. Pankhurst: 'Secular Themes in Ethiopian Ecclesiastical Manuscripts II', *J. Ethiop. Stud.*, xxiv (1991), pp. 47–69
P. O. Scholz, ed.: *Orbis Aethiopicus: Archaeologia et artes: Festschrift S. Chojnacki*, Bibliotheca nubica, iii/2 (Albstadt, 1992)
Le Roi Salomon et les maîtres du regard: Art et médecine en Ethiopie (exh. cat., ed. M.-C. Bianchini; Paris, Mus. A. Afr. & Océan., 1992)
D. Appleyard: *Ethiopian Manuscripts* (London, 1993)
African Zion: The Sacred Art of Ethiopia (exh. cat., ed. R. Grierson; Baltimore, MD, Walters A.G.; New York, Schomberg Cent. Res. Black Cult.; Houston, TX, Menil Col.; and elsewhere; 1993–6)
M. E. Heldman: *The Marian Icons of the Painter Frē Ṣeyon: A Study in Fifteenth Century Ethiopian Art, Patronage and Spirituality*, Orientalia biblica et christiana, vi (Wiesbaden, 1994)

20TH-CENTURY TRADITIONAL, POPULAR AND 'ACADEMIC' PAINTING

R. Pankhurst: 'Some Notes for a History of Ethiopian Secular Art', *Ethiopia Observer*, x (1966), pp. 5–80
S. Chojnacki: 'A Survey of Modern Ethiopian Art', *Z. Kulturaustausch* (1973), pp. 84–94 [special edition devoted to Ethiopia]
G. Fisseha, W. Raunig and W. Stein: 'Mensch und Geschichte', *Äthiopiens Volksmalerei* (Innsbruck, 1985)
R. Pankhurst: *Afewerk Tekle* (Addis Ababa, 1987)
E. Biasio: *The Hidden Reality: Three Contemporary Ethiopian Artists, Zerihun Yetmgeta, Girmay Hiwet, Worku Goshu* (Zurich, 1989)
L. Ricci: *Pittura etiopica tradizionale*, Istituto Italo-Africano cat. (Rome, 1989)
B. Benzing: 'Investigations into Contemporary Ethiopian Art with Special Reference to Painting', *Proceedings of the Eleventh International Conference of Ethiopian Studies: Addis Ababa, 1991*, pp. 29–39
Taye Tadesse: *Short Biographies of Some Ethiopian Artists, 1869–1957* (Addis Ababa, 1991)
J. Kennedy: *New Currents, Ancient Rivers: Contemporary African Artists in a Generation of Change* (Washington, DC, and London, 1992), pp. 125–39
E. Biasio: 'Twentieth-century Ethiopian Paintings in Traditional Style: "Traditional", "Folk", or "Popular" Art?', *Proceedings of the Third International Conference on the History of Ethiopian Art: Addis Ababa, 1993*

6. Zarihun Yatemgētā: *Research from the Art of Magic*, mixed media on bamboo strips, 1105×640 mm, 1988 (Zurich, Universität Zürich, Völkerkundemuseum)

W. Kindred: 'Skunder and Modern Ethiopian Art', *Aspects of Ethiopian Art from Ancient Axum to the 20th Century*, ed. P. B. Henze (London, 1993), pp. 126–33

Seyoum Wolde: 'Gebre Kristos Desta: Painter and Poet', *Aspects of Ethiopian Art from Ancient Axum to the 20th Century*, ed. P. B. Henze (London, 1993), pp. 134–40

E. Biasio: 'The Burden of Women: Women Artists in Ethiopia', *New Trends in Ethiopian Studies: Papers of the Twelfth International Conference of Ethiopian Studies: East Lansing, MI, 1994*, i, pp. 304–34

——: 'Zerihun Yetmgeta and Ethiopian World Art', *Ethiopian Traditions of Creativity*, ed. R. Silverman (East Lansing, MI, in preparation)

Girma Fisseha and R. Silverman: 'Religion, History and the Other: The Paintings of Qangeta Jembere Hailu', *Ethiopian Traditions of Creativity*, ed. R. Silverman (East Lansing, MI, in preparation)

III. Sculpture.

Very early examples of rock art are the undated incised drawings and high reliefs of cattle in a gorge at Chabe (*c.* 10 km west of Dilla) in southern Ethiopia. In northern Ethiopia pre-Aksumite (*c.* 5th century BC–1st century AD) sculpture shows Southern Arabian, Sabaean, influence. Important examples of stone reliefs in the Temple of Melazo (*c.* 5th century BC) are incense altars decorated with the crescent and disc of the Moon God and Sabaean inscriptions. At Hawelti, near Melazo, a 1.4 m-high stone baldachin resting on bull feet was found, probably a throne and votive gift (*c.* 5th–4th century BC; Addis Ababa, National Museum). Each of the two lateral panels is decorated with low reliefs showing a figure bearing a fan or a whisk following a smaller figure. The smaller figures, one of which is identified by South Arabian syllabary, are probably the donors. The representation of the figures recalls reliefs from Persepolis. The throne is also decorated by a frieze of crouching ibexes with coiled horns. The bull, ibex, crescent and moon were attributes of the Sabaean moon god Almaqah. Also found at Hawelti was a stone statue of a seated woman, probably of high rank, wearing a pleated dress and elaborate jewellery (h. 800 mm; Addis Ababa, National Museum). In all pre-Aksumite sites stone slabs and fragments with South Arabian inscriptions were found, probably from unexcavated buildings.

During the Aksumite period (*c.* 1st–10th centuries AD) the art of stone-carving continued, but no large statues have yet been found. Examples, which also show South Arabian influences, are the thrones, stelae and stone slabs with inscriptions, all in or near Aksum. Twelve thrones are at the entrance of the city and fifteen more near the old cathedral of Maryam Seyon (Māryām Ṣeyon; the Virgin of Zion). They consist of a rectangular granite base surrounded by four columns and are thought to have been votive gifts for Aksumite deities. The stelae show a progression from crude, unhewn stones to six monuments, dating from around the late 3rd century AD to the 5th, carved to represent multi-storey palaces. The third-largest of these stelae (h. 21 m), representing a ten-storey building, is still standing; four, including the largest (h. 33.5 m), lie broken; and one (h. 24 m) was moved to Rome and erected in the Piazza di Porta Capena in 1937, during the Italian occupation of Ethiopia (1936–41). Numerous inscriptions on stone slabs, found in various sites, tell of the military expeditions of the kings; one of the most important is the trilingual inscription of King Ezana (*reg c.* AD 320–40) in epigraphic South Arabian, unvocalized Ge'ez and Greek. Further finds are the carved lioness,

over 2 m long, on the rock of Gobedra, near Aksum, and stone waterspouts on Aksumite buildings in the shape of lion or bull heads. The large rock sculpture of a lion at Kombolcha (near Dessie) may be an Aksumite or later creation.

Pre-Aksumite and Aksumite sites, especially tombs, are also rich in other artefacts; the Aksumite objects demonstrate contacts with the Nile Valley, the Mediterranean region and the Byzantine empire. There are stone bowls, such as those from élite Aksumite palaces; elaborate pottery, for example jars with necks depicting women (6th–7th century), found near the Aksumite stelae; and metalwork, for example an incense burner or lamp (h. 410 mm) in bronze with a handle depicting a dog chasing an ibex, found at Matara. Especially important for the reconstruction of Aksumite history are the coins in gold, silver and bronze (*c.* 3rd–9th century). They show half-length portraits of the Aksumite kings, inscriptions, up to the 4th-century symbols of South Arabian gods, and later variously shaped Christian crosses.

The earliest built (as opposed to rock-cut) churches doubtless contained an abundance of carved ornament on capitals, arches, coffers and wooden rood screens. A few surviving examples can be seen in the basilica of the monastery of Debre Damo (*see* §I above). They include the blind windows of the wooden frieze showing ornaments including interlace, knots, swastikas, arabesques, rosettes, zigzag lines and diversely shaped crosses as well as the representations of wild and tame animals on the wooden coffered ceiling (?7th–11th century). These carvings, probably Aksumite in origin, recall ancient Eastern motifs, which may have entered Ethiopia by way of southern Arabia or of Coptic art. From around the 11th century the influence of Arabic art is also visible.

Later, stone sculpture is mainly evident in the rock-cut churches of Lalibela and Tigray. These churches, especially the monolithic churches, are more important sculptures than built architecture, and geometric patterns, similar to those carved earlier in wood, decorate their pillars and arches. The windows are provided with wood and stone fillings in the shape of a variety of crosses and arches; other windows, such as those of Beta Giyorgis (see fig. 1 above), are topped with ornamental tendrils. Much of this ornament is preserved in the carved wooden consecrated slabs (*tābot*) that are the essential element of a church, in carved portable 'altars' (*manbara tābot*), in the carved decorations of the wooden covers of diptychs and triptychs, in hand- and processional crosses, and in manuscript paintings.

The fact that early Christianity favoured painting explains the relative neglect of figural sculpture, particularly free-standing works. Only a few reliefs are known. In Maryam Church on Mount Qoror (Tigray) on a frieze below the cupola is a relief showing the *Virgin and Child Flanked by Two Archangels* (*c.* 14th century), and in the Maryam Church of Lalibela a relief with equestrian saints fighting a dragon is located above the porch of the main entrance (*c.* 13th century). The Sellasē (Śellāsē; Trinity) Chapel of the church of Beta Golgota contains three monolithic stone altars with low-relief carvings showing crosses, representing the centre of the cosmos, and, on the central altar, the Four Living Creatures, according to the vision of Ezekiel 1:10 the bearer of the throne of God.

In the two-nave church of Beta Golgota, reliefs of over life-size, unidentified saints are represented in arched niches of the wall.

Especially in southern Ethiopia, in traditionally non-Christian regions, stone and wooden sculptures can be found. In the partially islamicized Arsi–Oromo area (especially between lakes Shala and Awasa) there are stone tombs surrounded by standing slabs, often with engraved ornament. They show an affinity with tombs, statues and decorative and symbolic motifs found among other southern and south-western Ethiopian peoples (see §IV below). Although often characterized as prehistoric, they seem not to pre-date the 20th century. Later, engraved ornamentation gave way to reliefs depicting the deceased and, later still, to painted humans and animals. The approximately life-size wooden statues (waga) of the Konso, living south of Lake Chamo, are also erected after the death of a high-status person, especially a brave fighter or hunter. They represent the dead person, who has a phallic symbol on his forehead and is flanked by wives and victims.

In Addis Ababa, the capital founded in 1886 by Emperor Menelik II (reg 1889–1913), public monuments were needed; the earliest were the work of foreign artists. The equestrian statue of Emperor Menelik II was produced by the German sculptor H. (Rudolf) Härtel in 1930, and the Lion of Judah (1955) is the work of the French sculptor Maurice Colka. In 1968 the Ethiopian artist Afawarq Taklē (b 1932) created an equestrian statue of Ras Makonnen (d 1906; father of Emperor Haile Selassie I, and governor of Harar from 1887) in Harar. Contemporary Ethiopian sculptors, most of them educated at the Fine Arts School in Addis Ababa and in foreign art academies, favour three-dimensional figural sculpture in wood, plaster or concrete, often with impressionistic overtones, as in Pregnant, a work in concrete by Taddasa Māmača (b 1941). The trend towards abstraction did not result in a rejection of natural forms, as exemplified in the sculptures in concrete Fatigue, by Alamāyyahu Bezunah (b 1934), and Mother and Child, by Tāddasa Balāynah (b 1943). The wooden sculpture Mother and Child by Bekele Abebe (b 1943) suggests the influence of sub-Saharan African sculpture. The abstract compositions assembled from metal components by Tāddasa Gezāw (b 1935) are in a category of their own; and the same can be said of the works of Mikā'ēl Bēta Śellāsē (b 1951), who lives in Paris and creates imaginative compositions of animals and human beings in glaringly painted papier mâché.

BIBLIOGRAPHY

E. Haberland: Galla Süd-Äthiopiens (Stuttgart, 1963), pp. 495–500
G. Gerster, ed.: Kirchen im Fels (Stuttgart, 1968, rev. Zurich and Freiburg im Breisgau, 2/1972); Eng. trans. as Churches in Rock: Early Christian Art in Ethiopia (London, 1970) [excellent pls]
J. Leclant: 'Archäologie der äthiopischen Frühgeschichte', Kirchen im Fels, ed. G. Gerster (Zurich and Freiburg im Breisgau, 2/1972), pp. 29–35
Ethiopie millénaire (exh. cat., ed. A. Cacan and J. Leclant; Paris, Petit Pal., 1974)
C. R. Cowen: 'Wooden Sculpture among the Konso and Gato of Southern Ethiopia', Proceedings of the Fifth International Conference of Ethiopian Studies: Chicago, 1978, pp. 217–32
S. Munro-Hay: Aksum: An African Civilization of Late Antiquity (Edinburgh, 1991)
Taye Tadesse: Short Biographies of Some Ethiopian Artists, 1869–1957 (Addis Ababa, 1991)

P. B. Henze: 'Oromo Tomb Architecture and Art', Aspects of Ethiopian Art from Ancient Axum to the Twentieth Century, ed. P. B. Henze (London, 1993), pp. 120–25
Künstler der Welt: Mickaël Béthe-Sélassié (exh. cat. by P. Bianchi and others, Berlin, Haus Kult. Welt, 1994)

IV. Megalithic art.

Megaliths dating from prehistoric, early historical and later times occur in various regions in Ethiopia and Eritrea. Dolmens, forming necropolises, exist in the highland west of Harar, dating from c. 1500 BC, and monolithic stelae, which had a funerary function, are widespread, for example in Eritrea, in the mountains west of Harar, and especially in southern Ethiopia, where thousands of monolithic stelae were erected. Some are undecorated, some have a phallic or anthropoid shape, sometimes with stylized faces, limbs and ornaments. Others have low reliefs of uninterpreted symbols and swords or engravings of weapons, human beings and symbols. The size of the stelae varies considerably, from about 0.5 m to 8.0 m. In the region of the Sidama, especially east of Lake Abaya, mostly phallic stelae (mainly 3–4 m, the tallest 8 m) or anthropomorphic stelae with carved faces and ornaments (c. 2 m) are found; in the region called Soddo, west of lakes Koka and Zway, there are different types of stelae: anthropomorphic and phallic, some decorated with carvings and low reliefs. The stelae of the site of Tiya (Soddo) date from the 12th and 13th centuries.

BIBLIOGRAPHY

R. P. Azaïs and R. Chambard: Cinq Années de recherches archéologiques en Ethiopie, 2 vols (Paris, 1931)
R. Joussaume: 'Les Dolmens éthiopiens', An. Ethiopie, x (1976), pp. 41–52
F. Anfray: 'Recherches dans le Soddo: Eléments d'Archéologie', Proceedings of the Fifth International Conference of Ethiopian Studies: Chicago, 1978, pp. 295–307
R. Joussaume: 'Tiya: Cimetière aux stèles décorées dans le Soddo (Ethiopie)', Proceedings of the Eleventh International Conference of Ethiopian Studies: Addis Ababa, 1991, i, pp. 23–46
R. Joussaume, ed. Tiya—L'Ethiopie des Mégalithes—Du biface a l'art rupestre dans la Corne de l'Afrique (in preparation)

V. Patronage, museums and collections.

The first patrons of the arts in Ethiopia were religiously motivated rulers and nobles, who supported architecture and donated paintings (illuminated manuscripts (see AFRICA, fig. 117), wall paintings and paintings on wood) to churches and monasteries. The painters were primarily priests, monks and debteras (dabtarās), who worked in the scriptoria of the monasteries or of the rulers, or in their own studios. They were educated at traditional church schools, where painting was also taught, and through apprenticeships to a master. A son often inherited the profession of painter from his father (a married priest or debtera). As painting was regarded as an act of worship rather than as art, most paintings do not carry an artist's signature.

In 20th-century Ethiopia the State and the Church have continued to be important patrons of the arts, commissioning both traditional and academic painting. Non-Ethiopians have also often bought traditional and popular paintings to sell to foreign ethnological museums. Since 1931, popular painting has been commissioned by the

Empress Menen Handicraft School (from 1978 Handicrafts of Ethiopia; *see* §II above) or made for private souvenir shops and sold to tourists. At the Ethiopian Tourist Trading Enterprise (founded in the early 1970s as the Ethiopian Tourist Trading Corporation and renamed in 1992), disabled artists trained at the art academy produce popular paintings and handicrafts. Since the 1960s, academic Ethiopian art has been bought mainly by foreign residents.

The Museum of the Institute of Ethiopian Studies at Addis Ababa University has a large collection of 20th-century secular and religious paintings on canvas and parchment, displayed alongside paintings on wood, manuscripts and other traditional art and ethnographic items. The other major permanent exhibition in Ethiopia is at the National Museum, Addis Ababa, where paintings and sculptures by academy-trained artists supplement the Museum's archaeological and ethnographic collections. Temporary exhibitions of academic and, more rarely, popular art are held at the new National Museum building, the City Hall gallery, and such foreign cultural institutes as the Alliance Française, the Deutsches Kulturinstitut or the Istituto Italiano di Cultura, all in Addis Ababa. The Cultural Center (founded in 1963 as the Creative Arts Center) and the J. F. Kennedy Library, both of which are part of Addis Ababa University, are also used.

Outside Ethiopia, important collections of manuscripts are held in Paris (Bib. N.), London (BL), Oxford (Bodleian Lib.), Berlin (Staatsbib. Preuss. Kultbes.), Munich (Bayer. Staatsbib.) and Rome (Bib. Accad. N. Lincei & Corsiniana; Vatican, Bib. Apostolica). In Munich (Staatl. Mus. Vlkerknd.) and Salem, MA (Peabody Essex Mus.), there are notable collections of paintings on wood, and in Paris there are two significant collections (Bib. N.; Mus. A. Afr. & Océan.) of magic scrolls and manuscripts with magical subject-matter. Fine collections of 20th-century popular painting are held in Rome (Mus. Afr.), Zurich (U. Zürich, Vlkerkndmus.) and Frankfurt am Main (U. Frankfurt, Frobenius-Inst.). A smaller collection, with works by a variety of academy-trained artists, can be seen in Zurich (U. Zürich, Vlkerkndmus.) and Munich (Staatl. Mus. Vlkerknd.).

Art education is centred on the Fine Arts School, founded in 1957. The four-year course provides training for professional artists, school art teachers, designers and museum restorers. The subjects taught are painting, sculpture, mosaic, woodcut, applied graphics, mural art, photography, book illustration and academic subjects. For many artists this training is supplemented by further studies abroad.

ELISABETH BIASIO

Ethnographic photography. Term for the use of photographs in the recording of cultures. In the 19th century, parallel to the Industrial Revolution and the development of technological processes such as photography, European and American travellers systematically explored the colonial territories of the world. Among these were anthropologists untrained in photography, who were usually affiliated to scientific societies and museums and who pursued the natural sciences, including the study of technologically less advanced cultures. Soon after the invention of the first practical photographic process in 1839, travel photography became a popular photographic genre. In the 1860s scientists began to take photographs of other cultures and developed forms of photographic representation closely linked to their interests in documenting the ways of life of foreign peoples and classifying the races of mankind. By 1870 ethnographic photography had grown into a well-delineated photographic genre.

Two forms of ethnographic photography were most widely practised in the 19th and early 20th centuries. The first was photography of a human subject referred to as the 'type'. This provided racial evidence on human physical evolution, then a major field of study that had grown out of 19th-century positivism. These anthropometric photographs attempted to follow rigid guidelines, requiring frontal, half-profile or profile poses of the human subjects, often nude, so that measurements could be taken from the photograph. Such depersonalized, generic 'type' images were most often made of people (prisoners, for example) that were completely dominated and intimidated by the photographer's culture. The second form was photography that showed the scientists' interest in material aspects of 'exotic' cultures. Such visual inventories allowed the study of architecture, art, craft production and rituals. Inventory-type photography was particularly common in the German-speaking part of Europe, where anthropologists such

1. Benedicte Wrensted: *Logan Appenay, a Bannock, in Grass Dance Regalia*, 1905–8 (Washington, DC, National Archives and Records Administration)

2. Eliot Elisofon: *Kuba king Mbop Mabiinc ma Kyen, Zaïre*, 1947 (Washington, DC, Eliot Elisofon Photographic Archives, National Museum of African Art)

as Adolf Bastian (1826–1905) and Theodor Koch-Grünberg (1872–1924) worked in museum and university settings emphasizing the study of material culture. In North America the photographs of Native Americans by Franz Boas, George Dorsey (1868–1931), James Mooney (1861–1921) and others documented dances, ball-games, house construction and crafts. Native American photographers such as Louis Shotridge, a Tlingit, also documented material culture, especially as it related to artefacts that museums were considering purchasing.

In the late 19th and early 20th centuries the majority of photographers had adopted ethnographic conventions in cross-cultural photography. Professional photographers would produce sets of ethnographic images, for example when they were hired to accompany expeditions. Amateur photographers, among them missionaries, military men and merchants, also worked in the ethnographic style. Besides the scholarly purpose that most photographers wanted to fulfil when recording ethnographic subjects, many shared a passion for exotic themes. They often composed their photographs to enhance stereotypical aspects of their subject that the purchaser of the image, the viewer, demanded. Many missionary photographers and colonial administrators also used photography in their efforts to justify and demonstrate the civilizing and converting effect of their presence.

Various regions of the world—the Himalaya in India, Ceylon [now Sri Lanka], the Southwest and the Plains of North America, the ancient kingdoms in Africa—attracted the image-makers more than others because they were the focus of fantasies of the exotic and the unknown. Because photography was felt to be a direct reflection of nature and reality, the photographers attempted to make the unknown known by securing the image. In India a photographic record of castes and tribes was produced in the second half of the 19th century and the early 20th by European photographers such as William Louis Henry Skeen and Samuel Bourne and by indigenous photographers such as Deen Dayal & Sons and C. Mull & Co. In North America a prolific body of work was produced by Edward S. Curtis, William Henry Jackson, John K. Hillers (1843–1925), Richard Maynard (1832–1907) and Hannah Maynard (1834–1918), David F. Barry (1854–1934), Benedicte Wrensted (1859–1949; see fig. 1) and many others. Numerous Europeans photographed in Africa, the so-called 'dark' continent partitioned into colonies during the age of imperialism. Photographic studios existed in many of the big coastal towns, and the photographers ventured along the coast and into the hinterlands. One such professional, the Portuguese J. A. da Cunha Moraes, served the family photographic firm in Luanda (Angola) from about 1863 to 1889. His images were widely distributed in Europe. Among the German anthropologist photographers were Bernhard Ankermann (1859–1943) in Cameroon and Gustav Fritsch (1838–1927) in South Africa. The Austrian merchant Rudolf Oldenburg photographed in Guinea and Cameroon between 1900 and 1913, while the French traveller Marcel Monnier worked in the Ivory Coast in 1890–91.

South America had its share of ethnographic photographers, among them the English botanist and anthropologist Sir Everard im Thurn (1863–1932) in Guyana. In Brazil Marc Ferrez (1843–1923) captured the life of Brazilian blacks, as well as photographing cities and landscapes and members of the Brazilian élite. In Peru Martín Chambi (1891–1973) photographed the Europeanized élite as well as the descendants of the Inca. In Australia and New Guinea the studio photographer John William Lindt (1845–1926), who worked from about 1860 to 1890, specialized in views of the aborigines. The English administrator Edward Horace Man (1836–1929) captured the Andaman Islanders on commission from the Royal Anthropological Institute in London. A substantial photographic record was left by Henry B. T. Somerville (1863–1932), who served on a British Navy expedition to the Solomon Islands. In the late 19th century Richard Parkinson (1844–1909), a German national, spent 30 years in the South Seas, documenting his stay there with photographs. Hugo Adolf Bernatzik (1897–1953), a Viennese anthropologist and journalist, travelled and photographed extensively in many parts of the world.

In the mid- to late 20th century the photographic study of the Balinese (1942) by the American photographers Gregory Bateson (1904–80) and Margaret Mead (1901–78), and the Japanese photographers Tadao Kano and Kokichi Segawa's illustrated ethnography of the Formosan Yami (1956), opened an active disciplinary debate on the role of photography in anthropological research. Other photographers, such as Eliot Elisofon (1911–73; see fig. 2), who worked mainly in Africa, Helga Teiwes (b 1930), who photographed Southwest American Indians, and Carol Beckwith (b 1945), who photographed the Maasai and Fulbe of Africa, continued to produce ethnographic images of great value in anthropological inquiry. Both 19th- and 20th-century ethnographic photographs were used by visual anthropologists of the 1980s and 1990s, who carefully contemplated the implications of the photographic encounter and the meaning of the images as multilayered sources. Ethnographic photographs can be found in many older publications, including the series on the peoples of India (1868–75) by James Forbes Watson (1827–92) and Sir John William Kaye (1814–76), Dammann's work on the races of man (1873–6) and Blackmore's North American Indian delegation views (1857–8).

BIBLIOGRAPHY

J. F. Watson and J. W. Kaye: *The People of India: A Series of Photographic Illustrations, with Descriptive Letterpress, of the Races and Tribes of Hindustan*, 8 vols (London, 1869–75)

R. Parkinson: *Dreissig Jahre in der Südsee* (Stuttgart, 1907)

G. Bateson and M. Mead: *Balinese Character: A Photographic Analysis* (New York, 1942)

T. Kano and K. Segawa: *An Illustrated Ethnography of Formosan Aborigines: The Yami* (Tokyo, 1956)

J. C. Scherer: 'You Can't Believe your Eyes: Inaccuracies in Photographs of North American Indians', *Stud. Anthropol. Visual Communic.*, ii (1975), pp. 67–9

R. Poignant: *Observers of Man* (London, 1980)

M. B. Blackman: *Window on the Past: The Photographic Ethnohistory of the Northern and Kaigani Haida*, National Museum of Man, Mercury sec. no. 74 (Washington, DC, 1981)

J. M. Gutman: *Through Indian Eyes: 19th and Early 20th Century Photography from India* (New York, 1982)

C. Beckwith: *Nomads of Niger* (New York, 1983)

G. Ferrez: *A Fotografia no Brasil, 1840–1900* (Rio de Janeiro, 1985)

M. Banta and C. Hinsley, eds: *From Site to Sight: Anthropology, Photography and the Power of Imagery* (Cambridge, 1986)

C. M. Geary: *Images from Bamum: German Colonial Photography at the Court of King Njoya (Cameroon)* (Washington, DC, 1988)

T. Theye, ed.: *Der geraubte Schatten: Photographie als ethnographisches Dokument* (Munich and Lucerne, 1989)

R. Rudisill: 'Directories of Photographers: An Annotated World Bibliography', *Photographers: A Sourcebook for Historical Research*, ed. P. Palmquist (Brownsville, CA, 1991)

E. Edwards, ed.: *Anthropology and Photography: 1860–1920* (New Haven and London, 1992)

J. C. Scherer, ed.: *Benedicte Wrensted: An Idaho Photographer in Focus* (Pocatello, ID, 1993)

CHRISTRAUD M. GEARY, JOANNA C. SCHERER

Etienne [Estienne] **de Bonneuil** (*fl* 1280–*c*. 1300). French architect, active in Sweden. In a letter dated 30 August 1287, the provost of Paris attests that Etienne de Bonneuil, 'stone mason and master', had received payment for the support of assistants to accompany him to Sweden to build Uppsala Cathedral. Another document, lost by 1719, purportedly guaranteed that 'the said French architect would build the church in the same form as that of Notre-Dame of Paris'. Although the Swedish cathedral is of brick and steatite as well as limestone, construction at Uppsala dating to the late 13th century reflects knowledge of the most recent developments at Notre-Dame, Paris, which has led to speculation about a direct connection between Etienne and Notre-Dame.

Etienne's arrival in Uppsala apparently coincided with a change in the design of the cathedral, which was probably completed up to the top of the nave aisle walls. Only the north transept façade is universally attributed to Etienne. His responsibility for the choir with its five radiating chapels and the crossing has also been suggested, although according to Zeitler they are less definitively French in their execution. The upper nave, nave chapels and the lower level of the west façade may owe something to his influence, although Zeitler argued for the importance of Westphalian techniques and mendicant church design. The participation of other French artisans, particularly sculptors, is evident at Uppsala Cathedral, and sculptures have been attributed to Etienne himself (*see* UPPSALA, §2). The duration of Etienne's stay in Sweden is uncertain, but the Parisian tax rolls record 'Estienne de Bonneuil, stone mason' in the parish of St Gervais by 1300.

BIBLIOGRAPHY

M. Aubert: 'Les Cathédrales de Paris et d'Upsal', *Ksthist. Sällskapets Pubn* (1924), pp. 5–17

V. Mortet and P. Deschamps: *Recueil de textes relatifs à l'histoire de l'architecture et à la condition des architectes en France au moyen âge*, ii (Paris, 1929), pp. 305–6

G. Boethius and A. Romdahl: *Uppsala Domkyrka 1258–1435* (Uppsala, 1935), pp. 43–62 [with app. on Etienne de Bonneuil's contract by K. Michaëlsson, pp. 212–25]

F. Nordström: *Studier i Uppsala domkyrkas äldsta byggnadshistoria, från grundläggning en fram till 1300-talets första årtionden* [A historical study of the early construction of Uppsala Cathedral, from its foundation through the first decades of the 14th century] (diss., Uppsala U., 1952)

R. Zeitler: 'Die Baugeschichte des Doms zu Uppsala', *Aspekte zur Kunstgeschichte von Mittelalter und Neuzeit: Karl Heinz Clasen zum 75. Geburtstag*, ed. H. Müller and G. Hahn (Weimar, 1971), pp. 359–85

ELLEN M. SHORTELL

Etienne-Martin [Martin, Etienne] (*b* Loriol-sur-Drôme, 4 Feb 1913). French sculptor. He studied sculpture at the Ecole des Beaux-Arts in Lyon from 1929 to 1933 and while in Lyon met the writer Marcel Michaud (1898–1958). In his last year at the Ecole he won the Prix de Paris, which allowed him to travel to Paris to continue his studies under Charles Malfray, at the Académie Ranson (1934); in the same year he met Duchamp. In 1936 Michaud founded the Témoignage group in Lyon, which Etienne-Martin joined together with François Stahly, Alfred Manessier and others. Etienne-Martin's sculptures of this period consisted largely of bronze and stone heads, such as *Head of Andrée* (1935; see 1971 exh. cat., pl. 2). From 1939 to 1941 he was first mobilized and then held prisoner in Germany. After his release, he returned briefly to Nyons, Drôme, before moving in 1942 to the community at Oppède, Vaucluse, where Stahly was also living. In 1943 he moved to Dieulefit, Drôme, and there met the writer and art collector Henri-Pierre Roché. With Roché he sculpted the huge 8 m-tall *Virgin* (1943, destr.; see Le Buhan, p. 21) in a sand quarry in Beauvallon, a work showing the influence of Egyptian sculpture.

From 1944 to 1947 Etienne-Martin lived with Stahly and Manessier at Mortagne, Orne, where he produced a number of large wooden sculptures, such as the *Large Couple* (1946; see Le Buhan, p. 31). This totem-like, near symmetrical work was much praised by the influential critic Michel Tapié in his famous book *Un Art Autre* (Paris, 1952). Etienne-Martin returned to Paris in 1947 where through Roché he met Brancusi, Dubuffet and Henri Michaux. Establishing a reputation for himself by then, in 1948 he won the Prix Blumenthal and the following year the Prix de la Jeune Peinture. In 1949 he also produced the innovative *Passementerie* series of three sculptures, *Passementerie 1–3* (1949; Paris, Pompidou), from a mixture of materials including cloth, rope and wood. These have the appearance of liturgical robes for some primitive, magical religion, a quality enhanced by the skull included in the first of the series.

In the mid-1950s Etienne-Martin began work on the *Habitation* series of sculptures. Characteristic of these is *Habitation 2* (1958–9; Saint-Germain-en-Laye, Mus. Mun.), which is a labyrinthine structure with phallic protrusions through the holes in its side creating the sense of a protective shelter. The theme of protection permeates much of the series, and the mixed media *The Cloak* (1962; Paris, Pompidou; *see* FRANCE, fig. 41), for example, is similar to the *Passementerie* series, here offering shelter through the capacious robes. Such protection amid clothing suggests maternal shelter and, by implication, that of the womb. He continued to add to this series, later examples including the oak *Passage or Tower of Shadows (Habitation 12)* (1969; Paris, Mus. N.A. Mod. Ville Paris), which is roughly carved into a similar reclusive shelter structure.

After the 1970s the most important of Etienne-Martin's sculptures was *Wall-Mirror (Habitation 15)* (1979; Paris, Pompidou) made from a large piece of chestnut wood cut into two, near symmetrical halves. On the top and bottom of each half is a face: one pair looking at the Earth, the other at the Sky. On each of the inner sides are two pairs of hands separated by the thick rubber wall between the two halves, through which a phallic cross-piece passes. The work is brightly painted in some areas and both halves are cut through with holes in a manner characteristic of other pieces in the series. This arcane sculpture symbolizes the male and female, the two female parts split apart by the male wall with its double phallus. As also suggested by Etienne-Martin it depicts that internal wall or mirror by which the individual views him or herself. In his later work Etienne-Martin continued the *Habitation* series, as in the mixed media *Le Mur-Verseau* (1982–3; artist's col., see 1984 Pompidou exh. cat., p. 87), which confirmed his interest in varied materials and their contrasting textures.

BIBLIOGRAPHY

Etienne-Martin (exh. cat. by J. Dypréau, Saint-Etienne, Mus. A. & Indust., 1966)
M. Ragon: *Etienne-Martin* (Brussels, 1970)
Etienne-Martin (exh. cat. by J. Lassaigne, Paris, Mus. Rodin, 1971)
D. Le Buhan: *Les Demeures-Mémoires d'Etienne-Martin* (Paris, 1982)
Etienne-Martin: Les Demeures (exh. cat. by H. Szeeman and others, Paris, Pompidou, 1984)
Etienne-Martin: Sculptures/passementeries (exh. cat. by E.-D. Allemand, Calais, Mus. B.-A., 1984)

□

Etowah. Site in north-west Georgia, USA, where a densely occupied, haphazardly planned agricultural village flourished in the Mississippian period (*c.* AD 1000–*c.* 1600). It covers 21 ha at the junction of the southern Appalachian Mountains and the piedmont, at the major fork of the Coosa River. The site was surrounded by palisades with outworks. Within the village area were three large mounds arranged around an open plaza. Mound A, the largest, has a ramp. Both it and Mound B are flat-topped pyramidal structures, presumably built to support temple buildings. Excavations in Mound C (intermittent since 1884) reveal it to have been built in at least three stages, during the construction of which over 300 burials were interred.

In the last stage, after *c.* AD 1400, only a few socially élite burials (including rather impoverished retainers) were placed in a tomb dug below the floor of a temple on Mound C's final summit. Large carved stone cult statues marked the entrance to the burial chamber. The élite individuals were fully dressed in ritual costumes and were accompanied by ceremonial objects and badges of office marking their personal and lineage status in what is known as the Southeastern Ceremonial Complex (*see* NATIVE NORTH AMERICAN ART, §I, 4(v)). Objects included decorated shell-bead necklaces, bracelets and anklets; shell cups and dippers and gorgets; repoussé copper plaques, rattles, staves, ear ornaments and headdresses; polished, painted (and occasionally copper-covered) stone effigies of composite weapons; and stone pipes (Cartersville, GA., Etowah Mounds Archaeol. Area). The raw materials both for these objects and for the cult statues were obtained by exchange with the rulers of other, more distant Southeast societies also participating in this ceremonial complex.

BIBLIOGRAPHY

D. S. Brose, J. A. Brown and D. W. Penney: *Ancient Art of the American Woodland Indians* (New York, 1985)
L. Larson: 'The Etowah Site', *The Southeastern Ceremonial Complex: Artifacts and Analysis*, ed. Patricia Galloway (Lincoln, 1989), pp. 133–41
G. E. Stuart, L. Johnson and H. T. Hall: 'Etowah: A Southeast Village in 1491', *N. Geog.*, clxxx/4 (1991), pp. 54–67

DAVID S. BROSE

Etrog, Sorel (*b* Jassy [now Iaşi], Romania, 29 Aug 1933). Canadian sculptor, film maker, costume designer, playwright and poet of Romanian birth. His formal art training began in 1945 but in 1950 he emigrated to Israel. From 1953 he studied at the Institute of Painting and Sculpture in Tel Aviv. Etrog's first one-man exhibition took place in 1958 and consisted of *Painted Constructions*, wood and canvas objects blurring the distinctions between painting and low relief (see Heinrich). In these works he tried to embody uncertainties that stemmed from his experience of Nazi aggression as a boy. The results were loosely expressionistic versions of geometric abstraction, derived in part from the work of Paul Klee.

Assisted by the painter Marcel Janco, Etrog went on a scholarship to New York, where he was inspired by Oceanic and African artefacts he saw in the collections there. This led to a preoccupation with organic abstractions, flowing totemic forms, and metaphors of growth and movement, seen in *Sunbird II* (1962–4; Toronto, A.G. Ontario). His work had similarities with that of Jacques Lipchitz, whom he met in 1959.

After a period of travel between New York and Toronto, Etrog became a Canadian citizen in 1966. His works were at this time large-scale bronzes exploiting a favourite motif, a type of chainlike linkage that he saw as expressive of both physical and psychic tensions, for example *Olympia Hand* (1972; Toronto, A.G. Ontario). The same principle underlies later works, which are often more mechanical in appearance and enormous in size; most are untitled (see Bentley Mays, p. 11).

In the 1970s, Etrog's friendship with the media analyst Marshall McLuhan led to a widening of his interests, and he has since explored his central concerns in nearly all media, from poetry and play writing, to film and even costume design. Nevertheless, he is known chiefly as a sculptor.

BIBLIOGRAPHY

W. Withrow: *Sorel Etrog: Sculpture* (Willowdale, 1967)
T. A. Heinrich: *The Painted Constructions, 1952–60, of Sorel Etrog* (Berne, 1968)
Sorel Etrog (exh. cat., Toronto, Marlborough Godard Ltd; Montreal, Marlborough Godard Ltd; New York, Marlborough Gal. Inc.; 1976)
J. Bentley Mays: 'Sorel Etrog Unveils a Surprise', *Toronto Globe and Mail*, (10 Jan 1981), p. 11
R. J. Belton: *Sorel Etrog's Drawings and the Human Condition* (diss., U. Toronto, 1983)

ROBERT J. BELTON

Etruscan. Civilization of Italy that flourished from the 9th century BC to the 1st. Ancient Etruria is usually defined as the area bounded by the Tyrrhenian Sea, the River Arno, the Tuscan–Umbrian Apennines and the River Tiber (see fig. 1).

I. Introduction. II. Architecture. III. Sculpture. IV. Pottery. V. Painting. VI. Metalwork. VII. Other arts. VIII. Rediscovery. IX. Forgeries. X. Collections, museums and exhibitions.

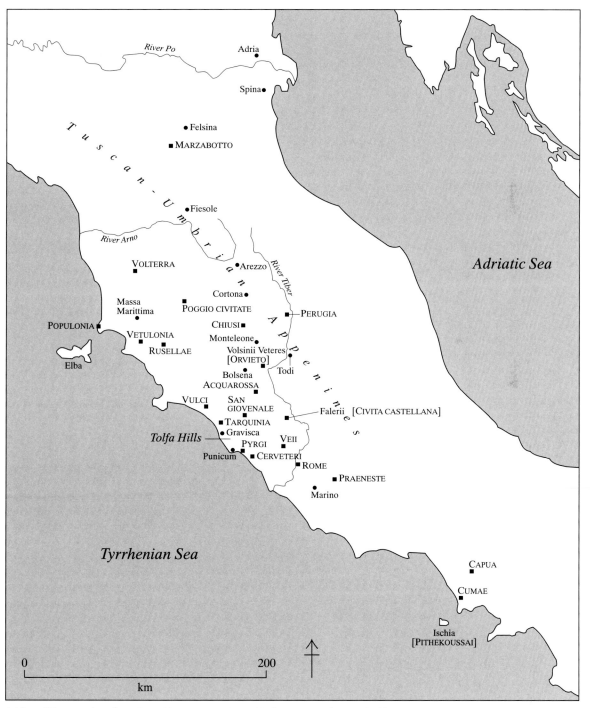

1. Map of Etruscan sites; those sites with separate entries in this dictionary are distinguished by CROSS-REFERENCE TYPE

I. Introduction.

1. General history. 2. Major periods. 3. Religion. 4. Trade. 5. Subject-matter.

1. GENERAL HISTORY. Etruria is a varied, predominantly hilly region with a low-lying, marshy coast and hence few natural ports, although its rivers provide good internal communication routes. In ancient, as in modern, times, the climate and terrain favoured agriculture, and Etruria also had rich mineral resources, especially iron and copper. Throughout its history certain main urban centres, each with a dependent territory, maintained a consistent cultural and political importance.

(i) Early development. (ii) Expansion. (iii) Decline.

(i) Early development. Etruscan civilization originated during the Late Bronze Age (12th–11th century BC), when the region's sparse population began to establish settlements on naturally defensible tufa plateaux in the south and hilltops in the north. Archaeological evidence from these sites, which later became the historical cities of Etruria, suggests that by about the 9th century BC they already accommodated quite populous communities and that a distinct regional culture, generally termed Villanovan (*see* §2(i) below), was emerging, with peripheral evidences in transappennine regions (Bologna, Verucchio, Fermo) and in Campania (Pontecagnano).

Despite numerous attempts, the archaeological evidence cannot be satisfactorily reconciled with an influential tradition, which is derived from ancient literary sources (e.g. Herodotus: I.xciv), that the Etruscans migrated to Italy from the eastern Mediterranean or Asia Minor. The conflict between this and Dionysios of Halikarnassos' claim (I.xxv–xxx) that the Etruscans were an indigenous people encouraged numerous exotic legends about their origins, but it is now clear that any original migration of the Etruscans to Italy must have predated existing archaeological remains.

The Etruscans spoke a non-Indo-European language, a rare survival from the prehistoric Mediterranean world before the Indo-European invasions of the 2nd millennium BC, the genealogy of which is common with the pre-Greek idiom of the Aegean island of Lemnos. Documentary evidence does not occur before c. 700 BC, when the Greek alphabet was introduced into Etruria. The absence of significant differences in dialect, however, suggests that Etruscan was already deeply rooted by this time. Its later development shows the influence of other languages, notably Greek.

During the 9th and 8th centuries BC the growth of Etruria's population and the formation of the main urban centres were accompanied by secondary settlements and farmsteads along the southern river courses. The territories of CERVETERI (Caere) and VEII were extended to the south and east, bringing control of fords across the River Tiber. At Cerveteri, TARQUINIA and VULCI systems of exchange were established with Greek and Phoenician merchants, and these centres thus became distribution points both for imported goods and for foreign cultural influences (*see also* §4 below).

Between c. 775 and c. 750 BC Greek pioneers from Euboia founded a trading-post on the island of Ischia (*see*

PITHEKOUSSAI) followed by a colony at CUMAE. They made use of existing Etruscan trading routes throughout central and southern Italy and to Sardinia and Corsica. The mineral wealth of northern Etruria in particular was a stimulus to trade, since the expansion of the Assyrian empire meant that the Greeks could no longer obtain metals easily from the Near East. Contact with the Greek colonists acted as a cultural catalyst in the centres of southern Etruria, where new technologies were introduced alongside the imported luxury goods prized by an emergent aristocracy. At the same time, there may have been military encounters between Greeks and Etruscans: several 8th-century BC Etruscan helmets offered at the Greek sanctuaries of Dodona, Olympia and Samos are possible evidence. As Eastern and Greek craftsmen began to set up workshops in Etruria, local artistic culture was profoundly altered, and luxury goods based on Near Eastern models were produced in Etruria itself in the Orientalizing style (see §2(ii) below).

The readiness of Etruscan communities to accept foreigners may be reflected in the story of Demaratos of Corinth, an aristocratic merchant said to have arrived at Tarquinia around 657 BC (Dionysios of Halikarnassos: *Roman Antiquities* III.xlvi–xlvii), and by Greek-derived names found in Etruscan inscriptions of the mid-7th century BC. There also seems to have been a degree of social mobility at this time: Demaratos' son, Lucumo, moved to Rome and later became its fifth king, Tarquinius Priscus (*reg c.* 616–579 BC; see Livy: *History of Rome* I.xxxiv.2). Under the Tarquin dynasty the political organization of Rome appears to have reflected the contemporary Etruscan pattern of an aristocratic élite, centred on a single leader in an essentially urban context.

(ii) Expansion. The period from *c.* 600 to the mid-5th century BC was one in which Etruscan power expanded, both on the Italian mainland and, notably, at sea. The exploitation of raw materials in southern Etruria was complemented by the establishment along the Tyrrhenian coast, from Cerveteri to Pisa, of numerous port-like settlements, each dependent on a larger city slightly inland. These ports provided facilities both for commerce and for military expeditions, and at some (e.g. Gravisca, port of Tarquinia) the foreign traders, especially the Greeks of the Ionia, were able to settle, interact with the local community and even institute cults. Through the role of the ports as emporia, the Etruscan cities inland soon adopted Greek styles and methods in areas as diverse as religion and myth, arts and crafts, agriculture and naval engineering.

During the 6th century BC, as finds of transport amphorae and bucchero pottery attest, Etruscan trade extended to southern France, Campania, Sicily, Carthage and the Phoenician colonies in Sardinia. It must have been accompanied by confrontations, for example with the Greek interests represented by the Phocaean colony at Massalia (Marseille), its sub-colonies from Emporiae (Catalonia) to Mainake (Monaco), and another Phocaean colony at Alalia (Aleria) on the Tyrrhenian coast of Corsica, founded *c.* 565 BC.

A naval clash some 20 years later was inevitable. It took place in the Sardinian Sea, with an Etrusco-Punic alliance against the Greek fleet (Herodotus: *Histories* I.clxv–clxvii),

and brought about the flight of the Phocaeans from Corsica and an ensuing Etruscan domination of the island's Tyrrhenian side. Etruscan relations with the Phoenician cities of Sardinia and with Carthage itself were tempered by mutual trading interests.

The Etruscans, meanwhile, established themselves along the Campanian coast, revitalizing the southern Bay of Naples and Salerno with a series of settlements at Pompeii, Stabiae and Fratte di Salerno, which in turn became linked with communities in the Campanian plain (Capua, Suessula and Nola), where groups of Etruscans may have arrived via the internal caravan routes. The occupation of Campania gave the Etruscans new bases for naval expeditions towards the lower Tyrrhenian coast. Greek records are patchy, but one naval encounter occurred off the island of Lipari (Diodorus Siculus: *Library of History* V.ix.3–4), where the Greek community suffered raids, sieges and perhaps temporary occupation. Such events led to Greek accusations of Etruscan piracy, although from the Etruscan point of view they represented a reasonable military strategy. The outlook of the later Greek historians similarly made it impossible for them to understand the ritual significance of the killing of prisoners, which earned the Etruscans a reputation for cruelty. Known during the 6th century BC as 'masters of the sea', the Etruscans themselves were confident enough to erect dedications in the great Greek sanctuaries; for example a tripod to Apollo at Delphi, where the Caeretans had their own treasury (Strabo: *Geography* V.ii.3), and an ivory throne to Zeus at Olympia (Pausanias: *Guide to Greece* V.xii.3). Etruscan expansion obviously posed a threat to the western Greeks, and naval conflicts are recorded. In 474 BC the Cumaeans succeeded, with Syracusan help, in defeating the Etruscan fleet in the Battle of Cumae (Diodorus Siculus: XI.li).

The maritime expansion of the 6th century BC was complemented by the extension of Etruscan power on the Italian mainland. The primary centres formed a twelve-city league comprising Veii, Cerveteri, Tarquinia, Vulci, RUSELLAE, VETULONIA, Volsinii Veteres (see ORVIETO, §1), CHIUSI, Perugia, Cortona, Arezzo and Volterra (see VOLTERRA, §1). Each of these cities had a dependent territory, and their representatives would have gathered annually at the pan-Etruscan Sanctuary of Voltumna at Volsinii Veteres.

Few political figures are known from literary and epigraphic sources (e.g. the Vibenna brothers from Vulci, related to Mastarna (the Servius Tullius of Roman tradition); Velthur Spurinna of Tarquinia, leader of an expedition to Sicily; Thefarie Velianas, King of Cerveteri and ally of Carthage), but even the little known of these suggests that the Etruscans organized large-scale enterprises by collective decision. Beyond the Apennines in Emilia-Romagna, already inhabited by the Etruscans, new arrivals from Volsinii Veteres and Chiusi brought a more structured settlement of the territory: the region south of the River Po centred on Felsina (Bologna), becoming an area of farmsteads and market-towns grouped near the major Apennine passes (MARZABOTTO) or by the Po delta (Spina), or else by transalpine routes to a river artery (Mantua). Spina grew during the 5th century BC to displace the Venetic emporium of Adria, attracting merchants from

Kerkyra (Corfu), Aigina and Athens, the latter seeking new trade outlets after the closure of the Egyptian grain market by the Persian conquest. Internal routes led down to Campania and the Etruscans who settled there maintained political links with those on the coast. During the reign of the last Tarquin at Rome (Tarquinius Superbus, *reg* 534–510 BC) relations between Rome and the southern Etruscan cities intensified, leading to the annexation of south Latium, territory of the Volsci and the Aequi. Tarquin's forced exile provoked the descent to Rome by Laris Porsenna, King of Chiusi, and Rome fell once again, if only temporarily, into Etruscan hands (Livy: II.ix–xv).

Living standards in the Etruscan cities during this phase of expansion rose markedly. The luxurious lifestyle of the Etruscan nobility attracted comment from Greek writers (Athenaeus: *Deipnosophists* XII.517d, 519h). The cities flourished at the expense of the rural hinterland, which underwent depopulation at the turn of the 6th century BC. The ruling families depended on large numbers of slaves and jealously guarded their own political privileges against rising middle-class groups, such as the merchants. In contrast to the political influence of an artisan class, the plebeians, in Rome, their Etruscan equivalents never achieved autonomy, and this lack of internal flexibility, coupled with the pressure exerted by an expanding Rome, contributed to the Etruscan decline of the later 5th century BC and 4th.

(iii) Decline. Veii, which during the 5th century BC was in conflict with Rome over the control of the River Tiber, fell in 396 BC. Successive Celtic incursions into Lombardy affected northern Etruria, and in 390 BC the Celts reached Rome and burnt the city. This possibly prompted a Roman–Caeretan alliance (Livy: V.xl.9). In Campania, the key Etruscan city of Capua fell into Samnite hands *c.* 430 BC, effectively marking the end of an Etruscan presence in the region, though some influence lingered at such coastal sites as Pontecagnano, where documents in Etruscan occur later than 300 BC.

From this period onwards Etruscan history concerns the smaller orbit of central Italy, with power increasingly devolving to Rome. From the main Etruscan cities attempts were made to repopulate the hinterlands abandoned in the 5th century BC and to revive agriculture. Closer links were created between ruling élites of different cities, but social imbalance remained, causing internal revolt (Livy: X.iii.2, XXXVI.xxxiii.1–3). It is not clear how the army and the fleet were managed, given that political and administrative functions within the aristocratic magisterial bodies seem to have been separate. The attacks of Dionysios the Old of Syracuse on both Tyrrhenian and Adriatic coasts during *c.* 400–*c.* 375 BC mostly took the form of guerilla raids, and Syracusan colonies were set up only at Ancona, and possibly at Adria. Both the Tyrrhenian and the Adriatic seas were infested by Sicilian-sponsored pirates preying on the Athenian traders approaching Spina, the hinterland of which was by now under Celtic control.

Preoccupied with expansion to the south, the Romans only turned their full attention to the conquest of Etruria after gaining extensive military experience, which was certainly superior to that of the Etruscans, who still had no real political unity to match their ethnic and religious identity. The paintings from the François Tomb, Vulci (*c.* 330 BC; *see* §V, 5(ii) below) testify to an intense antagonism towards Rome. Despite alliances with the Umbrians, the Gauls and the Samnites, the Etruscans suffered serious reverses and the loss of Chiusi (295 BC), Volsinii Veteres and Vulci (280 BC), Cerveteri (273 BC) and Falerii (CIVITA CASTELLANA; 241 BC); the last two towns were destroyed and their inhabitants resettled in new towns (Volsinii Novi (Bolsena), Falerii Novi). The lack of archaeological remains from the cities (except Rusellae, taken in 294 BC) makes it difficult to assess the damage done during the conquest. But the cemeteries evince an increasing impoverishment in tomb groups and a decline in funerary art concordant with the trauma of defeat, especially in southern Etruria.

The coastal territory of Vulci became host to a series of Roman colonies over a period of 30 years; from COSA in the north (273 BC) to Fregenae in the south (245 BC). The cities of northern Etruria, on the other hand, enjoyed a new phase of prosperity. They were linked to Rome by unilateral treaties after the fall of Volsinii Veteres, but left unmolested. Coinage of the 3rd century BC demonstrates fiscal subservience to Rome and some economic unity between Volterra, Vetulonia and the settlements along the Val di Chiana (*see* §VII, 1 below). Volterra became the urban focus of a large dependent territory, with secondary centres along the river courses leading to the River Arno or into the Tyrrhenian coast, where ports were founded (e.g. Vada, Castiglioncello). At POPULONIA the refining of Elban iron ore reached industrial levels, possibly serving an arsenal for the Roman army. In 205 BC the allied autonomous Etruscan cities furnished help to the fleet organized by Scipio against Carthage (Livy: XXVIII.xlv). The general economic revival in Italy in the 2nd century BC did not exclude Etruria, especially in the north, around Chiusi and Perugia, where large landowners entrusted farming to tenants, possibly with leasehold rights. The non-participation by the Etruscans in the revolt of the Italian peoples trying to secure Roman citizenship (90–88 BC) reveals just how close the links with Rome had become, although many Etruscan cities in the north paid a high price for their support of Marius in the civil war with Sulla that followed. The concession of Roman citizenship rights to Etruria in 90 BC paved the way for a definitive process of Romanization, and Etruscan institutions, customs and even language fell into disuse.

BIBLIOGRAPHY

M. Pallottino: *Etruscologia* (Milan, 1942, 7/1984)
J. Boardman: *The Greeks Overseas* (Harmondsworth, 1964, London, 3/1980)
J. Heurgon: *Rome et la Méditerranée Occidentale jusqu'aux Guerres Puniques* (Paris, 1969); Eng. trans. as *The Rise of Rome to 263 BC* (London, 1973)
W. V. Harris: *Rome in Etruria and Umbria* (Oxford, 1971)
R. M. Ogilvie: *Early Rome and the Etruscans* (Glasgow, 1976)
M. Torelli: *Storia degli Etruschi* (Bari, 1981)
M. Cristofani: *Gli Etruschi del mare* (Milan, 1983)
M. Pallottino: *Storia della prima Italia* (Milan, 1984)
Civiltà degli Etruschi (exh. cat. by M. Cristofani, Florence, Mus. Archeol., 1985)
M. Cristofani: *Saggi di storia etrusca arcaica* (Rome, 1986)
N. Spivey and S. Stoddart: *Etruscan Italy: An Archaeological History* (London, 1990)
M. Cristofani, ed.: *Gli Etruschi: Una nuova immagine* (Florence, 2/1993)

MAURO CRISTOFANI

2. MAJOR PERIODS. The conventional chronology of Etruscan art broadly follows that applied to ancient Greek art, by which it was profoundly influenced from the Orientalizing period onwards.

(i) Early Iron Age (9th century–c. 675 BC). The Early Iron Age art of Etruria is often termed VILLANOVAN, after the settlement of Villanova near Bologna, and it marks the beginnings of Etruscan civilization. The inhabitants of Etruria at this time were farmers and herdsmen; nevertheless their simple wattle-and-daub dwellings included some relatively advanced technical features, such as perimeter drainage channels to prevent flooding. The appearance of these huts is reproduced in the characteristic pottery hut urns of the period (see fig. 9 below). Early Iron Age artefacts fall into three main categories: impasto urns with incised decoration, painted Geometric vases and bronze implements with incised decoration. From early in the period, non-utilitarian funerary pottery and metal ornaments were placed in burials, and Etruscan art was to retain throughout a markedly funerary focus, in contrast to Greek and other contemporary Mediterranean art. Metalwork in particular seems to have been a speciality of this period, although most metal artefacts, such as fibulae, razors and statuettes, were small. Terracotta statuettes, especially those of animals, display the naive spontaneity characteristic even of later Etruscan art. Both metal and terracotta figurines served mainly as decorative attachments for vases and other containers, rather than as sculptures in their own right.

(ii) Orientalizing (c. 675–c. 575 BC). During this period Etruscan art developed rapidly, absorbing influences primarily from Greek and Near Eastern art. The increase in foreign trade stimulated by the mineral resources of Etruria brought imports of luxury goods. These in turn created a demand that was in part supplied by locally produced imitations, often made in the Etruscan workshops of immigrant Greek craftsmen. Thus three main categories of artefacts can be identified: Orientalizing art of Greek origin and its local imitations; Near Eastern art and its local imitations; and a continuation of the indigenous Villanovan tradition. Typical Orientalizing features include the use of vegetal and animal motifs (particularly palmettes and lions), and an altogether more representational emphasis. In this period also wealthy Etruscans in the main urban centres, notably Vetulonia, Cerveteri and Tarquinia, began to be buried in elaborate tombs containing rich burial goods (e.g. the Bocchoris Tomb, Tarquinia, *c.* 670 BC; the Regolini-Galassi Tomb, Cerveteri, *c.* 650–*c.* 630 BC; and the Pietrera Tomb, Vetulonia, *c.* 650–*c.* 630 BC). The structure and decoration of the tombs themselves provide valuable evidence of the nature of the houses and palaces on which they were clearly modelled (*see* §II, 1 below). Other innovations of the Orientalizing period include the introduction of the potter's wheel, the development of a distinctively Etruscan style of vase painting and the production of Bucchero pottery (*see* §IV, 4 below). Etruscan metalworkers produced particularly fine small artefacts in precious metals, using the newly introduced techniques of granulation and embossing (e.g. a fibula from the Barberini Tomb, Praeneste; *c.* 675–*c.* 650 BC; Rome, Villa Giulia).

(iii) Archaic (c. 575–c. 480 BC). The increased prosperity and artistic activity in Etruria continued throughout the 6th century BC. The most noticeable feature of the Archaic period is the even stronger influence exerted by Greek art, which supplanted the eastern influences of the Orientalizing period and, more gradually, extended from luxury goods to popular art. Political conflict between the Etruscans and the Greeks during this period, when Etruscan expansionism was at its height (*see* §1(ii) above), does not seem to have inhibited the spread of Greek artistic standards in Etruria.

Archaic Etruscan art is marked by a steadily increasing emphasis on the representational, with the emergence of human figural scenes and narrative art, often based on Greek mythological iconography (e.g. the Monteleone Chariot; *c.* 550 BC; see fig. 31 below). Etruscan vases still imitated the finest imported wares, and Greek craftsmen continued to establish workshops in Etruria, particularly following the conquest of Ionia by the Persians (*c.* 546 BC). Greek-born vase painters also contributed to the growth of Etruscan wall painting: the first examples occur in tombs at Cerveteri and in the Campana Tomb, Veii (early 6th century BC). Many of the finest 6th-century BC wall paintings come from the Monterozzi necropolis, Tarquinia (*see* §V below). Other new art forms that began to develop *c.* 600–*c.* 550 BC include grave monuments with figural decoration (e.g. stele of Avle Tite, from Volterra, *c.* 575–*c.* 550 BC; Volterra, Mus. Etrus. Guarnacci) and architectural terracottas. The terracotta statues from the roof of the Portonaccio Temple, VEII (*c.* 515–*c.* 490 BC; Rome, Villa Giulia), are among the greatest of all Etruscan sculptures. Stone sculpture, by contrast, shows less expertise, but several important works were produced at Vulci in the first half of the 6th century BC (*see* §III, 3 below).

The earliest substantial architectural remains also date from the Archaic period, including Temple B at Pyrgi (*c.* 520–*c.* 500 BC), the Capitoline Temple at Rome (ded. 509 BC), the Portonaccio Temple, Veii (*c.* 515–*c.* 490 BC) and the important remains of a planned town at MARZABOTTO (late 6th century BC). The end of the Archaic period constituted one of Etruria's most lively cultural and artistic periods.

(iv) Classical (c. 480–c. 300 BC). Etruscan art of this period shows far fewer parallels with the development of contemporary Greek art than does that of the Archaic period, and was produced in the context of gradual political decline. Between *c.* 480 and *c.* 450 BC production in most arts, with the exception of bronze sculpture, seems to have abated and the dominant traits remain Archaic. Large, hollow-cast bronzes such as the Capitoline *She-wolf* (early 5th century BC; Rome, Mus. Conserv.; *see* ROME, ANCIENT, fig. 60) or the *Spear Thrower* (*c.* 470 BC; Paris, Louvre) mark the introduction of this important new technique. From the mid-5th century BC comes evidence of revitalized contact with Greek art, perhaps through new Adriatic trade routes. The cities of maritime Etruria (e.g. Veii, Cerveteri, Tarquinia and Vulci) underwent economic decline, while those in the interior (e.g. Chiusi, Cortona, Arezzo, Perugia and Fiesole) gained increasing prominence. Etruscan towns in the Po valley (e.g. Adria, Spina and Felsina) flourished as never before. The earliest

Etruscan Red-figure vases date from this time, and a revival of interest in stone sculpture towards the end of the 5th century BC is evinced by elaborate stone sarcophagi, first produced at Cerveteri and later at other centres (see fig. 16 below).

During the 4th century BC levels of production again seem to have increased, equalling those of the Archaic period. With the exception of the engraved cists from Praeneste (*see* §VI, 2(iii) below), however, there were few major innovations in the types of artefacts produced. Instead, existing forms were developed and enriched, notably wall painting, Red-figure vase painting, bronze-work (both in smaller engraved artefacts and in large hollow-cast sculptures) and stone sculpture (in particular, monumental cinerary urns from Chiusi and sarcophagi from Tarquinia and Vulci). Stylistically, the Classical trends evident in the mid-5th century BC continued to develop. Etruscan art attained considerable cultural unity, with many active centres of production.

(v) Hellenistic (c. 300–c. 50 BC). By the end of the 4th century BC Rome was already becoming the dominant power in central Italy, with Veii under its control from *c.* 396 BC. Further victories by Rome in the early 3rd century BC meant the progressive loss of independence and Romanization of the great Etruscan cities. The last painted vases were produced at Volterra and Chiusi, to be replaced by Black-glaze pottery. Otherwise many standard types of artefact familiar from the 4th century BC continued to be made. Etruscan art remained, however, a far less public art than that of Greece and the Hellenistic eastern Mediterranean, with stone sculpture still reserved for funerary monuments. The construction of large painted tombs (e.g. Tomb of the Typhon, Tarquinia; *see* ITALY, fig. 26) continued into the 2nd century BC. Good examples of Etruscan funerary sculpture of this period include the urn of Arnth Velimnas (Tomb of the Volumnii, Perugia; *c.* 150–*c.* 100 BC) and the sarcophagus of Seianti Thanunia Tlesnasa (from Chiusi; mid-2nd century BC; London, BM). Many small urns, resembling miniature sarcophagi, with individual figures on the lids and figural friezes around the caskets, were also produced in both stone and terracotta (see fig. 4 below).

An innovation in the sculptural decoration of Etruscan temples was the introduction, long after its development in Greek art, of the closed pediment with figural groups in high relief (e.g. the *Seven against Thebes* from Talamone; Florence, Mus. Archeol.). Impressive city fortifications were erected during this period, for example at Perugia. Among the last important works of Etruscan art are bronzes from Arezzo, including replicas of Greek statues (e.g. the *Athena of Arezzo*; ?1st century BC), and innovative works such as the *Arringatore* (*c.* 90–*c.* 50 BC; Florence, Mus. Archeol.). The pose and expression of the latter, in particular, testify vividly to the extent to which Etruscan art and society of the 1st century BC had adopted Roman standards.

BIBLIOGRAPHY
G. Dennis: *Cities and Cemeteries of Etruria* (London, 1848; rev. by P. Hemphill, Princeton, 1985)
P. Ducati: *Storia dell'arte etrusca* (Florence, 1927)
G. Q. Giglioli: *L'arte etrusca* (Milan, 1935)
M. Pallottino: *Etruscologia* (Milan, 1942, 7/1984)
H. Müller-Karpe: *Beiträge zur Chronologie der Urnenfelderzeit nördlich und südlich der Alpen* (Berlin, 1959)
L. Banti: *Il mondo degli Etruschi* (Rome, 1960)
J. Heurgon: *La Vie quotidienne chez les Etrusques* (Paris, 1961)
H. H. Scullard: *The Etruscan Cities and Rome* (London, 1967)
H. Hencken: *Tarquinia, Villanovans and Early Etruscans* (Cambridge, MA, 1968)
I. Strøm: *Problems Concerning the Origin and Early Development of the Etruscan Orientalizing Style* (Odense, 1971)
R. Bianchi Bandinelli and A. Giuliano: *Etruschi e Italici prima del dominio di Roma* (Milan, 1973, rev. 2/1979)
R. Bianchi Bandinelli and M. Torelli: *Etruria–Roma* (1976), ii of *L'arte dell'antichità classica* (Turin, 1976)
M. Cristofani: *L'arte degli Etruschi: Produzione e consumo* (Turin, 1978)
M. Torelli: *Storia degli Etruschi* (Rome, 1981)
——: *L'arte degli Etruschi* (Rome, 1985)

GIAMPIERO PIANU

3. RELIGION. Our fragmentary information about Etruscan religion comes from two sources, one literary (references by Greek and Roman writers), the other archaeological. The information they contain is widely disparate. The archaeological evidence, which begins in the 7th century BC, includes remains of temples, votive deposits and inscriptions; the much later literary evidence concentrates on portents, their meanings and how to cope with them.

(i) Deities. The oldest known Etruscan temple, on the Piazza d'Armi at Veii, is a small, single-cella structure built in the early 6th century BC and dedicated to an unknown deity. (This may be antedated by the complex at Poggio Civitate (*see* §II, 3 below).) Excavations at the Portonaccio Temple outside one of Veii's city gates have produced a votive deposit with material that dates from the later 6th century BC to the 3rd, including dedicatory inscriptions to Menrva or Menerva, the Etruscanized form of the Roman goddess Minerva. A fine terracotta head of a helmeted young woman from the same deposit has the arched eyebrows, slanting almond-shaped eyes and crescent smile of the late 6th century BC (h. 190 mm; Villa Giulia; see Sprenger and Bartolini, fig. 124) and indicates that the Etruscans, like the Romans, gave Menrva the appearance of the Greek Athena. The famous Portonaccio Group of large terracotta sculptures (*c.* 515–*c.* 490 BC; Rome, Villa Giulia; *see also* §III, 1 below), which originally stood on the roof of the temple, includes figures identifiable as Apollo, Herakles and Hermes. The deities of most Etruscan temples are unknown, but two temples at Pyrgi, a port of Cerveteri, in the sanctuary of a goddess called by the Greeks Leukothea or Eileithyia, were dedicated to the Etruscan goddess Uni, the equivalent of the Greek Hera and the Roman Juno. She and Menrva seem to have been especially important.

Small temples, rustic sanctuaries and favissae (underground offering pits) also yield votive artefacts. A rural shrine at Punta della Vipera, on the coast north of Punicum (Santa Marinella), was dedicated to a version of Menrva whose cult included healing rites and sacrifices to the underworld. The offerings, mostly of terracotta, comprised heads of Minerva, votive masks of men and women, anatomical parts and gilded jewellery. A sanctuary in the Cannicella necropolis at Volsinii Veteres (Orvieto) (see Colonna, 1985, pp. 116–21, no. 6.1) contained not only temple terracottas, an altar, bronze and terracotta votive figures and an inscription on a bronze strip to 'Thval of

Veii' (*c.* 5th–1st century BC; Orvieto, Mus. Etrus. Faina)
but also the cult image, a half life-size nude female figure
(see fig. 2). Although carved in Greek island marble, she
does not look Greek. With feet together, she is erect and
frontal, her long, slender legs carrying a stocky torso, and
her broad, egg-shaped head is supported on a short, thick
neck. Her left arm is missing; the right is brought forward,
elbow bent. Her hair hangs in a flat mass down her back,
its surface covered with wavy striations; it is held at the

2. Marble statue of a nude goddess, h. 765 mm, from a sanctuary in
the Cannicella necropolis, Volsinii Veteres (Orvieto), late 6th century
BC (Orvieto, Museo Etrusco Faina)

back by a ribbon that once continued across the forehead
as a metal diadem; originally she also wore earrings and a
necklace. Nude female figures are uncommon in Greece
and Italy in the Archaic period, and those that exist are
musicians or dancers. But in the Near East Aphrodite
does appear nude, and this marble figure is an Aphrodite,
here as the goddess of a burial ground. She is the Etruscan
equivalent of the Aphrodite Epitumbios worshipped at
Delphi and the Venus Libitina at Rome.

A favissa found on the western shore of Lake Trasimene
contained five statuettes (untraced): two male worshippers
in togas and three women in chitons and cloaks. All are
inscribed with the words 'I belong to Mother Cel here'
(see Colonna, 1976–7, pls 1–4). Cel is an Etruscan name,
and the goddess is probably the equivalent of Mother
Earth. On a mirror from Populonia (*c.* 450–400 BC;
Florence, Mus. Archeol.) a bare-headed warrior with a
barbarian face turns to hurl a huge rock at his pursuer.
The name of the latter is Laran; the rock-thrower is
Celsclan ('son of Cel'). In Greek iconography, warriors
whose weapons are rocks are commonly the giants, sons
of Earth; the scene on the mirror seems to be a fragment
of a gigantomachy in which Laran (?Ares) attacks a fleeing
giant.

Several ritual inscriptions list the ceremonies to be
performed at certain times to certain gods. The longest,
the *Liber linteus* (?1st century BC; Zagreb, Archaeol. Mus.),
is the only surviving book written on linen; it names the
deities Aisera, Crapsti, Nethuns, Thanr, Thesan, Tins, Tiur
and Uslan. A tile found at Capua (5th or 4th century BC;
Berlin, Pergamonmus.) is inscribed with another ritual
text, which names the gods Calus, Laruns, Lethams, Tinian
and Uni. A lead plaque (5th century BC; Florence, Mus.
Archeol.) from Magliano in the Albegna valley names the
gods Aisera, Calus, Maris, Thanr and Tin.

Some of these gods appear on the backs of Etruscan
bronze hand mirrors, which are often engraved with scenes
from Greek myths (*see also* §VI, 2(ii) below). As the
mirrors add the names of the characters portrayed, they
provide evidence of the Etruscan equivalents of Greek
gods. Thus, Tin is identified as Zeus. A mirror in Bologna
(Bologna, Mus. Civ. Archeol.; see Pfiffig, fig. 112) shows
the birth of Athena from the head of Zeus, who sits, half-
draped, on a rocky throne; his flowing hair and beard and
the thunderbolt in his lowered right hand identify him.
Here his name is spelt Tina. A young man with a double
axe, evidently Hephaistos, is named Sethlans, and the two
female figures assisting at the birth are Thalna and Thanr
(the name of the latter appears on the *Liber linteus* and
the Magliano plaque). Another mirror (4th century BC;
London, BM) illustrates the same subject: here Tinia gives
birth to Menrva; the midwives are Ethausva and Thanr.
A mirror in the Vatican (second half of the 4th century
BC; Rome, Vatican, Mus. Gregoriano Etrus.; see Pfiffig,
fig. 107) shows three divinities, Nethuns, Usil and Thesan,
in conversation. Nethuns' trident identifies him as
Neptune/Poseidon. Usil wears the halo of Helios and
carries the bow of Apollo: he is a sun god. The elegantly
dressed young woman leaning on his shoulder, Thesan, is
Eos/Aurora. All three names (with Usil spelt as Uslan)
appear in the *Liber linteus*.

3. Inscribed bronze model of a sheep's liver, h. 60 mm, from near Piacenza, 2nd–1st centuries BC (Piacenza, Museo Civico)

(ii) Ritual. The earliest Etruscan rulers appear to have been Lucumones, or priest-kings, whose staff of office was the characteristic curved *lituus* (e.g. bronze *lituus*; 1.360 mm; early 6th century BC; Rome, Villa Giulia) and who are represented by many statuettes (e.g. bronze statuettes from Isola di Fano; late 6th century BC; Florence, Mus. Archeol.). With the development of the Etruscan city states during the 6th century BC, the role of a specifically priestly class seems to have become more clearly defined.

Detailed literary evidence, however, does not begin until the 1st century BC, and comes mostly from Roman sources. The Romans were interested not in the Etruscan pantheon, but in Etruria's way of protecting men against circumstances. Such knowledge was collected in the books of the *Disciplina etrusca*, divided into the Books of Divination (*Libri haruspicini*), of Lightning (*Libri fulgurales*) and of Rituals (*Libri rituales*) (Cicero: *On Divination* I.lxxii). These were supposedly the revelations of a certain Tages, who sprang from a furrow in the fields of Tarquinia in the form of a young boy but with the wisdom of an old man (*On Divination* II.l). The *Libri rituales* detailed the rites required to found a city or build a temple, the way to organize the civilian population and the army, and all other things pertaining to war and peace. The *Libri fulgurales* dealt with the highly significant portents of thunder and lightning. The *Libri haruspicini* were concerned with divination by the inspection of the liver of a sacrificial animal.

Extispicy was practised by Greeks and Romans too, but for them the liver merely indicated whether an action was approved or not. In Etruria it was far more complicated. The priest, the haruspex, taking the liver in his left hand, put his left foot on a raised surface, stretched the left forearm across his left knee and with the right forefinger traced out the liver's complexities. Two mirrors depict this practice: on one (*c.* 400 BC; Rome, Vatican, Mus. Gregoriano Etrus.; see Pfiffig, fig. 47) the Greek seer Kalchas, represented as a winged haruspex, performs this rite in a rocky landscape; on the other (3rd century BC; Florence, Mus. Archeol.), a figure named Pavatarchies in ritual dress takes the same pose as he explains the liver's evidence to Tarchunus (i.e. Tarchon, the legendary founder of Tarquinia; see Pfiffig, fig. 3).

A bronze model of a sheep's liver found near Piacenza (see fig. 3) is divided by incised lines into 40 areas. Sixteen of these are a border; the rest cover the interior surface. One or two names of divinities are inscribed in each area, and a transverse ridge divides the convex lower surface into two lobes, on each of which a single name is inscribed. The liver is a chart showing which gods govern which parts of it; from the condition of the parts the priest can tell which gods are favourable and which are not. It is also a microcosm of the universe; the 16 areas of the border represent the 16 divisions of the heavens, the inner 24 areas the earth's surface. Thus Tin controls three regions of the heavens and two adjacent ones on earth, Uni and Cel each have one and Neth (i.e. Nethuns) governs two. On the underside, Usil governs one lobe, while the name on the other lobe is Tivs, probably the moon. Altogether some 28 divinities are named, and dedications to many of them have been found elsewhere. They do not, however, comprise all the gods worshipped in Etruria: Menrva, for all her importance, does not appear on the liver, nor do Turan (Aphrodite), Aritimi (Artemis) or Turms (Hermes). Although these are Etruscanized foreign gods, so are Neth and Uni, who do appear. Many aspects of the Etruscan religion are still obscure.

BIBLIOGRAPHY
Livy: *History of Rome*
A. Andrén: 'Il santuario della necropoli di Cannicella ad Orvieto', *Stud. Etrus.*, xxxv (1967), pp. 41–85
A. J. Pfiffig: *Religio etrusca* (Graz, 1975)
G. Colonna: 'La dea etrusca Cel e i santuari del Trasimeno', *Riv. Stor. Ant.*, vi–vii (1976–7), pp. 45–62
M. Sprenger and G. Bartolini: *Die Etrusker: Kunst und Geschichte* (Munich, 1977); Eng. trans. by R. Wolf as *The Etruscans: Their History, Art and Architecture* (New York, 1983)
G. Colonna, ed.: *Santuari d'Etruria* (Milan, 1985)
F. Roncalli and others: *Scrivere etrusco* (Milan, 1985)
L. B. van der Meer: *The Bronze Liver of Piacenza: Analysis of a Polytheistic Structure* (Amsterdam, 1987)

EMELINE RICHARDSON

4. TRADE. Although each Etruscan city state set its own commercial and foreign policies, trade accounts in great part for the unique character of their art, since Etruscan craftsmen eagerly assimilated Levantine, Greek and barbarian media and decorative styles. Initially, Etruscan metal ores and agricultural products were offered to merchants from Greece, Ionia and Phoenicia in exchange for manufactured trinkets and luxury goods. Later, Etruscan bronze implements and artefacts became valued commodities, particularly by the Greeks of the Classical period. Commercial relations were generally less hampered by political constraints than in modern times.

(i) Phoenician contacts (8th–6th centuries BC). (ii) Greek contacts (8th–4th centuies BC). (iii) Punic contacts (7th–2nd centuries BC). (iv) Contacts with Iberia, Gaul and northern Europe.

(i) Phoenician contacts (8th–6th centuries BC). Canaanite prospectors visited the Tyrrhenian coast before the end of the 2nd millennium BC, and in the 8th and 7th centuries BC Phoenicians plied the Etruscan coast from colonies in Sardinia and Sicily, distributing Oriental curiosities both imported and manufactured at local trading posts: decorated ostrich eggs, faience and shell amulets and jewellery, ivories, glass vessels and perfume flasks, and large bronze and silver plates and bowls. Metal vessels from the Barberini and Bernardini tombs at Praeneste (both *c.* 675–

c. 650 BC) and the Regolini-Galassi Tomb at Cerveteri (*c.* 650 BC) are characteristically Phoenician in style, with repoussé and engraved friezes of hybrid Assyrian-Egyptian royal hunts and warfare. Finds of raw and worked ivory, some from the workshop of the Nimrud ivories (*see* ANCIENT NEAR EAST, §II, 3(ii)(c)), some produced by itinerant craftsmen, suggest commercial ties between north Syria and princely society in Latium and Etruria. Assyrian glass (some from Nimrud) apparently inspired the development in the 7th century BC of a native Etruscan industry producing beads and tiny 'porcupine' perfume flasks. Other local workshops arose to manufacture objects in faience and precious metals.

This influx of Near Eastern manufactured goods inspired the Orientalizing style of Etruscan art (*see* §2(ii) above), in which Oriental devices such as heraldic animals and stylized floral motifs dominated the surfaces of Etruscan metalwork, bucchero vases and painted pottery. Etruscan costume also adapted some Near Eastern styles (*see* §VII, 4 below). The development of monumental stone sculpture at Cerveteri, Vulci, Tarquinia and Chiusi may be traced to Near Eastern influence. Etruscan Orientalizing jewellery, many pieces so large and heavy with granulation that they must have been intended for funerary deposition, testifies to the new-found wealth of the Etruscan aristocracy. Phoenician cargoes included perishable items, such as exotic pets, precious woods, dyed or embroidered textiles and agricultural products. The use of such Oriental luxuries as parasols and fans soon distinguished the Etruscan élite (as seen in funerary portraits), while Phoenician military innovations, for example in the development of the war chariot, were also incorporated into Etruscan culture.

Although small amounts of Etruscan fine bucchero pottery have been found at Phoenician trading posts in Sardinia, Sicily, Syria and North Africa, other Etruscan exports rarely survive. Most must have been perishable goods or raw materials such as iron and copper ores and, to a lesser extent, tin, gold and silver. Etruria probably exported foodstuffs and leather; Etruscan shoes were sought by women in Classical Greece.

(ii) Greek contacts (8th–4th centuries BC). The Greek colonies founded in Italy and Sicily from the mid-8th century BC onwards had to be located outside the Phoenician and Etruscan spheres of influence, hence the siting of the Euboian colony of Pithekoussai (Ischia) in the Bay of Naples. Early colonies, however, were emporia based on cottage industries; they soon established trading links with the local peoples. Etruscan metal votive offerings, such as personal ornaments and arms and armour, began to appear in the Greek sanctuaries of Delphi, Olympia, Dodona and Samos, souvenirs of successful Greek voyages, and the Etruscan King Arimnestus was the first foreigner to make a dedication (a throne) in the Sanctuary of Zeus at Olympia (Pausanias: *Guide to Greece* V.xii.5). Euboian and Pithekoussan painted pottery reached Italy *c.* 760 BC, following river routes through Campania and Latium. In the late 8th century BC Etruscan and Italic bronze fibulae were dedicated by sailors at Samos, Rhodes, Perachora, Aigina and Olympia. North Syrian imports and craftsmen probably arrived in Italy via Euboian emporia

in the Levant. Demand for Greek painted pottery was high throughout Etruria in the later 7th century BC and the 6th, with drinking vessels, perfume flasks and large display vases from Ionian, Corinthian and Lakonian workshops placed in tombs at Vulci, Cerveteri and Tarquinia.

Trade with Greece led to the introduction of the alphabet, and the earliest coins in Etruria are of late 6th-century BC Phocaean type, though early 5th-century BC Etruscan mints used the Attic-Euboian weight standard. Permanent Greek emporia were established as ports near Cerveteri, Tarquinia and Vulci in the 7th century BC, where Greek artisans supplemented imports by producing wares locally. These colonists were integrated into Etruscan religious practice, as numerous Greek inscriptions attest. Greek artists, perhaps from Ionia, inspired the burgeoning of Etruscan tomb painting (*see* §V, 1 below) and Etruscan painted pottery at Cerveteri and elsewhere (*see* §IV, 3 below). Many of the finest monuments of Greek vase painting were discovered in Etruria, including the Corinthian Chigi Vase from Formello (*c.* 650–*c.* 625 BC; Rome, Villa Giulia) and the François Vase (*c.* 570–*c.* 560 BC; Florence, Mus. Archeol.) made in Athens. Pieces such as these inspired Etrusco-Corinthian drinking vessels and perfume vases from several workshops, and Etruscan Black- and Red-figure wares. The Athenian NIKOSTHENES produced Black-figure table amphorae imitating Etruscan metal vases specially for the lucrative Italian market, while Attic Tyrrhenian amphorae were also designed for export (*see* GREECE, ANCIENT, §V, 5(ii)(a)). Etruscan kyathoi and kantharoi (one- and two-handled drinking cups) inspired Greek, and especially Attic, potters during the 6th century BC, and Etruscan Bucchero pottery—mainly the distinctive kantharoi—was distributed throughout the Greek colonies, mother-cities and sanctuaries.

On the evidence of Tarquinian tomb paintings, Etruscan aristocrats eagerly adopted Greek customs, such as symposia, athletic contests, fashions and arms and armour, though usually with Italic modifications. Much Greek mythology and iconography was adopted piecemeal or adapted to fit local myths and legends, and appears, often with Etruscan labels, in the decoration of bronze mirror backs (*see* §VI below), sculptured urns and painted vases from the 6th century BC onwards. Some myths are so obscure that it is assumed that the Etruscans were following lost works of Greek literature. In fact, the volume of Greek goods, especially vases, in the tombs of Etruria was so great that 19th-century scholars mistook them for Etruscan originals.

Etruscan metalwork, including bronzes, lampstands and gold cups, was praised by 5th-century BC Greek authors, while Etruscan statuettes were collected by the Romans. Vulci was the source of many exported bronzes, including a tripod (6th century BC; Athens, N. Archaeol. Mus.) found on the Athenian Acropolis, beaked wine pitchers and high-quality utensils found throughout the Mediterranean and northern Europe. Perhaps part of their attraction is due to the fact that whereas fine Greek pieces have hollow handles, Etruscan utensils have solid-cast attachments.

By the 5th century BC the Etruscans were clashing with Greek colonists throughout the western Mediterranean, in piratical raids and full-scale invasions, such as the destruction of the sanctuary at Pyrgi by Dionysios I of Syracuse (384 BC). Nevertheless, imports of Attic Red-figure vases occurred on a large scale in the 5th century BC, with Etruscans exercising preferences for certain artists (e.g. Euphronios), as evidenced in the tomb goods of Vulci, Cerveteri and Tarquinia. Indeed, Etruscans and Greeks co-founded the new Adriatic ports of Spina and Adria to facilitate trade with Athens. Immigrants such as Arnth Praxias created Etruscan red-figure workshops, while Attic vase paintings such as those by the Meidias Painter inspired 4th-century BC and later Etruscan painting and sculpture. Throughout the 4th century BC vase painting workshops at Vulci, Chiusi, Perugia and Volterra were dependent upon prototypes, or even artists, from Tarentum and Syracuse.

(iii) Punic contacts (7th–2nd centuries BC). Etruria also had close commercial and political ties with Carthage, which grew from a 9th-century BC Phoenician trading post eventually to succeed the Phoenician maritime empire. Trade goods were raw materials and Oriental-style luxuries, as well as a few distinctive Punic items such as coarse dish-lamps and glass Semitic-head beads.

Etruscan bronze vases, bucchero pottery and some Etrusco-Corinthian and later painted wares were found in tombs in Carthage and its dependent states, while Punic merchants and scribes settled in Etruria, where their famous piety led to participation in local cults. In the remains of the Etruscan Temple of Uni (Juno) at the Caeretan coastal sanctuary of Pyrgi, three gold plaques were found, one in Punic, bearing a dedication to Astarte (*c.* 500 BC; Rome, Villa Giulia). The name of another Caeretan port, Punicum, attests to further Carthaginian settlement. Aristotle (*Politics* III.v.10–11) referred to treaties between unspecified Etruscan cities and Carthage, concerning commerce and military alliance, but historical events and the distribution of trade goods do not suggest extensive cooperation.

In the 4th and 3rd centuries BC commerce with Greece lessened, though Greek traders still operated at the notoriously philhellenic Cerveteri. Punic connections, however, continued. Punic amphorae and coins reached the Caeretan port of Punta della Vipera and the towns of Rusellae (Roselle) and Sesto Fiorentino in the interior. A grotesque Punic-type mask (Ferrara, Mus. N. Archaeol.) associated with the worship of Tanit was placed in a 3rd-century BC tomb at Spina, and small Etruscan ceramics (Caeretan 'Genucilia' plates) and bronzes were exported to Carthage and Malta. In the late 3rd century BC the wealthy Tarquinian Laris Partiunu was buried in a sarcophagus bearing the effigy of a Punic priest (Tarquinia, Pal. Vitelleschi). Identical sarcophagi in the same Greek island marble were found in a priestly necropolis at Carthage (Carthage, Mus. N.; Paris, Louvre). Laris Partiunu may, therefore, have been an Etruscan merchant initiated into a Carthaginian cult, and though his sarcophagus was probably an import with painted decoration added in Etruria, it may be the work of an itinerant, hellenized Punic artist. There was little subsequent contact between Etruria and Carthage, and the Etruscan cities did not actively support Hannibal's invasion of Italy (218–203 BC).

(iv) Contacts with Iberia, Gaul and northern Europe. As trade with Greece and Carthage decreased, Italy was increasingly dominated by Rome, but Etruscan influence to the north and west, begun in the 6th century BC, remained important. Bucchero ware, coarse wine amphorae and bronze utensils were exported throughout the Greek coastal colonies of France and Spain (e.g. Marseille and Ampurias) and traded up the river valleys to Iberian Tartessos and to the Hallstatt rulers of Gaul. Mid-6th century BC Etrusco-Corinthian pottery was popular and even imitated in Iberian towns where real Corinthian ware was not available. The volumes of cargo must have been considerable, on the evidence of wrecks such as that at Cap d'Antibes, which yielded Etruscan wine amphorae, some Bucchero pottery (e.g. Marseille, Mus. Borély; Marseille, Mus. Docks Romains) and a Punic lamp (Antibes, G. Pruvot priv. col.). Many bronzes were exported from Vulci. Trade declined in the 5th and 4th centuries BC, due to the rise of Marseille and the naval supremacy of the western Greeks. Hellenistic Etruscan fashions for Gallic-inspired jewellery (e.g. gold torques) and arms and armour probably arose from warfare rather than trade.

In the late 6th century BC the Etruscans made concerted efforts to reach markets in Illyria and central and eastern Europe, through their settlements in northern Italy such as that at Marzabotto. Some trade routes were probably pioneered by Chiusine merchants. Baltic amber and other natural materials were exchanged for Etruscan bronzes (the German word for bronze, *Erz*, is a corruption of Arretium, modern Arezzo) and other manufactured goods. The SITULA ART of Illyria shows the influence of Etruscan metalwork in its depiction of symposia, banquets, fine furniture, sports, costumes (much Etruscanized from the Greek) and arms and armour. The runic alphabets of Germany and Scandinavia, and even the development of urban society in northern Europe, are the result of commercial relations with Etruria, so that although the Etruscans eventually became subject to Rome (*see* §1 above), their lasting cultural legacy extended well beyond Italy.

BIBLIOGRAPHY

J. Boardman: *The Greeks Overseas* (Harmondsworth, 1964, London, 3/1980)

A. Rathje: 'Oriental Imports in Etruria in the 8th and 7th Centuries BC: Their Origins and Implications', *Italy before the Romans: The Iron Age, Orientalizing and Etruscan Periods*, eds. D. Ridgway and F. R. Ridgway (London, 1979), pp. 145–83

B. Bouloumié: *L'épave étrusque d'Antibes et le commerce en Méditerranée occidentale au VIe siècle av. J.-C.* (Marburg, 1982)

M. Cristofani: *Gli Etruschi del mare* (Milan, 1983)

M. Cristofani and others, eds: *Il commercio etrusco arcaico* (Rome, 1985)

M. Gras: *Trafics tyrrhéniens archaïques* (Rome, 1985)

J. M. Turfa: 'International Contacts: Commerce, Trade and Foreign Affairs', *Etruscan Life and Afterlife*, ed. L. Bonfante (Warminster and Detroit, 1986)

P. Pelagatti, ed.: *Le anfore da trasporto e il commercio etrusco arcaico*, 2 vols (Rome, 1990–)

N. Spivey: 'Greek Vases in Etruria', *Looking at Greek Vases*, eds T. Rasmussen and N. Spivey (Cambridge, 1991), pp. 131–50

D. Ridgway: *The First Western Greeks* (Cambridge, 1992)

JEAN MacINTOSH TURFA

5. SUBJECT-MATTER. Etruscan art has usually been surveyed in terms of its stylistic development (*see* §I, 2 above) and its subject-matter is rarely given independent consideration. It is an area in which the Etruscan debt to foreign ideas is consistently evident. The influence was primarily from Greece and its western colonies, even in the Orientalizing period when direct Etruscan contact with the Near East was most pronounced. Crucially, it was from Greek models that Etruscan craftsmen learnt the art of narrative; they applied this both to retelling Greek myths and to depicting more specifically Etruscan scenes and legends. The resulting taste for narrative distinguishes Etruscan art of the 7th to the 2nd century BC from that of all other contemporary native Italian cultures. In the overview that follows an attempt is made to keep chronological and geographical distinctions in focus, and to relate subject-matter to the varying functions of Etruscan art.

(i) Geometric and floral decoration. (ii) Animal decoration. (iii) Human figures. (iv) Scenes of daily life and the afterlife. (v) Scenes of Etruscan history and legend. (vi) Scenes inspired by Greek mythology. (vii) Inscriptions.

(i) Geometric and floral decoration. As in Greece, geometric styles prevailed in the 9th and 8th centuries BC, notably on pottery and metalwork, on which metopal schemes were especially common, often containing patterns based on the swastika. Later, floral motifs appeared, some based directly on Near Eastern forms, but most on Greek versions. They form a particularly important element on architectural terracottas, where they were treated either in painted relief or in openwork, or were simply painted. Continuous floral designs were commonly used on revetment plaques of horizontal and raking cornices to create effects of great richness on Etrusco-Italic temples throughout Etruria and Latium, as on the Hellenistic temples at Civita Castellana and Alatri. Geometric and floral motifs were also used ubiquitously as framing devices, such as the meander on pottery and gold jewellery, guilloche on ivories and stone reliefs and palmettes on Black-figure pottery.

(ii) Animal decoration. Animals and birds were staple subjects of art of the Orientalizing and Archaic periods, whether shown singly or, in the two-dimensional arts, in files or heraldic dispositions. They constitute the main decorative subjects for Etrusco-Corinthian and incised Bucchero ware, and on other wares of the 7th century BC stylized birds ('herons') feature prominently. Of the large quadrupeds, horses, goats and bulls were the most often depicted, and lions were a favourite subject derived from the eastern Mediterranean. There was a marked penchant for fabulous beasts: for example sphinxes (occasionally kilted in the Near Eastern fashion, or bearded), griffins, hippocamps and centaurs. In funerary contexts these may have represented guardians of the dead, as in Greece, and hence, in stone sculpture, they were sometimes placed at the entrances of chamber tombs (especially sphinxes and lions). This may also explain the animals and monsters frequently painted on the pediments of chamber tomb interiors. On Hellenistic relief ash urns, hippocamps and other sea-creatures suggest the journey to the underworld. In earlier art such hybrids as horses with clawed feet, the chimera and double-bodied creatures sharing a single head abound. The fantasy element in the depiction of animals and monsters was sometimes given further emphasis in Archaic tomb painting and vase painting by the application

of various non-naturalistic colours to different parts of the same animal. Nor is the actual species of animal always obvious, due to strange body proportions, anatomical markings and facial features. An element of cruelty and violence is often apparent: animals attacking and drawing blood; lions parading with a human leg dangling from their jaws.

(iii) Human figures. These entered the Etruscan decorative repertory in the 7th century BC. Early examples, mainly on decorated pottery, include 'horse-tamers', riders, hunters and files of dancers. Also to the 7th century BC belong the earliest mythological scenes. A little later, the Greek forms of standing male kouros and female kore had their counterparts in Etruria, but these were mostly on a small scale (though the bulk of monumental sculpture is lost). Many of these and other small-scale sculpture were given as votive offerings at sanctuaries.

Much of the larger-scale sculpture was funerary, the object apparently being to perpetuate an image of the deceased inside the tomb. The mode of representation varied from region to region, from the stark 'Canopic' masks and urns from the area around CHIUSI, sometimes placed on elaborate thrones, to the deceased shown as banqueters on 6th-century BC terracotta ash urns from Cerveteri. Also at Cerveteri the Tomb of the Five Chairs (second half of the seventh century BC) was furnished with terracotta figures seated on carved stone thrones (e.g. figure of seated man; Rome, Pal. Conserv.), the whole arrangement strongly suggestive of ancestor worship. In the Hellenistic period the deceased continued to be shown

4. Alabaster ash urn, showing a duel (?between Eteokles and Polyneikes), h. 490 mm, from Chiusi, 2nd century BC (London, British Museum)

in the banqueting pose on many lids of ash urns (see fig. 4). Less often they were represented as stiffly horizontal on sarcophagi from southern Etruria (see fig. 16 below). Even in later Etruscan art the dead were represented in most cases symbolically rather than by individual portraits, although some heads, both funerary and votive, show degrees of individualization from the 4th century BC onwards (*see* §III, 4 below).

(iv) Scenes of daily life and the afterlife. Just as details of domestic architecture can be gleaned from rock-cut tomb interiors, so many daily activities were represented on funerary monuments of sculpture and painting showing scenes of banqueting, sports, hunting and dancing. Much Etruscan art, especially funerary art, reflects the preoccupations and lifestyles of the aristocratic class. Artists often showed Greek styles of dress, modes of behaviour and types of entertainment, but it is not clear to what extent these were actually adopted in Etruria, or how far down the social scale they penetrated.

The banquet scenes, with their paraphernalia of couches, cups and kraters, were taken wholly from Greek art and usage. On tomb paintings (*see* §V, 4 and fig. 24 below) and funerary reliefs these no doubt represent part of the funeral celebrations, and in some cases possibly scenes of a hoped-for festive afterlife. On the terracotta revetment plaques of Poggio Civitale (Murlo) (see fig. 38 below) and Acquarossa, however, they appear to have more of a civic connotation. Generally there is much emphasis on the preparation and serving of food and on the display of vessels for food and drink. Women are shown reclining on the couches with men, and in most cases they are probably wives rather than courtesans, an Etruscan practice that shocked contemporary Greeks. Figures of husbands and wives also recline together on cinerary urns as if at banquet and are occasionally shown in eternal sleep under the same coverlet on stone sarcophagi (e.g. two sarcophagi; mid-4th century BC; Boston, MA, Mus. F.A.). Dancing was often depicted alongside the banqueting in tomb paintings; the dancers, male and female, may have been professional performers, as may the musicians accompanying on flute and lyre, together with the jugglers and acrobats shown on revetment plaques at Acquarossa. Performing troupes like these are known to have been called to Rome for their skills. Music and musicians occur frequently on Etruscan monuments, fully bearing out their centrality in Etruscan life as claimed by ancient writers. Music apparently accompanied even such activities as cooking (which is indeed illustrated) and the beating of slaves.

Hunting was a favourite aristocratic pursuit. It is shown on the grandest scale in the line-fishing and fowling scenes in the Tomb of Hunting and Fishing at Tarquinia (*c.* 540–*c.* 530 BC; see fig. 25 below). All the sports developed by the Greeks are also illustrated (see fig. 5), but whereas in Greece the great sporting occasions formed part of the major religious festivals, in Etruscan the usual context is the funeral celebrations. As in Greek art, the contestants often seem to be professionals and include wrestlers and boxers of especially bulky physique. Boxing is shown in the Greek fashion with oxhide thongs. Chariot-racing, though its origins lie in Greece, shows some native

5. Black-figure amphora showing a sporting scene by the Micali Painter, h. 460 mm, late 6th century BC (London, British Museum); the main frieze shows (from left to right) two officials, two boxers, a youth holding an aryballos and a sponge, a flute-player and an umpire

Etruscan features, such as the dangerous practice of tying the reins behind the back, and there are vivid illustrations of its sensational aspects.

The gaiety and celebratory atmosphere of early Tarquinian tomb paintings seem to disappear after the Archaic period; later scenes of the underworld may have been conditioned by the menace of Rome's growing power (e.g. Tomb of Oreus II; late 4th century BC). There may be much truth in this, although the first glimpse of these horrific visions is already visible in the Tomb of the Augurs (*c.* 530 BC) in the scene of Phersu directing grisly tortures. Whether or not Phersu is indeed a figure from the underworld is not made explicit; but such figures have a clear iconography in later funerary art, in which the Etruscan underworld is peopled with beings such as Charu(n), hook-nosed and wielding a hammer (see fig. 29 below), and the equally fearsome Tuchulcha. Impending death or bloodshed is heralded by Lasa and Vanth, the goddesses of fate, who may be added to the more bloody scenes from Greek mythology on the Hellenistic ash urns of northern Etruria, in which episodes of murder and death in battle proliferate. Also common on these urns are scenes of the journey to the underworld, sometimes represented as a family procession (*see* §III, 3 and fig. 16 below).

From domestic life there are some charming scenes on Archaic Chiusine funerary reliefs of women examining and holding up fabrics and garments, possibly for dressing the deceased. Otherwise, scenes involving women are most common on engraved mirrors, where they are frequently shown in a boudoir setting. Erotic scenes are much less numerous than in Greek art: on decorated pottery they are rare, but a few are found, oddly, in funerary contexts, for example in the Tomb of the Bulls (6th century BC) at Tarquinia, and on Archaic stone reliefs from Tarquinia and Chiusi. Male nudity occurs slightly less often than in Greek art and almost always shows strong Greek influence. In Greece it was fostered through the athletic ideal, and it is athletes who are most often portrayed nude in Etruria. Female nudity had a vogue in the Orientalizing period, where the influence was from depictions of Oriental love-goddesses. Later it was mainly restricted to scenes on mirrors, but even here accessories such as boots, jewellery and headgear are frequently shown.

Battle scenes are common in all periods. As in Greece they were found to be suitable for architectural sculpture, where pediment corners could be filled with lunging and falling warriors. Vases and ivories with scenes of fighting and combat, and of the armed dance, show that Greek hoplite armour was adopted in Etruria in the 7th century BC.

Finally, it must be admitted that many scenes remain obscure. The precise significance of the gestures of the painted figures on the back wall of the Tomb of the Baron, Tarquinia, of the little figures who plough (?and dance) their way around what may be a chained bear on an early bronze urn from Bisenzio (Rome, Villa Giulia), of figures emerging from wells on late ash urns (e.g. a monstrous animal; a man with wolf-skin cap), and of other enigmatic incidents, are still a matter for speculation.

(v) Scenes of Etruscan history and legend. Indisputable illustrations of Etruscan history are rare. The most famous is the painting in the François Tomb from Vulci (4th century BC), which shows battles between named warriors from various Etruscan cities (*see* §V below). The episodes apparently refer back to the 6th century BC, for it includes the death of one of the Roman Tarquin family. Interestingly, two of the characters, Avle and Caile Vipinas, also appear on ash urns and on a mirror (see fig. 6). Avle Vipinas was an historical figure, as an inscription from Veii proves, so there seem here to be remnants of a cycle of stories about great Etruscan leaders of the past. A mirror from Tuscania shows a scene of a haruspex interpreting a sacrificed animal's liver in the presence of Tarchon, legendary founder of the city of Tarquinia (*see* §3(ii) above). It is on engraved mirrors that many of the specifically Etruscan figures known from representations appear. They are mainly deities, most of them goddesses in attendance in childbirth and boudoir scenes. Unnamed figures also appear on a number of mirrors and ash urns in what are probably narrative scenes. These may have more to do with local Etruscan stories and legends than with lost or unidentified Greek myths.

(vi) Scenes inspired by Greek mythology. The Etruscans must have encountered Greek myths almost as soon as first contacts between the two peoples were made. In the 7th century BC a depiction of *Odysseus and his Companions Escaping from Polyphemos' Cave* occurred on a relief ivory

pyxis (box) from Chiusi (Florence, Mus. Archeol.; *see* §VII, 3 below); a possible *Menelaos and Helen* on a painted vase from Cerveteri (Cerveteri, Mus. N. Cerite); and an array of fabulous beasts, such as sphinxes, of Greek type. The importation of large quantities of Greek works, especially painted vases, and the establishing of Greek traders and artists in Etruria in the 6th century BC, speeded up this dissemination of ideas. The Etruscans showed a greater receptivity to Greek culture than any other race with whom the Greeks came into contact. Where possible, the Greek gods, together with their iconography and mythology, were eagerly assimilated into the Etruscan pantheon (*see* §3(i) above), producing a rich amalgam of Greek and local traditions. Thus Athena (Menrva) is shown in a peplos or armed with aegis, spear and helmet in the Greek manner; but she may also be winged and on one mirror she fights off Akrathe (?a giant) with his own severed arm. Menrva is one of the deities most frequently depicted, and her birth from the head of Zeus (Tinia) remained popular in Etruscan art far longer than in Greece. Herakles (Herkle) was the most popular Greek hero in Etruria; but although he was shown performing many of his labours, he was also depicted in new contexts, such as holding a baby (sometimes named Epiur), carrying off a woman named Mlacuch (see fig. 33 below), being suckled by Hera (Uni) to symbolize his deification, or even threatening a fleeing Minotaur. A beautiful mirror (4th century BC; Berlin, Pergamonmus.) shows a youthful Dionysos (Fufluns) embracing his mother Semele (Semla), a version of events not seen in Greece, where the usual story was that Semele perished before her son's birth. One of the earliest representations of the tale of Dionysos' transformation of the Tyrrhenian pirates into dolphins is

6. Bronze mirror showing *Cacu and Artile Ambushed by Avle and Caile Vipinas*, diam. 150 mm, from Bolsena, 3rd century BC (London, British Museum)

on a late 6th-century BC Etruscan Black-figure vase (Toledo, OH, Mus. A., 82.134).

Some of the above examples, and many others, suggest that Greek mythology was not invariably copied blindly but that it was often retold with embellishments and variations. What complicates matters further is that Etruscan artists could also be vague and inconsistent about details not only of Greek figures but also of their own gods. Some of the latter, for example, may change their sex from one scene to another or may be shown twice in the same scene. It is then perhaps not so surprising that Theseus may be shown winged, Pegasus and the Gorgons may be wingless and Medusa may have tiny Gorgon children. To describe such examples as 'errors' may be to miss the point; illogicalities also occur in Greek representations. Greek mythology seems to have been vital and constantly adapted in Etruria, rather than passively accepted in a fixed form, although it is also true that some artists had a much firmer grounding in it than others. Etruscan art was, in fact, produced in a mixed milieu: some artists were themselves Greek, others were trained by Greeks, still others may have consulted Greeks working in their own workshops or neighbouring ones. Sometimes the detailed knowledge shown is exceptional, as in the 5th-century BC relief sculpture on Temple A at Pyrgi where the episode from the Theban cycle of the *Seven against Thebes*, with Tydeus biting Melanippos' head, to the horror of Athena running up behind (*c.* 510–*c.* 485 BC; Rome, Villa Giulia; *see also* §III, 1 below), is not attempted in any extant Greek work. In the slightly earlier Black-figure vase painting of Aeneas at Troy being made invisible by Aphrodite and so rescued from the onslaught of Diomedes the only Etruscan element is the pair of wings given to Aphrodite.

In the two most extensive series of Archaic funerary works, mythology plays only a minor role. In the relief cippi from Chiusi it is confined to rare Amazonomachies. The only early mythological tomb painting of note shows the *Ambush of Troilos* (Tomb of the Bulls; 6th century BC; Tarquinia; see fig. 27 below), a subject that might well have been appropriate for the deceased. Yet tomb painters did not turn to mythology again until the 4th century BC and later, when, wishing to show visions of death as vividly as possible, they displayed the slaughter of the Trojan prisoners at Patroklos' tomb in the presence of Charun and Vanth (François Tomb, Vulci), and the underworld itself peopled with ghosts of Greek heroes and ruled over by Hades and Persephone (Tomb of Orcus II; *c.* 325–*c.* 300 BC; Tarquinia). Greek mythology also seems to fulfil a need on the ash urns of northern Etruria, the relief sides of which portray some of the more savage incidents: Pelops' murder of Myrtilos after the contest with Oenomaos (where a single wheel held by Myrtilos signifies the chariot-race); the sacrifice of Iphigenia; and a duel (?between Eteokles and Polyneikes; see fig. 4 above). Attempts have been made to connect these episodes shown on the urns with Greek, Roman and Etruscan drama, with little consensus reached, although many of them may have their ultimate origin in Euripidean tragedy.

It is difficult to say much about the choice of subjects for the exterior sculptures of temples. In Greece there was often no close thematic connection between the architectural sculpture and the deity of the temple, and it is likely to have varied similarly in Etruria. In the case of the Portonaccio Temple at Veii (*c.* 515–*c.* 490 BC), dedicated to Menrva, there are probably cult reasons why Apollo (Aplu) is shown prominently among the sculptures on the roof (for illustration *see* VEII). It is not the only sanctuary where this god and goddess are closely associated. Apollo is conspicuous too in the sculptures from the temple at Lo Scasato, Civita Castellana, but the mythological context is uncertain and there is no means of knowing to whom the temple was dedicated. As for Temple A at Pyrgi, mentioned above, the subject may have been chosen to reflect the Theban origin of Leukothea, goddess of the sanctuary. But why episodes from the Theban cycle were again selected for the pediment of the temple at Talamone is less clear. It may be partly explained by the great popularity of the subject at this time (2nd century BC) among Volterran artists, who may have carried out the work. For most temples the data is simply inadequate: either the deity is not known, or the sculptures are too fragmented to reconstruct the story, or both.

(vii) Inscriptions. Inscriptions labelling figures are common on mirrors, gems and tomb paintings, and the lids of sarcophagi and ash urns often name the deceased. In all other media inscriptions are rare. There are occasional captions explaining the action of a whole scene, and, again on mirrors, a few that report the utterances of the figures portrayed. On portable works inscriptions commonly give details of ownership, gift-giving or dedication to a god. Artists' signatures are exceptional except on Praenestine bronze-engraving, where they are in Latin. In the 7th century BC, when the art and knowledge of writing were known to few, inscriptions were sometimes given special decorative prominence, notably the alphabets and syllabaries incised on Bucchero pottery.

BIBLIOGRAPHY

S. De Marinis: *La tipologia del banchetto nell'arte etrusca arcaica* (Rome, 1961)
F.-H. Pairault: *Recherches sur quelques séries d'urnes de Volterra à représentation mythologique* (Rome, 1972)
I. Krauskopf: *Der thebanische Sagenkreis und andere griechische Sagen in der etruskischen Kunst* (Heidelberg, 1974)
M. Sprenger and G. Bartolini: *Die Etrusker: Kunst und Geschichte* (Munich, 1977); Eng. trans. by R. Wolf as *The Etruscans: Their History, Art and Architecture* (New York, 1983)
O. J. Brendel: *Etruscan Art*, Pelican Hist. A. (Harmondsworth, 1978)
N. de Grummond, ed.: *A Guide to Etruscan Mirrors* (Tallahassee, 1982)
E. Richardson: *Etruscan Votive Bronzes: Geometric, Orientalizing, Archaic* (Mainz, 1983)
G. Camporeale: *La caccia in Etruria* (Rome, 1984)
J.-R. Jannot: *Les Reliefs archaïques de Chiusi* (Rome, 1984)
S. Steingräber, ed.: *Etruscan Painting* (New York, 1985)
J.-P. Thuillier: *Les Jeux athlétiques dans la civilisation étrusque* (Paris, 1985)
TOM RASMUSSEN

II. Architecture.

In contrast to the architecture of ancient Greece, even important Etruscan buildings were seldom constructed in stone, and most are known only from foundation remains. From the 7th century BC onwards, however, the underground tombs of wealthy Etruscans, of which many well-preserved examples survive, provide detailed architectural evidence. Such tombs were generally modelled on domestic interiors, and the large necropoleis of the Etruscan cities reveal aspects of urban planning. The excavation of houses, urban areas and sanctuaries has now begun to receive more attention. While ancient literary sources provide little general information, specific aspects of Etruscan temple construction were addressed by Vitruvius (*On Architecture* IV.vii; *see also* VITRUVIUS, §2), who outlined rules for two main types of temple (*see* §3 below). (For the Tuscan order *see* ORDERS, ARCHITECTURAL, §I, 1(v).)

1. Funerary. 2. Domestic. 3. Religious. 4. Cities, fortifications and other structures.

1. FUNERARY. The first monumental Etruscan tomb structures evolved in the urban necropoleis of the 7th century BC. The earlier funerary customs of cremation with urn burial or simple graves partially gave way, at least for wealthy Etruscans, to interment in large chamber tombs. These structures consist typically of an extended entrance corridor (dromos), an anteroom and a main burial chamber, and, in many cases, side chambers flank the dromos and the anteroom. The chambers flanking the dromos have stone doors. The tufa in southern Etruria was easy to carve when moist and thus particularly suitable for rock-cut tombs. The exact nature of Etruscan grave

cult and ritual remains unclear, although the ramps, stairs and dromos must presumably have played a role in cultic practices.

The development of Etruscan tomb architecture from the 7th to the 5th century BC is exemplified by six types of tomb found in the Banditaccia necropolis of CERVETERI (Caere).

(i) The corbel type (c. 700–c. 650 BC). These were hollowed from the tufa with an upper section, built of ashlar and roofed with a corbel vault, as in the rectangular-plan Regolini-Galassi Tomb (*c.* 650 BC). The long dromos of this type later developed into a single extended burial chamber.

(ii) The arch door type (c. 650–c. 600 BC). These spacious structures were entirely hollowed out from the tufa in monumental grave mounds raised over them (e.g. the Campana Tomb, Cerveteri; early 6th century BC). The rock-cut interiors clearly imitate such features of houses as wooden roofs, arched doors and even wall decoration and furniture. The plan of this type is generally rectangular with the broad burial chambers now clearly separated from the dromos (e.g. the Tomb of the Dolia; early 6th century BC).

(iii) The lunette type (c. 600–c. 550 BC). Characterized by a semicircular arch in low relief above rectangular doors

7. Tomb of the Painted Reliefs, Cerveteri, late 4th century BC–early 3rd

and windows, these relatively small structures have a short dromos. The chambers themselves are less spacious, having only two burial places (e.g. the Tomba dei Letti e Sarcofagi).

(iv) The three-cell type (6th century BC). These have a broad burial chamber that leads to three adjacent cells, and the whole structure is thus broader and longer (e.g. the Tomba degli Scudi e Sedie; 6th century BC). The decoration of the chambers is particularly varied, including different roof formations, mouldings, columns with developed capitals and furniture carved from tufa. The relatively short dromos often gives access to further cells. In both earlier and later examples of this type the tombs were still dug into large tumuli (e.g. the Tomb of the Greek Vases), though in the mid-6th century BC single tombs in cube form occurred.

(v) The two-cell type (mid–later 6th century BC). This was essentially similar to the three-cell type, though with only two other burial chambers leading from the main chamber. Cells on either side of the dromos also became rare, and internal decoration almost totally disappeared from tombs of this type in the later 6th century BC.

(vi) The caditoia type (late 6th century BC–early 5th century BC). These tombs have a cube-shaped entrance façade, an entry shaft giving access from above and one or two chambers inside. They too have little internal decoration.

With the exception of the caditoia type, these Caeretan tombs are carved into tumuli, some monumental examples of which have a diameter of over 40 m. The cylindrical base of the tumulus, the Krepis, is generally carved from tufa, surmounted by an earthen mound and probably crowned with a cippus. The Krepis usually finishes with a profile of tori and rectangular elements, also common in Etruscan sacred buildings. Tumuli could be entered via a ramp at the side, which was probably connected with certain rituals, the grave itself perhaps functioning as an altar. Towards the end of the 6th century BC monumental tumuli ceased to be built, being largely superseded by small cube-shaped tombs, which were orientated on the grid plan of the necropolis, as at the Crocefisso del Tufo necropolis, Volsinii Veteres (*see* ORVIETO, fig. 1). Unlike 7th-century BC tombs, they no longer faced west or north-west, traditionally the direction of the Etruscan under-world. These tombs are relatively small, generally with one chamber, and have modest 'architectural' internal decoration. Initially the chambers were within the cuboid structure itself, but during the 4th century BC their usual position shifted to below the façade, and these undeco-rated, low, rock-cut chambers could contain up to 20 sepulchres (e.g. at Castel d'Asso, near Viterbo). As a result, the façades themselves became increasingly monumental, and finally, in the 3rd and 2nd centuries BC, became mock entrance façades, with false doors in relief, entablature and sometimes porticos (e.g. the Tomba Sottofacciata). These elaborate façade tombs were entered via ramps and stairs at the side, again suggesting the association of cult practices with tombs (e.g. the rock-cut tombs at Norchia, northern Latium). Rock-cut chamber tombs continued to be built, however, with their established features of layout and decoration, as in the Tomb of the Volumnii near Perugia (second half of the 2nd century BC). Their large halls with several side chambers may reflect the layout of contem-porary palaces of wealthy Etruscans.

While external tomb architecture generally took the form of a tumulus with a crowning cippus, by the 7th century BC tomb chambers were receiving ornate internal decoration, and this illustrates many features of Etruscan domestic architecture. Various forms of roof are clearly imitated, for example the hip roof, which also appears on Early Iron Age hut urns. The different elements of roof

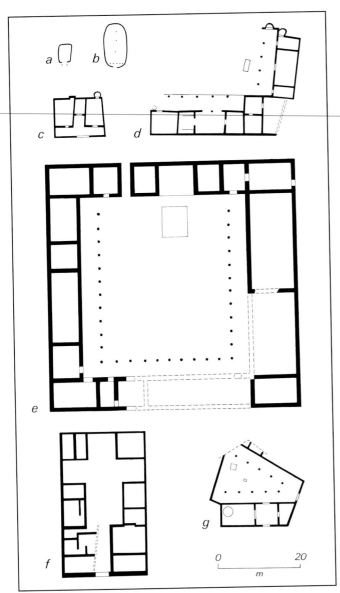

8. Etruscan domestic architecture: (a) Hut A, Palatine Hill, Rome, *c.* 8th century BC; (b) Hut D, San Giovenale, *c.* 8th century BC; (c) House A, Zone B, Acquarossa, 6th century BC; (d) Complex A–C, Zone F, Acquarossa, second half of the 6th century BC; (e) building complex, Murlo, Poggio Civitate, second quarter of the 6th century BC; (f) House 6, Marzabotto, *c.* 500 BC; (g) Regia, Forum Romanum, Rome, late 6th century BC

construction were carved from the tufa and probably highlighted in paint. Some tomb 'roofs' were supported by pillars and columns with fully developed shafts and capitals (e.g. the Tomba dei Capitelli, Cerveteri; 6th century BC). Where the antechamber is separated from the main chamber by a wall, the two are connected by windows and doors with clearly sculpted frames. In early tombs of the first half of the 7th century BC the furniture, such as couches and chairs, was generally of wood and bronze. From the second half of the 7th century BC onwards these and other objects were carved from tufa. The sculpted imitations of the baskets, seats, shields and other weapons and implements hung as wall decoration (e.g. the Tomba degli Scudi e Sedie; or the Tomb of the Painted Reliefs, Cerveteri; see fig. 7) are to some extent carved differently from purely funerary furniture, which suggests that they reflected the actual appearance of domestic interiors.

2. DOMESTIC. The architecture of Etruscan houses has been directly studied mainly through excavations of middle-sized and smaller settlements, and from some early houses at Veii. Nevertheless, it is possible to trace the course of its general development. Remains of early Italian houses survive primarily in southern Etruria and the neighbouring regions. Most of these display either an oval ground-plan or a square one with rounded corners (see figs 8a and 8b). They were made of perishable materials such as wood and mud-brick, and apparently usually had an entrance on the shorter side, in some cases protected by a small canopy. The Early Iron Age huts, up to 10 m long and 5 m wide, usually had no interior partition (e.g. at San Giovenale, northern Latium; see fig. 8b), but there seem to have been regional differences in plan. In addition to rectangular and oval huts there were circular structures, and some huts were totally or partially hollowed into tufa. Hut urns (see fig. 9) provide invaluable evidence for the reconstruction of Early Iron Age dwellings and roof structures, showing in particular the ridge-beams, rafters and lengths of wood to hold the thatch in place, with an opening for smoke above the entrance. Such urns also confirm the lasting connection between Etruscan funerary and domestic forms. The wattle and daub walls probably had one or more windows.

From the mid-7th century BC onwards, a house type with a long, rectangular plan occurs. In the 6th century BC this was superseded by the 'broad house' type. Excavations at Acquarossa suggest that this type of house had two or three adjacent rooms, in front of which, set at an angle, was a vestibule, generally with a colonnade (see fig. 8c). The front rooms can be identified as kitchens and store-rooms. The single-storey 'broad houses' (c. 10–15 m×c. 6–10 m) tended to be grouped haphazardly. The foundations were of tufa blocks, and the walls of wood, mud-brick or wattle and daub, generally stuccoed and painted, as were the relatively heavy gabled roofs. These projected considerably beyond the walls and had ornamental terracotta revetments. In the second half of the 6th century BC in Acquarossa, a larger, possibly sacred, type of complex structure was built (see fig. 8d). Its plan consists of two almost orthogonal wings abutting one another, each having three chambers behind a long, colonnaded area. These

9. Hut urn, impasto, h. 280 mm, from Marino, c. 8th century BC (Rome, Museo Nazionale Preistorico ed Etnografico Luigi Pigorini)

porticos open on to a kind of courtyard. They do not connect with each other but are separated by rooms between the two wings. It is impossible, therefore, to call this a peristyle building type, and its piecemeal character suggests it was not conceived as a unified complex.

It is slightly predated by the large Archaic building at Poggio Civitate (Murlo; see fig. 8e). This has an almost square plan with sides c. 60 m long and an inner courtyard surrounded by rooms, of different sizes and externally aligned. Along three sides of the courtyard runs a portico, and some of the entrances are axially aligned. Despite its monumentality, this complex shows a clear relationship to the tripartite division of space characteristic of Etruscan temples. As a building outside the Etruscan tufa zone, its foundations consisted of a layer of gravel, the walls of mud-brick with timber reinforcement. For weather protection the walls had a clay coating, and remains of both this and the roof covering show traces of painting. The roof-ridge, like that of the Portonaccio Temple at Veii (late 6th century BC; see fig. 10), was adorned with a row of terracotta figures. The function of the complex at Poggio Civitate has, however, not yet been determined. It may have been a sanctuary, although there are no finds of obvious votive offerings or sanctuary furnishings to confirm this (see also §3 below), or it may have been an aristocratic palace with an adjacent small sacred area. In foundations from c. 500 BC excavated at Marzabotto a further development of the house complex with courtyard can be seen (see fig. 8f). The plans of separate complexes, arranged on a regular grid plan of streets, are different but share certain features, including entrances on the shorter side and, leading from these, a long narrow corridor ending in a large central courtyard. These courtyards were sometimes partially paved and contained either a fountain or a

10. Portonaccio Temple, Veii, late 6th century BC (Rome, Università degli Studi di Roma, 'La Sapienza'); reconstruction

rectangular stone impluvium. Around the corridor and courtyard are rooms of different sizes, the whole having a rectangular plan of *c.* 20×35 m. The foundations are of large pebbles, and the walls were presumably of mud-brick reinforced with stones since a mud-brick wall alone would probably not have been able to support the roof. The Marzabotto settlement with this house type, probably a development of the 'broad house', dates from *c.* 500 BC. In two houses the courtyard is cross-shaped, suggesting a relation to the early Roman atrium house type found in 4th-century BC Pompeii. It is therefore possible that the buildings at Acquarossa, Poggio Civitate and Marzabotto provided models for the Roman atrium house (*see* ROME, ANCIENT, §II, 1(i)(c)).

The 6th-century BC three- and two-cell tombs (see §1 above) have plans comparable with those of the 'broad houses' at Acquarossa (see fig. 8c). Thereafter, although the relation between tomb and house architecture became less close, the idea of the house is nevertheless still discernible in the tombs of the 2nd and 1st centuries BC; for example the Tomb of the Volumnii near Perugia. Some funerary urns of this period (e.g. the marble house urn of P. Volumnius; late 1st century BC; see Brendel, fig. 320) represent palatial dwellings, with columns, capitals, pediments and other ornate architectural features.

3. RELIGIOUS. Unlike Egyptian and Greek temples, Etruscan temples were generally built of mud-brick and wood. Their podia and foundations, however, were of stone, and these, along with terracotta roof-tiles and ornaments, provide more archaeological evidence than in the case of houses, so that conjectural reconstruction is possible (e.g. the Portonaccio Temple, Veii; see fig. 10). Tomb interiors and façades also sometimes imitated temple architecture, as did votive artefacts (e.g. a cippus from Chiusi (Clusium), *c.* 500 BC; Berlin, Altes Mus.). Vitruvius' description of the ideal Etruscan temple (*On Architecture* IV.vii) is an important source, even given that by the early 1st century AD, when Vitruvius was writing, most Etruscan temples no longer survived intact.

From the outset Etruscan temples were architecturally quite distinct from their Greek counterparts, and they eventually provided the model for Roman sacred buildings (*see* ROME, ANCIENT, §II, 1(i)(a)). In contrast to Greek temples, Etruscan temples had only one access, the direction of which was usually determined through observation of a bird's flight by the priest or augur. The podium on which the temple generally stood was likewise accessible only from the front. The origins of this form are still not entirely clear. The complex at Poggio Civitate is important here (*see* §2 above and fig. 8e); it contains a three-cell suite with the central room opening on to a rectangular enclosure, possibly the remains of an altar, and its ornate terracotta decoration also indicates a sacred function. If so, it represents the oldest Etruscan sacred building so far discovered, although remains of an older, 7th-century BC structure discovered under its foundations have not yet been explained. The Regia in the Forum Romanum at Rome was certainly a sacred building (see fig. 8g). Traditionally perceived as the official residence of the Pontifex Maximus, it had a three-cell suite opening on to a courtyard with a rectangular altar. According to Vitruvius, the three-cella structure was characteristic of the Etruscan temple. In the Capitoline Temple at Rome (ded. 509 BC), begun by the Etruscan king Tarquinius Priscus in the first half of the 6th century BC and completed by Tarquinius Superbus, for the worship of the Roman triad of Jupiter, Juno and Minerva, each of the three divinities had its own cell (see further below).

Vitruvius' rules for Etruscan temples (*tuscanicae dispositiones*) prescribe proportions for a three-cella type, which are partially exemplified by such remains as those of the Belvedere Temple at Volsinii Veteres (see fig. 11) and Temple A at Pyrgi. According to him, the length-to-width ratio of the quadrangular building plot should be 6:5. This rectangle is divided equally, the rear part being occupied by the cellae (or, in Vitruvius' second main type of Etruscan Temple, by a single cella with alae (side chambers)), and the front of the pronaos. The central cella and each of the smaller side cellae open towards the temple front and could thus also function as alae. The pronaos should contain two rows of columns aligned with the cella walls.

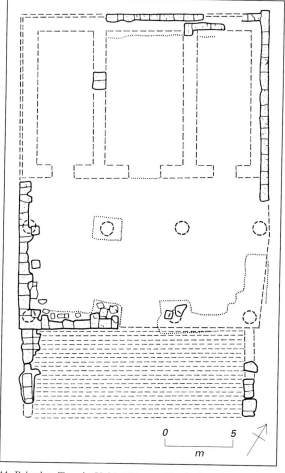

11. Belvedere Temple, Volsinii Veteres (Orvieto), early 5th century BC; reconstructed plan

Vitruvius' *tuscanicae dispositiones* are clearly an attempt to establish a theoretical model rather than a comprehensive description, and some sacred structures in Etruria suggest strong Greek influence. The Roman Capitoline Temple is the largest-known Etruscan temple, with a podium of 62.25×53.30 m; it can be compared in scale only with the large Archaic Greek temples at Didyma and Ephesos in the East and with those in Agrigento and Selinunte in the West. Its three-cella plan with two rows of columns in the pronaos is unequivocally Etruscan; the peristyle surrounding three sides and excluding only the closed back wall recalls Greek sacred buildings (see Boëthius, 1970, rev. 2/1978, fig. 34). It thus partially neutralizes the strict frontality of the Etruscan temple. The three-sided peristyle occurs in other Italian, single-cella sacred structures, a form described by Vitruvius as *peripteros sine postico*. It is exemplified by several buildings in Etruria, southern Latium and even Paestum, with more elongated plans adapted from Greek models. Greek influence also affected the decoration of Etruscan temples, with the extensive use of pedimental sculpture and roof ornament, although again the preferred material remained terracotta rather than stone, even in late temples such as that at Talamone (later 2nd century BC; pediments reconstructed in Florence, Mus. Archeol.; *see also* §III, 1 below.)

Etruscan temples were part of larger sanctuaries containing several sacred structures. The whole sanctuary area was surrounded by a temenos wall, as at PYRGI. Other sacred structures included many free-standing altars; some survive and others are documented in numerous depictions on funerary artefacts. Most were step-form altars, both rectangular and circular in plan, constructed in the characteristic profile (a sequence of such mouldings as torus and trochilus, echinus and abacus), which is also known from the funerary architecture.

4. CITIES, FORTIFICATIONS AND OTHER STRUCTURES. The sites of most Early Iron Age settlements can so far only be ascertained from the locations of necropoleis. They were probably loose accumulations of oval or rectangular huts, usually in a defensible place such as the Palatine Hill at Rome. For larger settlements the geology of southern Etruria offered almost ideal conditions, with its easily fortified tufa plateaux (e.g. Volsinii Veteres and Veii). Access to the sea was also important, and even though many cities, such as Tarquinia, Cerveteri and Vulci, were not coastal but on more secure inland sites, they had dependent seaports. Cerveteri, for example, had the three ports of Alsium, Punicum and Pyrgi on the coast of the Tyrrhenian Sea. The territories of the major Etruscan cities also extended far into the hinterland.

In addition to natural defences, city walls played an important role. The earliest known Etruscan defensive structure is probably a wall (?8th century BC) discovered at the foot of the Palatine Hill, which is of clay or sun-dried clay bricks. Beneath the 6th-century BC city wall at Rusellae (Roselle), which is over 3 km long, of rough polygonal ashlars and probably equipped with five gateways, are the remains of an earlier, 7th-century BC wall consisting of a foundation of several layers of stone and an upper section of sun-dried clay bricks. This technique was Eastern in origin and may well have been used more widely in Etruscan defensive architecture.

Some cities had both outer and inner ramparts. Thus, during the 6th century BC, the centre of Volterra was encircled by a wall some 1.8 km long, while a much longer city wall protecting the entire settlement was erected in the 4th century BC. This, like the inner wall, took advantage of the terrain. Of the gateways in the later wall, the best preserved is the Porta all'Arco, although its keystone arch must be a later addition, as is probably also the case with gateways at Perugia and Falerii Novi (outside Civita Castellana).

The original appearance of Etruscan cities is less easy to reconstruct than that of the necropoleis. Again, this results from the use of mostly perishable building materials, and from alterations and accretions of later structures, in some cases continuing up to modern times (e.g. Volsinii Veteres, Volterra, Chiusi and Cortona). Even so, the orthogonal city-plan, with its two intersecting main streets, the cardo (north–south) and the decumanus (west–east), is traditionally regarded as an Etruscan invention; it is found mainly in Roman colonies. There is little direct evidence of Etruscan city-plans, although Veii appears to have conformed to the orthogonal model. Marzabotto has been more thoroughly studied. It was established in the 5th century BC, and its streets have a rectangular plan (for illustration see MARZABOTTO) relating to the points of the compass. However, it is not possible to distinguish individual streets within the broader plan, and the whole scheme may represent a version of the hippodamic system derived from Greece (see HIPPODAMOS).

Ancient writers praised the Etruscans for their water-conduits and drainage systems. These include the Ponte Sodo at Veii, which was hollowed into the rock and served as a water-channel, and the Cloaca Maxima at Rome. This was probably built by the Etruscans, although its history is still disputed. It served to dry out the marshy valleys between the hills of Rome, channelling water to the River Tiber near by. An important contribution to the urbanization of ancient Rome, it has continued functioning up to modern times.

BIBLIOGRAPHY

A. Åkerström: Studien über die etruskischen Gräber (Uppsala, 1934)
A. Minto: 'Pseudocupole e pseudovolte nell'architettura etrusca delle origini', Palladio, iii (1939), pp. 1–20
L. Pareti: La tomba Regolini-Galassi (Vatican, 1947)
E. Gjerstad: Early Rome, 4 vols (Rome, 1953–66)
A. Boëthius: 'Vitruvio e il "Tempio Tuscanico"', Stud. Etrus., xxiv (1955–6), pp. 137–42
M. Bizzarri: 'La necropoli di Crocefisso del Tufo in Orvieto', Stud. Etrus., xxx (1962), pp. 1–109
G. A. Mansuelli: 'La casa etrusca di Marzabotto', Mitt. Dt. Archäol. Inst.: Röm. Abt., lxx (1963), pp. 44–62
H. Boëthius: Etruscan and Early Roman Architecture, Pelican Hist. A. (Harmondsworth, 1970, rev. 2/1978)
F. Boitani, M. Cataldi and M. Pasquinucci: Etruscan Cities (London, 1975)
C. E. Östenberg: Case etrusche di Acquarossa (Rome, 1975)
F. Prayon: Frühetruskische Grab- und Hausarchitektur (Heidelberg, 1975)
M. Sprenger and G. Bartoloni: Die Etrusker (Munich, 1977)
O. J. Brendel: Etruscan Art, Pelican Hist. A. (Harmondsworth, 1978)
E. Colonna di Paolo: Necropoli rupestri del Viterbese (Novara, 1978)
E. Colonna di Paolo and G. Colonna: Norchia, i (Rome, 1978)
M. Torelli: Etruria, Guida archeologiche Laterza (Rome, 1980)
S. Steingräber: Etrurien: Städte, Heiligtümer, Nekropolen (Munich, 1981)
G. Morolli: 'Templi etruschi "o di etrusco nome" tra archeologia e trattatistica architettonica', Secondo congresso internazionale. Atti: Firenze, 1985, i, pp. 173–89
F. Prayon: 'L'architettura funeraria etrusca: La situazione attuale delle ricerche e problemi aperti', Secondo congresso internazionale. Atti: Firenze, 1985, i, pp. 441–3
—: 'Architecture', Etruscan Life and Afterlife, ed. L. Bonfante (Detroit, 1986)
M. P. Baglione: 'Il santuario del Portonaccio a Veio: Precisazioni sugli scavi Stefani', Scienza dell'Antichità, i (1987), pp. 381–417
G. Sassatelli: La città etrusca di Marzabotto (Casalecchio di Reno, 1989)
F. Roncalli: 'Nuove osservazioni sulle mura etrusche di Perugia', Welt der Etrusker (Berlin, 1990), pp. 81–7
M. Torelli: Storia degli Etruschi (Rome and Bari, 1990)
F. Prayon: 'Deorum sedes: Sull'orientamento dei templi etrusco-italici', Archeol. Class., 43 (1991), pp. 1285–95
G. Camporeale: 'Architettura e decorazione architettonica', Gli Etruschi e l'Europa (Milan, 1992), pp. 72–7
—: 'Le città: Produzione e creazione artistica', Gli Etruschi e l'Europa (Milan, 1992), pp. 62–71
F. Prayon and others: 'Orvieto: Tübinger Ausgrabungen in der Cannicella-Nekropole, 1984–1990', Archäol. Anz. (1993), pp. 5–99

MICHAEL EICHBERG

III. Sculpture.

Etruscan sculpture includes votive figures, funerary monuments and architectural embellishments. Terracotta and bronze were used in all these contexts, but stone was used only for funerary sculpture. Stone included volcanic tufa in southern Etruria, sandstone and travertine around Chiusi (Clusium), sandstone at Fiesole and, occasionally, marble around Volterra in the north-west. (For utilitarian bronze ornaments and gold and ivory artefacts see §§VI, 2 and 3, and VII, 3 respectively.)

1. Terracotta. 2. Bronze. 3. Stone. 4. Portraiture.

1. TERRACOTTA. The earliest sculptures from the Iron Age in Italy were small figurines in terracotta and bronze, meant as ornaments or offerings for the dead. A free-standing terracotta figurine of a woman from San Lorenzo Vecchio in the Alban Hills (mid-9th century BC; Rome, Mus. N. Preist. & Etnog.; see Bianchi Bandinelli and Giuliano, fig. 23) was found in a cremation burial. She holds a bowl on the palm of her right hand, while her left is held open in a gesture of offering or prayer repeated by many later figures. Her body is heavy and shapeless, and the small head on a long tapering neck is featureless apart from a jutting nose and ears, the latter pierced for earrings. Also stylistically rudimentary, a somewhat later terracotta figure forms the handle of a three-legged cup from Bisenzio (Rome, Mus. N. Preist. & Etnog., 51762).

Etruscan Orientalizing sculpture shows a marked increase in scale. Figures were given full, rounded contours suggestive of mass and weight, as in the carefully modelled terracotta ash urns from CHIUSI. While some Early Iron Age ash urns had lids in the form of helmets, to indicate that the ashes were a warrior's, the Orientalizing Canopic urns from Chiusi carried this personification further: the lid became a head, the urn itself a body. Another example from Chiusi (h. 445 mm; c. 650–c. 600 BC; Florence, Mus. Archeol.) combines the ample curves of the new style with such Early Iron Age features as deeply cut eyes, slit mouth and prominent ears with spiral earrings. A rare form of ash urn has a lid carrying a large terracotta statuette surrounded by a ring of griffin protomes and figures of mourning women (see fig. 12). The main figure on this urn, raised on a circular base, has a round head too large for her body, with a conical projection on top. The hair

12. Terracotta ash urn (Gualandi Urn), h. 880 mm, from Chiusi, mid-7th century BC (untraced)

makes a striated pattern on the skull and hangs in a long braid at the back. Two little tresses in front of the ears fall to the shoulders. The back braid is an Early Iron Age fashion, while the tresses are Eastern features. The face is round, with a long narrow nose and small slit mouth; the eyes are blank oval bosses. The dress is of chequered material, belted and falling short of the ankles, and a small rectangular cloak fastened at the shoulders hangs down the back. The elbows of her bare arms are bent, the right hand closed as if holding something, the left raised to the chin. This figure may be an effigy of the dead, a mourning woman or an underworld deity.

During the second half of the 7th century BC, terracotta tomb monuments were produced for burials at Cerveteri (Caere). The Tomb of the Five Chairs (c. 600 BC) contained fragments of five small, seated figures: one male, almost complete (h. 470 mm; Rome, Mus. Conserv.); the trunks of two others; and two female heads now attached to the headless male bodies (London, BM). All three bodies wear a long tunic of chequered material and a cloak fastened on the right shoulder and covering the left arm. The heads are masterpieces of the Orientalizing style, with rounded skulls, ovoid faces, arched eyebrows and heavy eyelids framing oval eyes, and large noses, soft mouths and high cheekbones. The inspiration for these features may have been the bronze heads on cauldrons imported from the East.

In the second half of the 6th century BC the Ionian style of the Greek cities of Asia Minor captivated the Mediterranean world, and Cerveteri produced some of the finest examples of the new style. Caeretan ash urns now took the form of couches, sometimes the funeral couch, more often the banquet couch, on which figures of the dead reclined, smiling. The two finest (c. 525–c. 500 BC; Rome, Villa Giulia; Paris, Louvre) have life-size figures of a man and woman reclining together, the man's right arm around the woman's shoulders, both smiling and gesticulating animatedly. They have egg-shaped heads, long, oval faces with arched eyebrows and slanting eyes, short noses with rounded nostrils, and the 'Archaic smile'. Fine temple terracottas, female mask antefixes, and revetment plaques showing horse and chariot races were also produced at Cerveteri. The finest Archaic temple terracottas, however, are those from the Portonaccio Temple at Veii (c. 515–c. 490 BC; Rome, Villa Giulia). These include splendid antefixes, including a gorgon's head in a shell of curving tongues (h. 485 mm) and free-standing over life-size statues of Apollo (for illustration see VEII), Hermes, Herakles and a female figure holding a baby in her arms, which originally stood on the ridge of the temple roof. The heads are still Ionian, but the line of cheek and jaw has filled out and the smiles are less serene.

Fewer temples were given elaborate terracotta decorations in the Classical period than in the Archaic, and none rivalled the magnificent Late Archaic figures at Veii. On Temple B at Pyrgi, however, the projecting end of the ridge pole carried a relief showing a combination of two episodes from the story of the Seven against Thebes (c. 510–c. 485 BC; Rome, Villa Giulia). In the background Zeus hurls his thunderbolt at Kapaneus; Tydeus and Melanippos sprawl mortally wounded across the foreground, Tydeus biting into Melanippos' skull while Athena draws back in horror. The figures, which overlap and intertwine, are modelled in high relief on a flat background, and their heads are in the round. Every face, except that of Zeus, shows intense feeling, and both the composition and its emotional charge suggest comparison with the west pediment of the Temple of Zeus at Olympia (c. 470–c. 457 BC).

Fine terracottas were also produced at Volsinii Veteres (Orvieto) in the Classical period. The figures from the Belvedere Temple (late 5th century BC–early 4th; Orvieto, Mus. Etrus. Faina) are not grouped in scenes, but isolated, standing or seated. Their effect resembles that of the east pediment of the Temple of Zeus at Olympia, but their style is later, based on High Classical Greek statues such as the Borghese Anakreon and the Farnese Diadoumenos. A bearded man, nude except for a cloak fastened at the throat by a round brooch, stands with the weight on the left leg, the left hand resting on the hip, the right arm hanging easily at the side. His head, with staring eyes and a rather unpleasant open mouth, is lifted towards the left, as though he were watching something. There are several young men in armour: one, who wears a moulded cuirass over a full tunic, stands in the same pose but with the back

13. Terracotta head of a young man, h. 200 mm, from a temple pediment at Arezzo, *c.* 175–*c.* 150 BC (Florence, Museo Nazionale Archeologico)

of the right hand on his hip; his head was apparently turned to the right. Another, in a cuirass of small rectangular plates, stands with the weight on the right leg, the left arm lowered, the hand stretched forward to hold a spear, now missing. Like the figures from Pyrgi, the bodies are in high relief against a flat surface, the heads worked in the round. They are about half life-size (800–870 mm) and thus inadequate for the pediment of the Belvedere Temple (w. 16.3 m), though they may have been revetments for beam ends either side of the ridge-pole, perhaps two figural groups looking towards the ridge-pole where something dramatic was displayed.

Greater numbers of temple terracottas survive from the 3rd and 2nd centuries BC. Some of the finest come from the temple at Lo Scasato, Civita Castellana (Falerii). These include figures modelled in the round at three-quarters life-size, large figures in relief, and fragments of small figures, presumably parts of antefixes. The most spectacular of these is the 'Apollo', the head and torso of a nude youth (h. 560 mm; late 5th century BC; Rome, Villa Giulia). The head is turned to the right and lifted. The broad face with its deep-set eyes, high cheekbones, strong jaw and half open mouth, is crowned by a mass of curly hair brushed up in the centre above the forehead and falling loosely to the shoulders. The effect recalls portraits of Alexander the Great. The broad, muscular torso bends forward to the left and the left arm is stretched forward. Other important fragments of temple statuary come from

Arezzo, though again the pieces are too few to tell their location on the temple or the story they illustrate. The two finest heads are an *Athena* and a young man wearing a Phrygian cap (*c.* 175–*c.* 150 BC; Florence, Mus. Archeol.). The cap suggests that the whole scene may have been the Judgement of Paris. The gentle face of the helmeted goddess has deep-set eyes shadowed by heavy bulges under the outer corners of the thin eyebrows; her nose is short, her lips full and soft. Thick locks of hair straggle from under the visor of the helmet. The head of the young man (?Paris) must have been modelled by the same hand (see fig. 13). His face is longer and thinner, but otherwise the heads are alike. The contrast between the man's smooth face and the rough, lively texture of his hair is more noticeable because more of the hair is visible, modelled in high relief and striated, wavy rather than curling, in the manner adopted for portraits of Hellenistic heroes and princes.

2. BRONZE. Early Iron Age bronzes are more elegant than their terracotta equivalents; their spindly Geometric style depends as much on space as on form for its effect. A bronze cup from Bisenzio (see Proietti, figs 81–2) has a vertical handle ending in an openwork disc. This makes a double circle enclosing a nude female with a rod-like torso, arms and legs, and a big round head with loop earrings. The face is slightly flattened, with a long narrow nose, drilled holes for eyes and no mouth. It exemplifies the Wiry Geometric Early Iron Age figural style of the 8th century BC and early 7th. The figure, clearly a 'Mistress of Animals', is accompanied by two Geometric ducks and two four-footed beasts, and two large birds' heads adorn the rim of the disc. The 'Mistress of Animals' was derived ultimately, via Greece, from Minoan iconography, and the pose of this figure, with raised arms and straddled legs, suggests Geometric Greek representations of deities appearing to worshippers. Some Early Iron Age ash urns were also of bronze; one from Tarquinia has a real bronze helmet for a lid (Florence, Mus. Archeol.).

During the 7th and 6th centuries BC bronzes tended to be small votive figures or ornaments for utensils. Large funerary bronzes also survive, apparently made as images of the dead. The oldest is a hammered bronze bust from Marsiliana d'Albegna (Florence, Mus. Archeol.; Cristofani, 1985, fig. 109). The head is a globe decorated with repoussé lines and bosses in Early Iron Age style, set on a cylindrical neck attached to the broad shoulders of the torso. Early bronze busts were also produced at Vulci and were perhaps intended to represent figures rising from the underworld. During the second half of the 7th century BC, bronze human figurines dedicated at sanctuaries developed two distinct types: a male figure with long hair, armed with a sword or lance, often shown stepping forward, dressed in short trunks; and a female figure in a full-length dress or cape, with hair in a single long tress at the back, making a gesture of offering. Some of these figurines have the flat bodies and crudely articulated limbs reminiscent of Geometric forms; others, presumably the products of a more cosmopolitan urban culture, show Orientalizing influences.

Bronze reliefs of the 6th century BC are numerous and splendid. They almost always illustrate Greek myths, or mythological creatures, and are used in the decoration of tripods, furniture and chariots (e.g. the Monteleone Chariot; *c.* 550 BC; see fig. 31 below). Archaic votive figurines continued to be produced in quantity, with new types appearing: the Greek-influenced figures of the kouros, kore, hoplite, athlete, and mythological deities and heroes; and the more specifically Etruscan figures of the augur, haruspex, toga-clad male, and various animals and anatomical bronzes. Hollow-cast bronzes of the 5th century BC also show the influence of the Archaic Greek types of the Attic kore and nude kouros (e.g. statuette of a spear thrower, *c.* 470 BC; Paris, Louvre). Large collections of bronze statuary were assembled in Etruscan cities, although few of these pieces now survive. Two statuettes from Monteguragazza (*c.* 470 BC; Bologna, Mus. Civ. Archeol.) represent votaries. The man carries a libation bowl and wears a short cloak around his waist; the fully-clothed woman carries a flower and a fruit and wears Etruscan shoes.

The Etruscan Classical style is exemplified by the Todi *Mars* (see fig. 14), which is so close in style to the terracottas from the Belvedere Temple, Volsinii Veteres, that it has been assigned to the same workshop. It was hollow cast in seven pieces: head, arms and legs in piece moulds; the torso in two sections, cast directly from a wax model. It represents a warrior in a cuirass of overlapping plates, its lower part made of two rows of lappets, and worn over a full tunic like that of the Belvedere warrior in the moulded cuirass. The *Mars* stands with the weight on the right leg, hip thrown out, the left leg rather too far to the side, knee bent; both feet are firmly on the ground. The broad, blank face has thin eyebrows, a long nose, full mouth and heavy chin, recalling a terracotta head from Volsinii Veteres (see Roncalli, pl. 12, figs 3–4; p. 85, fig. 88). The left eye is a small travertine cone with a pupil of black resin; the right is modern. A libation bowl rests on the palm of his right hand; his left once grasped an iron spear, fragments of which are preserved, on which he leaned. His head is turned to the right, as though looking upwards. Attic Red-figure vases depict similar figures of warriors pouring libations before battle, but these are not part of the usual repertory of Greek sculpture. They do appear, however, among Etruscan and Italic votive bronzes of the Late Classical and Hellenistic periods. The *Mars* too is a votive bronze, and a dedicatory inscription in Umbrian is incised on the centre lappet of the cuirass.

A life-size head of a young man, found on an island in Lake Bolsena, also exemplifies Etruscan adaptation of a Greek style (h. 250 mm; London, BM). The long face has a sober expression; forehead and nose make a single line; iris and pupil are incised. The heavy cap of hair has flamboyantly swirling locks, parted on the forehead and shortened in the centre, framing the forehead like the hair of the *Doryphoros* of Polykleitos (*see* POLYKLEITOS, §1). A young beard is lightly chased, not a Polykleiten detail. The bronze is hollow cast, broken probably from a votive statue. Another important Classical votive bronze is the Arezzo *Chimaera* (h. 650 mm; *c.* 375–*c.* 350 BC; Florence, Mus. Archeol.; *see* ITALY, fig. 47). The wounded beast appears dangerous, snarling and crouching to spring, the mane and the hair along the back bristling in sharp spikes with slightly curved points and deeply striated surfaces, a

14. Bronze statue of *Mars*, h. 1.41 m, from Todi, late 5th century BC (Rome, Vatican, Museo Gregoriano Etrusco)

stylish archaism. Except for these the body is smooth; ribs and muscles are clearly articulated under its shining surface. On the right foreleg is a votive inscription, 'offering'. The serpent-headed tail is an 18th-century addition.

In the late 4th century BC Etruscan bronzeworkers took inspiration from LYSIPPOS: figures became taller and slimmer, with small heads and long legs, sometimes in gracefully sinuous attitudes, the heel of the free foot lifted, for example a bronze representing a young man offering a libation (h. 288 mm; Florence, Mus. Archeol.). Later bronzes are even more elongated (e.g. a togate figure from Volsinii Veteres; h. 270 mm; Rome, Villa Giulia). One series of elongated bronze figures has nothing to do with Lysippos. They are excessively tall, straight and flattened; very much like yardsticks equipped with heads, hands and feet. They represent men, women, priests or perhaps divinities. The oldest of these is a female figure from the

Sanctuary of Diana at Nemi (h. 500 mm; *c.* 350–*c.* 300 BC; Paris, Louvre). In a related series the elongated bodies are three-dimensional, and the women's dresses are more detailed and modelled in relief. The best known of these figures is a nude boy from Volterra, the 'Evening Shadow' (h. 570 mm, 2nd century BC; Volterra, Mus. Etrus. Guarnacci). The body has an attractive young boy's head with wavy hair straying over his cheeks and the nape of his neck. He has a snub nose, a smiling mouth and a rounded, childlike forehead. These figures seem strangely out of place in the generally philhellenic history of Etruscan sculpture. They may be descendants of an early Italic votive type, wooden and terracotta examples of which have been found in Campania. (For further discussion of Hellenistic bronzes *see* §4 below.)

3. STONE. Stone sculpture began to be produced in the 7th century BC, a clear indication that Etruria was becoming a major centre in the Mediterranean world. This new craft was probably learnt from Near Eastern and Greek immigrant craftsmen. Early stone figures are large, imposing and immobile, and were connected exclusively with the cult of the dead. The oldest surviving statues are two almost life-size seated male figures in the vestibule of a mid-7th century BC rock-cut tomb at Ceri in the territory of Cerveteri. They are carved in high relief in the tufa of the tomb and sit enthroned, facing one another, just within its entrance. Their heads are mutilated, but were obviously once bearded. They wear long tunics and their sandalled feet rest on footstools; one wears a slanting mantle over the tunic and his right hand holds a sceptre topped by a stylized lotus flower. Their forms are stocky, with the vertical and horizontal surfaces emphasized. They may have been carved by an Anatolian or north Syrian craftsman (see Colonna and von Hase). Throne, footstool and sceptre were signs of rank in the Near East, but Etruscan seated figures were usually images not of living potentates but of the dead. These dignitaries of Ceri are not effigies of the couple whose bodies lay in the tomb chamber beyond, but are perhaps ancestors, doing honour to their descendants.

The Pietrera Tomb at Vetulonia (*c.* 650–*c.* 630 BC; see Hus, pls 1–3, 17–18) contained parts of at least 18 standing figures, some in high relief, some apparently free-standing. The best preserved head, a woman's (h. 280 mm; Florence, Mus. Archeol.), suggests a Greek model, despite its non-Greek features, as it has similarities with early kouroi from Attica and Boiotia. It has a long, solemn face widening into the jaw, a shallow skull with flattened back and long ears set high and far back. The thin, sharp ridge of the eyebrow is separated from the upper lid by a shallow channel; the eye is a swelling oval framed by a fine line of shadow. The torso that probably belongs with this head has no Greek counterpart; but one of the male figures had the stance of a Greek kouros, with arms at the sides, hands half closed, left leg advanced. Unlike Greek kouroi, however, this figure wears a loincloth, as do other Etruscan male figures of the 7th and 6th centuries BC.

By the second quarter of the 6th century BC at Vulci handsome stone figures were being produced in close imitation of the post-Daidalic style of early 6th-century BC Greece. A gypsum figure from the Isis Tomb may be the

15. Stone statue of a woman, gypsum, h. 850 mm, from the Isis Tomb, Vulci, *c.* 600–*c.* 580 BC (London, British Museum)

earliest of these (see fig. 15). It represents a woman standing erect in a frontal pose with feet apart but parallel, upper arms pressed to the body, forearms held out. The head is cubic; the body, except for the forearms, a single mass. Details, however, are softly and delicately worked. The low-crowned head has a deep profile, the face is trapezoidal, with a low forehead, and the horizontal eyes, mouth and chin characteristic of Daidalic figures (*see* GREECE, ANCIENT, §IV, 2(i)(c)). The hair is arranged in a row of snailshell curls across the forehead, two curls fall on each shoulder and nine braids bound together hang down the back. A band circles the head and the hair at the back bulges slightly over this. Under a shawl she wears a long, belted dress; these are smooth, without folds, although the dress bulges a little over the belt. The dress, like the curls and the sandalled feet, is Greek. The shawl has three lappets; one at the back, two falling over the shoulders. This is an Etruscan garment, worn by small votive bronzes of the early 6th century BC. The elaboration of the back braid is also Etruscan, and the pose of the hands recalls some votive bronzes: the right hand open as if to hold a flat bowl, the left closed as if around the handle of a jug or cup. The gesture is that of a libation pourer, and the statue may represent the deceased, a mourner or a deity. It stands on a low, profiled base. Stone tomb guardians were also produced at Vulci. A centaur in local tufa is among the best (h. 770 mm; c. 590 BC; Rome, Villa Giulia). Seen from the front he resembles a bearded kouros with a sub-Daidalic head, enormous eyes, stunted arms, the open hands pressed to the thighs; the hindquarters of a horse are attached to the buttocks.

At Chiusi, stone tomb guardians and busts of mourning women for tomb doorways were produced in imitation of Vulci's post-Daidalic style. The finest early carving from Chiusi is a warrior with a pot helmet and a round shield with a gorgoneion in high relief (h. 490 mm, first half of the 6th century BC; Munich, Staatl. Antikensamml.), presumably a tomb guardian. In the Late Archaic period at Chiusi a long series of finely carved grave monuments of a new type appeared, comprising gravestones, ash urns, and some sarcophagi, decorated with low-relief panels, with numerous figures on quite a small scale but in elaborate detail. The scenes are of Etruscan funerary rites, mourners, funeral games and banquets, a repertory like those of the painted tombs of Tarquinia and Chiusi. The reliefs also recall early Attic Red-figure pottery styles. Also of a new type were the stone ash urns made at Chiusi from the mid-6th century BC; monumental seated figures with removable heads and cavities in the upper torso for the ashes. The earliest represent solemn, bearded men with heavy bodies, distantly related to the seated figures that lined the sacred way at Didyma. In the second half of the 5th century BC, the time at which true Classical art began in Etruria, the seated figures were female. Some sit on thrones with arms shaped like sphinxes; some hold a pomegranate in the left hand; one carries a baby (h. 900 mm; Florence, Mus. Archeol.). They look more like underworld deities than mortal women. Classical ash urns from Chiusi in the shape of banquet couches may have imitated the Late Archaic terracotta urns from Cerveteri. One shows a couple, the woman sitting, in the Greek manner, at the foot of her husband's couch (late 5th century BC; Florence, Mus. Archeol.). On others the foot of the couch is occupied by a messenger from the other world, who summons the banqueter away (e.g. limestone urn; c. 400 BC; Florence, Mus. Archeol.).

By the end of the 5th century BC, burial rather than cremation was almost universal in the cities of southern Etruria, particularly Cerveteri, Tarquinia and Vulci. The oldest stone sarcophagus comes from Cerveteri (see fig. 16). The lid is shaped like a couch, the head and foot like temple pediments with sphinxes for acroteria. A bearded man crowned with an elaborate wreath lies on the couch; around his neck is a garland, which he grasps with the left hand, and a necklace with five *bullae*; three more hang from a bracelet on the left upper arm. His upper torso is bare; a cloak covers him from waist to ankles; his right hand grasps a libation bowl. Head and feet are turned slightly to his left, towards the front of the sarcophagus. Although his couch seems to be a funeral

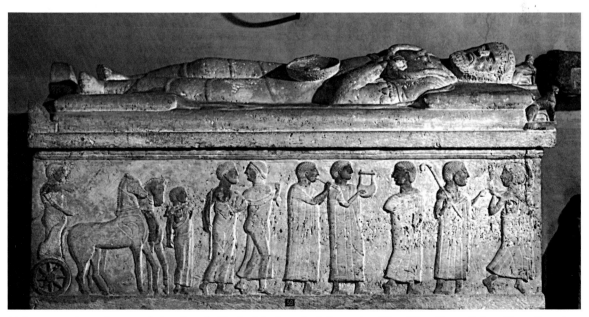

16. Stone sarcophagus, limestone, h. 1 m, from the Tomb of the Sarcophagi, Cerveteri, *c.* 450–*c.* 400 BC (Rome, Vatican, Museo Gregoriano Etrusco)

couch, the man is not dead, nor even sleeping; his eyes are open. Figural scenes in low relief adorn the front and right end of the sarcophagus itself. On the front, a procession moves to the right, headed by three men in long cloaks. The first carries a large circular trumpet framing his head and walks briskly with both heels off the ground, turning back towards the man who follows, evidently at a slower pace. His heels are firmly on the ground and his right hand holds a staff with a curved end, the Etruscan *lituus*, an emblem of priests and magistrates including those who supervised funeral games, which may be this man's function. Next comes a man with his arms muffled in his cloak except for the left hand, which holds a rod with a twisted top, rather like a cadeuceus; he is hurrying, and looks back at the two men who follow. These have the long, sleeved tunics of musicians; one plays a lyre, the other a double pipe; they walk slowly. Behind them hurry two figures: a bearded man in a long cloak carrying a staff or sceptre in his right hand, preceded by a woman turning her head towards him and laying her hand on his shoulder. Her jewels indicate high rank, and her dress and cloak are diaphanous. Both figures are wreathed; the man may represent the bearded man on the lid, the woman either his wife or her ghost, who has come, like the winged messengers on the urns from Chiusi, to escort him. Behind them stands a boy in a long cloak, carrying a stool and blocking the advance of the two-horse chariot driven by the final figure, a young man in tunic and cloak. Except for the boy and the horses, the heads of all the figures touch the upper frame of the chest and, except for the charioteer's, all their feet are on its lower frame. Attendants and musicians have large square heads and broad flat bodies; the figures of the old man, his wife, the boy and the charioteer are more shapely and detailed. The scene is a curiously disorganized procession, and a further scene, on the end of the sarcophagus, reveals its destination. It shows a man with a *lituus* on the left, a lyre player on the right and between them two nude boys preparing for an athletic contest. Thus the procession is on its way to the funeral games and includes the bearded man for whom they are given.

Figures of attendants, musicians, servants and chariots all appear on friezes on later sarcophagi from Tarquinia and on Hellenistic ash urns from Volterra, but these represent the cortèges of magistrates, who often drive the chariots themselves, accompanied by lictors. These processions move forward steadily; sometimes an underworld spirit and mourning women take part, but the magistrates are not accompanied by their wives or their ghosts. The destinations are not funeral games but the underworld itself. On early sarcophagi the figures lay supine on the funeral couch, as if dead or sleeping. Later, head and shoulders were half raised on cushions, the left hand supporting the head. Early in the Hellenistic period the figures were shown lifting themselves as if on banqueting couches, looking out at the world. The figures on Hellenistic ash urns assume all of these poses, but the one preferred was that of the banqueter (see fig. 4 above). Sarcophagi and ash urns with such figures continued to be produced well into the 1st century BC. The latest dated sarcophagus (Viterbo, Mus. Civ.), a lamentable work, was made for a burial in 23 BC.

4. PORTRAITURE. In Archaic and Classical Greece, statues honouring the living were uncommon. Portraiture only became important with Alexander the Great and his successors, especially on coins; it became important in Etruria at much the same time, and probably under Greek influence. But it was not used for the same purpose: it honoured the dead. Etruria had a long history of what may be called symbolic portraiture, beginning with the Early Iron Age urns with helmets as lids. Chiusi's Canopic jars carried on this tradition, and then the figures on Archaic ash urns and sarcophagi from Cerveteri. The earliest stone sarcophagus (see fig. 16 above) still presents a symbolic portrait, that of a bearded old man. Perhaps the first sarcophagus to carry a genuine portrait is the fine example from Vulci that shows an elderly man and his wife lying on their marriage couch (mid-4th century BC; Boston, MA, Mus. F.A.). Thereafter, such portraits and near-portraits became common, although, of course, there is no way of verifying that they were actually portraits.

The Greeks, and later the Romans, set up their funeral monuments as public memorials; Etruscan portraits of the dead were hidden in tombs. Public portraits were, however, set in Etruscan sanctuaries. In the Late Classical and Hellenistic periods terracotta heads were popular offerings throughout Italy: most of these are stereotypes, but a few look like individuals. Several splendid Hellenistic bronze portrait heads have been found in central Italy; the Capitoline *Lucius Junius Brutus* (h. 320 mm; Rome,

17. Bronze portrait head of a young man, h. 300 mm, from Fiesole, mid-2nd century BC (Paris, Musée du Louvre)

Mus. Conserv.; *see* ROME, ANCIENT, fig. 72), the 'Young General' from San Giovanni Lipioni near Chieti (h. 280 mm; Paris, Bib. N.), a young boy (h. 230 mm; Florence, Mus. Archeol.) and a plump young man from Fiesole (h. 300 mm; Paris, Louvre; see fig. 17). These heads have much in common: a cubical solidity, broad face, flat profile, hair in a thick cap of longish locks brushed forward from the crown of the head to fall in strands on the forehead. The greatest difference from the heads on sarcophagi and ash urns is their animated expression. They are not like the terracotta votive heads, either, but are more like parts of free-standing statues such as the Todi *Mars*. They too may have been votive, or honorary, as were the bronzes in the Forum Romanum described by Pliny (*Natural History* XXXIV.xx–xxx). These are true portraits, idealized but strongly individual; *Brutus* and the 'Young General' have the vigour and intensity of the best of the Greek princely portraits; they may well come from honorary statues. The portrait of the young boy in Florence is less individual and may have been part of a votive statue. The head from Fiesole is the least idealized and most realistic of the four. He looks straight ahead, two vertical frown lines between his heavy eyebrows. His small eyes once had inset irises and pupils; plump cheeks frame his short, broad nose, there is a roll of fat under his chin and his full lips are tightly closed. It is an impressive face, for all its quietness, recalling the head of the 'Magistrate' (Tarquinia, Pal. Vitelleschi) and anticipating Roman heads. It may also be from a votive statue, representing a private citizen who knows his own importance, but does not flaunt it, and thus more Roman than Greek in both feeling and form.

BIBLIOGRAPHY

Pliny: *Natural History*

R. Herbig: *Die jungeretruskischen Steinsarkophage* (Berlin, 1952)

A. Hus: *Recherches sur la statuaire en pierre étrusque archaïque* (Paris, 1961)

S. Haynes: 'Zwei archaisch-etruskische Bildwerke aus dem "Isis Grab" von Vulci', *Ant. Plast.*, iv (1965), pp. 13–25, pls 6–11

R. Bianchi Bandinelli and A. Giuliano: *Etruschi e Italici prima del dominio di Roma* (Milan, 1973, rev. 2/1979)

R. D. Gempeler: *Die etruskischen Kanopen: Herstellung, Typologie, Entwicklungsgeschichte* (Küsnacht, 1973)

F. Roncalli: 'Il "Marte" di Todi', *Atti Pont. Accad. Romana Archeol.*, 3rd ser., xi (1973) [whole issue]

M. Cristofani: *Statue-cinerario chiusine di età classica* (Rome, 1975)

M. Cristofani, ed.: *Il Museo Guarnacci, parte prima: Corpus delle urne etrusche di età ellenistica* (1977), ii of *Urne volterrane* (Florence, 1975–)

M. Sprenger and G. Bartolini: *Die Etrusker: Kunst und Geschichte* (Munich, 1977); Eng. trans. by R. Wolf as *The Etruscans: Their History, Art and Architecture* (New York, 1983)

G. Proietti, ed.: *Il Museo Nazionale Etrusco di Villa Giulia* (Rome, 1980)

G. Colonna and F.-W. von Hase: 'Alle origini della santuaria etrusca: La tomba delle statue presso Ceri', *Stud. Etrus.*, lii (1984), pp. 13–59

M. Cristofani: *I bronzi degli Etruschi* (Novara, 1985)

E. Hostetter: *Bronzes from Spina*, i (Mainz, 1986)

F. Jurgeit: *Le Ciste prenestine*, II/i (Italy, 1986)

J. Swaddling, ed.: *Italian Iron Age Artefacts in the British Museum* (London, 1986)

B. van der Meer: *The Bronze Liver of Piacenza*, Dutch Monographs on Ancient History and Archaeology, ii (Netherlands, 1987)

F. Buranelli: *La Tomba François di Vulci* (exh. cat., Rome, 1987)

The Gods Delight (exh. cat., Cleveland, OH, Mus. A., 1988)

G. Bordenache Battaglia and A. Emiliozzi: *Le Ciste prenestine*, I/ii (Italy, 1990)

M. Bentz: *Etruskische Votivbronzen des Hellenismus* (Florence, 1992)

EMELINE RICHARDSON

IV. Pottery.

For Etruria, as for the Classical world generally, pottery represents the largest and best defined body of available archaeological material. Scholarly attention has been mostly taken up by figured and decorated vases, even if they constitute only a fraction of all pottery production. The excavation of domestic settlements has demonstrated that the utilitarian pottery in everyday use was mostly coarse or undecorated. Pottery production as a specialized craft sector began in the 8th century BC through the acquisition of techniques from the Greek world and the settlement of immigrant craftsmen (*see* §I, 4 above). Workshops were set up in many Etruscan centres to meet the demand for pottery, a demand fuelled by the influx of Greek vases, which were imported continuously into Etruria from the first half of the 8th century BC to the mid-4th. As Etruscan trade developed, Etruscan pottery was itself widely exported; its distribution reveals patterns of trade and communication that are invaluable for reconstructing economic history. (A number of shapes are of purely local origin, but for the identification of the Greek-influenced shapes of Etruscan vases *see* GREECE, ANCIENT, §V, 1(ii) and fig. 71.)

1. Impasto ware. 2. Etrusco-Geometric. 3. Orientalizing. 4. Bucchero. 5. Red ware. 6. Etrusco-Corinthian. 7. Black-figure. 8. Red-figure. 9. Black-glaze.

1. IMPASTO WARE. During the Iron Age (9th–8th century BC) impasto was the fabric used for vases. It consisted of unpurified clay containing calcareous, siliceous and other matter, which was fired at low temperatures. It was either hand-modelled or slow-turned, and air-dried before being smoothed and sometimes decorated, then fired in an open kiln at about 800°C. This method produced robust vessels of irregular shape, in a range of earth colours from black to red.

During the 8th century BC finer wares began to be made (*see* §2 below), but impasto remained in use for domestic vessels. Many impasto vases were decorated with pointing tools and combs, or impressed *a cordicella* (given moulded cordons and pseudo-cordons). Punched impressions, notches, grooves and fingerprints also occur. Such decoration, mostly on the body and neck, emphasized the vases' structural features, and the formulaic geometric patterns include concentric circles, meanders, zigzags and other motifs. Less frequently, amber overlays (Verucchio), bronze chains and rings, bronze bosses and tin sheets were also used, the latter especially at Vulci, continuing into the Orientalizing period. Painted impasto ware, again with geometric decoration, was found at Veii, Tarquinia, Vulci, Poggio Montano and Civitavecchia. Stamped impasto occurs more commonly at northern Etruscan sites, such as Vetulonia and Populonia, and especially Felsina (Bologna) and Verucchio. Modelled decoration included human and animal figures, singly or in various configurations.

Impasto was used for both domestic and ritual, often funerary, vessels, and such shapes as the biconical urn (see fig. 18) clearly belonged in both contexts. Hut urns (see fig. 9 above) were obviously funerary, as were urns with peaked or crested helmet-shaped lids, miniature ships and

18. Impasto biconical urn with a helmet-shaped lid, h. 520 mm, from Vulci, late 9th century BC (Rome, Museo Nazionale di Villa Giulia e Soprintendenza alle Antichità per l'Etruria Meridionale)

miniature three-footed tables. Shapes mainly for domestic use included multiple vases, cups, saucers, pitchers, beakers, jugs, amphorae, plates and zoomorphic askoi, such as an example from Bologna (Benaccì necropolis) in the form of a bull-bird surmounted by an armed warrior on horseback (Bologna, Mus. Civ. Archeol.). The warrior wears the characteristic triangular-crested Villanovan helmet and has a round shield at his back. The stoves and dolium-jars, the latter used for containing foodstuffs, were also made of impasto, as were models of wagons and miniature horses, thrones, spindle whorls and loom weights. The shape range is conservative, but regional specialities occur: 'candelabra' from Tarquinia; from Felsina situlae, cists and so-called *presentatoi*; from Latium small ollas (jars) with modelled lattice decoration; and from Sardinia askoid jugs. With the introduction of the fast potter's wheel more regular shapes were produced, including spiral amphorae, jugs with oblique spouts and chalices with hemispherical or carinated bowls. Some impasto vases, ribbed phialai and stands (*holmoi*) have been influenced by metallic Oriental shapes: the three-footed plates produced at Cerveteri (Caere) derived from Levantine tripod-bowls, while skyphoi and kotylai are essentially Greek shapes.

In the 7th century BC a distinctive type of carved decoration with the design filled in with white or red ochre occurs alongside more traditional techniques, and impasto wares show the influence of Etrusco-Geometric and Bucchero pottery shows new figural, floral and geometric motifs. From the first half of the 7th century BC several impasto vases had their Etruscan names inscribed (e.g. chalices (*thafna*) and plates (*spanti*)). A dedicatory inscription on an olla with horseshoe cordons certainly made at Vulci (*c.* 675–650 BC; Rome, Villa Giulia, 63189) has letters formed from clay lines applied before firing, and surely relates to a special commission. A particularly fine local variety of 7th-century BC impasto with a red sheeny slip was produced at Cerveteri. It was used for pithoi, ollas, amphorae, oinochoai, chalices, plates, large pyxides and cinerary urns with sloping roofs, and it was decorated with motifs in added white (so-called 'white-on-red'). It is distinct from the Caeretan Red ware (*see* §5 below), generally used for pithoi and braziers.

2. ETRUSCO-GEOMETRIC. Vases in this style were produced from *c.* 775 to *c.* 630 BC. They were wheelmade from purified clay, and their painted decoration, in black, brown or orange-red, directly derives from Greek Geometric pottery (*see* GREECE, ANCIENT, §V, 3). Until *c.* 675 BC Euboean-Cycladic pottery of the Middle–Late Geometric style was a main model. From *c.* 675 to *c.* 630 BC more exotic, Orientalizing motifs occurred, along with Protocorinthian, Protoattic and Western Greek influence.

The first imports of Greek Geometric pottery to Etruria, the Faliscan region and Latium occurred at the beginning of the 8th century BC, before the founding of the Greek colonies in South Italy. With the establishment between *c.* 770 and *c.* 760 BC of the Euboean settlements at PITHEKOUSSAI and CUMAE, imports greatly increased, with drinking vessels predominating. The few larger vases may be evidence of gift-exchanges between Greeks and Etruscan leaders. From about 730 BC Etruscan imitations of Greek wares proliferated, with the increasing refinement both of the clay used and of the painted decoration. In fact it is sometimes difficult to distinguish imported Greek originals from south Etruscan imitations, many of which were in any case probably made by immigrant Greek craftsmen, who set up workshops and introduced new shapes, such as the skyphoi and round-mouthed jugs that occur at Veii, Cerveteri, Tarquinia, Poggio Montano, Vulci, Bisenzio and around Rome and Felsina. New decorative formulae such as groups of chevrons or vertical strokes, rows of concentric circles, and dotted rosettes also appeared. From about 730 BC workshops at Vulci assumed a leading role in producing Etrusco-Geometric pottery to judge by the quantity of pots recovered from the city and its territory. Other regional centres were Bisenzio, Veii (probably the earliest centre), Cerveteri and Tarquinia. The range of vases, apparently mainly for ceremonial or ritual functions, includes Greek shapes (e.g. kraters with stirrup handles, amphorae, high-stemmed dinoi, hydriai, oinochoai, a type of ring kernos) and Etruscan ones (e.g. ollas, holmoi, plastic or bottle-shaped askoi and biconical urns).

Decorations became richer from the third quarter of the 8th century BC, with elements from the Euboean–Boiotian–Cycladic common style of the Late Geometric period. Metopes frames enclosing hatched birds, swastikas, asterisks, chequers, zigzags, star-rosettes, running or isolated meanders, sequences of dots, crosshatched triangles and lozenges appeared, as did grazing horses, recumbent goats and rampant beasts. These were followed by the first narrative scenes: deer hunts, on foot (bird-shaped askos; Norbert Schimmel priv. col., see Martelli, 1987, pp. 247–8, no. 11) and horseback (holmos; see fig. 19); horsemen on parade (dinos; Los Angeles, CA, Co. Mus. A.); and an armed dance led by a phorminx player (krater; Basle, Antikenmus., BS 403.1963), all of which originate from Vulci workshops, as may the first possibly mythological scene, the *Crane-dance of Theseus and Ariadne*, on the neck of an oinochoe (London, BM, 49.5–18.18). A boat, with helmsman and two oarsmen perhaps hunting a deer (olla; Rome, Villa Giulia, 57069A), and a chorus scene, presumably threnodic (olla; Florence, Mus. Archeol., 85629), both come from Bisenzio. The so-called 'Metopengattung' shows the development of some Euboean motifs, such as squares enclosing chequered lozenges, and horizontal wavy lines, used routinely in the decoration of domestic vessels produced around Vulci and Tarquinia from the last quarter of the 8th to the mid-7th century BC.

19. Etrusco-Geometric holmos, h. 315 mm, *c.* 725–*c.* 700 BC (Rome, Museo Nazionale di Villa Giulia e Soprintendenza alle Antichità per l'Etruria Meridionale)

Again, the vase shapes are both Greek influenced (stamnoid ollas, oinochoai) and indigenous (e.g. biconical urns, ollas without handles, cups on high feet). Contact with Corinth is attested by a few Late Geometric Corinthian vases occurring at Veii, Tarquinia and Narce, and an increased number of early Protocorinthian vases, including kotylai, conical lekythoi, oinochoai, low pyxides and squat aryballoi, found at Narce, Veii, Tarquinia, Vulci and most notably at Cerveteri. At Tarquinia a workshop was set up specializing in oinochoai and kotylai of Protocorinthian–Cumaean type. The Bocchoris Painter and Palms Painter were both active here from *c.* 700 to 690 BC, and added a number of Orientalizing elements, such as hybrid bird-felines and palm leaves, to the stock Protocorinthian–Cumaean motifs. The latter also depicted maritime experiences (e.g. on oinochoai; St Louis, MO, Mus. A., 71.114; Haifa, N. Mar. Mus.).

3. ORIENTALIZING. The Orientalizing style succeeded Etrusco-Geometric gradually, the latter continuing in evidence into the 7th century BC. Early Orientalizing pottery includes much stereotyped work with Corinthian-derived linear decoration organized in registers or concentric zones, often alternating with files of fish and marsh birds. Parallels with contemporary metal and Bucchero vessels appear in vase shapes (e.g. kylikes imitating Protocorinthian types, bridge-handled situlae and vertical-handled cups). Although produced in southern Etruria, these vases were distributed widely within central Italy. Cerveteri was a major centre, producing the distinctive 'Heron class' vases, which show elongated aquatic birds with filiform beaks and silhouette bodies and tails, and a series of large vases, predominantly amphorae, dated *c.* 700–*c.* 625 BC. An important krater (Rome, Mus. Capitolino) depicting a *Sea-battle* and the *Blinding of Polyphemos* was signed by its craftsman, Aristonothos, a Greek immigrant, and it exemplifies a new Caeretan decorative approach, which introduced figural scenes executed in outline drawing filled in with dots entailing the break-up of traditional zoomorphic motifs. Effectively, the routine sub-Geometric schemata were relegated to filling motifs, and the principal decorative field was occupied by real or fantastic animals and narrative scenes, either from real life or from Greek myth and epic. One amphora (*c.* 650–*c.* 630 BC; Amsterdam, Allard Pierson Mus., 10188) shows a female figure confronting a three-headed serpent: this scene must be *Medea and the Dragon of Kolchis*. Two individual painters identified in this school are the Heptachord Painter and the Cranes Painter (both active *c.* 680–*c.* 670 BC). These developments are to some extent paralleled by work in fine impasto (so-called 'white-on-red'). Scenes painted in cream-white on a reddish slip include the *Birth of Athena* and the *Hunt of the Kalydonian Boar* (pyxis; *c.* 630 BC; Paris, Louvre, D151) and naval fights (pyxis; Paris, Louvre, D150). Stylistic affinities between impasto and fine ware production are also shown by two fine-ware amphorae from Caeretan tombs, made by the same potter as a pair of impasto pithoi (all four vases in Rome, Villa Giulia).

4. BUCCHERO. Produced continuously between *c.* 675 BC and the beginning of the 5th century BC, this

distinctively Etruscan ware was made from a clay similar to that of impasto but purer, which fired to a black tone with a lustrous, almost metallic brilliance. Bucchero was in fact produced as a deliberate substitute for metal vases, and its shapes and decoration were based, especially at first, on metallic prototypes. Bucchero was extremely versatile and was used for a wide range of shapes. Etruscan Bucchero is usually divided into three types: fine (*c.* 675–*c.* 625 BC), transitional (*c.* 625–*c.* 575 BC) and heavy (*c.* 575–*c.* 500 BC), according to the thickness of the pottery walls. Northern Etruscan Bucchero followed a different development: the oldest was a type of buccheroid impasto, which gave way in the Archaic period to a heavy Bucchero. 'Grey' Bucchero appeared only in the second half of the 6th century BC and was used for less than a century for a limited range of shapes.

Fine Bucchero production in southern Etruria began in Cerveteri, followed by Veii and Tarquinia. The vase shapes partly conformed to types established in the impasto repertory: double spiral amphorae, 'Phoenician-Cypriot' oinochoai, hemispherical or carinated chalices, kotylai, skyphoi and kylikes based on Protocorinthian types, olpai, plates, kantharoi and kyathoi with crested handles. Decoration also followed impasto techniques, being impressed, incised, stamped, relief and occasionally carved. Specific to Bucchero, however, are motifs of open and closed fans, and the 'diamond-point' notching that underlines carinations and relief cordons, both derived from metalwork. Towards the mid-7th century BC a workshop at Cerveteri produced relief decoration with human and animal figures, in clear imitation of metal embossed vases, with iconographic formulae taken from Syro-Phoenician models. The shapes on which such decoration appears include pyxides, situlae, kotylai, plates, kantharoi and kyathoi, and some of these have been found at Chiusi and even Vetulonia. Mid- to late-Orientalizing relief-decorated Bucchero was produced at Vulci, and possibly also in northern Etruria at Rusellae (Roselle) and Populonia. At Cerveteri some one-off commissions were produced, including the 'ink pot' inscribed with a syllabary (*c.* 650–*c.* 640 BC; Rome, Vatican, Mus. Gregoriano Etrus.) and the phiale from the Tomb of the Painted Lions (Rome, Villa Giulia) that, with its human heads, reproduces a prestigious Levantine metal type. Bucchero gradually acquired its own range of shapes, but new ones derived from ivory and metal vessels, or indeed from Protocorinthian, Transitional and Corinthian pottery (e.g. oinochoai, olpai, kylikes and aryballoi) and East Greek shapes (e.g. bird bowls), were constantly added.

The frieze-like incised decoration that was first produced at Cerveteri in the early 7th century BC derived from metal originals and featured an Orientalizing bestiary supplemented by horsemen, hunters, boxers, chariots and combat scenes, where influences from the Near East and, later, from Corinth are to be seen. Such decoration was also produced after *c.* 630 BC at Veii, Tarquinia and Vulci (see fig. 20). Some of these vases, particularly kantharoi, were exported at least as far afield as Naxos and Megara Hyblaea in Sicily, and Bucchero ware in general has been found throughout the Mediterranean region. Furthermore, it sometimes exerted its own morphological influence on Attic Black-figure vases, which were mainly exported in

20. Incised bucchero oinochoe showing a warrior on a chariot and hoplites, h. 280 mm, from Ischia di Castro, late 7th century BC–early 6th (Rome, Museo Nazionale di Villa Giulia e Soprintendenza alle Antichità per l'Etruria Meridionale)

Etruria (*see* GREECE, ANCIENT, §V, 5(ii)): amphorae produced in the workshops of NIKOSTHENES and Pamphaios around 530–510 BC clearly reflect a Caeretan shape of *c.* 575–*c.* 550 BC, with a stemmed foot, two relief cordons around the top half of the body, and a pair of band-shaped handles, vertically decorated with openwork or stamped animals. These were exported back to Cerveteri, and Nikosthenes' workshop also adapted both the high- and low-footed kyathos from Bucchero prototypes typical of Vulci, carefully imitating both the modelled projections at the top of the handle and the peculiar relief ornament inside it.

Transitional Bucchero was produced in Campania and probably Latium too. Towards the end of the 7th century BC a new technique of decoration was developed, and used primarily on chalices: carved wooden cylinders were run over the pot before firing. They impressed the negative areas of the desired design, resulting in small, shallow relief friezes, crudely executed, with simple motifs or a motley of schematic human and animal figures, the former seated, running, riding chariots, fighting, hunting or dancing. The technique persisted at Tarquinia up to the early 6th century BC and into the second half of the 6th century BC at Volsinii Veteres (Orvieto) and Chiusi.

The increased availability of imported Greek painted pottery during the Archaic period meant the relegation of Bucchero to ordinary domestic use, except in certain sanctuaries, where Bucchero vessels served cult purposes (e.g. a 'chest' dedicated to Menerva at the Portonaccio Sanctuary, Veii; Rome, Villa Giulia). The main shapes were oinochoai, including the beaked type, chalices, kantharoi (usually low-footed) and kyathoi. The influence of metal forms persisted, reasserting itself around the second quarter of the 6th century BC, first at Vulci and then at Tarquinia, Volsinii Veteres and especially Chiusi, with the manufacture of complete table services in heavy Bucchero with plastic decoration in the forms of human heads, 'acorns', animal protomes or relief motifs, clearly imitating contemporary bronzework. From the mid-6th century BC Bucchero undecorated plates, bowls and cups were widely made. Specialized vessels included 'filter' vases and libation cups. Occasionally, extra ornament was in the form of silver or gold foil, and polychrome decoration was painted after firing.

Northern Etruscan Bucchero had a more limited range of shapes and only local distribution. Decoration was dominated by geometric or linear motifs continuing the Iron Age tradition and small stamps with swastikas, rosettes, human and animal figures etc. Inland centres such as Chiusi and those in the Florence-Fiesole district produced from the late 7th century BC onwards chalices, kantharoi and kyathoi, and also perfume vases, alabastra, ring-askoi and kotyle-pyxides, with inscriptions attesting gift-exchange, and special objects such as the 'incense burner' or, more likely, lamp from Artimino (Artimino, Antiqua.), made up of a number of interlocking components and with an inscription denoting either its owner or maker. Although some imitations of southern Etruscan fine Bucchero with stamped figures were produced at Chiusi, most of the consistent output was heavy Bucchero, which, from the mid-6th to the beginning of the 5th century BC, had abundant modelled decoration, such as human masks, heads and figures of cocks and 'doves', and stamped relief ornament. The shapes made were predominantly local ones and only occasionally related to South Etruscan or Greek types: kraters, amphorae, hydriai, oinochoai, handled trays, foculi, simpula, infundibula, cylindrical stands, cups etc. The stamped relief ornaments, whether floral or figural, show Greek and some specifically Ionic influence.

5. RED WARE. A slightly purified impasto, granular in texture, with a blackish core and a shiny red surface, Red ware was used for stamped pithoi and braziers produced at Cerveteri and in the Caeretan hinterland from the late 7th century BC throughout the Archaic period to *c.* 500 BC. The pithoi are *c.* 700–900 mm high, with flat bases, flared mouths and ovoid bodies with vertical ribbing, bounded by relief cordons in such forms as zigzags, connected bows or double circles on the shoulders. Around the shoulder, and sometimes beneath the ribbing as well, there is often subsidiary decoration, whether stamped or cylinder-impressed. The braziers, in two typical sizes from 300 to 600 mm in diameter, have only cylinder-impressed ornament around the border. While pithoi were

food containers, braziers might be used for the presentation of cooked food. The stamped or cylinder-impressed decoration relates technically to that of both transitional and heavy Bucchero, and the variety of subjects is rich, including a wide range of both animal and human scenes. Horsemen, archers, hoplites, gorgoneia, centaurs and Acheloos all feature, showing clear late Orientalizing and Corinthian influence. In the more complex subjects (e.g. hunting, chariot-racing, banquets, sacrifices, Apollo and Tityos, Achilles and Troilos), Ionic influence is evident. At a lesser workshop at San Giovenale, in Caeretan territory at this time, the owner added his name, Larice Crepu, to the stamped decoration. At Cerveteri, a good deal of pithoi and braziers was found in both the settlement site and the necropolis; they have also been found at Pyrgi, Tuscania and various settlements in the Mignone Valley, the Tolfa Hills and the area around Lake Bracciano, and, less frequently, at Veii, Tarquinia, Graviaca and Vulci.

6. ETRUSCO-CORINTHIAN. Southern Etruscan pottery was copiously produced in imitation of Protocorinthian and Corinthian vases imported into Etruria from the 8th century BC to the first half of the 6th. It was in its own turn exported, both within central Italy and to other Mediterranean sites. Its initial phase (*c.* 630–*c.* 600 BC) shows shapes and decoration influenced by late Protocorinthian and Transitional, with the familiar filling motif of dot-rosettes. One of the Dot-rosette group artists, the Bearded Sphinx Painter, may have trained at Corinth, and was active at Vulci, being attributed with the decoration of more than 100 vases. He is notable not only for his predilection for the masculine sphinx, but also for his animal friezes; his dot-rosettes gradually degenerated into mere blobs and discs. His rare narrative scenes include the *Sack of Troy* on an oinochoe (Paris, Bib. N., 179), and warriors and chariots on an olpe (Ischia di Castro, Antiquarium Com. Pietro Lotti). He decorated mostly olpai and oinochoai, with a few alabastra, amphorae and large amphorae of the 'scale' type (*anforoni squamati*; see below). His contemporary, the Swallow Painter, also active at Vulci, was from East Greece and has been ascribed ten vases including oinochoai, olpai, amphorae, an alabastron and a large kylix similar to the Type A Ionic cup. He painted files of steinbock and geese and subsidiary decoration, essentially East Greek designs drawn from the Wild Goat style, to which he added some elements from the local repertory. At Cerveteri many large amphorae with scale decoration were produced between *c.* 620 and *c.* 590 BC. These have animal decoration of Late Protocorinthian–Transitional Protocorinthian type yielding to that of early Corinthian, with its files and heraldic schemata. Below these animal friezes, expansive areas of scales were incised on a dark background, although this repetitive format was occasionally altered by the Pilgrim Flask Painter, who sometimes included human subjects, for example in a hunting scene (see fig. 21).

In the last quarter of the 7th century BC the Etrusco-Corinthian Black-figure technique coexisted with the more widely practised polychrome technique involving incised figures, almost invariably animals, on a brownish surface glaze, heightened by white and purple overpaint. This technique is related to the incised decoration employed at

21. Etrusco-Corinthian dinos by the Pilgrim Flask Painter, showing a hunting scene, h. 273 mm, *c.* 620–*c.* 590 BC (Basle, Antikenmuseum)

the same time in Bucchero and impasto, and possibly also metalwork. It is exemplified by the Polychrome group of vases, made at Veii, Cerveteri and Vulci. At Veii the Castellani Painter painted small vases, preferring the piriform aryballos; at Cerveteri the style was applied to amphorae with large but incoherent figures by the Monte Abatone cycle; slightly later, at Vulci, the main centre of Black-figure production, artists such as the Pescia Romana Painter, the manneristic Painter of the Polychrome Bows and the Garovaglio Painter used some polychrome decoration. During the early 6th century BC simple linear or floral polychrome decoration was used for a relatively wide range of vases.

The middle phase of Etrusco-Corinthian (*c.* 600–*c.* 560 BC) was marked by the predominance of Vulci and the development of an industry to meet growing demand. The range of shapes was extended, with olpai remaining the most popular, while ring-askoi and kraters are very few. Modelled balsamaries in many forms (e.g. monkey, fawn, dead hare, swan, head of Acheloos, eagle's head, human leg, porcupine, piglet) came into vogue, inspired by East Greek and Corinthian models. Among the many groups of pottery identified from this period are the Olpai and Rosoni cycles. All employed repetitive animal friezes and filling motifs, but some exceptional pieces exist, including a krater by the Painter of the Rosoni Kraters depicting *Herakles and Alkyoneus* (Paris, Louvre, E631) and a krater (Cerveteri, Mus. N. Cerite) with *Herakles Stealing the Cattle of Geryon* and, possibly, the *Sacrifice of Polyxena*. The Feoli Painter depicted some of the few human subjects of Etrusco-Corinthian, notably a male and female couple (olpe; Turin priv. col.; see Szilágyi, 1992, pl. 82). The bilingual Pescia Romana Painter was distinguished by vigorous and fluid drawing, and the Boehlau Painter produced exuberant and undisciplined work. The Carnage Painter and the Wolf Heads Painter apparently initiated production at Tarquinia, where the Vitelleschi group, the Grasmere group and the 'Senza Graffito' Painter and his workshop specialized in plates, phialai and bowls from *c.* 590 to *c.* 560 BC.

During the third and final phase of Etrusco-Corinthian (*c.* 560–*c.* 540 BC) fewer small-scale vases such as cups, alabastra, globular aryballoi and plastic balsamaries were decorated and the formulae derived from the Vulci workshops in the preceding phase were rigidly applied. The Bobuda Painter, one of the 'Little Masters', was an uninspired imitator of the Pescia Romana Painter, and the Human Mask group simply transferred to Cerveteri and brought to an end the Rosoni group. Also possibly from Cerveteri were the artisans of one of the latest groups, the Heraldic Cocks cycle, which, with the Bird cycle, produced the banal stereotypes that marked the end of the Etrusco-Corinthian.

7. BLACK-FIGURE. Etruscan Black-figure ware was produced from *c.* 550 to *c.* 480 BC, and coincided with the highest percentage of importation of Athenian Black-figure and Red-figure (*see* GREECE, ANCIENT, §V, 5(ii) and 6(i) respectively). It was probably introduced by East Greek immigrants, who came to Vulci from the early 6th century BC, though in much greater numbers after the Persian invasions in the East. Their presence explains the exclusively Etruscan provenance of Caeretan hydriai and dinoi of the Campana group, and the Ionic quality of some Etruscan tomb paintings from 540–500 BC. The first phase (*c.* 550–*c.* 520 BC) is notable for the Pontic style developed by the Paris Painter and his followers. Over 200 vases are attributed to the Pontic painters, who were apparently based at Vulci and included the Paris Painter, the Amphiaraos Painter, the Tityos Painter, the Silen Painter and the Painter of Bibliothèque Nationale 178. They specialized in neck-amphorae, influenced by the 'Tyrrhenian' amphorae produced in Attica from *c.* 575 to *c.* 550 BC, mainly for the Etruscan market. They adopted the Tyrrhenian partitioning of the vase-space: a shoulder scene often depicting Greek myths (e.g. Herakles episodes connected with Troy and Thebes cycles), while the body of the vase was filled with animal files and friezes of subsidiary ornament, such as partridges, meanders, stars, ivy leaves and lotus buds. The effect is fluid and eclectic and shows strong North Ionic influence, such as the Caeretan painted plaques and Archaic architectural terracottas. The genre scenes include departure and arming, the hunt, horsemen, fights, symposia and centaurs. The shape range may have been influenced by local Bucchero, and includes chalices, kantharoi, kyathoi, oinochoai, lydia, plates, and also types that were uncommon, such as hydriai, nikosthenic amphorae, phialai and dinoi.

The Ivy Leaf group and the La Tolfa group, at Vulci and Cerveteri respectively, are slightly later. The Ivy Leaf group, named after a decorative motif frequently used, includes more than 50 vases, mostly Type B amphorae. Greek themes appear on both sides of these amphorae (often involving Dionysos, but also Herakles, Bellerophon and Odysseus), and apotropaic eyes, dancers and animals also occur. The predominant influence is that of Attic Black-figure, in particular the work of the AFFECTER and the AMASIS PAINTER (for both *see* VASE PAINTERS, §II). The La Tolfa workshop, to which some 30 vases have been attributed, produced neck-amphorae influenced by the North Ionic or 'clazomenian' winged, running figures, animals and hippocamps, as well as rare mythological

22. Black-figure hydria by the Micali Painter: *Apotheosis of Herakles*, h. 520 mm, *c.* 510–*c.* 500 BC (Florence, Museo Archeologico di Firenze)

scenes (e.g. Achilles and Troilos). The style is monumental and may owe something to the Caeretan hydriai.

In the second phase of production (*c.* 530–*c.* 500 BC) the Micali Painter ran a workshop, again at Vulci. His work shows signs of early contact with the Pontic painters, but clearly soon developed its own idiom of fantastic themes dominated by sphinxes and sirens. He painted athletes (see fig. 5 above), chariot-racing and, occasionally, mythological subjects including Herakles (see fig. 22), Achilles and Troilos, and the *Suicide of Ajax*. His mature style reveals a more conscious study of contemporary Attic style, with more added white and subsidiary vase-space filled with palmette florals. Among his followers the Painter of Vatican 238 is notable for his hydria depicting the *Transformation of the Tyrrhenian Pirates into Dolphins* (Toledo, OH, Mus. A., 82.134).

A third phase (*c.* 500–*c.* 480 BC) is characterized by shoddier work, only dependent on Attic models of the late 6th and beginning of the 5th century and manufactured at Vulci, Volsinii Veteres and Chiusi. Some of the painters who trained at Vulci may have set up the inland workshops as well as others in Campania. The uniform conventionality of these products makes attribution difficult. There are rarely more than three figures and ornament is restricted to palmette chains and lotus buds, all executed mostly in silhouette, with touches of white. The subject-matter is unambitious. More than 100 vases can be assigned variously to the Painter of Munich 892, the group of Munich 883 and the group of Vatican 265, with many more still unattributed. The Orvieto group is distinguished by the

coarse vigour of its style. It can be divided into patterned vases (geometricizing and floral decoration on chalices, plates, oinochoai and stamnoi) and vases with figural decoration, rarely mythological, ultimately inspired by Attic models. Minor groups include the local Chiusi pyxides, two non-figural groups of vases from Vulci, the 'Dot-wreath plates', and the bowls and plates of the Spurinas group, the latter with pre-fired onomastic inscriptions. Finally, the more individualistic work of the Painter of the Dancing Satyrs, probably active at Caere, includes depictions of satyrs and actors impersonating satyrs, the *Killing of the Minotaur* with Herakles, not Theseus, as the hero, and the instruction of the armed dance.

8. RED-FIGURE. The earliest examples are not strictly Red-figure but applied red painting and belong to the Praxias group, named from a signature on one amphora (Paris, Bib. N., 913). Arnthe Praxias was probably a Greek artisan naturalized in Etruria, active at Vulci from *c.* 480 to *c.* 460 BC. Some 80 vases are ascribed to the Praxias group, distributed well into the Etruscan inland (Volsinii Veteres, Chiusi). These may not all have come from a single workshop, but they share a common dependence on Late Archaic Attic style, and the inscriptions that occur for mythological subjects are in Greek.

Red-figure proper did not fully develop in Etruria until the end of the 5th century BC or the beginning of the 4th, a generation after the rise of the South Italian Red-figure workshops. In the first of its phases (*c.* 400–*c.* 350 BC) production centred at Civita Castellana (Falerii), Vulci and in northern Etruria; from Civita Castellana about 300 vases survive. Late Attic influence, especially that of the Meleager Painter and Jena Painter, is evident in the kylikes. Kraters and stamnoi show Attic floridness and intricacy, with a basic repertory of Dionysiac and erotic subjects. As the Faliscan style evolved, it absorbed elements of South Italian, notably Apulian vase painting, as in the work of the Aurora Painter and the Nazzano Painter. Vases believed to be from Vulci are less easy to classify. The large-scale vases of the Painter of London F 484, the Vatican Biga Painter and the Perugia Painter seem influenced by the work of the MEIDIAS PAINTER (*see* VASE PAINTERS, §II), but curious archaizing also occurs (Rodin kylix, Vich amphora). Overall, however, the dominant influence is South Italian, whether in the accessory decoration or in the subjects of the main scenes (see fig. 23). A South Italian theatricality is evident in the work of the Poggio Sommavilla Painter (e.g. Oedipus, satyr dramas), the Paestan-style stamnoi of the Settecamini Painter and the Campanizing group vases. Workshops in northern inland Etruria produced smaller vases, in particular kylikes, decorated with stock figures derived from late 5th-century BC Attic vases. One such painter, Pheziu Paveś, signed before firing a cup found at Grotti, near Siena (Siena, Mus. Archeol.).

In the second phase (*c.* 350–*c.* 300 BC) a marked increase in quantity occurred, as some workshops began to specialize in funerary vases. Quality, however, declined, with one or two exceptions. Workshops proliferated at Civita Castellana, Cerveteri, Tarquinia, Vulci, Volsinii Veteres, Chiusi and Volterra. At Civita Castellana and Cerveteri, a repetitive series of vases was produced featuring Dionysiac

23. Red-figure krater (the 'Argonaut krater'), h. 395 mm, early 4th century BC (Florence, Museo Archeologico di Firenze)

or erotic subjects or simply female heads. The Caeretan vases were distributed to Liguria, Gaul, Corsica, Sardinia, Carthage, Malta, Cyrene and elsewhere. At Vulci funerary themes predominated, for example the kraters of the Funnel group. From c. 330 to c. 300 BC the decorative style became less rigid. The Clusium group is perhaps the most representative of later Etruscan Red-figure: it includes at least five painters, who concentrated at first on kylikes decorated with Dionysiac subjects but then extended their repertory to large funerary vases (calyx kraters) as well as askoi and skyphoi. In the later phase compositions were more complex. At Volterra the Hesione Painter specialized in kelebai and stamnoi for cinerary purposes, and was followed by lesser Red-figure painters active into the early 3rd century BC (e.g. Asciano Painter and Pygmy Trumpeter Painter).

9. BLACK-GLAZE. Black-glaze ware was widely produced in Etruria from the mid-4th century BC, after import of Attic pottery had halted. As in Apulia, the vases were only occasionally decorated with added paint, and so classification depends on clay and glaze features and shape. The shapes produced range from vases for large domestic services to miniaturistic votive vessels, made in both southern and northern Etruria. At Volterra the fine Malacena class vases were produced in a beige-pink clay coated with an ink-blue glaze obviously intended to imitate metal vases. These were distributed throughout northern Etruria and Corsica. Overpainted decoration was less common than relief decoration, but the Sienese workshop produced many kylikes with painted ornament, and the Ferrara T 585 group specialized in skyphoi with a swan between floral motifs or with palmettes. There is evidence that Red-figure painters worked on Black-glaze overpainted vases: a Black-glaze kelebe is attributable to the Asciano Painter, one of the later masters of Volterran Red figure. Production of Black-glaze continued up to c. 200 BC, with lesser centres established at Arezzo, Rusellae, Vulci-Sovana and Bolsena.

Overpainted Black-glaze fabrics from the south include the Sokra group at Civita Castellana, named from a Greek signature on a kylix, workshops at Tarquinia, and the Phantom group at Cerveteri (c. 300–c. 280 BC), specializing in oinochoai with a single figure. But by the early 3rd century BC Rome was becoming the dominant presence: the Roman cups of the 'Atelier des petites estampilles' were widely distributed throughout Etruria, and *pocola deorum* ('cups of the gods') with polychrome overpainted decoration, were also distributed in Etruria. The Hesse group of vases, produced perhaps at Vulci in the early 3rd century BC, marks the end of local figured pottery production.

BIBLIOGRAPHY

Å. Åkerström: *Der geometrische Stil in Italien* (Lund-Leipzig, 1943)
J. D. Beazley: *Etruscan Vase-painting* (Oxford, 1947)
G. Camporeale: *Buccheri a cilindretto di fabbrica orvietana* (Florence, 1972)
M. Bonamici: *I buccheri con figurazioni graffite* (Florence, 1974)
F. Canciani: *Corpus Vasorum Antiquorum Italia*, LV/iii (Rome, 1974)
L. Hannestad: *The Paris Painter* (Copenhagen, 1974)
J. G. Szilágyi: *Etruszko-korinthosi vázafestészet* (Budapest, 1975)
L. Hannestad: *The Followers of the Paris Painter* (Copenhagen, 1976)
T. B. Rasmussen: *Bucchero Pottery from Southern Etruria* (Cambridge, 1979)
J.-P. Morel: *Céramique campanienne, les formes* (Rome, 1981)
J. M. Hemelrijk: *Caeretan Hydriae* (Mainz, 1984)
M. Cristofani, ed.: *Contributi alla ceramica etrusca tardo-classica* (Rome, 1985)
B. Adembri: *La più antica ceramografia falisca a figure rosse* (Rome, 1987)
S. S. Leach: *Sub-geometric Pottery from Southern Etruria* (Göteborg, 1987)
M. Martelli, ed.: *La ceramica degli Etruschi: La pittura vascolare* (Novara, 1987)
N. J. Spivey: *The Micali Painter and his Followers* (Oxford, 1987)
Un artista etrusco e il suo mondo: Il Pittore di Micali (Rome, 1988)
L. Cerchiai: *Le officine etrusco-corinzie di Pontecagnano* (Naples, 1990)
J. G. Szilágyi: *Ceramica etrusco-corinzia figurata, Parte I: 630–580 a.C.* (Florence, 1992)
M. Micozzi: *'White-on-Red': Una produzione vascolare dell'orientalizzante etrusco* (Rome, 1994)

MARINA MARTELLI

V. Painting.

The sheer quantity of extant Etruscan painting, from the 7th to the 2nd century BC, on tombs and terracotta slabs, makes it unique in Classical art.

1. Introduction. 2. Techniques and conservation. 3. Subsidiary ornament. 4. Subject-matter. 5. Historical survey.

1. INTRODUCTION. Most equivalent Greek painting has perished, although such examples as do survive suggest that its thematic and stylistic features can be related to contemporary Etruscan work. Detailed study of paintings on Greek vases, many of which were deposited in Etruscan tombs, has helped to establish the chronology of Etruscan wall painting.

How far Etruscan painting reflects the innovations of the great Greek painters, such as Polygnotos of Thasos, Zeuxis and Parrhasios, is uncertain. Ironically, while the names of the Greek artists survive, along with detailed descriptions of their works, their paintings have disappeared entirely. Conversely, although no Etruscan painter's name is known and no Etruscan painting is described in contemporary literature, many original works remain. The only possible ancient allusion to Etruscan painting occurs in Pliny (*Natural History* XXXV.xliii.152), who related that three craftsmen accompanied the Corinthian Demaratos when he settled in Etruria. One of these, Eugrammos ('the good draughtsman') sounds like a painter, even though Pliny actually credited the trio with the introduction of sculpture to Etruria. Significantly, Pliny went on to refer to Damophilus and Gorgasus, the artists who decorated the Roman Temple of Ceres in the Circus Maximus, as renowned sculptors and painters, implying early links between terracotta sculpture and painting. Otherwise, Pliny only recorded that he admired some 'extremely old' paintings in buildings at Ardea, Lanuvium and Cerveteri (Caere), without giving details (*Natural History* XXXV.vi.17–18).

Etruscan painting helps towards an understanding of wider developments in Classical art, but its location in religious and burial sites makes it primarily valuable in reconstructing the socio-religious history of Etruria itself, including details of funerary rituals, changes in beliefs in the afterlife and the status of those who commissioned the paintings. Only a small proportion of Etruscan tombs are painted, which implies that they were confined to the wealthy élite. There is evidence that paintings also adorned Etruscan sanctuaries, but almost all that survive occur on the walls of rock-cut family tombs (*see* §II, 1 and fig. 7 above).

Most of the painted tombs occur in southern Etruria, at Veii, Cerveteri, Tarquinia, Vulci, Volsinii Veteres (Orvieto) and moreover at Chiusi (Clusium), with isolated examples in San Giuliano, Blera, Orte and elsewhere. There are significant regional variations in both quantity and date. The oldest extant fresco occurs in the Tomb of the Ducks (*c.* 680–*c.* 670 BC), at Veii. The painted tombs at Tarquinia are all later, but they are far more numerous than at any other site, so that the history of Etruscan tomb painting is largely a history of Tarquinian tomb painting. The tombs discussed below are all Tarquinian, unless stated otherwise. At Tarquinia itself the painted tombs belong to a single necropolis on the Monterozzi hillside, which has attracted attention at least since the Middle Ages (*see* §VIII below).

Tomb paintings should ideally be viewed in their original setting. The Tarquinian tombs themselves were reached by way of a staircase and dromos (passageway) leading via a vestibule to the main rectangular or squarish chamber. In the Archaic and Classical periods this rarely exceeded 14 sq. m in area, and it contained two or three funeral couches. However, in the 4th and 3rd centuries BC the main chambers became larger and sometimes had pillars, and they were supplemented by further rooms. This reflected the development of the concept of an extended family and the internal layout of the houses of the living. Inscriptions in such tombs often specify family links and provide evidence for dating. Tomb robbing at Tarquinia and elsewhere left few intact tombs, so that the chronology of Etruscan painting is based more on stylistic than on archaeological evidence.

2. TECHNIQUES AND CONSERVATION. Tomb paintings are especially vulnerable when accessible to the public and their effective conservation involves detailed study of how they were executed. In the earliest tombs the paintings were made directly on the smoothed rock walls of the burial chamber. However, most Etruscan paintings are a form of fresco, which was applied in various stages. First, the soft volcanic tufa in which the tombs were cut was roughened and prepared for the application of plaster. This was made of clay and powdered stone, and was often coated with a final layer of lime wash. The plaster varied in thickness, tending to be thinner in Archaic tombs (*c.* 575–*c.* 480 BC). Coated plaster was also used to fill cracks in the rock, but it was not usually applied to ceilings. The origins of the technique are uncertain, but the admixture of peat and plaster, as in the Tomb of the Chariots at Tarquinia (*c.* 490 BC) also occurred in Asia Minor and Mesopotamia. The damp underground conditions and the use of a lime wash, which reacted with groundwater, created a constant level of humidity and paintings could thus be executed without any interruption in the process (unlike later fresco techniques).

The basic decorative scheme on tomb walls consists of three horizontal zones: an upper panel of geometric motifs; a large central zone bearing the principal figural frieze, which occupies about two-thirds of the height of the wall; and a base line. Cords soaked in paint were used to define each area. The figures in the main frieze were first sketched or incised in outline. Cartoons may sometimes have been used as models, as was probably the case for the drawing of the boxers on the Tomb of the Monkey, Chiusi (*c.* 480–*c.* 470 BC), where the artist possibly reversed a cartoon to produce identical profiles for both fighters. Some figures were apparently sketched in red outline with inner details, especially clothing, picked out, and many were clearly painted freehand. Once outlined, the figures were filled with broad brushstrokes, while the outline itself was often improved. When this colouring in was completed, both the inner details and the outlines were revised with a black outline, and at this stage a 'master' probably took over, if assistants had been responsible for other aspects of the work. Artists probably worked from 'pattern books' with figures sketched on a small scale. In the Archaic period the craftsmen who painted vases sometimes also decorated tombs, and it is possible to observe that they were accustomed to painting smaller surfaces, such as vases.

The Archaic and Classical painters, in particular, used a restricted palette of white, yellow, black, red, blue and green, with some intermediate tones. Some pigments were easy to obtain (e.g. red from earth containing oxidized iron); others, which were used more sparingly, had to be imported. Thus blue was made from an artificial compound known as Egyptian frit, traces of which have been found at Gravisca, the ancient port of Tarquinia.

Decorating a tomb cannot have taken more than a few days. Paintings may not have been commissioned until after a death by members of the deceased's family, to be completed during the *prothesis* (lying in state).

Etruscan painting techniques underwent certain changes between the 7th and the 2nd century BC. The most important was the shift from Archaic and Classical colour-based painting to a Hellenistic system based on light and shadow. Greek influence resulted in the use of crosshatching (e.g. Orcus Tomb II; *c.* 375–*c.* 350 BC), chiaroscuro highlighting (e.g. Tomb of the Charuns; *c.* 250–*c.* 200 BC), the 'stain' process (e.g. Tomb of the Garlands; *c.* 300–*c.* 250 BC) and the use of swift brushstrokes to paint figures (e.g. later frieze of the Tomb of the Cardinal; *c.* 240 BC). References in Pliny (*Natural History* XXXV.xxxvi.110) and Petronius (*Satyricon* II.ix) to Roman *picturae compendiariae* (shorthand methods of painting) have led some scholars to describe late Etruscan painting as 'impressionistic'.

The conservation of tomb paintings is problematic. Insects, plant roots and micro-organisms can cause extensive damage, but changes in humidity are the most crucial factor. Damp, caused by groundwater infiltration as well as condensation, can make the paintings swell and the plaster come away from the rock, while dryness causes flaking of pigments and plaster and surface growths of crystalline salts. Thus the tombs need to be kept at constant temperatures. Even short visits by small groups of people can have dramatic effects on their microclimates. Thus, restoration involves not only fixing the colours of the paintings but also coating them with a protective film, as at the Tomb of the Augurs (*c.* 530–*c.* 520 BC) and the Tomb of Hunting and Fishing (*c.* 520–*c.* 510 BC), among others. Previously, the only effective remedy was to transfer the paintings to museums, as in the case of the Tomb of the Chariots, the Tomb of the Olympic Games (*c.* 530–*c.* 520 BC), the Tomb of the Triclinium (*c.* 470 BC), the Tomb of the Funeral Couch (*c.* 460 BC), the Tomb of the Black Sow (*c.* 460 BC), the Tomb of the Ship (mid-5th century BC) and the Bruschi Tomb (3rd century BC; all Tarquinia, Pal. Vitelleschi).

3. SUBSIDIARY ORNAMENT. A continuous series of tomb paintings at Tarquinia from the second half of the 6th century BC onwards provides vital evidence for the general characteristics of funerary decoration. Subsidiary ornament served two main functions, emphasizing the architectural structure of the tomb and breaking up the wall space into distinct areas. The latter is achieved by the series of polychrome bands above the main figural frieze, and the further polychrome bands, or dado, that form a base line below it. Sometimes the dado is accompanied by figural decoration, such as dolphins leaping over a wave pattern.

24. Wall painting with banquet scene, Tomb of the Leopards, Tarquinia, *c.* 480–*c.* 470 BC

The sloping ceilings of the tombs were sometimes untreated, or simply whitewashed, but often they were painted. The decoration may consist merely of bands of red and white, imitating rafters, or it may take the form of chequers or small floral motifs, petals, dots and circles on a white background, probably based on textile designs. The fake ridge beam (*columen*) was simply painted on in red, but sometimes it was decorated with large discs and bands running lengthways.

The front and back walls of the tombs provided three decorative areas: dado, main frieze and 'pediment'. The latter was divided into two parts by a fake king-post under the end of the *columen*. The king-post's outer corners may be filled with volutes and circles and sometimes animal protomes, while the body of the pediment depicts either heraldic animals (lions, panthers, hippocamps, and deer being savaged by felines) or banqueting scenes. The long triangular space suits the recumbent figures of banqueters, but creates problems of consistency of scale. In some tombs (e.g. the Tomb of the Leopards; *c.* 480–*c.* 470 BC) the painted king-post is omitted, while the lower pitch of Hellenistic roofs meant that the pediment was then no longer decorated.

Some tombs contain more elaborate painted architectural elements. The Tomb of the Lionesses (*c.* 520 BC), for example, has six decorative Tuscan columns at its corners and in the middle of its side walls, rising from floor to ceiling. Some Classical tombs (e.g. Tomb of the Triclinium and Tomb of the Black Sow) have vines painted on their roofs and pediments, and painted props for a bower or pergola at their corners. The Tomb of the Funeral Couch is festooned with painted drapes, while the Tomb of the Hunter (*c.* 500 BC) resembles a tent, so that both probably mimic the awnings and temporary structures that covered the corpse during the *prothesis* and apparently sheltered the guests at the funeral banquet.

4. SUBJECT-MATTER. From the late 6th century BC to the early 4th, the content of Etruscan tomb paintings remained fairly consistent. Since they were closely associated with funerary ceremonies which were themselves the prerogative of aristocratic families, they probably represented both a form of perpetuated homage and an emblematic assertion of status. Certain themes had particularly strong symbolic values. The banquet was one of the most often repeated, especially during the 5th century BC (see fig. 24). The theme of the banquet may relate not only to funeral feasts but also to the Etruscan love of 'luxury' in general. Ancient sources are confirmed by the subject-matter of the tomb paintings: Diodorus Siculus might almost have been describing one of these when he wrote:

> They spread their tables for sumptuous meals twice daily, so that the tables groan with the weight of the luxurious fare, while they are shaded by canopies woven with flowers. The services are of solid silver, and the banqueters are waited on by countless slaves, some remarkable for their beauty, others for their lavish costumes. (*Historical Library* V.xl.3)

Typically, banquet scenes show between one and five couches, each bearing two recumbent banqueters. The couches are elaborate, with finely turned legs and embroidered covers. In front of them are small stands for the diners' sandals. The youths in attendance are naked or in loincloths, and hurry to and fro with jugs of wine, filled from large kraters on tables in the corner. Under the couches, domestic animals (e.g. dogs, cats, pigeons, hens and sometimes more exotic felines) wait for scraps of food. The banqueters, wearing garlands and intricately decorated cloaks, lie propped on cushions. They are shown talking, eating, drinking and playing *kottabos*, a messy game which involved flicking wine from a cup into a saucer balanced on a bronze stand. Both sexes participated at these banquets, a fact that aroused the indignation of the Greeks and Romans, who regarded it as a sign of immorality in Etruscan women, who were also reputed to be formidable drinkers. However, it actually reflects the higher legal status enjoyed by Etruscan women, who could inherit property in their own right in the absence of a male heir.

The 'banquet' in tomb paintings usually represents not the feast itself but the symposion that followed it, when guests drank, sang and talked under the supervision of a master of ceremonies. Thus minstrels are depicted beside the couches, usually playing some form of lyre or flute. Again this corroborates ancient literary sources, which not only credit the Etruscans with the invention of certain instruments, but state that they did everything to musical accompaniment, including boxing, kneading bread and even beating their slaves.

Dancing also occurs frequently, either as an element in the funerary ceremonies or simply as part of the general festivities. Dancers in fine costumes and apparently performing the *tripudium* (three-step jig) sometimes seem from inscriptions to be not 'actors' but members of aristocratic families. Whenever the inner wall of a tomb is taken up by the main symposion scene, the side walls are painted with dancing figures, sometimes alternating with trees and shrubs.

The iconography of Etruscan banquets derives from representations of symposia on Athenian vases, while the banquet in its ideological aspects may be Near Eastern in origin. Another funerary ritual often depicted in Etruscan tombs is the athletic contest held in honour of the dead. This may have originated in prehistoric times and the events involved are similar to those described at the funeral of Patroklos (*Iliad* XXIII). Scenes of boxing predominate, and though the combatants sometimes perform to flute music, these are brutally vivid: one competitor in the Tomb of the Funeral Couch is offered a sponge to mop up a spectacular nose-bleed. Wrestling also occurs, as in the Tomb of the Augurs, and bronze bowls or tripods are shown as prizes. Running, long-jumping and discus-throwing appear in the Tomb of the Olympic Games, so-called both for this reason and because it was discovered shortly before the 1960 Rome Olympics. This tomb also features a race between four chariots: the leading charioteer is shown glancing back over his shoulder to assess the size of his lead or to watch a dangerous crash involving the last chariot. The Tomb of the Chariots depicts preparations for a similar race, with grooms and judges milling about. Some spectators sit attentively on the canopied grandstand, while others make love underneath

25. Wall painting with hunting and fishing scene, Tomb of Hunting and Fishing, Tarquinia, *c.* 510 BC

it. The Etruscan armed dance, midway between ballet and athletics, was related to the Greek Pyrrhic dance and the Roman dance of the Salii. It is depicted in the Tomb of the Funeral Couch, where the dancer has a mantle knotted about his chest and wears a plumed helmet, while similar dancers appear in the Tomb of the Monkey and the Poggio al Moro Tomb (*c.* 480–*c.* 470 BC) at Chiusi.

Certain games in Etruscan tomb paintings suggest country fêtes rather than athletic competitions; for example the tug-of-war depicted on the entrance wall of the Tomb of the Augurs, and the quoit-throwing and balancing acts that give its name to the Tomb of the Jugglers (*c.* 520–*c.* 510 BC). Various equestrian sports are also depicted, as might be expected given the social prestige attached to horse ownership. Riders demonstrate their prowess by leaping from one galloping horse to another. Hunting also features as a sport of the Etruscan aristocracy, the pursuit of fierce prey giving ideal opportunities for displaying courage and practising military skills. According to one literary source (Athenaeus: *Deipnosophists* I.xviii.1), Macedonian youths had to hunt wild boar alone and without nets or traps, as a rite of passage before being admitted to the banqueting table, and the same custom may have been followed in Etruria. Boar hunts are vividly depicted in the Tomb of the Black Sow and the Querciola I Tomb (*c.* 450 BC), which show beaters and hounds along with hunters on horseback and on foot. The return from the hunt is shown on the pediment of the first room of the Tomb of Hunting and Fishing. The mounted hunters are followed by pairs of valets carrying the carcasses slung on poles. In one corner a dog worries a hare. In the second room youths are shown aiming slingshots at flocks of multicoloured birds and lowering nets into the sea from a boat (see fig. 25).

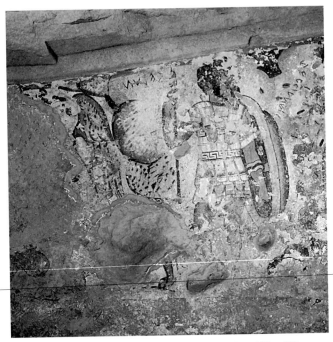

26. Wall painting with *Geryon*, Orcus Tomb II, Tarquinia, *c.* 375–*c.* 350 BC

Representations of the aristocratic way of life predominated during the Archaic and Classical periods, but the subject-matter favoured in tomb paintings changed markedly in the Hellenistic period, with vivid depictions of the underworld. The walls of the Orcus Tomb II (see fig. 26) are covered with paintings of the gods and heroes of Hades, and in the Golini Tomb I at Volsinii Veteres (*c.* 350 BC) they even participate in the funerary banquet. This is apparently meant to be located in the underworld, and from about this time ceases to feature in painted tombs and is transferred instead to the decoration of cinerary urns and sarcophagi. The banquet was replaced in tomb painting by more explicit emblems of status, such as magisterial insignia, files of toga-clad figures led by lictors, and inscriptions listing public offices held by the deceased. The inscriptions are sometimes so extensive that they cover the walls of an entire room; they include genealogies and may be accompanied by portraits, creating a detailed record of the family's achievements. The change in subject-matter may stem in part from the vicissitudes of Etruscan politics during the 5th and 4th centuries BC, and partly from the spread of Orphic–Pythagorean doctrines concerning the afterlife. The latter clearly influenced the decoration of Orcus Tomb II, which shows small souls scattered among the asphodels.

At this time, some aristocratic families apparently died out, while other, new names came to the fore and the painted tombs became a means of asserting acquired political and social status. Good examples of this are the Pumpu family with the Tomb of the Typhon (first half of the second century BC; *see* ITALY, fig. 26) and the eponymous Aninas family with its tomb used for a long period (3rd century BC). Etruscan tomb painting eventually ceased altogether when even these families' fortunes waned after the Roman conquest of Etruria (3rd century BC).

5. HISTORICAL SURVEY.

(i) *c.* 675–*c.* 500 BC. (ii) *c.* 500–*c.* 150 BC.

(i) c. 675–c. 500 BC. Orientalizing tombs of the 7th century BC mark the beginning of Etruscan painting. The earliest example is the Tomb of the Ducks at Veii, which depicts a file of five ducks painted in a style so close to that of Italo-Geometric vase painting that it may be by a vase painter, especially since close connections existed between Archaic tomb painting and vase painting. However, the late 7th-century BC Campana Tomb, also at Veii, is more significant. The end wall of the first of its two rooms is covered with registers of men, animals and monsters, with an abundant filling of floral and geometric designs. The second room contains six painted shields, which imitate the huge bronze shields frequently hung on tomb walls. The paintings are now faded, but watercolours by Luigi Canina suggest that they recalled Corinthian and Etrusco-Corinthian vase painting in both composition and colour. Several painted tombs of the 7th century BC occur at Cerveteri, but again they are poorly preserved. Their subjects were typical of the Orientalizing style: animal friezes containing lions, panthers, dogs, deer, dolphins, griffins, centaurs and sphinxes. The sarcophagus (*in situ*) in the Tomb of the Painted Animals (*c.* 650–*c.* 625 BC) had similar decoration to that on the tomb walls. In the Tomb of the Painted Lions (*c.* 650–*c.* 625 BC) the animal friezes included a 'Master of the Beasts' standing between two white-and-red lions, and, finally, the coeval Tomb of the Ship I (not the 5th-century BC tomb of the same name at Tarquinia) had an unusually early representation of a ship. Further Orientalizing tombs occur in various places, including Chiusi, San Giuliano, Cosa and Magliano.

Caeretan plaques are a separate but related development in the 6th century BC. These are a series of painted rectangular terracotta plaques from Cerveteri, measuring *c.* 1200×600 mm, which were once attached to the walls of sacred buildings or tombs to make a unified frieze. Some may have been transferred from buildings to tombs, since one has been sawn to fit its tomb's sloping roof. The technique used in decorating the plaques resembles vase painting: a stylus was used to incise the bands of decoration and figures on the white ground. The tops of the plaques may be painted with a frieze of tongues, guilloches or meanders and the bases are usually decorated with vertical two-tone stripes. Some of the earliest group (*c.* 560 BC; Rome, Villa Giulia) have two figural friezes, while others depict the Gorgons fleeing after Perseus' killing of Medusa. Of the five funerary Boccanera slabs (*c.* 560–*c.* 550 BC; London, BM), two show squatting sphinxes, while the remaining three each depict three figures. The identity of these is uncertain and interpretation depends largely on the order in which the plaques are juxtaposed. The Judgement of Paris is one possible subject, but at least two slabs may depict a funerary rite. Stylistically, they already show Ionic influence. The final group (*c.* 530–*c.* 520 BC; Paris, Louvre) were clumsily restored, and one may not even be authentic. Their subject is again uncertain, though the presence of an altar with a fire on it suggests a sacrifice scene.

The great period of Etruscan tomb painting began in the mid-6th century BC, although it was anticipated at Tarquinia by the Tomb of the Panthers (*c*. 600 BC), still in the Orientalizing style, and the Tomb of the Hut (*c*. 575–*c*. 550 BC). The former features two large felines on either side of a mask, a motif paralleled on many Etrusco-Corinthian vases; the latter an architectural design in brown wash, including a false door and rafters. Several later 6th-century BC tombs only have pedimental decoration or simple polychrome bands at the tops of their walls. These can be dated on the basis of stylistic comparisons with vase painting. Thus the Tomb of the Lotus Flower (*c*. 520 BC), the Tomb of the Jade Lions (*c*. 530–*c*. 520 BC), the Tomb of the Red Lions (*c*. 530 BC) and the Tomb of the Tritons (*c*. 520 BC) show affinities with the La Tolfa group of vases produced at Cerveteri (*see* §IV, 7 above).

The most significant Tarquinian Archaic painted tomb is the Tomb of the Bulls (*c*. 530 BC; see fig. 27). Two of its three rooms have pedimental decoration alone, in the form of animal friezes, but the main chamber features the *Ambush of Troilos by Achilles*. This is one of the few depictions of a known Greek myth in an Etruscan tomb and both subject and style connect it to the 'Pontic' vases produced at nearby Vulci. The Ionic influence on Etruscan vase painting in the second half of the 6th century BC also affected tomb art and may reflect the arrival of East Greek artists and craftsmen. Thus Phocaean artists have been credited with the paintings in the Tomb of the Augurs, the Tomb of the Jugglers and the Tomb of the Olympic Games, because of stylistic affinities with both Anatolian painting, exemplified by the frescoes at Gordion in Phrygia, and Caeretan hydriai, which were clearly produced by an East Greek immigrant in Etruria itself.

In addition to funeral games, the Tomb of the Augurs depicts two professional mourners on either side of a mock door symbolizing the passage between the living and the dead, as well as a gory scene involving a figure labelled Phersu. The latter represents a form of punishment inflicted on the condemned and prisoners. (The Roman gladiatorial games probably derived from this form of punishment.) Phersu, masked and dressed like a harlequin, incites a dog on a long lead to attack a naked man with a sack over his head. The man has a club with which to beat off the dog, but he can only do so blindly. The Tomb of the Jugglers depicts acrobats entertaining the deceased, who sits on a folding stool. It also includes an oddly scurrilous scene of a man defecating, identified in an inscription as the slave of Heracanas. This figure may represent the artist himself, adding a humorous touch to his signature.

The Tomb of the Olympic Games again in East Greek style possibly reflects familiarity with East Greek mythology, since the five figures at sides of the mock door resemble protagonists in the Judgement of Paris. Stylistic connections explain resemblances between the Tomb of Hunting and Fishing and works by the Samian Little Master cup painters. Influences of the Ionic style and of the workshop of 'Pontic' vases appear in the Bartoccini Tomb (*c*. 520 BC), with its elegantly tapestried ceiling and walls, and almost miniaturistic banquet scene in white and

27. Wall painting with the *Ambush of Troilos by Achilles*, Tomb of the Bulls, Tarquinia, *c*. 530 BC

red on a dark background. The painting in the Tomb of the Lionesses (*c*. 520 BC) seems less accomplished, not only because of inconsistencies in scale, but also because of discrepancies between the preliminary design and what was actually painted, especially in the figure of the dancer with her index and little finger raised in an apotropaic gesture. Finally, despite retouching done in the 19th century, the painting in the Tomb of the Baron (*c*. 510–*c*. 500 BC) still retains an impressive Ionic, perhaps Klazomenian clarity.

(ii) c. 500–c. 150 BC. Athenian Black-figure and Red-figure vase painting influenced Etruscan tombs at the start of the 5th century BC. Old tradition and new stylistic solutions are illustrated by the Tomb of the Hunter, which is painted to resemble a hunter's tent, so that the animal friezes on the upper zones of its wall become herds of game. In the Tomb of the Chariots a frieze of dark figures on a light background is placed directly above another with light figures on a dark background, suggesting the influence of Attic bilingual vases (i.e. with both Red-figure and Black-figure work on a single vase). The draughtsmanship resembles that of early Attic Red-figure vase painters such as EUPHRONIOS, EUTHYMIDES and EPIKTETOS (*see* VASE PAINTERS, §II), while some foreshortenings and three-quarter views recall the *katagrapha* ascribed to KIMON OF KLEONAI (Pliny: *Natural History* XXXV.xxxiv.56). Subsequently, the painters of the Tomb of the Triclinium and the Tomb of the Leopards (see fig. 24 above) must have been familiar with the developments in Athenian vase painting made by DOURIS and the KLEOPHRADES PAINTER (*see* VASE PAINTERS, §II). Thus the arrangements of the couches in the banqueting scenes recall the compositions of Douris, and several tombs (no. 994, of the Varnie family, and nos 4255, 4260 and

4021; all first half of the 5th century BC) share the same delicate workmanship.

The Tomb of the Monkey and the Tomb of the Hill (*c.* 475–*c.* 450 BC) at Chiusi both perpetuate earlier Tarquinian themes and styles. The Tomb of the Monkey contains scenes of chariot racing, wrestling, boxing and armed dancing, while the Tomb of the Hill features both banqueting and athletics. However, the friezes are significantly lower than in Tarquinian tombs.

Two important Tarquinian tombs of the second quarter of the 5th century BC are the Tomb of the Funeral Couch and the Tomb of the Black Sow. In the former the banquet takes place on either side of an imposing catafalque, and the scene, involving ballerinas, armed dancing and athletics, is composed with the same finesse as in the Tomb of the Triclinium. The Tomb of the Black Sow is named after a pedimental scene depicting the hunting of a great sow with prominent pink teats. In the banquet scene the diners are entertained not only by professional musicians, but also by a young female guest playing the zither. Several other tombs belong to the same workshop tradition. The figures in tomb no. 3697, which contained a cup signed by the potter Hieron, have similar profile-view eyes to those in the Tomb of the Black Sow, while tomb no. 5187 and the Tomb of the Stag Hunt both show similar hunting scenes, and tomb no. 5517 features another armed dancer. A hunt also occurs in the Querciola I Tomb, which is related to tomb no. 6071 and the four-roomed tomb no. 1560 (all *c.* 470–*c.* 450 BC).

The mid-5th-century BC Tomb of the Ship contains several banqueting scenes as well as its eponymous picture of a merchant vessel about to set sail. The execution is accomplished and suggests familiarity with the work of POLYGNOTOS OF THASOS. However, Tarquinian tomb painting in the later 5th century BC was undistinguished.

Only a few works demonstrate any originality. Thus in the Tomb of the Maiden (*c.* 430–*c.* 420 BC) a painted temple façade, complete with a palmette acroterion and a pediment containing a winged gorgoneion, forms a framework for a burial niche containing the first burial. On the back wall of the niche is a pair of winged genii of the sort that first appear in tomb no. 4813 (first half of the 5th century BC), reappear in the Tomb of the Warrior (*c.* 420–*c.* 400 BC) and become common in the 4th century BC. Here they are shown preparing a shroud for the deceased. The painter of the Tomb of the Cock (*c.* 420–*c.* 400 BC) coordinated his colours well but was a poor draughtsman. The Tomb of the Blue Demons, discovered in 1985, is the oldest representation in Tarquinian funeral painting of the world of the dead (*c.* 420–*c.* 400 BC); it is clearly derived from Greek models, particularly the *Nekyia* painted at Delphi by Polygnotus of Thasos. On the end wall the banquet is depicted; on the left is the journey of the deceased; and on the right is his arrival in the other world among blue demons.

The earliest 4th-century BC tomb at Tarquinia is the Tomb of Orcus. It is in fact two tombs, the earlier designated Orcus I (*c.* 400–*c.* 375 BC) and the later Orcus II (*c.* 375–*c.* 350 BC; see fig. 26 above), linked by an intermediate chamber. It belonged to the Spurinna family, whose most celebrated member was Velthur Spurinna, the *praetor Etruriae* who took the Etruscan fleet to help Athens in the battle against the Syracusans in 413 BC. The paintings are accomplished: Orcus I features a banquet, laid out under a pergola but apparently located in the underworld in the presence of demons; Orcus II contains a form of *nekyia* (summoning of the dead) which includes Hades and Persephone, the three-bodied Geryon and Kerberos on the end wall, and Agamemnon, Ajax, Tiresias, and winged demons on the left. The entrance wall depicts

28. Wall painting with *Achilles Slaughtering Trojan Prisoners*, François Tomb, Vulci, *c.* 350 BC (Rome, Museo di Villa Albani)

Sisyphos and his boulder, and the right wall shows Theseus and Perithoos, guarded by the winged demon Tuchulcha, with a rapacious look and snakes for hair. Finally, the intermediate room is decorated with the blinding of Polyphemos by Odysseus. Features of technique include a restrained use of crosshatching to give depth to the figures in Orcus I, while Orcus II evinces complete mastery of this device. The Tomb of the Shields (*c.* 340–*c.* 330 BC), named after the shields painted in its end room, belonged to the Velcha family, and its central room contains portraits of its first incumbent, Larth, and his father Velthur. Both are shown with their wives, and are represented twice, on different panels. Larth is also depicted on his journey to the underworld, accompanied by buglers and lictors. The painting is less sophisticated than in the Orcus complex, recalling contemporary Etruscan Red-figure vase painting.

The extent to which 4th-century BC Etruscans had assimilated Greek culture is clearly apparent in the François Tomb, Vulci (*c.* 350 BC; paintings in Rome, Villa Albani). Here the tomb's founder, Vel Saties, is depicted in a richly decorated toga, about to take auspices from the flight of a bird, and several scenes from Etruscan history are interspersed with a host of Greek mythological figures. In one room amid scenes that include the *Duel between Eteokles and Polyneikes*, the *Rape of Kassandra* and *Sisyphos with his Boulder*, the Etruscan Marce Camitlnas is shown killing one of the Roman Tarquins. In the adjacent room Achilles is depicted slaughtering Trojan prisoners to avenge the death of Patroklos (see fig. 28) and, on the opposite wall, the Etruscan leader Mastarna liberates Caile Vipinas amid combats between Etruscans from various named cities. The Etruscan scenes probably allude to the same events: the struggle that brought Servius Tullius (possibly identified with Mastarna) to the throne of Rome in place of the Tarquins. The scene with Achilles probably represents a piece of contemporary propaganda. Rome was beginning to take control of Etruria, capturing Veii in 396 BC, and the painting is doubtless intended to contrast Etruscan claims to be descended from the (victorious) Greeks with Roman claims of descent from the (defeated) Trojans.

Three painted tombs at Volsinii Veteres (Orvieto) belong to the second half of the 4th century BC. The best preserved, Golini I (*c.* 350 BC), is also the most interesting because, in addition to a fairly conventional banquet scene showing the Leinie family dining with Hades and Persephone, it also depicts the meal being prepared. Thus servants are shown in the kitchens, including one grinding something with a pestle and mortar to the accompaniment of a flute, while the entrance walls depict an ox, a hare, a kid, and various fowl suspended from hooks.

Highlighting was introduced into Etruscan painting under Greek influence. The *splendor* referred to by Pliny (*Natural History* XXXV.xi.29) took the form of brushstrokes of white paint which were first used to represent gleaming metallic objects and later figures. Shadows were created by crosshatching and depth was suggested by 'staining' the luminous areas. The results are illustrated by the paintings in the Giglioli Tomb (*c.* 300 BC) at Tarquinia, although they only depict a frieze of arms, which appear to hang on hooks in the walls. The tomb belonged to the Pinie family, and the shield blazons are especially interesting. They include not only magisterial insignia but also the

29. Wall painting with demons and a mock door, Tomb of the Charuns, Tarquinia, *c.* 250–*c.* 200 BC

symbols used on Tarquinian coinage (*see* §VII, 1 below). Powerful chiaroscuro depictions of shields also occur in the Tomb of the Garlands, belonging to the Curunas family, framed by a continuous band of wreaths. The flat ceiling of this tomb has blue panels, decorated with strands of foliage and erotes in the 'stain' technique. Its entrance is guarded by serpent-haired demons.

In the Aninas Tomb two winged demons standing on guard either side of the entrance perform a similar function. One, Vanth, is female and carries a torch; the other, Charun, bears a hammer. The tomb was used for some generations, and decoration, mostly in the form of garlands, was added with each new burial. Consequently, the painting is disorganized and stylistically disparate. The lack of planning in this and similar tombs has also been attributed to the status of their owners: middle-class 'new men' who assumed positions of power, such as the *zilath* (prime magistrate) Larth Aninas. However, the owners of the Tomb of the Cardinal, which was also restructured several times, were the illustrious Vestarcnie family, and its painting also inevitably varies in style. Thus the painting on the pilasters is more accurate than that on the walls. The subject-matter is of considerable interest, since it probably illustrates Etruscan eschatological texts. Further images of the afterlife occur in the Tomb of the Charuns (see fig. 29), named after the green-fleshed demons standing either side of the mock doors, which are carved in relief and painted. The doors and the Charuns, which are labelled with names and epithets, decorate a vestibule probably used for cult rituals, while the actual burial chambers are at a lower level.

Only detached painted panels survive from the Bruschi Tomb (3rd century BC) depicting processions of toga-clad figures, including members of the Apuna family, bearing insignia and musical instruments. Some figures are painted in a chiaroscuro technique, exploiting subtle changes of colour and tone, while others are simply drawn in outline. The whale and dolphin frieze on the dado recalls Archaic models. Funerary processions also occur in the Tomb of the Congress (third century BC; no longer accessible) and an elderly, white-haired man features particularly prominently. He is represented twice, each time in the centre of a toga-clad throng of people carrying various emblems of office, including whips and double axes. None of the figures overlaps and, while the heads are painted carefully, the bodies are treated more sketchily, with cursive brushstrokes used for the togas. Even the heads show little modelling, though some, in three-quarter view, have an air of pathos. Also among the last significant Tarquinian painted tombs is the Tomb of the Typhon, which belonged to the Pumpu family and is named after the two typhons on the sides of its central pillar. It too portrays a toga-clad procession, but here the figures do overlap, giving some impression of depth. A secondary frieze again depicts waves and dolphins.

BIBLIOGRAPHY

M. Pallottino: *Etruscan Painting* (Geneva, 1952)
F. Roncalli: *Le lastre dipinte da Cerveteri* (Florence, 1965)
M. Moretti: *Nuovi monumenti della pittura etrusca* (Milan, 1966; Eng. trans., Philadelphia, 1970)
——: *Pittura etrusca in Tarquinia* (Milan, 1974)
E. Poulsgaard Markussen: *Painted Tombs in Etruria: A Bibliography* (Odense, 1979)
S. Steingräber, ed.: *Etruskische Wandmalerei* (Stuttgart, 1985); Eng. trans. as *Etruscan Painting* (New York, 1986)
H. Blanck and C. Weber-Lehmann: *Malerei der Etrusker in Zeichnungen des 19. Jahrhunderts* (Mainz, 1987)
M. A. Rizzo, ed.: *Pittura etrusca al Museo di Villa Giulia* (Rome, 1989)

SIMONETTA STOPPONI

VI. Metalwork.

Etruria was the primary metal-producing region in Italy, and Etruscan metalwork was of the highest quality.

1. Introduction. 2. Bronze. 3. Gold and silver.

1. INTRODUCTION. Literary sources refer to the extraction of iron and copper on Elba and around Populonia, and there are actual remains of open-cast workings, quarries and tunnels, although these are difficult to date precisely and some are undoubtedly not of the Etruscan period. There are also extensive traces of metalworking activities, such as the finds of slag and furnaces at Populonia, Campiglia Marittima and on Elba, and large quantities of metal artefacts have been found at Etruscan sites. Metalwork was presumably traded abroad, along with Etruscan ore, for luxury goods such as painted vases, decorated textiles, jewellery and ivories. The main mining areas in Etruria were apparently the Monti Rognosi near Arezzo (copper and possibly iron), the regions around Volterra (copper), Campiglia (iron, copper, tin, lead and silver) and Massa (iron, copper, lead and silver), Elba (iron and possibly copper) and the Tolfa Hills (iron, copper, lead and silver). These indigenous sources may have been supplemented by imports of tin from the 'Cassiterides' Islands off the Cornish coast and of copper from the south of France and, in the 4th and 3rd centuries BC, perhaps also from Sardinia and the Iberian peninsula.

Bronze was apparently the metal most often used. It was employed for statues and statuettes, wagons, horse-bits, urns, tools and utensils, weapons, domestic and funerary furniture, vases for both ordinary and ceremonial use, clothing accessories and coinage. Iron, too, must have had many applications. Apart from being used to make arms, utensils and fitments, it was employed in the 7th century BC as a decorative inlay for bronze objects, such as belt buckles or laminas attached to carts. Iron objects are, however, rarely found intact, since they rust away, especially in the damp conditions of Etruscan tombs. Early Etruscan lead objects are rare, but from the 6th century BC lead was sometimes used for votive figurines, sling shots and, especially at Populonia and on Elba in the 4th century BC, for imitations of some established bronze types of object, for example, plates, bowls, jugs, candelabra and grapnels. Silver was used for personal ornaments, for small urns and for plating. Like iron, it does not conserve well. Etruscan silver was probably mined locally: gold, however, did not occur naturally, though it was widely used by Etruscan craftsmen. It was almost certainly imported from Egypt, and perhaps also from central Europe.

Etruscan tombs often contained sophisticated metal objects, and these were clearly valued for their craftsmanship as well as for the intrinsic value of their metal. Pottery vases often imitated metal originals, and some surviving metal vases show signs of having been carefully repaired in antiquity. Diodorus Siculus (*Historical Library* V.xl.3) attests their function as status symbols in his description of the luxurious banquets of the Etruscan aristocracy (*see also* §V, 4 above). Similarly, the first narrative scenes in Etruscan art, depicting hunts, duels and armed dances, occurred on bronze objects such as scabbards, incense burners and cinerary urns. These scenes allude to the power and status of an object's owner. It is also significant that innovations in the depiction of human and animal figures are invariably first evidenced on metal objects, probably because decorating metal usually requires a finer discipline than painting pottery and thus tended to attract the best craftsmen.

Most extant Etruscan metalwork comes from tombs and sanctuaries, while the little so far recovered from domestic contexts is of modest quality. Nonetheless, it is clear both from literary sources (see Diodorus Siculus quoted above and Athenaeus: *Deipnosophists* I.28 b; XV.700 c) and from evidence of usage and repair on metal objects themselves that they were not exclusively reserved for rituals or special celebrations.

2. BRONZE. As engraved bronze mirrors and cists were a speciality in Etruscan art, they are accorded sections to themselves. For bronze sculpture *see* §III, 2 above.

(i) General survey. (ii) Mirrors. (iii) Cists.

(i) General survey. The great quantity of Etruscan bronzework that survives only represents a fraction of what was originally produced, much of which has been melted down. In 1546, for example, Cardinal Alessandro Farnese obtained some 6000 pounds of ancient bronzes from the inhabitants of Tarquinia (then called Corneto) to melt down for decorations for the columns of the basilica of S

Giovanni in Laterano in Rome. It is also clear that bronzework from Etruria was widely distributed in the ancient world. The bronze dinner-services and candelabra used by 5th-century BC Greeks (see Athenaeus quoted above) were apparently Etruscan, and Pliny (*Natural History* XXXIV.xvi.34) spoke of Etruscan bronze statues being exported to places far away from Etruria. He also stated that when the Romans took Volsinii Veteres (Orvieto) in 264 BC they looted 2000 bronze statues. Pausanias (*Guide to Greece* V.xii.5) recorded a bronze throne at Olympia donated by Arimnestus, 'an Etruscan king, who was the first barbarian to make a votive offering to Zeus'. Archaeological evidence confirms that from the 8th century BC Etruscan bronzes, such as fibulae, razors, cauldrons, tripods, jugs and votive figurines, were exported not only around the Mediterranean but also to central Europe. The quality of Etruscan bronzework was noted by ancient writers, and Horace (*Epistles* II.ii.180) recorded that Roman connoisseurs included Etruscan bronzes among their interests.

Etruscan bronzework can be classified fairly precisely on stylistic grounds, but the frequent lack of accurate information on the original context and provenance of individual pieces imposes severe limitations on an interpretation of their cultural significance and function. Specialist study in this field tends to concentrate on questions of typology, attribution and technique, focusing on objects that demonstrate artistic achievement, such as statues, decorated utensils, laminated items and incised mirrors, rather than more mundane objects. Techniques of bronzeworking varied. Statuettes and utensils were cast solid, while larger statues are hollow. After casting, both types were smoothed and finished with scrapers and hammers, and decorative details were incised with a graver. Larger statues and complex utensils were cast in separate parts which were later soldered together. Bronzes were often clad in laminas, which could either be left smooth, or embossed or incised. Bronze products frequently demonstrate a combination of techniques, with some parts cast and others laminated, beaten or soldered together. Tripods, for example, have cast feet but beaten basins, which were sometimes made from a single sheet of bronze.

From the 7th century BC, Etruscan metalworkers occasionally used the sphyrelaton technique, which involved cladding a wooden figure with bronze laminas. The cut-out lamina technique was sometimes used for figurines, notably the mass-produced votive gifts at sanctuary sites in Umbria and Latium, and it was also employed after the end of the 7th century BC for other objects in tombs, such as the series of small griffin protomes from the Montefortini tumulus at Comeana. Lastly, there is the technique of 'enriching' bronze with precious metals: gold strands were wound around the bows of fibulae, statuettes were gilded and urns laminated with silver.

The earliest Etruscan bronzework comes from the 9th-century BC tombs of the Villanovan culture. It includes fibulae, pins, razors, helmets, swords, scabbards and spearheads. During the 8th century BC, tomb contents became richer and the bronzework more varied, encompassing biconical cinerary urns, tripods, bowls, flasks, wide belts, bracelets, pins, shields and horsebits. Such objects were, however, still rare possessions and arms and armour in particular seem to have been the status symbols of a ruling warrior class.

The decoration of these Villanovan bronzes usually consists of embossed or incised geometric patterns: dots, straight and wavy lines, angles and triangles, squares and boxes, hooked crosses, meanders, circles and semicircles. Designs tend to reflect the shape of the object itself, running lengthwise along the border of a scabbard or concentrically on a shield or flask. Figures are rare and extremely schematic. Animals occur more often than humans, and distinctive features are emphasized: the beak of a duck, the horns of a deer, a boar's bristles or a dog's tail. Three-dimensional human figurines were, however, occasionally used to embellish prestige objects, for example a male and female on the scabbard of a sword from Vulci (8th century BC; Rome, Villa Giulia, 64487). Figures engaged in various activities, such as ploughing, hunting and fighting, occur on the base of an incense burner (*c.* 750–*c.* 725 BC; Rome, Villa Giulia, 57022/2) and on the shoulder and top of a biconical vase from Bisenzio (*c.* 725–*c.* 700 BC; Rome, Villa Giulia, 57066). Even though the figures probably allude to the pastimes and privileges of

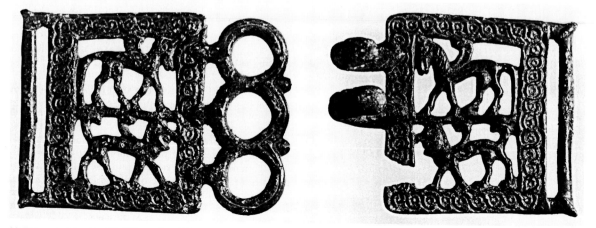

30. Bronze belt buckle, 57×125mm, from Massa Marittima, 7th century BC (Massa Marittima, Museo Archeologico)

the aristocratic owners of the objects, they are crudely executed, with over-large heads, monkey-like features and accentuated genitals. They recall terracotta figurines from tombs in Early Iron Age Latium (9th century BC).

Nonetheless, the technical accomplishment of early Etruscan bronzeworking should not be underestimated. Several techniques had already been developed in the Bronze Age; cast pieces have been found in Manciano, in the valley of the River Fiora, and 'panels' of bronze and axes occur at various localities in Tuscany and Latium. Immigrant craftsmen probably exerted an influence: the use of incised details may have originated in the Danube area, and the figural scenes suggest Aegean antecedents. During the 8th century BC the western Mediterranean was frequented by Greek and Phoenician traders and colonists, and, while Etruria's mineral resources ensured both economic and political independence, Etruscan culture altered rapidly through foreign commercial contacts. Imports of sophisticated artefacts, not only from the Near East, but also from Greece, central Europe and Sardinia, were accompanied by foreign potters, ivory and gold workers, and bronzesmiths, who profoundly changed the techniques and repertory of Etruscan art. Geometric patterns were replaced by lively floral motifs, including palmettes, lotus buds and rosettes, real and imaginary animals, and the first identifiable mythical scenes. This Orientalizing period in Etruscan art coincided with the construction of the first great 'princely' tombs at various sites along the central Tyrrhenian coast. One of these, the Regolini-Galassi Tomb (c. 670–c. 630 BC) at Cerveteri (Caere) yielded a series of laminated bronzes, with both embossed and engraved decoration, attributed to a local workshop. From the same tomb came a cauldron, a conical stand, various discs, and laminas, decorated with typically Orientalizing felines, monsters and lotus chains (all Rome, Vatican, Mus. Gregoriano Etrus.). The lion on these bronzes, for example, with its protruding tongue, pricked-up ears and serpent-like tail, exactly matches the lions depicted on gold and silver bowls imported to Cerveteri

from some Phoenician–Cypriot source (Rome, Vatican, Mus. Gregoriano Etrus., 20207). A similar lion appears on an incised and embossed bronze skyphos from the Barberini Tomb (c. 675–c. 650 BC) at Praeneste (Rome, Villa Giulia, 13132). From the Near East, probably North Syria, came the great bronze cauldrons with laminated protomes of griffins and lions riveted to the lips of the bowls. These were imitated locally in both bronze and terracotta. Also from this period is the handle on the cover of a bronze cinerary urn from the Tomb of the Cone at Vetulonia (Florence, Mus. Archeol., 6980), made of two solid cast griffins with elongated equine ears, gaping beaks and long curving necks, executed in a fluent, almost mannerist style.

Some forms of geometric decoration survived through the Orientalizing period. Lines and circles, for example, accompany floral and animal motifs on some large bronze 7th-century BC shields. Schematized figurines continue to be used to adorn certain bronze objects. Examples include the little horsemen on the feet of Vetulonian tripods, the human figures and dogs on a tripod from the Bernardini Tomb (c. 675–c. 650 BC) at Praeneste (Rome, Villa Giulia, 61619) and the mythical beasts on a belt buckle from Massa Marittima (7th century BC; see fig. 30). The facial details of female figures at the top of two vase stands from the 7th-century BC Tomba del Duce at Vetulonia (Florence, Mus. Archeol., 7053, 7054) are less schematic than those of their precursors, although their bodies remain geometric.

Important 6th-century BC bronzes from tombs in the Perugia area (San Valentino di Marsciano, Castel San Mariano) and Monteleone di Spoleto include chariots, tripods and thrones. The quantity, nature and artistic quality of these bronzes suggest that they belonged to 'princely' burials, which themselves imply the existence of a provincial pre-urban culture. Their place of manufacture remains uncertain, although north-east Etruria, Perugia, Chiusi (Clusium), Vulci and Cerveteri have all been suggested. Whatever the case, they must have originated from a region with an established tradition of metalworking. Some, at least, probably came from the same workshop; for example the Monteleone Chariot (see CHARIOT, fig. 4) and the Loeb Tripod C (c. 550–c. 500 BC; Munich, Staatl. Antikensamml., Br SL 68; see fig. 31), both of which feature similar versions of the *Combat of Achilles and Memnon*. Between c. 550 and c. 450 BC, workshops at Vulci produced bronzes for use at symposia and ceremonial banquets. These include jugs, rod tripods (e.g. a bronze rod tripod, from Populonia, made at Vulci, c. 530 BC; see fig. 32), candelabra and incense burners, and the decoration of these pieces combines patterned motifs and mythological scenes. The latter were sometimes expanded or adapted to suit the surface available, and both their style and iconography reflect Greek influence. Vases and other high quality bronze utensils and ceremonial objects were produced in large quantities and widely exported. The long-spouted jug, for example, not only occurs throughout Etruria and in other parts of Italy, but also in north-central Europe. Some bronze objects were monumental in size and appearance. This is true of the lamp from Cortona (Cortona, Mus. Accad. Etrus.), which probably came from a workshop in central Etruria around the mid-5th century BC. This consists of a large circular

31. Loeb Tripod C, detail depicting the *Combat of Achilles and Memnon*, bronze, diam. 230 mm, c. 550–c. 500 BC (Munich, Staatliche Antikensammlungen)

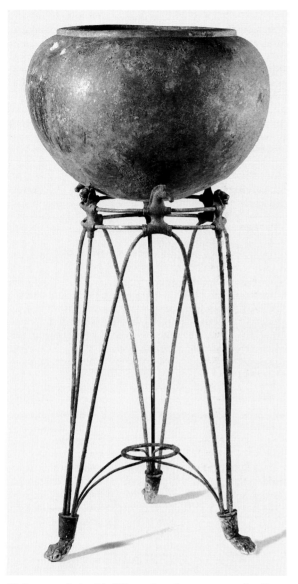

32. Bronze rod tripod, h. 900mm, from the area surrounding Populonia, made at Vulci, c. 530 BC (Copenhagen, Nationalmuseum)

basin, cast in a single block (57.72 kg; diam. 600 mm), with rich, detailed relief decoration on the outer surface, of obscure symbolic religious meaning. A central Gorgonesque mask, of Archaic type, is surrounded by a series of concentric friezes with animals fighting, dolphins leaping over waves, and sileni playing the double aulos or the syrinx alternating with sirens, with busts of Achelous behind.

Between the mid-5th century BC and the 2nd century BC the production of banquet vessels continued, including large stamnoi to contain wine, situlae with spouts in the form of lions' heads and jugs with elongated spouts. Candelabras consist of a three-footed base, a stem about 1 m tall and a top part with three or four prongs for candles and a statuette (a dancer, a musician, a satyr, an

athlete, Herakles) or a pair of statuettes. The main workshops were located at Vulci, Orvieto, Chiusi, Populonia and Spina. Incense burners stood on tables, and so were smaller than the candelabras. Their three-legged bases consist of the hind legs of animals, and they have a little pan on top where the incense burned. The workshops producing these were probably in Vulci, Tarquinia and Civita Castellana. A painting in the 4th-century BC Golini Tomb I in Orvieto clearly shows the use of these utensils during a banquet. Kottaboi also have a base with feet and a long stem (about 2 m), but at the top there is a small disc held by a statuette. In the game of *kottabos* during the banquet, the guest had to throw the wine from a goblet at the disc; if he hit the mark he was awarded a prize that might be a young man or woman. The known examples, datable to the 3rd century BC come from Perugia and Vetulonia.

(ii) Mirrors. The production of incised mirrors began during the second half of the 6th century BC and continued uninterrupted until the 3rd and 2nd centuries BC. Some 2000 mirrors survive. They were classified by early antiquarians and collectors of Etruscan relics as *paterae* (shallow dishes), then interpreted by Francesco Inghirami in 1824 as mystical mirrors and finally identified by Eduard Gerhard in 1840 as ordinary hand-mirrors. There are two main types: one with a disc and handle, the other with a hinged cover. There are far fewer examples of the second type, which were developed later, between the Late Classical era and the Hellenistic period (*see also* MIRROR, §I, 2).

Disc mirrors were first cast and then heated to 600°–700°C and hammered into either flat or convex surfaces which were polished with emery. The reverse, non-reflective side was often decorated with engraved designs or, more rarely, reliefs, although it was also frequently left plain. The discs vary in diameter between 110 and 200 mm. The mirror handle was either made of some other material, such as bone, ivory or wood, which rarely survives, connected by means of a tang; or it could be cast in one piece with the mirror, as a baton-shape ending in an animal head (a ram or a deer). Occasionally the handle takes the form of a bronze statuette. The edge of the mirror was normally folded back and decorated with motifs of beads, dentils, ovules or small tongues. The earliest examples have flat surfaces, later ones convex. On the reflective side the decoration of spirals, palmettes or other plants is restricted to the extension that connects the disc to its tang, sometimes extending to the frame of the mirror surface. On the reverse, however, it covers the whole area and is surrounded by a border of wave, meander, ropework or S-shaped patterns, floral or plant motifs or groups of animals, and divided horizontally by a lower and/or upper exergue. The whole scheme of decoration unites carefully designed devices to emphasize and enhance the form of the object itself.

Most Etruscan mirrors are of uncertain provenance and they have generally been classified on a stylistic basis. Attribution of groups or individual specimens to a particular centre of manufacture has been based largely on the sites where they were discovered, even though mirrors may well have been used far from their place of origin. It

33. Mirror with relief depicting the *Rape of Mlacuch by Herkle*, bronze, diam. 180 mm, *c*. 500–*c*. 450 BC (London, British Museum)

The circular form of the mirrors posed problems of composition for engravers, similar to those encountered by vase painters in the decoration of a plate or the tondo of a cup, and the vertical of the handle imposed a strong axial emphasis. These features caused no difficulties in the rare cases when the figural scene was modelled on some other circular composition, as in the case of a mirror portraying the *Rape of Mlacuch by Herkle* (Herakles; see fig. 33), which echoes the scenes of rape on early Attic Red-figure cups. Scenes involving only one figure were also quite straightforward, but when several figures were included the circular space proved less easy to fill. Some of the earliest engraved mirrors demonstrate the search for a satisfactory solution to this problem. A late 6th-century BC example (Paris, Bib. N., 1300) has the figures of Apollo-Helios and Artemis placed on two bases and framed by twisting vines, while the space above them is occupied by a walking panther.

Mirrors dating from the end of the 6th century BC show decorative motifs along the sides already taking the form of a frame, with the figures placed on the edge of the lower exergue. This lower section of the mirror-back later developed its own decoration. Sometimes a base or pedestal, perhaps supporting the figures in the original version of a scene, was rendered on the mirror as a decorative motif on the exergue (e.g. an Archaic example: London, BM, 543; and a 5th-century BC example: Boston, MA, Mus. F.A., 95–73).

Only two mirrors have been discovered at pre-Archaic sites in Etruria: one, from a Villanovan grave at Tarquinia, was possibly imported from Sicily or from the Aegean-Cypriot area; the other came from a late Orientalizing tomb at Populonia. Neither has any decoration. Thus large-scale production of Etruscan mirrors began only in the later 6th century BC. The development of their figural decoration follows that in other areas of Etruscan art. Successive Ionian, Attic and Italic influences are evident, with frequent archaisms, misinterpretations and adaptations by Etruscan craftsmen. The origin of incised decoration is uncertain, although it was certainly not Hellenic. Disc mirrors were widely used in Greece from the first half of the 6th century BC, but they were not ornamented in this way. According to one view they were an Etruscan innovation; another suggests that they derived from Egypt, despite the fact that few Egyptian mirrors have been discovered, none of them in Etruria.

From the period between *c*. 530 and *c*. 450 BC, a few dozen Etruscan mirrors survive. These generally have a flat disc and always end in tangs. The extension between disc and tang is either absent or in the form of a rectangle or circle. The design is of a high quality and the subjects depicted (banquets, dances, games, satyrs, maenads and Greek myths) echo those found in contemporary Etruscan tomb painting, vase painting and relief bronzes. It seems evident that the mirrors too belonged to the same wealthy members of society who commissioned the more lavish tombs. Moreover, the new popularity of mirrors in Etruria coincided with the appearance of other luxury goods, probably introduced through contacts with Greek Asia Minor. These contacts became even closer and more productive after the fall of Asia Minor to the Persians (546 BC), when East Greek craftsmen settled in Etruria.

is also unclear whether the casting and engraving were carried out in a single workshop: they obviously required different skills and standard patterns were possibly used in several workshops. This inconclusive picture has been remedied to some extent through analysis of other factors. These include the shape and size of the disc; the form of its border, extension and handle; the mirror's weight; the style of decoration; the palaeographic and phonetic characteristics of any inscriptions; and the stylistic, thematic and iconographical parallels between the mirror and other figural works of art, such as painted pottery.

The few mirrors of known provenance come exclusively from tombs. This does not, however, imply that they had a purely funerary significance. On the contrary, they were almost certainly used in ordinary domestic life. Mirrors are clearly depicted in numerous Etruscan scenes of women at their toilet, while several examples show evidence of having been repaired during use. Many others bear the inscription 'suthina' (i.e. for the tomb) on the reflective surface, written in a different script with a different tool from those used for other inscriptions. This suggests that their original, daily purpose had been deliberately cancelled. Many scholars now believe that these mirrors, and the cists discussed below, were made in the first place as marriage gifts.

Sometimes the subjects portrayed on the mirrors provide unique insights into the development of Etruscan culture. The typically Greek satyr and maenad on a mirror in Brussels (*c.* 470 BC; Mus. A. Anc., R1270), for example, were given the Etruscan names Chelphun and Munthuch, indicating that Greek mythology was now subject to Etruscan interpretation.

In the later 5th century BC and, to an even greater extent, during the 4th century BC, there was a marked increase in the production of mirrors, which were doubtless manufactured at several centres, one of which was certainly Vulci. Mirrors of this period have an enlarged (diam. 180–200 mm) and convex reflecting surface, with a wider, trapezoidal extension and slightly longer tang. At the same time, the scenes on the reverse tend to portray more figures. These compositions were adapted so well to the circular field, through devices such as varying the figures' heights or placing curving figures at the sides, that the lower exergue was often omitted. A recurrent composition involved a central seated figure with numerous others grouped around it. This was adapted to various different subjects (e.g. *Gods Performing their Toilet*, *Uni Suckling Herkle*, the *Birth of Menrva* and the *Judgement of Paris*). Sometimes mirrors can be directly compared with the tondi of Etruscan Red-figure cups. Thus one (late 5th century BC–early 4th century BC; Berlin, Pergamonmus., Fr. 36) depicts the naked youth Fufluns (Dionysos) being embraced from behind by the draped figure of his mother, Semla (Semele), a composition that is used on other mirrors and on cups for scenes depicting lovers.

The first mirrors to have the handle cast as one piece with the disc appeared during the second half of the 4th century BC. They are much smaller than the mirrors with tangs (sometimes only diam. 110–120 mm), their reflective sides are more markedly convex and their extensions have two tips. Their decorated sides may have an exergue or an architectural background, and the most common scenes show either four figures in conversation (two Dioscuri flanking two other figures), two Dioscuri facing each other or a Lasa (goddess of Fate). Many examples survive, but they are generally poorly executed, with repetitive subjects and layouts. Mirrors were clearly no longer the prestige objects they had been during the 6th and 5th centuries BC. Workshops were located at various centres, particularly in the hinterland of central Etruria. One group, thought to have been made at Praeneste (second half of 4th century BC–3rd century BC) and mostly found there, have pear-shaped discs with cast handles. They bear Latin inscriptions and, in both theme and style, resemble other objects made at Praeneste. Several depict the myth of Amykos which also appears on certain cists found at the site. These mirrors also include the only examples signed by their maker, and, since another engraved object found at Praeneste, the Ficoroni Cist (see fig. 34), carries a similar maker's signature, that of Novios Plautios, it seems possible that Latin engravers enjoyed a higher status than their Etruscan counterparts. Despite their artistic quality Etruscan disc mirrors were apparently made almost exclusively for the local market, as only about 20 examples have been found outside Etruria, in Italy and elsewhere in Europe.

34. Ficoroni Cist signed by Novios Plautios, with engraving depicting the myth of *Amykos*, bronze, h. 740 mm, from Palestrina, *c.* 325–*c.* 300 BC (Rome, Museo Nazionale di Villa Giulia e Soprintendenza alle Antichità per l'Etruria Meridionale)

The Etruscan mirrors with hinged covers were either circular or rectangular. The circular type, of which only a few dozen examples survive, all date from the late 4th century BC and the 3rd century BC. Greek mirrors of this type, however, were already in production by the late 5th century BC. The outside of the cover was decorated with relief figures generally in mythological scenes featuring Aphrodite, Dionysos or Ganymede, or depicting *Odysseus and Penelope*, *Thetis and the Armour of Achilles*, the *Acknowledgement of Paris* and the *Death of Troilos*. The last two subjects also occur frequently in reliefs on the small funerary urns produced during Hellenistic times at Chiusi, Perugia and Volterra. Even so, the mirrors were again primarily intended for everyday use and only secondarily as funerary objects.

Rectangular covered mirrors ('book mirrors') are known only from ancient representations on the covers of small urns from Volterra of the 2nd and 1st centuries BC, which show them held by reclining female figures. There is one extant example of a circular, convex mirror, with no decoration and no handle, possibly from a tomb at Volterra of the late 2nd century BC or early 1st century BC, which may originally have been cased (London, BM, Br. 731). If so, the case was presumably made of wood or some other perishable material.

(iii) Cists. Etruscan mirrors were closely associated with the cists used for women's toilet items. The two were often depicted together and with such objects as strigils, hairpins and containers for balsam, and both have been found together. The provenance of most Etruscan cists, however, is again usually uncertain. Their chronology is based mostly on a stylistic examination of their figural decoration, cast feet and handle figurines. Since the container itself was made from a thin metal sheet, often only the feet and handle, which were cast, survive. Cast feet, however, could also come from other containers, such as situlae and cauldrons, so that attribution is problematic if they are found without other evidence.

The earliest type of Etruscan cist was cylindrical and had three feet and a slightly convex cover. The container was made by hammering metal into a sheet, bending it so that the two vertical edges overlapped, and riveting them together. It was lined with wood and sometimes had a band of pierced foliar decoration half way up. The circular base was joined to the body by folding up its edges, while the handle on the cover was formed either by a single figurine in a 'wrestler's bridge', or by a more complex group. The feet were formed as claws surmounted by a narrow moulded band, often adorned with volutes, supporting a small sculpted element. The latter was usually carved in openwork, although it was sometimes in relief, and was riveted or soldered to the outside of the cist below the main field of decoration. The earliest examples of feet have been attributed to early 5th-century BC workshops at Vulci. The small sculptures on them depict scenes from Greek myths (*Herakles and Iolaos Fighting the Hydra, Herakles and Apollo Fighting for the Tripod, Europa and the Bull*), chariot races or heads of satyrs. Other feet, decorated with individual mythological figures (demons with snake-like legs, winged figures and sirens) or with a palmette between two volutes, have been attributed to 5th-century BC workshops in northern Etruria, notably at Chiusi. The earliest examples from a series of cists from Praeneste are also of this date. These have distinctive feet consisting of claws on a low cylindrical base surmounted by a beaded rim and supported by a four-sided plinth. The group also includes the first four-footed cists with ovoid bodies.

The greatest period of cist production at Praeneste seems to have been during the 4th and 3rd centuries BC, since more than 100 examples of this date survive. Their bodies can be cylindrical, ovoid or parallelepipedal; the decoration either pierced, engraved or executed in embossed dots, although this last method seems confined to the covers of a few ovoid examples. Engraved figural friezes are bounded at the top and bottom by borders of ornamental motifs, such as plants, waves and ropework, similar to those used in the borders of the Praeneste mirrors. The range of subject-matter is extensive, encompassing scenes of everyday life; battle scenes involving warriors, Amazons, giants and animals; Greek myths featuring Dionysos, Helen, Achilles, Peleus and Thetis, Bellerophon, Amykos (see fig. 34), Iphigenia and other

figures; and historical events. All show iconographical and stylistic resemblances to 4th-century BC Etruscan and Italic vase paintings. The appropriateness of these scenes is not always evident, and, although the numerous toilet scenes relate to the use of the cists, they normally only occupy the spaces left by the main subjects.

With the exception of a fine example from Vulci (Rome, Vatican, Mus. Gregoriano Etrus., 327) with an *Amazonomachy* in relief that shares some features with Praenestine works, most other Etruscan cists of the 4th and 3rd centuries BC are of poor quality. Their bodies are cylindrical, with bands of decoration near the base and mouth, with carrying handles in the form of quadrupeds (h. 150–180 mm, including handle). Examples occur virtually throughout central Etruria.

For bronze coins *see* §VII, 1 below.

3. GOLD AND SILVER. The intrinsic value of precious metals such as gold and silver profoundly influenced developments in their working, especially since gold had to be imported. At the same time, it also made gold and silver objects vulnerable to looting. According to the ancient authors, about 1500 talents of gold and silver were seized during the sack of the sanctuary of Pyrgi (384 BC) and later depredations often involved the removal of all gold and silver objects from rediscovered tombs for melting down. A cardinal was sent to Tarquinia by Pope Innocent VIII (*reg* 1484–92), after news of the discovery of a rich tomb, expressly for this purpose. Although Greek writers maintained that Etruscan aristocrats had gold and silver vessels for everyday uses (see Athenaeus: *Deipnosophists* I.28b and Diodorus Siculus: *Historical Library*

35. Gold disc fibula, h. 315 mm, from Cerveteri, *c.* 650 BC (Rome, Vatican, Museo Gregoriano Etrusco)

V.xl.3), such objects as do survive (mainly jewellery, ceremonial vases, coins and ingots) generally come from exceptional tombs and dedications at sanctuaries.

The gold used by the Etruscans was not pure, but contained some copper (0.1–10%) and some silver (15–37%). Goldworking techniques included beating, hollow or solid casting, the making of gold thread or wire and the application of thin gold leaf to other metals, ceramics or ivory. Gold objects were decorated with embossed and engraved designs, filigree, granulation or gold dust. A few were made from several pieces, soldered together with bronze. From the earliest times, Etruscan goldsmiths and silversmiths displayed considerable technical skill, although some of their products, for example fibulae, evidently reproduced objects previously made in bronze. Knowledge of the techniques of granulation (see GOLD, fig. 3), filigree and gold leaf spread throughout Etruria around the turn of the 8th and 7th centuries BC, possibly as a result either of Oriental influence or the arrival of Oriental craftsmen displaced by Assyrian expansion in the Near East. A suggestion that early Etruscan goldwork should be attributed to the Greek colony of Pithekoussai has gained little support.

In Early Iron Age times gold and silver were used only for personal ornaments: fibulae, hairgrips, discoid pendants (bullae), small rings, necklace charms, triangular and swastika-shaped plaquettes for clothes. Their decoration was geometric and they occur only in the richest tombs. With the advent of the 'princely' culture and Orientalizing styles in Etruria and Etruscan-influenced areas of Italy (Emilia, Latium, parts of Campania), exquisite imported and locally made gold and silver objects became more plentiful. Even so, extant 7th-century BC jewels and fine vases come from only a few rich tombs, including the Gesseri Tomb near Volterra; the Tomba del Duce, the Tomb of the Lebetes and the Tomb of the Lictor, all at Vetulonia; the Perazzeta and Fibula tombs at Marsiliana d'Albegna; the Regolini–Galassi Tomb at Cerveteri; the Aureli II Tomb at Felsina (Bologna); the Bernardini, Barberini, Castellani and Galeassi Tombs at Praeneste; and tombs nos 926 and 928 at Pontecagnano. These have yielded Cypriot piriform silver jugs, which inspired local imitations in bronze and in bucchero (see §IV, 4 above), as well as Phoenician–Cypriot silver-gilt bowls with figural decoration that deeply influenced Etruscan Orientalizing styles and iconography.

Locally produced works reflect diverse influences. The profiles and costumes of the figures in the decorative friezes of a gilded silver bucket from Chiusi (c. 650 BC; Florence, Mus. Archeol., 2594) recall Phoenician–Cypriot models, but their helmets are distinctly Corinthian. A silver kotyle (cup) from the Tomba del Duce (Florence, Mus. Archeol., 73582) displays all the incised decorative motifs typical of Phoenician–Cypriot work (files of real and fantastic animals, vegetable motifs), but is Protocorinthian in form. This creative eclecticism led to innovations that heralded a genuine Etruscan artistic tradition. This is apparent in the comparison of a locally made silver scabbard with an imported Phoenician–Cypriot cup, both from the Bernardini Tomb (c. 675–c. 650 BC). Both depict a deer hunt, but, where the scene on the cup (Rome, Villa Giulia, 61565) is set in a landscape, that on the scabbard

(Villa Giulia, 61705) is simply framed by files of animals, a device that eliminates any impression of depth while still achieving a strong decorative effect.

Etruscan jewellery took many forms, including fibulae, pins, hairgrips, diadems, necklaces, bracelets, pectorals, clasps and various ornamental plaquettes. The finesse of the decoration varied according to the technique chosen. Motifs include local geometric patterns and Orientalizing or Greek-inspired floral and animal designs, as on a gold disc fibula of c. 650 BC (see fig. 35), as well as scenes of hunts, duels and the Mistress of Animals. Gold and silver necklaces were sometimes decorated with amber or glass.

Ceremonial vases in precious metals either adhered to local shapes (e.g. silver spiral amphorae) or copied Oriental imports (e.g. silver cups and plates with scale decoration) or Protocorinthian models (e.g. silver and gold skyphoi and kotylai). Provenance, typology and certain stylistic features seem to imply that goldsmiths were active at Cerveteri and Vetulonia in the 7th century BC, and probably also at Tarquinia and Vulci. Their patrons were clearly local aristocrats. Silver vases from the Tomba del Duce and the Regolini-Galassi and Bernardini tombs are inscribed with their owners' names, and a gold fibula from Chiusi (c. 630 BC; Paris, Louvre, Bj 816) was clearly a gift, since the names of both giver and recipient form part of its granular decoration.

Changes in social structure and funerary practices meant that in the 6th century BC less jewellery was buried with the dead, even though precious metals were probably being traded in greater quantity. After the Persian conquest of Asia Minor in the mid-6th century BC, however, many Greek craftsmen fled to Etruria and began to produce increasingly sophisticated female jewellery. This was achieved less through technical innovation than through more ingenious use of existing devices. The usual clasps and fibulae were supplemented by earrings in the shape of discs or small caskets, and rings with oval or lozenge-shaped bezels, or inset stones. The latter were perhaps directly inspired by Asiatic models, but the figural decoration on the oval bezels, which includes hieratic animals, animals in three or four vertical registers, and various narrative scenes, closely resembles contemporary vase

36. Pair of gold bunch earrings, 60×40 mm, from Populonia, second half of the 4th century BC (London, British Museum)

paintings and wall paintings, as well as laminate and cast bronzes from Vulci and the tombs near Perugia. The main workshops were probably at Cerveteri and Vulci. Cerveteri may have produced the casket earrings decorated with human figures; Vulci those with floral clusters.

With the Syracusan domination of the Tyrrhenian seaboard in the mid-5th century BC, Etruria received fewer Greek imports and probably less gold. Jewellery from this period is virtually confined to sites such as Bologna, Spina and Etruria Padana, which had access to Greece, in particular to Athens, across the Adriatic. Populonia was alone among Etruscan cities on the Tyrrhenian coast in importing Attic pottery during the second half of the 5th century BC, and was also able in the 5th and 4th centuries BC to issue gold and silver coinage.

By the end of the 5th century BC, however, Etruria was producing more jewellery than ever. This included seal-stones (*see* GEM-ENGRAVING, §I, 3), bunch earrings (see fig. 36), diadems and heavy pendants of the bulla type, often decorated with mythological scenes. Figures depicted in the great 4th-century BC tomb paintings show the extent to which jewellery was worn at this time. Good examples are the figure of Velcha in the Tomb of Orcus and the banqueters in the Tomb of the Shields (both at Tarquinia), who wear crowns, bunch earrings, necklaces and bracelets. By the 3rd and 2nd centuries BC, Baroque tendencies are manifest: even bronze votive figures and statues on sarcophagus covers appear decked out in necklaces, rings and pectorals, or hold such jewels in their hands. The drinking vessels (cups, horns and rhyta) proferred by recumbent male figures on funerary urns or sarcophagi probably represent the precious metal table-ware referred to by Diodorus Siculus.

BIBLIOGRAPHY

S. Haynes: *Etruscan Bronze Utensils* (London, 1965)
I. Mayer-Prokop: *Die gravierten etruskischen Griffenspiegel archaischen Stils* (Heidelberg, 1967)
D. Rebuffat-Emmanuel: *Le Miroir étrusque* (Rome, 1973)
G. A. Foerst: *Die Gravierungen der pränestinischen Cisten* (Rome, 1978)
G. Bordenache Battaglia: *Le ciste prenestine* (Rome, 1979, rev. 1990)
U. Fischer-Graf: *Spiegelwerkstätten in Vulci* (Berlin, 1980)
R. Adam: *Recherches sur les miroirs prénestins* (Paris, 1982)
N. de Grummond, ed.: *A Guide to Etruscan Mirrors* (Tallahassee, 1982)
U. Höckmann: *Die Bronzen aus dem Fürstengrab von Castel San Mariano* (Munich, 1982)
M. Cristofani and M. Martelli: *L'oro degli Etruschi* (Novara, 1983)
A. M. Adam: *Bibliothèque Nationale: Bronzes étrusques et italiques* (Paris, 1984)
G. Camporeale, ed.: *L'Etruria mineraria* (Milan, 1985)
E. Formigli: *Tecniche dell'oreficeria etrusca e romana: Originali e falsificazioni* (Florence, 1985)
S. Haynes: *Etruscan Bronzes* (London, 1985)
E. Mangani: 'Le fabbriche di specchi nell'Etruria settentrionale', *Boll. A.*, lxx (1985), pp. 21ff
F. Jurgeit: '*Cistenfüsse': Etruskische und Praenestiner Bronzewerkstätten* (Rome, 1986)
U. Höckmann: 'Die Datierung der hellenistisch-etruskischen Griffspiegel des 2. Jahrhunderts v. Chr.', *Jb. Dt. Archäol. Inst.*, cii (1987), pp. 247ff
I. Jucker: 'Bemerkungen zu einigen etruskischen Klappspiegeln', *Mitt. Dt. Archäol. Inst.: Röm. Abt.*, xcv (1988), pp. 1ff
S. Haynes: 'Muliebris Certaminis Laus: Bronze Documents of a Changing Ethos', *Secondo congresso internazionale etrusco. Atti* (Rome, 1989), pp. 1395ff
U. Höckmann: 'Zur Datierung der sogennanten Kranzspiegel', *Secondo congresso internazionale etrusco. Atti* (Rome, 1989), pp. 713ff
B. B. Shefton: 'Etruscan Bronze Stamnoi', *Secondo congresso internazionale etrusco. Atti* (Rome, 1989), pp. 729ff
A. Testa: *Candelabri e thymiateria* (Rome, 1989)
F. Catalli: *Monete etrusche* (Rome, 1990)
G. C. Cianferoni: 'I reperti metallici', *Populonia in età ellenistica e romana. I materiali dalle necropoli* (Florence, 1992), pp. 13ff

GIOVANNANGELO CAMPOREALE

VII. Other arts.

1. Coins. 2. Furniture. 3. Ivory and bone. 4. Textiles and dress.

1. COINS. The minting of coinage occurred only late, and then sporadically, in Etruria. It was preceded by the use of metal, especially bronze, in the form of lumps and bars. From *c.* 550 to *c.* 400 BC a type of 'proto money' circulated in central Italy, consisting of ingots marked with a recognizable motif (*ramo secco*) and defined in units of weight. These ingots, sometimes found in Sicily or Croatia, far from their sites of production in central Italy, functioned as an 'international' but pre-monetary means of exchange based on established values. Etruscan silver coinage first occurred in the 5th century BC and was based on units of *c.* 5.5 g. Most examples of such coins come from the metal-producing coastal areas of Etruria and bear a variety of motifs on one side (e.g. wild boars, chimeras, sea-lions and lions' heads). Small tokens of similar weight, with a winged horse or gorgoneion on the obverse and a stamped square on the reverse, apparently originated near Volterra, where a number of such pieces were found in a hoard together with some Phocean and Massaliot coinage. From southern Etruria, perhaps minted at Vulci, come examples of a silver coinage carrying the name of an issuing authority, Thezi or Thezle. Decorative emblems include a running Gorgon and a wheel, a seated sphinx and a man's head in three-quarter view, and an ox-head and a sea monster, all deriving from Late Archaic and Classical models. The scarcity of these coins suggests that they were issued by an aristocratic faction, rather than by city authorities.

The earliest regular public coinage comes from Populonia, where mineral exploitation took place under city-state authority, in the second half of the 5th century BC. Certain gold coins, bearing a lion's head and modelled on types from Knidos in Asia Minor and Leontinoi in Sicily, appear to have had denominations equivalent to 50, 25, and 12.5 units, but probably served as prestige acquisitions, rather than as general currency. The more common silver coins, with a gorgoneion on one side, came in units of 10, 5 and 2.5. The silver drachma of Populonia weighing *c.* 7.8–8.2 g. relates to Euboian standard weights. Successive silver issues from Populonia reflect changes in both value and iconography. The classicizing gorgoneion motif

37. Silver didrachm with gorgoneion and value XX (obverse) and cross marks (reverse), diam. 22 mm, from Populonia, 3rd century BC (London, British Museum)

persisted (see fig. 37). Heads of Athena and Herakles, derived from Syracusan types and perhaps intended as symbols of divine patronage or protection, were also used. The role of the city state is underlined by the Etruscan name Pupluna on the reverse of such coins. Bronze coinage was also minted in the late 4th century BC, with similar images of Athena and Herakles and their appropriate attributes on the reverse. Based on a unit of 40–90 g., and unrelated to contemporary Roman standard weights, these coins had denominations of a sixth, a quarter and a third. Later issues carried motifs of Hermes and Hephaistos, the latter particularly suitable for Populonia as a metalworking centre. These correspond to types of coinage issued by Vetulonia, also in the metal zone, which carried the name Vatl and images of localized marine deities. But while the distribution of the Populonian coins was wide, from Tarquinia in the south to Pistoia in the north, and as far as Aleria in Corsica to the west, Vetulonian coinage circulated strictly within central Etruria. It was not, however, the sole currency of the area, and alternative bronze issues, ranging from 100 to 1 unit in value, were introduced, probably by Etruscans who had served as mercenaries for the Sicilian tyrants in the second half of the 4th century BC.

At Tarquinia, Volterra and the Val di Chiana, a standard bronze token was in use. The Tarquinian issues were few and circulated strictly within the city and its dependent territory as far as Tuscania. One series contains tokens equivalent in value to the Roman *as*, *semis*, *quadrans* and *uncia* (a unit, a half, a quarter and a twelfth respectively), and represents a consistent minting, with the symbols on obverse and reverse related to local industries. The average weight of the late 4th-century BC Tarquinian *as* (c. 295 g.), however, does not correspond to the Roman standard, and suggests an autonomous Tarquinian mint at this time. The frescoes of the Tarquinian Giglioli Tomb (late 4th century BC) depict a set of painted shields, the inner motifs (the boar and the surveyor's level) of which recall those on the local *as* and *uncia* coins. In the cities of the Val di Chiana (Chiusi (Clusium), Cortona and Arezzo) several bronze issues circulated, bearing the wheel motif on the obverse but otherwise without a legend. Three of these issues are based on an *as* weighing c. 204 g., four on an *as* weighing c. 150 g. These reflect two distinct phases of coinage; the first based on the Etruscan pound (212 g.), the second on the Roman *as* established in 286 BC. An eighth issue in these series is iconographically more interesting: on the obverse is the head of an augur; on the reverse, the sacrificial dagger and axe. The mint at Volterra operated during the 3rd century BC, producing a coinage based upon an *as* with a mean weight of c. 157 g. There were three series: the obverse of each bears the double-headed image of Culsans, divine protector of ports (the equivalent of the Roman Janus), while the reverse is alternately stamped with a sign of value, or a club or dolphin. Whichever it is, the city's Etruscan name, Velathri, always appears, a reminder that the coinage of northern Etruscan towns was primarily designed for use within the immediate territory.

All Etruscan coinage of the 3rd century BC gradually moved into line with Roman coinage, at least in terms of standard units of weight. As the Etruscan cities lost political autonomy they were compelled to supply military aid and other goods to Rome. It first became necessary to align Etruscan weights with the Roman system; eventually, however, the Etruscan mints were forced to close, leaving only Roman coinage in circulation in Etruria.

BIBLIOGRAPHY
A. Sambon: *Les Monnaies antiques de l'Italie* (Paris, 1903)
E. J. Haeberlin: *Aes grave* (Frankfurt, 1910)
Atti del V convegno internazionale di studi numismatici (Rome, 1976)
M. Cristofani: 'Economia e società', *Rasenna* (Milan, 1986), pp. 139–45, 147–51, 156
F. Catalli: *Monete etrusche* (Rome, 1990)

MAURO CRISTOFANI

2. FURNITURE. Some original examples of Etruscan furniture exist, but most evidence comes from painted or modelled representations of aristocratic households. For such families, furniture functioned as a status symbol as well as for utilitarian purposes. Fragments of ivory and wooden stools, tables and couches, and ivory, metal and terracotta decorative plaques from lost wooden originals are known. Liberal use of metal is characteristic of Etruscan work; much tomb furniture is of sheet bronze, intended to support offerings or urns. Etruscan homes would appear sparsely furnished to modern eyes, with no upholstery, and belongings stored in small chests or hung on walls, as represented in the Tomb of the Painted Reliefs at Cerveteri (see fig. 7 above).

The distinctive cylindrical throne appeared in the 7th century BC. Its flared base and curved high back (see fig. 38a) suggest wicker construction, but extant originals are of bronze-clad wood with round decorative bosses.

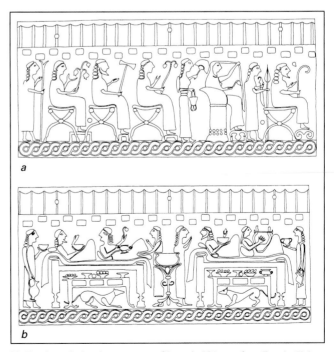

38. Furniture depicted on terracotta friezes, h. 234 mm, from Poggio Civitate, early 6th century BC: (a) cylindrical throne, folding stools and footstools used by divinities; (b) couches and three-legged tables used by banqueters (Murlo, Antiquario di Poggio Civitate)

Full-size carved stone versions appear in the anterooms of Caeretan tombs (e.g. the 6th-century BC Tomb of the Five Chairs), suggesting the later Roman custom of receiving *clientes*. The stone, relief-decorated Corsini Throne (2nd–1st century BC; Rome, Pal. Corsini) was designed for religious rituals. The *cathedra* of medieval bishops may have descended from the cylindrical throne.

The folding or camp-stool, with four double-curved animal legs and probably a leather seat, is represented in assemblies of gods and mortals. A folded example is carried by a servant in a painting in the 6th-century BC Tarquinian Tomb of the Augurs. (Such a stool-bearer is a stock figure in funeral and wedding scenes, an indicator of the master's wealth.) A fragmentary ivory original (Florence, Mus. Archeol.) from the Montagnola Tomb, Quinto Fiorentino (*c.* 600 BC) perhaps symbolized political office, the antecedent of a Roman senator's *sella curulis*. Such 'curule chairs' appear on the funeral urns of magistrates in Volterra (e.g. late 2nd century BC–early 1st; Volterra, Mus. Etrus. Guarnacci).

Footstools were often depicted as elaborately carved with feline claw feet and apotropaic eyes, as in the Tomb of the Monkey, Chiusi (early 5th century BC). Footstools and parasols recall Near Eastern traditions exalting gods and kings.

39. Ivory pyxis, from the Pania Tomb, Chiusi, *c.* 600 BC (Florence, Museo Archeologico di Firenze)

Sarcophagi for women can occur as simple rectangular beds, although commoner are couches shown heaped with pillows and covers, with legs carved in volute patterns. Wooden originals were painted or inlaid and were adopted by the Etruscans in the 6th century BC with the assimilation of the Greek customs of the symposion.

Three-legged tables with trapezoidal tops and ornate feet also occur in the context of banquets (see fig. 38b), as do smaller, round occasional tables with three animal legs, which are forerunners of feline marble and bronze examples from Pompeii.

The exact role played by foreign influence in Etruscan furniture is hard to assess: imported originals and manufacture by resident aliens account for its early development, but these combined with native innovation to produce a repertory of basic forms that were simply enriched with greater detail as the Etruscan period progressed.

BIBLIOGRAPHY

G. M. A. Richter: *The Furniture of the Greeks, Etruscans and Romans* (London, 1966)
J. MacIntosh: 'Representations of Furniture on the Frieze Plaques from Poggio Civitate (Murlo)', *Mitt. Dt. Archäol. Inst.: Röm. Abt.*, lxxxi (1974), pp. 15–40
S. Steingräber: *Etruskische Möbel* (Rome, 1979)
O. Wanscher: *Sella curulis: The Folding Stool: An Ancient Symbol of Dignity* (Copenhagen, 1980)
H. Blanck and G. Proietti: *La Tomba dei Rilievi di Cerveteri* (Rome, 1986)
G. Camporale: 'Vita Privata', *Rasenna: Storia e civiltà degli Etruschi* (Milan, 1986), pp. 241–308 [includes many colour illustrations]
T. Schäfer: 'Imperii insignia: Sella curulis und fasces', *Mitt. Dt. Archäol. Inst.: Röm. Abt.* xxix (1989) [supplement]

JEAN MACINTOSH TURFA

3. IVORY AND BONE. For the Etruscans, Oriental luxury was a sign of wealth and an emblem of power. Ivory, an exotic material, is a distinguishing mark of those in power: royal sceptres and folding stools were made from it. From the 7th century BC prestige objects were imported from Syria and also imitated locally. Fan handles in the shape of arms covered in superimposed decorative friezes, goblets, cylindrical caskets with lines of fabulous animals among lotus flowers, and sophisticated combs decorated with confronted lions all appear among the possessions of princes. Soon local aristocrats, at Poggio Civitate (Murlo) and elsewhere, had resident artisans who worked ivory for them, sculpting griffins or the sacred union of Tinia and Uni in the Orientalizing style. In the Pania Tomb at Chiusi, a small cylindrical pyxis (box), is decorated in the Greek style (*c.* 600 BC; see fig. 39). Its engraver represented themes beloved of local aristocrats: a procession of hoplites following their leader mounted on a chariot, a scene of armed dancers accompanied by the Aeolian harp, and on the upper level, a depiction of *Odysseus and his Companions Escaping from Polyphemos' Cave* and the first representation of a ship skirting Skylla, the sea monster guarding the Strait of Messina. This may be an Etruscan reference to a famous passage of the *Odyssey*, but the ship is carrying amphorae which probably simply evoke the lucrative trade in Tuscan wine on which many aristocratic fortunes were based.

In the last quarter of the 6th century BC ivory was no longer imported in tusk form, but in small tablets of standard dimensions. Objects of solid ivory are no longer found; instead, decorative ivory plaques were used to face small, square wooden caskets. These small plaques were sometimes replaced by bone strips which looked rather similar but could be treated in a more perfunctory fashion. The plaques were most often framed by gadroons and engraved in low relief with the silhouette of an animal or of a reclining banqueter. In order to make the composition occupy the whole space, some liberties were taken with posture. Like the sculptors of Chiusi, the craftsmen drew on a repertory of East Greek forms, their elegance of line compensating for their conventional character. These toilet boxes were transported widely throughout the Mediterranean, from the Balearics to Cyprus.

In the 5th century BC joined plaques often covered larger objects. A large casket depicting athletic games and armed dancers was dedicated at Paestum. About 470 BC a toilet box depicting a procession of young women carrying offerings was placed in a tomb at Chiusi (London, BM, and Paris, Louvre): it is decorated with rare elegance, embellished with gold, red and blue, and has the refinement of the Early Classical style of Attic sculpture. The joined plaques technique was used until the 3rd century BC, but the silhouettes of gods and warriors became coarse, their execution crude and their postures heavy. Mirror handles seem to remain the sole original products of a craft that was no longer innovative.

BIBLIOGRAPHY
Y. Huls: Ivoires d'Etrurie (Rome and Brussels, 1957)
M. Cristofani: 'Per una lettura della pisside della Pania', Stud. Etrus., xxxix (1971), pp. 63–89
——: 'Un gruppo di plachette eburnee etrusche', Rev. Archéol. (1979), pp. 73–86
——: 'Gli avori tardo arcaici: Botteghe e aree di diffusione', Il commercio etrusco arcaico (Rome, 1985), pp. 207ff
J.-R. Jannot: 'Sur les ivoires clusiniens de la collection Dutuit', Mnmts Piot, lxvi (1985), pp. 1–17
——: 'Sur les coffrets archaïques étrusques', Italian Iron Age Artefacts, ed. J. Swaddling (London, 1986), pp. 405–16
M. F. Briguet: 'Remarques sur les plaques de coffret de Tarquinies du Musée du Louvre', Studia Tarquiniensia (Rome, 1988), pp. 7–11

J.-R. JANNOT

4. TEXTILES AND DRESS. Evidence for ancient Etruscan dress and textiles comes mainly from contemporary artistic representations and from references in Greek and Roman literature, as material remains are few. Etruscan fashions—the way they dressed and the way they represented clothes, hairstyles, jewels and textiles in their art—both reflected their relations with other cultures and expressed their own originality.

Styles of the Early Iron Age, such as the wide, leaf-shaped bronze belts found in tombs, are illustrated in figural art of the later, Orientalizing period. A vase from Cerveteri (Caere) (c. 650 BC; Cerveteri, Mus. N. Cerite) shows an Etruscan couple, the man wearing the broad belt with short trunks or *perizoma* (the Etruscans never embraced the Greek convention of male nudity in real life, though they often did in art), the woman a long dress with a mantle at the back. All the garments seem to be of heavy wool decorated with the favourite pattern of the period, a chequer-board or 'plaid' design (see also fig. 12 above). Near Eastern influences in dress appear on representations of seated male figures wearing heavy robes or chitons (a Greek word; the Latin word *tunica* may come from an Etruscan term) and mantles, of figures dressed in

three-quarter-length chitons of a kind rarely seen in Greece, or pleated linen chitons, and a variety of hats—sugar-loaf shaped, or decorated with plumes or wing-like 'petals'—worn by both men and women. The patterns on Phoenician precious textiles were also important in the development of the Orientalizing style. Large quantities of Baltic amber from the Orientalizing period have been found in Etruria and Latium, where women of princely rank were buried with chariots, dressed in sumptuous pieces of gold jewellery and, at times, even in robes with amber and glass paste plaques sewn together with silver thread in a chequer-board design. Such a decoration was perhaps inspired by Near Eastern divine and royal garments decorated with gold plaques, since in Etruria, as in Greece, textile designs were woven rather than appliqued or embroidered, as they were in the Near East. Etruscan weaving was an advanced craft by c. 600 BC, since a bronze pendant of that date (see fig. 40) bears a scene of women, dressed in chequer-board-patterned robes and mantle, carding, spinning and weaving wool on a 'two-storey' loom, the most ambitious loom known from antiquity.

In the Archaic period there developed the most characteristically Etruscan 'look'. Around 550 BC Etruscan men and women adopted a number of Ionian fashions: long hair, pointed hats and hairstyles, pointed shoes, diagonally draped mantles and long linen chitons. The semicircular *tebenna* (Etrus.: the rounded ancestor of the Roman toga) was a new shape of mantle for men. Easily distinguishable from the rectangular Greek mantle (the himation), the shape of the *tebenna* may have originated in northern Europe, where woollen mantles were woven or

40. Woolworking scenes on a bronze pendant, h. 115 mm, from the Tomb of the Gold Objects, Bologna, c. 600 BC (Bologna, Museo Civico Archeologico)

cut to rounded shape as early as 1200 BC. The similarity of costume worn by men and women in this period was due perhaps to the greater liberty enjoyed by Etruscan women compared with their Greek contemporaries. The richness and variety of cloth, colour and pattern is illustrated on the wall paintings of Tarquinia—those in the Tomb of the Hunter imitated the decorated textiles of great tent-like pavilions set up for Etruscan banquets and ceremonies—and on other monuments, such as the terracotta sarcophagus with the married couple from Cerveteri (*c.* 525–*c.* 500 BC; Paris, Louvre). Purple-bordered tunics and rounded mantles, laced shoes and a high chignon hairstyle for women were introduced to Rome at the time of the last Etruscan kings, in the later 6th century BC; these were eventually adopted as the ritual dress for Roman citizens, priests, priestesses and magistrates.

In the Classical period Etruscan fashions conform more closely to those of the Greeks, although characteristic features include the men's rounded *tebenna*, a tunic with tassels for important women, heavier garments and more accessories (jewellery, diadems, garlands and shoes). There was a continuing reluctance to show male nudity. Laced, pointed shoes of earlier style were reserved for goddesses and aristocratic female funerary portraits. Items of jewellery included the bulla, a locket-shaped pendant of gold, silver or bronze, worn by men, women and children (the Romans used it for children, as a badge of free or noble birth); and the twisted necklace or torque adopted from the Gauls. Some fashions were shared with the Romans: in the François Tomb at Vulci (*c.* 330 BC) Vel Saties is shown dressed in the decorated mantle of a general celebrating a triumph.

In the Hellenistic period sculptured urns, sarcophagi and engraved bronze mirrors often represent scenes of daily life and 'portraits', illustrating both general dress and special costumes, such as an actor's dress with long sleeves and trousers. Everyday dress consisted of lighter, less heavily draped robes and mantles; women belted their tunics high, in 'Empire style', as in Greece. Silk was probably beginning to be used. Hair was worn long, and much jewellery appears, of a simpler style than the heavy Classical pieces. The *Arringatore*, or *Orator*, a life-size Etruscan bronze statue of *c.* 80 BC (Florence, Mus. Archeol.), wears what is by now symbolic Roman dress: bordered, rounded toga over tunic, laced high shoes (*calcei*) and a ring. Only the Etruscan inscription on the border of his toga, and the relative shortness of the garment, mark him as Etruscan rather than Roman. Etruria had by then been absorbed into the Roman world, and the rounded *tebenna* had become the toga worn by all Romans or Italians, including the Etruscans, as a sign of Roman citizenship.

Etruscan textiles were in demand not only for garments, but also for blankets, sheets, cushions, rugs, armour padding, sails and other objects of everyday use. One Etruscan speciality was linen books containing prayers and religious texts, which were used by priests and depicted on their sarcophagi as attributes of office. One of these, the *Liber linteus* (?1st century BC; Zagreb, Archaeol. Mus.), was subsequently taken to Egypt, cut into strips and used to wrap a mummy. The restoration and scientific analysis of this and other textiles provide evidence of, for example,

the origin of the flax and the methods of manufacture of both wool and linen, the two fabrics used most by the Etruscans. It is also possible to analyse 'pseudomorphs', the thread marks caused by the chemical reaction of bronze objects with cloth, for example when bronze mirrors were protected by cloth mirror-cases, the latter no longer surviving. Further information on Etruscan textile manufacture comes from finds of all periods, both tombs (women were buried with distaffs and spindles, sometimes made of precious materials) and dwelling sites (thousands of loom weights have been found, some still in place where they were used, tied to the threads of the cloth on the loom).

BIBLIOGRAPHY
L. Bonfante: *Etruscan Dress* (Baltimore, 1975)
J. Stage: *Etruscan Textiles* (MA thesis, Tallahassee, FL State U., 1981)
L. Bonfante: *Etruscan Life and Afterlife* (Detroit, 1986)
——: 'Aggiornamento: Il costume etrusco', *Atti del II congresso internazionale di studi etruschi: Firenze, 1985*
E. Barber: *Prehistoric Textiles* (Princeton, 1992)
L. Bonfante: 'Etruscan Nudity', *Source: Notes Hist. A.*, xii (1993), pp. 47–55

LARISSA BONFANTE

VIII. Rediscovery.

The first Etruscan scholar was apparently the monk Annio of Viterbo (1432–1502). He claimed that the Etruscans were descendants of Osiris or of Noah, who came to Italy after the Flood, led by mythical city-founders such as Vertumnus. To confirm these theories Annio was sanctioned by Pope Alexander VI to excavate at Cipollara, near Viterbo. He invented spurious etymologies connecting the Etruscan and Aramaic languages and inserted apocryphal texts into his book *Antiquitates* (Rome, 1498), which was reprinted throughout Europe in the 16th century (*see also* §IX below). He regarded Etruscan culture as the authentic legacy of Noah, less fanciful than Greek and more refined than Roman.

Annio's theories were revived in 16th-century Tuscany for political purposes, with attempts to promote Florentine as the original language of Italy, supposedly derived from Etrusco-Aramaic origins. The French orientalist Guillaume Postel (1510–81) dedicated *De Etruriae regionis . . . moribus* (Florence, 1551) to Cosimo I de' Medici, Grand Duke of Tuscany. In this bizarre monograph he linked the Tuscan heritage directly to Noah, and the Etruscan myth became an instrument of propaganda and a source of heraldic symbolism exploited by Cosimo during his consolidation of the Tuscan state. The discovery in 1553 of the Arezzo *Chimaera* (5th century BC; Florence, Mus. Archeol.), which Cosimo immediately acquired, changed attitudes towards Etruscan art, causing Vasari to reflect on its superiority to that of Greece and Rome. Shortly afterwards, however, even the Tuscans were drawn into the contemporary obsession with Classical history, culture and collecting of statuary, and this largely supplanted the interest in Etruscan questions.

The first major scholarly work on the Etruscans, *De Etruria regali* (written 1616–19), was commissioned by Cosimo II de' Medici from a Scotsman, THOMAS DEMPSTER, then teaching at the University of Pisa. In 1716 the manuscript was acquired by Thomas Coke, 1st Earl of Leicester, and first printed at his expense, in seven books, in Florence in 1723–5. Several Florentine scholars collaborated on the text, in particular Filippo Buonarroti (1661–1733), who added information and procured most of the illustrations. The book thematically assembled a collection of references, including 15th-century apocrypha, which emphasized the Etruscan heritage of the contemporary Tuscan nobility. However, it also inaugurated a genuine reawakening of interest in Etruscan history, antiquities and decorative forms throughout 18th-century Europe.

Learned societies were established for the study of Etruscan culture (e.g. the Accademia Etrusca at Cortona, founded in 1729), as were public collections of Etruscan antiquities (e.g. at Volterra, Siena and Cortona). ANTONIO FRANCESCO GORI encouraged the collection of Etruscan relics and promoted publications such as *Museum etruscum* (Florence, 1737–43) which generated scholarly controversy both within Italy and beyond, especially on behalf of Scipione Maffei. Academic arguments focused mainly on the language problem and on the asserted pre-eminence of Etruscan culture in the ancient world, but they also reflected a new evaluation of the position of the Etruscans among the peoples of pre-Roman Italy. At the same time, actual discoveries of archaeological remains during random excavations, especially at Volterra, not only stimulated a growing market for antiquities, but also aroused some sense of collective responsibility for safeguarding Tuscany's cultural inheritance.

As interest in the Etruscans spread from Tuscany to the more cosmopolitan ambience of Rome, foreign visitors, particularly the English, were attracted by the vogue for Etruscan research and dilettantism. Connoisseurs and art dealers such as THOMAS JENKINS and JAMES BYRES were among the first to explore the tombs at Tarquinia. Byres, who studied and sketched at Tarquinia c. 1780, provided the best information from this period, although his book *'Hypogaei' or the Sepulchral Caverns of Tarquinia* (London, 1842) was not published until much later. Several of the tombs recorded by Byres and others (e.g. the Tomb of the Biclinium, the Tomb of the Ceisinie Family and the Tomb of the Tapestry) have disappeared, while others (e.g. the Tomb of the Cardinal, 3rd–2nd century BC; drawn by both Byres and Giovanni Battista Piranesi) are badly damaged.

The re-evaluation of both Etruscan and Egyptian figural art in the second half of the 18th century prompted Johann Joachim Winckelmann to undertake the first chronological survey of Etruscan art (*Geschichte der Kunst des Alterthums*, Dresden, 1764), although as a Classical purist he condemned what he saw as its formal excesses. These 'flaws' did not undermine the popularity of Etruscan taste or the ETRUSCAN STYLE, particularly in England, where the decorative schemes of Robert Adam (e.g. his Etruscan Room, Osterley Park House, Middlesex, 1775), and the pottery of Josiah Wedgwood (who in 1769 named his Staffordshire factory 'Etruria') were widely appreciated. Both in fact owed more to Roman and Greek influences, such as the wall paintings at Pompeii and Herculaneum; the 'Etruscan' vases discovered in Campania were later gradually accepted as Greek.

In 1775 LUIGI LANZI became curator of the antiquarian section at the Uffizi, Florence, with special responsibility for reorganizing the collections. A new section devoted to Etruscan civilization was formed mainly of material from Volterra and Chiusi (Clusium). Lanzi was free from dilettante preconceptions and applied the same scientific method to his classification of Etruscan works as to Italian paintings. His book *Saggio di lingua etrusca* (Rome, 1789) is the first 'modern' work of Etruscan scholarship, uniting as it does advances in deciphering the Etruscan language with a systematic presentation of Etruscan civilization. It created a basis for further historical research, especially in Italy, where the intellectuals of the Risorgimento were obsessed by a romantic vision of free and independent Italian republics (e.g. G. Micali: *L'Italia avanti il dominio dei Romani*, Florence, 1810), and in Germany, where interest was focused on the Etruscan influence on Roman constitutional history and the theory that the Etruscans originated north of the Alps (e.g. K. O. Müller: *Die Etrusken*, Breslau, 1828). Linguistic research was based mainly on the collection and interpretation of funerary inscriptions.

A series of excavations in the early 19th century at the great southern Etruscan centres, first at Tarquinia and Vulci, then at Cerveteri, aroused considerable academic interest, especially in the Tarquinian tomb paintings, but a trade in antiquities also developed, chiefly involving bronzes, jewellery and Greek pottery recovered from the tombs. The Istituto di Corrispondenza Archeologica, founded in Rome in 1829, encouraged scientific debate but also stimulated the dispersal of finds, particularly to the newly established museums in Berlin and Munich, which bought large collections from professional excavators based at Vulci. One group of excavators, the Campanari family, organized an exhibition in London in 1836–7, which generated wide interest, in turn prompting new publications (e.g. Mrs Hamilton Gray: *Tour of the Sepulchres of Etruria in 1839*, London, 1841, a tourist guide, and G. Dennis: *The Cities and Cemeteries of Etruria*, London, 1848, the first major topographical study).

The Vatican, which had so far shown little interest in the excavations, established the Museo Gregoriano Etrusco in 1837. This acquired some of the finds from Vulci in the huge collection of Lucien Bonaparte, Prince de Canino, part of which was also acquired by the British Museum in London in addition to material from Cerveteri, where Giampietro Campana had collected prolifically. Campana was the foremost collector in Rome between 1835 and 1859, but his collection included forgeries and heavily restored pieces; most of it was later acquired by Napoleon III for the Louvre in Paris, although part went to the Hermitage in St Petersburg.

Although excavation remained unregulated and was initiated mainly by the owners of private collections, some serious archaeologists were active in the first half of the 19th century. Alessandro François (1796–1857) conducted important excavations at Cortona, Chiusi and Vulci between 1824 and 1857. In the wake of these and other discoveries, increasing numbers of publications appeared, notably works by Francesco Inghirami (1772–1846), Luigi Canina and Eduard Gerhard (1813–88). Moreover, the impact of the Tarquinian painted tombs on decorative taste is evident in schemes devised by Pelagio Palagi for the Etruscan Room of the Savoia's Castello di Racconigi (northern Italy) in the 1830s, and by Leo von Klenze for the Glyptothek in Munich in 1837.

In the second half of the 19th century, after the unification of Italy, the archaeological collections in the Uffizi Galleries in Florence began to be split into groups and distributed to separate museums. A special central collection was formed between 1898 and 1912 in the Museo Topografico dell'Etruria (since closed after the flood of 1966). This featured an integrated exhibition of material from tombs and temples from various Etruscan sites, set in the new positivist context of prehistoric archaeology. Similar methods were used in the museum at the Villa Giulia in Rome, opened in 1889. This collection of antiquities from pre-Roman Latium and the Ager Faliscus later received finds from Veii and Cerveteri. The continuing discovery and display of finds from Tarquinian tombs and elsewhere were complemented by changes in the methodology of Etruscan scholarship, and after the discovery of the Iron Age cemeteries at Tarquinia and Bologna greater efforts were made to trace the origins of the Etruscans. The publication of the inscription on the binding of the Zagreb mummy (*Liber linteus*, ed. J. Krall, Vienna, 1892; *see* §I, 3(i) above), the important inscription on the Capua Tile (ed. F. Bücheler, *Rheinisches Museum für Philologie*, lv, 1900) and the first fascicle of the *Corpus inscriptionum etruscarum* (Leipzig, 1893) all assisted Etruscan linguistic studies.

Between the 1890s and the 1950s fewer discoveries were made, although public interest was aroused between the two world wars by the terracotta statues from the Portonaccio Temple *c.* 510–*c.* 490 BC; Rome, Villa Giulia) found at Veii. New debate on Etruscan art considered it in terms of modern artistic experience and, kindled by nationalistic interpretations of history, revived the idea of two opposed cultures, the Greco-Roman and the Etrusco-Italic. Etruscan art influenced the work of various anti-Classical and expressionist artists, including Erich Heckel and the Italian sculptors Arturo Martini and Marino Marini, while the bronzes of Alberto Giacometti clearly recall Etruscan models.

The scale of systematic research at Etruscan sites increased, in particular at Cerveteri, Vulci and Populonia. In 1928 the first International Etruscan Congress was staged and in 1932 the Institute for Etruscan Studies was set up in Florence, its journal *Studi etruschi* reflecting a wide range of specialist interests within an academic discipline whose frontiers were definitively drawn up in the pioneering work of Massimo Pallottino (see especially *Etruscologia*, Milan, 1942). The most striking new discoveries after World War II were made in the late 1950s using survey techniques developed by C. M. Lerici, which revealed a further 6000 tombs on the Monterozzi ridge at Tarquinia, including several painted hypogea. Other developments during this period were advances in linguistic analysis and the reconsideration of crucial historical questions relating to the origins of Etruscan culture. Formerly Etruscanized areas, hitherto poorly documented (e.g. Spina on the Adriatic coast, Capua and Salerno) were investigated and research became concentrated on urban sites rather than cemeteries. At Pyrgi, the port of Cerveteri, excavations begun in 1959 uncovered gold plaques dedicated by the local king Thefarie Velianus, inscribed in both Etruscan and Punic (*c.* 500 BC; Rome, Villa Giulia). Work was also undertaken at Volterra and several minor inland centres such as Acquarossa near Viterbo, Poggio Civitate (Murlo) near Siena and, later, at Tarquinia and its port Gravisca, Populonia and Cerveteri. Important exhibitions in Milan (1955), Florence (1985; *see also* §X below) and Paris and Berlin (1992–3) reflected and intensified Etruscan research, which included such major publishing projects as the *Thesaurus linguae etruscae* (Rome, 1978–) and catalogues of mirrors and Hellenistic urns. Historical questions that have aroused particular interest include the impact of Greek culture on Etruscan civilization, the origins of urban development in Etruria and at Rome and the disintegration of Etruscan society during the Roman conquest of Etruria. Ancient Etruria is now regarded as having played a vital part in the development of Classical civilization by constituting a cultural intermediary between Greece and Rome.

BIBLIOGRAPHY
G. Vasari: *Vite* (1550, rev. 2/1568); ed. G. Milanesi (1878–85), i, pp. 221–2
J. Heurgon: *La Découverte des Etrusques au début du XIX siècle* (Paris, 1973)
D. E. Rhodes: *Dennis of Etruria* (London, 1973)
G. Cipriani: *Il mito etrusco nel rinascimento fiorentino* (Florence, 1980)
M. Pallottino, ed.: *Annio da Viterbo: Documenti e ricerche* (Rome, 1981)
M. Cristofani: *La scoperta degli Etruschi: Archeologia e antiquaria nel '700* (Rome, 1983)
P. Barocchi and D. Gallo, eds: *L'Accademia etrusca* (Milan, 1985)
G. Morghen, ed.: *Bibliotheca etrusca* (Rome, 1985)
Les Etrusques et l'Europe (exh. cat., Paris, Grand Pal.; Berlin, Altes Mus.; 1992–3)

MAURO CRISTOFANI

IX. Forgeries.

Forgeries have accompanied the rediscovery of Etruscan art and civilization. The Domenican friar Giovanni Nanni, known as Annio of Viterbo (*see* §VIII above), produced apocryphal Greek texts inscribed on marble (the 'Tabulae Cybelicae') and the 'Osiris Stone' (Viterbo, Mus. Civ.), which furnished hieroglyphic 'proof' of the arrival at Viterbo of Osiris, bringing civilization to Etruria. This type of forgery was intended not for the antiquities market but to corroborate a factitious account of early Tuscan history.

With the widespread collecting of curiosities and *objets d'art* in the 18th century, forgery became a craft in its own right. Specialist interest, commerce in and exhibitions of antiquities resulted in such 18th-century forgeries as the group of small bronzes and urns, some genuine but with false inscriptions added (Pesaro, Bib. & Mus. Oliveriani), which purported to have been found at Todi in the mid-18th century. Authentic antique pieces were often 'enhanced' with extra inscriptions and designs, for example certain vase fragments and Hellenistic urns with false graffiti in the Museo Etrusco Guarnacci, Volterra, and plain mirrors, later engraved with figural scenes, such as *Oedipus and the Sphinx* (Rome, Vatican, Bib. Apostolica) or the *Dioscuri* (Paris, Bib. N., 1308). Fragmentary bronze statuettes of human figures were completed to conform to the prevailing classical style (examples in Florence, Mus. Archeol.) and small bronzes were produced from casts of ancient originals (e.g. Vienna, Ksthist. Mus.; early 19th-century copies in London, BM, produced from originals).

Such forgeries, usually readily detectable, include the spurious frames designed by Piranesi for plates in his *Parere sull'architettura* (1763) and the 'Pasticcio Piranesi' in the Villa Albani, Rome.

From the second quarter of the 19th century, interest aroused by the extensive discoveries at Vulci, Tarquinia, Cerveteri and Chiusi combined with a flourishing antiquities market to encourage forgeries. The abundance of fragmentary remains yielded by these excavations stimulated trade in heavily repaired objects. At Chiusi in particular in the mid-19th century, the restorers kept pace with the rate of local finds, often adding to these the 'antique' features sought by speculators and collectors. Many such objects passed through the Romano-German Istituto di Corrispondenza Archeologica (founded 1829). Funerary relief sculpture (cippi, urns and sarcophagi) and three-dimensional sculpture, the so-called 'cinerary statues', were subject to considerable addition and alteration and disguised with an artificial patina. Indiscriminate assemblages of ancient pieces were put together as though forming genuine groups, edges and breaks were regularized, and plaster or stone (the latter sometimes matched with the original) was used for additions. The discovery of ancient quarries in the 1840s facilitated the production of large-scale forged pieces (examples in Paris, Louvre; Chiusi, Mus. Archeol. N.; and Perugia, Mus. Archeol. N. Umbria). The subjects of forgery extended to the anthropomorphic Canopic urns characteristic of Chiusi and its territory, and to pottery. Painted vases were often repainted and Bucchero vessels assembled from disparate fragments with painted plaster filling (examples in Paris, Louvre; London, BM; Florence, Mus. Archeol.; and elsewhere).

In Rome, restorers working for the foremost collector of the period, Marchese Giampietro Campana, who owned a terracotta factory, used the above methods to forge sculpture, vases and painted terracotta plaques (examples in Paris, Louvre, and St Petersburg, Hermitage), and even bronze pastiches. The CASTELLANI family were skilled goldsmiths and active collectors, and from 1814 to 1890 they produced declared forged Etruscan necklaces, as well as copies, imitations and elaborations of original Etruscan goldwork. For this they also used filigree and granulation techniques, further refined after 1826 by Fortunato Pio Castellani's discovery of an electrolytic process, which gave gold an 'ancient' appearance (so-called 'giallone'). The occurrence of forged incision on bronze mirrors increased during the 19th century, aided by the illustrations of mirrors in Gerhard's *Etruskische Spiegel* (1840–97). The tumultuous excavations at Palestrina (Praeneste) from 1855 stimulated the trade in mirrors and cists, and some originally plain examples were given additional ornament. Several of these (including examples in Paris, Louvre; London, BM; and Kraków N. A. Cols) can be attributed to the antiquarian restorer and gem-engraver Francesco Martinetti, who collaborated with certain experts (see Guarducci) and who decorated the Pasinati Cist acquired by the British Museum, London, in 1884, with its slightly too erudite scene of *Aeneas in Latium* incised on the lid.

The effrontery of 19th-century forgers is well demonstrated by the terracotta sarcophagus, once with Castellani and of supposed Caeretan provenance, sold to the British Museum in 1873. Despite the absurd couple reclining on the lid, the incongruous relief frieze on the chest and the unlikely inscription, this parody was only unmasked in 1930 and removed from display some five years later. It was the work of Pietro Pennelli, a former custodian and restorer of the Campana collection, who, with his brother Enrico, was also responsible for some barbarous restoration of the painted terracotta plaques and the sarcophagus *Degli sposi* acquired by the Louvre, Paris, together with the Campana collection. The Pennelli brothers may also have made the two Bucchero masks with relief and incised decoration donated to the British Museum in 1866: supposedly from Chiusi, they in fact show the influence of the Cerveteri material familiar to Pennelli. Forgers active in southern Tuscany, probably Chiusi, in the 1880s produced clumsy statuettes adorning Canopic urns from Chiusi (examples in Orvieto, Mus. Etrus. Faina; Florence, Mus. Archeol.), and some 'cinerary statuettes' (examples in Arezzo, Mus. Archeol. Mecenate Eunghini Col.; Florence, Mus. Archeol.; Copenhagen, Ny Carlsberg Glyp.). In the late 19th century the market for forgeries expanded and production intensified. The discoveries at Marzabotto and Monteguragazza inspired many forged bronzes, probably from Bologna (examples in Worcester, MA, A. Mus.; Perugia, Mus. Archeol. N. Umbria; Swiss Col.). Incised mirrors show a predilection for scenes featuring Dionysos, Semele and Apollo, and Peleus and Thetis. Some silver examples in an unusual relief technique show Zeus, Apollo and Hermes (e.g. Florence, Mus. Archeol.). On a group of gold bullae, probably also late 19th century and by a single forger, are incised Dionysos, Semele and Apollo (e.g. Arezzo, Mus. Archeol. Mecenate, Eunghini Col., 1954/B). Pieces of goldwork, some in an incongruous, fine dust (It. *pulviscolo*) technique, were made at the end of the 19th century or beginning of the 20th and acquired in 1911 by the Museo Archeologico, Florence, among them a fibula clearly modelled on one from Vetulonia, discovered in the Tomb of the Lictor in 1897.

During the 20th century some large-scale terracotta forgeries were produced. Between 1915 and 1921 the Metropolitan Museum of Art, New York, bought two giant warriors and a massive helmeted head, reassembling them from the parts in which technical limitations had forced the forgers to make them. Exhibited in 1933 in the new Etruscan Gallery and fully published in 1937 (but condemned in the same year by M. Pallottino), they were not admitted by the museum authorities to be forgeries until 1961. They were made in 1914 at Orvieto by Riccardo Riccardi and his cousins Teodoro and Virgilio, the sons of Pio Riccardi, a Roman goldsmith who collaborated with Francesco Martinetti and W. Helbig; a fourth accomplice, Alfredo Fioravanti, made a belated confession, producing the missing thumb from the left hand of one of the warriors as proof. Fioravanti was also responsible for another terracotta statue, more subtle than the warrior–puppets but clearly derived from the 1916 finds from the Portonaccio Sanctuary, Veii. This female figure, acquired in 1930 by the Ny Carlsberg Glyptotek, Copenhagen, supposedly from Veii or, more likely, Conca, has the face of the *Apollo* of Veii but a body copied from the marble korai of the Athenian acropolis. Similarly inspired by the Portonaccio groups, and also made in Rome during the 1920s and 1930s, is the abominable 'Diana with Deer' assembled by the Cremonese sculptor Alceo Dossena, who was equally at home with fake statues of Greek, Gothic and Renaissance styles. After some lustre on the antiquities market, during which there was a failed attempt to sell it to the Italian government, the piece was bought in 1953 by the Art Museum, St Louis, MO, for £50,000. Countless lesser 20th-century forgeries include terracotta statues, statuettes and gorgoneion antefixes; bronze figurines, mirrors and cists; and objects in bone, ivory and amber, gemstones and jewellery. The practice of altering and 'enhancing' originals continued: witness the marble sarcophagus discovered at San Giuliano in 1906 and bought in 1927 in Rome for the Heidelberg University collection. The Dionysiac decoration painted on the sides of the lid was declared fake by the dealer.

The travelling exhibition, 'Etruscan Art and Civilization', shown in several European cities between 1955 and 1956, undoubtedly sparked off a new wave of technically accomplished forgeries. In the early 1960s about 30 terracotta plaques appeared on the market, pedestrian copies of the type originally found at Cerveteri, but in this case with decoration based on Tarquinian tomb paintings. Most were acquired by American collections (e.g. Boston, MA, Mus. F. A., 62.362–363). Female head antefixes were readily available, as were bronze figurines, including the elongated 'Evening Shadow' type (see §III, 2 above), unwisely executed in silver (examples in Basle, Hess priv. col.). Bronze weapons, tools and personal ornaments (including fibulae) were forged, and vases included a Caeretan hydria showing *Juno Sospita*, the motif taken from a Pontic amphora by the Paris Painter (London, BM). Brown and red impasto vessels, especially pithoi and braziers of Caeretan type, and Bucchero ware, remain favourite objects for forgers, and the industry shows no signs of slackening. In 1985 the Stadtmuseum of Linz organized an itinerant exhibition of a local private collection to honour the 'Year of the Etruscans'; but this contained more than one forgery, including a clay urn with sloping-roof lid copied from a Caeretan type and figured decoration modelled on the Corinthian animal style. The post-war extension of the antiquities market on a global scale has inevitably sustained the craft of forgers, who collaborate closely with the tomb-robbers, smugglers and dealers. Mixing consignments of authentic and false pieces is a standard ruse, and technical advances make precise copies possible, especially of pottery, either painted or plain, which can even pass thermoluminescence tests. Even so, most forgeries can be detected by expert eyes and solid competence.

BIBLIOGRAPHY

M. Martelli: 'Il cippo 2269 del Museo Archeologico di Chiusi: Commento al restauro e rilettura', *Prospettiva*, xiii (1978), pp. 78–82
M. Pallottino: *Saggi di antichità*, iii (Rome, 1979), pp. 1173–92
M. Guarducci: 'La cosiddetta Fibula Prenestina: Antiquari, eruditi e falsari nella Roma dell'ottocento', *Mem. Cl. Sci. Mor., Stor. & Filol.*, 8th ser., xxiv (1980), pp. 415–545
M. Martelli: 'Il Sarcofago Campana del Louvre', *Prospettiva*, xxii (1980), pp. 99–101
M. Cristofani: 'Il cratere François nella storia dell'archeologia "romantica"', *Boll. A.*, special ser. i (1981), pp. 11–23
——: *La scoperta degli Etruschi: Archeologia e antiquaria nel '700* (Rome, 1983)
G. C. Munn: *Les Bijoutiers Castellani et Giuliano: Retour à l'antique au XIXe siècle* (Fribourg and Paris, 1983; Eng. trans., London and Fribourg, 1984)
M. Guarducci: 'La cosiddetta Fibula Prenestina: Elementi nuovi', *Mem. Cl. Sci. Mor., Stor. & Filol.*, 8th ser., xxviii (1984), pp. 127–77
Fortuna degli Etruschi (Milan, 1985), pp. 130–34
J. G. Szilágyi: 'Fälschungen etruskischer Kunstwerke', *Die Welt der Etrusker: Archäologische Denkmäler aus Museen der sozialistischen Länder* (Berlin, 1988), pp. 393–6
M. Guarducci: 'Per la storia dell'Istituto Archeologico Germanico, I: 1887: La Fibula Prenestina e Wolfgang Helbig', *Mitt. Dt. Archäol. Inst.: Röm. Abt.*, xcix (1992), pp. 307–13

MARINA MARTELLI

X. Collections, museums and exhibitions.

The three most comprehensive collections of Etruscan material are in Italy. That of the museum at the Villa Giulia, Rome, is drawn from all over southern Etruria and Latium, and here the prize exhibits are the material from the sanctuary at Pyrgi and the Orientalizing tomb-groups from Praeneste. The Museo Gregoriano Etrusco, part of the Vatican Museums, Rome, is especially rich in funerary objects from Vulci (the Gugliemi Collection) and Cerveteri (material from the Regolini-Galassi Tomb and others). The Museo Archeologico, Florence, is the centre for finds from northern and central Etruria, and the arrangement of its topographical section was quite revolutionary when it opened in 1898. Since the disastrous flood of 1966, however, this part has remained inaccessible, although the necessary reorganization has provided opportunities for modern scientific restoration and study of the affected material.

The many local museums in the area that once constituted ancient Etruria include those at Cerveteri (Mus. N. Cerite), notable for its 7th- and 6th-century BC pottery; Tarquinia (Pal. Vitelleschi) for tomb paintings and for material from 19th- and early 20th-century excavations; Vulci (Mus. N.), for later discoveries of tomb-groups; and Grosseto (Mus. Archeol.) for material from various sites in central Etruria. In northern Etruria the museums at Chiusi (Mus. Archeol. N.) and Volterra (Mus. Etrus. Guarnacci) are notable, the latter especially for its unrivalled series of sculptured cinerary urns. There is also a considerable body of work from Chiusi (the Casuccini Collection) in Palermo (Mus. Reg.). The architectural and other non-funerary finds from Poggio Civitate (Murlo) and Acquarossa are given fine displays in Siena (Pal. Pub.) and Viterbo (Mus. Civ.) respectively. Outside Italy many of the larger European and American museums have representative collections of Etruscan sculpture, bronzes, jewellery and pottery, from which the British Museum, London, and the Ny Carlsberg Glyptotek, Copenhagen, must be singled out for their richness. Also outstanding are the Louvre, Paris, the Boston Museum of Fine Arts, and the Metropolitan Museum of Art, New York.

The earliest international interest in Etruscan culture was created by the exhibition 'Etruscan and Greek Antiquities' organized in London in 1836–7 by the Campanari brothers (see §VIII above), which recreated Etruscan tombs and their contents. No further comparable exhibition was staged until the 'Mostra dell' arte e della civiltà etrusca' in 1955, which was shown in Switzerland, Italy, France, Holland, Norway and Germany, and marked a resurgence of interest in the Etruscans. It was followed in

1967 by the exhibition 'Arte e civiltà degli Etruschi' (1967), shown at Vienna, Stockholm and Turin, and two exhibitions of Etruscan art in North America, at Worcester, MA, and Santa Barbara, CA. In 1980–81 the exhibition 'Prima Italia', covering the whole of the Italian peninsula in the first millennium BC, toured several European capitals. More restricted in scope were the exhibitions on the cemetery archaeology of Cerveteri ('Gli Etruschi di Cerveteri') in Milan (Civ. Mus. Archeol.) in 1980; on mirrors ('Reflections on the Etruscan Mirror') at Tallahassee, Florida (1981); and on luxury arts ('Cento preziosi Etruschi') at Arezzo (1984). The huge 'Civiltà degli Etruschi' display in Florence (Mus. Archeol.) in 1985 dwarfed all previous exhibitions. It covered almost all aspects of material culture and, as the centrepiece of the Progetto Etruschi, it was held simultaneously with eight other exhibitions in Tuscany and Umbria, of which the most important covered domestic and civic architecture (Siena), sanctuaries (Arezzo) and ash urns and other aspects of late Etruscan crafts (Volterra and Chiusi); it was followed by 'Gli Etruschi di Tarquinia' at Milan in 1986, on the art and archaeology of Tarquinia, and then 'Gli Etruschi al nord del Po', on the settlements in northern Italy. Two later exhibitions were on a lavish scale: 'La grande Roma dei Tarquini' (1990; Rome, Pal. Espos.), on the Etruscan impact on early Rome and Latium, and 'Les Etrusques et l'Europe', shown in 1992–3 in Paris (Grand Pal.) and Berlin (Altes Mus.), which focused on Etruscan contacts with northern and western Europe. These exhibitions testify to the growing strength of interest in Etruscan civilization.

BIBLIOGRAPHY
[Campanari]: *A Brief Description of the Etruscan and Greek Antiquities Now Exhibited at No. 121 Pall Mall opposite the Opera Colonnade* (London, [1837])
M. Pallottino, ed.: *Arte e civiltà degli Etruschi* (Turin, 1967)
G. Proietti, ed.: *Il Museo Nazionale Etrusco di Villa Giulia* (Rome, 1980)
M. Cristofani, ed.: *Civiltà degli Etruschi* (Milan, 1985)
E. Macnamara: *The Etruscans* (London, 1990)
Les Etrusques et l'Europe (Paris, 1992)

TOM RASMUSSEN

Etruscan school [It. Scuola etrusca]. Group of Italian and English landscape painters. It was formally associated in Rome only during the winter of 1883–4; the name of the group was never widely accepted and came to refer retrospectively to the landscapes that artists in this circle painted and exhibited together from the 1860s. They were united by an affection for the countryside of Italy. Under the influence of GIOVANNI COSTA they revived the tradition of landscape painting that derived from Claude Lorrain and Nicolas Poussin and that Thomas Jones, Pierre Henri Valenciennes and Jean-Baptiste-Camille Corot had explored. The aesthetic principles that determined the nature of the paintings of the Etruscan school were first discussed by Costa with GEORGE HEMING MASON and FREDERIC LEIGHTON, whom he had met in 1852 and 1853 respectively. From 1877 Costa exhibited landscapes at the Grosvenor Gallery, London, in the company of George James Howard (later 9th Earl of Carlisle; *see* HOWARD (ii), (4)), Matthew Ridley Corbet (1850–1902), Edith Corbet (*c.* 1850–1920), William Blake Richmond (*see* RICHMOND (ii), (2)), Edgar Barclay (1842–1913) and

Walter Maclaren (*fl* 1869–1903) and the Italians Gaetano Vannicola (1859–1923) and Napoleone Parisani (1854–1932). These painters, with the addition of Norberto Pazzini (1856–1937), were the original members of the Etruscan school. Their style of painting is characterized by breadth of handling and a fondness for the subdued tonalities of panoramic distances. Costa instructed his followers that the purpose of the landscape artist is to evoke and describe the emotions and affections felt for his native land; sentiment is to be regarded as the most important element in a painting; 'the study which contains the sentiment, the divine inspiration, should be done from nature,' he is recorded as saying. Then, 'from this study the picture should be painted at home, and, if necessary, supplementary studies be made elsewhere' (Agresti, p. 213). From 1888 the members of the group transferred their allegiance from the Grosvenor Gallery to the New Gallery, London, exhibiting there until 1909. Other painters who joined the Etruscan school or were influenced by Costa include Walter Crane, Thomas Armstrong and the American Eugene Benson (1839–1908). (*See also* ROME, §III, 7)

BIBLIOGRAPHY
O. R. Agresti: *Giovanni Costa: His Life, Work and Times* (London, 1904)
The Etruscan School (exh. cat., ed. P. Skipwith; London, F.A. Soc., 1976)
Nino Costa ed i suoi amici inglesi (exh. cat. by S. Berresford and P. Nicholls, Milan, Circ. Stampa, 1982)
The Etruscans: Painters of the Italian Landscape, 1850–1920 (exh. cat. by C. Newall, York, C.A.G.; Stoke-on-Trent, City Mus. & A.G.; London, Leighton House A.G. & Mus.; 1989)

CHRISTOPHER NEWALL

Etruscan style. Type of delicate, painted Neo-classical decoration, derived mainly from the shapes, motifs and colours of antique vases. It was part of the quest in Europe in the last quarter of the 18th century for a contemporary expression in interior design and the applied arts. The term is applied loosely to various schemes of decoration inspired by Classical sources, involving Renaissance GROTESQUE ornament, as well as themes inspired by discoveries made at HERCULANEUM and Pompeii (*see* POMPEII, §VI) in the 18th century, or frequently a mixture of these sources. This fact serves to underline the complex antecedents of this style, which was originally based on the misidentification of imported Greek vases dug up in southern Italy and thought to have been made by ancient Etruscans (*see* ETRUSCAN, §VIII), a culture promoted in some quarters as having been the original fount for the whole of Classical antiquity. Indeed, the Etruscan style derived little direct artistic influence from that culture as such, except for certain potent historical associations promoted by the controversies concerning cultural debts. Initially represented by Josiah Wedgwood's black basaltes ware, the Etruscan style was developed by James Wyatt and the Adam brothers during the 1770s as a means of embellishing their intimately scaled rooms. Apart from scattered manifestations on the Continent and the use of the term for classicizing furniture of the Louis XVI period, this style remained substantially an English phenomenon. It survived until the last decades of the 18th century when it was eclipsed by the more vigorous and archaeologically exact taste of the mature POMPEIAN REVIVAL.

1. Historical accounts of Etruscan art. 2. Wedgwood. 3. Interior design. 4. Decline.

1. HISTORICAL ACCOUNTS OF ETRUSCAN ART. One of the earliest discussions of Etruscan art since antiquity occurred in Vasari's preface to his *Vite* (1550), to support his claims for the outstanding creative history and destiny of Tuscany. However, it was a Scottish historian, Sir Thomas Dempster, who produced the pioneering study of Etruscan culture in *De Etruria regali*, written in 1616–25 but not published until 1723–5 by Thomas Coke, later 1st Earl of Leicester. This work, and the writings of the Neapolitan philosopher Giambattista Vico, who first suggested the autonomy of Roman civilization as derived from the Etruscans in his *Scienza nuova* (Naples) of 1725, helped to promote a growing patriotic movement in 18th-century Italy. Encouraged by this 'Etruscheria', early excavations were followed by the foundation of the Accademia Etrusca at Cortona in 1726 and the Museo Guarnacci at Volterra in 1750. During the same period, new finds were evaluated in a substantial body of publications by such Italian scholars as Filippo Buonarroti, Anton Francesco Gori, Giovanni Battista Passeri, Abbé Mario Guarnacci (1701–85) and the Comte de Caylus. By the early 1760s this material had assumed a new significance for early Neo-classical designers searching for fresh sources of inspiration.

Around 1760 the British dealer Thomas Jenkins began excavating tombs at Corneto (Etruscan Tarquinia), accompanied on occasion by his associate, the architect and engraver Giovanni Battista Piranesi. In 1761 Piranesi portrayed the Etruscans as Rome's chief source of inspiration, when he countered the arguments of Johann Joachim Winckelmann and the Philhellenic cause in his *Della magnificenza ed architettura de' Romani*. 'Etruscheria' was swiftly transformed into 'Etruscomania' and, from the confusion of evidence, extravagant claims were made concerning the influence of Greek or Etruscan culture on the Romans. In 1765 Piranesi issued three etched plates of wall decorations derived from tombs at Corneto and Chiusi in a further polemical work, grandly entitled *Della introduzione e del progresso delle belle arti en Europa ne' tempi antichi*. At this time the Scottish antiquarian James Byres was inspired by the idea of preparing a 'History of the Etruscans'. The engraved plates based on his drawings of Etruscan tombs were in circulation by the later 1760s, although not actually published until 1842 as *'Hypogaei', or the Sepulchral Caverns of Tarquinia*.

Among Byres's correspondents concerning these plates was Sir William Hamilton (i), the eminent connoisseur and Envoy Extraordinary at Naples, who had been accumulating a major collection of antiquities, mainly found in southern Italy. This included a quantity of painted vases (London, BM) that were widely believed to be Etruscan. Between 1766 and 1776 Hamilton published this material in a lavish four-volume *Collection of Etruscan, Greek and Roman Antiquities* (discussed and illustrated with coloured plates by the scholar Baron d'Hancarville), with the explicit intention of providing model designs for contemporary artists and craftsmen.

2. WEDGWOOD. Proof plates of Hamilton's collection were in circulation in the 1760s, and they were seen not only by Piranesi but also by the potter Josiah Wedgwood. He was then experimenting with a traditional form of Staffordshire blackware or basaltes, as it subsequently became known. Initially 'Etruscan' was Wedgwood's term for certain basalt vases in a substance meant to imitate that civilization's bronze vessels, made through a process involving lightly fired metallic gold. He soon went on to use basaltes as the basis for other wares decorated with encaustic and enamel paintings; these he also described as being in the 'Etruscan style', and they were closely based on Hamilton's plates. In 1769 Wedgwood and his partner Thomas Bentley (1731–80) celebrated the opening of Etruria, their new factory at Burslem, Staffs, by producing six commemorative 'First Day' painted vases, each inscribed *Artes Etruriae renascuntur* ('The arts of Etruria are reborn'; for illustration *see* WEDGWOOD). The resulting range of objects in basaltes was to parallel in extent and to become even more popular than Wedgwood's other stoneware, called Jasper, being cheaper to produce and offering an ideal medium for displaying shape and fine modelling. Wedgwood followed up his vases with antique plaques and large cameos, advertised as in 'black basaltes with Etruscan red burnt-in grounds, and in polished Biscuits with brown and grey grounds'. By 1773 the first *Catalogue of Cameos, Intaglios, Medals, and Bas Reliefs, with a General Account of Vases and Other Ornaments after the Antique* included 'Etruscan' ornaments as 'fit either for inlaying, as Medallions, in the Pannels of Rooms, as Tablets for Chimney Pieces, or for hanging up as ornaments in libraries. . .or as Pictures for Dressing Rooms'.

3. INTERIOR DESIGN. Hamilton's ideals and Wedgwood's initiatives were extended to interior design as a whole. From the 1760s a succession of painted interiors that combined grotesque ornaments with designs based on new material recovered from Herculaneum were undertaken in close rivalry by James Stuart and Robert Adam and James Adam. James Wyatt followed suit with his Cupola Room at Heaton Hall (1775–8), Lancs, and he appears to have been the first to have devised an Etruscan-style interior. This was for a modest fishing-pavilion at Fawley Court, Bucks, in 1771. Its pale green walls were given the appearance of being hung or inlaid with Antique terracotta figures, medallions and plaques in the Wedgwood manner. The scheme was probably executed by Biagio Rebecca (1735–after 1784), who was to be closely associated with the diffusion of the Etruscan style.

Predictably, the Adam brothers were swift to adopt Wyatt's idea and in 1773 they decorated the Dressing Room of the Countess of Derby's house in Grosvenor Square, London, in the new taste. They published engraved designs (frequently issued in colour) for the ceiling and chimney-piece in the second volume of their *Works in Architecture* (1779). While flagrantly claiming to have invented the style, they did for the first time identify by name this decorative system and attempted a definition of its essentials as involving 'colour [i.e. terracotta and black]. . .both evidently taken from the vases and urns of the Etruscans'.

Despite the characteristic opportunism of the Adam brothers, their work in at least eight interiors designed between 1773 and 1780 should also be seen as a considered response to Piranesi's call for a modern style in interior design, based on a broadly eclectic use of antique sources. In his *Diverse maniere d'adornare i cammini ed ogni altra parte degli edifizi* (1769), much of Piranesi's lengthy preface further developed his theories concerning the Etruscan creative genius and its Roman legacy. Piranesi, like Wedgwood, had recognized the possibilities for transposing vase motifs for use in other decorative functions. At least two of Piranesi's opening plates, demonstrating this principle in wall compositions with chimney-pieces, clearly influenced Robert Adam's Etruscan interiors, particularly the finest to survive, at Osterley Park House, near London (see fig.). This was carried out mainly around 1775–6 as a dressing room for the banker Robert Child (1739–82) and his wife Sarah. Over 35 surviving drawings (1772–9; London, Soane Mus.) are devoted to this integrated scheme, one that involved not only the room's four walls, two doors and ceiling, but also its carpet (no longer extant), eight chairs, a chimney-board, a firescreen and the curtain cornices of the two windows. The painted wall decoration, on sheets of paper pasted on to canvas, was executed mainly in colours of terracotta and black on a pale blue-grey ground and incorporates highly coloured medallions of Classical subjects. Apart from Antonio Zucchi's central roundel on the ceiling, the painting, which extended to the furniture, was carried out by Pietro Maria Borgnis (1739/43–after 1810).

Contemporaries were swift to identify Adam's sources for Osterley's Etruscan Room; Horace Walpole in 1778 acidly noted resemblances to Wedgwood's ware, while in 1788 Mrs Lybbe-Powys noted debts to Herculaneum. Adam's wall compositions certainly owed much to the pergola or trellis-like themes of Pompeian second-style wall paintings, and the intermingling of Roman and 'Etruscan' contributions reflected the fertile complexity of Piranesi's own eclectic system.

In addition to those at Derby House and Osterley Park, Etruscan Rooms by Adam included the partially surviving scheme at Home House (20 Portman Square), London, and a small room under the stairs of Osterley's garden front. Others are recorded for Cumberland House (1780) and 'Mr Adamson's Parlour' (possibly at the Adelphi), both in London, as well as at Harewood House and Byram House, both in Yorkshire. Furthermore, a particularly striking example of the application of the Adam system by another designer can be seen at Woodhall Park, Herts, where in the 1770s Thomas Leverton provided the India administrator, Sir Thomas Rumbold (1736–91), with a marble-floored saloon in the Etruscan taste. There, the main emphasis was placed on a striking umbrella dome with appropriate terracotta and black ornaments, matched by walls with panels and medallions probably painted by Borgnis. The marble chimney-piece was enriched not only with painted panels but also with a form of scagliola inlay.

By the 1780s in France painted interiors after the Antique had been fully absorbed by the Louis XVI style, introduced by such designers as Charles-Louis Clérisseau. There is no trace of the 'Etruscan Room' Clérisseau is recorded in 1764 as having produced for Cardinal Alessandro Albani in Rome; he subsequently designed grotesque schemes for Laurent Grimod de la Reynière in Paris in the 1770s. A more specifically Etruscan manner

The Etruscan Dressing Room, designed by Robert Adam, with painted decorations by Pietro Maria Borgnis and Antonio Zucchi, Osterley Park House, London, *c.* 1775–6

appeared in interiors by F.-J. Bélanger and J.-D. Dugourc, and it was also applied to furniture by Georges Jacob (1739–1814), profusely embellished with palmettes and other ornaments. A set of Jacob's chairs, made to Hubert Robert's designs in 1787 for Marie Antoinette's Laiterie at Rambouillet, was described by Jacob as 'de forme nouvelle de genre étrusque'. Similarly, in Italy the 'Etruscan' dinner service (examples in Windsor Castle, Berks, Royal Col.) produced at the Royal Neapolitan Porcelain factory in 1785–7 justified the epithet only insofar as it was decorated with paintings of antique vases.

In England the Etruscan style underwent a new and astringent interpretation by Wyatt in a small anteroom at Heveningham Hall, Suffolk, completed before 1784. This was part of an extensive scheme for the interior of Sir Robert Taylor's building, commissioned by the banker Sir Gerard Vanneck. In what may be regarded as the purest expression of the Etruscan style, Wyatt (probably in close collaboration with Rebecca) purged the residual traces of illusionistic devices derived from Herculaneum and from the grotesque. Pale green walls with white wood or plaster enrichments offered an austere context for terracotta-coloured, figurative panels. Included in the accompanying suite of painted furniture was a pair of idiosyncratic candelabra set in opposing niches. Each took the form of a tapering pedestal surmounted by a vase with metal branches attached to ram's heads at the angles. The achieved balance between ingenuity of detail and overall restraint at Heveningham makes the later Etruscan interiors of Adam appear by comparison overwrought and somewhat effete.

4. DECLINE. Hamilton published his second collection in 1791, illustrated by Wilhelm Tischbein's severe line-engravings. Recent scholarship had identified his vases as largely Greek in origin, and Hamilton justified his own change of opinion in the text. Nevertheless, misconceptions persisted, even among such specialist designers as C. H. Tatham: writing from Rome to Henry Holland in 1796 Tatham described illustrations he had made as being 'in the Etruscan style, precisely copied from Sir Wm. Hamilton's Vases and applied to small rooms and cabinets'. By then fresh revelations at Pompeii had begun to replace those at Herculaneum as a new focus of interest, encouraging a taste for bolder, more strongly coloured interior schemes, as supported by archaeological evidence. This was vividly demonstrated by the remarkable Pompeian Gallery at Packington Hall, Warwicks, executed in 1785–8 to the combined designs of Heneage Finch, 4th Earl of Aylesford, and Joseph Bonomi (for illustration *see* POMPEIAN REVIVAL).

The waning of the Etruscan style's popularity by 1790 was closely paralleled by a change from Etruscomania to the sober discipline of Etruscology. This was largely established by the researches in Florence of the Abbé Luigi Lanzi, author of the magisterial *Saggio di lingua etrusca e di altre antiche d'Italia* of 1789. This work was followed in 1806 by *Dei vasi antichi dipinti volgarmente chiamati Etruschi*, his highly systematic analysis of vase paintings, which categorically refutes those persisting errors that had originally done so much to promote the Etruscan style. When it made one rare reappearance in Italy during the 19th century, the Etruscan style was by then sufficiently distant from earlier emotive associations to be treated as just one among many historicist modes of expression. In 1834 Pelagio Palagi and Carlo Bellosio (1801–49) created an Etruscan Room (complete with antique vases) in the Castello Reale di Racconigi, near Turin, as one of the refashioned interiors for King Charles-Albert of Piedmont (*reg* 1831–49). In this small room, richly painted themes from vases were framed by a highly eclectic vocabulary of ornament with all the heavy opulence of the late Empire Style.

BIBLIOGRAPHY
T. Dempster: *De Etruria regali*, 7 vols (Florence, 1723–5)
A. F. Gori: *Museum Etruscum exhibens insignia veterum etruscorum monumenta*, 3 vols (Florence, 1737–43)
——: *Museum Cortonense* (Florence, 1750)
C.-P. de Caylus: *Recueil d'antiquités égyptiennes, étrusques, grecques, romaines et gauloises*, 7 vols (Paris, 1752–67)
M. Guarnacci: *Origini italiche ossiano memorie istorico-Etrusche sopra l'antichissimo regno d'Italia*, 3 vols (Lucca, 1767–72)
G. B. Passeri: *Picturae etruscorum in vasculis*, 3 vols (Rome, 1767–75)
L. A. Lanzi: *Saggio di lingua etrusca e di altre antiche d'Italia*, 2 vols (Rome, 1789)
——: *Dei vasi antichi dipinti volgarmente chiamati etruschi* (Florence, 1806)
J. Byres: 'Hypogaei', or the Sepulchral Caverns of Tarquinia (London, 1842)
W. Mankowitz: *Wedgwood* (London, 1953)
R. Bloch: 'The History of Etruscology', *The Etruscans* (London, 1958), pp. 19–47
F. J. B. Watson: *Louis XIV Furniture* (London, 1960)
E. Harris: *The Furniture of Robert Adam* (London, 1963)
D. Stillman: *The Decorative Work of Robert Adam* (London, 1966)
B. Fothergill: *Sir William Hamilton* (London, 1969)
E. Croft-Murray: *Decorative Painting in England, 1537–1837*, ii (London, 1970)
J. Wilton-Ely, ed.: *G. B. Piranesi: The Polemical Works* (Farnborough, 1972) [reprints Piranesi's main publications on the Greco-Roman debate]
J. Wilton-Ely: 'Vision and Design: Piranesi's 'Fantasia' and the Graeco-Roman Controversy', *Piranèse et les français, 1740–90*, ed. G. Brunel (Rome, 1978), pp. 529–52
E. Harris and J. M. Robinson: 'New Light on Fawley', *Archit. Hist.*, xxvii (1984), pp. 263–5
J. Hardy and M. Tomlin: *Osterley Park House*, V&A guidebook (London, 1985)
L'accademia etrusca (exh. cat., ed P. Barocchi and D. Gallo; Cortona, Pal. Casali, 1985)
R. Reilly: *Wedgwood*, 2 vols (London, 1989)
J. Wilton-Ely: 'Pompeian and Etruscan Tastes in the Neo-classical Country-house Interior', *The Fashioning and Functioning of the British Country House*, ed. G. Jackson and others (Washington, DC, 1989), pp. 51–73

JOHN WILTON-ELY

Etselo. *See* HEZELO.

Et-Tell. *See* AI.

Ettinger, Pavel (Davydovich) [Pinkwas Beniamin; Lyubitel'] (*b* Lublin [now Poland], 10 Oct 1866; *d* Moscow, 15 Sept 1948). Russian critic and collector. Having completed his studies at the Commercial Faculty of Riga Polytechnic (1887) he began a career as a banker in Moscow. Simultaneously he took up writing on art and in 1903 became art critic for the newspaper *Russkiye vedomosti*. He subsequently wrote for several of the leading European art journals of the early 20th century, such as *The Studio* (1904–29), for which he was Moscow correspondent, *Mir iskusstva* ('World of art'; 1904), *Vesy* (1905–8), *Die Kunst* (1907–14), *Der Cicerone* (1909–30), *Russkiy bibliofil* (1912–16), *Sredi kollektsionerov* (1921–4) and *Apollon* (1910–17), for which he was in charge of the 'Rossica' and 'Artistic news from the West' sections. This work, together with his copious correspondence with many leading artists and other cultural figures from all over Europe, made him one of the foremost informants, for both Eastern and Western Europe, on artistic developments across the continent. In 1909 he also began to work for U. Thieme and F. Becker's *Allgemeines Lexikon* (Leipzig, 1907–50), ultimately contributing about 500 entries on Russian painters, graphic artists and sculptors. The nature of these articles, with the need for concise, factual information, allowed Ettinger to develop a distinctive and laconic style of writing. This was further in evidence in his monographs dedicated to Polish and Russian artists (Stanisław Noakowski, Ignaty Nivinsky (1881–1933), Vladimir Favorsky and Artur Fonvizin). His preference for graphic art, as seen in these books, was further embodied in his own vast collection of drawings and engravings, mainly of old and modern Russian artists such as Mikhail Vrubel', Leonid Pasternak, Yelizaveta Kruglikova, Mstislav Dobuzhinsky, Konstantin Bogayevsky, Mikhail Larionov, Kazimir Malevich, Georgy Vereysky and Vladimir Tatlin, now in the Pushkin Museum of Fine Arts, Moscow. Ettinger began to establish his collection in the late 1890s, first acquiring art posters, then drawings and engravings (and, to a lesser extent, paintings), many of which were given to him by the artists as a gesture of friendship.

WRITINGS

Stanislav Noakovsky: Opyt kharakteristiki [Stanisław Noakowski: an attempt at a description] (Moscow, 1922)

I. I. Nivinsky: Krymskaya syuita [I. I. Nivinsky: Crimean suite] (Moscow, 1925)

V. A. Favorsky (Kazan', 1926)

Knizhnyye znaki V. A. Favorskogo [The bookplates of V. A. Favorsky] (Moscow, 1933)

A. V. Fonvizin (Moscow, 1940)

BIBLIOGRAPHY

A. Demskaya and N. Semyonova: *P. D. Ettinger: Stat'i, iz perepiski, vospominaniya sovremennikov* [P. D. Ettinger: articles, from his correspondence, reminiscences of his contemporaries] (Moscow, 1989)

JEREMY HOWARD, SERGEY KUZNETSOV

Ettinghausen, Richard (*b* Frankfurt am Main, 5 Feb 1906; *d* Princeton, NJ, 2 April 1979). American curator and art historian of German birth. He received his PhD in Arabic from the University of Frankfurt in 1931 with a dissertation on Koranic references to anti-paganism. His first position (1931–3) was as assistant to ERNST KÜHNEL in the Islamic Department of the Berlin Museum. In 1933 he left Germany to study for a year in London and then moved to the United States. As a research associate with the American Institute of Persian Art and Archaeology, he worked as an author and editor for *A Survey of Persian Art*; much of his later research focused on the arts of Iran. He taught at the University of Michigan (1938–44) and then moved to the Freer Gallery of Art in Washington, DC, where he was Associate in Near Eastern Art (1944–58), Curator (1958–61) and Head Curator (1961–7). The Freer collection of Near Eastern Art, both Islamic and pre-Islamic, and many other collections of Islamic art were shaped by his eye and his advice. He consulted to the Los Angeles County Museum of Art and the L. A. Mayer Memorial Institute for Islamic Art in Jerusalem and was Consultative Chairman of the Islamic Department at the Metropolitan Museum of Art in New York (1969–79). On leaving the Freer, he was also named professor at the Institute of Fine Arts of New York University where he helped to secure an important bequest for teaching and research in Islamic studies from the Hagop Kevorkian Fund. A member of international academies in the USA, Europe and Turkey, he received the Iranian Decoration of the Imperial Crown (1965) and 'Pour le Mérite' from West Germany (1976).

Ettinghausen wrote fundamental studies in almost every category of Islamic art except architecture and archaeology, virtually all in the form of articles. His work includes enormous numbers of book reviews and review articles, introductions to catalogues, dictionary and encyclopedia articles, appreciations, obituaries and bibliographies. He edited many collective works and journals, including *Ars Islamica* (1938–50), *Ars Orientalis* (1954–7) and *Kunst des Orients* (1968–79). Two basic concerns emerge from his scholarship: iconography, which for Islamic art necessarily includes a consideration of the content and style of any inscription on an object or a building; and the stylistic analysis of painted images. Both derived from his early museum training and his innate sympathy for objects, often of the humblest materials. His interest in painting extended from the western Islamic lands to Turkey, Iran and India. His studies of objects are his true intellectual legacy: they begin with a careful and precise description and then develop into a far-reaching examination of a problem, an issue or a phenomenon, which always vibrates with an underlying iconographical resonance and illuminates an entire period or region.

WRITINGS

Studies in Muslim Iconography I: The Unicorn (Washington, DC, 1950)

ed.: *Aus der Welt des Islamische Kunst: Festschrift für Ernst Kühnel* (Berlin, 1959)

Paintings of the Sultans and Emperors of India in American Collections (New Delhi, 1961)

Persian Miniatures in the Bernard Berenson Collection (Milan, 1961)

Arab Painting (Geneva, 1962)

From Byzantium to Sasanian Iran and the Islamic World (Leiden, 1972)

ed.: *Islamic Art in the Metropolitan Museum of Art* (New York, 1972)

ed. with E. B. MacDougall: *The Islamic Garden* (Washington, DC, 1976)

ed. with E. Yarshater: *Highlights of Persian Art* (Boulder, 1979)

Richard Ettinghausen: Islamic Art and Archaeology (Collected Papers), ed. M. Rosen-Ayalon (Berlin, 1984) [contains reprints of 58 of Ettinghausen's most significant articles]

with O. Grabar: *The Art and Architecture of Islam, 600–1250*, Pelican Hist. A. (Harmondsworth, 1987)

BIBLIOGRAPHY

P. Chelkowski, ed.: *Studies in Art and Literature of the Near East in Honor of Richard Ettinghausen* (New York, 1974) [bibliog. of writings to 1973 arranged by category]

O. Grabar: Obituary, *Artibus Asiae*, xli (1979), pp. 281–4

ELEANOR SIMS

Etty, William (*b* York, 10 March 1787; *d* York, 13 Nov 1849). English painter. Born into a Methodist family, he was the seventh child of a miller and baker in Feasegate, York, and in 1798 he was apprenticed as a printer to Robert Peck, publisher of the *Hull Packet*. Financial support from his uncle, a banker, allowed him to go to London in 1805, where he entered the Royal Academy Schools in 1806. For a year, in 1807–8, he was a pupil of Thomas Lawrence, who greatly influenced him. Following the death of his uncle in 1809 he became financially secure. From 1811 he exhibited regularly at the Royal Academy and the British Institution and in 1816 worked in the studio of Jean-Baptiste Regnault in Paris.

At the Royal Academy in 1820 Etty exhibited his first substantial figure composition, the *Coral Finders: Venus and her Youthful Satellites Arriving at the Isle of Paphos* (London, priv. col., see Farr, pl. 12). He visited France, Italy and the Low Countries and, in 1822–4, made a prolonged Grand Tour of France and Italy. This culminated in a stay of nine months in Venice, where he was honoured by the Accademia di Belle Arti. These travels enabled him to see and copy many works by the Old Masters, especially Titian, Veronese and Rubens. The rich, warm colouring of his work was modelled on that found in Venetian painting while his method of composition derived from that of Rubens. He filled his canvas with rhythmic groups of nude or semi-nude figures but, unlike Rubens, he rarely gave these groups any depth. Their frieze-like arrangement recalls Poussin and also the outline illustrations of John Flaxman, which he copied. In 1825 he met Delacroix, the near-contemporary with whom he is most often compared.

During the 1820s Etty achieved recognition: he was elected an ARA in 1824 and RA in 1825, defeating Constable by eighteen votes to five in the latter election. His success was due to such large history paintings as *The Combat* (exh. RA 1825) and *Benaiah* (exh. RA 1829; both

William Etty: *Benaiah*, oil on canvas, 3.05×4.00 m, exhibited 1829 (Edinburgh, National Gallery of Scotland)

Edinburgh, N.G.; see fig.). He was one of the few British artists to make a career out of this genre, an ambition that had driven others to despair and, in the case of Benjamin Robert Haydon, even suicide. The Classical or biblical subject-matter of the history works gave Etty the ideal pretext for painting the nude. He did, however, believe that they had a serious purpose and proclaimed that his intention in all his major paintings had been 'to paint some great moral on the heart'. In *The Combat* he sought to convey 'the beauty of Mercy' and in *Benaiah* the virtue of valour. These were two of a series of 'nine colossal pictures' that Etty came to regard as his life's achievement. The figures in Etty's large exhibition pieces were based on countless painted studies of the nude made in the life room of the Royal Academy, as in *Seated Female Nude* (*c.* 1825; Providence, RI Sch. Des., Mus. A.). These studies were normally executed on sized but unprimed millboard. On this brownish ground Etty worked in a very limited number of colours, first laying in the lights and shadows and subsequently achieving half-tints by glazing and scumbling. He sought to achieve 'much lustre, beauty and fleshiness'. Often the studies were almost directly transcribed, with the result that there can be a conflict between the solid realism of the figures and the lofty ideal of the subject.

During the 1830s and 1840s Etty generally concentrated on smaller, less ambitious works. In this he catered to the market, to the point that, in his later years, he risked being accused of selling out to the dealers. The change also reflected his different patronage: during the 1820s he had to some extent enjoyed the support of traditional patrons: the nobility and landed gentry. Increasingly, however, he came to depend on such professional men, merchants and industrialists as John Sheepshanks, the cloth merchant, Robert Vernon, the military supplier, and, most particularly, Joseph Gillot, the pen manufacturer.

Throughout his career Etty painted portraits, the more formal of which reveal the influence of Lawrence though without his virtuosity and panache. The most striking are such penetrating but less formal studies of close friends painted towards the end of his career as *John Brook* (1838) and *John Harper* (1839–41; both York, C.A.G.). In his later years he also produced such landscape paintings as *The Strid, Bolton Abbey* (1843; York, C.A.G.) and such still-lifes as *Still-Life: Dead Pheasant and Fruit* (*c.* 1829; York, C.A.G.), the latter belonging to a genre little explored by British artists before the 20th century. At their best his spontaneous oil sketches of landscape bear comparison with Constable's. Etty remained in touch with friends in York throughout his career in London. He campaigned for the establishment (in 1842) of a school of design in

York and, despite his shy, reticent nature, he was involved in campaigns to preserve the city's medieval walls and gateways, then under threat. In 1848 he retired to York, where he died in 1849, a bachelor, with a fortune of £17,000.

Etty is the only major British painter before the 20th century to have devoted his career to the nude. Remarkably, his public recognition and success were achieved in the face of vitriolic censure from a press that accused him of indecency. Doggedly determined, however, he was not deflected from his path by the prim critics he referred to as 'Noodles'. His contemporary reputation is attested to by the rare honour of a one-man exhibition at the Society of Arts in London in 1849, which brought together 133 of his pictures. However, this received a mixed reception, as Etty's painterly rhetoric was then being superseded by the detailed naturalism of the Pre-Raphaelites. Though famous and financially successful in his day, his reputation declined after his death and has never fully recovered, although his work has always had its admirers. In the 20th century his full-scale exhibition pieces have been regarded as over-ambitious works requiring intellectual and imaginative powers beyond Etty's capabilities. The smaller, informal works, however, have been valued for their painterly handling and immediacy. The life studies, in particular, have been admired for their colour and their ability to convey the sensuous qualities of the nude.

WRITINGS

'Autobiography', *A. J.* [London], xi (1849), pp. 13, 37–40

BIBLIOGRAPHY

A. Gilchrist: *Life of William Etty*, 2 vols (London, 1855/*R* in 1 vol., East Ardsley, 1978)
W. Camidge: *The Poet-Painter of York: William Etty* (York, 1899)
W. Gaunt and F. G. Roe: *Etty and the Nude* (Leigh-on-Sea, 1943)
J. M. Biggins: *Etty and York* (York, 1949)
William Etty (exh. cat. by D. Farr, ACGB, 1955, rev. with suppl. 1955)
D. Farr: *William Etty* (London, 1958)
B. J. Bailey: *William Etty's Nudes* (Pulloxhill, Bedford, 1974)
G. C. Curr: 'Who Saved York Walls?: The Roles of William Etty and the Corporation of York', *York Historian*, v (1984), pp. 25–38
The Artist's Model: Its Role in British Art from Lely to Etty (exh. cat., ed. M. Postle and J. Wright; U. Nottingham, A.G., 1991)

RICHARD GREEN

Etzatlán [Itzatlán; Ytzatlán]. Site in the highland lake district of Jalisco, Mexico. A Pre-Columbian settlement dating mostly to the Post-Classic period (*c.* AD 900–1521), it is partly overlain by the modern town of Etzatlán. Ruins surround the town and may represent wards of the ancient settlement: Rancho San Antonio (north-west), Ranchos Guaje and Cortijo (north-east), Huistla (west), Chirimoya and La Garita (east) and Santa Clara (south), together with Puerto de Veracruz, El Templo and others. The siting of the ancient town and its environmental setting facilitated communications with peoples on the Pacific coast. Data gathered during modern sewer and water-line excavations and from archaeological excavations in 1967 by M. Glassow at Huistla have contributed to a systematic understanding of ancient Etzatlán.

The most important ceremonial plaza, surrounded by low platforms, lies beneath a Franciscan convent (1534), which is one of the earliest in west Mexico. Another section is under the adjacent *capilla*. A second ceremonial complex was built at nearby Santa Clara, where a great hill was reshaped and terraced to form a monumental pyramid and court complex. Reused fragments of its elaborate stone veneer can still be seen in several modern buildings in Etzatlán. The site's ancient population has been estimated to have been *c.* 10,000, based on historical work by Fray Antonio Tello in 1891 and on modern archaeological surveys. Ancient Etzatlán may have been the most important centre in the region, and its prominence was partly based on its apparent ability to form alliances, enabling it successfully to resist the expansion of the TARASCAN peoples to the south and east. The data from the Huistla excavations, taken with the sewer and water trench surveys, indicate that there was a settlement 'hierarchy' in the region, involving mining sites for obsidian, copper, silver, opal and quartz, a fort at El Mirador, canoe ports at El Relíz and El Guaje, and outlying farms, isolated ceremonial centres and other small settlements (Weigand, 1985).

Characteristic artefacts from Etzatlán and the surrounding region (Guadalajara, Mus. Reg. Antropol. & Hist.) include huge numbers of prismatic obsidian blades, eccentrically shaped obsidian objects, mould-made clay figurines, locally made polychrome tripod ceramic vessels, fine stone sculptures, copper bells, needles, awls, projectile points, adzes, ingots and finely worked blue-green stone and quartz artefacts. Large quantities of imported polychrome ceramics, mostly from coastal Nayarit, probably represent trade goods exchanged for obsidian blades.

BIBLIOGRAPHY

N. Guzmán: *Cuatro crónicas de la conquista de Nueva Galicia en territorio de la Nueva España* (Guadalajara, 1963)
M. Glassow: 'The Ceramics of Huistla, a West Mexican Site in the Municipality of Etzatlán, Jalisco', *Amer. Ant.*, xxxii (1967), pp. 64–83
P. Weigand and M. Spence: 'The Obsidian Mining Complex at La Joya, Jalisco', *Anthropology*, vi (1982), pp. 175–88
P. Weigand: 'Evidence for Complex Societies during the Western Mesoamerican Classic Period', *The Archaeology of West and Northwest Mesoamerica*, ed. M. Foster and P. Weigand (New York, 1985), pp. 47–91

PHIL C. WEIGAND

Etzina. *See* KARAKHOTO.

Euboulides. Name of at least three Greek sculptors, apparently members of a single family. They were active in Athens during the Late Classical (375–323 BC) and Hellenistic (323–31 BC) periods.

The first Euboulides is known only from an inscribed base at Tanagra (late 4th or early 3rd century BC; *Inscr. Gr./2*, vii, no. 552) that once held a portrait of a certain *Klines*, victor in the festival of the Basileia, which was established in 371 BC.

The second Euboulides is named by Pliny (*Natural History* XXXIV.xix.88) as the sculptor of a statue of a man counting on his fingers ('digitis computans'), perhaps a seated portrait of the Stoic philosopher *Chrysippos* (*c.* 280–204 BC), who was usually represented in this pose (Sidonius Apollinaris: *Letters* IX.ix.14). A statue of *Chrysippos* was erected in the Athenian Kerameikos (Pausanias: *Description of Greece* I.xvii.2), presumably soon after his death, so that this sculptor is probably the Euboulides mentioned as an Athenian representative (*proxenos*) at Delphi in 191/90 BC. Statues of a type apparently based on this portrait have been identified (e.g. torso in Paris, Louvre, and head in London, BM; both Roman copies of a late 3rd-century BC original) and suggest that Euboulides portrayed the philosopher as an elderly man deep in thought, in a style typical of Hellenistic 'character' portraits (see GREECE, ANCIENT, §IV, 2(iv)).

The third Euboulides is known from numerous signatures on statue bases of the later 2nd century BC and from a passage in Pausanias (*Description of Greece* I.ii.5) referring to him as both sculptor and dedicator of a statue of *Apollo* and perhaps of several other statues (*Athena, Zeus, Mnemosyne* and the *Muses*). A marble *Head of Athena* discovered in the same area of Athens where Pausanias saw Euboulides' work(s) and not far from an inscription (*Inscr. Gr./2*, ii, no. 1645) that almost certainly includes Euboulides' signature has also been generally attributed to him. It recalls copies related to the *Athena Velletri* (Paris, Louvre; Roman copy of an original of *c.* 420–410 BC) and is often said to typify the dry 'Neo-Attic' classicism of the late 2nd century BC. Its association with Euboulides, however, has recently been questioned and its date brought forward to the Augustan period (31 BC–AD 14).

BIBLIOGRAPHY

J. Overbeck: *Die antiken Schriftquellen zur Geschichte der bildenden Künste bei den Griechen* (Leipzig, 1868), nos 2235–44
G. M. A. Richter: *Portraits of the Greeks* (London, 1965, rev. Oxford, 1984), pp. 101–8
J. J. Pollit: *Art in the Hellenistic Age* (Cambridge, 1986), pp. 69, 165
P. Karanastassis: 'Untersuchungen zur kaiserzeitlichen Plastik in Griechenland, II: Kopien, Varianten und Umbildungen nach Athenatypen des 5. Jhs. v. Chr.', *Mitt. Dt. Archäol. Inst.: Athen. Abt.*, cii (1987), pp. 323–428

MARK D. FULLERTON

Eugen (Napoleon Nicolaus), Prince (*b* Drottningholm Castle, 1 Aug 1865; *d* Waldemarsudde, Stockholm, 17 Aug 1947). Swedish painter and collector. The youngest son of King Oscar II of Sweden, he showed an aptitude for art while still at school. At 21 he decided to become an artist, a decision considered startling for a member of the royal family. In 1887 he became a pupil of Léon Bonnat in Paris. Apart from summer holidays in Sweden he remained in Paris until 1889, also studying under Henri Gervex, Alfred Roll and Pierre Puvis de Chavannes, who was an important model for him. Subsequently he worked mainly in Sweden, although he travelled widely, visiting Italy on several occasions. He was primarily a landscape painter.

During his years in Paris Prince Eugen was influenced by French *plein-air* Realism, producing such pastels as *Pont Royal* (1887; Stockholm, Prins Eugens Waldemarsudde). His Realist phase of the 1880s came to an end with the highly detailed *Spring* (1891; Stockholm, Prins Eugens Waldemarsudde). In the 1890s, under the influence of Symbolism, he adopted the National Romantic style that characterized his most famous works (e.g. *The Forest*, 1892; Göteborg, Kstmus.). Major works of the 1890s include *The Old Castle* (1893; Stockholm, Prins Eugens Waldemarsudde) and *The Cloud* (1895; Göteborg, Kstmus.); the latter marked Eugen's breakthrough as an independent artist and is among the best-known works in Swedish art. The grandeur of conception, the intense colour and great formal simplification of the cloud, hillside and trees are characteristic of his painting at that date. In spite of the clear summer theme, the atmosphere consciously expresses discord, reflecting the conflict Eugen felt at the time between his official royal duties and his career as an artist.

Above all, Prince Eugen portrayed the landscape of Stockholm and central Sweden. After moving to Waldemarsudde in Stockholm in the early 20th century, views over the city and approaches to the city became common, for example *Illuminated Steamboat* (1906; Stockholm, Prins Eugens Waldemarsudde). Eugen worked also in a freer impressionistic style at this time, parallel with greater stylization of forms. His National Romantic period concluded with *Night Cloud* (Stockholm, Thielska Gal.) and *Still Water* (Stockholm, Nmus.), both painted in 1901. They embody an essentially Symbolist conception of landscape, which has much in common with contemporary work by Richard Bergh. *Still Water*, like *The Cloud*, is characterized by a solemn, tense atmosphere, created here through emphasis on the heavy sky, simplified landscape and subtle light of Nordic dusk.

Between 1910 and 1920 Eugen evolved a clearer and finer sense of colour and a more solid depiction of volume, under the influence of Swedish Expressionism and André Lhote's version of Cubism, which Eugen encountered in Paris in 1913. He developed this style in the monumental projects (particularly in fresco) that became an important part of his later activity. His subject-matter was again chiefly landscape. The earliest was the triptych *Haga Moods* (1898) in the Stockholm Opera House, followed by *Hoar-frost* (1909) in the Royal Dramatic Theatre, Stockholm, *City on the Water* (1917–22) in Stockholm City Hall and *Land of Memories* (1938) in the Göteborg Concert Hall.

From his early days Prince Eugen had radical sympathies. Nicknamed the Red Prince, his liberal and unprejudiced view of contemporary political questions and the politics of art made him an important promoter of Swedish art. He formed one of the most extensive collections of Swedish late 19th- and early 20th-century art, which he bequeathed, together with the contents of his studio and his home at Waldemarsudde, to the Swedish state as a museum.

WRITINGS

Breven berätta [The letters narrate] (Stockholm, 1942)
Vidare berätta breven [The letters narrate further] (Stockholm, 1945)

BIBLIOGRAPHY

A. Gauffin: 'The Landscape Paintings of Prince Eugen of Sweden', *Int. Studio*, xlv (1912), pp. 173–85
——: *Konstnären Prins Eugen* [Prince Eugen, the artist] (Stockholm, 1915, rev. 1947)
G. Pauli: *Prins Eugen: Målningar, akvareller, teckningar* [Prince Eugen: paintings, watercolours, drawings] (Stockholm, 1925)
——: *Prins Eugen: Hans konst och konstnärsvänner* [Prince Eugen: his art and artist friends] (Stockholm, 1934)
G. M. Silfverstolpe: *Prins Eugens konst* [The art of Prince Eugen] (Stockholm, 1935)
G. Lindgren: *Prins Eugen* (Stockholm, 1944)
E. Wennerholm: *Prins Eugen: Människan och konstnären* [Prince Eugen: the man and the artist] (Stockholm, 1982)
B. Lindwall: 'Eugen of Sweden: Painter on a Princely Pedestal', *Scand. Rev.*, ii (1983), pp. 64–75

TORSTEN GUNNARSSON

Eugene [Smith], Frank (*b* New York, 1865; *d* ?Germany, 1936). American photographer, painter and teacher. After attending the City College of New York and the Bayerische Akademie der Bildenden Künste, Munich, during the mid-1880s, he began exhibiting his photography in New York. Around 1899 he came to the attention of Alfred Stieglitz, and was praised by the critic Sadakichi Hartmann for the intelligent combination of painterly and photographic effects in his work. He became a member of the influential transatlantic photographic society, the Linked Ring (1900), and was a founder-member of Stieglitz's PHOTO-SECESSION.

In 1906 he moved permanently to Germany, where he became a lecturer at the Lehr- und Versuchsanstalt für Photographie und Reproduktionstechnik, Munich. He also began to paint, and to design tapestries influenced by *Jugendstil*. When Stieglitz visited him in 1907 the two made some of the first artistic experiments in colour photography with the newly developed autochrome process (*see* PHOTOGRAPHY, §I). In 1913 Eugene was appointed to the chair in pictorial photography at the Akademie für Graphische Künste, Leipzig.

With the exception of a few landscapes made in Egypt in 1901, Eugene's photographic oeuvre consists almost exclusively of allegorical images, as well as straightforward portraits and female nudes. His finest work, which brought him to the attention of the Stieglitz circle, was done within the decade around 1900. It included *The Horse* (1895; see Hartmann, 1978, p. 176) and a series of nude studies made around 1898, particularly *Adam und Eva* (1898; New York, Met.) and *Dido* (*c.* 1898; see Naef, 1978, p. 163). Here, as earlier, Eugene approached photography like a printmaker, substantially altering his negatives with oils and etched cross-hatching before printing them, which resulted in lively backgrounds to his main figures.

See also PICTORIAL PHOTOGRAPHY.

BIBLIOGRAPHY
S. Hartmann: *The Valiant Knights of Daguerre* (Berkeley, 1978)
W. J. Naef: *The Collection of Alfred Stieglitz* (exh. cat. by W. J. Naef, New York, Met., 1978)
TERENCE PITTS

Eugene of Savoy, Prince. *See* SAVOY, §II(10).

Eugénie, Empress of the French. *See under* BONAPARTE, (8).

Eumaros (*fl* ?late 6th century BC). Greek painter. He is the earliest Athenian painter named in ancient literature, known from a single reference in Pliny (*Natural History* XXXV.56), who listed him among painters in monochrome. None of his work survives. It is unlikely, however, that early artists used only one colour, later artists many, and that a fuller palette always indicates a later date. In any case, Eumaros was not a strictly monochrome painter, because he was given credit for first distinguishing between men and women and that distinction would have been in the colour of flesh, men being darker than women. He was also said to have depicted every sort of figure, perhaps a reference to experiments in pose. KIMON OF KLEONAI further developed the advances of Eumaros, who was perhaps his master. A statue base from the Athenian Acropolis is signed Antenor son of Eumares. This may be the same man as Pliny's Eumaros.

BIBLIOGRAPHY
F. Studniczka: 'Antenor der Sohn des Eumares und die Geschichte der archaischen Malerei', *Jb. Dt. Archäol. Inst.*, ii (1887), pp. 135–68
K. Jex-Blake and E. Sellers: *The Elder Pliny's Chapters on the History of Art* (London, 1896/R Chicago, 1976)
C. HOBEY-HAMSHER

Eumorfopoulos, George (*b* Liverpool, 18 April 1863; *d* London, 19 Dec 1939). English collector. The eldest son of a Greek merchant, Eumorfopoulos worked for the merchant firm of Ralli Brothers. He initially collected European porcelains and Japanese tea bowls but then turned to Chinese objects, which became his largest collection, emphasizing pottery and porcelains. His second interest was metalwork, and he formed a fine collection of Chinese bronzes; he was also interested in other media, such as jade. He chose items based on his aesthetic response rather than archaeological or rarity value, and he thus placed himself at the forefront of Western taste for Chinese art. From 1924 he also began to acquire Islamic art and formed a separate Chinese collection for the Benaki Museum, Athens, so that the museum eventually had nearly 800 examples of Chinese pottery and porcelain. Eumorfopoulos was elected the first president of the Oriental Ceramic Society in 1921 and retained this position until his death, his house becoming central to the activities of the society. In 1935, having retired from Ralli Brothers the previous year, he visited the Far East to select objects for the *Exhibition of Chinese Art* (London, RA), in which his own collection also figured prominently. In the same year, the bulk of his Chinese collection—apart from items duplicated in the British Museum and the Victoria and Albert Museum—was purchased by the British nation for £100,000 (about half the market value), and some of his remaining items were sold by Bluett and Sons. In the final years of his life, however, he continued to acquire Chinese and European art. He gave his books to the Courtauld Institute of Art, and his remaining collections were sold at Sotheby's on 28–31 May and 5–6 June 1940, and in 1944 after his widow's death.

BIBLIOGRAPHY
DNB
R. L. Hobson: *The George Eumorfopoulos Collection: Catalogue of the Chinese, Corean and Persian Pottery and Porcelain*, 6 vols (London, 1925–8)
L. Binyon: *The George Eumorfopoulos Collection: Catalogue of the Chinese Frescoes* (London, 1927)
——: *The George Eumorfopoulos Collection: Catalogue of the Chinese, Corean and Siamese Paintings* (London, 1928)
W. Perceval Yetts: *The George Eumorfopoulos Collection: Catalogue of the Chinese and Corean Bronzes, Sculpture, Jades, Jewellery and Miscellaneous Objects*, 3 of 6 vols published (London, 1929–)
R. Ettinghausen: Obituary, *A. Islam.*, vii (1940), p. 123
W. Perceval Yetts: Obituary, *J. Royal Asiat. Soc. GB & Ireland* (1940), pp. 253–8
S. J. VERNOIT

Euphranor (*b* Isthmia, *c.* 390 BC; *d* ?Athens, *c.* 325 BC). Greek painter and sculptor. An exact contemporary of Praxiteles, he seems to have been state artist at Athens in the mid-4th century BC, perhaps playing a role comparable to that of PHEIDIAS a century earlier. Along with NIKIAS, who trained in his workshop, Euphranor was among the foremost members of the 4th-century BC Attic school of painting and was exceptional also in producing marble and bronze statues as well as marble reliefs. Pupil of the painter Aristeides the elder and teacher not only of the painters Leonidas, Antidotos and Charmantides but also of his own son, the sculptor Sostratos, Euphranor also wrote treatises on his painting (*On Colours* and *On Proportions*), which were quoted by ancient writers; none of his own paintings survive. His preoccupation with proportions was criticized, and he was considered not quite on a level with Lysippos and Apelles, since the heads of his figures were allegedly rather large for their bodies.

Though he was renowned for his versatility and his experiments with proportions and colour, Euphranor worked wholly in the Classical tradition, depicting grandiose heroic themes. His surviving sculptures recall works associated with Pheidias, and he seems to have taken special pains to distinguish his paintings from those of PARRHASIOS, who had painted similar subjects, including Theseus, Odysseus and Demos.

Euphranor's paintings were praised for their high moral tone and heroic subjects, as was appropriate for works commissioned by the Athenian state. His earliest and most famous group of panel paintings (360s BC) decorated the Stoa of Zeus in the Athenian Agora. His reportedly novel colouristic effects are difficult to visualize, and these panels are now mainly of interest for their political content. In addition to depicting the Twelve Gods, whose cult had special significance for Athens, Euphranor painted an allegory of *Theseus Accompanied by Demos* [the citizens] *and Demokratia* [the constitution]. Euphranor was quoted as having contrasted his robust Theseus with a languid representation by Parrhasios. Another picture in the Stoa of Zeus conflated two separate events in the Battle of Mantinea (362 BC) to serve Athenian anti-Theban propaganda.

The only extant sculpture by Euphranor appears to be the mutilated cult statue of *Apollo Patroos* (Athens, Agora Mus.; *see* ATHENS, fig. 17), mentioned by Pausanias (*Description of Greece*, I.iii.4). It is a colossal work in Pentelic marble, and, though only the draped torso and right foot survive, it can be reconstructed from later copies. It is a late work (*c.* 330 BC), made for the temple in the Athenian Agora where Apollo was worshipped as the Athenians' ancestral deity. To emphasize his Ionian origin, the god is represented playing the kithara and wearing a laurel crown and a long, elaborate theatrical costume. The toes of the right foot are highly polished and shaded with a dark patina to suggest suntanned male flesh, and the costume was presumably originally decorated with patterns painted in the encaustic technique for colouring marbles, which was particularly associated with Euphranor's school. The statue is a skilfully executed blend of tradition and innovation. Despite its elongated proportions, pyramidal structure and twisting pose, the high belt-line, the realistic rendering of the drapery texture and the play of light and shadow, the work displays a clear debt to Pheidias' *Athena Parthenos*.

The *Apollo Patroos* has served as a basis for attributions of further works to Euphranor. The bronze *Athena* from Piraeus (4th century BC; Piraeus, Archaeol. Mus.; *see* GREECE, ANCIENT, fig. 65) has similar drapery, pose and proportions to the *Apollo*, though it is rather earlier. The figure wears its *peplos* in a fashion similar to 5th-century BC works. It seems, moreover, to have been designed for viewing from below and must thus have stood on a high base, perhaps a column, while its somewhat informal appearance implies that it was a dedication rather than a cult statue. It was accidentally buried in a warehouse in the 1st century BC, but a later marble copy (the *Athena Mattei*; Paris, Louvre) suggests that there were two bronze originals. Closely related to the Piraeus *Athena* is a somewhat austere female figure, known from a number of Roman copies based on a Greek original (e.g. Rome, Vatican, Gal. Candelabri; Copenhagen, Ny Carlsberg Glyp.). The copies are usually three-quarter life-size and were used as fountain ornaments, sometimes leaning on a pillar. The figure's resemblance to one of the three Graces/Seasons on the base of Pheidias' *Athena Parthenos* reinforces the impression that it was by an artist imitating the High Classical tradition.

Knowledge of Euphranor's other bronze works is based largely on Pliny's list of those that were famous in Rome in the 1st century AD (*Natural History*, XXXIV.xix.77–8), none of which is now identifiable with any certainty. His *Paris* was an unusual subject for free-standing sculpture, and his *Bravery and Hellas* anticipated Roman personifications of Virtus and Roma. His *Priestess Holding a Temple Key* and *Female Worshipper* were surely private portraits, while the *Alexander Rondanini* (2nd century AD; Munich, Glyp.), depicting Alexander the Great in a heroic but remarkably lifelike manner, may recall his portrait group of *Philip II and Alexander in a Chariot*.

BIBLIOGRAPHY
H. A. Thompson: 'The Apollo Patroos of Euphranor', *Archaiol. Ephemeris*, iii (1953/4), pp. 30–44
W. D. E. Coulson: 'The Nature of Pliny's Remarks on Euphranor', *Class. J.*, lxvii (1971/2), pp. 323–6
O. Palagia: 'Euphranoros Techne', *Athens An. Archaeol.*, vi (1973), pp. 323–9
R. Vasić: 'Some Observations on Euphranor's *Cavalry Battle*', *Amer. J. Archaeol.*, lxxxiii (1979), pp. 345–9
O. Palagia: *Euphranor* (Leiden, 1980)
R. Vasić: '*Odysseus Feigning Madness* by Euphranor', *Boreas*, x (1987), pp. 81–6

OLGA PALAGIA

Euphronios. *See* VASE PAINTERS, §II.

European School [Hung. Európai Iskola]. Hungarian artistic group formed in 1945 and active in Budapest until 1948. It was modelled on the Ecole de Paris and founded on the belief that a new artistic vision could only be established from a synthesis of East and West. According to its programme, it represented Fauvism, Cubism, Expressionism, abstract art and Surrealism in Hungary. The aim of its members was to organize exhibitions, publish writings and encourage contact between artists. Members included the art historians and critics Ernő Kállai, A'rpád Mezei and Imre Pán, and painters in the group included, among others, Margit Anna, Jenő Barcsay, Endre Bálint, Béla Czóbel, József Egry, Jenő Gadányi, Dezső Korniss, Tamás Lossonczy, Ferenc Martyn and Ernő Schubert. Among the sculptors were Dezső Bokros Birmann, Erzsébet Forgách Hahn, Etienne Hajdu (in Paris), József Jakovitz and Tibor Vilt. Marcel Jean, the Surrealist theorist who lived for a while in Budapest, was an honorary member, while Imré Amos and Lajos Vajda were looked to as role models. The group did not adhere to a unified style; for example, while Jenő Gadányi's *Fantastical Landscape* (1948; Budapest, N.G.) was Expressionist, Jenő

Barcsay's *Street* (1946; Budapest, N.G.) was influenced by Cubism. The members sought to use both organic and inorganic forms to balance rationalism and intuition in their work. The majority of them started from the Constructivist–Surrealist scheme introduced by Lajos Vajda. Some of them produced 'bioromantic' work after World War II. Others worked towards monumentality through Expressionist–Constructivist works. They organized 38 exhibitions of members' (and some foreign) work.

The group published a series of books on aesthetics under the titles *Index Röpirat* ('Index leaflet') and *Vitairatkönyvtár* ('Debate library') and the periodical *Európai Iskola Könyvtáta* ('European School library', 1946–7). Stalinist cultural policy denounced the European School as decadent for its relationship with 20th-century artistic trends, and in November 1948 all further exhibitions by the group were banned; the members either withdrew to the countryside or pursued their activities abroad.

WRITINGS
Index Röpirat [Index leaflet] (Budapest, 1946)
Vitairat-könyvtár [Debate library] (Budapest, 1946)

BIBLIOGRAPHY
B. Hamvas, K. Kemény: *Forradalom a müvészetben: Absztrakció és szurrealizmus Magyarországon* [Revolution in fine art: abstraction and surrealism in Hungary] (Budapest, 1947)
E. Kallai: *A természet rejtett arca* [The hidden face of nature] (Budapest, 1947)
P. Kiss: *Az ember felé* [Towards the man] (Budapest, 1948)
A. Mezei: 'Vajda Lajos és az Európai Iskola' [Lajos Vajda and the European School], *Müvészettörténeti Tanulmányok* (1960), pp. 215–19
S. Mándy: *Az Európai Iskola és elözményei* [The European School and its antecedents] (Budapest, 1962)
S. Láncz: 'L'Ecole européenne', *Acta Hist. A. Acad. Sci. Hung.*, xxi (1975), no. 1–2, pp. 167–94
P. György and G. Pataki: *Európai Iskola* [The European School] (Budapest, 1990)
Wille zur Form (exh. cat., Vienna, Hochsch. Angewandte Kst, 1993)

ÉVA BAJKAY

Eusebi, Luis (*b* Rome, *c.* 1770; *d* Paris, 16 Aug 1829). Spanish painter and art historian. He acquired his artistic training through study trips in Italy, France and England, and around 1800 he worked as a copier in the Academia de San Fernando in Madrid. After the Peninsular War (1808–13) he was appointed court painter by King Ferdinand VII (25 Feb 1816). However, his importance in the history of Spanish art lies more in his role as art historian than in that of painter. His publications reveal an outstanding knowledge of the schools of art. The first is of special interest: as keeper of the Museo de Pinturas in Madrid (now the Museo del Prado) he wrote the first catalogue of the museum, indeed of any museum in Spain, in 1819, with subsequent editions in 1821, 1823, 1824 and 1828. In 1822 he published his *Ensayo sobre las diferentes escuelas de pintura*, an introductory manual for painting enthusiasts. Another work, unpublished, is preserved in the Museo Lázaro Galdiano in Madrid and bears the title *Introducción al conocimiento de los cuadros [del] Rey N.S.* The manuscript is dated 1826 and a note in the author's handwriting indicates that it was not meant for publication but for personal use. It includes biographies and profiles of more than 700 artists. In 1829 Eusebi travelled to Paris for health reasons and died there that year.

UNPUBLISHED SOURCES
Madrid, Mus. Lázaro Galdiano [*Introducción al conocimiento de los cuadros [del] Rey N.S.*]

WRITINGS
Catálogo del Museo del Prado (Madrid, 1819, 5/1828)
Ensayo sobre las diferentes escuelas de pintura (Madrid, 1822)

BIBLIOGRAPHY
N. Sentenach: 'Los grandes retratistas en España', *Bol. Soc. Esp. Excurs.* (1 Sep 1913)
J. A. Gaya Nuño: *Historia de la crítica de arte en España* (Madrid, 1975)

M. DOLORES JIMÉNEZ-BLANCO

Eusebio (di Jacopo di Cristoforo) da San Giorgio (*b* Perugia, between 1465 and 1470; *d* Perugia, after 1539). Italian painter and sculptor. The son of an apothecary, he was a pupil of Perugino. His work reveals the influence not only of the young Raphael but also of Bernardino Pinturicchio, who often employed him as his journeyman. In 1493 Eusebio received payment from the monastery of S Pietro, Perugia, for a panel (untraced) depicting *St Benedict*. He was treasurer of the Perugian painters' guild for the first term of 1494, and in 1496 he took a year's lease on a workshop in the parish of S Maria del Mercato, Perugia, with Berto di Giovanni, Sinibaldo Ibi, Lattanzio di Giovanni (*fl* 1484; *d* 1534) and Lodovico di Angelo (*fl* 1481–1522). His earliest surviving work of importance is the *Adoration of the Magi* (Perugia, G.N. Umbria) executed for the Oddi Chapel in S Agostino, Perugia. The year MDV or MDVI is inscribed on the hem of the Virgin's robe. The crowded procession of figures and the gentle, finely drawn landscape with the characteristic arched rock testify strongly to the influence of Pinturicchio. Subsequently, in company with Matteo Balducci (*fl* 1509–54), Giovan Battista Caporali and Giovanni di Francesco Ciambella (*fl* 1495–1510), Eusebio assisted Pinturicchio with the frescoes (1502–8) for the Piccolomini Library, Siena Cathedral.

Pinturicchio's influence continued in Eusebio's frescoes depicting *St Francis Preaching* and the *Stigmatization of St Francis* for the cloisters of S Damiano, near Assisi, and in the altarpiece executed for S Andrea, Spello (*in situ*). The contract of March 1507 for the Spello painting stated that Eusebio was to receive 100 gold ducats for a representation of the *Virgin and Child with the Infant St John the Baptist and Four Standing Saints*. Pinturicchio executed the preparatory drawing and was bound by the contract to paint the heads himself. He also promised to produce designs for the predella. In 1508 Eusebio was commissioned by the Baglione family to paint an *Adoration of the Magi* for S Pietro dei Cassinensi, Perugia. In this work the influence of Raphael, his contemporary under Perugino, is evident as well as his debt to Pinturicchio. In the *Virgin of the Masts* (Perugia, G.N. Umbria), painted for the oratory of the confraternity of St Benedict, the overall disposition of the figures recalls Raphael's *Virgin and Child Enthroned with SS John the Baptist and Nicholas of Bari* (1505; London, N.G.). One of Eusebio's finest panels, comparable in quality to the Spello altarpiece, is the *Virgin and Child with SS Anthony of Padua, John the Evangelist, Andrew and Nicholas of Tolentino*, painted for S Francesco, Matélica, near Fabriano, with scenes from the *Miracle of St Anthony* on the predella.

Eusebio was also active as a sculptor, though he was less prolific in this medium. In 1525 he executed a relief of St Roch. In 1530 he made two candlesticks in the form of angels for the high altar of the confraternity of St Benedict, Perugia, and a figure of *St Roch* for Guido di Meo d'Antonia. Eusebio always preserved his links with Perugia. In 1516, 1526 and 1537 he was again treasurer of the Perugian painters' guild, and in 1509 he held the office of prior. In 1527 he was a member of the 100-man authority that was elected for each district of Perugia. He is last documented, gravely ill, in 1538. As he is not entered in the register of deaths for Perugia it can be presumed that he died after 1539. Eusebio ranks next to Raphael as the most important representative of the Perugian school of painting as it developed after Perugino and Pinturicchio.

BIBLIOGRAPHY

Thieme-Becker

J. A. Crowe and G. B. Cavalcaselle: *A New History of Painting in Italy* (London, 1866/*R* New York, 1980), pp. 241–3, 339–41

W. Bombe: 'Geschichte der Peruginer Malerei', *It. Forsch. Kstgesch.*, v (1912), pp. 234–5, 238–9

C. Ricci: *Pintoricchio* (Perugia, 1912), pp. 299–303

E. Jacobsen: *Umbrische Malerei* (Strasbourg, 1914), pp. 123–33

G. Urbini: *Arte umbra* (Rome, 1925/*R* 1974), pp. 55–121

SUSANNE KIEFHABER

Eusebios of Caesarea [Eusebios Pamphili] (*b c.* AD 265; *d c.* AD 340). Bishop of Caesarea in Palestine, church historian and prominent supporter of Constantine the Great. Eusebios studied under the learned presbyter Pamphilus (*c.* 240–309), whose name he adopted, in Caesarea, an important centre of Christian learning since the time of Origen (*c.* 185–254). He achieved a formidable reputation as a scholar, yet managed to escape harm during the Great Persecution of the Church (AD 303–12). In 313 he was appointed Bishop of Caesarea, which position he held until his death. When the Arian controversy broke out *c.* 318, Eusebios attempted to present Arianism in a more acceptable form. At the Council of Nicaea (325), however, it was condemned as a heresy and Eusebios was required to recant his position and to accept the doctrine of the Council. From this time he gave full support to Constantine's drive for unity in the Church, and in return he enjoyed considerable imperial favour.

He was a prolific author of dogmatic and historical works, panegyrics and sermons. Among the numerous texts that survive, his *Ecclesiastical History* provides the earliest account of the first centuries of Christianity and culminates in the triumph of the Church under Constantine. His panegyrical *Life of Constantine* was almost certainly revised after his death. Both works offer invaluable documentation of works of art of the Constantinian age. Eusebios describes the Emperor's campaign of eradicating pagan forms of worship, his embellishment and aggrandizement of Constantinople, and his vast programme of church building both in the east and west of the empire. Some individual churches are described, and their size and wealth of decoration repeatedly emphasized. Many of his descriptions help towards the reconstruction of churches no longer standing, or surviving only in fragments, such as the church of the Holy Sepulchre in Jerusalem (*see* JERUSALEM, §II, 2(i)), the church (*c.* 317, destr.) of Tyre and the church of the Holy Apostles in Constantinople

(*see* ISTANBUL, §III, 9(i)). They also elucidate the complex symbolic significance attached to the various features of these churches and provide information concerning the existence of, and attitude to, Christian imagery.

Like most early Fathers of the Church, Eusebios condemned the worship of images of Christ and the Apostles, which he rightly saw as an inheritance of pagan practices. When Constantia, sister of Constantine, wrote to him requesting an image of Christ, he replied in a letter that survives in part, giving the first theologically elaborated argument against Christian portraiture. This letter was later cited as a key text against icon-worship during the Iconoclast controversy (726–843). His *Ecclesiastical History* provides an early testimony to the widespread circulation of unofficial painted icons of Christ and SS Peter and Paul among the Christian communities. In the *Life of Constantine* he also mentions, but does not condemn, depictions of Christian narrative scenes decorating public fountains (III, 49) and a portrait of Constantine and his sons triumphing over the enemy of humankind that hung over the palace gate at Constantinople (III, 3).

WRITINGS

Eusebius Werke, ed. I. A. Heikel and others, 9 vols (Leipzig-Berlin, 1902–56)

Ecclesiastical History, Eng. trans., ed. K. Lake, J. E. L. Oulton and H. J. Lawlor, 2 vols (London, 1926–32)

BIBLIOGRAPHY

F. J. Foakes-Jackson: *Eusebius Pamphili: A Study of the Man and his Writings* (Cambridge, 1933)

J. D. Breckenridge: 'The Reception of Art into the Early Church', *Atti del IX congresso internazionale di archeologia cristiana: Roma, 1975*, i, pp. 361–9

T. D. Barnes: *Constantine and Eusebius* (Cambridge, MA, and London, 1981)

SARAH MORGAN

Euston Road School. Name given by Clive Bell in 1938 to a group of English painters associated with the School of Drawing and Painting established in October 1937 by William Coldstream, Claude Rogers (*b* 1907) and Victor Pasmore, in a review of the exhibition *15 Paintings of London* (Oct-Nov 1938; London, Storran Gal.). The school was initially in Fitzroy Street, but it moved soon after to premises at 314/316 Euston Road. The term was quickly broadened to describe a movement encompassing as many as 30 other painters, many of them former students of the Slade School of Fine Art, including Rodrigo Moynihan, Lawrence Gowing (*b* 1918), William Townsend (1909–73), Graham Bell, Anthony Devas (1911–58) and Geoffrey Tibble (1909–52).

The Euston Road painters worked essentially in a realist tradition, reacting in part against modernist tendencies (especially Surrealism and abstract art) but also responding to the conditions engendered by the Depression, which they felt called for a socially committed art. These political concerns led Coldstream and Bell to work briefly in Bolton in 1938 in association with the MASS OBSERVATION investigative project, resulting in paintings such as Coldstream's *Bolton* (1938; Ottawa, N.G.). They spoke of being guided by an aesthetic of verification, rather than one of discrimination, using restrained colours and brushwork and applying strict procedures of measurement to their treatment not only of landscapes and cityscapes but also of interior scenes with figures, such as Graham Bell's *The*

Café (1937–8; Manchester, C.A.G.). The school closed shortly after the outbreak of World War II, and an exhibition at the Ashmolean Museum, Oxford, in 1941, marked the official end of the movement. Many of the painters, however, remained active after the war, teaching and (with the exception of Pasmore, who turned to abstract art) continuing to work in a similar manner. Their aesthetic had a long currency in England, particularly through Coldstream's role as Slade Professor from 1949 to 1975.

BIBLIOGRAPHY

C. Harrison: *English Art and Modernism, 1900–1939* (London, 1981), pp. 333–43

B. Laughton: *The Euston Road School: A Study in Objective Painting* (Aldershot, 1986)

British Art in the 20th Century (exh. cat., ed. S. Compton; London, RA, 1987)

DAVID CAST

Euthymides. *See* VASE PAINTERS, §II.

Eutresis. Site south-west of Thebes, in central Greece, where Hetty Goldman's major excavation campaign (1924–7) revealed a long and informative prehistoric sequence, running from the later Neolithic period through almost the entire Bronze Age. Indications of later occupation are present but sparse. Early Helladic (EH; *c.* 3600/3000–*c.* 2050 BC) strata make up the bulk of deposit, while Middle Helladic (MH; *c.* 2050–*c.* 1600 BC) is poorly represented until near its end. There are important building levels covering the MH to Late Helladic (LH; *c.* 1600–*c.* 1050 BC) transition (the abundance of Mainland Polychrome in the third 'MH' level demonstrates its equivalence to LH I) and, although few LH buildings were uncovered, a fortification wall, enclosing much unoccupied territory as well as the settlement, was identified, dating to LH IIIB (*c.* 1335–*c.* 1180 BC). The rather small quantity of LH pottery originally documented has been considerably increased (see Mountjoy), which presents plausible evidence for a LH IIIC phase (*c.* 1180–*c.* 1050 BC). Although the site is unlikely to have been of major importance, it was probably a significant local centre, as demonstrated by the rich range of decorated pottery in the earlier phases, the presence of likely Cycladic imports and the late fortification wall. Many complete house plans were recovered, and there are other features of interest, notably a possible EH II ritual pit and shrine (*c.* 2900–*c.* 2400 BC) and a workroom for bone, boar's tusk and, apparently, mother-of-pearl, in a late MH house. All finds are in the Thebes Museum.

BIBLIOGRAPHY

H. Goldman: *Excavations at Eutresis in Boeotia* (Harvard, 1931)

J. L. Caskey and E. G. Caskey: 'The Earliest Settlements at Eutresis: Supplementary Excavations 1958', *Hesperia*, xxix (1960), pp. 126–67

P. A. Mountjoy: *Mycenaean Pottery from Orchomenos, Eutresis and Other Boeotian Sites* (Munich, 1983)

O. T. P. K. DICKINSON

Eutychides (*fl* late 4th century BC–early 3rd). Greek sculptor. He was a pupil of Lysippos and, like him, worked in bronze. He was particularly noted for his large statuary group representing the *Tyche* (Fortune) of Antioch with the River Orontes at her feet (*see* ANTIOCH (i), fig. 1). The Tyche is represented wearing a crown of the city walls on her head, seated with legs crossed and one elbow resting on her knee. The complex pose is resolved into a pyramidal composition, which is admirable from many points of view. As Antioch was founded in 300 BC the statue was probably made around this time. It was a distinctive and impressive image of which numerous copies were made in a variety of reduced scales (e.g. marble copies in Rome, Vatican, Gal. Candelabri and Budapest, Mus. F.A.; bronze copies in Paris, Louvre and Florence, Uffizi; and a silver copy in London, BM). Eutychides was also said to have made a statue of *Timosthenes* at Olympia (Pausanias: *Guide to Greece* VI.ii.6–7), presumably an athlete, a statue of *Dionysos* (Pliny: *Natural History* XXXVI.34) and an image of *Eurotas*, the river god, praised by Pliny (*Natural History* XXXIV.78) as making 'the art more liquid than the water'. No original works by Eutychides survive.

BIBLIOGRAPHY

Enc. A. Ant.

J. Malalas: *Chronographia* IX.cclxxvi.4–9

T. Dohrn: *Die Tyche von Antiochia* (Berlin, 1960)

J. J. Pollitt: *The Art of Ancient Greece* (Cambridge, 1990), pp. 109–10

Evangeliary. *See under* SERVICE BOOK.

Evangelista da Reggio, Fra (*b* Reggio Emilia, *c.* 1440; *d* before 15 Jan 1495). Italian scribe, illuminator and Franciscan friar. Between 1477 and 1487 he wrote three, and partially decorated six, large Antiphonaries for the cathedral of Ferrara (Ferrara, Mus. Duomo). In a series of eleven Antiphonaries and six Graduals commissioned in 1490 for the convent of S Francesco, Brescia (Brescia, Pin. Civ. Tosio-Martinengo, MSS 1–17), he illuminated initials as well as border decoration. In both enterprises Fra Evangelista probably had a controlling hand and used JACOPO FILIPPO D'ARGENTA as a close collaborator. Attributions of cuttings in Berlin (Kupferstichkab.) and a miniature with *St Jerome* (Cleveland, OH, Mus. A.) are inconclusive.

Fra Evangelista emulated the styles of Guglielmo Giraldi, Martino da Modena and Jacopo Filippo d'Argenta, all three active on the two series of choir-books. Like most contemporary painters in Ferrara, he was greatly influenced by the works of Cosimo Tura. His own style is characterized by a geometrically structured, balanced page layout that includes strong acanthus decoration bound within frames, and wooded or rocky scenes with large figures draped in bulky garments and with smallish heads. When working directly with Jacopo Filippo d'Argenta (best exemplified in Ferrara, Mus. Duomo, MS. Corale VI), he tended to be more inventive, his acanthus leaves stylishly framing medallions.

BIBLIOGRAPHY

H. J. Hermann: 'Zur Geschichte der Miniaturmalerei am Hofe der Este in Ferrara', *Jb. Ksthist. Samml. Allhöch. Ksrhaus.*, xxi (1900), pp. 117–271

M. Salmi: *Pittura e miniatura a Ferrara nel primo rinascimento* (Milan, 1961)

PATRICK M. DE WINTER

Evangelista di Pian di Meleto (*b* Pian de Meleto, nr Urbino, *c.* 1460; *d* Urbino, 18 Jan 1549). Italian painter. He is first documented in 1483 as a 'pupil of Giovanni Santi of Urbino', and he later worked for Timoteo Viti. He received commissions for chalices, candelabra, epitaphs and other similar work (untraced), sharing the more prestigious commissions with other artists. For example, he was named with Ottaviano Prassede (*c.* 1480–*c.* 1537) in connection with the decoration of the chapel of the Holy Sacrament in Urbino Cathedral (*in situ*) and as Raphael's assistant in executing the altarpiece of *St Nicholas of Tolentino* (1501; Paris, Louvre; Naples, Capodimonte; Brescia, Pin. Civ. Tosio-Martinengo) for the church of S Agostino in Città di Castello, commissioned in 1500. Although some works formerly accredited to Evangelista are now indisputably attributed to Giovanni Santi, he is still attributed with an oil-on-panel *Virgin and Child Enthroned with Saints* and frescoes depicting *Christ Crucified between SS Lawrence, Roch and Sebastian* (all Sassocorvaro, Pal. Com.) and *Christ Crucified with the Virgin and SS John the Evangelist and Mary Magdalene* (Pian di Meleto, parish church).

BIBLIOGRAPHY

A. Venturi: *Storia* (1901–40), VII/ii, pp. 188–221
E. Scatassa: 'Evangelista di Pian di Meleto', *Rass. Bibliog. A. It.*, vi (1903), pp. 110–21
L. Calzini: 'Raffaello ed Evangelista di Pian di Meleto', *Rass. Bibliog. A. It.*, xii/10–11 (1909), pp. 145–51
P. Zampetti: *L'arte marchigiana del '400* (Milan, 1969), p. 230
——: 'Per Raffaello', *Not. Pal. Albani*, xi/1–2 (1982), pp. 47–62
F. Martelli: *Giovanni Santi e la sua scuola* (Rimini, 1984), pp. 51–4

Evans, Allen. *See under* FURNESS, FRANK.

Evans, Sir Arthur (John) (*b* Hemel Hempstead, Herts, 8 July 1851; *d* Oxford, 11 July 1941). English archaeologist and historian. He is best known as the discoverer of the Palace of Minos at KNOSSOS and the inventor of the term MINOAN to designate the Bronze Age civilization of Crete. His father ran a paper-milling business and was also a prominent antiquary. Evans studied modern history at Brasenose College, Oxford (1870–74), during which time he also travelled widely, from war-torn France to the Turkish-occupied Balkans (1871) and Romania (1872). His sympathies for the Slavs and his interest in the ancient remains of the region led him to settle at Ragusa (now Dubrovnik) in 1875. There he divided his time between investigating the political turmoil of the area, assisting refugees, visiting numerous historical sites, producing a series of books and scholarly articles and working as a reporter for the *Manchester Guardian* (from 1877); but as Austrian involvement in the Balkans increased, he was accused of mixing with nationalistic elements, arrested, imprisoned and expelled (1882).

Forced back to England, Evans eventually became Keeper of the Ashmolean Museum, Oxford (1884). In this capacity he obtained a series of important archaeological collections, including that of Charles Drury Fortnum, and, with the help of a substantial endowment from the latter, he transformed the collection (1890–96). He studied numismatics and British antiquities but continued to travel (Greece and the Black Sea, 1885; Sicily, 1887 and 1891). Inspired by Heinrich Schliemann's discoveries in the Aegean, he visited Crete in 1894, 1895, 1898 and 1899, becoming particularly interested in scripts and seal-stones. In 1900 he finally succeeded in purchasing the site of Knossos and began to excavate it in the spring of that year. Lacking experience, he hired Duncan Mackenzie

(1859–1935) to run the excavation, while bearing most of its high cost himself. The results were immediate and staggering: much of the Minoan palace was uncovered in 1900–03, and in 1904 Evans first propounded his broad chronological framework for the Minoan civilization, which remains in general use. After inheriting a substantial fortune (1908) he resigned as Keeper of the Ashmolean but continued to excavate at Knossos and to work on his definitive publication, *The Palace of Minos*. Although excavation and reconstruction work continued at Knossos into the 1930s, Evans donated the site to the British School at Athens in 1927 and indulged his unassuaged passion for travel. In 1938 his health and memory began to fail and he was forced to go into retreat at his estate at Youlbury, near Oxford. Evans was made an FRS in 1901 and knighted in 1911.

WRITINGS

Essai de classification des époques de la civilisation minoenne (London, 1906)
The Palace of Minos, 4 vols (London, 1921–35)

BIBLIOGRAPHY

J. Evans: *The Palace of Minos: Index* (London, 1936)
——: *Time and Chance: The Story of Arthur Evans and his Forebears* (London, 1943)
A. C. Brown: *Arthur Evans and the Palace of Minos* (Oxford, 1983)
D. B. Harden: *Sir Arthur Evans, 1851–1941: A Memoir* (Oxford, 1983)

D. EVELY

Evans, Edmund (William) (*b* Southwark, London, 23 Feb 1826; *d* Ventnor, Isle of Wight, 21 Aug 1905). English printer. He established his printing firm (still operating in the late 20th century) in 1847. Working with Routledge Publishers he specialized in illustrated children's books, including the 'toy books' of Walter Crane, and also printed a range of illustrated textbooks, poetry and novels. His sensitive line and capacity to translate effects from drawing to woodblock while retaining the style and spirit of the original made him justly popular with his clients. His ingenious combination of pigments and engraving techniques made him a pioneer in colour printing, greatly enlarging the scope of the art.

See also BOOK ILLUSTRATION, §V.

WRITINGS

R. McLean, ed.: *The Reminiscences of Edmund Evans* (Oxford, 1967)

BIBLIOGRAPHY

M. Hardie: *English Coloured Books* (London, 1906), pp. 266–82

JUSTINE HOPKINS

Evans, Frederick H(enry) (*b* London, 26 June 1853; *d* London, 24 June 1943). English photographer and writer. He took up photography in the early 1880s out of his interest in the 'study of the beautiful' while a bookseller in London. In 1887 he received a medal from the Royal Photographic Society for his microscopic photographs of shells, which to his dismay were categorized as scientific photographs. In 1889 he met Aubrey Beardsley and was instrumental in getting Beardsley his first assignment illustrating Tennyson's *Morte d'Arthur*. Evans's portrait of *Aubrey Beardsley* (1894; Rochester, NY, Int. Mus. Phot.), showing the artist holding his head in his hands, is one of his finest.

Around 1890 Evans began to photograph English and French cathedrals; it was on his architectural photography that his reputation was established. One hundred and twenty of his platinum prints were exhibited at the Architectural Club, Boston, in 1897. The next year, aged 45, Evans retired from his bookshop to devote his time to photography. In 1900 two achievements helped to consolidate his reputation: he had his first one-man exhibition of 150 prints at the Royal Photographic Society and was elected to the exclusive photographic brotherhood, the LINKED RING. As one of its most important members, he was responsible from 1902 to 1905 for the innovative hanging of the annual Salons. In 1903 Alfred Stieglitz featured Evans's photographs in his new journal *Camera Work*, accompanied by an appreciation by George Bernard Shaw. Evans's a *Sea of Steps (Wells Cathedral)* (1903; Rochester, NY, Int. Mus. Phot.) is one of his greatest images of that period. The wave of steps to the chapter house that engulfs the viewer prompted such a rash of camera-club imitations that indentations were made in the floor for the amateur to erect his tripod in the correct spot.

In 1905 Evans took on assignments from *Country Life* that enabled him to photograph further afield, such as his commission in 1906 to photograph English parish churches and French châteaux. This period marked a shift in his style to solid, more sculptural architectural elements that contributed to his eventual distancing from the Ring. Around 1909 Evans turned increasingly to landscape photography, in which he explored effects of light in forested areas. In 1912 he began to publish privately platinotype editions of his collections of works by William Blake, Hans Holbein the younger and Beardsley. He was a master of the platinum print, then called the platinotype, which created an image of clear grey tones whose subtlety of range allowed for exceptional realistic detail. When combined with the precision allowed by his exposure, sombre corners of medieval churches became marvels of discriminating detail. His output declined by the 1920s due to the high price of platinum, his dissatisfaction with the new silver paper and his dislike of the photographic avant-garde's interest in abstraction.

Evans was described by Alfred Stieglitz as 'the greatest exponent of architectural photography'. Evans aimed to create a mood with his photography; he recommended that the amateur 'try for a record of emotion rather than a piece of topography'. He would spend weeks in a cathedral before exposing any film, exploring different camera angles for effects of light and means of emotional expression. He always tried to keep the camera as far as possible from the subject and to fill the frame with the image completely, and he used a small aperture and very long exposure for maximum definition. Equally important to the effect of his photographs were his printing methods; he rejected the fashion for painterly effects achieved by smudging, blowing or brushing over the surface of the gum paper print. His doctrine of pure photography, 'plain prints from plain negatives', prohibited retouching.

Evans was a prolific writer on photography, regularly contributing essays and photographs to *Camera Work* until 1907 and to the weekly *Amateur Photographer* between 1902 and 1910, where he explained his philosophy of 'pure' photography. In 1928 he was made an honorary fellow of the Royal Photographic Society. Evans is represented in the collections of the Boston Museum of Fine Arts, the Philadelphia Museum, the International Museum of Photography at Rochester, NY, and the Royal Photographic Society, Bath.

BIBLIOGRAPHY
Frederick H. Evans (exh. cat., ed. B. Newhall; Rochester, NY, Int. Mus. Phot. 1964; rev. Millerton, NY, 1973)
Pictorial Photography in Great Britain, 1900–1920 (exh. cat., ed. J. Taylor; ACGB, 1978)
M. F. Harker: *The Linked Ring: The Secession Movement in Photography in Britain, 1890–1910* (London, 1979)
The Golden Age of British Photography, 1839–1900 (exh. cat., ed. M. Haworth-Booth; London, V&A, 1984)

MARY CHRISTIAN

Evans, Merlyn (Oliver) (*b* Llandaff, nr Cardiff, 13 March 1910; *d* London, 31 Oct 1973). Welsh painter and printmaker. Although born in Wales, he grew up in Glasgow. He first produced abstract paintings in 1930 while a pupil at Glasgow School of Art (1927–31), in part after scientific drawing, and, despite discouragement, continued to do so secretly at the Royal College of Art (1932–4), inspired by visits to Paris. He was a peripheral member of the Surrealist group in London and showed three paintings at the International Surrealist Exhibition (1936), although his work had Cubist elements. In 1938 he moved to South Africa to teach at the Natal Technical College in Durban, where he lived until he became an engineer with the South African army in North Africa and Italy (1942–5). He then began to paint anti-war subjects, depicting violent allegories of World War II in a style that was an idiosyncratic development of Vorticism. In part abstract, and in lurid colours, these were sometimes based on specific incidents, for instance *The Chess Players* (1940; Eldred Evans priv. col., see 1985 exh. cat., p. 36), which takes as its subject the non-aggression pact between Germany and Russia signed in August 1939. Others were about aggression in general, as in *The Conflict* (1940; M. O. Evans estate, see 1956 exh. cat., pl. IV). After the war he returned to London and held his first large exhibition at the Leicester Galleries in February 1949.

In the 1950s Evans examined the expressive power of abstract shape and became a leading British printmaker, reviving the technique of mezzotint for large-scale prints. His six aquatints *Vertical Suite in Black* (1958) used shapes from primitive art, while the *Pentaptych* mezzotints (1961) shared the geometrical abstraction of his paintings of the 1960s. Evans's large post-war paintings were often based on the patterns made by crowds of people and were intended as a public art on an architectural scale. *The Meeting* (1.83×2.92 m, 1950; London, N. Westminster Bank) was taken from a trades union meeting, and *Metropolitan Crowd Forming into a Procession* (3.15×3.76 m, 1954; AC Eng) from the start of a protest march in London. From 1965 to 1973 he taught painting at the Royal College of Art. His work became increasingly abstract and geometrical but retained a feeling of confrontation or movement by means of black outline and colour contrast.

BIBLIOGRAPHY
Merlyn Evans (exh. cat., intro. R. H. Wilenski; London, Whitechapel A.G., 1956)
The Graphic Work of Merlyn Evans (exh. cat. by R. Erskine and B. Robertson, London, V&A, 1972)
Merlyn Evans, 1910–1973 (exh. cat. by F. Laws, Cardiff, N. Mus., 1974)

The Political Paintings of Merlyn Evans (exh. cat. by D. F. Jenkins and M. Evans, London, Tate, 1985)

DAVID FRASER JENKINS

Evans, Walker (*b* Saint Louis, MO, 3 Nov 1903; *d* New Haven, CT, 10 April 1975). American photographer and writer. He grew up in Kenilworth, a suburb of Chicago, but moved to New York with his mother after his parents separated. Primarily interested in literature, he sat in on lectures at the Sorbonne in Paris (1926–7), visited museums and bookshops, and thought of becoming a writer. In 1928 he acquired a camera and, out of frustration over his inability to find work and develop a literary means of expression, he decided to become a photographer. Intermittent assignments instigated by friends such as Lincoln Kirstein made it possible for him to live a bohemian life in Greenwich Village, where he met the writers Hart Crane (1899–1932) and James Agee (1909–55) and the artist Ben Shahn, with whom he worked and shared a house for a short time. Within this circle he found his early influences.

Evans began the work that brought him recognition and a modest living in 1935. In 18 months he completed all of the images for '*Let us now praise famous men*' (Cambridge, MA, 1941), a collaborative project with James Agee devoted to the lives of the sharecropper families of the south, and a large portion of the plates for *American Photographs* (New York, 1938), his panorama of the USA. At the same time he was active with the Farm Security Administration (FSA) photographic team (*see* UNITED STATES OF AMERICA, §XII) under the directorship of Roy Stryker (1893–1975). *Allie May Burroughs, Hale County, Alabama (Alabama Cotton Tenant Farmer's Wife)* (1936; Chicago, IL, A. Inst., see *First and Last*, pl. 73) became a lasting symbol of the victims of poverty caused by the Depression.

Evans was often in disagreement with Stryker over the goals of the FSA programme and left in 1937, but the following year MOMA, New York, recognized his work with a major exhibition at the time of the publication of *American Photographs*, a book that would have a profound influence on the work of younger photographers such as Robert Frank and on documentary photography as a whole. His carefully composed views, ranging from exterior and interior still-lifes, for example *Burroughs Kitchen, Hale County, Alabama* (1936; New York, MOMA, see *First and Last*, pl. 77), to tattered billboards, are testimony to the beauty and vivid presence he found in the most common themes. Evans's preference for light that illuminated flat, frontal, almost airless images can be seen in *Moundville, Alabama (Corrugated Tin Façade)* (1936; Washington, DC, Lib. Congr.; see fig.).

In 1943 Evans went to work for *Time* magazine as a writer but soon moved to *Fortune*, where he was both a writer and a photographer (1945–65). The *Fortune* years spanned almost half of his career, and more than 400 of his photographs were published by the magazine; *Fortune* had in fact commissioned Evans as early as 1936. However,

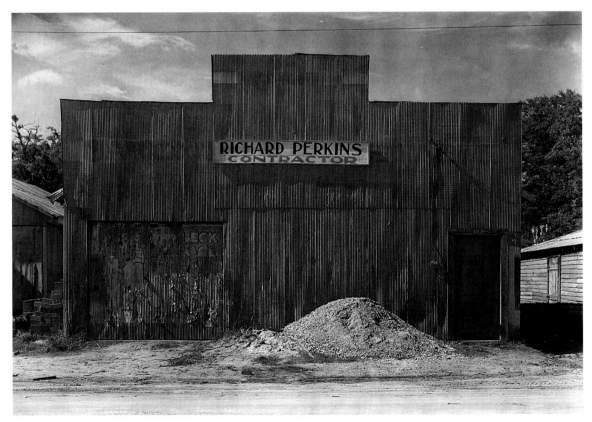

Walker Evans: *Moundville, Alabama (Corrugated Tin Façade)*, photograph, 1936 (Washington, DC, Library of Congress)

much of Evans's work for *Fortune* was less accessible and often denigrated by Evans himself, who never accepted his role in commercial photography. Among the portfolios that *Fortune* did publish, many accompanied by Evans's own texts, were *Labor Anonymous* (Nov 1946) and *Chicago: A Camera Exploration* (Feb 1947). Relative autonomy at the magazine allowed him to continue and amplify his work of the 1930s. His subject remained the American vernacular, the changes wrought by the passage of time and the grandeur of simple things. He produced his first colour work for *Fortune* in 1945, although he later rejected it, asserting that colour was vulgar. After 1950 he created 27 portfolios, 14 of which included colour work. However, one of his most extraordinary portfolios was the black-and-white *Beauties of the Common Tool* (July 1955; see 1977 exh. cat., nos 43–8). For the project he used an 8×10 view camera and made his own prints for the almost full-page reproductions. Astonishing icons, these works remain among the most arresting artists' photographs ever to appear in a commercial publication.

In 1965 Evans retired from professional photography and became a professor at Yale University. If a particular body of his work pointed the way for photographers of the 1950s and 1960s, it was probably the street and subway photographs of the 1930s and 1940s, such as *Corner of State and Randolph Streets, Chicago* (1946; see Szarkowski, p. 161), which embraced the element of chance long before it became a central issue in American art during the late 1950s, rather than the still, powerful evocations of a passing America. Towards the end of his life he returned to poignant interior still-lifes, such as *Walpole, Maine* (1962; see *First and Last*, pl. 192), which evoked his early FSA images and testified to an extraordinarily constant vision that seemed to distil the essence of time and place.

PHOTOGRAPHIC PUBLICATIONS
First and Last (New York, 1978)

BIBLIOGRAPHY
J. Szarkowski: *Walker Evans* (New York, 1971)
D. Farmer and W. Stott, eds: *Walker Evans: Photographs from the 'Let us now praise famous men' Project* (Austin, TX, 1974)
Walker Evans at Fortune, 1945–1965 (exh. cat. by L. K. Baier, Wellesley Coll., MA, Jewett A. Cent., 1977)
Walker Evans and Robert Frank: An Essay on Influence (exh. cat. by T. Papageorge, New Haven, CT, Yale U. A.G., 1981)
Walker Evans: The Hungry Eye (exh. cat. by G. Mora and J. Hill, New York, MOMA, 1993)
G. Mora: *Walker Evans: The Hungry Eye* (London, 1994)
J. Keller: *Walker Evans: A Catalogue of the Collection at the J. Paul Getty Museum* (Malibu, 1995)

CONSTANCE W. GLENN

Eveillard, Pierre-Louis. *See* LIVOIS, Marquis de.

Evelee, Henry. *See* YEVELE, HENRY.

Evelyn, John (*b* Wotton, Surrey, 31 Oct 1620; *d* Wotton, 27 Feb 1706). English diarist, writer and collector. He is remembered principally for his journal, a mixture of reminiscence and record, first published in 1818. Evelyn, the second son of a gentleman, was born at Wotton House near Dorking. In 1637 he was admitted to the Middle Temple and in the same year went up to Balliol College, Oxford. In 1640, following his father's death, he abandoned the study of law and travelled in Holland and Belgium, immersing himself in art, architecture, horticulture and 'curiosities', interests that he was to pursue for the rest of his life. He returned to England in 1641, during the Civil War, and after an abortive attempt to join the Royalist army, thought it prudent to leave the country once again. He left in 1643 on a Grand Tour that was to last four years. He travelled via France to Italy, where he stayed in all the principal cities, studying languages, gardening, art and anatomy, antiquities and 'curiosities'. In 1646 he travelled from Venice to Paris, where he renewed his friendship with the English Resident Sir Richard Browne, whose daughter Mary he married the following year. Leaving his wife in France, Evelyn returned to England, where he appears to have worked clandestinely in the Royalist cause. In 1648 he sat to Robert Walker for his portrait 'in which there is a death's head' (London, N.P.G.): a portent not only of his own mortality, but also of that of Charles I, who was executed in 1649.

Evelyn joined the Stuart court in exile in Paris, returning with Mary in 1653 to Sayes Court, Kent, where he indulged his passion for gardening (*see also* GARDEN, §I). For the next seven years he lived as a gentleman scholar. In 1656 he published a translation of *De rerum natura* by Lucretius (?96–55 BC), with a frontispiece by Mary Evelyn, engraved by Wenceslaus Hollar; and in 1658 a translation of a work on horticulture by Bonnefons. On the Restoration of the Stuart monarchy in 1660, Evelyn resumed public life, serving both Charles II and James II loyally, despite his pious distaste for the excesses of the court. In 1662 he was appointed a founder-member of the council of the Royal Society, in which he was active and influential. In 1664, while serving on an Admiralty Commission, he met Pepys, who became a valued friend. Two years later Evelyn advised Sir Christopher Wren on the scheme to rebuild St Paul's; and, after the Great Fire of 1666, he devised a plan for a new City of London (*see* LONDON, §II, 3). His highest public office, as one of three Commissioners of the Privy Seal, was granted him by James II in 1685.

Evelyn wrote a number of political works in the Stuart cause, but his own prevailing interests are the subjects of three books: *Sculptura* (London, 1662); *Sylva* (London, 1664); and *Numismata* (London, 1697). *Sylva*, a treatise on arboriculture for which in his lifetime he was best known, sprang from the practical needs of naval shipbuilding and was probably intended as part of an encyclopedia of gardening. Prints and medals, the subjects respectively of *Sculptura* and *Numismata*, were an abiding interest; Evelyn was an inveterate collector and also executed a small number of etchings (London, BM). In 1649, while living in Paris, he had visited Abraham Bosse for advice on perspective and patronized Stefano della Bella and Gabriel Pérelle; in 1650 he sat for his engraved portrait (London, N.P.G.) to Robert Nanteuil. In 1653 he visited the medallist Thomas Simon, who was to design in 1660 the gold Coronation medal of Charles II.

Evelyn's interest in prints and medals, which to him were largely interchangeable, lay more in the subjects than in the execution. He helped both Edward Hyde, 1st Earl of Clarendon, and Pepys to form and arrange collections of portraits of historical and contemporary heroes. Writing to the latter in 1689 he extolled the virtue of medals over paintings, because they emphasized the sitter rather than the artist; he preferred prints to paintings on grounds of convenience and expenditure. *Sculptura* was probably the direct result of Evelyn's introduction by Prince Rupert of the Rhine in 1661 to the technique of mezzotint engraving. The book contains a plate engraved by Rupert of the *Head of the Executioner of John the Baptist* from a painting (Munich, Alte Pin.) then thought to be by Jusepe de Ribera. This plate is now the only virtue of *Sculptura*, in which the account both of the history and the practice of printmaking is unreliable and the style discursive and inelegant.

Although paintings interested Evelyn less than engravings, he translated in 1688 Roland Fréart's *Idée de la perfection de la peinture* (1662) as *Perfection of Painting*. He knew Francis Barlow and John Michael Wright and admired Antonio Verrio. As well as to Walker, he sat for his portrait (1641; London, N.P.G.) to Hendrik van der Borcht the younger (*b* 1614) and was also painted by Godfrey Kneller in 1685 (Stonor Park, Oxon) and 1689 (priv. col.; copy, London, Royal Soc.). The latter portrait, 'holding my *Sylva* in my hand', was painted for Pepys. Like many of his contemporaries, Evelyn was fascinated by 'curiosities' and assembled his own 'cabinet' (London, Geffrye Mus.). He visited the leading collectors of his day, John Tradescant (ii), Elias Ashmole and Hans Sloane, thus becoming tangentially involved with the foundation of public museums. He was responsible for persuading Henry Howard, 6th Duke of Norfolk (1628–84), to give the Arundel Marbles, collected by the Duke's grandfather, Thomas Howard, 2nd Earl of Arundel, to Oxford University (Oxford, Ashmolean) and the Arundelian Library to the Royal Society. Evelyn's championship of Grinling Gibbons in the 1670s probably owes more to his delight in the 'curious' than to aesthetic appreciation. In 1699 he inherited Wotton House from his brother and remained there, devout, inquisitive and active, until his death, aged 86.

WRITINGS

Sculptura, or the History of the Art of Chalcography (London, 1662)
Sylva, together with Pomona and Gardener's Almanack (London, 1664)
Numismata, or a Discourse of Medals (London, 1697)
E. S. de Beer, ed.: *Diary*. 6 vols (London, 1955)

BIBLIOGRAPHY

A. Dobson: 'Life of Evelyn' [preface to his 1906 edition of *Diary*]
H. C. Levis: *Extracts from the Diaries and Correspondence of John Evelyn and Samuel Pepys relating to Engraving* (London, 1915)

DAVID RODGERS

Evenepoel, Henri(-Jacques-Edouard) (*b* Nice, 3 Oct 1872; *d* Paris, 27 Dec 1899). Belgian painter and printmaker. His mother died when he was two, and he was brought up by his severe but cultivated father, a senior civil servant and musicologist. He studied in Brussels under the architect Ernest Acker (1852–1912) at the Académie des Beaux-Arts (1889–90), the painter Ernest Blanc-Garin (1843–1916) and the decorative painter Adolphe Crespin (1859–1944), then entered the Ecole des Beaux-Arts in Paris on 21 October 1892 as a pupil of P. V. Galland. Galland died in November 1892, and Evenepoel was admitted to Gustave Moreau's atelier on 14 March 1893. There he came into contact with Georges Rouault and became friendly with Henri Matisse, Paul Baignères (1869–1945), Charles Milcendeau (1872–1919),

Simon Bussy (1869–1954) and Charles Hoffbauer (1875–*c*. 1957). For more than four years Evenepoel was very close to Moreau, a demanding teacher who appreciated his sensitivity and determination and encouraged him to develop a distinct artistic personality.

Evenepoel made his début at the Salon des Artistes Français in 1894 with one of his finest portraits of his cousin Louise De Mey-van Mattemburgh, *Madame D.* (or *Louise in Mourning*, 1894; Antwerp, Kon. Mus. S. Kst.). The following year he exhibited four portraits at the Salon du Champ-de-Mars, including the striking full-length *Paul Baignères* dressed in red (1894; Brussels, Mus. A. Mod.), and he continued to show there every year for the rest of his life. His first solo exhibition took place at the Brussels Cercle Artistique (Dec 1897–Jan 1898), while he spent the winter in Algeria. On his return in May 1898 he painted Paris street scenes and interiors (e.g. *Fête at the Invalides*, 1898; Brussels, Mus. A. Mod.). In 1899 he worked feverishly on such paintings as *Henriette in a Large Hat* (1899; Brussels, Mus. A. Mod.), *Spaniard in Paris* (1899; Ghent, Mus. S. Kst.) and *Sunday Walk in the Bois de Boulogne* (1899; Liège, Mus. A. Mod.). His work was finding increasing support among critics, and he was on the point of being able to marry Louise and recognize their son Charles, when he died from typhoid.

Evenepoel's favourite subjects were his family and friends, whom he painted with tenderness and insight. His full-length portraits, usually simply posed against a neutral background, owe much to the example of Edouard Manet and James McNeill Whistler. His scenes of contemporary Parisian life were particularly influenced by Jean-Louis Forain and Henri de Toulouse-Lautrec. In his early Parisian pictures he generally preferred a somewhat sombre palette. The paintings he brought back from Blidah and Tipaza, for example *Orange Market, Blidah* (1898; Brussels, Mus. A. Mod.), were in a radically different style that foreshadowed the heightened colours of Fauvism. In his more important works he used flat areas of bold colour, emphatic outlines and flattened space. Despite his short life he produced a sizeable oeuvre that includes drawings, lithographs, etchings, poster designs, photographs and a vast correspondence, which is a valuable source for the art history of this period in Paris.

WRITINGS

F. E. Hyslop, ed.: *Henri Evenepoel à Paris: Lettres choisies* (Brussels, 1972)
D. Derrey-Capon, ed.: *Henri Evenepoel, lettres à mon père* (Brussel, 1994)

BIBLIOGRAPHY

P. Lambotte: *Henri Evenepoel* (Brussels, 1908)
P. Haesaerts and L. Haesaerts: *Henri Evenepoel* (Brussels, 1932)
M.-J. Chartrain Hebbelinck: 'Henri Evenepoel: A Belgian Precursor of Fauvism', *Apollo*, xciv (1971), pp. 293–9
F. E. Hyslop: *Henri Evenepoel: Belgian Painter in Paris, 1892–1899* (University Park, 1975)
P. Roberts-Jones and others: *Henri Evenepoel* (Brussels, 1994) [with cat. rais. and complete bibliog.]

DANIELLE DERREY-CAPON

Everdingen, van. Dutch family of painters and draughtsmen. The brothers (1) Caesar van Everdingen and (2) Allart van Everdingen were the sons of Pieter van Everdingen, a notary and solicitor in Alkmaar; their mother, Aechte Claesdr., was a midwife in the city. Houbraken claimed that Caesar was a pupil of the Utrecht artist Jan van Bronchorst; though there is no documentary evidence to prove this, the noticeable influence on his work of paintings by Utrecht artists does seem to suggest that he served his apprenticeship in that town. Moreover, the van Everdingen family had long-standing ties with Utrecht, and Allart also eventually trained with a painter from Utrecht. Caesar is best known as a history painter who worked in the classicizing style that became fashionable in Haarlem in the mid-17th century, while Allart made his name as a landscape artist, the first to depict Scandinavian motifs in his paintings and drawings.

(1) Caesar (Bovetius) [Boetius] **van Everdingen** (*b* Alkmaar, 1616 or 1617; *bur* Alkmaar, 13 Oct 1678). In 1632, at a very early age, he entered Alkmaar's Guild of St

Luke. There are a number of unsigned but dated works by him from the 1630s. The earliest signed and dated painting is the group portrait of the *Officers of the Orange Company of the Alkmaar Civic Guard* (1641; Alkmaar, Stedel. Mus.), both the execution and the composition of which are rather weak. From 1641 to 1643 Caesar lived in Amersfoort, where, under the supervision of the painter and architect Jacob van Campen, he worked on a modello for the exterior decoration of the organ shutters of Alkmaar's Grote Kerk. The size and shape of these shutters, as well as the great height at which they were to be placed, forced the artist to make allowances for possible distortions of perspective. The highly successful finished result, representing the *Triumph of Saul after David's*

Caesar van Everdingen and Pieter Post: *Count William II of Holland Issuing the Charter*, oil on canvas, 2.18×2.12 m, 1655 (Leiden, Rijnlandshuis)

Victory over Goliath (1644; *in situ*) was partly executed on panel and partly on canvas. The figures forming the procession and the women playing music behind the balustrades have much in common with figures that appear in paintings by the Utrecht Caravaggisti.

In 1646 Caesar van Everdingen married Helena van Oosthoorn in Heiloo; they had no children. After 1648 Caesar lived in Haarlem, where he probably worked on two paintings for the Oranje Zaal in the Huis ten Bosch (*see* THE HAGUE, §IV, 3), commissioned through van Campen. Of Caesar's two contributions to this vast collaborative programme, the *Birth of Frederick Hendry* and the *Rewards of Parnassus* (both *in situ*), the second is the better of the two: it has a well-balanced composition showing the winged horse Pegasus and four muses with musical instruments.

During the 1650s Caesar painted several splendid works in the classicizing style that became typical of Haarlem history painting at that time, such as *Count William II of Holland Issuing the Charter* (1655; Leiden Rijnlandshuis; see fig.), in collaboration with Pieter Post, and *Jupiter and Callisto* (1655; Stockholm, Nmus.). The actual event in these pieces—the granting of privileges in 1255 to the Rhineland district water-control board in the first instance—is presented rather statically, and the large figures are idealized; the rendering of details is meticulous, and the colours tend to be bright. The same is true of paintings by Pieter de Grebber and Salomon de Bray, who together with Caesar van Everdingen are sometimes referred to as the Haarlem Classicists or Haarlem Academics. Apart from these stately history pieces, they also produced genre pictures; Caesar van Everdingen repeatedly depicted courtesans, for instance playing musical instruments or combing their hair.

Caesar was dean of the Haarlem Guild of St Luke in 1655 and 1656. A year later he returned to Alkmaar, where—apart from a brief stay in Amsterdam in 1661—he remained until his death. Quite a few signed and dated works from this Alkmaar period have survived, including the portrait of the *Officers and Ensigns of the Old Civic Guard* (1657; Alkmaar, Stedel. Mus.), a successful composition in which the members of the Civic Guard are rendered with an air reminiscent of the elegant portraits of Bartholomeus van der Helst. In 1662 van Everdingen finished his *Lycurgus and the Fruits of Education* (Alkmaar, Stedel. Mus.), destined for the Prinsenkamer in the town hall at Alkmaar. Of the many other portraits from this period, especially touching is that of a *Child with an Apple* (1664; Barnsley, Cannon Hall Mus.).

Caesar van Everdingen usually signed his work with the monogram CVE. After 1655 he signed various documents *Caesar Bovetius van Everdingen*. References in old inventories suggest that he also made many drawings, but no signed examples are known at present. Various civil actions seem to indicate that Caesar van Everdingen was reasonably wealthy.

BIBLIOGRAPHY
A. Houbraken: *De groote schouburgh* (1718–21), ii, p. 94
D. van der Poel: *Caesar van Everdingen (1617–1678)* (diss., Rijksuniv. Utrecht, 1975)
Gods, Saints & Heroes: Dutch Painting in the Age of Rembrandt (exh. cat. by A. Blankert and others, Washington, DC, N.G.A.; Detroit, MI, Inst. A.; Amsterdam, Rijksmus., 1980–81), pp. 214–19
Nieuw licht op de Gouden Eeuw: Hendrick ter Brugghen en tijdgenoten (exh. cat. by A. Blankert and L. J. Slatkes, Utrecht, Cent. Mus.; Brunswick, Herzog Anton Ulrich-Mus., 1986–7), pp. 252–6

D. B. HENSBROEK-VAN DER POEL

(2) Allart [Allaert, Allert] **van Everdingen** (*b* Alkmaar, *bapt* 18 June 1621; *d* Amsterdam, *bur* 8 Nov 1675). Painter, draughtsman, etcher and dealer, brother of (1) Caesar van Everdingen. According to Houbraken, Allart was the pupil of Roelandt Savery in Utrecht and Pieter de Molyn in Haarlem; both painters certainly influenced his work. In 1644 Allart travelled to Norway and Sweden, a trip that was to have profound consequences on his art; his annotated sketches document visits to the south-east Norwegian coast and to Bohusland and the Göteborg area in western Sweden. He returned to the Netherlands by 21 Feb 1645, when he married Janneke Cornelisdr Brouwers in Haarlem. He became a member of the Reformed Church in Haarlem on 13 Oct 1645, joined the Haarlem Guild of St Luke in 1646 and, along with his brother Caesar, enlisted in the Haarlem Civic Guard of St George in 1648. From 1646 to 1651 four of Allart's children, a son and three daughters, were baptized in Haarlem; four additional children were born later in Amsterdam. In 1652 he moved to Amsterdam and on 10 April 1657 became a citizen. A visit he made about 1660 to the Ardennes in the southern Netherlands is documented by his painting *View of Montjardin Castle* (The Hague, Mauritshuis) and by his drawings and etchings of Spa and its surroundings. The artist probably forwent a return trip to Sweden in order to execute the commissions he received from the Trip family in the 1660s to paint the four overdoors decorating the Trippenhuis in Amsterdam (*in situ*), as well as the large *Cannon Foundry of Julitabroeck, Södermanland* (Amsterdam, Rijksmus.). In 1661 van Everdingen joined Jacob van Ruisdael and Willem Kalf to judge the authenticity of a seascape by Jan Porcellis; Meindert Hobbema served as a witness to the proceedings. The sale of his widow's estate on 16 April 1709 suggests that the artist, like many of his colleagues, had a second profession as an art dealer; the sale catalogue lists works by Raphael, Giorgione, Annibale Carracci, Titian, Veronese, Holbein, Savery, Porcellis, Hals and Rembrandt. The master's only known pupil was the seascape painter Ludolf Bakhuizen.

Allart's earliest dated painting, *Rough Sea* (1640; untraced), establishes his beginnings as a marine painter in the tradition of Jan Porcellis. Although his production of seascapes was small (19 are known) and occurred early in his career, his contribution to the genre was notable. His monochrome paintings emphasized the dramatic aspect of heaving waves and darkened sky, both at open sea, as in the small *Stormy Sea* (Leipzig, Mus. Bild. Kst.), and in topographical views, such as the *Stormy View of Flushing* (St Petersburg, Hermitage). The impact of his naturalistic marine paintings on van Ruisdael's seascapes is especially significant.

In 1644, the year of his trip north, van Everdingen painted a Dutch dunescape in the style of his second teacher, de Molijn (1644; untraced; with the dealer A. van der Meer, 1964). The earliest known date on a Nordic landscape is 1646 (sold, Stockholm, 1981; untraced). The influence of Savery's Tyrolean views on van Everdingen's Scandinavian landscapes is clear in his next dated works, the four majestic mountain views of 1647, exemplified by the *Mountain Landscape with a River Valley* (Copenhagen, Stat. Mus. Kst.). By 1648 van Everdingen had introduced his countrymen to his full repertory of Nordic motifs—mountain views, rock and water scenes, and waterfalls. He continued to paint rocky terrains, fir trees, cascades, water-mills and blockhouses for the remainder of his career.

His early Nordic works are characterized by a Flemish landscape colour scheme (soon followed by a monochromatic grey-brown), by delicate touches of thinly applied paint and by the diagonal organization of overlapping light and dark planes (possibly indebted to Hercules Segers) in a horizontal format. The Haarlem painter Cornelis Vroom probably inspired his silhouettes of dark trees against a light sky. One dated *Waterfall* (1648; priv. col., on loan to Hannover, Niedersächs. Landesmus.) has a vertical design, which became the artist's preferred and most influential composition type. His early upright waterfalls, best represented by the *Scandinavian Waterfall with a Water-mill* (1650; Munich, Alte Pin.; see fig.), had a formative effect on Jacob van Ruisdael, who started painting the subject shortly after his own move to Amsterdam *c.* 1657. The *Swedish Scenery* (1655; Amsterdam, Rijksmus.) shows van Everdingen's next shift to a more decorative style relying on fluid brushwork and a lighter palette; his occasional collaborator Nicolaes Berchem probably added the staffage. The overwhelming majority of van Everdingen's paintings after 1660 were waterfalls, some pastel in colour and others predominantly brown, with the paint applied broadly in large zones. The *Scandinavian Landscape* (1670; Rouen, Mus. B.-A.) reveals the artist's working methods, as it exactly repeats the composition of a sketch he executed 26 years earlier during his visit to the waterfall at Mölndal (Mölndal, Gunnebo). Van Everdingen also painted topographical Dutch landscapes, such as the *View of Zuylen Castle in Winter* (Haarzuilens, Kasteel de Haar) and the *View of Alkmaar* (Paris, Fond. Custodia, Inst. Néer.), but these are exceptional cases (9 examples are known).

Allart was a talented and prolific draughtsman; over 500 Scandinavian and Netherlandish landscape drawings by him are found in European public collections. At least seven sets of drawings of the *Twelve Months* are known. The artist's reputation as an innovative printmaker rests largely on his experiments with mezzotint. His 166 catalogued etchings include a set of illustrations for the fable *Reynard the Fox* (drawings, London, BM) and landscapes exclusively devoted to Nordic subjects.

Besides van Ruisdael, Allart van Everdingen's waterfalls influenced Jan van Kessel, Roeland Roghman, Pieter de Molijn and the 19th-century Norwegian painter J. C. Dahl. In his own day they were appraised at relatively high values. Although his prices and regard fell in the 18th century, when Dutch Italianate landscapes were favoured, by the end of that century his drawings and watercolours were highly prized, and van Everdingen was singled out for praise by Goethe in 1784 and enjoyed a revival of interest by 1820.

BIBLIOGRAPHY

Hollstein: *Dut. & Flem.*
A. Houbraken: *De groote schouburgh* (1718–21), ii, pp. 95–6

Allart van Everdingen: *Scandinavian Waterfall with a Water-mill*, oil on canvas, 1.12×0.88 m, 1650 (Munich, Alte Pinakothek)

W. Drugulin: *Allart van Everdingen: Catalogue raisonné de toutes les estampes qui forment son oeuvre gravé* (Leipzig, 1873)
C. W. Bruinvis: 'De van Everdingens', *Oud-Holland*, xvii (1899), pp. 216–22
O. Granberg: *Allart van Everdingen och hans 'Norska' landskap: Det gamla Julita och Wurmbrandts kanoner* [Allart van Everdingen and his 'Norwegian' landscape: the old Julita and Wurmbrandt's cannons] (Stockholm, 1902)
K. E. Steneberg: *Kristinatidens måleri* [Painting in the time of Queen Christina] (diss., Malmö U., 1955), pp. 118–25
A. I. Davies: *Allart van Everdingen* (New York, 1978)
Hollandse schilderkunst: Landschappen 17de eeuw (exh. cat. by F. J. Duparc, The Hague, Mauritshuis, 1980), pp. 29–31
Masters of 17th-century Dutch Landscape Painting (exh. cat., ed. P. C. Sutton; Amsterdam, Rijksmus.; Boston, MA, Mus. F.A.; Philadelphia, PA, Mus. A.; 1987–8), pp. 307–12

ALICE I. DAVIES

Evergood, Philip (*b* New York, 26 Oct 1901; *d* Bridgewater, CT, 11 March 1973). American painter. He was educated largely abroad, studying art at the Slade School of Fine Art, London (1921–3), and in Paris with André Lhote and others (1924–5). After a brief period in New York, he returned to Paris in 1930 and the next year spent six months in Spain where he was much influenced by the work of El Greco and Goya. On his return to the USA in 1931, during the depths of the Depression, he married and supported his family by odd jobs while painting for the Federal Art Project of the Works Progress Administration. He was a militant supporter of workers and was jailed several times for his part in strikes and protests. To attack what he saw as events of social injustice or the exploitation of the poor, he developed a strident expressionist style, which resulted in violent paintings such as the *Pink Dismissal Slip* (1937; Ithaca, NY, Cornell U., Johnson Mus. A.) and *Don't Cry Mother* (1938–44; New York, MOMA). His first of three murals, commissioned in 1936 by the Works Progress Administration for a library in Richmond Hill, NY, was intended to glorify an ideal community of working families, although it offended many of them.

After the mid-1940s Evergood turned more towards private fantasies, some erotic, some playful, some nearly surrealist. In these his touch was lighter and his expressionist style was tempered by deliberate borrowings from naive art, especially that of children. In 1952 Evergood moved to Connecticut, where he spent the rest of his life.

WRITINGS
'Sure, I'm a Social Painter', *Mag. A.*, xxxvi (1943), pp. 254–9

BIBLIOGRAPHY
Philip Evergood (exh. cat. by J. I. H. Baur, New York, Whitney, 1960)
Philip Evergood: Selections from the Hirshhorn Museum and Sculpture Garden, Smithsonian Institution (exh. cat. by K. Taylor, Washington, DC, Hirshhorn, 1978)

JOHN I. H. BAUR

Evers, Henri (Hendrik Jorden) (*b* Ellecom, 24 Nov 1856; *d* Wassenaar, 21 Nov 1929). Dutch architect, teacher and writer. He was trained by his father, J. Brink Evers, and attended the Academie voor Bouwkunst in The Hague and in Antwerp. He then worked on the Gerechtshof (built 1871–9) in Antwerp with the architects François Baekelmans (1827–96) and his brother Louis Baekelmans (1835–71), before moving to Brussels, where he worked with J. Naet. Between 1883 and 1885 he worked in Vienna and Budapest, but he returned to the Netherlands and set up in 1885 as an independent architect in Amsterdam. Two years later he was appointed lecturer at the Academie voor Bouwkunst in Rotterdam, and in 1902 he became a professor at the Technische Hogeschool in Delft. He rejected the use of historical revival styles, believing that the past could not be copied but could only inspire. Evers felt that the architecture of his time was undergoing a crisis: one possible way of overcoming this was through the study of history; another solution lay in the study of different architectural traditions, such as the architecture of East Asia. His most important architectural work is the Stadhuis (1914–20) in Rotterdam.

WRITINGS
'Stroomingen' [Movements], *Bouwknd. Wkbld*, xi (1891), pp. 206–9, 211–16, 219–22
'Het oriëntalisme in de westersche architectuur', *Bouwknd. Wkbld*, xiv (1894), pp. 93–5, 107–10, 124–6, 146–8, 150–3, 184–7
'Het nut der historische studiën tot de vorming van den architect' [The use of historical studies in the development of an architect], *Bouwwereld*, i (1902), p. 325
De architectuur in hare hoofdtijdperken [Architecture in the main periods] (Groningen, 1905–11)

BIBLIOGRAPHY
G. Fanelli: *Architettura moderna* (1968)
M. Bock: *Anfänge einer neuen Architektur: Beilages Beitrag zur architektonischen Kultur der Niederlände im ausgehenden 19. Jahrhundert* (Wiesbaden, 1983)

DIANNE TIMMERMAN, FRANK VAN DEN HOEK

Evers, Tönnies [Antonius], **II** (*b* Lübeck, 1550–52; *d* Lübeck, 1613). German wood-carver. He trained in the workshop of his father, Tönnies [Antonius] Evers I (*d* 1584), who belonged to the guild of master builders and joiners in Lübeck from 1556 to 1580, using (from 1559) an escutcheon showing a lily and a boar's head. From 1567 the younger Evers travelled widely and in 1576 was as far south as Konstanz; his later work showed the influence of his contact with South German craftsmen and with Netherlandish works of art. In 1580 he returned to Lübeck and took over his father's workshop; a year later his first apprentice, Hans Weydmann, joined him. Tönnies Evers II was an active member of his guild but was brought to trial by fellow members for having defied its rules by employing more journeymen and apprentices on contracted work than was permitted. Although there was animosity towards him within the guild, he was widely accepted by his contemporaries as the leading wood-carver. His surviving works are well documented and bear the lily-and-boar's head emblem; they include the rood loft (1587) in the church of St Egidius in Lübeck, the wooden pulpit created for the church of St Mary in Wismar (1587; since 1746, Neustadt, Mecklenburg) and the interior decoration (*c.* 1607) of the boardroom in the Merchants' House in Lübeck. His strength lay in his ability to assimilate and synthesize the stylistic trends with which he came in contact before and after his return to Lübeck. He was indebted to the Netherlandish school, notably to the older style of Cornelis Floris and the newer one of Hans Vredeman de Vries. In the organ façade (1587–9) of the church of St Peter in Lübeck he combined the two styles, adding other elements that can be traced back to the Netherlanders Hendrick Goltzius and Adriaen Collaert (*c.* 1560–1618) and to the Nuremberg master Peter Flötner. These influences appeared less evident in his work in the war cabinet room (1594–1613; destr. 1942) of the Rathaus in Lübeck, the most important Renaissance room of its time in Germany (*see* GERMANY, §V, 1). His inspiration, especially for the figurative work, may have come from German prints by the Goltzius school, Jost Amman and Virgil Solis, or small-scale sculpture. The room's decoration demonstrated his ability to harmonize immensely rich and varied architectural and sculptural details with the intarsia of the wood panelling, conveying an impression of splendour and power. After his death his son Tönnies Evers III carried on the workshop tradition but never achieved the same success as his father.

BIBLIOGRAPHY
K. Hinrichsen: *Tönnies Evers, 1550–1613: Ein Beitrag zur Geschichte des Stilwandels in der deutschen Plastik um 1600* (Hamburg, 1937)
L. Wilde: *Die Bau- und Kunstdenkmäler der Hansestadt Lübeck*, i (Lübeck, 1974)

HANNELORE HÄGELE

Evesham, Epiphanius (*b* ?1570 or earlier; *fl* 1589–*c.* 1623). English sculptor and painter. He was born (probably at Epiphany) into a family of Herefordshire gentry, the fourteenth and youngest child of William Evesham of Wellington. He is said to have been a pupil of the Southwark sculptor Richard Stevens, but the source of this information is unreliable. His earliest recorded work is an engraved sun-dial (1589; Hereford, City Mus. & A.G.); during the 1590s he made at least two minor memorial tablets. In 1591 he was apparently in London, and by 1600 he had moved to Paris, where he remained until at least 1615. The extensive documentation of his time abroad indicates that he was an artist of considerable versatility (see Jurgens, 1960). In 1601 he subcontracted the metal-casting of a model of Neptune on three sea-horses. Five years later he undertook to make the black marble tomb slab of the *Archbishop of Sens* (untraced), to be installed in the cathedral of Notre-Dame, Paris, and in 1611 he contracted for the stone and marble monument to *Jacques de Poyanne* at the Grands-Augustins Church (destr.), Paris; it included an approximately life-size effigy kneeling at a prayer-desk and painted in natural colours. Evesham also designed six plaster chimney-pieces for a house near Melun (*c.* 1611). In several documents he is described as a painter as well as a sculptor, and he probably did the sketches of three paintings, two of a religious and one of a Roman historical subject, which in 1611 he handed over to an artist called Jehan Le Roy for completion.

Evesham may have become a French citizen, for he is recorded as a 'stranger' living in London in 1621. All his known work after his return to England was tomb sculpture, and it is all highly distinctive. His monument to *Edmund West* (*c.* 1618; Marsworth, Bucks, All Saints) consists of a chest, on one side of which an effigy of the deceased on his deathbed is incised on a brass plate; on the front, incised slate figures alternate with alabaster panels, two of them bearing emblems of death and resurrection in relief. One of the figures is a risen Christ, an image that was still deeply offensive to Protestant sensibilities in Britain and therefore rarely used. Evesham's talent for relief sculpture appears very clearly on memorials in Kent to members of two recusant families, *Sir Thomas and Lady Hawkins* (*c.* 1617; Boughton under Blean, SS Peter and Paul) and *Christopher Roper, 2nd Lord Teynham* (*c.* 1622; Lynsted, SS Peter and Paul). Both have alabaster panels set into the chest showing the children of the deceased grouped in a remarkably free pictorial fashion, doubtless influenced by the artist's knowledge of painting, while Evesham's acquaintance with the religious art of the Continent appears in the daughters' open display of grief. The small alabaster wall tablet that Evesham began but did not complete for his kinsman Richard Boyle, 1st Earl of Cork, to commemorate the Earl's son Roger (*d* 1615; Deptford, London, St Nicholas) also has a relief panel, in this case with an effigy of the young man. Evesham pawned his part of the work, and the Earl was obliged to redeem it.

Of the monuments attributed to Evesham only those of *c.* 1619–23 can be assigned to him with confidence. The dignified, full-size effigy of *Lady Teynham* kneeling by her husband's side is matched by that of *Lady Lewin* (*c.* 1620; Otterden, Kent, St Lawrence), while the relief panels of sons and daughters have counterparts below the effigy of *Sir Adrian Scrope* (*c.* 1623; South Cockerington, Lincs, St Leonard's). *Richard, Lord Rich* (alabaster with black and green veined marble, *c.* 1620; Felsted, Essex, Holy Cross), is oddly portrayed, twisting round to look at his eldest son; episodes from his life and death are shown as panels behind and below him. Rich's grandson Robert, 2nd Earl of Warwick, is commemorated with his wife, Frances, by

a novel and charming medallion portrait in alabaster, touchstone and pink marble (*c.* 1619; Sharford, Lincs, St Lawrence), a type also used for *Captain John Troughton* (alabaster and yellow stone, *c.* 1621; Ingatestone, Essex, SS Edmund and Mary) and Cicile and Ellenor, wives of Sir John Denham (1619; Egham, Surrey, St John the Baptist). John Penkethman described Evesham in 1624 as a 'most exquisite artist', and for the England of his day in which much sculpture was dull and repetitive the epithet is fully justified.

BIBLIOGRAPHY
M. Jurgens: 'Quelques actes inédits concernant Epiphanius Evesham', *Bull. Soc. Hist. A. Fr.* (1960), pp. 175–82
M. Whinney: *Sculpture in Britain, 1530–1830*, Pelican Hist. A. (Harmondsworth, 1964, rev. 2/1988), pp. 56–60
E. Esdaile: '"A Most Exquisite Artist": The Work of Epiphanius Evesham', *Country Life*, clxix (11 June 1981), pp. 1690–93

ADAM WHITE

Évora. Portuguese city, capital of the Alto Alentejo province. It was a Roman city, given the name of Liberalitas Julia in the time of Julius Caesar, and owed its importance to its position dominating the junction of several routes of communication. The seat of an archbishopric since 1540 and of a university between 1559 and 1759, Évora has for centuries been the chief city of southern Portugal. It was also a favourite residence of the kings of the first and second dynasties, who held *cortes* (parliaments) there 12 times. The frequent presence of the royal household led to the construction of many civic and religious buildings, so that the city represents an architectural and artistic heritage unique in Portugal for its richness, diversity, compactness and state of preservation. Through the centuries Évora has functioned as the natural capital of the large and distinctive region of the Alentejo, in which agriculture is still the basic activity. The city today has some 40,000 inhabitants.

Within its ancient walls can be found examples of almost all the artistic styles that have prevailed in Portugal, particularly those of the medieval and Renaissance periods, during which many outstanding works of art were executed in Évora. Among the most notable buildings are the well-preserved Roman temple (3rd century AD) traditionally known as the Temple of Diana, an emblem of the city. It is hexastyle, with 14 Corinthian columns remaining, and is related to the Maison Carrée at Nîmes. The cathedral, on the highest point of the city, which it dominates majestically, is the most important building south of the River Tagus. Built on the site of a Moorish mosque, it is believed to have been begun in 1186, consecrated in 1204 and almost completed by *c.* 1250. The building marks a transitional stage between Romanesque and Gothic; the ground-plan and arrangement of space belongs to the first style and the lighting, roofing and decoration to the second. It has a nave without a tribune, higher than the two aisles and with a triforium; the domed crossing is supported by pendentives, and an octagonal lantern, with the rose windows at either end of the transept, floods the cathedral with light. The chancel, which was rebuilt between 1716 and 1746 during the reign of John V, is perhaps the most harmonious construction of Italian-influenced Portuguese Baroque, designed by João Frederico Ludovice, the court architect. At the end of the north transept is a triumphal

Évora, Nossa Senhora da Graça, attributed to Diogo de Torralva, *c.* 1524–9

arch with Renaissance decoration leading to a funerary chapel with a ribbed vault. On the main west front is a deeply recessed ogival portal (14th century) flanked by marble columns bearing statues of the apostles, and on either side are two dissimilar towers completed in the early 16th century during the Manueline period. The lantern tower is French in inspiration and is also related to the lanterns of the Old Cathedral at Salamanca, but it is unique in Portugal.

The church of S Francisco (1480–1500) is a royal foundation built to the design of Martim Lourenço (*d* 1524–5). It is of particular interest and originality in the context of Mediterranean late European Gothic for the combination of Manueline and Moorish elements, the majestic proportions (36×34×24 m), the asymmetrical narthex and the spacious vaulting of the crossing on ogival arches. Adjoining the church is the Chapel of Bones, a late 16th-century construction the interior of which is covered with human bones, exemplifying the macabre taste (*memento mori*) fostered by the Counter-Reformation in certain areas of southern Europe. The church of S João Evangelista (1485), adjacent to the Monastery dos Lóios (the pantheon of the Duques de Cadaval, now a hotel), is Gothic in structure with *mudéjar*, Renaissance and Baroque elements in its decoration and important *azulejo* (glazed tile) panels depicting the *Life of St Lawrence Giustiniani, Patriarch of Venice* and signed in 1711 by António de Oliveira Bernardes (for illustration *see* BERNARDES, (1)).

The Espírito Santo University was founded in 1559 by Henry I of Portugal, Cardinal Infante Dom Henrique (Archbishop of Évora before his accession in 1578), for the Jesuits, who controlled it until the expulsion of the order by Sebastian Carvalho e Mello, 1st Marquis de Pombal, in 1759. For two centuries the Jesuit University of Évora rivalled that of Coimbra, and outstanding philosophers and theologians from the Iberian peninsula, such as Luis de Molina (1535–1600) and Pedro de Fonseca (1528–99), taught there. The most interesting feature of the interior is the two-storey, Tuscan-arched cloister, dominated by the Baroque façade of the Sala dos Actos, where formal functions took place (restored in 1973). Adjoining the university is the church of Espírito Santo, which is the finest example of Jesuit architecture in southern Portugal. It is the work of the royal architects Afonso Alvares and Manuel Pires (who with DIOGO DE TORRALVA were also responsible for the complex of the University buildings). It was built between 1566 and 1574 and thus anticipates Il Gesù (begun 1568) in Rome, which was to serve as a model for Jesuit churches throughout the world. It has a severe façade, a narthex inspired by that of S Francisco and a single barrel-vaulted nave with communicating lateral chapels and tribunes. The church had considerable influence on the development of the *estilo-chão* (plain style), the austere provincial style between Mannerism and Baroque that distinguished Portuguese architecture between the middle of the 16th century and the beginning of the 18th. A building with an unusual Mannerist façade is Nossa Senhora da Graça (*c.* 1524–9), attributed to Diogo de Torralva (see fig.).

The Museu de Évora, housed in the former Archbishop's Palace (late 16th to early 18th century), contains collections of archaeology, epigraphy, painting, the decorative arts and sculpture, the last being particularly rich with examples dating from the 1st century AD to the present day; medieval funerary carving is exceptionally well represented. The paintings are mainly from the collection of the celebrated patron and Archbishop of Évora, Dom Frei Manuel do Cenáculo Vilas Boas.

BIBLIOGRAPHY

A. F. Barata: *Évora antiga* (Évora, 1909)
A. Franco: *Évora ilustrada* (Évora, 1945)
T. Espanca: *Évora, arte e historia* (Évora, 1980)

JOSÉ ALBERTO GOMES MACHADO

Evrard d'Orléans (*fl* 1292–1352). French architect, painter and sculptor. He is first mentioned in the Parisian tax rolls of 1292, and a document of 1304 refers to him as 'peintre du roi'. Between 1308 and 1328 he was employed as painter and architect at various royal châteaux, but his most important commission involved the additions ordered by Philip IV to his palace on the Ile de la Cité in Paris. Guérout concluded that Evrard designed the portal of the Galerie des Merciers with facing statues of *Philip IV* and his minister, *Enguerrand de Marigny* (both destr.), and that he was in charge of the decoration in the Grand'Salle, which ran parallel to the river. The great vaulted hall was the setting for a series of life-size painted statues of the *Kings of France* (destr.), an ensemble that reflected Philip's programmatic image of the French monarchy. The statues themselves, doubtless planned if not all executed by Evrard, impressed contemporaries with their 'lifelike' aspect. Evrard may have been a specialist in creating donor images that preserved the convincing presence, if not an actual likeness, of their subjects. He continued to supervise the work at the Palais de la Cité under Philip VI (*reg* 1328–50), and in 1352 he directed restorations at the Sainte-Chapelle.

Evrard also executed many works for Mahaut, Comtesse d'Artois: in 1313 he directed the work at her mansion in Paris, and in 1314 he was at her château at Conflans. In the same year he collaborated with others on the tomb of *Otto IV, Count of Burgundy* (mostly destr. 1793) and received payment for a *Calvary* group and a statue of *Robert d'Artois* for Maubuisson Abbey. The sculpted retable that was given by Joanna of Evreux, Queen of France (*d* 1371), to Maubuisson *c.* 1340 is also attributed to him. His last known commission was for a *Virgin and Child* with Guy Baudet, Chancellor of France (*d* 1338), in prayer before St Mammès (Langres Cathedral), which was ordered by Baudet's executors.

The scope of Evrard's commissions and the range of his talents indicate that he was the head of one of the workshops that dominated Parisian sculpture during the first decades of the 14th century. Aside from his documented activity it has been suggested that he was a participant in the decoration executed for the choir of Notre-Dame and that he might also have been among those sculptors employed by Philip IV at the priory of St Louis at Poissy. Given the conservative nature of the works commissioned by Philip IV and his immediate successors, it is difficult to make attributions on the basis of style. The *Virgin and Child* of Guy Baudet and the altar of Maubuisson remain the only works that can be securely associated with his name.

BIBLIOGRAPHY

Lami; Thieme–Becker
J. M. Richard: *Une Petite-nièce de Saint Louis: Mahaut, comtesse d'Artois et de Bourgogne, 1302–29* (Paris, 1887)
J. Guérout: 'Le Palais de la Cité à Paris dès ses origines à 1417', *Mem. Féd. Soc. Hist. & Archéol. Paris & Ile-de-France*, i (1949), pp. 55–212; ii (1950), pp. 21–204
A. Erlande-Brandenburg: 'La Priorale Saint-Louis de Poissy', *Bull. Mnmtl*, cxxix (1971), pp. 85–112
Les Fastes du gothique: Le Siècle de Charles V (exh. cat., Paris, Grand Pal., 1981–2), nos 29, 31, p. 430
M. Beaulieu and V. Beyer: *Dictionnaire des sculpteurs français du moyen âge* (Paris, 1992), pp. 78–80
D. Gillerman: *A Contract for Paradise: Enguerran de Marigny and the Church of Notre-Dame at Ecouis* (University Park, PA, 1994)

DOROTHY GILLERMAN

Evreux Cathedral. Cathedral dedicated to Notre-Dame at Evreux, in the département of Eure, France, 80 km west of Paris, known primarily for its collection of stained-glass windows. Begun after fire destroyed its predecessor in 1119, it was not completed until the 17th century, and its appearance reflects several phases of the Gothic style, with richly decorated Flamboyant traceried windows and a late 16th-century west façade. The cathedral has an aisled nave with a two-tower façade and transepts leading to a chevet with ambulatory and chapels. It was severely damaged in 1940 and was subsequently restored.

Although glazing survives from building campaigns from the late 13th century (south nave chapels, parts of the nave clerestory) to the 16th (north transept clerestory and rose window), the most important windows date from the 14th and 15th centuries, in particular the choir clerestory, whose glass is dated *c.* 1320–1400. The exact dating, patronage and original disposition are controversial. The iconographic emphasis is on the Virgin Mary and the patron saints of the donors. The latter constitute some of the most powerful Normans of 1320–40 (Raoul de Ferrières, Guillaume d'Harcourt, Regnault de Moulins, Jean Duprat, Geoffroy Faé) and some enigmatic royal figures from the end of the century. Stylistically, the gently modelled forms, courtly poise and pearly tonalities of the earliest windows have been related to contemporary manuscript painting in Paris, whereas the flatter, drier, but more decorative and refined style of the hemicycle windows of the 1330s are affiliated with the other great monuments of 14th-century Norman glass painting at Jumièges and Rouen (both the cathedral and St-Ouen) and should probably be assigned with them to a single, large, exporting workshop (Lafond, 1955). Notable 15th-century stained glass includes the grisaille Guillaume de Cantiers window (*c.* 1400, nave clerestory) and the glazing (*c.* 1470) of the axial Virgin Chapel (built to commemorate the coronation of Louis XI in 1461) with windows portraying the lives of Christ and the Virgin.

BIBLIOGRAPHY

J. Lafond: 'Les Vitraux royaux du XIVe siècle à la cathédrale d'Evreux', *Bull. Mnmt.*, ci (1942), pp. 69–93
——: 'Le Vitrail en Normandie de 1250 à 1300', *Bull. Mnmt.*, cxi (1953), pp. 345–6
——: 'Le Vitrail du XIVe siècle en France: Etude historique et descriptive', *L'Art du XIVe siècle en France*, ed. L. Lefrançois-Pillon (Paris, 1954), pp. 189–207
——: 'La Peinture sur verre à Jumièges', *Jumièges: Congrès scientifique du XIIIe centenaire: Rouen, 1955*, ii, pp. 531–2
L. Grodecki: 'La Restitution des vitraux "royaux" de la cathédrale d'Evreux', *Mnmts Hist. France*, n.s., ii (1956), pp. 201–16
M. Baudot and R. Dubuc: 'Les Verrières de la cathédrale d'Evreux: Cinq siècles d'histoire', *Nouv. Eure*, xxvii (1966), pp. 26–55
L. Grodecki, M. Baudot and R. Dubuc: 'Les Vitraux de la cathédrale d'Evreux', *Bull. Mnmt.*, cxxvi (1968), pp. 55–73

M. Beucher: 'Les Verrières du choeur d'Evreux', *Doss. Archéol.*, xxvi (1978), pp. 63–75

MICHAEL W. COTHREN

Ewer and basin. A matching jug and bowl used for hand washing during and after meals and for toilet purposes. They were made in precious and base metals, ceramics, glass and enamel. Early medieval ewers are usually in the form of animals or figures (*see* AQUAMANILE). In the Middle Ages their use was ceremonial as well as practical. From the 15th century ewers and basins were acquired by institutions and corporations for ceremonial presentation and as ambassadorial gifts, becoming prized display objects. In form and decoration the ewer and basin altered with stylistic developments, and they were always of the most elaborate design and finish. With the increased use of cutlery from the late 17th century, ewers and basins had less function, although mainly ceramic examples were used as an accoutrement for toilet use until the advent of widespread domestic plumbing in the early 20th century.

Eworth, Hans [John] (*b* Antwerp; *fl* 1540–73; *d* ?London). Flemish painter, active in England. 'Jan Euworts' was listed in 1540 as a freeman of the Guild of St Luke in Antwerp, but by 1545 he had moved to England, where until 1571 his name, spelt in a wide variety of ways (e.g. Eeworts, Eottes, Euertz, Evance, Eworts, Ewotes, Ewout, Ewoutsz., Eywooddes, Hawarde, Heward, Huett etc), appeared in numerous naturalization, tax and parish documents. About 35 paintings are generally attributed to him, consisting primarily of dated portraits of the English gentry and nobility. The majority are signed with the monogram HE, which led to their being attributed to the Flemish painter Lucas de Heere during the 18th and 19th centuries. Cust reattributed the paintings to Eworth on the basis of an inventory (1590) of the collection of John, 1st Baron Lumley, in which three monogrammed portraits were listed as being by 'Haunce Eworth'.

Eworth's earliest known work is the unusual signed and dated *Turk on Horseback* (1549; Brocklesby Park, Lincs), which is smaller in scale (571×483 mm) than most of his later panels. The representation of the Turk is derived from a woodcut by Pieter Coecke van Aelst. Eworth's earliest known portrait is of *Sir John Luttrell* (1550; U. London, Courtauld Inst. Gals), a work that may commemorate the Treaty of Boulogne between England and France, with the captain depicted as a Triton restrained by the personification of Peace; the allegorical inset at the upper left is perhaps by another hand, possibly an artist from the school of Fontainebleau (Yates).

Eworth was the principal court portrait painter during the reign (1553–8) of the Catholic queen Mary Tudor. Strong (1966) attributed five portraits of her to Eworth, and these established one of the two official patterns for the Queen's image, the other being by Anthonis Mor. Eworth's variations on the royal portrait range from a miniature (Duke of Buccleuch priv. col.), attributed to 'Hanc Seward' in the inventory of Charles I's collection, to an almost life-size three-quarter-length figure (London, Soc. Antiqua.), with a monogram HF that may be a later addition to suggest the hand of Holbein. Eworth also received the large majority of his portrait commissions from Catholic patrons. This close association with the Roman Church was a major reason for his fall from court favour during the reign of Elizabeth. Millar and Strong (1969) questioned the traditional attribution to Eworth of the allegorical *Elizabeth I and Three Goddesses* (1569; London, Hampton Court, Royal Col.). There are significant stylistic discrepancies with Eworth's portraits and a slightly different monogram; also the notable lack of commissions for Eworth from the Elizabethan court during the 1560s makes his association with this particular work unlikely.

Eworth's painting style shows the influence of a number of artists. Strong (London, N.P.G., 1965 exh. cat.) emphasized the similarities to some of Jan van Scorel's portraits, especially in the quality of the light and the highly glazed surfaces. The impact of Holbein's paintings was of paramount importance, as it was to the development of 16th-century English portraiture in general. Eworth borrowed poses and motifs from Holbein, as in his portrait of *Lady Dacre* (*c.* 1555–8; Ottawa, N.G.; see fig.). Although more awkward spatially than Holbein's works, the plasticity of form and variety of texture are reminiscent of the earlier artist. As with many English portraits of the period, there is a wealth of detail in costume and setting, but in this instance it does not overwhelm the personality of the sitter. As compared with his portrait of *Margaret Audley, Duchess of Norfolk* (1562; Audley End, Essex), in which the figure is flattened by and becomes part of the decorative patterning, there is still a powerful physical presence in *Lady Dacre*, who dominates the portrait of her first

Hans Eworth: *Lady Dacre*, oil on panel, 737×578 mm, *c.* 1555–8 (Ottawa, National Gallery of Canada)

husband (probably by Holbein) on the wall behind her. There is a similar immediacy in the double portrait of *Frances Brandon, Duchess of Suffolk, and Adrian Stokes* (1559; England, J. C. Wynne Finch priv. col., see Strong, 1965 exh. cat., pl. 3). The basis of the relationship between this implausible couple—a plump 36-year-old noblewoman and her 21-year-old second husband, formerly her master of horses—is suggested by the richly ornamented costumes (over-elaborate in the case of the young man) and the delicate fingering of necklaces and rings. Eworth's mature style, formed under the influence of Holbein, is seen at its best in the sobriety and monumentality of the pendant portraits dated 1566 of *Richard Wakeman* (England, J. B. Gold priv. col., see Strong, 1965 exh. cat., pl. 23b) and *Mrs Wakeman* (Cornbury Park, Oxon). Iconic formality is combined with a sense of character that is heightened by the *memento mori* inscriptions in the background. Eworth's experimentation with pose and scale, ranging from miniatures to life-size portraits and from bust-length to full-length, may also be due to the variety found in Holbein's works. Certainly his indebtedness is evident in his copy (1567; Cambridge, Trinity Coll.) of Holbein's full-length portrait of *Henry VIII* in Whitehall. Eworth's style is also reminiscent at times of the stiff formality of the court portraits of William Scrots and may have been affected as well by the brief visit of Anthonis Mor to England *c.* 1554–5.

A more complex and full-blown allegorical interest is revealed in Eworth's last dated work, *Allegory of the Wise and Foolish Virgins* (1570; Copenhagen, Stat. Mus. Kst.). Wilenski suggested that the landscape may have been added by another painter specializing in such topographical views. This unusual work, an elaborate illustration of the parable in Matthew 25, can be related stylistically to later continental mannerism, in particular to the figural proportions, crisp profiles, expansive gestures and clinging drapery of the School of Fontainebleau. His awareness of this style is also suggested by the haughty aloofness and elegant contours in the somewhat earlier portraits of the *Earl of Moray* and the *Countess of Moray* (1561; Darnaway Castle, Grampian).

Only towards the end of his life did Eworth again work for the court. In 1572, after the death of the Serjeant painter who would customarily have been in charge of royal festivals, he was called in to design decorations and costumes for an allegorical representation of Parnassus, part of the celebrations in honour of the arrival of the French ambassadors. In 1573–4 he continued to design masques for the Office of Revels.

BIBLIOGRAPHY

Thieme-Becker

L. Cust: 'The Painter HE', *Walpole Soc.*, ii (1913), pp. 1–44
E. Auerbach: 'Holbein's Followers in England', *Burl. Mag.*, xciii (1951), pp. 44–51
E. Waterhouse: *Painting in Britain, 1530–1790*, Pelican Hist. A. (Harmondsworth, 1953)
E. Auerbach: *Tudor Artists* (London, 1954)
R. H. Wilenski: *Flemish Painters, 1430–1830*, 2 vols (New York, 1960)
O. Millar: *The Tudor, Stuart, and Early Georgian Pictures in the Collection of Her Majesty the Queen*, 2 vols (London, 1963)
Hans Eworth: A Tudor Artist and his Circle (exh. cat., ed. R. Strong; London, N.P.G., 1965)
R. Strong: 'Hans Eworth Reconsidered', *Burl. Mag.*, cviii (1966), pp. 225–33
F. A. Yates: 'The Allegorical Portraits of Sir John Luttrell', *Essays Presented to Rudolf Wittkower* (London, 1967), pp. 149–50
R. Strong: *The English Icon: Elizabethan and Jacobean Portraiture* (London, 1969)
D. Piper, ed.: *The Genius of British Painting* (New York, 1975)

ELISE L. SMITH

Exat-51 [Eksperimentalni atelje; Croat.: 'experimental atelier']. Croatian group of artists active in Zagreb from 1950 to 1956. Its members were the architects Bernardo Bernardi (1912–85), Zdravko Bregovac (*b* 1924), Zvonimir Radić (1921–83), Božidar Rašica (1912–92), Vjenceslav Richter (*b* 1917) and Vladimir Zarahović, and the painters Vlado Kristl (*b* 1922), IVAN PICELJ and Aleksandar Srnec (*b* 1924). On 7 December they united officially at the plenary meeting of the Association of Applied Artists of Croatia (Croat. Udruženje likovnih umjetnika primijenjenih umjetnosti Hrvatske (ULUPUH)), at which time they proclaimed their manifesto. The group was formed to protest against the dominance of officially sanctioned Socialist Realism and the condemnation of all forms of abstraction and motifs unacceptable in Communist doctrine as decadent and bourgeois. In its manifesto, Exat-51 emphasized that such an attitude contradicted the principles of Socialist development, that the differences between so-called 'pure' art and 'applied' art were non-existent and that abstract art could enrich the field of visual communication. The activity of the group was therefore to spring from the existing social situation and, as such, to contribute to the progress of society. The principal intention was to attain a synthesis of all branches of the fine arts and to encourage artistic experimentation. At the first Exat-51 exhibition in February 1953, held in Zagreb at the Hall of the Architects' Society of Croatia, works by Picelj, Kristl, Srnec and Rašica were featured; the exhibition was later shown in Belgrade. The group made an important contribution in helping to free Yugoslav artists from predominant Stalinist dogmas, and its members later continued to work in a more individual manner, still adhering, however, to the main ideas set out in the manifesto.

BIBLIOGRAPHY
J. Denegri and Ž. Koščević: *Exat-51, 1951–56* (Zagreb, 1979)

JURE MIKUŽ

Exchange. Building where merchants, bankers or stock-brokers assemble to transact business. The origins of the exchange can be traced back to Roman market basilicas (*see* BASILICA; *see also* ROME, ANCIENT, §II, 1(i)(b)), and to the market squares and loggias of medieval Italy, while its history is inextricably linked to the development of trade and banking. Exchanges are differentiated from market halls in that they are used for the sale of products through samples only, exchanges having no storage space for merchants' goods. Markets and exchanges were sometimes housed in the same buildings, and many exchanges had shops attached to them in some form or another. The existence of exchanges, however, was dependent on the location of financial and trade centres. During the 14th century trade and commerce were firmly in Mediterranean hands. The first exchanges are recorded in Italy (Bologna, Loggia dei Mercanti, 1382) and Spain (Barcelona, Lonja, 1383). Their design reflected that of other civic buildings, such as town halls; business was transacted in a large hall, which was often in the same building as the law courts and the actual market.

In the 16th century a distinct building type was created with the exchange (1531; destr.) at Antwerp by Domenicus van Waghemakers (1490–1542), which consisted of a large, square courtyard surrounded by a gallery or cloisters, reminiscent of market squares surrounded by loggias. This type of courtyard exchange was quickly adopted in most important European cities, for example in London, where the Royal Exchange (1566–8; destr. 1666) was designed by Henryk van Passe of Antwerp and based on the Antwerp exchange; in Seville (1585–98; *see* HERRERA, JUAN DE, fig. 2); and in Amsterdam (1608–11; destr. 1838) by Hendrick de Keyser (*see* KEYSER, DE, (1), §2). The courtyard scheme remained popular: the Royal Exchange in London was rebuilt twice along the lines of its original plan, once in 1667–71 to a design by Edward Jerman (*d* 1668), and a second time in 1839–44 by William Tite. An important circular version of the courtyard exchange was the Halle au Blé (1763–9; destr. 1885), Paris, by NICOLAS LE CAMUS DE MÉZIÈRES, which was later covered over (1781 and 1808–13; see below). Some smaller towns built more modest exchanges that drew on the models of municipal building types, usually guild or town halls. Examples include the exchange in Copenhagen (1619–40) by Lourens van Steenwinckel II; the very small exchange

(1683; now the Customs House) in Kings Lynn, Norfolk; and the Loge du Change (1747–9), Lyon, by JACQUES-GERMAIN SOUFFLOT. During the 18th century a number of exchanges were designed as part of larger urban planning schemes, as at Bordeaux (1736) by Jacques Gabriel V, and at Bristol Exchange and Market (1743; *see* BRISTOL, fig. 2) and Liverpool Exchange and Town Hall (1749–54), both by John Wood (i) the elder. Although these buildings were designed according to Palladian principles, in their plans they still adhered to the open courtyard type.

Two developments influenced the building of exchanges in the late 18th century and after: the industrial revolution, with the resulting increase in world trade, and the popularity of Neo-classicism. The former created a diversification of exchanges, for stocks and shares as well as for corn, coal and cotton. The increase in share dealings, particularly with the growth of the railway companies, created a heavy demand for stock exchanges, more than 250 being founded in the USA alone during the 19th century. Neo-classicism led to the abandonment of the open courtyard exchange in favour of the basilica type. This idea was introduced in the writings of Nikolaus Goldmann (e.g. in his *Vollständige Anweisung zur Civil-Bau-Kunst* (Brunswick, 1696)). He published a design for an exchange that referred back to the market basilicas of

Stock Exchange (Beursgebouw), Amsterdam, by H. P. Berlage, 1896–1903; interior view showing exposed steel roof structure

antiquity, citing Palladio's basilica at Vicenza as the immediate source; in this design the courtyard was replaced by an oblong, two-storey hall. Not until the end of the 18th century, however, did the architectural world and, above all, French academics take up the model of the basilica. The basilica exchange is essentially a cubic structure, surrounded by columns or two-tier arcading, with a large, usually galleried hall inside. It was first developed through designs for the French Académie and finally realized in the exchange (1805–10) by THOMAS-JEAN DE THOMON at St Petersburg (now the Central Naval Museum; see RUSSIA, fig. 11).

In the surge of exchange building in the early 19th century the basilica type was universally adopted, and many of the old rectangular courtyard exchanges were roofed over, thus becoming basilicas. There was initially an adherence to strict Neo-classical motifs, for example in such designs as the Bourse (1808–13; much altered), Paris, by ALEXANDRE-THÉODORE BRONGNIART, surrounded by a Corinthian colonnade, and the Philadelphia (or Merchants') Exchange (1832–4) by WILLIAM STRICKLAND. Later in the 19th century a more eclectic approach developed. As in the case of bank buildings and warehouses, Italian Renaissance and Baroque styles were usually preferred, no doubt because of their mercantile and commercial associations; examples include exchanges at Manchester (1845; by Alexander W. Mills); Frankfurt (1844; destr.; by Friedrich August Stüler), with a classical exterior but Gothic fan vaults inside; and Vienna (1871–7; by Theophilus Hansen). Other styles were sometimes employed, such as Gothic (e.g. Bradford Wool Exchange; 1864–7; by Lockwood & Mawson) or French Renaissance (e.g. the Bourse, 1857, Lyon; by René Bardel). Some buildings followed the circular design of the Halle au Blé: these included Dublin's Royal Exchange (1769; by Thomas Cooley; see DUBLIN, §I, 2), the London Coal Exchange (1846–9; destr.; by J. B. Bunning) and the Leeds Corn Exchange (1860–62; by Cuthbert Brodrick).

The large, open space at the heart of the exchange provided a particularly suitable opportunity for the use of new structural materials and techniques, notably iron and glass. The Halle au Blé, which had been covered with a timber dome in 1781, was later given a pioneering cast-iron dome (1808–13) by FRANÇOIS-JOSEPH BÉLANGER; it was rebuilt as the Bourse de Commerce in 1889. Bunning's London Coal Exchange featured three tiers of iron balconies and a glazed, iron-ribbed dome; and Brodrick's Leeds Corn Exchange has an oval dome framed in iron and partially glazed (see IRON AND STEEL, fig. 3). The Amsterdam Stock Exchange (Beursgebouw; 1896–1903) by H. P. Berlage has a fully exposed trussed iron roof structure (see fig.), an early example of structural rationalism. Italianate influences nevertheless continued well into the 20th century: arcaded loggias, for example, featured as a façade element in the Essen exchange (1922–6; by Edmund Körner). Technological developments, including the introduction of the telegraph (1840s), telephone (1870s) and computer networks (1980s), subsequently facilitated a centralization of trading, a tendency increased by the growing internationalization of business in the late 20th century. This concentrated most important business transactions within a handful of exchanges with

highly technological requirements, which are overtly expressed in the High-Tech Lloyds Building (1985; for illustration see ROGERS, RICHARD), London, focused on a huge market room. At the same time, the new technology curtailed demands for space, allowing such 19th-century buildings as the Baroque-style exchange (Börse; 1874–9; by Oskar Sommer and Heinrich Burnitz) at Frankfurt to remain in use.

BIBLIOGRAPHY
N. Pevsner: *A History of Building Types* (London, 1976)
R. Dixon and S. Muthesius: *Victorian Architecture* (London, 1978, rev. 1985)
R. C. Michie: *The London and New York Stock Exchange, 1850–1914* (London, 1987)

Exchange Club [Amateur Photographic Exchange Club]. American photographic society founded in 1861 and open only to amateur photographers. The three founder-members, all from New York, were Henry T. Anthony (1814–84) as President, F. F. Thompson as Secretary and Correspondent, and Charles Wager Hull. Its membership was originally restricted to 20, and, though this rule was later dropped, the members never numbered many more than this. Nevertheless they were from all over the USA and soon included most of the prominent American amateurs of the day. Among them were August Wetmore and Lewis M. Rutherford of New York; Coleman Sellers, Professor Fairman Rogers and Constant Guillou of Philadelphia; Titian R. Peale of Washington; Robert Shirner of Cumberland, Maryland; John Towler of Geneva, New York, author of *The Silver Sunbeam* (New York, 1864), and Professor E. Emerson of Troy, New York. The physician and writer Oliver Wendell Holmes (1809–94) was an honorary member on the strength of his achievements as a photographic pioneer. The Club's existence reflected the enormous popularity of photography in the USA in the 1860s.

One of the main interests of the Exchange Club's members was stereoscopic photography; Wendell Holmes was the inventor of the most widespread version of the stereoscopic viewer, though single plate images were also produced. While the exact activities of the Club are not clear, its rules stated that 'every member shall forward each other member on or before the 15th of January, March, May, July, September and November, at least one stereoscopic print, a copy of which has not been sent before, mounted and finished'. Anyone failing to fulfil this condition would be struck off the membership list. Each member was required to keep an account-book showing all the prints sent and received. On 1 February 1863 Thompson published the first of seven issues of the Club's official journal, *The Amateur Photographic Print*, the last of which appeared on 1 September 1863.

The photographs produced by members of the Exchange Club were of variable interest, often consisting of single and group portraits and landscapes (see Taft, p. 206). As a mark of membership each member designed his own label, which was stuck on to the back of any print sent. The contents of the labels varied from basic descriptions of the subject, as in those of John Towler (see Darrah, fig. 9), to more detailed technical records about how the work was taken, as in those of Coleman Sellers (see Darrah, fig. 10). The Club was active only until late 1863, by which time the American Civil War and the increased availability of commercial prints had virtually brought it to an end. References to the activities of the Club appeared in Wendell Holmes's article 'The Doings of the Sunbeam' in *Atlantic Monthly*, though it was not mentioned by name. In 1888 a more detailed account was published by one of its most energetic members, Sellers, in a series of articles in *Anthony's Photographic Bulletin*.

BIBLIOGRAPHY

O. Wendell Holmes: 'The Doings of the Sunbeam', *Atlantic Mthly*, xii (1863), no. 69, pp. 1–15

C. Sellers: 'An Old Photographic Club', *Anthony's Phot. Bull.*, xix (1888), no. 10, pp. 301–4; no. 11, pp. 338–41; no. 12, pp. 356–61; no. 13, pp. 403–6

R. Taft: *Photography and the American Scene: A Social History, 1839–1889* (New York, 1938, R/1964), pp. 213–16, 222

W. Culp Darrah: *Stereo Views: A History of Stereographs and their Collection* (Gettysburg, 1964), p. 4, figs 9–11

Exedra. In Greek architecture, a room in a GYMNASIUM provided with benches where visitors could relax and converse in comfort (see fig.). From the 5th century BC onwards the gymnasia of Athens, the Academy, the Lykeion and the Kynosarges, all had a great hall provided with benches that served as an *apodyterion* or changing-room for the ephebes; here, according to Plato, Socrates and his companions liked to sit, admire the athletes and discuss philosophical problems. The first type of exedra found in the gymnasium was thus both utilitarian and a site of intellectual activity.

In the earliest surviving gymnasium, at Delphi (*c.* 350 BC), the single large exedra built in the south-west corner of the peristyle court also fulfilled the dual function of changing-room and meeting place (for illustration *see* GYMNASIUM). In the more elaborate gymnasia of the Hellenistic period the number of exedrae was greater and a distinction could be drawn between the rooms intended for relaxation, the conference rooms and the changing-room, although the latter nevertheless continued to be the place for informal conversation and was often the most luxurious of the exedrae. Exedrae were rectangular rooms reached through wide entrances inside the portico of the peristyle. The entrance architrave was usually supported by two columns, but sometimes—as in the case of Olympia (late 2nd century BC)—by as many as nine. A continuous stone bench was built along the walls, which were sometimes painted with hunting scenes, with scenes from the myths of Bacchus or with Victories driving four-horse chariots, as in the granite palaestra of Delos (*c.* 150 BC). If some generous patron—the gymnasiarch, for example—had paid the costs of construction or decoration his name was carved on the entablature over the entrance or his statue was erected in a niche in the far wall of the exedra. Semicircular exedrae were rare, although better suited for conversation, because they were more expensive to build and more difficult to incorporate into the quadrangular layout of the gymnasium. They foreshadowed the apses of Early Christian churches, which had their inside walls lined by the tiers of the synthronus and which were, for this reason, also sometimes called exedrae.

When, from the 4th century BC onwards, the gymnasium ceased to be for physical education only, exedrae served as classrooms (on the walls of which the ephebes often carved their names) where philosophy, rhetoric, grammar, music and various sciences were taught. The teachers included Plato at the Academy and Aristotle at the Lykeion. The gymnasia and their exedrae were thus the forerunners of today's universities. Vitruvius (*On Architecture* V.xi.2) prescribed that the gymnasium should have several 'spacious exedrae, provided with benches, in which philosophers, rhetors and all those who enjoy studying should have the possibility of discussing while seated'. The exedrae of the gymnasia thus played the same part in the development and dissemination of Greek thought as did the STOA. The Stoa of Attalos at Delphi was a kind of monumental exedra (*see* DELPHI, §1). The houses of wealthy Romans, such as Cicero, also had exedrae, rooms designed for philosophical discussion, and from the Roman period on, the word was imbued with intellectual connotations.

Exedrae of the gymnasium at Delos, *c.* 150 BC

On a more modest level the exedra could be no more than a stone bench, either straight or curved, erected in the open air in a public place. These benches became common during the Hellenistic period in the great sanctuaries at Delos, Delphi, Epidauros and Olympia, where statue bases often served as back-rests, their donors thus being able to combine the evidence of their piety with that of their care for the comfort of their contemporaries. The marble exedra on Mt Tmolos above Sardis that afforded a superb view over the Lydian landscape (Strabo) was probably a simple bench of this general type.

BIBLIOGRAPHY

J. Delorme: *Gymnasion* (Paris, 1960)
S. Settis: *Esedra e nynfee nella terminologia architettonica del mondo romano*, i/4 of *Aufstieg und Niedergang der römischen Welt*, ed. H. Temporini (Berlin and New York, 1972–), pp. 661–745
M. C. Hellmann: *Recherches sur le vocabulaire de l'architecture grecque* (Paris, 1992), pp. 126–30 [exedrae at Delos]

GEORGES ROUX

Exekias. *See* VASE PAINTERS, §II.

Exeter [Lat. Isca Dumnoniorum; Anc. Brit. Caerwysc]. Cathedral city, port and county town of Devon, on the River Exe in south-western England. It first became important under the Romans, who, about AD 55, constructed a legionary fortress close to an earlier auxiliary fort on a hill commanding the lowest point at which the Exe could be bridged. The fortress was abandoned *c.* AD 70–79, but from *c.* AD 80 much of its site was occupied by a settlement known as Isca Dumnoniorum. Its civic buildings, part of which were excavated in 1971–3 under the cathedral green, were converted from the legionary bathhouse. The ramparts, which extended for 3.2 km, were built in the late 2nd century.

Little survives of Anglo-Saxon Exeter. The most impressive surviving Norman buildings are the house-keep of Rougemont Castle (*c.* 1068) and the transept towers of the cathedral (*see* §1(i) below). The present cathedral is an impressive and almost complete example of the English Decorated style. A few domestic buildings from the late medieval period survive around the cathedral green. Exeter's growing importance as a cloth centre during the 15th century is most clearly seen in the flamboyant Guildhall (rebuilt late 15th century; porch added in the 16th century).

In the 18th century the Assembly Rooms (1769, now the Royal Clarence Hotel) were built opposite the cathedral in a new French style, and a Palladian sessions house was constructed in the castle precincts (1773). Around this time an important workshop for the production of carpets was established in the town (*see* §2 below). At the same time an ambitious residential development within the city, the Bedford Circus, was begun under the direction of Francis, 5th Duke of Bedford. Much of this was destroyed by bombing in World War II, leaving a few buildings near the castle and in Bartholomew Street. Rebuilding programmes immediately after World War II resulted in an unremarkable façade for the upper High Street. The development of the Guildhall Shopping Centre in the 1960s involved the destruction of the best surviving medieval frontage, though a small fragment survives as a shop frontage. Subsequent building programmes in the city have been more sensitive and have attempted to retain some of the medieval character of the city; the area around the quay has been redeveloped and houses a museum and craft centre.

BIBLIOGRAPHY

N. Pevsner: *Devon*, Bldgs England (Harmondsworth, 1952); rev. by B. Cherry (Harmondsworth, 1989)
W. G. Hoskins: *Two Thousand Years in Exeter* (Chichester, 1960, 2/1989)

FRANCES WILSON

1. Cathedral. 2. Centre of carpet production.

1. CATHEDRAL. Exeter Cathedral, dedicated to St Peter, is outstanding for its Romanesque transept towers, for the completeness of its Decorated architecture and for its high vaults uniquely stretching the whole length of the church.

(i) Architecture. (ii) Sculpture.

(i) Architecture.

(a) Saxon and Romanesque cathedrals. Traditionally a monastery of SS Mary and Peter was founded in Exeter *c.* 670, and re-established *c.* 932 and 1018. The Lotharingian bishop Leofric (*reg* 1046–72) moved his seat to Exeter from Crediton (Devon) in 1050, and introduced regular canons. By the 12th century they had become a secular chapter, so no conventual buildings exist except the chapter house. The Saxon church probably stood west of the present cathedral on the site of St Mary Major (destr.). Saxon remains have also been found further east (see fig. 1a).

The new Romanesque cathedral (*c.* 1112–60) was begun by Bishop William de Warelwast (*reg* 1107–37) and was sufficiently complete for the canons to enter in 1133, when it was consecrated. The nave and towers may not have been finished until *c.* 1150–60; the upper stages of the towers are highly ornamented with chevron decoration. In plan and size, the nave and transept were similar to the existing church (1i). The eastern arm was shorter, consisting of three bays plus a deep apse; foundations found under the floor indicate that the latter was polygonal externally. The liturgical choir occupied the crossing and east bay of the nave. Romanesque fabric survives up to the window sills in the outer walls of the present nave and the two west bays of the choir, indicating that the cathedral was aisled. The eastern arm had large circular piers, about 1.8 m in diameter, as in such buildings of western England as Tewkesbury Abbey. A scalloped capital from the piers was reused in the Gothic construction of St James's Chapel. Other loose fragments suggest that the aisles were rib-vaulted. Evidence from the fabric of the towers implies that there was no space for a gallery in the main elevation. The towers over the transepts (1f and 1g) are the most enduring reminders of the 12th-century cathedral and a unique survival in British Romanesque architecture. The idea probably derived from Lotharingia and may relate to customs introduced earlier by Leofric. A similar arrangement may have existed at Old Sarum, Wilts, another cathedral with a Lotharingian bishop in the 11th century.

(b) Gothic cathedral. The first surviving Gothic architecture is in the new chapter house (*c.* 1225), built when the chapter was reorganized. The interior has stiff-leaf foliage capitals and detached shafts (originally of blue lias) typical

The present building is 125 m long internally and 20.75 m high. The work falls into three main phases. The first, c. 1275–85, consisted of laying out the plan of the new extension to the east of the Romanesque cathedral incorporating a Lady chapel (1b), east chapels and rectangular ambulatory as at Salisbury Cathedral. The Romanesque presbytery was probably not demolished in this phase but at some stage between 1288 and 1299. During the second phase, c. 1285–1328, the presbytery was built (complete 1304; 1c), together with the choir (complete 1310; 1d), the crossing, the east bay of the nave and the remodelling of the transept (c. 1310–25). These were mainly the work of Master Roger (*fl* 1296–1310) and William Luve (*fl* 1310–13). Most of the features of the eastern aisles and Lady chapel (c. 1285–1300) belong to the second campaign, as also do the magnificent furnishings, such as the sedilia, bishop's throne and pulpitum (1313–26; 1e; *see also* THRONE, fig. 3), inspired by the patronage of Bishop Walter de Stapledon (*reg* 1307–26) and designed by THOMAS OF WITNEY. The dedication of the high altar in 1328 completed this phase. In the third campaign, c. 1328–60, the rest of the Romanesque nave (1k) was demolished to permit the six west bays to be rebuilt under the patronage of Bishop John Grandisson (*reg* 1327–69; see fig. 2). These were structurally complete by 1342, though it is uncertain whether the vault was erected before 1346 or after 1353. This phase included the north porch, the completion of St Edmund's chapel c. 1330 and the minstrels' gallery in the nave c. 1350. The west front was built c. 1329–42, and the image screen was added in the 1340s, incorporating Bishop Grandisson's mortuary chapel (1j) and three porches, mainly the work of William Joy.

The predominant style was established in the second building phase, in the elevation of the presbytery (from 1288). The original interior design was of only two storeys (arcade and clerestory), but its simplicity proved unsatisfactory, and a narrow triforium was included in the choir, c. 1300–10, as at Chester Cathedral and St Albans Abbey (now Cathedral), and was added in the presbytery, 1318–19. The exterior has prominent flying buttresses and battlemented parapets. The latter are mainly for display, the first example of this court fashion applied to a great church in England. The rich combination of coursed Purbeck marble piers and tierceron vaults derives mainly from Old St Paul's Cathedral, London (c. 1280–1315; *see* LONDON, §V, 1(i)(a)), but treated here with an exuberance typical of western masons.

Once established, the elevation and mouldings remained remarkably consistent throughout the rebuilding, but changes in style appear in window tracery, the furnishings and foliage carvings. The main windows from the first phase are the lateral windows of the eastern chapels and ambulatory bay, which are geometrical compositions of oculi. The second phase introduced more sophisticated Rayonnant patterns from London, for example impaled trefoils and intersecting tracery, as at St Etheldreda's, Ely Place, London (c. 1285); but they were used differently at Exeter in the Lady chapel, clerestory and choir aisles to stress variety of design. The first ogee arches appear in the windows of the transept chapels (1310–11) and then in Thomas of Witney's choir furnishings. He introduced

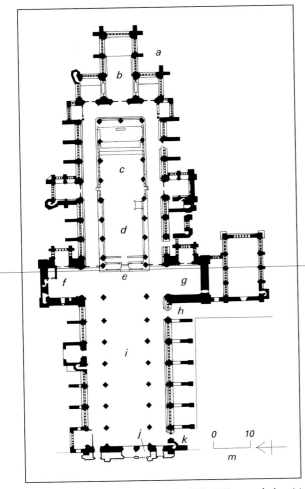

1. Exeter Cathedral, 12th century and c. 1279–1360, ground-plan: (a) site of Saxon remains; (b) Lady chapel; (c) presbytery; (d) choir; (e) pulpitum; (f) St Paul's tower (north transept); (g) St John's tower (south transept); (h) processional door to cloister; (i) nave; (j) Bishop Grandisson's mortuary chapel; (k) presumed western termination of Norman nave

of south-west England. It is a rare survival of a rectangular chapter house in an English cathedral. The processional door to the cloister (1h) also dates from the early 13th century.

The rebuilding (c. 1279–1360) of the cathedral in the Decorated style, conceived by Bishop Bronescombe (*d* 1280) and endowed by Bishop Quinil (*reg* 1280–91), has removed all obvious traces of the earlier church except the towers. The primary reason for rebuilding was to provide a longer eastern arm to accommodate the ritual life of the chapter entirely east of the crossing, following the Use of Sarum. The work is better documented than for any other European cathedral in this period, because of the relatively complete fabric accounts between 1299 and 1353 (Erskine). There is also a summary account for 1279–87, but references in it and in other early records to work going on in various parts of the cathedral do not always correspond to surviving features and give a misleading impression of rapid progress in the early stages.

2. Exeter Cathedral, view of nave looking west, *c.* 1328–60

some of the earliest lierne vaults in the pulpitum and sedilia (from 1316) and in St Edmund's Chapel (*c.* 1330). The windows of his period (1316–42), especially in the nave, display a dazzling variety of later Decorated tracery, for example mouchette wheels, propeller patterns and complicated geometrical roses. His most personal design is a series of curved triangles in a distinctive reticulated pattern, which is similar to the Lady chapel at Wells Cathedral and the nave of Malmesbury Abbey. The predominance of non-Flamboyant motifs shows an affinity to the work of the Kentish masters in London and Canterbury and to continental Rayonnant.

The presbytery east window was rebuilt 1389–90 by Robert Lesyngham (*fl* 1376–94), who also continued work from 1377 on the new cloister (begun 1318) and designed the early fan vault in the north porch of the west front. Some of the upper statues on the west front may be of the 15th century, and other works in this century included new windows and a roof (*c.* 1470) in the chapter house, and the reconstruction of the south transept window. The cloister was demolished in 1656–7. The main Victorian restoration was by Sir George Gilbert Scott, from 1870 to 1877. St James's Chapel was destroyed by bombing in 1942 and rebuilt in replica.

BIBLIOGRAPHY

H. E. Bishop and E. K. Prideaux: *The Building of the Cathedral Church of St Peter in Exeter* (Exeter, 1922)
A. W. Everett and V. Hope: 'The Rebuilding of Exeter Cathedral, *c.* 1270–1360', *Trans. Devon Assoc.*, c (1968), pp. 179–90
V. Hope and J. Lloyd: *Exeter Cathedral: A Short History and Description* (Exeter, 1973); rev. A. Erskine (Exeter, 1988)
J. P. Allan and B. Jupp: 'Recent Observations in the South Tower of Exeter Cathedral', *Proc. Devon Archaeol. Soc.*, xxxix (1981), pp. 141–54
A. Erskine: *The Accounts of the Fabric of Exeter Cathedral, 1279–1353*, Devon & Cornwall Rec. Soc., xxiv (Torquay, 1981); xxvi (Torquay, 1983)
C. G. Henderson and P. T. Bidwell: 'The Saxon Minster at Exeter', *The Early Church in Western Britain and Ireland*, ed. S. M. Pearce (Oxford, 1982), pp. 145–75
F. Kelly, ed.: *British Archaeological Association Conference Transactions, xi. Medieval Art and Architecture at Exeter Cathedral: Exeter, 1985*
N. Pevsner and P. Metcalf: *The Cathedrals of England: Southern England* (Harmondsworth, 1985), pp. 103–23
C. Brooks and D. Evans: *The Great East Window of Exeter Cathedral: A Glazing History* (Exeter, 1988)

R. K. MORRIS

(ii) Sculpture. Little sculpture of the cathedral before the 1270s survives apart from the series of misericords of *c.* 1250–70 and the tombs of the early bishops. The Decorated cathedral has, however, been unusually fortunate in its preservation of sculpture, despite some notable losses, including the figures in stone, wood and precious metal that adorned Thomas of Witney's furnishings of the choir (1313–26). With the reconstruction of the eastern limb from the 1270s Exeter provides the best-documented sequence of Decorated sculpture in Britain.

The earliest (late 1270s–*c.* 1300), in the eastern chapels, Lady chapel and those adjoining, is characterized by sharply cut, naturalistic and botanically precise foliage. In the vaults of the Lady chapel and presbytery human and animal motifs are interspersed, sometimes arranged in geometric patterns. The figural sculpture of the presbytery bosses, which were painted in 1301–2, is characterized by comfortable poses, stocky bodies with plump faces and rolling, but still fairly simple, draperies. Following the building break between the presbytery and choir there is a marked change of style. The great variety of figural subjects disappears, and swirling, seaweed-like leaves, precisely comparable to bosses in Wells Cathedral chapter house, come into vogue. Interest in rippling surfaces is evident in more exuberant form on the wooden bishop's throne (1313–20; *see* THRONE, fig. 3), followed by the intensely convoluted foliage style of the pulpitum (*c.* 1318–24, now the organ screen). The corbels and bosses of the choir and transepts are of variable quality. Some of the finest, such as a corbel in the choir with a delicate depiction of the *Virgin and Child* below censing angels, has been attributed on uncertain grounds to William of Montacute, recorded as a mason from 1301 to 1312.

The nave vault similarly displays a variety of styles. A group of bosses at the west end of the nave—centred on the murder of St Thomas Becket—is calm, almost reserved, in mood; the same style is found at Ottery St Mary, Devon. A second distinctive group displays the features of the west front's kings (see below). The bosses in the western bays of the nave and in the crossing preserve extensive traces of medieval colour; all the other bosses of the high vaults have been repainted.

On the image screen that straddles the west front are 69 near life-size figures arranged in two tiers of niches, the lower one supported by smaller angels. The figures, carved from limestone quarried at Beer in south-east Devon, are now badly eroded, but evidence of their former character is recorded in a series of drawings by John Carter (London, BL, Add. MS. 29931, fols 76–86), which were the basis of the engravings published in his *Specimens of Ancient Sculpture and Painting now Remaining in this Kingdom*

(London, 1780–94). The primary design consisted of the lower major tier of figures—seated kings and mailed figures, some cross-legged—supported by angels in various poses. Scenes of the *Nativity* and the *Annunciation* (see fig. 3) in the south porch belong to the same group, which is characterized by vigorous, highly animated, often asymmetrical poses and extremely elaborate costumes, the draperies spiralling downward in fantastically complex tubular folds; the origins of the style have been traced to northern French fashions of *c.* 1300. Faces are long and solemn, with hair rolling down to the shoulders. Figures in precisely this style survive in the reredos of Christchurch Priory (Hants), the architectural details of which are also closely comparable. The image screen was commissioned by Bishop Grandisson. Although these sculptures have been dated variously between *c.* 1330 and *c.* 1360–65, payments to William Joy for the porches between 1342 and 1346 almost certainly document the work; the carver R. Crocke is named.

Seated kings in a quieter, simpler style fill the niches of the screen's northern sector. Clearly later in date, they may be the work of 'John Pratt imaginator' who worked 'at the front of the church' in 1375. The higher tier of standing figures and niches was added *c.* 1450–80; their dating depends upon style and dress, the sharp angularity of the draperies, the fancy hats worn by the figures above the aisles, and details of a purse, Christ's crown etc. The central pair were Christ and the Virgin (removed), seated above shields commemorating the foundation of the see of Exeter, and probably representing the *Enthronement* or *Coronation of the Virgin*. The twelve Apostles and four Evangelists, identifiable by their emblems, surrounded them. The figures over the aisles could have been prophets and saints: their identities were formerly proclaimed on scrolls, now decayed. Only St Michael trampling a dragon, now formless, was once identifiable (Carter). Both figures and niches were once painted: tiny fragments of orpiment, azurite etc survive. Small metal fixtures further enriched the niches.

The front has been much repaired. The Exeter mason John Kendall (1766–1829) replaced figures and recarved decayed detail between 1803 and 1829. E. B. Stephens (1815–82) added two figures in 1869. The architectural surrounds were heavily restored under E. H. Harbottle (mainly 1899–1913). A programme of conservation and restoration was also undertaken in 1979–85.

Of the medieval monuments, the Purbeck marble tomb-chest of *Bishop Marshall* (*d* 1206) was of advanced design, if not subsequently remodelled. The sensitive and powerful effigy of *Bishop Bronescombe* and the original composition of the tomb of *Sir Robert Stapledon* (*c.* 1320), which incorporates standing figures of his squire, groom and horse, deserve particular note.

BIBLIOGRAPHY

J. Carter: *Specimens of Ancient Sculpture and Painting now Remaining in this Kingdom*, 2 vols (London, 1780–94, rev. 1838/*R* 1887)
E. K. Prideaux and G. R. Holt Shafto: *Bosses and Corbels of Exeter Cathedral* (Exeter, 1910)
E. K. Prideaux: 'Figure Sculpture of the West Front of Exeter Cathedral', *Archaeol. J.*, lxix (1912), pp. 1–35
N. Pevsner: 'A Note on the Art of the Exeter Carvers', *Medieval Carvings in Exeter Cathedral*, ed. C. J. P. Cave (Harmondsworth, 1953), pp. 25–32
L. Stone: *Sculpture in Britain: The Middle Ages*, Pelican Hist. A. (Harmondsworth, 1955, rev. 2/1972)
M. Swanton: *Roof-bosses and Corbels of Exeter Cathedral* (Exeter, 1979)
J. Givens: *The Garden outside the Walls: Botanical Naturalism in English Gothic Sculpture* (diss., Berkeley, U. CA, 1985)

J. P. ALLAN

3. Exeter Cathedral, west front, south porch, *Annunciation*, Beer limestone, mid-14th century

(iii) Stained glass. Several windows in the choir aisles and their eastern chapels contain grisaille glass of *c.* 1300, but they are hybrids, incorporating shields (including those of Bishop Grandisson and of the Montacutes and Courtenays and their families), as well as a 15th-century kneeling donor (canon). One of the windows of the choir clerestory, opposite the Bishop's throne, retains original glass with fragments of four Apostles, set against blue backgrounds under Decorated canopies set in grisaille.

In the summer of 1303–4 Master Walter the Glazier was paid £4 10s. in wages 'for setting the glass of the high gable and eight high windows and six windows in the aisles of the new work'; he was still employed in 1310–11. His great east window contains two-dimensional canopy-work, similar to that of the choir glass, placed over *St Margaret*, *St Catherine* and *St Mary Magdalene*, with *St Peter*, *St Paul* and *St Andrew* now in the outer main lights. Three prophets, *Abraham, Moses* and *Isaiah*, at the top of the window are of the same date. The rich colouring includes blue, purple, white and yellow. In the 1390s the window was reconstructed in the Perpendicular style: in 1391 Robert Lyen is documented as glazier. He added figures of *St Edward the Confessor*, *St Sidwell*, *St Helena* and *St Edmund*. The handling of draperies and facial features is comparable with the style of Thomas the Glazier at New College, Oxford (*see* OXFORD, §3(ii)), and at Winchester College. The canopies and bases were replaced by Frederick Drake in his restoration of 1884–96. The window was restored in 1764–7 by William Peckitt of York, who also executed glass for the great west window, which was removed in 1904.

The cathedral contains excellent 16th-century south Netherlandish and French glass. There are many modern windows, as most of the Victorian glass was destroyed by bombing in 1942.

BIBLIOGRAPHY

F. M. Drake: 'The Fourteenth Century Stained Glass of Exeter Cathedral', *Trans. Devon Assoc.*, xliv (1912), pp. 231–51

The Age of Chivalry: Art in Plantagenet England, 1200–1400 (exh. cat., ed. J. Alexander and P. Binski; London, RA, 1987), cat. no. 739, p. 532

C. Brooks and D. Evans: *The Great East Window of Exeter Cathedral: A Glazing History* (Exeter, 1988)

M. Q. SMITH

2. CENTRE OF CARPET PRODUCTION. The workshop that produced hand-knotted carpets in Exeter seems to have lasted only six years, from 1755 to 1761, and yet the three signed and dated surviving carpets are among the most important English carpets. In 1750 two weavers from the Savonnerie, with the help of Pierre Parisot, a fellow émigré, started to weave a carpet under the patronage of William Augustus, Duke of Cumberland, in premises in London (*see* CARPET, §II, 2(iii)). The enterprise did not meet with lasting success, and in 1755 the entire workshop was sold at auction to a Swiss Huguenot, Claude Passavant, of Exeter. Passavant took many of the Fulham weavers to Exeter, and it seems probable that they also took with them actual designs that they had brought from France. The three surviving carpets from Exeter incorporate distinctly French Rococo motifs, including the French preference for such colours as red, deep blue and a blackish brown. The earliest carpet, dated 1757, is in the Victoria & Albert Museum, London (*see* CARPET, fig. 10). The second, dated 1758, is in a private collection, and the third, also dated 1758, is at Petworth House, W. Sussex, NT. This last carpet may have been the one for which Passavant was awarded a joint prize by the Royal Society of Arts in 1758. He valued his entry at an exorbitant 80 guineas, and it may have been the high cost of his carpets that precipitated the closure of his workshop in 1761.

For further illustration *see* ENGLAND, fig. 95.

BIBLIOGRAPHY

A. F. Kendrick and C. E. C. Tattersall: *Handwoven Carpets: Oriental and European* (London, 1926)

C. E. C. Tattersall and S. Reed: *British Carpets* (London, 1966)

B. Jacobs: *Axminster Carpets* (Leigh-on-Sea, 1969)

C. Gilbert, J. Lomax and A. Wells-Cole: *Country House Floors*, Temple Newsam Country House Stud., iii (1987)

JENNIFER WEARDEN

Exeter, 5th Earl of. *See* CECIL, (3).

Exhibition. The temporary display of works of art for pleasure, instruction, the enhancement of scholarship or for sale. The earliest regular exhibitions were often conducted to show the wealth of existing collections rather than to promote or sell new works of art. As patronage declined, exhibitions of newly executed work became more necessary, and their institution was further encouraged by the foundation of academies, societies and museums. This article deals with Western exhibitions; for other traditions *see* AFRICA, §XIII; CHINA, §XIX; INDIAN SUBCONTINENT, §XIII; ISLAMIC ART, §XIII; and JAPAN, §XXI.

1. Before *c.* 1700. 2. *c.* 1700–*c.* 1850. 3. *c.* 1850–*c.* 1907. 4. After *c.* 1907.

1. BEFORE *c.* 1700. In Greece in the late 5th century BC or early 4th the painter Zeuxis of Heracleia charged an admission fee for viewing his *Helen* (destr.). Towards the end of the 4th century BC a picture gallery for the exhibition of works by local artists was founded in Sikyon, and by the 2nd century AD the Pinacotheca in the Propylaia of the Athenian Acropolis was open to the public. Pilgrims might be given guided tours of the statues in Greek temple sanctuaries and were able to purchase reproductions; Praxiteles' *Aphrodite of Knidos* (copy, Rome, Vatican, Mus. Pio-Clementino) was one of the great tourist attractions of the ancient world. Artistic COMPETITIONS were also organized: according to the Roman writer Pliny (*Natural History* XXXIV.liii), Polykleitos' statue was accepted for the Temple of Artemis at Ephesos following an exhibition by rival sculptors.

Whereas Greek art was intended primarily for public and religious display, in Rome an art market developed in the 2nd century BC. With the rise of collecting, works of art were exhibited for sale or for public appreciation. An important element of Roman triumphs was the exhibition of plunder in parades and at religious festivals; in 180 BC Marcus Fulvius Nobilior had 785 bronze and 230 marble statues carried in his triumphal procession, and in 168 BC Lucius Aemilius Paullus (*d* 160 BC) exhibited paintings. Portrait busts of ancestors (e.g. a statue of a *Roman Patrician Carrying Two Ancestral Portrait Busts*, late 1st century BC; Rome, Mus. Conserv.) were paraded in public in religious rites. This processional tradition was revived in the Middle Ages. When Duccio's *Maestà* (Siena, Mus. Opera Duomo), the altarpiece of Siena Cathedral, was completed in 1311, it was transported through the streets to public acclaim.

Until the establishment of public museums (largely from the 18th century onwards) works of art not in churches were unavailable except to those with permission to view private collections. In 1501 Leonardo exhibited his cartoon (untraced) of the *Virgin and Child with St Anne and a Lamb* at the monastery of SS Annunziata in Florence, so anticipating the later idea of the 'one-man show'. This was allied to the rising concept of the work of art as a virtuoso performance. In the 16th century, competitions between artists produced exhibitions in a rudimentary sense. These were encouraged by such patrons as Cardinal Giulio de' Medici, who in 1516 commissioned from Raphael and Sebastiano del Piombo altarpieces that were exhibited together to attract critical discrimination.

The expansion of the art market in the 17th century encouraged the development of auction houses and dealers and, concomitantly, of exhibitions. The establishment of

1. *Exhibition of the Académie Royale in the Grande Galerie of the Louvre*, engraving, 1699 (Frankfurt am Main, Städelsches Kunstinstitut und Städtische Galerie)

societies and academies of art also led to the institution of regular exhibitions by their members. In Rome, where there was a thriving art market, the Accademia di S Luca (founded 1577) inveighed against the degradation of art by its display in shops or in the streets; exhibitions offered a more dignified opportunity for the artist to show his work to the public. In Italy, pictures had traditionally been shown on Corpus Domini and other holy days, when they were exhibited indiscriminately with other works of art. Such exhibitions were primarily held in glorification of the saint but were exploited by artists keen to establish their reputations. Pictures were generally not for sale, but could be bought thereafter. On 29 August from 1620, at S Giovanni Decollato in Rome, annual exhibitions were held under the patronage of prominent families, who used the occasion to promote their favourite painters or to show their own art collections. The exhibitions held in S Salvatore in Lauro, Rome, on 10 December from 1669, were organized (1678–1719) by the Permanent Secretary of the Accademia di S Luca, Giuseppe Ghezzi, whose methodical arrangements for transport, lighting and security anticipated the administrative requirements of modern exhibitions. Each exhibition consisted of an average of five or six large canvases and two hundred smaller ones. Old Masters were more numerous than contemporary works, and certain masterpieces were shown repeatedly.

The forerunner of the French Salon, an exhibition instituted in 1667 by the Académie Royale de Peinture et de Sculpture (founded 1648), was held for a three-week period in the Louvre in Paris. The right to exhibit was limited to members of the Académie, whose royal foundation ensured conformity to the canons of taste laid down by Louis XIV, his chief minister, Jean-Baptiste Colbert, and the Académie's Director (from 1663), Charles Le Brun. An engraving (Frankfurt am Main, Städel. Kstinst. & Städt. Gal.; see fig. 1) of the exhibition of 1699 shows the pictures in the course of arrangement in the Grande Galerie of the Louvre. They were hung on Gobelins tapestries after Raphael's *Acts of the Apostles*, which were borrowed from the Royal Collection to provide a *mise-en-scène*. A portrait of *Louis XIV* hung at the entrance to the Galerie, which also contained sculpture. The prestige of the exhibition was augmented by the publication of a catalogue.

2. *c.* 1700–*c.* 1850. By the beginning of the 18th century there were four regular exhibitions in Rome. In 1706 in Florence, Ferdinando de' Medici, Grand Prince of Tuscany, organized a loan exhibition of 250 pictures in SS Annunziata, where they were hung in groups of eight or less in the lunettes of the cloister. A portrait of the Grand Prince, hung over the entrance to the chapel, proclaimed his patronage of the exhibition, which was notable for one of the first printed catalogues in Italy. The exhibition was held under the auspices of the Accademia del Disegno, which held similar exhibitions between 1715 and 1767. Ferdinando wished to promote Venetian painting, and the idea for this exhibition may have derived from Venice, where exhibitions were held at the Scuola di S Rocco. These developed from the processions that the Doge and Senate made to the church on the saint's feast day, 16 August (see fig. 2). However, the S Rocco exhibitions never attained the prestige or influence of the Salons in Paris.

Between 1715 and 1774 there were 26 Académie exhibitions, and from 1774 to 1792 they were held in alternate years. From 1725 the exhibition was staged in the Salon Carré and adjoining rooms of the Louvre—hence the name 'Salon'. Works were displayed according to the artist's rank and were arranged by the *tapissier* or *décorateur*, who, in mid-century, was Jean-Siméon Chardin. Paintings were tightly packed from ceiling to floor, and until later in the century, sculpture and cabinet pictures were displayed on tables, as depicted in the *Salon of 1767*

(1767; see Conisbee, 1981, p. 22) by Gabriel de Saint-Aubin and the engraving of the *Salon of 1785* by Pietro Antonio Martini (1738–97). By the 1780s, 20,000 catalogues were sold to 500–1000 visitors per day during the three weeks of the exhibition. By the mid-18th century the Salons had become a focus for distinguished art criticism by Diderot and others. Because of the official sanction of the Salon, there were few other exhibitions in France. The Exposition de la Jeunesse was held *en plein air* in the Place Dauphine or on the Pont Neuf, Paris, annually on the feast of Corpus Christi. Its catalogues reveal that Chardin first exhibited there in 1728. The Académie de St-Luc arranged exhibitions (1751–77), and an exhibiting society, the Salon de la Correspondance (1779–87), staged a retrospective exhibition of Joseph Vernet in 1783.

In England, before the foundation of the Royal Academy in 1768, exhibitions were mainly commercial, staged by dealers and auctioneers. However, the pictures painted by Hogarth and others for the Foundling Hospital (*in situ*), London, after 1740 had by 1760 begun to attract a daily crowd of spectators. From 1760 the first public exhibitions were held in London at the Society of Arts, forerunners of the annual Royal Academy summer exhibitions. At the first exhibition, held between 21 April and 3 May, 6582 catalogues describing 130 works by Reynolds, Louis-François Roubiliac, Richard Wilson and others were sold. In 1762 the works were on sale, despite Reynolds's claim that the purpose of the exhibition was 'not to enrich the artists, but to advance the art'. From 1769 the Royal Academy proposed 'an annual exhibition of paintings, sculpture and designs, which shall be open to all artists of distinguished merit'. Views of the Academy exhibitions of 1771 at Pall Mall (mezzotint by Richard Earlom after Michel Vincent [Charles] Brandoin (1733–1807)) and of 1788 at Somerset House (engraving by Pietro Antonio Martini after Johann Heinrich Ramberg; see fig. 3) show the pictures hung frame to frame from floor to ceiling in toplit rooms. The Great Room at Somerset House (16.2×13.1×9.8 m), completed by Sir William Chambers in 1780, was the finest picture gallery of its date in England. Its design was derived from Roman models via such increasingly lucrative commercial galleries as Christie's auction rooms at 83–4 Pall Mall. These were built in 1767 and incorporated one of the earliest toplit exhibition spaces in London, followed by John Boydell's Shakespeare Gallery, opened in 1789 and later used by the British Institution, and the galleries of the printsellers Fuller's and Ackermann's. The number of exhibits increased at Somerset House, reaching 672 paintings by 1791. The crowded, roughly symmetrical hang was dictated by sheer numbers. Artists often complained that their works had been allotted an obscure position, the strongest objection being that they had been 'skied'. This style of exhibition persisted

2. Canaletto: *Venice: The Feast Day of St Roch*, oil on canvas, 1.48×1.99 m, *c.* 1735 (London, National Gallery)

3. *Their Majesties and the Royal Family Viewing the Exhibition at the Royal Academy, London, 1788*, engraving by Pietro Antonio Martini after Johann Heinrich Ramberg, 315×489 mm, 1788 (London, Royal Academy of Arts Library)

throughout the 19th century (as seen in William Powell Frith's engraving of the Royal Academy exhibition of 1881) and continues to be a feature of the Academy's exhibitions.

The Royal Academy provided a focus for the exhibition of contemporary work, but until the foundation of the British Institution in 1805, the works of Old Masters could be seen only in commercial and private galleries. With the purchase of the Orléans collection (probably the finest private collection in the world at the time) by a syndicate of three English noblemen came the first opportunity in London to see (for three months at the end of 1798) an exhibition of important Old Masters. The British Institution not only provided a setting for the exhibition of such works from private collections but also organized displays of contemporary pictures. The winter exhibitions of Old Masters (open to the public from 1813) were the first major loan exhibitions in Britain and, according to Gustav Friedrich Waagen (1838), were of a quality that would have been impossible elsewhere in Europe. Their popularity encouraged the more widespread opening of private collections, and they were supplemented by retrospectives of individual artists, beginning with that of the work of Reynolds in 1813. In 1867 the Institution's functions were incorporated into the Royal Academy.

In France, Napoleon's plunder of works of art was paraded through the streets of Paris in a revival of the Roman triumph. Until 1815, when the majority of the loot was returned, the Louvre (renamed the Musée Napoléon, 1803–15) housed the greatest unofficial loan exhibition

that the world had yet seen. The exhibition of French manufactures was also initiated. In 1797 the Marquis d'Avèze formulated a scheme for the exhibition of the porcelain of Sèvres and the textiles of the Gobelins and the Savonnerie factory. In 1798 the first Exposition de l'Industrie was organized by the French government. A series of ten exhibitions followed between 1801 and 1849. The exhibitions in Paris led to the first German exhibition of art and industry at Stuttgart in 1812 and subsequent exhibitions in Munich from 1815, Düsseldorf and Leipzig from 1816, Nuremberg and Augsburg from 1818 and Dresden from 1824.

3. *c.* 1850–*c.* 1907.

(i) *England.* The success of the French and German exhibitions encouraged emulation in England. In 1845 Prince Albert, President of the Society of Arts, set up a committee with the aim of improving British design by means of exhibitions. The exhibition in Birmingham in 1849 presaged Prince Albert's ambitious plan for the first truly INTERNATIONAL EXHIBITION: the Great Exhibition of 1851. A total of 13,937 exhibitors from the British Isles and the Empire and 6556 foreign exhibitors displayed over 100,000 exhibits in 92,146 sq m of space. All the industrial and decorative arts as well as sculpture were represented, but paintings were excluded. The exhibition, open from 1 May to 11 October, was seen by 6,039,195 people and produced a profit of £186,437. Four further international exhibitions took place in London in 1862

4. Manchester Art-Treasures Exhibition, The Great Hall, 1857; engraving from the *Illustrated London News* (30 May 1857)

and from 1871 to 1874, when the concept of an annual international exhibition was abandoned. The design reforms initiated by the Great Exhibition and its successors were continued in England through the Arts and Crafts Exhibition Society (founded 1888).

Queen Victoria and Prince Albert also patronized the Manchester Art-Treasures Exhibition of 1857 (see fig. 4). This gigantic enterprise was the inspiration of three Germans: the Prince Consort, Gustav Friedrich Waagen and George Scharf. The greenhouse architecture used for the exhibition—a glass roof supported by cast iron—was inspired by Joseph Paxton's Crystal Palace (destr.), built in Hyde Park, London, for the Great Exhibition. Both were conceived as temporary, purpose-built, toplit spaces and established a style of EXHIBITION ARCHITECTURE that was copied throughout the 19th century. In four months, nearly a million people saw modern and Old Master paintings, sculpture, watercolours, drawings, engravings, decorative arts and photographs—all from British collections. The exhibition was notable for the presence of early Italian and Netherlandish pictures as well as the more familiar works of the High Renaissance and the 17th-century Italian, Dutch and Flemish schools. The British Institution had first shown such early works as a novelty in 1848, and William Ward, Lord Ward of Birmingham (1817–85; Earl of Dudley from 1860), attracted 50,000 visitors a year to the exhibition of early paintings that he held in the Egyptian Hall in London, a public gallery. The exhibition in Manchester initiated an intense interest in 18th-century English portraiture, which became both popular and highly expensive until the 1920s.

In the 19th century Thomas Agnew, the founder of Thos Agnew & Sons Ltd, was typical of the new breed of dealers, owning their own premises and staging regular exhibitions. The upstairs exhibition gallery at Agnew's in Bond Street, London, designed by Edward Salomons (1828–1906) and Ralph Wornum (1847–1910) in 1877, with its red-velvet walls and toplighting, is typical of the galleries built by dealers benefiting from the boom in the art market after 1860. Others include the Fine Art Society (1876), the Grosvenor Gallery (1877), the New Gallery (1888), the Grafton Gallery (1893) and Colnaghi's (1913), all in London.

(ii) France. In Paris (and on the Continent in general) Old Master exhibitions were less numerous than in England. The works of the Galerie Espagnole, collected for King Louis-Philippe and displayed from 1838 to 1848 in the Louvre, encouraged French interest in Spanish pictures. 18th-century French art was exhibited at the Bazar Bonne-Nouvelle in Paris in 1848, but it was not until 1860 that an exhibition of Old Masters on the scale of the annual British Institution displays was held. 300 paintings and drawings were lent by French collectors and shown in Paris: this was the first occasion that substantial numbers of works by Boucher, Watteau, Chardin, Greuze, Jean-Honoré Fragonard and other painters of the *ancien régime* were made available to the public, and their prices subsequently rose as their reputations were re-established.

The Salon continued to dominate the French artistic scene, but artists (e.g. Greuze from 1770) also held independent exhibitions. In 1855 Courbet built, at his own expense, a Pavillon du Réalisme for the exhibition of his own paintings at the Exposition Universelle in Paris. It was in part the exhibition of 14 of Manet's works at the Parisian gallery of the dealer Martinet in 1863 that inspired Monet, Renoir and Sisley to leave the studio of Charles Gleyre that year to paint on their own. In 1863 Napoleon III set up a Salon des Refusés in Paris in reaction to complaints about the doctrinaire attitude of the Salon judges. Manet's painting *Déjeuner sur l'herbe* (*see* MANET, EDOUARD, fig. 1) caused a scandal, as did his *Olympia* (both 1863; Paris, Mus. d'Orsay) at the Salon of 1865. In 1873 the Salon jury rejected pictures by Pissarro, Monet, Renoir, Cézanne and Sisley, who took the then unusual step of setting up their own exhibitions. At their first exhibition in 1874 the artists were dubbed 'Impressionists' after Monet's painting *Impression, Sunrise* (1873; Paris, Mus. Marmottan; *see* IMPRESSIONISM, fig. 1). There were eight Impressionist exhibitions between 1874 and 1886. In 1884 Seurat's *Bathers at Asnières* (London, N.G.) was refused by the Salon, and he, Paul Signac and other artists set up the Salon des Indépendants in the same year. The constitution allowed any artist to exhibit for a fee, and there was no selection committee. Exhibitions were held until World War I and were of great significance for the development of modern art. The one-man exhibition, usually at a dealer's premises (e.g. Ambroise Vollard, Gimpel, Adolphe Goupil and Léopold Zborowski), served to promote the reputations of artists. Paul Durand-Ruel held exhibitions of Renoir (1883) and Pissarro (1892), and Picasso was taken up by Daniel-Henry Kahnweiler *c.* 1907.

4. AFTER *c.* 1907. Displays by innovative artists were often conducted in an atmosphere of controversy, and the titles of some artistic movements—Fauvism and Cubism among others—derived from critical reviews of their exhibitions. Exhibitions carried the word about new movements throughout the world. In 1908 the work of Russian avant-garde painters was hung alongside that of the French Impressionists in the Russian Golden Fleece exhibition arranged by Mikhail Larionov and others in Moscow. Roger Fry organized two Post-Impressionist exhibitions at the Grafton Galleries, London, in 1910–11 and 1912, including works by Cézanne, Gauguin, van Gogh, Picasso and Braque. In 1913 the ARMORY SHOW, an international exhibition of modern art, was held at the 69th Regiment Armory in New York. Its forerunners were the anti-academic exhibitions of American paintings organized by Robert Henri, who founded the Eight (i) (exhibited at Macbeth Galleries in New York in 1908) and staged the Exhibition of Independent Artists in New York in 1910. The Armory Show included 1300 works by American and foreign artists, concentrating on the Ecole de Paris (German Expressionism was poorly represented, and the Italian Futurists refused to participate). From New York the exhibition travelled to Chicago and Boston. It was seen by 250,000 people, and 300 pictures were sold. Although the initial public reaction was critical, the exhibition achieved its aim of reviving interest in modern American art, which thereafter remained a living issue in the USA. At the show, Duchamp's *Nude Descending a Staircase, No. 2* (Philadelphia, PA, Mus. A.) had a *succès de scandale*. With his subsequent exhibition of ready-mades,

most notably a urinal entitled *Fountain* (1917; untraced), Duchamp anticipated the similar eccentricities of many later artists. Among others, his ideas were adopted by the Surrealists, who founded their Galerie Surréaliste, Paris, in 1926. Important international Surrealist exhibitions were held in London (New Burlington Gals) in 1936 and Paris (Gal. Maeght) in 1947.

Duchamp's ready-mades mark the beginning of one important attitude towards exhibitions in the 20th century. This is to make parasitic use of the established association between an exhibition and its contents: objects are exhibited because they are works of art, though they remain thus whether or not they are in fact exhibited. In the 20th century, however, certain artists suggested that a work of art could only be defined as such through the act of exhibiting it in a gallery or museum. By implication, therefore, anything that is given this privileged treatment is art. Though Duchamp's work is, in the Dadaist spirit, often ironic, later artists took this approach more seriously (though their intentions are frequently ambiguous). For example, the Pop artists of the 1960s exhibited banal, mass-produced objects as art, suggesting that they embodied the most distinctive and appealing aspects of contemporary consumer society.

Despite the continued use of exhibitions by many 20th-century artists, some rebelled against what they saw as the élitist, commercial atmosphere of the exhibiting system, particularly that centred on dealers' galleries. This led to the production of various forms of ephemeral, public art that by its very nature could not be exhibited in the traditional manner. Notable among them were the products of PERFORMANCE ART in the 1960s and 1970s, which, consisting solely of live events, left no art object to be exhibited. Another aspect of performance art was Body Art, in which the artist's body was both art object and exhibiting space. The works of LAND ART are site-specific and usually of vast scale, so that they can be exhibited only secondhand, through photographs, documents and fragments of material. The French artist Yves Klein subverted the normal exhibition format in 1958 by holding an exhibition of *Le Vide* at the Galerie Iris Clert in Paris. He removed all the furniture and painted the walls white, so in effect exhibiting an exhibiting space. In 1959 he printed a number of *Receipts for the Immaterial*, which were given to anyone purchasing a 'zone of immaterial pictorial sensibility' for a given weight of gold. The receipt was the only material remnant of the work bought. The very non-existence of such 'works' denied any genuine possibility of exhibition.

As well as exhibitions of contemporary art, loan exhibitions of the art of the past continued to develop in the 20th century. Though the scale of such Victorian exhibitions as the Manchester Art-Treasures exhibition of 1857 has never been surpassed, the frequency and the internationalism of exhibitions have been on the increase since the late 19th century. A peak was reached in the great exhibitions of the 1930s at the Royal Academy in London. The Academy staged loan exhibitions mainly of works of the Old Masters from 1870. The exhibitions of Dutch Art (1929) and Italian Art (1930) were remarkable for their content of masterpieces. Attendances were enormous— Italian Art attracted 600,000 visitors. Persian Art (1931),

French Art (1932) and Chinese Art (1935–6) were also of signal importance, the last reintroducing the taste for chinoiserie. Since World War II exhibitions on every conceivable subject have been held at museums and commercial galleries throughout the world. As well as promoting contemporary art, they have provided a vehicle for the rediscovery of individual artists, periods, styles and countries. This has gone hand in hand with the development of scholarship, confirmed by comparison between the basic lists published by the Royal Academy in the 1930s and the comprehensive apparatus of the modern exhibition catalogue (see CATALOGUE, §4). The risk to works of art in the process of exhibition has led to sophisticated requirements for packing, transport, environmental control, lighting, insurance and security. Certain categories of object (e.g. panel paintings) are no longer lent, or only in exceptional circumstances if their preservation can be assured. Travelling exhibitions are rarer. Despite these restrictions, exhibitions continue to multiply in number and in theme, and an exhibition about the history of exhibitions would seem to be the only conceivable new departure.

See also DISPLAY OF ART.

BIBLIOGRAPHY

J. Lavallée, ed.: *Galerie du Musée Napoléon*, 11 vols (Paris, 1804–28)
Catalogue Raisonné of the Pictures Now Exhibiting at the British Institution (London, 1815)
An Account of All the Pictures Exhibited in the Rooms of the British Institution from 1813 to 1823, Belonging to the Nobility and Gentry of England: With Remarks, Critical and Explanatory (London, 1824)
G. F. Waagen: *Works of Art in Great Britain*, 3 vols (London, 1838)
A. Graves: *The Royal Academy of Arts: A Complete Dictionary of Contributors and their Work from its Foundation in 1769 to 1904*, 8 vols (London, 1905–6)
——: 'The British Institution', *A. J.* [London] (1910)
——: *A Century of Loan Exhibitions, 1813–1912*, 5 vols (London, 1913–15)
W. T. Whitley: *Artists and their Friends in England*, 2 vols (London, 1928/R New York, 1968)
N. Pevsner: *Academies of Art Past and Present* (Cambridge, 1940)
The Great Exhibition of 1851 (exh. cat. by C. H. Gibbs-Smith, London, V&A, 1950)
F. Haskell and M. Levey: 'Art Exhibitions in 18th Century Venice', *A. Ven.*, xii (1958), pp. 179–85
F. Haskell: 'The Market for Italian Art in the 17th Century', *Past & Present*, 15 (April 1959), pp. 48–59
——: 'Art Exhibitions in 17th Century Rome', *Stud. Seicent.*, i (1960), pp. 107–21
N. von Holst: *Creators, Collectors and Connoisseurs* (London, 1967)
S. C. Hutchison: *The History of the Royal Academy, 1768–1968* (London, 1968)
A. Boime: 'The Salon des Refusés and the Evolution of Modern Art', *A. Q.* [London], xxxii (1969), pp. 411–26
J. Gage: *Colour in Turner* (London, 1969)
W. I. Homer: *Robert Henri and his Circle* (Ithaca, 1969)
F. Herrmann: *The English as Collectors* (New York, 1972)
F. Borroni Salvadori: 'Le esposizioni d'arte a Firenze dal 1674 al 1767', *Mitt. Ksthist. Inst. Florenz*, xviii/1 (1974), pp. 1–166
W. H. Friedman: *Boydell's Shakespeare Gallery* (New York and London, 1976)
F. Haskell: *Rediscoveries in Art* (Oxford, 1976)
——: *Patrons and Painters* (New Haven and London, 1980)
H. Zmijewska: *La Critique des Salons en France du temps de Diderot, 1759–89* (Warsaw, 1980)
J. Bayard: *Works of Splendour and Imagination: The Exhibition Watercolour, 1770–1780* (New Haven, 1981)
P. Conisbee: *Painting in 18th Century France* (London, 1981)
L. Lippincott: *Selling Art in Georgian London: The Rise of Arthur Pond* (New Haven and London, 1983)
D. P. Curry: 'Total Control: Whistler at an Exhibition', *James McNeill Whistler: A Reexamination* (Washington, DC, 1984), pp. 67–82
G. Waterfield: 'The Gallery as Exhibition Space', *'Soane and After': The Architecture of Dulwich Picture Gallery* (exh. cat., ed. G. Waterfield; London, Dulwich Pict. Gal., 1987), pp. 10–13
I. Pears: *The Discovery of Painting: The Growth of Interest in the Arts in England, 1680–1768* (New Haven and London, 1988)
A. Tinniswood: *A History of Country House Visiting: Five Centuries of Tourism and Taste* (Oxford, 1989)
L. M. Fink: *American Art at the 19th Century Paris Salons* (Cambridge, 1990)
Palaces of Art: Art Galleries in Britain, 1790–1800 (exh. cat., ed. G. Waterfield; London, Dulwich Pict. Gal., 1991–2)
Metropole London: Macht und Glanz einer Weltstadt, 1800–1840 (exh. cat., ed. C. Fox; Essen, Kultstift. Ruhr, 1992) [P. Funnell: 'Die Londoner Kunstwelt und ihre Institutionen', pp. 155–66; A. Wilton: 'Die Malerei im London des frühen neunzehnten Jahrhunderts', pp. 167–86]

CHRISTOPHER ROWELL

Exhibition architecture. The great international exhibitions (often called expositions), the first of which was held in London in 1851, are intended to feature displays by nations and large companies of current developments in areas ranging from science and industry to the arts and trade. Since temporary buildings are necessary to house the displays and enhance the sites, exhibitions have provided opportunities for architects, engineers and industrial designers to demonstrate their skills. Although such structures are usually temporary, intended only for the duration of the exhibition, a number of them remain *in situ*, the best-known example of which is the Eiffel Tower, built for the Paris Exposition of 1889.

1. Early exhibitions in London, Paris and Vienna, 1851–73. 2. France and the USA, 1876–1915. 3. Exhibitions of 1925–40. 4. Developments since 1945.

1. EARLY EXHIBITIONS IN LONDON, PARIS AND VIENNA, 1851–73. The ephemeral quality of most buildings constructed for international exhibitions in the second half of the 19th century often encouraged highly experimental approaches to materials and style. After an inconclusive international competition, the building commission for the Great Exhibition held in Hyde Park, London, in 1851 opted for a design belatedly submitted by Joseph Paxton. Paxton's Crystal Palace was not only the first building to house an international exhibition but also a significant early essay in prefabrication and modular construction in iron and glass. Erected by the contracting firm of Sir Charles Fox (1810–74) and George Henderson (1783–1855), the Crystal Palace was 564 m long, 124 m wide and covered 70,000 sq. m. It was constructed in 7.3-m modules from standardized cast- and wrought-iron components and sheathed in panels of glass 1.2 m in length (the largest capable of being mass-produced at the time). The central transept, with a span of 22 m, was fabricated with a laminated wooden framework. The Crystal Palace was actually far from a pure iron and glass structure, since wood was extensively employed for the flooring, sash-bars and gutters. Nevertheless, it was remarkably novel in the transparency of its interior space and in its relative lack of the historicist ornament that so permeated High Victorian architecture. (After the Great Exhibition it was re-erected at Sydenham in south London but destroyed by fire in 1936.)

1. Exhibition architecture: main building of the Exposition Universelle, Paris, 1867; view from the west

Nearly 100 exhibitions organized in major cities between 1851 and 1900 claimed some sort of international status, but in architectural terms few were truly significant. Paris was by far the most important venue, hosting five major exhibitions between 1855 and 1900. The Palais de l'Industrie, built on the Champs-Elysées for the Exposition Universelle of 1855, was a joint effort by the engineer Alexis Barrault (1812–67) and the architect Victor Viel (1798–1863). Barrault's solution for the frame and roof of the building was similar to several large railway stations constructed in this period and consisted of a large nave with two structurally supportive aisles. The nave was 192 m long, and its unprecedented 48-m span (more than twice that of the Crystal Palace transept) was not supported by supplementary tie-bars, although enormous lead abutments had to be used to handle the lateral stress. Viel's massive stone exterior was, however, a regression from the straightforward functionalism of Paxton's Crystal Palace. A shortage of space in the main building necessitated the addition of a separate barrel-vaulted Galerie des Machines running 1200 m along the banks of the River Seine.

The London International Exhibition of 1862 was housed in a building designed by the military engineer Captain Francis Fowke. This massive, stone-clad structure, erected in the heart of South Kensington, featured a nave 244 m in length with two wide transepts at either end, each crowned by an enormous dome 76 m high. Compared to its predecessors, Fowke's building did not represent an advance, either in building technology or in style. It was judged so unsuccessful that, although originally intended to become a permanent museum, it was soon pulled down. The main building for the next major international event, held in Paris in 1867, was by contrast daringly experimental (see fig. 1). Situated on the Champ-de-Mars, it was an elliptical structure with semicircular ends constructed of corrugated iron and glass, measuring 490×386 m. The precise origin of this unusual design is unclear, although it has frequently been attributed to Frédéric LePlay (1800–82), an eminent economist and engineer and the exhibition's commissioner-general. Jean-Baptiste Krantz was the engineer and Leopold Hardy (1829–94) the managing architect for the building. It was laid out in seven concentric galleries, each representing a different category of products displayed. The outermost gallery was for exhibiting machinery; 35 m wide and 25 m high, it was twice the height and width of the others. The calculations for this Galerie des Machines were prepared by the young Gustave Eiffel. Another novel feature of this exhibition was the host of smaller national and corporate pavilions that quickly sprouted in the gardens surrounding the main structure. Indeed this was the last time any attempt was made to house a major exhibition within one building.

The only major international exhibition to be organized in a German-speaking country in the 19th century was held in Vienna in 1873. The main building, 907 m long and 206 m wide, was composed of a central aisle from which 32 rib pavilions radiated at right angles. At its centre was a square court capped by a huge rotunda and lantern, which measured 85 m from the floor to the ceiling of the dome, designed by the English architect John Scott Russell (1808–82). The machinery hall was again a separate structure, a three-aisled building 800 m long. Apart from the dramatic height of its central rotunda, there was little to be seen in the way of technical innovation, and the liberal use of Baroque-inspired ornament did not indicate any new stylistic directions.

2. FRANCE AND THE USA, 1876–1915. As a celebration of the USA centennial, the Philadelphia Exposition of 1876 was immense and included 249 buildings. There were large halls for machinery, the arts, horticulture, agriculture and, for the first time in the history of international exhibitions, a women's building. This was the first attempt to create an international exhibition in a carefully integrated landscape setting. Herman J. Schwarzmann (1843–91), a little-known German immigrant, was its supervising architect. Schwarzmann was responsible for landscaping the enormous site in Fairmount Park and designed 34 of the buildings, including the permanent Memorial Hall. The most ambitious structure was the main exhibition hall; 573 m long and 141 m wide, it was at that time the largest building in the world. As with several other buildings at the Exposition, its squared towers and large expanses of small-paned windows gave it a vaguely Elizabethan quality. As in Paris in 1867, many of the exotic non-Western structures, especially the Japanese pavilion, made a strong impression on architectural commentators of the time. For the Paris Exposition of 1878, the elliptical plan used in 1867 was abandoned in favour of a quadrilateral complex measuring 300×725 m, which occupied virtually all of the available space on the Champ-de-Mars. Jean-Baptiste Krantz, the Exposition's commissioner-general, assigned the architectural planning of this complex to Leopold Hardy, his collaborator in 1867. The emphasis throughout was on cost-saving, recyclable, metal components, but as the giant metal pylons Hardy designed to support the corner domes of the complex could not be supplied by French foundries,

masonry pillars were employed instead. The most technically innovative elements of the Champ-de-Mars complex, designed by the engineer Henri de Dion (1828–78), were the two galleries displaying machinery, which longitudinally flanked and enclosed the remainder of the exhibition space. Instead of using simple barrel vaults he covered these galleries with non-rigid, transverse ogee arches; although spanning 35 m, these needed neither buttresses nor tie-bars. The iron and glass main façade and entrance vestibule facing the Seine were engineered by Gustave Eiffel. On the other side of the Seine, the Palais du Trocadéro by the architect Gabriel Davioud and the engineer Jules Bourdais (1835–1915) was a strange assortment of historicist and vaguely Oriental references. Unlike the Champ-de-Mars complex, this massive stone and brick monument remained as a city-owned facility after the Exposition; it was finally destroyed to make way for the Palais de Chaillot, built for the Exposition of 1937.

Although several smaller exhibitions were held in various cities in the 1880s, none of great architectural significance occurred until the Paris Exposition of 1889. Organized as a centennial celebration of the French Revolution, this was perhaps more important as a showcase of engineering technology than any other international exhibition of the 19th century. It boasted not only the highest structure then ever built, Gustave Eiffel's 300-m tower, but also that with the widest clear span, the Galerie des Machines (destr. 1910), a collaborative effort by the architect Charles-Louis-Ferdinand Dutert and the engineer Victor Contamin (1840–98). The Galerie was 420 m long and had an unprecedented clear span of 115 m, accomplished with a novel system of thrice-articulated arches without intermediate supports. Even in much more eclectic structures, such as the Palais des Beaux-Arts and the Palais des Arts Libéraux by Jean-Camille Formigé, deliberately exposed metal structural components were much in evidence. The Exposition of 1889 was also notable for its collection of 48 buildings illustrating the history of human habitation, a display organized by Charles Garnier, architect of the Paris Opéra.

The architectural character of the World's Columbian Exposition held in Chicago in 1893 was largely due to the overriding influence of its Director of Works, Daniel H. Burnham, who chose the five prestigious architectural firms—none of which was from Chicago—entrusted with the design and placement of the major buildings. Richard Morris Hunt designed the Administration Building; Robert Swain Peabody and John Goddard Stearns (1843–1917) the Machinery Hall; McKim, Mead & White the Agricultural Building; Henry Van Brunt and Frank Maynard Howe (1849–1909) the Electricity Hall; and George Browne Post the Manufactures and Liberal Arts Building. No previous exhibition had shown such a deliberate singularity in architectural style: Burnham and his colleagues created a consistent if flamboyant classicism for the buildings, all of which were painted in the same shade of cream-white. The 'White City', as the World's Columbian Exposition was popularly known, was a conscious denial of the iron and glass functionalism of 1878 and 1889. Ironically, while the style of the buildings implied a timeless permanence, this was perhaps the least permanent of major 19th-century exhibitions. Most of the structures

were constructed primarily of 'staff', a cheap composite of plaster of Paris, glue and fibre, and they were demolished immediately after the exhibition closed. There were some notable engineering feats, however, the most obvious of which was Post's Manufactures and Liberal Arts Building, the span of which outdistanced Dutert and Contamin's Galerie des Machines by approximately one metre. A notable exception to the otherwise rigorous classicism of this exhibition was the Transportation Building, designed with a zestful decorative flair by Dankmar Adler and Louis H. Sullivan.

The Paris Exposition of 1900 was also characterized by the predominance of staff and other temporary materials. Unlike the uniformity of the Chicago exhibition, however, it included a chaotic assortment of styles. As in 1889, many of those who designed the principal structures were relatively young; most were former students of the Ecole des Beaux-Arts, an institution whose teaching at that time encouraged the concealment of structural elements behind sculpture-laden façades. This tendency is evident in the two buildings that survive: the Grand Palais, principally the work of Henri Deglane (1855–1931), and the Petit Palais by Charles-Louis Girault. Like the Palais de l'Industrie of 1855, which it replaced, the Grand Palais has a vast iron and glass roof; this is most impressive when seen from within, since exterior views of it are considerably obscured by conservative stone façades. Surprisingly, Art Nouveau influence was little in evidence in the larger buildings, although in some of the smaller structures, most notably the Finnish Pavilion by Eliel Saarinen, there were some highly imaginative combinations of Art Nouveau and vernacular building styles.

In early 20th-century Europe, the emphasis shifted from comprehensive international events to those of a more specialized and localized nature. These were, however, often highly significant as showcases for new experiments in architectural design, as was apparent in the 1901 exhibition in DARMSTADT by the artists' colony. The first ever specifically to feature domestic architecture, it included highly original structures by Joseph Maria Olbrich and Peter Behrens and represented a major stylistic departure from the prevailing Art Nouveau. In Cologne, the 1914 Deutscher Werkbund exhibition was particularly important for revealing the new functionalist aesthetic of Walter Gropius, seen particularly in his model factory and administration building. This Werkbund exhibition also featured some of the first manifestations of Expressionist architecture, most notably in the Glashaus by Bruno Taut.

Certain international exhibitions organized in the USA in the early 20th century were very large, but generally there was little to be seen in the way of architectural innovation. The largest exhibition in history, the Louisiana Purchase Exposition held in St Louis, MO, in 1904, included 1576 buildings; its focal point was the Beaux-Arts style Festival Hall by Cass Gilbert, the only major building still extant. The Panama-Pacific Exposition held in San Francisco in 1915 similarly relied on a long-established Beaux-Arts vocabulary, although it demonstrated a particular flair for lighting effects and gargantuan scale, evident in the surviving Palace of Fine Arts by the Californian architect Bernard Maybeck. The Panama-California Exposition, held in San Diego, CA, in the same year, was principally the work of a New York architect, Bertram Grosvenor Goodhue. Designed in a colourful Spanish Colonial style, this exhibition had a major impact on subsequent public architecture in southern California.

3. EXHIBITIONS OF 1925–40.

(i) *Paris, Barcelona and London*. After World War I the Exposition Internationale des Arts Décoratifs et Industriels Modernes, held in Paris in 1925, revealed a sharp contrast between the ornate character of the predominantly French Art Deco style and more radically modernist trends. By far the most adventurous buildings were the starkly functional Pavillon de l'Esprit Nouveau by Le Corbusier and the Soviet pavilion, designed by Konstantin Mel'nikov. The exterior of Mel'nikov's pavilion was a particularly aggressive statement in radical Constructivist design; it also contained a model workers' club by Aleksandr Rodchenko. The only large international exhibition held in Europe during the 1920s was in Barcelona in 1929; its major buildings remain, virtually unchanged. Although international, many of the Barcelona exhibition buildings showed strong Spanish influence, and they were distinctly anachronistic in style. There was also, however, the small but lavishly financed German pavilion by Ludwig Mies van der Rohe. In this pivotal statement of Modernist architecture, Mies rejected any traditional sense of room organization, using the walls not as structural supports but to regulate space freely. Although the original pavilion was dismantled after the exhibition, a reconstruction (1987) now stands on the original exhibition site.

When early 20th-century European exhibitions were not based on particular artistic or industrial themes, they were often centred on cultural aspects of colonial imperialism. Such was the case with the British Empire Exhibition held in London in 1924–5 (for which Wembley Stadium was built in 1922–3), and the Exposition Coloniale Internationale organized in Paris in 1931, which bequeathed the present Musée des Arts Africains et Océaniens. As political instability and international tensions grew in the 1930s, however, faith in the viability of international exhibitions rapidly waned in Europe. The only one of major importance was the Exposition Internationale des Arts et Techniques dans la Vie Moderne, held in Paris in 1937. Although physically the largest ever organized in that city, it showed little of contemporary trends in international modernist architecture. As with the German pavilion, designed by the official architect of the Nazis, Albert Speer, it more frequently reflected increasing conservative retrenchments in national architectural styles. A marked exception to this tendency was the Finnish pavilion by Alvar Aalto, in which strikingly modern uses of wood prefigured later 20th-century Scandinavian innovations in that medium. The still extant Palais de Chaillot by the team of Jacques Carlu, Louis-Hippolyte Boileau and Léon Azéma (*b* 1898) provided ample evidence of an increasingly restrained classicism in French architecture compared to the previous decade.

(ii) *Chicago and New York*. Despite the Great Depression, two very ambitious international exhibitions were organized in the USA in the 1930s, both of which emphasized a confident, if somewhat fantastic, interpretation of future

technology. In Chicago, the 'Century of Progress' Exposition was open for 12 months during 1933 and 1934. Official participation by European nations was meagre, but the exhibition nonetheless reflected various currents in European Modernism and influences from the Paris Exposition of 1925 in particular. This was due in part to the early managerial role of the Austrian architect Joseph Urban, who employed the latest technological building materials and orchestrated sensational coloured lighting effects to enhance the buildings. Examples of particular ingenuity included the Hall of Science by Paul Cret, and the Travel and Transportation Building by John Holabird (1886–1945), Daniel H. Burnham jr and Edward H. Bennett (1874–1954), a highly innovative structure with a roof spanning 200 m suspended from 12 steel towers.

Even more than its predecessor in Chicago, the 'World of Tomorrow' Exposition held in New York in 1939–40 stressed consumer technology and the popularization of science. Although a record number of nations participated, their presence was dwarfed by the pavilions of large American corporations; those of the large automobile companies were especially ambitious. The planning of this exhibition was dominated as never before by a new generation of industrial designers led by Walter Dorwin Teague, head of the Board of Design. Teague was largely responsible for the interior of the Ford Building, designed by Albert Kahn, a pioneer in expressive uses of concrete in industrial architecture. The General Motors complex, also supervised by Kahn, contained what was undoubtedly the most popular attraction, the 'Futurama', by the industrial designer Norman Bel Geddes, which offered visitors a panoramic view of the future—the model city of 1960. Throughout the exhibition, widespread use of air-conditioning allowed for the first time the creation of unprecedented expanses of unbroken wall surfaces and a more fluid, curvilinear treatment of building surfaces than had been evident in Chicago six years earlier. In their emphasis on corporate structures and on entertainments often thinly veiled as consumer education, both the Chicago and the New York exhibitions anticipated the direction to be taken by many later 20th-century international exhibitions.

4. DEVELOPMENTS SINCE 1945.

After World War II no major international exhibitions were held until the one that took place in Brussels in 1958. Dedicated to peaceful uses of atomic energy, its thematic centrepiece was the 'Atomium', a model of an iron molecule magnified 165 million times and standing 110 m in height. The Brussels exhibition included an ambitious representation by the European Communist states. The enormous pavilion of the Soviet Union, constructed with aluminium cantilever trusses anchored by cables and with a curtain façade in glass and aluminium, was especially innovative. Undoubtedly the most expressive building at Brussels was a corporate one, the Philips pavilion by Le Corbusier. Formed by a series of dramatically flaring concrete ribs over which the architect stretched a tent of reflective metal alloy, this structure, unlike most of the other modernist buildings at the exhibition, was avowedly temporary in character. Le Corbusier's novel solution to enclosing exhibition space clearly anticipated similar experiments in other materials at later exhibitions.

More than any other exhibition of the post-war period, Expo 67, held in Montreal in 1967, offered a variety of opportunities for architectural experiment, particularly as it pertained to questions of urban planning and design and the use of alternative building technologies. Perhaps the most novel structure was the pavilion of the Federal Republic of Germany (see fig. 2) by Frei Otto, with Rolf Gutbrod. This consisted of an enormous tent roof of steel cable mesh held up by a group of masts as much as 15 storeys tall. The USA was represented by a geodesic dome 76 m in diameter by Buckminster Fuller. While both Otto and Fuller had built such structures before, they had never been seen by so wide a public as in Montreal. In the area of urban housing, the Canadian architect Moshe Safdie produced 'Habitat 67', an experiment in high-density urban housing in which each of the 158 factory-produced, reinforced-concrete units was hoisted into place to form a huge complex of terraced apartments.

At the Osaka International Exposition, held in Japan in 1970, space-frame construction and pneumatically supported structures were prominently featured. The dominant example was the gigantic space-frame roof by Kenzo Tange covering the Festival Plaza. The United States pavilion by Lewis Davis (*b* 1927) and Samuel Brody (*b* 1926) featured a huge inflated roof over a subterranean complex. Anchored by steel cables, this roof was held up by air alone and was the largest such structure ever to be attempted. The Fuji Group pavilion by Yutaka Murata was shaped from 16 inflated tubes bent to form a nave 10 storeys high. Osaka was perhaps the last major exhibition to display significant new directions in architectural technology. The trend away from national pavilions to those sponsored by large corporations, already evident at Osaka, was a continuing pattern in the scattered exhibitions held after 1970 that claimed international status. As support by central governments and broad participation by foreign nations faltered, international exhibitions rapidly lost their former significance, as well as their role in demonstrating new and experimental technologies in architecture.

2. Exhibition architecture: Pavilion for the Federal Republic of Germany, Expo 67, Montreal, by Frei Otto, with Rolf Gutbrod

BIBLIOGRAPHY

A. Démy: *Essai historique sur les expositions universelles de Paris* (Paris, 1907)
R. Isay: *Panorama des expositions universelles* (Paris, 1937)
S. Giedion: *Space, Time and Architecture* (Cambridge, 1941, rev. 5/1967), pp. 243–90
K. Luckhurst: *The Story of Exhibitions* (London, 1951)
E. Cornell: *De stora utställningarnas arkitektur historia* (Stockholm, 1952)
R. Poirier: *Des Foires, des peuples, des expositions* (Paris, 1958)
J. F. Davis: 'International Expositions, 1851–1900', *Pap. Amer. Assoc. Archit. Bibliographers*, iv (1967), pp. 49–129
E. Schild: *Zwischen Glaspalast und Palais des Illusions: Form und Konstruktion im 19. Jahrhundert* (Berlin, 1967)
C. Beutler: *Weltausstellungen im 19. Jahrhundert* (Munich, 1973)
E. Kroker, ed.: *Die Weltausstellungen im 19. Jahrhundert* (Göttingen, 1975)
N. Pevsner: *A History of Building Types* (Princeton, 1976), pp. 235–56
J. Allwood: *The Great Exhibitions* (London, 1977)
W. Plum: *Weltausstellungen im 19. Jahrhundert: Schauspiele des soziokulturellen Wandels* (Bonn and Bad Godesberg; Eng. trans., Bonn and Bad Godesberg, 1977)
P. Ory: *Les Expositions universelles de Paris* (Paris, 1982)
J. J. Bloch and M. Delort: *Quand Paris allait à l'expo* (Paris, 1983)
W. Friebe: *Architektur der Weltausstellungen: 1851–1970* (Stuttgart, 1983; Eng. trans., Leipzig 1985)
Le Livre des expositions universelles 1851–1939 (exh. cat. by R. Bordaz and others, Paris, Mus. A. Déc., 1983)
P. Greenhalgh: *Ephemeral Vistas: The Expositions Universelles, Great Exhibitions and World's Fairs, 1851–1939* (Manchester, 1987)

E. G. Holt, ed.: *Universal Expositions and State Sponsored Fine Arts*, The Expanding World of Art, 1874–1902, i (New Haven and London, 1988)
ROBERT JAY

Existentialism. A movement in mid-20th century Continental philosophy that cannot be identified with any single set of philosophical doctrines but tends to emphasize the human individual in the analysis of being. Setting aside the tradition of Christian existentialism, the best-known exponents of existentialism in its non-religious form are MARTIN HEIDEGGER and JEAN-PAUL SARTRE.

Existentialism derived from various sources in 19th-century philosophy and took contemporary inspiration from Edmund Husserl (*see* PHENOMENOLOGY). The concept of the 'individual' proposed by Søren Kierkegaard (1813–55) is usually regarded as the prototype for the existentialist conception of the human subject. Kierkegaard's disparagement of systematic conceptual thought as a means of truth and his insistence on the lack of rational grounds for religious belief may also be claimed to have provided a model for several characteristic features of existentialist writings: a predilection for nuanced description of the particular instance, a tendency to privilege abnormal and extreme experience over the quotidian, a preference for broadly anthropological over narrowly epistemological modes of investigation, and the appearance of endorsing some degree of irrationalism in the spheres of belief and action. From renewed discussion of the work of Georg Wilhelm Hegel by Alexandre Kojève and Jean Hyppolite in Paris in the 1930s, existentialism drew its manner of formulating philosophical issues anthropocentrically, in terms of a dramatic confrontation between man and the world. Husserl's phenomenology provided a new philosophical discourse for the description of the mind that seemed to guarantee logically that human beings cannot be assimilated to the objects of scientific explanation.

Existentialism remained closely associated with the ambitions of traditional metaphysics but reflected disappointment at its failure rather than any renewed hopes for its success, and in this respect existentialism has seemed to many to give crucially appropriate intellectual expression to the social experiences and atrocities of 20th-century Europe. The moral dimension of existentialism is usually identified with Sartre's ethics, popularly considered the acme of voluntaristic subjectivism, in particular his concept of 'authenticity', which Sartre never fully elaborated. The political commitments of individual existentialists have, however, been diverse: while Karl Jaspers (1883–1969) remained a liberal, Heidegger endorsed National Socialism, and Sartre and MAURICE MERLEAU-PONTY each undertook major philosophical revisions of Marxism.

It may be claimed with justice that the relation of existentialism to the arts has been more intimate than that of any other 20th-century philosophical movement. Existentialism's claim that the individual necessarily and fully transcends his culture implies that the critical assessment of art objects should be freed from historical ways of understanding. Existentialism may be thought to have provided a suitable *post facto* rationale for such avant-garde practices as experimentation, ceaseless innovation and the artist's cultivation of a highly individual style, through its validation of the artist's personal autonomy and right to recast reality, precisely because it had itself been formed in part by avant-garde influences. A strong affinity may also be discerned between existentialist descriptions of the content of human subjectivity as tragically conflicted and the levels and qualities of experience explored in various forms of 20th-century expressionism. The reciprocal relation between existentialist philosophy and artistic modernism ultimately becomes a matter of their sharing the same broad cultural outlook.

Existentialist writings on art have tended to fall short of providing a systematic aesthetic, but they converge in emphasizing the cognitive role of art, adopting the position of the spectator rather than considering the work of art's expressive relation to the psychological states of the artist. A precedent had been set for treating art as a way of furthering authentic existence by Friedrich Nietzsche, whose *Die Geburt der Tragödie* (1872) went so far as to accord a semi-theological role of metaphysical world-justification to the aesthetic, and again by Kierkegaard, who in the first volume of *Enten-Eller* (1843) described the aesthetic, which he closely associated with hedonism, as a wholly distinctive and autonomous form of human existence, albeit one that is in the end inferior to the ethical.

Heidegger's philosophical interests had led him in search of ways of formulating answers to questions of a radical ontological kind, which he considered to have been elided by traditional metaphysics. In the course of a meditation on the nature of 'thinghood', he claimed for art, using the examples of Greek architecture and van Gogh's painting of peasants' shoes, the power to provide access to a deeper philosophical understanding of the nature of truth and being than had been available to conceptual thought since Plato. This revelatory power Heidegger also detected in Romantic poetry, declaring that 'the poetic' is in fact the essence of all forms of art. Sartre,

by contrast, through his restrictive account of the function of imagination, evidenced a contrary strain in existentialism, voicing a suspicion of at least those forms of aesthetic experience bound up with the value of beauty as too closely intertwined with 'unreality' to be allowed to qualify as authentic.

Mikel Dufrenne, whose *Phénoménologie de l'expérience esthétique* (1953) paralleled Merleau-Ponty's attempts to give phenomenology an existential import, attempted to press further and make applicable to all the arts the kind of phenomenological analysis that had been supplied for literary works by the Polish philosopher Roman Ingarden. Dufrenne opposed Sartre's claim that the work of art is grasped only in imagination, reinstating it as a real object of perception, and proceeded to give a detailed and systematic account of the differentiation of the work of art from ordinary objects, crediting the aesthetic object with the capacity to generate an 'expressed world'. Dufrenne proposed that the ontological significance of art lies in its authentication of an *a priori* affective dimension to reality; the specific concern of pictorial works he considered to be the exploration of spatiality and temporality.

BIBLIOGRAPHY

V. Eremita [S. Kierkegaard]: *Enten-Eller*, i (1843); Eng. trans. as *Either-Or* (London and Princeton, 1944)

F. Nietzsche: *Die Geburt der Tragödie aus dem Geiste der Musik* (Leipzig, 1872); Eng. trans. in *Complete Works*, i, ed. O. Levy (London, 1909)

M. Heidegger: 'Der Ursprung des Kunstwerkes', *Holzwege* (Frankfurt, 1950; Eng. trans., New York, 1971)

M. Dufrenne: *Phénoménologie de l'expérience esthétique* (Paris, 1953; Eng. trans., Evanston, 1973)

A. B. Fallico: *Art and Existentialism* (Englewood Cliffs, 1962)

SEBASTIAN GARDNER

Ex-libris. *See* BOOKPLATE.

Experimental Atelier. *See* EXAT-51.

Experimental film [avant-garde; fine art film]. Term referring to films that are distinguished by their concern to analyse and extend the medium, not only by means of new technology or subject-matter but also in terms of new formal or aesthetic ideas. Work of this kind is generally produced on a small budget and is screened in galleries and specialized film venues; it maintains close links with avant-garde forms of literature and art. The first decade of film making (after 1895) necessarily involved a great deal of experiment, although most participants saw film as a medium for entertainment rather than art. The work of two early French directors, Georges Méliès (1861–1938) and Émile Cohl (1857–1963), was later singled out by film makers. Méliès, a professional magician, showed the power of the film medium to transform time and space in *An Up-to-date Conjuror* (1899) and *Voyage to the Moon* (1902). In *The Joyous Microbes* (1909) Cohl demonstrated the linear freedom possible in film animation. In the 1910s and 1920s many artists associated with modernism were drawn to film as a product of new technology and a medium unencumbered by tradition. It also offered artists the opportunity to animate their images. The Italian Futurists issued a manifesto about the possibilities of 'Futurist cinema' in 1916. The major Futurist films appear to have been lost, although an essay of 1912 by Bruno Corra (1892–1976) provided a detailed description of

Still from the Surrealist film *Un Chien andalou* by Luis Buñuel and Salvador Dalí, 1928 (London, British Film Institute)

animation work. He and Arnaldo Ginna (1890–1982) bypassed the camera by painting directly on celluloid. Their work attracted so little attention that this method of direct film making was reinvented two decades later.

In the early 1920s artists in Germany developed the 'absolute' or 'non-objective' film. Their animated films featured geometrical forms that moved and changed rhythmically, and their titles implied a parallel between abstract art and music. Between 1921 and 1925 Walther Ruttmann (1887–1941) made *Opus One* to *Opus Four*; Viking Eggeling made *Diagonal Symphony*; and Hans Richter made *Rhythmus 21* and *Rhythmus 23*. Richter and Oskar W. Fischinger were the first to build up long careers as experimental film makers. Fischinger continued to develop new methods of animation, from his abstract studies of the 1920s to his film *Motion Painting No. 1* (1947), which followed the development of an oil painting through thousands of images. Other films of the 1920s demonstrated the variety of ways in which live action could be transformed by an artist's framing, editing and processing. In *Ballet mécanique* (1924) Fernand Léger created an abstract vision of everyday objects. His collaborators were the American cameraman Dudley Murphy (*b* 1897) and the American composer Georges Antheil (1900–59). *Anemic Cinema* (1925) by Marcel Duchamp

was an important forerunner of structural or conceptual film making. Duchamp based the film on his experiments with 3-D and kinetic sculpture. Many artists' films have similarly grown out of installations or kinetic sculpture, for example *Light-play: Black and White and Grey* (*c.* 1930) by László Moholy-Nagy (*see* MOHOLY-NAGY, LÁSZLÓ, fig. 1). Man Ray created *Return to Reason* for a Dada event in 1923 (*see* DADA). The film was a vivid demonstration that the 'rayograph' method of making exposures directly on photographic paper without a camera could be applied to cinematography. Another notable Dada film was *Entr'-acte* (1924) by Francis Picabia and the French film maker René Clair (1898–1981) with the involvement of Ray, Duchamp and the composer Erik Satie. The Surrealists also took an intense interest in films, which they saw as closely related to dreams. The best-known Surrealist films included two made in 1928: *The Seashell and the Clergyman*, based by the French film maker Germaine Dulac (1882–1942) on a script by Antonin Artaud, and *Un Chien andalou* (see fig.) by the Spanish film maker Luis Buñuel (1900–82) and Salvador Dalí, which began with the slicing of a person's eye, one of the best-known of all film images. Buñuel and Dali's other film, *L'Age d'or* (1930), was confiscated by the police.

By the late 1920s there were enough 'cine poems' or examples of 'pure cinema' to justify the claim that film had become a fully independent art. In Europe the audience was expanded by cine clubs, film societies and art cinemas. In the 1930s, however, experimental film making declined as Fascist governments suppressed modernism. Also, the introduction of sound had considerably increased the cost of film making. Some artists were able to fund abstract films set to music by including a sponsor's message. Such 'prestige commercials' were greeted by cinema audiences with a mixture of delight and bewilderment. Both Fischinger and Len Lye used this genre to experiment with the artistic possibilities of colour. Lye created new styles of direct or cameraless animation as he painted and stencilled such films as *Colour Box* (1935) and *Swinging the Lambeth Walk* (1939). The fluid nature of animation lent itself particularly well to experiment, shown also by the work of the German Lotte Reiniger (1899–1981), the American Mary Ellen Bute (1906–83) and the Scot Norman McLaren (1914–87).

After World War II the USA became an important centre of experimental film making. One of the catalysts was the presence of Fischinger, Lye, Richter and other European artists. The Russian film maker Maya Deren (1917–61) and the Czech film maker Alexander Hammid (*b* 1907) created the poetic *Meshes of the Afternoon* in California in 1943. Deren applied her interest in modern dance and magic to five other dream-like films. Her genre of 'psychodrama' or 'personal film' was central to this first phase of the New American Cinema. Another powerful example was *Fireworks*, made in 1947 by Kenneth Anger (*b* 1930). Stan Brakhage (*b* 1933) made psychodramas in the 1950s but then concentrated on exploring new forms of perception 'unruled by man-made laws of perspective', as demonstrated by *The Art of Vision* (1961–5). This approach has been described as 'lyrical' or 'visionary', although it is difficult to categorize a body of work that includes more than 200 films. Brakhage experimented with material aspects of the medium (*Mothlight*, 1963) as well as new ways of seeing (*Text of Light*, 1974). In the late 1950s and early 1960s a strong 'underground film' movement developed in the USA, combining artistic experiment with cultural and political radicalism. Its connections with the Beat movement in literature were represented in *Pull my Daisy* (1959) by Robert Frank and Alfred Leslie (*b* 1927). *Flaming Creatures* (1962) by Jack Smith (1932–89) was one of many films that challenged sexual taboos. The underground had learnt a great deal from Dada and Surrealist films and from a few American precedents such as *Rose Hobart*, which Joseph Cornell started to work on in 1936, reducing a Hollywood feature film to a bizarre 13-minute short.

France had its own underground movement during the 1950s. *Un Chant d'amour*, made in 1950 by Jean Genet (1910–86), was an experiment in the representation of homosexuality as startling as Anger's *Fireworks*. The Lettrist movement challenged all aspects of established culture, provoking audiences with *The Film Has Already Started?* (1951), by Maurice Lemaître (*b* 1926) and *Howls in Favour of Sade* (1952) by Guy-Ernest Debord (*b* 1931). Lettrist work was introduced to the USA in 1962 by the Fluxus movement, which created its own 'anti-films' such

as Nam June Paik's imageless *Zen for Film*. In the 1960s Pop art and conceptual art formed close links with experimental film making. Andy Warhol created films of 'real time', in which a static camera was trained on a person (*Sleep*, 1963) or object (*Empire*, 1964). His production-line approach ignored the assumption that experimental films were personal in style and emotion. Emphasis shifted to the concept of the film and the activity of the viewer. Warhol was an important influence on the development of 'structural film', which became the leading tendency of the 1970s (see below). Other predecessors included two Austrians: Peter Kubelka (*b* 1934), who made films such as *Schwechater* (1958), in which a few images were put through complex variations; and Kurt Kren (*b* 1929), who shared Kubelka's interest in mathematical styles of editing, as in *Trees in Autumn* (1960).

Structural film, also known as 'formal' or 'materialist' film, was a broad range of work that questioned the physical nature of the medium and the arbitrariness of its codes of representation. American examples included *Film in which There Appear Edge Lettering, Dirt Particles, Sprocket Holes, etc.* (1965) by George Landow (*b* 1944) and *Tom, Tom, the Piper's Son* (1969) by Ken Jacobs (*b* 1933). Jacobs began with a ten-minute film from 1905, which he then fragmented and reworked for 90 minutes, revealing an astonishing wealth of detail before once again screening the original. Other American structural film makers included Ernie Gehr (*b* 1943), Hollis Frampton (*b* 1936) and Paul Sharits (*b* 1943). In Canada Joyce Wieland made *Sailboat* (1967), exploring subtle variations in the movement of boats across the screen. In the same year her husband Michael Snow completed *Wavelength*, a 45-minute camera zoom towards the far wall of a loft. This has remained the best known of all structural films, although Snow went on to such other extraordinary projects as *The Central Region* (1971), in which he programmed a camera to explore a landscape in ways that challenged normal perception. The structural-materialist film was developed in England by Malcolm Le Grice (*b* 1940) in films such as *Yes No Maybe Maybe Not* (1967) and *Little Dog for Roger* (1967–8), and by Peter Gidal (*b* 1946) in *Hall* (1968) and *Condition of Illusion* (1975). Other film makers included Annabel Nicholson (*b* 1946), who experimented with film loops and elements of live performance (e.g. *Precarious Vision*, 1973). Important work was also done in other countries, as illustrated by the multi-screen films (1971–3) and *Three Colour Separation Studies* (1976) by the Australian film makers Arthur Cantrill (*b* 1938) and Corinne Cantrill (*b* 1928).

Animation continued to be a strong area of experiment, with the American Robert Breer (*b* 1926) emerging as a major figure. His rapid juxtaposition of images and styles in *Recreation* (1956) and *Fist Fight* (1964) anticipated some of the concerns of structural films. In 1958 Len Lye summed up a lifetime of experiment in direct animation when he scratched the black-and-white patterns of *Free Radicals*, reducing the medium to its most basic and powerful elements. In the 1960s computers became an important area of research for animators such as the American brothers John Whitney (*b* 1917) and James Whitney (1921–82), who had been making abstract films since 1940. Their most important computer work included

Lapis (1966) by James Whitney and *Permutations* (1967) by John Whitney.

Experimental film making has often been energized by political ideas. In the 1970s, for example, there was a strong development of feminist film theory that encouraged a radical approach to the language of film. A variety of new forms emerged, as shown by British work such as *Riddles of the Sphinx* (1976) by Laura Mulvey (*b* 1941) and Peter Wollen (*b* 1938), *Light Reading* (1978) by Lis Rhodes (*b* 1942), *Thriller* (1979) by Sally Potter (*b* 1949), and *I Dish* (1982) by Jayne Parker (*b* 1957); or American work such as *Film about a Woman who . . .* (1974) by Yvonne Rainer (*b* 1934) and *Double Strength* (1978) by Barbara Hammer (*b* 1939). In general the 1980s was a more eclectic period than the 1970s, with film makers freely combining lyricism with structural concerns. Influential examples include the films of the Peruvian film maker Rose Lowder (*b* 1941), such as *Sunflowers* (1982) and *Impromptu* (1989), or those of the French film maker Yann Beauvais (*b* 1953), who explored visual deconstruction in *Untitled* (1984), verbal politics in *VO/ID* (1985) and complex diary form in *Divers épars* (1987). One tendency that continued to grow in strength was the interest in SEMIOTICS, shifting attention from material aspects of the medium to its use of signs. Many film makers returned to traditional genres and mainstream imagery to play subversively with them, in such films as *Mayhem* (1987) by the American film maker Abigail Child (*b* 1948) and *Cruises* (1989) by the French film maker Cécile Fontaine (*b* 1957).

See also VIDEO ART.

BIBLIOGRAPHY
B. Corra: 'Musica cromatica', *Il pastore, il gregge e la zampogna*, i (1912)
P. Adams Sitney, ed.: *Film Culture Reader* (New York, 1970)
U. Apollonio, ed.: *Futurismo* (Milan, 1970); Eng. trans. as *Futurist Manifestos* (New York, 1973)
D. Curtis: *Experimental Cinema* (London, 1971)
P. Adams Sitney: *Visionary Film* (New York, 1974)
——: *The Essential Cinema* (New York, 1975)
S. Dwoskin: *Film Is: The International Free Cinema* (Woodstock, 1975)
S. D. Lawder: *The Cubist Cinema* (New York, 1975)
P. Gidal, ed.: *Structural Film Anthology* (London, 1976)
R. Russett and C. Starr: *Experimental Animation* (New York, 1976, rev. 1988)
M. Le Grice: *Abstract Film and Beyond* (London, 1977)
Film as Film: Formal Experiment in Film, 1910–75 (exh. cat., ed. D. Curtis and R. Francis; London, Hayward Gal., 1979)
Trente ans de cinéma expérimental en France (1950–1980) (exh. cat., ed. D. Noguez; Paris, A.R.C.E.F., 1982)
The Elusive Sign: British Avant-garde Film and Video, 1977–1987 (exh. cat., ed. D. Curtis; ACGB, 1987)
R. E. Kuenzli: *Dada and Surrealist Film* (New York, 1987)
P. Gidal: *Materialist Film* (London, 1989)

ROGER HORROCKS

Expert, Roger-Henri (*b* Arcachon, 18 April 1882; *d* Château de Calvimont, commune of Cérons, 13 April 1955). French architect, urban planner and teacher. In 1906 he entered the Ecole Nationale des Beaux-Arts, Paris, initially under Gustave Umbdenstock and from 1909 with Odilon Redon. On leaving the school in 1912 he worked for André Granet, a fellow student and the nephew of Gustave Eiffel. He participated from 1912 to 1914 in drawing up the Cité Mondiale design, financed by the sculptor Hendrick Christian Andersen (*b* 1872), as part of a team directed by the architect Ernest Hébrard. He also submitted a plan (1919), with Léon Jaussely and Louis Soller, for the expansion of Paris, which won first prize. Expert's mature work was a distillation of disparate strands in French art between the wars, when he became regarded as an ambassador of French taste. Most importantly, he blended the logical and scientific undercurrent of the architecture of the period with a retrospective affinity for Hellenism. His use of tall, slender Doric columns, with neither base nor capital, in the Villa Tethys (1924), and Villa Kypris (1926), both at Arcachon, and the French Legation (1928–33) in Belgrade illustrate his particularly 20th-century neo-classicism.

Expert's well publicized projects of the 1930s included luminous fountains at the Exposition Coloniale of 1931 in Paris, the design, with Richard Bouwens van de Boijen (*b* 1863), of the promenade deck (1932–5) of the *SS Normandie*, which was intended as a travelling exhibition of contemporary French art, and the French pavilion at the World's Fair of 1939, New York. The academic complex (1931–4) on the Rue Kuss, Paris, echoed the steamship aesthetic in its superimposition of stepped volumes, gangways and masts, and led him to be associated with the International Style. He collaborated in most of his projects with painters and sculptors, notably the group of neo-classicist architects active in Bordeaux from the 1930s to the 1960s: Alfred Janniot (1889–1965), Jean Dunand, Paul Landowski (1875–1961), Jean Dupas (1882–1964) and especially the sculptor Carlo Sarrabezolles (1881–1971). After World War II he designed several projects (unexecuted) for the reconstruction of parts of the old port of Marseille. He taught at the Ecole des Beaux-Arts, Paris, from 1919 to 1953.

BIBLIOGRAPHY
M. Culot and others: *Roger-Henri Expert, 1882–1955* (Paris, 1983)

MAURICE CULOT

Exposition universelle. *See* INTERNATIONAL EXHIBITION.

Expression. Etymologically, the term can be traced back to Latin roots meaning to press or to press out. Today 'expression' indicates the outward manifestation in behaviour of an inward state of mind. People are said to express a variety of psychological states—feelings, moods, attitudes and emotions—as well as more discursive states—beliefs, ideas, credos and convictions. Objects and artefacts are also deemed expressive, among them works of art. When we say paintings express anger, we sometimes put this by saying they are angry.

The paradigm case of expression is that of a person expressing an emotion. Emotions can be expressed verbally; they are also revealed in behaviour. They are marked by various involuntary changes as well as by a variety of gestures and responses that may vary from culture to culture and that are to some extent under our conscious control. Clearly the expressiveness of works of art (and of other inanimate objects) is not literal. No painting has beliefs or feelings to express, or behaviour in which to express them. Our ascriptions of expressiveness to such objects must then be understood in some extended way: as tied to the expressiveness of those who produced the objects, those who regard them or those who are represented in them, or as marking some correspondence between the object and human expressive behaviour.

1. Western. 2. Chinese.

1. WESTERN.

(i) Expression as representation. (ii) Expression as arousal. (iii) Expression as clarification. (iv) Expression as a property of the work. (v) Later accounts of expression.

(i) Expression as representation. One way in which works of art become expressive is by showing humans in the throes of emotion. In such cases, the predominant feeling or emotion portrayed often comes to characterize the overall work as well. A painting of sad people is, more often than not, a sad painting. This sort of expressiveness, achieved through the *representation* of expression and therefore limited to representational, indeed to figurative, art, was considered a desideratum of painting from the time of the very first aesthetic treatises.

In *Della pittura* (1435–6), LEON BATTISTA ALBERTI identified the history painting or *istoria* as the painter's greatest work. Such paintings, which take their themes from Classical literature, gain emotional power by representing a number of people reacting to the central event portrayed. Alberti wrote that 'the *istoria* will move the soul of the beholder when each man painted there clearly shows the movement of his own soul ... we weep with the weeping, laugh with the laughing, and grieve with the grieving. These movements of the soul are made known by movements of the body' (trans., p. 77).

Leonardo da Vinci's treatise on painting has not survived, but Leonardo too emphasized the importance of expression. In a famous remark he derided any painting without expression as 'twice dead', and he advised artists to study dumb and mute people, since they are likely to emphasize and exaggerate expressive gestures. Later Italian artistic treatises (e.g. that of Giovanni Paolo Lomozzo (1538–1600): *Trattato dell'arte della pittura, scoltura, et architettura*, Milan, 1585) continued this emphasis on the representation of emotion. The interest of artists in representing human emotion reached a zenith, however, in 17th-century France. CHARLES LE BRUN devised an

elaborate system for painting the passions, pairing each passion with a unique facial expression (see fig.). He based these correspondences, which he presented in lectures in 1668, on a physiological theory outlined by the philosopher René Descartes in *Les Passions de l'âme* (Paris, 1649). Le Brun's theory was very popular in its time; a version of it is defended in André Félibien's *Entretiens* (1666–8). Above all, the theory helped to elevate the status of painting, which had hitherto been considered a mechanical art.

(ii) Expression as arousal. Another body of theory has connected art with emotion in two respects, through its capacity to arouse emotion and through its capacity for catharsis. Both views derive from the practice of Romanticism, which valued individual feeling, freedom and responsiveness as opposed to Classicism's emphasis on shared forms and canons. LEV TOLSTOY construed expression as arousal in *Chto takoye iskusstvo?* ('What is art?'; 1898). He believed that art exists only when an artist knowingly communicates an emotion to his audience in such a way that it ends up experiencing that very same emotion, and he often spoke of becoming *infected* with another's emotion in this situation. Tolstoy placed certain restrictions on this basic model, stipulating, for instance, that the emotion transmitted must be one connected with the religious perception of the time. Serious problems arise with this theory, however, when we ask whether the artist must actually feel the emotion as he expresses it in his work of art. Must the emotion be sustained if the work takes several months to complete? And what sense can we make of the artist and audience experiencing the *same* emotion? If Leonardo felt love for the mysterious woman he painted as the '*Mona Lisa*' (*see* DRESS, fig. 22), must we feel love as well, and if so must it be love for that very woman? Despite these difficulties, Tolstoy's theory is valuable in many respects. It makes us think deeply about the relation between artist and audience, and it places a welcome insistence on the accessibility of art.

(iii) Expression as clarification. Two theorists writing after Tolstoy dispensed with the arousal aspect of his triadic theory—artist, work of art, audience—and concentrated instead on the relation between the artist and his work. BENEDETTO CROCE, in *Estetica* (1902), and R. G. Collingwood (*see* COLLINGWOOD, (2)), in *The Principles of Art* (1938), construed art not as a conduit between artist and audience but as a means for the artist to clarify his or her own emotional state. Collingwood wrote: 'Until a man has expressed his emotion, he does not yet know what emotion it is'. The artist is conscious first only of a perturbation, which is clarified and individualized in the course of being expressed. Art is thus a form of knowledge. But Croce stressed that the work of art need not exist as a physical object. It is complete once it is expressed as a sensuous intuition in the artist's imagination. In relocating works of art from the physical world to the artist's head, this theory does violence to our everyday conceptual scheme. It also clashes with our notions of artistic creativity.

Two American philosophers developed distinctive accounts of expression that resemble the Croce-Collingwood view in certain respects. In his early work *The Sense*

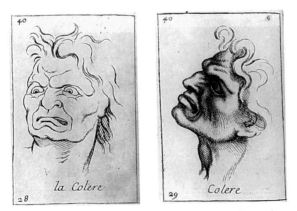

Charles Le Brun: *Anger*, frontal (left) and profile (right) versions after a painting by the author; engravings from *Conférence . . . sur l'expression générale et particulière* (Amsterdam and Paris, 1698), pl. XCI

of Beauty (1896), GEORGE SANTAYANA defined beauty as pleasure objectified: 'Beauty is pleasure regarded as the quality of a thing' (p. 31). He identified expression as one of three varieties of beauty (the other two are matter and form) and analyzed it in terms of association. An expressive object is one that suggests another and thereby acquires that object's emotional character. Thus for Santayana expression is pleasure doubly distanced. It involves emotions that we feel, attribute to one object and then associate with another. If our attention passes entirely to the suggested object, expression has not occurred, but if feelings associated with that object cloak the first object like a sort of halo, then the result is expressive and has aesthetic value.

The account of expression by JOHN DEWEY in *Art as Experience* (1934) resembles that of Santayana in its emphasis on a fusion of past and present experience. For Dewey, expression requires 'meanings and values extracted from prior experiences and funded in such a way that they fuse with the qualities directly presented in the work of art' (p. 98). Dewey's description of expression as the clarification of turbid emotion recalls Croce's position, but this is leavened by the emphasis Dewey placed on the interaction between organism and environment. Dewey insisted that emotional discharge is necessary but not sufficient for expression. Expression and art occur only when material is employed as medium. An expressive object, then, clarifies and reorganizes experience for both creator and beholder.

(iv) Expression as a property of the work. A number of theorists have proposed accounts of expression that emphasize neither audience arousal nor creative catharsis. Rather, they analyse the expressiveness of works of art in terms of the actual features of those works themselves. Two American aestheticians who pursued this line are O. K. Bouwsma (*b* 1898) and Monroe Beardsley (*b* 1915). In 'The Expression Theory of Art' (1954), Bouwsma maintained that the statement 'The music is sad' is to be assimilated to the statement 'The apple is red', not to the statement 'Carrie is sad'. Bouwsma also claimed that 'the sadness is to the music rather like the redness to the apple than it is like the burp to the cider'. Yet his paper does not do much to flesh out these claims. Beardsley, in *Aesthetics* (1958), analysed matters a little more fully, claiming that the term 'express' applies to human regional qualities of works of art.

An intransigent metaphor remains at the heart of Beardsley's theory. The claim that a human regional quality applies to an inanimate object is as much in need of clarification as the claim that such objects express feelings and emotions. One philosopher who tried to explain exactly how objects acquire expressive power is Susanne Langer. In a series of books published in the 1940s and 1950s (*Philosophy in a New Key* (1942), *Feeling and Form* (1953), *Problems of Art* (1957)) Langer developed a theory of expression, first for the art of music, then extended to all the arts. Briefly, Langer claimed objects become expressive when they acquire forms congruent with the feelings and behaviours that express human emotion: 'Artistic form is congruent with the dynamic forms of our direct sensuous, mental, and emotional life' (*Problems of Art*, p. 25). Speaking of music, Langer noted various affinities with the forms of human feeling: 'forms of growth and of attenuation, flowing and stowing, conflict and resolution, speed, arrest, terrific excitement, calm, or subtle activation and dreamy lapses' (*Feeling and Form*, p. 27). Such patterns transfer to the other arts as well. For Langer, artistic expression is not symptomatic. That is, works of art need not express emotions actually felt by the artist at the time of creation or at some previous time. Nor need such works arouse any emotions in their viewers.

(v) Later accounts of expression. From the 1960s on, a number of aestheticians put forward theories of expression that do not fit neatly into any of the categories adduced above. The art historian Ernst Gombrich developed an account of expression in *Art and Illusion* (1960) and subsequent essays, particularly those collected in *Meditations on a Hobby Horse* (1963). Gombrich challenged those who defend a 'natural resonance' theory, according to which, colours, shapes, sounds and so on are inherently charged with feeling tones and thus serve as the currency of artistic expression. Indeed for artists to communicate feeling and emotion all they have to do is to select appropriately charged constituents and incorporate them into their work. Against this theory Gombrich argued persuasively that, although there is striking agreement about some of these natural equivalences, if we are to grasp the expressive value of a work of art, we have to interpret the choices that the artist has made. A given pairing has significance only against the background of the alternatives that the artist allows himself. That is, the meaning of a given colour, shape, texture, etc. depends largely upon that part of the scale which the artist had adopted as his repertory and from which it was selected.

In *Languages of Art* (1968), Nelson Goodman (*b* 1906) defined expression as metaphorical exemplification. For Goodman traits are exemplified when they are both possessed and referred to. Thus a tailor's swatch exemplifies the colour, pattern and texture of the fabric it displays but not the fabric size or shape. Metaphorical exemplification involves perspicuous properties that are possessed not literally but metaphorically: the grief of a poem, the hopefulness of a symphony's second theme. Thus Goodman's account of expression rests on his theory of metaphor. Goodman insisted that metaphorical possession, though not literal, is indeed actual (p. 68), and he held that metaphorical statements can be true, though not literally true; it follows that, for example, sad pictures really are sad. Goodman's theory applies to the synaesthetic transfers that engaged Gombrich—sad music, cold colours, angry lines—but Goodman would classify these as frozen metaphors (p. 68). He held that metaphors can be effective or ineffective, and that successful metaphors are those that convey new and notable insights. Yet Goodman did not discuss whether entirely fresh metaphors are forged by particular paintings. He did insist that the properties a work of art expresses are its *own* properties. They have no connection with the artist's emotions or ideas, nor with those of the viewer, nor with those of the persons, if any, depicted in the work.

In *The Transfiguration of the Commonplace* (1981), Arthur Danto (*b* 1924) took up Goodman's claims about expression and metaphor. Danto offered certain narrow criticisms of Goodman's theory of expression, then adapted its larger outlines to his own purposes. Danto noted that metaphorical and literal exemplification are not mutually exclusive, and he contended that Goodman, like other theorists before him, construed expression too narrowly, taking into account only the psychological. Danto traced the expression of individual properties—of power, sadness, verticality and so on—not to the content of a work but to the *way* that content is represented. This is neither a psychological nor a causal matter. We can recognize expressive properties in art without necessarily knowing anything about the artist. Rather, artistic expression arises from the 'gap' between the actual painting and an illusionistic ideal (a 'transparent' representation of that same content). Danto concluded *The Transfiguration of the Commonplace* with speculation about a broader sort of expression, according to which every work of art expresses a way of seeing the world. Danto here treated the notions of style, metaphor and expression as intertwined.

Two theorists offered accounts of expression that emphasize the artist's role. In *Mind and Art* (1972), Guy Sircello (*d* 1992) pointed out that some anthropomorphic properties belong to works of art in virtue of what those works represent, describe, depict or portray (p. 24). Sircello introduced the notion of artistic acts to account for such cases, claiming that, for example, the *Rape of the Sabine Women* is aloof and detached in part because Poussin *observes* and *paints* in an aloof and detached way. Sircello also invoked artistic acts to explain how works of art can express subjective factors or forms of sensitivity (p. 54) such as the love of nature in Cretan painting and the sense of power and mass in Roman architecture. Artistic acts are truly acts of the artists in question, they are things that artists *do*, but they have the peculiarity that they 'are not identifiable or describable independently of the works "in" which they are done' (p. 29). Overall, Sircello maintained that anthropomorphic properties apply to works of art not on the model of an object and its qualities but rather on that of a face and its expressions. However, since Sircello acknowledged various circumstances in which one can exhibit, say, an angry scowl yet not be angry, his use of the facial expression model does not reduce his enterprise to one of 'artist biography'.

In *Painting as an Art* (1987) Richard Wollheim (*b* 1923) went against prevailing fashion and defended a psychological account of the art of painting. Wollheim traced a painting's meaning or content to the fulfilled intentions of the artist who paints that painting. The artist intends to produce certain experiences in his audience, and his intentions are fulfilled if those spectators who are sufficiently sensitive and informed have the requisite experiences *in looking at* the painting. Wollheim grounded artistic expression, both logically and historically, in our prior capacity for expressive perception. This is a species of seeing in which emotions flow from us to what is perceived but do so in a manner that is responsive to features of the perceived scene (pp. 82–3). Expressive perception gives rise to expression proper when standards of correctness are imposed on individual projections. These standards are given by the artist's fulfilled intentions. Though Wollheim's account of expression is a causal one, the final upshot of his theory depends upon how the standards of correctness are specified. If it is conceded that some of the factors highlighted by other theorists—convention, congruence, resemblance, natural resonance, the artist's repertory and so on—play a role in determining just what painted passages can express what feelings and emotions, then Wollheim's would not be a purely psychological account of artistic expression, and expressive perception would be, by the time expressive art draws upon it, no longer a form of seeing in any straightforward sense.

BIBLIOGRAPHY

L. B. Alberti: *Della pittura* (1435–6); Eng. trans. by J. R. Spencer as *On Painting* (New Haven, 1956)
C. Le Brun: *Conférence sur l'expression générale et particulière* (Amsterdam and Paris, 1698)
G. Santayana: *The Sense of Beauty* (New York, 1896)
L. Tolstoy: *Chto takoye iskusstvo?* [What is art?] (Moscow, 1898; Eng. trans. by A. Maude, Oxford, 1930)
B. Croce: *Estetica come scienza dell'espressione e linguistica generale* (Palermo, 1902, rev. Bari, 3/1909; Eng. trans. by D. Ainslie, London, 1922)
J. Dewey: *Art as Experience* (New York, 1934)
R. G. Collingwood: *The Principles of Art* (Oxford, 1938)
S. Langer: *Philosophy in a New Key* (Cambridge, MA, 1942)
——: *Feeling and Form* (New York, 1953)
O. K. Bouwsma: 'The Expression Theory of Art', *Aesthetics and Language*, ed. W. Elton (New York, 1954), pp. 73–99
S. Langer: *Problems of Art* (London, 1957)
M. Beardsley: *Aesthetics: Problems in the Philosophy of Criticism* (New York, 1958, 2/Indianapolis, 1981)
E. Gombrich: *Art and Illusion* (Princeton, 1960)
——: *Meditations on a Hobby Horse* (London and New York, 1963)
N. Goodman: *Languages of Art* (Indianapolis, 1968)
G. Sircello: *Mind and Art: An Essay on the Varieties of Expression* (Princeton, 1972)
R. Wollheim: *Art and its Objects* (Cambridge, 1980)
A. Danto: *The Transfiguration of the Commonplace* (Cambridge, MA, 1981)
R. Wollheim: *Painting as an Art* (Princeton, 1987)

STEPHANIE ROSS

2. CHINESE. Chinese pictorial art can be divided into two broad categories: *gongbi* ('detailed manner') and *xieyi* ('sketching the idea', freehand) paintings. The former is a decorative and strongly illustrative style, which normally does not claim to express the thoughts and feelings of the artist. In contrast, the aim of *xieyi* painting is not to create a precise pictorial representation, but rather to give an image of the 'ultimate truth' or 'soul' of the subject or theme, and so portray what cannot be expressed in words. *Xie* means writing or committing to paper, and it is determined by calligraphic rules; *yi* means sense as well as expression and refers to the 'soul' of that which is depicted and the painter's understanding of the cosmic forces, as well as the literary quality of a painting. *Xieyi* is a central tenet of literati painting (*see* CHINA, §V, 4(ii)) and informs the work of scholar–officials such as SU SHI, Mi Fu (*see* MI, (1)) and LI GONGLIN, who set themselves apart from the detailed painting manner of professional and court artists such as LI CHENG, FAN KUAN and GUO XI.

The painters who were most successful at mastering *xieyi* were described in the following terms by the painter and art critic JING HAO in his *Bifa ji* ('Notes on brush method'; *c.* AD 925): 'A divine (*shen*) painter penetrates and grasps the nature of all phenomena between heaven and earth in his mind and so there is harmony between that which flows from his brush and the object he is depicting. On this level heavenly inspiration is very strong and thoughts are in harmony with the spirit.' According to the *Shitao* ('Record on talks about paintings') by Yuan Qi (*c.* 1642–1718), perfection is achieved when one produces 'beyond all rules, effortlessly obeying the rules, the relationship between the artistic creation and the mystic unity with the *Dao* ['way']'. But the painter could not achieve this highest freedom of unconstrained creativity until he had completely mastered the rules of painting. Only then would art critics and educated viewers be ready to accept a painter's emotional outpourings.

Naturally, there have been painters throughout Chinese history who, because of their strong personalities and their consciously non-conformist artistic struggle, cannot be measured by these very rigid criteria. The critics called these artists *guai* ('mad', 'funny', 'peculiar') and placed them at the bottom of the hierarchy. It appears paradoxical that, unlike any other art form, Chinese painting is determined by precise rules concerning aspects ranging from the smallest dot in the painting, through brush-strokes, to the finished work, and that almost all element of chance is excluded. Before an art critic or viewer would assess the value of a painter's expression, he made sure that several criteria were met, the most important of which was the brushwork or painting technique. Such a painting must have *qi* ('spirit'), a concept that illuminates the meaning of expression. In the *Gu huapin lu* ('Classification of painters'), the critic Xie He (*fl c.* AD 500–35) established a set of painting rules, the Six Laws, including *qiyun shengdong* ('spirit resonance, vital movement/producing movement') (*see* CHINA, §V, 5). Alongside the notion of *qi* are two other principles that play a role in painting: *li*, the highest metaphysical principle in Neo-Confucianism, and the Daoist concept of *ziran* ('nature').

BIBLIOGRAPHY
O. Sirén: *The Chinese on the Art of Painting* (Beijing, 1936)
Wen Fong: 'Ch'i-yün sheng-tung: Vitality, Harmonious Manner and Aliveness', *Orient. A.*, n. s., xii (1966), pp. 159–64
S. Bush: *The Chinese Literati on Painting: Su Shih (1037–1101) to Tung Ch'i-ch'ang (1555–1636)* (Cambridge, MA, 1971)
E. Coleman: *Philosophy of Painting by Shih-tao* (The Hague, 1978)
FRIEDRICH ZETTL

Expressionism. International movement in art and architecture, which flourished between *c.* 1905 and *c.* 1920, especially in Germany. It also extended to literature, music, dance and theatre. The term was originally applied more widely to various avant-garde movements: for example it was adopted as an alternative to the use of 'Post-Impressionism' by Roger Fry in exhibitions in London in 1910 and 1912. It was also used contemporaneously in Scandinavia and Germany, being gradually confined to the specific groups of artists and architects to which it is now applied.

1. Painting, graphic arts and sculpture. 2. Architecture.

1. PAINTING, GRAPHIC ARTS AND SCULPTURE. Expressionism in the fine arts developed from the Symbolist and expressive trends in European art at the end of the 19th century. The period of 'classical Expressionism' began in 1905, with the foundation of the group DIE BRÜCKE, and ended *c.* 1920. Although in part an artistic reaction both to academic art and to Impressionism, the movement should be understood as a form of 'new Humanism', which sought to communicate man's spiritual life. It reflected the deep intellectual unrest *c.* 1900, reflected in contemporary literary sources, about the destruction of the traditional relationship of trust between man and the world. This was set against 19th-century notions of reality. Art took on a new and crucially different role, no longer being used, as previously, to reproduce that which was visible, but rather to 'make things visible' (Paul Klee). The motivating forces or 'inner communication' were considered to be the only concepts worth portraying. A young generation of artists believed that the traditional artistic medium was inadequate to enable them to do this. In order to communicate the human spiritual condition the Expressionists made use of new, strong, assertive forms, often violently distorted, symbolic colours and suggestive lines. Their work also showed an interest in Primitivism (*see* PRIMITIVISM, §2).

(i) Origins and developments in Germany. (ii) International developments and legacy of Expressionism.

(i) Origins and developments in Germany.

(a) Origins. (b) Artists' groups. (c) Printmaking. (d) Sculpture.

(a) Origins. The roots of Expressionism lay in international developments of the late 19th century, although the German Expressionists always emphasized their independence from every foreign influence. Crucial impulses came, for example, from Norway, the Netherlands and Belgium, countries that had, like Germany, an old tradition of expressive art. Gauguin and the Nabis as well as the Swiss artist Ferdinand Hodler, were also involved with its pioneering ideals. In Germany before 1900 such local schools as those at the artists' colonies of Dachau or Worpswede developed intensely expressive landscape painting, in which stylized depictions of nature represented overpowering emotional experiences, as in German Romantic painting. These lyrical images of nature, linked to similar ideas in *plein-air* painting and *Jugendstil*, significantly influenced Expressionism. Another important influence during the first phase of Expressionism was the use of pure colours developed in Neo-Impressionism and Fauvism.

The work of Vincent van Gogh, Edvard Munch and James Ensor was still more important. These artists inspired a feeling of spiritual kinship in others and promoted several ideas, which were as yet unclear, about an art that could express spiritual dimensions. This potential was exemplified by van Gogh, in both his tragic life and work, characterized by an intensely expressive use of pure colours, and dynamic brushstrokes and outlines. Munch's work transformed people and landscapes into images representing dramatic tensions arising from areas of the psyche that had hitherto been taboo. The expressive strength of the symbolic colours and lines developed traditional motifs into images of the artist's psychological world. The tormented, hallucinatory view of the world of masks and phantoms painted by Ensor was equally characteristic of the Expressionists' sense of alienation. Expressionism developed in Germany not as a 'style', but rather as an 'ideology' formed by a sense of spiritual unity, although with no theoretically defined goal. It arose simultaneously in many places in Germany and was not confined to one generation: even such an established artist as Lovis Corinth responded to its impulses.

(b) Artists' groups. One of the early Expressionist centres was in northern Germany, the home of such painters as EMIL NOLDE, CHRISTIAN ROHLFS and PAULA MODERSOHN-BECKER, and of the sculptor Ernst Barlach. Their intuitive, untrained art was inspired by an awareness of the close link between man and nature, and eschewed both literary and classical influences. A second, stronger impulse came from central Germany. Here the artistic revolution after 1900 was a conscious, more intellectual process. Its focal-point was Die Brücke, founded in Dresden with the aim of 'attracting all the elements of revolution and unrest'. The founder-members were ERICH HECKEL, ERNST LUDWIG KIRCHNER, KARL SCHMIDT-ROTTLUFF and Fritz Bleyl (1880–1966), who were later joined by others, including MAX PECHSTEIN, Cuno Amiet, KEES VAN DONGEN, OTTO MUELLER and (briefly) Nolde. They were interested in the work of such artists as the French Neo-Impressionists, van Gogh and Munch. Like other Expressionists, their rejection of traditional Western aesthetic values led to an interest in non-European art, in particular from Africa and the Pacific islands, where both Nolde and Pechstein travelled. They also turned to the literature of Scandinavia (e.g. Henrik Ibsen and August Strindberg) and Russia (e.g. Fyodor Dostoyevsky) as sources of inspiration. They were passionate graphic artists, like the northern Germans.

Die Brücke was the essential catalyst for German Expressionism. It reached its artistic climax after its members moved between 1910 and 1914 to Berlin. There they drew on contemporary themes, depicting the bright and dark sides of city life: people living under psychological pressure or with an eroticism that often had morbid overtones, as well as scenes from the circus and music-halls. All their themes expressed the human condition under extreme stress prior to the outbreak of World War I. Such psychologically intense subjects demanded a painting of extraordinary communicative force. The Berlin works document the mature Expressionism of Die Brücke at its most intense. Even after the group's dissolution in 1913, Kirchner continued to produce some of the most powerful Expressionist paintings, for example the self-portrait *The Drinker* (1915; Nuremberg, Ger. Nmus.; see fig. 1).

The artists of Die Brücke exemplified certain qualities that came to characterize Expressionism as a whole. Henceforth, the extent of an artist's heightened emotional involvement was seen as an important element in determining the status and quality of the work of art. The role of the artist in society was also altered. Expressionist artists considered themselves to be both provocative and esoteric. They not only demanded publicity, asking others to join together under the revolutionary banner, but also espoused elitist principles, as expressed in the quotation *'odi profanum vulgus'* used by Kirchner in *Chronik der Künstlergemeinschaft Brücke* (Berlin, 1913). This double role formed part of the Expressionist artist's image as a 'wild' person, a destroyer of traditional values. In future the public became

1. Ernst Ludwig Kirchner: *The Drinker*, oil on canvas, 1195×905 mm, 1915 (Nuremberg, Germanisches Nationalmuseum)

used to seeing the artist no longer as a sacred guardian of traditions but rather as a prophet, who ruthlessly broke social conventions.

Although Die Brücke was widely influential, the Expressionism of southern Germany diverged from the exalted form of personal expression prevalent among the artists in northern and central Germany. For the BLAUE REITER group in Munich, imagination was the source of inspiration in a pantheistic world-view: the group's members expressed a new poetry about nature and an urge towards mystical spiritualization, which included a strong eastern European element, as interpreted by the Russian artists, VASILY KANDINSKY and ALEXEI JAWLENSKY. The painters in Munich aimed to create an image that would portray the 'mystic inner construction' of the world, a notion that FRANZ MARC developed. This spirituality became the basis for a move towards complete abstraction, completed by Kandinsky in 1910. There was also a strong French influence in Munich, particularly from Robert Delaunay and the Fauves, which brought with it an openness towards foreign influences. This was in contrast to north German Expressionism, which was introverted by nature and tended to concentrate on its own problems. Both tendencies were, however, linked by the sense of a need to find the point where the outer and inner worlds met—their common inheritance from German Romanticism. This was, however, achieved pictorially in different ways. The northern artists concentrated on elementary, pictorial qualities that were expressive, rather than aesthetic, for example strong colours without much tonal subtlety. The Blaue Reiter painters developed a luminous, sensitive palette, rich in different tonal values, analogous to music, which was an aspect that greatly interested Kandinsky.

Western German Expressionism comprised the 'Rheinische Expressionisten' (AUGUST MACKE, Walter Ophey (1882–1930), HEINRICH CAMPENDONK and others) and the 'Westfälische Expressionisten' (Eberhard Viegener (*b* 1890), Wilhelm Morgner, and Heinrich Nauen). Unlike the close association of Die Brücke, these were loose alliances of artists with fundamentally different characters and temperaments, who came together for various lengths of time. Expressionism was also promoted in Berlin by HERWARTH WALDEN's periodical *Der Sturm* (founded 1910), and by his Sturm-Galerie (founded 1912). These played an important role in furthering the Expressionist cause, as well as the whole of the modern art movement in Berlin. The group Die Pathetiker (founded 1912 by Ludwig Meidner, Jacob Steinhardt and Richard Janthur (*b* 1883)) also worked there, as did Otto Dix, George Grosz and Max Beckmann periodically: the latter three artists all experimented with Expressionism, before developing more realistic styles. The Austrian artist EGON SCHIELE also exhibited in Berlin in 1916.

(c) Printmaking. The image of northern and central German Expressionism was determined not only by painting but also by graphic art, in particular woodcuts. This technique was used by such precursors of Expressionism as Munch and Gauguin, and culminated in the printed graphic work of the painters of Die Brücke, and Rohlfs and Nolde (e.g. *The Prophet*, 1912; Seebüll, Stift. Nolde; see fig. 2). No other medium was as well suited as the woodcut to evoking strong emotional tensions by contrasting black-and-white planes or two basic colours, or to making such expressive use of its rudimentary roughness, without any pictorial illusion of bodies, shadows or space. Like Gothic woodcutters, they both designed and cut the blocks, even printing the copies themselves. Like Munch, they preferred the texture of blocks cut along the grain. The resistance of the brittle material was exploited for its expressive potential. Some of the best Expressionist woodcuts were produced during the Berlin years of Die Brücke. The urban themes of people, cityscapes, the circus and variety-hall, as well as the hectic and abnormal life-style of the city, are closely linked with the paintings of that era. Around 1910 their painting was influenced by the printmaking: the colours crowded on to the surface and were heavily outlined in black, as on woodcuts.

Despite the dominance of woodcuts, etching and lithography also played a vital role in Expressionism. Lithography could be quite graphic or painterly in its effect. It was made by applying brush, pen or chalk on to stone and printed in black-and-white or colour. This technique was already fully developed in the work of Die Brücke by 1907. Lithography was also important in the work of the sculptor Barlach, and in that of the Austrian OSKAR KOKOSCHKA, who became known in Berlin through his lithographs. Some of the numerous colour prints of the period resemble watercolour, which was also one of the Expressionists' favourite techniques and exceptionally successful in the hands of Nolde and Rohlfs.

2. Emile Nolde: *Prophet*, woodcut, 346×267 mm, 1912 (Seebüll, Stiftung Ada-und Emil Nolde)

Nolde was one of the greatest Expressionist masters of etching. Other significant practitioners included Heckel and Kirchner, and later Beckmann, who were also particularly interested in drypoint. However, the paramount importance of Nolde started at the latest from the time of the famous *Hamburg Harbour* series (1910). His skilful pictorial compositions are among the most important achievements in 20th-century European graphic art.

(d) Sculpture. The success of Expressionist sculpture was achieved by a few important sculptors, above all ERNST BARLACH, WILHELM LEHMBRUCK and Bernhard Hoetger, who was also an architect. Their portraits penetrated, with striking depth, into the sitter's state of mind, as this was considered more important than any superficial similarity. They also took as themes extreme psychological states and human situations, including works inspired by experience of World War I (e.g. *The Avenger*, 1914; for illustration *see* BARLACH, ERNST). The artists' spirituality also led to religious imagery, which extended to represent general truths. The forms and expressive purpose of the sculpture are sometimes reminiscent of German Gothic art. Apart from the works of Barlach and Lehmbruck, Expressionist sculpture did not gain the international level of recognition of the painting and graphic work of this period.

Significant sculpture was also made by artists who otherwise practised painting and graphic arts, particularly the members of Die Brücke and their circle: for example,

Kirchner was inspired to produce large sculptures after his meeting with Hermann Scherer in 1923. Such work was not known until relatively late and was seldom shown during their lifetimes. The favourite material was wood (also preferred by Barlach), since this was cheaper and easier to work than bronze. The Die Brücke artists' interest in sculptures from Africa and the Pacific islands, which they had seen in the collections of the Völkerkundemuseum in Dresden, clearly inspired their own sculpture in its formal aspects. Their works, which were almost exclusively figurative, adapted, rather than copied the non-European art, in order to intensify the power of their own designs; they were later often painted. The sculptures can also often be found as motifs in the artists' paintings.

(ii) International developments and legacy of Expressionism.
Although Expressionism particularly flourished in Germany, significant developments occurred in other European countries. The principal Austrian Expressionists were Schiele and Kokoschka, both of whom had been influenced by *Jugendstil* and especially Gustav Klimt. Kokoschka produced powerful Expressionist portraits, including some drawn for *Der Sturm*. Other important work was done before 1908 by Richard Gerstl, who was influenced by Arnold Schoenberg. Outside German-speaking countries, some Expressionist art was produced in Scandinavia (e.g. by Henrik Sørensen in Norway). However, the most important other group was based in the artists' colony of LAETHEM-SAINT-MARTIN in Belgium, which from 1905 developed an Expressionism dominated by rural and religious themes. Albert Servaes created a vigorous style characterized by schematic forms and sombre colours, which also informed the work of CONSTANT PERMEKE, GUSTAVE DE SMET and FRITS VAN DEN BERGHE. French art was dominated by other trends, although individual painters produced some work that showed Expressionist influences, for example that of André Dunoyer de Segonzac before World War I. GEORGES ROUAULT combined Expressionism with more traditional drawing techniques. Although such artists as Marcel Gromaire rejected the Expressionist label, their art betrayed an obvious debt: for example, work by Gromaire after World War I was heavily influenced by Flemish and (to a lesser extent) German Expressionism. The painting of CHAÏM SOUTINE was also highly expressionistic, characterized by violent brushwork. Among sculptors active in Paris, the work of Alexander Archipenko and Ossip Zadkine also showed Expressionist influences.

The legacy of Expressionism was widespread. In Germany the period of 'Sturm und Drang' ended *c.* 1920, although a younger generation, formed by the disorders of the period of World War I, were vociferous for a long time in their support of certain Expressionist positions: in particular, the Expressionists' social criticism inspired NEUE SACHLICHKEIT. It can be argued that all later stylistic tendencies in German art have in some way been involved with Expressionism, even if only by clearly defining themselves in contrast to its formal and ideological arguments. Internationally the innovations of the Blaue Reiter undoubtedly influenced the development of later expressive abstraction. A more direct link between later movements and Expressionism was evident from *c.* 1980 in the figurative work of artists sometimes termed neo-Expressionists. These included the German Georg Baselitz and the so-called 'Neue Wilden', and the American Julian Schnabel and the *Nieuwe Beelding* movement.

BIBLIOGRAPHY

H. Bahr: *Expressionismus* (Munich, 1920)
P. Fechter: *Der Expressionismus* (Munich, 1920)
G. Hartlaub: *Die Graphik des Expressionismus in Deutschland* (Stuttgart, 1947)
V. Apollonio: *'Die Brücke' e la cultura dell'Espressionismo* (Venice, 1952)
L.-G. Buchheim: *Die Künstlergemeinschaft Brücke* (Feldafing, 1956)
H. Neumayr: *Expressionismus* (Vienna, 1956)
B. S. Myers: *Die Malerei des Expressionismus* (Cologne, 1957)
P. Selz: *German Expressionist Painting* (Berkeley, CA, and Los Angeles, 1957)
L.-G. Buchheim: *Graphik des Expressionismus* (Feldafing, 1959)
J. Willet: *Expressionism* (London, 1970)
E. Langri: *Expressionism in Belgium* (Brussels, 1971)
E. Roters: *Europäischer Expressionismus* (Gütersloh, 1971)
W.-D. Dube: *Die Expressionisten* (Frankfurt am Main and Vienna, 1973)
P. Vogt: *Expressionismus* (Cologne, 1978; Eng. trans., New York, 1980)
R. Brinkmann: *Expressionismus* (Stuttgart, 1980)
L'Identité flamande dans la peinture moderne (exh. cat. by L. M. A. Schoonbaert and K. Peereboom, Tampa, FL, Mus.; Atlanta, GA, High Mus. A.; Lyon, Mus. B.-A.; 1980–81)
P. Kreiger and L. Reidemeister: *Meisterwerke des Expressionismus aus Berliner Museen* (W. Berlin, 1982)
S. E. Bronner and D. Kellner, eds: *Passion and Rebellion: The Expressionist Heritage* (London and South Hadley, MA, 1983)
B. Herbert: *German Expressionism: Die Brücke and Der Blaue Reiter* (London, 1983)
German Expressionist Sculpture (exh. cat., ed. S. Barron; Los Angeles, CA, Co. Mus. A.; Washington, DC, Hirshhorn; Cologne, Josef-Haubrich-Ksthalle; 1983–4)
H. Jahner: *Künstlergruppe Brücke* (Berlin, 1984)
S. Sabarsky: *Graphics of the German Expressionists* (Milan and New York, 1984)
D. E. Gordon: *Expressionism: Art and Idea* (New Haven and London, 1987)
E. A. Powell III and B. Davis, eds: *German Expressionist Prints and Drawings: The Robert Gore Rifkind Center for German Expressionist Studies*, 2 vols (Los Angeles and Munich, 1989)
S. C. Trauger, ed.: *Bibliography of German Expressionism: Catalog of the Library of the Robert Gore Rifkind Center for German Expressionist Studies at the Los Angeles County Museum of Art* (Boston, MA, 1990)
J. Lloyd: *German Expressionism: Primitivism and Modernity* (New Haven and London, 1991)

PAUL VOGT

2. ARCHITECTURE. Expressionist architecture, especially in the German-speaking area, developed during the years of political crisis preceding and following World War I. It was a protest movement in architecture with sociopolitical overtones and was fuelled by a solemn and euphoric belief in the future, which it strove to realize. Architecture was perceived as a substantial educational tool in refashioning human society. Pioneering developments in the fields of engineering and technology using such new building materials as steel, concrete and glass smoothed hitherto unexplored paths and seemed to open up new doors to the realization of Utopian ideas of society. The Expressionist generation of architects aimed to free form from the confines of the norm, replacing it with a direct, spontaneous communication between the idea and the product. The traditional building-unit principle was to be resolved in flowing or crystalline distortions of space. The mood of the period was reflected most radically in the Utopian phantasmagorias of Paul Scheerbart. In many written works from the turn of the century on he evoked an architecture made of glass, the light, crystalline, curving, floating images of which would transform the ways of

living and thinking of the 'Old European'. However, the movement's dependence on clients who were willing to experiment, in addition to other external factors, meant that architectural practice was able to match the visionary start of Expressionism in only a restricted way. Many of its most creatively original contributions never went beyond sketches of ideas on paper. The inherently Utopian character of Expressionist architectural sketches systematically points forward to future possibilities in the development of architecture.

Significantly, the first examples of Expressionist architecture to be constructed were industrial buildings. In such commissions architects discovered what might be described as 'fallow land' which offered less resistance to experimentation. The transition to Expressionism was effected in Peter Behrens's buildings for AEG in Berlin (1903–13; for example, *see* BEHRENS, PETER, fig. 1). They have a ceremonial character and developed as a new force from Romantic, national architecture, which was turning away from the eclecticism of the period of Emperor William II. The AEG turbine factory (1908–9; *see* MODERN MOVEMENT, fig. 1) was the first German building to introduce the combination of steel and glass. Even though Behrens's buildings went far beyond pure functionalism in their expressive monumentalism, they already indicated rationalist tendencies. In this they differed considerably from the contemporaneous buildings of Hans Poelzig. His water-tower (1911) in Posen (now Poznań, Poland) and his chemical factory at Luban (1911–12; for illustration *see* POELZIG, HANS) were distinguished by a sculptural, dynamic, almost lyrical Expressionism, which culminated after World War I in his conversion of the Zirkus Schumann into the Grosses Schauspielhaus (1919) for Berlin. By the use of applied stalactite shapes he transformed the interior into a fantastic visionary cavern (see fig. 3). The Jahrhunderthalle (1912–13) in Breslau (now

3. Hans Poelzig: interior of Grosses Schauspielhaus, Berlin, 1919

Wrocław, Poland) by Max Berg can also be counted as one of the few projects realized before World War I that can be described as Expressionist (for illustration *see* BERG, MAX). As a steel-and-concrete structure with a cupola with a bold 67 m span, it pointed in the direction of an Expressionism that was completely in the grip of new technical achievements.

One of the important stylistic roots of Expressionism was *Jugendstil* or Art Nouveau architecture. Having begun with a formal language that was confined to surface decoration, *Jugendstil* evolved towards sculptural three-dimensionality. Such buildings as the Hochzeitsturm (1907) in Darmstadt by JOSEPH MARIA OLBRICH, the Werkbund Theater (1914) in Cologne by HENRY VAN DE VELDE or the Casa Milà (1906–10) in Barcelona by ANTONI GAUDÍ indicated a smooth transition from Art Nouveau to Expressionism. They were signposts on the way towards a new type of concrete architecture using cast sculptural shapes, though they themselves did not yet use concrete. At this point Erich Mendelsohn made his contribution; during his student years he had been closely connected with artists of the Blaue Reiter (*see* §1 (i)(b) above) and was decisively influenced by them. In numerous drawings before and during World War I he conjured up a new monolithic architecture using concrete, which aimed at overcoming the traditional structural laws relating to support and loading to achieve an organically flowing internal space. His first 'built sketch' was the Einstein Tower (1919–21) in Potsdam (*see* MENDELSOHN, ERICH, fig. 1). It gave the impression of being a freely formed abstract sculpture. Even though it is renowned as a famous example of Expressionist architecture, at the same time it demonstrated the engineering and technical limitations of cast-concrete structures; large sections of the tower had to be made of rendered brick. Recognizing that his sketches were not (yet) able to be built, in his subsequent buildings Mendelsohn reverted at first tentatively and later more explicitly to the rectangular building unit, confining himself to 'Expressionist touches' in dynamic resolutions of corners, with a strong emphasis on a built mass that had been conceived three-dimensionally.

The political basis of the Expressionist avant-garde in Germany came to a head after World War I. The ARBEITSRAT FÜR KUNST was founded in Berlin in 1918 and shortly afterwards joined forces with the Novembergruppe, which had been set up along the same lines. Under the leadership of Walter Gropius, Bruno Taut and the architectural critic Adolf Behne, it became a political and artistic mouthpiece for architects such as Otto Bartning, Max Taut, Bernhard Hoetger, Erich Mendelsohn, Adolf Meyer and Hermann Finsterlin (1887–1973). In March 1919 the Arbeitsrat launched its manifesto under the heading: 'Art and the people must be united. Art should no longer be for the enjoyment of the few, but for the happiness and life of the masses. The objective is to bring the arts together under the wing of the great art of architecture.' The suppression of the Spartacist Revolution a few months later brought about a growing feeling of disillusionment, which ultimately smoothed the way for the advent of Neue Sachlichkeit and Functionalism. The Utopian visionary spirit of Expressionism lived on in reminiscences in the letter sequences emanating from the Gläserne Kette, a correspondence group that included the Taut brothers, Gropius and Finsterlin among its members. In Finsterlin's many sketches and in Taut's *Alpiner Architektur* (Hagen, 1919), Expressionism was shown at its most extreme, fully independent of any considerations as to whether it could actually be built.

The early Weimar Bauhaus, founded and directed by Walter Gropius, is also rooted in the climate of Expressionism. Its overall teaching concept was based on Expressionist ideas. Taut's concept of 'Die Stadtkrone', a Utopian secular cathedral of the people for every city, was echoed in the woodcut by Lyonel Feininger in the first Bauhaus manifesto (1919), which used the motif of the Gothic cathedral to idealize mediaeval craftsmanship and symbolize the Expressionist Utopia of the 'cathedral of the future'. Thus many of the later masters of 'Neues Bauen' (see below) went through a youthful 'Sturm und Drang' phase that had affinities with Expressionism. Ludwig Mies van der Rohe created his first design for the Friedrichstrasse office building (1919) in Berlin as a crystalline glass body, which seems to hark back in a refined form to Paul Scheerbart's visions. The same liking for acute angles and over-emphasis of verticals can be found in the Chilehaus (1921–3) in Hamburg by Fritz Höger (see fig. 4), although here the idea is conveyed in decorated bricks. The buildings of RUDOLF STEINER in Dornach, near Basle, come into a special category (first Goetheanum, 1913–20; second Goetheanum, 1924–8).

Flowing spatial distortion is an aspect they share with Expressionism, but in Steiner's buildings this derives directly from anthroposophical philosophy. Towards the mid-1920s a new trend and direction became apparent among the German architectural avant-garde under the designation 'Neues Bauen', moving away from Utopia towards reality, precise data and practical functionalism (*see* GERMANY, §II, 7).

While the number of buildings constructed along uncompromisingly Expressionist lines in Germany remained small in the final analysis, there were countless examples in Dutch architecture, especially in Amsterdam. The AMSTERDAM SCHOOL with its publicity organ *Wendingen* (1918–31), directed by Hendrik Th. Wijdeveld, maintained close contact with the Expressionist avant-garde in Germany. Urban-planning development in Holland, however, was not subject to the drastic interruptions experienced in Germany, and the socio-political commitment of the Expressionist protest that was of prime importance in Germany was a subsidiary factor. Rather, a delight in experimenting in exotic forms was at the forefront. Among the most outstanding buildings by the Amsterdam school are the block of flats for the builder Klaas Hille (1911–12) and the Eigen Haard estate (1915–16; 1917–21), both in Amsterdam, by MICHEL DE KLERK; the Minder Marine-personeel (Minor marines) building (1911–13; destr.) in Den Helder by P. L. Kramer; and the Scheepvaarthuis (1912–16) in Amsterdam by J. M. van der Meij (with de Klerk and Kramer). The heyday of Dutch Expressionism was expressed in sometimes bizarre brick sculptures. In a certain respect it came to an end in 1923 with the early death of de Klerk, who had undoubtedly been the scintillating centre of the Amsterdam school. The group of architects associated with *De stijl*, who were at the opposite pole from the Amsterdam school, took over the artistic leadership of the Dutch avant-garde, influencing Functionalism, which was becoming established in Europe in the mid-1920s. Certain tendencies or aspects of Expressionism were revived in the 1950s in Brutalism and also in the poetic shell constructions of such architects as Jørn Utzon or Eero Saarinen.

BIBLIOGRAPHY

P. H. Endt: 'Amsterdamse school', *Wendingen*, i (1918), no. 7, pp. 3–5
A. Behne: 'Wiedergeburt der Baukunst', *Die Stadtkrone*, ed. B. Taut (Jena, 1919), pp. 113–31
E. M. Hajos and L. Zahn: *Berliner Architektur der Nachkriegszeit* (Berlin, 1928)
W. Mueller-Wulckow: *Deutsche Baukunst der Gegenwart* (Leipzig, 1929)
A. Whittick: *European Architecture in the Twentieth Century*, 2 vols (London, 1950–53)
V. Gregotti: 'L'architettura dell'espressionismo', *Casabella Cont.*, 254 (1961), pp. 24–50
P. Scheerbart: *Dichterische Hauptwerke* (Stuttgart, 1962)
M. Taut and O. M. Ungers: *Die gläserne Kette: Visionäre Architektur aus dem Kreis um Bruno Taut, 1919–1920* (Berlin, 1963)
U. Conrads, ed.: *Programme und Manifeste zur Architektur des zwanzigsten Jahrhunderts* (Munich, 1964)
D. Sharp: *Modern Architecture and Expressionism* (London and New York, 1966)
W. Pehnt: *Expressionist Architecture* (London, 1973/R 1979)
Planen und Bauen in Europa, 1913–1933. Von der futuristischen zur funktionellen Stadt (exh. cat. by P. Pfaukuch, W. Berlin, Akad. Kst, 1977)
M. Tafuri and F. Dal Co: *Architektur der Gegenwart* (Stuttgart, 1977)
K. Frampton: *Modern Architecture. A Critical History* (London 1980; rev. and enlarged, 1985)

4. Fritz Hoger: Chilehaus, Hamburg, 1921–3

W. de Witt, ed.: *The Amsterdam School: Dutch Expressionist Architecture, 1915–1930* (New York and London, 1983)

W. Pehnt: *Expressionist Architecture in Drawings* (New York, Melbourne and Agincourt, 1985)

ITA HEINZE-GREENBERG

Exter [Ekster; née Grigorovich], **Alexandra (Alexandrovna)** (*b* Belostok, Russia [now Białystok, Poland], 6 Jan 1882; *d* Fontenay-aux-Roses, Paris, 17 March 1949). Russian painter and designer of Polish birth. After graduating in 1906 from art school in Kiev, Exter married in 1908 and went to Paris, where she studied at the Académie de la Grande Chaumière. The following year she rented a studio in Paris and became acquainted with Picasso, Braque, Guillaume Apollinaire, Max Jacob and with the Italian Futurists Filippo Marinetti, Giovanni Papini and Ardengo Soffici (with whom she shared a studio in 1914). In Paris she also attended the Vasil'yeva Free Russian Academy, where Fernand Léger gave two important lectures on modern art. In the years 1909–14 Exter travelled extensively between Paris, Moscow and Kiev, playing an important role in disseminating Cubist and Futurist ideas among the Russian avant-garde. She participated in many important avant-garde exhibitions in Russia and the Ukraine, including David Burlyuk's *Link* (Kiev, 1908), the first and second Izdebsky Salons (Odessa, 1909–10; Kiev and St Petersburg, 1910–11), and the first and last shows of the Union of Youth in St Petersburg (1910 and 1913–14). She also exhibited in Paris at the *Section d'Or* (1912) and at the Salon des Indépendants (1912 and 1914), and in Rome at the International Futurist Exhibition (1914).

In Exter's work the gradual assimilation of Cubist and Futurist ideas was never divorced from a decorative interest in colour and rhythm. This is clear in works such as *Composition (Genoa)* (1912–14; Cologne, Mus. Ludwig), where the cityscape is fragmented into a system of small geometric planes, enlivened by variations of tone and colour. In *Firenze* (1914–15; Moscow, Tret'yakov Gal.) fragments of urban architecture are more boldly juxtaposed with passages of brightly coloured patterning to create a taut and dynamic composition analogous to the work of Exter's friends Robert and Sonia Delaunay.

From the summer of 1914 Exter was based in Russia, exhibiting with the avant-garde at the exhibitions *Tramway V: Pervaya futuristicheskaya vystavka kartin* ('Tramway V: The first Futurist exhibition of paintings'; Petrograd, March 1915) and *Magazin* ('The store'; Moscow, 1916). Her paintings became totally abstract, exploring a personal interpretation of Malevich's Suprematist style. In *Colour Dynamism* (1916–17; Cologne, Mus. Ludwig; see fig.) the interpenetrating geometric elements seem to explode outwards from the core of the composition, while the sense of dynamic energy is reinforced by contrasts of black, white and strong colour, of curved against rectilinear shapes, and by the vibrant freedom of the brushwork.

In 1916 Exter began working for Aleksandr Tairov's Kamerny Theatre in Moscow. Her experiments in theatrical design included treating the costumes almost as abstract sculptures, reducing the set to movable three-dimensional geometric forms and using mobile coloured lights to dramatize the effects (e.g. the set for Innokenty Annensky's *Thamira Khytharedes*, 1916; some costume

Alexandra Exter: *Colour Dynamism*, oil on canvas, 895×540 mm, 1916–17 (Cologne, Museum Ludwig)

designs in Moskow, Bakhrushin Cent. Theat. Mus.). She introduced a more dynamic organization of the stage, using complex arrangements of brightly coloured curtains to intensify the action (e.g. the set for Oscar Wilde's *Salome*, 1917; costume and set designs in Moskow, Bakhrushin Cent. Theat. Mus.), and also used bridges to create different levels for the action (e.g. the set for Shakespeare's *Romeo and Juliet*, 1920–21; set designs and some costume designs in Moskow, Bakhrushin Cent. Theat. Mus.; see 1986 exh. cat. for illustrations of Exter's set and costume designs).

Exter's pedagogical interests developed in Odessa, where from 1917 to 1918 she taught four- to eight-year-olds the abstract study of form and rhythm. She then taught in Kiev (1918–21), and among her students were Isaak Rabinovich (1894–1961) and Pavel Tchelitchew. Exter's studio also produced decorations for the revolutionary festivals of May Day 1918 and the first anniversary of the October Revolution, and enormous abstract designs for agitprop ships travelling on the River Dnieper.

In 1921 Exter moved to Moscow and joined the staff of the Higher Artistic and Technical Workshops (Rus. Vkhutemas), where she taught for a year. In 1921 she contributed to the important $5 \times 5 = 25$ exhibition, together with Aleksandr Vesnin, Lyubov' Popova, Aleksandr

Rodchenko and Varvara Stepanova. Exter showed five paintings, each called *Planar and Colour Structure*, which she described in the catalogue as 'colour constructions based on the laws of colour'. A characteristic work from this period is *Construction* (1922–3; New York, MOMA), which uses the flat application of black, white and primary colours and shows a great simplicity and purity in the arrangement of the geometrical elements. Formal contrasts combine with the diagonal composition to create an effect of dynamism and spatial ambiguity.

Exter was one of the most experimental women artists among the avant-garde of 1910–30, but she was not affiliated to any particular movement. She never shared the Russian Constructivists' involvement with real materials, their disdain for easel painting or their ideological and utilitarian objectives. Yet she did accept the idea that art could contribute to everyday life, and in 1921 she began working in fashion design. She produced some very economical and austere prototypes for mass production, but in general her designs were decorative, individualistic and within the traditions of *haute couture*. In 1923 she was one of the artists responsible for the painted decorations on the pavilions at the *All Russian Agricultural Exhibition* in Moscow. She designed and decorated the International Pavilion, and together with Vera Mukhina and Boris Gladkov produced a superstructure of brightly coloured skeletal arches and steps for the kiosk of the newspaper *Izvestiya*. That same year she began designing the sets and costumes for the Martian scenes in the film *Aelita*, based on the novel by Aleksey Tolstoy and produced by Yakov Protozanov. Her sets were spatially exciting, using multicoloured structures (sometimes skeletal openwork constructions) and expressive mechanistic imagery. Her tubular costumes exploited the transparency and vibrancy of new materials such as celluloid (see Lodder, pls 5.7, 5.8 and 1972 exh. cat., pp. 27, 28, 31).

In 1924 Exter emigrated and settled in Paris, teaching with Fernand Léger and in her own studio. She returned to a figurative style of painting, producing still-lifes influenced by Purism. She worked extensively in the theatre and continued to experiment, beginning, at this time, to make inventive theatrical puppets. In 1929 she used tubes of light to create an elegant, almost dematerialized spatial setting for the ballet *Don Juan* (set design in Moskow, Bakhrushin Cent. Theat. Mus.) produced by Elsa Kruger in Cologne.

BIBLIOGRAPHY

V. Tugendkhold: *Aleksandra Ekster kak zhivopisets i khudozhnik tseni* [Alexandra Exter as painter and theatrical designer] (Berlin, 1922)
Alexandra Exter (exh. cat. by A. Nakov, Paris, Gal. Jean Chauvelin, 1972)
Artist of the Theatre: Alexandra Exter (exh. cat., New York Pub. Lib., 1974)
Russian Women Artists of the Avant Garde, 1910–30 (exh. cat., Cologne, Gal. Gmurzynska, 1979), pp. 111–30
C. Lodder: *Russian Constructivism* (New Haven, 1983)
Aleksandra Ekster: Eskizy dekoratsiy i kostyumov iz sobraniya Gosudarstvennogo Teatral'nogo Muzeya imeni A. A. Bakhrushina [Alexandra Exter: sketches for decor and costumes from the collection of the Bakhrushin Theatre Museum] (exh. cat., Moscow, Bakrushin Cent. Theat. Mus., 1986)

CHRISTINA LODDER

Extrados. Outside curve or upper edge of an arch or voussoir (*see* ARCH, fig. 1f).

Exultet rolls. Long scrolls, usually of parchment, containing the music and words of the liturgical chant for the Easter Vigil. Named after the opening word of the chant announcing Easter, 'Exultet iam angelica turba coelorum . . .', these rolls were used during the ceremony of the blessing and lighting of the Easter Candle, which symbolizes both the Pillar of Fire that led the Israelites through the wilderness and the Resurrection of Christ, the Light of the World, on Easter Day. This liturgy, derived from the Pontifical, is attributed to Bishop Landolfo I of Benevento (*reg* 957–82) and became widespread among the churches in southern Italy dominated by Montecassino Abbey. As a result, such scrolls were prevalent in the Benevento and around Montecassino from the 10th to the 13th centuries (*see* MONTECASSINO, §2 (i)).

Although they served a liturgical function, these scrolls were primarily ceremonial display pieces. Decorated with large elaborate interlace initials in the Beneventan style, they also contain miniatures painted in a Byzantinizing style. The miniatures were often painted upside down in relation to the text, so that when the scrolls were draped over the pulpit and the deacon intoned the words of the chant, the congregation could see the succession of illustrations right side up (e.g. Bari, Mus. Dioc., Cod. 1; see fig.).

Exultet roll, *Deacon Reading the Easter Chant* and *Earth*, 619×390 mm; miniatures from a roll 5.30×0.39 m, 11th century (Bari, Museo Diocesano, Cod. 1)

About 40 Exultet rolls have survived. Three of the most elaborately decorated examples are the scroll in Bari and two in Rome (Vatican, Bib. Apostolica, MS. Vat. lat. 9820, and Bib. Casanatense, MS. B.I.13). Although the subject-matter and even the sequence of miniatures vary from scroll to scroll, the opening miniature before the preface is usually a Christ in Majesty. A large decorative E for the opening of the *Exultet* is usually followed by angels blowing horns ('turba angelica') and the Descent into Limbo where Christ wrests Adam and Eve from purgatory, symbolizing the salvation of mankind through his sacrifice on the cross. In some Exultet rolls a personification of Earth, clothed in a flowery garment, signifies the renewal of life in spring, appropriate at Easter (see fig.). Sometimes the image of Christ triumphant appears, signifying his victory over death and evil. Interspersed among these are miniatures introducing commemorative prayers, which show praying clerics, the congregation of the Church, a bishop between two apostles to commemorate St Peter and St Paul, and sometimes the prayer for a ruler is introduced by a depiction of the emperor. Occasionally, as in the Bari scroll, the unusual image of the Rose of the Winds, a reference to the winds of the angels in St Paul's Letter to the Hebrews (1:7) is used. An image of bees around a beehive, the 'laus apum', refers to bees not only as a symbol of virginity but also, since they gather in a hive, to the congregation of the faithful in the church. Along the borders of some Exultet rolls medallions containing the portrait busts of Old Testament prophets and of saints are painted.

Although limited to southern Italy and pertinent only to the liturgy as developed by Montecassino, the Exultet roll was nevertheless a particularly rich and evocative liturgical artefact that embodied the essence of hope, rejuvenation and life after death celebrated at Easter.

BIBLIOGRAPHY
A. M. Latil: *Le miniature nei rotoli dell'Exultet: Documenti per la storia della miniatura in Italia*, iii (Montecassino, 1899–1901)
M. Avery: *The Exultet Rolls of South Italy*, ii (Princeton, 1936) [pls]
A. Grabar and C. Nordenfalk: *Romanesque Painting* (New York, 1958), p. 147

ROBERT G. CALKINS

Ex-voto [Lat.: 'by reason of a vow']. Term for a panel painting, usually small, or, more rarely, a statue, donated as a token of remembrance, entreaty or thanks by individual believers or communities and hung at sites of pilgrimage or holy places. In the Latin and Greek churches certain written formulae—*ex voto* or its equivalent, *hyper euchēs*—recur repeatedly on votive panels, on votive gifts of every kind and in entries in books of miracles. (Other wordings, often reduced to initials, include *Votum feci, gratiam accepi* in Italy and Spain and *Milagre que fez* in Portugal.)

1. THE TRADITION. Although stereotyped *ex-voto* expressions and formulations occur in all the languages of the Catholic world, there are also statements that the donor has 'placed his trust' in a certain saint or miraculous image or at a particular miraculous site; that he has 'taken refuge'; that he has appealed to a saint 'in full confidence'. This offering and public presentation (*promulgatio*) of an image can best be seen within a broad framework of consecrated acts and the giving of oblations. Written

documents, oral traditions and concrete objects, in conjunction with primary written testimonies, reveal a characteristic form of pious conduct: in acute or protracted states of suffering, misfortune, danger or fear, the believer appeals to God, to a saint or other supernatural powers, for protection and help, promising that once his entreaty has been granted he will bear witness to the help and grace he has received with an act of devotion, an offering or the presentation of a sign at the place at which the sacred act has been performed.

In the pre-Christian and pre-Islamic religions of Asia Minor, North Africa, the Mediterranean and the western and western central regions of Europe, comparable or identical forms of cult and ritual can be demonstrated or inferred from written and concrete traditions since the second millennium BC. The same is true of the more recent traditions of the popular, the high and the universal religions of India, Tibet, China and Japan. The custom of making votive offerings was disseminated in its Western, Christian form, especially through Spanish and Portuguese colonization and the Roman Catholic missions, flourishing above all in Central and South America.

Art historians are interested in the origins and meaning of the votive image in the form of frescoes and mosaics from the 6th to the 13th century and in its relation to the history of the portrait, the image of the dead, the donor's image, dedicatory images and those used for worship and veneration. These terms for comparable types of image represent only very roughly the diverse and highly complex religious ideas that underlie them. Among these ideas are beliefs in the constant activity of the Creator within earthly existence; in the power and capability of the saints to mediate divine help in all affairs; in the presence and efficacy of God and divine goodness in nature both animate and inanimate (sacred springs, flowers, stones) and thus also in the remains left by saints (relics) in the community of believers, as well as in artificial structures (cult objects, miraculous images).

2. THE IMAGE. Well-preserved early votive images are to be found in the church of Hagios Demetrios (6th–7th century) in Thessaloniki (see THESSALONIKI, §III, 3) and in the catacomb of Commodilla (6th century) in Rome (see ROME, §V, 13). The formal structure of the votive image was developed in the Eastern Church and partly in the West up to the 16th century and also appears in individual examples of the emerging popular votive image from c. 1400. Christianity took over ancient cult forms, such as the offering of clothes, strips of cloth and wreaths. From the early Middle Ages specifically Western votive forms also evolved, such as the offering of a staff (of the same size as the votant or intended beneficiary), a live domestic animal representing an illness, or a wax candle or torch, sometimes having the weight or size of the intended beneficiary.

Within the religious customs of the West, a special type of votive image has developed since the 14th century in conjunction with founders' images, depictions of miracles and images of the dead. In the lower half of this image the votant (the person appealing for help or protection with a vow to God or a saint, placing his fate at their mercy) is depicted in a posture of prayer and veneration, within an interior that is usually only indicated or in an expansive landscape (the world landscape). Beside him the cause of the vow is shown, realistically or as a reduced, conventional sign. In the middle or upper half of the image the supernatural personage invoked appears (in the form of a traditional depiction or miraculous image), dominating the supplicant in size and mounted on a throne, socle or altar, in a conch or apse, or floating full-length or half-length on a cloud or in an aureole of fire and light within a cloudy sky. The pictorial representation is often supplemented by a written *ex-voto* formula and by a verbal account. The elements of the image are varied in form and structure in many ways.

In aesthetic quality the images range from the works of great masters to products of traditional, popular image-making and very simply produced signs. The votive panel painting is only one of the many traditional objects used to manifest the act of vow-making and the granting of aid and grace.

Instead of a more or less detailed two-dimensional representation, three-dimensional treatments, small to life-size sculptures of the votant or intended beneficiary in wax (see fig.), precious metal, bronze, clay, stone or forged iron can be offered. Other conventional two- or three-dimensional signs indicate the seat or symptoms of the illness (head, arm, heart etc) or the implement that has caused the injury (e.g. a broken sword or today the steering wheel of a crashed car). The importance of the large-figure *ex-voto* and votive sculptures for the emergence of the free-standing three-dimensional figure, for portrait painting and for the portrait figure as a full-length or half-length figure or bust has not yet been dealt with in art history. Such votive figures can be traced in records (lives, miracle books and descriptions of sites, votive offerings and pilgrimages) from the 8th century, and isolated examples have been preserved, usually in fragments, since the 15th century.

BIBLIOGRAPHY

J. von Schlosser: 'Geschichte der Porträtbildnerei in Wachs', *Jb. Ksthist. Samml. Allhöch. Ksrhaus.*, xxix (1910), pp. 171–258
A. Warburg: *Die Erneuerung der heidnischen Antike: Kulturwissenschaftliche Beiträge zur Geschichte der europäischen Renaissance* (Berlin, 1932)
——: 'Bildniskunst und florentinisches Bürgertum (1902)', *Gesammelte Schriften*, i (Leipzig, 1932), pp. 99–100, 116–19, 346–50
L. (Kriss-)Rettenbeck: 'Zur Phänomenologie des Votivbrauchtums', *Bayer. Jb. Vlksknd.* (1952), pp. 75–8
——: 'Heilige Gestalten im Votivbild', *Kultur und Volk: Festschrift Gustav Gugitz* (Vienna, 1954), pp. 330–60
W. Brückner: 'Volkstümliche Denkstrukturen und hochschichtiges Weltbild im Votivwesen: Zur Forschungssituation und Theorie des bildlichen Opferkultes', *Schweizer. Archv Vlksknd.*, lix (1963), pp. 186–203
L. Kriss-Rettenbeck: *Ex-voto: Zeichen, Bild und Abbild im christlichen Votivbrauchtum* (Zurich, 1972)
F. Yates: *L'Art de la mémoire* (Paris, 1975)
G. B. Bronzini: 'Fenomenologia dell'ex-voto', *Puglia ex voto* (Bari, 1977), pp. 249–71
E. Chorherr: 'Zur religiösen Volkskunde Italiens: Ein Literaturbericht', *Jb. Vlksknd.*, n. s. 1 (1978), pp. 227–35
G. B. Bronzini: 'Ex-voto e cultura religiosa popolare: Problemi di interpretazione', *Riv. Stor. & Lett. Relig.*, xv (Florence, 1979), pp. 3–27
D. Arasse: 'Entre dévotion et culture: Fonctions de l'image religieuse au XVe siècle', *Faire croire: Modalités de la diffusion et de la réception des messages religieux du XIIe au XVe siècle* (Rome, 1981), pp. 131–46
P. Brown: *Society and the Holy in Late Antiquity* (London, 1982) [on belief in relics and miraculous images]
R. Griebel: 'Die Votivbrauchforschung in Frankreich: Geschichte, Bibliographie und thematischer Aufriss', I: *Jb. Vlksknd.*, vi (1983), pp. 208–29; II: *Jb. Vlksknd.*, vii (1984), pp. 159–78
L. Carlen: *Wallfahrt und Recht im Abendland* (Fribourg, 1987), pp. 185–204
D. Freedberg: *The Power of Images: Studies in the History and Theory of Response* (Chicago and London, 1989)
H. Belting: *Bild und Kult: Eine Geschichte des Bildes vor dem Zeitalter der Kunst* (Munich, 1990), pp. 100–03

LENZ KRISS-RETTENBECK

Ex-voto, wax votive statue of *Prince Maximilian Philipp Hieronymus of Bavaria*, h. 960 mm, 1644 (Munich Cathedral)

Eybl, Franz (*b* Vienna, 1 April 1806; *d* Vienna, 29 April 1880). Austrian painter and lithographer. He entered the Vienna Akademie at the age of ten, studying sculpture under Josef Klieber and landscape painting (1817–20) with Joseph Mössmer (1780–1845), from whom he also learnt the new technique of lithography. He then spent three years with Johann Baptist Lampi (i) and Franz Caucig (1762–1828), drawing after antique statues and casts. He studied history painting (1823–8), during which period he came under the influence of Johann Peter Krafft, who introduced him to the principles of realism, suggesting that he work directly from nature and reflect contemporary, everyday subject-matter in his painting. Together with Josef Danhauser and Matthias Ranftl (1805–54), Eybl was among the most significant followers of Krafft's ideas, also becoming one of the principal Viennese painters of the Biedermeier period.

On leaving the Akademie, Eybl embarked on a career as a portrait painter. His portraits, executed with the detail of a miniaturist, gradually became larger but remained constant in character: they tend to depict their subject in a rather stiff, formal pose, but draw attention to the mood and feelings of the sitter as well as his or her physical characteristics. Eybl's technical virtuosity enabled him to reproduce warm skin tones and the texture of different materials, as in *The Landscape Painter Franz Wipplinger, Looking at a Picture of his Dead Sister* (1833; Vienna, Belvedere). Eybl also produced outstanding lithograph portraits. With Josef Kriehuber (1800–76), he is considered the main representative of this genre, which flourished in Vienna between 1830 and 1860. Over the years Eybl produced portraits of a complete cross-section of Austrian society, from peasants to the emperor himself. From 1840 he received many commissions from the patrons Joseph Winter and Rudolf von Artaber for both portraits and copies from Old Masters. He was also a popular genre painter: his pictures usually contain a single figure or a small group placed in a modest interior (see fig.) or in front of a landscape. In his skill at rendering light, Eybl may be compared with Ferdinand Waldmüller, but his greatest concern was always with the depiction of human beings. Eybl combined his sharp eye for detail, especially in his depiction of varieties of material, with his ability to convey a sense of the sitter's mental state. His portraits are often contained within genre scenes, as in *The Old Beggar* (1856; Vienna, Belvedere). Occasionally he depicted more unusual subjects, with figures set, for example, in places of work, though he did not use such scenes for social criticism. In 1853 Eybl was appointed curator of the Kaiserliche Gemäldegalerie, and thereafter his own artistic activity decreased; after the mid-1860s he scarcely painted at all, occupying himself with the copying and restoration of the gallery's collection. In 1867 he became a teacher at the Kaiserliche Restaurierungsanstalt.

BIBLIOGRAPHY

Thieme–Becker
Unvergängliches Österreich: Ferdinand Georg Waldmüller und seine Zeit (exh. cat., Essen, Villa Hügel, 1960)
B. Grimschitz: *Die Alt-Wiener Maler* (Vienna, 1961)
R. Feuchtmüller and W. Mrazek: *Biedermeier in Österreich* (Vienna, 1963)
I. Kastel: *Franz Eybl (1806–1880)* (diss., U. Vienna, 1983)
Wiener Biedermeiermalerei zwischen Kongress und Revolution (exh. cat., Vienna, Kunstforum der Bank Austria, 1992)

MARIANNE FRODL-SCHNEEMANN

Eyck, van. Netherlandish family of artists. The brothers (1) Hubert van Eyck, (2) Jan van Eyck and (3) Lambert van Eyck were all painters; a sister, Margaret, was also identified as a painter by van Vaernewijck (1568), who recorded that she was unmarried and was buried next to Hubert in Ghent. The tradition that the family originated in Maaseick [Maeseyck], near Maastricht, seems confirmed by the dialect of Jan van Eyck's motto and colour notes on his portrait drawing of a man (Dresden, Kupferstich-kab.) and by his gift of vestments to a convent in Maaseick, where his daughter Lievine became a nun. The family belonged to the gentry: the armorials of Jan's epitaph in St Bavo's, Ghent, showed that his father or grandfather came from Brabant, perhaps near 's Hertogenbosch, and married a woman from a Mosan family. It is possible that Barthélemy d'Eyck, court painter to King René I of Anjou, belonged to the same family.

Hubert van Eyck, probably the eldest of the three brothers, was one of the first Netherlandish painters to free himself from the conventions of the Late Gothic

Franz Eybl: *Farmer's Wife with Spinning-wheel*, oil on paper, mounted on panel, 380×290 mm (Vienna, Österreichische Galerie)

style. He used angular drapery folds to enhance the volume of the figures, achieving a monumentality rare in Netherlandish painting. Jan van Eyck worked at the courts of Holland and Burgundy and produced secular paintings as well as religious works and portraits, many containing sophisticated symbolism. He is best known for his harmonious and highly finished compositions in which the figures are integrated into convincing three-dimensional settings, whether exquisitely detailed landscapes, domestic or church interiors. His technical mastery, combined with acute observation of nature and the effects of light and shadow, was so legendary that he was later credited with the invention of oil painting. In fact the use of oil is documented as early as the late 13th century, and Jan van Eyck was one of several early 15th-century Netherlandish painters who sought to obtain rich saturated colours by applying transparent oil glazes over lighter opaque underpaints. What is true is that he used the technique with unprecedented consistency and unequalled refinement.

(1) Hubert [Hubrecht; Lubrecht] **van Eyck** (*b c*. 1385–90; *d* Ghent, 18 Sept 1426). Painter.

1. LIFE. A *Magister Hubertus, pictor* was paid in 1409 for panels for the church of Onze Lieve Vrouwe, Tongeren, and a Master Hubert painted a panel bequeathed by Jan de Visch van der Capelle to his daughter, a

Benedictine nun near Grevelingen, in 1413; considering the rarity of this given name among painters of the time, the artist may well have been Hubert van Eyck. The designation of Hubert as 'Master', his absence from guild records, the childlessness revealed in his heirs' living outside Ghent and his sister's burial beside him, all suggest that he was in minor orders, perhaps attached to the abbey church of St Bavo, Ghent (Dhanens, 1980). He must have settled in Ghent by c. 1420 and shortly afterwards begun his only surviving documented work, the retable with the *Adoration of the Lamb* or Ghent Altarpiece, which was commissioned for St Bavo's by Jodocus Vijd (d 1439) and his wife Elisabeth Borluut (d 1443); to judge from its advanced state at the time of Hubert's death it must have been designed c. 1423. The following year Hubert made two designs for a picture for the town magistrates of Ghent, some of whom visited his shop in 1425. He was probably commissioned to paint the retable with a painted or carved figure of *St Anthony* (untraced) for the altar in the church of the Saviour, Ghent, which Robbrecht Portier and his wife endowed on 9 March 1426. This can hardly have been started, however, since the retable for St Bavo's must have occupied most of his time until his death six months later. The painter was buried in St Bavo's before the altar on which the retable was to stand, a sign of the patrons' esteem. The tombstone is still in the cathedral museum, bereft of the brass plaque with its inscription declaring that Hubert's painting had won him fame and the highest honour.

2. WORKS. According to the doubtless reliable inscription on the frame of the Ghent Altarpiece, the great work was begun by Hubert, 'than whom no greater was found', and finished by Jan, 'his brother, second in art', at Vijd's behest; the chronogram in the last line gives the date of the dedication, 6 May 1432. The text implies that large

Hubert van Eyck, completed by Jan van Eyck: *Christ, the Virgin and St John the Baptist*, detail of the Ghent Altarpiece, oil on panel, 3.65×4.87 m (wings open), c. 1423–32 (Ghent, St Bavo)

areas of at least the lower layers of paint could be seen at the time of Hubert's death. The homogeneous execution of the finished work has made it difficult to distinguish the share of each painter, but technical studies by van Asperen de Boer and Brinkman have added new data to an emerging consensus on the iconography and style.

The programme of the 12 panels comprising the polyptych is complex but essentially coherent; the apparent discrepancies were probably mitigated, and in some instances required, by the original architectural frame (Dhanens, 1972). Three christophanies, the Incarnation, the Mass and the final Triumph, follow the terms of the Vijds' endowment, which provided for a daily Mass 'dedicated to God, his blessed mother and all saints'. The altarpiece has two tiers, each with four hinged wings. When closed for weekday Masses and in Lent, it represents the moment of the Incarnation, depicted as an *Annunciation* set in a low-ceilinged room filling the top four panels, with prophets and sibyls in the lunettes above the beams. On the lower tier Vijd and his wife are shown kneeling in traceried niches before statues of *St John the Baptist*, the church's original patron, and *St John the Evangelist* (see GRISAILLE, fig. 2), the putative patron of the chapel. These are depicted in identical niches to those of the donors, but they are painted in grisaille to resemble sculpture. When the upper tier was open on ordinary Sundays, it showed *Christ, the Virgin and St John the Baptist* (see fig.). The Baptist, reading a Bible with the first words of Isaiah 40:1 ('Comfort ye'), points to the Lord who wears a papal tiara, while the Virgin is absorbed in a book that resembles a missal. At their side are music-making angels, while the tops of the outer wings bear illusionistic 'reliefs' of *Cain* and *Abel* in grisaille, representing the sin from which *Adam* and *Eve*, below them, have been redeemed. When the retable was fully opened for a major feast, these great figures presided over a paradisical scene below of the *Adoration of the Lamb*, with patriarchs, prophets, Apostles and confessors around a fountain, and processions of saints and martyrs appearing from a distance, with the *Soldiers of Christ* and *Just Judges* on one pair of wings and *Hermit Saints* and *Pilgrim Saints* on the other. Van Vaernewijck mentioned a *Hell* scene on a predella (untraced), but this was probably a later addition because it was painted, unlike the panels, in tempera on parchment. The original framework was lost probably in the 16th century during the religious wars; the panels have been restored on several occasions and were dispersed in the 19th century. They are now reunited in the chapel, but the *Just Judges* panel, stolen in 1934, has been replaced by a modern copy.

Throughout the retable, inscriptions and invocatory words from the Bible, the Book of Revelation, the Little Office of the Virgin, the writings of St Augustine, St John Chrysostom and Hugh of St Victor, and other sources glorify Christ and exalt the main figures represented. Many of the texts are combined in the pictorial writings of the 12th-century Mosan commentator Rupert of Deutz, which informed a Netherlandish tradition of Eucharistic explication that stressed Christ as the Supreme Priest, the Mass as a fountain and the Virgin's acceptance of the promise to Adam that God would become man, and declared that the reading of the epistle signifies the Baptist's preaching (Dhanens, 1965).

While the programme must have been devised by a learned cleric, Hubert was responsible for the designs. Infra-red photographs of the ceiling of the *Annunciation* chamber revealed an underdrawing of Gothic arches identical to those of the lower niches, which suggests that he planned to simulate a sculptured retable such as those of the Rhineland (e.g. that in the Liebfraukirche, Oberwesel). The design of the interior of the altarpiece also follows a monumental tradition, the combined *Triumph of the Church* and *All the Saints* which, beginning in the Early Christian period and continuing on Italian 14th-century panels, also existed in Romanesque Germany (e.g. St Klemens, Schwarzrheindorf, Bonn).

Except on the panels of *Adam* and *Eve*, which are probably entirely by Jan van Eyck, the underdrawing is sparsely executed in long hatching strokes gathered along the contours. Modifications in the drawing fall into two categories: those that change the two-dimensional composition, found under the isolating layer, and those on top of the layer that conform to Jan's later increasing plasticity of forms. Hubert's style is essentially planar, unlike the fusion of rounded forms and the ambient in Jan's independent works and in the *Adam* and *Eve*. The recession is structured by overlapping planes with a varied perspective. The figures are lost in deep folds of drapery and, also planar, are shown in profile or a flattened three-quarters view with an advancing farther contour. On the left wings, X-rays have revealed a northern forest under the present Mediterranean vegetation. Since Netherlandish panels were painted in layers, the painting must have been well advanced by the time of Hubert's death. The interior was probably largely covered with underpainting, including the northern trees, and the gold of the brocades and backgrounds was in place (van Asperen de Boer, 1979). The central panel probably had only the underdrawing for the background and no indication of the fountain or dove. The exterior probably had much of the final painting on the figures and lower niches.

Other work by Hubert is naturally hard to identify. There are reasons to see him as the painter, before he left his native valley of the Meuse, of the oldest Eyckian miniatures in the prayerbook and missal known as the TURIN–MILAN HOURS (Turin, Bib. N. U., MS. K.IV.29, destr. 1904; Turin, Mus. Civ. A. Ant., Inv. No. 47). The same artist seems to have been responsible for the lost *Captivity of Christ* copied in a drawing (London, BM). Hubert may also have begun the *Three Marys at the Tomb* (Rotterdam, Boymans–van Beuningen), whose underdrawing and chevron-shaped composition of figures round the open tomb and vertical rocks resemble the older panels in the Ghent Altarpiece. He seems to have left the work unfinished, however, because light falls on the city from the left and on the figures from the right; and the women and the tomb are more archaic than the angel and the soldiers, whose weapons and helmet include, with some imaginary features, shapes not seen until the middle of the century. Hubert's style is also found in the study figures in drawings of the 12 Apostles (Vienna, Albertina).

(2) Jan van Eyck (*b* ?Maaseick, *c*. 1395; *d* Bruges, 22/23 June 1441). Painter and illuminator, brother of (1) Hubert van Eyck.

1. Life and work. 2. Working methods and technique. 3. Iconography. 4. Character and personality. 5. Critical reception and posthumous reputation.

1. LIFE AND WORK.

(i) Training and early works in The Hague, to 1425. (ii) Early works in Flanders, 1425–30. (iii) Mature works in Ghent and Bruges, 1430–41. (iv) Other lost works.

(i) Training and early works in The Hague, to 1425. According to a 16th-century Ghent tradition, represented by van Vaernewijck and Lucas d'Heere, Jan trained with his brother Hubert. Pietro Summonte's assertion (1524) that he began work as an illuminator is supported by the fine technique and small scale of most of Jan's works, by manuscript precedents for certain of his motifs, and by his payment in 1439 for initials in a book (untraced) for Philip the Good, Duke of Burgundy. Jan is first documented in The Hague in August 1422 as an established artist with an assistant and the title of 'Master', working for John III, Count of Holland (John of Bavaria; *reg* 1419–25), who evidently discovered the artist while he was bishop (1389–1417) of the principality of Liège. Jan became the court's official painter and was paid, with a second assistant when the work increased in 1423, continuously, probably until the count's death in January 1425.

The earliest known work by Jan van Eyck is an *Adoration of the Magi* (untraced) copied in a drawing (Berlin, Kupferstichkab.) and in several Dutch manuscripts, in which the kings wear clothes datable to *c*. 1420. The elongated and extremely delicate figures stand in a comprehensive landscape remarkable for this time. A *Fishing Party at the Court of Holland* centred possibly on John and his wife, Elizabeth of Görlitz, probably a wall painting or a tapestry for the Count's residence, is also reproduced in a drawing (Paris, Louvre). Its archaic composition, with a frieze of figures flanking a vertically depicted stream, as well as the fashions, indicate a date *c*. 1420. A slightly later date is suggested by the Dutch costumes in most of the illuminations of Hand G, almost certainly Jan, in the Turin–Milan Hours. The technique of tiny strokes is similar to that of the small works in Jan's accepted oeuvre, for example the flickering light and reflections in water, as in the somewhat later *Virgin and Child with Chancellor Rolin* (*see* §(iii) below).

(ii) Early works in Flanders, 1425–30. After the death of John of Bavaria, Jan van Eyck moved to Bruges, where, on 19 May 1425, he became court painter and 'varlet de chambre' to Philip the Good, who knew the quality of his work personally and from reports of his familiars who also vouched for the artist's loyalty and honesty. The *Crucifixion on a Hill* (untraced) that is copied both on a panel (Venice, Ca d'Oro) and in a miniature by Hand H in the Turin–Milan Hours (*c*. 1440; Turin, Mus. Civ. A. Ant., MS. 47, fol. 48*v*) must have dated from these months. The composition still uses the device of a hill to cover a missing middle ground in front of an exotic representation of Jerusalem, with small houses and enormous towers. The same device was used in a many-figured *Building of the*

Tower of Babel (untraced; fragmentary copy, The Hague, Mauritshuis), which included a giant Nimrod in armour like that of the archangel Michael in the somewhat later *Last Judgement* (see below).

Jan moved to Lille in the summer, but soon began to travel for the Duke, making a pilgrimage in his name and at least two secret voyages. One of these may have been with an embassy that was absent for four months in 1425, enough time to go to Italy, which would account for the Alpine views and reflections of Italian art in some of Jan's pictures. Jan spent most of 1426 and 1427 in Lille, probably decorating the walls of the ducal residence, which was then being rebuilt. Contrary to previous assertions, he did not accompany the embassy to Aragon that failed to negotiate a marriage for the Duke in 1427: he was in Lille in July and in Bruges in August (Paviot). But he may well have travelled to Tournai in October, where on Saint Jude's day the municipality give a gift of wine to a painter named John.

In October 1428 Jan did accompany a Burgundian embassy, this time for the hand of Isabella, eldest daughter of John I of Portugal (*reg* 1385–1433). After a storm forced them to spend four weeks in England, the Burgundians arrived in Lisbon in December. In January they met the King in the castle of Aviz, and van Eyck painted the Infanta's portrait, probably in two versions to accompany the two separate groups who left by sea and by land on 12 February to report the terms to the Duke. The portraits are untraced, but one is preserved in a drawing (Germany, priv. col., see Sterling, fig. 42), which reveals that Jan used the princess's Portuguese dress for the Erythrean sibyl on the Ghent Altarpiece. While awaiting the Duke's answer, the group made a pilgrimage to Santiago de Compostela and visited John II of Castile at Valladolid and the Duke of Arjuna and Muhammad IX in Granada. After the favourable answer, the embassy re-embarked with the bride in September, but the voyage was so rough that they arrived only on Christmas Day. The wedding was celebrated in Bruges on 8 January 1430, and van Eyck undoubtedly contributed to the elaborate decorations for the week-long festivities. It seems that Jan painted the original of the *Fountain of Life* (untraced) during his stay in Portugal. Both of the known copies are Spanish (Madrid, Prado; Oberlin, OH, Oberlin Coll., Allen Art Mus.), the time is right for the style of the clothing, and the theme, the Jews confounded by their own scriptures, recalls the disputation of Tortosa of 1414 in which the Christian debaters attacked the Jews with rabbinic texts that were claimed to demonstrate the truth of Christianity. The history of the Bible of the Duke of Alba (Madrid, Pal. Liria, Col. Casa Alba) suggests that this idea persisted in Castile in the 1420s even as the government exercised greater tolerance towards the Jews, and the King or a member of his court could have commissioned the panel when they received the Burgundians in March 1429.

Other works attributed to Jan during this period are the wing panels of the *Crucifixion* (see fig. 1) and *Last Judgement* (both New York, Met.), which repeat the narrative mode of the Turin manuscript with crowds of small figures in a panoramic landscape. The distant river winding back to a pale alpine horizon in the *Crucifixion*, and the clothing similar to that in the *Virgin and Child*

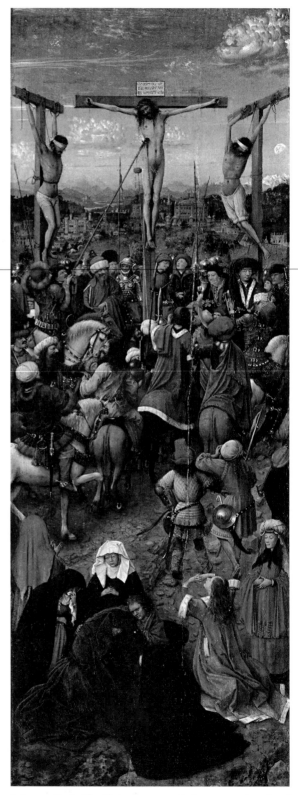

1. Jan van Eyck: *Crucifixion*, tempera and oil on canvas, transferred from panel, 565×197 mm, *c.* 1425–30 (New York, Metropolitan Museum of Art)

with Chancellor Rolin, suggest a date of *c.* 1428. The viewpoint is lower than in the earlier *Crucifixion on a Hill* and the middle ground is extended so that the crowd and setting flow smoothly behind the crosses almost to the distant city. A *Road to Calvary* (untraced), preserved in a copy on panel with an unusual horizontal format (Budapest, Mus. F.A.), also displayed fashions of the late 1420s and landscape devices similar to those in the New York *Crucifixion*.

Most of the early panels, like the miniatures in the Turin–Milan Hours, are narrative scenes that no longer present the sequence of episodes found in earlier narrative art, but epitomize the story in one significant scene (Belting and Eichberger), in which many little figures are massed together in a glancing light that suggests a particular and ephemeral time of day.

(iii) Mature works in Ghent and Bruges, 1430–41. Jan settled in Bruges, where he is documented in 1431, and spent much of the next two years in finishing the panels of his brother's retable (*see* (1) above), which were apparently transported from Ghent. Technical and stylistic analyses suggest that Jan painted the impossibly low-ceilinged room over the underdrawn arches in the *Annunciation*, turned the ewer in the niche to emphasize its volume and was entirely responsible for the lunette figures, perhaps with an assistant for the Prophets. Inside, he increased the angle of the angels' furniture and revised the fingering of the musicians to correspond to the playing of actual music, painted the Mediterranean vegetation over Hubert's northern woods and added the fountain and the crown at Christ's feet. His *Adam* and *Eve* are modelled on those of Masolino in the Brancacci Chapel in S Maria del Carmine, Florence.

In 1432 Jan bought a house, on which he paid a quit-rent each midsummer to the chapter of St Donatian. On 17 July he received the two burgomasters and some of the aldermen, inspecting some work, perhaps a panel similar to the *Virgin of the Councillors* (1443–5; Barcelona, Mus. A. Catalunya) of Lluís Dalmau, who was then in Bruges, which combines motifs from the Ghent retable with some used in Jan's later works. Jan received a similar visit from the Duke in the autumn, but what Philip came to see remains unknown. Recently married, he became a father in 1434, naming the child after its godfather, the Duke, who made his customary present of six silver cups. In 1435 Jan gilded and painted six statues and tabernacles for the façade of the town hall, while two more were executed by painters who may have been his assistants, Willem van Tongeren and Jan van der Driessche. He also went to Arras at the Duke's behest, where he probably painted the original of *St Jerome in his Study* (untraced; copy in Detroit, Mus. A.) as a gift from the Duke to the papal legate, Cardinal Niccolò Albergati, who presided at the congress. Since no baptism is mentioned, the panel may have been the reason for another gift of silver cups, smaller ones this time.

Except for the visit to Arras and a long journey to a distant region, probably the Holy Land, in 1436, Jan spent his remaining years in Bruges. He painted at least two portraits of Philip the Good (untraced; copies in Gotha, Schloss Friedenstein; Madrid, Pal. Real; Ghent, Mus. S.

2. Jan van Eyck: *Man in a Red Chaperon*, oil on panel, 257×190 mm, 1433 (London, National Gallery)

Kst.) and a *Mappa mundi* (untraced), perhaps to further Philip's plans for a crusade. Calling the last 'the most perfect work of our age', Bartolomeo Fazio reported that the distances between the atmospherically depicted sites could actually be calculated, presumably by means of coordinates. To paint these small pictures, probably on parchment, required experience as an illuminator. Like all ducal servants, Jan served as the Duke's agent in the realm of his expertise, in 1439 hiring Jean Creve of Bruges (*fl* 1427–40) to come to Lille and paint hundreds of gold initials, the only decoration, in a book for the Duke. In 1441, he bought Philip some paintings on panel, together with 'other secret things'. He was still, however, producing paintings; the *Holy Face* of 30 January 1441 (modern dating; untraced; copies in Bruges, Groenigemus., and ex–U. Durham, Swinburne Coll.) was probably a ducal commission because every one of Philip's devotional manuscripts contains a replica.

Jan van Eyck's service for Philip the Good did not prevent him from receiving commissions from other patrons. The *Virgin and Child with Chancellor Rolin* (Paris, Louvre) was ordered by Nicolas Rolin (*see* ROLIN, (1)) for his family chapel in Autun. The clothing styles and an indulgence granted by Cardinal Albergati to encourage visitors to the chapel in 1432, probably because the decoration was complete, suggest that Jan painted the picture around 1431. Jan also painted portraits of members of the nobility, *Baudouin de Lannoy* (*d* 1474), one of the leaders of the delegation to Portugal (Berlin, Gemäldegal.),

3. Jan van Eyck: *Giovanni Arnolfini and Giovanna Cenami*, oil on panel, 818×597 mm, 1434 (London, National Gallery)

and a Lord of Berlaimont, identified by the collector Peter Stevens (1590–1668) as the sitter of the signed and dated portrait of the *Man in a Red Chaperon* (traditionally known as the *Man in a Red Turban*, 1433; London, N.G.; see fig. 2). The direct gaze has caused the painting to be seen as a self-portrait, but the sitter is older than Jan's probable age at the time.

Many of Jan van Eyck's patrons belonged to the Italian colony in Bruges. The earliest known full-length double portrait, of *Giovanni Arnolfini and Giovanna Cenami* (traditionally known as the *Arnolfini Marriage* or *Betrothal*, 1434; London, N.G.; see fig. 3), was painted to commemorate the betrothal of this successful Lucchese merchant (*d* 1472), who supplied most of Philip the Good's enormous purchases of silk and velvet. The inscription on the wall of the richly furnished room recording that Jan 'was here' may mean that he was a witness to the agreement, one of the two men reflected in the mirror (*see* BELGIUM, fig. 27). The picture also contains allegorical allusions to the marriage bond. Arnolfini is also the probable sitter in a later portrait (Berlin, Gemäldegal.). The Genoese Battista Lomellini commissioned a triptych (untraced) described by Fazio as showing the *Annunciation* with *St John the Baptist* and *St Jerome in his Study* on the wings and lifelike portraits of the donor and his wife on the exterior. The little signed and dated triptych with the *Virgin and Child*

as the central panel (1437; Dresden, Gemäldegal. Alte Meister; *see* TRIPTYCH, fig. 1) may have borne, before they were overpainted by the arms of Michele Giustiniani of Genoa, those of Michiel Bollemard, or Burlamacchi, a son-in-law of the Duke's banker, Filippo Rapondi (Dhanens, 1980). The Virgin and Child are set in a church, the aisles of which are continued on the wings where the attendant figures of *St Michael and the Donor* (left) and *St Catherine* (right) are depicted. On the reverse of the wings is the *Annunciation*, painted in grisaille (*see* TRIPTYCH, fig. 2). Anselm Adornes, a member of a Genoese family settled in Bruges, acquired the *Stigmatization of St Francis* (Turin, Gal. Sabauda) together with an excellent smaller replica from the painter's shop (Philadelphia, PA, Mus. A.). The composition includes a fairly accurate representation of the cliff at La Verna, which Jan may have visited during one of his foreign journeys.

For his own milieu Jan painted isolated portraits. In 1432 he portrayed a man identified by the inscription on the parapet as 'Tymotheos', probably Philip's court composer Gilles Binchois (London, N.G.; *see* RENAISSANCE, fig.4), in 1436 the goldsmith *Jan de Leuw* (Vienna, Ksthist. Mus.; *see* BRUGES, fig. 3) and in 1439 his wife *Margaret van Eyck* (Bruges, Groeningemus.). Like his portraits of more exalted sitters, they represent an important advance,

4. Jan van Eyck: *Virgin and Child with SS Donatian and George and the Donor*, oil on panel, 1.22×1.57m, 1436 (Bruges, Groeningemuseum)

with the bust- or half-length figure filling a plain background and turned three-quarters towards a light source from the left that leaves the nearer cheek in shadow. The sitter's steady gaze is usually averted, the personality held in powerful reserve.

Among the clergy, Georg van der Paele (*d* 1443), canon of the church of St Donatian, Bruges, ordered a large picture, the *Virgin and Child with SS Donatian and George and the Donor* (1436; Bruges, Groeningemus.; see fig. 4), to commemorate his founding of a chaplaincy two years earlier. The composition of the Virgin and Child between the patron saints of the church with the kneeling donor conforms to local tomb reliefs, indicating that the panel was planned to hang by the canon's grave in the church.

Nicholas van Maelbeke (*d* 1445), provost of the cathedral of St Martin, Ypres, commissioned a triptych (possibly Warwick Castle; drgs Nuremberg, Ger. Nmus. and Vienna, Albertina), the execution of which may have been interrupted by the painter's death since it was still unfinished in the 16th century (d'Heere, van Vaernewijck). The central panel showed the kneeling cleric and a standing Virgin and Child in an arcade opening on to a landscape while the wings contained typological scenes from the *Speculum humanae salvationis* alluding to the Virgin's purity. In Jan's mature works richly clothed figures are generally surrounded by objects and settings depicted with an illusionism that makes them more splendid than in life. Although some include a distant panorama, all present one or two large figures immobile in unchanging sunlight. The evolution of the style is hard to discern, because of the short period in which they were made, their difference from the early narrative scenes and the use of a harder technique for the large church panels than in the small private works (Sterling, see below). Nevertheless, the technique becomes even lighter and the figures are smaller and more fused with the atmosphere in the latest of the finished works: the small Dresden triptych; the *Madonna at the Fountain* (1439; Antwerp, Kon. Mus. S. Kst.); and the *Virgin and Child in a Church* (Berlin, Gemäldegal.; see fig. 5), which in the 19th century had a date, 1440, on a brass plate that may have been copied from the inscription on the original frame. The painting is the left half of a small devotional diptych, the other half of which (untraced) contained, judging from the most faithful copy (Antwerp, Kon. Mus. S. Kst.), by the Master of 1499, a portrait of the owner praying in his bedroom.

(iv) Other lost works. The religious nature of those works that survive besides portraits should not obscure the importance of Jan's lost secular creations. His scenes of women bathing were particularly popular. A lost picture of one being helped by a maid to take a sponge bath, formerly in the collections of Cornelis van der Geest and Peeter Stevens, was reproduced in Willem van Haecht (ii)'s *Archduke Albert Visiting the Cabinet of Cornelis van der Geest* (1628; Antwerp, Rubenshuis) and copied on a panel (Cambridge, MA, Fogg). Fazio described another, of beautiful women emerging from a bath, their intimate parts veiled in fine linen, including one in half-length whose whole back is seen in a mirror, against a background that included a lantern in the chamber, an old woman, a puppy lapping water and, presumably through a window, horses, men, mountains and woods with villages and castles. The mysterious German *Spell of Love* (Leipzig, Mus. Bild. Kst.) may be a copy of an Eyckian original: a woman standing nude before an open hearth on a flower-strewn floor sprinkles a powdery substance into a casket as a young man peers through a door at the rear. Jan seems also to have started the long tradition of the commerce picture: Marcantonio Michiel saw one in Milan of a merchant going over accounts with his agent, dated 1440, the year before the painter's death, which, according to chroniclers, occurred at an early age. As a ducal servant, Jan was buried in St Donatian, Bruges, at first in the

5. Jan van Eyck: *Virgin and Child in a Church*, panel, 320×140 mm, ?1440 (Berlin, Gemäldegalerie)

cloister and then inside the church, near the font. The tombstone, destroyed with the church, bore a brass shield with the emblem of the painters' guild in the centre and inscribed banderoles carved on a rim.

2. WORKING METHODS AND TECHNIQUE. The survival of both the preparatory drawing (Dresden, Kupferstichkab.) for a portrait of an unknown man, whose secular gown and haircut contradict the usual identification as Cardinal Niccolò Albergati, and the finished painting (1431–2; Vienna, Ksthist. Mus.), combined with microchemical stratigraphic studies and photographs in various kinds of light, provide insights into Jan van Eyck's working methods. In the drawing, in silverpoint on prepared paper, the head is fully developed through many short strokes. These are multiplied along the contours and laid down in an overall web of parallel hatching that gives mobility to the face, suggesting the sitter's detached humour. In the more summarily drawn body and background, the strokes are limited to the contours and parallel hatching is used only for shadows and the rounding of the shoulder. Next to the head the painter inscribed colour notes concerning the sitter's features. Such portrait drawings were transferred to the panel with a good deal of freedom, although there appear to be pouncing marks in the underdrawing of the head of Canon van der Paele. The more complicated compositions were drawn directly on the chalk ground of the panel, while some ruled lines for perspective in the architecture and what may be a module in the floor tiles have been found under the *Annunciation* (Washington, DC, N.G.A.). In this and other interiors the orthogonals lead to as many as four vanishing areas, which reduces the depth and slows the rate of foreshortening (Elkins). Using a pen or brush and an aqueous solution of black pigment and glue, Jan frequently drew on top of the isolating layer of brownish drying emulsion. In the early authenticated works, such as the Rolin *Virgin and Child*, the drawing is similar to Hubert van Eyck's, but contains more modelling at the centre of forms; this increases in later works, where a full web of hatching creates volume in areas of flesh and drapery. The hatching is intensified in areas of shadow and a wash of ink or watercolour is often added for the darkest ones. This technique, on a polished chalk ground (the sulphurous colours in the sky being a later addition), almost certainly reveals the signed and dated *St Barbara* (1437; Antwerp, Kon. Mus. S. Kst.; see fig. 6) as an unfinished painting, which Jan then elaborated, adding figures to the landscape, to make an independent picture. Any modifications in the underdrawing usually enhance the solidity of forms or the movement of figures, particularly in hands and feet, although others expose more of a nude body or bare head. Both types betray the overriding concern for realism that is the essence of Jan's style.

The forms were then broadly modelled in a base of translucent greyish underpainting, reserving sections of the light beige ground in the areas of sky. Local colours were then applied in tinted glazes of oil, exploiting the reflection through these glazes of natural light striking the underpainting. Small amounts of lead white were added in flesh areas to increase the reflection. The first of the individually coloured layers was a middle tone and as many as six glazes were superimposed in lighter and darker

6. Jan van Eyck: *St Barbara*, brush and ink on panel, 340×185 mm, 1437 (Antwerp, Koninklijk Museum voor Schone Kunsten)

shades, to reinforce the modelling and to add density to the medium. The finished painting, varnished for protection, reflected light like a jewel.

The brushwork varies according to the size of the picture (Sterling). In small works made for close perusal, Jan used the apparently more congenial technique of tiny strokes of colour to represent scintillating water, fine hair and gold. Large-scale works—the foreground of the Rolin *Virgin and Child*, the van der Paele *Virgin and Child* and the triptych of which the Washington *Annunciation* was the left wing—were painted in a technique similar to Hubert's, with invisible strokes that created a perfectly smooth surface. The two techniques are combined in such middle-sized works as the Rolin *Virgin and Child* and the Lucca *Virgin and Child* (Frankfurt am Main, Städel. Kstinst. & Städt. Gal.), with visible strokes for the painterly forms in the background.

To assist him, Jan had a workshop, which was probably responsible for the *Crucifixion* (Berlin, Gemäldegal.), the *St Jerome in his Study* (1442; Detroit, MI, Inst. A.), which is the best replica of Albergati's panel, the *Virgin and Child with SS Barbara and Elizabeth and Jan Vos* (New York, Frick), and the copy on parchment (Philadelphia, Mus. A.) of the *St Francis*. About 1440 the painter joined a group of Bruges illuminators in the first of the Flemish campaigns to complete the Turin–Milan Hours. The shop, whose paintings contain motifs from original works by Jan probably found in the shop's collection of patterns, seems to have continued for a while after his death.

3. ICONOGRAPHY. The content of Jan van Eyck's works is as many-layered as their physical structure. Their meticulous realism is only what the viewer first encounters: for Jan's contemporaries the paintings resonated with theological overtones. Inscriptions proliferate. Throughout Jan's career he painted full inscriptions on the frame, but in the early paintings there are also words on banderoles, emerging from the mouths of figures, worked into the hem of a garment or chiselled in the stone of a parapet. While most of the texts are derived from the medieval commentaries or compendia of St Augustine, Honorius Augustodunensis and Gerhard van Vliederhoven as well as Rupert of Deutz, a high proportion from the Old Testament and the Book of Revelation reflects the renewed interest in them that began *c.* 1400. The content is exalted and metaphorical: these pictures were made to be read as well as seen.

They also abound in pictorial metaphor or, less exactly, 'disguised symbolism'. Fountains, flowers and enclosed gardens symbolize the Virgin's purity; church portals illustrate her epithet, 'Gate of Heaven'. Reliefs on capitals and thrones show Old Testament types of the Church's teaching or liturgy. The tower, the attribute of St Barbara, is behind her in the Antwerp picture, shown under construction in a vivid depiction of current building practice, and the mirror in the Arnolfini double portrait is surrounded by Passion and Resurrection scenes in glass roundels that may refer to the analogy of the relationship between Christ and the Church and that of husband and wife in the epistle reading for the nuptial Mass (Ephesians 5:22–31). Other metaphors are more subtle. The setting of the Rolin *Virgin and Child* is a watchtower in the Heavenly Jerusalem; the church in the van der Paele *Virgin* recalls the Holy Sepulchre in Jerusalem; the Romanesque clerestory above a Gothic arcade in the Washington *Annunciation* may signify the descent of the Holy Spirit through the Jewish and Christian eras.

Many of Jan van Eyck's extant pictures depict the Virgin. Although the subject was chosen by the patron, Jan's presentation shows him as a considerable Mariologist (Purtle). She appears serene and immobile, even when receiving the news of her election. She is usually shown as a queen amid the trappings of royalty, but her motherhood is occasionally emphasized, in nursing the child in the Lucca *Virgin and Child*, or teaching him to read, as in the Ince Hall *Virgin and Child* (Melbourne, N.G. Victoria), a copy of an Eyckian original. The most striking images, however, identify her with the Church. She replaces the altar in the van der Paele and Dresden *Virgins* and personifies the Church in the Berlin *Virgin and Child*, where, as a painted version of the sculpted figure on an altar behind her, she stands to triforium height. In the last, there is one remarkable exception to the meticulous realism of the building. The north windows are unnaturally pierced by a shaft of light, illustrating a current metaphor for her virginity (Panofsky) and supporting the inscription on her hem that pronounces her more beautiful than the sun. In the choir vested angels sing Mass before a candlelit altar and the rood screen displays, beside the usual *Crucifixion*, reliefs of the *Annunciation* and *Coronation of the Virgin*, flanking a statue of Simeon, who prophesied the Virgin's suffering at the Crucifixion.

4. CHARACTER AND PERSONALITY. Jan van Eyck's paintings reveal him to have been well-educated. Familiar with liturgical and devotional texts, he became acquainted with the commentaries at least in the course of his work. Schooled in Latin, he could reproduce Greek and Hebrew letters, and the language and calligraphy of his signed works indicate that he knew something of legal procedures. He also knew enough geography to make his world map, and Fazio supposed that he learnt about colour from Pliny's *Natural History*. A 17th-century description reports a quotation from Ovid on the frame of the Arnolfini double portrait, but the frame may not have been original.

Jan was conscious of his exceptional powers. The signatures and use of a motto are almost unique at this time. The motto, 'As I can', in the tradition of medieval scribal humility, is also a statement of pride in his accomplishment, and the careful dating and signing of his works suggest that he saw them as documenting his creativity. Furthermore, a remarkable self-assurance guided his relations with Philip the Good. Already in 1428 the Duke exempted Jan from the reduction in salary that a currency reform had made him order for most of the other retainers. In 1434 he not only changed Jan's appointment into an exceptional one for life, but raised his salary by 720%. The receiver of Flanders sending the documents to the duchy's receivers at Lille warned that the painter would institute proceedings with the Duke if they rejected the enormous increase. They did hesitate and Jan not only went to the Duke, but threatened to leave his service. Philip then wrote to the receivers himself, ordering them to comply: because, he wrote, he could not find another painter so much to his liking or so excellent in skill and knowledge as Jan van Eyck.

5. CRITICAL RECEPTION AND POSTHUMOUS REPUTATION. The Duke of Burgundy's high opinion of Jan van Eyck was universal not only in the Netherlands, where Jan's epitaph reported that he was the most ingenious painter who ever lived there, but also in Italy, where writers expressed similar praise, and copies of his paintings in many lands reflect the esteem of fellow artists. His influence in the Low Countries was long lasting and more important than has been realized. In Bruges a group of illuminators used patterns from his shop until the early 1460s and other painters made imitations on panel, such as the *Virgin and Child* in Covarrubias (Burgos, Colegiata de San Cosme y San Damian) and the original of the Ince Hall *Virgin and Child* (Melbourne, N.G. Victoria). The more independent Petrus Christus, arriving after Jan's death, probably lacked access to the Eyckian patterns, but studied panels more or less publicly visible in town. His early works reproduce a few figures and compositions and much of Jan's style. In Ghent, where the *Adoration of the Lamb* remained one of the town's major monuments and was enacted in a *tableau vivant* for the ducal entry in 1458, the Eyckian style seems to have influenced the panels,

usually but probably erroneously attributed to Robert Campin, from Flémalle and the lost *Descent from the Cross* (Frankfurt am Main, Städel. Kstinst. & Städt Gal.; copy in Liverpool, A. Mus.). Hugo van der Goes modelled his *Fall of Man* (Vienna, Ksthist. Mus.) on the *Adam* and *Eve* and used illustrated metaphors in the Portinari Triptych (Florence, Uffizi); according to one tradition, his fatal depression was caused by his failure to equal the great Ghent Altarpiece. During these years the Master of Mary of Burgundy created deep crowd scenes in a style resembling Jan's early works.

The copying of originals by Jan van Eyck, such as the *Madonna at the Fountain* and the *Holy Face*, became an industry in Bruges. Dendrochronological evidence that the *Man with the Pink* (Berlin, Gemäldegal.) was painted *c.* 1475 means that the imitation continued throughout the century, but the practice blossomed around 1500. Gerard David and illuminators of the Ghent-Bruges school copied Eyckian works. The Berlin *Virgin and Child* was copied not only by the Master of 1499 for Abbot Christian de Hondt but also by Jan Gossart for the diplomat Antonio Siciliano. Gossart also copied the central figures of the Ghent Altarpiece in his *Christ between the Virgin and St John the Baptist* (Madrid, Prado). In Antwerp, Quinten Metsys imitated one of Jan's lost commerce pictures in the *Money Changer and his Wife* (1514; Paris, Louvre; *see* METSYS, (1), fig. 2), to be followed by Marinus van Reymerswaele (e.g. that of 1538; Madrid, Prado).

In Holland, the Master of Zweder van Culemborg continued the style of Jan van Eyck's Hague period in manuscripts of the 1420s and 1430s, as did a few panel painters. The illuminators of the next generation continued to use the Hand G compositions of the Turin–Milan Hours in the new hard style and, in Haarlem, Albert van Ouwater adopted Eyckian motifs, including the round, arcaded choir of the van der Paele *Virgin and Child* in his *Raising of Lazarus* (Berlin, Gemäldegal.). As in the southern Netherlands, there was a revival of Jan's multi-figured style in the late 1470s, influencing first the Master of the Virgo inter Virgines and then Hieronymus Bosch, whose early *Tabletop of the Seven Deadly Sins* (Madrid, Prado) contains Eyckian motifs, while the composition of the vertical *Carrying of the Cross* (Ghent, Mus. S. Kst.) resembles the *Crucifixion* of the New York diptych.

Jan's art also made a considerable impact in the upper Rhineland. Konrad Witz isolated solid figures in low rooms in his altar of the *Mirror of Human Salvation* (*c.* 1435; Basle, Kstmus.; Berlin, Gemäldegal.; Dijon, Mus. B.-A.); an unknown master of *c.* 1450 copied the lost *St George and the Dragon* (Munich, Alte Pin.) and Martin Schongauer made an engraving after the untraced *Road to Calvary*. Elsewhere in Germany, however, the emotional art of Rogier van der Weyden seems to have been more congenial. In France, the Bedford Master copied the background of the Rolin *Virgin and Child* in the Dunois Hours (London, BL, MS. Yates Thompson 3) and the whole *Madonna at the Fountain* in another Book of Hours (San Marino, CA, Huntington Lib., MS. HM 1100), but these are isolated instances. The court preferred the cooler art of Jean Fouquet. The single exception is in Provence, where Barthélemy d'Eyck painted his early panels and manuscripts in a definitely Eyckian style. Since a *Virgin* in

his early Book of Hours (New York, Pierpont Morgan Lib., MS. M. 358) is based on Jan's late *Madonna at the Fountain*, the affinity is due not to their common homeland but to the younger artist visiting Flanders and possibly spending time in Jan's shop.

Jan van Eyck was the first of several south Netherlandish painters to influence Spanish art. The *Fountain of Life* was imitated in the Bible of the Duke of Alba, while both Lluís Dalmau, who returned in 1436, and the Netherlandish painter Lodewijk van Hallynckbroot [Louis Alimbrot] (*fl* 1432–63), who arrived from Bruges in 1439, were active in Valencia; the latter was probably responsible for a triptych with scenes from the *Life of Christ* (Madrid, Prado) that shows an assortment of Eyckian motifs. Valencia was also the market where Jan's *St George and the Dragon* was purchased in 1444 for King Alfonso V. In 1468, a south Netherlandish version of this composition may have inspired the main panel of the altarpiece of *St George* by Pere Nisart (Palma de Mallorca, Mus. Dioc.).

Jan van Eyck's influence in Italy was extensive. In Naples, painters learnt the oil technique *c.* 1440, and Eyckian motifs appear in *St Francis Giving the Rule to the Franciscans* (Naples, Capodimonte) by Niccolò Colantonio. Slightly later, Alfonso V, ruling Naples from 1442, acquired not only van Eyck's *St George* (untraced) but also the Lomellini triptych and a copy, or the original, of Philip the Good's *Mappa mundi* (Sterling). Describing these works, Fazio expressed admiration for Jan's magic realism, effects of light and learned skill. The paintings were frequently copied by local artists, illuminators as well as Colantonio and his pupil Antonello da Messina, who painted the Eyckian *St Jerome in his Study* (*c.* 1465; London, N.G.; *see* ANTONELLO DA MESSINA, fig. 1).

In Ferrara, Cyriac of Ancona learnt of Jan van Eyck's distinction on visiting the Este collection in 1449. In Urbino, Ottaviano Ubaldini delle Carda, nephew of Federigo da Montefeltro, owned the bathing picture described by Fazio. In 1465 Piero della Francesca painted the *Triumphs* of Federico and his duchess in front of Eyckian mountains and winding streams, and in 1485 Giovanni Santi, praising their colour, wrote that Rogier van der Weyden had been the pupil of the great 'John of Bruges' (*La vita e le geste di Montefeltro, duca d'Urbino*, ed. L. Michelino Tocci, Vatican City, 1985). In Padua, the Ca d'Oro copy of the *Crucifixion on a Hill* (Padua, Mus. Civ.) was copied by an unknown painter and reproduced more freely by Andrea Mantegna. In Florence, the *St Jerome in his Study*, in the Medici collection almost certainly before Piero's death in 1456, was imitated by Lorenzo's favourite illuminator, Francesco di Antonio del Chierico, from 1457 onwards, and by other illuminators after him; the composition was also used by Sandro Botticelli and Domenico Ghirlandaio in 1480 in their frescoes of *St Augustine* and *St Jerome* in the church of Ognissanti, Florence. Botticelli had already copied the landscape of the *Stigmatization of St Francis* in his *Adoration of the Magi* (London, N.G.), and Verrocchio reproduced the representation of La Verna in his *Baptism* (Florence, Uffizi).

Although the influence of south Netherlandish art subsequently declined in Italy, Jan's reputation persisted in the Low Countries, where the Ghent humanists and van Mander revered him as the founder of their great school of painting. In the 19th century Jan was the first of the so-called Flemish primitives to be studied by the developing critical methods. The oeuvre attributed to him was pared down in the early 20th century, after which scholars turned to the study of his complex iconography. More recent studies have concentrated on the pictures' technique, patronage and devotional or social function.

For further discussion of works by Jan van Eyck, *see* FRAME, §V, and THE NETHERLANDS, §III, 2.

(3) Lambert [Lambrecht] **van Eyck** (*fl* 1431–42). Painter, the brother of (1) Hubert and (2) Jan van Eyck. He performed some unspecified tasks for Philip the Good in Bruges in the early months of 1431. The following year he went to Voorhout, in southern Holland, to paint a portrait of Jacqueline of Bavaria, Countess of Holland (*reg* 1417–33), which he completed on 3 August (untraced); this was copied in a drawing (Frankfurt am Main, Städel. Kstinst. & Städt. Gal.) and a panel (Vienna, Ksthist. Mus.). In March 1442 Lambert obtained permission for the reburial of Jan's remains inside the church of St Donatian, Bruges. As a painter and evidently Jan's executor, he probably directed the shop in completing some of the unfinished commissions. These apparently included the *Virgin and Child with Saints and Jan Vos*, because Jan's hand in the underdrawing appears limited to the figure of the Virgin, and the stock figures and motifs and the stiff execution confirm the possibility that Vos commissioned the picture when he became prior of the Carthusian monastery at Bruges only three months before Jan died. The picture would therefore be almost entirely by Lambert van Eyck.

BIBLIOGRAPHY

ARCHIVAL DOCUMENTS

W. H. J. Weale: *Hubert and John van Eyck: Their Life and Work* (London, 1908) [incl. most of the documents; some dates are incorrect]

V. van der Haeghen: 'Autour des van Eyck: Cartulaire', *Hand. Maatsch. Gesch. & Oudhdknd. Gent*, xv (1914), pp. 1–68

J. Duverger: 'Jan van Eyck voor 1422: Nieuwe gegevens en hypothesen', *Handelingen van het 3e Congres voor allgemeene kunstgeschiedenis: Ghent, 1936*, pp. 13–20

J. Pariot: 'La Vie de Jan van Eyck selon les documents écrits', *Rev. Archéologues & Historiens A. Louvain*, xxiii (1990), pp. 83-93

EARLY SOURCES

B. Fazio: *De viris illustribus* (MS., 1456); ed. L. Mehus (Florence, 1745); Eng. trans. in M. Baxandall: 'Bartolomeus Facius on Painting: A Fifteenth-century Manuscript of *De viris illustribus*', *J. Warb. & Court. Inst.*, xxvii (1964), pp. 90–107

M. Michiel: *Notizia d'opere del disegno* (MS., *c.* 1520-30); ed. T. Frimmel in *Quellenschriften für Kunstgeschichte* (Vienna, 1888), pp. 16, 54, 98

P. Summonte: Letter to Marcantonio Michiel (MS., 1525); ed. F. Nicolini: *L'arte napoletana del rinascimento e la lettera di Pietro Summonte a Marcantonio Michiel* (Naples, 1925)

G. Vasari: *Vite* (1550, rev. 2/1568); ed. G. Milanesi (1878-1906), ii, pp. 565-6

L. d'Heere: *Ode, den hof en boomgaerd der poesien* (Ghent, 1565); ed. W. Waterschoot (Zwolle, 1969), pp. 35-8

M. van Vaernewijck: *Den spieghel der Nederlandscher audtheyt* (Ghent, 1568), fols cxvij–cxix

K. van Mander: *Schilder-boeck* ([1603]-1604), fols 199–203

MONOGRAPHS

A. Brignetti and G. T. Faggin: *L'opera completa dei van Eyck*, Class. A. (Milan, 1968) [complete colour pls]

E. Dhanens: *Hubert en Jan van Eyck* (Antwerp, 1980; Eng. trans., New York, n.d.); reviews by M. J. H. Madou in *Oud-Holland*, xcv (1981), pp. 258-60; J. Giltaij in *Simiolus*, xiii (1983), pp. 54-7

O. Pächt: *Van Eyck: Die Begründer der altniederländischen Malerei* (Munich, 1989) [lectures delivered in 1972]

SPECIALIST STUDIES

L. Mirot and E. Lazzareschi: 'Un mercante di Lucca in Fiandra, Giovanni Arnolfini', *Boll. Stor. Lucchese*, xii (1940), pp. 81–105

E. Panofsky: *Early Netherlandish Painting*, 2 vols (Cambridge, MA, 1953)

K. Bauch: 'Bildnisse des Jan van Eyck', *Sber. Heidelberg. Akad. Wiss.* (1963), pp. 96–142; also in *Stud. Kstgesch.* (Berlin, 1967), pp. 79–122

E. Dhanens: *Het retabel van het Lam Gods in de Sint-Baafskathedraal te Gent* (Ghent, 1965) [with documents and text of the account of the *tableau vivant* of 1458]; Eng. trans. as *Van Eyck: The Ghent Altarpiece* (London, 1973) [Eng. version omits documents]

E. C. Hall: 'Cardinal Albergati, St Jerome and the Detroit van Eyck', *A. Q.* [Detroit], xxxi (1968), pp. 2–34

E. Dhanens: 'Dewijze waarop het Lam godsaltaar war opgesteld', *Gent. Bijdr. Kstgesch. & Oudhdknd.*, xxii (1969–72), pp. 109-50

E. C. Hall: 'More about the Detroit van Eyck: The Astrolabe, the Congress of Arras and Cardinal Albergati', *A. Q.* [Detroit], xxxv (1971), pp. 181-201

R. Haacke: *Programme zur bildenden Kunst in den Schriften Ruperts von Deutz* (Siegburg, 1974), pp. 18–33; summarized by H. Silvestre as 'Le Retable de l'Agneau mystique et Rupert de Deutz', *Rev. Bénédictine*, lxxxviii (1978), pp. 274–86

C. Sterling: 'Jan van Eyck avant 1432', *Rev. A.* [Paris], xxxiii (1976), pp. 7–82

J. Duverger: 'Jan van Eyck as Court Painter', *Connoisseur*, 194 (1977), pp. 172–9

A. H. van Buren: 'The Canonical Office in Renaissance Painting, Part II: More about the Rolin *Madonna*', *A. Bull.*, lx (1978), pp. 617–33

E. Hall and H. Uhr: '*Aureola* and *Fructus*: Distinctions of Beatitude in Scholastic Thought and the Meaning of some Crowns in early Flemish Painting', *A. Bull.*, lx (1978), pp. 249–70

U. Panhans-Bühler: *Eklektizismus und Originalität im Werk des Petrus Christus* (Vienna, 1978), pp. 92–108

J. R. J. van Asperen de Boer: 'A Scientific Re-examination of the Ghent Altarpiece', *Oud-Holland*, xciii (1979), pp. 141–214

R. Terner: 'Bemerkungen zur *Madonna des Kanonikus van der Paele*', *Z. Kstgesch.*, xlii (1979), pp. 83–91

D. Goodgal: 'The Central Inscription in the Ghent Altarpiece', *Le Dessin sous-jacent dans la peinture, Colloque IV: Louvain-la-Neuve, 1981*, pp. 74–86

T. W. Lyman: 'Architectural Portraiture and Jan van Eyck's Washington Annunciation', *Gesta*, xx (1981), pp. 263–71

C. J. Purtle: *The Marian Paintings of Jan van Eyck* (Princeton, 1982); review by D. Goodgal in *Ren. Q.*, xxxvi (1983), pp. 590–94; L. Silver in *Pantheon*, xli (1983), p. 397; C. Eisler in *A. Bull.*, lxviii (1986), pp. 676–9

H. Belting and D. Eichberger: *Jan van Eyck als Erzähler: Frühe Tafelbilder im Umkreis der New Yorker Doppeltafel* (Worms, 1983); reviews by J. C. Smith in *Speculum*, lx (1985), pp. 638–41; C. J. Purtle in *A. Bull.*, lxix (1987), p. 651

J. K. Steppe: 'Lambert van Eyck en het portret van Jacoba van Beieren', *Acad. Anlct.: Kl. S. Kst.*, xliv/2 (1983), pp. 55–86

——: 'De mappemonde geschilderd door Jan van Eyck voor Filips de Goede', *Acad. Anlct.: Kl. S. Kst.*, xliv/2 (1983), pp. 87–131

D. de Vos: 'Nogmaals Als ich can', *Oud-Holland*, xcvii (1983), pp. 1–4

E. E. Lowinsky: 'Jan van Eyck', *Studi Musicali*, xiii (1984)

E. K. Reznicek: 'De overlevering van en verloren gegaan schildereij van Jan van Eyck', *De arte et libris: Festschrift Erasmus, 1934–84*, ed. A. Horodisch (Amsterdam, 1984), pp. 387–93

P. W. F. Brinkman and others: 'Het Lam Godsretabel van Van Eyck: Een heronderzoek naar de materialen en schildermethoden, 1. De plamuur, de isolatielaag, de tekening en de grondtonen', *Bull. Inst. Royal Patrm. A.*, xx (1984-5), pp. 137–66 [Fr. summary]

P. Klein: 'Dendrochronologische Untersuchungen an Bildtafeln des 15. Jahrhunderts', *Le Dessin sous-jacent dans la peinture, Colloque VI: Louvain-la-Neuve, 1985*, pp. 29–40 (31-2)

C. Périer d'Ieteren: *Colyn de Coter et la technique picturale des peintres flamands du XVe siècle* (Brussels, 1985), pp. 13–42

D. Eichberger: *Bildkonzeption und Weltdeutung im New Yorker Diptychon des Jan van Eyck* (Wiesbaden, 1987)

H. Verougstraete-Marcq and R. van Schoute: 'Les Cadres de l'*Agneau mystique* de Van Eyck', *Rev. A.* [Paris], lxxvii (1987), pp. 73–6

P. W. F. Brinkman and others: 'Het Lam Godsretabel van Van Eyck: Een heronderzoek naar de materialen en schildermethoden, 2. De hoofdkleuren. Blau, groen, geel, en rood', *Bull. Inst. Royal Patrm. A.*, xxii (1988-9), pp. 20–49 [Fr. summary]

M. H. Butler: 'An Investigation of Two Paintings of The Stigmatization of Saint Francis Thought to Have Been Painted by Jan van Eyck', *Le*

Dessin sous-jacent dans la peinture, Colloque IX: Louvain-la Neuve, 1989, pp. 95–102

D. Hammer-Tugendhat: 'Jan van Eyck—Autonomisierung des Aktbildes und Geschlechterdifferenz', *Krit. Ber.* (1989), pp. 78–99

J. R. J. van Asperen de Boer and M. Faries: '*La Vierge du chancelier Rolin* de Van Eyck: Examen au moyen de la réflectographie à l'infra-rouge', *Rev. Louvre*, i (1990), pp. 37–49

J. R. J. van Asperen de Boer, B. Ridderbos and M. Seldenrust: 'The Portrait of a Man with a Ring by Jan van Eyck', *Bull. Rijksmus.*, xxxix (1991), pp. 8–35

J. Elkins: 'On the Arnolfini Portrait and the Lucca Madonna: Did Jan van Eyck Have a Perspectival System?', *A. Bull.*, lxxiii (1991), pp. 53–62

E. Bosshard: 'Revealing van Eyck: The Examination of the Thyssen-Bornemisza *Annunciation*', *Apollo*, cxxxvi (1992), pp. 4-11

J. C. Hall: *The Arnolfini Betrothal* (Berkeley, 1994)

INFLUENCE

R. Weiss: 'Jan van Eyck and the Italians', *It. Stud.*, xii (1956), pp. 1–15; xiii (1957), pp. 7–21

G. Panhans: 'Florentiner Maler verarbeiten ein Eyckisches Bild', *Wien. Jb. Kstgesch.*, xxvii (1974), pp. 188–98

J. Bruyn: 'Antonello en de Nederlanden', *Oud-Holland*, xcvi (1982), pp. 240–43

A. S. Fuchs: 'The *Virgin of the Councillors* by Luis Dalmau (1443–1445): The Contract and its Eyckian Execution', *Gaz. B.-A.*, 6th ser., xcix (1982), pp. 45–54

L. Castelfranchi-Vegas: *Italia e Fiandra nella pittura del quattrocento* (Milan, 1983); review by A. Roberts in *A. Bull.*, lxix (1987), pp. 470–72

L. Silver: 'Fountain and Source: A Rediscovered Eyckian Icon', *Pantheon*, xli (1983), pp. 95–104

E. Dharens: 'Tussen de van Eycks en Hugo can der Goes', *Acad. Anclt.: Kl. S. Kst.*, xlv/1 (1984), pp. 1–98

A. Garzelli: 'Sulla fortuna del *Gerolamo* mediceo del van Eyck nell'arte fiorentina del quattrocento', *Scritti di storia dell'arte in onore di Roberto Salvini* (Florence, 1984), pp. 347–53

For further bibliography, see M. Comblem-Sonkes: *Guide bibliographique de la peinture flamande du XVe siècle* (Brussels, 1984)

ANNE HAGOPIAN VAN BUREN

Eyck, Aldo van (*b* Driebergen, 16 March 1918). Dutch architect, writer and teacher. He attended Dutch and English schools and received his architectural training at the Eidgenössische Technische Hochschule in Zurich (1939–43). He worked as an architect in the Publieke Werken, Amsterdam (1946–51), and then established his own office in 1951. Van Eyck was a talented Functionalist of the younger generation and the Dutch delegate to CIAM from 1947, but one of his early concerns was for a freer imagination in architecture in place of the rigid Functionalism of CIAM. Like the Cobra group, he found a source of inspiration in the imagination of children, expressed in the 730 playgrounds he designed in Amsterdam between 1947 and 1974, and in traditional cultures, particularly in Africa. These experiences, and contact with a new generation of modern architects in the Netherlands including Jacob Bakema and Herman Hertzberger, led him to play an important role in TEAM TEN, the group that emerged from CIAM in 1956 to promote the importance of individual architectural and social identity, scale and meaning in place of the mechanical and generalized ideology of CIAM's Charte d'Athènes (1933).

Van Eyck envisaged the dwelling as a spiritual core that would continually interact with the individual lives of its inhabitants and the community to which they belonged. An early example of his ideas was the group of 64 houses for senior citizens (1951–4; with Jan Rietveld), Amsterdam, which incorporated striking spatial innovations to make life more pleasant for the occupants. The Burgerweeshuis (1957–60; see fig.), Amsterdam, a municipal orphanage arranged as a cellular cluster of individual,

Aldo van Eyck: Burgerweeshuis, Amsterdam, 1957–60

domed spaces and open courts, is perhaps the best-known expression of his concept of the house as a small city: it allowed its inhabitants to live in their own spaces, in their own imaginative worlds, as well as in the larger communal areas and the covered passageways that served as streets. In 1991 van Eyck converted the building for use by the Berlage Institute, a post-graduate school of architecture.

Another well-known work, the temporary sculpture pavilion (1966) in the Sonsbeek park in Arnhem, allowed for the interaction between sculpture and people; designed as a 'labyrinth', a series of narrow parallel corridors separated by walls built of simple stone blocks, it incorporated many unexpected circular niches to give each work its own individual space, as well as cross-connections to give the visitor a sense of security. The idea of circular niches is echoed in the Pastoor Van Ars church (1968–9) in Loosduinen, The Hague; inside the simple, rectangular building there are rows of cylindrical skylight drums in the roof placed directly over the roof beams, creating a complex fall of light.

A later building that summarizes van Eyck's architectural and social ideals is the Hubertushuis (1973–8), Amsterdam, a home for single mothers and their children. Planned around a rear courtyard, the building is full of unexpected details and in-between spaces that allow the occupants to lead their own lives within the community, and it is painted in bright colours to articulate the spaces and make a small, kaleidoscopic city of the house.

From 1971 to 1982 van Eyck was in partnership with Theo Bosch and produced several housing developments in Amsterdam as well as the Faculty of Arts building (1975–85) for the University of Amsterdam, a large structure that is fitted into the context of the old inner city. In 1982 he established a partnership with his wife, Hannie van Eyck; their buildings include complexes for the European Space, Technology and Energy Centre (ESTEC) near Noordwijk and residential blocks for Padua psychiatric hospital near Eindhoven, both completed in 1989. He became internationally known as editor (1959–67) of the Dutch journal *Forum* and for his contributions to the writings of Team Ten. He was also well known as a teacher in the Netherlands and overseas, particularly in the USA, and he became a professor at the Technische Hogeschool in Delft in 1968. His thoughtful and expressive work had a great influence on the evolution of modern architecture in The Netherlands, providing a rich alternative to the rigid Functionalism and monotony of the International Style.

WRITINGS
A. Smithson, ed.: *Team 10 Primer* (London, 1968) [several contributions]

BIBLIOGRAPHY
O. Newman, ed.: *CIAM '59 in Otterlo* (Stuttgart, 1961)
J. van de Beek, ed.: *Aldo van Eyck: Projekten, 1948–1961* (Groningen, 1981)
H. Hertzberger, A. van Roijen-Wortmann and F. Strauven: *Aldo van Eyck: Hubertushuis* (Amsterdam, 1982)
J. van de Beek, ed.: *Aldo van Eyck: Projekten, 1962–76* (Groningen, 1983)
'New Amsterdam School: Aldo van Eyck', *Archit. Rev.* [London], 1055 (1985), pp. 14–17 [special issue on The Netherlands]
P. Buchanan, L. Lefaivre and A. Tzonis: *Aldo & Hannie van Eyck: Recent Work* (Amsterdam, 1989)

PIETER SINGELENBERG

Eyck [de Ayck; Deick; Deyck; de Eck; van Eyck], **Barthélemy d'** (*fl* 1444–69). Netherlandish painter, active in France. The son of Ydria Exters 'd'Allemagne' (*d* 1460) and the stepson of Pierre du Billant, he is first recorded on 19 February 1444 as a witness with Enguerrand Quarton in Aix-en-Provence and described as 'magister Bartolomeus de Ayck pictor', inhabitant of Aix. From *c.* 1447 he was 'peintre et varlet de chambre' at the court of René I, King of Naples (*reg* 1438–42) and Duke of Anjou (*reg* 1434–80). Between 1447 and 1449 Barthélemy worked at René's château of Tarascon (Bouches-du-Rhône) in a room close to the Duke's own apartments. There his activities may have included supervising fellow artists, providing designs and perhaps painting the ceiling decoration of the Royal Apartments in the east wing of the château (de Mérindol). In 1451 Barthélemy travelled in the Duke's entourage to Guyenne, and in 1456 he was at Angers, which he visited on a number of other occasions. Existing accounts show that Barthélemy was responsible for paying painters and illuminators, purchasing materials for manuscripts and obtaining gold to be made into jewellery for René's second wife, Joanna of Laval. The last document relating to Barthélemy is dated 26 December 1469, when he received wages for himself, three servants and three horses. The high esteem in which he was held may be deduced from Jean Pélerin's third edition of his treatise *De artificiali perspectiva* (Toul, 1521), which ends with a French poem mentioning a 'Berthelemi' together with Jean Fouquet, Jean Poyet and Coppin Delf.

There are no known works by Barthélemy, and the documents make no reference to the precise nature of works he executed. His presence in Aix in 1444 has prompted the suggestion that he may be identified as the Master of the Aix Annunciation, author of the panel of the *Annunciation* (Aix-en-Provence, Ste Marie-Madeleine; for illustration *see* MASTERS, ANONYMOUS, AND MONOGRAMMISTS, §I: MASTER OF THE AIX ANNUNCIATION), which was executed 1443–5. In addition, because of his long and close association with René of Anjou, Barthélemy has been suggested as the author of the 16 miniatures in the manuscript of the *Livre du cueur d'amour espris* (Vienna, Österreich. Nbib., Cod. 2597), together with the other works traditionally attributed to the MASTER OF KING RENÉ OF ANJOU (*see* MASTERS, ANONYMOUS, AND MONOGRAMMISTS, §I). One further hypothesis is that the Master of the Aix Annunciation and the Master of King René of Anjou were both Barthélemy d'Eyck, representing different phases of his career.

BIBLIOGRAPHY
M. Laclotte and D. Thiébaut: *L'Ecole d'Avignon* (Paris, 1983), pp. 218–22
C. de Mérindol: 'Nouvelles données sur Barthélemy d'Eyck, peintre du roi René: Les Plafonds peints du château de Tarascon', *Bull. Soc. Hist. A. Français* (1983), pp. 7–16
C. Sterling: *Enguerrand Quarton: Le Peintre de la Pietà d'Avignon* (Paris, 1983), pp. 173–83
N. Reynaud: 'La Lettre de la veuve de Barthélemy d'Eyck au roi René', *Bull. Soc. Hist. A. Français* (1984), pp. 7–10
Les Manuscrits à peintures en France, 1440–1520 (exh. cat. by F. Avril and N. Reynaud, Paris, Bib. N., 1993–4)

HELEN GEDDES

Eykens, Frans. *See* YKENS, FRANS.

Eynde, van den. Flemish family of sculptors. (1) Hubert van den Eynde taught the son of his brother and fellow sculptor Cornelis van den Eynde (1586–1664), (2) Sebastian van den Eynde; he also taught another nephew, Sebastian de Neve, as well as his own son (3) Norbert van den Eynde. The works of Hubert and his pupils all demonstrate an adherence to the High Baroque style of Rubens.

(1) Hubert van den Eynde (*b* Antwerp, 11 Nov 1594; *d* Antwerp, 1661). He trained with an unknown master before joining the Antwerp Guild of St Luke in 1620. During the 1630s he received numerous civic commissions, including sculptural decorations for the Vierschaar, the Beurs (destr.), the Jorispoort and Waterpoort (destr.; reconstruction of original, 1883), as well as for a monumental *Madonna* (destr.), which stood near the town hall, the base (destr.) of the Meirbrugge *Crucifixion* (*c.* 1635; now Antwerp Cathedral) and the figures for the 'Arch of the Emperors', part of the temporary decoration designed by Rubens for the entry of Ferdinand of Austria into the city in 1635.

Despite the destruction of a number of works in the 18th century, including the marble figure of *St Matthew* (1649–50) for the Schipper–van den Broeck epitaph in St Walburga's, Hubert van den Eynde is still well represented in the Antwerp churches. In the cathedral is his altar of St Michael (marble, *c.* 1640–60; completed after his death by Artus Quellinus (ii)), while his later works include two figures of saints for the upper niches of the choir in St Carlo Borromeo (marble) and, possibly, the altars of the Virgin and of St Roch (both marble, *c.* 1660) for St Jacob's. His commissions from churches outside Antwerp include the altar (marble, 1629) for the church of Onze Lieve Vrouw, Dendermonde, and the designs for that church's rood screen (red-and-black marble, 1659–66; both *in situ*), which were executed by Adriaan van Ronse, with some figures attributed to Matheus van Beveren. He was also responsible for the altar of St John the Baptist (1640) at Averbode Abbey, the altar of St Bernard (marble, 1648) at St Rumoldus, Steenokkerzeel, and an altar (marble, 1653–5) in the church of Onze Lieve Vrouw, Duffel (all *in situ*), which was commissioned from his brother Cornelis in 1641 but mostly carried out by Hubert and his son (3) Norbert.

(2) Sebastian van den Eynde (*b* Antwerp, *bapt* 20 June 1624; *d* Antwerp, 1702). Nephew of (1) Hubert van den Eynde. He studied with his uncle and with his cousin Sebastian de Neve. He may have travelled to Italy before 1656. In 1661–2 he became a master in the Antwerp Guild of St Luke. Sebastian van den Eynde is best represented by the numerous works he executed for St Jacob's, Antwerp, including the altar in the chapel of Onze Lieve Vrouw (black-and-white marble, 1664), that in the Trouwkapel (Marriage Chapel; red-black-and-white marble, 1669–71), for which he also executed the architectural decoration in 1669–74, and the altar (marble and white stone, 1665) and gates for the chapel of SS Peter and Paul (all *in situ*). He was also responsible for the altar in the chapel of St Anthony Abbot (marble; originally the high altar at the convent of the Victorinnen, Antwerp). His decorative skills are best displayed in his marble and alabaster commemorative plaques in St Jacob's, Antwerp, for the van Weerden–van Severdonck family (*c.* 1660), for

the Fourment–Piqueri and Fourment–Stappaert families (*c.* 1661–7), with busts of *Christ* and the *Virgin*; and for the Bollaert–Alardi family (*c.* 1664–70), including busts of *St Cornelia* and *St James*. His epitaph for *Cornelis Lantschot* (*c.* 1660) in the Kapel van de Zoete Naam Jezus, also in St Jacob's, includes a portrait attributed to Cornelis de Vos or Abraham van Diepenbeeck, which may be related to Sebastian van den Eynde's bust of *Lantschot* (*c.* 1660; Antwerp, Maagdenhuismus.). His black-and-white marble epitaph for *Octavius Franciscus Tensini* (1674; destr.) for Antwerp Cathedral also included a medallion portrait (see Jansen and van Herck, p. 77).

(3) Norbert van den Eynde (*b* Antwerp, 11 Dec 1628; *d* Antwerp, 7 Oct 1704). Son of (1) Hubert van den Eynde. He was trained by his father and collaborated with him on an altar in the church of Onze Lieve Vrouw, Duffel (marble, 1653–5; *in situ*). He became a master in the Antwerp Guild of St Luke in 1662. The majority of his commissions were for furniture and decoration in the Antwerp churches. The more important examples include several altars (destr.) for St Joris's, among them the altar for the chapel of St Roch (before 1671), with a figure of the *Virgin and Child*, that for the chapel of the Holy Sacrament (1671) and the high altar (1677; with Artus Quellinus (ii)). The altars of St Catherine (1681) and of St Eligius (1693) in Antwerp Cathedral are also attributed to him. Norbert also created the choir-stalls (wood, 1663) in the church at Vilvoorde; a throne (1663) for the priory at Groenendael; the altars (both red-black-and-white marble) of Onze Lieve Vrouw (1658–9) and of St Nicholas (1664 and 1668; with figures of St Nicholas and St Roch) for the church of St Nicholas in Waas; and, again in collaboration with Artus Quellinus (ii), a temporary high altar at St Michael's, Ghent (*c.* 1674; replaced with a permanent altar, 1679).

BIBLIOGRAPHY

A. Jansen and C. van Herck: 'De Van den Eynde's: Antwerpsche bouwmeesters and beeldhouwers uit de XVIIe eeuw', *Jb. Antwerpens Oudhdknd. Kring*, xx–xxi (1944–5), pp. 5–90

H. Nauts: 'Beeldhouwwerk van Huybrecht en Norbertus van den Eynde, en van Lucas Faydherbe in de hoofdkerk te Sint-Niklaas', *An. Oudhdknd. Kring Land van Waas An. Cerc. Archéol. Pays de Waes*, lxxii (1969), pp. 37–49

CYNTHIA LAWRENCE

Eynde, Jan van den (*fl* Antwerp, second half of the 17th century). Flemish architect, possibly related to the Antwerp family of sculptors of the same name. His major work was the new abbey church at Averbode, for which he was awarded the commission in 1644 after Lucas Faydherbe's plans had been rejected. The ground-plan of this Baroque church combines a centralized cruciform space to the west for the laity with a deep choir, necessary for Norbertine choral services. Van den Eynde probably based this combination of central and axial plans, resulting in an imposing and spacious interior, on other Flemish Baroque churches, such as the abbey church of St Pieter (1629–1722), Ghent, by Peter Huyssens. The design combined Gothic structural forms, such as ribbed vaults, with Renaissance ornamental details. No dome was built over the central section because in January 1668 one of the major piers and a portion of the vault collapsed, indicating that van den Eynde did not have sufficient knowledge of the structure of domes based on Roman models. The church, built entirely of natural white stone, was completed in 1672; the tower in 1700. Van den Eynde may also have designed the church of St Jean Baptiste (begun 1657) in the Beguinage in Brussels, which displays a stylistic affinity with the Averbode church (see Plantenga).

BIBLIOGRAPHY
J. H. Plantenga: *L'Architecture religieuse dans l'ancien duché de Brabant depuis le règne des archiducs jusqu'au gouvernement autrichien, 1598–1713* (The Hague, 1926), p. 231–7, 272
T. de Maisières: *L'Architecture religieuse à l'époque de Rubens* (Brussels, 1943)

J.-P. ESTHER

Eyre, Wilson (*b* Florence, 31 Oct 1858; *d* Philadelphia, PA, 21 Oct 1944). American architect. He was born to a prominent Philadelphia family and spent his first 11 years in Italy, where his father was serving as a US consular official. Eyre's architectural training came principally through an apprenticeship in Philadelphia under James Peacock Sims (1849–82), whom he joined in partnership just before Sims's sudden death. Sims's last works and Eyre's own early works show the impact of Richard Norman Shaw's Queen Anne and Old English styles, aspects particularly notable in The Anglecot, 401 East Evergreen Avenue, Philadelphia (1883; altered), and in the H. Genet Taylor house in Camden, NJ (1885). By the late 1880s, however, his designs were moving towards greater stylistic freedom, a departure comparable to that in the works of that decade by McKim, Mead & White, Lamb & Rich and Peabody & Stearns. Some works, particularly suburban houses, were clearly influenced by the Shingle style, such as the Charles L. Freer house, in Detroit, MI (1890). In his town houses Eyre achieved an almost unmatched type of free and flowing design, effortlessly eclectic, without the effect of a 'shotgun marriage' of styles. This is particularly evident in his Rodman Wistar house, 1014 Spruce Street, Philadelphia (1887; altered), and his C. B. Moore house, 1321 Locust Street, Philadelphia (1891). In many ways such houses represent an urban equivalent to the American achievement in the creation of the Shingle style. They were vaguely anglophile in derivation and self-consciously artistic but were usually reliant upon the horizontal continuity of thin brick courses and the warmth of buff-toned brick in the place of more rustic materials. Often a more formal, cosmopolitan note was introduced by historically allusive stone carving. In rural settings or for 'bohemian' clubs Eyre often turned to an engaging Arts and Crafts manner, as in his Mask and Wig Club, 311 South Camac Street, Philadelphia (1893), or his Neilson Brown house in the Torresdale section of Philadelphia (1900), but only rarely, as in the University of Pennsylvania Museum, Philadelphia (begun 1893), did these qualities feature in his larger urban projects. The Museum was designed in collaboration with his likeminded peers Frank Miles Day (1861–1918), Walter Cope and John Stewardson, but Eyre's hand is the most evident.

By the mid-1890s the self-consciously artistic stylization of his early work, along with the signs of the Aesthetic Movement generally, began to diminish, and Eyre's subsequent designs embodied such values only more subtly, in more nominally historicist modes. At first his reference to such historicist styles had been remarkably free, as in

his quirkily American Colonial Revival Neill and Mauran houses, 315–17 South 22nd Street, Philadelphia (1891), but he later settled into a more plausibly authentic but equally picturesque manner evident in such imposing houses as his W. T. Jeffords house at Glen Riddle, PA (1917). Country houses such as these, often Colonial Revival or 'Jacobethan', were the mainstay of his practice after 1912, when he formed a partnership with J. Gilbert McIlvaine (1880–1939).

Eyre's work had a profound influence on more than one generation, first in the 1880s among the young Philadelphia architects who showed and discussed their designs in the T-Square Club (founded 1883), and later in the less formal but historicizing stone-built suburban houses near Philadelphia that established the reputations of early 20th-century firms such as Mellor, Meigs & Howe (1916–27), Duhring, Okie & Ziegler (1899–1918), and individual architects including Edmund B. Gilchrist (1885–1953) and Robert R. McGoodwin (1886–1967).

BIBLIOGRAPHY
A. M. Githens: 'Wilson Eyre, jr: His Work', *Architectural Annual, 1900*, ed. A. Kelsey (Philadelphia, 1900), pp. 121–84
J. Millard: 'The Work of Wilson Eyre', *Archit. Rec.*, xiv (1903), pp. 279–325
V. J. Scully, jr: *The Shingle Style and the Stick Style* (New Haven, 1955, rev. 1971), pp. 121–5
E. Teitelman: 'Wilson Eyre in Camden: The Henry Genet Taylor House and Office', *Winterthur Port.*, xv (1980), pp. 229–55
B. Fahlman: 'Wilson Eyre in Detroit: The Charles Lang Freer House', *Winterthur Port.*, xv (1980), pp. 257–70
S. Tatman and R. Moss: *Biographical Dictionary of Philadelphia Architects, 1700–1930* (Boston, 1985), pp. 253–61

JEFFREY A. COHEN

Eysen, Louis (*b* Manchester, 23 Nov 1843; *d* Munich, 21 July 1899). German painter and engraver. His family, which had moved to England in the 1840s, returned to Frankfurt am Main in 1850. He studied wood engraving with Alexander Stix (1819–93) at the Städelsches Kunstinstitut in Frankfurt and later achieved considerable success in this medium (e.g. *Glade*, 1868; see Zimmermann, p. 9). He was taught painting by Karl Hausmann (1825–86) and was influenced chiefly by contemporary French art. He first worked mainly in Berlin and then in Munich, where he met Otto Scholderer and Wilhelm Leibl, who painted his portrait (*c*. 1870; Frankfurt am Main, Städel. Kstinst.). He studied with Léon Bonnat in Paris from 1869 to 1870. In 1873 he settled at Kronberg, in the Taunus mountains, and after visiting Italy in 1876–7 he settled in Obermais, near Meran (now Merano), where he hoped the climate would cure his tuberculosis.

Eysen had two main periods of creativity, the first in Frankfurt and Kronberg and the second in Meran (1879–99). In the landscapes he painted while at Kronberg, for example *The Middle of the Forest* (*c*. 1875; Nuremberg, Ger. Nmus.), he was largely influenced by Courbet. However, Eysen soon began to absorb the influence of the more atmospheric *paysage intime* of the Barbizon school. His most mature works, such as *The Wildflower Meadow* (1877; destr., see Ruhmer, 1960), reveal the influence of the Impressionists, particularly Auguste Renoir. In Meran his subject-matter and composition returned to the Romantic concept of landscape painting, executed in a moderately Impressionist style, for example *Landscape at Meran* (1882; Mannheim, priv. col., see Ruhmer, 1960). Eysen worked in Meran in complete seclusion, holding occasional exhibitions in Berlin, which attracted little interest. The year after his death, a touring exhibition, which visited Meran, Karlsruhe, Munich, Frankfurt and Berlin, aroused interest in his work.

BIBLIOGRAPHY

Thieme–Becker
E. Ruhmer: 'Louis Eysen', *Kst & S. Heim*, lviii (1960), pp. 404–7
W. Zimmermann: *Der Maler Louis Eysen* (Frankfurt am Main, 1963)
E. Ruhmer: *Der Leibl-Kreis und die Reine Malerei* (Rosenheim, 1984)
Louis Eysen (exh. cat., Frankfurt am Main, J. P. Schneider jr, 1990)

EBERHARD RUHMER

Eytan, Dan (*b* Palestine, 28 June 1931). Israeli architect, teacher and urban planner. He graduated from the Technion (Israel Institute of Technology), Haifa, in 1954, winning two housing competitions in that year. His early influences were the post-war architecture of Le Corbusier and then the architects who developed New Brutalism, including Peter and Alison SMITHSON. This brand of Modernism, with its austere Minimalist appearance and total exposure of materials, particularly concrete, was viewed as appropriate for the socialist-oriented and economically straitened Israel of that time. Other related early influences were traditional Japanese architecture and Louis Kahn's notion of servant and served parts of a building. In 1966 Eytan was appointed professor of architecture at the Technion, and in the late 1960s he demonstrated his assimilation of his early influences in both housing and public buildings, most notably in the Tel Aviv Museum (1965–70) and the Mexico Building (1968) for the Arts Department of Tel Aviv University, both with Yitzhak Yashar (*b* 1921). In both buildings the structural skeleton and the servicing parts, especially the lift and stair towers of the museum, are clearly expressed in rough exposed concrete. The wall infill consists of slabs of white marble in the museum, and, in the Mexico Building, rough brown–grey cobblestones or glass. This clear distinction between structure and infill is also manifest in his buildings in Jerusalem, notably the National Police Headquarters (1970), the City Tower (1972) and Clal Centre (1972–80) office blocks and the Faculty of Social Sciences (1975) at the Hebrew University. In these the infill is glazed or of stone or marble, to comply with a city bye-law. During a period of greater national affluence in the 1980s, with his new partner Eri Goshen (*b* 1945), Eytan shifted to an extensive use of glazed curtain walls, mainly for office buildings in Tel Aviv, and later towards Post-modernism, for example in the Tel Aviv University Gallery (completed 1987; with Bracha Chyutin (*b* 1950)). Here he included a peach-coloured curving wall and false columns in what is nevertheless a restrained and clearly planned design. His extensive urban planning includes projects in Jerusalem, Tel Aviv and Iran, where his office planned, designed and supervised the construction of the new towns Bandar-e Abbās and Būshehr (1972–7).

BIBLIOGRAPHY

'Buildings for the Arts', *Archit. Rec.* (1978), pp. 132–5
M. D. Levin: *The Modern Museum* (Tel Aviv, 1983)
Tvai, 24 (1985), pp. 30–31
D. Kroyanker: *Jerusalem Architecture—Periods and Styles: Modern Architecture outside the Old City Walls* (Jerusalem, 1991)

ADAM A. MAZOR

Eyüboğlu, Bedri Rahmi (*b* Rize, 1911; *d* Istanbul, 1975). Turkish painter and writer. He studied at the Fine Arts Academy in Istanbul (1927–31) and then under André Lhôte in Paris (1931–2). On returning to Istanbul he joined the D Group in 1934, and at the end of 1936 became assistant to Léopold Lévy (1882–1966) at the Fine Arts Academy. Although influenced by the work of such European artists as Matisse and Dufy, he also appreciated from an early date the arts of Anatolia. Under the Turkish government's policy to send artists to work in the provinces, he went to Edirne in 1938 and to Çorum in 1942, where he studied the folk culture. Thereafter themes relating to Anatolian life became prominent in his work. He also taught younger artists to appreciate folk art, and with this aim some of his students at the Academy formed the Group of Ten in 1947. In his own works he experimented with various styles and media. In *Peasant Woman* (or *Night Train*, 1954; Istanbul, Mimar Sinan U., Mus. Ptg & Sculp.) small, brightly coloured dots appear like mosaics on a dark background. From the late 1950s he occasionally produced abstract works in mosaic, graphite, stained glass and ceramics, with stylized folk and calligraphic motifs, for example a mosaic panel (227 sq. m; 1958) of stylized figural and geometric elements for the façade of the Turkish pavilion at the Exposition Universelle et Internationale in Brussels and a mosaic panel (50 sq. m; 1959) for the restaurant in the NATO Building in the Palais de Chaillot, Paris. He was a visiting artist at the University of California from 1960 to 1963, and in 1969–70 he worked on murals for the Turkish Embassy in Bonn. Eyüboğlu's late works included the *Yellow Saz* (1966; Ankara, Mus. F.A.). He was also a successful poet and wrote articles on art. His wife Eren Eyüboğlu (*b* 1913), who entered the Academy of Fine Arts at Iaşi in Romania in 1928, and studied under André Lhôte in Paris from 1930 to 1932, was also a notable figure in Turkish painting, producing figurative paintings, portraits, landscapes and large-scale murals, including mosaic panels.

BIBLIOGRAPHY

Z. Güvemli: *The Sabancı Collection of Paintings* (Istanbul, 1984) [Eng. and Turk. texts]
S. Tansuğ: *Çağdaş Türk sanatı* [Contemporary Turkish art] (Istanbul, 1986)
G. Renda and others: *A History of Turkish Painting* (Geneva, Seattle and London, 1988)

Eyvan. *See* IWAN.

F

Faber, Johann, II (*fl* Leipzig, 1592; *d* after 1617). German painter, illustrator and printmaker. In 1592 he was granted the freedom of Leipzig, where he worked mainly as an illustrator for the publisher Henning Gross. He specialized in views and plans of towns, including Moscow, Wrocław, Venice, Istanbul and Jerusalem. His etchings illustrated the *Persianische Reise* (Leipzig, 1609) by Karasch and a book on horse-breeding, *Deliciae ordinum equestrium* (Leipzig, 1617). He also produced a few costume engravings and genre scenes. His etchings have the lightness of sketches but are coarser in detail than works by comparable engravers, such as the Leipzig artist Andreas Bretschneider (*fl* Leipzig, 1611; *d* after 1640).

BIBLIOGRAPHY

G. Wustmann: *Geschichte der Malerei in Leipzig* (1879)

ANNETTE FABER

Faber, Johann Joachim (*b* Hamburg, 12 April 1778; *d* Hamburg, ?2 Aug 1846). German painter and printmaker. He studied first in Hamburg under the painter Carl Waagen (1800–73), moving to Dresden in 1797 and subsequently to Prague. From 1802 until 1804 he lived and worked in Vienna, where he supplemented his earlier training by attending classes at the Akademie der Bildenden Künste. In 1806 he made the customary journey to Italy, where there already existed a thriving colony of German and Austrian artists. In Rome he seemed destined for a career as a history painter, making his début with a religious composition entitled *Christ Blessing the Children*. On his return to Hamburg in 1808 he discovered that there was little demand for historical compositions, and in order to earn a living he was obliged to turn to portraiture. In addition to portraits in oils, during this period he also worked extensively in aquatint, at which he was particularly adept. In 1816 the financial support of wealthy patrons enabled him to undertake a second visit to Italy, where he remained for 11 years. In Rome he kept company with Ludwig Richter and Johann Heinrich Schilbach (1798–1851), and under the joint influence of Joseph Anton Koch and Johann Christian Reinhart he devoted himself to landscape painting, executing a prodigious array of oil sketches, for example the *Serpentara at Olevano* (1824; Hamburg, Ksthalle). In 1827 he returned to Hamburg, where he resumed his career as a portrait painter and taught at the drawing school of the Patriotische Gesellschaft.

BIBLIOGRAPHY

Thieme–Becker

H. Ehl: 'Zwei unbekannte Hamburger Romantiker-Landschaften', *Kstrundschau*, i/4 (1942), pp. 65–7

COLIN J. BAILEY

Faber, John, the elder (*b* ?The Hague, *c.* 1660; *d* Bristol, 1721). Dutch draughtsman, printmaker and calligrapher, active in England. He first worked as a portrait draughtsman in ink on vellum, in a refined but somewhat archaic manner; accompanied by florid calligraphic inscriptions, these portraits belong to a tradition established in the Low Countries and represented by such artists as Ludolf Bakhuizen and Crispijn van den Queboorn (1604–52). Although he is variously reported as going to England in 1687 or 1695, inscriptions on his drawings show that Faber was in Amsterdam in 1693 and 1696; his earliest London portrait, of the Dutch theologian *Simon Episcopius* (pen and ink on vellum; London, BM), is dated 1698.

In London, Faber adopted the indigenous medium of black lead on vellum, as used by David Loggan and John White; like most portrait draughtsmen of his generation, he experimented with mezzotint, sometimes to reproduce his own drawings. These were not always taken from life—for example, *William III* (1697) was probably adapted by Faber from an oil painting of the King—but can sometimes be associated with prototypes by recent and contemporary painters. Faber's dated mezzotints, which include portraits of divines, the Native American chiefs who visited England in 1710 and founders of Oxford and Cambridge colleges, cover the period 1707 to 1719. His son John Faber the younger (*c.* 1695–1756) adopted his mezzotint practice and became one of the most prolific engravers of the first half of the 18th century.

BIBLIOGRAPHY

DNB

E. Croft-Murray and P. Hulton: *British Drawings: 16th and 17th Centuries,* London, BM cat., i (London, 1960), pp. 309–10

DAVID BLAYNEY BROWN

Faber, Martin Hermansz. (*b* Emden, *c.* 1587; *d* Emden, 13 April 1648). German painter, draughtsman and architect. The son of a goldsmith, he apparently studied mathematics at Groningen, where he came into contact with French, Italian and Netherlandish painting. In 1611 he travelled to Rome and Naples, encountering the Dutch painter Louis Finson, through whom he came under the powerful influence of Caravaggio's style. He followed Finson to Aix-en-Provence in 1613, then to Toulouse and Bordeaux, and is thought to have contributed some of the landscapes in Finson's works. In Provence they painted matching self-portraits (1613; Marseille, Mus. B.-A.). In Paris the collaboration ended, and in 1616 Faber returned to Emden, where he joined the painters' guild in 1618 and was elected Ratsherr in 1628 and 1631. He became known for his Italianate landscapes and religious paintings, such as the Caravaggesque *Liberation of St Peter* (after 1616; Emden, Rathaus).

Faber's drawings, however, mainly of landscapes, are typical of the Central European international style stemming from the court at Prague. The subject-matter of his *Ruins on a Hill* (1629; Rotterdam, Mus. Boymans–van Beuningen) and the light pen strokes in two shades of brown are close to the style of Roelandt Savery. His *Cupid, Mars and Venus in a Landscape* (Edinburgh, N.G.), in white ink and coloured washes on a dark grey ground, recalls Bartholomäus Spranger. As state architect to the city of Emden from 1634, Faber's most notable building was the Neue Kirche (1643), executed in a serviceable classical Baroque.

BIBLIOGRAPHY
H. Siebern: *Die Kunstdenkmäler der Stadt Emden*, xlviii of *Kunstdenkmä-lerinventare Niedersachsens* (1927/*R* Hannover, 1980), pp. 51–72; pl. viia
B. Nicolson: *The International Caravaggesque Movement: Lists of Pictures by Caravaggio and his Followers throughout Europe from 1590–1650* (Oxford, 1979), p. 47   □

Fabergé, (Peter) Carl (Gustavovitch) (*b* St Petersburg, 30 May 1846; *d* Lausanne, 24 Sept 1920). Russian goldsmith and jeweller. He was descended from Huguenot stock, and his family had fled France after the Revocation of the Edict of Nantes in 1685 and had settled in eastern Germany. In the 18th century a goldsmith from Württemberg with the name of either Faberger or Fabiger settled in St Petersburg; he may have been a relative. Fabergé's father, Gustav (Petrovitch) Fabergé (1814–72), moved *c.* 1830 to St Petersburg, where he served his apprenticeship as a goldsmith and became a master in 1841 with an independent workshop. In 1842 he opened a jewellery shop. Carl toured Europe between 1860 and 1864; he returned to St Petersburg as a master goldsmith and joined his father's firm, which he took over in 1870. In 1882 his brother, Agathon Fabergé (1862–95), joined the firm.

At the beginning of his career Fabergé produced bracelets and medallions decorated with stones and enamels. He transformed the conventional jewellery business

Carl Fabergé (workshops of) (clockwise from top left): (a) frame, enamel, red gold and green-gold swags; (b) seated gorilla, agate set with rose-diamond eyes; (c) lilies of the valley flowerpot, pearls, rose diamonds, gold stalk, nephrite leaf, in rock-crystal bowl; (d) candlestick in the form of a toad, nephrite set with carbuncle eyes, green-gold mount, rock-crystal drip-tray; (e) jabot brooch, gold and enamel, with a rose-diamond border; (f) Easter egg pendant, platinum and rose diamonds; (g) bowenite dish with gold mounts; (h) pair of cufflinks, enamel with diamond centres and borders; (i) aquamarine brooch with gold basketwork mount set with rose diamonds; (j) cigarette box, gold and opaque white enamel with rose-diamond thumb piece, l. 99 mm; (k) blue tit, various hardstones with rose-diamond eyes and gold legs; (l) crochet hook, nephrite, opalescent oyster enamel and gold mounts set with rose diamonds (London, Wartski Ltd and various private collections)

by insisting that the value of an object should reside in its craftsmanship rather than its materials. Under his direction, the firm moved away from the contemporary custom of setting large gemstones in shoddy settings and produced elaborate diamond-set pendant brooches, ribbon-knot necklaces and trelliswork bracelets. From 1866 he was one of a number of jewellers selling pieces to the Russian imperial household, and the items produced were linked to contemporary French designs.

Fabergé perfected a wide palette of translucent enamels that were applied over a guilloche ground with sunburst, wave or moiré effects among others (*see* ENAMEL, colour pl. IV, fig. 3), and he revived *quatre-couleur* goldwork. Under the influence of Agathon Fabergé, the most attractive compositions—typical of Fabergé production from 1882 onwards—were the animals, flowers and objects of vertu produced in hardstones or precious metals; such functional objects as cigarette and cigar boxes, photograph-frames, pencil-cases, note-pads and letter-openers (see fig.) were also made. The hardstone carvings of animals, birds and fish, usually measuring between only 25 and 75 mm in length or height, were never signed by the individual lapidary but must nevertheless be regarded as original works of sculpture. The natural resources of Siberia, the Caucasus and the Urals provided a rich variety of materials for these models and for larger pieces, including many types of agate, Siberian jade (nephrite), rhodonite, malachite, aventurine quartz, rock crystal, obsidian and bowenite (a variety of serpentine). Some of the most enchanting compositions of the firm, and characteristic of its output, are the pots of flowers. The flowers, supported on engraved gold stalks and often enamelled and set with gemstones, and the leaves carved from nephrite, are placed in rock crystal skilfully carved to simulate a bowl filled with water (e.g. bowl of cornflower and oat sprays with blue enamel petals and rose diamond pistils; St Petersburg, Hermitage).

Czar Alexander III (*d* 1894) patronized the Fabergé firm and on 1 May 1885 awarded Fabergé the title Supplier to the Imperial Court. The first of the sensational series of Imperial Easter Eggs, each concealing a surprise, was commissioned by Alexander III in 1884 or 1885, and he even collaborated to some extent with Fabergé on its design. Later examples were commissioned by Nicholas II for the Dowager Tsarina Marie Feodorovna and the Tsarina Alexandra Feodorovna (e.g. Lilies of the Valley Egg, 1898; New York, Forbes Mag. Col.).

The Fabergé workshops produced pieces in many different styles. Some of the most successful silver was made in the Moscow workshop (est. 1887) in a typically medieval Russian style (e.g. cigar box shaped as a helmet, 1899–1908; Doorn, Huis Doorn), and some pieces also reflect the influences of Renaissance Italy (e.g. rock-crystal dish with enamel, 1896; St Petersburg, Hermitage) and the contemporary Art Nouveau style (e.g. silver mounts of trailing peapods on a Doulton vase, 1899–1908; St Petersburg, Peter & Paul Fortress).

The St Petersburg branch was composed of a number of separate workshops, whose responsibility it was to oversee each item from its initial design through all the different stages of manufacture. A number of workmasters operated in each workshop, who were entitled to stamp

their initials beside the firm name on the pieces they supervised. The Moscow branch was run more as a commercial enterprise, and its pieces bear the firm's name beneath the Imperial Warrant of Appointment, the Romanov double-headed eagle. Other branches were founded in Odessa (1890), London (1903) and Kiev (1905), and, in all, *c.* 500 people were employed. With the start of the Russian Revolution in 1917, a Committee of Employees was formed; it managed the firm until 1918, when Fabergé closed the workshops and left the country.

See also RUSSIA, fig. 47.

BIBLIOGRAPHY

H. C. Bainbridge: *Peter Carl Fabergé* (London, 1949)
A. K. Snowman: *The Art of Carl Fabergé* (London, 1953, rev. 1962/*R* 1968)
Fabergé, 1846–1920 (exh. cat. by A. K. Snowman, London, V&A, 1977)
H. Waterfield and C. Forbes: *Fabergé: Imperial Eggs and Other Fantasies* (New York, 1978)
G. von Habsburg-Lothringen and A. von Solodkoff: *Fabergé: Court Jeweller to the Tsars* (Fribourg, 1979, rev. 1984)
A. K. Snowman: *Carl Fabergé: Goldsmith to the Imperial Court of Russia* (London, 1979, rev. 1983)
A. von Solodkoff and others: *Masterpieces from the House of Fabergé* (New York, 1984/*R* 1989)
Fabergé: Juwelier der Zaren (exh. cat., ed. G. von Habsburg; Munich, Ksthalle Hypo-Kultstift., 1986–7; Eng. trans., Geneva, 1987)
A. K. Snowman: *Fabergé: Lost and Found: The Recently Discovered Jewelry Designs from the St Petersburg Archives* (London, 1993)
Fabergé: Imperial Jeweller (exh. cat. by G. von Habsburg and M. Lopato, St Petersburg, Hermitage; Paris, Mus. A. Déc.; London, V&A; 1993–4)

A. KENNETH SNOWMAN

Fabiani, Max (*b* Cobdil [now Kobdilj, Western Slovenia], 1865; *d* Italy, 1962). Slovene architect. He studied at Otto Wagner's Spezialschule in the Akademie der Bildenden Künste, Vienna, in the late 1880s and was soon marked out for a promising career in Vienna. He designed the opulent Rococo Revival-style Artaria house (1900) in the Kohlmarkt in Vienna, and he was commissioned to construct the headquarters of the Portois & Fix interior design company (1899), also in Vienna. This Jugendstil design was remarkably simple, with a plain façade of encaustic green tiles on which the company's trademark was picked out. Fabiani seems, however, to have been more than willing to turn his back on Jugendstil Modernism. He developed a fine Baroque Revival style, exemplified by the picturesque Urania headquarters and observatory (1905–9) on the Ringstrasse in Vienna, which reflected the tastes of the more conservative elements of the Habsburg court. Archduke Franz Ferdinand (1863–1914), heir to the throne and a man of unyielding and reactionary taste, was particularly impressed by Fabiani's work in this style, which suited his aim to re-create the late Baroque splendour of Maria Theresa's reign (*reg* 1745–80). Fabiani was commissioned to restore and extend the archducal castle at Konopiste in Bohemia (1910–12). It was also through imperial patronage that he became the principal architect employed by the Slovene authorities in Ljubljana after the earthquake of 1895.

In Ljubljana, however, Fabiani eschewed tradition and set about reconstructing squares in a form of Jugendstil that was largely inspired by contemporary developments in Prague. In this he was encouraged by the mayor, who had studied in Prague. At the same time Fabiani became interested in Camillo Sitte's ideas on urban planning and developed his own concept of the urban square and its relationship to the city. On the collapse of the Habsburg Empire he withdrew to Italy. There he worked with enthusiasm on a number of projects in Gorizia, rebuilding the city after damage caused by World War I.

Fabiani grew increasingly eccentric with age; he published several treatises and philosophical works, but some of his ideas—such as the innate superiority of people with red hair—could be dismissed as the misguided ramblings of an old man out of place in the new order of Europe. His other theories, however, especially with regard to urban planning, continued to merit the respect of Italian architects, and he was justly honoured by the Italian state a few years before his 100th birthday.

BIBLIOGRAPHY

M. Pozzetto: *Max Fabiani* (Vienna, 1985)

RICHARD BASSETT

Fable of the Ancients, the. *See* MASHEL HA-KADMONI.

Fables. Literary genre characterized by the combination of a brief fictional narrative featuring non-human, anthropomorphized actors (typically animals, less frequently plants or other inanimate objects) with a generalized moral lesson usually made explicit in a proverb-like epimyth. It differs from the more episodic animal epic in its brevity and explicitly didactic intention, and from animal allegory (e.g. the *Physiologus*; *see* BESTIARY) in the contrived behaviour of its non-human characters. By the end of the 5th century BC the fable tradition in the West was generally attributed to Aesop, who is thought to have been a slave on Samos in the 6th century BC.

1. Manuscript. 2. Printed.

1. MANUSCRIPT. The earliest preserved Western fable manuscripts are unillustrated Greek fragments from the 1st century AD. The first surviving Latin collection is the verse compilation by the freed Roman slave Phaedrus (*c.* 15 BC–*c.* AD 50), and shortly thereafter, Babrius, a Roman citizen living in Syria, exploited the same sources for his collection in Greek verse; both were immediately imitated and paraphrased. Although neither was available in its original form in the Middle Ages, the Babrius corpus was represented in the Latin distichs of Avianus (*c.* AD 400), and the fables of Phaedrus were transmitted in a variety of adaptations, beginning with the Latin prose paraphrases (5th century AD) attributed to Romulus (whose name is found in the prefatory letter). Avianus' 42 poems were generally transmitted with their author's name, but in the Middle Ages the Romulus collections were invariably known as 'Aesop'.

It can be presumed—given their subject-matter and audience—that these fable collections were furnished with illustrations soon after their composition. The only pictorial representations of fable material preserved from Late Antiquity, however, are scenes on vases and tombstones, some dating to the 3rd century BC, while the oldest known illustrated manuscripts are medieval. A manuscript from northern France (late 9th century AD; Paris, Bib. N., MS. nouv. acq. lat. 1132) preserves an illustrated Apocalypse and 11 drawings illustrating Avianus. The retention of archaic details of dress and architecture in both picture cycles suggests that they were copied from a manuscript model of the mid-6th century AD. The earliest known

1. *Fable of the Aged Hunting Dog*, tinted drawing, 175×245 mm, from the Romulus LGB, *c.* 1300 (Hamburg, Staats- und Universitätsbibliothek, MS. in scrinio 47, fol. 54*r*)

illustrations to a Romulus collection are found in a manuscript (*c.* 1030; Leiden, Bib. Rijksuniv., MS. Voss. lat. 8° 15) copied by Ademar of Chabanais (*d* 1034) at the monastery of St Martial in Limoges. The archetype of this series is also presumed to have been Late Antique: although Ademar's immediate model already had the schematic details of landscape, dress and gesture associated with Carolingian style, the compositional techniques (above all the symmetrical confrontation of fable actors and the simultaneous representation of chronologically distinct events) are characteristic of Late Antique practice. These simple drawings were not used in any other extant medieval manuscripts, but their influence is evident in the woodcuts for the Ulm *Vita Esopi et fabulae* of Heinrich Steinhöwel (1412–82; *see* §2 below). In addition to these two manuscripts, the fable scenes of the 11th-century Bayeux Tapestry (Bayeux, Mus. Tap.) provide further evidence for an early European tradition of fable illustration. Both Avianus and various Romulus collections were widely used in the Middle Ages for teaching Latin. These inexpensive school-books were only rarely illustrated (e.g. late 15th century; Trier, Stadtbib., MS. 1108). The only Latin text frequently illustrated was the 12th-century Romulus redaction known as the *Anonymus Neveleti*, a collection of 60 fables in elegiac distichs that was both a standard scholastic text and a principal source for vernacular collections, in which illustration was integral from the first.

The earliest preserved vernacular fable collection is the *Esope* of Marie de France (*fl c.* 1160–90), an Anglo-Norman noblewoman who translated into French a lost Anglo-Saxon collection of 103 fables ultimately derived from the Romulus material. The epimyths are marked by a generally conservative political stance, and the success of the collection among the medieval upper classes is reflected in the provenance of most of the 23 known manuscripts, all of which date from the 13th to the 15th centuries. Marie's rhymed collection was translated into Italian and, early in the 13th century, into Latin prose; known as the 'Romulus LBG', the Latin text was in turn the direct source of further vernacular collections. The Romulus LBG is itself illustrated in one north German manuscript (*c.* 1300; Hamburg, Staats- & Ubib., MS. in scrinio 47; see fig. 1).

Throughout Europe, however, the *Anonymus Neveleti* was the most frequently translated of the Romulus collections. The first of these in French verse, the *Ysopet-Avionnet*, is dated to the 13th century. It combines renderings of all 60 *Anonymus* poems with 19 fables translated from Avianus and is transmitted in 6 extant manuscripts that divide into 2 groups. In the three closely related 14th-century manuscripts (e.g. Paris, Bib. N., MS. fr. 1594), each of the French translations is preceded by the text of the corresponding Latin fable, and each is illustrated by a miniature. In dress, architecture and composition these illustrations are thoroughly medieval, and it is likely that they were designed specifically for the *Ysopet*'s archetype. The three 15th-century manuscripts (e.g. Paris, Bib. N., MS. fr. 1595), on the other hand, contain the French text alone and are illustrated only by historiated initials showing the protagonists. The earliest prose fable translations in any European vernacular are the 29 Romulus fables translated by Jean de Vignay *c.* 1330 from the *Speculum historiale* of Vincent of Beauvais (*c.* 1190–*c.* 1264). Their illustrations, even more so than in the case of the *Ysopet-Avionnet*, are characterized by the abandonment of traditional models in favour of innovative compositions.

The close connection between the vernacular and the illustration of fable literature in the later Middle Ages is especially apparent in Germany, where the most popular collection was the rhymed work of the Swiss Dominican Ulrich Boner (*fl c.* 1324–49). Called the *Edelstein* after the introductory fable of the foolish cock who found a precious pearl, it contains 100 fables from Avianus, the *Anonymus Neveleti* and other, minor sources. Of the 36 extant manuscripts and fragments, 18 illustrate all or part of the fables, and 4 others have space for illustrations.

Two of the earliest and most lavishly illustrated manuscripts (*c.* 1420; Basle, Off. Bib. U., MS. A. N. III. 17; 1449; Augsburg, Ubib., Cod. Oettingen-Wallerstein I.3.2° 3) were commissioned for members of the Swiss nobility and urban patriciate. Simpler illustrations were more usual, however, and their unsophisticated style and uniformity are typical of the products of workshops offering vernacular books for popular consumption; indeed, listed in the inventories of the 15th-century Hagenau 'publisher' Diebolt Lauber are illustrated *Aesop*s likely to have been Boner's work. Like the French *Ysopet*s, the *Edelstein* was occasionally copied with the Latin fables it translated, so that the vernacular text and its illustrations together elucidate the original for readers less expert in Latin.

Throughout most of the Middle Ages, the fable corpus remained essentially Classical in origin; in the 15th century such new collections as the Indian *Panchatantra* and the fables in the *Speculum sapientiae* attributed to Cyrillus were introduced into Europe. Translated into the vernacular, these collections were accompanied by illustrations modelled on those in popular Aesopic manuscripts; the miniatures in some manuscripts of Ulrich von Pottenstein's German translation (*c.* 1410) of the Cyrillic fables, for example, recall illustrations to similar fables in manuscripts of the *Edelstein*.

In 1461 Boner's *Edelstein* became the first printed German book (*see* §2 below); its woodcut illustrations were based closely on a contemporary manuscript model. With the publication 15 years later of Steinhöwel's innovative version, however, the manuscript illustration tradition came to an end. Although fables continued to be copied by hand into the 16th century (e.g. Paris, Bib. N., MS. fond. Smith-Lesouëf 68), such late manuscripts were based on the new printed sources, the woodcut illustrations of which they copied in rough sketches.

BIBLIOGRAPHY

L. Hervieux: *Les Fabulistes latins* (Paris, 1883, rev. 1893) [Lat. texts and lists of MSS]
G. Thiele: *Der illustrierte lateinische Aesop in der Handschrift des Ademar* (Leiden, 1905)
K. McKenzie and W. Oldfather, eds: *Ysopet-Avionnet: The Latin and French Texts* (Urbana, 1919)
H. Chefneux: 'Les Fables dans la Tapisserie de Bayeux', *Romania*, lx (1934), pp. 1–35, 153–94
A. Goldschmidt: *An Early Manuscript of the Aesop Fables of Avianus and Related Manuscripts* (Princeton, 1947)
K. Grubmüller: 'Elemente einer literarischen Gebrauchssituation', *Würzburger Prosastudien*, ed. K. Matzel (Munich, 1975), pp. 139–59

D. Peil: *Der Streit der Glieder mit dem Magen* (Frankfurt, 1985)
G. Dicke and K. Grubmüller: *Die Fabeln des Mittelalters und der frühen Neuzeit* (Munich, 1987) [MS. lists and comprehensive bibliog.]

2. PRINTED. The first programmatic illustrations extant in any printed book accompany the fables of Ulrich Boner's *Edelstein* (see BOOK ILLUSTRATION, fig. 1) in its *editio princeps*, printed in Bamberg by Albrecht Pfister in 1461; although no single immediate model can be identified, the 101 woodcuts reveal clearly the influence of earlier manuscript illustrations. Similarly based on a much older tradition—going back at least to the 11th century and the manuscript of Ademar—are the 197 woodcuts (see fig. 2) prepared for Heinrich Steinhöwel's bilingual *Vita Esopi et fabulae* (or *Aesop*) issued by Johann Zainer in Ulm, 1476–7 (see §1 above). Imitated and adapted for *Aesop*s printed in Bohemia, France, Spain, the Netherlands and England, the Ulm cycle was for nearly a century the standard in European fable illustration, effectively rendering obsolete the competing models still offered in manuscripts. The influence of the Ulm series continues in such depictions of the fabulist as Antonio

2. Fable frontispiece illustration of *Aesop* with elements recalling episodes from his life, woodcut, 190×115 mm; from Heinrich Steinhöwel: *Vita Esopi et fabulae* (Ulm, 1476–7) (Wolfenbüttel, Herzog August Bibliothek, 10.2 Eth. 2°)

Frasconi's 1954 linoleum block, in which Aesop is still the rustic hunchback of the Ulm woodcuts.

The enormous success of Steinhöwel's *Aesop* was due not only to its illustrations but also to the authenticity of its Latin fables, which, deriving in part from ancient and authoritative redactions since lost, offered clearly superior texts for translation. Only in Italy did the Ulm tradition meet with resistance; there the favoured collections were compilations entitled *Aesopus moralizatus*. Like Steinhöwel's collection, these bilingual works combine both Latin verse and prose fables with vernacular paraphrases, most notably by Accio Zucco and Francesco del Tuppo (*fl c.* 1478–98). Illustration was integral to these collections from the beginning; the earliest such text, printed at Mondovi (Piedmont) by Dominicus de Vivaldis in 1476, contained 67 woodcuts, and the most successful series, introduced in the 1479 Verona version of Giovanni Alvise and Alberto Alvise, was modified and reused in dozens of further editions, the latest printed by Giolito in Vercelli (1578).

Although the descendants of these few cycles dominated fable illustration well into the 16th century, the texts they accompanied changed, most strikingly by the assimilation of the fable to emblematic genres (*see* EMBLEM BOOK). The earliest of these, published in Paris by Denis Janot in 1542, contains 100 texts in French verse by Gilles Corrozet (1510–68), each faced by an engraved illustration in emblem form, ornately framed and flanked by lemma and epigraph; several of these icons are unmistakably drawn from the Ulm-influenced series of the turn of the century. These illustrations provided the model for at least 12 further French editions of Corrozet, and they were also adapted for editions of Latin and Greek fable texts published in more traditional formats in Italy and the Netherlands.

An English translation by William Caxton, the *Subtyl Historyes and Fables of Esope* (London, 1484), was accompanied by copies of the Ulm woodcuts. Following this, the first new collection to be illustrated in England was the *Fables of Aesop Paraphras'd in Verse* by John Ogilby (1600–76) with etchings by Francis Cleyn, which was printed in London by Thomas Warren in 1651. Ogilby's collection was twice expanded and reprinted, in 1665 with illustrations by Wenceslaus Hollar and in 1668 by Francis Barlow. Barlow's engravings, strongly influenced by Marcus Gheeraerts the elder's plates in the Flemish version, *De warachtighe fabulen der dieren* (Bruges, 1567) published by Pieter de Clerck, appeared in two other English fable collections in the artist's lifetime, and they were used into the 19th century for *Aesop*s printed in France, Germany and the Netherlands, including an edition of *Recueil de fables d'Esope et autres mythologistes* (Paris, 1799) by Jean de La Fontaine (1621–95).

La Fontaine's first collection of 124 rhymed texts (issued in Paris by Claude Barbin in 1668) was illustrated by François Chauveau. This was ultimately expanded to 12 books of fables and didactic tales from outside the Aesopic tradition, and it was reprinted throughout the 18th century in increasingly extravagant luxury editions. The most lavish of these was the four-volume set (printed in Paris by Desaint & Saillant, 1755–9) comprising all 237 fables accompanied by 485 galant engravings, 276 of which are after Jean-Baptiste Oudry. In the 19th century the *Fables* were illustrated in their entirety by such artists as J. J. Grandville and Gustave Doré, while selected texts of La Fontaine have more recently provided subjects for Chagall, Dali and Gus Bofa (1885–1968) among others.

The primacy of illustration, apparent in both the emblematic fable and in the artists' books of the early 20th century, is most pronounced in the modern large-format *Aesop*s intended for children. Begun in the 19th century, this transformation of the fable into a chiefly juvenile literature made possible collections that were based not on a complete and authoritative text, but on a selection of the most familiar, most obviously edifying and most easily illustrated fables. Their usually colourful illustrations range in style from the realistic to the grotesquely anthropomorphized and typically occupy an entire page facing the text, which is often simplified or reduced to a concise statement of the fable's moral lesson.

BIBLIOGRAPHY

E. Levêque: *Iconographie des fables de La Fontaine, La Motte, Dorat, Florian* (Paris, 1893)
A. Mauro: *Francesco del Tuppo e il suo 'Esopo'* (Città di Castello, 1926)
J. Landwehr: *Fable-books Printed in the Low Countries: A Concise Bibliography until 1800* (Nieuwkoop, 1963)
J. McKendry: *Aesop: Five Centuries of Illustrated Fables* (New York, 1964)
B. Quinnam: *Fables from Incunabula to Modern Picture Books: A Selective Bibliography* (Washington, DC, 1966)
C. Küster: *Illustrierte Aesop-Ausgaben des 15. und 16. Jahrhunderts* (diss., U. Hamburg, 1970)
D. Fouquet: *Der Edelstein: Faksimile der ersten Druckausgabe Bamberg 1461. 16.1 Eth. 2° der Herzog August Bibliothek Wolfenbüttel* (Stuttgart, 1972)
A. Hobbs: *Illustrated Fables: A Catalogue of the Museum's Holdings*, London, BM cat. (London, 1979)
E. Hodnett: *Aesop in England: The Transmission of Motifs in Seventeenth-century Illustrations of Aesop's Fables* (Charlottesville, 1979)
Fabula docet: Illustrierte Fabelbücher aus sechs Jahrhunderten (exh. cat., ed. U. Bodemann; Wolfenbüttel, Herzog August Bib.; Düsseldorf, Goethe-Mus; Zurich, Zentbib.; Karlsruhe, Bad. Landesbib.; 1983–5) [excellent bibliog.]
P. Carnes: *Fable Scholarship: An Annotated Bibliography* (New York, 1985)
R. Ash: *Aesop's Fables: A Classic Illustrated Edition* (San Francisco, 1990) [sel. illus. from var. 19th- and 20th-century edns]
N. Holzberg and others, eds: *Der Äsop-Roman: Motiv-Geschichte und Erzählstruktur* (Tübingen, 1992)
G. Dicke: *Heinrich Steinhöwels 'Esopus' und seine Fortsetzer* (Tübingen, 1994)

A. E. WRIGHT

Fabre, François-Xavier, Baron (*b* Montpellier, 1 April 1766; *d* Montpellier, 16 March 1837). French painter, printmaker and collector. He was taught by the painter Jean Coustou (1719–91) in Montpellier before entering, in 1783, the studio of David, to whose artistic principles he remained faithful all his life. His career as a history painter began brilliantly when, in 1787, he won the Prix de Rome for *Nebuchadnezzar Ordering the Execution of Zedekiah's Children* (Paris, Ecole N. Sup. B.-A.). This early success was consolidated by the four years he spent at the Académie de France in Rome and by the enthusiastic reception of his *Death of Abel* (1790; Montpellier, Mus. Fabre; see fig.) at the Salon of 1791.

In 1793 his royalist sympathies forced him to move to Florence, where the poet Vittorio Alfieri and his mistress the Countess of Albany, estranged wife of the Young Pretender, introduced him to the artistic and social life of the city. In the years preceding the French invasion of Tuscany in 1799, he worked for members of the cosmopolitan aristocracy of the region, including the Swede Gustaf Armfelt and the 3rd Lord Holland and his circle. He turned increasingly to producing society portraits, often in landscape settings, as in *Allen Smith Seated above the Arno* (1797; Cambridge, Fitzwilliam). Fabre survived the various political upheavals of his time without mishap, changing his patrons and the nature of his production as conditions demanded. His portraits include *Lucien Bonaparte and his Wife* (1808; Rome, Mus. Napoleonico), *Maréchal Clarke, Duke of Feltre* (1810; Nantes, Mus. B.-A.) and *Mme Clarke with her Children* (1810; Paris, Mus. Marmottan).

Fabre was a prominent figure in Florentine society, being a member of the Academy, teacher of art and collector and dealer. He nevertheless remained in contact with French artists, notably Girodet, and with artistic bodies in Paris, becoming a corresponding member of the Institut in 1804. His voluminous correspondence is in the Bibliothèque Municipale at Montpellier. Changing fashions and bad health due to gout gradually forced him to abandon history painting and to concentrate on portraiture, landscape and printmaking (both etching and aquatint). He also intensified his activity as a collector, amassing an important group of 16th- and 17th-century Italian paintings, Poussin's *Landscape with Venus and Adonis*, drawings and paintings by his French contemporaries, as well as prints, books and manuscripts; his collection was further enriched by those of Alfieri and the Countess of Albany. After the Countess's death, in 1824, Fabre donated his collection to the city of Montpellier (resulting in the foundation of the Musée Fabre); the library and school of fine art in Montpellier were also created at his instigation. The title of Baron was conferred upon him by Charles X.

Although he was only a mediocre printmaker, his numerous drawings, of which there are about 500 examples in the Musée Fabre and in the Uffizi, Florence, show him to be an expressive and dynamic as well as a meticulous and accurate draughtsman. His paintings are characterized by a sound technique, a precise line and a delicacy of detail

François-Xavier Fabre: *Death of Abel*, oil on canvas, 1.46×1.98 m, 1790 (Montpellier, Musée Fabre)

that borders on preciousness. They also show a certain stiffness and an occasionally defective perspective. The combination of elegance, realism and precision in his portraiture can be seen in the various paintings of Alfieri and of the Countess of Albany (e.g. Montpellier, Mus. Fabre; Florence, Uffizi) and in that of *Canova* (1812; Montpellier, Mus. Fabre). The *Vision of Saul* (1803; Montpellier, Mus. Fabre) and the *Judgement of Paris* (1808; Dayton, OH, A. Inst.) are good examples of his achievements in religious and mythological painting. The former was commissioned by the Countess of Albany and inspired by Alfieri's tragedy *Saul* (1784). Its style is firmly within the French Neo-classical tradition: the composition and use of dramatic gesture owe much to Poussin, of whose work Fabre assembled a fine set of prints; the meticulous technique and careful illumination of the central figure against a dark background show the influence of early David. *Oedipus at Colonus* (1808) and *Death of Narcissus* (1814), both in the Musée Fabre, exemplify his treatment of mythological subjects in landscape settings. Fabre is one of the most interesting representatives of French Neo-classicism and its links with Italy.

BIBLIOGRAPHY

P. de Baudicour: *Le Peintre-graveur français*, ii (Paris, 1859–61/*R* Paris, 1967), pp. 319–25
L. G. Pelissier: 'Les Correspondants du peintre Fabre (1808–1834)', *Nouv. Rev. Rétro.*, iv (1896)
——: 'Le Fonds Fabre-Albany à la Bibliothèque de Montpellier', *Centbl. Bibwsn*, xvii (1900)
A. Joubin: 'Comment fut fondé le Musée de Montpellier', *Ren. A. Fr. & Indust. Luxe* (June 1926), pp. 237–45
P. Marmottan: 'La Jeunesse du peintre Fabre', *Gaz. B.-A.*, xv (Feb 1927), pp. 93–113
F. Boyer: *Le Monde des arts en Italie et la France de la révolution et de l'empire* (Turin, 1969)
P. Bordes: 'Girodet et Fabre, camarades d'atelier', *Rev. Louvre*, vi (1974), pp. 393–9
——: 'François-Xavier Fabre, peintre d'histoire', *Burl. Mag.*, cxvii (1975), pp. 91–8; cxviii (1975), pp. 155–61
Actes du colloque: Florence et la France. Rapports sous la révolution et l'empire: Florence, 1977 [with papers by P. Bordes, pp. 187–208, and L. Pellicer, pp. 159–86]
L. Pellicer: 'François-Xavier Fabre et les sources littéraires antiques', *Bull. Assoc. Guillaume Budé*, no. 4 (1983), pp. 378–98
——: *Le Peintre François-Xavier Fabre (1766–1837)* (diss., U. of Paris-Sorbonne, 1983)
François-Xavier Fabre (exh. cat., Spoleto, Palazzo Racani-Arroni; Florence, Uffizi; 1988)

LAURE PELLICER

Fabre, Jaume [Jaime] (*fl c.* 1313–38). Spanish architect. He came from Mallorca and was active mainly there and in Barcelona. He is documented *c.* 1313 at the Dominican convent in Palma de Mallorca (destr. 1837), the plan of which was probably similar to that of S Catalina, Barcelona (destr.), with a single-cell nave and side chapels between the buttresses. In 1317 Fabre was called to Barcelona to supervise the construction of the new cathedral (begun 1298), probably to someone else's design. In Barcelona he received a salary, a house and an annual stipend, but he was forbidden to work on other projects without permission from the Bishop and the Chapter. He was still in charge at Barcelona in 1338, and he must have designed the crypt, which houses the tomb of St Eulália. It has a centralized, polygonal plan and a very low vault, with 13 ribs radiating from a boss carved with figures of the *Virgin* and *St Eulália*. It has been suggested that Fabre also contributed to other churches in Barcelona, such as S María del Mar and S María del Pi.

BIBLIOGRAPHY

W. von Lohneysen: 'Jaime Fabre: Ein katalanischer Baumeister des 14. Jahrhunderts', *Sp. Forsch. Görres-Ges.*, x, pp. 23–54

M. ROSA TERÉS I TOMÀS

Fabrés, Antonio (*b* Barcelona, 27 June 1854; *d* Rome, 23 Jan 1938). Catalan painter, sculptor and teacher. He was the son of the draughtsman Cayetano Fabrés. He studied at the Academia Provincial de Bellas Artes in Lonja (1867–75) and in the studio of the sculptor Andrés Aleu y Teixidor. With his sculpture in plaster the *Dead Abel* (1875; Barcelona, Real Acad. Cat. B.A. San Jordi), he won a scholarship to study in Rome. There he was attracted to the work of the sculptor Vincenzo Gemito and at the same time to the paintings of Mariano José Bernardo Fortuny y Marsal; and eventually he abandoned sculpture to devote himself completely to painting. He worked in a similar Orientalist genre, inspired by North African subject-matter, in paintings such as the *Warrior's Repose* (1878), the *Sultan's Present* (1877–8; both Barcelona, Mus. A. Mod.), and *On the Sultan's Order* (*c.* 1902; Mexico City, Mus. N. A.). His painting of musketeers, *The Drunkards* (1896; Mexico City, Mus. N. A.), a subject also popularized by Jean-Louis Meissonier, displays a compositional virtuosity in keeping with the academic realism of the time. When in 1895 he showed the *Offering to the Virgin Mary* at the Paris Salon, he had a magnifying glass placed beside the painting so that the viewer might observe the minute details.

In 1892 Fabrés settled in Paris, where he showed regularly at the Salon and submitted work to international competitions. His Paris dealer was Goupil. In 1900 Jesús F. Contreras invited Fabrés to Mexico City to run the department at the Escuela Nacional de Bellas Artes. Finally he acquiesced and moved to Mexico in 1902. The Mexican government acquired *The Drunkards* and commissioned a painting on the subject of local history to decorate a room in the Palacio Nacional, Mexico City (*in situ*), entitled *Hidalgo after the Victory of Monte de las Cruces* (*c.* 1903–4). He also designed the arms room (destr., see Moreno, pp. 61–5) of the president's private residence. In Mexico Fabrés abandoned exotic themes in favour of realistic depictions of the daily milieu. His principal formative influence on his students, among whom were Diego Rivera, Saturnino Herrán and José Clemente Orozco, was to develop an interest in the life of ordinary people. In 1907 Fabrés left Mexico to settle once more in Rome.

WRITINGS

'Verdades', *An. Inst. Invest. Estét.*, lvi (1986), pp. 173–204

BIBLIOGRAPHY

S. Moreno: *El pintor Antonio Fabrés* (Mexico City, 1981)

FAUSTO RAMÍREZ

Fabri, Francesco Saverio [Francisco Xavier] (*b* Medicina, Bologna, 1761; *d* Lisbon, 1807). Italian architect, active in Portugal. He qualified after studying at the Accademia Clementina, Bologna, where he was influenced by the great tradition of the Bolognese school as well as by the Palladianism that was current when he received his artistic and technical training. A visit to Rome was also important; while there he was invited by the Oratorian, Francisco Gomes de Avelar, who in 1789 had become Bishop of the Algarve, to go to Portugal and work in his diocese.

Fabri arrived in the Algarve in November 1790 and lived with his cultured and enlightened patron in the Episcopal Palace at Faro. There he designed a hospital and seminary and was active in planning the reconstruction of many churches that had been ruined or destroyed by the Lisbon earthquake of 1755. Fabri also built the city arch, the Arco da Vila (c. 1792), at one end of the old harbour, where he framed the original gate with a majestic double architectural composition. The arch itself is framed by two Ionic columns and crowned by a niche with a triangular pediment in which stands a fine Italian statue of St Thomas Aquinas. This composition is in turn framed by another, divided by four Tuscan pilasters and surmounted by a bell-tower, also with pediment and wings. Adjoining the triumphal arch, Fabri built the new hospital incorporating the 16th-century Misericórdia Church, to which he added a façade with a triangular pediment, and at one side of this a Tuscan arcade open to the Ria (all 1790–94). The plan of the hospital interior was new to the region of the Algarve and showed a knowledge of Italian hospital planning as well as Fabri's ability to adapt to local conditions, such as using false ceilings made of cane for coolness.

The seminary (1790–94) is a functional and utilitarian building that nevertheless enhances the fine urban space of the cathedral square (Largo da Sé) that it faces. Here Fabri gave continuity to the existing buildings by using the same scale and a simplified arrangement of openings, and he completed the new construction with a refectory of fine proportions, using a Neo-classical façade that maintains the dignified simplicity of a large wing of the cathedral square.

Fabri rebuilt the church of S Maria at Tavira, which had been virtually destroyed in 1755. He strengthened the outer walls and was able to retain the earlier ogival doorway and the Gothic, Manueline and Renaissance side chapels. He gave a strong Palladian feeling to the new interior as well as to the façade, the central section of which is framed by Tuscan pilasters and surmounted by a pediment bearing urns. He appreciated the qualities of simplicity, proportion and rhythm, often emphasized by the use of whitewash, that were characteristic of the local architecture of the Algarve. He often restricted himself to strengthening pre-existing structures, as at Cacela, or remodelling earlier structures while at the same time retaining their essential feeling, as at Tavira and as is seen in the bold integration of the Manueline church at Alcantarilha. Elsewhere he retained or restored 16th-century buildings and only made additions, as at São Brás, or remodelled the capitals with a new Ionic design, as at Estoi, Algarve. For the church at Alzejur, however, which has a Greek-cross plan, he made new designs.

In 1794 Fabri went to Lisbon, and through Bishop Gomes de Avelar he was patronized by the court and nobility. He designed the palace of the Marquês de Castelo Melhor (c. 1795; unfinished), remodelled in the 19th century by the Marquêses de Foz, by whose name it is now known. He designed the Hospital Real da Marinha (Royal Naval Hospital, 1797) and the mausoleum of Christian August, Prince of Waldeck), inspired by Giovanni Battista Piranesi.

Fabri was appointed Architect of Public Works (Arquitecto das Obras Publicas), and the design of the severe Neo-classical monument to *Queen Mary I* (1797; now Queluz, Pal. N.) executed by João José de Aguiar has been attributed to Fabri. His last work was the important new Ajuda Palace, Lisbon, begun 1802, on which he worked in collaboration with José da Costa e Silva, who had made the plans. They replaced the Baroque architect, Manuel Caetano de Sousa, who had previously been in charge of building at court. A more monumental programme was envisaged at Ajuda, which is strongly influenced by Luigi Vanvitelli's design for the palace at Caserta, Naples, and incorporates ideas from the rebuilding of Lisbon in Pombaline style, seen at its most palatial form in the Praça do Comércio. The great central pavilion at Ajuda has an arcade that echoes the Villa Albani-Torlonia in Rome and a vista through a courtyard that evokes the engravings of Piranesi. The formal qualities and great dignity of the Palace express political values in Portugal at the beginning of the 19th century, and Ajuda is considered the finest example of Neo-classical architecture in the country.

BIBLIOGRAPHY
J.-A. França: *A arte em Portugal no século XIX*, i (Lisbon, 1966)
G. Rimondini and L. Samoggia: *Francesco Saverio Fabri, architetto* (Medicina, 1979)
A. de Carvalho: *Os três arquitectos da Ajuda* (Lisbon, 1979)
                                    JOSÉ EDUARDO HORTA CORREIA

Fabriano. Italian town and the site of the earliest known European papermill. Fabriano became a centre of paper manufacturing in 1276 and still produces a brand of quality handmade paper, which carries the name of the town. ☐

Fabriano, Antonio da. *See* ANTONIO DA FABRIANO.

Fabriano, Gentile da. *See* GENTILE DA FABRIANO.

Fabriano, Giovanni Andrea Gilio da. *See* GILIO DA FABRIANO, GIOVANNI ANDREA.

Fábrica da Vista Alegre. Portuguese ceramics and glass factory. It was founded in Ílhavo, near Aveiro, in 1824 by José Ferreira Pinto Basto (1774–1839), and the licence obtained on 1 July 1824 permitted the manufacture of earthenware, porcelain and glass (*see* PORTUGAL, §VIII). Pinto Basto's son Augusto Valério Ferreira Pinto Basto (1807–1902) was the first managing director and spent some time at the Sèvres porcelain factory, where he learnt the various processes and techniques involved in porcelain production from the director Alexandre Brongniart (1770–1847). In 1826 Pinto Basto was granted a 20-year monopoly for his enterprise. However, as only very small deposits of kaolin were available in the early stages, the factory produced creamware, stoneware and a few pieces of poor-quality porcelain. Two Neo-classical enamelled and gilded cups and saucers (1827; Lisbon, Mus. N. A. Ant.) have inscriptions indicating that they were fired in the first kiln of ware from this factory and were painted by João María

Fabre (1805–29). The special type of enamel decoration used at this stage was devised by both Fabre and the artist, sculptor and engraver Manuel de Morais de Silva Ramos (1806–72). During this period Pinto Basto also employed the potter Joseph Scorder from Saxony, who took charge of the production of porcelain at the factory.

In 1832 the first significant deposits of kaolin were located in Vale Rico, at the village of Feira in the district of Aveiro, by Luís Pereira Capote (*d* 1870), a potter's apprentice at the Fábrica da Vista Alegre. The factory was then in a position to produce porcelain on an industrial scale, and a period of intense activity began. The factory's artistic standards and fame were aided by the work of the French portrait painter Vitor François Chartier Rousseau (*d* 1852) and his successor Gustave Fortier (*fl* 1853–69). The latter was particularly notable for his excellent draughtsmanship and his landscape and flower painting in polychrome enamels and gilding (e.g. pair of jardinières, 1851; Lisbon, Mus. N. A. Ant.). He is also credited with the introduction of pen painting and transfer printing. A teapot attributed to the artist Manuel Francisco Pereira shows the influence of the Sèvres porcelain factory at Vista Alegre in the mid-19th century in its use of a deep blue underglaze ground (*see* PORTUGAL, fig. 17). The factory also participated in such international exhibitions as the Great Exhibition of 1851 in London and the Exposition Universelle of 1855 in Paris, where they showed a statue called 'Nossa Senhora da Penha de França', made in biscuit porcelain. The painter Joaquim José da Oliveira (*fl* 1869–81) was painting master between 1869 and 1881 and trained such skilful artists as Manuel Fernandes Barros ('Padre Noche') and Duarte José de Magalhães, who became painting master in 1889.

From *c.* 1870 to the first quarter of the 20th century the factory went through a difficult period and artistic standards declined. However, from 1922 to 1947 the factory prospered under the administration of João Teodoro Ferreira Pinto Basto (1870–1947), and such designers as Ângelo Simões Chuva (1883–1973) and Palmiro da Silva Peixe produced Art Deco-style domestic and ornamental wares. In the late 20th century the factory maintained its importance as a manufacturer of hard-paste porcelain, distinguished by its production of both industrialized and well-executed hand-painted ware.

BIBLIOGRAPHY

M. Gomes: *Vista Alegre: Apontamentos para a sua história* (Oporto, 1883)
J. T. F. Pinto Basto: *A Fábrica da Vista Alegre: O livro do seu centenário* (Lisbon, 1924)
V. Valente: *Porcelana artística portuguesa* (Oporto, 1949)
R. de Plinval-Salgues: 'La Contribution française à la porcelaine portugaise', *Museu*, ser. 2, ii (1961), pp. 5–14
Portugal and Porcelain (exh. cat., ed. I. Arez, M. Azevedo Coutinho and J. McNab; New York, Met., 1984)

Fábrica de Viana [Fábrica de Darque]. Portuguese ceramics factory. It was founded in Darque near Viana do Castelo in 1774 by João Araújo Lima and Carlos de Araújo Lemos, in partnership with João Gaspar do Rego and António Alves Pereira de Lemos. Although there is a lack of dated pieces three stylistic periods of production have been recognized. During the early years (before 1790) the factory produced tureens, octagonal plates, tankards and large jars that were influenced by wares from the REAL

FÁBRICA DO RATO in Lisbon and imported wares. Decoration was executed in blue or manganese-purple. During the second period (1790–1820) a wide range of wares was manufactured, characterized by well-shaped forms, perfect milky white ground and polychrome decoration dominated by blues, greens, canary-yellow, orange and violet. Delicately executed floral motifs predominate, with very few figurative compositions. Variously sized pear-shaped vases were inspired by East Asian wares and were decorated with finely drawn weeping willows and pagodas. Other characteristic wares included English-style 'Toby' jugs, toothpick holders, figures in the form of negroes, tankards shaped as negro heads, mugs, washbowls, pitchers and a variety of tableware, some of which was enamelled in light blue and green in the manner of faience produced at the Fábrica de Miragaia (*see* OPORTO, §2). During the third period (1820–55) there were successful attempts in the use of transfer printing, but artistic standards declined and the factory closed in 1855.

BIBLIOGRAPHY

L. A. de Oliveira: *A extincta fábrica cerâmica de Viana* (Lisbon, 1915)
A. Cardoso Pinto: *Faiança da antiga fábrica de Viana: Colecção Dr Alfredo Queiróz* (Lisbon, 1954)
A. Matos Reis and J. Cepa Machado: 'Museu municipal de Viana do Castelo: Catálogo da faiança de Viana', *Patrimonio*, i (1982), pp. 9–24

Fábrica do Juncal. Portuguese ceramics factory. It was founded in the borough of Porto de Mós, near Leiria, in 1770 by the painter and architect José Rodrigues da Silva e Sousa (*d* 1824). In 1784 the factory received the designation 'Royal' and the protection of Sebastião de Carvalho e Melo, the 1st Marquês de Pombal. The factory had two very distinct periods of production. During the first 30 years it produced blue-and-white tableware that was influenced in style and decoration by the REAL FÁBRICA DO RATO. Many pieces are distinctive for their recurring semi-abstract, leaf-like motifs, shaded in blue or manganese-purple, surrounded by chains of beads. During the second period, under the direction of José Luís Fernandes da Fonseca, wares were decorated with more sober decoration in manganese-purple. Important painters who worked at the factory at this time included João Coelho Pó and Manuel Coelho. Fonseca's son Bernardino José da Fonseca directed the factory from 1837, and he was succeeded by his nephew José Calado da Fonseca. In addition to faience the factory also produced some rather poorly designed tiled panels of religious themes, many of which are signed and dated. The factory closed in 1876.

BIBLIOGRAPHY

J. Queirós: *Cerâmica portuguesa* (Lisbon, 1907, rev. in 2 vols, 1948/*R* 1987)
R. dos Santos: *Oito séculos de arte portuguesa: História e espírito*, iii (Lisbon, 1970)
A. de Sandão: *Faiança portuguesa, séculos XVIII, XIX* (Oporto, 1976)

BERNADETTE NELSON

Fabriczy, Cornelius [Kornél] **von** (*b* Löcse, Hungary [now Levoča, Slovakia], 3 Sept 1839; *d* 5 Oct 1910). Hungarian engineer and art historian. He trained as an engineer and became a senior manager in the Hungarian railways. Following a two-year study trip to Italy (1876–8), he resigned his post and embarked upon a new career as an art historian. He visited Paris and London and in 1880 settled in Stuttgart.

Fabriczy devoted the greater part of his life to the study of Italian, and in particular Florentine, Renaissance art. In 1892 he published a major study of the life and work of the Florentine architect and engineer Filippo Brunelleschi. At the same time, after research in the Biblioteca Nazionale of Florence, most notably on 16th-century documents (the Codice Strozziano and Codice Petrei) containing notes on Florentine artists of considerable art historical value, he published the so-called *Libro di Antonio Billi* (1891; *see* BILLI, ANTONIO) and the *Codice dell'Anonimo Magliabechiano* (1893). Fabriczy's research had been undertaken in consultation with the Florentine art historian Gaetano Milanesi, but he was careful to correct the German scholar Karl Frey, whose own interpretation of the same manuscripts (1892) did not always agree with Fabriczy's, when Frey wrote that Milanesi had helped Fabriczy to discover the Codices. In the later 1890s Fabriczy began to collaborate with WILHELM BODE on a revised edition of Jakob Burckhardt's guidebook to Italian art, *Der Cicerone* (1855). In 1903 Fabriczy published his study of Italian Renaissance medals, a work which, by bringing together the results of scholarship to date and combining the numismatic approach with an appreciation of medals as works of art, may rank as his most original and perhaps most valuable contribution to art historical study.

WRITINGS
Zur Kunstgeschichte der Hohenstaufenzeit (Leipzig, 1879)
'Il libro di Antonio Billi e le sue copie nella Biblioteca Nazionale di Firenze', *Archv Stor. It.*, 5th ser., vii (1891), pp. 299–368; repr. (Farnborough, 1968)
Filippo Brunelleschi: Sein Leben und Seine Werke (Stuttgart, 1892)
'Il codice dell'Anonimo Gaddiano (Cod. magliabechiano XVII, 17) nella biblioteca nazionale di Firenze', *Archv Stor. It.*, 5th ser., 3 and 4 (1893); repr. (Farnborough, 1968)
Die Handzeichnungen Giuliano da Sangallo (Stuttgart, 1902)
Niccolo di Piero Lamberti d'Arezzo (Florence, 1902)
Medaillen der italienischen Renaissance (Leipzig, 1903), Eng. trans. as *Italian Medals*, Mrs Gustavus W. Hamilton, intro. G. F. Hill (London, 1904)

BIBLIOGRAPHY
C. Frey: *Il libro di Antonio Billi esistente in due copie nella Biblioteca Nazionale di Firenze* (Berlin, 1892)
J. Szinnyei, ed.: *Magyar írók* (Budapest, 1894/*R* 1980–81), pp. 67–70
JANET SOUTHORN

Fabri de Peiresc, Nicolas-Claude. *See* PEIRESC, NICO-LAS-CLAUDE FABRI DE.

Fabris, Emilio De. *See* DE FABRIS, EMILIO.

Fabris, Pietro (*fl* Naples, 1756–79). Italian painter and engraver. He worked in Naples for most of his life, but frequently added the phrase 'English painter' to his signature. His genre scenes and landscapes, of which the earliest are four large canvases of *Scenes of Popular Life* (1756–7; Naples, priv. col., see 1990 exh. cat., p. 79), illustrate events at the royal court as well as picturesque scenes of Neapolitan life with pedlars, fishermen, picnickers and dancers; they were popular with those making the Grand Tour. Two paintings representing the *Departure of Charles III of Bourbon for Spain* (Aranjuez, Pal. Real) were presumably painted in 1759, when this event occurred. In 1768 Fabris exhibited in London at the Free Society and accompanied the British envoy, Sir William Hamilton, to Sicily; he included a portrait of this enthusiastic patron in one of two genre scenes showing the *Drawing-room in Lord Fortrose's Apartment in Naples* (1770; Edinburgh, N.P.G.). He exhibited again in London in 1772 at the Society of Artists.

Fabris was one of the first artists in Naples in the 18th century to use gouache, and he was commissioned by Hamilton to provide 58 gouache paintings to illustrate his publication *Campi phlegraei* (1776; supplement 1779). The plates, engraved and hand-coloured after the original gouaches, range from landscape views (e.g. *Hamilton Shows the King and Queen of Naples Vesuvius Erupting*) to more scientific illustrations of volcanic minerals. Later works, which include the *Scene of Popular Life on the Frisio Beach at Posilippo* (1778; priv. col., see Spinosa, no. 309), are close to the tightly polished, somewhat stilted manner of Philipp Hackert.

BIBLIOGRAPHY
The Golden Age of Naples: Art and Civilization under the Bourbons, 1734–1805 (exh. cat., Detroit, MI, Inst. A., 1981)
F. Powell-Jones: 'A Neo-classical Interior in Naples', *NACF Rev.* (1985), pp. 104–7
N. Spinosa: *Pittura napoletana del settecento dal rococo al classicismo* (Naples, 1987)
In the Shadow of Vesuvius: Views of Naples from Baroque to Romanticism, 1631–1830 (exh. cat., London, Accad. It. A. & A. Applic., 1990)
PETER WALCH

Fabritius. Family of Dutch artists. Pieter Carelsz. (1598–1653) was a teacher and talented amateur painter, who apparently used the nickname 'Fabritius' (from Lat. *faber*: 'craftsman'). His son (1) Carel Fabritius was one of Rembrandt's most gifted and imaginative pupils, who, despite his early death, had a great influence on late 17th-century Dutch painting. Pieter's second son (2) Barent Fabritius was a lesser artist, much influenced by Rembrandt and by his own brother. A third son, Johannes Fabritius (1636–after 1693), was a still-life painter.

(1) Carel Fabritius (*bapt* Midden-Beemster, nr Hoorn, 27 Feb 1622; *d* Delft, 12 Oct 1654). Painter. His oeuvre consists of a scant dozen paintings, since research has rigorously discounted many previously attributed works. These few paintings, however, document the painter's unique development within his brief 12-year career. He is often mentioned as being the link between Rembrandt and the Delft school, particularly Pieter de Hooch and Jan Vermeer, whose depiction of light owes much to Fabritius's late works in which his use of cool silvery colours to define forms in space marks a radical departure from Rembrandt's use of chiaroscuro.

1. LIFE AND CAREER. Carel Fabritius was probably taught painting by his father, after having first learnt the craft of carpentry and worked in Midden-Beemster, a rapidly expanding suburb of Hoorn. In October 1641 Carel married his neighbour's daughter, Aeltge Hermannsdr., moving shortly after the wedding to Amsterdam, where he lived until his wife's premature death in April 1643. During this short period he trained in Rembrandt's studio: his presence there is documented by Samuel van Hoogstraten, who was also an apprentice with Rembrandt and mentioned Fabritius in his notes on studio conversations.

Following the death of his wife (and both their children), Fabritius moved back to his parents' home in Midden-Beemster. He lived there for the next few years, except for the occasional visit to Amsterdam. Little is known about the years from 1643 until 1650, when he married his second wife, Agatha van Pruyssen, a widow from Amsterdam. Fabritius may have worked exclusively as a painter or as a carpenter again. There are only three known paintings from this period: the portrait of *Abraham Potter* (1648; Amsterdam, Rijksmus.), who was a close friend of Fabritius's family, the *Mercury and Argus* (c. 1645–7; New York, Richard L. Feigen) and a *Portrait of a Family* (1648; ex-Boymans Mus. Rotterdam, destr. by fire, 1864). Fabritius lived with his second wife in Delft, where on 29 October 1652 he joined the Guild of St Luke. The couple must have been badly off financially, as on 4 July 1654 Fabritius was commissioned by the town council to paint both a large and a small version of the city arms, for which he was paid the meagre sum of 12 guilders. Fabritius no doubt accepted the small salary because of the prospect of further commissions from the town. Tragically, however, he was killed only three months later, when there was an explosion at the gunpowder warehouse in Delft, which was situated close to Fabritius's house. He was buried in the Oude Kerke in Delft.

2. WORK. In his early works, Fabritius adopted Rembrandt's thick, impastoed brushstrokes, but he was quick to move away from the chiaroscuro colours of Rembrandt's scenes to his own characteristic lighter palette. The *Raising of Lazarus* (c. 1642–3; Warsaw, N. Mus.), probably painted during Fabritius's stay in Rembrandt's studio, already shows the beginnings of the artist's painterly style. The composition adopts the main motifs from Rembrandt's *Raising of Lazarus* (c. 1630–31; Los Angeles, CA, Co. Mus. A.) and the '*Night Watch*' (1642; Amsterdam, Rijksmus.). Fabritius employed a wealth of different poses in this picture; however—unlike Rembrandt's biblical themes—the link between the inner meaning and the action is missing. The figures remain isolated, scarcely reacting to one another. Nevertheless, even in this early work Fabritius adopted a palette that is luminous and achieves new effects from surprising colour combinations.

In the exceptionally large *Portrait of a Family* (1.61×2.37 m) of 1648, now known only from a 19th-century watercolour copy by Victor de Steurs (Rotterdam, Mus. Boymans–van Beuningen), Fabritius again concentrated on the composition, which was unprecedented in the 17th century. The portrait was divided into three distinct groups in front of an elaborate architectural background: three people are walking down a staircase in the background; on the right a young man is sitting at a table covered with *vanitas* symbols and behind him there is a view of a palatial property; on the left are two small girls. The loose grouping of the sitters opened up new possibilities for portraiture, later taken up by Pieter de Hooch in particular. Surpassing by far traditional Dutch family portraits, the composition anticipates the 'conversation pieces' of the 18th century. The detail with which Fabritius depicted the interior is also completely new, as is the distant view in the right-hand background.

The painter's artistic development can be clearly followed in his series of individual portraits from 1648 to 1654. In the portrait of *Abraham Potter*, also of 1648, the sitter is depicted in dark tones in front of a light background. This treatment was used again in two portraits traditionally thought to be self-portraits—the *Portrait of a Man* (c. 1648–50; Rotterdam, Mus. Boymans–van Beuningen) and the *Portrait of a Man in a Fur Cap and a Breastplate* (1654; London, N.G.). The earlier self-portrait is completely innovative in both form and concept. The head was placed relatively low down on the canvas, with almost a third of the picture above it devoted to the background. More importantly, the idea of portraying himself with an open collar and as a worker and artisan (perhaps a play on the name Fabritius) was new compared to traditional portrayals of an artist either as a 'gentleman', in half length, or as a painter standing by his easel. The later self-portrait is often considered to be a pendant to a *Portrait of a Woman with a Feather Cap and Pearls* (1654; Hannover, Niedersächs. Landesmus.), which is assumed to represent Agatha van Pruyssen, Fabritius's second wife. The attribution of the latter was doubted by Brown (1981), but the handling and colouring of the picture fit in with other known examples of Fabritius's work from this year.

Besides portraits, there are three other late paintings, dating from the artist's last years of activity, which demonstrate his skill as a painter. All three focus on problems of perspective and illusionism, problems that Fabritius tried to solve with new painting techniques rather than with the help of traditional mathematical solutions. This is most clearly illustrated in *The Sentry* (also known as '*The Guard*', 1654; Schwerin, Staatl. Mus.), in which the deep perspective of a staircase at upper right is conveyed by graduated colour tones going from light to dark. The rest of the picture is painted in very light tones, predominantly white and shades of grey, which, blended with strong local colours, give the impression of intense, bright sunlight. Such effects appear to anticipate the work of Vermeer. The spatial arrangement, with the architecture framing a distant view in the background, also had a decisive influence on the work of Pieter de Hooch.

Fabritius seems to have tackled the problem of illusionism in a different way in *The Goldfinch* (1654; The Hague, Mauritshuis; see fig.). Although there has been much discussion about the interpretation of the picture's iconography, it does not appear to hold any special meaning, since the goldfinch is depicted alone, without any attributes. It is more plausible that it was simply an exercise in *trompe l'oeil*. The realistic play of light and shadow, which plays so important a role in *The Sentry*, also features prominently here.

In the slightly earlier *View of Delft* (1652; London, N.G.), Fabritius had confronted quite another problem of perspective. It is now assumed that the unusual and distorted perspective of this picture of a Dutch street and church is due to the fact that it came from a diorama with a curved back wall. Fabritius was certainly interested in paintings that united science and artistic aims, as was his fellow pupil van Hoogstraten, who painted similar pictures (*see* PERSPECTIVE, fig. 5) and also described Fabritius's picture in his *Inleyding tot de hooge schoole der schilderkonst* (1678). The *View of Delft* is the only example of this type

Carel Fabritius: *The Goldfinch*, oil on panel, 335×228 mm, 1654 (The Hague, Mauritshuis)

of work in Fabritius's oeuvre; however, since the workshop was destroyed in the explosion, it is possible that he produced similar works.

Fabritius apparently painted some large-scale frescoes in Delft (all destr.), and the single documentary reference to them alludes to the fact that he dealt with problems of foreshortening and perspective, obviously more so than is evident in the few easel pictures that have survived. After his death, his widow reported that he was also commissioned to paint some large-scale perspective murals for the Prince of Orange. Unfortunately, however, there is no longer any record of this sort of commissioned work. According to van Hoogstraten, Fabritius's wall paintings were comparable to those of Baldassare Peruzzi or to Guilio Romano's work in the Palazzo del Te, Mantua; he further reported that Fabritius had painted pictures like them in the house of the art lover and connoisseur Dr Valentius.

3. CRITICAL RECEPTION AND POSTHUMOUS REPUTATION. It is interesting to note that when Fabritius joined the Delft Guild of St Luke in 1652, he described himself as a history painter; he obviously considered himself to be capable of the highest type of painting, history painting, although only two examples survive: the *Raising of Lazarus* and the *Mercury and Argus*. There are also no fully

authenticated drawings by Fabritius (for a catalogue of sheets falsely attributed to him see Sumowski, 1981). During Fabritius's short period of activity in Delft, he apparently did not have any pupils, and although a certain Matthias Spoor presumably helped him in his workshop, he also died in the gunpowder explosion and no works by him have survived.

Jan Vermeer is often named as a 'successor' to Fabritius, but he was almost certainly not his direct pupil, as Fabritius did not come to Delft until 1650, when Vermeer was 18 years old. Vermeer was nonetheless impressed and influenced from an early age by Fabritius's luminous, light colouring in his work. The inventory of Vermeer's estate lists two works by Fabritius, which were kept in the younger artist's studio. Fabritius's approach to painting perspective was adopted mainly by Pieter de Hooch and his own brother, Barent.

In the 17th century Fabritius's work was scarcely known outside Delft. Within Delft, however, even in the 1660s he was praised, alongside Vermeer, as the most outstanding painter of his time. For the next 200 years his pictures were ignored by art historians, until Théophile Thoré [Wilhelm Bürger] mentioned them again in the introduction of the Arenberg collection in 1856. It was also Thoré (1864) who first distinguished the work of Carel and Barent Fabritius, which was still often confused. Thoré, who himself owned *The Goldfinch*, described Fabritius as a first-rate artist. Research on Fabritius in the 20th century has shown him to be one of Rembrandt's most brilliant pupils.

(2) Barent Fabritius (*bapt* Midden-Beemster, nr Hoorn, 16 Nov 1624; *d* Amsterdam, 20 Oct 1673). Painter and draughtsman, brother of (1) Carel Fabritius.

1. LIFE AND CAREER. Like Carel, he was first taught painting by his father, also learnt carpentry and practised as an artisan in Midden-Beemster in 1641. He is documented in Amsterdam in 1643 and 1647, though it is not known if, like his brother, he was also a pupil of Rembrandt. Nevertheless, his style is similar to that of the Rembrandt school. He must have been trained in the second half of the 1640s. His work is reminiscent of the style of his brother, who clearly influenced and may also have instructed him. In 1652 Barent lived in Amsterdam and married Catharina Mussers [?Mutsart] in Midden-Beemster. In the following years he is documented alternately in Midden-Beemster and Amsterdam. He painted a group portrait of the town master builder, *Willem Leenderstsz. van der Helm and his Family* (1656; Amsterdam, Rijksmus.), in Leiden, and in 1660–61 he received further commissions for the Lutheran church in Leiden. From 1669 Barent lived with his family in Amsterdam, where he died at the age of 49. He was buried in the churchyard in Leiden that was usually reserved for the poorer inhabitants of Amsterdam. He left behind a wife, who lived until 1701, and six children.

2. WORK. Barent's surviving oeuvre of at least 44 paintings is substantially more extensive than Carel's. It is dominated by history paintings with biblical or mythological themes; in addition, there are several allegories and a few portraits, including his first dated work, a *Self-portrait*

(1650; Frankfurt am Main, Städel. Kstinst. & Städt. Gal.), in which the composition was influenced by Rembrandt but the lightening of the background recalls the work of Barent's brother, Carel. Like Rembrandt, Barent also painted numerous individual figures, mainly half-length studies of characterful heads known as *tronies*, carried out mostly in the 1660s.

Barent often chose unusual or rarely depicted biblical themes, some of which he used repeatedly, for instance the *Naming of John the Baptist* (London, N.G., and Frankfurt am Main, Städel. Kstinst. Städt. Gal.), *Roman Charity* (e.g. York, C.A.G.) and the *Satyr with Farmers* (Hartford, CT, Wadsworth Atheneum, and Bergamo, Gal. Accad. Carrara). His earliest history painting depicts the *Expulsion of Hagar* (*c.* 1650; San Francisco, CA, de Young Mem. Mus.; additional versions, New York, Met., and Hull, Frerens A.G.). Like Carel, Barent concentrated first and foremost on colour: the figures are depicted in clear local colours (red, yellow, black and white) in front of a

chiaroscuro landscape. The composition and individual motifs, on the other hand, were borrowed from other masters. For example the motif of the group around Hagar and the background elements recall Lastman's version of the theme (1612; Hamburg, Ksthalle), which Barent must have known through a drawn copy by Rembrandt (Vienna, Albertina).

In the 1652 version of *Satyr with Farmers* (Hartford, CT, Wadsworth Atheneum) Barent seems already to have moved away from Rembrandtesque brushwork. Instead, the pigments are applied evenly across the surface, and the way in which light is depicted is more refined. A year later Barent painted a family group portrait in a historicizing mode, *Peter in the House of Cornelius* (1653; Brunswick, Herzog Anton-Ulrich-Mus.), in memory of the family's father, who had just died and who was portrayed as the Apostle Peter. By treating the family portrait as a history painting, it was possible to depict a larger variety of action poses, which would not have been the case with a

Barent Fabritius: *Blind Tobias with his Wife and the Goat*, oil on canvas, 640×700 mm, *c.* 1654–60 (Innsbruck, Tiroler Landesmuseum Ferdinandeum)

traditional family portrait. The 15 people in the picture—some standing, some kneeling—form a rhythmic composition that is high on each side and low in the middle. The classicizing style of dress, with long folds and linear curves, already points to Barent's late style. The whole work appears rather archaic, as if Barent were using a late Mannerist style to break away completely from all of his earlier models. Another striking characteristic of this picture is the exaggerated vanishing-point, a feature also found in the work of other Delft masters in the early 1650s. This interest in painting perspectives also clearly links Barent's work to that of his brother Carel.

Carel's influence is also evident in Barent's *Blind Tobias with his Wife and the Goat* (*c.* 1654–60; Innsbruck, Tirol. Landesmus.; see fig.), in which Barent has succeeded in creating a picture with an atmosphere similar to that of *The Sentry* by Carel, even down to the way in which the wall behind Tobias is painted. The picture was long thought to be by Carel (e.g. Bode, 1882, and Hofstede de Groot, 1907). Valentiner (1932) and Pont (1958) correctly recognized it as Barent's work, drawing attention in particular to the typical way in which the folds of the clothes were painted by applying dark lines to a coloured background (not by colour gradations, as Carel would have done).

The five paintings of *Parables* commissioned for the Lutheran church in Leiden are among Barent's most important works of the 1660s (see Liedtke, 1977). Only three of the five *Parables* survive (all Amsterdam, Rijksmus.). They are distinguished by their 'strip format' (0.93×2.85 m) and were originally installed in 1661 on the western choir loft, under the organ. Their vivid colour has occasionally been attributed to Venetian influences, but this has not been proven and, in any case, the strong, colourful impression must have been necessary for the pictures to be effective from a great distance. The *Parables* are arranged to be read from left to right, like a book, with the moment of healing and relief always on the right-hand side. A uniform horizontal line contributes to the effect of overall coherence, an effect not impaired by a deep perspective more strongly emphasized in some places than in others.

Among Barent's last history paintings is the signed and dated *Presentation in the Temple* (1668; Copenhagen, Stat. Mus. Kst), a masterpiece comparable to *Peter in the House of Cornelius* in terms of the maturity of the composition. The following year Barent painted four large-scale murals in the triangular spandrels at Zwaansvliet, a country house near Beemster (2.8×4.3 m; 1669; now on movable wooden panels, Haarlem, Frans Halsmus.); these decorations consisted of putti and allegorical and personified images of the Seasons, with their attributes, on fields of clouds.

Carel Fabritius's influence, while not so apparent in Barent's history paintings, was much stronger in the case of his few known portraits and genre pieces. This is certainly true of Barent's *Self-portrait in an Exotic Costume* (*c.* 1656–7; Munich, Alte Pin.) and the *Self-portrait as a Shepherd* (*c.* 1658; Vienna, Gemäldegal. Akad. Bild. Kst.). The light colours in the background and the lighting of the head in the latter are reminiscent of Carel's presumed self-portrait of 1654 (London, N.G.). Barent's *Smoking Sentry* (1653–4; Rome, Pal. Barberini) definitely refers back

to Carel's picture in Schwerin or to a similar untraced composition. Finally, Barent's two versions of the *Butchered Pig* (Rotterdam, Mus. Boymans-van Beuningen, and Berlin, Gemäldegal.) also show a clear debt to Carel's work. Barent seems also to have been inspired by the paintings of Nicolas Maes, whom he knew in the 1650s, as can be seen in the late *Visit to the Doctor* (1672; Bremen, Ksthalle), which should be interpreted as an allegory of the *natura passiva*.

Unlike Carel's, Barent's personality as a draughtsman has begun to be identified and his drawings distinguished from those by Maes and van Hoogstraten. Barent's drawings, as catalogued by Sumowski (1981), relate closely to the subjects and style of his paintings; they use relatively wide brushstrokes and are frequently washed. A few of the drawings are preparatory studies for his pictures.

3. CRITICAL RECEPTION AND POSTHUMOUS REPUTATION. Though Carel was already honoured by academics in the 17th century, Barent and his work were forgotten almost immediately. None of the important early sources mentions his name, and his work was not rediscovered until Théophile Thoré studied it and Bredius wrote an essay (1883) about the *Parables*. In the course of the 20th century his artistic output was gradually distinguished from that of his more important brother and its quieter nature was revealed.

BIBLIOGRAPHY

S. van Hoogstraten: *Inleyding tot de hooge schoole der schilderkonst* [Introduction to the high school of painting] (Rotterdam, 1678), pp. 11–12
W. Bürger [T. Thoré]: 'Notes sur les Fabritius', *Gaz. B.-A.*, ii (1864), pp. 100–04
C. Hofstede de Groot: *Holländischen Maler* (1907–28)
—: *Jan Vermeer en Carel Fabritius* (The Hague, 1930)
H. F. Wijnman: 'De schilder Carel Fabritius (1622–1654): Een reconstructie van zijn leven en werk', *Oud-Holland*, xlviii (1931), pp. 100–41
K. E. Schuurman: *Carel Fabritius* (Amsterdam, [1947])
D. Pont: *Barent Fabritius* (Utrecht, 1958)
W. Sumowski: 'Zum Werk von Barent und Carel Fabritius', *Jb. Kstsamml. Baden-Württemberg*, i (1964), pp. 188–98
A. K. Wheelock jr: 'Carel Fabritius: Perspective and Optics in Delft', *Ned. Ksthist. Jb.*, xxiv (1973), pp. 63–83
W. A. Liedtke: '*The View of Delft* by Carel Fabritius', *Burl. Mag.*, cxviii (1976), pp. 61–73
—: 'The Three *Parables* by Barent Fabritius with a Chronological List of his Paintings Dating from 1660 Onward', *Burl. Mag.*, cxix (1977), pp. 316–27
C. Brown: *Carel Fabritius: Complete Edition with a Catalogue Raisonné* (Oxford, 1981)
W. Sumowski: *Drawings of the Rembrandt School*, iv (New York, 1981)
The Impact of a Genius: Rembrandt, his Pupils and Followers in the 17th Century (exh. cat. by A. Blankert and others, Amsterdam, Waterman Gal.; Groningen, Groninger Mus.; 1983)
W. Sumowski: *Die Gemälde der Rembrandt-Schule*, ii (Landau-Pfalz, 1983)
C. Brown: '*Mercury and Argus* by Carel Fabritius: A Newly Discovered Painting', *Burl. Mag.*, cxxviii (1986), pp. 797–9
F. J. Duparc: 'A *Mercury and Aglauros* Reattributed to Carel Fabritius', *Burl. Mag.*, cxxviii (1986), pp. 799–802
D. R. Smith: 'Carel Fabritius and Portraiture in Delft', *A. Hist.*, xiii (1990), pp. 151–71

IRENE HABERLAND

Fabro, Luciano (*b* Turin, 20 Nov 1936). Italian sculptor, conceptual artist and writer. He frequented artistic circles in Udine in the mid-1950s. In 1958 Fabro saw Lucio Fontana's contribution to the Venice Biennale and the following year moved to Milan, where he discovered the work of Yves Klein and Francesco Lo Savio and was closely associated with Piero Manzoni and Enrico Castellani. Their investigations of matter and space influenced

Fabro's idea of the artist as a facilitator of experiences without preconceived categories. After tentative early works, he embarked upon austere pieces that encapsulated phenomenological problems, such as *The Hole* (1963; artist's col.), a mirror with the reflective coating partially scraped away. While the scraping mimicked the techniques of *Art informel*, the fusion of reflection and the recession, seen through the suspended glass, was indebted to Duchamp. His first one-man show (1965; Milan, Gal. Vismara) combined mirror pieces with the *Spatial Lines*, which demarcated their environment with tubular metal (e.g. *Cross*, 1965; Rotterdam, Boymans–van Beuningen). He included the physical participation of the observer in *In Cube* (metal rods and canvas, 1966; artist's col.), a cubical enclosure tailored to a person's height, and in *Theatrical Production* (1967; see 1987 exh. cat., p. 52), a mirrored cube that reflected the expectant audience. The series culminated in the cosmic space of the photographic wall *In Front, Behind, Right, Left (Sky)* (1967–8; artist's col.). He grouped all these works together as *Tautologies*.

In 1967 Fabro exhibited with Paolini, Kounellis and Pino Pascali in *Arte Povera/In spazio* (Genoa, Gal. La Bertesca). Responding to their unorthodox materials, Fabro began to diversify into silk, molten glass and marble for the gigantic bird-like *Feet* (1968–71; artist's col.). He employed the craftsmanship of funerary sculpture for *The Deceased* (marble, 1968–73; artist's col.), which facilitated the seamless absence of the head from the shrouded figure. By 1971, feeling that purely group activity was restricting, Fabro attempted (unsuccessfully) to have the *Arte Povera* show at the Kunstverein, Munich, retitled to a simple list of names. By this time he had begun the series of *Italys*, which continued for the next two decades. They constituted differing visions of the nation, reflecting a period of political and social upheaval; Fabro commented upon the geographical and historical accidents of the north/south divide by hanging the country by the toe in *Golden Italy* (gilded bronze, 1971; artist's col.); or he segmented it along provincial lines in *Puppet Italy* (1975; priv. col., see 1991 exh. cat., no. 40). Alongside these were more private themes, such as the sexual connotations of hanging cloth captured in the undulating *Clothes-Hangers* (1976; artist's col.), with their allusions to Apollo and the laurel-garlanded Daphne. Cloth was also used in the subsequent *Habitats*, which recalled the cubes of the 1960s (e.g. *Habitat*, 1983; artist's col.). In the late 1980s massive stone pieces such as the *Double Face of the Sky* (steel cable and marbled-blue rock, 1986; see 1987 exh. cat., pp. 30–31) were made light by means of their suspension, which was typical of Fabro in its paradox and whimsy.

WRITINGS
Regolo d'arte (Milan, 1980)
Luciano Fabro: Works, 1963–1986 (exh. cat., Edinburgh, Fruitmarket Gal.; Paris, Archvs A. Contemp. and Mus. A. Mod. Ville Paris; Villeurbanne, Nouv. Mus.; 1987)
Arte torna arte lezioni (Milan, 1987–8; Ger. trans., Berlin and Berne, 1990)

BIBLIOGRAPHY
Luciano Fabro: Sehnsucht (exh. cat. by Z. Felix, Essen, Mus. Folkwang; Rotterdam, Boymans–van Beuningen; 1981)
J. de Sanna: *Luciano Fabro* (Ravenna, 1983)
Luciano Fabro (exh. cat. by J. Gachnang, R. Fuchs and C. Mundici, Rivoli, Castello, 1989)
Luciano Fabro (exh. cat. by M. Rowell, Barcelona, Fund. Joan Miró, 1990)
Luciano Fabro (exh. cat. by J. Caldwell, M. Rowell and R. Fuchs, San Francisco, MOMA, 1991)

MATTHEW GALE

Fabry, Emile (*b* Verviers, 30 Dec 1865; *d* Woluwe-Saint-Pierre-lez-Bruxelles, 1966). Belgian painter and designer. He studied at the Académie Royale des Beaux-Arts in Brussels under Jean-François Portaels, and worked with the designer Cir Jacques. His early Symbolist work, influenced by Maurice Maeterlinck (1862–1949), expresses anguish through its depiction of wild-eyed and deformed figures. He described this as his 'nightmare period', exemplified by *The Offering* (1894; Brussels, Mus. A. Mod.). In 1892 Fabry took part in the first exhibition of the group 'Pour l'Art', which he founded with Jean Delville, and in 1893 and 1895 exhibited at the Salons de la Rose+Croix, established by Joséphin Péladan. In the late 1890s he began to work with the Art Nouveau architects Victor Horta and Paul Hankar. At this point his work became more serene and increasingly monumental. He designed the interior of the sculptor Philippe Wolfers's villa, built by Hankar, and also the interior of Horta's mansion Aubecq (destr.).

Fabry became drawing teacher at the Académie Royale des Beaux-Arts in Brussels in 1901. In 1904 he began work on decorative panels on canvas for the Théâtre de la Monnaie in Brussels depicting *Dance* and *Musical Inspiration*; in 1905 he decorated the provincial Palais du Gouvernement in Brabant, and in 1912 the Musée Royal de l'Afrique Centrale. His new post-Pointillist technique created bright, light-filled spaces, as in *The Harvest* (1912; Brussels, Mus. A. Mod.). In 1916 he took refuge in England and painted *War and Peace* (untraced) for Cardiff University. He was a member of the Groupe d'Art Monumental together with Delville and took part in work on the mosaics of the Arcade du Cinquantenaire in Brussels from 1926 to 1930. He also taught mural and decorative art at the Académie Royale.

BIBLIOGRAPHY
Rétrospective Emile Fabry, 1865–1965 (exh. cat., Brussels, Hôtel Com. Woluwe-Saint-Pierre, 1965)
F.-C. Legrand: *Le Symbolisme en Belgique* (Brussels, 1971)
R. Dalemans: *Emile Fabry* (Brussels, 1986)

FRANCINE-CLAIRE LEGRAND

Façade decoration. Some of the earliest civilizations are known to have attempted to improve a building's aesthetic appearance by forms of decoration, including the use of coloured materials or the application of colour (*see* POLYCHROMY, §1 and colour pls I–V). This article concentrates on Western façade decoration; for other civilizations see the appropriate country or culture heading.

I. Painting. II. Sgraffito. III. Sculpture.

I. Painting.

Outer walls have for centuries been painted with figured, architectural or ornamental elements, deliberately commissioned and intended to last. Ephemeral decorations of the type made for special festivities, for instance, do not count as façade decoration in this strict sense, any more than do the pictures of condemned men on the walls of court-houses ('pillory pictures'), which were common in

Italy from the 14th to the 16th century. Because of the deterioration caused by climatic effects, mainly the alfresco or *sgraffito* methods were used (*see* §II below). As a rule façade paintings were polychrome; in the first half of the 16th century monochrome light–dark paintings (chiaroscuri) were also popular in Italy, especially in Rome. Today only meagre remains of this once important genre have survived. Because of weathering, building conversions and changes in taste, the stock of such façades has been greatly reduced.

1. History and development. 2. Subject-matter. 3. Function. 4. Documentation and designs. 5. Theory and criticism.

1. HISTORY AND DEVELOPMENT. There is very sparse evidence of façade decoration in the Middle Ages. The oldest paintings on external walls that have survived or can be shown to have existed were on the façades of churches, which displayed portraits of saints, St Christopher in particular, in the 13th century. As for secular buildings, town gates and towers were often decorated with frescoes, mainly of coats of arms, patron saints, standard-bearers and gate watchmen. There are reports of decorative paintings in the courtyards and on the outer walls of castles in the Alpine region; painted rectangles suggesting stonework or patterns similar to textiles were widespread. Coats of arms and house signs also decorated the walls. In Toruń, Poland, it can be demonstrated that the blind niches at the town hall were covered with illusionary tracery as early as the 13th century. In 1307 a *domus picta* ('painted house') was mentioned in Worms, an indication that certain houses were decorated with paintings. Façade painting was documented in the 14th century, especially in Italy, with remains in Treviso, Florence, Verona and elsewhere.

The exploitation of the wall surface as a backing for a prominent picture area continued to be current practice in the 15th and 16th centuries, although by this period the painting of façades with figures and ornamental and architectural features had become customary. This became a crucial element in the overall appearance of many European towns and cities, its popularity due to the greater importance attached to the secular town house and to the newly kindled desire for impressive display. In many cases a stone façade was replaced by painted pilasters, cornices and friezes. From the late 15th century illusionary architectural techniques were evolved, which were applied to the wall as a system complete in itself (*see* ILLUSIONISM). Often areas between the architectonic elements were left free and could be used for representations of figures in simulated relief or as illusionistic scenes in simulated spaces or openings. From the late 15th century there was a noticeable tendency to transfer the illusionistic motifs to the figures as well by making them appear to go about their business in front of the actual façade, as in Pordenone's hovering Mercury or Marcus Curtius leaping up from the depths (*c.* 1530; Venice, Palazzo d'Anna) or to hover on clouds in front of the façade.

The architectural conceit of opening up the façade by means of perspectives, creating illusionistic spaces and thereby negating the flatness of the wall surface, was particularly popular north of the Alps; at the Harnaschhaus (1505) in Innsbruck an open spiral staircase with a man and a little dog climbing up it is painted on the façade. Artists who worked in this style include Hans Holbein (ii), Hans Bock I (*c.* 1550–1623), Tobias Stimmer and the

1. Detail of design for the painted façade decoration of the Palazzo dell'Antella, Florence, by Giovanni da San Giovanni, watercolour, 165×930 mm, 1619–20 (Florence, Galleria degli Uffizi)

Bocksbergers. Often architectural fantasies with artificial openings into the wall surfaces, lavishly supported by architectonic elements, were applied to already existing buildings. This also sometimes allowed a house to look more up-to-date in style. Perspective effects continued to be associated with façade decoration for a long time, as at the château of Marly, France, where the pavilions were painted in 1686.

Façade painting reached its peak in the 16th century, both in Italy and north of the Alps, as an important branch of work for painters, some of whom specialized in it; Bernardino Poccetti in Florence, for example, was nick-named 'Bernardino delle facciate'. It was particularly popular in northern and central Italy. Genoa, Brescia, Verona, Trento, Venice and Bologna had a great many painted façades; in Florence *sgraffito* was used more, and in Rome both methods were used. Among the major Italian examples of façade painting are Donato Bramante's frescoes at the Palazzo del Podestà, Bergamo (*c*. 1480), those by Giorgione and Titian at the Fondaco dei Tedeschi in Venice (1508) and in Rome those by Baldassare Peruzzi at the house of Ulisse da Fano (*c*. 1515) and by Polidoro da Caravaggio at the Palazzo Gaddi (*c*. 1525). Further examples include the work of Marcello Fogolino at the Case Rella in the Piazza del Duomo, Trento (1531), that of Giorgio Vasari at the Palazzo Almeni in Florence (1554), Lelio Orsi's façade paintings in Novellara and Reggio (*c*. 1560) and the later work by Giovanni da San Giovanni at the Palazzo dell'Antella in Florence (1619–20; see fig. 1).

The popularity of façade decoration spread to the lands adjoining Italy to the north, extending to Austria, Bavaria and Swabia and on to Bohemia, Silesia and Saxony. Notable examples include that in Basle by Hans Holbein the younger at the Haus zum Tanz (*c*. 1525), and in Germany the work of an anonymous artist at the Haus zum weissen Adler, Stein am Rhein (*c*. 1525), the work of Giulio Licinio at the Rehlingerhaus in Augsburg (*c*. 1560; see fig. 2) and that of Tobias Stimmer at the Haus zum Ritter, Schaffhausen (1567–70). The painted façades of certain towns in Switzerland and Germany presented an appearance similar to those of towns in Italy. Thus Aeneas Silvius Piccolomini, later Pope Pius II, commented with regard to Vienna: 'The painted house and interior are splendid. Entering this house you will think you have come into the home of a prince' (*Historia Austrialis* (1454–8)). Munich, Ulm, Nuremberg and Frankfurt am Main were also adorned by numerous painted façades. About 50 still survive at Augsburg, and formerly there would have been far more. In Austria, Bohemia and Silesia there were many examples of whole streets with decorative façades, although they were mainly in *sgraffito* (*see* §II below).

In the 17th century there was a general decline in the popularity of façade decoration in Italy but also an increase in its use in connection with the dimensions and forms of Baroque architecture. North of the Alps the use of façade decoration was to some extent reduced by the Thirty Years War (1618–48). The preferences of the Baroque movement were adopted in its form and application, but the discrepancy between what was built and the ideas of architectural theorists became increasingly pronounced.

2. Design for the painted façade of Rehlingerhaus, Augsburg, by Giulio Licinio, *c*. 1560

Although façade decoration spread in the 18th century, particularly in the Tyrol and Upper Bavaria, the illusionistic qualities of façade painting were out of tune with the period's classically inspired taste. Especially in the late 18th century it was therefore generally confined to the sparing representation of architectural elements such as pilasters and window surrounds. The historicism of the 19th century brought about a limited revival of façade decoration; in the 20th century it came back into fashion in many countries, for example in Mexico and the United States, with illusionistic *trompe l'oeil* paintings covering large areas. (*See also* MURAL.)

2. SUBJECT-MATTER. Religious subjects were obviously a main influence on façade decoration in the late Middle Ages (Jacob Burckhardt believed that the origins of façade decoration were to be found in religious pictures), and probably genre figures, satires and humorous scenes were also popular; a 14th-century jousting scene in Augsburg might indicate that it was based on a romance of chivalry. Mythological and allegorical subjects were widely represented with the onset of humanism. Scenes from Roman history, in so far as they could serve as examples of virtue or courage, were also popular; Livy (59 BC–AD 17) and Ovid were the most important sources. As a rule the function of the building was a determining factor for the iconographic programme of the decoration.

As early as the 14th century Ambrogio Lorenzetti painted the façade of the Ospedale Chapel in Siena with scenes from the *Life of the Virgin* (1335) but that of the prison with episodes from Roman history.

In the late 15th century and particularly in the 16th, multipartite picture programmes became popular on town halls and mansions; for example, Augsburg's Altes Rathaus (destr.) was painted by Jörg Breu (i) in 1516, and at the Palazzo Almeni in Florence Giorgio Vasari produced frescoes of the *Active Life* and *Contemplative Life*, the *Seven Liberal Arts*, the *Virtues*, the *Ages of Man* and the *Planets* (1554). The painting of allegories, historical episodes and examples of virtue was a basic feature of humanist-inspired culture. They were found in many variations and mainly on public buildings. Themes from literature were also adopted; for example, scenes from Giovanni Boccaccio's *Decameron* (1358) and from the *Gesta Romanorum* (Feats of the Romans; *c*. 1340) were depicted on the Haus zum weissen Adler in Stein am Rhein (*c*. 1525). One popular satirical theme was the 'world in reverse', in which hares roast the hunter, as at the Haus zum Wachtelkorb in Legnica, Poland, and at the Hasenhaus in Vienna (?1594), and in the representation of monkeys in human disguise depicted at Berchtesgaden on the Gasthaus zum Hirschen (1600–10).

Contemporary references or references to the person commissioning the façade are rare. The façade paintings (1567) on the inner court of Schloss Ambras are an exception: the court life of Schloss Ambras is outlined using heroic models and virtuous ideals from antiquity and the Old Testament, emphasizing the nurture of art and science. Similarly, scenes from the *Life of David* (*c*. 1580–90) were depicted at the Palazzo dal Borgo in Florence and linked by an inscription with the deeds of Cosimo I de' Medici, Grand Duke of Tuscany. At Dresden the decorations at the castle (1550–52) and Stallhof (1587–91) should presumably be understood as referring to court life there; they depicted Roman warriors, the labours of Hercules, battle scenes and a triumphal procession that extended over the entire length of the building.

In 16th-century Italy biblical subjects gave way in popularity to themes from Classical antiquity; in the north they retained their significance as a result of the religio-political conflict following the Reformation. In 1525 Martin Luther expressly recommended façade paintings as a means of keeping the knowledge of scenes from the Bible alive: 'Would to God that I could persuade the ruling classes and the rich to have the whole Bible painted inside and outside their houses for all to see; that would be a Christian work' (*M. Luthers Werke, kritische Gesamtausgabe*, xviii (Weimar, 1883), p. 83). However, on several occasions he spoke against paying excessive respect to pictures.

From the early 16th century printed graphic matter was often used as a pattern for façade decorations, especially north of the Alps. In 1518 Holbein adopted themes from engravings made after Andrea Mantegna's *Triumph of Caesar* (London, Hampton Court, Royal Col.) for the decoration of the Hertensteinhaus in Lucerne. Illustrations by Hans Schäufelein and Hans Burgkmair from two publications by Johann von Schwartzenberg (1463–1528),

the *Officia Ein Buch so Marcus Tullius der Römer* (Augsburg, 1531) and *Büchle Memorial der Tugent* (Augsburg, 1534), with subjects from the Old and New Testaments and Roman history, were used at the Rathaus in Ulm (1539–40). In Eggenburg, Austria, an extensive programme of decoration was implemented using scenes from Hans Burgkmair's series on the planets (1510) and illustrations from Lucas Cranach (i)'s 1534 Bible. At the Haus zum Wachtelkorb in Legnica, an engraving by or after Virgil Solis was the prototype for the armed hares roasting the hunter and his dog; at the same house the *Triumph of Ceres*, an allegory for summer, is also after an engraving by Virgil Solis. At the Haus zur Minute in Prague (*c*. 1603) the portraits of 15 French kings were copied from the *Effigies regum francorum omnium* (1576), with engravings by Virgil Solis and Jost Amman; the allegories on the same house were based on descriptions by Cesare Ripa. The didactic character of 16th-century northern façade decoration is sometimes stressed by explanatory inscriptions; some are taken from the prints that served as models for the painting, others from the appropriate matching texts, as at the Rathaus in Ulm, the Haus zum Wachtelkorb in Legnica and Hauptplatz 15 in Retz, Austria.

3. FUNCTION. Hardly any category of art is so strongly determined by its social function as façade painting. In painting his house the owner is turning towards the public and can use the decoration to underline not only his civic status but also his way of thinking, his religious convictions or his scholarship. The ambivalence between its private inspiration and public effect is a characteristic of façade painting. On public buildings the towns were able to appeal to social conscience by means of heroic or virtuous models and to place the ideal of a good government before the eyes of the public, as at the Altes Rathaus in Augsburg, and Ulm, Basle, Mulhouse (Alsace) and Wrocław, Poland.

Didactic, humanist-inspired tendencies in façade painting were associated with the need felt by the increasingly powerful townspeople to create an impression. This public genre was in fact closely linked with the theatrical nature of social life in the Renaissance. Other powerful incentives for façade decoration were 'conspicuous consumption', self-advertisement through a display of splendour and, not least, the possibility of winning renown. Usually references to the person commissioning the painting were disguised in allegorical or mythological themes so that it is rarely possible to decode them. On occasions knowledge of the meaning was lost soon after the façade was created. Even in his day Vasari lamented that no-one in Venice could explain Giorgione's and Titian's façade paintings (1508) on the Fondaco dei Tedeschi. One of the important functions of façade decoration was the dissemination of Renaissance motifs, and the paintings also kept a knowledge of mythological and biblical stories alive.

Sometimes façade painting was seen as a less expensive way of creating a façade. In 1537 Sebastiano Serlio (fol. 33) was already recommending painting as a substitute for stone elements: 'If because of the cost you do not want to use marble or another stone, it is quite possible to supplement the ornamentation of many things with painting, imitating the genuine article with the artificial.' Josef

Furttenbach the elder made a similar point in 1640 (ii, fol. 2 f). Such an argument is proposed almost only in connection with purely architectural painting. Further, Lodovico Dolce valued a well-painted façade more highly than an ostentatious stone façade. However, the popularity of façade painting in the 16th century clearly rested on its special ability to represent illusionistic make-believe spaces, spatial perspectives and animating figures, and wide-ranging figural scenes. The broad spectrum of decorated buildings, from town houses to public buildings and castles, suggests that façade painting was not always a surrogate for built architecture.

4. DOCUMENTATION AND DESIGNS. Only a fraction of the façade painting that once existed has been preserved, and a documentary source or a mention in books on art or tourist literature is rare. In some cases drawings or engravings made after the façade, views or photographs are available. Systematic compilation of façade decorations in some towns has been attempted, such as Treviso (Botter), Rome (*Le case romane con facciate graffite e dipinte*), Florence (Thiem and Thiem), Verona (Schweikhart) and Regensburg (*Farbige Architektur, Regensburger Häuser: Bauforschung und Dokumentation*).

Among the few designs that have been preserved and that can impart an idea of the painters' intentions are Domenico Beccafumi's design (1514; London, BM) for the façade decoration of the Casa dei Borghesi in Siena, Hans Holbein (ii)'s design (*c.* 1525; Basle, Kstmus.) for the façade painting of the Haus zum Tanz in Basle and Pordenone's design (*c.* 1530; London, V&A) for the façade of the Palazzo d'Anna in Venice. Also of value are Giorgio Vasari (i)'s design (*c.* 1565–70; Florence, Uffizi) for a façade decoration, the design (1571–2; Basle, Kstmus. see fig. 3) for the façade of Haus Zwinger in Basle, by Hans Bock I (*c.* 1550–1623), Melchior Bocksberger's designs (1573–4; Regensburg, Stadtmus.) for painting the town hall in Regensburg and the design (1643; Wasserburg, Mus. Wasserburg) for the façade of the town hall in Wasserburg by Wolfgang Pittenhart (*c.* 1590–before 1643).

5. THEORY AND CRITICISM. No theory relating specifically to façade decoration has been developed; admiration for certain examples can be inferred from biographical literature, such as that by Vasari and Giovanni Paolo Lomazzo. Writers on the theory of architecture have been more inclined to express reservations; Sebastiano Serlio, for example, warned that the dignity of architecture might be diminished by the use of illusionistic effects (fol. 192). There is a comparative assessment of good façade painting and lavish stone cladding on the façade by Lodovico Dolce (p. 37): 'Likewise externally those houses or mansions with façades painted by a skilled master offer a greater feast to the eyes than those which are covered with white marble, porphyry or serpentine decorated with gold.' In architectural theory in the 17th century and first half of the 18th, façade decoration was regarded more as architectural painting, and decoration with figures was recommended partly as easily understandable allegory and partly to supply simulated stone or bronze reliefs; pictures using perspective were to be

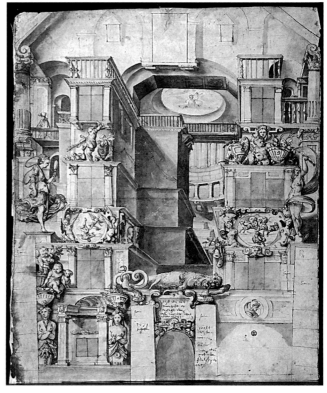

3. Design for the painted façade of Haus Zwinger, Basle, by Hans Bock I, pen and ink and grey wash, 494×394 mm, 1571–2 (Basle, Kupferstichkabinett)

avoided and if they were used were to be clearly distinguished as pictures on the façade by the insertion of painted frames, according to Josef Furttenbach the elder and Leonhard Christoph Sturm.

RDK

BIBLIOGRAPHY

S. Serlio: *Sette libri dell'architettura*, iv (Venice, 1537/*R* 1544)
G. Vasari: *Vite* (1550, rev. 2/1568); ed. G. Milanesi (1878–85)
L. Dolce: *Dialogo della pittura intitolato l'Aretino* (Venice, 1557); ed. R. Eitelberger von Edelberg (Vienna, 1871)
J. Furttenbach: *Architectura ricreationis* (Augsburg, 1640)
L. C. Sturm: *Vollständige Anweisung zu der Civil Bau-Kunst* (Wolfenbüttel, 1696)
——: *Vollständige Anweisung grosser Herren Paläste* (Augsburg, 1718)
J. Burckhardt: *Die Baukunst der Renaissance in Italien* (Stuttgart, 1867)
W. Lübke and A. Haupt: *Geschichte der Renaissance in Deutschland*, iii (Esslingen, 1914)
H. Phleps: *Die farbige Architektur bei den Römern und im Mittelalter* (Berlin, 1930)
L. Foscari: *Affreschi esterni a Venezia* (Milan, 1936)
M. Botter: *Ornati a fresco di case trivigiane, secoli XIII–XV* (Treviso, 1955)
Le case romane con facciate graffite e dipinte (exh. cat., Rome, Pal. Braschi, 1960)
G. Thiem and C. Thiem: *Toskanische Fassaden-Dekoration in Sgraffito und Fresko, 14.–17. Jahrhundert* (Munich, 1964)
A. Marabottini: *Polidoro da Caravaggio* (Rome, 1969)
C. Klemm: 'Der Entwurf zur Fassadenmalerei am Haus "Zum Tanz" in Basel', *Z. Schweiz. Archäol. & Kstgesch.*, xxix (1972), pp. 165–75
G. Schweikhart: *Fassadenmalerei in Verona: Vom 14. bis zum 20. Jahrhundert* (Munich, 1973)
M. Baur-Heinhold: *Bemalte Fassaden: Geschichte, Vorbild, Technik, Erneuerung*, ii (Munich, 1975)
Genua picta: Proposte per la scoperta e il recupero delle facciate dipinte (exh. cat., Genoa, Commenda S Giovanni Pré, 1982)

Urbs picta: La città affrescata nel Veneto. Atti del convegno di studi: Treviso, 1982

Farbige Architektur, Regensburger Häuser: Bauforschung und Dokumentation, Bayerisches Landesamt für Denkmalpflege (Munich, 1984)

P. Burke: *Städtische Kultur in Italien zwischen Hochrenaissance und Barock: Eine historische Anthropologie* (Berlin, 1987)

II. *Sgraffito*.

This form of ornamentation is produced by scratching the surface of a plastered façade to uncover the coloured plaster below. Whenever outer walls are plastered, a first rendering coat (*rinzaffo*) is required to cover and fill joints and holes in the rough masonry. For *sgraffito* the wall is then coated with a dark-coloured plaster (*arricciato*) made of slaked lime mixed with sand. When burnt straw or powdered charcoal is added, it colours the plaster silvery black; there were also isolated instances in the 15th and 16th centuries of bright-coloured grounds being used. A white lime wash, usually made from pure travertine and sometimes mixed with sand (*malta*), was applied to the *arricciato* before the latter was dry. If the wash did not contain sand, several coats were needed. On this white layer a sketch was made or a cartoon used to scratch the outlines of the decoration. Using a stylus, or on larger surfaces a pointed trowel or scraper, the top white layer was scratched away. The contrasting colours of the light, smooth outer surface and the darker, rough, lower layer of plaster allowed figures or patterns to appear. *Sgraffito* is not only weather resistant but also requires less artistic skill than alfresco painting.

The colouring of the background plaster followed a refined technique developed during the Renaissance. Earlier examples of scratch work did not use coloured plaster, and it was only with the introduction of differentiated colouring that finer patterns and lively figures with internal drawing could be effectively achieved. In the introduction to the second edition of *Vite*, Vasari gave a precise technical description of the process. After Gottfried Semper had revived *sgraffito* decoration in the 19th century, artists also used other materials to give colour, such as coal cinders, manganese dioxide, iron oxide and powdered coke.

Although scratch work was used in Germany from the 13th century (e.g. Magdeburg Cathedral, cloisters), true *sgraffito* developed in Italy and spread from there. Decoration of a plastered façade with simulated regular stonework existed in Florence from the late 13th century, two-tone decorations from the 15th century. The early *sgraffito* decorations follow on from the medieval practice of using overlay and ornamentation on buildings and reflect the way in which stone is worked. The tendency to suggest illusionary architecture with pilasters, window surrounds, ledges and infilled panels developed in the 15th century (*see* ILLUSIONISM).

Sgraffito was popular in Rome from the late 15th century until *c.* 1520; in 1960 there were about 60 *sgraffito-*

4. *Sgraffito* façade decoration of the Palazzo dei Cavalieri, Pisa, by Giorgio Vasari, 1562–6

decorated façades in Rome. In Florence *sgraffito* decoration was common until *c.* 1630. Italian decorations consisted almost exlusively of geometric or ornamental shapes until the mid-16th century, when representations of figures become more prevalent. In the most extensive preserved example, that by Giorgio Vasari on the Palazzo dei Cavalieri in Pisa (1562–6; see fig. 4), a humanist programme glorifies the Knights of the Order of St Stephen in allegorical form.

In the 16th century *sgraffito* spread to Central and Northern Europe, where it was used as ornamental decoration conforming to popular local traditions. Sometimes it was combined with fresco paintings using several colours, although façades were usually characterized by contrasts between light and dark, well suited to reproducing scenes from prints. Whole streets were sometimes decorated with *sgraffito*. The most predominant type was the decoration of façades with stone rustication and friezes, which can be found on virtually every type of building. After the 16th century *sgraffito* persisted as a popular art, particularly in Lower Austria and Grisons. In Switzerland traditional signs and symbols were widely used in the 14th and 15th centuries, and Renaissance motifs in the 16th century, especially copies of architectural elements. Peculiar to the Engadine is the undulating frieze, the basic structure of which was scratched into the wet plaster with a compass.

Sgraffito decorations were particularly common in Lower Austria, the earliest examples dating from the 1540s. Although *sgraffito* was used there mainly on window surrounds and to extend architectural features by ornamentation using plants or figures, there are also some scenes with figures. Façades with *sgraffito* were created largely along the same lines: single, simply framed pictures are separated by scrolls, festoons or panels with inscriptions, the series tied into a layer that covers the whole façade and overrides the architecture. In 16th-century Bohemia whole streets were decorated with *sgraffito*, and rows of such houses are extant in Krumlov, Tábor, Jindřichův Hradec, Telč, Třebíč, Prague, Prachatice and Slavonice, many decorated with picture panels, often with Old Testament scenes (e.g. Slavonice). In Bohemia *sgraffito* almost completely superseded fresco painting.

In Germany the *sgraffito* technique was widely practised in Ulm, though confined to ornamental decorations, ashlars and decorative window surrounds. Only one composition with figures has been preserved in Bavaria, the court façade of the west wing of the castle at Neuburg an der Donau (1562), on which figures are depicted between the windows and scenes from the Old Testament between the pilasters. It is also the only surviving example of a mixture of fresco and *sgraffito* in Germany. A model of the castle in Dresden (mid–late 16th century, destr.; Dresden, Grünes Gewölbe) shows its façade decoration between 1534 and 1620, designed and executed by Benedikt da Thola (*fl* 1550–72) and Gabriel da Thola (*fl* 1550–69), on which figures, pictures and ornamental work cover all available wall surfaces. In 16th-century Silesia (Poland) *sgraffito* was used on castles, public buildings and town houses. At Pohlwitz Castle (after 1584–6) the gable decoration on the manor house depicts allegorical figures, characters from the Old Testament, saints and animals. In

Legnica on the Haus zum Wachtelkorb is a picture of a stag hunt, Ceres in triumphal procession, motifs from the 'world in reverse' (hares as huntsmen) and other scenes (heavily restored).

BIBLIOGRAPHY
G. Vasari: *Vite* (1550, rev. 2/1568); ed. G. Milanesi (1878–85)
S. Vögelin: 'Geschichte der Fassadenmalerei in der Schweiz', *Anz. Schweiz. Altertknd.*, iii (1879), pp. 931–2, 955–7/33–5, 50–56; iv (1880), pp. 33f; pls v, vi
K. Weber: 'Das englische Haus in Danzig', *Denkmalpflege*, xv (1912), pp. 113–16
W. Lubke and A. Haupt: *Geschichte der Renaissance in Deutschland*, 3 vols (Esslingen, 1914)
H. Urbach: *Geschichtliches und Technisches vom Sgraffitoputz* (Berlin, 1928)
Le case romane con facciate graffite e dipinte (exh. cat., Rome, Pal. Braschi, 1960)
G. Thiem and C. Thiem: *Toskanische Fassaden-Dekoration in Sgraffito und Fresko, 14.–17. Jahrhundert* (Munich, 1964)
W. Bertram: 'Die Restaurierung der Sgraffito-Fassade im Schlosshof zu Neuburg an der Donau', *Dt. Kst- & Dkmlpf.*, xii (1966), pp. 37–62
I. U. Kunz: *Sgraffito im Engadin und Bergell* (Zurich, 1977), p. 51
H. Hickel: *Mittelalterliche Wandmalerei in der DDR* (Leipzig, 1979)
G. Klimesch: *Beiträge zu Fassadenmalerei der Renaissance an Profanbauten in Österreich* (diss., U. Vienna, 1984)

GUNTER SCHWEIKHART

III. Sculpture.

The use of sculpture on façades has been almost universal, both as decoration and, more importantly, to convey information about the purpose, content, builders or users of the structure. Sculpture has the advantage over other forms of decoration, such as painting or *sgraffito*, of being more durable and often more legible, owing to the fall of light and shadow. It has frequently been painted to enhance its effect. Such decorative sculpture is normally in relief and carved directly on to the blocks of stone, trunks of wood or moulded bricks that were used for the building. Less frequently, figures carved in the round—or virtually so—have been placed just in front of or against the façade: for example the colossal statues of pharaohs that flank the doors of Egyptian temples, or the sculptures from the two pediments of the Parthenon, Athens, which form part of the Elgin Marbles (London, BM). Statues carved completely in the round were occasionally incorporated into a structure, instead of columns: most famous are the caryatids at the Porch of the Maidens at the Erechtheion in Athens (*see* CARYATID, fig. 1), which have given rise to an enormous progeny, right down to 18th- and 19th-century chimney-pieces. Similarly, the column figures that flank Gothic portals often function as physical supports, and were carved *in situ*.

1. Ancient Egypt and Ancient Near East. 2. Ancient Greece and ancient Rome. 3. Medieval and early Renaissance. 4. High Renaissance and Baroque. 5. Neo-classical and modern.

1. ANCIENT EGYPT AND ANCIENT NEAR EAST. In ancient Egypt the vast external wall surfaces of the pylons that mark the entrances to the temple enclosures were frequently carved in sunken relief with enormous individual figures of gods or pharaohs, and narratives with many much smaller figures enacting ritual processions, battles etc, as in the temples of Luxor (*see* THEBES (i), §III), Karnak (*see* THEBES (i), §II, 1) and EDFU. Still more impressively sculptural is the façade of the Great Temple

of Abu Simbel (after 1290–*c.* 1265 BC), in which four heroic, colossal seated figures of pharaohs were hewn out of the rock in extremely deep relief: the plinths on which they sit project below, so that their front edges, the knees and the headdresses of the figures above all adhere to the sloping surface of the original rock face, which was flattened round them so as to create a frame (for illustration *see* ABU SIMBEL). Many variations of façades occur during the long history of Egypt. Some were columniated but had large, squarish panels of relief carving set between the columns, rising to half their height, as in the Temple of Horus at Edfu (begun 237 BC), while others had figures engaged with the front of their piers, so that they resembled caryatids. Almost all of the internal façades of the courts of Egyptian temples were similarly treated, with any large flat areas of wall being incised with sunken narrative reliefs (or true reliefs), which were then brightly coloured for realism and splendour.

In Mesopotamia in the Babylonian empire, stone was scarce; consequently bricks, manufactured from the alluvial mud of the Tigris and Euphrates, were frequently moulded and sometimes glazed to form great low reliefs. Less durable than stone, these bricks have mostly not survived, but in general Babylonian façades seem not to have been so liberally decorated with sculpture as those in Egypt. In the Assyrian kingdom alabaster and limestone, which were readily available, were brilliantly incised with low reliefs: those from the palaces of Nineveh, Nimrud and Khorsabad (8–7th century BC) showing warlike pursuits, hunts and building (London, BM) are of high artistic quality. Human-headed, winged lions or bulls were frequently used to flank main entrances, usually in relief, facing forwards and with one flank exposed down a side wall. In Persian buildings similar motifs were employed; thus the façades at Persepolis and Susa (5th century BC), executed in bricks glazed green, yellow and blue, represented processions of ambassadors, archers or roaring lions (examples Paris, Louvre; *see also* PERSEPOLIS, fig. 2).

2. ANCIENT GREECE AND ANCIENT ROME. The Greeks of the 6th and 5th centuries BC codified the application of sculpture on their façades (*see also* GREECE, ANCIENT, §IV, 1(i)(b)); unlike the Egyptians, they did not allow it to spread anarchically over every available flat surface. Plain architectural components acted as a foil for the carvings that were contained in particular areas: the low, but often quite deep triangular gable of the pediment was used to house three-dimensional statues, carved elsewhere and arranged frequently in a symmetrical progression of poses of human figures, from the outward-pointing toes of recumbent statues conveniently filling the awkward, low corners, through crouching and kneeling figures, to standing figures at the lofty centre (*see also* PEDIMENT, §2(i)). A series of metopes below the pediment, running round the entablature between the triglyphs, provided fields for relief carving (*see* POLYCHROMY, colour pl. I, fig. 1). These were often used to depict single episodes from a greater narrative, such as the Labours of Hercules on the Temple of Zeus at Olympia (*c.* 470–457 BC). Inside the colonnade, round the upper edge of the cella, ran a FRIEZE of continuous relief carving, which often depicted a religious or victorious procession, such as would in

reality have come to the temple on special occasions. Statues or other ornaments were set at the apex of the pediment and at the corners (*see* ACROTERION): they were frequently made of terracotta rather than marble, for the sake of lightness, as well as to match more closely the surrounding tiled roof. The capitals of the columns below were also carved into various shapes, conforming with the various orders or architecture: of these the Corinthian, with its curly acanthus leaves, was most sculptural. The Classical Greek façade has continued to be used ever since.

As well as using statues and reliefs to adorn the façades of buildings (*see* ROME, ANCIENT, §IV, 1(iv)(b)), the Romans found, around the beginning of the Christian era, another use for decorative statues and reliefs—to form part of a triumphal arch, commemorating a victorious campaign. Panels in relief showing martial trophies or particular episodes of a campaign or triumphal ceremony, and set in rectangular or circular frames, were carved on the façades and returns of the archways; allegorical female figures of winged Fame or Victory filled the spandrels on either side of the arch; while the structure was often crowned by a free-standing bronze group of the victorious general on a *quadriga*. Bronze statues with trumpets might adorn the four corners. Most celebrated among many such arches are those of Titus (AD 81), Septimius Severus (AD 203; *see* ROME, ANCIENT, fig. 34) and Constantine (AD 315; *see* ROME, fig. 30), all in Rome, that of Tiberius at Orange in France (*c.* AD 21), and those of Trajan in Ancona (AD 115) and Benevento (AD 114). (*See also* TRIUMPHAL ARCH, §1.)

3. MEDIEVAL AND EARLY RENAISSANCE. Apart from occasional inserted reliefs and minor ornaments such as bosses and capitals, sculpture was not a major feature of Early Christian or Byzantine façades, partly owing to suspicion attaching to 'graven images', which led to periodic bouts of iconoclasm. Around AD 1000 sculpture again began to appear on the façades of churches all over western Europe and in the following centuries it proliferated, as the Romanesque style gave way to the Gothic. In Romanesque arcuated architecture, sculpture tended to be clustered round the doorways, often in series of reliefs running up the jambs and across the lintels, round the archivolts and in the semicircular tympanum. Furthermore, the door itself was employed as a field for narrative reliefs cast in bronze. In Italy, Romanesque church portals were often protected by porches supported on columns, which customarily rested on the backs of pairs of recumbent lions; these usually faced slightly inwards and were shown roaring, sometimes with prey beneath their forepaws (example *c.* 1138; Verona, S Zeno Maggiore). Sculpture might also spread sideways from a portal and on to the adjacent walls, as in S Zeno Maggiore and in St Trophîme, Arles. The tympanum might provide a field for a large narrative relief, often portraying the Last Judgement, with the central figure of God the Father dividing the chosen from the damned, as in the narthex of Ste Madeleine, Vézelay (*c.* 1120–40) and in St Lazare, Autun (*see* AUTUN, fig. 2). It could also provide a plain foil against which statues in the round were set; often the Virgin and Child would be placed at the centre, carved on a larger

scale than the flanking saints or raised above them on a plinth, to take advantage of the greater height in the centre of the lunette. These figures were usually supported by a carved lintel resting on a central trumeau, which itself was often carved with a figure acting as a caryatid (Beaulieu-sur-Dordogne, Corrèze), or related in some way to the Last Judgement scene on the tympanum: for instance, St Michael the archangel weighing souls in the balance. This also became a classic position for a life-size sculpture of the *Virgin and Child*, as on the Vierge Dorée portal (*c.* 1260) of Reims Cathedral. A later Gothic example by Claus Sluter (1383) appears on the portal of the Virgin of the Charterhouse of Champmol, Dijon. Such a central group would sometimes appear to be responding to figures flanking the doorway; at Champmol these represent the *Duke and Duchess of Burgundy with their Patron Saints*.

The Camposanto of Pisa is the major complex of buildings in the Tuscan Romanesque style, but its exteriors are not rich in sculpture; a few pictorial reliefs, including the foundation date of 1174, are carved at the foot of the campanile by Bonanus of Pisa. The capitals of the rows of superimposed columns on the campanile, cathedral and baptistery are carved, but otherwise statuary on the façade of the cathedral is limited to a *Virgin and Child* on the apex of the gable, flanked by angels at the ends and a pair of *Evangelists* above the side aisles, with associated carved gargoyles; the central portal is flanked by two great marble columns gorgeously carved with acanthus scrolls and crowned by a pair of boldly projecting lion gargoyles. (The Romanesque bronze doors by Bonanus, destroyed in 1595, were replaced *c.* 1600 by a series made under the aegis of Giambologna.) The exterior of the baptistery is richer in sculpture: the jambs of its east portal (*see* PISA, fig. 6) are richly carved with 13th-century reliefs of the *Labours of the Months* on the left and the *Twelve Apostles* on the right. The architrave depicts the *Life of St John the Baptist*, while above is a *Virgin and Child* by Giovanni Pisano. The most important sculptures, however, are the colossal half-length statues of the *Virgin and Child, Christ*, prophets and saints (Pisa, Mus. Opera Duomo), carved by Nicola Pisano for the gables of the arcade above the portal, and subsequently replaced by copies. Giovanni Pisano, whose style was becoming distinctly Gothic, decorated the lower zone of the façade of the cathedral of Siena with numerous reliefs and, more important, a series of highly expressive statues of *Prophets* (1284–96; Siena, Mus. Opera Duomo, and London, V&A; copies on cathedral façade).

In the great Gothic cathedrals of Germany, France and England carved figures were often substituted for the engaged columns that flanked the portals in serried ranks, although slim colonnettes occasionally survived to recall the architectonic function of support. Sometimes sculpture spread from the portals to the whole façade; occasionally there were series of more or less life-size statues, set under the arcades of great galleries running the full width of the façade and round the flanking towers. Examples are Notre-Dame, Paris, and the cathedrals of Exeter and Lincoln. In Wells Cathedral such statues were also disposed in vertical series of niches flanking the great lancets. Milan Cathedral (*c.* 1385) has much in common with northern Gothic edifices, owing to its geographical proximity; it is therefore richer in sculpture than was the norm in central Italy. The

sculptors were often of German or Burgundian extraction, but Italian masters, such as Matteo Raverti, Jacopino da Tradate (*fl* 1401–25) and Antonio Briosco (*fl* 1414–57) also worked there. In the cathedral of Orvieto, Lorenzo Maitani carved serried ranks of figures expounding the Christian faith, from the Creation to the Last Judgement (1310), covering all the surfaces of the lower zone of the façade (*see* ORVIETO, figs 3 and 4). The same *horror vacui* is apparent on some Renaissance façades, for example those by Agostino di Duccio on S Bernardino, Perugia (1461), and those by Giovanni Antonio Amadeo for the Certosa di Pavia (1473; *see* PAVIA, fig. 1). In Florence a Late Gothic, ogival design for the façade of the cathedral, embodying much sculpture by Arnolfo di Cambio and his school (*see* ARNOLFO DI CAMBIO, fig. 3), was transmuted early in the 15th century by sculptures of the *Four Evangelists*, two of which, *St John* (1415) by Donatello and *St Luke* (1413) by Nanni di Banco, were in the novel Renaissance style. The façade was never completed, although its appearance is known from a drawing (1587) by Bernardino Poccetti, and it was finally demolished (fragments and drawing, Florence, Mus. Opera Duomo).

Venetian architecture is noted for its façades, which were always enlivened with sculpture. The skyline of S Marco is a forest of pinnacles bearing statues of saints, virtues or angels, and its frontons are encrusted with agitated leaf mouldings. Some of the sculptural adornments on the façade were booty from other cities: notably the four gilt-bronze ancient Greek horses from a *quadriga* on the Hippodrome of Constantinople (now Istanbul), plundered in 1204 and erected in 1265, and the porphyry group of *Tetrarchs* at the south-west corner (*see* ROME, ANCIENT, fig. 82). The quadrilateral of the Doge's Palace was marked at its corners by prominent sculptures, which on the two adjacent flanks were halfway between being reliefs and fully in the round. In chronological sequence from the south-east corner they were the *Drunkenness of Noah*, the *Temptation of Adam and Eve* (see fig. 5), the *Judgement of Solomon* and an allegorical figure of *Justice*. The capitals of the colonnade were carved, although without the finesse of northern European Gothic, and the portal was marked by a life-size statue of a doge kneeling before the symbolic winged lion of St Mark, with allegorical statues of the Venetian Republic's virtues above. Other Venetian Gothic façades, such as those of the Ca' d'Oro or Palazzo Pisani, rely for their ornamental effect on a filigree of tracery and are not particularly sculptural, apart from the usual carvings on capitals, balconies etc, and occasional Byzantine decorative panels built into the wall.

Spanish Gothic and early Renaissance façades tend to follow the example of the medieval Pórtico de la Gloria (1188) of the cathedral of Santiago de Compostela (*see* SANTIAGO DE COMPOSTELA, fig. 3) in being much more heavily ornamented with sculpture than Italian ones. Numerous statues within niches and other decorations create an ebullient, if rather un-architectural, effect, as in the Colegio de S Gregorio (Museo Nacional de Escultura) in Valladolid (1488; for illustration *see* VALLADOLID), where a vast central rectangular panel of relief depicts the family tree of Ferdinand II of Aragon and Isabella I of Castile, with their conjoined coats of arms displayed above. A similarly overladen façade is to be seen on S Pablo,

5. Sculptural façade decoration, the *Temptation of Adam and Eve*, the Doge's Palace, Venice, mid-14th century

Valladolid (*c.* 1463). This rich sculptural embellishment, divided by abstract geometrical shapes, tends to submerge or completely disguise the actual structure. Considered as sculptures, however, these embellishments, in which Moorish influence has been noted, are magnificent creations. In England the principal application of sculpture on the façades of grand secular buildings was in elaborate armorial bearings set over the gateways, with the supporters being given great prominence; an example is the arms of Beaufort supported by Yales over the gateway of St John's College, Cambridge. Statues in niches, such as those of founders, also featured occasionally.

4. HIGH RENAISSANCE AND BAROQUE. The great Italian architects of the High Renaissance tended to eschew sculpture on their façades, or at least to limit the sculptural elements strictly to statues of saints or virtues symmetrically disposed in niches, which were interspersed with rectangular panels of narrative or decoration, neatly framed, and thus integrated into the underlying system of proportions, as in Andrea Palladio's S Francesco della Vigna, Venice. However, architects who had begun as sculptors tended to favour their original métier. Thus when Jacopo Sansovino was called on to design the loggetta at the foot of the campanile in Venice (*c.* 1537–42), a structure that was little more than a façade (*see* SANSOVINO, (1), fig. 3), he utilized a Roman triumphal arch as his model: bronze statues in niches were complemented by narrative reliefs above, framed in variously coloured stones or marbles to create a sumptuous effect of polychromy. Friezes and panels of relief continued to be applied all over façades in Venice; Sansovino's library (1536) had over life-size statues punctuating its skyline, colossal caryatids flanking its doors and reliefs encrusted on every available wall surface. In the work of other architects sculpture tended to be clustered only round the portals, apart from small ornamental figures in spandrels, and so forth. Elsewhere in Italy the triumphal arch provided a format for the façades of churches; the most influential such design (even though it was never executed) was by Michelangelo for S Lorenzo, Florence.

In Milan Cathedral the Renaissance style emerged in the 16th century, with façade sculptures such as Cristoforo Solari's *Adam and the Infant Abel* or *Jonah*. Later in that century Angelo de Marinis (*fl* 1550–84) contributed beautifully draped, voluptuous female statues of *St Helena* and *St Mary Magdalene* (*c.* 1565). In the Baroque period several boldly modelled low reliefs of Old Testament subjects (*c.* 1635) by Gaspare Vismara, inspired by grisaille paintings by Cerano, were added, as well as some statues (*c.* 1658) by Dionigi Bussola. In that period sculpture on façades tended to play a more significant role, although one similar in kind to what had gone before. There was more implicit movement in the rhetorical poses of statues and their windswept draperies, and it became more common to adorn gables and roof-lines in general with statues with strikingly dramatic silhouettes, such as Bernini's series of saints on the colonnade of the Piazza of St Peter's, Rome (*see* BERNINI, (2), fig. 5). The most brilliant façade of the whole Baroque era, also derived from that of a triumphal arch, is the Trevi Fountain (1732–62) designed by Nicola Salvi, with its rich complement of gigantic statues carved by Pietro Bracci from models by Giovanni Battista Maini (for illustration *see* SALVI, NICOLA). Contrasting with the comparatively restrained statues by Angel Della Valle in the flanking niches of the lower façade, the central figure of *Oceanus* is shown standing in an amazingly curvilinear sea-shell chariot, which is being drawn by seahorses and tritons towards the pool of water below and in front. Simulated rock-pools, formed from blocks of Travertine marble, are integrated with the basement of the façade behind the fountain, and the whole is crowned with the escutcheon of Clement XII, supported by angels with outspread wings, boldly silhouetted against the sky.

In France, Renaissance façades were often more highly sculptural than was normal in Italy, although not as much as in Spain; a typical example is the Cour Carrée of the Palais du Louvre, Paris (1546–1654), built by Pierre Lescot and embellished with sculpture by Jean Goujon and his workshop (for illustration *see* LESCOT, PIERRE). On the Pavillon Henri II, in between the notionally structural framework of columns, pilasters and their entablatures, all the wall surfaces, especially on the second storey, are adorned with massive figures of gods, heroes and other mythological characters. The same effect may be seen on other Parisian façades of the 1550s that Goujon decorated: the Hôtel Carnavalet and the Fountain of the Innocents, the famous panels of which represent nymphs carrying urns, clad in classicizing 'wet' drapery that reveals their voluptuous forms (originals Paris, Louvre; *see* GOUJON, JEAN, fig. 1). The façade of the Porte Dorée of the château of Fontainebleau was to have been adorned with a stupendous bronze lunette by Benvenuto Cellini of the *Nymph of Fontainebleau* (Paris, Louvre); there it would have been flanked by leering satyrs functioning as caryatids, with winged victories in the spandrels (1540–45). Such buildings were, however, exceptional; very few of the châteaux of this period had sculptural adornments on their façades other than the decorative frontons, friezes, coats of arms or emblems that were usual in Renaissance Mannerist architecture. Occasionally, busts or statues (sometimes equestrian) of the reigning monarch or of the château's owner were set over the entrance gateways.

In Germany statues in niches of Classical gods or rulers were not uncommon. Such sculptures by Alexander Colin were a principal feature of the façade of both Schloss Ottheinrichsbau (1556; *see* GERMANY, fig. 5) and of the Friedrichsbau (1601–7) in Schloss Heidelberg. During the Baroque period sculpture tended to invade the whole façade, as on the parish church of Bückeburg (1613), and the late Baroque Neumünster, Würzburg (1711–19). The façades of town halls and guild houses in Germany and the Low Countries were generally embellished with sculpture in the Mannerist style, often chosen from examples in the engraved pattern books of great architects such as Peter Cocke, Cornelis Floris and Hans Vredeman de Vries. Statues were sometimes set centrally in the façade or on top of its gable, while architecturally oriented figures, such

as herms and caryatids, set amid strapwork decoration, were greatly in vogue. In Antwerp the Stadhuis (*see* ANTWERP, fig. 9) was lavishly decorated by Floris in 1565, while a century later the Stadhuis of Amsterdam (now the Royal Palace) was adorned (1650–65) with Rubensian Baroque figures by Artus Quellinus (i) (*see* TOWN HALL, fig. 3). Several guild houses on the Grand-Place in Brussels are decorated with Baroque sculpture (see fig. 6). Also in the Low Countries, an interesting development during the early Baroque period was the insertion on the façades of public buildings of statuary or reliefs referring to their function: thus weigh-houses would show merchandise on large scales, orphanages would show weeping children, penitentiaries, shackled prisoners, and madhouses, lunatics suffering fits.

5. NEO-CLASSICAL AND MODERN. In the Neo-classical style and the revival of the High Renaissance style in the late 18th century, followed in the 19th century by the Gothic Revival, the sculptural decoration of the façades tended simply to echo earlier styles. Examples of Neo-classical façades are Leo von Klenze's Walhalla (1830–42) near Regensburg; the British Museum, London (1823–48), designed by Robert Smirke; and La Madeleine (1806–42), Paris, designed by Alexandre-Pierre Vignon. In the Neo-classical period triumphal arches reappeared to celebrate military victories. Among them were the Arc de Triomphe de l'Etoile, Paris (1806–36), by Jean-François-Thérèse Chalgrin, and the Marble Arch, London. All embodied sculptural decoration based on ancient models, and often imitated Grecian standards of economy and austerity in the narrative friezes. Innovative on the Arc de Triomphe were the four groups of colossal statuary engaged with the architecture; of these, François Rude's *La Marseillaise* (1833–6) is the most dramatic and memorable. This idea was translated into a less aggressive mode a generation later, when JEAN-BAPTISTE CARPEAUX was commissioned to enliven the façade of the Paris Opéra with his group, *Dance* (1867–8; *see also* TRIUMPHAL ARCH, §2). In the 1920s many Art Deco buildings were given an Egyptian flavour by the application of stylized low reliefs. Token sculptures have been used to enliven the blank, geometric façades of many edifices of the Modern Movement. Some, in bronze, are attached like brooches, for example Jacob Epstein's *St Michael Vanquishing the Devil* (1960; Coventry Cathedral). Others, carved in the same stone as the building, relate more homogeneously, through their cubist or abstract forms, with the façade, an example being Henry Moore's *Screen* (1952) on the façade of the Time-Life Building in New Bond Street, London.

See also RELIEF SCULPTURE.

BIBLIOGRAPHY
B. Fletcher: *A History of Architecture on the Comparative Method* (London, 1948)

For further bibliography *see* the bibliographies of individual articles on specific regions and periods, and of individual biographical articles.

CHARLES AVERY

6. Sculptures on the façade of Le Sac, the 17th-century guild house of the Joiners and Coopers, Grand-Place, Brussels

Faccini, Pietro (*b* Bologna, *c.* 1562; *d* Bologna, 1 April 1602). Italian painter, draughtsman and printmaker. He began to paint around the age of 30 and produced only about a dozen paintings, datable between 1590 and 1602.

Malvasia mentioned his training in the Carracci Academy in Bologna, which ended *c.* 1594 when Faccini, envious of Annibale Carracci's rapid success, opened his own school. Until his last works, Faccini remained basically faithful to the tenets of the Carracci, and, gradually adding ideas gathered in diverse artistic circles, he developed a language of his own, characterized by great formal freedom and a lively, full-bodied use of colour.

The only surviving dated painting by Faccini is the *Martyrdom of St Lawrence* (1590; Bologna, S Giovanni in Monte; see fig.). The warm, rich colour recalls the Carracci paintings in the Palazzi Fava and Magnani (now Salem) in Bologna, while the dense, thickly applied paint is reminiscent of Venetian painting. Faccini's creation of a space teeming with bizarre humanity, with exaggerated facial expressions, however, shows a very personal taste already distanced from the academic idealizations of his early training. Venetian influence is even more striking in the light-saturated colour, reminiscent of Titian, of the *Martyrdom of St Stephen* (Bologna, Budrio, S Maria del Borgo). The style of Parma, on the other hand, can be seen in the darting rhythms, suggestive of Parmigianino, of the *Virgin of Loreto and SS Bonaventura, Agatha, Lucy and Blaise* (Mirándola, Pal. Com.), of the *Rest on the Flight into Egypt* (Guastalla, Pal. Vescovile) and *Christ and the Virgin Appearing to SS Francis and Antoninus* (Bologna, S Domenico), all painted after 1593. Other Venetian elements, derived from Jacopo Tintoretto, occur in the patchy brushwork and the division of colours into warm and cold hues in the *Annunciation* (Bologna, Pin. N.), considered to be one of the artist's finest works. Faccini's knowledge of the work of Correggio is evident in a series of paintings of *c.* 1600, characterized by a greater freedom of execution and softer, more fluid brushwork. Correggio's influence is perceptible especially in the loose, expansive style of the *Assumption of the Virgin* (Bologna, S Maria dei Servi) and in the delicate use of paint in the *Mystic Marriage of St Catherine* (Rome, Pin. Capitolina). The same influence can be seen in the beautiful painting of *St Francis Receiving the Child from the Hands of the Virgin* (Modena, priv. col., see Squellati Brizio, fig. 95a) and the small painting on copper of the *Mystic Marriage of St Catherine* (Bologna, Rac. Molinari–Pradelli). Faccini's last work is perhaps the *Virgin with St Dominic* (Bologna, Quarto Inferiore, Parrochiale): the colouring is dark and sober, but the greater luminosity and richer texture seem to presage the work of Domenico Fetti.

In his prints Faccini developed the taste for the grotesque already noted in his paintings. Etchings such as the *Blind Beggar* and the *Blind Man Guided by a Dog* (both Bologna, Pin. N.), based on a drawing by Annibale Carracci, emphasize the most brutal and extravagant aspects of reality. His drawings were reportedly abundant, and there are examples in many major museums. Most are sketches from the nude, usually executed with rapid, restless strokes, in pen and watercolour with red chalk. Nine drawings (Florence, Uffizi) are all that remain from the rich collection owned by Leopoldo de' Medici.

BIBLIOGRAPHY

Thieme–Becker

C. C. Malvasia: *Felsina pittrice* (1678); ed. M. Brascaglia (1971), pp. 325–32

Bolognese Drawings in North American Collections, 1500–1800 (exh. cat., ed. M. Cazort and C. Johnston; Ottawa, N.G., 1982), pp. 73–6

P. Squellati Brizio: 'Per Pietro Faccini, "irregolare", bolognese', *Fond. Stor. A. Roberto Longhi, Firenze: An.*, i (1984), pp. 115–37

Correggio and his Legacy: Sixteenth-century Emilian Drawings (exh. cat. by D. De Grazia, Washington, DC, N.G.A., 1984), pp. 135–7, 374–88

MARINA GAROFOLI

Faccioli, Girolamo. *See under* MASTERS, ANONYMOUS, AND MONOGRAMMISTS, §III: MASTER H.F.E.

Facht [Fachgt; Feucht; Keul; Voÿgh], **Jacob** (*b* ?Andernach; *fl* 1590s; *d* before 1598). German carpenter and copyist. He made a craftsman's copybook (Cologne, Hist. Archv, Hs. Wf°. 276*) that reproduced important verbal and graphic evidence on particular design techniques of Late Gothic master masons in Germany. He included a few biographical details, such as variant spellings of his name and the fact that he was known in his home town of Andernach as Jacob Keul. On one page of architectural drawings he wrote, 'Drawn in Vienna in the year 1593', and on another, 'Drawn in Breslau in Silesia in 1593'. By 1596 he had returned to Andernach and inscribed one of his drawings accordingly. The Andernach archives have revealed that he was the son of Jacob Keul, who may also have been a carpenter. In 1596 the younger Jacob Keul was paid from the accounts of the Watch and Artillery Master for working with several other carpenters at the 'stone lodge on the Rhine' (Koblenz, Landeshauptarchv, MS. 612. III. H. 4, fasc. 5, p. 215). In 1598 the 'widow of Jacob Keulen' appeared in the city tax register under the rubric of the carpenters' craft (Koblenz, Landeshauptarchv, MS. 612. III. H. 12, fasc. 1, anno 1598).

Pietro Faccini: *Martyrdom of St Lawrence*, oil on canvas, 2.0×1.4 m, 1590 (Bologna, S Giovanni in Monte)

It is curious to discover that Facht was a carpenter, since the technical information that he included in his copybook primarily concerned the masons' craft. He made copies of Mathes Roriczer's *Büchlein von der Fialen Gerechtigkeit* (*see* RORICZER, (3)) and the 'Instructions' by LORENZ LECHLER for his son, Moritz Lechler (*fl* 1538–55). Until 1975 Facht's manuscript copy was the only known source of Lechler's text, and it remains the most complete and the only one to be accompanied by copies of Lechler's illustrations (for illustrations *see* TEMPLATE and SETTING OUT, fig. 2). Facht's copybook also contains valuable technical drawings of Late Gothic vaults showing the methods of projecting the elevations of the ribs from the ground-plan of the vault.

BIBLIOGRAPHY

A. Reichensperger: *Vermischte Schriften über christliche Kunst* (Leipzig, 1856), pp. 133–55 [slightly transliterated version of Facht's copy of Lechler's 'Instructions']
K. Menne: 'W. f° 276*', *Mitt. Stadtarchv Köln*, x/1, pt 5 (1937), pp. 218–21
W. Müller: 'Technische Bauzeichnungen der deutschen Spätgotik', *Technol. Gesch.*, xl (1973), pp. 281–300
——: 'Einflusse der österreichischen und der böhmisch–sächsischen Spätgotik in den Gewölbemustern des Jacob Facht von Andernach', *Wien. Jb. Kstgesch.*, xxvii (1974), pp. 65–82
U. Coenen: *Die spätgotischen Werkmeisterbücher in Deutschland als Beitrag zur mittelalterlichen Architekturtheorie* (Aachen, 1989), pp. 21–5, 175–6
W. Müller: *Grundlagen gotischer Bautechnik* (Munich, 1990), pp. 170–81

For further bibliography *see* LECHLER, LORENZ.

LON R. SHELBY

Facia. *See* FASCIA.

Facio [Fazio], Bartolomeo (*b* La Spezia, nr Genoa, before 1410; *d* Naples, Nov 1457). Italian humanist and writer. From a family of Ligurian notaries, he received his early education at Verona with Guarino Guarini (i) in the early 1420s and at the end of the decade studied Greek at Florence. After holding various minor positions in Genoa and Lucca, he was appointed official Genoese envoy to Naples in 1443 and 1444, entering the service of King Alfonso of Naples the following year. At Naples, where he remained for the rest of his life, he obtained the highly paid position of Royal Historiographer and served as tutor to Prince Ferrante.

Among Facio's works are treatises on happiness and the dignity of man and translations of Isocrates and Arrian. He is best known for his historical writings, in particular *De rebus gestis ab Alphonso primo libri X* (1455) and *De viris illustribus* (1456), a collection of 92 brief lives of contemporary figures, classified according to their professions. He included Leon Battista Alberti in the category of orators and referred to his *De pictura* and *De re aedificatoria*. The section of *De viris illustribus* devoted to painters and sculptors probably reflects the artistic taste and standards of the Neapolitan court, as well as Facio's own knowledge of Tuscan and Venetian art. It is introduced by a comparison of literature and art, based on Horace's *Ars poetica* and the *Prooemium* by Philostratus the younger to the *Imagines*. Importing a number of rhetorical terms into his discussion of art, Facio placed the highest value in painting, as in poetry, on the vivid and lifelike representation not only of external, physical traits but also, and more importantly, of interior feelings and character. It was primarily on the basis of their ability to convey emotional expressiveness that he judged what he considered to be the four outstanding painters of his day: Gentile da Fabriano, Jan van Eyck, Pisanello and Rogier van der Weyden.

Among the paintings of Gentile da Fabriano, Facio singled out the *Adoration of the Magi* painted for Santa Trinita, Florence (Florence, Uffizi; *see* GENTILE DA FABRIANO, fig. 3), the fresco of the *Virgin and Child* in Orvieto Cathedral painted in 1425 and an unidentified painting of *Pope Martin V and Ten Cardinals*, whose images he claimed 'seem to differ in no respect from the living'. His account of JAN VAN EYCK provides important evidence for the popularity of this Flemish artist in 15th-century Italy. He particularly admired van Eyck's illusionistic realism, as seen in the *St Jerome* panel of the Lomellini Triptych (untraced), then in the private apartments of King Alfonso, and a painting of women bathing (untraced), in which the artist used the reflection from a mirror to spectacular effect. Facio praised Pisanello's naturalistic depiction of horses and other animals, his powerful portrayal of *St Jerome* (untraced) and his medals of King Alfonso, Filippo Maria Visconti and other Italian princes. In his life of Rogier van der Weyden, Facio described paintings and tapestries (all untraced), which particularly impressed him on account of their realistic but decorous rendering of emotion and character.

Facio gave biographies of three sculptors: Lorenzo Ghiberti and his son Vittorio, mentioning the bronze *Gates of Paradise* for the Florentine Baptistery (*see* GHIBERTI, (1), fig. 4), and Donatello, who, he said, approached the ancients in his ability to turn marble into living faces and exhibited equally marvellous workmanship in his bronze equestrian statue of *Gattamelata* in Padua (*see* DONATELLO, fig. 4).

WRITINGS

De viris illustribus (MS. 1456); ed. L. Mehus (Florence, 1745); partial Eng. trans. in M. Baxandall: 'Bartholomaeus Facius on Painting: A Fifteenth-century Manuscript of *De viris illustribus*', *J. Warb. & Court. Inst.*, xxvii (1964), pp. 90–107

BIBLIOGRAPHY

R. Weiss: 'Jan van Eyck and the Italians', *It. Stud.*, xi (1956), pp. 1–15
P. O. Kristeller: 'The Humanist Bartolomeo Facio and his Unknown Correspondence', *From the Renaissance to the Counter-Reformation: Essays in Honor of Garrett Mattingly* (New York, 1965), pp. 56–74
C. Marchiori: *Bartolomeo Facio tra letteratura e vita* (Milan, 1971)

JILL KRAYE

Facio, Sara (*b* Buenos Aires, 18 April 1932). Argentine photographer. She trained as a painter at the Escuela Nacional de Bellas Artes, Buenos Aires (1947–53), and took up photography only in the late 1950s. She studied in Buenos Aires first in the studio of Luis d'Amico and then in 1960 under Annemarie Heinrich. In 1960 she opened a studio in Buenos Aires with the Argentine photographer Alicia d'Amico (*b* 1933). She contributed to *La Nación* and *Autoclub*, and in 1973, together with María Cristina Orive, she co-founded La Azotea, a publishing house specializing in Latin American photography. She was primarily a documentary photographer, whose reputation did not depend on the recording of sensational events. Her photographs were realistic portrayals of the Argentine way of life; they were taken using natural light and were not modified in the laboratory.

PHOTOGRAPHIC PUBLICATIONS

Buenos Aires, Buenos Aires (Buenos Aires, 1968)
Retratos y autorretratos (Buenos Aires, 1973)
Seven Voices (New York, 1973)
Geografía de Pablo Neruda (Buenos Aires, 1974)
Humanario (Buenos Aires, 1976)
with M. C. Orive: *Actos de fe en Guatemala* (Buenos Aires, 1980)
with Alicia d'Amico: *25 años de fotografía* (Buenos Aires, 1985)

BIBLIOGRAPHY

Fotografie Lateinamerika: 1860 bis heute (exh. cat. by E. Billeter, Zurich, Ksthaus, 1981)
J. Potenze: *Sara Facio* (Buenos Aires, 1982)

ERIKA BILLETER

Factory. Building for the commercial and usually mechanical production of goods. The modern factory was developed in the course of the Industrial Revolution in the 18th century, and its subsequent architectural development was linked to advances in technology. Previously, goods had been produced, usually by hand, in the home or in specialized workshops ('manufactories'). Nevertheless, some early manufacturing premises were substantial in size, such as the glass works at Saint Gobain, France, which received its royal patent in 1695, where workers' housing was built concurrently with the workshops. Another early example of large-scale premises was the Real Fábrica de Tabacos, Seville (1728–57; *see* SEVILLE, fig. 3). However, it was only during the Industrial Revolution, with increases in the use of machinery and in the scale of production, that the factory as a distinct building type came into existence.

Pioneered in England, the early textile (and especially cotton) mills of Derbyshire and Lancashire served as stylistic models for the rest of the world from the 18th century until the early 20th. The first such building was John Lombe's silk mill (1718; destr.) in Derby. It consisted of a five-storey, plain rectangular masonry structure with long rows of evenly spaced windows, and it was powered by a water wheel. It was the invention of the water-frame (1769), the power loom (1785) and most importantly the steam engine (1769), however, that allowed mass production, and the new factories universally adopted Lombe's building type. Richard Arkwright (1732–92), the inventor of the water-frame, was one of the early cotton entrepreneurs and factory builders (e.g. Cromford Mill, 1771; Belper Mill, Derbys, 1776). Water-powered factories were dependent on a ready water supply, and many of the early mills were in isolated valleys, but the advent of the steam engine ensured a steady supply of power and production, and factories began to expand and move to the cities. They retained, however, their utilitarian style and mostly consisted of multi-storey rectangles, originally of stone and later of brick, with rows of windows and usually a small cupola or belfry to call the workers. Fireproofing was the main concern, and only a very few mills had some form of Georgian or Palladian decorative elements, such as a pediment (e.g. Cressbrook Mill, Millers Dale, 1815) or Serlian windows (e.g. Masson Mill, Cromford, 1783). Whereas in Britain factory building was left to private individuals, on the Continent there was a greater degree of royal patronage. For example, in France CLAUDE-NICOLAS LEDOUX designed the semicircular factory complex of the Saline de Chaux (1774–9), near Besançon, for Louis XV.

In the 1790s British builders and engineers began to experiment with the use of cast iron to replace timber. Charles Bage (1752–1822) built the first iron-frame building, the Marshall, Benyon & Bage Flour Mill (1796–7), Ditherington, Shrewsbury, Salop, with iron colonnettes and beams but still load-bearing walls, and this system was quickly taken up throughout Britain. As the industrial processes pioneered in Britain were readily adopted elsewhere, so were the building types. American mills in particular (e.g. Pawtucket, RI, 1793) closely followed English examples, but they remained reliant on timber construction rather than cast iron until the mid-19th century. In continental Europe industrial development was delayed by political instability. The first mechanized cotton-spinning mill on the Continent was reputedly at Ratingen (1783–4), near Düsseldorf.

In the early 19th century little stylistic development took place. Continued advancement of civil engineering as a profession and the continual development of technological aspects of factory building led to the rise in Britain of such specialized factory designers as William Fairbairn (1789–1874). In Germany a large number of salt works were built in the early 19th century (e.g. Staatssalinen Dürrheim and Rappenau, 1823–7), and they were mostly large, formal complexes that followed the functional classical tradition propagated by such writers as Jean-Nicolas-Louis Durand. Most continental designs, however, followed English examples in their interior organization, while their exteriors often continued local traditions (e.g. Meinert Mill, Lugau, 1812) or followed an austere classicism. By the 1840s iron-frame construction was widely adopted in Europe, and two distinct forms of factory evolved: the multi-storey mill and the single-storey shed. The former consisted of a chimney, an often decorative water-tower and an architecturally distinct engine house (e.g. Hawthorne Mill, Chadderton, 1878). With the increase in private shareholders, these buildings began to be used as advertisements for the company, with large lettering and showy details. The close proximity of mills and factories to urban centres also meant that they often determined the face of a town (e.g. Pittsburgh, PA). The style chosen for factories was usually Italianate, reflecting historical associations with trade and commerce (e.g. Ravensberg Spinning Mill, Bielefeld, Germany, 1854). Buildings for heavy industry, for example steel or iron works, were usually single-storey sheds, often top-lit. The prime consideration here was to achieve a span as wide and as uninterrupted as possible. In the second half of the 19th century Britain's technological and structural initiative was taken over by France. The first externally steel-framed building in the world was the Menier Chocolate Factory (1871) at Noisiel in the Marne Valley by JULES SAULNIER. In the 1890s the French engineer FRANÇOIS HENNEBIQUE finally overcame the problem of the monolithic joint in reinforced concrete with his development of stirrup girders (*see* CONCRETE, §II, 1(iii)), and the prototype of his Charles VI spinning mills (1895) in Tourcoing was soon copied all over the world.

Towards the end of the 19th century a few factories adopted revivalist styles, such as William Leiper's Templeton Carpet Factory (1889), built in a Venetian Gothic style, or the Benedictine liqueur factory (1893–1900),

Hoover Factory, Perivale, Middlesex, by Wallis, Gilbert & Partners, 1931–5

Fécamp. With the development of Modernism in the early 20th century, though, factory design became the subject of serious architectural theory. The fascination with technology and its appropriation in factory design became one of the catalysts of the MODERN MOVEMENT. The technical expertise that facilitated the replacement of load-bearing outer walls had existed since the 1850s, but the aesthetic aspects of this type of design had so far been unexplored. This changed fundamentally in the early 20th century. The key buildings of the Modern Movement included such factories as the AEG Turbine Factory (1909; *see* MODERN MOVEMENT, fig. 1) in Moabit, Berlin, by PETER BEHRENS, the Fagus Factory (1911–13) at Alfeld, Germany, by WALTER GROPIUS and ADOLF MEYER, and the Van Nelle Factory (1925–31) at Rotterdam, by Brinkmann & Van der Vlugt. These buildings pioneered the new aesthetic of lightness and transparency, achieved through the use of steel frames and walls with large areas of glass. However, appearance and style were not the only areas developed in these years. ALBERT KAHN, who designed over 2000 factories in his career, built the first concrete-frame factories in the USA (e.g. Packard Motor Company Factory, Detroit, MI, 1903) and developed a type of factory planning and design that accommodated Henry Ford's ideas of industrial mass production. His factories were single-storey, roof-lit with flexible interiors and built of steel and glass (e.g. Dodge Half-Ton Truck Factory, Detroit, MI, 1937; *see* UNITED STATES OF AMERICA, fig. 9).

In the inter-war years, Art Deco factories made a brief appearance, mostly in Britain and the USA. Their use of highly decorative façades was best exemplified by the Firestone Tyre Factory (1928–9; destr. 1980), Brentford, Middx, or the Hoover Factory (1931–5; see fig.; now Tesco's Supermarket), Perivale, Middx, both by Wallis, Gilbert & Partners. The economic depression of the 1930s produced a functional utilitarianism in factory-building, with glass and steel and simple cubic shapes predominating. Industry gradually moved to the outskirts of cities with the advent of the industrial estate, a design scheme that predominated in the late 20th century. William Holford's innovative government-backed Team Valley Trading Estate (1936), Gateshead, Tyne and Wear, with factories laid out on a grid of roads, was most influential (e.g. Dorstfeld West, Dortmund; Brook Hollow, Dallas, TX). In the mid-20th century, factories were designed as the heart of architectural programmes of almost urbanistic scope (e.g. Olivetti Plant, Ivrea, Italy, 1942, by Figini and Pollini). In the later 20th century industrial development largely moved away from the large-scale heavy industries of the 19th century, and there was a growing emphasis on High Tech industries. This gave rise to High Tech architecture, firmly based on modern technology. Its use of complicated structural systems and a fully fledged 'machine aesthetic' is best illustrated in the work of Richard Rogers (e.g. INMOS Microprocessor Factory, Newport, Gwent, completed 1982) and Norman Foster (Renault Parts Centre, Swindon, Wilts, 1984; for illustration *see* HIGH TECH).

BIBLIOGRAPHY

RDK: 'Fabrikbau'

C. G. Holme, ed.: *Industrial Architecture* (London, 1935)

J. M. Richards: *The Functional Tradition in Early Industrial Buildings* (London, 1958)

J. Tann: *The Development of the Factory* (London, 1970)

J. Winter: *Industrial Architecture: A Survey of Factory Building* (London, 1970)

N. Pevsner: *A History of Building Types* (London, 1976), pp. 273–88

E. Jones: *Industrial Architecture in Britain, 1750–1939* (London, 1985)

H. C. Schulitz, ed.: *Constructa-Pries '86: Industriearchitektur in Europa/ Industrial Architecture in Europe* (Brunswick, 1986)

Fadrusz, János (*b* Pozsony, Hungary [now Bratislava, Slovakia], 2 Sept 1858; *d* Budapest, 26 Oct 1903). Hungarian sculptor. A professional locksmith and woodcarver, he was sponsored to go to Vienna and work in Viktor Tilgner's studio, where he executed several busts. In 1887 he became Edmund Hellmer's pupil at the Akademie der Bildenden Künste in Vienna and while there produced his first major work, a *Crucifixion* (bronze, 1891; Budapest, N.G.). His first tentative steps as an artist coincided with the preparations for the millennium celebrations in 1896 of the founding of Hungary, and thus his most important commissions were related to this event. As his aim was to immortalize Hungary's history and its national leaders and heroes; his thorough training in the neo-Baroque style and his commitment to nationalism helped him to achieve his goals. At this time the town of Pozsony commissioned from him an equestrian statue of *Maria-Theresa Accompanied by Two Hungarian Aristocrats* (marble, 1892–7; destr. 1921; fragments in Budapest, N.G.). In 1894 he won the commission to design a twice life-size equestrian bronze statue of *King Matthias Corvinus* for Kolozsvár (now Cluj-Napoca, Romania). It was erected in 1902, and depicts the mounted ruler on a plinth, flanked by four well-known leaders of his army. The work is a major example of historicizing monumental sculpture, for which Fadrusz won the Grand Prix at the Exposition Universelle in Paris in 1900. His life-size bronze equestrian statue of *Béla Wenckheim* (1901) in Kisbér (Hungary) and his bronze monument to *Wesselényi* (1902) in Zilah, Hungary (now Zalău, Romania) are located in the main squares of these towns. He also produced sculptures for the Parliament Building, the former Curia and the former Royal Palace (now containing the Hungarian National Gallery), all in Budapest.

BIBLIOGRAPHY

K. Hercsuth: *Fadrusz János élete és művészete* [János Fadrusz's life and art], Iparosok Olvasótára [Artisan Library], xvii/4 (Budapest, 1911)

B. Lázár: *Fadrusz János élete és művészete* [János Fadrusz's life and art] (Budapest, 1924)

G. Soós: *Fadrusz János* (Budapest, 1960) [extensive bibliog.]

S. KONTHA

Faed. Scottish family of artists. The three Faed brothers were the sons of James Faed sr, a skilled millwright and the tenant of Barlay Mill, Gatehouse of Fleet.

(1) John Faed (*b* Gatehouse of Fleet, Dumfries & Galloway, 31 Aug 1819; *d* Gatehouse of Fleet, 22 Oct 1902). Painter. He was self-taught and received early encouragement from an Edinburgh collector who had settled locally. He painted miniatures until 1840, when he moved to Edinburgh, and he attended classes at the Trustees' Academy there. Being hard-working and cautious he continued in the 'cramped minuteness' of miniature painting against his true inclination. The *Evening Hour (Children of Dr Archibald Bennie)* (1847; Edinburgh, N.G.), painted on a piece of ivory 330×241 mm, shows his portrait style at the height of his success as a miniaturist. By the late 1840s he had begun to exhibit oils at the Royal Scottish Academy, of which the *Trysting Place* (1848; Glasgow, A.G. & Mus.) was among his earliest. During the 1850s he received two commissions from the Royal Association for the Promotion of the Fine Arts in Scotland

for illustrations to Robert Burns, including *Tam O'Shanter* (1856). *A Wappenschaw* (1863; Edinburgh, Offices of the NT Scotland), an ambitious work depicting a feudal shooting contest with some 40 figures, reveals his compositional weaknesses, due perhaps to his miniaturist training. In 1864 John followed his brother (3) Thomas Faed to London. In later life John was free to indulge his early ambition to become a history painter. In order to paint the *Warning before Flodden* (1875; Wolverhampton, A.G.), he first borrowed historical costumes from Mme Tussaud's waxworks. He settled at Gatehouse in 1880.

(2) James Faed (*b* Gatehouse of Fleet, 4 April 1821; *d* Edinburgh, 23 Sept 1911). Painter and engraver, brother of (1) John Faed. He inherited his father's mechanical aptitude, and after James sr's death he joined (1) John and (3) Thomas in Edinburgh *c*.1846, intending to take engineering classes. However, he was drawn into the painting activities of his brothers and after experimenting with oils took up mezzotint engraving, inventing a machine for speeding the process. James specialized in engraving portraits after Francis Grant and other eminent painters. He also painted landscapes and miniatures.

(3) Thomas Faed (*b* Gatehouse of Fleet, 8 June 1826; *d* London, 17 Aug 1900). Painter, brother of (1) John Faed and (2) James Faed. He showed an early inclination for painting. At 16 he was apprenticed to a draper but left Gatehouse for Edinburgh to join John some time after his father died in 1843. The intention was that he should assist with John's miniatures, but his success as a student at the Trustees' Academy, where he won the life drawing prize in 1847, changed his course. The *Art Journal* [London] praised his paintings exhibited at the Royal Scottish Academy in 1849. Two years later Thomas moved to London. The *Mitherless Bairn* shown at the Royal Academy, London, in 1855 (Melbourne, N.G. Victoria) was an outstanding triumph. The humble cottage interior, the carefully studied expressions and the strong narrative element were features that established his popularity in London as they had for David Wilkie in his Scottish genre paintings earlier in the century. He painted the topical theme of emigration several times. *Sunday in the Backwoods of Canada* (exh. RA 1859; Wolverhampton, A.G.) elicited a favourable, if condescending, comment from Ruskin. The *Last of the Clan* (1867; Glasgow, A.G. & Mus.) deals movingly with human anguish and shows Thomas's compositional strength; the void left by the departing emigrants is emphasized by his grouping of those left behind. He also painted a number of single female figures set in landscapes: *Evangeline* (1856; Manchester, C.A.G.), the heroine of Longfellow's poem, was among the earliest and became widely known through the engraving of James Faed.

UNPUBLISHED SOURCES

Edinburgh U., Lib. [Letters of John and Thomas Faed]

D. Faed Macmillan: *The Artists Faed* [five copies for private circulation, 1965; property of the writer's estate]

BIBLIOGRAPHY

D. Irwin and F. Irwin: *Scottish Painters at Home and Abroad, 1700–1900* (London, 1975), pp. 300–04

M. McKerrow: *The Faeds: A Biography* (Edinburgh, 1982)

FRANCINA IRWIN

Faenza. Italian centre of maiolica production. It is one of the most famous centres of Italian maiolica production and from the 17th century lent its name to this particular category of ceramics made throughout Europe ('faience'). Ceramic production in Faenza is referred to in records and documents dating from as early as the 14th century. Early products are solid and heavy in shape and decorated with rather frugal, severe ornamentation, mostly in brown and green. For this reason they are generally considered 'archaic' medieval products. Only during the 15th century did the production of ceramics in Faenza begin to develop a specifically individual style. Faenza maiolica was technically more refined than that produced in other centres and incorporated a rich, varied palette. In particular the decoration was enriched with fashionable subjects, including Gothic-Moorish motifs, coats of arms, heraldic devices and portraits of *belle donne* painted on *coppe amatorie* (love dishes). These features remained during the 16th century when the *istoriato* (narrative) genre was often combined with *berettino* (blue) glaze decoration, with grotesques and arabesques (e.g. plaque, *c.* 1525–30; London, BM). From the mid-16th century and through most of the 17th Faenza was involved in the development of the so-called *bianchi di Faenza* (white ware). In this period skilful craftsmen and such heads of workshops as Francesco Mezzarisa, Virgiliotto Calamelli and Leonardo Bettisi (*fl* 1570–80) created relief surfaces, which became increasingly Baroque in style and were covered with a thick, white glaze onto which they applied a sparse, sketchy form of decoration known as *compendiaria* (e.g. pierced dish, *c.* 1550–70; London, BM). During the 18th and 19th centuries the Conti Ferniani Factory continued this style and became the leading producer in Faenza. Its production, however, unlike those of the past, reflects a repertory common to many European centres.

BIBLIOGRAPHY
F. Argnani: *Il rinascimento delle ceramiche maiolicate in Faenza* (Faenza, 1898)
G. Liverani: 'La rivoluzione dei bianchi nella maiolica di Faenza', *Faenza*, xliv (1958), pp. 27–32
E. Golfieri: 'Il cenacolo della Fabbrica Ferniani e i pittori di genere a Faenza', *Faenza*, liii (1967), p. 58
CARMEN RAVANELLI GUIDOTTI

Faenza, Antonio Gentili [Gentile] **da** (*b* Faenza, 1519; *d* Rome, 29 Oct 1609). Italian goldsmith. He was the son of Pietro Gentili, a goldsmith. By *c.* 1549 he was active in Rome and by 1552 he had entered the goldsmiths' guild as a master craftsman, holding several offices during his lifetime. His fame enabled him to move in high circles. Records indicate that he executed various works in gold for the Medici, pieces ranging from vases and lamps to keys and bedwarmers. It was for Cardinal Alessandro Farnese that Antonio created his acknowledged masterpiece, consisting of two silver-gilt candlesticks and a cross (1582; Rome, St Peter's, Treasury), for which he received 13,000 *scudi*. The objects, which contain rock-crystal tondi by Giovanni Bernardi and inlay work of lapis lazuli, were then donated by the Cardinal to St Peter's. Antonio signed the work yet authorities have often attributed it to Benvenuto Cellini or Michelangelo, among others. Part of the difficulty in identifying Antonio's work is the confusion caused by his habit of borrowing motifs from other artists, especially those employing a style similar to that of Michelangelo. This practice was highlighted when the 90-year-old goldsmith testified in an inheritance lawsuit brought by Guglielmo della Porta's son, Teodoro della Porta, regarding casts and models missing from his father's workshop. During testimony Antonio stated that he owned and used casts by Michelangelo and others. His adoption of others' designs in his pieces, a common practice among 16th-century goldsmiths, did not hinder his versatility. In 1580 he fashioned a miniature gold bust of the armoured *Emperor Augustus* on a small agate base (h. 210 mm; Florence, Pitti). In 1584 he became an assayer for the papal mint. Antonio also created a silver book cover for Cardinal Farnese's Book of Hours (1600; New York, Pierpont Morgan Lib.). The richly decorated cover portrays the *Annunciation* bordered by a pattern of cherubim heads and acanthus leaves. Famous in his own day, Antonio's influence extended to 18th-century France and England, where the candlesticks in St Peter's inspired such figures as Jean-Louis Prieur, Matthew Boulton and Josiah (i) Wedgwood to incorporate elements of Antonio's masterpiece in their own works.

BIBLIOGRAPHY
G. Baglione: *Vite* (1649); ed. V. Mariani (1935)
A. Bertolotti: *Artisti bolognesi, ferraresi ed alcuni altri* (Bologna, 1885)
W. Volbach: 'Antonio Gentili da Faenza and the Large Candlesticks in the Treasury of St Peter's', *Burl. Mag.*, xc (1948), pp. 281–6
H. Honour: *Goldsmiths and Silversmiths* (New York, 1971)
A. Chadour: *Antonio Gentili und der Altarsatz von St Peter* (diss., Münster, Westfäl. Wilhelms-U., 1980)
A. Chadour: 'Der Altarsatz des Antonio Gentili in St Peter zu Dom', *Wallraf-Richartz-Jb.*, xliii (1982), pp. 133–98
ROBIN A. BRANSTATOR

Faesch. Swiss family of artists and collectors. Claus [Clewi, Nicolaus] Faesch (*d* 1475) joined the stone masons' guild of Basle in 1438 and is reported to have been working for the Bishop of Basle in Porrentruy in 1465. He was probably the father of (1) Remigius Faesch (i), who worked on a number of buildings in Basle and Thann. The latter's son, Paul Faesch (*d* Basle, 1524), rebuilt Basle Minster's Pfalz terrace (1510), which overlooks the Rhine. Johann Rudolph Faesch (*b* Basle, 1510; *d* 1564), Paul's son, was a renowned goldsmith and the founder of a dynasty of Basle goldsmiths who contributed to the city's art life until well into the 18th century. Collectors in the family included (2) Remigius Faesch (ii), who was Johann Rudolph's great-grandson, and (3) Johann Jakob Faesch.

(1) Remigius [Ruman; Rumiger; Romey] **Faesch (i)** (*b* Basle; *d* Thann, Alsace, 1533–4). Architect and mason. According to the local tax records, he started working in Basle in 1476. His first known building is the Engelhof (Nadelberg 4), a splendid town house commissioned *c.* 1480 by the Junker Mathias Eberle. In 1485 Faesch built the Haus zum Schlüssel (Freiestrasse 25) for the merchants' guild. The last building in Basle connected with his name is the church of the Charterhouse Carthusian Church (mostly destr.; now orphanage), the flat ceiling of which he vaulted elaborately in 1487–8. Having won considerable fame with his works, he held a number of public offices after 1487. In 1490 he was commissioned to finish St Thiébaut (begun *c.* 1330), Thann, on which work had come to a halt. This summons to Thann was probably a result of his work at the Charterhouse Carthusian Church, since the highly elaborate vaulting scheme that he applied to the previously flat ceiling of St Thiébaut's north aisle is very similar. Not only the vaults' ribs and bosses but also the corbels were carved. The easternmost boss bears Faesch's maker's mark and the date 1492. From that year he was no longer registered in Basle. He moved to Thann, was appointed master builder for life and given a considerable pension. He finished St Thiébaut's nave in 1493–5, adding buttresses and then vaulting it. In 1496–8 he added the gable of the west façade, which also bears his initials and the date of completion, as do most of his later works. In 1506–16 he erected a splendid openwork spire, which is highly indebted in style to the cathedrals of Freiburg im Breisgau and Strasbourg. Besides finishing the work on St Thiébaut, the last additions being the vaulted treasury (1520) and a small staircase (1521), he also built a number of Thann's secular buildings, such as the poor asylum (1518), the granary (1519) and Mint (1533), as well as a city gate (1532; destr.). Although based in Thann, he was head of the workshop of Basle Minster between 1503 and 1509. It seems that he accepted the assignment only in order to pass it on to his son Paul. Remigius Faesch was buried in St Thiébaut and his tomb, along with others there, was demolished in 1781.

BIBLIOGRAPHY

Thieme–Becker

K. Stehlin: 'Basler Baumeister des 15. Jh.', *Basl. Z. Gesch. & Altertknd.*, v (1905), pp. 100–06

Inventaire Général des Monuments et des Richesses Artistiques de la France, Commission Régionale d'Alsace, *Haut-Rhin: Canton Thann* (Paris, 1980)

(2) Remigius [Rémy] **Faesch** [Fäsch] **(ii)** (*b* Basle, 12 May 1595; *d* Basle, 1 March 1667). Collector and lawyer, great-great-great-grandson of (1) Remigius Faesch (i). His family was well established in Basle and his father was the city's burgomaster. He studied law in Switzerland, France and Germany, and earned his doctorate at Basle University in 1620. During 1620–21 he travelled extensively in Italy, where his interest in Antiquity was aroused during a long stay in Rome. He returned to Basle to practise law and was appointed a professor at the university in 1628. He continued to teach there throughout his career, while also acting as legal adviser to the Duke of Württemberg, the Margrave of Baden and the city's noble families.

Faesch was a keen and passionate collector with wide interests, demonstrated in the range of his collection. Although it is generally known for its paintings, it mainly comprised prints, drawings, books, manuscripts, curios and coins, in the manner of the *Kunstkammer*. In 1619, for example, he commissioned François Perragod (*d* 1629) to build a cabinet (Basle, Hist. Mus.) to display part of his collection. Some works were inherited through his family, notably Hans Holbein (ii)'s portraits of *Jakob Meyer* and his wife *Dorothea Kannengiesser* (both 1516; Basle, Kstmus.), together with their preparatory metalpoint studies; by the time that Faesch started collecting, however, the Meyer Altarpiece (*c.* 1526; Darmstadt, Hess. Landesmus.; *see* HOLBEIN, fig. 1) had been sold, leaving only the preparatory sketches. He appreciated and collected the works of the Upper Rhine school and of such early 16th-century German masters as Urs Graf, Niklaus Manuel Deutsch and Hans Baldung. Among the 191 woodcuts,

engravings and etchings by Albrecht Dürer listed in his 1648 inventory was the series of 132 woodblocks, with drawings by Dürer and his assistants, that were prepared *c.* 1492 to illustrate an unexecuted edition of the comedies of Terence; only five of the woodblocks were carved at some point and a number of the illustrations survive only as prints.

Faesch's approach to collecting was specific and carefully directed. Every acquisition was preceded by a long period of investigation and negotiation, and followed by the writing of a careful description and essays. The two earliest records of his possessions, both of which were first compiled in 1628, combine an inventory with an encyclopedic disquisition. In *Humana industriae monumenta* he attempted to unite all that was then known on art, artists, crafts and collecting, while the *Thesaurus rei numerae*, which lists 3400 coins, contains all the available information on coins, collectors and collections. He continued to update these records, producing inventories of his graphic collection, for example, in 1641 and 1648.

Returning to earlier terminology, Faesch referred to his collection as a 'museum', a name that it fully deserved when it was displayed on the first floor of the large house on the Petersplatz to which he moved in 1653. This became renowned throughout Europe and the 'museum' was highly praised by Joachim von Sandrart and other travellers. In 1661 he helped to persuade the Basle Council to purchase the cabinet of Basilius Amerbach for 9000 thalers. Since he never married, his collection was inherited in 1667 by his brother and was handed down until the last doctor of law in the family died in 1819. By the terms of Remigius's will, however, the 'museum' was then to be bequeathed to Basle University. The enforcement of these conditions led to a long and costly dispute between the university and the heirs to the estate. In 1823 the whole collection was finally transferred to the university, which then directed the city's art collections and library: the paintings, drawings and prints form the core of the Kunstmuseum's collections, while the rest is housed in the Historisches Museum.

UNPUBLISHED SOURCES

Basle, Ubib. [papers include *Humana industriae monumenta*, *Thesaurus rei numerae* and inventories]

BIBLIOGRAPHY

E. Major: 'Das Fäschische Museum und die Fäschischen Inventare', *Öff. Kstsamml. Basel, Jber.*, lix (1907), pp. 1–69

O. Fischer: 'Geschichte der öffentlichen Kunstsammlung', *Festschrift zur Eröffnung des Kunstmuseums* (Basle, 1936), pp. 7–118

H. C. Ackermann: 'The Basle Cabinets of Art and Curiosities in the Sixteenth and Seventeenth Centuries', *The Origins of Museums: The Cabinet of Curiosities in Sixteenth- and Seventeenth-century Europe*, ed. O. Impey and A. MacGregor (Oxford, 1985), pp. 62–8

A. Berchtold: 'La Collection Faesch', *Bâle et l'Europe: Une Histoire culturelle*, 2 vols (Lausanne, 1990), pp. 761–3

CHRISTINA MAURER

(3) Johann Jakob Faesch (*b* Basle, 1732; *d* Basle, 1796). Merchant and collector, descendant of (2) Remigius Faesch (ii). As a merchant in Amsterdam, from 1751, he started a small collection of paintings. In 1765 he returned to Basle, where he lived in the palatial Seidenhof. On his travels in 1779 the art critic Johann Georg Meusel (1743–1820) recorded Faesch's collection of paintings in the Seidenhof. Apart from a *Holy Family* by Andrea del Sarto (untraced), it consisted of 30 to 40 works from the Netherlands, by such artists as Ludolf Bakhuizen, Gerrit Berckheyde, Pieter de Hooch, Meindert Hobbema, Aert van der Neer, Rembrandt, Teniers and Philips Wouwerman. The identification of Faesch's collector's monogram (wrongly ascribed by Lugt to Ignazio Enrico Hugford) has enabled the reconstruction of his collection of drawings, the contents of which were hitherto unknown. In contrast to his paintings, the drawings were mainly by 16th- and 17th-century Italians, though the most outstanding item was a *Crucifixion of St Peter* (Basle, Kstmus.), attributed to Rubens, formerly in the Everhard Jabach, Crozat and Mariette collections. Faesch acquired other drawings from the auction of the collection of Gerard Michael Jabach (1688–1751) in Amsterdam in 1753. So far 22 of the drawings in Faesch's collection have been identified (some unpublished), including works by Annibale Carracci, Giuseppe Cesari, Battista Franco, Michelangelo (presumed), Raphael, Parmigianino, Titian (presumed) and Taddeo Zuccaro. The collection may have been small, but its quality was far from negligible. As with almost all private collections in Basle from the Enlightenment era, his collection was dispersed in the 19th century: six drawings were, however, donated to the Kupferstichkabinett, Basle, by his great-granddaughter in 1865.

BIBLIOGRAPHY
J. G. Meusel: *Miscellaneen artistischen Inhalts*, ii (Erfurt, 1779), pp. 26–33
D. Burckhardt: 'Die baslerischen Kunstsammler des 18. Jahrhunderts', *Basl. Kstver.: Berstatt.: Jahr 1901* (1902), pp. 29–30
T. Falk: 'An Unknown Collection of Drawings in the 18th Century', *Drawing: Masters and Methods. Papers Presented to the Ian Woodner Master Drawings Symposium at the Royal Academy of Arts: London, 1992*, pp. 177–96
F. Lugt: *Marques*, suppl. (1956), no. 1468a

TILMAN FALK

Fagan, Robert (*b* London, 5 March 1761; *d* Rome, 26 Aug 1816). English painter, archaeologist and dealer, of Irish origin. A Roman Catholic, he was the son of a prosperous London baker, originally from Cork. He entered the Royal Academy Schools in 1781; two years later he travelled to Italy via Flanders and Paris, reaching Rome in January 1784. There, under the influence of Andrea Appiani and François-Xavier Fabre, he evolved an individual and original Neo-classical style of portrait painting, with an emphasis on contour, clear colour and psychological penetration. By the early 1790s he had become a fashionable painter of English visitors and a prominent member of Roman artistic society. His portraits often include evocative Italian landscape settings, as in *Elizabeth, Lady Webster* (1793; priv. col.), which shows Mt Vesuvius in the background, and the double portrait of his friend *Sir Corbet Corbet with his Wife and Dogs in the Roman Campagna* (*c.* 1797; priv. col., see Crookshank and Glin, 1978, pl. 17). His most unusual work is his *Self-portrait with Maria Ludovica Flajani* (*c.* 1803; priv. col., see Crookshank and Glin, 1978, fig. 91), in which the lady, his second wife, appears bare-breasted, *à la Grec*. Another striking portrait is *General Taszychi with his Family* (1803; Warsaw, N. Mus.). He also painted copies of Old Master paintings and *trompe l'oeil* grisailles (two grisailles, 1793–5; Attingham Park, Salop, NT).

Fagan was an enthusiastic archaeologist: during his excavations at Ostia between 1794 and 1800 he discovered a Mithraeum; he also worked at Laurentum with Corbet and Prince Augustus Frederick (later Duke of Sussex), a son of George III. He recovered numerous antiquities which were to find their way into British, Italian and other museums and private collections, such as that of Thomas Hope. Fagan was also active as a dealer in Old Master paintings. His major coup came in 1797 with two paintings by Claude Lorrain from Gasparo Altieri: *Landscape with the Father of Psyche Sacrificing at the Temple of Apollo* and the *Landscape with the Arrival of Aeneas at Pallanteum* (both Anglesey Abbey, Cambs, NT; *see* CLAUDE LORRAIN, fig. 6); they were shipped back to England, escorted by one of Admiral Horatio Nelson's frigates. Regarded as among Claude's finest works, they were bought by William Beckford for the vast sum of 6500 guineas. In 1798 the French invaded Rome; many of Fagan's possessions were confiscated, including statues and busts. Fagan fled to Sicily, where he entered the circle of Lord Nelson and Sir William and Lady Hamilton; later he went to Florence and in 1799, following the French withdrawal, back to Rome. He resumed his activities as a dealer, supplying pictures to Beckford, Frederick Augustus Hervey, 4th Earl of Bristol and Bishop of Derry, William Penn and others. Meanwhile, indiscriminate archaeological excavations in Rome were stopped in 1801 by order of Pius VII.

Fagan's political activities forced him once more to leave Rome in 1807 and he settled at Palermo in Sicily. In 1809, through the agency of his son-in-law, William Baker, Fagan was appointed British Consul-General for Sicily and Malta, in which role he became a confidant of Caroline of Naples and the Two Sicilies. He resumed his archaeological activities, excavating at Tyndaris in 1808 and at Selinunte in 1809–10. He continued to paint (e.g. the double portrait of *Jeffrey and Sarah, Children of Lord Amerherst*, 1811; Dublin, N.G.), but there is a noticeable falling-off in quality in his later work. He committed suicide in Rome in 1816 while in ill-health.

BIBLIOGRAPHY
Strickland
T. Ashby: 'Thomas Jenkins in Rome', *Pap. Brit. Sch. Rome*, xi (1913), p. 224
The Art of Claude Lorrain (exh. cat., ACGB, London, Hayward Gal., 1969), nos 32, 37
Irish Portraits, 1660–1860 (exh. cat., ed. A. Crookshank and the Knight of Glin; London, N.P.G.; Belfast, Ulster Mus.; Dublin, N.G.; 1969), pp. 64–5
B. de Breffney: 'Robert Fagan, Artist', *Irish Ancestor*, cxi/2 (1971), p. 71
R. Trevelyan: 'An Irish Bohemian in Italy', *Apollo*, xcvi (1972), p. 298
A. Crookshank and the Knight of Glin: *The Painters of Ireland, c. 1660–1920* (London, 1978), pp. 100–01

JOHN TURPIN

Fage, Raymond La. *See* LAFAGE, RAYMOND.

Fagel. Dutch family of government officials and collectors. In 1763 the art collection of 'Griffier Fagel' was labelled as 'superior a tous les autres' (in Holland), and the same year it was described by Joshua Reynolds as 'walls hung round with thoughts'. At this time the collection belonged to Griffier Hendrick Fagel (*b* The Hague, 7 Dec 1706; *d* The Hague, 1790). Trained as a lawyer, Hendrick was appointed registry clerk (Dut. *griffier*) at the Dutch States General in 1728, following the resignation of his uncle, the famous Griffier François Fagel (1659–1746), who was the most powerful politician of the second stadholderless era (1702–47). Hendrick, who remained in the office until his death, was a confidant of the stadholders William IV and William V and a passionate Orangist. His collection, described in a catalogue of 1752, may well have contained some pieces acquired by his uncle and father, Cornelis Fagel (1663–1746), who was also a lawyer.

In 1790 Hendrick's namesake and great-grandson Hendrick Fagel (*b* Amsterdam, 21 March 1765; *d* The Hague, 22 March 1838) succeeded him as clerk, the sixth and last member of the family to hold the post. (Hendrick the younger married the same year, but the marriage remained childless.) When the French invaded the northern Netherlands five years later, Hendrick the younger was on a political mission in England, where he stayed. His possessions in Holland were confiscated, including the Fagel family house at Noordeinde 140 in The Hague, which contained a substantial library (now mostly Dublin, Trinity Coll.), as well as a collection of prints, drawings and paintings by Italian, early Netherlandish and numerous 17th-century Dutch masters. On 22–3 May 1801 (the delay caused by the war), 106 paintings from the Fagel collection ('emporte de La Haye') were sold at auction in London, among them works by Jan Steen and Gabriel Metsu (e.g. *Two Men with a Sleeping Woman*, early 1660s; London, N.G.). The books were sold the same day, and the drawings on 27–30 May. On 6 March 1802 there followed the sale of the collection of the Countess of Holderness who, according to the description in the catalogue, had acquired her 81 paintings from the Fagel collection. Two years later Hendrick Fagel became a naturalized British citizen, though in 1813 he returned to the Netherlands with Crown Prince William (later King William I), who offered him a baronetcy.

BIBLIOGRAPHY
F. Lugt: *Ventes*, i (1938), nos 5935, 6229, 6260, 6269, 6270
L. Brummel: *Miscellanea libraria* (The Hague, 1957), pp. 204–33

B. P. J. BROOS

Fahlcrantz, Carl Johan (*b* Stora Tuna, Dalarna, 29 Nov 1774; *d* Stockholm, 9 Jan 1861). Swedish painter. He began his artistic training in Stockholm as a pupil of the theatre painters J. G. Brusell and E. Limnell (1764–1861). He also studied under the French landscape painter Louis Belanger (1736–1816). In 1805 he was awarded a scholarship to go to Italy, but he preferred to use it to travel within Sweden, as this corresponded more with his interest in painting his native landscape in a National Romantic style. Fahlcrantz settled permanently in Sweden, never travelling outside the Nordic countries. In 1819 he became a professor at the Royal Academy of Arts in Stockholm and in the 1820s Karl XIV commissioned a series of major works from him. Oscar I followed suit, as did numerous other buyers inside and outside Sweden. In this way, Fahlcrantz's paintings were distributed as far as Denmark, Bavaria, Russia and America.

Fahlcrantz's lyrical Romantic style of landscape painting is characterized by a warm, often very dark range of colours, dominated by brown and violet. This was succeeded by violet and blue in a lighter range, together with an often rose-coloured tone, which continued into the 1820s. His compositions often included water and are greatly simplified in the details. From the 1820s his works also included numerous views of castles and mansions, such as *Kalmar Castle in Moonlight* (1835; Stockholm, Nmus.). Fahlcrantz was the founder of the Swedish school of landscape painting. Yet in spite of his central position in the Swedish art world, he had few pupils, and only P. G. von Heideken (1781–1864) can be considered a direct successor. Fahlcrantz is best represented in the Nationalmuseum, Stockholm, the Konstmuseum, Göteborg, and the Swedish Royal Collections.

BIBLIOGRAPHY
Obituary, *Ill. Tidning* (26 Jan 1861)
G. Nordensvan: *Svensk konst och svenska konstnärer i det 19 århundradet* [Swedish art and artists of the 19th century] (Stockholm, 1925), pp. 203–9
D. Widman: *Carl Johan Fahlcrantz' måleri* (diss., Uppsala U., 1953)

TORSTEN GUNNARSSON

Fahlström, Öyvind (*b* São Paulo, 28 Dec 1928; *d* Stockholm, 8 Nov 1976). Swedish painter. Following a childhood spent in Brazil, he moved to Sweden in 1939. He studied archaeology and the history of art, specializing in pre-Columbian manuscripts, and he showed an interest in the theatre. In the early 1950s he worked as a journalist, wrote plays and poems and in 1952 began to paint his first composite pictures. In 1953 Fahlström published a manifesto, *Hipy Papy Bthuthdth Thuthda Bthuthdy: Manifesto for Concrete Poetry* (Stockholm), which manipulates language irrespective of the meanings of words. He saw an unexploited wealth, both sensual and intellectual, in its phonetic materials and in the distortions that occur when letters are transposed. In the following years he worked mainly on a large painting entitled *Ade-Ledic-Nander II* (oil, 1955–7; Stockholm, Mod. Mus.; *see* SWEDEN, fig. 11), where little hieroglyphic signs are arranged in major, antagonistic groups. Next, he appropriated images from such comic strips as *Krazy Kat* (for illustration *see* COMIC-STRIP ART) and *Mad*, successively shattering and recycling the figures so as to render them almost unrecognizable. The absurdity of events and absence of any moral sense in *Krazy Kat* held a particular appeal. Fahlström used language as basic material and unexpected angles of vision to reveal hitherto hidden contexts.

In 1961 Fahlström resettled in New York. His painting *Sitting* was executed in 1962 in several versions. In the second of these (1962; Stockholm, Mod. Mus.) Fahlström introduced loose forms that, with the aid of magnets, could be moved anywhere across the picture's surface, creating what he termed his 'variable paintings'. In such works as *The Planetarium* (tempera on vinyl-covered magnets, 1963; Paris, Pompidou) the variable forms still remain on the surface of the painting, but in *Dr Schweitzer's Last Mission* (installation, 1964–6; Stockholm, Mod. Mus.) the parts have left the picture surface and float in space. Fahlström wished to draw no lines between the media he used. Besides painting he organized happenings and designed plays and films. Sometimes he abandoned his artistic pursuits in favour of newspaper and television journalism. The pseudo-journalistic content of his late paintings is concerned with the struggle for the wealth of the Third World and other political issues (e.g. *World*

Politics Monopoly, acrylics, magnets and metal, 1970; priv. col., see 1979–82 exh. cat., p. 82).

BIBLIOGRAPHY

Öyvind Fahlström, Svezia (exh. cat., ed. P. Hultén; Venice, Biennale, 1966)
P. Hultén: *Öyvind Fahlström* (Milan, 1976)
Öyvind Fahlström (exh. cat., ed. O. Granath and P. Hultén; Stockholm, Mod. Mus.; Paris, Pompidou; Rotterdam, Boymans–van Beuningen and elsewhere; 1979–82)
Öyvind Fahlström (exh. cat., ed. B. Springfeldt and D. Feuk; Valencia, IVAM Cent. Julio Gonzalez, 1992)

OLLE GRANATH

Fahrenkamp, Emil (*b* Aachen, 8 Nov 1885; *d* Düsseldorf, 24 May 1966). German architect and teacher. He studied architecture at the Technische Hochschulen in Aachen and Düsseldorf and then taught at the Kunstgewerbeschule and Kunstakademie, Düsseldorf, where he directed the master studio for house building and interior design. He first became well known as the architect of the industrial buildings (1921–3) for Rheinstahl A.G. in the Ruhr area. Other work of the 1920s included the Stadthalle (1925), Mülheim an der Ruhr; a block of flats (1926–7) in Emser and Pariser Strasse, Berlin; the multi-storey Shell-Haus (1930–31; now the BEWAG administration centre), Berlin; and an administration building (1931–2) for the Deutsche Versicherungskonzern, Berlin, and its extension (1935). His projects of the 1920s reveal expressionistic, decorative elements in their clear and simple forms; decoration was a significant part of his work in this period. After 1933 he subordinated his earlier style to the monumental and large-scale architectural approach of the Nazis, which neglected decorative detail. He produced designs for an extension to the Reichsbank (1933–4), for a main building for the Deutsche Arbeitsfront (1935; executed 1936-8), Fehrbelliner Platz, and for the German Tourist Board (1937; building inc.), Unter den Linden, all in Berlin, and he built the German pavilion at the International Water Exhibition (1939) in Liège, Belgium. Fahrenkamp was also involved in various projects for Albert Speer's monumental plans to redesign Berlin, including a housing block (1939–40; unexecuted) with a traditional, representative façade on the projected North–South Axis. In 1939 Fahrenkamp was appointed Director of the Kunstakademie, Düsseldorf, and after World War II he contributed to the rebuilding programme in Berlin.

BIBLIOGRAPHY

Vollmer
A. Hoff: *Emil Fahrenkamp* (Stuttgart, 1928)
E. Bender: 'Das Deutsche Haus aus der internationalen Wasserausstellung in Lüttich, 1939', *Zentbl. Bauverwalt.*, lix (1939), pp. 779–87
——: 'Das Ehrenmal des Baues Essen', *Zentbl. Bauverwalt.*, lix (1939), pp. 1093–6

BRIGITTE JACOB, WOLFGANG SCHÄCHE

Faichtmayer. See FEUCHTMAYER.

Faidherbe, Lucas. See FAYDHERBE, LUCAS.

Faience (i). Term used to describe a material widely employed in antiquity consisting of a sintered-quartz body covered with an alkaline glaze. This material is sometimes also referred to as 'composition' or, if unglazed, as FRIT.

See also EGYPT, ANCIENT, §XVII, 5 and ANCIENT NEAR EAST, §II, 5.

Faience (ii). Term probably derived from the Italian town of Faenza, famous for its popular maiolica. It is often used to describe French, German and Scandinavian tin-glazed earthenware but is also interchangeable with the terms maiolica and delftware.

□

Failaka. *See under* ARABIA, PRE-ISLAMIC, §§II, III, IV.

Fairbairn, Sir Thomas (*b* Manchester, 18 Jan 1823; *d* Bishopstoke, Hants, 12 Aug 1891). English industrialist, patron, collector and exhibition organizer. Having developed the London businesses of his father, William Fairbairn (1789–1874), the pioneer engineer and manufacturer of industrial machinery, he settled in Manchester in the 1850s and began collecting contemporary paintings. He is particularly associated with William Holman Hunt, whose *Awakening Conscience* (1853; London, Tate) Fairbairn bought from the artist in 1854, although he requested that the woman's apparently anguished expression be repainted. Hunt was also persuaded to modify *The Scapegoat* (1854; Port Sunlight, Lady Lever A.G.). In 1864, Fairbairn commissioned Hunt to paint the *Children's Holiday* (1864; Torre Abbey, Torbay, Devon), a group portrait of the Fairbairn family taking tea in a landscape setting. In 1873 he negotiated the sale of the *Shadow of Death* (1870–3; Manchester, C.A.G.) to Thos Agnew & Son's.

Otherwise Fairbairn preferred landscapes and historical genre scenes in a precise Pre-Raphaelite style, for instance Augustus Egg's *Beatrix Knighting Esmond* (1857; London, Tate). Hunt introduced Fairbairn to the sculptor Thomas Woolner, from whom he commissioned the group *Constance and Arthur* (marble, 1857–62; Tunbridge Wells Borough Cemetery), which portrays the patron's two deaf and dumb children. Part of his collection was sold at Christie's on 7 May 1887.

A commissioner on the Great Exhibition of 1851, Fairbairn was the most influential advocate of the 1857 Manchester Art-Treasures Exhibition, serving as chairman of the organizing committee. He was particularly concerned with selecting the contractors for the exhibition building, C. D. Young & Co., who were then completing the Museum of Science and Art, South Kensington. He was probably responsible for appointing his friend Egg as Director of the Gallery of Modern Masters at the exhibition, and he took a keen interest in the choice of contemporary artists. The Pre-Raphaelites and other favourites of Fairbairn such as Frederick Goodall and F. R. Pickersgill were well represented. He bought the important Jules Soulages collection of decorative arts for £13,500 to display at the exhibition and thereafter sold it by instalments to the South Kensington Museum. Subsequently, Fairbairn worked on the International Exhibitions of 1862, 1867 and 1871, and in 1860 advocated a new art gallery for Manchester (opened as the City Art Gallery in 1882).

BIBLIOGRAPHY

A. J. [London], n. s., vi (1860), pp. 71, 112 [rep. of Manchester gal. proposals]
J. Bronkhurst: 'Fruits of a Connoisseur's Friendship: Sir Thomas Fairbairn and William Holman Hunt', *Burl. Mag.*, cxxv (1983), pp. 586–97

OLIVER GARNETT

Fairfax Murray, Charles. *See* MURRAY, CHARLES FAIRFAX.

Fairn, Leslie (Raymond) (*b* Waterville, Nova Scotia, 26 June 1875; *d* Wolfville, Nova Scotia, 11 Aug 1971). Canadian architect. He attended Acadia College, Wolfville, and then studied architecture at Harvard (from *c.* 1895). In 1900 he was apprenticed to Edward Elliott, architect of Halifax City Hall, and was then Principal (1901–4) of the Manual Training Department, Horton Academy, Annapolis, Nova Scotia. In 1904 he founded his practice, launching a 65-year career that had a major impact on the region's architectural life. Early commissions included court-houses at Kentville (1903) and Digby (1910), both in Nova Scotia, and Newcastle (1913), New Brunswick. Although his early work is in a Beaux-Arts style mixed with colonial elements, the court-house at Newcastle is Gothic Revival. He received major commissions throughout the area, including the Administration Building at Acadia University, Wolfville, the Grace Maternity Hospital (1923) and the Killam Library (1971) at Dalhousie University, both in Halifax. He was also a pioneer in establishing the professional status of architects in Canada, being one of the founders of the Nova Scotia Association of Architects.

BIBLIOGRAPHY
J. Conwell and B. Russell: *Nova Scotia Blue Book and Encyclopedia* (1932)
H. B. Jefferson: 'Leslie R. Fairn, FRAIC, FRSA, the Distinguished Architect of the Atlantic Provinces', *Mar. Advocate & Busy E.*, xliv/4 (1953)
Architectural Drawings by Leslie R. Fairn, 1875–1971 (exh. cat. by P. Latta, Halifax, NS, Mt St Vincent U., A.G., 1980)
J. B. Weir: *The Lost Craft of Ornamented Architecture: Canadian Architectural Drawings, 1850–1930* (Halifax, NS, 1983)
GRANT WANZEL, AARON BOURGOIN

Fairweather, George Earnest. *See under* MCKEAN & FAIRWEATHER.

Fairweather, Ian (*b* Bridge of Allan, 29 Sept 1891; *d* Brisbane, 20 May 1974). Australian painter of Scottish birth. He studied at the Academie in The Hague in 1918 and at the Slade School, London, from 1920 to 1924. Fairweather had a reclusive, nomadic nature. He lived in Shanghai (1929–33), Beijing (1935) and in Bali, the Philippines and India. After surviving a raft voyage from Darwin to Bali in 1952, he settled on Bribie Island, in northern Australia. Fairweather was a pioneer in mixing with the cultures of Australasia and was one of the few who successfully assimilated Aboriginal painting. Of his surviving works (*c.* 500) scarcely a dozen have Australian subjects. His years in China and his interest in calligraphy and the Chinese written language had a decisive influence, shifting him from tonal figures, as in *Bathing Scene, Bali* (1933; London, Tate), to an open linear style and a restrained use of colour. His oils exhibited in London from 1935 were mostly Chinese landscapes in a Post-Impressionist manner. From the 1940s he turned to gouache, thickly applied, often on poor materials, until 1958 when he used synthetic polymer paint. To evoke experiences long past he developed his own distinctive calligraphy, with traces of Cubism, as in *Monastery* (1961; Canberra, N.G.) and *Monsoon* (1961; Perth, A.G. W.

Australia). His meditative grey abstracts of 1959–61 remain among the most impressive in Australian art.

BIBLIOGRAPHY
M. Bail: *Ian Fairweather* (Sydney, 1981)
MURRAY BAIL

Faistauer, Anton (*b* Saint Martin bei Lofer, Salzburg, 14 Feb 1887; *d* Vienna, 13 Feb 1930). Austrian painter. He began his studies at the Akademie der Bildenden Künste in Vienna in 1906. As a protest against the conservatism of his professor, the German painter Christian Griepenkerl (1839–1916), he left with some like-minded students in 1909 to establish the NEUKUNSTGRUPPE, which exhibited for the first time in Vienna in the same year. A second exhibition in 1911 with the Hagenbund group was an important event for modern Austrian painting, but Faistauer himself was unable to gain public recognition. In the first period of his work he remained in the European tradition of colouristic painting with a strong affinity to Cézanne; he used colour in his landscapes and still-lifes to build the picture in a tectonic way, as in *Still-life with Apples, Jug, Wine Bottle and Glass* (*c.* 1912; Salzburg, Mus. Carolino-Augusteum). In his portraits he neglected individual, psychological characterization of his models, for example in *Ida, the Painter's First Wife on a Red Sofa* (1913; Vienna, Belvedere). An exhibition that had already been arranged with Paul Cassirer in Berlin had to be cancelled when World War I broke out. After the war he lived for a few years in Salzburg, where he was involved with the foundation of the artistic group Der Wassermann in 1919.

From 1922 onwards Faistauer created monumental wall and ceiling paintings dealing with religious and symbolic or allegoric subject-matter. These included the fresco cycle of 1926 for the Festspielhaus in Salzburg (*see* SALZBURG, fig. 6); the work had to be removed during the National Socialist regime in 1939, and it was not replaced until 1956. Presumably because of his involvement with the techniques of fresco painting, Faistauer's later works reveal a lighter palette and a thinner coat of paint, which allowed the structure of the paintings a greater role. In addition to his practical work he was also a theorist of note. His book *Neue Malerei in Österreich* (Vienna, 1923) is one of the most important contemporary documents on modern Austrian painting.

BIBLIOGRAPHY
F. Fuhrmann: *Anton Faistauer* (Salzburg, 1972)
A. Rohrmoser: *Anton Faistauer, 1887–1930: Abkehr von der Moderne: Untersuchung zur Stilentwicklung* (Salzburg, 1987)
EDWIN LACHNIT

Faistenberger [Feistenberger]. Austrian family of painters and sculptors. Balthasar Faistenberger was a stuccoist in Hall in the Tyrol, *c.* 1560, and subsequently moved to Kitzbühel. His son Andreas Faistenberger I (*b* Hall, 1588; *d* Kitzbühel, 1625), a painter, had two sons, the sculptor Benedikt Faistenberger (*b* Kitzbühel, 1621; *d* Kitzbühel, 1693) and the painter Wilhelm Faistenberger (*b* Kitzbühel, 1623; *d* Salzburg, *c.* 1690). While Benedikt had nine artist sons (including the sculptor Andreas Faistenberger II (1647–1736)) and five artist grandsons, Wilhelm had only two: the painters Joseph Faistenberger (*b* Salzburg, *c.* 1675; *d* Salzburg, 1724) and (1) Anton Faistenberger.

(1) Anton Faistenberger (*b* Salzburg, 1663; *d* Vienna, 29 Feb 1708). Painter. After studying with his father, between 1680 and 1694 he visited Italy, where he encountered the landscape painting of Poussin and Salvator Rosa and met Johann Carl Loth in Venice. Subsequently he worked mainly in Vienna, probably in part for the Esterhazy family. He produced numerous imaginary and heroic landscapes, in which the figure staffages were generally painted by other artists, such as Loth, Hans Graf (1653–1710) and Jean Pierre van Bredael II (1683–1735). His works include a *Mountain Landscape with Nymphs* (*c.* 1680–90; Dresden, Gemäldegal. Alte Meister), *Landscape with the Parable of the Good Samaritan* (*c.* 1700; Nuremberg, Ger. Nmus.), *Landscape after a Thunderstorm* (after 1700; Vienna, Belvedere) and *Classical Mountain Landscape* (*c.* 1690–1700; U. Würzburg, Wagner-Mus.).

BIBLIOGRAPHY

E. Schaffran: 'Anton Feistenberger und die mittelitalienische Landschaftsmalerei des Hochbarock', *Alte & Mod. Kst*, vi (1961), pp. 21–2, no. 42

I. Strnadt: *Anton und Josef Faistenberger* (diss., U. Innsbruck, 1964); extract in *Mitt. Ver. Vergl. Kstforsch.*, xx (1967–8), p. 38

G. Adriani: *Deutsche Malerei im 17. Jahrhundert* (Cologne, 1977), pp. 108, 180, no. 92

E. Baum: *Katalog des Österreichischen Barockmuseums in Unteren Belvedere in Wien*, i (Munich, 1980), pp. 156–61

C. HÖPER

Faithorne, William (*b* London, ?1616; *d* London, 1691). English engraver and portrait draughtsman. The son of a London bitmaker, Faithorne was first apprenticed to the goldsmith William Veale in 1635 but chose instead to train as an engraver. His earliest master was Robert Peake; from *c.* 1636–9 he worked for the engraver John Payne and later for Peake's son, Sir Robert Peake (?1592–1667), himself a print-seller and engraver.

During the Civil War, Faithorne served under Peake's command in the royalist garrison at Basing House, Hampshire. He was taken prisoner when the besieged house surrendered in 1645. Although imprisoned in Aldersgate he was permitted to engrave portraits, but, presumably having refused to swear allegiance to Oliver Cromwell, he was banished to France. There he resumed his engraving career, winning the patronage of Abbé Michel de Marolles; he fell under the powerful influence of Philippe de Champaigne and Robert Nanteuil, both of whom are said to have instructed him, though this seems unlikely.

On returning to England *c.* 1650, Faithorne established an engraving and print-selling business in London, near Temple Bar. Whatever the reason for his previous banishment, he was now patronized by such prominent Commonwealth leaders as Sir Robert Fairfax, whose likeness he engraved and which Faithorne holds in his own portrait by Robert Walker (London, N.P.G.). After the Restoration, he continued to serve the court, adopting the sobriquet 'Painter to Prince Rupert'; despite this there is no evidence that he practised as an easel painter. Bainbridge Buckeridge's assertion that he was 'a great proficient...in painting' may refer to work as a miniaturist, but his main business continued to be engraving and, later, crayon drawing.

In 1662 Faithorne published his own translation of Abraham Bosse's *Traité des manières de graver en taille douce*, retitled *The Art of Graveing and Etching*; it was the first practical account of the subject to appear in England, and it prompted John Evelyn to abandon an addendum to his *Sculptura* (London, 1662) for fear of repetition. Faithorne's own numerous engravings set a new standard, George Vertue judging him the first to have 'arrived to any perfection' in the art. His production was chiefly portraits, some of them taken from William Dobson and others after his own drawings, but he also engraved a number of frontispieces and book illustrations for such works as Jeremy Taylor's *Life of Christ* (1663) as well as large maps of London and Westminster (1658) and Virginia and Maryland (1673). He published the last two himself and in 1673 issued Francis Barlow's *Multae et diversae avium species* with etchings by Wenceslaus Hollar.

About 1680 Faithorne moved to Printing House Yard, Blackfriars, and relinquished his print-selling to concentrate on engraving and making chalk drawings from life. He was a prolific and swift draughtsman, working both in chalk and in combinations of chalk and wash or India ink, as he had seen in France. His handling of the latter method recalls that of Nanteuil; it is seen at its best in a portrait of his friend *John Aubrey* (1666; Oxford, Ashmolean; see fig.). He also drew in chalk on copper, the plates having been roughened with a rocker to hold the chalks, a method also used by Edward Luttrell.

William Faithorne: *John Aubrey*, black chalk and wash on vellum, the face tinted with red chalk, retouched in pencil, 196×145 mm, 1666 (Oxford, Ashmolean Museum)

Faithorne's associates included the mezzotint-engraver John Smith and many contemporary writing-masters and calligraphers. He may have taught the engraver John Fillian (*fl* 1660–80) and the portrait painter Thomas Hill, as well as his own son, William Faithorne the younger (1655–*c*. 1710), a mezzotint-engraver.

DNB

BIBLIOGRAPHY

B. Buckeridge: 'An Essay towards an English School of Painters', *The Art of Painting*, ed. R. de Piles (London, 1706, 3/1750), pp. 371–2

L. Fagan: *A Descriptive Catalogue of the Engraved Works of William Faithorne* (London, 1888)

C. F. Bell and R. L. Poole: 'English Seventeenth Century Portrait Drawings in Oxford Collections', *Walpole Soc.*, xiv (1926), pp. 43–64

J. Woodward: *Tudor and Stuart Drawings* (London, 1951)

E. Croft-Murray and P. Hulton: *British Drawings: 16th and 17th Centuries*, London, BM cat., i (London, 1960), pp. 314–15

DAVID BLAYNEY BROWN

Faiyum. Egyptian semi-oasis region *c*. 80 km south-west of Cairo on the Bahr Yusuf, an ancient channel of the Nile (see fig.). In the north-west is Lake Qarun, a remnant of the ancient Lake Moeris, an important part of ancient Egyptian cosmogony since it was reputed by some to be the site of Nun, the primeval ocean. Throughout the Dynastic and Greco-Roman periods (*c*. 2925 BC–AD 395) the major god worshipped in the Faiyum was the crocodile-headed Sebek (Gr. Suchos), but the region had a large Jewish community from the 3rd century BC, and Christianity probably arrived in the 1st century AD. Major sites in the Faiyum include the Middle Kingdom monuments at Hawara, el-Lahun and Qasr el-Sagha, and Greco-Roman towns at Qasr Qarun and Kom Ushim. The principal Coptic monuments are the monasteries of Deir el-Azab and Deir el-Malak, and there is a 15th-century mosque in the regional capital of Medinet el-Faiyum.

1. DYNASTIC. Early records in the form of toponyms and administrative titles show that the Faiyum was settled and under the control of central authority from the very beginnings of Egyptian history. When civil war broke out during the First Intermediate Period (*c*. 2150–*c*. 2008 BC), the new rulers of the 9th and 10th dynasties built their capital city at HERAKLEOPOLIS MAGNA to the south. However, few records have survived from the site, and little is known about this period in the Faiyum. With peaceful conditions re-established in the Middle Kingdom (*c*. 2008–*c*. 1630 BC) and the founding of a new capital city at EL-LISHT to the north-east of the region, the Faiyum was once again the focus of royal attention. Existing monuments were restored, and a new temple was built at QASR EL-SAGHA in the north (a). Sesostris I of the 12th Dynasty (*reg c*. 1918–*c*. 1875 BC) erected an obelisk near Medinet el-Faiyum (Gr. Crocodilopolis), site of the main temple of Sebek (b). His grandson Sesostris II (*reg c*. 1844–

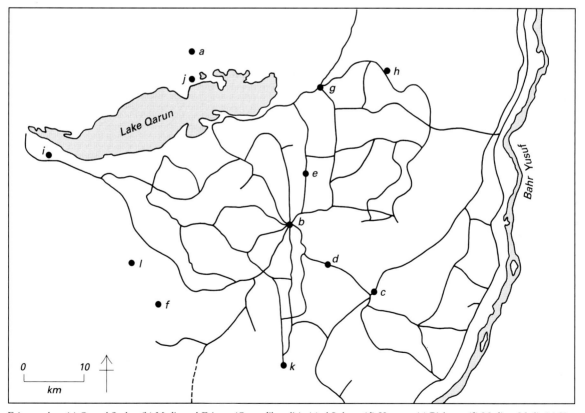

Faiyum, plan: (a) Qasr el-Sagha; (b) Medinet el-Faiyum (Crocodilopolis); (c) el-Lahun; (d) Hawara; (e) Biahmu; (f) Medinet Madi; (g) Kom Ushim (Karanis); (h) Kom el-Asl (Bacchias); (i) Qasr Qarun (Dionysias); (j) Dimai (Soknopaiou Nesos); (k) Umm el-Baragat (Tebtunis); (l) Deir el-Malak

c. 1837 BC) built his pyramid at EL-LAHUN in the south (c); a nearby tomb yielded a cache of exquisite jewellery and toilet objects belonging to the princess Sithathoriunet (New York, Met.; *see* EGYPT, ANCIENT, fig. 91). In Kahun, a government-created settlement next to the pyramid, a hoard of papyri yielded a wealth of information on the town and its economic life during this period.

The royal name most closely associated with the Faiyum, however, is that of King AMMENEMES III (*reg c.* 1818–*c.* 1770 BC), who built his pyramid at HAWARA, between el-Lahun and Medinet el-Faiyum (d). To the south of the pyramid was a mortuary temple, which became famous in Classical times as the 'Egyptian Labyrinth'. A seated limestone statue of Ammenemes found there (Cairo, Egyp. Mus., CG 385) exemplifies the royal statuary of the time: departing from his father Sesostris III's weary and melancholic look, the young king wished to be shown in a slightly more idealized way, yet retaining a brooding, meditative appearance (*see* EGYPT, ANCIENT, §IX, 3(v)(a)). At the site of Biahmu (e), he erected two seated colossi surrounded by their own courtyards; the incline of their walls probably explains Herodotus' description of these monuments as 'two pyramids . . . each surmounted by the stone image of a man sitting on a throne' (*Histories* II.cxlix). Ammenemes added to the main temple of Sebek and also built another temple to Sebek and the snake-headed harvest goddess Renenutet at Medinet Madi in the south-west of the region (f). The latter is fairly well preserved and is in fact one of the only temples extant from this period. The ubiquity of Ammenemes' monuments in the Faiyum must account for his deification there in the Greco-Roman period (332 BC–AD 395).

The next period of intense artistic activity was the Ptolemaic era (304–30 BC), when the artificial lowering of Lake Moeris and the construction of new irrigation systems made more land available for cultivation, leading to increased settlement and the founding of new towns. Archaeologists excavating these sites have discovered a wealth of papyri, including administrative, legal and religious documents.

BIBLIOGRAPHY
LÄ: 'Fajjum'; 'Medinet el-Fajjum'
H. E. Winlock: *The Treasure of el-Lahun* (New York, 1934)
K. Parlasca: *Mumienporträts und verwandte Denkmäler* (Wiesbaden, 1966)
D. Arnold and D. Arnold: *Der Tempel Qasr el-Sagha* (Mainz, 1979)
M.-E. Lane: *A Guide to the Antiquities of the Fayyum* (Cairo, 1985)
J. Śliwa: 'Siedlung des Mittleren Reiches bei Qasr el-Sagha', *VI Congresso internazionale di egittologia: Torino, 1992*, i, pp. 565–71

R. J. LEPROHON

2. ROMAN. Architectural activity in the Faiyum continued from the Ptolemaic into the Roman period, the additions under Nero to the temple at Kom Ushim (Gr. Karanis) being some of the most visible projects (g). The temples at Kom el-Asl (Gr. Bacchias (h)) and Qasr Qarun (Gr. Dionysias (i)) were also expanded in the Roman period, and numerous Roman statues have been recovered from the Ptolemaic temple at Dimai (Gr. Soknopaiou Nesos (j)). Private building and settlement in the Faiyum continued, and many towns experienced great growth and expansion. Karanis is one of the best-preserved urban sites in the Faiyum; excavations, undertaken by the University of Michigan's Kelsey Museum of Archaeology

at Ann Arbor (directed by J. L. Starkey and E. E. Peterson) from 1924 to 1935 have yielded extensive urban remains and masses of Greek papyri, which enable the reconstruction of an active and prosperous economy (*see* EGYPT, ANCIENT, §VIII, 4(vi)). Several wall paintings from Karanis are important as examples of decorative paintings (often of religious subjects) in secular buildings. The ceramic series from Karanis is unusually complete and important for dating finds of pottery vessels and lamps from elsewhere. Most of the finds from Karanis (approximately 45,000 objects, including pottery, glassware, basketry, textiles and coins) are in the collection of the Kelsey Museum of Archaeology. Decorated household objects, including utensils, devotional images, cosmetic articles and textiles, are also known from several sites in the Faiyum.

The region is best known, however, for the Faiyum 'mummy portraits' (collections in Cairo, Egyp. Mus.; London, BM; London, U. Coll., Petrie Mus.; Paris, Louvre). Although not geographically limited to the region, most of the nearly 600 paintings from this corpus come from cemeteries in the Faiyum and represent an important stage in the development of portraiture and Roman Egyptian art. Painted in encaustic or tempera on wooden panels, the life-size Faiyum portraits show a degree of realism hitherto unknown in Egyptian art (*see* ENCAUSTIC PAINTING, fig. 2, and TEMPERA, colour pl. V, fig. 1). These portraits were commemorative but also served cultic and funerary functions. Unfortunately, many of the portraits have, in modern times, been detached from the mummy, depriving them of their original context as part of an overall iconographic scheme with complex religious significance (*see* MUMMY, EGYPTIAN).

BIBLIOGRAPHY
B. P. Grenfell and A. S. Hunt: *Fayûm Towns and their Papyri* (London, 1900)
E. K. Gazda, ed.: *Karanis: An Egyptian Town in Roman Times* (Ann Arbor, 1983) [extensive bibliog., photographs and plans]
K. Parlasca, ed.: *El Fayyum* (Milan, 1985)
L. Corcoran: *Portrait Mummies from Roman Egypt* (diss., U. Chicago, IL, 1988)
D. Montserrat: 'The Representation of Adolescent Males in "Fayyum Portraits"', *J. Egyp. Archaeol.*, lxxix (1993), pp. 289–97 [extensive bibliog.]

3. COPTIC. Changes in agricultural conditions resulted in the depopulation of certain areas of the Faiyum in the 3rd and 4th centuries AD. The coming of Christianity to the Faiyum resulted in, among other things, the conversion of temples to Christian churches, but as it became better established, new churches were constructed, good examples being the 6th–9th-century complex at Medinet Madi. A poorly preserved church at Umm el-Baragat (Gr. Tebtunis (k)) contained several wall paintings (untraced) from the 10th century; in addition to typical portraits of saints, these murals included otherwise unparalleled scenes of the punishment of sinners in the afterlife. The Faiyum and the desert region to the west became an important area for monasteries: several are known from ruins and literary references, and the modern monastery of Deir el-Azab appears to conceal remains of a much earlier building. Little is known of the architecture or history of Deir el-Malak (l), near el-Hamuli, but unofficial excavation of the site yielded a large collection of manuscripts from the 9th to the 10th century, most now in the Pierpont Morgan

Library, New York. Some of these manuscripts contain important examples of Coptic manuscript illuminations, including several biblical scenes and extensive marginalia. Decorated textiles are the most characteristic products of the Faiyum in the Coptic period; a representative collection of these is in the Musée du Louvre, Paris. Certain styles of weaving were the specialities of individual cities, the most distinctive being the textiles from Medinet el-Faiyum (Gr. Arsinoe).

BIBLIOGRAPHY

N. Abbott: *The Monasteries of the Fayyûm*, Studies in Ancient Oriental Civilization, 16 (Chicago, 1937)

P. du Bourguet: *Musée National du Louvre: Catalogue des étoffes coptes*, i (Paris, 1964)

C. C. Walters: 'Christian Paintings from Tebtunis', *J. Egyp. Archaeol.*, lxxv (1989), pp. 191–208

T. G. WILFONG

Fa Jo-chen. *See* FA RUOZHEN.

Fake. *See* FORGERY.

Falaise, Jean de. *See* CHENNEVIÈRES, CHARLES-PHILIPPE.

Falangcai. *See under* FAMILLE ROSE.

Fałat, Julian (*b* Tuligłowy, nr Lwów [now Lviv, Ukraine], 30 July 1853; *d* Habelschwerdt, Silesia [now Bystrzyca Kłodzka, Poland], 9 July 1929). Polish painter. He studied (1869–71) at the Kraków School of Fine Arts before working as a draughtsman for the archaeologist Stanisław Krzyżanowski (1841–81) on excavations in the Ukraine, then for the architect Feliks Ģsiorowski. With the latter's support, Fałat was able to study architecture in Zurich and Munich, but he gave up his studies to work as a technical draughtsman in Zurich. He continued with his painting studies in Munich (1877–80) under Alexander Strähuber (1814–82) and Georg Raab (1821–85). Fałat's early work shows the influence of the watercolourists Hubert von Herkomer and Ludwig Passini (1832–1903), and of Eduard Grützner (1846–1925). Fałat's own watercolour work was soon acclaimed both by the large group of Polish painters in Munich and also by those at home. In 1882–6 Fałat lived in Warsaw painting realistic genre scenes and landscapes and contributing illustrations to Polish and German periodicals, such as the Viennese Secession journal *Ver Sacrum*. He enjoyed living in style and travelled extensively, incorporating new settings into his work. During a journey to the East in 1885 he executed a series of 'oriental' watercolours, being among the first Polish artists to adopt Japanese motifs.

In January 1886, at a hunt given by the Radziwiłłs at their palace at Nieśwież (now in Lithuania), Fałat met the future Prussian Emperor William II. Several months later, at William's invitation, Fałat went to Berlin and spent eight years at various imperial residences, where he painted many hunting scenes, including a series of watercolours showing the hunt at Nieśwież (destr.) and others usually in winter settings. Among his most representative works is *Return from a Bear-hunt* (1892; Warsaw, N. Mus.). From December 1894 to April 1896, together with Wojciech Kossak and a group of assistants, Fałat painted the famous panorama showing *Napoleon's Army Crossing the Berezina in 1812* (mostly destr.; fragments in Warsaw, N. Mus.; Kraków, N. Mus.; Poznań, N. Mus.; Opole, Sil. Mus.; Lublin, Distr. Mus.). This was exhibited with great success in Berlin in April 1896.

In 1895 Fałat was appointed Director of the Kraków School of Fine Arts and undertook its radical reform, altering the curriculum and recruiting professors among young and innovative artists. In 1897 Fałat took part in the founding of the Polish Artists' Society, Sztuka (Art) and exhibited with it abroad with some success. He was also a member of the Vienna Secession and the Berlin Akademie der Künste. Fałat continued to paint hunting pictures but he also produced nostalgic landscape scenes, often of forests in Polesie and Lithuania, such as *Landscape with Elks* (*c.* 1899; Poznań, N. Mus.) and landscapes with the motif of a dark stream against snow. His subject-matter broadened to include townscapes (e.g. *Montmartre Cemetery in Paris*, 1893; Warsaw, N. Mus.). His scenes from the Kraków region often stressed picturesque and folkloric elements, such as traditional costume or religious customs. He also produced some fine portraits, the most popular, *Self-portrait with Palette* (1896; Warsaw, N. Mus.), remarkable for its artist's scrutinizing look directed at the spectator.

In 1910 Fałat resigned his post at the Kraków Academy and settled in the village of Habelschwerdt in Silesia. During World War I he fought in the Polish-Austrian Legion and painted watercolour portraits of his fellow soldiers. In 1919, with the restoration of Polish independence, he settled in Toruń where, in 1920, he set up a Confraternity of Artists. In 1922 he settled again in the country where he lived on a modest pension. During the last years of his life he painted little.

WRITINGS

Pamiętniki [Diaries] (Warsaw, 1935)

BIBLIOGRAPHY

SAP; Thieme–Becker

M. Masłowski: *Julian Fałat* (Warsaw, 1964)

W. Juszczak: *Modernizm: Malarstwo polskie* [Modernism: Polish painting] (Warsaw, 1977) [biog. notes by M. Liczbinska]

Polnische Malerei von 1830 bis 1918 (exh. cat., Kiel, Christian-Albrechts U., Ksthalle; Stuttgart, Württemberg. Kstver.; Wuppertal, von der Heydt-Mus.; 1978–9)

La Peinture polonaise du XVIe au début du XXe siècle (exh. cat., Paris, Grand Pal., 1979)

J. Malinowski: *Julian Fałat* (Warsaw, 1985) [good illus., extensive bibliog.]

JANINA ZIELIŃSKA

Falca, Pietro. *See* LONGHI (iii), (1).

Falcini, Mariano (*b* Campi Bisenzio, Florence, 10 May 1804; *d* Florence, 11 Nov 1885). Italian architect. He studied at the Accademia di Belle Arti in Florence under Giuseppe Cacialli and Pasquale Poccianti, winning the prestigious triennial prize in architecture with his project for a boarding-school for 200 pupils. With a scholarship from the Accademia, he continued his studies in Rome and Venice, returning to Florence in 1835. His subsequent career, during which he established himself as a prolific and eclectic architect, can be divided into three periods. The first (1836–50) includes his competition entry for the parish church of S Stefano in Genoa, the hospital (1847, built 1852) at Pietrasanta, near Lucca, the monuments to Felice Matteucci in La Badia, to Pietro Benvenuti (1844) in S Lorenzo, and to the Marchese Tempi in SS Annunziata, all in Florence, as well as numerous restorations of Florentine palazzi. For most of this first period he was working for the Scrittoio delle Regie Fabbriche. In the second period (1851–60), Falcini planned the Palazzo Comunale of Dicomano, near Florence, some marble refacings for the Collegiata at Pietrasanta and the enlargement in Romanesque style of S Margherita (1856) at Cortona. He also won the international competition (1858) for the new theatre in Alexandria, Egypt. In the last period (1860–80), he was an unsuccessful contender in the competition to design the new façade for Florence Cathedral. His executed projects of this period include the fountain (1861) in the Piazza del Duomo in Prato; the completion (1865) of the monumental cemetery of S Miniato al Monte; the main hall of the Post Office (1865) in the Old Mint building in the Piazzale degli Uffizi; and the senate hall in the Palazzo degli Uffizi (during Florence's brief period as capital of Italy, 1865–70). Perhaps his most celebrated work, however, was the synagogue (1874–82) in the Via Giosuè Carducci, Florence, a Moorish and Byzantine Revival design built in collaboration with Marco Treves (1814–97) and Vincenzo Micheli (1814–97).

WRITINGS

Alcune osservazioni sul dipinto prospettico della facciata del duomo di Firenze (Florence, 1856)
Cenni intorno ai due progetti della facciata del duomo di Firenze (Florence, 1867)

BIBLIOGRAPHY

G. Maffei: *Dell'architetto Mariano Falcini* (Florence, 1888)
C. L. V. Meeks: *Italian Architecture, 1750–1914* (New Haven and London, 1966), pp. 224–5, 265, 399
C. Cresti and L. Zangheri: *Architetti e ingegneri nella Toscana dell'ottocento* (Florence, 1978), pp. 88–9
C. Cresti, M. Cozzi and G. Carapelli: *Il duomo di Firenze, 1822–1887: L'avventura della facciata* (Florence, 1987), pp. 77–80, 112–13
Due granduchi, tre re e una facciata, Opera di S Maria del Fiore di Firenze (Florence, 1987), pp. 115–17, 154–6, 180, 182

MARIO BENCIVENNI

Falck [Falckius; Falk; Falque], **Jeremias** [Jeremiasz; Jeremij] (*b* ?Gdańsk, *c.* 1610; *d* Gdańsk, 1677). Polish engraver. Between 1639 and 1645 he worked in Paris for the publishers Justus van Egmont, Justus Leblond, François Langlois and Pierre-Jean Mariette, producing a series of engraved allegories, for example the *Five Senses*, the *Four Seasons*, the *Twelve Months* and the *Four Elements*. He engraved portraits of Louis XIII and his family and surroundings, after paintings by van Egmont, while for the Leblond print publishers he produced portraits of actors in the manner of Jacques Callot.

Falck was active in Gdańsk from 1646, producing engravings of the triumphal arches erected for the entry of Queen Marie Louise de Gonzague in 1646 (plates, Gdańsk, Lib. Pol. Acad. Sci.) and drawings (1648–9; Gdańsk, N. Mus.) of the sculptures by Peter Ringering (1612–50) on the Golden Gate in Gdańsk. In 1646–55 Falck engraved his mature portraits of Swedish and Polish dignitaries and magnates and of Gdańsk scholars and patricians, which were based on paintings by David Klöcker Ehrenstrahl and Daniel Schultz, among others. Falck used the oval-framed, bust-length format he had developed during the years he had worked in Paris; the background was made up of concentric lines, the shading

giving an illusion of depth, and at the bottom of each engraving was a tablet-form inscription. He occasionally alluded to his origins by signing himself *Polonus* or *Gedanesis*. His French training led to some idealization of his models' features, although without eclipsing the Dutch realism that characterized the paintings he imitated. In 1650 he was appointed court engraver to Queen Christina in Stockholm. However, he continued to collaborate with Gdańsk circles, above all with the printing house of G. Förster, for whom he produced illustrated title-pages. Around 1655, Falck was in Copenhagen, at which time he engraved the portrait of *Frederick III of Denmark*, after the painting by Karel van Mander III. He later worked in Amsterdam on the set of 18 reproductive engravings of the Italian Old Master paintings in the collection of Gerrit Reynst, in which he subtly conveyed the qualities of light and shade of the original paintings. From 1657 he lived for several years in Hamburg, where he published his own drawings in *Novae et exquisitae florum icones . . .* (1662) as well as templates for goldsmiths. Falck's graphic output (around 300 engravings in all) made him a model for other Central European engravers.

SAP

BIBLIOGRAPHY

E. Rastawiecki: 'Ryciny Jeremiasza Falcka, gdańszczanina Polaka' [The engravings of Jeremiasz Falck, a Polish native of Gdańsk], *Bib. Warszaw.*, i (1856), pp. 525–50
J. C. Block: *Jeremias Falck: Sein Leben und seine Werke* (Danzig [Gdańsk], 1890)
E. Iwanoyko: *Jeremiasz Falck Polonus* (Poznań, 1952)

BOŻENA STEINBORN

Falcó, Jacobo Fitz-James Stuart y, 17th Duque de Alba. *See* ALBA, (2).

Falcone, Andrea (*b* Naples, ?1630; *d* Naples, before 23 March 1675). Italian sculptor. He was the great-nephew of the painter Aniello Falcone and probably trained in the workshop of Cosimo Fanzago. During a visit to Rome in 1659 he executed two marble putti for the altar of the sacristy in S Agnese in Agone and studied the works of François Duquesnoy (e.g. *St Susanna*, S Maria di Loreto) and those executed by Jacques Sarrazin, such as the stucco telamones of the Porfirio Chapel in S Lorenzo in Miranda. These examples of Roman classicism were decisive for the future development of Falcone's style when he finally returned to Naples and renewed contact with the Baroque tradition of Fanzago. Six stucco *Angels* (1668; Naples Cathedral, Cappella del Tesoro) and the monumental statues depicting *Prudence*, *Temperance* and *Divine Justice* (*c.* 1672–5) that stand before the Cappella della Purità in S Paolo, Maggiore, are examples of his work that are outside the pure Baroque tradition. The tomb of *Giulio Mastrilli* (1672; Naples, S Maria del Purgatorio ad Arco) and the *Virgin and Child* and two *Allegories of Charity* (Naples, Pio Monte della Misericordia) show the balanced combination of the two components of his style, the classical elements tempered by 'picturesque' modelling, with broad areas of light and shade.

Falcone made use of Andrea Bolgi's composition for the tomb of *Vittoria de Caro* (1652; Naples, S Lorenzo Maggiore) in his tomb of *Isabella Guevara* (1673; Naples, Gesù e Maria), which consists of the kneeling effigy of the deceased sculpted in white marble, almost entirely in the round and set in a sumptuous framework of polychrome marble. Falcone added, however, a formal dynamism that constituted a new development in his art, and this was in turn to serve as a model for Lorenzo Vaccaro and other Neapolitan sculptors until the beginning of the 18th century.

Falcone also produced models for silver sculptures, but the only surviving example is the bust of *St Cajetan of Thiene* (1671; Naples, S Gennaro, Treasury).

BIBLIOGRAPHY
B. de Domenici: *Vite* (1742–5), iii, pp. 186–7
G. Borrelli: *Il presepe napoletano* (Rome, 1970), pp. 141–3
O. Ferrari: *Le arti figurative* (1970), vi of *Storia di Napoli* (Cava dei Tirreni and Naples, 1967–78), pp. 1302–4
V. Rizzo: 'Scultori della seconda metà del seicento', *Seicento napoletano*, ed. R. Pane (Milan, 1984), pp. 165–75
R. Lattuada: 'Andrea Falcone, scultore a Napoli tra classicismo e barocco', *Stor. A.*, liv (1985), pp. 157–81

ORESTE FERRARI

Falcone, Aniello (*b* Naples, 1607; *d* Naples, 1656). Italian painter and draughtsman. He trained briefly with Jusepe de Ribera, the Caravaggesque Spanish painter. He quickly won fame as a specialist in scenes of battle, and his contemporaries nicknamed him the 'oracle' of this genre.

Falcone created the 'battle scene without a hero' (Saxl): he showed the battle as a brutal, confused struggle between anonymous troops, without heroes, without defeats and without particular historical incidents. The *Battle between Turks and Christians* (1621; Paris, Louvre; see fig.) is one of the earliest. The frieze-like composition is elaborately structured, yet the picture is rich in intensely naturalistic, vividly coloured details of armour and weapons and precisely observed expressions of anger and pain. The famous dealer and collector Gaspar Roomer and other Neapolitan collectors commissioned many battle pictures from him, and these were soon introduced throughout Europe. He was especially favoured by Ferrante Spinelli, Prince of Tarsia, who gave Falcone a residence in his palace after 1651. The genre was developed by artists in his workshop: Micco Spadaro, Marzio Masturzio, Carlo Coppola (*fl* 1640–60), Andrea di Lione and Salvator Rosa.

De Dominici records a journey to Rome, and Falcone's early works include genre paintings influenced by artists working in Rome, such as Pieter van Laer and Michelangelo Cerquozzi, and, equally importantly, by works painted by Diego Velázquez in Italy (1629–30); it was perhaps through Falcone that the painting of *bambocciate* (low-life

Aniello Falcone: *Battle between Turks and Christians*, oil on canvas, 136×168 mm, 1621 (Paris, Musée du Louvre)

scenes) spread to Naples. His early *Schoolmistress* (New York, Wildenstein's; see Spinosa, fig. 314) is a harshly naturalistic work with strong contrasts of light and dark. The theme of *St Lucy Distributing Alms* (Naples, Capodimonte) is religious, yet Falcone painted a scene from everyday life. The saint and her companions give alms to tattered, crippled beggars in a Neapolitan street, and the group is portrayed with a warmth and dignity reminiscent of Velázquez and Louis Le Nain.

Falcone also painted in fresco and received several official commissions. In the frescoes in the chapel of St Agatha in S Paolo Maggiore in Naples and in the signed *Rest on the Flight into Egypt* (1641; Naples Cathedral) Falcone began to move towards an academic style influenced by Romano-Bolognese classicism, developing it further in frescoed scenes from the *Life of St Ignatius* in the sacristy of the Gesù Nuovo in Naples and in paintings (around 1645) for Philip IV of Spain for various rooms in El Buen Retiro in Madrid (now Madrid, Prado). In these pictures, and in the battle scenes of the 1640s, Falcone's handling became more painterly, and his richer colour and warmer light suggest a response to Nicolas Poussin and to Giovanni Benedetto Castiglione.

Falcone was an important draughtsman. His favoured medium was red chalk, and he interpreted the red chalk drawings of Ribera in a more subtle and more pictorial manner. By 1636 he was holding a life drawing class in his studio over the winter months, and his academic nude drawings (for example, Paris, Louvre, 7623) are forcefully modelled and sharply outlined. Many preparatory studies for the battle scenes survive, among them copies of drawings by Leonardo da Vinci; they include horsemen and strongly characterized heads of shouting men and warriors. He also made landscape drawings, and the naturalism of the landscape backgrounds in his battle scenes is indebted to these informal studies.

BIBLIOGRAPHY
B. de Dominici: *Vite* (1742–5), iii, pp. 70–87
A. von Bartsch: *Le Peintre-graveur* (1803–21), pp. 93–109 [B.]
F. Saxl: 'Aniello Falcone, "Oracolo delle battaglie"', *Ein Wiederbelebung: Festschrift für Walter Friedländer* (1933), pp. 478–526
——: 'The Battle Scene without a Hero: Aniello Falcone and his Patrons', *J. Warb. & Court. Inst.*, 3 (1939/40), pp. 70–87
G. de Vito: *Ricerche sul '600 napoletano: Aniello Falcone* (Milan, 1982), pp. 7–36
N. Spinosa: *La pittura napoletana del '600: A cura di Nicola Spinosa* (Milan, 1984) [with good illus.]
Civiltà del seicento a Napoli (exh. cat., Naples, Capodimonte, 1984), i, pp. 135, 260–66
A. Brejon de Lavergnée: 'Autour de Falcone, de Rosa et de Micco Spadaro: Quelques tableaux napolitains conservés dans les musées de province français', *Scritti di storia dell'arte in onore di Raffaello Causa* (Naples, 1988), pp. 195–202

ARNAULD BREJON DE LAVERGNÉE

Falcone [Falconi; Faldoni], **Bernardo** (*fl* 1659–94). Italian sculptor. He probably came from Lugano. By tracing his sculptures, it is possible to gain intermittent knowledge of his whereabouts. In 1659 he was in Venice, where he carved a *Virgin*, a *St Dominic* and a *St Thomas* for the high altar of SS Giovanni e Paolo. From 1664 to 1671 he was in Turin. He contributed to the sculptural decoration of the Palazzo Reale's park with a marble *Hercules* (?1699–71; Turin, Mus. Civ.), which originally formed part of a group (untraced), executed in collaboration with Bernardo

Paleari and Bernardino Quadri. The figure, 3.3 m high, is related stylistically to Falcone's contemporaneous *St Sebastian* (?1669; Venice, church of the Scalzi). An exaggerated musculature, typical of late Mannerist style, characterizes both. Falcone left Turin *c.* 1671 and by 1676 was again in Lugano, where he faced unsettled debts. Documents of 24 November 1676 and April 1677 record that officials there inventoried his possessions in this connection and the lists show that the artist was an eclectic collector of paintings, sculpture and diverse *objets d'art*. By 1682 he was in Padua, completing the signed and dated marble group of *SS Thomas and Matthew with Two Angels* (Padua, S Giustina). The final mention of Falcone occurred in 1694 when, with Siro Zanelli (*d* 1724), he created a colossal (23 m high) bronze statue of *St Carlo Borromeo* in the town of Arona. Begun originally in 1614, to a design by Grattarolo and Giovanni Battista Cerano ('il Crespi'), the image was destined to be part of an ambitious complex of chapels and statuary forming a sacromonte at Borromeo's birthplace, but it was never completed. Falcone and Zanelli altered certain of the original specifications, producing the towering, somewhat static figure that is the only remaining evidence of the ill-fated project.

BIBLIOGRAPHY
F. Bartoli: *Le pitture, sculture ed architetture della città di Rovigo* (Venice, 1743/*R* 1974)
'Arte ed artisti luganesi', *Boll. Svizzera It.*, xxi (1899), pp. 119–21
L. Mallé: *Le sculture del Museo d'Arte Antica* (Turin, 1965)
P. Cannon-Brookes: 'The Sacri Monti of Lombardy-Piedmont', *Connoisseur*, clxxxvi (1974), pp. 286–95

□

Falconet, Etienne-Maurice (*b* Paris, 1 Dec 1716; *d* Paris, 24 Jan 1791). French sculptor, designer and writer. He was one of the foremost French sculptors of the mid-18th century and is best known for his small-scale marble sculptures on gallant and allegorical themes, as well as for his widely reproduced models for the porcelain factory at Sèvres. From 1766 to 1778, however, he lived in Russia, and his most interesting work is the monumental bronze equestrian statue of *Peter the Great* that he designed for St Petersburg. Falconet was an autodidact of fiercely independent and moralistic spirit; he wrote a number of essays on the theory of art and left notable correspondences with the philosopher Denis Diderot and with Catherine the Great of Russia. He was made a professor at the Académie Royale in 1761. His son Pierre-Etienne Falconet (1741–91) was a minor draughtsman and engraver, whose most notable achievement was the illustrating of his father's article on sculpture for the *Encyclopédie* of Diderot.

1. Sculpture. 2. Writings.

1. SCULPTURE.

(i) Early career and commissions for the Bâtiments du Roi. Falconet was of humble origin; he entered the Paris studio of Jean-Baptiste Lemoyne (ii) at the age of 18 and remained there for almost 10 years. He never went to Italy, but in spite of this was profoundly influenced by Bernini and the Baroque. In 1744, seeking acceptance into the Académie Royale, he presented the group *Milo of Crotona* (marble; Paris, Louvre), but it was thought to be too like the famous work on the same theme by Pierre Puget. The following

year he was given a different subject, but it was on the strength of the *Milo* that he was eventually received (*reçu*) into the Académie in 1754. During this period Falconet worked to fill the gaps in his education, and no other sculptor of his time was to display such an inquiring mind. The inventory of his library shows the breadth and depth of his reading, much of which can be found more or less assimilated in his theoretical and polemical works (*see* §2 below).

The first commission Falconet received from the Bâtiments du Roi dates from 1748. It was for a marble, *France Embracing the Bust of Louis XV*, after a drawing by Charles-Antoine Coypel. Abandoned by Falconet, the work (Libourne, Hôtel de Ville) was not finished until 30 years later by Augustin Pajou. In 1750 Lenormant de Tournehem, Directeur des Bâtiments du Roi, commissioned a marble *Genius of Music*, the small model of which appeared at the Paris Salon of 1751. The statue (h. 2.08 m; Paris, Louvre), intended as a pendant to Lambert-Sigisbert Adam's *Lyric Poetry* in the entrance hall of the château of Bellevue, is an allegorical portrait of the *Marquise de Pompadour*. Falconet enjoyed further official patronage; in 1753 he was commissioned to execute *La Jardinière*, a stone statuette for the dairy at the château of Crécy, in 1758 the *Duck Shoot*, a plaster relief for the salon of the château of Saint-Hubert, and in 1759 a statue of *Minerva* for the gardens of the château of Choisy (all untraced or never executed). His last commission for the Bâtiments was in 1764, for a statue of *Winter* (St Petersburg, Gatchina Pal.), which was intended for the gardens of the Petit Trianon, Versailles, but was instead purchased by Catherine the Great.

(ii) Work for the Marquise de Pompadour; small models and groups. The Marquise de Pompadour was Falconet's greatest patron. In 1757 she appointed him as director of the sculpture studios at the porcelain factory at Sèvres, an office that he filled until his departure for Russia in 1766. During this period he either executed or supervised the making of about 100 models for statuettes or groups. These fall into two categories, original creations and works made from designs by FRANÇOIS BOUCHER. Of the figurines inspired by Boucher one series is devoted to trades, and a subsequent series, dating from several years later, is on the theme of the attractions of the fair. Several other loosely connected groups, also the result of collaboration with Boucher, were based on the fables of Jean de La Fontaine. The subjects attributable solely to Falconet are either those that are reductions of his marble statues or compositions specially designed for manufacture in biscuit. Some of these charming miniatures preserve the memory of statues that have been destroyed or have disappeared, such as *Erigone* or *Sweet Melancholy*; others are based on contemporary theatrical entertainments: there is a cycle of dances from the Opéra ballet, subjects from the comic operas of Charles-Simon Favart, and from the pastoral works of Jean François Marmontel; others illustrate the repertory of the Comédiens Italiens.

Falconet owed his greatest popularity to his small marble works, groups such as his *Venus and Cupid*, or figures such as his seated or crouching female *Bathers*, which were widely used for ornamenting clock cases. Initially these were produced in a number of versions in his studio, then imitated by commercial copyists during his lifetime and into the 19th and 20th centuries. He also provided models for some of the most famous goldsmiths of his time, including Thomas Germain, Robert-Joseph Auguste and the Roettier family. Furniture signed FALCONET is, however, the work of the *ébéniste* Louis Falconet.

(iii) Exhibits at the Paris Salon. During the same period of 1757 to 1765, Falconet exhibited regularly at the Paris Salon, where he showed a series of light-hearted works of which the best-known are the *Threatening Cupid* (see fig.) and the famous *Standing Bather* (both marble, exh. Salon 1757; Paris, Louvre), both of which gave rise to an extraordinary number of copies. At the Salon of 1763 Falconet showed the marble group of *Pygmalion at the Feet of his Statue* (Paris, Louvre), of which there are many marble replicas, as well as reduced versions in Sèvres biscuit. His 1765 exhibit, a relief of *Alexander Offering One of his Concubines to the Painter Apelles* (priv. col.) is, by contrast, a unique work.

(iv) Monumental and ecclesiastical works. Falconet executed a number of monumental works before leaving Paris for

Etienne-Maurice Falconet: *Threatening Cupid*, marble, h. 900 mm, 1757 (Paris, Musée du Louvre)

St Petersburg, including four tombs, although only that of *Mme La Live de Jully* (1754) is known, both from a drawing of the whole monument (Paris, Carnavalet) and from the dull marble portrait medallion that is all that survives *in situ* in St Roch, Paris. He also carved seven statues for the same church, but only *Christ in Agony*, the terracotta model for which was shown at the Salon of 1757, survives; its pose recalls that of Bernini's *St Teresa* (Rome, S Maria della Vittoria). Falconet was in the process of completing a model for a statue of *St Ambrose* for the Dôme des Invalides, Paris, when he left for Russia in 1766. Through Denis Diderot he was introduced to the Empress Catherine the Great, who commissioned from him a bronze equestrian statue in honour of *Peter the Great* in St Petersburg (Pl. Dekabristov; for illustration *see* EQUESTRIAN MONUMENT), an opportunity at last to give full scope to his talent. Initially much in favour with Catherine, Falconet saw his position gradually deteriorate, and he had to leave Russia before his work was unveiled in 1782. The originality of his conception—which combines a horse rearing on the summit of a steep rock with a hero represented as legislator rather than conqueror, eliminates any allegorical figure apart from the serpent of envy crushed beneath the horse's hoofs, and has an inscription of only four words—makes the statue striking in its grandeur and simplicity. The head of the statue was modelled by his pupil MARIE-ANNE COLLOT. Beside this masterly success the other works Falconet executed in St Petersburg seem of little importance. These were copies of his early works, the completion of roughed-out marbles, and the making of models for goldsmiths and the Imperial porcelain factory. His output came to an abrupt end after the statue of *Peter the Great*. He was completely taken up with the revision of his writings during a visit to The Hague, when a stroke deprived him of the use of his right side, and he was unable to take up his chisel again.

BIBLIOGRAPHY

L. Réau: *Etienne-Maurice Falconet*, 2 vols (Paris, 1922)
G. Levitine: *The Sculpture of Falconet* (New York, 1972) [with an Eng. trans. of Falconet's 'Réflexions sur la sculpture']

2. WRITINGS. All of Falconet's essays and some of his correspondence were published in his *Oeuvres complètes* in 1781. The earliest item, the 'Réflexions sur la sculpture' (1760), was written at the request of Diderot for the *Encyclopédie*. It espouses traditionally accepted academic standards. Falconet's most persistent ideas are set forth in essays such as the 'Observations sur la statue de Marc-Aurèle' and 'Quelques idées sur le beau dans l'art'. Volumes iii and iv of his *Oeuvres* are devoted to his translation of and commentary on the books of Pliny's *Natural History* that deal with painting and sculpture. Falconet claimed that Pliny was incompetent to discuss the visual arts, and he directed the same charge repeatedly throughout his writings against other critics and commentators on art, including Pausanias, Cicero, Shaftesbury, Winckelmann and Voltaire. He consistently expressed enmity towards any attempt to infringe on artists' autonomy and authority.

The polemical tone and haphazard organization of Falconet's ideas make many portions of the *Oeuvres complètes* difficult for the reader. Their contents were in fact largely inspired by a controversy between Falconet and Diderot. The latter claimed that even vanished works of art could achieve enduring glory if they had been praised by a writer. Falconet resentfully denied that a desire for the admiration of posterity motivates artists' production. This debate furnished the primary content for the Falconet–Diderot correspondence (1765–73), which contains some of the most important ideas of both men. Falconet also maintained an extensive correspondence (1767–78) with Catherine the Great. It deals with artistic, literary, philosophic, religious and political questions.

WRITINGS

Oeuvres complètes, 6 vols (Lausanne, 1781)
L. Réau, ed.: *Correspondance de Falconet avec Catherine II* (Paris, 1921)
Y. Benot, ed.: *Diderot et Falconet: Le Pour et le contre* (Paris, 1958) [corr. dealing with the dispute on posterity]

BIBLIOGRAPHY

H. Dieckmann and J. Seznec: 'The Horse of Marcus Aurelius', *J. Warb. & Court. Inst.*, xv (1952), pp. 198–228
A. B. Weinshenker: *Falconet: His Writings and his Friend Diderot* (Geneva, 1966)
Diderot et l'art de Boucher à David (exh. cat., ed. M.-C. Sahut and N. Volle; Paris, Hôtel de la Monnaie, 1984–5), pp. 448–54

□

Falconetto, Giovanni Maria (*b* Verona, 1468; *d* Padua, 1535). Italian painter and architect. He was one of the foremost painters working in the Renaissance style in Verona in the early 16th century and is notable for his employment of antique themes. His later architectural works are an important feature of the city of Padua. His work prepared the architectural climate for the large-scale shift of interest to antiquity, which reached a climax in the next generation of architects in northern Italy, especially in the work of Andrea Palladio.

1. Verona, before 1517. 2. Padua, 1517–35.

1. VERONA, BEFORE 1517. According to Vasari, Giovanni Maria Falconetto's father Jacopo Falconetto (1396–1472), also a painter, was his first teacher, although Michiel (more plausibly) named Melozzo da Forlì as his teacher. During a long stay in Rome, Falconetto seems to have come into close contact with Bernardino Pinturicchio. In his painted work northern Italian influences are mingled with central Italian and Roman elements from the late 15th century.

The earliest work securely attributed to Falconetto is the painting of the chapel of S Biagio (1497–99) in the church of S Nazaro, Verona. The two spandrels on the right wall are signed by Falconetto. Several other painters were involved in the decoration of the chapel, including Domenico Morone, Zuane Giacomo (*c*. 1444–1502), Francesco Morando, Paolo (Morando) Cavazzola and Girolamo Mocetto. The design for the decoration of the dome and drum of the chapel, and the painted architectural articulation, are probably by Falconetto. The painted pillars, architraves and coffered arches below the dome, the column-embellished drum and the dome itself make the chapel one of the most important works of Renaissance architecture in Verona. The details of the painted architecture and the figural decoration show that by this date Falconetto already had extensive knowledge of Roman architecture and sculpture. The frieze with Tritons and

1. Giovanni Maria Falconetto: *Augustus and the Sibyl*, tempera on panel, 1.52×1.53 m, ?*c.* 1509–17 (Verona, Museo Civico di Castelvecchio)

nereids, and other small chiaroscuro scenes, incorporate reliefs in an antique style, which Falconetto can have seen only in Rome. Vasari's statement that Falconetto spent 12 years in Rome in his youth would appear to be confirmed by such early work.

In 1498 Falconetto married Elena di Provalo, a weaver's daughter from Verona. In the early 1500s he produced further wall decoration in the form of painted architecture around two chapels, the Cappella Calcasoli and the Cappella Emilei in the southern aisle of Verona Cathedral. Falconetto made use of motifs from Roman triumphal arches, filling the painted niches and false architectural spaces with figures. Above the Cappella Calcasoli he incorporated on two tablets his signature and date in the manner of Roman inscriptions. This style of decoration had parallels in the local tradition of decorating chapels with sculptural or painted frames, evident in other chapels in the cathedral and those in the church of S Anastasia, Verona, but Falconetto's repertory of forms and proportions reveals an influence of Roman architecture greater than that of any other artist. For the cathedral at Trento, in collaboration with his brother Tommaso Falconetto, he painted in 1507–8 organ shutters depicting *SS Peter and Paul* when closed and the *Annunciation* when open (now in Trento, S Maria Maggiore). Here, too, Falconetto made numerous allusions to ancient Roman architecture.

In the following years Falconetto decorated several houses in Verona with frescoes. Those on the façade of the Casa Trevisani–Lonardi on the Vicolo S Marco in Foro are partly preserved and show numerous illusionistic reliefs painted in stone colour against a colourful background between painted pilasters and friezes. Almost all the illustrations can be traced back to Roman reliefs, such as those found on sarcophagi, on the Arch of Constantine

or Trajan's Column. Sacrificial and hunting scenes, illustrations of battles and triumphs, as well as such mythological scenes as the *Rape of Proserpine* and *Daedalus and Pasiphae*, were shown in the individual picture panels. The preference for Classical themes and images affected even the details of the decoration of the house. His paintings (destr.) at the Palazzo Sanbonifazj–Tedeschi in the Via Scala were equally fine. Falconetto also executed the frescoes on the Palazzo Franchini in the Via Emilei. Only parts of the frieze below the eaves have survived, revealing sacrificial, triumphal and cavalry scenes. The frieze in the Casa Vignola is a well-preserved example of his interior fresco style. It also incorporates copies and variations of ancient reliefs, repeated in laterally inverted form and grouped symmetrically around coats of arms.

During the occupation of Verona in 1509–17 by the troops of Maximilian I, the Holy Roman Emperor, Falconetto painted the east wall of the small church of S Giorgetto, of which only the lunette decoration has survived. The patrons were two counsellors of the Emperor, and they are both portrayed as donors. The lunette decoration depicts an allegory of the Annunciation. Many Marian themes, including the *Unicorn Hunt*, the *Hortus conclusus*, the *Porta clausa* and *Moses and the Burning Bush*, show that Falconetto must have had an exact model from northern Europe, where such pictures were widely disseminated. The closest parallels are to be found in a contemporary Swiss tapestry of the *Hortus conclusus* (Zurich, Schweiz. Landesmus.). Falconetto's panel picture from the church of Santa Trinità, depicting *Augustus and the Sibyl* (now Verona, Castelvecchio; see fig. 1), may also be from this period. The figures and setting are strongly influenced by Classical antiquity. Several architectural ruins in the painting can be joined together to form a *frons scenae*, which has parallels in contemporary theatre illustration. Falconetto omits a complete *frons scenae*, however, in favour of a 'perspective stage'. From this picture it is apparent that he had detailed knowledge of contemporary work on the Vitruvian and the modern perspective stage. This knowledge played an important part in his later works for Alvise Cornaro (*see* §2 below).

About 1515 the canons Francesco Maffei and Girolamo Maffei had a chapel built in Verona Cathedral, in which Falconetto painted a *Resurrection* in the upper lunette. He incorporated painted arcaded arches with *all'antica* coffers in the existing Gothic architecture. Vasari refers to the work in the Maffei chapel, adding that Falconetto himself recognized his limitations as a painter.

2. PADUA, 1517–35. As a supporter of the imperial party, Falconetto was forced to leave Verona in 1517 when the Venetians returned. According to Vasari, he first went to Trento, although no works by Falconetto from this period have been traced there. The frescoes in the Palazzo d'Arco in Mantua, however, were probably produced soon after 1517. Falconetto divided the four walls of a room (9.7×15.4 m) on the first floor into 12 compartments (one compartment destr. through the later addition of a fireplace). These display a broad spectrum of Classical allusions with rich architectural articulation and diverse figural scenes. The pictures show typical occupations of the calendar months along with the mythological stories of

the associated signs of the zodiac. For the figures Falconetto drew on ancient reliefs and statues, on such contemporary works as that by Andrea Riccio, and even on the graphic works of Lucas van Leyden. The chamber is one of the most important surviving frescoed rooms of the early 16th century in northern Italy, demonstrating more clearly than almost any other the predilection of the period for Classical themes and forms.

At the beginning of the 1520s Falconetto seems to have come to the notice of ALVISE CORNARO, who was in the process of transforming his house in Padua, with an extensive garden, into a splendid estate on the Classical pattern. Michiel relates that Falconetto painted the chapel and the staircase in Cornaro's house, which suggests that Falconetto first worked as a painter for Cornaro and became an architect in his circle at a later date. Falconetto's first architectural work in Padua was the loggia (1524; see fig. 2) in the courtyard of the Cornaro house (now the Palazzo Giustiniani). The architrave is inscribed and dated. The building originally had a single storey and served as a *frons scenae* at theatrical performances, for example of works by Angelo Beolco (called Ruzzante). It consists of five arcaded bays divided by Tuscan semi-columns, which support a richly decorated frieze. The central bay projects slightly and has carved figures of Victories in the spandrels. The upper storey is architecturally more reticent. The central and terminal bays have shallow, rectangular, pedimented niches, which frame statues of Classical figures, including Apollo, appropriate to the theatrical use of the loggia. A few years later the courtyard was extended by a further building—the so-called Odeo (1530)—which was built to Cornaro's own plans, although Falconetto, along with other artists, can be assumed to have been involved in the decoration, which includes lavish stucco and fresco work comparable to that in the Villa Madama, Rome.

Although in 1529 and 1531 Falconetto is mentioned in the registers and the estimates of Verona, works from this period cannot be traced there. In the same period in Padua he had a rich architectural output, including numerous civic buildings. The Porta S Giovanni is signed and dated 1528 and combines motifs of the Classical triumphal arch with the function of a city gate. The Porta Savonarola followed in 1530, making still greater use of Classical motifs. The ground-plan presents a variation on the Classical idea of an octagonal room with niches in the diagonal sides, as used in the Odeo Cornaro. On the outer façades there are stone tondi copied from analogous pieces on the Porta Aurea in Ravenna, showing busts of the *Four Seasons*.

About 1530 Falconetto was commissioned by the Consiglio of the city of Padua to reshape the upper floor of the Monte di Pietà on the Piazza del Duomo. Falconetto's articulation of the façade with pilasters, socles, window pediments and entablatures reveals an intensive study of Classical and contemporary Roman architecture. In the same year he was put in charge of work on the Loggia del Consiglio, which had been planned since 1496 and was built to a design by Annibale Magi da Bassano (*d* 1504). In 1531–2 the main entrance to the Palazzo del Capitanio, the seat of the Venetian governor on the Piazza dei Signori, Padua, was rebuilt to a design by Falconetto. It is an enlarged version of the central bay of the Loggia Cornaro,

2. Giovanni Maria Falconetto: loggia of the Cornaro house (now Palazzo Giustiniani), Padua, 1524

with the addition of paired Tuscan semi-columns. Instead of an antique frieze the architrave bears the inscription of the Doge of Venice, Andrea Gritti, and also the insignia of the two administrators Badoer and Moro, who represented Venice in Padua from 1531 to 1532. The entrance is thus a visible sign of Venetian sovereignty next door to the Loggia del Consiglio, in which the local Paduan assembly met. The portal recalls the form of the triumphal arch, while particular motifs, for example the double columns, allude to such Classical buildings as the Arch of the Sergius family at Pula. Falconetto's advice was also sought outside Padua in this period. In 1532 the Scuola Grande della Misericordia in Venice commissioned him to design a new building for the Scuola, planned since 1505 and already partly constructed. In 1533 Falconetto was commissioned to complete the Cappella del Santo in the Basilica di S Antonio, Padua. He designed a lavish stucco ceiling, based on Roman models and making particular use of motifs from the Domus Aurea.

Only a small part of Falconetto's undoubtedly large output of drawings has so far been identified. The inventory of his legacy of 9 January 1535 mentions a portfolio of preparatory drawings for paintings. In addition, some drawings are mentioned separately, probably the ones of ancient monuments (London, BM, inv. no. 1911–10–18–1, and Vienna, Albertina, inv. nos 13247–8). The numerous attributions of drawings to Falconetto by G. Zorzi cannot be substantiated. Of his designs for frescoes or panel paintings, only one of *St Peter* (Verona, Mus. Miniscalchi Erizzo) has survived. More numerous are the drawings that are reproductions or variations of ancient illustrations. Designs for tombs or altars are among the most interesting works, especially the careful design for a monument on which many bronze figures and reliefs were to be mounted (Paris, Louvre, RF 1075). Also from Falconetto's last years is the large design for an altar and tomb monument (Florence, Uffizi, UA2194), attributed to him by Burns (1980 exh. cat.; see *Palladio e Verona*).

BIBLIOGRAPHY

M. Michiel: *Notizia d'opere del disegno* (MS.; *c.* 1520–40); ed. P. Barocchi in *Scritte d'arte del cinquecento*, iii (Milan, 1977), pp. 2867–8

G. Vasari: *Vite* (1550, rev. 2/1568); ed. G. Milanesi (1878–85), v, pp. 318–26

G. Biadego: 'La cappella di S Biagio nella chiesa SS Nazaro e Celso di Verona', *Nuovo Archv. Ven.*, xi (1906), pp. 91–134

E. Lovarini: 'L'eredità di Gian Maria Falconetto', *Boll. Mus. Civ. Padova*, n. s., i (1925), pp. 122–32

G. Fiocco: 'Le architetture di Giovanni Maria Falconetto', *Dedalo*, xi (1931), pp. 1203–41

R. Brenzoni: 'Nuovi dati d'archivio su G. M. Falconetto, pittore e architetto, detto il Rosso da San Zeno e i due Ridolfi plasticatori', *Atti Ist. Ven. Sci., Lett. & A.*, ii (1953), pp. 269–95

R. Wyss: 'Vier Hortus-conclusus-Darstellungen im schweizerischen Landesmuseum', *Z. Schweiz. Altertknd.*, xx (1960), p. 113

T. Buddensieg: 'Die Ziege Amalthea von Riccio und Falconetto', *Jb. Berlin. Mus.*, v (1963), pp. 121–50

W. Wolters: 'Tiziano Minio als Stukkator im "Odeo Cornaro" zu Padua: Ein Beitrag zu Tiziano Minios Frühwerk: Der Anteil des Giovanni Maria Falconetto', *Pantheon*, xxi (1963), pp. 20–28, 222–30

G. Zorzi: 'Gli antichi archi veronesi nei disegni palladiani di Verona e di Londra attribuiti a G. M. Falconetto', *Atti & Mem. Accad. Agric., Sci. & Lett. Verona* (1965), pp. 169–91

——: 'Le filigrane dei disegni palladiani delle antichità e alcune attribuzioni a G. M. Falconetto', *Atti Ist. Ven. Sci., Lett. & A.*, (1964), pp. 303–42

G. Schweikhart: 'Studien zum Werk des Giovanni Maria Falconetto', *Boll. Mus. Civ. Padova*, lvii (1968), pp. 17–67

T. Buddensieg and G. Schweikhart: 'Falconetto als Zeichner', *Z. Kstgesch.*, xxxiii (1970), pp. 21–40

F. E. Keller: 'Alvise Cornaro zitiert die Villa des Marcus Terentius Varro in Cassino', *L'Arte*, xiv (1971), pp. 29–53

G. Schweikhart: *Fassadenmalerei in Verona: Vom 14. bis zum 20. Jahrhundert* (Munich, 1973), pp. 215–18

——: 'Giovanni Maria Falconetto', *Maestri della pittura veronese* (Verona, 1974), pp. 123–32

——: 'Antike Meerwesen in einem Fries der Casa Vignola in Verona: Ein unbekanntes Werk des Giovanni Maria Falconetto', *A. Ven.*, xxix (1975), pp. 127–33

P. Carpeggiani: 'Giovanni Maria Falconetto: Temi ed eventi di una nuova architettura civile', *Padova, case e palazzi*, ed. L. Puppi and F. Zuliani (Vicenza, 1977), pp. 71–99

L. Venier: 'Falconetto: Astrologia e cultura antiquaria', *Piranesi e la cultura antiquaria: Atti del convegno: Rome 1979*, pp. 111–21

Palladio e Verona (exh. cat. by P. Marini, Verona, 1980), p. 99

R. Signorini: 'Due fonti iconografiche di affreschi mantovani: La conversione di S Paolo di Luca di Leida e due dettagli della sala dello zodiaco in Palazzo d'Arco a Mantova', *Civiltà Mant.*, n. s. ii (1984), pp. 9–11

G. Schweikhart: 'Un artista veronese di fronte all'antico: Gli affreschi zodiacali del Falconetto a Mantova', *Roma e l'antico nell'arte e nella cultura del cinquecento*, ed. M. Fagiolo (Rome, 1985), pp. 461–88

P. Brugnoli: *La cattedrale di Verona nelle sue vicende edilizie dal secolo IV al secolo XVI* (Verona, 1987)

'La casa Trevisani-Lonardi', *Affreschi del rinascimento a Verona: Interventi di restauro*, ed. P. Brugnoli (Verona, 1987), pp. 15–53

R. Signorini: *Lo zodiaco di Palazzo d'Arco in Mantova* (Mantua, 1987)

GUNTER SCHWEIKHART

Falconi, Giovanni Battista (*fl c.* 1630–58). Italian stuccoist, active in Poland. Documentary evidence attributes only two decorative schemes to Falconi with any certainty: the Oświęcim Chapel (1647) in Krosno and the collegiate choir (*c.* 1647) in Klimontów. On the basis of stylistic analysis, however, at least 14 other schemes, mostly in southern Poland, can be ascribed to him and his workshop. His earliest works date from about 1630. These largely involve the decoration of cupolas, chapel vaulting and chambers in palaces. Only rarely did his stuccowork extend from the vaulting to the walls, and an example of rare scale and splendour was the early Baroque interior of the church of the Discalced Carmelites (1633–5; destr. *c.* 1939–44) in Wiśnicz Nowy. A document (13 Nov 1639; Warsaw, Cent. Archvs Hist. Rec.) admitting him to the group of royal craftsmen and artists records his marblework. At first Falconi worked for voivode Stanisław Lubomirski (*see* LUBOMIRSKI, (1)) and he subsequently worked for other leading magnates of the kingdom. Other projects included chapels in the Camaldulensian church at Bielany, Kraków, and the Jesuit church of SS Peter and Paul in Kraków (1630–33). Falconi's work is stylistically closest to the Mannerist Baroque art of Genoa and Milan. Balanced compositions included floral motifs, cartouches, shells, putti and festoons of fruit. Although these forms could have derived from Rome or Florence, they were always interpreted and arranged in a north Italian manner; some of them are particularly close to the stuccos of Giovanni Battista Serodine and indicate an early link between his studio, working in the region of Ascona and Locarno, and Falconi. As his career progressed, the forms of Falconi's stuccos became increasingly weighty and flowing, and his cartouches assumed the characteristics of pulpous shells. His last work was the decoration (1654–8) of the vast chapel of the Holy Cross in the Dominican church, Lublin, and here there are exceptionally large wall figures that are not of the highest artistic quality. Falconi was the most distinguished stuccoist working in Poland in the 17th century, his influence persisting to the 1680s. Work by his studio was also influential in the countries of the Habsburg empire.

BIBLIOGRAPHY

A. Bochnak: *Giovanni Battista Falconi* (Kraków, 1926)

J. Kowalczyk: 'Architektoniczno-rzeźbiarskie dzieło Falconiego w Lublinie' [Architectural-sculptural work by Falconi in Lublin], *Biul. Hist. Sztuki*, xxiv (1962), pp. 27–43

A. Miłobędzki: *Architektura polska XVII wieku* [Polish architecture of the 17th century] (Warsaw, 1980), pp. 219–21

M. Karpowicz: *Artisti ticinesi in Polonia nel '600* (Agno and Lugano, 1983), pp. 100–02

J. Gajewski: 'Falconi w Podkamieniu oraz jego dzieło architektoniczno-rzeźbiarskie' [Falconi at Podkamień and his architectural and sculptural work], *Ikonotheka*, v (1993), pp. 23–81

ADAM MIŁOBĘDZKI

Falconieri. Italian family of patrons and collectors. They were a distinguished Tuscan family, well established in Florence by the 13th century when SS Alessio and Giuliana Falconieri figured among the early promoters of the Servite Order, a mendicant order approved by the Pope in 1249. By the late 16th century, the Falconieri had established themselves in Rome, where they played a conspicuous role in the Tuscan community. The businessman Paolo di Pietro Falconieri (*b* 1538) subscribed in 1583 to the construction of S Giovanni dei Fiorentini, the Florentine national church in Rome, which was built under the supervision of Giacomo della Porta.

Three of Paolo di Pietro Falconieri's children were of particular dynastic importance: Lelio, Orazio and Pietro. Lelio (*d* 1648) was elected cardinal in 1643. (1) Orazio Falconieri made a fortune and initiated a series of ambitious projects that were to occupy his descendants for several generations.

Orazio's son Paolo Francesco (1626–96) was one of the most opulent figures in later 17th-century Rome. He continued his father's work on the family chapel in S Giovanni dei Fiorentini according to revised plans by Ciro Ferri and commissioned a scenographic high altar from the sculptor Antonio Raggi in the late 1660s. In these years, Paolo Francesco also began an extensive rebuilding of the Villa Falconieri (previously Villa Rufina) at Frascati after plans by Borromini and later commissioned frescoes there by Ciro Ferri and Carlo Maratti. He was an active collector and is considered the last great patron of Claude Lorrain, from whom he acquired four paintings between 1666 and 1673 (Roethlisberger, LV 166, 168, 180, 183). Paolo Francesco's son Cardinal Alessandro (d 1734) employed the architects Ferdinando Fuga and Niccolo Michetti at the family palace and villa, and embellished the latter with frescoes by Pier Leone Ghezzi.

Another influential if less affluent branch of the Falconieri family is represented by Ottavio (1636–75) and Paolo (1636–1704), who were sons of Pietro and grandsons of Paolo di Pietro. Monsignor Ottavio resided primarily in Rome, where he made an ecclesiastical career and figured prominently in scientific, literary and antiquarian circles. From the early 1660s he supervised Leopoldo de' Medici's collecting of Classical antiquities, particularly coins and engraved gems (see ROME, ANCIENT, §XI), and in 1674 was a founder-member of the Academy in Rome of Queen Christina of Sweden. Paolo divided his activities between Rome and the Medici court in Florence, where he enjoyed great authority in artistic matters. He played a decisive role in the early patronage of Grand Duke Cosimo III and during the 1670s and 1680s was a crucial link between artistic circles in Rome and Florence. Paolo was involved in the foundation of the Tuscan Academy in Rome (1673–86), promoted Cosimo's purchase in 1674 of Michelangelo's late *Pietà* (Florence Cathedral), assisted with the project for the reliquary chapel of S Maria Maddalena de' Pazzi in Florence (begun by Ciro Ferri in 1674) and helped to arrange the transfer of three celebrated Classical sculptures (*Venus de' Medici*, *Knife Sharpener* and *Wrestlers*) from the Villa Medici in Rome to the Uffizi in 1677. The Roman–Florentine line of the Falconieri family became extinct in 1865, when their holdings passed to the Princes of Carpegna.

BIBLIOGRAPHY
P. Portoghesi: 'L'opera del Borromini nel Palazzo della Villa Falconieri', *Quad. Ist. Stor. Archit.*, xiv (1956), pp. 7–20
L. Salerno, L. Spezzaferro and M. Tafuri: *Via Giulia* (Rome, 1973)
M. Roethlisberger: *Claude Lorrain: The Paintings*, i (New Haven, 1981)
E. Goldberg: *Patterns in Late Medici Art Patronage* (Princeton, 1983)
L. Giovannini, ed.: *Lettere di Ottavio Falconieri a Leopoldo de' Medici* (Florence, 1984)
EDWARD L. GOLDBERG

(1) Orazio Falconieri (*d* Rome, 15–17 Feb 1664). In the early 17th century he established his family's fortune in Rome, making his money as a collector of the salt tax. In 1646 he commissioned Borromini to rebuild the Palazzo Falconieri on the Via Giulia for himself and his brother Cardinal Lelio Falconieri. Borromini's falcon-herms on the façade are a reference to the family's heraldic bird; inside, many of the rooms are dominated by richly ornamented stucco ceilings, which give the impression of hovering domes that have temporarily alighted on the walls. Orazio also commissioned the Cappella Maggiore of the church of S Giovanni dei Fiorentini: begun in temporary materials by Pietro da Cortona in 1634, the scheme was altered by Borromini between 1656 and 1664; it was finished by Ciro Ferri for Orazio's son Paolo Francesco Falconieri in 1674. In the 1660s Orazio had the Villa Rufina at FRASCATI rebuilt and extended; although usually attributed to Borromini, the alterations bear none

of the hallmarks of his style and are probably the work of Ferri.

BIBLIOGRAPHY
A. M. Ferretti: *I fatti e le persone più illustri della famiglia Falconieri* (Rome, 1906)
C. A. Bertini: *La storia delle famiglie romane*, i (Rome, 1910), pp. 388–90
E. Rufini: *S Giovanni de' Fiorentini*, Chiese di Roma illustrate (Rome, 1957), pp. 65–8
K. Noehles: 'Architekturprojekte Cortonas', *Münch. Jb. Bild. Kst*, xx (1969), pp. 171–206
M. Tafuri and others: *Via Giulia: Una utopia urbanistica del 500* (Rome, 1973)
E. Howard: *The Falconieri Palace in Rome* (New York, 1981)
A. Blunt: *Guide to Baroque Rome* (London, 1982), pp. 51, 267
JOSEPH CONNORS

Falda, Giovanni Battista (*b* Valduggia, Novara, 7 Dec 1643; *d* Rome, 22 Aug 1678). Italian draughtsman and printmaker. Best known for architectural views, many of which celebrate Pope Alexander VII's role in the renovation of Rome, he contributed significantly to Rome's pre-eminence as a centre for this genre of print. While Florentine contemporaries such as Stefano della Bella employed delicately etched line and Giovanni Battista Galestruzzi and Ercole Bazzicaluva used the picturesque, formulaic landscape conventions of Remigio Cantagallina, Falda developed a more realistic style that greatly influenced Roman printmakers, from Giovanni Francesco Venturini and Alessandro Specchi to Giuseppe Vasi. Falda's training remains unknown but his etchings are distinguished by deeply bitten line and shadow in the manner of Jacques Callot and Israël Silvestre, and by accuracy in topographical and genre details. His catalogue of prints, greatly expanded from 80 (Bartsch) to 298 (Bellini), includes views of the buildings, gardens and fountains of Rome (the earliest dated 1655), detailed plans of Rome and representations of ceremonial events. Best known among his works are the *Giardini di Roma* (1670; B. pp. 329–49) and the *Fontane di Roma* (1675; B. pp. 278–328; *see* FRASCATI, figs 1 and 2).

BIBLIOGRAPHY
Thieme–Becker [with bibliog. to 1915]
A. von Bartsch: *Le Peintre-graveur* (1803–21) [B.]
H. Keller, ed.: *Das barocke Rom in Kupferstich-veduten* (Dortmund, 1979)
R. Assunto and A. Tagliolini: *Ville e giardini di Roma nelle incisioni di Giovan Battista Falda* (Milan, 1980)
P. Bellini: *Italian Masters of the Seventeenth Century*, 47 [xxi–xxii] of *The Illustrated Bartsch*, ed. W. Strauss (New York, 1983), pp. 274–373
——: 'Per una definizione dell'opera di G. Battista Falda', *A. Crist.*, lxxi/695 (1983), pp. 81–92
R. d'Amico: 'La veduta nell'incisione tra '600 e '700: G. B. Falda and G. Vasi', *Ric. Stor. A.*, 1–2 (1986), pp. 81–102
P. A. Wilson: *G. B. Falda's 'Il nuovo teatro' as an Urban and Political Document* (diss., Charlottesville, U. VA, 1993)
MILES L. CHAPPELL

Faldoni [Faldon], **Gianantonio** [Giovanni Antonio] (*b* Asolo, Treviso, 24 April 1689; *d* ?Rome, *c*. 1770). Italian engraver. He moved to Venice at the beginning of the 18th century and in 1723 engraved a portrait of the procurator *Giovanni Emo* (see 1941 exh. cat., no. 27). Between 1724 and 1735 he engraved a series of the elder Anton Maria Zanetti's copies of drawings by Parmigianino. As a youth he had visited Paris and come to know the prints of Claude Mellan, whose technique of selectively emphasized parallel lines he imitated. From 1726 Faldoni engraved a large number of plates for the sumptuous two-volume publication entitled *Delle antiche statue greche e romane*, published in Venice (1740–43) by the Zanetti cousins. His irascible character caused him to be involved in numerous violent incidents and in 1765 he was banned from the territories of the Venetian Republic. An engraver of impeccable quality, he produced some outstanding portraits of famous artists, including *Marco Ricci* (see 1983 exh. cat., no. 180) and *Anton Maria Zanetti the elder* (1983 exh. cat., no. 178), both after Rosalba Carriera, *Sebastiano Ricci* (see Daniels, fig. 103), from a self-portrait, and *Luca Carlevaris* (1983 exh. cat., no. 179), after Bartolomeo Nazari (1699–1758). Faldoni also engraved religious subjects after Giuseppe Camerata I, Sebastiano Ricci, Palma Giovane and Stefano Pozzi, three portraits of Jesuit priests and a picture entitled *Holiday* (*c.* 1748; see 1983 exh. cat., no. 181), derived from a lost painting by Pietro Longhi (ii). With Marco Alvise Pitteri, he was one of the best reproductive engravers working in 18th-century Venice.

BIBLIOGRAPHY

C. Le Blanc: *Manuel de l'amateur d'estampes* (Paris, 1854–90), ii, p. 217
G. Moschini: *Dell'incisione in Venezia* (Venice, 1924), pp. 88–90
R. Gallo: 'L'incisione nel '700 a Venezia e a Bassano', *Ateneo Ven.*, v–vii (1941), pp. 153–214
Mostra degli incisori veneti del settecento (exh. cat., ed. R. Pallucchini; Venice, 1941)
L. Comacchio: *Giovanni Antonio Faldoni incisore asolano* (Castelfranco Veneto, 1976)
J. Daniels: *Sebastiano Ricci* (Hove, 1976)
Da Carlevarijs ai Tiepolo: Incisori veneti e friulani del settecento (exh. cat. by D. Succi, Venice, Correr; Gorizia, Mus. Prov. Pal. Attems; 1983), pp. 161–5

DARIO SUCCI

Falerii. *See* CIVITA CASTELLANA.

Falguière, Alexandre (*b* Toulouse, 7 Sept 1831; *d* Paris, 19 April 1900). French sculptor and painter. His father, a cabinetmaker, sent him in 1844 to the Ecole des Beaux-Arts in Toulouse, where he won the city's major prize and was awarded a grant to study at the Ecole des Beaux-Arts in Paris. There he was François Jouffroy's pupil but considered himself a follower of François Rude. In order to have enough to live on while studying, he also worked for Albert-Ernst Carrier-Belleuse and Jean-Louis Chenillion (1810–78). In 1859 he was joint winner with Léon Cugnot (1835–94) of the Prix de Rome, for the bas-relief of the *Wounded Mezentius aided by his Son Lausus* (plaster, Paris, Ecole N. Sup. B.-A.). While studying at the Académie de France in Rome, he came under the influence of his fellow student Jean-Baptiste Carpeaux. He remained in Italy until 1865.

The spontaneity of Falguière's approach to composition, and his handling of materials, were in tune with the official taste of the period; in spite of protests from the Académie Impériale about an excess of 'realism' in his works, the sculptures he sent to Paris were readily purchased by the State. They included the *Winner of the Cockfight* (bronze, exh. Salon 1864; Paris, Mus. d'Orsay); *Nuccia the Trasteverine Girl* (bronze, 1864; untraced); and *Omphale* (marble, exh. Salon 1866; Paris, Min. Indust., garden). This last work initiated the magnificent series of female figures with mythological names but modern bodies, such as *Eve* (marble, 1880; Copenhagen, Ny Carlsberg Glyp.), *Diana* (1887) and *Hunting Nymph*

(1888; both marble, Toulouse, Mus. Augustins). At the same time he continued the Salon tradition of slender youths in his recumbent figure of the Christian martyr *Tarcisius*; its plaster version was awarded a medal at the 1867 Salon, and the marble version (Paris, Mus. d'Orsay) was awarded the medal of honour at the 1868 Salon.

Falguière worked fast; thus in December 1870 he modelled in snow a statue of *Resistance* on the ramparts of Paris while the city was being besieged by the Prussians (bronze cast of later sketch model, Los Angeles, CA, Co. Mus. A.). He subsequently received the Légion d'honneur and other official honours, being appointed a professor at the Ecole des Beaux-Arts in 1882 and being elected that same year to the Académie des Beaux-Arts. He always completed his commissions punctually and exhibited regularly from 1857 to 1899. He was immensely popular and prolific (with the help of five workshops), and his work was to be seen everywhere, in public and private sites.

Among Falguière's many sculptures for public buildings, to which his spirited, neo-Baroque style was well suited, were the statue *Drama* (stone, 1869; Paris, Opéra); the group the *Seine and its Tributaries* (plaster, 1878; Paris, Pal. Trocadero, destr.); the great quadriga group the *Triumph of the Revolution* (plaster, 1882; Paris, Arc de Triomphe de l'Etoile, destr. 1886; wax maquette, Paris, Mus. d'Orsay); the statue *Heroic Poetry* (marble, 1893; Toulouse, Capitole); and the huge and ambitious *Monument to the French Revolution* (plaster, 1890–1900; Paris, Panthéon, destr.). He produced other allegorical monuments, not linked with buildings, as well as providing many of the monuments to great Frenchmen past and present set up by the Third Republic as part of its programme of public education. These included the monuments to *Alphonse de Lamartine* (bronze, 1877; Macon, Promenade du Sud); *Pierre Corneille* (marble, 1878; Paris, Comédie-Française); and *Ambroise Thomas* (marble, 1900; Paris, Parc Monceau). What might have been among his most attractive works in this vein, the monument to *Claude Lorrain*, intended for Nancy, never got beyond the stage of a sketch model (plaster, 1886–9; Nancy, Mus. B.-A.). Falguière also executed a certain amount of religious sculpture, but this is on the whole less successful than his secular monuments or even his monuments to churchmen, for example that to *Dom Calmet* at Senones (stone, red granite and black marble, 1873; Senones, St Pierre–St Gaudelbert).

Falguière was a productive and accomplished portraitist. Among his numerous busts was that of the painter *Carolus-Duran* (bronze, 1876, untraced) and of the actress *Marie Heilbron* (bronze, 1851–86; Paris, Montparnasse cemetery, funerary chapel of Marie Heilbron). He also produced a number of paintings and, though this was a secondary activity, he enjoyed considerable contemporary success with them. Some, such as *Cain and Abel* (1876; Carcassonne, Mus. B.-A.), reflected sculptural themes being explored at the same time. Others, such as *Begging Dwarfs, Souvenir of Granada* (1888; untraced), were independent productions and underline his predilection for 17th-century Spanish painting.

Falguière was one of the most successful and productive sculptors of the late 19th century in France, his salon exhibits being widely reproduced in bronze by the founders Thiebaut Frères, Fumière & Gavignot; in 1898 he had his one-man exhibition at the Nouveau Cirque, Paris. His robust style combined elements of fleshy realism with neo-Baroque verve of composition, and he found many imitators, particularly among those of his pupils who came from south-western France and were known as 'les Toulousains'; they included Paul Gasq, Laurent Marqueste (1848–1920), Antonin Mercié, Denys Puech and Felix Soulés.

Lami

BIBLIOGRAPHY
G. Barbezieux: 'L'Art au Panthéon', *La Paix* (20 Aug 1897)
La Plume (1 June 1898) [issue pubd. at the time of Falguière's exh.]
A. Pingeot: 'Le Fonds d'atelier Falguière au Musée du Louvre', *Bull. Soc. Hist. A. Fr.* (1978), pp. 263–90
The Romantics to Rodin: French Nineteenth-century Sculpture from North American Collections (exh. cat., ed. P. Fusco and H. W. Janson; Los Angeles, CA, Co. Mus. A.; Minneapolis, MN, Inst. A.; Detroit, MI, Inst. A.; Indianapolis, IN, Mus. A.; 1980–81)
M. Scuitti: *L'Oeuvre sculptée de Falguière à Toulouse* (diss., U. Toulouse II, 1985)
Les 'Toulousains': Plâtres originaux et sculptures du XIXe siècle (exh. cat., ed. D. Milhau; Toulouse, Mus. Augustins, 1992), pp. 22–30

ANNE PINGEOT

Falier, Antonio [Antonio da Negroponte] (*fl* Venice, second half of the 15th century). Painter of Greek origin, active in Italy. In a document of 3 March 1469, Jacopo Bellini nominated his attorney, Alvise Sagundino, Chancellor of the captain of the Venetian fleet, to recover money owed to him by 'Antonio Falirio, painter, resident of Negroponte', threatening the latter with legal proceedings if he failed to pay. Jacopo's death (1470–71) and the fall of Negroponte to the Turks in 1470 make it likely that no further action was taken. Two other documents, one a Venetian missive sent to Crete that mentions a 'frate Antonio da Negroponte' (7 June 1497) and the other a will made by Antonio da Negroponte in Venice (24 July 1449), presumably refer to the same person.

It seems possible to identify this painter with the author of an altarpiece of the *Virgin and Child Enthroned with Angels* painted for the Morosini chapel in S Francesco della Vigna, Venice (*in situ*) and signed *Frater Antonius de Nigroponto pincsit*. It is a bizarre painting, combining highly decorative Gothic elements derived from Pisanello and Jacopo Bellini with Renaissance elements derived from Antonio Vivarini and Squarcione's Paduan school. The former include carefully painted birds, flowers and fruit, while the latter is evident in the elaborate canopied throne decorated with fictive relief panels. The composition may have influenced Bartolomeo Vivarini's *Virgin and Child Enthroned with SS Augustine, Roch, Louis of Toulouse and Nicholas of Bari* (Naples, Capodimonte), dated 1465, and consequently Antonio's altarpiece has been tentatively dated slightly earlier. It is his only known work.

BIBLIOGRAPHY
DBI; *Enc. It*: 'Antonio da Negroponte'
B. Cecchetti: 'Saggio di cognomi ed autografi di artisti in Venezia: Secc. XIV–XVII', *Ateneo Veneto*, 17 (1887), p. 209
P. Paoletti: *Raccolta di documenti inediti per servire alla storia della pittura veneziana nei secoli XV e XVI*, i: *I Bellini* (Padua, 1894), pp. 10–11
L. Venturi: *Le origini della pittura veneziana, 1300–1500* (Venice, 1907), pp. 94–7
L. Testi: *Storia della pittura veneziana*, ii: *Il divenire* (Bergamo, 1915), pp. 547–51

M. Cattapan: 'Nuovi documenti riguardanti pittori cretesi dal 1300 al 1500', *Atti del 2° convegno internazionale di studi cretesi: Athens, 1968*, iii, pp. 35–6
E. Merkel: 'Una ricerca per frate Antonio Falier da Negroponte, pittore girovago', *Quad. Sopr. Beni A. & Stor. Venezia*, 7 (1979), pp. 45–56

ETTORE MERKEL

Falize, Lucien (*b* Paris, 4 Aug 1839; *d* Paris, 4 Sept 1897). French jeweller. He was the son of the jeweller Alexis Falize (1811–98) and received his training (1856–71) in his father's firm. His early work was influenced by East Asian art, which he saw at the International Exhibition of 1862 in London and at the Exposition Universelle of 1867 in Paris. About 1867 the firm began to produce cloisonné-enamelled jewellery in the Japanese manner, which was made in collaboration with Antoine Tard (*fl c.* 1860–*c.* 1889). It cannot be determined how much of this work was by Falize, even with marked pieces, as both jewellers used the firm mark AF, with a fusee hook in a lozenge. In 1875 the symbol was changed to a cross of St Andrew. In 1878 Falize exhibited an eclectic range of work in his own name for the first time: wares included silver statues, clocks, Japanese-inspired jewellery enamelled by Tard and jewellery in the Renaissance Revival style. From 1880 to 1892 he was in partnership with Germain Bapst (1853–1921). Their mark, BF, accompanied by a ring with a pearl, was not registered until 1892 but was used during this period, sometimes as a decorative device. Falize made extensive use of historical, chiefly Renaissance, traditions and incorporated architectural and sculptural elements, as well as different enamelling techniques, into his designs. He made frequent use of calligraphy in his designs, especially his bracelets, which are compositionally formal and complex and are notable for the clarity and vividness of enamelling and contrast between colour and texture. Among his many collaborators were Emmanuel Fremiet and Albert-Ernest Carrier-Belleuse. Falize's last major work was the Hanap de la Vigne et des Métiers (1896; Paris, Mus. A. Déc.), an enamelled gold goblet in which Renaissance and more naturalistic styles were combined. Falize also contributed articles on Japanese art and on his own work to contemporary journals.

WRITINGS
M. Josse [L. Falize]: 'L'Art japonais', *Rev. A. Déc.*, iii (1882–3), pp. 329–38, 353–63
'Une Conférence sur les bijoux', *Rev. A. Déc.*, vi (1885–6), pp. 342–50, 367–78
'Exposition universelle de 1889: Orfèvrerie et bijouterie', *Rev. A. Déc.*, x (1889–90), pp. 1–12
BIBLIOGRAPHY
K. Purcell: 'Falize', *The Master Jewelers*, ed. A. K. Snowman (New York, 1990), pp. 61–76

CLARE LE CORBEILLER

Falk, Jeremij. *See* FALCK, JEREMIAS.

Fal'k, Robert (Rafailovich) (*b* Moscow, 8 Nov 1886; *d* Moscow, 1 Oct 1958). Russian painter. He studied under Konstantin Yuon and in the studio of Il'ya Mashkov (1904–5), then at the Moscow School of Painting, Sculpture and Architecture under Valentin Serov and Konstantin Korovin. In 1909 he exhibited with Golden Fleece and in 1910 was a founder-member of the avant-garde exhibiting society, the JACK OF DIAMONDS, of which he remained an active member until its dissolution in 1916.

Fal'k was well known for his portraits and still-lifes of this period. His elongated seated figures of 1913 reveal a study of Cézanne, while the portraits and still-lifes of 1914 betray the influence of Picasso's early Cubist work. The *Portrait of the Tatar Journalist Midkhata Refatov* (1915; Moscow, Tret'yakov Gal.) shows his mature style in the Cubist idiom.

After the 1917 Revolution, Fal'k taught painting at Svomas (Free Art Studios) (1918–20) and Vkhutemas (Higher Artistic and Technical Workshops) (1920–28). He participated in many exhibitions at home and abroad including the Erste Russische Ausstellung in Berlin, 1922, and the Exposition Internationale des Arts Décoratifs in Paris, 1925. At this time he eschewed the Cubism of earlier years and specialized in intimate portraits painted in subdued colours with subtle lighting effects.

During the years 1928–38 Fal'k lived and worked in Paris. His brushwork became more vivacious, and portraits such as *The Cook* (1932; St Petersburg, A. F. Chudnovsky priv. col., see Sarabjanow, 1974, pl. 59) are reminiscent of the work of Chaïm Soutine. His last years in Moscow were devoted to teaching and to the painting of wistful portraits, evocative landscapes and mysterious still-lifes.

R. R. Fal'k: *Besedy ob iskusstve, pis'ma, vospominaniya o khudozhnike* [Talks on art, letters, reminiscences about the artist], ed. A. V. Shchekin-Krotova (Moscow, 1981)

D. Sarab'yanov: 'Zhivopis' Fal'ka' [The painting of Fal'k], *Tvorchestvo* [Creative Work], ii (1967), pp. 2–17
——: 'Stanovlenie Fal'ka' [The development of Fal'k], *Russkaya zhivopis' kontsa 1900–kh nachala 1910–kh godov: Ocherki* [Russian painting of the end of the first and the beginning of the second decade of the 20th century: essays] (Moscow, 1971), pp. 117–39
D. Sarabjanow: *Robert Falk* (Dresden, 1974)

ANTHONY PARTON

Falke, Jakob von (*b* Ratzeburg, Schleswig-Holstein, 12 June 1825; *d* Lovrana [now in Croatia], 8 June 1897). German writer and art historian. He studied Classical philology at the universities of Erlangen and Göttingen. In 1855 he joined the staff of the Germanisches Nationalmuseum in Nuremberg and in 1858 entered the service of the Princes of Liechtenstein as archivist and director of their art collections in Vienna. In 1860 he published a study of contemporary design, *Das Kunstgewerbe*, basing his theories on those current in Henry Cole's circle in England and published in Cole's *Journal of Design and Manufactures*. He made contact with the art historian Rudolf von Eitelberger-Edelburg (1817–85) and together they were responsible for the foundation in 1864 of the Kaiserliches Königliches Österreichisches Museum für Kunst und Industrie (now Österreiches Museum für Angewandte Kunst) in Vienna, modelled on the South Kensington Museum (now Victoria and Albert Museum) in London. This was the first museum of applied arts in continental Europe; Eitelberger-Edelburg was its first director and was succeeded (1885–95) by Falke. Writing at the same time as Gottfried Semper, he developed in such works as *Geschichte des modernen Geschmacks* (1866) and *Aesthetik des Kunstgewerbes* (1883) his own aesthetic of applied art, building on Georg Wilhelm Friedrich Hegel's ideas in establishing the principle of standards in design. In *Die Kunst im Hause* (1871) he propounded this principle to a general readership (as Charles Locke Eastlake had propounded his in 1868 in *Hints on Household Taste*). It was the first book of this kind on interior decoration to be published in German. Concerned not only with reform in the applied arts, Falke also wrote on garden history and the history of dress.

Das Kunstgewerbe (Vienna, 1860)
Geschichte des modernen Geschmacks (Leipzig, 1866)
Die Kunst im Hause (Vienna, 1871)
Aesthetik des Kunstgewerbes (Stuttgart, 1883)
Lebenserinnerungen (Leipzig, 1897)

E. B. Ottillinger: 'Konzept eines "zeitgenössischen" Möbels im Wiener Historismus', *Österreich Z. Dkmlpf.*, xli (1987), pp. 32–40
——: 'Jakob von Falke (1825–1897) und die Theorie des Kunstgewerbes', *Wien. Jb. Kstgesch.*, xlii (1989), pp. 205–23

EVA B. OTTILLINGER

Falkenstein, Claire (*b* Coos Bay, OR, 1909). American sculptor and painter. She studied at the University of California, Berkeley, gaining a degree in Letters and Science, and then taught at Mills College, Oakland, CA, and at the California College of Fine Arts in San Francisco until 1950. Initially she was interested in painting, producing works influenced by Cubism and Constructivism, but *c*. 1942 she began to devote herself to sculpture. Her sculptures of the 1940s are mainly in wood, often painted, in abstract or in simplified figurative forms as in *Polychrome Set Structure* (1942; New York, Guggenheim). After turning to more organic forms in the late 1940s, in 1950 she went to Paris to work and travel around Europe.

While in Paris, Falkenstein abandoned wood and began to use metal wire to build up her sculptures. The first of these was the *Sign of Leda* (1953; Paris, M. Tapié priv. col., see 1957 exh. cat.), followed by the series of *Sun* sculptures, again built up from metal wire. In 1957 she produced a portal for Princess Pignatelli at her villa in Santa Marinella near Rome, and in 1962 she designed a set of gates for Peggy Guggenheim's Palazzo Venier dei Leoni in Venice. She moved to Los Angeles in 1963 and in the 1960s and early 1970s made a number of fountains from an open construction of copper tubes, as in *Structure and Flow No. 3* (1970; Long Beach, CA, Mus. A.). After her stay in Paris she made increasing use of fused glass in her sculptures, as in *Yellow Fusion* (1978; see 1989 exh. cat., p. 20). In the 1970s she created a number of sculptures using stainless-steel constructions suspended in a metal frame, as in *Rolling* (1976–7; see 1989 exh. cat., p. 27). Among her various public commissions were the three-dimensional window-screens (1979) for St Basil's Cathedral, Los Angeles.

Claire Falkenstein (exh. cat. by M. Tapié and K. B. Sawyer, Paris, Rodolphe Stadler, 1957)
Claire Falkenstein (exh. cat. by A. Temko, Palm Springs, CA, Desert Mus., 1980)
Claire Falkenstein (exh. cat. by M. Henderson, Los Angeles, CA, Jack Rutberg F.A., 1989) □

Falknov [Ger. Falkenau]. Czech centre of glass production. In 1530 a glass factory was established by Paul Schürer (1504–94) of Aschberg, and during the 16th and

17th centuries it was one of the most important glassworks in Bohemia. It was evidently associated with the beginnings of enamel decoration, because as early as 1562 it was commissioned to supply enamelled glass to the Imperial Vice-Regent in Prague, Archduke Ferdinand of Tyrol. At the end of the 16th century and beginning of the 17th it supplied glass to the Imperial court. One of the glassworks' products is a tankard decorated in enamel depicting the Virgin Mary (1647; Prague, Mus. Dec. A.). In the second half of the 16th century glass painters began to concentrate in the area around the Falkenau works and were joined in the last quarter of the 17th century by glass engravers, who since 1683 had been associated with the guild of painters and glass engravers at Polevsko. In 1732 the works were sold to Johann Josef Kittel of Polevsko, and in 1748 his son Johann Anton Kittel transferred them elsewhere, but subsequently production ceased for lack of wood. During the second half of the 19th century new coal-fired glassworks were started but later ceased production.

BIBLIOGRAPHY

E. Schebek: *Böhmens Glasindustrie und Glashandel: Quellen zu ihrer Geschichte* (Prague, 1878)

K. R. Fischer: *Die Schürer von Waldheim* (Prague, 1924)

O. DRAHOTOVÁ

Falla, Julián (*b* Guatemala City, 4 Sept 1787; *d* Guatemala City, 22 March 1867). Guatemalan painter and printmaker. He was a pupil of the Guatemalan painter Juan José Rosales (1751–1816) and of Pedro Garci-Aguirre. He studied in the Escuela de Dibujo of the Sociedad de Amigos del País in Guatemala City, and he later taught there for more than 45 years; his role in training many artists was perhaps his greatest contribution. One of the first etchers and lithographers in Guatemala, in 1834 he was in charge of the lithographic reproduction of views of the indigenous ruins of Iximché and Utatlán published as illustrations (each 115×175 mm) in the *Atlas geográfico del Estado de Guatemala* (1835).

In 1835 Falla and other artists were commissioned to produce a collection of model drawings for the Academia de Estudios. In the same year he received a Guatemalan government award for one of his etchings and a commission for a portrait of General Francisco Morazán, the president of the Federation of Central America. Most of his pictures, almost all of them portraits, have been lost, but the quality of his brushwork and Neo-classical style can be appreciated in his portrait of *Canon José María Castilla* (oil on canvas, 612×501 mm, 1845; Guatemala City, Acad. Geog. & Hist.).

BIBLIOGRAPHY

R. Toledo P.: 'Julián Falla (1787–1867), maestro e impulsor de la pintura en Guatemala', *El Imparcial* (21 March 1967)

E. Núñez de Rodas: *El grabado en Guatemala* (Guatemala City, 1970), pp. 77–8

JORGE LUJÁN-MUÑOZ

Falloppi, Giovanni di Pietro. *See* GIOVANNI DA MODENA.

Falque, Jeremij. *See* FALCK, JEREMIAS.

Faltz [Falz], **Raimund** [Raymund] (*b* Stockholm, 4 July 1658; *d* Berlin, 21 May 1703). Swedish medallist, wax-modeller, sculptor and miniature painter, also active in France and Germany. From 1674 to 1678 he trained in Stockholm under his father, a German immigrant goldsmith. For three years from 1680 he travelled around Europe, finally settling in Paris, where he entered the studio of Charles-Jean-François Chéron before establishing his own workshop. In Paris he took part in producing Louis XIV's *histoire médallique* and received from the King an annual stipend of 1200 livres. After leaving France for Sweden in 1688 he produced medals for Karl XI (*reg* 1660–97) and Queen Ulrica (1656–93). In 1690 Faltz entered the service of Frederick III, Elector of Brandenburg (later Frederick I of Prussia) and settled in Berlin for the rest of his career, producing a large number of medals for the Prussian court.

The hard-edged medallic style of Faltz's French period became softer in his later works, with the increased use of wax models; the effect is notable in such works as the portrait medals of *Aurora von Königsmarck* (*c.* 1690) or the reverse of the medal of *Queen Sophia Charlotta of Brandenburg* (1693), which depicts her seated with a putto. Faltz's technique was greatly admired. He also executed ivory-carvings, miniature paintings and silverpoint drawings (all untraced), as well as making a collection of medals. After his death his collection of wax models was donated to the Münzkabinett in Berlin. His tomb in the Petrikirche, Berlin (damaged 1730) was designed by Balthasar Permoser.

BIBLIOGRAPHY

Forrer; *SVKL*; Thieme–Becker

C. Theuerkauff: 'Raimund Faltz (1658–1703): Wachsbossierer und Medailleur des Kürfursten von Brandenburg und Königs von Preussen in Berlin', *Kst & Ant.*, i (1984), pp. 34–44

——: *Die Bildwerke in Elfenbein des 16.–19. Jahrhunderts*, ii (Berlin, 1986), pp. 78–116

ANTONIA BOSTRÖM

Famagusta [Gr. Ammochostos; Turk. Magosa]. City and port on the east coast of Cyprus.

1. HISTORY AND URBAN DEVELOPMENT. Although there is evidence of Roman occupation, Famagusta became important only after the sack of Salamis in AD 848. It was the seat of an Orthodox bishop, and under the Lusignans from 1192 it was also a diocese of the Latin Church, the two cathedrals existing side by side. The harbour began to flourish after the fall of Acre in 1291, and the city's most prosperous period was from then until the late 14th century; the ruins of many late medieval churches survive inside the walls. Famagusta was occupied by the Genoese from 1372 to 1464, and by the Venetians from 1469 until the Turkish siege of 1570–71. The Venetians rebuilt the Lusignan walls on a vast scale, with 15 bastions, land and sea gates and the citadel beside the harbour. The symbol of Venice, a lion sculpted in relief, survives over the entrance. Before the Turkish invasion of Cyprus in 1974, the old city, contained within the walls, was exclusively occupied by Turks, the modern Greek suburb (Varosha) lying to the south. Of the churches, the most prominent ruins are those of SS Peter and Paul and the Orthodox cathedral, St George of the Greeks, a large

14th-century structure alongside its diminutive predecessor (for illustration *see* CYPRUS, fig. 26). The Latin cathedral was preserved as the main mosque; it introduced a new, Late Gothic style of architecture that strongly influenced not only other buildings in Famagusta but also became the basis of late medieval architecture throughout Cyprus.

2. CATHEDRAL [now Lala Mustafa Mosque]. Former Latin cathedral of St Nicholas. Once part of a group of buildings, including the Bishop's Palace, the medieval cathedral faced the Royal Palace across a square in the centre of the city. It was built from *c.* 1300 and was used as the coronation church of the Lusignan rulers in their role as kings of Jerusalem.

An inscription placed near the south door in 1311 by Bishop Baldwin states that three bays of the aisles had been vaulted, but that the nave was yet to be roofed in. The homogeneity of the work suggests that if there was a delay in building it was not a long one, but the next documentary reference to the cathedral is to the coronation there of the Lusignan King Peter II in 1360. The building was damaged by earthquakes in 1546 and 1568 and badly holed by the Turkish bombardment of 1572, after which it was converted to a mosque, and its stained glass and interior fittings were stripped out. A major restoration was carried out by G. Jeffery in 1908, but the modern rebuilding, mostly on the south side, is easily distinguishable from the original, and the bulk of the medieval building remains intact.

The style closely reflects the Rayonnant developments in France and the Rhineland of the late 13th century and early 14th. The cathedral is built of limestone and has three parallel apses at the east, seven straight bays and no

Famagusta, former cathedral of St Nicholas (now Lala Mustafa Mosque), view from the east, first half of the 14th century

transept. The church is *c.* 36 m long internally and is vaulted throughout in quadripartite rib vaults. There are north and south doors in the fourth straight bay and three west doors set into a two-tower façade; the towers rise only one storey above the flat roof and were probably never intended to go higher. The north-west minaret was rebuilt by Jeffery. Chapels were added to the north and south sides.

The cathedral has a two-storey elevation, a columnar arcade with moulded capitals and bases and a clerestory of four-light, traceried windows. The vault shafts rise from the abaci of the capitals. The aisle windows also have four lights. The central apse has two levels of windows and a traceried piscina in the lower wall. The vault and arch mouldings are simple, but light and slender.

The decoration of the cathedral is concentrated on the exterior, with sufficient traces to reconstruct the original appearance. The window tracery, comprising oculi and pointed foil shapes, some double-cusped, is identical in style and position on the building to the cathedrals of Amiens and Cologne; other details suggest that the Rhineland, rather than France, was the main stylistic source. A jutting walkway encircles the main apse between the upper and lower windows. Throughout the building the clerestory was enriched with foliage ornament and surmounted by crocketed gables, each containing a circle of florid leaves. Moulded pinnacles rose between the gables, and the interstices were filled by an openwork parapet (see fig.). The south door, which was a ceremonial entrance, has three orders of continuous mouldings enframed in a foliate arch with a traceried gable above, and enriched variations on this theme are found on the west front. The traceried gables over the three west doors overlap the windows above, which are set back behind a narrow gallery or passage, fronted by an openwork parapet. Crocketed gables, pinnacles, foliate arches and cornices combine with the tracery to give an air of elaboration. The outer doors have continuously moulded jambs; the central door has embrasures for statues. The tympana are glazed and traceried.

The ground plan without a transept and the columnar arcade are typical of Lusignan Cyprus, but other details show that Famagusta Cathedral is a faithful provincial version of such Rhineland buildings as the cathedrals of Strasbourg and Freiburg-im-Breisgau. It represents a style introduced to Cyprus *c.* 1300, and it was extremely influential, both in Famagusta itself, where several buildings, including the Greek Orthodox cathedral, were built by the same workshop, and in Nicosia and at Bellapais Abbey.

BIBLIOGRAPHY

C. Enlart: 'Cathédrale Saint-Nicolas de Famaguste', *L'Art gothique et la Renaissance en Chypre* (Paris, 1899; Eng. trans., ed. D. Hunt, London, 1987), pp. 268–300, pls xxiii–xxvi

G. Jeffery: *A Description of the Historic Monuments of Cyprus* (Cyprus, 1918), pp. 116–25

N. Coldstream: 'The Church of St George the Latin, Famagusta', *Rep. Dept. Ant., Cyprus* (1975), pp. 147–51

NICOLA COLDSTREAM

Famille jaune. *See under* FAMILLE VERTE.

Famille noire. *See under* FAMILLE VERTE.

Famille rose. Term applied to Qing-period (1644–1911) overglazed enamel porcelain characterized by a delicate rose pink derived from colloidal gold. All the *famille rose* colours (*see* CHINA, §VII, 3(vii)(a), and figs 217 and 219) are opaque and stand proud of the surface. The wide palette and manageable qualities of these enamels facilitated a meticulous style of painting. The term *famille rose*, coined by the artist and art historian Jules Jacquemart in the 19th century, embraces *yangcai* ('foreign colours'), *fencai* ('powdered colours'), *ruancai* ('soft colours') and *falangcai* ('enamel colours').

Famille verte. Term applied to Qing-period (1644–1911) translucent overglaze enamel wares on which the predominant colour is green. *Famille verte*, a term coined by Jules Jacquemart in the 19th century, is known also as *yingcai* ('strong colours'; *see* CHINA, §VII, 3(vii)(a)). *Famille jaune* and *famille noire*, characterized by the predominant use of yellow and black respectively, are effectively variants of *famille verte*.

Famin, Charles (*fl* Paris, 1863–74). French photographer. He left a collection of numbered prints (highest number 209), signed either with his surname or initials, which were deposited in the Bibliothèque Nationale, Paris, in 1863 and 1874. His favoured subjects were aspects of rural life—peasants, farming scenes (e.g. *The Horse*, *c.* 1874; see Berger–Levrault, pl. 27)—and also scenes photographed in the forest of Fontainebleau. He is known to have had two studios in Paris.

BIBLIOGRAPHY
Berger–Levrault: *Regards sur la photographie en France au XIXe siècle* (Paris, 1980)

PATRICIA STRATHERN

Fāmiya. *See* APAMEIA.

Fan. Cooling or winnowing device. It was known to earliest civilizations and served utilitarian, ceremonial, ritual and decorative purposes. Infinite variations of fan shapes have evolved throughout the ages in most countries in the world. There are, however, two main types of fan: the screen or fixed fan, and the folding fan. The screen fan consists of a handle that can vary in length, design and material, on to which is fixed a rigid leaf or mount. The folding fan is composed of a set of sticks, which can be made in a variety of materials, on which is fitted a pleated leaf that allows the fan to be opened and closed. A rivet or pivot holds the sticks together, either at the base or, as in a cockade fan (see fig. 6 below), in the centre; the *cabriolet* fan consists of two or more concentric leaves. Overlapping sticks secured at the top by a ribbon or thread, with no leaf, constitute a *brisé* fan.

BIBLIOGRAPHY
S. Blondel: *Histoire des éventails chez tous les peuples et à toutes les époques* (Paris, 1875)
G. Buss: *Der Fächer* (Bielefeld and Leipzig, 1904)
Fans (1975–)
Il Ventaglio (1984–)
Eventails (exh. cat., ed. M. Volet and A. Beentjes; Geneva, Mus. A. & Hist., 1987)

I. Ancient world. II. East Asia. III. Indian subcontinent. IV. Southeast Asia. V. Africa. VI. Pacific Islands. VII. Pre-Columbian Americas. VIII. Europe.

I. Ancient world.

Fans are depicted in Egypt as early as the Late Predynastic period (*c.* 3000 BC), on the maceheads of such kings as Narmer and Scorpion, and appear in wall paintings and low reliefs in tombs and temples throughout the Dynastic period. The artefacts themselves survive, for example the fans found in the tomb of Tutankhamun (*reg c.* 1332–*c.* 1323 BC; see fig. 1). Designed as cooling devices, ancient Egyptian fans were of the fixed type, with a rigid handle on to which a large flat surface of woven straw or overlapping feathers was attached. The large, semicircular ceremonial fans carried by bearers could also provide shade and often had highly decorated handles over 2 m long; various smaller types were carried by noblemen and officials as insignia of their rank. Everyday fans were small enough for easy manipulation and may have doubled as fly-whisks or served to ventilate cooking fires.

The Assyrians used fans, and the ancient Greeks put fans to a variety of uses. In their more sophisticated form fans were carried by men and women throughout Magna Graecia (South Italy). Terracotta figurines (*c.* 200 BC) from Boiotia show circular and leaf-shaped fans that were probably made of straw, plaited fibres or leather. These fans can sometimes be seen in Etruscan funerary art. The Romans, who are known to have used peacock-feather fans, introduced new art forms into western Europe; a circular cockade-type fan was carried by Romano-British women in the 2nd and 3rd centuries AD. Cockade fans and fans of similar design were used in the Early Christian era, allegedly to keep insects from the Eucharist. Fans are attested in liturgical use by the 4th century AD and are described as being made of fine skin, peacock feathers or linen. These liturgical fans are known as rhipidia. The soft pennant of the fan was later replaced by a metal disc; the earliest known examples, dated AD 577, are from the

1. Fan, ostrich feather and ivory, from the tomb of Tutankhamun, *reg c.* 1332–*c.* 1323 BC (Cairo, Egyptian Museum)

Kaper Koroan Treasure (Washington, DC, Dumbarton Oaks) and are made of silver. The early 6th-century consular diptych (Paris, Bib. N. Cab. Médailles) shows Consul Philoxenus accompanied by eunuchs holding fans that comprise a staff with a square piece of tissue depicting a laurel wreath. Recent studies on the flabellum of Monza, known as Queen Theolinda's fan (*c.* AD 600, the later leaf *c.* AD 1000), suggest a continuing secular use of fans at this date. The flabellum at Canosa suggests that fans were widely known and used in the Russian Orthodox Church. The flabellum of Tournos (Florence, Bargello) was probably made in France *c.* AD 836–40.

HÉLÈNE ALEXANDER-ADDA

II. East Asia.

Within East Asia, the fan probably originated in China and from there spread to Japan via Korea. The earliest known Chinese examples are two woven bamboo side-mounted fans dating from the 2nd century BC from Mawangdui, Hunan Province. Chinese influence on the Japanese fan is suggested by a 6th-century AD tumulus painting in TAKEHARA TOMB, Fukuoka Prefecture, illustrating large upright fans resembling those that appear in Chinese Eastern Han (AD 25–220) depictions and a painting (*c.* late 7th century) on the west wall at TAKA-MATSUZUKA, Nara, in the Chinese Tang (AD 618–906) style depicting a circular screen fan. There are three types of Chinese fan: the screen (see fig. 2), the ceremonial and the folding fan. The screen or fixed fan (Chin. *bianmian*)

2. Chinese screen fan, 'mandarin' type with cockatoo and peonies, mid- to late 19th century (Cambridge, Fitzwilliam Museum)

was made of feathers or silk stretched on an oval frame, often painted or embroidered, frequently with bird-and-flower scenes. Some later screen fans were made from silk tapestry. The ceremonial fan (Chin. *tuanshan*) is larger than the screen fan and mounted on a long handle. Painted silk fans of the 5th century appear to have been decorated with landscape scenes, and by the Song period (960–1279) fan painting was an established branch of Chinese painting. In Japan, ceremonial or screen fans (Jap. *uchiwa*) were still in use at the end of the Heian period (794–1185).

The folding fan was invented in Japan in the 7th century. Two types developed there: the *hiōgi* or *brisé* fan, usually made of cypress wood, and the paper folding fan, sometimes called *kōmori ōgi* ('bat fan'). *Hiōgi* fans consist of thin wooden strips, riveted at one end and pierced at the other, with a thread running through the holes to control the spread of the sticks. They were developed for ceremonial court use. Initially reserved for the emperor, they were eventually used at all levels and remained important items of court dress until the 19th century. *Hiōgi* fans became highly decorated: their faces were painted with designs of pines, chrysanthemums, plum or cherry blossom or birds, and their edges were decorated with artificial flowers and long streamers. Paper folding fans were also based on a number of flat sticks, riveted at one end, and with paper stuck to one side. By the 10th century, paper folding fans had become so popular in Japan that sumptuary laws were introduced to restrict their decoration. Fans were painted, sometimes by artists commissioned by courtiers, but were also left plain. Among the earliest surviving Japanese folding fans are a group of 115 *sūtra* fans dating from the 12th century (e.g. *sūtra* fan leaf, second half of the 12th century; Osaka, Shitennōji), painted with genre scenes over which texts from the Lotus *sūtra* are written (*see also* JAPAN, §VI, 3(iii)(e)). The few fans that survive from the Muromachi period (1333–1568) are mostly painted with landscapes and have thicker sticks. The two end sticks became guards with pierced decoration.

The date of the appearance of the folding fan in China is uncertain. Some sources suggest as early as AD 960; certainly by the 11th century the Japanese folding fan was attracting much interest among the Chinese literary classes. A Korean history of 1445 describes large numbers of Japanese folding fans sent to China and Korea; but only in the early 15th century did the folding fan with painted decoration become fashionable in China. According to one report, Korean ambassadors presented a folding fan to the Yongle emperor (*reg* 1403–24), who then ordered large numbers to be made. The popularity of the folding fan may have been due to the fact that it was less cumbersome than the screen fan and could be closed up and tucked into a sleeve or boot. It became fashionable among the Chinese literati to buy a blank fan and commission an artist to paint it, usually to mark a special occasion or for presentation as a gift. Highly prized folding fans had sticks of mottled bamboo (Chin. *xiangfei*), ivory, or sandalwood, and were kept in lacquered cases or embroidered pouches when not in use.

Early Chinese folding fans, unlike Japanese ones, consisted of two semicircular paper leaves pasted one to each side of the sticks; this innovation was taken up by the Japanese in the 15th century. The Japanese court and *nō* theatre also began to use a folding fan known as a *suchiro* (wide-ended fan) with a large number of wooden sticks, sometimes jointed to allow for splaying, lacquered in red or black with a design called 'cat's-eyes' (Jap. *nekome*). When closed, the fan formed a Y-shape. Another type of fan, known as a *bonbori* ('hand lantern'), was made with guards curving inwards to accommodate the extra thickness of a double layer of paper.

Fans became an important painting medium in both China and Japan, with many leading artists producing fan paintings. Fans were also inscribed with poems and calligraphy (e.g. folding fan, Qing Dynasty, 1721–5; London, V&A). Such works were highly prized and were frequently removed from their sticks or frames for mounting in albums. Indeed some fan leaf paintings were so highly prized that they were never used as fans at all (e.g. fan painting by Mori Sosen; Oxford, Ashmolean). In Japan, two artists are particularly associated with fan painting: Tawaraya Sōtatsu and Ogata Kōrin. Sōtatsu was chiefly known for his folding fan paintings, whereas Kōrin, although acknowledging Sōtatsu's influence, preferred the rigid fan as a medium (e.g. fan painted with scenes from the *Tales of Ise* and chrysanthemums and water; Washington, DC, Freer; *see also* OGATA, (1), §1(ii)).

The development during the Edo period (1600–1868) of *ukiyoe* woodblock printing (*see* JAPAN, §IX, 3(iii)) led to the printing of fan leaves in large numbers for mass consumption, both as folding and rigid fans. The work of many famous *ukiyoe* artists such as Utamaro occurs on fans. Prior to the Edo period, a popular type of fan for prints was introduced to Japan from Korea. It was made from a length of bamboo split above a joint into 50–60 splints splayed to form a base for the fan leaf on either side, with a handle formed by the un-split bamboo below the joint. These fans depict scenes from the brothels, theatres, restaurants and tea houses of Edo and were particularly popular with merchants and townspeople. Chinese fans were usually painted with brush and ink outline, with faint colour washes; landscapes were especially popular. Japanese fans tended to have brighter colours and more varied subject-matter.

Distinctive types of fan developed in local areas and for special uses. In China, in Hangzhou, a black oiled folding fan decorated with gold splashes and composed of up to 50 sticks was produced, and in Zhejiang Province the type known as a 'jade-plaque' fan was carved from a giant bamboo. The Taiwanese made a rigid fan from the dried leaf of the betel palm, which was engraved with a hot poker. The Japanese made a folding fan known as a war fan (*gunsen*) or iron fan (*tessen*), composed of 10–12 lacquered wood or iron sticks with thick paper attached, decorated with a red sun on a gold ground on one side, and a silver moon on a black ground on the other. The military fan (*gunbai uchiwa*) was made from iron and hardened leather or from heavily lacquered wood and was usually decorated with sun, moon and stars (see fig. 3). It was used like a baton to give military commands, as a weapon, and to ward off blows.

As trade between Europe and East Asia developed, fans became popular in the West. The Chinese began producing fans for export featuring a combination of traditional Chinese and Western elements. Black and gold

3. Japanese military fan (*gunbai uchiwa*), chased in low relief with gold, probably 17th century (Cambridge, Fitzwilliam Museum)

lacquer fans with a design enclosing the owner's monogram were common. More sophisticated materials and techniques were used than for fans for the domestic market: gold and silver filigree, cloisonné, lacquer, mother-of-pearl and tortoiseshell. Export fans were usually *brisé* fans, a type never very popular in China. Some of the earliest export fans, dating from the 18th century, are of pierced ivory painted with decorations similar to those on contemporary export *famille verte* and Chinese Imari porcelain (*see* CHINA, §VII, 4(v)), and pierced ivory fans, with designs of flowers or geometric patterns, continued to be popular in the West. Neo-classical designs also became common. By the 19th century, there were depictions of carved figures in landscape settings on a ribbed ground. Generally, fan paintings for the Western market depicted either Western scenes, usually awkward in execution, or Eastern scenes, featuring domestic, ceremonial or social life, or flowers, fruit, birds or insects.

From the mid-19th century, the Japanese also made large numbers of export fans. Although these differed from fans for the domestic market, they utilized traditional skills and materials. Mostly inexpensive, many were folding fans, generally much larger than those used by the Japanese, although there were also such new forms as the *cabriolet* fan, consisting of two or more concentric leaves. Finer, more expensive export fans included *brisé* fans with ivory sticks decorated with gold and silver *hiramakie* and *takamakie* (*see* LACQUER, §I, 1(ii)(d)) and guards enriched with tortoiseshell and mother-of-pearl (e.g. export fan, late 19th century; London, Fan Mus.). Depictions on fan leaves tended to be of the type considered typically Japanese by Europeans, such as *ukiyoe* scenes, bird-and-flower paintings and representations of Mt Fuji. In both China and Japan, the manufacture and use of fans continues in the late 20th century.

See also KOREA, §IX, 2.

BIBLIOGRAPHY
J. Earle: 'The Fan in Japan', *Fans from the East* (London, 1978), pp. 37–45
J. Hutt: 'Chinese Fans and Fans from China', *Fans from the East* (London, 1978), pp. 27–35
S. Mayor: *Collecting Fans* (London, 1980)
J. Hutt and H. Alexander: *Ogi: A History of the Japanese Fan* (London, 1992)

III. Indian subcontinent.

The Hindi term for a fan is *pankha*, which derives from *pankh*, meaning a feather or bird's wing. Feather fans were often used in ancient India to signify status, and important personages were cooled by means of long peacock-feather fans called *marchal*, which were held by attendants. These fans comprised a bunch of feathers either simply tied together or mounted in a handle of carved wood or ivory. Lengths of cloth, usually fine gauze, were waved, fan-like, by servants, and whisks (*caurīs*) were also used in this context: early Hindu sculptures commonly show deities accompanied by attendants carrying whisks (*see* INDIAN SUBCONTINENT, fig. 139). Many Mughal and Deccani court paintings also depict whisk-bearers. These whisks commonly had fronds of Yak tails, horsehair, grass or feathers, set into handles of metal, ivory or wood; the latter could be plain or carved and were sometimes jewelled. One particularly ornate 18th-century whisk (London, V&A) has fine ivory fronds gathered into an ivory handle carved with poppy and iris motifs and ending in a pineapple finial.

Fixed fans were made in a great variety of shapes: round, heart-shaped, spade-shaped and flag-shaped. Crescent- or axehead-shaped fans usually have side-mounted handles. *Brisé*, cockade and folding fans were also produced, and large ceiling fans operated by a rope are common. The materials employed vary greatly: south Indian fans are often made from reed, bussa-palm and bamboo, while cloth fans are more common further north. Cotton, silk and velvet were all used and were often embroidered with coloured silks, gold and silver metallic threads, tinsel, spangles and fragments of mica. In Kashmir, papier mâché was used to produce fixed fans. Handles and fan-sticks were generally of wood (especially sandalwood), sometimes coated with lacquer or ivory (carved, veneered, inlaid or stained).

BIBLIOGRAPHY
Fans from the East (London, 1978), pp. 59–71
S. Mayor: *Collecting Fans* (London, 1980), p. 91

IV. South-east Asia.

In many parts of South-east Asia fans, like parasols, are often used to denote rank and status. Palm-leaf and peacock-feather fans are used in rituals and carried by royal and other high-ranking persons in processions in Burma, Thailand, Cambodia, Laos and Malaysia. They are also frequently shown in wall paintings and carried by statues of deities to indicate the rank of the subject. Buddhist monks in South-east Asia sometimes carry large fans made from pleated bamboo or palm leaf, which they may use to screen their faces when addressing women. Pierced sandalwood fans are used in South-east Asian Buddhist temple ceremonies. They are first dipped in water and then waved about, their scent being regarded as a form of homage to the deities. Fans made of gold and silver and of pierced leather are used throughout Indonesia and Malaysia, mainly for the dance and ritual ceremonies. Typically, they are pear- or leaf-shaped and mounted on horn sticks. Rarer are fans made of folding hide. These usually have painted and gilt decoration and, particularly in Java, depict figures from the shadow plays. Fans made from woven rattan, bamboo and bark are used as fire-fans or for carrying throughout the region. They may be decorated or plain, and flag- or kidney-shaped or in a wide variety of other shapes.

BIBLIOGRAPHY
Fans from the East (London, 1978)
S. Mayor: *Collecting Fans* (London, 1980)

V. Africa.

In Africa fans are used to denote status as well as to provide shade or act as cooling devices. Woven or plaited vegetable fibre fans are common. Paddle-shaped palm leaf fans are used in dances by the Tallensi of northern Ghana. Flag fans, sometimes bound with leather, are used for fanning fires. In the later 20th century natural coloured, plaited straw flag fans, with wood handles and coloured raffia designs, have been produced for the tourist market. Round straw fans have also been made with brightly coloured patterns incorporated in the weave, often with feathers attached. Less commonly, coloured wool has been used to weave flag fans. Round leather fans are popular throughout West Africa. They are attached to hide-covered wooden handles and may have coloured hide or cloth appliqué designs stitched on with hide thread. In Benin, particular appliqué designs were reserved for certain ranks of chiefs and their wives. In the late 20th century these fans were also made for the tourist trade and sometimes incorporated ostrich feathers. The leather appliqué is sometimes cut away to reveal silver paper underneath.

Carved wooden fans were used as screens by the queen mothers of West African kingdoms and were often incised and decorated with poker-work. Benin craftsmen made bronze copies of fans as ceremonial objects and Asante gold-weights sometimes took the form of miniature fans. In Niger fans in the form of ostrich feathers attached to hide-covered wood handles were carried by chiefs as a symbol of rank. Beaded fans form part of Yoruba royal regalia. Brass fans with incised designs are also used by Yoruba, for example by the priestesses of Osun, Osogbo.

Fly-whisks might also be considered under the category of fan. They are used throughout Africa as status symbols and are made from a variety of materials, including animal tails, vegetable fibre and hair. Handles are made of bone, wood, beads or animal teeth.

BIBLIOGRAPHY

L. Mowat: 'Ethnic Fans at the Pitt Rivers Museum, Oxford', *Fans*, xli (1989), pp. 15–25

VI. Pacific Islands.

The main materials used for making fans in the Pacific Islands are coconut and pandanus palm-leaf, and plaited grass and cane. Fans of hide, feather and wood are less common. Chiefs' fans were often larger than those of commoners. They also often had ornate handles, old whalebone handles in particular being intricately carved. In the Marquesas Islands wooden handles were carved with religious figures. Pandanus-leaf fans with handles of plaited coconut-leaf fibre and human hair were carried by the attendants of Hawaiian chiefs. In Tahiti and the Cook Islands fly-whisks and fans with carved double figures were used by chiefs. In general Polynesian fans tend to be spade- or hatchet-shaped, often with wood handles covered with stringwork. Openwork wooden fans are known from Tonga (e.g. London, BM).

Throughout Melanesia kite- and diamond-shaped palm-leaf fans are common. In Papua New Guinea coloured and natural palm are used, and circular fans are often edged with feathers. Dance fans from Bougainville may be more than 1 m across, and many incorporate coloured fibre. The spatula-shaped fans of Fiji were copied by the peoples of other islands. Fijian missionaries also introduced fan-making to the Aborigines of Arnhemland. Traditionally no one Fijian was permitted to manufacture a complete fan; moreoover, certain fibres were reserved for chiefs' fans. Wood-handled Micronesian fans were often of palm-leaf decorated with feathers, cowries or tortoiseshell. Ornamental Marshall Island fans have elaborately woven borders, and crocheted fans were also made there. The islanders of Kiribati and Tuvalu make ephemeral circular fans for use at gatherings. A tear-shaped fan is used on Arorae for special occasions. In the late 20th century machine-stitched tapa fans were being manufactured on Tonga.

BIBLIOGRAPHY

A. North: *Australia's Fan Heritage* (Brisbane, 1985)
L. Mowat: 'Ethnic Fans at the Pitt Rivers Museum', Oxford, *Fans*, xli (1989), pp. 15–25

SIAN E. JAY

VII. Pre-Columbian Americas.

The paucity of extant examples of fans from the Pre-Columbian Americas belies their probable widespread use. Fan-shaped decorations of bound feathers were used in

4. Aztec fan with butterfly motif, flower motif on reverse, feathers and bamboo, circumference 0.68 m, h. with shaft 1.19 m, *c.* 1350–1521 (Vienna, Museum für Völkerkunde)

headdresses in all the high civilizations of Mesoamerica and the Andes. The tropical bird feathers used were a regular trade item from the Gulf and Pacific coasts, Yucatán and Central America to the Central Highlands and Southern Highlands of Mesoamerica, and from the Amazon Basin to the Andes. Aztec tribute lists depict quotas of feathers and of finished fans, and figures in the codices are shown holding small, whisk-like fans of feathers and circular or oval fans of paper or basketwork (e.g. Codex Nuttall, London, BM; Codex Mendoza, Oxford, Bodleian Lib.).

The Maya used bark paper fans that folded up: in the wall painting at BONAMPAK (*c.* AD 800), a noblewoman watching the victory celebrations after a battle wears a white robe and holds an opened fan in her left hand. In the same murals, two members of a processional group hold aloft two circular, presumably feather, parasols above a richly dressed figure. In a fragment of wall painting at Las Higueras, Veracruz, one figure holds the shaft of what must be a similar parasol over the figure in front of him. A gold fan handle of cast openwork ending in a serpent head (Oaxaca, Mus. Reg.) was found in Tomb 7 at MONTE ALBÁN.

Of eight surviving pieces of Aztec featherwork, one is a large circular fan on a delicate bamboo shaft (Vienna, Mus. Vlkerknd; see fig. 4). The central design shows a butterfly on one side and a flower on the other. Around this are V-shaped designs in many colours and finally a fringe of long, dark blue cotinga feathers set at right angles to the circumference. Folded bark paper fans were also much used by the Aztecs, and probably by earlier cultures, in their headdresses, as shown for example in a ceramic incense burner representing the maize god, from Tlatelolco (Mexico City, Mus. N. Antropol.).

In Peru, up to 16 copper shafts (c. 200–300 mm) with remains of cane splints for feathers were found at the unlooted Sipán burial of a Moche lord in the Lambayeque Valley. Some have flattened triangular ends and others round ends; they may be headdress ornaments and/or the handles of small whisk-like fans (Lambayeque, Museo Arqueol. Reg. Brüning). Accompanying a featherwork square said to have been found in a Chancay burial, possibly at Caqui in the Chancay Valley, was a silver 'straight piece' (370 mm; New York, Met.) that may have been a fan handle. Three objects of Amazonian parrot tail feathers bound to wooden shafts with camalid and vegetable fibres (280 mm; New York, Amer. Mus. Nat. Hist.) could possibly be fans although they are more likely to be headdress plumes; they are said to be from Chan Chan, found in the 1890s.

In North America, Plains Indians used feather fans in the Peyote cult. Known as 'singing fans', they were shaken gently to accompany prayer singing and were held in the smoke of burning incense and struck against the body to transfer spiritual power to the user (see NATIVE NORTH AMERICAN ART, §XII, 2).

BIBLIOGRAPHY
M. D. Coe: *The Maya* (London and New York, 1966, rev. 4/1987)
M. P. Weaver: *The Aztecs, Maya and their Predecessors: Archaeology of Mesoamerica* (New York, 1972, rev. 3/1993)
D. Heyden and P. Gendrop: *Pre-Columbian Architecture of Mesoamerica* (New York, 1975)
D. Snow: *The Archaeology of North America: American Indians and their Origins* (London and New York, 1976, rev. 1980)
W. du Solier: *Indumentaria antigua mexicana* (Mexico City, 1979)
P. R. Anawalt: *Indian Clothing Before Cortés: Mesoamerican Costumes from the Codices* (Norman, 1981)
E. Pasztory: *Aztec Art* (New York, 1983)
A. P. Rowe: *Costumes and Featherwork of the Lords of Chimor* (Washington, DC, 1984)
W. Alva and B. Ballenberg: 'Discovering the New World's Richest Un-looted Tomb', *N. Geog.*, clxxiv (1988), pp. 510–49 [Sipán]
M. E. Moseley: *The Incas and their Ancestors: The Archaeology of Peru* (London, 1992)

DAVID M. JONES

VIII. Europe.

Fans are documented in royal wills and inventories from the 14th century; in France they were known as *esmouchoirs*. At this date fans were also used in agriculture for winnowing. Visual evidence of fans exists in such paintings as the *Birth of the Virgin* by Pietro Lorenzetti (completed 1342; Siena, Mus. Opera Duomo; see LORENZETTI, (1), fig. 2). These fans appear to be fixed fans and are usually flag-shaped. Feather fans, set in plain or jewelled handles, date from the 16th century. Few examples survive, however, and evidence derives mainly from portraits and contemporary descriptions. Folding fans, of the type made in China and Japan (see §II above), were made in Europe during the 16th century and were considered luxury items. The early European fan-makers seem to have encountered technical difficulties in the manufacture of these folding fans. They were in fashion concurrently with fixed feather fans, which varied in size, splendour, shape and colour. A list (1589) of Queen Elizabeth I's New Year gifts describes two feather fans set in jewelled handles. During the 16th century fans were used by royalty at first, and later by the court; only at the end of the century did the merchant class own them. The use of fans spread from Italy to the rest of Europe.

In the 17th century feather fans were superseded at court by folding fans, but they were still used by the middle classes and children. The sticks and guards of the folding fan were made from a range of materials that included ivory, bone, mother-of-pearl, tortoiseshell, horn and wood. They could be decorated with silver or gold pins (*piqué*);

5. Fan leaf with central vignette of the *Judgement of Paris* engraved by Abraham Bosse, 74×540 mm, 1637 (London, Fan Museum)

other types were of pierced (*posé*) or carved mother-of-pearl. The leaves, or mounts, were made of the finest kid, vellum, paper, silk or parchment or, in some cases, strips of mica, and they could be decorated in diverse ways. Elegant fans were painted with mythological subjects copied from engravings of contemporary or earlier works by such artists as Raphael and Titian, members of the Carracci family, Domenichino, Guido Reni and Abraham Bosse (see fig. 5). The appearance in France of such costly items, coming mainly from Italy, prompted the formation in 1668 of a guild, with statutes approved by royal patronage. The revocation of the Edict of Nantes in 1685 resulted in the dispersal of many of these highly skilled French craftsmen throughout Protestant countries.

By the early 18th century there were numerous fan-makers and fan merchants in England, the Netherlands and Germany. Fans and fan sticks were brought to Europe by the East India companies, which also supplied European patterns and designs for Chinese craftsmen. In England, the Worshipful Company of Fan Makers was granted its charter by Queen Anne in 1709 and still flourishes. England produced both finely carved ivory sticks for high-quality fans and larger quantities of printed fan leaves for a much wider clientele. France specialized in elaborate, costly fans. Small *brisé* fans made of ivory and lacquered in *vernis Martin* were popular in the earlier part of the 18th century. Favourite subjects were the *fêtes galantes*, *fêtes champêtres* and compositions based on the paintings of Antoine Watteau, Jean-Baptiste Pater and Nicolas Lancret, often incorporating chinoiserie motifs and designs by such artists as François Boucher and Jean Pillement. In the second half of the century France initiated the vogue for fabric leaves, usually of silk. These could be painted, embroidered or embellished with sequins, ribbon, applied feathers or straw-work. The Netherlands had a prolific fan industry, and by the mid-18th century there were 30 fan shops in Amsterdam. High quality, finely painted *brisé* fans of ivory were produced, but later a somewhat stereotyped composition for fan leaves developed, which depicted Old Testament themes, usually in a central medallion flanked by two smaller vignettes in reserve on a lightly painted floral background. Many of the German states produced fans, as did Austria, Sweden and Switzerland, where the best-known fan-maker was Johannès Sulzer (1748–94) of Winterthur. Italy continued to produce fine quality fans, using 'chicken skin' (fine, papery looking skin) for the leaves, and specializing, after the mid-18th century, in reasonably good quality fans depicting subjects popular with tourists. Among the most favoured themes were copies of such popular paintings as *Aurora* (1614) by Reni in the Palazzo Rospigliosi-Pallavicini and the fresco (1508–11) by Raphael, in the Stanza della Segnatura in the Vatican, depicting *Fortitude, Prudence and Temperance*. Views of ancient buildings and of Vesuvius in eruption against backgrounds ornamented with classical motifs copied from Pompeian prototypes were also used frequently. Sticks of tortoiseshell and *piqué* work were produced more often in Italy than elsewhere. France and Portugal produced most of the fans for use in Spain, but Portugal also imported fans from Macao. By the end of the 18th century America was importing fans from East Asia and from Europe.

6. Cockade fans, *c.* 1808–12: (left): horn, with applied gold leaf and silver and steel spangles containing a spy glass in the pivot, diam. 150 mm; (right) horn, pierced and painted, diam. 190 mm; both probably from France or Switzerland (London, Fan Museum)

During the first part of the 19th century economic and political factors made the importation of rare goods into Europe difficult. Fan-makers found themselves obliged to work with such readily accessible materials as horn, bone, wood and steel (see fig. 6). Pierced designs of sticks in *brisé* fans echoed the Neo-classical style and the later Gothic Revival. With the new interest in romantic and historical subject-matter, polychrome lithographic and chromolithographic printed fan leaves were manufactured in France in vast quantities and distributed throughout Europe and the rest of the world, making France's exports of fans the largest of any European country. By the mid-19th century a greater variety of materials was used for the sticks and guards, and new inventions were patented to improve the technology and speed of the production of fans and fan sticks. These attempts to compete with cheap imported fans from East Asia never really succeeded, although Spain and Italy produced cheap fans in great quantity. The Great Exhibition in London in 1851 brought French fans to the attention of an international public, and they became synonymous with the best. Alexandre and Duvelleroy, gold medallists at the Great Exhibition, attracted the most distinguished clientele and the most skilled craftsmen. Specialist retail shops were set up, for example the world-renowned Maison Duvelleroy, established in 1827, which was patronized by royalty and continued in business in Paris and London well into the second half of the 19th century. The finest sticks and guards of ivory and mother-of-pearl were carved by artists working in the Méru and S Geneviève areas of Paris. Among those artists who painted fan leaves are Ingres, Corot, Rosa Bonheur, Philippe Rousseau, Veysserat, Vibert, Diaz, Eugène Lami, Luigi Calamatta, Boutry, Gavarni and Dumarecq. Throughout the second half of the 19th century professional painters specialized in fan painting, among them Charles Conder, M. Soldé, the Donzel family of father, son and uncle, who had a school of painting and design in Paris, Cécile Chenevière, Sailly, Lazellas, Ostolle, Van Garden, Billotey, Louise Abbeme, Maurice Leloir and many others. The influence of *Japonisme* was particularly strong, and Degas, Gauguin, Monet, Toulouse-Lautrec and others discovered in the fan a new stimulus for composition. Fans became fashionable decorative motifs, used extensively in interior decoration, textiles and objects of vertu.

Feather fans in every shape and form were popular at all levels of society throughout the 19th century. As the feather industry developed, so did its application in fans. Feathers came from all over the world and from every type of animal and were cured, dyed, curled and fashioned into spectacular objects. Feather fans remained popular well into the 20th century. Alongside the majestic ostrich-feather fans were smaller fans made from the plumes of different birds with the colours blending harmoniously. In the 1920s and 1930s, one or two long, tinted feathers attached to a handle complemented fashionable dress. Another type of fan developed in the 19th century was the lace fan. Due to the additional skill required in creating a circular form, lace fans were costly and prized objects, many intended as wedding gifts. They could be mounted on sticks of amber, tortoiseshell or beautifully carved mother-of-pearl. It was customary at this time among the wealthy for initials, made of gold, diamonds, or a combination of precious materials, to ornament the guards. Less costly lace-trimmed fans were also produced, as were fans made up with either hand- or machine-made lace insertions. Such manmade materials as pressed ivory, Bakelite and other plastics were also used for making fan sticks and guards.

Fans have always reflected the latest styles, from the gauze-painted or bespangled fans popular in the Directoire period, to those whose leaves held an overlying symbolism characteristic of Art Nouveau. Fans also became a popular form of advertising, with the more unsual *fontange* (bow) leaf inspired by Art Deco replacing the traditional form. Fans were used to promote products ranging from restaurants and tea-rooms to department stores, beverages, perfume and haute couture. By the end of the 19th century world-renowned collections had been assembled, for example that of Lady Charlotte Schreiber (now in the British Museum, London), the Burdett Coutts and the Walker collections. A revival of fan collecting among the aristocracy of Europe took place in the early 20th century; Queen Mary (1867–1953) assembled an important collection in England, as did Queen Margaret (1902–29) in Italy. The Messel Collection (now in the Fitzwilliam Museum, Cambridge) was formed around this period. Collecting and exhibiting regained popularity in the 1970s, with regular specialized auctions taking place in London and New York, and a revival in the art of fan-making began in the 1980s in England. Spain remains the only country in Europe to have a fan-making industry, and it has retained the fan as an object for both ceremonial and everyday use.

BIBLIOGRAPHY
S. Blondel: *Histoire des éventails chez tous les peuples et à toutes les époques* (Paris, 1875)
C. Schreiber: *Fans and Fan Leaves*, 2 vols (London, 1888–90)
L. Cust: *Catalogue of the Collection of Fans and Fan Leaves Presented to the Trustees of the Collection of the British Museum of the Lady Charlotte Schreiber* (London, 1893)
E. Petit: *Le Passé, le présent et l'avenir: Etudes sur la fabrication de l'éventail* (Versailles, 1895)
G. Buss: *Der Fächer* (Bielefeld and Leipzig, 1904)
G. W. Rhead: *History of the Fan* (London, 1910)
M. Percival: *The Fan Book* (London, 1920)
C. Baro: *Eventails anciens* (Lausanne, 1957)
N. Armstrong: *A Collector's History of Fans* (London and New York, 1974)
B. de Vere Green: *A Collector's Guide to Fans over the Ages* (London, 1975)
M. Gostelow: *The Fan* (Dublin, 1976)
S. Mayor: *Collecting Fans* (London, 1980)
H. Alexander: *Fans* (London, 1984)
L'Eventail: Miroir de la Belle Epoque (exh. cat., Paris, Mus. Mode & Cost., 1985)
Royal Fans (exh. cat., Fan Circle International, 1986)
Eventails (exh. cat., ed. M. Volet and A. Beentjes; Geneva, Mus. A. & Hist., 1987)

HÉLÈNE ALEXANDER-ADDA

Fancelli, Cosimo (*b* Rome, 1620; *d* Rome, 3 April 1688). Italian sculptor. He was one of four sons of Carlo Fancelli (*c.* 1566–1640), a stonecutter from Arezzo. He and his older brother, Giacomo Antonio Fancelli (1619–71), also a sculptor, were trained by Bernini and often worked together on the same projects. Cosimo may have helped his brother to carve reliefs for the decoration of pilasters in the nave of St Peter's, Rome (1647), and the colossal statue of the Nile for the Fountain of the Four Rivers (1648–50; Rome, Piazza Navona); both projects were designed and supervised by Bernini. Cosimo also worked closely with Pietro da Cortona from 1648 until the latter's death in 1669, and between 1667 and 1669 with Bernini, Carlo Rainaldi and Johann Paul Schor. He was one of the most prolific Roman sculptors of his generation, and he specialized in providing stucco sculpture for large projects designed by architects and decorators. His style was derived from that of the artists with whom he collaborated.

For Cortona, Cosimo provided marble, bronze and stucco reliefs and statues for such Roman churches as SS Martina e Luca (*c.* 1648–*c.* 1660) and S Maria della Pace (1656). He was one of several sculptors involved in the decoration of the Spada Chapel, S Girolamo della Carità, Rome (1657–9), for which he carved the figure of *Giovanni Spada* reclining on a black marble bench. For Cortona he carved the marble portrait, two putti and an eagle for the tomb of *Cardinal Widman* (*c.* 1660; S Marco) and continued to work on such churches as S Maria in Vallicela (1662–5) and S Carlo al Corso (1668–9). His colossal marble *Angel Carrying the Sudarium* (1668–9) on the Ponte Sant'Angelo, Rome, was carved at the request of Bernini, whose model it rather dryly follows. It was one of a series of standing angels each designed by Bernini and carved by several different sculptors. The pose and drapery of Cosimo's angel heighten the emotional tension by reflecting and reinforcing the form of the sudarium. The short, robust proportions of the angel are reminiscent of the angels in two paintings by Cortona, the *Guardian Angel* (1656; Rome, Pal. Corsini) and the *Annunciation* (1665; Cortona, S Francesco).

Other works by Cosimo include the figure of Faith for the tomb of *Clement IX* (1671; S Maria Maggiore) and, for the Palazzo Borghese, models for fountains, a porphyry bust of *Vitellus*, stucco figures and reliefs for the vault of the gallery (1772–6). He trained a number of assistants, including Francesco Cavallini (*fl* 1684–1700).

BIBLIOGRAPHY

L. Pascoli: *Vite* (1730–36), ii, pp. 467–77
R. Wittkower: *Gian Lorenzo Bernini, the Sculptor of the Roman Baroque* (London, 1955, rev. 2/1966), pp. 202, 216, 246
H. Hibbard: 'Palazzo Borghese Studies, I: The Garden and its Fountains', *Burl. Mag.*, c (1958), p. 206
——: 'Palazzo Borghese Studies, II: The *Galleria*', *Burl. Mag.*, civ (1962), pp. 9–20
G. Drago and L. Salerno: *SS Ambrogio e Carlo al Corso* (Rome, 1967), pp. 64, 92, 96–7
K. Noeles: *La chiesa dei SS Luca e Martina nell'opera di Pietro da Cortona* (Rome, 1970), p. 104, n. 216; p. 108, n. 239; p. 165, n. 345; pp. 184–5, doc. 165
M. Weil: *The History and Decoration of the Ponte S Angelo* (University Park, PA State U., 1974)
M. Heimburger Ravalli: *Architettura, scultura e arti minori nel barocco italiano, ricerche nell'Archivio Spada* (Florence, 1977), pp. 105–230
R. Enggass: 'New Attributions in St Peter's: The Spandrels of the Nave', *A. Bull.*, lx (1978), pp. 96–108
J. Montagu: *Alessandro Algardi*, 2 vols (New Haven, 1985)

MARK S. WEIL

Fancelli, Domenico (Alessandro) (*b* Settignano, 1469; *d* Saragossa, 21 April 1519). Italian sculptor, active in Spain. He came from a family of artists and trained as a sculptor in marble under an unidentified Florentine master. In 1508 he is recorded in Carrara buying marble, possibly for the tomb of the Cardinal of Spain, *Diego Hurtado de Mendoza, Archbishop of Seville*, who died in 1502, a commission from the deceased's brother, Iñigo López de Mendoza, Conde de Tendilla. The latter was influential in introducing the Renaissance to Spain and was Spain's ambassador to the Holy See. The tomb was made in Genoa in 1509, and Fancelli went to Spain to supervise its installation in the Capilla de la Antigua, in the south transept of Seville Cathedral. It is designed in the form of an arch set against the wall and decorated with niches housing small statues, the front with garlands and the base with shallow low reliefs, all reminiscent of the 15th century. From Seville, where the cathedral chapter tried to retain him, Fancelli went to Granada and contracted again with Tendilla to make the tomb of *Prince John* (1478–97), son of the Catholic monarchs Ferdinand II, King of Aragon, and Isabella, Queen of Castile and Leon, and in 1512 Fancelli returned to Carrara to purchase the materials.

The document of payment to Fancelli, dated 21 October 1513 and despatched by Ferdinand in Barcelona, suggests that the tomb had already been completed. The white marble monument (see fig.), installed in front of the high altar of the convent of S Tomás in Ávila, is free-standing, with a base in the form of a truncated pyramid on which there is a second simple construction supporting the recumbent figure of the Prince. Fancelli followed the structure used by Antonio del Pollaiuolo for the monument of *Sixtus IV* (1493; Rome, Vatican Tesoro S Pietro), and his increasing ability is seen in the design of the griffins that adorn the corners of the tumulus as well as in the exquisite carving. The beauty of the monument led to the important commission for the tomb of *Ferdinand and Isabella* for their Capilla Real (1506–21; for illustration *see* ARAGON (6)), Granada. The dating for this is indicated by Fancelli's stay in Carrara in 1514, and the work may have been completed by 26 March 1517 when he made a revision of his first will before returning to Spain. There is no record of his stay in Granada while the tomb was being installed. The tomb is similar in form to that of Prince John but is more monumental, due to the increased height and the more elaborate sculptured decoration of the second section, with figures of the Church Fathers at each corner; the effigies of the two monarchs are portrayed

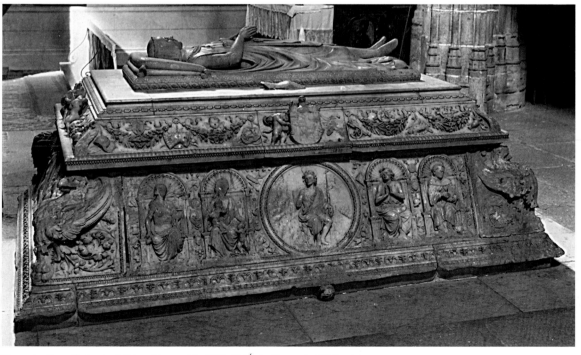

Domenico Fancelli: tomb of *Prince John*, marble, 1512–13 (Ávila, Convent of S Tomás)

with idealized features. On 14 July 1518 Fancelli was contracted to make the tomb of *Cardinal Francisco Jiménez de Cisneros*, who acted as the Regent of Spain from 1516 until the arrival of Charles V. On 21 December 1518 in Saragossa Charles V commissioned the tomb of his parents, *Joanna the Mad and Philip the Fair*, through the Contador Mayor of Castile, Antonio Manuel de Fonseca. Fancelli fell ill in Saragossa, dictated a will on 19 April 1519 and died without completing these contracts, which were later given to Bartolomé Ordóñez. Parts of the sepulchral monuments of the Fonseca family in Coca (Segovia) are attributed to Fancelli on stylistic grounds and because of his links with that family.

Fancelli's art, characteristic of Florentine sculpture after Donatello, with influences of Benedetto da Maiano and Desiderio da Settignano, is of great formal beauty although without originality. His work could be said to be rather old-fashioned for the date, considering his contact with the work of Michelangelo and such artists as the sculptor Antonio Giusti. However, Fancelli's sculpture was decisive in the diffusion of Renaissance forms in Spain as much for its technical quality as for the standing of his patrons, and it was very influential in the change of aesthetic taste then taking place in Spain.

BIBLIOGRAPHY
Ceán Bermúdez

P. Andrei: *Sopra Domenico Fancelli, fiorentino, e Bartolomeo Ordognes, spagnuolo* (Massa, 1871)

P. de Madrazo: 'Mausoleo de los reyes católicos, don Fernando y doña Isabel: Capilla Real de Granada de Bartolomé Ordoñez', *Mus. Esp. Ant.*, i (1872), pp. 431–47

M. Assas: 'Sepulcro del principe don Juan, hijo de los reyes católicos', *Mus. Esp. Ant.*, x (1882), pp. 105–28

V. Polero: 'Bultos sepulcrales de los reyes católicos', *Bol. Soc. Esp. Excurs.*, xii (1904), pp. 166–8

J. Martí Monso: 'Noticias: Sepulcro de los reyes católicos', *Bol. Soc. Castell. Excurs.*, ii (1905–6), pp. 387–8

E. Tormo: 'El brote del renacimiento e los monumentos españoles y los Mendozas del siglo XV', *Bol. Soc. Esp. Excurs.*, xxv (1917), pp. 51–65

M. Gomez Moreno: 'Sobre el renacimiento en Castilla, *Archv Esp. A. & Arqueol.*, i (1925), pp. 253–6

——: 'En la Capilla Real de Granada', *Archv Esp. A. & Arqueol.*, ii (1926), pp. 99–128

V. Garcia Rey: 'El sepulcro del Cardenal Cisneros y los documentos de los artífices', *A. Esp.*, viii (1926–7), pp. 483–6

J. M. Madurell Marinon: 'Bartolomé Ordoñez', *An. & Bol. Mus. A. Barcelona*, vi/3–4 (1948), pp. 365–8

J. Hernandez Perera: *Escultores florentinos en España* (Madrid, 1957)

J. M. Azcárate: *Escultura del siglo XVI*, A. Hisp. (Madrid, 1958)

MARGARITA ESTELLA

Fancelli, Luca (*b* Settignano, *c.* 1430; *d* after 1494). Italian architect and sculptor. He trained as a stonecutter but was involved more with architecture than sculpture. Several contradictory references by Vasari relate to Fancelli's early career and attribute to him the construction of the Palazzo Pitti, the tribune of SS Annunziata and other Florentine buildings designed by Brunelleschi and Alberti. Vasari's proposal, however, lacks documentary confirmation, since Fancelli moved *c.* 1450 to Mantua, where he entered the service of Ludovico II Gonzaga, 2nd Marquis of Mantua. While there he supervised the construction of Alberti's churches of S Sebastiano (from 1460) and S Andrea (from 1472); his personal contribution to these buildings, especially S Andrea, which was begun only shortly before Alberti's death, should not be underestimated.

For approximately 35 years Fancelli supervised building work for the Gonzaga family, including improvements to the castle at Mantua, numerous country residences, fortresses and even the construction of the Marchese's Bucentaur, a luxurious river vessel. During the 1450s Fancelli was responsible for Revere, the Gonzagas' fortified palace on a rectangular plan, which was not completed. The military allusions are limited to the vertical emphasis of the corner towers, the outward slope of the socle and the blind crenellation of the roofline. The paired columns of the open loggia of the courtyard have bases and capitals in the Gothic tradition. The main entrance has classical qualities, with fluted Corinthian pilasters, trabeation in the form of an antique frieze, and a triangular pediment in strong relief. The rectangular windows surrounded by denticulated frames are characteristic of Fancelli's work. Many of his buildings have been destroyed or radically transformed. Certain of his characteristic features, however, such as blind crenellation and denticulated window-frames, are found on little-documented buildings, such as the Palazzo Pastore built for Francesco Secco at San Martino Gusnago. Fancelli's influence is also evident in the reconstruction (early 1470s) of the medieval Palazzo del Podestà, Mantua, although the project was supervised by the engineer Giovanni Antonio d'Arezzo.

Fancelli's career as a sculptor is difficult to define. He is generally credited with the sculptural embellishment of the buildings on which he collaborated, such as the entrance and a fireplace in the Revere castle, the transennae on the façade of S Sebastiano, the fireplace in the Camera del Sole of the Ducal Palace at Mantua, but these designs are more probably attributable to Mantegna or Alberti. In 1482 he produced a design for the funerary monument to Ludovico's wife, Barbara of Brandenburg (*d* 1481), but this was rejected in favour of a model by Mantegna. In the early 1480s Federico I Gonzaga, 3rd Marquis of Mantua, offered Fancelli his most prestigious commission: to design a monumental new palace within the confines of the Mantuan court. The Nova Domus differed from Fancelli's other palace designs with the introduction of superimposed architectural orders, although the corner towers were retained and opened up into roof terraces. After the death of Federico Gonzaga (1484), the palace remained unfinished (the façade towards the lake is largely the result of 20th-century restoration), and Fancelli's fortunes at the Mantuan court rapidly declined.

During the following decade Fancelli left Mantua on several occasions to take up prestigious but temporary commissions. In 1487 he spent some time in Milan studying the structural problem of the cathedral's lantern and evaluating the solutions put forward by Leonardo, Bramante and other famous architects. Subsequently, thanks to the intervention of Lorenzo de' Medici, he was appointed superintendent of the dome of Florence Cathedral. As an architect he achieved an original synthesis of elements, some Florentine in origin, as well as archaeological references and themes traditional to the Po region, from which he created compositional solutions that were widely diffused and contributed to the establishment of Mantua's civic image during the second half of the 15th century.

WRITINGS

C. Vasić Vatovec, ed.: *Luca Fancelli, architetto: Epistolario gonzaghesco* (Florence, 1979)

BIBLIOGRAPHY

G. Vasari: *Vite* (1550, rev. 2/1568); ed. G. Milanesi (1878–85), ii, pp. 373, 545–6

W. Braghirolli: 'Luca Fancelli: Scultore, architetto e idraulico del secolo XV', *Archv Stor. Lombardo*, iii (1876), pp. 610–38

E. Marani: 'Luca Fancelli', *Dall'inizio del secolo XV. alla metà del XVI.*, ed. E. Marani and C. Perina (1961), ii/2 of *Mantova* (Mantua, 1958–65), pp. 63–115

C. Perina: 'L'attività scultoria di Luca Fancelli', *Dall'inizio del secolo XV. alla metà del XVI.*, ed. E. Marani and C. Perina (1961), ii/2 of *Mantova* (Mantua, 1958–65), pp. 511–16

M. Salmi: 'La "Domus Nova" dei Gonzaga', *Arte, pensiero e cultura a Mantova nel primo rinascimento in rapporto con la Toscana e con il Veneto: Atti del VI convegno internazionale di studi sul rinascimento: Firenze, Venezia, Mantova, 1961*, pp. 15–21

C. Cottafavi: 'Saggi inediti su edifici della corte di Mantova: La Nova Domus', *Atti & Mem. Accad. N. Virgil. Mantova*, n. s., xxxiv (1963), pp. 8–18

P. Carpeggiani: 'Luca Fancelli architetto civile nel contado mantovano: Ipotesi e proposte', *Civiltà Mant.*, 20 (1969), pp. 87–114

——: *Il palazzo gonzaghesco di Revere* (Mantua, 1974)

C. Vasić Vatovec: 'La villa di Rusciano', *Filippo Brunelleschi: La sua opera e il suo tempo: Firenze, 1977*, pp. 663–7

A. Calzona: *Mantova città dell'Alberti: Il San Sebastiano: Tomba, tempio, cosmo* (Parma, 1979)

M. Palvarini Gobio Casali: 'La "Ghirardina" di Motteggiana ovvero la "casa di Saviola" del marchese Ludovico II Gonzaga', *Civiltà Mant.*, n. s., 8 (1985), pp. 37–57; 11 (1986), pp. 5–34

AMEDEO BELLUZZI

Fancy picture. Term current in 18th-century England to describe contemporary genre pictures of a sentimental realism, in which the artist's own whimsy played a substantial part. Samuel Johnson defined 'fancy' in his *Dictionary of the English Language* (1755) as a synonym for 'imagination' but also in the subsidiary senses of 'taste' and of 'something that pleases and entertains'. The usual subjects for fancy pictures are children and young women represented life-size or slightly smaller, though the term, never used very precisely, has also been applied to landscape paintings having a predominant figural element of a sentimental nature. The keynote in fancy paintings is a sort of contrived innocence, sometimes with erotic overtones. In style and treatment, though not in mood, they were often inspired by the genre scenes and character studies of such 17th-century masters as Rembrandt and Murillo; analogous works by 18th-century French artists, most notably Chardin and Greuze, were also influential in the development of the type. The fancy picture is now most commonly associated with works of this kind by Thomas Gainsborough.

The term was in use by 1737, when Vertue noted that Philip Mercier was painting 'conceited plaisant Fancies & habits, mixt modes really well done—and much approvd off' ('The Note-books of George Vertue', *Walpole Soc.*, xxii, 1934, p. 82). The tone of this type of picture by Mercier ranged from the moral or sentimental, as in the *Bible Lesson* (*c.* 1743; priv. col., see 1969 exh. cat., no. 58), to the playful, as in *Children Blowing Bubbles* (*c.* 1747; priv. col., see 1969 exh. cat., no. 66), or the mildly erotic, as in the *Lady at her Toilet* (priv. col., see 1969 exh. cat., no. 34), in which a pretty girl admires herself in a mirror while displaying her bosom. There is a Rococo pertness about a number of these pictures that reveals Mercier's affinities with contemporaneous French art. Some became well

known through mezzotints made after them by John Faber the younger (1695–1756). Certain paintings, such as the *Bible Lesson*, were clearly influenced by the contemporary domestic realism of Chardin, whose work was also a possible influence on Joshua Reynolds's earliest fancy picture, the *Boy Reading* (1747; priv. col., see 1985–6 exh. cat., no. 7). Other English painters producing fancy pictures in the 1740s included Francis Hayman, for example *May Day, or the Milkmaid's Garland* (*c.* 1741–2; London, V&A), one of Hayman's series of decorative paintings for the supper-boxes at Vauxhall Gardens (*see* LONDON, §V, 6), and William Hogarth, for example his *Shrimp Girl* (*c.* 1745; London, N.G.).

By the 1760s the leading French artist working in the vein of sentimental realism was Greuze. He introduced a new note in such pictures as the *Girl with a Dead Bird* (1765; Edinburgh, N.G.), in which tearful emotion was combined with more than a hint of eroticism. With a revival of pastoral motifs in England during the same period, settings shifted from town to country and from interiors to the open air. Examples include *A Piping Boy* (exh. RA 1769; Dublin, N.G.) by Nathaniel Hone (i) and Reynolds's *Piping Shepherd Boy* (1773; Antony House, Cornwall, NT). Such pictures transposed into a mode of sentimental realism the thoroughly artificial French Rococo pastorals popularized most notably by François Boucher (e.g. *Shepherd's Idyll*, 1768; New York, Met.), which were widely circulated in engravings.

By the 1770s another important influence in England was the work of the mid-17th-century Spanish painter Murillo. Enthusiasm for the sweet sadness of his genre scenes of beggar children (e.g. *Two Peasant Boys*, late 1660s; London, Dulwich Pict. Gal.) coincided with the new mood of seriousness verging on melancholy that characterized late 18th-century sensibility. The influence of Murillo is apparent in such works as Reynolds's *Beggar Boy and his Sister* (*c.* 1775; Buscot Park, Oxon, NT) and several pictures by Gainsborough. It was Reynolds who established the enduring link between the fancy picture and Gainsborough's name, in the obituary comments concerning his former rival given to the Royal Academy in 1788 and published the following year as his 'Fourteenth Discourse' (see Reynolds's *Discourses on Art*, ed. R. R. Wark, London, 1959/*R* 1975, pp. 253–4):

> Whether he most excelled in portraits, landskips or fancy-pictures, it is difficult to determine.... In his fancy-pictures, when he had fixed on his object of imitation, whether it was the mean and vulgar form of a wood-cutter, or a child of an interesting character, as he did not attempt to raise the one, so neither did he lose the natural grace and elegance of the other.

Gainsborough's work in this manner consists of rustic scenes of beggar children and humble families at work or play outside tumbledown Picturesque cottages. His *Girl with Pigs* (exh. RA 1782; Castle Howard, N. Yorks) was bought by Reynolds for 100 guineas; others made around this time include *Two Shepherd Boys with Dogs Fighting* (exh. RA 1783; London, Kenwood House) and *Cottage Girl with Dog and Pitcher* (1785; Dublin, N.G.; see fig.), which was sold to Sir Francis Basset for the high price of 200 guineas. It was 'little simple subjects' such as these, as

Fancy picture by Thomas Gainsborough: *Cottage Girl with Dog and Pitcher*, oil on canvas, 1.74×1.25 m, 1785 (Dublin, National Gallery of Ireland)

Gainsborough's fancy pictures were described in the *Morning Herald* (2 May 1786), 'that awakened in the heart the most pathetic sensations'; and William Hazlitt was later to note that it was 'the fancy pictures, on which Gainsborough's fame chiefly rests' (*The Champion*, 31 July 1814).

The mood of fancy pictures in the later 18th century was not always serious, and although the poor were frequently represented, albeit at one or more removes from the real circumstances of rural life, such pictures were not meant as criticisms of social conditions; the sole intention was to move the beholder's affections. Those who specialized in this type include Henry Robert Morland, whose pretty laundresses smirk coyly in the Mercier tradition (e.g. *A Lady's Maid Soaping some Fine Linen*, 1770s; sold London, Christie's, 19 June 1970, lot 52; for illustration see Waterhouse, *18th C.*, p. 247), and Francis Wheatley. Wheatley's fancy pictures painted after 1783 were popularized through engravings by Charles Knight among others and strongly reflect the influence of Greuze and his imitators. His single works reproduced in engravings include the *Industrious Cottager: Girl Making Cabbage Nets* (1786); others he painted as pairs, such as the *Sailor's Return* (London, N. Mar. Mus.; for illustration see Webster, p. 164) and the *Soldier's Return* (1786; see Webster, p. 164), or in sets, for example the *Happy Fireside* set: *Maidenhood*, *Courtship*, *Marriage* and *Married Life* (1791; priv. col., see Webster, figs 96–9). A similar spirit of simple

innocence pervades the work of William Redmore Bigg who, as his *Girl at a Cottage Door Shelling Peas* (1782; Plymouth, City Mus. & A.G.) indicates, concentrated on a small-scale and neatly finished full-length type of fancy picture that was founded, in Samuel Redgrave's words, 'upon the simplest incidents of domestic life, and always with a benevolent and moral tendency'.

The fancy picture reached its height of popularity in the late 18th century and the early 19th. To the modern spectator these coy young women and ragged children seem excessively sentimental. Nevertheless, such pictures continue to be admired for their painterly qualities of rich brushwork and powerful chiaroscuro.

BIBLIOGRAPHY
Redgrave; Waterhouse: *18th C.*
C. B. Tinker: 'Gainsborough: Return to Nature', *Painter and Poet: Studies in the Literary Relations of English Painting* (Cambridge, MA, 1938), pp. 70–99
E. K. Waterhouse: 'Gainsborough's "Fancy Pictures"', *Burl. Mag.*, lxxxviii (1946), pp. 134–40
——: *Painting in Britain, 1530–1790*, Pelican Hist. A. (Harmondsworth, 1953, rev. 4/1978), pp. 188–98, 262–3
Philip Mercier, 1689–1760 (exh. cat., ed. R. Raines and J. Ingamells; York, C.A.G.; London, Kenwood House; 1969)
M. Webster: *Francis Wheatley* (London, 1970)
Reynolds (exh. cat., ed. N. Penny; Paris, Grand Pal.; London, RA; 1985–6)

DAVID MANNINGS

Fanelli, Francesco (*fl* 1608–?1661). Italian sculptor, active in England. He was, by his own account, a Florentine, but is first recorded in Genoa, where he rented a house in 1608. In that year he carved a wooden figure of the *Dead Christ* (Genoa, S Luca) under the supervision of Giovanni Battista Paggi and Stefano Rezza, and in 1609 Giovanni Domenico Spinola contracted with him for a small bronze Crucifix (untraced). In 1620 he undertook to provide unspecified bronze decorative features for the chapel of the Virgin Mary in the church of S Maria delle Vigne, Genoa, and in a further contract, of 1627, he agreed to cast the capitals of the columns there. Fanelli is next documented in England, at the court of Charles I, who paid him a pension in 1635; he later described himself as 'Sculptor to the King of Great Britain', a title that may have been officially conferred. Joachim von Sandrart wrote that the King had summoned him to his service mainly on the strength of an ivory figure of *Pygmalion* (untraced), but Fanelli's chief attraction for Charles probably lay in his talent as a maker of bronze statuettes, there being apparently no artist in Britain at the time with a particular skill in this type of sculpture.

Abraham van der Doort listed two groups of figures in the royal collection by 'ffrancisco the one eyed Italian': from this and an 18th-century list, compiled by George Vertue, of sculpture at Welbeck Abbey, Notts, it has been possible to identify at least five types of bronze statuette for which Fanelli was responsible. They are *St George and the Dragon*, *Nessus and Deianira*, *A Turk on Horseback Attacked by a Lion*, *Cupid on Horseback* and a single *Horse*. All are represented at least once in the collection of the Victoria and Albert Museum, London (e.g. A.5–1953, A.7–1953, A.4–1953, A.37–1952, A.20–1978) and have been recognized in many versions and variants, showing that their author must have practised a type of high-quality mass production.

Fanelli's skill in portraiture is revealed by the only signed work that has come to light, a powerfully characterized bronze bust of *Charles II as Prince of Wales* (1640; Welbeck Abbey, Notts). This may be compared with the memorial bust of the poet and courtier *Sir Robert Aiton* (*c.* 1638) in Westminster Abbey, London, which is probably by the same hand. Other convincing attributions are a small bronze bust of *Charles I* (Miss Daphne Ionides priv. col.) and sets of plaques representing *Orpheus Singing to the Beasts*. The latter comprise a relief of the subject and varying numbers of smaller reliefs of individual animals, and they were probably made to be set in cabinets. This was done with the most famous of the sets by the diarist John Evelyn, who at some time between 1646 and 1652 appears to have commissioned special modifications to the main *Orpheus* plaque so that it would fit a Florentine cabinet that he had acquired previously (London, V&A). At this time Evelyn was in Paris, where Fanelli appears also to have moved in or after 1641. There two suites of engravings were published under his name, *Dessins de grottes* and *Fontaines et jets d'eau d'après les plus beaux lieux d'Italie*.

Fanelli's work was not of the first rank, by contemporary Italian standards, but in northern Europe it drew extravagant praise. Stylistically his work is most notable for the pronounced Baroque characteristics that are especially apparent in many of his statuettes.

BIBLIOGRAPHY

J. Pope-Hennessy: 'Some Bronze Statuettes by Francesco Fanelli', *Burl. Mag.*, xcv (1953), pp. 157–62
A. Radcliffe and P. Thornton: 'John Evelyn's Cabinet', *Connoisseur*, cxcvii (1978), pp. 254–62

ADAM WHITE

Fang. Culture in west Central Africa that flourished in the late 19th century and early 20th, noted for its production of wooden sculpture and masks.

1. Geography and cultural history. 2. Statues. 3. Masks. 4. Other arts.

1. GEOGRAPHY AND CULTURAL HISTORY. The Fang people form the southern part of a large ethnic group defined by language and culture, the Yaunde–Fang. The northern part of this entity consists essentially of the Beti (Bene and Ewondo), Eton and Bulu peoples, who occupy south-western Cameroon. The German term 'Pangwe', the French 'Pahouin' and the Spanish 'Pamue' convey the same inclusive meaning as does 'Yaunde–Fang'. In arthistorical parlance the term 'Fang' is often imprecisely used to designate all of the Yaunde-Fang, as well as an unrelated neighbouring people, the Ngumba, whose statuary style resembles and has probably influenced that of the Fang.

The Fang extend southward from the basin of the Middle Ntem River, which takes in the most southerly part of south-western Cameroon, through the basins of the Benito and Muni rivers in Equatorial Guinea. In Gabon the Fang occupy almost all of the basins of the Noya, Mbé, Como, Remboué and Upper Ntem rivers, while they command the northern bank of the Ogowe River's lower reaches and most of the northern tributaries of its middle course. They reach their southernmost point in a spur that takes them across the lower Ngounié River and slightly past Lake Oguemoué. Most of their territory lies some distance inland; only in their southern sector do they reach the sea. Today they number about 200,000 people, and their wide dispersal is manifest in the great cultural and ethnic diversity of the peoples who adjoin them.

Interest in Fang art centres mainly on wooden statues traditionally used to protect the supernatural power of relics sacred to family groups. A considerable interest in wooden masks that played a number of societal roles has grown out of the high regard for the Fang sculptor's representation of the entire human form. Fang traditional art is probably of relatively recent development, largely a product of massive and extensive migrations that began some time in the 18th century and continued for most of the 19th. Its florescence began towards the last quarter of the 19th century and continued into the first two decades of the 20th. Within this period the Fang received and modified cults and iconographies from the peoples they met as they travelled west and south from their homeland. This country was probably in the woodland–savannah zone north of the Sanaga River and quite possibly east of its headwaters, most likely in the west of the present-day Central African Republic.

It is likely that the Fang did not act as culture-bringers. They would have travelled more as learners than as teachers. A large bloc of their formidable relatives—mainly the Beti—stood between them and the sea, peoples who differed considerably from the Fang in material culture and religion. The Fang had two kinds of cult statuary: one acquired from the Ngumba to their south; the other from the Sanaga-speakers to their north, Tsinga and Mangisa. These borrowings could indicate that the Yaunde–Fang had no distinctive style of statuary before they left their homeland or that they abandoned it in the course of their journeys.

The Beti claim to have received *melan*, the cult of family skulls, from the Ngumba around the second quarter of the 19th century. This involved both a body of ritual procedures and its accessories, mainly wooden statues to be used either as reliquary guardians or as puppets in an initiatory sort of theatre. The statuary style of the Tsinga and Mangisa differs markedly from that of the Ngumba. It is most closely related to the figures that the Beti and Eton used in contexts other than the guarding of *melan* reliquaries.

The original position of the Ngumba to the south of the Fang enabled them to teach the newcomers the skills needed to survive in the forest and succeed in trade: religious systems as well as technological. The essential similarities between Ngumba and Fang statues strongly suggest that the formation of a Fang style owes much to Ngumba instruction. Their southward passage brought the Fang into contact with other peoples and, most likely, other styles. These mainly would have been members of the Kele language group, especially the Ngom and Sekiyani, who lived in small scattered groups in the basin of the Rio Muni system. In its westward sweep the Fang vanguard reached the Gabon Estuary and the Lower Ogowe River between 1860 and 1870. There they found Myéné peoples—Orungu, Galoa and Nkomi—settled. Fang contact with the trade-enriched Myéné doubtless led to their borrowing some features of their religion, thereby adding to the complexity of the influences implicit in the development of Fang traditional art.

The Fang ability to displace and absorb other decentralized societies did not help them against the military force of the European nations moving in from the coast to protect European trading companies from pillage. This served to check the Fang advance, leading its components to establish themselves where they were or, in some cases, to recoil towards less contested parts. The period of containment before strong European influence began in the 1870s and lasted into the 1910s.

As the Fang moved through the stages of their migration they entered into the trading-systems of the regions they traversed. Adept at killing elephants and industrious in the collecting of African rubber and other forest products, they became affluent and competed among themselves for greater wealth and power. Lineages—social units consisting of brothers, sons and their wives—attempted to forestall increasing internal fission, and its consequence of dispersal, by observing a family cult of skulls, *byeri*. Although the name of this cult is cognate with those of the cults practised by the Ngom and other Kele-speakers, its ritual pattern and iconography show it to be a reduced version of the *melan* cult that the Ngumba taught the Beti as an avenue to wealth through European trade. It is likely that the Fang adopted *byeri* in the hope of gain through exploiting the supernatural forces controlling the trading systems of their new lands, and later in the hope that it offered protection against hostile witchcraft. They believed that the jawless skulls kept stacked in cylindrical bark reliquaries retained supernatural power for some time. These reliquaries were guarded by carved wooden statues.

Knowledge of Fang traditional culture is the legacy of Günter Tessmann (1884–1969), a German ethnologist whose study of the Fang of the Upper Rio Benito Basin (then Spanish Guinea and French Gabon) from 1907 to 1909 culminated in a profusely illustrated and, for its time, ethnologically sophisticated monograph, *Die Pangwe*, published in 1913. His work was both corroborated and complemented by the observations of Father H. Trilles, a missionary who some time earlier had worked to the south of Tessmann's field. During the 1910s and 1920s the hasty and unreflective removal of Fang guardian statuary from its loci of origin for the European art market effectively forestalled any primary research into the question of ethnic styles. The virtual abandonment of the *byeri* cult—partly because of its failure to provide protection against European domination—and the acceptance of new religions greatly reduced Fang interest in the art of their past, little of which remained among them.

2. STATUES. The primary function of the reliquary guardian figure remains uncertain. The earliest interpretation regarded it as a device to warn the uninitiated, mainly women and children, away from the contents of the reliquary. Later field investigators saw it as either a symbol of the collectivity of ancestors materialized in the barrel or as a physical evocation (?portrait) of the first ancestor

of the lineage. Guardian figures are of moderate size, only occasionally higher than 550 mm. They differ from statues of the wider region in several ways. Their treatment tended to be rounded rather than angular, the roundness of limbs and trunk often lending itself to swelling effects that impart a quality of segmentation. The schematic use of geometric forms to represent the monoxylic (made of one piece of wood) body can contrast strikingly with the treatment of the face, which, although itself fashioned of simple conventionalized elements, can often produce an affecting expressiveness.

Fang statuary style shows a distinctive concern with balance. The figure is usually symmetrical and frontal. Its three main masses—head, shoulders and arms, and thighs and shanks—play off against each other rhythmically, and details within these masses often echo each other in subtle ways. This interplay depends considerably upon the Fang selection of the coiffure as a coordinate component in the scheme. Its idealization and expansion give the figure a sense of fullness and self-containment. The arms usually merge with the body or connect with each other at a distance from the body. Most Fang reliquary guardian figures have a distinctive finish: dark, monochromatic and lustrous.

Although many of these statues can seem of indifferent quality, there are numerous series of outstanding examples

1. Fang sculpture of a crouching male figure, wood and brass, h. 340 mm, from Gabon, Equatorial Guinea or south-west Cameroon, *c.* 1900 (New York, Metropolitan Museum of Art)

that suggest a professionalism transcending occasional *ad hoc* attempts to meet ritual requirements within the confines of a lineage. But insufficient data would seem to limit the prospect for the attribution of important statues to anonymous masters distinguished more by features and details of their oeuvre than by the localities in which they worked. Preliminary reduction—the felling of the tree, the removal and trimming of branches and the roughing out of the primary mass—was the work of the woodsman's large axe. The following major stages—the defining of secondary masses and the subsequent bringing out and refining of the major features—were done with an adze. Finer features and decorative details were the work of small knives. The smooth finish desirable in all figures throughout the wider region was attained by the rough-textured leaves of a kind of fig tree.

A number of moderately hard woods served as the material of the statues. The Fang finished their figures in uniformly applied colours ranging from black through dark brown to a reddish mahogany-like shade. The use of brass and, less frequently, copper for apotropaic and decorative purposes was generally limited to the eyes of statues, generally those with a secular function rather than guardian figures themselves (see fig. 1). Guardian figures usually wore crowns of plumes, which had both martial significance and aesthetic value.

The poses and surface enhancement of some figures may provide insight into their roles. The arrangement of the arms and the shape and interrelationship of the facial features sometimes seem to correspond to an apotropaic intent. For example, the simple position of the arms in most figures is sometimes changed to accommodate the holding of a vessel. Some authors have seen in this gesture a request for offerings, although the role of guardian seems to be at odds with an act of petition. On the other hand, the proffering or displaying of a vessel might refer to a defensive act: inviting an intruder to drink the ordeal poison that would reveal witchcraft and destroy its host. Perhaps where the guardian figure holds a head (see fig. 2), the warning power was considered to have been enhanced.

Tessman proposed a sequence of formal development in Fang sculpture through an undefined time-span, perhaps implicitly corresponding to the settling down in the present territory. He conducted his intensive studies only among groups in the region of the Upper Benito River in what was then Spanish Guinea. There he found guardian images of three kinds: independent heads on long necks (see fig. 3), half-figures ending above the hips, and full figures. Finding the heads to be rarest of all, he inferred that they came first, that their use led gradually to the invention of the half-figure and, finally, to that of the full figure.

However, the prevailing style of coiffure and the shape of the face in the inventory of guardian heads is at variance with most Fang half- and full figures. The coiffure of crests and sidelocks running down into long points is easier to reconcile with non-Fang figures collected on the coast of what was then Spanish Guinea. These correspondences suggest that the presence of guardian heads among the Fang is more the result of external influence and internal diffusion than of independent invention.

The essential Fang image would be the reliquary guardian figure, essential in the sense of having integral features

2. Fang sculpture of a seated female figure holding a head, wood, h. 495 mm, from Gabon, Equatorial Guinea or south-west Cameroon, *c.* 1900 (New Haven, CT, Yale University Art Gallery)

that distinguish it sharply from analogous figures in other cultures. This distinctiveness can fall away at the north-western edge of the Fang range, where interaction between the Fang and the Ngumba apparently led to the exchange of a considerable number of style-elements. Fang and Ngumba guardian-figure styles agree closely in their basic features: somewhat contracted posture, rounded masses, self-contained body-parts, lustrous finish and the sitting-stalk by which they are fixed in the lid of the bark reliquary-barrel. These attributes separate them from most of the other major styles in the wider region. The sitting-stalk had another purpose among the Fang and probably among the Ngumba. Considerably longer in its traditional use

3. Fang head, wood and mirror, h. 260 mm, from Gabon, 1902 (Neuchâtel, Musée d'Ethnographie de Neuchâtel)

than is the case in figures mounted for display in Western collections, it served as a handle to animate the figure as it took part in theatrical performances during convocations of the *byeri* cult.

The distinctiveness of Fang figure style is best presented through its contrast with Ngumba style. One of the more striking differences is found in modes of coiffure: both peoples had diverse ways of dressing or covering the hair, but the styles seem not to have overlapped much in their guardian figures.

At the turn of the century the central Fang chose a low series of front-to-back, subequal crests that coalesced to form a wide havelock, usually descending at least below the middle of the nape. At this time the north-eastern Fang developed a coiffure in the form of a hemispherical cap with a moderately high, sagittal crest flattened at the top and sides. The prevailing Ngumba coiffure was then based on a low, keeled crest of ovoid outline. This was constructed in life either singly over the mid-line of the head or at each side of the head, the inner edges joining at the mid-line. These seem to have been prevailing choices, as seen in the statuary; a number of other distinctive styles appear less frequently among known examples.

The faces of Fang figures vary from deeply concave to moderately convex; convexity prevails in those of the Ngumba, although the depth of the element representing the lips and mouth in some substyles can create the illusion of concave cheeks. Most Fang styles tend toward prognathism and prominent mouths. This feature is less consistent across the Ngumba substyles. Both styles treat the body and limbs as a composition of rounded units, even though they may assume angular poses. Ngumba style tends towards attenuation, while the Fang at its most characteristic is frontal and massive, partly through the swelling quality of shoulders, arms, trunk and legs.

Nearly all Ngumba figures show an openwork treatment of the arms. These are held away from the trunk, with the hands brought either together in the vertical plane of the face or straight down separately to each thigh. The former mode is often made distinctive by asymmetry: the hands are placed one above the other as they hold such objects as flutes and medicine-filled antelope horns. Some Fang substyles follow the openwork plan, but the hands hold various kinds of receptacles, both always at the same level.

Except for rare examples in ebony, the colour of Ngumba guardian figures is rarely darker than dark brown. A mahogany shade, perhaps attained through the use of powdered barwood, is common. While some Fang substyles employ this range of colour, others tend towards black, often with reddish undertones. This preference remains to be explained, but it has come to be thought of as an intrinsic part of Fang style.

Byeri was apparently not the only religious context for free-standing figures of moderate size. A number of whitened wooden figures in a style appreciably different from that of the reliquary guardians were collected at unspecified localities around the end of the 19th century. They might exemplify the kind of wooden figure that Trilles found guarding crossroads near Fang villages. Trilles also saw numerous small images of animals and birds, carved in *musanga* wood or constructed of raffia pith, hanging from the roofs of men's houses, which were lineage-limited buildings used as guard-houses, eating places, workrooms and dormitories. He guessed that such figures would have harboured the spirits of slain animals.

A major rite, *so*, for the initiation of youths into manhood provided another religious context for statuary among the northern Fang, borrowed from the Beti. In addition, *so* (and a number of lesser cults among the northeastern Fang) fashioned earthen figures representing such animals as elephant, antelope and bush-pig in prone positions. Another cult, *ngi* (a men's association intended to protect its members and their families against harm from witchcraft), constructed large, sometimes heroic, human figures in earth. These usually supine figures were modelled in varying degrees of relief, but showed less reduction of form than *so* animal figures. They contained magical materials thought to reveal the guilt of those who falsely swore before them that they were innocent of witchcraft.

The secular, prestige-motivated field of Fang art takes in a number of masterfully carved human figures, usually standing more erect than those of the *byeri* reliquary. Such relatively small statues—and independent heads—served as the finials and handles of wooden objects, lending distinction to their owners. These status-enhancing artefacts included leaders' staffs, men's spoons, bow-harps, side-blown horns and smiths' bellows. Some spoons and possibly a few horns were carved out of ivory.

3. MASKS. Most Fang masks fall into three formal categories. The simplest of all reproduces an ovoid mass longitudinally bisected and hollowed out; it covers only the face and often has concave cheeks. The second design mediates between the first and third categories. Its outline reproduces a solid right triangle on point; its mass is hollowed out and its inverted base rests on top of the wearer's head. It can be thought of as a partial helmet mask. The third category is a true helmet mask, schematically viewed as a solid elliptical form cut transversely in half, of which one half is hollowed out and adapted for wear. It completely conceals the head of the wearer (see fig. 4). The manner of representing the eyes in Fang masks is distinctive: they are small round or oval perforations

4. Fang helmet mask, wood, pigment and fibre, h. 340 mm, from Gabon or south-west Cameroon, c. 1900 (Paris, Musée d'Art Moderne de la Ville de Paris)

cut into the flush surface of the face. Some styles render the eyelids in relief.

Masks seem to have surpassed sculptures of human figures in their decorative effects. They were usually made of softer kinds of wood with the same tools as were used for making statues (see §2 above). Their colours were confined to the regional triad of pigments—red, white and black (including dark brown)—but were designed in various geometric patterns. The masks bore crowns and aureoles of long plumes, sometimes trimmed into toothed and tufted shafts. European mirrors fixed to their faces flashed as they moved.

The corpus of Fang masks, unlike that of reliquary guardian figures, comprises a number of distinct canons, some of which grade into each other. Types explicitly representing animals, or endowed with animal attributes, are rare, a trait that contrasts with the masking traditions of some adjacent groups; the presence of zoomorphic features usually seems to attest to borrowing from those groups. The horned masks found among the Fang tend to occur at the northern edge of this people's range, which suggests that they might have been borrowed from the Ngumba and, perhaps indirectly, from the Kwele. Among the more central Fang, the presence of helmet masks with diverse horn- and wing-like additions almost certainly reflects their interaction with a number of Kele-speaking groups. These appendages do not explicitly refer to real animals but were probably intended initially to contribute to the fantastic aspects of the forest spirits that the masks represent.

The Fang *so* rite (see §2 above) brought the use of masks into its ceremonies. These masks were carved in a number of styles, but all show a pair of horns, usually curved and often more reminiscent of those of a goat than those of any forest antelope. Their faces were predominantly white and showed some degree of modelling in their features. Masks used in the *ngi* cult of the northern Yaunde–Fang peoples had longer and usually thinner horns, and their facial features were greatly simplified, consisting mainly of a flat nose of triangular outline rising out of a facial plane that was long, flat and usually rectangular. These masks, which were distinctively coloured in squares or stripes of black and white, were worn by the master of a cult lodge when interrogating initiands, supervising their ordeals and leading witch-finding campaigns. It is possible to discern a formal relationship between the *ngi* mask of the Beti and Bulu and the *so* mask of the northern Fang. Indeed, certain Fang frontal masks with long, narrow and predominantly white faces now make up a category attributed, probably erroneously, to the Fang version of the *ngi* cult. The Fang *ngi* apparently did use masks, but not consistently, and in some accounts the master's disguise consisted only of pigments applied to his face and body.

Masks also had a role centred in primarily secular play, though perhaps having strong religious and political implications. These masks, made predominantly of wood, belonged to individuals or to associations that could include members of different lineages, and were used to entertain villagers and their guests. The custom of rewarding dancers, masked or otherwise, with gifts according to their beauty and skill—or in some cases their fearsomeness—led to the development of a number of distinct masked personages throughout Fang country. Certain Fang groups in Equatorial Guinea developed a distinctive use for masklike forms. In several dances the dancers (mostly women) performed with a small replica of a mask attached to one of their upper arms. The dances spread into adjacent parts of Gabon and Cameroon, probably around the 1920s.

4. OTHER ARTS. The Fang obsession with coiffure provides the most apparent link between secular art and *byeri* iconography. The first migrants observed by Europeans around the 1860s wore their hair in several arrangements of simple braids that did not follow any particular design and were minimally decorated. During the late 19th century, this style changed drastically, giving way to a fashion of one or more comparatively high front-to-back crests, complemented at the outset by pendent sidelocks that in due course became subordinate elements. The style began with the working of hair over 'rats' of false hair to form ridged crests. Later, helmetlike prestige caps were fashioned from animal hide or palm-leaf strips, on to which were sewn braids of plant fibre and then crests of raffia pith. These caps served to display European-manufactured shirt-buttons, brass tacks, glass beads, mirrors and cowries affixed to their surfaces. The form and volume of these headdresses contribute importantly to the sculptural composition and the aesthetic effect of the *byeri* guardian.

Human images sometimes decorated the pillars that held up the beams of men's houses. Heads and mastoids in varying degrees of relief ran along the shaft. Occasionally a massive full-figure in the round would represent the base of the column; its style was not likely to be as finely conceived and executed as that of the *byeri* guardian, but the stance was similar. Non-representational motives, both sculptural and two-dimensional, distinguished other pillars. The enhancement of objects to symbolize social status was not consistent through Fang society: some families and individuals strove for distinction while others had more prosaic concerns.

The Fang use of diverse non-representational motifs, usually of a geometric nature, in the surface decoration of many kinds of artefact complemented their high attainments in sculpture. The main techniques used to decorate wooden objects—not just *byeri* guardian figures and masks—were incised fretwork, chip-carving and low relief. In some instances red, white and black or brown pigments intensified the contrast between forms in low relief and their backgrounds. Chip-carving and scraping scorched surfaces away also achieved striking decorative effects. The sculptural rendering of such three-dimensional non-representational forms as spheres, ovoids, oblong tetragons and radially arranged vanes strengthened the impression of temporal power implicit in leaders' staffs and men's house pillars.

Fang women were competent potters, but their work, although pleasantly and simply decorated, has not received the recognition accorded to the non-representational ceramic traditions of other Central African peoples. The same is true for other domestic arts: basketry, mat-plaiting and the decoration of house exteriors. The Fang, unlike many of their new neighbours, did not take to weaving

raffia cloth, preferring instead to wear bark-cloth of their own manufacture or, later on, cotton trade cloth.

The Fang inclination towards adornment followed through into the decoration of their weapons. The first Europeans to meet the migrating groups noted their characteristic short sword and small all-purpose axe. These arms did not vary greatly in their grace of form, but their blades were often profusely engraved with small geometric motifs in individualized patterns, contrasting in this regard with the traditions of their new neighbours. The distinctiveness of these forms and their ornament seem to point to pre-migration origins. Even so, the intensity and variety of Fang engraving appear to surpass analogous ironwork of the peoples who might have lived near them in earlier times. Fang skill in casting and chasing brass circlets was also notable but likely to have been influenced by the circumstances of the migration.

UNPUBLISHED SOURCES

London, BM, and Geneva, Mus. Ethnog. [MS of F. Grébert: *Monographie ethnographique des tribus Fang: Bantous de la forêt du Gabon, Afrique Equatoriale Française* (1940)]

BIBLIOGRAPHY

T. E. Bowdich: *Mission from Cape Coast Castle to Ashantee with Statistical Account of that Kingdom, and Geographical Notices of Other Parts of the Interior of Africa* (London, 1819)

J. L. Wilson: *Western Africa* (New York, 1856)

P. B. Du Chaillu: *Explorations and Adventures in Equatorial Africa* (New York, 1861)

V. D., Marquis de Compiègne: *L'Afrique équatoriale*, 2 vols (Paris, 1876)

M. Hartert: 'Ein Besuch bei den M'Pangwes am Muni', *Globus*, lx/14 (1891), pp. 209–12

A. L. Bennett: 'Ethnographical Notes on the Fang', *J. Anthropol. Inst. GB & Ireland*, n. s., ii (1899), pp. 66–98

R. H. Nassau: *Fetishism in West Africa* (New York, 1904)

E. Poutrin: 'Etude des documents anthropologiques recuellis à la Mission Cottes par le docteur Gravot', *La Mission Cottes au Sud-Cameroun (1905–1908)*, ed. A. Cottes (Paris, 1911)

A. F., Duke of Mecklenburg: *Vom Kongo zum Niger und Nil*, 2 vols (Leipzig, 1912)

G. Tessmann: 'Die Kinderspiele der Pangwe', *Baessler-Archv*, ii/5–6 (Berlin, 1912), pp. 250–80

R. P. H. Trilles: 'Le Totémisme chez les Fang', *Anthropos-Bibliothek*, i/4 (Münster, 1912)

G. Tessmann: *Die Pangwe: Völkerkundliche Monographie eines west-afrikanischen Negerstammes* (Berlin, 1913)

P. Guillaume and T. Munro: *Primitive Negro Sculpture* (New York, 1926)

F. Grébert: *Au Gabon (Afrique Equatoriale Française)* (Paris, 1928)

——: 'Arts en voie de disparition au Gabon', *Africa*, 7 (1934), pp. 82–8

I. Dugast: 'Inventaire ethnique du Sud-Cameroun', *Mém. Inst. Fr. Afrique Noire: Cent., Cameroun, 'Populations'* (Dakar, 1949)

M. Guthrie: *The Bantu Languages of Western Equatorial Africa* (London, 1953)

P. Alexandre and J. Binet: *Le Groupe dit Pahouin (Fang–Boulou–Beti)* (Paris, 1958)

H. Pepper: *Anthologie de la vie africaine* (Paris, 1958) [text accompanying an album of ethnomusicological records]

Abbé T. Tsala: 'Moeurs et coutumes des Ewondo', *Etud. Cameroun.*, 56 (Yaoundé, 1958), pp. 8–112

A. Panyella: *Esquema de Etnologia de los Fang Ntumu de la Guinea Española* (Madrid, 1959)

H. Deschamps: *Traditions orales et archives au Gabon* (Paris, 1962)

G. Balandier: *The Sociology of Black Africa: Social Dynamics in Central Africa* (Paris, 1963; Eng. trans., 1970)

C. Gonzales Echegaray: 'Aportación al estudio de las canciones y danzas de la provincia española de Rio Muni', *Instituto de Estudios Africanos, Estudios Guineos*, ii (Madrid, 1964), pp. 115–60

K. Krieger: *Westafrikanische Plastik*, i, Veröff. Mus. Vlkerknd. Berlin, n. s., 7 (1965), pp. 1–148

Masks and Sculptures from the Collection of Gustave and Franyo Schindler, Museum of Primitve Art (New York, 1966)

W. B. Fagg: *Miniature Wood Carvings of Africa* (Bath, UK, and Greenwich, CT, 1970)

Arts africains: Musée Cantini (Marseille, 1970)

J. W. Fernandez: 'Principles of Opposition and Vitality in Fang Aesthetics', *Art and Aesthetics in Primitive Societies*, ed. C. F. Jopling (New York, 1971), pp. 356–73

J. Binet: 'Sociétés de danse chez les Fang du Gabon', *Travaux et documents de l'ORSTOM*, 17 (Paris, 1972)

Peoples and Cultures, Lisbon Overseas Museum of Ethnology (1972)

L. Perrois: *Statuaire Fan(g): Gabon* (Paris, 1972)

J. W. Fernandez: 'The Exposition and Imposition of Order: Artistic Expression in Fang Culture', *The Traditional Artist in African Societies*, ed. W. L. d'Azevedo (Bloomington, 1973), pp. 194–220

J. W. Fernandez and R. L. Fernandez: 'Fang Reliquary Art: Its Quantities and Qualities', *Cah. Etud. Afr.*, xv/4 (1975), pp. 723–46

L. Siroto: *African Spirit Images and Identities* (New York, 1976)

——: 'Njom: The Magical Bridge of the Beti and Bulu of Southern Cameroun', *Afr. A.*, x/2 (1977), pp. 38–51, 90–91

M. E. Joseph: *African Art: The Spirit Manifest* (Lincoln, MA, 1978)

L. Perrois: *Arts du Gabon* (Paris, 1979)

L. Siroto: 'Witchcraft Belief in the Explanation of Traditional African Iconography', *The Visual Arts: Plastic and Graphic*, ed. J. M. Cordwell (The Hague, 1979), pp. 241–91

J. W. Fernandez: *Bwiti: An Ethnography of the Religious Imagination in Africa* (Princeton, 1982)

J.-L. Paudrat: 'The Arrival of Tribal Objects in the West: From Africa', *'Primitivism' in 20th Century Art: Affinity of the Tribal and the Modern*, ed. W. Rubin, 2 vols (New York, 1984), pp. 124–75

P. Laburthe-Tolra: *Initiations et sociétés secrètes au Cameroun: Essai sur la religion Beti* (Paris, 1985)

L. Perrois: *Ancestral Art of Gabon from the Collections of the Barbier-Mueller Museum* (Geneva, 1985)

J. McKesson: 'Réflexions sur l'évolution de la sculpture des reliquaires Fang', *A. Afrique Noire*, 63 (1987), pp. 7–21

C. Falgayrettes-Leveau and P. Laburthe-Tolra: *Fang* (Paris, 1991)

LEON SIROTO

Fang Chao-ling. *See* FANG ZHAOLING.

Fang Congyi [Fang Ts'ung-i; *zi* Wuyu; *hao* Fanghu] (*b* Guixi, Jiangxi Province; *fl c.* 1340–80). Chinese painter who became a Daoist priest in his youth; he joined the Zhengyi sect, whose main temples were situated in the Shangqing Temple (Shangqing si) on Mt Longhu in his home district, and studied under the priest Jin Pengtou. During the early 1340s, after the death of his teacher, he travelled from Xinzhou to many areas along the River Yangzi and in 1343 visited the capital, Dadu (Khanbaligh, now Beijing), where he became acquainted with many officials and scholarly men and established a reputation as a painter. He is reported to have visited many famous sites along the Great Wall and may have made several trips to the scenic mountains that were considered the home of the Daoist immortals; these included the Taihang range, on the border of Henan and Shanxi provinces, Mt Heng (Shanxi), Mt Tai and Mt Huafouju (Shandong), Mt Zhong in Nanjing (Jiangsu), Mt Kuanglu (Jiangxi) and Mt Wuyi (Fujian). During his time in the capital he seems to have attracted the attention of the Princess of Lu, known as a great patron of art, and of another Daoist painter, Zhang Yanfu (*fl* 1340–50), who was connected with the court. However, he soon returned to Xinzhou and set up his own temple. Later he was said to have lived in mountain temples in Jinhua, in western Zhejiang Province. During the last period of his life he is thought to have travelled extensively in south China, including various parts of Jiangxi, Jiangsu, Zhejiang and Fujian provinces, visiting many of the Daoist sacred mountains. According to his contemporaries, he had an unearthly manner and bearing that recalled the qualities of a Daoist immortal. This characteristic ethereality is reflected in such paintings as *Boating under Mt Wuyi* (hanging scroll, 1359; Beijing, Pal. Mus.) and *Divine Mountains and Luminous Woods* (hanging scroll, 1365; Taipei, N. Pal. Mus.), in which the landscape appears to change and evolve, without clearly defined shapes and images. Influenced by the atmospheric monochrome ink-wash manner of Mi Fu and Mi Youren of the Song period (960–1279), his paintings may be grouped, with those of Ni Zan, in the untrammelled category (*yipin*) of painters (*see* CHINA, §V, 5(ii)). Fang was also part of the tradition developed in the early Yuan period (1279–1368), when literati painters such as Gao Kegong were increasingly concerned with developing personal modes of expression and with the depiction of more than objective reality (e.g. *Clouds and Snow on the Shanyin Mountains, after Gao Kegong*, hanging scroll, n.d.; Taipei, N. Pal. Mus.). However, his life as a Daoist priest and the individuality of his style set him apart from his contemporaries.

BIBLIOGRAPHY

DMB: 'Fang Ts'ung-i'

O. Sirén: *Chinese Painting: Leading Masters and Principles*, iv (London, 1958), pp. 58–9

J. Cahill: *Hills beyond a River: Chinese Painting of the Yuan Dynasty, 1279–1368* (New York and Tokyo, 1976), pp. 127–8

Chen Gaohua: *Yuan dai huajia shiliao* [Literary sources of Yuan period painters] (Shanghai, 1980), pp. 483–94

M. G. Neill: *Mountains of the Immortals: The Life and Works of Fang Ts'ung-i* (diss., New Haven, CT, Yale U., 1980)

CHU-TSING LI

Fangor, Wojciech (*b* Warsaw, 15 Nov 1922). Polish painter and poster designer. He studied at the private studios of Tadeusz Pruszkowski (1888–1942) and Felicjan Kowarski in Warsaw between 1940 and 1942. From 1966 he lived in the USA. In 1949 Fangor exhibited his early portraits of *Lenin* and *Einstein*, among others. They were garish in colour and intentionally primitivist and brutalist in form. The Socialist Realist works from between 1950 and 1955 (e.g. *Bricklayers*, 1950, and *Korean Mother*, 1951) are monumental academic, programmatic paintings of a propagandist, poster-style character, occasionally featuring ambiguity and irony, as in *Figures* (1950). Fangor gained popularity as a poster designer, and when Socialist Realism went into decline he switched from programmatic simplifications to experimental simplicity (e.g. the street decorations for the 5th International Festival of Youth, Warsaw, 1955).

Fangor achieved fame in 1958 with the Warsaw exhibition *Studium Przestrzeni* ('Study of Space'), in which he presented an environment operating on the principle of the after-image. He produced spatially interdependent abstract canvases and explored a temporal sequence of colour perception. This was further developed in the *Colour in Space* environment, prepared with S. Zamecznik (Amsterdam, Stedel. Mus., 1959). In the 1960s he produced technically refined Op art works: hazy multi-coloured circles and waves that throb and pulsate when viewed, making it impossible to gain a clear perception of shape and colour. In the 1970s Fangor produced a series of paintings analysing mass images from illustrated magazines and television (akin to the work of the German

'Capitalist Realists'), series of *plein-air* sculptures and archaizing, brutalist head masks.

BIBLIOGRAPHY
Fifteen Polish Painters (exh. cat. by P. Setz, New York, MOMA, 1961), pp. 9, 20–21, 57–8
R. Kenedy: 'Notes on Fangor', *A. Int.*, x/4 (1966), pp. 53–6
B. Kowalska: *Polska awangarda malarska 1945–1970* [Polish avant-garde painting, 1945–70] (Warsaw, 1975)
J. Bogucki: *Sztuka Polski Ludowej* [The art of the people's Poland] (Warsaw, 1983)

EWA MIKINA

Fang Ts'ung-i. *See* FANG CONGYI.

Fang Zhaoling [Fang Chao-ling] (*b* Wuxi, Jiangsu Province, 17 Jan 1914). Chinese painter and calligrapher. Born into a prosperous and well-educated family, Fang developed an early interest in art. She studied at the University of Hong Kong and Oxford University before devoting herself to art from the 1950s onwards. The foundations of her art were traditional. A student of Qian Songyan (1899–1985), Zhao Shao'ang (*b* 1905) and Zhang Daqian, she grasped firmly the spirit and techniques of her native tradition, especially the expressive calligraphic line. In addition to studying Chinese literature and philosophy, she 'walked 10,000 miles' to visit scenic landscapes in China and elsewhere. She was also open to influences from modern developments in Western art. Her personal and individualistic style evolved from a synthesis of these factors, expressing her profound empathy for the joys and sorrows of life and her refreshing vision in bold compositions and powerful brushwork.

BIBLIOGRAPHY
Wucius Wong: 'Fang Zhao-ling', *Orientations*, xiii/11 (1982), pp. 44–55
The Paintings and Calligraphy of Fang Zhao-ling (Hong Kong and Shanghai, 1986) [Eng. and Chin. text]

MAYCHING KAO

Fan Kuan [Fan K'uan; *ming* Zhongzheng; *zi* Zhongli] (*b* Huayuan [now Hua xian, Shaanxi Province], *c.* AD 990; *d c.* 1030). Chinese painter. He was one of the most important representatives of the monumental tradition of Northern Song (960–1127) landscape painting, which at that time was becoming established as the most important category of painting in China (*see* CHINA, §V, 3(iv)(b)). About 1024 Guo Ruoxu (*fl* 11th century), a minor court official at Bianliang (modern Kaifeng), the capital of the Northern Song dynasty, wrote in the *Tuhua jianwen zhi* ('Experiences in painting') that Fan Kuan was the equal of Li Cheng and Guan Tong and that these three masters stood 'like the legs of a tripod' and would serve as models 'for a hundred generations'. About 20 years later, Liu Daochun (*fl* mid-11th century) wrote in the *Shengchao minghua ping* ('Critique of famous painters of the present dynasty') that the only landscapists deserving absolute praise were Li Cheng and Fan Kuan and that there was no-one, past or present, who compared with them.

Fan Kuan was not a scholar, nor did he pass any examinations or hold any official position. Guo Ruoxu wrote that 'Kuan's manner and appearance had an antique severity, that his behaviour was rude and rustic and that it was his nature to crave wine and love the Daoist Way'. His earlier work was based on the paintings of LI CHENG, which he studied as a young man, as well as on those of JING HAO. As he matured, however, Fan introduced innovations obviously based on direct and careful observation of nature. According to the *Xuanhe huapu* ('Xuanhe collection of paintings'; the catalogue of the paintings of the Song emperor Huizong (*reg* 1101–26); preface dated 1120), he believed that, like those before him who had made it their rule never to be detached from things, he too should learn, not from other men but from things themselves or, better still, from their inner nature. In order to accomplish this he isolated himself from society and lived alone in the mountains, exactly where is not known. His artistic activity, temperament and way of life are clearly reflected in the character of his landscapes. They have a rational order and inherent structural precision that reflect a Neo-Confucianist cosmic view, and surface textures and atmospheric effects that could only have been based on careful observation of nature in all its moods.

As early as the beginning of the Song period (960–1279), critics distinguished between two major schools of painting originating with either Li Cheng or Fan Kuan. The comparison involved not only their general styles but also their brush techniques. According to Mi Fu, in the *Hua shi* ('History of painting'; completed 1103), Fan Kuan's work was 'as dark as nightfall on a gloomy day', and his excessive use of ink in his later years made it impossible to distinguish the earth from the rocks in his paintings. Mi Fu went so far as to rank Fan Kuan as superior to all the landscape painters of his period, but other critics generally regarded Fan Kuan and Li Cheng as equals, and both as belonging to the 'divine' (*shen*) category of painters.

Sternness and independence were the qualities most frequently associated with Fan Kuan. Throughout his career, his creative genius was patently nurtured by his communication with nature. It was felt that his paintings revealed no sense of the soft or mellow aspects of nature, but his attention to realism earned him a reputation for 'showing the very bones of the mountains' (Miyagawa, p. 176); and Mi wrote that 'in Fan Kuan's landscapes you can hear the water' (Loehr, p. 100). According to Alexander Soper, the commentaries of Liu Daochun referred to the 'real rocks and ancient trees which thrust themselves up, alive, under his brush. One finds in him a spirit consonance (*qiyun*) that goes beyond the surface of things and an indifference to ornamental beauty' (*see* 1961–2 exh. cat., no. 18). Fan's sense of order came to be regarded as characteristic of the Northern Song tradition of landscape painting. He introduced the principle of *sanfen gefa* ('three-division method') of staggered depth to establish a logical, three-part organization: foreground, middle ground and background—the 'three distances' (*sanyuan*). High distance (*gaoyuan*) perspective set off towering peaks in monumental settings against tiny human forms. These cliff faces were given form as well as a rocklike sense of mass by a brushstroke known as *yudian cun* ('raindrop texture stroke'). This technique may have been used earlier but Fan was the first to develop it systematically on a large scale.

The only authenticated example of Fan Kuan's work is *Travellers among Mountains and Streams* (see fig.), one of the most famous of Chinese paintings. Originally believed to have been unsigned, this hanging scroll bears a signature

Fan Kuan: *Travellers among Mountains and Streams*, hanging scroll, ink and colours on silk, 2.06×1.03 m, early 11th century (Taipei, National Palace Museum)

(rediscovered in 1958) in the lower right-hand corner. Additional authentication is provided by an inscription on the mount by Dong Qichang, which attributes the work to Fan and gives the title. The painting is monumental both in conception and in size. At the centre of the composition and dominating it is a massive vertical cliff viewed in the high distance, which creates a visual barrier to movement beyond the middle ground. Only the mountain crests have vegetation. Space provided for movement is limited to the foreground, where the tiny figures of travellers, dwarfed by the central mass, are seen on a road. Clustered at the base of the cliff, and thus providing a transition between middle ground and background, are mists, created by light ink washes, which silhouette the roofs of a temple barely visible above the densely wooded

hill. The entire composition emphasizes rational organization and the unmistakable sense of nature's dominant relationship with man. It also strongly reflects the severity identified with Fan's style. Several other paintings in the National Palace Museum in Taipei are attributed to Fan Kuan but none is signed.

Fan Kuan exerted enormous influence on contemporary artists such as Yan Wengui as well as on subsequent generations. The later Song master Li Tang made persistent references to him in such compositions as *Whispering Pines in the Gorges* (hanging scroll; ink and light colour on silk; 1.88×1.39 m; 1124; Taipei, N. Pal. Mus.). Even though the balance of foreground to background and the sense of space have been modified, as has the brushstroke, a dependence on the earlier heroic style is clearly evident. Copies made in the later part of the Ming (1368–1644) and early Qing (1644–1911) periods were increasingly removed from the original in their depiction of space, the relationships between pictorial elements and the different brushwork, although the original conception remained.

BIBLIOGRAPHY

Franke: 'Fan K'uan'
Xuanhe huapu [Xuanhe collection of painting] (compiled before 1119), ed. Yu Jianhua (Beijing, 1964)
Guo Ruoxu: *Tuhua jianwen zhi* [Experiences in painting] (c. 1024), ed. Huan Miaozi (Shanghai, 1963); Eng. trans. in A. C. Soper: *Kuo Jo-hsü's Experiences in Painting (Tu-hua chien-wen chih)* (Washington, DC, 1951/R 1971)
O. Sirén: *Chinese Painting: Leading Masters and Principles*, i (London, 1956), pp. 201–7
Chinese Art Treasures: A Selected Group of Objects from the Chinese National Palace Museum and the Chinese National Central Museum, Taichung (exh. cat., Washington, DC, N.G.A.; New York, Met.; Boston, MA, Mus. F.A. and elsewhere; 1961–2), no. 18
Li Lincan: 'Fan Kuan Qishan xinglu tu' [Fan Kuan: Travelling in the Qi mountains], *Zhongguo minghua yanjiu* [A study of famous Chinese paintings], i (Taipei, 1973), pp. 39–49
M. Loehr: *The Great Painters of China* (New York, 1980), pp. 98–102
T. Miyagawa, ed.: *Chinese Painting* (Tokyo, 1983), pp. 121–3, 175–6

MARY S. LAWTON

Fano, Giovanni da. *See* GIOVANNI DA FANO.

Fanon. *See under* VESTMENTS, ECCLESIASTICAL, §1(i).

Fanta, Josef (*b* Sudoměřice u Tábora, 7 Dec 1856; *d* Prague, 19 June 1954). Bohemian architect, designer and teacher. He studied at the Czech Imperial Polytechnic, Prague, and then became assistant to Josef Zítek, who designed the National Theatre, Prague. After the theatre burnt down in 1881, Fanta became assistant to Josef Schulz, who was in charge of its reconstruction, contributing mainly to the design of the interiors. Fanta then gained a grant to spend a year in Italy studying ancient and Renaissance architecture, which influenced the decoration of his first works, minor domestic buildings in Prague. During this period he was also assisting with the interiors of other major buildings in Prague designed by Schulz, such as the Rudolfinum (1876–84) and the National Museum (1886–90). He also took part in the establishment of the Náprstek Museum of Asian, African and American Culture and the Czech ethnography exhibition in Prague in 1895, and he designed interiors for the Czech pavilion at the Exposition Universelle in Paris in 1900 (*see* CZECH REPUBLIC, §V, 4). His later works were strongly influenced by Art Nouveau: for example the main railway station

(1901–9), the Hlahol community house (1905), Hálek's hall of residence (1903), all in Prague, and a number of country houses, such as Kořínek's villa (1909–10) in Poděbrady. In addition, he laid out several cemeteries and designed several tombs and memorials, the most notable of which is the memorial to the Battle of Austerlitz (1906–12), Slavkov, Moravia. From 1909 to 1926 he was a professor of medieval architecture in the Czech university, Prague, and was active in Prague's religious and cultural life, designing ecclesiastical vestments and belonging to the Czech Academy of Science and Art. He also undertook museum work and was involved in the protection of historical monuments.

BIBLIOGRAPHY

P. Toman: *Nový slovník československých výtvarných umělců* [New dictionary of Czech fine artists] (Prague, 1936)

——: *Slovník českých výtvarných umělců* [Dictionary of Czech fine artists] (Prague, 1947)

YVONNE JANKOVÁ

Fantastic Realism. *See* PHANTASTISCHER REALISMUS.

Fantin-Latour. French artists. (1) Henri Fantin-Latour painted in a wide variety of genres, from portraits and still-lifes to allegorical and mythological works. He also produced lithographs. His wife, (2) Victoria Fantin-Latour, painted some portraits but is best known for her still-lifes.

(1) (Ignace-)Henri(-Théodore) Fantin-Latour (*b* Grenoble, 14 Jan 1836; *d* Buré, Orne, 25 Aug 1904). Painter and printmaker. He studied with his father, Jean-Théodore Fantin-Latour (1805–75), from 1846 and then with Horace Lecocq de Boisbaudran at the Petite Ecole de Dessin in Paris from 1850 to 1856. His apprenticeship was based on copying the Old Masters before beginning to study from nature. He had a growing enthusiasm for the Italian painters, particularly Titian and Veronese, whom he copied in the Louvre, Paris, from 1852. *The Dream* (1854; Grenoble, Mus. Grenoble) is one of the first of a series of imaginary scenes in which Fantin-Latour concentrated on the theme of vision, which he later continued in his representations of scenes from various operas. He met François Bonvin and Félix Bracquemond in 1853 and went to the Ecole des Beaux-Arts in 1854, but he left before the end of the year. He began to paint the life around him and did a series of self-portraits from 1854 to 1861, such as *Self-portrait Seated at the Easel* (1858; Berlin, Alte N.G.) and *Self-portrait* (1859; Grenoble, Mus. Grenoble). These two directions—Realism and fantasy—were already clearly defined when he met Gustave Courbet in 1859. For several months in 1861 he was a pupil at Courbet's studio, but from the start he tempered the brutal Realism of his master with a discreet intimacy in such works as the *Two Sisters* (1859; St Louis, MO, A. Mus.), *Woman Reading* (1861; Paris, Mus. d'Orsay) and *Reading* (1863; Tournai, Mus. B.-A.). By rejecting the anecdotal aspect of genre, Fantin-Latour heightened the tension inherent in a contrast between the physical proximity of the models and their psychological distance, creating a sense of solitude.

Through James McNeill Whistler, whom he met in 1858, Fantin-Latour made a succession of trips to England (1859, 1861, 1864, 1881). He met Whistler's brother-in-law, Seymour Haden, who taught him to etch; he exhibited at the Royal Academy, London, in 1862; and he sold his first still-lifes through the collectors Ruth Edwards (*c.* 1833–1907) and Edwin Edwards (1823–79), whom he portrayed on several occasions (e.g. 1875; Washington, DC, N.G.A.). Fantin-Latour's commissioned portraits, such as *Mlle Marguerite de Biron* (1868; Paris, priv. col., see 1982–3 exh. cat., p. 112), also date from this period.

Fantin-Latour's aesthetic is not easily defined: his friendship with Edouard Manet, whom he met in 1857, and the future Impressionists led him to exhibit in the Salon des Refusés in 1863; but he refused to exhibit with them at Nadar's studio in 1874. Although he was rejected at the Salon of 1859, he appeared there regularly from 1861 to 1899, and his works were generally well received by the critics.

Like his friends, Fantin-Latour had a taste for modern life and contemporary scenes, while rejecting anecdote; he had the same sensitivity to light effects, although he was not attracted to *plein-air* painting. From 1864, in an evident desire to become better known, he began exhibiting group portraits, which brought together avant-garde painters and writers: Edouard Manet and Charles Baudelaire in *Homage to Delacroix* (exh. Paris Salon, 1864; Paris, Mus. d'Orsay); Whistler in *The Toast* (exh. Paris Salon, 1865; destr.); Emile Zola, Claude Monet and Auguste Renoir in *Studio in the Batignolles* (exh. Paris Salon, 1870; Paris, Mus. d'Orsay); the 'accursed' poets Paul Verlaine and Arthur Rimbaud in *Corner of the Table* (exh. Paris Salon, 1872); and finally *Around the Piano*, a homage to Richard Wagner (1885; both Paris, Mus. d'Orsay). Fantin-Latour transformed the traditional apotheosis into a bourgeois homage, a friendly gathering even, but the static composition isolates each immobile figure in a monochrome space. This absence of triteness is also typical of his portraits, such as *Edouard Manet* (1867; Chicago, IL, A. Inst.; see fig.) or *Reading* (1877; Lyon, Mus. B.-A.). Lack of facial expression enhances the rigour of the composition and the austerity of the mourning worn by the *Dubourg Family* (1878; Paris, Mus. d'Orsay).

Fantin-Latour was similarly far from Impressionism in his still-lifes. He cut flowers and brought them indoors to paint in the studio. He studied the relationship of tones and colours in compositions based on a balanced pyramid, as in *Autumn Bouquet* (1862; Philadelphia, PA, Mus. A.). He achieved complete control of the composition in *Double Chrysanthemums and Fruit* (1865; Boston, MA, Mus. F.A.). He was able to link a precise rendering of plants with the objective of the overall pictorial effect in *Primulas, Pears and Pomegranates* (1866; Otterlo, Kröller-Müller Sticht.) and in *Tea Roses and a Blue Glass Carafe* (1889; Lyon, Mus. B.-A.). In *White Rambler Roses* (1870; Houston, TX, Mus. F.A.) he depicted only flowers, concentrating on the subtle variations of colour. From the late 1870s he and his wife, (2) Victoria Fantin-Latour, spent the summers in Buré, Orne, and vegetation became accordingly more prominent in his paintings (e.g. *Annual Chrysanthemums*, 1889; Kansas City, MO, Nelson–Atkins Mus. A.).

During the Siege of Paris and the Commune (1871), Fantin-Latour gave up portraiture for more literary pursuits, which he had already tried with the lithographs for

Henri Fantin-Latour: *Edouard Manet*, oil on canvas, 1175×900 mm, 1867 (Chicago, IL, Art Institute of Chicago)

Tannhäuser: Venusberg (1862; Paris, Bib. N., see 1982–3 exh. cat., p. 153), a theme he also painted (1864; Los Angeles, CA, Co. Mus. A.). This allegory of hedonistic love fitted in with a growing interest in 18th-century painting, particularly *fêtes galantes*, a genre taken up again by Narcisse Diaz and Adolphe Monticelli. From 1870 Fantin-Latour's output was punctuated with such mythological scenes as Danae, Auroras, the *Toilet of Venus* (Geneva, Petit Pal.) and nymphs illustrating an edition of poems by André Chénier (Paris, 1902).

Through such friends as Otto Scholderer, a painter and violinist from Frankfurt, Edmond Maître (*d* 1898), a pianist and dilettante, Adolphe Jullien (1840–1932), his biographer, and the judge Antoine Lascoux, Fantin-Latour discovered the contemporary German music of Robert Schumann, Johannes Brahms and Richard Wagner. He was imbued with the spirit of Romanticism, as underlined by his choices, celebrating in turn Schumann in *Reflections of the Orient* (1864–9; destr.) and Hector Berlioz in *The Birthday* (exh. Paris Salon, 1876; Grenoble, Mus. Grenoble). Music provided a reservoir of ideas in which Fantin-Latour's escapism could find imaginative expression; he discovered the dreaming idealistic side of life that he did not find in contemporary society. Using the flexible technique of tracing with lithographic chalk, later reworked by rubbing or scratching the stone, he created the *Witch of the Alps* (1873; see 1982–3 exh. cat., p. 223) after Schumann and the *Trojan Duet* and the *Apparition of Hector* (both 1879) after Berlioz. From Wagner he took the legendary romanticism of the eternal temptations and great myths, illustrating *Tannhäuser* with the *Evening Star*

(1884; see 1982–3 exh. cat., p. 299), *Lohengrin* with *Lohengrin's Prelude* (1882; see 1982–3 exh. cat., p. 117), *Parsifal* with the *Evocation of Kundry* (1883) and above all *The Ring* (all Paris, Bib. N., Cab. Est.). He depicted the same scenes several times, and the definitive versions appear in Adolphe Jullien's biographies of *Richard Wagner* (Paris, 1886) and *Hector Berlioz* (Paris, 1888). Fantin-Latour's tastes never evolved; only a single journey to Bayreuth in 1876 allowed him to enrich his sources of inspiration by developing such new themes as *Das Rheingold: Opening Scene* (pastel and charcoal on lithography, 1876–7, Paris, Mus. d'Orsay; painting, 1888, Hamburg, Ksthalle), in which he showed an Impressionist sensitivity to light and the technique of applying colour in broken strokes.

UNPUBLISHED SOURCES

Paris, Bib. N., Cab. Est. [V. Fantin-Latour: *Notes prises par Mme Fantin-Latour du vivant de H. Fantin-Latour, 1836–1860*]

BIBLIOGRAPHY

Catalogue des lithographies originales de Henri Fantin-Latour (exh. cat. by L. Bénédite, Paris, Mus. Luxembourg, 1899)

G. Hédiard: *L'Oeuvre de Fantin-Latour: Recueil de cinquante reproductions d'après les principaux chefs-d'oeuvre du maître* (Paris, 1906/*R* Geneva, 1980)

A. Jullien: *Fantin-Latour: Sa vie et ses amitiés* (Paris, 1909)

V. Fantin-Latour: *Catalogue complet, 1849–1904, de Fantin-Latour* (Paris, 1911, rev. Amsterdam and New York, 1969)

Centenaire de Henri Fantin-Latour (exh. cat., Grenoble, Mus.–Bib., 1936)

D. Druick: *The Lithographs of Henri Fantin-Latour: Their Place within the Context of his Oeuvre and his Critical Reputation* (diss., New Haven, CT, Yale U., 1979)

Fantin-Latour (exh. cat. by D. Druick and M. Hoog, Paris, Grand Pal.; Ottawa, N.G.; San Francisco, CA Pal. Legion of Honor; 1982–3)

V. M. C. Bajou: *Les Sujets musicaux chez Fantin-Latour* (diss., Paris, Ecole Louvre, 1988)

(2) (Marie-Louise-)Victoria Fantin-Latour [née Dubourg] (*b* Paris, 1 Dec 1840; *d* Buré, 30 Sept 1926). Painter, wife of (1) Henri Fantin-Latour. She studied under the portrait painter Fanny Chéron (*b* 1830) and probably met Fantin-Latour at the Louvre, Paris, where they were both copying in the mid-1860s. Around 1867–8 she was associated with the circle of Edouard Manet, Berthe Morisot, Fantin-Latour and Edgar Degas; it was at this time that Degas painted a very frank and unflattering portrait of her (Toledo, OH, Mus. A.). While it may be impossible to prove that she was actually a pupil of Fantin-Latour, the early works she exhibited at the Salon are in a style close to his, in particular the portrait of her sister *Charlotte Dubourg* (exh. Paris Salon, 1870; Grenoble, Mus. Grenoble). In this intimate indoor portrait the neutral background recalls the austerity of Fantin-Latour's early portraits. The position of the model is a little stiff, and her expression is like that of a spectator. After exhibiting two portraits at the Salons of 1869 and 1870, she showed only still-lifes of fruit and flowers, often signed *V. Dubourg* or monogrammed *V. D.* From Fantin-Latour she derived a simplicity of composition, an absence of detail and neutral but vibrant backgrounds; her flowers, grouped in generous bouquets, stand out from backgrounds of sustained greyish scumbling or red-brown tones. Her brushstrokes, in long flecks of colour or in tight scumbling, emphasize the play of light and shade.

Soon after their marriage on 16 November 1876, the Fantin-Latours began each summer to paint still-lifes (e.g. 1884; Grenoble, Mus. Grenoble) at Buré in Orne. In 1880 they inherited a house there, which Victoria Fantin-Latour depicted in two paintings, the *House at Buré* (Alençon, Mus. B.-A. & Dentelle) and the *Garden at Buré* (Grenoble, Mus. Grenoble). Whereas Henri Fantin-Latour developed a more direct approach to nature in his still-lifes from the 1880s, no such change is apparent in the work of Victoria Fantin-Latour. After her husband's death she continued to paint, with a supple, freer brushstroke. Her colours are very lively in such traditional compositions as *Chrysanthemums* (1908; Grenoble, Mus. Grenoble). She compiled *Notes prises par Mme Fantin-Latour du vivant de H. Fantin-Latour, 1836–1860* (Paris, Bib. N. Cab. Est.) and published a catalogue raisonné (Paris, 1911) of her husband's work. In March 1905, in collaboration with the dealer Gustave Tempelaere, she organized a sale of her husband's drawings and prints, and she subsequently gave numerous works to various museums, especially to the Musée de Peinture et de Sculpture, Grenoble, and the Palais du Luxembourg, Paris.

BIBLIOGRAPHY

Fantin-Latour: Une Famille de peintres au XIXe siècle (exh. cat., Grenoble, Mus. Peint. & Sculp., 1977)

E. Hardouin-Fugier and E. Grafe: *French Flower Painters of the Nineteenth Century: A Dictionary* (London, 1989), p. 179

VALÉRIE M. C. BAJOU

Fantoni, Andrea (*b* Rovetta, Bergamo, 26 Aug 1659; *d* Rovetta, 25 July 1734). Italian sculptor, architect and furniture-maker. He was the eldest son of the sculptor and carver Grazioso Fantoni (1630–93) and trained in his father's flourishing workshop, which played a leading part in the supply of church furnishings in Bergamo, Parma and the surrounding provinces. In 1674 documents record Andrea in Parma, but in 1675 he was at Edolo, where he is recorded as an apprentice in the workshop of Pietro Ramus (?1639–82), a sculptor active in Valcamonica. It is thought that around 1678 he went to Venice to work in the workshop of the Genoese sculptor Filippo Parodi, a pupil of Bernini and a friend of Pierre Puget. Certainly Fantoni's work gives stylistic evidence of contacts with Genoese and Venetian circles. In 1679 he returned to Rovetta, taking part from the early 1680s in a process of extensive stylistic modernization in the family workshop. This change can be seen in the contrast between Grazioso's carved and inlaid wooden decorations and furnishings in the first sacristy (1679) at S Martino, Alzano Maggiore, which are Baroque in form and Counter-Reformation in their iconography, and Fantoni's in the second sacristy (1692), which is already Rococo in form and more allusive in its language.

Andrea Fantoni displayed a particular gift for wooden furniture, which he made for churches, convents and private houses. Because of their characteristically rich ornamentation (drapery, volutes, leaves, flowers and putti), these works have been called 'living furniture' and they, too, display a typically 18th-century taste, with a tendency towards blurring the line between objects designed for religious purposes and those intended for lay use. Two outstanding examples of these virtuoso achievements, both originally designed for Bergamo Cathedral, are the confessional (1704; Bergamo, S Maria Maggiore) and the bishop's throne (1705; *in situ*). Both are made of walnut,

inset with figured reliefs in boxwood. The celebrated pulpit (1711) designed by Giovanni Battista Caniana (1671–1754) in S Martino at Alzano Lombardo was decorated by Fantoni with rich, coloured marble reliefs, medallions and statues of telamones. This work, the wooden model of which is preserved in the Museo Fantoni, Rovetta, gave rise to a series of similar pulpits in the Bergamo region (e.g. Ardesio, parish church; Castione della Presolana, parish church).

Another major part of the varied range of activities undertaken by Fantoni and the workshop was the production of devotional works. An important example of this genre is the sepulchre with scenes from the Passion in polychromed wood made for the parish church at Zone in 1691. Also mentioned in contemporary documents is a considerable output of ivory and boxwood Crucifixes, several fine examples of which have survived, such as those in the parish church at Romano Lombardo (1700, boxwood) and in the Accademia Carrara di Belle Arti, Bergamo (*c.* 1699–1711; wood). In these works Fantoni used models inspired by the works of Bernini and Alessandro Algardi to create a typology in keeping with 18th-century taste.

Fantoni also worked as a monumental sculptor—his statues of *St John the Baptist* and *Mary Magdalene* (both 1716; marble) in the sanctuary of the Grazie at Crema show the influence of Parodi's style—and he is known to have been active as an architect, producing schemes for the churches at Onore and Cerete, and for S Andrea in Val di Scalve, as well as an unrealized project for the façade of S Martino at Alzano. Drawings for these, influenced by Giovan Battista Caniana (1671–1754), and for his sculptural work are in the Museo Fantoni at Rovetta. The Fantoni workshop continued to be active until *c.* 1817.

BIBLIOGRAPHY

Thieme–Becker

G. Rota: *Andrea Fantoni nei documenti d'archivio e nella storia dell'arte* (Bergamo, 1934)

G. Cesarano: 'Formelle inedite di Andrea Fantoni', *A. Figurativa*, iii (1959), pp. 36–7

P. Tirloni: *Andrea Fantoni scultore* (Milan, 1961)

G. Mandel and M. Zanardi: *Andrea Fantoni: Confessionale in Santa Maria Maggiore Bergamo Alta* (Bergamo, 1974)

R. Bossaglia, ed.: *I Fantoni: Quattro secoli di bottega di scultura in Europa* (Vicenza, 1978)

I Fantoni e il loro tempo: Atti del convegno di studi: Bergamo, 1978

A. M. Pedrocchi: 'Il coro ligneo della Parrocchiale di Vertova: Caniana e Fantoni', *A. Lombarda*, li (1979), pp. 57–61

U. Pilon: 'La bottega di scultura dei Fantoni lungo quattro per cento anni', *A. Crist.*, lxvii (1979), pp. 59–68

A. Nava Cellini: *La scultura del settecento* (Turin, 1982)

M. Lorandi: 'Il *De martyrum cruciatibus* della seconda sacristia di Alzano e l'iconografia della scultura fantoniana', *Ant. Viva*, xxii (1983), pp. 35–48

MARIA IDA CATALANO

Fantoni, Giacomo [Colonna, Jacopo] (*fl* Venice, *c.* 1530; *d* Bologna, *c.* 1543). Italian sculptor. He was the son of a sculptor from Bergamo, Venturino Fantoni (*fl c.* 1517; *d c.* 1524). Vasari and Francesco Sansovino mention him as a disciple of Jacopo Sansovino, and his earliest surviving work, a statuette of *St Lawrence* (1530) made in competition with a *St Jerome* by Danese Cattaneo (both Venice, S Salvatore), is a modest work showing the influence of Sansovino. His other surviving Venetian work, *Christ*

Showing his Wounds, made for the now destroyed Santa Croce, Venice (*c.* 1535; Venice, Ca' d'Oro), is a more accomplished performance in the same vein. Fantoni made an equestrian statue probably also dating from the 1530s for S Marina in Venice, as well as figures of *St Dorothy, St Lucy* and *St Catherine* (all destr.) for S Giovanni Novo.

In 1532 Fantoni was engaged on relief decoration for the Scuola di S Rocco, and by 1533 he had completed two stucco figures of *St Anthony of Padua* and *St Daniel* for the façade of the chapel of St Anthony in the Santo in Padua. He probably gained this commission through the influence of Sansovino, on whose *Virgin and Child* for Verona Cathedral Fantoni based the *St Daniel*. Sansovino introduced Fantoni to the circle of the humanist Alvise Cornaro in Padua, for whom he created three colossal stucco figures of *Minerva, Venus* and *Diana* (all destr.) as well as smaller figures such as a terracotta nude *Mars* (destr.) based on the antique bronze *Spinario* (Rome, Mus. Conserv.). By 1536 Fantoni had moved to Forlì, where he provided decorations for the chapel of the Conception in S Mercuria, and at the end of the decade he was engaged on the marble decoration of the high altar of the church of the Madonna di Galliera in Bologna, a composition designed by Serlio, on which Niccolò Tribolo and Danese Cattaneo also collaborated.

BIBLIOGRAPHY

G. Vasari: *Vite* (1550, rev. 2/1568); ed. G. Milanesi (1878–85)
A. Venturi: *Storia* (1901–40)
R. Bossaglia, ed.: *I Fantoni, quattro secoli di bottega di scultura in Europa* (Vicenza, 1978), pp. 74–5
S. Wilk: 'La decorazione cinquecentesca della cappella dell'Arca di S Antonio', *Le sculture del Santo di Padova*, ed. G. Lorenzoni (Vicenza, 1984), pp. 119, 159, 162

For further bibliography *see* SANSOVINO, JACOPO.

BRUCE BOUCHER

Fantuzzi, Antonio (*b* ?Bologna; *fl* Fontainebleau, 1537–50). Italian painter and printmaker. He was one of Francesco Primaticcio's main assistants at Fontainebleau. Although no painted work or drawing by him can be identified, he is recorded as having designed some of the grotesques for the vault of the Galerie d'Ulysse. From 1542 to 1545 he was one of the principal etchers of the Fontainebleau school, producing more than 100 etchings in that short time. Around 1542–3 he reproduced many drawings by Giulio Romano and Rosso Fiorentino, recording many of the latter's compositions for the palace of Francis I. Because he always worked from preparatory drawings rather than from the frescoes themselves, Fantuzzi's etchings are an invaluable source of information about lost drawings by Rosso. Later he worked from Primaticcio's designs, especially his drawings after antique statues. While Fantuzzi's earlier etchings are violent in their handling and light effects (e.g. his etching after Rosso's *The Sacrifice*; see Zerner (1969), no. 27), his *maniera* later became more careful and softer (e.g. *Apollo and Marsyas*, after Parmigianino; see Zerner (1969), no. 77). Fantuzzi has often been mistakenly identified with Antonio da Trento.

BIBLIOGRAPHY

F. Zava-Boccazzi: *Antonio da Trento, incisore* (Trent, 1962)
H. Zerner: 'L'Eau-forte à Fontainebleau: Le Rôle de Fantuzzi', *A. France*, iv (1964), pp. 70–85
——: *Ecole de Fontainebleau: Gravures* (Paris, 1969)
Rosso Fiorentino (exh. cat. by E. Carroll, Washington, DC, N.G.A., 1987)

HENRI ZERNER

Fanzago [Fansago], **Cosimo** (*b* Clusone, Bergamo, 1591; *d* Naples, 13 Feb 1678). Italian architect, sculptor and interior designer. His prowess in many fields of art and his remarkable facility of production led him to a position of unchallenged supremacy in 17th-century Neapolitan architecture, where his styles exhibit every nuance, from the severe classicism of Early Baroque via an exuberant use of coloured marbles and the occasional exploitation of Mannerist detail, to a scenographic Late Baroque.

1. Architectural works. 2. Sculptural works.

1. ARCHITECTURAL WORKS. Fanzago came from a patrician family whose members included engineers, architects and bronze-casters. In 1608 he went to Naples, where he trained as a mason and sculptor in the workshop of Geronimo d'Auria. From 1612 to 1620 he ran a workshop in partnership with his father-in-law, the marble-worker Angelo Landi (*d* 1620), and during that time produced many works of sculptural decoration, in particular for Neapolitan churches and chapels (e.g. three *stremmi* for the façade of the Palazzo degli Studi in 1614–16; unspecified works for Naples Cathedral), but also at Catanzaro and Barletta (e.g. the decoration of the Gentile Chapel in Barletta in 1620). In the early 1620s he became an assistant to Giovanni Giacomo di Conforto, one of the leading architects in Naples, and soon extended his scope from details to more complex architectural tasks, for example in Santa Trinità delle Monache, where he designed the church porch and external flight of steps, and at the Certosa di S Martino (*see* NAPLES, §IV, 3), where he assumed control of the extensive building works after Conforto's death in 1631. From then until 1656 he created some of his finest work at the Certosa, including the completion and decoration of the Chiostro Grande (1623–43), with seven large portals containing imaginatively decorated frames and busts of Carthusian saints (see fig. 1 and NAPLES, fig. 9), the church façade (1636–50) and the decoration of certain apartments.

The first church built entirely by Fanzago, the church of the Ascensione a Chiaia in Naples, was begun in 1626 but only completed, with its dome, in 1662; it has a simple central structure over a Greek cross and is much less ambitious in design than his oval church of S Sebastiano (1628). In 1629 he executed another important commission, the bronze gate of the Cappella del Tesoro, Naples. Fanzago also designed numerous richly inlaid altars, in which his virtuosity as a marble-worker was greatly enhanced by his formal inventiveness as an architect. Fanzago's altars are mostly free-standing, of the box or aedicule type, have offertory doors at the sides and are surmounted by statues to form a semi-transparent division between the sanctuary and the choir. The most important are at S Nicola al Lido, Venice (1629–34), S Maria la Nova, Naples (1632–4), SS Severino e Sossio, Naples (1635–41), at the Benedictine Abbey, Montecassino (1636), and at the Neapolitan churches of S Maria di Costantinopoli (1639–45), S Pietro a Maiella (1640–47) and S Domenico Maggiore (1640–52).

1. Cosimo Fanzago: *The Blessed Nicola Albergati*, marble, portal of the Chiostro Grande, Certosa di S Martino, Naples, 1623–43

Fanzago's workshop was responsible for extensive chapel decorations and much building and rebuilding of churches in Naples (e.g. S Giuseppe dei Vecchi, from 1634; S Maria degli Angeli alle Croci, from 1639), as well as palaces (e.g. façade of the Palazzo Firrao, 1636–40) and public fountains (e.g. Fontana Medina, 1634–40; Fontana del Sebeto, 1635–7). About 1636 Fanzago and his assistants were engaged on a wall altar and pulpit for the church of the Agustinas Descalzas at Salamanca, commissioned by the Viceroy of Naples, Don Manuel de Acevedo y Zúñiga, 6th Conde de Monterrey. In 1636–60 Fanzago executed the *Guglia di St Gennaro*, a votive column in honour of the patron saint of Naples: built in the style of an ephemeral festive structure, this work became a prototype for similar monuments throughout southern Italy and may also have served as a model for Central European plague columns in the Baroque style. From 1630 Fanzago worked for the Neapolitan Jesuits, who commissioned him to build the altar of *St Francis Xavier* in the Gesù Vecchio; about 1634–6 he planned the church of S Francesco Saviero (now S Ferdinando), which was completed according to modified plans in 1665. His original design (Paris, Bib. N.) shows the spatial concept of an elongated cruciform church with a dome; the three square bays of the nave combine with the side compartments to form a type of *Wandpfeilerkirche*. In S Giorgio Maggiore, begun in 1640 for the Order of the Padri Pii Operari,

Fanzago brought this idea of space to artistic perfection by a series of three domes increasing in size towards the centre of the church—a form of articulation subtly attuned to his aim of creating a centralized space—and a shaping of the apse derived from Andrea Palladio's Redentore in Venice (1576–80). He also worked at the Gesù Nuovo, the principal Jesuit church in Naples built by Giuseppe Valeriano S. J. in 1584–95, creating the two transept altars with their large niche figures (from 1637) and at the same time embarking on a campaign of decoration which continued for decades, and in which all the columns and walls were covered with precious marble incrustations.

Another outstanding work of decoration was the Cappella di S Teresa (1640–50) in S Teresa degli Studi, Naples. The façade of that church is also by Fanzago, but while it is richly decorated, it gives an architecturally weak effect. His treatment of the façades of the Neapolitan churches S Maria della Sapienza (1639–49) and S Giuseppe delle Scalze a Pontecorvo (1643–60) was much more creative. In both cases he had to place a porch before the front wall with a flight of steps within it so as to overcome a considerable difference of level between the street and the church interior, while the crypts could be approached at ground level. The Sapienza façade features a three-arch loggia—in effect three overlapping Serlian windows—set above a podium storey and between end bays with rectangular openings, reached by steps from the street, which give access to a double ramp staircase behind the façade. This leads to the nave, which is at a higher level than the street. At S Giuseppe delle Scalze the openings in the wall correspond to the complicated layout of the steps: structural and decorative elements merge into an effective scenographic whole. The spatial conception of this church combines the basic form of a trough-vaulted rectangular hall, divided rhythmically into three, with the idea of a cruciform centralized layout closed by an apse at the choir and entrance ends. Fanzago's most important secular building, the Palazzo di Donn'Anna (*c.* 1640–44) at Posillipo, is a massive structure relieved by loggias, niches and corner turrets, spectacularly sited on a rocky promontory. The problem of approach is solved in a remarkable way: the upper floors at the back form a *cour d'honneur* facing on to the coastal road above, while arches in the reinforced base allow direct access to the sea.

On 25 January 1645 Fanzago was appointed Ingegnere Maggiore del Regno but two years later, at the time of the Neapolitan revolution led by Tomaso Masaniello, he was threatened with the death penalty and fled to Rome, where he lived until 1650, and again *c.* 1660. He received some minor commissions there (redesigning the interior of S Lorenzo in Lucina and S Maria in Via Lata; decorative and sculptural work in S Agostino, S Isidoro and Santa Trinità dei Pellegrini), and for a time took part in the planning of S Agnese in Piazza Navona. His plan for S Maria Egiziaca a Pizzofalcone (begun 1651; completed by Arcangelo Guglielmelli, 1717; see fig. 2), one of the three churches he designed shortly after returning to Naples, is closely connected with S Agnese in its organization of space: it is an octagonal domed structure with wide apses radiating in the form of a cross and shallow niches on the smaller diagonal sides. Another perfectly centralized building is S Teresa a Chiaia (1650–64), a cruciform church

2. Cosimo Fanzago: section and plan of S Maria Egiziaca a Pizzofalcone, Naples, begun 1651

commissions included various works at Avellino and collaboration in some monuments that became landmarks of Naples: the *Guglia di St Domenico* (1657–8), the *Guglia di St Gaetano* (1657–70), and the Fountain of Monteoliveto (1668–76). In his architecture, Fanzago turned functional problems to scenographic effect, concentrating and simplifying the volumetry of his church interiors by the steep proportions he achieved through lengthening the floor plan of his cruciform domed structures while preserving the balance between centralization and longitudinal stress, often screening the choir with an altar arcade to accentuate the feeling of spatial progression.

2. SCULPTURAL WORKS. By 1612 Fanzago had achieved the status of 'maestro di scoltura di marmo'. His technical virtuosity derived from his training among Tuscan sculptors such as Pietro Bernini, who certainly contributed to his formation as an artist. However, the highly expressive quality of Fanzago's oeuvre finds its closest parallel in the work of Milanese sculptors active about 1600 (e.g. Annibale Fontana), with which he would have become acquainted in early youth. The tension felt in their work between an exaggerated naturalism of human forms and a free treatment of drapery contrasting with the physical structure beneath was developed by Fanzago to a high degree of subjective expressiveness. His sculptures demonstrate psychological insight, dramatic effect and forceful monumentality, with a subtle delicacy apparent in his relief and surface work.

Like Bernini, Fanzago was concerned to synthesize sculpture and architecture, but without acknowledging the innovations of Roman High Baroque. His main preoccupation was with a formal and material fusion, using newly developed organizational schemata. An essential factor is the highly dynamic ornamentation, the vocabulary of which combines geometrical and floral elements of Mannerist pietra dura with naturalistic scrollwork; in its free and fluent development it seems at times to anticipate aspects of the Rococo style. Stacked, sawn marble slabs (recalling Wendel Dietterlin's abstract ornamentation), elegantly cut lancet shapes, repeatedly broken scrolls mutating from strict linearity to organic solidity, and skilfully carved three-dimensional rosettes, festoons, putti and cherubs' heads are the recurrent set pieces of this decorative art—the trademarks of a mass production based on the craftsmanlike organization of a large workshop, yet full of the master's artistic inspiration. Of primary importance to the overall impression is the polychromy of the different sorts of marble. Fanzago's sublime intarsia work aims at a refinement of nuances (either with grisaille-type combinations or with glowing coloration) and in this way achieves painterly values that give an illusion of atmosphere, light and shade. The result is a charming interplay between *trompe l'oeil* and a surface pattern, which is one of the artist's most individual achievements.

BIBLIOGRAPHY

Macmillan Enc. Architects
B. De Dominici: *Vite* (1742–5), iii, pp. 176–89
R. Pane: *Architettura dell'età barocca a Napoli* (Naples, 1939)
P. Fogaccia: *Cosimo Fanzago* (Bergamo, 1945)
F. Strazzullo: *Architetti e ingegneri napoletani dal '500 al '700* (Naples, 1959), pp. 181–4

with a dome where the square corner chapels inserted between the arms of the cross are linked to the main space by high openings with architraves and the supports consist of rectangular pillars intersecting one another at right angles. In addition, the choir wall is perforated and decorated with statues in the manner of a triumphal arch. In his last great church building, S Maria Maggiore (1653–75), Fanzago achieved a harmonious synthesis of his most original ideas for the treatment of space. An elongated cruciform church and dome of the type of Rosato Rosati's S Carlo ai Catinari in Rome (1612), the centralizing effect at S Maria Maggiore is accentuated by the much enlarged and lofty crossing under the dome, while the symmetrical unity of the whole scheme is perfected by the longitudinal spatial components having an apse at each end. An altar arcade open to the monks' choir provides a delightful scenic progression along the main axis. Fanzago's final

M. A. De Cunzo: 'I documenti sull'opera di Cosimo Fanzago nella Certosa di San Martino', *Napoli Nob.*, vi (1967), pp. 98–107

R. Mormone: 'Sculture di Cosimo Fanzago', *Napoli Nob.*, ix (1970), pp. 174–85

F. Brauen: *Cosimo Fanzago and Seventeenth Century Neapolitan Marble Decoration* (diss., New York, Columbia U., 1973)

R. Causa: *L'arte nella Certosa di San Martino a Napoli* (Naples, 1973)

G. Cantone: 'Cosimo Fanzago e l'arredo urbano: Le guglie e le fontane', *Napoli Nob.*, xiii (1974), pp. 41–58

A. Blunt: *Neapolitan Baroque and Rococo Architecture* (London, 1975), pp. 59–89, 179–86

R. Bösel: *Studien zur Sakralarchitektur Cosimo Fanzagos* (diss., U. Vienna, 1975)

F. Brauen: 'Fanzago's Commission as Royal Chief Engineer', *Stor. A.*, xxvi (1976), pp. 61–72

R. Bösel: 'Cosimo Fanzago a Roma', *Prospettiva*, xv (1978), pp. 29–40

——: 'Neue Materialien zur Sakralarchitektur des neapolitanischen Seicento: Die Kirche S Francesco Saverio', *Röm. Jb. Kstgesch.*, xviii (1979), pp. 113–71

G. Cantone: *Napoli barocca e Cosimo Fanzago* (Naples, 1984)

G. Salvatori and C. Menzione: *Le guglie di Napoli: Storia e restauro* (Naples, 1984)

RICHARD BÖSEL

Fara, Tell [anc. Shuruppak]. Site of an ancient Sumerian city beside the Euphrates, in the middle of Sumer (now in Iraq). The city flourished *c.* 3000–*c.* 2000 BC, although the Babylonian King List mentions a dynasty at Shuruppak 'before the flood'. All versions of the Babylonian flood story name Shuruppak as the home of the Babylonian 'Noah'. Under the Ur III kings (2112–2004 BC), Shuruppak was an administrative centre with its own *ensi* (ruler). The city was eventually abandoned when the Euphrates changed course. Tell Fara was excavated by the Deutsche Orient-Gesellschaft in 1902–3 (finds in Istanbul, Archaeol. Mus. and Berlin, Pergamonmus.) and by the University of Pennsylvania in 1931 (finds in Baghdad, Iraq Mus., and Philadelphia, U. PA, Mus.). The excavations of 1902–3 recovered little architecture but many objects, most belonging to the Early Dynastic period (*c.* 2900–*c.* 2334 BC). Altogether over 900 cuneiform tablets of Early Dynastic IIIa were excavated by both expeditions.

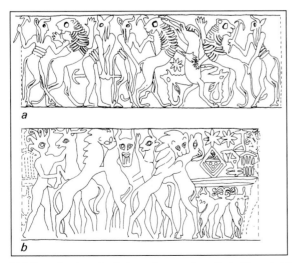

Tell Fara, drawing of cylinder seal impressions, Early Dynastic II (*c.* 2750–*c.* 2600 BC): (a) impression of seal from refuse deposit in trench I d–e, h. *c.* 27 mm; (b) impression of seal of Anzu Súd from trench XIII f–g, h. 34 mm (original seals Berlin, Pergamonmuseum)

Fara is noted for its cylinder seal impressions (Berlin, Pergamonmus.). A refuse deposit at the site yielded at least 838 impressions ranging from Jemdet Nasr to Early Dynastic II styles (see fig. (a)). Early Dynastic IIIa buildings contained over 350 impressions together with cuneiform tablets. These include seals of Late Early Dynastic II with stylized crossed figures and Anzu Súd style seals (named after the owner of the seal in fig. (b)). The terms 'Fara-style seals' and 'Fara-period tablets' are sometimes used to mean Early Dynastic II seals and Early Dynastic IIIa tablets. Some German chronologies describe the phase from Late Early Dynastic II to Early Dynastic IIIa as the Fara period.

For further discussion of cylinder seals *see* ANCIENT NEAR EAST, §II, 1(ii).

BIBLIOGRAPHY

E. Heinrich: *Fara, Ergebnisse der Ausgrabungen der Deutschen Orient-Gesellschaft in Fara und Abu Hatab 1902/3* (Berlin, 1931)

E. Schmidt: 'Excavations at Fara, 1931', *U. PA Mus. J.*, xxii (1931), pp. 193–235

H. Martin: *Shuruppak: A City of the Third Millennium BC* (Birmingham, 1988) [includes Heinrich on microfiche]

HARRIET MARTIN

Farab. *See under* OTRAR.

Farain, Tell el- [Arab. Tall al-Fara'īn; anc. Egyp. Pr-Wadjit; Copt. Puoto; Gr. Buto]. Ancient Egyptian city in the western Delta that flourished during the Predynastic and Saite periods. The ancient Egyptian name of the city was Pr-Wadjit ('House of Wadjit'), and its principal deities were Wadjit, the snake-goddess, and Horus, the falcon-god. More commonly known as Buto, the site was a sacred place of great iconographic importance.

British excavations (1964–9) revealed a major temple, probably dating from the Saite period (664–525 BC). Egyptian excavations (1987–8) have also uncovered stelae and statues dating to the New Kingdom (*c.* 1540–*c.* 1075 BC) and the Late Period (*c.* 750–332 BC), in the area around the temple. Grants of land were made to the temple according to an early Ptolemaic stele, later received in a Cairo mosque. Apart from a hoard of bronze hawks (Cairo, Egyptian Mus.), few other objects of artistic importance have been found, due to the wet climate, the salty soil and the fact that surface remains are of an industrial city of the Ptolemaic and Roman periods. Since 1983 German excavations have uncovered remains of occupation dating to the 4th millennium BC, thus supporting the traditional identification of the site with the twin cities of Pe and Dep, the Predynastic capital of Lower Egypt. This evidence raises hopes of the eventual discovery of the Predynastic royal palace and necropolis. In Old and New Kingdom tomb paintings, the necropolis at Buto is frequently depicted as a place with palms and a winding waterway, which was the destination of a notional pilgrimage by the deceased. Several New Kingdom tomb paintings (such as those of Reneni and Sobknakht at Elkab) show the arrival of the dead at Buto, where they were received by *mww*-dancers (mythical beings who guided the mummy through funerary rites) wearing wickerwork royal crowns. There are many examples of statues and reliefs of the hawk-headed 'souls of Pe', who seem to have represented the Predynastic kings and could legitimize later rulers. The nearby site of Khemmis, the exact location of which is unknown, was revered as the island in the marshes where Isis suckled Horus, a frequent motif in Egyptian religious art.

BIBLIOGRAPHY

LÄ: 'Buto'

B. Porter and R. Moss: *Topographical Bibliography*, iv (Oxford, 1934), p. 45

PETER FRENCH

Faraj. *See* MAMLUK, §II, 2(8).

Farakhshah. *See* VARAKHSHA.

Farangī, 'Alīqulī. *See* 'ALIQULI JABBADAR.

Faras [Egyp. Sehetepneterw; Copt. Pachoras]. Site in Egypt on the west bank of the Nile, 35 km north of Wadi Halfa. Since the completion of the Aswan High Dam in 1970, Faras has been submerged beneath Lake Nasser. There were three important phases in the history of Faras: the later New Kingdom (*c.* 1540–*c.* 1075 BC), when it was rebuilt by Tutankhamun (*reg c.* 1332–*c.* 1323 BC) as the administrative capital of Lower Nubia; during the Meroitic period (*c.* 300 BC–AD 360), when it was again a regional capital; and Christian times (8th–15th centuries AD) when it was the seat of a bishop.

In terms of Nubian art the Meroitic and Christian phases at Faras are the most important. The large Meroitic cemetery has produced a great quantity of pottery vessels in fine painted wares, and painted pottery has long been recognized as one of the most important aspects of Meroitic art, revealing influences from Pharaonic, Hellenistic and Roman Egypt in its forms and the decorative motifs employed (*see* NUBIA, §IV, 4). These influences, however, combine with an ancient indigenous pottery tradition to create a unique style. Although the dating of the pottery is still debated, some groups can be recognized as the work of individual artists; pottery painted by the same artist has been discovered both at Faras and in the cemetery of Karanog, some 70 km further north. Many fragments of New Kingdom stonework were discovered reused in the buildings and cemeteries of the Meroitic and Christian periods. These were originally believed to belong to New Kingdom temples at Faras, but it has now been established that they derive from the temples of Hatshepsut (*reg c.* 1479–*c.* 1458 BC) and Tuthmosis III (*reg c.* 1479–*c.* 1426 BC) at Buhen and of Ramesses II (*reg c.* 1279–*c.* 1213 BC) at Aksha (*see* NUBIA, §III).

The Faras cathedral contained one of the largest collections of Nubian Byzantine painting, revealing a continuous tradition from the 8th to 15th centuries AD. Many layers of paintings were separated and conserved by a Polish excavation team working in the 1960s. These are now on display at the Muzeum Narodowe, Warsaw, and the Sudan National Museum, Khartoum. The paintings are not frescoes, as they were applied to dry plaster. This collection is particularly important, since paintings from other Nubian churches are either fragmentarily preserved or confined to specific periods. The Faras paintings can be divided into nine styles, which may then be compared with other Nubian and Byzantine material. There seem to be strong influences from painting styles in Palestine and Coptic Egypt. As a result of the study of the Faras paintings it is possible to distinguish local traditions and adaptations as well as favoured compositions and colour ranges, all suggesting the importance of the Faras school within Nubia.

BIBLIOGRAPHY

J. Karkowski: *Faras*, v: *The Pharaonic Inscriptions from Faras* (Warsaw, 1981)

M. Martens-Czarnecka: *Faras*, vii: *Les Eléments décoratifs sur les peintures de Faras* (Warsaw, 1982)

——: 'Nubian Wall Painting', *Nubian Culture Past and Present*, ed. T. Hägg (Stockholm, 1987), pp. 261–74 [useful summary of styles and significance of cathedral ptgs]

L. Török: 'Nubian Christianity, North and South: The Historical Background, Meroe North and South', *Nubian Culture Past and Present*, ed. T. Hägg (Stockholm, 1987), pp. 139–229 [incl. valuable study of chronology and stylistic dev. of Meroitic painted pott.]

R. G. Morkot: *Faras: The Meroitic Cemetery* (London, in preparation)

R. G. MORKOT

Farelli, Giacomo (*b* Rome, ?1624; *d* Naples, 26 June 1701). Italian painter. After a literary education in Rome, he moved to Naples to study painting in the workshop of Andrea Vaccaro. Nevertheless, his early work was in the classical style of Guido Reni and Domenichino and he occasionally collaborated with Francesco di Maria, the main exponent of this style in Naples. His first documented works are a *St Gennaro* and a *Massacre of the Innocents* (both 1651; untraced) executed for Cesare Zattara. The large altarpiece depicting *Christ and the Virgin Appearing to St Bridget* (1655–6; Naples, S Brigida), executed in rivalry with Luca Giordano (who was completing at the same time and for the same church the altarpiece with the *Miracle of St Nicholas*) showed that Farelli had by then created an independent style. In 1661 he painted a *St John the Evangelist* for the church of S Giovanni at Sulmona, near L'Aquila in the Abruzzi, and in 1664 the frescoes with the *Life of the Virgin* in the sacristy of the Cappella del Tesoro in Naples Cathedral (finished 1673). He then worked until 1671 on the frescoes (untraced) in the Palazzo dei Duchi Acquaviva in Atri (Teramo) and in the church of S Filippo at L'Aquila.

Once more in Naples, Farelli had further important commissions, including the altarpiece depicting the *Virgin Interceding for the Liberation of Slaves* (1672; Redenzione dei Cattivi) and canvases with the *Angel Telling Joseph of the Flight into Egypt* and the *Death of St Joseph* (1673; S Giuseppe a Chiaia). In 1676 he was again in Abruzzi, where he executed the frescoes in the sanctuary of S Maria di Roio (L'Aquila). Finally he is documented in Pisa, in 1693, when he painted two frescoes celebrating military episodes, the *Conquest of the Balearics* and the *Sardinian Campaign*, in the Palazzo Gambacorti. These late works are in a Baroque manner close to that of Luca Giordano and show how far Farelli had moved during the course of his career from his early classical style.

BIBLIOGRAPHY

G. Roselli: 'Preface to P. Sarnelli', *Guida de' Forastieri . . . di Pozzuoli Baja* (Naples, 2/1697)

B. de Dominici: *Vite* (1742–5), iii, pp. 457–66

I. Gallichi Schwenn: 'Note su Giacomo Farelli pittore napoletano del seicento', *Partenope*, i (1961), pp. 200–13

E. Borea: 'Farelli o Fardella: Questioni relative a due pittori meridionali in Toscana', *Scritti di storia dell'arte in onore di Ugo Procacci*, ii, ed. M. G. Ciardi-Dupré and P. dal Poggetto (Milan, 1977), pp. 554–66

Civiltà del seicento a Napoli (exh. cat., ed. S. Cassani; Naples, Capodimonte, 1984), i, pp. 135–88

O. Ferrari: 'Ein neu entdecktes Werk des Giacomo Farelli', *Niederdt. Beitr. Kstgesch.*, xxiii (1984), pp. 157–62

ORESTE FERRARI

Farès, Bishr (*b* Zagazig, 20 Dec 1906; *d* Cairo, 21 Feb 1963). Egyptian historian, sociologist, playwright, literary critic, linguist and art historian. He attended secondary school at the Jesuit Collège de la Sainte-Famille, Cairo, and then pursued his higher education under Ahmad Zaki Pasha in Cairo and at the Sorbonne in Paris under the Orientalists Louis Massignon and Maurice Gaudefroy-Demombynes. In 1932 he completed two doctoral theses on pre-Islamic Arabia, one on the concept of honour, the other on the nature of linguistic exposition. He travelled widely in Britain, France, Germany, Italy, Lebanon and Turkey, and in the 1940s began to dedicate more time to writing plays, short stories and literary criticism. He was also editor of the literary journal *Al-Muqtaṭaf* and researched Egyptian folklore. From 1948 he was consultant to the Egyptian delegation to UNESCO and from 1958 secretary-general of the French Institut d'Egypte. From 1942 he wrote about Islamic art, especially illustrated manuscripts of the 12th to the 14th century from Iraq and Syria, from the point of view of aesthetics and Christian and Muslim iconography. He also wrote about the lawfulness of painting in Islam. He discovered several important Arabic manuscripts with illustrations, and his interpretation of Arab painting was enriched by his extensive knowledge of history and literature. He published academic works and drama in French and Arabic and was one of the first Arab historians to write about Islamic art. He also supported modern art movements, publishing an open letter to the Soviet president Khrushchev in 1962 in response to his condemnation of abstract art.

WRITINGS
Une Miniature religieuse de l'école arabe de Bagdad (Cairo, 1948)
Essai sur l'esprit de la décoration islamique (Cairo, 1952)
Le Livre de la thériaque (Cairo, 1953)
'Philosophie et jurisprudence illustrées par les Arabes', *Mélanges Louis Massignon* (Damascus, 1957), pp. 77–109
Vision chrétienne et signes musulmans, autour d'un manuscrit arabe illustré au XIIIe siècle (Cairo, 1961)

BIBLIOGRAPHY
C. Vial: 'Hommage à Bichr Farès (1906–1963)', *Arabica*, x (1963), pp. 113–20
P. Anawati, R. Ettinghausen and M. F. Gabrieli: 'In memoriam Bichr Farès', *Mél. Inst. Dominicain Etud. Orient. Caire*, viii (1964–6), pp. 499–506
Y. Moubarac: 'L'Oeuvre scientifique et littéraire de Bishr Farès (1906–1963)', *Rev. Etud. Islam.*, xxxvi (1968), pp. 319–30

S. J. VERNOIT

Farfa. Italian village in the Lazio region, *c.* 50 km northeast of Rome. Its Benedictine abbey was one of the most important monastic centres of the period between the 9th century and the early 12th, although far-reaching alterations make it difficult to reconstruct its medieval appearance, which was much extolled in documentary descriptions. According to the Farfa Register, compiled largely by the local monk Gregorio di Catino in 1092–9, the abbey was founded in AD 369 by a certain Lorenzo Siro but sacked by the Lombards in the 6th century. A second foundation, which probably included the abbey church of S Maria, was established *c.* 680 by S Tomaso di

Maurienne, and the community, originally mainly Franco-Germanic, became increasingly prosperous with the support of Farwald II, Duke of Spoleto (*reg* 703–24), and Pope John VII, who granted it a degree of autonomy in 705. In the Carolingian period Farfa reached its peak: declared an imperial abbey and enjoying exemption from civil and episcopal rule and taxes, its independence from the Church grew, and it became the most significant political and economic power in northern Lazio. During this period Abbot Sichartus (830–41) undertook the refurbishment of the abbey's buildings. A transept and an apse with an annular crypt, similar to those in S Prassede (817–24), Rome, were added at the west end of the church, and the east end of the porticoed atrium was adapted so that it curved around the new western apse (see fig.), as at Fulda Abbey Church (now Cathedral). This unusual combination of German and Roman features is also found in the nearby Benedictine monastery of S Giovanni in Argentella. McClendon and Whitehouse have suggested a reconstruction of the monastic layout that relates primarily to the Carolingian period, when all the component parts (lay cemetery, priests' cemetery and the abbot's palace,

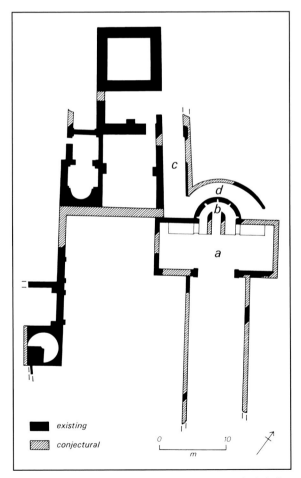

Farfa, abbey church, late 7th century to the 9th, hypothetical plan: (a) transept; (b) western apse with annular crypt; (c) atrium; (d) portico

including a large tower) appear to be aligned with the main church in regular fashion.

Farfa was overrun by the Saracens after a bitter siege, forcing the monks to take refuge in Rome and Rieti and near Fermo, where they founded S Vittoria in Matenano. After its restoration to the Benedictine Order, the abbey was troubled for many years by internal divisions. The moral and architectural revival of the monastery began in earnest with the Cluniac reforms under Abbot Hugo (997–1039) and his successor, Berardus I. It has been suggested by McClendon that in the 11th century the east end of the church was rebuilt, with the addition of a square presbytery and twin bell-towers over the north and south projecting side chapels. Only the presbytery and the north bell-tower survive.

The output of the scriptorium, which was inaugurated by Berardus, is now dispersed in various libraries. The Farfa manuscripts have immense documentary value: the *Farfa Customary* (1043), in particular, is noted for its detailed description, with dimensions, of the entire monastery of Cluny II. In addition, the manuscripts were at the forefront of painting in the Lazio region between the 11th and 12th centuries; the paintings in one Evangeliary (Rome, Vatican, Bib. Apostolica, MS. F.13), for example, are very close in style to the wall paintings in S Silvestro at Tivoli and in the crypt of the cathedral at ANAGNI.

With its reversion to ecclesiastical jurisdiction under the Concordat of Worms (1122), Farfa entered a phase of unbroken decline. Boniface IX (*reg* 1389–1404) granted it *in commendam* to the Tomacelli family, who were succeeded by the Orsini (1421–1553), the Farnese, the Barberini and the Lante della Rovere. The abbey church itself was rebuilt in 1492 on a completely different axis to its predecessor: the present church is on a north–south axis, at right angles to the earlier one. The Renaissance church, into which numerous Romanesque and Gothic remains are integrated, contains interesting late 16th-century painted decorations, including those (1597–9) by Orazio Gentileschi. Nearby was the rebuilt palace of the abbot, similar in form to the stables (1512) of the Farnesina in Rome, designed by Raphael. The abbey was abandoned from 1870 until 1919 and was declared a national monument in 1928.

BIBLIOGRAPHY
I. Giorgio and U. Balzani, eds: *Il regesto di Farfa compilato da Gregorio di Catino*, 5 vols (Rome, 1879–1914)
Farfa Customary [MS.; 1043]; *Consuetudines farvensis* (1900), i of *Consuetudines monasticae*, ed. B. Albers, 5 vols (Stuttgart, 1900–12), pp. 137–9
I. Schuster: *L'abbazia imperiale di Farfa* (Rome, 1921)
N. Franciosa: *L'abbazia imperiale di Farfa* (Naples, 1964)
R. Enking: *Cenni storici sull'abbazia benedettina di S Giovanni in Argentella* (S Giovanni in Argentella, 1976)
C. McClendon: *The Medieval Abbey Church of Farfa* (Ann Arbor, 1978)
C. McClendon and D. Whitehouse: 'La Badia di Farfa, Fara in Sabina (Rieti): Terza nota preliminare', *Archeol. Med.*, ix (1982), pp. 323–9
C. B. McClendon: *The Imperial Abbey of Farfa: Architectural Currents of the Early Middle Ages* (New Haven and London, 1987)

GIUSEPPE PINNA

Farghana. *See* FERGHANA.

Färg och Form [Swed.: 'colour and form']. Swedish informal association of painters and sculptors, active from 1932. The two dominant artists were Bror Hjorth and Sven Erixson: the former created sculptures of forceful primitivism and some epic paintings in bold primary hues that echoed the decorative traditions of rustic art; the latter painted works in a naive but spontaneous, earthy, colourful style. Other artists included Ivan Ivarson (1900–39), Ragnar Sandberg (*b* 1902), Albin Amelin (*b* 1902), Inge Schiöler (*b* 1908) and Åke Göransson (1902–42); the latter two declined into mental illness at early ages. Amelin's paintings often expressed a socio-political concern or represented sensual scenes of primitive violence.

BIBLIOGRAPHY
R. Soderberg: *Introduction to Modern Swedish Art* (Stockholm, 1962)
O. Granath: *Another Light: Swedish Art since 1945* (Stockholm, 1982)

☐

Fargue, La. *See* LA FARGUE.

Farhad-Beg Yailaki. *See under* KHOTAN.

Faria Lobo, Silvestre de. *See* LOBO, SILVESTRE DE FARIA.

Farigoule, Louis(-Henri-Jean). *See* ROMAINS, JULES.

Farinati [Farinato]**, Paolo** (*b* Verona, 1524; *d* Verona, 1606). Italian painter and draughtsman. He was the son of a painter, Giambattista, but probably trained in the workshop of Nicola Giolfino (Vasari). His earliest documented painting, *St Martin and the Beggar* (1552; Mantua Cathedral), was commissioned by Cardinal Ercole Gonzaga along with works by Battista dell'Angolo del Moro, Veronese and Domenico Brusasorci for Mantua Cathedral, newly restored by Giulio Romano. As is evident in his chiaroscuro and figure types, Farinati had absorbed certain Mannerist influences from the frescoes of scenes from the *Life of the Virgin* (1534) in the choir of Verona Cathedral, executed by Francesco Torbido to Giulio's design. Giolfino's eccentric style would also have encouraged Farinati to emphasize line over colour and to restrict his palette to rather opaque greys, browns, mauve and rust. His two-canvas *Massacre of the Innocents* (1556; Verona, S Maria in Organo) displays the muscular figures, sharp foreshortenings and posed attitudes of Mannerism and has a more polished finish than his earlier work. Its strong, plastic qualities are also evident in *Christ Walking on the Water* and the *Supper of St Gregory* (1558) in the choir of the same church. These characteristics are united with a more defined architectural space, derived from Veronese, in his *Ecce homo* (1562; Verona, Castelvecchio). In 1566 Farinati painted two frescoes—one of *Elijah Ascending into Heaven*, the other (damaged) of uncertain subject—on the walls flanking Veronese's altarpiece in the Cappella Marogna, S Paolo, Verona. His use of somewhat brighter colours is probably due to the influence of Veronese. Farinati's mythological and allegorical frescoes in the Palazzo Giuliari, Verona, were completed before he began his journal in 1573. Around 1575 he executed the cycle of canvases and frescoes depicting the *Lives of SS Nazarius and Celsus* in the choir of SS Nazaro e Celso, Verona. While his altarpiece of *SS Francis and Nicholas* (1588; Verona, S Paolo) is among the more colourful, his style did not change radically. His late works include the *Miracle of the Loaves and Fishes* (1603; Verona, S Giorgio in Braida). Drawings form a significant part of Farinati's oeuvre, especially his numerous chiaroscuro drawings on tinted paper, which were often used as modelli (e.g. New York, Met.; Vienna, Albertina; Washington, DC, N.G.A.).

WRITINGS

Giornale, 1573–1606 (Verona, Archv Stato, MS. Comune, n. 604); ed. L. Puppi (Florence, 1965)

BIBLIOGRAPHY

G. Vasari: *Vite* (1550, rev. 2/1568); ed. G. Milanesi (1878–85), vi, pp. 374–5
C. Ridolfi: *Meraviglie* (1648); ed. D. von Hadeln (1914–24), ii, pp. 127–34
B. dal Pozzo: *Le vite de' pittori, degli scultori et architetti veronesi* (Verona, 1718), pp. 122–9
L. Simeoni: 'Il giornale del pittore Paolo Farinati', *Madonna Verona*, i (1907), pp. 123–9; ii (1908), pp. 49–53, 90–101, 130–40; iii (1909), pp. 125–30, 151–70, 222–7
G. Fiocco: 'Paolo Veronese und Farinati', *Jb. Ksthist. Samml. Wien*, i (1926), pp. 123–36
U. G. Tessari: *S Tomaso C., S Paolo, S Fermo Minore* (Verona, 1955)
F. dal Forno: *Paolo Farinati, 1524–1606* (Verona, 1965)
B. Berenson: *Central and North Italian Schools* (1968), pp. 124–7
D. DeGrazia Bohlin: 'Paolo Farinati in the Palazzo Giuliari: Frescoes and Preparatory Drawings', *Master Drgs*, xx (1982), pp. 347–69, pls 1–11
G. Baldissin Molli: 'Paolo Farinati e gli affreschi della chiesa dei Santi Nazaro e Celso a Verona', *A. Ven.*, xxxviii (1984), pp. 31–45
——: 'Qualche riflessione su un quadro poco noto e un disegno inedito di Paolo Farinato', *A. Ven.*, xxxix (1985), pp. 47–54

DIANA GISOLFI

Farinelli, Carlo Broschi (*b* Andria, Puglia, 24 Jan 1705; *d* Bologna, 16 Sept 1782). Italian singer, choreographer and collector. He was castrated as the result of an accident at an early age, following which he dedicated himself to singing, studying with the great teacher Nicola Antonio Porpora (1686–1766), who took him to Rome in 1722. He enjoyed a series of triumphs in the musical circles of Naples and Bologna and at the courts of Vienna and London.

In 1737 he went to the Spanish court in Madrid, where he was warmly welcomed by Philip V and the queen, Isabel Farnese, and his success there continued under Ferdinand VI, from whom he received the title of Royal Servant (Criado Real), an annual salary of 1500 English guineas and in 1750 was further honoured with the Order of Calatrava. He was an influential and cultivated figure in court circles; the King, who was prone to hypochondria, found relief only in Farinelli's singing. His privileged position enabled him to help the impoverished family of the Italian architect Santiago Bonavía. He was a friend of the powerful minister Somodevilla y Bengoechea, whom he emulated in dress and luxurious living. He was also a friend of Metastasio (Pietro Trapassi; 1698–1782), the Italian poet, and interpreted many of his works.

Farinelli organized festivals and opera at the Madrid palace of El Buen Retiro during the reign of Ferdinand VI and left a manuscript record of them (*Fiestas reales en el reinado de Fernando VI;* see Morales Borrero). During his residence in Spain he collected Spanish and Neapolitan works of art, including paintings by Bartolomé Esteban Murillo, Luis Morales and Corrado Giaquinto, who painted his portrait (Bologna, Conserv. Stat. Musica). He also owned 18 landscapes, contemporary Venetian works and the *Self-portrait*, possibly by Diego de Velázquez (Valencia, Mus. B.A.). He possessed many works by his friend Jacopo Amigoni, and Farinelli's own features are known from Amigoni's portraits, including *Farinelli and his Friends* (*c.* 1747–52; Melbourne, N.G. Victoria) and *Farinelli* (1747–52; Paris, Carnavalet).

When Ferdinand died in 1759, Farinelli considered remaining with the Spanish court and moved to Saragossa, where Charles III resided. But the new king was not fond of music, and Farinelli returned to Italy, where from 1762 he lived near Bologna surrounded by his princely portrait gallery and his magnificent collection of 318 paintings, his silver, tapestries, porcelain, chinoiserie and engravings.

BIBLIOGRAPHY

G. Sacchi: *Vita del cavaliere Don Carlo Broschi* (Vinagia, 1784)
L. Carmena y Millan: *Crónica de la ópera italiana en Madrid* (Madrid, 1878), pp. xlv–lv, 11–26
C. Morales Borrero: *Fiestas reales en el reinado de Fernando VI: Manuscrito de Carlos Broschi Farinelli* (Madrid, 1972)
J. Urrea Fernandez: *La pintura italiana del siglo XVIII en España* (Valladolid, 1977), pp. 70–71, 225
G. degli Esposti: 'La galleria dei ritratti', *Collezionismo e storiografia musicale nel settecento: La quadreria e la biblioteca di padre Martini* (Bologna, 1984), pp. 37–8

MERCEDES AGUEDA

Farington, Joseph (*b* Leigh, Lancs, 21 Nov 1747; *d* Didsbury, Manchester, 30 Dec 1821). English painter and diarist. In 1763 he moved to London to train under the landscape painter Richard Wilson, who taught him always to paint from nature and to refine his impressions through studying the work of Claude Lorrain. In 1764, 1765 and 1766 Farington received premiums from the Society of Arts, and in 1765 he joined the newly formed Incorporated Society of Artists, with which he exhibited until 1773. He also enrolled in the Royal Academy Schools at their inception in 1769. Elected ARA in 1783 and RA in 1785, he exhibited intermittently at the Royal Academy until 1813. Between 1776 and 1781 he lived in the Lake District at Keswick, producing numerous topographical sketches, such as *Gilsland, Cumberland* (1780; Newcastle upon Tyne, Laing A.G.), some of which he worked up into exhibition pieces for the Academy (1779–82). A number of his sketchbooks survive (London, V&A), and a collection of prints after his sketches was published as *Views of the Lakes in Cumberland and Westmorland* (1789). His *Stoke Park, Buckinghamshire* (1801; priv. col., see Harris, pl. 328), a country-house portrait in oils commissioned by the owner, John Penn, is influenced by Wilson in its composition but with a late 18th-century Neo-classical emphasis on distinct outlining and smooth brushwork.

Farington's early interest in topography and antiquities was developed further by a growing appreciation in Britain for native landscape. He contributed to many publications, notably William Combe's *An History of the River Thames* (1794–6), the illustrations for which were engraved by Joseph Constantine Stadler. Published by John Boydell, this Picturesque topographical history of the banks of the Thames was the only part to appear of an ambitious project intended to cover the principal rivers of Great Britain.

Farington made many sketching tours in the British Isles and one excursion to the battlefields of Flanders in 1793; his itineraries and impressions of the sights he viewed and sketched are described in his *Diaries*. It is these *Diaries*, spanning 1793–1821, that comprise his main contribution to the historiography of art in England. They are an invaluable chronicle of day-to-day affairs at the Royal Academy, of its development and of the rivalries and alliances among its members. Although he never held a major official post within the Academy, he was intermittently on its Council and served on many influential committees. These included those revising the Academy's rules, establishing a pension fund and advising on the decoration of St Paul's Cathedral, London. His support seems to have been considered of paramount importance to most would-be exhibitors, and for the two or three months that preceded each annual exhibition he recorded many pleas for admission and for the favourable placing of works. More approachable than the *Diaries* might suggest, Farington was always sympathetic to the hopes and ambitions of younger artists. He was closely involved with the Academy's charitable distributions; he took infinite pains to help such artists as the melancholic John Robert Cozens, also sorting out the financial affairs of Francis Wheatley and William Hodges.

Farington was often approached to arbitrate on disputed attributions of works. He attended and commented on sales and often acted as an agent for collectors, among whom were industrialists and merchants from the Midlands and further north. He played a major role, for example, in the dispersal of Sir Joshua Reynolds's collections on behalf of Mary, Lady Inchiquin, after Reynolds died in 1792. Farington knew, and recorded his impressions of, numerous dealers and restorers, and he was deeply interested in the techniques and processes of art. In 1796, for example, he was one of the moving spirits behind experiments made in 'Venetian' colour, the recipe for which Mary Anne Provis (Ann Jemima Provis; *b c.* 1770) claimed to have rediscovered. Farington's appetite for news was omnivorous and the net he cast to gather it very wide. He drew not only on his extensive family connections, but also on his assiduous attendance at meetings of the Society of Antiquaries, the Royal Society and various clubs. It was his attention to every sort of conversational topic that gives the *Diaries* their richness, and they remain an invaluable source.

Among Farington's pupils was his brother George Farington (1752–88), who went on to study history painting with Benjamin West; he also provided landscapes (exh. London, Soc. Antiqua. 1771, 1780) and portraits (exh. London, RA 1782). In 1782 George settled in India, remaining active as a painter.

WRITINGS

Diaries (1793–1821); ed. K. Garlick and A. Macintyre (i–vi) and K. Cave (vii–xvi) as *The Diaries of Joseph Farington*, 16 vols (New Haven and London, 1978–84)

BIBLIOGRAPHY

F. V. P. Rutter: *Wilson and Farington* (London, 1923)
Joseph Farington: Watercolours and Drawings (exh. cat., ed. W. Ruddick; Bolton, Mus. & A.G., 1977)
J. Harris: *The Artist and the Country House* (London, 1979, rev. 2/1985), pl. 328

EVELYN NEWBY

Farmakovsky, Boris (Vladimirovich) (*b* Vyatka, 12 Feb 1870; *d* Pargolovo, Leningrad [now St Petersburg] province, 29 July 1928). Russian archaeologist and art historian. He graduated from the historical philology department at Novorossiysk University in 1892 and then visited museums and studied the results of excavations in Greece, Italy, France and Turkey (1894–7). From 1896 to 1900 he was academic secretary of the Russian Archaeological Institute in Istanbul. From 1901 to 1918 he was a member of the Archaeological Commission in St Petersburg (Petrograd from 1914) and academic secretary of the Russian Archaeological Society (1906–19). He became a corresponding member of the Russian Academy of Sciences in 1914 and a professor at Petrograd University in 1919. In 1921 he was appointed academic secretary of the State Academy for the History of Material Culture and curator of the State Hermitage Museum in 1924. He began independent excavations of the necropolis at OL'VIYA and on Berezan' Island in 1896 and followed this with a systematic study of Ol'viya in 1901–15 and 1924–6. During excavations at Ol'viya he made a particular study of its architecture, town planning and sculpture. His interests included Classical vase painting (the subject of his master's thesis in 1902); the links between Archaic Greek art and that of the Ancient Near East; and Greek art of the Classical period (5th century BC).

BIBLIOGRAPHY

Kratkiye soobshcheniya Inst. Istor. Mat. Kult., xxii (1948) [whole volume on Farmakovsky, including a list of writings and articles by V. D. Blavatsky and M. M. Kobylina]
T. I. Farmakovskaya: *Boris Vladimirovich Farmakovsky* (Kiev, 1988)

V. YA. PETRUKHIN

Farnborough, 1st Baron. *See* LONG, (1).

Farnese. Italian family of rulers, ecclesiastics, patrons and collectors. The family originated in Lazio, possessing much territory in the region of Lake Bolsena. During the 13th and 14th centuries they distinguished themselves chiefly as civic leaders in Orvieto and as condottieri, usually in the service of the papacy. They became prominent in Rome under Martin V, who made Ranuccio Farnese (*d c.* 1450) a senator in 1417. In 1435 Ranuccio was made Gonfalonier of the Church by Eugenius IV, and his service was rewarded with grants of land in Lazio. The family entered the Roman aristocracy when Ranuccio's son Pier Luigi Farnese married Giovanna Caetani. From this union was born Alessandro Farnese (*see* (1) below), who later became Pope Paul III and was the true founder of the family's fortunes. During the 15 years of his pontificate (1534–49) he pursued an energetic policy of nepotism to make the Farnese one of the leading families of Europe. His son (2) Pier Luigi Farnese was made papal Gonfalonier, created Duke of Castro in 1537 and Duke of the newly created duchy of Parma (*see* PARMA, §I) and PIACENZA in 1545. Paul's eldest grandson, (3) Alessandro Farnese, was made a cardinal (1534) and Vice-Chancellor of the Church (1535) and showered with lucrative benefices. Alessandro's younger brother (4) Ranuccio I Farnese was also made a cardinal (1545). Important dynastic marriages were arranged for Paul's other two grandsons: in 1538 Ottavio Farnese (1525–86) married the illegitimate daughter of Emperor Charles V, Margaret of Austria (Alessandro de' Medici's widow), while in 1552 Orazio Farnese (*c.* 1531–53) married Diane de Valois, illegitimate daughter of the French king Henry II. Paul III was a patron on a lavish scale, a family tradition that was continued by Alessandro and Ranuccio.

With the death of Alessandro in 1589, the family began to decline as a Roman power, although (5) Cardinal Odoardo Farnese was an important artistic patron. Alessandro's brother Ottavio established Parma as the centre where the family continued to flourish. His son, Alessandro Farnese (1545–92), 3rd Duke of Parma and Piacenza, the hero of the wars in the Low Countries, was not an active patron of the arts (for illustration of Francesco Mochi's statue of Alessandro *see* PIACENZA), although his son, Ranuccio I Farnese (1569–1627), 4th Duke of Parma and Piacenza, continued the family tradition in this area. Ranuccio I's second son, Odoardo Farnese (1612–46), 5th Duke of Parma and Piacenza, reconstructed the city walls of Parma. The family's final defeat in the Second War of Castro (1641–9) against Pope Urban VIII resulted in its withdrawal from Rome. In 1649 the paintings in the family collection were transferred to Parma from the Palazzo Farnese, despite the instruction in Cardinal Alessandro's will that they should be kept in Rome *in perpetuo*. The Farnese line became extinct on the death of Antonio Farnese (1679–1731), and their entire estate passed to the Bourbon Don Carlos (later Charles III of Spain), son of Philip V of Spain and Elizabeth Farnese, Antonio's niece. The family collection was transferred to Naples, where the majority of the antiquities are housed in what is now the Museo Archeologico Nazionale, while the pictures are in the Museo e Gallerie Nazionali di Capodimonte.

BIBLIOGRAPHY

F. de Navenne: *Rome, le Palais Farnèse et les Farnèse* (Paris, 1914)

——: *Rome et le Palais Farnèse pendant les trois derniers siècles* (Paris, 1923)

G. Drei: *I Farnese* (Rome, 1954)

E. Nasalli Rocca, ed.: *I Farnese* (Milan, 1969)

F. da Mareto, ed.: *Bibliografia generale delle antiche province parmensi* (Parma, 1974) [full bibliog.]

Le Palais Farnèse, Ecole française de Rome (Rome, 1981)

CLARE ROBERTSON

(1) Pope **Paul III** [Alessandro Farnese] (*b* Canino, nr Viterbo, 29 Feb 1468; elected 1534; *d* Rome, 10 Nov 1549). He received a humanist education at the University of Pisa and at the court of Lorenzo de' Medici (the Magnificent), where he came into contact with such leading scholars as Angelo Poliziano, Marsilio Ficino, Pico della Mirandola, Cristoforo Landino and probably with the young Michelangelo. In 1491 he entered the curia in Rome as an apostolic notary and in 1493 was made a cardinal by the Borgia pope, Alexander VI, who was said to have had Alessandro's sister, Giulia Farnese, as one of his mistresses. Cardinal Farnese's career prospered; he accumulated 16 bishoprics and finally realized his ambition to become pope in 1534. Despite a licentious past, which had produced at least four illegitimate children, he worked devotedly and with the skill of a consummate politician to repair the devastations of the Sack of Rome (1527) and to overcome problems caused by the Reformation.

In this context, Michelangelo's *Last Judgement* (*see* ROME, fig. 43) on the altar wall of the Sistine Chapel (commissioned by Clement VII but executed under Paul III and completed in 1541) was of extreme iconographic and spiritual importance. Perhaps the most important event during Paul III's early reign was the triumphal entry into Rome of Emperor Charles V on 5 April 1536 in the wake of his African campaigns. This provided the pretext for repairing the damages of the Sack as well as for an ambitious urban restructuring of the city with new axial thoroughfares (*see* ROME, §II, 3(ii)). Many churches were destroyed to create processional routes and to expose to view important monuments of antiquity. The special temporary decorations (triumphal arches etc) were executed to a sophisticated programme based on the triumphs of the Emperor as the Defender of the Faith and, as the route approached the Vatican palace, on the glories of the papacy. Baldassare Peruzzi was initially in charge of artistic supervision, and after his death (6 Jan 1536) was succeeded by Antonio da Sangallo the younger. The Emperor's itinerary carefully omitted a visit to the Capitoline Hill, which had not yet felt the effects of the urban renewal programme and, moreover, was the city's most important political centre. Paul's own patronage was soon to extend to this area: in January 1538, at the Pope's insistence, Michelangelo transferred the ancient equestrian monument of *Marcus Aurelius* (*see* ROME, ANCIENT, fig. 61) from the Lateran to the Capitol, where its central placement provided the nucleus for the development of the Piazza del Campidoglio, one of the most spectacular and influential urban schemes of the 16th century (*see* MICHELANGELO, §I, 4).

From 1540 Paul stressed the papal presence on the Capitol by his villa near Aracoeli, designed by JACOPO MELEGHINO and connected by a walkway to one of his favourite residences, the Palazzo di S Marco (now Palazzo di Venezia). The gardens had select views over some of the remains of Republican and Imperial Rome, and the complex therefore indicated a re-assertion of papal authority after the disaster of the Sack. In a similar vein, and again anticipating the triumph of papal authority during the Baroque, Paul developed an entire area in the Campus Martius around the Campo dei Fiori. Here he built the Palazzo Farnese (*see* ROME, §V, 25). He had already started on the construction, with Sangallo as architect, in 1514–15 while still a cardinal. After Farnese's accession to the papacy, plans were created on a grander scale to include the great atrium, whose 12 main columns are ancient spoils of great quality. The Via dei Baullari, begun by Leo X, was completed to connect the new palace with the Campo dei Fiori, the Massimi palaces and the main papal processional routes. On the death of Sangallo in 1546 the commission was transferred to the 71-year-old Michelangelo. His changes to the façade included a more dynamic emphasis to the central axis, a raised upper floor and a massive cornice, *c.* 3 m deep, which gave the palace a more overpowering appearance and made it a prototype for many future palaces in Rome and elsewhere (*see* MICHELANGELO, §I, 4). Michelangelo wanted to create a grand vista involving a bridge across the Tiber to connect with the Farnese gardens on the other side, but nothing came of this. The third important architect was Giacomo della Porta, who abandoned the rear façade in favour of the present loggia. Other commissions in palace architecture for which Paul III was responsible include the palace at Gradoli (1517–26) in northern Lazio, designed by Sangallo, and the Palazzo Farnese at Capodimonte (both decorated with frescoes), the 'tempietti' on the Bisentina island in Lake Bolsena, the development of the Palazzo del Drago in Bolsena (under Simone Mosca and Raffaello da Montelupo, 1542–5) and, above all, the villa at Caprarola, begun (1520–21) by Sangallo and Baldassare Peruzzi and completed (1559–73) after the Pope's death by JACOPO VIGNOLA.

It was Pope Paul III who appointed Michelangelo architect-in-charge of the new St Peter's after the death of Sangallo (1546). Michelangelo rejected much of Sangallo's design (based on having a nave) and returned again to a central plan, which developed Bramante's original project (*see* MICHELANGELO, §I, 4 and ROME, §V, 14(ii)(d)). He also designed the dome, but the proportions he devised were altered later by Domenico Fontana (iv) in order to give the structure added height and therefore better visibility from the Piazza S Pietro. By that time a longitudinal section with a massive nave had again been adopted. Paul III also commissioned Michelangelo's last frescoes, the *Crucifixion of St Peter* and the *Conversion of St Paul* (1542–50; Rome, Vatican, Pauline Chapel). These images of suffering and conversion are fully in the spirit of the Counter-Reformation and make few concessions to conventional aesthetic tradition (*see* MICHELANGELO, §I, 2). Their themes, featuring the patron saints of Rome—Peter, Christ's appointed successor, and Paul, who convened the first council of the Christian Church—represent a further acclamation of papal authority. Another outstanding expression of the inviolability of papal authority was the replacement of the angel on the summit of the Castel Sant' Angelo (destroyed in the Sack of Rome) with a new one (1544) by Montelupo. Tiberio Crispi (1497–1566), papal castellan of the Castel Sant' Angelo (1542–5), commissioned Raffaello da Montelupo (*see* MONTELUPO, (2)) to build a series of new apartments and other rooms for Paul III in the fortress. These were decorated (from 1545) by PERINO DEL VAGA, including the vast Sala Paolina, for which he executed an elaborate fresco scheme.

Paul III also strengthened the military defences in Rome and the papal states. His costly fortifications of Rome concentrated on the left side of the Tiber and on the Aventine. The fortifications on the right side of the Tiber, at the Vatican and the 'borgo', were the work of Sangallo and Meleghino; Michelangelo completed the Belvedere bastion in 1548. Paul had already (in 1536) fortified Ancona and Civitavecchia against the Ottoman threat, and after the 'Salt War' in 1540 against Perugia, which crushed the power of the Colonna clan, he erected the formidable Rocca Paolina (designed by Sangallo) above that city. The most famous portrait of Paul III is that by Titian: *Pope Paul III with his Grandsons* (1546; Naples, Capodimonte). The two had first met in Bologna in 1543, when Titian made his earliest portrait of the Pope (Naples, Capodimonte; *see* TITIAN, fig. 9). Paul III's tomb in St Peter's, with his image in bronze, is by Guglielmo della Porta (*see* PORTA, DELLA, (3)).

BIBLIOGRAPHY
C. Capasso: *Paolo III, 1534–1549*, 2 vols (Messina, 1924)
W. Friedensburg: *Kaiser Karl V und Papst Paul III, 1534–1549* (Leipzig, 1932)
W. H. Edwards: *Paul der Dritte, oder der geistliche Gegenreformation* (Leipzig, 1933)
R. Harprath: *Papst Paul III als Alexander der Grosse: Das Freskenprogram—der Sala Paolina in der Engelsburg* (Berlin and New York, 1978)
Gli affreschi di Paolo III a Castel Sant' Angelo: Progetto ed esecuzione, 2 vols (exh. cat., ed. F. M. Aliberti Gaudioso and others; Rome, Castel S Angelo, 1982)

TILL R. VERELLEN

(2) Pier Luigi Farnese, 1st Duke of Parma and Piacenza (*b* Rome, 19 Nov 1503; *d* Piacenza, 10 Sept 1547). Son of (1) Paul III. He became a professional soldier at an early age and in 1528 fought in Italy as an ally of Emperor Charles V against the papal forces, to the embarrassment of his father. Nonetheless, after his election as pope, Paul III pardoned Pier Luigi and made him papal Gonfalonier (1537). His violent character has generally obscured the fact that he was an energetic and adventurous patron, often favouring young and relatively unknown artists rather than those patronized by his father. Most of his architectural commissions were for military projects. Paul III granted him the duchy of Castro in 1537, and Pier Luigi undertook extensive fortifications both there and at Nepi, employing his father's architect, Antonio da Sangallo the younger. In both locations he also commissioned much domestic architecture: at Castro, indeed, a complete town was built, which was destroyed in 1649 during the Second War of Castro. He employed Francesco Salviati as his court painter during the 1530s and early 1540s. Salviati designed a set of tapestries illustrating the *Life of Alexander the Great*, one of which, *Alexander Sacrificing*, survives (Naples, Capodimonte). Salviati also frescoed a bathroom at Nepi and designed temporary decorations for the Duke's entry into Castro in 1543. A portrait of Pier Luigi, long attributed to Titian but now thought to be by Salviati, is in the Palazzo Reale, Naples. Another portrait, probably by Titian (Naples, Capodimonte), is greatly damaged. In 1545 Pier Luigi employed Girolamo Siciolante as court painter, but only one of the works painted for him, a *Virgin and Child with Saints* (1545; Parma, G.N.), can be identified. In the same year Paul III made Pier Luigi Duke of Parma and Piacenza, whereupon he started planning major building projects for both towns. However, these plans were abruptly curtailed when he was murdered in Piacenza.

BIBLIOGRAPHY
I. Affò: *Vita di Pier Luigi Farnese* (Milan, 1821)
I. Cheney: *Francesco Salviati (1510–1563)* (diss, U. New York, 1963), pp. 42–3
H. Giess: 'Die Stadt Castro und die Pläne von Antonio da Sangallo den Jüngeren', *Röm. Jb. Kstgesch.*, xvii (1978), pp. 47–88; xix (1981), pp. 85–140

(3) Cardinal **Alessandro Farnese** (*b* Valentano, nr Viterbo, 7 Oct 1520; *d* 2 March 1589). Son of (2) Pier Luigi Farnese. He was the most important private patron of mid-16th century Rome. He entered the Church very young and was made a cardinal at the age of 14 by his grandfather, Pope Paul III, although he was not ordained as a priest until 1564. In 1535 he was made Vice-Chancellor of the Church for life and was showered with lucrative benefices. Even after the death of Paul III in 1549 he remained one of Rome's most powerful men, and his enormous wealth enabled him to commission an immense number of artistic projects, including the Villa Farnese at Caprarola and the church of Il Gesù in Rome. His earliest artistic experience was gained acting as an intermediary between Paul III and his artists: for example, conveying Paul's instructions and receiving reports from Antonio da Sangallo the younger and JACOPO MELEGHINO about the fortification of Rome and additions to the Vatican palaces. During the 1540s he began to commission works of art for himself. Paolo Giovio introduced Giorgio Vasari to Cardinal Alessandro and arranged for him to paint a *Justice*

(1543; Naples, Capodimonte) for the Cardinal. In 1546 Vasari frescoed the Sala dei Cento Giorni in the Palazzo della Cancelleria (*see* ROME, §V, 23(ii)) with a cycle glorifying Paul III's achievements, the programme for which was devised by Giovio. Also in 1546 Alessandro suggested that Vasari should help Giovio to compile biographies of artists, and Giovio, in turn, suggested that Vasari should do this on his own. In the same year Titian was invited to Rome to paint portraits of members of the Farnese family, including the unfinished *Pope Paul III with his Grandsons*; he also painted the *Danäe* (both Naples, Capodimonte). Francesco Salviati, who had already worked as Pier Luigi's court painter, decorated (1548) the Cardinal's private chapel in the Cancelleria, the Cappella del Pallio, and painted two angels for his titular church, S Lorenzo in Damaso, Rome. ANNIBAL CARO, who had also earlier worked for Pier Luigi, became Alessandro's secretary and chief artistic adviser on Pier Luigi's death.

Alessandro was particularly interested in the minor arts, and many of his early commissions were for engraved gems by Giovanni Bernardi, medals by Alessandro Cesati and miniatures by GIULIO CLOVIO, including the celebrated Book of Hours (*c.* 1540–46; New York, Pierpont Morgan Lib., MS. M. 69). Among his most important commissions was for the Farnese Casket (Naples, Capodimonte), executed between 1543 and 1561, in which six crystals engraved by Bernardi, some after designs by Perino del Vaga, were set in a silver-gilt frame by Manno Sbarri (1536–76).

In 1558 Alessandro commissioned JACOPO VIGNOLA to convert the pentagonal fortress at Caprarola, begun by Baldassare Peruzzi and Sangallo, into a sumptuous villa; Vignola did this with conspicuous success, creating what was thereafter known as the VILLA FARNESE, CAPRAROLA. It was Vignola's first project for his major patron and involved extensive remodelling of the town to provide a suitably grand approach road. From *c.* 1561 Taddeo Zuccaro decorated the interior with an elaborate and sophisticated series of images described by Caro, who devised some of the programmes, as 'suitable to the place and out of the ordinary'. On Taddeo's death in 1566, the work was taken over by his brother, Federico Zuccaro, who worked there until his dismissal in 1569. The remaining apartment was frescoed by Jacopo Bertoia, Giovanni de' Vecchi and Raffaellino da Reggio (1550–78), following programmes by various advisers, including Fulvio Orsini and Onofrio Panvinio. The Villa Farnese also had fine gardens designed by Vignola and Giacomo del Duca and containing a palazzina by the latter. Alessandro also owned extensive gardens in Rome: the Palatine Hill was transformed into the Orti Farnesiani by Vignola and later by del Duca. He was given the Villa Madama by the Medici family in 1555 and housed some of his antique sculpture there; and he bought the Villa Farnesina from the heirs of Agostino Chigi, planning to revive Michelangelo's scheme to connect it to the Palazzo Farnese with a bridge across the Tiber.

After the conclusion of the Council of Trent in 1564, religious commissions became far more significant in Cardinal Farnese's patronage. The reasons for the change were several: there was great papal pressure on cardinals at this period to reform and refurbish their religious foundations, but Alessandro was also anxious to forward his ambitions to become pope himself. Furthermore, he became closely involved with the Jesuit Order around this date. In 1568 he commissioned from Vignola designs for a new church for the order: Il Gesù. The façade and cupola were designed by Giacomo della Porta, who succeeded Vignola as Alessandro's architect. This was the largest church to be built in Rome since the Sack of 1527, and it became an influential model of the Counter-Reformation church (*see* ROME, §V, 16). Throughout the project Alessandro was eager to impose his own architectural ideas on the Jesuits, often against their wishes. He also commissioned the decoration of the cupola and drum with frescoes by Andrea Lilli and Giovanni de Vecchi (destr. during the 17th century). His extensive programme of religious patronage also included refurbishing S Lorenzo in Damaso, for which he commissioned a new altarpiece, the *Martyrdom of St Lawrence*, from Taddeo Zuccaro (completed by Federico Zuccaro), and frescoes (destr.) from de' Vecchi, Niccolò Pomarancio and Giovanni Cesari. He restored the abbeys of Grottaferrata and Farfa and the cathedral at Monreale. After the death of his brother (4) Cardinal Ranuccio I Farnese in 1565 he substantially assisted the Arciconfraternità del SS Crocefisso attached to S Marcello, Rome, in the construction of the façade of their oratory and the piazza in front. He apparently also contributed to the oratory of the Gonfalone, Rome, where his coat of arms features on a wooden ceiling. His last major religious commission was the building of S Maria Scala Coeli (1581–4), Rome, designed by della Porta, with mosaic decoration by de' Vecchi.

Alessandro inherited the Palazzo Farnese on Ranuccio's death but continued to live in the Cancelleria. This circumstance, and his commitment to several costly commissions, explains his reluctance to complete the building of the palace, although the rear section was finally finished in accordance with designs by della Porta in 1589. The palace housed the vast family collection of paintings and antique sculpture, including Gianfrancesco Ponni's *Madonna del Divin Amore* (Naples, Capodimonte), El Greco's *Christ Healing the Blind Man* (Parma, G.N.), the Farnese *Hercules*, Farnese *Flora* and Farnese *Atlas* (all Naples, Mus. Archeol. N.). Artists were occasionally allowed to make copies of works in the collection, and friends seem to have had access, but the palace was inhabited only by a few familiars such as Fulvio Orsini and Giulio Clovio.

As a patron, Alessandro was particularly interested in architecture and was well-versed in the technicalities of this art and able to influence the ultimate appearance of a project to a considerable degree. This was demonstrated by his intervention over the Il Gesù plans, which resulted in the decision to build the church with a single nave, to have a vault rather than a wooden ceiling and to orientate the building so that it could have a piazza in front of it. He apparently took much less interest in painting, and it is difficult to discern any particular stylistic preferences in his choice of artists. Rather, he delegated much responsibility for both the selection of subject-matter and even of painter to advisers such as Caro and Orsini. It is largely their taste that is revealed in the surviving Farnese commissions for paintings.

BIBLIOGRAPHY

C. Trasmondo Frangipane: *Memorie sulla vita e i fatti del Cardinal Alessandro Farnese* (Rome, 1876)

F. Zeri: *Pittura e controriforma* (Turin, 1957), pp. 44–61

C. Riebesell: *Die Sammlung des Kardinal Alessandro Farnese: Ein 'studio' für Künstler und Gelehrte* (Weinheim, 1989)

C. Robertson: *Il Gran Cardinale: The Artistic Patronage of Alessandro Farnese* (New Haven and London, 1992)

(4) Cardinal **Ranuccio I Farnese** (*b* Rome, 11 Aug 1530; *d* Parma, 28 Oct 1565). Son of (2) Pier Luigi Farnese. Like his elder brother, (3) Cardinal Alessandro Farnese, he entered the Church at an early age and was made Prior of the Knights of Malta and Archbishop of Naples before becoming a cardinal in 1545. The magnificence of Alessandro's artistic patronage has somewhat overshadowed the achievements of the short-lived Ranuccio. Their patronage was, moreover, intertwined since they frequently commissioned work from the same artists, and after Ranuccio's death Alessandro took over several of his ecclesiastical commissions. Ranuccio visited Venice in 1542, where Titian painted the magnificent portrait of him wearing the cloak of the Knights of Malta (Washington, DC, N.G.A.). In 1544 he commissioned Giorgio Vasari, who had already worked for Alessandro, to paint a pair of organ-shutters for Naples Cathedral (*in situ*). They show *Paul III among the Patron Saints of Naples* and a *Nativity with Cardinal Ranuccio Farnese and his Entourage*. Francesco Salviati, who had worked for both Pier Luigi and Alessandro, was commissioned to paint a fresco cycle in the *salotto* (Sala dei Fasti Farnesiani) of the Palazzo Farnese, depicting scenes from the Farnese family history. Possibly the artist was chosen in this case by Annibale Caro, then Ranuccio's secretary. Salviati may also have painted a portrait of Ranuccio: a sheet survives with sketches of both him and Caro (Venice, Accad.). At Salviati's death in 1563 the *salotto* was incomplete, and the commission for the remaining two walls was awarded to Taddeo Zuccaro, who was simultaneously working at Alessandro's villa at Caprarola. In 1561 Ranuccio also commissioned a *Last Judgement* from Hendrik van den Broeck for Farfa Abbey, which was one of his benefices. Although he purchased a villa at Frascati (now the Villa Ricci) in 1562 from Cardinal Giovanni Ricci of Montepulciano (1497–1574), he effected few changes there before his death. The young Cardinal was protector of the Arciconfraternità del SS Crocefisso attached to S Marcello, Rome, at the time when they began building their oratory in 1562, later completed under Alessandro's patronage. Ranuccio was buried in the family mausoleum on Isola Bisentina, Lake Bolsena. Alessandro later had Giacomo della Porta erect a monument to him in S Giovanni in Laterano (the Lateran basilica), Rome.

BIBLIOGRAPHY

P. Litta: *Famiglie celebri italiani* (Milan, 1819–83), x, pl. xii

C. Pietrangeli and C. d'Onofrio: *Abbazie del Lazio* (Rome, 1971), p. 163

(5) Cardinal **Odoardo Farnese** (*b* Parma, 8 Dec 1573; *d* Parma, 11 Feb 1626). Great-nephew of (4) Cardinal Ranuccio I Farnese. He was educated for an ecclesiastical career in Rome under Fulvio Orsini and became a cardinal in 1591. He is most notable as a patron for his advanced taste in painting, which led him to encourage both Annibale Carracci and Agostino Carracci. He invited them to Rome in 1594, planning to have them paint a fresco cycle of the deeds of his father, Alessandro Farnese, the 3rd Duke of Parma, but this project did not materialize. Instead he commissioned the Camerino in the Palazzo Farnese (*see* ROME, §V, 25) and Annibale's masterpiece, the Galleria Farnese (1597–1601; *see* CARRACCI, (3), figs 5–6, and ITALY, fig. 36). His support for Annibale and his pupils was demonstrated in numerous further commissions: from Annibale himself, among other works, a *Bacchus* (1590–91) and a *Pietà* (1599–1600; both Naples, Capodimonte), a *Christ and the Woman of Cana* (*c.* 1594–5; Parma, Municipio), a *Christ in Glory with Four Saints and the Donor* (1597–8; Florence, Pitti) and a *Venus with a Satyr* (Rome, Pal. Montecitorio). The Palazzetto that Odoardo arranged to be built behind the Palazzo Farnese was decorated with Annibale's *Sleeping Venus* (Chantilly, Mus. Condé), *Rinaldo and Armida* (Naples, Capodimonte), *Dawn* and *Night* (both Chantilly, Mus. Condé), as well as frescoes by Giovanni Lanfranco and Domenichino. On Annibale's advice, Odoardo also commissioned Domenichino to paint the chapel of S Nilo at the abbey of Grottaferrata, which was one of his benefices. As a patron of architecture Odoardo was less adventurous, partly because his income was modest in comparison with that of his great-uncle, (3) Cardinal Alessandro Farnese, and partly because the latter had in any case left him several grand buildings. His projects were mainly extensions of Alessandro's schemes, such as Girolamo Rainaldi's work on the Orti Farnesiani and on the palazzina at Caprarola. He also had Rainaldi build S Teresa at Caprarola and the Casa Professa, adjoining Il Gesù (Rome), thus continuing the family tradition of support for the Jesuits.

BIBLIOGRAPHY

J. R. Martin: *The Farnese Gallery* (Princeton, 1965)

C. Robertson: 'The Artistic Patronage of Cardinal Odoardo Farnese', *Les Carrache et les décors profanes* (Rome, 1988), pp. 359–72 [see also articles by C. Riebesell (pp. 373–417) and R. Zapperi (pp. 335–58)]

CLARE ROBERTSON

(6) Ranuccio II Farnese, 6th Duke of Parma and Piacenza (*b* 1630; *d* 11 Dec 1694). Great-nephew of (5) Cardinal Odoardo Farnese. His strongest interest in the arts was for opera and the architecture associated with it. He instigated the construction of several theatres, among them the large Nuovo Teatro Ducale (1687–8; destr. 1830) in the Palazzo di Riserva, Piazzale Marconi, Parma, and the Teatrino di Corte (1689; destr. 1822), next to the Teatro Farnese, Parma, both designed by the architect Stefano Lolli (1685–1714). The painter Sebastiano Ricci was employed by Ranuccio, producing a *Pietà* (completed 1686) for the church of the Cappuccine Nuove, Parma, a convent founded by Ranuccio, and contributing to the decoration of the Palazzo Farnese (known as the Cittadella), Piacenza, where he painted a series of 19 canvases (12 remain) of scenes from the *Life of Pope Paul III* (1687–8; Piacenza, Mus. Civ.) for the duchess's apartments. Ferdinando Galli-Bibiena and Francesco Galli-Bibiena entered Ranuccio's service initially as fresco painters and later as stage designers. Ferdinando, who was at Ranuccio's court for 30 years from 1687, acknowledged his patron's generosity in his *Direzioni della prospettiva teorica* (Bologna, 1732, pp. 115–17). Ferdinando was also employed at the Villa Ducale, Colorno, designing the external walls with four towers. Between 1660 and 1728 the villa was remodelled from the *rocca* of the Sanseverino family to serve as a pleasure retreat for the Duke and his court.

Ranuccio's reign was noted for lavish theatrical spectacles, the most celebrated and well-documented being the nine-day celebration in May 1690 in Parma for the marriage of his son Odoardo II (1666–93) to Dorothea Sophia, princess of Neuburg-Pfalz. This included a splendid *naumachia*, a spectacle recorded in a painting (*c.* 1700; Parma, Pal. Com.) by Pier Ilario Spolverini (1657–1734). There were also numerous performances in the Teatro Farnese, with painted sets produced by the Galli-Bibiena brothers and Domenico Mauro (*fl* 1669–1707). On Ranuccio's death Ferdinando Galli-Bibiena designed the temporary mausoleum that was erected in the Chiesa Palatina (S Maria di Campagna), Piacenza, for the funeral oration. Frans Denys (1610–70) painted Ranuccio's portrait (Parma, G.N.), as did Spolverini (1710–20; Cremona, Mus. Civ. Ala Ponzone), an unknown miniaturist (first half of 18th century; Piacenza, Mus. Civ.) and Giusto Suttermans (untraced; copy Piacenza, priv. col.).

BIBLIOGRAPHY

L. Balestrieri: *Feste e spettacoli alla corte dei Farnese: Contributo alla storia del melodramma* (Parma, 1909/*R* 1981), pp. 31–49
V. Consoli Mandracci: 'Le "Delizie Farnesiane" di Colorno', *A. Lombarda*, xi (1965), pp. 107–14
M. Pellegri: *Colorno, Villa Ducale* (Parma, 1981), pp. 37–83
I. Mamczarz: *Le Théâtre Farnese de Parme e le drame musical italien (1618–1732)* (Florence, 1988), pp. 311–75
G. Cirillo and G. Godi: *Il trionfo del barocco a Parma nelle feste farnesiane del 1690* (Parma, 1989)

□

Farnese, Elizabeth. *See* BOURBON, §II(2).

Farnese Bull. Ancient Roman sculptural group. An enormous work in marble (h. 3.7 m; Naples, Mus. Archeol. N.), it is considered by modern scholars to be an enlarged and modified version of a group described by Pliny (*Natural History* XXXVI.iv.34) in connection with the myth of Dirke and attributable to APOLLONIOS AND TAURISKOS of Rhodes. This re-elaborated copy seems to have been made by Roman sculptors in the 3rd century AD for the Baths of Caracalla in Rome, where the group was found in August 1545. It depicts the punishment of Dirke, by being tied to a wild bull, exacted by her stepsons Amphion and Zethus for her mistreatment of their mother Antiope. In 1546 the group was restored and placed in the second court of the Palazzo Farnese, where it was to be made into a fountain. This project was never carried out while the group remained in Rome. In 1788 it was taken by sea to Naples, where it was again restored. In 1791 it was used as the centrepiece of a fountain in the gardens of the Royal Villa of Chiaia. Since 1826 it has been on display in the Museo Archeologico Nazionale. This 'marvellous mountain of marble' was praised by the most exacting critics, and together with the LAOKOON it was long considered one of the best works of sculpture to have come down from ancient times. More recently, admiration for the Farnese *Bull* has been based on its exceptional size rather than on the quality of the sculpture.

BIBLIOGRAPHY

U. Aldrovandi: 'Delle statue antiche, che per tutta Roma in diversi luoghi & case si veggono', *Le antichità della città di Roma*, ed. L. Mauro (Venice, 1556), pp. 115–316 (162–3)
R. Lanciani: *Storia degli scavi di Roma e notizie intorno le collezioni romane di antichità*, ii (Rome, 1906)
M. Robertson: *A History of Greek Art*, i (Cambridge, 1975), p. 608
F. Haskell and N. Penny: *Taste and the Antique: The Lure of Classical Sculpture, 1500–1900* (New Haven and London, 1981), pp. 165–7

Farnese Hercules. Large marble statue by the ancient Greek sculptor Glykon. It is 3.17 m high and represents a heavily muscled Hercules leaning on his club. According to the inscription, it is probably a version of a work by Lysippos or his school made in the 3rd century AD for the Baths of Caracalla in Rome, where it was found in 1546. When discovered, the statue had no head or legs. The sculptor Guglielmo della Porta, a pupil of Michelangelo, worked on the restoration. He replaced the original head, which had been found six years before, and provided the statue with new legs. The original legs were discovered a few years after the restoration, but it was not until 1787 that they were restored by Carlo Albacini (*fl* 1780–1807). The *Hercules* was exhibited in the court of honour of the Palazzo Farnese until 1787, when it was brought to Naples and set up in the old porcelain factory of Capodimonte. In 1792 it passed to the Museo degli Studi, now the Museo Archeologico Nazionale. The significance of the pose has been interpreted in different ways. Some scholars, noting the apples that Hercules clutches in his right hand, have seen him as resting after taking them from the Hesperides. Others have supposed that the hero was depicted after killing the Nemean lion. This statue has been hugely admired and studied by artists, antiquaries, archaeologists and travellers since the year of its discovery. Among the many copies and modern versions, a notable example is the one in copper executed between 1713 and 1717 by the goldsmith Johan Jacob Anthoni, three times the height of the original (h. 9.20 m; Kassel, Schloss Wilhelmshöhe).

BIBLIOGRAPHY

U. Aldrovandi: 'Delle statue antiche, che per tutta Roma in diversi luoghi & case si veggono', *Le antichità della città di Roma*, ed. L. Mauro (Venice, 1556), pp. 115–316 (157–8)
F. Haskell and N. Penny: *Taste and the Antique: The Lure of Classical Sculpture, 1500–1900* (New Haven and London, 1981), pp. 229–32
                                                          LUCA LEONCINI

Faro, António da Costa (*b* Carregueira de Vilar de Besteiros; *fl* 1757–86). Portuguese master mason. All his work is in the diocese of Viseu. He lived for some time near the town of Mangualde, where it is likely that he worked as a mason on the church of the Misericórdia and the palace of the Condes de Anadia. In 1757 he was contracted to build the tower for the church at Moledos. In 1763 he worked on S Miguel de Papízios with Francisco Cabral, an artist from the province of Minho. Other early works include S Pedro de Lardosa (1769) and the church of Ribafeita (1778), where he collaborated with João Martins, another artist from the Minho: hence the rocaille elements of the building. In 1768 Faro completed work on S João de Areias and S Pedro de França. Faro began work on the church of the Misericórdia in Viseu in 1775. In his contract he undertakes to remain true to the plans, which were undoubtedly drawn up by António Mendes

Coutinho, the city architect in Viseu. The Misericórdia's white Baroque façade, with its two towers and balcony surmounting the broad granite portal, is the finest work by this eminently capable craftsman, who appears never to have practised as an architect.

BIBLIOGRAPHY
A. Alves: 'António da Costa Faro', *Beira Alta*, xxxviii (Viseu, 1979)
M. L. de Freitas: *A igreja da Misericórdia de Viseu* (Lisbon, 1985)
JOSÉ FERNANDES PEREIRA

Faroe Islands. Group of 22 sparsely vegetated volcanic islands in the North Atlantic, approximately midway between Scotland and Iceland. Settled by Vikings in the 8th century AD, the islands became part of the kingdom of Norway in the 11th century, coming under Danish rule in 1380. The islands became a self-governing region of Denmark in 1948 and had a population in the late 20th century of *c.* 44,000. The capital, Tórshavn, is situated on the island of Streymoy.

The earliest known Faroese paintings were executed by Didrikur of Karastovu in the mid-19th century. After the early stages of modern Faroese pictorial art, represented by the pioneering Samuel Joensen-Mikines, whose work sometimes depicted violent and dramatic situations, the work of Ingálvur av Reyni (*b* 1920) came to epitomize the depth and range of modernism in the islands' art. He studied at the Kongelige Danske Kunstakademi in Copenhagen (1943) and quickly established himself as a forceful Nordic Expressionist, demonstrating also the influence of Cézanne and Braque. His mature work was marked by a vibrant and distinctive combination of essentially post-Cubist principles of construction, broadly and freely handled, with a colour-sense that conveys both the emotional intensity of Expressionism and the swirling play of light and mist on northern seashores (e.g. *Girl*, 1980; priv. col., see Irve, p. 349).

In the late 1950s, with the Danish-born painter Jack Kampmann and the sculptor Janus Kamban, Reyni founded an art school at Tórshavn, which, although it closed after only a few years, was of great significance to the generation of students that included the multi-media artist Tróndur Patursson (*b* 1944). Patursson studied applied arts, sculpture and painting at Voss and Oslo in Norway in the late 1960s and early 1970s and had his first one-man show in 1973 at the Listaskálin in Tórshavn. He received his first official commission in 1978 from the Faröya Sparkassi (Faroe Islands Savings Bank) in Tórshavn, for which he built a water sculpture. In his later work as a painter, collagist and illustrator, Patursson displayed both intimate lyricism and gestural power; his semi-abstract language is full of bold but subtly nuanced colour and improvisatory élan, and it conveys the power of immense natural forces. Among his many monumental sculptural commissions are a relief in copper and steel (1986) for Vågø airport and an imposing polychrome glass sculpture (1987) in the SMS shopping centre in Tórshavn, made in collaboration with the Danish glass artist Per Steen Hebsgaard.

Such artists as Amariel Nordoy, Zakarias Heinesen, Thomas Arge (1942–78) and Bárdur Jákupsson have also developed an impressive series of Faroese variations on the modern Nordic landscape tradition, within a social context in which institutional support for the arts is both strong and imaginative. Heinesen's *Walldecoration* (tripartite polychrome wood-relief, 1982; Tórshavn, Eyrsturskúlin) is exemplary in its emblematic combination of elements from Faroese folk legend with modernist simplicity and clear spatial rhythms. A similar blend of the atavistic and the avant-garde marks the work of the sculptor Hans Pauli Olsen (e.g. *Sculpture*, mixed media, 1985; see Irve, p. 363). The overriding feature of Faroese art throughout the 20th century, whatever the medium and whether the work be naturalistic or abstract in conception, has been, however, the representation of the metamorphosing power of nature.

BIBLIOGRAPHY
K. Williamson: *The Atlantic Islands: A Study of the Faroe Life and Scene* (London, 1948) [add. chap. by E. Kallsberg]
Faerøsk kunst (exh. cat. by H. Bramsen and others, Copenhagen, 1955–6)
Faerøsk kunst (exh. cat. by W. Heinesen, K. Hoydal and O. Jacobsen, Copenhagen, 1976)
W. Heinesen: *Faerøsk kunst* (Tórshavn, 1982) [Ger., Eng. and Fr. text]
M. Arvidsson, L. Hamberg, B. Jakupsson and B. Irve: *Føroysk list* [Faroese art] (Sveaborg, 1983)
B. Irve: 'The Faroe Islands', *Northern Poles: Breakaways and Breakthroughs in Nordic Painting and Sculpture of the 1970s and 1980s*, ed. T. Bløndal (Copenhagen, 1986), pp. 346–65
P. S. Hebsgaard: *Ny dansk glaskunst: The Art of Modern Danish Glass* (Copenhagen, 1988), pp. 90–94, 103 [Dan., Ger., Eng. and Fr. text]
L. Funder, P. S. Hebsgaard and G. Hoydal: *Tróndur Patursson* (Copenhagen, 1991) [Dan. and Eng. text]
MICHAEL TUCKER

Farquharson, Joseph (*b* Edinburgh, 4 May 1846; *d* Finzean, Grampian, April 1935). Scottish painter. He combined a career as a painter with his inherited role as laird of Finzean. His father, the 10th laird, was a doctor with an Edinburgh practice, and a competent amateur artist who encouraged Joseph. Much of his childhood was spent at Finzean. He trained at the Trustees' Academy, Edinburgh, and during the 1860s he was strongly influenced by the landscape painter Peter Graham (1836–1921). The watershed in his career was marked by three or four winters spent from 1880 onwards in Paris in the studio of Carolus-Duran. An admirer of Velázquez, Carolus-Duran taught his students to use the brush straight away and think in terms of form and colour. As a result Farquharson's work was always characterized by richly handled paint. Landscape was not taught, but Farquharson would have been aware of the Barbizon painters.

Back at Finzean he adapted French *plein-air* techniques to the Scottish climate. He designed a painting hut on wheels, fitted with large windows and a stove. From this hut he painted the great snowscapes on which his reputation rested. *The Sun Had Closed the Winter Day* (1904; Burnley, Towneley Hall A.G. & Mus.) is a good example of his mature style. A shepherd drives his flock through a gateway down a snow-covered track already printed with hooves and wheel ruts. A dramatic sunset sky seen between winter trees creates pink reflections on the snow. Pictures such as this earned him the nickname 'frozen mutton Farquharson', and a large number of prints after his work increased his popularity.

BIBLIOGRAPHY
W. M. Sinclair: 'The Art of Joseph Farquharson, ARA', *A. J.* [London] (1912), pp. 1–32

Joseph Farquharson of Finzean (exh. cat., by F. Irwin, Aberdeen, A.G., 1985)

FRANCINA IRWIN

Farrand [née Jones], **Beatrix Jones** (*b* New York, 19 June 1872; *d* Bar Harbor, ME, 27 Feb 1959). American landscape designer. She was born to a well-connected family, and her cultural mentor was her aunt, Edith Wharton, who introduced her to the great gardens of Europe. Farrand studied horticulture with Charles Sprague Sargent (1841–1927) at the Arnold Arboretum, Boston, MA, and after a period of European travel established a practice in New York (1895). She was a founder-member of the American Society of Landscape Architects (1899). Farrand received commissions for work throughout the north-eastern USA, creating sophisticated gardens that combined formal elements of Italian villa gardens with the naturalism of the English tradition, but that were appropriate to American conditions. Her approach compared with Gertrude Jekyll's because of her understanding and imaginative use of plants. As well as private gardens, she also designed the campuses of a number of colleges, including Yale University, New Haven, CT, and Vassar College, Poughkeepsie, NY. Her most important extant designs are at Princeton University (*c.* 1913–41), NJ, Dumbarton Oaks (1922–33; *see* GARDEN, fig. 61), Washington, DC, for which she wrote a plant book to guide its development after it was deeded to Harvard University (1940), and The Eyrie (1926–late 1930s), at Seal Harbor, ME, where a moon gate, Korean tomb figures and balanced design approach demonstrate familiarity with the gardens of East Asia. In 1927, when her husband, the historian Max Farrand, became Director of the Huntington Library in San Marino, CA, she began to undertake projects on the West Coast of the USA. She also worked on the gardens of Dartington Hall (1933–8), Totnes, England. Farrand believed that maintenance was inseparable from creation, and in 1955 she demolished her own garden at Reef Point in Bar Harbor, ME, rather than trust its stewardship to others.

WRITINGS

The Plant Book for Dumbarton Oaks (Washington, DC, 1980)

BIBLIOGRAPHY

D. K. McGuire and L. Fern, eds: 'Beatrix Jones Farrand: Fifty Years of American Landscape Architecture', *Dumbarton Oaks Colloquium on the History of Landscape Architecture: Washington, DC, 1980*
D. Balmori, D. K. McGuire and E. M. McPeck: *Beatrix Farrand's American Landscapes* (New York, 1985)

WILLIAM MORGAN

Farrar. Canadian family of potters of American origin. They were descended from English colonists and were potting in Vermont by 1795. They made two important contributions to Canadian pottery: they introduced stoneware potting and promoted Canada's first whiteware pottery. In 1840 Moses Farrar (*b c.* 1810) and Isaac Newton Soule built the first stoneware pottery in Canada in St Johns (now St Jean, Quebec), importing the necessary American clay for salt-glazed wares via the Lake Champlain-Richelieu River waterway. In the 1850s Ebenezer Lawrence Farrar (*d* 1857), proprietor of potteries in both Fairfax, VT, and St Johns, acquired the assistance of his brother George Whitfield Farrar (1812–81). When Ebenezer Farrar died, George Farrar remained in St Johns to make earthenware and stoneware and to enlarge the scope and nature of Canadian ceramics by vigorous promotion in 1873 of the St Johns Stone Chinaware Co. for white-bodied earthenware. Though only briefly connected with the final organization of this company, George Whitfield Farrar had been the prime mover behind it. In 1876, after a fire, his own yellow ware and stoneware factory, in which his sons joined him, was relocated across the river in Iberville, Quebec. The Farrars encouraged the ceramic industry in an area that became known as the Staffordshire of Canada and brought innovation to Canadian potting in general. George Farrar's son George Henry Farrar (1843–1927) eventually succeeded his father, but stoneware was being replaced by newer materials. He sold the pottery just before his death, and within five years it was closed.

DCB

BIBLIOGRAPHY

E. Collard: *Nineteenth-century Pottery and Porcelain in Canada* (Montreal, 1967, rev. 2/1984)
H. H. Lambert: *Two Centuries of Ceramics in the Richelieu Valley* (Ottawa, 1970)

ELIZABETH COLLARD

Farrell, Micheal (*b* Kells, Co. Meath, 3 July 1940). Irish painter. From 1957 to 1961 he studied at St Martin's School of Art, London, and at Colchester College of Art. In 1971 he settled in Paris at the La Ruche studios. His distinctive style, combining hard-edge pattern and figurative references in a soft-sprayed background, dates from 1965, when he consciously introduced Celtic motifs. *Thourables Wake* (1965; Dublin, A.C. Ireland), the title of which refers both to James Joyce's work and to the coils of smoke emitted by a censer or thurible, is one of a series using coils and intertwined circles. In 1970 Farrell commenced his most dramatic group of paintings, the *Pressé* series, in which two hatchet shapes meet and squirt out what might be wine or blood; one such work, *Pressée politic* (1973; Dublin, Trinity Coll.), is painted on wood and spills out from the wall on to the floor. *Madonna Irlanda* (1977; Dublin, Hugh Lane Mun. Gal.), a variation on Boucher's *Miss O'Murphy*, gave Farrell a gentler but no less witty vehicle for his feelings about Ireland. During the 1990s, he renewed his obsession with Joyce in the *La Rencontre* canvases (1994; Dublin, Taylor Gals).

BIBLIOGRAPHY

Micheal Farrell (exh. cat. by C. Barrett, Dublin, Trinity Coll., Hyde Gal., 1979) [retro.]
Irish Art, 1943–1973 (exh. cat. by C. Barrett, Cork, Crawford Mun. A.G., 1980)
Works (exh. cat., Dublin, Taylor Gals, 1994), no. 9

□

Farrell, Terry (*b* Sale, Cheshire, 12 May 1938). English architect. He studied architecture at the University of Newcastle (1956–61) and was a Harkness Fellow at the University of Pennsylvania, Philadelphia (1962–4). Returning to England after further travel in the USA and Japan, he established the practice of Farrell Grimshaw with Nicholas Grimshaw in 1965. The buildings designed in partnership, such as the Herman Miller Factory (1976), Bath, were in a High-tech modernist style, but after 1980, when he began to practise independently, his work began to display the influence of Post-modernist American architects, particularly Michael Graves. His small but expressive buildings of this period make flamboyant use of ornament and historical imagery; examples include Clifton Nurseries at Bayswater (1979–80) and Covent Garden (1980–81), both in London, and Henley Royal Regatta headquarters (1983–5). His principal work of this period is the TVam headquarters (1981–2), London, a conversion of a 1930s garage, which reflects Farrell's particular enthusiasm for Art Deco ornament. Other notable conversions of industrial buildings include Limehouse Studios (1982–3), a former rum and banana warehouse; his own offices (1985–8) at Hatton Street in North London, a former aero-tyre factory; and Tobacco Dock (1985–90) in London's Docklands. Farrell's later large-scale buildings in London are stylistically more refined, combining elements of historicism with High-tech modernism. His significance lies not in matters of style, however, but in his commitment to the urban context of buildings and the restoration of urban life in declining areas. He was especially concerned with repairing the damage that the isolated structures of the Modern Movement had caused to the traditional urban fabric. His commercial redevelopment above Charing Cross Station (1987–90; for illustration see LONDON, fig. 11), for example, has a powerful curved skyline that evokes the former train shed and is designed to revive the Thames waterfront. Other major office complexes include Alban Gate (1987–92), 125 London Wall, and Vauxhall Cross (1988–92), a government headquarters building fronting the River Thames.

BIBLIOGRAPHY
Terry Farrell, Architectural Monograph (London, 1985)
Terry Farrell in the Context of London (exh. cat. by R. Moore, London, RIBA, Heinz Gal., 1987)

MICHAEL FORSYTH

Farrell, Sir Thomas (*b* Dublin, 1827; *d* Dublin, 2 July 1900). Irish sculptor. He was the third son of Terence Farrell (1798–1876), a sculptor who headed a family workshop and earned fame carving miniature portrait busts. Thomas Farrell trained with his father and at the Royal Society School, Dublin. In 1852 he won a competition that resulted in a prestigious commission for his kneeling figure of *Archbishop Murray* (1855; Dublin, St Mary's Pro-Cathedral); he went to Italy to choose the marble and while there studied a range of sculpture, most particularly Neo-classical. Farrell received notable patronage from the Catholic and Nationalist communities, and a second important commission is the marble figure of *Cardinal Cullen*, the first Irish cardinal (1882; Dublin, St Mary's Pro-Cathedral), which is positioned on a drum of high-relief figures, a method of presentation seen in European monumental sculpture of the first half of the 19th century.

Unlike his contemporaries, absentee artists John Henry Foley and John Hogan, Farrell pursued his career in Ireland. Among his numerous public monuments are the bronze statues of *William Dargan* (erected 1864; Dublin, N.G.) and *Lord Ardilaun* (erected 1892; Dublin, St Stephen's Green). One of his finest works is the monumental figure of *Captain Boyd* (1864; Dublin, St Patrick's Cathedral), a rugged marble carving that combines realism and drama. Farrell was the first sculptor appointed President of the Royal Hibernian Academy in 1893 and was knighted in 1894. He was a diffident and retiring man, qualities perhaps best demonstrated by his request that three days elapse after his death before any notice was placed in the newspaper.

BIBLIOGRAPHY
Strickland
B. Read: *Victorian Sculpture* (New Haven, 1982)
P. Murphy: 'Terence Farrell, Sculptor', *Irish A. Rev. Yb.* (1991–2), pp. 73–9
——: 'Thomas Farrell, Sculptor', *Irish A. Rev. Yb.* (1992–3), pp. 196–207

PAULA MURPHY

Farreras, Francisco (*b* Madrid, 7 Sept 1927). Spanish painter. He studied painting at the Escuela de Bellas Artes de San Fernando in Madrid before travelling in 1952 to Paris, London and the Netherlands. His first one-man exhibition, at the Galería Biosca in Madrid in 1952, consisted of figurative paintings, although even at that stage he appeared to be more concerned with the richness of his impasto and colouring than with his subject-matter. In Madrid he came into contact with the El Paso group, whose example led him in the late 1950s to adopt Art Informel in pictures such as *Collage No. 139* (1961; London, Tate); he also began at this time to execute commissions for murals, mosaics and stained-glass windows.

After living in New York from 1964 to 1966, Farreras settled in Madrid where, like other Spanish artists of the time, he explored the possibilities of different materials. He executed collages using different types of paper (Japanese, silk-based, printed, tinted and manipulated), and in the late 1960s he moved from abstraction to more specific signs, notably letters and numerals from printed material and fragments of posters; he also broadened his range of colours. *Collage No. 477: La Frisa* (1971; Madrid, Fund. Juan March) is a typical example. In 1982 he used collage to create a mural at Barajas airport in Madrid. In 1984 he abandoned collages completely, realizing in three dimensions the volumes previously suggested by their plane surfaces. As these works were sewn rather than glued together, he called the technique 'coudrage'.

BIBLIOGRAPHY
J. Marín-Medina: *Farreras: Proceso y análisis de su pintura* (Madrid, 1979)
Coudrage (exh. cat., Madrid, Gal. Theo, 1984)
Farreras: Oleos, temples, arenas, collage, coudrage, técnicas mixtas, 1953–1985 (Madrid, 1985)
Dossier: 1955–1988 Farreras (Granada, 1988)

PILAR BENITO

Farrukh Beg (*b c.* 1547; *d* after 1615). Persian painter, active in India. He went to India at the age of 39. His year of birth, AH 954–5 (AD 1547–8), has been calculated from an inscribed painting, executed when he was 70 in AH 1024. His ethnic origin has been given by Abu'l Fazl as Qalmaq and elsewhere as Qaqshali (a misreading of Qashqa'i?). He evidently received his training in Khurasan, probably from artists associated with the production of a manuscript of Jami's *Haft awrang* ('Seven thrones'; Washington, DC, Freer) for Prince Ibrahim Mirza, governor of Mashhad 1564–77. His earliest surviving work comprises four miniatures in a simplified Khurasani style in a manuscript of

Farrukh Beg: *The Mughal Emperor Babur Receiving a Courtier*, opaque watercolour on paper, 414×270 mm; from the *Bāburnāma*, *c.* 1589–1590 (Washington, DC, Arthur M. Sackler Gallery)

Amir Khusraw's *Khamsa* ('Five poems'; Cambridge, King's Coll.) dated AH 978–9 (AD 1571–2) at Herat. This manuscript evidently travelled to India because the attributions include the title Nadir al-'Asrī ('wonder of the age') bestowed on him by the Mughal emperor Jahangir (*reg* 1605–27) before AH 1024 (AD 1615). Farrukh Beg went to Kabul and entered the service of Muhammad Hakim, half-brother to the Mughal emperor Akbar (*reg* 1556–1605). On 13 March 1580 he negotiated the sale, to Akbar's library, of a manuscript, recently illustrated with two miniatures in Khurasani style, possibly by him. After the death of his patron in July 1585 he travelled with Muhammad Hakim's son and others to the court at Rawalpindi and entered Akbar's service.

The first evidence of Farrukh Beg's work for the Mughal court is found in a *Khamsa* of Nizami (Pontresina, Keir priv. col.). Two of the miniatures were fully painted by him, and five others, coloured by other artists, were based on his compositions. The fully painted works are heavily indebted to the Safavid court style in which he was trained, with jewel-like brilliance of colouring, an elegant use of line and restraint in the posing of figures. These qualities are also found in three paintings that he made for the *Bāburnāma* of *c.* 1589–90 (Washington, DC, Sackler Gal.; see fig.), and the *Akbarnāma* of about the same date (London, V&A). The outline drawings for two miniatures in the *Tīmūrnāma* ('History of Timur'; *c.* 1584–8; Bankipur, Patna, Khuda Bakhsh Lib.) ascribed to 'Farrukh the elder' appear to be his work, differentiated from 'Farrukh the younger', who is evidently the artist otherwise known as FARRUKH CHELA. After this burst of activity (1585–*c.* 1590) Farrukh Beg played no part in the production of any known manuscript of Akbar's reign other than his illustration of the *Sufi Pir at the Tavern Door* in an undated *Dīvān* (collected poems) of Hafiz (Rampur, Raza Lib.). This is similar to the painter's earliest works under Mughal patronage and cannot be later than *c.* 1590. In 1590 he took part in Akbar's Kandahar campaign, no doubt owing to his local knowledge, but he seems to have been absent from the Mughal court until after 1605. This is significant because Farrukh Beg's early work prefigures the refined output of a series of important poetical manuscripts in which one would have expected his participation: *Bahāristān* ('Spring garden') of Jami (1595; Oxford, Bodleian Lib.), *Khamsa* of Nizami (1595–6; London, BL), *Anvār-i Suhaylī* ('Lights of Canopus'; 1596; Varanasi, Banaras Hindu U., Bharat Kala Bhavan), *Khamsa* of Amir Khusraw (1597–8; Baltimore, MD, Walters A.G.) and *Nafaḥāt al-uns* ('Fragrant breezes of friendship') of Jami (1603; London, BL).

It has been suggested (Skelton), contested (Ahmad) and accepted (Hájek, Knížová, Welch—see 1985 exh. cat.) that during this period Farrukh Beg worked at Bijapur and is the same person as Farrukh Husayn, who executed a portrait of his patron *Muhammad Hakim* in Kabul (AH 992, AD 1584; Tehran, Gulistan Pal. Lib.) shortly before Farrukh Beg left Kabul for India in December 1585. Farrukh Husayn is otherwise unknown except for praise as the leading artist of Bijapur at this time in the *Sih Naṣr* ('Three essays') of Zahuri. Works in Bijapuri style have been attributed to Farrukh Beg/Husayn on the basis of his style up to *c.* 1590 and after January 1609, when

Jahangir rewarded him with 2000 rupees and commended him as *az bī badalān-i 'aṣr* ('unrivalled in the age'). These have also been attributed to Farrukh Husayn and subsequently to the 'Leningrad painter' by Mark Zebrowski, who sees the same hand in an equestrian portrait of *Ibrahim 'Adil Shah II*, although an inscription on the portrait identifies the artist as Farrukh Beg. A slightly later portrait of *Ibrahim* (*c.* 1595) as a master musician from Jahangir's album (Prague, Náprstek Mus. Asian, Afr. & Amer. Cult.) bears an attribution to Farrukh Beg dated AH 1019 (AD 1609–10). Other attributions to the artist at Bijapur include the celebrated elephant portrait stolen from the Sahu Collection, Varanasi, another on loan to the Harvard University Art Museums and a *Horse and Groom* (London, V&A). The style of the Leningrad equestrian portrait, with heavy facial shading and distinctive colouring, is exactly mirrored in several paintings of young men made by Farrukh Beg for Jahangir *c.* 1610–15 (Tehran, Gulistan Pal. Lib.; Dublin, Chester Beatty Lib. (done in his 70th year); and San Diego, CA, Mus. A., Binney Col.). His adaptation of *Dolor* by Raphael Sadeler after Marten de Vos, in an American private collection, confirms that Jahangir had given him the title Nadir al-'Asr before 1615, when the artist was 70. The portrait of *An Aged Mulla* (London, V&A) was also painted at the age of 70, and Farrukh Beg's *Self-portrait* in old age (formerly Bombay, A. C. Ardeshir priv. col.) is clearly contemporary with these other late works.

BIBLIOGRAPHY
R. Skelton: 'The Mughal Artist Farrukh Beg', *A. Orient.*, ii (1957), pp. 393–411
L. Hájek: *Indian Miniatures of the Moghul School* (London, 1960), pp. 48, 70–73, pls 10–14
Nazir Ahmad: 'The Mughal Artist Farrukh Beg', *Islam. Cult.*, xxxv/2 (1961), pp. 115–29
——: 'Jahangir's Album of Art—Muraqqa-i-Gulshan and its Two Adilshahi Paintings', *Indo Iranica*, xxx (1977), pp. 25–43
A. K. Das: *Mughal Painting during Jahangir's Time* (Calcutta, 1978), pp. 173–83
M. Zebrowski: *Deccani Painting* (London, 1983), pp. 92–9
India: Art and Culture, 1300–1900 (exh. cat. by S. C. Welch, New York, Met., 1985), pp. 221–5, 291–2
K. K. Khandalavala: 'Farrukh Beg the Artist and the Deccani Problem', *Rupañjali: In Memory of O. C. Gangoly*, ed. K. K. Gangoly and S. S. Biswas (Calcutta, 1986), pp. 163–73
H. Knížková: 'Notes on the Portrait of Ibrahim 'Adil Shah II of Bijapur in the Naprstek Museum, Prague', *Facets of Indian Art* (London, 1986), pp. 116–23
M. C. Beach: *Mughal and Rajput Painting* (Cambridge, 1992), pp. 48–9
A. Okada: *Le Grand Moghol et ses peintres* (Paris, 1992), pp. 116–24
ROBERT SKELTON

Farrukh Chela (*fl c.* 1580–*c.* 1604). Indian miniature painter. Not to be confused with the contemporary master FARRUKH BEG, he was a middle-rank, prolific painter who contributed to most of the major illustrated manuscripts produced for the Mughal emperor Akbar (*reg* 1556–1605), starting from the *Dārābnāma* ('Story of Darab'; *c.* 1580; London, BL, OR 4615) and ending with the *Akbarnāma* ('History of Akbar'; *c.* 1602–4; London, V&A). His personal style can be detected in certain leaves of the *Hamzanāma* ('Tales of Hamza'). He seems to have been a disciple (*chela*) in Akbar's new religion, the Tauhid-i Ilahi.

Like other painters of Akbar's court, Farrukh Chela must have been fully trained in the given style when he entered the imperial studio, yet he retained his personal (perhaps traditional) style, which is well projected in his paintings. A single-handed painting from the *Dārābnāma* (fol. 32a) shows the pre-Akbari Indian tradition in his treatment of clouds. Some of his characteristics were: highly finished architecture with dry modelling; a deep landscape with rocky vistas, usually of boulders punctuated with hairy plants or shrubs; and in later stages a deep ink-blue strip as sky, other colours ranging from brick red to a pale mauve. The space is divided in horizontal platform-like plateaux, sometimes with perpendicular drops and vertical, regular, panel-like shading. His human figures lacked vitality and were sometimes finished or touched up by such celebrated painters as Basawan, Manohar and Dhanraj. His animal figures on the other hand are quite animated, as in an illustration from an *Anvār-i Suhaylī* ('Lights of Canopus'; 1596–7; Varanasi, Banaras Hindu U., Bharat Kala Bhavan, 9069/6): *The Lion's Court* has an unprecedented liveliness both in the animal figures and in the depiction of nature. The Layla and Majnun scene from the so-called Dyson Perrins manuscript of Nizami's *Khamsa* ('Five poems'; 1595; London, BL; see fig.) contains practically the same animal group but the figures are milder. Possibly the artist improved upon his composition, or he may have been helped by a superior artist.

Farrukh Chela: *Layla and Majnun Fainting*; illustration from Nizami: *Khamsa* ('Five poems'), 1595 (London, British Library, MS. OR12208, fol. 123a)

His rocky landscape in a page from the *Dīvān* (collected poems) of Hafiz (*c.* 1595–1600) showing an old shepherd with his flock is a desolation of arid brown patches in which the man and his animals are set like enamelled pieces in a mosaic. Farrukh Chela painted several elephant studies and scenes.

He was the designer of illustrated leaves of the *Tārīkh-i khāndān-i Tīmūriyya* ('History of the house of Timur') and of the *Akbarnāma*, where he was assisted by such lesser painters as Narayan, Anant and Surjan. He himself assisted Mukund in an illustrated leaf of the *Razmnāma* ('Book of wars'; 1582–6; Jaipur, Maharaja Sawai Man Singh II Mus.). At times the influence of Mukund and Miskin is apparent in his work.

BIBLIOGRAPHY

R. Skelton: 'The Mughal Artist Farrukh Beg', *A. Orient.*, ii (1957), pp. 393–411

A. Krishna: 'A Study of the Akbari Artist Farrukh Chela', *Chhavi*, i (Banaras, 1971), pp. 353–73

D. N. Verma: 'A Painting by the Mughal Artist Farrukh Chela', *Islam. Cult.* (1984), pp. 151–9

ANAND KRISHNA

Farsetti, Filippo (*b* Venice, 13 Jan 1703; *d* Venice, 22 Sept 1774). Italian financier. He was the most important Venetian collector and patron during the first half of the 18th century. His aim was to develop in Venice a new international art, directly inspired by Greek and Roman Classical models. He was educated in Venice about 1720 under the guidance of Father Carlo Lodoli. From 1734 he lived for some time in Paris, frequenting the court of Louis XV and the château of Versailles. There, he particularly admired the marble copies of the most famous Roman statues, and a series of plaster casts of sculptures at the Académie de France in Rome, which Louis XIV had commissioned. Under the pontificate of Clement XII (*reg* 1730–40), Farsetti began commissioning copies of antique statues in Rome; later, from Benedict XIV (*reg* 1740–58), he obtained casts of the most celebrated works in the Vatican. This nucleus was transformed into a rich and well-organized collection under Pope Clement XIII (*reg* 1758–69), Farsetti's cousin, who gave him his protection. Farsetti commissioned Luigi Pozzi to copy Raphael's frescoes (untraced) in the Vatican loggias, and those of Annibale Carracci in Palazzo Farnese (untraced). He also ordered from Antonio Chichi reproductions (also untraced) in cork of the arches of Constantine, Titus and Septimius Severus. Most of Farsetti's plaster casts were made by the Roman Bonaventura Forlani, who in 1770 became curator of his collection, which also included copies of famous Renaissance and Baroque sculptures.

Farsetti displayed his collection of casts in his Palazzo di S Luca, Venice. He conceived of it as an ideal museum, open to scholars and artists, and it became a meeting-place for supporters of Francesco Algarotti's theories. In 1764 Abbot Natale delle Laste published the catalogue of the museum, which Goethe visited and praised in 1786. Among the young artists who copied ancient art in the collection was Antonio Canova, between 1768 and 1779. In 1774 his cousin Daniele Farsetti bought the two *Baskets of Fruit* (Venice, Correr), sculpted by Canova for Giovanni Falier, and placed them on the palazzo's stairway. In the same building he also maintained the picture gallery started by his ancestors. This held mainly Venetian works from the late 16th century to the early 18th, as well as Dutch and Flemish paintings.

With the pontificate of Clement XIII, Farsetti decided to construct a villa–museum on the family estate at Santa Maria di Sala, near Padua, where he could bring together the beauties of nature, architecture and the figurative arts. In 1758 he obtained permission from the Pope to transport 42 antique marble columns from Rome to the estate. He then commissioned Paolo Posi to construct a villa (1759–62), in which part of his collection was installed. The building departed from the traditional Venetian style, being closer to northern European Rococo taste. It was placed in a landscaped setting with tempietti, ruins and artificial lakes, dominated by the glass-houses of the botanic garden to which Farsetti dedicated his last years. The villa's enormous costs burdened Filippo's relatives with debt. Daniele Farsetti (1725–87), an amateur painter, managed to keep the Venetian museum open, but, after the fall of the Republic, his son Antonfrancesco Farsetti (1760–1808) disposed of the picture gallery. In 1805 he sold the largest plaster casts to the Accademia di Pittura e Scultura, Venice, and in 1807 he sold the villa at Santa Maria di Sala. He presented the rest of the museum to the Tsar in St Petersburg. The villa was partially restored in 1965, although its garden and most of its outbuildings have been destroyed.

BIBLIOGRAPHY
Catalogo de' quadri esistenti nella galleria della casa eccellentissima Farsetti in Venezia (Venice, n.d.)
N. Lastesii: De musaeo Philippi Farsetti patricii Veneti epistola ad clarissimam C tonensem academiam (Venice, 1764)
T. G. Farsetti: Notizie della famiglia Farsetti (Venice, 1778)
Museo della casa eccellentissima Farsetti in Venezia (Venice, 1788–)
E. De Tipaldo: Descrizione della deliziosa villa di Sala di proprietà del Sig. Demetrio Mircovich (Venice, 1833)
G. Sforza: Il testamento di un bibliofilo e la famiglia Farsetti a Venezia (Turin, 1911)
E. Vio: La villa Farsetti a S Maria di Sala (Venice, 1967)
M. Brusantin: Venezia nel settecento: Stato, architettura, territorio (Turin, 1980), pp. 55–8

LAURA MATTIOLI ROSSI

Faruffini, Federico (*b* Sesto San Giovanni, nr Milan, 1833; *d* Perugia, 16 Dec 1869). Italian painter and printmaker. Obliged by his father to study law at the University of Pavia, he also enrolled at the local art school. When he abandoned his legal studies he received essential financial support from his two brothers. With the painting *Cola di Rienzo Contemplating the Ruins of Ancient Rome* (1855; Pavia, Castello Visconteo), Faruffini relinquished the academic Romanticism of Francesco Hayez and of Giacomo Trécourt (1812–82), head of the art school in Pavia, adopting instead a style clearly influenced by the work of Giovanni Carnevali.

Faruffini apparently first visited Rome in 1856, remaining there until 1858. During this period he received his first official commission, the *Immaculate Conception* for Pavia Cathedral (*in situ*), and also painted *Cardinal Ascanio Sforza Examining the Model of Pavia Cathedral* (Pavia, Castello Visconteo). In 1860 he went to Venice, probably to visit the painter Tranquillo Cremona, whom he had known in Pavia. The impact of the colour in Venetian painting was immediately apparent in Faruffini's *Titian's Gondola* (Milan, Brera), in which he attempted a new form

of history painting. The intimate, almost romantic atmosphere of the scene is emphasized by soft forms, achieved through interesting juxtapositions of light, shade and colour. The work was received favourably at the annual exhibition at the Accademia di Brera in 1861. In 1863 he was invited to send a group of watercolours to the Société des Aquarellistes in Brussels and he was nominated for several official positions in Italy. His best-known work, *The Reader: Clara* (1864; Milan, Gal. A. Mod.), was followed by the less successful *Virgin Being Sacrificed to the River Nile* (1865; Rome, G.N.A. Mod.), one of his few paintings of exotic subject-matter.

In 1865 Faruffini began experimenting with etching, usually following the compositions of his previous paintings. He also produced a series of illustrations for Francesco Pagnoni's edition (1865) of Dante's *Divine Comedy*. The following year Faruffini went to Paris, where his *Legation of Niccolò Machiavelli, Citizen and Secretary of Florence, to Cesare Borgia, Duke Valentino* (1864, see 1985 exh. cat., p. 67) received a gold medal at the Exposition Universelle of 1867. The *Orgy of Messalina* (1867; Milan, priv. col., see 1985 exh. cat., p. 21) reflects the influence of the French painter Thomas Couture. In 1867 Faruffini returned to Italy and in 1868 he became interested in photography, using the collodion process and favouring a large-scale format, simplified settings and well-defined spacing.

BIBLIOGRAPHY
Federico Faruffini (exh. cat. by A. Finocchi, Spoleto, Rocca Albornoziana, 1985)
A. Finocchi: Federico Faruffini: Un pittore tra romanticismo e realismo (Sesto San Giovanni, 1989)

CLARE HILLS-NOVA

Fa Ruozhen [Fa Jo-chen; *zi* Hanru; *hao* Huangshi] (*b* Jiaozhou (modern Jiao xian), Shandong Province, 1613; *d* 1696). Chinese painter and government official. Fa was active mostly in Anhui Province and is often loosely associated with the ANHUI SCHOOL of the early Qing period (1644–1911), but he is best grouped with the eccentrics or individualists of the period rather than with the more conservative traditions of the ORTHODOX SCHOOL. The 19th-century text *Tongyin lun hua* ('Discourses on painting in the shade of the paulownia tree'), referring to his highly original painting style, noted that Fa 'followed a path of his own'. Nevertheless he is seldom ranked among the foremost painters of the period, his output and influence being limited.

Fa gained his *jinshi* degree in 1646 and joined the Hanlin Academy in Beijing in the same year. He held a number of government posts and even helped repel Ming loyalist attacks on the Manchus in Fujian Province. He served as a judicial commissioner in Zhejiang (1662–4) and became Lieutenant-Governor of Anhui Province in 1668. After losing that post (allegedly for concealing a shortage in a friend's accounts), he tried to enter service again in 1679 but failed the *boxue hongci* examination, which brought his official career to an end.

A large hanging scroll, *Misty Mountain Landscape* (Stockholm, Östasiat. Mus.), exemplifies Fa's painting style. Composed almost exclusively of a rocky slope and mist-enshrouded trees, it suggests a primeval volcanic wilderness with vapours escaping from fissures and swirling masses. The nervous line of Fa's rock contours, his ambiguous rendering of landscape forms (which can sometimes be read as hollows rather than crags and hillocks) and the pronounced contrast of light and shadow animate his images, producing an effect of strangeness. Like most of his other landscapes, this painting represents a mountainside after heavy rain (some examples portray the landscape in rain). Fa's own inscriptions and other evidence reveal that this was a longstanding pictorial metaphor for good government—the effective and benevolent administrator brings benefits to the people he governs as rain brings good crops to farmers. In painting numerous depictions of this theme, presumably for others who, like himself, held positions under the Manchus and so were open to accusations of collaboration from Ming loyalists, he was asserting the virtuousness and wisdom of such practice and justifying his own decision to serve the Manchu regime (a course some considered dishonourable, even turncoat).

BIBLIOGRAPHY

Hummel: 'Fa Jo-chen'
Qin Zuyong: *Tongyin lun hua* [Discourses on painting in the shade of the paulownia tree] (preface 1865/*R* 1883)
O. Sirén: *Chinese Painting: Leading Masters and Principles* (London and New York, 1956–8), v, pp. 121–2
Chinese Calligraphy and Painting in the Collection of John M. Crawford, Jr. (exh. cat., ed. L. Sickman; New York, Pierpont Morgan Lib., 1962), pp. 152–3
J. F. Cahill: *Fantastics and Eccentrics in Chinese Painting* (New York, 1967), pp. 64–5
Shadows of Mt Huang: Chinese Painting and Printing of the Anhui School (exh. cat., ed. J. F. Cahill; Berkeley, U. CA, A. Mus., 1981)

VYVYAN BRUNST, with JAMES CAHILL

Fäsch, Remigius. *See* FAESCH, (2).

Fascia [facia]. Architectural term for a plain horizontal band. In the Classical orders, it refers to the planes into which the architrave is subdivided (*see* ORDERS, ARCHITECTURAL, fig. 1xxiv). In modern architecture, the fascia (or fascia board) is the flat wooden board used to mask the ends of rafters, which serves as an attachment for guttering around the eaves. This same vertical surface, when above a shop window, is conventionally used to carry the lettering of the shop's name. By extension, the term is also employed for the whole of a shop-front.

Fascism [It. *Fascismo*]. Political movement and philosophy, founded in 1919 by Benito Mussolini in Italy, which spread to other European and Latin American countries. The name was derived from the Latin word (*fasces*) for the bundle of rods and axe that symbolized authority in Imperial Rome, an emblem taken up by the Fascists.

1. Introduction. 2. Art and architecture.

1. INTRODUCTION. Italian Fascism developed in the wake of the aggressive nationalism of FUTURISM and FILIPPO TOMMASO MARINETTI. However, in the 1920s and 1930s it became associated with a more conservative ideology, which it attempted to impose on both popular and élite culture. Its anti-individualist philosophy stressed the supremacy of the 'totalitarian' state, nationalism and the organization of different sectors of the economy into 'corporations'. Although Fascism was ideologically closely related to NAZISM in Germany, it had a far more pluralistic artistic policy, with no equivalent of the Nazi campaign against ENTARTETE KUNST. Mussolini became prime minister in 1921 and dictator in 1926. The alliance between Italy and Germany in the 1930s and during World War II eventually resulted in his fall from power in 1943; he then headed a puppet regime in northern Italy under German control until executed by Communist partisans in 1945. Other Fascist governments included those of Spain, Romania and various Latin American countries, and Fascist movements arose throughout Europe in the 1930s. Fascist art must be seen in the context of the post-World War I *rappel à l'ordre*, in which various forms of Neo-classicism spread throughout Europe. Some European figurative artists, for example Maurice Denis, were attracted to Fascism; others, including Picasso, who also produced some classical painting, bitterly opposed it. After World War II Fascist art in Italy was censured by historians, but it was later reappraised.

2. ART AND ARCHITECTURE. On 26 March 1923 Mussolini inaugurated in Milan an exhibition of the Sette pittori del Novecento, sponsored in the Galleria Pesaro by Margherita Sarfatti. In his speech he declared: 'In such a country as Italy, a government uninterested in art and artists would be lacking in its duty' (*Popolo Italia*, 27 March 1923). The Fascists encouraged the qualities of structure and clarity supposedly inherent in Italian art. Such traditional values were presented, paradoxically, as a means of bringing the old, liberal culture up to date. The regime supported in particular the movement NOVECENTO ITALIANO, which developed from the Sette pittori del Novecento. Its pluralistic, progressive nature contrasted with the more old-fashioned works celebrating Fascism in various public sites, which were attacked as 'trash' in 1927 by Giovanni Bottai (later a Fascist minister).

It was architects who realized most fully the possibilities offered by the reorganization of the Fascist state infrastructure, creating for themselves the role of urban-planning specialists. Architecture followed new paths in Turin and Milan, where GIOVANNI MUZIO became the leader of a 'return to order'. Muzio's buildings (e.g. the headquarters of the Banca Popolare di Bergamo (or Bergamasca; 1924–7), Bergamo; see fig.) displayed an ironic Neo-classicism, also practised by Gio Ponti, Giuseppe De Finetti and others, broadly influenced by the values of *Novecento Italiano*. In Rome, architecture was traditionally more closely linked to a monumental classicism, which expressed itself in this period through the leadership of Marcello Piacentini (*see* PIACENTINI, (2)). He showed a cautious experimentation, also evident in the work of such architects as Innocenzo Sabbatini (1891–1983). More radical innovation resulted from a new awareness by the younger generations of professionals of modern European architecture. For example, in 1926 the Milanese GRUPPO 7 was established, founding the movement known as razionalismo (*see* RATIONALISM (ii)), to some extent influenced by international Rationalism.

In this rich variety of hypotheses, Fascism did not express clear preferences. This pluralism was challenged

Giovanni Muzio: headquarters of the Banca Popolare di Bergamo (Banca Bergamasca), Bergamo, 1924–7

by Pier Maria Bardi (*b* 1900) at the inauguration of the second *Esposizione dell'architettura razionale* organized by the MIAR in Rome (1931). Bardi, a journalist and writer, handed to Mussolini his famous polemic *Rapporto sull'architettura (per Mussolini)*. In this he underlined the value of *razionalismo* as the sole form of architecture capable of transforming and representing the new Italian reality. He also further developed the sense of the central importance of the state in Italian culture, which Mussolini had set in motion in the 1920s.

During the 1930s the reorganization of the state's participation was represented by the control of such important exhibitions as the Biennale in Venice, the Triennale in Milan and the Quadriennale in Rome and in the perfection of a support network in the visual arts. This included exhibitions of the Sindicato Fascista degli Artisti; the 2% law, which deducted that proportion of the total expenditure on all public buildings to be given to works of art; and the Ufficio per l'Arte Contemporanea, which functioned as an archive of contemporary Italian artists and encouraged experimentation by the younger generation. The work of artists and architects was thus directed towards the production of a new iconography of public power, combining the myth of Fascism as a popular movement with signs of modernity.

In 1932 the *Mostra della rivoluzione fascista*, in the Palazzo delle Esposizioni in Rome, was one of the most effective Fascist artistic events. It included work by such architects and artists as Giuseppe Terragni, MARIO SIRONI, Enrico Prampolini and Achille Funi. While the exhibition showed the open-mindedness of the regime towards different types of avant-garde art, the event was unified by the ideology that equated the Fascist 'revolution' and artistic revolutions as expressions of the same 'need for change'. The exhibition also tested the new, privileged role given to the artist by the state. Furthermore, the public found a new rite of association with the exhibition's contents and a sense of national identity.

The joint participation of artists and architects in the exhibition indicated a desire for the synthesis of art forms, especially art and architecture. This was the subject of a heated debate during the first decade of the Fascist period, but it was officially sanctioned in Rome in 1936 at the international Convegno di Arti, which included Denis, Le Corbusier, Marinetti, Piacentini, Severini and Sironi. The need to integrate art and architecture, in particular through murals, was strengthened in the early 1930s through the apparent triumph of the Rationalists in architecture (e.g. for the design of the railway station in Florence, 1932–5). This was characteristic of the climate of euphoria that created *Quadrante* (1933), which stated: 'Today. . .the centre of expression lies in architecture.' This feeling was echoed by Corrado Cagli who in the same publication claimed: 'Walls are what is needed to act as supports for the force of contemporary painting.' Yet this was perhaps most definitively expressed by Sironi—the spokesman of the heroic conception of the 'new man' dreamt of by the Rationalists. He was the leader and a signatory of the *Manifesto della pittura murale* (1933), together with Carlo Carrà, Massimo Campigli and Funi. This declared: 'Mural painting. . .works on the imagination of the people more directly than any other form of pictorial art. . . .Indeed, the actual location of mural painting (public buildings. . .), together with the laws which govern it. . .and its intimate association with the architecture, prevent the artist from giving in to improvisation and facile virtuosity.'

Not by chance, the Fifth Triennale of Milan in 1933 sanctioned this union, by housing in the rooms of the new Palazzo dell'Arte (1932–3), built by Muzio, one of the most complete collections of Italian murals and mosaics, including works by Severini (*The Arts, in situ*), Campigli, Giorgio De Chirico and Sironi (mostly destr. after the exhibition). Shortly afterwards, the completion of the Palazzo di Giustizia in Milan by Piacentini offered a less ephemeral opportunity to many artists to decorate the interior spaces.

Although such projects employed *Novecento* artists, no movement could monopolize official art. Indeed, the 1930s were one of the most intense decades in the history of 20th-century Italian art with regard to critical debate. It was the most lively period in the Italian development towards abstract art, especially in Como and Milan, where such artists as Carlo Belli (1903–91), Gino Ghiringhelli (1898–1964), Alberto Magnelli, Fausto Melotti and Lucio Fontana practised. They found important common ground with a group of architects (including Figini and Pollini in Milan). Abstract art was promoted by Belli, who in 1935 published *Kn*, almost the manifesto of the northern Italian abstract style, and by Gino Ghiringhelli and his brothers Giuseppe ('Peppino') and Virginio, who organized the Galleria Il Milione in Milan. Futurism also continued, concentrating on decoration and applied arts as well as on the new subjects of AEROPITTURA.

It was only in the second half of the decade that the illusions about Fascism were shattered by the regime's increasing brutality, in particular by the alliance with Germany, the racial laws and the aid given, together with Germany, to the Fascist Falange Española Tradicionalista led by General Francisco Franco. This eventually defeated the Spanish Republic in the Spanish Civil War (1936–9). The war created strong anti-Fascist feeling among many European artists and intellectuals, most notably expressed in Picasso's *Guernica* (1937; Madrid, Prado). In Spain, Franco's regime promoted conservative styles that drew on national traditions. In particular it supported the idealized realism of Ignacio Zuloaga, José Solana, Daniel Vásquez Díaz and others, and academic depictions of commemorative and religious subjects (e.g. the work of José Maria Sert). The first Director General of the Fine Arts was Eugenio d'Ors, whose classicizing theory of art had been developed during long periods in Fascist Italy. After Franco's victory such avant-garde artists as Baltasar Lobo left the country, while others living in Spain (including Joan Miró) detached themselves from artistic life. The major example of the official aesthetic was the monumental cemetery, the Valle de los Caídos (1940–58), near Madrid, commemorating the Nationalist dead, with a basilica excavated into a hillside by Republican prisoners. Supervised by the architects Pedro Mugurza (until 1950) and Diego Méndez Gonzalez, it included a monumental cross with heroic sculptures by Jean de Avalos and murals in the basilica by Carlos Saenz de Tejada. Only in the late 1940s did a degree of artistic liberalization begin, although the official Exposición Nacional di Bellas Artes, Madrid, continued to favour realism into the 1950s.

As in other parts of Europe, the intellectual class in Italy began in the later 1930s to react to the development of Fascism with anxiety or even open refusal, as in the case of Giuseppe Pagano. Faith in the construction of the 'new man' dwindled, and artists concentrated more on the anti-heroic and private aspects of life. This was apparent in the softening of the Rationalists' intransigence, in favour of 'Mediterranean' evocations with a classical tone, as well as the adoption in architecture and the decorative arts of a more fantastic, 'organic' dimension. The later 1930s were characterized in particular by the opposition to the official style by the SCUOLA ROMANA and the CORRENTE movement. From 1939 the Premio Bergamo (dominated by Corrente) supported a new political autonomy for the artist. In contrast the Premio Cremona dictated propagandist subjects with an easily understood iconography. In 1942 the Premio Bergamo was controversially won by the *Crucifixion* (1941; Rome, G.N.A. Mod.) of Renato Guttuso. Inspired by Picasso's *Guernica*, this proposed itself—with its crude expressionistic style—as a prophetic metaphor of a tragedy destined, with the worsening of World War II, to become an atrocious reality.

BIBLIOGRAPHY

G. Bottai, ed.: *Crit. Fascista*, Opinioni sull'arte fascista (1926–7) [series of articles]
P. M. Bardi: *Rapporto sull'architettura (per Mussolini)* (Rome, 1931)
Fillia: *La nuova architettura* (Turin, 1931)
A. Sartoris: *Gli elementi dell'architettura razionale* (Milan, 1932)
M. Sironi, C. Carrà, M. Campigli and A. Funi: 'Manifesto della pittura murale', *La Colonna* (Dec 1933), pp. 10–11
C. Belli: *Kn* (Milan, 1935, rev. 1972)
Convegno di arti, Fondazione Volta, Reale accademia d'Italia. Rapporti dell'architettura con le arti figurative: Roma, 1937
M. Bontempelli: *L'avventura novecentista* (Florence, 1938)
G. Bottai: *Politica fascista delle arti* (Rome, 1940)
Diez años de cultura española, 1939–1948 (Madrid, 1949)
C. De Seta: *La cultura architettonica in Italia tra le due guerre* (Rome and Bari, 1972)
L. Patetta: *L'architettura in Italia, 1919–1943: Le polemiche* (Milan, 1972)
R. Bossaglia: *'Il Novecento italiano': Storia, documenti, iconografia* (Milan, 1979)
Anni trenta: Arte e cultura in Italia (exh. cat. by R. Barilli and others, Milan, Com. Milano, 1982)
F. M. Martin: *El pabellón español en la Exposición Universal de Paris en 1937* (Seville, 1983)
S. Lux and E. Coen: *1935: Gli artisti nell'università e la questione della pittura murale* (Rome, 1985)
M. Fagiolo dell'Arco: *Scuola Romana: Pittura e scultura a Roma dal 1919 al 1943* (Rome, 1986)
L'Europa dei razionalisti: Pittura, scultura, architettura negli anni trenta (exh. cat., ed. L. Caramel; Como, Com. Valmorea, 1989)
G. Ciucci: *Gli architetti e il fascismo: Architettura e città, 1922–1944* (Turin, 1989)
P. Barocchi: *Dal Novecento ai dibattiti sulla figura e sul monumentale, 1925–1945*, iii of *Storia moderna dell'arte in Italia* (Turin, 1990)
K. Vernon, ed.: *The Spanish Civil War and the Visual Arts* (Ithaca, NY, 1990)

FULVIO IRACE

Fashion plate and costume book. Fashion plates are images made specifically to illustrate to people types of clothes that they should wear to keep up to date with fashions; they also give instructions or guidance on whether the clothing shown would suit the taste and style of the individual wearer. They evolved in the 18th century in Europe and have their origin in 16th-century *Trachtenbücher* (Ger.: 'clothing books'), which in turn grew out of a desire for more knowledge about costume and the development of printing. For the first time such books gathered together and illustrated information about costume, jewellery and many decorative motifs, such as embroidery. They declined during the 19th and 20th centuries when they were superseded by photography. While text was minimal, the illustrations they contained were a record of what was being worn, with particular reference to nationality and rank. The most important of the costume books for the history of costume is considered to be Cesare Vecellio's *De gli habiti antichi et moderni di diverse parti del mondo* (Venice, 1590). It was the first of the illustrated costume books to have meticulously written descriptions to accompany 500 carefully drawn woodcuts, and it covers Europe, Africa, Asia and America. Particularly significant are the records of textiles made and sold by merchant drapers, who plied their trade at, for example, the Italian courts, and who, therefore, would have been *au fait* with current tastes. Vecellio was a cousin of Titian, to whom his costume book was attributed for two centuries, a wonderful testament to Vecellio's artistic and historical achievement.

Tractenbücher continued to be published well into the 18th century, by which time French fashion had established an ascendancy over the rest of Europe. The illustrated costume book reached its apogee during the last quarter of the 18th century with *Le Monument du costume physique et moral de la fin du dix-huitième siècle* (Paris, 1775, 1777 and 1783; see fig. 1), published by Prault. With plates after designs by Jean-Michel Moreau, one of the outstanding artists of late 18th-century France, and a text by Nicolas E. Restif de la Bretonne (1734–1806), it is the most complete example of the elegant and refined taste of the French nobility at the end of the *ancien régime*. After Prault's work the Parisian publishers Jean Esnauts and Michel Rapilly then astutely conceived the idea of disseminating prevailing French fashions through a series of hand-coloured fashion plates. *La Gallerie des modes et costumes français* (Paris, 1778–87) was published in more than 70 portfolios, usually containing 6 exquisitely hand-coloured engravings. The fashions of French men and women were accurately drawn by some of the most celebrated artists of the time: Claude-Louis Desrais (1746–1816), Pierre-Thomas Le Clère (*fl c.* 1740–c. 1796), François Watteau and Augustin de Saint-Aubin. The clothes were carefully commented upon, some singled out for commendation, others for ridicule and much of the commentary supplied by contemporary newspapers.

While not exclusively a fashion magazine, *La Gallerie des modes et costumes français* broke new ground, with the result that during the last quarter of the 18th century, especially in France, a flood of magazines appeared devoted exclusively to fashion, containing sumptuous hand-coloured fashion plates that rendered the travelling fashion dolls obsolete. *Le Cabinet des modes* (Paris, 1785–6), the first periodical devoted to news about fashion, was published fortnightly, usually with three hand-coloured fashion plates. To keep up with the demand for British fashions, it changed its name in 1786 to *Le Magasin des modes nouvelles françaises et anglaises*; in 1790 its international standing was recognized when it became simply *Le Journal de la mode et du goût*. This periodical continued until 1793, proving that French fashions continued apace during the Revolution (1789–99). The last of the great 18th-century French fashion magazines, *Le Journal des dames et des modes*, was launched in 1797 by the Oratorian priest and professor of philosophy Pierre de La Mésangère

1. Fashion plate, *La Petite Toilette*, engraved by P. A. Martini after designs by Jean-Michel Moreau, 250×180 mm, 1777 (London, University of London, Courtauld Institute of Art); from *Le Monument du costume physique et moral de la fin du dix-huitième siècle* (Paris, 1777)

(1759–1831; see fig. 2). At first he supplied his readers unfailingly with at least one hand-coloured fashion plate every five days; in June 1798 he announced the addition of a second in each issue, so rapid were changes in fashion. The dress of the *élégantes* of the Directoire proved so fertile that a month or even a week saw greater changes in fashion than several decades under the *ancien régime*. As fashion became an industry in its own right, the publication of fashion plates drawn by leading artists became fully established in journalism.

At the beginning of the 19th century the fashion plate continued to be an important branch of fashion journalism, but the genre degenerated, especially with the closure of *Le Journal des dames et des modes* in 1839. Fashion plates became increasingly stereotyped, with wooden poses and masses of detail. French fashion continued to dominate, with the development of *haute couture* significantly expanding the fashion industry. Couturiers were, however, rather reluctant at first to publicize their models through fashion plates, as it meant they had to give up their total exclusivity over their individual creations. The decline of the fashion plate grew with the invention of photography, with some of the leading magazines, including *Les Modes* (Paris, 1901–37), devoting themselves entirely to photographic fashion studies. A revolution in fashion and fashion illustration was effected in the early 20th century

2. Engraved fashion plate, 190×115 mm; from *Le Journal des dames et des modes*, February 1798 (London, private collection)

by the couturier PAUL POIRET, whose bold use of simple classical line in fashionable dress created an elegance and freedom of movement reminiscent of the Directoire. Poiret recognized the need for a rejuvenation of fashion plates along the lines of *Le Journal des dames et des modes*. *Les Robes de Paul Poiret racontées par Paul Iribe* (1908) was followed by *Les Choses de Paul Poiret vues par Georges Lepape* (1911). The importance accorded to artists is immediately recognizable in the titles of the works. The colours in the plates have a jewel-like brilliance achieved through a special technique, the pochoir process, whereby a monochrome print was hand-coloured using a series of bronze or zinc stencils. The enormous success of Poiret's albums sparked off a veritable renaissance in fashion plates and fashion literature. A new *Journal des dames et des modes* (Paris, 1912–14) followed the tradition of the lavish periodical of La Mésangère in both title and appearance. *La Gazette du bon ton* (Paris, 1912–25), a luxurious monthly, united the couturier and the artist in the same way as Poiret's enterprises. The fashions of such couturiers as Jacques Doucet, Jeanne Lanvin (1867–1946), Madeleine Cheruit (*fl* 1898–1935) and Poiret were drawn by, among others, Georges Barbier (1882–1932), Pierre Brissaud (*b* 1885; *fl* 1929), Paul Iribe (1883–1935), Georges Lepape (1887–1971), André Edouard Marty (1882–1974) and Edouard Garcia Benito (*b* 1892; *fl* 1934). Fashion plates of the quality of *La Gazette du bon ton* were expensive because of the manual pochoir process. In 1925 *La Gazette*

du bon ton was purchased by Condé Nast and merged with *Vogue* (New York, 1892–7). This marked the end of the era of the de luxe fashion plate. Fashion photography became pre-eminent, although *Vogue* did also successfully promote the graphic tradition.

See also DRESS.

BIBLIOGRAPHY

C. Vecellio: *De gli habiti antichi et moderni di diversi parti del mondo* (Venice, 1590); *R* as *Vecellio's Renaissance Costume Book* (New York, 1977)
F. J. Lipperheide: *Katalog der Freiherrlich von Lipperheideschen Kostumbibliothek*, 2 vols (Berlin, 1905/*R* 1965)
Les Robes de Paul Poiret racontées par Paul Iribe (Paris, 1908)
G. Schefer: *Documents pour l'histoire du costume de Louis XV à Louis XVIII*, 5 vols (Paris, 1911)
Les Choses de Paul Poiret vues par Georges Lepape (Paris, 1911)
P. Cornu: *Préface à l'impression de La Gallerie des modes et costumes français, 1778–1787* (Paris, 1912)
J. Laver: *Fashions and Fashion Plates, 1800–1900* (London, 1943)
S. Sitwell: *Gallery of Fashion, 1790–1822* (London, 1949)
V. Holland: *Hand-coloured Fashion Plates, 1770 to 1899* (London, 1955)
R.-A. Weigert: *Debucourt: Modes et manières du jour à Paris à la fin du dix-huitième siècle et au commencement du dix-neuvième siècle* (Paris, 1957)
Modes et costumes français, 1574–1815: Gravures et dessins (exh. cat., Paris, Louvre, 1966)
C. L. White: *Women's Magazines, 1693–1968* (London, 1970)
D. Langley Moore: *Fashion through Fashion Plates, 1770–1970* (London, 1971)
A. Adburgham: *Women in Print: Writing Women and Women's Magazines from the Restoration to the Accession of Queen Victoria* (London, 1972)
J. Olian: 'Sixteenth-century Costume Books', *Dress*, iii (New York, 1977)
French Fashion Plates in Full Color from the Gazette du Bon Ton (1912–1925) (New York, 1979)
Hollar to Heideloff: An Exhibition of Fashion Prints Drawn from the Collections of Members of the Costume Society (exh. cat., London, V&A, 1979)
M. Ginsburg: *An Introduction to Fashion Illustration* (London, 1980)
Fashion in Paris from the 'Journal des dames et des modes' (London, 1980)
S. Blum, ed.: *Eighteenth-century French Fashion Plates* (New York, 1982)
R. Gaudriault: *Répertoire de la gravure de mode français des origines à 1815* (Nantes, 1988)
W. Packer: *Fashion Drawing in Vogue* (London, 1989)

ALICE MACKRELL

Fasolo, Giovanni Antonio (*b* Mandello del Lario, 1530; *d* Vicenza, 23 Aug 1572). Italian painter. Of Lombard origin, he was initially a pupil of Paolo Veronese and subsequently had a short but successful career as a fresco and portrait painter in and around Vicenza. In 1551–2 he collaborated with Battista Zelotti and Veronese on frescoes for the Castello Porto-Colleoni, Thiene. Scenes such as the *Meeting of Sophonisba and Massinissa* are executed in the style of Veronese, but with a noticeably harder and drier edge and lacking Veronese's rich luminosity and effortless control of space. In 1955–6 Fasolo was employed as a minor assistant to Veronese at S Sebastiano, Venice, but emerged in his own right towards the end of the decade (1557–61), when he began producing stage designs for the Accademia Olimpica, Vicenza. In the 1560s he executed frescoes at several country villas: at the Villa Roberto (Brugine, nr Padua; *c.* 1564–5), the Villa Campiglia (Albettone, nr Vicenza; *c.* 1565–7) and the Villa Caldogno (Caldogno, nr Vicenza; *c.* 1568–70). These last (e.g. the *Stolen Embrace*) are characterized by their contemporary air and informality, reproducing on a large scale the naturalistic tendencies—a possible Lombard inheritance—that underpin his style and become increasingly apparent in his portraiture.

In the companion portraits of *Paola Gualdo Bonanome with her Daughters Laura and Virginia* and *Giuseppe Gualdo with his Sons Paolo Emilio and Paolo* (*c.* 1566–7; Vicenza, Mus. Civ. A. & Stor.), Fasolo's most original works, penetrating individualization is combined with Veronese's firmness of structure, but the twisting, elongated forms of the sitters with their delicately spread fingers also demonstrate Fasolo's increasing interest in the stylizations of Parmigianino's *maniera*. Fasolo also produced altarpieces, for example the *Virgin of the Rosary* (*c.* 1570; Vicenza, Mus. Civ. A. & Stor.), although these typically lack the strength of his portraits and frescoes.

BIBLIOGRAPHY

G. Zorzi: 'Giovanni Antonio Fasolo pittore lombardo-veneto emulo di Paolo Veronese', *A. Lombarda*, vi (1961), pp. 206–26

L. Crosato: *Gli affreschi nelle ville venete del cinquecento* (Treviso, 1962), pp. 77–8

R. Pallucchini: 'Giambattista Zelotti e Giovanni Antonio Fasolo', *Boll. Cent. Int. Stud. Archit. Andrea Palladio*, x (1968), pp. 203–28

THOMAS NICHOLS

Fassbender, Joseph (*b* Cologne, 14 April 1903; *d* 1974). German painter. He studied from 1926 to 1928 at the Werkschule in Cologne with the German painter Richard Seewald (*b* 1889). As early as 1929 he received the Villa-Romana prize from the Deutschen Künstlerbundes, which gave him a grant to study for a year in Florence. At this stage in his career, while working as a typographer, he concentrated on portraits, figurative compositions, landscapes and still-lifes; most of his early work is lost. During World War II he served as a cartographer in the Wehrmacht, and in 1946 he established his studio in Bornheim, near Bonn, where he was one of the founders of the so-called Alfterer Donnerstagsgesellschaft, an association of artists and intellectuals who wanted to create a new cultural identity following the Nazi era. He was a lecturer at the Landeskunstschule in Hamburg (1953–4) and at the Werkkunstschule in Krefeld (1955–8), and from 1958 to 1968 he was professor of painting at the Künstakademie in Düsseldorf. He was a member of the Neuen Rheinischen Sezession, the Zen 49 group, the Deutschen Künstlerbundes and the Akademie der Künste in Berlin.

After the war Fassbender's work became more abstract; until around 1955 he worked with mixed media, which were based on typefaces and were strikingly linear, though later on he worked almost exclusively on large-scale oil paintings and on prints. In the 1950s and 1960s he also made wall paintings (such as in the Beethovenhalle in Bonn from around 1958) and tapestries, such as that for the Staatskanzlei in Düsseldorf (1965–6) and in 1971 for the Muschelsaal in the Rathaus, Cologne.

BIBLIOGRAPHY

G. Aust: *Joseph Fassbender* (Recklinghausen, 1961)

Joseph Fassbender (exh. cat., Hannover, Kestner-Ges., 1961)

Joseph Fassbender: Malerei zwischen Figuration und Abstraktion (exh. cat., ed. W. Herzogenrath and U. Haupenthal; Cologne, Kstver., 1988)

UWE HAUPENTHAL

Fassett & Stevens. *See under* STEVENS, JOHN CALVIN.

Fassin, Nicolas Henri Joseph, Chevalier de (*b* Liège, 1728; *d* Liège, 1811). Franco-Flemish painter and draughtsman. He was born into a wealthy and cultured family, and for amusement he frequented the studio of Jean-Baptiste Coclers (1698–1772), where he probably met Léonard Defrance. Fassin joined the French army in 1748 but resigned and returned to Liège in 1754. He studied at the Antwerp Académie and made copies of the work of such Dutch Italianate painters as Jan Both, Nicolas Berchem and Philips Wouwerman. He went to Italy, where he made studies after the Antique and landscape sketches (e.g. drawing of the *Mole at Gaete*, Liège, Mus. A. Wallon, and the painting *Cascatelles of Tivoli*, Wörlitz, Schloss).

In 1769 Fassin visited Geneva and met François Tronchin, who owned a famous collection of Dutch and Flemish landscapes. While in Geneva Fassin exhibited three works in the Salon and founded a school of drawing known as the Académie Fassine. On his return to Liège, together with Léonard Defrance, he founded an academy in 1773, which was officially recognized the following year by the Prince-Bishop Count Velbrück (1719–84). In 1776 Fassin settled in Spa, where he resumed his military duties in 1791, but he spent winters in Brussels and continued to paint. His technique was typically 18th-century and was characterized by a certain dryness. His work shows little development and continued to reflect his debt to the Dutch Italianates (e.g. *Noon*, 1802; Liège, Mus. A. Wallon).

UNPUBLISHED WRITINGS

Geneva, Bib. Pub. & U. [correspondence with François Tronchin, 1771–92, full of reflections on art]

BIBLIOGRAPHY

D. Coekelberghs: *Les Peintres belges à Rome de 1700 à 1830* (Brussels and Rome, 1976)

1770–1830: Autour du Néo-classicisme en Belgique (exh. cat., Brussels, Mus. Ixelles, 1985–6), pp. 293–5

BERNADETTE THOMAS

Fassler, John (*b* Potchefstroom, Transvaal, 21 April 1910; *d* Johannesburg, 18 June 1971). South African architect and educator of Swiss parentage. His outstanding draughtsmanship brought him early prominence as a student under G. E. Pearse at the University of the Witwatersrand and led to a teaching appointment in 1934, a year after graduating. His intimate contact as student and colleague with Rex Martienssen and his circle was the dominant influence on his career. His early affiliation with the Modern Movement was balanced by a love of architectural history: his design, in Pearse's office, of the University Library (1933), with its classical portico and restrained modern interior, was prophetically ambivalent.

In 1934 Fassler began a brief association with Martienssen and Bernard Cooke, which in an intense burst of creativity produced some of Johannesburg's pioneer major modern works, notably House Stern and Peterhouse (1934–5). His Joubert Park project for a block of flats (1934) was a striking contribution. Fassler first visited Europe in 1936: the most powerful influences were Classical Greece and Rome, and his first personal encounter with Le Corbusier, but he later also appreciated the immaculate detailing of modern Swiss architecture and its humane symbiosis of building and landscaping. These characteristics typified his later approach to architecture, from the second Dental School (1951) to his last unfinished work, at the University of the Witwatersrand, exemplifying his technical mastery of precast concrete, his sensitivity to detail and his innate classicism. He was also a dominant force in architectural education for over three decades.

WRITINGS

'Realising the Abstract: Creation', *S. Afr. Archit. Rec.*, xxi/7 (1937), pp. 314–23
'Contemporary Building', *Archit. Rev.*, 10 (1944) [S. Afr. issue]

BIBLIOGRAPHY

W. D. Howie: 'John Fassler, 1910–1971', *Plan*, lvi/9 (1971), pp. 14–20
G. Herbert: *Martienssen and the International Style: The Modern Movement in South African Architecture* (Cape Town, 1975), pp. 109–35
M. F. Kamstra: 'John Fassler, 1910–1971: John Fassler, 1920–1940', *Archit. S. Africa*, 7–8 (1985), pp. 28–35

GILBERT HERBERT

Fassola. *See* FAZOLA.

Fatehpur Baori. *See under* RAWALPINDI.

Fatehpur Sikri [Faṭhpur Sīkrī; Fatehpur Sīkri]. Town in Uttar Pradesh, India, 40 km from Agra. It is situated adjacent to a lake (now dry) on a long narrow ridge (see fig. 1); red sandstone of fine quality was quarried from the ridge from an early date, and the town is known mainly for a red sandstone palace complex built by the Mughal emperor Akbar (*reg* 1556–1605).

1. History. 2. Town planning. 3. Buildings.

1. HISTORY. Temple fragments and sculptures attest the settlement of Fatehpur Sikri in the pre-Muslim period. It was probably a stronghold of the Sikarwar Rajputs around the 12th century and may have acquired the name Sikri at that time. During the Sultanate period (*c.* 1206–1526), Sikri played a strategic role as a stopping place on the route to Bayana and other important centres in Rajasthan. Inscriptions and early mosques from the 13th and 14th centuries indicate that it was a significant provincial town.

Babur (*reg* 1526–30), founder of the MUGHAL dynasty, mentioned in his memoirs that he stopped at Sikri on the eve of the Battle of Khanwah (1527). After his victory he camped on the banks of the lake and began a garden and stepwell, probably on the north-west side of the ridge, and an octagonal pavilion in the middle of the lake. A stepwell,

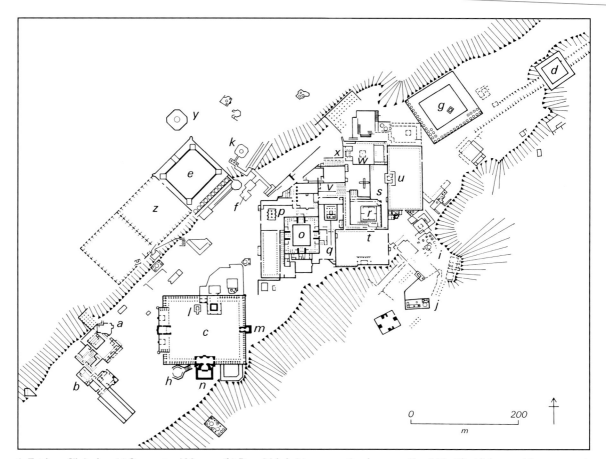

1. Fatehpur Sikri, plan: (a) Stonecutters' Mosque; (b) Rang Mahal; (c) congregational mosque (Jami' Masjid); (d) bazaar; (e) caravanserai; (f) Hathi Pol ('Elephant Gate'); (g) workshops; (h) reservoir; (i) well; (j) stepwell of southern waterworks; (k) stepwell of northern waterworks; (l) tomb of Shaykh Salim Chisti; (m) Badshahi Darvaza ('Emperor's Gate'); (n) Buland Darvaza ('Lofty Gate'); (o) Jodh Bai's Palace, possibly main harem quarters or Akbar's residential palace; (p) Birbal's House; (q) Sonahra Makan ('Gilded House'); (r) Anup Tala'o pavilion ('Turkish Sultana's Palace'); (s) Anup Tala'o ('Peerless Pool'); (t) Kutub Khana ('Library') and Khwabgah; (u) Divan-i 'Am ('Hall of Public Audience'); (v) 'Panch Mahal'; (w) building with central column, possibly Divan-i Khas; (x) 'Ankh Michauli', possibly treasury or Divan-i Khas; (y) Hiran Minar ('Deer Tower'); (z) garden

probably attributable to Babar, survives. A decade later, the Sufi holy man Shaykh Salim Chisti established his hermitage on the ridge at Sikri. Born in Delhi in AH 884 (AD 1479–80), he came to Sikri as a child with his family; in later life he travelled in the central Islamic lands for 13 years and returned to Sikri in AH 944 (1537–8). One of the oldest buildings at the site, the Stonecutters' Mosque (see figs 1a and 2), was apparently built for the Shaykh *c.* 1560–69 by workers quarrying stone from the ridge for Akbar's fort at Agra. Later the mosque was extended to include the Shaykh's cell. The mosque's red sandstone serpentine brackets (see fig. 2) served as the prototype for the white marble brackets of the Shaykh's tomb (*see* §3(i) below). Akbar, worried because he had no son and heir, visited the Shaykh and, according to court historian Abu al-Fazl, was assured that he would have three sons. The first, Prince Salim (the future emperor Jahangir), was born at Sikri in 1569 in a palace known as the Rang Mahal (extant but damaged; see fig. 1b), built especially for Akbar's pregnant queen near the Stonecutters' Mosque and the Shaykh's hermitage.

The congregational mosque (1c) at Fatehpur Sikri was commissioned about this time and completed in AH 979 (1571–2). Also in 1571 Akbar commissioned a palace complex to be built adjacent to the mosque—possibly due to his association with the Shaykh or the site's strategic position. The city was named Fatehpur (Ind.-Pers.: 'City of Victory'), a reference to the conquest of Malwa, the Rajput princes and Gujarat. Fatehpur Sikri was Akbar's residential headquarters from 1572 to 1585, an experimental and innovative period during which he initiated numerous political, administrative and religious reforms.

In 1585 Akbar left Fatehpur Sikri for Lahore in order to secure the north-west border of his empire. The city was never again fully inhabited, though the tomb of Shaykh Salim Chisti remained a pilgrimage centre, maintained by his descendants. When Akbar returned from Lahore in 1598 he took up residence in his palace at Agra. His brief visit to Fatehpur Sikri in 1601 on his return from the Deccan seems to have been the last before his death in 1605.

Akbar's son Jahangir spent three months in Fatehpur Sikri in 1619 to avoid a plague at Agra. By this time houses that had been built for nobles in Akbar's time had fallen into disrepair and had to be renovated for Jahangir's courtiers. The emperor Shah Jahan made a number of visits to Fatehpur Sikri but never resided there.

Some buildings were damaged in the late 18th century by Jats and other groups rising against the weakened Mughal house. In the early 19th century the British East India Company established an administrative subdivision at Fatehpur Sikri. Conservation efforts under the British government were begun in 1876; repairs were carried out in 1881, at which time some structures were demolished. On Akbar's departure in 1585 most of the craftsmen migrated to Delhi and Agra; the only industry that survives is the production of *darī*s (Hindi: flat-woven floor coverings).

2. TOWN PLANNING. The layout of Fatehpur Sikri was carefully planned to make use of the terrain. The ridge was reserved for religious and royal buildings. Mansions

2. Fatehpur Sikri, Stonecutters' Mosque, serpentine brackets supporting the eaves (*chajjā*) on the façade, *c.* 1560–69

for nobles were constructed on its eastern and western slopes; their large family houses (Ind.-Pers. *havelī*) and gardens were also scattered in the surrounding plains. A stone paved bazaar (1d) with shops for public use was laid out at the foot of the ridge. Land on both sides of the bazaar was allotted for the houses of ordinary citizens against a small fee. Stables for elephants, camels and horses were built mainly on the north-west side of the ridge in close proximity to the lake. Two caravanserais were established: one near the bazaar and the other (1e) near the Hathi Pol ('Elephant Gate'; 1f). On all but the lake side, the town was enclosed within battlement walls with bastions and gateways at intervals.

Workshops (Pers. *kārkhānā*) for artists and craftsmen were set up; some structures (1g) near the palace complex may have served this purpose. The imperial establishment created a significant call for manuscript illuminators, calligraphers, jewellers, enamellers, perfumers, workers of ivory, wood and leather, as well as weavers of silk, wool and cotton.

Provisions for water were a fundamental aspect of planning; devices for draining, collecting and storing water were built into the complex. The river Khari Nadi was dammed, creating (according to Abu al-Fazl) a huge lake with a circumference of 40 km. It provided a supply of water year round, and breezes from it made summer more comfortable. In addition the lake illustrates the Mughal use of water for architectural landscaping. Rainwater was also collected and stored in an open stepwell-cum-reservoir (Hindi *jhālrā*; 1h). Two underground reservoirs (Pers. *birkā*) and a number of tanks were provided, and stepwells (Ind.-Pers. *bā'olī*) were positioned on either side of the ridge (1j and k) with a complex system worked out for raising water and conveying it to the palaces. Water channels, cascades, pools and tanks were used to beautify and cool the palace area. It is often said that Akbar abandoned Fatehpur Sikri due to a shortage of water, but the elaborate provisions make this unlikely. (Political problems in the north-west were probably an important factor in Akbar's decision to move the court to Lahore.)

The best-preserved buildings are those on the ridge. These are grouped mainly into three enclosures, originally separated by walls. The sacred complex (*see* §3(i) below) includes the congregational mosque and tomb of Shaykh Salim Chisti (*d* 1572); this area was open to the public. The residential area (*see* §3(ii) below), which included the women's apartments, was the most restricted. The civic area (*see* §3(iii) below) included buildings where state business was conducted; the degree of access to this zone varied. The sacred complex occupies the highest part of the ridge with the two other enclosures on lower terraces.

3. BUILDINGS.

(i) *Sacred complex.* The congregational mosque (Jami' Masjid; 1c), the focus of this complex, is one of the largest and most ornately finished mosques in India. Built on a high plinth, it has a vast central courtyard (133.73×109.68 m) with a prayer hall on the west and arcades on the other three sides. The prayer hall (87.78×19.81 m) has three domes, one over the central bay and the others over square bays that form part of the wings. In these, beautifully designed corbelled pendentives are used in lieu of squinches (see fig. 3). The façade is dominated by the central bay's high recessed arch, which is set within a rectangular frame surmounted by a parapet and a line of domed pavilions or *chatri*s.

The mosque's rich and varied decoration includes bold geometric patterns of white marble and black slate inlaid in a red sandstone background—a precursor of the exquisite inlay with hardstones on a white marble ground that

appears in the Shah Jahan period (1628–58). Glazed tile mosaic has been used for borders, for example in some subsidiary mihrabs, where the tile colours include green, blue, turquoise and white. Carved calligraphic compositions outline arches and panels. Much of the interior is painted with floral designs in opaque watercolours applied directly on the rough stone surface.

The north arcade accommodates the graves of members of Shaykh Salim Chisti's family. The Shaykh's tomb (see fig. 11 above; *see also* TOMB, fig. 5) is situated near by on the north side of the open courtyard. The tomb bears a date of 1581–2, but its present white marble exterior was probably commissioned *c.* 1605 by Jahangir (*reg* 1605–27) and constructed under the supervision of Qutb al-Din Khan Kokaltash, grandson of the Shaykh. The tomb is square in plan (14.63 m each side) with a porch at the front reminiscent of the porches of Hindu temples. The central chamber is enclosed by a screened verandah, serving as a circumambulatory. Its white marble lattice screens (*jālī*) are among the finest examples in India. The building is shaded by a broad slanting stone projection (Hindi *chajjā*) supported by graceful serpentine brackets. Each bracket is monolithic with lacelike floral and geometric patterns carved in the spaces between the curves.

The sacred complex has two gateways: the Badshahi Darvaza ('Emperor's Gate'; 1m) on the eastern side, through which Akbar entered from the palace area, and the more magnificent Buland Darvaza ('Lofty Gate'; 1n) on the southern side. The Buland Darvaza (h. 53.64 m) is a structure of monumental scale and great dignity. Its most prominent feature is a high central recessed arch set within a rectangular frame crowned by a parapet composed of thirteen *chatri*s. Three larger *chatri*s rise behind. The central face of the gateway is flanked by two narrower faces, receding at an angle, with recessed arches on two levels. Panels of fawn-coloured sandstone outline the frame, contrasting with the warm red stone seen throughout Fatehpur Sikri. The gateway has been variously dated *c.* 1585 or 1601. An inscription with the date 1601 records Akbar's triumphant return from the Deccan. Either the inscription was added to the gateway to mark that occasion or the original gateway was demolished and the present one built to celebrate Akbar's victories.

(ii) *Residential quarters.* The identification of buildings in both the residential and civic areas is problematic. They have been given fanciful names (such as 'Turkish Sultana's House') that bear no relation to their use in the 16th century. Furthermore, efforts to assign a specific purpose to each structure probably distort a more flexible court life where some buildings were put to varied uses. The building traditionally known as Jodh Bai's Palace (1o) is generally thought to be either the main harem quarters or Akbar's residential palace. It has a guardhouse near its portal and a crooked entrance to ensure security and privacy. The quarters are disposed around a spacious inner courtyard providing a light and airy yet secluded environment. The suites around it are architecturally separated yet interconnected.

Construction throughout is trabeated, relying on the pillar, bracket and lintel. A *chajjā* shades the façade facing the inner courtyard; *chatri*s and windows with balconies

3. Fatehpur Sikri, congregational mosque (Jami' Masjid), corbelled pendentives in the prayer hall's south wing, 1571–2

add variety to the scheme. Two upper chambers have sloping roofs covered in blue-glazed tiles, a distinctive feature of this building. The palace is furnished with toilets and baths (*ḥammām*), essential requirements for living-quarters. Buildings without such facilities would not have been suitable as residences and were probably reserved for formal uses.

A two-storey structure, popularly known as Birbal's House (1p), is located near by to the north-west of the principal residential palace. It has been suggested that this was the palace of Akbar's two chief queens, mainly due to its proximity to the royal residence. It lacks, however, both bathing facilities and a private inner courtyard. The site of the building at the edge of the royal complex overlooking the lake suggests a special use. An inscription in devanagari script reads: '[*Vikrama*] *year 1629* [AD 1572] *royal mansion of initiation*'. This may suggest the structure was built for some of Akbar's religious discussions and initiation into his new order, the Din-i Ilahi.

Standing independently to the north-east of the main residential palace is a single-storey building known as either Maryam's Palace, the Rangin Mahal ('Painted Palace') or the Sonahra Makan ('Gilded House'; 1q). The most splendid and surprising feature of this building is its paintings: the interior and exterior walls were originally covered with figurative works painted in opaque water-colour on the stone. The faded remains of elephant fights and processions are still visible. It seems likely that no other building at Fatehpur Sikri was gilded and painted with figurative work on such a scale. According to a popular but fanciful view, this was the house of a Portu-guese wife of the Emperor, named Maria. It has also been suggested that it was the private residence of Akbar's mother, Hamida Banu Begum, known as Maryam Makani ('equal in rank to Mary') or of his Rajput queen, who was the mother of the future emperor Jahangir and known as Maryam Zamani ('Mary of the age'). Like 'Birbal's House' the building does not, however, have bathing or other residential facilities; it may have been reserved for cultural events and used by Akbar to receive poets, musicians and painters.

(iii) Civic enclosure. A third structure unlikely to have had the residential role traditionally assigned to it is a pavilion (1r) known as the Turkish Sultana's Palace, situated within the third part of the complex where the business of state was conducted. It is located near a square pond known as the Anup Tala'o ('Peerless Pool'; 1s). The pavilion is profusely decorated and exquisitely embellished with carv-ings of geometric patterns, naturalistic vegetal motifs (including grape vines and pomegranate plants carved on pillars) and low-relief figurative panels (now damaged) delicately carved in imitation of painting. This superb work is a distinctive feature of the building. It was possibly created next to the pool as a retreat for repose and discussion. On the south side of the pool is a colonnaded building (1t), which may have been the Kutub Khana ('Library') housing the Mughal collection of manuscripts. The chamber on the upper level is known as the Khwabgah ('Sleeping Apartment'; see fig. 4); inscriptions there state it was intended for the king to sit in. It has been suggested

4. Fatehpur Sikri, Khwabgah ('Sleeping Apartment'), upper pavilion, 1572–85

that two adjacent chambers on the ground level served as the Divan-i Khas ('Hall of Private Audience').

The Divan-i 'Am ('Hall of Public Audience'; see fig. 1u above) has been firmly identified. It was on the perimeter of the civic enclosure and consisted of a courtyard with colonnades on all sides. A throne chamber set off by beautifully carved red sandstone screens occupies the middle of the western side. The enthroned emperor faced east, possibly to associate him with the rising sun and underscore that he was an emanation of divine light.

The highest building of the civic area is the so-called 'Panch Mahal' (1v), a five-storey structure of trabeated construction. Each of its five receding tiers is open on all sides. The fifth level consists of a large domed *chatrī*. The building's balanced pyramidal form is reflected in its measurements: the total height is equal to the length of the ground floor. This imposing structure overlooks the great courtyard around which the civic buildings are positioned. It was possibly intended as a place to catch cool breezes while watching the activity below—a place from which Akbar could see and be seen. Facing east, it may have been associated with the daily viewing of the emperor at sunrise, a practice that Akbar instituted.

At the north end of the civic enclosure stands a unique double-storey building (1w), its distinctive feature being an elaborate column in its centre that culminates in a cluster of brackets supporting a circular platform. Radiat-ing out from the platform at the diagonal are bridges joining balconies lining the four sides of the room. It seems likely that the composition was symbolic, repre-senting the *axis mundi* separating the heavens from the earth and creating cosmic order. Sitting atop the unitary pillar, Akbar was symbolically identified with the ancient Indian concept of world sustenance.

Situated to the west is a simple structure known as the 'Ankh Michauli' (1x). This building may have been the imperial treasury, or it may have been the Divan-i Khas. A kiosk outside with elaborately carved brackets may have been the treasurer's seat.

Visible from the upper storeys of the various buildings is a distinctive tower (1y) some 21 m high, the Hiran Minar ('Deer Tower'; see fig. 5). It stands near the now dry lake

5. Fatehpur Sikri, Hiran Minar ('Deer Tower'), 1572–85

and the Hathi Pol ('Elephant Gate'; see fig.1f above) to which it is connected by a stone-paved ramp. The lower part of the tower is octagonal, the middle section circular. At the top is a balcony supported by stone corbels and a crowning octagonal *chatrī*. Access is by an inner spiral stair. The circular portion of the tower is spiked with stone projections resembling elephant tusks. Local lore has it that this is the burial place of Akbar's favourite elephant. It was probably a measuring point for a chain of mileage markers (*kos minār*) that were set along main roads. It may also have served as a viewpoint for matches on the polo ground, laid out along the lake, or elephant fights, held near by. The name seems to date to the time of Jahangir, who is recorded as having established a deer park in the open area around the tower. Possibly the Persian *ḥayr* ('enclosure' or 'park') was transmuted to *hiran* (Hindi: 'deer').

See also INDIAN SUBCONTINENT, §III, 7(i)(a).

BIBLIOGRAPHY
E. W. Smith: *The Moghul Architecture of Fathpur Sikri* (Allahabad, 1894–98)
S. A. A. Rizvi: *Fatehpur Sikri* (New Delhi, 1972)
S. A. A. Rizvi and V. Flynn: *Fatehpur Sīkrī* (Bombay, 1975)
R. Nath: 'The Dīwān-Khāṣṣ of Fatehpur Sikri: A Symbol of Akbar's Belief in Sūrya-Puruṣa', *Some Aspects of Mughal Architecture*, ed. R. Nath (New Delhi, 1976), pp. 7–21
M. Brand and G. D. Lowry: *Akbar's India: Art from the Mughal City of Victory* (New York, 1985)
——: *Fatehpur-Sikri: A Sourcebook* (Cambridge, MA, 1985)
R. Nath: *Akbar: The Age of Personality Architecture* (1985), ii of *History of Mughal Architecture* (New Delhi, 1982–5)
——: 'Unidentified Tomb at Fatehpur Sikri (so-called Todarmal's Baradari): A Landmark in Sepulchral Architecture', *J. Res. Soc. Pakistan*, xxiii/4 (1986), pp. 35–47
——: 'Khaprel-Roof and Chhappar Ceiling: Folk Elements in Mughal Architecture', *Archvs Asian A.*, xl (1987), pp. 69–73
——: 'Ladao Ceiling in Early Mughal Architecture', *Indologica-Jaipurensia*, i (1987), pp. 117–27
A. Petruccioli: *Fathpur Sikri città del sole e delle aque* (Rome, 1988)
R. Nath: 'Panch Mahal of Fatehpur Sikri: Architectural Derivation and raison d'être', *Ajay Mitra Sastri Felicitation Volume*, ii (1989), pp. 515–25

R. NATH

Fath 'Ali Shah. *See* QAJAR, (1).

Fathy, Hassan (*b* Alexandria, 23 March 1900; *d* Cairo, 30 Nov 1989). Egyptian architect, teacher and writer. He graduated in architecture (1926) from the High School of Engineering, University of King Fuad I (now University of Cairo), and then worked at the Department of Municipal Affairs, Cairo (1926–30). He subsequently began to teach at the Faculty of Fine Arts at the university (1930–46 and 1953–7) while working independently as an architect. Fathy's work can be considered in five main phases (see Steele, 1988). His early projects (1928–37) reveal his interest in the classical Beaux-Arts tradition, Art Deco and other trends fashionable in Europe at the time. In his second phase (1938–56) he developed the interest in indigenous building that made him internationally known. Starting with villas, the use of mud-brick and a preoccupation with the rural poor, Fathy evolved a new aesthetic that irrevocably linked him to local vernacular building traditions. This new direction was expressed in a series of beautiful gouaches and coloured pencil drawings (see Richards, Serageldin and Rastorfer, pls 1–8) exhibited in Mansoura and Cairo in 1937, and in a number of individual houses that typified his work: examples include Hamid Said House (1945) and the Stopplaere House (1952), both on the outskirts of Cairo. They were generally built around a courtyard and constructed with mud-blocks or brick in vaulted and domed forms; careful attention was paid to climate control through the size and arrangement of openings, and to the application of traditional crafts, for example in the use of timber lattice screens (*mashrabiyas*).

Fathy's best-known project of this period is the village of New Gourna (1948; see fig.), near Luxor, later made famous through his book *Architecture for the Poor* (1973). He produced a master-plan and designs for public buildings and housing, including an influential design for the mosque, which drew upon traditional Nubian architecture. About a quarter of the entire scheme was executed, using mud-brick and domed and vaulted forms similar to those of his houses, with mouldings and tracery in mud (claustrawork), timber lattice screens and patterned doors (*sabra*s) made from small pieces of wood. There has been much discussion about the success of the village in social terms, but it remains a powerful architectural model for rural areas, emulated by architects around the world, from Morocco to New Mexico.

Between 1946 and 1953, Fathy held several government posts, and from 1957 to 1962 he was a consultant with Doxiadis Associates in Athens. This marked the third period of his work, when he experimented with other materials, such as concrete, and worked on a number of

Hassan Fathy: New Gourna Market, near Luxor, 1948

buildings in other countries, including the Sudan, Pakistan, Greece and Saudi Arabia. He also worked on several urban plans and projects for a 'city of the future'. Following his return to Egypt, he was again appointed to government posts (1963–5) and he also produced a substantial body of writings. This fourth period (1963–79) was his most productive: in addition to a typically large proportion of residential projects, for example the Riad House (1967) in Shabramant, his own house (1971) at Sidi Krier and the Samy House (1979) in Dashour, he also designed such communities as New Baris (1970) in the Kharga Oasis. Fathy's late works (1980–89) were relatively few but revealed a greater diversity of approach, illustrating his ability to reflect the variations of each client's personality. Examples include 'Mit Rehan' on the outskirts of Cairo and the Sadat Rest House (both 1981) in Gharf Hussain, and the Greiss House (1984) in Abu Sier. The project most published abroad is probably Dar al-Islam (designed 1980), a small rural village for an American Muslim community in Albiquiu, near Albuquerque, New Mexico. The settlement, around an elegant mosque and a religious school, was planned by function and was heavily influenced by his earlier Gourna project.

Fathy has often been referred to as the 'poet of the mud-brick' but he also designed buildings in other materials. Although his approach was developed for the poor, his work found considerable patronage among the wealthy,

and he became known abroad (mainly through his book) before he was greatly recognized in Egypt itself; nevertheless only about 35 of his many projects were actually built. He never established a formal architectural practice but worked with young architects at his 14th-century house in Cairo, Bait al Fan. He lectured widely around the world and was a member of the steering committee of the Aga Khan Award for Architecture (1977–80), which bestowed on him its first Chairman's Award (1980). Other distinctions included honorary fellowship of the American Institute of Architects (1976) and the Gold Medal of the Union Internationale des Architectes (1984).

See also ISLAMIC ART, §II, 8.

UNPUBLISHED SOURCES

Geneva, Aga Khan Trust for Culture [projects and writings]

WRITINGS

'Rural Self-Help Housing', *Int. Labour Rev.*, 85 (1962), pp. 1–17
Gourna: A Tale of Two Villages (Cairo, 1969); *R* as *Architecture for the Poor: An Experiment in Rural Egypt* (Chicago, 1973)
Urban Architecture in the Middle East (Beirut, 1971) [in Arabic]
Natural Energy and Vernacular Architecture (Tokyo and Chicago, 1985)

BIBLIOGRAPHY

J. M. Richards: 'Gourna: A Lesson in Basic Architecture', *Archit. Rev.* [London], cxlvii (1970), pp. 109–18
J.-P. Cousin: 'Hassan Fathy', *Archit. Aujourd'hui*, 195 (1978), pp. 42–78
R. Holod and D. Rastorfer, eds: 'Hassan Fathy: Chairman's Award', *Architecture and Community: Building in the Islamic World Today* (New York, 1983), pp. 235–45

J. M. Richards, I. Serageldin and D. Rastorfer: *Hassan Fathy* (Singapore and London, 1985)
J. Steele: *Hassan Fathy* (London, 1988)
——: *The Hassan Fathy Collection: A Catalogue of Visual Documents at the Aga Khan Award for Architecture* (Geneva, 1989)
H.-U. Khan: 'Poète de l'architecture: Hassan Fathy', *Conn. A.*, 459 (1990), pp. 144–51
                                    HASAN-UDDIN KHAN

Fatimid. Islamic dynasty that ruled in Ifriqiya (now Tunisia) from AD 909 to 972 and in Egypt from AD 969 to 1171. The Fatimids were Isma'ili Shi'ites who traced their ancestry back to Fatima, the daughter of the Prophet Muhammad, via Isma'il, the seventh Shi'ite Imam. They believed that their rightful position as leaders of the Muslim community had been usurped by the Umayyad and Abbasid caliphs. The first Fatimid success was the toppling of the Aghlabid rulers of Ifriqiya in 909. The Fatimid leader 'Ubayd Allah assumed the title of caliph and the regnal name al-Mahdi (*reg* 909–34). He soon moved his capital from the hostile religious environment of Kairouan to MAHDIA on the Mediterranean coast, a base more appropriate for the expected Fatimid conquest of the rest of the Islamic world. The port soon became a centre for Mediterranean commerce, whose revival was one of the cornerstones of Fatimid prosperity. The indigenous Berber population of North Africa rose in repeated rebellions, often fomented by the Fatimids' Umayyad rivals in Spain. In 947 the caliph al-Mansur (*reg* 946–53) moved the capital again, to a splendid palace complex near Kairouan called Sabra or Mansuriyya. A fine ivory casket (Madrid, Mus. Arqueol. N.) made there by (?Ahmad) al-Khurasani gives some substance to the high reputation of its court workshops.

In 969 the Fatimid general Jawhar conquered Egypt and settled his army a short distance to the north of the old capital, Fustat, thus founding the city of Cairo (*see* CAIRO, §I, 1). The caliph al-Mu'izz (*reg* 953–75) soon decided to move the capital to Egypt, which was at the centre of the empire he expected to conquer. North Africa was left in the hands of Zirid and Hammadid princes, who continued to recognize Fatimid authority for nearly another century, while to the east Syria and the Hejaz (western Arabia) came under Fatimid control. During the late 10th century Fatimid prosperity was at its height, as the regular flooding of the Nile provided a strong agricultural base for the Egyptian economy.

Although Egypt was often technically at war with its neighbours, commercial and diplomatic ventures made Cairo an important centre of Mediterranean trade. Muslim, Christian and Jewish traders brought the products of East and West to the city, while Egyptian luxury goods, particularly lustre ceramics, rock crystals and textiles (*see* ISLAMIC ART, §§V, 3 (i); VI, 2(i)(a); and VIII, 13), were highly prized abroad. In Europe they were placed in church treasuries, where several important examples have remained, for example the rock crystal ewer (Venice, Mus. S Marco; see fig.) inscribed with the name of the caliph al-'Aziz (*reg* 975–96). The prosperity of the period allowed building on a large scale. Under al-Mu'izz, his son al-'Aziz and his grandson al-Hakim (*reg* 996–1021) magnificent mosques and palaces were built in Cairo (*see* ISLAMIC ART, §II, 5(ii)(c)).

Rock crystal ewer inscribed with the name of the Fatimid caliph al-'Aziz, h. 230 mm, AD 975–96 (Venice, Museo S Marco); the enamelled gold mount dates to the 16th century or later

In the middle of the 11th century Fatimid fortunes changed. North Africa declared itself independent, and in retaliation the caliph al-Mustansir (*reg* 1036–94) encouraged bedouin tribes to devastate the region. The Nile repeatedly failed to flood, leading to widespread famine and recurrent social crisis. Meanwhile, the Saljuq Turks attacked Syria and Palestine from the east, capturing both Jerusalem and Damascus. The Caliph was forced to sell his treasures to pay the hungry troops. A functionary recorded these as they were removed from the palace, where separate rooms housed precious manuscripts (*see* ISLAMIC ART, §III, 4(iv)(a)), gold and silver automata studded with jewels, rich textiles and rare curios. In order to restore order in Egypt, al-Mustansir appointed the governor of Damascus, Badr al-Jamali, as vizier. Badr and his successors assumed more and more power at the expense of a sequence of young and ineffectual caliphs, who barely retained even their spiritual authority once a series of succession crises had split their diminishing following. Apart from new stone fortifications for Cairo, parts of which still stand, large public building projects were no longer undertaken. Instead, the caliphs, viziers and others built small mosques and restored the shrines of Shi'ite saints. These testify to the continuing vitality of Fatimid art, as do other, less expensive, tokens of piety, such as portable wooden mihrabs for mosques and shrines (examples in Cairo, Mus. Islam. A.; *see* ISLAMIC ART, §VII, 1(i)).

The Fatimids also had to face the new challenge of the Crusaders, who by 1124 controlled the entire coast of the Levant except for Ascalon (now Ashqelon). In the 1160s a Crusader army reached the gates of Cairo but was repulsed by an army from Syria under the command of Salah al-Din (Saladin), who remained in Egypt first as governor and then, after 1171, as the first Ayyubid sultan of Egypt. To prevent its falling into the hands of the Crusaders, Fustat, the oldest part of Cairo, was set on fire. The excavations of its ruins have yielded important information about material culture in the Fatimid period.

In the Fatimid art of Egypt many of the materials and techniques that were developed under the Tulunid dynasty (*reg* 868–904) continued to be used, but Tulunid abstraction, based on the art of the Abbasid capital at Samarra', was replaced by antique figural motifs as well as a more casual interest in naturalism, seen in both book illustration and ceramics. The painted *muqarnas* ceiling of the Cappella Palatina in Palermo is thought to represent Fatimid court techniques and representational style (*see* ISLAMIC ART, §II, 5(ii)(b)). This figural art would have been out of place in religious buildings, which were decorated with inscriptions in a particularly elegant and distinctive form of kufic script elaborated with foliate and floral elements.

See also JEWELLERY, colour pl. III, fig. 1.

BIBLIOGRAPHY
*Enc. Islam/*2: 'Fāṭimids', 'Fāṭimid Art'
J. Amer. Res. Cent. Egypt, iv– (1965–) [preliminary reports on the excavs at Fustat by G. T. Scanlon]
O. Grabar: 'Imperial and Urban Art in Islam: The Subject Matter of Fatimid Art', *Colloque international sur l'histoire du Caire: Caire, 1973*, pp. 173–89
J. M. Bloom: 'The Origins of Fatimid Art', *Muqarnas*, iii (1985), pp. 20–38
JONATHAN M. BLOOM

Fatsan. *See* FOSHAN.

Fattah, Ismail [al-Turk] (*b* Basra, 1934). Iraqi sculptor and painter. He studied sculpture and painting at the Institute of Fine Arts in Baghdad under Jawad Salim, and after graduating in 1958 went to Rome where he studied at the Accademia di Belle Arti e Liceo Artistico and the Accademia di San Giacomo. Fattah began to work in a style that combined elements of realism and expressionism, as well as influences from Sumerian and Assyrian art. On returning to Baghdad he became active in the artistic life of the city and in 1967 joined the group Al-Zāwiya ('The Religious Fraternity'), led by the painter Faik Hassan; Fattah also became a member of the New Vision group, formed in 1969. He had one-man shows in Rome and Beirut, as well as Baghdad, and from the 1960s participated in a number of national and international exhibitions. At the first Indian Triennale held in New Delhi (1968), for example, he exhibited the bronze sculpture *Two Figures* (360×180 mm, 1964; Baghdad, N. Mus. Mod. A.). He

produced sculptures and murals for public buildings and squares in Baghdad and in the 1970s taught ceramics at the Academy of Fine Arts, Baghdad University (established 1962). In the early 1980s, under the patronage of President Saddam Hussein, he designed the *Martyr's Monument* (1981–3; for illustration *see* IRAQ) for Baghdad, to commemorate the nation's dead in the Iraq–Iran War. This large monument, which brought Fattah international recognition, consists of a 40-m high turquoise dome, split into halves, with a 5-m high sculptural rendering of the Iraqi flag in twisted metal in the centre. The monument rests on a circular platform 190 m in diameter, beneath which is an underground museum, and the entire ensemble is located in the middle of an artificial lake. The monument was built by the Mitsubishi Corporation to the specifications of Ove Arup and Partners.

BIBLIOGRAPHY
Contemporary Arab Artists, i (exh. cat. by D. al-Azzawi, London, Iraqi Cult. Cent., 1978)
S. al-Khalil: *The Monument: Art, Vulgarity and Responsibility in Iraq* (London, 1991), pp. 23–6

Fattore, il. *See* PENNI, (1).

Fattori, Giovanni (*b* Livorno, 6 Sept 1825; *d* Florence, 30 Aug 1908). Italian painter and etcher. Initially established as a painter of military subjects, he came to be one of the leading Italian *plein-air* painters of landscape with figures. Towards the end of his life he produced many excellent etchings, mainly of rural subjects.

1. Training and early paintings, to 1860. 2. Middle period paintings, 1861–83. 3. Etchings and later paintings, 1884–1908.

1. TRAINING AND EARLY PAINTINGS, TO 1860. He studied in Livorno under Giuseppe Baldini (*b* 1807), a minor painter of religious and genre subjects. In 1846 he moved to Florence where he lodged in Via Condotti with Constantino Mosti, an ex-pupil of Baldini's. Here he attended first the school of Giuseppe Bezzuoli and then, late in 1846, the Accademia itself. A rebellious pupil, Fattori preferred reading novels on medieval themes by Ugo Foscolo, Francesco Domenico Guerrazzi and Walter Scott to the academic study of art; but at this time he developed the practice of annotating his observations in pencil and pen sketches in pocket-sized notebooks. During the anti-Austrian movement in Tuscany from 1846 to 1848, Fattori distributed leaflets for the conspirators but was prevented by his family from enrolling in the army. After the war of liberation (1849), he continued his course at the Accademia until 1852 and began to frequent the Caffé Michelangiolo in Florence, collaborating in the subversive activities of various patriotic friends.

Fattori's first paintings date from the early 1850s when, still supported by his father, he lived with the sculptor Giovanni Paganucci in Via Nazionale, Florence, and used a studio in Piazza Barbano. At this time he met Settimia Vannucci, his future wife, and earned money by making illustrations for newspapers. His first landscapes were probably painted in the company of Andrea Gastaldi (1826–89) from Piedmont, while around 1857 his style assimilated the influence of Ingres through the painter Enrico Pollastrini from Livorno. Fattori's early works include *Farewell to the World* (*c.* 1857; priv. col., see Malesci, pl. 10, p. 28), taken from T. Grossi, and *Mary Stuart at the Battlefield of Crookstone* (1861; Florence, Pitti), taken from Walter Scott. In 1859 Giovanni Costa, a member of the MACCHIAIOLI, visited Fattori's studio. Costa's instruction was a formative influence on Fattori's work of the 1860s, and Fattori's first essays in the *macchia* technique are evident in a series of paintings of 1859 that show French troops encamped by the Cascine Gardens in Florence. This radical revision of Fattori's means of expression was strongly encouraged by Costa, who also spurred Fattori into entering the competition for a patriotic battle scene, organized by the Ricasoli government. With his design for the *Italian Camp during the Battle of Magenta* (1859; priv. col., see Malesci, pl. 129, p. 91) he was awarded the commission in 1860, and he completed the painting in 1860–61 (Florence, Pitti). The financial rewards of this success enabled Fattori to marry in July 1859 and also to visit the battle site in Lombardy during the spring of the following year. The journey took him and his wife to Genoa, Turin, Magenta, Milan, Lake Como, Montebello, Bologna and back to Florence, where he was finally able to settle in Via Maglio.

2. MIDDLE PERIOD PAINTINGS, 1861–83. In work carried out at Livorno during the early 1860s, and initially in Costa's company, Fattori first demonstrated his mastery of the *macchia* technique. Between 1864 and 1866 he painted a series of landscapes, often on small panels taken from cigar-boxes, directly observed from nature and characterized by their arrangement of contrasted areas of broad colour, as in the *Palmieri Terrace* (1866; Florence, Pitti; see fig. 1). The geometrical simplicity of these works recurs in Fattori's larger compositions such as *Water-carriers from Livorno* (1865; priv. col., see Malesci, pl. 631, p. 268) and the *Brush Gatherers* (*c.* 1867; priv. col., see Malesci, pl. 643, p. 293), a painting that provoked official criticism for its lack of decorative qualities but that was warmly defended by the painter and critic Telemaco Signorini. After his wife's death in March 1867 Fattori retired to the estate of the critic Diego Martelli at Castiglioncello. The painter Giuseppe Abbati (1836–68), for some time already a guest there, was stirred into fresh activity by Fattori's arrival and the two worked together, often painting the same motif, as in Fattori's *Oxen Hitched to a Cart* (*c.* 1870; Florence, Pitti) or the many studies of market gardens with peasants at work. These paintings are distinguished by their bold design and intense luminosity. Fattori's portrait of *Diego Martelli*, seated reading near his house (*c.* 1870; priv. col., see Malesci, pl. 347, p. 34), also belongs to this period, as does *Horses on the Tombolo Marsh* (*c.* 1867; priv. col., see Malesci, pl. 644, p. 274).

While continuing to paint landscapes, portraits and episodes of rustic life in his new *Macchiaiolo* manner, Fattori proceeded with his commissions for other Risorgimento battle scenes. Late in 1866 he took a new studio in Via Rosa, Florence, to accommodate larger canvases, and there he finished the *Storming of the Madonna della Scoperta* (1864–8; Livorno, Mus. Civ. Fattori), an episode in the Battle of San Martino, which was acquired for the city of Livorno by public subscription. Another large, although less dramatic, battle scene, *Prince Amedeo Wounded at Custoza* (*c.* 1870; Milan, Brera), received an award at the Parma exhibition of 1870. Fattori travelled to Rome in 1872 and there made studies for *Horse Market at Terracina* (*c.* 1872; destr., see Malesci, pl. 646, p. 275), exhibited at the Weltausstellung in Vienna in 1873, where he received a bronze medal, and also at the Philadelphia World's Fair in 1876. In May 1875 Fattori accompanied Francesco Gioli, Niccolò Cannicci (1846–1906) and Egisto Ferroni (1835–1912) to Paris, where he exhibited a composition entitled *Repose* (untraced) at the Salon, registering as Costa's pupil. In Paris he met many French artists, visited the Louvre and showed particular interest in the work of painters of the Barbizon school.

In 1877 Fattori's financial resources were at a low ebb: he was unable to sell his military paintings, and he taught painting privately to earn a living, pinning his hopes on a sale at the Esposizione Nazionale in Naples, which he visited in May with Alfonso Testi (*c.* 1825–*c.* 1915) and Stefano Bruzzi (1835–1911). On his return to Rome, he was particularly impressed by the recent paintings of Costa, who gave him photographs of them. Further depressed by a spell in hospital for a broken kneecap and by the confiscation of his property in Florence for unpaid taxes, Fattori planned to hold a lottery of his works to ease his accumulated debts. In 1878y Fattori exhibited two paintings at the Exposition Universelle in Paris but was too impoverished to afford to be able to attend, despite offers

1. Giovanni Fattori: *Palmieri Terrace*, oil on panel, 120×350 mm, 1866 (Florence, Palazzo Pitti, Galleria d'Arte Moderna)

2. Giovanni Fattori: *Sheep Jumping*, oil on canvas, 895×1740 mm, 1887 (Florence, Palazzo Pitti, Galleria d'Arte Moderna)

of hospitality from Diego Martelli, now resident there. Martelli's close friendship with Camille Pissarro and Federico Zandomeneghi nevertheless brought Fattori into direct, if unfruitful, contact with Impressionism. Assailed by the burden of recurring debt, frequently relieved by the hardly less indigent Martelli, Fattori attempted to procure an official sale for his largest canvas, the *Battle of Custoza* (1880; Rome, G.N.A. Mod.; not on display), which the King of Italy, Humbert I, came to see in his studio in November 1878; it was exhibited unsuccessfully at the Promotrice in Turin in 1880. Fattori, however, obtained regular employment as a Professor at the Accademia in Florence, where he taught twice weekly. In the household where he continued to give private tuition, he met Amalia Nollenberger, a German girl who became his close companion for the next four years.

During the late 1870s Fattori's work entered a phase of harsher realism, reflecting his disillusionment with political events under the centralized government in Rome. This change may be seen, for example, in *Caught by the Stirrup* (c. 1879; Florence, Pitti), or *Explosion of a Bomb during the Italian War of 1866* (c. 1880; Venice, Ca' Pesaro). In October 1881 and August 1882 Fattori visited the estate of the Princes Corsini in Maremma, where the life of the cowherds inspired a new cycle of paintings culminating in the three major works exhibited at the Esposizione Nazionale in Venice in 1887: the *Branding of the Colts* (1887; priv. col., see Malesci, pl. 699, p. 295), *Sheep Jumping* (1887; Florence, Pitti; see fig. 2) and *Repose, c.* 1885; Milan, Brera). The mood of melancholy detachment of this period, which distinguishes even these works, reflects Fattori's own embittered spirit of resigned isolation. Fattori visited the Esposizione Internazionale di Belle Arti in Rome in 1883, staying part of the time with Costa. He was fiercely critical of Francesco Paolo Michetti (1851–1929) and disgusted by the intrigues behind the official purchases. However, Fattori's own earlier composition, the

Battle of Custoza (1880) was finally sold, thanks to the help of Ferdinando Martini who also offered Fattori a decoration, an offer characteristically declined.

3. ETCHINGS AND LATER PAINTINGS, 1884–1908. In 1884 Fattori began etching enthusiastically. The results were much approved by other artists, and he exhibited them at the Promotrice in Florence in 1886 and at the Esposizione Nazionale in Bologna in 1888. The Galleria Nazionale in Rome acquired the work shown in 1888, and Fattori also produced an album of phototype reproductions: *20 Ricordi del veto* (Pistoia, 1884). During his later years, Fattori devoted much energy to etching (he produced only a few engravings) and brought to this work a good deal of innovation, both in technique and composition. In December 1888, with the long-awaited ministerial reform of the Accademia in Florence, Fattori was named Resident Professor of Drawing; he also became Professor of Figure Study at the School of Architecture. He exhibited in Bologna, Turin, Florence and Milan; and his painting the *Brush Gatherers* was shown at the Italian Exhibition in London.

In 1890 Fattori found renewed inspiration, in both painting and etching, in a series of rural subjects, and in June the following year he married his second wife, Marianna Bigozzi Martinelli, who had already been his companion for some time. However, he was forced by rising debt and a reduction in his salary to give private tuition, and for the same reason he entered the competition announced in 1895 by the publisher Ulrico Hoepli for illustrations to Alessandro Manzoni's historical novel *I promessi sposi*. The following year Fattori also contributed illustrations to *Fiammetta*, a satirical newspaper founded by Diego Martelli. Fattori clung obstinately to tradition in the face of innovation. In 1891 he had taken issue with Plinio Nomellini, his favourite pupil and an emerging champion of Divisionismo. When Fattori sent some paintings to Paris for sale in 1896, at the instigation of Martelli, they proved too remote from current French work to attract interest. Fattori's decline was further hastened by the death in November of Martelli himself, his closest friend. However, Fattori's work did not go entirely without recognition: he received awards for work sent to several exhibitions, for example to Cologne in 1889, to Paris in 1900 and to Saint Louis in 1904. He also received honorary nominations to the Accademia di Brera in Milan in 1891 and to the Accademia Albertina in Turin in 1900. Symptomatic of his condition, however, was the fact that he did not exhibit at Dresden in 1896 simply because he lacked money to pay for frames. The strength of Fattori's work from the 1890s is largely concentrated in his etchings: in his many scenes of rural life, the animals—especially cattle—take on a mysterious hieratic quality, as in *Oxen* (1893–6). Fattori's second wife died in 1903, and he took a third wife, Fanny Marinelli, three years later. In order to earn a living, he continued to teach at the Accademia where he was held in affection by his pupils, but he was no longer receptive to new ideas, and his late painting is characterized by the repetition of his favourite themes, now drained of their former intensity.

WRITINGS

F. Errico, ed.: *Giovanni Fattori: Scritti autobiografica editi e inediti* (Rome, 1980)
P. Dini, ed.: *Giovanni Fattori: Lettere a Diego* (Florence, 1983) [letters to Diego Martelli]
——: *Lettere ad Amalia* (Florence, 1983) [letters to Amalia Nollenberger]

BIBLIOGRAPHY

O. Ghiglia: *L'opera di Giovanni Fattori* (Florence, 1913)
Onoranze a Giovanni Fattori nel centenario della sua nascita (exh. cat., Florence, Soc. B.A., 1925) [extensive retro.]
M. Tinti: *Giovanni Fattori* (Rome, 1926)
Giovanni Fattori: Dipinti, disegni, acqueforti (exh. cat., ed. D. Durbé; Livorno, Villa Fabbricotti, 1953)
M. De Micheli: *Giovanni Fattori* (Busto Arsizio, 1961)
G. Malesci: *Catalogazione illustrata della pittura a olio di Giovanni Fattori* (Novara, 1961)
L. Bianciardi and B. Della Chiesa, eds: *L'opera completa di Fattori* (Milan, 1970)
Fattori: Disegni nel Museo Civico di Livorno (exh. cat., ed. D. Durbé; Rome, G.N.A. Mod., 1970–71)
K. Lankheit: 'Giovanni Fattori und die europäische Malerei seiner Zeit', *Toskanische Impressionen: Der Beitrag der Macchiaioli zum europäischen Realismus* (exh. cat., Munich, Haus Kst, 1975–6), pp. 36–43
La giovinezza di Fattori (exh. cat., ed. V. Durbé and D. Durbé; Livorno, Cisternino, 1980)
D. Durbé, ed.: *Giovanni Fattori e i suoi 20 ricordi dal vero* (Rome, 1981)
D. Durbé and C. Bonagura, eds: *I Macchiaioli*, VI, i (Rome, 1981) [Fattori, 1825 to 1859]
L. V. Masini: *Giovanni Fattori* (Florence, 1982)
D. Durbé: *Fattori e la Scuola di Castiglioncello*, i–ii (Rome, 1982–3) [well illus.]
A. Baboni and A. Allegranza Malesci, eds: *Giovanni Fattori: L'opera incisa* (Milan, 1983) [illus. in facs.]
Fattori, da Magenta a Montebello (exh. cat., ed. C. Bonagura, L. Dinelli and L. Bernardini; Livorno, Cisternino, 1983–4)
Giovanni Fattori: Dipinti, 1854–1906 (exh. cat., ed. G. Matteucci, R. Monti, E. Spaletti; Florence, Pitti, 1987) [well illus.]

PAUL NICHOLLS

Fattorini. *See* SCHIAVON.

Fauchier, Laurent (*b* Aix-en-Provence, 11 March 1643; *d* Aix-en-Provence, 25 March 1672). French painter. He was the son of a prosperous goldsmith, Balthazar Fauchier, who in 1657 entrusted him to the painter Bernardin Mimault (*fl* 1650–64). Fauchier worked as an apprentice for three years in Mimault's studio and then completed an apprenticeship as a goldsmith with his father. He became an independent *maître-peintre* in 1664.

Fauchier's surviving works are almost all portraits, which are unsigned and undated and belong together only by virtue of their stylistic similarities. They are in the realistic, psychologically expressive tradition of Jean Clouet, Robert Nanteuil and Philippe de Champaigne but have a distinctive Caravaggesque quality, along with certain weaknesses. His subjects' uniformly melancholy facial expressions contrast with the high technical quality of the portraits, which render textures and facial features in a detailed, lifelike way. This trait of elegant sadness is especially apparent in the *Portrait of a Young Man* (Brussels, priv. col., see exh. cat., pl. xiii) and two portraits of unknown ladies (Chartres, Mus. B.-A. and Nantes, Mus. B.-A.), as well as in the portrait of *Prince Mario Piccolomini* (Orléans, Mus. B.-A.). The *Portrait of a Young Gentleman* (Nantes, Mus. B.-A.) is livelier and more authentic, despite its typically static bust-length composition.

BIBLIOGRAPHY

Thieme–Becker
N. Coste: 'Le Peintre Laurent Fauchier', *Réun. Soc. B.-A. Dépt.*, xxiii (1899), pp. 222–33; xxviii (1904), p. 167
Les Peintres de la réalité (exh. cat. by C. Sterling, Paris, Mus. Orangerie, 1934)

CATHRIN KLINGSÖHR-LE ROY

Faulchot. French family of masons. Several generations were active in Troyes in the late 15th century and much of the 16th. Colleçon Faulchot ('de Châlons') worked from the 1460s to the end of the century under the direction of Anthoine Colas and Jehançon Garnache (*fl* c. 1485; *d* c. 1529) on the completion of Troyes Cathedral nave, for much of the time at a daily wage of three sous and four deniers. His son, Gérard [Girard] Faulchot I (*d* 1540), was at first an apprentice in the cathedral workshop, but after working with Garnache on the now-demolished St André at Montier-la-Celle, he graduated to become an important master mason. Gérard's principal work was on the parish church of St Nicolas, Troyes, which was badly damaged by the great fire of 1524. Gérard devised plans for the new church and began construction (1525–6) at the east end. The boxlike exterior wall enclosing chapels and the trapezoidal east end recall the earlier St Jean, Troyes. Features of the design of St Nicolas were also borrowed from the cathedral, where work was directed by Martin Chambiges; these elements were ingeniously adapted, especially in the reduced aisles and in the decorative vaults. The unusual pilgrimage centre (with representations of Calvary, the Mount of Olives, the Holy Sepulchre and the place of Resurrection) at the west end of the church was probably part of Gérard's plan, although not constructed until the end of the 16th century. Two further members of the family, Jean Faulchot and Gérard [Girard] Faulchot II, were both active in work on Troyes Cathedral and on Troyes parish churches, including St Nicolas and St Pantaléon.

BIBLIOGRAPHY

A. Assier: *Les Arts et les artistes dans l'ancienne capitale de la Champagne, 1250–1680* (Paris, 1876)
M. E. Poulle: 'Eglise Saint-Nicolas de Troyes', *Congr. Archéol. France*, cxiii (1955), pp. 71–84

A. Lance: *Dictionnaire des architectes français* (Paris, 1972)
S. Murray: *Building Troyes Cathedral* (Bloomington, 1987)

STEPHEN MURRAY

Faulkner, John (*fl* 1848–90). Irish painter. Having trained at the Dublin Society's Art Schools, he exhibited regularly at the Royal Hibernian Academy from 1853, becoming an Academician in 1861. He also exhibited at the Royal Academy. His earliest works are scenes of south Co. Dublin and the Wicklow coast. In the 1860s he spent some years in Scotland, dividing his time between the mountain areas and the western seaboard (e.g. watercolour views of Argyllshire in Dublin, N.G., and U. Manchester, Whitworth A.G.). For unknown reasons he lost his status as an Academician in 1880 and seems to have spent his latter years in England, producing views of Warwickshire. Faulkner was a gifted watercolourist and at his best conveys a finely attuned feeling for the soft dampness of the Irish climate as seen in his watercolour of *Slievemore, Achill Island* (*c.* 1850–60; U. Manchester, Whitworth A.G.).

Strickland

BIBLIOGRAPHY
A. Crookshank and the Knight of Glin: *The Painters of Ireland, c. 1660–1920* (London, 1978), pp. 203, 207
A. Stewart: *Royal Hibernian Academy: Index of Exhibitors, 1826–1979*, i (Dublin, 1985), pp. 255–7

FINTAN CULLEN

Faulte, Jean (*b* Bruges, *bapt* 26 Sept 1726; *d* Brussels, May 1766). Flemish architect. He studied at the Academy in Bruges and became a master cabinetmaker. After a short trip to Italy he established himself in Brussels, where, after a brief stay in England, he was taken on at the court of Charles of Lorraine as an ebony-worker, draughtsman, engraver, decorator and, above all, as an architect. In 1752 he succeeded the court architect Jan Anneessens and directed the execution of Anneessens's designs for the annexes to Charles's country seat, the castle at Tervuren, near Brussels. Charles commissioned Faulte to build a new palace on the site of the earlier Hôtel van Nassau in Brussels; Faulte supervised the work from 1757 until his death. Of this palace, for which he also designed the interiors, only the garden façades and the court chapel remain. The façades, which now form part of the Musées Royaux des Beaux-Arts, are designed according to a sober classicism in the French style, in which ornament and sculpture are subordinated to architectural severity. In this Faulte was probably influenced by the French architect Barnabé Guimard, who assisted him in the design. He was succeeded as court architect by Laurent Benoît Dewez.

BIBLIOGRAPHY
S. Ansiaux: 'Jean Faulte: Architecte de Charles de Lorraine', *Bull. Soc. Royale Archéol. Bruxelles* (1935), pp. 135–40
C. Lemaire: *Het paleis van Karel van Lorreinen, 1750–1980* (Brussels, 1981)

J.-P. ESTHER

Faure, Jean-Baptiste (*b* Moulins, 15 Jan 1830; *d* Paris, 9 Nov 1914). French singer and collector. He began his career in 1840 as a chorister in Paris; he made his début as an operatic baritone in 1852 at the Opéra-Comique, Paris, and in 1861 at the Paris Opéra, where he was the principal baritone until his retirement in 1878. He also performed regularly in London and Brussels. Financed by his successful career and a small inheritance, Faure began in the early 1850s to collect paintings of the Barbizon school. Following his first sale (Paris, Gal. Durand-Ruel, 7 June 1873), he turned to Manet, Degas and the 'new school', later known as the Impressionists, to whose work he had been introduced by his close friend the dealer Paul Durand-Ruel. Faure's collection, which he constantly upgraded, consisted of approximately 67 paintings by Manet, including the *Déjeuner sur l'herbe* (1863; Paris, Louvre; *see* MANET, EDOUARD, fig. 1) and the *Spanish Singer* (1861; New York, Met.) and 63 paintings by Monet, as well as 30 works by Alfred Sisley, 11 by Degas, including the *Ballet Scene from Meyerbeer's Opera 'Robert le Diable'* (1876; London, V&A) and a number of paintings by other contemporaries. Faure was seen as a speculator, but by purchasing paintings directly from the artists, he was helping Durand-Ruel, with whom he was often in partnership, to maintain their support. Faure's gallery in his house on the Boulevard Haussmann provided one of the few places where the public could view large numbers of contemporary French paintings. The 1902 catalogue of his collection further helped to stimulate appreciation of the Impressionists. Following the death of his wife in 1905, Faure sold a large part of his collection, especially works by Manet and Monet, through Durand-Ruel, who exhibited them in London, Berlin, Stuttgart and Paris. Faure was awarded the Légion d'honneur in 1881.

BIBLIOGRAPHY
DBF; *Grove 6*
R. Ménard: 'Collection Faure', *Gaz. B.-A.*, n. s. 1, vii (1873), pp. 459–67
Notice sur la collection J.-B. Faure, suivi du catalogue des tableaux formant cette collection (Paris, 1902)
H. de Curzon: *J.-B. Faure, 1830–1914* (Paris, 1923) [pages 126–8 concern his collection]
A. Callen: 'Jean-Baptiste Faure, 1830–1914' (MA thesis, Leicester U., 1971) [on deposit U. London, Courtauld Inst.]
——: 'Faure and Manet', *Gaz. B.-A.*, n. s. 5, lxxxiii (1974), pp. 157–78
S. Monneret: *L'Impressionisme et son époque: Dictionnaire international illustré*, i (Paris, 1978), pp. 207–8
Degas (exh. cat., Paris, Grand Pal.; Ottawa, N.G.; New York, Met., 1988)

Faust, Séverin. *See* MAUCLAIR, CAMILLE.

Fautrier, Jean (*b* Paris, 16 May 1898; *d* Châtenay-Malabry, Seine-et-Oise, 21 July 1964). French painter, printmaker, illustrator and sculptor. An illegitimate child, he was given his mother's surname but was brought up by his grandmother. On the death of both his father and grandmother in 1908 he joined his mother in London, where he entered the Royal Academy Schools in 1912. Finding the teaching too traditional, he left to enrol at the Slade School of Fine Art, which had a reputation for being more avant-garde, though he was again disappointed. He then decided to work alone and devoted himself to painting, concentrating on nudes and still-lifes. He also regularly visited the Tate Gallery, where he was particularly impressed by the works of Turner. In 1917 he was called up for the French Army, but because of his poor health he was soon transferred to the auxiliary corps. Suffering from a pulmonary complaint, he lived in the Tyrol from 1920 to 1921 and was finally discharged from the army in 1921.

In 1922 Fautrier moved to Paris. Later that year, at the Salon d'Automne, he exhibited works in a proficient realist technique, such as *Tyroleans in Sunday Dress* (1921–2; Paris, Mus. A. Mod. Ville Paris) and *Portrait of my Concierge*

(1922; Tourcoing, Mus. Mun. B.-A.). Later that year he travelled to Corsica, returning in 1923 to Paris, where he exhibited works at the Galerie Fabre; there he met the dealer Jeanne Castel, who soon became his friend and first collector. In the same year he started to produce engravings and etchings, for example *Self-portrait: Fautrier Etching* (1923; see Mason, pl. 8), in which he shows himself at work on a plate. Other prints from that year included several inspired by texts by Charles Baudelaire and Edgar Allen Poe. His first one-man show, held in Paris at the Galerie Visconti in 1924, attracted several reviews, some of them favourable. In 1926 he met the dealer Léopold Zborowski, who exhibited his works alongside those of Amedeo Modigliani, Moïse Kisling and Chaïm Soutine. His paintings at this time were dark and violent, taking as their subject-matter dead animals, flowers and mountain landscapes and often incorporating linear marks scratched into the paint surface, as in *Flayed Wild Boar* (1927; Paris, Pompidou). His mountain landscapes, such as *Blue Lake II* (1926; Paris, Pompidou), recall Turner in their suggestions of the power and majesty of nature.

Through Castel, in 1928 Fautrier met André Malraux, who asked him to illustrate a text of his choice. Copyright problems prevented him from using Arthur Rimbaud's *Les Illuminations*, so he settled on Dante's *Inferno*, producing 34 lithographs, one for each canto. Since many of these, such as *Inferno, Canto XXV* (1928; Paris Mus. A. Mod. Ville Paris), came close to abstraction, the proposed publication by Gallimard was deemed impossible and finally abandoned in 1930. A similar trend towards abstraction was apparent in Fautrier's pastels and in oil paintings such as *The Trees* (1928; Paris, Mus. A. Mod. Ville Paris), executed in an expressive gestural style. In fact, much of his work of that year foreshadowed his later *Art informel*. From 1927 to 1930 he produced a number of paintings in sombre tones of female models, such as *Large Nude from the Front* (1930; Amiens, Mus. Picardie); these women with mask-like faces are often shown nude or undressing. Concurrent with these were his first bronze sculptures,

Jean Fautrier: *Sunset in Alabama*, oil on paper glued on to canvas, 600 × 810 mm, 1957 (Paris, Musée d'Art Moderne de la Ville de Paris)

again of female figures, such as the roughly modelled *Large Torso* (h. 660 mm, 1928; Paris, Pompidou).

During most of the 1930s, with his life straitened by poor financial circumstances, Fautrier's output was very slight. In order to earn a living, from 1934 to 1936 he lived in the mountain resort of Tignes, where he worked as a ski-instructor and also set up a jazz club; in 1936 he moved to Val d'Isère and again set up a club. His exclusion from *L'Art indépendant: Maîtres d'aujourd'hui*, a large exhibition of modern art organized by Raymond Escholier in Paris in 1937, caused him considerable indignation. At the outbreak of World War II in 1939 he left the mountains and lived in Marseille, Aix-en-Provence and Bordeaux before returning in 1940 to Paris, where he began to paint again. In Paris he soon became acquainted with the writers and poets Jean Paulhan, René Char, Robert Ganzo, Francis Ponge and Paul Eluard, later illustrating works by them, such as Paulhan's *Les Causes célèbres*.

After being arrested and briefly imprisoned by the Germans in January 1943, Fautrier settled in the outskirts of Paris in Châtenay-Malabry, where in 1945 he bought an old château in which he remained until his death. There he began work on a series of paintings on paper entitled *Hostages* (e.g. *Head of Hostage No. 3*, 1943; Sceaux, Château, Mus. Ile de France), executed with tactile blocks of colour of thick impasto. Although consisting of highly simplified, almost abstract forms, these despairing, fugitive heads and figures reflected the events of the war. The mood of such works by Fautrier and other painters of his generation gave rise to their characterization in the early 1950s as ART AUTRE. The simplification of form and method of execution of these paintings, exhibited together in 1945 at the Galerie Drouin in Paris with a catalogue preface by Malraux, characterized all his subsequent production and proved highly influential in the development of ART INFORMEL in the following decade. A similar tactile quality can be found in the bronze heads made from 1940 to 1944, such as *Large Tragic Head* (1942; Paris, Pompidou), in which the left side of the face has been all but scratched away, culminating in *Hostage* (bronze, h. 485 mm, 1943; Gunter Sachs priv. col., see Engelberts, pl. 22), which bears virtually no facial features.

In 1947 Fautrier worked on a number of etchings to illustrate Paulhan's *Fautrier l'enragé* (Paris, 1949), and in the latter half of the 1940s he painted several still-lifes, for example *The Key* (1949; Paris, Mus. A. Mod. Ville Paris). His prints at this time, such as *Violent Head* (1947; Geneva, Mus. A. & Hist.), are often more overtly figurative than his paintings. Together with his mistress Jeanine Aply, in 1950 he developed a technique of 'multiple originals', combining elements of printing and painting, which enabled him to produce numerous variations of a work. His exhibition of such pictures in Paris (1950 and 1953) and New York (1956), although designed as a means of attracting a wider public, proved a commercial failure.

After the Soviet crackdown in Hungary in 1956, Fautrier painted a number of works entitled *Head of Partisan* in homage to the tragic courage of its victims, for example *Head of Partisan, Budapest* (1957; Paris, Paul Haim priv. col., see 1989 exh. cat., pl. 134). Other works of the 1950s included landscapes such as *Sunset in Alabama* (1957; Paris, Mus. A. Mod. Ville Paris; see fig.), in which he

adopt Fauvism, for in it he discerned 'the miracle of the imagination translated into line and colour' (A. Werner: *Raoul Dufy*, London, 1970, pp. 24–5).

Matisse and Derain freed themselves from Neo-Impressionism and carried the exaltation of saturated colour to its extreme at Collioure during the summer of 1905. In *Collioure* (1905; Troyes, P. Levy priv. col.; see 1976 exh. cat., p. 50) and *View of Collioure with the Church* (1905; New York, MOMA) Derain used Neo-Impressionist-derived dots or bars of colour but linked them to strips of pure colour which enriched each other in a carefully planned composition. These landscapes, along with his contemporary views of London and the Thames such as *Pool of London* (1906; London, Tate) or the *Houses of Parliament* (1905; St Tropez, Mus. Annonciade), are as intense in colour as Vlaminck's work but less instinctive; the vibrations of separate brushstrokes against primed canvas sometimes appear to shatter the surface of the work.

Both Matisse's portrait of *André Derain* and Derain's portrait of *Henri Matisse* (both 1905; London, Tate) reveal a determined use of pure colour for expressive purposes. In Matisse's *View of Collioure* (1905; St Petersburg, Hermitage) colours appear to radiate from the picture with extraordinary power. The paint is applied in broad uninhibited strokes and sometimes in large flat areas that play a key role in the spatial organization of the canvas and also mark Matisse's increasing distance from Neo-Impressionism.

Fauvism's debt to Gauguin was especially evident in the cases of Matisse and Derain, who saw a group of his late Tahitian pictures at the home of his executor, Daniel de Monfried, at Corneille-en-Conflans near Collioure. For Matisse, in works such as *Woman on a Terrace* (1906; St Petersburg, Hermitage), the influence of Gauguin can be seen in the anti-naturalistic and decorative use of colour arranged in flat planes and enclosed by a contour line. Gauguin's interest in symbolism and his search for a lost paradise away from civilization are also discernible influences in works by Matisse such as *Joy of Life* (*see* MATISSE, HENRI, fig. 1). The lessons of Gauguin's work for Derain were largely formal ones. Derain's *Charing Cross Bridge* (*c.* 1906; Paris, Mus. d'Orsay), for example, reveals his sensitivity to the formal and linear values of Gauguin's *Vision after the Sermon: Jacob Wrestling with the Angel* (1888; Edinburgh, N.G.), both in its organization of space by coloured masses in pure synthetic hues ringed with black and in the curving composition with rising perspective.

The impact of Gauguin's art on Fauvism was reinforced by that of French 15th-century painting, which was the subject of an acclaimed exhibition, *Primitifs français*, held in Paris in 1904 at the Pavillon de Marsan and the Bibliothèque Nationale. One of the most celebrated of such works, the Avignon *Pietà* (*c.* 1450), was acquired by the Louvre at that time. The Fauves found a sort of moral justification for their work in this French art, which was newly appreciated and officially condoned, yet which treated space without recourse to conventional perspective by using flat areas of saturated colour bounded by a linear style of drawing.

3. ASSOCIATED DEVELOPMENTS. The appearance in 1905 of Fauvism in France was paralleled in Germany by the formation in that year of the group Die Brücke, whose art tended towards an exacerbated form of Expressionism deriving from the work of Munch, van Gogh and from much earlier sources such as Matthias Grünewald. Ernst Ludwig Kirchner, Emil Nolde, Max Pechstein, Karl Schmidt-Rotluff and Erich Heckel did have some dealings with the French Fauves, but their intense colours and expressive forms conveyed a dramatic inner anguish that was far removed from the painterly preoccupations of the French artists.

Rouault, one of Matisse's fellow students in Moreau's studio, took part in the dazzling manifestation of 1905, but his preference for compassionate and religious subject-matter and for a restricted palette of blues and blacks distanced him from the mainstream of the movement. The Dutch painter Kees van Dongen also took part in the Salon d'Automne of 1905 with daring works in glowing colours that continued to characterize his art long after the demise of Fauvism. An Expressionist strain in his subject-matter and his treatment of the human figure identify him as an important link between the two movements.

4. TRIUMPH AND DISSOLUTION OF FAUVISM, 1905–8. On his return to Paris from Collioure, Matisse continued to use colour in what seemed a brutal way, for example in *Woman with a Hat* (1905; San Francisco, CA, W. A. Haas priv. col.; see Muller, p. 36), a portrait of his wife in which planes of shrill colour are matched for expressive and constructive purposes. It was this painting in particular that caused a scandal at the Salon d'Automne of 1905. The slightly later *Portrait with the Green Stripe* (1905; Copenhagen, Stat. Mus. Kst), in which the picture is subdivided into powerful zones of pure complementary colour, is even more concentrated in its formal organization and expressive effect.

The full flowering of Fauvism in 1906 was marked by its triumph at the Salon d'Automne, in which all the participants of the group exhibited, and by the work produced not only by the instigators of the style but by some of its more recent adherents. Manguin and Camoin painted dazzling light-filled works during the summer of 1905 at St Tropez, for example Manguin's *Fourteenth of July at Saint-Tropez, the Harbour—Left Side* (1905; Paris, Gal. Paris; see 1976 exh. cat., p. 78). Camoin painted a lively, straightforward *Portrait of Marquet* (1904–5; Paris, Pompidou) at about this time. Marquet worked briefly in the company of the Fauves, recording their sense of common purpose in *Matisse Painting a Nude in Manguin's Studio* (1904–5; Paris, Pompidou) and then going on to work in Normandy with Dufy, a recent convert to Fauvism. Like Marquet, Dufy favoured subjects that had intrinsically brilliant colouring, as in *Street Decorated with Bunting, Posters at Trouville* and *Fourteenth of July at Le Havre* (all 1906; Paris, Pompidou). The Fourteenth of July, with its joyful fanfare of flags of red, white and blue, proved an irresistible Fauve subject; in 1906 Marquet also painted such a scene, *Fourteenth of July at Le Havre* (Bagnols-sur-Cèze, Mus. Bagnols-sur-Cèze). Marquet's friend Othon Friesz adopted Fauvism at Auvers-sur-Oise in 1906, and in *Landscape at La Ciotat* (1907; Troyes, Mus. A. Mod.) he employed a violent range of colours and a freedom of handling reminiscent of van Gogh in its twisting lines of trees and rocks. Braque's most typically Fauve works, such as *Little Bay at La Ciotat* (1907; New York, Sidney Janis Gal.), were painted in the south of France.

A memorial exhibition of the work of Cézanne held at the 1907 Salon d'Automne, which proved a major influence on the birth of Cubism, also caused the Fauves to question the continuing viability of a style based on saturated colour and expressive line. They were particularly sensitive to Cézanne's late works, such as *Mont Sainte-Victoire* (1902–6), *Large Bathers* (*c*. 1906; both Philadelphia, PA, Mus. A.) and *Château noir* (1904–6; Washington, DC, N.G.A.), in which a visionary element had been added to the search for order and harmony between man and nature.

From 1908, Fauvism ceased to exist both as a style and as a coherent group. Vlaminck abandoned his use of bright primary colours, as did Derain, who experimented briefly with Cubism before turning in the 1920s to classicizing elements. Braque's study of Cézanne and his meeting with Picasso led towards the foundation of Cubism. Matisse likewise developed his style with reference to Cézanne as early as 1899 and particularly after buying the *Three Bathers* (1905–6; Paris, Petit Pal.) from Vollard, adapting its rigorous compositional structure to his own concern for simplification. The increasing harmony of Matisse's work, however, particularly after his discovery of Persian miniatures and other examples of non-Western art, in no way diminished the expressive and constructive role of colour in his work.

BIBLIOGRAPHY

G. Duthuit: *Les Fauves* (Geneva, 1949; Eng. trans. 1950)
Les Fauves (exh. cat. by J. Rewald, New York, MOMA, 1952)
M. Rayal: *Peinture moderne* (Geneva, 1953)
A. Salmon: *Le Fauvisme* (Paris, 1956)
B. Dorival: *Les Peintres du XXème siècle: Nabis, Fauves, Cubistes* (Paris, 1957)
L. Vauxcelles: *Le Fauvisme* (Geneva, 1958)
J. Leymarie: *Le Fauvisme* (Geneva, 1959)
J.-P. Crespelle: *The Fauves* (London, 1962)
Gustave Moreau et ses élèves (exh. cat. by J. Cassou, Marseille, Mus. Cantini & Gal. Faience, 1962)
C. Chassé: *Les Fauves et leur temps* (Lausanne, 1963)
Le Fauvisme français et les débuts de l'Expressionnisme allemand (exh. cat. by B. Dorival, M. Hoog and L. Reidemeister, Paris, Mus. N. A. Mod., 1966)
J. E. Muller: *Fauvism* (London, 1967)
J. Laude: *La Peinture française et 'l'art nègre': Contribution à l'étude des sources du Fauvisme et du Cubisme* (Paris, 1968)
G. Diehl: *Les Fauves* (Paris, 1971; Eng. trans. 1975)
Fauves et Cubistes (exh. cat., Paris, Grand Pal., 1972)
Les Fauves (exh. cat. by F. Daulte, Osaka, Seibu-Takatsuki Gal., 1974)
E. C. Oppler: *Fauvism Reexamined* (New York, 1976)
The 'Wild Beasts': Fauvism and its Affinities (exh. cat. by J. Elderfield, New York, MOMA; San Francisco, CA, MOMA; Fort Worth, TX, Kimbell A. Mus.; 1976)
Les Fauves (exh. cat., London, Lefevre Gal., 1978)
M. Giry: *Le Fauvisme: Ses origines, son évolution* (Neufchâtel, 1981)
Nabis und Fauves (exh. cat., ed. U. Perucchi; Zurich, Ksthaus; Bremen, Ksthalle; Bielefeld, Städt. Ksthalle; 1982–3)
James D. Herbert: *Fauve Painting: Making of Cultural Politics* (New Haven, 1992)

DORA PÉREZ-TIBI

Favanne, Henri(-Antoine) de (*b* London, 3 Oct 1668; *d* Paris, 1752). French painter. His parents were French, resident in England, and his father was Master of the Hunt to James, Duke of York (later James II). Favanne was destined to succeed him, but in 1686 he moved to France instead. His intention was to study under Charles Le Brun, but on discovering that the aging master no longer accepted pupils, he went to René-Antoine Houasse. In 1695 he won the Prix de Rome and left Paris for Rome, where he spent five years. There, according to Cousin de la Contamine, he chose for his models 'the quiet painters' (i.e. the classicizing painters of the 16th and 17th centuries), in particular Raphael. Shortly after Favanne's return from Rome, Jean Bouteroue d'Aubigny, equerry of Marie-Anne de la Trémouille, Princesse des Ursins, took him to Spain to execute copies of pictures in the Spanish royal collections, a task that occupied him for ten years. Approved (*agréé*) by the Académie Royale in 1701, he was received (*reçu*) in 1704 with an allegory of the *Presentation of Philip V to Spain by France* (Versailles, Château). He continued to enjoy the protection of the Princesse des Ursins in France, and in 1715 he executed the painted decoration of her sumptuous château, built by Robert de Cotte, at Chanteloup, near Tours, the major work of his career. Although most of the pictures from Chanteloup were destroyed during the French Revolution, at least two compositions for the chapel survive: an *Arrival of the Holy Family into Egypt* (Charleville, Mus. B.-A.) and a *Presentation of the Virgin in the Temple* (Saint-Symphorien-les-Tours, nr Tours, convent of La Bretèche); there are also surviving oil sketches for other parts of the decoration (Lille, Mus. B.-A.; Orléans, Mus. B.-A.; Tours, Mus. B.-A.; Paris, Louvre; Detroit, MI, Inst. A.). It is possible that Favanne retained some links with England, for in 1717, according to Cousin de la Contamine, he entered a competition for the decoration of the cupola of St Paul's Cathedral. In 1724 he collaborated with Jean-Baptiste Oudry, Charles-Antoine Coypel, Louis Galloche, Ernest Christophe, Jean Restout (ii), Pierre-Jacques Cazes and Jean-François de Troy (ii) in the decoration of the Hôtel du Grand Maître at Versailles, for which he produced *Rinaldo and Armida* (Versailles, Hôtel de Ville). Other representative works of this period are *Coriolanus Taking Leave of his Family to Fight against his Country* and its pendant, *Coriolanus Entreated by his Wife and Mother* (*c*. 1725; Auxerre, Mus. A. & Hist.). Favanne exhibited irregularly at the Salon between 1704 and 1751 (e.g. the *Separation of Telemachus and Eucharis* and the *Nymphs Setting Telemachus' Ship on Fire*, both exh. Salon 1746; both Moscow, Pushkin Mus. F.A.), and he was made rector of the Académie Royale in 1748.

Favanne produced more than 150 pictures, including portraits, religious, mythological and historical compositions and landscapes, as well as numerous drawings. His style betrays the combined influence of the painters he had studied in Italy and of Houasse, from whose poised compositions he inherited a distinctive silvery tonality. The general effect is of a somewhat austere classicism, which provides an unexpected link between Nicolas Poussin and the Neo-classical painting of the later 18th century.

BIBLIOGRAPHY

O. Cousin de la Contamine: *Mémoire pour servir à la vie de M. de Favanne, peintre ordinaire du roi et recteur de l'Académie royale de peinture et de sculpture* (Paris, 1753); also in *Rev. Univl. A.*, xiv (1861), pp. 245–60

G. Rouches: 'Henri de Favanne (1668–1752), illustrateur des fastes du gouvernement de Philippe V, roi d'Espagne, à son début', *Bull. Soc. Hist. A. Fr.* (1950), pp. 133–6

A. Schnapper: 'Deux tableaux de Henri de Favanne', *Rev. Louvre*, xxii (1972), pp. 361–4

——: 'Traces du décor peint par Henri de Favanne (1668–1752) pour le château de Chanteloup', *Rev. Louvre*, xxxiv (1984), pp. 349–52

J.-P. Marandel: 'Two Sketches by Henri de Favanne for the Chapel at Chanteloup', *Bull. Detroit Inst. A.*, lxiii (1987)

J. PATRICE MARANDEL

Favorsky, Vladimir (Andreyevich) (*b* Moscow, 1886; *d* Moscow, 1964). Russian engraver, draughtsman and theorist. He trained with Konstantin Yuon in Moscow, with Simon Hollósy in Munich (1906–7) and in the Art History Department at Moscow University (1907–12). He made his first engraving in 1907 and started exhibiting his work in 1911. After experimenting with a Neo-primitivist style, as in, for example, *St George* (1911), and a simplified academicism (e.g. *Bombardier Sviridenko*, 1916–18), Favorsky developed a mature style that was bold yet highly disciplined (e.g. *October 1917*, 1928). He was particularly deeply influenced by the ideas of Adolf von Hildebrand, with their tendency towards a type of Neo-classicism and faultless architectonic precision in form. (In 1914 Favorsky translated Hildebrandt's famous work, *Das Problem der Form in der bildenden Kunst*, into Russian.) He taught at the second Svomas (State Free Art Studios) in Moscow (1918), served in the Red Army (1919–21) and taught drawing (1921–9) in the Graphics Faculty of Vkhutemas (Higher Artistic and Technical Workshops) in Moscow. He was popular as the Director of Vkhutemas (1923–5) because of his commitment to technical skill, his lack of dogmatism and his tolerance of experimentation of all kinds. In 1930 he joined the staff of the Moscow Graphics Institute. Although he was sympathetic to avant-garde ideas, Favorsky's own work was firmly representational and he was a member of the moderate FOUR ARTS SOCIETY OF ARTISTS, together with Lev Bruni and David Shterenberg. He produced designs and illustrations for numerous publications (e.g. the cover of the magazine *Makovets*, 1923). His engravings, along with his theoretical analyses of the artistic and technical bases of wood-engraving, had a great influence on the development of modern Russian graphics.

WRITINGS

Ob iskusstve, o knige, o gravyure [Concerning art, the book and engraving] (Moscow, 1986)

BIBLIOGRAPHY

Yu. Khalaminsky: *V. A. Favorsky* (Moscow, 1964)

V. A. Favorsky (exh. cat., ed. Y. Levitin; Moscow, 1964)

Yu. Molok, ed.: *Kniga o Vladimire Favorskom* [A book on Vladimir Favorsky] (Moscow, 1966)

V. A. Favorsky, 1886–1964: Katalog ystavki k 100-letiyu so dnya rozhdeniya [V. A. Favorsky, 1886–1964: Catalogue of the exhibition on the centenary of his birth] (exh. cat. by E. A. Anferova, Moscow, Tret'yakov Gal., 1986)

E. B. Murina and D. D. Chebanova, eds: *Literaturno-teoreticheskoye 'naslediye* [Literary-theoretical heritage] (Moscow, 1988)

E. S. Levitin and G. Zagianskaya: *V. Favorsky: Vospominaniya o khudozhnike* [V. Favorsky: Reminiscences about the artist] (Moscow, 1990)

——: *V. A. Favorsky: Vospominaniya sovremennikov: Pis'ma khudozhnika: Stenogrammy vystupleniy* [V. A. Favorsky: Reminiscences by his contemporaries: The artist's letters: Stenographic reports of his speeches] (Moscow, 1991)

CHRISTINA LODDER

Favray, Antoine de (*b* Bagnolet, nr Paris, 1706; *d* Malta, *c.* 1792). French painter. He is not documented until 1738, when he was mentioned as a private pupil of Jean-François de Troy (ii), who was then director of the Académie de France in Rome; in 1739 he became an official student at the Académie. Among his student works is a copy (untraced) of Raphael's *Fire in the Borgo* (Rome, Vatican, Stanza dell'Incendio), which was mentioned by Charles de Brosses and exhibited in Paris in 1741. In 1744, for reasons that are not clear, he left Rome for Malta, remaining there for much of the rest of his career and devoting himself primarily to portraiture and genre painting. His ambition as a history painter, however, was fulfilled to a certain extent as a result of the patronage of two Grand Masters of the Order of the Knights of Malta, Manoel Pinto da Fonseca and Emmanuel de Rohan. His first dated picture executed in Malta is a *Portrait of a Maltese Lady* (1745; Paris, Louvre). Portraits and island scenes showing the inhabitants in local costume assured him a certain notoriety in France; he reserved a less exotic portrait style for his official Maltese clientele.

Favray's ties with France remained strong: in 1762 he was both approved (*agréé*) and received (*reçu*) by the Académie Royale with his *Maltese Ladies Paying a Call* (1751; Paris, Louvre); he made his début at the Salon in 1763 (when Diderot described his work as 'miserable') and exhibited there irregularly until 1788. By 1762 he had left Malta for Constantinople, where he remained for nine years, enjoying the patronage of the French Ambassador, Charles Gravier, Marquis de Vergennes, and painting portraits of the Marquis as well as of *Madame de Vergennes in Oriental Costume* (France, priv. col.; see Boppe, 1902). He also executed many views of the city (e.g. *View of the Bosphorus and the Golden Horn*, 1763; Château de Lantheuil, nr Caen) and recorded specific events such as the *Audience Given by the Sultan to Mr de Saint-Priest on Tuesday November 29, 1768* (untraced). In 1771 the war between Turkey and Russia obliged Favray to return to Malta by way of Marseille. The only important commission recorded between his return and his death is that for his *Self-portrait* (Florence, Uffizi) for the gallery of Leopold, Grand Duke of Tuscany, devoted to self-portraits of artists.

Favray himself thought highly of his religious compositions; the *Submission of the Antipope Victor IV to Pope Innocent III* (1743; Los Angeles, CA, Norton Simon Found.) reveals the influence of Carle Vanloo as well as de Troy. He was an able portraitist and a delightful genre painter. Although he did not introduce a Maltese fashion into France, his work was admired and collected by his contemporaries. His appealing style bears a touch of naivety that is akin to that of Pietro Longhi (ii) in Venice (see 1970 exh. cat.). The largest holding of his work, including many drawings, is in Malta (Valletta, N. Mus.).

BIBLIOGRAPHY

A. Boppe: 'La Mode des portraits turcs au XVIIIe siècle', *Rev. A. Anc. & Mod.*, ii (1902)

——: *Les Peintres du Bosphore au dix-huitième siècle* (Paris, 1911), pp. 57–100

The Order of St John in Malta (exh. cat. by P. Rosenberg, Valletta, St John's Mus., 1970), pp. 93–9, 314–16

J. PATRICE MARANDEL

Favretto, Giacomo (*b* Venice, 11 Aug 1849; *d* Venice, 12 June 1887). Italian painter and draughtsman. He studied at the Accademia in Venice from 1864 to 1875. He lost an eye through a blood infection in 1877, but he recovered his general health and stayed on at the Accademia as an assistant until 1878. Favretto's early interiors and portraits were influenced by the chiaroscuro realism of Michele Cammarano (1835–1920). In 1878 he became a national celebrity at the Brera exhibition with his charming and amusing genre scene *The Mouse* (Milan, Brera). The same year he showed *The Prescription* (priv. col.; see Perocco and Trevisan, pl. 45) and *At the Tailor's* (priv. col.; see Perocco and Trevisan, pl. 43) at the Exposition Universelle in Paris, which he visited with Guglielmo Ciardi (1842–1917).

While in Paris, Favretto was apparently much impressed by the work of Ernest Meissonier and Mariano Fortuny y Marsal. Back in Italy again, he was influenced by Pompeo Molmenti's 'rediscovery' of Giambattista Tiepolo. Favretto turned to 18th-century genre themes and ironic interpretations of popular life in Venice (*see* VENICE, fig. 9). These were often enriched by the authentic detail of his collection of antiques, as in *Two Paintings for Sale* (Milan, Gal. A. Mod.), and are striking for their brilliant use of colour. In the late 1880s Favretto returned to purely contemporary subjects, as in the three works he exhibited in Venice in 1887, of which a *Modern Promenade* (untraced; sold at auction 19 Oct 1989, Milan, Finarte; see Perocco and Trevisan, pl. 192) was an updated version of his 18th-century scene of Piazza San Marco in Venice, *The Promenade* (1884; Rome, G.N.A. Mod.). Favretto also produced fine drawings in pencil and in pen and ink; these are mostly still in private collections (see Perocco and Trevisan, pp. 196–215).

BIBLIOGRAPHY
L. Obici Talamini: 'Ricordi favrettiani: Primi passi sulla via maestra', *La lettura*, xli/12 (1941), pp. 1155–60
Venezia nell'ottocento: Immagini e mito (exh. cat., ed. G. Pavanello and G. Romanelli; Venice, Ala Napoleonica and Correr; 1983–4)
G. Perocco and R. Trevisan: *Giacomo Favretto* (Turin, 1987)

PAUL NICHOLLS

Favro, Murray (*b* Huntsville, Ont., 24 Dec 1940). Canadian sculptor. He studied from 1958 to 1964 at Beal Technical School in London, Ontario, and began working as a painter in that city in the mid-1960s. Soon, however, he questioned the relationship between life experience and traditional artistic methods, as a result of which he produced a wide range of constructions (representing guitars, aircraft and inventions) as well as installations using film or images projected from slides.

Such interests led Favro to engage in ambitious projects such as the *Flying Flea* (1976–7; Ottawa, N.G.), built from the plans of a light aircraft designed by Alfred Mignet in 1934, and *Sabre Jet* (1979–83; Ottawa, N.G.), a model just over half-scale that reproduces not only the form but also the construction methods of the original aircraft. For the latter sculpture he drew on childhood memories and also paid tribute, through the process itself, to the anonymous workers who built the original aeroplane. In *Van Gogh's Room* (1973–4; Toronto, A.G. Ont.), one of a series of *Projected Reconstructions* initiated in 1970, he created an installation formed by a three-dimensional replica of van Gogh's painting on to which he projected a reproduction of the original painting.

BIBLIOGRAPHY
Murray Favro: A Retrospective (exh. cat. by M. L. Fleming, Toronto, A.G. Ont., 1983)

DAVID BURNETT

Fayaz Tepe. *See* TERMEZ, §2(ii).

Faydherbe [Fayd'herbe; Faidherbe], **Lucas** (*b* Mechelen, 19 Jan 1617; *d* Mechelen, 31 Dec 1697). Flemish sculptor and architect. His father, Hendrik Faydherbe (1574–1629), a painter and sculptor, died when Lucas Faydherbe was 12, so it was his stepfather, Maximiliaan Labbé (*d* 1675), who between 1631 and 1634 trained him as a sculptor. Faydherbe then travelled to Antwerp to continue his training in the studio of Peter Paul Rubens, under whose guidance he executed a number of ivory-carvings, such as *Leda and the Swan* (Paris, Louvre). Abandoning a planned trip to Italy, Faydherbe in 1640 married and settled in Mechelen.

Faydherbe's work can be divided into three periods. The first, from 1640 to 1660, is characterized by the strong influence of Rubens but lacks his vigour and dynamism. Faydherbe's attempts during this period to develop a personal style are seen most clearly in his over life-size statue of *St James the Greater* (white stone, h. 3 m, 1650) for Brussels Cathedral. It is a lifelike work with a powerful anatomy; the heavy folds of the draperies add a further impression of strength to the figure. The statue is more ponderous in appearance than contemporary sculptures inspired by Italian Baroque prototypes, so stressing the Flemish character of Faydherbe's art.

In the second period, from 1640 to 1660, Faydherbe's popularity increased. He was overwhelmed with commissions, not only for sculptures but also for building projects. His most important architectural works are the church (1662) of Leliendael Abbey at Mechelen and a chapel (1663) for the Hanswijk Church in the same town. His sculptures include one of his best works, the tomb of *Archbishop Andreas Cruesen* (white and black marble, 1660) in the cathedral of St Rombout, Mechelen. It is closely modelled on the monument designed by Jérôme Du Quesnoy (ii) for Bishop Antoine Triest (1654; Ghent, St Bavo's Cathedral). The Archbishop, naturalistically portrayed, kneels directly in front of the figure of the *Risen Christ*, who appears more elegant and serene than Faydherbe's other sculptures, thanks to Du Quesnoy's influence. The figure of *Time*, standing on the left, is more like the general run of Faydherbe's sculptures: heavily built, with accentuated anatomy, a long curly beard and high cheekbones.

Faydherbe's best-known work, made barely two years later, is in the same cathedral: the high altar of black touchstone, white marble and gilded wood, ordered in 1660 by Archbishop Cruesen and installed in 1665. In its execution Faydherbe had the collaboration of Matheus van Beveren and of his own son, Jan Lucas Faydherbe (1654–1704). It is a markedly decorative, dramatic and moving sculpture. Between the four marble columns there is a large pair of gilded doors, with a broken, segmental pediment above, inside which is placed the base of the gigantic (3.75 m) statue of *St Rombout*. The saint's two murderers, who flank him, are innovatorily placed: not on top of the pediment but fitted inside it. The altar's good proportions, simple composition and well-organized division of surfaces make it a masterpiece of Baroque art. After 1676 Faydherbe's most productive years were over: his few subsequent works lack originality.

BIBLIOGRAPHY
Thieme–Becker
A. Vanderpoel: *Notice sur la vie et les oeuvres de Lucas Fayd'herbe, sculpteur et architecte malinois* (Mechelen, 1851)
E. Neeffs: 'Sculpteurs malinois du XVIIe siècle: Les Fayd'herbe', *Messager Sci. Hist. Belgique* (1875), pp. 164–210
M. Libertus: *Lucas Faydherbe, beeldhouwer en bouwmeester: 1617–1697* (Antwerp, 1938)
La Sculpture au siècle de Rubens (exh. cat., Brussels, Mus. A. Anc., 1977), pp. 96–115 [good bibliog.]
IRIS KOCKELBERGH

Faylaka. *See under* ARABIA, PRE-ISLAMIC, §§II, III, IV.

Fazio, Bartolomeo. *See* FACIO, BARTOLOMEO.

Fazio, Gano di. *See* GANO DI FAZIO.

Fazola [Fassola; Fassole]. Hungarian family of metalworkers of German origin. Henrik Fazola (*b* Würzburg, *c.* 1730; *d* Diósgyőr, 18 April 1779) came to Hungary in 1758 at the invitation of Ferenc Barkóczy, Bishop of Eger, and established his workshop in the county of Heves. Henrik made all the wrought ironwork for the new County Hall, the Archepiscopal Palace and monasteries, as well as all the steelwork and wrought ironwork for the ecclesiastical estates in the county. After discovering iron ore in the surrounding mountains, he established iron smelting works in Omassa, Hámor and Diósgyőr; the last continues to operate. His most important works are the wrought-iron gates of the County Hall of Eger, decorated with acanthus leaves (*see* HUNGARY, fig. 24). Lénárd Fazola (*b* Würzburg, 1737; *d* Eger, 11 Oct 1805) was the younger brother of Henrik Fazola and settled in Eger in 1768. He made the great gates of the Archbishop's Palace and the gates of its park, the latticework wrought-iron balcony of the Liceum and the lattice ironwork of the door of the Observatory and its revolving cupola. He worked in a similar style and used similar techniques to those of his brother, but his later work incorporates geometric forms.

BIBLIOGRAPHY
I. Soós: 'Fazola Henrik és Lénárd egri vasművesek' [Henrik and Lénárd Fazola of Eger: wrought ironworkers], *Archeologiai értesitő* (1955), pp. 29–46
FERENC BATÁRI

Fazzini, Pericle (*b* Grottammare, Ascoli Piceno, 4 May 1913). Italian sculptor. The son of a wood-carver, he moulded his first figures in clay in his father's studio. In 1929 he moved to Rome, where he attended free courses in drawing and specialized in portraits. In 1931 he won the Cardinal Dusmet competition in Catania with his design for the Cardinal's tomb and met the painters Fiorenzo Tomea (*b* 1910), Renato Birolli and Atanasio Soldati (1896–1953). In 1932 he won the Pensionato Artistico Nazionale with *Leaving the Ark* (Rome, artist's

priv. col., see Mohr, nos 7–9) and *Woman in the Storm* (Rome, Gal. Accad. N. S Luca), which enabled him to rent a studio in Villa Caffarelli on the Campidoglio; his bursary ended in 1935 and he moved to Via Margutta. Between 1937 and 1952 he taught at the Museo Artistico Industriale and at that time his future wife Anita Buy became the subject of many of his compositions. During World War II he continued to work with various materials, from clay to bronze, and in 1942 he won the Accademia d'Italia prize. Between 1930 and 1950 he exhibited widely and in 1951 he had a retrospective at the Palazzo Barberini. In 1952 he won an award at the Quadriennale in Rome and the Alexander Jolas Gallery in New York was inaugurated with an exhibition of his work. He taught from 1953 to 1958 at the Accademia di Belle Arti in Florence and then at the Accademia di Brera in Milan.

Fazzini established the motifs of his later works between 1929 and 1935, and his association with established artists, such as Gino Bonichi Scipione, Mario Mafai, Arturo Martini (whom he met in 1935), Fiorenzo Tomea, Renato Birolli and Atanasio Soldati, led him to react against the rhetoric of the Fascist regime. He refuted academicism and supported creative freedom, seeing sculpture as 'not a cliff, but water and sky ... not an object, but an extension'. He made sober compositions in wood in which he celebrated their 'unfinished' quality so as to exploit effects of light. In opposition to Fascist monumentalism he preferred bas-reliefs imbued with light, movement and plastic strength, for example *The Dance* (1933–5; Capri, Malaparte priv. col., see Bellonzi, 1987, pp. 82–3). In *Woman in the Storm* movement is represented through volume. In 1936–45 Fazzini appeared to reflect on his ideas of the 'unfinished' and on the effects of movement; this resulted in a more thoughtful plasticity and a more sober style. In his figures depicting movement and in his portraits Fazzini strove to achieve complete coherence and a sense of humanity. His portrait of *Ungaretti* (Rome, G.N.A. Mod.) is typical of this period. At the same time, memories of his childhood on the Adriatic coast lend a poetic air to works that are characterized by a renewed sense of the baroque in unusual poses, contortions and rhythms.

The period 1946–55 is characterized by fantastic ideas and creations even though Fazzini wavered between reason and emotion and between constructed forms and free plasticity. His *Wounded Partisan* (1945–6; artist's priv. col., see Mohr, nos 26–8) is typical of this trend in that emotion is not overtly displayed but 'contained' in form. A new baroque tendency can be seen in the *Deposition* (1951) in the chapel of Santa Francesca Cabrini in Rome and in the *Execution of a Partisan* (1953–5; Tokyo, Universe Gal.). Figures of acrobats, of youths and of fantastic characters influenced by European neo-Cubism appear together with geometric patterns from ancient Mediterranean cultures and create plastic rhythms of harmony and vitality. After 1956 Fazzini achieved his best solutions: he elaborated well thought-out relationships of mass and revived the idea of the 'unfinished'. By using free expression and reflecting on ancient cultures he produced forms tinged with a restrained sensuality and resolved in light and aerial rhythms. His later work included the *Monument to the Resistance* (1956) in Ancona, the model for the *Monument to Kennedy* (1965, artist's priv. col., see Mohr, no. 73), the *Fountain* (1964–5) for the EUR in Rome and especially the *Resurrection* (1972–7) for the Sala Paolo VI in the Vatican, in which the figure of Christ dominates a dramatic landscape resembling the aftermath of a nuclear explosion.

Fazzini gained attention without a set programme or manifesto, and he regarded any kind of theory with mistrust. He believed in a methodical and disciplined approach to his work and described himself as 'both a pagan and a Christian, a heretic and a mystic'. His development as an artist was uneven and he was influenced by different cultural stimuli, while retaining an interest in his own time. A romantic using lively and expressive imagery, he gained his sense of equilibrium from classical sculpture. His most original work derived from the observation of natural phenomena, and the poet Giuseppe Ungaretti described him as 'a sculptor of the wind'.

BIBLIOGRAPHY
Pericle Fazzini (exh. cat. by G. Ungaretti and R. Lucchese, Rome, Pal. Barberini, 1951)
R. Lucchese: *Pericle Fazzini* (Rome, 1952)
F. Bellonzi: *I campi di P. Fazzini* (Rome, 1956)
G. Carandente: *Scultura italiana del XX secolo* (Rome, 1957)
P. Volponi: *Album di Grottammare* (Rome, 1964)
R. Pallucchini: *Pericle Fazzini* (Rome, 1965)
B. Mohr: *Fazzini* (Florence, 1969)
Fazzini (exh. cat. by D. Durbé, M. Faggiolo dell'Arco and V. Rivosecchi, Rome, G.N.A. Mod., 1984)
F. Bellonzi: *Fazzini* (Rome, 1987)

PIERO PACINI

Fazzolari, Fernando (*b* Buenos Aires, 28 Sept 1949). Argentine painter and stage designer. After a series of pictures featuring hallucinatory images of disembodied mouths and orifices, bodies and pits, he began to treat circus scenes, exploiting their symbolic suggestiveness by representing candles, ladders, insects and animals of arbitrary size alongside ambiguous human forms. Falling somewhere between the merry and the tragic, they have a theatrical aspect consonant with his experience as a stage designer. Combining a lively, almost festive palette with thick paint, sometimes violently applied, Fazzolari emerged in the 1980s as one of the leading Neo-Expressionist painters in Argentina.

BIBLIOGRAPHY
Fernando Fazzolari (exh. cat., intro. H. Safons; Buenos Aires, A. Nue., 1983)
J. Glusberg: *Del Pop-art a la Nueva Imagen* (Buenos Aires, 1985), pp. 520–22

HORACIO SAFONS

Fea, Carlo (*b* Pigna, Liguria, 4 June 1753; *d* Rome, 17 March 1836). Italian archaeologist and churchman. He went when young to Rome, where he studied philosophy and civil and canon law at the Sapienza. He took priestly orders, but after working briefly as a lawyer devoted himself entirely to archaeology. His first written work was *Sulle rovine di Roma*, a dissertation appended to the third volume of his translation (Rome, 1783–4) of Johann Joachim Winckelmann's *Geschichte der Kunst des Altertums*. He became librarian of the Biblioteca Chigiana and was appointed by Pope Pius VII (*reg* 1800–23) commissioner for Roman antiquities. Numerous excavations were carried out under his direction: he took a particular interest in those on the Roman Forum. Apart from his many writings about Roman antiquities, Fea published editions of Horace, G. L. Bianconi's *Descrizione dei circhi particolarmente di quello di Caracalla* and the works of Anton Raphael Mengs. He was one of the founders of the modern law for the protection of artistic heritage.

WRITINGS
Progetto di una nuova edizione di Vitruvio: L'integrità del Panteone di Marco Agrippa (Rome, 1801)
Relazione di un viaggio ad Ostia, e alla Villa di Plinio (Rome, 1802)
Della statua di Pompeo Magno del Palazzo Spada (Rome, 1812)
Iscrizioni di monumenti pubblici trovate nell'attuali escavazioni (Rome, 1813)
Notizie degli scavi nell'Anfiteatro Flavio (Rome, 1813)
Frammenti di fasti consolari e trionfali (Rome, 1820)
Descrizione di Roma e dei contorni con vedute (Rome, 1822)
La fossa Traiana (Rome, 1824)
Aneddoti sulla basilica ostiense di S. Paolo, riuniti nel 1823 dopo l'incendio e recitati nell'Accademia di Archeologia il 27 genn. 1825 (Rome, 1825)
Miscellanea antiquario-idraulica (Rome, 1827)

BIBLIOGRAPHY
P. E. Visconti: *Biografia dell'abate don Carlo Fea, commissario dell'antichità* (Rome, 1836)
E. Re: 'Brumaio dell'abate Fea', *Nuova Antol.*, v (1929), pp. 216–31
G. de Angelis d'Ossat: 'Carlo Fea e lo studio dei monumenti romani', *Boll. Reale Deput. Stor. Patria Liguria: Sez. Ingauna & Intemelia*, ii (1936), pp. 3–36

LUCA LEONCINI

Fearnley, Thomas (*b* Frederikshald [now Halden], 27 July 1802; *d* Munich, 16 Jan 1842). Norwegian painter. He was descended from a Yorkshire merchant who had settled in Norway in 1753. In 1819 he went into business but at the same time entered the Kongelige Tegneskole in Christiania (now Oslo) and received further training at the art colleges in Copenhagen (1821–3) and Stockholm (1823–7), where Karl XIV commissioned work from him. Fearnley spent much of his life travelling. In Norway in the summer of 1826 he met J. C. Dahl, with whom he later studied in Dresden (1829–30), learning especially to observe nature. After two years in Munich (1830–32), Fearnley's style was also influenced by the local school of landscape painters, which stressed more atmospheric effects.

In Italy (1832–5) Fearnley produced charming light-filled studies of local vegetation and popular life and harmoniously composed pictures of the landscape around the Bay of Naples (e.g. *From Sorrento*, 1834; Bergen, A.G.). He then spent three months in the Swiss Alps where he depicted such romantic subjects as the *Grindelwald Glacier* (1838; Oslo, N.G.). From 1836 to 1838 Fearnley was in England. In August and September 1837 he toured the Lake District, and several of his pictures from this time show an intimate knowledge of the English landscape (e.g. *Patterdale Church*, 1837; Oslo, N.G.). *Labro Waterfall* (exh. RA 1837; Oslo, N.G.), based on studies made at the falls at Numedal and painted in London, is a typical example of how the artist combined faithful observation of reality with a heightened and idealized interpretation of nature. In his most famous painting, the *Birch Tree at Slinde* (1839; Oslo, N.G.), Fearnley gave to his impression of a Norwegian summer evening an elevated symbolic meaning by emphasizing the huge tree on the burial mound; he also included two minute figures turning away from the viewer to contemplate the greatness of nature, in a manner that recalls the art of Caspar David Friedrich, whom Fearnley had met in Dresden. Fearnley died of typhus at the age of 39.

NKL   BIBLIOGRAPHY
S. Willoch: *Maleren Thomas Fearnley* (Oslo, 1932)
H. Alsvik and S. Willoch: *Thomas Fearnleys Tegninger* [Thomas Fearnley's drawings] (Oslo, 1952)
Thomas Fearnley (exh. cat. by S. Willoch, Åmot, Stift. Modums Blaafarveværket, 1986)
                                          ERNST HAVERKAMP

Featherwork. Collective term for artefacts made of or decorated with feathers.

1. MATERIALS AND TECHNIQUES. Feathers are composed of the protein keratin and form the protective covering of birds; they make flight possible (in most species), provide protection from wetting, regulate body temperature and provide insulation. They grow in follicles, arranged in tracts over a bird's body. When fully grown, feathers, like hair, have no connections to the blood supply or nervous system and are dead material. Most bird species moult and regrow their feathers at least once a year.

There are three main types: contour feathers, semiplumes and down. Contour feathers form the visible outer covering of most birds (see fig. 1). They have a well-developed hollow quill (a) and a shaft (b) with a vane (c) on either side. The vane consists of barbs, which are subdivided into interlocking barbules. It is the fine structure of hooks and hollows on the barbules that holds the vane together (d). Semiplumes have a less cohesive vane: the hooks and hollows are poorly developed, so the barbs remain largely unconnected (e), as in ostrich feathers. Down feathers lack any shaft, the barbs spring directly from the short quill and have no significant barbules (f).

Feathers exhibit an extremely wide range of colours, from blacks and browns to vivid reds and metallic blues and greens. The principal pigments are melanin, which is synthesized within the bird's body, and carotenoids, which are absorbed from food. Melanin is responsible for shades from black to pale yellow, and carotenoids for some of the brightest reds and yellows. Other colours are the result of optical effects caused by the reflection or refraction of light on the outer layers of the feather keratin, modified by the presence of pigments in the underlying layers.

Birds maintain their feathers, mainly through preening: they rearrange the feathers and apply preen oil, a greasy substance largely composed of monester waxes that lubricates the feather keratin to retain suppleness and repel water. Feathers are generally strong and resilient, but they may be damaged on the bird through dietary deficiencies, wear and tear or parasite attack. Once incorporated into an object, feathers should be protected from such insects as clothes-moths and carpet beetles and from strong light, which may cause colours to fade and fibres to become embrittled.

Flight contour feathers appear most frequently on featherwork artefacts, but body contour feathers, semiplumes and down have also been used. They are rarely used to form objects on their own and are commonly found in combination with such materials as textiles, fibre netting, basketwork, skins and wood. Individual feathers or bunches of feathers are attached to each other and to a foundation in a variety of ways, including tying, binding, sewing, weaving and sticking. Techniques of attachment may be very simple, pushing the quills through basketwork for example, or they may be complex systems of bending and tying. Rows of feathers are often laced together through their shafts to create semi-rigid structures, as seen in many Native American war bonnets. Animal and fish glues and natural resins have also been used to stick feathers to paper, wood and textiles; much Amazonian featherwork, for example, utilizes resin-impregnated thread to bind feathers to decorative objects.

The visual qualities of feathers may be enhanced by such techniques as splitting the shaft to give a softer effect, stripping off part of the vane or cutting it into decorative shapes. The careful arrangement of natural and artificial shapes and colours to create patterns and collage is widespread. Feathers can be dyed easily and curled with the use of heat or steam. In some cultural groups bird quills have been used in place of porcupine quills to produce a form of decorative quillwork. Bird skins with the feathers still attached have been used, for example in Hawaii and South America. This technique is most often found where the feathers are very small or where the dramatic effect of the natural feather arrangement was valued. Bird parts, for instance wings, heads and plume sprays, and even whole birds, are frequently incorporated into artefacts.

2. USES. Feathers have been used to decorate the human body in a wide variety of ways. In one of its simplest forms, down feathers were stuck directly to the skin (*see* ABORIGINAL AUSTRALIA, §II, 4), but such objects as necklaces, bracelets, ear and nose decorations and head ornaments are more widespread. Fine examples can be seen from Hawaii, Papua New Guinea (*see* PAPUA NEW GUINEA, figs 8 and 14) and the Amazonian tribes of South America. Elaborate forms of featherwork headdress are

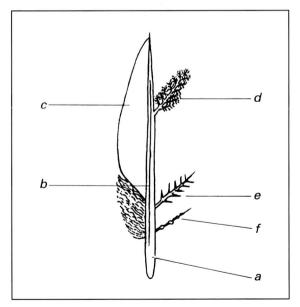

1. Contour feather: (a) quill; (b) shaft; (c) vane; (d) strong barbs and barbules; (e) poorly developed hooks; (f) no true barbules

found among the Maasai in Kenya, and the Mende of Sierra Leone use feathers in some of their masks. In Hawaii helmets and headdresses were produced incorporating millions of feathers that completely covered complex cane foundations. Costumes and headwear incorporating feathers were often designed to display the wearer's status, as in the outstanding feathered cloaks and gorgets created in Polynesia and by the Incas and Aztecs in Mesoamerica (*see* MESOAMERICA, PRE-COLUMBIAN, §IX, 3). In Maori cloaks the feathers were usually incorporated in the weaving rather than being tied on afterwards, as was the practice elsewhere in Polynesia (*see* MAORI). In Japan feathers were also used to decorate the garments of high-ranking individuals, although few examples survive. In China blue kingfisher feathers were used with hardstones, gems, gold and silver in the ceremonial headdresses or crowns of emperors, empresses and courtiers (*see* CHINA, §XIII, 16), and Chinese immigrants in South Africa have produced capes with feather patterns and swans' down linings. In Europe, particularly in the 18th and 19th centuries, the decorative value of feathers in self-adornment was exploited for the trims of gowns and for elaborate millinery, often including whole birds (*see* DRESS, fig. 47).

In many cultures feathered objects embody a ritual or sacred element. This is true of many Native North American examples where eagle feathers or skins are incorporated in sacred headdresses, medicine pipes and charms (*see* NATIVE NORTH AMERICAN ART, §XII). Dance masks and costumes frequently include featherwork for ritual and decorative value, for example in West Africa (*see* EJAGHAM, fig. 1). The trophy heads of the Jívaro and Mundurucú in South America were often embellished with feathers (*see* SOUTH AMERICA, PRE-COLUMBIAN, §VIII, 3). In the Hawaiian Islands feathers formed an integral part of god images (see fig. 2), sacred bundles and temples. Some bird species, such as the quetzal in Mesoamerica, had an extremely powerful ritual value, and the use of its feathers was fiercely controlled.

Feathers have been used to decorate everyday objects from the earliest times. The use of feathers to fletch arrows and to decorate spear shafts and shields is widespread (Europe, South America, New Guinea). Utilitarian clothing has sometimes been made from feathers, although it is generally too delicate for everyday use. Some Inuit groups have made parkas using eider-duck skins stitched together with the feathers on the inside for warmth; more commonly, utilitarian garments are decorated with feather trimmings. Feathers have been used to decorate hammocks (Amazonia), baskets (Pomo Indians, North America), ceramic vessels (New Guinea) and canoes (Maori, New Zealand); in Europe they have been used for such diverse purposes as writing quills (*see* PEN, §2), fans (*see* FAN), stuffing for mattresses, bedcovers and pillows and as decorative plumes for military headgear, four-poster beds and hearses. The use of feathers to create decorative features in interiors is infrequent, but impressive where it survives: largely as a women's pastime of the 18th and 19th centuries (particularly in Britain), feathers were stuck on to card to make panels and friezes (e.g. *c.* 1795; drawing-room and gallery, A la Ronde, Devon, NT; *see* SHELL, fig. 1). The gilt-leather wall coverings found in some German

2. Featherwork image of a god, feathers, cane, vegetable fibre, dog teeth and shell, h. 1 m, from the Hawaiian Islands, *c.* 1778 (London, British Museum)

castles of the same period occasionally incorporate featherwork.

BIBLIOGRAPHY
R. W. Doughty: *Feather Fashions and Bird Preservation* (London, 1975)
H. Cobbe, ed.: *Cook's Voyages and Peoples of the Pacific* (London, 1979)
V. Elbin: *The Body Decorated* (London, 1979)
D. S. Farner and J. R. King, eds: *Avian Biology* (London, 1982)
J. C. Welty: *The Life of Birds* (London, 1982)
A. P. Rowe: *Costumes and Featherwork of the Lords of Chimor* (Washington, DC, 1984)
E. Carmichael and S. Hugh-Jones: *The Hidden People of the Amazon* (London, 1985)
The Spirit Sings: Artistic Traditions of Canada's First Peoples (exh. cat. by J. D. Harrison and others, Calgary, Glenbow–Alta Inst., 1987)
Feather Masterpieces of the Ancient Andean World (exh. cat., ed. T. Gibson; London, Gibson F.A., 1990)

ALLYSON RAE

Fechter, Paul (*b* Elbing, E. Prussia [now Elblag, Poland], 14 Sept 1880; *d* Berlin, 9 Jan 1958). German writer. He studied architecture, natural science and the humanities, graduating as a DPhil at Erlangen in 1905, and then worked for newspapers in Dresden and Berlin. From 1918 to 1933 he was arts correspondent for the *Deutsche*

Allgemeine Zeitung. In 1908 he read Wilhelm Worringer's *Abstraktion und Einfühlung* (Munich, 1908), and Worringer's ideas and terminology underlie Fechter's pioneering study of German Expressionism (1914) as well as his stimulating survey of the development of architecture in *Die Tragödie der Architektur* (1921). He remained in Germany after 1933, although quite out of sympathy with the Nazi regime: his books on Expressionism and on Ernst Barlach (1935) were included in the infamous exhibition of *entartete Kunst* in Munich in 1937. He also joined the Wednesday Club in Berlin, several members of which died after taking part in the attempt on Adolf Hitler's life in July 1944. Fechter not only benefited from personal contact with many artists in Dresden and Berlin but also aimed to trace the general artistic trends of the time. In addition to his writings on art, he produced novels, stories and works on drama.

WRITINGS
Der Expressionismus (Munich, 1914, rev. 3/1919)
Das graphische Werk Max Pechsteins (Berlin, 1921)
Die Tragödie der Architektur (Jena, 1921, rev. Weimar, 2/1922)
intro.: *Ernst Barlach: Zeichnungen* (Munich, [1935])
Deutsche Backsteingotik (Königsberg, 1937)
Kleines Wörterbuch für Kunstgespräche (Gütersloh, 1951)
Ernst Barlach (Gütersloh, 1957)
Regular contributions to *Dt. Allg. Ztg* (1918–33)

BIBLIOGRAPHY
Dank und Erkenntnis: Paul Fechter zum 75. Geburtstag am 14. September 1955 (Gütersloh, 1955)

N. A. FURNESS

Feddes van Harlingen, Petrus (*b* Harlingen, *c*. 1585; *d* ?1623). Dutch etcher, painter and poet. Like his fellow townsman Simon Frisius, Feddes was one of the few early 17th-century Dutch printmakers to practise etching rather than engraving. He etched in soft-ground but sometimes also used the engraver's burin on his plates. The earliest dated prints of 1611–15 include the frontispiece for a drawing booklet and a number of apparently related, etched copies of drawings. These sheets were associated in a hypothetical reconstruction of the second oldest drawing book in the Netherlands (Bolten). His other etchings depict allegories, biblical and mythological scenes, (royal) portraits, townscapes and Frisian costumes, from which the book illustrations stand out as a group. They were published mainly in Leeuwarden (1614, 1619), where he lived from 1615, and Fraeneker (1619, 1620 and 1622). Of his paintings, a number of portraits have survived as well as a *Diana and her Nymphs Surprised by Satyrs* (Hoorn, Westfries Mus.).

BIBLIOGRAPHY
A. Wassenbergh: *De portretkunst in Friesland in de zeventiende eeuw* [The art of portraiture in Friesland in the 17th century] (Lochum, 1967)
J. Bolten: *Dutch and Flemish Method and Practice Drawing Books, 1600–1750* (Landau in der Pfalz, 1985; Eng. trans. of diss., U. Amsterdam, 1979)

CHRISTIAAN SCHUCKMAN

Fede, Conte (Giuseppe) (*b* ?Rome, *c*. 1700; *d* before 1777). Italian land-owner and excavator. He owned much of the land that constituted the Villa of Hadrian at Tivoli (*see* TIVOLI, §2). He was called 'Romano' by the noble Tiburtine historian Francesco Bulgarini in his history of Tivoli (1848), who also recorded that around 1730 Fede planted the pines and the cypresses and built the various

small buildings that dot the grounds of the villa, thus forming a single large estate. From this estate he excavated many precious marbles. Some of these were sold directly to Pope Pius VI (*reg* 1775–1800), entering the collections of the Vatican and Capitoline Museums, and others were shown in the Palazzo Fiorenza in the Campo Marzo, Fede's residence in Rome. A tablet set into the wall of the Casino Fede (the present entrance to the excavations at Hadrian's Villa) records the visit of the Emperor Joseph II and his cousin Pietro Leopoldo, Grand Duke of Tuscany, on 20 March 1769, when they were shown the villa by the Conte. In 1803 the estate passed into the hands of the Duca Braschi-Onesti who joined to it the Roccabruna, part of the original villa formerly in the possession of the Jesuits.

BIBLIOGRAPHY
F. Bulgarini: *Notizie storiche, antiquarie, statistiche ed agronomiche intorno all'antichissima città di Tivoli e suo territorio* (Rome, 1848)
C. Pietrangeli: *Scavi e scoperte di antichità sotto il pontificato di Pio VI* (Rome, 2/1958)
F. Haskell and N. Penny: *Taste and the Antique* (London and New Haven, 1981)

EUGENE DWYER

Fedeli. *See* MAGGIOTTO.

Federal style. Architectural and decorative arts style that flourished in the USA from shortly after the acknowledgement of independence in the Treaty of Paris (1783) until *c*. 1820. The term is derived from the period surrounding the creation of the federal constitution in 1787 and was in use in a political sense by that year. Essentially it was a form of Neo-classicism, strongly influenced by manifestations of that style in England and, to a lesser extent, in France; but at times certain more conservative qualities inherited from the previous Colonial period are also present. The inspiration of European, and especially English, Neo-classical architecture was to be expected in a society grounded in that of 18th-century England; but an added impetus was the association often cited at the time between the fledgling American republic and the ancient Roman one.

Although a few indications of European Neo-classical influence are found in the American colonies before the Revolution began in 1776, these were almost exclusively restricted to an occasional appearance in such interior decorative details as ceiling patterns, as in the stair-hall ceiling of the Chase-Lloyd House in Annapolis, MD (*c*. 1769–72), and in silver. Generally a Palladian style with certain Baroque and Rococo decorative treatments characterized American architecture in the third quarter of the 18th century. After the Revolution, in the second half of the 1780s, a substantial infusion of Neo-classical taste reached the USA, and this began to mix with and in some cases replace the Colonial style.

1. Architecture. 2. Decorative arts.

1. ARCHITECTURE. The importation of newer architectural books, the influence of patrons directly acquainted with European Neo-classicism and the arrival of craftsmen and architects trained in this new manner all helped to establish the Federal style. The earliest examples of the new approach include: John Penn's Solitude (*c*. 1784–5)

and William Hamilton's Woodlands (1787–8), both country houses outside Philadelphia; William Bingham's town house in that city (c. 1786–7, destr.), probably by the English architect John Plaw; and the Virginia State Capitol, Richmond (c. 1785–96; see UNITED STATES OF AMERICA, fig. 5), designed by the statesman and architect Thomas Jefferson with some help from the Frenchman Charles-Louis Clérisseau. Shortly thereafter the style appeared throughout the country, from Salem, MA, to Charleston, SC.

The specific adaptation of Roman buildings (as in the Virginia Capitol, based on the Maison Carrée, Nîmes) is relatively rare. Much more common is the transformation of the Colonial Palladian style by the introduction of attenuated proportions and flatter surfaces, as well as such Neo-classical decorative details as fanlights, chimneypieces and, occasionally, oval rooms and projections. This type of Neo-classicism is found extensively from Maine to Georgia and as far west as Indiana and Kentucky. Among its leading practitioners were Samuel McIntire in Salem, Charles Bulfinch in Boston, Asher Benjamin in western Massachusetts and later in Boston, John McComb jr in New York and Gabriel Manigault (1758–1809) in Charleston, SC.

Still another form of Neo-classicism, derived not so much from the work of Robert Adam as from the more austere aesthetic popularized in the 1790s by George Dance (ii) and John Soane in England and by Claude-Nicolas Ledoux and Etienne-Louis Boullée in France, reached the USA with the arrival from London in 1796 of Benjamin Henry Latrobe, the first professionally trained architect to practise in the USA. In buildings such as the Bank of Pennsylvania, Philadelphia (1799–1801; destr.), and the Roman Catholic Cathedral, Baltimore (1805–20; see fig. 1), Latrobe introduced not only the powerful plain walls, saucer domes and concealed lighting effects of Dance or Soane but also certain more archaeological

features, including the Greek Ionic order of the Erechtheion. This brand of Neo-classicism, though derived more from Ledoux and Boullée, was also brought to America by the Frenchman Maximilian Godefroy, as in his Unitarian Church, Baltimore (1817–18). It was practised as well by Latrobe's pupil Robert Mills, for example in his Monumental Church, Richmond (1812–17).

Although he supported Latrobe and his interpretation of Neo-classicism, Jefferson created yet a different facet of the Federal style. Apart from his Virginia Capitol, which was an exercise in Roman Revivalism tempered by the needs of the state government, he also transformed (1796–1809) his own house, Monticello, near Charlottesville, VA; built a number of other houses in Virginia for himself and friends, including Poplar Forest (1806–12); and both laid out the plan and designed the buildings for the University of Virginia, Charlottesville (1817–26). In all of these other works he combined the Palladian influences of his youth with such Neo-classical features as curved and canted projections, saucer domes and an appreciation of certain archaeological details.

Among the other major monuments of the Federal style are the plan of the city of Washington, DC, and its two principal public buildings, the Capitol and the President's House (the White House; see WASHINGTON, DC, figs 1, 5 and 6). The city itself was laid out in 1791 by Pierre Charles L'Enfant, utilizing grand French Baroque allées and rondpoints overlaid by a grid. The Capitol (1792–1835; wings and dome, 1850–65) was designed by William Thornton, but various changes were made by a series of executing architects, the most important of whom was Latrobe. The White House was designed by James Hoban and completed by him in 1802 (altered by Latrobe and Hoban, 1807 and 1824).

Although various characteristics of the Federal style, especially its modified simplifications of the Adam style, continued into the 1830s and beyond, it had begun to be supplanted by the Greek Revival by 1820 (see GREEK REVIVAL, §3). Motivated more strongly by both archaeology and Romanticism, this new style became dominant in the second quarter of the 19th century.

BIBLIOGRAPHY

F. Kimball: Domestic Architecture of the American Colonies and of the Early Republic (New York, 1922)
——: Mr. Samuel McIntire, Carver: The Architect of Salem (Portland, ME, 1940/R Gloucester, MA, 1966)
T. Hamlin: Greek Revival Architecture in America (New York, 1944)
S. Boyd: The Adam Style in America, 1770–1820 (diss., Princeton U., 1967)
——: 'The Adam Style in America, 1770–1820', Amer. Assoc. Archit. Bibliog.: Pap., v (1968), pp. 47–68
W. H. Pierson: American Buildings and their Architects: The Colonial and Neo-classical Styles (Garden City, NY, 1970)
J. Quinan: The Architectural Style of Asher Benjamin (diss., Providence, RI, Brown U., 1973)
W. H. Adams, ed.: The Eye of Thomas Jefferson (Washington, DC, 1976)
L. Craig and others: The Federal Presence: Architecture, Politics and Symbols in the United States Government Buildings (Cambridge, MA, 1978)
B. Lowry: Building a National Image: Architectural Drawings for the American Democracy, 1789–1912 (Washington, DC, 1985)
C. E. Brownell and J. A. Cohen, eds: The Architectural Drawings of Benjamin Henry Latrobe (London and New Haven, 1994)
P. Norton: The Papers and Drawings of Samuel McIntire (in preparation)
D. Stillman: Neo-classicism in America: The Architecture of the Young Republic, 1785–1825 (in preparation)

1. Benjamin Henry Latrobe: Roman Catholic Cathedral, Baltimore, MD, 1805–20

2. DECORATIVE ARTS. Like the architecture in which they were used, the decorative arts of the Federal period reflect the inspiration of Classical antiquity, and even more of Neo-classical England and France, tempered by existing, often conservative traditions. This can be seen most readily in metalwork and furniture, but it is also true of glass, ceramics and textiles. The appeal of antiquity is clearly indicated by the use of such classical motifs as urns, garland swags and fasciae and such antique shapes as the klismos chair or urn- or helmet-fashioned teapots and sugar bowls. Specific motifs associated with the new American republic are less common than those reflecting antiquity, but they were sometimes employed (eagles, for example, inspired by the Great Seal, were especially popular). Such other patriotic motifs as the liberty cap were used occasionally, and there is even a card-table (Winterthur, DE, Du Pont Winterthur Mus.), made in New York, with a glass decorative panel featuring the names of the Democratic-Republican party candidates for President and Vice-President in 1800, Thomas Jefferson and Aaron Burr. As with architecture, a new lightness and delicacy first appeared, modified towards the end of the period by an increased heaviness and a somewhat more archaeological approach. Again, as with buildings, there is a heightened homogeneity in the decorative arts made in different areas of the new country, but regional differences and the individual characteristics of specific artist-craftsmen can be detected.

Although in general the new style did not appear until after the conclusion of the American Revolution in 1783, it can be found before then in metalwork, especially silver, as in a presentation tea urn (Philadelphia, PA, Mus. A.; see fig. 2) made in 1774, on the eve of the Revolution, in Philadelphia by Richard Humphreys (1750–1832) and inscribed to Charles Thomson, the secretary to the Continental Congress. Fashioned in the shape of an urn and ornamented with fluted bands and rosettes, as well as having a square base and squared handles and spout, it epitomizes the Neo-classical taste that is synonymous with the Federal style. After the Revolution a similar taste could be found, for example, in tea services made in Boston by Paul Revere in 1792 (Minneapolis, MN, Inst. A.) and in Philadelphia by Simon Chaudron (1758–1846) and Anthony Rasch (1778–1857) in 1809–12 (Winterthur, DE, Du Pont Winterthur Mus.), as well as in such objects as a jug shaped like a wineskin, made for Jefferson by Anthony Simmons (d 1808) and Samuel Alexander (d 1847) in Philadelphia in 1801 (Monticello, VA, Jefferson Found.), or a plateau (or tray) executed in New York by John Forbes (1781–1864) and presented to De Witt Clinton in 1825 (priv. col., on loan to New York, Met.).

In furniture the Federal style flourished throughout the country from Salem, MA, to Charleston, SC, and westward into Kentucky and Louisiana. The most direct inspiration was from the pattern books of George Hepplewhite and Thomas Sheraton, but later influences include Thomas Hope (ii), George Smith (ii) and Pierre La Mésangère (1761–1831). The presence of French as well as English source books was paralleled by the activity of a number of French-trained cabinetmakers working in Federal America, including Charles-Honoré Lannuier in New York and Michel Bouvier (1792–1874) in Philadelphia, just as

2. Federal style presentation tea urn by Richard Humphreys, silver, h. 546 mm, 1774 (Philadelphia, PA, Museum of Art)

Chaudron represents French silversmiths working in the latter city.

Indications of the new style are found in oval- and shield-back chairs, often with delicately tapered or sabre legs; a host of Neo-classical motifs from urns and Classical orders to putti and paterae; and refined inlay and exquisite ormolu mounts (see WOOD, colour pl. II, fig. 2). Such mounts were employed especially by French émigrés, but Americans and cabinetmakers from Britain also used them. Representative examples of chairs include those with carved shield-backs made in Salem by Samuel McIntire in the 1790s (e.g. Winterthur, DE, Du Pont Winterthur Mus.); scroll-back and sabre-leg models created by Duncan Phyfe in New York in 1807 (Winterthur, DE, Du Pont Winterthur Mus.); painted oval-backed chairs with Prince of Wales feathers (e.g. New York, Met.) ordered from Philadelphia in 1796 by Salem merchant Elias Haskett Derby (1739–99); and rectangular ones enlivened with scenes of country houses near Baltimore (*c.* 1800–10; Baltimore, MD, Mus. A.) executed by John Finlay (1777–1840) and Hugh Finlay (1781–1831). Tables range from delicately inlaid Pembroke or breakfast tables made in Salem by Elijah Sanderson (1751–1825) and Jacob Sanderson (1757–1810) in the 1780s or 1790s (Winterthur, DE, Du Pont Winterthur Mus.), to card-tables with gilded winged figures by Lannuier (*c.* 1815; Baltimore, MD Hist. Soc. Mus.; New York, Met.). Examples of Federal style cabinets include an inlaid semicircular commode by John Seymour and Thomas Seymour of Boston (*c.* 1809; Boston, MA, Mus. F.A.); a carved double chest with numerous Neo-classical motifs on top and a more Rococo bombe-shaped lower half, made by William Lemon (*fl c.* 1796–1827) and carved by McIntire (*c.* 1796; Boston, MA, Mus. F.A.); or a lady's dressing-table with inlay of fine woods and painting on glass, topped by urns and an eagle (Baltimore, MD Hist. Soc. Mus.), made in Baltimore in the first decade of the 19th century and attributed to William Camp (1773–1822).

The most noteworthy glass of the period was that made by John Frederick Amelung at his New Bremen Glass-manufactory near Frederick, MD. Established in 1784, this glassworks produced a number of high-quality pieces between *c.* 1788 and 1792. These are not characterized by Neo-classical motifs but rather by a refined elegance, as in an amethyst-covered sugar bowl (Winterthur, DE, Du Pont Winterthur Mus.) or a clear glass tumbler of 1792 (priv. col., see Cooper, 1980, fig. 175), which sports an engraving of the Great Seal of the USA. Other Federal period glass includes the products of Bakewell & Co., founded in Pittsburgh in 1808; the New England Glass Co., established in Cambridge, MA, in 1818; and a number of glasshouses in southern New Jersey.

Neo-classical ceramics used in the USA during the Federal period were mostly wares imported from England, France and China. Earthenwares were made, some of which, such as a black-glazed coffeepot by Thomas Haig & Co. of Philadelphia (*c.* 1825; New York, Met.), reflect the influence of English Regency and French Empire silver and porcelain. Only in 1826 did the china manufactory founded by William Tucker in Philadelphia begin to produce similarly inspired porcelain wares. The most fashionable textiles in the Neo-classical taste were also imported from England and France, but both hand-embroidered and machine-printed fabrics, notably the printed calicoes of John Hewson (1744–1821) of Philadelphia, were produced in the USA during this era.

BIBLIOGRAPHY
B. Tracy and W. H. Gerdts: *Classical America, 1815–1845* (Newark, NJ, 1963)
C. F. Montgomery: *American Furniture: The Federal Period* (New York, 1966)
19th-Century America: Furniture and Other Decorative Arts (exh. cat., New York, Met., 1970)
W. Cooper: *In Praise of America: American Decorative Arts, 1650–1830* (New York, 1980)
B. Garvan: *Federal Philadelphia, 1785–1825: The Athens of the Western World* (Philadelphia, 1987)
S. Feld: *Neo-classicism in America: Inspiration and Innovation, 1810–1840* (New York, 1991)
W. Cooper: *Classical Taste in America, 1800–1840* (Baltimore, New York and London, 1993)

DAMIE STILLMAN

Federation style. Term applied to domestic designs of Australian architecture from around the turn of the 20th century, when the Commonwealth of Australia (1901) was created. It was first proposed by Professor Bernard Smith (1969) to replace the use of 'Queen Anne', which he argued was inappropriate and misleading in the Australian setting. The context of the original suggestion applies the name to a particular domestic picturesque idiom developed from the 1880s until *c.* 1914. These designs featured red bricks, turned wood ornament, half-timbering with rough-cast in the gables, shingled walls and striking terracotta tiles. Externally the designs derive from the English Domestic Revival pioneered by architects such as Richard Norman Shaw and from American sources such as the Shingle style, while internally there is an affinity with Arts and Crafts ideals. The designs developed within a ferment of discussion on the creation of an Australian style, partly as an offshoot of the English Arts and Crafts movement's concern with the uniqueness of place, materials, climate and local culture, and partly as a response to the excitement caused by the recognition in Australia of an American style in the work of architects such as H. H. Richardson.

The rediscovery of this Australian work began in the 1960s, firstly by the architectural historian David Saunders (1928–86) in Melbourne, who later became Professor of Architecture at the University of Adelaide, South Australia. He prompted a resurgence of interest in architectural nationalism. The architectural aspect was quickly absorbed within a broader cultural nationalism that had been developing in all the arts since World War II and that reached its high point in the 1970s. A desire to create new descriptive terms, such as 'Federation style', independent of the British heritage of terms, was an enduring legacy. In the same spirit of creating an Australian nomenclature, Conrad Hamann used 'Federation villa' and 'Federation bungalow' to refer to picturesque hip-roof examples. Federation style was also adopted into usage by property agents as a substitution for Edwardian. Later the term was being applied broadly to any buildings using red bricks and expressing Arts and Crafts sympathies in decoration, even to previously ignored commercial and industrial work.

BIBLIOGRAPHY
B. Smith: 'Architecture in Australia', *Hist. Stud.*, xiv (1969), pp. 85–92
C. Hamann: 'Nationalism and Reform in Australian Architecture, 1880–1920', *Hist. Stud.*, xviii (1979), pp. 393–411
G. Tibbits: 'The So-called Melbourne Domestic Queen Anne', *Hist. Envmt*, ii/2 (1982), pp. 4–44
R. Apperly: 'The Federation Period', *The History and Design of the Australian House*, ed. R. Irving (Melbourne, 1985), pp. 86–116

GEORGE TIBBITS

Federici, Domenico Maria (*b* Verona, 1739; *d* Treviso, ?Oct 1808). Italian monk and historian. He was a member of the Dominican Order and taught theology at parish schools in Udine and Padua before being assigned (*c.* 1785) to the Dominican college in Treviso. He became a passionate expounder of the history and culture of that city and the province of the Trevigiano—the 'Marca trivigiana' or 'gloriosa Marca' of chivalric history and romance. His first work, *Istoria de' cavalieri gaudenti* (1787), clearly displays his interests as well as his weaknesses: his discussion of a minor Franco-Italian chivalric order of the 13th to the 16th century (and 'of the illustrious widows and ladies connected with it') involves such evident pursuit of novel narrative effects as to render its historical methodology uncritical. However, his *Commentario sopra la vita e gli studi del conte Giordano Ricco* (1790) is a more restrained publication. His most important work, *Memorie trevigiane sulle opere di disegno dal 1100 al 1800, per servire alla storia delle belle arti d'Italia* (1803), again suffers from Federici's overenthusiasm for his subject but contains much important information, especially about such lost monuments as the villas destroyed in the Napoleonic era. His last books are more problematic: *Memorie trevigiane sulla tipografia del secolo XV* (1805) argues implausibly that movable type had been developed by Panfilo Gastaldi in Treviso before 1456 but also includes a useful list of 95 Trevisan incunabula of 1471–1500. *Della letteratura trevigiana del secolo XVIII sino a nostri giorni* (1807) again champions Trevisan accomplishments but was energetically rebutted by Giannantonio Moschini's work on Venetian literature. A generation after Federici's death, Trevisan historiography (especially of its art and architecture) was put on a much firmer footing by the Canon of Treviso Cathedral, Lorenzo Crico (1764–1835), in particular in his *Lettere sulle belle arti trevigiane* (1833), which corrected many of Federici's misattributions.

WRITINGS

Istoria de' cavalieri gaudenti, 2 vols (Venice, 1787)
Commentario sopra la vita e gli studi del conte Giordano Ricco (Venice, 1790)
Memorie trevigiane sulle opere di disegno dal 1100 al 1800, per servire alla storia delle belle arti d'Italia, 2 vols (Venice, 1803)
Memorie trevigiane sulla tipografia del secolo XV (Venice, 1805)
Della letteratura trevigiana del secolo XVIII sino a nostri giorni (Treviso, 1807)

BIBLIOGRAPHY

Michaud
L. Crico: *Lettere sulle belle arti trevigiane* (Treviso, 1833)

DOUGLAS LEWIS

Federighi, Antonio (*b* ?1420; *d* Siena, 15 Jan 1483). Italian sculptor and architect. He served as *capomaestro* of the cathedral workshop in Siena for three decades (1450–81). During this period he was involved in almost every major public artistic enterprise undertaken in the city, which was revitalized following the election (1458) of Aeneas Silvius Piccolomini, a Sienese, as Pope Pius II. First mentioned as an apprentice in the cathedral workshop, Federighi was employed by Jacopo della Quercia in 1438 just before the latter's death. This brief association with Quercia was crucial to the development of Federighi's robust, classicizing style.

In 1444 Federighi played a minor role in carving the tomb of *Bishop Carlo Bartoli* (Siena Cathedral) designed by Pietro del Minella (1391–1458). In 1445 he was paid for work on the Cappella di S Ansano at Castelvecchio; this was probably limited to the design of four windows and a doorway (Mantura). In May 1451 Federighi received his first independent commission to create a marble intarsia for the exterior pavement of the central portal of the Sienese Baptistery. In September of the same year he was commissioned to carve three statues of saints for the Loggia di Mercanzia (Loggia di San Paolo), Siena, but the monies advanced to him were withdrawn in 1453, when he failed to deliver the figures within the specified time. From 1451 to 1456 Federighi served as *capomaestro* of Orvieto Cathedral, which, no doubt, contributed to his failure to fulfil his Sienese obligations. He contributed some work to the cathedral façade, including the addition of niches to the topmost edge of the rose window, and designed a holy water basin for the interior. A statue mentioned in the documents cannot be identified, as has been customary, with the *Sibyl* on the left flank of the cathedral.

Federighi returned to Siena in 1457, lured, perhaps, by a more lucrative contract for the Loggia di Mercanzia, the decoration of which had remained dormant in his absence. In March 1457 his statue of *St Peter* (untraced) was already installed in a niche on the first pier of the Loggia. A second, documented, figure of *St Ansano* (*c*. 1458–9), on the adjacent pier, is reminiscent of Quercia's *Angel Gabriel* (San Gimignano, Collegiata). The treatment of the massive tubular folds of S Ansano's robe recalls Quercia's handling of the garments of the saints in the Trenta altarpiece (Lucca, S Frediano). The figure of *St Vittore* (*c*. 1457–8; see fig.) on the third pier is less subtle but more dramatic; barely contained within the niche, the warrior saint gazes defiantly into the distance. The intensity of his expression is accentuated by the straining tendons of his neck and the exaggerated folds of his voluminous mantle. In spirit, the saint is reminiscent of Donatello's *St George* (Florence, Or San Michele). Donatello was in Siena at this time (1457–61) and was offered the commission to carve a statue of *St Bernardino* (unexecuted) for the same Loggia.

A marble bench (*c*. 1459–64; *in situ*) for the Loggia, ornamented with reliefs of ancient Roman heroes on the front and the nursing she-wolf with her human charges on the reverse, has also been attributed to Federighi. The heavy foliated carving of the *all'antica* garlands demonstrates the sculptor's assimilation of both classical form and technique.

In 1459 Federighi was paid for a marble intarsia of the *Parable of the Blind* for the pavement of the choir of Siena Cathedral. The following year he began work on the Loggia del Papa, Siena (*c*. 1460–62), for Pius II. The small, three-bay loggia is exceptional for its lack of sculptural detail. The Pope's sister, Caterina, selected Federighi to work on the Palazzo Piccolomini, Siena (1462–3). It was probably designed by Bernardo Rossellino, with Federighi assuming a largely supervisory role. Federighi also executed the tomb monument to *Vittoria Fortiguerra and Silvius Piccolomini* (Siena, S Francesco, destr. 1655), the parents of the Pope. Pius composed the Latin epitaph located below the half-length posthumous portraits for which Federighi was paid in 1460.

Two holy water basins (Siena Cathedral), described as newly made in an inventory of 1467, are also attributed to Federighi. They resemble antique candelabra and are richly decorated with lush garlands, palmettes, sphinxes and dolphins. They combine antique motifs with contemporary fantasy; the four bound, nude figures ornamenting the neck of one of the basins are sometimes cited as the modest precursors of Michelangelo's *Slaves* (Paris, Louvre; Florence, Accad.) for the tomb of *Julius II*. A marble statuette of *Bacchus* (Siena, Monte dei Paschi) is related to

Antonio Federighi: *St Vittore*, marble, *c.* 1457–8 (Siena, Loggia di Mercanzia)

perhaps the first sculptural image of Bacchus since antiquity, represents a further development of Federighi's assimilation of the Classical vocabulary.

In 1468 Federighi was involved in the construction of the upper storey of the Cappella del Campo, Siena. He designed the intarsia panel depicting the *Seven Ages of Man* for the cathedral (Siena, Mus. Opera Duomo) in 1475. In 1480 he was appointed supervisor of the water pipes that service the fountains of Siena. Federighi's increased civic responsibilities and absences due to illness meant that he spent less time in the cathedral workshop, and he was relieved of his duties as *capomaestro* in 1481. His last commission was to design a marble intarsia of the *Erythraean Sibyl* (1481–2) for the south aisle of the cathedral. An octagonal font for the Cappella di S Giovanni Battista (Siena Cathedral) can no longer be regarded as an autograph work since the chapel was constructed after 1482. Various wooden sculptures, including the statuettes of *St Ambrose* and *St Augustine* and the larger *St Nicholas of Bari* (all Siena, Pal. Pub.), have been attributed to Federighi, but none of these figures is stylistically consistent with the sculptor's marble works.

BIBLIOGRAPHY

Thieme–Becker

G. Milanesi: *Documenti per la storia dell'arte senese*, 3 vols (Siena, 1854–6)
A. Schmarsow: 'Antonio Federighi de' Tolomei, ein sienesischer Bildhauer des Quattrocento', *Repert. Kstwiss.*, xii (1889), pp. 277–99
R. H. H. Cust: *The Pavement Masters of Siena, 1369–1562* (London, 1901)
P. Schubring: *Die Plastik Sienas im Quattrocento* (Berlin, 1907)
E. Carli: *La scultura lignea senese* (Milan and Florence, 1951)
B. Mantura: 'Contributo ad Antonio Federighi', *Commentari*, xix (1968), pp. 98–110
C. Del Bravo: *Scultura senese del quattrocento* (Florence, 1970)
A. Bagnoli: 'Antonio Federighi', *Jacopo della Quercia nell'arte del suo tempo* (Florence, 1975), pp. 294–305
J. T. Paoletti: 'Antonio Federighi: A Documentary Re-evaluation', *Jb. Berlin. Mus.*, xvii (1975), pp. 87–143
E. Carli: *Il Duomo di Siena* (Genoa, 1979)
——: *Gli scultori senesi* (Milan, 1980)
E. Richter: *The Sculpture of Antonio Federighi* (diss., Columbia U., New York, 1984)
L. Martini: 'Antonio Federighi', *Donatello e i suoi* (Florence, 1986), pp. 221–4

ELINOR M. RICHTER

Federigo Parmense. *See* BONZAGNA, GIAN FEDERIGO.

Feders [Fedders; Feder], **Jūlijs (Voldemars)** [Yuly (Ivanovich); Yuly (Bogdanovich)] (*b* Koknese, Latvia, 19 June 1838; *d* Nezhin, Ukraine, 14 Feb 1909). Latvian painter and teacher. He was the first artist to concentrate on the representation of the Latvian landscape and as such is considered the founder of the Latvian school of landscape painting. Assigned (1856–62) to the studio of Sokrat Vorob'yov (1817–88) at the St Petersburg Academy of Arts, he developed an approach to landscape that moved away from academic romanticism towards *plein-air* realism and that was more akin to that of his fellow students Ivan Shishkin and Lev Kamenev (1833–86), founder-members of the WANDERERS, than to his teacher's. However, on the death of his father in 1863, he lost his means of support and was forced to teach art and photography in Mitava (now Jelgava), thereafter principally maintaining contact with the Academy by sending works to its spring exhibitions. He maintained a lifelong attraction to the local countryside in Latvia, which he depicted in many paintings (e.g. *Landscape with Storm-clouds*, 1873; *After the Storm*,

the heroic, struggling nudes on the basin. All exhibit the same widespread stance, sinewy limbs, locked knees, ample pelvises and broad, muscular shoulders. The modelling of the *Bacchus* is, however, considerably softer as befits his inebriated, self-indulgent state. This faunlike creature,

1874; the *Ruins of Koknese Castle*, 1904; all Riga, Latv. Mus. F.A.). From 1874 he travelled extensively, visiting Norway, France, Spain and, in 1875–6, Germany, where he studied with his fellow Balt Eugen Dücker, a professor of landscape painting at the Kunstakademie in Düsseldorf. Feders then moved to Belgorod (now in Russia), north of Kharkiv (Ukraine), where he worked for ten years as art teacher at the Pedagogical Institute. During this time he became an academician (1880) and made many studies of the Ukrainian landscape (e.g. *Near Svyatogorsk Monastery*, 1882; Moscow, Tret'yakov Gal.). In 1886 he was appointed to teach art at St Petersburg Commercial School, a position he held until 1898. His studio became a meeting-place for the younger generation of Latvian artists then studying in the Russian capital, among them the founders of the new progressive Latvian nationalist group THE GNOME (Rūķis), whose members included Ādams Alksnis (1864–97), Janis Rozentāls, Vilhelms Purvītis and Jānis Valters. This contact and environment proved significant not only for the young artists but also for Feders, who visited Latvia almost every summer and painted some of his most atmospheric scenes and his finest studies of light and shade during these years, for example *Gauja Valley* (1891; Riga, City A. Mus.), *Fishermen's Nest* (1886) and *Pērse River* (1894; both Riga, Latv. Mus. F.A.). In 1898 he retired to Belgorod.

BIBLIOGRAPHY

A. Eglītis and A. Lapiņš: *Jūlijs Feders* (Riga, 1956), Rus. trans. as A. Eglit and A. Lapin': *Yu. Fedders* (Riga, 1958)

J. Siliņš: *Latvijas māksla, 1800–1914* [Latvian art, 1800–1914], ii (Stockholm, 1979), pp. 227–36

JEREMY HOWARD

Fedotov, Pavel (Andreyevich) (*b* Moscow, 4 July 1815; *d* St Petersburg, 26 Nov 1852). Russian painter and draughtsman. He was noted for his satirical critique of Russian life of the mid-19th century. He attended the First Moscow Military School (1826–33), then served in St Petersburg in the Finnish Regiment Life-Guards. While earning a reputation as an honest and hard-working officer, he drew a great deal, played the flute and took part in amateur theatrical performances. Having become established as the regimental artist, in 1834 he began to attend evening classes at the St Petersburg Academy of Arts. In November 1843, after a long period of doubt, he resigned his commission in the army in order to become a professional artist. He began to attend the Academy regularly and joined the battle-painting class of Aleksander Zauerveid (1783–1844), but he was soon attracted to genre painting. He was greatly helped by the painter Karl Bryullov, who recognized his talent.

Fedotov's pictures from the 1830s, when he had not yet mastered the technique of oil painting, are largely concerned with military life, although Fedotov also made copies of Classical and Romantic works, and sketches from life. Many of Fedotov's early watercolours are painted skilfully and with an engaging freedom, for example the *Arrival of Grand Prince Mikhail Pavlovich at the Camp of the Finnish Regiment Lifeguards* (1837), the *Grenadier Lifeguards' Bivouac* and the *Pavlovsk Regiment Lifeguards' Bivouac* (1841–2; St Petersburg, Rus. Mus.). A new stage in his creative work, marking the emergence of a critical

spirit, is seen in a series of eight sepia drawings on the manners of the day. These were largely produced in 1844, immediately after Fedotov's departure from military life. They show scenes of town life with people of various ranks and classes: functionaries, merchants, doctors, artists, officers, aristocrats and paupers; in short, a cross-section of a typical Russian town of the mid-19th century. The sharpest criticism is seen in the exposure of the manners of the poorer people, as in *Fido's Last Illness* (1844), *Beauty for the Poor Girl is the Scythe of Death* or *The Shop* (1844–6; all Moscow, Tret'yakov Gal.). The anecdotal richness and moral clarity of such scenes renders commentary almost superfluous.

In the first of his oil paintings, the genre scene *A Newly Decorated Knight* (1846; Moscow, Tret'yakov Gal.), Fedotov remained stylistically close to his work in sepia, although the composition is notably more compact. The picture shows a functionary who has been given his first medal, which he is proudly showing to the cook, who is also his mistress. He is ridiculously wrapped up in a dressing-gown showing traces of the previous evening's drinking, also suggested by many other details in the picture. The scene is both comic and deplorable and very effectively exposes the empty conceit of officialdom. Aesthetically, it has weaknesses: abundance of detail detracts from its impact. However, in his next oil painting, the *Fastidious Bride* (1847; Moscow, Tret'yakov Gal.), Fedotov showed clear advances in style and technique. The picture shows a woman, no longer young, forced to accept an ugly, hunchbacked suitor. The scene, however, does not aim to provoke censure but rather to elicit sympathy. Fedotov does not exaggerate the ugliness of the figures, and his overall treatment argues for their vindication. Details of dress and decor are finely executed.

In 1848 Fedotov painted the picture for which he is best known: *The Major's Marriage Proposal* (1848; Moscow, Tret'yakov Gal.; version *c*. 1851, St Petersburg, Rus. Mus.; see fig.), for which he was made an Academician. In this painting Fedotov successfully combines the bitter and the absurd in the subject of the courtship of a rich merchant's daughter by an elderly, ruined officer. The setting, the merchant's house, is attractive and the characters are depicted in a world of splendid things, very beautifully painted. The scene is reminiscent of a lively theatrical performance and has been associated with the play *Zhenit'ba* (The marriage), by Nikolay Gogol', first performed in 1842. Fedotov reveals, in the sudden eruption of disorder, the inhuman social conventions that may distort human relationships. Fedotov's use of the marriage motif is typical of Russian painting in the mid-19th century; he also used card games, social festivities and meals, as in the *Poor Aristocrat's Breakfast* (1849–50; Moscow, Tret'yakov Gal.), where proof of the aristocrat's hypocrisy is found in his attempt to hide from arriving visitors the coarse slab of bread that is evidence of his poverty.

Fedotov's drawings from these years are closely linked to his paintings in their themes. With the artist Yevstafy Bernadsky (1819–89), he intended to publish prints based on a series of satirical scenes of everyday life, to be accompanied by inscriptions, often in verse form. This series was especially critical of the world of functionaries, contractors and small-minded townspeople. The plan,

Pavel Fedotov: *The Major's Marriage Proposal*, oil on canvas, 583×754 mm, *c.* 1851 (St Petersburg, Russian Museum)

however, came to nothing: the two artists were found to have links with a revolutionary group, the *petrashevtsy*. Fedotov was severely reprimanded, and he spent the remaining years of his life alone, in poverty and increasing mental instability, though still managing to paint.

In his last years, however, Fedotov abandoned satirical subjects. In *The Widow* (1851; Ivanovo, Reg. A. Mus.; two versions in Moscow, Tret'yakov Gal.) he is not concerned to tell a story or point a moral but rather to show the sadness of the woman's fate in a spirit of compassion. The subject is personal rather than social, although the woman is also able to represent the condition of all women. In Fedotov's late work there are also Romantic themes, notably the ideas of solitude, opposition to society and the refusal to accept the painful aspects of reality. These are especially clear in *Encore, Again Encore* (1851–2; Moscow, Tret'yakov Gal.): the painting shows an officer training a dog in the semi-darkness of a peasant's hut, but the scene is imbued with a feeling of frustration and sadness at the meaninglessness of life and the tragedy of inaction. The figure of the officer, dissolving in the shadows, is deprived of any individual features. The colouring contains a mixture of warm and cool tones that induces an effect of instability. Fedotov's last picture, *The Gamblers* (1852; Kiev, Mus. Rus. A.), conveys a sense of a world transformed into a realm of shadows. The painting's restless composition plays on the alternation of

the seated and standing figures of the gamblers in the candlelit room, their unsteady poses casting flickering shadows on the walls and ceiling. The melodramatic element is increased by the dark corners, the corridors and the empty picture frames on the wall.

Fedotov also painted portraits in both watercolour and oils. Among his best watercolour works are a *Group of Colleagues* (1840; Moscow, Tret'yakov Gal.) and the *Druzhinin Brothers* (1840; St Petersburg, Rus. Mus.). In these the use of line is refined, precise and gentle. Among Fedotov's oil portraits, his treatment of women is poetic, and the sitters have an air of ingenuousness, gentleness and trustfulness. The most important of these works is the portrait of *N. Zhdanovich at the Piano* (1849; St Petersburg, Rus. Mus.). Here genre and portrait combine in Fedotov's attempt to convey the complexity of the sitter's character. Late works, such as the portrait of the *Zherbin Children* (*c.* 1851; St Petersburg, Rus. Mus.), do not differ greatly in style from works of the 1840s.

Fedotov's love of the Dutch painters of the 17th century is reflected in his own work, in particular his interest in the principles by which Dutch genre scenes were constructed and the means by which narrative was carried in gesture and movement. An even more important influence, however, was the work of the English 18th-century genre painter William Hogarth, who interested many European artists in the 19th century. Commentators have also referred to the printmakers Paul Gavarni and Honoré Daumier, and Fedotov was, indeed, sometimes called the 'Russian Gavarni'. Fedotov also clearly paid attention to the Russian popular print (*lubok*) linking image and text, and he naturally absorbed the traditions of Russian painting, particularly the elements of genre painting in the 1820s in the work of Aleksander Orlovsky, Vasily Tropinin and, in particular, Aleksey Venetsianov. He has, however, proved more popular with a very large public than any of these.

BIBLIOGRAPHY

G. Nedoshivin: *Pavel Andreyevich Fedotov, 1815–1852* (Moscow, 1945)
Ya. Leshchinsky: *Pavel Andreyevich Fedotov, khudozhnik i poet* [Pavel Andreyevich Fedotov, artist and poet] (Leningrad, 1946)
D. V. Sarab'yanov: *P. A. Fedotov i russkaya khudozhestvennaya kul'tura 40-x gg. XIX v.* [P. A. Fedotov and Russian art in the 1840s] (Moscow, 1973)
G. A. Zagyanskaya: *P. A. Fedotov* (Moscow, 1977)
D. V. Sarab'yanov: *Pavel Andreyevich Fedotov* (Leningrad, 1985)

G. A. PRINTSEVA

Fehling, Heinrich Christoph (*b* Sangerhausen, *bapt* 23 April 1654; *d* Dresden, 1725). German painter, draughtsman and teacher. He was a cousin and pupil of SAMUEL BOTTSCHILD, to whom he was apprenticed until 1672 and with whom he travelled to Italy in 1673–7, to study the works of Italian masters and ancient sculptures. After his return he settled in Dresden, where he was appointed court painter by Elector John-George IV (*reg* 1691–4). With Bottschild he worked on three ceiling paintings (completed after 1693; destr. 1945) in the Palais in the Grosser Garten (destr. 1945) in Dresden. He also produced wall paintings (destr.) in the Dresden palaces of Lubomirski (destr. 1760) and Vitzthum (destr. 1786).

After Bottschild's death in 1706, Fehling was made chief court painter and inspector of art works by Elector Augustus II, who also put him in charge of the Malerakademie. His pupils here included Christian Friedrich Zincke (1687–1770), Paul Christian Zincke (1687–1770) and Christian Benjamin Müller (1690–1758). Probably after 1717, when it was completed, he took over the ceiling painting in the Marmorsaal in the French pavilion of the Dresden Zwinger (destr. 1945). A mythological allegory of Augustus II, this ceiling was decorated with animated, isolated figures in the bright colours of the Rococo style, floating in a nebulous expanse.

As a portrait painter, Fehling favoured the full-length or three-quarter-length portrait, as in his depictions of the electors of Saxony and members of their families. Characteristic examples have survived in the group portrait of *Aurora von Königsmark and her Sisters* (Moritzburg, Jagdschloss) and the portrait of master builder *Wolf Caspar von Klengel* (1691; Dresden, Gemäldegal. Alte Meister). Other portraits by Fehling are reproduced in engravings by Johann Martin Bernigeroth (1713–67), Johann Christian Boecklin (1657–1709) and Johann Georg Wolffgang (1662/4–1744). Few of his drawings have survived (Berlin, Kupferstichkab.; Windsor Castle, Berks, Royal Col.; Dresden, Kupferstichkab.).

BIBLIOGRAPHY

Thieme–Becker
F. Löffler: 'Die Monumentalmalerei des Barock in Dresden', *Jb. Pf. Kst.*, iv (1956), pp. 5–23
H. Menz: 'Ein Bildnis von Christoph Fehling', *Dresdn. Kstbl.* (1962), pp. 151–3

H. Marx: 'Der Zwinger und die Farbe', *Jb. Staatl. Kstsamml. Dresden*, xiv (1982), pp. 7–35

CHRISTIAN DITTRICH

Fehling, Hermann (*b* Hyères, France, 10 Sept 1909). German architect. He studied architecture at the Baugewerkschule in Hamburg, although he first worked as a joiner's apprentice. He was in private practice in Berlin from 1945 until 1953, when he formed a partnership with Daniel Gogel (*b* 1927), also working with Peter Pfankuch (1925–77), a former assistant to Hans Scharoun until 1958. Fehling and Gogel made their name in Berlin with the pavilion for the *Interbau* exhibition (1956–7) at Hansaviertel, Berlin, and by winning second prize in the Berlin Philharmonie competition (1956). Thereafter came a series of distinctive buildings, including seven private houses, two churches, two parish centres and a student village, as well as housing, shops, offices and exhibitions. A worklist of 1980 contains 18 competition entries, of which 12 gained prizes, eight being firsts.

Rooted in the architectural culture of Berlin, the work of Fehling and Gogel is neither well known nor well understood elsewhere. With its functional articulation of elements, its emphasis on space and transparency, and its frequent departures from orthogonal convention in plan, it suggests affinities with the work of such architects as Hans Scharoun and Erich Mendelsohn (for whom Fehling worked between 1929 and 1930), but detailed comparison reveals crucial differences in planning, geometry and construction, which make their work innovative and unique. Some of the greatest critical acclaim for the practice centred on a number of scientific institutes, including the Max-Planck-Institut für Bildungsforschung in Berlin (1965–74), the Max-Planck-Institut für Astrophysik at Garching near Munich (1975–9) and the offices for the European Southern Observatory (1976–80), also at Garching. Their dramatic multi-level foyer spaces are also used for concerts and parties.

BIBLIOGRAPHY

P. Bucciarelli: *L'architettura di Fehling e Gogel, Vitalità dell'espressionismo* (Bari, 1981)
Fehling+Gogel (exh. cat., ed. J. Conrads and M. Sack; Berlin and Brunswick, 1981)
J. Janofskei: 'Renunciation of Form in the Interest of Life', *Archit. Rev.*, clxxvii/2060 (June 1985), pp. 56–64
Fehling+Gogel, Grundrissanalysen (exh. cat., Berlin, Gal. Aedes, 1986)

PETER BLUNDELL JONES

Fehn, Sverre (*b* Kongsberg, 14 Aug 1924). Norwegian architect. He graduated from the Oslo School of Architecture in 1949 and joined a group of young architects who, under the leadership of Arne Korsmo, founded a Norwegian division of CIAM. Their aim was to oppose the New Empiricism dominant in Scandinavia after World War II, and to continue the endeavours of the Modern Movement. From the beginning Fehn stood out as the most important talent in Norwegian post-war architecture. The House of Crafts (1949–56), Maihaugen, Lillehammer, and the Økern Home for the Elderly (1955), Oslo, were both built in collaboration with Geir Grung (*b* 1926). The Økern Home (since enlarged) was built as a large, low, concrete-and-glass block in an old manorial park. It enclosed two gardens, each *c.* 1 km square. The pensioners lived in rooms with direct access either to one of the gardens or to balconies with views out over the park. Villa Bødtker (1967), the Bøler Civic Centre (1972) and the Skådalen Residential School (1976–7) are all in Oslo. In contrast to the monolithic home for the elderly, the school was built as a cluster of small blocks, an arrangement that gave the students some variety when walking from their rooms to class. The variety and visual interest were enhanced by the mixture of building materials: wood, red brick and raw concrete. In the Hedmarksmuseet at Hamar (1973), Fehn harmoniously combined the remains of the medieval building with his own modern addition. Fehn's talent found a particularly convincing expression in the mounting of art exhibitions, including the Norwegian Pavilion at the Brussels Exposition Universelle of 1958 and the Scandinavian Pavilion at the Venice Biennales of 1959 and 1964.

NKL

BIBLIOGRAPHY

U. Grønvold: 'Linjer Hos Fehn' [Projects by Sverre Fehn], *Bygkst*, lxvi/1 (1984), pp. 15–40

——: 'Det presise Uttrykk' [The precise expression], *Bygkst*, lxvii/6 (1985), pp. 332–53

C. Norberg-Schulz: *Modern Norwegian Architecture* (Oslo, 1986)

CHRISTIAN NORBERG-SCHULZ

Fehr [née Fuld], **Gertrude** (*b* Mainz, 5 March 1895). German photographer. She studied photography from 1918 to 1921 with Eduard Wasow. After this she ran a photographic portrait studio in Munich until 1933, specializing increasingly in theatre photography. After her marriage to the Swiss painter Jules Fehr (1890–1971) in 1939 she went to Paris, where she opened the photography school Publi-Phot. During this period she became prominent through her experiments with solarization, double exposure, photomontage and the photogram. In the same year she founded the Ecole Fehr in Lausanne, training well-known photographers such as Jeanloup Sieff. After the incorporation of the school into the Ecole des Arts et Métiers in 1945 she withdrew from full-time teaching and worked as a freelance photographer in Territet, Switzerland.

BIBLIOGRAPHY

Gertrude Fehr, Fotografien seit 1918 (exh. cat. by O. Ruppen and W. Boje, Munich, Stadtmus., 1980)

R. Misselbeck: 'Gertrude Fehr zum 90. Geburtstag', *Intern: Vjschr. Dt. Ges. Phot.*, iii (1985), pp. 133–6

Deutsche Lichtbildner–Wegbereiter der zeitgenössischen Photographie (exh. cat. by R. Misselbeck, Cologne, Mus. Ludwig, 1987), p. 124

REINHOLD MISSELBECK

Fei, Alessandro (di Vincenzio) [Barbiere, Alessandro del] (*b* Florence, ?1538–43; *d* ?Florence, 1592). Italian painter. As a youth he was an apprentice in the workshops of the Florentine painters Ridolfo Ghirlandaio and Pierfrancesco Foschi. From 1564 he was enrolled at the Accademia del Disegno in Florence and in 1565 he began to work for Giorgio Vasari, painting a series of canvases for the decoration of the Salone del Cinquecento (Florence, Pal. Vecchio). Fei collaborated with Maso da San Friano, whose work in S Pietro in Gattolino, Florence, is linked stylistically to Fei's *Virgin Suckling the Infant Christ with Two Angels* of 1568. Around 1570 he painted one of his most famous works, the *Goldsmith's Workshop*, in the *studiolo* of Grand Duke Francesco I de' Medici in the Palazzo Vecchio (*in situ*), in which Tuscan late Mannerism

is combined with an almost Flemish attention to narrative detail. In 1571, following Vasari, he was in Rome, where he worked in the Vatican on the papal chapels in the Torre Pio. After his return to Florence he worked at Santa Croce, where he painted the signed and dated *Flagellation* (1575; *in situ*), which shows a mixture of Tuscan and Roman influences, particularly from the Zuccaro brothers. Other paintings from this period are the fresco for the great cloister of S Maria Novella, Florence, the *Annunciation* of S Nicolò Oltrarno and the *Virgin and Saints* in S Maria delle Grazie, Pistoia. In 1585 he painted four canvases of *Christ and the Apostles* for S Giovannino degli Scolopi, Florence. A year later he was commissioned by Lorenzo de' Medici to do his portrait. The *Virgin of the Rosary* (Vicchio di Mugello, S Giovanni Battista) and *S Pancrazio* (Valdelsa, Parrochiale di S Pancrazio) are also from this period. In 1589 he collaborated on the festive decorations for the wedding of the Grand Duke Ferdinand I de' Medici and Christine of Lorraine. According to Borghini and Baldinucci (confirmed by Susinno), Fei spent some time in Messina, producing a cycle of 12 painted stone tiles set in the mosaic of the *Virgin of the Ciambretta* (Messina, S Gregorio). Following this, five stone tiles painted with scenes from the *Life of the Virgin* (*c.* 1582; Messina, Mus. Reg.) have been attributed to Fei.

BIBLIOGRAPHY

G. Vasari: *Vite* (1550, rev. 2/1568); ed. G. Milanesi (1878–85), vii, pp. 620–21

R. Borghini: *Il riposo* (1584); ed. M. Rosci (Milan, 1967), pp. 632–7

F. Baldinucci: *Notizie* (1681–1728); ed. F. Ranalli (1845–7), rev. P. Barocchi (Florence, 1974), iii, pp. 527–8

F. Susinno: *Le vite de' pittori messinesi* (MS.; 1724); ed. V. Martinelli (Florence, 1960), p. 94

A. M. P. Tofani: 'Firenze e la Toscana dei Medici nell'Europa del cinquecento', *Il primato del disegno* (exh. cat., ed. L. Berti; Florence, Pal. Strozzi, 1980), p. 111

F. Campagna Cicala: 'Presenze fiorentine a Messina nella seconda metà del cinquecento', *Quad. Ist. Stor. A. Med. & Mod.*, 9–10 (1985–6), pp. 21–37

GIOVANNA FAMA

Fei, Paolo di Giovanni. *See* PAOLO DI GIOVANNI FEI.

Feibush Ashkenazi. *See* JOEL BEN SIMEON.

Feichtmayer [Feichtmeyr]. German family of stuccoists and sculptors. This extensive family from Wessobrunn in upper Bavaria were, along with the FEUCHTMAYERs (a distinct family), the ZIMMERMANNs and the SCHMUZERs, leading figures in the Wessobrunn school, which played a leading role in south German architecture and decoration in the 18th century. The first major artists in the family were the sons of Michael Feichtmayer (1667–1706): (1) Johann Michael Feichtmayer and (2) Franz Xaver Feichtmayer (i), who often worked with their younger brother Anton Feichtmayer (*b* 1700). Franz Xaver Feichtmayer (i) married four times and had three children by his third wife: Maria Theresia (*b* 1729), who married Jakob Rauch; Simpert Feichtmayer (1732–1806), a stuccoist and barrel-painter; and (3) Franz Xaver Feichtmayer (ii), a stuccoist at the court in Munich.

BIBLIOGRAPHY

NDB; Thieme–Becker

P. von Stetten: *Kunst-, Gewerb- und Handwerksgeschichte der Reichs-Stadt Augsburg*, i (Augsburg, 1779), p. 443

F. J. Lipowsky: *Baierisches Künstler-Lexikon* (Munich, 1810), p. 70

G. Hager: 'Die Bautätigkeit und Kunstpflege im Kloster Wessobrunn und die Wessobrunner Stukkatoren', *Oberbayer. Archv Vaterländ. Gesch.*, xliv (1893–4), pp. 195–512

B. Pfeiffer: 'Die Künstlerfamilie Feichtmayer', *Schwäb. Archv*, xxix (1911), pp. 177–87

S. Grän: *Wallfahrts- und Klosterkirche Grafrath* (Munich and Zurich, 1981)

K. Kosel: 'Augsburger Barockkünstler in Stams', *Jb. Ver. Augsburg. Bistumsgesch.*, xviii (1984), pp. 383–407

H. Schnell and U. Schedler: *Lexikon der Wessobrunner Stukkatoren* (Munich, 1988), p. 70

(1) Johann Michael Feichtmayer (*b* Haid, 17 Oct 1696; *d* Augsburg, 4 June 1772). He settled in Augsburg with his brothers and was apprenticed to the Augsburg master mason Johann Paulus from 1722 to 1725. He became one of the town's foremost Rococo craftsmen, generally working in a large communal workshop with other artists. On his first authenticated job (1721–4), at the former Dominikanerkirche in Augsburg, he worked with his brothers. His workshop association with (2) Franz Xaver Feichtmayer continued until *c.* 1745. Between 1736 and 1749, and from 1759, he worked regularly with JOHANN GEORG ÜBLHER. When engaged on large commissions outside Augsburg, he collaborated with regional sculptors, such as Johann Joseph Christian at Zwiefalten and Ottobeuren or Johann Georg Weckenmann at Haigerloch and Sigmaringen. Possible contacts with the workshop of Joseph Anton Feuchtmayer would explain the increasing frequency with which the latter's motifs appear in Feichtmayer's later work.

In 1736–7 Feichtmayer did stuccowork in Diessen am Ammersee Abbey Church in association with his brother Franz Xaver and Üblher, working presumably from François Cuvilliés's designs. His works at Münsterschwarzach (1736–49) have been destroyed. He worked with Üblher on stuccos in the transepts and choir at Wilhering Abbey Church from 1741 to 1746, producing powerful rocaille forms interspersed with gnarledwork; Feichtmayer is also recorded as the altar builder and as a sculptor in plaster, though the plaster sculptures on the altars are by Üblher. Between 1745 and 1751 he did work in the former abbey at Amorbach, emerging for the first time as the leading force in the association consisting of his brothers and Üblher.

Between 1747 and 1758 Feichtmayer was engaged on the decoration of Zwiefalten Abbey. Deep-relief cartouches composed of broad S-shaped gnarledwork cover all the wall and ceiling surfaces above the main cornice. The big cartouches on the spandrels anchor Franz Joseph Spiegler's large frescoes within the spatial structure. The altars in stucco marble are also by Feichtmayer, while the sculptures are by Johann Joseph Christian. The broad-based altar is developed along the lines of a triumphal arch, with heavy rocaille and gnarled ornamentation, introduced in a way that evokes architectural forms: coiled rocaille motifs in place of capitals and bases, and very extended, long drawn-out prongs of gnarledwork as pilasters. This concept of the altar, still basically founded on the classic, architecturally constructed retable, also shapes Feichtmayer's other altars. Thus even in the side altars that do not mimic architectural forms, where the gnarledwork is drawn out into long, deeply curving pilaster strips, there is still a feeling of architecture. The visually distracting use of ornament does not mask the basic construction of the altar, as was the case in more or less contemporaneous altars by Joseph Anton Feuchtmayer.

After work at Bruchsal (Schloss and St Peter, 1751–6; destr. 1945) and a number of smallish commissions, from 1754 Feichtmayer was engaged on the masterpiece of his maturity, the stuccowork and altar decorations for the abbey at Ottobeuren (see fig.). Here the flowing stuccos with their expansive curves consist of gnarledwork using S-shapes, which is interspersed with plaques and flower tendrils; they are concentrated on a small number of surfaces and accentuate the architecture of Johann Michael Fischer. Larger-than-life plaster figures on the main cornice are documented as Feichtmayer's, as are the plaster reliefs above the confessional boxes and in the nave. The stucco marble altars are partly created by heavy ornamentation and bear sculptures by Christian. The way in which the side altars are framed with far-projecting gnarledwork brackets is typical. Feichtmayer's superstructure above the choir-stalls and the organ front seems influenced by Joseph Anton Feuchtmayer's series of engravings.

In 1757–60 Feichtmayer decorated the altars at Sigmaringen Pfarrkirche. His last major work was the stuccowork in the interior and for the altars at the pilgrimage church,

Johann Michael Feichtmayer: stuccowork at the abbey at Ottobeuren, begun 1754

Vierzehnheiligen, which is more restrained than that at Zwiefalten and Ottobeuren. The figures were strongly influenced by Üblher, who was Feichtmayer's associate for the contract but died before work began; his workshop associates continued their work under Feichtmayer's direction. The Gnadenaltar here must be the Feichtmayers' most original. A canopy supported by concave brackets of gnarledwork rises over slanting rocaille consoles that project in wide outward curves. The altar is surrounded by a heart-shaped gallery, which is emphasized by the placing of statues on the diagonal axes. The high altar and the side altars have an architectural superstructure, with numerous references to Feuchtmayer's engravings.

Three series of copper engravings of rocaille cartouches by Feichtmayer are known.

BIBLIOGRAPHY

A. Buff: 'Die Anfänge der Stuccatorkunst in Augsburg bis in das 18. Jahrhundert', *Z. Hist. Ver. Schwaben & Neuburg*, xxiii (1896), pp. 1–72
W. P. Fuchs: 'Die Tätigkeit des Wessobrunner Stukkators Johann Michael Feichtmayer in Württemberg', *Archv Christ. Kst*, xxxiv (1916), pp. 12–21
R. Guby: 'Die Stiftskirche zu Wilhering und Engelszell: 2 unbekannte Werke der Wessobrunner Stukkatoren im oberösterreichischen Donautal', *Jb. Ksthist. Inst. Wien*, xii (1918), pp. 76–114
E. Michalski: *Joseph Christian* (Berlin, 1926), pp. 49–59
N. Lieb: 'Die Feichtmayr–Christian Frage in Ottobeuren', *Z. Bayer. Landesgesch.*, iv (1931), pp. 175–87
E. Lutze: *Barockplastik im Germanischen Nationalmuseum Nürnberg* (Nuremberg, 1935), pp. 83–91
E. Petri: *Johann Michael Feichtmayer: Ein Beitrag zur Geschichte des deutschen Rokoko* (diss., U. Munich, 1935)
U. Huber: *Die Zusammenarbeit des Joseph Christian und des Johann Michael Feichtmayer in Zwiefalten und Ottobeuren* (diss., U. Tübingen, 1949)
H. Bauer: *Die Rocaille* (Munich, 1962); reviewed in *J. Soc. Archit. Hist.*, xxvi (1967), pp. 158–60
B. Hubensteiner: 'Die Donauklöster Wilhering und Engelszell: Glanzlichter des bayrisch-österreichischen Barock', *Ostbair. Grenzmarken*, x (1968), pp. 5–11
K. Kolb: *Käppele: Rokoko-Kleinod in Würzburg* (Würzburg, 1976)
H. Huth: *Schloss Bruchsal: Die ehemalige Residenz des Fürstbischofs von Speyer* (Königsstein, 1977)
E.-C. Vollmer: 'Zur Stuckdekoration der Wallfahrtskirche Maria Steinbach an der Iller', *A. Bavar.*, ix (1978), pp. 41–50
H.-R. Heyer: *Der Dom zu Arlesheim* (Arlesheim, 1981)
H. D. Ingenhoff: 'Die Münsterkirche in Zwiefalten: Beobachtungen am barocken Gesamtkunstwerk', *Pantheon*, xi (1982), pp. 201–10
N. Jocher: 'Die Stuckatoren von Vierzehnheiligen', *Die Restauration der Wallfahrtskirche Vierzehnheiligen*, ser. 49/1, Bayerisches Landesamt für Denkmalpflege (Munich, 1990), pp. 113–18

(2) Franz Xaver Feichtmayer (i) (*b* Wessobrunn, 11 Aug 1698; *d* Augsburg, before 21 Aug 1763). Brother of (1) Johann Michael Feichtmayer. Apart from him, he was the foremost stuccoist of the Rococo period in Augsburg. He presumably trained in his father's workshop; from 1721 to 1724 he was working for Georg Paulus, mason and clerk of works for Augsburg. In his early years he shared a workshop with Johann Michael and Johann Georg Üblher. In 1721–4 he worked with his brothers to create delicately wrought strapwork stuccos at the Dominican church in Augsburg. In 1731–4 he decorated the Cistercian abbey church at Stams with rich strapwork stucco, working this time with Joseph Fischer from Füssen. He again worked with Johann Michael at Diessen am Ammersee (1736–7). He also frequently worked with the fresco painter Matthäus Günther.

From *c.* 1740 Feichtmayer worked with powerful rocaille motifs, composed of numerous C-curves, often with leaves and plants applied on to them, as at the Herrgottsruh Pilgrimage Church (1737–53) and St Alban at Diessen (1739). From 1743 to 1751 he worked on the stucco decorations and high altar at Fiecht Abbey Church, and between 1743 and 1749 on stuccos (destr.) in the abbey church at Münsterschwarzach. In the many churches subsequently decorated by Feichtmayer the rocaille ornamentation was often built up from minute shapes superimposed on regular basic structures. After 1752 he regularly collaborated with his son-in-law, Jakob Rauch, who finally took over the major part of his work.

BIBLIOGRAPHY

M. Mayer: *Kleine Beiträge zur Kunstgeschichte Tirols* (1902), pp. 20ff
F. Wolf: 'Johann Michael Fischers Kirchenpläne von Ottobeuren', *Z. Dt. Ver. Kstwiss.*, xvii (1963), pp. 221–30
A. Lohmüller: *Wallfahrt zur Schmerzhaften Mutter Gottes Violau* (Munich and Zurich, 1964)
F. Wolf: 'Der Stuckator Franz Xaver Feichtmayer der Ältere und sein bedeutender Mitarbeiter Jakob Rauch', *Z. Hist. Ver. Schwaben & Neuburg*, lix–lx (1967), pp. 251–69
A. Maier: *Die Herrgottsruh* (Friedberg, 1968)
K. Diemer: 'Die Barockisierung der Klosterkirche Gutenzell, 1755–1770: Ein Beitrag zur Geschichte des oberschwäbischen Barock', *Z. Württemberg. Landesgesch.*, xli (1982), pp. 530–40
G. Paula: 'Die Barockisierung der Klosterkirche Indersdorf nach den Rechnungsbüchern von 1753–1755', *Amperland*, xviii (1982), pp. 326ff
F. Caramelle: 'Die Restaurierung der Stiftskirche Stams', *Österreich. Z. Kst & Dkmlpf.*, xxxviii (1984), pp. 110–17
M. Koller: 'Untersuchungsergebnisse zur Innenausstattung der Stiftskirche Stams', *Österreich. Z. Kst & Dkmlpf.*, xxxviii (1984), pp. 142–55
N. Jocher: *Johann Georg Üblher (1703–1763): Ein Beitrag zur Geschichte des Ornaments und der Stuckplastik Süddeutschlands im 18. Jahrhundert* (diss., U. Munich, 1986), pp. 54ff, 69ff, 98ff, 130ff

(3) Franz Xaver Feichtmayer (ii) (*b* Augsburg, 17 Oct 1735; *d* Munich, 6 Jan 1803). Son of (2) Franz Xaver Feichtmayer (i). His first training took place in the workshop of his father, then from 1752 he worked under Johann Baptist Zimmermann at the court in Munich. He did stuccowork in Schäftlarn Klosterkirche in 1754–6, perhaps with Zimmermann, and in 1756 worked at Freising on the Neustiftskirche under Zimmermann's direction. The Steinerne Saal (1756) at Schloss Nymphenburg in Munich is attributed to him. In 1758 he married Johann Baptist Zimmermann's widow and became stuccoist to the court in Munich.

Following designs by François Cuvilliés, Feichtmayer did work at the Munich Residenz (1760–63; destr. 1944), decorated the Festsaal at Schloss Sünching with elegant rocaille stuccowork (1761) and in 1763–9 did further work at Schloss Nymphenburg. Apart from much work in Augsburg town houses, in 1765 he did stuccos at Thierhaupten Klosterkirche, and in 1767 he decorated the Festsaal in the Schaezlerpalais in Augsburg. In 1766 the sculptor Roman Anton Boos, the painters Thomas Christian Winck and Andreas Seidl and Feichtmayer together founded a private drawing school; at first it was held in Feichtmayer's house, then in 1770 Elector Maximilian III Joseph proclaimed it a public art school.

Feichtmayer's stuccos were strongly influenced by the work of François Cuvilliés the elder and Zimmermann until *c.* 1770, when he adopted a Neo-classical repertory of forms; he integrated these into his systems of decoration, which were still rooted in Munich Rococo. The stuccos at Schloss Zell an der Pran (*c.* 1772) are an early example of work in a Louis XVI style. He decorated the

Bürgersaal in Munich in 1773–4 (destr. 1944). The stucco decoration and altars in the Klosterkirche of Rot an der Rot (1774–86) are mature works in the Neo-classical style.

In his sculptural work Franz Feichtmayer reveals the influence of Johann Georg Üblher. He published a series of copper engravings of rocaille and chinoiserie motifs in Augsburg.

BIBLIOGRAPHY
L. Hager: 'Instandgesetzte Stuckdecken in Schloss Nymphenburg und ihre Meister', *Dt. Kst- & Dkmlpf.*, xi (1953), pp. 58–62
F. Zimmermann: 'Die Künstler des Damenstiftsgebäudes in München (1784/85)', *S. Heimat*, xlv (1956), pp. 250–53
K. Kosel: 'Ein Spätwerk des François Cuvilliés: Neue Archivalien über bayerische Rokokokünstler', *Verhand. Hist. Ver. Oberpfalz & Regensburg*, cvii (1967), pp. 103–20
H. E. Millig: 'Zu den süddeutschen Schiffskanzeln', *Alte & Mod. Kst*, xiii (1968), pp. 19–26
R. Schneider and R. Kempter: *Bad Wurzach: Geschichte und Denkmäler* (Bad Wurzach, n.d.)

ULRICH KNAPP

Feichtmayr. *See* FEUCHTMAYER.

Feilden, Sir Bernard (Melchior) (*b* London, 11 Sept 1919). English architect and conservator. He studied at the Bartlett School of Architecture, University of London (1938), and the Architectural Association School, London (1946–9). After working in architects' offices in London and Norwich (1949–54), he entered private practice in Norwich and, in partnership (1954–77) with David Mawson, designed several buildings in the area such as Trinity Presbyterian Church (1954), some warehouses, housing and educational buildings including a group (1969) for the University of East Anglia, Norwich. Feilden was more widely known for his conservation and restoration work on historic buildings. In 1955 he took charge of a restoration programme for Norwich Cathedral and was subsequently appointed Cathedral Architect (1963–77). He also served as Surveyor to York Minster (1965–77), carrying out a major restoration programme, and as Surveyor to St Paul's Cathedral, London (1969–77), where he planned and supervised repair and restoration work at a time when the fabric of the cathedral was in increasing danger from ground settlement, pollution and traffic vibration. His conservation work was notable both for its technical expertise and its scholarship. A member of the Ancient Monuments Board from 1964–7, Feilden was later appointed the first director of the International Centre for Conservation (ICCROM), established in 1977 in Rome. He returned to England in 1982 to become an architectural consultant specializing in historic buildings and chairman of the English branch of the International Council on Monuments and Sites (ICOMOS). He also served on many other historical and conservation committees and was knighted in 1985.

WRITINGS
The Wonder of York Minster (York, 1976)
An Introduction to Conservation of Cultural Property (Paris, 1979)
Conservation of Historic Buildings (London, 1982)

BIBLIOGRAPHY
V. Tapner: 'Conservation Profile 4: Bernard Feilden', *Bldg Refurb. & Maint.*, ii/10 (1980), p. 42

J. M. RICHARDS

Feilding, Basil, 2nd Earl of Denbigh (*b c.* 1608; *d* Dunstable, 28 Nov 1675). English agent, connoisseur and diplomat. He acquired his interest in pictures through his father, William, 1st Earl of Denbigh (*c.* 1582–1643), a modest patron and collector whose full-length portrait by Anthony van Dyck (London, N.G.) ranks as one of that artist's masterpieces. Feilding was also influenced by the example of his uncle, George Villiers, 1st Duke of Buckingham, who in the 1620s had one of the finest collections in England. In 1635 Feilding was appointed English ambassador to Venice, and for three years he corresponded with his brother-in-law James Hamilton, 3rd Marquess of Hamilton, about possible acquisitions for Hamilton's collection. Their correspondence constitutes a rich source for the history of collecting in 17th-century England. Feilding's purchases for Hamilton included the Bartolommeo della Nave, Priuli and Renier collections, and he thus acquired Raphael's *St Margaret* and Giorgione's *Three Philosophers* (both Vienna, Ksthist. Mus.; *see* GIORGIONE, fig. 4), but the collection was dispersed after Hamilton's execution in 1649. A number of his pictures were later bought by Leopold I and came to form the basis of the Habsburgs' imperial collections in Vienna. Feilding was equally enthusiastic about contemporary art: in addition to acquiring Guido Reni's *St Peter* (Vienna, Ksthist. Mus.) for Hamilton, he tried to interest him in works by Giovanni Lanfranco, Giovanni Baglione and Valentin de Boulogne. He had his own portrait painted by Tiberio Tinelli.

BIBLIOGRAPHY
E. Waterhouse: 'Paintings from Venice for Seventeenth-century England', *It. Stud.*, vii (1952), pp. 1–23
P. Shakeshaft: ' "Too much bewiched with thoes intysing things": The Letters of James, Third Marquis of Hamilton, and Basil, Viscount Feilding, Concerning Collecting in Venice, 1635–1639', *Burl. Mag.*, cxxxviii (1980), pp. 114–32
D. Howarth: *Lord Arundel and his Circle* (New Haven, 1985)

DAVID HOWARTH

Feininger. American family of artists. (1) Lyonel Feininger was active as a painter and printmaker in Germany from the 1890s to 1937 and was involved in the Bauhaus from its foundation. His sons (2) Andreas Feininger and (3) T. Lux Feininger also studied at the Bauhaus before eventually moving to the USA.

(1) Lyonel Feininger (*b* New York, 17 July 1871; *d* New York, 13 Jan 1956). Painter, printmaker and illustrator. Although he was sent to Germany as a teenager to study music, a drawing class at the Kunstgewerbeschule in Hamburg instead sparked an interest in art, which led to further training at the Akademie der Künste in Berlin and in 1892–3 at the Académie Colarossi in Paris. Returning to Berlin, he was a prominent illustrator by the mid-1890s for *Ulk*, *Lustige Blätter* and other leading German satirical magazines. His work also appeared in the USA, first for *Harper's Round Table* in 1894 and 1895 and in 1906–7 in the comic strips 'The Kin-der-Kids' and 'Wee Willie Winkie's World' for the *Chicago Sunday Tribune*, by which time he was again in Paris. There he was also in contact with Wilhelm Uhde, Jules Pascin and other members of the circle that met at the Café du Dôme and produced a series of drawings for *Le Témoin*. While often alluding to serious contemporary issues, the style of his illustrations and drawings was fanciful rather than grotesque.

Lyonel Feininger: *Glorious Victory of the Sloop 'Maria'*, oil on canvas, 546×851 mm, 1926 (St Louis, MO, Art Museum)

Seeking more creative freedom after first-hand exposure to the French avant-garde, Feininger gave up illustration for painting when he returned to Germany in 1908. Most of his early oil paintings, such as *Emeute* (1910; New York, MOMA), are street scenes with numerous figures, which combine his already sensitive use of line and shape with the spatial exaggeration and bold colours favoured by the Fauves and his fellow Berlin Secessionists (with whom he had first exhibited in 1903–4). After his first experience of Cubism at the Salon des Indépendants in 1911 and subsequent contact with major German Expressionist groups, including Die Brücke in 1912 and the Blaue Reiter, with whom he exhibited in the *Erster Deutscher Herbstsalon* a year later, he concentrated on landscapes; although they remained intensely luminous, they were more formally ordered by an underlying network of precisely modulated, intersecting planes (e.g. *Bridge I*, 1913; St Louis, MO, Washington U., Gal. A.). Despite difficulties as a foreigner during World War I, he held his first one-man show at Herwarth Walden's Sturm-Galerie in 1917 and showed with other innovators at the Galerie Dada, Zurich.

After the war Feininger joined the NOVEMBERGRUPPE, through which he met Walter Gropius. When Gropius established the Bauhaus in Weimar in 1919 he invited Feininger to become the first form master in charge of the school's printmaking workshop. Feininger's prints, especially his woodcuts, enhanced many Bauhaus publications, including the cover of its original manifesto, *Cathedral of Socialism* (1919; New York, MOMA). Despite the demands of teaching, his skills as a painter also evolved. His landscapes increasingly featured architectural motifs that ranged from picturesque village buildings, as in *Ober-Weimar* (1921; Rotterdam, Boymans–van Beuningen), to monumental medieval churches, such as *Gelmeroda VIII* (1920–21; New York, Whitney). In these, he effectively coupled a penetrating vision of the contemporary world characteristic of Cubism with romantic patches of colour that affirmed his personal reverence for such subjects; moreover, the contrapuntal tenor of this imagery reflected his enduring interest in music and, more specifically, the 13 fugues for organ that he composed during the same period.

In 1925, with Alexei Jawlenski, Paul Klee and Vasily Kandinsky, Feininger formed the BLUE FOUR, which made its début at the Charles Daniel Gallery in New York. When the Bauhaus moved to Dessau a year later, Feininger followed as artist-in-residence without teaching responsibilities, so that he was free to concentrate on painting. His architectural landscapes, such as *Church of the Minorites II* (1926; Minneapolis, MN, Walker A. Cent.), and a growing number of seascapes inspired by the Baltic or memories of the American coast, such as the *Glorious Victory of the Sloop 'Maria'* (1926; see fig.), assumed a physical and emotional grandeur unprecedented in his work. Important recognition ensued when he was included in MOMA's inaugural *Paintings by 19 Living Americans* (1929) and given a large solo exhibition by the Nationalgalerie, Berlin (1931). However, later seascapes, some set at night with storm-tossed ships (e.g. *Four-Mast Bark and Schooner*, 1934; New York, Guggenheim), others strangely vacant except for small isolated figures (e.g. *Dunes at Eventide*,

1936; New York, Guggenheim), seemed to express a deepening concern over the forced closing of the Bauhaus, the spread of Fascism across Europe and ultimately the Nazis' public display of his own and other modern art as 'degenerate' (*see* ENTARTETE KUNST).

In 1937 Feininger left Germany for California, where he taught for a term at Mills College, Oakland, before resettling permanently in New York. Except for murals designed for two buildings at the World's Fair in 1938, *Marine Transportation* and *Masterpieces of Modern Art* (destr.; sketches, *ARTnews*, 1939), two years passed before he resumed painting. The rough texture, grainy contours and relatively subdued colour of his late German style at first carried into his American work, which varied from wistful recollections of pre-war Europe, for example *Cathedral (Cammin)* (1942; Cleveland, OH, Mus. A.), to tentative efforts to pictorialize the vast scale and new energy of his native city, as in *Manhattan I* (1940; New York, MOMA). Encouraged by Curt Valentin and by major prizes from the Metropolitan Museum of Art, New York, and Worcester Art Museum, MA, Feininger's confidence gradually returned. By 1944, the year of his joint retrospective with Marsden Hartley at MOMA, his New York imagery, for example in *Manhattan, The Tower* (1944; San Francisco, CA, MOMA), showed a graphic purity and aerial radiance akin to the mystical 'white writing' of his friend Mark Tobey. The following summer he accepted his former Bauhaus colleague Josef Albers's invitation to serve as guest instructor at BLACK MOUNTAIN COLLEGE, Lake Eden, NC. Late in his career he was elected president of the Federation of American Painters and Sculptors and honoured with membership in the National Institute of Arts and Letters.

BIBLIOGRAPHY
'Art at the World's Fair: I', *ARTnews*, xxxvii (1939), no. 32, p. 7
L. Schreyer: *Dokumente und Visionen* (Munich, 1957) [incl. extracts from letters, writings]
H. Hess: *Lyonel Feininger* (Stuttgart, 1959, rev. New York, 2/1961)
E. Scheyer: *Lyonel Feininger: Caricature and Fantasy* (Detroit, 1964)
L. Prasse: *Lyonel Feininger: A Definitive Catalogue of his Graphic Works, Etchings, Lithographs and Woodcuts* (Cleveland, 1972)
J. Ness: *Lyonel Feininger* (New York, 1974)
P. Mies: 'Lyonel Feininger: Painting and Music', *Z. Ästh. & Allg. Kstwiss.*, xxi/1 (1976), pp. 123–9
J. Hughes: 'The Cathedral of Socialism', *Preview: York A.G. Bull.*, xxx (Oct 1977), pp. 1035–9
D. Rosenthal: 'Lyonel Feininger', *A. Mag.*, li/9 (1977)
Lyonel Feininger: Caricatures, Comic Strips, Illustrations, 1888–1915 (exh. cat. by U. Luckhardt, Hamburg, Mus. Kst & Gew., 1981)
K. Hartley: 'Lyonel Feininger for Scotland', *Burl. Mag.*, cxxvii/993 (1983), pp. 893–5
U. Luckhardt: *Lyonel Feininger* (Munich, 1989)
P. Romanus, ed.: *Lyonel Feininger: Die Halle-Bilder* (Munich, 1991)
For further bibliography *see* BLUE FOUR.

JEFFREY R. HAYES

(2) Andreas (Bernhard Lyonel) Feininger (*b* Paris, 27 Dec 1906). Photographer, son of (1) Lyonel Feininger. He studied at the Bauhaus in Weimar (1922–5) and received a degree in architecture from the Bauschule in Zerbst (1929). Rejecting the abstract nature of Bauhaus photography, he developed a realist style, preferring black-and-white to colour. His work typically examines both the structural forms of nature, emphasizing the relationship between function and form, and the city, which he treats in a similar way, as a dynamic living organism. As a staff photographer for *Life* magazine (1942–62), Feininger documented such diverse subjects as the American war industry and the structures built by insects. He produced over 30 books on photographic subjects.

PHOTOGRAPHIC PUBLICATIONS
The Image of Women, text J. Bon (London, 1961)
The World through my Eyes: 30 Years of Photography (London, 1964)
New York, text K. Simon (London, 1964)
Trees (London, 1968)
Andreas Feininger: Photographer (New York, 1986)
WRITINGS
Successful Color Photography (Englewood Cliffs, 1957)
A Manual of Advanced Photography (London, 1962)
The Complete Photographer (London, 1966)
BIBLIOGRAPHY
R. Hattersley: *Andreas Feininger* (New York, 1973)

DORA APEL

(3) T(heodore) Lux Feininger (*b* Berlin, 11 June 1910). Photographer and painter, son of (1) Lyonel Feininger. He studied at the Bauhaus under Josef Albers, Paul Klee and Vasily Kandinsky. While there he collaborated on theatre and music projects with Oskar Schlemmer. He studied photography with László Moholy-Nagy, creating visual experiments with oblique angles, solarization and close-ups, as, for example, in his portrait of *Clemens Röseler* (1920s; New York, Prakapas Gal.). From 1927 to 1932 he photographed for the agency Dephot in Berlin. Some of his photographs were included in the important exhibition *Film und Foto* in Stuttgart in 1929. In 1932 he left the Bauhaus to live in Paris, giving up photography and working and exhibiting as a painter. In 1935 Feininger returned to Germany, then emigrated to the USA, where, after study at the Institute of Fine Arts, New York, he taught at various art colleges between 1950 and 1975. He continued to paint in a semi-abstract style, developing a dreamy, atmospheric manner for depicting ships and trains. His work was shown in the *American Realists and Magic Realists* exhibition at the Museum of Modern Art, New York, 1943, in *Four American Painters* at Massachusetts Institute of Technology, Cambridge, MA, 1954, and received a retrospective at Harvard University (see 1962 exh. cat.).

BIBLIOGRAPHY
T. Hess: 'Lux Feininger: Through the Telescope', *ARTnews*, xlv (1947), pp. 35, 60
T. Lux Feininger (exh. cat., Cambridge, MA, Busch-Reisinger Mus., 1962) [retro.]
Photographie und Bauhaus (exh. cat. by G. Gluber and S. Pastor, Hannover, Kestner-Ges., 1986)

SHERYL CONKELTON

Feinstein, Daniel Isaac. *See* SPOERRI, DANIEL.

Feistenberger. *See* FAISTENBERGER.

Feitama, Sybrand (*b* Amsterdam, 10 Dec 1694; *d* Amsterdam, 3 June 1758). Dutch poet, draughtsman and collector. He trained as a preacher but was forced to choose a career in commerce because of ill health. The family fortune, however, enabled him to devote himself to poetry and to assembling a remarkable collection of mostly 17th-century Dutch drawings; his poems were 'simple and edifying exercises in the art of rhyming', and he was a good translator of verse (e.g. *Telemachus* and *Henry the Great* from Voltaire). Feitama also took drawing lessons from Abraham Rademaker; his own works were mostly watercolours after paintings from the early Netherlandish school. Feitama described the history of his collection in a manuscript that contains the accounts of three generations of collectors, beginning with his grandfather Sybrand Feitama the elder (1620–1701), a chemist who began collecting in 1670. Feitama's father, Isaac (1666–1709), extended and improved the collection until, after his death, it reached its apogee in the hands of Sybrand the younger, providing an overview of the art of drawing in the Golden Age. There were excellent drawings by such artists as Ludolf Bakhuizen, Nicolaes Berchem, Jan de Bisschop, Allert van Everdingen, Adriaen van Ostade, Jacob van Ruisdael, Herman Saftleven and Adriaen van de Velde (as well as by his own contemporaries). The family had a liking for finished drawings, and in certain cases Feitama would ask friendly artists to 'make up' (complete) sketchy compositions or to add figures to them. For a long time it was unknown, for example, that many of the drawings by Jacob van Ruisdael (e.g. *High Bridge in Alkmaar Harbour*; Amsterdam, Hist. Mus.) had been 'made up' soon after the artist's death by Dirck Dalens, at the request of grandfather Sybrand. Sybrand Feitama the younger died childless, and his collection was sold at auction; among the buyers at the sale, which took place on 16 October 1758 and the following days, were famous collectors, including Johann Goll van Franckenstein the elder and Cornelis Ploos van Amstel.

UNPUBLISHED SOURCES
The Hague, Rijksbureau Ksthist. Doc. [MS., *Notitie der teekeningen, uit de oudste en latere aanteekeningen, sedert de jaren 1685 en 1690, tot 1746. . .opgemaakt* (Notes on the drawings, based on the earliest and later notes, made since the years 1685 and 1690, until 1746. . .)]

BIBLIOGRAPHY
NNBW
F. Lugt: *Ventes*, i (1938), no. 1019
B. P. J. Broos: 'Notitie der Teekeningen van Sybrand Feitama', *Oud-Holland*, xcvii (1984), pp. 13–39; xcix (1985), pp. 110–54; ci (1987), pp. 171–217 [with Eng. summaries]

B. P. J. BROOS

Feito, Luis (*b* Madrid, 31 Oct 1929). Spanish painter. He studied at the Escuela de Bellas Artes de San Fernando in Madrid (1950–54) and held his first one-man exhibition in 1952, at the Galería Buchholz in Madrid, showing both figurative and abstract paintings. His later work, however, was entirely abstract. In 1953 he travelled to Paris on a French Government grant, making it his home in 1957 after exhibiting there with great success in 1955 but still visiting Madrid frequently. Along with other Spanish practitioners of *Art informel*, he helped found El Paso in 1957, taking part in all the group's activities until its dissolution in 1960. The most characteristic feature of Feito's early work, for example *Painting No. 460A* (1150×890 mm, 1963; Cuenca, Mus. A. Abstracto Esp.), was his dramatic division of the chromatic field into two sections, one of them sometimes nearly monochromatic, with a pronounced contrast between smooth and encrusted surfaces. In later paintings, for example *Painting 608* (1.8×2.6 m, 1968; Madrid, Mus. A. Contemp.), he continued to use this format of two conjoined canvases but created a rhythmic movement from one half to the other through the deliberate echoing of the coloured shapes. Feito left Paris for Montreal in 1981 and in 1983 moved to New York, where he continued to live and work even after renewing his contacts in Spain in 1988. In his later paintings he adopted a purer, flatter technique and demonstrated a tendency towards elegant geometric forms.

BIBLIOGRAPHY
J. J. Levêque: *Feito: Une Peinture tauromatique* (Paris, 1971)
C. Arean: *Feito* (Madrid, 1975)
S. Sarduy and A. Aguilera-Cerni: *Luis Feito* (Seville, 1982)
F. Huici: 'Luis Feito, ecos de una conversación', *Feito* (exh. cat., Madrid, Mus. A. Contemp., 1988)

PILAR BENITO

Feke, Robert (*b* Oyster Bay, NY, ?1707; *d* ?1752). American painter. He was the son of a Baptist preacher. Only one portrait of a small child (Media, PA, R. F. Cox priv. col., see Foote), dated to the 1730s, is associated with his years in the New York area. In 1741 he moved to Boston, MA, where he painted an ambitious group portrait, *Isaac Royall and his Family* (1741; Cambridge, MA, Harvard U., Portrait Col.); the composition relies on John Smibert's *The Bermuda Group* (1729; New Haven, CT, Yale U. A.G.) as a model, which suggests a degree of contact with the elder artist. Although somewhat stiff and rigid in its palette and freshness, the portrait is the most provocative development in colonial painting since Smibert's arrival 12 years earlier. From 1742 to 1744 Feke may have been in England or Europe, where he would have been exposed to contemporary developments in painting, but this is unsubstantiated.

Approximately 60 portraits by Feke survive, of which 12 are signed and dated. His career reached its zenith in 1748, when he painted numerous impressive three-quarter-length portraits for a number of Boston's leading families. Although their sequence is not known, it is conceivable that they followed his success with a grand portrait of the land speculator and military leader *Brigadier General Samuel Waldo* (*c.* 1748; Brunswick, ME, Bowdoin Coll. Mus. A.). This portrait, which is skilfully drawn and forcefully coloured, is generally accepted as the consummate full-length portrait painted in America during the first half of the 18th century. Other three-quarter-length portraits, painted about the same time, include *James Boutineau* and *Susannah Faneuil Boutineau* (Halifax, NS Mus.) and two Boutineau cousins, the brothers *James Bowdoin* and *William Bowdoin*, and their wives, *Elizabeth Erving Bowdoin* and *Phebe Murdock Bowdoin* (all 1748; Brunswick, ME, Bowdoin Coll. Mus. A.). These last four are all signed and dated. Feke's younger patrons, presumably tired of the sombre-toned palette of artists of John Smibert's generation, found his preference for silver and pastel shades of blue, pink and yellow appealing.

After Feke's success in Boston, he went to Philadelphia, PA, where he painted several documented portraits, the best of which is *Margaret McCall* (1749; Dietrich Corp., on loan to Philadelphia, PA, Mus. A.). The last record of his whereabouts is 26 August 1751. Early biographers said that he made his way to Barbados or Bermuda, where he is thought to have died, although no evidence has been found to substantiate this suggestion. Feke's impact on the development of colonial painting was substantial, and his pictures set a new standard by which the work of the next generation of aspiring colonial artists was judged.

BIBLIOGRAPHY

H. W. Foote: *Robert Feke: Colonial Portrait Painter* (Cambridge, MA, 1930)

R. P. Mooz: *The Art of Robert Feke* (diss., Philadelphia, U. PA, 1970)

——: 'Robert Feke: The Philadelphia Story', *American Painting to 1776: A Reappraisal* (Charlottesville, 1971), pp. 181–216

M. Elwood: 'Two Portraits Attributed to Robert Feke', *Antiques*, cxvi (1979), pp. 1150–52

W. Craven: *Colonial American Portraiture* (Cambridge, 1986), pp. 281–95

RICHARD H. SAUNDERS

Felaert, Dieric. *See* VELLERT, DIRK.

Felber, Hans [Felwer, Hanns], the elder (*b* ?Nördlingen, before 1400; *d* ?Nördlingen, before 3 June 1439). German architect. He was one of the versatile specialists of the 15th century who was sought after for his experience as architect, mason, military and hydraulics engineer or caster of cannon. He was probably the son of the Hans Velber mentioned in 1382 and as a taxpayer in Nördlingen between 1404 and 1410. In the tax register for 1415 a Master Hans Felber is mentioned, notably as being exempt from taxation. This suggests some special consideration, usually granted only to people in important positions or with unusual duties, in an attempt to secure their continued presence in the city. The absence of tax entries from 1416 to 1434 indicates that Felber was then living away from Nördlingen. His second marriage, in 1428, was to Magdalena Medinger of Nördlingen, but he did not reside there permanently, even after he started paying taxes again. Felber owned land and his father's bath house in Nördlingen. In Ulm he purchased the mill in Werd next to the premises of the Teutonic Knights and was by means of it enfeoffed to Emperor Sigismund on 11 November 1430. From 1434 Felber paid an annual tax of 8 florins and was still able in 1438 to pay a rent of 50 florins to Konrad Stenglin, the Master of the Works in Ulm.

Felber probably first became known for his work in Ulm. In 1423–4 and again in 1426 he is mentioned in the registers of the tax office as 'Meister Hanns Felwer', serving as master metal-caster and Master of the Ordnance. As a military engineer and arms technician, he was called to Nuremberg, first in autumn 1426, to give specifications for the construction of military machines and buildings, and again in 1427, 1428 and 1430, when Nuremberg was threatened by large Hussite forces. In 1427 Felber worked with the contingent from Ulm in the siege of the Bohemian city of Mies (now Stříbro). On 1 October 1429 Emperor Sigismund wrote from Pressburg (now Bratislava, Slovakia) to Ulm, seeking Felber's services as an experienced gunmaker and military technician. Felber may have resided at the imperial court from October 1429 to January 1430.

Felber also undertook considerable civil engineering commissions in, for example, hydraulics. As early as 1423 he had contact with Nuremberg over the city's long-standing plans to divert the River Röthenbach into the city for manufacturing purposes, and between December 1425 and January 1426 he was paid by the city council for his recommendations. In 1433 he was called to Augsburg to construct a water tower and a new water conduit.

Felber is first recorded as a Master of the Works in Nördlingen in 1425–6. In collaboration with Hans Kun, the 'Kirchenmeister' from Ulm, he oversaw the construction of the so-called Nördlingen Kürschnerhaus (the Furriers House), one of the oldest fair houses and stores in Germany (destr. 1955). It was a large half-timbered building with a small interior court and two spacious storage cellars with barrel vaults. In 1427 Kun and Felber produced plans for the church of St Georg, Nördlingen, the new choir of which had already been begun in that year. Felber's contribution can no longer be identified. Both masters were already working together on Ulm Minster, Felber being paid for his 'recommendations' in Ulm in 1427. He directed the building works in Nördlingen until his death.

Felber's great specialist knowledge and considerable abilities would presumably have found many applications. He was, for example, employed in the service of Baron Johann von Öttingen in 1433–4, but the task was not specified in the records.

BIBLIOGRAPHY

K. Hassler: 'Meister Hans Felber von Ulm', *Anz. Knd. Dt. Vorzeit*, n.s. 6, xii (1859), pp. 443–5

A. Gümbel: 'Der Baumeister und Stückegiesser Hans Felber von Ulm, dessen Beziehungen zu Nürnberg und Todesjahr: Nachträgliches zur Biographie Konrad Heinzelmanns', *Repert. Kstwiss.*, xxxiv (1911), pp. 232–54

G. Wulz: 'Beiträge zur Nördlinger Baugeschichte', *Jb. Hist. Ver. Nördlingen & Umgebung*, xix (1936), pp. 33–8

K. Gröber and A. Horn: *Die Kunstdenkmäler v. Bayern: Die Kunstdenkmäler von Schwaben und Neuburg, ii: Stadt Nördlingen* (Munich, 1940; R 1981), pp. 21, 224–5

E. D. Schmid: *Nördlingen: Die Georgskirche und St Salvator* (Stuttgart and Aalen, 1977), pp. 27–30, 90, 99, 148

W. Baer and others: *Augsburger Stadtlexikon* (Augsburg, 1985), pp. 105, 194

FRANZ BISCHOFF

Felbinger, Bartol (*b* Cheb, Bohemia [now Czech Republic], 15 Sept 1785; *d* Zagreb, 17 Feb 1871). Croatian architect of Bohemian birth. He qualified as a builder in Vienna with Franz Wipplinger (*fl* 1803–12) and in 1809 settled in Zagreb, where he took up the position of city architect. His career began during the period of late Viennese Baroque architecture, but Felbinger developed his own path towards a Neo-classicism that was lyrical, unlike the abstract classicism of Schinkel or Friedrich Weinbrenner, and characterized by simplicity and functional logic. His work commanded great respect in Zagreb, to the extent that the city was dominated by his Neo-classical architecture for almost the whole of the first part of the 19th century. Felbinger built private houses, palaces, manor houses, villas and garden pavilions. He also took part in the ambitious project (1812–43) to develop Maksimir Park, Zagreb, eventually landscaped in the English style. Among his most notable buildings is Januševac (1828), a manor house in Novi Marof, near Zagreb. Within a simple overall volume there is a two-storey central domed space; externally each façade is treated somewhat differently, according to its particular aspect. Felbinger's use of classical architectural elements was always functional rather than decorative, as can be seen in the Drašković-Jelačić Palace (1830) in Zagreb, which has a façade of four Ionic columns of the major order supporting a heavy entablature, while the plain wall attached behind them has an arcaded portico on the ground and the articulation of only three vertical windows on the first floor.

Felbinger's principal buildings in Zagreb are the residential palaces at nos 7 and 10 Ilica, with courtyard pavilions; the Domotörffy Palace (1815), 32 Radićeva Street; Felbinger House (1820–24), 15 Jelačić Square; and Alagović Villa (1824), 87 Nova Ves. Perhaps the most outstanding is Karlo Draškovic (now Dvorana) Palace (1837–40), 18 Opatička Street, which has a portico on the eastern façade. The interior of this palace is one of the finest in Zagreb. A particular skill of Felbinger's was his ability to integrate new elements with an existing historical context, and a pragmatic feature of his architecture is his use of the ornate Corinthian order in residences for bourgeois clients, while his palaces for the aristocracy are marked by the use of more modest Ionic and Tuscan columns and almost functional wrought-iron balustrades. This symbolizes the power balance between the two classes after the revolution of 1848 and is reflected in the development of the bourgeois Biedermeier style in interior design.

BIBLIOGRAPHY

A. Albini: 'Naša architektura u prošlosti i sadašnjosti' [Our architecture in the past and today], *Obzorova Spomen Knjiga* (1935), p. 170
L. Dobrović: 'Kovano željezo u radu zagrebačkog arhitekta Bartola Felbingera' [Fabricated iron in the work of the architect Bartol Felbinger], *Urb. & Arhit.*, 5–8 (1951), pp. 88–9
G. Jurišić: 'Bartol Felbinger i gradnja dvorca Januševac' [Bartol Felbinger and the building of Januševac manor house], *Peristil* (1954), pp. 170–73
P. Tvrtković: 'Shades of Zagreb', *Bldg Des.*, 895 (1988), pp. 14–17

PAUL TVRTKOVIĆ

Felderhoff, Reinhold Karl (*b* Elbing, 25 Jan 1865; *d* Berlin, 18 Dec 1919). German sculptor. He attended the Akademische Hochschule für die Bildenden Künste, Berlin, in 1881 to train as a sculptor. In 1885 he was accepted by Reinhold Begas as a pupil in his studio, and he participated in some of Begas's large commissions, including the monument to *Emperor William I* (1892–7). Felderhoff's first works bear close resemblance to his teacher's style and were from then on regularly presented at exhibitions in Berlin. As early as 1885 he won a state prize enabling him to make a first study trip to Italy. A second journey followed in 1890–91. During this stay the artist met Louis Tuaillon, through whom he took part in topical discussions on art with artists who had gathered around Hans von Marées (by then dead) and Adolf von Hildebrand.

Felderhoff established himself as an independent sculptor in Berlin. His first public commissions included works for the Zeughaus (1889) and the *Röntgen* monument for the Potsdamer Bridge (1899). He won competitions in other German towns as well (e.g. for a fountain in Stettin, 1895; for a *Bismarck* monument in Essen, 1899). His participation in the Siegesallee in Berlin with the group of *Margrave John II* (unveiled 1899) indicated membership of the group of 'official' sculptors who represented the state art and style of Emperor William II. In Felderhoff's free works there was a gradual tendency away from the idiom of the neo-Baroque. If *Diana* (1890; several versions including Berlin, Dahlem, Skulpsamml.) still owed much to the style of Begas, the works that followed reveal the first signs of a reduction in form and content: *Girl with Dead Youth* (1910; Essen, Mus. Flkwang) largely dispenses with picturesque surface treatment. Busts formed a major part of his work, and in them his development is clearly reflected. Although Felderhoff never joined the Berlin Secession, he sympathized with their aims.

UNPUBLISHED SOURCES

Berlin, Akad. Kst., Archv [personal rec.]

BIBLIOGRAPHY

Die Bildwerke seit 1800 (exh. cat., Cologne, Wallraf-Richartz-Mus., 1965)
P. Bloch and W. Grzimek: *Das klassische Berlin* (Berlin, 1978), pp. 318–20
Berlin und die Antike (exh. cat., intro. P. Bloch; W. Berlin, Schloss Charlottenburg, 1979)
P. Bloch and B. Hüfler: *Rheinland Westfalen und die Berliner Bildhauerschule des 19. Jahrhunderts* (Berlin, 1984)
S. Einholz: 'Sepulkralplastik in Stahnsdorf', *Frühlicht in Beton*, eds C. Fischer and V. Welter (Berlin, 1989)

SIBYLLE EINHOLZ

Felguérez, Manuel (*b* Hacienda de Valparaíso, Zacatecas, 12 Dec 1928). Mexican painter and sculptor. He grew up in Zacatecas and achieved recognition as a sculptor in Mexico City *c.* 1953, after briefly attending courses there at the Escuela Nacional de Pintura y Escultura, better known as La Esmeralda. He worked as a ceramicist and travelled throughout Mexico to study the country's archaeology, art, geography, customs and traditions. After studying medicine briefly at the Universidad Nacional Autónoma de México in Mexico City, he decided to devote himself to art, travelling for the first time to Europe in 1947 in order to visit museums, churches and monasteries. On his return to Mexico he obtained a scholarship from the French government, which allowed him to study in Paris for two years. There he met Brancusi, frequently visiting his studio, but he was especially close to Ossip Zadkine.

Felguérez returned definitively to Mexico in 1956, teaching sculpture in Mexico City at the Escuela de Arte y Diseño of the Universidad Iberoamericana and later at the Universidad Nacional Autónoma de México. Together with his first wife, Lilia Carrillo, whom he married in 1960, he initiated a movement, Ruptura, which (as its name suggests) consciously broke with the selfconsciously Mexican identity pursued by other painters. In 1958 his first important one-man exhibition of painting and sculpture in Mexico was held at the Galería Antonio Souza in Mexico City, a meeting-place for dissident artists. While he established a reputation (both as a painter and sculptor) as perhaps the strictest exponent of geometric abstraction in Mexico, he also made daring excursions into other styles, although he continued to incorporate geometric elements. After 1979, in particular, he emphasized painterly qualities of colour, touch and surface texture, for example in *Light Path* (oil on canvas, 1.15×1.35 m, 1987; see D. Bayón and R. Pontual, *La Peinture de l'Amérique latine au XXe siècle*, Paris, 1990, p. 97). He is also credited with the first abstract mural, painted in earth and tar in the Diana cinema in Mexico City, and with initiating a new phase of mural painting in Mexico. He was influential in many ways on the public sphere of Mexican cultural life: he was active as a polemicist, lecturer and theoretician, instigating changes in the course of study at the Escuela Nacional de Artes Plásticas; he frequently served on exhibition juries and planned and promoted a free forum for exhibitions and discussions, the Salón Independiente, which was in operation between 1968 and 1971; and in 1975 he was the first Mexican artist to win one of the grand prizes at the São Paulo Biennale.

WRITINGS
El espacio múltiple (Mexico City, 1978)
La máquina estética (Mexico City, 1983)

BIBLIOGRAPHY
Manuel Felguérez: El espacio múltiple (exh. cat., intro. O. Paz; Mexico City, Mus. A. Mod., 1973)
J. A. Manrique and others: *El geometrismo mexicano* (Mexico City, 1977)
Manuel Felguérez: Muestra antológica (exh. cat., essays T. del Conde and L. M. Schneider; Mexico City, Inst. N. B.A., 1987)

TERESA DEL CONDE

Félibien, André, Sieur des Avaux et de Jàversy (*b* Chartres, May 1619; *d* Paris, 11 May 1695). French administrator, art historian and critic. He belonged to the minor provincial nobility and received an excellent education, completed in Paris, where he moved in literary and artistic circles. Among his friends were the frequenters of the Hôtel de Rambouillet and the artists Sébastien Bourdon, Louis du Guernier, Charles Le Brun and Nicolas Loir. In 1647 he was named secretary to the Marquis de Fontenay-Mareuil, Louis XIV's ambassador to the Holy See, and spent the period from May 1647 to August 1649 in Rome. There Félibien occupied his leisure hours in studying monuments and works of art and in meeting artists such as Claude Lorrain, Pierre Mignard, Charles-Alphonse Du Fresnoy, Pietro da Cortona, Lanfranco and, above all, Nicolas Poussin. This experience played a part in putting Félibien's taste for the fine arts in context, as he acquired more extensive knowledge both of theory and practical matters.

After his return to France, Félibien was introduced to the powerful finance minister Nicolas Fouquet, and in 1660 dedicated to him his *De l'origine de la peinture*, the first part of a projected history of painting designed to replace Vasari's famous work. When Fouquet was disgraced the following year, Félibien prudently withdrew to Chartres but was recalled to Paris by Jean-Baptiste Colbert. In March 1666, after Félibien had first written a number of preliminary essays describing Le Brun's works, Colbert appointed him historiographer of the Bâtiments du Roi. From then on his activities increased rapidly: he was made Conseiller Honoraire to the Académie Royale de Peinture et de Sculpture, was a founder of the Académie des Inscriptions et Belles-lettres in 1663, a member and secretary of the Académie Royale d'Architecture from its creation in 1671 and keeper of the king's antiquities at the Palais Brion. He wrote descriptions of various royal festivities, such as *Relation de la feste de Versailles du 18e juillet 1668* and *Les Divertissements de Versailles donnez par le Roy au retour de la conqueste de la Franche-Comté en l'année 1674*, as well as the well-known *Description sommaire du château de Versailles* (1674). His various official pamphlets on some of the paintings and tapestries made for Louis XIV and on aspects of the royal collections, published from 1663 to 1674, were reprinted as the *Recueil de descriptions de peintures et autres ouvrages faits pour le Roy* in 1689. They mark an important stage in the development of art criticism. In addition to these texts advertising the merits of the royal collections and numerous devotional works, Félibien also published *Conférences de l'Académie Royale de Peinture et de Sculpture pendant l'année 1667* (1668), an edited collection of lectures given at the Académie designed to present a coherent body of theory, and *Principes de l'architecture, de la sculpture, de la peinture et des autres arts qui en dépendent* (1676). In 1674 he started work on a never completed *Histoire des maisons royales et bastimens de France*, which drew on many contemporary documents. These major works reveal Félibien's vast erudition, his concern with the teaching of techniques and his capacity for defining an artistic and aesthetic theory.

Félibien's most famous work is the *Entretiens sur les vies et les ouvrages des plus excellens peintres anciens et modernes*, published in ten volumes from 1666 to 1688 and later translated into English (1705), German (1711) and Italian (1755; for illustration *see* LIGHT). The *Entretiens*, which constitute a history of European painting from antiquity to the 17th century, display his intellectual curiosity and his lively and sensitive observation of works of art, both highlighted by his literary talent. In addition, Félibien's qualities as a theoretician are given authoritative expression in the 8th *Entretien*, which is devoted to Poussin, and in which he defined 'the classical doctrine' in art, a doctrine shared by Poussin, Le Sueur, Bourdon and Le Brun. The *Entretiens* earn Félibien his place as the father of art criticism and art history in France. They remain a resource of great value today.

Félibien's learned studies were later pursued by two of his sons. Jean-François Félibien des Avaux (*d* 1733) was historiographer of the Bâtiments du Roi, treasurer of the Académie des Inscriptions et Belles-lettres and a member of the Académie Royale d'Architecture. Among his works is the *Recueil historique de la vie et des ouvrages des plus célèbres architectes* (1699), the first general history of architecture up to the Renaissance, which is noteworthy for his interest in Arab and medieval architecture. Michel Félibien (1666–1719) was a Benedictine monk of the Congregation of Saint-Maur and wrote *Histoire de l'abbaye royale de Saint-Denis en France* (1706) and *Histoire de la ville de Paris*, the latter completed after his death and published by Dom Lobineau (1725).

See also POUSSINISME.

WRITINGS
De l'origine de la peinture (Paris, 1660)
Entretiens sur les vies et les ouvrages des plus excellens peintres anciens et modernes, 5 vols (Paris, 1666–88, rev. 6 vols Trévoux, 1725/*R* London, 1967)
Conférences de l'Académie royale de peinture et de sculpture pendant l'année 1667 (Paris, 1668)
Description sommaire du château de Versailles (Paris, 1674)
Principes de l'architecture, de la sculpture, de la peinture et des autres arts qui en dépendent, avec un dictionnaire des termes propres à chacun de ces arts (Paris, 1676)
Recueil des descriptions de peintures et autres ouvrages faits pour le Roy (Paris, 1689)
Mémoires pour servir à l'histoire des maisons royales (Paris, 1874) [part of the lost MS. of *Histoire des maisons royales et bastimens de France*]

Mariette

BIBLIOGRAPHY
'Eloge funèbre d'André Félibien', *Le Journal des sçavans* 39 (Paris, 1695), pp. 459–65
P.-J.-P. Nicéron: *Mémoire pour servir à l'histoire des hommes illustres de la république des lettres*, ii (Paris, 1727), pp. 342–52
Y. Delaporte: 'André Félibien en Italie', *Gaz. B.-A.*, n. s. 5, lii (1958), pp. 193–214

B. Tessèydre: 'Félibien et Roger de Piles: Historiens de la peinture française avant Poussin', *Inf. Hist. A.*, vi/3 (1961), pp. 72–81

A. Niderst: 'Préciosité, esthétique mystique dans les *Entretiens* de Félibien', *La Critique artistique, un genre littéraire* (Rouen, 1983), pp. 197–204

J. Thuillier: 'Pour André Félibien', 'Lettres familières d'André Félibien', *XVIIe siècle*, 138 (1983), pp. 67–95, 141–57

ALEXANDRE SKLIAR-PIGUET

Felice, Matteo [Mazzeo] (*fl* 1467–93). Italian illuminator. He commanded a sizeable patronage at the Aragonese court and among religious institutions of the Kingdom of Naples–Sicily. His colourful miniatures are eclectic with characteristic boldly outlined, child-like figures. He apparently trained with Cola Rapicano, and such manuscripts as Albertus Magnus's *Summa* (U. Valencia, Bib., MS. 820) seem to have been cooperative ventures by the two men. The earliest record concerning a manuscript that Felice illuminated independently is a payment in 1467 for a volume combining Boethius's *Consolation of Philosophy* and Vergerio's *De ingenuis moribus* (Rome, Vatican, Bib. Apostolica, MS. Pal. lat. 1470). Here he adopted the white intertwined vine-scroll borders that had become the trademark of Gioacchino de Gigantibus de Rottenburg, who was active in Naples at the same time.

Felice, to a greater degree than Rapicano, sought his own style in Catalan versions of south Netherlandish modes that Lleonard Crespi, Alfonso di Cordova (*fl c.* 1442–58) and others had developed, creating miniatures with open, luminous landscapes inhabited by many figures. His borders are constructed of short, symmetrical flower sprigs in which nestle putti, fauna and medallions. Single initials are enlivened with delicately painted vine-scrolls. Most appealing among his many works is a series of Books of Hours: that made for Isabella di Chiaromonte (Cambridge, MA, Harvard U., Houghton Lib., MS. Typ. 463), for her son Alfonso when Duca di Calabria (London, V&A, MS. 2397) and a third now in Trieste (priv. col.). As accomplished are a Breviary (U. Valencia, Bib., MS. 662) and a Psalter (New York, Pub. Lib., Spencer MS. 130). Felice also contributed six miniatures to the Codex of S Marta (Naples, Archv Stato, MS. 99.C. I.) and decorated a number of theological and Classical texts, such as Duns Scotus's *Commentaries* (Berlin, Staatsbib. Preuss. Kultbes., MS. 52), St Thomas Aquinas's Commentary on the book of Isaiah (Paris, Bib. N., MSS lat. 495 and 674) and works of Plato (London, BL, Harley MS. 3481).

BIBLIOGRAPHY

T. De Marinis: *La biblioteca napoletana dei re d'Aragona*, 4 vols (Milan, 1947–52); *Supplement*, 2 vols (Verona, 1969) [with additions by J. Ruysschaert]

——: 'Codici miniati a Napoli da Matteo Felice nel secolo XV', *Contributi alla storia del libro italiano: Miscellanea in onore di Lamberto Donati* (Florence, 1969), pp. 96–103

A. Daneu Lattanzi: 'Di alcuni codici miniati attribuibili a Matteo Felice e bottega (e di qualche altro codice della scuola napoletana del quattrocento)', *La Bibliofilia*, lxxv (1973), pp. 1–43

A. Putaturo Murano: *Miniature napoletane del rinascimento* (Naples, 1973)

PATRICK M. DE WINTER

Feliciano, Felice [Felix Antiquarius] (*b* Verona, Aug 1433; *d* ?La Storta, nr Rome, after Aug 1479). Italian calligrapher, writer and antiquary. He was the son of a wine-tax collector but, despite his relative poverty, he received sufficient education to allow him to earn a living copying texts and to develop a lifelong interest in Classical antiquity. He developed a distinctive calligraphic style and his interest in writing extended to the preparation of a treatise on the construction of the Roman alphabet, the *Alphabetum Romanum* (*c.* 1460). He also wrote several poems and a novella (*c.* 1474), which he illustrated with his own miniatures (1474). He is best known, however, as an antiquary, especially as a collector of inscriptions, in which he was inspired by the example of the collector and traveller CYRIAC OF ANCONA, concerning whom Feliciano assembled a number of papers and biographical details (Treviso, Bib. Capitolare). His antiquarian interests were shared by Giovanni Marcanova Antenoreo, the Paduan physician and collector, whose *Collectio antiquitatum* Feliciano inscribed on vellum (Modena, Bib. Estense), and Andrea Mantegna, to whom in 1463 Feliciano dedicated an edition of his own collection of inscriptions, the *Epigrammaton* (now known only from copies). During his life Feliciano travelled widely in Italy, including Rome and Ravenna, and he settled in Bologna from 1470 to 1473. On his return to Verona he set up a printing house with his financial backer Innocente Zileti, in an apparent attempt to confront the threat that printing represented to his livelihood. Their sole publication was *Degli uomini famosi* (Pojano, 1476), an Italian translation by Donato degli Albanzani (*c.* 1326–1411) of Petrarch's *De viris illustribus*. In 1478 Feliciano went to Rome and it is possible that he died of the plague at La Storta, where he had gone to escape it.

See also THE ANTIQUE.

WRITINGS

Alphabetum Romanum [*c.* 1460; Rome, Vatican, Bib. Apostolica, cod. Vat. lat. 6852]; Eng. trans., ed. R. H. Boothroyd (Verona, 1960), pp. 14–30

Epigrammaton ex vetustissimis per ipsum fideliter lapidibus inscriptorum ad splendis [1463]

La gallica historia di Drusilla intitulata Justa Vittoria [1474]; ed. G. Papanti in *Catalogo dei novellieri italiani . . .*, ii (Livorno, 1871)

BIBLIOGRAPHY

DBI

F. S. Maffei: *Verona illustrata*, ii (Verona, 1731), pp. 98–9

G. Tiraboschi: *Storia della letteratura italiana*, vi (Modena, 1790), pp. 208–9

JANET SOUTHORN

Felipe V, King of Spain. *See* BOURBON, §II(1).

Felípez de Guzmán, Diego. *See* GUZMÁN, (1).

Felix. *See* BERNABÉ, FELIX.

Felix V, Pope. *See under* SAVOY, §II(1).

Felixmüller [Felix Müller], **Conrad** (*b* Dresden, 21 May 1897; *d* W. Berlin, 24 March 1977). German painter and printmaker. He had drawing lessons at the Kunstgewerbeschule in Dresden in 1911. The following year he joined the painting class of Carl Bantzer (1857–1941) at the Königliche Kunstakademie and had his first training as a painter at the school run by Ferdinand Dörsch (*b* 1875), both in Dresden. By this point he had taught himself various printmaking techniques. After leaving the Kunstakademie in 1915, he settled as an independent artist in Dresden, continuing to study printmaking techniques in line with academic tradition. Through several visits to Berlin he came into contact with the artistic and literary

Expressionist circles. Nearly a third of his graphic work from this period was published in various magazines devoted to this artistic trend, including Herwarth Walden's *Der Sturm*; from 1917 until 1928, 55 works appeared in Franz Pfemfert's *Aktion*. In 1917 Felixmüller joined the bookseller Felix Stiemer as co-editor of a short-lived art and literature magazine *Menschen*, in which he was represented by 22 works, mostly portraits and self-portraits.

Until 1916 the simple composition of the works, built up of large surfaces, recalled the early graphic work of Die Brücke. Around 1917 Felixmüller developed an increasingly dynamic pictorial space, divided up into facets as if exploding. This moment of motion, in which aspects of time such as hectic pace, confusion and collapse are translated into image, unites his work with that of the Expressionists. However, he connected it with the formal qualities of Cubism, the parcelling of spatial forms into a surface area, which became characteristic of his work. In this combination there are parallels with Orphism. In the 'Postulat' published in 1918 by the Felix Stiemer Verlag,

he added a written statement of his conviction that Synthetic Cubism was his only means of attaining 'absolute form' (see Söhn, 1977, pp. 12–13).

In works depicting Felixmüller's vision of life at the end of World War I, fragmented angles, sharp-edged distorted forms and the meshing of foreground and background evoke the impression of torment, disturbance and conflict. The woodcut *Dejection in the Studio* (1917; priv. col., see Söhn, 1975, rev. 1987, no. 99) portrays the problems he saw confronting him: the solitude of the artistic struggle, financial need and the uncertainty that followed war. The conflicts between the individual and the city, internal and external space, the personal and the anonymous are typical themes during this period. He returned to this imagery and also to his formal means of the earlier period, when he portrayed the *Death of the Poet Walter Rheiner* (1925; Beverly Hills, CA, Rifkind Found.), a friend who had killed himself with an overdose of cocaine; he symbolized the desperate artist confronted with the hectic and destructive thrust of the city.

Conrad Felixmüller: *The Widower (the Artist's Father)*, oil on canvas, 860×970 mm, 1920 (Halle, Staatliche Galerie Moritzburg Halle)

Around 1919 Felixmüller broke from the Cubist–Expressionist endeavours that he had been working with, which he had come to see as too formalistic and unsuited to contemporary events. He subsequently devoted himself to two groups of works, completely different in their iconography: one was about the everyday life of coal miners; the other concentrated on his family and closest friends, for example the portrait of *The Widower (the Artist's Father)* (1920; Halle, Staatl. Gal. Moritzburg; see fig.). In 1918 Felixmüller married Londa Freiin von Berg, moved with her briefly to Wiesbaden and then to Klotzsche near Dresden until 1931. The new experience of domestic isolation and harmony fed into his painting and graphic work. *Self-portrait with my Sons* (*c.* 1921; priv. col., see Herzog, p. 61) shows clearly the retreat into the private sphere and the artist's spiritual peace. The painting also demonstrates the stylistic break with the Expressionistic distortion of form, while at the same time retaining use of strong colour.

While he was painting these works, Felixmüller was involved in several, often politically oriented artists' groups. In 1919 he joined the NOVEMBERGRUPPE and took over the leadership of the newly founded Dresdner Neue Sezession Gruppe 1919, leaving it again the following year. In 1918 he also joined the Kommunistische Partei Deutschlands, remaining a member until *c.* 1926. The artist's social commitment was demonstrated in the works that resulted from a lengthy study-tour in the Saxon coal-mining region and the Ruhr, made possible by the Staatliche Akademie der Künste in Dresden. In the resulting works, for example *Coal Miners* (colour lithograph, 1920; see Söhn, 1975, rev. 1987, no. 211), the emphasis is less on the class struggle than on sympathy with suffering and need. He continued to depict the treatment of human life on a more objective level. The confusions of perspective in the earlier works make way for a clear linear pictorial organization.

Towards the end of the 1920s Felixmüller abandoned his previous colouring of strong yellow, deep pink and blue tones and thus broke completely with his first Expressionist period. In the years leading up to the seizure of power by the Nazis his works, predominantly portraits, came close to Neue Sachlichkeit, although they express an empathetic romantic undertone. The portrait of the actress *Pamela Wedekind* (1929; Von der Gabelentz Col., on loan to Altenburg, Staatl. Lindenau-Mus.) makes a clear division between the individual, pictorial objects portrayed in detail, isolating the subject not in a clinical way, but rather bringing it into a harmonious union with the softly blurred background. Wedekind was married to the Expressionist writer Carl Sternheim, with whom Felixmüller had a lasting friendship, documented by numerous portraits.

The painting style of these years resulted from the artist's struggle to make the connection between portrayals that are both expressive and close to nature and life. The *Artist at Dresden* (woodcut, 1930; see Söhn, 1975, rev. 1987, no. 393), one of the few woodcuts from this period, is a programmatic symbol of these efforts according to Felixmüller (see Herzog, p. 88).

In contrast to Felixmüller's immediate success during his first period of work, there was no public recognition in the following decades. Under the Nazis his work was shown in 1933 at the exhibition of *Spiegelbilder des Verfalls in der Kunst* in the Stadtmuseum in Dresden (*see* ENTARTETE KUNST), and 151 of his publicly owned works were confiscated and destroyed in 1937–8 by the Reichskammer der Bildenden Kunst. From 1941 until 1944 he was evacuated to Damsdorf in Fläming, finally moving to Geithain near Leipzig. In 1949 he was made professor of drawing and painting at the Martin-Luther University in Halle, where he taught until he moved to Köpenick, near Berlin in 1961. His later work deals, in a naturalistic, often anecdotal form of representation, almost exclusively with his private and immediate circles. From 1967 he lived in Zehlendorf, West Berlin.

BIBLIOGRAPHY
G. Söhn, ed.: *Conrad Felixmüller: Das graphische Werk, 1912–1977* (Düsseldorf, 1975, rev. 1987)
G. H. Herzog, ed.: *Conrad Felixmüller: Legenden, 1912–1976* (Tübingen, 1977)
G. Söhn, ed.: *Conrad Felixmüller: Von ihm—über ihn* (Düsseldorf, 1977)
Conrad Felixmüller, 1897–1977 (exh. cat., Dortmund, Mus. Ostwall, 1978)
Conrad Felixmüller: Werke und Dokumente (exh. cat., Nuremberg, Ger. Nmus., 1981)
Conrad Felixmüller: Das druckgraphische Werk 1912 bis 1976 im Kunstmuseum Düsseldorf, Schenkung Titus Felixmüller und Luca Felix Müller (exh. cat., Düsseldorf, Kstmus., 1986)
Conrad Felixmüller: Die Dresdner Jahre, 1913–1933. Zum 90. Geburtstag des Künstlers (exh. cat., Düsseldorf, Gal. Remmert & Barth, 1987)
Conrad Felixmüller: Retrospektive (exh. cat., Düsseldorf, Kstmus., 1990)

BEATRICE V. BISMARCK

Fellerer, Max (*b* Linz, 15 Oct 1889; *d* Vienna, 27 March 1957). Austrian architect, furniture designer and teacher. He trained first in Linz and from 1909 at the Technische Hochschule, Vienna, under the Neo-classicist Karl König (1841–1915). He completed a year in Josef Hoffmann's studio at the Wagnerschule in 1913–14, and after World War I he returned to work with Hoffmann, rising to be his senior assistant and helping with the development of the WIENER WERKSTÄTTE. In 1926 he left to work in Clemens Holzmeister's studio, teaching with him at the Akademie der Bildenden Künste, Vienna. Active in the Österreichischer Werkbund during the 1920s and 1930s, Fellerer built two houses (1932) for the Werkbundsiedlung in Vienna. In 1934 he was appointed Director of the Kunstgewerbeschule and succeeded Hoffmann as head of its architectural section until he was dismissed by the Nazis in 1938. From 1934 he was also in private practice with Eugen Wörle (*b* 1909) and won a Grand Prix at the Exposition Internationale des Arts et Techniques dans la Vie Moderne in Paris in 1937. In 1945 he returned to his former post at the Kunstgewerbeschule, Vienna, becoming its first president in 1946, and from 1945 to 1951 he was president of the Zentralvereinigung der Architekten Österreichs. His post-war architectural projects included a number of public housing developments, such as the Per-Albin-Hansson Siedlung (1947–51), Vienna, and alterations (1955–6) to the Parliament Building, Vienna. He was also active as a furniture designer during this period.

BIBLIOGRAPHY
G. Harbers: 'Hotelrestaurant auf dem Tulblinger Kogel', *Baumeister*, xxxi (1933), pp. 82–4
F. Achleitner: *Neue Architektur in Österreich, 1945–1970* (Vienna, 1970), pp. 72–4, 168

NICHOLAS BULLOCK

Felletin. French centre of tapestry production. *See under* AUBUSSON, §1.

Fellig, Arthur [Usher]. *See* WEEGEE.

Fellner, Ferdinand (*b* Vienna, 19 April 1847; *d* Vienna, 22 March 1916). Austrian architect. He was the son of a theatre architect, also called Ferdinand Fellner, and in 1873 he formed a partnership with the German architect HERMANN HELMER. The firm subsequently became one of the most active and successful companies in the field of theatre architecture, building 47 theatres all over the Austro-Hungarian Empire, in Germany and in south-east Europe. Fellner and Helmer were originally influenced by the architecture of Fellner the elder. However, new regulations for fire protection, issued in the 1880s as a result of frequent and disastrous theatre fires, came to influence strongly the exterior and interior construction. Each theatre was required to have an isolated site, a clear separation of the whole structure into an auditorium and a stage with separate roofs, iron stage construction and electric lighting. To meet these requirements, Fellner and Helmer divided their theatres into three parts: a front block containing the vestibule, foyers and staircases; a lower auditorium; and a dominating stage tower. This is best seen in the Neues Deutsches Theater (1886–7), Prague, and the Deutsches Volkstheater (1888–9) in Vienna. Inside, the arrangement of the staircases and the auditorium was crucial. Fellner and Helmer adapted elements from the central staircase of the Vienna Opera House in Brno (1881–2), in the Theater unter den Linden (1891–2), Berlin, and in Graz (1898–9); in Odessa (1884–7), Fiume (now Rijeka, 1883–5) and Bratislava (1885–6), they tried such experimental designs as diagonal stairs. For the auditorium, they often used the traditional system of boxes, often combined with circles and galleries, but their best solution was found in the Deutsches Volkstheater, where two wide circles offer the spectators the best possible view of the stage.

Other commissions undertaken by Fellner and Helmer included many private houses, castles, villas and commercial and public buildings. Of these, the Observatory (1874–80; *see* OBSERVATORY, §2) in Vienna is particularly noteworthy. It is a huge structure, rising on a Latin cross plan. The dominating central dome is accompanied by three smaller cupolas, and there is a dramatic interior staircase. Here, as elsewhere in the early part of his career, the architectural and decorative forms used by Fellner were based on Renaissance and Baroque models and displayed a splendour and richness typical of this period of late historicism. After 1905 Fellner gradually began to show the influence of Art Nouveau in theatres at Giessen (1906–7), Germany, Jablonec (1906–7), in what is now the Czech Republic, Baden (1908–9), near Vienna, and Klagenfurt (1909–10), Carinthia.

WRITINGS
Die Entwicklung des Theaterbaues in den letzen 50 Jahren (Vienna, 1909)
with H. Helmer: *Sammelwerk der ausgeführten Bauten und Projekte, 1870–1914* (Vienna, 1914)

BIBLIOGRAPHY
Macmillan Enc. Architects
A. von Wurm-Arnkreuz: Obituary, *Z. Österreich. Ingen.-&-Architekten-Ver.*, lxviii (1916), p. 416
——: *Der Architekt Ferdinand Fellner und seine Bedeutung für den modernen Theaterbau* (Vienna and Leipzig, 1919)
H. -C. Hoffmann: *Die Theaterbauen von Fellner und Helmer*, Studien zur Kunst des 19. Jahrhunderts, ii (Munich, 1966)

SUSANNE KRONBICHLER-SKACHA

Fellner, Jakob (*b* Nikolsburg, Moravia [now Mikulov, Czech Republic], 25 July 1722; *d* Tata, Hungary, 12 Dec 1780). Austrian architect. He moved to Tata in 1744 and spent 16 years there, carrying out most of the construction work for the Esterházy estates in the regions of Pápa, Devecser, Ugod and Tata, and for villages in the diocese of EGER under the control of Bishop Károly Esterházy. He designed many buildings—some functional, some decorative—that are still *in situ* in and around Tata. His most important work is the twin-steepled parish church (1774–83) in the town of Pápa, which was commissioned by Esterházy and reflects Esterházy's nostalgia for Francesco Borromini's S Agnese in Rome. Fellner also designed the modification of the Lyceum in Eger (1765–85; *see* HUNGARY, fig. 3) for Esterházy. This imposing, four-winged building (now the Pedagogical Seminary) was originally intended to be a university, and work had already begun to the designs of Joseph Gerl. Fellner invested it with a distinctly classical appearance in the style of Louis XVI. In 1761 he took over work on the twin-spired parish church of Tata, begun in 1751 by Franz Anton Pilgram, and building was continued after Fellner's death by Jozsef Grossman (1747–85). Fellner worked on the Cifra watermill (1755; Tata, now Ger.-Speaking Peoples Mus.) and designed the Nepomucenus Bridge (1770). He also built the graceful Lamberg Palace (1762–76) at Mór, the E-shaped Episcopal Palace in Veszprém in the contemporary French manner (1767) and the extension (1765–9) of the Esterházy Palace at Tata (now the District Hospital) in a style sympathetic to the Hungarian vernacular. Because Fellner employed several draughtsmen in his office at Tata, it is difficult to draw a sharp distinction between his work as a designer and as a builder. Recent research has shown that many buildings previously attributed to him can be attributed to Franz Anton Pilgram.

BIBLIOGRAPHY
P. Lukcsics and J. Pfeiffer: *A veszprémi püspöki vár* [The Episcopal Palace in Veszprém] (Veszprém, 1933)
I. Genthon: *Az egri liceum* [The Lyceum of Eger] (Budapest, 1955)
E. Hempel: *Baroque Art and Architecture in Central Europe*, Pelican Hist. A. (Harmondsworth, 1965)
J. Soós: 'Az egri liceum épitéstörténete' [The architectural history of the Lyceum of Eger], *Heves megye műemlékei* [Historical monuments of County Heves], ed. P. Voit, ii (Budapest, 1972)
P. Voit: *Franz Anton Pilgram* (Budapest, 1982)

PÁL VOIT

Fellowship of St Luke [Brotherhood of St Luke; Pol. Bractwo Świetego Łukasza]. Polish group of painters that flourished in 1925–39. It emerged from the studio of Tadeusz Pruszkowski (1888–1942) at the School of Fine Arts (Sekoła Sztuk Pięknych), Warsaw, and was the first post-war group in Warsaw's largest art school. The fellowship's 14 members, all pupils of Pruszkowski, included Bolesław Cybis (1895–1957), Jan Gotard (1898–1943), Antoni Michalak (1902–75) and Jan Zamojski (1901–85). The fellowship modelled itself on the medieval guilds (*see* GUILD), and the 'Master' Pruszkowski ceremoniously emancipated his pupils. The leadership of the group rested with the 'Chapter' (Kapituła). The members of the fellowship received special diplomas of emancipation. The group's artistic programme was also based on former models, primarily on 16th- and 17th-century Dutch painting, although the group was essentially held together by ties of friendship. The artistic character of the fellowship was largely influenced by the personality of Pruszkowski, an admirer of Frans Hals and Diego Velázquez and a colourful character in the Warsaw art world.

The fellowship's first exhibition in Warsaw's Zachęta Gallery in 1928 was enthusiastically received by the critics, but subsequent exhibitions, held more or less annually, met with increasing criticism. The members of the fellowship were attacked by the Polish colourists and the avant-garde. The cult of drawing and of the studio, which the fellowship espoused, was not approved of by the circles of innovative artists. On the other hand this cult did meet with the approval of the State, the group's members receiving commissions to decorate the interiors of passenger ships and government buildings. In 1934 the artists of the Fellowship of St Luke jointly organized the Bloc of Professional Plastic Artists (Blok Zawodowych Artystów Plastyków), an association firmly in favour of the concept of national art. The Bloc also included artists from other groups of painters founded by Pruszkowski in his studio who shared similar attitudes, for example the 'Warsaw School' Association of Plastic Artists (Stowarzyszenie Plastyków 'Szkoła Warszawska'; 1929), the Freepainters' Lodge (Loża Wolnomalarska; 1932) and the Fourth Group (Grupa Czwarta; 1936).

BIBLIOGRAPHY

W. Bartoszewicz: *Buda na Powiślu* [Cabin on the bank of the Vistula] (Warsaw, 1966)
Z. Baranowicz: 'Bractwo św. Łukasza', *Polskie życie artystyczne w latach 1915–39* [Polish artistic life in the years 1915–39], ed.A. Wojciechowski (Wrocław, 1974)
Malarze kręgu Pruszkowskiego [Painters of Pruszkowski's circle] (exh. cat., Warsaw, N. Mus., 1978)

WOJCIECH WŁODARCZYK

Felsina. *See* BOLOGNA.

Felt. Non-woven textile used as a practical material, particularly in Central Asia, and as an artistic and craft medium. Felt is the end product of a process whereby fibres or staples of animal hair are subjected to friction and pressure under moist, hot conditions. The action enables the fibres to matt owing to their ability to 'creep' in a tip to root direction. The scales on the outer covering of the fibres (*see* TEXTILE, §I, 1) then become enmeshed in the natural crimp of the twisted fibres.

1. Materials and techniques. 2. History and uses.

1. MATERIALS AND TECHNIQUES. Felt is usually made from sheep's wool and from goat or camel hair, but the hair or wool from many other animals can be used, even that of humans. It is also possible to incorporate such vegetable fibres as jute. The wool is used in its natural colours—ivory, light brown and dark brown—or it is dyed. Traditionally, the dyes were such locally obtainable plants as madder and pomegranate, but widely traded dyes, indigo

and cochineal for example, were introduced in many areas; all have now been replaced by synthetic dyes.

The methods by which felt is made vary in different countries. On the Asian steppe felt is usually, but not exclusively, made by women. A reed mat is placed on the ground, and the shorn wool is beaten or teased by a felting bow made of a length of gut attached to an L-shaped piece of wood. The worker holds the bow firmly over the wool with one hand and with the other hand strikes the tautened gut with a mallet. The vibration causes the wool fibres to loosen and disentangle. The Turkoman tribes card the fibres through a large comb standing on the ground, its metal teeth pointing upwards. The wool is then laid in clumps on the mat and spread evenly, without gaps, to the required depth. The thickness required of the final product dictates the amount of wool put down on the mat; it may be as much as 400 mm deep. The wool is sprinkled with warm water and an alkaline solution (e.g. urine or soap powder), then rolled tightly in a bundle and tied. Depending on the width of the piece being made, up to ten women, elbow to elbow, roll it for several hours. The larger and thicker the material required, the more pressure, workers and time are needed. In Turkey men make the felt. Having tied up the bundle, they roll it with their feet, standing in a row, their hands pressing on one knee to give the greatest weight. They work to music, singing in rhythm. In Afghanistan both sexes make felt: normally, the women lay out the pattern, and the men do the heavy work.

In finer pieces, the work is sometimes unrolled for inspection and adjustment before completion; the edges are tidied, and then it is rolled again. When dried, the surfaces are smoothed by a burnishing stone or roller. Rougher rugs are not inspected, just unfolded and put out to dry. The finished felt varies in thickness from 15 mm, when used for tents, to 2 mm for fine appliqué.

In hat-making, the felt is prepared in a shallow dish, kneaded until soft and pliable, then moulded around a block to form the required shape. It is then pressed until ready. A hatter in Iran can make up to 30 hats a day, before putting them outside to dry and finally polishing them.

There are a number of ways of patterning and decorating felt. Two or more colours can be felted together at random. Alternatively, predyed clumps of fibre, arranged in a pattern, are placed on the mat, and the rest of the wool laid on top of them; the wool will felt together in one piece. If a pattern is to appear on the back of the finished felt, more coloured wool is placed on the top of the mass. If layers of different coloured felt are superimposed, contrasts of shape may be achieved with, for example, incisions and saw-tooth edges. Plain felts can be decorated by painting, stencilling or block-printing.

Sewing techniques are also used to decorate felt. In Afghanistan it is common to find appliquéd motifs of felt, silk, cotton, feathers, bark or leather. A mosaic effect can be achieved by sewing small pieces of felt together, with the stitches hidden in the seams. This technique is often found in Afghanistan and the Commonwealth of Independent States. Edges can be applied as decoration and to strengthen the article. These may be of cord, silk or leather and surround either the complete article or individual design motifs. Further protection is afforded by decorative quilting stitches, often zigzags or spirals: these are used on such items as camel, horse and donkey trappings, which come under great strain. Sometimes felts are richly embroidered, which reinforces the fabric as well as enhancing its appearance.

2. HISTORY AND USES.

(i) Asia. (ii) Elsewhere.

(i) Asia. In large areas of Central Asia felt was once ubiquitous; indeed in the 4th century BC the northern steppes were known by the Chinese as the 'land of felt' (Gervers and Gervers, p. 15). Most of the steppe peoples, from Anatolia to the eastern borders of Mongolia, were nomads, and for them felt was an ideal material. The wool was readily available; no special equipment was needed for its manufacture; it was easy to pack, roll up and transport; and it was warm, waterproof and resilient in the face of wind, rain, snow and sun. Felt provided the fabric for tents (*see* TENT, §II), rugs, bedding mats, bags, saddlery, animal trappings, shepherds' mantles and countless other items. Its utilitarian nature, however, has meant that little has survived.

Because felt was essential to the nomadic way of life, it was considered to have symbolic and ritual significance. European writers, including Marco Polo, described idols and ritual images made of felt, and also its use in funerary rites in Iran and Mongol China. This tradition appears to have a very ancient history: it is recorded that when Hephaistion, the companion of Alexander the Great, was interred at Babylon in 324 BC, the pyre was draped in purple or scarlet felt.

It is likely that in Central Asia felt-making predates weaving, but it is not known when it first evolved. Excavations at the Anatolian site of Çatal Hüyük suggest that it was already in use *c.* 6500 BC. Wall paintings show curvilinear designs outlined in black very similar to those used on felt appliqué. The earliest known felts (St Petersburg, Hermitage) were found in Pazyryk, in the Altai Mountains of Siberia, and date from between the 6th century BC and the 4th. It is clear that the art was already highly developed, both technically and visually. The felts are sometimes extremely fine (*c.* 2 mm thick), and all the decorative techniques—inlay, mosaic, appliqué and embroidery—were employed with great skill. These felts were found in burial mounds where they had been preserved by the permafrost. They include carpets, shrouds, linings for sarcophagi, socks and stockings, cushion covers, hair accessories, saddle and mane covers, blankets and masks. The largest and most significant piece, the 'Great Felt', is 4.5×6.5 m in size and was probably a hanging. It is a multicoloured mosaic depicting a female ruler seated and holding a branch while a male rider approaches her. This motif is repeated on two rows separated by bands of stylized floral decoration. On the right edge there appears to have been a border with representations of a griffin-like bird and a sphinx. Four sculptural figures of swans (for illustration of three of these see fig. 1), stuffed with deer hair, were also found. It has been suggested that they decorated a grave canopy or ceremonial carriage.

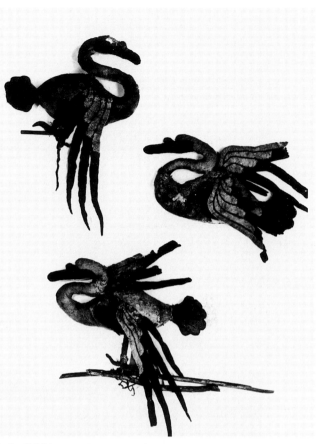

1. Stuffed felt swans, l. *c.* 300 mm, from Pazyryk, Siberia, 5th–4th century BC (St Petersburg, Hermitage Museum)

Knowledge of early felt-making, however, is derived largely from documentary evidence rather than from surviving examples, which are exceedingly rare. Chinese dynastic histories reveal that in the 3rd century BC the Xiongnu, the warrior nomads of the northern steppes, were living in felt tents and wearing felt hats and boots. Felt appears to have spread to China by *c.* 230 BC: Aurel Stein, during his excavations in Eastern Central Asia, unearthed written evidence in the Kharoṣṭhī scripts of felts being used in the Han period (206 BC-AD 220) for rugs and saddle covers.

The next significant find was at Noin Ula in northern Mongolia. The felts, which have been dated by the presence of a lacquer bowl to the first decade of the 1st century AD, comprise floor and ceiling carpets, with appliqué of felt and other materials. The largest piece has a central panel of 24 spirals and a frieze of animals in combat. An important collection of Chinese felts of the Tang period (AD 618–907) was found in Japan, in the Shōsōin at Nara (*see* NARA, §III, 3). Of the thirty-one pieces in the repository, five are square and over 1×1 m in size, the rest rectangular and *c.* 2×1 m. Many are on a white ground, but the most exotic and brightly coloured is on a dark blue ground with a white reverse. Each side has floral medallions between which there are flowers; there is a white wavy border. Other designs include polo players and such floral motifs as peonies. The colours used are dark and pale blue, bluish green and dark and pale pink. The backs of some of the rugs are stamped with the seals of the Tōdaiji.

Hereafter it is necessary to refer again to documentary evidence. Marco Polo in the 13th century travelled in a rain-proof felt-covered wagon, as did Ibn Battuta in the 14th century (similar wagons are still used in Mongolia and can be seen in the Toy Museum, Kecskemét, Hungary, and in Gertrude Bell's photographs of the early 20th century). Willem van Rubruck described the felt-covered tents and finely decorated felt doors that he observed among the Turkic tribes north of the Caucasus in 1253. These, and other writers, described the way in which the nomads transported the tents between their summer and winter pastures. Several writers gave full accounts of the use of felt in China when the Mongols ruled as the Yuan dynasty (1279–1368). Doors, tent walls and carpets, some of enormous size, were made for the imperial court in multicoloured and embroidered felt (Bidder, 1964, pp. 87–91).

Later European writers, for example John Smith in 1630 and John Chardin in 1670, made further references to felt. It continued to be used in the 18th and 19th centuries, when, for example, the floors of Persian homes were covered with a knotted carpet while felt rugs lay around the extremities of the room. Its utilitarian nature is indicated by R. Shaw's account in 1874 of a single caravan travelling from Kashgar to Kokand in Eastern Central Asia with 120 loads of felt valued at 7000 *tungas* and 25 loads of Khotan carpets valued at 16,500 *tungas* (Bidder, 1964, pp. 37–9). This suggests both the commercial value of felt in comparison with carpets and also the extent of its use. It could still be seen in the richest circles in the early 20th century: in the emirate of Bukhara, for example, felt hangings were used in ceremonial tents.

Later in the 20th century, however, when many of the customs of the sophisticated classes were eroded by outside influences and modernization, felt became exclusively the fabric of the poorer nomads. In Iran the manufacture of felt rugs, which had taken place particularly in Isfahan, Yazd and Kirman died out, and the village and tribal production of rugs, hats and shepherds' coats greatly declined by the end of the century. In Turkey and Iraq, too, felt-making virtually disappeared, and only the production of shepherds' coats and some mats remained. However, the tradition continued in Georgia and among the Turkoman, Kazakh and Kirghiz peoples (*see* KAZAKHSTAN, §4, and KYRGYZSTAN, §3) and in Afghanistan, where rugs, hangings and animal trappings were made by

2. Kirghiz felt rug, probably from Alma Alta, 20th century (London, Doris Rau private collection)

the tribal people in a variety of techniques, including appliqué, mosaic and inlay.

The designs on Central Asian felts are generally abstract and, given the significance of the material, were probably once symbolic as well as decorative. The Turkoman, Kazakh and Kirghiz, the major felt-makers of Asia, continue an ancient visual tradition using spirals, hooks, animal horns, scrolling bands, lattice and other geometric motifs (see fig. 2). Often these create reciprocal images, with contrasts of light and dark. In contrast to weaving, where the interaction of the warp and weft creates a structured effect, the felting process allows considerable freedom in the flow of designs. Often, however, there has been an interchange of designs between the two methods, felt-makers borrowing motifs from carpets and weavers adapting felt designs, for example scrolls, to their work.

In India felt mats (*numdah*s) with embroidered floral designs are still made for export to the West. Little is known of felt-making in Tibet. It was first mentioned by Chinese writers of the Tang period, being used for plates, tents and clothing; high-quality painted felt rugs survive from the late 19th century or the early 20th; and in the late 20th century it was still used for clothing (see TIBET, §V, 10). In Outer Mongolia there is no history of pile weaving, and tents, carpets, bags and saddle rugs are traditionally made of felt (see MONGOLIA, §IV, 4). Only undyed natural colours are used, and the ornamentation is done purely by quilting stitches all over the surface.

(ii) Elsewhere. There are numerous references to felt in Classical literature, particularly to felt hats, which seem to have been especially popular in Greece. The Romans, too, wore felt hats, as well as using the material inside armour and for larger items; a mural (*in situ*) outside Verecundus' workshop at Pompeii shows felt-makers at work.

There is evidence for the use of felt socks, boots and hats in Britain, Germany, Scandinavia and Iceland from the 5th century AD to the early 20th. The making of felt hats was initially a cottage industry, but it became more formalized in the 16th century, and in 1604 the Worshipful Company of Feltmakers of London was incorporated by royal charter. In the 19th century the process became fully mechanized. The felt often incorporated rabbit, hare or beaver fur along with the wool. In Bohemia and Slovakia, too, there was a long tradition of hat-making, and here, as in other eastern countries and in Lapland, felt was used for folk dress.

Before the 20th century, the only part of the world in which felt could be found outside Asia and Europe was Morocco. It was introduced in the 8th century AD, probably from Turkey, and was considered to be of good quality. The craft died out in the 18th century.

In the West felt has usually been considered a humble material, but since *c.* 1975 its possibilities as an art form have been recognized. This revival has taken place chiefly in Scandinavia, the Netherlands, Britain, the USA, Australia and New Zealand. Artists have been able to use modern industrial machinery (e.g. needle-punching machines) or small motorized hand-felting machines to speed up the felting process. Vegetable, metallic and synthetic fibres have been incorporated into the felt, and hard materials, for example metal and stone, have been used to contrast

3. *Felt 29* by Jenny Cowern, 914×1219 mm, 1984–5 (London, Victoria and Albert Museum)

the padded quality of the fabric. Sculptural effects have been achieved by cutting back layers of felt or by building up projections from the surface; wire has been used by such artists as Magdalena Abakanowicz to form armatures. Other techniques exploit felt in a more painterly fashion, graduating the colours by superimposing thin layers of colour or by 'felting-in' precut shapes. Some artists, such as Inge Dorothea Evers in the Netherlands and Tuula Nikulainen in Finland, use felt for hats, boots, garments and installations, while others make hangings (e.g. *Felt 29* by Jenny Cowern; see fig. 3). Two artists in particular were interested in the symbolic qualities of felt. For Robert Morris (ii) it formed part of his exploration of ephemera, while for Joseph Beuys it had personal, autobiographical associations as well as wider social and sculptural implications. The International Felt Symposium held in Århus, Denmark, in 1990, showed the work of various makers of art felts, including Annie Sherburne in England and Karen Page and Chad Alice Hagen of the USA. In June 1994 an important International Felt Conference was held in Tilburg in the Netherlands, and the International Felt Association put on a major exhibition at the Collins Gallery, Glasgow, in the summer of 1994. A Museum of Felt has also been opened in Mouzon, France, associated with the last felt factory in that town.

See also FIBRE ART and SOFT ART.

BIBLIOGRAPHY

J. Smith: *True Travels, Adventures and Observations in Europe, Asia and America from 1593 to 1629* (London, 1630)

J. Chardin: *Voyages du chevalier Chardin, en Perse, et autres lieux de l'orient,* ed. Langlès, iv (Paris, 1811), pp. 18–19

C. Tomlinson, ed.: *Tomlinson's Cyclopedia of Useful Arts and Chemical Manufactures, Mining and Engineering* (London and New York, 1854)

W. W. Rockhill, ed.: *The Journey of William of Rubruck to the Eastern Parts of the World* (London, 1900)

J. H. Hawkins: *History of the Worshipful Company . . . of Feltmakers of London* (London, 1917)

A. Stein: *Serindia,* v (Oxford, 1921), pp. 246–50

B. Laufer: 'The Early History of Felt', *Amer. Anthropologist*, xxxii (1930), pp. 1–18

J. Harada: *English Catalogue of Treasures in the Imperial Repository, Shōsōin* (Tokyo, 1932)

W. Meister: 'Zur Geschichte de Filzteppichs im I. Jahrtausend n. Chr.', *Ostasiat. Z.*, n. s., xii (1936), pp. 47–61

L. Olschki: *The Myth of Felt* (Berkeley and Los Angeles, 1949)

S. I. Rudenko: *Kultura naseleniya gornogo Altaya v. skifskoe vremya* (Moscow and Leningrad, 1953); Eng. trans. as *Frozen Tombs of Siberia: The Pazyryk Burials of Iron Age Horsemen* (London, 1970)

'Felt', *Ciba Z.* (1958), no. 129 [Gesellschaft für chemische Industrie]

J. F. Haskins: 'The Pazyryk Felt Screen and the Barbarian Captivity of Tasi Wei Chei', *Bull. Mus. Far E. Ant.*, xxxv (1963), pp. 141–60

H. Bidder: *Teppiche aus Ost-Turkestan, bekannt, als Khotan-, Samarkand- und Kansu-Teppiche* (Tübingen, 1964; Eng. trans., London, n.d.)

K. Jettmar: *Kunst der Welt: Die frühen Steppenvölken* (Baden-Baden, 1964); Eng. trans. as *Art of the Steppes: The Eurasian Animal Style* (London, 1967)

J. P. Wild: *Textile Manufacture in the Northern Roman Province* (Cambridge, 1970), p. 171

V. Gervers-Molnar: *The Hungarian Szur: An Archaic Mantle of Eurasian Origin*, Textile, Royal Ont. Mus. (Toronto, 1973)

V. Gervers and M. Gervers: 'Felt-making Craftsmen of the Anatolian and Iranian Plateau', *Textile Mus. J.* (1974), iv, pp. 14–29

R. Michaud and S. Michaud: *Caravanes de Tartarie* (Chêne, 1977; Eng. trans., London, 1985)

The Art of the Felt Maker (exh. cat. by M. E. Burkett, Kendal, Abbot Hall A.G., 1979) [extensive bibliog.]

H. Bidder and I. Bidder: *Filzteppiche: Ihre Geschichte und Eigenart* (Brunswick, 1980)

B. Gordon: *Feltmaking* (New York, 1980)

Felting, American Craft Mus. (New York, 1980)

M. E. Burkett: 'A Knotted Rug with a Felt Motif', *Feltmaker's Assoc. J.* (Jan 1986), p. 5

Internationalt Filtsymposium (exh. cat., Århus, Studenternes Hus, 1990)

E. J. W. Barber: *Prehistoric Textiles: The Development of Cloth in the Neolithic and Bronze Ages, with Special Reference to the Aegean* (Princeton, 1991)

M. E. BURKETT

Fel'ten, Yury (Matveyevich) [Velten, Georg Friderick] (*b* St Petersburg, 1730 or 1732; *d* St Petersburg, 1801). Russian architect and teacher. The son of a German from Danzig, West Prussia (now Gdańsk, Poland), he studied mathematics at Tübingen University before turning to architecture. After gaining practical experience during the building of the Neues Schloss (1747–8), Stuttgart, for the Duke of Württemberg, he returned to St Petersburg to study (1749–52) at the Academy of Arts. He subsequently worked under Bartolomeo Francesco Rastrelli, assisting him at the Winter Palace and later succeeding him there as architect (1762). He designed part of the Small Hermitage (1765–6) and new interiors (1770–79) for Peterhof in a style that combined classical and Baroque features. His finest work was executed in the 1770s and demonstrates his twin approach to classicism. His churches, such as St Catherine (1768–71), the Armenian Church (1770–77) and St Anne (1775–9), all in St Petersburg, are enriched with sculpture, plasterwork and porticos, giving them a splendid and stately appearance. He preferred, however, a less ornamented style, using pilasters rather than columns. Often his large public buildings were astylar (without columns), for example the Alexander Institute (1765–75) and the Old Hermitage (1771–87) in St Petersburg and the Foundling Hospital (1765–74) in Moscow. He was also responsible for the delicate, wrought-iron railing (1770–84) for the Summer Garden, St Petersburg, one of the masterpieces of 18th-century Russian ironwork. Fel'ten was involved in the architectural transformation of St Petersburg, replacing the wooden fences along the River Neva with mighty granite quays (1762–80), with parapets and steps running down to the water. Other works included the reconstruction of Palace Square (1779) and the installation (1782) in Decembrists' Square (Ploshchad' Dekabristov) of Etienne-Maurice Falconet's bronze statue of *Peter the Great* (for illustration *see* EQUESTRIAN MONUMENT), as well as town houses and such industrial buildings as the paper-mill (1787–9) at Peterhof. For estate buildings he was happy to work in various fashionable, exotic or revival styles popularized by William Chambers, evident, for example, in the Ruined Tower (1771–3), the Gothic Gates (1777–80) and the Chinese Creaking Pavilion (1778–86), all at Tsarskoye Selo (now Pushkin). Fel'ten also taught for many years (from 1772) at the Academy of Arts, serving as its director from 1789 to 1794. His career spanned the change from Baroque to Neo-classicism in Russia.

BIBLIOGRAPHY

N. P. Sobko: 'Fel'ten, Yury Makhiylovich', *Russkiy biograficheskiy slovar'*, xxi (St Petersburg, 1901), pp. 47–9

I. E. Grabar', S. S. Bronshteyn and G. G. Grimm: 'U istokov russkogo klassitsisma' [At the origins of Russian classicism], *Istoriya russkogo iskusstva*, vi, ed. I. E. Grabar' and others (Moscow, 1961), pp. 76–84

Arkhitektor Yury Fel'ten: K 250-letiyu so dnya rozhdeniya: Katalog vystavki [The architect Yury Velten: catalogue of an exhibition for the 250th anniversary of his birth] (exh. cat. by M. F. Korshunova, Moscow, 1982)

N. A. YEVSINA

Felton, Alfred (*b* Maldon, Essex, 8 Nov 1831; *d* Melbourne, 8 Jan 1904). Australian philanthropist and businessman of English birth. In Britain he was apparently apprenticed to an apothecary before migrating to Victoria in 1853, where he profited from transporting supplies to the gold-fields in a horse-drawn dray. This enabled him to go into business in Melbourne, where by 1857 he was established as an importer and agent, and four years later he was recorded as a wholesale pharmacist. In 1867 in partnership with F. Grimwade he acquired control of a chemical supply company of which Grimwade had been manager. They prospered as Felton Grimwade & Company, dominating the market and establishing subsidiaries in other Australasian colonies. They also expanded into related fields of manufacturing such as acid works, glass making, eucalyptus oil extraction and salt production. Felton also personally invested in several rural properties.

Although probably largely self-educated, Felton had a keen interest in art and literature. He is recalled as a moderately eccentric bachelor who lived frugally in modest lodgings at the Esplanade Hotel in St Kilda, where he kept his large collection of books and works of art. He was a dedicated philanthropist, and during his lifetime he regularly donated large sums to various charitable causes. He bequeathed his fortune for the equal benefit of the National Gallery of Victoria and established charities, especially those devoted to the relief of women and children. The estate was valued at £497,248, and the residue after probate duties and minor legacies was used to establish a trust fund that later appreciated to more than £2,000,000 under the management of a Felton Bequests Committee. Only interest on the accrued capital was used to fulfil the terms of the bequest, which in the case of the National Gallery of Victoria provided for acquisition of works of art with artistic and educational value likely to enhance public taste, for example Giambattista Tiepolo's *Banquet of Cleopatra* (1743) and Nicolas Poussin's *Crossing of the Red Sea* (mid- 1630s). It was the Gallery's major benefaction.

BIBLIOGRAPHY

C. Bage, ed.: *Historical Record of the Felton Bequests*, 2 vols (Melbourne, 1923–7)

Alfred Felton and his Art Benefactions (Melbourne, 1936)

R. Grimwade: *Flinders Lane: Recollections of Alfred Felton* (Melbourne, 1947)

E. Lindsay, ed.: *The Felton Bequest: An Historical Record, 1904–1959* (Melbourne, 1963)

J. Poynter: *Alfred Felton* (Melbourne, 1974)

ROBERT SMITH

Feltre, Morto da. *See under* LUZZO, LORENZO.

Feltre, Vittorino da. *See* VITTORINO DA FELTRE.

Feltrini, Andrea (di Giovanni di Lorenzo) [Andrea di Cosimo] (*b* Florence, 1477; *d* 12 May 1548). Italian painter. Vasari noted that Andrea was a student of Cosimo Rosselli and then of Lorenzo Luzzo, whose names he appended to his own. Through the latter, who arrived in Florence from Rome *c.* 1505, he became aware of the archaeological classicism dominant in Rome from at least the 1480s. He mastered the vocabulary of Classical motifs, especially the grotesques inspired by examples in the newly excavated Domus Aurea, and Vasari credited him with the idea of using them in *sgraffito* decorations of palace façades, which brought him fame among his contemporaries. He was much in demand in Florence to decorate houses in what was believed to be the fashion of imperial Rome, and the façades of the Palazzo Lanfredini (1515) and Palazzo Sertini (1515–20), both now restored, indicate the extremes to which Classical motifs were developed in Florence. Andrea was also in demand by his fellow artists: in 1515, for example, he collaborated with Ridolfo Ghirlandaio and Jacopo Pontormo on the decoration of the Cappella dei Papi in S Maria Novella, Florence. The grotesques on the walls and vault can be attributed to Andrea and, perhaps, the *all'antica* organization of the latter. For the execution of these large projects, he formed a partnership with Mariotto di Francesco and Raffaello di Biagio, who assisted him in his later years in the preparation of decorations for festivals and Medici weddings.

BIBLIOGRAPHY

G. Vasari: *Vite* (1550, rev. 2/1568); ed. G. Milanesi (1878–85), v, pp. 201–10

C. Thiem and G. Thiem: 'Andrea di Cosimo Feltrini und die Groteskendekoration der Florentiner Hochrenaissance', *Z. Kstgesch.*, xxiv (1961), pp. 1–39

——: *Toskanische Fassaden-Dekoration in Sgraffito und Fresko: 14. bis 17. Jahrhundert* (Munich, 1964), pp. 31–3

J. Cox-Rearick: *Dynasty and Destiny in Medici Art: Pontormo, Leo X and Two Cosimos* (Princeton, 1984)

MARJORIE A. OCH

Fémes Beck, Vilmos. *See* BECK (ii), (2).

Feminism and art. Feminist art is work that is rooted in the analyses and commitments of contemporary feminism and that contributes to a critique of the political, economic and ideological power relations of contemporary society. It is not a stylistic category nor simply any art produced by women.

1. THE 'WOMAN QUESTION' AND WOMEN ARTISTS IN THE 19TH CENTURY. 'Feminism' (Lat. *femina*: 'woman') referred originally to the qualities of women. It did not come into use as a term denoting 'advocacy of the claims and rights of women' (OED) until 1895, after a century of debate on 'the woman question' or 'women's rights'. It cannot be coincidence that a flurry of books devoted to women artists, the first exhibitions that grouped them together as women and the first opportunities for their serious education and employment all accompanied the rise and influence of the Victorian women's movement. Both as professionals and as amateurs, women became artists in large numbers for the first time in the 19th century: what Virginia Woolf called the 'battle of the Royal Academy' was one among many: the battle of Westminster, the battle of Whitehall, the battle of Harley Street. Art was open to women in a way that the institutionalized professions of politics, religion, law and (until the 1870s) medicine were not. The idea of the woman artist, if increasingly familiar, was, however, still deeply uncomfortable. The serious pursuit of art was understood to be incompatible with the demands of femininity, just as the attributes of femininity were incompatible with the production of good art.

A keen awareness of these contradictions made many women artists feminists, and feminists were interested in the woman artist, not only because she was a type of the

1. Emily J. Harding Andrews: *Convicts and Lunatics*, poster published by the Artists' Suffrage League, printed paper, 988×737 mm, 1908–9 (London, Guildhall University, Fawcett Library)

skilled and independent woman but because women's supposed lack of cultural creativity was often given as a reason for denying them the vote. In 1897 the Central Committee of the National Society for Women's Suffrage published a list of suffrage supporters that included the names of 76 women painters, among them Lady Butler, Henrietta Rae, Annie Louisa Swynnerton and Lucy Madox Rossetti. From 1907, after the foundation of the Artists' Suffrage League (followed in 1909 by the Suffrage Atelier), women lent their artistic skills to the propaganda of an elaborate political campaign, seen, for example, in a poster of 1908–9 (London, Guildhall U., Fawcett Lib.; see fig. 1) by Emily J. Harding Andrews. This was the most polemical feminist work produced before the Women's Movement of the late 1960s. Until then women, in flight from the newly insistent and inferior category of the female artist, tended to concede the conventional wisdom that 'art has no sex'.

2. THE WOMEN'S LIBERATION MOVEMENT AND ART INSTITUTIONS. Feminism's 'second wave' emerged in the USA at the end of the 1960s. Women were fed up with drudgery and isolation at home, inferior pay and conditions at work and secondary status in the Civil Rights Movement and anti-war campaigns. The first British women's groups were formed in 1968, and the first Women's Liberation Movement (W.L.M.) National Conference took place in Oxford in 1970. The seven demands of the W.L.M. were formulated between 1970 (at Oxford) and 1978 and included equal pay for equal work; equal education and job opportunities; legal and financial independence for women; the right to a self-defined sexuality and an end to discrimination against lesbians; freedom from intimidation by male violence and an end to the laws and institutions that help to perpetuate male dominance and men's aggression towards women. The emphasis on equal opportunity led women artists to organize against institutional discrimination. The emphasis on a self-defined sexuality encouraged feminists to challenge the images of femininity then current in advertising, pornography and the mass media; it also led to exploration of alternative representations of and for women, and ultimately into an analysis of how representation itself produces social definitions of femininity and determines the way experiences are perceived.

In 1969 women from the Art Workers' Coalition in New York formed Women Artists in Revolution or WAR. This was followed by a second breakaway group in 1970, the Ad Hoc Committee (of women artists), which was organized to fight institutional discrimination, beginning with the picketing of the Whitney Museum of American Art. At the Whitney Annual of 1969 less than 6% of the work had been by women; the exhibition of 1970 included 22% of work by women. Further demonstrations took place at the County Museum of Art, Los Angeles (1970), the Corcoran Gallery of Art, Washington, DC (1971), and the Museum of Modern Art, New York (1972). In 1971 WAR and Women Students and Artists for Black Art Liberation (W.S.A.B.A.L.) observed in a letter to the Human Rights Commission that women constituted 52.5% of the American population, 60–75% of the art students, but only 5% of the artist population in galleries

and 3% of that in museums. The early editions of H. W. Janson's standard text-book *A History of Art* (1962 and 1977) ignored women, and Arnold Hauser's multi-volume *Social History of Art* (1951) included only one in a list of 450 names.

Women were also poorly represented in contemporary reviews. This led feminist artists to organize independent exhibitions and women's cooperatives and galleries such as the feminist A.I.R. (founded in 1972 and housing the Women's Art Registry) and SoHo 20 (opened in 1973). Redstocking Artists produced the first issue of *Women and Art* in December 1971, but political disagreements led to a splinter group publishing the *Feminist Art Journal* (1972–7). The *Feminist Art Journal*, *Chrysalis* (1977–80), *Heresies* (from 1977) and the *Woman's Art Journal* (from 1980), together with the dedicated efforts of Lucy Lippard in the art press, provided a critical context for the public discussion of feminist work. The Guerrilla Girls, unidentified activists who constituted themselves as the feminist conscience of the New York art world, nevertheless claimed that the mainstream coverage of women's art was little improved (see their advertisements in *A. Mag.*, xi/5, 1987, pp. 104, 128; for further discussion of feminist literature *see* WOMEN AND ART HISTORY).

Artists in New York emphasized equal representation and economic parity, but during the 1970s there was also an active women's art movement in California, which placed greater emphasis on what it perceived as specifically female content (related to women's bodies and female experiences) and feminine sensibility. In 1970 JUDY CHICAGO established a female art class at Fresno State College, which used consciousness-raising techniques from the women's movement to help students 'make art out of the things with which they were really involved'. With Miriam Schapiro, she established the Feminist Art Program at the California Institute of the Arts (1971). Their principal project was Womanhouse, a mansion in Los Angeles, restored and transformed in a series of environments and performances that opened to the public in January 1972. Womanspace, a gallery in Los Angeles, run by women and exhibiting women artists' work, opened in January 1973.

In London the first Women's Liberation Art Group exhibition was held at the Woodstock Gallery in 1971; the first to make a public impact, however—and bring upon Monica Sjoo the threat of obscenity and blasphemy charges for her painting *God Giving Birth*—was the *Womanpower* exhibition held at Swiss Cottage Library in April 1973. The London Women's Liberation Art Group had formed in 1970, the Women's Workshop of the Artists' Union in 1972, and a splinter-group of the Women's Workshop became the Women Artists' Collective in 1975. The Women's Free Arts Alliance was planned in 1972 and registered as a charity in 1974. In 1976 the Women Artists Slide Library was founded. The Women's Art History Collective, which began meeting in 1972, joined women artists' groups to picket the Hayward Gallery *Condition of Sculpture* exhibition in 1975, after the model of the Whitney demonstrations, demanding 50% representation in state-housed and subsidized exhibitions and on Arts Council selection panels; in 1978 the Hayward Annual was selected, controversially, by an all-woman panel and reviewed in the press, as 'The Girls' Own Annual' and 'Ladies' Night at the Hayward', in terms that reiterated the 19th-century category of 'feminine' creativity. Thereafter it was tacitly recognized that women should be represented on major grant-awarding bodies and selection committees, although a level of institutional discrimination remained.

Special issues of *Art and Artists* (Oct 1973), *Studio International* (cxciii/987, 1977) and the *Oxford Art Journal* (iii/1, 1980) were devoted to women artists, and feminist work was covered regularly in *Spare Rib* (from 1972). The quarterly *Feminist Art News* was published from 1979. Parallel developments took place in Germany, Sweden, Denmark, France and Italy; from 1976 *Lip* was published in Australia. From the mid-1970s groups, exhibitions and publications proliferated beyond the point of tidy summary. Among the most significant in Britain were the exhibitions *Women's Images of Men*, *About Time* and *Issue* (all 1980; London, ICA); *Sense and Sensibility in Feminist Art Practice* (1982; Nottingham, Midland Group); *Beyond the Purloined Image* (1983; London, Riverside Gal.); *Pandora's Box* (1984; Bristol, Arnolfini Gal.); *Difference: On Representation and Sexuality* (1985; London, ICA); and *The Thin Black Line* (1985; London, ICA).

Much feminist work was exhibited in libraries, women's centres or other non-gallery spaces, sometimes from necessity but often as a matter of principle. For some, 'art' was primarily a form of expression and communication between women rather than something to put in a gallery. The *Feministo Postal Event* (1975), which developed from an exchange of objects through the post between a network of women, both professional and amateur artists, was characteristic of collaborative work only later exhibited as *Portrait of the Artist as a Housewife* (1976–7). Jo Spence's 'photo-therapy' was based on a refusal to acknowledge traditional distinctions between photography, communication, therapy and 'art'. For others, the point was to reach an audience in the overlap between avant-garde interests and those of the women's movement, to address feminist and art-world constituencies at the same time. May Stevens suggested that where their political intent is unrealized, feminist works in museums and galleries 'hang like unopened letters, unanswered invitations' (Robinson, p. 181).

3. FEMINISM AND REPRESENTATION, THE 1970s. At the same time that feminist artists struggled for equal rights in existing institutions and set up alternatives of their own, they worked at developing a political culture that would intervene in the 'interlocking network of images, values, identities which saturate our daily living' (Parker and Pollock, 1987, p. 79). This has involved transformations or role reversals at the level of content (e.g. Sylvia Sleigh's male nudes and other images by women of men); cultural 'heroism', exemplified by Judy Chicago's *The Dinner Party* (installation, 1974–9; see fig. 2); and great goddess and matriarchal imagery (Mary Beth Edelson, Monica Sjoo). The Red Poster Workshop produced overtly propagandist graphics, while the social position of working-class women was treated in works by Kay Hunt, Mary Kelly and Margaret Harrison from the Women's Workshop of the Artists' Union and the Hackney Flashers. The subject of women's health was tackled by Peter Dunn and Lorraine Leeson, and particularly explicitly in Jo

2. Judy Chicago: Elizabeth Blackwell (1821–1920), the first woman in America to graduate from medical school and become a licensed physician; detail from *The Dinner Party*, mixed media installation, triangular table 14.63 m each side with 39 place settings, 1974–9

Spence's photographs. Women's relation to the unconscious and the unspoken was treated by Susan Hiller. An emphasis on such uniquely female experiences as menstruation and motherhood and on domesticity was made in work by Judy Chicago, Vivienne Binns and Kate Walker. Artists such as Lynda Benglis, Hannah Wilke and Suzanne Santoro celebrated the female body in its difference, often using parodied glamour imagery, or what the American critic Barbara Rose termed 'vaginal iconology'. Through performance and video Valie Export, Carolee Schneemann, Ulrike Rosenbach, Jana Sterbak, Eleanor Antin and Adrian Piper attempted to analyse or manipulate gendered identities and to confront or critique the male gaze; Marianne Wex and Annette Messager treated similar themes using photographs and texts. Work by Kate Walker and Joyce Weiland exploited an alternative sub-cultural tradition of domestic production in quilting and needlework. Lippard referred to a recognizable expression of a (controversial) feminine sensibility in central-core imagery, or in 'circles, domes, eggs, spheres, boxes, biomorphic shapes—maybe a certain striation or layering' (Lippard, 1976, p. 81). Artists such as Mary Kelly, Victor Burgin and Marie Yates deconstructed 'femininity' as something fixed and essential rather than as something precarious and fluid, the product of psycho-social representations. Among artists, as in the Women's Movement itself, there existed a plurality of feminist positions and strategies. Feminist art drew on the possibilities of conceptual, environmental, scripto-visual, film, video and performance work, or on

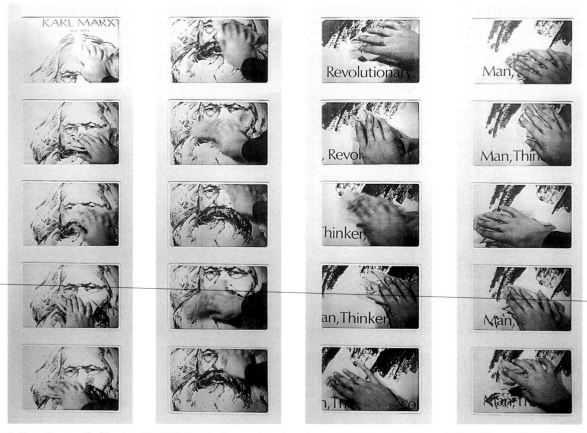

3. Alexis Hunter: *The Marxist's Wife (Still Does the Housework)*, colour photocopies in 4 panels, each panel 368×1207 mm, 1978 (Auckland, City Art Gallery)

more traditional techniques of painting and sculpture. In certain circumstances it may not be the intention of the producer but the eye of the beholder and the context in which the work appears that secures its political reading: Georgia O'Keeffe's flower paintings were, to her dismay, perceived as celebratory sexual images by feminists; in the context of the *Women's Images of Men* exhibition, Elisabeth Frink's bronze heads lost their generalized humanism and became pointedly masculine. 'Feminism' is not necessarily a consciously determined ingredient of the work but a product of the relation between the work and the representations of a dominant culture, a particular audience, and the uses to which it is put. It has also been argued (Partington in Robinson, p. 228) that there is no feminist art but only art that can be read as feminist.

Judy Chicago claimed that she had 'wanted to speak out of my femaleness, to make art out of the very thing that made me the "other" in male society' (Chicago, 1975, p. 203). Much feminist art began with the search for a female subject-matter and form. Form could be interpreted as a matter of feminine sensibility, medium or style; a tendency to centralized, veiled or grid-like compositions was often interpreted as specific to women's art. If femaleness was the repressed 'other' of male society, feminism had to locate it (in the body or the kitchen) as the basis for a shared women's culture. Different textual strategies in feminist art of the 1970s articulated 'the feminine' for different audiences in different ways. Work based on the rhythms, pleasures and reproductive capacities of the female body, like matriarchal and 'goddess' imagery, implied an essential feminine power that could be released into creativity. Work on the alienation and pain of women's physical experience invited identification in the experience of oppression and expanded the category of legitimate sexual subject-matter to include menstruation, rape and abortion. The exploitation of a sub-cultural and domestic tradition led to the celebration of women's nurturing capacities or, alternatively, to the denigration of their drudgery depicted by Alexis Hunter's *The Marxist's Wife (Still Does the Housework)* (1978; Auckland, C.A.G.; see fig. 3). These are not exclusive categories, and Chicago's *The Dinner Party*, a collaborative installation, joined matriarchal celebration to vaginal iconography and the use of needlework and china-painting as domestic techniques. The power of these strategies lay in their revaluation of despised or neglected feminine attributes. They were accessible (Chicago said of her work, 'you didn't have to read *Artforum* to appreciate it'). They offered a sense of identity and community to their audiences and unsettled the criteria for orthodox 'art'. To the extent that they dealt in the fixed signs of femininity, however, they produced a 'reverse-discourse' that accepted the terms on which difference had already been laid down. The paradox for feminism has always been that it speaks from a feminine position that it is simultaneously trying to transform.

Another more deconstructive practice refuses to oppose a 'masculine' culture with a (largely domestic) 'feminine' one. It assumes, first, that the patriarchal culture inhabited by men and women is riven with contradictions that feminists can expose and explore; and, second, that masculinity and femininity are not fixed categories, founded on anatomy, but unstable identities psycho-socially produced. The contrast between what is some-times called 'cultural feminism' and feminist work on

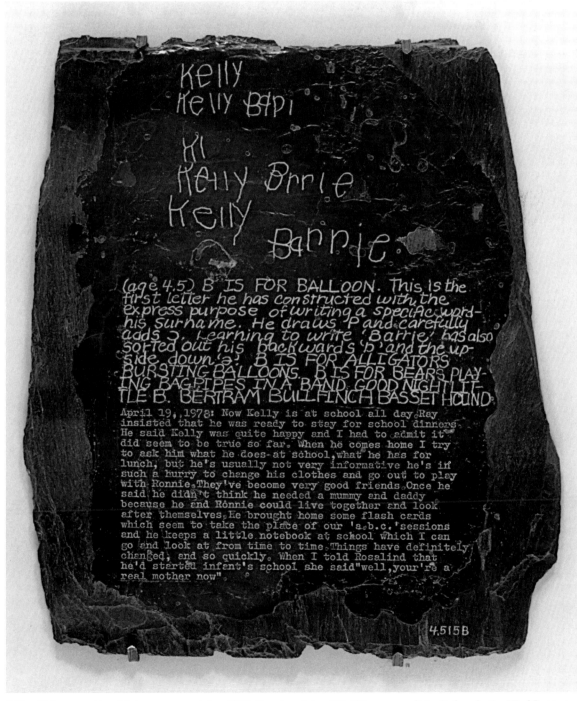

4. Mary Kelly: pre-writing alphabet, exergue and diary (1978–9), resin and slate, 254×203 mm, one of 15 units from Section VI of *Post-partum Document*, mixed media installation in six sections of 135 frames, 1973–9 (London, Arts Council of England)

sexual difference is starkest in a comparison of Chicago's *The Dinner Party* and Mary Kelly's *Post-partum Document* (1973–9; ACEng; see fig. 4). The 'feminine' is not a problem for the *The Dinner Party*, which produces and celebrates a coherent sexual identity; the *Post-partum Document* takes as its subject-matter the processes by which, in the early years of motherhood, an unstable femininity is provisionally secured. Arguments have been advanced for each strategy at the expense of the other. A political reading of either depends on the relative weight accorded to textual strategies on the one hand, or to accessibility through an appeal to the 'reading competences' of a large audience on the other (see Partington in Robinson).

4. (?)POST-FEMINISM, THE 1980s AND THE 1990s. The three exhibitions at the ICA in 1980 represented a turning-point in the institutional visibility of feminist art in Britain. The influence of theories of ideology and the subject (in particular the impact of Freudian and Lacanian psychoanalysis) encouraged a shift away from 'cultural feminism' towards a recognition of the processes of sexual differentiation and of the hopelessness of excavating a free or original femininity beneath the layers of patriarchal 'oppression'. The vexed question of whether men could make feminist work was answered in the 1980s by an increase in the number of men making work about masculinity (e.g. Victor Burgin and Sunil Gupta). A younger generation of women came to take the insights of feminism for granted, dealing with gender and identity through parody and masquerade: Laurie Anderson used a voice coder to heighten her sexual ambiguity; Cindy Sherman presented herself as the object of the look while refusing, in a mobility of self-constructed identities, to be discovered in it; Barbara Kruger's montages offered women the pleasure of answering back. Despite a use of neutral pronouns, the posited spectator is invariably male (*We Won't Play Nature to Your Culture*).

Feminism is no longer (necessarily) marginal. Jenny Holzer and Rebecca Horn (in 1989 and 1993 respectively) have had solo exhibitions at the Guggenheim Museum; Jenny Holzer was selected for the American Pavilion at the Venice Bienniale (1990); Rachel Whiteread became the first woman to win the Turner Prize (1993) at the Tate Gallery. At the same time, and perhaps significantly, the visceral strand in 1970s feminist art has re-emerged in work by such artists as Annie Sprinkle, Karen Finlay, Sue Williams and Kiki Smith, and in publications including *Angry Women* (1991) and *Bad Girls* (1993). The foreword in *Bad Girls* claims to chart a reaction against the puritanism and 'hard-edged didactic work' of the 1980s in favour of a return to 'the surrealist traditions of Louise Bourgeois and Meret Oppenheim' and 'the aggressive camp of Judy Chicago's *Dinner Party*'. It is now almost impossible to generalize about feminist art, a term uncomfortably stretched to cover the work of rigorous but marketable New Yorkers, a collective of peace campaigners like Sister Seven, and black artists organizing and exhibiting 'at a critical distance to the white-dominated feminist movement' (Chila Burman in Robinson, p. 195). Artists such as Lubaina Himid, Maud Sulter, Sutapa Biswas, Chila Burman and Sonia Boyce (see fig. 5) are concerned with 'positive

5. Sonia Boyce: *She Ain't Holding Them up, She's Holding on (Some English Rose)*, crayon, chalk, pastel and ink on paper, 2180×990 mm, 1986 (Middlesbrough, Cleveland Gallery)

images of black women ... reclaiming history, linking national economics with colonialism and racism, with slavery, starvation and lynchings ... the challenging of racial stereotypes, and breaking through tokenism and sexism' (Himid in Betterton, p. 261). New and challenging work on 'race' and identity has also emerged in the USA (Adrian Piper, Lorna Simpson, Carrie Mae Weems).

Feminism was one of the forces that threw modernism into crisis, and feminist work of the 1970s was part of a broad rejection of modernist aesthetics. French feminists such as Hélène Cixous and Luce Irigaray emphasized the disruptive potential of the feminine as the enemy of authority and fixity; they also argued for 'l'écriture féminine' as a form of writing that erupts from the pulsions of a female sexual body, recasting the link between body and culture in a way that has been taken up by NANCY SPERO. Attempts to bring feminism under the umbrella of 1980s Post-modernist pluralism are, however, strained and ambiguous. Neo-expressionist painting reinstated the male artist–hero. Feminist politics' concern with the emancipation of women and the transformation of society meant that feminist cultural activities were not to be reduced to a single aspect of Post-modern diversity (even to what has been designated 'a postmodernism of resistance'). There is no perfect marriage between feminism (as a political ideology) and art (as a cultural activity). Feminism promises at the same time to enrich the products of art, to expose the pretensions and vested interests in art and to break open the category of art altogether.

BIBLIOGRAPHY

E. Baker and T. Hess: *Art and Sexual Politics* (New York, 1973)
J. Chicago: *Through the Flower: My Struggle as a Woman Artist* (New York, 1975)
L. Lippard: *From the Center: Feminist Essays on Women's Art* (New York, 1976)
J. Chicago: *The Dinner Party: A Symbol of our Heritage* (New York, 1979)
J. Chicago and S. Hill: *Embroidering our Heritage: The Dinner Party Needlework* (New York, 1980)
L. Lippard: 'Sweeping Exchanges: The Contribution of Feminism to the Art of the 1970s', *A. J.*, xl/1–2 (1980), pp. 362–5
G. Nobakowski, H. Sander and P. Gorsen: *Frauen in der Kunst*, 2 vols (Frankfurt, 1980)
About Time (exh. cat., London, ICA, 1980)
Issue: Social Strategies by Women Artists (exh. cat., London, ICA, 1980)
Women's Images of Men (exh. cat., London, ICA, 1980)
I. de Courtivon and E. Marks, eds: *New French Feminisms* (Brighton, 1981)
R. Parker and G. Pollock: *Old Mistresses: Women, Art and Ideology* (London, 1981)
M. Barrett: 'Feminism and the Definition of Cultural Politics', *Feminism, Culture and Politics*, eds R. Brunt and C. Rowan (London, 1982)
N. Broude and M. D. Garrard: *Feminism and Art History: Questioning the Litany* (New York, 1982)
Sense and Sensibility in Feminist Art Practice (exh. cat., Nottingham, Midland Group, 1982)
M. Kelly: *Post-partum Document* (London, 1983)
C. Owens: 'The Discourse of Others: Feminists and Others', *The Anti-aesthetic*, ed. H. Foster (Washington, DC, 1983)
M. Roth, ed.: *The Amazing Decade: Women and Performance Art in America, 1970–1980* (Los Angeles, 1983)
C. Lyle, S. Moore and C. Navaretta: *Women Artists of the World* (New York, 1984)
Difference: On Representation and Sexuality (exh. cat., New York, New Mus. Contemp. A.; London, ICA, 1984–5)
S. Kent and J. Moreau, eds: *Women's Images of Men* (London, 1985)
Kunst mit Eigen-Sinn: Aktuelle Kunst von Frauen (exh. cat. by S. Eiblmayer, V. Export and M. Prischl-Maier, Vienna, Mus. 20. Jhts, 1985)
The Thin Black Line (exh. cat., London, ICA, 1985)
R. Betterton, ed.: *Looking On: Images of Femininity in the Visual Arts and Media* (London, 1987)
T. Gouma-Peterson and P. Mathews: 'The Feminist Critique of Art History', *A. Bull.*, lxix/3 (1987), pp. 326–57
S. Nairne: 'Sexuality, Image and Identity', *State of the Art: Ideas and Images in the 1980s* (London, 1987)
R. Parker and G. Pollock, eds: *Framing Feminism: Art and the Women's Movement, 1970–1985* (London, 1987)
H. Robinson, ed.: *Visibly Female: Feminism and Art* (London, 1987) [valuable anthology]
L. Tickner: 'Nancy Spero: Images of Women and *la peinture féminine*', *Nancy Spero* (exh. cat., London, ICA, 1987)
——: *The Spectacle of Women: Imagery of the Suffrage Campaign, 1907–1914* (London, 1987)
G. Pollock: *Vision and Difference: Femininity, Feminism and the Histories of Art* (London, 1988)
A. Raven: *Crossing Over: Feminism and the Art of Social Concern* (Ann Arbor, 1988)
W. Chadwick: *Women, Art and Society* (London, 1990)
A. Juno and V. Vale, eds: *Angry Women* (San Francisco, 1991)
Bad Girls (exh. cat., London, ICA, 1993; New York, New Mus. Contemp. A., 1994)
N. Broude and M. D. Garrard, eds: *The Power of Feminist Art: Emergence, Impact and Triumph of the American Feminist Art Movement* (London, 1994)

LISA TICKNER

Fencai. *See under* FAMILLE ROSE.

Fendi, Peter (*b* Vienna, 4 Sept 1796; *d* Vienna, 28 Aug 1842). Austrian painter, engraver and lithographer. In autumn 1810 he entered the Vienna Akademie to study drawing with Johann Martin Fischer, Hubert Maurer (1738–1818) and Johann Baptist Lampi (i). After the death of his father in 1814, Fendi was forced to leave the Akademie and become a clerk to earn his living, although he still received occasional lessons. However, he was soon taken up by the doctor and art collector Joseph Barth, who recommended him to Anton, Graf von Lamberg-Sprinzenstein; Fendi was thus able to copy the Classical and Etruscan vases in the latter's collection. In 1818 he was appointed engraver and draughtsman of the imperial coin and antiquities collection, where his copies of the objects were valued not only for their precision but for their attractive 'still-life' quality. In the 1820s Fendi started making lithographic prints, still a new technique at that time; these were mostly designs for illustrations in almanacs, albums or pocket-books, for example, *Wien, seine Geschichte und seine Denkwürdigkeiten*, edited and published by Josef Freiherr von Hormayr in Vienna (1823–5). Fendi drew a great deal after the works in the Kaiserliche Gemäldegalerie and the Lamberg collection, paying particular attention to the Dutch genre painters of the 17th century. His development as an artist was further enhanced by a journey in 1821 to Venice, where he studied the art collections and drew local people and street scenes.

Although Fendi suffered poor health as a result of a spinal injury, he was anxious to be more than a copyist to the court. He was known in Vienna as an engaging personality and was much sought after socially; he frequented salons, for example that of Karoline Pichler, and never married. In 1826 he painted his first significant work, the *Open-air Mass in the Outer Palace Square, 13 April 1826* (Vienna, Belvedere), in which the mood of a wet spring day is both realistically and impressionistically evoked; it is painted mainly in pale green and grey, and attention to the view as a whole, filled with clouds of gunpowder smoke, is combined with a focus on anecdotal details in the crowd of spectators and soldiers. In 1829 Fendi painted his first genre picture, *Girl at the Lottery* (Vienna, Belvedere), a type of painting frequently found in Viennese art of the Biedermeier period. It is characterized by the mixture of social stereotype, emotional intensity and a moralizing tone that typifies Fendi's genre paintings in oil.

Fendi's preferred medium was watercolour, in which he did his best work. Like his contemporaries, he produced works of moralizing social criticism, though he raised genre subjects to a higher aesthetic level through his personal vision of reality, using pale, luminous tones, carefully and subtly attuned, to depict anecdotal scenes with gentle humour or melancholy. Fendi's watercolours are also notable for their flowing lines and the neat, attractive forms of the figures, especially in his studies of children. In these paintings he created an 'idyll', one of the principal characteristics of Biedermeier art. Fendi found the themes and models for his pictures in the outskirts of Vienna, where he lived, and in the imperial and aristocratic families who commissioned work from him and to whom he also gave tuition. In *Evening Prayer* (1839; Vienna, Albertina) the children of the Emperor and their mother are shown in an intimate setting, suffused with tender affection more readily associated with scenes of bourgeois family life. Fendi's work influenced Karl Schindler, Albert Schindler and Friedrich Treml.

BIBLIOGRAPHY

Thieme–Becker

E. H. Zimmerman: *Das Alt-Wiener Sittenbild* (Vienna, 1923)
H. Adolf: *Peter Fendi* (diss., Innsbruck, Leopold-Franzens U., 1951)
——: 'Die Druckgraphik Peter Fendis', *Mitt. Österreich. Gal.*, li (1963), pp. 54–89
Peter Fendi (exh. cat., Vienna, Belvedere, 1963)
H. Fuchs: *Die österreichischen Maler des 19. Jahrhunderts*, i (Vienna, 1972)
Das Jahrhundert des Wiener Aquarells, 1780–1880 (exh. cat., Vienna, Albertina, 1973)
Bürgersinn und Aufbegehren: Biedermeier und Vormärz in Wien, 1815–1848 (exh. cat., Vienna, Hist. Mus., 1987–8)
Wiener Biedermeier: Malerei zwischen Wiener Kongress und Revolution (exh. cat., ed. G. Frodl and K. A. Schroder; Vienna, Belvedere, 1992)

MARIANNE FRODL-SCHNEEMANN

Fénelon, François de Salignac de La Mothe- (*b* Château de Fénelon, Périgord, 6 Aug 1651; *d* Cambrai, 7 Jan 1715). French writer and theologian. Born into the nobility, he was educated by the Jesuits in Cahors, and at the college of Le Plessis and the seminary of St Sulpice in Paris. After his ordination Fénelon worked in the parish of St Sulpice until he was made superior of the convent of Nouvelles Catholiques, Paris, in 1678. He was appointed tutor to the young Louis de Bourbon, Duc de Bourgogne (grandson of Louis XIV) in 1689. For the duke's edification he wrote the *Fables*, the *Dialogues des morts* and *Les Aventures de Télémaque*, a novel in which the search is recounted of the eponymous hero for his father, Ulysses. Fénelon was elected to the Académie Française in 1693, and he became Archbishop of Cambrai two years later. His friendship with Marie de La Mothe Guyon led to suspicions that he was sympathetic to the heterodox devotional mysticism of Quietism; subsequent disputes with a leading prelate, Jacques Bossuet, resulted in Fénelon's banishment to Cambrai in 1697, where he remained.

Fénelon's writings on art contributed to the most prominent debate of that time, the QUARREL OF THE ANCIENTS AND MODERNS. In his *Dialogues des morts* (written in the early 1690s), famous men from antiquity and more recent times meet for discussions in the underworld. Two of the dialogues (published as 'Dialogues sur la peinture' in an appendix to the Abbé de Monville's *La Vie de Pierre Mignard*, 1730) feature Nicolas Poussin. In the first Poussin discusses the relative artistic achievements of the ancients and the moderns with the Greek painter Parrhasius and gives a detailed account of his *Funeral of Phocion* (Paris, Louvre). Poussin impresses Parrhasius by describing the architectural accuracy of his depiction of Athens in the background of this picture, the balance of colours and forms in the landscape and the expressions of emotion in the figures. In the second dialogue Poussin is joined by Leonardo da Vinci, who is annoyed that a French painter should presume to challenge the reputation of the Italians; Poussin attempts to show that he painted the *Landscape with a Man Killed by a Snake* (London, N.G.) in harmony with Leonardo's own theories. He admits that this picture is a caprice rather than a history, denies that he is exclusively reliant on Italian models and emphasizes his independent study of the Antique.

Fénelon's critical position is clarified by his *Lettre sur les occupations de l'Académie Française* (written in 1714 in response to the request of the Académie Française for suggestions for future projects), in which he occasionally used analogies from the visual arts to further arguments about literature. He maintained in his *Lettre* that the natural is to be preferred to the artificial in the choice of both subject and form: painters should strive for accuracy in the imitation of nature and the representation of history, and architects should eschew the use of ornament which, when employed for its own sake, is always superfluous. He also pointed to the excesses of Gothic architecture as a reminder of the folly of those who attempt to surpass antiquity. His suspicion of the moderns did not extend to painting, however: he made appreciative references to the works of Raphael, Titian and several 17th-century artists, both in his *Lettre* and in his brief notes on paintings seen by him in the Condé family's collection at the château of Chantilly, Picardy.

Fénelon's *Les Aventures de Télémaque* (1699) was widely read in the 18th century and episodes were sometimes illustrated. There is a portrait of Fénelon by Joseph Vivien in Munich (Alte Pin.); his funerary monument (1719–24) by Jean-Louis Lemoyne in Cambrai Cathedral was destroyed along with the cathedral in 1794, but the bust (Cambrai, Mus. Mun.) was recovered.

WRITINGS

J. E. A. Gosselin, ed.: *Oeuvres complètes*, 10 vols (Paris, 1848–52/*R* Geneva, 1971)

BIBLIOGRAPHY

DBF; Souchal

A. Fontaine: *Les Doctrines d'art en France: Peintres, amateurs, critiques, de Poussin à Diderot* (Paris, 1909)
H. Brémond: *Apologie pour Fénelon* (Paris, 1910)
J. von Schlosser: *Die Kunstliteratur* (Vienna, 1924); It. trans. as *La letteratura artistica* (Florence, 1956/*R* 1976)

MALCOLM BULL

Fénéon, Félix (*b* Turin, 29 June 1861; *d* Châtenay-Malabry, 29 Feb 1944). French art critic, dealer and collector. After completing his education, he moved to Paris in 1881. A clerk in the War Ministry, he made a name for himself by writing for the numerous literary magazines of the period. In 1884 he was co-founder of the *Revue Indépendante*, and he swiftly became one of the dominant personalities in Symbolist circles, befriending a number of writers (he was a regular visitor to Mallarmé's Tuesday gatherings) and artists, notably Georges Seurat and Paul Signac. A period of prodigious activity followed: he collaborated on magazines such as the *Revue Wagnérienne*, *Le Symboliste* and *L'Art Moderne* from Brussels, and he edited works by Arthur Rimbaud (1886, 1887), Jules Laforgue (1890) and Lautréamont (1890). As an art critic, by 1886 he was championing the work of his Neo-Impressionist friends, whose anarchist political views he shared. In 1892 he became editor of *L'En Dehors*, one of the main anarchist reviews, and published articles in Didier Pouget's *Le Père Peinard*. He was among those charged for their anarchist beliefs in the 'trial of thirty' (1894). Despite his acquittal he was forced to resign his post at the Ministry. He worked at the Natanson brothers' *Revue Blanche* as editor-in-chief from 1896 to 1903, and organized the great Seurat retrospective exhibition of 1900. From 1906 he was a correspondent for *Le Figaro* and *Le Matin*, but he devoted himself primarily to art dealing: until 1925 he was director of the modern art section of the Galerie Bernheim-Jeune. He put under contract such minor Neo-Impressionists as Henri Edmond Cross, and the young Fauves (Albert Marquet and Matisse) whose early work was indebted to Neo-Impressionism. He introduced Kees van Dongen in 1904, and in 1912 organized the first Futurist exhibition in Paris. A discerning collector, he bought work by both André Derain and Georges Braque, and owned Signac's *Portrait of Fénéon* (1890; priv. col., see *Post-Impressionism*, exh. cat., London, RA, 1979–80, p. 138). From 1919 he began assembling a considerable collection of African art. It was only in 1919 that he once again began to write on art in the *Bulletin de la vie artistique*, published by Bernheim. The last 20 years of his life were passed in a comparatively inactive retirement, preparing the catalogue raisonné of Seurat's work with César M. de Hauke (published in 1961).

Fénéon's creative period as an art critic was limited to the years 1883 to 1896, his articles decreasing in number from 1892. After 1904 he wrote only catalogue introductions. His criticism was determinedly modernist: from 1883 he totally rejected academic art and treated it with contempt. His criticism was essentially descriptive and he only began theorizing in 1886, when he published the first of his texts on Neo-Impressionism, some of which were republished in his anthology *Les Impressionnistes en 1886*. In 1884 he discovered Seurat, who was exhibiting *Bathers at Asnières* (London, N.G.) at the Salon des Indépendants. 'I was fully aware of the importance of this painting', he wrote later; Neo-Impressionism had found its most brilliant champion, although he did not begin to proclaim his support publicly until 1886. In a dated but precise style, he tirelessly developed the aesthetic credo of Divisionism as it was explained to him by Seurat and the colour theorist Charles Henry. At a time when the greatest confusion reigned in the minds of critics and public alike concerning avant-garde trends in art, he at once placed Neo-Impressionism in historical perspective, coining the term to distinguish it from the Impressionism of Claude Monet, while stressing the connection between the two. At the same time he defined Impressionism as a school of colour and light, from which he excluded Edgar Degas and Mary Cassatt, who were then showing their work in Impressionist exhibitions. His discerning eye and his attention to chronology mark him as a valuable historian of contemporary art. However, his vision was not neutral: he believed in scientific determinism in art, incarnated in Neo-Impressionism. In his view, an artist such as Monet had gone astray.

His thorough analysis of pictorial surface texture and his search for a vocabulary with which to describe the material nature of the work of art made him the first critic to consider the work as an autonomous object, independent of its subject; indeed this is what opposes him to J.-K. Huysmans, whom he considered too tarnished with literary preoccupations. Nonetheless, he never totally lost sight of the subject, which he believed should conform to the modern aesthetic: he favoured scenes from contemporary life as painted by Degas, Henri de Toulouse-Lautrec, or even Jean François Raffaëlli. His rejection of literary painting gave his analysis of Symbolism a modernist slant which concentrated on Odilon Redon and Pierre Puvis de Chavannes, to the exclusion of Gustave Moreau and the followers of Josephin Péladan. In Paul Gauguin's work he acknowledged only its qualities of strictly formal innovation.

WRITINGS

Les Impressionnistes en 1886 (Paris, 1886)
F. Cachin, ed.: *Au delà de l'Impressionnisme* (Paris, 1966)
J. U. Halperin, ed.: *Oeuvres plus que complètes* (Geneva, 1970)

BIBLIOGRAPHY

J. Rewald: 'Félix Fénéon', *Gaz. B.-A.*, n.s. 6, xxxi (1947), pp. 45–62; xxxiii (1948), pp. 107–26
J. U. Halperin: *Félix Fénéon and the Language of Art Criticism* (Ann Arbor, 1980)
——: *Félix Fénéon, Aesthete and Anarchist in fin-de-siècle Paris* (London and New Haven, 1988)

For further bibliography see J. Rewald: *Post-Impressionism: From van Gogh to Gauguin* (London, 1978), pp. 525–7

RODOLPHE RAPETTI

Fenestella. Term for a small window or window-like opening. It may be a small glazed opening in a shrine to afford a view of the relics, an aperture in an altar or confessional to allow the contents to be visible at times or a small niche above a *piscina* or credence.

□

Fengshui. *See* GEOMANCY.

Feng Tse-kai [Feng Tzu-K'ai]. *See* FENG ZIKAI.

Feng Zikai [Feng Tzu-K'ai; Feng Tse-kai] (*b* Shimenwan, near Changde, Zhejiang Province, 9 Nov 1898; *d* Shanghai, 15 Sept 1975). Chinese cartoonist, teacher, translator and writer. He is best known for the lyrical cartoons he created from the 1920s to the 1960s, which explored themes of Buddhist philosophy and the innocence of childhood through humorous observations of daily life. He trained as a teacher at the First Teacher Training College in Hangzhou, where he was taught by Li Shutong, a Buddhist monk who was to prove influential in Feng's conversion to Buddhism in 1927 and in the development of his artistic career.

In 1921 Feng left Shanghai, where he had founded a teacher training college, and went to study Western art in Japan. However, as he later acknowledged in his book *The Art of the Cartoon*, he became fascinated by the popular Japanese *manga* (Chin. *manhua*; cartoon). On his return to China ten months later he joined the editorial staff of the Kaiming Book Company and began to publish his cartoons in the journal *We* ('Women') and in Shanghai's literary review. Feng's early cartoons were based on lines of classical Chinese poetry, but from 1924–5 he fused the poetic with vignettes of family life drawn from direct observations of his own children. Using the traditional Chinese brush and ink, Feng captured in a few deft brushstrokes the charm of a child's uncomplicated existence. Drawings such as *First Step* (1925), *Putting on Father's Clothes* (1925) and *When Father is Away* (1926) are typical of the warm, spontaneous style that made Feng a household name.

In 1925 Feng published his first collection of cartoons under the title *Zikai manhua* ('Zikai's cartoons') and a year later began to teach at institutions of higher learning around Shanghai. He also began to write and publish informal essays, of which the best known are *A Teacher's Diary* and *Dr X Sees Ghosts*, as well as books on art such as *History of Western Art* and *The ABC of Composition*. Although never an orthodox Buddhist, Feng nevertheless expressed his compassion for all living things and, in collaboration with Li Shutong, illustrated a set of fables with Buddhist morals entitled *A Collection of Sketches of the Floating Life*. To highlight the insensitivity, hypocrisy, injustice and cruelty of the adult world, he used contrasting images, as in *Today and Tomorrow*. In the same vein were such later works as *There is a Beggar on the Roadside*. The years of the Sino-Japanese war (1937–45) were disruptive, but Feng returned to teaching at Zhejiang University, then at Yishan, and continued to draw. In 1939 he illustrated Lu Xun's famous character Ah Q for the Kaiming Book Company.

After 1949 Feng's art began to be used as a propaganda tool for the new regime, and he was constrained to produce works that presented a world of idyllic happiness and harmony. In such pictures as *Careful Economy at Home* (1958) and *The Enthusiastic Workers: II* (1960) even his use of colour washes did not redeem a lack of vigour and freshness as compared with his earlier work. In 1952 Feng was forced to write a public self-criticism, although he retained enough status to be appointed head of the Institute of Chinese Painting in Shanghai in 1960 and to be elected President of the Shanghai branch of the Chinese Artists' Association in 1962. Nevertheless, by 1961 Feng had become primarily a translator, his most significant contributions being translations of the 11th-century Japanese novel *Genji monogatari* ('Tale of Genji') and the *Treatise on the Rise of the Mahayana Faith*. Condemned as a bourgeois intellectual, Feng was sent to work in the countryside in 1969 and died six years later at a hospital in Shanghai.

WRITINGS
Zikai Manhua [Zikai's cartoons] (Shanghai, 1925)
Goutu fa ABC [The ABC of composition] (Shanghai, 1928)
Xiyang meishu shi [History of Western art] (Shanghai, 1928)
Today and Tomorrow (Shanghai, 1928)
with Li Shutong: *A Collection of Sketches of the Floating Life* (Shanghai, 1929)
Gui tu ougan [There is a beggar on the roadside] (Shanghai, 1940)
Manhua di miaofa [The art of the cartoon] (Guilin, 1943)
Jiaoshi riji [A teacher's diary] (Chongqing, 1944)
Boshi jian gui [Dr X sees ghosts] (Shanghai, 1948)

BIBLIOGRAPHY
Wang Zhaowen, ed.: *From Feng Tse-Kai's Drawings of Children* (Beijing, 1956)
Bi Keguan: 'On Feng Zikai's Cartoons', *Chin. Lit.* (1981), no. 8, pp. 73–80
C. Harbsmeier: *The Cartoonist Feng Zikai* (Oslo, 1984)

DEBORAH NASH

Feni, Zwelidumile Geelboi Mgxaji Mslaba [Feni, Domile]. *See* DUMILE.

Fenoglio, Pietro (*b* Turin, 1865; *d* Corio Canavese, 22 Aug 1927). Italian architect. He studied civil engineering at Turin Polytechnic under Carlo Ceppi, graduating in 1886. He worked in the practice of Brayda, Boggio and Reycend and then began in private practice in 1889. Through Ceppi he had become aware of the most up-to-date architectural developments. Several of his early buildings are in the Piedmontese medieval tradition, brick with stone dressings, for example the Ansaldi Factory (1899), Via Modena, Turin, a sparse brick building with stone cornices to broken gables, or the Villino della Società Finanziaria Industriale (1900), Via Beaumont, Turin. The eclectic mode was not entirely limited to industrial buildings, however: the Casa Besozzi (1904), Corso Siccardi, is like an early Renaissance palazzo with a rusticated, red granite base flanked by five-storey pavilions with medieval castellations and neo-Romanesque openings. Fenoglio achieved official recognition with his election to the Artistic Committee of the Esposizione Internazionale d'Arte Decorativa (1902) in Turin. In the following years his practice was extremely busy, undertaking more than 140 projects in the first decade of the new century. Fenoglio's search for new formal solutions made him particularly attentive to the styles of Art Nouveau and of the Deutscher Werkbund. Of well over 100 executed buildings, the most significant are perhaps Fenoglio's vigorous and elegant contributions to the *Stile Liberty*: curvilinear stone window heads and balconies with floral decoration in iron balustrades and window bars. Among the most remarkable are the Palazzina Scott, Corso Lanza, with flowing stonework and ironwork to bow windows and an enclosed loggia, and the Casa Fenoglio on the corner of the Corso Francia and Via Principi d'Acaja (both 1902). He returned to traditional references for the public housing in the Via Marco Polo (1903), although elements of *Stile Liberty* remain in the Villino Raby (1905) and the Istituto Beneficenza Denis (1907). His appointment as coordinator for the Technical Committee of the Esposizione Internazionale dell'Industria e del Lavoro (1911) in Turin coincided with the unexpected abandonment of his professional practice. In 1912 he joined the management committee of the Banca Commerciale and, in the following year, he also took over the post of Director of the Società Commerciale d'Oriente, which was active in Libya, Egypt and Turkey. In his new profession as financier he was mainly concerned with projects geared to developing the heavy engineering industry, both civil and military, and the hydroelectric industry. In 1920, having become Director General of the Banca Commerciale, he opposed Luca Beltrami's project for its Rome office, accusing it of being out of date. He favoured instead a project by Marcello Piacentini.

BIBLIOGRAPHY
A. Galvano: 'Per lo studio dell'Art Nouveau a Torino', *Boll. Soc. Piemont. Archeol. & B.A.*, n. s., xiv/xv (1960–61), pp. 125–34

M. Leva Pistoi: *Torino, mezzo secolo di architettura, 1865–1915* (Turin, 1969)
R. Nelva and B. Signorelli: *Le opere di Pietro Fenoglio nel clima dell'Art Nouveau internazionale* (Bari, 1979)
R. Bossaglia: 'Archivi del Liberty Italiano', *Architettura*, ed. F. Angeli (Milan, 1987), pp. 58–84, 569
R. Nelva and B. Signorelli: *Avvento ed evoluzione del calcestruzzo armato in Italia* (Milan, 1990)

AMEDEO BELLINI, SANDRO CALLERIO

Fenollosa, Ernest Francisco [Tei shin; Kanō Yeitan Masanobu] (*b* Salem, MA, 18 Feb 1853; *d* London, 21 Sept 1908). American historian, curator and teacher. He had a highly influential career in Japan, where he taught Japanese and Chinese art and literature. The son of a Yankee and a Spanish musician, he studied philosophy and sociology at Harvard, graduated at the head of his class in 1874 and continued studies in divinity and drawing. The American zoologist and Orientalist EDWARD SYLVESTER MORSE brought him to Tokyo Imperial University in 1878 to teach. His growing interest in Japan's then neglected and crumbling ancient temples, shrines and art treasures led him to study and collect traditional art and to become a practising Buddhist. He and contemporary painters Kanō Hōgai (*see* KANŌ, (16)) and HASHIMOTO GAHŌ became pioneers in the revival of the *Nihonga* (Japanese) style of painting (*see* JAPAN, §VI, 5(iii)). In the 1880s he made Japanese art more accessible to the Japanese themselves by helping to found the Tokyo Art Academy and by preserving art treasures. In 1886 he sold his superlative art collection to Charles Goddard Weld of Boston, on the understanding that it was to remain permanently in the Boston Museum of Fine Arts. The collection, subsequently called the Fenollosa–Weld Collection, arrived in Boston in 1889, and in 1890 Fenollosa returned to Boston as curator of the new Department of Oriental Art at the Museum, which became a training centre for generations of scholars. He was dismissed in 1895 after his divorce and immediate remarriage had scandalized Boston. He then moved to New York, lectured across America and Europe, writing, art dealing and revisiting Japan. In his last years he assembled for the Detroit railway magnate and aesthete CHARLES LANG FREER the basis for what became the Freer Collection, Smithsonian Institution, Washington, DC.

WRITINGS

Mural Painting in the Boston Public Library (Boston, 1896)
The Masters of Ukiyoe (Boston, 1896)
M. M. Fenollosa, ed.: *Epochs of Chinese and Japanese Art*, 2 vols (London, 1912)

BIBLIOGRAPHY

V. W. Brooks: *Fenollosa and his Circle* (New York, 1962)
L. W. Chisholm: *Fenollosa: The Far East and American Culture* (New Haven and London, 1963)
S. Yamaguchi: 'Fenollosa: A Bibliography (1)', *J. Saitama U. (For. Lang. & Lit.)* (1971)

DIANE TEPFER

Fenton, Roger (*b* Bury, Lancs, March 1819; *d* London, 8 Aug 1869). English photographer. Born into a family of bankers and cotton merchants, he attended University College, London, in 1838 but left having been attracted to painting. After studying for a year with the historical genre painter Charles Lucy, he went to Paris in 1841 and entered the studio of Paul Delaroche. Delaroche, as early as 1839, had recognized the importance of the new daguerreotype for artists and followed the development of photography in the 1840s with interest.

After Delaroche closed his studio in 1843, Fenton returned to London and studied law. In 1847 he was married and qualified as a solicitor and four years later was called to the Bar. He did not, however, abandon his artistic aspirations and exhibited at the Royal Academy in 1849 and 1851.

It has been suggested that Fenton's interest in photography arose from an association with the Calotype Society, founded in 1847; but it is not until 1851 that there is firm evidence of his active role. Influenced by the display of photographs in the Great Exhibition of 1851, a committee was organized to consider ways of promoting the medium in England. Fenton, as honorary secretary, went to Paris late in 1851 to study the newly constituted Société Héliographique and visited his friend Gustave Le Gray, who may have introduced him to the waxed-paper negative process. Returning to London, he published a paper advocating the formation of a gentlemanly society for the cultivation of this 'branch of the natural sciences' and became the honorary secretary of the new Photographic Society in January 1853 (a position that he held until 1856).

During the summer of 1852 Fenton made his first photographic experiments and recorded the landscape and architecture of South Wales, Windsor Forest and London. In the autumn he accompanied his friend Charles Vignoles, an engineer, to Kiev to document the construction of a bridge across the Dnieper River. He also used the waxed-paper negative process to record the exotic onion-shaped domes and wooden architecture of Moscow and St Petersburg.

Between 1853 and 1855 Fenton worked almost exclusively as a photographer. In 1853 he became official photographer to the British Museum and in 1854 he began photographing Assyrian tablets, Classical busts and relief sculpture, using full sunlight and dark backdrops set up on the roof of the museum. At the first exhibition of the Photographic Society in January 1854, he met Prince Albert and Queen Victoria, who as influential patrons invited him to Windsor that spring to photograph the royal family.

After the outbreak of the Crimean War, Thomas Agnew, a Manchester print dealer and publisher, commissioned Fenton to travel to the Crimea. In December 1854, accompanied by his assistant Marcus Sparling, Fenton embarked for the front with a photographic van of his design and letters of introduction from his royal patrons. During the next six months he took over 360 collodion-on-glass plates of the officers, troop divisions and terrain around Sebastopol. Even though there was little military action during his stay, he portrayed a rosy picture of camp life that contradicted his own letters, which recorded the widespread disease and inefficient management that plagued the British war effort. Prints from his negatives were exhibited in the Gallery of the Old Water-Colour Society in London in September 1855 and were later published in elegant portfolios by Agnew & Sons. However, the conclusion of the war in 1855 meant that Fenton's images were no longer topical, which resulted in significant losses for his publisher.

During the next six years, Fenton marketed and exhibited views of rushing mountain streams, Gothic abbeys and cloisters and landscapes peopled by the urban bourgeois, subjects that attracted his eye and fitted neatly within the Victorian canon of 'art'. He also produced a beautiful series of elaborate still-lifes in 1860–62 that were sold as larger-than-life albumen prints and stereoscopic views. Confronted by the increasing competition of the collodion plate, the loss of prestige and novelty that had formerly surrounded photography and failing health, Fenton sold his equipment and negatives in 1862 and served as a barrister in provincial court circuits and legal adviser to the stock exchange until he retired in 1865. His work is included in the collections of the Royal Photographic Society, Bath, the National Army Museum and the Victoria and Albert Museum in London and the Harry Hunt Ransom Humanities Research Center, University of Texas at Austin.

WRITINGS
'Narrative of a Photographic Trip to the Crimea', *Phot. J.* (21 Jan 1856), pp. 284–91

BIBLIOGRAPHY
H. Gernsheim and A. Gernsheim: *Roger Fenton: Photographer of the Crimean War* (London, 1954)
J. Hannavy: *Roger Fenton of Crimble Hall* (Boston, 1975)
Roger Fenton: Photographer of the 1880s (exh. cat., intro. V. Lloyd; London, Hayward Gal., 1988)
ELIZABETH ANNE MCCAULEY

Fényes, Adolf (*b* Kecskemét, 29 April 1867; *d* Budapest, 15 March 1945). Hungarian painter. He was a pupil of Bertalan Székely at the School for Design Drawing in Budapest, and he studied under Max Thedy (1858–1924) in Weimar and at the Académie Julian in Paris. On his return to Hungary he attended classes by Gyula Benczur. From 1894 he participated in exhibitions at the Art Hall in Budapest and from 1903 he spent his summers painting mainly at Szolnok (*see* SZOLNOK COLONY). Some anecdotal genres from the beginning of his career, such as *Gossip* (1895; Budapest, N.G.), show the influence of his stay in Weimar, but this was short-lived.

In 1898 Fényes began a series of paintings, the *Life of Poor People* (e.g. *Old Man*, 1898 and *Farm Hand*, 1901; both Budapest, N.G.), in which tension is suggested by dark tones in monumental yet succinct representations of one or two figures. In the later paintings of the cycle the colour becomes livelier, and the last pictures, such as *Bean Huskers* (1904; Budapest, N.G.), are in almost total harmony with the vibrant colours of his contemporary post-Impressionist small town scenes in Tabán and Szentendre. At Fényes's first one-man exhibition in 1905 this series was hailed as the expression of Socialist art, although, apart from zeal for acute observation, his portrayal of poor peasant and agrarian types was not driven by any kind of political conscience, and the pictures form a cycle only by virtue of their common theme.

In 1907 a new phase in Fényes's art began when, in line with several other Hungarian painters of the period, he gravitated towards a more Secessionist style. He now paid more attention to fine drawing as well as to the hues of decorative elements. This is apparent even in paintings that in subject-matter seem to belong to his previous period, and the same general traits dominate the lively yet disciplined still-lifes (e.g. *Poppy-seed Cake*, 1910; Budapest,

N.G.) and the playfully symmetrical palace interiors painted with a virtuoso technique (e.g. the *Salon of Mme de Maintenon*, 1911; priv. col.).

The year 1913 was a turning-point in Fényes's career: he started reading the Bible and consequently began painting biblical scenes and mythical landscapes, mostly with symmetrical compositions (e.g. *The Jews Defeat the Army of Amalik*, 1915; Budapest, N.G.). In 1918 he exhibited nearly 70 canvases as a retrospective of his work, but from this point onwards pre-1913 paintings no longer figured in his exhibitions. Although critics noted the change, they did not look for any specific reasons for his introspection. The stylized landscapes of the years following 1913 portray small mobile figures under a low horizon. The increasing refinement in shapes and lines and the strict discipline observed in the choice of hues counteract any possibility of objective depiction, and the fabulous character of the paintings is emphasized by the contrasting use of light and shade, lending the composition a tragic tone. The growing feeling of anguish became overt, as in *Unsettling Times* (1929; Budapest, N.G.).

Fényes's last important exhibition was held in 1936 and consisted of a selection of mythical landscapes, including his earliest biblical scenes. His last known pictures unveil his personal tragedy during World War II. The *Dream of the Painter* (late 1930s; priv. col.) is a romantic, symbolic composition featuring in the centre an easel with a landscape canvas, around which real and fictitious birds gather, while in the bottom left-hand corner the painter is depicted lying on his back. In the self-portrait *Old Painter in Winter Landscape* (1940; priv. col.), the artist, carrying a portfolio and leaning on his umbrella on the edge of a snowy, inhospitable village painted in glassy hues, looks back from the foreground on to an estranged world, which he is about to leave. Fényes was found dead in a hideaway, after declining the help of friends in saving him from persecution for being Jewish.

BIBLIOGRAPHY
K. Lyka: 'Adolf Fényes', *Művészet* (1905), pp. 353–69
Fényes Adolf romantikus képei [Romantic paintings of Adolf Fényes] (exh. cat., foreword E. Kállai; Budapest, Fränkel Gal., 1936)
Fényes Adolf emlékkiállítás [Adolf Fényes: commemorative exhibition] (exh. cat., essay A. Oelmacher; Budapest, N.G., 1960)
A. Oelmacher: *Fényes 1867–1945* (Budapest, 1962)
N. Aradi: *Fényes Adolf* (Budapest, 1979)
NÓRA ARADI

Feodosiya. *See* KAFFA.

Feofan Grek. *See* THEOPHANES THE GREEK.

Ferabosco [Ferrabosco]**, Pietro** (*b* Laino, nr Como, ?1512; *d* ?Como, ?1599). Italian painter, architect and fortification designer. He entered the service of the Habsburg court in Vienna in 1544 and undertook military service for five years in Hungary. His first documented works are the painted decorations (1549–54) in several rooms of the Hofburg, Vienna, and one of the gates (1553). In 1552 he began the reconstruction of the Royal Castle in Bratislava (Slovakia), and from 1555 to 1587 he supervised the construction of fortifications in Hungary, Slovakia and Gorizia, making use of the contemporary system of bastions and ravelins. He designed the town defences of Győr, Komáro and Kinzsa, as well as working on those of Vienna. From 1554 he was sent to Prague on several occasions, once with Bonifaz Wolmut, to survey Hradčány Castle. He was probably involved in the design of the Stallburg (1559–69), built for Maximilian II as part of the Vienna Hofburg. The four-wing palace has a central courtyard framed by three storeys of identical round-headed arcades between massive pilasters. Ferabosco worked on Bučovice Castle (Moravia), for which he may have made a model to Jacopo Strada's plan. For Archduke Charles of Habsburg (*reg* 1564–90) he designed part of Graz Castle, probably the east wing (1570). He worked on the Hofburg once more in 1581–3, on Rudolf II's Amalienburg and on the Hlavenec and Sadská (nr Prague) hunting lodges for Rudolf II. In 1582 he designed the Königinnenkloster, Vienna.

BIBLIOGRAPHY
M. Dreger: 'Baugeschichte der k.k. Hofburg in Wien', *Österreich. Ksttop.*, xv (1914), pp. 104–6, 113–15, 125
J. Krčálová: 'Pietro Ferrabosco und sein Schaffen im Königreich Böhmen', *Ostbair. Grenzmarken*, xi (1969), pp. 183–96
——: *Zámek v Bučovicích* [The mansion at Bučovice] (Prague, 1979)
J. KRČÁLOVÁ

Ferapontov Monastery. Monastery in the Vologda region of the Russian Federation, *c.* 500 km north of Moscow and 20 km north of the Kirillo-Belozersky Monastery. It was founded in 1398 on the summit of a small hill near the White Lake by Ferapont, a monk from the Simonov Monastery in Moscow. In the mid-15th century the monastery became a major religious and cultural centre in the Russian north, with a scriptorium and a large library. It played an important role in the social and political life of the Moscow state and became a place of honourable exile for disgraced higher-ranking members of the clergy. At the end of the 17th century the monastery fell into decline, and it was dissolved in 1798, when its churches became parish churches. It was briefly revived as a convent between 1903 and 1923, and from 1908 to 1915, and in 1920–21 it was restored by the architects P. P. Pokryshin, K. K. Romanov and V. V. Danilov. The monastery houses a museum devoted to the frescoes of the painter Dionisy.

The present buildings were begun after a fire in 1488 destroyed the wooden church of Rozhdestvo-Bogoroditsy ('Birth of the Mother of God') and the monastic buildings. The patron was Ioasaf, Archbishop of Rostov and a former monk, who brought in masons from Rostov and, probably, Dionisy and his workshop. The oldest building is the brick Rozhdestvo-Bogoroditsy Cathedral, constructed in 1490. In plan and structure it follows the traditional formula of a domed, cruciform church within

Ferapontov Monastery, founded 1398; present buildings begun after the fire of 1488

a cubic structure, the height of which lends verticality to the whole (see fig.). This was emphasized by the crowning pyramid of two tiers of keel-shaped *zakomary* (gables) and rows of *kokoshniki* (onion-shaped gablets) around the base of the drum (now hidden under lean-to roofs). The cathedral is surrounded on three sides by a covered gallery, with apses on the fourth (east) side. To harmonize the balance of the masses of the building, the architect positioned the drum of the cupola in the centre of the whole plan, including the apses, so that the eastern pair of piers was displaced eastwards. Owing to this the external pilasters ceased to correspond with the internal members and became purely decorative, a characteristic trait of the Moscow architectural school at the turn of the 14th century and early 15th. The exterior faces of the cathedral are magnificently decorated with broad bands of decorative terracotta balusters, tiles with foliate ornament and bands of *begunets* and *porebrik* (vertical and lateral hatching).

The interior of the building was painted in 1502–3 by the workshop of Dionisy and his sons Vladimir and Feodosy. The paintings, which are dated by inscription, are executed in fresco, with tempera added in secco. The iconographic programme is a Marian cycle in keeping with the cathedral's dedication. Of the well-preserved exterior paintings on the west wall around the entry portal, the scenes of the *Birth of the Virgin* and *Mary Caressed by her Parents* are outstanding. The paintings on the north, west and south walls of the nave are in four registers: the upper registers are devoted to scenes from the Akathistos hymn to the Mother of God, including one in the north lunette illustrating the versicle *Rejoice*. Worship of the Virgin is further intensified in the central apse, where, in addition to the enthroned *Virgin and Child* in the conch, she appears as *Virgin of the Sign* in the upper altar arch and *Intercessor* in the lunette. In style the paintings develop features of the Moscow school founded on the work of ANDREY RUBLYOV. The compositional rhythm of both individual scenes and the whole ensemble parallels the architectural members of the interior. At the same time Dionisy and his sons executed icons for the cathedral's iconostasis (Moscow, Tret'yakov Gal.; St Petersburg, Rus. Mus.; Kirillov, Kirillo-Belozersky Monastery).

The church of Martinian with its pyramidal roof adjoins the cathedral to the south and was built in 1640–41 over the tomb of Ferapont's successor Martinian, the Father Superior until 1483. Covered two-storey passages link the cathedral with the refectory buildings and the church of the Annunciation (Blagoveshcheniye), built in 1530–34. The exterior of the refectory is laconic and monumental; the central square of the interior has a powerful central pillar supporting the striking vaults. The most original aspect of the church of the Annunciation is its upper tier, where several of the *zakomary* served as arched recesses for bells. Within the monastery complex to the west of the cathedral are the brick Holy Gates, with two equally large arched passageways and two small churches with pyramidal roofs over them: the church of Christ of the Epiphany (Bogoyavleniye) and the church of St Ferapont (1649).

BIBLIOGRAPHY

I. I. Brilliantov: *Ferapontov Belozersky: Nyne uprazdnyonnyy monastyr', mesto zatocheniya patriarkha Nikona* [Ferapontov Belozersky: the now abolished monastery and place of the imprisonment of Patriarch Nikon] (St Petersburg, 1899/*R* 1994)
V. T. Georgiyevsky: *Freski Ferapontova monastyrya* [Frescoes of the Ferapontov monastery] (St Petersburg, 1911)
I. Y. Danilova: *Freski Ferapontova monastyrya* (Moscow, 1970)
G. Bocharov and V. Vygolov: *Vologda, Kirillov, Ferapontovo, Belozersk* (Moscow, 1979)
Ferapontovskiy sbornik [Ferapontov collection] (Moscow, 1985–)

M. I. ANDREYEV

Ferber (Silvers), Herbert (*b* New York, 30 April 1906). American sculptor and painter. He began his independent artistic studies in New York in 1926 at evening classes at the Beaux Arts Institute of Design, while attending Columbia University Dental School. The institute was a free school for academic architectural sculptors, where students' work was assessed monthly. In 1930 he attended the National Academy of Design, and that summer he was awarded a scholarship to work at the Tiffany Foundation, Oyster Bay, Long Island. He also began part-time work as a dentist. Impressed by an exhibition of African sculpture from the Guillaume collection at the Valentine Gallery (1930), New York, he purchased his first piece of African art in 1931.

Between 1931 and 1944 Ferber carved wood and stone sculptures, influenced by the contemporary work of William Zorach, Ernst Barlach and Aristide Maillol, and by a mixture of African, Pre-Columbian and Romanesque sources. He travelled to Mexico in 1935 and bought several pieces of Pre-Columbian sculpture. His direct carved and cast work of the 1930s often reflected the social consciousness of the times, as in *To Fight Again* (granite, 1936–7; New York, MOMA). He participated in the First American Artists' Congress in 1936 and belonged to the Artists' Union and the John Reed Club; in the same year he joined the Federation of Modern Painters and Sculptors, an anti-Stalinist splinter group from the Artists' Congress. Ferber's first one-man exhibition was held at the Midtown Galleries, New York, in 1937. A year later he travelled to Europe for the first time, admiring the Romanesque sculptures at Moissac, Carcassonne and Souillac, as well as Italian Renaissance sculpture. In New York he attended Meyer Schapiro's weekly art lectures at the New School for Social Research.

During 1945 Ferber turned to drawing in order to work through the influence of Henry Moore, whose work he had seen on exhibition at the Brummer Gallery (1944). By the end of the year he began to sculpt in welded metal, which allowed for a lighter, more open, formal vocabulary. Ferber created Surrealist-influenced works, infused with images of the prehistoric skeletal forms that he knew from the Museum of Natural History, such as *Hazardous Encounter* (bronze, 1947; Pittsfield, MA, Berkshire Mus.); he also developed vertical, totemic sculptures, for example *He is Not a Man* (bronze with welded metal rods, 1950; New York, MOMA). The imagery and forms of such metal sculptures as the portrait of *Jackson Pollock* (lead, 1949; New York, MOMA) and the *Action is the Pattern* (lead and brass rods, 1949; priv. col., see Goossen, 1983, p. 66) aligned him with the Abstract Expressionist painters whom he befriended.

In 1950 Ferber was awarded his first architectural sculpture commission for the façade of the B'nai Israel

Synagogue, Millburn, NJ; '. . . *and the bush was not consumed*', an openwork metal sculptural relief made of soldered copper, brass, lead and tin, was installed in 1952. In 1953 he was an award winner in the American section of the international competition for a monument to the unknown political prisoner with *Spheroid I* (soldered lead, brass and copper, 1951; priv. col., see Goossen, 1983, p. 76), a spiked, multidirectional, open metalwork piece. In 1954 he made his first 'roofed' sculpture in which organic forms threatened to explode out of the rational 'cage' framework that contained them; by 1958 he began to think of these works as environments. He devoted the summer of 1958 and most of the next year to painting large canvases. The spatial explorations of the 'roofed' sculptures reached fruition in 1959 when he began to create maquettes for *Sculpture as Environment*, exhibited as a large-scale, indoor sculptural installation at the Whitney Museum of American Art, New York, in 1961 (original installation in papier mâché, permanent installation in fibreglass; New Brunswick, NJ, Rutgers U., Zimmerli A. Mus.). The *Homage to Piranesi* series, consisting of linear 'cages' containing thrusting calligraphic forms, was begun in 1961.

By the 1970s Ferber's sculptural compositions of boldly simplified curvilinear forms, designed to be viewed outdoors in urban and rural settings, were often horizontally orientated, as in *Konkapot II* (Corten steel, 1972; Mountainville, NY, Storm King A. Cent.). His impatience with sculpture in the late 1970s led to a deeper involvement with painting. His multicoloured relief paintings, begun in 1977, and the *Semaphore* series, begun in 1983, which incorporated sculptural sail-like canvas elements, further developed his synthesis of painting and sculpture.

BIBLIOGRAPHY
R. Goldwater, E. C. Goossen and I. Sandler: *Three American Sculptors: Ferber, Hare, and Lassau* (New York, 1959)
The Sculpture of Herbert Ferber (exh. cat. by W. V. Anderson, Minneapolis, Walker A. Cent., 1962)
E. C. Goossen: *Herbert Ferber* (New York, 1983)

JOAN H. PACHNER

Ferdinand. *See* ELLE.

Ferdinand, Archduke of Austria. *See* HABSBURG, §I(9).

Ferdinand, Cardinal-Infante. *See* HABSBURG, §II(9).

Ferdinand, Duke of Guarda. *See* AVIZ, (10).

Ferdinand I, Holy Roman Emperor. *See* HABSBURG, §I(6).

Ferdinand [Fernando; Ferrante] **I**, King of Naples. *See* ARAGON, (3).

Ferdinand II, Holy Roman Emperor. *See* HABSBURG, §I(16).

Ferdinand II, King of Aragon and Sicily. *See* ARAGON, (5).

Ferdinand II, King of Portugal. *See* BRAGANZA, (13).

Ferdinand III, Holy Roman Emperor. *See* HABSBURG, §I(17).

Ferdinand V, King of Castile. *See* ARAGON, (5).

Ferdinand [Fernando] **VI**, King of Spain. *See* BOURBON, §II(3).

Ferdinand [Fernando] **VII**, King of Spain. *See* BOURBON, §II(7).

Ferdinand Maria, Elector of Bavaria. *See* WITTELSBACH, §I(6).

Ferdinando, Grand Prince of Tuscany. *See* MEDICI, DE', (28).

Ferdinando I, Grand Duke of Tuscany. *See* MEDICI, DE', (17).

Ferdinando II, Grand Duke of Tuscany. *See* MEDICI, DE', (22).

Ferdinand-Philippe, Duc d'Orléans. *See* ORLÉANS, (8).

Ferdinand the Catholic, King of Aragon and Sicily. *See* ARAGON, (5).

Feré, Pierrot (*fl* Arras, 1395–1429). Burgundian tapestry-weaver. He is notable as the only documented 14th- or 15th-century high-warp weaver whose part in the production of an extant tapestry is certain. The tapestries of *SS Piat and Eleuthère* (Tournai, Notre-Dame Cathedral) were made and finished at Arras by Feré in December 1402, according to a lost inscription woven above four scenes and now preserved only in a 17th-century copy by Canon Dufief (Brussels, Bib. Royale Albert 1er, MS. 13762, p. 82). The same inscription stated that Feré made this work for Toussaint Prier (*d* 1437), a canon of Tournai Cathedral, to which he donated the tapestries. It is not clear from the inscription whether Feré was personally responsible for all or part of the weaving or acted as the overseer of a workshop. The tapestry itself, however, appears in its simplicity of materials, scale and design to conform with the documentary evidence for Feré's life.

First recorded in 1395 as a resident of the parish of Saint-Géry, Arras, Feré reappears in 1415–29 as a man of modest influence and status serving on two elected municipal bodies, in one of which he was jointly responsible for maintaining the town's regulations relating to the making of high-warp tapestry. Feré's only son, Jean (*d* 1454), and Jean's two sons, Pierrot (*d* 1448) and Jean (*d* 1447), are also recorded at Arras as weavers of high-warp tapestry. None appears to have sold tapestries to any of the important noble collectors of their times.

BIBLIOGRAPHY
A. Guesnon: 'Le Hautelisseur Pierre Feré d'Arras, auteur de la tapisserie de Tournai', *Rev. N.*, i (1910), pp. 201–15

SCOT MCKENDRICK

Ferenczy. Hungarian family of artists. The painter (1) Károly Ferenczy was one of the first modern Hungarian artists and a leading figure in the NAGYBÁNYA COLONY. He introduced a generation of young Hungarian artists to *plein-air* painting and led the reaction against conventional academic art. All of his important works are in Hungary, and he is consequently little known outside his native land.

Károly married his cousin, the Austrian painter Olga von Fialka (1848–1930). Their son (2) Béni Ferenczy was primarily a sculptor and medallist. He spent many years in Vienna and his mature work shows a successful reinterpretation of Classical sculpture. His twin sister (3) Noémi Ferenczy specialized in making tapestries and was the greatest influence on Hungarian tapestry in the 20th century. Another son, Valér Ferenczy (*b* Körmöczbánya, 22 Nov 1885), having studied with his father and with Simon Hollósy at Nagybánya, became a painter and etcher. The Ferenczy Museum in Szentendre (the birthplace of Béni and Noémi) is devoted to the work of the family.

BIBLIOGRAPHY

J. Muradin: *A Ferenczy művészcsalád Erdélyben* [The Ferenczy family of artists in Transylvania] (Bucharest, 1981)

(1) Károly Ferenczy (*b* Vienna, 8 Feb 1862; *d* Budapest, 18 Mar 1917). Painter.

1. EARLY YEARS, TO 1896. He came from a well-to-do middle-class family, who owned a small estate in southern Hungary. Influenced by his cousin, Olga von Fialka, whom he subsequently married, he turned to painting at the comparatively late age of 22. He and Olga travelled to Italy in 1885 and stayed for some time in Naples, where Ferenczy began to study at the Accademia di Belle Arti. On a short visit to Munich in 1887 he met the young Hungarian painters studying there, all of whom were heavily influenced by Juks Bastien-Lepage; this encouraged Ferenczy to study in Paris (1887–9), where he attended the Académie Julian. He was taught by Tony Robert-Fleury and Adolphe-William Bouguereau, but the greatest influence on him remained that of Bastien-Lepage.

Returning to Hungary in 1889, Ferenczy settled in Szentendre and embarked on a series of large compositions in the style of Bastien-Lepage. An outstanding example is *Ducks and Drakes* (1890; Budapest, N.G.), which radiates an every day tranquillity. Ferenczy's works of this period is characterized by the use of a unifying pearl grey tone that binds together the pale tints and lends a gentle, pensive mood to the whole composition. He rapidly became dissatisfied with his work and in 1893 renounced the seclusion of Szentendre for the lively artistic milieu of Munich, where he hoped to gain new inspiration. Although he was not a natural mixer in Munich's Bohemian circles, he did immediately respond to the *plein-air* style then in fashion. The greyish colours of the Munich school, so popular with Hungarian painters, were abandoned; although Ferenczy retained a preference for overcast scenes, his colours became fresher and more vivid, and his brushwork softer. *Birdsong* (1893; Budapest, N.G.) is the first example of his more colourful approach. In this work Ferenczy succeeded in harmonizing the human figure and the natural environment, a feature that became the leit-motif of his subsequent work. His most successful pictures show an idealized harmony between man and nature, placing the figures among luxuriant foliage in woods or gardens, and balancing tone, colour and light to endow them with equal compositional weight to the natural world.

2. THE NAGYBÁNYA COLONY. In 1896 Ferenczy decided to leave Munich and return to Hungary. Together with a small group of other Munich Hungarians, students and friends of Simon Hollósy, he moved to Nagybánya (now Baia Mare, Romania). Hollósy became the first leader of the Nagybánya artists' colony, and almost at once the colony attracted the attention of intellectuals in Budapest. The artists were given a shared commission to illustrate the poems of a contemporary popular poet, József Kiss. Ferenczy's contributions—four drawings and four paintings, the most lyrical of which is *Memory of Naples* (1896; Budapest, N.G.)—are among the finest Hungarian book illustrations. Together with the earlier poster-like *Archaeology* (1895; Budapest, N.G.), they are a rare example of his use of Art Nouveau.

By this time Ferenczy had three years' experience of *plein-air* painting, whereas the other Hungarians were at first somewhat nonplussed by their new surroundings. When Hollósy suffered a creative crisis, his mantle passed to Ferenczy, whose artistic achievements, steadiness and self-discipline made him a natural figure of authority. Embittered and jealous, Hollósy left Nagybánya in disgust in 1902. Although the public did not instantly take to the *plein-air* style, which was as yet unfamiliar in Hungary, fellow artists and leading critics responded warmly. Like many other artists in Munich at the turn of the century, Ferenczy periodically tried out new styles on large-scale biblical themes, traditionally the most demanding. This had little or nothing to do with conventional piety, or even with securing commissions. Most contemporary religious paintings were naturalistic, often either pathetic or banal, while attempts at Symbolist interpretations tended to be rigid and imbued with an air of self-conscious archaism.

Károly Ferenczy: *October*, oil on canvas, 1.25×1.07 m, 1903 (Budapest, Hungarian National Gallery)

However, Ferenczy's *Three Magi* (1899; Budapest, N.G.) is unusually successful. Only the title reveals the identity of the three mysterious riders who are enveloped in the dark green shadows of dense woodland as darkness falls. They appear as mystical, enigmatic figures, melting into the trees as if in a dream. The effect is that of a profound and tranquil harmony, a pantheistic idyll.

Around 1901 Ferenczy began to lighten his palette and to paint sunlit scenes with large blocks of intense greens, blues and yellows. These brightly coloured paintings radiate a joy in the beauty of life and nature similar to that found in the work of the French Impressionists. *October* (1903; Budapest, N.G.; see fig.) is one of his finest works from this period; a simple lyrical depiction of a man reading a newspaper under a sunshade in a garden, the scene is bathed in the autumnal glow of a typical Central European Indian summer. Despite the bold asymmetry of the large brilliantly coloured areas of the sun-shade and tablecloth, the composition possesses a sophisticated and reassuring balance. Its magic lies not only in the evocation of a soft autumnal atmosphere, but also in the integration of figure and background.

3. LATE YEARS, 1903–17. In December 1903 Ferenczy held a first, highly successful retrospective in Budapest; it marked the high point of his career. In the preface to the catalogue of the show, he defined his style as 'colouristic naturalism on a synthetist basis'. Somewhat later the naturalistic elements became more stylized, developing into a highly formal organization of shape and colour. The gestures and poses of his figures became forced and unnatural, and his palette grew darker and more intense. The double portrait of his children, *Noémi and Béni* (1908; Budapest, N.G.), is a good example of this new approach to portraiture, in which he incorporated strong decorative elements akin to the late Art Nouveau style that was flourishing at the time. In 1906 he was invited to teach at the Academy of Fine Arts in Budapest, and from that time on he divided his time between the capital and Nagybánya. This influenced his output; he produced many more portraits and still-lifes, which were painted in his winter studio. After 1910 he underwent a creative crisis and produced only a few works, mainly female nudes and still-lifes. Although he tried to regain his inspiration, his *fin de siècle* aestheticism made him increasingly isolated in an artistic milieu that was moving towards Expressionism and Constructivism.

The new generation was no longer interested in *plein-air* naturalism, and from 1912 Ferenczy was increasingly alienated from his contemporaries, both artistically and personally. Even two of his children, the artists Noémi and Béni, turned against his treasured principles of truth to nature. Although he struggled to come to terms with the new theories, ultimately they meant little to him, although some of his works did exhibit fleeting signs of their influence. His last works are dominated by black backgrounds and dullish colours, reflecting an atmosphere of oppressive melancholy. Illness, war and alienation from the younger generation determined the mood of these works, most uncompromisingly in the *Pietà* (1914), which he slashed to pieces before his death.

Although Ferenczy's ideals had come to seem outdated by 1907, just at the point when he began teaching, the artistic aims of the Nagybánya landscape painters were revived after 1918 and set the tone for art education in Hungary between the two world wars. Ferenczy's friends and followers, such as Aurel Bernáth, Istvan Szőnyi and Jozsef Egry in the Gresham group, maintained and furthered his philosophy—a pantheistic approach to nature and a strongly ethical dedication to art.

WRITINGS
Előszó a kiállításhoz. Nemzeti Szalon (Budapest, 1903) [Preface to his exhibition at the National Salon]
I. Genthon, ed.: 'Ferenczy Károly tizenneg levele' [Fourteen letters of Károly Ferenczy], *Magyar Muveszettorteneti Munkaközösség Évkönyve* (Budapest, 1952), pp. 192–9

BIBLIOGRAPHY
V. Ferenczy: *Ferenczy Károly* (Budapest, 1934) [Biography by his son; an important source]
E. Petrovics: *Ferenczy Károly* (Budapest, 1943)
I. Genthon: *Ferenczy Károly* (Budapest, 1963/R 1979) [with catalogue of the works]
I. Réti: *A Nagybányai Művésztelep* [The Artists' Colony of Nagybánya] (Budapest, 1954), pp. 153–72
M. Jacobs: *The Good and Simple Life: Artists' Colonies in Europe and America* (Oxford, 1985), pp. 131–42
A Golden Age: Art and Society in Hungary, 1896–1914 (exh. cat. by G. Éri and Z. Jobbágyi, London, Barbican, A.G.; Miami, FL, Cent. F.A. 1989)

ILONA SÁRMÁNY-PARSONS

(2) Béni [Benjámin] **Ferenczy** (*b* Szentendre, 18 June 1890; *d* Budapest, 2 June 1967). Sculptor, medallist, watercolourist and draughtsman, son of (1) Károly Ferenczy. He studied drawing at the Free School at Nagybánya. In 1909 he travelled to Florence, where he studied modelling with Joseph Beer and Giuseppe Cassioli (*b* 1865), and at the Akademie der Bildenden Künste in Munich he studied wood-carving with Balthasar Schmidt (*b* 1858). His interest in medals was aroused by another Hungarian student in Munich, József Reményi (1887–1977). Between 1911 and 1913 Ferenczy continued his studies in Paris under Emile-Antoine Bourdelle and later, at the Académie Libre Russe, under Alexander Archipenko. During this period he spent his summers at Nagybánya. Throughout World War I he lived in Budapest. Ferenczy's début as an artist coincided with the appearance in Hungary of Cubism and Futurism, and with the emergence of two groups: the Neos at Nagybánya and the Group of Eight, while his later work developed parallel to that of the Activists. Although his early work displays close similarities with these trends, it also shows a conscious link with the Classical Greek tradition and other major periods of European sculpture. The main features of his style at this time can best be seen in one of his large-scale male nudes, *Dévi* (bronze, h. 605 mm, 1918) and his portrait of *János Wilde* (bronze, h. 410 mm, 1918; both Budapest, N.G.).

After the downfall of the Council Republic in 1919, Ferenczy was forced to emigrate. He went via Nagybánya and Pozsony (now Bratislava) to Vienna where, apart from a brief spell in Berlin (1922–3) and in Moscow (1932–5), he lived and worked until 1938. His circle of friends included major Viennese cultural figures as well as exiled leaders of the Hungarian labour movement. His work grew more versatile, though for a while it was still dominated by Cubism. He constructed his portraits and nudes from geometric shapes and exaggerated their proportions. These traits were particularly marked during his stay in Berlin, where he had an exhibition in 1924 at the Sturm-Galerie with Aurél Bernáth. From this time onwards he strove towards monumentality, and his large-scale statues, tombstones and building reliefs, mostly in stone, show increased consolidation of his style (e.g. the tomb for *Egon Schiele*, 1928; Vienna, Ober St Veit cemetery). His most significant medals while in Vienna, such as *Lenin* (bronze, diam. 130 mm, 1930; Vienna, Ksthist. Mus.), stress his commitment to the labour movement. While in Moscow he began a series of medals devoted to great artists (e.g. *Daumier*, 1933; *Goya*, 1934). On the obverse he portrayed the head of the subject, on the reverse a detail of one of the artist's best-known works. Later he continued the series, and his initiative was widely imitated. Apart from medals he drew portraits of his second wife (e.g. *Artist's Wife*, 1935; Budapest, N.G.), who became central in his oeuvre as a model. He also drew a number of Moscow scenes and produced two memorial reliefs for *Valery Bryusov* (Moscow, House of Poets) and for *Jenő Landler* (ex-Moscow, Emigrés Club), as well as a portrait of *Karl Marx* (untraced) on commission. In 1935 he returned to Vienna, where he continued to produce commemorative medals and also sculpted a female figure with soft, rounded shapes, entitled *Woman with Raised Arms* (bronze, h. 215 mm, 1936; Budapest, priv. col.). He remodelled the same subject in a number of variations (e.g. *Atalanta*, 1937; Budapest N.G.; see fig.). Such works show his successful reinterpretation of Classical form and spirit. In 1937 he produced a sculpture of an adolescent male nude, *Miklós* (bronze, h. 860 mm; Budapest, N.G.), which he later recast in several variations.

Ferenczy returned to Budapest in 1938. In spite of World War II he worked a great deal and exhibited widely. He began a series of medals devoted to Hungarian artists of the past and also at about this time he made a sculpture of a squat female nude, *Youth* (bronze, h. 325 mm, 1944; Szentendre, Ferenczy Mus.). At the end of the war his studio burnt down, destroying a number of his drawings and sculptures. In 1947 and 1948 he spent a considerable time in Switzerland; later he worked at the Hungarian Academy in Rome, where he created a statue with an archaic, upright stance entitled *Young Athlete* (bronze, h. 1.92 m, 1947; Budapest, N.G.) in commemoration of his son who had died during the war. From this period Ferenczy's work was dominated by sculptures with two figures, of which he had already made several examples. He worked gradually on *Playing Boys* (bronze, h. 640 mm, 1947; Budapest, N.G.), a work of visionary power, and *Lovers* (bronze, h. 520 mm, 1948; Szentendre, Ferenczy Mus.).

In 1946 Ferenczy was appointed professor at the College of Fine Arts in Budapest and in 1948 he was awarded the Kossuth Prize. He sculpted the state-commissioned memorial to the poet *Sándor Petőfi* (bronze, h. 2.02 m) in 1948–9, but it was only erected in a public square ten years later in Gyula, and only in 1973 in the place originally intended for it: the courtyard of the Biblioteca Ambrosiana (*in situ*) in Milan. In 1949 Ferenczy was dismissed from his teaching post and thereafter received large commissions only from the Church. Despite this he continued to work, producing such notable sculptures as the portrait of the conductor *János Ferencsik* (bronze, h. 370 mm, 1952; Budapest, N.G.), the tomb of the poet *Mihály Babits* (bronze, 1954; Budapest, Kerepesi cemetery) and a sculpture of his wife entitled *Genius* (bronze, h. 665 mm, 1955; Szentendre, Ferenczy Mus.). He also produced illustrations for novels by Thomas Mann (e.g. *Egy szélhámos vallomásai* [Bekentnisse des Hochstaplers Felix Krull] (Budapest, 1957)) and Zsigmond Móricz, among others. In November 1956 he suffered a stroke that paralysed his right side and took away his power of speech, but he started to draw again with his left hand, and to do some modelling.

WRITINGS
Irás és kép [Writings with illustrations], postscript I. Genthon (Budapest, 1961) [with cat. of works]
S. Kontha, ed.: 'Ferenczy Béni tiz levele' [Ten letters by Béni Ferenczy], *Művészete* (1983), no. 9, pp. 54–7; no. 10, pp. 49–53

BIBLIOGRAPHY
I. Genthon: 'Béni Ferenczy', *Acta Hist. A. Acad. Sci. Hung.*, 1–2 (1959), pp. 194–214
G. Illyés: *Ferenczy Béni* (Budapest, 1967)
K. Szabó: *Ferenczy Béni* (Budapest, 1967)
T. Katana, ed.: *Béni Ferenczy: Fák könyve* [Béni Ferenczy: book of trees] (Budapest, 1976) [with verses by E. Ady and Gy. Juhász]
J. Murádin: 'Ferenczy Béni Erdélyben' [Béni Ferenczy in Transylvania], *Művészettörténeti Értesítő*, 3 (1976), pp. 234–41
S. Kontha: 'Béni Ferenczy', *Acta Hist. Acad. Sci. Hung.*, 3–4 (1979), pp. 253–80
——: *Ferenczy Béni* (Budapest, 1981)
G. Illyés: *Ferenczy Béni rajzai* [Drawings of Béni Ferenczy] (Budapest, 1982)
M. Illyés: 'Ferenczy Béni: A keresés évei 1917–25' [Béni Ferenczy: the years of searching, 1917–25], *Művészettörténeti Értesítő* (1982), pp. 34–40
P. Réz, ed.: *Ferenczy Béni arcképe* [A portrait of Béni Ferenczy] (Budapest, 1984)

Béni Ferenczy: *Atalanta*, bronze, h. 350 mm, 1937 (Budapest, Hungarian National Gallery)

M. Illyés: 'Béni Ferenczy', *Wechsel Wirkungen: Ungarische Avantgarde in der Weimarer Republik* (exh. cat., Kassel, Neue Gal., 1986), pp. 147–55
'Szaz éve született Ferenczy Béni és Ferenczy Noémi', *Új Iras*, ix (1990), pp. 19–50

S. KONTHA

(3) Noémi Ferenczy (*b* Szentendre, 18 June 1890; *d* Budapest, 20 Dec 1957). Tapestry artist and textile designer, sister of (2) Béni Ferenczy. She trained as an artist by visiting major European museums and by studying (1912) tapestry-weaving at the Manufactures des Gobelins in Paris. She worked partly in Budapest and at the Nagybánya colony until 1932, when she settled permanently in Budapest.

Ferenczy was among the few artists who did not come to tapestry design from a background in painting. She preferred to weave the tapestries herself, so that she could modify the techniques wherever necessary to suit the design. For example, she did not weave in complete rows but finished an entire motif before proceeding, which gave her more freedom to concentrate on details. This 'free' style of weaving allowed her to develop distinctive decorative and monumental compositions. Initially, her work resembled the plant- and animal-filled verdure of 16th-century Flemish and French tapestry. She had a lifelong love and respect for nature, which she gained from her family background. Her first monumental tapestry, *Creation* (2.23×2.19 m, 1913; Budapest, Mus. Applied A.), was inspired by the stained-glass windows of Chartres Cathedral. A fairy-tale atmosphere infuses the tapestry, which depicts God, the Garden of Eden and Adam and Eve, with stylized forms and deep, flaming colours—various shades of blue, brown, claret, red and green. The *Flight into Egypt* (1915–16; Budapest, Mus. Applied A.), the other major work of her early period, is also characterized by much decorative detail, particularly lush vegetation, and a rich use of colour. She first exhibited, with her father and brothers, in Budapest in 1916.

From 1917 Ferenczy was involved in the labour movement, and she was imprisoned for her part in the arts administration of the Council Republic of 1919. Her subsequent work was largely determined by this involvement: the rich backgrounds of nature give way to monumental, decorative depictions of man and work. In these compositions she used simple forms and fewer colours, the hues becoming deeper and warmer in tone, with reds and browns dominating. *White Man with an Axe* (1923–4; Budapest, N.G.) was conceived as a portrait. In the centre of the composition a man dressed in white holds an axe, with mallows and a rotten tree trunk behind him. The large sweep of the composition points to Ferenczy's growing inclination towards monumentality, developed to the full in her tapestries of the 1930s. *Stonemason* (1933; Budapest, N.G.) is a fine example on the theme of labour, while *Spring Work* (1943; Budapest, Hist. Mus.) stands out among her landscapes. After World War II Ferenczy began to give equal expression to internationalist and patriotic convictions. *Joining Forces* (1948; Budapest, Mus. Applied A.) portrays two workers, one with a hammer and one with a pair of callipers, joining hands. Two enormous wheels in the background make clear reference to industrial workers, while the chains running round the border represent their exploitation. Patriotism inspired

Centenary (1948; Budapest, Mus. Applied A.), which commemorates the 1848 Revolution and depicts a female figure holding up a tablet with the words of a patriotic song of the time. In 1948 Ferenczy was awarded the Kosuth Prize, and from 1950 to 1954 she taught at the College of Applied Arts in Budapest. In her last works she returned to the luxuriant portrayal of nature. *Ring of Girls* (1952–4; ex-Patriotic Popular Front priv. col., Budapest, see Jankovich, pl. 157), for example, shows girls in a green meadow forming a circle by holding hands against a background of extraordinarily rich and detailed hills and woods.

BIBLIOGRAPHY
K. Tolnay: *Ferenczy Noémi* (Budapest, 1934)
M. Cseh: *Ferenczy Noémi* (Budapest, 1963)
É. Kovács: 'Noémi Ferenczy', *New Hung. Q.*, iv/9 (1963), p. 212
Ferenczy Noémi, intro. J. Jankovich (Budapest, 1983) [contains cat., Ferenczy's diary and photographs of herself and her family]

IDA BOD-BOBROVSZKY

Ferenczy, István (*b* Rimaszombat [now Rimavska Sobota, Slovakia], 23 Feb 1792; *d* Rimaszombat, 4 July 1856). Hungarian sculptor. He began his career as an apprentice locksmith in his father's workshop and then, from 1810, worked independently in Budapest. Between 1814 and 1818 he worked as a locksmith in Vienna while also studying steel engraving and minting at the Sunday school of the Akademie der Bildende Künste. It was around this time that he formed the ambition to become a sculptor, embarking on a course of self-education and travelling to Rome, where from 1818 to 1824 he worked in the studio of Bertel Thorvaldsen. During this period he produced a portrait of the poet *Vitéz Mihály Csonokai* (marble, 1818–19) and his most important work, *The Shepherdess: The Beginning of Fine Art* (marble, 1820–22; both Budapest, N.G.). The latter work, depicting a girl drawing the image of her departing lover in the sand and derived from Pliny's *Natural History*, was intended to mark the beginning of Hungarian sculpture. The influence of Canova's statue of *Paolina Borghese Bonaparte as Venus Victorious* (1804–8; Rome, Gal. Borghese) is evident in it, particularly in the poise of the hand and the sensual modelling of the arms, while the naked upper body is devoid of any sensuality. The drapery is very delicately carved to suggest the form of the body beneath.

The portrait of *Csonokai* and *The Shepherdess* were both highly acclaimed when they were sent to Hungary in 1822. Ferenczy was therefore optimistic about his artistic prospects when he returned to Hungary in 1824. He immediately drew up a proposal for a national school of sculpture and put much energy into the search for high-quality marble, which he eventually found in Ruskicza in Transylvania. In the decade that followed his return, Ferenczy was deluged with orders for portrait busts, tombstones and altarpieces, and his workshop employed several apprentices. The collection of small sculptures that he had purchased in Rome also formed the basis of the sculpture collection of the Museum of Fine Arts in Budapest. However, without the artistic inspiration that he had found in Rome, and artistically isolated, his technical uncertainties as a sculptor became increasingly evident. He still managed to produce some notable portraits, for example *Ferencz Kazinczy* (1828) or the statue of the poet and statesman

Ferencz Kölcsey (1841–6; both Budapest, N.G.), all generally within the realist tradition of Roman portrait sculpture, but as the Hungarian aristocracy (who provided him with the bulk of his commissions) began to decline, Ferenczy's fortunes began to wane. Particularly galling was the failure of his plan for a memorial to King Matthias, and in 1846 he abandoned his career, selling the house that he had bought in Buda Castle and returning to his birthplace, where he undertook only minor commissions.

BIBLIOGRAPHY
S. Meller: *The Life and Work of István Ferenczy* (Budapest, 1906)
P. Cifka: *István Ferenczy* (Budapest, 1969)
——: 'The Early István Ferenczy', *Art and Enlightenment* (Budapest, 1978), pp. 465–513
                                                    C. NAGY

Feretory. Term used in church architecture for the space in which major portable relics are kept; it is often treated as a chapel behind the main altar.

☐

Ferg, Franz de Paula [Franz Josef; Paulus] (*b* Vienna, 2 May 1689; *d* London, 1740). Austrian painter, draughtsman and printmaker. He studied landscape painting with his father, Adam Pankraz Ferg (1651–1729), and with Josef Orient (1677–1747) and staffage painting with Johann (Hans) Graf (1653–1710). He also studied the engravings of Jacques Callot and Sébastien Leclerc (i). His early works show such subjects as harbours, markets and villages as wide vistas with many figures, trees and buildings, for example *Fair with Temple and Maypole* (Vienna, Belvedere). These scenes combine landscape and genre and are characteristic examples of early 18th-century Austrian panel painting, showing the influence of Dutch, Flemish and Italian models. The colours are dark, and the staffage figures in the manner of Graf are slender, with small heads and peculiarly wooden poses.

In 1718 Ferg left Vienna and went to Franconia, Bamberg, and Leipzig. There he met Johann Alexander Thiele (1685–1752), whom he accompanied to Dresden. A small self-portrait (untraced) from this period was bought by the painter Christian Wilhelm Ernst Dietrich. Later Ferg travelled to Lower Saxony and from about 1724 lived in London, where he made an unfortunate marriage and died in misery. In 1726 he created a series of eight etched *Capricci* (preparatory sketches in Vienna, Albertina), which help to date many smaller pictures to the London period. His late cabinet pieces contain fewer, clearly drawn figures, set in Italianate landscapes with ruins; their Arcadian mood, brilliant colour and Rococo manner are particularly pleasing.

BIBLIOGRAPHY
M. Huber: *Catalogue raisonné du Cabinet d'Estampes de feu M. Winkler*, i (Leipzig, 1802), p. 165
Österreichische Barockmaler aus der Nationalgalerie in Prag (exh. cat. by P. Preiss, Vienna, Belvedere, 1977), pp. 66–8
E. Baum: *Katalog des österreichischen Barockmuseums im Unteren Belvedere in Wien*, i (Vienna, 1980), pp. 163–6
                        ELISABETH HERRMANN-FICHTENAU

Ferghana [Farghana; Fergana; Pers. Farghānā]. Valley (300×70 km) of the middle Syr River in Uzbekistan and Kyrgyzstan. The fertile region has been inhabited by farmers and pastoralists for millennia, and numerous archaeological sites from the Bronze Age onwards have been found there. The nearly inaccessible site of Saimaly Tash, at an altitude of 3000 m in the Ferghana Mountains north of Uzgend, has produced over 100,000 petroglyphs dating from the Bronze Age to the 1st millennium AD. The 25 ha Bronze Age settlement at Dalverzin included a citadel, residential buildings and an enclosure for livestock, and yielded many clay vessels and stone, bone and bronze objects. Eylatan (7th-3rd century BC) contained small pisé structures surrounded by two rows of walls with towers. At Aktam the dead were buried in shallow earth tombs on small stone mounds; finds included modelled, painted and thrown vessels, everyday objects of iron, stone and bone, jewellery and weapons.

In 101 BC Ferghana was at war with the Han Chinese, who received a tribute of 3000 horses as part of a peace treaty. The small (1 ha) settlement at Ark Tepe (2nd–3rd century AD) near Ferghana had defensive walls and oval towers of mud-brick. The cruciform citadel at the centre contained a courtyard enclosed by vaulted rooms forming a sort of corridor. The rectangular towers had lancet-shaped embrasures in their outer sides, and a staircase or ramp gave access to the roof or second storey. Excavations yielded thrown pottery and stone weapons. In the Kara-bulak burial (2nd–4th century) the dead were laid in circles in lined graves, more rarely in catacombs and earth tombs, some in troughs or coffins. Finds included ceramics, female jewellery, metalwares, weapons, fabrics (including embroidered cloth) and clothes. Kayragach (5th–6th century), a residential estate with complexes of houses and service quarters and a domestic sanctuary with ornamental wall painting and an altar, yielded painted statues of clay and plaster, ceramics, everyday items of stone and iron, jewellery and arrow heads.

Ferghana came under Turkish dominion in the 7th century, and Kasan became the capital of the princes of Ferghana. Excavations at KUVA, occupied from the last centuries BC to the 13th century AD, revealed a Buddhist temple (7th century), residential and commercial quarters and iron workshops, as well as remains of painting, sculpture, ceramics, everyday objects, weapons, jewellery and coins. Muslims occupied Ferghana in the early 8th century, but Islamization of the region was only completed under the Samanid dynasty (*reg* 819–1005), when Ferghana was the frontier between the Islamic lands and those of the unconverted Turks. Akhsikath (Rus. Akhsyket), the capital of Ferghana in this period, has revealed cultural layers dating from the first centuries AD to the 13th. Rectangular in plan, the site comprised a citadel, two urban centres and a suburb, each surrounded by walls with towers. Residential and trading quarters and iron workshops have also been excavated. Finds include glazed and unglazed ceramics and other objects.

Following the collapse of the Samanid state, Ferghana came under the control of the Qarakhanids (*reg* 992–1211), who made UZGEND their capital, and three important mausolea survive from this period. After the region fell to the Mongols in the 13th century, rulers of the Timurid, Shaybanid and local dynasties contested for power in the valley. In the 18th century the region became the centre of the khanate of KOKAND; it was annexed by Russia in 1876.

BIBLIOGRAPHY
Enc. Islam/2: 'Akhsīkath', 'Farghānā', 'Khokand'
V. A. Bulatova: *Drevnyaya Kuva* [Ancient Kuva] (Tashkent, 1972)
N. G. Gorbunova: *The Culture of Ancient Ferghana, VI Century BC–VI Century AD*, Brit. Archaeol. Rep. (London, 1986)

N. G. GORBUNOVA

Ferguson, William Gouw (*b* Scotland, *c.* 1633; *d* Scotland, after 1695). Scottish painter, active also in the northern Netherlands. He was probably trained in Scotland but went to the Continent as a young man and worked in Utrecht, The Hague and Amsterdam; he also visited Italy. He painted accomplished still-lifes in the style of such Dutch painters as Jan Vonck (1630–after 1660) or Willem van Aelst. A distinguished early example, the *Still-life with Birds* (1662; Amsterdam, Rijksmus.), has a distinctive pale background, while a later *Still-life with Dead Game* (1684; Edinburgh, N.G.) exploits a shadowed background. Ferguson also painted landscapes with ruins and figures, generally under a dark sky and often sinister in mood, for instance a *Ruined Altar and Figures* (Edinburgh, N.G.). He was probably in London in the 1670s, when John Maitland, 2nd Earl and 1st Duke of Lauderdale, and his wife commissioned him and other artists to produce pictures for the decoration of Ham House, Surrey. Two of these, *Classical Ruins* and a *Sorceress among Classical Ruins*, were inset as overdoors in the Duchess's private closet. Ferguson's choice of subject-matter was probably partly influenced by Dutch painters, for instance Thomas Wijck, who was also in the service of the Lauderdales, or earlier artists such as Jacob de Wet.

BIBLIOGRAPHY
M. R. Apted and S. Hannabus: *Painters in Scotland, 1301–1700: A Biographical Dictionary* (Edinburgh, 1978), p. 39
R. J. Holloway: *Patrons and Painters: Art in Scotland, 1650–1750* (Edinburgh, 1989), pp. 43–5

OLIVER MILLAR

Fergusson, James (*b* Ayr, Scotland, 22 Jan 1808; *d* London, 9 Jan 1886). British art historian, active in India. His interest in the study of architecture was formed and developed in India, where he went at an early age to join a merchant firm with which his family had connections. He left this mercantile establishment to begin his own indigo factory in Bengal, and in the course of his career as an indigo merchant began a pioneering survey of Indian architecture. Travelling extensively across India between 1835 and 1842, armed with a draughtsman's pad and a camera lucida, he acted as a 'one-man architectural survey' making drawings and taking notes and measurements. The labours of these years not only produced all his major writings on Indian architecture but also formulated his basic methods on the study of architecture in general.

Although firmly committed to European classical standards of artistic excellence, Fergusson, unlike most Western scholars of his time, did not impose these on Indian architecture. Rather, he applied to European and world architecture a set of analytical principles he had evolved through a direct, detailed study of Indian monuments. For instance, in all his studies, his reliance on pure architectural evidence for his conclusions grew out of his intimate survey of old Indian buildings. His strong criticism of all post-1500 Western architecture as 'copying or imitative styles' was also centrally premised on his admiration of Indian architecture as one of the alternative 'true styles'. Drawing out its lessons for contemporary England, he found in Indian architecture a 'living tradition' and a truly 'natural production' where materials, form and function were in perfect alignment and ornaments grew naturally out of the constructions.

Fergusson's first paper (presented to the Royal Asiatic Society in 1843) and book concerned the 'rock-cut' or cave temples of India as the earliest architectural specimens in the country. This work led to the presentation of a memorial to the Court of Directors of the East India Company and the appointment of persons for the measurement and drawing of antiquities in all the Indian presidencies. Fergusson's travels and studies found shape in his *Picturesque Illustrations of Ancient Architecture in Hindostan* (1848), where a synoptic survey and classification were accompanied by large lithographs (prepared meticulously from Fergusson's own on-the-spot drawings) of temples and buildings of varied regions of India ranging from Orissa to Rajasthan and the far south.

In the 1840s Fergusson also began his parallel studies of Greco-Roman and western Asian architecture. It was in the course of investigating the source of Islamic architecture in India that Fergusson moved westwards to the mosques of Egypt and Syria and delved further into the Romanesque and Byzantine styles, out of which much of Islamic architecture was seen to have arisen. In his *Essay on the Ancient Topography of Jerusalem* (1847), he argued, through a close analysis of architectural structures, that the Mosque of Omar at Jerusalem was in origin the church called the Dome of the Rock, built by Constantine the Great over the tomb of Christ, and constituted the true site of the Holy Sepulchre. Alongside, he pursued his special interest in the perfect 'harmonic proportions' and the special mode of lighting in Classical Greek buildings, such as the Parthenon or the restored mausoleum at Halikarnassas. In this period Fergusson also wrote on general principles of beauty in art, especially architecture, applying to a sketch of ancient Egyptian, Assyrian, Greek, Roman and Etruscan architecture 'a theory of art', which he admitted to have been 'elaborated from a study of Indian, Mahomedan and Gothic architecture'.

In subsequent decades, Fergusson produced not only the first 'quasi-exhaustive' history of Indian architecture but also the first universal history of architecture in English. In both instances, a main aim was to establish architecture as an 'art' and a distinct discipline of study, quite separate from archaeology. His first *Illustrated Handbook* (1855) was followed by a sequel, *History of the Modern Styles of Architecture* (1862), with the two later combined into a *History of Architecture in All Countries from the Earliest Times to the Present Day*. In 1876 his *History of Indian and Eastern Architecture* appeared as a third volume to this compendium.

In a lecture delivered to the Society of Arts in 1866, Fergusson set out the basic principles and the central importance of the study of Indian architecture. While it offered the West the example of superior norms of design and craftsmanship, Indian architecture, he believed, also provided the most vital and reliable source for reconstructing the history, religions, culture and ethnology of a country where few written records existed. The twin needs were sought to be fulfilled by Fergusson's pioneering and comprehensive history. Here, he elaborated a theory, propounded earlier, of the inverted evolution of Indian art from its highest point in early Buddhist architecture to the 'decadence' of the later excessively ornate Hindu styles. This theory was argued out through a racial periodization of the history of Indian art, in terms of the greater and lesser purity of the Aryan race—through his notion of the progressive corruption of the Aryans by their mixture with the culturally inferior Dravidians and Turanians, and the resultant decline in artistic achievements. Classifying architectural styles in racial and ethnic categories, for example classing the Orissan temples of the 12th and 13th centuries as the 'Dasyu' style, Fergusson also introduced to the study of Indian architecture the broad denominational groupings of Buddhist, Jaina, Hindu and Muhammadan that would long linger.

In 1867–8 Fergusson's only work on Indian sculpture emerged from his discovery of some Buddhist sculptures of Amaravati, lying abandoned in the old India Museum at Fife House, London. Exhibiting these at the Paris International Exhibition of 1867, he combined a study of the Amaravati sculptures with earlier examples from the stupas at Sanchi, using a rich body of drawings and photographs. Once again, his prime interest in these sculptures was as illustrations of Indian ethnology, and of the religious faith and customs of the people illustrated in these panels. His admiration of the Bharhut and Sanchi sculptures as thoroughly original was woven in with his idea of the intervention of Greco-Bactrian influences on the art of Amaravati. For this was the only way he could account for the continued excellence of these later sculptures in his structure of the continuous decline of Indian art.

Indian architecture, for Fergusson, notwithstanding all its merits, would always pale in comparison with European Classical art. This innate racial prejudice led to his attack on the Bengali scholar, Dr Rajendralal Mitra, who challenged his views regarding the introduction of stone architecture in India by the Greeks. Nonetheless, Fergusson's singular achievement lay in transcending the standard British involvement with the 'exotic' and 'picturesque' in India to provide the first thorough and systematized study of Indian architecture, evaluated on its own architectural principles.

In London, where he lived from the 1840s until his death, Fergusson was also actively involved in such architectural projects as the decoration of St Paul's Cathedral, the restoration of Westminster Hall and the designing of an exhibition gallery at Kew Gardens.

WRITINGS
Illustration of the Rock-cut Temples of India (London, 1845)
An Essay on the Ancient Topography of Jerusalem (London, 1847)
Picturesque Illustrations of Ancient Architecture in Hindostan (London, 1848)
The Palaces of Nineveh and Persepolis Restored, an Essay on Ancient Assyrian and Persian Architecture (London, 1851)
The Illustrated Handbook of Architecture, Being a Concise and Popular Account of the Different Styles of Architecture Prevailing in All Ages and Countries (London, 1855)
History of the Modern Styles of Architecture (London, 1862)
The Mausoleum at Halicarnuss Restored (London, 1862)
The Rock-cut Temples of India (London, 1864)

History of Architecture in All Countries from the Earliest Times to the Present Day, 2 vols (London, 1865–7)
On the Study of Indian Architecture (London, 1867)
Tree and Serpent Worship or Illustrations of Mythology and Art in India in the First and Fourth Centuries after Christ from the Sculptures of the Buddhist Topes at Sanchi and Amaravati (London, 1868)
History of Indian and Eastern Architecture (London, 1876)
with J. Burgess: *The Cave Temples of India* (London, 1880)
Archaeology in India, with Special Reference to the Works of Babu Rajendralal Mitra (London, 1884)

BIBLIOGRAPHY
DNB
N. Pevsner: 'James Fergusson', *Some Architectural Writers of the Nineteenth Century* (Oxford, 1972), pp. 238–51
P. Mitter: *Much Maligned Monsters, History of European Reactions to Indian Art* (Oxford, 1977)
P. Chandra: *On the Study of Indian Art* (Cambridge, MA, 1983)

TAPATI GUHA THAKURTA

Fergusson, J(ohn) D(uncan) (*b* Leith, 9 March 1874; *d* Glasgow, 30 Jan 1961). Scottish painter. He abandoned the idea of a career in medicine to devote himself to art *c.* 1894. Self-taught, his earliest works were small impressionistic sketches of his native Edinburgh and studies of his family. Influenced by the work of the Glasgow Boys, in particular Alexander Roche (1863–1921) and Arthur Melville, he travelled in northern Africa and paid regular summer visits to northern France from *c.* 1898 (and from the early 1900s in the company of S. J. Peploe). Friendships with artists in France, including the American graphic illustrator Anne Estelle Rice (1879–1959), encouraged him to settle in Paris *c.* 1907, where he associated with a circle of progressive French, American and British artists and was elected a member of the Salon d'Automne. Strongly influenced by the Fauves, his work from this date was characterized by strong colour, thick impasto and free brushwork. He also executed sculpture. While teaching at the Académie de la Palette run by Jacques-Emile Blanche, a more structured approach began to enter his work, both in his choice of imagery and in the formal qualities of his composition. This reached a climax in a group of life-size nude compositions executed between 1910 and 1912, including *Rhythm* (1911; U. Stirling, J. D. Fergusson Col.), and a series of still-lifes (1912–14). These accompanied his brief art editorship of Middleton Murry's London journal *Rhythm* in 1911–12.

In the company of Rice and Peploe, Fergusson painted scenes of Royan, near La Rochelle, in the summers of 1910 and 1911. He spent the summer of 1912 in Cassis, near Marseille, where he settled briefly in 1913–14. Living in wartime London with the dancer Margaret Morris, his portraits and paintings of Portsmouth docks showed his interest in stylized pattern and a more muted colour range, anticipating his Scottish and French landscapes of the 1920s. On Fergusson's return to France *c.* 1929 his figural work such as *Megalithic* (1931; London, F.A. Soc.) reflected the prevalent neo-classicism and reduced tonality of the period.

In 1940 Fergusson founded the New Scottish Group in Glasgow where he and Morris spent the remainder of their lives. Bonded by neo-romantic Celtic allegiances with France, where several members of the group spent their post-war summers, their work maintained a preoccupation with colour, spontaneity and sincerity of approach. The general call for a Scottish national identity was reflected in

Fergusson's published view of his own work and Scottish affairs, *Modern Scottish Painting* (1943).

The colour and exuberance of much of Fergusson's work has led some critics to associate him with the SCOTTISH COLOURISTS. Although he was omitted from their number (which included his friend Peploe) in T. J. Honeyman's study of 1950, as he was also from the major Edinburgh Festival exhibition of 1949, later small-scale shows included his work, leading to his subsequent ranking as the fourth Colourist.

For illustration *see* SCOTLAND, fig. 12.

WRITINGS
Modern Scottish Painting (Glasgow, 1943)

BIBLIOGRAPHY
M. Morris: *The Art of J. D. Fergusson* (Glasgow, 1974)
J. D. Fergusson, 1874–1961 (exh. cat., intro. R. Billcliffe; London, F.A. Soc., 1974)
Colour, Rhythm & Dance: Paintings and Drawings by J. D. Fergusson and his Circle in Paris (exh. cat., intro. E. Cumming, S. Macgregor and J. Drummond; Edinburgh, Scot. A. C., 1985)
R. Billcliffe: *The Scottish Colourists* (London, 1989)

ELIZABETH CUMMING

Ferlov Mancoba [née Ferlov], **Sonja** (*b* Copenhagen, 1 Nov 1911; *d* Paris, 1985). Danish sculptor, draughtswoman and painter, active in France. She trained in Copenhagen with Bizzie Høyer (1930–31) and at the Kongelige Danske Kunstakademi (1932–4). In 1936 she moved to Paris, marrying the South African painter ERNEST MANCOBA in 1942. She lived the rest of her life in Paris, apart from the years 1947–52, when she returned to Denmark. She developed an early connection with the artists' group Linien (The Line) in 1937–9. Around this time she produced abstract drawings incorporating graffiti-like masses of calligraphic shapes (e.g. *Drawing*, 1939; Copenhagen, Stat. Mus. Kst) and paintings using flat areas of contrasting colour and shape (e.g. *Painting*, 1939; Silkeborg, Kstmus.). In the 1940s she formed part of the COBRA group.

At the heart of Ferlov Mancoba's abstract sculptures were simple formal elements that never altered significantly. Her meeting with Alberto Giacometti in Paris was decisive; the influence of Giacometti's work from the 1920s was evident in her work there. An interest in concave and convex forms is already discernible in such early sculptures as *The Owl* (1936; destr., see Andersen, no. 7). At the same time she worked with images of masks, a preoccupation that could produce the intensity of the *Outbreak of War* (1939). Mask motifs, in plaster or wood, were a natural result of her contact with African art and the inspiration she drew from it. In spite of its abstract character, Ferlov Mancoba's work in wood, plaster and iron was infused with organic form. She also worked with unaltered natural materials: for example branches of trees were incorporated into her sculptures in the form of *objets trouvés*.

As a member of Cobra, and a participant in the Autumn Exhibition, the Høst (Harvest) group exhibition (1948) and the Frie Udstilling (1968) in Copenhagen, she maintained her connections with Denmark. She also executed a number of decorative commissions in Copenhagen, including those for the Zealand Landsarkiv building, Copenhagen (1969), and the County Hospital in the suburb of Søllerød, near Copenhagen (1978). In the early 1960s Ferlov Mancoba worked on several large plaster sculptures and exhibited *Trust* (1963; bronze version, Holstebro, Kommune) at the Galerie Denise René in Paris in 1963. In the last 20 years of her life Ferlov Mancoba concentrated on sculpture but also made a few abstract collages and drawings (e.g. *Collage*, ink and paper on paper, Fru N. Munkvad priv. col., see Andersen, no. 39). Many of her works of the 1960s and 1970s were characterized by the social indignation with which she treated contemporary issues, as in the bronze *Solidarity* (1966; Copenhagen, Stat. Mus. Kst). She also continued to produce occasional abstract paintings.

BIBLIOGRAPHY
C. Dotremont: *Sonja Ferlov Mancoba*, Cobra Bibliotheket (Copenhagen, 1950)
T. Andersen: *Sonja Ferlov Mancoba* (Copenhagen, 1979)

MICHAEL FLINTHOLM

Fermo da Caravaggio. *See* GHISONI, FERMO.

Fernande [Ferdinande; Fernandes; Fernandi], **Joseph** (*b* Bruges, *bapt* 1 Oct 1741; *d* Bruges, 10 Aug 1799). Flemish sculptor. He was a pupil of the painter Matthias de Visch (1702–65) and in 1755 of the sculptor Jan van Hecke (1699–1777) at the academy in Bruges. In 1763 Fernande travelled to Paris, where he studied at the Académie de Saint-Luc and later at the Académie Royale, where he won several medals. The Empress Maria-Theresa of Austria became his patron and sent him to study in Rome, where he stayed from 1772 to 1775. He returned to the Netherlands via Vienna and in 1776 was appointed court sculptor to Prince Charles of Lorraine (1712–80) at Brussels. Fernande's oeuvre consists of somewhat idealistic portraits, such as that of *Marie-Antoinette, Queen of France* (1779; Vienna, Schloss Schönbrunn), which he executed in Paris. His style is markedly influenced by the classical tradition of strong, heavily carved sculpture. From 1780 until his return to Bruges in 1794 he was court sculptor to Archduchess Marie Christine (1742–98) in Brussels.

BIBLIOGRAPHY
BNB; Thieme–Becker
J. Immerzeel: *De levens en werken der Hollandsche en Vlaamsche kunstschilders, beeldhouwers, graveurs en bouwmeesters* [The lives and works of Dutch and Flemish painters, sculptors, engravers and architects] (Amsterdam, 1843), iii, pp. 172–3
E. Jacques: 'Joseph Fernande, sculpteur brugeois (1741–1799) et le mécénat autrichien au XVIIIe siècle', *Mém. Acad. Royale Belgique: Cl. B.-A.*, x/4 (1957)

IRIS KOCKELBERGH

Fernandes, Eduardo (Manuel) Batarda. *See* BATARDA, EDUARDO.

Fernandes, Garcia (*fl* 1518–40; *d* ?Lisbon). Portuguese painter. He was the son-in-law of the Luso-Netherlandish painter Francisco Henriques, and with CRISTÓVÃO DE FIGUEIREDO, with whom he may have collaborated (1533 and 1537), and Gregório he dominated Portuguese painting during the reigns of Manuel I (*reg* 1495–1521) and John III (*reg* 1521–57). Among Portuguese painters of the first half of the 16th century, Fernandes was the most closely related to Italian artists, and he often used engravings by Marcantonio Raimondi. His painting shows the changes that were apparent in the 1540s, when Portuguese art began to move slowly away from Netherlandish and towards more Italian influences.

In 1540 Fernandes made an inventory of some of his most important works (see Raczyński, 1846): this document refers to panels made for Coimbra, Leiria, Montemor, the Tribunal de Relação in Lisbon (destr.), Évora, S Eloy in Lisbon, and for India. It has enabled the identification of his works, including a series of saints: among others there are *St Sebastian*, *St Vincent* and *St Roch* (Coimbra, Santa Cruz, Sacristy). An *Immaculate Conception* (Lisbon, Mus. N. A. Ant.) was part of a group of paintings made for S Francisco, Évora, where among those still *in situ* are *St Michael* and *St Bernardino of Siena*. Other works cited in the inventory of 1540 are the altarpiece of *St Catherine* (Old Goa, Goa Cathedral), which recalls the capture of Goa by Afonso de Albuquerque on St Catherine's Day, 1510.

Fernandes does not refer in 1540 to the altarpiece of the *Holy Trinity* (*c.* 1540; Lisbon, Mus. N. A. Ant.), one of his most noted works, which was painted for the Convento da Trinidade, Lisbon. The composition of the central panel of the *Holy Trinity* recalls the tympanum of a Gothic portal. In the predella of the altarpiece of *St Bartholomew* (1537) in Lisbon Cathedral, Fernandes copied the *Last Supper* from an engraving by Raimondi of about 1515 or 1516, after a drawing attributed to Raphael.

BIBLIOGRAPHY

A. Raczyński: *Les Arts en Portugal* (Paris, 1846), pp. 212–13
A. Gusmão: *Os primitivos e a renascença in arte portuguesa: Pintura* [The primitives and the Renaissance in Portuguese art: Painting] (Lisbon, 1950), pp. 253–4
L. Reis-Santos: *Garcia Fernandes* (Lisbon, 1957)

DAGOBERTO L. MARKL

Fernandes, Mateus, I (*fl* 1490; *d* 10 April 1515). Portuguese architect. He was master of works at the monastery of Batalha from at least 1490. He enjoyed the confidence of King Manuel I, who appointed him to supervise other works throughout the country. His most important work is at Batalha, on the Capelas Imperfeitas (unfinished chapels; for illustration *see* BATALHA PRIORY), which represent the Manueline contribution to the monument. Fernandes was responsible for the magnificent entrance portal, completed in 1509, the cornice of the lower storey, the beginning of the upper storey (unfinished) and possibly some of the chapel vaults.

The portal belongs to the traditions of Late Gothic yet shows some distinctly Portuguese characteristics in its decorative treatment. Using the space available to the full, Fernandes decorated the portal with a series of intersecting arches of varied shapes (trefoil, ogee) and filled the jambs and arches with complex decorative devices, including plant motifs (thistle, ivy) combined with suggestions of textiles and basketwork, as well as geometric decoration evocative of Late Gothic and *Mudéjar* ornament, with either individual lettering or whole phrases. The most original aspect of the work lies, however, in the deep undercutting and the predominance of sculptural over architectural forms. It was one of the first and most influential examples of the Manueline style, which spread from Batalha throughout the rest of Portugal.

Fernandes's son, also called Mateus Fernandes, worked with him on the construction of Batalha, deputizing in his absence. In 1516, following his father's death, he was appointed master of works at the monastery. The full extent of his contribution to the work remains unknown.

See also HUGUET.

BIBLIOGRAPHY

F. São Luís: *Memoria historica sobre as obras do real mosteiro de Santa Maria da Victoria* [A historical record of the works of the royal monastery of S Maria da Victoria] (Lisbon, 1872)
F. M. S. Viterbo: *Diccionario*, 3 vols (Lisbon, 1922)
V. Correia: 'Arte: Ciclo manuelino', *História de Portugal*, ed. D. Peres and E. Cerdeira, iv (Barcelos, 1948), pp. 433–74
R. Santos: *O estilo manuelino* [The Manueline style] (Lisbon, 1952)

JOSÉ CUSTODIO VIEIRA DA SILVA

Fernandes, Vasco [Grão Vasco] (*b* ?Viseu; *fl* 1475–1542). Portuguese painter. He was the leading painter of northern Portugal during the first half of the 16th century, and it is probable that he received his training abroad. Fernandes is the best-documented Portuguese artist of the period; there are nearly 100 works attributed to him, some of which are securely documented and record his activity either alone or in collaboration with the Viseu painter GASPAR VAZ. Fernandes's most important work was carried out in Lamego and in Viseu, where the term *Grão* ('Great') used in praise of him is first recorded (Ribeiro Botelho Pereira). In 1753 the Director of the Dresden Gallery, Pietro Guarienti, first used the epithet when he referred to Fernandes by the name of Gran Vasco. The many myths about the painter and his work developed from this date and were not clarified until 1846, when Conde Athanasius Raczyński listed works by Fernandes that he considered authentic.

Fernandes is first recorded in Viseu 1501–2, when he collaborated on the high altar of the cathedral (1500–06; dispersed). Attributed to Fernandes are the *Adoration of the Magi* (Viseu, Mus. Grão Vasco), in which the dark-skinned king is portrayed as a Brazilian Indian, a reference to the discovery of Brazil by the Portuguese in 1500; and the central, larger panel depicting the *Assumption of the Virgin* (Lisbon, Mus. N. A. Ant.). Documented between 1506 and 1511 are the 20 panels for the high altar of Lamego Cathedral. The five existing panels, *Creation of the Animals*, *Annunciation*, *Visitation*, *Circumcision* and *Presentation in the Temple* (Lamego, Mus. Reg.), show that Fernandes was influenced by the art of northern and central Europe. This is particularly apparent in the *Annunciation*, which has affinities with an *Annunciation* (*c.* 1480; Kraków Cathedral) by the Polish painter Stanislav Durink (*fl* 1426–82). Fernandes also used elements for these panels taken from the engravings of the chronicle *Neue Weltchronik* by Hartmann Schedel (Nuremberg, 1493) and illustrated by Michael Wolgemut and Wilhelm Pleydenwurff. This adaptation of German iconographic models was combined with a Netherlandish aesthetic, derived from artists influenced by the Haarlem painter Geertgen tot Sint Jans, to which Fernandes added details that are Portuguese in character, such as the pottery brazier in the *Annunciation*.

In 1515 Fernandes was in Lisbon and in contact with the workshop of the court painter Jorge Afonso, but his style remained unaffected by this brief stay in the capital.

Vasco Fernandes: *St Peter*, oil on panel, 314×265 mm, *c*. 1535–40 (Viseu, Museu de Grão Vasco)

Around 1520 he painted the triptych of the *Lamentation*, with side panels representing *St Francis Receiving the Stigmata* and *St Anthony* (Lisbon, Mus. N. A. Ant.). The fact that he signed the central panel VASCO FRZ. indicates a sense of independence unprecedented among Portuguese painters at this date. Shortly after 1521 he painted the *Descent from the Cross* (Viseu, Mus. Grão Vasco) after an engraving of 1520–21 by Marcantonio Raimondi.

Between 1520 and 1525 he painted the retable for the parish church of Freixo-de-Espada-à-Cinta, for which he again turned to engravings, in this instance by Albrecht Dürer. This is most apparent in the panel *Christ in the House of Martha and Mary* (Viseu, Mus. Grão Vasco), in which he used the engraving of *Melancholy I* for the figure of Mary and the background of Dürer's *Prodigal Son* for the landscape. In 1535 he signed his name in Latin,

Velascus, on the *Pentecost* (Coimbra, Santa Cruz, Sacristy), a late work expressing intense emotion through the agitated Mannerist poses.

A more monumental style is seen in the late *St Peter* (*c.* 1535–40) painted on panel for Viseu Cathedral (Viseu, Mus. Grão Vasco; see fig.). A knowledge of Renaissance forms is apparent in the modelling of the powerful head, the sweep of the drapery, the Italianate shell on the top of the throne and the ordering of space, which continues beyond the figure to the landscape seen through a pair of arches. Fernandes's first version of this work, in S João, Tarouca, shows the hieratic figure seated on a Gothic throne. Other late works include the great *Calvary* (panel; Viseu, Mus. Grão Vasco), with a composition more influenced by a German aesthetic, which may have been inspired by the 15th-century Master of Laufen, active in Salzburg; and *Pentecost*, which is close to Fernandes's painting of the same subject in Santa Cruz, Coimbra; a *Martyrdom of St Sebastian*, which suggests the influence of Luca Signorelli; and a *Baptism of Christ* (all 1535–40; Viseu, Mus. Grão Vasco).

BIBLIOGRAPHY
M. Ribeiro Botelho Pereira: *Dialogos moraes historicos e politicos. Fundação da cidade de Vizeu. Historia de seus Bispos, genealogia de suas familias. Relações sobre muitos successos que tiveram logar nesta cidade, diversas antiguidades e factos curiosos* (Viseu, 1630), chaps i, iv, x
P.-A. Orlandi [P. Guarienti]: *Abecedario pittorico* (Venice, 1753), p. 49
A. Raczyński: *Les Arts en Portugal* (Paris, 1846), pp. 107–91, 297–308 and references under Vasco, Grão Vasco and Vasco Fernandes do Casal
V. Correia: *Vasco Fernandes: Mestre do retábulo da Sé de Lamego* (Coimbra, 1924)
L. Reis-Santos: *Vasco Fernandes e os pintores de Viseu do século XVI* (Lisbon, 1946)
D. L. Markl: *Duas gravuras de Albrecht Dürer no painel 'Jesús em casa de Marta e Maria' atribuído a Vasco Fernandes* (Lisbon, 1988)
DAGOBERTO L. MARKL

Fernández, Agustín (*b* Havana, 16 April 1928). Cuban painter. He studied at the Academia de S Alejandro in Havana from 1946 to 1950 and the Art Students League, New York, in 1949. He had his first one-man exhibition at the Lyceum in Havana in 1951. In 1959 he left Cuba for Paris, from where he moved to San Juan, Puerto Rico, in 1968 before settling in New York in 1972 as a political exile.

During the 1950s Fernández painted luminous pictures that combine still-life elements with landscapes, as in *Landscape and Still-life* (1956; New York, MOMA). In such works he made elements of the still-life dissolve into the distant landscape forms in order to coalesce the expansiveness of landscape with the still-life interplay of form and light. In the 1960s he developed his mature style, characterized by images of body parts and armour on large canvases painted in earth tones, greys, and black and white. Like his Brazilian contemporary Antonio Henrique Amaral, he explored unflinchingly the interrelationship of sexuality and aggression without sensationalism or vulgarity, as in *The Large Skin* (1964; Detroit, MI, Inst. A.), in which the multiplication of breasts and blades is used to explore how violence and eroticism parallel each other in affirming and subverting the integrity of the self. Fernández's work is formal and lyrical, almost metaphysical, rather than cathartically expressionist.

BIBLIOGRAPHY
R. C. Kenedy: *Agustín Fernández* (New York, 1973)
Outside Cuba/Fuera de Cuba (exh. cat. by I. Fuentes-Perez, G. Cruz-Taura and R. Pau-Llosa, New Brunswick, NJ, Rutgers U., Zimmerli A. Mus.; New York, Mus. Contemp. Hisp. A.; Oxford, OH, Miami U., A. Mus.; and elsewhere; 1987–9)
RICARDO PAU-LLOSA

Fernández, Alejo [Alexo] (*b* ?Germany, *c.* 1475; *d* Seville, 1545). Spanish painter. Alejo Fernández (a hispanicized version of his original name) is first documented of at the end of the 15th century in Córdoba. In 1508 he moved with his brother Jorge (1470–1533 or 1553), a sculptor, to Seville, where they had been commissioned by the cathedral chapter to carry out painting, gilding and *estofado* (tooling) work on the figures of the reredos of the main altar. His work there won him a prominent and authoritative position among painters in Seville, and within a few years he had also become well established financially. His style reflects the influence of northern European painting, and echoes of 16th-century Flemish style are clearly visible in his work, as well as of Italian painting of the same period, which suggests that he spent some time in Italy before moving to Córdoba.

A painting of *St Peter Praying before Christ at the Column* (*c.* 1500; Córdoba, Mus. Prov. B.A.), in which Flemish and Italian elements are harmoniously combined, survives from Fernández's Córdoban period. His first important commission in Seville was for four large panel paintings contracted by the chapter of the cathedral to hang on the beam crossing the roof space of the Capilla Mayor in the cathedral. The pictures portray the *Conception of the Virgin*, the *Birth of the Virgin*, the *Nativity* and the *Purification of the Virgin* (all *c.* 1509–12). All these works show monumental figures against architecturally composed backgrounds opening on to deep landscapes. In about 1520 Fernández executed the altarpiece in the convent of S María de Jesús, the *Virgin of Antigua*, which is one of his best works. Another important painting is the *Virgin of the Rose* in S Ana, Triana (near Seville), which exemplifies his characteristic female type, gentle and meditative. In collaboration with some of his pupils he painted the *Virgin of Seafarers* (*c.* ?1531–6; Seville, Alcázar), in which the figure of the Virgin appears to float, her mantle protecting the Spanish sailors who took part in the discovery and conquest of America—among whom can be identified Christopher Columbus and Hernán Cortés.

BIBLIOGRAPHY
D. Angulo Iñíguez: *Alejo Fernández* (Seville, 1946)
——: 'Pintura del renacimiento', *A. Hisp.*, xvii (1955), p. 128
E. Valdivieso: *Historia de la pintura sevillana* (Seville, 1986), p. 93
ENRIQUE VALDIVIESO

Fernández, Antonio Arias. *See* ARIAS FERNÁNDEZ, ANTONIO.

Fernández, Antonio Susillo. *See* SUSILLO, ANTONIO.

Fernandez, Armand. *See* ARMAN.

Fernández, Gregorio (*b* Sarria, Galicia, 1576; *d* Valladolid, 22 Jan 1636). Spanish sculptor. He moved from Galicia to Valladolid, drawn by the presence of the Spanish court, and there he was the disciple and collaborator of FRANCISCO RINCÓN. Fernández's work in Valladolid is first documented in 1605. He created a style based on strong, vigorous figures and garments with broken, angular folds. His great ability is apparent in the carving of the hair and beards of his figures. He integrated the formal beauty found in the academic Mannerism of Pompeo Leoni and the idealized beauty of the Classical nude with deep Christian feeling. The nude figure of his *Ecce homo* (1610–12; Valladolid, Mus. Dioc. y Catedrálicio) is based on Classical models. However, his work gradually evolved into a forceful naturalism. He was a skilled narrator of subjects from the Gospels, but he placed greater emphasis on the expressive qualities of the episodes than on the narration. His work also shows a high degree of mysticism. Fernández never visited Italy, so his art is essentially Spanish in style and expression.

The sculptures produced by Fernández were admired and greatly sought after, and his patrons included Philip III, who commissioned a *Reclining Christ* (1614) and gave it to the Capuchin convent of El Pardo (*in situ*). Around 1606 the Duque de Lerma, Francisco Gomez de Sandoval y Rojas, had donated a *Reclining Christ* to the convent of S Pablo in Valladolid (*in situ*), and in 1617 Fernández completed the alabaster tombs of the *Condes de Fuensaldaña* (Valladolid, S Miguel). In 1635 Philip IV stated that the archangel *St Michael* for the Colegiata, Alfaro, Logroño (*in situ*), had been executed 'by the hand of the most highly skilled sculptor in my kingdom' (*de mano del escultor de mayor primor que hay en estos mis reinos*; Martín González, 1983, p. 43). Fernández's other patrons were the religious orders, principally the Carmelites and the Franciscans and Jesuits, and the various penitential brotherhoods (*cofradías penitenciales*).

Fernández directed a large and well-organized workshop in Valladolid, which at the time produced the largest output of sculpture in Spain. He carved the principal sculptures himself, as well as the heads and hands, and the rest was executed by assistants working from his models. The production of his workshop is widely dispersed in Spain. It reached the Basque country (Aranzazu, Vergara, Eibar and Vitoria: *retablos* in S Antonio), Madrid (the convents of La Encarnación and S Plácido), Plasencia (Cathedral), Saragossa (Convento de Facetas), Valencia (Colegio del Corpus Christi), Salamanca, Avila, Segovia, Palencia, León, Burgos and especially Valladolid.

An important part of Fernández's production was the making of *retablos*. An early commission, Mannerist in style, was the retable (1606) for S Miguel in Valladolid. An important and highly expressive work is the monumental relief of the *Assumption of the Virgin* (1610), part of the principal retable of the cathedral of Miranda do Douro (Portugal), which shows the sculptor's ability to handle a large-scale subject and to make his sculpture effective alongside large paintings. The principal retable (1613), composed entirely of sculpture, in Santos Juanes, Nava del Rey, was executed after the design of the sculptor Francisco de Mora (*see* MORA, (1)). A significant work is the high relief of *Christ Embracing St Bernard* (1613) in the principal retable of Las Huelgas Reales, Valladolid, which depicts the supreme moment of a mystical experience. In 1624 Fernández was working on the principal retable of S Miguel, Vitoria, adorned with statues and reliefs including the *Immaculate Conception, St Michael* and *Calvary*. The principal retable of Plasencia Cathedral,

Cáceres province, devoted to the *Life of Christ, Life of the Virgin* with *Evangelists* and *Saints*, is the southernmost point of Spain to which the sculpture of Fernández was dispersed, and this commission, executed in Valladolid and completed in 1632, was his major work. The cathedral chapter, who wanted a work of the highest quality, hesitated between commissioning the retable from Juan Martínez Montañés or from Fernández. The architecture was by Juan Velázquez and Cristóbal Velázquez of Valladolid, and the paintings were commissioned in 1635 from the school of Madrid (especially from Francisco Rizi; *see* RIZI, (2)).

The processional *pasos* carved by Fernández and conceived as scenes with numerous life-size figures followed the type created by his master, Francisco de Rincón. In the *Raising of the Cross* (1604–12; Valladolid, Mus. N. Escul.) by Rincón, in which Fernández may have collaborated, the near foreground scene of *Thirst* depicts the

Gregorio Fernández: *St Dominic*, polychromed wood, h. 1.87 m, 1625 (Valladolid, S Pablo)

casting of lots for Christ's tunic, but the emotive tension gradually rises towards the top of the *paso*, where the executioner is shown placing the inscription *INRI*. The daring conception of this *paso* aims to present diverse viewpoints. In 1623 Fernández contracted the more complex *paso* of the *Descent from the Cross* (Valladolid, Vera Cruz). This skilful composition, with two figures standing on the ladder to take down the body of Christ, successfully resolves the difficult problems of balance and the placing of the figures in space.

Fernández's treatment of incidents from the Passion include the *Flagellation* (before 1619; Valladolid, Vera Cruz; Madrid, convent of the Encarnación; Ávila, convent of S Teresa), a large series of *Crucifixions* (Valladolid U., La Luz; León, S Pedro de las Dueñas) and a large series of *Christ Reclining* (Madrid, S Plácido; Medina de Pomar; Valladolid, Mus. N. Escul.). Among themes taken from the life of the Virgin are the *Immaculate Conception*, where Fernández created a type of Virgin with long hair and wearing a rigid cloak, and with the use of rich polychromy (León, S Marcelo and 1626; Astorga Cathedral), and the example in the Franciscanas Descalzas in Montforte de Lemos, where the sumptuous appearance of the Virgin resembles the work of the goldsmith.

Among Fernández's numerous sculptures of saints are the standing *St Francis of Assisi*, depicted, following tradition, as he was found in his tomb (Valladolid, convent of las Descalzas Reales) and the fine, dramatic *St Paul* (1624) and *St Dominic* (1625; see fig.), who is shown in ecstasy contemplating a crucifix (both Valladolid, S Pablo). Fernández used the death-mask and the portrait by Alonso Sánchez Coello (life-size; 1614) for various images of *St Ignatius Loyola*, including those in Bergara, Semin.; San Luis; Villagarcía de Campos; and S Miguel, Valladolid (1622). He depicted *St Teresa de Jesús* writing with pen and book, the earliest example of which is in 1614, the year of her beatification (Valladolid, convent of Carmen Extramuros); a late version of before 1625 is the *St Teresa* for the convent of Carmen Calzado (Valladolid, Mus. N. Escul.). He also executed many figures of patron saints including *St Antolín* (*c*. 1605–10; Palencia Cathedral) and *St Marcelo* (1628; León, S Marcelo), who is shown contemplating a crucifix. The lifelike quality of these statues was praised at the time and is seen in the *St Peter* (Valladolid, Mus. N. Escul.), who appears as if he were about to speak. Fernández's fame was such that throughout the 17th century sculptors were required to copy his models, which resulted in a certain lack of initiative among his followers.

BIBLIOGRAPHY

J. Martí y Monsó: *Estudios histórico-artísticos* (Valladolid, 1901)
E. García Chico: *Escultores* (Valladolid, 1914), ii of *Documentos para el estudio del arte en Castilla*
J. Agapito y Revilla: *La obra de los maestros de la escultura vallisoletana*, ii (Valladolid, 1929)
F. J. de la Plaza Santiago: 'El pueblo natal de Gregorio Fernández', *Bol. Semin. Estud. A. & Arqueol.* (1973), pp. 505–09
J. J. Martín González: *El escultor Gregorio Fernández* (Madrid, 1980)
M. A. Fernández de Hoyo: 'Oficiales de Gregorio Fernández y ensambladores que trabajaron con él', *Bol. Semin. Estud. A. & Arqueol.* (1983), pp. 347–74
J. J. Martín González: *Escultura barroca en España, 1600–1700* (Madrid, 1983), pp. 42–68
J. Urrea: 'Escultores coetáneos y discípulos de G. Fernández en Valladolid', *Bol. Semin. Estud. A. & Arqueol.* (1984), pp. 349–70

J. J. MARTÍN GONZÁLEZ

Fernández, Juan (i) (*b* ?Seville; *d* Seville, between 12 May and 17 May 1572). Spanish architect. He was descended from Moorish architects. He was appointed Maestro Mayor of the Alcázar of Seville (*see* SEVILLE, §IV, 2) by Emperor Charles V on 30 June 1537; all his known work is connected with this building. He directed the restoration of the Patio de las Doncellas, building its upper galleries (1540–72) to a new plan from the designs by Luis de Vega, with paired Ionic columns imported from Genoa and Plateresque stuccowork. The old supports in the lower galleries (1560–69) were replaced by elegant marble Corinthian columns, also from Genoa. Here the original *Mudéjar* stuccowork was repaired, and Fernández introduced new stucco and possibly helped in the design. His models were disseminated and influenced the planning of other palaces in Seville. He was also responsible for the plan of the Cenador de Carlos V (1543–6), which he transformed from the original Moorish *qubba* or room into a beautiful garden pavilion with a fine coffered ceiling, in a composition that effectively combines Andalusian and Florentine influences. Fernández's style expresses the taste that characterized the reign of Charles V rather than the more austere, rigid forms that were prevalent during the reign of Philip II.

BIBLIOGRAPHY

J. Gestoso y Pérez: *Sevilla monumental y artística*, i (Seville, 1889), pp. 464, 516–17, 520–21
A. Marín Fidalgo: *El Alcázar de Sevilla bajo los Austrias: Estudio arquitectónico e histórico*, 2 vols (Seville, 1990)

ANA MARÍN FIDALGO

Fernández, Juan (ii). *See* LABRADOR, EL.

Fernández, Juan Antonio Ribera y. *See* RIBERA (ii), (1).

Fernandez, Louis [Fernández, Luis] (*b* Oviedo, 29 April 1900; *d* Paris, 1973). Spanish painter and writer. He moved in 1924 to Paris, where he met Picasso, Georges Braque, Amédée Ozenfant, Le Corbusier and other avant-garde artists and became associated first with Purism and in 1928 with Neo-plasticism. He apparently exhibited in 1934 with Abstraction-Création, writing a text for their magazine. During the 1930s he wrote a series of texts on formal and technical aspects of painting and produced abstract geometrical images characterized by their flatness and great simplicity, such as *Abstraction* (1933; see Picón and others, p. 8) and *Sketch for Grey Abstraction No. 51* (1933; Saint-Etienne, Mus. A. & Indust.).

During the 1940s Fernandez abandoned geometrical abstraction in favour of an intense search for figurative and expressive reality, partly under the influence of Picasso, as can be seen in works such as *Bullfight* (1940; see Picón and others, p. 18). In the late 1940s and early 1950s he produced still-lifes in which he subjected ordinary objects to a process of geometric stylization, as in *Vase, Bread Rolls and Fruit on a Table* (1948; see Picón and others, p. 23), before turning to simplified landscapes and to studies of the human figure or animals, such as *Cows in the Stable* (1955; see Picón and others, p. 66). Among his later works are a group of *Skulls* dating from 1953 to the early 1970s (see Picón and others, pp. 79–85). He held his first one-man exhibition at age 50 in the Galerie Pierre in Paris, but in spite of further shows and an extensive exhibition of his work in Spain more than a decade after his death he continued to be appreciated by only a small public.

BIBLIOGRAPHY

J. Paez Vilaro: *Concentración y obra de Louis Fernandez* (Montevideo, 1954)
G. Picon and others: *Louis Fernandez*, CNAC Archives 4 (Paris, 1972) [published on the occasion of his exhibition at Paris, Cent. N. A. Contemp.]
Luis Fernández (exh. cat., Madrid, Col. Banco Exterior España, 1984)

M. DOLORES JIMÉNEZ-BLANCO

Fernández, Luis (*b* Madrid, ?1594; *d* Madrid, 1654). Spanish painter. He trained in Madrid as a pupil of Eugenio Cajés and specialized in fresco and tempera painting. He executed a series of scenes from the *Life of the Virgin* (destr.) in Santa Cruz, Madrid. In 1625 he painted episodes from the *Life of St Raymond Nonnatus* (destr.) in the cloister of the convent of the Merced Calzada, Madrid. Most of his work has been lost, and only three works definitely by him survive: two of these, *St Joachim* and *St Anne* (both 1630; Pastrana, Guadalajara province, collegiate church), are voluminous and monumental figures; the third, *St Lawrence* (1632; Madrid, Consejo Estado), is also solemn and monumental with an intense and spiritual facial expression. In all these works the brushwork is free and firm. A retable with paintings signed *Luis Fernández* and dated 1634, in the parish church of Cebreros, Ávila province, is probably by a different artist of the same name (very common in Spain), since the technique is less spontaneous and more conservative.

BIBLIOGRAPHY

D. Angulo Iñíguez and A. E. Pérez Sánchez: *Pintura madrileña del primer tercio del siglo XVII* (Madrid, 1969), pp. 266–70
D. Angulo Iñíguez: *Pinturo del siglo XVII*, A. Hisp., xv (Madrid, 1971), p. 48

ENRIQUE VALDIVIESO

Fernández de Castro Andrade y Portugal, Pedro. *See* LEMOS, Conde de.

Fernández de Córdoba Folch de Cardona y Aragón, Luís de la Cerda. *See* MEDINACELI, (1).

Fernández de Córdoba y Figueroa de la Cerda, Luís de Soledad. *See* MEDINACELI, (2).

Fernández de la Vega, Luis (*b* Llantones, Gijón, *c.* 1601; *d* Oviedo, 1675). Spanish sculptor. He was probably a pupil of Gregorio Fernández in Valladolid, whose influence shows in his style and compositions. His earliest documented work is a *St Nicholas* for S Nicolás de Bari, Avilés (1634; untraced). In 1636 he carved the *St Joseph* and *St Anthony* (both untraced), commissioned by Don Fernando Valdés for the Capilla de Nuestra Señora de Guadalupe in Gijón; the sculptures were highly praised by Jovellanos. In 1638 he was established in Oviedo, where in 1641 he collaborated on the principal retable in S Vicente, and where in the same year he signed a contract for the funeral effigy of Bishop Don Juan Vigil de Quinones (Bishop of Valladolid in 1614) and for a relief of the *Annunciation*, both in Oviedo Cathedral. From then he worked in Oviedo Cathedral with the support of Bishop Don Bernardo Caballero de Paredes and carved the *St Teresa*, an *Immaculate Conception* and *St Roque* (all 1658)

and the *St Barbara* (1658) in the chapel of the same dedication.

Outside Asturias, Fernández de la Vega carved the *St Joseph* (*in situ*) on the side altar in the Iglesia de Agustinas Recoletas (now Carmelites) at Medina del Campo (documented in 1650) and part of a commission from Bishop Caballero de Paredes in this church. In 1645 he had been commissioned by the same bishop to carve the figures for the principal retable in Nuestra Señora de Carrasconte, León (mainly untraced), two of which may be reliefs of the *Annunciation* and *St Roch* (Barcelona, Mus. Marés).

BIBLIOGRAPHY

Ceán Bermúdez
G. M. de Jovellanos: *Obras completas*, Biblioteca de Autores Españoles (Madrid, 1952); Carta décima a don Antonio Ponz, p. 308; Cartas a Ceán, p. 364, dated 10 Oct 1775
G. Ramallo Asensio: *Luis Fernández de la Vega, escultor asturiano del siglo XVII* (Oviedo, 1983)

G. RAMALLO ASENSIO

Fernández del Campo, Pedro. *See* MEJORADA, Marqués de.

Fernández de Medrano, Sebastián (*b* Spain, 24 Oct 1646; *d* Brussels, 18 Feb 1705). Spanish engineer and writer. He was an expert mathematician and in 1675 was appointed a master in the Military Academy, Brussels, of which he became director in 1692. He was a leading military engineer and the author of important theoretical works, mostly written after he became blind. His writings on military architecture demonstrate that engineering was becoming an increasingly exact science and moving away from the humanistic and aesthetic considerations of the 16th-century treatises on the subject. He represents the culmination of the process of specialization in engineering and his broad knowledge embraced geography, techniques of warfare, the training of new practitioners of the profession in academies and the formulation of new scientific possibilities.

WRITINGS

Rudimentos geométricos y militares (Brussels, 1677)
El práctico artillero (Brussels, 1680)
Descripción del mundo o guía geográfica (Brussels, 1686)
El ingeniero: Primera parte de la moderna architectura militar, 2 vols (Brussels, 1687)
El ingeniero práctico (Brussels, 1690)
El architecto perfecto en el arte militar (Brussels, 1700)

BIBLIOGRAPHY

J. Almirante: *Bibliografía militar de España* (Madrid, 1876)
J. Vigón: *Historia de la artillería española* (Madrid, 1947)
J. M. López Piñero: *Ciencia y técnica en la sociedad española de los siglos XVI y XVII* (Barcelona, 1979)

ALICIA CÁMARA MUÑOZ

Fernández de Velasco, Juan (*b c.* 1550; *d* Madrid, 15 Mar 1613). Spanish statesman, soldier, diplomat and collector. After studying at the Universidad de Salamanca under the humanist El Brocense, he fought against the English fleet, which was harrying the Spanish coast, and in the war in Flanders. He was Condestable de Castilla, twice governor of Milan and was a member of the Consejo de Estado and President of the Consejo de Italia. As leader of the Spanish delegation at the conclusion of the peace between Spain and England in 1604, James I of England presented him with the splendid gold and enamel 14th-century Royal Gold Cup of the Kings of France and

England (London, BM; *see* ENAMEL, colour pl. III, fig. 1), valued at 4323 reales.

During his travels he amassed an important collection of *objets d'art*. This was especially strong in tapestries but also included sculpture, mostly on Classical themes, some antiques and paintings. The paintings were probably by important artists to judge by the valuation put on them. Many were on religious subjects, outstanding among which were works by Bassano: *Moses* (36 ducats), *Agony in the Garden* (300 reales), *Arrest of Christ* (550 reales) and *Burial of Christ* (500 ducats). Besides a series of family portraits, there were also portraits of sovereigns and illustrious figures of antiquity and of his own time. There were mythological paintings, landscapes, still-lifes and genre paintings, including a panel and a canvas by Bosch of unknown subjects, which were valued at 100 reales and four ducats respectively. He also collected an important library, largely of Italian provenance, which included manuscripts (some in Madrid, Bib. N.). Outstanding among his manuscripts was the 15th-century illuminated Breviary of Isabel la Católica (Madrid, Bib. N.), valued at 3800 reales. Many items in the collection were sold after his death.

WRITINGS
Inventario del Condestable de Castilla a la muerte de su primera mujer, doña María Girón, duquesa de Frías (1608; Madrid, Archv Hist. Protocolos, protocolo 24,850)
Inventario del Condestable de Castilla (1613; Madrid, Archv Hist. Protocolos, protocolo 24,851)
Almoneda del Condestable de Castilla (1613; Madrid, Archv Hist. Protocolos, protocolo 4,719) [record of sale]

BIBLIOGRAPHY
J. Scheper: *Panegírico y compendio de la vida y hazañas del Condestable* (Milan, 1612)
F. López de Mendicorroz: *Observaciones de la vida del Condestable Juan Fernández de Velasco* (Vigebano, 1625)
G. de Andrés: 'La biblioteca manuscrita del Condestable Juan Fernández de Velasco († 1613)', *Cuad. Bibliog.*, xl (1980), pp. 1–18
NATIVIDAD SÁNCHEZ ESTEBAN

Fernández-Jardón, César Portela. *See* PORTELA FERNÁNDEZ-JARDÓN, CÉSAR.

Fernández Ledesma, Gabriel (*b* Aguascalientes, 30 May 1900; *d* Mexico City, 26 Aug 1984). Mexican painter, printmaker, teacher, writer and ceramicist. He enrolled at the Escuela Nacional de Bellas Artes, Mexico City, in 1917 and soon became active in the post-revolutionary nationalist cultural movement, attempting to recuperate folk-art motifs and techniques. In 1920 he designed a ceramic frieze for the Colegio Máximo de San Pedro y San Pablo, Mexico City. He edited the influential art magazine *Forma* (1926–8) and was involved in creating the Escuela Libre de Escultura y Talla Directa, Mexico City, the ¡30–30! group (which promoted the democratization and de-academization of the arts), and the Centros Populares de Pintura, which offered art education to people in industrial areas, encouraging the representation of their surroundings without academic constraints. In the 1930s he directed an exhibition space funded by the Ministerio de Educación Pública, for which, with Roberto Montenegro and Francisco Díaz de León, he designed posters and catalogues noted for their innovative typography. Fernández Ledesma also produced prints inspired by popular graphics and

figurative paintings influenced by Picasso and by Pittura Metafisica; he also wrote several books on popular traditions and stage and costume designs.

BIBLIOGRAPHY
Exposición homenaje a Gabriel Fernández Ledesma (exh. cat., Aguascalientes, Mus. Aguascalientes, 1981)
Gabriel Fernández Ledesma: Artista y promotor cultural (exh. cat., Mexico City, Mus. Pal. B.A., 1982)
J. Alanís: *Gabriel Fernández Ledesma* (Mexico City, 1985)
KAREN CORDERO REIMAN

Fernández Muro, José Antonio (*b* Madrid, 1920). Argentine painter of Spanish birth. He moved to Argentina in 1938, studying under the Spanish Catalan painter Vicente Puig (1882–1965) and holding his first one-man exhibition in 1944. In 1952 he joined the ARTISTAS MODERNOS DE LA ARGENTINA. He took Constructivism as his starting-point, preserving its rigour and severity but moving towards a lyrical and highly personal form of abstraction. In the late 1950s he began to create rhythmic patterns of circles on geometric shapes by means of perforated sheets of metallic foil, an impressed effect which he was the first to use in Argentina, for example in *Penetrating Black* (1962; Washington, DC, Mus. Mod. A. Latin America).

Fernández Muro moved to New York in 1962 and from 1969 divided his time between Madrid and Paris. From *c.* 1970 he made reliefs in which he displayed an inexhaustible imagination, consistently offering the observer a renewed vision of geometry through a sensitivity towards materials, a refined elaboration of texture and an incomparable assurance in composition. He won many awards for his work, including the Guggenheim International Prize in New York in 1960.

BIBLIOGRAPHY
A. Pellegrini: *Panorama de la pintura argentina* (Buenos Aires, 1967), pp. 61, 69–70
Fernández Muro (exh. cat., preface L. Castedo; Madrid, Mus. A. Contemp., 1985)
NELLY PERAZZO

Fernández Noseret, Luis (*fl* Madrid, 1793–1828). Spanish engraver. He trained at the Real Academia de S Fernando, Madrid, where he was a pupil of Manuel Salvador Carmona. In 1795, under Salvador Carmona's direction, he copied Gerard Edelinck's print of the *Holy Family*, a painting (Venice, Pin. Manfrediniana) formerly attributed to Leonardo. Fernández Noseret engraved *St Cecilia* (Madrid, Pal. Real) by Guido Reni, after the drawing by León Bueno (1793); *St Joseph* and *St Lawrence* after the paintings by Alonso Cano; and 13 plates after drawings by Antonio Carnicero for *Colección de las principales suertes de una corrida de toros* (Madrid, 1795). He collaborated on *Brigada de artillería volante* (Madrid, 1796) and in 1828 copied two 18th-century prints: *St Barnabas* by Francisco Muntaner Moner and *St Ferdinand* (Madrid, Prado) by Murillo, the latter after the engraving by Salvador Carmona.

BIBLIOGRAPHY
E. Paez Rios: *Repertorio de grabados españoles de la Biblioteca Nacional*, i (Madrid, 1981), p. 344
A. Tomas and M. S. Silvestre: *Estampas y planchas de la Real Academia en el Museo de Bellas Artes de Valencia* (Valencia, 1982)

J. Carrete Parrondo: *La Real Calcografía de Madrid: Goya y sus contemporáneos* (Madrid, 1984)

J. Carrete, F. Checa and V. Bozal: *El grabado en España, siglos XV al XVIII*, Summa A., xxxi (Madrid, 1987), pp. 575, 579, 594–5

BLANCA GARCÍA VEGA

Fernandi, Francesco. *See* IMPERIALI.

Fernando, Duke of Guarda. *See* AVIZ, (10).

Ferneley, John (*b* Thrussington, Leics, 18 May 1782; *d* Melton Mowbray, Leics, 1860). English painter. He was apprenticed to his father, a master wheelwright, until 1801 when, encouraged by John, 5th Duke of Rutland, he went to study in London with the sporting artist Benjamin Marshall. At various intervals from 1806 to 1853 Ferneley's work was exhibited at the Royal Academy, but he set up his main painting practice in Melton Mowbray, which was rapidly developing as a centre for the sporting fraternity. The records of his busy studio were kept in account books from 1807 to 1860. Ferneley's group painting *John, Henry and Francis Grant at Melton* (1823; Melton Mowbray, Carnegie Mus.) is typical of his finest compositions, depicting huntsmen, horses and hounds. He also specialized in large panoramas of hunt scurries at full stretch, for example *The Quorn Hunt* (*c.* 1830; priv. col.).

Ferneley's *The Artist and Family with Nursemaid in the Studio* (*c.* 1822–3; Melton Mowbray, Carnegie Mus.) portrays his family. Several of his children were painters, including Claude Lorraine (1822–91), John Junior (1815–62) and Sarah (1811–1903). Sarah married an artist, Henry Johnson (*c.* 1800–50), whose portrait of Ferneley (1838) is in the National Portrait Gallery, London.

BIBLIOGRAPHY
G. Paget: *The Melton Mowbray of John Ferneley* (Leicester, 1931)
R. Paisey: *John Ferneley* (Leicester, 1983)

ROBIN PAISEY

Fernhout, Edgar (Richard Johannes) (*b* Bergen, Noord-Holland, 17 Aug 1912; *d* Bergen, 4 Nov 1974). Dutch painter. He was the son of Charley Toorop (*see* TOOROP, (2)). Until 1931 he lived in Schoorl, Bergen, Amsterdam and Paris. At the suggestion of Hendricus Petrus Bremmer, he started to paint interior still-lifes. In addition he painted self-portraits and later landscapes, as well as commissioned portraits. Because of its bright realism, his early work, detailed and documentary in character, could be categorized with Neue Sachlichkeit. Between 1936 and 1939 he worked with Rachel Fernhout-Pellecaan (*b* 1905) in Alassio, Italy. At the outbreak of World War II they returned to the Netherlands. During the war his work became more expressive and darker in tone. He moved from one place of hiding to another, painting portraits on commission. From 1945 until 1956 he lived and worked in Amsterdam. The move to the studio-house De Vlerken in Bergen in 1956 signalled a change in his work. Partly using sketches as a basis, he painted the landscape around his house: polders, dunes, woods, beach and sea, for example *Beach* (1957; Eindhoven, Stedel. Van Abbemus.). He represented their abstract characteristics, with the result that the naturalistic depiction of the scenes disappeared from his work. In 1963 he started teaching at the Ateliers 63, which led to another acceleration in the development of his work. The paintings that he produced during the last years of his life consist of canvases with monochrome fields of colour on which blocks are painted on top of and alongside each other, creating trellis patterns, for example *Silence* (1972–3; Amsterdam, Stedel. Mus.). He always maintained a link with reality in his work.

BIBLIOGRAPHY
G. J. P. Cammelbeeck: *Edgar Fernhout* (Amsterdam, 1969)
A. van den Berk, J. Moerbeek and J. Steen: *Edgar Fernhout, schilder/painter* (The Hague, 1990) [bilingual text]

JOHN STEEN

Fernkorn, Anton Dominik (*b* Erfurt, 17 March 1813; *d* Vienna, 16 Nov 1878). Austrian sculptor. He came from craftwork to art; he was apprenticed as a mechanic and brazier in Thuringia and there acquired a good deal of his knowledge in modelling, casting and chasing. In 1832 he became a volunteer in the artillery, but three years later he had to quit service after a bad fall, which left him with a permanent limp. He then moved to Munich, where he joined the Königliche Erzgiesserei (Royal foundry), the leading German enterprise in the field of bronze-casting. He also attended the Munich Akademie, although he did not pursue regular study there. He appears to have had a marked autodidactic talent and did not need a special teacher but maintained contact with artist friends such as Ferdinand von Miller (1813–87) or the Viennese Hans Gasser. Moreover, his work in the foundry brought contacts with such sculptors as the Dane Bertel Thorvaldsen, whose models he helped to realize and, sometimes, also copied.

Having gained a solid reputation as a founder, chaser and artist, though his independent creations were still few, Fernkorn went to Vienna in 1841. He worked first at the foundry of Joseph Glanz (1795–1866) and then with Johann Preleuthner (1807–97); but, while still realizing Preleuthner's designs, he became strongly interested in executing his own. His first truly independent works date from 1845: portrait busts in an unbiased, realistic manner influenced by the Berlin tradition of Gottfried von Schadow and Christian Daniel Rauch (e.g. *Duchess Elizabeth of Bavaria*, 1845; Vienna, Hofburg-Schauräume). In the following years Fernkorn turned to equestrian subjects and produced a bronze statuette of *Archduke Charles on Horseback* (1847; Vienna, Heeresgesch. Mus.), which he later turned into a monument design. Further commissions from the court were impossible during the disturbances of 1848, and meanwhile Fernkorn worked with the Salm foundry in Blansko, which was noted for its zinc-casting. Among works cast there was Fernkorn's statue of the *Immaculata* (1853; *in situ*) for the façade of Miklós Ybl's church at Fót near Budapest. The sculptor's style now often resembled that of his friend Gasser, aiming at dramatic expression and less passive than the Biedermeier ideal, although Fernkorn was inclined to think on a more monumental scale. Both artists carved figures in wood for Queen Victoria's bookcase (1851; London, V&A). It is sometimes hard to tell their work apart (see for example the bronze figures of the Donauweibchen Fountain, 1861; Vienna, Pal. Ferstel).

With the commission for a truly monumental zinc fountain group *St George and the Dragon* (1851–3; Vienna, Pal. Montenuovo), Fernkorn was able to reveal his skill in establishing a perfect synthesis between the harmonious appearance of the whole and the energy of the main action. The powerful modelling with its rich sculptural and pictorial values helped to balance realism with romantic idealization. The same could be said of Fernkorn's large-scale bronze monument to *Archduke Charles* (1853–9; see fig.), erected in the Heldenplatz in front of the Hofburg. The Archduke is shown raising a flag and calling his troops to follow him into the final victorious attack against Napoleon at the Battle of Aspern (1809). Concentrating on one dramatic moment, with rider and horse forming a single dramatic gesture, Fernkorn's monument recalls François Rude's *Marseillaise* of 1833. In the free and open silhouette, however, and in the masterful command of the colossal dimensions (h. *c.* 20 m, incl. socle) Fernkorn successfully revived the spirit of Baroque models to which he had turned. From a technical point of view the monument was especially impressive, particularly with regard to the position of the horse, which rests entirely on its hind legs without any other support. As a reward for his achievement Fernkorn was knighted in 1860, although he himself remained dissatisfied with his work because he had had to cancel the four corner groups, figures symbolic of Love of the Fatherland, Fidelity, Charity and Valour; these are found in smaller versions (see Aurenhammer, cat. no. 14, pl. 41), which alone Fernkorn considered authentic.

In 1856 Fernkorn had taken over the old cannon foundry in Vienna, which he turned into the K. K. Kunst-Erzgiesserei, the undertaking developing quickly into an internationally renowned centre for bronze-casting. This activity did not, however, lead to his neglecting other materials. In 1858 he finished a large sandstone sculpture, the *Lion of Aspern* (Aspern, former cemetery), a memorial

to those fallen at the Battle of Aspern. The mourning, wounded lion surpasses similar monuments, such as Thorvaldsen's *Dying Lion* near Lucerne (1821), in its vigour and psychological realism. Immediately after the monument to *Archduke Charles* was unveiled, Fernkorn started work on a bronze equestrian monument to *Prince Eugene*, to be erected opposite it in the Heldenplatz. Finished in 1865, the second monument marks a stylistic shift towards strict Historicism: no action, but a quiet pose modelled in such a way that the figure's disciplined energy is not hidden; it thus conveys a greater sense of substance, both visually and morally, than the monument opposite.

In 1861 Fernkorn also began a third bronze equestrian monument, to *Count Josef Jellačić*, for the main square in Zagreb (unveiled 1866). Having suffered a stroke in 1857, however, Fernkorn had little strength for the work he had undertaken, which included several portraits and memorials. A second stroke in 1863 forced him more or less to retire from work, and a third, in 1864, resulted in increasing malady and mental aberration. He produced several competent portrait busts (e.g. *Beethoven*, bronze, 1862–3; Vienna, Hist. Mus.), but at the unveiling of his *Prince Eugene* monument (1865) he was under constant medical supervision. After Christmas 1866 he was confined to a lunatic asylum, and during the last 12 years of his life his students executed his last designs.

BIBLIOGRAPHY

Thieme–Becker
H. Aurenhammer: *Anton Dominik Fernkorn* (Vienna, 1959)
R. Wagner-Rieger, ed.: *Die Wiener Ringstrasse*, i: *Das Kunstwerk im Bild* (Vienna, 1969); ix/1, G. Kapner and others: *Die Denkmäler der Wiener Ringstrasse* (Wiesbaden, 1973); ix/3, W. Krause: *Die Plastik der Wiener Ringstrasse von der Spätromantik bis zur Wende um 1900* (Wiesbaden, 1980)
H. W. Janson: *19th-century Sculpture* (New York, 1985)

WALTER KRAUSE

Ferrabosco [Ferabosco], **Martino** (*b* Capolago, Ticino; *d* Rome, *bur* 3 Aug 1623). Italian architect, stuccoist and engraver. He arrived in Rome by 1613 and worked on a number of commissions sponsored by Pope Paul V (Borghese). From 1613 until 1621 he was papal *fontaniero*, responsible for the embellishment and maintenance of the fountains in the Vatican and Quirinal gardens and in the Borgo. In 1616 he supervised the execution of the elaborate stucco coffering in the vault of the Cappella Paolina in the Palazzo del Quirinale, and in 1620–21 he led one of several teams of stuccoists at work on the vaults of the choir and sacristy in St Peter's.

Only one of Ferrabosco's architectural projects was ever realized. This was the clock-tower entrance to the Vatican Palace, which he built (with the participation of Giovanni Vasanzio) between July 1617 and September 1618. This ornate architectural frontispiece was known as the tower of Paul V and consisted of four tiers of diminishing width, fortified below with buttresses and quoins and decorated above with a pre-existing mosaic flanked by marble angels, a clockface and belfry. Emphasis on surface ornament was clearly a salient feature of the architect's style, no doubt stemming from his training as a stuccoist. The tower was located in front and to the right of the façade of St Peter's. Ferrabosco originally planned

Anton Dominik Fernkorn: monument to *Archduke Charles*, bronze, 1853–9 (Vienna, Heldenplatz)

to build a second tower to the left, as part of an even more ambitious scheme for a vast enclosed piazza surrounding the basilica. This project was never executed, and in 1659 the tower of Paul V was pulled down to make way for Gianlorenzo Bernini's monumental portico.

Ferrabosco was also a skilled printmaker, specializing in architectural engravings. Under the auspices of his friend and protector Giovanni Battista Costaguti, *maggiordomo* to Paul V, he produced a set of 30 engravings of St Peter's and its surroundings, eventually issued under the title *Architettura di San Pietro in Vaticano*. He began work on these prints no later than 1615 (one of them shows a marble relief by Taddeo Landini that was removed from the church in that year) and had them ready for publication by 1620 (the date on the original title page). They seem to have been intended as illustrations to Ferrante Carlo's *Templum Vaticanum*, an erudite history of St Peter's and the Vatican Palace commissioned by Paul V. Carlo's text was left unfinished, however, and Ferrabosco's engravings, several of which were reworked after his death, were published in 1684. The volume includes detailed views, plans and elevations of the interior and exterior of the basilica. It also includes illustrations of several unexecuted projects by Ferrabosco. One of these is a design for a ciborium screen over the high altar, evidently modified after Ferrabosco's death to include the coat of arms of Urban VIII as well as several details gleaned from Bernini's first project for the baldacchino. Other prints illustrate his proposals for a choir in the main tribune and for the enlargement and decoration of the *confessio* beneath the high altar.

WRITINGS
Architettura della basilica di S Pietro in Vaticano. . .fatta esprimere e intagliare in più tavole da Martino Ferrabosco e posta in luce l'anno MDCXX (Rome, 1684)

BIBLIOGRAPHY
A. Muñoz: 'Martino Ferabosco architetto: Il baldacchino di S Pietro; gli stucchi del Quirinale', *Vita A.*, vii (1911), pp. 83–103
G. Beltrami: 'Martino Ferabosco architetto', *L'Arte*, xxix (1926), pp. 23–37
H. Egger: 'Der Uhrturmbau Pauls V', *Meded. Ned. Hist. Inst. Rome*, ix (1929), pp. 71–110
C. Thoenes: 'Studien zur Geschichte des Peterplatzes', *Z. Kstwiss.*, xxvi (1963), pp. 97–145 (118–19)
I. Lavin: *Bernini and the Crossing of Saint Peter's* (New York, 1968), pp. 43, 45–6
H. Hibbard: *Carlo Maderno and Roman Architecture, 1580–1630* (London, 1971)
C. Delcorno: 'Un avversario del Marino: Ferrante Carli', *Stud. Seicent.*, xvi (1975), pp. 69–155 (103–4)

LOUISE RICE

Ferrand, Jacques-Philippe (*b* Joigny, Yonne, 25 July 1653; *d* Paris, 5 Jan 1732). French painter and writer. The son of a doctor to Louis XIII, he was a pupil of Pierre Mignard and the miniature and still-life painter Jacques-Samuel Bernard. His highly-finished, decorative miniature portraits in enamel quickly found favour at the court of Louis XIV and abroad. He was Peintre du Roi from 1680 to 1688. He travelled widely, working in England and Germany as well as in Turin, Genoa, Florence and Rome. In 1690 he was received (*reçu*) as a member of the Académie Royale on presentation of an oval miniature of *Louis XIV* (untraced) surrounded by a decorated copper border in the form of a trophy. A rectangular miniature portrait of *Anne of Austria* (Duke of Buccleuch priv. col.) suggests that Ferrand's miniatures followed the style of such court portrait painters as Mignard and Hyacinthe Rigaud. But the exquisite delicacy and minute handling of the drapery, and the silhouetted leaves of the tree in the background underline the artist's debt to his predecessor, the miniaturist Jean Petitot I. In 1721 he published a treatise on enamel painting, *L'Art du feu ou de peindre en émail*, dedicated to his former pupil, Louis XV.

WRITINGS
L'Art du feu ou de peindre en émail (Paris, 1721)

BIBLIOGRAPHY
'Notice biographique', *Mercure France*, 763 (March 1732), p. 550
L. Dussieux: *Les Artistes français à l'étranger: Recherches sur leurs travaux et sur leur influence en Europe* (Paris, 1856), pp. 370–73
G. C. Williamson: *History of the Portrait Miniature*, ii (London, 1904)
H. Clouzot: *Dictionnaire des miniaturistes sur émail* (Paris, 1924)

THOMAS NICHOLS

Ferrant, Angel (*b* Madrid, 1 Dec 1891; *d* Madrid, 25 July 1961). Spanish sculptor and writer. Both his father and grandfather were painters, and he started drawing when still a child. He later recalled that he became a sculptor because he was always more attracted by volumes than planes, responding to a piece of cardboard with a pair of scissors rather than with a pencil. He studied at the Escuela de Bellas Artes de San Fernando in Madrid from 1904 to 1908, and in 1913 he travelled through Belgium, Germany and Italy, also spending a period in Paris. His residence abroad brought him into contact with Cubism and Futurism, and he became a great admirer of Boccioni and Filippo Tommaso Marinetti. In 1918 he began teaching modelling and moved to La Coruña; there, together with some friends, he began publishing the review *Alfar* and exhibited his first sculptures.

In 1920 Ferrant moved to Barcelona, a more cosmopolitan city, to take up a teaching post at the Escuela de Artes y Oficios, and he formed links with other artists such as Manolo and Joan Miró. He took part in the Exposición de Artistas Ibéricos held in Madrid in 1925, and in the following year he was awarded the Premio Nacional de Escultura for his carved relief *The Schoolgirl* (limestone, 810×1320 mm, 1925; Madrid, Inst. Ramiro de Maeztu). In 1931 he joined the newly formed Els Evolucionistes, a group of painters whose stated aim was to overcome the prejudice against the modern style. Soon afterwards he was a founder-member of the society Amics de l'Art Nou, which likewise sought to promote modernism.

Ferrant was melancholic and full of self-doubt. His art did not establish its momentum until he was in his mid-30s, and his work did not follow a straightforward line of development: figurative and abstract groups of sculptures alternated without any apparent continuity. Avoiding repetition and favouring stylized or geometric shapes, he was as likely to idealize representations made from life as to humanize essentially abstract forms. He rejected realism and the academic traditions favoured in public monuments. Until the 1930s he expressed his ideas clearly and with a refined elegance in works such as *Woman's Head* (marble, 220×310×150 mm, 1930; Madrid, Mus. A. Contemp.), and it was during this first phase also that he made terracotta figures, such as the polychromed *Wise Man*

(390×270×140 mm, 1931; Madrid, Mus. A. Contemp.), and primitive masks in which he achieved great expressiveness and simplicity.

In 1935 Ferrant returned to Madrid as professor of sculpture at the Escuela de Artes y Oficios, and during the Spanish Civil War (1936–9) he strove to save the country's artistic heritage from destruction as president of the Alianza de Intelectuales Antifascistas. He was imprisoned for his Republican activities in 1939 but on his release continued his artistic activity.

Ferrant experimented with numerous media and techniques in later years. In the late 1930s, for example, he produced a series of wall-hanging reliefs representing bullfights, such as *Ovación y arrastre* (330×520 mm, 1939; Madrid, Mus. A. Contemp.), which shows the dragging of the dead bull before the crowd; movement is implied here by the repetition and superimposition of images. He also made Surrealist-influenced assemblages using *objets trouvés*, such as *Water Sprite* (355×290×90 mm, 1945; Madrid, N. Gómez Moreno priv. col., see 1983 exh. cat., no. 56), and abstracted figures, either in wood alone (e.g. *Girl with Mantilla*, 1947; Bilbao, Mus. B.A.; see fig.) or in wood and steel (e.g. *Mannequin*, 1700×850×530 mm, 1946; Madrid, Mus. A. Contemp.). In 1944 he exhibited a series of carvings of female heads collectively entitled the *Human Comedy*, such as *Woman's Head* (1940; Madrid, priv. col., see 1983 exh. cat., no. 28), at the Galería Estilo in Madrid.

Consistently constrained by economic difficulties and by the demands of commissioned work, Ferrant was unable to complete some of his most ambitious projects, such as the enormous reredos animated by coloured figures in movement that he designed in 1943 for the façade of the Teatro Albéniz in Madrid (see 1983 exh. cat., p. 48). Another unexecuted project was his *Cyclopean Series* of 1947–8, which was to consist of a sequence of carved figures housed in large spaces but which ultimately took the form only of scale models, such as *Three Women* (stone, 1948; Madrid, Mus. A. Contemp.).

The idea of representing movement, or of creating sculptures animated in space, was constant throughout Ferrant's work. In the late 1940s he produced a series of ingenious mobiles using geometric forms; although he acknowledged the example of Alexander Calder, whom he had met years earlier in Barcelona and whose mobiles were the first he had seen, his own experiments with the medium were free of any direct imitation. A particularly light-hearted example is *Happy and Flirtatious Woman* (wood, string and wire, h. 1.2 m, 1948; Madrid, priv. col., see 1983 exh. cat., no. 74).

In spite of an accident in 1954, which left him with serious physical problems, Ferrant was at his most inventive in his last years. He conceived of an 'infinite sculpture' realized in the form of abstract assemblages made of iron, such as *Venice Series 10* (h. 1.2 m, 1958; Madrid, priv. col., see 1983 exh. cat., no. 119), which consist of a number of separate elements that can be repositioned in different configurations. These were exhibited in a room of their own at the Venice Biennale in 1960, where they were awarded a prize. Ferrant was also a prolific writer on

Angel Ferrant: *Girl with Mantilla*, wood, h. 305 mm, 1947 (Bilbao, Museo de Bellas Artes)

sculpture, including his own work, as early as the 1920s, using his texts to espouse his theories on the medium.

WRITINGS

Naturalizes de los móviles (Santander, 1950)
Dónde está la escultura? (Barcelona, 1955)
Ante una escultura infinita (Madrid, 1960)

BIBLIOGRAPHY

R. Gullón: *Angel Ferrant* (Santander, 1951)
V. Marrero: *La escultura en movimiento de Angel Ferrant* (Madrid, 1954)
J. Romero Escassi: *Angel Ferrant* (Madrid, 1973)
J. E. Cirlot: *Las esculturas de Ferrant, Ferreira, Oteiza y Serra* (Barcelona, 1975)
Angel Ferrant (exh. cat., ed. A. Vázquez de Parga; Madrid, Pal. Cristal, 1983)

PILAR BENITO

Illustration Acknowledgements

We are grateful to those listed below for permission to reproduce copyright illustrative material and to those contributors who supplied photographs or helped us to obtain them. The word 'Photo:' precedes the names of large commercial or archival sources who have provided us with photographs, as well as the names of individual photographers (where known). It has generally not been used before the names of owners of works of art, such as museums and civic bodies. Every effort has been made to contact copyright holders and to credit them appropriately; we apologize to anyone who may have been omitted from the acknowledgements or cited incorrectly. Any error brought to our attention will be corrected in subsequent editions. Where illustrations have been taken from books, publication details are provided in the acknowledgements below.

Line drawings, maps, plans, chronological tables and family trees commissioned by the *Dictionary of Art* are not included in the list below. All of the maps in the dictionary were produced by Oxford Illustrators Ltd, who were also responsible for some of the line drawings. Most of the line drawings and plans, however, were drawn by the following artists: Diane Fortenberry, Lorraine Hodghton, Chris Miners, Amanda Patton, Mike Pringle, Jo Richards, Miranda Schofield, John Tiernan, John Wilson and Philip Winton. The chronological tables and family trees were prepared initially by Kate Boatfield and finalized by John Johnson.

Egypt, ancient *77–9*, *97*, *102–3*, *107*, *109*, *112*, *116* Trustees of the British Museum, London; *81*, *88* Ashmolean Museum, Oxford; *82*, *92–3*, *96*, *98*, *101*, *105*, *118* Egyptian Museum, Cairo; *84*, *94–5*, *99* Photo: © RMN, Paris; *86*, *89* Staatliche Museen zu Berlin, Preussischer Kulturbesitz; *87* Petrie Museum of Egyptian Archaeology, University College, London; *90* Museum Expedition/Museum of Fine Arts, Boston, MA; *91* Metropolitan Museum of Art, New York (Rogers Fund and contributions from Henry Walters, 1916); *104* Museum of Fine Arts, Boston, MA; *106* University of Pennsylvania Museum, Philadelphia, PA (neg. no. S4-140360); *108* Corning Museum of Glass, Corning, NY; *110*, *120* Metropolitan Museum of Art, New York; *111* Museo Egizio di Torino, Turin; *113* Petrie Museum of Egyptian Archaeology, University College, London (no. UC 14365); *114* Rijksmuseum van Oudheden, Leiden; *115* Pelizaeus-Museum, Hildesheim; *119* Deutsches Archäologisches Institut, Cairo

Egyptian Revival British Library, London

Eiffel, Gustave Photo: Arch. Phot. Paris/© DACS, 1996

Eigtved, Niels *1* Kunstakademiet, Copenhagen; *2* Royal Academy of Fine Arts Library, London (Art Documentation)

Eilbertus of Cologne Staatliche Museen zu Berlin, Preussischer Kulturbesitz

Einhard Bibliothèque Nationale de France, Paris

Eisen: (2) Charles Eisen British Library, London (no. 11474.e.34)

Eisenman, Peter D. Photo: Eisenman Architects, New York

Ejagham *1–2* Photo: Keith Nicklin

Ekman, Robert Wilhelm Art Museum, Turku

Ekphrasis Photo: Warburg Institute, London

Electroplating *1* British Library, London; *2* Photo: Dr P.T. Craddock

Eleusis National Archaeological Museum, Athens (Archaeological Receipts Fund)

Ellora Photo: M. Soar

Elmalı Photo: M.J. Mellink, Bryn Mawr College, Bryn Mawr, PA

El Salvador *2* Photo: D. Donne Bryant, DDB Stock photo, Baton Rouge, LA

Elsheimer, Adam *1* Trustees of the National Gallery, London; *2* Städelsches Kunstinstitut und Städtische Galerie, Frankfurt am Main/ Photo: Ursula Edelmann; *3* Historisches Museum, Frankfurt am Main; *4* Bayerische Staatsgemäldesammlungen, Munich

Elsner, Jakob Niedersächsische Landesgalerie, Hannover

Eltham Palace Photo: RCHME/© Crown Copyright

Elvas Photo: Robert Harding Picture Library, London

Ely Cathedral *2–3* Photo: Anthony Kersting, London; *4* Photo: Mrs Faith Johnson; *5* Photo: James Austin, Cambridge

Elymais Trustees of the British Museum, London

Emblem book *1* British Library, London (no. C.40.b.31); *2* British Library, London (no. 11556.g.361)

Embossing © DACS, 1996

Embriachi Photo: Archivi Alinari, Florence

Embroidery *1* Photo: © ACL Brussels; *2* Board of Trustees of the Victoria and Albert Museum, London

Empire style Photo: British Architectural Library, RIBA, London

Empoli, Jacopo da *1* Kunsthistorisches Museum, Vienna; *2* Photo: Archivi Alinari, Florence

Enamel *1* Trustees of the British Museum, London; *2* Kunstindustrimuseet, Oslo/Photo: Teigen Fotoatelier; *3* Trustees of the Wallace Collection, London

Encaustic painting *1* British Library, London (no. 7856.d.25); *2* Trustees of the British Museum, London; *3* Trustees of the National Gallery, London

Encyclopedia, manuscript Universiteitsbibliotheek, Ghent

Engebrechtsz., Cornelis Stedelijk Museum De Lakenhal, Leiden

Engel, Carl Ludwig *1* National Board of Antiquities, Helsinki; *2* Museum of Finnish Architecture, Helsinki/Photo: N.E. Wickberg

Engelberg, Burkhard Photo: Franz Bischoff

England *2*, *26*, *31*, *43* Photo: Conway Library, Courtauld Institute of Art, London; *3*, *5* Photo: RCHME/© Crown Copyright; *4* British Library, London (no. Maps C.26 b.8); *6*, *8–9*, *11*, *13*, *25* Photo: Malcolm Watson; *7*, *35–6* Photo: Anthony Kersting, London; *10* Architectural Association, London/Photo: Adrian Forty; *12* Photo: © City Hall, Norwich; *14* Master and Fellows of Corpus Christi College, Cambridge/Photo: Conway Library, Courtauld Institute of Art, London; *15*, *17* National Portrait Gallery, London; *16* Woburn Abbey, Bedfordshire; *18*, *21–2* Tate Gallery, London; *19* Trustees of the British Museum, London; *20*, *38*, *46*, *48–56*, *59–69*, *71*, *74–9*, *81–2*, *84–8*, *91*, *93–5* Board of Trustees of the Victoria and Albert Museum, London; *23* Photo: © Angela Verren-Taunt, 1996. All rights reserved, DACS, 1996; *24* British Council, London; *27* © Maurice H. Ridgway/ Photo: Fred H. Crossley); *28* Bodleian Library, Oxford; *29–30* Photo: Malcolm Crowthers, London; *32* Board of Trustees of the National Museums and Galleries on Merseyside, Liverpool; *33* Courtauld Institute Galleries, London; *34* Arts Council Collection, London; *37* Masters and Fellows, Magdalene College, Cambridge; *39*, *41* Photo: National Trust Photo Library, London; *40* Yale Center for British Art, New Haven, CT; *42* Guildhall Library, Corporation of London; *44* Photo: Country Life Picture Library, London; *45* Photo: Colefax and Fowler, London; *47* National Trust Photo Library, London/Photo: John Bethell; *57* Royal Pavilion, Art Gallery and Museums, Brighton; *58* Photo: Winchester Research Unit, Winchester; *70* Syndics of the Fitzwilliam Museum, Cambridge; *72* Broadfield House Glass Museum, Kingswinford, West Midlands/Photo: Lawrence Whistler, Oxford; *73* Borough Council of King's Lynn and West Norfolk/Photo: P.M. Goodchild and Son; *80* Royal Collection, Windsor Castle/© Her Majesty Queen Elizabeth II; *83* Castle Museum, York; *89* Photo: A. Kenneth Snowman; *90* Mobilier National, Paris; *92* National Trust Photo Library, London/Photo: Bill Batten

Engraving *1* Photo: Amy N. Worthen; *2* Bibliothèque Nationale de France, Paris; *3–4, 8* Trustees of the British Museum, London; *5* Photo: © RMN, Paris; *6* Rijksmuseum, Amsterdam; *7* British Library, London (no. 64.g.1-65); *9* Brooklyn Museum, New York (Brooklyn Museum Collection; no. 43.238.4.1-8)/© DACS, 1996

Enkomi Department of Antiquities, Cyprus Museum, Nicosia

Enlightenment, the Trustees of the National Gallery, London

Ensinger: (2) Matthäus Ensinger Photo: Bildarchiv Foto Marburg

Ensor, James *1* Museum voor Schone Kunsten, Ghent/© DACS, 1996; *2* © DACS, 1996

Environmental art Photo: Salvatore Licitra

Ephemera, printed *1* Bodleian Library, Oxford (Douce S. 848, p. 71; Covent Garden Playbill, John Johnson Playbills 1813–14); *2* Trustees of the British Museum, London; *3* Foundation for Ephemera Studies, London

Ephesos *2* Photo: Anton Bammer; *3* Photo: Ulrike Müss; *6* Trustees of the British Museum, London

Epidauros *2* National Archaeological Museum, Athens (Archaeological Receipts Fund)

Epitaph *1* Photo: Conway Library, Courtauld Institute of Art, London; *2* Bibliothèque Nationale de France, Paris

Epstein, Jacob Tate Gallery, London

Equestrian monument Photo: Charles Avery

Eretria Photo: Hirmer Fotoarchiv, Munich

Erevan Photo: VAAP, Moscow

Erfurt *1* Photo: Helma Trefz; *2* Photo: Bildarchiv Foto Marburg

Erhart: (1) Michel Erhart Staatliche Museen zu Berlin, Preussischer Kulturbesitz

Erhart: (2) Gregor Erhart Photo: © RMN, Paris

Erickson, Arthur Archaeology Museum, University of British Columbia, Vancouver, BC

Erlitou Metropolitan Museum of Art, New York (on loan from the People's Republic of China)/Photo: Seth Joel

Ernst, Max *1* Museum of Modern Art, New York/© SPADEM/ADAGP, Paris, and DACS, London, 1996; *2* © SPADEM/ADAGP, Paris, and DACS, London, 1996; *3* British Library, London (no. 7872.bb.16)/© SPADEM/ADAGP, Paris, and DACS, London, 1996; *4* Wadsworth Atheneum, Hartford, CT/© SPADEM/ADAGP, Paris, and DACS, London, 1996

Erotic art *1* Ephesos Archaeological Museum, Selçuk; *2* Staatliche Museen zu Berlin, Preussischer Kulturbesitz; *3* Photo: RCHME/© Crown Copyright; *4* Photo: Peter Webb, London; *5* Trustees of the National Gallery, London; *6, 8, 10* Trustees of the British Museum, London; *7* Maclean Gallery, London; *9* Private collection, Italy/Photo: Anthony D'Offay Gallery, London

Escorial *1* British Library, London; *2* Photo: Anthony Kersting, London; *3* Photo: Bildarchiv Foto Marburg; *4* British Library, London (no. 1899.e.15)

Eski Mosul region Department of Antiquities and Heritage, Baghdad

Esna Trustees of the British Museum, London

Espinosa, Jerónimo Jacinto Photo: Ampliaciones y Reproducciones MAS, Barcelona

Esquivel, Antonio María Photo: Enrique Valdivieso

Esselens, Jacob Amsterdams Historisch Museum, Amsterdam (Fodor Collection)

Essen Photo: Bildarchiv Foto Marburg

Este (i): (6) Isabella d'Este Photo: © RMN, Paris

Esterházy, §I: (4) Miklós Esterházy II Photo: István Barkoczi

Estève, Maurice Musée Estève, Bourges

Estonia *2* Estonian Museum of Architecture, Tallinn; *3* Photo: Kunst Publishers, Tallinn; *4* Art Museum of Estonia; *5* Tallinn Art Hall Archive

Esztergom *1* Photo: © Interfoto MTI, Budapest; *2* Photo: Dr Ernö Marosí

Etampes, Notre-Dame Photo: Hirmer Fotoarchiv, Munich

Etching *1–4, 6–7* Trustees of the British Museum, London; *5* British Library, London (no. 146.i.23(1))

Etching, lift-ground Trustees of the British Museum, London

Etching, relief Photo: Raymond Lister

Etching, soft-ground Trustees of the British Museum, London

Ethiopia and Eritrea *1* Photo: Georg Gerster, Zumikon; *2–3* Bibliothèque Nationale de France, Paris; *4* Völkerkundemuseum der Universität Zürich; *5* Völkerkundemuseum der Universität Zürich/Photo: Peter R. Gerber; *6* Völkerkundemuseum der Universität Zürich/Photo: Peter Nebel

Ethnographic photography *1* National Archives and Records Administration (Still Pictures Branch; no. 75-SEI-59), Washington, DC; *2* National Museum of African Art, Smithsonian Institution, Washington, DC (Eliot Elisofon Photographic Archives)/Photo: Jeffrey Ploskonka and Eliot Elisofon

Etruscan *2* Photo: Johannes Felbermeyer; *3* Deutsches Archäologisches Institut, Rome (neg. no. 81.862); *4–6, 15, 33, 36–7* Trustees of the British Museum, London; *7* Photo: Hirmer Fotoarchiv, Munich; *9* Laboratorio Fotografico, Museo Nazionale Preistorico ed Etnografico 'Luigi Pigorini', Rome; *10* Deutsches Archäologisches Institut, Rome; *12* Gabinetto Fotografico, Soprintendenza ai Beni Artistici e Storici, Florence; *13, 18–20, 22–3, 34* Soprintendenza Archeologica della Toscana, Florence; *14, 16, 35* Vatican Museums, Vatican City, Rome; *17* Photo: © RMN, Paris; *21* Antikenmuseum Basel und Sammlung Ludwig, Basle; *24, 28* Photo: Archivi Alinari, Florence; *25* Deutsches Archäologisches Institut, Rome (neg. no. F.82.608); *26* Deutsches Archäologisches Institut, Rome (neg. no. F.82.634); *27* Deutsches Archäologisches Institut, Rome (neg. no. F.81.4277); *29* Deutsches Archäologisches Institut, Rome (neg. no. F.81.4359); *30* Museo Archeologico, Massa Marittima (GR)/Photo: © Foto Marzio, Cresci; *31* Staatliche Antikensammlungen und Glyptothek, Munich; *32* Nationalmuseum, Copenhagen (Department of Near Eastern and Classical Art); *39* Photo: Scala, Florence

Etruscan style Photo: Anthony Kersting, London

Etty, William National Gallery of Scotland, Edinburgh

Evans, Walker Library of Congress, Washington, DC

Everdingen: (1) Caesar van Everdingen Hoogheem Raadschap Van Rijnland, Leiden

Everdingen: (2) Allart van Everdingen Bayerische Staatsgemälde-sammlungen, Munich

Évora Photo: Conway Library, Courtauld Institute of Art, London

Eworth, Hans National Gallery of Canada, Ottawa

Exchange Photo: Jan Derwig, Architectuur Fotografie, Amsterdam

Exedra Ecole Française d'Archéologie, Athens

Exeter *2* Photo: RCHME/© Crown Copyright; *3* Exeter City Museums

Exhibition *1* Bibliothèque des Arts Décoratifs, Paris/Photo: J.-L. Charmet, Paris; *2* Trustees of the National Gallery, London; *3* Permanent Collection, Royal Academy of Arts, London; *4* Photo: Illustrated London News Picture Library, London

Exhibition architecture *1–2* Photo: British Architectural Library, RIBA, London

Experimental film Contemporary Films Ltd, London

Expression British Library, London (no. 1043.d.13)

Expressionism *1* Germanisches Nationalmuseum, Nuremberg; *2* Photo: © Nolde-Stiftung Seebüll; *3* Photo: Bildarchiv Foto Marburg; *4* Staatliche Landesbildstelle, Hamburg/Photo: W. Beutler, 1954

Exter, Alexandra Photo: Rheinische Bildarchiv, Cologne

Exultet rolls Soprintendenza ai Beni Ambientali, Architettonici, Artistici e Storici della Puglia, Bari

Ex-voto Munich Cathedral

Eybl, Franz Österreichische Galerie im Belvedere, Vienna

Eyck, van: (1) Hubert van Eyck Photo: © ACL Brussels

Eyck, van: (2) Jan van Eyck *1* Metropolitan Museum of Art, New York (Fletcher Fund, 1933; no. 33.92a); *2–3* Trustees of the National Gallery, London; *4* Groeningemuseum, Bruges; *5* Staatliche Museen zu Berlin, Preussischer Kulturbesitz; *6* Photo: © ACL Brussels

Eyck, Aldo van Photo: Jan Derwig, Architectuur Fotografie, Amsterdam

Fabergé, Carl Photo: A. Kenneth Snowman

Fables *1* Staats- und Universitätsbibliothek, Hamburg (Cod. 47 in Scrin.); *2* Herzog August Bibliothek, Wolfenbüttel (inv. no. 10.2 Eth 2)

Fabre, François-Xavier Musée Fabre, Montpellier

Fabritius: (1) Carel Fabritius Mauritshuis, The Hague

Fabritius: (2) Barent Fabritius Tiroler Landesmuseum Ferdinandeum, Innsbruck

Façade decoration *1* Photo: Bardazzi Fotografia, Florence; *2* Städtische Kunstsammlungen Augsburg; *3* Öffentliche Kunstsammlung Basel, Basle; *4* Photo: Conway Library, Courtauld Institute of Art, London; *5* Photo: Osvaldo Böhm, Venice; *6* Photo: Robert Harding Picture Library, London

Faccini, Pietro Photo: Archivi Alinari, Florence

Factory Photo: Conway Library, Courtauld Institute of Art, London

Faithorne, William Ashmolean Museum, Oxford

Falcone, Aniello Photo: © RMN, Paris

Falconet, Etienne-Maurice Photo: © RMN, Paris

Falconetto, Giovanni Maria *1* Photo: Umberto Tomba, Verona; *2* Photo: Archivi Alinari, Florence

Famagusta Photo: Anthony Kersting, London